ROLL OF THE GRADUATES OF THE UNIVERSITY OF ABERDEEN 1956–1970

PREVIOUS VOLUMES OF
ROLL OF THE GRADUATES OF THE
UNIVERSITY OF ABERDEEN

I

1860–1900
Compiled by Colonel William Johnston
Published by subscription as no 18 in Aberdeen University
Studies series. Aberdeen 1906

II

1901–1925
with Supplement 1860–1900
Compiled by Theodore Watt
Published by Aberdeen University Press 1935

III

1926–1955
with Supplement 1860–1925
Compiled by John Mackintosh
Published by University of Aberdeen 1960

ENQUIRIES ABOUT AVAILABILITY TO
ABERDEEN UNIVERSITY PRESS

ROLL OF THE GRADUATES OF THE UNIVERSITY OF ABERDEEN 1956–1970

WITH *SUPPLEMENT*
1860–1955

Compiled by
LOUISE DONALD MA LLB
W S MACDONALD MBE MA

PUBLISHED FOR THE UNIVERSITY OF ABERDEEN
BY ABERDEEN UNIVERSITY PRESS

First published 1982
Aberdeen University Press
A member of the Pergamon Group

The University of Aberdeen gratefully acknowledges
the assistance of the F. E. Bruce Bequest and the C. J. Weir Fund
in the production of this volume of the Roll of Graduates

British Library Cataloguing in Publication Data
University of Aberdeen
Roll of the graduates of the University of
Aberdeen 1956–1970: with supplement 1860–1955
1. University of Aberdeen—Alumni
I. Title II. Donald, Louise III. Macdonald, W. S.
378.412′35 LF968

ISBN 0-08-028469-8

PRINTED IN GREAT BRITAIN AT
ABERDEEN UNIVERSITY PRESS

PREFACE

In 1972 the University Court approved the proposal from the General Council that a fourth volume of the Roll of Graduates covering the period 1956–1970 should be compiled and that, as in the two previous volumes, a Supplement should be included bringing information up to date for graduates of the earlier periods. Mrs Louise Donald (née Turner) MA 1923 LLB 1972 was appointed editor and worked on the task from early 1973 until her death in December 1980. By that time all material for the 1956–1970 graduates had been edited and printer's galley proofs had partly been read and amendments made. The material for the Supplement had partly been edited and had begun to go into the printing stage.

The name Louise Donald had for many years been associated with Aberdeen University, notably as a member of the Business Committee of the General Council, as writer of a history of *Alma Mater* for the *Aberdeen University Review* and of a history of the General Council for the publication *The Fusion of 1860*. This volume of the Roll may well be seen to be her memorial as it is largely the result of her work during the last eight years of her life. Her successor as editor had worked closely with her from 1976 and was very willing to continue and bring her work to fruition.

Some information about the Roll as a whole may be appropriate. Volume I, published in 1906 the year of the University's Quatercentenary celebrations, dealt with graduates from 1860 to 1900, 1860 being the year of the 'fusion' of King's College and Marischal College to form the University of Aberdeen; volume II, published in 1935, dealt with graduates 1901–1925; volume III, published in 1960 the year of the celebrations marking the centenary of the 'fusion', dealt with graduates 1926–1955; and now volume IV covers the period 1956–1970. Each of volumes II, III and IV has a Supplement updating information about graduates in the previous volumes. As it has been the practice not to repeat in one volume material printed in an earlier volume, the information concerning the older graduate may start in volume I, continue in II and III and finish in volume IV. Where in the present volume *qv* is followed by (I), (II), (III) or (IV), or a combination of these, the numbers in parentheses refer to the respective volumes.

About 20,000 questionnaire forms were prepared for the initial mailing for this volume. Accompanying the forms for the pre-1956 graduates were copies of the information printed about them in volume III so helping them when updating the particulars of their careers. On the return of the completed forms the information supplied was condensed, typed and a copy sent to the graduate concerned for approval or amendment.

Section I (1956–1970)

It was decided to include in the main list the names of all graduates of the period. To achieve this Graduation Lists for the years 1956 to 1970 were checked against the 1971 General Council Register. There are close to 9,000 entries and about 35% of these show only names and degrees with dates, being all the information available. This is explained by the facts that many forms were never sent out as the Register showed no addresses; forms were returned marked 'gone away'; or the forms were never returned to the editor. In the case of many of the women graduates in this 35% category the Register showed a married surname and this has been printed. At a later stage addresses were found for some of these 'lost' graduates and a second issue of questionnaire forms was made up to as late as 1980. This proved relatively productive in replies.

Following precedent, married women graduates are recorded under their maiden names and identification of these, including any who graduated under their married names, may be aided by reference to the Section I list of Married Women Graduates on pp 374 to 392.

Information is presented in a standard pattern under five headings:

(1) Name and degree(s) with date(s) (Aberdeen University degrees only)
(2) Names and occupations of parents, and place and date of birth
(3) Further qualifications (other than those gained at Aberdeen University) and conferred honours
(4) Details of career
(5) Details of marriage with name and place of residence of father-in-law unless the spouse is an Aberdeen graduate when the degree and *qv* follows the name.

First degrees only have been given for parents, spouses of graduates and fathers-in-law. In connection with the death of graduates references are given to obituary notices in the *Aberdeen University Review* (*AUR*).

Section I concludes with the Honorary Graduates 1956–1970 (pp 393 to 399). Their designations at the time of the conferring of the honorary degrees are as shown in the University Graduation Lists and a follow-up of the *AUR* references to the laureation addresses will give further information as to the sphere in which each gained distinction.

Section II (1860–1955)

Here are listed the names of those from volume I who graduated after 1890 and of all graduates from Sections I of volumes II and III—unless death has been intimated in one of these volumes. This Section contains approximately 11,600 names many with only basic information as they are in the Register without addresses or no replies have been received. Some are stated to be no longer on the General Council Register as contact has been completely lost for many years. While it is impossible to say if they are still alive, it is hazardous to assume they are dead.

A list of Married Women Graduates whose marriages have not been intimated in a previous volume of the Roll is included (pp 738 to 740) and the Section ends with a list of the Honorary Graduates for the volume III (1926–1955) period (pp 741 to 745).

The Appendix consists of a detailed analysis of the degrees and diplomas granted by the University during the period 1956–1970. The figures have been obtained from the Annual Statistics published by the University. One noticeable feature is the threefold increase in the annual number of degrees awarded over the period—from approximately 400 in 1956 to approximately 1,200 in 1970.

The structure of this volume of the Roll is similar to that of the earlier volumes but, to keep printing costs down, information has been condensed and words abbreviated without, it is hoped, leading to loss of intelligibility. The lists of Abbreviations and Degrees supplied should be material aids to the avoidance of ambiguity or misunderstanding. Punctuation has been reduced to a minimum as has the use of capital letters. An oblique line separates occupations which are thought to be contemporaneous, a comma if they follow on each other. A semicolon is used as the dividing device between posts held. The preposition 'from' has been used in front of the year when a graduate started in a post and so far as is known is still in that post unless a note to the contrary follows, e.g. 'retd'. In only a few cases have county names been added after place names.

In a book of this kind compiled over the long period of nine years errors of omission and commission and variations in style of recording and typographical presentation are almost inevitable and for this indulgence is claimed. From the very nature of the work the information given cannot be up-to-date. The main source of information has, of course, been the questionnaire forms, for the completion of which the editor expresses sincere thanks to the graduates concerned. Other information has been found in University records and the editor is indebted to the University Archives Department and the Registry for their willing cooperation and response to any enquiry. The personalia, obituary and marriage announcements in the *Aberdeen University Review* have been extensively drawn upon and for this there is further indebtedness.

A number of people have helped in the work. Miss Nora F. Glennie MA 1924, Lady Taylor (née Helen M. Jardine) MB ChB 1920, Dr Beatrix B. Law MA 1920, Miss Florence Mackenzie secretary to Principal Wright, and Miss Agnes M. Pittendrigh BSc 1926 helped in the preliminary years getting the volume under way. Mrs Flora M. Anderson (née Burley) MA 1923 acted as typist for some years. Mrs Roberta Morgan (née Gordon) MA 1932, Miss E. Ashley Scott MA 1930 and Mr Ian MacLean Smith MA 1931 were involved in the early stages and continued throughout. To all these the editors owe thanks. The office used by the editors was, conveniently, adjacent to that of the General Council and Mrs Ursula Price, assistant registrar, readily made records available and contributed to the work by typing and assisting in research. Guidance from Mr Harold M. R. Watt MA 1942 of Aberdeen University Press was a source of encouragement to both editors.

Aberdeen, January 1982 W. S. MacDonald

CONTENTS

ABBREVIATIONS

Explanations of some of the abbreviations and terms used

A period follows an abbreviation which in itself forms a word e.g. 'man.' for 'manager.'
An asterisk (*) indicates that the abbreviation is for the name of a university.
Note the difference between 'Aber' meaning Aberdeen city and 'Aberd' meaning Aberdeen University, 'Dun' Dundee city and 'Dund' Dundee University. In other cases the same abbreviation has been used in the text for city and university where it was thought no ambiguity would arise.

Aber	Aberdeen
*Aberd	Aberdeen
*Acad	Acadia (Canada)
acad	academ-y-ic-ical-icus
acct	account-s-ing-ant-ancy
*Adel	Adelaide
admin	administrat-ion-or
adv	advanced
advis	advis-er-ory
advoc	advocate-s
advt	advertis-ing-ement
AEC	Army Educational Corps
AERE	Atomic Energy Research Establishment
Af	African
ag	agen-t-cy
agr	agricultur-e-al-alist
AGS	Aberdeen Grammar School
AHA	Area Health Authority
*Alex	Alexandria
*Alta	Alberta
alum.	aluminium
amb	ambulance
anaest	anaesthe-tics-tist-sia
anat	anatomy
anim husb	animal husbandry
*ANU	Australian National University Canberra
app	apprentice
arch	architect-ural
archae	archaeolog-y-ist
ARI	Aberdeen Royal Infirmary
assoc	associat-e-ion
asst	assistant
assur	assurance
*Aston	Aston in Birmingham
ATS	Auxiliary Territorial Service
*Auck	Auckland
AUP	Aberdeen University Press
AUR	Aberdeen University Review
Aust	Australia-n
auth	authority
aux	auxiliary
av med	aviation medicine
AWRE	Atomic Weapons Research Establishment
b	born
BAC	British Aircraft Corporation
bact	bacteriol-ogy-ogist-ogical
BAOR	British Army of the Rhine
*BC, BrCol	British-Columbia
B of R	Book of Remembrance
*Belf	Queens University Belfast
BFES	British Forces Educational Service
BICC	British Insulated Callenders Cables
BIM	British Institute of Management
biochem	biochem-ist-istry-ical
biol	biolog-y-ist-ical
*Birm	Birmingham
bld(g)(r)	build-ing-er
BLMC	British Leyland Motor Corporation
BMA	British Medical Association
bn	battalion
BOCM	British Oil and Cake Mills
*Bom	Bombay
bor	borough
bot	botany
BP	British Petroleum
br	branch
*Brad	Bradford
BR	British Rail
brig.	brigad-e-ier
*Brist	Bristol
Brit	Brit-ain-ish
bs	building society
BSBI	Botanical Society of the British Isles
BSIP	British Solomon Island Principality
bus.	business
c	council-lor, county
CAA	Civil Aviation Authority
*Cai	Gonville and Caius College Cambridge

*Calc	Calcutta
*Calg	Calgary
*Calif	California
*Cantab	Cambridge
*Cape T	Cape Town
cardiol	cardiolog-y-ist
cas	casualty
cath	cathedral
cc	county council
CEGB	Central Electricity Generating Board
cent.	central
ch	church child-ren
chap.	chaplain
chem	chem-ist-istry-ical
chirop	chiropod-y-ist
chmn	chairman
civ	civil-ian
C of E	Church of England
C of S	Church of Scotland
cler	clerical
clin	clinic-al-ian
CMA	Canadian Medical Association
CNAA	Council for National Academic Awards
col	colon-el-ial
*Col	Columbia (NY)
coll	colleg-e-iate
comm	committee, command-er-ing, commer-ce-cial, commission-ed-ers
commun	commun-ity-ications
comp	company, comprehensive
compar	comparative
cong	congregation-al
conserv	conserv-ancy-ation-ative-ator
constit	constit-uency-utional
construct.	construction
consult.	consult-ant-ing-ancy
contr	contract-ing-or
*Corn	Cornell
corp	corporation
cott	cottage
CSIRO	Commonwealth Scientific and Industrial Research Organisation
cult.	cultural
curric	curriculum
d	daughter
d	died
DAFS	Department of Agriculture and Fisheries for Scotland
DDMS	Deputy Director of Medical Services
def	defence
dem	demonstrat-ion-or
dent	dent-al-ist-istry
dep	deput-e-y
dept	department-al
dermat	dermatolog-ist-y
des	design-er
dev	development-al
DHSS	Department of Health and Social Security
DIH	Department of Industrial Health
Dip.	diploma-tic
dir	director
diss	dissolved (marriage)
dist	district
distrib	distribution
div	division-al-divinity
D o E	Department of the Environment
doct	doctor-al
dom	domestic
DRI	Dundee Royal Infirmary
DSIR	Department of Scientific and Industrial Research (*see* SRC)
DTI	Department of Trade and Industry
DTp	Department of Transport
*Dub	Trinity College Dublin
Dun	Dundee
*Dund	Dundee
*Durh	Durham
dyn	dynamics
*E Ang	East Anglia
ecol	ecolog-y-ist
econ	econom-y-ist
*Edin	Edinburgh
edit.	edit-or-orial-ing
educ	educat-ion-ional-or
EIS	Educational Institute of Scotland
elect.	electric-al-ian
emb	embassy
EMS	Emergency Medical Service
eng	engineer-ing
Eng(1)	England (English)
ENT	Ear Nose and Throat
entomol	entomolog-y-ist
epis	episcopal
ERI	Edinburgh Royal Infirmary
esn	educationally sub-normal
estab	establishment
estim	estimat-ing-or
ESU	English Speaking Union
eval	evaluation
exam	examin-ation-er
*Exe	Exeter
exec	executive
exped	expedition
exper	experiment-al
ESTB	Employment Service Training Board
fac	faculty
fam	fam
FAO	Food and Agricultural Organisation
farm.	farm-er-ing
FCO	Foreign and Commonwealth Office
fd	field
f e	further education
fed.	federal
fell.	fellow-ship
fin.	financial
for.	forest-er-ry, foreign
FPA	Family Planning Association
Fr	French
GATT	General Agreement on Tariffs and Trade
GC reg	General Council Register
g d	general duties
gen	general
GEC	General Electric Company
geog	geograph-y-er
geol	geolog-y-ist-ical
geophys	geophysic-s-al-ist
Ger	German-y
geriat	geriatric-ian
*Glas	Glasgow
Glasg	Glasgow

gov(t)	govern-or-(ment)
g p	general pract-ice-itioner
grad	graduat-e-ion
*Greg	Gregorian University Rome
g s	grammar school
GTC	General Teaching Council(Scotland)
guid	guidance
gyn	gynaecolog-y-ical-ist
haemat	haematology
*Harv	Harvard
HIB	Herring Industry Board
HIDB	Highlands and Islands Development Board
hist	histor-y-ical
h o	house officer
hon	honorary
h, hosp	hospital-s
h p	house physician
h s	house surgeon, high school
husb	husband-ry
hyg	hygiene
HMFO	Her Majesty's Foreign Office
HM(C)IS	Her Majesty's (Chief) Inspector of Schools
HNC	Higher National Certificate
HSC	Hospital for Sick Children
*H-W	Heriot Watt
I	infirmary
IAEA	International Atomic Energy Agency
IBA	Independent Broadcasting Authority
i/c	in charge
ICI	Imperial Chemical Industries
ICL	International Computers Ltd
ICS	Indian Civil Service
ILEA	Inner London Education Authority
ILO	International Labour Organisation
IMA	International Mineralogical Association
indust	indust-ry-rial-rialist
inf	infirmary, infant
infect.	infectious
info	information
Inl Rev	Inland Revenue
insp	inspector
inst	institut-e-ion
instr	instruct-or-ion
insur	insurance
Inv	Inverness
invest.	investment
Ital	Ital-y-ian
ITA	Independent Television Authority
ITE	Institute of Terrestrial Ecology
JMB	Joint Matriculation Board
JP	Justice of the Peace
juris	jurisprudence
*Kar	Karachi
*Kent	Kent at Canterbury (UK)
kg	kindergarten
*Khart	Khartoum
Kt(d)	Knight(ed)
l a	local authority
lab	labour (politics)-er, laboratory
*Lake	Lakehead Canada
*Lanc	Lancaster
lang	language-s
Lat	Latin
lect	lecturer
leg.	legal
*Leic	Leicester
lib	librar-y-ian-ianship
ling.	linguist-ic-ics
lit	liter-ary-ature
*Liv	Liverpool
loc	local
LMC	London Medical Council
*Lond	London
LSE	London School of Economics
lt	lieutenant
*Luck	Lucknow
m	married
*Macq	Macquarie
MAFF	Ministry of Agriculture, Fisheries and Food
mag	magazine
man.	manag-er-eress-ement-ing
*Manc	Manchester
*Manit	Manitoba
manuf	manufactur-e-ing
marr	marriage
*Mass	Massachusetts
mat.	maternity
*McG	McGill
*McM	McMaster
MDC	Metropolitan District Council
mech	mechan-ic(s)-ical-isation
med	medic-al-ine
*Melb	Melbourne
mem	memorial
merch	merchant
met.	meteorolog-y-ist-ical
metall	metallurg-y-ical
meth	methodist
metro	metropolitan
m h	mentally handicapped
MHSS	Ministry of Health and Social Security
microbiol	microbiolog-y-ical
min	minist-er-ry, mineral-s-ogist
miss.	missionary
MIT	Massachusetts Institute of Technology
MN	Merchant Navy
mod lang	modern languages
MoD	Ministry of Defence
mo(h)	medical officer (of health)
MoH	Ministry of Health
*Montr	Montreal
MoT	Ministry of Transport
MoW	Ministry of Works
MPNI	Ministry of Pensions and National Insurance
MRC	Medical Research Council
munic	municipal
mus	music-al-ian, museum
NAB	National Assistance Board
NAMH	National Association of Mental Health
NASA	National Aeronautics and Space Administration(US)
nat	natural, national
NATO	North Atlantic Treaty Organisation
NCB	National Coal Board
*N'cle	Newcastle
NCR	National Cash Registers
NE	North East (Scotland)
NERC	Natural Environment Research Council
NESDA	North East of Scotland Development Association
neurol	neurolog-y-ical-ist

*New Br	New Brunswick
*Nfld	Newfoundland
NFU	National Farmers' Union
NHS	National Health Service
NIAB	National Institute of Agricultural Botany
NOSCA	North of Scotland College of Agriculture
*Nott	Nottingham
NPL	National Physical Laboratory
NRC	National Research Council
NSHEB	North of Scotland Hydro Electric Board
*NUI	National University of Ireland
nurs	nurs-ery-ing
nutrit	nutrition-al-ist
NZ	New Zealand
obst	obstetric-s-al-ian
occup	occupation-al
ODA	Overseas Development Administration
ODM	Ministry of Overseas Development
OECD	Organisation for European Economic Development
off.	offic-e-er-ial
oper	operat-ing-ion-or
ophth	ophthalm-ic-ology-ologist
ordin	ordinance
org	organic
organis	organis-er-ation
orthop	orthopaedic
*Osm	Osmania
*Ott	Ottawa
*OU	Open University
OUP	Oxford University Press
O & M	Organisation and Method
*Oxon	Oxford
p a	personal assistant
paediat	paediatric-s-ian
*Panj	Panjab (Pakistan)
par	parish
path.	patholog-y-ist-ical
p e	physical education
*Penn	Pennsylvania
pers	person-al-nel
petr	petrol-ogy-eum
p h	public health, physically handicapped
pharm	pharmac-y-ist-eutical-ology
phc	pharmaceutical chemist
phil	philosoph-y-ical
*Phil	Philadelphia
phys	physic-s-ian-al-ist
physiol	physiolog-y-ical-ist
physioth	physiotherap-y-ist
plan.	plann-er-ing
PMG	Post Master General
PNEU	Parents' National Educational Union
pol	politic-s-al
poly	polytechnic-al
pop.	population
pract	pract-ice-itioner
prep	preparat-ion-ory
pres	president
presb	presbyter-y-ian
prevn	prevention
p or prim.	primary
prin	principal
pr(o)	public relations (officer)
prob	probation-er-ary

prod.	produc-tion-er-tivity-ts
prof	profess-or-ional
progr.	progr-amme(r)-ess
proj	project-ion-ionist
prop.	prop-erty-rietor-rietress
prot	protestant
prov	provinc-e-ial
p s	private secretary, primary school
psych	psycholog-y-ical-ist
psychiat	psychiat-ry-rist
ptnr	partner
publ	publi-c-city-cations-sher
QARANC	Queen Alexandra's Royal Army Nursing Corps
QEH	Queen Elizabeth Hospital
qv	which see
RA	Royal Academy
radiol	radiolog-y-ist
RAE	Royal Aircraft Establishment
RAEC	Royal Army Educational Corps
RA(E)HSC or	Royal Aberdeen (Edinburgh) Hospital for Sick Children
RACH	Royal Aberdeen Children's Hospital
RAI	Royal Alexandra Infirmary
RAM	Royal Academy of Music
RAMC	Royal Army Medical Corps
RANR	Royal Australian Naval Reserve
RASC	Royal Army Service Corps
RCAF	Royal Canadian Air Force
RCAMC	Royal Canadian Army Medical Corps
RCT	Royal Corps of Transport
*R'dg	Reading
RE	Religious Education
reg	regular, region-al
regist	regist-er-rar-ered-ration
regt	regiment-al
remed	remedial
rep	representative
reprod	reproduct-ion-ive
res	research
resid	resid-ent-ential-ing
retd	retired
RGC	Robert Gordon's College, Aberdeen
RGIT	Robert Gordon's Institute of Technology, Aberdeen (previously RGTC)
RGN	Registered General Nurse
RGS	Royal Geographical Society
RGTC	*see* RGIT
RHA	Regional Health Authority, Royal Horse Artillery
rheumat	rheumatology
*Rhodes	Grahamstown (SAf)
RHM	Rank, Hovis, McDougall
rly	railway
RMN	Registered Mental Nurse
RN	Royal Navy
RNI	Royal Northern Infirmary (Inv)
ROC	Royal Observer Corps
RRE	Royal Radar Establishment
RSPB	Royal Society for the Protection of Birds
RST	Rhodesian Selection Trust
s	son, school
S	South
SAf	South Africa
*St And	St Andrews
SAI	Scottish Agricultural Industries
*Salf	Salford

*Sask	Saskatchewan
sc	science
SCE	Scottish Certificate of Education
schol	scholar-ship
scient	scient-ific-ist
SCM	Student Christian Movement
Scot.	Scot-land-tish
sec	secondary
sect.	section-al
secy	secretar-y-ial
SED	Scottish Education Department
sen	senior
serv	serv-ant-ice-ing
*S Fraser	Simon Fraser Vancouver
*Sheff	Sheffield
SHHD	Scottish Home and Health Department
*Sing	Singapore
soc	soci-ety-al
sociol	sociolog-y-ist
solic	solicitor
spec	special-ist-isation
SRC	Science Research Council (previously DSIR)
s s	secondary school
SSEB	South of Scotland Electricity Board
stat	station
statist	statisti-cs-cian-cal
*Stir	Stirling
*S'ton	Southampton
*Strath	Strathclyde
struct	structur-es-al
stud.	stud-ent-ied-ies
subj	subject-s
subsid	subsidiary
superv	supervisor
supt	superintendent
*Sur	Surrey
surv	survey-or-ing
*Sus	Sussex
*Syd	Sydney
syst	system-s
TARO	Territorial Army Reserve of Officers
tech	techn-ical-ician-ology-ologist
TEFL	Teaching (er) of English as a Foreign Language
TESL	Teaching of English as a Second Language
tel	tele-phone-phonist-graph
telecom(m)	telecommunications
tv	television
temp	temporary
theol	theolog-y-ical
therap	therap-y-ist-eutics
*Tor	Toronto
trans	transport
trav	traveller
treas	treasurer
trg	training
*Trin	Trinidad
trop	tropical
trust.	trustee
TSB	Trustee Savings Bank
tut.	tutor-ial
UAE	United Arab Emirates
UCH	University College Hospital
*UCNW	University College of North Wales (Bangor)
*UCW	University College of Wales (Aberystwyth)
UKAEA	United Kingdom Atomic Energy Authority
*UM(W)IST	University of Manchester (Wales) Institute of Science & Technology
univ	university
URC	United Reformed Church
urol	urolog-y-ist
util	utilisation
Vanc	Vancouver
vd	venereal disease
vet.	veterinary
*Vic BC	Victoria British Columbia
virol	virolog-y-ist
vis	visual
VSO	Voluntary Service Overseas
WAIT	West Australian Institute of Technology
*Warw	Warwick
*Wash	Washington Seattle
WCC	World Council of Churches
WEA	Workers' Educational Organisation
*Well	Victoria Wellington NZ
WHO	World Health Organisation
*Wind	Windsor Ontario
*Wis	Wisconsin
*WOnt	Western Ontario
WRNS	Women's Royal Naval Service
WS	Writer to the Signet
YESTB	Youth Employment Service Training Board
zool	zoolog-y-ist

DEGREES ETC

Degrees, Diplomas, Titles and Memberships of professional bodies

An asterisk (*) in front of an Aberdeen University degree indicates a degree with honours.
c or **d** indicates 'commendation' or 'distinction'. These indications are given *only* for the Aberdeen University degree(s) shown in bold type in line with the graduate's name. Throughout the text degrees not followed by a university name in brackets are usually Aberdeen degrees.

ABPsS	Associate Member of the British Psychological Society
ABSI	Associate Member of the Building Societies Institute
ACA	Articled Chartered Accountant
ACCA	Association of Certified and Corporate Accountants
ACGI	Associate of the City and Guilds of London Institute
ACII	Associate of the Chartered Insurance Institute
ADMS	Assistant Director of Medical Services
ADPA	Advanced Diploma in Public Administration
AFIMA	Associate Fellow of the Institute of Mathematics and its Applications
AFRAeS	Associate Fellow of the Royal Aeronautical Society
AHA	Associate of the Health Service Administration
AInstBM	Associate Member of the Institute of Builders' Merchants
AICMA	Associate of the Institute of Cost and Management Accountants
AICSA	Associate Member of the Institute of Chartered Secretaries and Administrators
AIInfS	Associate of the Institute of Information Scientists
AIL	Associate of the Institute of Linguists
AILA	Associate of the Institute of Landscape Architects
AInstP	Associate of the Institute of Physics
AIRI	Associate of the Institute of the Rubber Industry
AIWSc	Associate of the Institute of Wood Science
ALA	Associate of the Library Association
AMBIM	Associate Member of the British Institute of Management
AMInst F	Associate Member of the Institute of Fuel
AMICE	Associate Member of the Institution of Civil Engineers
AMIChemE	Associate Member of the Institute of Chemical Engineers
AMIEE	Associate Member of the Institute of Electrical Engineers
AMIHE	Associate Member of the Institute of Highway Engineers
AM(A)IMM	Associate Member of the (Australian) Institute of Mining and Metallurgy
AMIMSW	Associate Member of the Institute of Medical Social Workers
AMIStructE	Associate Member of the Institute of Structural Engineers
AMIWE	Associate Member of the Institute of Water Engineers
AMIWPC	Associate Member of the Institute of Water Pollution Control
ARAChem Soc	Associate of the Royal Australian Chemical Society
ARCM	Associate of the Royal College of Music
ARCO	Associate of the Royal College of Organists
ARCST	Associate of the Royal College of Science and Technology
ARIBA	Associate of the Royal Institute of British Architects
ARIC	Associate of the Royal Institute of Chemists
ARICS	Associate of the Royal Institute of Chartered Surveyors
ARMCM	Associate of the Royal Manchester College of Music
ATCL	Associate of the Trinity College of Music London

ATPL	Civil Pilot's Licence
BASc	Bachelor of Applied Science
BCL	Bachelor of Civil Law
BD	Bachelor of Divinity
BDS	Bachelor of Dental Surgery
BEd	Bachelor of Education
BL	Bachelor of Law
BMedBiol	Bachelor of Medical Biology
BPharm	Bachelor of Pharmacy
BSA	Bachelor of Agricultural Science
BSc	Bachelor of Science
BSocSc	Bachelor of Social Science
BTh	Bachelor of Theology
BVMS	Bachelor of Veterinary Medicine and Surgery
BVS	Bachelor of Veterinary Surgery (or Science)
CA ca	Chartered Accountant
Cand Med	Graduate in Medicine (Oslo)
CASS	Certificate in Applied Social Studies
CBE	Commander of the Order of the British Empire
CChem	Chartered Chemist
CCFP	Certificate of the College of Family Physicians, Canada
CD	Canadian Forces Decoration
C Dip AF	Certified Diploma in Accounting and Finance
CE	Civil Engineer
CEng	Chartered Engineer
ChB	Bachelor of Surgery
ChM	Master of Surgery
CIH	Certificate in Industrial Health
CMG	Companion of St. Michael and St. George
CRP(S)(C)	Certificate Royal College of Physicians (Surgeons) (Canada)
CRK	Certificate of Religious Knowledge
CS	Clerk to the Signet
CStJ	Commander of The Order of St John of Jerusalem
DA	Diploma in Art; Diploma in Anaesthesia
DABOS	Diplomate of the American Board of Orthopaedic Surgeons
Dip Ag Ex	Diploma in Agricultural Extension
DABPysch & Neurol	Diplomate of the American Board of Psychiatry and Neurology
DABS	Diplomate of the American Board of Surgery
DADMS	Deputy Assistant Director Medical Services
DBE	Dame of the Order of the British Empire
DBEA	Diploma of the British Esperanto Association
DC	District Commissioner
DCH	Diploma in Child Health
DCMT	Diploma in Clinical Medicine of the Tropics
DCP	Diploma in Clinical Pathology
DD	Doctor of Divinity
Dip Ed	Diploma in Education
DEP	Diploma in Educational Psychology
Dip FM	Diploma in Farm Management
Dip FMBO	Diploma in Farm Management & Business Organisation
DIC	Diploma of the Imperial College
DIH	Diploma in Industrial Health
Dip H&TEng	Diploma in Highway and Traffic Engineering
DL	Doctor of Laws; Deputy Lieutenant
Dip LA	Diploma in Landscape Architecture
Dip LD	Diploma in Landscape Design
Dip Lib	Diploma in Librarianship
DMJ	Diploma in Medical Jurisprudence
DMR	Diploma in Medical Radiology
DMRD	Diploma in Medical Radiological Diagnosis
DMRT	Diploma in Medical Radio Therapy
Dip Man St	Diploma in Management Studies
DO	Diploma in Ophthalmology
DOMS	Diploma in Ophthalmic Medicine & Surgery

Dip OR	Diploma in Operational Research
DObstRCOG	Diploma in Obstetrics of the Royal College of Obstetricians and Gynaecologists
DPath	Diploma in Pathology
DPA	Diploma in Public Administration
DPE	Diploma in Physical Education
DPH	Diploma in Public Health
DPM	Diploma in Psychological Medicine
Dip Pers Man	Diploma in Personnel Management
Dip R Ed	Diploma in Religious Education
DRSS	Diploma of the Royal Statistical Society
DSc	Doctor of Science
Dip Sec St	Diploma in Secretarial Studies
Dip Soc Ad	Diploma in Social Administration
DSCHE	Diploma of the Scottish Council for Health Education
Dip Soc Med	Diploma in Social Medicine
DSS	*see* DRSS
Dip Soc St	Diploma in Social (Sociological) Studies
Dip Stat	Diploma in Statistics
DTA(Trin)	Diploma in Tropical Agriculture
Dip TCP	Diploma in Town and Country Planning
DTM&H	Diploma in Tropical Medicine & Hygiene
Dip TP	Diploma in Town Planning
DUP	Docteur de l'Université de Paris
DVM	Doctor of Veterinary Medicine
DVSM	Diploma in Veterinary State Medicine
EdB	Bachelor of Education (later changed to MEd)
ERD	Emergency Reserve Decoration (Army)
FAAAS	Fellow of the American Association for the Advancement of Science
FAAP	Fellowship of the American Academy of Paediatrics
FACA	Fellow of the American College of Anaesthetists
FACCP	Fellow of the American College of Chest Physicians
FACMA	Fellow of the Australian College of Medical Administrators
FACOG	Fellow of the American College of Obstetricians and Gynaecologists
FACP(R)(S)	Fellow of the American College of Physicians(Radiologists)(Surgeons)
FAI	Fellow of the Chartered Auctioneers and Estate Agents Institute
FAMA	Fellow of the Aerospace Medical Association
FANZCP	Fellow of the Australian & New Zealand College of Psychiatrists
FAPA	Fellow of the American Psychological Association
FAPsS	Fellow of the Australian Psychological Society
FAS	Fellow of the Association of Surgeons of Great Britain and Ireland
FASA	Fellow of the American Statistical Association
FASCE	Fellow of the American Society of Civil Engineers
FASCP	Fellow of the American Society of Clinical Pathologists
FBA	Fellow of the British Academy
FBCS	Fellow of the British Computer Society
FBOA	Fellow of the British Optical Association
FBPsS	Fellow of the British Psychological Society
FCCP	Fellow of the College of Chest Physicians
FCFP	Fellow of the College of Family Physicians, Canada
FCIPA	Fellow of the Chartered Institute of Patent Agents
FCIT	Fellow of the Chartered Institute of Transport
FCMA	Fellow of the Institute of Cost and Management Accountants
FCS	Fellow of the Chemical Society
FCS(WAf)	Fellow of the West African College of Surgeons
FCSP	Fellow of the Chartered Society of Physiotherapy
FDSRCS	Fellow in Dental Surgery, Royal College of Surgeons of England
FEIS	Fellow of the Educational Institute of Scotland
FFA	Fellow of the Faculty of Actuaries
FFARACS	Fellow of the Faculty of Anaesthetists, Royal Australian College of Surgeons
FFARCS	Fellow of the Faculty of Anaesthetists, Royal College of Surgeons of England
FFARCSI	Fellow of the Faculty of Anaesthetists, Royal College of Surgeons in Ireland
FFB	Fellow of the Faculty of Building
FFCM	Fellow of the Faculty of Community Medicine
FFR	Fellow of the Faculty of Radiologists
FGAC	Fellow of the Geological Association of Canada

FGS	Fellow of the Geological Society
FHA	Fellow of the Institute of Hospital Administrators
FIA	Fellow of the Institute of Actuaries
FIB	Fellow of the Institute of Banking
FIBiol	Fellow of the Institute of Biology
FICeram	Fellow of the Institute of Ceramics
FICE	Fellow of the Institute of Civil Engineers
FICS	Fellow of the International College of Surgeons
FIDP	Fellow of the Institute of Data Processing
FIE (Aust)	Fellow of the Institute of Engineers (Australia)
FIEE	Fellow of the Institute of Electrical Engineers
FIEEE	Fellow of the Institute of Electrical and Electronic Engineers of America
FIEI	Fellow of the Institute of Engineering Inspection
FIFor	Fellow of the Institute of Foresters (GB)
FIFST	Fellow of the U.K. Institute of Food Science and Technology
FIHE	Fellow of the Institute of Highway Engineers
FIL	Fellow of the Institute of Linguists
FIMA	Fellow of the Institute of Mathematics and its Applications
FIME	Fellow of the Institute of Mechanical Engineers
FIMM	Fellow of the Institute of Mining and Metallurgy
FIMunE	Fellow of the Institute of Municipal Engineers
FIOB	Fellow of the Institute of Builders
FInstP	Fellow of the Institute of Physics
FInstPet	Fellow of the Institute of Petroleum
FIPHE	Fellow of the Institute of Public Health Engineers
FIRI	Fellow of the Institution of the Rubber Industry
FIStructE	Fellow of the Institution of Structural Engineers
FIWE	Fellow of the Institution of Water Engineers
FIWSc	Fellow of the Institute of Wood Science
FLA	Fellow of the Library Association
FLAS	Fellow of the Chartered Land Agents' Society
FLS	Fellow of the Linnaean Society
FMFCM	Foundation Member Faculty of Community Medicine
FMSA	Fellow of the Mineralogical Society of America
FPS	Fellow of the Pharmaceutical Society
FPhysS	Fellow of the Physical Society
FRACGP	Fellow of the Royal Australian College of General Practitioners
FRACI	Fellow of the Royal Australian Chemical Institute
FRACP(S)	Fellow of the Royal Australian College of Physicians (Surgeons)
FRAI	Fellow of the Royal Anthropological Institute
FRAS	Fellow of the Royal Astronomical Society or Royal Asiatic Society
FRAeS	Fellow of the Royal Aeronautical Society
FRCGP	Fellow of the Royal College of General Practitioners
FRCO	Fellow of the Royal College of Organists
FRCOG	Fellow of the Royal College of Obstetricians and Gynaecologists
FRCPath	Fellow of the Royal College of Pathologists
FRCP(C)	Fellow of the Royal College of Physicians, London (Canada)
FRCPE	Fellow of the Royal College of Physicians, Edinburgh
FRCPSGlas	Fellow of the Royal College of Physicians and Surgeons, Glasgow
FRCPysch	Fellow of the Royal College of Psychiatrists
FRCR	Fellow of the Royal College of Radiologists
FRCS(C)	Fellow of the Royal College of Surgeons, London (Canada)
FRCSE	Fellow of the Royal College of Surgeons, Edinburgh
FRCVS	Fellow of the Royal College of Veterinary Surgeons
FRES	Fellow of the Royal Entomological Society
FRGS	Fellow of the Royal Geographical Society
FRIAS	Fellow of the Royal Incorporation of Architects of Scotland
FRHistS	Fellow of the Royal Historical Society
FRIBA	Fellow of the Royal Institute of British Architects
FRIC	Fellow of the Royal Institute of Chemistry
FRICS	Fellow of the Royal Institute of Chartered Surveyors
FRIPHH	Fellow of the Royal Institute of Public Health and Hygiene
FRLS	Fellow of the Royal Literary Society
FRMS	Fellow of the Royal Microscopical Society
FRMetS	Fellow of the Royal Meteorological Society

FRS(C)	Fellow of the Royal Society (Canada)
FRSA	Fellow of the Royal Society of Arts
FRSE	Fellow of the Royal Society of Edinburgh
FRSGS	Fellow of the Royal Scottish Geographical Society
FRSH	Fellow of the Royal Society for the Promotion of Health
FRSM	Fellow of the Royal Society of Medicine
FRSS	Fellow of the Royal Statistical Society
FRSTM&H	Fellow of the Royal Society of Tropical Medicine and Hygiene
FSAScot	Fellow of the Society of Antiquaries, Scotland
FSAO	Fellow of the Scottish Association of Opticians
FSCA	Fellow of the Society of Company and Commercial Accountants
FSS	*see* FRSS
Grad BIM	Graduate British Institute of Management
Grad IEE	Graduate Institute of Electrical Engineers
Grad MechE	Graduate Institute of Mechanical Engineers
Grad Inst P	Graduate Institute of Physics
GMIPM	Graduate Member Institute of Personnel Management
Grad RIC	Graduate Royal Institute of Chemistry
idc	on staff Imperial Defence College
jssc	Joint Services Staff Course
LCP	Licentiate of the College of Preceptors
LDS	Licentiate in Dental Surgery
L-ès-L	Licencié-ès-lettres
LGSM	Licentiate Guildhall School of Music and Drama
LHA	Licentiate of the Institute of Health Service Administrators
LLA	Lady Literate in Arts
LL B	Bachelor of Laws
LLCM	Licentiate London College of Music
LLCO	Licentiate London College of Osteopathy
LL D	Doctor of Laws
LL M	Master of Laws
LM	Licentiate in Midwifery
LMCC	Licentiate of the Medical Council of Canada
LRAM	Licentiate Royal Academy of Music
LRCP	Licentiate of the Royal College of Physicians, England
LRCP(S)E	Licentiate of the Royal College of Physicians(Surgeons) Edinburgh
LTCL	Licentiate Trinity College of Music London
LTh	Licence in Theology
MA	Master of Arts
MAAPG	Member of the Association of American Petroleum Geologists
MANZCP	Member of the Australian & New Zealand College of Psychiatrists (Practitioners)
MAPLE	Member of the Association of Public Lighting Engineers
MASCE	Member of the American Society of Civil Engineers
MB	Bachelor of Medicine
MBA	Master of Business Administration
MBCS	Member of the British Computer Society
MBE	Member of the Order of the British Empire
MBIM	Member of the British Institute of Management
MBKS	Member of the British Kinematograph Sound & Television Society
MBNES	Member of the British Nuclear Energy Society
MBPS	Member of the British Psychoanalytical Society
MCEA	Member of the Canadian Electrical Association
MCFP	Member of the College of Family Physicians, Canada
MCIMM	Member of the Canadian Institute of Mining & Metallurgy
MCIT	Member of The Chartered Institute of Transport
MCPS	Member of the College of Physicians and Surgeons
MCRA	Member of the College of Radiologists, Australia
MCSP	Member of the Chartered Society of Physiotherapy
MD	Doctor of Medicine
MEd	Master of Education
MEIC	Member of the Engineering Institute of Canada
MF	Master of Forestry
MFCM	Member of the Faculty of Community Medicine
MFCP	Member of the Faculty of Community Physicians
MFHom	Member of the Faculty of Homoeopathy

MFO	Member of the Faculty of Ophthalmologists
MIA	Master of International Affairs (U.S.)
MIBiol	Member of the Institute of Biology
MICA	Member of the Institute of Chartered Accountants
MICE	Member of the Institution of Civil Engineers
MIEA	Member of the Institute of Engineering of Australia
MIEE	Member of the Institution of Electrical Engineers
MIERE	Member of the Institution of Electronic & Radio Engineers
MIFor (GB)	Member of the Institute of Foresters (GB)
MIH	Member of the Institute of Hygiene
MIHE	Member of the Institution of Highway Engineers
MIHVE	Member of the Institution of Heating and Ventilating Engineers
MILGA	Member of the Institute of Local Government Administrators
MILocoE	Member of the Institution of Locomotive Engineers
MIM	Member of Institute of Marketing
MInstMC	Member of the Institute of Measurement & Control
MIMechE	Member of the Institution of Mechanical Engineers
MIMH	Member of the Institute of Material Handling
MIMM	Member of the Institute of Mining & Metallurgy
MIMSW	Member of the Institution of Medical Social Workers
MIMunE	Member of the Institution of Municipal Engineers
MInstP	Member of the Institute of Physics
MIPHE	Member of the Institution of Public Health Engineers
MIPlantE	Member of the Institution of Plant Engineers
MIPM	Member of the Institute of Personnel Management
MIPR	Member of the Institute of Public Relations
MIQ	Member of the Institute of Quarrying
MInstR	Member of the Institute of Refrigeration
MIRSE	Member of the Institute of Railway Signal Engineers
MIStructE	Member of the Institute of Structural Engineers
MITAA	Member of the International Transactional Analysis Association
MIWES	Member of the Institution of Water Engineers and Scientists
MIWPC	Member of the Institute of Water Pollution Control
MIWSP	Member of the Institute of Works Study Practitioners
M Jur	Master of Jurisprudence
M Litt	Master of Letters
MMSA	Master of the Midwifery Society of Apothecaries
MNZIE	Member of the New Zealand Institute of Engineers
MPH	Master of Public Health (Yale)
MPS	Member of the Pharmaceutical Society
MRACGP	Member of the Royal Australian College of General Practitioners
MRCGP	Member of the Royal College of General Practitioners
MRCM	Member of the Royal College of Medicine
MRCOG	Member of the Royal College of Obstetricians & Gynaecologists
MRCP	Member of the Royal College of Physicians
MRCPE	Member of the Royal College of Physicians, Edinburgh
MRCPGlas	Member of the Royal College of Physicians & Surgeons, Glasgow
MRCPath	Member of the Royal College of Pathologists
MRCPsych	Member of the Royal College of Psychiatrists
MRCS	Member of the Royal College of Surgeons of England
MRCSE	Member of the Royal College of Surgeons, Edinburgh
MRCVS	Member of the Royal College of Veterinary Surgeons
MRI	Member of the Royal Institution
MRIC	Member of the Royal Institute of Chemistry
MRSForS	Member of the Royal Scottish Forestry Society
MRSH	Member of the Royal Society for the Promotion of Health
MRTPI	Member of the Royal Town Planning Institute
MRWEA	Member of the Royal West of England Academy
MS	Master of Surgery (of Science(USA))
MSA	Master of Science Agriculture
MSc	Master of Science
M Soc Pet Eng AIM & Mech Eng	Member of the Society of Petroleum Engineers of the American Institute of Mining and Mechanical Engineers
MSocW	Master of Social Work
MTAI	Member of the Institute of Travel Agents

MTh	Master of Theology
MVO	Member of the Victorian Order
MVSc	Master of Veterinary Science
MWD	Ministry of Works Department (NZ)
NDA(D)	National Diploma in Agriculture(Dairying)
NP	Notary Public
OBE	Officer of the Order of the British Empire
OStJ	Officer of the Order of St. John of Jerusalem
psc	Graduate of Staff College
PhD	Doctor of Philosophy
QHP(S)	Queen's Honorary Physician (Surgeon)
RD or VRD	Reserve Decoration Royal Navy
RGN	Registered General Nurse
RMN	Royal Mental Nurse
RSA	Royal Society of Arts
RSCN	Registered Sick Children's Nurse
SCM	State Certificated Midwife
SRN	State Registered Nurse
SSC	Solicitor before the Supreme Court(Scotland)
STB(M)	Bachelor (Master) of Sacred Theology
TD	Territorial Efficiency Decoration
ThM	Master of Theology

SECTION I

ROLL OF GRADUATES 1956–1970

ABBEY Heather Diane MA 1966
m Bulmer

ABBOTT Ann Pringle *MA 1967
d of Thomas P. A. CA and Christina Reid civ serv; b Perth 2.5.45
Dip Lib (Lond) 1969
lib: arch. res unit Edin univ 1969–72, Roskilde univ Denmark 1973–74; Danish min of environment from 1974
m Aber 9.6.72 Graham D. Caie MA 1968 *qv*

ABBOTT David Reid *BSc(eng) 1965
s of Thomas P. A. CA and Christina Reid civ serv; b Edin 26.11.42
MICE 1973
asst eng Scott Wilson Kirkpatrick & Ptnrs: Lond 1965–69, Brunei 1969–72, Lond 1972–74; res eng Crouch & Hogg Inv from 1974

ABBOTT Derek Graham Cameron *MA 1968

ABBOTT Elizabeth Margaret *MA 1962
ward of Elizabeth R. A.; b Gloucester 29.5.41
teacher Stirling 1963–72
m Lossiemouth 12.4.69 Norman A. Black site eng s of Albert Z. B. Stirling

ABBOTT John Granville *BSc(agr) 1969
s of Kenneth G. A. civ serv MoH and Margery Brakell; b Southport 9.8.45
sen res off. I, II Canberra 1969–73; Gaberone Botswana: market. off. (agr)/res consult. dev 1973–78; educ plan. Maseru Lesotho from 1978
marr diss

ABBOTT Susan *MA 1969 Dip Ed 1970
d of Thomas P. A. CA and Christina Reid civ serv; b Buckie 7.5.47
teacher: Cults acad 1970–73, Golspie h s from 1973
m Inv 27.7.73 Norman J. D. Wright MA 1969 *qv*

ABDELNOUR Hassan Osman BSc(for) 1967
s of Osman Abdelnour Adam and Zeinab Mohamed Ahmed; b Abu Usher Sudan 1.1.44
MSc(Khart) 1972
utilization off. for. dept Khartoum 1967–72; vice-prin Forest Rangers' coll Soba Sudan from 1972
m Aber 3.2.65 Shane Moscati MA 1974 *qv*

ABDEL-TAWAB Gamal El Dín Mohamed PhD 1957
BSc(Cairo)

ABDEL-WAHED Joseph *MA 1959

ABDULAZIZ Abdullah *MA 1963

ABDULAZIZ Mohammad Annuar Bin BSc(for) 1960

ABDULMANAN Othman Bin BSc(for) 1961

ABEL George BSc 1965
s of George A. gas man. and Rose A. McRobb; b Inverurie 13.8.42
jun tech off. inst of cancer res Lond from 1966

ABEL Joyce Audrey Katherine MB ChB 1964

ABEL Patricia Margaret MA 1969
d of John W. M. A. tel eng and Margaret B. Cooper; b Aber 9.12.47
teacher Engl/hist Aber: Kaimhill s s 1970–71, Kincorth acad 1971–73, Harlaw acad from 1974
m Aber 13.4.73 Arthur V. Duncan tech off. PO telephones s of Lawrence D. Aber

ABEL Scott Adam BSc(eng) 1964

ABELL Trevor Michael Barry BSc(for) 1968
s of Kenneth W. A. HM insp taxes and Patricia E. Turner; b Leicester 10.8.46
stud. ODM Oxon 1968–69; asst conserv for. Kitwe Zambia 1969–75; scient off. land res div (for.) Tolworth from 1976
m Wigtown 3.7.71 Helen F. B. McKay BSc 1970 *qv*

ABERDEIN James Douglas BSc(agr) 1959
s of James A. radiographer and Christina Pope; b Aber 25.2.38
flying off. RAF 1959–63; helicopter pilot Bristow's England, Pers Gulf 1963–65; farm. New Deer 1965–69; teacher: Monquhitter 1966–68, Aboyne acad 1968–72; head Lumphanan p s 1972–75
m Aber 17.10.64 Ethel Jamieson MA 1961 *qv*

ABERDEIN John Henry *MA 1970
s of James M. A. lect in elect. installation and Marion Smith shorthand typist; b Aber 23.3.46
teacher Fife from 1972
m Kirkcaldy 10.3.73 Penelope A. Shircore drama teacher d of Winston S. Croydon

ABERNETHY Douglas Grieve LLB 1970
s of Douglas G. A. mech and Agnes B. Grieve; b Aber 27.10.48
law app Edin 1970–72; Glasg: law asst 1972–75, ptnr in law firm from 1975
m Aber 4.8.73 Pamela Green MB ChB 1974 med pract d of Raymond G. Aber

ABOU AKKADA Abdelkadir Rashid PhD 1961
BSc(agr) MSc(Alex)

ABOUL-KHAIR Sidky Abdallah PhD 1964
MB ChB DCH(Alex)

ABUSAQ Muhammad Osman *MA 1965
BA(Khart) PhD(Edin) 1971
s of Osman A. and Aishah; b Sudan 20.11.36
teacher Sudan 1961–62; lect teacher trg coll Khart 1965; lect politics univ Khart 1965–74; secy for thought Sudanese Socialist Union from 1974
m Khart 12.8.64 Safia M. Arabi BA(Khart) head community dev Khartoum d of Muhammad A.

ACQUAYE David Kpakpoe PhD 1960
s of Samuel A. A. carpenter and Madam Kordey Annan trader; b Accra 14.9.28
BSc(agr)(Mich)
res off. cocoa res inst Tafo Ghana 1960–66; univ of Ghana: sen lect 1966, acting head dept of crop sc 1969, dean fac of agr from 1972
m 23.12.62 Eugenia Quarty-Papifio sen tel superv d of Samuel Q.-P. Kumasi Ghana

ACRES Bryan Douglas MSc 1963
s of Ian S. A. MB BS(Lond) g p and Eileen O. L. Bunday secy/missionary; b Bolobo Zaïre 9.5.37
BA(Lond) 1961
contr with Nigerian govt Ibadan 1964–66; sen scient off. Sandakan Sabah 1967–72; with ODM Sana'a Yemen 1974–76
m Lond 28.9.63 Jannice M. Goode BSc(Lond) teacher d of Alfred G. BSc(eng)(Birm) Sunbury-on-Thames

ADAM Alasdair Hugh Macqueen LLB 1969
s of Robert J. A. MA(Oxon) univ prof and Frances

M. A. Macqueen; b Glasg 15.11.47
WS 1971
law app Edin 1969–71; solic: Kirkcaldy 1971–74, Alloa and Alvah from 1975
m Edin 17.3.73 Judith A. Steele RGN d of John D. T. S. MB ChB(Edin) Dumfries

ADAM Albert William *MA 1970
s of Keith C. R. A. BR signalman and Elizabeth Hodgkinson GPO tel; b Alloa 19.11.48
trainee Ford Motor Co Warley and Richardson-Merrell Lond 1970; trainee Conserv party ag 1972–73; ag for Stirlingsh group from 1972
m Edin 16.7.71 Jennifer M. Saxby hotel man. trainee d of George K. B. S. Hexham

ADAM Brian James *BSc 1970

ADAM Hazel May *MA 1966
d of Peter A. foreman and Violet Watt; b Aber 27.11.42
teacher Fr Ashford s Kent 1967–71; inf teacher various schools Ashford 1971–72
m Aber 12.8.67 Stuart G. McRae BSc 1965 *qv*

ADAM Helen Margaret MB ChB 1967
m Cason

ADAM John MA 1966
s of John A. BR plant maintenance eng and Georgina Keddie; b Perth 2.6.44
teacher Engl/mod stud. Hawick h s 1967–70; head Engl dept Breckenbeds j h s Gateshead 1970–71; sen Engl master Blaydon c s Co Durham 1971–73; dep head Brumby c s Scunthorpe from 1973
m Aber 5.9.66 Lorna R. Cheyne MA 1966 *qv*

ADAM John Alexander *MA 1962

ADAM Kirsten *MA 1959
d of Archie D. A. MA 1929 *qv*(III) and Muriel M. Cheyne MA(Edin) teacher; b Edin 22.7.37
Cert Ed(Leeds) 1960
teacher mus: Datchet 1960–63, Inverurie acad 1963–65; prin mus Braehead s Buckhaven 1965–70; Fife: asst organis mus 1970–74, organis arts from 1974

ADAM Malcolm MB ChB 1958

ADAM Margaret Eleanor *MA 1961 PhD 1967
d of Hyacinth A. G. A. chief p o RN and Eleanor M. E. Fancourt secy; b Portsmouth 11.8.39
teacher mod lang Zurich 1961–64; temp asst lect: St Michael's coll Toronto 1964–65, Magee univ coll Londonderry 1967–68; lect tech coll Londonderry 1969–74, head dept arts/soc stud. from 1974
m Aber 7.8.61 Walter Baumann DPhil(Zür) sen lect Ger s of Jakob M. B. Switzerland

ADAM-SMITH Margaret Elphinston MA 1968
(conferred for long service of exceptional merit)
d of George A. S. MA(Edin) C of S min, prof Hebrew, Principal & Vice-Chancellor Aberd 1909–35 and Alice L. Buchanan; b Old Aber 3.9.10
advis to women stud. Aberd 1946–75
m Aber 7.8.34 Ian A. Clarke (*d* 1939) MA 1911 *qv*

ADAMS Angela Clare PhD 1970
d of William E. A. MB ChB prof anat and med dean and Ena N. Mathewson typist; b Leeds 27.11.40
BSc(Otago) 1961
BECC res fell. Christchurch NZ 1961–63; res worker Euratom Institut für Strahlensforschung Freiburg i Br. Germany 1964–67
m Athens 28.3.71 Kosmas A. Kiossoglou MB ChB(Athens) assoc prof paediat s of Anastasios K. Bourdourion Asia Minor

ADAMS Christopher John *BSc(eng) 1968

ADAMS Frederick George MB ChB 1961
s of Lawrence A. and Catherine M. M. McPherson fish curer; b Aber 24.9.38
DMRD 1968 (Lond) FRCR 1970
res hosp posts Aber 1961–63; g p Ilkeston 1964–66; trainee radiol Sheffield 1966–70; consult. radiol Western I Glasg from 1971
m Aber 4.10.63 Allison E. Richardson d of Joseph B. R.

ADAMS James Alexander *BSc 1960
s of William A. farm. and Jessie Chapman; b New Aberdour 27.10.37
marine lab Torry Aber: scient off. 1960–66, sen 1966–72, prin from 1972
m Aber 16.7.65 Elizabeth M. Elliot MA 1961 *qv*

ADAMS James Thomas Ward ᵈLL B 1967 *1968
s of William S. A. MA(Glas) solic and Maisie T. Ward; b Glasg 30.11.46
Hawker Siddeley Aviation: asst to leg. man. 1968–69, sen contr off. 1969–71, asst contr man. from 1971
m Sanderstead 16.1.71 Rosemary C. Baker LL B 1968 *qv*

ADAMS John *BSc(agr) 1970
s of William A. BSc(agr) 1941 *qv* and Annie R. Pirie MA 1941 *qv*; b Aber 16.7.47
auditor Ford Motor Co Brentwood from 1970
m Peterculter 30.10.71 Rosemary Henderson teacher dom sc d of James H. St Cyrus

ADAMS John Mervyn *BSc(agr) 1969
s of George M. A. comp dir and Betty C. Davies loc govt employee; b Walsall 14.4.46
MSc(Lond) 1970 DIC 1970 FRES(Lond) 1970
attached Oxfam grain storage proj as entomologist Limbe 1971–72; sc off. grain storage Slough 1972–73; proj leader ODA econ of storage proj Lusaka 1973–74; FAO consult. Pakistan 1975; storage losses spec. ODM from 1976

ADAMS Roy Douglas *BSc(for) 1966
s of Ronald S. W. A. and Edna W. Elton; b Wimbledon 7.3.44
MF(Vanc) 1969; PhD(Wash) 1974
univ instruct. Moscow Idaho 1969–71; stud. Washington 1971–76; wood scient Houghton Mich from 1975
m Aber 12.7.66 Fiona B. Clark MCSP physioth d of Thomas M. C. BSc(Glas) Aber

ADAMS William Arthur *MA 1970

ADAMSON Helen Clark *MA 1960

ADAN George Edward MB ChB 1957
s of Edward A. carpenter and Isabella F. Lumsden; b Aber 14.11.32
h o City hosp, Woodend hosp Aber 1957–58; army nat serv Cyprus, Malta 1958–60; g p Cruden Bay 1960–62, Spennymoor from 1962
m Blechingley 17.9.60 Patricia M. Murray SRN lieut QARANC d of Thomas A. M. Blechingley

ADATIA Manharlal Harjivandas MSc 1965
BSc(Bom)

ADDISON Barbara *MA 1967
m Bancroft

ADDISON Eileen Patricia MA 1964

ADDISON Jack Thomson MA 1957
s of John T. A. comp owner and Violet Thomson; b Cullen 22.5.32
Dip BA(Strath) 1968
Glasg: admin asst 1958–60; factory man. 1960–62; gen man. 1962–66; man. dir from 1968

ADDISON James Lochore *MA 1969
s of John A. man. and Elizabeth A. Lochore; b Aber 27.7.47
ergonomist Pilkington Bros St Helens 1969–70; temp posts 1971–72; teacher Glasg 1973–74; exec off. DHSS Glasg from 1974
m Glasg 7.4.73 Judith M. Deacon lib d of David G. D. Southampton

ADDISON John Douglas *BSc(eng) 1970
s of Douglas J. A. boilermaker/welder and Gladys I. Stuart; b Wartle 20.1.48
site eng Taylor Woodrow Construct. Lond 1970–73; des eng: Kinnear & Gordon 1973–74, R. H. Cuthbertson & Ptnrs Edin 1974–76, Steensen, Varming, Mulcahy & Ptnrs from 1976
m Inverurie 6.11.71 Moira Ledingham staff nurse d of Alfred F. L. Inverurie

ADDISON Marcus Leopold Gabriel MB ChB 1960

ADDISON Margaret Ogilvie MA 1964
d of John W. A. fisherman and Jeannie Hadden; b Inv 19.12.44
teacher: Fr/Ger Keith g s 1965–73, prin guid from 1973

ADDISON Violet Thomson MB ChB 1957
m Coutts

ADDISON William George BSc(agr) 1957
s of Alexander A. master baker and Mary Addison; b Portknockie 12.9.35
Dip Agr(Cantab) 1958 DTA(Trinidad) 1959
Nyasaland: agr off. Rumpi 1959–62, soil conserv off. Blantyre 1962–64; agr advis Elgin 1964–73; spec advis crop husb NOSCA Aber from 1973
m Aber 12.6.59 Dorothy C. M. Stewart bus. asst d of John H. S. Stonehaven

ADDO Stephen BSc(for) 1959

ADEN Sandra MA 1967
m Wilson

ADEOYE Isaac Adebayo BSc(for) 1966
s of Emanuel A. A. ch worker and Julianah Adepate trader; b Ibadan 11.9.37
CPA(Unife) 1974
sen asst conserv for. Ibadan, Oyo state, Nigeria from 1966
m Dun 11.4.63 Odunola O. Mipon nurse d of Adebola M. Lagos

ADEY Gillian Dalton MB ChB 1968
b Hull 27.8.44
FFARCS 1975
h o Aber 1968–69; sen h o Aber 1969–71; regist anaest Aber 1971–75; res fell. biochem Aberd from 1975
m Kirkby Lonsdale 1973 Norman B. Bennett MB ChB 1963 *qv*

ADEYEMI Benjamin Omotunde *BSc(eng) 1958

ADOMAKOH Christian Charles MB ChB 1960
s of John Y. A. farm. and Rebecca Onemeng; b Ghana 14.1.31
DPM 1964 Dip Psych(Edin) 1965 MRCP(Edin) 1965 MRCPsych 1972
m o Accra 1961–71; sen lect med s Accra from 1971
m Accra 30.6.62 Victoria K. B. Davies nutrit/teacher d of James B. D. Accra

ADU Samuel Victor *BSc 1958 PhD 1968
b Abebifi Ghana 4.7.23
Ghana: scient off. min of agr 1959–63; inst soil res: res off. 1963–69, sen res off. 1969–74, chief res off. from 1974
m Kumasi Ghana 1964 Victoria R. Larbi home sc tut.

AETHERIS Phoebus Sophroniou MB ChB 1962

AFFLECK Georgina Stoddart BEd 1969
d of George A. eng and Jean Blaikie; b Edin 15.1.42
teacher Engl Lasswade 1969–70, Glasg 1970–74, Fort William from 1974
m Oban 14.6.74 Victor J. Scott elect eng s of Douglas S. Glasg

AGBEKO Bertha Perpetua Bake BSc 1966

AGBIM Charles Chuba *BSc(eng) 1958
s of Felix O. A. civ serv and Grace A. Ilodigwe; b Nimo Nigeria 6.10.34
DIC(Lond) 1959 PhD(Lond) 1961
site eng Tolworth Lond; Nigeria: exec eng min of works Lagos 1963–64, lect univ of Lagos 1964–65, prin consult. Agbim & Ptnrs (consult. eng) Lagos, Enugu, Kaduna, Calabar from 1965
m Lond –.12.60 Ukamaka Okeke d of A. O. Arondizogu Nigeria

AGBLE Theodore Komla MB ChB 1959
s of Erastus L. A. storekeeper and Kate Ama Apo; b Hohoe Ghana 21.7.31
BSc(Lond) 1954 MRCOG 1965 FCS(W. Af) 1974
m o Ghana 1960–62; sen h o obst/gyn: Southern gen hosp Glasg 1963–64, St James hosp Leeds 1964–65; Kumasi Ghana: sen m o 1965–70, spec gyn from 1970
m Leeds 1.10.65 Yolande Garraway nurse/midwife

AGERBAK Gullan Susanne BSc 1966
d of Harry E. A. counsellor to Danish Embassy Lond and Gudrun Rysgaard; b Stockholm 20.7.43
res asst (embryology) agr res council Edin 1966–67; microbiol genetics (MRC) Lond 1967–68; Novo pharm div, res inst Bagsvaerd Denmark 1968–73; scient prod. man. from 1973

AGNEW John McMurray MA 1969
s of James McG. A. ploughman and Mary C. McMurray; b Stranraer 19.3.48
teacher maths: Stranraer acad 1970–72, St George's s Vanc 1972–74, Stranraer acad 1974–75, Nanaimo B.C. 1975–76, Upper Canada Coll from 1976
m Vanc 6.7.74 Sharon Maclean

AH-SEE Antoine Kim-nen MB ChB 1965 ChM 1975
s of Wong A. shopkeeper and Sin Y. Sew; b Mauritius 1.6.38
FRCS(Edin) 1970

h o Aber 1965–66; sen h o: Sidcup 1966–67, Bournemouth 1967–68; sen h o and regist Aber 1968–70; res fell. Uppsala Sweden 1970–71; regist Aber 1971–72; lect surg Aberd 1972–75; res fell. RN physiol lab Alverstoke 1975–77; sen lect surg Aberd/consult. ARI from 1977
m Aber 22.6.63 Catherine R. Matheson MA 1964 *qv*

AHMED Abul Hasan Moinuddin MSc 1967 PhD 1969
BSc(Calc) MSc(agr)(West Bengal)

AHMED Fouad BSc(for) 1959

AHMED Shammim Jehangir PhD 1968
BSc MSc(Dacca)

AHMED Siddik Mohamed Shaheen MSc 1970
BSc(Khart)

AHMED Tawfig Hashim MSc 1964
s of Hashim A. acct and Zahra A. Rahman; b Omdurman 5.3.33
agr econ Khartoum 1964–67; agr econ advis Tripoli 1967–71; asst under-secy for plan., min of agr Khartoum 1971–74, dir dept of plan. from 1974
m Omdurman 28.3.60 Fathia el Baghir d of El Baghir Admed Ibrahim Omdurman

AHMED Yehia Youssef PhD 1964
MB(Cairo) BSc(Lond)

AIDLEY Susan Mary *BSc 1965

AIKEN Laura Jane MA 1963 *1965
d of Agnes H. Aiken secy; b Bucksburn 10.3.43
Dip Ed(Lond)
teacher: Fort George Quebec 1966–68, Punnichy Sask 1968–71; peripatetic remed teacher Kincardine 1971–72; educ psych Aber and Kincardine 1972–73
m Burlington Vermont USA 17.12.73 David D. Blanchard BSc(Lehigh univ) headmaster s of Roger W. B. BA (Boston) NY USA

AIKEN Marigold Helen BSc 1961
m Hall

AIKEN William Alexander BSc(agr) 1967
s of Alexander F. A. farm. and Ella Scott; b Aber 14.3.45
Dip in Crop Protection (Edin) 1968
asst insp (GD) DAFS Oban from 1968
m Aber 23.8.68 Anne Davidson d of Hugh D. Lyne of Skene

AIKMAN David Powrie *BSc 1961
s of Thomas S. A. BCom 1928 *qv*; b Aber 14.5.39
PhD (E Ang)
lect Univ of E Ang from 1965
m Aber 3.10.62 Margaret R. Morrice clerkess/typist d of Forbes M. M. M. Footdee

AIKMAN Peter Ramsay BSc 1966
s of Thomson S. A. BCom 1928 *qv*; b Aber 18.4.43
prod. asst Erith 1966–68; Wrexham: prod. supt materials controller from 1969
m Huntly 14.7.66 Cathleen A. Munro MA 1964 *qv*

AIRD Iain Campbell *MA 1968

AITKEN Alistair James MA 1965
s of Walter J. A. and Isabella Black; b Fraserburgh 27.5.43
teacher Fr/Ger AGS 1966–69; prin teacher Powis acad from 1969
m Aber 4.7.70 Yvonne M. Mutch teacher d of Alexander F. M. Aber

AITKEN Gordon Brown *BSc 1967 PhD 1970
s of Archibald B. A. man. and Dorothy A. Fraser; b Aber 15.3.45
ARIC 1970
res fellow: univ of Delaware 1970–71, Strath 1971–72; trained as teacher Aber 1972–73; lect chem univ Sains Malaysia from 1973

AITKEN Gordon Graham MB ChB 1967
m Doreen L. Rettie MB ChB 1965 *qv*

AITKEN James Meff MA 1967

AITKEN Joseph Caldwell MA 1970
(conferred for long service of exceptional merit)
provisor univ union Aberd from 1950; retd 1970
d Aber 2.8.74

AITKEN Robin Elliot Guild MB ChB 1963
s of Andrew A. civ eng and Isabella L. G. Guild teacher; b Edin 7.11.39
h o ARI, Inv RI 1963–64; regt m o 23rd Parachute Field Ambulance, Aldershot, Bahrain, Adelaide 1964–67; army health spec (major), York and Germany 1968–72; asst sen m o NE reg hosp board 1972–74; spec commun med Grampian health board from 1974
m Lond 26.7.69 Gillian A. Odell SRN d of Brig Benjamin A. O. Stanmore

AKALOO Nuvinchund MA 1964
s of Ramnarain A. prop. and Sonia Beeharry; b Vacoas 3.10.37
educ off. Mauritius 1964–66; diplomatic off. freelance radio and tv broadcaster and interviewer in Engl with Mauritius Broadcasting Corporation from 1966; chief of protocol min of external affairs (Mauritius) from 1973
m Mauritius 11.2.66 Nalini D. Jhowry comp man. d of Ramroop J. Mauritius

AKHIDIME Samuel Olatunde *BSc(eng) 1956

AKINKUGBE Ajibayo Mb ChB 1957
s of E. A. A. trader and Victoria O. Akinnagbe; b Ondo 3.2.29
MRCOG 1965 FMCOG(Nigeria) 1971
m o W. Nigeria 1958–62; regist mat. hosp Aber 1962–66; consult. obst/gyn 1966-69; sen consult. & prin m o Ile-Ife hosp Nigeria 1969–74; assoc prof coll of med Lagos from 1974
m Lagos 15.12.60 Obafunke Femi-Pearse barrister d of J. T. F.-P. MB ChB(Edin) Lagos

AKPOM Cyril Amechi Odiakosah MB ChB 1963

AL-AWADI Abdul Raman Abdulla MB ChB 1963
s of Abdullah M. H. Al.-A. bus. man. and Mariam; b Kuwait 18.12.36
BSc(Beirut) 1958 DTM&H(Harv) 1965 FRCP(Dub) 1978 hon PhD(Si Chang Bon Korea) 1977
MoH Kuwait: h o, regist, member reporter of plan. comm 1963–69; asst dir, dir preventive serv 1969–75; min of health from 1975
m Kuwait 14.8.69 Sadika A. Al-wadi MD(Cairo) paediat d of Ali Al-A.

ALBERT Michael *MA 1970

ALCOCK John Wright BSc(for) 1956
s of Ralph T. A. comp dir and Edith D. Wright; b Morecambe 28.12.34

nat serv R.E.; trainee for. estates Lowther Castle Penrith; Queensland for. comm 1960
m Brisbane 1.10.66 Carole Baldwin d of Alexander B. Brisbane

ALCOCK Stephen Robert MB ChB 1969
s of Leonard G. A. eng and Marjorie I. Davis; b Sutton Coldfield 24.6.45
h o ARI 1969–70; lect dept bact Aberd from 1970
m Tighnabruiach 30.6.72 Jean M. D. Paterson MA 1969 *qv*

ALDER Clive Philip *BSc 1970
s of Philip A. civ serv and Joan Murphy; b Romford 15.7.48
teacher chem Peebles h s from 1971
m Aber 31.7.71 Kathleen S. Paton BEd 1969 *qv*

ALEXANDER Anita June BSc 1963
d of Alfred A. farm. and Annie Rennie asst matron; b Marykirk Laurencekirk 11.6.42
teacher biol Telford coll of f e Edin 1964–72, 1973–75
m Marykirk 26.8.73 William B. Hayton detective s of James B. H. Wishaw

ALEXANDER Anne Elizabeth BSc 1960
m Normand

ALEXANDER Charlotte Mary Margaret MA 1958

ALEXANDER Christine Moira MA 1966
d of John T. A. OBE MA(Edin) comp dir and Moira G. Macdougall BSocSc(Edin); b Lanark 21.3.46
market res investigator Procter & Gamble Lond 1966–68; res asst Procter & Gamble (Scandinavia) Lond 1968–69; market res exec: L'Oreal Lond 1969–74, CPC (UK) Ltd 1974–76
m –.3.76 Ian A. Walker MA (St And)

ALEXANDER Dianne Marion *LLB 1970
d of Alfred H. A. butcher and Margaret L. Sproul secy; b Aber 15.1.47
law app Edin 1970–72; sen conveyancing asst private WS firm Edin 1972–75; solic, sen solic off. of Solic to Secy of State for Scotland Edin from 1975
m Edin 18.10.76 Maurice M. Howieson man. dir eng comp s of James S. H. Broxburn

ALEXANDER Donald Gerald *MA 1962

ALEXANDER Duncan Kennedy *BSc 1960
s of John D. A. bank off. and Isabella D. Kennedy shorthand typist; b Banchory 15.3.38
teacher sc Mackie acad Stonehaven 1961–66; prin sc Lochaber h s Fort William 1966–69; prin chem Mackie acad 1969–73; asst rector Elgin acad from 1973

ALEXANDER Elizabeth Margaret MA 1963
d of John D. A. bank acct and Isabella D. Kennedy secy; b Banchory 5.9.42
teacher Fr/Ger Knox acad Haddington 1964–68; tut./teacher Inv from 1969
m Aber 14.7.67 Neil A. Campbell MA 1967 *qv*

ALEXANDER Eric Richardson MB ChB 1957 MD 1973
s of James A. farm worker and Annie B. Smith reg nurse; b Aber 31.3.33
DPM(Lond) 1969 MRCPsych 1972
h o Aber 1957–58; army Germany 1958–60; asst lect Dun 1960–63; army Germany 1963–67; regist Dumfries 1967–70; sen regist Aber 1970–74, consult. Aber from 1974

m Orkney 15.1.60 Elizabeth I. S. Gray reg nurse d of Robert G. Orkney

ALEXANDER George BSc 1963
s of George A. fisherman and Alexina C. Lamb; b Peterhead 6.6.42
pilot RAF from 1964
m Old Deer 17.4.65 Dorothy M. Webster teacher d of Henry W. Stuartfield

ALEXANDER Gwynyth Margaret BSc 1970
d of Alfred H. A. butcher and Margaret L. Sproul secy; b Aber 26.6.49
teacher geog Johnstone from 1971, asst guid from 1973; prin guid Renfrew h s 1975–78; teacher Furze Platt c s Maidenhead 1978–79
m Aber 25.8.78 Kenneth R. Abernethy acct s of Thomas A. Langbank

ALEXANDER Ian Kemp BSc 1969
s of Harry W. A. MA 1921 *qv* and Mabel Kemp MA 1929 *qv*; b Aber 15.5.47
comm asst ICI HOC div Lond 1969–70; rep ICI petrochem div Lond 1971–73; raw materials man. ICI petrochem div Billingham 1973–74; petrol prod. and bulk sales man. ICI petrochem div Wilton from 1975
m Northwich 18.12.71 Susan A. Frith MA 1969 *qv*

ALEXANDER James Bremner BSc(eng) 1957
s of James A. farm serv and Anne B. Smith nurse; b Cuminestown 27.9.35
grad trainee Scot. elect. trg scheme Glasg 1957–58; nat serv REME sgt Cyprus 1958–60; teacher maths/sc Hilton acad Aber 1961–62; computer customer eng IBM Edin 1962–68; sen plan. rep Greenock IBM from 1968
m Aber 15.8.61 Marina A. Main typist d of John A. M. Cuminestown

ALEXANDER James Irving BSc(agr) 1956
s of John A. MA(Glas) C of S min and Jane H. Irving; b Kirkwall 8.12.31
DTA(Trin) 1958
dist agr off. Balovale N Rhod 1958–62; agr res off. Fort Jameson N Rhod 1962–64; prin agr res off. Mount Makulu Zambia 1964–68, asst chief agr res off. 1968–69; farm. on own account Wigtown from 1969
m Balovale 3.11.59 Anne Lowrie SRN d of Wilfred L. L. Halesworth

ALEXANDER John Ross *MA 1968

ALEXANDER Margaret Jean MA 1959
d of Edward S. A. man. dir and Robina K. Ellis cashier; b Aber 13.3.38
teacher Fr/Ger: Fraserburgh acad 1960–67; lect coll of comm Aber from 1968

ALEXANDER Muriel Elizabeth cLLB 1966
d of Alastair I. L. A. acct and Muriel Gorman; b Aber 6.5.46
law app Arbroath 1966–68; leg. asst: Dun 1969–72, Montrose 1972–75, ptnr 1975
m Montrose 21.10.72 Christopher R. C. Hardy journalist s of Ronald H. Montrose

ALEXANDER Patricia Anne PhD 1967
b Glasg 12.11.42
BSc(Glas) 1963
biochem: Dun RI 1967–69, St Joseph's hosp Sarnia Canada 1969–70; post doct res fell. Tor 1971–74, res assoc since 1974
m Glasg –.12.66 Rae

ALI Faisal Mirghani MSc 1966
s of Mirghani A. retd off. and Nagia Mohamed; b Sudan 31.1.38
BSc(agr)(Alex) 1961; course maths Norwood tech coll Lond 1963; pt I Dip Stat(Aberd) 1964
agr res corp Sudan: exper off. Sudan 1961–66; res worker Wadmedani from 1966

ALI Zaffar *MA 1962
s of Ameer A. and Nuroon Khan; b Trinidad 8.9.38
Dip Stat(Lond) 1964
statist Trinidad 1964; Univ of WI Jamaica: lect 1965–72; educ statist from 1972
m Woking 27.7.63 Moira A. R. Fachie MA 1962 *qv*

ALLAM Hassan Nashaat Abdel Fattah PhD 1967

ALLAN Alexander *BSc 1966 PhD 1969
s of Alexander A. motor mech and Margaret I. Hay; b Forres 26.2.44
scient Unilever res lab Port Sunlight from 1969
m Nairn 15.7.67 Margaret M. Baikie teacher d of John B. Nairn

ALLAN Alexander Moir *MA 1968

ALLAN Anne Mary *MA 1963
d of John R. A. driver and Mary H. McRae; b Beauly 22.9.41
teacher geog: St Audrey's s mod s Hatfield 1963–64, Loreto coll St Albans 1964–66, Harrytown h s Romiley 1966–72; prin St Bernard's g s for girls Slough from 1972
m Beauly 7.8.65 William A. Anderson BSc 1963 *qv*

ALLAN Barbara Gunn BSc 1958
d of Donald A. farm. and Barbara G. Mathieson; b Thurso 12.9.37
asst scient off. Wales 1958, Torry res stat 1959; teacher p s Castletown 1960
m Castletown 1.6.61 Donald M. Sutherland civ eng/comp dir s of Hugh D. S. Thurso

ALLAN Charles Maitland *MA 1962
s of John R. A. MA 1928 *qv* and Jean A. Mackie MA 1929 *qv*; b Stirling 19.8.39
lect: Glas 1962–63, Dund 1963–65; lect, sen lect Strath 1965–74; farm. Methlick, writer, broadcaster from 1975
m Banchory-Devenick 23.2.61 Fiona Vine BSc(St And) lect d of Reginald V. Dun

ALLAN Christine Susan MA 1969
d of George D. A. CA and Blanche M. Eddie; b Aber 8.2.48
exec off. DHSS Dunfermline 1970–73
m Aber 13.4.71 Roger M. Needler civ serv s of William H. N. Dun

ALLAN David Cameron *MA 1969

ALLAN David Martin *LLB 1968
s of Alexander J. A. comp dir and Margaret I. Caldwell teacher; b Aber 25.10.46
law app, leg. asst Glasg 1968–73; ptnr Fergusson Robertson & Norrie Dun 1973–76; sen lect conveyancing/prof pract of law Aberd from 1976
m Aber 16.6.69 Evelyn M. Black teacher d of Alan F. B. BL(Edin) Elgin

ALLAN Dorothy May MA 1968 DipEd 1969
d of John C. E. A. driving instr and Kathleen M. Coutts; b Aber 29.4.47
teacher Engl/r e Lenzie acad 1969–72
m Aber 16.7.71 Sinclair B. Ferguson MA 1968 *qv*

ALLAN Douglas Kinmonth BSc(agr) 1969 *1971
s of Charles P. A. printer and Jean K. Keay; b Perth 4.7.46
teacher W. Lothian from 1972

ALLAN Duncan Shearer MB ChB 1966
s of Robert F. A. acct and Laura J. Fettes teacher; b Insch 17.11.43
h o Aber: City hosp, cas dept ARI 1966–67, g p from 1967
m Aber 3.4.67 Valerie P. Allan MA 1966 *qv*

ALLAN Eric Robert *BSc 1964
s of John C. E. A. driving instr and Kathleen M. Coutts; b Aber 9.2.42
teacher sc West Calder h s 1965–66; Edin: teacher chem George Heriot's 1966–71, prin chem from 1971
m Darlington 9.7.66 Valerie Cawthorn teacher d of John C. Darlington

ALLAN Grant Alexander Thomas *MA 1964
PhD(Alta)

ALLAN Helen Adcock MA 1958
m (1) Imray
(2) O'Neill

ALLAN Ian Malcolm Thomson *MA 1957
s of John A. BSc(Glas) headmaster and Marjory Thomson BSc(St And) teacher; b Fraserburgh 5.8.35
man. trainee Rugby 1957–61; works study eng Glasg 1961–63; man. bldrs and civ eng Aber from 1963
m Aber –.9.59 Mary Stewart radiogr d of Donald C. S. Ellon

ALLAN Irene Pirrie MA 1962

ALLAN Isobel Rose Campbell MA 1964 Dip Ed 1965

ALLAN Keith Kellas Armstrong *BSc 1962

ALLAN Lesley Marion *MA 1965
d of Bertie A. theatre stage dir and Ellen M. Green civ serv; b Aber 31.8.43
Charles McGregor mem prize for teaching 1966
teacher Engl Aber h s for girls 1966–72, year mistress Northfield acad Aber from 1972

ALLAN Leslie Stewart *MA 1965

ALLAN Mellis *BSc 1962

ALLAN Patricia Margaret Isabella MA 1967
d of Cecil E. A. A. bank teller and Annie C. Cunningham secy; b Glasg 3.2.46
teacher: Engl/hist 1968–70, Engl from 1970 Hermitage acad Helensburgh
m Inveraray 30.10.71 Andrew W. Wiseman ACMA internal audit. s of Andrew W. Pittenweem

ALLAN Roderick James *BSc 1965
s of James A. mus teacher/piano tuner/mus and Mary H. Mitchell; b Huntly 23.6.43
MSc(Wis) 1967 PhD(Dart) 1969
res geochem geol surv Ottawa 1969–74; chief nat water res inst Western and Northern reg, Govt of Canada from 1974
m Quebec 28.12.72 Sandra E. Casey BA(Carleton) res asst d of Joseph M. C. Ottawa

ALLAN Terrence William *BSc(eng) 1970
s of William A. mason and Margaret L. M. McLeod insur ag; b Forres 8.10.47

teacher coll of comm Aber from 1970
m Aber 5.8.72 Linda M. J. Low MA 1972 d of William J. L. MA 1937 *qv*

ALLAN Thomas *MA 1967
s of Thomas A. clerk and Eileen Blain; b Glasg 29.7.45
asst teacher/dep head Worsley Canada 1968–71; prin hist: Dumfries 1971–72, Fraserburgh from 1972
m Glasg 12.8.67 Anne Howatson teacher d of Robert H. Glasg

ALLAN Valerie Pearl MA 1966
d of Duncan A. salesman/man. dir and Pearl Robinson; b Aber 24.4.46
teacher private nurs s 1968–71
m Aber 3.4.67 Duncan S. Allan MB ChB 1966 *qv*

ALLAN William Craig *BSc 1964
s of William A. and Doris C. Bowman art teacher; b Aber 8.11.42
PhD(Edin) 1971 AMA 1976
res stud. Edin 1965–68; res asst Hunterian Museum Glasg 1968–72; dep curator and keeper of geol County Museum Warwick
m Lighthorne 2.4.66 Ann M. Miller radiogr d of Robert A. M. Gaydon

ALLAN William Sinclair MB ChB 1957

ALLANACH Ian Gordon *BSc 1969
s of John A. and Jessie A. Cunningham; b Inv 1.11.47
teacher chem Dunf 1970–71; prin chem Glenrothes from 1972
m Inv 12.9.69 Patricia M. Loudon

ALLARDYCE Janette Harper MA 1962
m Taylor

ALLARDYCE Raymond Joseph Michie *MA 1969
s of Charles A. head porter Stir and Janet Michie; b Crieff 3.1.46
teacher: Hanover Germany 1970–73, Stirling from 1973

ALLATHAN Alexander George BSc(agr) 1960
s of Alexander G. M. A. farm. and Roberta T. Rettie; b Peterculter 8.9.37
asst agr advis Caithness 1960–62, acting agr advis Skye 1962–65, area agr advis Caithness from 1965
m Muir of Ord 25.10.68 Myra J. Johnstone secy d of Archibald K. J. Invergarry

ALLATHAN Ronald Ewen BSc(agr) 1964
s of Alexander G. M. A. farm. and Roberta T. Rettie; b Skene 26.6.43
agr advis Aber 1965–72; man. consult Aber from 1972
m Aber 22.3.66 Marilyn E. Simpson d of William S. Rosehearty

ALLBROKE Raymond *BSc(agr) 1968
s of William A. farm. and Mary I. D. A. Mackie; b Aber 25.4.45
agr advis W of Scotland agr coll: Campbeltown 1968–72, Stirling from 1972

ALLEN Alistair Roy *BSc 1969

ALLEN Hilary *MA 1965
d of Thomas W. A. C Eng and Florence E. Ironmonger; b Yorks 8.10.43
MA(Alta) 1967 PhD(Alta) 1972 Canada Council doct fell. 1968–69
univ of Alta teaching asst 1965–68; Acadia univ: lect 1969–73, asst prof from 1973
m Halkirk 12.9.66 Raymond H. Thompson PhD(Alta) asst prof head Engl dept Acadia univ s of Victor H. T. Belf

ALLINSON Derek Wilfred *BSc 1963

ALLISON James BSc(agr) 1957

ALLISON Judith Elizabeth MA 1970
d of Thomas A. sales rep and Olive K. Matthew instr spastic adolescents; b Newport-on-Tay 22.4.49
secy Lond 1971–73; teacher Engl Stuttgart W Ger 1973–75; secy Lond 1975–77, Ingolstadt W Ger from 1977

ALLISON Margaret McGregor *MA 1968 Dip Ed 1969
d of Thomas M. A. dep secy board of man. Inv hosp and Elizabeth L. Hunter; b Inv 2.11.45
teacher mod lang Greenock acad from 1969
m Elderslie 14.4.73 Ronald K. Thomson BSc(Strath) teacher maths Johnstone h s s of Samuel J. T. MA(Glas) Johnstone

ALLISON Stuart Norwood MB ChB 1969 DMRD 1974
s of Thomas B. A. shop man. and Ghislaine Turner ladies' outfitter; b Annfield Plain 19.2.43
h o Woodend hosp, ARI 1969–70; trainee g p Aber 1970–71; regist radiol/hon clin tut. ARI from 1974
m Aber 20.7.68 Marguereta M. F. Davie MA 1966 *qv*

ALLISTON John Charles BSc(agr) 1969 *1970
s of Gordon C. A. man. dir and Margaret T. Hay; b Twyford 30.6.46
PhD(UCNW) 1974
lect anim prod. royal agr coll, Cirencester 1974–76; sen scient off. animal breeding res organis Edin from 1976

AL-NAJAR Muthafar Haider MLitt 1968
BA(Cairo)
d 1976

ALPINE George LLB 1968
s of George D. L. A. MA(Cantab) marketing dir and Josephine Azrak teacher; b Irvine 11.5.46
law app, leg. asst Paul & Williamsons advoc Aber from 1968
m Aber 17.9.71 Margaret A. Morrison secy d of Roderick G. M. Huntly

ALSOP Gillian Eileen Margaret BEd 1969
d of William J. A. civ serv and Maud Arnold; b Nuneaton 12.7.47
teacher: Summerhill acad Aber 1969–71, Heart of England s Balsall Common from 1975
m Edin 28.6.69 Robin G. Peacock MA 1970 *qv*

ALSTON Alastair Summers *BSc(for) 1961
s of Thomas A. and Margaret R. Wilson art teacher; b Glasg 27.9.39
dept of for. Fiji: div for. off. Lautoka 1962–64; util off. Suva 1964–71; prin util off. Suva from 1971

ALVIS Patricia Ann MA 1967
m Robertson

AMAR Satya Swarup MB ChB 1965 DMRD 1969
s of G. S. A. MA(Punjab) dep dir educ; b Mathura India 13.2.41
FRCR (1971)
ARI: m o 1965–66; regist 1967–69; sen regist 1969–72; Nott gen hosp: consult. radiol from 1972
m Aber 1965 May E. Skinner MA 1967 *qv*

AMATRUDA Janina Maria Celeste MA 1969
d of George A. shop owner and Celeste R. Vettraino shop owner; b Dun 3.6.44
teacher Ital/Engl Lawside acad 1970–72; temp posts Scot. and USA 1972–73; course shorthand/typing Dun 1974

AMOS Lilias Teresa BEd 1969
d of William A. area man. E Scot. bus group and Jean M. S. S. Lothian; b Edin 23.4.46
teacher Engl Galashiels acad 1969–70; res asst educ psych univ of Virginia Charlottesville Va USA 1970–71; asst s psych Exeter 1971–72
m Galashiels 25.7.70 James B. Reary BSc 1967 *qv*

AMOS Valerie Anne MA 1967

AMSTELL Anthony David LLB 1967
s of R. J. A. bus. man and Margaret Nathan numismatist; b Lond 6.1.45
AIL
barrister-at-law Lincoln's Inn from 1970
m Tonbridge 12.8.72 Ingrid J. Woodgate secy d of Harold W. BDS(Lond) Tonbridge

AMUJO Stephen Jimo BSc(for) 1964
s of Bale A. farm. and Dada Amujo Dada; b Odo-Ere 20.12.38
MSc(Oregon St Univ USA) 1970
posts in Nigeria: for. man. off. Bornu Prov 1964–65; prov for. off. Bauchi 1965; res off. soil surv N Nigeria 1965–68; for. admin Kwara State 1970–71; acting chief conserv for. Kwara State 1971–73; chief conserv for. Kwara State from 1973
m Odo-Ere 23.12.65 Rachel I. Amujo d of Amujo Okejan Odo-Ere

ANAKWENZE Francis Nwoye BSc(for) 1958
s of Umeano O. A. farm. and Mgbeke Okafor; b Nigeria 1926
conserv for. Calabar: asst 1958–60, sen asst 1961–63; Enuga: dep chief 1963–69, chief from 1970; post grad course at Commonwealth For. Inst Oxford 1964–65
m Akure, Nigeria 1951 Rebecca N. Ikeme d of Patrick I. Awka Nigeria

ANDERSEN Ragnar Peter Axel MB ChB 1962
s of Ragnar K. D. A. Cand Med (Oslo) surg and Borghild Odegaard; b Harstad Norway 28.10.35
Cand Med (Oslo) 1962
asst dis g p/lt army med corps Oslo 1964–65; asst res dept anaest various hosps Norway; asst anaest Sweden 1969, Canada 1969–70, Oslo 1970–71; head dept anaest Honefoss Norway 1971–73; asst chief dept anaest Aker hosp Oslo from 1973
m Oslo 8.7.61 Merethe Mjelstad hosp pharm d of Hjalmar A. M. Oslo

ANDERSON Aileen Anne MA 1963
d of Alexander A. joiner and Annie S. Whitley; b Aber 31.7.42
teacher: Fr Aber 1964–68, Fr/Lat Colchester from 1975
m Aber 5.4.66 Alexander D. Murray tech buyer s of Archibald M. Aber

ANDERSON Alan Bain *MA 1969

ANDERSON Alan John Bruce *MA 1964 MSc 1966
s of John A. civ eng and Mary W. Moir; b Aber 14.1.41
FSS 1967
scient off. statist dept Rothamsted exper stat 1966–70; chief statist MRC clin and pop. cytogenetics unit Edin 1970–74; lect statist Aberd from 1974
m Edin 26.6.74 Bridget I. Lowe BA(Hull) res off. SHHD d of Patrick J. L. Carlow Eire

ANDERSON Alexander BSc 1958
s of Alexander A. master mariner and Winifred D. Riddell french polisher; b Aber 19.9.27
res asst Aberd 1958–66; res off. (grade I) from 1972
m Edin 25.3.61 Norma S. Hunter physioth d of John N. W. H. MA(Edin) Edin

ANDERSON Alexander BEd 1970
s of Alexander W. A. plumbing warehouse and trans man. and Jessie T. B. Falconer secy; b Banchory 12.11.40
teacher sc Peterhead acad from 1970
m Longside 14.7.66 Moyra D. Henderson teacher home econ d of William G. H. Inverurie

ANDERSON Alexander McRobert MA 1958 ᶜLLB 1960
s of William M. A. farm. and Isabella Fyfe tailoress; b Leochel Cushnie 11.7.36
leg. asst: Adam Thomson & Ross advoc Aber, ptnr 1967–71; secy supreme court leg. aid comm, Law Soc of Scot. from 1972
m Aber 10.2.68 Brenda Main shorthand typist d of Charles J. M. Dyce

ANDERSON Ann Ogilvie MA 1963
b Elgin 24.2.42
secy Glas 1964–66; Apia W Samoa: teacher 1966–68, admin asst 1968–70; careers off. Aber from 1970
m Aber 19.12.64 Alexander L. Walker BSc 1962 *qv*

ANDERSON Anne Barbara Michie MB ChB 1960 ᶜMD 1965
d of James M. M. A. pharm and Jane A. Anderson teacher; b Forres 10.2.37
D.ObstRCOG 1962 PhD (Univ of Wales) 1972
h o Inv, Aber, Glasg 1960–62; res fell. obst Aber and Cardiff 1962–70; lect clin repro physiol Welsh Nat s of med Cardiff from 1970

ANDERSON Arthur BL 1958
d 1.3.68

ANDERSON Brian Alexander MA 1963
s of John A. A. joiner and Isabella W. Davie bookkeeper; b Aber 8.1.42
DPE 1967
teacher geog/Engl/hist Northfield acad Aber 1965–66; dip. in p e post grad course Scot. s of p e Jordanhill 1966–67; teacher p e/geog Northfield acad; prin p e Powis acad Aber from 1973
m (1) Aber Marianne E. H. Mackay MA 1964 *qv*
(2) Aber 27.7.73 Mary R. Flockhart MA 1970 *qv*

ANDERSON Bryce Alexander MA 1959 BD 1963
s of Alexander A. weighing machine mech and Maggie Gaunt shop asst; b Aber 10.1.39
STM 1964
trainee urban training centre Chicago 1964–65; soc res C of S Aber 1966–69; dir action res proj Youth dev trust Manchester from 1969
m Aber –.10.69 Morag A. Booth cler asst d of Alexander B. Aber

ANDERSON Catherine MA 1964
d of Alexander H. A. teacher and Elizabeth M. D. Smith teacher; b Airdrie 12.6.43
teacher hist Fort William 1965–69, spec asst 1969–72; prin guid Lochaber h s 1972–75; prin hist Alness acad from 1975

ANDERSON Catherine Mary *BSc 1969
d of William A. BSc 1940 *qv* and Agnes W. Kerr BSc 1940 *qv*; b Aber 31.7.49
teacher VSO Shendam and Vom, Nigeria 1969–72; market. man. Unilever Lond 1972; proj acct J. R. McDermott Aber from 1977
m Aber 22.10.72 Thomas L. Mason BSc(eng)(Lond) civ eng/contr man., corporate plan., comm dir s of Harold P. M. Bishop's Stortford

ANDERSON Cecilia Patterson MA 1970
d of James P. A. fisherman and Cecilia C. Patterson; b Edin 23.1.49
teacher: p s Dalry 1971–74, New South Wales from 1974

ANDERSON Christopher David BSc(eng) 1970
s of Alexander G. A. BSc(eng) 1945 *qv*; b Aber 27.3.48
civ eng William Tawse Aber from 1970

ANDERSON Colin *MA 1966 Dip Ed 1967
s of Simon P. A. factory worker, dustman and Amelia S. Steele factory worker; b Forfar 10.5.43
teacher Fr/Ger: Arbroath h s 1967–68, Grantown g s 1969–71, Elgin acad 1971–74; asst prin Fr/Ger Denny h s 1974–78; prin mod lang Deans Community h s Livingston from 1978
m Aber 1.8.69 Moyra M. Robertson teacher p e d of Alastair M. R. Bromley

ANDERSON Colin Henry BSc 1970

ANDERSON David BSc(eng) 1970
s of David A. chief for. and Jessie W. Taylor; b Torphins 12.4.48
civ eng: Taylor Woodrow construct. Heysham 1970–73; James Williamson & Ptnrs Glasg from 1973

ANDERSON David George *MA 1968
s of Adam G. A. and Winifred N. Haworth; b Orpington 31.5.45
res fell. geog univ of Newfoundland 1968–70; tut. asst Aberd 1970–71; lect geog Luton coll of tech from 1971
m Aber 3.8.70 Joy E. E. Ogston d of James A. O. Aber

ANDERSON David George MA 1970

ANDERSON David John Boyd MA 1970 BD 1973
s of John B. A. author and Jessie M. Begg; b Glasg 23.6.49
asst C of S min Douglas & Angus ch Dun from 1973, min Bainsford ch Falkirk from 1974
m Edin 20.7.73 Eleanore St V. Dick MA 1970 *qv*

ANDERSON David Rae *MA 1958
s of David A. marine eng and Alice M. Rae; b Stonehaven 27.1.36
LLB(Edin) 1960 LLM(ANU) 1966 WS 1961 NP 1969
Aust fed publ serv 1962–65; lect leg. and constit hist Canberra; asst solic Edin 1965–67; ptnr leg. firm Alloa and cent. Scot. from 1967
m Aber 6.1.62 Jean Strachan MA 1957 *qv*

ANDERSON David Sinclair *MA 1970
s of Hope V. A. area controller Scot. (telephones) and Jean T. Sinclair cler off.; b Glasg 30.6.48
McGraw Hill Book Co Maidenhead: rep 1970; acad spec Dusseldorf from 1971

ANDERSON David William MB ChB 1965
s of John W. L. A. mining eng and Ivy E. H. Butler; b Nott 11.7.39
houseman ARI 1965–66; g p Aber from 1967
m Banchory 20.6.62 Janie W. F. Durward d of Lloyd G. D. Banchory

ANDERSON Dennis *BSc(eng) 1957
s of James A. painter/decorator and Bella M. Middleton; b Aber 22.4.35
electronic des & dev eng Liverpool 1957–66; f e teacher elect./electronics Falkirk from 1966
m Aber 1960 Shirley Gray d of John S. G. Aber

ANDERSON Elizabeth Margaret Bain *BSc 1962
d of Robert J. A. auctioneer/estate ag/factor/farm. and Laura M. Ligertwood MB ChB(Edin); b Aber 27.9.39
teacher Summerhill acad Aber 1964–65
m Aber 28.7.64 John Y. L. Hay BL 1962 *qv*

ANDERSON Eric *BSc 1957
s of Robert H. A. eng and Eveline A. M. Kindness; b Aber 8.10.35
DPhil(Oxon) 1961
metallurgist group man. Geneva from 1961
m Geneva 21.12.63 Renate M. Kollrack metall tech d of Fritz K. Berlin

ANDERSON Frances Mary MA 1970
d of James M. A. farm. and Phyllis A. Taylor teacher dom sc; b Elgin 18.6.49
teacher Maisondieu s Brechin 1971–73
m Alves 30.12.72 Dennis Holland farm acct s of Charles C. H. Leeds

ANDERSON Gladys Margaret *BSc 1967
m Watt

ANDERSON Gordon Ingram MA 1967

ANDERSON Grant Mackenzie MA 1966

ANDERSON Hamish Alexander *BSc 1962 PhD 1966
s of Alexander J. A.; b Aber 8.5.40
Brit Council fell. faculté de sciences, Orsay France 1965–66; ICI fell. org chem Liverpool 1966–68; Macaulay inst for soil res Aber from 1968
m Aber 1964 Maureen L. Woollard MA 1959 *qv*

ANDERSON Hazel MA 1969

ANDERSON Iain Howe *BSc 1958 PhD 1962
s of John A. foreman (dyeing & cleaning) and Elizabeth March; b Glasg 8.2.37
FRIC 1971
lect chem H-W Edin 1961–71; asst secy Scottish assoc for nat certif and diplomas Glasg 1971–73; Scottish tech educ council Glasg: educ off. 1973–74, sen educ off. from 1974
m Stornoway 27.12.62 Anne I. Morrison BSc 1960 *qv*

Anderson Ian MB ChB 1969
s of William A. carpenter and Mary McDonald; b Aber 6.6.45
intern Vict Hosp, Lond, Ontario 1969–70; g p Pembroke, Ontario 1970–76; radiol Vict hosp London, Ont from 1976
m Turriff –.12.68 Lorna V. Elvin psychiat res worker d of William E. Turriff

ANDERSON Ian *LLB 1970
s of Robert A. eng and Helen Marshall; b Paisley 4.7.43
LLM(Cape T) 1974
bar app Edin 1970–71, 72–73; advoc of sup courts of Scot.; member of coll of Justice 1973; lect in Roman Law, Witwatersrand 1973–74; advoc S. Af 1976

ANDERSON Ian Robert *BSc(agr) 1968
s of Robert E. A. off. man./comp secy and Margaret E. Baxter shop man.; b Elgin 6.11.45
MSc(Edin) 1970
pers trainee Shell Chem UK Carrington nr Manc 1970–72, pers off. Shell R and M Stanlow 1972–74; remun advis: Shell Venezuela Caracas 1975–78, Shell Internat Pet. Co Lond from 1978
m Edin 13.8.71 Jane R. Langlands MA(Edin) Brit Council off., BBC sen asst educ liaison d of Charles B. L. BSc(agr) (Edin) Edin

ANDERSON Ian William White MB ChB 1959
s of Alfred W. A. sales rep and Annabella M. Lyall; b Aber 1.2.35
DObstRCOG 1965
h o ARI 1959–60; RAMC Brunei 1960–64; h o Raigmore Hosp Inv 1964–65; g p: Saltcoats 1965–69, Kirkcaldy from 1969
m Aber 13.12.60 Doris A. S. Leith physioth d of James L. Aber

ANDERSON Isabel Barrie BSc 1962

ANDERSON Isabella Ann MA 1970
d of Herbert A. A. farm. and Isabel Walker; b Tough 14.5.49
teacher geog: Fife 1971–73, Ross-shire 1973–76
m Ballater 28.7.73 Ian D. Fraser mus instr s of Ernest F. Crathie

ANDERSON James Allan *MA 1964

ANDERSON James Andrew *MA 1967
s of Gilbert A. crofter, fisherman and Robina S. Williamson; b Whalsay 19.11.45
Dip Ed (Makerere Univ of E Africa) 1968
ed off. Kenya 1968–70; teacher Kaweran Coll NZ 1971; sen town plan. asst Hamilton NZ from 1971

ANDERSON James Hugh LLB 1966
s of David M. A. banker and Muriel E. Micklem MA (Cape T) teacher; b Gwelo, Rhodesia 11.10.45
CA 1970
Johannesburg: comp acct subsid of Unilever SA 1970–72; reg acct Western Bank (Anglo-Amer Group Co) 1972–75; gen man. admin Ryan Niger corp (U.D.T. Group Co) 1975–76, dir from 1976
m Johannesburg 20.7.74 Anne V. Adcock p r consult. (travel) d of R. A.

ANDERSON James Hunter *BSc 1956 PhD 1959
s of Kenneth J. A. rly trans off. and Jessie R. S. Hunter; b Romford 28.9.34
scient off. Long Ashton res stat Brist 1959–63; jun res fell. univ of Brist 1963–66; sen res biochem, Fisons Pharmaceuticals Loughborough 1966–69; sen scient off. microbiol res estab Wilts 1969–71; teacher biol/chem Lossiemouth h s from 1972

ANDERSON James Terry MB ChB 1957
d Aden 14.5.67 *AUR* XLII 375

ANDERSON John *MA 1960
s of George W. A. C of S min; b Oyne 20.11.37
teacher: RGC Aber 1961–65, prin geog Buckie h s 1965–70; rector Speyside h s Aberlour from 1970
m Aber 17.7.63 Christina M. Murray MA 1958 *qv*

ANDERSON John MB ChB 1964
s of Francis J. A. pharm and Elsie Falconer; b Lond 6.10.37
FRCSE 1968
hosp med pract Aber 1964–73; sen reg orthop surg from 1973
m Gatley 1966 Jennifer M. Brownhill nurse d of Albert B. Gatley

ANDERSON John Leeds *MA 1969
s of John L. A. foreman elect. welder and Alison Jolly; b Aber 2.9.46
Lond: res asst inst for soc stud. in med care 1970–72, Middx hosp med s 1972–75, lect in sociol 1975–78; lect med sociol univ of Hong Kong from 1978
m Aber 25.7.69 Alison E. Grant MA 1969 *qv*; marr diss

ANDERSON John Peter George MA 1968

ANDERSON Kathleen Guild MA 1967

ANDERSON Margaret *MA 1968
d 15.1.75

ANDERSON Margaret Louise Mary *BSc 1966
d of George J. C. A. farm. and Margaret B. Barrie MA 1930 *qv*; b Aber 6.12.44
PhD(Lond) 1970
post doct. fell. Cold Spring Harbor lab Long Island USA 1970–73; scient staff Imp Cancer Res Fund Lond from 1973

ANDERSON Margaret Rosemary MB ChB 1961
d of Thomas E. A. MB ChB 1926 *qv*; b Aber 17.11.37
m Aber 21.6.63 Murdoch W. MacLean MB ChB 1961 *qv*

ANDERSON Marvin Walter PhD 1964
s of Walter R. A. BA(Pacific Lutheran univ) bapt min, air force chap, coll pres and Faith E. Bennett; b Montevideo Minn 12.1.33
BA(Wash) 1955 BD(St Paul) 1959
asst to assoc prof ch hist Bethel Seminary St Paul Minn 1964–73, prof from 1973, visiting schol Cantab 1970–71 and 1977–78
m Spring Lake Park Minn 9.6.62 Ann M. Welin d of Elmer C. W. Alvarado Minn

ANDERSON Myra Gordon *MA 1964
d of James C. A. comm trav and Nellie G. Stables saleswoman; b Aber 10.5.41
teacher mod lang Aber 1965–69; participation in MA course Russian at Aberd 1965–67; teacher Engl centre for British teachers in Germany, Wipperfürth W. Ger 1969–71; dep dir of Centre for British Teachers in Europe 1971–74, admin from 1974

ANDERSON Nancy Lyons *MEd 1966
d of David M. A. joiner/undertaker and Mary J. Kelly nurse; b Kirkcaldy 23.10.11
BCom(Edin) 1932 DipEd(Edin) 1953 Dip RE(Edin) 1966
teacher: sen asst coll of comm Aber 1959–67; head comm studies, Stranmillis coll of educ Belf from 1967

ANDERSON Peter George *BSc(eng) 1969

ANDERSON Philip Edward LLB 1969
s of Robert E. journalist and Catherine Martin; b Glasg 9.6.49
Milne & Mackinnon Advoc Aber: app 1969–71, asst solic 1971–73, ptnr from 1973
m Aber 28.6.68 Elizabeth M. Levie secy d of James M. L. Aber

ANDERSON Raymond Kennedy MA 1964 *1966
s of Francis W. A. police insp and Florence Kennedy secy/bookkeeper; b Elgin 13.8.42
fin. exec: Ford Motor Co Essex 1966–72, BLMC Lond from 1972

ANDERSON Robert LLB 1966 MA 1969
s of James S. A. acct and Tony Levine nurse; b Chelmsford 26.9.45
teacher: Adelaide 1969–71, coll of comm Aber from 1972

ANDERSON Robert BSc 1970
s of Alexander A. agr worker and Maria J. Gordon; b East Clyth 27.11.29
lect maths coll of comm Aber from 1971
m Exeter 14.2.63 Alison Black nurse d of Frederick B. Devon

ANDERSON Robert John *BSc 1966

ANDERSON Robert Moir Lechmere MA 1962 MB ChB 1967
s of David L. A. police off. and Mary Boyle head teacher; b Doncaster 17.9.40
DPM 1974 MRCPsych 1975
major RAMC Germany, spec in psychiat
m Southport 1971 Mary T. Gavin MA 1970 *qv*

ANDERSON Roderick Stuart *BSc 1969

ANDERSON Rosemary *BSc 1966
m Smith

ANDERSON Sheila Buchan MA 1964

ANDERSON Sheila Margaret *BSc 1958
d of James C. A. coastguard and Alice M. A. Cocker; b Aber 9.1.37
MSc(Manit) 1960
sc lib Manit 1960–61; dem bot: Sir George Williams Univ Montreal 1961–62, Manit 1962–63; Manit: Lect bot 1965–66 and 1975, res asst bot 1975–76
m Winnipeg 7.7.62 Charles W. Anderson BSA(Manit) farm./corporate secy grain exporting comp s of William F. A. Manitoba

ANDERSON Violet MB ChB 1962

ANDERSON William Alexander *BSc 1963
s of William A. insur ag and Flora B. P. Christie; b Forres 22.10.41
O R scient De Havillands Hatfield 1963–66; ICI paints div: syst analyst Hyde 1966–69, bus. analyst Hyde 1969–72, Slough from 1972
m Beauly 7.8.65 Anne M. Allan MA 1963 *qv*

ANDERSON William Craib MA 1958 LLB 1961

ANDERSON William Peter *BSc 1962
PhD(Edin)

ANDERSON-SMITH Gordon MA 1966 *1969 BD 1971
s of Andrew M. F. S. master hairdresser and Nora N. Forsyth; b Aber 29.12.40
ThM(Phil) 1972
asst min C of S Edin and Aber 1972–73; res stud. for PhD Manc from 1973
m Aber 24.9.73 Myrtle I. Matthew MA 1964 *qv*
d Aber 4.3.80

ANDREW George Cassie BSc MB ChB 1969

ANDREW Thomas Duncan BSc 1962
s of William A. A. bus driver and Christina D. Ewen; b Aber 7.10.35
teacher: maths/sc Robert Douglas mem s Scone 1963–72, maths Perth g s from 1972
m Aber 4.4.64 Edith A. Wattie shorthand typist d of Robert W. Aber

ANDREWS Peter John BSc(for) 1961

ANGASTINIOTIS Michael Antoniou MB ChB 1966
s of Anthony M. A. BEd(Athens) headmaster and Helen Christaforou teacher; b Famagusta Cyprus 10.4.41
DCH(Glas) 1976
h o Aber 1966–67; regist neonatal paediat DRI 1968–69, regist paediat Churchill hosp Oxford; paediat Famagusta h from 1970
m Famagusta 27.8.61 Demetra McDonald d of James McD. Glasg

ANGUS David *MA 1969
s of George H. S. A. plumber and Jamesina Dalgarno hosp cleaner; b Aber 7.12.46
clerk IPC bus. press London 1969–70; trainee journalist IPC Mags 1970–71; asst edit. W. H. Smith & Son 1971–72; sub edit. IPC Mags 1972–73; edit. Williams Mags 1973–74; free lance journalist from 1974
m Islington Sheila W. M. Fowlie secy d of James F. Aber

ANGUS David Nicol MA 1958
s of James A. MA(Glas) teacher and Stella Nicol MA(Glas) teacher; b Bettyhill 24.1.35
rly operating exec Lond from 1958

ANGUS Elizabeth Robb MA 1970
d of John A. bus. man. and Agnes Shepherd; b Aber 23.10.18
teacher Engl Aber: coll of educ 1972–73, St Margaret's s for girls 1973–74, Fr s of Total Marine 1974–78
stud. Aberd for M Litt from 1978
m Aber 8.4.41 J. Fergus Watt BL(Edin) town clerk Aber s of James Watt CBE Aber

ANGUS George BSc 1968
s of John A. sheet metal worker and Ethel Milne; b Aber 6.2.47
teacher maths Huntly from 1969

ANGUS Jean MA 1962

ANGUS Jeanette Alison BEd 1970
d of Donald A. master butcher and Elizabeth M. Hendry; b Wick 8.1.47
teacher Fr Wick h s 1970–72; man. staff Marks & Spencer 1972–74; teacher Fr/asst prin guid Wick h s from 1974
m Wick 23.12.77 Alan G. Mackenzie teacher, bus. man. s of John G. M. Wick

ANGUS Jennifer Ann MA 1967
d of Hector J. A. joiner and Ann M. Murphy shorthand typist; b Aber 3.4.44
teacher geog: Portobello s s 1968–69, Breadalbane acad Aberfeldy 1969–74
m Aber 27.12.67 Michael Cooper MA 1968 *qv*

ANGUS Margaret Gardner BSc 1960
d of Walter Angus police serg and Isabella Angus; b Aber 2.10.38
Aberd: res asst med phys Foresterhill 1960–62; computing asst Richard Thomas & Baldwins Newport Mon 1962–64; teacher maths Glasg from 1973
m Aber 6.8.62 David Coutts BSc(eng) 1964 *qv*

ANGUS Michael George Noel *BSc 1962

ANGUS Zena June *MA 1964
m Wight

ANNAND Gideon Scott MA 1962 *MEd 1967
s of James S. A. banker and Wilhelmina E. A. Scott MA 1932 *qv*; b Tullynessle 28.9.41
CA app 1962–64; educ off. Kenya 1967–72; teacher Bannockburn h s Stirling from 1972
m Nairobi 7.2.72 Margaret R. Steer MA 1964 *qv*

ANNAND Patricia Ruth MA 1965
m Somerville

ANNELLS Jane-Ann Ward *MA 1968
d of Alfred G. M. A. and Dorothy J. Adsett; b Brampton 6.3.45
m Aber 23.3.68 Ian K. M. Cameron MA 1966 *qv*

ANSTEY Clive BSc(for) 1968
s of Frank F. Y. A. NZ rly publ and Nancy M. Fairway; b Wellington 24.1.44
BSc(Well) 1965
dist for. Dunedin from 1968

ANTAO Anthony Juno Orlando MB ChB 1967
s of Anthony J. P. A. MBE MBBS(Bom) 1937 and Jesuina L. Carvalho; b Blantyre Malawi 4.6.43
DCMT(Lond) 1969 MRCP 1972
jun med off. Qn Eliz cent hosp Blantyre 1967–68; sen h o infect. diseases E Birmingham hosp 1969–70; sen h o med Knightswood hosp Glasg 1970; Milesmark hosp Dunfermline 1970–71; regist renal and gen med S Teesside hosp group 1971–73; med regist and m o Westminster hosp London 1973–75; sen asst consult. med min of publ. health Doha Qatar from 1975

ANUMUDU David Ndubuisi MB ChB 1967
s of Mathais O. A. merch and Janet Nwsahalu; b Nigeria 25.11.37
h o: surg Ashington, med York, obst/gyn Leicester 1968–69; sen h o obst/gyn Beverly 1968–69; sen h o genetic med Sheffield 1969–70; regist obst/gyn Stockport 1970–71; g p Warrington from 1971
m Aber 1.11.68 Alison J. Finnie DA d of David F. Cullen

ANWAR Ahmed PhD 1957
MSc(Cairo)

APPERLEY Marion Barbara BSc 1970
d of Eric R. A. estim eng and Dorothy A. Rowley; b Birm 27.6.49
MSc(CNAA) 1974
metall chem Biometals Birm from 1970

APPIAH Robert Kwasi *BSc(eng) 1965

APPLIN Josephine Mary *BSc 1965
m Corke

ARANDA Jose Martin PhD 1960

ARAP-SANG Francis Kiptorus BSc(for) 1968
s of Barkoiyet Chepkeitany peasant and Kabon Barkoiyet; b Kenya 27.3.42
MSc(for)(Tor) 1971
asst conserv of for. Kenya 1968–69; for. path. Kenya from 1971
m Kenya 16.8.69 Mary Jepkorir secy d of Jeremiah Kipyab, Kenya

ARBUTHNOTT Gordon William *BSc 1964 PhD 1968
s of Roy G. A. rly fitter and Maggie Lobban dom serv; b Ellon 14.3.42
temp lect physiol Aberd 1968–69; Wellcome res fell. Stockholm 1969–70; lect physiol Aberd 1970–73; MRC staff scient Edin from 1973
m Aber 10.9.65 Joan E. Minto MA 1968 *qv*

ARCHEAMPONG Emmanuel BSc(for) 1963
s of Robert Asiedu-Dentu min of relig and Madam Adwoa Pokuaa farm.; b Larteh-Akwapim, Ghana 21.9.38
Ghana: asst conserv of for. 1964–67; for. supt Ashanti Goldfields 1967–68; sen sc tut. Prempeh Coll 1968–73; stocks supt State Gold Mines Corp, Tarkwa Goldfields from 1973
m Bekwai-Ashanti –.12.65 Dorothy Kyei teacher d of John D. K. Bekwai-Ashanti

ARCHER Rudolph MB ChB 1962

ARCHIBALD James Kennedy *BSc(eng) 1966
resid Aber

ARDERN Richard John *BSc 1969
MA(Sheff) 1971 ALA 1973
trainee univ lib St And 1969–70; lib HIDB Inv from 1971
m Inv 1970 Eileen M. Rhind BEd 1969 *qv*

ARGO Frances Elizabeth MA 1964
d of John A. farm. and Annie I. Barron; b Ellon 22.2.44
teacher maths: Northfield s s Aber 1966–67, Duncanrig s E Kilbride 1967–70, Ardersier s 1970–71, Victoria Drive s Glasg 1971–74; asst prin maths Duncanrig s 1974–78
m (2) Glasg 20.7.73 Antony F. H. Henry CA comp secy s of Samuel G. H. Cupar

ARGO Kenneth Barclay BSc(agr) 1970
s of Douglas D. D. A. farm. and Edith Barclay MA 1944 *qv*; b Aber 19.8.48
MSc(N'cle) 1972
farm man. Cadbury/Typhoo/Schweppes Brechin 1972–76; farm. Weldon Northants from 1976
m Aber 6.10.72 Helen M. Blyth teacher d of Robert B. Laurencekirk

ARIDEGBE Michael Ojo BSc(for) 1961
s of Josiah F. A. painter and Grace Ajayi dyer; b Igbajo Oyo State Nigeria 4.11.22
Western and Oyo State Nigeria: asst conserv for. I and II 1961–67, sen asst 1968–72, conserv for. 1973–75, asst chief conserv 1975–76, dep chief conserv from 1977
m Ibadan Nigeria 10.8.52 Grace Eyinade dressmaker d of Daniel Adetona, Ogbomoshe Nigeria

ARKHURST Eustace MB ChB 1963
BSc(McG)

ARKLEY Kenneth Ian *BSc(eng) 1966
s of Alexander A. teacher and Victoria M. Grant; b Laurencekirk 22.12.42
ICI Billingham: grad app 1966–67; plasterboard plant man. 1967–69, plan. man. 1969–72, workshops man. 1972–76, comm man. waste water treatment from 1976
m Aber 10.4.64 Elizabeth S. Thomson secy d of James I. F. T. MA 1936 *qv*

ARLIDGE Ernest Zane *PhD 1958
BSc MSc(NZ)

ARMSTRONG Alison Margaret MA 1970
s of William A. A. paper mill worker and Alexandrina Smith; b Aber 22.11.48
teacher: Fr/Ger Hazlehead acad Aber 1971–72, St Joseph's s s Workington from 1972
m Aber 22.7.72 James K. Murdoch MA 1971 soc worker s of James K. M. Aber

ARMSTRONG Colin Maxwell *BSc 1970
s of James M. A. MA 1936 *qv*; b Dun 19.10.47
MSc(N'cle) 1971
teacher chem St Andrews from 1972

ARMSTRONG Duncan BSc(eng) 1958
s of Allan A. MA 1925 *qv*; b Carrbridge 14.8.36
asst city eng dept Aber 1958–62; des eng pulp and paper mills Vanc 1962–64; head of munic des dept corp for 1967 world exhib Montreal 1965–67; eng man. Warnock Hersey Montego Bay 1967–69; proj eng Assoc Eng Services Edmonton 1970–74; sen resid eng Cohos Evamy & Ptnrs Fort McMurray from 1974
m Shetland 5.4.60 Jemima A. Peterson MA 1958 *qv*

ARMSTRONG Shona Inglis MA 1970
d of Matthew A. hotelier and Jessamy W. Hall; b Burton-on-Trent 1949
secy posts S & E Africa 1971–72; secy: Amer consulate, Edin 1972–73, Amer emb Lond from 1973

ARMSTRONG William George *MA 1963
s of William S. A. paper mill worker and Rena Smith; b Aber 20.3.41
teacher: Whitehaven g s 1963–66, Longton h s 1967–70; Stoke on Trent sixth form coll from 1970
m Aber –.7.64 Patricia Callum teacher d of Douglas C. Aber

ARNOT Alexander Ian LLB 1968
s of Robert A. insur insp and Margaret E. O. Forbes teacher; b Bridge of Allan 9.10.46
law app 1968–70; leg. asst 1970–72 Edin; solic Dunfermline from 1972

ARNOT Katharine Agnes Kinmond BSc 1960
d of Arthur W. A. BL(Edin) lawyer and Agnes M. Watt MA(St And) teacher; b Forfar 8.6.40
asst biochem hosp lab Aber 1960–62; part time teacher remed reading Stockton-on-Tees 1968–73; teacher biol/chem Callander from 1975
m Strathpeffer 11.7.62 George H. Haddock RAF off./sales eng s of Francis A. H. Coulsdon

ARRELL Margaret Olive MA 1967

ARULANANTHAM David Cumaresan *BSc(eng) 1969
s of Daniel C. A. BSc(Calc) headmaster and Grace E. A. Sathianadhan BA(Osm) teacher; b Jaffna Sri Lanka 2.6.44
plant eng Grangemouth from 1969
m Edin 1.6.74 Diana M. Knight BSc 1969 *qv*

ASARE Emmanuel Broni BSc(for) 1957
s of Isaac K. A. headmaster and Mary Afra Hemaa; b Oda Ghana 7.3.33
Ghana: asst conserv for. Kumasi 1957–61; sen asst 1961–63; conserv for. Koforidua 1963–71; dep chief conserv for. Takoradi 1971–73; dir/dep chief exec Guksten (WA) Sefwi Wiawso from 1973
m (1) Koforidua –.7.60; marr diss 1967
(2) Koforidua –.8.70 Dora O. Kwane d of Emmanuel O. Dapaa Agogo

ASHCROFT Thomas MB ChB 1957

ASHCROFT William Alexander *BSc 1958
s of William G. A. BSc(Glas) schoolmaster and Margaret S. Anderson; b Urquhart 16.6.36
MSc(Birm) 1963 PhD(Birm) 1967
geophys Seismograph Service, south Arabia, Nigeria 1959–62; res stud. Birm 1962–65; lect geol/mineral. Aberd from 1966
m Lond 1961 Margaret J. Cotching BA(Liv) lect d of Charles J. C. Carshalton

ASHER Lilian Stass MA 1965
d of William A. soldier/motor mech/commissionaire and Maria E. H. Stass; b Inv 13.3.44
teacher Engl Inv h s from 1966

ASHFORD Anne Margaret BSc 1965
m Wolk

ASHFORD Judith MA 1963

ASHLEY Michael John MEd 1964
s of John R. A. gold mine off. and Maud E. Darlow; b Boksburg Transvaal 11.8.37
BA(Witwatersrand) 1958
lect educ: Johannesburg coll of educ 1964–66, Rhodes univ Grahamstown 1967–71, sen lect 1972–78; prof educ univ of Cape Town from 1978
m Aber 9.5.64 Angela M. D. Cort d of Frank C. MB ChB (Manc) Brook I of W

ASHTON Robert William *BSc(eng) 1970
m Helen M. Barclay MA 1969 *qv*

ASHTON Shirley Elliott MEd 1970
d of Harry T. A. BSc(Adel) asst dir Aust bureau of met and Melva G. V. Elliott Dip Com(Adel) teacher; b Adelaide Aust 22.7.44
BA(Melb) 1965 AASD 1965 DipEd(Melb) 1966
teacher: Engl Bristol 1967–69; Engl/commun Aber from 1970
m Bristol 26.7.69 Charles R. A. Earl BSc 1971 scient off. Rowett inst Aber

ASHUN Joseph Enimil MB ChB 1958
BSc(Lond)

ASIBEY Emmanuel Osei Agyeman BSc(for) 1960 PhD 1974
s of Kwaku O. A. farm./cocoa broker and Ama Omenaa farm./ornamental beadworker; b Kwaso (Ashanti) 21.11.35
Ghana: Damongo- asst conserv for. 1961–62, asst, sen asst game warden 1962–65, game warden 1965–67; chief game and wild life off. from 1967; member: internat comm park syst plan, 1963–65; Soc/agr/econ sub-comm Volta Lake res proj from 1970; survival serv comm/nat parks comm of internat union for conserv of nature and nat resources (IUCN) from 1972; IUCN exec board from 1975
m Aburi 18.12.71 Joyce L. K. Kyei BA(R'dg) headmistress d of Thomas E. K. DipEd(Oxon) Kumasi

ASIEDU Emanuel Ransford MB ChB 1959
d Ghana 8.2.72

ASKEW James Alan MSc 1963
s of James E. and Gladys Askew; b Preston 10.7.39
BSc(eng)(Salf) 1962 CEng MIEE 1967
lect Harris Coll Preston 1964–68: sen lect 1968–73; sen lect Preston poly from 1973
m Penwortham Preston 17.4.65 Joyce Ravenscroft

ATHANAS Christopher Nicholas MA 1962 LLB 1964
s of Nicholas A. BA(Columba NY) comp dir and Elizabeth C. Tasker nurse; b Aden Arabia 26.8.41
WS 1969
law app Aber 1964–66; leg. asst: Aber 1966–68, Edin 1968–69; ptnr leg. firm Edin from 1969
m Aber 30.6.64 Sheena A. Stewart teacher p e d of Peter M. S. Perth

ATKINSON Adrian Paul Charles *MA 1960
s of Edward P. F. A. naval off. and Christina C. M. MacArthur; b Gourock 28.7.44
MSc(Aston) 1970 PhD(Aston) 1974
indust consult. Birm 1970–72; lect psych Aston from 1974
m Kingsley 1970 Christine L. Jones MA 1968 *qv*

ATKINSON Alison Mary LLB 1969
d of James E. M. A. safety off. and Heather A. Young; b Edin 7.8.48
solic Edin from 1971
m Alloa 27.5.78 Douglas K. Tullis LLB 1971 solic s of Ramsey T. BA(Oxon) Dollar

ATKINSON Douglas BSc(eng) 1960
s of John R. R. A. trans insp and Lizzie M. Will; b Aber 1.9.39
MICE 1968
BR: Glasg—civ eng 1960–62, eng asst 1962–65, sen eng asst 1965–67; Perth—asst (works & bridge) from 1968
m Clydebank 20.9.63 Elizabeth I. McKay d of John McK. Clydebank

ATKINSON Geoffrey Eric *MA 1969
s of Eric A. A. loc govt off. Muriel E. Wicks; b Epsom 23.8.43
BA(econ)(Sheff) 1965 ARCO 1968
dir property comp Aber 1971–73; dir sports goods outlet Aber from 1973; mus critic *Press and Journal* from 1968
m Aber 1967 Mary E. Macdonald BSc 1975 d of Thomas K. M. BL 1937 *qv*

ATKINSON John Edmund PhD 1967
s of John G. A. eng and Eliza M. Burrell; b Barnard Castle 19.8.40
BPharm(Lond) 1964 FCS 1965 MPS 1969 MIBiol 1970 ARIC 1972
post doct fell. chem dept Belf 1967–68; lect pharm RGIT Aber from 1968
m Felling 7.4.66 Joan V. Nicholson teacher d of John D. N. Gateshead

ATKINSON Kenneth MSc 1963
BA PhD(Durh)

ATKINSON Margaret May BSc 1969
d of Edmund A. MA(Cantab) income tax insp and Kathleen Taylor teacher; b Renfrewsh 11.5.46
careers off. Teesside 1969–71; careers advis off. Darlington 1971–74; sen careers off. S Shields 1974–75; area careers off. Crawley from 1975

ATMOWIDJOJO Sumadi MSc 1966
s of Tukardi A. police off. and Sajem Karsowidjojo; b Yogyakarta Indonesia 21.1.36
PhD(Corn) 1978
jun res worker: Nat Biol Inst Bogor Indonesia 1966–72 and from 1978

ATTIN Kathleen Mary MA 1967
d of John A. tech and Cynthia Y. Young; b Trinidad WI 25.3.44
secy Brit emb Helsinki Finland 1968; stud. soc work univ of Alabama from 1976
m Helsinki 9.3.68 Mauri Valtonen MSc(Helsinki) res astronomy s of Yrjo V. Kiljava Finland

AU NYUK CHENG Dorothy MB ChB 1968
d of William Au Ahwah LLB(Lond) and Mary Vu; b Malaya 4.5.43
m o Malaysia from 1969
m Aber 25.7.66 Liew Meng Leong MBBS(Sing) consult. obst/gyn s of Liew Him Yaw

AUCHINACHIE Isobel Margaret Taylor MA 1960
d of Henry W. A. bank man. and Edith R. Taylor teacher; b Old Aber 8.7.39
teacher: Engl/hist Fochabers 1961–66, Castle Hill NSW Aust 1966–68, Engl Tumut NSW Aust 1968–76
m Adelong NSW John L. Crain grazier s of William P. C. Adelong

AUCHINACHIE Keith Taylor MB ChB 1970
s of Henry W. A. bank man. and Edith R. Taylor teacher; b Kincardine 7.9.46
MRCGP 1974 D Obst RCOG 1973
h o ARI 1970–71; sen h o dept g p Aberd; fam phys Brantford Ontario from 1977
m Aber 9.7.70 Gwen Porter teacher d of Peter P.

AULD Alan Graeme *MA 1963
s of Alan T. A. LLD 1970 *qv*; b Aber 14.8.41
BD(Edin) 1966 PhD(Edin) 1976 ordained Edin presb C of S 1973
res in OT studies Edin, Jerusalem, W Germany 1966–69; asst dir Brit s of archae Jerusalem 1969–72; lect Heb and OT stud. Edin from 1972
m Sparkford 23.9.67 Sylvia J. Lamplugh secy d of Stephen L. Sparkford

AULD Alison Mary BSc 1969
d of Alan T. A. LLD 1970 *qv*; b Aber 28.5.47
teacher: West Lothian 1970–73, Renfrewsh 1973–75
m Aber 2.7.73 Graham P. Angus arch. s of William A. Aber

AUNG Maung Gyaw MB ChB 1963
s of Tha T. A. barrister and Daw Nee; b Akyab Burma 19.1.38
h s ARI 1964; h p Birkenhead 1964; h s Stracathro hosp 1964–65; regist path.: Mayfield 1966–69, Castleford from 1969
m Stracathro 1967 Margaret M. Ritchie SRN d of John R.

AUSTIN Euphemia Hall Hope (Fay) MB ChB 1967
d 20.12.70 *AUR* XLIV 216

AVENT Yvonne Gladys MA 1962 Dip Ed 1963
d of Douglas J. A. pilot RAF and Muriel J. Murray; b Perth 25.12.40
teacher: Pulteneytown acad Wick 1963–64, Halkirk j s 1964–67, Mt Pleasant s Thurso 1967–74; head: Bower p s Wick 1974–76, Pulteneytown acad Wick from 1976
m Perth 3.8.63 Robert M. Gunn BSc(eng) 1961 *qv*

AVERY Moira-June Ingram MA 1968

AWAD Mahmoud Mohamed Hassan MSc 1963
s of Mohamed H. A. and Sabah A. Nawar; b Kaha Egypt 2.3.29
BSc(Ein Shams) Dip Soil Mech (France)
eng Monopia 1964; eng in min of irrig (barrages and dams) Cairo 1964–68; chief eng from 1968
m Doki-Giza 5.7.52 Zinab A. E. R. Nawar d of Abd El R. A. Elbaki N. Doki-Giza Egypt

AWON Ann Patricia MA 1965

AWOUDA El Hag Makki BSc(for) 1964

AWUNOR-RENNER Charles MB ChB 1965

AYERST John Michael BSc(for) 1961
s of William H. A. salesman and Muriel E. P. Stillwell secy; b Perivale 10.12.38
asst for. comm Keith 1961–62; teacher sc: Kiltarlity 1963–64, Larkhall acad 1964–66; lect biol David Dale coll f e Glasg 1966–69; sen lect environment stud. Crewe & Alsager coll Cheshire from 1969
m Aber 31.8.63 Alice M. Cobb MA 1961 *qv*

AYERST Peter William BSc(for) 1957 *1958
s of William H. A. comm trav and Elsie M. P. Stilwell secy; b Perivale 10.12.38
asst conserv for. Tanganyika 1959–60; teacher: Hemel Hempstead 1960–63, Nairobi 1963–73, Cape Town from 1973
m Aber –.8.60 Doreen E. Mitchell teacher d of Gordon M. Aber

AYIVOR Gabriel Kodzovi MB ChB 1964
s of Albert Y. A. tailor/storekeeper and Comfort Amegashie; b Denu Ghana 29.9.31
BSc(McG) 1959 DPM 1971
h o Bridge of Earn 1965–66, sen h o, regist psychiat Ross clin Aber 1966–71; Ghana: sen m o Ankaful psychiat hosp 1971–77, psychiat spec from 1977
m Aber 8.10.71 Betty P. Thomson nurse d of William F. T. Perth

AYLWARD Nigel Nunn PhD 1967
BSc MSc(Birm)

AYRE John Fearnley BSc(eng) 1970

BABALOLA Alexander Akinade Ajibola *BSc(eng) 1969

BABBÉ Jean Evelyn Mary BSc 1968
d of Peter M. F. B. horticulturalist and Vera E. Guilbert; b Guernsey 26.7.46
Derby: computer progr 1968–70, sen progr 1970–72; teacher maths: g s Burton-on-Trent 1972–74, Moreton Wirral 1974–76; trg man. Transaction Data Syst Dawlish from 1976
m (1) Derby 2.4.70 Rodney A. Firth dir Joshua Tetley s of Norman F. Huddersfield; marr diss 1.1.76
(2) Newton Abbot 26.7.76 John M. Watkins prod. rep Marlow Ropes s of Leonard W. Dawlish

BACKETT Anne Louise *BSc 1965 PhD 1969
d of Edward M. B. BSc(Lond) prof commun med Nott and Shirley P. Thompson teacher; b Lond 17.10.43
res fell. pharm Aberd 1969–70; information scient in pollution at MBA Plymouth from 1977
m Aber 21.6.66 James Cowie BSc 1964 *qv*

BADAWY Ahmed Mahmoud PhD 1957
BSc(agr)(Alex) MSc(Alex)

BAGLEY Alexander John *MA 1966 MLitt 1968
BA(Oxon)

BAHZAD Abdulla MSc 1970
s of Abdulla Abdul-Kader lect mech and Sabiha Fawzi; b Baghdad 12.3.36
BSc Comm(Baghdad) 1960
statist: Aber & dist milk marketing board 1971–72, USA 1972, self employed from 1973
m Aber 12.4.71 Christobel G. Terris MB ChB 1971 obst/gyn d of David G. T. Grantown-on-Spey

BAILEY Colin David Howard MB ChB 1968

BAILEY Mary Jane Greenlaw BSc 1969
d of Gordon J. B. attendant nat phil dept Aberd and Jane K. Hamilton beauty consult.; b Crowthorne 22.7.47
teacher sc Aber: Hazlehead acad 1970–73, Harlaw acad 1974–75, Hazlehead acad 1975–77
m Aber 9.8.69 David R. Franks MB ChB 1970 *qv*

BAILEY Warren Peter Neal MSc 1969
MA(Oxon)

BAILEY-SMITH Robin BMedBiol 1970 MB ChB 1973
b 11.4.48
resid Clackmannan

BAILLIE Alister Cameron *BSc 1963 PhD 1966
s of Hugh B. mill worker and Margaret S. Macdonald cook; b Brora 17.7.41
res fell. Atlanta, Georgia 1966–67; Chesterford Park res stat: res chem 1968–72, sect. leader from 1972
m Dunphail 12.9.64 Elizabeth MacPherson MA 1963 *qv*

BAILLIE Ian James BSc 1967

BAILLIE Kenneth Cameron *MA 1963
s of Hugh B. mill worker and Margaret S. MacDonald cook; b Brora 17.7.41
MSc(Lond) 1979
journalist: trainee Thurso 1963–65, sub edit. *The Scotsman* Edin 1965–67; Lond: media res Gallup Poll 1967–71; stud. Birkbeck coll 1971–73, trg advis printing/publ ITB 1973–75; self-employed pers and res consult. from 1975
m Wallington Marion Collins secy d of John R. C. Wallington

BAILLIE Rita Marion MB ChB 1959
d of Alexander M. B. MB ChB 1915 *qv*; b Eire 12.2.31
DCH 1962 (Lond) DPM 1964 (Lond) MRCPsych 1971
consult. psychiat Monyhull hosp Birm from 1972, consult. from 1969

BAILLIE-HAMILTON Alexander Buchanan MB ChB 1956
s of John B.-H. tea planter and Bridgett E. Baker; b Ceylon 2.11.32
DIH 1959
h o Aber and Stracathro 1956–57; chief m o tea estates Peermade India 1957–58; sen h o Truro 1958–59; g p Barbados 1959–64; indust m o Standard Telephones 1964–65; g p Maidenhead from 1965
m Caxton Hall 1964 Lilia M. J. Peters or Eaton boutique owner d of Alan P. West Indies

BAIN Alexandrina Mary MA 1963
d of Donald B. bldg contr and Johan C. Mackenzie post mistress; b Tore 9.5.42
teacher maths: Bridge of Earn 1964–69, Penzotti s for missionaries' children Lima Peru 1969–73, Invergordon from 1974

BAIN Alison Anne MA 1969

BAIN David Robertson BSc 1960 *1964
b Thurso 8.4.39
PhD(Glas) 1968
res chem: UKAEA Dounreay 1960–63, 1964–65, univ of

Dayton Ohio 1968–70, Liv 1970–74; scient Unilever res lab Port Sunlight from 1974
m Aber 10.8.64 Elizabeth R. Baikie BSc(St And) teacher

BAIN Denis Warburton MA 1961
s of James B. master slater and Jane Warburton; b Bolton 11.6.37
teacher: Engl/hist Grange s Alloa 1962–64, Engl Elgin acad 1964–67; instr lt RN Arbroath, Shotley Gate, Fareham 1967–72; teacher Aber: Hazlehead acad 1972–73, Craighill p s 1973–75, asst head Kittybrewster p s from 1976
m Aber 31.8.60 Jennifer B. Jack teacher d of James K. J. Aber

BAIN Derek Charles *BSc 1966 PhD 1974
s of James B. blacksmith, insur ag and Jessie B. Taylor; b Buckie 30.4.44
mineralogist Macaulay inst for soil res Aber from 1966
m Fochabers 2.3.68 Grace M. Mackenzie BSc 1970 *qv*

BAIN Donald Straiton *MA 1966
s of Donald B. MRCVS(Edin) vet surg and Isobel J. T. Finlay teacher dom sc; b Lanark 16.6.44
MSc(Strath) 1972
Dafoe fell. internat relations Manit 1966–67; res off. SNP Edin 1968–71; man. dir Res and Intelligence serv Stirling 1971–74; dir of res SNP Edin 1974–77; econ advis joint res centre of Europ communities Ispra Italy

BAIN Douglas John Geddes MB ChB 1964 MD 1974
s of Douglas H. B. rly clerk and Margaret Geddes MA 1923 *qv*; b Aber 18.8.40
DObstRCOG 1966 DCH 1968 MRCGP 1970
res m o RACH, ARI, mat. hosp Aber 1964–66; g p Edin 1966–68; regist med, paediat Bangor and Kirkcaldy 1968–71; g p Livingston from 1971
m Sandra M. Souter p e teacher d of George M. S. LDS(Edin) Elgin

BAIN Edmund Donald Bruce MA 1965
s of Robert B. BSc(Glas) lect agr and Christina M. Kirkman SRN; b Aber 7.6.40

BAIN Elizabeth Walker MA 1969 Dip Ed 1970
d of John M. B. ship's steward and Isamay M. Logie; b Westray Orkney 27.7.48
teacher: Aber 1972–73, Engl Inv from 1975
m Orkney 12.6.68 Douglas A. Thomson MA 1973 teacher s of Douglas T. Kirkwall

BAIN George William *MA 1963
s of George B. fishmerchant and Anne H. Gibb ptnr in fishmerchant's bus.; b Aber 4.11.40
articled CA app Aber 1963–64; asst res econ White Fish auth Hull 1965–67; econ Dunlop, Lond 1967–70; man. consult. Urwick Orr & Ptnrs Lond 1970–72; fish merchant Bain Bros Aber

BAIN John MA 1970

BAIN Laurence Douglas *MA 1962

BAIN Nigel Bruce *MA 1967
BD(Glas)

BAIN Norman Brander MB ChB 1968
s of Peter J. B. gamekeeper and Elizabeth Geddes; b Lossiemouth 2.1.41
DObstRCOG 1970
h o: King's Lynn, Norwich 1968–69, obst Gt Yarmouth, anaest Worcester, York 1969–70, paediat Abergavenny 1971; g p/anaest Bromsgrove 1971; civ m o 1st regt RHA BAOR W Ger 1972–73; g p/anaest Wonthaggi Aust from 1973
m York 25.2.67 Anne M. Crichton MCSP Aber d of William S. C. Keswick

BAIN Priscilla Anne MA 1969
d of Logie S. B. MB ChB 1937 *qv*; b Aber 30.11.48
Dip St Godric's secy coll Lond 1970
pa/secy to gen man. Ferranti Edin
m Aber 11.9.76 Robert J. M. Fraser prod. eng s of Robert F. Bathgate

BAIN Robert *BSc 1956 PhD 1959
s of Robert Bain BSc(Glas) lect Aberd and Christina M. Kirkman; b Aber 17.2.34
paper indust in Scot. 1959–68; pulp and paper res Inst of Canada, Pointe Claire 1968–75; paper indust res assoc Leatherhead from 1975
m Aber 19.7.60 Helen C. Shirreffs MA 1955 *qv*

BAIN Sheila Margaret *MEd 1965 PhD 1974
d of James M. B. wine and spirit merch and Isabella S. Robertson; b Dun 3.5.29
MA(Edin) 1952 Dip Ed(St And) 1954
lect Stockholm 1955–56; teacher Dun and Angus 1956–62; Aberd: asst, res fell. 1962–67, res asst, res off. from 1967

BAIN Stanley *BSc 1960
s of Charles H. B. lab and Euphemia Curran; b Huntly 24.3.31
teacher biol: asst Dumfries 1960–62; prin Huntly from 1962
m Huntly 20.9.58 Irene M. Morrison health visitor d of Eric M. Huntly

BAINES William Robertson BSc(eng) 1957
s of Sydney B. teacher of mus and organist; b Glasg 6.10.35

BAIRD Elizabeth MA 1969
d of Alexander S. B. eng and Mary McWilliam teacher; b Buckie 12.3.46
m Aber 1969 Alexander W. L. Joss BSc 1967 *qv*

BAIRD Gabrielle Anne MB ChB 1959
d of James A. B. BSc 1932 *qv* and Elizabeth M. Petrie MA 1936 *qv*; b Holyhead Anglesey 22.9.35
g p: Rhynie 1968–73, Aber from 1973
m Aber 22.9.59 George S. Sorrie MB ChB 1957 *qv*

BAIRD Jennifer Naomi
see Pinnock

BAIRD Margaret Davidson MA 1962
d of David D. B. master plumber and Margaret M. Law; b Ellon 10.4.41
teacher Strichen 1963–67, Forres from 1967
m New Pitsligo 19.7.67 James A. Grant shopkeeper s of John G. Forres

BAKER Dennis Anthony *BSc 1963 PhD 1966
MIBiol 1968
post doct fell. Nott 1966–67; sen lect biol Leic poly 1967–68; Sus: lect biol/sub dean biol sc 1968–72; reader biol from 1972

BAKER Penelope Anne *MA 1969
d of Paul B. B. physioth and Alice M. M. Penney nurs. off.; b Walton-on-Thames 8.6.47
teacher: Christ's hosp girls' h s Lincoln 1970–72; Lubavitch House s London 1972–73; Lond: temp cler and

bank work, Queen's secy coll 1973–74; edit. asst/secy Wiedenfeld & Nicolson, Clapham from 1974
m –.9.75 O'Grady

BAKER Rosemary Clare LLB 1968
d of Norman H. B. tech illustrator GPO and Constance E. Whiting bankruptcy clerk; b Croydon 31.1.47
asst solic Caterham 1971–72; lect law Ewell 1972–74; private pract from 1974
m Sanderstead 16.1.71 James T. W. Adams LLB 1968 *qv*

BAKER Susan Jenifer MA 1965 BSc 1969
m Haddock

BAKIE Elspet Mitchell MA 1960
d of Joseph B. master joiner and Marie L. Gault; b Lossiemouth 12.5.39
teacher: maths Forres 1961–63, Hopeman 1963–64; prim and remed Kirkcaldy from 1972
m Aber 19.7.63 Donald C. Halliday BSc 1960 *qv*

BALAKRISHNAMURTI Thampu Saravanamuttu MSc 1966
s of Thampu Saravanamuttu teacher/law stud. and Mangayarkarasy Thamotharampillai; b Colombo, Sri Lanka 19.10.21
BSc(Lond) 1947
teacher Colombo 1946–50; res off. Lunuwila, Sri Lanka from 1950

BALD Lilian Urquhart MA 1968
d of David B. civ eng and Annie B. Urquhart; b Dingwall 22.2.46
Lond: teacher Brixton 1969–72, audio-visual aids/head remed dept Charlton from 1972
m Aber 3.7.69 David M. W. Martin BSc 1969 *qv*

BALDERSTON Mary Stewart BSc 1966
d of James B. eng and Mary Stewart; b Glasg 4.4.49
teacher geog: Johnstone h s 1967–70, Buenos-Aires 1970–72, Lond 1972–73, Hyndland s s Glasg 1973–76; prin geog Kirkintilloch h s from 1976
m Paisley 4.4.77 Richard H. Thomas MA 1968 *qv*

BALDWIN David Kenneth John *MA 1970 Dip Ed 1971
s of Kenneth J. B. chlorination dept metrop water auth and Lilias M. S. Cruickshank superv racecourse tot. board; b Esher 3.11.47
MEd(Birm) 1976
asst teacher Aylesbury 1971–74; Cleveland educ auth: trainee educ psych 1974–75, educ psych from 1976
m Aber –.9.70 Carol J. L. Martin MA 1970 *qv*

BALDWIN Jaroslav Raymond *BSc(agr) 1963
s of Anthony H. B. BMus(Durh) mus and Miluse Policka; b Dun 9.8.39
teacher biol: Linlathen s Dun 1963–64, 1965–66; Kirklands s Methil from 1966
m Dun 1964 Daisy Sibbald lib, secy d of Archibald S. Dun

BALDWIN John Alexander *MB ChB 1958 *MD 1969
s of John A. B. LDS(Liv) dent surg and Margaret E. Sewell SRN; b Lond 11.12.27
BA(Oxon) 1951 MA(Oxon) 1958 MRCPsych 1971 FFCM 1972
h o ARI 1958–59; clin & res fell. in psychiat Massachusetts gen hosp and Harvard 1959–61; regist Kingseat hosp 1961–62; dept ment health Aberd: sen res fellow 1962–64, Scot. hosp endow res trust fell. 1964–69; dir unit clin epidemiology Oxon, med dir Oxon record linkage study Oxford reg hosp board now RHA hon consult. Oxon AHA(T) from 1969

m Aber 2.10.62 Joy H. Tremlett occup therap d of Alfred J. T. Bristol

BALFOUR Anne Allan MA 1964
d of William Balfour eng BBC and Anne A. Ford; b Sutton 20.7.42
f/lt WRAF educ branch UK and Ger 1965–71; p a to dir educ Cumbria from 1972

BALFOUR Bernard Maitland *MA 1966
s of William C. B. trade union organis and Henrietta Mitchell; b Aber 21.7.28
FSAScot 1976
teacher: spec asst lib stud. Summerhill acad Aber 1967–73, prin hist Hazlehead acad Aber from 1973
m Aber 25.9.52 Isobel Davidson teacher d of Harry D. Aber

BALFOUR Donald James Howland *BSc 1970
s of Walter B. insur ag and Margaret W. Howland secy; b Fearn 29.4.48
post grad res Sheff 1970–73; teacher Isle of Harris from 1974

BALFOUR Walter Joseph *BSc 1963
s of Walter B. insur ag and Margaret W. Howland secy; b Fearn 1.5.41
PhD(McM) 1967
post doct fell. Ottawa 1967–69; Vic BC: asst prof chem 1969–73, assoc prof from 1973
m Victoria BC 10.5.74 Rosemary Picozzi BA(Rdg) assoc prof Ger lang and lit, Vic B.C. d of Nicholas P. MA(Glas) Thorpe Bay

BALFOUR William John BSc 1964
s of Walter B. insur ag and Margaret W. Howland secy; b Fearn 20.1.44
Surrey: insur clerk: actuarial 1964–67, pensions 1967–68, work study off. 1968–70; computer progr from 1970
m Lond 16.9.74 Rosemary A. Philpot secy d of John W. P. Lond

BALL Derrick Frank PhD 1962
s of Frank B. driver and Gladys Hanley; b Lond 7.5.30
BSc(Sheff) 1950 MBSc(Manc) 1975
lect chem Teesside poly 1962–66; sen lect chem Salf from 1966; visiting sen res fell. Manc bus. s 1973–74
m Stockton-on-Tees 25.2.56 Joyce Coffield d of John F. C. Stockton-on-Tees

BALL John Christopher PhD 1957

BALL Matthew Curry PhD 1962
ARIC

BALLANTYNE David Ferguson LLB 1965

BALLANTYNE David John *BSc 1970

BALLARD Peter *BSc 1964
s of Frederick B. rly eng dr and Ellen E. M. M. B. Benton; b Crathie 15.9.41
post grad res Aberd 1964–65; teacher sc: Keith g s 1966–68, RGC Aber 1968–73, prin phys/chem Turriff acad 1973–76, prin chem from 1976

BALLARD Sylvia Teresa MB ChB 1959
b Aber 14.7.35
h o RACH 1959–60; res asst lab City hosp Aber 1960–61; res stud. Newham coll Cantab 1961–62
m Aber 10.8.60 Derek G. Land PhD(Liv) res biochem

BAMFORD John Michael BSc(for) 1966
BSc(NZ)

BAMFORTH Malcolm MB ChB 1957
s of Stanley B. woollen manuf and Lilian Pitchforth; b Brighouse 20.10.31
FRSM 1966
g p Halifax 1958–66; med dir: Berk Pharm Godalming 1966–69, Winthrop Pharm Surbiton and USA 1969–72; g p Halifax from 1972
m Halifax 13.7.57 June Hiller Dip Ed(Lond) teacher d of Fred H. Halifax

BANCROFT David William MA 1959
s of Sidney B. newsagent and Marion Schofield; b St Helen's 29.3.38
nat service R.A. Hong Kong 1959–61; teacher Liv 1962–63; betting off. man. Liv 1963–73, ptnr Wigan 1973–74; civ serv HM customs & excise Liv from 1975
m Liv 10.10.70 Irene G. Wood off. superv d of Henry W. Liv

BANG Ove MB ChB 1961
s of Oscar B. Cand Med(Oslo) distriktslege and Johanne C. Hammer; b Nore Norway 12.3.35
Cand Med(Oslo) 1961
distriktslege Norway: Gildeskal 1964–68, Bodo from 1968
m Trondheim 1962 Eva Andersen teacher d of Thorlief A. Oslo

BANKS David Michael *BSc(eng) 1967 MSc 1970

BANKS Diane MB ChB 1962

BANKS Dorothy Anne BSc 1962
d of David B. watchmaker/optician and Margaret Mackenzie; b Forres 13.7.41
teacher maths: Inv 1963–68, London 1968–71, Cowdenbeath 1971–72; prin guid Cowdenbeath from 1972
m Dunfermline 10.4.71 David J. G. Scott BSc(S'ton) teacher s of John T. S. Dunfermline

BANKS Ernest Alexander LLB 1970
s of Ernest R. B. site clerk and Robina G. Tolan; b Dun 5.1.49
law app Edin 1970–71; Dun: leg. asst 1971–74, self-employed solic from 1974
m Dun 13.7.74 Ann V. Reilly teacher d of James R. Dun

BANKS Hazel Manson *MA 1969
d of William J. B. master draper and Kathleen Coghill shopkeeper & confectioner; b Thurso 9.10.46
housemother: Camphill village for handicapped adults Yorks 1970–73; s for handic adolescents Napier NZ 1974–75; stud. Emerson coll, Sussex 1975–76

BANKS James Andrew MA 1968
s of James A. B. prod. eng and Irene C. Stephen; b Aber 13.1.45
DLC Loughborough coll 1969
teacher p e: Aber acad 1969–71, Queen's coll Nassau 1971–74, Kincorth acad Aber from 1975
m Aber 5.4.71 Jennifer S. Leslie teacher p e, d of Douglas F. L. Stonehaven

BANNERMAN Emily *MA 1966
d of Marcus B. crofter and Georgina Mackay; b Bettyhill 27.6.44
teacher: prin hist Farr s Bettyhill from 1967, dep head
m Thurso 14.4.65 Marcus M. Campbell farm. s of Donald C. Tongue by Lairg

BANNERMAN James Patrick Cochrane *BSc 1969

BANNERMAN Roslyn MA 1969
m Johnston

BANNISTER Peter PhD 1963
s of John B. window cleaner and Gretchen A. S. Taubald teacher; b Preston 2.5.39
BSc(Nott) 1960
Glasg: asst lect bot 1963–65, lect 1965–69; Stir: lect biol 1969–72, sen lect from 1972
m London 26.8.61 Margaret E. Hockley BSc(Nott) teacher d of Reginald H. Lond

BARBER Elizabeth Anne MA 1968
d of Henry C. B. agr seedsman and Winifred M. Brocklehurst; b Grappenhall 30.6.45
teacher Fr and Ger: Huyton coll Liv 1969–71, Tenbury s s Worcs 1971–73
m Stretton 11.8.71 Barnaby K. G. Miln man. dir seed garden centre comp s of William W. G. M. Weaverham

BARBER Jennifer MA 1967
d of John B. baker/confect and Gladys Milne shop asst; b Aber 16.4.46
teacher Arbroath acad 1968–72, asst prin guid. from 1972

BARBER William MA 1961 MEd 1972

BARBOUR Neil McLaurin *BSc(eng) 1962

BARCLAY David John Chalmers MB ChB 1969
s of John J. B. sales rep and Ruby B. Syme; b Aber 23.4.44
DObstRCOG 1974
h o, sen h o ARI 1969–71; S. Af: regist Durban 1971–72, m o Ernest Oppenheimer hosp Welkom 1973–74; g p Mudgee NSW Aust from 1974
m Edin 5.7.69 Jennifer A. Bryce MA 1967 *qv*

BARCLAY David Stewart *BSc 1957
s of Hector G. B. foreman baker and Elizabeth Summers; b Hatton of Cruden 20.11.32
teacher: gen subj Peterhead acad 1957–58, maths/sc Insch 1958–59; Perth h s: 1959–63, spec asst phys 1963–72, asst prin phys from 1972
m Aber 28.3.72 Sheila C. Benzie MA 1966 *qv*

BARCLAY Gordon MB ChB 1967
s of David B. MB ChB 1936 *qv*; b Pontardawe nr Neath 3.11.42
DRCOG 1969 MRCGP 1972/3
h o; casualty med, obst, paediat Aber 1967–69; g p Braintree from 1969
m Aber 1.9.67 Meriel Gordon MA 1969 *qv*

BARCLAY Gordon Campbell *BSc 1970
s of William R. B. stockbroker and Enid A. Strathern; b London 25.1.49
Dip Stat(UCW)(Aberyst) 1974
Lond: asst statist/civ serv cadet Cabinet off. 1973–74, asst Home off. from 1974

BARCLAY Hazel Doreen Emilie BSc 1960
d of James B. farm worker and Emily Angus; b Turriff 25.9.38
teacher biol: Powis s s Aber 1961–63, Vincent Massey h s Brandon Canada 1966–69; lab superv bot Brandon univ from 1969
m Aber 5.7.61 James M. Skinner MA 1955 *qv*

BARCLAY Helen Margaret *MA 1969 Dip Ed 1970
m Robert W. Ashton BSc(eng) 1970 *qv*

BARCLAY Ian Malcolm Taylor BSc 1969

BARCLAY James Quarry BSc 1958

BARCLAY John Edward BMedBiol 1968 MB ChB 1971
s of John W. B. elect. eng and Margaret B. Begg; b Aber 25.5.46
MRCP 1974
h o Woodend hosp Aber, ARI 1971–72; g p Aber, Orkney 1972; lect chem path. Aberd 1972–73; regist Wessex reg renal unit Portsmouth from 1973
m Aber 22.9.67 Alicia G. A. Cunningham speech therap d of John C. Aber

BARCLAY Margaret BSc 1958
d of Hector G. B. foreman baker and Elizabeth Summers; b Hatton of Cruden 21.4.36
teacher sc: Goodlyburn j s s Perth 1959–63, Pitlochry h s from 1963, prin guid
m Aber 12.10.63 John Brydone free-lance reporter s of Archibald S. B. Pitlochry

BARCLAY Mitchell BSc(Eng) 1958

BARCLAY Moira Todd *BSc 1968

BARCLAY Peter Gordon MA 1961

BARCLAY Rodney Gretton Esslemont MA 1970
s of Alfred G. B. banker and Margaret K. Beedie; b Aber 4.11.48
BAC Weybridge: computer progr 1970–71, organis and methods off. 1971, jun syst analyst 1971–72; syst analyst Nestlés Croydon 1972–74; bus. syst analyst BP Chemicals Mayfair Lond from 1975
m Aber 2.8.71 Patricia E. Thomson teacher d of Lesley J. T. Aber

BARCLAY Sheena Mary *MA 1964
d of William A. B. MA 1939 *qv*(III) and Jean P. Buchan MA 1941 *qv*; b Buckie 20.5.42
teacher Fr h s for girls Aber 1965–68
m Penang Malaysia 13.4.68 Karl D. Frankish elect. eng

BARCLAY William BSc 1960 *1962
s of Adam S. H. B. elect. eng and Gudbjorg Jonsson; b Aber 17.2.38
oil and gas exploration: geophys eng GSI Bromley 1963–64; jr–sen geophys Mobil Oil Canada, Calgary 1964–73; geophys Union Oil of GB Richmond 1973–74; sen geophys Oil Exploration (Holdings) Edin from 1974
m Calgary 13.6.70 Leona D. Skibo BA(Calg) med res tech d of Daniel N. S. Calgary

BARCLAY William Hector *MA 1967
s of William P. B. lab and Ann C. McKenzie; b Aber 5.3.40
teacher: Engl Fraserburgh acad 1968–71, prin Engl: Larkhall acad 1971–73, Peterhead acad 1973–76; asst rector Craigie h s Dun from 1976

BARCLAY William John *BSc 1966
s of William B. pharm and Margaret C. Florence; b Aber 15.9.43
FGS
geol Anglo-Amer corp Kabwe Zambia 1966–68; field geol Inst of Geol Sciences Lond from 1968
m Aber 16.5.69 Rachel T. B. Taylor MA 1965 *qv*

BARCLAY William Wilkie MA 1970
s of William G. B. policeman and Isabella H. Wilkie nurse; b Stonehaven 23.1.49
dairy farm worker Tønsberg Norway 1970–71; teacher Liberton s s Edin from 1972

BARCLAY Win Flora Margaret MA 1962
d of James B. livestock auctioneer and Williamina M. Duncan; b Insch 1.4.41
teacher Aber: Willowpark inf s 1963–69, St Margaret's s for girls 1969–74
m Aber 9.10.74 Robert G. Strathdee s of Alfred G. S. Milltimber

BARCLAY-ESTRUP Paul PhD 1966
s of John B.-E. motel owner and Gudrun Kristensen nurse/motel owner; b Calgary 13.2.31
BA(Br Col) 1957
Lake Thunder Bay Canada: asst prof 1966–72, assoc prof from 1972
m Victoria B.C. Patricia M. Westwood BA(Br Col) 1958 book reviewer/radio drama critic d of Albert N. W. Victoria B.C.

BARDEN Nicholas *BSc 1967
s of Frank B. clerk and Mabel Nendick insur ag; b Rotherham 8.7.46
D Phil(Sus) 1970
MRC stud. Sus 1967–70; Laval univ Canada: fell. 1970–73, asst prof from 1973
m Rotherham 1968 Anne C. Chapman teacher d of Henry C. Rotherham

BARKER Joyce BSc 1970
d of Percy S. B. bricklayer and Janet M. Mackay cashier; b Rotherham 16.10.47
teacher: Liberton s s Edin 1971–75, Windsor girls' s Hamm W Ger from 1975

BARKER Veronica Frances *MA 1968
d of James W. B. guard/motorman and Florence M. West tailoress; b Worcester Park 3.4.37
ALA 1972 AIInfS 1974 MIInfS 1976 FLA 1977
asst lib Dund 1968–74; asst med lib Ninewells hosp/med s Dund 1974–76; sen information off. centre for med educ Dund from 1976

BARLATT Daphne Victoria Olakumbi MA 1966

BARLOW Colin Hastings PhD 1964
BSc(Lond) MS(Corn)

BARLOW William BSc 1962

BARNES Keith Frederick BSc 1968
s of Frank A. B. civ serv and Phyllis N. Vince; b East Grinstead 27.5.43
MRIC 1973
lab tech: Inst of Cardiol Lond 1969–70, Kingston poly 1970–72; RIC course Medway and Maidstone coll of tech Chatham 1972–73; res asst chem Thames poly Lond 1973–75; res stud. agr chem Wye coll(Lond) from 1976

BARNES Mavis MA 1962 MLitt 1980
m Gray

BARNETT Bryanne Ethel Waldie MB ChB 1961

BARNETT James BSc 1966

BARNETT John *MA 1970
s of Joseph B. sheet metal worker and Rosina Wilson quality control superv electronics factory; b Glasg 2.10.48
teacher hist Fraserburgh acad 1971–74, prin hist from 1974
m Aber 13.12.69 Angela M. Bray teacher d of John A. B. Scrabster

BARNETT John Keith Ross *MA 1959

BARR Archibald John *MA 1964
s of Archibald J. B. publ and Grizel P. Alexander; b Glasg 25.11.42
CA 1968
man. dir McNaughton & Sinclair Glasg from 1968; dir and secy Munro-Marr publ Glasg from 1972, N Pitglassie Farm. Co Abdnsh from 1973, Scotgolf Serv Glasg from 1973
m Helensburgh 10.1.71 Helen R. Dundas physioth d of Ralph M. D. Helensburgh

BARR Kirsteen Holmes MA 1969
d of Archibald J. B. printer and publ and Grizel P. Alexander; b Kilmacolm 25.12.48
secy: Edin 1970–72, Glasg 1972–73; off. man. Aber from 1974
m Kilmacolm 9.9.72 Robert Davidson syst analyst s of Henry W. D. MA(Glas) Aber

BARR Margaret *MA 1967
d of Archibald J. B. man. dir/publ and Grizel P. Alexander; b Kilmacolm 26.2.45
teacher/lib Minden Germany 1968–69
m Kilmacolm 6.8.67 David H. White major s of Harry A. W. Upper Hatfield

BARR Peter BEd 1969
s of Thomas B. signalman RN, boot and shoe operative and Jean S. Dunlop off. worker, shop asst; b Northants 25.4.45
teacher geog Cumnock 1969–74; asst prin geog Ayr from 1974
m Lerwick 17.7.69 Maureen E. Hobbin BEd 1969 *qv*

BARR William *MA 1963

BARRACK Dianne Margaret MA 1961
d of Ian W. B. bank man. and Emily M. Anderson nurse; b Aber 11.3.40
pers asst: trg off. Nestlé Co Lond 1961–63, prof biochem and prof oceanography MIT USA 1963–69
m Aber 29.6.63 Jon A. McCleverty BSc 1960 *qv*

BARRACK Frances Mary MA 1966
d of William C. B. bank man. and Frances E. Wilson secy; b Ellon 21.5.45
teacher: Kirkhill p s Aber 1967–68, maths Kidderminster 1968–70, Bridge of Allan p s 1970–71
m Aber 27.7.68 Peter G. Morrison MA 1967 *qv*

BARRACK Iris Patricia MA 1966
d of Lewis B. farm. and Violet Moir; b Kinellar 1.11.43
teacher: Engl/Lat Inverurie acad 1968–70, Engl Glenrothes h s 1970–71 tut. Engl: Basil Paterson coll Edin from 1977
m Rayne 25.12.65 Frederick D. F. Shewan MA 1966 *qv*

BARRACK James White *BSc(eng) 1964
s of James R. B. farm. and Margaret S. White; b Ellon 6.10.41
MSc(eng)(Lond) 1972 DIC(Lond) 1972 MICE 1969 FRSA 1973
Sir R. McAlpine & Sons: civ eng on site—jun and sect. eng York 1964–65, Doncaster 1965–67; civ des eng Knutsford from 1967
m Aber 21.7.65 Betty T. Hardie MA 1963 *qv*

BARRASS Kenneth Neil BSc 1970

BARRETT William *MA 1963
s of Frederick B. operative cotton spinner, sheet metal worker and Bertha Bradley dressmaker; b Ashton-under-Lyne 1.11.29
psych: Belfast 1963–65, Sleaford 1965–66, Portsmouth 1966–67, Chichester 1967–73; clin psych St James hosp Portsmouth from 1973
m Lancaster 31.8.63 Kristin Maclennan MA 1962 *qv*

BARRETT-AYRES Ross BSc(eng) 1969
s of Reginald B.-A. Bac Mus(Edin) head mus dept Aberd and Elizabeth J. D. Ewing; b Edin 26.10.47
MICE
civ eng Aber c c 1970–74; asst lect (VSO) univ Benin, Nigeria 1974–75; civ eng Grampian reg from 1975
m Aber 21.12.70 Alexandra Berry MB ChB 1971 d of Alistair B. Stirling

BARRIE Gordon MB ChB 1968

BARRIT Derek Swaine MB ChB 1959
s of Jeffrey B. pharm and Gladys M. Swaine; b Hull 8.3.32
h o Aber, Perth, Middlesbrough 1960–61; g p Cold Lake Alberta 1961–62, Goodsoil Sask 1963–74; hosp m o Winnipeg from 1975
m Aber 6.7.56 Catherine W. G. Wood teacher d of George W. Aber

BARRON Aileen Ann MA 1968
d of James B. grocer and Mary B. B. Ferguson; b Edin 30.11.46
teacher Aber, Glasg from 1968
m Aber 4.7.69 James A. I. MacEwan MA 1969 *qv*

BARRON Anne Alexandra *BSc 1965 PhD 1978
d of Thomas B. gamekeeper and Lily Ross dom serv; b Dingwall 18.2.43
MSc(UCNW) 1971
res asst human cytogenetics Sheff 1966–69; jun tech off. MRC Harwell 1969–70; res asst immunology Aberd 1972–75
m St Albans 24.11.76 Malcolm Dye PhD 1976 res microbiol s of Jack E. D. Hunstanton

BARRON Charles Aitken *MA 1958
s of Charles F. B. storekeeper and Elizabeth M. Aitken; b Aber 11.1.36
teacher Engl Inverurie 1959–63; lect Glasgow 1963–70; head of drama coll of educ Aber from 1970
m Aber 1961 Margaret M. Shand MA 1961 *qv*

BARRON David James *MA 1965

BARRON Edward James MB ChB 1961
s of Edward B. stationmaster BR and Mary W. Dawson; b Keith 10.6.38
h o ARI, City hosp Aber 1961–62; Burnie Tasmania: sen h o 1962–63, g p 1963–70; g p Somerset Tasmania from 1970
m Aber 25.4.62 Elizabeth L. Lindsay nurs sister d of Charles D. L. Ballater

BARRON Hugh Wilson Taylor *BSc 1964 PhD 1971
s of Edward B. stationmaster BR and Mary W. Dawson b Portgordon 25.3.43
nat phil dept Aberd: asst lect 1968–70, lect from 1970
m Aber 11.12.71 Grace M. Scott secy, aux nurse d of Ernest J. S. Aber

BARRON Joan Louise MA 1970 CASS 1972
d of Douglas H. B. welfare off. for the blind and Helen L. Ironside; b Aber 22.5.49
soc worker Aber assoc of soc serv from 1972
m Aber 5.7.72 Leslie Hutton teacher s of Alexander H. Aber

BARRON Kathleen Elizabeth *MA 1960
d of Charles F. B. storekeeper and Elizabeth M. Aitken shop asst; b Aber 26.10.37
secy/translator STC Lond 1961–62; teacher: Fr/Ger Woodford county h s 1962–64; Wombourne: teacher Westfield jun s 1973–76, prin Fr Westfield middle s from 1976
m Aber 11.8.62 David A. Watkins BA(Birm) teacher s of Frederick W. Luton

BARRON Margaret MA 1969
d of John B. fisherman and Mary B. MacLean; b Nairn 8.3.48
teacher: Forres acad 1971–73; Ludenscheid W Ger 1973–74; Forres acad from 1974
m Senior

BARRON Norma Margaret BSc 1957
d of Norman J. B. MA 1923 *qv*; b Aber 31.1.36
res asst zool: Nott 1958–61, Wye coll Ashford Kent 1962–63
m Aber 17.7.61 David J. Hannant BSc(Nott) lect civ eng s of Eric L. H. New Barnet

BARRON Patricia BSc 1959 *1960 PhD 1963
d of Norman J. B. MA 1923 *qv*; b Aber 1.1.39
res asst: anat Aberd 1963–64, biol Middx hosp med s Lond 1964–66; res fell. genetics Edin from 1967
m Aber 21.3.64 Iain B. R. Bowman BSc 1959 *qv*

BARRON Philip Thomson MB ChB 1962
s of Robert T. B. civ serv and Ann Philip clerkess; b Aber 18.5.38
FRCS(Can) 1971
h o ARI 1962–65; dem dept anat Manc 1965–66; res surg Ottawa civic hosp 1967–72; lect dept surg Ott from 1973; consult. surg Ottawa civic hosp
m Elgin 1963 M. Joan Mavor radiogr d of James M. Elgin

BARRON Richard William *MA 1970 Dip Ed 1972
s of James W. B. lect and Muriel T. Kennedy; b Aber 19.1.49
1st year div course Edin 1970–71; teacher classics Dumbarton from 1972

BARRON Rosemary MacLean MA 1970
d of John B. fisherman and Mary MacLean; b Nairn 30.8.49
teacher Fr Perth h s from 1971

BARRON Thomas James *MA 1962
s of Thomas L. B. eng storeman and Mary A. Urquhart; b Peterhead 20.1.40
PhD(Lond) 1969
post grad stud. Lond 1962–65; lect Edin from 1965

BARRON Veronica Moira MA 1970
d of Stanley D. B. joiner and Moira M. Mann; b Aber 10.3.49
cler asst DHSS Aber 1971–72
m Aber 15.1.72 James P. Robertson bldg mason s of Alan R. Aber

BARRY John BSc(eng) 1961
s of John B. B. mason/draughtsman and Alice E. L. Wilson; b Aber 30.7.40
CEng MICE 1967
eng: asst Crouch & Hogg consult. Glasg, Angus 1961–63, Williamson & Ptnrs consult. Glasg, Edin 1963–66; sen eng Mitchell Construction Co Glasg, Peterborough 1966–67; asst, sen, resid eng Lanark c c from 1967
m Aber 14.9.63 Marjory A. Stalker teacher d of William S. Aber

BARTON Anne Margaret BEd 1969
d of Roy B. carpet fitter/salesman and Margaret H. Vass; b Inv 16.9.47
teacher Engl: Niagara Falls collegiate Ont 1969–71, Dumfries h s 1971–73, Buckhaven h s 1973–76
m Inv 4.4.69 John G. Reid MA 1966 *qv*

BARTON Rae Colledge MA 1958 ᶜLLB 1960
s of George E. C. B. MA 1929 *qv*; b Aber 6.2.39
part time asst law Aberd 1960–68; ptnr Stronachs, advoc Aber
m Glasg 10.7.63 Eileen E. D. Goodall teacher d of David G. MA(Glas) Thornliebank

BASHAM Ian Reginald BSc 1961 *1964 PhD 1968
s of Reginald J. B. (retired) and Flora Denoon; b Quendon 8.12.39
FGS 1961
asst exper off. Macaulay inst Aber 1961–63; geol surv: mineralogist Ghana 1964–65, mineralogist/tech aid expert Sierra Leone 1969–70; prin scient off. in applied mineralogy unit inst of geol sc Lond from 1970
m Aber 8.8.63 Sheena A. Macpherson teacher d of William P. M. Huntly

BASIT Mohammed Abdul MSc 1966 PhD 1969
MSc(Kar)

BATCHELOR Martyn Aubrey *MA 1969
s of Aubrey R. B. OBE secy and Dorothy G. M. Ford; b Sutton Coldfield 22.10.46
Dip LD(N'cle) 1971 AILA 1974
land arch. asst Derek Lovejoy & Ptnrs N'cle 1971; sen city arch. dept N'cle 1971–74; prin landscape arch. S Tyneside metro bor South Shields from 1974
m Sutton Coldfield 25.3.72 Lindsay J. Faulconbridge BA(Durh) 1969 land. arch. d of Robert C. F. Glamorgan

BATES Russell *MA 1969 Dip Ed 1970

BATESON John David MSc 1968
BA(Durh)

BATSON Gerald Audley ᶜMB ChB 1960 MD 1969
s of Frederick E. B. gen man. Trinidad Sugar Estates and Iris Pearce; b Trinidad 3.2.35
regist: cardiol N'cle gen hosp 1966–68, gen med Royal Victoria I N'cle 1968–70; sen regist: cardiol N. gen hosp Sheffield 1970–72, gen med Sheffield RI 1972–74; consult. phys Scunthorpe health dist from 1974
m Gateshead 28.1.69 Pamela M. Scott SRN d of Archibald T. S. Gateshead

BAXTER Aldon Thompson *MA 1966
d of Gordon A. B. MA(St And) teacher, headmaster and Margaret S. A. Thompson MA(Edin) teacher; b Fordyce 19.6.44

teacher Lond 1967–71 and from 1978
m Aber 16.7.66 James Williamson PhD 1965 *qv*

BAXTER Colin Henry MB ChB 1966
s of Henry R. B. lect and Iris B. Young; b Jarrow 3.1.42
MCFP 1971 LMCC 1972
h o Stirling RI, ARI 1966–67; lect chem path. Aberd 1967–69; trainee g p Aber 1969–70; Toronto: g p Yorkview med centre, m o Pilkington Glass Co from 1970; active staff York Finch gen hosp
m Aber 23.12.65 Margaret E. Tough teacher art/artist d of William T. Aber

BAXTER Kenneth BSc 1961

BAXTER Margaret McLaren MA 1961
d of John F. B. garrison works off. DoE and Margaret M. Campbell; b Perth 28.11.39
teacher Perth 1962–66, Stirling 1966–72, Episkopi Cyprus 1972–74, Gütersloh W Ger 1974–75; asst prin Engl Kirkcaldy from 1975
m Dollar 29.7.66 Duncan M. Kennedy MA 1964 *qv*
marr diss 1972

BAXTER Margaret Sophia MA 1961 Dip Ed 1962
m Alford 19.9.64 Geoffrey M. Telling MSc 1965 *qv*

BAYFIELD Neil Gillan PhD 1967
BSc(Bangor)

BAYNE Rowan Stewart Ian Yelland *MA 1970 PhD 1977
s of James I. B. tv eng man. and Edna Wilder nurse; b Reading 16.8.47
res stud. Aberd 1970–74; psych civ serv dept Lond 1974–79; lect NE Lond poly from 1979
m Aber –.12.70 Elma Garden teacher d of Alister G. Aber

BEAR Keith Patrick *MA 1965
s of Robert T. B. hairdresser and Kathleen A. Mugan; b Stafford 1.11.42
Dip Ed(Edin) 1966
teacher Engl: Trinity acad Edin 1966–69, spec asst Kirkcaldy h s 1969–71; prin Engl St Patrick's h s Dumbarton 1971–74; asst rector St Saviour's h s Dun from 1974
m Aber 1.8.72 Jean E. Gray MA 1965 *qv*

BEATON Alasdair William Stewart BSc(eng) 1966

BEATON George Alexander LLB 1968
s of John G. B. and Nancy S. Milne; b Banff 22.7.47
law app, leg. asst Aber 1968–71; leg. asst Dun 1971–72; leg. asst, ptnr Edin 1972–75; dep chief exec Sutherland dist c Golspie from 1975
m Aber 18.7.70 Deirdre A. Smith LLB 1971 d of Richard S. Kingussie

BEATON John McCall *BSc 1966 MSc 1969
s of Walter W. B. man. dir and Elizabeth H. S. McCall; b Huntly 21.6.44
PhD(Alabama) 1973
sen res asst addiction res foundation Toronto 1969–71; univ of Alabama Birm USA: instr 1971–73, asst prof psychiat/psych 1973–76, assoc prof from 1976
m Aber 20.4.68 Eleanor Rose d of James R. Aber

BEATON Margaret Hamilton MA 1970
d of Kenneth B. upholst/house furn and Catherine M. Hamilton secy; b Dingwall 20.3.50
asst lib Aber from 1972
m Dingwall 17.7.70 Norman M. Macrae des eng s of Farquhar M. Strathcarron

BEATON Mary BEd 1968
d of David W. B. fishmonger and Mary A. Watt; b Aber 22.12.17
Aber: teacher Engl/hist Summerhill acad 1968–72 and careers mistress 1972–73; teacher Engl and year mistress Torry acad from 1973
m Aber 15.10.41 John M. Loggie merch N off. s of George R. L. Torphins; husb *d* 29.10.66

BEATTIE Alan Gordon BMedBiol 1968 MB ChB 1971
s of Alexander G. B. MB ChB 1939 *qv*; b Aber 24.9.47
MRCP 1974
h o ARI 1971–72; res fell. dept med Aberd 1972–73; sen h o gen med Aber city hosp 1973–74; regist gen med Woodend hosp Aber 1974; res fell. therap Aberd 1974–75; g p Aboyne 1975–76; regist gen med Aber from 1976
m Newton Mearns Christine A. Uytman nurs sister d of Harold B. U. Newton Mearns

BEATTIE Alastair MA 1958 LLB 1960
s of Archibald B. rly lengthman and Evelyn S. Bennett; b Aber 11.10.37
leg. asst, sen, prin asst Dumfries c c 1961–67; dep clerk Caithness c c Wick 1967–75; chief exec Caithness dist council from 1975
m Dumfries 21.1.65 Rosaline Wright secy d of George W. W. Dumfries

BEATTIE Eileen Margaret MB ChB 1958

BEATTIE George *BSc 1959

BEATTIE James Alexander Gordon MB ChB 1967 DMRD 1972
s of Alexander G. B. MB ChB 1939 *qv*; b Aber 23.4.43
DObstRCOG 1970
ARI: h o 1967–69, sen h o, regist radio diagnosis 1970–72; g p Edin 1972–74, Inverurie from 1974
m Aber 1.8.68 Jennifer B. Nichols teacher d of Walter M. N. MB ChB(Glas) Glasg

BEATTIE Marilyn Watson *MA 1964
d of Bruce B. mill worker, masseur and Mary Watson; b Forfar 13.10.41
MA(Manit) 1965
teacher: Turriff 1966–67, Monifieth 1967, teacher Fr: Bottisham 1967–68, Exeter 1969–71
m Aber 12.8.67 William F. Hunter MA 1964 *qv*

BEATTIE Maureen Joan MA 1970
d of David B. acct and Maud MacGillivray audit asst; b Inv 14.6.49
teacher: Maisondieu s Brechin from 1971
m Inv 12.7.74 Iain A. Bain MA 1971 s of Alastair I. R. B. Nairn

BEATTIE Robert Dennis MA 1957

BEATTIE Sheena Margaret MA 1963
d of Robert A. B. farm. and Margaret D. Skinner; b Insch 10.9.42
teacher Gordon s Huntly 1964–67
m Kennethmont 23.7.66 George J. McConachie farm. s of Robert McC. Wardhouse

BEAVINGTON Frank MSc 1967
s of Edward N. B. farm. and Eva Shotbolt; b Hulcote 6.10.27
BA(Lond) 1954 PhD(Lond) 1961
visiting lect geog: univ of New Eng Aust 1967, univ of Ibadan 1967–68; sen lect Wollongong univ coll Aust from 1969, prof geog Ahmadu Bello univ Kano 1974

m Sydney 20.6.70 Ruth B. Rainsford BA(Syd) teacher d of Milton J. J. R. Turramurra NSW

BECERRA Luis Arcadio MSc 1965
BSc(agr)(Puerto Rico)

BECK Thelma Cecilia PhD 1968
d of Walter N. B. comm trav and Elsie F. Beresford; b Lond 25.10.34
BSc(Lond) 1959 and 1961
Lond: tech King's coll hosp med s 1959, res asst univ coll 1959–63; Aber: res asst univ 1963–65, scient off. inst marine biochem 1965–73, prin scient off. from 1973
m Lond 11.8.62 Hugo J. Fletcher BSc(Lond) lect s of Walter J. F. Lond

BECKETT Edward George MA 1967

BECKLEY Sandra Jane MA 1966
d of Vernon E. W. B. banker and Alma M. Houlgate; b Sanderstead 25.4.44
m Sanderstead 6.8.66 John McQuillan MA 1965 *qv*

BECK-SLINN Iain *MA 1970
s of George A. B. S. banker and Hilda J. Gordon prob off.; b Aber 1948
MSc(H-W) 1972 MRTPI 1974
plan. asst W Lothian c c 1972–73; sen plan. Banff c c 1973–75, Grampian reg from 1975
m Insch 1970 Elaine Cowie teacher d of William C. Insch

BEDDARD Susan Rydal MA 1967
d of Frederick D. B. MB BS(Lond) med admin and Anne Porter teacher; b Windermere 13.2.45
secy: Ferranti Edin 1968–69, dept psych Edin 1969–70, dept arch. Edin from 1973
m (1) Aber 3.8.68 Jeremy O'Regan MA 1967 *qv*
marr diss 1.9.74
(2) Weymouth 22.10.76 Michael S. Spring MA(Cantab) computer consult. s of Albert E. S. Warrington

BEDDOE Michael Richard LLB 1968
s of Jack E. B. BA(Cantab) chief exec Severn water auth; b Aber 3.5.45
law app, solic Aber 1970–73; solic Edin from 1973

BEECH Maureen Theresa MA 1964

BEGBIE Olivia Margaret Murdoch BEd 1969
b Edin 30.7.44
teacher geog Bellevue s Edin 1969–74, remed Drummond h s Edin from 1974

BEGG Alan George MA 1967

BEGG Alan John MA 1969
s of James B. paper-finishing man. and Gladys E. Chilles lib; b Aber 19.11.48
Aber: app CA 1969–73, div acct from 1973
m Aber 24.1.72 Sheena E. Newby accounts clerkess d of Albert W. N. Aber

BEGG Alistair Hendry Emslie BSc 1956

BEGG Ian Stewart Darroch MB ChB 1967 DMRD 1971
s of Norman D. B. MB ChB 1929 *qv*; b Harrowby 21.7.44
DMRD(Lond) 1972
h o Inv and ARI 1967–69; trainee radiol Aber hosp 1969–71; regist radiol Aber 1971–72; g p Aber from 1972
m Aber 15.7.67 Carolyn I. Magee MA 1967 *qv*

BEGG Ingrid Edith MA 1969
d of William G. A. B. MB ChB(Glas) consult. psychiat and Lucy M. R. Clarkson; b Ayr 22.10.45
teacher Engl: Kilmarnock 1970–71, Ayr from 1973; Hodder & Stoughton publ Lond 1971–73

BEGG John Alexander Sutherland MA 1959
s of Daniel A. B. grocer and Elizabeth B. Sutherland; b Castletown 2.7.38
BCom(Edin) 1961
man. posts Lewis's/Selfridge's dept store group Glasg 1961–73; dep chief exec Supa Centa (subsid of Lewis's) Lond 1973–75; man. dir Supa Centa Northampton 1975–76; chief exec Lewis's Saverstore Ellesmere Port 1976–79; dir Lewis's Liv from 1979
m Irby 21.10.78 Lesley D. Nicol secy d of Donald N. Thingwall

BEGG Lorna Marion MA 1959
d of Robert W. A. B. min of relig and Jessie H. Notman nurse; b Unst 26.1.38
Dip R E 1960
teacher: Aber 1960–62, Stirling 1962–66; admin asst Strath 1966–68; dep acad secy Stir from 1968
m Paterson

BEGG Norman Roderick Darroch MA 1962 LLB 1964
s of Norman D. B. MB ChB 1929 *qv*; b Islington 23.12.41
admin asst: E Ang 1964–66, Aberd 1966–68; asst secy (acad) Aberd 1968–76; registry off. Aberd from 1976
m Aber –.7.65 Elizabeth J. Davidson teacher d of Alexander M. D. Cults

BEGG Wilma Ann Cattanach *MA 1962
d of Alexander M. B. master butcher, hotelier and Christina E. Bruce caterer, hotelier; b Montrose 7.5.40
teacher hist: Kinross 1963–66, Aber 1964–69
m 18.8.69 John K. L. MacLean BSc(St And) des and dev eng s of Lindsay M. BSc(St And) Sandwick Shetland

BELL Agnes Davidson BEd 1969

BELL Alfred Alan *MA 1967

BELL David Scott *MA 1970
s of David B. MA(Edin) bus. man. and Irene S. Page; b Edin 7.5.47
MSc(S'ton) 1971
post grad stud. Wolfson coll Oxon 1971–74; res fell. centre for Europ stud. Sus from 1974

BELL Eileen Jessica BEd 1969
d of James A. B. shepherd and Margaret Nisbet; b Kelso 4.4.48
teacher Engl Newbattle h s Dalkeith 1969–75
m Dalkeith 13.7.74 Charles B. S. Gibson MA(Edin) teacher maths s of John E. G. Musselburgh

BELL Gavin Clement *MA 1967
s of Clement W. B. MA 1942 *qv* and Margaret I. R. Angus MA 1942 *qv*; b Aber 14.4.44
res stud. Selwyn coll Cantab 1967–68; teacher George Watson's coll Edin 1969–73; asst prin Ger Arbroath h s 1973–75; prin Ger Harlaw acad Aber from 1976
m Altrincham 29.12.70 Patricia M. Scott BA(Com) (Manc) univ careers advis d of W. F. S. Cheshire

BELL Jennifer MA 1970

BELL John Douglas Gordon *MA 1969
s of Douglas B. MB ChB(Edin) phys and Rose

Gordon nurs sister; b Aber 4.12.46
LRAM 1968
freelance arranger/composer Lond from 1969
m Aber 21.8.70 Angela M. James MA 1969 *qv*

BELL Kathleen Eleanor *MA 1967

BELL Kathleen Taylor MA 1969
d of Joseph B. aircraft fitter (Brit aerospace) and A. J. Kathleen Taylor; b Elgin 5.6.48
teacher: Elgin 1970–75, BFPO Münster W Ger 1976, Lossiemouth 1976–78, itinerant mus 1978, Lossiemouth from 1978
m Elgin 25.3.78 Nigel S. Robinson flying off. RAF s of Kenneth R. Whitby

BELL Margot MA 1970
civ serv: Lond 1971–72, Elgin from 1973
m Edin 12.9.69 Graham Tuley BSc(for) 1970 *qv*

BELL Mary Rose MB ChB 1967
d of Douglas B. MB ChB(Edin) chest phys and Rose Gordon nurs sister; b Cairo 21.7.43
DA 1969
h o ARI 1967–68; regist anaest Falkirk 1969; occasional locums from 1969; part time res work for NCB on pneumoconiosis in miners inst occup med from 1974
m Aber 23.11.68 Peter H. Fettes MB ChB 1968 *qv*

BELL Thomas Matthew PhD 1962
s of Thomas M. B. headmaster and Kate G. Lindsay; b Greenock 22.8.36
BSc(Glas) 1959 MRCPath 1968 BA(OU) 1975
lect Aberd 1959–63; leader Afr proj imp cancer res fund Entebbe 1963–69; sen virol MRC demyelinating dis unit and hon lect N'cle 1969–72; lect virol N'cle 1973–74; sen lect from 1974
m Glasg Fiona M. Downie civ serv d of Archibald D. Dunoon

BELL Wendy Erskine Wetherly MA 1963
d of Harold F. B. policeman, hotelier and Mary E. Wetherly nurse; b Aber 19.5.43
secy: Lond 1964, Edin 1965–72, Houston Texas 1972–76, Raleigh NC from 1976
m Aber 20.3.65 Gordon B. Burnett MB ChB 1964 *qv*

BELLIS Joanna Christine MB ChB 1965
d of Herbert H. B. retailer and Marjorie D. Charlton writer; b Woodford 31.10.39
DA 1968
h o RACH, City hosp Aber 1965–66; sen h o: med Woodend hosp Aber 1967, sen h o, regist Guildford 1967–69; clin asst anaest Lancaster 1970–74; dept m o commun health Barrow from 1974
m Ilford 3.9.67 David K. Lindley BSc(for) 1963 *qv*

BELLRINGER Alan Wayland PhD 1968
s of Clarence W. B. carpet des and Edith G. M. Sayer secy; b Croydon 26.8.32
MA(Glas)
lect Engl univ coll of N Wales Bangor 1968–74, sen lect from 1974
m Bangor 5.7.65 Jean W. Taylor BA(Wales) tech coll lect d of Thomas A. T. Belper

BELTON Sidney James MA 1966

BEMBRIDGE Peter Christopher LLB 1967

BENECKE Udo BSc(for) 1961
s of Joachim A. B. PhD(Berlin) diplomat and Wilfriede L. H. Brackemann; b Lemgo Germany 1.4.40
M Agr Sc(Canterbury NZ) 1968 Dr oec publ(München) 1972
NZ: scient Rangiora 1962–76, Christchurch from 1976
m Christchurch 1.5.65 Jennifer A. Jack nurse d of Gordon D. J. Hokitika NZ

BENJAMIN Michael Ian BSc 1969 MB ChB 1969
s of Cyril A. B. chem and Florence H. Warshowski; b Leeds 15.7.44
Dip Psycho-therap(Tel-Aviv) 1978
Israel: h o Asof Marofe 1970–71; resid Beit Yam 1971–72; army psychiat I.D.F. 1972–76; consult. psychiat: nat insur/Israel milit industries/nat road safety council from 1976
m Tel-Aviv 10.11.78 Patricia R. Kelly admin (Hotel-Sheraton T.A.), teacher of art

BENNET Anne Margaret *MA 1961
m Chandler

BENNETT Colin *MA 1963
d Glasg 5.8.73 *AUR* XLV 322

BENNETT David Stephen BSc 1968

BENNETT James Roy *BSc 1962 PhD 1967
s of Norman S. B. eng/man. dir and Mary Gowans; b Perth 9.4.40
teacher: Falkirk h s 1967–69; head biol Graeme h s from 1969
m Brechin 5.8.66 Barbara M. Eunson BSc 1965 *qv*

BENNETT John David MA 1970

BENNETT John Michael PhD 1966

BENNETT Norman Bruce MB ChB 1963 MD 1967
s of Norman S. B. eng and Mary Gowans; b Gorakphur India 5.7.38
MRCP 1969 MRCPath 1973
Aberd: Ashley Mackintosh res fell. med 1964–65, MRC jun res fell. med 1965–67, lect med 1967–70, Wellcome res fell. and sen lect med from 1973; Eli Lilly internat fell. Cleveland Ohio 1970–73
m Kirkby Lonsdale 1973 Gillian D. Adey MB ChB 1968 *qv*

BENNETT Peter James *BSc(for) 1967

BENNETT Peter Norman MB ChB 1963 *MD 1967
s of Norman B. tea planter and Jane E. Ogston teacher; b Calcutta 25.11.39
MRCP(UK)
res fell., lect med Aberd 1964–71; Wellcome res fell. clin pharm UCH med s Lond 1971–73; lect clin pharm Royal post grad med s Hammersmith hosp Lond from 1973
m Kirkella 31.8.63 Jennifer M. Brocklehurst MB ChB 1963 *qv*

BENNETT Richard Dawson *MA 1964 Dip Ed 1965

BENNETT Valerie MA 1963

BENNISON George Mills PhD 1959
BSc(Durh) 1943 MSc(Durh) 1951
lt REME 1943–45; asst geol Glas 1947–49; lect geol: Aberd 1949–60, Birm 1960–71, sen lect from 1971
m Lond 11.7.43 Gwendoline McQueen secy, teacher d of William McQ. Lond

BENTINCK Susan Joyce *BSc 1969
d of Gordon T. B. p o telecomm and Joyce Mearns wages clerk; b Middlesbrough 15.5.47

teacher: Farnham Common 1970–71, Honiara Sol Is 1971–72
m Leeds 28.8.71 Christopher J. Lomas BSc(agr) 1970 *qv*

BENZIE Alexander Stewart MB ChB 1970
s of Alexander B. farm. and Margaret S. Harcus MA (Edin) teacher; b Glasg 24.11.46
DObstRCOG 1973 MRCGP 1976
h o Aber hosps 1970–71; sen h o Inv hosps 1971; m o RAF 1971–77; g p Jeddah Saudi Arabia from 1977
m Aber 15.7.70 Dorothy C. Lunney MB ChB 1970 *qv*

BENZIE Carmen Hill Elmslie MA 1957
d of Athol B. man. dir dept store and Carmen H. Allan teacher, secy; b Aber 8.4.37
secy: export/import firm Lond 1958–59, to dir J. Lyons & Co Lond 1959–63, to dir of prop. comp Glasg 1963–65
m Aber 1.5.65 George Ritchie man. dir dept store s of William R. Glasg

BENZIE Heather Aileen BSc 1956
d of James S. B. housing factor and Helen M. Rattray loc govt off.; b Aber 12.5.35
teacher: sc Aber 1957–58, Wick 1958–62, Halkirk p s from 1970
m Aber 6.8.58 Hamish I. Gunn BSc 1955 *qv*

BENZIE Helen MA 1962
m Welham

BENZIE Ronald John MB ChB 1961

BENZIE Sheila Clark MA 1966
d of James B. and Isabella Clark; b Perth 28.4.45
Dip Ed(Glas) 1967
teacher: Engl/Fr Perth 1968–73, asst prin guid from 1973
m Aber 1972 David S. Barclay BSc 1957 *qv*

BERG Peter Jack BSc(for) 1969
s of Jack H. B. for. contr and Muriel E. Gray; b Palmerston North NZ 23.9.45
BSc(Auck) 1966
NZ for. serv: for. Kaikohe, Thames 1969–70, dist for. Waitemata 1970–75; chief for. off. Apia Samoa from 1978
m Waimate North 7.3.70 Glenda A. Hoult shorthand typist d of Ralph W. H. Ohaeawai NZ

BERGER Jennifer *BSc 1967
d of John B. MRCVS(Lond) vet surg and Leslie M. Stewart; b UK 10.9.44
MA(Calif) 1969 (Zool) MPH(Calif) 1971
co-ordinator freedom commun clin Calif 1971; Nairobi: Frederikson pop. fell./guest auxil FAO 1971–73, pop. educ and eval spec in progr for better family living FAO from 1974

BERGER Vere *MA 1969
d of John B. MRCVS(Lond) vet surg and Leslie M. Stewart; b Wilmslow 8.1.46
MSocW(Sus) 1971
soc worker Berks c c from 1971

BERRIDGE Paul MB ChB 1964
b Blackburn 23.9.39
DObstRCOG 1966

BERROW Michael Lloyd PhD 1958
s of Leslie L. B. pharm and Winifred D. Brown; b Norwood 20.7.32
BSc(Wales) 1955
soil chem agr dev and advis serv Bristol 1959–60; res staff Macaulay inst for soil res Aber from 1960
m Aber 30.9.66 Sylvia M. Hartley asst scient off. d of Harold B. H. Aber

BERRY Mary Alice Jane *MA 1965

BERRYMAN Julia Clare *BSc 1968
d of Eric R. B. solic and Jerameane R. Garnett; b Luton 6.5.45
PhD(Leic) 1974
Leic: res asst dept psych 1969–74, res fell. dept psych 1974–75, lect psych dept adult educ from 1976

BERTRAM Barbara Costie MB ChB 1956
d of William B. marine eng (insur) and Mabel Flett; b S Shields 12.12.31
h o RI Inv 1956, S Shields 1957; sen h o: paediat Sunderland 1958, mat. N Shields 1958; g p trainee Inv 1959
m Inv 2.4.60 Duncan Livingstone LRCPGlas m o h Kincardine s of George L. Inv

BERTRAM Julia Stanley *BSc 1969
d of James S. B. eng and Evelyn Buchanan clerkess; b Glasg 9.2.47
geol Zeehan Tasmania 1969–71, Perth W Aust from 1971
m Bearsden 7.8.69 Kenneth M. Ferguson BSc 1969 *qv*

BERY Jawaharlal BSc(eng) 1957
s of Cate A. R. B. and Kaushalaya Handa; b Lahore 28.9.35
BSc(Calc) 1955 MIE(India) 1972
trainee Mitchell eng co Lond 1957–59; Bery Bros eng workshop Calcutta: asst works man. 1959–67, purchase off. 1969–76; commercial off. Bery Machin Manuf Calcutta from 1976

BETTRIDGE Ann Elizabeth BSc 1969
d of Robert C. B. man. sales eng and Audrey Weeder playgroup organis; b Evesham 6.7.48
teacher: Elton county jun s Bury 1970–71, Hillside middle s Skelmersdale 1971–72, games Oakdale middle s Poole 1972–75
m N'cle-u-Tyne 14.9.68 Neil W. Sharp MA 1970 *qv*

BEVERIDGE Thomas MB ChB 1969
BSc(Glas)

BEVERLY Eric Angus *MA 1967
s of Edwin A. B. bank off. and Alice Fleming teacher; b Aber 18.11.43
res stud. Aber 1967–70; lect Fr: Warw 1970–71, poly Plymouth from 1971

BEVERLY Gordon Maxwell *BSc 1963 PhD 1966
s of John B. painter and Mary D. Bowie; b Huntly 18.3.41
post doct fell.: univ of Maine 1966–67, univ of N Carolina 1967–68; res chem ICI plastics div Welwyn Garden City from 1969
m Huntly 17.9.66 Irene G. Brander dent nurse d of Charles B. Huntly

BEWS Alan Alexander MA 1966
s of James B. farm man. and Mary J. Robertson; b Rhynie 6.9.45
Aber: CA app F. A. Ritson & Co 1966–72, acct JGB Oil Serv Centres and assoc comps from 1972

BEWS Isobel Mary MA 1962

BEWS Neil Davidson BSc 1963
s of Donald B. tech advis and Adeline E. Davidson clerkess; b Aber 9.4.43

Carshalton: shift man. chem firm 1963–70; asst prod. man. from 1970
m Aber -.9.65 Joyce M. Reid secy d of Albert M. R. Aber

BEY Norman Stewart MA 1968

BEYTS Diana Mary *MA 1968 Dip Ed 1973
d of Clement E. B. asst lib Aberd and Edna M. Davidson; b Aber 13.2.47
field asst geog field centre Dale Fort 1968–70; teacher Ashington 1971–72
m Bainbridge 5.9.72 Nigel Dower lect

BHATT Gunvant Shankerprasad MB ChB 1966
s of S. M. B. MBBs(Bom) and Vidya Dave; b Nairobi 8.9.38
LMCC 1970
h o Kilmarnock I and Ballochmyle hosp 1967–68; g p Prescott Ont from 1968

BHATTI Perveen Akhtar MB ChB 1965
d of Abdul K. B. army off. and Feroza Janjua; b Rawalpindi Pakistan 3.12.41
DObstRCOG 1967
h o Aber 1965–66, Cambridge 1967; g p Sudbury Canada from 1968
m Manc 27.5.69 Iftikhar Hosain MSc(McG) geophys s of Tassaduq H. MBBS(Punjab) Rawalpindi

BHATTY Muhammed Salabat Yar PhD 1969
MSc(Panj)
in USA

BICHAN Herbert Roy *BSc 1964

BICHAN Robert Miller MB ChB 1957

BICHAN Sydney John Eunson BSc(agr) 1968
s of Sydney B. farm. and Myrtle Tait; b Kirkwall 2.11.46
farm. ptnrship Drumoak and Swanbister, Orkney from 1968

BICKERTON Judith Carol BSc 1967
d of Richard S. B. MA(Cantab) eng and Ethel M. Cheetham; b Farnborough 11.8.44
res asst Alta 1967–68; tech Calgary 1968–69; progr: Lond 1969–71, (MRC) Lond and Edin 1971–74, Ferranti Manc from 1974
m Siddington 21.9.74 James P. S. Bell BSc(Leic) s of George T. B. BA(Cantab) Mobberley Nr Knutsford

BIDE Richard Willan PhD 1964
MSc(Alta)

BIGGAR Susan Mary MA 1968
d of Walter A. B. BSc(Edin) farm. and Patricia M. I. Elliott; b Aber 18.2.47
Lond: BBC tv prod. asst 1968–72; Guinness Superlatives publ res 1972–75; freelance sports res from 1975
m St Boswells 2.10.76 Michael R. Browne MA(Cantab) oyster farm. s of Francis B. R. B. MA(Cantab) Pewsey

BIGGINS Peter MB ChB 1969
s of Sidney J. B. retailer and Doris Walters; b Mansfield 14.7.43
Jersey: h s gen hosp 1969–70; g p St Helier from 1970
m Guernsey 11.12.71 Mary E. Hamon SRN d of A. G. H. Guernsey

BIGNELL Peter *MA 1962 Dip Ed 1963
s of Charles E. B. ship's eng and Isabella N. Hodgson clerkess; b Lond 16.5.36
teacher: Tabora Tanzania 1963–65, Lond 1966–68, Nairobi 1968–74; insp s Nairobi from 1974
m Aber 28.9.60 Patricia S. Morrison nurse d of George J. M. Aber
marr diss 24.10.75

BIGWOOD Winifred Katherine *MA 1957
m Main

BILLAU Frances Joy BEd 1969

BINNIE David Chalmers *MA 1968

BINNIE, Lorna MA 1966
m Mitchell

BINNS Paul Edward *BSc 1969
s of Percy E. A. B. MA(Oxon) clerk in holy orders and Edith Barker; b Greywell 27.7.42
PhD(Edin) 1975
geol Inst of geol sc Edin; scient off. 1969–71; sen scient off. 1971–74, prin scient off. 1974–75; geol RD Shell Explor and Prod. lab The Hague from 1975
m Richmond Surrey 13.8.66 Ceri L. Nelson airline clerkess d of Brian N. Whitton

BINNS Richard Henry Fieldwick BEd 1969

BIRCHALL Paul Malcolm Anthony *BSc 1968

BIRD David Graham LLB 1969
s of Herbert B. process engraver and Muriel M. Adams; b Aber 11.8.48
law app Henry J. Gray & Connochie Aber 1969–71; solic Russell & Dunlop Edin 1971–73; solic and attorney-at-law W. S. Walker & Co Grand Cayman BWI from 1973
m Dunblane 7.4.73 Catherine J. MacNaught d of David C. MacN. Dunblane

BIRKBECK Helen Margaret Ann MB ChB 1967
d of John E. H. B. B. min of religion and Peggy Simpson secy; b Aber 4.11.43
h o Woodend hosp Aber, RACH 1967–68; g p Aber 1969–76
m Aber 30.9.67 Gethyn Burgess univ lect

BIRKBECK Valerie Elizabeth Renner MA 1956
d of Philip L. B. ironmonger's man. and Elizabeth D. Fraser; b Darlington 15.10.33
JP Denbighsh (now Clwyd) 1972
teacher: Quarryhill p s Aber 1957–60, Aber h s for girls 1960–61
m Aber 9.9.60 Michael A. Shields MB ChB 1954 *qv*

BIRNIE Alison Forbes Hunter MB ChB 1959
d of James A. B. MA 1927 *qv*; b Oldham 17.4.35
h o: RACH 1959–60; part-time g p Aber from 1970
m Aber 16.7.59 Frederick P. Lynch MB ChB 1955 *qv*

BIRNIE Donald James Forbes MB ChB 1962
s of James A. B. MA 1927 *qv*; b Farnworth 15.7.37
DA 1965 MRCGP 1972
h o ARI 1962–63; trainee asst Inverbervie 1964–65; g p Aber from 1965
m Aber 1.12.62 Allison M. Tait d of James T. Aber

BIRNIE Gordon William Valentine *BSc 1968
s of William B. MB ChB 1936 *qv*; b Edin 15.10.43
teacher: Perthsh 1969–70; Abdnsh: asst 1970–71, spec asst biol 1971–72, prin teacher from 1972
m Bridge of Earn 10.4.71 Margaret S. Paton health visitor

BIRNIE Mae Lorimer MA 1956
d of Allan B. baker and Elsie M. Buchan hotel worker; b Glasg 13.12.34
teacher mod lang Fraserburgh 1957–64, Ellon 1964–71
m New Deer 29.12.71 William Mitchell farm. s of John M. Ellon

BIRNIE Mary Jean MA 1966
d of James B. farm./shop prop. and Christina J. Robertson nurse; b Aber 15.9.45
teacher Engl Macduff h s 1967–69, New Deer j s s 1969–73; private tut: Engl Varberg Sweden 1973–74; teacher Engl Brierton c s Hartlepool, Cleveland 1975–76, New Deer s from 1977
m Aber 21.3.66 Gordon T. Whyte elect. eng s of Charles G. W. Cuminestown

BIRNIE Myrtle Elise BSc 1960
m McGregor

BIRRELL Brian William *BSc 1968
s of Alexander B. actuary and Anne S. Deuchars; b Kircaldy 26.10.46
teacher chem Armadale 1969–72; prin chem Kirkcaldy from 1972
m Dun 28.12.74 Bronwyn M. Lauder BSc(Dund) teacher d of George O. L. Dun

BIRRELL Elizabeth Fergusson MA 1968
d of George D. B. motor mech and Christina F. S. Ellis tel; b Edin 18.4.48
advt copywriter Edin 1968–69; teacher N'cle 1970–72
m Edin 27.6.70 Christopher J. Adams BSc 1968 *qv*

BIRSE Douglas James MA 1960
s of Charles B. rly shunter and Elsie Wildgoose; b Oyne 1.7.37
teacher Latin/Engl Creetown 1961–64; head: Lumphanan 1964–70, Dunecht 1970–74, Auchterellon 1974–76, Upper Westfield s Bridge of Don from 1976
m Aber 25.7.61 Phyllis J. Third secy d of George T. Premnay

BIRSE Muriel Jean *MA 1960
d of George B. B. elect. eng and Agnes M. McLean; b Dun 5.5.38
teacher geog Kirkton h s Dun 1961–62, Greycotes Oxon 1962–63, Headington 1963–64; part-time geog coll of comm and mainly mus in p s Aber from 1970
m Dun 28.7.62 Ian J. Patterson BSc 1961 *qv*

BIRSE Sheila Margaret MB ChB 1965
m Leslie

BIRSS James Gordon MA 1961

BIRSS John Alexander Fullarton MB ChB 1968
s of James F. B. CA and Dorothea H. Coutts MA 1932 *qv*; b Aber 28.7.45
h o: ARI, Woodend hosp Aber 1968–69; Tasmania: resid m o NW gen hosp Burnie 1969–70, Mersey gen hosp Latrobe 1970–71; g p Devonport Tasmania from 1971
m Devonport –.2.70 Heather D. Turner SRN d of John G. R. T. Quoiba Tasmania

BIRSS Sheila Smith MA 1964
d of William A. B. joiner and Isabel T. Smith; b Aber 1943
teacher: Currie 1965–70; prin guid Gorebridge from 1970

BISHOP Frances Margaret *MA 1958
d of John B. bank teller and Margaret Dougherty MA 1928 *qv*; b Aber 19.11.36
teacher Engl: Morgan acad Dun 1958–59, Aber h s for girls 1959–62, Peterhead acad from 1973
m Aber 13.7.60 Frederick Crawford MA 1958 *qv*

BISHOP Hugh William MA 1968

BISHOP Iain Ritchie *BSc 1959
s of John B. bank teller and Margaret Dougherty MA 1928 *qv*; b Aber 23.2.38
MSc(S'ton) 1962 OBE 1969
res asst S'ton 1959–63; lect: Guy's hosp med s Lond 1963–66, Leic 1966–72; on secondment to RGS exped Mato Grosso Brazil 1967–69; dept zoology Brit Mus (nat hist) from 1972

BISHOP Janet Margaret BSc 1965
d of Frank B. nurse, eng and Frances S. Wallace tailoress; b Whalley 26.10.41
res asst Aberd 1965–69
m Aber 22.6.68 Alan J. Hay BSc 1966 *qv*

BISHOP Margaret Elizabeth MA 1968

BISHOP Marigold Rehan MA 1968
m Cannings

BISHOP Prudence Margaret *BSc 1968
m Vipond

BISSET Catherine Hutcheon *BSc 1962
d of James B. B. sailmaker and Catherine H. Matthews; b Aber 4.2.40
MSc(Exe) 1964
scient information off. Commonwealth mycological inst 1964–66
m Aber 16.9.66 Donald W. H. Stewart BSc 1960 *qv*

BISSET Derek MA 1959

BISSET Gladys Margaret MA 1958
m Hart

BISSET Iain Muir Fraser MA 1961

BISSET James Martin *MA 1956

BISSET Katrine McKenzie MA 1959
m McLean

BISSET Morag Jane *MA 1967
d of Robert D. N. B. MB ChB(Dunedin) surg and Janet N. Sloan or Smillie radiographer; b Edin 1945
DipEd(Edin) 1968
teacher Engl Stirling h s 1968–72
m Auchterhouse Dun 25.8.67 Daniel S. Macleod MA 1967 *qv*

BISSET Raymond George BSc 1963
s of William B. shop asst and Jean Thom clerkess; b Ellon 16.8.42
teacher: Ellon 1963–64, sc Insch 1965–75; head Keithhall p s from 1975
m Peterhead 10.4.47 Heather M. Smith teacher d of James S. Peterhead

BISSET Reid Fyfe MB ChB 1964
s of James B. PO eng and Mary L. Chasser shop asst; b Aber 10.1.41
DObstRCOG 1967
h o: Woodend hosp Aber, ARI, Craigton mat. hosp St

Andrews 1964–65; Perth RI; sen h o 1966–68, regist anaest 1968–70; g p Perth from 1970
m Inv 26.5.66 Annette M. Mackenzie nurse d of David M. Foyers

BISSET Richard Alexander *MA 1969
s of Thomas B. letterpress machineman and Dorothy M. Cardno; b Aber 26.3.47
teacher: Mackie acad Stonehaven 1970–72, prin geog Mackie acad 1972–79; asst rector Banchory acad from 1979
m Banff 23.3.78 Joyce A. Weir dental surg asst d of William W. Banff

BISSET Roderick Bruce BSc 1968
s of George B. B. BSc(agr) 1924 *qv*; b Reading 31.8.47
electronic test eng Chelmsford 1968–70; electronic eng Inv from 1970

BISSETT George Norman *MA 1963
s of George B. elect. and Johanna M. Shirsinger; b Burntisland 19.7.38
MPhil(Yale) 1969
lect Br Council Beirut 1964–66, head Engl dept pol sc fac Ankara Univ 1969–71; Anglo-Uruguayan cult. inst Montevideo: dir gen 1971–74 and cult. attaché Brit emb 1974–75; Br inst Barcelona: dir stud. from 1975
m Aber 9.8.65 Faith L. Svajian MA (Middlebury Vt) teacher Spanish d of George S.

BJØRNSON Leif Jan MB ChB 1964
s of Olav B. grad pharm Oslo dir pharm comp and Liv Pallesen; b Oslo 6.11.39
spec intern. med 1974 MD(Oslo) 1978
Norway: h o Drammen, dist g p Senja 1965–66, milit m o 1966–67; Ulleval hosp Oslo univ clin: jun regist 1967–70, sen regist 1970–73, res fell. univ of Oslo 1973–77, sen regist from 1977
m Oslo 22.6.67 Elisabeth Bang teacher d of Hans B. Oslo

BLACK Adam Mackenzie BSc(for) 1958
s of William J. L. B. teacher and Isabella Mackenzie secy; b Wick 7.11.34
nat serv BAOR 1956–58; teacher Wick 1958–59, prin biol Thurso h s from 1960
m Aber 1956 Anne S. Duthie shorthand typist d of Kenneth A. M. D. Aber

BLACK Alison Agnes Rankine MA 1968 DipEd 1969
d of Archibald D. B. and Alice Rankine; b Loch Awe 12.9.47
teacher mod lang: Dunbarton 1969–70, spec asst Edin 1970–72; TEFL Unna W Ger from 1972

BLACK Allan William *BSc 1965

BLACK David Alexander BSc(for) 1958
s of Thomas A. B. preventive off. Customs & Excise and Mary T. Ferguson; b Edin 8.7.37
N Nigeria: asst conserv for. Maiduguri 1958–60, Bauchi 1960–64; NZ: for. Christchurch 1964–68, sen for. Auckland from 1968
m Darfield 3.9.60 Jeanette Barnes teacher d of Thomas S. B. Darfield nr Barnsley

BLACK Elizabeth Myrna Dowdy MA 1957
d of James J. B. stat supt BEA Sumburgh and Mary A. Burgess; b Sumburgh 4.4.35
teacher: Lossiemouth 1958–61, Sandwick Shetland 1966–71, Dunrossness 1972–73, Sandwick from 1973
m Dunrossness 22.7.58 Andrew L. B. Flaws agr advis NOSCA s of Magnus F. Virkie Shetland

BLACK Francis Montgomery *BSc 1970 PhD 1974

BLACK Gavin Thomas BSc(eng) 1959

BLACK Gordon MacPherson MB ChB 1956

BLACK Hugh Leggat BSc(agr) 1957
s of Thomas B. LDS(Glasg) dent. surg and Agnes Leggat; b Huddersfield 31.5.35
Winston Churchill mem trust trav schol (Europ countries) 1971
man. Tarriebank estate Angus 1957–60; NOSCA: agr county and area advis from 1960 and farm man. from 1968
m Aber 21.7.61 Doreen M. Jeans teacher home econ d of Alexander J. Laurencekirk

BLACK Ian Macintosh MA 1963
s of George S. B. civ serv, hotelier, prop. man. and Isabella R. Tait civ serv; b Inv 27.6.41
Aber: man. trainee 1964–65, sales man. 1965–66, dir 1966–68; Canada: teacher Winnipeg 1968–69, Port Alberni 1969–70, Victoria from 1970
m Aber 12.11.66 Alison M. Walker d of John W. Aber

BLACK James Howard Smith MB ChB 1964

BLACK John Alexander Gordon BSc(eng) 1968
s of J. Gordon B. MB ChB 1929 *qv*; b Camberley 7.1.44
BBC tv Lond from 1969
m Lond 3.6.72 Mary S. Kelly film/tv make-up artist d of James K. Telford

BLACK Margaret Catherine BSc 1969
d of Charles D. B. farm./sub-contr and Mary H. Mathers; b Ellon 13.7.46
teacher sc Beauly 1970–74; prin guid Moray s Grangemouth 1974–78
m Aber 4.7.70 Allistair G. Matheson fin. acct s of Robert M. Tomintoul

BLACK Norval Marshall Burns *MA 1966

BLACK Robert Leitch LLB 1965

BLACK Robert William *MA 1969

BLACK Ronald MA 1970
s of Albert B. bus driver and Pearl J. D. Irvine off. worker; b Aber 3.7.49
housefather m h youths Pembury 1971–72; teacher: Dalmellington 1973–74, Lossiemouth from 1974
m E Kilbride 8.8.75 Kathleen M. Collier teacher dom sc d of Peter C. E Kilbride

BLACK Roy Peter BSc 1968
s of Horace A. C. B. asst distillery man. and Isabella M. Bremner; b Knockando 3.12.46
Dip OR(Strath) 1969
Strath: res asst 1969–70, res fell. from 1970
m Johnstone 11.8.73 Eileen E. Townsend secy d of George A. T. Johnstone

BLACK William Broad MA 1967
s of William J. B. joiner and Ella Broad; b Edin 7.4.46
BD(Edin) 1970
C of S min: asst Bathgate High ch 1970–72; min Durness linked Kinlochbervie from 1972

m Edin 18.7.70 Kathleen Clarkson MA(Edin) teacher d of William H. C. Huntly

BLACKBURN Alan Henry Hugh BSc(agr) 1959

BLACKBURN Thomas Henry PhD 1965
s of Thomas H. B. MA(Dub) headmaster and Mabel G. Shankey; b Sligo Ireland 8.8.33
BA MSc(Dub)
scient off. Rowett inst Aber 1957–67, assoc prof Br Col from 1967
m Aber –.4.63 Sheila E. Bell d of George B. Aber

BLACKHALL Margaret Isobel MB ChB 1956 MD 1970
d of William G. B. master tailor and Jane S. Fowlie; b Tarland 17.12.32
DCH 1959 DObstRCOG 1960 MRCPE 1964
h o: RACH, Dumfries and Galloway RI, Cumberland I, Carlisle, Aber mat. hosp 1956–58; sen h o, regist paediat Duchess of York hosp Manc 1958–61; regist paediat RACH 1961–65; sen regist, res fell. Alderhey ch hosp Liv 1965–69; Aust: sen lect ch health Queensland univ 1970–73; visiting paediat Prince Charles hosp Brisbane/post-grad superv Royal ch hosp Brisbane from 1973
m Brisbane 23.10.72 Kenyon G. Fry MBBS(Queensland) s of Kenyon M. V. F. Brisbane

BLACKIE Ruth Violet *MA 1967
d of Walter G. B. publ and F. Nancy S. Kerr; b Glasg 2.3.45
Dip Ed(Glas) 1968
teacher: Clydebank h s 1968–72; Dunbartonsh curric dev centre Clydebank from 1972
m Rhu 18.10.75 Andrew M. Currie MA (Edin) cartographic publ s of Robert E. C. Edin

BLACKIE Sheila Murray MA 1970
d of Ian A. J. B. bus driver and Edith Murray; b Montrose 2.6.49
teacher Engl Arbroath h s 1971–72
m Hertford 11.10.73 John R. P. Abbott farm. s of Alexander I. A. Cape Town

BLACKLAW William MA 1956

BLACKMORE Ian Raymond *MA 1970
s of Donald I. B. solic clerk and Dorothea P. Corcoran; b Perth 26.10.46
pers off. Ford Motor Co Dagenham 1970–73; div pers and trg man. Lex Tillotson Manc from 1974
m Dunfermline 25.3.72 Moira F. McNeill teacher d of R. M. McN. Dunfermline

BLACKSTONE Anita Maureen MB ChB 1963

BLADES Alexander William MA 1959

BLAIR Alastair BEd 1969
s of Duncan M. B. off. man. and Jessie L. Douglas; b Glasg 21.9.33
LGSM 1971
peripatetic teacher speech and drama Aber 1969–71; lect sp and drama Callendar Park coll of educ Falkirk from 1971

BLAIR David Antony James *MA 1963
s of Alexander Y. B. master printer and Anne Smith; b Aber 27.7.40
teacher mod lang Arbroath h s 1964–68, Kirkcaldy tech coll from 1968
m Glasg 19.7.69 Laura M. A. Lees teacher p e, d of David L. MA(Glas) Glasg

BLAIR David Howie LLB 1969
s of Alastair C. B. BA(Cantab) solic and Catriona H. Orr MA(St And); b Edin 10.4.48
trainee Swiss Bank Corp Lausanne 1969–70; Lond: invest. man. J. Henry Schroder Wagg 1970–74, invest. banker Dev West from 1974
m Arbroath 8.7.72 Carol L. Forbes MB ChB 1972 med pract d of Atholl G. F. MB ChB(St And) Arbroath

BLAIR Frances *MA 1964
d of Francis B. dock lab and Alice Donaldson; b Aber 5.12.41
teacher: Dun 1965–67, Kirkcaldy 1973–74; educ off. Kano Nigeria 1967–70, Nairobi 1971–72, Maiduguri Nigeria from 1974

BLAIR Jennifer Ann BSc 1970
d of Donald D. W. B. dir and Betty Cruickshank; b Lutterworth 14.1.49
Dip Exec & Secy Skills (Lond) 1971
clerk/tracer Brit Waterways Lond 1971–73; plan. asst: Hants c c Lyndhurst 1973–74, Winchester 1974–76; plan. off. Berks c c Reading from 1976

BLAIR Mary Stewart *BSc 1970
d of William B. MB ChB(Glas) med pract and Alexina M. Paterson MB ChB(Glas) med pract; b Glasg 3.7.48
teacher: Glasg 1971–72, N'cle 1972–74, Louth from 1974
m Glasg 21.7.72 Ian R. Cubitt BSc(agr) 1971 plant breeder s of James C. Athens

BLAIR Robert PhD 1960
b Beith 29.5.33
BSc(agr)(Glas) 1956
scient off. Rowett inst Aber 1957–60; Aberd: asst anim husb 1960–61, sen res fell. 1961–66; prin scient off. ARC poultry res centre Edin 1966–75; res assoc Corn. Ithaca NY USA 1969–70; dir nutrit Swift Canadian Co Toronto from 1976

BLAIRS Margaret Chalmers MA 1967
m Chalmers

BLAKE Ian Kerr *BSc(eng) 1970
s of James B. comp dir and Catherine Kerr comp dir; b Watford 7.4.48
civ eng from 1970

BLAKEMORE Marie MSc 1970
d of Sydney R. B. blacksmith and Florence M. Morris; b Shrewsbury 13.7.31
BSc(Lond) 1953
res asst soil sc dept Aberd 1970–72
m Grinshill Shrewsbury 28.7.71 Christopher D. Bristow MSc 1969 *qv*

BLANCE George Gilbert *BSc 1960
s of George W. B. MA 1927 *qv*; b Lerwick 21.7.36
teacher Fraserburgh 1961–64, spec asst 1964; Kirkwall: prin chem 1964–72, asst then dep rector from 1972
m Aber 1.4.63 Morag C. Smith teacher d of James S. Peterhead

BLANE William *MA 1969
s of David B. miner and Helen Walker; b Cumnock 26 4.47
teacher: Ger/Russian Cumnock acad 1970–71, prin Ger from 1971

BLANKSON Henry Richard Sagoe BSc(for) 1962

BLENCH Sheena Margaret *BMedBiol 1969 MB ChB 1972
d of Ian B. MRCVS(Glas) vet surg and Jeanie Mactaggart; b Aber 12.9.47
h o ARI, King's Cross hosp Dun 1972–73; sen h o psychiat royal Dun Liff hosp 1973–74, regist psychiat Aber from 1974
m Oldmeldrum 10.7.72 John E. Pollet BMedBiol 1969 *qv*

BLITZ Nicolas Martin *BSc(agr) 1967 ᶜMB ChB 1978
s of Thomas J. Weihs MD(Basle) med consult. and Marie Blitz teacher; b Aber 30.3.43
PhD(McG) 1970
res fell. McG univ 1970–71, Imp coll Lond 1971–73
m Peterculter 20.3.65 Karin G. Kunzer remed educ d of Ernst K. Berlin

BLUM Alfred Ernest Gustav BSc(eng) 1961

BLYTH Angus Campbell MB ChB 1970
s of Joseph O. B. BR ticket coll. and Christina Campbell; b Oban 6.5.45
h o: RACH, Woodend hosp Aber 1970–71; obst Royal Free hosp Lond 1971–72; med off. Nsambya hosp Kampala 1972–73; sen h o anaest Southend gen hosp from 1973

BLYTH John Francis *BSc(for) 1968 PhD 1974
s of Francis G. H. B. PhD(Lond) lect and Margaret G. Crowley mus teacher; b Watford 18.1.46
area for. Fountain Forestry Cheddar 1968–70; res asst soil sc Aberd 1970–73; land husb off. min of agr and nat resources Karonga Malawi from 1974

BOA Donalda Forbes MA 1957
d of Peter B. crofter and Elizabeth Forbes; b Kiltarlity 9.2.36
teacher: Engl Northfield acad 1958–59, Elm Tree House s Cardiff 1971–74, supply S Glamorgan from 1977
m Aber 20.7.59 Alan R. Beattie BSc 1955 *qv*

BOA Hugh Forbes MA 1962 LLB 1965
s of Peter B. crofter and Elizabeth Forbes; b Kiltarlity 20.2.40
law app, qualif asst Inv 1964–71; resid magist/dep regist high court Kenya from 1971

BOA Mary Isobel MA 1958
m Reinhardt

BOAG Ian Francis BSc(eng) 1959
s of William J. B. rly clerk and Alexandrina Mackenzie shop asst; b Inv 20.4.37
site eng (Wm Tawse) Skye, Harris 1959–62; Ross & Cromarty c c: asst eng Ullapool 1962–67, Dingwall 1967–70, dist surv Black Isle 1970–73, asst county surv maintenance Dingwall 1973–75; prin eng Highland reg from 1975
m Inv 6.10.67 Anne M. Fraser teleph d of Donald F. Kyle

BOAL David BSc 1959
b Edin 21.5.38
teacher sc: Northfield s Aber 1960–62, Auchterarder 1962–67, Oakbank approved s 1967–75, Northfield acad from 1975
m Peterculter 21.1.61 Isla F. Douglas teacher d of Crawford E. D. Peterculter

BOLLAND Allan BSc 1963

BOLLINGTON David Ian LLB 1967

BOLTON Alan BSc(for) 1968 Dip Ed 1969
s of John B. dir and Muriel B. Galloway; b Manc 16.4.46
Bankhead acad Aber: teacher 1969–72, prin guid from 1972
m Aber 20.12.67 Isabella T. MacKay MA 1970 *qv*

BOND Margaret Jane MA 1967
d of Robert B. farm. and Sophia Rimmer; b Southport 2.11.46
BA(St Albans) 1970
Ambassador coll of St Albans: secy to coll regist 1970–71, secy to dir estate dept 1971–74

BONE Alan Barclay BSc(agr) 1962
s of Robert B. B. marine eng and Betsy G. W. Nicoll; b Calcutta 23.2.39
asst insp dept agr for Scot Aber from 1963
m Elgin 6.8.65 Frances Morrison teacher d of John M. M. Fochabers

BONE Jessie Muir *MA 1963
d of Alexander H. B. MA(Edin) min of relig and Margaret L. Macpherson BSc(Edin) teacher mus; b Barrhill 5.3.42
LTCL(Lond) 1964
teacher mus: St Denis s Edin 1964–67, Tarbert s s 1967–68
m Ruthwell Dumfries 2.6.67 John D. Sutherland MA (Edin) min of relig s of John S. Edin

BONNICI Joseph John MA 1960
s of S.B. and Catherine Barton; b Glasg 13.4.28
teacher Holy Cross p s Glasg 1961–66; housemaster: St Mary's Hall Stonyhurst 1966–71, St Aloysius prep s Glasg 1971–72; head St Joseph's p s Peebles 1972–74; housemaster St Mary's Hall Stonyhurst from 1974

BONNYMAN Sheena Dutton MB ChB 1965
d of James B. mason and Williamina J. Philip; b Keith 29.3.42
DPM(Lond) 1970
Aber: h o 1965–66; sen h o, regist psychiat 1966–70; asst prof psychiat and neurol, Creighton univ Omaha USA 1971–72; regist psychiat Aber 1972–73; asst prof psychiat/behavioural sc Omaha from 1973

BONOMY Christine Margaret *BSc 1969
d of William B. BD(Glas) C of S min and Margaret M. Lindsay MA(Glas) teacher; b Chinsali, Zambia 9.6.47
scient edit. Oss Holland 1969–71; asst m o Beerse Belgium 1971–72; prod. registration off. Ware Herts 1972–73; teacher Kano Nigeria 1975–78
m Perth 4.12.71 Rex A. H. Laycock BSc(Eng) 1969 *qv*

BOOTH Catherine Mary BSc 1968
d of Ernest M. B. hydraulic eng and Mary A. Duncan; b Cove Bay 20.6.47
teacher: maths/geog Stonehaven 1969–72
m Aber 25.7.70 Colin G. Berry joiner/carpenter s of John B. Aber

BOOTH George Davidson BSc(agr) 1967
s of George E. R. B. auctioneer/farm. and Annie J. Davidson; b Aber 25.12.44
ptnr in fam farm. bus. Bucksburn from 1967
m Aber 19.6.70 Patricia Spence nurse d of John P. S. Aber

BOOTH James Connon Donald MB ChB 1956
s of Alfred B. pharm and Agnes J. Connon shop asst; b Aber 25.12.29
DPM(Lond) 1962 MRCPE 1969 MRCPsych 1971

h o Brechin, Bishop Auckland, Aber 1956–58; g p trainee Coatbridge 1958–59; jun psychiat posts Edin 1959–64; jun posts med psychiat Sedgefield, Bradford, Glasg 1964–69; consult. psychiat Glasg from 1969
m Edin 11.4.64 Rosemary H. Fraser MB ChB(Edin) med/psychiat posts d of Alexander F. Edin

BOOTH Kathleen Margaret Dawson MA 1964
m Thomson

BOOTH Mary Ellen MA 1961

BOOTH Michael John *MA 1961

BOOTH Peter Frank *MA 1964

BOOTH Rupert Guy Tempest *MA 1968 Dip Ed 1969

BOOTH Thomas Calvin BSc(for) 1970

BOOTHBY Patricia Mary MA 1966
m Greig

BOOTHBY Robin John *BSc 1969
s of Kenneth A. B. sales man. and Hilda M. Pardoe; b Lond 17.12.47
syst eng International Computers Lond from 1969

BORRIE John Peters BSc 1964
s of Alexander P. B. arch. and surv and Vera E. Holdcroft; b Dumfries 5.1.40
teacher phys Perth acad 1965–74; prin phys Millburn acad Inv from 1974

BORTHWICK Leslie John MB ChB 1969

BORTHWICK Sheila Ross BSc 1970

BOSTOCK Fred Allan PhD 1964
s of Horace B. painter/decorator and Adelaide Pegg; b Nott 27.9.30
BSc(Nott) MSc(Nott)
lect S'ton from 1965
m Nott 9.8.56 Margaret M. Thorpe d of William J. T.

BOTCHWAY Theophilus *BSc(eng) 1965

BOULIND Peter Rodney MB ChB 1969

BOURNER Sybil Audrey MA 1968
d of Albert M. B. cler off. BR and Caroline B. Morgan; b Aber 27.2.47
TEFL Berlitz s of lang Paris 1969–76; translator/exec secy Beauté, Hygiène et Soins (Boots Co) Paris from 1976
m Aber 4.9.75 Jean-Luc J. Popineau (degree in econ (Paris)) res dept min of environment Paris s of Etienne P. Paris

BOUSFIELD Ivan John PhD 1969
BTech(Brad)

BOWDEN Alexander Barclay BSc 1970

BOWDEN Elizabeth Margaret Mitchell *MA 1961 Dip Ed 1964
d of T. Mitchell B. LRAM mus organis Orkney, Moray and Nairn and Margaret W. Turner; b Ceres 27.4.39
teacher Aber from 1964

BOWDEN Thomas Neil *BSc 1965
s of William L. B. admin man. and Ethel Howarth; b Blackpool 19.7.43
MSc(Manc) 1967 FRAS 1969
res stud. Manc 1965–69; analyst/progr Plessey Telcomms Liv 1970–73; sen syst progr Burroughs Machines Cumbernauld from 1973
m Aber 6.4.48 Margaret H. Horne BSc 1967 *qv*

BOWEN Gwladys Margaret *BSc 1959

BOWEN Ian Hamilton PhD 1967
s of Herbert L. Bowen p s v conductor and Sarah A. Hamilton; b N'cle-u-Tyne 3.11.42
BPharm(Lond) 1964 MPS 1970
res fell. chem Strath 1967–68; s of pharm Sunderland poly: lect pharmacognosy 1969–74, sen lect from 1974
m Sunderland 3.4.65 Margaret Hanson audio secy d of Reginald H. Sunderland

BOWEN Jennifer Ellen *MA 1969
d of Edward L. B. bank man. and Alice M. Simpson; b Edin 5.3.46
Dip Ed(Edin) 1970
teacher Fr: Bathgate 1970–71, Edin 1971–72, coach Rudolph Steiner s Edin 1972–73; off. man. anim feed supplements York from 1974
m Edin 20.12.69 Keith S. Castell army off. s of Reginald T. C. C. Windlesham

BOWERS Anthony BSc(for) 1960
s of Reuben O. B. banker and Esther I. Dando; b Stockton-on-Tees 29.6.33
Tokoroa NZ: investigation for. (silviculture) NZ Forest Products 1962–78, estab for. from 1978
m Findochty 19.7.55 Grace A. Campbell MA 1955 *qv*

BOWIE James Frederick Rognvald MB ChB 1960
s of Frederick J. T. B. MB ChB 1924 *qv* and Victoria H. Reid BSc 1921 *qv*; b Aber 3.3.35
FRCP(C) 1972
h o ARI, Woodend hosp Aber 1960–61; sen h o Cromer/Aylsham 1961–65; regist phys med and rheumat Norfolk and Norwich area 1965–67; consult. Winnipeg 1967–72; prof and dir s med rehab Univ of Manit Winnipeg from 1972
m Aber 5.8.61 Lena C. Stephen d of John B.S. Aber

BOWIE Kenneth *MA 1968
s of John B. eng and Jessie Duthie; b Fraserburgh 17.6.45
AICMA 1974
fin. analyst Lond 1968–71; Greenock: internal then materials audit. 1971–74; oper res analyst from 1974
m Aber 29.6.68 Yvonne Mathieson d of Nathaniel M. Aber

BOWIE Raymond Alexander *BSc 1961 PhD 1964
s of Alexander B. civ serv and Catherine H. Watt; b Aber 23.12.38
post doc fell. (Fulbright schol) Wash USA 1964–65; res chem ICI pharm div Cheshire from 1965
m Aber 12.7.63 Sheila E. M. MacLeod BSc 1960 *qv*

BOWKER Christine *BSc 1965

BOWLING Dudley James Francis PhD 1961
s of Geoffrey B. eng and Ethel G. Smith; b Ganstead, Hull 20.5.37
BSc(Nott) 1958
asst bot Aberd 1961–63, lect from 1963
m Aber 9.4.62 Sheila M. Daun MA 1959 *qv*

BOWMAN Iain Bell Ramsay *BSc 1956 PhD 1959
s of Alexander S. R. B. master baker and Agnes A. Bell; b Arbroath 8.10.34

NATO res fell. Wash USA 1959–61; sen res fell. Aberd 1961–62; scient staff MRC Mill Hill Lond 1962–65; Edin: lect biochem 1965–70, sen lect from 1970
m Aber 21.3.64 Patricia Barron BSc 1960 *qv*

BOWMAN Robert Miller *BSc(eng) 1956

BOWTHORPE Michael *BSc 1959
s of Leonard A. B. mus dir and Nancy Dickinson; b Belfast 26.11.37
FRMetS 1968
Aust: scient off. weapons res estab Adelaide 1959–63; phys Tasmania 1963–66 (Austral nat antarctic res exped Wilkes 1964–65) lect phys univ coll Townsville 1966–71; sen scient off. sc res council Lond from 1971
m Aber 12.9.59 June M. Ingram admin exec d of John I. Aber

BOWYER Elizabeth Alice MA 1956

BOWYER Leonard William BSc 1970

BOYACK Patricia Alison MA 1967 *1969
d of George W. B. tea planter and Agnes G. Johnston secy; b Dun 3.10.45
civ serv inl rev Edin and Blackpool from 1971
m Carnoustie 26.8.72 Christopher D. Smith MA 1966 *qv* marr diss

BOYCE Francis Angus BSc 1970
s of Anthony B. steamfitter and Margaret H. Angus saleslady; b Aber 11.4.45
teacher maths Aber from 1971

BOYD John Minto MA 1961
s of John M. B. comp dir and Margaret A. Gordon; b Huntly 20.1.40
trainee man. Glasg 1961–71; dir Boyds (Huntly) from 1971
m Edin 15.5.64 Jennifer A. G. Black d of John M. B. MB ChB(Edin), Edin

BOYD Joseph Ian PhD 1970
s of John A. B. LLB(Dalhousie) barrister and Thyrza J. McManus teacher; b Blaine Lake Sask Canada 23.1.35
BA(Sask) 1956 STB(Tor) 1964 MA(Tor) 1965
asst prof Engl Sask 1970–75, assoc prof from 1975; edit. *The Chesterton Review*

BOYD Peter David Armstrong *BSc 1970
s of James C. B. eng and Elaine C. Armstrong; b Woodford 4.5.46
Sheff: res geol 1970–74; cert educ 1975
m Aber 17.7.69 Evelyn Y. Fox MA 1969 *qv*

BOYD Rognvald *BSc 1969 PhD 1973
s of James H. T. B. MA(Glas) C of S min and Margaret Logie; b Glasg 22.7.46
geol Norway 1972–74; proj geol English Clays Lovering Pochin & Co St. Austell from 1974
m Petersham 3.4.71 Susan J. Reece agr d of Henry W. W. R. Basingstoke

BOYES Pamela Ann Margaret MA 1963
d of George B. MA(Edin) bus. man., admin asst in educ and Edith M. Abernethy MA(Edin) teacher; b Aber 22.3.43
teacher Fr: Perth h s 1966-67, Walthamstow Hall, Sevenoaks 1967–70
m Perth 3.8.68 Alan R. Crook BA(Cantab) teacher s of Reginald W. C. Bournemouth

BOYLE Douglas McKenzie BSc 1969

BOYLE John Garrett LLB 1969
s of James M. B. MA(Glas) solic/town clerk and Margaret Garrett; b Fraserburgh 27.5.48
law app Aber c c 1969–71; Lyall & Wood solic Turriff: qual asst 1971–73, ptnr from 1973
m Aber 2.6.72 Heather Green clerkess d of James N.G. Aber.

BRACEWELL Margaret Jeanette BSc 1968
d of George H. B. prod. worker and Margaret G. Morrice factory worker; b Aber 12.9.47
scient off. crop analysis Macaulay inst for soil res Aber 1969–72; tech dept pharm Aberd from 1976
m Aber 15.9.67 John D. Gray MA 1971 teacher s of George G. Aber

BRACK John Angus *MA 1964
s of John B. cashier and Agnes E. Dick shop asst; b Aber 14.10.42
MSc(Econ)(Lond) 1965
lect Warw from 1965

BRACK Margaret Holland BSc 1964
m Husband

BRADFORD Ann Patricia MB ChB 1960
d of Thomas B. army off. (killed WW II) and Annie Gossop clerk; b York 11.3.36
DPH(N'cle) 1966 MS(Prev Med)(Wash.) 1969 Prize soc epidemiologic res 1969
h o Derbysh RI 1960–61; g p trainee Leabrooks 1961–62; asst county m o Derbysh 1963–64; asst m o h S Shields 1964–66; Seattle: post doct fell. 1967–69, assoc dir Washington/Alaska reg med program 1969–74, asst prof epidemiology Wash. from 1969, dir mat. and inf care dept publ health from 1974
m York 11.10.58 Clive S. Carter BSc(Leeds) res metall s of Harry S. C. York

BRADFORD Helen Margaret BEd 1969
m Scott

BRADFORD Nial Charlton MB ChB 1969 *BSc 1972
s of Ernest F. B. BSc(Lond) geol and Phoebe Charlton MB ChB(Lond) med pract; b Lond 30.5.46
h o ARI 1972–73; MRC fell. res Aberd 1973–76; lect Dund from 1976

BRADFORD Richard Halsey Gordon *BSc 1970
s of Kenneth G. B. chartered surv and Helen G. Thompson; b Belfast 17.4.47
Mannlife Toronto: progr 1970–72, syst superv 1972–74, proj man. from 1974

BRADLEY Robert PhD 1965
s of Robert B. farm. and Frances A. Denny; b Blackburn Lancs 12.4.39
BSc(agr)(Leeds) 1962
field dev off.: white fish auth, fish farming Ardtoe 1965–68; farms man. fish farming Marine Harvest Lochailort from 1968
m Slaidburn Dorothy Wood SRN d of Wilfred W. Slaidburn

BRADSHAW Ian Robin MacDonald *MA 1967

BRADY Colin John PhD 1962
MSc(agr)(Syd)

BRAMLEY Paul Scotson PhD 1970
s of David S. B. farm./comp dir and Marjorie S.

Duckett; b Liverpool 21.5.40
BVSc(Liv) 1963
lect vet physiol Nairobi 1970–71; sen vet res off. ARC inst Compton 1971–73; comp vet surg Glasg from 1973
m Cartmel 20.4.67 Fiona C. Townley nurse d of Humphrey C. T. BSc(agr)(Edin)

BRAND John Arthur *MA 1956
s of John W. B. civ eng and Mary M. Anderson; b Aber 4.8.34
PhD(Lond) 1962
asst politics Glas 1959–61, asst lect politics: R'dg 1961–63, Lond 1963–64; sen lect politics Strath from 1964

BRAND Norrie Gordon BSc 1967

BRAND Winifred Campbell Duncan MA 1968
m Reid

BRANDER Colin *MA 1970
s of Joseph M. B. riveter and Georgina S. Milne; b Aber 7.9.32
teacher hist: Harlaw acad Aber from 1971

BRANDER Heather MA 1963
d of William R. B. farm. and Isabel B. Innes; b Nairn 16.7.42
teacher: Liberton h s Edin 1964–65, E Calder 1965, W Calder 1965–67; Aust: Coffs Harbour NSW 1968–69, Albury NSW 1970–71, Shepparton Victoria 1973–74, Wodonga Victoria 1974
m Aber 20.11.71 Frank D. Holden master mariner/ grazier s of Arthur C. H. Bright Victoria Aust

BRANDER John Gordon MA 1969
s of John M. B. aircraft eng and Sheila Smith; b Aber 29.12.48
Dip Bus Stud(H-W) 1970
invest. analyst P & O shipping group Lond 1970–71; airline pilot: Oxon CSE aviation 1970–71, BA Heathrow Lond from 1971
m Aber 14.4.72 Elizabeth Naysmith BEd 1969 *qv*

BRANDIE WILLIAM *BSc(eng) 1960
s of William B. naval off. and Nettie Bowie; b Aber 25.11.36
Edin: res eng electronics & computer syst 1960–64, group leader computer syst 1964–69; sen electronics eng E Lothian 1969–73; syst analyst-computer Edin from 1974
m Edin 21.7.62 Margot J. Wright teacher d of Frederick W. Aber

BRANDS Sheila Johnston Campbell MB ChB 1961
m Wiseman

BRANDT Halvor MB ChB 1969
s of Olav B. min and Emma L. Midtbø; b Oslo 11.3.44
Norway: Mo i Rana h o 1970–71; g p 1971–72; army m o Heistadmoen 1972–73; regist anaest Skien from 1973
m Mo i Rana 17.2.71 Eva Gronseth d of Torstein G. MB ChB(Oslo) Mo i Rana

BRANSON Raymond Albert * MA 1968
AFC

BRATT John Dudley BSc(eng) 1962

BRAY Beverley Jane MA 1970
m Hunter

BRAY John Terence BSc 1958
s of George H. B. wholesale fish merch and Maggie M. E. Crancher; b Grimsby 5.2.36
petr eng Kirkuk Iraq 1958–68; sen petr eng: Dukhan Qatar 1969–74, Abu Dhabi UAE from 1974
m Glasg 5.8.63 Ann Johnson MA(Glas) teacher d of Thomas R. J. Glasg

BRAZENDALE Anthony Henry *MEd 1969
s of Henry B. sales rep and Bessie Connor; b UK 31.3.36
MA(Cantab) 1958
sen lect educ/psych Berks coll of educ Reading from 1969

BREBNER Alan MA 1970

BREBNER Barbara Anne MA 1957
d of John T. B. civ serv MoT traffic off. and Elsie A. McKay; b Cruden Bay 2.9.35
teacher: Seaton p s Aber 1958–61, Albyn s for girls Aber from 1968
m Aber 5.8.61 Gordon H. Turner MA 1958 *qv*

BREBNER Eileen MA 1966
d of William B. and Isabella A. Troup; b Turriff 15.3.45
Ibadan Nigeria: teacher/head dept arts Our Lady of Apostles' g s 1968–75, vice-prin Isabatudeen girls' g s from 1975
m Dun 9.11.67 Bandele A. Olusanya MB ChB(St And) g p s of Allen O. O. Ijebu-Ode Nigeria

BREBNER George Grieve BSc 1970
(conferred for long service of exceptional merit)
s of William G. B. haulage contr and Johan McLennan; b Aber 30.4.11
elected fell. inst of sc tech 1963
Aberd: member of staff from 1938, res asst dept geol & mineral. 1965–70, sen res asst 1970–76; retd
m Aber 7.6.33 Christina Main d of John M. Portlethen

BREBNER John Main Thomson *MA 1957
s of John M. T. B. trawl skipper and Lydia Buchan shop asst; b Aber 17.5.35
PhD(Exe) 1965 PhD(Adel) 1970
res psych RAF Farnborough 1957–59; Nuffield res asst Exe 1959–62; MoD res fell. Dund 1962–64; lect psych Dund 1964–69; lect, sen lect psych Adel Aust from 1969
m Rolleston 29.7.59 Mary J. Fawkes BSc 1958 *qv*

BREBNER Ronald Martin MA 1961 Dip Ed 1962

BRECHIN Derek Masson *MA 1960

BRECHIN Neil Stuart *MA 1957

BREED William Godfrey *BSc 1965
s of Arthur W. B. MA(Cantab) schoolmaster and Annie D. L. Marchant LRAM mus; b Redruth 27.6.41
DPhil(Oxon) 1968
fell: Calif 1968–69, Birm 1969–73; lect Adel Aust from 1973
m Hexham 7.8.72 Esther Richardson SRN d of Herbert R. Hexham

BREMNER Alan MB ChB 1960
s of David R. B. MA(Glas) HMIS and Alison L. Kent MA(Glas) teacher; b Glasg 8.3.36
DObstRCOG 1962 MRCGP 1964
hosp jun posts Wales, Aber, Inv 1961–62; g p: trainee Peebles 1962–63; asst Kemnay 1963–64; lect Edin 1964–68; ptnr Market Drayton from 1968
m Aber 16.1.61 Shirley Jones MB ChB 1960 *qv*

BREMNER Catherine Margaret MA 1965
d of Gerald F. B. MA 1968 *qv*; b Aber 29.11.44
teacher Ayr 1967–71
m Aber 12.8.67 John Brown BSc 1967 *qv*

BREMNER David Malcolm *BSc(eng) 1966
s of James S. B. works man. and Florence Leslie; b Aber 12.5.44
contr site eng Perth 1966–69, plan. site eng Anglesey 1969–71, plan. eng head off. Wallington 1971–76; UAE: asst man. Sharjah and Dubai 1976–77, br man. Dubai from 1978
m Aber 27.7.68 Alice S. Gibson BSc 1968 *qv*

BREMNER Douglas *BSc 1960
s of David R. B. MA(Glas) HMIS and Alison L. Kent MA(Glas) teacher; b Glasg 18.9.38
jun whaling insp/biol S Georgia sub-Antarctica 1960–61; res asst W Norwood tech coll Lond 1961–62; asst warden, warden Malham Tarnfield centre Yorks 1962–69; prin Culzean country park Maybole 1969–75; chief ranger Nat Trust for Scotland from 1975
m Kirkby Malham 11.6.66 Vivien Caton secy d of Frank C. Otterburn

BREMNER Gerald Falconer MA 1968
(conferred for long service of exceptional merit)
s of James B. pharm and Margaret Shearer; b Oldmeldrum 27.6.10
Aberd: admin off. 1927–57, asst finance off. 1957–75; retd
m Stornoway 3.3.43 Catherine I. Macdonald d of John M. Stornoway

BREMNER Harold Alan MB ChB 1964
s of Harold A. B. pharm and Sarah Craib; b Lond 23.2.40
DRCOG 1969
h o Scotland 1964–68; g p Nairn from 1968
m Inv 27.3.65 Alison M. Maclean MA 1961 *qv*

BREMNER Ian *BSc 1960 PhD 1963
s of George P. B. joiner and Alexina M. Thomson; b Aber 19.2.39
res fell. Stockholm 1963–64; biochem: Fisons Holmes Chapel 1964–66, Rowett inst Aber from 1967
m Elgin 22.9.62 Kathleen Stewart teacher d of John S. Elgin

BREMNER Joan Ann MB ChB 1960
d of Harold A. B. pharm and Sarah Craib; b Lond 25.1.37
DObstRCOG 1962 DA 1964
h o Aber, Perth 1960–62; sen h o Aber 1963–64; govt m o: Nandi Hills Kenya 1967–70, Blantyre Malawi from 1971
m Aber –.9.64 Alexander C. McLean tea factories supt s of Daniel P. M. McL. Peterhead

BREMNER Maureen Anne MB ChB 1969

BREMNER Williamina MA 1957
m Ross

BRENNAN Donald Macrae MA 1968

BRENNAN Patricia Ann MA 1967
d of Kevin P. B. cler asst and Annie Stuart bookkeeper; b Forres 15.5.46
Dip Sec St(Strath) 1968
secy/pa: Fochabers 1968–72, N'cle 1973; admin asst Fochabers 1973–74; secy/pa: Lond 1974–76, Aber 1976; marketing asst Aber 1976–77
m Forres 24.10.70 William A. Dalgarno MA 1969 *qv*

BREW Eric James Collie *BSc 1967 PhD 1971
s of Frank B. shoemaker, hosp theatre orderly and Agnes D. Collie clerkess; b Aber 19.3.44
res fell. Lond 1970–73; teacher: Marr coll, Troon 1973–75, prin chem Inverurie acad from 1975
m Aber 21.11.70 Marjory G. Mitchell MA 1966 *qv*

BREWSTER William David MA 1968

BRIDGE Christopher John LLB 1968
s of Joseph E. B. OBE TD Lt-col and Jeanne M. Pryor; b Cambridge 30.4.48
indust rel off. Rolls Royce Glasg 1968–71; pers off., sen pers off. BBC Lond from 1971

BRIERLEY John Clegg LLB 1964
s of John B. B. CA and Ruth Clegg; b Oldham 2.8.42
CA art. clerk Lond 1964–67, tax/audit man. 1967–70; CA self-employed Oldham from 1970
m Oxon 30.9.67 Susan J. Plummer MA 1965 *qv*

BRIGGS Peter Kemp PhD 1961
BSc(agr)(Syd)

BRIGGS Valerie Ann MB ChB 1961

BRIGGS William BSc(for) 1964

BRIGHT Peter Duncan *BSc 1970
s of Alec C. B. CA
MIBiol 1978
VSO teacher Vanua Levu Fiji 1972–73; teacher biol 6th form coll Ashford Middx from 1974

BRINKMAN David *BSc(eng) 1970

BRISTOW Christopher David MSc 1969
s of Arthur W. S. B. comm trav and Julie E. I. Cartwright teacher; b Worthing 1.8.39
BSc(S'ton) 1961 Dip Ed(S'ton) 1962
teacher Hounslow Lond 1962–63; geol: NCB opencast exec S Wales 1964–65, De Beers Consol Mines Cape Province S Africa 1965–67, Rio Tinto Zinc Abdnsh 1969–71; teacher: Aber 1971–73, Acton Reynold s Shropshire from 1973
m Shrewsbury 28.7.71 Marie Blakemore MSc 1970 *qv*

BRISTOW Peter Harold William *MA 1966
s of Harold E. W. B. comp dir and Marjorie N. Harper secy; b Bristol 21.10.43
admin asst univ E Ang 1966–67; asst lect Hunterian Mus Glas 1967–68; tech writer and computer syst progr and des Lond 1969–71; asst secy St Thomas's hosp med s univ Lond 1971–76; asst secy(acad) OU from 1976
m St And 28.6.69 Gillian Howey MA(St And) d of John H. Seaham

BRITTAIN John Michael *MA 1963
s of Harold B. banker and Dorothy Johnson; b Lincoln 14.8.38
res asst univ of Illinois USA 1963–64; res fell. S'ton 1964–68; sen res fell. Bath 1968–74; sen lect Loughborough from 1975
m Freshford 26.12.69 Hilary W. James marketing exec d of Harold J. MB ChB(Brist) Cardiff

BROCKIE Colin Glynn Frederick BSc(eng) 1963 BD 1967
s of Donald A. B. mech eng and Vera R. Thompson shop superv; b Westcliff-on-Sea 17.7.42
ordained prob Mastrick par ch Aber 1967–68; min St Martin's par ch Edin from 1968
m Richmond Surrey 28.9.68 Barbara K. Gordon BSc 1968 *qv*

BROCKLEHURST Jennifer Mary MB ChB 1963
d of Eric A. B. pharm and Henrietta S. Taylor pharm; b Hull 23.7.39
h o Woodend hosp Aber, ARI 1963–64; res Woodend hosp 1964–66; g p Aber, Rickmansworth from 1970
m Kirkella 31.8.63 Peter N. Bennett MB ChB 1963 *qv*

BROCKS Ashley Margaret MB ChB 1968
d of Basil E. B. MB ChB 1941 *qv*; b Aber 14.5.44
DCH 1971 FRCS 1974
h o Aber 1968–69; sen h o: paediat surg Carshalton 1970–71, cas and surg St George's hosp Lond 1971–72; regist gen surg Orpington from 1972

BRODIE Andrew Francis *BSc(eng) 1957

BRODIE Donald Ian Fordyce BSc(eng) 1961
s of Ian F. B. plasterer and Kathleen Macleod; b Nairn 25.9.36
jun eng Switchgear des Manc 1961–63; transmission plan. SSEB Glasg 1963–69; transmission plan. eng Belf 1969–76; power stat man. Kilroot Carrickfergus from 1976
m Huntly 19.8.61 Christine MacBain teacher d of Alexander MacB. Huntly

BRODIE Iain Keith *MA 1966 Dip Ed 1968
s of Stanley F. B. signalman in Royal Can Corps Signals—killed in action Italy July 1944 and Agnes W. S. Keith lib asst; b Edin 4.6.44
MSc(Edin) 1971
teacher: (VSO) Vidya Bhawan s Udaipur Rajasthan India 1966–67; Bearsden acad 1970–72; prin maths Cumbernauld h s from 1972
m Aber 26.7.68 Gillian I. MacLean MA 1968 *qv*

BRODIE Isobel Francis BSc 1959
d of William B. sales supt Shell Oil and Agnes G. Thomson teacher; b Brechin 2.2.39
lab tech GEC Coventry 1959–61; teacher: Coventry 1961–64, Brampton Ont 1964–66, Montreal 1966–67
m Forfar 27.7.63 Peter R. Fisher BSc(Warw) elect. eng s of Frederick R. F. Southport

BROMFIELD Ian Derek *BSc 1969
s of Leslie E. B. radio & tv eng and Dorothy T. Nicol secy; b Aber 24.1.47
elect. eng: Loughton 1970–72, Leicester from 1972

BROOKS Alexander *MA 1958

BROOKS David Wilson BSc(eng) 1966

BROOKS Elizabeth Ada BSc 1966 Dip Ed 1967
d of Alexander R. B. joiner, shipwright and Wilhelmina I. Irvine; b Aber 1.11.44
teacher Munda Solomon Is 1968–69
m Aber 31.7.67 Michael B. Self BSc(for) 1966 *qv*

BROOKS Elizabeth Catherine BSc 1970
m Petrie

BROOKS Marjorie MA 1968 Dip Ed 1969
d of James B. and Sarah J. Wilson MA 1926 *qv*; b Edin 13.12.47
Nassau Bahamas: teacher Engl 1969–70 and year co-ordinator 1973–75; lect Engl in coll of the Bahamas from 1975, lit co-ordinator, humanities div from 1978
m Aber 14.9.70 Winston G. Jones arch s of Geoffrey J. Nassau

BROOKS Simon Alan Lawrence MA 1969 MB ChB 1974

BROOMFIELD Sinclair George *MA 1965

BROOMFIELD William McIntyre BSc(eng) 1959
s of William P. B. comp dir and Eliza M. McIntyre; b Aber 1.6.35
grad app Morris-Commercial cars Birm 1959–61; Aber: asst serv man. Town & County motor garage 1961–63, serv man. 1963–71, man. dir 1971–73; chmn Aber Motors from 1973; dir Campbell & Sellar, T and C serv stat, Grampian serv stat, County Garage (Fraserburgh) from 1976
m Aber 7.10.61 Mary C. Reid MA 1957 *qv*

BROUGH Alexander Hardie BSc 1968

BROWN Aileen MA 1969
d of Thomas A. B. bus driver, insur ag and Violet McLeod shop asst, clerk; b Aber 17.8.48
Dip Pers Man.(RGIT) 1970
UKAEA: exec off. 1970–73, higher exec off. 1973–76
m Leigh 1973 Gordon C. B. Bull BSc(Brad) s of William G. B. Sheffield

BROWN Alastair Nisbet MB ChB 1961
s of Thomas R. B. airship des, teacher tech subj and Marjorie S. D. Fowlie bank teller; b Aber 22.8.36
DObstRCOG(Lond) 1963
h o: ARI, city hosp Aber 1961–62, Motherwell mat. hosp 1962–63; g p: Crieff 1963, Aber/asst m o Craiginches prison Aber from 1963
m Aber 28.1.63 Joan M. Garden med res asst d of Albert E. G. Aber

BROWN Alastair William Scott
see Scott-Brown

BROWN Allan Guildford PhD 1965

BROWN Anne Gordon MA 1968
d of James B. overseer/custodian and Myra J. Stephen; b Fyvie 6.5.47
teacher biol/geog Saltus g s Bermuda
m Aber 27.12.67 Leonard G. Cruickshank BSc 1968 *qv*

BROWN Anne McLean Gray MA 1969

BROWN Anthony Leslie LLB 1963
s of John W. B. police supt and Edith M. Goodwin; b Banff 14.9.41
Dip Indust Ad(Strath) 1964
admin asst Glas 1964–65; res off. man. serv unit G. K. N. Steel Co Cardiff, Scunthorpe 1966–68; lab relations off. Yorks TV Leeds 1968–70; indust relations man. BL Leeds 1970–74; div pers man. The Weir Group Leeds 1974–75; dir indust relations and pers: Weir Pumps Glasg 1976–80, Weir Foundries Leeds from 1980
m Glasg 10.9.66 Sandra K. Graham photogr d of James G. Glasg

BROWN Audrey Beckett *MA 1968

BROWN Barclay MB ChB 1968
s of Alfred B. prod. eng and Helen B. Murray; b Forfar 18.2.43
DObstRCOG(Lond) 1973
cas off. ARI 1968; h o geriat med Woodend hosp Aber 1969; med off. RAF Eng, Germ, Scot. 1969–74; fam pract Simcoe Ontario 1974–76; g p Aber from 1976
m Aber 28.9.68 Patricia W. Angus d of Edward M. A. Canada

BROWN Caroline Elizabeth *MA 1967
m Davidson

BROWN Catherine Anderson MA 1969
d of Adam B. mech eng and Catherine D. T. Anderson secy; b Aber 27.11.22
cler off. Edin from 1972

BROWN Charles *BSc 1963 PhD 1966
s of Charles B. civ serv and Margaret A. Gunn; b Aber 13.5.42
FCS(Lond) FCS(USA)
res assoc Wis 1966–67; res fell. Kent; lect: Dund 1968–69, univ Kent from 1969
m Aber 30.7.64 Margaret R. Downie BSc 1963 *qv*

BROWN David Lawrence Keddie *MA 1969
s of David K. B. water filtration plant oper and Frances McElroy accts clerkess; b Kennoway 17.5.47
teacher Ayr from 1970
m Aber 2.10.70 Margaret H. Burnett MA 1971 teacher d of Robert C. B. Fraserburgh

BROWN David Raymond BSc 1970
s of Raymond T. B. printer and Mary H. E. Albans shop asst; b Nottingham 2.10.48
computer syst analyst Liverpool from 1970
m Bury 29.8.70 Rona G. Howarth BSc(Hull) teacher d of Charles H. Bury

BROWN David William *BSc 1966

BROWN Dorothy May MA 1968
d of Robert J. B. master draper and Jean A. Smith cashier/bookkeeper; b Aber 2.5.46
MIPM(RGIT Aber)
hosp soc worker Bilbohall hosp Elgin 1969–73

BROWN Duncan John Moir BSc 1961

BROWN Edward Massie *MA 1967

BROWN Eileen MA 1965

BROWN Eric Macpherson MA 1967

BROWN Evelyn Kaye BSc 1964
d of Neil G. B. wine and spirit merch and Evelyn Simpson publican; b Aber 20.8.43
asst exper off. Nature Conserv Bangor Wales 1965–66; asst, later ptnr fam bus. from 1966

BROWN Frank Howell MB ChB 1957
s of Frank L. B. secy and gen man. friendly soc and Emily B. Shaw; b Romiley 26.2.33
DTM&H(Liv) 1962 MRCGP 1966
med off. col serv Falkland Is 1958–62; g p: Stoke-on-Trent 1962–68, Isle of Mull 1968–70, Oban from 1970
m Aber 17.5.58 Margaret M. Stewart MA 1954 *qv*

BROWN Gordon Macdonald *BSc 1970
s of Robert G. B. BSc(Edin) civ eng and Eleanor C. Macdonald; b Nigg Easter Ross 16.11.46
Dip TCP(H-W) 1975 MRTPI 1976
asst res off. Scot. dev dept Edin 1971–74; geog/plan. asst Inv c c 1974–76; plan./geographer Highland reg c from 1976

BROWN Graham Leslie *MA 1968

BROWN Iain Alexander BSc(for) 1961
s of John A. B. MA(Glas) schoolmaster and Elizabeth Killin teacher; b Glasg 10.2.40
asst plantation man. Guthrie Corp Malaysia 1961–65; Plant Protection (ICI) overseas tech serv Fernhurst Surrey, Canada, Israel, Aust, Asia 1965–67; ICI (Japan) agr advis 1968–70, Plant Protection (ICI) head tech serv Asia 1970–72; ICI (Malaysia) spec duties Kuala Lumpur 1972–73; Twiga Chem Indust (ICI assoc) agr coordinator E Africa Nairobi from 1974
m Midhurst 25.3.67 Diana Edwards d of Harold E. Midhurst

BROWN Ian Ross BSc(for) 1957 *1958
s of William M. B. insur ag and Mary Ross; b Aber 16.2.36
MS(NY state coll of For. at Syracuse) 1960 PhD(Edin) 1964
Aberd for. dept: asst lect 1964–67, lect from 1967
m Aber 1.2.63 Madeline Morrison MB ChB 1962 *qv*

BROWN Irene MA 1963
m Martin

BROWN James David Kingsley MB ChB 1966

BROWN Janet Kathleen Thomson MA 1969
d of Ian E. B. bank man. and Janet F. Spowart; b Ballater 6.1.49
teacher geog: Montrose acad 1970–73, St Andrew's h s Kirkcaldy from 1973

BROWN Jean *BSc 1969 Dip Ed 1970
d of Henry B. gardener/chauffeur and Rebecca MacLennan; b Gourock 8.10.47
Renfrewsh: educ psych 1971–73, sen from 1973

BROWN John *BSc 1967
s of Charles B. civ serv and Margaret A. Gunn; b Aber 11.3.44
res phys Stevenston 1967–71; coll lect Ayr from 1971
m Aber 12.8.67 Catherine M. Bremner MA 1965 *qv*

BROWN John Boyter *BSc 1970
s of John B. aeroplane mech (RAF) civ serv and Margaret Boyter; b Cellardyke 13.2.48
teacher maths/geol: George Watson's coll Edin 1971–72, Mhlume cent s Swaziland 1972–73, St Augustine's s Edin 1973, Strathallan s from 1973
m Anstruther 4.8.73 Jennie E. Smith secy d of James W. S. Cellardyke

BROWN John Peter BSc(agr) 1967
s of Peter J. G. B. civ serv and Mary Ross; b Inv 15.3.45
Dip FM(NOSCA) 1968
asst insp dept agr Scot. Aber from 1968
m Aber 15.8.69 Irene Taylor teacher dom sc d of Alexander T. Auchnagatt

BROWN John Robert MA 1970

BROWN John Stuart *BSc 1967 PhD 1972
MSc(Imp Coll)

BROWN Josie BSc 1970
d of Leslie A. B. stoker and Olive Key; b Holbrook 5.2.49
Dip Ed(Leic)
teacher maths: Churchill Somerset 1971–72, Stockbridge 1972–73; computer progr Worthy Down 1973–74, Crossgates Leeds from 1974
m Shipham 22.7.72 Christopher D. Jackson BA(Durh) town plan. s of Ronald E. J. BSc(Nott)

BROWN Joyce Mary *MA 1969

BROWN Karl Aubrey Leslie *MA 1956
b Georgetown Guyana 9.6.24
Dip Ed(Edin) 1957
Guyana: teacher geog Queen's coll 1957–60, head s s Essequibo coast s 1960–65; teacher gen stud. tech coll Aber from 1965
m Georgetown –.12.57 Moira H. McRobb MA 1954 *qv*

BROWN Kenneth *MA 1964
s of Stanley W. B. eng machine oper and Ann P. I. Pirie; b Forfar 28.7.41
Aberd: tut. stud. psych 1964–65; asst lect psych 1965–67, lect 1968; lect psych Queen's univ Belf 1968–75, sen lect from 1975
m Brechin 3.8.64 Erica M. Johnston teacher d of John J. Lerwick

BROWN Kenneth Joseph *BSc 1968
s of Charles H. B. farm grieve and Dorothy Duncan shop asst; b Torphins 20.12.45
PhD(Dund) 1971
lect maths H-W Edin 1970–72; res fell. Sus Brighton 1972–73; lect maths H-W from 1973
m Aber 6.10.71 Elizabeth T. Lobban BSc 1967 *qv*

BROWN Linda Jane MB ChB 1964
d of William C. B. DA HMIS and Jane R. Lothian teacher art; b Loanhead 10.6.40
FRCP(Aust) 1977
h o Aber 1964–66; lect path. Aberd/hon sen regist ARI 1968–70; NZ: regist path. Cook hosp Gisborne 1970–71, part time g p Tapanui 1971–74, lect path. univ of Otago from 1975
m Rangiora NZ 30.5.70 John S. Holloway BSc 1969 *qv*

BROWN Margaret MB ChB 1956
d of James H. B. butcher and Christina H. McCall linen fact. worker/dom serv; b East Wemyss 7.2.31
DObstRCOG 1959
h o: Stracathro hosp, City hosp Aber 1956–57, obst & gyn: Perth RI, Br of Earn 1957–58; sen h o Leic gen h 1958–59; g p: Leith 1959–60, Musselburgh 1961–63, Peterhead from 1963

BROWN Margaret Jean Vernon *MA 1962
d of Alister B. pharm/optic. and Jean V. Halliday PO clerk/tel; b Fraserburgh 29.6.40
teacher Engl/hist Inverurie acad 1963–65; sixth form mistress county h s for girls Romford 1965–67; part-time tut. Engl S Havering coll adult educ 1968; part time teacher Engl Maylands s s for girls Hornchurch from 1976
m Aber 22.7.64 Alexander J. Kemp BSc 1961 *qv*

BROWN Mary BEd 1970

BROWN Matthew Stephen Ross *MA 1961 Dip Ed 1962
s of Matthew B. and Isabella S. Ross; b Aber 1.1.33
Ruthrieston s s: teacher Engl/hist/geog 1962–66; spec asst lib and careers master 1966–70; prin asst lib 1970–71; prin teacher Engl 1971–73; prin teacher Engl Arbroath acad from 1973

BROWN Michael LLB 1967
s of Rowland B. comp dir and Mona Furness; b Blackpool 20.5.46
law app Glasg 1967–69; solic: Hamilton 1969–71, Ayr 1971–75; asst dir of admin Kyle and Carrick dist council Ayr from 1975
m Lenzie 20.1.72 Elaine R. Emmerson home serv advis/dom supt d of John R. E. Bishopbriggs

BROWN Pamela Alison MA 1968
d of Robert P. M. B. MB ChB 1935 *qv*; b Aber 13.4.45
teacher: Fernielea s Aber from 1969

BROWN Pamela Margaret BSc 1970
d of Robert S.B. BSc(Glas) teacher, lect and Ada M. Preece SRN; b Glasg 18.7.49
teacher biol: Tranent from 1971
m Aber 28.7.72 John R. Hart BSc 1971 teacher s of Rupert A. H. Leeds

BROWN Patricia Helen MA 1968
m Shea

BROWN Peter Alan *BSc 1970
s of Norman M. B. BSc(Edin) for. and Sheila Cunningham teacher; b Hawick 22.5.45
MSc(Nfd) 1973
grad stud. St John's Nfd 1970–73
m Cullen 1971 Margaret G. Wilson MB ChB 1971 d of John F. W. Cullen

BROWN Richard Alexander John MA 1966 *MEd 1968

BROWN Robert Edward *LLB 1969
s of Albert E. B. customs & excise off. and Joan B. Powton tracer; b Newcastle-on-Tyne 25.12.47
law app, asst Aber 1969–72; part time lect Scots Law Aberd 1970–72; proc fiscal depute Dumbarton 1972–74; solic Rutherglen from 1974; prosp Liberal candidate Rutherglen from 1974

BROWN Robert Morris MB ChB 1969
s of John H. B. headmaster and Rachel M. Clark secy, nursery teacher; b Grantham 26.10.43
DCM 1976
QEH Barbados: h o med obst/gyn 1969–70, sen h o obst/gyn, regist paediat 1970–72; m o Chivenor UK and Malta 1972–75; clin asst St George's hosp Lond 1975–76; sen m o RAF N Ireland from 1976
m Aber 1.2.69 Patricia A. Swanson BSc 1969 *qv*

BROWN Ronald Scott
see Scott-Brown

BROWN Rosalind Ann *MA 1969
d of Frederick C. B. BSc(Lond) schoolmaster and Edith M. Goodhall teacher; b Middlesbrough 2.10.46
grad secy course Aber coll of comm 1969–70; various secy posts from 1970
m Aber 30.5.70 Alan D. M. B. Samuel MA 1971 res sociol s of John M. S. Edin

BROWN Ruby MA 1968
d of Christopher W. B. crofter/road foreman and Barbara C. Gray; b Shetland 27.12.46
teacher maths: Whitburn acad 1969–72, Dunbar g s 1972–75, Kirkwall g s from 1975

BROWN Ruth Mary MA 1956
d of George W. B. paper mill worker and Margaret A. McPherson SRN; b Aber 22.9.35
teacher Aber: St Clement St p s 1958–59, Springhill p s 1960–66, remed reading centre (ch guid serv) 1966–72; head Carden House s for maladjusted pupils from 1972

BROWN Samuel Grieve *BSc 1969
s of Henry D. P. B. naval arch. and Mary G. M. Currie; b Glasg 21.11.46
exploration geol Mount Morgan Queensland 1969–70; mine geol Tennant Creek NT Aust 1970–71; exploration/

mine geol King Is Tasmania from 1972
m Mackay Queensland 4.1.74 Denise O. Tunnah teacher d of John D. T. North Mackay Queensland

BROWN Sheila Anne *MA 1962
b Aber 23.6.41
resid Manc
m Aber 1963 Neil A. Simpson MA 1962 *qv*

BROWN Thomas Ian Spowart MB ChB 1968
s of Ian E. B. bank man. and Janet S. D. F. Spowart; b Dunfermline 22.11.44
DObstRCOG(Lond) 1970 FRCSE 1973
h o, sen h o Bridgend, Glamorgan, Hexham, Newcastle, Musselburgh 1968–71; Edin: regist surg 1971–74, orthop surg from 1974

BROWN William *BSc 1965 PhD 1969

BROWN William Alan *BSc(agr) 1970
s of Stanley B. agr worker and Jane Thornber; b Fulwood Preston 24.11.45
consult. off. (MMB) Lancs from 1970
m Penwortham Preston 7.10.72 Juliet C. Taylor sales superv Marks & Spencer d of Michael T. Penwortham Preston

BROWN William Barton BSc(eng) 1961
s of William J. B. master bldr and Ethel M. Rutherford; b Aber 6.5.39
MICE 1968
Glasg: asst eng Crouch & Hogg consult. eng 1961–64, site eng and des Reema (Scotland) contrs 1964–67; sect eng: W. A. Fairhurst & Ptnrs consult. Glasg Inner Ring Road, Kingston Bridge 1967–69, Charing Cross 1969–72; resid eng WAF on N Ayrshire District gen hosp Kilmarnock 1972–73; dep resid eng WAF on Renfrew Motorway Stage II Glasg 1974–76, resid eng from 1976
m Aber 21.3.62 Helen C. S. Hepburn shorthand typist d of John S. H. Aber

BROWN William Campbell MA 1969
s of Joseph B. bldg contr and Flora Campbell; b Banff 25.5.48
stud. lang Frankfurt 1974

BROWN William Peddie *MA 1956 PhD 1959
s of William B. BL 1926 *qv*; b Aber 7.12.34
Dip Ed(Edin) 1960 FBPsS 1973 FPsSoc of Ireland 1973
Bedford coll Lond: asst lect psych 1960–62, lect 1962–64; lect psych: Aberd 1964–68, Queen's Univ Belf 1969–70; reader psych Queen's Univ from 1970

BROWNE Bernard James Forbes *MA 1968
s of Bernard L. B. teacher and Margaret Watson teacher; b Aber 8.7.43
teacher Engl Dun from 1969
m Dunfermline 24.7.71 Frances E. Reid d of David R. MA (St And) Dunfermline

BROWNE Felicia Ibironke MB ChB 1963 MD 1972
m Akinsete

BROWNE Michael MB ChB 1970

BROWNING Matthew Peter *MA 1966
s of James B. grocer and Rowina S. Taylor; b Paisley 8.6.43
Dip Ed(Edin) 1967
teacher geog: South Eastham s s Newham Lond, Prince Rupert s (BFES) Wilhelmshaven & Rinteln W Ger; teacher geog/Engl Königin Mathilde Mädchen Gymnasium 49 Herford W Ger

BROWNLEE Norman Robert *MA 1969
s of James B. and Margaret N. Young MA(Edin); b Markinch 16.2.47
teacher maths Cults acad Aber from 1970
m Aber 26.3.75 Elizabeth H. F. Hay d of A. D. F. H Kintore

BROWNLIE Kathleen Anne MA 1969
d of Thomas A. C. B. BSc(Edin) civ eng and Marjorie Bennetts; b Dumfries 16.6.48
post grad course statist LSE 1970–71; res asst prod. assessment (food) Unilever Bedford 1969–70; asst statist hosp board Cambridge 1971–74; statist sect. hosp auth Croydon 1974–75; sen statist NW Thames reg health auth from 1975
m Edin 28.8.72 Paul V. Griew BSc(Birm) computer syst analyst, eng s of David G. Lond

BRUCE Alexander MB ChB 1961

BRUCE Alexander Cobban *BSc 1968

BRUCE Alexander Ritchie BSc 1963

BRUCE Annie (Anne) MA 1959
d of Robert B. master baker and Charlotte N. Suttar; b Peterhead 2.4.38
invest. asst Standard Life Assur comp Edin 1959–60; secy Lindsay Jamieson & Haldane CA Edin 1960–62; dir Thomas Murison Peterhead from 1969
m Aber 3.1.62 Thomas Murison MA(Edin) comp man. dir s of Thomas M. Peterhead

BRUCE Audrey Bevin *MA 1969
d of Robert B. and Ethel Sim; b Ellon 4.10.47
plan. asst: Banff c c Buckie 1970–71, Coatbridge t c from 1972
m Aber 14.10.71 John R. T. Breckenridge off. customs and excise s of John W. B. OBE Woking

BRUCE Carol Isabel MA 1958
d of David T. B. fish merch/comp dir and Isabella Massie; b Aber 3.9.37
secy course Lond 1958–59
m Aber 27.6.59 William J. A. Innes MA 1956 *qv*

BRUCE Carole MA 1966
m Preshaw

BRUCE Charles John *BSc 1959

BRUCE Charlotte *MA 1961
d of Robert B. master baker and Charlotte N. Suttar; b Peterhead 10.12.39
m Singapore 11.11.61 Allan M. Thomson MB ChB 1957 *qv*

BRUCE Christine Flora Helen *MA 1969
m Thayer

BRUCE Clive *MA 1967
s of Robert B. master baker and Charlotte N. Suttar; b Peterhead 10.7.43
teacher Grange acad Kilmarnock 1968–72; prin soc stud. Queen Victoria s Dunblane from 1972
m Aber 14.9.66 Irene Guthrie teacher d of Alexander G. Peterhead

BRUCE David Woodland *MA 1956

BRUCE Donald McBeath *BSc 1966

BRUCE Donald McCaskill *MA 1969

BRUCE Dorothy Elinor MA 1963
d of Alexander B. trawl owner and Helen M. Knowles; b Aber 12.9.41
stewardess: BEA 1963–65; Caledonian 1965–71
m Aber 6.11.71 Charles J. Bell bus. man (eng) s of Frederick B. North Walsham

BRUCE Elizabeth Jane Rose MA 1960

BRUCE George Ian Copland *BSc(eng) 1970 MSc 1972
s of George M. B. farm. and Christina M. Copland; b Aber 22.11.48
des and dev eng (electronic) Ferranti Edin from 1972

BRUCE George Kerr BSc(for) 1964
s of George O. B. merch/electronics expert and Amy M. Kerr; b Aber 18.2.41
reg for. off: asst conserv, acting sen asst conserv for Malawi 1964–70; branch man. Tilhill Forestry (Scot.) Ripon 1970–72, Gifford E. Lothian 1972–74; for. consult. Umtali Rhodesia from 1975

BRUCE George Leonard BSc(eng) 1958
s of George R. B. cycle ag/shopkeeper and Kathleen S. Murray cashier; b Aber 4.10.36
AMInstF 1966 MIME 1969
res eng Babcock & Wilcox Renfrew 1958–66; des eng Clarke Chapman Wolverhampton from 1966
m Birm 20.7.68 Jean F. Knight BSc(Lond) computer progr d of Leonard F. C. K. Birmingham

BRUCE Gordon McKay MB ChB 1960
s of William B. MB ChB 1925 *qv*; b Aber 30.8.33
DObstRCOG 1962
h o: ARI, mat. unit Raigmore hosp Inv 1961–62; g p Dingwall from Dec 1962
m Inv 12.8.66 Rosemary M. Souter nurse d of James P. S. Fort William

BRUCE Graeme Maclean *MA 1958 BD 1961

BRUCE Henry Thomson MB ChB 1967
s of Henry T. B. hotelier and Elizabeth Selbie hotelier; b Insch 25.10.43
h o: Maryfield hosp Dun, ARI 1967–68; regist path. WI Glasg 1968–72; g p Glasg from 1972
m Glasg 27.9.68 Ellen J. Bishop MB ChB(Glas) d of William B. Clydebank

BRUCE Iain Charles *BSc 1969
s of John B. MB ChB 1941 *qv*; b Aber 17.1.46
PhD(Calg) 1975

BRUCE Iain Gordon *BSc 1965
s of Robert B. farm. and Elizabeth Shand; b Methlick 6.5.43
BSc(Lond)) 1973
teacher: Perthsh 1966–71, Adelaide Aust from 1971
m Aber 19.2.66 Elizabeth A. Whyte nurse d of Robert W. Aber

BRUCE Irene Margaret Jessie MA 1958
d of Robert J. B. farm. and Jessie M. I. Collie; b Nairn 2.1.37
teacher: Kinloss 1959–61, Lochside s Dumfries 1961–63; comp secy Annan 1967–75; teacher Hecklegirth p s Annan from 1975
m Findhorn 17.8.61 Raymond C. MacDonald civ eng/comp dir s of Donald A. MacD. Elgin

BRUCE James Masson MSc 1968 PhD 1971

BRUCE Jane Isabel MB ChB 1960
d of Alexander G. B. MA(Edin) teacher and Ellen Manson MA(Edin) teacher; b Wick 4.1.37
h o Inv, Perth, Inv 1960–61; g p Inv from 1970
m Aber 8.9.61 Ian Macpherson MB ChB(Glas) med asst bact s of John M. Diabaig

BRUCE John MA 1963

BRUCE John Clark *BSc(eng) 1963
s of John M. B. blacksmith and Catherine J. Clark secy; b Tarves 2.4.41
MICE 1969
eng: James Williamson & Ptnrs (power stat des) Glasg 1963–65, Tarmac Civ Eng (road and bridge construct.) Hamilton and Cumbernauld 1965–67; Scott Wilson Kirkpatrick & Ptnrs bridge des Glasg 1967–68, tunnel des Lond 1968–69, sen eng in des of cross-harbour tunnel and gen civ eng works Hong Kong from 1969

BRUCE Joseph Alexander George BSc 1957

BRUCE Kate Margaret *MA 1967
d of Douglass B. CA and Kate Hurrell BSc(Durh) teacher; b Gravesend 23.12.43
secy Butterworths Lond 1968–70; prod. controller Macmillan Lond 1970–72, prod. man. Maddox Editorial 1972–74; sales promotion exec The Radiochemical Centre Amersham 1974–76
m Gravesend 25.3.72 Anthony A. Mortimer BSc(Lond) marketing plan. s of Alexander M. Rickmansworth

BRUCE Lawrence MA 1967

BRUCE Margaret Anne Mary MA 1968
d of Allan M. B. haulage contr and Margaret B. Moffatt; b Inverurie 16.3.47
teacher: Perth 1969–71, Rheindahlen W Ger 1971–73, asst prin guid S Queensferry from 1973
m Aber 5.4.77 Peter R. Henderson CA s of Thomas W. H. Edin

BRUCE Michael George *MA 1966

BRUCE Michael Stewart Rae MA 1959 ᶜLLB 1961
s of Alexander E. B. MA 1921 *qv*; b Aber 26.7.38
law app: L. McKinnon & Son advoc Aber 1959–61, Brodie Cuthbertson & Watson Edin 1961–62; member of fac of advoc 1963
m Edin 27.12.63 Alison M. M. Stewart d of Alastair M. S. Edin

BRUCE Patricia Helen MA 1968
d of George R. B. motor/cycle ag and Kathleen Murray secy; b Aber 13.1.47
teacher geog Kilmarnock acad 1969–72
m Aber 19.7.69 Robert G. Thomson tv film cameraman s of William T. Edin

BRUCE Peter BSc(eng) 1960 *1961
s of George B. fisherman and Jane Bruce; b Buckie 5.6.38
Edin: dev eng Ferranti 1960–68, tech writer ISI 1969–70, dir Advanced Des Dev 1970–74, man. dir Bruce Anchor from 1972

BRUCE Robert Gordon *BSc(agr) 1963
s of Robert B. policeman and Isabella M. Gordon

hotelier; b Aber 19.1.41
PhD (Cantab) 1967
Glasg: asst lect 1966–70, lect zoology from 1970
m Camb 1963 Moira M. Christie MA 1960 *qv*

BRUCE Rosaleen Anne BSc 1966
m Norman D. Deans BSc 1966 *qv*

BRUCE Sheila MA 1963

BRUCE William Craik MA 1958 BD 1961
s of William B. crofter and Elizabeth M. Craik; b Dun 9.9.29
C of S min: asst St Giles Elgin 1961–62, min: St Andrews ch Lochgelly 1962–68, Dalziel par ch Motherwell from 1968
m Forfar 20.9.58 Euphemia T. Sturrock secy d of William S. Forfar

BRUNNEN Rosemary Ann *MA 1968
d of Peter L. B. MB ChB 1939 *qv* and Margaret C. T. Brown MA 1942 *qv*; b Aber 1.11.46
MA(Nott) 1969
dem Nott 1969–71; Lond: soc worker 1972–76, sen clin psych Charing Cross hosp/Gt Ormond St hosp 1976–78; lect handicapped in commun OU Milton Keynes from 1978
m (1) Jones
(2) Lond –.5.78 Derek M. Brechin MA 1960 *qv*

BRUNTON Jennifer Margaret *MA 1970
m Taylor

BRYANT Carl Leonard BSc(for) 1957 MSc 1971
s of Leonard B. steelworker and Marjorie A. Dixey; b Coventry 12.10.35
Tanzania: asst conserv for. 1959–64, for. man. off. hardwoods Dar-es-Salaam 1964–66, res off. hardwoods Lushoto 1966–68; sen asst reg off. SWOAC Castle Douglas from 1968
m Aber 23.7.62 Audrey M. Noble MA 1957 *qv*

BRYANT Jeremy Joseph BSc(eng) 1964

BRYCE Andrew Bonner BSc(eng) 1958 *1959
s of Donald P. B. soldier, admin and Patricia I. Bonner d of Thomas I. B. MA 1889; *qv*(I, II); b Yorks 6.6.36
MIEE CEng
grad app Rugby 1959–61; asst elect. eng HMTS *Alert* 1961–62; elect. eng RRS *Discovery* 1962–64; professional eng Rolls Royce & Assoc at HMS *Vulcan* Thurso from 1964
m Lerwick 19.4.65 Elizabeth M. Inkster MA 1963 *qv*

BRYCE Graeme Findlay *BSc 1960
s of William C. B. master plumber and Veda M. H. Findlay; b Aber 1.5.38
PhD(Lond) 1963
USA: res fell. univ of Indiana 1963–65, Yale 1965–69; asst member Roche Inst of Molec Biol 1969–74; sen scient Hoffmann–La Roche 1974–76, res fell. from 1976
m Connecticut 13.4.67 Mary A. Addelson BA(Hofstra) secy d of Arthur E. A. New York

BRYCE Jennifer Anne MA 1967
d of George C. B. sports dealer and Annie M. Smith civ serv, pharm; b Edin 23.6.45
Dip Soc Work(Glas) 1968
soc worker Aber 1968–71; almoner Durban hosp S Af, dept ch welfare, Bantu Indian children 1971–73; hosp soc worker Mudgee NSW Aust from 1975
m Edin 5.7.69 David J. C. Barclay MB ChB 1969 *qv*

BRYCE Judith Helen *MA 1970 PhD 1977

BRYDON Brenda Valerie *BSc 1965 PhD 1969
m Imlach

BRYER Kenneth Robert *BSc 1967
s of Robert G. B. BA(OU) res and des eng and Joan Wallbank; b Hillingdon 18.10.43
CPA
tech asst chartered patent ag Lond 1967–70; chartered patent ag Plymouth from 1970
m Aber 18.3.67 Patricia Nicholls d of Frank N. Aber

BUCHALA Antony Joseph *BSc 1968 PhD 1971
s of Stefan J. B. teacher, prof photogr and Anne Dick nurse; b Aber 31.10.46
ARIC 1971
res fell. (Royal Society) Inst plant biol univ of Fribourg Switzerland 1971–73; doctoral asst inst Cardiovascular Res Fribourg from 1973

BUCHAN Alan Fraser BSc(agr) 1968

BUCHAN Alexander *BSc 1961 PhD 1965
s of Robert B. bldr and Mary K. McDonald civ serv; b Aber 4.9.39
res associate St Thomas hosp Lond 1964–67; lect Birm from 1967
m Aber 12.8.65 Jennifer A. Cutt BSc 1962 *qv*

BUCHAN Alexander MA 1970
s of Alexander B. fisherman and Mary Crawford; b Fraserburgh 1.4.35
BD(Edin) 1974
C of S min Stonefield and Burleigh with Anderson ch Blantyre from 1974
m Paisley 1.5.67 Isabel C. Black BSc(Strath) d of David C. B. Glasg

BUCHAN Alexander Greig MA 1960 LLB 1962
s of Charles B. fishselling man. and Mabel Greig; b Fraserburgh 15.12.38
Aber: law app 1960–63, law asst 1963–65, ptnr J. & G. Collie advoc from 1966
m Aber 11.7.62 Marie Marioni teacher d of Giulo A. M. Fraserburgh

BUCHAN Alexander James MB ChB 1959
s of Alexander B. marine eng and Isabella Buchan; b Fraserburgh 6.9.34
DObstRCOG 1964
ed off. RAMC Singapore, Maralinga Aust, Hong Kong 1960–63; h o mat. hosp Aber 1963; g p: Dagenham, Airdrie 1963–64, Hobart Tasmania from 1964
m Aber 4.4.64 Aileen S. Dewar nurs sister d of Andrew D. Aber

BUCHAN Alexander Reid *BSc(eng) 1956
s of Alexander R. B. fisherman and Davina C. Cruickshank; b Peterhead 6.9.33
MICE AMIHE CEng
asst BR Glasg 1956–58; nat serv (commissioned in Royal Eng) RMCS Shrivenham 1958–60; chief asst eng capital works Dumfries 1960–64; asst road eng Livingston dev corp. 1964–65; lect: Napier coll of sc and tech Edin 1965–67, struct eng Strath from 1967
m Peterhead 22.12.56 Myra Booth secy d of George B. Peterhead

BUCHAN Alexander Strachan BSc(eng) 1969
s of George W. B. shipwright and Mary T. Ironside; b Fraserburgh 22.6.48
asst civ eng: Invergordon 1969–71, Lond from 1971

m Lochwinnoch 26.9.70 Sharon A. Smith secy d of Robert B. S. Lochwinnoch

BUCHAN Ann MA 1962
d of Arthur B. factory man. and Elsie R. Duncan; b Ellon 29.11.41
teacher: Engl/hist Peterhead acad 1963–66, p s Lagos 1967–69, p s Peterhead 1973–74, remed teacher
m Aber 3.4.64 Robert S. S. Summers asst buyer s of Gilbert S. Fraserburgh

BUCHAN Barbara Bruce MA 1969
m Thomas

BUCHAN Charles Cummin BSc 1967
s of Charles B. ship's capt, fisherman etc and Jeannie McGee; b Peterhead 13.10.45
G Inst P 1975
teacher Fraserburgh acad: maths/sc 1968–73, asst prin phys from 1973
m Fraserburgh 17.8.68 Georgina S. Buchan MA 1966 *qv*

BUCHAN Christina Sutherland MA 1966

BUCHAN David Duncan *MA 1960 PhD 1965
s of Joseph D. B. civ serv/marine scient and Elsie A. Robb; b Aber 7.1.39
Gordon Bottomley fell. Aberd 1960–61, 1963–64; instr Engl univ Victoria Canada 1961–63, 1964–65; asst prof Engl Mass USA 1965–68; lect Engl stud. Stir 1968–71, sen lect from 1971
m Aber 2.9.65 Moyra J. Nisbet MA 1963 *qv*

BUCHAN Elizabeth Jean BSc 1961
d of James B. motor mech and Jessie A. A. Milne; b Huntly 19.12.35
res asst Lond 1961–64; teacher Aber from 1975
m Aber 21.12.61 John R. Sargent PhD 1961 *qv*

BUCHAN Georgina Stephen MA 1966
d of Gilbert M. B. fisherman and Christian Stephen; b Cairnbulg 10.4.44
teacher Fraserburgh acad: maths/sc 1967–69, r e 1971–72, prin guid from 1972
m Fraserburgh 17.8.68 Charles C. Buchan BSc 1967 *qv*

BUCHAN Jennifer Rosemary MB ChB 1969
d of Campbell B. MB ChB(Edin) surg and Marjorie Clark nurse; b Edin 27.9.45
DCH 1971
h o Aber, Inv 1969–70; sen h o Lond, Glasg 1970–72; g p Glasg 1972–73; Ayrsh: clin m o 1974–75, fam plan. off. from 1975
m Edin 28.4.73 John Cleland MB ChB(Glas) g p s of Gavin C. MB ChB(Edin) Mauchline

BUCHAN Joan Crawford BSc 1970
b Fraserburgh 12.11.48
clerkess NSHEB 1971–73
m Fraserburgh 14.8.71 Alan Rafferty bricklayer

BUCHAN John MA 1968
s of Alexander B. master butcher and Barbara S. Duthie teacher; b Fraserburgh 22.11.46
Dip Pers Man.(RGIT Aber) 1969
man. father's bus. Fraserburgh 1969–70; labour off. MoD Bishopton 1970–73; pers off. Ethicon Edin from 1973
m Aber 5.4.72 Ruth C. McInnes Dip Sp and Drama (Glas) drama teacher d of William D. McI. LLB(Glas) Aber

BUCHAN Kathleen Ina MacNicol BSc 1964 MB ChB 1967
d of William A. E. B. teacher and Janet W. MacNicol teacher; b Ballater 21.2.43
DPM(Scot. conjoint) 1970 MRCPsych 1973
h o ARI/Woodend hosp Aber 1967–68; sen h o psychiat Ross Clinic Aber 1968–69; regist psychiat Cornhill and assoc hosps Aber 1969–73; locum regist RACH 1974–75; med asst psychiat Malvern Worcs from 1975
m (1) 1964
(2) 1975 Richard E. Mackie BA(Cantab) psychotherap, writer s of Frederick P. M. MBBs(Brist) Mark Somerset

BUCHAN Leonard BSc 1957

BUCHAN Mabel MA 1969
d of Charles B. fish salesman and Mabel Greig; b St Combs 11.1.48
teacher Peterhead 1970–74
m Rathen 6.7.71 Karl J. T. Revel BEd 1970 *qv*

BUCHAN Margaret Elizabeth *BSc 1966
d of William B. farm. and Margaret J. Shearer; b Turriff 12.11.44
teacher Queen Margaret acad Ayr 1967–71
m Aber 20.7.67 James A. Goodlad MA 1965 *qv*

BUCHAN Maynard Cowe BSc 1968
s of Samuel M. B. stat off. HM coastguard and Margaret J. Bowie; b Rattray Head 10.8.47
teacher maths Peterhead acad from 1969
m Peterhead 14.4.73 Lilian F. Melford MA 1969 *qv*

BUCHAN Muriel MA 1958
d of Charles M. B. installation insp and Alice W. Tocher; b Aber 4.5.38
teacher Aber 1959–66
m Aber 1.7.64 John W. Sim MB ChB 1964 *qv*

BUCHAN Neil BSc(eng) 1961
s of Alexander J. B. off. man. and Mabel Watson; b Aber 2.4.39
grad eng Crouch & Hogg consult. civ eng Glasg 1961–62; asst eng Glasg corp 1962–65; site eng/ag George Wimpey civ eng contr 1965–70; chief eng Scot. Myton civ eng/bldg contr 1971–72; sen eng, asst prin eng roads Strathclyde reg c from 1972
m Aber 26.7.62 Lesley H. Tough teacher d of Robert J. S. T. Knockando

BUCHAN Nigel Gordon MB ChB 1966
s of John B. trawl skipper and Jeannie Gray; b Aber 26.6.43
FRCSE 1972
h o Aber 1966–67; sen h o: Lincoln 1967–68, rotating surg Leeds 1968–70; regist surg Hull 1970–71; regist plastic surg Lond 1972–75
m Leeds 12.7.69 Verona Clemens nurse Thurscoe

BUCHAN Patricia Ann Bruce MA 1960
m Noble

BUCHAN Peter MA 1967

BUCHAN Robert *BSc 1959 PhD 1972

BUCHAN Robert MB ChB 1960 MD 1965
s of Robert A. B. b Peterculter 24.6.36
FRCSE 1968
h o ARI 1960–61; res fell. Aberd 1961–63; regist surg ARI 1966–69; sen regist Cardiff 1969–71; lect surg Edin 1971–74; consult. surg Kirkcaldy from 1974

BUCHAN Ronald MacDonald MB ChB 1959
BDS

BUCHAN Sandra MA 1966
d of Alexander B. journalist and Jane E. Ritchie; b Peterhead 14.12.44
teacher Peterhead North s 1967–69; stud. Moray House dip. in educ of the deaf 1969–70; nurs teacher Aber s for deaf 1970–73; peripatetic teacher of deaf Aber county from 1973

BUCHAN Sinclair MA 1958 *BSc 1961
s of John M. B. B. JP man. fish-selling and ship chandler's bus. and Robina Sinclair; b Fraserburgh 14.4.36
FRGS 1970
UCNW Menai Bridge: asst hydrographer 1961–64, res asst 1964–68, temp lect 1968–69, lect phys oceanography from 1969
m Garnfadryn nr Pwllheli 12.4.69 Sarah C. Hughes nurs sister d of Griffiths J. H. Garnfadryn

BUCHAN William Arthur *BSc(eng) 1961

BUCHANAN Jane Ann Macintosh *MA 1969
d of Samuel M. B. insur insp and Margaret MacBean; b Glasg 3.6.47
Dip Lib(Lond) 1971 ALA 1972
asst Sus lib Brighton 1969–70; audio visual aids lib Newcastle-u-Tyne poly from 1971
m Newcastle-u-Tyne 28.7.73 Nigel M. G. W. Davey BSc (Hull) res chem, materials tech s of Neville W. D. Maidstone

BUCHANAN Maria Theresa MB ChB 1969
m Stoker

BUCHANAN William Andrew Petrie MA 1970

BUCHANAN-SMITH Jock Gordon BSc(agr) 1962
s of Rt Hon Lord Balerno MA 1922 *qv*; b Edin 9.3.40
BS(Iowa state univ USA) 1963 MS(Texas tech coll USA) 1965 PhD(Oklahoma state univ USA) 1969
USA: res asst: Lubbock Texas 1963–65, Stillwater Okla 1965–69; asst prof Guelph Ont Canada 1969–76, assoc prof from 1976
m Dallas Texas 26.8.64 Virginia L. Maxson d of John S. M. Dallas

BUCHMANN Karoly Francis Joseph MB ChB 1969
s of Othar L. K. B. BSc(Budapest) indust pharm and Erzsebet S. Varga secy; b Budapest 17.4.43
DA 1972 FFARCS 1975 DObstRCOG 1975
h o, trainee anaest ARI 1969–75; trainee anaest Stobhill hosp Glasg 1975; consult anaest Tygerberg Cape Town from 1975
m Glasg 14.9.73 Elizabeth R. Ewing SRN d of Walter E. Glasg

BUCHMANN Othmar Laszlo Karoly Attila *BSc 1967

BUCK Francis Norman *BSc 1968
s of Alfred G. B. comp chmn textile trade and Cicely Jackson; b Carlisle 16.4.45
prod. man. British Gypsum 1971–75, asst works man. from 1976
m Carlisle 15.6.74 Janice Marshallsay d of James M. Whitley Bay

BUCKLE Donald James BSc(for) 1960
s of Hector D. B. comp secy and Doris M. Clark; b Southampton 4.2.38
surv asst for. co New Forest 1960–61; for. man.: Yattendon Estate Berks 1961–64, English Woodlands Kent, Sussex, Surrey from 1964
m Aber 15.7.60 Verity M. Hutchison teacher d of Gordon H. MB ChB 1930 *qv*

BUCKLE Ernest Roy *PhD 1958
s of Ernest H. B. police constable, civ serv and Florence M. Sinclair pianist; b Lond 23.9.26
ARIC 1955 FRIC 1961 CChem 1975 FIM 1976 CEng 1978
asst chem Aberd 1957–58; sen res asst Imp Coll Lond 1958–68; Sheff: lect metall 1968–75, sen lect 1975–77, reader from 1977
m Sundridge 4.2.56 Shirley A. Brown bank clerk d of John B. Sundridge

BUCKLEY Graham Peter BSc(for) 1968
s of Frederick W. B. headmaster and Eileen Street teacher; b Oswestry 11.4.47
MSc(Wales) 1970
res asst Leeds univ 1970–73; lect landscape/horticulture/ecology Wye coll Lond from 1973

BUDDHOO Jayraz BSc 1968

BUDGE Margaret *BSc 1970
m Youngson

BUDGE Rosemary Kathleen *MA 1964
d of James B. farm. and Ada M. Halcrow; b Bigton Shetland 25.10.42
exec off. W. Pacific high commission Brit Solomon Is 1970–72; commissary superv Uniroyal Plantations Liberia W. Af 1973–75; teacher Swaziland 1975–78
m Bigton 22.7.64 Ian W. Skea MSc(R'dg) anim prod. off. ODM s of James S. Rendall Orkney

BUICK Ronald Nicoll *BSc 1970 PhD 1974
s of Douglas S. B. consult. eng and Isobel J. Nicoll teacher; b Dun 10.3.48
res biochem: Wis Madison USA 1973–76; inst of cancer res Toronto from 1976
m Aber 3.7.70 Susan M. Wright BSc 1970

BUIE Christine Margaret MA 1965
m Grant

BULLOUGH Frances Stewart PhD 1967
d of Arthur S. B. MB ChB (Manc) consult. surg and Margaret B. Stewart MA(Glas) foreign correspondent; b Bellshill 10.12.41
BSc(Leeds) 1963 Dip Ed(Oxon) 1964
Brit Council Lond 1967–68; teacher Napier tech coll Edin 1968–71
m Timperley 18.12.70 Peter J. Lindsay tech off. s of David W. L. MB ChB(Glas) Edin

BULMER Susan Rosalind BMedBiol 1969 MB ChB 1972
d of Gerald B. BA(Cantab) rector Liv poly from 1970, dir RGIT Aber 1965–70 and Greta L. Parkes BA(Cantab) plant path.; b Herne Bay 23.12.47
h o RACH, Southampton gen hosp 1972–73; sen h o clin path. United Sheffield hosp from 1973

BUNTING John Allen *BSc 1969
s of Thomas A. B. RAF and Mary J. Massie teacher; b Aber 12.11.46
geol with geol surv of W Aust from 1969
m Aber 1.9.69 Ann G. Sinclair MA 1968 *qv*

BUNTING Ronald Strachan *BSc 1957
s of George B.; b Aber 18.10.34
jun geol, div explor supt several oil companies Calgary Alberta from 1957
m Aber 29.6.57 Maureen A. W. Leslie

BURGESS Alexander Sharp *MA 1970 Dip Ed 1971
s of John B. and Elizabeth J. Donaldson; b Elgin 29.4.48
teacher hist/mod stud: Elgin acad 1971–75, Arbroath acad from 1975

BURGESS Anna Margaret *MA 1956
d of Douglas B. BBC eng i/c and Evelyn Mackie; b Aber 26.11.34
teacher Engl Perth acad 1957–63; prin Engl Dover g s for girls 1963–65; lect Engl/commun New coll Durh from 1970
m Aber 10.8.63 Brian A. S. Primmer BMus(Cantab) lect mus Durh s of Harold P. Southsea

BURGESS Charles Smith MB ChB 1964
s of Alexander G. B. farm. and Agnes Singer; b Newmachar 28.1.41
MRCGP 1975
h o: ARI, city hosp, mat. hosp Aber 1964–65; g p Aber 1966–69, Ellon from 1969
m Aber 8.5.65 Doris M. Riddell teacher dom sc d of James R. Whiterashes

BURGESS John Moncrieff BSc(agr) 1958
s of George B. crofter and Catherine Moncrieff; b Scousburgh 8.9.36
nat serv UK, Germany 1959–61; lect NOSCA Aber 1961–64; DAFS: asst lands off., lands off. Shetland, Edin 1964–75; dir of res and dev Shetland Is Lerwick from 1975
m Aber 31.7.65 Patricia M. Smith teacher d of Robert W. S. Cults

BURGESS William Steven *BSc 1962
s of William S. B. baker and Joey West; b Scalloway Shetland 22.7.40
teacher chem: Perth h s 1963–66, spec asst 1966–72; prin chem Galashiels acad from 1972
m Perth 29.9.63 Carmelita E. Brady secy, nurse d of Joseph P. E. B. Aber

BURGHER George Stevenson BSc(agr) 1960
b Ness, Westray 7.12.37
Orkney: teacher 1961–69, NFU area secy from 1969
m 10.7.63 Winifred S. Urquhart

BURN John Campbell LLB 1966

BURN-MURDOCH Nigel Alexander Spencer *BSc 1966

BURN-MURDOCH Noel Gray *BSc(for) 1965

BURNETT Alan Robertson *BSc 1964 PhD 1968
s of Alexander B. bus prop. and Jeannie B. Cruden; b Mintlaw 6.10.42
dem org chem Liv 1967–69; teacher chem/housemaster Stirling h s 1970–73, prin chem Denny h s from 1973
m Larbert 27.2.72 Helen I. Mitchell BSc(Glas) teacher d of George E. M. Larbert

BURNETT Alexander Walker MA 1966
s of Alexander C. B. insp of works (col serv) and Jessie F. Walker clerkess; b Aber 27.6.27
ALA 1970
trainee lib nat lending lib Boston Spa and Durham lib 1966–67; stud lib N'cle poly 1968–69; sc lib St And from 1969
m Aber 14.8.68 Marjory S. Middleton MA 1967 *qv*

BURNETT Alistair George Murray LLB 1970
s of George M. B. BSc 1943 *qv* and Anne E. Bow MA 1946 *qv*; b Birmingham 18.5.50
NP 1972 WS 1974
Edin: law app Shepherd & Wedderburn 1970–72; asst Baillie & Gifford WS from 1972
m Edin 10.6.72 Jennifer Edwards occup therap

BURNETT Frances Elizabeth MA 1963

BURNETT Frances Helen MA 1960
d of William J. B. mech eng and Helen J. Benzie; b Insch 1.10.39
teacher Engl girls' s s Chesterfield from 1973 after various part-time posts
m Aber 4.7.61 Robert D. Porter BSc(eng) 1960 *qv*

BURNETT Gordon Bernard MB ChB 1964 MD 1976
s of Joseph S. F. B. insur ag and Georgina C. Main bookkeeper; b Aber 26.7.37
DPM(Edin) 1968 MRCPsych(Lond) 1972
h o Aber hosp 1964–65; regist royal Edin hosp 1965–68, sen regist 1968–69; res fell. psychiat Edin 1969–72; asst prof psychiat Baylor coll med Houston Texas; assoc prof psychiat univ of N Carolina Chapel Hill from 1976
m Aber 20. 3.65 Wendy E. W. Bell MA 1963 *qv*

BURNETT Ian Anthony Julian BSc(agr) 1969

BURNETT Irene Mary BSc 1969
d of Robert B. joint prop. drapery store and Monica M. Vincent cashier; b Nairn 3.3.46
Dip Comput Sc(Glas) 1970
analyst, progr Lucas Birm 1970–74
m Birm 6.4.74 Philip G. Grant maintenance plumber Alberta govt tel s of Joseph G. Staffs

BURNETT James Brodie Crawford MB ChB 1961
s of James W. M. B. wine & spirit merch and Elizabeth S. McIntosh millinery/man. buyer; b Victoria BC Canada 3.3.31
DObstRCOG 1963 DA 1963
h o: Dumfries, Aber 1961–63; sen h o: Aber, Dumfries 1963–65; regist obst/gyn Aber 1965–67; g p Kirkwall 1967–68, med advis John Wyth & Son, Taplow 1968–70; g p Caversham from 1970
m Aber 21.11.64 Josephine F. Stewart SRN nursing sister d of William S. Ballater

BURNETT Janet Christine MA 1967
d of Joseph B. BOAC radio oper, tv eng and Isabella B. Arnott secy; b Aber 20.9.46
teacher: Lossiemouth h s 1968–69, Fr/Ger 1969–72
m Elgin 17.7.68 Charles M. Grant NDA farm. s of Ian H. G. Lochhills Elgin

BURNETT Lorna Mary MA 1964
d of David J. B. police sgt and Catherine Smith; b Aber 3.1.43
teacher: Inv 1965–69, Aber 1969–71, Brechin 1973–78, Inv from 1978, acting asst head Holm s
m Aber 29.6.65 Nichol Thomson tech teacher

BURNETT Madeleine Anne MA 1960
d of Joseph B. tv eng and Isabella B. Arnott secy; b Lockerbie 26.8.40
teacher p s: h s for girls Aber 1961–64, Valley p s Kirkcaldy 1964–66, Mauricewood p s Penicuik 1974–76,

asst head from 1976
m Aber 12.8.64 James R. Wight MA 1960 *qv*

BURNETT Panton Ironside MA 1957

BURNETT Patricia Anne BSc 1969
d of George M. B. BSc 1943 *qv* and Anne E. Bow MA 1946 *qv*; b Aber 30.8.47
edit. asst journal clin and exper immunol Edin 1970–71; secy asst vice-dean fac sc Edin 1971–73; med secy univ St John's Newfoundland 1973–75
m Aber 29.9.73 Richard G. Cawthorn BSc(Durh) sen lect geol univ Witwatersrand Johannesburg s of Thomas H. C. Bingley

BURNETT Sandra Mary Margaret MA 1960

BURNETT William John MA 1961
s of John W. B. farm. and Lizzie I. Panton; b Fraserburgh 13.3.40
teacher Aber from 1962
m Aber 7.8.67 Katharine J. M. West MA 1964 *qv*

BURNHAM Bruce *MA 1965
s of Thomas C. B. headmaster and Margaret Ronald; b Hartlepool 27.3.43
BLitt(Oxon) 1971
teacher: Harrogate g s 1967–71; head hist Norwich h s from 1971
m Harrogate 19.12.70 Dorothy J. Hudson BA(Leeds) teacher d of Charles H. Leeds

BURNS Alasdair Michael BSc 1969
s of Alexander S. B. art teacher and Kathleen McLean art teacher; b Aber 9.5.46
teacher: maths/phys/chem Peterhead acad 1969–70, phys/geol/sc Kincorth acad from 1971
m Milngavie 2.7.69 Sheila M. Garvie BSc 1970 *qv*

BURNS Alexander Julius MA 1967
s of William A. B. MRCVS vet off. and Ilse Wohl; b Mpwapwa Tanganyika 8.7.45
Dip PE(Leeds) 1968 Cert Indust Man. (Hull coll of comm) 1975
teacher Span/Engl/Fr/PE Stockport s Cheshire 1968–70; Palma Mallorca: frogman ASA 1970–71; frogman/ptnr OSAN 1971–74; teacher Span Dartmouth h s, Birm from 1976
m Beverley 18.12.71 Ruth M. Whitfield BEd(Leeds) teacher d of Alfred H. W. Hull

BURNS James MB ChB 1956

BURNS Marilyn Raynor MA 1969
m Mackenzie

BURNS Philip *BSc 1969
s of Denis B. boilermaker and Mary Stewart; b Glasg 24.1.31
Glasg: teacher biol 1970–72, prin biol from 1972

BURNS Robert Bruce *MA 1962 *MEd 1965
s of Robert B. B. trans clerk and Mabel Cleminson; b Greenwich 17.6.39
PhD(Manc) 1973 ABPsS
teacher geog St Peter's s s Aber 1963–65; Manc: lect educ Didsbury coll of educ 1965–67, sen lect 1967–71, prin lect Mather coll 1972–74, lect educ Brad univ from 1974
m Manchester 17.12.66 Patricia M. Jackson d of Albert J. Levenshulme Manc

BURNS Robert John *MA 1969

BURNS Rosalind Anne *MA 1965
d of Arnold M. B. MA 1931 *qv* and Winifred Neilson MA 1930 *qv*; b Aber 20.7.43
teacher Kingston Surrey 1966–67
m Aber 3.9.65 David P. G. Williams MA(Cantab) sen prod. BBC(radio) s of David G. W. BSc(Bangor) Worcester Park

BURNS Sheila Anne Valentine MA 1969
d of Norman B. chief supt police and Grace I. Valentine shorthand typist; b Aber 23.5.47
teacher maths: Aber 1970–72, Lossiemouth from 1972
m Elgin 8.7.72 Geoffrey Hanson RAF, insur broker s of John H. Rugby

BURNS William BSc 1959
s of Adam B. gardener and Margaret D. Gibb teacher; b Insch 1.8.38
teacher maths: Knox acad Haddington 1960–64, Tillicoultry s s 1964–66; prin guid Alva acad from 1966
m Musselburgh 25.7.64 Elizabeth K. Thomson MA (Edin) teacher d of Thomas T. Musselburgh

BURR Robert John MA 1956 *1958
s of Ebenezer B. shoemaker, estate employee and Helen A. Donald; b Tarves 10.4.34
teacher Engl: Leith acad 1959–63; prin Engl: Plockton h s 1963–66, Denny h s 1966–69, Peterhead acad 1969–72; head Plockton 1972–76; prin Engl Peterhead acad from 1976
m Aber 20.7.66 Eileen M. Strachan MA 1956 *qv*

BURROWES Esther Elizabeth Ann *MA 1956 *EdB 1961
d of Ernest E. B. bus. man and Olivia Nichols secy; b Georgetown, Guyana 31.5.32
Georgetown: teacher, sen mistress/dep head (ag) Bishop's h s 1957–71; asst chief educ off. (Min of Educ) 1971–74; dep chief educ off. (dev) (Min of Educ & Soc Dev) from 1974

BURT Cynthia Kinloch MA 1956 *MEd 1958
m Dixon

BURT Michael William *BSc 1970
s of Ernest H. W. B. MA(Glas) teacher and Margaret S. W. McCreath; b Glasg 2.8.48
various geol exploration posts Aust 1970–73; sen geol in field explor: Angola SW Af 1974–75, SW Af, S Af 1976–78; stud. chem univ of Natal in Durban from 1978

BURT Susan Helen Hay MA 1967
d of Robert H. B. draughtsman and Eileen S. Singer; b Huntly 25.4.47
syst analyst, progr: Burmah Castrol Co Lond 1967–68, Aberd 1968–70, Philips Eindhoven Neths 1971–72, Lond 1972–73, Manc from 1973
m Lond 7.7.73 Christopher J. Davies BSc(eng) 1968 *qv*

BURT William Johnston MA 1967
s of George A. T. B. police insp and Mabel G. Johnston secy; b Aber 14.11.45
Lond: exec off. min of publ bldg and works 1967–71, exec off. DOE 1971–72, higher exec off. oper res DOE 1972–78, sen exec off. from 1978

BURTON Richard Keith BSc 1959 *1962

BUSBY Roger John Nicholas BSc(for) 1960 *1961
s of Alfred E. G. B. teacher and Elsie E. Millward; b London 3.8.37
MSc(Sur) 1974

field asst Murphy chem co Wheathampstead 1961–62; dist off. for. comm Thetford & Princes Risboro' 1962–66; asst conserv for. (on secondment) Suva Fiji 1966–68; dist off. for. comm Cardiff, Malvern 1969–71; econ for. comm: Alice Holt 1971–75, Edin from 1975

BUSSEY Kenneth John *MA 1969
s of John G. B. secy Brit Legion (Scot.) and Catherine Jamieson sales asst; b Inv 16.6.42
MPhil(Glas) 1971
res asst HIDB Inv 1971–1972; lect Paisley coll tech from 1972
m Hawick 4.12.71 Jennifer R. Johnstone teacher d of Gavin J. Hawick

BUTCHART Dorothy Anne Grace MA 1967
m Yusuf

BUTLER Eileen Ann *MA 1959
d of Sydney W. B. workshop superv and Annie I. Smith shorthand typist; b Aber 18.8.37
teacher: Engl Bell Baxter h s Cupar, Fife 1960–61, Leith acad 1961–64, part time remed subj Arbroath acad 1974–76
m Aber 28.7.60 John A. L. Cheyne MA 1957 *qv*

BUTLER Elizabeth Olive *MA 1966

BUTLER James Sutherland MA 1962

BUTLER Joyce Edith MA 1969 Dip Ed 1970
d of Sydney W. B. PO superv and Anne I. Smith clerkess; b Aber 20.4.48
teacher Engl: Sidcup 1970–71, Harpenden 1971–74
m Aber 8.10.70 Ian A. Clegg MA 1970 *qv*

BUTLER Marilyn MA 1961
m Watson

BUTLER Morgan *BSc 1969
s of Alexander M. B. clerk and Anne C. Forman; b Ellon 29.10.46
GSM(Rhodesia)
software eng Marconi Space & Defence Hillend 1970–73; computer progr Lond 1973–74; comp dir Poole 1974–76; computer eng Johannesburg 1976–77; infantry off. Rhodesian army from 1977

BUTLER Noreen Isabel *MA 1962
d of Sydney W. B. motor mech and Ella Smith shorthand typist; b Aber 6.8.40
teacher: Glasg 1963–67, remed Wigan 1969–71; ch guid Glasg from 1972
m Aber 3.4.63 William G. Thompson MA *qv*

BUTT Walter Dion PhD 1959

BUTTERWORTH Ian Eric *MA 1967
s of John B. and Vera M. Mellor; b Oldham 20.5.44
asst curate All Saints & Martyrs Church Middleton, diocese of Manc 1969–72; precentor St Andrew's episc cath Aber 1972–75; vicar St Matthew with St Barnabas Bolton diocese of Manc from 1975
m Manc 24.4.71 Valerie M. Storer

BUTTERWORTH Marilyn Holt PhD 1960

BUTTLER Frank George PhD 1958

BUXTON Ian William Derek *MA 1958
s of William F. A. B. BA(Lond) HMIS and Janet A. Mitchell teacher; b Alexandria Egypt 4.2.36
MBE 1972
Uganda govt: audit. Jinja, Kabale, Fort Portal 1958–62, sen audit. Gulu 1962–65, prin audit. Kampala 1965–68, dir of audit. Kampala 1968–71; loc govt off. Lond borough of Redbridge 1971–75; admin Commission for Local Admin in England from 1975
m Jinja 15.8.59 Elizabeth M. Gillies med lab res asst d of Neil G. Aber

BUXTON Neil Keith *MA 1962
s of William F. A. B. BA(Lond) HMIS and Janet A. Mitchell teacher; b Alexandria Egypt 2.5.40
asst dept pol econ Aberd 1962–64; lect dept econ: Hull 1964–69, H-W Edin 1969–72, sen lect from 1972
m Aber 8.12.62 Margaret G. Miller d of William F. M. Aber

BUXTON Rosalind Carissa Clarence MA 1968
d of Clarence E. V. B. BA(Cantab) col serv, farm. and Mavis J. B. Bromhead farm.; b Nairobi 21.7.46
Cert Ed TEFL(Lond) 1974
p r o Lond 1969–70; fam plan. asst Lond 1970–72; VSO teacher Engl Vientiane Laos 1972–73
m Limuru Kenya 7.9.74 Peter R. Nightingale BA(Cantab) indust man. s of Edward H. N. BA(Cantab) Lond

BUYERS William James Leslie *BSc 1959 PhD 1963
s of William B. banker, rubber planter and Williamina B. McBey; b Aboyne 10.4.37
Aberd: asst lect 1962–64, lect 1964–65; AECL Chalk River Canada: NRC fell. 1965–66, assoc res off. 1966–74, sen res off from 1975; sen res fell. Oxon 1971–72, guest scient Oak Ridge 1972, AEC Denmark 1975, vice chmn Div Cond Matter Phys (Can Assoc Phys)
m Deep River Ontario 1.10.66 Marilyn J. Cliff BA(West. Ont) secy d of Walter C. S. Porcupine Ont

BYIERS Robert *MA 1966
s of Robert B. porter univ hall of resid and Ellen W. Minty clerkess/typist; b Aber 26.12.42
MEd(Glas) 1972
teacher mod lang Glasg h s 1968–72; prin mod lang Kingsridge h s Glasg 1972–75; lect mod lang Notre Dame coll of educ Glasg from 1975
m Oban 6.7.68 Anne A. Irving MA(Glas) teacher d of Cunningham B. I. MA(Glas) Oban

BYRES Terence James *MA 1958
s of James H. B. salesman and Annabelle Elder shop asst, shorthand typist; b Aber 6.10.36
BLitt(Glas) 1962
School oriental/Af stud. Lond: res fell. econ 1962–64, lect from 1964
m Aber 10.9.60 Anne C. MacKenzie lib d of Kenneth J. MacK. Crathie

BYRNE Pauline Jeannie MA 1968

BYTH Robert William LLB 1964

BYTH William *MA 1962 PhD 1969
s of Alexander S. B. MA 1928 *qv*; b Edin 3.4.40
Aberd asst lect: psych 1965–66, lect 1966–71; lect psych Belf from 1971
m Aber 4.8.63 Irene B. Noble MA 1962 *qv*

BZDEGA Elizabeth Maria *BSc 1969

CABLE William James Angus MA 1966
s of James E. C. MB ChB 1915 *qv*; b Forfar 11.8.29
teacher: Hazlehead acad Aber 1967–70, spec asst 1970–

73; asst prin teacher 1973–74, prin teacher from 1974
m Perth 20.11.54 Elizabeth D. Smith asst warden school of dom sc Aber d of John A. S. Lundin Links

CADENHEAD Alexander Thomson *MA 1970 Dip Ed 1971

CADGER John Mitchell Pirie *MA 1969

CAIE Christina *MA 1970
d of John F. C. customs watcher and Katie B. Morrison; b Aber 6.12.48
Dip Lib(Strath) 1974
teacher Engl St Mungo's RC h s Falkirk 1971–72; stud. asst Glas lib 1972–73; asst lib Andersonian lib Strath from 1974
m Aber 18.9.70 John N. McSween chem s of Finlay MacS. Is of Scalpay

CAIE Colin Fraser *MA 1969

CAIE Dorothy Elizabeth MB ChB 1966
d of William C. group secy Aber gen hosps and Adeline Donald shop asst; b Aber 9.12.42
MRCGP 1973
h o ARI, RACH 1966–67; MRC res worker The Gambia W Af 1967–68; g p: Portlethen 1972–73, Skene 1974–77
m Aber 12.7.66 Alexander W. Logie MB ChB 1963 *qv*

CAIE Graham Douglas *MA 1968
s of William C. secy/treas gen hosp Aber and Adeline M. Donald; b Aber 3.2.45
MA(McM) 1969 PhD(McM) 1974
asst Engl dept McM univ Hamilton Canada 1968–72; lect Engl univ Copenhagen from 1972
m Aber 9.6.72 Ann P. Abbott MA 1967 *qv*

CAIE Ronald Webster *MA 1960 Dip Ed 1963
s of William W. C. supt marine eng and Elizabeth Grant shorthand typist; b Aber 22.9.38
teacher Engl: London 1960–62, Aber 1963–68; spec asst Kincardine 1968–70, prin teacher Aber from 1970
m Aber 19.8.61 Mary E. Stewart BSc 1960 *qv*

CAIRNCROSS Robert George MB ChB 1968
s of George G. C. dir and Mary McInroy; b Dundee 6.7.44
MRCP 1974 MRCGP 1976
h o, sen h o ARI 1968–70; sen h o Birm, Dun 1970–72; regist med Edin 1972–76; lect med educ Dund from 1976

CAIRNIE Alan Bruce PhD 1958
s of John B. C. MA(Edin) teacher and Isabella Moodie; b Ayr 18.11.32
BSc(Glas)
lect Aberd 1958–61; scient Inst of Cancer Res Lond 1961–67; assoc prof Queen's univ Kingston Canada 1967–76; head Radiation Biol defence res estab Ottawa from 1976
m Troon 21.8.58 Agnes A. Blackwood

CAIRNS David Stitt MA 1968
s of James G. C. bank man. and Margaret M. S. Hunter teacher dom sc; b Aber 22.1.45
invest. analyst: JCI; Martin & Co Inc stockbrokers Johannesburg 1968–71, asst to gen man. 1971–72; S Af Cane Growers Assoc Durban from 1972
m Johannesburg 12.2.72 Susan J. Clews receptionist d of Raymond A. C. Johannesburg

CALDER Alan *BSc 1965 PhD 1969
s of John C. lorry driver and Margaret Goodbrand; b. Wick 22.3.44
ICI organics: chem Stevenston 1968–72, sect leader from 1972
m Wick 8.7.66 Jean F. S. Sinclair tax off. d of Alexander S. S. Wick

CALDER Alexander Charles *MA 1940
s of Alexander C. master slater and Hilda Liddell; b Aber 30.8.48
MA(Liv) 1974 BA(Lond) 1976
res Engl lang Liv 1970–72; civ serv DHSS Aber from 1977

CALDER Charlotte Newman BEd 1970
b Aber 7.9.23
Biggar h s: teacher Engl from 1970, asst prin guid 1975–77, prin guid from 1977
m Peterhead 1942 Skelsey

CALDER Hector John *MA 1959 *MEd 1968
s of Charles C. man. and Helen Spalding; b Aber 8.6.37
teacher mod lang: Alloa acad 1961–65, AGS 1965–67; Perth and Kinross: asst dir educ 1967–68, dep dir 1968–75; div educ off and dep dir educ Tayside reg council from 1975
m Falkirk 1.5.65 Diane M. Moore teacher d of Samuel J. M. Falkirk

CALDER Iain Alexander Hamilton BSc 1969
s of John H. C. surv customs and excise and Martha G. Hamilton organis N of Scot FPA; b Asmara Eritrea 27.2.47
control chem i/c quality control lab/res and dev work Edin from 1969
m Edin 12.5.72 Sheila N. Thomson lab asst d of William T. Edin

CALDER Ian Mollison *BSc 1965 Dip Ed 1966
s of Ronald M. C. hotelier and Athlene M. Henry hair stylist, hotel prop; b Aber 12.7.43
teacher phys: RGC Aber 1966–69, spec asst 1969–70, prin teacher from 1971

CALDER James Moir *BSc(agr) 1967
s of John C. farm. and Annie Grant; b Dunphail 2.2.44
advis off. min of agr Armagh N. Ireland 1967–69; NOSCA: asst econ Aber 1969–72, agr advis Keith from 1972
m Forres 6.8.66 Mary M. Ross teacher d of Archibald R. Forres

CALDER James Rose MA 1958 *BSc 1961 PhD 1964

CALDER James Stewart Winton *MA 1962

CALDER Joan Christine MA 1965
m Cumming

CALDER Stanley Shearer MA 1965

CALDER William James BSc 1961

CALLANDER James Dickson MA 1970
s of John S. C. postmaster and Jessie M. M. Cross secy; b Motherwell 9.6.48
Dip Bus Admin(Edin) 1973
postal h q (Scot): exec off. Edin 1970–72, asst postal controller from 1973
m Aber 11.8.73 Jean Maxwell prod. secy d of Alexander M. Edin

CAMERON Alan Graham MB ChB 1964

CAMERON Douglas Martin BSc 1970
s of Thomas M. C. burgh chamberlain Kilmarnock and Marion Anderson cler worker; b Kilmarnock 25.4.45
teacher maths Inverurie acad from 1971
m Aber 8.4.74 Moreen A. Simpson MA 1970 *qv*

CAMERON Elizabeth MA 1968
d of William C. slater and Florence Sutherland; b Nairn 2.8.47
asst housemother children's home Rhynie 1968–69
m Forres 3.5.69 George A. M. Shaw porter-driver s of Donald S. Forres

CAMERON Elizabeth Jane MA 1968

CAMERON Graham John *BSc(eng) 1969

CAMERON Hamish William *BSc 1969
s of William D. C. farm. and Hannah Gillies; b Cromarty 27.1.47
Glasg: proj leader 1970–78, syst man. from 1978
m St Cyrus 9.8.75 Edna Johnston BSc 1970 *qv*

CAMERON Henry Gordon MA 1966
s of James H. C. cabinetmaker, univ tech and Florence Dey; b Aber 27.5.43
teacher: hist/mod stud Oban h s 1967–69, econ/mod stud Rosyth h s 1969; computer progr Nairn Williamson Kirkcaldy 1969–70; NCR(Mfg) Dun: computer progr 1969–70, progr, head EDP Operations, syst des 1970–73, computer proj controller 1973–76; sen syst des NSHEB from 1976
m 12.8.67 Mary M. Stewart MA 1966 *qv*

CAMERON Henry Ogilvy BL 1961
s of Henry O. C. police insp and Marion M. Burnett; b Aber 9.12.39
app CA Aber 1961–64; dir agr and motor eng firm Aberdeensh 1964–68; law app Aber 1968–70, ptnr C. & P. H. Chalmers advoc Aber 1971–78; ptnr Cameron & Thom advoc Aber from 1978
m Kent 25.7.64 Fiona C. Grant MA 1962 *qv*

CAMERON Hugh McKenzie MA 1967
b Edin 3.4.46
teacher Engl Lockerbie 1969–71, asst prin Engl Craigshill h s Livingston from 1971

CAMERON Ian Alexander ^{d}LLB 1961
MA (Edin)

CAMERON Ian Kenneth Mackenzie *MA 1966
s of Kenneth M. C. and Eileen Wright; b Fremington 15.8.40
Edin: journalist *Evening Post* 1966–68; labourer Scot. Construct./supply teacher 1968; teacher Engl: Bankhead acad 1969–72, Ingiliz Lisesi, Istanbul 1972–74; lang instr univ petr and min Dhahran Saudi Arabia from 1974
m Aber 23.3.68 Jane-Ann W. Annells MA 1968 *qv*

CAMERON James *BSc 1969 PhD 1973

CAMERON Jean Nicol MA 1970 Dip Ed 1971
d of John G. C. letterpress foreman and Catherine M. Nicol; b Kilmarnock 11.2.49
teacher Latin/Engl Dunfermline h s 1971–76
m Aber 3.7.73 Archibald Bennett BSc(Edin) teacher s of John S. B. Kelty

CAMERON Joan MA 1965 Dip Ed 1966
d of Alexander G. C. killed in action 1.7.44 and Evelyn Fraser; b Aber 18.12.43
teacher Engl: Dunoon 1966–68, Aboyne 1968–74, asst prin teacher from 1974

CAMERON John Francis MA 1967 Dip Ed 1969
b Stanley 4.3.39
teacher Clydebank h s: Engl 1969–71, asst prin guid 1971–72, asst prin Engl 1972–74; prin Engl Dumbarton acad from 1974
m Aber 6.8.69 Diana M. Douglas MA 1967 *qv*

CAMERON John Mowat BSc 1956
s of Kenneth J. C. MA(Edin) C of S min and Barbara J. S. Mowat teacher; b Aber 27.1.35
RAF: educ off. Cosford 1957–62, Halton 1962–64; teacher sc Stranraer from 1964
m Coulsdon 31.12.60 Patricia M. Pink secy d of Joseph E. P. Coulsdon

CAMERON Kathleen Isabel MA 1964

CAMERON Kenneth John *MA 1967
s of John C. Sudan govt off. and Kathleen M. Skinner chirop; b Perth 27.4.45
PhD(Edin) 1971 Dip Lib(Strath) 1972
Dund: grad lib asst 1970–71, asst lib from 1973, res asst dept mod hist Dund 1972–73

CAMERON Mairi Henrietta MA 1965

CAMERON Margaret Elspeth Milne *MA 1961
d of Norman A. C. MA 1929 *qv* and Elspeth M. Milne MA 1969 *qv*; b Elgin 15.7.39
Dip Ed(Edin) 1964
Kansas univ USA: schol stud. 1961–62, lect Greek 1962–63; St Andrews: teacher classics St Leonard's s 1964–66, Madras s from 1970
m Stirling 15.8.64 Martin S. Smith MA(Glas) univ lect s of Alexander D. S. Glasg

CAMERON Marie Sylvia MA 1963

CAMERON Marion Brown *MEd 1967
d of Thomas R. C. driver and Margaret T. Russell waitress; b Edin 15.9.35
MA(Edin) 1957 Dip Ed(Edin) 1958
res assoc dept educ Manc 1967–68; lect educ psych coll of educ Dun from 1968
m Edin 20.7.72 John E. C. de Quincey BA(Durh) s of Arnold de Q. BA(Durh) Warwicksh

CAMERON Marjory Martin MA 1961 Dip Ed 1962
d of John G. C. letterpress printer and Catherine M. Nicol leg. secy; b Kilmarnock 2.4.40
teacher: Aber 1962–64, Manc 1964–66, Dun 1973–75, Barrhead h s from 1975
m Aber 14.7.64 Alexander B. Wilson BSc 1962 *qv*

CAMERON Mary MB ChB 1970

CAMERON Neil Duncan *BSc 1970

CAMERON Rhona Cumming LLB 1969

CAMERON Robert Ward BSc 1970
s of Evan R. C. BSc(Glas) shipbuilding consult. and Dorothy P. Ward; b Glasg 19.7.48
Lloyds broker Lond from 1970
m Exeter 4.9.71 Norma P. Edwards MA 1971 d of Norman F. J. E. Exeter

CAMERON Roderick Francis MA 1966
s of Stanley C. small tool worker and Gwendoline M. C. Jackson; b Wolverhampton 26.4.44

teacher Craighill p s Aber 1967–73; asst head Tullos p s Aber 1973–77; head Inverurie Market Pl p s from 1977
m Aber 9.8.68 Catherine Ross MA 1966 *qv*

CAMERON Ruth Elizabeth LLB 1969
m Wilkie

CAMERON Seonaid Ealasaid MA 1970
d of John C. MA 1939 *qv* and Elizabeth W. Eddie BSc 1940 *qv*; b Inverness 15.9.49
Dip Soc Work(Edin) 1971
soc worker: Midlothian c c 1971–73, Roxburgh c c from 1973
m Aber 24.10.74 Richard D. Hollands BVMS(Edin) vet surg s of Frank G. H. LRCP(Lond) Derby

CAMERON Wilfred *MA 1965
m Dun 1969 Alison M. Low BSc 1965 *qv*

CAMERON-MACKINTOSH, Elizabeth BSc(agr) 1956

CAMPBELL Alan *MA 1965
b Thurso 6.12.42
teacher Thurso 1966–72; prin geog Montrose acad from 1972
m Wick 8.7.72 Maura C. Morrison teacher p e

CAMPBELL Alan Braidwood *MA 1970

CAMPBELL Alan Grant LLB 1968
s of Archibald G. C. master plumber and Catherine M. Morrison; b Aber 4.12.46
Aber c c: law app 1968–70, solic 1970–75; asst dir law/admin Grampian reg c from 1975
m Aber 29.6.74 Susan M. M. Black res worker d of John M. B. MB ChB(Edin) Aber

CAMPBELL Alan Tormaid MA 1967

CAMPBELL Alasdair *BSc 1968
s of William C. and Marion Morrison; b Struan 9.6.47
electronics eng Chelmsford 1968–73; des eng Nott 1973–74; computer syst analyst Somercotes from 1974
m Levenshulme Manc 12.6.71 Sylvia Wagstaff computer progr d of Francis T. W. Stockport

CAMPBELL Alasdair James *BSc 1963 MSc 1964
s of John R. C. joiner and Mary Grant; b Balmoral, Crathie 22.7.41
Assoc Fell. Inst Maths 1967
lect maths RGIT Aber from 1964
m Aber 23.8.68 Doris M. McLean MB ChB 1967 *qv*

CAMPBELL Alexander John MA 1968

CAMPBELL Alistair Robert MacBrair *BSc 1968
s of Bruce C. BSc(for)(Edin) author, broadcaster and Margaret Gibson-Hill MA(Edin) soc worker, writer; b Cardiff 9.5.46
Oxford: sub-edit. Blackwell scient publ 1968–69, edit. 1969–78; dir micromedia 1973–78, chmn Oxford microfilm publ 1975–78; dir Blackwell scient publ Oxford and vice-presid Blackwell scient publ N Amer/NY/Delaware from 1978; also writer
m Oxford 7.9.68 Frances R. Kirkwood teacher d of Kenneth K. BA(Wits) Oxford

CAMPBELL Angus BSc 1969
s of Angus C. gardener and Christine Tuach; b Plockton 6.4.48
MIBiol(Paisley tech) 1973
teacher biol Newton Stewart 1971–75; prin biol Eyemouth from 1975
m Stranraer 15.7.71 Elizabeth Purdie teacher home econ d of Stephen P. Stranraer

CAMPBELL Angus Iain Lionel *LLB 1969

CAMPBELL Calum Mackenzie *MA 1966
s of Tormaid C. MA 1933 *qv*; b Corgarff 14.10.43
PhD(Leeds) 1973
teacher: Malaskolinn Mimir Reykjavik 1966–73, Inverurie acad 1968; lect univ Iceland Reykjavik 1972–73; teacher Edin from 1974
m Strathdon 5.4.75 Sigridur Oladottir d of Oli K. Gudmundsson Cand. Med. (Laeknisprof Reykjavik) Reykjavik

CAMPBELL Cameron Robb Dixon MB ChB 1966
s of Peter C. Dip Ed(Durh) teacher, admin and Elizabeth H. Dixon; b S Shields 24.10.41
Dip Anaest RCS(E) 1969
h o Shotley Bridge 1966–67; sen h o, regist anaest Aber 1967–69; g p Norwich from 1969
m Aber 29.9.67 Patricia E. Morrice p e teacher d of Peter M. Aber

CAMPBELL Catherine Maciver *MA 1965
d of Norman M. C. joiner and Margaret J. Ross; b Avoch 22.1.43
teacher geog Aber h s for girls 1966–70
m Ullapool 2.4.68 Douglas P. Willis MA 1965 *qv*

CAMPBELL Clair MA 1969

CAMPBELL Colin Balnaves BSc 1964
s of Albert C. eng, works man. and Lizzie J. W. Balnaves saleswoman; b Aber 5.5.43
Dip Indust Man.(Strath) 1965
jun explor geol Sierra Leone 1966–67; Canada: staff geol INCO Sudbury 1969–70, proj geol Cerro mining comp Vancouver 1970–71; oper man. IRSCO Toronto 1971–78, VP marketing Crinan Toronto from 1979
m Toronto 30.6.69 Sandra L. Bromwich teacher d of H. Frederick B. Toronto

CAMPBELL Colin Grant BSc 1960
s of Wilson C. police janitor and Alice M. J. Grant; b Aber 17.6.38
teacher, spec asst Kaimhill s s Aber 1961–68; prin sc St Columba s s Kilmacolm 1968–73; prin chem Linlathen h s Dun from 1973
m Aber 3.7.65 Sandra V. T. Clements d of Frederick D. C. Aber

CAMPBELL Colin Kerr *MA 1964
s of Alan A. C.; b Edin 9.3.42
MA(Br Col) 1967 PhD(Brist) 1971
teaching asst Simon Fraser univ Vanc 1966–67; res fell. Strath 1967–68; asst prof geog Vict BC 1971–73; head res sect. BC parks branch Vict BC from 1973
m Victoria B.C. 1966 Linda Carol BSc(UBC) phys and occup therap

CAMPBELL Colin Murray LLB 1967
s of Isabel C. secy; b Aber 26.12.44
lect law: Dund 1967–69, Edin 1969–73; prof juris Belf from 1974

CAMPBELL Colinne BSc 1964
m Souter

CAMPBELL David Craig MA 1960

CAMPBELL David John BSc 1959
s of David R. M. C. civ serv and Dorothy M. Elgin clerkess; b Inv 29.8.38

teacher: AGS 1960–62, Hemel Hempstead g s 1962–66, Carleton Place h s Canada 1966–68, Niagara Falls adult educ centre 1968–70, Sundon Park j s Luton from 1970
m Aber 1.8.73 Gloria J. K. Whyte hosp cler off. d of Patrick W. Aber

CAMPBELL David Murdoch Armstrong *MA 1962
s of Murdoch C. MA(Edin) min of religion and Mary A. Fraser; b Glasg 11.8.39
asst lect, lect moral phil Glas from 1965

CAMPBELL David Stanley *BSc 1959 PhD 1962

CAMPBELL, Dorothy Mildred MA 1969
d of Donald C. gamekeeper and Mona Curr; b Aber 15.7.47
teacher: Inverallochy 1970–74, Aber 1974–75, Inv 1975–76
m Aber 15.7.75 Robert A. Masson BSc 1968 *qv*

CAMPBELL Duncan William BSc(agr) 1956
s of Duncan C. farm. and Helen R. Allan; b Elgin 28.5.33
farm man. Elgin 1956–60; teacher sc Forres acad 1961–66; farm. Elgin from 1966
m Perth 8.4.63 Glenda McDonald secy d of Gilroy B. M. Scone

CAMPBELL Frances Balnaves MA 1958
d of Albert C. eng, works man. and Lizzie J. W. Balnaves saleswoman; b Aber 22.5.36
Dip Pers Man.(Strath) 1966
teacher: Aber 1959–61, Glasg 1961–62; various posts Berlin, Paris 1962–63; teacher Glasg 1963–65; pers off., trg off. Lond 1966–69; tut., head of courses dept nat inst of indust psych Lond 1969–73
m Aber 30.12.71 Mohammed Y. Manjra BA(Rangoon) CA s of Yacoob M. M. Gujrat India

CAMPBELL Gillian Agnes *MA 1965
d of George A. C. shopkeeper and Jessie Macdonald nurs sister; b Dingwall 19.3.43
teacher geog/hist: Convent of Sacred Heart s s Aber 1966–71, Torry acad 1971–72
m Aber 23.3.67 John S. Smith MA 1963 *qv*

CAMPBELL Grace Stewart MA 1968 Dip Ed 1969
m Allanach

CAMPBELL Ian BSc(agr) 1959
s of William G. C. farm. and Isabel B. Steven; b Wick 31.12.36
dept agr: temp field off. Elgin 1960, asst insp Edin 1960–62, Kirkwall 1962–68, Dumfries 1968–74, insp Dumfries from 1974
m Kirkwall 25.3.65 Sonja M. O. Graham RGN d of Joseph O. G. Rimington Sheffield

CAMPBELL Ian James MA 1970

CAMPBELL Ian McDonald *MA 1964
s of Donald C. MA 1929 *qv* and Mary B. Cruickshank MA 1930 *qv*; b Lausanne 25.8.42
PhD(Edin) 1970 FSAScot 1970
Edin: res stud. 1964–67, univ lect from 1967; visiting lect Germany 1971; visiting lect, prof Canada, USA 1971, 1973, 1976

CAMPBELL James Buchan *BSc 1962
s of James B. C. eng and Janie T. Hugginson; b Fraserburgh 1939
PhD(Alta) 1965
post doct fell. Alta 1965–66; US publ health serv Wistar Inst Philadelphia: post doct trainee 1966–67, res asst 1967–68; univ of Toronto: asst prof virol 1968–70, assoc prof virol from 1970
m Aber 3.8.66 Sheena G. Hunter MA 1964 *qv*

CAMPBELL Jean Elizabeth MA 1968
b Aber 9.8.46
Edin: teacher 1968–71; civ serv from 1971

CAMPBELL Jean McEwen MA 1964
d of George C. master plasterer and Agnes Webster secy; b Fraserburgh 3.11.42
teacher hist: Inverurie acad 1965–68, St Mark's s s Mbabane Swaziland 1968–70
m Aber 16.7.68 George I. M. Martin BSc(Glas) agronomist/sen tut. coll of agr s of George M. Aber

CAMPBELL Jean Macrae MA 1964
d of Roderick M. C. MA 1929 *qv*; b Edin 20.3.43
teacher: Montreal, Weybridge, Fort William, Pereira (Colombia), Koratti, Kerala (India) 1965–75; head Glenelg p s from 1975

CAMPBELL Jessie MA 1964
d of James C. gardener/janitor and Isabella McArthur; b Perth 25.3.43
Cert Secy St (Strath) 1965
teacher secy stud. Moray & Nairn 1966–67; Perth: off. supervis 1969–73, asst acct from 1976
m Aber 15.5.65 John Hogg MA 1966 *qv*

CAMPBELL Joan Glen MA 1960
m Harding

CAMPBELL John Dugald *MA 1963
s of John C. C. MA(Edin) C of S min and Dorothy T. Torrance nurse; b Aber 19.2.41
teacher: Glenwood j h s Glenrothes 1964–66, Glenrothes h s 1966–69, prin hist Fortrose acad from 1969

CAMPBELL Joseph Mitchell MA 1969
s of Joseph M. C. fisherman and Margaret Main; b Lossiemouth 15.10.27
teacher geog Forres from 1971
m Lossiemouth 12.8.68 Isa Mackenzie d of Alexander B. M. Lossiemouth

CAMPBELL Kathleen Christine MA 1967

CAMPBELL Kenneth Murdoch MA 1967
s of Donald C. policeman and Ishbel Campbell; b Isle of Skye 26.8.40
BD(Penn USA) 1970 ThM(Penn USA) 1971 PhD(Manc) 1975
stud. res: Philadelphia 1967–71, Manc 1971–72, Tübingen, Germany 1972–73; Kampen, Holland 1973–74; Manc from 1974
m Aber 16.8.67 Christina MacLeod teacher d of Murdoch MacL. Stornoway

CAMPBELL Lachlan Alexander MA 1959 *1961

CAMPBELL Lawrence Curwen BSc 1960

CAMPBELL Lennox Hamilton *BSc 1970 PhD 1975

CAMPBELL Margaret Christine *MA 1967
d of James P. C. MB ChB(St And) orthop surg and Catherine A. Duncan MA(St And) teacher; b Nott 9.2.45

teacher: geog Bathgate acad 1968–69, soc stud./Engl Howe Sound s s Canada 1969–70; England: geog Rushcliffe s s 1970–71, Congleton girls' s s 1971–73, humanities Rothwell s s 1973–74
m Nott 28.8.71 Jeremy Nigel Sands prod. man. s of John W. S. Edin

CAMPBELL Mary Ann MA 1959 Dip Ed 1960
d of Malcolm C. crofter; b Arnol Barvas Is of Lewis 13.3.35
teacher: Ruthrieston s Aber 1960–62; Longhope Orkney 1965–67; Brora h s 1969–73
m Perth 8.8.61 Charles Abel min of religion

CAMPBELL Mary Fraser MA 1958 Dip Ed 1959
d of Murdoch C. MA(Edin) Free C of S min and Mary A. Fraser PO clerk/co-owner newsag bus.; b Glasg 21.9.37
teacher Cullicudden p s Black Is 1959–61; relief teacher Aber 1961–62
m Aber 13.9.61 James D. MacMillan MA 1963 *qv*

CAMPBELL Mary Slater MA 1957
d of William C. fisherman/skipper and Margaret Liebnitz cook/dom worker; b Lossiemouth 4.4.37
teacher: Hopeman 1958–59, Elgin acad 1960–61; supply Elgin acad, Lossiemouth h s, Elgin h s from 1974
m Aber 17.7.59 Norman M. Stewart BL(Edin) solic s of George S. Lossiemouth

CAMPBELL Moira Ann *MA 1957 Dip Ed 1958
d of George A. C. elect. contr and Margaret J. Niven; b Aber 29.8.35
CRK(Lond) 1965
teacher: hist/geog Fort William 1958–59, geog Inv r acad 1959–63; stud. Bible Training Inst Glasg 1963–65; Lond: teaching/ch work 1965–66, linguistics/missionary trg 1966–67; Taiwan: overseas missionary fell./lang study 1967–69, stud. work with Campus fell. 1969–70, work with tribal stud. from 1970

CAMPBELL Morag Clayton MA 1969

CAMPBELL Myra Anne MA 1965
m Jacobs

CAMPBELL Neil Andrew *MA 1967
s of Frederick C. C. maintenance eng and Josephine M. Read BA(Leeds) teacher; b Durban 19.12.43
Dip Gen Ling(Edin) 1968
Inv royal acad: teacher Fr/Ital 1969–73, asst prin Fr/Ital from 1973
m Aber 14.7.67 Elizabeth M. Alexander MA 1963 *qv*

CAMPBELL Norma MA 1970
d of Norman J. C. weaver and Christina Smith; b Brasar Is of Lewis 11.10.49
hotel man. Perth 1971–72, Aviemore from 1972
m 10.7.73 Kenneth P. MacKenzie hotelier s of W. H. MacK. Turriff

CAMPBELL Norman *BSc 1966 MSc 1970

CAMPBELL Norman MA 1966
s of Kenneth C. sub-postmaster and Rachel A. MacLeod; b Scalpay Harris 12.6.32
BA(Strath) 1972
teacher: Engl Kilmarnock tech coll 1967–74, asst prin Engl Ayr acad from 1974

CAMPBELL Norman *BSc 1966

CAMPBELL Peter Ian *MA 1959
d 6.10.63 *AUR* XL 304

CAMPBELL Richard Ewen BSc(for) 1964

CAMPBELL Roy Hutcheson PhD 1956

CAMPBELL Ruth Macdonald MA 1956 Dip Ed 1957
d of John C. pharm and Hilda Manson LRAM mus; b Lerwick 29.3.34
teacher Richmond: h s 1957–59, convent s 1959–60; head dept sec mod s Uppingham; lect liberal stud. Beverley 1964–66; asst prin Engl Norwood comp s Lond; year mistress Croydon from 1974
m Cambridge 19.12.59 Peter G. Fletcher BA(Cantab) prof mus s of Eric F. Combe Martin

CAMPBELL Sheila Mary MA 1959
d of Donald C. MA 1929 *qv* and Mary B. Cruickshank MA 1930 *qv* b. Lausanne 20.2.39
teacher: Mackie acad Stonehaven 1960–61, Culcabock p s Inv 1962–67, Inv h s from 1971, asst prin from 1976
m Inverbervie 27.12.61 Brian D. J. Denoon MA 1959 *qv*

CAMPBELL Sherry Elizabeth *MA 1970 Dip Ed 1971
d of Keith B. C. judge and Betty J. Muffet; b Lond 18.7.47
m Lond 22.7.72 Thomas J. Wilkie civ serv

CAMPBELL Stewart James *BSc 1966

CAMPBELL William James *BSc 1959 MSc 1960

CAMPBELL William John MA 1965
s of William C. MA(Glas) min of religion and Christina MacLean; b Garrabost Isle of Lewis 18.11.33
Grad Dip Theol(Free Ch Coll Edin) 1968
ordained Glasg 1968
min Detroit 1968–72, Park (Scot.) from 1972
m Glasg 24.8.64 Margaret M. Morrison RGN d of John A. M. Stornoway

CANNON Dorothy May Susan MA 1970
d of John C. comp dir and Jane A. Keillor; b Galashiels 4.9.49
teacher Engl: Edin 1971–72, Perth W Aust from 1973
m Galashiels 14.7.71 Leo V. M. Forsyth struct eng tech s of Vincent H. F. Stow M'Lothian

CANT Derek George MA 1966

CANT Helen Elaine MA 1969
m Peterson

CANTLAY Evelyn Mary *MA 1963

CANTLAY Jean Lesley MA 1970
d of Leslie T. C. farm. and Mary B. Davie; b Ellon 23.2.49
teacher geog: Alford 1971–73, Vale of Leven acad Alexandria from 1973
m Cruden 30.7.73 Charles A. Murdoch LLB 1972 solic s of Robin M. MB ChB(Glas) Bearsden

CANTLAY John Simon MB ChB 1969 DMRD 1973

CANTLAY Kenneth George BSc(eng) 1969
s of William S. C. joiner and Elizabeth J. C. McRae clerkess; b Aber 29.1.48
CEng MICE 1974
asst eng Glasg: Babtie Shaw & Morton 1969–71, Scott

Wilson Kirkpatrick 1971–72; sect. eng Whatlings 1973–76; des eng Blyth & Blyth FFICE Inv from 1976
m Aber 4.4.72 Valerie A. Copland MA 1970 *qv*

CANTLAY Leslie Stuart MB ChB 1969
s of William J. C. BSc 1943 *qv* and Sheila V. Innes MA 1966 *qv*; b Aber 14.7.45
Aber: h o 1969–70, sen h o psychiat 1970–71, psychiat regist 1971–72; milit serv r m o Belfast, Edin, Folkestone, S'ton (psychiat) and BAOR from 1972
m Aber 28.6.69 Sheila J. MacKenzie d of Hugh F. MacK. Inv

CANTLAY Valaine Innes *MA 1967
m Middleton

CANTLAY William Shirras MA 1966 LLB 1969
s of William R. C. teacher and Jane F. Shirras; b Aber 25.2.45
law app Elgin 1969–71; ptnr Cantley & Caithness solic St Andrews from 1971
m Aber 24.10.69 Rosemary J. Greig MA 1967 *qv*

CARBY-HALL Joseph Roger Rahbé MA 1959 LLB 1961
s of Daniel C-H army off., arch. and Nina A. Caruana; b Lydda Palestine 1.12.33
BA(Lond) RD 1974
asst leg. advis David Brown Indust Melham 1961–63; lect law Brist poly 1963–69; milit serv RA(TA) Sarawak and N Borneo 1965–66; RNR Intelligence from 1967; res stud. faculty of law Brist 1968–70; lect law univ Hull from 1970; author: *Principles of Industrial Law*, *Studies in Labour Law*, *Labour Relations and the Law*, *Cases in Managerial Law*, *Worker Participation in Europe;* edit. *Managerial Law*
m Southampton 3.3.62 Hilary V. Rudd stud. Aberd d of Thomas N. R. MB(Lond) Southampton

CARDEN Christopher Robert BSc(for) 1970
s of Henry C. C. army off. and Jane StC. Daniell; b Lond 24.11.46
Papua, New Guinea: attached helicopter surv unit, for. dept 1970–71; asst dist for. off. Hoskins 1971; dist for. off. Nantambu 1972–73; sen lect utilization for. coll Bulolo 1973–74; Fiji: self-employed farm., relief estate worker NLDC 1975; car assembly worker NZMC Nelson NZ; man. off. Fiji pine commission from 1976
m Suva, Fiji 29.12.72 Sainimere Rokotuibau nurse, cosmetician, secy d of Isei R. Fiji

CARDNO David Donn *MA 1962

CARDNO Edith Christina Jane MA 1964
d of Andrew C. clerk and Lily Watt auxil nurse; b Fraserburgh 1.11.42
teacher Engl/Lat Fraserburgh acad 1965–76
m William T. Downie MA 1960 *qv*

CARDY James Charles BSc 1970

CAREY Cynthia Laird MA 1968 *1970
d of Bruce T. C. RN off. and Margaret Smith; b Aber 6.11.47
bilingual lexicographer Victoria, Canada 1971–74; Engl lang asst Paris 1974–75

CAREY Frances Elizabeth Gordon *MA 1967
d of Gordon H. M. C. flt/sgt RAF (killed June 1944) and Barbara E. Thomson teacher; b Aber 24.8.44
secy/ling. course City of Westminster coll 1967–68; secy/pa London branch of Fr comp 1968–69; teacher Fr/Ger St Margaret's s Aber from 1970

CAREY Susan Veronica MA 1963
d of B. John R. C. dir paper-making tech and Agnes B. Porteous secy; b Edin 11.3.43
sen secy course Wycombe coll 1963–64; pers secy to hosp admin Wycombe gen hosp from 1964

CARGILL Margaret Mary MA 1961
d of George M. C. farm. and Margaret N. Forbes nurse; b Aber 30.4.40
Dip Soc St(Edin) 1962 Dip Child Care(Dund) 1968
disablement off. Stirling 1962–63; Edin: ch care off. 1963–67, 1968–70; soc worker 1970–73
m Aber 8.5.70 Myles M. Dryden BSc(Lond) univ prof Glas s of Robert P. D. Kirkcaldy

CARIDIS Dimitri Taki PhD 1968
MD(Istan) FRCSE FRCAS

CARLE Alexander Robert MA 1962 LLB 1964
s of Alexander R. C. clerk and Helen L. Rennie; b Aber 27.4.41
Aber: law app 1964–66, solic from 1966
m Aber 22.7.66 Judith M. Findlay MA 1965 *qv*

CARLISLE Eleanor McLaren *MA 1964
d of Sydney S. C. CA and Elizabeth M. Webb; b Bombay 9.3.42
m Aber 15.9.65 James H. Stalker stationer/newsagent s of James M. S. Elgin

CARMICHAEL Barbara Morag MA 1970
m Hamilton

CARMICHAEL David Alan *MA 1968 Dip Ed 1969

CARMICHAEL Flora Christine Campbell LLB 1963
d of William C. C. MA(Glas) chem and Elizabeth P. MacRae; b Glasg 19.8.41
Edin, Glasg: law app 1963–66; stud. Europ univs—Nancy, Düsseldorf, Hamburg 1966–68; lect compar law Glas 1968–71; jurist ling. Council of Min Brussels 1972–73; sen leg. asst, solic off. St Andrew's House Edin from 1973
m Edin 28.7.78 Leslie Hunt prod. man (aero. eng) s of Walter H. Alfreton

CARMICHAEL John Allan BL 1965
s of John C. CA and Margaret R. F. Allan pharm; b Elgin 15.11.40
CA 1967
Aber: audit man. 1967–74; man. acct from 1974
m Aber 26.2.66 Kathleen Dutch staff nurse d of Norman D. Aber

CARMICHAEL Rosemary Catherine Dilys MA 1962 LLB 1964
d of John H. C. MA 1929 *qv* and Alexandrina G. Dunlop MA 1932 *qv*; b Trawsfynydd Merioneth 2.11.40
law app: Aber 1964–66, Motherwell 1966; leg. asst: Carluke 1970–74, Glasg from 1975
m Aber 9.4.65 Ernest R. D. Smart MA 1958 *qv*

CARNEGIE Hazel May *BSc 1969 PhD 1975
d of Alexander N. C. mech eng des and Betty Hampton; b Aber 16.3.47
res asst for. Aberd 1970; res stud. s of agr Aber 1970–73; scient off. natural envir res council Brathens res stat Banchory 1974; dem NOSCA from 1974

CARNEGIE Patrick Robert PhD 1963
s of Robert Y. C. farm. and Catherine M. Leslie; b Kirkcaldy 16.12.34
BSc(St And) 1955

scient off. Ruakura NZ 1959; lect biochem univ Singapore 1960–64; sen res fell. Leeds 1964; sen lect biochem Melb Aust 1965–75, reader from 1975
m Hamilton NZ 1960 Mary E. Thompson p e teacher d of Robert M. T. Rutherglen Aust

CARNEGIE-SMITH Kaetrin MB ChB 1966
d of George C-S. BSc(eng) 1934 *qv*; b Shrewsbury 23.5.42
m John E. Black MB ChB(Belf) surg

CARNIE Ann *BSc 1964
MSc(Manit)
m Russell

CARNIE David Robertson BSc 1958
s of Thomas D. C. grocer and Edith Ross; b Laurencekirk 13.11.37
BA(OU) 1974 G Inst P(IOP) 1975
teacher sc: Montrose acad 1959–66; Dingwall acad 1966–68, spec asst sc 1968–72; prin phys Dingwall acad from 1972
m Collieston 15.4.60 Isobel F. Cowie lab asst d of John C. Collieston

CARNIE Dorothy Frances MA 1967
d of Frank A. C. BSc 1935 *qv* and Anne J. S. Scroggie MA 1935 *qv*; b Stonehaven 29.4.47
m Aber 10.7.68 Alexander S. Craig BSc 1968 *qv*

CARNIE James Thomas MA 1962

CARNIE John Allan BSc 1958 PhD 1961
b Aber 12.12.35
Manc: asst lect 1961–64, lect from 1964
m Aber 16.4.62 Marjorie I. Taylor

CARNIE Patricia Anne MA 1965
d of Frank A. C. BSc 1935 *qv* and Anne J. S. Scroggie MA 1935 *qv*; b Aber 15.5.44
m Aber 14.10.65 Jack R. Webb

CARNIE Thomas Ross *BSc 1959
s of Thomas D. C. grocer and Edith Ross; b Laurencekirk 30.10.36
teacher math/sc Bell-Baxter h s Cupar 1960–62, spec asst phys 1962–65; prin phys: St Andrew RC h s Kirkcaldy 1965–67, Inverurie acad from 1967
m Aber 15.9.55 Elspeth J. G. McHardy d of Charles McH. Stonehaven

CARPENTER David William BSc(eng) 1969
s of K. N. C. schoolmaster and M. S. Sumner; b Newport, Mon 22.9.46
grad app Rolls-Royce aero div Glasg 1969–71; RAF coll Cranwell—pilot trg 1971–72; further flying trg Varsity and Hercules aircraft Oakington, Thorney Is 1972–73; Lyneham: Hercules co-pilot RAF 1973–76, Hercules capt RAF (flt-lt) from 1976

CARR Timothy Dominic Stephen BSc(eng) 1964 *1965
s of John M. C. BA(Cantab) solic and Edith M. Vincent; b Cambridge 27.5.43
Montreal: method eng Northern Elect. Co 1965–66, des eng United Aircraft of Canada 1966–69; Bristol: des eng Rolls Royce 1969–72, sales man. from 1972
m Hordle 30.8.75 Julia P. Child speech therap

CARRIE Brian James *BMedBiol 1968 MB ChB 1971
s of William W. C. BL 1940 *qv*; b Aber 16.4.47
MRCP 1975
h o ARI 1971–72; lect path. Aberd 1972–73; ARI: sen h o gen med 1973–74, regist gen med from 1974

CARROLL Helena Mary MA 1964

CARRUTHERS David Robert MA 1966 LLB 1968

CARRUTHERS James Philip *MA 1967 Dip Ed 1968

CARSON Graham Margaret Gilston *MA 1968
d of William G. C. LRCPE g p and Margaret G. Munro nurs sister; b Edin 15.12.46
Dip Gen Ling(Manc) 1969
teacher Engl/Fr Montrose acad 1971–75
m Montrose 5.4.69 James P. Stevenson tel eng s of James P. S. Montrose

CARSON Joyce Marilyn *MA 1960
d of John M. C. estate gardener, school jan and Alice A. A. M. Thomson private serv/companion; b Aber 23.5.38
visiting lect relig kn/stud. Aber coll of educ 1960–61; part-time lect Engl/gen stud. Loughborough coll of f e 1962–64; lect Engl: coll of f e, tech coll Nott 1966–69, Burton-on-Trent tech coll 1969–74; sen teacher i/c career based courses Sixth Form coll Nott from 1974; TA: lieut WRAC 1958–62, 1965–66, capt 1967–76
m Aber 20.8.60 Arnold G. Fogg PhD 1961 *qv*

CARSS Alison Henderson MB ChB 1958

CARTER Alyson Mary MA 1968
d of Andrew M. C. sheriff's off. and Mina M. Thomson; b Banff 1.10.46
teacher: Helensburgh 1969–70, Paisley 1970–71, Linwood 1972–75, Erskine from 1975
m Aber 6.12.69 Michael J. O'Leary MA 1969 *qv*

CARTER Caroline Katherine Horne *BSc 1970
d of William C. health phys monitor and Elizabeth Macdonald; b Wick 15.4.48
res asst Aberd 1970–71; teacher biol Edin from 1972
m Wick 29.3.75 Harold M. Gillespie BA(Cantab) s of John B. G. Currie

CARTER Jennifer Mary Talbot *MA 1966

CARTER Peter Eric Graham MB ChB 1968
s of Eric T. G. C. army off. and Violet G. Penney; b Solihull 2.6.22
Croix de Guerre 1945 BA(Cantab) 1949 MBE 1960 MA(Cantab) 1968 DObstRCOG 1972
off. RE 1941–62, retd as major; h o ARI 1968–69; g p trainee Culter 1969–70; sen h o ARI: cas 1970–71, obst 1971–72; med off. stud. health serv 1972–74; phys i/c stud. health serv Aberd from 1974
m Accra 3.5.58 Alison C. Hare BBC secy d of Ivan L. O. H. Rottingdean

CARTER Robert Nattress MB ChB 1958
s of James V. C. acct and Gladys Nattress; b Trimdon Colliery Co Durham 9.8.34
DObstRCOG MRCGP
h o, sen h o Hartlepool 1958–60; trainee g p Edin 1960–61, lect g p Edin 1961–62; prin trainer in g p Easington, Peterlee (univ N'cle) from 1962
m Horden 13.8.59 Sheila Johnson teacher d of Frederick C. J. Horden

CARTNEY Michael William BSc(eng) 1966
s of William S. C. civ serv and Marjorie Rushton; b Maryport 18.9.43
MICE 1970
asst civ eng Cumberland c c highways dept Carlisle

1966–71; sen civ eng Stirling c c central reg highways from 1971
m Sulby I of M 12.8.67 Elaine B. Radcliffe MA 1967 *qv*

CARTWRIGHT Hugh MacLean MA 1966
s of Thomas C. soldier, miner, for. and Margaret MacLean nurse; b Motherwell 22.10.43
Dip Free Ch coll(Edin) 1969
min Urquhart, Conon Bridge from 1969
m Daviot Inv, Mina M. Mackintosh farm. d of Alexander M. Dores

CASELEY Jane Rosamond MB ChB 1956
d of John R. C. BSc(eng)(Lond) civ eng and Katherine C. Spence MB ChB 1921 *qv*; b Singapore 15.4.31
h o: Aber, Brighton, Loughborough 1956–58; sen h o: Elizabeth J. Anderson hosp Lond 1958–59, Radcliffe I and Churchill hosp Oxford 1959–60; N Lond blood transfusion centre Edgware from 1960
m Lond –.7.61 Kurt Hellman DM(Oxon) cancer res

CASS David Roger Thoday MA 1965

CASSELS Christine Thompson MA 1968
d of Kenneth J. C. retail man. and Jessie T. Lockhart; b Lanark 24.6.47
teacher geog/Engl/mod stud. Bearsden acad from 1969

CASSIDY John Edward PhD 1968
s of Edward C. and Elizabeth McDermott; b Manc 6.1.39
ARCST(Salf) 1962 ARIC 1962
res scient sect. leader ICI Runcorn 1966–77; tech man. ICI lime group Buxton from 1977
m Altrincham 6.6.64 Kathleen O'Connor

CASSIE Elizabeth Anne *MA 1967
d of William C. security advis and Isobel K. Reid; b Huntly 27.6.45
Dip Ed(Edin)
teacher Engl: Kirkcaldy h s 1968–71, Inv r acad 1971–74
m Aber 2.8.69 Peter N. Grainger BA(Durh) lect s of Francis L. G. BA(Lond) Upminster

CASSIE George *BSc 1968
s of Charles T. C. radio mech and Ella Ritchie; b Fraserburgh 31.1.46
army off. (capt) England, Germany 1968–78
m Grasmere 10.4.71 Marilyn A. Metcalfe teacher d of Joseph B. M. Whitburn

CASSIE Ralph MB ChB 1964

CASTRO José López MSc 1969
s of Alejandrino C. vet surg and Nelida López teacher; b Tacuarembo 10.4.31
Ing Agrónomo(Uruguay) 1959
Uruguay: tech plan agropecuario Montevideo 1961–62, tech asst dept soil Sei Centro de Inv Agricolas La Estanzuela 1962–69, head dept soil sc agr res center 1969–74, head dept integrated res from 1974
m Tacuarembo 8.11.63 Violeta Albernaz d of Ursino A. Tacuarembo

CATER Alan John LLB 1969

CATTANACH Helen Barlow MB ChB 1962
m Cooper

CATTO Christian May MA 1966

CATTO Doreen Mary BSc 1970
d of William R. C. trackman and Maggie M. Thomson nurse; b Maud 28.10.49
nurse auxil Maud 1970–73; stud. nurse Edin from 1973

CATTO Graeme Robertson Dawson *MB ChB 1969 *MD 1975
s of William D. C. MB ChB 1939 *qv*; b Aber 24.4.45
MRCP(UK) 1971
h o Aber 1969–70; dept med Aberd: res fell. 1970–73, lect from 1973
m Aber 14.7.67 Joan Sievewright LLB 1966 *qv*

CATTO Leslie Urquhart Macdonald BSc 1969

CATTO Sheila Mary MA 1964
d of Patrick C. farm. and Mary Herd MA 1937 *qv*
b Fraserburgh 20.12.42
teacher Daviot Aberdeensh from 1965

CAWTHORN Nigel George *BSc 1970
s of James E. C. master tailor and Mary Monseair; b Pontefract 12.6.47
MSc(BC) 1973
mine geol Tungsten Canada from 1973
m Vancouver 7.5.71 Mary I. Florence BSc 1970 *qv*

CENTER Alexander Ross *MA 1959

CEREXHE Ian BSc 1970
s of Ernest A. G. C. contr and Sophia M. M. McCracken nurse; b Portpatrick 9.9.46
UK, North Sea, Europe: operative, chargehand civ eng 1970–74, jun man., sen man. from 1974
m Shipley 1975 B. Lesley Anderson teacher d of James A. Shipley

CHADHA Rajendra Nath PhD 1959
s of Beant R. C. army off. and Krishna W. Suri; b Rawalpindi 1.8.30
BSc(Luck) 1951 MSc 1953 PhD(Luck) 1957
USA: post doct fell. Brooklyn poly New York 1959–60; sen chem W. R. Grace & Co 1960–63; dir res and dev Staufer Chem Co 1966–69; man. chem and polymers Marbon Chem Co 1966–69; chmn of board and chief exec off. Carroll Products Inc from 1969
m Washington D.C. Ajit Kaur Behl MD(Amritsar) phys d of S. Kundan S. B. Chandrigarh Punjab

CHADWICK Beryl MA 1968
d of Vincent C. eng and Ada Smith; b Accrington 28.12.45
careers off.: Prescot 1969–71, Middlesbrough 1971–73
m Aberfeldy 23.10.71 Robert T. Third MA 1966 *qv*

CHAINA Perviz PhD 1968
BSc MSc(Bom)
m Clifford

CHALLINOR Ronald MA 1966
s of Ronald C. and Mary Macleod; b Stornoway 25.5.45
teacher: Greenock 1967–73, Denny 1973–79; prin Engl Falkirk from 1979

CHALLIS-SOWERBY Loraine *MA 1969 CASS 1975
d of Derek C-S. teacher and Florence A. Bedworth shop asst; b Newton-le-Willows Lancs 2.8.47
commun worker Aber 1970–71; soc worker: Lancs 1971–74, Peterhead from 1974
m Aber 1.4.70 William Donaldson MA 1968 *qv*

CHALMERS Alastair MA 1966 *MEd 1970

CHALMERS Anthony Alan *BSc 1960 PhD 1964

CHALMERS David Johnstone *BSc 1962 MSc 1964

CHALMERS George Lovie MB ChB 1957
s of Roderick M. C. stonemason and Annabella Strachan; b Aber 12.1.33
MRCPGlas 1965 MRCPE 1964
h o Inv R I, Victoria I Glas 1957–61; regist: gen med Aber 1961–63, geriat med Dun 1963–65, sen regist 1965–67; consult phys geriat med WI Glasg from 1967
m Inv 25.3.60 Jean Sutherland SRN d of William S. Fearn

CHALMERS John Colin *BSc 1960
s of Alan C. banker and Dorothy M. Polkinghorn; b Tientsin 17.12.34
Belfast, Min of Agr, NI: asst prin 1960–64, dep prin 1964–68, prin 1968–74; asst secy dept agr from 1974
m Aber 11.7.61 Freda S. Rae teacher d of Harry R. Cults

CHALMERS Margaret Mitchell MA 1969
d of Robert C. bus driver and Agnes H. M. Hepburn shop asst; b Aber 11.7.48
teacher: Aber 1970–73, asst prin Engl Aber from 1973
m Aber 28.12.70 Ian T. Brodie teacher s of Daniel B. Aber

CHALMERS Robert Alexander DSc 1968
s of Alexander C. steelgrinder and Maud R. Nickolls; b Birm 17.6.20
BSc(Manc) 1950 PhD(Edin) 1953 FRSE 1978
ICI res fell. Durh 1953–56; Aberd: from 1956 lect, sen lect, reader
m Aber 4.8.62 Grace C. Turner MB ChB 1958 *qv*

CHALMERS William Skea BSc(for) 1956
s of William S. C. BSc(agr) 1922 *qv*(II) and Violet E. Richards; b Co. Durham 10.7.31
jun res fell. bot univ coll WI Jamaica 1956–58; Trinidad and Tobago: res off. govt for. dept 1959–65, acting dep conserv for. 1965–66 Port of Spain; UWI: res fell. cocoa 1966–73, asst regist 1973–76, sen asst regist from 1976
m 3.12.57 Alisha O. Westmaas d of Vivian O. W. Arima Trinidad

CHAMBERLAIN Brian Richard PhD 1965
s of Joseph H. S. C. aircraft eng and Ivy L. Bradshaw; b Oxford 30.6.35
ARIC (1965)
res chem Pilkington Bros Ormskirk from 1964
m Aber 28.8.64 Helen S. Gilmour BSc 1962 *qv*

CHAMBERLAIN Janet Mary PhD 1957
d of Clifford C. radio eng and Eva D. Curtis; b Desborough 14.5.31
BSc(Lond) 1952 MSc(Lond) 1953
res fell. dept of materia med Aberd 1963–68; res assoc dept of internal med univ of Virginia USA 1965–66; asst res dept biochem Cantab/fell. Lucy Cavendish coll Cambridge
m Desborough 22.7.53 W. Peter G. Stein PhD 1955 *qv*

CHAMBERS Marcus Rex *BSc 1965 MSc 1966
s of Laurence R. C. cotton manuf and Nellie C. Law; b Rawtenstall 28.1.43
PhD(Liv) 1971
Edin: res asst nature conserv 1966–67; lect biol Napier Coll 1967–68; res fell. zool Liv 1968–71; res fell. Aberd 1971–74; lect biol univ Sains Malaysia Penang from 1975
m Aber 18.1.75 Phyllis W. Booth SRN d of James B. Aber

CHAMBERS Martin Alexander LLB 1968 *1969
s of Alexander M. C. cabinetmaker and Robina H. T. Sinclair; b Glasg 7.10.46
lang teacher Swaziland 1969–70; Glasg: law app 1970–72, solic 1972–74; geol asst Namibia 1974–76; solic Melbourne from 1976
m Melbourne 18.3.78 Inez B. A. Prasad d of Andrew G. P. Fiji

CHAN Edwin Wai BSc 1970

CHAN Kwok Thye *MA 1960
s of Chan Ah Hong AMN; b Malaysia 29.3.25
Kuala Lumpur: educ off. 1960–64, secy tariff advis board Malaysia 1964–70, dir tariff div fed. indust dev auth from 1970
m Kuala Lumpur 18.8.62 Eleanor M. Berry teacher d of P. P. B. Lundin Links

CHANDLER David Brendan MA 1961

CHANDRASENAN Kochukunju PhD 1966
BSc(Trav) MSc(Luck)

CHAPMAN Dianne Heald BSc 1967

CHAPMAN Elizabeth Anne Mary MA 1967

CHAPMAN Gwendoline Mary MA 1969 CASS 1972
d of James P. C. garage prop. and Jessie A. de S. Morison teacher; b Kirriemuir 22.8.48
soc worker Dun from 1972 (trainee 1969–70)

CHAPMAN John Sangster *MA 1963
s of Harry C. and Lilias M. Sangster; b Aber 6.6.41
HM insp taxes Glasg 1964–65; Lond: salesman 1965–66, town planning res off. 1966–70, computer progr from 1974

CHAPMAN Margaret Anne MA 1965

CHAPMAN Martin John *BSc 1967
s of Richard J. C. chem and Madeleine Rushforth teacher piano; b Stanford-le-Hope 14.7.45
PhD(Lond) 1970
res asst Middx med s 1967–70, fell. Oklahoma city USA, 1970–72, publ health serv San Francisco 1972–74; res investigator Paris from 1974

CHAPMAN Robert Sutherland *MB ChB 1962
s of Robert C. bank man. and Edith G. Sutherland teacher; b Cults 4.6.38
MRCPE 1965 (Lond) 1967
res fell. therap Aberd 1963–66, regist, sen regist dermat ARI 1966–69; sen regist dermat Middx h Lond 1969–71; consult dermat Glasg northern h and Stirlingsh/hon clin lect Glas from 1971
m Meonstoke Rosalind S. Slater BSc(Leeds) scient res worker (atherosclerosis) d of Ian G. S. BSc(Birm) Meonstoke

CHAPMAN William *MA 1963
s of George G. C. bank man. and Jane A. Cameron; b Peterhead 26.1.40
teacher geog: Blairgowrie 1964–71, prin geog Perth g s from 1971
m Perth 28.3.75 Kathryn L. Mackay MA(St And) teacher d of G. L. M. Perth

CHARITONOWSKY Ariene MA 1964
d of Nicolau C. LLB(Riga) barrister and Astrid von der Pahlen secy, bus. prop.; b Riga Latvia 29.4.39
Dip Ed(Syd) 1972
shop asst to Fr consul, audit asst, clerk Blantyre Malawi

1961–62; teacher: Fr Kumasi Ghana 1964–65, mod lang NSW Aust from 1968
m Aber 5.9.60 Alastair J. McLean BSc 1960 *qv*

CHARLES Benedict Augustine MB ChB 1957
s of Richard C. farm. and Maude A. Batt; b St Andrews Grenada WI 15.1.19
BSc(Wash) 1951
h o Stracathro h 1957–59; g p Grenada 1959–75; private pract St Andrews Grenada from 1975

CHARLES Gaynor Barbara MA 1969
d of Bryn C. teacher and Aileen F. Hutchison receptionist; b Rossett Wales 28.7.48
teacher: Aber 1970–71, Hastings NZ 1972–78
m Aber 28.12.71 Ian G. Cotching BSc 1971 teacher s of John W. C. Aber

CHARLES Lauchlan Munro BSc 1964
b Inv 8.10.39
sen biochem (NHS) Aber from 1964

CHARLESON Euphemia Barbara BSc(agr) 1958
d of Charles W. C. crofter/postman and Jemima Cheyne; b Shetland 11.8.36
asst exper off., exper off. Rowett inst Aber 1958–66
m Aber 27.6.62 Gordon M. Philip master butcher s of Patrick C. C. P. Aber

CHARLTON Maureen *BSc 1969
m Rose

CHAYTOR Daniel Emanuel Babatunji *BSc 1958
s of Daniel A. H. C. civ serv and Adeline L. Lisk; b Sierra Leone 13.4.31
PhD(Lond) 1961
Sierra Leone: lect zool Fourah Bay coll 1961–65; Njala univ coll: sen lect 1965–66, dean sc 1966–67, vice-prin 1967–68; visiting prof biol Mass inst tech USA 1968–71; prof zool Fourah Bay coll from 1971; dir inst marine biol oceanog from 1973
m Lond 28.9.55 Trixie M. Thomas nurs sister d of Emanuel H. T. MA(Durh) Freetown Sierra Leone

CHEADLE Yvonne Ada MA 1961

CHEE Sek Por PhD 1961
BCE(Melb)

CHEONG-LEEN Philip MB ChB 1964
s of Edward C-L. merch and Elvira Low; b Hong Kong 8.3.38
FRCSE 1970
h o Aber 1964–65, sen h o Dun 1966–67; regist: Inv 1967–71, Lond 1971–74; sen orthop regist St George's hosp Lond 1974–75; clin lect orthop univ of Hong Kong from 1975; consult. orthop surg Queen Mary's hosp for ch Carshalton/St James's hosp Lond from 1975
m Perth –.9.67 Dorothy J. Jackson nurse d of James J. Newburgh Fife

CHERIYAN Joseph Kottukapally MB ChB 1960

CHERMSIRIVATHANA Chirayupin MSc 1964
BSc(Thaild)

CHESTER Michael Peter *BSc(eng) 1968

CHEW Kenneth John *BSc 1968 PhD 1978
s of John C. and Margaret M. MacEwan MA(St And) statist; b Edin 24.8.45
sen asst geol Ontario dept mines Toronto 1968–69; Aberd: res stud. geol 1968–69, 1971–73, SRC secy 1969–70, pres 1970–71, rector's assessor univ court 1970–72; geol BP Petr Dev 1974–76; lect geol univ coll Galway from 1976
m Aber 6.4.71 Gillian G. Robertson MA 1966 *qv*

CHEW Moh-Koon MB ChB 1961

CHEYNE Colin Fitzroy MA 1970
s of George D. C. MA 1927 *qv*; b Edin 21.3.48
indust eng: Wiggins Teape S Wales 1970–71, MBO advis St Neots 1971–72; Appleyard(Aber) p a to man. dir 1972–73, marketing man. 1973–74; gen man, 1974–76; quality control man. Simpson Wright & Lowe Notts from 1976
m St Neots 9.9.72 Hilary K. Sheffield d of Ernest W. S. St Neots

CHEYNE David George Mitchell *MA 1969

CHEYNE Denis BSc 1970

CHEYNE Gordon McLeod MB ChB 1961
s of Robert G. C. banker and Margaret McLeod teacher; b Insch 11.3.37
DObstRCOG 1963 MRACGP 1967
h o Aber, Nantwich 1961–63; g p Aber 1963–64; res m o Burnie hosp Tasmania; Melbourne: g p 1965–69, anaest from 1969
m Elgin 28.9.73 Sheila Telfer nurse d of James L. T. Elgin

CHEYNE John Alexander Leitch *MA 1957
s of Charles D. C fish merch and Rosaline Leitch typist; b Aber 5.10.34
BA(Oxon) 1959 MEd(Edin) 1970
secy Christian Council for overseas stud. Edin 1960–64, min St Andrews cong ch St And 1964–65; chaplain Royal h s Edin; lect educ dept coll of educ Dun from 1970
m Aber 28.7.60 Eileen A. Butler MA 1959 *qv*

CHEYNE Laurence Alexander *MA 1970
s of James C. civ serv and Joyce L. Grant secy; b Aber 5.12.47
teacher hist Glasg: Kingsbridge s s 1971–73, Bellahouston acad 1973–74, prin hist Lochend s s from 1974
m Aber 6.2.71 Pamela A. Milne MA 1970 *qv*

CHEYNE Lorna Ruth *MA 1966
d of William B. C. cost acct and Lila Mackenzie; b Aber 22.8.44
teacher Engl: Hawick h s 1967–70, Riddings comp s Scunthorpe from 1975
m Aber 5.9.66 John Adam MA 1966 *qv*

CHEYNE Muriel May *MA 1959
m Nicol

CHEYNE William Mackenzie *MA 1961 PhD 1965
s of William B. C. acct and Lila Mackenzie; b Aber 8.11.38
asst lect dept psych Strath 1964–66, lect from 1966
m Cumbernauld 10.5.74 Rona J. G. Lamont BA(Strath) teacher d of John L. Glasg

CHIEDU Sylvester Okafor BSc(eng) 1957

CHILD Mary Elizabeth MA 1968
d of George C. BSc(Leeds) res chem ICI and Kathleen Stevenson BSc(Leeds) magistrate; b Stockton-on-Tees 6.9.46
shorthand typist dept educ Stir 1969–70; secy Nott 1970–71, Aston 1971–72
m Stockton-on-Tees 17.7.68 Graham T. Maybank BSc 1966 *qv*

CHILMAN Paul Thomas BSc(eng) 1964

CHILTON Kenneth John *BSc 1968
s of John A. C. clerk and Joyce Borrill; b Aber 10.5.46
MSc(Essex) 1972
computer progr with ICL from 1968
m Lond 11.12.71 Linda M. Barnes BEd(Lond) teacher d of Eric B. Downton

CHIN Leslie *BSc 1962
PhD(Lond)

CHIN Sherlock Syn Lok MB ChB 1966
s of Chin C. C. chief acct and Betty K. H. Tong teacher; b Brunei 25.12.36
DTM&H(Liv) 1972
h o RNI Inv, RACH 1967–68; gen hosp Brunei: m o 1968–77, sen m o from 1977
m Aber 9.7.66 Vivienne M. Douglas MA 1955 *qv*

CHINNOCK John Henry MB ChB 1959
s of William H. C. policeman and Eliza Whiston; b Tamworth 26.10.33
DObstRCOG 1962
h o: N Staffs RI and ARI 1959–60, obst N Staffs mat. hosp 1960–61; g p Stourbridge from 1961, clin asst obst/gyn from 1966
m Tamworth –.8.63 Margaret L. Downing SRN d o Arthur H. D. Stoke-on-Trent

CHIPHANGWI John David MB ChB 1966
s of P. David C. farm. and Esther Z. Nsoma; b Malawi 17.12.36
DObs 1971 and MMed 1973(Makerere) MRCOG 1973
Malawi: h o Blantyre cent h 1966–67, dist m o Dedza 1967–69, acting med supt Zomba 1969–70; Uganda: Mulago h Kampala 1970–73; Malawi: consult. Blantyre cent h from 1973
m Blantyre 1974 Stella Thewe nurse

CHISHOLM Allan Donald *MA 1967
s of Roderick C. MA(Edin) headmaster and Flora Finlayson; b Grantown-on-Spey 16.6.45
econ: plan consult. Epsom 1967–68, Scot. dev ag Edin 1968–72; man. construct. comp Edin from 1973
m Inv 10.7.70 Anne L. Parkhill MA 1967 *qv*

CHISHOLM Duncan Douglas MB ChB 1965 Dip Psychother 1970
s of Roderick C. MA(Edin) headmaster and Flora Finlayson; b Grantown-on-Spey 8.10.41
DPM 1968 MRCPsych 1972
Aber: h o Glenburn Wing, ARI 1965–66; sen h o, regist, Royal Cornhill h 1966–69; regist Ross Clinic 1969–70, sen regist child psychiat RACH from 1970 (seconded Clarke inst of psychiat Tor 1973–74)
m Aber 6.10.66 Rosemary G. Doyle MA 1964 *qv*

CHISHOLM James Alan *BSc 1970
s of James C. tech UKAEA and Robina L. R. Brown; b Edin 31.12.47
CEng MIEE 1977
PO exec eng telecom dev Lond from 1970
m Aber 22.12.70 Ruebena A. Duncan MA 1969 *qv*

CHISHOLM John Martin BSc 1969

CHISHOLM Mairi MA 1970
b Dingwall 20.5.48
teacher classics Millburn acad Inv 1971–75, asst prin classics from 1975

CHISHOLM Neil William Thomas BSc 1968

CHIZEA Leonard Governor BSc(for) 1960
s of Obi C. Egumkonye farm. and Mary Elikwu; b Asaba Nigeria 8.11.19
Nigeria: prov for. off. Ibadan 1960–63, for. off. Benin 1963–67, off. i/c regeneration Bendel State 1970–71, biol master St Patrick's coll Asaba from 1976
m Benin city 9.1.45 Elizabeth Mokolo d of John O. M. Asaba

CHONA Walter Dyson MSc 1967
BSc(Rhodes)

CHOW Pak Shan PhD 1970
b China 26.11.41
BSc(Chu Hai) MSc(R'dg)
lect Aberd from 1966
m Dun 25.9.71 Man C. Chiu MSc(Dund) computer progr

CHOY Stephen Tze Leung MSc 1968 PhD 1969
BSc(Sun-Yat-Sen)

CHRISTIAN Glenda Angela MA 1964
m Bastien

CHRISTIANSON Aileen Barbara *MA 1966
d of Alan C. and Muriel Barker; b Colwyn Bay 8.8.44
res Engl dept Edin from 1966

CHRISTIE Alexander Ogilvie *BSc 1956 PhD 1960

CHRISTIE Brenda Air MA 1965
d of Robert E. C. off. man. and Agnes A. Young clerkess; b Aber 17.10.44
teacher maths: Kaimhill s s Aber 1966–68, Queen Anne s Dunfermline 1968–69, Douglas acad Milngavie 1970–72, Summerhill acad Aber 1972, Mackie acad Stonehaven 1972–73
m Aber 18.10.68 Neil Robertson BSc(eng) 1967 *qv*

CHRISTIE Bryce *BSc 1959
b Aber 27.6.37
prin teacher biol sc Peterhead acad from 1964; prin examiner SCE exam board from 1976
m Aber 24.7.67 Priscilla Robb

CHRISTIE Colin MA 1963

CHRISTIE Derek James MA 1969

CHRISTIE Dorothy MA 1968
m Riviere

CHRISTIE Dorothy Louise MA 1968
m Kelso

CHRISTIE Evelyn Jane Campbell MA 1968
d of William C. banker and Evelyn Dempster; b Edin 19.7.47
Dip Sec St(Strath) 1969
teacher ILEA from 1973

CHRISTIE Frances Mary MA 1970

CHRISTIE Gayre *MA 1970 MEd 1972
s of David C. eng and Isobel Gair; b Arbroath 16.3.45
teacher Arbroath acad 1972–73; educ psych Dun 1973–75; lect psych Kelvingrove coll Brisbane Aust from 1975
m Aber 14.2.75 Carol A. Mullin d of Henry W. M. Arbroath

CHRISTIE Gordon *MA 1969
s of William G. C. chief supt E of Scot. Water Board

and Doris Thompson play s supt; b Aber 8.9.46
Dip Ed(Edin) 1970
teacher hist Ardrossan acad from 1970

CHRISTIE James McLean BSc 1963
s of Martin H. C. rly porter and Mary M. McLean landscape artist; b Inverbervie 17.5.42
teacher maths/sc Laurencekirk 1964–66; RAF educ off. SW Britain from 1966
m Laurencekirk Arlene E. H. Polson teacher, sales rep

CHRISTIE Janet Frances MA 1961
d of Richard N. C. army off. (G.H.) and Norah Elsmie; b Gibraltar 30.1.36
secy: Collins publ London 1961–63, to Warden Rhodes House Oxford 1963–70; secy/asst to prin Aberd 1971–73; secy to prin Royal Holloway Coll univ Lond Egham from 1974

CHRISTIE Jessie Mary MA 1958

CHRISTIE John Alexander MA 1956 LLB 1959
s of John C. lic grocer/gen merch and Mary W. B. Sangster; b Tarland 2.6.35
solic Huntly from 1959, town clerk from 1970
m Huntly 17.3.63 Elizabeth M. Whitehouse d of Joseph W. Huntly

CHRISTIE John Grant *BSc(eng) 1960
s of William C. MA 1929 *qv* and Isobel G. Bain MA 1923 *qv*; b Aber 12.4.38
MS(Harv) 1961
ICI: eng Billingham 1961–63, plastics Welwyn 1963–69; Thetford: chief eng Vacuum Res 1969–73, dir Camvac from 1973
m Aber 22.12.61 Patricia M. Shannon teacher d of William P. S. MA(Glas) Aber

CHRISTIE John Lindley MB ChB 1961

CHRISTIE Kathleen Hardie MA 1962
d of Alexander C. insur man. and Catherine B. Hardie secy; b Arbroath 9.7.41
teacher Engl Dalkeith h s 1963–68
m Aber 28.12.66 Forbes Marr BArch(Edin) arch./plan. s of Archibald M. Aber

CHRISTIE Linda Sylvia Matthew MA 1966
m Hargrave

CHRISTIE Malcolm Andrew Bain *MA 1958
s of William C. MA 1929 *qv* and Isabel G. Bain MA 1923 *qv*; b Aber 9.7.36
dist off. N Rhodesia 1959–64; econ cent. plan. off. Lusaka 1964–66; dev stud. Sus 1966–68; sen econ M o Dev/Fin. Lusaka 1969–70, dir Walkover Estates (irrigated farm. comp) Lusaka 1970–75; dir Landells Mills Assoc (agr res and man. consult.) Lond, Bath from 1975
m Aber 3.11.62 Christian D. Fraser MA 1957 *qv*

CHRISTIE Margaret Barbara Anne MA 1965 Dip Ed 1966
d of Alexander C. farm. and Elizabeth M. Berry nursery nurse; b Torphins 2.6.43
Dip. to teach deaf(Edin) 1978
teacher: Viewforth s s Kirkcaldy 1966–68, Elgin acad 1968–72, New Elgin p s 1972–73, Milltimber p s 1973–74, Aber s for deaf from 1974

CHRISTIE Michael George Alexander MA 1966 cLLB 1968 *1969
m Margaret R. Sharp MA 1970 *qv*

CHRISTIE Michael James BSc 1970
s of James G. C. sheep man. and Rebecca M. M. Ross; b Nigg Tain 15.6.49
Plessey telecomm Liv: tel syst des eng 1970–77, computer facilities man. from 1977
m Liv 14.2.74 Sandra Y. Martin clerkess d of George S. Liv

CHRISTIE Moira Macleod MA 1964
d of Alexander C. civ serv and Louise H. Johnston cashier; b Aber 2.6.43
Dip Soc Ad(St And) 1965
soc welfare off. C of S Langlands Park s Port Glasgow 1965–66; Fraserburgh: asst to children's off. Aberdeensh 1966–69, soc worker counties of Aber & Kinc 1969–72; Aber: sen soc worker Aberdeensh/Kinc 1972–75; soc work man. Grampian reg council (Aber city div) from 1975

CHRISTIE Moira Margaret MA 1960
m Bruce

CHRISTIE Moyra Margaret MA 1958
m Burness

CHRISTIE Peter George Smith BSc(eng) 1965
s of Laurence S. postman/crofter and Magdalen Christie knitter (cottage indust); b Skibhoull Cunningsburgh Shetland 28.6.41
trainee/jun eng Eng Elect. Co Burton-on-Trent and Edin 1965–69; steam turbine eng GEC Turbines Liddell Power Station NSW Aust 1970–76; eng Construction Div GEC (Aust) from 1976
m Lond 11.3.67 Lynette A. Wilson bank clerk d of Reginald W. Southport

CHRISTIE Peter Laurie BSc(eng) 1959

CHRISTIE Reginald George LLB 1969
s of Reginald C. C. MA 1946 *qv* and Flora Barclay MA 1942 *qv*; b Aber 1.7.48
Aber: law app, asst A. C. Morrison & Richards advoc 1969–72; ptnr Christie, Buthlay & Rutherford advoc from 1972
m Aber 9.9.71 Yvonne M. H. Alden MA 1971 secy d of Charles T. A. Dyce

CHRISTIE Robert Philip MA 1967
BSc(Lond)
res fell. occup guid proj sponsored by DES and DE Hatfield poly 1974–76; prin off. psych/trg advis Hants c c from 1976, consult. psych dyslexia remed organis from 1979

CHRISTIE Roy David BSc 1970
s of David A. C. publ works contr and Mabel F. Will; b Aber 10.11.48
BVMS MRCVS(Glas) 1974
vet stud. Glas 1970–74; vet surg Grange, Adelaide S Aust from 1974

CHRISTOPHER Moira Anne BEd 1969
d of David B. C. auto-elect. and Jean R. Bowie audio-typist; b Elgin 8.5.48
teacher Mosstodloch 1969–72; relief teaching from 1978
m Aber 20.6.70 James L. Wilson farm worker/grieve, self-employed contr s of William W. Keith

CHRYSTAL Kathleen May Robertson *MB ChB 1958
d of William A. C. law acct and Agnes M. Robertson typist; b Aber 23.10.34
FRCSE 1964

h o ARI 1958–59; sen h o gen and orthop surg Inv hosps 1959–61; ARI: res fell. SHERT 1961–62, regist cas traumatic surg 1962–63, regist gen surg 1963–67; plastic surg: regist Westminster & Roehampton h Lond 1967–70, sen regist United Cardiff h 1970–71, SERHB Scot. Edin 1971–72; consult plastic surg N'cle RHB from 1972

CHU Cheong Wai MA 1970

CHUA Dorothy Poh Luan MB ChB 1958
d of Keh H. C. bank man. and Swee H. (Annie) Lee; b Singapore 9.7.30
Lond: h o 1960–61, cas off. 1961–62, sen h o paediat 1962–63; part-time m o Wandsworth 1964–73; clin asst Kingston hosp 1969–73, med asst from 1973
m Lond 31.1.59 Albert C. K. Looi comp dir s of Eng L. Penang; marr diss 1974

CHUNG Arthur Frederick MB ChB 1967
s of Albert C. and Myrtle M. Minott; b Portland, Jamaica 12.10.42
h o Aber 1967–68; New York: resid obst/gyn 1968–72, fell. mem Sloan Kettering cancer centre 1972–74, asst prof coll phys and surg Columbia univ from 1974
d NY 16.12.78 *AUR* XLVIII 234

CHUNG PIN YONG Susan Sanne Hing BSc 1968
m Lanhinglit

CHURCHARD Graeme Ogg *BSc 1969
s of John C. C. head storekeeper and Jeannie E. Ogg; b Aber 19.9.47
geol: St And 1969–72; S Africa: geol surv Zululand 1973–74, Union Corp Orange Free State from 1974 (St Helena Gold Mines)

CIESLA Michael John *MA 1969
s of Josef C. welder and Isabella Thomson; b Montrose 7.3.47
teacher, asst prin guid Arbroath 1970–72; prin geog Penicuik 1972–78; asst head S Queensferry from 1978
m Montrose 14.6.69 Patricia A. Beattie secy d of William F. B. Montrose

CLARK Adam Alexander *BSc(eng) 1968
s of Adam A. C. farm. and Jessie I. Barclay; b Turriff 9.5.46
Dip Man Stud(Derby) 1969
Rolls-Royce: trainee aero-eng div Derby 1968–70; nuclear reactor course R.N. coll Greenwich 1970; operating eng RR & Associates Thurso 1970–76; asst resid eng RR & A Clyde submarine base Faslane from 1977

CLARK Alan Peter *BSc 1970
s of Albert C. civ serv; b Cheshire 18.8.46
MSc(Stir) 1971 PhD(Stir) 1973
res fell. (SRC) theoret phys Stir 1973–77; prin res off. BSRA Wallsend N'cle-u-Tyne from 1977

CLARK Alastair James *BSc 1962
s of James B. C. farm. and Barbara H. Rae; b Insch 29.5.40
chem tech BP Co Grangemouth 1962–68; res chem Arthur D. Little res inst Edin 1968–70; sen dev scient M.S.A.Co. Glasg 1970–72, res/dev man. from 1972

CLARK Alistair Verne MA 1963 BD 1966
s of Alexander C. Christian missionary Bolivia, fin. secy to YMCA Aber and Mary O. Wood Christian missionary Bolivia; b Samaipata Bolivia 18.6.41
Baptist min: Oban 1967–71, Lossiemouth from 1971
m Aber 9.7.65 Audrey Smith teacher d of James S. Aber

CLARK Cecilia Marie MB ChB 1962
d of William C. C. tech off. GPO tel and Cecilia Black; b Aber 2.1.38
h o ARI, RACH 1962–63; res fell. Brit heart foundation Aberd 1964–67
m Aber 19.7.63 Derek Ogston MB ChB 1957 *qv*

CLARK Christopher Geoffrey Hood *MA 1966
s of Geoffrey B. H. C. barrister-at-law and Raymonde G. Gouache; b Fulmer 5.10.42
bank trainee, asst bank vice-pres New York 1966–71; bank man. Lond 1971–76, bank dir from 1977
m Lond 18.7.72 Fenella H. Bullen int decorator d of Paul G. B. Aboyne

CLARK David *BSc 1969
s of John C. shipbuilder's yard man. and Helen S. Simpson; b Forfar 26.8.47
Aber: CA app Meston & Co 1969–73, asst acct W. G. Wilson & Co from 1973
m Aber 9.12.72 Mhairi D. Middleton bank clerkess d of William D. M. Aber

CLARK David Alexander *BSc 1957
s of Alexander C. pharm and Sybil G. Paxton; b Aber 11.11.34
geol: Canada: Regina 1957–59, Calgary 1959–63 and from 1964; Tripoli 1963
m Aber 8.3.58 Jean M. Kirk lib d of Alexander K. MB ChB(Glas) Birmingham

CLARK David Arbuckle MA 1969

CLARK David Mitchell MA 1961 LLB 1964
s of Ronald M. C. comp dir and Clara Melville; b Aber 9.3.40
Aber: law app 1962–65, leg. asst 1965–67, ptnr Clark & Wallace advoc from 1967
m Aber 7.8.64 Lorna C. Ritchie receptionist d of Alexander R. Aber

CLARK David Robertson *BSc 1965
s of William R. C. civ eng and Margaret E. Davies BSc(Aberystwyth) teacher: b Aber 7.10.43
MSc(Sus) 1967 FSAScot 1976
asst lect maths univ of sc and tech Kumasi, Ghana 1965–66; admin UKAEA Harwell 1968–73, Lond from 1973
m Dornoch 26.8.67 Genefer G. F. Wright MA 1966 *qv*

CLARK Denise Framar MA 1961
d of Franck J. H. C. clerk and Marie T. MacDonald; b Aber 19.4.41
teacher Aber: Deeview p s 1962–67, Ferryhill p s 1974–78, nursery Walker Dam s from 1978
m Aber 12.7.63 Thomas A. Steele ARIBA arch. s of Douglas A. S. Coventry

CLARK Derek William LLB 1967

CLARK Doris Helen BSc 1964
d of James B. C. farm. and Barbara H. Rae farm.; b Chapel of Garioch 18.3.43
teacher maths Brechin h s 1965–73, asst prin maths from 1973

CLARK Dwight Bothwell MSc 1968
s of Harold G. C. BS(Calif) chem and Lois H. Bothwell BA(Calif) teacher; b Long Beach Calif 1.2.38
BSc(Calif) 1961
progr man. (operational testing) Monterey Calif from 1968
m Minneapolis Minnesota 21.6.70 Margaret J. Kylander BS(Minn) teacher d of John B. K. Minneapolis

CLARK Eileen Mackenzie BSc 1961
d of John A. S. C. bank teller, man. and Margaret H. Mackenzie; b Aber 1.10.41
teacher maths, spec asst Aber 1962–70; part time/temp teacher maths Methlick, Aboyne, Banchory from 1972
m Aber 8.8.69 Robert Paterson civ eng Aber c c s of Robert M. P. Aber

CLARK Frances Mary MA 1958
d of Frank Reid insur ag and Ann M. Fraser; b Aboyne 19.7.30
teacher Aber: Engl/hist Powis s s 1958–68 Beechwood spec s 1968–71
m Aber 5.4.65 John F. Smith, Lord Kirkhill LLD 1974

CLARK Gerald Charles BSc 1967

CLARK Gordon Milne MA 1968
s of George A. C. golf club steward and Jessie Robertson golf club stewardess; b Glasg 30.4.47
foreign lang asst Munich 1969–70; teacher Bathgate 1970–71; foreign lang asst Lyon 1971–72; teacher: Stirling 1972–78, asst prin mod lang Wallace h s Stirling from 1978

CLARK Graham Sturrock *MA 1965
s of John M. C. agr sales rep and Catherine M. Sturrock sub-postmistress; b Forfar 21.8.42
Dip Ed(Edin) 1966
Edin: teacher 1967–72, civ serv from 1972
m Haddington 24.7.71 Elizabeth A. M. Collins-Young MA(Edin) d of Joe R. Collins BA(Chicago) Philippines

CLARK Hamish *MA 1970
s of David C. clerk/acct OS map agency man. and Mary D. Guthrie med secy; b Blantyre Malawi 27.12.47
post-grad stud. geog Belf 1970–72; res off. Scot dev dept, Scot. off. Edin from 1973
m Edin 15.9.73 Lynda J. Henderson BA(Belf) civ serv, lib d of Albert H. H. LLB(Belf) Belfast

CLARK Iain Mackinnon MA 1961
s of Donald C. master mariner and Mary F. Mackinnon; b Glasg 24.11.33
teacher: Campbeltown 1962–66, Glasgow 1966–67, asst head Kirkconnel from 1967
m Helensburgh 1967 Anne V. C. Shuttleworth journalist d of Francis A. S. Broughty Ferry

CLARK Ian Anderson MA 1965 BD 1971
s of John C. BR rep and Margaret Anderson; b Aber 19.7.38
teacher Lusaka s s Zambia; asst min N & E ch of St Nicholas Aber 1971–72; C of S min New Restalrig par ch Edin 1972–78; prin St Colm's coll Edin from 1978
m Aber 25.9.61 Elizabeth M. Cruden wages clerkess d of James C. Aber

CLARK Ian Cameron BSc(eng) 1968
s of John Clark MA 1923 *qv*; b Aber 25.4.47
MS(eng) (Ohio) 1972
dev eng Goodyear Tyre & Rubber Co Glasg 1969–70; (stud. univ of Akron Ohio 1970–71) Goodyear International Tyre Tech Center Luxembourg: based Glasg 1972–74, based Wolverhampton from 1974, worked France, Germany, Luxembourg, Morocco, Philippines
m Aber 21.12.73 Teresita Lisano BBA (univ of E. Manila), exec secy d of Jose L. Philippines

CLARK Ian Douglas *BSc 1956
s of James C. MA 1917 *qv* and Mary J. Rae MA 1921 *qv*(II); b Dingwall 7.2.34
teacher: Morgan acad Dun 1957–61; prin maths: Grantown g s 1961–63, Annan acad 1963–65, Aber (later Hazlehead) acad from 1965
m Dun 3.4.59 Christine Fitzwalter teacher d of Leslie C. W. F. Dun

CLARK Ian Illingworth *MA 1966 Dip Ed 1967
s of John A. S. C. bank man. and Margaret H. McKenzie; b Aber 23.5.43
teacher: RGC Aber 1967–73, prin mod lang Kincorth acad Aber from 1973
m Aber 5.4.68 Joan G. Walker teacher d of Alexander W. Aber

CLARK John *BSc 1966 MSc 1968 PhD 1970

CLARK John Kydd MA 1969
s of William K. C. shopkeeper and Barbara B. Andrews bookkeeper; b Invergordon 24.3.48
teacher geog Loudon acad Ayrsh 1970; shopkeeper Invergordon from 1971
m E Kilbride 7.4.71 Elizabeth M. Murdoch MA 1969 *qv*

CLARK John Stuart Borthwick BSc 1964
MSc(Edin)

CLARK Kathleen McKenzie MB ChB 1968

CLARK Kenneth *MA 1970
s of William C. butchery worker, prod. man. and Jessie A. F. Smith shop asst; b Aber 24.3.48
DPhil(Glas) 1972 Dip Commun Work(Aber) 1976
group worker in therap commun Lond 1972–74; voluntary commun work Aber 1974–75; commun worker Powis Aber 1976–77; dev off. with Langstane housing assoc Aber from 1978
m Aber 6.4.79 Helen J. C. Noble BSc 1975 lab tech d of Charles C. N. Longside

CLARK Margaret Elizabeth *BSc 1964 PhD 1968
d of George C. machinist and Florence Robinson; b Sunderland 17.4.42
asst lect Belf 1967–69; dem univ coll Dub 1969–70
m N Ireland 24.5.69 William N. Osborough LLB(Belf) prof s of William T. O. Bangor Co Down

CLARK Margaret Jane MA 1969
d of George S. C. comp dir and Elizabeth W. Brown; b London 22.4.48
ICL Lond 1969–72
m Lond 31.7.71 David J. Ewles haulage contr s of Douglas J. E. Lond

CLARK Margaret Smith MA 1968 Dip Ed 1969
d of John S. C. publican, despatch clerk and Betsy G. de G. Garland restaurateur; b Broughty Ferry 7.6.47
invest analyst with advis serv to merch banks, insur co, stockbrokers etc. Lond 1969–71
m Dun 13.9.68 Kenneth M. Peebles lect civ eng Dund s of John A. P. Dun

CLARK Moira MA 1966
d of James C. polit constit ag/agr show secy and Margaret S. Cruickshank MA 1936 *qv*; b Turriff 8.11.45
Dip Sec Sc(Strath) 1967
Lond: edit. secy *Architect and Building News* 1967–68; p a group insur man. De La Rue Co 1969–72; insur off. from 1973
m Aber 28.9.68 Robert W. George MA 1967 *qv*

CLARK Moira Grant *MA 1960
d of Arthur C. oil drilling superv and Mary G. Fleming; b Aber 2.1.38
teacher mus Aber 1961–63, Aberdeensh from 1973

m Aber 5.7.63 Francis I. J. Fraser farm. s of Francis W. V. F. Findhorn

CLARK Peter William BSc(for) 1960

CLARK Ronald George [c]MB ChB 1956
s of George C. rly traffic controller and Gladys Taylor; b Aber 9.8.28
FRCSE 1960
h o ARI 1956–57; regist surg Western I Glasg 1958–60; res fell. surg Harv 1960–62; lect surg Glas 1962–66; Sheff: sen lect surg 1966–73, prof surg from 1973
m Dunbartonsh –.9.60 Tamar W. Harvie physioth d of Walter H. Duntocher

CLARK Ronald Thomson BSc(eng) 1967
s of John C. comm trav and Elsie Thomson shopkeeper; b Elgin 17.1.46
computer: logic des/progr Chelmsford 1967–70, syst des Stockholm 1970–72; computer consult.: Helsinki 1972–73, Lond 1973–75; banking res Lond from 1975
m Kirkwall 1.4.70 Sandra R. Lloyd teacher d of Douglas L. Kirkwall

CLARK Sally Ann LLB 1970

CLARK Stanley Ross MSc 1961
s of Cecil C. C. elect. and Gertrude C. Beazer nurse; b Berwyn Alta 8.3.37
BASc(Br Col) 1959 PhD(Manc) 1967
Athlone fell. 1959–61
def scient serv off. DRB Canada 1962–64; Commonwealth schol 1964–67; univ of Manit: res off. 1967–68, asst prof 1968–69; univ of Victoria: asst prof 1969–73, assoc prof c sc from 1973
m Nanaima BC 12.8.62 Mary Carney teacher d of Dennis C. Bradford

CLARK Thomas Fetzer PhD 1957
AB BD(USA)

CLARK Vivien Mary Pamela LLB 1970
d of Charles C. MB ChB 1943 *qv*; b Woolwich 19.1.49
law app, solic Clark & Wallace advoc Aber 1970–77; lect law Aberd from 1977
m Aber 26.2.72 Graeme L. Ogston LLB 1970 *qv*

CLARK William Gladstone Bartle MB ChB 1960
s of Evan C. civ serv and Lottie Johnston; b Invergordon 23.11.34
DA(Lond) 1963 FFARCS(Lond) 1967
h o ARI 1960–61; sen h o Leic RI 1961–62; resid anaest Charing Cross hosp Lond 1962–63; lect anat Brist 1963–65; anaest posts Brist, Manc, Salford, Stockport 1965–71; consult. anaest N Birm health dist from 1971
m Aber –.6.62 Margaret Hepburn nurs sister d of Alexander H. Aber

CLARK William James BSc 1970
s of William G. C. lorry driver and Jeannie A. Cheyne; b Fraserburgh 22.11.47
sen assoc syst progr with IBM (UK) Greenock from 1970
m Greenock 12.5.79 Anne S. McNelis youth/commun leader d of Roderick McN. Greenock

CLARK William Sneddon Reid *MA 1965

CLARK Winifred Campbell MA 1959
d of Ronald M. C. comp dir/haulage contr and Clara Melville; b Aber 29.6.38
teacher: Muirfield s Aber 1961–62, Middlefield s Aber from 1969
m Aber 22.12.61 Charles S. A. W. Levitt MB ChB 1961 *qv*

CLARKE Alexander Gordon MA 1965

CLARKE Audrey MB ChB 1961

CLARKE Avril Robertson MA 1965
d of William R. C. eng and Janet Anderson; b Glasg 4.7.44
Bangkok: teacher Engl 1966–68, Mrs Clayton's s 1968–74, Pattana s from 1974
m Aber 14.4.65 Prida Sananikorn BSc(agr) 1965 *qv*

CLARKE Mrs Margaret Elphinston
see Adam-Smith

CLARKE Muriel MB ChB 1957
d of Charles R. C. shopkeeper and Maggie D. Stewart; b Aber 15.9.33
h o, regist RACH 1957–60; trainee asst g p Aber 1960–61
m Aber 12.9.60 Donald A. Aitken MB ChB 1954 *qv*

CLARKE Peter Lawrence *BSc 1969

CLARKSON Susan Trevor MA 1964
m Adam

CLEGG Ian Alston *MA 1970
s of Alan C. secy NFU and Eva Leaver; b Burnley 8.4.47
posts Nat West. Bank Lond from 1970
m Aber 8.10.70 Joyce E. Butler MA 1969 *qv*

CLEGG John Roger BSc(eng) 1969
s of William F. C. dir and Catherine I. Kane; b Rochdale 25.12.46
CEng 1972 MIMunE 1972 MIStructE 1974
eng: in loc govt Carlisle 1969–73, with consult. eng Liv from 1973
m Rochdale 6.7.68 Judith H. Kirby d of Henry A. K. Rochdale

CLEGG Kathleen Mary PhD 1956
b Lancs 12.12.27
BSc(Manc) 1948 MSc(Manc) 1952
sen lect food sc and nutrition Strath from 1960

CLEMENTS Cyril George BSc 1970

CLERK Donald Edwin *BSc(agr) 1970
s of Archibald Clerk BSc(Glas) elect. eng and Cecilia M. Hay; b Elgin 2.7.46
ARICS 1974
VSO Mazabuka Zambia 1970–71, asst Moray Estates dev co Forres 1972–74; young farm. sponsored study tour NZ and Aust 1974–75; farm/estate man. Hayes Henderson & Co Elgin from 1975

CLOUSTON Erlend David Roger *MA 1970
s of David S. C. vet surg and Sheila M. Roger teacher; b Lerwick 3.5.46
sports journalist/arts correspondent *Liverpool Daily Post* from 1970

CLOUSTON Robert William BSc 1968
s of Rognvald C. caterer and Catherine H. E. Sinclair caterer; b Stromness 18.3.44
ALA 1970
Leeds: trainee lib 1967–70, lib inst geol sc 1970–73; Glos tech information serv Cheltenham: tech serv lib 1973–74, dep county tech information off. from 1974
m Aber 6.9.68 Vera F. Simpson MA 1966 *qv*

CLOWRY Brendan Patrick Michael *MA 1969

CLUBB Dawson Robert MB ChB 1964
s of William G. C. eng and Hannah M. Ironside; b Ellon 5.12.39
h o Aber hosp 1964–66; sen h o 1966–67; g p Edin 1967–70, Shetland 1970–73, Mintlaw from 1973
m Aber 2.7.65 Roberta Ratter art teacher d of Gilbert R. Lerwick

CLUNESS Anne Maureen MB ChB 1958
d of Alexander J. C. excise off. and Ann H. Garriock; b Lerwick 22.6.35
m Aber 5.7.58 Andrew P. Watt BSc 1955 *qv*

CLUNESS Sheila Margaret MA 1957

CLURE Ann Elizabeth LLB 1970
d of Denis J. C. civ serv and Elizabeth A. Brodie; b Aber 22.1.49
law app Balfour & Manson SSC Edin 1970–72; leg. asst James & George Collie advoc Aber 1972–73; solic Scot. Health Serv central leg. off. Edin 1973–78
m East Saltoun 8.10.77 Nigel J. Pollock LLB 1970 *qv*

CLYNE Isobel Anne MA 1956
d of William W. C. farm. and Isabella B. Forgie; b Boddam 2.1.35
teacher: Markinch s Inv 1957–62, St Peter's RC s Aber 1962–69, Northfield acad 1969–72
m Aber 4.7.72 Roy Will farm. s of Robert W. W. Fordoun

COAD George Nicholas MB ChB 1966
s of Evelyn Coad AMIEE chartered elect. eng and Gladys Hodgson teacher; b Bowdon 2.10.33
h o ARI 1967–68; g p Newhaven from 1969; part-time surg lt RNR 1969–73, dep police surg Seaford from 1969, div surg Newhaven div St John's ambulance from 1971, loc civ serv m o Newhaven from 1976
m Eastbourne 21.11.59 Barbara C. Welch d of Cuthbert C. W. MD(Lond) Eastdean

COATES Eileen Susan MA 1970

COBB Alice Margaret MA 1961 LLB 1963
d of Thomas G. C. police off., security off. and Jane Torrie; b Aber 25.4.41
leg. asst: c clerk Inv 1963–64, c clerk Lanarksh 1964–66; self-employed solic E Kilbride 1966–69; lect publ law N Staffordsh poly 1970–72, sen lect from 1972
m Aber 31.8.63 John M. Ayerst BSc(for) 1961 *qv*

COBB Ian BSc 1967

COBB Judith Mary BSc 1965
d of Martin Y. C. actuary and Mary Hay-Smith; b Esher 15.4.43
pers asst-syst analysis Shell Internat Petr Lond 1965–67; syst analyst Queen Eliz h Birm 1967
m Shere 15.4.67 John Cartmell BA(Cantab) chartered mech eng s of Geoffrey S. C. BA(Cantab) Brampton

COBBAN Alan Balfour *MA 1961
s of William C. fire off. and Annabella M. M. Balfour; b Aber 25.9.39
MA PhD(Cantab) 1965 FRHistS
Trinity Coll Cantab: res hist 1961–63, fell. 1963–67; lect med hist Liv 1966–75, sen lect from 1975

COBBAN Marion McArthur *MA 1970
d of Robert J. A. C. baker and Marion M. McArthur clerkess/typist; b Aber 24.2.49
Aber: cler off. HM Customs & Excise 1971–73; gen admin asst hosp man. from 1973
m Aber 13.9.71 Alasdair G. Roberts off. MN, BSc 1975 s of George A. R. Aber

COCHRAN Francis Gordon LLB 1960
s of David G. C. LLB 1925 *qv*; b Aber 7.4.34
BA(Oxon) 1957
advoc Aber from 1961
m Canford Cliffs 12.9.63 Ann J. S. Reynolds d of Leslie R. Dorset

COCKBURN George Gordon MB ChB 1956
s of George R. C. MA 1923 *qv*; b Aber 14.11.32
MRCGP 1962 DMJSoc Apoth(Lond) 1971
capt RAMC Dover, Edin 1957–60; h o mat. hosp Aber 1960–61; g p Aber from 1961; forensic med Aberd: hon asst 1963, lect path. 1969, part time asst from 1974
d Aber 28.1.79 *AUR* XLVIII 234

COCKBURN John Alasdair Murray LLB 1968
s of James R. M. C. MA(Cantab) indust man. and Evelyn M. Mathieson BCom(Edin); b Glasg 10.7.46
CA 1972
Coopers & Lybrand: Glasg 1968–73, Montreal 1973–74, Lond 1974–76, sen man. Glasg from 1976

COCKBURN John Shearer MB ChB 1966 ChM 1973
s of James C. shoemaker and Olive J. Shearer nurs sister; b Turriff 25.8.42
FRCSE 1970
h o, sen h o Aber 1966–68; sen h o Cardiff 1968–69; surg regist Aber 1969–71; res fell. surg Uppsala Sweden 1971–72; regist cardiac surg Glasg 1973–74; sen regist cardothoracic surg: Lond 1974–75, S'hampton from 1975
m Keith 30.4.69 Ethel M. M. Duncan shoe buyer d of George A. D. Keith

COCKBURN Sarah Caudwell *MA 1960

COCKER James Ian Burnett BSc 1964
s of John W. C. joiner and Jeannie M. Allan shop asst; b Banchory 6.3.42
teacher maths Banchory acad from 1965
m Stonehaven 1.7.67 Winifred C. C. Hopper teacher p e d of Noel B. H. MB ChB 1950 *qv*

COCKERHAM Barry *BSc(eng) 1969
s of George C. MA(Cantab) civ serv and Winnefred Graver; b Edgeware 4.2.47
CEng MICE
asst eng(struct) with consult. eng Lond from 1969
m Ashtead 14.11.70 Mary M. Cooper bank clerkess d of John C. Kirkwall

COCKSHOOT Ian BSc 1968

COHEN Daniel LLB 1966
s of Eli C. missionary and Olive M. Mackay nurse; b Leeds 22.5.46
teacher: VSO Jaiama s s Sierra Leone 1966–67, grad contract 1967–68; Aber: law app 1968–71; solic Fraser & Mulligan advoc 1971–75, ptnr 1975–78; ptnr Cohen & McCaw advoc from 1978
m Aber 10.4.72 Kathleen M. Buchan d of John W. B. Aber

COHEN Grant Irving MB ChB 1959
s of Sam N. C. MB ChB(Leeds) g p and Joyce Gillow; b Sunderland 14.3.33
LRCSE LRCPE LRFPSGlas 1960
Sunderland: h o gyn gen hosp 1959–60; h o gen med RI 1960; g p from 1960; also clin asst diabetes in pregnancy antenatal clin gen hosp 1973–76

m Newcastle 29.3.60 Laura Osterman lib asst d of Myer O. Newcastle

COLE Andrew John Latham MB ChB 1969
s of John G. L. C. MB ChB(Birm) med pract and Peggy C. Bryant MB ChB(Birm) med pract; b Birm 30.12.43
h s Charles Johnson mem hosp Nqutu Zululand 1969; h p Gulson hosp Coventry 1970; E Birm hosp: sen h o 1970–71, sen h o infect. diseases 1971–72, sen h o path. 1972–73; regist radiol United Birm hosps 1973–75, sen regist radiol 1975–78; consult. radiol Dudley Rd hosp Birm from 1978

COLE James Kolawole *BSc(eng) 1956

COLE John MA 1967
s of John G. C. eng and Margaret I. H. Campbell nurse; b Buckie 2.12.45
teacher: spec asst Portessie 1968–72, asst prin guid Buckie h s from 1972

COLLERAN Ethel Mary BSc 1958
d of James C. labourer/storeman and Mary J. Ingram; b Fochabers 20.12.35
lab tech biol Unilever Sharnbrook 1958–61; Bedford: lab asst agr Mander coll 1967–68; part-time teacher: Putnoe j s 1968–69, biol Mander coll 1969–70; full-time supply teacher from 1973
m(1) Bedford 18.2.61 Gordon W. Cruickshank nav off. s of Arthur L. C. BSc 1928 *qv*; husb *d*
(2) Bedford 30.3.70 Terry Westgarth carpenter s of William A. W. Bedford

COLLERAN Nan Park Dunbar BSc 1959
d of James C. labourer/storeman and Mary J. Ingram; b Ellon 20.11.37
exper off. geol surv of Gt Britain Edin 1959–66
m Edin 30.10.65 Robert Jackson BSc(eng)(H-W) civ eng, lect coll tech Dun s of Robert H. J. Edin

COLLEY Reginald James PhD 1965
s of William H. C. BA(Cantab) headmaster and Martha-Jane O. Hayton; b Woodford Green 22.5.29
BSc(agr)(Leeds) 1951 Dip Agr(Leeds) 1952
internat civ serv OECD Paris from 1966

COLLIE George Scott *MA 1961 Dip Ed 1962
s of George S. C. lab tech and Priscilla Hart teacher; b Liverpool 18.1.40
AFIMA 1971 MSc(Dund) 1974
teacher maths: St Andrew's h s Kirkcaldy 1962–65, spec asst Berwicksh h s Duns 1965–67; lect coll of tech Dun from 1967
m Aber 19.7.65 Barbara Gall MA 1960 *qv*

COLLIN Peter Paterson MA 1968
s of George C. fisherman/security guard and Agnes Buchan; b Peterhead 24.1.46
teacher Clerkhill s Peterhead 1969–71, dep head 1971–75; head Hatton (Cruden) p s from 1975
m Peterhead 27.9.72 Anne M. Melville shop asst d of Ronald M. Peterhead

COLLINS Edwyn Patrick MB ChB 1956
s of Edwin G. C. MB ChB(Edin) ENT surg and Elizabeth M. Baird art teacher; b Inv 31.10.31
h o ARI, Dr Gray's hosp Elgin 1956–57; RAF m o from 1957; wing comm from 1971
m Aber 9.2.60 Thelma K. McIntosh radiogr d of Robert P. McI. Aber

COLLINS Pamela Joy BSc(agr) 1970

COLLINS Peter Munro *BSc(eng) 1970
s of Herbert D. C. MB ChB 1941 *qv*; b Aber 1948
site eng Lond 1970–71; des eng Cardiff from 1971

COLMAR Kenneth Edwin BSc(eng) 1957
s of Geoffrey C. C. lect and Agnes T. Forrester; b Aber 5.12.34
MIHE 1959 MICE 1961
grad asst eng Cumberland c c Carlisle 1957–60; asst eng Argyll c c Lochgilphead 1960–63; asst div surv W Perthsh Dunblane 1963–64; Ross & Cromarty c c: dist surv Black Isle Muir of Ord 1964–71, dep county surv Dingwall 1971–75; div eng (roads/trans) Ross & Cromarty div Highland reg Dingwall from 1975
m Lossiemouth 11.7.59 Morag C. Hardie teacher d of George A. H. Lossiemouth

COLQUHOUN Robert *BSc(eng) 1965

COLVILLE Christine Peters *MA 1970 CASS 1974
d of John C. nurseryman and Jessie Nichol; b Alloa 19.1.49
soc worker Aber 1974–75; lib asst Aberd 1976; res asst educ Aberd from 1977
m Aber 12.6.73 David W. Stewart MA 1973 journalist s of David L. S. MA 1930 *qv*

COLVILLE Penelope Mary MA 1965
d of Duncan J. F. C. farm. and Catriona M. MacLean; b Campbeltown 9.2.45
educ edit Blackie & Sons Glasg 1966–69; teacher Mombasa Kenya 1971–72
m(1) Campbeltown 2.7.65 Ian G. Grossert BSc 1966 *qv*; husb *d* 10.11.73
(2) Johannesburg 12.12.75 Quentin D. Grearson BSc (Glas) prod. man. Ayliffe Cables, Edenvale S Af s of Lester D. G. Parkstone

COLVIN Michael Bruce BSc(eng) 1969

COLWELL John Henry Murray *BSc 1969 PhD 1977
s of Henry C.; b Buckie 22.4.47
ABPsS 1977
res stud. Aberd 1969–72; sen lect psych Middx poly from 1972
m Lond 4.9.71 Jennifer Fitzpatrick BSc 1972

COMLOQUOY Sheena MA 1970
d of John H. C. MB ChB(Edin) g p and Christina H. Allan; b Edin 25.3.49
civ serv HIDB Inv 1970–71; teacher Dumfries 1972–77
m Edin 27.12.72 Alexander Wilson farm. s of Alexander W. Dumfries

CONDIE Adrian Peter ᶜMB ChB 1956
s of Robert H. C. art teacher and Margaret G. Rennie art teacher; b Brechin 1.11.32
DObstRCOG 1959 MRCOG 1963
h o Aber hosps 1956–57; nat serv m o Singapore 1957–59; sen h o Durh, N'cle hosps: 1959–61, regist obst and gyn 1961–64; sen regist obst/gyn Birm hosps 1964–68; consult. obst/gyn NW Thames reg health auth—Edgeware gen hosp Middx from 1968
m Dun -.9.64 Marjorie R. Sword med secy d of Percy S. Dun

CONDIE Roy Gordon MB ChB 1966 ᶜMD 1975
s of Robert H. C. DA artist/teacher and Margaret G. Rennie DA teacher art/dom sc; b Aber 6.3.42
DObstRCOG 1968 MRCOG 1971
h o, sen h o Aber 1966–70; regist obst Dun 1970–72; res fell. Aberd 1972–73; sen regist/lect Aber teaching hosps 1973–76; visiting sen lect univ of Brisbane 1975–76;

consult./sen lect obst/gyn Birm area health auth/Birm univ
m Aber 4.1.65 Wilma M. P. Cruickshank MA 1967 *qv*

CONN Brian Gordon *BSc 1968 MSc 1971

CONNOCHIE Henry John Gray BL 1957
s of William D. C. advoc in Aber and Muriel Milne; b Aber 17.2.29
NP 1962
Henry J. Gray & Connochie advoc in Aber: law asst 1957–59, ptnr 1961, sen ptnr from 1966; dir N of S board Eagle Star group from 1976
m Aber 29.8.57 Marguerita C. Cowie radiogr d of George C. Aber

CONNON Alexander MA 1964
s of George C. cooper and Mary A. M. Morrison weaver; b Peterhead 1.4.26
Aber coll of comm: teacher 1965–74, asst stud. advis from 1974
m Aber 26.9.52 Jessie C. Duthie secy, teacher shorthand typewriting d of Gilbert D. Aber

CONNON Gylymn John Douglas MA 1967

CONNON Rhoda Anne Elizabeth *MA 1961
d of John H. C. agr contr and Annie Barrack; b Daviot Aberdeensh 10.5.39
teacher: Fyvie 1962–65; part-time Wick h s 1969–74, Anna Ritchie s Peterhead from 1974
m Aber 21.4.62 Douglas M. Fraser BSc 1961 *qv*

CONNOR Richard Bridges *MA 1970
s of Richard C. bus conductor and Nellie Bridges; b Aber 4.5.38
teacher Engl: Summerhill acad Aber 1971–73, Studierrat-Gymnasium Nordhorn W Ger 1973–74, asst prin Engl Balwearie h s Kirkcaldy from 1974
m Aber 8.12.62 Audrey Porter

CONROY James William Hendry *BSc 1966 MSc 1971
s of William C. driver/timekeeper and Beatrice Munro receptionist; b Elgin 2.10.43
biol i/c ornithol res with Brit Antarctic Surv Aber, Lond, Huntingdon, Antarctica 1966–74; establishment div BAS 1974–77; inst terrestrial ecology Monks Wood exper stat from 1977

CONSTANTINIDES Costas Costa MB ChB 1956
s of Costas C. merch and Joanna Karletti; b Cyprus 10.2.28
DO(Lond) 1961 FRCS(Glas) 1965 FRCSE 1966
h o: Stracathro hosp 1957–58, ARI 1958–59; Glasg eye infirm: sen h o 1960–61, regist 1961–63, sen regist 1963–66; consult. ophth: Kuwait 1967–68, Abu Dhabi from 1968
m Aber 26.7.63 Dorothy M. Thorburn MA 1963 *qv*

COOK Aileen Barrie Swankie MA 1969 MEd 1971
d of John H. C. policeman, miner and Annie B. E. Swankie dispensing chem, teacher; b Dunfermline 20.4.47
teacher handicapped infants Aber 1970–76, asst head from 1976

COOK Archibald Noel *MA 1966

COOK David Ashley MB ChB 1967
s of Henry B. C. MB ChB 1921 *qv*; b Leeds 28.3.43
Aber: h o geriat, orthop, ophth 1967–68, ENT, dermat 1968–69; Hull sen h o: gen med 1969, neurol 1969–70, g p and neuro surg 1970; Dun: sen h o gen med renal med 1971, regist gen med chest med 1971–73; Leeds: s h o obst and gyn 1973–74; g p: Beauly 1974–75, Thirsk from 1975
m York 2.4.71 Elaine P. Warren nurs sister d of Gerald W. York
d Thirsk 12.3.78 *AUR* XLVII 360

COOK Gordon James *MA 1970
s of Wilfred C. gen man. and Josephine Bartle; b Aber 1.4.48
DMS(Edin) 1973 AMBIM
salesman Edin from 1970
m Aber 1971 Maureen C. Thomson teacher d of James T. Aber

COOK Gordon Watt *MA 1961
s of Robert C. banker and Rose J. Wight; b New Deer 4.2.39
DRSS 1963
statist Cardiff 1962–65; lect statist: univ of Essex 1965–67, St And 1967–68, Aberd from 1968
m Aber 19.8.67 Frances O. Williamson MA 1962 *qv*

COOK Graham George BSc 1970

COOK Irene Brodie MA 1958
d of Andrew C. police off. and Isabella G. Brodie; b Lonmay 3.3.37
teacher Leeds 1959–63 and from 1973
m Aber 9.6.62 Alan Tiffany eng man. s of Frank T. Leeds

COOK Jennifer Valerie BEd 1970
d of Norman C. painter/decorator and Catherine Leslie shop asst; b Aber 30.7.49
teacher Engl Sir John Cass Redcoat s Lond 1970–73, head careers dept from 1973
m Aber 21.12.70 Roderick S. Anderson BSc 1969 *qv*

COOK Josephine Anne Harlow MA 1961
d of Harold H. C. RN, teacher and Mira S. Gyte teacher/authoress; b Settle 28.8.40
WRNS Reading and Petersfield 1961–62; radio oper Cornwall 1962–63, Gibraltar 1963–64
m Brazil 29.5.64 Michael J. Robinson telecomm eng (Cable & Wireless) s of Frank J. R. Tunbridge Wells

COOK Martin Robert MA 1968

COOK Ramsay *BSc(agr) 1964

COOK Richard Keith Daxon BSc(eng) 1969
s of Douglas R. J. C. mech eng/comp dir and Phyllis E. M. Smith; b Hillingdon 22.4.46
BAC Bristol: R & D test eng 1969–71, syst eng from 1971
m Amersham 3.8.68 Michelle M. Stoessl BSc(eng) 1969 *qv*

COOKMAN Gerald Philip *BSc(for) 1961
s of Giles C. CA and Laura E. Haines; b Devizes 9.10.39
MSc(Syracuse NY) 1964
agronomist Mexico, S America from 1964

COOKSON Henry John Angus BSc 1970
s of Robert P. C. LRCP med pract and Barbara A. Mair SRN; b Huntly 24.8.47
invest. analyst: stockbrokers Lond 1970–73, pension fund man. York from 1974

COOMBS Janet MA 1966
d of Ronald P. C. cutler and Jean H. Sanders nursing auxil; b Sheffield 4.3.45

Engl lang asst Arles 1967–68; teacher: Sheffield 1968–70, head mod lang 1970–73, Bassaleg Wales from 1973
m Sheffield 4.8.73 Peter B. Giles ship's off. MN s of Bernard G. Sheffield

COONEY Eileen *MA 1970
d of Robert H. C. political organis, bldr, crane slinger and Annie McPherson; b Aber 18.3.48
teacher Engl Cumbernauld 1971–72
m Aber 1971 Alan B. Grant MA 1968 *qv*

COONEY Neil *MA 1965 Dip Ed 1966
s of George T. C. watchmaker and Joan F. Howie comb-polisher; b Aber 17.8.43
teacher: hist Harlaw acad Aber 1966–70, prin hist Cults acad from 1970
m Aber 10.8.62 Aileen J. Thomson cashier d of David T. Aber

COOPER Alan Gordon *MA 1968

COOPER Elaine Hilda MA 1966
m Stalker

COOPER Gillian Anne MB ChB 1968
m Robin F. Johnston MB ChB 1962 *qv*
killed in accident in Aust along with her two children

COOPER Ingrid Margaret Jane MA 1969
d of Harry J. C. C. physioth and Margaret J. Hay teacher; b Aber 8.12.47
teacher Fr/Ger: Stonehaven 1970–71, Stromness from 1971
m Orphir Orkney 2.4.74 Ronald E. Tait boatbuilder/ chief steward, purser P & O ferries Orkney s of Edwin C. T. Toab Orkney

COOPER Kathleen Stuart MA 1958
d of James C. farm. and Georgina E. Wilson teacher; b Buckie 9.2.39
teacher: Aber 1959–63, W Lothian 1963–64, Moray 1964–66, Renfrewsh 1966–69
m Buckie 3.3.66 Robert J. Shiach aircraft eng s of Robert S. Kingston

COOPER Michael *MA 1968
s of Alexander S. C. clerk and Elsie Milne staff nurse; b Aber 13.10.43
teacher: asst prin Engl Breadalbane acad Aberfeldy from 1969
m Aber 27.12.67 Jennifer A. Angus MA 1967 *qv*

COOPER Robert Gary MB ChB 1961

COOPER Simon John BSc 1968

COOPER Stephanie MA 1970
m Wright

COOPER William David *MA 1959 *MEd 1970
s of William D. C. bookbinder and Florence M. Brown bookbinder's asst; b Aber 14.11.36
teacher: Engl Morgan acad Dun 1960–61, r e Waid acad Fife 1961–66, spec asst Engl RGC Aber 1966–71, prin Engl Bankhead acad 1972–74, asst head 1974–75; asst dir of educ Grampian reg council from 1975
m Edin 11.7.64 Gillian F. A. Porteous MA(Edin) teacher d of Norman W. P. MA(Edin), Edin

COOTE Audrey Elizabeth BSc 1970
d of William C. bus. man. and Janetta Agnew; b Omagh Co Tyrone 21.11.47
teacher maths Bearsden acad from 1971
m Omagh 5.8.71 Robert H. B. Gardiner BSc 1970 *qv*

COPEMAN Mary Evelyn BSc 1963
m Michie

COPLAND Alison Anne *MA 1968 PhD 1971
d of Gordon S. C. eng draughtsman and Agnes Fraser secy; b Aber 2.10.46
teacher mus: West Calder h s 1972–74, Mary Erskine s Edin from 1974; part-time tut. OU from 1974
m Aber 12.4.75 David H. Guest BSc(H-W) eng s of John H. G. Balerno

COPLAND Annabel Moira *MA 1956

COPLAND Graeme McAllan ᶜMB ChB 1956

COPLAND John Murray *MA 1957
MA(Oxon)

COPLAND Robert James MA 1970

COPLAND Valerie Agnes MA 1970
d of Gordon S. C. draughtsman and Agnes Fraser secy; b Aber 20.7.49
teacher: Garrowhall 1971–73, Park s Glasg 1973–74, Crown s Inv 1975
m Aber 4.4.72 Kenneth G. Cantlay BSc(eng) 1969 *qv*

CORBETT Catherine Mary BSc 1967 Dip Ed 1968
d of Alexander R. C. bldg contr and Jessie A. Fraser nurse/asst matron; b Tain 6.3.46
teacher: maths/sc Inv 1968–71, maths Birm 1971–73, maths/sc Lond from 1973
m Tain 10.7.71 Alexander C. Skinner BSc 1968 *qv*

CORBETT Daniel Ferguson BSc 1965

CORBETT Ian Leslie BSc(eng) 1959

CORBETT James BSc 1965

CORDINER Ian Callan BSc 1965
s of John H. C. MA 1935 *qv*; b Dalbeattie 11.10.42
teacher: Aboyne acad 1966–75, prin phys from 1975
m Huntly 29.7.67 Margaret R. MacDonald MA 1967

CORDINER Peter Stephen *BSc 1970
s of George L. C. and Janet C.; b Aber 5.10.42
Dip Ed(Belf) 1971
teacher: Kirkton h s Dun 1971–72, Kirkcaldy h s 1972–73; 2nd elect. off. MN 1973–74; teacher Summerhill acad Aber 1974–77; educ psych Elgin from 1977
m 6.8.77 Catherine Cameron hosp secy d of Hugh C.

CORDINER Sheila Elizabeth West MA 1968
d of Robert W. C. MA 1948 *qv*; b Aber 21.11.45
edit. asst D.C. Thomson Dun 1968–69; teacher Engl Joensun Finland 1969–71
m Peterhead 20.7.71 Thomas F. Taylor chief tech RAF

CORDINER Stella BSc 1970
m Sykes

CORFIELD John Richard MSc 1970
s of Ronald A. C. acct and Gladys E. Smith; b Stratford-upon-Avon 15.12.40
BSc(Brist) 1962
hosp physicist Lond 1963–65; med physicist: Copenhagen 1965–66, Aber 1966–69, Canterbury from 1969
m Copenhagen 1966 Agnes D. Seehuusen computer progr d of Sven T. R. S. Copenhagen

CORMACK Arthur Paterson BEd 1969
s of Arthur P. C. and Jane E. Glass; b Aber 5.10.34
teacher Aber from 1969

CORMACK Elizabeth Anne MA 1970
d of Robert J. C. shopkeeper and Ivy Sanders; b Dingwall 22.5.49
Aber: teacher trg 1970–71, shop asst 1971–72, clerkess computer changeover 1972–73
m Strathpeffer 6.8.71 Peter G. Savage MA 1972 s of George G. S. Edin

CORMACK Elspeth MacDiarmid MA 1968
d of Alexander C. C. MA 1950 *qv* and Moira N. J. MacDiarmid MA 1941 *qv*; b Aber 7.5.47
RGN 1975
Engl lang asst Bonn 1968–69; Edin: teacher Engl Portobello s s 1970–72, Royal h s 1972–73; stud. nurse ERI 1973–75, staff nurse ERI 1975–76; Aber: dist nurse trg from 1977

CORMACK Geoffrey George MA 1966

CORMACK Ian Richard *BSc 1967 Dip Ed 1968
s of Alexander C. C. furniture store man. and Mary J. Farquharson; b Aber 24.3.45
teacher AGS 1968–75, prin geog Cults acad from 1975
m Aber 7.7.73 Moira Hunter teacher p e d of Sydney H. Cults Aber

CORMACK Ingrid Alexandra Jane MA 1964 LLB 1966
d of Alexander K. C. insur off. and Elsie M. Dickson shorthand typist; b Dun 24.1.43
RGN 1973
law app Aber 1966–68; leg. asst: Edin 1968–71, Aber c c, Grampian reg c 1974–77
m Aber 2.12.77 John K. M. Dodds BSc(eng) 1967 *qv*

CORMACK James Gordon MA 1961
s of James E. C. master carpenter/joiner and Jessie G. Smith MA 1930 *qv*; b Newmachar 15.3.40
Dip Bus St(Strath) 1965
syst rep Dun 1961–64; pers man. Linwood 1965–67; man. consult. UK and overseas; Lond: pers dir 1971–73, self-employed man. consult. from 1973
m Guisely 10.5.69 Carol A. Wood secy d of Alfred W. Guisely

CORMACK Jennifer Anne MA 1970
d of John C. under-secy DAFS and Jessie M. Bain; b Edin 3.10.48
Dip Secy Ling(Westminster coll Lond) 1971
secy: Rank Xerox Lond 1971–73, conference asst *Financial Times* Lond 1973–74, pers asst joint res centre Ispra Italy from 1974

CORMACK John *BSc 1967
s of George A. W. C. labourer and Ethel M. Youngson; b Aber 3.2.45
working in nuclear med in Aust
m Adelaide Aust 4.1.74 Jane Shearer d of James S.

CORMACK John Dickson MB ChB 1962
s of Alexander K. C. insur off. man. and Elsie M. Dickson secy; b Aber 18.9.38
DObstRCOG 1965 DCH(Glas) 1971 LMCC 1972
h o: Aber hosps 1963–64, Bellshill mat. hosp 1964–65; g p Aber 1965–67; paediat regist Aber/clin tut. ch health Aberd 1967–71; g p Oakville Ont 1971–76; asst med dir Canada Life Ass. Co Toronto from 1976
m Laurencekirk 12.9.65 Katherine L. Spalding RGN d of David M. S. Laurencekirk

CORMACK Marjorie Forbes MA 1961
d of Joseph C. castings controller and Janet S. Erskine pianist; b Fraserburgh 9.10.40
teacher: Aber 1962–64, Surrey 1964–65, Grangemouth part-time from 1973
m Aber 5.8.64 Allan J. Macarthur BSc 1961 *qv*

CORMACK Patricia *MA 1957
d of James C. shopkeeper and Betty McKay; b Peterhead 19.7.35
teacher: Fr St Margaret's s Aber 1958–60, mod lang Aber acad 1960–63; housemistress Windsor girls' s BFES Hamm Germany 1963–66; dep head Downs s Compton Newbury 1966–69; lady advis Bellshill acad 1969–70; dep rector Hazlehead acad Aber from 1970

CORMACK Richard Melville PhD 1961
s of William S. C. BSc(Glas) prin tech coll and Jean W. Niven teacher; b Glasg 12.3.35
BSc(Lond) 1954 BA(Cantab) 1955 MA 1962 Dip Math Stat(Cantab) 1956 FRSE 1974
Aberd: asst statist 1956–58, lect 1958–66; visiting asst prof univ of Wash. 1964–65; sen lect Edin 1966–72; prof statist St And from 1972
m Aber 1.9.60 Edith Whittaker BSc 1957 *qv*

CORMACK Robert John *MA 1969

CORMIE David Ian *MA 1962
s of David E. D. C. chartered surv and Jessie T. Brown; b Aber 18.8.38
trainee pers off. Lond 1962–66; pers off. Brentwood 1966–67; Lond: pers man. 1967–72, group indust relations advis from 1972

CORMIE Gordon David *MA 1965
s of James C. C. painter and Nora M. Blandford lib; b Sleaford 15.4.43
Dip Town Plan(Leeds) 1970 MRTPI 1973
res off. min of housing and loc govt Leeds 1965–71; sen plan. asst Edin city plan. dept from 1971
m Worsbrough Bridge 2.12.67 June Mitchell town plan. d of Donald M. Worsbrough Bridge

CORMIE Stewart Dufton BSc 1970

CORNER Alexander Wallace *MA 1967 Dip Ed 1968
s of Alexander M. C. army off., ironmonger and Joan T. Paterson; b Bangalore India 19.9.44
teacher: Macduff 1968–69, Banff acad 1969–74, prin history Peterhead acad from 1974
m Aber 2.8.72 Sheila M. C. Bell teacher p e d of James B. Dumfries

CORNFORTH Hazel MB ChB 1961

CORSE Douglas Alexander *BSc 1963
s of David W. C. and Janet Tulloch; b Orkney 16.2.40
MS(Corn) 1966 PhD(Corn) 1968
grad asst Corn. 1963–68; England: res scient Nat Inst res in dairying 1968–73, nat cattle exec Cooper Nutrit Products Witham 1973–75; man. sales advis centre BP Nutrit (UK) Witham from 1975
m Kirkwall 5.8.65 Jennifer A. S. Harcus d of Edward S. H. H. Kirkwall

CORSE John Oliver MB ChB 1968

CORSER Charles McKenzie MB ChB 1959
s of James R. C. MA 1928 *qv* and Mona Meldrum MA 1928 *qv*; b Pluscarden 18.2.36
DObstRCOG 1960 MRCPsych 1975
h o: Woodend Hosp Aber 1959–60, Raigmore hosp Inv

1960–61; g p Bolton 1961–65, Elgin 1965–73, g p, psychiat Livingston 1973–76; consult. psychiat Bangour village hosp from 1977
m Aber 1.10.60 Sheila M. R. McKechnie nurse d of Duncan McK. Aber

CORSIE Edward Ogilvie MA 1962
s of Robert G. C. bank man. and Jane A. O. Mattewson; b Hopeman 11.5.41
teacher: Engl/hist Newmill s s 1963–65, hist Lossiemouth h s 1965–69; head Boharm p s 1969–72; dep head Kinloss p s 1972–73; head Mosstodloch p s from 1973
m Buckie 5.8.67 Kathleen A. Hargreaves teacher d of John S. H. Elgin

CORSIE Mary MA 1970
m Reid

COSTELLO Heather Pauline McKenzie MA 1965
m Long

COTHLIFF Margaret Maud *MA 1968

COULL Alexander Bruce MB ChB 1957
s of David C. MRCVS(Edin) vet surg and Janetta Bruce MA 1921 *qv*; b Buckie 21.1.33
DObstRCOG(Lond) 1962
h o ARI 1957–58; short serv comm RAMC Ghana, Belgian Congo 1958–61; h o obst/gyn St Alfese's hosp Greenwich 1961; g p Thorpe Bay from 1961
m Aber Elizabeth J. L. Baxter civ serv d of William B. Turriff

COULL Dorothy Carnegie MB ChB 1965 MD 1970
b Aber 27.3.42
MFCM 1974
Aberd: res fell. therap 1966–69, lect commun med 1970–79; commun med spec Grampian health board from 1979
m Aber 21.8.70 Moir

COULL Douglas MA 1962

COULL Isobel Ronald MA 1961
d of David B. C. mech and Isabella E. Ronald shop asst; b Aber 12.6.40
teacher: Glasg 1961–63, Leeds 1964–65, Hull 1965, Leeds 1967, W Wickham 1974–78; prin Lat/housemistress W Wickham from 1978
m Aber 9.3.63 Alexander W. Still BSc(eng) 1961 *qv*

COULL James Alistair Bruce *MA 1966
s of James C. burgh surv and Isabella Bruce; b Aber 13.3.44
teacher classics: Brechin h s 1967–68, AGS 1968–71; prin classics Turriff acad from 1971

COULL James Reid *MA 1957 PhD 1962
s of William C. fisherman and Jeannie Reid; b Peterhead 18.2.35
dept geog Aberd: asst 1959–61, lect 1961–71, sen lect from 1971

COULL James West MA 1967

COULL John Taylor MB ChB 1958
s of John S. C. fish merch and Ethel M. Taylor; b Aber 4.3.34
FRCS 1965
h o Aber 1958–60; sen regist: surg Edin 1963–65, traumolology Birm 1967–70; lect orthop Edin 1970–71; serv RAMC, later consult. orthop surg BAOR from 1971, consult advis Br army orthop surg Lond from 1977
m Aber 27.12.58 Mildred Macfarlane MA 1956 *qv*

COULL Sandra Margaret MA 1965
m Smart

COULL William BSc 1961 MA 1962 MEd 1971
s of William C. fisherman and Jane R. Reid; b Peterhead 27.1.39
teacher Aber 1963–71; Elgin: educ psych 1971–74, teacher from 1974
m Buckie 17.7.68 Charlotte M. Thoresen teacher d of Otto T. Buckie

COUPER Alastair Dougal *MA 1962 Dip Ed 1963
s of Daniel A. C. bldr and Devina Riley; b Aber 4.6.31
PhD(ANU) 1967 FCIT 1974
lect Durh 1966–69; prof UWIST Cardiff from 1969
m Aber 30.8.58 Norma Milton civ serv d of Clifford M. Aber

COUPER James Alexander MA 1957
s of James W. C. butcher and Georgina Walker shop asst; b Aber 3.6.35
nat serv sergt instr RAEC, chief instr Engl app chef school Aldershot 1957–59; teacher Engl: Fernhill s mod s Farnborough 1959–60, Hilton s s Aber 1961–66; Aber: dep head Airyhall p s 1966–73, head Cloverfield p s from 1973
m Port Glasg 3.8.63 Jean R. Kane teacher d of George A. K. Port Glasg

COUPER Laureen Margaret MA 1970
d of James C. clerk and Margaret A. Williamson; b Lerwick 18.12.49
teacher Engl/Fr: Webster h s Kirriemuir 1971–73, Aith j h s Shetland from 1973
m Voe Shetland 20.7.73 Allan Johnson bldr s of George J. Girlsta

COURT Roger James *BSc 1963

COURT-BROWN Charles Michael BSc 1970
s of William M. C-B. MB ChB(St And) prof genetics and Caroline G. S. Thom radiogr; b Edin 3.2.48
MB ChB(Edin) 1975
m Edin 6.7.74 Jacqueline Y. Q. Mok MB ChB(Edin) g p d of Mok To Leong BA(Nanking) Kuala Lumpur

COUSAR Charles Blanton PhD 1960
s of Robert W. C. ThD(Virg USA) min and Irving Blanton; b Charlottesville Virg USA 7.2.33
AB(Dav Col NC) USA 1955 BD(Col Theol Sem) USA 1958
Col Theol Sem Georgia USA: asst prof NT 1960–64, assoc prof 1964–66, prof from 1966, dean of acad affairs from 1971
m Tallahassee Florida 10.9.55 Elizabeth C. Bowen AB (Oglethorpe) d of Reeves B. Tallahassee

COUSINS John Alexander BSc(eng) 1958

COUSINS Roger Lee *BSc(agr) 1969
s of Leonard H. C. sub-postmaster and Anne Eustace clerkess; b Coulsdon 11.6.46
MS(Corn) 1973
lect Corn. New York 1970–71; res assoc Edin 1973–74; sen res assoc E Ang 1974–75; sen res off. Dartington Amenity Res Trust (Dart) from 1975

COUTINHO Maria de Lourdes Pamela MB ChB 1963
d of Basil M. T. C. auditor and Timothea D'Souza teacher; b Aden 11.2.38

BSc(Bom) 1956 DTM & H(Liv) 1965
h o: Ontario, Aber, Dun, Banstead, Lond, Nott 1962–69; regist Lond: Whittington hosp, Royal Free hosp, St Ann's 1969–72, g p from 1972; FPA clin from 1970

COUTTS Alan Maxwell MA 1967
s of William C. comm trav and Janet M. Barclay; b Edin 28.7.45
CA 1971
Glasg: app 1967–71, audit asst 1971–73, taxation asst 1973–75, man. from 1975
m Bearsden 11.1.74 Dorothy Baird teacher d of William N. B. Glasg

COUTTS David *BSc(eng) 1962
s of George C. newsagent, hosp porter and Joan Gray; b Aber 8.5.40
MIHE 1964 MICE 1965
asst site eng Newport Wales 1962–64; bridge eng: asst Carlisle 1964–66; Glasg: chartered eng 1966–68, superv from 1968
m Aber 6.8.62 Margaret G. Angus BSc 1960 *qv*

COUTTS Elizabeth Anne *BSc 1962
d of Gordon C. farm. and Bella Taggart; b Durris 13.10.40
teacher biol High s for girls Aber 1963–66; lect biol Cambridge coll of f e from 1966
m Aber 27.7.65 Alan J. Thomson BSc(agr) 1963 *qv*

COUTTS Evelyn Margaret *MA 1959
d of Thomas C. pharm and Evelyn Gordon teacher; b Aber 23.1.38
PhD(St And) 1972
teacher: Leeds 1960–61, Dublin 1961; asst lib Irish cent lib and TCD Dublin 1962; teacher: Madras coll St And 1964–66, Bell Baxter h s Cupar 1966–68; univ lect Columbia Mo USA 1969; prin geog Madras coll from 1970
m Aber 3.8.61 John A. Soulsby MA 1959 *qv*

COUTTS Findlay MacRury MA 1964 LLB 1966
s of William L. C. barman and Kathleen Findlay secy; b Aber 16.3.43
law app Hamilton t c 1966–69; town clerk Cupar 1969–75; dir admin Dunferm dist c from 1975
m Aber 16.4.68 Christina G. Leathem MA 1966 *qv*

COUTTS Hamish Michael BSc(agr) 1970

COUTTS Ian George Cormack *BSc 1960 PhD 1964
m Aber 1968 Fiona Wood MB ChB 1968 *qv*

COUTTS John Gordon MB ChB 1969

COUTTS John Isbister MB ChB 1958
s of Thomas C. master mariner and Mary A. Peterson nurse; b Aber 29.3.34
h o Woodend hosp Aber 1958–59; Tasmania: NW gen hosp Burnie 1959–62, g p Somerset from 1963
m Wynyard Tasmania 7.3.69 Susan E. Harris nurse d of Geoffrey P. H. Burnie

COUTTS Kathleen Margaret BSc 1969
d of Frank Coutts PO worker and Jean A. T. Mackie; b Stonehaven 29.8.48
Dip Ed(Edin) 1970
teacher Craigie h s Dun 1970–71; civ serv DHSS Dun from 1971

COUTTS Penelope Ann MA 1970
d of Alexander D. C.; b London 16.5.48
Cert for teachers of deaf(Manc) 1971
remed teacher s for deaf Aber from 1974
m Herts 9.1.71 Jeremy C. L. Saunders Stonehaven

COWAN George Sheppard Marshall MB ChB 1964

COWAN Torquil Hamish MA 1967
s of Robert J. C. civ eng/elect. consult./hotelier and Agnes P. B. Borley secy; b Invergordon 10.9.46
Dip Ed(UCNW) Cert Curric Stud(Keele) 1974
Wales: teacher Holywell c s 1968–70; St David's h s Saltney: head Engl 1970–74, head fac of commun and lang from 1974
m Lloc 21.8.70 Enid W. Hughes loc govt clerk d of Samuel H. H. Lloc

COWAP Sheila Mary Leslie MA 1968
d of William L. C. film lib naval base and Mary Strachan shop asst; b Ellon 3.6.46
Lond: Chelsea and Kensington hosp man. comm: various admin posts 1968–72, New Charing Cross hosp Fulham: admin off. equipping new hosp 1972–73; Civil Aviation auth temp typing 1973; City and Guilds of Lond Inst prod. of craft level exam papers and syllabus dev from 1973

COWARD Helen Mary MA 1967

COWE (Cowan) James McDonald MA 1957
s of Andrew B. C. fisherman and Maggie McDonald; b Fraserburgh 17.1.36
nat serv 1958–60; teacher Fraserburgh acad 1960–65; dep head Fraserburgh centr s 1965–67; head: Kininmonth p s 1967–71, Fraserburgh South Park p s 1971–75, Fraserburgh Central from 1975
m Aber 4.8.59 Kathleen J. Dey teacher d of George A. D. Fraserburgh

COWE Sybil Norma MA 1957 Dip Ed 1958

COWELL Susan Elisabeth MA 1965
d of John C. headmaster and Florence J. Atkinson teacher; b Allerton Bywater 20.12.43
teacher Castleford 1966–68 and from 1975
m Leeds 5.8.67 Harry Cox headmaster s of Harry C. Castleford

COWIE Alan *MA 1959 Dip Ed 1960

COWIE Alexander Bertram MA 1968

COWIE Alison Kilgour MA 1965
d of John M. C. bank man. and Norah R. Kilgour; b Aber 18.1.44
teacher Fr: Aber acad 1966–69, Perth acad 1970–72
m Aber 29.12.69 Hugh M. Smith asst man. insur s of Hugh S. Aber

COWIE Alistair Gordon *BSc(eng) 1970
s of Gordon C. nursery man. and Jessie Reid; b Portgordon 12.7.48
proj eng-struct Lowestoft 1971–72, Lond 1973–74; struct des eng Sarawak Malaysia from 1975

COWIE Carol Ann Cummings BSc 1966
d of James R. C. boardinghouse owner and Helen McBeth shop man.; b Aber 27.6.45
exec off.: spectrochem Macaulay inst Aber 1966–67, computer progr econ div NOSCA Aber from 1979
m Durris 7.1.67 Hugh M. Shepherd agr eng instr and advis s of Kenneth J. S. Durris

COWIE Carol Mary MA 1964
d of George A. C. master plumber and Caroline S. Masson; b Glasg 9.5.43

teacher: Brandon 1965–67, Princes Risborough 1974–76, High Wycombe from 1976
m Stanley 24.7.65 Andrew Nall BSc(for) 1964 *qv*

COWIE Doris MA 1960

COWIE Ethel Margaret *MA 1957 Dip Ed 1958
d of Alexander E. C. upholsterer and Jessie A. Murray; b Aber 19.3.35
teacher: Montrose 1958–61, Lond 1962–66, Falkirk 1966–72, Lond from 1972

COWIE Frederick Cleveland Fulton MA 1962
s of Frederick M. C. eng and Evelyn M. Fulton; b Aber 7.4.41
teacher: RGC Aber 1963–67, Services p s Accra 1968–69, head humanities dept Gatow m s Berlin 1970–76, 4th yr co-ord Derby m s Osnabrück from 1976
m Aber 3.8.67 Jeanette I. Jack MA 1966 *qv*

COWIE Gordon Manson *BSc(for) 1966
s of Charles G. C. grocery man. and Flora M. Manson; b Insch 30.4.44
dist for. off. II Fort William 1966–68; asst educ off. Dean Foresters Training s; dist off. man. serv div For. Comm res stat 1971–74; dist off. I Fort Augustus from 1974
m Tidenham 6.3.71 Elizabeth M. O. Hewitt teacher ballet d of Arthur R. J. H. Chepstow

COWIE Isabell Catherine MA 1960
d of John M. C. bank man. and Norah R. Kilgour; b Aber 15.3.39
teacher Engl/Fr Perth 1961–62
m Aber 1.9.62 David Jack BSc(agr) 1954 *qv*

COWIE James BSc 1964 MB ChB 1969
s of James C. security off. and Annie Buchan; b Banbury 9.2.42
MRCP(UK) 1972
h o ARI 1969–70; sen h o, regist Lond 1970–73; sen regist Oxford 1973–77; consult. phys Plymouth from 1977
m Aber 21.6.66 Anne L. Backett BSc 1965 *qv*

COWIE James D. MA 1967
s of Patricia A. C. canteen asst; b Aber 6.8.45
MSc(Lond) 1974
res off. min of agr Leeds 1967–73, 1974–75, N'cle-u-Tyne from 1975
m Leeds 27.5.69 Mandy R. Ure teacher, civ serv

COWIE Jeannie Reid MA 1956
d of James C. farm. and Agnes Farquhar; b Cornhill 21.9.35
teacher maths: Keith 1957–58, Powis s s Aber 1958–61, remed maths Dun 1973–76
m Aber 2.8.58 Hance Fullerton BSc 1956 *qv*

COWIE John *BSc 1964 MEd 1978

COWIE Margaret Stephen *MA 1968

COWIE Marion Patricia *MA 1957 Dip Medieval St 1968 MLitt 1970
d of George S. C. men's outfitter and Edna M. Littlechild bus. acct; b Aber 25.5.36
Dip Ed(Lond) 1958
teacher: Chatelard s Les Avants Switzerland 1958–59, Abbey s R'dg 1959–62, Engl lang Athens 1963, Kingsley s Leamington Spa 1964–67
m Aber 11.8.69 John H. Swogger BA(Kansas) Dip Medieval St Aberd 1969 s of Leo G. S. MA(Kansas) Topeka Kansas

COWIE Maureen Menzies MA 1970
d of Joseph C. journalist and Annie B. Menzies secy; b Aber 1.10.48
Dip Youth ESTB 1971
careers off. Stirlingsh 1971–72; soc worker Fraserburgh 1972–73; careers off. Aber from 1973
m Aber 15.8.72 James Murray BSc 1971 med res tech s of James M. Aber

COWIE Michael MA 1969
s of James C. credit ag and Vera T. Sutherland; b Aber 10.12.47
MEd(Glas) 1977
teacher St Thomas Aquinas s s Glasg 1971–73; housemaster Bellshill acad 1973–75; asst prin mod stud. Camphill h s Paisley 1975–79; prin mod stud. Hawick h s from 1979
m Glasg 7.4.73 Jennifer A. Lake teacher d of Cecil C. F. L. Glasg

COWIE Nettie Isabella MA 1957

COWIE Stanley Windsor MA 1961
s of James C. trawl skipper and Agnes A. Smith; b Aber 25.7.37
teacher: Summerhill acad Aber 1962–64, Dailly p s Ayrsh 1965–68, Shortlees p s Kilmarnock 1969–75; trained as teacher of deaf 1975–76; teacher West Park s for partially hearing Crosshouse from 1976

COWIE William Pirie *BSc 1958

COWKING Thomas Leonard *MA 1968
s of Thomas C. bldr and Alice A. Harrison; b Settle 24.3.47
banker Lond from 1969
m Giggleswick 18.7.69 Philippa J. S. Jackson MA 1969 *qv*

COWLING Geoffrey John PhD 1968
BSc BD(Syd)

COWLING Terence Ian *BSc 1968
s of William C. motor mech and Edna M. Hook; b Aber 29.11.45
computer progr Winchester from 1968

COWN David John *BSc(for) 1967
s of William J. C. bldr and Isobel W. Diack MA 1933 *qv*; b Huntly 21.12.44
PhD(B Col) 1976
asst br man. Tilhill for. Elgin 1967–69; res scient for. res inst Rotorua NZ 1969–73 and from 1976
m Rotorua 19.12.70 Paula C. Hutton MA(Canterbury) teacher d of William M. H. BSc(Birm) Marapara

COWPER Hugh William MA 1968
s of John C. marine eng and Catherine M. P. Chisholm teacher; b Forres 10.9.46
teacher maths: Nairn acad 1969–73, Elgin acad 1973–74; asst prin maths Forres acad from 1974, asst prin guid from 1976
m Dallas Moray 16.7.76 Elizabeth Campbell MA 1977 museum asst d of Peter C. Kellas

COWPER Rosemary Hartell MA 1970
d of James A. C. cler off. Scot. gas and Joan S. Smith secy; b Penicuik 7.8.48
Dip Secy (coll of comm Aber) 1971
Edin: secy southern hosp board of man. 1971–72, to group eng 1973, to matron Elsie Inglis mat. hosp 1973–76, to gen admin Lothian health board s dist from 1976

COX Anthony Raymond Cole BEd 1969

COX Cecil Joseph MB ChB 1961
s of Henry C. prop. and Iris D. Hughes; b Trinidad 6.1.25
WHO fell. 1964 DPH(Tor) 1965 LMCC 1972
h o Aber hosps 1961–62; Trinidad: gen med, surg 1962–64, county m o h 1965–67; reg dir med serv Tobago 1967–69; m o h Port of Spain 1969–71; m o h Renfrew county Canada 1971–73; g p Cambridge Canada from 1973
m Aber 3.11.58 Franziska M. Nottelmann midwife d of Johann N. Gross-Reken Germany

COX Eric Frank *BSc 1963
s of Albert C. grocer and Lillian L. Frost teacher; b Ely 3.2.41
PhD(Nott) 1966
res scient nat veg res stat Wellesbourne Warwick from 1966
m Nott 7.6.65 Avril H. Redfern nurs nurse d of Albert R. Nott

COXON Philip Stanley MA 1970
s of Stanley C. ord surv and Ivy I. Rosher play s superv; b Derby 6.12.44
Aber: stud. teacher, stud. lib 1970–71; Inv: for. worker Dochfour estate, reindeer herder Aviemore 1971–72; asst warden Royal Soc Protection Birds Wales, England, Outer Hebrides from 1972

CRABB David Iain Charles BSc(eng) 1961

CRAIB Margaret *MA 1961
d of Andrew A. C. trawl skipper and Margaret R. Mair; b Aber 21.6.34
Aber: teacher Engl Aber acad, Hazlehead acad, St Margaret's s for girls, Rubislaw acad 1963–74; asst prin Engl Harlaw acad from 1975
m Aber 9.10.59 Anastasius Eleftheriou BSc 1964 *qv*

CRAIG Alexander Souter *BSc 1968
s of Joseph C. fish merchant and Mary R. Souter; b Gourdon 20.12.46
phys: field trials Hawker Siddeley Dynamics Hatfield 1968–70, inst dev dept Barr & Stroud from 1970
m Aber 10.7.68 Dorothy F. Carnie MA 1967 *qv*

CRAIG Alison Margaret *MA 1969
d of George A. C. acct and Dorothy Forbes telephonist; b Aber 10.4.47
Dip Ed(Edin) 1970
teacher: hist Dumbarton acad 1970–74, Jeddah prep s Saudi Arabia from 1975
m Aber 18.7.73 Robert H. Thomson BSc(Strath) civ eng s of James T. Dumbarton

CRAIG Alison Mary MA 1958
d of Joseph C. and Mary R. Souter; b Gourdon 31.12.36
teacher: Mackie acad Stonehaven 1959–60, Killin s 1960–64, Prince Charles' s Kitwe Zambia 1964–66, Thurso h s 1968–74, Oban h s from 1974
m Aber 23.12.59 Ronald Mackay MA 1957 *qv*

CRAIG Amber Margaret MA 1967
d of Andrew C. MA 1932 *qv*; b Aber 26.6.45
Dip Lib St(Belf) 1968; ALA 1970; Dip Hist of Art(Belf) 1972
sen lib asst Greenisland 1968–69; Down Co library 1969–70; asst lib Down Co 1970–71; sen asst lib Down Co Lib (later S-E Educ Lib Board) from 1971
m Peterhead 27.12.69 James R. R. Adams lib s of Alexander A. Ballybofey

CRAIG Andrew MA 1966
s of Andrew C. MA 1932 *qv*; b Stonehaven 17.1.43
teacher-trg 1966–67; instr off. RN HMS *Ganges* 1967–69; transfer to gen list seaman spec HMS *Plymouth* Far East 1969–71, HMS *Lincoln* Far East 1971–73, HMS *Kent*, Medit 1973, HMS *Phoebe* 1973–74, RNC Greenwich 1974, HMS *Dryad* 1975, HMS *London* 1975–76, HMS *Excellent* 1976–77, HMS *Ark Royal* 1977–78
m Inv 13.4.68 Jennifer M. Hutchinson teacher d of Laurence H. BSc(Durh) Inv

CRAIG Cecilia *MA 1966
d of Alexander M. C. fisherman and Elizabeth K. Gray; b Forfar 10.11.43
Lucy Fell(Aberd) 1966; MLitt(Cantab) 1972
univ teacher Waterloo Lutheran univ Ontario 1966–67 and 1972–73; teacher Wellshot s Glasg Jan–June 1972; lect Wilfrid Laurier univ Waterloo Ontario (formerly Waterloo Lutheran univ) 1973–74; teacher Mackie acad Stonehaven from 1975

CRAIG Evelyn Rose MA 1962
m Scott

CRAIG Isobel Milne MB ChB 1966
d of John C. civ serv and Gertrude M. Milne; b Aber 22.2.42
h o, sen h o gyn, dermat, gen med, psychiat Aber 1967–70; m o FPA: Teesside 1971–72, Birm 1973–75
m Aber 21.7.67 Peter A. Slater MB ChB 1966 *qv*

CRAIG James Alexander MB ChB 1958

CRAIG James Boyle PhD 1963
s of Albert C. machinist and Jessie Boyle; b Aber 12.7.32
CChem MRIC
post-doct res asst Oxford univ 1963–64; scient off. Macaulay inst for soil res Aber 1964–66; post-doct res fell. Aberd 1966–67; lect chem Aberd from 1967
m Aber 11.11.70 Ann M. Bannerman telecomm traffic supt d of Charles L. B. Aber

CRAIG John Austin BSc 1963

CRAIG Joseph BSc(eng) 1960

CRAIG Lesley Catherine *MA 1967 *MEd 1969
d of William G. W. C. comp man. and Catherine S. Ewen; b Aber 2.1.44
teacher Fr Hazlehead acad Aber 1969–75, asst prin mod lang Summerhill acad Aber from 1975

CRAIG Margaret Patricia MA 1956

CRAIG Norma Rennie *MA 1959
d of Daniel F. C. co-op soc man. and Jean A. Anthony secy; b Glasg 25.8.37
teacher hist: Keith 1960–62, Aber 1962–64; lib asst Glasg from 1974
m Aber 8.9.62 James G. Kellas MA 1958 *qv*

CRAIG Peter Michael *BSc 1967
s of John P. Craig MA 1927 *qv*; b Ballater 13.8.45
govt geol: Honiara Br Solomon Is 1968–70, Edin from 1970
m Aber 22.11.47 Marjory A. Gall BSc 1966 *qv*

CRAIG Robert MA 1960

CRAIG Robert Lawrence *BSc 1970
s of Robert E. C. BSc(Edin) marine phys and Dorothy A. Lawrence MA 1967 *qv*; b Edin 16.8.48
phys Barr & Stroud Glasg from 1970
m Aber 17.7.71 Kathleen E. M. Robertson MA(Glas) teacher d of Robert R. BSc 1965 *qv*

CRAIG Robin Alexander MB ChB 1969
s of James L. C. LLB(Glas) county clerk Aberdeensh and Annie H. McCulloch; b Dumfries 18.12.44
Aber: h o ARI and city hosp 1969–70; sen h o Cornhill hosp 1970–71, g p from 1971
m Aber 10.4.74 Lynda M. Sutherland teacher d of William S. BL 1935 *qv*

CRAIG Roger Kingdon *BSc 1970 PhD 1974

CRAIGHEAD Peter Bruce BSc 1961 *1963
s of Peter C. journalist and Eliza B. L. Bruce typist; b Aber 19.1.40
ARIC 1968
teacher Aber: chem RGC 1964–71, prin chem Kincorth acad from 1971
m Aber 5.4.65 Margaret Hay teacher d of David H. Aber

CRAIGHEAD William Arthur MA 1957

CRAIGIE Alasdair Shaw BSc(eng) 1966
s of Hugh H. C. farm. and Margaret Shaw; b Inv 21.1.43
asst eng: Geo Wimpey & Co. Helensburgh 1965–66; W. Tawse: asst eng Clacton-on-Sea 1966–68, site ag Aber, Edin, Laurencekirk 1968–73, contr man. Aber 1973–76; dir CHAP Construct. (Abdn) from 1976
m Aber 4.4.74 Ada J. Newlands RGN d of William N. Buckie

CRAIGIE James Alexander BSc(agr) 1961
s of James R. L. C. farm. and Tina S. Matheson teacher; b Sandwick 15.1.39
poultry man. Inv 1961–64; farm. Cawdor 1964–67 and from 1969; tech rep Isaac Spencer Aber 1967–69
m Nairn 6.10.62 Doreen Allan secy d of James A. Nairn

CRAIGIE Jean Roberta MA 1956
d of William I. C. master grocer and Jane S. Wilson; b Fraserburgh 29.8.34
teacher: Middlefield s Aber 1957–62, Inverallochy 1962–69, Fraserburgh inf s from 1969

CRAIGIE Peter Campbell MTh 1968
s of Hugh B. C. MB ChB(Manc) CBE chief m o mental health Scot. and Lilia C. Murray SRN; b Lancaster 18.8.38
MA(Edin) 1965 Dip Th(Durh) 1967 PhD(McM) 1970
asst prof: Carleton univ Ottawa 1970–71, McM Hamilton Ontario; assoc prof Calg Alberta from 1974, head of dept from 1977; author *The Book of Deuteronomy* (Eerdmans) 1976
m Edin 5.9.64 Elizabeth Alexander MB ChB(Edin) phys d of Charles A. Edin

CRAIGMILE Arthur Brown MA 1957

CRAIK Ian William *MA 1970

CRAMB Maurice Quentin *MA 1962 Dip Ed 1963
s of Maurice C. MA 1932 *qv*; b Aber 4.2.40
teacher Engl: Gordon s Huntly 1963–64, AGS 1964–69 (spec asst from 1967), prin Engl Madras coll St And 1969–72; HMIS: W of Scot 1972–75, national spec Engl, convener Engl panel of HM Insp from 1975
m Aber 31.3.64 Diane P. Lawrie MB ChB 1967 *qv*

CRAMB Thomas James BSc(for) 1957

CRAN George Castle *MA 1969
s of William C. and Minnie Cran; b Inverurie 30.6.47
PhD(R'dg) 1973
operations analyst MoD Sevenoaks from 1973
m Prudhoe-on-Tyne 22.12.73 Catherine J. Harrand

CRAN Gordon William *BSc 1963
s of George W. C. cashier and Annie C. Scroggie; b Aber 3.9.41
Dip Stat(Oxon) 1965 PhD(Belf) 1972 FRSS 1966
Queen's univ Belf: asst lect 1965–67, lect from 1967
m Belfast 4.8.73 Elizabeth A. Riddell staff nurse d of William R. Belfast

CRAN James Douglas *MA 1969
s of James C. and Jane McDonald; b Kintore 28.1.44
Lond: res off. Conservative res dept 1970–71; secy nat assoc of pension funds from 1971
m Lond 7.4.73 Penelope B. Wilson d of Richard T. P. W. Lond

CRANE Nicola Hilary Francis *MA 1970
d of Bryant F. F. C. MA(Cantab) clerk in holy orders and Gwendoline M. Hughes BA(Cantab) teacher; b Brighton 6.4.47
Dip Secy St(Strath) 1971
secy to Inst fin. and invest. Stir 1971–72; admin asst Midlothian c c Edin 1972–75; secy to acad board and dir sixth form stud. Newton Abbot Devon group of s s from 1976
m Congleton 15.7.72 Robin M. Orr BSc(agr) 1971 post grad stud. s of Robert M. O. MA(Edin) Kirknewton

CRAVEN Janet Margaret MA 1970
d of Stanley N. A. C. BSc(eng)(Lond) C eng and Margaret L. French, teacher; b Wakefield 29.3.49
ASO Dunstaffnage marine lab Oban 1971; ASO hill farm. res organis: Edin 1971–73, Bush Estate, Penicuik from 1974
m Oban 20.6.70 Robert M. Brown BSc(St And) elect. eng s of Robert B. Tayport

CRAVEN Linda Joan Mary *MA 1969
d of Edward C. bank man. and Alice F. McWhor comm artist; b Meols Wirral 6.9.46
Dip Soc Ad(Liv) 1970
Kirkby: asst playleader 1970–71; asst commun dev off. 1971–73; area commun dev off. Huyton Knowsley from 1974
m Huyton N Liverpool 18.12.71 Colin A. Brown instrument mech. s of George S. B. Maghull

CRAW William *MA 1967 Dip Medieval St 1968
s of Alexander M. C. turner and Jane H. Bain carpet des, clerkess; b Paisley 10.3.38
post grad/part-time tut. Aberd 1968–69; res Paris 1969–70; Rennes: lecteur d'Anglais univ de Haute-Bretagne 1970–72, lecteur in Institut universitaire de technologie, univ of Rennes 1972–73; lect Fr Glas from 1973

CRAWFORD Derick Alexander BSc(agr) 1956
s of Theodore A. C. MB ChB(Edin) med pract and Marjorie E. Leith; b London 5.12.31
Macheke Rhodesia: conserv and extension off. 1956–58, tobacco farm asst 1958–63, man. 1963–65; Belfast: asst man. cigarette dev 1965–71, prod. des man. 1971–73; Montreal: gen man. res and dev 1973–74, dir res and dev from 1974
m Aber 5.10.57 Elizabeth L. Donald MA 1957 *qv*

CRAWFORD Frederick *MA 1958
s of Frederick A. C. rly clerk and Alice C. Barron; b Aber 13.8.36
teacher Engl Ellon from 1959; Ellon town councillor 1972–75
m Aber 13.7.60 Frances M. Bishop MA 1958 *qv*

CRAWFORD George Patrick Mitchell *MB ChB 1970 *MD 1975
s of George C. insur comp man. and Nellie Mitchell MA 1932 *qv*; b Aber 12.10.46
MRCP (UK) 1972
h o Aber 1970–71; res fell. dept med Aberd 1971–72; MRC jun res fell. Aberd 1972–75; lect med Aberd 1975–76; sen lect med haematol post grad med s univ Lond 1976–77; sen lect med univ W Aust from 1977
m Aber 27.7.67 Allison M. Irvine BSc 1967 *qv*

CRAWFORD John Richard PhD 1958
BA(KCTenn) BD(Theol Sem Richmond Virg)

CRAWFORD Sarah Herdman MA 1965
d of Ronald C. biscuit manuf and Isabel Herdman; b Edin 23.11.43
secy course Lond 1965–66
m Kinloch Rannoch 21.5.66 Lionel G. D. Barclay farm. s of Charles B. Dess

CRICHTON Rhoda BSc 1961

CRICHTON Ronald MA 1957 *1959

CRICHTON Roy Williamson *BSc 1968
s of Alexander M. C. MA 1932 *qv*; b St And 8.4.46
Dip Ed(Makerere coll univ E Af) 1969
teacher: Kapsabet s Kenya 1969–71, housemaster Bishopbriggs h s Glasg 1971–74; prin guid Craigroyston h s Edin from 1974
m Glasg 2.7.73 Hazel P. Barker MA(Glas) teacher d of Benjamin B. Torrance

CRIGHTON Barbara Anne Moncrieff MA 1964
d of David M. C. advoc Aber and Eileen A. Troughton; b Portadown NI 31.5.43
teacher: Prestonpans p s 1965–70
m Aber 4.8.67 John H. McLaren arch./plan. consult. s of John McL. Aber

CRIGHTON George Innes BSc(eng) 1960

CRIGHTON Joan Beveridge MA 1967 Dip Ed 1968
d of William C. C. postal and tel off. and Annie B. S. Beveridge; b Glasg 7.12.46
teacher maths Mackie acad Stonehaven 1968–75
m Stonehaven 16.8.75 William M. Steele MB ChB 1971 g p s of Edgar W.S. Loth

CRIGHTON John Watson BSc(eng) 1960
s of Thomas T. C. county road surv/civ eng and Mary D. Watson governess; b Elgin 15.5.39
MIMunE 1963 MICE 1966 MIHE 1978
asst eng Argyll c c 1960–64; asst eng, sen eng Perth & Kinross joint c c 1964–75; team leader Tayside reg c from 1977
m Aber 17.7.64 Helen M. L. Kerr teacher dom sc d of Joseph T. K. Aber

CRIGHTON Maureen Ross MA 1965
m Smith

CRITCHLEY Carol Mary MA 1966
d of Thomas A. C. civ serv/under secy and Margaret C. Robinson; b Lond 24.12.43
teacher: Leyton Lond 1966–67, Basildon 1967–69, Kidderminster from 1969
m Hampstead 23.7.66 Alexander W. Mathieson MA 1966 *qv*

CROALL Margaret Matheson *MA 1967
d of Peter S. C. man. dir and Peggy Matheson secy; b Stornoway 5.1.45
gen admin asst NE reg hosp board Aber 1967–68; secy Belford hosp Fort William 1968–69; sen admin asst NE reg hosp board 1969–71
m Kelso 9.5.70 Alexander Halliday BSc(Glas) prod. man. s of Alexander H. Wishaw

CROCKETT Edward John *MA 1962

CROCKETT George Watt MA 1964

CROCKETT Isobel Margaret BSc 1967
d of Alexander S. C. BSc(eng) 1942 *qv*; b Aber 4.8.45
teacher Broughton s Edin 1968–72
m Edin 21.3.72 Michael S. Fisher MB ChB(Edin) g p s of J. L. F. Huddersfield

CROCKETT Raymond Hughes *MA 1965 *MEd 1969
s of George C. RNat Mission to Deep Sea Fishermen Aber and Bessie Hughes ch sister; b Aber 10.5.43
teacher Engl West Calder from 1970

CROFTS Gillian Mary *BSc 1965
d of Richard B. I. C. comp dir and Vera R. Bland; b Shrewsbury 4.11.43
teacher: Liv 1965–66, Bebington 1966–69
m Aber 5.8.66 Alexander S. Philip BSc 1965 *qv*

CROFTS Harold Robert MB ChB 1959

CROLL Hugh MacArthur *MA 1965
s of John M. C. MB ChB 1929 *qv*; b Lincoln 3.7.42
ALA 1969
lib asst Aberd 1965–66; stud. s of librarianship Manc coll of comm 1966–67; Edin univ lib: sen lib asst 1968–69, asst lib from 1969

CROLL Neil Macarthur *BSc 1960
s of John M. C. MB ChB 1929 *qv*; b Sheffield 6.7.37
health phys Manc 1960–66; Rolls Royce Derby: computer progr 1966–69, information analyst from 1969
m Stretton-on-Dunsmore 18.3.61 Veronica M. Hill MA 1959 *qv*

CROMAR Neil LLB 1966
s of Peter C. lab and Isabella Leys; b Aber 24.5.45
law app 1966–68; solic A. C. Morrison & Richards advoc Aber from 1969
m Aber 4.4.70 Catherine F. H. Ross MA 1968 *qv*

CROMBIE Alan Shaw BSc(eng) 1960
s of Theodore C. construct. eng and Jessie T. Shaw MA 1931 *qv*; b Duns 19.10.38
Aber: asst eng city eng dept 1960–62, county eng dept 1962–64; Ross & Cromarty c c: asst eng 1964–70, sen asst 1970–74; comp dir Dingwall from 1974
m Aber 2.4.62 Anne M. Wood bank clerkess d of John J. W. Banff

CROMBIE Elspeth Mary MA 1961
d of David L. C. BSc(eng)(Glas) man. dir and Barbara C. Cumming; b Aber 14.4.40
shorthand typist: Ferranti Edin 1962–63, William Tawse Aber 1964–65, secy soil sc dept Aberd from 1965

CROMBIE Margaret Harben *MA 1961
m Ferguson

CROMPTON-NICHOLAS Eunice Lucinda *MA 1969
d of Carlton A. C. C-N. civ serv Jamaica and Margaret L. Lidstone saleswoman; b England 18.1.46
interpreter/private secy Argentine emb Jamaica 1969–71; exec asst/p r ag for private artist (painter) Jamaica, USA, S Amer from 1971

CROOK Ian Clitherow BSc(agr) 1968
s of Sidney C. med rep and Ida C. Clitherow; b Liv 8.8.45
Dip FMBO(NOSCA) 1969
rural dev off. dept agr Papua New Guinea 1969–71; W Aust: educ off. farm man. foundation of Aust Perth, farm man. consult. Dowerin from 1974
m Prestatyn N Wales 22.8.69 Gillian M. Hughes teacher d of Gwilym F. H. BA

CROOKSHANKS Noreen Meredith MB ChB 1958
d of George C. C. MA 1923 *qv* and Jean S. Gorrod BCom 1923 *qv*; b Aber 18.3.35
h o Hairmyres hosp E Kilbride, RAHC, Yorkhill hosp Glasg 1958–60; g p Stockport from 1971
m Aber 5.2.60 Hugh D. Baillie MB ChB(Glas) vascular surg s of Hugh B. Glasg

CROSGROVE Torrance Pringle MB ChB 1960

CROSKERRY Patrick George *BSc 1968

CROSSLEY Peter John *BSc 1968

CROW Charles Gordon David MA 1965 MEd 1973

CROW Timothy John PhD 1970
s of Percy A. C. BSc(Lond) loc govt off. and Barbara B. Davies; b Lond 7.6.38
MB BS(Lond) 1964 DPM 1971 MRCP 1972 MRCPsych 1972
lect mental health Aberd 1970–72; sen lect psychiat Manc 1973–74; head div of psychiat, clin res centre Northwick Park hosp Harrow from 1974
m Lond 22.1.66 Julie C. Carter BSc(Lond) med pract d of Eric G. H. C. PhD(Lond) Orpington

CROWE Walter Pressler MA 1969

CROXSON Jeremy Peter Gover BSc(eng) 1963
s of John A. G. C. oil comp exec, press and p/r and Jessica J. I. White, secy to MP; b Sutton 25.9.41
MICE 1968 AMIHE 1969
Sir Frederick Snow & Ptnrs: asst eng Lond 1963–66, resid eng 1968; site eng M62 Motorway Sir Alfred MacAlpine & Sons Yorks 1967; civ eng Brit Petr Co based in Lond from 1969
m Kenley Felicity Wilson-Brown airline receptionist d of Malcolm W-B. Kenley

CRUDDAS John Wilfred *MA 1963
s of John W. C. and Mary A. T. Herron; b Shotton Colliery 2.10.40
asst lect Engl and liberal stud. Darlington coll of f e 1963–64; liberal party organis for parl constit Roxburgh, Selkirk, Peebles 1964; secy to fac of soc sc St And 1964–67; secy to fac of soc sc and letters Dund 1967–68; admin asst N'cle 1968–70; gen asst to secy/prin admin asst univ coll Lond from 1970

CRUDEN John McNab BSc 1958 *1960

CRUDEN Norma Jeannette Margaret MA 1968
m Macdonald

CRUICKSHANK Alexander Esson BSc 1969
s of John C. hosiery mech and Agnes Esson; b Aber 3.4.48
Turriff: cost acct 1970–72, cost/wages man. 1972–74; acct Aber from 1974
m Aber 30.6.72 Alison E. Merson MA 1971 teacher d of John M. Aber

CRUICKSHANK Alfred Ian Duncan MA 1967

CRUICKSHANK Alistair Ronald *MA 1966
m Aber 29.3.67 Alexandra M. Noble MA 1965 *qv*

CRUICKSHANK Charles Ian *BSc(eng) 1961
s of Charles C. marine eng and Mabel Eddie; b Singapore 30.8.39
CEng MICE 1966 MIEA 1972 MIE(Hong Kong) 1978
civ eng: site eng Lond, R'dg 1961–63, des eng Edin 1963–66, des eng Vancouver, Calgary 1966–69, assoc Sydney 1969–77, ptnr John Connell & Assoc Hong Kong from 1977
m Tomintoul 26.3.66 Jane A. Stuart SRN d of William S. Glenlivet

CRUICKSHANK Colin James MA 1966

CRUICKSHANK David Keir Ross BSc(agr) 1957
s of Peter J. C. master butcher and Dorothy J. Ross SRN; b Fochabers 11.6.34
Dip Agr(Cantab) 1958 DTA(Trin) 1959
Zambia: agr off. 1959–63, anim husb off. 1963-64, anim husb res off. 1964–72, prin res off. from 1972

CRUICKSHANK Diana Christina *MA 1956
d of Ernest W. H. C. MB ChB 1910 *qv*; b Halifax Nova Scotia 21.3.34
BA(Cantab) 1958
lect: Bergen univ Norway 1959–62, Engl City of Leeds and Carnegie coll Leeds 1962–71, drama coll of educ Aber from 1971

CRUICKSHANK Don William *MA 1965
s of William C. lab tech and Mary E. Duncan nurse; b Fettercairn 16.8.42
PhD(Cantab) 1968
res fell. Emmanuel coll Cantab 1968–70; lect univ coll Dub from 1970
m Aber 12.8.67 Margrit R. Ritchie MA 1965 *qv*

CRUICKSHANK Donald Gordon MA 1963
s of Donald C. C. MA 1933 *qv*; b Elgin 17.9.42
CA 1967 MBA(Manc) 1972
corporate plan. Alcan Alum Newport 1967–70; McKinsey & Co Lond: man. consult. from 1972
m Aber 17.10.64 Elizabeth B. Taylor MA 1966 *qv*

CRUICKSHANK Edith Elsie *BSc 1964
m McBoyle

CRUICKSHANK Francis Robertson *BSc 1963 PhD 1966
s of Francis G. N. C. wood machinist and Margaret I. Robertson secy; b Aber 30.1.41
res fell. Stanford res inst USA 1966–68; lect phys chem Strath from 1968
m Aber 3.10.66 Joyce Muir cashier/telephonist d of James W. M. Aber

CRUICKSHANK Gordon Dyce MA 1969
s of John C. factory stoker and Maggie A. H. Dyce papermill worker, net braider; b Aber 29.9.26
teacher AGS from 1970
m Aber 23.3.51 Marion M. Stott MA 1946 *qv*

CRUICKSHANK Hugh Ogilvie Campbell *MA 1962
s of James C. rubber planter and Agnes Sherrif; b Malaya 13.12.16
teacher geog Aberfeldy 1963–68; prin geog/mod stud. from 1968
m Portsoy 2.8.58 Helen Wylie teacher home econ d of William J. W. Port Glasg
d 10.12.75

CRUICKSHANK Ian MA 1962
d Ayr 20.2.67 *AUR* XLII 376

CRUICKSHANK Isobel MA 1961
d of Duncan J. C. pharm and Isobel Milne; b Insch 29.9.40
teacher: Dunf 1962–63; Ashton in Lancs, Makerfield 1963–64; Bowdon 1971–72
m Aber 12.8.63 George M. Bath dent surg s of George B. Wigan

CRUICKSHANK James George *BSc 1957
s of Charles C. marine eng and Mabel Eddie receptionist; b Singapore 15.3.35
scient off. Macaulay inst for soil res Aber 1957–59; lect geog Belf 1959–72, sen lect from 1972; visiting lect: McM Ontario 1966–67, univ New England Armidale NSW Aust 1973
m Rotherham 22.9.62 Margaret M. Bower BSc(Lond) univ lect d of George B. Greasbrough

CRUICKSHANK John McRae cMB ChB 1966
s of William C. farm. and Mabel A. Cruickshank secy; b Ellon 17.12.42
DObstRCOG 1971
h o ARI 1966–67; Perth RI: sen h o, regist med 1967–70, sen h o obst and gyn 1970; g p Northallerton from 1970
m Beith 10.9.68 Ann L. Smith occup therap d of Robert N. S. Beith

CRUICKSHANK Leonard George *BSc 1968
s of Donald C. C. MA 1933 *qv*; b Banff 15.8.46
teacher maths/geog Saltus g s Bermuda from 1969
m Aber 27.12.67 Anne G. Brown MA 1968 *qv*

CRUICKSHANK Marna MA 1959 Dip Ed 1961
d of James C. auctioneer and valuator and Grace M. Boddie; b Cruden Bay 13.6.38
teacher: Engl/gen subj Kaimhill s s Aber 1961–66; classics Peterhead acad 1966–77, asst prin classics (i/c dept) from 1977

CRUICKSHANK Muriel Bremner MA 1962
d of George A. C. draper and Isabella Bremner; b Cornhill 9.12.41
Norway: lab sister Tana 1967–69, Askim 1970–77; soc worker Askim from 1977
m Aber 17.2.62 Per Spenning MB ChB 1965 *qv*

CRUICKSHANK Nancy Patricia MB ChB 1957
d of Robert C. MB ChB 1922 *qv*; b Milngavie 24.4.32
h o: Woodend hosp Aber, Farnham 1957–58; g p locum work Edin from 1958; g p Dalkeith from 1977
m Edin 7.3.58 Kenneth McLean MB ChB 1956 *qv*

CRUICKSHANK Ruth Alexander MA 1966

CRUICKSHANK Sheila MA 1964
d of John C. timber contr and Helen F. Davidson; b Aber 1.10.42
Dip Sec Sc(Strath) 1965
secy: to dir shipping comp Leith 1965–66, Edin univ 1966–73
m Aber 14.4.67 Robert H. C. Somerville shipbroker s of Peter C. S. BCom(Edin) Edin

CRUICKSHANK Stanley MB ChB 1963
s of Robert C. foreman painter LNER and Mary A. G. Aitken; b Insch 17.11.32
h o ARI, mat. hosp Aber 1963–64; g p Hull from 1965
m Aber 3.8.57 Mary E. Wallace MA 1954 *qv*

CRUICKSHANK William James BSc 1959 *1960

CRUICKSHANK Wilma Margaret Philip MA 1967
d of William C. farm. and Mabel A. Cruickshank; b Aber 24.6.46
teacher: Mile-End p s Aber 1968–70, Fr Aber 1973–75, Brisbane Aust 1975–76, Birm 1976–78; TEFL lang centre Birm from 1978
m Aber 4.1.65 Roy G. Condie MB ChB 1966

CUDDEFORD Derek MSc 1968
s of Charles W. C. civ serv and Janet N. Williams; b Hayes 10.5.45
BSc(Lond) MIBiol 1973
lect Edin from 1968
m Aber 17.2.68 Alison Lyall BSc 1966 *qv*

CULLEN Catherine Fraser *MA 1968 MLitt 1974
d of James C. teacher and Mary C. Fraser; b Hamilton 28.11.45
teacher Ger Harlaw acad from 1970
m Aber 12.7.74 Dirk Nikodem MA 1970 *qv*

CULROSS Brian Richard *BSc 1966
s of Kenneth A. C. printer's estimator and Marjorie E. Savournin; b Lond 12.9.43
Dip Indust Chem Pract & Man 1966
market res exec: Berk, Lond and Harlow 1966–69, Baird & Tatlock Chadwell Heath Essex 1969–70; E region Brit Gas Corp, Potters Bar: sen marketing res asst 1970–75, market res man. from 1975
m Lond 11.9.66 Lynn S. Davis secy d of Edgar H. D. Lond

CUMINE Patrick Gerrie BSc(eng) 1963
s of Joseph G. C. bank man. and Elizabeth G. Peterkin: b Dun 26.9.41
Aust: Sydney drawing off. 1965–67, Gladstone alum. smelter 1967–70; alum. smelter Invercargill NZ 1970–71; iron-ore conveyor belt Dampier W Aust 1971–73; cement factory Jacarta Indonesia from 1973
m Brisbane 26.12.69 Heather Lawrie

CUMMINE Duncan Penny MB ChB 1957
s of John M. C. MRCVS(Edin) vet surg and Annie S. Penny teacher; b Aber 17.3.34
DObstRCOG 1961 DCH(Lond) 1962 MRCGP 1976
h o ARI 1957–58; capt RAMC Nicosia Cyprus 1958–60; sen h o royal hosp for sick ch Brist 1962–63; regist Aber gen hosp 1963–65; g p Bo'ness 1965–69, Edin from 1970
m Edin 10.7.65 Sally J. Harris RGN nurse

CUMMINE John Anderson MA 1956

CUMMING Alastair McConnachie *BSc 1967
s of Alick C. fitter eng and Mary M. Innes; b Keithhall 19.8.45
res scient Whitehaven 1969–70; med genetics res asst Aberd from 1971
m Aber 2.8.69 Kathryn A. Cole d of Harry C. Aber

CUMMING Alexander James *MA 1968
s of Alexander G. C. MA 1938 *qv*; b Aber 7.3.47
ACMA 1973

teacher VSO Calcutta 1968–69; trainee acct Fort William 1970–72; comp secy Aber 1972–76; acct Grampian health board from 1976
m Perth 21.7.73 Margaret A. Callan MA(Edin) teacher d of John A. C. Perth

CUMMING Ann Patricia MA 1966
d of Patrick C. MA 1928 *qv*; b Broughty Ferry 6.11.43
Dip Sec St(Strath) 1967
m Aber 6.9.68 Malcolm S. Murray BSc(St And) brewer s of Randolph S. M. West Mersea

CUMMING Anne Davidson BSc 1965
d of William G. D. C. CA and Jane G. Golightly; b Inv 22.6.44
teacher maths: Morrison's acad for girls Crieff 1966–72, Kincorth acad Aber 1972–73
m Inv 2.8.71 Brian A. Stalker BCom(Edin) CA s of Anthony S. Crieff

CUMMING Arthur *MA 1960

CUMMING Elsie Jean MA 1968
d of Leslie D. C. comm trav and Jeannie T. Morrison secy; b Aber 29.10.47
teacher Springburn p s Glasg 1969–70
m Aber 15.6.68 Russell D. J. Pollock-Smith granite merch s of David P-S. Lenzie

CUMMING Francis BSc(agr) 1956 *1957

CUMMING Harold Greenfield PhD 1966
s of Roy E. C. BScA(Guelph)agr and Alburtta A. Greenfield piano teacher; b Gore Bay Ontario 1928
BA(Tor) 1951 MWM(Mich) 1953
Ontario: superv big game man. 1967–71; moose/caribou biol 1971–73; assoc prof fish and wildlife man. Wakehead univ Thunder Bay from 1973
m Gore Bay 31.7.71 Wilma L. Nothrop BA(Melb) teacher d of Wilmot N. farm. Lake Rowan Victoria Aust

CUMMING Jean Elizabeth MB ChB 1965
d of Alexander G. C. MA 1937 *qv*; b Lossiemouth 11.10.40
DObstRCOG 1967
h o: ARI, Woodend hosp 1965–66, paediat Inv RI 1966–67, obst Aber 1967; sen h o obst/gyn Taplow 1967–68; m o FPA clin Middx and Surrey from 1970
m Lond 27.12.67 Thomas G. Taylor MB ChB 1965 *qv*

CUMMINGS Leslie Peter Clement *MA 1960
s of James D. C. taxi driver and Winifred C. Briggs; b Guyana 14.4.33
PhD(Iowa) 1967 FRGS 1956
various posts Guyana, Canada, USA 1960–67; sen lect, head geog univ Guyana 1967; commonwealth fell./visiting asst prof univ Iowa USA 1968–70; visiting prof univ Papua N Guinea 1971; prof/dean fac Arts univ Guyana 1972–75; dir Mirev proj govt Guyana 1976; univ Guyana: dep vice chancellor 1976–79, vice chancellor 1979; Fulbright res fell. univ Puerto Rico from 1979
m(2) Guyana 22.12.78 Marva Scholl banker d of Cecil S. Guyana

CUNDILL Erica Dorothy MB ChB 1960
d of Eric T. C. LLB(Rhodes) lawyer and Kate V. Lamsley teacher; b Komgha Cape S Af 15.11.16
BA(S Af)
h o Aber 1960–61; g p Bolsover and Claycross 1961–62; S Af: hosp m o Lovedale 1962–68; Frere hosp E Lond 1968–69, Lovedale 1969–74, Grey hosp King Williamstown 1974–75; prin m o/actg supt Victoria hosp Lovedale from 1975

CUNNINGHAM Alison Jane *MA 1967
d of Alexander K. C. CA and Edith M. Dickson MB ChB(Glas); b Huddersfield 22.1.46
teacher Engl Ashington g s Northumberland 1968–70; caseworker Shelter Housing aid centre Edin 1970–71; asst reporter children's panel Lothian from 1972

CUNNINGHAM Donald Ian Alexander MB ChB 1956
s of Donald E. S. C. MB ChB(Glas) g p and Barbara S. Hinds; b Wolverhampton 18.2.33
DObstRCOG 1963
Stourbridge: h o 1956–57, regist gen med 1957–58; SSC RAF med branch, mass radiography München Gladbach Germany 1958–61; sen h o obst/gyn Wolverhampton 1961–62; g p: Dudley 1962–71, Dufftown from 1971
m Dudley 14.1.57 Mary K. Malvena civ serv Rowett inst Aber d of Alexander M. Bucksburn

CUNNINGHAM Elizabeth Mary MA 1968
resid Auchterarder
m Carmichael

CUNNINGHAM Gerald Andrew MA 1956 LLB 1958
s of John C. sawmaker and tool dealer and Mary Degnan; b Aber 6.3.35
nat serv Bordon 1959–61; Aber: leg. asst: town council 1961–64, Burnett & Reid 1964–68; Hunter & Gordon from 1968—firm later amalgamated with others as Stronachs, ptnr from 1969
m Aber 30.9.61 Lyn Carragher tv announcer d of Norman G. C. Aber

CUNNINGHAM Heather MA 1969
m Stern

CUNNINGHAM Margaret MB ChB 1960

CURNOW Robert Nicholas PhD 1959
s of Dr Reginald N. C. and Olive E. Curnow; b Derby 9.3.33
BA(Cantab) 1954 Dip Math Stat(Cantab) 1955
scient off. agr res council unit of statist Aberd 1955–61; Harkness fell. commonwealth fund USA 1959–60; R'dg: lect, reader, prof/head of dept applied statist 1961–74 and from 1977; dean faculty agr and food 1974–77
m Cornwall 1957 Vera J. Bull BA(Cantab) clin biochem

CURRIE Bruce McKenzie *MA 1970

CURRIE Ian Fraser *BSc 1961
s of John H. C. painter and Helen Murray; b Brechin 8.6.38
scient civ serv RRE Malvern 1961–72 and from 1973; Maitre de conference associé Grenoble univ 1972–73
m Brechin 1959 Evelyn F. Findlay art teacher d of Robert F. Glenlivet

CURRIE Kathleen Isobel *MA 1969
m Harry

CURRIE Mairi Morrison *MA 1969
d of George A. C. teacher and Ruth Bain; b Buckie 1.10.47
Dip YESTB(Napier coll) 1974
teacher Engl/Fr: Portree h s 1970–71, Grantown g s 1971–72; surv cler work Inv 1973; stud. careers off. Napier coll Edin 1974–75; careers off. Highland reg council Dingwall from 1975

CURRIE William Dawson *BSc(eng) 1965

CURRY David John *BSc(eng) 1965
s of Kenneth E. C. ARIBA arch. and Isabel L. Cox secy; b Lond 18.4.42
eng AEI Leic 1965–68; SRC res stud. Loughborough univ 1968–71; asst elect. eng RN eng serv 1971–76; elect. eng RCNC from 1976
m Lond 23.7.66 Katharine G. Murray MA 1966 *qv*

CURTIS David John MA 1966
s of P. Arthur C. man. dir indust plumbing contr and E. Kathleen Lees prop. comp dir; b Wolverhampton 6.9.42
exec off. inland rev Birm 1966–70; Lond: higher exec off. board of inl rev secys' off. 1970–73; sen exec off. organis div inl rev from 1974
m Tettenhall Wolverhampton 3.5.69 Josephine G. Bate loc govt off. d of Joseph J. B. Wolverhampton

CURTIS Kathleen Mary MA 1964
d of Ronald F. C. and Marjorie S. Polson; b Lybster 26.6.44
Dip Sec Sc(Glas)
secy: Edin 1965–67, Cambridge 1967–68, Copenhagen 1968–73; translator: Brussels 1973–74, Luxembourg from 1974

CURTIS Robert Bryan BSc(for) 1960

CUSA Rosalind Jane BSc 1967
d of Noel W. C. BSc(Lond) chem, patent off., artist and Mary B. Oliver; b Cheadle Hulme 14.4.44
lab tech univ of Alberta Edmonton 1967–68; scient edit. oceanographic inst DSIR Wellington NZ 1968–77
m Wellington 1976 Neil M. Robertson marine eng, farm. s of Jock R. Nelson NZ

CUSHNIE Jennifer Anne Baird *MA 1963
d of Albert P. D. C. comm trav/warehouseman and Constance J. Stables hairdresser; b Aber 11.9.40
dir res and publ at an internat stud. house and conference centre Geneva 1964–68; enrolled in MA programme Span. dept Santa Barbara Calif 1969–71; teacher re-evaluation counselling San Francisco from 1971
m Santa Barbara 10.10.70 Dennis W. Allen MA(Princeton) asst dean for. stud. and peace educ and organis s of Lewis C. A. Arcadia Calif

CUTBUSH Elizabeth Ann MA 1966
d of Richard C. BMus(Lond) prin teacher mus Aber h s for girls and Doris Furlong radiographer; b Leeds 5.2.45
Huddersfield: part time lect Ger adult educ 1970–72; head mod lang Almondbury s s from 1972
m Oxford 1965 Alan J. Foubister BSc 1966 *qv*

CUTHBERT John Alexander Mitchell LLB 1968
s of Alan D. C. shipowner and Elspeth M. Mitchell; b Glasg 19.5.46
Edin: law app 1968–70, asst solic 1970–71; Glasgow: leg. asst 1971–73, ptnr from 1974
m Skene 28.8.71 Kirsty M. Frazer MA 1969 *qv*

CUTHBERT Mary McLaren Gordon *MA 1956

CUTHBERTSON Alastair BSc(agr) 1958
s of Sir David P. C. MB ChB(Glas) hon res fell. Glas and Lady Jean P. Telfer; b Glasg 1.3.36
Dip Agr(Cantab) 1959
Cantab: res schol pig indust dev auth 1959–62, res fell. 1962–64; carcase evaluation off. pig indust dev auth Hitchin 1964–68, head of carcase and meat quality, meat and livestock comm Milton Keynes from 1968
m Reigate 24.8.63 Caroline L. Ferguson BSc(St And) teacher d of Sir Gordon F. Reigate

CUTLER Timothy Robert BSc(for) 1956
s of Frank R. C. bus. exec and Jeannie E. Badenoch teacher dom sc; b Bihar India 24.7.34
nat serv 2nd lt RE Farnborough 1956–58; asst conserv for. col for. serv Kenya 1958–64; NZ for. serv from 1964, now dir prod. for. man. div head office Wellington
m Grangemouth 11.10.58 Ishbel W. M. Primrose teacher d of James P. Grangemouth

CUTT Jennifer Allan BSc 1962
d of James R. C. MA 1926 *qv*; b Aber 1.11.41
teacher maths: Montrose acad 1963–64, Lond 1965–67, Birm 1967–68, home teacher Birm 1974–75; teacher ch hosp s Birm from 1975
m Aber 12.8.65 Alexander Buchan BSc 1961 *qv*

DADI Samuel Olorun Femi BSc(for) 1962
s of Elisha G. D. farm. and Racheal A. Oyo petty trader; b Ikare W Nigeria 3.6.35
Nigeria: asst cons for. W State 1962–70; vice prin Bassa Nge anglican g s Bibololeo Kware State 1971–76; sen for. Skoup & Co assoc bus. consult. Enugu from 1976
m Aber 24.7.61 Josette Y. Lecafette teacher d of Leon L. Tourcoing Nord France

DAFALLA Dafalla Ahmed MSc 1965
s of Ahmed D. Abdelbagi merch and Aziza Hamadelniel; b Elodayia Sudan 1.1.36
BSc(agr)(Khart) 1960 PhD(N'cle) 1979
agr res corp Sudan: agronomist 1966–70, sen agronomist 1970–74, chief agronomist from 1974
m Sudan 7.11.68 Mahassin Suleiman d of Suleiman I. Elbitain Sudan

D'AGOSTINO Laurence Cormack BSc(eng) 1960
s of Louis D'A. shopkeeper and Gertrude S. Cormack; b Torphins 9.1.39
grad app Ferranti Edin 1960–61; IBA: tech asst Durris transmitting stat 1961–62, eng Durris 1962–68, sen eng oper Lond 1968–72, sen eng methods/oper Winchester from 1972
m Banchory 25.8.62 Maurelle L. Coutts soil analyst d of Arthur D. C. Banchory

DAHL Peter Henry *MA 1970
d of Peter C. D. hotelier and Edith M. K. Weierter; b Edin 18.9.45
MSc(H-W) 1972
plan asst Notts c c 1972–74; sen plan. asst Bassetlaw dist c Worksop 1974–75; sen plan. N'cle-u-Tyne metr d c from 1975
m Aber 28.8.72 Dorothy M. Goldie BSc 1970 *qv*

DAILEY William Sebastian PhD 1962
ARIC(Upminster)

DALE Brian Graeme LLB 1968
s of Reginald C. D. chartered elect. eng/factory man. and Marjorie A. Vousden; b Hanwell Lond 20.11.46
Edin: law app Shepherd & Wedderburn WS 1968–70; solic Stuart & Stuart Cairns & Co WS from 1970, ptnr 1972–75; ptnr Brooke & Brown Dunbar from 1975; treas diocese of Edin Epis Church 1971; chapter clerk Cath Ch of St Mary 1972–75; dep regist of diocese 1973–75; regist/secy of diocese 1975
m Felton Common 23.5.70 Judith G. de B. Franklin SRN d of Henry L. F. BA(Oxon) Felton

DALGARNO Frederick George Scott LLB 1964
s of Frederick D. depot superv and Winifred H. Scott clerkess; b Aber 17.6.43
Dip Indust Man(Strath) 1965 CA 1968
Aber: law app 1968–71; solic acting as invest. man. from 1971
m Aber 5.9.69 Moyra Ellis bank clerk d of William E. Aber

DALGARNO Gordon *BSc 1963
s of William W. D. clerk and Jean Gordon secy; b Aber 15.3.40
tech off. ICI Billingham 1963–64; York: phys Rowntree 1964–67, head phys Rowntree-Mackintosh from 1967

DALGARNO Laraine Massie MA 1967
m Brown

DALGARNO Melvin Taylor *MA 1966 PhD 1972
s of William W. D. clerk and Jane A. M. Gordon shorthand typist; b Aber 4.12.43
asst moral phil dept Aberd 1969–70; lect phil inst of extension stud. Liv 1970–71; lect moral phil Aberd from 1971

DALGARNO William Alexander MA 1969
s of John A. D. fruit salesman and Mary Morrison; b Elgin 26.9.46
entertainments ag Elgin 1969–72; trainee man. 1972–78; retail store man. Harrogate from 1978
m Forres 24.10.70 Patricia A. Brennan MA 1967 *qv*

DALGETTY Yvonne Anne MA 1958 Dip Ed 1959
d of Ian R. D. ARIBA arch. and Emma Sime secy; b Alyth 22.8.37
teacher Blairgowrie 1959–62; resid Malaysia
m Blairgowrie 16.2.63 James G. Taylor rubber estate man. s of Robert T. Buckie

DALRYMPLE John Allan *MA 1961

DALZIEL Francis Robert *MA 1956 PhD 1958
s of Francis D. capt MN and Agnes Shand; b Aber 30.7.34
lect: Indiana 1959–61, Adelaide univ Aust from 1961

DANBURY David John BSc(for) 1958 *1959

DANIEL Anne Rosemary MA 1967
d of William D. farm. and Louisa Smith; b Kirkcaldy 2.1.46
teacher mod lang Bo'ness acad from 1968

DANIEL James Donaldson MA 1967

DANIELS Samuel Bannerman Martin BSc(eng) 1962
s of Edwin P. D. gen merch and Faustina Coleman dressmaker; b Cape Coast Ghana 22.3.35
DIC(Lond) 1964 MBA(Windsor univ Ont) 1976
M Gh IE 1976
asst eng: Oscar Faber & ptnrs Lond 1962–63, Tahal consult. eng Tel Aviv 1964–65; Ghana: reg man. GWSC 1965–77, proj eng IISC Accra from 1977
m Ghana 18.8.68 Margaret R. Isliker secy d of Frederick I. Accra

DARGIE Bryan Alfred *MA 1963
s of Robert C. D. city chamberlain and Mary K. Bryan; b Dun 24.9.41
stud. RAM Lond 1964–66; freelance violinist 1966–68; teacher violin Aber from 1969
m Aber 17.7.70 Elizabeth M. Witte MA 1970 *qv*

DARLING Alan Jeffrey BSc(eng) 1967 *1970
s of John N. Q. D. pers man. Hong Kong & Shanghai Bank Lond and Elvira M. de Magistris teacher; b Sutton 13.11.48
MICE 1974
eng: civ des Lond 1970–72, resid construct. Aber 1972–73; Rendel Palmer & Tritton consult. eng Lond: des Thames Barrier 1973–74, resid construct. Thames Barrier from 1974

DAUBE Jonathan Mahram *MA 1957
s of David D. PhD(Cantab) univ prof and Herta B. Aufseesser; b Cambridge 23.11.37
Acad Dip(Lond) 1960 EdD(Harvard) 1968
teacher: Engl/maths Watford g s 1958–60, Engl Manc g s 1960–63, Engl Newton h s Mass. USA 1963–65; teaching fell. in educ Harvard univ 1965–67; asst to supt Newton Mass. 1967–68; sen lect educ univ of Malawi Limbe 1968–70; supt schools Martha's Vineyard Mass. USA 1970–75; dir grad progr in educ Union Grad s Yellow Springs Ohio from 1975
m Newton Mass. 29.8.64 Linda C. Lindquist BA(Minn) d of Charles G. L. Minnesota

DAUN Sheila Mary MA 1959 Dip Ed 1960
d of James C. D. bus driver and Mary R. Leven; b Aber 11.6.38
teacher Torry acad Aber 1960–62
m Aber 9.4.62 Dudley J. F. Bowling PhD 1961 *qv*

DAVEY Brian Gregor PhD 1957
BSc(agr)(Syd)

DAVIDSON Aileen Elizabeth MA 1969
d of Thomas B. D. MB ChB 1940 *qv*; b Aber 12.7.48
teacher: Inchgarth p s Aber 1970–72, Tower coll Rainhill 1972–73
m Aber 8.7.72 Ian R. Gemmell elect. eng BICC s of Stanley M. G. Aber

DAVIDSON Alan Ingram MB ChB 1959 ChM 1973
s of Joseph D. shoemaker and Jean Dunbar; b Aber 25.3.35
DObstRCOG 1963 FRCSE 1968
h o ARI 1959–60; m o RAMC Jamaica/Brit Guiana 1960–62; sen h o ARI 1962–63; lect path. Aberd 1963–65; ARI: regist surg 1965–70, sen 1970–74, consult. surg from 1974
m Aber 14.10.67 Margaret E. Mackay nurs sister d of Eric R. M. Inv

DAVIDSON Alexander *BSc 1956

DAVIDSON Alexander Melvin *BSc 1964 Dip Ed 1965
s of Alexander D. paperworker and Helen R. Duffus; b Aber 15.3.42
Dip Stat(Strath) 1970 FRSS
teacher maths Langside coll Glasg 1965–67, lect maths/statist Paisley tech coll from 1967

DAVIDSON Alicia Rose MA 1969
d of George I. D. MB ChB 1935 *qv*; b Aber 9.12.47
teacher: kindergarten Edin acad 1970–74, nursery class St Margaret's Aber from 1974
m Aber 11.3.78 Richard G. Brown comp dir s of Geoffrey R. B. Westcott

DAVIDSON Angus William Black *MA 1966

DAVIDSON Arthur Ian Greenwood MB ChB 1960 *ChM 1965 PhD 1969
s of Arthur D. civ eng/tea plantation man. and Sarah F. Greenwood SRN; b Aber 29.1.37

FRCSE 1965
h o ARI 1960–61; lect anat Aberd 1961–62; lect/regist surg Aberd 1962–66; res fell. Western Reserve univ Cleveland USA 1963–64; sen regist surg Aber hosp 1966–71; consult. surg/sen lect surg Dund from 1971
m Montrose 27.4.67 Doreen R. Long SRN theatre sister d of Thomas L. MA(Glas) Ferryden

DAVIDSON Bennett Erskine MA 1963
s of John B. D. cinema proj, film edit. and Raechel Erskine; b Aber 26.6.42
teacher phys: Aber acad 1964–68, prin phys: Albyn s for girls Aber 1968–73, Hilton acad from 1973
m Aber 26.12.67 Eileen Gordon CA civ serv d of Leslie W. G. Aber

DAVIDSON Brian John *BSc 1966
MSc(Sheff)

DAVIDSON Catherine Mary BSc 1962
d of James W. D. BR worker, caretaker Christ's coll Aber and Catherine E. Mutch; b Whitehouse 5.2.40
scient off. Torry res stat Aber 1962–63; teacher sc Forfar acad from 1970
m Aber 17.8.63 John F. Shepherd sales rep s of David S. Brechin

DAVIDSON Donald Allen *BSc 1967

DAVIDSON Dorothy Hanna MA 1956
d of Sydney G. D. MA 1920 *qv* and Gertrude C. McDonald MA 1922 *qv*; b Aber 29.10.35
teacher: Victoria Rd p s Aber 1960–62, Fernielea p s Aber 1962–64, part-time Oakfield s Lond 1966–67
m Aber 11.9.65 William P. Gill MA 1953 *qv*

DAVIDSON Elaine BSc 1966
d of William L. D. g p o tel superv and Mabel Carr shop asst; b Aber 30.8.45
res asst: chem path. med s Aberd 1966–67, G. D. Searle res lab High Wycombe 1967–68
m Aber 23.9.66 James G. Knowles PhD 1967 *qv*

DAVIDSON Eleanor Fraser MA 1956
b Aber 7.8.35
teacher: Kinneff p s 1957–59, Dumfries 1959–60
m Aber 27.6.59 Thomas G. Milne MA 1956 *qv*

DAVIDSON Elizabeth Joan MA 1964
m Lingard

DAVIDSON Elizabeth Waiter BSc 1960
m Hall

DAVIDSON Elsie Patricia Jane *BSc 1969
d of William M. D. MB ChB 1934 *qv*; b Aber 2.3.45
post-grad stud. bot Aberd 1969–70; teacher biol Edin: Portobello s s 1971–72, Broughton h s 1972–77, prin biol from 1977
m Dirleton 8.7.72 Hugh M. Gordon BSc 1970 *qv*

DAVIDSON Eric George *BSc(eng) 1966

DAVIDSON Fred Leith MA 1960
s of Annie B. Davidson; b Oyne 2.8.39
BA(Lond) 1972
teacher: mod lang/Lat Dalbeattie h s 1961–73; Engl Bayonne France 1973–74; mod lang/Lat Dalbeattie from 1974
m Aber 19.8.61 Heather A. Duncan shorthand typist/ cler off.

DAVIDSON Ian Alexander MA 1970

DAVIDSON Ian Douglas MA 1970

DAVIDSON Ian Gillespie *MA 1967 *MEd 1969

DAVIDSON Irene Mary *BSc 1962 MSc 1963
d of Alexander D. salmon fisherman and Eva E. Erskine; b Auchencairn 14.6.40
teacher sc: Nicolson inst Stornoway 1964–65, Bankhead acad Bucksburn 1965–66
m Aber 29.3.65 Alexander Matheson pharm/man. dir s of Alexander M. MB ChB 1931 *qv*

DAVIDSON Irene Urquhart MA 1958

DAVIDSON James Alexander BSc(agr) 1970
s of Thomas D. surv chainman and Catherine D. Lobban; b Aber 28.4.29
Fiji: sen agr off. Suva 1970–73, prin agr off. Lavtoka from 1973
m 2.6.56 Margaret H. Ross admin secy d of Douglas R. Lond; wife *d* Athens –.3.76

DAVIDSON James Russell *BSc 1962

DAVIDSON Janice Mary *MA 1970 Dip Ed 1971
d of John G. D. arch. and Frances M. Alexander teacher; b Aber 27.6.47
teacher Fr/Ger Mackie acad Stonehaven from 1971

DAVIDSON Jean Cooper *MA 1968
d of James D. CA and Jean M. Cooper; b Aber 3.9.44
bilingual secy course City of Lond coll 1968; asst edit. dictionaries Collins & Sons publ Glasg 1969–70; teacher part-time coll of comm Aber 1972–73
m Aber 27.6.70 Christopher J. Gossip MA(Edin) univ lect s of Robin A. J. G. MA 1927 *qv*

DAVIDSON Jennifer MA 1970
d of James H. D. comm cashier and Rosalie Menzies clerkess; b Aber 27.1.49
Dip Ed(Lanc)
teacher mod lang Carlisle from 1971
m Aber 10.8.73 Stewart Hudson plan. eng s of Kenneth H. Jarrow

DAVIDSON John Cunningham MB ChB 1970
s of George I. D. MB ChB 1935 *qv*; b Aber 15.7.46
h o ARI 1970–71; sen h o, regist anaest Aber hosps 1971–73; g p in father's pract Aber from 1973
m Aber 10.7.73 Lorne M. McRoberts nurs sister d of James M. McR. MA 1962 *qv*

DAVIDSON John Forsyth MB ChB 1957
s of John F. D. MA 1923 *qv*; b Lumphanan 11.1.34
MRCPE 1965 FRCPE 1974
h o ARI 1957–58; surg lieut RN UK and east of Suez 1958–61; med regist ARI 1961–65; Glasg RI: res regist 1965–66, sen regist haemat 1966–69, consult. haemat from 1969
m Paisley 30.7.59 Laura G. Middleton schoolmistress d of James E. M. Glasg

DAVIDSON John Gordon *BSc(agr) 1967
s of John G. W. D. CA and Isabella Kemp art teacher; b Aber 17.4.44
agr advis Ayr/Wigtown 1967–72; gen man. farms, heavy plant hire and butchery Stranraer from 1972
m Aber 5.8.67 Margaret H. S. Robertson MA 1967 *qv*

DAVIDSON John Gregory Gordon MB ChB 1968
s of Sydney G. D. MA 1920 *qv* and Gertrude C. McDonald MA 1922 *qv*; b Aber 21.11.43
h o ARI 1968–69; g p: Willesden 1969–71, Enfield 1972–78 Aber from 1978

DAVIDSON John Grieve MA 1969
s of Samuel F. D. farm. and Mary Salter; b Torphins 14.3.46
teacher mus Walsingham s Kent 1970–71: actor as David Grieve: Argyle Theatre for youth 1971–72, Adeline Genée theatre E Grinstead 1972, Grand Theatre Swansea 1972–73, *At the End of the Day* Savoy Theatre Lond 1973–74; touring from 1974

DAVIDSON Joseph BSc 1967
s of Joseph D. soldier and Ellen Harrison; b Birm 14.1.32
teacher: Rosemount s s Aber 1968–70, Kaimhill s s 1970–71, Castle Toward s 1971–73; asst prin maths Summerhill acad Aber from 1973
m Newhills Helen E. Raitt d of Walter R. Bucksburn

DAVIDSON June Rebecca Smith MA 1969
m Mutch

DAVIDSON Kathleen MA 1957
m Day

DAVIDSON Margaret Sharp MA 1966

DAVIDSON Margarita Masson MA 1962
d of John M. D. master mariner and Margaret E. Hynd MA 1933 *qv*; b Ellon 20.7.41
teacher: mod lang Elgin acad 1964–67, S Queensferry 1967–68, mod lang Morgan acad Dun 1968–69
m Huntly 5.10.68 Alexander G. Cooper comp rep s of Robert C.

DAVIDSON Marischal William BSc 1963
s of Alexander M. D. civ serv and Jessie Brown civ serv; b Aber 18.9.37
teacher sc Aber from 1964

DAVIDSON Neil *BSc 1963
s of Charles D. sen scient off. civ serv and Isobel Wood; b Aber 17.9.41
PhD (NY State) 1967
Downstate med center New York: teaching asst dep physiol 1963–64, res foundation fell. State univ NY 1964, asst instr 1966–67; grass foundation fell. marine biol labs Wood Hole Mass USA 1964; lect physiol Aberd from 1967
m NY 1965 Geraldine A. Fisher secy d of William J. F. The Wirral

DAVIDSON Peter Ian LLB 1968
s of Peter D. C of S min and Elizabeth M. Winder; b Halifax 19.7.46
law app Aber 1968–70; asst solic Aber, Montrose 1970–74; ptnr T. Duncan & Co solic Montrose from 1974
m Kirkhill Invsh 3.11.73 Rosalind E. Munro RGN d of Alexander J. M. Kirkhill

DAVIDSON Rachel Chattan *BSc 1969
d of William D. MB ChB(Leeds) consult. radiol and Jean M. Kerr; b Bradford 24.5.46
res chem ICI Billingham 1969–72; teacher sc Cleveland educ dept Middlesbrough 1972–76
m Hexham 6.9.69 Stuart L. Smith BSc(eng) 1967 *qv*

DAVIDSON Robert Hugh Clifford MA 1968
s of Clifford A. D. rubber planter, farm. and Helen M. C. Buchanan nurse; b Malacca Malaya 27.1.47
RAF pilot from 1968
m Aber 24.12.68 Johan G. Whyte MA 1968 *qv*

DAVIDSON Roger George Leith *MA 1963
s of George Davidson comp man. and Winifred Leith; b Glasg 2.10.41
fin. admin: Shell internat Lond 1963–66, Brunei, Sarawak 1966–68, Thailand, Laos 1968–70, Lond 1971–74, Lagos 1974–76, Lond from 1976
m Aber 27.7.64 Valerie E. Strang teacher d of Gavin S. Dinnet

DAVIDSON Ruth Isobel BSc 1958 *1959
d of Sydney G. D. MA 1920 *qv* and Gertrude C. McDonald MA 1922 *qv*; b Aber 20.12.37
teacher Alberni Canada 1960–61; lib asst UBC Vancouver 1961–62; blood transfusion serv Edin 1963–64
m Aber 6.3.64 Malcolm Sutherland FSA Scot. merch s of Norman S. MBE Cults

DAVIDSON William BSc(agr) 1958
s of F. W. D. farm. and Ada I. Norrie farm.; b New Deer 15.2.35
MSc(Durh) 1960
Glasg: lect agr eng 1960–68, sen mech advis from 1968
m Aber 15.12.60 Isobel McLean teacher d of John McL. Dinnet

DAVIDSON-LAMB Richard William MB ChB 1968
s of William D.-L. MB ChB 1938 *qv*; b Bedford 26.11.42
DObstRCOG 1972 FFARCS 1975
h o Aber 1968–69; lect bact Aberd 1969–70; g p Aber 1970–71; h o obst 1971–72; s h o, regist anaest Aber 1972–75; sen regist anaest Edin RI 1975–78; consult. anaest ARI from 1978
m Aber 19.8.69 Nanette J. Flockhart MB ChB 1968

DAVIE Ann Margaret MA 1967
d of James C. D. master mariner and Ellen M. E. Smith; b Montrose 22.4.44
Dip Sec St(Strath) 1968 ACII 1972
dealing with leg. documents Life assur co. Edin from 1968; later in Aust

DAVIE Anne *MA 1968
m Paterson

DAVIE Fredric *BSc 1967 PhD 1971
s of Percy D. asst pharm and Margaret S. Muir; b Aber 26.1.45
ICI: res chem Welwyn Garden City 1970–71, market dev off. 1971–76, proj man. 1976–79, gen man. RN plastics Leeds from 1979
m Aber 1.7.67 Carol C. Murray BA(Strath) teacher d of William M. Aber

DAVIE Isobel Marlene MA 1964
d of George H. D. farm. and Christian Buchan; b Mufulira Zambia 27.8.42
teacher Engl/Lat: Inverurie acad 1965–66, Boroughmuir h s Edin 1966–68, Liberton h s Edin 1968–72
m Aber 26.7.69 Ian S. Mackay s of Donald M.

DAVIE Kathleen Fiona *MA 1961
d of John W. D. barkeeper/chief steward Brit Leg. club and Bessie Donald; b Aber 1.7.37
Norway; part time teacher Fr/Ger Sandnessjøen 1966–71, teacher: Geir Borresen comp s Drammen 1971–72, Fr g s Sandnessjøen from 1973; also teacher Fr Norwegian corresp s (Engl dept) from 1972
m Münster Westfalen Germany 18.12.58 Tore Walen MB ChB (Münster) consult. surg s of Sigmund W. LLB(Oslo) Tromsø Norway

DAVIE Margaret Helen BSc 1960
d of James D. ironmonger and Jeannie Morrison; b Nairn 10.11.38
teacher maths: Peterhead, Forres 1960–61, Chatham 1961–63; tech lib Camberley 1963–64; cardiol tech

Montreal 1965–67; ch welfare teacher Carshalton 1973–76; med rep from 1976
m Forres 28.12.61 Richard N. F. Dunbar BSc 1961 *qv*

DAVIE Marguereta Mary Ferguson MA 1966
m Allison

DAVIE Ramsay Anderson Gove BSc 1960

DAVIE Victoria Frances BSc 1956 Dip Ed 1957
d of Alexander F. D. schoolmaster and Victoria E. Laing teacher dom sc; b Dun 27.5.35
teacher: sc Blairgowrie 1957–60, sc/maths Methven 1960–61, sc/maths Tain r h s 1961–62
m Perth 1960 Francis Young BSc 1956 *qv*

DAVIES Andrew Neil Brett BSc(for) 1959

DAVIES Bronwen Veronica MA 1969 Dip Ed 1970
d of George L. D. civ serv MoD and Irene M. Macie; b Wyke Regis 3.2.48
civ serv Inl Rev Manc 1970–71; teacher mod lang Perth from 1972

DAVIES Christopher John BSc(eng) 1968
s of John A. D. civ serv and Phyllis Wiltshire secy; b Exeter 19.1.46
MICE 1973
Taylor Woodrow: site eng 1967–71, des eng (sect. leader) Southall 1971–73; des eng with consult. Sale from 1973
m(2) Lond 7.7.73 Susan H. Burt MA 1967 *qv*

DAVIES David Lewis *BSc 1970

DAVIES Dorothy Valerie Ann BSc 1969
d of Frank E. D. toolmaker and Doris A. Vickers; b Wolverhampton 16.9.47
teacher: Birm 1969–70, Wolverhampton 1970–71, head maths dept Bradford 1972–73, temp Fleet from 1973
m 26.12.71 Martin C. P. Burke BSc(Aston) phys, prod. man. s of Michael B. Birm

DAVIES Eileen Joan Alfreda MA 1959
m Flavill

DAVIES Elisabeth Shona MA 1969
m Raitt

DAVIES Ian Munro *MA 1967
s of Joseph G. D. factory man. and Betty Munro; b Elgin 26.7.44
buyer Rootes Motors Coventry 1967–70; teacher Cheshire c c: Hyde 1970–72, 5th year tut. Bredbury 1972–77; dep head Macclesfield from 1977
m Hyde 8.5.71 Anne Shepley teacher/artist d of Peter K. S. Charlesworth

DAVIES James Andrew MB ChB 1966

DAVIES Janet Elizabeth BSc 1965
d of John H. D. BA(Sheff) area prin f e and Annetta Hough secy; b Stockton Brook 8.1.43
Cert Envir Sc(S'ton) 1974
teacher biol: Victoria Vancouver Is 1966–67, Poole 1967–68, Southampton from 1968

DAVIES Joan Margaret MA 1968
m Macleod

DAVIES John Norman MA 1966

DAVIES June Amelia PhD 1967
d of John G. D. trans man. and Ethel A. Hutchings; b Cardiff 26.5.43
BSc(Wales) 1964
lect univ coll S Wales 1967–70; edit. CEGB Leatherhead 1970–71
m Cardiff 25.7.69 David Byrom BSc (Cardiff) res Beechams res labs, ICI Teesside s of Tom B. Manc

DAVIES Lesley Ceridwen MA 1970
m Golbourn

DAVIES Patrick Protheroe LLB 1965
s of Kenneth D. D. MB ChB(Brist) med pract and Ethel G. Protheroe; b Cheltenham 5.10.44
Aber: law app 1965–67, solic, leg. asst 1967–70, solic, ptnr Milne & Mackinnon advoc from 1970
m Aber 19.9.80 Caroline Jane Gray LLB 1973 d of J. Hector Gray MA 1932 *qv*

DAVIS Betsy Maud Annies Ada MB ChB 1959
d of Samuel D. teacher and Amy K. Speid teacher; b Priestman's River Jamaica 30.8.33
univ of Milan: Med Chir 1966 Dip Dent. 1969
h o Warrington 1959–60, Liv 1960–61, Kingston Jamaica 1961–70; g p Monza Italy from 1970
m Aber 1.10.58 Marcello Cavallo Med Chir(Milan) cardiol s of Alfredo C. Milan

DAVIS Elizabeth Ann MA 1969
d of George W. E. D. tel sales rep and Isabella Beaton clerkess; b Aber 10.10.47
computer progr Manc reg hosp board 1969–70; computer progr (analyst) NW elect. board 1970–73
m Aber 26.12.69 Russell Milne MA 1970 *qv*

DAVIS Godfrey Peter *MA 1969
s of Eustace B. D. BA(Brist) clerk in holy orders and Eva Henshall; b Liv 21.6.45
ARCO ARCM LRAM ATCL 1974
head mus St Andrew's s and organist/choirmaster Christchurch cath Nassau Bahamas 1970–73; stud. royal s of ch mus Croydon 1973–74; dir mus St George's s Clarens Montreux Switzerland 1974–76; dir mus Adams' g s Newport Salop from 1976 and organist/choirmaster collegiate ch of St Mary Stafford from 1977
m Aber 4.7.70 Stella R. Smith MA 1968 *qv*

DAVIS Lionel John *MA 1966 Dip Ed 1967
s of Eustace B. D. BA(Brist) clerk in holy orders and Eva Henshall missionary in China; b Tachu Szechwan China 9.6.42
teacher: mod lang AGS 1967–70, prin mod lang Banchory from 1970
m Aber 14.7.67 Ingeborg I. Konig MA 1966 *qv*

DAVISON Elizabeth Armstrong *BSc 1967 MSc 1970
d of Meredith H. A. D. MD(N'cle) consult. anaest and Ida F. Evans nurse; b Bicester 5.3.44
lect tech coll Aber 1970–72
m Chillingham 5.4.69 John P. Blakeman BSc(Wales) univ lect s of John C. B. Cranleigh
d N'cle 28.11.73

DAW Michael Richard *BSc(for) 1962
s of William R. D. mental welfare off. and Florence L. C. Sampson; b Bath 23.5.40
for. man. Messrs. Clutton chartered surv Wells from 1963
m Inv 15.9.61 Anne P. L. Richards secy d of Robert L. R. MB ChB 1932 *qv*

DAWE Michael Charles Stewart BSc(agr) 1965
s of Eric C. S. D. MRCVS(Edin) vet surg and Kathleen Barr hosp matron; b Johannesburg 9.11.40

Ukiriguru, Mwanza, Tanzania: pasture res off. 1966–73, also acting sen res off. Western res centre 1971–73; agronomist lower Shire valley proj Ngabu Malawi from 1974
m Mwanza 8.7.66 Jennifer A. Beveridge d of Andrew W. B. Edin

DAWSON Alexander Richard LLB 1968
s of Alexander D. comp chmn and Elisabeth G. W. Lakin MA(Glas) teacher; b Milngavie 23.1.47
law app Glasg 1968–70; solic, leg. asst Aber 1970–73; solic loc govt Aber from 1974
m Aber 7.9.70 Jennifer M. Maclean MA 1968 *qv*

DAWSON Audrey Anne *MB ChB 1956 *MD 1966
d of Henry J. D. MA 1916 *qv*; b Aber 27.1.33
MRCPE 1959 FRCPE 1970 MRCPath 1971
h o: ARI 1956–57, Hammersmith hosp Lond 1957–58; Aberd: lect med 1958–67, sen lect haemat from 1967

DAWSON David George *BSc 1963 PhD 1966
s of Robert G. D. BSc 1929 *qv* and Annie E. Adams MA 1928 *qv*; b Aber 28.7.41
res fell. chem: univ of W Ontario 1966–68, Aberd 1968–69; scient res dept ICI (paints div) Slough from 1969
m Aber 17.7.65 Caroline H. Munro MA 1963 *qv*

DAWSON Donald George MB ChB 1959

DAWSON Elizabeth Helen MA 1965
d of Robert G. D. BSc(eng) 1929 *qv* and Anne E. Adams MA 1928 *qv*; b Aber 31.7.44
Cert Sec Sc(Strath) 1966
asst lib inst chartered acct of Scot. Edin 1966–67; secy to advt man. Henry Birks & Sons, Montreal 1967–69; asst advt man. inst chartered acct of Scot. Edin 1969–70; secy Galashiels: to Bernat Klein des consult. 1970–72, J. & J. Hall & Co arch. 1972–73
m Aber 16.9.70 William T. M. Cleghorn CA s of William T. C. Galashiels

DAWSON Gavin Robert MB ChB 1958

DAWSON Gordon Shepherd *BSc 1963

DAWSON Margaret Caroline MA 1956

DAWSON Margaret Jane *MA 1961
d of Robert G. D. BSc(eng) 1929 *qv* and Anne E. Adams MA 1928 *qv*; b Berkhampstead 15.4.39
teacher Engl: Brechin acad 1962–67, Peterhead acad 1967–68
m Aber 5.4.66 Norman G. F. Russell MA(Edin) teacher s of George Y. R. Leven

DAWSON Moira LLB 1965

DAWSON Robert Leslie *MA 1958

DAWSON Ronald Peter Bond *BSc(eng) 1970
s of Thomas F. D. lect tech coll and Elizabeth L. M. Brodie; b Aber 21.3.48
grad trainee tech eng Elgin 1970–72; Aber: gen eng NSHEB 1972–73, 4th eng 1973–74, 3rd eng 1974–76, 2nd eng from 1976

DAWSON William James MA 1959

DAY Michael James John *MA 1966
s of Hector J. D. wall and floor tiler and Winifred Myatt pottery decorator/clerk; b Manc 27.3.43
teacher Engl: Stamsund Lofoten Norway 1967–68, Peebles 1968–70; prin Engl Slidre Norway from 1970

DAY Nicholas Edward PhD 1967
BA(Oxon)

DAYAL Radha Raman PhD 1965
s of Amar S. Mathur lawyer and Jag R. Mathur; b Agra India 19.1.41
BSc(Agra) 1957 MSc(Agra) 1959
res assoc Penn state univ USA 1965–66; defence sc lab Delhi: pool off. 1966–69, sen scient off. 1969; NRC (Canada) fell. energy mines and resources Ottawa 1969–71; sen scient off. defence sc lab Delhi from 1972
m New Delhi 12.12.68 Rama Mathur MA(Luck) d of Govind N. M. Lucknow

DE JONCKHEERE Cyril Gustave *BSc 1965
s of Cyril J. De J. civ serv/clerk of works and Mary B. Bremner; b Wick 20.11.41
FRMetS
scient off., sen scient met. off. Bracknell from 1968

DE SILVA Angela Rosemary MA 1961
d of William de S. CA and Rhéa Parcon teacher; b Seychelles 17.2.38
MSc(Makerere) 1972
sen tut. zoology/bot univ of Makerere 1967–72; W Aust inst of tech dept of med tech Perth WA: lect: Engl/anat 1973–74, anat/physiol from 1974
m Aber 11.4.58 Gordon A. German MB ChB 1958 *qv*

DE SILVA Nihal Nemichandra PhD 1960
BSc(Ceylon)

De SILVA William Raymond *BSc(eng) 1968

DEADMAN Andrew James MSc 1969 PhD 1973
BSc(Lond)

DEAN Alexander William *MA 1968

DEAN Helen Millicent MB ChB 1957
d of Charles A. Dean MB ChB 1925 *qv*; b Hull 13.7.32
DCH(Glas) 1960
h o St Luke's hosp Bradford 1957–58; Glasg: resid m o paediat royal mat. hosp 1958–59, royal hosp for sick ch 1959, jun h m o paediat Southern gen hosp 1959–62; school m o 1963–68; W Aust: m o intell handic serv Perth 1968–70 and from 1972; g p Kondinin 1970–72
m Renfrew 25.7.61 Henry Thornton Scott-Pillow s of Edward E. S-P; marr diss 1974

DEAN Peter Alexander MA 1963 LLB 1966

DEANS Andrew MA 1963
s of Andrew D. hotel prop. and Margaret R. Crozier; b Galashiels 3.5.40
superv with brewery 1963–67; teacher Galashiels acad from 1968
m Hawick 10.8.65 Evelyn Farish fashion des d of George F.

DEANS Isabella McDonell MA 1962
m Pennington

DEANS Norman Dickson *BSc(eng) 1966
m Rosaleen A. Bruce BSc 1966 *qv*

DEANS Thomas MA 1962
s of Alexander S. C. D. head beekeeping dept NOSCA and Mary Young; b Edin 24.8.38
instr RA Nuneaton 1963–65; OCS S Arabian army Aden; instr Highland Bde depot Aber 1967–70; staff off. HQ 4 div Herford W Ger 1970–73; o c Sandhurst wing

Beaconsfield 1973–76; group educ off. Oxon Bucks & Berks Bicester 1976–79; staff off. SW dist Bulford from 1979, major RAEC
m Salisbury 23.5.79 Sybil M. Bromham d of Henry B. Acton

DEAR Alasdair George Wilbert MA 1956 LLB 1959
s of Sidney W. D. BSc(St And) headmaster and Margaret E. Matheson teacher; b Crathie 14.9.35
Diplôme de Droites Comparées (univ of Luxembourg) 1959 WS 1972 TD 1976
parachute regt M East 1959–62; Edin: private leg. pract 1962–72, on own account from 1972
m Cockpen 30.7.67 Lesley A. Robertson d of Donald R. Edin

DEAR Elizabeth Margaret Anne BSc 1962
d of Sydney W. D. BSc(St And) headmaster and Margaret E. Matheson teacher; b Crathie 15.1.42
res asst physiol Aberd 1962–66, sen tech physiol univ of Tor. Canada 1967–69
m Aber 23.12.64 Ian S. Hay MA 1963 *qv*

DEAS-DAWLISH Christopher Malcolm Keith MA 1966

DEATON Mairi Rose MA 1970
d of Leslie H. D. civ eng and Janet Wood; b Edin 11.6.49
teacher: Hawick 1971–76, Derby middle s Osnabruck W Ger from 1976

DEHDASHTY Akbar BSc(agr) 1963

DELANEY Thomas MA 1957

DEMIRALAY Ibrahim PhD 1970
BSc(Ankara)

DEMPSEY Mary Henderson MA 1959
m MacCallum

DEMPSTER Albert George MA 1966

DEMPSTER Elaine Alexandria MA 1970
d of Alexander J. D. bldg estimator/valuer and Irene C. Summers; b Caversham 20.10.48
visiting exec off. DHSS Manc 1970–72
m Huntly 1.8.70 Philip J. Coombes sheet metal worker/welder s of William C. Chester

DEMPSTER Walter MA 1958
s of Walter D. acct Royal Bank of Scotland and Catherine Robertson clerkess; b Aviemore 4.3.37
teacher: Echt s 1959–69, head Arnage s from 1969
m Banchory 18.4.64 Annie Duncan nurse d of John D. Cullerlie

DENHAM Neil Leicester MB ChB 1956

DENHOLM Alexander Carle MB ChB 1957
s of Robert D. Scot. epis clergyman and Doris E. Dixon teacher dom sc; b Fraserburgh 23.3.31
h o Edin RI 1958–59; Royal Aust Air Force 1959–63; g p Perth W Aust from 1964 and clin tut. g p W Aust univ from 1976
m Edin 23.8.58 Myfanwy G. Owen occup therap d of John L. O. MB ChB(Edin)

DENNISTON Alexander Hastie *MA 1966

DENOON Brian Donald James MA 1959
s of Robert A. D. MA(Edin) teacher and Robina M. MacPhee MA(Edin) teacher; b Inv 23.1.37
teacher Inv h s from 1960, asst prin from 1973
m Inverbervie 27.12.61 Sheila M. Campbell MA 1959 *qv*

DENOON Charles Alexander Royston MA 1962

DENOON Deirdre Margaret Ann MA 1962

DENT John Barry PhD 1964
s of Cyril D. eng and Barbara R. Jackson; b Barrow-in-Furness 11.10.37
BSc(R'dg) 1960 MAgricSc(R'dg) 1962
lect R'dg 1964–70; reader Nott 1971–74; prof univ Canterbury NZ from 1974
m Sutton 1965 Sandra C. Webb BA(R'dg) teacher d of Edward W. W. Sutton

DENT Lesley Scott PhD 1957 DSc 1972
d of Hugh A. D. civ serv and Marjorie Lord; b Grimsby 19.5.32
BA(Cantab) FInstP 1974
res fell.: Penn state univ USA 1957–59, Aberd 1959–66; Aberd: lect 1966–74, sen lect 1974–80, reader from 1980
m Pa USA 17.5.58 Fredrick P. Glasser DSc 1968 *qv*

DENTON Nigel George Martin *MA 1966

DERIA Abdillahi MB ChB 1966

DESOUGI Mohamed Abdo BSc(for) 1970
BSc(Khart)

DEWAR Anne Armstrong BSc 1970
d of Christopher A. D. dairyman and Elizabeth B. Wilson caterer; b St Andrews 24.3.50
teacher biol: Kirkland h s Methil 1971–73, Maltby g s Yorks 1973–74; analyst progr Sheff from 1974
m Denbeath 31.7.73 Andrew N. Brown BSc(St And) oper res scient s of George B. N. B. Methil

DEWAR Brenda Louise *LLB 1969
d of Peter F. D. proof reader and Emily P. Dorian MA 1936 *qv*; b Aber 21.12.47
NP 1972
Edin: law app 1969–71, leg. asst Balfour & Manson 1971–76, ptnr from 1976
m Glasg 10.9.71 Donald G. Rennie MA 1968 *qv*

DEWAR David BSc(eng) 1957

DEWAR Ian Alexander *MA 1963
s of James A. D. civ serv and Mary Jessiman; b York 14.4.40
Ottawa: pers off. Canadian broadcasting corp 1964–66; pers off. dept fin. 1966–68; dept nat defence: dir labour relations 1968–70, dir biling programs 1970–72; dir biling programs Treasury 1972–74; dir exec staffing civ serv comm 1974–76; asst secy to Cabinet (pers) from 1976
m Aber 17.8.63 Julie Pack MA 1961 *qv*

DEWAR James Graham BEd 1970
s of George D. butcher and Annie Graham; b Alloa 3.4.39
teacher geog RGC Aber from 1970

DEWAR James Wilson *BSc 1956
s of John D. eng and Margaret H. Wilson teacher; b Maud 9.8.34
teacher geog: Montrose acad 1957–58, Forfar acad 1958–59, prin geog Kirkwall g s from 1959
m Kirkwall 15.7.66 Mary M. Hercus teacher of mus d of George H. Kirkwall

DEWAR John Willocks MB ChB 1969
s of John M. D. insur ag and Mary F. Willocks; b Dun 31.1.39
BSc(St And) 1964 DA(Dub) 1975 FFARCSI 1977
resid m o: geriat Dun 1969–70, paediat Aber 1970–71, Burnie Tasmania 1971–72; g p locums NSW Aust 1972–73; regist anaest Perth, Ninewells hosp Dun from 1973
m Dun 1966 Alison J. R. Duncan lab asst d of Peter J. D. Dun

DEWAR Peter Saunders *BSc 1968 PhD 1972
s of William D. poultry farm./market gardener/museum attendant and Doris C. Stevenson milk off., lab steward; b Perth 15.12.45
FCS 1970
res fell. org chem S'ton 1971–73; org chem in chem process dev The Boots Co Nott 1973–75; chief chem Broomchemie: Almelo Neths 1975–77, Terneuzen Neths from 1977
m Aber 15.4.70 Anne H. Bowman insur clerkess, lib asst d of Albert H. B. Aber

DEWAR Robert BSc(eng) 1959

DEY Elizabeth Milne *MA 1967 Dip Ed 1968
m Moir

DEY Elizabeth Wilson MA 1967
m Trevena

DEY Neil Alexander *MA 1969

DHALL Dharan Pal PhD 1968 cMD 1970
MB(Manc) FRCSE

DIACK Alistair Angus BSc 1959

DIACK William George Hendry MB ChB 1963
s of William D. MA 1930 *qv*(III); b Dunfermline 3.7.39
h o: City hosp Aber, ARI 1963–64; g p: Insch 1964–65, Inverbervie from 1965
m Aber 26.10.63 Patricia A. Bain lab tech d of William B. Aber

DIAMENT Morton Leonard *MB ChB 1964 MD 1967
s of Robert D. bus. man. and Betty Gang; b New York 13.7.29
BA(Col) 1951
h o ARI 1964–65; Aberd: Garden res fell. med 1965–66, lect physiol 1966–69, h o obst, anaest 1969–70; g p: Stromness 1970–76, Dounby from 1976
m Edin 11.12.54 DeLille M. M. Porter MA(Edin) teacher d of James G. P. Aber

DIAMOND Anthony William MSc 1968 PhD 1971
s of William H. D. BA(Cantab) civ eng and Dorothy G. Powell; b Calcutta 5.9.44
BA(Cantab) 1966
grad res asst to Dr Black FRS Oxford 1970–72; scient admin Cousin Is nature reserve Seychelles from 1973
m Canada 27.9.69 Elizabeth P. McIntyre MLitt 1968 *qv*

DIAZ Elgin *MA 1969
s of Loyola E. D. teacher and Mavis Schumacher teacher, dressmaker; b Colombo 15.9.45
res assoc Leic 1969–73; stud. Derby coll of art 1973; potter Nott from 1973
m Leic 1971 Christina J. Schule BA(Leic) d of Freidrich S. Teneriffe and Hamburg

DICK Andrew Duthie BSc 1959
s of Henry D. fishcurer and Elspeth Duthie; b Peterhead 27.9.36
teacher sc Peterhead acad 1960–68; head St Andrew's s Inverurie; advis prim educ Aber c c 1971–75; div educ off. Gordon div Grampian reg c from 1975
m Peterhead 1959 Olive McConachie d of Andrew McC. Peterhead

DICK Douglas McDonald *BSc 1956 PhD 1959
s of Walter R. D. secy board of man. Moray hosps and Grace McDonald secy; b Elgin 22.1.35
chief analyst ICI Slough from 1959
m Aber 27.7.60 Irene E. Davidson secy d of Arthur G. D. Aber

DICK Eleanore St. Vernal *MA 1970 Dip Ed 1971
d of William D. BSc(Glas) civ eng and Maisie M. Brown nurse; b Glasg 6.5.48
asst educ psych Angus c c 1971–74
m Edin 20.7.73 David J. B. Anderson MA 1970 *qv*

DICK Elizabeth Marjory MA 1967
d of Thomas M. D. MA(Glas) headmaster and Petronella J. M. Roojackers; b Bellshill 8.3.47
teacher: Engl Eshwege Germany 1968, Ger/Fr asst Kaimhill s s Aber 1969–70, asst prin mod lang Holyrood s s Edin/oral examiner Ger for SED 1970–74; teacher Ger Melbourne from 1975
m Aber –.6.70 Robert Stevenson BSc(eng)(H-W) elect. s of Alfred S. Aber

DICK William Alexander *MA 1958
s of James D. quarry worker and Isabella M. Barclay; b Elgin 11.3.35
man. trainee T. Wall & Sons Edin 1959–60; man. Simplicity Patterns Blantyre 1960–62; man. consult. F. B. Trethewey & Ptnrs Manc 1962–64; lect Strath from 1964
m Dun 3.4.65 Ruth Knight lect d of William L. K. Dun

DICK William Graham *MA 1970

DICKIE Agnes MA 1957 LLB 1959

DICKIE Arthur Coull *BSc 1962 PhD 1965
s of Arthur J. D. marine eng and Elizabeth Coull; b Aber 2.2.40
res fell. St And 1965–67; sen biochem Aberd from 1967
m Aber 24.8.66 Barbara J. Thain tv prod. asst d of John T. Aber

DICKIE David Murray *BSc 1968 Dip Ed 1969

DICKIE Douglas Sutherland *BSc 1968
s of Douglas D. pharm and Sheila M. Wood; b Aber 6.1.47
BSc(City univ Lond) 1972
ophth optician Aber from 1973

DICKIE Gordon Lindsay MB ChB 1968
s of James L. T. D. MB ChB 1942 *qv* and Alma C. Ritchie MB ChB 1942 *qv*; b Aber 25.2.45
DObstRCOG 1970 CCFP 1973
post grad g p training 1968–71; geog lect dept fam med univ of W Ontario Lond Ontario 1971–73, asst prof from 1973
m Aber 21.7.69 Margaret C. Leiper MA 1969 *qv*

DICKIE John Keay *MA 1957
s of Alexander J. D. agr eng and Margaret I. Keay teacher; b Bankhead 17.5.35
nat serv RAF 1957–59; trainee acct man. chartered bank Lond 1959–60; teacher Renfrewsh 1961–64; prin teacher Turriff 1964–66; lect coll of educ Aber from 1966
m Aber 15.8.61 Anne H. W. Foley lib d of Augustine F. Dunfermline

DICKIE William Wood *MA 1968
s of Douglas D. pharm and Sheila M. Wood; b Aber 12.5.41
Dip Ed(Edin) 1969
teacher hist St Mirins acad Paisley 1969–71; stud. phil pontifical Greg Rome 1972; lect lib stud. Peterborough 1973–75; head sixth form St Benedict's s Bury St Edmunds from 1975

DICKSON Alexander MB ChB 1969
s of Alexander D. master tailor and Mary A. Thom tailoress; b Girvan 30.3.45
DObstRCOG 1971
h o Scot. and Eng 1969–73; g p New Cumnock from 1973
m Aber 30.4.71 Murdina V. MacInnes nurse d of Murdoch MacI. Gourock

DICKSON David Alexander *BSc(for) 1958

DICKSON Fiona Jane *BSc 1960
m Mellanby

DICKSON James Grant MA 1959 LLB 1962
s of Lewis G. D. banker and Eleanor Ellis MA 1929 *qv*; b Glasg 17.6.38
leg. asst: Oban 1962–63, Edin 1963–66, Edin corp 1966–75; prin solic Lothian reg c from 1975
m Edin 14.10.66 Shirley Gray secy

DICKSON James Henderson BSc 1964

DICKSON John MA 1970

DICKSON Thomas *BSc(eng) 1967

DICKSON William John *MA 1968
s of George D. fruit merch and Magdalene Black; b Edin 5.6.45
res Paris 1968–70; lect Fr Glas from 1970
m Glasg 3.10.70 Michèle Bassi LèsL (Paris) teacher

DILLON Geoffrey MB ChB 1958
s of John T. D. pers off. and Beatrice M. Smith; b York 17.9.28
MRCGP 1968
h o gen hosps Aber 1958–59; g p Cockermouth 1959–61; s h o gen hosps Aber 1961–63; g p Spalding from 1963
m 10.7.58 Helen F. B. Grieve MB ChB 1956 *qv*

DINNES James Annand *MA 1956
s of Robert D. master butcher and Jane A. Keith; b Peterhead 25.8.27
FSAScot 1963 Dip TCP(H-W) 1964 Assoc M Royal Town Planning Inst 1965; Assoc M BIM 1975
farm man. spec Victoria BC 1957–59; plan. res off. Cupar 1960–64, county dev off. Buckie 1964–70; dep dev off. NESDA Aber from 1970
m Aber 22.9.52 Nancy R. C. Davidson MA 1949 *qv*

DINDA Paritosh Kumar PhD 1960
BSc(agr)(Calc)

DINWIDDIE Robert MB ChB 1969
s of Noel A. W. D. MA(Edin) master printer and May Kennedy MA(Edin); b Dumfries 23.2.45
DCH(Lond) 1971 MRCP(UK) 1974
h o Dumfries and Galloway RI 1969–70; paediat h p RACH 1970–71; res fell. ch health Aberd 1971–73; paediat regist RACH 1973–74; asst chief res phys ch hosp Philadelphia 1975–76; regist, sen regist hosp for sick ch Gr Ormond St Lond 1975–77; consult. paediat Gr Ormond St, Queen Charlotte's hosp from 1977; hon sen lect inst of ch health, inst of obst/gyn univ of London from 1977
m Dumfries 23.10.71 Mary M. Saunderson RGN d of James S. Dumfries

DINWOODIE John Macmillan Walter *BSc(for) 1957 PhD 1960
b Ayr 29.3.35
MTech(Brunel) 1976
Princes Risborough lab BRE: jun res fell. scient civ serv 1960–62, sen scient off. 1963–70, prin scient off. from 1970
m Aber 15.7.58 Margaret Johnson BSc 1957 *qv*

DIOMI Pierre PhD 1969
MD(Paris)

DISBURY William Harold BSc 1970
s of H. C. J. D. civ serv and Winifred E. Ryder; b Bootle 2.1.48
Thurso: barman 1970–71, UKAEA (SO) from 1971
m Thurso 4.2.71 Emily A. Barrons

DIX, Helen Main BSc 1960
d of Harry W. D. civ serv and Nellie Lees civ serv; b Aber 5.2.39
teacher maths: Berwicksh h s 1961–64, Aber h s for girls 1964–65, Grove acad Dun 1965–66, Aber acad 1968–74
m Aber 2.10.65 Archibald B. Allan Anglican clergyman s of Archibald W. G. A. Glasg

DIXON Geoffrey Arthur MB ChB 1965 Dip Psychother 1970
DPM(Scot. Conj)

DIXON George Andrew *MA 1957
s of James W. D. and Beatrice R. Reid MA 1925 *qv*; b Grantown-on-Spey 12.5.36
BSc(Edin) 1967

DIXON John Michael Martin *MA 1969
s of John M. D. journalist (killed on active service 1941) and Ena J. Harland; b Lossiemouth 25.3.42
Lond: O & M off. 1969–70; pers work from 1970
m Aber 30.1.71 Anne S. Murray MA 1968 *qv*

DIXON Margaret Doreen *MA 1968

DIXON Roy George Ogilvie *MA 1968

DOAK Noreen Mary Henderson MA 1970
d of Matthew M. D. master butcher and Mary T. Sommerville; b Bellshill 3.8.49
RGN 1972 SCM 1975
staff nurse Aber and Edin 1973–74; stud. midwife Bellshill 1974–75
m Aber 14.6.75 John A. Young MB ChB 1973 s of Archibald G. Y. Longniddry

DOBSON Alan PhD 1956
s of Albert P. D. clerk and Dorothy B. Hougham nurse; b Bethnal Green 20.12.28
BA(Cantab) 1952 MA 1970
Rowett inst Aber: scient off., sen scient off. 1952–61; sen scient off., prin scient off. 1962–64; Cornell univ Ithaca USA: visiting prof NYS coll vet med 1961–62, assoc prof 1964–71, prof vet physiol from 1971; Wellcome fell. Cantab 1971–72
m Aber 29.3.54 Marjorie J. Masson BSc 1948 *qv*

DOCHERTY Alistair George *LLB 1969
s of James S. D. cashier and Jessie Burnett; b Dun

13.4.47
ACA 1974
Leeds: cashier/securities clerk Barclays Bank 1969–71, CA Guiseley from 1975
m Bradford 21.3.70 Wendy Howard secy d of Joseph E. H. Bradford

DOCHERTY Margaret Isabella MA 1968
d of Robert H. D. head postmaster and Alexia M. Niven cler off.; b St And 9.5.47
teacher Banff acad 1969–71
m Banff 5.4.69 William R. McRobert insur insp s of Grant McR. Stonehaven

DODD Bernard Thomas *MA 1962
s of Sydney T. D. caterer and Frances V. Stewart; b Lond 11.4.34
res DSIR, SSRC, Min of Lab Sheff univ 1962–71; Learning Syst (training des consult.) Richmond 1971–73; prin psych Admiralty res lab 1973–76; sen psych (Navy) div from 1976
m Lond 16.8.58 Hazel A. Moore bank clerk d of Edwin L. M. Lond

DODD Ingrid Helena MA 1967
d of John A. A. D. comp dir/eng and Brenda C. Vale MB ChB(Edin) phys; b Kingsdown 25.6.47
MBBS(Lond) 1975 MRCS LRCP 1975
interpreter/teacher Rome 1967–68; med stud. Guy's hosp Lond 1968–75

DODD Sarah Margaret *MA 1968
m Dukes

DODDS John James Anderson *BSc 1965 PhD 1968
s of John Dodds coal miner and Lena Anderson; b N'cle-u-Tyne 9.6.41
teacher biol Dingwall acad 1968–73; prin biol Lochaber h s Fort William from 1973
m Aber 29.8.66 Anne Sinclair MA 1966 *qv*

DODDS John Keith Mathieson BSc(eng) 1967
s of John M. D. MA 1928 *qv* and Anna L. McDonald MA 1934 *qv*; b Timperley 12.6.44
DMS (RGIT Aber) 1968 ACMA 1972
grad app Girling Cwmbran Wales 1968–70; trainee Connal & Co Glasg 1970–72; Lond: dir Imperial Cold Stores 1972–73, man. dir Bermondsey Cold Stores 1973–75; dir Charles Alexander & Ptnr (Transport) 1975–76; prop. Netherley bus. serv from 1977
m Aber 2.12.77 Ingrid A. J. Cormack MA 1964 *qv*

DOHERTY James *MA 1962 *MEd 1965

DOHERTY Mary Margaret MA 1967
m Murray

DOIG Dorothy Margaret MA 1967

DOIG Jonathan David *MA 1969
s of David T. D. journalist and Katherine W. Watters; b Dun 12.6.47
teacher Kirkintilloch from 1974
m Ullapool 9.4.74 Helen M. Hennessy BSc 1971 nurse d of Jeremiah D. H. MB ChB(Cork) Sweetly

DOIG Robert Jules MB ChB 1956 MD 1973
s of Robert S. D. MB ChB(Glas) m o h Isle of Lewis and Lucienne Nizart teacher; b Lennoxtown 12.5.30
MRCPsych 1973
h o Aber 1956–57; resid phys Paris 1963–66; Lond: regist 1966–71, sen regist 1971–73, consult. psychiat from 1973

m Lond 9.8.73 Ruth Watson BSc(Lond) soc worker d of Robert W.

DONAGHEY Sean Francis O'Brien *BSc 1969
s of Cyril F. O'B. D. BSc(eng)(Lond) eng, soc worker and Lois A. M. Daniels drama organis; b Sunderland 25.2.44
res stud. applied biol Cantab 1969–72; lect chem/biol Newark tech coll from 1972
m Nott 6.12.69 Margaret J. Ingram BSc 1969 *qv*

DONALD Alice Margaret *MA 1958
d of David D. MA 1927 *qv* and Alice B. Morrison MA 1927 *qv*; b Aber 20.7.36
teacher maths: Bell-Baxter h s 1959–62; Edin: spec asst Trinity acad 1962–70, Ainslie Park s s 1970, spec asst Craigmount c s 1970–71
m Aber 30.7.70 Thomas B. S. Campbell MA(Edin) teacher s of William C. MA(Glas) Edin

DONALD Anne Fiona LLB 1969
d of Douglas A. D. BA(Oxon) sheriff and Flora M. Macdonald; b Glasg 24.3.49
Edin: law app 1969–71, leg. asst from 1971

DONALD David MB ChB 1965 PhD 1973
s of Maxwell A. W. D. garage prop. and Barbara A. Mearns; b Huntly 28.4.41
MRCPath
h o ARI 1965–66; lect path. Aberd 1966 and 1974–77; MRC travelling fell. res in USA and visiting asst prof path. Boston univ 1973–74; sen lect path. Aberd from 1977

DONALD David Alexander BSc(agr) 1967
s of David A. D. MA(Cantab) teacher and Sheila C. M. Scott; b Dun 21.8.44
DFMBO(NOSCA) 1968
sales advis BOCM Aber 1968–69; farm man. Inverurie 1969–70; comp man. agri/hort co-op Fettercairn from 1970
m Inv 27.12.69 Lesley A. Ledingham MB ChB 1972 anaest d of Leslie A. L. MB ChB 1934 *qv*

DONALD David James Thomson BSc(eng) 1961

DONALD Elizabeth Louise MA 1957
d of Robert T. D. MA 1914 *qv*(II, III) and Louise Turner MA 1923 *qv*; b Aber 9.9.36
resid Montreal
m Aber 5.10.57 Derick A. Crawford BSc(agr) 1956 *qv*

DONALD Ethel Margaret *MA 1963
d of William D. grocer/storeman and Maggie Ritchie; b Rhynie 23.7.40
res stud. for univ Lanc, Geneva, Paris 1963–65; lect Fr Glas 1965–71
m 27.7.76 Alistair H. Blyth MA(Glas) univ lect s of Henry M. B. Welwyn Garden City

DONALD George Francis John *MA 1957
s of George C. D. lorry driver and Margaret J. U. Shand; b Huntly 16.6.34
teacher mod lang RGC Aber 1958–69; prin Ger Perth acad from 1969 and asst rector from 1973
m Aber 4.4.61 Isabella M. Roe MB ChB 1958 *qv*

DONALD Ian Benzies *MA 1970
s of Forbes M. M. D. acct and Violet L. Benzies; b Aber 26.5.47
Dip Ger for foreigners(Hamburg) 1974
BP: supply asst Lond 1970–71, Hamburg 1971–74; oil trader Mabanaft Hamburg from 1974

DONALD John Gordon MB ChB 1960

DONALD John Henry *BSc(eng) 1963
s of Norman D. electro-plater and Isabella Short; b Aber 6.12.41
Lond: electronic dev eng 1963–65, sen eng 1965–66, proj eng 1966–68, man. proj eng 1968–71, tech dir from 1971
m Aber 28.5.66 Eileen McGrory MA 1964 *qv*

DONALD Leslie Forrest *MA 1967 Dip Ed 1968
s of Robert R. D. shop asst and Helen F. Donald; b Aber 7.4.44
teacher mod lang Mackie acad Stonehaven 1968–70, spec asst 1970–72; prin mod lang Cults acad from 1972
m Aber 30.3.72 Mary K. Smith secy d of John S. Aber

DONALD Margaret Jessie MA 1963
m Finnie

DONALD Maureen BSc 1963
m Reid

DONALD Morag Russell MA 1969
d of Charles R. D. and Hilda M. Russell; b Aber 19.3.49
ALA 1971
children's lib Bridge of Allan 1971–74; branch lib Stirling from 1974
m Aber 16.3.73 Kenneth S. MacSween BSc(for) 1968 *qv*

DONALD Muriel Elizabeth MA 1964

DONALD Robert *LLB 1968
s of Robert S. D. van driver and Eleanor C. Findlay; b Aber 26.2.46
law app Clark & Wallace advoc Aber 1968–70, leg. asst Lefevre & Co advoc Aber 1970–74, ptnr from 1974
m Aber 25.6.69 Judith H. Stuart MA 1967 *qv*

DONALD Ruth Alicia BSc 1966
d of Charles J. D. plumber and Alice Ewen teacher; b Echt 25.10.45
teacher Muthill p s 1967–71
m Aber 13.7.68 Donald S. McLusky BSc 1966 *qv*

DONALD Sheila Elizabeth *BSc 1968 Dip Ed 1969
m Welsby

DONALD Sylvia Margaret Bisset MA 1961
d of George L. D. master mariner and Margaret B. Gardiner; b Aber 27.11.40
teacher: Engl/Lat Possil s s Glasg 1962–63, Engl/commun coll of comm Aber from 1963
m Aber 1.8.61 Norman A. Donald wholesaler/caterer s of Alexander D. Aber

DONALDSON Alan Eunson MB ChB 1967
s of Hector A. D. MA 1927 *qv*: b Aber 28.5.44
DObstRCOG 1969 MRCGP 1973
Aber: h o med City hosp, cas dept Woolmanhill, ENT dermat and ophth Foresterhill and Woodend hosps, obst mat. hosp 1967–69; g p Portlethen 1969, Ellon from 1970
m Aber 24.1.70 Christina J. Melhuish chiropodist d of John W. M. Newtonhill

DONALDSON Anne Forbes MA 1969
d of James I. D. hotelier and Elizabeth A. Robertson teacher; b Kiel W Ger 8.5.48
teacher Edin 1970–71; secy Goethe inst Dublin 1971–73; lect Engl univ of Jyväskylä Finland 1973–76
m Aber 29.12.71 Douglas C. Riach MA 1968 *qv*

DONALDSON John Dallas *BSc 1956 PhD 1959
s of John D. chief welfare off. and Alexandrina M. R. Dallas; b Hopeman 11.11.35
DSc(Lond) 1970 FRIC 1971
asst lect chem Aberd 1958–61; lect, sen lect inorg chem Chelsea coll Lond 1961–72, reader 1972–80; prof indust chem City univ Lond from 1980
m Aber 22.3.61 Elisabeth A. Forrest nurse d of George E. F. Aber

DONALDSON Marjorie Ann *MA 1970
d of Henry C. D. MA(Glas) min of relig and Kathleen R. Anderson MA(Glas) SCM secy; b Glasg 7.4.48
careers advis in schools: Lytham 1970–71, Aber 1971–73; secy course Edin 1973–74; secy Scottish Council of soc serv 1974–76; volunteers organis Edin Council of soc serv from 1976

DONALDSON Marjory Anne Russell MB ChB 1970
d of James A. F. D. PO superv and Frances A. Russell optician; b Aber 1.5.46
ARCM 1964
h o ARI and Woodend hosp Aber 1970–71; teacher violin: Berks 1971–72, Downehouse s Berks 1974–75
m Aber 5.8.71 Douglas G. Fowlie MB ChB 1970 *qv*

DONALDSON William *MA 1968 PhD 1974
s of William D. man. and Margaret G. Buchan nurse; b Ellon 19.7.44
mobile lib Aberdeensh 1974–75; archivist Aber from 1976
m Aber 1.4.70 Loraine Challis-Sowerby MA 1969 *qv*

DONKIN Jean BSc 1965

DONN George Cormack *BSc 1966

DONNELLY Margaret Mary BSc 1970
d of John P. D. soc worker and Mary Fox; b Barrhead 8.8.49
teacher: St Luke's h s Barrhead 1971, Nandom s s Ghana 1972–74, Holyrood s s Glasg from 1974

D'ORBAN Paul Theodore MB ChB 1956
s of Charles D'O. landowner and Constance E. Hill; b Lond 26.5.30
DPM 1961 MRCPsych 1972
m o publ hosp Georgetown Br Guyana 1956–59; psychiat regist Friern hosp Lond 1959–62; psychiat Kingston Jamaica 1962–65; Lond: m o HM prison Holloway 1966–74, consult. psychiat St. George's and Tooting Bec hosps from 1974
m Aber 15.10.55 Laura S. F. Ho-A-Shu MA 1956 *qv*

DORCEY Anthony Hugh Joseph *MA 1969

DORIS Coreen Wilma BEd 1970

DORMAN David Kennedy BSc(agr) 1968
b Cambridge 11.7.45
Dip Man St(Birm) 1972
Ely: man. trainee Dorman Sprayers 1968–69, marketing asst, man. 1970–72; dir marketing and sales Dorman Sprayers, A.C. Mouldings from 1973
m Birm 11.4.72 Pamela Small SRN

DORN Tola *BSc 1969

DORWARD Gordon John *BSc 1967 PhD 1978
s of John D. gen man. coachbuilding comp and Elizabeth S. Easton; b Aber 28.3.45
ACMA 1973 MBA(New Jersey)
direct exchange schol Kansas USA 1967–68; res chem

Aberd 1968–71; trainee acct, marketing prod. group acct T. Wall & Sons (ice-cream) Gloucester from 1971
m Denver Colorado 22.12.74 Rebecca C. Ashley BA (Kansas) syst analyst d of Thomas E. A. BSc Aurora Colorado
d California 27.1.79 *AUR* XLVIII 234

DORWARD Lloyd Forbes PhD 1962
b Dublin 15.6.26
BSc(Lond) 1946 FIEE 1967
prin lect elect. eng Rutherford coll of tech N'cle-u-Tyne 1963–65; head eng dept Oxford poly from 1965
m Aber 14.8.50 Christina Munro secy d of John M. Aber

DOTT Harold Edwin Morton BSc 1967 *1968
s of Eric F. D. MB ChB(Edin) consult. phys (paediat) and Sarah D. Alexander artist; b Edin 5.3.45
res agr Brit overseas dev Cochabamba Bolivia 1969–71; teacher biol: Edin 1972, Lornshill acad Alloa 1972–73; collecting wild life specimens (self-employed) Cochabamba from 1974
m Cochabamba 3.10.74 Teresa Steinbach secy d of Franz S. Cochabamba

DOUDELL John Owen *BSc 1970 Dip Ed 1971
s of Herbert D. clerk and Mary J. Owen; b Liv 11.9.39
NDA 1960
teacher Huntly from 1971

DOUGHERTY Alan John *MA 1961

DOUGHTY Flora Mary Scorgie MA 1963
d of William F. D. MA(Edin) headmaster and Flora Scorgie teacher; b Haddo 30.12.42
teacher: Mintlaw s 1964–70, Westfield s from 1970
m Tarves 6.8.65 Fergie Allan farm. s of William T. C. A. Mintlaw

DOUGLAS Alasdair Henry Mercer *BSc 1970
s of Alan D. MB ChB(St And) med pract and Alexandra D. Murray nurse; b Broughty Ferry 3.3.47
BR man. trainee 1970–71; lect Aberd from 1973
m Aber 23.7.74 Linda J. Forsyth MA 1971 d of Stanley F. MA 1939 *qv*

DOUGLAS Diana Margaret MA 1967
b Edin 27.2.46
secy mod lang dept Strath 1968–72
m Aber 6.8.69 John F. Cameron MA 1967 *qv*

DOUGLAS Ian MA 1968

DOUGLAS John Forbes *BSc 1965

DOUGLAS Lois Ernesta MB ChB 1956
d of Ernest G. D. LRCP(Edin) med pract and Mildred A. Case PO exec; b Jamaica 2.10.28
m o: Bridgetown Barbados 1958, Kingston publ hosp Jamaica 1959–62, Buea West Cameroon 1963, Jamaica 1963–67; asst m o h Bridgetown Barbados 1967–70, m o h from 1970
m Jamaica 8.2.58 Frederick G. Smith QC, SC, BA attorney-at-law Barbados s of Cecil S. Christchurch Barbados

DOUGLAS Louise Munro MA 1970
d of Percy R. D. eng and Muriel M. Sandison nurse; b Insch 24.9.49
teacher hist/mod stud.: Peterhead acad 1971–72, Dingwall acad 1972–73; relief teacher
m Inverurie 25.7.70 Neil F. Grant MA 1968 *qv*

DOUGLAS William Henderson MA 1968
s of Adam F. D. master bldr and Mary J. Cowie; b Elgin 1.12.36
teacher: Engl/hist Lossiemouth h s 1969–71; asst prin guid Buckie h s from 1971
m Buckie 12.10.60 Caroline Thomson d of William A. T. Buckie

DOUGLASS Lesley Helen *MA 1969 *MEd 1973
d of Edward E. D. bus. man. and Helen Brebner postmistress; b Sidcup 23.1.47
teacher: Livingston 1970–71, Aber 1972–73, educ psych Aberdeensh from 1973
m Aber 8.9.73 Harvey J. Aberdein LLB 1976 s of James A. Aber

DOULL Peter John Uilleam *BSc 1962

DOUSE Michael John *MEd 1964
BSc(econ)(Belf) Dip Ed(Belf)

DOW Alexander Crawley PhD 1957
s of James M. D. c c arch. Renfrewsh and Elsie D. Crawley; b Paisley 12.10.05
MA(Glas) 1928 MC(Italy) 1945
C of S min Kelty 1932–48; chap. 8th Army Africa, Italy 1940–45; min East St Clements Aber 1948–50; chap. to forces Ger, Scot, Eng, Ireland 1950–58; min Stoneywood 1958–71, Westray and Papa Westray from 1971
m Paisley 20.7.32 Marion C. Anthony

DOW Gordon Edwards MA 1965 Dip Ed 1966
s of Alan B. D. joiner, store man., printer and Mary Edwards; b Glasg 19.4.44
teacher: Glenrothes p s 1966–68, Arbroath from 1968
m Aber 20.8.66 Linda J. Anderson d of Alister A. Aber

DOW Marion Baird Anthony BSc 1960
d of Alexander C. D. PhD 1957 *qv*; b Kelty 21.10.34
teacher: maths/sc Hilton s Aber 1961–64, sc Bankhead acad 1964–67, maths/sc Westray from 1967
m Bucksburn 8.7.63 Sydney M. Cooper lay missionary C of S s of William C. Bucksburn

DOW Michael Gillean Cameron McDonald *BSc 1957

DOW Robin James *MA 1970
s of Alexander J. D. rly clerk, cost acct and Dorothy D. Muir s secy; b Glasg 10.5.39
teacher Balloch 1971–73, Rothesay s s from 1973
m Aber 1970 Wendy J. Gaffron MA 1969 *qv*

DOWDEN Hugh George Martin BSc(for) 1956

DOWDS Stephen LLB 1970

DOWER Michael James BSc 1968
s of James D. clerk civ serv and Doris M. Forsyth; b Aber 28.2.44
med copy-writer: Oss Holland 1968–71, Welwyn Garden City, Dagenham 1971–75; Lond: acct exec 1975–76, acct superv from 1976
m Aber 18.7.69 Moira Mackenzie MA 1968 *qv*

DOWEY Paul Wilson MA 1967

DOWNIE Isobel Mary *MA 1968
d of Alexander J. D. post./tel off. and Eleanor H. Hay clerk; b Banff 13.8.46
Oxford: OUP gen catalogue 1969–70; copyright edit. and lib 1970–74; Sask Canada: sessional lect 1974–75, teaching fell. 1975–76
m Aber 26.7.68 Leonard M. Findlay MA 1967 *qv*

DOWNIE James Ritchie *BSc 1958
s of George D. fisherman and Sarah W. Ritchie; b Rosehearty 23.9.36
Zambia: field geol Chartered Exploration Lusaka 1958–68; asst chief geol NCCM Chingola div 1968–71; chief geol NCCM: Broken Hill div Kabwe 1971–75, Konkola div Chililabombwe from 1975
m Aber 5.1.62 Millicent M. Garrioch nurse d of David B. G. MA(Edin) Milltimber

DOWNIE Margaret Rosaline *BSc 1963
d of William J. D. fisherman and Margaret M. West teacher; b Rosehearty 22.7.41
teacher Aber acad 1964–66; res asst Wisconsin 1966–67; various part-time teaching posts and at Simon Langton g s Canterbury from 1968
m Aber 30.7.64 Charles Brown BSc 1963 *qv*

DOWNIE Mary Christine BSc 1970
d of Maxwell D. marine eng and Barbara A. Taylor nurse; b Rosehearty 7.6.48
teacher biol: Lasswade 1971–75; Aber: Summerhill acad 1975–76, Hazlehead acad from 1976
m Rosehearty 10.8.74 Donald Maclean loc govt off. s of Donald G. M. Dingwall

DOWNIE Norman William *MA 1966 Dip Ed 1967
s of William S. D. MA 1922 *qv*; b Aber 4.7.44
Lond: lect International Computers 1967–69; syst man. Glaxo 1969–73; computer man. Oxford reg health auth from 1973
m Aber 15.8.69 Cyndy A. Eastman dep computer man. d of John F. Heasman Surbiton

DOWNIE Robert Taylor *MA 1964

DOWNIE Robert William Mackenzie MB ChB 1960
s of Robert D. auctioneer/valuator and Elizabeth R. C. Mackenzie; b Aber 1.2.36
FRCSE 1966 Dip Laryngology & Otology(Lond) 1968
h o Woodend hosp Aber, ARI 1960–61; trainee g p Ballater 1961–62; temp lect anat Aberd 1962–63; regist ARI: surg 1963–65, ENT 1965–68; sen regist ENT 1968–72
m Durris 4.9.68 Aileen J. McHardy MB ChB 1966 *qv*
d Aber 9.5.72

DOWNIE Sheena Elizabeth MA 1965
d of Robert W. D. sales rep and Lillian E. Ferries; b Aber 4.2.32
teacher Engl Aber: Northfield acad 1966–67, Kaimhill s s, Kincorth acad 1967–73; asst prin Engl Kincorth acad from 1973
m Aber 7.7.55 John L. C. Duthie sales rep s of John D. Aber; husb *d* 1972

DOWNIE Susan Margaret MA 1964

DOWNIE William Alexander MA 1969
s of Alexander J. D. post./tel off. and Eleanor H. Hay cashier/bookkeeper; b Banff 6.3.44
computer spec Lond from 1969
m Aber 11.10.68 Sandra G. Reid telex oper d of Alfred R. Huntly

DOWNIE William Tytler MA 1960
s of William T. D. baker and Gertrude Leask; b Rosehearty 1.5.35
teacher Engl/hist: Possilpark s s Glasg 1963–66, Fraserburgh acad from 1966 and housemaster from 1972
m Fraserburgh 6.7.73 Edith C. J. Cardno MA 1964 *qv*

DOWNING Andrew John *BSc 1969

DOWNING Charles Stephen *BSc 1969

DOWNING Peter William BSc(eng) 1970

DOWNING Ronald Ernest *BSc 1969

DOWSETT Anthony Peter BSc(eng) 1965
s of Joseph D. loc govt off. and Irene D. Gould; b Epsom 2.10.42
post grad app Bristol Siddeley Engines Watford 1964–66; Carreras-Rothmans Belf: mech eng 1966–67, packing dept man. 1967–71, prod. man. Unilever Croydon 1971–73; fin. analyst Brit Leyland Birm from 1973
m Oxborough 8.10.66 Theresa M. Smith secy d of David R. E. S. FRCS Norfolk

DOYLE Rosemary Galloway MA 1964
d of James M. D. hairdresser and Mary M. Sutherland teacher; b Aber 16.6.41
teacher: Engl/Fr Fraserburgh acad 1966–67, Engl/hist Mackie acad Stonehaven 1967–68; Aber: Engl/Fr Kaimhill s s 1968–69, Cornhill p s 1969–72
m Aber 6.10.66 Duncan D. Chisholm MB ChB 1965 *qv*

DRANE John William *MA 1969
PhD(Manc)

DRAPER Ivan Thomas MB ChB 1956
s of Thomas G. D. cost acct and Ethel A. Pearson; b Derby 11.9.32
MRCPE 1959 FRCPE 1966
h o med, surg, neurosurg Aber 1956–58; sen h o gen med Glasg 1958–59; regist and sen regist neurol Edin 1959–65; Fulbright fell. Wellcome fell. and fell. clin physiol Johns Hopkins univ Baltimore USA 1962–63; consult. neurol inst of neurol sc S gen hosp Glasg from 1965
m Aber 4.7.56 Muriel M. Monro journalist d of John M. Aber

DRAYSON Geraldine Munro BSc 1968
d of Eric G. D. loc govt off. and Marjory B. White; b Ealing 20.9.46
teacher: sc Cults acad Aber 1968–69, Peterhead acad 1969; ptnr George C. McGowan (Contracts) civ eng contr Banchory from 1969
m Aber 12.8.69 George C. McGowan BSc(eng)1966 *qv*

DREVER Michael James Flett MA 1963
s of Thomas A. D. clerk of works and Helen S. Flett; b Harray 14.3.41
teacher Kirkwall g s from 1964
m Orkney –.7.68 Inga Tulloch bank clerk d of James T. Kirkwall

DREW Elizabeth Helen MA 1969
d of Sidney F. D. radio and tv eng and Helen A. Buchan shorthand typist; b Swindon 11.8.47
teacher Fr/Ger: Aberfeldy 1970–75, Fraserburgh 1975–76; prin Fr/Ger Aberfeldy from 1976
d road accident 16.2.80 *AUR* XLVIII 443

DRINKWATER Barry William *MA 1966
s of Kenneth D. foreman joiner and Alice M. Broadley distribution area man.; b Manc 6.9.42
grad pers off., man. recruitment of Standard Telephones and Cables, part of ITT, Amer multinational corporation based in NY mainly Lond 1966–77; pers man. LRC International Lond 1977; recruitment dir Cambridge recruitment consult. from 1977
m Epping 28.4.73 Christine Draine secy d of John F. A. D.

DRUMMOND Bruce Mackenzie MA 1968
s of John A. D. ophth optician and Olive B. Parkinson; b Aber 5.10.48
BSc(Ophth Optics)(Manc inst of sc and tech) 1971
ophth optician Aber from 1971

DRUMMOND Elizabeth Margaret MA 1963
m Miller

DRUMMOND Iain Roderic MA 1962
s of Henry T. H. D. MA(Cantab) lib Aberd and Dorothea O. Mackintosh; b Stirling 22.5.41
acct/audit clerk Aber 1962–65; Inl Rev: exec off./computer progr Aber, Perth, E Kilbride, Carlisle 1965–72; insp of taxes/syst analyst Lond from 1973
m Aber 23.9.67 Ann E. Robertson d of William R. Milltimber

DRUMMOND John Parkinson MA 1961

DRUMMOND Neil MA 1958
s of Robert H. D. supt eventide home and Christina MacLeod matron eventide home; b Stornoway 21.11.36
MBCS 1973 FIDP 1973 MSc(N Lond poly) 1974
teacher Gordon s Huntly 1959–64; lect, sen lect coll of comm Aber from 1964
m Dufftown 7.7.61 Winifred D. Shearer teacher d of John S.

DRUMMOND Peter John *MA 1970

DRUMMOND Sheelagh Margaret BSc 1970
d of Charles W. D. bank man. and Kathleen A. Reid teacher p e; b Galashiels 1.4.50
res asst microbiol MRC Edin 1970–71
m Cupar 7.8.70 George L. McQuitty LLB(Edin) solic s of Gordon R. McQ. Cupar

DRY Frank Thomas *BSc 1965
s of Jesse B. D. eng and Louisa Pilkington; b Manc 2.12.42
Macaulay inst Aber: soil surv off., scient off. 1965–72; sen scient off. from 1972
m Aber 16.4.71 Helen M. Paterson MA 1966 *qv*

DRYDEN William Alexander Fraser *MA 1970
s of William D. acct, bus. man. and Mary Mackay tailoress; b Inv 24.3.48
Dip LA(Edin) 1972 Assoc Landscape Inst 1977
plan. asst (landscape) E Kilbride dev corp 1972–74; landscape arch. Warrington dev corp from 1974
m Thurso 7.8.71 Sheila R. Chisholm teacher

DUCAT Thomas Nicholas *MA 1965

DUDMESH Yvonne Margaret MB ChB 1968
d of Stanley D. and Lilian M. Robins hotel prop.; b Bournemouth 11.2.43
DRCOG 1970
h o Salisbury gen infirm. 1968–69; h o obst/gyn Odstock hosp Salisbury 1969–70; trainee asst g p Teignmouth 1970–71; asst g p Hugglescote/cas off. Loughborough gen hosp 1971–73; g p Hugglescote from 1973
m Teignmouth 12.6.71 Frederick A. Bladon spec eng s of Frederick R. B. Teignmouth

DUFF Ernest Melvin *MA 1964
s of Alexander D. tinsmith and Lily Kinsley; b Peterhead 21.4.39
teacher: Aber 1965–74; asst head p s from 1974
m Aber 21.5.66 Margaret M. Collier teacher/free-lance writer d of John C. C. Aber

DUFF John MA 1965

DUFF William Strath *MA 1968
s of William D. elect. and Jeannie M. Cheyne; b Aber 9.2.45
teacher: Salford 1969–71, Corowa NSW Aust from 1972; salesman NCR Manc 1971–72
m Alnwick 11.11.67 Lesley J. Meyer Dip Ed(Manc) art teacher d of Wilfred H. M. Alnwick

DUFFTY Paul MB ChB 1970
s of Stanley D. acct and Joan M. Pitman teacher; b Leeds 1.9.46
MRCP 1976
h o: RACH, ARI 1970–71, Scarborough hosp 1971–72; sen h o royal Manc ch hosp 1972; lect ch health Aberd from 1972
m Aber 14.8.69 Lesley M. Macdonald MB ChB 1970 *qv*

DUFFUS Anne MA 1959
m Clarke

DUFFUS Evelyn Elizabeth MA 1959
d of Alexander C. D. clerk and Caroline M. S. Olley; b Aber 19.7.39
teacher: Aber 1960–65 and from 1968
m Aber 2.8.63 Alistair Duncan BSc 1971 civ serv, teacher s of Charles D. Aber

DUFFUS Gillian Marjorie MB ChB 1964 MD 1969
d of George M. R. D. MB ChB 1931 *qv* and Marjorie A. S. Third MA 1934 *qv*; b Aber 30.4.40
DObstRCOG 1966 PhD(Glas) 1975 MFCM 1977
h o Aber hosps 1964–66; res asst mat. hosp Aber 1966–69; clin instr dept of obst/gyn Downstate med centre State univ NY Brooklyn 1969–70; Wellcome res fell. royal mat. hosp Glasg 1970–72; res fell. soc paediat unit Glas 1972–75; fell. commun med from 1975
m Aber 30.10.70 Ronald J. McIlwaine MB ChB(Belf) consult. psychiat s of Gilbert McI. Craigavon Co Armagh

DUFFUS John Logie Lyall *MA 1969
s of George M. R. D. MB ChB 1931 *qv* and Marjorie A. S. Third MA 1934 *qv*; b Aber 12.2.46
progr oper asst BBC radio Lond 1969–70; Scot. Opera Glasg: pers asst to gen admin 1971–73, asst gen admin 1973–76, tech controller 1976–79; gen man. Hong Kong Philharmonic Soc from 1979

DUFFUS Peter Ross Sinclair MB ChB 1970
s of George M. R. D. MB ChB 1931 *qv* and Marjorie A. S. Third MA 1934 *qv*; b Aber 18.8.47
DObstRCOG 1973 MRCGP 1974
h o ARI 1970–71; vocational trg scheme for g p Aberd 1971–74; g p from 1974; dep police surg from 1975
m Aber 25.9.70 Margaret M. Millar MA 1969 *qv*

DUFFY Gerard MA 1961

DUGDALE Jeffrey *MA 1970

DUGUID Eleanor Jean MA 1969
d of Adam D. psychiat nurse and Helen F. Donald; b Perth 22.3.48
teacher Dun 1970–72; civ serv Edin 1972–77
m Scone 14.10.72 Norman R. Weir civ serv

DUGUID Elizabeth Lillie MA 1970
d of Alexander J. D. comp exec and Elizabeth Lillie; b Aber 13.6.49
A Inst Pers Man 1975
teacher mod lang Surrey 1971–72; Lond: trg off. 1972–73, pers off. from 1973; Qantas Airways, Chiswick 1976

DUGUID George Robertson BSc 1966 Dip Ed 1967

DUGUID Hilda Margaret MA 1969
d of William H. D. papermaker and Elspet M. Hadden millworker; b Bucksburn 25.12.28
employment asst careers serv Aber town council, Grampian reg from 1970
m Aber 10.5.50 Swanson McKenzie MA 1969 *qv*

DUGUID Margaret Glegg MB ChB 1957
d of Alexander G. D. supplier off. equipment and Isabella C. Glegg; b Aber
DA(McG) 1966
h o, sen h o Aber 1957–59; rotating interneship Plainfield New Jersey USA 1959–60; resid anest Hartford Connecticut 1960–63; fell. anaest: Montreal 1963–66; fell. anest univ of Vermont Burlington USA 1966–68; attending phys anest Plainfield New Jersey USA from 1968
m Aber Denis Gorvett s of Samuel G. Pontyridd; marr diss

DUGUID Martin Neil MA 1969
s of John D. baker, gardener and Elizabeth Christie; b Weymouth 28.9.45
teacher Aber from 1970
m Elgin 19.8.70 Sheila G. Henderson teacher d of James H. Elgin

DUGUID Robert Watson BSc(eng) 1966
s of Robert H. D. BCom 1926 *qv*; b Calcutta 9.2.45
MICE 1973
site eng UK 1966–71; Birm: des civ eng 1971–72; prod. eng (site) 1972–73; site ag from 1973
m St Albans 27.3.71 Elizabeth M. Rees occup therap d of William R. St Albans

DUNBAR Ian James Cameron MB ChB 1961

DUNBAR John Manson BSc(eng) 1959
s of John M. D. civ serv dept agr(Scot.) and Jessie B. Manson; b Stirling 21.8.37
MICE 1965 PEng(Ont) 1966 AMIWPC 1968 MSc(Strath) 1968 MIPHE 1970
eng asst: Leeds 1959–62, Glasg 1962–66, London Ontario 1966; post grad stud. Glasg 1967; eng man. Paisley 1967; assoc ptnr consult. practice Glasg 1970–71, ptnr from 1971

DUNBAR Mary MA 1959
d of James D. omnibus driver and Mary Castle cook; b Aber 21.11.38
teacher maths: Northfield acad Aber 1960–62, Elgin acad 1963–66
m Aber 11.7.62 Andrew M. Philip civ serv s of Frank P. Aber

DUNBAR Patricia Mary BSc 1956
d of Alexander L. D. farm. and Margaret A. Watson; b Kemnay 19.8.34
AEO at AWRE Aldermaston 1956–57; res asst Milk Marketing Board Thames Ditton 1957–58; AEO at NIRD Reading 1958–61; part-time med phys tech Glasg S gen hosp from 1972
m Aber 21.7.59 Ronald H. Christie BSc(Glas) SSO at AWRE, lect Strath s of James C. Airdrie

DUNBAR Richard Neil Findlay *BSc 1961
s of James D. MA 1925 *qv*; b Margate 1.4.39
electronics eng: Chatham and Frimley 1961–65, Montreal 1965–67, Addlestone 1967–72; sales eng Dulwich 1972–74; sales man. Tolworth 1974–76, Slough from 1977
m Forres 28.12.61 Margaret H. Davie BSc 1960 *qv*

DUNCAN Alastair Barclay *MA 1966 PhD 1976
s of Eric M. D. MA 1929 *qv*; b Kirkpatrick Fleming 9.5.42
res stud. Aberd, Paris 1966–68; dem Fr Aberd 1968–69; temp lect Fr R'dg 1969–70; lect Fr Stir from 1970

DUNCAN Allan George *BSc 1963
s of Donald A. D. sales rep and Annabella Thom; b Aber 17.10.40
DPhil(Oxon) 1966
fell. univ of Calif Los Angeles 1966–67; res chem: US bureau of standards Colorado 1967–69; UKAEA AERE Harwell from 1969
m Aylesbury 5.5.73 Alison P. Reid occup therap d of Patrick R. Aylesbury

DUNCAN Allison Isabella BSc 1962
d of William D. paper millworker and Alice Lindsay; b Peterculter 24.11.41
prob. analyst Hawker Siddeley Hatfield 1962–64; teacher Dun 1964–65; free-lance progr NCR Dun 1965–66; part time progr Strath 1973–75; teacher: St Aldred's h s Paisley 1976–77, St Columba's s for girls Kilmalcolm from 1977
m Aber 30.3.64 Roy M. Johnson BSc(Brist) dynamics eng/lect s of Ernest A. J. Lond

DUNCAN Anne *MA 1968
m Noble

DUNCAN Anne Lawrence *MA 1968
m Cartshore

DUNCAN Brian Thomas Calder MA 1967

DUNCAN Catherine Rose MA 1962
d of James S. D. banker, coal merchant and Catherine McPherson; b Grantown-on-Spey 21.7.41
pers secy Shell internat petr Co Lond 1962–65; teacher Haslemere 1965–67; resid Lagos 1973–77, The Hague from 1978
m Elgin 12.6.65 Richard R. Rayner oil co exec s of Ralph E. R. Twickenham

DUNCAN Cecil John MA 1968

DUNCAN Charles George MB ChB 1967
s of Charles D. ship's carpenter and Margaret Smith; b Aber 6.7.43
CCFP 1974
Ont Canada: fam phys St Catharines 1970–72, Fonthill from 1972
m Aber 16.7.69 Patricia M. McAllister MA 1968 *qv*

DUNCAN Colin George *MA 1969
s of George M. D. gen merch and Nelly Forbes; b Torphins 28.8.47
Marks & Spencer: dept man. Aber 1969–70, Edin 1970–73; asst man. Stirling 1973–76, Preston from 1977

DUNCAN David Alexander *BSc 1969
s of William D. upholsterer and Elizabeth W. Anderson; b Elgin 12.4.47
FFA 1976
syst analyst Edin 1969–76, sen analyst from 1976

DUNCAN David Andrew McLaren *MA 1967
s of Andrew M. D. joiner and Ann H. Malcolm; b Auchtermuchty 13.2.43
L-es-L (Lettres Modernes) univ of Nancy France 1968
lect univ of Nancy 1967–68; teacher mod lang: Daniel Stewart's coll 1969–70, Schiller gym Hamelin 1970–71;

prin mod lang Alford acad from 1971
m Lindores 1967 Morag F. Rennie MA 1966 *qv*

DUNCAN David McPherson *BSc 1962 MSc 1964

DUNCAN Douglas *MA 1956
s of John D. garage prop. and Flora McBain; b Aber 13.11.32
Dip Russian Interpreter(Lond) 1958
teacher: George Watson's coll Edin 1959–68; prin Ger/Russian Elgin acad from 1968
m Edin 1.4.61 Ayline C. Kerr nurse d of John Y. K. Calcutta

DUNCAN Douglas James McKerrow PhD 1961
b St And 14.6.31
MA(Oxon) 1953
lect Engl S'ton 1958–64; prof and head dept Engl univ of Ghana 1964–67; visiting prof univ of Western Ontario Lond Ontario 1967–68; prof Engl McM univ Hamilton Ontario from 1968
m Stratford-on-Avon 18.9.65 Janet Hoskins

DUNCAN Douglas John Stewart *LLB 1966

DUNCAN Elaine Margaret MA 1968
d of Douglas D. bank admin and Clarice I. L. Fraser civ serv; b Aber 29.3.47
teacher: Fr Liberton Edin 1970–71, Westbourne Glasg 1971–72, Engl/Fr Lenzie acad Kirkintilloch 1972–74
m Aber 5.8.71 James Ross BSc(eng) 1970 *qv*

DUNCAN Eleanor Margaret Cormack MA 1970
d of Thomas S. D. MA 1938 *qv*; b Lossiemouth 5.12.48
teacher: East Barnet 1971–73, Ewell 1974–75, Peterhead acad from 1975
m Aber 24.6.70 Harris J. Lacey; marr diss 1976

DUNCAN Elizabeth Ann *MA 1966
m Mackie

DUNCAN Eric Thomson MA 1956
s of Nathaniel J. D. D. farm. and Margaret D. Noble teacher; b Newmachar 11.7.32
nat serv RAEC sgt/instr Harrogate 1957–59; teacher Crieff p s 1959–62; head: Findo-Gask p s Perth 1962–68, Errol p s from 1968
m Aber 29.6.57 Elaine M. C. Goodall bank clerkess d of Joseph G. Wigtown

DUNCAN Erica Barbara Anne Weir MB ChB 1962
d of Eric H. W. D. MB ChB 1931 *qv*; b Banff 7.9.38
DObstRCOG 1964 Dip Soc Med(Edin) 1969 MFCM 1973
h o: ARI, RACH 1962–63, Chase Farm hosp Enfield, Edin RHSC, Simpson Mem Mat. Pav 1964–65; trainee asst g p Edin 1965–66; res fell. Edin from 1966
m Aber 27.6.73 Hugh B. L. Russell MRCS(Lond) med pract

DUNCAN Esmé Félicité MA 1962
d of Harry F. D. tel and Elsie McKay off. man.; b Aber 3.8.41
teacher Engl/r e Aber 1963–70; staff member Scripture Union East Scot. from 1970

DUNCAN George BSc(eng) 1969
s of George D. man. ship bldrs and Josephine Wyness dist nurse; b Peterhead 26.1.49
civ eng county surv dept Lanarksh, Hamilton 1969–74; sen eng Mears civ eng Peterhead from 1974
m Longside Doreen Hutchison MA 1972 teacher d of Alexander M. H. Peterhead

DUNCAN George *BSc 1965
s of Peter R. D. fish merch and Barbara L. Simpson; b Peterhead 11.1.43
MSc(E Ang) 1966 PhD(E Ang) 1968
sen res asst Nijmegen Holland 1968–69; lect biol UEA Norwich from 1969
m Saxmundham 3.6.67 Margaret A. Daniels secy d of Bernard C. D. Saxmundham

DUNCAN Gordon Lindsay *BSc 1956 PhD 1959

DUNCAN Hazel MA 1958
d of William D. chief fisheries advis HIB and Isabella McLean; b Peterhead 23.3.38
teacher: Peterhead 1959–60, Redruth 1960–62, Peterhead 1972–76, remed Buchan dist from 1976
m Peterhead 19.8.60 John L. Craze acct s of John L. C. Redruth

DUNCAN Helen Pauline *MA 1966
d of Harold D. bank man. and Phoebe P. Hulse; b Kendal 16.6.44
res asst surv Engl dialects Leeds univ 1966–69; lect Sedgley Park coll of educ Manc from 1969
m Duncan-Austwick

DUNCAN Isobel Margaret *MA 1960
d of James D. bldg contr and Bessie I. Barclay MA 1924 *qv*; b Inverurie 26.6.38
BA(Cantab) 1962
res asst Nat lib of Scot. Edin 1962–64; part-time adult educ tut. Leic 1964–66; dep regist births, marriages deaths Ely from 1977
m Edin 3.4.64 George D. S. Galilee BA(Oxon) clerk in holy orders C of E s of George A. G.

DUNCAN Jean Davidson MA 1970
m Bryce

DUNCAN Jeanette Christina MA 1969 Dip Ed 1970
d of Maxwell L. D. joiner and Jeannie A. Murray teacher; b Torphins 22.10.48
teacher maths: Whitburn s s 1970–72, Boroughmuir s s Edin from 1972, asst prin maths from 1973
m Aber 27.6.70 Derek M. Turpie MA 1969 *qv*

DUNCAN Jennifer Ethel BSc 1964
m Steven

DUNCAN John *MA 1970

DUNCAN John *BSc 1960 MSc 1961
s of Albert G. D. joiner and Margaret B. Patterson shop asst; b Aber 10.8.38
PhD(N'cle) 1964 FRSE 1974
lect maths Aberd 1963–70, sen lect 1970–71; prof maths Stir from 1971
m Aber 8.8.63 Patricia Patterson BA(Mich) teacher d of Adam G. P. Cleveland Ohio

DUNCAN John Alan BSc 1970
s of John L. D. merch seaman and Joan E. Manson machine-knitting instr; b Lerwick 14.4.48
teacher maths Brae j h s Shetland from 1971

DUNCAN Kenneth MA 1960

DUNCAN Margaret Isobel MA 1959

DUNCAN Margaret Josephine MA 1966
d of Alfred J. D. bank man. and Margaret S. Willox; b Ellon 15.10.45
teacher: Engl/hist Woodhill h s Dunfermline 1967–71, Engl Ellon acad from 1971

DUNCAN Neil Alexander MA 1961 BD 1964
s of William D. bank teller, acct, man. and Isobel J. Moir bank clerk; b Aber 20.1.40
teacher: Glasg 1965–66, Banffsh 1966–68; field asst to Exploration Ventures UK 1969–70; C of S min Keiss from 1970

DUNCAN Nicolas Anne MA 1967
d of Robert B. D. teacher and Nicolas Geddes teacher; b Banff 5.5.45
teacher: Perth 1968–71, Dumbarton 1971–74, Alva from 1974
m Aber 28.12.71 John R. McIntosh BA(NSW) Aust teacher s of Alvan D. McI. Waverton NSW

DUNCAN Raymond Grierson *MA 1968
s of John C. D. man. and Margaret Coutts; b Aber 21.5.46
Dip Bus Admin(Edin) 1969
cadet dept of employment 1969–71; teacher Engl/hist Perth h s from 1972

DUNCAN Robert *MA 1969
s of George D. works man. and Josephine Wyness nurse; b Peterhead 3.9.47
teacher hist Airdrie acad from 1970 and housemaster from 1973

DUNCAN Robert Emslie *MA 1970 MLitt 1977
b Forres 28.8.48
res assoc centre for study of soc hist Warw 1972–74; joint author *Warwick Guide to British Labour Periodicals 1790–1970* 1977

DUNCAN Roderick MA 1967

DUNCAN Ronald Wallace MB ChB 1960
s of John D. master mariner and Jane Wallace; b Aber 21.3.35
MRCOG 1970
h o Aber hosps 1960–62; g p Aboyne 1962–65; HM Forces consult. gyn Hanover W Ger from 1965
m Aber 12.7.60 Brenda M. Simpson teacher d of William S. Cullen

DUNCAN Ruebena Ann MA 1969
d of Walter D. boat-bldr/carpenter and Thomasina Smith; b Lerwick 21.12.47
pers man. course RGIT Aber 1969–70
Lond: civ serv MHSS Blackheath 1970–72, Scot. off., Lord Advoc's off. Westminster 1972–75
m Aber 22.12.70 James A. Chisholm BSc 1970 *qv*

DUNCAN Sheila MA 1967
m Harrison

DUNCAN Stuart Henry Weir MB ChB 1965
s of Eric H. W. D. MB ChB 1931 *qv*; b Banff 7.9.41
DObstRCOG 1968 MRCGP 1976
h o ARI 1965–67; g p Peterculter from 1967 and clin asst dept orthop ARI from 1969
m Marykirk 11.8.66 Irene A. Robertson MA 1965 *qv*

DUNCAN Walter *BSc(eng) 1964
s of Walter D. boat-bldr/carpenter and Thomasina Smith; b Lerwick 12.11.42
Coventry: post grad trg course 1965–67; des draughtsman 1967–70

DUNCAN William MA 1957
s of Robert B. D. yard man. and Ethel Nicol; b Peterhead 4.2.36
teacher: Fraserburgh N s 1958–60; dep head Buchanhaven s Peterhead 1960–66; head: Ayton s 1966–70, Chirnside s 1971–74; Culter s from 1974
m Peterhead 11.7.60 Mary C. Taggart teacher d of George J. T. MA 1920 *qv*

DUNLOP James PhD 1970
s of James A. D. and Lo-Ioma E. Palmer; b Palmerston Nth NZ 4.6.42
BSc(Well) 1964 MSc(Well) 1966
scient DSIR Palmerston Nth NZ from 1970
m Palmerston Nth NZ 16.10.65 Frances M. Gerrand nurse

DUNLOP Katherine Louise MA 1966

DUNLOP Murray John MA 1969

DUNLOP Sally Margaret Doris *MA 1967
d of George G. D. lt col The Royal Scots, Scot. rep Guide Dogs for the Blind Assoc and Aline T. Arthur teacher; b Douglas I o M 16.4.45
edit asst Wm Collins Sons & Co publ Glasg 1967–69; Lond: asst edit. George E. Harrap publ 1969–70; assoc then dep edit. cookery books The Hamlyn publ group 1970–75; edit., publ man. Beaver books from 1975
m Edin 13.3.71 John N. Floyer MA(Cantab) oper res s of Martyn du B. F. Milverton

DUNLOP Stewart Brice *BSc(eng) 1964
s of John E. D. MB ChB(Edin) med pract and Ena P. Simpson; b Steeple Bumpstead 11.5.42
tech asst serv dept (aero-engine) Rolls Royce Glasg 1964–65; army off. (capt) REME 1965–69; PA man. consult.: man. consult. Edin 1969–73, Dublin from 1973
m Aber 23.4.69 Jennifer A. MacDonald MA 1964 *qv*

DUNN Elizabeth Ann *MA 1966
d of Alexander D. MA(Glas) C of S min and Florence M. S. Hourston nurse; b Portlethen 9.7.42
teacher geog: Bathgate 1965–67, St Serfs s Edin 1972–73; lib asst Napier coll Edin 1967–68
m Portlethen 9.7.66 Allan G. Dodds MA(Edin) sen med photogr s of Gilbert D. Edin

DUNN Euan Kennedy *BSc 1967
s of Henry G. D. journalist and Phyllis Campbell; b Aber 16.2.45
PhD(Durh) 1972
dept dem Edward Grey inst of field ornithology Oxon 1970–76; freelance writer Oxford from 1976

DUNN Marilyn Jennifer Lynette MA 1965
d of Alexander D. MA(Glas) C of S min and Florence M. S. Hourston nurse; b Portlethen 21.6.44
teacher Kaimhill s Aber 1966–70, Br of Don s from 1977
m Aber 20.7.68 Andrew F. Stronach BSc(eng) 1968 *qv*

DUNN William Dawson *BSc(eng) 1970

DUNNETT Charles William DSc 1960
s of William F. D. mech eng and Vera E. Holt; b Windsor Ontario 24.8.21
MBE BA(McM) 1942 MA(Tor) 1946 FASA 1965
statist: dept nat health and welfare Ottawa 1949–53; Lederle labs Pearl River NY 1953–74; prof biostatist McM Hamilton Ontario from 1974
m Windsor Ontario 14.6.47 Constance W. MacDonald nurse d of Roy S. MacD. Windsor Ontario

DUNSMUIR Martin Maxwell *MA 1968 Dip Ed 1969

DURNIN Kenneth James McDonald MA 1959 Dip Ed 1965
s of Joseph J. D. MA 1930 *qv*; b Aber 25.4.37
Cert Teacher of Deaf(Manc) 1969
teacher: p s Aber 1960–67, deaf Aber 1967–70, deaf Perth W Aust 1970–75; dep head p cath s Morley Perth W Aust from 1976
m Aber 26.12.62 Margaret A. Argo staff nurse d of William A. Aber

DURNIN Monica Mary *MA 1960
m Morales

DURNIN Patrick Joseph MA 1957
s of Patrick J. R. D. master slater and Muriel T. Keane; b Aber 13.3.29
teacher Aber 1958–64; head Selkirk p s 1964–65; dep head Dumfries p s 1965–71; head: Annan p s 1971–77, Brighouse from 1977
m Aber 3.1.55 Elizabeth A. Mutch MA 1952 *qv*

DURNO Denis MB ChB 1960 MD 1972
s of Robert D. comm trav and Mabel Taylor milliner; b Aber 19.5.36
MRCGP 1968
h o cas dept ARI, City hosp Aber 1960–61; g p Portlethen from 1961
m Aber 6.7.60 Audrey J. Angus cashier d of George A. Aber

DURNO Joyce MA 1964
d of Robert D. sales rep and Mabel D. Taylor milliner; b Aber 1.5.43
Dip Soc St(Edin) 1965 MSocW(Br Col) 1973
soc worker: Aber 1965–67, Lond Ontario 1967–69, Lions Gate hosp Vanc 1969–71 and from 1973
m Vanc 8.5.71 Edward G. Auld BASc(Br Col) prof phys Br Col Vanc s of George W. A. Chilliwack BC

DURWARD Ian George MA 1968
s of John Y. D. master confectioner and Nora Gordon nurse; b Crieff 10.4.22
teacher: hist/mod stud. Peterhead acad 1969–71, geog/mod stud. Cults acad Aber from 1971
m Fraserburgh 27.9.48 Margaret Donald catering superv d of William J. D. Fraserburgh

DURWARD Wilma Anne Margaret BSc 1963
d of Alexander F. D. master shoemaker/dir and Mary R. Andrew asst father's bus.; b Torphins 7.2.42
teacher maths: Lasswade h s 1964–67, Inverurie acad from 1977
m Aber 31.3.66 David S. Roberts BSc(H-W) teacher s of Peter S. R. Dalkeith

DUTCH Eileen Watson *MA 1957 Dip Ed 1958
m Gorie

DUTHIE Andrew BSc 1957

DUTHIE Andrew Stewart *MA 1968
s of Charles S. D. MA 1932 *qv*; b Edin 4.8.46
ACMA 1975
Vauxhall Motors Luton: grad induction course 1968–70, statist fin. forecast sect. 1970–71, budget co-ordinator 1971–73; gen superv final budgets 1973–75, Europ budget co-ordinator 1975–77, man. budgets/forecasts from 1977
m Lond 9.9.72 Joy Musgrave florist d of Joseph M. Gateshead

DUTHIE Anne Elisabeth MA 1961
d of Alexander D. wholesale grocer and Jessie Robertson nurse; b Aber 30.6.40
Dip Soc Ad(Dund) 1963 CASS(N'cle) 1966
soc worker educ dept Dun 1963–65; N'cle: psychiat soc worker RVI 1967–68, Nuffield ch psychiat unit 1968–69, sen psychiat soc worker 1969–72; sen soc worker Morpeth 1972–73
m Aber 26.8.72 Eric H. Fisher BSc(N'cle) mech eng, univ lect s of William H. F. Hartlepool

DUTHIE Ashley Mackintosh MB ChB 1959 ᶜMD 1976
s of Andrew M. D. MA 1920 *qv* and Christian M. McDonald MA 1918 *qv*; b Chesterfield 31.1.32
DRCOG 1961 DA(Lond) 1962 FFARCS 1966
h o med and neuro-surg ARI 1959–60; sen h o obst and gyn Scarsdale hosp Chesterfield 1960–61; ARI: sen h o neuro-surg 1961–62, sen h o and regist anaest 1962–66; sen regist anaest Westminster hosp Lond 1966–69; sen lect anaest univ of Rhodesia from 1969, then prof anaest Godfrey Huggins s of med, univ of Rhodesia
m Aber 19.9.60 Margaret S. Morrice radiogr d of Alexander M. M. Aber

DUTHIE Elizabeth Jean Watson MB ChB 1967

DUTHIE George MA 1970

DUTHIE Iain Fraser PhD 1961
BSc(Glas) BVMS

DUTHIE James Alexander MB ChB 1959
b Peterhead 1.2.35
m Airdrie 9.9.66 Christine F. M. Chalmers BSc(Glas) teacher

DUTHIE Jennifer Milne MA 1968
d of James D. cooper and Jeannie Milne herring worker; b Peterhead 29.3.47
m Peterhead 13.7.68 David E. Witts rly clerk s of Edgar A. W. Portobello

DUTHIE John MA 1965

DUTHIE John Scott MB ChB 1962 ChM 1973

DUTHIE John Simpson BSc 1969
s of Alexander D. D. butcher and Jane S. Simpson nurse; b Rosehearty 13.9.32
teacher sc Fraserburgh 1971–78; share fisherman from 1979
m Peterhead 28.1.56 Vera Strachan d of Alexander S. Peterhead

DUTHIE Joseph Graeme Munro *BSc 1957
s of Frederick S. R. D. insur assessor and Maggie B. Reid; b Aber 2.11.34
PhD(Brist) 1961
univ of Rochester NY: asst prof 1961–66, assoc prof 1966–74; visiting res assoc California inst of tech 1970–71; Alfred P. Sloan res fell. 1970–72; dir C. E. K. Mees observatory from 1974
m Hornell NY 11.8.62 Sue A. Roberts secy d of Clarence S. R. Bath NY

DUTHIE Margaret Bruce MA 1969
d of William C. D. joiner and Margaret B. Buchan; b St Combs 2.1.48
teacher: Saline p s Dunfermline 1970–72, Fraserburgh 1972–74, Livingston from 1974
m Lonmay 17.10.75 Norman Raven MA 1969 *qv*

DUTHIE Pamela Ann MB ChB 1962
d of Robert T. D. capt RFA, harbourmaster and Irene

King; b Fraserburgh 19.10.37
Co Durh: h o Shotley Bridge 1962–63; clin m o Bournemouth from 1972
m Aber 10.7.62 Kenneth Fleming MB ChB 1962 *qv*

DUTHIE Ruth MA 1970 MEd 1972
m(1) Trail
(2) Thom

DWORZAK Antoinette Elsie BSc 1970
d of Anton H. D. bus. man. and May M. Jones caterer; b Freetown Sierra Leone 31.12.40
MSc(Strath) 1972
forensic analyst Freetown from 1972
m Freetown 27.4.74 Kenneth A. B. Fergusson BSc(Lincoln USA) prin fisheries off. s of Adjai F. Freetown

DYAS John Charles MA 1967

DYER Hamish McMillan BSc 1964 MB ChB 1967 PhD 1976
s of Norman F. D. banker and Annie E. Rothnie banker; b Aber 17.11.42
h o Falkirk, Aber 1967–68; resid in g p Ottawa civic hosp/Ottawa univ 1968–69; m o Zambia flying doct serv Ndola 1969–70; Aberd: res fell. dept of embryology 1970–71; lect dept of dev biol from 1971

DYER Herbert Joseph *MA 1959

DYER James Archibald Thomson *MB ChB 1970
s of Thomas J. D. MA(St And) C of S min and Mary W. Thomson; b Arbroath 31.12.46
MRCPsych 1975
h o ARI, Woodend hosp Aber 1970–71; trainee g p Skene 1971–72; Royal Edin hosp: sen h o psychiat 1972–73, regist psychiat 1973–75, sen regist 1975–77; res psychiat MRC unit epidemiological stud. in psychiat Edin from 1977
m Aber 30.7.69 Lorna M. S. Townson MA 1969 *qv*

DYER Robin Maitland MA 1960 MEd 1971
s of Norman F. D. banker and Annie E. Rothnie banker; b Aber 29.9.39
Aber: teacher Old Aber s s 1961–66; teacher, careers master Hazlehead acad 1967–73; year master Northfield acad 1973–75; asst div educ off. Aber div Grampian reg from 1975
m Aber 20.7.63 Aileen M. Walker MA 1961 *qv*

DYKE Stanley Frederick PhD 1958
s of Albert E. D. BSc(Lond) metall and Kate E. Russell; b Woolwich 15.9.31
BSc(Lond) 1955 DSc(Lond) 1969 FRIC
lect chem Aberd 1957–58; Bristol coll of tech: lect org chem 1958–59, sen lect chem 1959–61, prin lect 1961–66; univ of Bath: sen lect chem 1966–69, reader org chem from 1969
m Aber 10.7.58 Alexandrina B. Sutherland MA 1954 *qv*

EADIE Jean Margaret PhD 1956
d of Robert G. W. E. BSc(Glas) indust chem and Florence A. C. Paterson; b Glasg 17.5.31
BSc(St And) 1953
res protozoologist Rowett res inst Aber from 1953

EADIE Patricia Ann BEd 1969
d of David L. E. slater/plasterer and May Reid; b Perth 24.10.44
teacher Fr Keith g s from 1969

EARL John Roderin BSc 1968

EARLS John Crawford PhD 1963
s of Archibald E. eng and Jean Thompson; b Glasg 11.6.31
BSc(eng)(Lond) 1953 CEng 1959 FIEE 1973
RGIT Aber: sen lect 1963–65, prin lect 1965–70, head of s of electronics and elect. eng 1970–76; asst prin (resources) Sheff city poly from 1976
m Pitlochry 11.7.59 Constance A. Miller teacher p e d of James A. M. Pitlochry

EASTLAKE John Jeffrey MA 1968

EASTMAN Donald Sidney MSc 1964
BSc(Br Col)

EASTON David John Courtney MA 1962 ᵈBD 1965
s of William C. E. missionary and Elizabeth Bennett missionary; b Bogota Colombia 7.10.40
C of S min: asst St Andrew's ch Inverurie 1965–67, Hamilton-Bardrainney ch Port Glasgow 1967–77, Burnside ch Glasg from 1977
m Port Glasgow 7.10.70 Edith Stevenson midwife d of James S. Greenock

EASTON Eugene Gervais *MA 1967 *MEd 1972

EASTON Thomas Bruce BSc 1961
d Aber 26.11.62 *AUR* XL 94

EATON Jane Patricia *BSc 1970 Dip Ed 1971
d of George E. dir environmental health/master of works and Patricia J. Martin; b Banff 27.1.48
teacher biol/gen sc Firhill h s Edin, prin biol from 1972
m Banff 1.4.72 Ralph C. Wylie BSc 1970 *qv*

EBBON Gordon Patrick *BSc 1965
b 24.5.43
PhD(Lond) 1970
scient off. radiochem centre Amersham 1965–67; dem St Thomas hosp med s Lond 1967–70; tech BP Grangemouth 1970–74; proj leader BP res centre Sunbury from 1974
m 31.8.68 Jean G. Shannon BSc 1966 *qv*

EBUADE-IYAMABO John Osoba BSc(for) 1958

ECCLESTON Donald MB ChB 1957
b Preston 18.12.31
DPM(Lond) 1960 PhD(Edin) 1965 MRCPsych 1973 DSc(Edin) 1976
Edin: mental health res fund fell. 1962–64, consult. psychiat royal hosp 1967–70; asst dir MRC brain metab unit 1970–77; prof psych med N'cle from 1977

EDDIE Fiona Elspeth *MA 1968 Dip Ed 1969
m Burnett

EDDIE George MB ChB 1962
s of Joseph N. E. disablement re-settlement off. and Euphemia C. Robertson; b Bradford 17.7.33
h o Aber: ARI, RACH 1962–64; h o Bellshill mat. hosp 1964; g p: Snaith 1964–69, Guernsey from 1969
m Aber 12.10.59 Mary I. Johnston MA 1959 *qv*

EDDIE Jean Lillian *MA 1956
m Wood

EDDIE Valerie Anne MA 1969 Dip Ed 1970
d of Robert M. E. tea planter and Elizabeth M. C. Ross teacher; b Wick 4.8.44
teacher Dumfries from 1970
m(1) Alasdair R. R. Leonard; marr diss 1971

(2) 29.12.71 Ian Callander valuation surv s of Robert C. Dumfries

EDDON David Howard *BSc 1969

EDEN Frederick John BSc 1970

EDGAR Alison Mary BSc 1960
d of William M. G. E. MA(Glas) C of S min and Isobel M. Marr teacher p e; b Rhynie 28.7.39
teacher maths Nairn acad from 1961, also prin guid 1972–77

EDGAR Ian Alfred BSc(agr)1970
s of Alfred E. aircraft eng and Edna Holden; b Kilbarchan 19.8.47
A Inst BM
employed Miller, Morris & Brooker Slough from 1970, contr man
m Slough Carol Smith d of K. C. L. S. Slough

EDGE Rosemary Anne *BSc 1968
m Thompson

EDMOND Carol Mackenzie MB ChB 1958
g p Chiswick Lond from 1968
m(1) Cowie; marr diss
(2) Lond 25.5.77 Ernest F. Roberts MA(Cantab) g p s of James B. R. MA(Oxon) East Grinstead

EDMOND David Michael *MA 1969

EDMOND Margaret Grant MA 1960
m Aber 3.8.63 Stuart A. Middleton MA 1961 *qv*

EDWARD Alexander Thomas Hutson BSc(Eng) 1964
b Huntly 11.11.43
MICE 1969 MIWE 1973
resid eng Baptie Shaw & Morton consult. civ & struct eng Glasg, Loch Braden water treatment works Ayrsh from 1972

EDWARD Alison Jean Elphinstone MA 1961
d of Ian D. E. MA 1927 *qv*; b S India 19.3.40
Dip Soc St(Edin) 1962
res asst dept criminology Edin 1962–70; res assoc tourism and recreation res unit Edin from 1974
m Edin 5.8.63 Sidney J. Arnott MB ChB(Edin) lect, consult. s. of George A. Leeds; marr diss 1976

EDWARD Ian MA 1956 LLB 1958
s of Charles E. E. civ serv and Isobel T. Kynoch; b Aber 3.9.35
cadet col serv Cantab 1958–59; dist. off. col serv Mkushi N Rhod 1959–62; ptnr C & P H Chalmers advoc Aber from 1962
m Aber 20.8.58 Marguerite A. Leiper teacher p e d of George L. Aber

EDWARD Janice Elizabeth MA 1967
m Hepburn

Edward John MB ChB 1965
s of John E. grocer and Barbara J. Cormack; b Aber 14.2.40
h o Aber gen hosps 1965–67; sen h o obst/gyn Groote Schuur hosp Cape Town 1967–68; regist obst/gyn Grey's hosp Pietermaritzburg 1968–69; sen h o anaest Aber gen hosps 1969–71; g p Aber from 1971
m Aber 8.4.71 Elizabeth C. Duncan art teacher d of George D. D. Aber

EDWARD Kenneth George *MA 1966 Dip Ed 1967

EDWARD Neil MB ChB 1961
s of Charles E. E. civ serv and Isobel T. Kynoch; b Aber 8.1.38
MRCPE 1965
Ashley MacIntosh res fell. med Aberd 1962–64; lect med Aberd 1964–73; sen regist Glasg RI 1971; tut. med Temple univ Philadelphia USA 1971–72; consult. phys Grampian area health board from 1973
m Aber 16.7.65 Vivien E. M. Smith MB ChB 1962 *qv*

EDWARD Patrick Duncan *BSc(agr) 1968
s of Duncan C. E. farm/grocer and Marjorie Duncan; b Methlick 19.5.45
res stud. Rothamsted 1968–70; field dev man. Yorksh 1970–73; lect NOSCA from 1973
m Udny 16.9.67 Mary A. Whyte civ serv d of Mormond W. Udny

EDWARDS David George Warrilow BSc(for) 1959
s of Richard H. E. paint tech and Gladys M. Lees; b Bloxwich 5.2.37
MF(Wash) 1963 PhD(Wash) 1969
res asst Wash 1959–60; lab tech for. comm Farnham 1961–62; teacher Walsall 1962–63; Wash: teaching asst 1963–65, res asst 1966–68; res scient Canadian for. serv Victoria BC from 1968
m Aber 14.8.61 Margaret H. Mitchell MA 1959 *qv*

EDWARDS John *BSc 1970

EDWARDS John Charles Seaman *MA 1957

EDWARDS Keith Ian Campbell *MA 1956
s of John G. E. grocer, security off. and Flora Jack; b Fort George 13.10.33
trg for C of S min Aber 1956–59; asst min Douglas and Angus ch Dun 1959–61; min Laurieston-Renwick ch Glasg 1961–68; warden Iona Abbey 1968–71; min the Michael ch Sheff from 1971

EDWARDS Meldrum Barclay *BSc(eng) 1964
s of Alfred J. M. E. MA 1924 *qv*; b Aber 2.12.42
MSc(Cantab) 1966 Dip H & T Eng(N'cle) 1967
res asst S'ton 1967–69; asst eng: Aber c c 1969–75, Grampian reg c from 1975
m Aber 28.10.72 Kareen A. M. Anderson soc worker d of Richard D. A. Aber

EDWARDS Michael Alexander *MA 1969

EDWARDS Peter Stewart MA 1969

EDWARDS Rex Richard Cyril PhD 1968
BSc(Hull)

EDWARDS Robert Norman *BSc(eng) 1970
s of Thomas C. E. BA(Wales) schoolmaster and Agnes H. M. Inglis; b Edin 14.8.47
MSc(Birm) 1973 MICE MIWE
asst civ eng R. H. Cuthertson & Ptnrs Edin 1970–72 and from 1974

EDWARDS Susan Mary MA 1970
d of Ronald D. E. prod. dev eng and Mary I. Smartt secy; b Woking 7.3.46
Dip Lib(UCW) 1978
Norway: teacher Lyngseidet 1971–72; Engl in s s/adult evening classes Tromsø 1972–74; lib asst univ lib Tromsø 1975–77

EDWARDS Timothy Drummond BSc(for) 1967
s of Colin C. E. MRCP consult. neurol and Lesley H.

Reynolds LRAM; b Lond 3.9.43
MA(Cantab) 1969
computer aided hist demographic res Cantab 1967–70; syst dev with IBM Lond from 1970

EFFA Columbus Nsor MB ChB 1965

EFOBI Onwuka Celestine *MA 1959

EGBUONU Francis James Chukwodi MB ChB 1963

EGLIN Stewart *MA 1967

EHRHARDT Johanna Elisabeth Ursula Margarete MB ChB 1960
d of Arnold A. T. E. LLB(Königsberg) lect law, clerk in holy orders, sen lect ch hist Manc and Edit R. G. H. Hahn MA(Königsberg) teacher; b Königsberg Pr Germany 6.9.34
h o: RACH 1960–61, Oldham 1961; m o Port of Spain Trinidad 1961–62; Kenya: m o Kakamega, Kisii 1963–67, g p Eldoret 1967–72, clin tut. med trg centre Nakuru from 1972
m Heywood 16.7.60 Roger W. Gray BSc(agr) 1960 *qv*

EL-ADEEMY Mahmoud Sadek Mahmoud MSc 1966
BSc(Ein Shams)

ELDER Elizabeth Fraser MA 1959
d of Ernest F. E. comp dir/hotel prop. and Isabella S. Watson hotel man.; b Buckie 24.8.38
teacher: Glasg 1960, Hilton s s Aber 1961–63, Turriff acad 1963–64, Macduff h s, Banff acad 1964–71, hist/Engl Turriff acad from 1971
m Aber 28.12.67 Trevor L. Kenrick RAF pilot, garage prop. s of Edward F. K. Llangollen

ELDER Keith Robert McMillan *BSc 1956 PhD 1959

ELDER Lilian McIntyre MA 1969 MEd 1977
d of Alexander R. E. trawl skipper and Johnann M. Cross fish worker; b Aber 8.7.42
part-time lect statist Aberd 1970–72, full-time from 1972
m Aber 14.11.59 James Gordon panel beater s of James G. Aber

ELDER Michael Robert MA 1969
s of Alan R. E. insur off. and Ivy L. Morgan clerkess; b Dun 16.4.47
Dip Lib(Wales) 1971 Ch Lib 1972
Luton: trainee lib 1969–70, sen asst lib Bedfordsh c lib from 1971
m Belmont 14.9.74 Pauline A. Wiltshire chartered lib d of Harold F. W. Sutton

ELDER Reynold Malcolm MA 1965

ELDER Susan Winifred *MA 1969
d of Albert G. E. civ serv and Kathleen Yates civ serv; b Aber 24.3.46
m Aber 29.8.69 Ronald C. Speirs MA 1969 *qv*

ELEFTHERIOU Anastasius *BSc 1964
s of Stephanos E. Eng Sc(Lausanne) chief telecomm advis to Greek govt and Helen Rangou; b Athens 14.9.35
marine lab DAFS Aber: govt scient exper off., sen scient off. 1964–74, prin scient off. from 1974
m Aber 9.10.59 Margaret Craib MA 1961 *qv*

ELERIAN Mohammed Kamal PhD 1964

EL-GARHY Mohammed Talaat PhD 1963
MD(Ein Shams)

EL HAG Gaafar Abbas MSc 1966 PhD 1969
BSc(Khart)

EL HASSAN Babiker Ahmed BSc(for) 1965

EL-HOSSADY Awad MSc 1967 PhD 1971
BSc(Libya)

ELKAROURI Mohamed Osman El Hassan MSc 1965
BSc(agr)(Khart)

ELLEN Judith Lesley *MA 1970
d of Eric M. E. Lloyds underwriter and Eunice Heath MB ChB(St And) med pract; b Woking 1.7.48
au pair Moscow 1971–72; TEFL Lond, Milan from 1973
m 15.5.75 Archie Lambourne

ELLEN Signa Anna Main MA 1968
d of William M. E. trawl man. and Margaret F. F. Baxter secy; b Aber 23.3.47
teacher Newtonhill p s 1969–76
m Aber 4.7.69 Ian V. Mackenzie hotelier s of Ian M. M. MPS(Edin) Cults

ELLINGTON Henry Irvine *BSc 1963 PhD 1969
s of Henry K. T. E. eng and Alice B. Coutts; b Aber 17.6.41
scient off. AERE Harwell 1963–65; RGIT Aber: lect phys 1966–73, lect i/c educ tech 1973–74, sen lect from 1974
m Aber 12.4.66 Lindsay M. Sheldon teacher d of James A. S. Aber

ELLINGTON Kathleen Alice Tester MA 1966
d of Henry K. T. E. eng and Alice B. Coutts; b Aber 24.3.45
teacher: Tullos p s Aber 1967–69, Walker Rd p s, Tullos p s 1974–78, Brit s Tripoli Libya from 1978
m Aber 30.6.67 John G. M. Sutherland BSc 1960 *qv*

ELLIOT Elizabeth Mary MA 1961
d of Richard E. teacher and Georgina C. McWilliam nurse; b Lossiemouth 21.6.40
teacher: Engl/hist Nairn acad 1962–64, Summerhill acad Aber 1964–66, part time remed dept Summerhill 1969–73; part-time res asst inst med sociol Aberd from 1975
m Aber 16.7.65 James A. Adams BSc 1950 *qv*

ELLIOT James Rowland MA 1970
s of Rowland E. g p and May Pearson; b Edin 16.6.48
Dip Soc Work(Edin) 1972
trainee soc worker Bromsgrove 1970–71; Droitwich Spa: soc worker 1972–74, asst team leader soc serv 1974–76; asst trg off. Birm soc serv from 1976
m Birm 16.9.72 Linda A. Downey BSc(Swansea) soc worker d of Thomas W. D. Birm

ELLIOTT James Montgomery BSc(for) 1959
s of James E. farm. and Katherine Maguire; b Tempo NI 5.2.39
dist for. off. counties Londonderry/Tyrone 1960–64; farm. Co Fermanagh from 1964

ELLIS Dennis George *BSc 1967 PhD 1970
s of George E. welder and Henrietta Simpson; b Aber 20.1.45
syst progr Bracknell from 1970
m Aber 15.7.72 Jennifer A. Irving staff nurse d of William I. Kirkwall

ELLIS Dorothy Johanne Margaret *MA 1968
d of Arthur J. E. agr rep and Jane A. Stewart; b Aber 25.11.45

Dip Ed(Edin) 1969
teacher maths Hazlehead acad Aber 1969–72; asst prin maths Hawick h s 1972–74; asst mistress Channing s Highgate Lond 1974–76
m Aber 23.11.74 James W. Walton police off. s of James W. W. Sunderland

ELLIS Ian Angus *BSc 1959 PhD 1962
s of John E. marine eng and Helen Watt; b Liv 12.3.37
visiting post doct fell. res univ of Indiana Bloomington USA 1962–64; Westfield coll Lond: asst lect 1964–66, lect 1966–74; teacher sc Aboyne acad from 1974
m Aber 24.8.62 Sheila A. Marr typist d of John M. Aber

ELLIS Janet Elizabeth *MA 1969
d of Richard T. E. MA 1939 *qv* and Jean B. M. Porter BSc 1940 *qv*; b Aber 25.4.47
computer progr Esso Petr Lond 1969–72; sales forecaster Scot. and Newc Breweries Edin 1972–73; computer syst des Scot. Widows' Fund Edin from 1973
m Aber 24.6.72 Malcolm B. Baldwin MA(Edin) oper res analyst govt statist s of John T. B. MB ChB(Edin) Penicuik

ELLIS Susan Terry PhD 1966
d of Humphry F. E. MA(Oxon) writer and Barbara P. Hasseldine; b Lond 28.6.39
BA(Oxon) 1961 MA(Oxon)
res stud. St Bart's hosp Lond 1961–62; res asst: Aberd 1962–66, Oxford 1966–70, Sydney 1972, sen res asst 1978
m Somerset 1.11.69 Bruce J. Roser MB BS(Syd)

ELLISON Travers David *MA 1967
s of Travers W. E. dir contr civ aviation auth and Enid M. Atkinson; b Sutton Coldfield 11.8.43
DMS 1970
comm app Stevenage 1967–70; Lond: sen buyer 1970–74, comm man. from 1974

ELLWAY Judith Margaret MA 1969
d of Graham A. E. office man. and Phyllis D. Porter cashier; b Lydney 31.3.48
post with task force Heanor 1970–71; soc worker Clay Cross 1971–74, Cardiff from 1979
m Aber 5.6.70 Brian S. R. Harman MA 1970 *qv*

ELMAHI Abdu Rahman Gorashi BSc(for) 1968
s of Gorashi E. farm. and Fatima Mahmoud; b Elrabwa Sudan 1.1.45
MS(Utah) 1976
Sudan: instruct. for. rangers coll Khartoum 1968–69, asst conserv for. 1969–75, conserv. for. Gezira from 1976
m Remaitab 25.7.74 Arafa Yousif d of Ahmed Y. Remaitab

ELRICK John Davidson BSc(agr) 1961

ELRICK Margaret Rose MA 1967
m Marshall

ELSTON David Thomas BSc(for) 1963

ELWELL-SUTTON Giles Paul *BSc 1970

ELWICK Susan Ann *MA 1970
d of Thomas H. E. plant eng and Constance A. Petty; b Middlesbrough 26.7.47
Middlesbrough: teacher Engl St George's s s 1970–71, St Peter's comp s 1972–73
m Middlesbrough 8.8.70 John A. Gardiner BA(OU) teacher s of Thomas G. South Bank Teesside

ELWOOD Richard *MEd 1963
MA(Edin)

ELY Elizabeth Mary Kidd MA 1962
d of George E. mech and Rachel Wedderburn; b Glasg 22.1.41
teacher: Engl/hist Northfield s s Aber 1964–67, SW Ross 1967–71; head Achmore p s from 1971
m Aber 29.6.62 Christopher Mackenzie MA 1963 *qv*

EMSLIE Gordon Ritchie *MA 1962
s of Charles R. E. arch. and Jessie K. Gordon; b Aber 30.6.40
Dip Psych(Lond) 1963 PhD(Queens univ Kingston Canada) 1971 Regist Psych(Ont) 1966
Ontario: res asst dept psychiat Queen's univ Kingston 1963–65, clin psych gen hosp Kingston 1965–69, chief psych commun psychiat hosp Guelph 1969–70; chief psych Waterloo county board of educ Kitchener 1970–72, Ryerson polytech inst Toronto: prof psych 1972–75, chmn dept psych from 1975
m Kingston Ont 6.8.66 Judith R. Cafley

EMSLIE Helen Grant MA 1959
m Wallace

EMSLIE Peter Forbes LLB 1964
s of William E. MA 1926 *qv* and Elizabeth M. Dugan MA 1926 *qv*; b Aber 11.12.41
law app Aber 1964–65; solic Edin 1965–72; solic Aber from 1972
m Aber 18.1.68 Alexandra S. Mackintosh teacher d of Alastair M. Insch

EMSLIE Ruth Anthea MA 1966
d of William I. E. MB ChB 1936 *qv*; b Kirkwall 16.8.43
Denmark: p r asst ITT 1966–67, Engl secy advt ag 1967–68, asst liaison off. W A & Bates advt ag 1968–70; Canada: secy JWT advt ag 1970–71, sales admin Knoll internat 1971; England: market res asst Beecham 1971–72; sen information off. Compton UK advt ag 1972–75; market. off. Barclays bank internat from 1975

EMSLIE William James Ingram MA 1962 LLB 1964
s of William I. E. MB ChB 1936 *qv*; b Aber 29.11.40
m Edin 9.9.67 Elizabeth K. Young tel d of John Y. Edin

ENDREDY Andrew Stephen MA 1960
s of Andrew S. E. PhD(Budapest) pedologist and Katalin Egressy; b Budapest 28.12.34
teacher maths: Alford s 1961–69, St Joseph's coll Dumfries 1969–70; sales rep CICA, SW Scot and N Eng 1970; prop. Dumfries stamp shop from 1970; founder Palmerston philatelic auctions 1974
m Aber 28.12.61 Ruth Richardson MA(St And) lib d of Alan R. BSc(Lond) Bridge of Weir

ENGESET Jetmund MB ChB 1964 *ChM 1970
s of Arne K. E. MD(Oslo) med pract and Marta Birkeland; b Vega Norway 22.7.38
FRCSE 1970
h o Aber hosps 1964–65; Aberd: res asst surg 1965–67, sen h o gen surg and orthop surg 1967–68, lect surg 1969–74, sen lect from 1974; seconded to dept surg univ of Gothenburg Sweden 1972–73
m Aber Anne G. Robertson SRN d of Allan G. R. Aber

ENGLAND Carol Susan *MA 1966
m Bagnall

ENGLAND Esther Morrison Reid MA 1970 Dip Ed 1971
d of William R. E. eng machine man and Esther

Morrison shop asst; b Aber 24.1.49
Bowthorpe s Norwich: teacher Engl/hist 1971–74, dep head Engl from 1974
m Aber 1971 Brian W. Henderson arch. s. of William J. H. Aber

ENGLISH Peter Roderick BSc(agr) 1959 *1961 PhD 1969
s of William R. E. bldr, man. meat processing factory and Lily MacDonald; b Glen Urquhart 9.3.37
NDA(Edin) 1960
farm man. Inverness-sh 1959–60; Aberd: asst lect 1961–66, sen res fell. 1966–68, lect 1968–78, sen lect from 1978
m Inv 19.10.63 Anne D. Mackay BCom(Strath) college regist/teacher d of James A. M. Balnain

ENNIS Elizabeth Jacqueline Ogilvy MA 1970

ENTWISTLE Noel James PhD 1967
s of Joseph E. leather merch and Gladys Jackson secy/man.; b Bolton 26.12.36
BSc(Sheff) 1960
lect, sen lect, prof dept educ res Lanc from 1968
m Hyde 8.8.64 Dorothy M. Bocking BA(Lanc) teacher d of John W. B. Hyde

ENYI Patrick Ogbogu MA 1963

ERRIDGE Robert MA 1960 *1972
s of Robert F. E. stone polisher and Emily Gauld; b Aber 11.10.38
Lucy Fell., Senatus Prize in Engl Lit, Minto Mem Prize in Engl 1971
teacher Engl: Peterhead acad 1961–62, Banchory acad 1962–63, Kaimhill s s Aber 1964–69; stud. Aberd 1969–72; teacher Engl Rubislaw acad 1972–73, prin Engl Linksfield acad from 1973
m Aber 15.7.60 Margaret C. H. Hossack asst scient off., teacher d of Robert H. Aber

ERSKINE-HILL Alexander Roger LLB 1970
s of Sir Robert E-H. BA(Cantab) CA and Christine A. Johnstone mus teacher; b Biggar 15.8.49
app CA Edin 1971–72; shipbroker Lond from 1972

ESPLEY Sally Marion *MA 1964
d of Thomas H. E. BA(Oxon) civ serv, head teacher and Marion M. J. Stott MA 1925 *qv*; b Chester 10.5.42
Dip Ed 1967 (Makerere coll univ of E Af)
VSO teacher Ibadan Nigeria 1964–66; teacher: Lond 1966, Korogwe and Machame Tanzania 1967–70, Swanley 1970–72
m Bromley 31.1.70 David C. Fletcher MSc(Lond) univ lect s of Arthur L. F. Ipswich

ESSLEMONT Anne Russell MA 1960
d of Harold E. draper/comp dir and Roberta R. Turnbull; b Aber 16.7.39
educ edit.: Lond 1961–64, Edin 1964–65; teacher p s Buckhaven 1967
m Aber 5.9.64 James J. Stott MA 1960 *qv*

ESSLEMONT Ean William McLennan *MA 1966

ESSLEMONT Elizabeth Mary MA 1961
d of J. Bryce E. BL 1929 *qv*; b Aber 17.10.40
teacher: Anderson S Carolina USA 1961–62, Dem s Aber 1963–65
m Aber 13.7.65 Michael G. H. Gibb paper mill supt s of Maxwell G. G. MB ChB 1928 *qv*

ESSLEMONT George Fowlie *BSc 1969 MSc 1971
s of Ernest J. E. man. dir and Marjory M. Duncan dir; b Aber 12.12.46
res asst chem: Aberd 1969–70, R'dg from 1971

ESSLEMONT Iain MB ChB 1956
s of John C. E. BCom 1925 *qv*; b Aber 2.9.32
DObstRCOG 1960 MRCGP 1973
h o: Ayr c hosp 1956–57, gen hosp Dewsbury 1957; Regt m o Gurkha Rifles Malaya, Hong Kong 1957–59; h o obst Ayrsh cent. hosp Irvine 1960; Malaya: g p Cha'ah 1960–62, Penang from 1962
m Penang 3.9.66 Mary G. Mars teacher d of James H. M. Bishopbriggs

ESSLEMONT Marjory Elizabeth Helen *MA 1959
d of Ernest J. E. ironmonger, man. dir and Marjory M. Duncan; b Aber 23.2.37
teacher hist: Aber h s for girls 1964–67, Powis acad 1970–71, prin guid Harlaw acad 1971–76; asst head Linksfield acad from 1976
m(1) Fort Jameson Zambia 5.12.59 Alexander F. Florence MA 1957 *qv* (*d* 31.3.63)
(2) Aber 12.8.65 John I. Rose MA 1953 *qv*

ESSLEMONT Norman MA 1964
s of Harold E. comp dir and Roberta R. Turnbull; b Aber 22.7.43
trainee store man. Bradford, Lond 1964–66; retail clothing buyer 1966–70; comp dir Aber from 1971; presid Jun Chamber Aber 1973
m Aber Rosalind M. MacAulay dom supt d of Robert G. MacA. Glasg

ESSON George Michael LLB 1969 *1970
s of George E. tel eng and Christine W. Paterson; b Aber 28.7.48
NP 1976
Aber: law app 1970–72, solic 1972, ptnr Esslemont & Cameron advoc from 1974
m Aber 3.9.74 Lindsey A. Cameron MA 1971 cartographer d of James C. Aber

ETHERIDGE Nicholas Haggar Rowse MLitt 1967
BA(Vic Tor)

ETTLES James Anthony BSc 1969
s of William A. E. MA 1941 *qv*; b Aber 10.4.48
lieut RN reserve 1970; teacher sc: Cargilfield s Edin 1970–73, Haileybury coll Melbourne 1973–74, Kerang g s Victoria Aust from 1974

EUNSON Barbara Miller *BSc 1965
d of George J. E. bank man. and Elizabeth G. Halbert; b Stromness 5.8.44
teacher Falkirk 1966–69; asst educ psych Stirlingsh ch guid centre 1969–72
m Brechin 5.8.66 James R. Bennett BSc 1962 *qv*

EUNSON John William MA 1966
s of Ellen Eunson; b Whalsay 31.5.20
teacher Engl Brumby comp s Scunthorpe from 1966
m Cleethorpes 26.8.41 Kathleen Webb d of Charles W. W. Cleethorpes
d Banchory 15.9.78

EUNSON Ronald John *MEd 1963
s of James A. E. preventive off. Customs & Excise and Madge Rodmell; b Kingston-u-Hull 28.1.38
BA(Durh) 1960
teacher mod lang Melville coll Edin 1963–66; lect educ N'cle-u-Tyne from 1967
m Newcastle-u-Tyne Susan C. Tansley BA(N'cle) teacher d of George E. T. BA(Birm) Newcastle-u-Tyne

EVANS Alexander Robert Matheson MB ChB 1966
s of Alexander C. E. civ serv and Gladys Hedley; b Aber 6.11.42
DMRD(Lond) 1971
various trg posts in NHS hosps mainly in W Midlands; consult. radiol NW Durham health dist from 1974
m Aber 2.8.76 Mary Linklater MB MS(Lond) med pract

EVANS David Victor *BSc(eng) 1968
s of Victor O. E. draughtsman, prod. man. and Beatrice J. Shuck; b Birm 9.5.46
MICE 1973
Taylor Woodrow construct.: sect. eng Nott 1968–70, des eng Southall 1970–72, chief site eng Derby 1972–76, dep proj man. from 1977
m Newmill 15.9.74 Daphne E. Mark secy d of Stanley B. M. Keith

EVANS Dita Marjorie Kaye *MB ChB 1957

EVANS Ruth Eileen Margaret BSc 1968
d of Noel W. E. civ serv and Mary F. Cross; b St Helens 15.2.42
BSc(Leeds) 1972
tech information off. Express Dairy Ruislip from 1978
m Guildford 14.10.78 David B. Clayton horticulturalist s of Oswald J.C. Wisley

EVANS Thomas Russell *MA 1970
s of Thomas A. E. newspaper distrib man. and Marion Russell; b Edin 20.11.47
HM insp taxes Dumfries, Leeds, York from 1970

EVERETT Richard John *MA 1969
s of John W. E. bldr and Hilda M. Hibling teacher; b Hilgay Norfolk 13.12.33
Dip Ed(Lond) 1970
teacher/traveller Lond and Aust from 1969; prin geog Woodlands g s Glenelg S Aust from 1979
m Lower Hutt NZ 25.7.64 Elaine M. Edridge teacher d of Allan G. E. Lower Hutt

EVERITT Brian MA 1960

EWBANK Corinna Valerie MA 1964
d of Henry V. E. BA(Cantab) army off. (col) and Joyce M. Barrett teacher sp and drama; b Meopham 19.12.41
teacher: Engl St Winefride's s s Liv 1965–66, hist/r e Stanley Park comp s Liv 1966–69, hist Sir William Nottidge s s Whitstable from 1974
m Meopham 31.7.65 Christopher F. Cowie scient information off. s of Samuel R. C. Deal

EWEN Alexander James *MA 1966 MSc 1968 PhD 1971 LLB 1979
s of Alexander S. E. house furnisher and Rosabell Nicoll; b Glasg 1.10.43
Aberd: asst lect maths 1967–70, lect 1970–77; part-time lect RAF Aber 1968–72; tut. OU Aber 1971–74
m Aber 8.7.75 Lindsay Watt B Ed 1975 teacher d of Robert J. M. W. BL 1952 *qv*

EWEN Cameron Archibald *BSc(eng) 1967
s of William A. E. MA 1928 *qv*; b Aber 1.12.45
MICE 1973
civ eng Glasg 1967–75, Perth from 1975
m Elgin 11.9.70 Margaret A. Shirran BSc 1969 *qv*

EWEN George BMedBiol 1970 MB ChB 1973

EWEN Graham *MA 1962
s of William A. E. MA 1928 *qv*; b Torphins 9.7.40
teacher Aber from 1963
m Tannadice 27.12.72 Jane A. Taylor midwifery sister d of James D. T. MA(St And) Tannadice

EWEN Jane Helen Esslemont MA 1968
d of Herbert J. E. admin BR, shop owner and Laura L. Geddie teacher sp and drama; b Aber 24.2.47
Dip Sec St(Strath) 1969
secy: educ trust careers res Lond 1969–70, univ admissions Lond 1971–72; p a to Brit judge at European Court of Justice Luxembourg 1973–77
m 25.6.77 Andrew Durand barrister/lect univ coll Buckingham

EWEN Norma Leslie MA 1962
d of Alexander L. E. member Shore Porters' Soc Aber and Annabella B. Middleton; b Aber 15.3.41
teacher Kittybrewster p s Aber 1963–65; visiting teacher mus Aber s 1967–68
m Aber 19.7.63 John Lockie BSc 1959 *qv*

EWEN Patricia Margaret *MA 1967 MSc 1969
d of George S. E. warehouseman and Elizabeth S. Harkin; b Aber 1.7.45
PhD(Stir) 1973
teacher: Glasg h s for boys 1970–72, prin maths Bathgate acad 1972–74, Mackie acad Stonehaven from 1974, asst rector from 1976
m Aber 2.7.69 Iain E. Maclean MA 1967 *qv*

EWEN Richard MA 1965

EWEN Robert *MA 1961
s of Robert E. insur ag and Helen L. McVie bank clerk; b Clydebank 3.3.39
grad app Engl Elect. Co Bradford 1961–63; asst to dir Glass Manuf Fed. Lond 1963–64; Aberd: admin asst (acad) 1964–66, asst secy (acad) 1966–73, sen asst secy (acad) and clerk to Senatus 1973–76, dep secy (acad) from 1976
m Glasg 2.7.63 Eleanor I. Grayson teacher p e d of John R. G. Glasg

EWEN Robert Robertson MA 1961

EWEN Sheila Barbara MA 1957
d of Alexander L. E. member Shore Porters' Soc Aber and Annabella B. Middleton; b Aber 17.9.35
teacher Kirkhill p s Aber 1958–60; teacher/lib Mitcham tech s Melbourne Aust from 1974
m Aber 17.7.58 Francis A. Macnab MA 1958 *qv*

EWEN Stanley William Barclay MB ChB 1964 PhD 1971
s of William B. E. pharm/optician and Jessie J. McCallum pharm; b Aber 20.5.39
MRCPath 1972
Aberd: lect 1965–72, sen lect from 1973
m Aber 1965 Doreen J. R. Morrice nurs sister d of Alexander M. Aber

EWIN Alison Margaret *MA 1970
d of Robert A. E. civ serv and Jean Burgess; b Farnworth 4.10.48
admin asst Lancs c c Preston 1970–71; teacher: humanities Kirkcaldy 1972–73, outdoor educ Hexham 1973–77; instr outdoor pursuits Crickhowell from 1977

EWING William Edward *BSc 1965

EYIUCHE Godwin Chukunweike MB ChB 1956
s of Charles U. E. fitter Nigerian Rlys and Dinah E. Odeluga; b Abacha Idemili ECS Nigeria 26.7.31

DTM & H(Liv) 1957 FRCSGlas 1963 FMCS(Nigeria) 1971 FICS 1974
Commonwealth schol in surg Glas 1961–63; h o; Elgin 1956, Windygates, Fife 1956–67; Nigeria: m o 1958–61, spec grade 1963–66, consult. surg 1967–72, sen consult. surg from 1972
m Arochukwu Nigeria 27.5.61 Rosaline Igomanta, stenog d of Kenrick N. I. Nigeria

FACHIE Moira Ann Ritchie MA 1962

FADL Osman Ahmed Ali PhD 1968
s of Ahmed Ali rly stationmaster and Zeinab A. Rahman; b Sudan 1.1.36
BSc(agr)(Khart) 1960 MSc(agr)(Khart) 1964
Wad Medani Sudan: scient, sen scient Gezira res stat 1968–78, asst res prof 1978, head soil sc sect. from 1978
m Sudan 30.5.66 Fatima d of Mohamed A. R. M. Kheir Jedda

FAIRBAIRN Ian Smith BSc 1967

FAIRLIE Isobel Anne MA 1969
d of Andrew K. F. MA(Glas) C of S min and Jane T. Buchanan; b Thurso 13.12.47
Dip Soc Ad(Manc) 1970 Dip Soc Work(Edin) 1975
trainee soc worker Dun 1970–71; Edin: clerical post 1972–74, trainee soc work 1974–75, soc worker from 1975
m Edin 20.10.75 John C. Lodge civ serv s of James O. L. Cape Town

FAIRWEATHER Keith John LLB 1970
s of Stanley J. F. crew supt, civ serv and Jessie M. Smith civ serv; b Edin 24.3.47
Linlithgow: law app, leg. asst, sen leg. asst W Lothian c c 1970–74; Haddington: sen leg. asst, asst dir of admin E Lothian dist c 1974–77; leg. asst NCB Edin from 1977

FAJEMIYO Akinleye *BSc(eng) 1965

FALCONER Alan David MA 1967 *BD 1970
s of Alexander F. publ prod. man. and Jean B. Littlejohn secy; b Edin 12.12.45
Cert of Fac of Theol(Geneva) 1971
C of S min asst St Machar's cath Aber 1972–74; lect syst theol Irish s of ecumenics Dublin from 1974
m Edin 6.8.68 Marjorie E. Walters children's resid houseparent, secy d of Frederick J. W. Edin

FALCONER Atholl George *BSc(eng) 1957
s of Robert F. and Eva Farquharson; b Aber 29.5.35
grad trainee Rolls Royce 1957–59; nat serv 1959–61; des eng Rolls Royce 1961–62; lect mech eng RGIT Aber from 1962
m Aber 9.8.67 Judith M. Weale

FALCONER Hugh Robert MB ChB 1956
s of Hugh F. cler off. and Elizabeth Rhind; b Inv 21.9.32
h o ARI, Woodend hosp Aber 1956–57; surg lt RN 1957–60; sen h o Aber mat. hosp 1960–61; g p Aber from 1961
m(2) Aber 29.2.80 Annita Smith d of George A. S. Portlethen

FALCONER Ian Robert PhD 1960
s of Robert H. F. elect. eng/dir and gen man. and Lilian W. Ball cashier; b Walton-on-Thames 12.5.35
BSc(Nott) 1957 DSc(Nott) 1971 FIBiol 1971 FRIC 1972
lect biochem Adelaide Aust 1960–64; reader animal biochem Nott 1965–71; univ of New England Aust: prof biochem from 1972, head s of biol sc from 1974
m Pavenham 20.9.58 Mary E. Roff BSc(Nott) res scient, teacher d of Joseph R. Pavenham

FALCONER James Parry BSc 1966
s of John F. rly guard and Jessie A. M. Parry; b Wishaw 1.7.28
teacher: Kaimhill s s Aber 1967–68; maths tech coll Aber from 1968
m Wishaw 18.3.49 Gerda Gerst fashion buyer, lang lab steward d of Paul G. Bad Oeyhnhausen W Ger

FALCONER Robert *MA 1963
s of David F. tel eng and Marjory M. U. Nixon; b Edin 28.12.40
market res exec: Cadbury Birm 1963–65, London Press Exchange 1965–67; dir market res subsid LPE Lond 1967–69; dir market res comp Commun Res Lond from 1969
m Aber 31.7.65 Eva M. Slessor BSc 1962 *qv*

FALK Alexander Jules BSc(eng) 1967
s of Ernest F. Dip Ing(Hanover) mech and man. eng and Eva B. Halberstadt SRN; b Hampton 22.2.44
Cert Trans Stud(Lond) 1971 MICE 1973 MCIT 1975
sen tech off. chief civ eng off. BR (Eastern Reg) York and London 1967–73; sen eng asst London Midland Reg Lond 1973–75; Van Niekerk, Kleyn & Edwards consult. eng Johannesburg 1975–76; chief res off. nat inst for trans and road res Pretoria from 1976
m 20.2.76 Marion H. Rosenthal

FALK Robert Samuel BSc(eng) 1968
s of Ernest F. Dip Ing(Hanover) mech and man. eng and Eva B. Halberstadt SRN; b Hampton 19.3.46
MIMechE
tech mech eng BP res centre 1968–73; trilingual tech eng Becorit (GB) Nott from 1973

FARQUHAR Dennis Alexander LLB 1969

FARQUHAR Doreen Meldrum MA 1969
m Mann

FARQUHAR Eric MA 1959
s of John F. fisherman and Jean F. Sinclair; b Dunbeath 25.5.38
teacher maths: spec asst Fort William 1960–68 and f e off. 1968–70; head Tomintoul s s 1970–74; teacher maths Wick h s 1974–76, asst prin maths from 1976
m Inv 6.12.58 Audrey F. Fraser MA 1967 *qv*; marr diss 1977

FARQUHAR Fiona Margaret MA 1966
d of H. Gordon F. BA(Oxon) consult. paediat phys and Jean Warden; b Oxford 31.3.45
Dip Soc St(Edin) 1967
secy Edin 1967–68; prob off./soc worker Cape Town 1968–72; med soc work Edin 1972–75; Oman: secy res dept Salalah 1975–76, secy palace dept of agr Seeb 1976, secy dairy proj Digdaga, Ras Al Khaimah 1976–79; resid N. Yemen
m Pittenweem 3.5.75 W. Alasdair S. Wyllie farm man. s of W.R.C.W. Bury St Edmunds

FARQUHAR Freda Jessie MA 1964
d of Alexander D. F. trans man. and Jessie S. Gillan; b Ellon 18.10.42
m Aber 29.8.64 Stephen J. Carr RAF pilot s of James T. P. C. Aber

FARQUHAR George *BSc 1970

FARQUHAR Ian Harry MB ChB 1967
s of Harry F. master mariner and Catherine Bruce; b Portgordon 22.12.41
DObstRCOG 1972 MRCOG 1972
h o Taunton, Aber 1967–68; m o med TTB Inv, obst Kirkcaldy 1968–70; h o paediat Inv, gyn Kirkcaldy 1970–73; sen h o obst Glasg, obst/gyn Edin 1972–74; regist obst/gyn: Lond 1974–75, Ninewells hosp Dun, Perth RI 1975/77, Ninewells hosp from 1977

FARQUHAR Ian James MA 1969
s of James M. F. bank man. and Irene M. Foot; b Banff 24.5.48
teacher VSO Mhlume Swaziland 1970–72; RAF off./pilot trg Cranwell 1972–74; teacher: geog Linwood 1975–78, asst prin outdoor educ Armadale from 1978

FARQUHAR Marian Donald BSc 1957
d of Donald F. stonemason and Mary O. Dalgetty; b Brechin 3.9.35
teacher: maths/sc Montrose 1958–62, maths St Austell 1962–65, head maths dept Fareham 1965–75, dep head maths Bracknell from 1975
m Portsmouth 23.2.70 Francis G. Langton RN, civilian instr off. MoD s of Francis G. L. Portsmouth

FARQUHAR Marjory Niven MA 1958
m Innes

FARQUHAR Mary Easter MA 1956
d of James F. farm. and Jane D. Scott; b Lhanbryde 21.4.35
teacher: p s Banchory acad 1957–60, Wellhouse p s Glasg 1960–65, Stepps p s Glasg 1971–76, asst head from 1976
m Aber 23.12.63 John L. Robertson journalist s of John G. R. Glasg

FARQUHAR William John *MA 1958
s of John C. F. gardener and Mary Whyte; b Maud 29.5.35
Dip Soc Ad(Manc) 1960 FHA 1963
NHS: nat trainee hosp admin Aber, Manc 1958–61; Whitehaven: hosp secy 1961–64, dep group secy 1964–66; reg staff off. Edin 1966–69; dep secy Eastern Reg hosp board Dun 1969–74; dist admin S dist Lothian health board Edin from 1974
m Aber 24.2.62 Isabel H. Rusk MA 1956 *qv*

FARQUHAR William Sinclair *MA 1963
s of William F. trawl eng and Williamina Sinclair; b Aber 4.10.40
teacher Engl Buckhaven h s 1964–67; prin teacher Brockley c s Lond; lect Engl Jordanhill coll of educ 1971–74; asst rector Beath h s Cowdenbeath from 1974
m Aber 17.8.63 Eileen Hather d of Jack H. Aber

FARQUHARSON Alistair James Dawson MB ChB 1959

FARQUHARSON Graham Gibb MA 1968

FARQUHARSON Malcolm James MB ChB 1968

FARQUHARSON William Charles BSc 1957
s of George F. carpenter and Lily Irvine; b Torphins 25.8.35
Dip Sc and Tech(Glasg) 1960 MICE 1964 CEng 1966
shop man. UKAEA 1960–65; process eng Demerara bauxite comp Guyana 1966–67; metall Broken Hill dev comp Zambia 1968–70; mill supt Sherbro Minerals Sierra Leone 1970–71; prod. eng Chilanga Cement Zambia 1972–73; sen chem eng Revere Jamaica Alumina 1974–75, sen process eng MMIC Surigao Nickel Project Philippines 1976–78

FARR Valerie MB ChB 1956 ᶜMD 1966
b Darlington 2.10.30
DCH(Lond) 1959
h o: paediat Aber 1956–57, med Barnstaple 1957–58; Aber: sen h o and regist paediat 1958–63, lect ch health 1963–66; asst obst from 1966

FARSI Ali Abdulla Suleh MA 1962
d Texas USA –.12.73

FASEHUN Frederick Isiotan MB ChB 1969
d car accident in 1977

FASHOLE-LUKE Edward William PhD 1969
s of William F-L. acct GPO Sierra Leone and Cecilia O. P. Macauley secy; b Freetown 6.12.34
BA(Durh)
visiting prof of relig Kalamazoo coll USA 1970; Fourah Bay coll Sierra Leone: lect theol 1970–72; sen lect theol/acting head and dean fac of arts from 1972
m Freetown 7.1.60 Henrietta A. P. Lynch-Shyllon teacher d of H. L-S. Freetown

FAULKNER Clive MA 1962

FAULKS James Neville Gardiner *BSc 1962

FAULKS Judith Mary MA 1967

FAULKS Norman Quinney BSc 1965

FAWKES Mary Jill BSc 1958
d of Harry I. F. schoolmaster and Lilian Broadhead teacher; b Rolleston 27.5.37
asst res chem Ind Coope (Brewers) Burton-on-Trent 1958–59; lab tech MRC carcinogenic substances res unit Exe 1959–61; teacher sc: Stover s Newton Abbot 1961–62, Morgan acad Dun 1962–63
m Rolleston 29.7.59 John M. T. Brebner MA 1957 *qv*

FEARNLEY Arthur Herbert *BSc 1967
s of Joseph E. F. BSc 1927 *qv*; b Banff 9.9.46
plan. asst Moray & Nairn joint c c Elgin 1967–74; sen asst res plan. dept N Yorks c c Northallerton from 1974
m Grantown-on-Spey 5.4.69 Maureen M. Macaulay teacher d of Alexander M. Grantown-on-Spey

FEATHER Elizabeth Ann ᶜMB ChB 1965
d of Herbert G. F. LLB(Lond) solic and Norah E. Warman; b Fulmer 14.7.41
MRCP 1972
sen regist paediat Queen Elizabeth hosp for ch Lond 1974–75
m Frankley 17.8.74 John Seager MB ChB(Liv) paediat s of Thomas S. MD(Liv) Heswall

FELL John Alexander BSc(for) 1968
s of John W. F. (Cantab) and Evelyn A. Case; b Edin 9.6.43
BA(Cantab) 1965 MA(Cantab) 1969
for. invest. advis Edin 1968–71; gen fin. advis stockbrokers Glasg 1971–74; for. invest advis Econ For. Edin from 1974
m Stenton 26.8.67 Mary A. H. Hunter MA(St And) d of Hon Lord Hunter LLB(Oxon) Stenton Dunbar

FELL Margaret Eleanor MA 1959
m Athawes

FELL Rosaleen Mabel MA 1967
m Bishop

FEMI-PEARSE Ayodeji MB ChB 1959 MD 1970
MRCPE DTM&H(Liv)

FENELON Anne Deirdre Sutherland MA 1968

FENNELL John Allinson BSc 1963

FENTON Winston *BSc(eng) 1964 MSc 1966 PhD 1968

FERGUSON Charles Alexander BSc(agr) 1970
s of George F. farm. and Barbara Wilson; b Elgin 1.11.47
MSc(N'cle) 1972
farm. Forres 1972–73; working Aust, NZ 1973–74; farm. Forres from 1974

FERGUSON David MacKay *BSc 1963
s of James M. M. F. loc govt off. and Margaret F. Eggie; b Duns 26.12.40
PhD(Edin) 1969
dem physiol med s Edin 1965–66; ICI Alderley Park: member physiol sect. indust hyg res lab 1966–70, head physiol unit 1970–72, head acute toxicity unit, Central Toxicology Lab 1972–75, toxicology advis Cent Med Group from 1975
m Aber 28.4.67 Lois King d of Angus H. K. Winchelsea Victoria Aust

FERGUSON Donald Ewen *MA 1965

FERGUSON Donald Hugh Nicolson BSc 1968
s of Hamish N. F. hotel porter and Anne Fraser MA (Edin) teacher; b Inv 4.7.47
ALA
salesman Farrington Data Processing Glasg 1968–69; stud. N'cle-u-Tyne poly tech 1969–70; lib AWRE Aldermaston from 1971
m Lond 20.4.71 Patricia M. Simpson MA 1968 *qv*

FERGUSON Elizabeth Susan MA 1970
m Stuart

FERGUSON Fiona Margaret MA 1970
d of John W. F. PO tel eng and Christina M. Munro nurs nurse; b Haslemere 25.9.49
teacher p s Lond 1971–76
m Invergordon 21.4.73 George D. Porter police sergeant s of Alexander P. Alness

FERGUSON Gail Cooper MA 1970

FERGUSON Iain Scoon *BSc(eng) 1970
s of Ian S. F. MB ChB(Edin) g p and Marjory H. Walker; b Edin 7.4.48
Vickers defence syst div N'cle-u-Tyne: syst eng 1971–73, tech asst to chief buyer 1973–76, purchasing off. from 1976
m Stocksfield 30.9.72 Mary E. Phillips d of Horace A. P. Stocksfield

FERGUSON Ian Russell *MEd 1956
MA(Glas)

FERGUSON Irene Ramsay MA 1960
d of James M. M. F. loc govt off. and Margaret F. Eggie civ serv; b Perth 25.6.39
teacher Fr: Stirling h s 1961–62, Aber acad 1962–64; ptnr in farm. bus. from 1965
m Aber 2.8.62 William R. Strachan BSc 1959 *qv*

FERGUSON Joanne Audrey Lorne BSc 1970
d of John A. F. farm. and Lorna F. Conway dom bursar; b Oban 30.4.48
teacher: Slough 1971–72, Brisbane Aust 1972–73, Honiara BSIP 1973–78
m Aber 13.8.71 Steven E. Watson BSc 1971 pasture agronomist s of George A. W. Strathtay

FERGUSON Kathryn Anne *BSc 1969
m Carmichael

FERGUSON Kenneth McIntosh *BSc 1969
s of David M. F. assur ag and Minnie T. MacDonald; b Dingwall 25.7.47
geol Renison Bell Tasmania 1969–71; Perth W Aust: univ stud. 1971–72, sen geol from 1973
m Bearsden 7.8.69 Julia S. Bertram BSc 1969 *qv*

FERGUSON Sinclair Buchanan MA 1968 *BD 1971
s of Robert B. F. manuf's ag and Emma H. S. S. S. Munro bookkeeper; b Glasg 21.2.48
C of S min: asst St George's Tron ch Glasg 1971–74, par of Unst 1974–76, asst edit Banner of Truth Trust Publ from 1976
m Aber 16.7.71 Dorothy M. Allan MA 1968 *qv*

FERGUSSON Marjorie Hill BSc 1964

FERNANDEZ-CARMONO Julio MSc 1969
Dr Ing Agr(Madrid)

FERRARI Leonella Lucia Anna Maria *MA 1958
d of Pietro F. restaurateur and Linda Acquistapace; b Aber 6.4.35
private secy to Italian consul gen Toronto 1958–60; TEFL European s Parma 1960–61; teacher Fr/Ital royal acad Inv 1961–71, asst prin Fr/Ital 1971–72, prin from 1972
m Inv 29.9.58 Alexander B. G. Longmore MA 1956 *qv*

FERRARIS Mary MA 1967
d of Alfredo F. LLB(Torino) man. dir and Teresa Santone; b Lond 27.1.47
MA (York univ Toronto) 1969
res asst Tor 1968–69; au pair, waitress Neuchatel, St Cergue Switzerland 1970–71; secy Lond 1971–72; teacher Ponteland Northumberland 1972–73; secy Tor 1974; teacher Mississauga Ont from 1974
m Lond 1.8.73 William M. Kennedy BA (York Toronto) teacher s of William M. K. Weston Ont

FERREIRA Robert Edwin Christopher PhD 1958
s of Edwin C. F. comp dir and Jessica G. Robinson farm; b Windermere 30.8.31
BSc(Lond) 1954
bot: Nature Conserv Edin 1960–67, seconded from DOS to govt of Uganda 1967–71, VSO Zambia 1972–74; conserv biol and ecological advis Zambia Lusaka 1974–76; plant ecol Nature Conserv Council Inv from 1977

FERRIES Isobel Jean MA 1965

FETHNEY Hilary Ann MA 1959
d of John R. F. pharm and Janet F. McDonald; b Bishopbriggs 16.4.39
m Aber 6.4.61 Robert I. Gloyer MA 1957 *qv*

FETHNEY Moira *MA 1957
d of John R. F. pharm and Janet F. MacDonald; b Glasg 19.1.36

teacher mus: Gordon s Huntly 1958–60, Ripon 1960, Moray from 1972
m Aber 4.7.60 John A. Dickson RAF off. s of George F. D. BL 1928 *qv*

FETTES Douglas James *BSc 1963
s of George F. F. fishmonger and Nellie Falconer; b Aber 24.12.40
PhD(Edin) 1968 FGS 1970
Edin: scient off. Inst of geol sc 1966–69, sen scient off. 1969–73, prin scient off. from 1973
m Dunfermline 8.11.68 Frances M. Hay secy d of William H. Dunfermline

FETTES Ian William MB ChB 1969

FETTES Peter Hugh MB ChB 1968
s of William Y. F. MB ChB 1938 *qv*; b Insch 1.5.42
h o ARI, City hosp Aber 1968–69; h o obst/gyn Falkirk and dist RI 1969–70; g p: Musselburgh 1970, Ardersier 1970–71, Gorebridge from 1971
m Aber 23.11.68 Mary R. Bell MB ChB 1967 *qv*

FIDDLER Alasdair Stuart *BSc 1968
s of John R. F. and Margat J. Banks; b Kirkwall 23.10.46
Dip Chem Eng(Sur)
tech BP: Sunbury-on-Thames 1970–74, Lond from 1974
m Sunbury-on-Thames 15.9.73 Mollie A. Deacon copytypist d of William E. D. Sunbury-on-Thames

FIELDING Jacqueline Anne BSc 1970
d of William F. furn salesman and Gladys Greenwood lab tech; b Kendal 10.6.49
VSO teacher Kenya 1971–72; lect Exeter coll 1973; VS organis Exe Vale psychiat hosp from 1973
m Broadstone 13.9.69 Hamish Henderson MA 1971 insp taxes s of James L. H. Huntly

FIFE Alistair Angus *BSc 1964
s of George F. MA 1930 *qv*; b Nairn 11.10.41
MSc(Alta) 1966 PhD(S Fraser) 1971
teaching asst: Edmonton 1964–66, S Fraser 1966–70; post doct fell.: S Fraser and Br Col 1971–72, univ Montr 1972–73; res phys CTF Syst Inc Port Coquitlam BC from 1973

FIFE William Alexander Anderson BSc(agr) 1962

FILBY Alan George *BSc 1969 PhD 1973

FINCH David William MA 1965
s of William G. F. prod. eng and Annie E. Bollans; b Carshalton 6.2.41
MSc(Kansas) 1967
Lond: sub edit. The Assoc Press 1967–69; sen sub edit. BBC external serv 1969–74; edit. in resid Kansas univ 1974; foreign desk edit. The Assoc Press NY 1974–75; edit. Reuters NY from 1975
m Carshalton 30.8.69 Louise A. Riller BA(Kansas) lab tech d of Lowell E. R. BA(Kansas) Kansas City Miss.

FINCH Maureen Frances Heneage *BSc 1970
d 19.8.70

FINDLAY Adam Herd *MA 1970
s of Adam H. F. trawl eng and Isabella Sinclair; b Aber 16.10.44
teacher: Engl Fraserburgh acad 1971–72, Rubislaw acad Aber 1972–73; Engl/hist Kedron h s Brisbane Aust 1974–75; asst prin Engl Inverurie acad from 1976
m Aber 22.7.66 Patricia Ritchie MA 1966 *qv*

FINDLAY Alan Grant Reid *MA 1964
s of William H. F. MB ChB(Glas) consult. phys, photographer and Marjorie J. Greenlees; b Stirling 10.8.42
BR: man. trainee Glasg 1965–67, asst to man. freightliner terminal Glasg 1967–68; traffic asst Auchinleck 1969; teacher geog Inv royal acad from 1970

FINDLAY Alice Dawson MA 1968 *MEd 1970 PhD 1974
b Aber 11.7.47
m Archbold

FINDLAY Angela Bisset *MA 1964 *MEd 1966
m Duncan

FINDLAY David *BSc 1957 PhD 1961
s of David F. cemetery supt and Frances Gordon; b New Pitsligo 30.5.35
FPhysS 1959
asst lect Aberd 1960–62; scient off. royal radar estab Malvern 1962–68; lect phys Queen's univ Belf 1968–72, sen lect from 1972
m Lerwick 14.7.60 Barbara E. Robertson teacher d of Thomas H. R. Mossbank

FINDLAY David Robert MB ChB 1957

FINDLAY James Alexander May MB ChB 1959
s of James W. F. water insp and Mary B. May; b Fraserburgh 1.1.35
FRCSE 1966
h o Aber hosps 1959–60; dem anat Aberd, Glas 1960–62; orthop: regist Glasg, chief resid Ottawa 1967–70, sen regist Leeds 1970–72; consult. orthop surg Paisley from 1972
m Hamilton 16.6.65 Mary E. W. Wright MB ChB(Glas) med pract d of William W. MA(Glas) Hamilton

FINDLAY James Slater *MA 1963

FINDLAY John Bell Cuthbert *BSc 1968
s of Robert F. dir sugar/rum prod. and Georgina Spence; b Georgetown Guyana 5.2.46
PhD(Leeds) 1972
univ Leeds: res assoc 1968–71, post doct fell. 1971–72; res fell./dept tut. Harvard univ USA 1972–74; lect Leeds from 1974

FINDLAY John William *BSc(eng) 1969

FINDLAY John William Addison *BSc 1966 PhD 1969
s of Alexander F. fisherman and Jessie R. Addison; b Buckie 27.3.45
USA: res assoc med chem Charlottesville Virginia 1969–72, clin res assoc Norfolk Virginia 1972–73; res scient Amersham 1973–75; USA: sen res scient (drug metabolism) Res Triangle Park N Carolina from 1975
m Aber 11.7.70 Jean M. Hey MB ChB 1970 *qv*

FINDLAY Judith Margaret MA 1965
d of James A. F. insur surv and Mary Shewan; b Aber 29.3.44
teacher Fernielea p s Aber 1966–69
m Aber 22.7.66 Alexander R. Carle MA 1962 *qv*

FINDLAY June Mary PhD 1959
d of Alexander F. master mariner and Miriam Stewart; b Hartlepool 8.6.31
BSc(Wales) 1952
teacher sc: Milford Haven g s 1953–54, James Gillespie's h s Edin 1954–56; res asst Rowett inst Aber 1956–60

m Aber 7.5.60 John S. Bevan-Baker FRCO(Lond) Sutton Coldfield

FINDLAY Leonard Murray *MA 1967
s of George F. ship's rigger and Irene Black; b Aber 14.12.44
DPhil(Oxon) 1973
Engl lit.: lect Birm 1972–74, asst prof Saskatoon Sask from 1974
m Aber 26.7.68 Isobel M. Downie MA 1968 *qv*

FINDLAY May Florence MA 1957
d of John F. county arch. Moray & Nairn and May S. Geddes; b Elgin 8.2.35
secy lit. side of *Journal* Glasg chamber of commerce 1958–60; prin teacher comm subj Brinnington s Stockport 1961–63; part-time nurs teacher Glasg from 1964
m Aber 17.8.60 Lewis A. Gunn MA 1957 *qv*

FINDLAY Neil Alexander *MA 1965
s of Thomas A. F. bank man. and Elspeth MacNeil; b Aber 1.7.42
Lond: teacher mus Beaufoy s 1968–69, head of mus Coopers' Company s 1969–73, head of mus Coopers' Company and Coborn s Upminster from 1973

FINDLAY Patricia Margaret MA 1966
d of James A. F. master butcher and Catherine Muldoon; b Selkirk 29.4.44
teacher: Engl Closeburn 1967–70, Engl/maths Melbourne, 1970, Toowoomba Aust 1970–72
m Dumfries 3.8.68 Christopher J. E. Newman BSc 1967 *qv*

FINDLAY Robert Campbell *MA 1962
s of Isaac M. F. taxi driver and Sarah J. Westland; b Aber 28.2.40
MA(Temple univ Philadelphia) 1967 PhD(Temple univ Phil) 1971
Philadelphia: staff psych ch hosp 1963–66, audiologist ch hosp 1966–68, audiol veteran's admin 1968–71; clin prof dept of speech univ of Pittsburgh from 1971
m Haddonfield NJ -.12.60 Judith G. Black MS(Drexel) lib d of Otis D. B. PhD(Ohio State univ) Haddon Hts NJ

FINDLAY Roderic Ian Garrioch *MA 1965
s of George I. G. F. MB ChB 1931 *qv*; b Ilford 21.12.41
Colston's s Bristol: teacher 1966–69, sen hist master from 1969

FINLAY Ian Chirnside BSc(eng) 1957 *1958

FINLAYSON Brenda Elizabeth BSc 1958
d of Eric C. F. MA 1926 *qv*; b Milltimber 27.7.37
teacher: Perth 1959–61, Reading 1961–64, Crediton from 1974
m Aber Wilson S. Mitchell livestock husb advis with ADAS s of A. Hunter M. Forfar

FINLAYSON Helen Rosemary BEd 1969 *MEd 1973
d of John F. fitter and Helen R. Findlay ch nurse; b Livingstonia Malawi 9.7.48
res asst educ surv and investig coll of educ Aber 1969–71; teacher Fr Rubislaw acad Aber 1972–75
m Aber 8.4.71 James H. Maycock BSc 1968 *qv*

FINLAYSON James *MA 1958
s of James F. master baker and Elsie Ogston embroiderer; b Stonehaven 28.3.36
educ off.: Sekondi Ghana 1959–61, Mbale Uganda 1961–71, Mackay Aust 1971–74; Toowoomba Aust from 1974
m(2) 14.8.67 Barbara Verest, Heeze Holland

FINLAYSON John *MA 1957
s of James F. master baker and Elsie Ogston embroiderer; b Aber 23.2.35
PhD(Cantab) 1962
res fell. Liv 1960–62; Canada: lect McG univ 1962–64; asst assoc prof Queen's univ Kingston from 1964
m Kingston Ont 4.8.67 Francien R. Mantin BA(Queen's univ) lib d of Joseph L. M.

FINLAYSON John Duncan MA 1969

FINNIE Helen Milne *MA 1968
b Banffsh 25.10.44
PhD(Edin) 1975
parliamentary res off. House of Commons Lond from 1974

FINNIE Ivor McIntosh MA 1969
s of William F. stationmaster BR and Betty S. Wilson; b Keith 23.1.45
Dip Man. St(RGIT Aber) 1970
marketing trainee Rowntree York 1970–72; Aber: C. E. Heath & Co insur brokers 1972–74, man. dir Crown Park estate agents and other companies from 1974
m Aber 15.4.68 Frances M. Buchanan secy d of Albert B. Aber

FINNIE Oswald Copland MA 1969
s of James S. F. agr eng and Clara W. Copland; b Fraserburgh 4.7.48
app CA Aber 1969–72; CA comp acct Edin from 1973
m Aber 21.7.72 Irene M. Ritchie MA 1969 *qv*

FINNIE William Wilson BEd 1970

FISH Melvin Raymond BSc(for) 1970 *MEd 1972
s of Joe F. fitter and Stella Caswell; b Bradford 26.12.47
teacher biol Prince Henry's g s Otley from 1972
m Bradford 19.8.72 Jean L. Wilson physioth d of Maurice W. Bradford

FISHER Peter McLaren MB ChB 1969 [c]MD 1976
s of James F. laundry prop. and Elizabeth F. McDonald MA(Edin) teacher; b Aberfeldy 24.4.44
MRCOG 1976

FISHER Stanley Finlayson *MA 1965
s of Stanley P. F. lab and Frances B. Tosh fish worker; b Fraserburgh 6.12.42
indust trg off. Manc 1965–67; teacher: Stonehaven 1968–73, Aber 1973–76; blaster, oil-rig worker 1976–77; gen contr from 1977
m Stockport 13.7.68 Joan C. Wolstenholme MA 1973 soc worker d of Tom W. Stockport; marr diss 1976

FISHER Stuart Timothy BSc(eng) 1970
s of Leonard R. F. BSc(Lond) marine zool and Jean I. Elliott; b Chelmsford 2.8.48
Costain civ eng: jun eng Lond, Reading 1970–71, seconded to J. D. & D. M. Watson High Wycombe 1971–73, asst eng Birkenhead 1973–74; civ eng Transport and Road res lab des and site eng Crowthorne 1974–76; proj eng J. D. & D. M. Watson High Wycombe from 1976

FITCH Peter James BSc(for) 1965
s of James H. F. acct and Doris C. V. Langley; b Carshalton 22.12.43
Malawi: asst conserv for. Mzimba 1965–70, acting sen asst cons for. Limbe 1970–71; for. man. Accra Ghana 1971–75; man. Tilhill For. (Scotland) from 1976
m Aber 12.9.68 Helen M. Gibb d of James A. G. Aber

FITCHIE Logan Rodney George BSc 1969
s of George F. army off., eng and Jean H. A. Webster; b Edin 25.8.46
S Af: trainee quality controller Vereeniging 1970–72, sen work stud. off. Lever Bros Boksburg 1972–74, work study off. Stewarts & Lloyds Vereeniging from 1974
m Vereeniging 6.2.71 Kathleen P. Mathers BSc 1969 *qv*

FITZROY Felix Rudolph MSc 1961
BSc(Lond)

FLANAGAN Elizabeth MB ChB 1959
b Aber
DPM(Dub) 1963 FRCPS(Can) 1968 LMCC 1969 MSc(Harvard) 1978
h o, regist, sen regist Aber 1960–68; spec psychiat Vancouver 1968; dir mental health centre Vancouver 1969–77; consult. psychiat mental health serv Brit Columbia from 1978
m Luke

FLEMING Christopher Alexander *BSc(eng) 1970
s of Brian A. F. insur comp dist man. and Marguerite G. Allingham; b Lond 14.8.48
grad eng consult. eng Lond 1970–72; site eng consult. eng Port Victoria Seychelles 1972; asst eng consult. eng Lond 1972–73, PhD stud. Rd'g from 1973
m Aber 17.7.70 Christeen Maclean BEd 1969 *qv*

FLEMING Eleanor Shearer *MA 1963

FLEMING Fiona Margaret MA 1969
m Moir

FLEMING Hamish Kirkpatrick MA 1962
s of William S. F. CA and Jean H. Kirkpatrick; b Aber 17.3.37
div course New Coll Edin 1961–64; C of S min: Barrhead South ch 1966–72, St Marnock's ch Kilmarnock 1972–75, St Mark's ch Aber from 1975
m Barrhead 20.6.67 Agnes Duncan nurse d of Robert M. D. Barrhead

FLEMING Jean BSc 1957
d of John F. farm. and Isabella Paterson; b Aber 24.12.35
biochem: Bangour hosp 1957–58, ch hosp Glasg 1958–60; res asst ch hosp Toronto 1960–61; biochem East gen hosp Toronto 1961–63; res asst univ of Pittsburgh USA 1963–64; biochem Homestead hosp USA 1964–66
m Aber 23.7.63 Ronald Gibson BSc(eng)(Belf) soils eng s of Charles G. Belf

FLEMING Joan Mairi MA 1967
d of John F. BSc(Glas) teacher and Murdina Macleod youth hostel warden; b Dunoon 12.6.46
teacher: Kirkhill p s Aber 1968–72, Banchory p s 1972–74, remed from 1974
m Ullapool 30.3.68 Michael D. Lowndes BSc(eng) 1966 *qv*

FLEMING John Leslie MA 1968 *1970
s of John S. F. shop owner and Helen Leslie; b Dufftown 24.9.47
O and M off. Gen Accident Insur Perth from 1970

FLEMING Kathleen MA 1964

FLEMING Kenneth MB ChB 1962
b N'cle-u-Tyne 10.7.38
DObstRCOG 1964
h o Shotley Bridge gen hosp 1962–63; Aber: h o obst mat. hosp 1963–64, sen h o, regist med ARI 1964–66; g p Broadstone from 1966
m Aber 10.7.62 Pamela A. Duthie MB ChB 1962 *qv*

FLEMING Mark Roger Patrick MA 1968
s of Roger J. C. F. timber merch and Judith A. Q. Jackson; b Aber 11.5.47
CA 1972
app CA Edin 1968–72, CA Paris 1972–73; timber merch Glasg from 1973

FLEMING Rosslyn Muriel BSc 1970
d of Roland M. F. comp dir and Muriel A. S. Watt nurse; b Redruth 4.10.49
progr Dublin 1970–72; syst progr Lond 1972–74; progr Buffalo NY 1975–76; syst progr Boston USA from 1976
m Aber 1.9.72 Peter M. Bradley BSc 1971 res scient s of Hunter W. B. MA 1946 *qv*

FLEMMING Christopher John MB ChB 1968
s of Clifford F. F. BSc(Manc) schoolmaster and Mary W. Monaghan schoolmistress; b Buxton 1.5.43
Royal Alexandra hosp Rhyl: h o 1968–69, sen h o paediat 1969; sen h o obst/gyn Gt Yarmouth 1969–70; g p Capel St Mary from 1970
m Rickmansworth 4.5.68 Lynda Ruff BSc 1968 *qv*

FLETCHER Alan McKay *BSc(for) 1960 PhD 1963
s of Sylvester T. F. comm trav and Annie M. Cook clerkess; b Aber 25.2.37
geneticist with for. comm res div Edin from 1963
m Aber 28.8.64 Isobel J. Ritchie clerkess d of William R. Dunecht

FLETCHER David James *MA 1960
s of Harry F. bank man. and Hilda Wood; b Burnley 20.12.37
res asst McG univ Montreal 1960–61; edit. asst D. C. Thomson Dun 1961–62; cartographic edit. Clarendon Press Oxford 1962–66; publ and edit. Wm Blackwood Edin 1966–76; co-dir/edit. *Blackwood's Magazine* from 1976
m Aber 25.8.62 Margaret M. Stoney MA 1961 *qv*

FLETCHER Jane Margaret *MA 1965
d of Randall J. F. lathe oper and Jessie S. A. Waugh midwife; b Birm 31.3.42
BA(Lond) 1968 MA(Toronto Ont) 1969
prof dept of Engl, Ryerson poly inst Toronto from 1970
m Tor Ont 22.6.74 Stanley T. J. Isherwood BTh(Tor) clergyman/teacher s of Thomas W. I. MTh(Oxon)

FLETCHER Joan MA 1968

FLETCHER Terrence Albert Claude BSc(eng) 1962
s of James A. F. headmaster and Beryl C. Bourne teacher; b Georgetown Guyana 15.2.39
MSc(Columbus Ohio) 1969
asst eng Lond 1962–63; Georgetown: eng 1963–68, spec eng 1970–72, consult. eng from 1972
m Georgetown 26.3.64 Greta Perreira secy

FLETT Alexander Paul MA 1967

FLETT Alistair Murray *BSc 1959 PhD 1964
s of George F. BSc 1928 *qv*; b Inv 29.9.37
M Inst P 1965 FRAS 1972 TD 1972
Aberd: res stud. nat phil 1959–62, asst 1962–64, lect from 1964
m Aber 16.9.61 Aileen E. Mackie MB ChB 1962 *qv*

FLETT Allan Munro BSc 1962

FLETT Douglas Stewart *BSc 1957 PhD 1960
s of George F. BSc 1928 *qv*; b Inv 3.6.36
sen phys chem Permutit Co. Lond 1960–62; scient off. DSIR Warren Spring lab Stevenage 1962–64; exch scient Nat Inst of Metall Johannesburg 1964–65; sen scient off. Warren Spring lab Stevenage 1965–66, 1968–71; guest res nat res inst for metals Tokyo 1967–68; visiting prof univ of Waterloo Ontario 1971; prin scient off. Warren Spring lab Stevenage from 1972
m Aber 6.5.68 Mitsuko Hirano BA(Tokyo) clerkess d of Torijiro H. BA(econ)(Tokyo) Fukioka City Japan

FLETT Hazel Margaret Gibb MA 1956
d of George S. F. harbour master and Isabel G. Paul insur ag; b Findochty 15.4.35
LTCL 1960
teacher: Aber 1957–60, Geilenkirchen Germany 1960–62, Wyton 1970–72, Bracknell 1973–75, dep head 1974–76, asst head Edin from 1976
m Finningley 22.12.62 Anthony G. Box BSc(Lond) RAF off. (pilot), secy Scot. council for health educ from 1978 s of Ernest R. B. Market Drayton

FLETT James Crichton Smith MA 1963

FLETT Joan BSc 1970
d of John F. marine eng RN, seine fishing boat skipper and Christina G. Edwards; b Lossiemouth 10.10.49
computer progr NCB computer centre Cannock 1970–73; teacher biol/gen sc Lornshill acad Alloa from 1974
m Lossiemouth 21.4.73 Philip Dyer BSc(Liv) computer progr, teacher s of Andrew D. Worsley

FLETT Joan Reid *BSc 1969
d of George R. F. BSc(for) 1933 *qv*; b Bathgate 26.8.47
res asst Unilever Bedford 1969–70; teacher: sc Bannockburn j s s 1970–71, biol Broxbourne 1972–74; NZ: trade-mark searcher at patent attorneys Wellington 1974, teacher biol Erskine coll Wellington 1974, Naenae coll Lower Hutt 1975–76
m Hertford 24.12.73 Neil W. Hindley BSc(Nott) civ eng s of William C. H. Lowton

FLOCKHART Mary Rattray MA 1970 Dip Ed 1971
d of Ian F. sales rep and Nan Allan; b Aber 13.11.49
teacher hist Northfield acad Aber 1971–76
m Aber 27.7.73 Brian A. Anderson MA 1963 *qv*

FLOCKHART Nanette Jamieson MB ChB 1968
d of Ian F. and Nan Allan; b Aber 10.8.44
h o ARI 1968–69; trainee g p Aber 1969–70; sen h o psychiat Aber 1970–71; clin m o Aber c c 1971–73; part-time g p Aber 1973–75; clin asst: gen med Edin 1976–77, part time paediat Aber from 1978
m Aber 19.8.69 Richard W. Davidson-Lamb MB ChB 1968 *qv*

FLORENCE Alexander Farquhar *MA 1957
dist off. col serv Zambia
d Lusaka Zambia 31.3.63 *AUR* XL 207

FLORENCE Anne McKenzie MB ChB 1962
d of Alexander A. F. police off., gen merch and Annie G. A. Mitchell MA 1931 *qv*; b Aber 12.11.38
FFARCS 1966 (Nuffield Prize)
h o: Woodend hosp Aber, Victoria hosp Keighley, paediat Edin 1962–63; sen h o anaest: Edin 1963–65, Broadgreen hosp Liv 1965–66, regist 1966–67; res fell. surg Liv 1967–68, sen regist paediat anaest 1968–69; consult. anaest Liv reg cardio-thor unit from 1969, clin lect Liv from 1969

FLORENCE Elizabeth May MA 1959
d of George F. insur off. and Elizabeth T. Smith teacher dom sc; b Aber 16.2.38
teacher maths/sc Mackie acad Stonehaven 1960–64
m Aber 1.10.64 Herbert D. Hay oil comp exec s of William H. Pitcaple

FLORENCE Margaret Maitland MA 1960
d of Kenneth S. F. law acct and Isabella L. Thomson; b Aber 19.7.38
RGN(ARI) 1964 CMB(Aber)
staff nurse ARI 1964–67; Lond: private nursing 1968–70; nurse Harley St clin 1970–71
m Lond 20.11.71 Salim H. Macki BSc(Moscow) petr eng, min plenipotentiary Sultanate of Oman s of Hassan Y. M. Muscat

FLORENCE Mary Isabel BSc 1970
d of Alexander A. F. policeman, shopkeeper and Annie G. A. Mitchell MA 1931 *qv*; b Braemar 1.12.47
geol Vancouver 1970–71 and 1973; part-time office work Tungsten NWT Canada from 1974
m Vancouver 7.5.71 Nigel G. Cawthorn BSc 1970 *qv*

FLORY Flora Ann MA 1966
d of Reid F. pharm and Sybil M. Lefleur tel; b Agra India 16.5.45
teacher Summerhill s s Aber 1967–68
m Huntly 17.8.67 Alexander S. Milne BSc(eng) 1967 *qv*

FLUX John Etheridge Cormack *BSc 1957 PhD 1962
s of Ronald C. F. BSc(eng)(Lond) civ eng and Charlotte S. Cormack; b Maymyo Burma 20.12.34
scient with ecology div NZ DSIR Lower Hutt NZ from 1960, NZ nat res fell. Nairobi Kenya 1967–68
m Aber 30.7.58 Margaret M. West BSc 1956 *qv*

FOAD Roger John Michael *MA 1969
s of John E. F. bank off. and Eileen M. Smeeton insur ag; b Tendring 23.7.45
immigration off. Heathrow airport from 1971
m St Albans 17.2.73 Rosalind A. Carpenter nurse, civ serv d of Alfred D. C. St Albans

FOGG Arnold George PhD 1961
s of Richard F. cemetery regist/parks supt and Edith Balmer; b Radcliffe 6.12.35
BSc(Lond) 1958 ARTCS(Salf) 1958
Loughborough coll of adv tech, Loughborough univ: asst lect inorg chem/sub warden 1961–64, lect 1964–66, lect analytical chem 1966–76, sen lect from 1976
m Aber 20.8.60 Joyce M. Carson MA 1960 *qv*

FOGG Lance Trevor *BSc(eng) 1967

FOLEY Terence *BSc 1968 PhD 1972
s of Michael F. RAF, antique dealer and Muriel Yellowlees; b Selkirk 6.4.44
res fell. Imp Coll Lond from 1971

FONG Weng Cheong MSc 1965
ARCFT

FOOT Janet Zoë PhD 1969
d of Arthur S. F. MSc(R'dg) res scient and Dorothy M. H. Irvine NDD; b Reading 7.7.46
BSc(R'dg) 1962 MAgrSc(Melb) 1965
scient with hill-farming res organis Edin from 1969; visiting res fell. univ Melb s of agr Aust 1974–75

FOOTE Robert Lewis MA 1970
s of Robert F. F. acct and Dorothy L. Forbes secy;

b Aber 5.3.42
teacher Engl Arbroath h s 1971–75; lect Engl Aber coll of commerce from 1975

FORBES Alan David *BSc 1956

FORBES Alan George LLB 1965

FORBES Alan Ritchie *MA 1956
s of James R. F. marine eng and Charlotte D. Kemp MA 1923 *qv*; b Edin 26.11.33
PhD(Otago) 1970
sen clin psych Crichton royal hosp Dumfries 1960–64; NZ: lect psych med Otago univ Dunedin 1964–67, lect, sen lect psych Otago univ 1967–75, prof psych Victoria univ Wellington from 1975, visiting prof Manc 1979
m Aber 7.8.58 Alison F. McCaskill teacher d of Francis W. McC. MA(Otago) Keith

FORBES Alexander *MA 1959
s of Alexander F. MA 1928 *qv*; b Lond 22.6.36
AInstLang(Madrid) 1957
teacher: Fr/Span Eastwood h s Glasg 1960–66, Harrison coll Bridgetown Barbados 1966–69; head Skinner comm coll Castries St Lucia 1969–71; teacher: guid Eastwood h s Glasg 1971–72, Internat s Singapore from 1972
m Aber 22.7.61 Moira Fraser teacher d of George F. Aber

FORBES Andrew King MA 1970
s of Frank M. F. MA 1947 *qv*; b Aber 7.5.49
police constable Lond from 1971

FORBES Anne MA 1960
d of John F. area off. Aber c c and Mary W. Duncan shop asst; b Keith 2.3.39
Dip Sec (Scot. coll of comm Glasg) 1961
p a to TU gen secy Lond 1961–65; admin asst MRC unit Edin 1965–67; pers secy to man. dir Lincs 1967–68; secy MRC med sociol unit Aberd 1968–74, admin asst from 1974

FORBES Atholl Roderick MB ChB 1966
s of Thomas F. bank teller and Annie H. A. Spain restaurateur b Aber 17.5.43
FRARCS 1970
h o Aber gen hosps 1966–67; sen h o, regist anaest united Sheff hosps 1967–71; sen regist anaest and tut. Hammersmith hosp Lond 1971–73; asst prof anaest univ Calif San Francisco from 1973
m Aber 2.8.67 Esmé Maxwell MA 1967 *qv*

FORBES Charles Leslie MB ChB 1957
s of Charles B. F. MA 1922 *qv*; b Aber 18.10.33
g p Aber from 1960
m Aber 10.3.58 Margaret M. Buthlay pharm d of Alexander B. Aber

FORBES David *MA 1965 Dip Ed 1969
s of Alexander F. MA 1928 *qv*; b Torphins 5.9.43
MA(Lond) 1968
exchange schol univ of Kansas USA 1965–66; trainee insp of taxes Aber 1966–67; teacher: Fraserburgh acad 1969–71, prin hist Golspie h s 1971–73; lect soc stud. Craigie coll of educ Ayr from 1973
m Aber 8.7.70 Marlene Chrystal tracer/draughtsman d of Robert C. Aber

FORBES Dorothy Kathleen *BSc 1966
m Richard W. Marriott BSc 1966 *qv*

FORBES Elspeth Ann *MA 1958
d of John S. F. (Bart) DSO R Eng farm. and Agnes J. Farquharson; b Bangalore S India 10.3.37
teacher mus: Aber 1959–60, Glasg 1960–61, Aber from 1969
m Glasg 1960 George M. Hardie comm artist/teacher art s of John H. Aber

FORBES Emily Coutts MB ChB 1969
d of William S. F. master draper and Rosanna Kelman dressmaker; b Insch 9.7.45
h o: med Greenock, gyn Aber 1969–70; sen h o Kingseat hosp 1970–71, regist 1971–72; regist Ross Clin Aber 1972–73, part time from 1973
m Aber 14.7.71 Peter G. Hamilton MB ChB 1972 g p s of Joseph S. H. MB ChB 1937 *qv*

FORBES Eric Alexander BSc(eng) 1966
s of John F. comp dir and Margaret J. Neish; b Forres 1.10.46
MICE 1974 CEng 1973
Aber: asst civ and struct eng (consult.) 1966–69, prin eng (consult.) 1969–72, dev eng (contr) from 1972
m Aber 22.9.66 Marguarite Urquhart d of Joseph U. Aber

FORBES Eric Simon *BSc 1956

FORBES Gordon Gorrod *BSc 1961

FORBES Hilda Mary MA 1969
d of Alexander F. agr worker and Isobella D. Simpson clerkess; b Insch 11.3.48
teacher geog/mod stud. Gordon s Huntly from 1970
m Aber 4.4.72 Brian T. Christie plant hire sales rep s of Thomas C. Banchory

FORBES Iain MB ChB 1968
s of John D. R. F. airline pilot and Elizabeth M. Macdonald; b Inv 23.10.42
LMCC 1976
h o Aber 1968–69; g p: Lond 1969–71, Lethbridge Canada 1971–76, Parksville Canada from 1976
m Lond 4.3.71 Anna D'Agostino DA teacher d of Louis D'A. Banchory

FORBES Iain Macdonald BD 1964
s of Alexander F. bank man. and Margaret F. Macdonald; b Johnstone 16.12.39
BSc(Edin) 1961
missionary/min Presb ch of E Africa Kiene settlement scheme Kenya 1966–69; home organis secy C of S overseas council Edin 1970–74; min Benbecula from 1975
m Aber 19.8.64 Margaret R. Macartney midwife d of William M. M. MA(Edin) Aber

FORBES Isabel Christina MA 1970
m Shearer

FORBES James Carnegie *BSc 1969 PhD 1973

FORBES Margaret Iris Stuart MA 1964
d of Alexander A. F. shop man. and Margaret C. Miller; b Grantown-on-Spey 9.7.43
teacher: Pitcairn p s Almondbank 1965–67, Causewayend p s Aber 1967–69
m Grantown-on-Spey 12.4.69 Harry D. McIntosh pharm s of Donald S. McI. Turriff

FORBES Margaret Xanthe Patricia MB ChB 1964
d of John S. F. (Bart) DSO R Eng farm. and Agnes J. Farquharson; b Lond 25.3.40
h o RACH, Perth RI 1964–65; regist rheumatology ARI/assoc hosps Aber from 1972
m Aber 16.7.64 James C. Petrie MB ChB 1964 *qv*

FORBES Michael Davidson MA 1964
d of Harry C. F. fish merch and Jessie Massie; b Aber 14.4.43
Aber: CA 1969, man. acct Claben from 1970
m Limerick 21.6.72 Una M. Tobin nurse d of Michael T. Limerick

FORBES Patricia MA 1963
m Ait-Hocine

FORBES Patrick Beaumont MB ChB 1956
s of William F. MA 1922 *qv* and Margaret P. Beaumont MA 1922 *qv*; b Aber 20.1.33
DObstRCOG 1967 FRACGP(Adel) 1972
h o Woodend hosp Aber 1956–57; m o BMH RAMC Singapore 1959–61; h o mat. hosp Aber 1961–62; Terrace clin Naracoorte S Aust 1962–72; dep dir accident dept Box Hill hosp Melbourne 1973–75; g p Blackburn Melbourne from 1975
m Aber 10.4.58 Dorothy E. Mortimer MA 1953 *qv*

FORBES Ruairidh Alasdair LLB 1970

FORBES Shona Macpherson *BSc 1968 MSc 1970

FORBES Sinclair Thomson *BSc 1960 MSc 1963

FORBES William Lithgow BSc(agr) 1961

FORDYCE Andrew Patrick LLB 1967
s of James P. F. lab/gen handyman and Minnie A. Thomson shop asst; b Unst 31.1.47
law app Aber 1967–69; Dumbarton: leg. asst 1969–71; ptnr firm of solic from 1971

FORDYCE Dennis Alexander *BSc 1966
s of James A. F. foreman ganger with bldg contr and Patricia Chittenden; b Ashford Kent 7.5.44
MSc(CNAA)(Teesside poly) 1977
res phys Head, Wrightson & Co Thornaby 1966–69; elect. eng ICI petrochem div Billingham 1969–77; dev man. Electronic Serv (Manc) Middlesbrough from 1977
m Aber 24.6.67 Isobel Fife d of George F. MA 1930 *qv*

FORDYCE George *BSc(eng) 1969
s of James F. farm worker and Violet Simpson; b Turriff 26.3.47
dynamicist Westland helicopters Yeovil 1969–70, des eng C. A. Parsons & Co N'cle-u-Tyne 1970–72; res eng CEGB Harrogate from 1972

FORDYCE James *BSc(agr) 1969 MSc 1970
s of James F. farm worker and Violet Simpson; b Turriff 18.4.46
anim nutrit Dorset from 1974
m Turriff 28.11.70 Annie H. Pirie

FORDYCE Jane Elizabeth MB ChB 1969
d of Gordon E. F. MB ChB 1932 *qv*; b Nunthorpe 5.2.45
DObstRCOG 1971 MRCOG 1974
h o ARI, Woodend hosp Aber 1969–70; h o and sen h o Elizabeth Garrett Anderson univ coll hosp Lond 1970–71; Glasg: sen h o Sick Ch hosp 1971–72, Vict Inf Samaritan hosp 1972–73, regist Queen Mother's hosp, Western I 1973–74; consult. genito-urinary med Glasg from 1974
m Middlesbrough 19.5.73 David T. Roberts MB ChB (Glas) dermat s of Trevor R. Llanelli

FORDYCE John MA 1969 Dip Ed 1970
s of James F. farm worker and Violet Simpson; b Rathen 2.10.48
teacher Fr Woodmill h s Dunfermline from 1970

FORDYCE William Cairns *BSc 1961 *MEd 1967
s of Lawrence S. F. indust chem and Euphemia D. Cairns; b Peterculter 27.8.39
res stud. Aberd 1961–63; teacher Aber: Northfield s, AGS 1964–66, prin teacher Albyn s for girls 1966–68; asst dir of educ: Dumfriessh 1968–69, Aberdeensh 1969–72, dep dir 1972–75; dep dir of educ (sec) Grampian reg Aber from 1975; member advis council on misuse of drugs from 1975
m Aber 13.7.61 Aileen M. Allan teacher d of Robert F. A. Aber

FORMAN Andrew LLB 1966
s of William F. trawl skipper and Helen S. Bruce; b Peterhead 16.1.42
law app Edmonds & Ledingham advoc Aber 1966–68; asst Donaldson & Henderson solic Nairn 1968–70, ptnr from 1970
m Aber 13.9.68 Agnes M. Lindsay clerkess/typist d of James L. Aber

FORMAN Jennifer Constance *MA 1968
m Kershaw

FORMAN Robert BSc(eng) 1964
s of Robert F. driving instr and Margaret Duncan; b Peterhead 29.3.40
Aber: civ eng city eng's off. 1964–67, contr man. Lewis Middleton 1967–72, dir Hunter Construction (Abdn) from 1972
m Aber 2.8.63 Norma Robertson teacher d of George R. Cruden Bay

FORNA Mohamed Sorie MB ChB 1962
d Freetown Sierra Leone 19.7.75 *AUR* XLVI 326

FORREST Alan Iain *MA 1967
s of John F. MA(Edin) schoolmaster and Anne L. T. Miller; b Aber 19.12.45
DPhil(Oxon) 1971
res stud. hist Balliol coll Oxon 1967–70; lect hist Stir 1970–73; lect Fr hist Manc from 1974

FORREST Irene Joan *MA 1969
m Oldman

FORREST James Tyson BSc(for) 1958

FORREST Jean PhD 1962
d of William F. eng and May E. M. Bennett; b Derby 29.8.26
BSc(Lond) 1951 MSc(Lond) 1957
tut. asst Queen's univ Belf 1963–66; tut./counsellor OU N Wales 1970–74; teacher John Bright's s Llandudno from 1974
m Aber 17.10.59 David W. M. Lindsay PhD 1962 *qv*

FORREST Robert Fowlie *BSc 1965
s of Alexander C. F. butcher/bacon curer and Chrissiebell Fowlie tel; b Dyce 8.11.43
teacher: Onthank j s s Kilmarnock 1966–68, geog Cumnock acad 1968–70, prin geog Auchinleck acad from 1970
m Inv 1968 Sheena M. Macdonald teacher d of Donald J. M. Inv

FORREST Rosalind Elizabeth *MA 1968

FORRESTER Alexander Robert PhD 1963 DSc 1977
s of Robert J. F. eng and Mary Gavin; b Fife 14.11.35
BSc(H-W) 1959 MRIC 1963
Aberd: asst lect chem 1963–65, lect 1965–77, sen lect from 1977

m Stirling 4.4.61 Myrna R. Doull d of James D. BSc(Glas) Stirling

FORRESTER William MSc 1967

FORSYTH Audrey Thoirs MA 1968
m Gibb

FORSYTH David James Cameron *MA 1962
s of Joseph S. M. F. bank man. and Margaret J. Smith; b Elgin 4.6.40
Thomas Jefferson fell. univ of Virginia USA 1962–63; lect: econ Strath 1963–64, pol econ Aberd 1964–65, econ Strath 1965–71; visiting sen acad univ of Ghana Legon (Accra) 1971–72; sen lect Livingstone Inst Strath from 1973
m Stockport 7.9.69 Gillian A. Dunmore teacher d of H. Eric D. Poynton

FORSYTH David Rae *BSc 1968
s of William A. F. sales rep and Gladys M. Rae secy; b Ellon 12.12.45
pilot plant man. St Helen's Lancs 1968–74; works man. Bolton from 1974
m Lancs 1968 Jane E. Anderson training advis d of Arthur A. Marple

FORSYTH Hope Glen Milne MB ChB 1967
d of James P. F. MA(Glas) HMCIS and Joan W. McCulley; b Edin 10.2.44
DCH(Lond) 1969
h o: Aber hosps 1967–68, St Mary's hosp Lond 1969–70; m o Save the Children Fund Nigeria 1970–71; regist: paediat Reading 1971–73, Nuffield centre Lond 1974; m o commun health serv Edin from 1974
m Aber 24.6.74 John A. Sills MA(Cantab) med pract s of Oliver A. S. MRCS MRCP(Lond) Cambridge

FORSYTH Janet Marian Gibb *MA 1969
d of James P. F. MA(Glas) HMCIS and Joan W. McCulley; b Edin 4.6.47
res asst sociol Aberd 1970–72
m Aber 28.12.70 David K. Yule MA 1969 *qv*

FORSYTH Kathleen Margaret MA 1969
d of Charles F. lorry driver and Margaret C. M. Cumming; b Fyvie 24.3.48
teacher p dept Turriff acad from 1973
m Oldmeldrum 6.12.69 Albert M. Reid distill. worker/maltman s of Albert R. Oldmeldrum

FORSYTH Keith Wilson BSc(agr) 1959
b Broughty Ferry 1.6.36
m Dumfries 20.12.69 Irene Hannay

FORSYTH Margaret Elizabeth MA 1965
m Booth

FORTUNE James Duncan MSc 1967
s of James A. F. livestock grader and Jessie G. F. Duncan; b Glasg 25.12.43
BSc(Glas) 1966 ARIC 1968 PhD(Glas) 1969
ICI polymer rheology(Glas) 1969–71; teacher chem Jordanhill s Glasg 1971–72, prin chem 1972–75; chem Strath reg council publ analyst's lab from 1975
m Glasg 15.6.74 Helen M. McLaverty BSc(Glas) teacher d of William McL. Glasg

FOSTER Charles Vincent *MA 1968

FOSTER David Deas MA 1970

FOSTER Jonathan Charles Brian *MA 1959
s of John F. MA(Edin) schoolmaster, clergyman and Barbara Ludwig LRAM teacher mus; b Aber 2.5.38
BPhil(Oxon) 1964
Liv: asst lect Latin 1962–65, lect from 1965
external examiner Humanity Aberd 1973–76
m Aber 17.8.68 Joan A. Reid ARMCM teacher mus d of Graham R. Aber

FOSTER Joseph Redman MA 1959

FOSTER Thomas *BSc(eng) 1969

FOSTER William Warwick PhD 1957
BSc(Lond)

FOTHERINGHAM Laurence James *MA 1958
s of James F. traffic supt and Annie King; b Stonehaven 25.7.36
ICI: marketing exec fibres div Harrogate 1958–67, marketing exec Zürich from 1967

FOUBISTER Alan John *BSc 1966

FOUBISTER Glenn MC ChB 1959
s of Thomas F. photographer and Elsie E. Glennie civ serv; b Peterhead 20.1.35
MRCPE 1967
h o Aber 1959–60; nat serv rmo Catterick garrison 1960–62; jun m o Lincoln, Oxford, Lond, Cambridge 1962–70; consult. geriat Reading from 1970
m Oviedo Spain 18.8.69 Adela A. Garcia stud. d of Antonio G. Rodriguez Oviedo

FOWDAR Youssouf MA 1966

FOWLE Heather Beatrice Antoinette White MA 1968

FOWLER Alexander Campbell *MA 1970

FOWLER Alexander Phillips MB ChB 1969
s of Alexander P. F. and Helen M. Henderson; b Aber 25.9.44
h o ARI 1969–70; temp lect path. Aberd 1970–72; g p Aber 1972, Benbecula 1972–76, Fraserburgh from 1976
m New Pitsligo 20.7.70 Helen M. Watson MB ChB 1970 *qv*

FOWLER Frank Macpherson *MA 1957
s of William A. F. bank man. and Jen C. Macpherson; b Inv 16.6.35
DPhil(Oxon) 1962
lect Ger: Aberd 1960–65, univ of Kent Canterbury 1965–66, King's Coll Lond 1967–70; Queen Mary coll Lond: reader Ger 1970–77, prof/head Ger dept from 1977

FOWLER Muriel Margaret BEd 1969
d of David F. butchery man., off. clerk and Catherine M. T. Ross teacher; b Aber 26.3.47
teacher maths: Northfield acad Aber 1969–71, part time Kincorth acad 1976
m Aber 19.7.69 Raymond Inkster MA 1967 *qv*

FOWLER Ruth Kathleen MA 1967 Dip Ed 1968
d of Neil H. C. F. foreman and Ruth A. Taylor; b Torphins 3.5.46
teacher hist/Engl/mod stud. Queen Anne h s Dunfermline 1968–72
m Torphins 1.8.70 Alan J. Campion prof and tech off. M o D s of John E. C. Rosyth

FOWLES Nathan Briggs *MA 1966
s of Lloyd W. F. BA(Bowdion) teacher and Jane Briggs

BA(Wellesley); b Hartford Conn USA 13.6.43
reporter/feature writer *Evening Express* Aber 1967–69; reporter *Evening Gazette* Middlesbrough 1969–74; Aber: reporter *Scottish Daily News* from 1974; freelance labour/indust reporter from 1975

FOWLIE Alan Smollett MA 1963 LLB 1966
s of Harold F. driving instr and Helen Smollett nurse; b Aber 8.3.42
syst analyst Sheepbridge Eng, Chesterfield 1967–68; Sheff: admin asst, sen admin asst 1968–72; asst regist Hull univ from 1972
m Coventry 17.4.71 Elizabeth A. Freeman BA(Sheff) soc worker/univ admin d of Kenneth H. F. MB ChB(Birm) Coventry

FOWLIE Douglas Gibb MB ChB 1970
s of Herbert F. MB ChB 1930 *qv*(III); b Aber 16.1.46
MRCPsych 1976
h o ARI, City hosp Aber 1970–71; unit m o RAF Marham, Benson 1971–72; trainee psychiat/spec in neuro-psychiat Wroughton 1972–76, sen spec neuro-psychiat Wegberg W Ger from 1976
m Aber 5.8.71 Marjory A. R. Donaldson MB ChB 1970 *qv*

FOWLIE Jean MA 1961 Dip Ed 1962
m Fisher

FOWLIE John Leslie BSc(agr) 1968

FOWLIE Peter BSc(agr) 1970
s of John F. farm. and Elizabeth M. Leslie; b New Deer 24.3.49
farm. New Deer from 1970
m Aber 31.8.72 Janet M. Mitchell teacher d of T. C. M. Fordoun

FOWLIE Sylvia Mary BEd 1969
d of Henry F. lorry driver and Mary B. Gow dom help; b Aber 17.5.48
teacher Aber 1969–72 and from 1975
m Aber 11.7.69 Charles F. Western DA draughtsman/off. man. s of Charles A. W. Aber

FOX Evelyn Yeats *MA 1969
d of William F. F. bank man. and Eleanor MacLean; b Buckie 7.4.47
ALA 1973
asst lib coll of educ Sheff 1970–71; Sheff univ: res worker s of lib 1971–73, sen lib asst from 1973
m Aber 17.7.69 Peter D. A. Boyd BSc 1970 *qv*

FOX Richard Henry *BSc(eng) 1970
s of Walter H. F. dep gen sales man. and Ethel A. Ambrose; b Birm 20.7.48
MSc(Birm)
asst eng/hydrologist Robert H. Cuthbertson & Ptnrs Edin from 1972

FRAME Ian Andrew *MA 1966
s of John W. F. policeman, JP and Barbara M. Grant; b Glasg 2.2.37
teacher geog Portobello 1967–70; prin geog: Tranent 1970–76, Lossiemouth from 1976
m Dunbar 18.10.75 Ann M. Ballantine DA art teacher d of Stanley B. B. LRCPSE Dunbar

FRANCIS Heather Rosamund Dalton MSc 1969
BSc(Rhodes)

FRANKLIN Andrew *BSc 1966
s of Andrew F. carpenter and Elspeth I. Pirie; b Aber 19.5.44
marine biol: scient off., sen scient off. MAFF fisheries lab Burnham-on-Crouch from 1967
m Maldon 8.4.72 Frances L. Hyam marine biol d of Laurence F. H. Burnham-on-Crouch

FRANKS David Robert MB ChB 1970 Dip Psychother 1977
s of Martin L. F. BSc(Brist) consult. civ eng and Gwendolen M. B. Bailey BA(Cantab); b N'cle-u-Tyne 3.4.46
h o ARI 1970–71; sen h o, regist, sen regist Royal Cornhill hosps Aber 1971–77; visiting prof psychiat Creighton univ Omaha Nebraska USA from 1977
m Aber 9.8.69 Mary J. G. Bailey BSc 1969 *qv*

FRASER Alan William *BSc 1969 PhD 1973
s of Alexander F. master butcher and Ann Ettles MA 1940 *qv*; b Forres 12.3.47
teacher chem: Buckhaven h s 1972–73, Kirkcaldy h s from 1973
m Forres 2.4.70 Edith H. Johnston MA 1969 *qv*

FRASER Alasdair James BSc(agr) 1956
s of John F. farm. and Annabella M. Howar; b Inv 14.7.32
lect agr Melton Mowbray 1956–58; asst insp DAFS: Inv 1959–66, Perth 1966–72; insp DAFS Stirling from 1972
m Groby 5.9.59 Averill Tweddle farm secy d of Joseph T. Groby

FRASER Alastair Ian BSc(for) 1957

FRASER Alexander *MA 1968 Dip Ed 1969
d 15.3.71 *AUR* XLIV 216

FRASER Alexander Leslie MA 1963
s of Alexander F. master draper and Maggie Chalmers MA 1926 *qv*; b Ellon 6.10.41
pers off. Colvilles Bellshill 1963–65; youth employ. off. Aber educ dept 1965–66; group trg off. Peterhead and dist group trg assoc Peterhead 1966–68; trg consult. indust trg serv Scot. 1968–71; trg man. Hiram Walker & Sons Dumbarton 1971–74; manpower and trg off. Scot. Eng Employers' Assoc from 1974
m Crail 26.9.64 Kathleen B. Riach teacher d of Ronald A. C. R. Crail

FRASER Alison *MA 1965
d of Alexander S. F. MA 1930 *qv*; b Aber 27.7.42
teacher: Lond 1966–67, Aber 1967–73
m Aber 25.11.73 John C. E. Allan driving instr s of J. A. O. A. Aber

FRASER Angela MA 1967
d of Orville L. P. F. comp secy and Williamina M. Menzies; b Aber 6.2.46
teacher: Fr St Ive s St Ives 1968–71; i/c Fr St Colette's s Cambridge 1971–75
m Aber 23.7.70 Roger W. Barlow MA(Cantab) lect s of Vernon H. B. Rottingdean

FRASER Angus Charles MA 1967

FRASER Archibald Kerr *BSc 1968 PhD 1971
s of Alexander M. F. dist off. for. comm and Agnes Kerr; b Stromeferry 27.8.46
teacher: sc Wishaw 1971–72, asst prin biol Peterhead 1972–74, prin biol Inv from 1974
m Inv 10.7.71 Kathleen M. Stewart MA 1970 *qv*

FRASER Arthur George *BSc 1968
s of Oliver G. L. F. bank cashier and Violet L. Persse hosp sister; b Golspie 26.1.47
geophys computer Tripoli 1968–70; computer progr: Lond 1970–75, IBM Portsmouth 1975, Teheran 1975–77, IBM Portsmouth 1977, Singapore 1977–78, Amsterdam from 1978

FRASER Arthur Gilmour *BSc 1959
s of William G. F. trav, bookbinder and Mary B. Wyllie; b Aber 1.8.37
PhD(Birm) 1964 FGS(Lond) 1965 Polar medal 1967
geol Brit antarctic surv: Antarctic penin Antarctica 1960–62, Birm 1962–64; res fell. geol Brit antarctic surv Birm 1964–67; lect geol Hull from 1967
m Dyke 20.10.62 Marion E. Snedden MA 1957 *qv*

FRASER Audrey MA 1967
d of Francis R. F. journalist/shopkeeper and Christina M. Fraser RAF (traffic control), hotelier; b Beauly 21.6.38
teacher: Lochaber h s Fort William 1968–70, Tomintoul 1970–76, Forres acad 1977
m Inv 6.12.58 Eric Farquhar MA 1959 *qv*; marr diss 1977

FRASER Callum BSc 1968
s of William A. F. bus driver and Mary M. Thain; b Aber 14.7.47
syst progr: E Midlands gas board Leic 1969–73, Brit gas corp Hinckley from 1973
m Banchory 3.6.72 Christina S. Sinclair MA 1969 *qv*

FRASER Callum George *BSc 1966 PhD 1969
s of Douglas C. F. eng and Bessie M. Johnstone secy; b Dun 3.1.45
res fell. NRC Ottawa 1969–70; lect chem path. Aberd from 1970
m Cults Aber 8.9.72 Stella Sim lib d of John S. Cults

FRASER Carole MA 1970
m Henderson

FRASER Christian Davidson MA 1957
d of Donald F. gamekeeper and Annie Davidson; b Fordoun 3.11.36
Dip Soc St(Edin) 1958
child care off. Aber 1959–62
m Aber 3.11.62 Malcolm A. B. Christie MA 1958 *qv*

FRASER Christine Mary *MA 1968
d of Cuthbert W. F. policeman, soldier and Catherine A. Crabb MA 1938 *qv*; b Fraserburgh 10.4.47
teacher Chapelpark s Forfar from 1973
m Forfar 8.6.68 Iain L. N. Dodds arch. draughtsman s of John D.; marr diss 1977

FRASER Colin Hugh Thomson *MA 1958
s of Thomas F. gas worker/trade union off. and Margaret R. Barron; b Aber 17.7.37
PhD(Brist) 1975
res stud. inst of psychiat Lond 1958–60; res assoc and lect psych MIT Cambridge Mass 1960–63; res assoc lab of soc relations Harvard 1962–63; lect: psych Exe 1963–64, soc psych Birm 1965–68, Brist 1968–74, Cantab from 1975, fell. Churchill coll from 1976
m Birm 14.7.65 Carole M. Bell occup therap

FRASER Cristabel MB ChB 1963
d of Farquhar F. sales rep and Isabel R. Mackenzie saleswoman; b Inv 13.9.38
DCH(Glas) 1969
h o RACH, City hosp Aber 1964–65; sen h o: clin path. paediat ch hosp Birm 1965–67, Worcester 1967–68, regist paediat Inv 1968–71; med asst mental subnormality Inv 1971–72 and from 1975
m Inv 11.7.70 William A. Macdonald bldg man. s of Charles D. M. Inv

FRASER Derek James *MA 1969

FRASER Doreen Catherine MA 1965
d of Angus F. master draper and Jean Y. S. Barclay; b Aber 1.10.44
teacher Aber 1966–70
m Aber 7.8.68 John Hutcheson CA s of Herbert C. H. MA 1929 *qv*

FRASER Douglas Morrison *BSc 1961 Dip Ed 1962
s of George F. BR foreman and Jane Balneaves; b Aber 17.1.39
teacher geog Turriff 1962–68, prin geog Wick 1968–74, Peterhead from 1974
m Aber 21.7.62 Rhoda A. E. Connon MA 1961 *qv*

FRASER Elspeth Gray Mackenzie MA 1963
d of Arthur F. farm worker, crofter and Elizabeth G. Gray farm worker; b Inv 2.9.41
teacher Engl/geog Banchory acad 1964–70, Tarradale p s 1971
m Nairn 30.7.70 John G. C. Weir BSc(agr) 1966 *qv*
husb *d* 22.3.74

FRASER Evelyn Mairi MA 1966
d of William A. F. bank off. and Emma A. Matheson stewardess MN; b Balmacara 28.5.44
teacher p s Aber 1967–74
m Aber William D. Topp offshore oper s of Alexander T. Aber

FRASER Finlay Christopher MA 1963

FRASER Frederick John Thomas BSc(eng) 1956

FRASER George Balneaves *BSc 1967 MSc 1971
s of George F. BR workshop superv and Jane Balneaves; b Inverurie 3.2.45
electronics eng: computers Borehamwood 1967–68, Dun 1968–69, commun Portsmouth 1970–73, servomechanisms Winchester from 1973
m Carnoustie 26.6.68 Catherine M. Clerk civ serv exec off. d of Archibald C. LDS(Glas) Carnoustie

FRASER George Leslie *BSc 1956
s of George F. MA 1917 *qv*; b Aber 21.6.31
prospecting geol Greenland, Fr Guinea 1956–58; educ rep Scot., Ireland 1958–61; prin teacher geog: Ross h s Tranent 1962–67, English s Nicosia Cyprus 1967–71, Penicuik 1971–72; comp dir Broxburn from 1972
m Aber 11.3.59 Frances C. Gordon MA 1957 *qv*

FRASER George Lewis BSc(eng) 1961
s of George M. F. market gardener and Jean S. Mowat; b Aber 10.9.40
grad app Mullard Radio Valve Co Mitcham 1961–63: Foxboro-Yoxall Redhill: lect customer trg centre 1963–65, digital support eng Foxboro USA 1965–67, digital syst eng Redhill 1967–69, application spec (consult.) 1969–72, syst spec 1972–76, man. market dev and sales support from 1976
m Aber 11.7.61 Rosemary P. Lowe secy

FRASER Gordon Alister *BSc 1957

FRASER Gordon Davidson MB ChB 1956
s of Robert J. F. farm. and Anne M. Fyfe; b Strichen

6.11.32
MRCGP 1973
h o ARI 1956–57; surg lt RN 1957–60; jun h m o ARI 1960–61; g p Aber from 1961
m Aber 10.8.59 Doreen A. Henderson physioth d of Alexander H. Aber

FRASER Graeme William *MA 1966 Dip Ed 1967

FRASER Graham Campbell MB ChB 1956
s of Eion R. F. bank man. and Dorothy S. Williams; b Inv 20.6.32
Keith gold medal surg
FRCSE 1962 FRCS(Lond) 1962 LMCC 1967 FRCS(C) 1972 FACS 1973 Member Brit Pacif & Canadian Assoc of Paediat Surgeons, American paediat surg assoc
h o ARI 1956–57: surg lt RN 1957–60, surg regist ARI 1960–63 resid asst surg HSC Lond 1963–67; consult. paediat surg Vancouver from 1967
m Cupar 15.8.58 Rae S. McCallum museum lect d of Thomas McC. Cupar

FRASER Helen Mary Alexander MA 1970
d of Robert S. F. MA 1925 *qv* and Kathleen M. B. Smith teacher; b Aber 8.6.49
Dip St Godric's secy coll Lond 1971
p a Lond: Ibbs & Tillett concert ag 1971–74, Phonogram 1974–75; mus asst Scot. Arts Council Edin from 1975

FRASER Hugh Ross MA 1966
s of Ian S. F. BSc(eng)(Glas) eng and Elizabeth W. Miller teacher; b Bath 2.9.43
journalist, staff reporter West Kirby 1967–68, Blackburn 1968, *Glasgow Herald* Edin 1968–69; San Francisco: asst, man. edit. *Western Construction* 1969–72, edit. *California Industry* 1972–73; *World Wood Magazine:* European edit. Brussels 1973–74, edit. Brussels 1974–77, Harrow from 1977
m Edin 26.7.67 Victoria A. Greenamyer

FRASER Ian Charles MA 1957
s of John O. F. motor mech/driver bldg comp and Edith I. Richardson; b Nairn 20.4.36
educ measurement univ of Melbourne 1963; Melbourne s of printing and graphic arts 1965–67
teacher Bryans s Midlothian 1958–61; Aust: teacher Taroona h s and Glenorchy state s Hobart Tasmania 1961–62; Aust council for educ res Melbourne: res off. test dev div 1962–64, off. i/c publ div 1964–73; exec asst to man. dir Thomas Nelson & Sons (spec proj) Sunbury Mddx from 1973
m Newton-Grange 1.4.61 Elizabeth M. Sinclair secy d of John B. S. Easthouses

FRASER Ian McGregor *MA 1969

FRASER Ian Simon MA 1957
s of John F. foreman joiner and Joan B. Copeland; b Aber 22.2.34
MTAI
Aber: clerk (bldg) 1957–59, trav salesman 1959–66; dept man. trav Glasg 1966–72, branch man. Carlisle 1972–77, Aber from 1977
m Aber 7.3.59 Ethel M. Reid d of Arthur R. Aber

FRASER, Irene MA 1968
m Rose

FRASER James Duncan Mackenzie LLB 1963

FRASER James Kenny *BSc(eng) 1967

FRASER Jean Elspet Elrick *MA 1969
m Smith

FRASER John MA 1956 LLB 1958

FRASER John *MA 1959
s of John F. retail man. and Jessamine E. Mathieson; b Inv 8.8.36
teacher Harris acad Dun 1960–66; prin teacher Buckie 1966–72; asst head Peterhead 1972–73, dep rector 1973–75; rector Mackie acad Stonehaven from 1975
m Monifieth 29.7.63 Judith H. Procter bank clerk d of Harold L. P. Dun

FRASER John MA 1970
s of John F. eng and Mary Bell; b Inv 30.7.47
Dip Soc Sc(S'ton) 1971 MSc(S'ton) 1972
lect govt: Fareham tech coll 1971–75, Isleworth poly 1975–76, sen lect Hounslow borough coll from 1976
m Aber 4.9.69 Pamela Brown teacher

FRASER John George Nevill MA 1958 ᶜLLB 1961
s of James F. F. MA 1914 *qv*; b Aber 31.1.38
admin asst: St And 1962–64, Edin 1964–67; Aberd: asst secy (acad) 1967–74, sen asst secy 1974–76, clerk to univ court from 1976
m Aber 9.1.65 Helen F. Simpson teacher d of Vincent J. A. S. Peterculter

FRASER John Watson MA 1968 Dip Ed 1969
s of John F. painter and Elsie Watson; b Forres 19.7.24
teacher: Allan Glen's s Glasg 1969–72; asst prin maths: Banff acad 1972–73, Auchenharvie acad Stevenston from 1973
m Forres 19.5.51 Margaret E. Morrison

FRASER John William PhD 1969
s of John F. sen dep c clerk Ross and Cromarty and Christina I. Jack; b Dingwall 9.10.18
BEM MA(Edin) 1947 BD(Edin) 1950 JP 1972
C of S min: Banchory Ternan 1950–59, Farnell and Kinnell 1959–67, Farnell only from 1967
m Edin 12.7.50 Mary E. Purves bank clerk d of Robert W. P. Edin

FRASER Julia Macphedran MA 1970
d of Alexander R. F. foreman steel erector and Margaret M. Breingan hotel man.; b Grantown-on-Spey 6.2.48
teacher Clydebank h s 1971–72; cler post hydro elect. Aber 1972–73; teacher Millburn s s Inv 1973–77
m Nethybridge 26.8.72 James Macadie quantity surv s of William B. M. Newtonmore

FRASER Julie *MA 1963
m Morris

FRASER Kathryn Joan *MA 1969
d of James W. F. army off. and Agnes Ford group VS organis; b Edin 21.4.46
MSc(Strath) 1973 Dip Adult Educ(Glas) 1977 ABPsS 1976
VSO Akure Nigeria 1970; educ psych, sen educ psych Fern Tower Glasg 1974–78; res fell. Stir from 1978

FRASER Leila Anne BSc 1970
d of William G. F. farm man. and Jean G. Milne hosp records off., hosp interviewer; b Aber 17.7.49
teacher biol Aber from 1971
m Aber 18.9.70 Andrew G. Littlejohn banker s of William L. Inverurie

FRASER Leslie William *MA 1969

FRASER Lorna Kinkaid MB ChB 1962
d of Andrew K. F. butcher and Elizabeth M. Munro; b Aber 20.8.39
h o Aber: City hosp, Woodend hosp, Ross clinic 1962–64, g p Aber 1964–68; part-time asst g p Colchester from 1968; m o FPA Wittam, Tiptree from 1971; clin asst venereology Colchester from 1973
m Aber 18.6.68 Gilbert Gray secy NE Essex commun health council s of Gilbert G. Ardersier

FRASER Margaret MA 1966 Dip Ed 1967
d of Kenneth W. F. HM insp of taxes and Isabella Low; b Coventry 3.4.45
teacher Ferryhill p s Aber 1967–71
m Aber 29.7.67 Alexander G. Garrow BSc 1966 *qv*

FRASER Margaret Baird *MA 1961
d of Alexander S. F. MA 1930 *qv*; b Aber 14.8.39
teacher geog Perth acad 1962–69, spec asst 1969; conserv off. Countryside Comm for Scot. Perth from 1969

FRASER Margaret Ethel *BSc 1967 Dip Ed 1968
d of James D. F. ophth optician and Maureen A. Anderson dom sc teacher; b Aber 4.2.45
teacher sc Parkstone s Poole 1967–70
m Aber 27.7.68 Peter M. MacIntosh BSc 1966 *qv*

FRASER Margaret McBoyle MA 1960
m Glass

FRASER Moira MA 1961
d of John A. F. shoemaker, postman, filling stat owner and Helen J. Reid shop asst; b Ellon 8.10.40
teacher: Cowie Stirlingsh 1962–65, Peterhead 1965–66, East Plean 1966–67
m Inverurie 23.9.67 Frederick B. Brown, Dip Agr (WOSCA) distrib superv (lamps & elect. appliances) s of Frederick B. B. Giffnock

FRASER Norman MA 1969 Dip Ed 1970

FRASER Norman Alexander LLB 1970

FRASER Pamela Margaret MA 1966
d of Henry F. MA 1927 *qv*; b Aber 8.2.45
Aber: teacher Hazlehead p s 1967–71, class singing in p s from 1971

FRASER Peter John *BSc 1970 PhD 1973
s of William E. F. MA 1935 *qv* and Margaret R. G. Ferguson MA 1938 *qv*; b Aber 7.11.48
fell. res schol biol sc ANU Canberra 1973–75; lect zool Aberd from 1975
m Largo 31.10.72 Patricia C. G. Rodger BSc(Dund) teacher d of Hamish G. R. DA(Edin) Lundin Links

FRASER Peter Kerr *MA 1969
s of Alexander S. F. MA 1930 *qv*; b Aber 20.5.47
syst analyst/progr Grampian Computer Facilities Aber 1970–73, syst and progr man. from 1974

FRASER Robert Alan *MA 1968

FRASER Robert Dunbar *MA 1967
s of Alexander W. F. FRIAS auctioneer and Christina Dunbar bus. woman; b Dingwall 30.11.45
teacher geog Dumfries 1968–71; prin geog: Thornhill 1971–73, Dumfries from 1974
m Aber 15.7.71 Annice P. Blackmore MA 1971 teacher d of Donald I. B. Tibbermore

FRASER Robin Charles MB ChB 1963 MD 1974
s of Albert G. F. motor/agr ag and Jean Beaton; b Aber 15.2.40
MRCGP 1969 FRCGP 1974
h o ARI, RACH 1963–65; trainee g p Aber 1965; m o stud. health serv Aberd 1965–66; g p Leicester from 1966; part time lect g p, dept of commun health Leic from 1975
m Aber 20.7.64 Mary E. S. McAfee DA d of Andrew M. McA. BSc(Belf) Inv

FRASER Ronald MB ChB 1970
s of Ronald F. farm. and Annie McCrae; b Inv 20.1.47
LMCC 1973
h o ARI, Woodend hosp Aber 1970–71; sen h o ARI 1971–72; asst m o Grand Bank Newfoundland 1972; private practice fam med Sault Ste Marie Ont from 1972
m Aber 14.1.71 Janette W. McCrone nurse d of James McC. Tighnabruaich

FRASER Rosemary Angela MA 1970
m McAndrew

FRASER Sheila Maclennan *MA 1966
d of Alexander F. master mariner and Muriel Harker; b Aber 9.5.44
teacher Engl Albyn s for girls Aber 1967–70
m Aber 24.7.68 Robin F. Scott MB ChB 1966 *qv*

FRASER Sheila Margaret *BSc 1967
m Russell

FRASER Sheila Mary *MA 1970
d of William R. D. F. LDS(St And) dent. surg and Mary Macdonald; b Aber 12.7.47
secy/p a to group trg off. Davidson Radcliffe group (paper indust) Bucksburn 1971–72; secy to head of Scott Sutherland School of Arch. Aber 1972–73; secy/p a to man. dir Borrell Sayward Burles Lond 1973–74; secy to dir and chief exec Bayer UK Richmond from 1974
m Aber 14.6.72 Colin G. E. Scotland LLB 1969 *qv*; separated 1978

FRASER Stephanie Ann MA 1970
d of Campbell C. F. warehouseman and Florence M. Sayers factory man.; b Northampton 5.2.50
Aber: cler asst city police 1970–72, pers asst Impulse Publ 1973, teacher Sunnybank p s from 1974

FRASER Sylvia Rebecca BEd 1970
d of Duncan F. livestock insp dept agr and Catherine Macdonald; b Drumnadrochit 7.12.48
teacher: Inv 1970–71, Drumnadrochit 1971–74
m Drumnadrochit 2.10.71 Kenneth J. Fraser mech s of Donald F. Glenurquhart

FRASER Wendy Paul MA 1970
d of Orville L. P. F. comp dir and Wilhelmina Menzies; b Aber 3.3.49
teacher King James's s Knaresborough from 1971
m Aber 30.5.75 Thomas R. Evans MA 1970 *qv*

FRASER William Alistair *BSc 1968
s of Roderick A. F. civ serv and Winifred G. F. Bristow teacher; b Dufftown 30.10.46
MPhil(Yale) 1972 PhD(Yale) 1972
res asst Imp Coll Lond 1972–73; radio pharm quality control Radiochem Centre Amersham from 1973
m New Haven Connecticut 27.12.69 Lynn C. Repsis BA(Colorado) reprod biol d of Anthony C. R. BA (Illinois) Denver

FRASER William Edward MA 1957
s of William G. F. bookbinder and Mary B. Wyllie;

b Aber 16.5.35
BD(Lond) 1959
Bapt ch min: St Andrews 1960–64, Crown Terrace ch Aber 1964–76, Victoria Place, Paisley from 1976
m Aber 1.8.59 Lillian J. House midwife d of Charles T. H. Aber

FRASER William Hamish *MA 1963
s of Hugh R. R. F. loom turner and Charlotte Milne shopkeeper; b Keith 30.6.41
DPhil(Sus) 1967
res stud. Sus 1963–66; lect Strath from 1966
m Aber 4.9.65 Helen Tuach MA 1965 *qv*

FRASER William Ross BSc 1966 MB ChB 1972
s of William A. F. lorry driver and Beatrice J. Ross nurse; b Aber 27.7.44
h o ARI 1972–73; sen h o g p vocational trg unit 1973–76; g p Aber from 1977
m Aber 17.7.73 Alison F. A. Knox MA 1970 *qv*

FRATER Susan Elizabeth MA 1967
m Sawyer

FRAZER George Bernard MB ChB 1963
s of Theophilus E. F. elect. and Martha M. Peters; b Freetown Sierra Leone 28.12.33
MRCOG 1968 FWACS
Aber mat. hosp: regist 1966–68, temp sen regist 1968–69; sen spec obst/gyn Freetown from 1969
m Lond 1961 Frances A. Bowen-Wright teacher d of Frank B-W. Freetown

FRAZER Kirsty Margaret MA 1969
d of Frederick Y. F. BSc 1928 *qv*; b Manc 4.2.47
trainee surv Aber 1970–71; teacher Fintry 1973–78
m Skene 28.8.71 John A. M. Cuthbert LL B 1968 *qv*

FRAZER William Murdoch BSc 1969
s of Robert F. eng and Agnes J. Murdoch; b Falkirk 28.12.46
RAF: trainee pilot 1969–72, pilot(Hercules) Cyprus 1972–75, careers off. N'cle-u-Tyne 1975–78, pilot (Andover) flight checking from 1978
m Falkirk 15.2.69 Margaret E. Ivory teacher home econ d of George I. Falkirk

FREELAND William John Walker MB ChB 1958

FREEMAN Alan George MSc 1960 PhD 1962
s of George R. F. bldr and Rose J. Bowater; b Birm 9.2.35
BSc(Birm) 1959
fell. Birkbeck coll Lond 1962–64; sen lect Victoria univ Wellington NZ from 1964
m Wythall 4.4.63 Annie Drever SRN d of John D. Papa Westray

FRENCH Catherine McLean MA 1969
m Murray

FRENCH Chris (Christopher Norman) *MA 1966
s of Frederick G. F. bldr and Kathleen R. D. Norman; b Letchworth 8.11.42
PhD(Exe) 1975 ABPsS MBCS
res stud. Exe 1966–70; lect exper psych optics dept UMIST from 1970
m Aber 18.2.65 Ann Watson BSc 1966 *qv*; marr diss 29.4.75

FRENCH Elspeth May MA 1968
d of William G. F. MB ChB 1942 *qv*; b Aber 10.5.47
teacher: Glenbervie s Drumlithie 1969–71, Milltimber p s Aber 1971–74, Croyland inf s Wellingborough 1974–75
m Aber 14.7.71 Peter J. Gordon MB ChB 1971 s of Ian G. BSc 1929 *qv*

FRENCH John Richard Joseph BSc(for) 1963
b Wallasey 7.11.35
MSc(Syd) 1968 PhD(Oregon) 1972
for. off. Millicent S Aust 1963–64; res off. entomol Sydney 1964–69, Corvallis USA 1969–72; res scient entomol CSIRO Melbourne from 1972

FREW Euan Malcolm Shearer MB ChB 1968
s of John F. M. F. MB ChB(Glas) consult. orthop surg and Elizabeth M. Jack; b Aber 11.10.44
FRCSE 1973
h o City hosp Aber, ARI 1968–69; Garden fell. path. Aberd 1969–70; sen h o surg rotation scheme Western Inf Glasg 1970–72, regist from 1973; surg Royal Alexandra Inf Paisley 1972–73
m Glasg 6.1.72 Anne I. Macdiarmid nurs sister d of Malcolm M. Glasg

FRITH Susan Agnes MA 1969
d of William F. acct clerk and Phyllis Rogerson; b Northwich 17.9.47
teacher lang: Kentwood boys' s s Penge 1969–71, South Norwood h s Lond 1971–73; head Ger dept Grange s Stockton-on-Tees from 1973
m Northwich 18.12.71 Ian K. Alexander BSc 1969 *qv*

FRONDIGOUN Edward Miller MA 1962

FROST Yvonne Marie MA 1970
d of William H. F. master baker and Grace M. Govetel, typist; b Montrose 29.11.49
teacher: Engl Forfar acad 1971–74, asst prin Engl 1974–76, Engl Oak Park h s Melbourne 1976–78; supply Engl Wheathampstead h s from 1978
m Montrose 2.7.75 Vincent A. Arpino asst factory man s of Vincent A. St Pauls Cray

FRYDMAN Anna BSc 1967
d of Kaziemierz F. eng and Mattie H. Dowie comp dir; b Nairn 9.12.45
MPhil(Lond) 1971 Dip Voc Guid(Kent coll for careers serv) 1974
Lond: res asst MRC Hammersmith hosp and List inst 1967–72; asst secy royal inst of publ health and hyg 1972–73; careers off. ILEA 1973–74; careers advis PCL from 1974
m Bolton 6.9.69 David M. Ewins acct s of William A. E. Bolton

FULLERTON Clare Elizabeth Oakes *MA 1964 PhD 1978

FULLERTON Hance BSc 1956
s of Robert F. fisherman and Jessie Smith; b Hamnavoe 6.12.34
Wiggins Teape: chem Stoneywood mill Aber 1959–63, chem and asst paper prod. man. Fort William mill 1963–67; prod. man. Caldwell paper mill Co Inverkeithing 1967–69; prod. man. Guardbridge Paper Co. 1969–72, man. dir 1972–76; mill man. Wiggins Teape Stoneywood mill Aber from 1976
m Aber 2.8.58 Jeannie R. Cowie MA 1956 *qv*

FULLERTON Michael John *MA 1968

FULLERTON Robert Keith Ross BSc(eng) 1967
s of Robert G. F. BSc 1924 *qv*; b Aber 12.1.46

CA 1971
sen acct Peat, Marwick, Mitchell & Co Paris/Lond 1971–73; man. Price, Waterhouse & Co Hong Kong 1974–75; group acct Swire Pacific Hong Kong from 1975

FULTON Anne Bradford Gray MA 1969
d of James F. MA(Glas) teacher, headmaster and Mary W. G. White; b Aber 31.3.48
Edin: computer progr 1969–73, sen progr 1973–77
m Aber 28.6.75 Ian G. Kirkpatrick BSc(Edin) syst des (computers) s of John K. Edin

FURNELL James Rupert Gawayne *MA 1968
s of Percy G. F. B Eng(Liv) elect eng and Margaret K. A. Wray journalist; b Lond 20.2.46
Dip Clin Psych(Glas) 1970 ABPsS 1971 PhD(Stir) 1977
clin psych: Dumfries, Glasg 1968–70, RHSC Glasg 1970–72; sen clin psych Stirling from 1972, hon lect Stir from 1978
m Glasg 14.9.74 Lesley A. Ross physioth d of John S. R. Glasg

FURNESS Anthony John *BSc 1969
s of Eric L. F. BSc(Lond) univ teacher and Enid B. Bacon BA(Cantab); b Lond 31.10.46
teacher Lond 1970–72; Stockholm: TEFL univ 1972–73; Engl St Erik's Folkhögskola from 1973
m Stockholm 15.6.73 Annika M. Erikson teacher d of Karl E. Solna

FURNIVAL Colin Mitchell MB ChB 1964
s of Ian M. F. acct and Martha R. Craik; b Edin 7.12.40
PhD(Leeds) 1971 FRCS 1972
h s ARI 1964–65; res asst physiol Leeds 1965–68; regist surg univ hosp of Wales Cardiff 1968–72; lect surg Glas 1972–75; univ of Queensland Brisbane: sen lect surg 1975–79, reader in surg from 1979
m Aber 21.7.64 Isobel G. Souter MB ChB 1964 *qv*

FURRIE Brian Lawrie MA 1963

FYDA Janina Cecilia Zofia MA 1968
d of Charles J. F. eng/prop. garage and precision eng comp and Jane D. King; b Ladybank 15.4.47
Aber coll of educ 1968–69
m Banff 22.3.69 John K. Walker bldg contr s of A. D. W. Banff

FYFE Beryl MA 1968
d of James F. clerk/stock controller and Rachel R. Stephen; b Aber 12.12.46
teacher: geog Glenrothes 1969–73, Engl/geog Sultan Omar Ali Saifuddin coll (sen), Bandar Seri Begawan, Sultanate of Brunei from 1975
m Aber 16.8.69 Colin R. Mowat MA 1967 *qv*

FYFE Eric *BSc(eng) 1970
s of Francis R. F. cashier/acct and Elizabeth R. Largue clerkess; b Aber 17.2.48
electronic circuit des eng space div Hawker Siddeley Dynamics Stevenage from 1970

FYFE Graham *MA 1967
s of John B. F. test pilot/pilot RAF and Katherine G. MacNab; b Frimley 14.6.37
teacher Kircudbright acad, Dalry s s, Castle Douglas h s and assoc p s 1968–70; mus teacher Städtische Musik und Singschule Heidelberg W Ger from 1971

FYFE Hans George Simpson MA 1967
d 18.4.69 *AUR* XLIII 218

FYFE James Johnstone MA 1957

FYFE John *MA 1965
b Forfar 10.4.43
Dip Ed(univ of E Af) 1966
teacher: TEFL King's coll Budo Uganda 1966–71, Engl St Joseph's coll Dumfries 1971–73, prin Engl Nairn acad from 1973
m Sale 30.8.65 Susan M. Beckett

FYFE Lindsay Audrey MA 1967
d of C. W. Kirkwood F. ophth optician and Audrey H. Davidson tel oper; b Aber 14.5.46
teacher Airyhall p s Aber 1968–70
m Aber 16.6.67 Alexander I. Mitchell BSc 1972 res biochem s of Alexander M. Kinellar

FYFE Ronald MA 1960 MEd 1971
s of Francis R. F. acct/cashier and Elizabeth R. Largue clerkess; b Aber 30.4.39
teacher: Northfield s s Aber 1960–62, Banchory acad 1963–66, Beechwood spec s Aber 1967–71; lect educ psych Aber coll of educ 1971–76, sen lect from 1976
m Aber 20.3.63 Doris Kelman off. man. d of William K. Aber

FYFFE Allen Frederick *BSc 1968
s of Allen F. F. stereotyper and Charlotte Whyte; b Dun 10.11.46
manual work 1968–69; teacher trg 1969–70; climbing instr Glencoe 1970–71; outdoor pursuits instr Glenmore Lodge Aviemore from 1971

FYSON Mary-Jean MA 1966
d of Roger F. F. garage prop. and Winifred M. Heath bookkeeper; b Dartford 15.8.42
secy Aber 1966–67; interviewer, man., pers off. employment ag Lond 1968–70; secy Guildford 1971; civ serv/cler off. Eltham 1971–74; crown serv/exec off. Lond 1974–78; pers off. UBAF Bank Lond from 1978
m Eltham 24.9.66 Andrew M. Stewart MA 1965 *qv*; marr diss 1.5.72

GACHARU Alex Micah MSc 1970
BSc(agr)(E Af)

GACOKA Philip MSc 1964
s of Ayub Githaiga farm. and Yunis Wambui farm.; b Kenya 8.8.30
BSc(Lond) Makerere univ coll of E Africa 1957
Kenya: res off. Nairobi 1964–66; chief tech off., asst gen man. Kenya tea dev auth 1967–74; gen man. nat irrigation board from 1974
m Kenya 1958 Damaris Njeri teacher d of James Kaberere, Limuru

GADDIE John MB ChB 1968 *MD 1975
s of John G. farm. and Elizabeth A. B. Wylie; b Orkney Is 21.12.43
MRCP(UK) 1977
ARI: h o 1968–69, res fell. 1969–73, regist 1973–77, sen regist respiratory med from 1977
m Aber 1.9.65 Patricia J. R. Kynoch d of James D. K. MB ChB 1937 *qv*

GAFFNEY James Stewart Pettigrew BEd 1969
s of Charles G. fisherman and Christina Pettigrew; b Dunbar 26.2.47
teacher Engl Hawick 1969–73; asst prin Engl Elgin from 1973
m Aber 3.4.67 Elizabeth A. Cooney teacher d of George M. C. MA(Edin) Invergordon

GAFFRON Wendy Jennifer *MA 1969
d of David J. G. MA 1948 *qv*; b Aber 26.12.46
teacher Engl: Vale of Leven acad Alexandria 1970–72, Rothesay acad from 1972
m Aber –.8.70 Robin J. Dow MA 1970 *qv*

GAIT Peter William Dixon MA 1966

GALBRAITH James Donald *MA 1967 MLitt 1970
s of James A. G. police off. and Ann G. Selbie; b Aber 26.4.43
res asst Scot Record Off. Edin from 1970

GALBRAITH Philip Andrew *BSc 1968 Dip Ed 1969
s of Andrew P. G. BSc(Edin) teacher and Dorothy Hetherington; b Edin 8.7.46
teacher geog: The Marr Coll, Troon 1969–71, prin geog from 1971; author *Geography in Action* I and II 1978
m Aber 1.8.69 Dorothy I. Liddle MA 1969 *qv*

GALL Barbara MA 1960
d of John G. farm. and Mary I. E. Strath; b Ellon 17.11.38
teacher classics: Woodmill h s Dunfermline 1961–65; Berwicksh h s Duns 1965–66; Dun: part time: Craigie h s 1971–75, Dun h s from 1975
m Aber 19.7.65 George S. Collie MA 1961 *qv*

GALL Elsie Mary MA 1962
d of Frank R. G. farm. and Elsie H. Booth; b Ellon 22.7.41
teacher Engl/hist/geog Crimond s Lonmay 1963–68; relief p s teacher Monifieth area 1969–70
m Aber 29.8.68 Bruce T. Welch seed merch s of Robert M. W. Monifieth

GALL Ian James BSc 1959

GALL Kathleen Mary MA 1966
d of Alexander N. G. insur ag and Agnes A. Smith; b Aber 2.4.43
m Aber 28.12.64 Kenneth M. Hutcheon syst progr s of Albert R. H.

GALL Marjory Anne BSc 1966
d of Alexander N. G. insur ag and Agnes A. Smith clerkess, shop asst; b Aber 21.7.45
teacher various short-term posts Edin 1967–74
m Aber 22.11.67 Peter M. Craig BSc 1967 *qv*

GALLACHER Jane Mitchell MA 1969
m Ross

GALLICKER Patrick MA 1961
s of Rose Gallicker textile worker; b Aber 3.11.39
Aber: teacher Engl Kaimhill j s s 1963–65, asst prin Engl Northfield acad from 1965
marr diss 1979

GALLIE Nicholas Ian *MA 1969

GALLIE Roger Douglas *MA 1964
s of Douglas G. comp dir and Catherine Y. Stephen; b Glasg 7.5.42
MLitt(Cantab) 1971
asst lect phil Leic 1966–69, lect from 1969
m Blandford Camp 12.8.72 Alison J. A. Lees asst dom bursar d of Albert J. L. Blandford Forum

GALLOWAY Ann MA 1960

GALLOWAY David Brian MB ChB 1964
s of Harold W. G. bus man and Evelyn A. Johnston teacher; b Aber 6.3.40
MRCP(Lond) 1971 DObstRCOG(Lond) 1966 FPA 1966
h o ARI 1964–65, Glasg Bellshill mat. hosp, Birm ch hosp 1965–66; sen h o, regist Lond teaching hosps 1966–70; regist, sen regist, lect Aber hosps/Aberd from 1970
m Lond 25.3.72 Diana E. Marshall MCSP(Lond) physioth d of William M. Lond

GALLOWAY Richard Melvin *BSc(eng) 1967
m Aber 27.10.69 Patricia A. Howard MA 1968 *qv*

GAMBLIN Alfred Joseph MB ChB 1969

GAMBLIN Sandra Anne MB ChB 1968
d of Richard E. G. civ eng and Bessie I. Gray clerkess/bookkeeper; b Aber 15.3.44
h o RACH, Woodend hosp Aber 1968–69; sen h o cas dept RACH 1969–71; g p Aber from 1971
m Aber 28.12.68 William E. McIntosh MA 1965 *qv*

GAMMACK Evaline Anne Joan MB ChB 1960

GAMMACK George Cooper MA 1968

GAMMIE Agnes Davidson Ogg MA 1956
d of Norman T. G. farm. and Elizabeth Davidson; b Bieldside 20.2.36
teacher Kelowna BC Canada 1958–60; prin Fr Palmerston Ontario 1963–73; farm. Harriston Ont from 1973
m Ontario 1.2.58 George Strachan farm. s of John S.

GAMMIE Eileen Marie Cameron MA 1968
m(1) Ledgard
(2) Tagart

GAMMIE Leslie *BSc 1968

GAMMIE Linda Rosemary *MA 1965

GAMMIE Michael John *MA 1968
MA(Glas)

GAMMIE Peter Alexander MA 1969 *MEd 1972
s of James W. G. farm. and Flora M. McGibbon nurse; b Aber 8.10.48
teacher Engl: Dumfries h s 1970–71, Arbroath acad 1971–72, Alloa acad 1972–75; asst prin Engl Alva acad from 1975
m Rabastens, Tarn, France 1.8.73 Maryse C. M. Marty BA(Stir) d of Jean R. B. M. Rabastens

GANSON Christine Jean *MA 1967

GANSON John Robert *BSc 1969

GARD John Alan PhD 1956
s of John S. F. G. BSc(Durh) chem and Eliza Ainsley teacher; b Washington, Co Durh 29.4.19
BSc(Durh) 1940 ARIC
res chem: Turners Asbestos Cement Co Manc 1940–45, Washington Chem Co Durh 1945–49, Ferodo Chapel-en-le-Frith 1949–52; Aberd: electron microscopist 1952–60, res lect from 1960
m Washington Co Durh 3.9.45 Millicent Radford secy d of Francis E. R. Heworth

GARDEN Brian BSc 1965
s of Frank G. shipwright and Isabella B. Birnie; b Aber 23.5.43
TD
Poole: progr 1966–69, syst analyst 1969–70; lect M o D from 1970
m Cromarty 28.3.67 Catriona H. Thomson staff nurse d of William T. Cromarty

GARDEN Eric Rae BSc(eng) 1966

GARDEN Gordon Henderson MA 1968
s of Alexander G. eng and Mary J. Towler; b Aber 3.7.23
teacher: tech coll Aber 1969-71, Beechwood s Aber from 1971
m Aber 1948 Ann Cardno nurse d of Alexander C. Aber

GARDEN Ian Allardyce MB ChB 1958
s of Norman W. G. pattern maker, trans insp and Ruth A. M. Allardyce tailoress; b Aber 6.2.33
h o Stracathro hosp Brechin 1959–60; m o RAMC Singapore 1960–63; regist anaest Bridge of Earn, Perth R.I. 1963–64; g p Kirkby-in-Ashfield from 1964
m Inv 7.5.60 Mary M. MacGruer SRN d of Thomas L. MacG. Fort Augustus

GARDEN Isabel Stewart MA 1962
m Gault

GARDEN Leonora *BSc 1962
d of Charles P. G. decorator/signwriter and Williamina M. Scroggie; b Aber 31.10.39
teacher: maths/geog Newtyle 1963–64, maths Ayr from 1972
m Aber 9.7.63 Hector R. Mackenzie MA 1956 *qv*

GARDEN Margaret Ann Flett MA 1956
d of George G. capt MN and Mary A. Geddes; b Portgordon 26.2.35
teacher: Fr/Engl Rhynie 1957–58, Fr Turriff 1958–59
m Aber 22.7.59 James W. Mackay master draper s of James B. M. Buckie

GARDEN Thomas Buchan MB ChB 1966
s of John A. M. G. capt MN and Martha Leadbetter; b Stonehaven 11.3.42
h o Aber hosps 1966–68; g p: Elgin 1968–70, Rugeley from 1970
m Aber 6.7.65 Alice T. Paterson teacher d of James H. P. Fraserburgh

GARDINER Alexander Quentin MB ChB 1962 PhD 1967
s of James M. G. OBE BCom 1926 *qv* and Nell W. Sutherland SRN; b Aber 5.5.35
DPM(Edin) 1966 MRCPsych 1971
h o ARI, Ross Clin 1962–64; MRC jun res fell. psych Aberd 1964–67; sen regist psych Royal Cornhill hosp Aber 1967–70; fell. commun psych Yale univ s of med New Haven, Conn 1970–71; consult. psychiat Grampian area health board/clin sen lect mental health Aberd from 1971
m Aber 18.7.62 Rhoda M. Primrose teacher d of Norman P. Aber

GARDINER Austen James Sutherland MB ChB 1960 MD 1974
s of James M. G. OBE B Com 1926 *qv* and Nell W. Sutherland SRN; b Great Bently 27.1.34
Anderson Medal 1960 MRCP(Lond) 1966 MRCPE 1977 FRCPE 1979
h o ARI 1960–61; res fell. surg, Garden res fell. med Aberd 1962–64; regist ARI 1964–68; res fell. McG Montreal 1968–70; sen regist, lect med Aberd 1970–76; phys i/c Monklands hosp Lanarksh from 1976
m Edin 27.7.61 Ruth Duncan SRN d of Leslie D. MA(Edin) Edin

GARDINER Celia Hamilton MA 1963
d of George H. G., BSc(Leeds) teacher, farm. and Diana M. Plummer; b Northallerton 25.5.42
ALA(Strath) 1964
sen lib asst Leeds univ med s 1964–66; dep lib Trinity and All Saints coll of educ Leeds 1966–70; lib Friarage hosp Northallerton from 1970

GARDINER James Kenneth MEd 1956
s of John G. and Margaret Fothergill; b Dunfermline 5.8.27
MA(Edin) 1949 Dip Ed(Edin) 1952
dep dir educ Fife from 1967
m Edin 1.9.54 Ellenor Currie MA(Edin) teacher d of James C. Edin

GARDINER Robert Hamilton Baxter BSc 1970
s of Thomas B. G. MB ChB(Glas) surg and Elizabeth H. Graham time and motion study observer; b Lennoxtown 8.10.48
chartering asst Glasg from 1970
m Omagh 5.8.71 Audrey E. Coote BSc 1970 *qv*

GARDINER William *BSc 1960 MSc 1962

GARDNER Allan Buchanan *MA 1958
s of Alexander B. G. arch.; b Aber 24.10.37
BA(Oxon) LLB(Cantab)
official Internat Labour Off. Geneva from 1964

GARDNER Elizabeth Charlotte Johnston MA 1969
d of William G. G. G. master butcher and Louie E. J. Reid MA(Glas) teacher; b Falkirk 29.11.48
staff man. Marks & Spencer S E England from 1969
m Falkirk 9.8.72 John D. Stevenson BA(Manc poly) insur broker, stud. s of John C. S. Romford

GARDNER Hugh MacCallum *BSc 1962

GARDNER Jean Stewart BSc 1969

GARLAND Michael Stanley Ogilvie MA 1959 Dip Ed 1960
s of Andrew W. G. comm trav and Barbara M. Moir teacher; b Dun 7.9.38
teacher Andover s Brechin 1961–64; serv children's educ auth: teacher Verden W Ger 1964–65, head p s Jever W Ger 1965–70; head p sect. AFCENT internat s Brunssum Holland 1970–72; head St Christopher's s Rheindahlen W Ger 1972–76; head of Langlands s Forfar from 1976
m Farnell 6.10.61 Margaret M. McNicol teacher d of Duncan McN. Farnell

GARRIOCH David Brown BMedBiol 1968 MB ChB 1971 MD 1978
s of David B. G. MA(Edin) headmaster and Millicent Milne teacher; b New Aberdour 12.3.47
MRCOG 1977
h o ARI 1971–72; Lond: obst h o Hackney 1972–73; regist obst/gyn St Thomas hosp and Pembury hosp Kent 1974–77, lect obst/gyn St Thomas med s from 1974

GARRIOCH Joanna Mackenzie MB ChB 1966
d of James G. clerk of works and Margaret Mackenzie nurse; b Kirkwall 13.5.42
h o Woodend hosp Aber 1966–67
m Aber 17.12.65 James A. Wattie MB ChB 1960 *qv*

GARRIOCK Kathleen Winifred Margaret MA 1969
d of Francis G. man. dir and Barbara M. Jamieson; b Lerwick 6.8.47
teacher Engl Landskrona Sweden 1970–71; teacher Fr: Lerwick 1971, Nairn 1971–74; timber manager's asst

Lerwick from 1974
m Aber 2.4.73 William H. Stubbings asst man.

GARRISON Frederick Charles *MEd 1970

GARROW Alexander George *BSc 1966 Dip Ed 1967
s of Alexander J. G. stone mason/blder and Elizabeth M. Burnett; b Elgin 22.8.44
teacher phys AGS 1967–72; prin phys Kincorth acad from 1972
m Aber 29.7.67 Margaret Fraser MA 1966 *qv*

GARROW Alice Anne BSc 1959
d of Frederick C. G. MA 1926 *qv* and Alice W. Stewart BSc 1928 *qv*; b Aber 8.2.39
teacher sc: sen h s Dartmouth Nova Scotia 1960–61, Sutton 1961–62, Shawlands acad Glasg 1963–64
m Aber 14.10.61 Alexander S. F. Mair BSc(eng) 1957 *qv*
d Worcester 29.12.75

GARROW Robert Stewart *BSc(eng) 1963
s of Frederick C. G. MA 1926 *qv* and Alice W. Stewart BSc 1928 *qv*; b Aber 23.5.42
Dip Man. St(Strath) 1972
app/0 & M asst AEI Rugby, Leic 1963–66; Glasg: O & M off. Rolls Royce 1966–67, man. serv off. SSEB 1968–69, bus. consult. Arthur Andersen & Co 1969–72; man. advis John Aird & Co Darvel 1972–73; bus. dev. exec Grampian Oil Serv Glasg 1973–75; asst chief man. serv off. Glasg dist c from 1975
m Milngavie 9.8.72 Christine W. McCracken inc tax insp d of Dugald C. McC. Clarkston

GARTH Jeremy Robinson *BSc 1970
s of Geoffrey W. G. power stat supt and Freda M. Robinson teacher; b Bradford 17.8.45
asst geol dept McM univ. Hamilton, Ont 1970–72; press oper/machinist Burnley 1972–74; geol/well logger based Aber from 1974

GARTMANN Jacqueline Hélène Elsbeth MA 1963
d of Anton G. confectioner and Alice R. L. Cugny concert pianist; b Safien Switzerland 4.4.39
post grad stud.: Besançon 1963-64, Madrid 1964–65, Berne 1965–66; Switzerland: teacher Engl Ftan 1966–69, Engl translator in a major trust comp Zürich 1969–78, free-lance translator Zürich from 1979

GARTSHORE Maurice John MA 1969

GARVIE Christopher Ludwig BSc 1962
s of Denis S. G. BSc(eng) 1935 *qv*; b Aber 15.10.40
computer progr with Elliot Automation Lond, Den Helder, Holland 1962–65; syst analyst: Seattle 1965–67, Houston 1967–70, Munich, 1970–73, Houston 1973–77, Friedrichshafen Germany from 1977
m Aber 2.4.65 Shirley R. J. Kidd d of Joseph I. K. Wick

GARVIE John Henry *BSc 1970
s of John G. butcher, factory sect. man. and Lydia M. Black clerkess; b Aber 9.3.48
teacher: Stornoway 1971–75, prin phys Balfron from 1974
m Aber 20.8.71 Fiona M. Clark lib asst d of Alfred C. Kingswells

GARVIE Sheila Margaret BSc 1970
m Milngavie 2.7.69 Alasdair M. Burns BSc 1969 *qv*

GARVIE William Hamilton Heslop MB ChB 1956
s of Hamilton A. G. bank man. and Elizabeth M. Heslop p e teacher; b Kirkcaldy 15.6.30
FRCSE 1961 FRCS 1963
sen regist surg: Dun 1965–66, Aber 1966–67; Aberd: lect surg 1967–68, sen lect 1968–69, consult. surg from 1969
m Aber 17.6.59 Katherine M. Matheson nurse d of Alexander M. Aber

GASCOIGNE Michael Neil Clifton LLB 1970
s of C. A. Hector G. chartered land ag and Jean Muller; b Inv 1.2.49
admitted WS; ptnr Messrs Brodies WS Edin from 1973

GASKIN Celeste Ellen MA 1966
d of Patrick G. dept store man. and Celesta M. Emslie; b Aber 24.9.45
teacher: Engl/hist Fyvie s 1967–69; Engl lang British s Milan 1969–72
m Aber 20.9.66 James H. Christie CA s of James C. Aber

GASTON Arthur Raymond Charles MA 1958 BD 1961
s of William J. G. min of relig(cong) and Mary M. Chaplin; b Atherstone 25.5.36
Dip Scot. Cong Coll(Edin) 1961
prin theol coll/prof NT stud. Fianarantsoa Malagasy Repub 1962–67; min Sauchie par ch Alloa 1969–75; min Dollar West with Muckhart and Glendevon from 1975
m Glasg 12.6.62 Evelyn W. Mather civ serv d of James M. Glasg

GAUKROGER Catherine Mary MB ChB 1968
d of Charles A. G. BA(Leeds) headmaster and Mary Turner teacher; b Dunfermline 26.8.44
DObstRCOG 1971
h o Whitehaven, Aber 1968–69; sen h o; obst, paediat Carlisle, Liv 1969–70, obst, med Wigan, Liv 1970–71; g p: Aber 1971–72, Alva from 1972

GAULD Alexander George *MA 1966
s of William G. lorry driver, bus driver and Nellie Manson; b Aber 11.2.43
teacher Fr/Span: Aber coll of comm 1967–69, AGS 1969–74, prin Span. Northfield acad Aber from 1974

GAULD George Alexander MA 1959

GAULD James Alexander BSc 1969

GAULD James Hendry *BSc 1966 PhD 1969
s of James G. insur man. and Dorothy I. Simpson; b Aber 8.2.44
Royal Soc Leverhulme Schol 1966–67
soil surv staff Macaulay inst soil res Aber from 1969
m Aber 12.10.72 Lesley Baxter teacher d of William B. Aber

GAULD Malcolm William Robertson LLB 1964
s of William R. G. MB ChB 1935 *qv*; b Cairo 10.10.43
CA 1967 AMBIM 1972
app Williamson & Dunn CA Aber 1964–67; audit sen Price Waterhouse & Co. Glasg 1967–70; fin. controller Hayward Tyler & Co eng E. Kilbride 1970–73; group acct and comp secy Auchinleck Invest. Co Glasg from 1973
m Aber 2.8.68 Lesley M. H. Riddel med secy d of Johnston R. Aber

GAULD Morton Alexander Edward *MA 1959
s of Charles G. G. naval off. and Gladys M. D. Eunson teacher piano; b Edin 3.6.37
teacher classics Inverurie acad 1960–71; prin classics Bankhead acad Aber from 1972

GAULD William *MA 1963
s of William G. elect. welder and Rose Merchant; b Aber 5.4.41
exec off. BoT Lond 1963–68, civil aviation Highlands and Islands Edin 1968–69; higher exec off. Glasg 1969–73; far east rep civ aviation auth Hong Kong from 1973
m Aber 5.8.64 Yvonne Cormack d of George C. Aber

GAVIN, Irene Sise MA 1963
m Cormack

GAVIN Kevin George *MA 1970 Dip Ed 1971

GAVIN Mary Teresa *MA 1970
m Southport 1971 Robert M. L. Anderson MA 1962 *qv*

GAVIN Neil Gow Sinclair MB ChB 1970

GAVIN Pamela Ethel *MA 1960
m Craig

GAVINE David Myles *MA 1969
BSc(St And)

GEALS Michael Forbes MB ChB 1968
s of James G. MA 1929 *qv*; b Aber 26.4.45
DObstRCOG 1972 MRCOG 1975
h o med, surg Woodend hosp Aber 1968–69; sen h o obst /gyn Dumfries 1969–71; regist: obst/gyn Inv 1971–73, surg St Leonard's hosp Lond 1973–74; obst/gyn Duke St hosp Glasg 1974–77; lect obst/gyn Aberd from 1977
m Aber 16.1.69 Jill Barker d of John B. Peterculter

GEAR Andrew David Davidson BSc 1956
s of David M. C. crofter/boatman and Jemima A. Henry crofter; b Foula 3.6.33
nat serv 1957–59; teacher Mid Yell j h s Shetland from 1959
m Mid Yell 9.7.57 Wilma A. Hughson MA 1955 *qv*

GEAR Christine Anne BSc 1960
d of John G. head postmaster and Margaret Dunbar teacher; b Lerwick 5.3.40
teacher: maths/sc Aberdeensh 1961–66, Kirkcudbrightsh 1966–67, maths Inverurie acad from 1977
m Aber 12.7.63 William F. Murdoch MA 1964 *qv*

GEDDES David Flett *BSc 1966

GEDDES David Stewart *BSc 1962 PhD 1967

GEDDES Elizabeth Marshall MA 1967
d of George G. quarrymaster/farm. and Barbara M. Whitelaw BA(Lond) teacher; b Elgin 21.3.46
Dip Soc Ad(Edin) 1969 Dip Soc Work(Glas) 1974
soc worker: Falkirk 1969–75, Moray 1975–77 and from 1979; various posts (including vine-training) NZ 1977–79

GEDDES Ian Mackie MA 1964

GEDDES James Clarke MA 1958 *1960 Dip Ed 1961
s of James G. town chamberlain Inverbervie and Marjory A. B. Clarke; b Inverbervie 19.12.22
teacher hist/Engl RGC Aber 1961–64; head lib stud. Elmwood coll Cupar 1964–67; dir adult educ and extra-mural stud. St And from 1967
m Aber 28.12.55 Muriel L. McNab MA 1952 *qv*

GEDDES Jean Munro MA 1966
d of William G. farm worker and Elizabeth W. Davidson; b Lintmill 22.5.46
teacher: Ayr 1967–68, Macduff 1968–71, Buckie from 1971
m Cullen 31.7.71 Alexander Watt acct s of Alexander W. Portknockie

GEDDES Margaret Elane BSc 1963
d of George A. G. teacher and Isabella Kelman teacher; b Aber 20.10.42
teacher sc: Tynecastle s Edin 1964–66, Longbrook s Feltham 1966–67, Davies, Lains & Dick Lond 1967–68, Dalkeith s 1968–69
m Aber 31.3.67 Roger Gordon MRCVS(Edin) vet surg s of Robert G. Ballymena

GEDDES William Charles *BSc 1959 PhD 1962
s of William R. G. farm. and Mary A. G. Anderson; b Buckie 2.9.38
Assoc Plastics & Rubber Ind 1975
asst lect chem Aberd 1962–63; sen scient off. rubber and plastics res assoc Shawbury 1963–67; sect. leader dev Nairn Floors Kirkcaldy 1967–70; lect polymer tech Napier coll of comm and tech Edin from 1970
m Fochabers 11.9.63 Barbara J. Morrison shorthand typist, hotel man. d of William M. Fochabers

GEE Isoline PhD 1958
BSc(Wales)
res grant Rowett inst Aber 1958–59; part-time teacher sc Royal h s Edin 1959–60
m Aberystwyth 4.10.58 James F. D. Greenhalgh PhD 1959 *qv*

GELLATLY Ian Findlay MA 1956 LLB 1958
s of John F. G. hairdresser, tobacconist, farm. and Janet Weir; b Stonehaven 18.4.35
teacher New Stevenston 1959–60; leg. asst Dunbarton c c 1960–65; leg. admin asst Stirling c c 1965–67; prin solic Motherwell & Wishaw t c 1967–69; prin dep town clerk, interim town clerk Coatbridge t c 1969–72, leg. advis 1972–75; solic (Scot.) British Airports Auth from 1975

GELLATLY Leonard James Weir MA 1967

GELMAN Aubrey Louis PhD 1967
s of Joseph G. rancher/mining comp dir and Ethel Smith; b Bulawayo Rhodesia 13.2.27
BSc(Cape Town) 1948 BSc(Rhodes univ S. Af.) 1949 Dip Agr Sc(Cantab) 1954
gen man. farming, ranching/mining Bulawayo 1949–53; jun exec Fisons Felixstowe 1954–57; consult. chem/gen man. farm./mining Bulawayo 1957–60; lect NOSCA Aber from 1961

GEMMELL Alastair Millar Duncanson *BSc 1968
s of Alan R. G. PhD(Glas) univ prof and Janet A. B. Duncanson; b Ayr 9.2.46
PhD(Glas)1971
dem geog Keele univ 1971–73; lect geog Aberd from 1973
m Stair 27.2.71 June Hannah acct asst d of Andrew H. Drongan

GENTLE Terence Alexander *BSc(eng) 1970
s of James A. G. taxi owner/driver and Lena I. Finlayson; b Aber 19.8.47
AMIEE
des eng Ferranti Edin 1970–72; eng/dir Pettamp Linlithgow 1972–74; sen eng Marconi space and defence syst Hillend 1974–76; instrument eng Kingsworth Marine Drilling Dun from 1976
m Aber 19.8.68 Ishbel M. Low MA(Edin) d of Robert A. L. Aber

GENTLES Myrna Grace MB ChB 1961

GEORGALA Douglas Lindley PhD 1957
BSc(agr)(Stellenbosch)

GEORGE Graham BSc 1959

GEORGE Kathleen Margaret MA 1970
d of Charles G. BSc 1939 *qv*; b Newcastle-u-Tyne 13.12.47
teacher Prestonpans 1971–74
m Newcastle-u-Tyne 6.4.74 Douglas I. Allan farm man. s of William A. Symington

GEORGE Robert Wilson *MA 1967
s of Robert W. G. loc govt off. and Elizabeth Newell loc govt off.; b Ayr 6.4.44
econ res asst Lond 1967–68; p a to gen man. Varese, Italy 1968–69; Lond: econ 1969–70, man. consult. 1970–73, fin. analyst 1973–74, corporate plan. 1974–77, invest. control from 1977
m Aber 28.9.68 Moira Clark MA 1966 *qv*

GEORGE Sheila Catherine MA 1967 Dip Ed 1968
d of Charles G. BSc 1939 *qv*; b Newcastle-u-Tyne 10.11.45
teacher Kirkhill p s Aber 1968–72
m Newcastle-u-Tyne 31.7.70 John N. Slater MB ChB 1971 med pract s of John S. MB ChB 1941 *qv*

GEORGESON James Arthur Hugh MA 1969
s of Kathleen E. Hunter or Georgeson crofter; b Shetland 18.11.47
teacher maths/geog Aith jun h s from 1970
m Aith 31.3.72 Evelyn H. Smith bank clerkess, comptometer oper d of George S. Aith

GEORGESON Vaila Mackenzie *BSc 1970
d of James S. F. G. supt insur comp and Janet O. Mackenzie; b Wick 10.12.48
vet regist off. (sect. head) pharm comp Dorking from 1973

GERMAN Gordon Allen ᶜMB ChB 1958
s of Gidley H. G. min of relig and Willeminia Gordon; b Inverurie 12.5.35
DPM(Lond) 1962 MRCPE 1963 FRCPE 1971 MRCPsych 1972 FRCPsych 1973 MANZCP 1973 FANZCP 1975
sen h o, regist psychiat ARI 1958–63; regist, sen regist psychiat The Maudsley hosp Lond; prof psychiat Makerere univ Kampala, Uganda 1966–72; prof psychiat univ of W Aust from 1972
m Aber 14.4.58 Angela R. de Silva MA 1961 *qv*

GERRARD Erica Margaret MA 1966
m Downie

GERRARD Helen *MA 1966
d of James G. and Jemima Kiloh; b Aber 5.9.43
lect geog Aber coll of comm 1967–74, sen lect gen stud. from 1974

GERRARD Margaret Elizabeth MB ChB 1968
m Herd

GERRARD Michael Alexander MA 1968

GERRIE Anne BSc 1959
d of John G. MB ChB 1929 *qv*(III); b Aber 13.11.38
RSA(Lond)
secy to man. dir Lloyds Pharmaceuticals Lond 1961; teacher Aber: RGC 1967, Albyn s 1967–70, Kincorth acad 1971; own bus. '*The Windmill*' Aber from 1972
m Aber 7.9.61 James F. Donald theatre man./comp dir s of James R. D. Aber

GERRIE Roy Marnoch *MA 1965
s of Alexander G. civ serv and Margaret Whyte; b Edin 21.9.42
asst exam. Estate Duty Off. Edin 1965–66; admin asst Strath 1966–74; asst regist univ of Kent Canterbury 1974–75; asst secy Dund from 1975

GERVAIS Lawrence Leonard MA 1968

GHANEM Azza Muhammed Abdo MA 1965

GHANEM Shihab Muhammad Abduh BSc(eng) 1964

GHAURI Arif Ali Khan MSc 1967
s of Hamid A. K. G. cloth merch and Fatima H. A. Hussain; b Pilibhit (U.P.) India 22.9.38
BSc(Kar) 1961 MSc(Kar) 1962 Dip Fr(Peshawar) 1968
Peshawar univ Pakistan: lect 1967–72, asst prof geol 1972–77, assoc prof from 1977
m Karachi 12.10.67 Orooj B. M. Ullah BSc (Peshawar) teacher d of Mohammad Ullah Khan, Karachi

GHAZALLI Baharuddin Bin Haji BSc(for) 1963

GIBB Elizabeth Jean MA 1959
d of John A. C. G. farm./hotel prop. and Jessie W. Davidson; b Aber 24.5.38
teacher Aber 1960–61; floral art dem Scot. area from 1972
m Aber 27.6.60 Gerald Mortimer MA 1958 *qv*

GIBB George Gordon BSc 1969

GIBB Jean *MA 1970
d of Andrew R. G. estate factor and Jean R. Ritchie; b Fraserburgh 19.3.48
teacher geog Perth acad 1971–75
m Fraserburgh 24.7.71 Duncan M. Pringle BSc 1970 *qv*

GIBB Jennifer Rosemary BSc 1970
m Anderson

GIBB Judith Anne MA 1967
d of Robert M. G. timber merch and Elspeth M. F. Grant; b Aber 31.3.46
Dip Bus St(Strath)
secy to educ off. Grampian TV Aber 1967–72
m Aber 11.4.69 David G. Millar MB ChB 1967 *qv*

GIBB Margaret Carr MA 1965
b Tarland 1.10.43
teacher mod lang: Inverurie acad 1966–67, Currie h s 1967–72
m Aber 5.8.66 Karl A. Linklater MRCVS(Edin) vet surg, lect

GIBB Marilyn Rosemary MA 1968
d of Robert M. G. timber merch and Elspeth M. F. Grant; b Aber 22.9.41
teacher Fr: Norfolk 1969–73, RGC from 1974
m Aber 24.6.61 James G. Lowdon GD navigator RAF s of James L. Elgin

GIBB Richard Alexander *BSc 1958
MSc(Birm) 1959 PhD(Birm) 1961

GIBBONS June Evelyn Kathleen MA 1970 *1972
d of Henry J. G. computer man. and Muriel Smith shop man.; b Aber 21.2.50
asst soc work. Bellsdyke psychiat hosp Stirlingsh 1972–73
m Aber 14.3.71 Eoin M. Ross s lib s of John R. Bucksburn

GIBBONS Neil Mackintosh BSc(eng) 1969

GIBSON Alastair *MA 1970 CASS 1975
s of Harold G. civ serv and Olive Hendry; b Aber 9.4.48
Aber: hosp admin 1970–72, soc worker 1973–77; sen soc worker: Gateshead 1977–79, Aber from 1979
m Aber 8.4.72 Maureen Simpson d of Maurice A. S. Muchalls

GIBSON Alice Sim BSc 1968
d of William G. clerk of works and Mary E. Ross; b Aber 22.5.47
progr Perth 1968–69; exec off. (DPS) Lond 1971–73; syst progr: Mitcham 1973–76, Dubai UAE from 1976
m Aber 27.7.68 David M. Bremner BSc(eng) 1966 *qv*

GIBSON Donald Mathieson *BSc 1964 PhD 1968
s of John M. G. warehouseman and Alice M. A. F. Clark; b Aber 13.2.42
Torry res stat Aber: scient off. 1964–71, sen scient off. 1971–75, prin scient off. from 1975
seconded Laboratorium voor Microbiol univ of Ghent, Belgium 1965–66
m Aber 12.12.66 Joan M. Cook secy d of Douglas C. Aber

GIBSON Hilary Marcia BSc 1963

GIBSON James George *BSc 1961
s of James S. G. delivery driver and May M. Nicol; b Ellon 1.4.39
Anglo-Amer Corp of SA: field geol Mwadui diamond mine Tanzania 1961–63, Lobatse, Botswana 1963–74; mine resid geol Orapa diamond mine Botswana from 1974
m Serowe, Botswana 9.3.68 Cynthia M. Pretorius secy d of Hendrik C. P. Serowe

GIBSON Joan Stephen Buchanan MA 1968
d of Donald S. G. asst eng PO tel and Phyllis Winstanley hairdresser; b Aber 28.4.47
TEFL: Berlitz s Rome 1971, Windsor centre ling. Monza, Italy 1974, NIOGATE Teheran from 1977
m Aber 23.9.70 Enrico G. R. Nicoletti computer field eng s of Leopoldo N. Forli Italy

GIBSON Peter James *BSc(eng) 1966

GIBSON Stewart Glen *BSc 1970

GIBSON Terence Michael MB ChB 1970
s of Patrick G. clerk and Edith J. Mason soc worker; b Newcastle-u-Tyne 6.3.47
RAF from 1970
m Leicester 17.7.71 Alison F. Kibble cartographer

GIDNEY Alan Russell BSc 1965 *1966 PhD 1970
b S Shields 19.2.44
MIBiol 1969 scient fell. zool soc Lond 1970
lect NE Lond poly from 1969
m S Shields 6.8.66 Anna Rippon

GIFFORD Rosalind Mary *MA 1969
m Gilbert

GILBERT Philip Stanley MA 1970

GILES Louise Fleming *MA 1970
d of Alan M. G. MB ChB(Glas) consult. obst and Winifred M. Hiddleston: b Glasg 19.9.48
Edin: asst res off. res and intell unit SHHD (now information serv div common serv ag Scot. health serv) 1971–74, res off. 1974–76, sen res off. from 1976

GILL Angela Margaret *MA 1958
d of Alexander G. ARIBA arch. and Gladys M. Bullock; b Oxford 8.4.36
teacher maths St Helen's girls' s Abingdon 1959–61; computer progr: Boeing aircraft comp Seattle USA 1961–64, ICT Lond 1964–65, Boeing aircraft comp Seattle 1965–66; sen applications analyst Control Data Corp Lond from 1966
m Lambeth 9.7.77 Patrick H. Barnes comp dir s of Harold A. B.

GILL Anna Berenice MA 1967
d of Thomas P. Gill MSc(Melb) lect and Kala R. Rudin res asst; b Melbourne 18.10.45
Dip Ed(Melb) 1972 BEd(Melb) 1977
Melbourne: lect RMIT 1969–70, asst to acad regist tech teachers' coll 1970–72, tech teacher Box Hill tech coll 1973–74, lect SCV Hawthorn from 1974
m Jean C. Pha MA 1967 *qv*; marr diss

GILL Brian MB ChB 1967
s of William G. blacksmith and Elsie Dickinson; b S Shields 27.8.43
DMRD(Lond) 1971 FRCP(C) 1976
h o ARI 1967–68; sen h o path. Manc 1968–69; regist radiol ARI 1969–72, sen regist 1972–74; consult. radiol Calgary from 1974
m Bathgate 27.3.68 Mary N. Roberts teacher d of William R. Bathgate

GILL Douglas Sutherland MB ChB 1960

GILL Elizabeth Ann MA 1963
d of Alexander G. G. shopkeeper, car salesman and Barbara Cruden; b Aber 1.2.43
children's nurse NY 1963–64; teacher Peterhead 1964; prob off. Aberdeensh/Kincardine 1964–68, soc worker 1968–72
m Aber 19.7.63 William Howie MA 1960 *qv*

GILL George Alastair Thomas MB ChB 1958
s of James W. G. MB ChB 1921 *qv*(II, III) and Margaret E. Anderson MA 1919 *qv*; b Montrose 10.7.33
FRCS(C) 1969 CD 1974
Canada: m o RCAF 1959–74; private med pract (ENT) Victoria BC from 1974
m St Hubert PQ 30.12.61 Marie A. Stewart secy d of Gordon W. S. Matsqui BC

GILL George Barbour MA 1966

GILL John Joseph Bisset *BSc 1959
s of George G. grain merch and Agnes A. Barbour clerkess; b Macduff 21.12.37
PhD(Liv) 1969
Liv: res asst 1960–61, asst lect, lect from 1961
m Aber 10.8.61 Sheila T. Urquhart teacher d of John U. Banff

GILL Malcolm Alexander MA 1962
s of Alexander G. ARIBA arch. and Gladys M. Bullock; b Oxford 22.3.40
TD 1972
exec The Thomson Organis Lond 1962–73; man. dir Thomson Publ Johannesburg from 1974
m Newton St Loe 13.7.68 Jane Q. Roberts d of William Q. R. CVO Newton St Loe

GILL Mark Andrew *MA 1964
s of Joseph G. aircraft eng and Rosemary Butcher weight and stress tech; b Lytham St Annes 3.1.42
Dip PE(Loughborough)

trainee NFU Lond 1964–65; teacher: Kenya 1966–68, Turks and Caicos Is BWI 1968–71, royal g s High Wycombe 1971–73, Chalvedon s Basildon 1973–77, Fairham s Nott from 1977
m Hounslow 23.7.66 Maureen Smith nurse d of Hubert S. S. Hounslow

GILL Norman John BSc(eng) 1959
s of James M. G. MB ChB 1927 *qv*; b Aber 14.4.36
ATPL(pilot civil licences) Qualified Pilot Instructor (Civil)
RAF pilot Germany, UK, Malta 1959–75; civil pilot from 1975
m Inverurie 21.8.65 Lesley J. Stephen d of James A. S. Inverurie

GILL Rhoda Catherine *MA 1966
m Peter J. Bennett BSc(for) 1967

GILL Robert Gerrard *BSc 1970
s of Robert G. and Elsie R. Still; b Aber 15.12.47
man. trainee Reed Corrugated Cases 1970–71; prod. foreman 1971, work stud. eng 1972, prod. controller 1973–74, asst sales man. 1975–76; p a to chmn and chief exec Reed International from 1976

GILLAN Christopher John Archibald LLB 1966
s of Archibald W. G. BL 1930 *qv* and Jane F. Mann teacher; b Stirling 4.9.45
Kinnear, Carlisle & Gillan solic Dun: app 1966–68, asst solic 1968–70, ptnr from 1970
m Dun 26.6.73 Carol A. Gordon teacher d of Arthur G. Dun

GILLAN Frances Leigh MA 1970
d of Andrew G. rlyman and Maria Holmes s auxiliary; b Edin 28.9.48
Dip Sec St(Edin) 1972
Edin: secy indust des & consult. 1972–75; admin asst Lothian reg educ dept 1975–78, publ off. f e Lothian reg educ dept from 1978

GILLAN Robert Fairweather MA 1958 LLB 1961
s of John F. G. advoc in Aber and Janet M. Thomson; b Aber 18.9.36
asst solic Alexander & Gillan advoc Aber 1961–66, ptnr from 1966
m Aber 29.6.67 Christian G. S. Gillan nursing sister d of Frederick R. G. Torphins

GILLANDERS Robert MA 1963
s of Robert M. G. hairdresser and Isabella McKay; b Aber 9.10.41
teacher Aber: Muirfield s 1964–71, dep head Cummings Park s 1971–73, asst head Kittybrewster s 1974–75, head from 1975
m Aber 20.7.67 Wilma Buchan teacher d of Charles L. B. Aber

GILLESPIE Graham Alexander Mackay *BSc 1968
s of Charles M. G. soldier, s attendance off. and Annie Mackay; b Lossiemouth 29.6.46
computer progr ICL Lond, Reading 1968–69; sen computer proj off. Brit Airways Lond 1970–76; real-time reservations syst controller Gulf Air Manama Bahrain from 1977
d 17.6.81

GILLESPIE Margaret Bella Dalgarno MA 1957
d of William G. G. trans insp and Jane M. M. Porter; b Aber 13.3.34
teacher maths: Aber 1958–65, Croydon 1965, part time Aber from 1969, full time from 1977
m Aber 13.3.65 Norman W. Martin soldier, police off. s of William M. Edin

GILLIES Angus Reid MA 1961 Dip Ed 1962

GILLIES Duncan Norman MA 1963

GILMER Joan Margaret Morton *MA 1969
d of James G. shop man., comp dir med serv and Elizabeth M. Morton teacher; b Glasg 26.6.47
scient asst anti-locust res estab Lond 1969–70; geol asst: site explor serv Aber 1970–72, R. C. Stewart 1972–73; exper off. geol country roads board Melb Aust from 1973

GILMORE George Malcolm BSc 1967

GILMORE Linda Adams PhD 1969
d of Allen A. G. BA(Amherst) univ prof and Althea Adams BA(Ohio State); b Boston USA 16.4.43
BS(Michigan State) 1965
Aberd: res fell. 1969–70, res asst 1970–72, res off. from 1972
m Aber 24.6.68 John E. Fothergill BSc(Brist) reader biochem Aberd s of Edward B. F. Bristol

GILMORE Stewart MA 1963
s of Robert J. G. eng and Elizabeth Stewart; b Aber 8.5.35
teacher Perth 1964–67, sen teacher from 1967
m Beckenham 31.3.62 Jane H. Dixon staff nurse d of Arthur W. D. Beckenham

GILMOUR Helen Shirran BSc 1962
d of Thomas G. master mariner and Margaret M. Bruce nurse; b Aber 20.1.41
analyst chem Aberd 1962–64; information scient Pilkington Bros Ormskirk 1965–71
m Aber 28.8.64 Brian R. Chamberlain PhD 1965 *qv*

GILMOUR Iain Fordyce *MA 1969
s of Robert J. G. MA(St And) CA and Elnora M. Fordyce MA(Glas) teacher; b Colombo Sri Lanka 18.2.46
buyer Ford Motor Co Dagenham 1969–73; inventory man. Black & Decker Spennymoor 1973–77; head of manufacturing Berkey Colortran (UK) Thetford from 1977
m Ayr 21.8.70 Marjorie Y. Smith MA 1969 *qv*

GILMOUR Quentin William LLB 1964
s of William G. solic and town clerk and Elizabeth B. Rennie; b Nairn 10.9.38
ptnr Gilmour & Co solic Lossiemouth from 1971

GILMOUR Tom Lister *BSc(eng) 1966

GILMOUR William Mayne MA 1965 BD 1968
s of George M. G. fitter BR and Ann R. Scott; b Glasg 18.10.42
C of S min: asst Cardonald par ch Glasg 1961–69, Coatbridge from 1969
m Glasg 22.8.69 Helen G. Dewar shorthand typist d of Ewan D. Glasg

GILROY Ian Shepherd MA 1968
s of Alexander G. maintenance eng and Ella Hall shop asst; b Dun 17.11.45
teacher Dun 1968–69; stud. div St And 1970–71; teacher Engl St Mungo's acad Glasg 1971–76; asst prin Engl St Margaret's h s Airdrie 1976–78; prin Engl St Andrew's h s E Kilbride from 1978

GINZ Beryl MB ChB 1964
d of Henry E. G. asst man. life insur and Winifred Welch; b Lond 12.1.39
MRCOG 1971 MSc(Leeds) 1974
h o Aber 1964–67; regist obst/gyn, paediat Auck NZ

1967–70; regist obst/gyn Cardiff 1970–73; MSc course steroid endocrinology Leeds 1973–74; lect obst/gyn Sheff from 1974

GIULIANI Maria Assunta *MA 1968
d of Edward G. shopkeeper and Maria Dalli; b Aber 10.11.46
TEFL Florence 1969–76
m Aber 14.2.70 Giustino Moni sales rep s of Giulio M. Gallicano Lucca Italy

GLADSTONE Patrick James *MA 1970
s of Archibald G. solic clerk and Mary J. Swanston; b Ayton 17.1.37
BSc(Edin) 1958
teacher: Engl Wick 1970–73, asst prin Engl from 1973
m Wick 29.10.71 Margaret M. Gunn BSc 1966 *qv*

GLASHAN Robin Wattie MB ChB 1958
s of Gordon M. G. bank man. and Alexandra Wattie art teacher; b Aber 8.9.33
FRCSE 1963 FRCSGlas 1964
h o Aber 1958–59; g p Dorset 1959–60; h o Angus 1960; dem anat Dund 1960–61; sen h o Bristol 1961–62; regist surg Glasg 1962–65; sen regist urol Glasg 1965–68; consult. urol Huddersfield from 1968
m Aber 21.7.59 Wilma M. R. Thomson nurse d of William J. T. Forgue

GLASS Duncan Alexander MA 1963
s of Duncan G. lab and Charlotte W. Jamieson; b Inv 9.8.30
teacher Engl Aber coll of comm from 1964
m Aber 14.7.58 Doreen Cumming hairdresser d of Robert W. C. Aber

GLASS Lesley Rose LLB 1966
m Davidson

GLASSER Fredrik Paul DSc 1968
s of David D. G. MSc(NY) teacher and Esther Glasser; b New Haven Conn USA 2.5.29
BA(Conn) 1952 PhD(Penn) 1958
res fell. Penn state univ USA 1957–59; Aberd: res fell. 1959–61, lect 1961–69, sen lect 1969–77, reader from 1977
m Pa USA 17.5.58 Lesley S. Dent PhD 1957 *qv*

GLASSMAN Robert Martin MB ChB 1969
s of Charles G. MB ChB 1934 *qv*; b Brooklyn NY 7.4.40
BSc(Penn) FACAnaest 1972 DA 1976
USA: intern med centre Nassau cty 1969–70, anaesthesiology resid 1970–72; attending and assoc prof anaesthesiology New Haven hosp Yale 1972–75; attending anaesthesiologist Waterbury hosp/St Mary's hosp Waterbury from 1975
m Aber 3.7.69 Kathleen J. Birnie MA(Edin) lib, proof reader d of George A. B. Aber

GLEN Eric Uprichard *MA 1966

GLEN Martyn Coulter BSc(agr) 1967
s of Robert S. B. G. estate factor and Williamina M. Combe; b Drymen 15.3.44
ARICS 1970
Inl Rev: valuation asst Aber 1967–70, main grade valuer to dist valuer's off. Aber from 1972
Rotary grad fell. Christchurch NZ 1970–72

GLENDINNING Catherine Milne MA 1957
d of Archibald D. G. acct and Mary M. Dewar; b Edin 19.4.36
teacher s for deaf Aber 1959–61; part time teacher: Kirkwall 1970–71, mus Aberdeensh s 1971–72, Logie Durno p s 1972–74; head Crathes p s from 1974
m Aber 23.7.60 George L. Parkinson MA 1957 *qv*

GLENDINNING Ian Archibald *BSc 1966 MSc 1968
s of Archibald D. G. acct and Mary M. Dewar; b Arbroath 24.9.44
field seismologist Sultanate of Oman and UK 1967–71; instrument eng Algeria 1972; geophys consult. Aber, Lond 1972–73; sen staff eng 1973–76 and operations man. from 1977 in geophys comp Swanley

GLENNIE Gwendoline Lorna *MA 1967
d of John A. S. G. MA 1928 *qv*; b Guildford 14.1.44
translator/interpreter Lond 1968–69
m Cruden Bay 5.10.68 Robin I. McConnachie MA 1961 *qv*

GLENNIE Hilda Isobel MA 1964
d of George G. shop asst and Hilda I. Mathieson teacher; b Aber 14.3.43
teacher: Ellon acad 1966–68, City of Lond s for girls 1968–70, Musselburgh g s 1970–71, Clydebank h s 1971–72, Northfield acad Aber 1972–75, asst prin Fr/Ger from 1975

GLENNIE James Harvey MA 1958

GLENNIE Janet Margaret *MA 1966
m Byth

GLENNIE John Alexander MB ChB 1962
s of James D. G. MA(Glas) teacher, headmaster and Alice Gammie secy; b Glasg 5.2.39
h o: Kilmarnock I, Ballochmyle hosp, Rotten Row hosp Glasg 1963–64; g p Wednesbury from 1964
m Kemnay 4.8.64 Frances M. Smart MA 1964 *qv*

GLENNIE John Moray McGregor BL 1961

GLENNIE William MA 1967
s of William R. G. farm. and Annabel Chalmers; b Dinnet 30.10.46
teacher: Chryston 1969–71, spec asst Rosehill h s Coatbridge 1971–73, asst prin hist Coatbridge h s 1973–77, prin hist Portree h s from 1977

GLENTWORTH Garth William *MA 1965
s of Robert Glentworth PhD 1941 *qv*; b Aber 27.11.43
MIA(Col) 1967 DPhil(Oxon) 1977
post-grad stud.: Columbia univ 1965–66, Edin 1966–67, Linacre coll Oxford 1967–68, 1972–73; lect/res fell. Makerere univ Kampala, Uganda 1969–72; lect univ of Botswana, Lesotho and Swaziland, Roma, Lesotho 1972; inst of loc govt stud. Birm from 1973

GLOVER David Robert MA 1970
s of George G. teacher and Frances M. J. Longhurst nurse; b Knolton 22.7.46
teacher Salop c c (Market Drayton, Wellington, Cleobury Mortimer) from 1971
m Shrewsbury 2.9.68 Eveline M. Hitzinger teacher

GLOVER Douglas Dwight BSc(eng) 1968

GLOYER Robert Irvine MA 1957 LLB 1959
s of Marshall H. G. photographer and Lizzie I. Whent; b Aber 7.1.36
short serv comm Royal Ulster Rifles 1960–63; asst Allan, Black and McCaskie solic Elgin 1963–65; ptnr Teague,

Leonard & Muirhead (later Leonards) Hamilton from 1965
m Aber 6.4.61 Hilary A. Fethney MA 1959 *qv*

GLUCK Martha BSc 1960

GODDEN Michael John MB ChB 1968

GODFREY Michael Eric Ray BSc(for) 1967
s of Rex G. storeman and Olive M. Young stenographer; b Wellington NZ 26.5.42
BSc(Victoria NZ) 1964
NZ; dist for. King country 1967–70, scient, anim biol Rangiora 1970–73; MSc/PhD candidate ecology Davis, Calif (NZ govt burs/Jastro schol) from 1973
m Palmerston North NZ Anne C. Harris teacher d of Gordon S. H. BSc(Auck) Palmerston North

GOGOI Paramananda PhD 1966
MBBS(Assam)

GOLBY Sean Anderton *MA 1970

GOLDFARB Peter Samuel Gabriel *BSc 1966

GOLDIE Dorothy Muirhead *BSc 1970
d of Alexander G. BSc (Glas) headmaster and Janet M. Muirhead lect; b Edin 4.4.48
Dip Ed(Edin) 1972
field biol asst Field Stud. Council Malham 1970–71; teacher biol comp s Notts 1972–74, prin biol 1974–75
m Aber 28.8.72 Peter H. Dahl MA 1970 *qv*

GOLDIE Muriel Jean *MA 1966 Dip Ed 1967
d of Alexander G. MA(Glas) headmaster and Janet M. Muirhead lect; b Doncaster 12.4.44
teacher mod lang Thurso h s 1967–72, prin mod lang 1972–75
m Aber 14.7.71 Donald A. K. Murray farm. s of George D. K. M. Castletown

GOLDING Harry Sutherland Walpole MA 1966 Dip Ed 1972
s of Harry F. G. mech eng and Helen Sutherland bookkeeper/clerkess; b Glasg 15.1.21
lect Engl/gen stud. tech coll Aber from 1967
m Aber 10.7.54 Elaine T. Findlater teacher d of William A. M. F. Aber

GOLDSPINK Christopher Raymond MSc 1967
s of Eric C. G. CA and Mary M. Smith; b Leicester 25.2.44
BSc(St And) 1966 PhD(Liv) 1971
res fell. limnological inst Neths 1967–70; lect: Didsbury coll of educ Manc 1971–76, Manc poly from 1976
m Maltby 19.9.70 Kathleen U. Hancox BA(York) med soc worker

GOLDSTRAW Brian Richard *MA 1970
s of Richard H. G. sales rep, off. machine spec and Isobel M. Robertson typist; b Aber 20.12.46
asst postal controller Edin 1970–79, head of group from 1979
m Gladsmuir 22.5.76 Catherine W. Bruce BSc(Edin) postal serv d of Daniel C. B. Longniddry

GOMES Errol Henry BSc 1967 MB ChB 1971
s of Frank G. and Lilian Nunes; b Singapore 4.8.41
MRCOG 1977
Aber: h o Woodend hosp, ARI, mat. hosp 1971–73; m o Kandang Kerban hosp Singapore 1974–76; g p Linden Clinic Bundaberg Queensland Aust from 1976
m Wokingham 31.8.68 Margaret Read MA 1968 *qv*

GONNELLA Frances BSc 1961
d of Joseph F. G. elect. eng and Eliza W. Yeaman; b Bendochy 26.12.40
teacher: Dun 1962–68, Dartmouth, Nova Scotia from 1968
m(1) Blairgowrie 11.9.61 Anthony S. Campbell art teacher s of Aldo N. C. Kirkmichael; marr diss
(2) –.4.76 Harry C. H. Wallace bank man.

GONZALEZ Carlos Adolfo MSc 1967
s of Darwin G. bank man. and Maria C. Perez; b Montevideo Uruguay 17.11.29
FRSS 1977
lect universidad de la republica Uruguay 1968–73; statist INTA Castelar Argentina 1974–75; sen statist CNP-GL Embrapa Brasil from 1975
m Montevideo 5.4.62 Marta Diaz d of Wallace D. Montevideo

GOODALL Charles Morrison MA 1956
s of William G. foreman finisher (textiles) and Margaret I. Morrison; b Keith 1.2.35
sgt/instr (RAEC) mod lang King Richard's s Cyprus 1957–59; Perth: teacher Craigie s 1959–68, dep head Letham p s from 1968

GOODALL James Alexander BSc 1970
s of James G. farm worker and Grace Alexander shop asst; b Huntly 13.6.48
teacher sc Aberlour 1970–72, asst prin sc 1972–78, prin chem from 1978
m Rothiemay 22.7.72 Margaret A. Reid teacher d of Joseph R. Rothiemay

GOODALL John Charles *BSc(eng) 1969
s of John G. police off., teacher and Ethel Goddard; b Garforth 3.3.47
CEng MICE 1975
site civ eng Wirral 1969–73; eng asst Chester 1973–76; sen asst eng Carlisle from 1976
m Wirral 6.11.71 Lynn B. Morgan BEd (Lanc) teacher d of Thomas J. M. Wirral

GOODALL Thomas MA 1961
s of William G. shipyard worker, salesman and Jean King; b Glasg 7.1.29
teacher maths/sc Rhynie j s s 1963–65; head Eday South j s s 1965–72; teacher remed/ROSLA Kirkwall g s 1972–73, p s based Aberchirder from 1973
m Rothiemay 12.8.58 Phyllis J. Shearer MA 1957 *qv*

GOODBRAND Theodore Allan MB ChB 1960
s of George D. G. hydraulics eng and Mabel B. N. Smith shop asst; b Aber 9.1.36
Aber: h o city hosp, Woodend hosp 1960–61; g p Longside 1961–62, Mintlaw from 1962
m Aber 1958 Isabella G. Mitchell man. d of William M. Aber

GOODFELLOW Carol Ann MA 1969
d of John M. G. eng and Isabella Sutherland: b Inv 31.12.48
ALA(RGIT) 1970
sen asst lib Glenrothes 1970–72; asst lib Inv publ lib from 1972

GOODFELLOW Margaret Selbie MB ChB 1965
d Glasg 31.7.67 *AUR* XLII 187

GOODLAD Charles Alexander *MA 1965 PhD 1968
s of Henry G. fisherman and Williamina Guthrie; b Yell 19.9.43
Newfoundland: asst prof/res fell. fisheries geog St John's 1968–70, fishing capt Stephenville 1970–71; fishing tech FAO of UN Rome 1971–73, Casablanca 1973–74; reg dir Arabco Bahrain from 1974
m Gibraltar 17.12.73 Myrtha Magloire d of Paul E. M. NY

GOODLAD James Adam *MA 1965
s of Robert G. bank man. and Jemima B. Halcrow; b Crayford 5.3.38
teacher: Ayr acad 1966–69, prin geog St Joseph's acad Kilmarnock 1969–71, Cumnock acad from 1971
m Aber 20.7.67 Margaret E. Buchan BSc 1966 *qv*

GOODLAD Williamina Catherine MA 1968
d of William G. fisherman and Robina Smith; b Hamnavoe 21.5.47
teacher: Bathgate 1969–71, Edin 1971–73, exchange teacher Aust 1973–74, Edin from 1974

GOPAUL Jaygobin *MA 1970
s of Ramkwar G. chmn publ serv comm and Sonia Billoo; b Mauritius 21.11.44
teacher Fr Qn Eliz coll and Royal coll Port Louis from 1970
m Mauritius –.4.77 Karini Bhunjun secy d of Tarkeshwar B. Quatre-Bornes

GORDON Alexander *BSc(eng) 1961
MEng(Glas)

GORDON Alexander Lobban *MA 1958
s of George G. G. farm. and Elizabeth M. Lobban; b Grantown-on-Spey 12.4.35
DUP 1965
univ of Manit: lect Fr 1961–65, asst prof 1965–70, assoc prof from 1970

GORDON Allan Tawse BSc(eng) 1964
s of Thomas T. G. rly eng(E Af) and Florence M. Edward; b Methlick 15.8.43
RAF off.(navigator) UK, Singapore from 1965
m Dyce 12.7.66 Alison M. Milne teacher

GORDON Andrew George *BSc(agr) 1963 PhD 1968

GORDON Anne MA 1966

GORDON Anthony John MSc 1970
s of Bruce C. H. G. farm. and Lorna M. Harris; b Orange NSW Aust 7.10.46
B Rur Sc(New Eng) PhD(Guelph, Ont) 1974
sessional lect Guelph 1974; res fell. Wageningen, Netherlands 1974; then res scient Aust Wool Corp, Prospect
m Hobart Tasmania 29.12.70 Gwendolyn Bull BA(New England) teacher d of Peter C. A. B. Midway Point Tasmania

GORDON Barbara Katherine *BSc 1968
d of G. A. Douglas G. MB ChB(Edin) ultrasonic radiol and Hildegard M. Middleton SRN theatre sister; b Ealing 15.8.46
biochem Western Gen Hosp Edin 1969–71
m Richmond 28.9.68 Colin G. F. Brockie BSc(eng) 1963 *qv*

GORDON Catherine Dillon MA 1969
m Davidson

GORDON David Hendry MA 1969
s of William H. G. LDS(Edin) dent. surg and Charlotte Gauld; b Forres 28.5.46
timber yard lab Gothenburg Sweden 1970–72; teacher Hazlehead acad Aber from 1972
m Gothenburg 10.6.72 Pia E. Ander midwife d of J. Evert A. Gothenburg

GORDON Donald Ian MA 1964
s of Forbes R. G. master signwriter, comm artist and Eliza R. Robertson; b Becontree 12.12.30
SRN 1954 RMN 1957 BA(Strath) 1972
teacher Engl Airdrie 1965–69, spec asst Engl Larkhall 1969–70, asst prin Engl 1970–74, asst prin Engl Airdrie from 1974
m Bankhead 26.3.55 Winifred Grier SRN d of Andrew G. Ramelton Co Donegal

GORDON Eileen BSc 1962
d of James S. G. farm. and Georgina Bruce; b Rothienorman 13.9.41
teacher: Perth acad 1963–65, Aber h s for girls 1965–66, h s NY state USA 1966–70, Old Aber s 1970–71, part-time Mackie acad Stonehaven 1976–77
m Aber 28.7.66 Donald MacLaren BSc(agr) 1966 *qv*

GORDON Elizabeth MA 1969
m Johnstone

GORDON Frances Christina MA 1957
d of Robert G. farm. and Frances C. Gauld; b Drumlithie 26.11.36
Dip Secy Pract(St Godric's coll Lond) 1958
secy classics dept Edin univ 1958–59; teacher Lasswade p s 1962–67; teacher Engl/lib The Engl s Nicosia Cyprus 1967–71
m Aber 11.3.59 George L. Fraser BSc 1956 *qv*

GORDON George Park Douglas *BSc 1960
s of George P. G. fish salesman and Chrissie A. Douglas; b Peterhead 23.10.37
Grad RIC 1963 MRIC 1975 CChem 1975
teacher: sc Peterhead 1961–64, prin sc Dornoch 1964–67; asst advis sc Glasg 1967–69; HMIS W Scot 1969–73; HMIS Headquarters' staff Edin 1973–77; HMIS nat spec sc from 1977
m Aber 16.7.63 Karein L. M. Fraser teacher d of Hector M. F. Aber

GORDON George Philip MA 1968
s of George G. G. hotel wine cellarman and Mary S. Philip; b Aber 15.7.37
teacher Aber: Kirkhill p s 1969–72, Seaton p s 1972–76, The Hillocks p s Bucksburn from 1976
m Aber 17.7.74 Joan M. S. MacLachlan MA 1963 *qv*

GORDON Hugh MacLeod *BSc 1970
s of Ronald G. tweed mill man. and Ann MacLeod; b Stornoway 28.8.47
teacher biol Craigmount h s Edin 1971–72, asst prin biol 1972–76; asst exam off. SCE exam board from 1976
m Dirleton 8.7.72 Elsie P. J. Davidson BSc 1969 *qv*

GORDON Ian LLB 1963

GORDON Ian Livingstone MA 1958
s of John D. G. MB ChB 1925 *qv*; b Bolsover 15.2.31
MA(Edin) 1968
teacher Dalkeith 1959–69, prin teacher from 1969 then TEFL Lure, France
m Edin 18.3.61 Patricia C. A. Laidlaw MA(Edin) teacher d of John W. L. MB ChB(Edin) Edin

GORDON Irving Philip BL 1961
s of Albert G. footwear retailer and Rachael Greenstein; b Aber 31.3.40
Cert Indust Ad(Glas) 1963
Geo Bassett & Co Sheff: grad trainee, prod. man. 1963–65, pers/trg off. 1965–69; chmn/man. dir IPG group selection and search consult. Lond from 1969
m Lond 15.11.70 Jacqueline Sinclair p a d of John T. S. FRICS Surbiton

GORDON Jennifer Mirabelle MA 1967
d of John A. S. G. grain merch and Margaret M. G. Mitchell MA 1930 *qv*; b Inv 1.1.46
teacher: Inv 1968–70, Aber 1970–71, remed Aviemore from 1977
m Inv 1.8.70 Angus MacNeill MB ChB g p s of Duncan H. MacN. MA(Glas) Inv

GORDON Joan Elizabeth MA 1969
d of James A. G. LDS(Sheff) dental surg and Dorothy S. Sim market res; b Sheffield 26.9.47
teacher Edin 1971
m Aber 1968 Michael J. R. Stephen dentist s of William R. S. MB ChB 1940 *qv*

GORDON John Fraser MB ChB 1967
s of Robert A. G. foreman eng and Victoria W. Cruickshank tailoress; b Aber 13.4.43
DObstRCOG 1968
h o ARI med, surg, obst/gyn 1967–69; g p: Aber 1969–70, Peterborough from 1970
m Aber 1.9.65 Maureen C. Rae SRN d of Alexander R. Aber

GORDON Kathleen Elisabeth *MA 1969

GORDON Kenneth Ian *BSc(eng) 1956

GORDON Malcolm Niall Duncan *MA 1960

GORDON Margaret Anne *MA 1970
d of Alexander G. gen merch and Christina B. M. Duggie MA 1938 *qv*; b Nairn 28.1.48
Dip Soc Ad(Dund) 1971
soc worker Lisburn NI; med soc worker Newtonards hosp NI 1973–75
m Huntly 3.4.72 James M. Maybin asst prin soc worker s of Robert J. M. Belfast

GORDON Margaret Jean MA 1956
d of James A. G. gen merch and Isabella Russell; b Aber 19.3.35
teacher: Aber 1957–59, Toronto 1959–62, Sydney Aust 1963–64, Woking 1964–66, Sydney from 1966
m Rhynie 1.8.64 Errol S. Ward teacher s of Albert J. W. Sydney

GORDON Martin *BSc 1969
s of William M. G. car showroom attendant and Jamesina H. Bruce; b Aber 17.3.47
CPA 1975
tech asst to chartered patent ag Lond 1969–72, Glasg 1973–75; chart. pat. ag Glasg 1975–77; chart. pat. ag/ European pat. attorney Worthing from 1977
m Lond 27.6.70 Jacqueline M. Simpson BSc 1969 *qv*

GORDON Meriel *MA 1969
d of Ian Gordon MB ChB 1932 *qv*; b Aber 1.9.47
res asst econ univ of Essex 1969–70
m Aber 1.9.67 Gordon Barclay MB ChB 1967 *qv*

GORDON Nanette Lilian Margaret cMB ChB 1965
d of Harold G. G. and Hannah L. C. Stephen; b Aber 27.4.42
FFARCS 1969
h o Woodend hosp Aber, ARI 1965–66; anaest Aber hosps 1966–73
m Aber 16.7.65 Alan D. Milne MB ChB 1964 *qv*

GORDON Pamela Jane MA 1962
d of Alexander M. G. timber merch and Violet Scorgie comp dir; b Laurencekirk 29.1.42
teacher maths: Netherwood s for girls New Brunswick Canada 1963–64, acad head 1964–65, Montrose acad 1965–68
m Laurencekirk 14.6.68 Ian D. Salmon farm. s of John O. S. Montrose

GORDON Patricia Fairlie Leith MA 1966
d of William G. tel eng and Williamina S. Leith; b Wick 15.1.46
teacher: maths/phys city h s Chester 1967–69, maths/sc Northmead s s Guildford 1970–71, maths Guildford C of E s from 1971
m Aber 16.8.68 Derek Patch BSc(for) 1965 *qv*

GORDON Patricia Mary MB ChB 1965
d of Alexander M. G. timber merch and Violet Scorgie; b Laurencekirk 29.1.42
Memb Amer Psychiat Assoc
h o: Woodend hosp Aber, RAHC, RSC hosp Melbourne 1965–69; fell. haemat Melbourne 1969–70; resid, chief resid ch psych Baylor coll of med Houston Texas 1975–79
m Adelaide S Aust 18.2.69 Ian J. Butler MB BS(Adel) ch neurol univ of Texas s of John A. B. Adelaide

GORDON Robert Emslie MSc 1970 PhD 1975
s of Samuel M. G. superv Scot. gas board, re-instatement off. Greenock corp and Agnes M. McMaster midwife; b Gourock 6.8.46
BSc(Glas) 1968
res asst med phys Aberd 1970–75; res fell. phys univ of Kent from 1975

GORDON Robert Lennox MB ChB 1960
s of Robert G. MA 1909 *qv*; b Aber 23.11.36
DObstRCOG 1963
h o ARI 1960–63; lect path. Aberd 1963–67; g p: Wednesbury 1967–72, Buchlyvie 1972, Wolverhampton from 1972
m Aber 1.4.65 Laura Wallace nurs sister d of Douglas W. New Pitsligo

GORDON Rosemary Ellen BSc 1968
m Michie

GORDON Ross Barclay MB ChB 1967
s of Thomas B. G. MB ChB 1936 *qv*; b Cambridge 4.9.41
h o Peterborough 1967–68; g p Peterborough from 1968
m Downham Market 14.8.65 Helen M. Feetham d of Frederick J. F. Downham Market

GORDON Sheila Edward *MA 1964
d of Thomas T. G., PW insp E Af rlys, security off. and Florence M. Edward; b Aber 17.8.41
teacher hist Whitburn j s 1965–67; spec asst Whitburn acad 1967–72; prin hist Armadale acad 1972–78; prin guid Penicuik h s from 1978
m(1) Dyce 4.8.65 John Ward designer/graphic artist s of Arthur L. W. Ringwood
(2) Edin 9.7.77 Philip K. Templeton stud. Edin s of John T. Kirkcaldy

GORDON Shelagh Ann Ormond MA 1967 CASS 1969
d of Kenneth G. O. G. MB ChB(Edin) med pract and

Eileen P. Biggar; b Walton-on-Thames 1.10.46
soc worker Falkirk 1969–70, Aber 1970–71; sen soc worker Falkirk from 1971
m Alloa 11.9.70 Ian M. Prentice LLB 1969 *qv*

GORDON Valerie MA 1966
d of William S. G. bus driver, bus conductor and Jessie Garden; b Aber 26.9.42
MA(N Carolina)
teaching asst univ of N Carolina USA from 1978
m Aber 22.9.61 Colin D. Hall MB ChB 1966 *qv*

GORDON William *MA 1969

GORDON William Cleveland MB ChB 1959
s of Sydney C. G. journalist and Georgina E. McKay; b Tarbrax 3.10.35
DPM(Lond) 1969 MRANZCP 1971
surg/lt RN 1960–65; regist psychiat Sunnyside hosp, Christchurch NZ 1966–69, consult. psychiat from 1971
m Aber 28.12.62 Adrien V. Fitch MA(Canterbury) clin psych d of Lewis C. F. LLB(NZ) Christchurch NZ

GORIE James Sinclair *MA 1959

GORMAN Hugh MA 1966
s of Hugh G. bricklayer and Catharine McCallum; b Milngavie 20.7.29
teacher Castle Douglas from 1967

GORMAN Martyn Lee *BSc 1967 PhD 1970
s of John J. M. G. farm worker and Edna Fisher; b Holmfirth 15.11.44
lect biol univ S. Pacific Fiji 1970–73; lect zool Aberd from 1973
m Peterhead 27.7.68 Margaret Duthie teacher d of Wilson D. Peterhead

GORMLEY George Donald MB ChB 1960
s of George A. G. foreman baker and Marion F. Ferguson nurse; b Elgin 13.6.36
h o Woodend hosp Aber 1960–61; g p Lossiemouth from 1961; part-time m o blood transfusion serv Aber from 1960; part-time cas off. Dr Gray's hosp Elgin 1962–67
m Aber 28.2.59 Grace E. McLeod teacher d of Thomas McL. Dufftown

GORROD Kenneth Michael BSc 1964
s of George G. comp dir and Jean Gibb; b Aber 18.7.43
CA 1968
Lond: fin. acct Glaxo Group 1968–72; man. consult. Coopers & Lybrand 1972–75; fin. dir Airfix Prod. from 1975
m Aber 17.6.72 Fiona L. Galloway d of Harold W. G. Aber

GOSS-CUSTARD John Douglas PhD 1967
BSc(Brist)

GOTTFRIED Herbert PhD 1963
ARIC

GOTTS Ian *MA 1969 MLitt 1975

GOUDIE John Charles BSc 1959

GOUGH Adrian Christopher *BSc 1970

GOULD Grahame Warwick PhD 1959
BSc(Brist)

GOULD Richard John BSc(for) 1960
s of Walter H. G. tool maker, flt serg RAF, factory man. and Eveline M. Philpott; b Lond 15.3.39
for. off. Queensland dept of for. Aust from 1961
m Brisbane 20.9.69 Charlene A. Reynolds-Thompson BEd(Queensland) teacher d of Maurice R. J. R.-T. Brisbane

GOULDING Christopher John *BSc(for) 1968
s of Harry G. BEM W/O RAF and Phyllis Clare; b Barnsley 13.10.46
PhD(Br Col) 1972
asst lect fac for. Br Col 1971–72; scient for. res inst Rotorua NZ from 1972
m Inv 1967 Isobel P. Reid teacher d of John R. Avoch

GOVAN Eileen Tennant BSc 1969
m Grant

GOVE Robert BEd 1970
s of Robert G. fisherman and Marjory A. Lownie; b Gourdon 19.7.35
FSA Scot 1973
teacher: Achnamara resid s Argyll 1970–73, hist/mod stud. Peterhead acad from 1973

GOW David Drummond MA 1964

GOW Elspeth Jean Ann *MA 1970
d of Patrick H. G. bus. man. and Mary C. Shand bus. ptnr; b Grantown-on-Spey 14.10.47
m Gt Yarmouth 27.6.70 Louis M. Smith MA 1969 *qv*

GOW Kenneth Shiach *BSc(eng) 1969 MSc 1971
s of James G. insur salesman and Catherine R. Milton; b Elgin 17.5.47
basic grade phys ERI 1971–74; dev eng Sonicaid, Livingston from 1974
m Elgin 1971 Christine M. Mathieson pers off.

GOW Sheena MB ChB 1965 MD 1971
d of John G. agr eng and Margaret A. Stewart; b Aber 22.8.42
h o Aber hosps, Orkney 1965–68; res asst: Aberd 1968–70, univ of Ottawa 1971–75
m Aber 29.12.70 Albert A. Tuttle MA 1969 *qv*

GOWAN Alastair Campbell *BSc 1956 PhD 1959
s of Alexander E. G. BSc(Edin) headmaster and Agnes C. Johnston; b Aber 30.3.35
res fell. univ of BC 1960; GEC NY: res and marketing man. positions in chem businesses Mass., NY 1961–70; gen man. polyester bus. 1971–72; pres GE Plastics BV, Bergen op Zoom, Neths/chmn subsid comps in UK, France, Germany, Italy from 1972
m Pittsfield Mass. 19.2.66 Silvia I. Kember

GOWANS David MEd 1967
s of John G. comp dir and Elizabeth S. Stewart bank clerkess; b St Monance 1.11.27
BSc(St And) 1949 Dip Ed(St And) 1950
educ off. RAF 1950–56; teacher maths/sc Buckhaven 1957–62; prin biol Aber acad 1962–67, dep head Ruthrieston s s Aber 1967–71; rector Menzieshill h s Dun from 1971
m St Monance 2.8.52 Margaret W. H. Fyall teacher d of Thomas E. F. St Monance

GRACE Kenneth Frederick BSc 1968
s of Howard F. G. distillery worker and Jessie Young;

b Montrose 19.12.45
teacher chem Montrose acad 1968–74; asst prin sc Balwearie h s Kirkcaldy from 1974

GRACIE Ian *MA 1966

GRAHAM Alexander James MA 1969
s of Alexander G. cooper and Helen Falconer; b Banff 9.6.48
Fraserburgh: teacher 1970–71, spec s (m h) teacher from 1971

GRAHAM Alexandrina Macdonald MA 1956

GRAHAM Alexina MA 1961
d of George G. tweed weaver and Margaret Campbell; b Back 26.10.39
teacher: Dingwall acad 1962, Nicholson inst Stornoway 1962–67, temp posts Back and Tolsta s 1969–73, Nicolson Inst from 1973
m Back 29.8.64 John Graham joiner s of John G. Portnaguran

GRAHAM, Ann Elizabeth MA 1956
m Mackenzie

GRAHAM Carolyn Wendy *MA 1970
d of Joseph L. G. bank off. and Sheila M. Blackburn; b Kendal 1.5.47
Dip Ed(Cantab) 1971
commun serv: volunt with spastics Lanarksh 1971, mentally handicapped Portsmouth 1972; teacher Friends' s Wigton from 1972

GRAHAM Christine MA 1958
d of Robson G. met. off. and Margaret M. Mouat; b Carshalton 20.11.36
teacher: Fraserburgh 1959–62, Shetland 1962–69, Berlin 1969–71, Shetland 1972–73
m Lerwick 18.3.69 Sidney J. Carey commun eng s of John F. C. Thornton Heath

GRAHAM Donald Roderick BSc(eng) 1963

GRAHAM Elizabeth Jane MA 1969
m Edin 2.8.69 Christopher J. Ogilvie MA 1967 *qv*

GRAHAM Fiona Margaret MA 1970

GRAHAM George Paterson MA 1963
s of George G. chem worker and Dora L. Watt tailoress; b Aber 2.7.41
teacher: Insch 1964–68, Arbroath 1968–70; head: Gartly 1970–74, Aboyne p s from 1974
m Aber 4.8.65 Jennifer A. Pyper teacher p e d of Douglas P. Aber

GRAHAM Ian Wilson *MA 1970
s of James W. G. colliery clerk and Sarah I. Mason civ serv; b Edin 17.11.47
Dip LA(Edin) 1972
asst landscape arch. Livingston dev corp 1972–74, landscape arch. E Sussex c c Lewes from 1974

GRAHAM James Gordon *BSc 1970

GRAHAM Janet Sutherland BEd 1968

GRAHAM Margaret MA 1962
d of George G. tweed weaver and Margaret Campbell; b Back 6.11.41
teacher: Engl Glasg 1963–69, part time from 1973
m Glasg 6.8.65 John A. MacLean catering off. s of Murdo MacL. N Tolsta

GRAHAM Marjory Helen MA 1956
m Mowat

GRAHAM Moray Keillour *MA 1960
s of Reginald M. G. BA(Oxon) for. off. Kenya and Vera I. Ogle; b Nairobi 7.10.33
Dip Trop Ag(Trinidad) 1958
asst man.: Lobe estate Brit Cameroons 1956–60, Pamol estate N Borneo 1960–63; man. Sabah Palm estate Sabah 1963–77; consult. Agrotech Assoc Kota Kinabalu Malaysia from 1978
m Moniaive 12.6.75 Alison W. Gourlay d of James G. Thornhill

GRAHAM Thomas Carmichael *MA 1956
s of John M. G. MA(Glas) prof of theol Aberd and Jessie H. Carmichael MA(Glas) teacher; b Clydebank 2.7.34
FI Pers Man. 1968
pilot RAF 1956–58; ICI pers man. posts Teesside, Grangemouth, Huddersfield, Manc, Ayrsh 1958–72, head of pers Hiram Walker (Scot.) Dumbarton 1972–74; pers man. Ciba-Cegy (UK) pigments div Paisley from 1974
m Aber 11.7.58 Jean J. Cran MA 1954 *qv*

GRAINGER Maureen Campbell MA 1966
m Morrow

GRANT Adrian *BSc 1970
s of Frederick A. G. off. serv and trans man. AA Manc and Winifred E. Pritchard; b Shawford 9.2.47
Manc: clerk dom contr dept NORWEB 1970–71, costing asst/stock controller HGV repair garage W. H. Cowburn & Cowpar chem mfrs Trafford Park from 1971
m Aber 20.8.71 Elizabeth D. Paterson teacher d of David P. Cumnock

GRANT Alan Bryce MA 1968 LLB 1970
s of Peter B. G. linotype oper and Margaret M. C. Bell; b Falkirk 17.8.47
estate duty off. Edin 1971; law app, solic Cumbernauld dev corp 1972–74; solic Aber town c 1974–75; prin leg. asst Gordon dist c from 1975
m Aber 1971 Eileen Cooney MA 1970 *qv*

GRANT Alan James BSc(eng) 1968 *1969
s of Kathleen M. Grant secy; b Cardiff 31.12.46
MSc(Cranfield inst of tech Bedford) 1971
Shell: res scient Thornton res centre Chester 1971–75, sen res scient The Hague from 1975
m Wilmslow 11.12.71 Elizabeth D. Saxon FSRTD teacher of radiography

GRANT Alasdair MacArthur *MA 1969
s of Kenneth G. estate handy man and Margaret MacArthur; b Glasg 2.12.35
teacher: Engl/Gaelic Daliburgh S Uist 1970–72, Engl Glasg 1972–74, Lochgilphead from 1974

GRANT Alasdair Reid BSc 1969

GRANT Alexander *MA 1957
s of John C. G. postman and Margaret L. Grant clerkess; b Rothes 13.10.35
DIC 1959
scient off. UKAEA Dounreay 1958–60; lect: Thurso tech coll 1960–63, Nat coll of agr eng Silsoe 1963–75; sen lect s of agr eng Cranfield inst of tech from 1975

m Silsoe 1.1.72 Anne J. Tucker dom bursar d of John R. T. Silsoe

GRANT Alexander MA 1964

GRANT Alexander James MA 1969
s of James G. acct and Maria Morales; b Colombia S Amer 28.6.48
distrib man.: Newcastle-u-Tyne 1969–70, Wakefield 1970–72; reg distrib man. Glasg 1972–75; Lond: plan. man. 1975–78, comm man. from 1978
m Durham Marian Appleby teacher

GRANT Alison Elizabeth MA 1969
d of Alexander N. G. post./tel off. and Annie M. Pirie typist; b Aber 12.1.48
asst edit.: *Hospital & Health Services Purchasing*, inst of health serv admin Lond 1970–78; stud. Aber coll of comm (post-grad biling secy course) 1979; admin asst Peacock Printmakers Aber from 1980

GRANT Calum Roderick *MA 1968 Dip Ed 1969
s of Calum M. G. bldg consult. and Elaine C. Fraser; b Edin 10.8.46
teacher: Stornoway p s 1969–72 and from 1974; remed teacher Is of Lewis 1972–74

GRANT David Iain Montgomery MA 1965 BD 1968
s of Clifford M. G. wholesale confectioner and Edith M. Taylor teacher; b Glasg 3.1.42
C of S min: asst Cathcart old parish Glasg 1968–69, Trinity ch Dalry from 1969

GRANT David Renwick MA 1963
s of Leslie R. G. timber ag and Amy B. Macdonald; b Edin 5.5.41
MSc(Edin) 1969
farm./sheep shearing Aust 1963–65; warden RSPB Loch Garten 1966; asst reg off. nature conservancy Perthsh 1969–73; exped leader Quest 4 Algeria, Niger, Mali, Upper Volta, Ivory Coast, Mauretania 1974–76; crofter/fisherman Is of Skye from 1977
m Portree 28.4.78 Catherine E. S. Cochrane d of George S. C. Southampton

GRANT Doris Margaret MA 1969
m Strachan

GRANT Elaine Margaret MA 1965
d of James C. G. edit. *Press & Journal* Aber and Hilda L. Gordon; b Aber 15.5.44
Dip Soc Ad(Dund) 1966 Cert Med Soc Work(Edin) 1967
med soc worker: Hull RI, Cardiff RI, Southampton RI, ARI, Lond, mat. hosp Aber 1968–72; generic soc worker Hammersmith soc serv Lond 1972–74; trg and recruitment off. Fulham Lond 1974–76
m(2) Lond 14.6.75 John M. King soc worker, trg off., child care man., lect Aberd s of Leslie K. Lond

GRANT Elizabeth Helen BSc 1967 Dip Ed 1968
d of James G. security off. and Elizabeth C. MacBeth quality controller; b Aber 12.1.46
teacher maths: Northfield s Aber 1968–69, Bellahouston acad Glasg 1969–72; part time Penilee s Glasg from 1972
m Glasg 30.12.71 Roderick A. C. Murray merch seaman s of Thomas G. M. Glasg

GRANT Elizabeth Jane MA 1967

GRANT Elspeth Anne *BSc 1967
m Cooke

GRANT Eric George *MA 1967

GRANT Fiona Christine *MA 1962
d of Ian W. G. navig off. merc marine and Emily W. Salmon restaurant man.; b Farnborough 22.9.40
teacher phys/maths: Aber 1963–65, f e 1965–66, part-time (mostly evening classes) 1968–74; part-time tut. phys OU from 1971
m Kent 25.7.64 Henry O. Cameron BL 1961 *qv*

GRANT Gordon Duncan BSc 1966
s of Duncan G. loc govt off. and Williamina Blackley; b Hamilton 12.10.43
MBA(W Aust) 1978
electronics eng Maidenhead 1966–68; computer syst eng Lond 1968–72; Perth Aust: sen syst analyst 1972–76, computer syst man. from 1976
m Perth W Aust 25.8.78 Lorraine J. Walker dep prin p s d of Clifford W. Geraldton W Aust

GRANT Gregory Vincent MA 1959 cLLB 1961
s of Gregory V. G. and Mary H. Dawson; b Aber 26.12.37
solic Milne & Reid Aber from 1961

GRANT Helen Isobel BSc 1956
d of Benjamin G. tailor and Jane A. Forbes; b Forres 24.4.34
teacher maths Perth h s 1957–60
m Forres 24.9.60 George A. W. Ferguson farm. s of William F. F. Forres

GRANT Ian BSc 1959 *1963

GRANT Ian MA 1960 LLB 1962
s of Archibald S. G. butcher and Elspeth Johnston; b Aber 11.11.38
law app Aber 1961–64; leg. asst Kincardine-on-Forth 1964–69; lands off. Blantyre Malawi from 1969
m Blantyre 5.5.73 Rahima Bhatti

GRANT Ian Alisdair Macgregor *BSc 1964
s of Ian G. lect Aber coll of educ and Gladys D. Tullo typist; b Edin 31.12.42
Kodak, Harrow: res 1964–66, prod. technol from 1966
m Aber 6.3.67 June M. Lumsden MA 1966 *qv*

GRANT Ian Herbert Wynne Macdonald *BSc 1964 Dip Ed 1965 MSc 1970

GRANT Ishbel Sinclair MA 1961
d of Paul G. bar man. and Margaret J. Watson; b Invergordon 15.9.40
teacher Torry acad Aber from 1962
m Aber 27.3.64 John Fraser letterpress machineman s of John F. Aber

GRANT James Alexander *BSc 1957

GRANT James Allister *BSc(agr) 1957
s of James A. G. slater and Margaret J. Walker; b Aber 14.11.33
BLitt(Oxon) 1959
lect Cheshire coll of agr from 1960
m 2.1.60 Sheila M. Johnston lib

GRANT Kathleen Margaret *BSc 1956
d of David H. S. G. coach bldr and Margaret L. Norrie clerk; b Aber 20.10.33
statist Coats res lab Paisley 1956–67; teacher maths/sc Westwood s Reading 1957–58; asst exper off. AWRE Aldermaston 1958–61; Basingstoke: teacher maths Richard Aldworth s 1972–77, N Foreland Lodge from 1977
m Aber 24.7.57 Thomas O. Young BSc 1956 *qv*

GRANT Leslie Craib *MA 1970 Dip Ed 1971
s of John G. master blacksmith and Annie Leslie; b Lumphanan 14.4.29
teacher Engl/hist Torry acad Aber from 1971
m Fraserburgh 10.9.53 Sheila Doig waitress d of Robert D. Fraserburgh
d Aber 19.2.76 *AUR* XLVI 418

GRANT Lilian Ann MA 1964
d of William W. G. lab and Lily A. G. Kinnaird; b Aber 19.3.43
teacher: Toronto 1966–70, Aber 1970–73
m Aber 6.8.65 John T. Brebner asst controller city police Aber s of John T. B. Aber

GRANT Linda Mary MA 1964
d of George R. G. MA(Glas) headmaster and Catherine M. Morrison MA 1933 *qv*; b Aber 4.4.43
teacher: St Faith's prep s for boys Cambridge 1965–66, Speedwell inf s Littlemore Oxon 1967, Albyn s for girls Aber 1967–69
m Grantchester 8.8.66 Donald J. Morrison MA 1965 *qv*

GRANT Lionel MB ChB 1956

GRANT Margaret Henrietta *MA 1967 Dip Ed 1968
d of Alexander J. G. farm. and Marjory P. Watt; b Dufftown 4.5.46
teacher: Bankhead acad 1968–71, part time Fleetwood 1974–75, Mytchett from 1975
m Aber 20.7.70 Charles W. Lyon Dean MB ChB 1971 army m o s of William J. L. D. MB ChB 1933 *qv*

GRANT Margaret Isabel *MA 1961
d of Ian H. G. farm. and Isabella Milne MA 1930 *qv*; b Elgin 28.2.39
Dip Sec St(Lond) 1962
prod./edit. asst OUP Lond 1962–64; teacher: Lond 1964–65, Bournemouth 1965–66
m Urquhart 22.12.64 Ralph J. Woodward BSc(City) syst analyst s of William H. W. Doncaster

GRANT Margaret Mary MA 1969
d of John G. gen merch and Mary J. Reid; b Tomnavoulin 19.12.25
med secy, translator, teacher Kinshasa univ Zaire 1970–73; teacher mod lang Lawside acad Dun 1974–76; asst prin mod lang St John's s Dun 1976–78, prin mod lang from 1978

GRANT Mavis *MA 1960
m Elrick

GRANT McGregor Thom BL 1958

GRANT Michael Murray MA 1964
b Aber 8.11.41
FRSA 1968
sales man. Birm 1972–73; group dev exec Lond 1973–75; teacher Staines 1975–77; bus. dev exec Colchester/Lond 1977–78; sen res exec Lond from 1978

GRANT Moira Booth MA 1959
m Ewen

GRANT Moira Elizabeth BSc 1968
d of James G. bank clerk, farm. and Patricia M. Newbery nurse; b Keith 9.3.48
teacher: Banff 1969–71, Aberlour, Tomintoul 1971–73, Tomintoul from 1974
m Tomintoul 14.8.71 Ian A. Mathieson farm. s of John M. Tomnavoulin

GRANT Morag Henrietta Kerr MA 1966
d of Robert G. van salesman and Maisie M. Martin factory superv; b Fyvie 23.2.46
teacher Ayr: 1966–69, hist and asst prin guid from 1969
m Ayr 5.7.71 Robert R. Gibson apron operative s of John G. Ayr

GRANT Neil Farquharson MA 1968

GRANT Norman Marshall MB ChB 1956
s of Robert F. G. man. dir/pharm and Doris M. Gable; b Aber 20.7.26
h o sen h o Woodend hosp Aber, Lond, Essex 1956–58; g p Grays 1958–59, Rochester from 1959
m Aber 5.12.53 Dorothy S. G. Banks DA med secy d of Robert B. St Margaret's Hope

GRANT Raymond James Shepherd *MA 1964
s of Bertie J. G. MA 1922 *qv* and Mabel S. Milne MA 1930 *qv*; b Aber 26.5.42
PhD(Cantab) 1971
Edmonton asst prof 1967–74, assoc prof dept Engl from 1974
m Vancouver 22.12.73 Pauline (Pieterke) Pearl Kits Dip Chr Educ (Emmaus coll, Oak Park Illinois) girls' club rep B.C. d of G. B. K. Red Deer Alta

GRANT Robert Morrison MB ChB 1970
s of George R. G. MA(Glas) headmaster and Catherine M. Morrison MA 1933 *qv*; b Aber 17.5.46
h o ARI 1970–71, res fell. surg Aberd 1971–72; regist path. Wester I Glasg 1972–74; lect path. Glas from 1974
m Irvine 15.1.73 Joan C. Paton teacher d of Andrew P. Irvine

GRANT Ronald Alexander BSc 1958 *1959

GRANT Ronald Clark *MA 1968
s of George A. G. insur off. and Margaret S. Clark; b Elgin 19.5.44
post-grad res Glas 1968–71; tut. hist Glas 1968–71; teacher AGS from 1972
m Aber 6.4.68 Audrey A. Menzies teacher d of John A. M. Elgin

GRANT Ronald William MB ChB 1967

GRANT Ruth Margaret MB ChB 1970
m Collins

GRANT Sheila Margaret MA 1965

GRANT Sheila Margaret MA 1966
d of Archibald G. H. G. MA(Edin) min of relig and Dorothy J. Paterson BSc(Glas) teacher; b Dunfermline 9.11.45
Dip Ed(Edin) 1967
teacher Peterculter p s 1967–74
m Aber 17.7.70 George E. Robertson MA 1970 *qv*

GRANT Victor Norman MA 1963

GRANT Wilma Forrest *MEd 1965
d of James W. G. bank off. and Mary B. Forrest; b Keith 1.11.37
BA(NZ) 1961 BSc(Auck) 1971 MB ChB(Auck) 1973
NZ: teacher Engl/Fr Wellington E girls' coll 1966–67; h o Cook hosp Gisborne 1974; m o NZ Red Cross S Vietnam 1975; h o RACH 1975; med pract NZ from 1976

GRANT Wilma Taylor MA 1970

GRASSICK Brian Douglas Miller MB ChB 1961
s of Charles D. G. comp rep and Joan Miller; b Aber 13.5.34
DObstRCOG 1965
h o ARI 1962–63, Kuching/Miri gen hosps Sarawak, Borneo 1963–64; sen h o obst Forth Park mat. hosp Kirkcaldy 1964–65; regist obst/gyn Princess Margaret hosp Nassau, Bahamas 1965–67; med advis Hoechst pharm Lond 1967–70; g p Slough from 1970 and part time indust m o with Slough indust health serv from 1970
m Aber 24.6.65 Annette Foo tel superv d of Francis F. Kuching

GRASSICK Kenneth Alan MB ChB 1966
s of Charles D. G. comp rep and Joan Miller; b Aber 7.6.35
h o Aber hosps 1967–68; m o, sen m o RAF Singapore, England 1968–73; g p Newcastle-u-Tyne from 1973

GRASSIE Alexander Donald Campbell *MA 1957
s of James C. G. DSc 1945 *qv*; b Aber 4.4.35
BA(Cantab) 1959 PhD(Cantab) 1962 FInstP 1979
lect phys Sus from 1962
m 1960

GRATTON Samuel Douglas Walls MA 1961
s of Samuel G. bldg contr and Priscilla L. Walls; b Glasg 5.3.37
tv prod.: Europe 1964–66, NYC, USA from 1966

GRAVES Peter Arthur *MA 1966

GRAVES Rodney James *MA 1970 Dip Ed 1971

GRAY Albert BSc(eng) 1960

GRAY Alexander *MA 1970

GRAY Alison Catherine MA 1969
d of Edward G. comp dir and Muriel W. Fraser MA 1938 *qv*; b Aber 3.9.48
teacher Aber from 1970
m Aber 7.8.70 Eric E. Lachowski BSc 1970 *qv*

GRAY Catherine Jennifer MA 1970
d of Robert A. A. G. stockbroker and Susannah I. H. Thomson; b Glasg 6.4.49
Dip Sec St(Strath) 1971
secy: Ethicon Edin 1971–72, to man. dir Noble Grossart from 1972
m Edin 22.6.74 Anthony D. D. MacIver LLB(Edin) solic s of Donald D. MacI. Edin

GRAY Daniel BL 1959
d Aber 11.6.61 *AUR* xxxix 205

GRAY Derek William George MB ChB 1963
s of William G. house carpenter and Helen R. Sherriffs; b Aber 28.4.38
h o ARI 1963–64; trainee g p Aber 1964–65; regist paediat RACH 1965–69; g p Aber from 1969
m Aber 1.4.64 Allison Easton teacher d of Charles C. E. Aber

GRAY Doreen Watson *MA 1966
d of James A. G. slater and Barbara J. Lovie factory worker; b Aber 18.11.43
HM insp taxes Aber, Lond 1966–72, higher grade from 1972

GRAY Elma *MA 1956
m Howitt

GRAY Evelyn Mary Stewart BSc 1967

GRAY Gordon *MA 1967

GRAY Helen BSc 1966
d of Alexander S. G. barman and Williamina Marr; b Aber 27.3.45
res poultry res centre Edin 1967–68; teacher: Armadale acad W Lothian 1968–69, Edin 1969–71
m Aber 19.7.69 Barry O. Hughes BA(Cantab) vet res off. s of Leslie E. H. Cambridge

GRAY Ian MA 1969 *1971
s of Charles G. P.O. tel and Elizabeth I. Kiloh; b Aber 20.6.48
teacher maths Rubislaw acad Aber 1972–75; asst prin maths Kincorth acad Aber from 1975

GRAY Ian Alexander MB ChB 1970
s of Alexander G. civ eng and Grace M. E. Jaffray; b Aden Saudi Arabia 28.1.45
LMCC
h o: Gilbert Bain hosp Lerwick 1970–71, city hosp Aber 1971; g p: Thompson Manitoba 1971–73, Alliston Ontario from 1973
m London –.10.65 Ellen M. McDonagh secy d of William McD. Lond

GRAY Ian Gibson MA 1965 LLB 1967

GRAY Ian Nicol MA 1968

GRAY Ian Sharp BSc 1956
s of John G. MA 1930 *qv* and Margaret C. Black MA 1929 *qv*; b Scalloway 27.4.36
soldier Munster Lager Germany 1956–58; teacher: Lerwick 1959–62, Scalloway from 1972
m Lerwick 4.4.60 Marina J. Burgoyne hairdresser, secy d of Robert C. M. B. Lerwick

GRAY Isabel Anne MA 1969
d of Robert G. MA(Glas) C of S min and Johanna I. M. Morison teacher dom sc; b Harthill 17.4.48
teacher Fr: Glenrothes 1969–71, Alloa 1972–73
m Stonehaven 29.12.71 David W. Hay BA(Stir) scient civ serv s of Andrew A. H. St Fillans

GRAY Isobel Stewart MA 1962
d of Alexander J. G. baker, NFU branch secy and Christina S. Stewart shop asst, secy; b Aber 18.11.41
teacher Engl/Lat Fraserburgh acad 1963–64, Alford s 1964–67; part-time remed teacher Alford acad 1972–77, full time from 1977
m Alford 7.8.65 William J. Balfour painter/decorator s of William J. B. Alford

GRAY James *BSc 1963 MSc 1965
s of James F. G. master painter and Gladys Robertson mus teacher; b Fort George 9.1.41
lect Aberd 1967–68; temp teacher Bervie 1968–69; div man. Rockfall, Glasg 1969–71, comp dir site explor serv Aber 1971–74; comp man. dir Grampian Soil Surv Aber from 1974
m Tomintoul 29.7.67 Rhoda V. Murray BSc 1968 *qv*

GRAY James Anthony MA 1959
s of James M. G. master draper and Monica M. McKay teacher; b Dufftown 20.6.37
teacher maths Hilton acad Aber 1960–70, Cults acad from 1970
m Huntly 12.7.61 Margaret G. Grant teacher home econ d of William M. G. Huntly

GRAY James Duncan *MA 1970
MSc(Wales) 1971
statist civ serv from 1971; resid Newport Gwent

GRAY James Millar *MA 1965
s of James M. G. chief eng MN and Jane W. Bate; b Dun 8.11.43
RN instr lt 1966–71; teacher: asst prin Engl Harris acad Dun from 1971

GRAY James Telfer *MA 1964

GRAY Janet McNaught *MA 1970
d of Colin M. G. civ serv and Murdina McArthur SRN: b Glasg 22.5.49
Dip Bible Coll of Wales 1976
teacher Gaelic Stornoway 1971–74, lang Barra 1976–78, Gaelic/r e Stornoway from 1978

GRAY Janice Margaret BEd 1970

GRAY Jean Elizabeth *MA 1965
d of John G. G. MA 1914 *qv* and Ida J. Cumming MA 1934 *qv*; b Aber 20.11.43
teacher Engl: West Calder h s 1966–70, Woodmill h s Dunf 1970–72, Notre Dame h s Dumbarton from 1972
m Aber 1.8.72 Keith P. Bear MA 1965 *qv*

GRAY John Alexander MA 1969
s of Robert G. prof and tech off. eng div M o D and Annie J. Shand civ serv D o E dept; b Colombo Ceylon 20.3.48
teacher Engl subj: Queen Anne h s Dunfermline 1970–73, St Andrew's Scots s Buenos Aires from 1973
m Kirkcaldy 3.4.72 Margaret A. Bogie BEd(Edin) teacher d of John B. Kirkcaldy

GRAY John Peter Shaw *MA 1970
s of John H. G. MA 1932; b Aber 11.3.47
LLB(Edin) 1972
law app Edin 1972–74, solic Gray & Kellas advoc Aber from 1974
m Larbert 4.6.77 Lesley A. Reid LLB(Glas) solic d of James B. R. Larbert

GRAY Joseph BSc(eng) 1964
s of Joseph G. motor eng and Anne J. Smith; b Lerwick 6.8.42
MICE 1976
asst eng Zetland c c Lerwick 1964–75; dep dir construct. Shetland Is c from 1975
m Hillswick 4.7.67 Agnes H. Williamson teacher d of Robert J. W. Ollaberry

GRAY Laurence MA 1966
s of John G. eng and Margaret S. Gibson; b Musselburgh 19.1.40
LTCL (speech) 1968 LGSM (drama) 1971 ADBEd (drama) 1973
Aber: teacher Engl 1967–69, sp and drama 1969–71; asst organis sp and drama 1971–76; advis drama Grampian reg c from 1976
m Aber 7.7.69 Elizabeth S. Whiteford MB ChB 1967 *qv*

GRAY Laurina Gilberta Elizabeth MA 1966
d of Robert G. quartermaster and Ann Christie; b Vidlin Shetland 10.12.43
lib asst Aber publ lib 1966–67; tax off. Inl Rev Welwyn Garden City from 1974
m Aber 4.3.67 Hennessey A. S. Thompson BA(Durh) CA s of James T. Freetown Sierra Leone

GRAY Margaret Reid Russell MA 1962
d of Andrew J. M. G. grocer, clerk and Margaret R. Russell comptometer oper; b Aber 23.3.41
teacher: Engl Aber acad 1963–64, jun s RGC Aber 1964–69, remed Kirkhill p s Aber from 1974
m Aber 6.8.65 Derek J. Murison marine biol s of David R. M. New Pitsligo

GRAY Marilyn MA 1969

GRAY Marjory MA 1968
d of Magnus H. G. fish merch and Elaine M. Martin; b Aber 12.5.48
m Aber 29.12.67 Myles D. G. Hardie MA 1969 *qv*

GRAY Monica Mary MA 1966
d of James M. G. draper and Monica McKay teacher; b Dufftown 18.1.46
welfare off. Ayrsh 1967–68; soc worker Highland reg from 1979
m Aber 6.8.69 Neil S. Campbell teacher s of Thomas S. C. Ayr

GRAY Patricia BSc 1963
d of John G. provender miller and Williamina S. Banks printer's asst; b Aber 4.3.42
teacher maths: Barstable s Basildon 1965–66, Kaimhill s Aber 1968, Portobello s 1969, Forester s Edin 1969–73, Kincorth acad Aber 1973–79, Westhill acad Skene from 1979
m Aber 7.8.64 John W. Ritchie BSc 1964 *qv*; marr diss 1972

GRAY Peter Stuart *BSc(eng) 1968

GRAY Roger Woodville BSc(agr) 1960
s of Donald G. MA(Oxon) headmaster Bootham s York and Janet K. Wright teacher: b York 30.8.34
Dip Agr(NOSCA) 1957 Nat Dip Agr 1957 DTA(Trin) 1962
Kenya: agr res off. min of agr Kakamega, Kisii 1962–67, res off. E Af Tanning Extract comp Eldoret 1967–72, man. seeds plant Kenya Seed comp Nakuru from 1972
m Heywood 16.7.60 Johanna E. U. M. Ehrhardt MB ChB 1960 *qv*

GRAY Russell MA 1968
s of Andrew J. M. G. clerk and Margaret R. Russell; b Aber 14.6.47
AGS: teacher, asst prin guid, prin guid, from 1969
m Aber 8.4.72 Sheila C. G. Baxter teacher d of Alexander B. Aber

GRAY Sandra BSc 1966 Dip Ed 1967
d of Alexander M. G. butcher shop man. and Agnes M. Stephen; b Aber 10.4.45
teacher maths Summerhill s s Aber 1967–70; teacher maths/asst house mistress Windsor g s Hamm Germany 1970–74, head maths dept from 1974

GRAY Sheenagh Mabel *BSc 1956
d of Thomas G. farm. and Elizabeth M. G. Scott tailoress; b Dyce 8.10.34
res biol: MRC AERE Harwell 1956–58, plant breeding Pentlandfield 1958–60; teacher sc Inv h s 1960–62
m Aber 1.10.60 James Fitzpatrick indust photogr s of Patrick F. Dun

GRAY Walter BSc 1966

GRAY Walter Bignell MA 1956

GRAY William Gavin MA 1969 LLB 1971
s of William G. eng and Gladys M. Taylor; b Aber 14.11.48
law app Aber 1972–73; ptnr Kinnear & Falconer solic Stonehaven 1973–75; dir Royal Deeside Inns (Northern) from 1975
m Aber 6.7.71 Pamela H. Jowett LLB 1970 *qv*

GRAY William Hugh BSc 1964
s of John Gray MA 1930 *qv* and Margaret C. Black MA 1929 *qv*; b Scalloway 13.8.40
phys: Glasg 1964–68, Leic from 1968
m Leicester 9.7.66 Anne P. Sharp lib d of Leonard E. S. Leicester

GRAY William Robert MA 1967
s of John H. G. carpenter/boat bldr and Mary S. Anderson; b Baltasound Shetland 21.12.44
teacher: Perthsh 1968–75, central reg Scot. 1975–77; head p s Cunningsburgh from 1977
m Killin 12.7.71 Margaret J. Lindsay teacher d of Michael L. Edin

GREEN Andrew Braham *MA 1968
s of Henry G. clerk and Edith Pinkus; b Lond 29.4.45
Dip Pers Man (LSE) 1969
pers off. Masson Scott eng Lond, Brist 1969–73; pers man.: J Blakeborough eng W Yorks 1974–78, Stone Platt eng Crawley from 1978
m Helsinki Finland -.7.71 Riitta K. Salonen

GREEN Anne Mitchell *MA 1970
d of James G. MA 1929 *qv*; b Buckie 26.5.47
PhD(Cantab) 1975
grad stud. Girton coll Cantab 1970–73; lect LSE from 1973
m 21.6.75 J. B. Bullen MA(Cantab)

GREEN Christopher Stephen BSc 1970
s of Frederick R. G. sales consult. and Dorothy E. T. Trobe; b Edgware, 29.8.48
Lond: articled clerk CA's off. 1970–73, exec off. in P.O. (telecomms fin.) from 1973

GREEN Dorothy LLB 1968
d of Raymond G. gen man. and Louise G. Strachan; b Aber 15.2.47
law app Aber 1968–70; leg. asst: Glasg 1970–74, part-time Aber from 1975
m Aber 5.9.70 Ronald S. C. Shanks CA s of Robert I. S. Dullatur

GREEN William Innes BSc(eng) 1964
s of Richard G. G. master joiner and Isabella Middleton, b Tarland 17.2.42
Birm: grad app 1964–65, prod. quality eng 1965–67; Dun: indust eng 1967–68, asst head indust eng 1968–72; man. MFG eng Waterloo, Canada 1972; head distribution Dun from 1973
m Ballater 25.9.65 Jennifer M. Bruce secy d of George O. B. Ballater

GREENHALGH James Francis Derek PhD 1959
s of Cecil G. sales man. and Phyllis Woodmass buyer in dept store; b Frodsham 4.10.32
BA(Cantab) 1953 MA 1957 MS(Illinois) 1954
lect agr chem Edin 1959–63; Rowett res inst Aber: head pasture util sect. 1963–66, head cattle sect. 1966–70, dep head of dept from 1970
m Aberystwyth 4.10.58 Isoline Gee PhD 1958 *qv*

GREENLEES Charles Victor MA 1967

GREENSHIELDS Irene MA 1969
d of Frank G. gents' outfitter and Williamina Fraser; b Cambuslang 3.5.48
Glasg: teacher 1969–70, 1971–73, asst prin mod lang from 1973
m Burnside 29.2.72 Alan S. Muir dir s of David M. Glasg

GREENSHIELDS Robert Archibald *BSc 1958

GREENSMITH Isobel Moyra *BSc 1968
d of Leonard A. G. BSc 1928 *qv*; b Fowlis Easter 19.1.46
teacher maths Aber acad later Hazlehead acad 1969–74
m Aber 3.1.69 Christopher B. Howard BSc 1966 *qv*

GREENWELL George Rodney Lyndon BSc(eng) 1965

GREENWOOD Duncan Joseph PhD 1957 DSc 1973
s of Herbert J. G. customs and excise and Alison Fairgrieve MA(Liv); b New Barnet 16.10.32
BSc(Liv) 1954 Sir Gilbert Morgan medal of soc of chem indust 1962
res fell. Aberd 1957–58; nat vegetable res stat Wellesbourne, Warwick: s o chem sect. 1959–62, s s o 1962–66, head chem sect. 1966–74 (hon lect Birm from 1969 and Leeds from 1974), s p s o and head soil sc from 1974

GREGORY Angela Christine BSc 1965
d of Andrew D. G. MA(Glas) acct, comptroller AEI (Rugby) and Isabel M. Johnston; b Rugby 10.2.44
asst market res Ilford, Ilford 1965–66; econ/corporate plan. Nairn Williamson (Holdings) Kirkcaldy 1966–68
m Kinross 28.9.68 John R. Crossland BA(Durh) market res off, marketing man. s of Harold C. Barnsley

GREGORY Tudor John *MA 1966
s of Griffith J. G. bank man. and Phyllis M. Jennings secy; b Bristol 20.9.42
pers man. ICI: Runcorn 1966–70, Brussels 1970–72, Runcorn 1972–77, Kenya 1977–79, Widnes from 1979
m Widnes 6.6.70 Brigid M. Roach secy, receptionist d of William R. Widnes

GREIG Allan BSc 1962
s of Thomas G. and Isabella McAllan; b Aber 1.12.40
teacher: S. Queensferry 1963–65, Chingola, Zambia 1965–68, Tripoli, Libya 1968–70, Corby from 1970
m Gorey 30.10.68 Breda O'Toole

GREIG Denis PhD 1958
s of Valentine G. bldg contr ag and Constance Cobban; b Fettercairn 31.8.32
BSc(St And) 1953
phys: post-doc fell. nat res council of Canada Ottawa 1958–60, lect Leeds 1960–70, sen lect from 1970
visiting assoc prof Michigan State univ E Lansing, Mich, USA 1969–70
m Brechin 4.9.57 Charlotte H. Webster MB ChB 1956 *qv*

GREIG Evelyn Margaret BSc 1965
d of Charles M. G. interior decorator and Evelyn A. Flett; b Aber 21.12.43
teacher: Inverurie acad 1965, coll of comm Aber 1966–67; air stewardess Lond 1967; teacher: Kampala Uganda 1968–71, Bauchi Nigeria 1972–73, Folkestone then Beaconsfield from 1976
m Aber 27.12.69 William D. Wilkie BSc(Glas) teacher, capt RAEC s of David G. W. Glasg

GREIG Irene Jean *MA 1962

GREIG Isobel Elizabeth MA 1961
m Cook

GREIG James Robertson MB ChB 1960
s of William H. G. police off. and Barbara M. Robertson civ serv; b Auchterless 14.5.36
MSc(Lond) 1973 DIH 1973
h o ARI and Aber city hosp 1960–61; lect Aberd 1961–62; m o RAF England, Aden, Scot., Guernsey, Lond from 1962
m Newton Mearns 1.8.63 Janet M. Morrison teacher p e d of Stanley M. Glasg

GREIG Linda Jean *MA 1970
d of Alfred W. G. dept man. paper mill and Jean R. D. Innes secy; b Aber 8.9.48
teacher: Kincorth acad Aber 1973, Turriff acad from 1978
m Aber 4.12.70 Edward Shand MA 1970 *qv*

GREIG Marion Graham BSc 1969
d of Alexander W. G. and Marion Graham; b Aber 25.4.48
teacher maths: Montrose acad 1970–72, Currie h s 1972–76
m Aber 31.7.72 David F. Goda MA(Oxon) statist (lect Aberd 1968–72) s of Lawrence G. Manc

GREIG Michael Andrew *MA 1964

GREIG Norma Ann Mitchell MA 1957
d of Charles G. bus driver and Mary M. McIntosh; b Fyvie 25.5.35
teacher: Ashley Rd p s Aber 1958–64, relief Crudie, Fyvie, Fintry, Ardmiddle p s 1972–73, Auchterless p s from 1973
m Fyvie 15.5.64 Harry P. Clark seeds exec s of Henry C. Turriff

GREIG Raymond BSc 1963
s of Thomas G. house painter and Isabella M. McAllan; b Aber 31.8.42
teacher maths: Bo'ness acad 1964–68, Jarvis coll, Toronto from 1968
m(2) Toronto 24.6.77 Isobel Anderson d of William Hamilton Greenock

GREIG Robert *MA 1958
s of Robert M. G. cattle dealer and Helen Y. Lumsden; b Aber 6.7.35
teacher mod lang Harris acad Dun 1959–64; prin mod lang Mortlach h s Dufftown 1964–66; Turriff acad: prin mod lang 1966–74, asst rector 1974–75, dep rector from 1975
m Aberlour 19.7.61 Isobel Miller MA 1958 *qv*

GREIG Rosemary Jeanette MA 1967
d of Alexander W. G. chief insp police and Jessie M. Calder; b Arbroath 30.3.46
teacher p s: Aber 1968–69, Elgin 1969–71, St Andrews 1972–74
m Aber 24.10.69 William S. Cantlay MA 1966 *qv*

GREIG William Rattray MB ChB 1959 *MD 1964
s of Hugh F. G. and Jessie Rattray; b Inv 28.9.35
MRCPGlas PhD(Glas)
sen lect Glas from 1969

GRENFELL James McNab BSc 1968

GRIBBLE Colin Duncan *BSc 1959
s of Joseph M. G. salesman and Elizabeth Duncan; b Lond 26.11.36
PhD(Edin) 1965 MIMM 1972
geol Williamson Diamonds Tanganyika 1959–62; lect Glas from 1965; consult. geol Scot. quarry comp (AQS) from 1968

GRIBBLE Elizabeth Jean MA 1960 ᶜLLB 1962

GRIEVE Alasdair Aitken Hume MB ChB 1965
s of William B. G. branch man. insur comp and Agnes Hume; b Glasg 31.12.39
h o RACH, city hosp Aber 1965–66; g p Aber from 1966
m Aber 1962 Irene H. Aitken hairdresser d of Alistair A. Aber

GRIEVE Alexander Millar MB ChB 1970
s of James A. G. acct GPO Aber and Helen R. M. Miller p o clerk; b Aber 4.7.46
DObstRCOG 1972
h o Aber hosps 1970–72; army m o: Catterick 1972–74, Farnborough 1974–76, Hereford from 1976
m Kirkintilloch 20.12.69 Alexandra W. C. Taig midwife d of James T. Kirkintilloch

GRIEVE Andrew Alexander MA 1970

GRIEVE David Rollo MB ChB 1958
s of Charles B. G. MB ChB(Edin) med pract and Isabella H. Brown teacher; b Aber 25.2.35
MRCGP 1972
h o Aber hosps 1958–59; m o RCAF 1959–62; g p Aber from 1962
m Switzerland 3.1.59 Madeleine H. I. Schumacher PhD(Zurich) d of Eugen S. Wangs KtSt Gallen Switzerland

GRIEVE George Brown *MA 1966
s of George G. painter and Mary Durham; b Glasg 20.2.35
teacher: geog Galashiels acad 1967–70, prin geog Campbeltown g s 1970–74; comp dir bldg comp Banffsh from 1974
m Aberlour 15.7.61 Patricia K. Munro comp secy d of Peter M. Carron Moray

GRIEVE Helen Ford Bayne MB ChB 1956
d of Charles B. G. MB ChB(Edin) g p and Isabella H. Brown teacher; b Aber 27.6.32
h s RACH 1956; Woodend hosp Aber: sen h phys Glenburn wing (geriatric) 1957–58; s h o med 1961–64; clin med off. Lincolnshire AHA Sleaford from 1965
m 10.7.58 Geoffrey Dillon MB ChB 1958 *qv*

GRIEVE Ian Barr MA 1963
s of William B. G. insur branch man. and Agnes Hume; b Glasg 22.2.42
teacher Engl: Hatton (Cruden) s 1964–69, Kaimhill s s Aber 1969–73, Kincorth acad Aber 1973–75, Bankhead acad from 1975

GRIEVE Kathleen Freda Seatter MA 1958
d of William A. G. farm. and Clara Craigie; b Rousay 2.2.37
clerkess Moffat from 1972
m Rousay 17.7.58 William Murray MA 1959 *qv*

GRIEVE Richard Andrew Francis *BSc 1965
MSc PhD(Tor)

GRIFFIN Anthony Roderick *BSc(for) 1967
s of Anthony G. artist and Diana B. Long; b Watford 17.4.45
PhD(Oregon) 1974
Traralgon, Vict, Aust: for. res off. 1967–70, for. res off.

with Commonwealth govt (genetics and breeding of pinus radiata) from 1973
m Rosewell 13.2.65 Lindsay Jack MA 1967 *qv*

GRIFFITH Margaret Anne *BSc 1967
m Davies

GRIFFITHS Arthur BSc(eng) 1957

GRIFFITHS Freda Elizabeth BSc 1962
d of Frederick N. G. machine oper and Elizabeth W. Nicol; b Lond 7.12.41
Govt actuary's dept Lond: cler off. 1964–70, exec off. 1970–76, higher exec off. from 1976

GRIFFITHS Peter Vernon *MA 1970
s of T. Vernon G. acct and Nora Taylor; b Edin 6.12.47
MSc(Glas) 1972
clin psych RHSC Glasg from 1972

GRIGGS Daphne Ellen MA 1967
m Vaughan

GRIGOR Norman MA 1961

GRIMBLE Ian PhD 1964
BA(Oxon)

GRIMES Katherine Mary Vincente BSc 1965
d of Leslie E. G. off. customs and excise and Frances M. Rettie; b Turriff 29.3.44
Dip Ed(Edin) 1966
teacher maths: Knox acad Haddington 1966–67, Lossiemouth 1967–70, Invernesssh 1971–72, Castle Douglas 1973, Nairn acad 1973–76
m Elgin 7.8.76 James M. Dixon flt lt RAF s of David F. D. Baldock

GRIMM Andrew Spalding *BSc 1962
s of Robert J. W. G. farm. and Jean H. E. Spalding physioth; b Forfar 22.5.40
PhD(Glas) 1965
post-doc fell. nat res council of Canada Halifax Nova Scotia 1965–67, lect zool UCNW from 1967
m Aber 11.10.65 Marion Gordon BSc(Glas) reg plan., teacher d of Ernest J. G. Aber

GRINLY David MA 1970
s of James G. civ serv and Anne W. M. Sharp textile worker; b Stirling 6.7.49
teacher geog Lornshill acad Alloa 1971–73 and from 1974; exec off. DTI Lond 1973–74
m Alloa 28.10.72 Eileen Mackison BSc(Edin) secy, civ serv d of Thomas M. Alloa

GRINSTED Carol Jean MSc 1970
b Tunbridge Wells 30.10.47
BSc(S'ton) 1969 Dip Lib(Aberystwyth) 1973 ALA 1975
asst lib univ coll of Wales Swansea from 1973

GRISEDALE Alfred Catto BSc(eng) 1957
s of Alfred G. shipyard worker and Stella D. Cardno; b Lancaster 8.8.36
MIEE 1970 CEng 1970
Bradford: grad app 1958–60; investigations eng Eng Elect. Co 1960–68; new prod. eng Lucas Aerospace from 1968

GRIVAS Jeffrey Peter BSc 1970

GROSS Eric *MA 1957 MLitt 1970 DMus 1975
s of Leo G. DL(Vienna) barrister and Ida Suchanek; b Vienna 16.9.26
LTCL 1958 FTCL 1963
Sydney, Aust: teacher conservatorium mus 1959–60, univ lect mus 1960–71, sen lect 1971–73, assoc prof from 1974; pres fellowship of Aust composers 1970–73, 1976–77
m Plymouth 28.3.55 Pamela M. M. Davies d of John D. Mutley

GROSSERT Ian Gillies BSc(eng) 1966
b 7.11.42
des eng Barclay Curle Glasg 1966–69; works man. John Grossert & Co Mombasa Kenya 1969–73
m Campbeltown 2.7.65 Penelope M. Colville MA 1965 *qv*
d Mombasa 10.11.73

GROSSET Arthur Early *MA 1967

GROUNDWATER Gordon Thomas MA 1967

GROUNDWATER James David MA 1970

GROUNDWATER Myra Cumming MA 1961
m Shearer

GROVE Eric John *MA 1970
s of Gordon E. B. G. MB ChB(Manc) med pract and Irene Wilshaw; b Bolton 3.12.48
MA(Lond) 1971
lect dept of hist/Engl Britannia royal naval coll Dartmouth from 1971
m Lond 14.4.73 Elizabeth J. Stocks ALA asst lib Dartington coll of arts Totnes d of Thomas H. S. Bridlington

GROVES Arthur *MA 1967

GRUBB Anthony Ainslie *BSc 1966
s of Anthony J. G. MA 1933 *qv*; b Wroxham 27.7.44
MIEE and CE 1975 MIRSE 1975
rly signal eng BR Glasg from 1966

GRUBB John Alexander *BSc 1964

GRUENLER Royce Gordon PhD 1957
s of Walter P. G. machinist and Maude E. Gordon; b Laconia, New Hampshire, USA 10.1.30
AB(Williams coll) 1955 BD(Philadelphia) 1955
Hiram coll Ohio, USA: asst prof phil and relig 1957–64; chmn dept phil and relig 1962–66, assoc prof 1964–67; chmn dept of relig 1966–69, 1972–75, prof relig from 1967
m Laconia 6.9.52 Grace L. Sansom Dip Bible inst Penn. USA d of Frank S. Laconia

GUHA Madhabendra Mohan PhD 1961
s of Surenda M. G. and Subarna Prava; b Barisal India 1.5.32
BSc(Calc) 1949 MSc(N Delhi) 1954
rubber res inst Malaysia: asst soils chem 1955–58 (study leave 1958–62) sen soil chem 1962–68; acting head of soils div 1968–70; dir agr res and advis bureau Malaysia from 1970
m Calcutta 1.5.64 Parul R. Paul BSc 1962 *qv*

GUNN Hugh James *BSc(agr) 1963
d Bottisham 14.8.68 *AUR* XLIII 86

GUNN John Barnetson LLB 1969

GUNN Lewis Arthur *MA 1957
s of Lewis H. G. master butcher and Jane Arthur; b Aber 10.4.35
teaching asst Engl-speaking union Cornell univ USA 1957–59; asst lect, lect govt Manc 1959–66; lect, sen lect

politics Glas 1966–72; prof of admin Strath from 1972 and civ serv prof of admin civ serv coll London 1974–79
m Aber 17.8.60 May F. Findlay MA 1957 *qv*

GUNN Mairi Anne Macdonald MA 1968

GUNN Margaret Mackay BSc 1966
d of David G. process superv UKAEA and Jane B. Nicolson; b Wick 2.10.44
teacher maths Wick 1967–73
m Wick 29.10.71 Patrick J. Gladstone MA 1970 *qv*

GUNN Nancy Sim MA 1959
d of Murdoch Y. G. asst area man. BR and Mary L. Boyes dent. recept; b Peterhead 9.1.38
teacher: maths Ellon acad 1960–65, spec asst from 1965
m Insch 28.7.62 Edward B. Wallace postman s of Edward B. W. New Pitsligo

GUNN Robert Morrison BSc(eng) 1961
s of Donald B. G. acct and Williamina Miller; b Wick 2.4.40
eng Aber corp 1961–63; asst eng Caithness c c Wick 1963–69; area eng N of Scot. water board Wick 1969–75; div eng Highland reg c water and sewerage dept from 1975
m Perth 3.8.63 Yvonne G. Avent MA 1962 *qv*

GUNN William MA 1959
s of William G. fish buyer and Isabella M. Webster; b Aber 18.6.36
FIL
teacher Westerton p s Aber 1960–62; lect Aber coll of comm 1962–70, sen lect Sp/Ital from 1970
m Aber 5.4.61 Moira I. Mitchell acct machine oper d of George A. M. Aber

GUNTON Tom William BSc(eng) 1967
d 26.8.69

GURNEY Jill Diana MB ChB 1967
d of John L. G. elect. eng and Molly B. Bracher; b Lond 8.3.42
FFARCS primary 1973
resid anaesthesiology NY USA 1969–71; regist anaest Charing Cross hosp Lond 1972–73; med advis Wellcome foundation from 1973

GUTHRIE Janet Margaret *MA 1970
d of Duncan D. G. MA(Belf) charity dir and Prunella S. B. Holloway organis secy; b Newcastle-u-Tyne 2.2.48
cler off. DHSS Lond 1970–71
m Wandsworth 24.10.70 Alan R. Mearns fishmonger s of Allan E. M. Aber; husb *d* 15.12.73

GUTHRIE John Mowat MA 1967
s of Henry F. G. farm. and Annie Mowat; b Pitsligo 17.2.41
teacher maths AGS 1968–74, asst prin maths from 1974
m Elgin 21.12.74 Kathleen E. Cantlie nurse, health visitor

GUY Alistair Ross MA 1970
d Dingwall 29.12.70 *AUR* XLIV 216

GUYAN Alice McKnight MA 1963
m Deans

GUYAN John McKnight *BSc(eng) 1963

GYANG Emmanuel Afiakwa MSc 1963 PhD 1965
s of Robert A. farm. and Emma Nyakoa farm.; b Ghana 21.10.23
BPharm(Lond) 1953
Ghana: lect univ of sc/tech Kumasi 1954–64, sen lect 1964–66, assoc prof from 1966
visiting prof pharm univ of Pittsburg USA 1972

HACKET Alastair MA 1970
b Aber 16.6.49
resid Edin

HADDEN Norman Alexander MA 1961
s of Alexander H. gardener and Ethel E. Ferguson; b Insch 18.10.38
teacher geog: Alford s s 1962–63, St John's j s s Dun 1963–65, also housemaster govt s s Yola, N Nigeria 1965–69, St Michael's s Dun; prin geog St Saviour's h s Dun from 1973
m Dun 10.7.63 Monica A. Feeney catering man. d of James F. Dun

HADDON Susan Mary *BSc 1970

HADDOW John Foulds BSc 1970

HAGGART David Ballantine *MA 1956
s of William G. H. life assur man. and Isabella M. Patrick secy; b Dun 15.3.34
JP 1971
nat serv R Corps Sig 1956–58; teacher Perth 1958–59; youth employment off. Aber 1959–63; sen careers advis off. Aberd from 1963
m Aber 1.9.64 Gwendolen M. Hall MA 1964 *qv*

HAIGH John Beverley *BSc 1970
s of William H. retailer and Nora Fern; b Huddersfield 22.7.46
syst analyst Lond 1970–73; teacher from 1974

HALCROW John Andrew BSc 1967

HALDON Carol Anne *BSc 1968

HALDON Robert Anthony *BSc 1962 PhD 1965

HALEY David BSc(for) 1961 *1962
b Goole 3.11.39
MF(Br Col) 1964 PhD(Br Col) 1966
Canada: lect for. econ Tor 1966–67, assoc prof for. Br Col Vancouver 1967–73; visiting reader for. econ univ of Ibadan, Nigeria 1973–74; assoc prof for. Br Col Vancouver from 1974

HALFHIDE Andrew George BSc(for) 1963

HALL Alan Richard *MA 1963
s of Francis C. H. comm trav and Winifred L. Low loc govt housing visitor; b Aber 28.8.40
admin off. govt N Nigeria, Gboko 1963–64; pers off. ICI agr div Stockton-on-Tees 1964–65; teacher econ Queen's Park s s, Glenwood s s Glasg 1966–68; Aber: lect econ coll of comm 1968–74; head of dept econ and acct AGS from 1974
m Glasg 16.2.68 Jean A. McIntyre art teacher d of Donald McI. Bathgate

HALL Alexander Urquhart MA 1968

HALL Alison Margaret *MA 1965
d of John K. H. bldg contr and Joyce Smith physioth; b Aber 15.12.42
UN Interpreters Dip(Holborn coll Lond)
m Paris 28.11.68 Patrick Giffin CA s of George W. G. BSc(eng) (Durh)

HALL Colin David MB ChB 1966
s of David H. MB ChB 1955 *qv*; b Chester 11.5.41
DABPsych & Neurol 1976
h o, regist Aber gen hosp 1966–69; dept of neurol univ of N Carolina USA; resid 1969–72, instr 1972–73, asst prof 1973–77, assoc prof from 1977, dir neuromuscular unit from 1977
m Aber 22.9.61 Valerie Gordon MA 1966 *qv*

HALL David John MSc 1967 PhD 1969
s of John W. H. loc govt off. and Gladys L. Briggs; b Farnborough 25.9.43
BSc(S'ton) 1962 FIMA 1973 MBCS 1972
Aberd: res fell. dept mental health 1967–74, syst dir mental health res unit 1970–74; sen lect Lond s of hyg and trop med from 1974
m Sidcup 25.7.64 Janet Wells MB ChB 1968 *qv*

HALL David John *BSc 1970
s of K. J. H. sales man. and S. M. Webb teacher; b NZ 2.2.47
teacher: biol/gen sc Hazlehead acad 1973, biol/phys Hulme g s Oldham from 1973
comm in RAF VR(T)
m Salford 25.9.70 Helen M. Murphy BSc 1970 *qv*

HALL Gwendolen Margaret MA 1964
d of John N. H. C of S min and Roberta R. Clark b Newport-on-Tay 12.5.43
teacher Ger Aber acad 1965–66
m Aber 1.9.64 David B. Haggart MA 1956 *qv*

HALL Hilda Rae MA 1960
d of Norman J. A. H. farm. and Jeannie Rae; b Udny 1.1.39
teacher: Fraserburgh cent s 1961–63, Hayshead s Arbroath 1963–68; Edin: Muirhouse s 1968–69, Gylemuir s 1969–74 asst head from 1974
m Aber 23.3.79 Ian S. Robertson farm. s of David M. R. Forfar

HALL Jean Valerie Aitken *MA 1967
d of Gilbert B. H. textile dyer and Elizabeth C. Andrew; b Dunbartonsh 15.2.45
teacher geog: Ainslie Park s s Edin 1968–69, Northfield acad Aber 1969–70, part time coll of comm 1971–72
m Aber 15.7.69 Richard A. North BSc MB ChB 1969 *qv*

HALL Joan Mary Robertson MA 1968
d of John K. H. comp chmn and Joyce R. Smith physioth; b Aber 5.7.47
SRN 1974

HALL John Thackray *MA 1968
s of John M. H. MA(Oxon) unitarian min and Hilda I. Thackray MA(Oxon) teacher; b Wigan 14.5.44
Brit Council: admin asst Edin 1968–71, Lond from 1971

HALL Linda Frances *MA 1970
d of Francis C. H. comm trav and Winifred L. Low housing visitor; b Aber 5.10.47
teacher s s Burnham-on-Crouch 1970–72; exec off. DHSS Chelmsford 1973–74
m Aber 13.9.69 Keith W. Wilson BSc 1967

HALL Maureen Yvonne *BSc 1967 Dip Ed 1968
m Lorimer

HALL Mildred Lillington MA 1970
b Newcastle-on-Tyne
MA(Oxon)
res fell. Aberd from 1970
m Kenneth L. Blaxter FRS Norfolk

HALL Pamela Mary MB ChB 1969
d of Willie H. traffic man. BEA and Helen Duguid; b Lisbon 26.4.45
DObstRCOG 1971 MRCOG 1977 FACOG 1978
h o Aber 1969–71; res fell. obst Aberd 1971–72; m o publ health/regist path. Lond 1972–74; sen h o obst/gyn Harrow 1974–75; regist obst/gyn Cape Town 1975–77; asst prof obst/gyn Case Western Reserve univ Cleveland Ohio from 1977
m Aber 12.7.69 Stewart M. Hamilton MB ChB 1968 *qv*

HALL Sandra MA 1970
m Kelman

HALL Wendy Muriel Adanma MB ChB 1968
m Amaechi

HALL William David *MA 1959

HALL William Fergusson MA 1968

HALLEY Jean *MA 1970
d of David B. H. and Ethel J. Scott; b Lanark 10.12.47
higher exec off. D o I: Lond 1971–73, N reg off. Newcastle-u-Tyne from 1973
m Sudbury 18.9.71 Robin C. Moss BA(Sus) s of Charles T. M. Sudbury

HALLEY Margaret Loosome MA 1958

HALLEY Mary Rosalind MA 1963
d of James R. H. insur supt and Mary M. Angus; b Perth 3.8.43
teacher: Aber 1964–66, Wick 1971–75, Cumbernauld 1976–77
m Aber 29.12.65 Alan R. Reid MB ChB 1966 *qv*

HALLIDAY David MSc 1967 PhD 1969

HALLIDAY Donald Catto BSc 1960
s of Archibald S. H. millwright and Margaret M. Catto; b Oldmeldrum 13.11.37
teacher maths Elgin 1961–72; prin maths Glenrothes from 1972
m Aber 19.7.63 Elspeth M. Bakie MA 1960 *qv*

HALLIDAY George Sime *MA 1966 MSc 1967
s of Archibald S. H. millwright and Margaret M. Catto; b Oldmeldrum 10.11.44
PhD(Cantab) 1970
geophys: NCB Burton-on-Trent 1970–72, geophys serv internat Croydon 1972–73; explor geophys Shell: Lausanne 1973–74, The Hague, Kinshasa Zaire from 1974
m Aber 16.11.67 Patricia M. H. Neill MA 1967 *qv*

HALSTEAD Peter Howard LLB 1968
s of Jack Halstead civ serv and Florence Howard; b Flete 22.3.47
BA(OU) 1975 solic supreme court 1972
Telford: articled clerk 1969–72, asst solic 1972–75, chief asst solic (loc govt) from 1975
m Cumbernauld 4.4.70 Margaret D. Leaker MA 1968 *qv*

HAMBANANDA Chumsri MSc 1963

HAMBLIN Caroline Anne *BSc 1967
m Taylor

HAMDARD Mohammad Siddique MSc 1970
BSc(agr)(W. Pak)

HAMID Hamid Ibrahim PhD 1964
MSc(N W Khart)

HAMILTON Angela Geraldine *MB ChB 1968
d of Ronald K. H. bank man. and Mary K. A. Lloyd-Hall, SRN; b Lond 22.12.42
FFARCS 1973 fell. prize
h o RACH, ARI 1968–69; intern Montreal 1969–70; h o anaest Westminster hosp Lond 1970, sen h o Royal Berks hosp Reading 1971; Lond: sen h o Westminster hosp 1971–72, regist Royal Marsden hosp 1972–73, hosp for sick ch Great Ormond St 1973; sen regist anaest Wessex area health auth Southampton and Winchester from 1973

HAMILTON Brian Wallace *MA 1970
s of David H. trans clerk and Mabel Todd; b Irvine 22.7.48
teacher mus: Aberdeensh 1971–73, Oldham from 1976

HAMILTON Elizabeth Ann *MA 1962
d of David A. H. MB ChB 1936 *qv*; b Aber 9.10.39
teacher Engl: Aber h s for girls 1963–64, New Engl s Kuwait from 1975
m Aber 27.12.63 Ian A. Olson MB ChB 1962 *qv*

HAMILTON Elizabeth Muriel Jane MB ChB 1957
d of Malcolm H. insur surv and Helen S. F. Henderson; b Aber 4.3.34
m Aber 26.7.57 James D. Rust granite merch s of James R. Aber

HAMILTON Frank Eric Graham *MA 1966

HAMILTON Gilbert Brown BSc(eng) 1969
s of Gilbert F. H. BSc 1933 *qv* and Margaret W. Monro MA 1934 *qv*; b Aber 21.12.45
grad eng BBC TV Lond 1969–74; man. (des/res) Aertech San Jose California from 1974

HAMILTON Ian Varcoe MTh 1969
BEng BD(Melb)

HAMILTON Joan Isobel Sinclair LLB 1967
d of David A. H. MB ChB 1936 *qv*; b Aber 23.10.46
solic Inv 1969–72; reporter to Inv burgh ch panel 1971–73
m Inv 20.1.68 Bruce A. Merchant LLB 1965 *qv*

HAMILTON Leslie William *BSc 1967 PhD 1971
s of Norman M. H. civ serv and Eileen M. Inder; b Aber 6.10.45
asst prin teacher sc Powis acad Aber from 1971

HAMILTON Margaret Vera MA 1969
d of Thomas H. chief off. MN and Margaret J. Marshall; b Aber 24.3.46
teacher Aber p s from 1970
m Aber 14.9.68 Thomas Wemyss MA 1969 *qv*

HAMILTON Stewart Maclean MB ChB 1968
s of Joseph S. H. MB ChB 1939 *qv*; b Aber 22.1.45
MSc(Lond) 1974 MRCP 1972 Dip Amer board internal med 1978
h o Woodend hosp Aber 1968–69; lect path., med Aberd 1969–71; regist Aber 1971–73, Harrow 1973–75; spec regist endocrinology Cape Town 1975–77; med firm dir/dir metabolic unit/consult. endocrin Cleveland metrop gen hosp/asst prof med Case Western Reserve univ Cleveland USA from 1977
m Aber 12.7.69 Pamela M. Hall MB ChB 1969 *qv*

HAMILTON William Farquhar Douglas MB ChB 1967
s of Douglas H. pharm/optic and Stella Farquhar MA 1931 *qv*; b Aber 24.7.43
DA 1970 FFARCS 1972
h o ARI 1967–68; res asst dept med Aberd 1968–69; sen h o (hon clin tut.) regist, sen regist (hon lect Aberd) 1969–75; consult. anaest (hon sen lect Dund) Tayside health board from 1975
m Aber 19.7.68 Frances T. Auchinachie teacher d of Henry W. A. Lonmay

HAMMERSTAD Bodil MB ChB 1965
d of Erling H. MD(Oslo) chief m o Innherred Sykeheim Verdal and Else M. Borch; b Oslo 16.11.40
spec internal med(Norway) 1974 spec gastroenterology (Norway) 1974
jun regist surg Oslo 1965–66, h o surg and intern med 1966–67; asst publ health off. Andøy 1967; Oslo: regist geriat 1967–69, jun regist intern med 1969–70, regist int med 1970–75, res fell. from 1976
m Stiklestad, Norway 13.5.67 Reidar Selbekk Cand Psych (Oslo) clin psych s of Arne S. Selbekken

HAMPTON Alexander William Matthew *MA 1964
s of Alexander J. C. H. marine eng and Isabella R. Matthew; b Aber 2.1.41
asst pers man. Peterhead 1965–67; Aber: welfare and accommodation off. 1967–73, stud. serv off. from 1973
m Aber 11.9.64 Kathleen Sangster d of William S. Aber

HAMSON Robin Barrington BSc 1970
s of William S. B. H. teacher and Cynthia I. Parrish lib; b Cambridge 26.5.49
teacher: Liv 1971–72, Droitwich 1972–73, Leic from 1974

HANCE Raymond John PhD 1961
BSc(R'dg)

HANKIN Ronald George *MA 1956 Dip Ed 1958

HANNAY Margaret Kerr MA 1968
m O'Hagan

HANSON Rosalind Irene MA 1965
d of Sydney W. F. H. BSc(Liv) scient (food & nutrit) and Irene Tomlinson teacher; b Liv 15.10.43
m Aber 2.6.66 Charles J. E. McIver MA 1962 *qv*

HANTON Douglas Alexander MB ChB 1964
s of Alexander P. H. bus. exec and Davinah A. Baxter; b Aber 25.4.38
DObstRCOG 1968
h o Woodend hosp Aber 1964–65; sen h o: DRI 1965–66, Bellshill mat. hosp Lanarksh 1966; g p: E Kilbride 1966–73, Strathpeffer from 1973
m Aber 22.10.66 Margaret I. McKendry banker d of William E. McK. Cults

HANTON William Baxter *MA 1958

HARBINSON Heather MA 1968

HARBOUR Anthony Bryan *MA 1966
s of Harold E. M. MA(Cantab) tech dir and Mary P. McManus MA(Edin) teacher; b Edin 26.6.43
grad trainee Metal Box Lond, Manc 1966–68; Mars Slough: div sales man. 1974–77, pers man. from 1977
m St Albans 23.7.66 Jacqueline E. M. Wright MA 1965 *qv*

HARCUS Mary Elizabeth MA 1960

HARDCASTLE Patrick David ***BSc(for) 1968**
s of Harold B. H. schoolmaster and Florence W. Taylor clerk; b Nott 11.6.47
Malawi: asst conserv for. Limbe 1968–70, reg for. off. Mzimba 1970–72, sen silviculturist Dedza 1972–75, sen for. res off. Zomba from 1975
m Blantyre Malawi 23.8.69 Moira A. G. Runcie MA 1969 *qv*

HARDIE Alexander Lewis **BSc 1968**

HARDIE Andrew David Kemp **BSc(for) 1958 *1959**
s of James M. H. estate factor and Isabella F. Kemp; b Fochabers 10.4.36
FIWSc 1973
asst conserv for. W reg Nigeria 1959–63; dist off. for. comm Ipswich, Hitchin, Princes Risborough 1964–66; Kitwe Zambia: market. off., timber util res off. 1966–72, chief for. prod. res off. 1972–73; temp lect for. and wood sc univ coll N Wales (Bangor); branch man. Tilhill for. (Scot.) Stirling 1974–76; indep for. consult. overseas from 1976
m Dublin 31.8.73 Kathleen Cleary BComm(NUI) teacher, indust trg off. d of John C. C. Ballylongford

HARDIE Audrey Fowler ***MA 1956**

HARDIE Betty Theresa **MA 1963**
d of George F. H. c c employee and Beatrice M. McGillivray; b Ellon 20.11.41
teacher: Boddam 1964–65, Dunscroft 1965–66
m Aber 21.7.65 James W. Barrack BSc(eng) 1964 *qv*

HARDIE Elsie McPherson **BSc 1964**
d of Hans H. garage owner and Maria A. Murdoch; b Aber 5.6.43
m Aberchirder 4.1.64 James H. W. Gray farm./wholesale dairyman s of James G. Dufftown

HARDIE Hamish McGregor ***BSc 1968**
s of Hugh G. M. H. PhD 1948 *qv*; b Aber 5.7.46
syst eng (computer tech) Lond, Edin from 1968
m Aber 9.8.69 Joy S. Riddell tel/receptionist, tourist asst d of Leslie R. Cults

HARDIE John David Morrison **MSc 1968**
BA(Cantab)

HARDIE Michael John **MB ChB 1965**
s of George M. H. col civ serv and Margaret G. F. Bell nurse; b Aber 18.10.41
Dip Amer brd of paediat 1971 FRCP(C) 1972
h o Aber 1965–67; resid paediat New Haven USA; Canada: fell. neo natal div hosp for sick ch Toronto 1969–72, asst prof paediat univ of W Ont 1972–77, asst prof paediat and obst/gyn univ of Ottawa from 1977
m Aber 26.7.67 Betty F. McDonald nurs sister d of Alexander McD. Inverurie

HARDIE Myles Douglas George **MA 1969**
s of George H. driver and Dorothy McIntosh; b Aber 19.6.45
teacher Engl Daniel Stewart's coll Edin 1970–73; prin Engl: Auchterarder s 1973–76, Torry acad Aber from 1976
m Aber 29.12.67 Marjory Gray MA 1968 *qv*

HARDIE Raymond Alfred **MA 1968**
b Aber 30.9.46
publ man. Hallam group of Nottingham

HARDIE Richard Henry **MB ChB 1963**
s of Henry C. H. bldr and Elisabeth B. Buchan; b Ellon 18.12.33
h o Aber 1963–64; capt RAMC r m o: 1st Tank regt Hohne W Ger 1964–66, 1st para Aldershot 1966–68; major RAMC: 2Ic 23rd Para Fd Amb Aldershot 1968–70, DADMS 4th div Herford, W Ger 1970–72; lt col RAMC: c o 23 Para Fd Amb Aldershot 1972–77, 1st armd div Fd Amb Hohne from 1977
m Aber 10.7.62 Janet G. Warren MA 1961 *qv*

HARDIMAN Michael John **MA 1964**

HARDING Robert Blythe ***BSc 1967**

HARDMAN Lorna **MSc 1968**
d of Thomas Hardman civ serv and Hilda A. France; b Edin 11.12.43
BSc(Edin) 1964
res asst chem dept Aberd 1964–69
m Dunfermline 25.7.67 Malcolm D. Ingram BSc(Liv) s of Arthur I. BSc(Liv) Wallasey

HARGRAVE Stuart Anthony **MB ChB 1968**

HARGREAVES John Wilson **BSc(for) 1967**

HARHARA Feisal Bin Abdullah **MB ChB 1967**
s of Abdullah H. land-owner and Alyah Bajrai; b Singapore 31.7.37
LMCC 1972 regd coll of phys and surg (Ont) 1972
h o med/surg Scot. 1967–68; Singapore: m o pass. ship 1968–69, publ health off. 1969–70; resid psychiat Kingston, Ontario 1970–71; fam pract Toronto from 1971

HARINCK Emmanuel **MB ChB 1964**

HARKINS Charles **LLB 1970**

HARLEY Roy MacGregor **LLB 1970**
s of John H. civ eng and Thelma D. MacGregor teacher p e; b Glasg 29.10.48
law app Edin 1970–71; leg. asst E.D.C., Menzies, Dougal & Milligan, Dan McKay & Norwell 1971–75; Drummond & Co from 1975, ptnr from 1978

HARMAN Brian Sydney Robertson ***MA 1970**
s of Albert C. H. insur insp and Winifred I. Findlay; b Aber 4.10.46
Cert Qual Soc Work (Keele) 1973
soc worker: Derbysh 1970–75, Northumberland 1975–78, Cardiff from 1978
m Aber 5.6.70 Judith M. Ellway MA 1969 *qv*

HARMON William McIntosh **BSc 1967**
s of Roy J. H. clerk and Catherine McIntosh; b Nigg Station by Tain 31.10.45
teacher: sc Glenrothes 1968–69, chem Dingwall from 1969

HARNDEN John Robert **MA 1969**
s of Noel J. H. Mus Bac(Edin) teacher and Agnes A. Bee MA(Edin) teacher; b Edin 12.5.46
vandriver/storeman Hazlehead garden centre Aber 1970–72; van driver gen store Lerwick 1973; exec off. Register House (civ serv) Edin 1973–74; author from 1974 (resid Alford, Orkney)

HARPER Douglas Ross **BSc 1962 MB ChB 1967 ᶜMD 1975**
s of Louis R. H. eng and Margaret H. Cartwright secy; b Aber 16.2.40
FRCSE 1971 FRCS 1972
h o ARI 1967–68; res fell. dept path. Aberd 1968–69; ARI sen h o, regist gen surg 1969–73, vascular surg fell. 1972–73; sen regist gen surg ERI 1973–76; consult. surg

Forth Valley health board Falkirk RI from 1976
m Aber 19.7.68 Dorothy C. Wisely MA 1966 *qv*

HARPER Elizabeth Mackay MA 1964
d of Donald H. soldier (*d* 1944) and Elizabeth J. Forbes school meals attend.; b Thurso 4.11.42
teacher Engl/allied subjs Lochyside s Fort William 1965–66, Pulteneytown acad Wick 1966–67 and in 1977; part-time tel Wick 1974–77; teacher remed/spec Engl and maths Wick h s from 1977
m Aber 28.7.64 Fredrick G. McBoyle BSc(eng) 1958 *qv*

HARPER Elizabeth Shearer MB ChB 1959

HARPER Hugh Alexander Barrie MA 1960 LLB 1962
s of John H. MA(Glas) BBC educ off. and Agnes F. N. Barrie teacher; b Glasg 29.3.39
MICA 1965 Dip Man. St BIM 1969 PhD(H-W) 1975
lect Aberd 1965; ptnr H. A. B. Harper & Co CA 1965–73; man. dir. Kildonnan Invest. 1973–74; ptnr H. A. B. Harper & Co solic from 1974
m Aber 26.8.67 Vivienne Eden secy d of Robert E. E. Aber

HARPER John Louis BSc(eng) 1958
s of Louis R. H. eng and Margaret H. Cartwright secy; b Aber 30.5.36
MIMechE 1966 MIProdE 1970 MEng(Glas) 1978
Babcock & Wilcox: grad trainee Renfrew 1958–60, proj eng Dalmuir 1960–64; contr eng John Brown Land Boilers Clydebank 1964–65; mech eng Babcock & Wilcox (operations) Renfrew from 1965 then prod. syst man.
m Aber 5.7.61 Fiona M. Hunter MA 1959 *qv*

HARPER Lillian Helen *MA 1964
d of Peter H. master butcher and Lily M. Murray cook; b Aber 7.4.42
teacher Engl Mackie acad Stonehaven 1965–68
m Aber 30.3.65 Alexander R. Gallacher arch. s of Alexander R. G. Aber

HARPER Robin Charles Moreton MA 1962

HARPER William *MA 1966
s of Harry H. miller, road trans driver and Margaret E. Clarke; b Norwich 15.4.44
asst plan. Norfolk c c 1966–68; head geog dept Langley s Langley Park from 1968
m Woodbastwick 14.4.73 Mary E. Le Fevre nurse/riding s prop. d of Donald Le F. Thorpe Hamlet Norwich

HARPER William Findlay MA 1959 Dip Ed 1960
s of William M. H. BR insp and Isabella R. B. Findlay; b Gartly 21.11.39
teacher: Aber 1960–61, Keith 1961–63, Banff 1963–71, prin maths Inv 1971–76, asst rector Cults from 1976
m Aber 24.7.61 Cathleen J. Ogston teacher d of Charles A. O. Botriphnie

HARRIES Harry Raymond *MA 1969
s of Harry P. H. clothier and Gwendoline Hill comp dir; b Cardiff 1.7.05
FIB
retd; resid Cheltenham
m Braintree 1.7.74 Mary F. Smithers lib Cheltenham ladies' coll d of Kenneth O. S. BA(Oxon) Braintree

HARRIS Gillian Margaret *MA 1968
d of Bernard F. D. H. BSc(Lond) teacher and Norah I. Campbell; b Southborough 3.2.47
teacher: Gatehouse-of-Fleet 1969–70, f e tech coll Clydebank 1970–74, Queensland Aust 1974–75, Helensburgh from 1976

HARRIS Iain Grant Nicolson *MA 1968
s of Ian Nicolson (stepfather James F. G. H.) and Christine Nicolson; b Edin 17.3.46
Lond: advt and p r man. 1968–74, dir, advt and p r comp from 1974; mayor Royal borough of Windsor and Maidenhead 1976–78
m Aber 8.8.69 Jane P. Robertson MA 1967 *qv*

HARRIS Paul Anthony *MA 1970
s of John D. H. collector HM customs and excise and Rita Harris; b Barnhurst 22.7.48
man. dir Impulse publ Aber from 1970

HARRIS Winifred Anne Charlotte *MA 1969
d of Leslie F. H. comp dir and Winifred M. B. Wilson MA(Glas) teacher; b Whyteleafe 1.1.47
Ford Motor Co (tractor oper) Essex: grad trainee 1969–70, admin asst 1970–71, trg off. 1971–72; pers asst GATT UNO Geneva 1973; dept employment UK home civ serv Lond: admin trainee 1973–75 H E O (A) 1975–77, prin from 1977

HARRISON Christopher Peter Motte *MA 1967

HARRISON Derek John BSc(for) 1959
s of George H. H. RAF off. and Ethel M. Hutchins; b Stoke Poges 11.6.26
FIFor 1969
Forres: woodlands man. Moray estates dev comp from 1959, man. Moray timber preserv (Forres) 1961–71, man. dir from 1972; for. consult. in private practice various estates in Scot. from 1964
m Edin 26.6.59 Janet L. M. Kennedy SRN d of A. E. K. BSc(Edin) Portobello

HARRISON Ian Rodger MA 1965

HARRISON Jacqueline Mary MA 1961
m Wheeler

HARRISON Moira Ann BEd 1969
b Aber 1.1.47
teacher Glenrothes from 1975
m Aber 11.11.67 James A. Wito BEd 1969 *qv*

HARRISSON John *BSc 1969

HARROW Andrew Lewis BSc 1960
b Aber 1.7.37
resid Milltimber

HARROW Iain Alastair Lewis MA 1965 LLB 1968
s of William B. H. CBE trawlowner/comp dir and Isobel W. Lewis; b Aber 3.3.32
app solic: Aber 1968–69, Stonehaven 1969–70
m Castle Eden 16.7.66 Diana Gordon-Russell MA(Edin) teacher d of Rognvald G.-R. OBE MB ChB 1931 *qv*

HARROWER Margaret Elizabeth Mary MA 1962
m Webster

HARRY Keith William *MA 1968 PhD 1975

HART Roderick *MA 1967

HART Stewart PhD 1967
BSc(Edin)

HARTNOLL Gillian Pauline MA 1967
m Tyrer

HARVAIS Gaëtan Hugues BSc 1957 MSc 1963 PhD 1966
s of A. Roger H. acct gen, dep fin. secy and S. Lucette Raffin; b Quatre-Bornes Mauritius 9.4.35
asst plant breeder sugar indust res inst Reduit Mauritius 1957–61; tut. dem Aberd 1963–65; res asst St And Dun 1965–66; Canada: asst prof biol: univ de Moncton NB 1966–67, Lakehead univ Thunder Bay Ont from 1967, then assoc prof

HARVAIS Georges Roland MB ChB 1957

HARVEY Lynette Patricia MA 1966

HARVEY Michael Douglas *MA 1968

HARVIE Thomas Gilchrist BSc(eng) 1970
s of Thomas G. H. mech eng and Sarah Hutchison; b Glasg 21.8.47
CEng MIMechE
stress eng Rolls Royce Hamilton 1970–71; mech des eng Weir Pumps Alloa from 1971
m Dedham 24.7.71 Janet L. Turner MA 1968 *qv*

HARVIE Winifred Ann MA 1966
m Thomson

HASAN Ghaziuddin MA 1967

HASSAM Sadruddin Esmail MLitt 1967
BA(Lond)

HASTIE Dennis MA 1969
s of Peter T. H. colliery man. and Agnes L. Fisher; b Edin 7.2.49
teacher Brechin from 1970
m Aber 24.7.71 Kathleen A. Owen MA 1970 *qv*

HASTIE Isobel Gerrard MA 1968
d of Walter H. van driver and Mary A. Gerrard; b Aber 4.4.47
teacher mod lang Banchory acad from 1969
m Aber 4.10.69 William S. Macdonald asst scient off. marine res s of William F. S. M. Aber

HASTON Douglas Donaldson MA 1958
s of Albert H. MA(Edin) teacher, headmaster and Elizabeth S. C. Donaldson teacher; b Aber 8.7.31
LTCL 1969
teacher Westerton p s Aber 1959–71; mus instrument (recorder) teacher Aber/Grampian from 1971
m Aber 6.8.55 Elspeth A. McMurtrie DA artist d of John McM. MA(Edin) Skene

HATEM Ali Abdulla MB ChB 1966

HATRICK Alan Arundel *BSc 1969
s of Thomas F. H. chief collector taxes and Mary E. Arundel; b Aber 13.2.47
Lic I Biol 1971
indust admin Glasg 1969–70; teacher biol Wolverhampton 1970–73; head s biol dept Walsall from 1973

HAUGLAND Anne *BSc(eng) 1970

HAWCO George Thomas BSc 1969

HAWKES Susan Gail *BSc 1968

HAWKSWORTH Peter George BSc(eng) 1968
s of Gerald G. H. aero eng fitter and Diana Davies; b Burton-on-Trent 19.6.46
Clarke Chapman internat combustion div Derby: grad app 1968–69, res and dev eng 1970–73 and fluid mech group sect. leader from 1974
m Tutbury 3.1.70 Kay Harding man. hair stylist d of Joseph B. H. Burton-on-Trent

HAWLEY John George *MA 1969
s of George W. H. clerk in holy orders and Annie W. Deans organist/accompan; b Insch 23.5.44
FRGS 1970
teacher: Queen Elizabeth's boys' s Barnet 1970–74, head geog St Nicholas g s Northwood 1974–77, sen year tut. Haydon s Northwood from 1977

HAWTHORN Lily Fleming MA 1970

HAY Abigail Lyon MA 1967
d of John L. H. eng fitter and Abigail F. S. Spence; b Stromness 29.7.46
Aber: teacher sp and drama 1968–70, geog Powis acad from 1970
m Aber 27.2.76 William G. Innes MA 1962 *qv*

HAY Alan James *BSc 1966 PhD 1969
s of William H. BSc(agr) 1938 *qv* and Margaret H. G. Crichton BSc(Glas); b Bexhill 16.10.43
post doct res fell. Duke univ USA 1969–71; res scient nat inst for med res Lond from 1971
m Aber 22.6.68 Janet M. Bishop BSc 1965 *qv*

HAY Alexander John *BSc(eng) 1969

HAY Alison Mary MA 1968

HAY Audrey Mary Wilson *MA 1970
d of Archibald H. LDS(Glas) chief dent off. Aber and Mary W. Thomson MA(Glas) teacher; b Hamilton 23.5.48
teacher Westbury Park s Brist
m Aber 28.12.70 Peter A. Mitchell MA(Oxon) prod. man. s of Eric R. M. MSc(Lond) Nott

HAY David Alexander *MA 1968
s of George A. H. civ serv and Patricia M. McGregor; b Aber 25.8.47
PhD(Birm) 1970
res fell. Birm 1970–72; lect La Trobe univ Victoria Aust from 1972, then sen lect

HAY David Sinclair BSc 1966
s of Alexander J. H. bus prop. and Catherine I. Davidson teacher; b Elgin 21.2.44
teacher sc Summerhill acad Aber 1967, asst prin sc from 1973
m Elgin 7.8.70 Isobel L. Stuart teacher d of Robert P. S. Elgin

HAY Douglas Middleton MB ChB 1964
s of Charles M. W. H. foreman stevedore and Mary H. Wyness; b Aber 21.4.41
DObstRCOG 1966 MRCOG 1973
h o RACH, Woodend hosp Aber 1965–66; Glasg: h o obst/gyn South gen hosp, g p 1966; locum g p Kilsyth 1967; m o Tawau, Sabah E Malaysia 1967–70; regist obst/gyn South gen hosp Glasg 1970–74; sen regist/hon lect obst/gyn Ninewells hosp Dun 1974–78; consult. obst/gyn Kingston-u-Hull from 1978
m Aber 23.7.64 Sheila R. Forsyth teacher d of John F. F. Aber

HAY Elizabeth Mary *BSc 1970
d of William E. H. MB BS(Durh) med pract and

Elizabeth Diericx BSc(Durh) teacher; b Newcastle-u-Tyne 22.3.48
lect biol coll f e Plymouth from 1971

HAY Gordon William *MA 1970
d of William W. H. clerk and Agnes M. I. Dickie; b Aber 25.4.47
teacher: mod lang Kincorth acad Aber 1971–74, prin mod lang Turriff acad from 1974

HAY Ian Morgan MA 1965

HAY Ian Stewart *MA 1963
s of James C. H. clerk and Margaret F. Stewart secy; b Aber 9.10.40
teacher: RGC Aber 1964–67, Jarvis coll inst Tor Canada from 1967
m Aber 23.12.64 Elizabeth M. A. Dear BSc 1962 *qv*

HAY James Leslie MB ChB 1959
s of Andrew L. H. MA 1925 *qv*; b Aber 13.4.35
g p: Kingston-u-Hull 1961–64, Aber from 1964
m Aber 10.12.75 Margaret Hurst health visitor d of Joseph H. London

HAY James Taylor Cantlay *BSc 1957
s of James H. farm serv and Elsie M. Cantlay; b Huntly 13.6.35
FGS FInstPet Amer Assoc Pet. Geol
geol (IPC) Kirkuk Iraq; head geol dept Abu Dhabi petr comp 1967–71; lect geol Aberd 1971–74; chief dev geol BODL from 1975
m Aber 21.8.59 Mary G. Davidson MA 1955 *qv*

HAY Jean Margaret *MA 1966
d of William H. garage owner and Hilda Martin teacher; b Birkenhead 11.4.44
Dip Ed(Lond) 1967
teacher: Lond 1967–69, Liv 1969–71, Cheshire 1971–73
m West Kirby 31.7.71 Ivor W. Phillips chauffeur

HAY John David Lumsden *BSc 1958
s of John P. H. merch seaman and Isabella A. Lumsden; b Aber 23.6.35
MSc(Nott) 1962 DipEd(Nott) 1966
Nott: res digestive physiol 1958–61, teacher biol 1962–66, lect educ 1966–75; dir religious experience res proj Nott univ
Educ Information Book of the Year award by Times Educ Sup for book *Human Populations* publ Penguin Educ
m Sleaford 1964 Felicity J. Dilley teacher p e d of Percy J. D. Sleaford

HAY John Munro *BSc 1959
s of William M. H. civ serv and Margaret I. M. B. Miller teacher; b Forres 7.10.38
PhD(Cantab) 1963 barrister at law of Gray's Inn
lect: Westfield coll Lond 1962–63, Aberd 1963–67, Imp coll Lond 1967–69; HM diplom serv: 1st secy Lond 1970–71, (AID) Vientiane Laos 1972–74, (chancery) Canberra from 1974
m Aber 16.8.60 Avril M. I. Menzies BSc 1960 *qv*

HAY John Yeaman Leslie BL 1962
s of Andrew L. H. MA 1925 *qv*; b Aber 25.2.38
leg. asst Cooper & Hay advoc Aber 1963–64, ptnr from 1964
m Aber 28.7.64 Elizabeth M. B. Anderson BSc 1962 *qv*

HAY Kathleen Margaret *MA 1968
d of Alexander J. H. bus prop. and Catherine I. Davidson teacher; b Elgin 25.12.45
teacher inf s Lond 1969–77
m Elgin 4.8.72 Gregory P. Hayes computer consult. s of Edward P. H. Regina Sask

HAY Margaret Jean Wilson *MA 1968
d of George H. master mariner, harbour master and Pearl G. Wilson; b Aber 24.6.45
ALA 1971
ref lib publ lib Aber 1968–69; rare books lib Glas 1971–75
m Aber 20.9.68 James A. Mellis MA 1968 *qv*

HAY Morag Cordiner *BSc 1969
d of James C. H. NALGO off. and Margaret F. Stewart secy; b Aber 9.7.47
anim feedstuffs chem Aber 1969–78; consult. chem Ellon from 1978
m Aber 1.8.70 James Taylor MA 1971 teacher s of James F. T. Aber

HAY Norman *MA 1956

HAY Robert King Miller *BSc 1967
s of William M. H. civ serv DHSS and Margaret M. J. B. Miller teacher; b Edin 19.8.46
MSc(E Ang) 1968 PhD(E Ang) 1971
MRC post doct res fell. zool dept Edin 1971, s of agr Edin 1972–74; lect: crop prod. dept Bunda coll of agr univ of Malawi 1974–76, crop prod. s of agr Edin 1976–77, soil sc dept of environmental sc univ of Lanc from 1977
m Monifieth 31.5.69 Dorothea H. Vinycomb MA 1968 *qv*

HAY Rosalind Anne MB ChB 1965
d of William M. H. civ serv DHSS and Margaret M. J. B. Miller teacher; b Edin 10.5.42
h o Bangour gen hosp, Leith hosp 1965–66; sen h o Bangour gen hosp 1966–68
m Aber 17.7.65 David G. Pyatt BSc(for) 1961 *qv*

HAY Sandra Yeaman *MA 1959
d of Andrew L. H. MA 1925 *qv*; b Aber 26.7.36
assistante école normale d'institutrices Amiens France 1959–60; teacher Europ lang and educ centre Bournemouth 1961–63; Glasg: lect Langside coll of f e 1964–72, coll of tech 1972–73; asst chief off. Scot. bus. educ council Edin from 1974

HAY Stuart Scott *MA 1969
s of Walter H. coll janitor and Annabella B. Scott shop man.; b Dun 6.4.47
Dip Ed(Dund) 1970
teacher hist/mod stud. Lawside acad Dun from 1970
m Dun 3.4.71 Eileen M. Ferguson machine oper d of Douglas M. F. Dun

HAY William Graham *MA 1965

HAY William Thomas MA 1970
s of William P. H. foreman slater and Lillian B. Hay; b Ellon 12.3.48
teacher: Peterhead acad 1971–74, Banksia Park h s Adelaide Aust from 1974
m Inverurie 7.8.71 Helen M. Minty d of George A. M. Inverurie

HAYES Norman Douglas PhD 1957
BSc(R'dg)

HAYFRON-BENJAMIN Jonathan MB ChB 1966
s of Charles F. H.-B. BA(Lond) barrister-at-law and Grace Sackey; b Elmina Ghana 11.8.36
h o med/surg Glasg 1966–67; sen h o obst and gyn Chatham 1967–68; m o min of health Tamale Accra 1968–73; resid paediat univ of Ott from 1973
m Leeds 1967 Ataa S. Koram nurse d of E. M. K. BSc(Cantab) Accra

HAYMAN Jarvis Rigden MB ChB 1966
s of Arthur G. R. H. w/off. RAF, civ serv, teacher violin and Elizabeth J. Smith teacher; b Shrewsbury 18.2.42
FRCSE 1973 FRACS 1974
h o surg, med ARI 1966–67; sen resid m o surg, med Ballarat Aust 1967–69; lect anat Aberd 1970–72; regist surg: Inv gen hosps 1972–74, NSW teaching hosps Sydney Aust 1974–76, private pract Goulburn NSW from 1976
m Inv –.3.67 Kathleen R. Melville RGN d of William M. Inv

HAYS Mark Stormont BSc 1965

HAZEL Alan Walter *BSc 1968
b Chelmsford 24.7.46
MBA(Harv) 1973
ESSO petr Co: marketing trainee 1968–69, salesman Coleraine 1969–73; Lond: motoring analyst, invest. analyst from 1973
m Cheadle Hulme 20.7.68 Jean M. Pepper MA 1968 *qv*

HEALEY Michael Charles PhD 1969
s of Arthur G. H. ship's wireless oper M o T and Elizabeth Clarke; b Prince Rupert BC Canada 31.3.42
BSc(BC) 1964 MSc(BC) 1966
Canada: leader fisheries man. res Winnipeg 1970–74, Nanaimo from 1974
m Vancouver 2.7.66 Judy A. Takahashi BSc(BC) d of Yosh T. Salmon Arm BC

HEAP Wilfrid *MA 1962 Dip Ed 1963

HEARD Sheila Marilyn MA 1970
m Macrae

HEATH Margaret Gowans MA 1970
d of William G. J. H. marine eng and Ruby Gowans shorthand typist; b Montrose 16.7.49
secy Montrose 1970–71; teacher Gourdon p s from 1972
m Aber 3.4.70 Graeme S. M. Calder asst mill man. s of Albert I. C. Inverbervie

HECTOR Moira Eilona Margaret MA 1970
m de Silva

HEDDLE Frederick William BSc 1958

HEDLEY Anthony Johnson MB ChB 1965 MD 1972
s of Thomas J. H. chem eng/man. dir and Winifred Duncan secy; b Greenmount 8.4.41
MRCP(UK) 1973 Dip Soc Med(Edin) 1973 MFCM 1974
h o ARI 1965–66; Aberd: Garden & Phillips fell. materia medica 1966–67, res fell. mat. med and therap 1967–69; med regist Maryfield hosp and hon asst dept of pharm Dund 1969–72; fell. dept commun med Edin 1972–74; lect commun med Aberd 1974–76; sen lect commun health Nott from 1976
m Aber 2.8.67 Elizabeth A. Walsh nurse/clin teacher d of William H. W. Houston Renfrew

HEGEDUS Istva'n Imre Zsolt MA 1966
s of I. I. H. DEcon(Budapest) lect maths and Klàra G. A. Salamon lang secy; b Budapest 2.10.42
Cert Biol(Tor) 1973
teacher: biol Lond 1967–69, maths/sc Toronto from 1969

HEGGS Glenville William *BSc(for) 1969
s of Thomas W. H. paintshop foreman and Mary J. Philips packer; b Leicester 7.3.47
for. off. with logging comp responsible for logging and for. progr Belize C America 1970–74; market. man. for. co-op N Wales 1975–76; for. advis Windward Is/gen man. Forest Indust Dev Corp Commonwealth of Dominica from 1977
m Urquhart 17.1.69 Jeanette Henderson MA 1968 *qv*

HEILPERN Jeffrey MB ChB 1964

HEINZMAN Colin *BSc 1968
s of George C. H. indust chem and Betty M. Auckland cler off., civ serv; b Newcastle 5.7.46
Dip Ed(Sheff) 1969 Dip Admin(W Aust) 1976
teacher: chem Rutherford s Newcastle-u-Tyne 1969–71, sc Perth W Aust from 1972
m Wilmslow 26.8.68 Lesley M. Short MA 1968 *qv*

HELGASON Bjarni PhD 1959
BA (Iceland)

HELLSTRØM Per Arvid MB ChB 1967

HENDERSON Aileen Jean Marshall MA 1965
d of William D. H. teacher and Jean G. Marshall; b Buckie 19.2.44
teacher Engl: Fraserburgh acad 1966–68, Aber acad 1968–71; remed Portlethen from 1978
m Aber 23.12.68 David N. Howie MA 1965 *qv*

HENDERSON Alasdair Ross BSc 1969

HENDERSON Alastair Andrew Ross *MA 1959

HENDERSON Alexander Scott MB ChB 1959 MD 1967
s of Alexander H. MB ChB(St And) phys and Mary E. Charlton nurs. sister; b Aber 7.12.35
DPM(Lond) 1962 MRACP(Melb) 1964 MRCP(Lond) 1965 MRCPsych 1969 FRACP 1971
h o ARI 1959–60; h o, regist Ross clin Aber 1960–62; regist psychiat Prince Henry hosp Sydney 1963–65; member scient staff MRC unit epidemiological stud. in psychiat Edin 1965–68; foundation chair of psychiat univ of Tasmania 1968–74; dir NH and MRC soc psychiat res unit ANU Canberra from 1975
m Sydney 1965 Priscilla H. Gill physioth d of William G. Drummoyne NSW

HENDERSON Anne MA 1968 Dip Ed 1969
d of James L. H. site ag and Alice M. Smith shop asst; b Huntly 10.5.47
teacher Engl/hist: Kelso h s 1969–71, Perth h s from 1971

HENDERSON Antoinette Margaret BSc 1957
d of Peter R. H. draper and Flora Cumming shop asst; b Aber 19.5.36
chem Esso res Abingdon 1957–59; teacher sc Forres acad 1960–63
m Aber 6.8.62 James Brown RAF/radio tech/telecommun tech off (MOD) s of James B. Haswell

HENDERSON Brian Alexander MA 1968

HENDERSON Charles Neil *BSc 1961
s of Charles S. H. MA 1930 *qv*; b Peterculter 24.3.39
trainee paper tech Dartford 1961–62; dev chem Wiggins Teape photogr paper mills 1962–66; tech man. Samuel Jones & Co. Tillycoultry 1966–72; tech and comm man. Guardbridge paper comp from 1972
m Birm 4.8.62 Susan M. Lambert BSc 1961 *qv*

HENDERSON Colin *BSc 1964 PhD 1968

HENDERSON David John MA 1968
s of David M. H. BSc(Glas) civ eng and Margaret G. Inkster; b Perth 3.6.47
RAF pilot 1968–72; airline pilot BA Heathrow from 1972
m Perth 10.8.73 Patricia Z. Hall airline stewardess d of Albert H. H. MB ChB(Lond) Stanley

HENDERSON David Munro *MA 1965
s of Roderick B. H. sales man., C of S min and Isabella C. Munro; b Inv 16.1.43
Dip Ed(Edin) 1968
post grad stud. univ of Virginia USA 1965–66; methods analyst Vancouver 1966–67; econ master Daniel Stewart's coll Edin 1968–69; lect bus. organis H-W 1969–72, lect econ 1972–75; reg econ HIDB Inv from 1975
m Strathdon 7.9.68 Anna M. C. Webster teacher d of Alexander W. Glenbuchat

HENDERSON David Scott *MA 1958

HENDERSON Elisabeth Agnes Ross MA 1967
m Gammie

HENDERSON Eric Alexander Macleod *MA 1966

HENDERSON Eric Watt BSc 1969
s of Charles B. H. foreman stonemason and Annabella Soutar; b Forfar 25.4.46
scient off. in phys oceanography Marine lab Aber 1969–73, higher scient off. from 1973
m Aber 27.7.79 Jennifer E. M. McLaren sales rep d of Ian McL. Braemar

HENDERSON Ernest Allan *BSc 1959

HENDERSON Fraser George BSc(eng) 1966
s of George M. H. RN and Gertrude Calder bus. woman; b Valetta Malta 27.4.39
MNZIE 1970 MICE 1971 Member Assoc Consult. Eng, NZ 1974
asst eng city Aber 1966; Marks, Stiles & Sedcole consult. eng and arch., Hamilton NZ: asst, sen des eng, assoc 1966–73, ptnr from 1973
m Hamilton NZ 1967 Elizabeth F. Grattan acct asst d of Denis F. G. Toronto

HENDERSON George *BSc 1967 MSc 1969

HENDERSON George William MA 1959

HENDERSON George William MA 1967

HENDERSON Hamish McNaughton LLB 1957
s of James S. H. MA(St And) schoolmaster and Kate M. McNaughton MA(St And) teacher; b Tannadice 19.9.26
BA(Cantab) 1949 MA(Cantab) 1957
lect Edin: constit law 1958–69, Scots law 1969–72; sen lect from 1972
m Edin 1.9.60 Kathleen M. Guthrie MA(Edin) univ lect, teacher d of Henry W. G. MA(Edin) West Linton

HENDERSON Ian Bruce *BSc(eng) 1965
s of Jonathan H. haulage contr and Sarah Bruce; b Oldmeldrum 30.7.43
MSc(Strath) 1971
ICI: plant eng agr div Billingham 1965–68, construct. eng dyestuffs div Ayrsh 1968–70, proj eng petroleum div Billingham 1970–75, sen staff from 1975
m Wick 5.6.70 Margaret G. Calder nurse d of John C. Wick

HENDERSON Iona Mairi Clark *MA 1967

HENDERSON James *MA 1968

HENDERSON Jeanette MA 1968
d of George H. H. master butcher and Elspeth M. Cruickshank; b Rothes 29.6.48
Belize City: teacher Engl/hist 1970–71, lect Eng lit. teachers' trg coll 1971; Wrexham: teacher Fr/Europ stud. 1975–76, Fr/Ger 1976, Engl/Fr 1976–79
m Urquhart 17.1.69 Glenville W. Heggs BSc(for) 1969 *qv*

HENDERSON Jennifer Jean BEd 1969
d of William H. farm. and Dorothy Barton; b Fyvie 20.8.47
teacher Fraserburgh North p s 1969–70, Cowie p s Stirlingsh 1970–73, stud. infant/nurs assoc and Froebel Callander Park coll of educ Stirlingsh 1973–74
m Aber 7.7.70 Douglas L. Stewart teacher, advis outdoor educ s of Douglas L. S. MA 1934 *qv*

HENDERSON Jonathan *MA 1963

HENDERSON Mabel Christina *MA 1967
s of David H. gamekeeper and Agnes A. W. Barr; b W Hartlepool 3.4.45
teacher mod lang Harlaw acad Aber 1968–78
m Tongue 24.7.71 Leslie M. Baxter asst man. s of Alexander L. B. Aber

HENDERSON Margaret MA 1957
d of George H. H. master butcher and Elspeth M. Cruickshank; b Rothes 12.4.37
teacher: Engl Stanley j s s 1958–62, Logie Easter p s 1964–65, Tain p s from 1975
m Aber 18.4.62 Lawrence D. R. Allan CA s of David A. Perth

HENDERSON Margaret Elizabeth LLB 1967
d of Gordon H. H. MA 1937 *qv*; b Lurgan NI 9.12.46
law app Aber 1967–68; solic Burnett & Reid advoc Aber from 1969
m Aber 3.7.71. John G. Sutherland estate fact. s of John M. S.

HENDERSON Mary Fletcher MA 1968
d of James H. customs and excise off. and Isabella H. Leitch; b Edin 30.1.47
teacher mod lang Inverurie acad 1969–73
m Balerno 26.12.69 Neil D. Morrison res tech s of Charles M. Aber

HENDERSON Michael George MB ChB 1970

HENDERSON Peter *MA 1960
s of Peter H. marine eng, TU off. and Mary Hepburn; b Aber 28.5.37
res asst labour party Lond 1960–61; lect: St And 1961–66,

univ of Otago Dunedin NZ 1966–70, sen lect from 1970
m Aber 14.10.67 Doreen J. Davies BA lib Middx

HENDERSON Peter George *BSc 1966

HENDERSON Reginald Laurence MA 1956 *MEd 1958
s of Andrew H. dep chief constable, comp rep and Johanna B. Gear secy; b Lerwick 8.8.34
2nd lt RAEC 1958–60; teacher Aber 1960–61; educ psych Durh 1961–63, admin asst Northumberland 1963–66; asst dir of educ Argyll 1966–72; dep dir of educ Banffsh 1972–75 interim dir 1975, div educ off. Keith from 1975
m Aber 12.7.61 Gladys Wilson MA 1958 *qv*

HENDERSON Robert Burnett Mackenzie BSc 1968
s of Robert G. B. H. man. and Elizabeth Burnett; b Fraserburgh 23.1.40
teacher chem Inverurie acad from 1969

HENDERSON Robert Rait *BSc(eng) 1962

HENDERSON Ronald Gordon MA 1962

HENDERSON Rosalind Lyra MA 1967 LLB 1970
d of David H. MA(Glas) jeweller, ex-hon sheriff and Lyra J. C. Gray; b Aber 26.5.46
law app Glasg 1970–72; leg. asst. Brander & Cruickshank advoc Aber 1972–73
m Aber 15.11.72 John Flett fishery off. s of James T. F. Buckie

HENDERSON Thomas William MA 1968 Dip Ed 1969
s of Thomas W. H. plumber and Eveline Evans; b Aber 28.5.27
teacher Aber: Rosemount s 1969–71, AGS 1971–73, year master from 1973
m Aber 27.5.63 Margaret R. Walker pharm d of James W. Aber

HENDERSON Vera Margaret MA 1970
d of John H. drainage insp and Vera M. McGovern; b Aber 1.10.46
teacher Glasg from 1972

HENDERSON William Hillyard *BSc 1969

HENDERSON William Lawrence MSc 1961
BSc(Edin)

HENDRIE Robert *BSc 1969

HENDRY Alastair David Morrice BSc(eng) 1962

HENDRY Albert Gordon MA 1962
s of Albert J. H. bakery vanman/man. and Helen H. Robertson shop asst, clerkess; b Ellon 30.10.40
teacher: dem s Aber 1963–69, RGC j s from 1969
m Bearsden 24.7.71 Morag Mason teacher d of William M. T. M. MA(Glas) Bearsden

HENDRY Alison Margaret MA 1964
d of John M. H. man. fishing comp and Amabel Tawse typist; b Aber 30.7.43
Dip Soc St(Edin) 1965
ch care off. Midlothian c c 1965–67
m Aber 28.12.66 Charles J. Forbes arch. draughtsman s of Charles F. Udny

HENDRY David Alexander Forbes *BSc 1968
s of Alexander F. H. MA(Glas) Scot. chmn conserv party and Margaret Whitehead; b Falkirk 12.3.46
PhD(Cantab) 1972
univ lect Syd Aust from 1971
m 9.10.72 Mary Collard

HENDRY David Forbes *MA 1966
s of Robert E. H. hotel prop. and Catherine Mackenzie hotel prop.; b Nott 6.3.44
MSc(Lond) 1967 PhD(Lond) 1970 fell. econometric soc
LSE: lect econ 1969–73, reader 1973–77; prof of econometric from 1977; USA: visiting assoc prof Yale 1975, UC Berkeley 1976
m Lond 7.10.66 Evelyn R. Vass MA 1966 *qv*

HENDRY Ian David BEd 1969
s of Norman D. H. MA(Edin) teacher and Annabella M. Reid; b Kempston 1.6.41
teacher: Engl Arbroath acad 1969–71, Hayshead p s Arbroath 1971–72; head: Carmyllie p s Arbroath 1972–76, Torphins p s from 1976
m Aber 30.9.67 Elizabeth A. Hay teacher d of Adam H. Newmachar

HENDRY Jacqueline Ann BSc 1966
m Simpson

HENDRY John Fraser LLB 1968
s of John M. H. asst progr controller and Amabel Tawse typist; b Cottingham 28.2.47
Aber: app solic 1968–70, asst solic 1970–73, ptnr Campbell Connon & Co advoc from 1974
m Aber 21.12.70 Margaret C. Robertson MA 1969 *qv*

HENDRY June Rennie MA 1959
d of George H. farm. and Maggie Rennie; b Banff 30.6.38
teacher: Fr/Engl/Lat Aberlour h s 1960–64, Linlithgow acad and p s from 1970
m Grange 27.7.62 Alexander N. Adam teacher p e s of Robert A. Aberlour

HENDRY Kathleen Anne *MA 1968
d of David H. mech eng merch N, oil comps and Margaret Johnston secy; b Iran 19.3.46
teacher: Kelso 1969–71, Dun 1971–72, head hist Dormem Wells h s Southall from 1972
m Dun 6.4.72 John A. Grocott landscape asst s of Edmund S. G. Lond

HENDRY Robert Duthie BSc 1959

HENDRY Sylvia Mattison *MA 1964
m Ramsay

HENEGHAN Kathleen Cecelia MA 1969

HENRY Agnes Christina *MA 1962

HENRY Michael Duff MA 1958 ᶜLLB 1960
s of Robert H. MA 1929 *qv*; b Harrow 29.8.37
leg./admin asst Renfrew c c Paisley 1962–65; leg. asst Aber c c 1965–67; Renfrew c c Paisley: p a to county clerk 1967–72, asst county clerk 1972–73, dep county clerk from 1973 and chief exec off. to new Eastwood dist council from 1974
m Aber 1962 Margaret C. Murray occup therap d of J. M. M. Gardenstown

HEPBURN Alan Anderson LLB 1965
s of William R. H. sen exper off. and Jean C. Thomson; b Kilmarnock 15.9.43
Dip Pers Man.(Strath) 1966 MIPM

Coventry: pers off. Bristol Siddeley Eng 1966–67; indust rel off. Rolls Royce 1967–68, Dunlop 1968–70; pers man. National Tyre Service Stockport; div pers man. Dunlop Semtex Brynmawr from 1974
m Aber 22.12.67 Olga F. Stephen catering man., teacher d of Robert J. S. BSc(Strath) Bieldside

HEPBURN Alexander Andrew BSc 1967

HEPBURN Ian Ronald *BSc 1969
s of Stuart D. H. acct and Joyce E. Huggins; b Aber 27.5.47
syst progr nat eng lab E Kilbride 1969–71; Sperry Univac: sen syst progr, proj leader, group leader Zagreb Yugoslavia 1971–74, Europ h q data processing consult. Madrid, other Europ. capitals 1974–76; European syst spec Sperry Univac internat div Lond from 1976
m Elgin 30.6.69 Irene E. Slowey

HEPBURN Margaret Rennie MA 1957

HEPBURN Robert BSc 1970

HEPBURN Sheila Doreen MA 1963
d of James R. H. chief insp CID and Mary Noble shorthand typist; b Aber 2.7.29
teacher Aber: Sunnybank p s 1964–70, asst head Kittybrewster p s 1970–77, head Balnagask p s from 1977
m 12.4.55 Nicol P. Patterson; husb *d* Lond 6.3.62

HEPBURN Stanley *BSc 1970

HEPBURN Stella *MA 1970

HEPBURN Stuart Philip *BSc 1967 PhD 1971
s of Stuart D. H. farm cost acct and Joyce E. Huggins; b Norwich 15.4.45
ARIC 1969
ICI: res/market dev Runcorn 1970–74, USA market dev Wilmington Delaware from 1974

HEPPLESTON Paul Bernard PhD 1968
BSc(Wales)

HEPWORTH, Joan Susan *MA 1970
m Evison

HERBERT Alan Gordon *BSc(eng) 1970

HERBERT David William *BSc(eng) 1963

HERBERT Rodney Andrew PhD 1970
s of Harold H. loc govt off. and Dora Scarth; b York 27.6.44
BTech(Brad) 1967
res fell. Edin 1970–71; lect microbiol Dund from 1971
m Carlisle 4.9.71 Helen J. M. Millard MSc 1968 *qv*

HERD David James *MA 1965

HERD Isabella Helen BSc 1965

HERD Patricia Margaret MA 1970
d of James H. MB ChB 1944 *qv*; b Aber 18.4.49
post grad. secy ling course Aber coll of comm; Lond: secy/information asst 1971–73, edit. asst 1973–74, sub edit. BBC from 1974

HERD Peter Bruce MA 1970
s of Birrell H. trawler skipper/owner and Jeannie Bruce; b Buckie 2.7.48
CA 1977
Aber: asst acct, acct 1976–79, acct/comp secy from 1979
m Fraserburgh 2.6.73 Maureen P. McDonald beauty therap d of James McD. Fraserburgh

HERFORD Penelope Jean PhD 1968
d of Philip H. H. mech eng and Elizabeth J. Hawkins; b Reading 26.11.40
BSc(Glas)
asst lect agr biochem s of agr Aber 1968–69; scient off., higher scient off. poultry res centre Edin 1970–72
m Glasg 13.12.69 Dorian J. Pritchard BSc(Wales) biol, res fell. s of Oliver L. P. Caerphilly

HERRICK Peter William BSc(for) 1966
s of Neil C. H. clerk and Betty F. Findlay; b Auckland NZ 28.2.40
BSc(Canterbury NZ) 1964
for. NZ for. serv Rotorua 1966–69, prin for. trg centre 1970–74; prin for. Kaingaroa for. from 1975
m Christchurch 15.1.64 Kaye E. Webley artist d of Kasper G. W. Christchurch

HERRINGTON Reginald Nicholas PhD 1966
MB(Birm) DPM(Glas)

HESLOP Jane Stuart MA 1964
m Macnamara

HESLOP Rodney Eric Faber *BSc(for) 1958
s of Eric T. H. army off. and Kathleen E. Faber; b Hurworth-on-Tees 11.6.36
nat serv 5th royal tank regt Catterick, W Ger 1958–60; dist off. for. comm Farnham 1960–62; scient off., prin scient off. dept of soil surv Macaulay inst Aber from 1963

HETHERINGTON Alison Ann MA 1967

HEWET Elizabeth Ann MA 1967
d of Alexander R. H. MA 1936 *qv*; b Aber 20.11.46
teacher: Aber 1968–69, Rosssh 1969–71
m Aber 1.8.69 Hugh G. J. Jamieson BSc(eng) 1967 *qv*

HEWINS Roger Herbert *BSc 1962
s of Herbert C. H. civ serv and Linda M. Marshall; b Farnham 29.11.40
PhD(Tor) 1971 NASA fell. 1972–75
geol: geol surv Georgetown Guyana 1963–65, Falconbridge Nickel Ontario 1965–67; grad stud., lect Tor 1967–72; USA: lunar sample co-investigator Lehigh univ Pa 1972–75, asst prof geol Rutgers univ NJ from 1975 (NASA grant to study meteorites)
m Georgetown 2.8.63 Catherine P. McDonald MA 1961 *qv*

HEWITT David Sword PhD 1969
MA(Edin)

HEWITT Michael Ross *BSc(eng) 1962 MSc 1964 PhD 1968
s of Robert G. H. soldier, civ serv and Anna R. Priest MA 1924 *qv*; b Aldershot 14.5.40
T.D.
Aber: scient off. Torry res stat 1964–68, sen scient off. 1968–73, head of eng sect 1970, prin scient off. Torry res stat from 1973; AUOTC major 1970 21c 1974
m Aber 14.10.63 Catherine A. Watt MA 1963 *qv*

HEY Jean Marjorie MB ChB 1970
d of George B. H. BA(Cantab) insur actuary and Elizabeth H. Burns BA(Cantab) teacher; b N Shields 16.4.47
USA: clin assoc paediat Charlottesville Virginia 1970–72,

intern paediat Norfolk Virginia 1972–73; h o surg Amersham 1973–74; USA: resid, sen resid paediat Durham N Carolina 1975–77, private practice paediat Durham from 1977
m Aber 11.7.70 John W. A. Findlay BSc 1966 *qv*

HICKIE John Frederick *MA 1968
m Hessle 13.9.69 Rosemary Hings MA 1969 *qv*

HICKIE Sheila *MA 1968 Dip Ed 1969
d of Charles H. distillery employee and Margaret R. Anderson; b Montrose 14.8.45
teacher: mod lang Stirling 1969–72, Munster W Ger with BFES 1972–75, Engl Stadthagen W Ger 1975–77

HICKSON Bryan MB ChB 1965
s of Frank P. H. cabinetmaker and Winifred Grundy; b Reepham 9.1.40
MRCP(UK) 1970
h o, regist Aber hosps 1965–71; sen med regist St Bart's hosp Lond from 1971
m Aber 13.7.65 Kathleen Russell BSc 1962 *qv*

HIGGINS Helen Ritchie *BSc 1967

HIGGINS Katharine *BSc 1968
m Jewitt

HIGSON John Michael LLB 1966

HILL Avril Nicol *MA 1956 Dip Ed 1957
d of Harold G. H. MA(Glas) teacher and Elizabeth A. H. Nicol; b Nairn 5.4.34
teacher Perth 1957–64; spec asst geog: Perth 1963–64, Merritt Canada 1964–65; teacher Toronto 1965–67, head geog from 1967

HILL Guy Anthony *MA 1966
s of Arthur H. H. and Gladys Coleman; b Dartford 16.2.43
Cert TEFL(Lond) 1969
VSO teacher Engl Vientiane Laos 1966–68; lect Engl: univ of Belgrade 1969–70, Chulalongkorn univ Bangkok 1970–76; Edin lang foundation 1976–77; educ off. Brunei from 1977
m Edin 26.8.70 Dorothy A. Hare MA(Edin) TEFL d of James H. Edin

HILL Harry Joseph Charles *MA 1963
s of Henry B. H. SAI and May Curle; b Aber 17.10.40
Canada: grad asst Alta 1963–64, instr Engl univ of Victoria 1964–66; artistic dir RPA Productions Victoria acting/directing assignments 1968–69; lect Winona state coll Minn USA 1969–70; chmn CEGEP Engl dept Loyola coll Montreal 1970–75

HILL Veronica Marianne *MA 1959
d of Ronald H. MA(Oxon) civ serv and Elizabeth M. Rawson; b Lincoln 18.4.37
statist asst Macaulay inst Aber 1959–60; res asst dept geol Nott from 1974
m Stretton-on-Dunsmore 18.3.61 Neil M. Croll BSc 1960 *qv*

HILMI Haluk Ahmed BSc(for) 1956

HILMY Yousef PhD 1959
BCom MSc(Cairo)

HILTON Anthony Victor *MA 1968
s of Raymond W. H. BSc(for) 1933 *qv*; b Ottringham 26.8.46
Lond: fin. journalist: *Guardian* 1968–69, *Observer* 1969–72, *Sunday Express* 1972–74; edit. *Accountancy Age* from 1974
m Bradford 29.3.69 Patricia Moore TV exec; marr diss 1974

HILTON John Geoffrey *BSc 1970

HILTON Susan Nola *MA 1964
d of Raymond W. H. BSc(for) 1933 *qv*; b Ottringham 18.2.42
asst prin Scot. dev dept Edin 1964–66; man. eng services Boston, Mass from 1969
m Edin 15.3.68 James M. Carifio BA(Col) univ teacher, consult. s of Luigi J. C. Bradford Mass

HINCH Barry *BSc(eng) 1969 MSc 1970

HIND Angela Joan *MA 1969
d of Francis P. H. physioth and Kate J. Page teacher; b Margate 25.6.47
teacher Engl girls' county h s Romford 1969–73
m Ramsgate 21.6.69 Richard S. Thomas MA(Oxon) prin home civ serv

HINDMARSH Paul Stewart *BSc(agr) 1967
s of Ralph H. hardware merch and Mabel P. Brigham; b Newcastle-u-Tyne 1.9.43
MSc(Lond) 1968 DIC 1968 MIBiol 1971
ODA stud. crop storage problems Yundum res stat The Gambia 1968–69; scient off. trop stored prod. centre 1970–72; sen scient off. from 1972 (seconded to Mt Makulu res stat Chilanga Zambia)
m Sunderland 16.8.67 Elizabeth A. Toyer MA 1965 *qv*

HINDOCHA Suresh Laljibhai BSc(eng) 1966
s of Laljibhai H. indust and Muktaben Lakhani; b Kakira Uganda 20.1.42
Pondicherry: dir New Horizon sugar mills from 1967; tech dir Auroville Electronics from 1968; man. dir Aummag Private from 1974

HINDS Enrique Roland MA 1964

HINDS Eric Arthur BSc(eng) 1969
s of Wilfred H. bus driver and Lilian M. McCue shop prop., man.; b Houghton-le-Spring 10.2.47
MICE 1973 MIWE 1974
eng asst mid-Scot. water board Falkirk 1969–73; asst eng NE Scot. water board Aber 1973–75; group leader (operations) Gordon div dept of water serv Grampian reg c from 1975
m Buckie 4.4.70 Cathleen H. Geddes teacher d of Alexander G. Buckie

HINGA Godfrey MSc 1964
BSc(agr) Lond

HINGE Peter Leonard Graham MA 1968

HINGS Rosemary MA 1969
d of Ronald H. tailor and Mavis Salmon; b Hessle 18.7.48
Southampton: acct asst Southern Gas 1969–70, p r asst 1970–71
m Hessle 13.9.69 John F. Hickie MA 1968 *qv*

HINTON Susan Jane *MA 1969

HIRD Marilyn BSc 1968
m Murray

HITCHING Alan Victor LLB 1968

HJORT Ove Johan MB ChB 1963
s of Sven K. H. MB(Oslo) consult. surg and Harriet Backer-Groendahl; b Egersund Norway 25.6.36
Norway: resid surg/med Gjoevik 1964–65; asst g p V Slidre 1965; sen h m o/regist med Oslo 1965–72; consult. med Hammerfest 1970; regist cardiol Oslo from 1972; lt-col Norwegian army med corps and part-time consult. Red Cross clin Oslo from 1975
m Drammen Norway 1.10.66 Tove Vilstad d of Ivar V. Drammen

HO-A-SHU Laura Shirley Jocelyn *MA 1956
d of David O. Ho-A-Shu acct and Dorothy A. Lee; b Guyana 29.4.32
teacher: Georgetown Guyana 1956–59, hist Kingston Jamaica 1962–65, hist Lond from 1965
m Aber 15.10.55 Paul T. d'Orban MB ChB 1956 *qv*

HOBBIN Maureen Elizabeth BEd 1969
d of Norman G. E. H. sub postmaster and Agnes Goudie dist nurse; b Lerwick 2.12.47
teacher mod lang/Engl St Conval's R.C. h s Cumnock 1969–72
m Lerwick 17.7.69 Peter Barr BEd 1969 *qv*

HOBBS Alexander *MA 1958
s of Alexander H. shopworker and Davidena Blacklaw hairdresser; b Aber 23.8.37
asst St And 1961–64; res fell. Strath 1965–67; lect: Edin coll of comm 1968–69, Jordanhill coll of educ Glasg 1969–75; sen lect Paisley coll of tech from 1975
m Aber 16.10.61 Mary L. Kemp BSc 1961 *qv*

HOBSON Christine Patricia MB ChB 1961
b Ashton-u-Lyne 19.9.27
DObstRCOG 1963
g p Saddleworth Oldham

HODD Keith Tobias Burnett MSc 1967
s of Frederick A. B. H. ophth optic. and Barbara J. Foster; b Hoddesdon 4.10.45
BSc(Lond) 1966
teacher sc Aberdeensh from 1973
m Hatfield 16.3.68 Patricia M. Berry BSc(Lond) res asst, teacher d of William B. Welwyn Garden City

HODGART Susan Wynne *MA 1966
d of Charles G. H. MIMechE man. dir eng works and Dorothy M. H. Gillespie WAAF, BBC tech; b Aber 1.11.44
Lond: admin asst dept Engl Bedford coll 1967; edit. asst, asst edit., proj edit., gen edit. Macdonald & Jane's book publ from 1967
m Lond 6.7.73 Ian Fleming art dir and des consult. s of Ernest F. Worthing

HODGES Timothy MA 1967
s of Thomas M. H. pers man. and Evelyn J. Foster; b Wolverhampton 18.5.44
lib Highfields s Wolverhampton 1970–73; teacher Engl Wood Green h s Wednesbury 1973–76; head Engl dept Pendeford h s Wolverhampton from 1976
m Aber 25.7.70 Angela J. G. Whyte BSc 1969 *qv*

HODGSON Ronald Arthur BSc 1970

HOGAN James Philip PhD 1957
BSc(agr)(Syd)

HOGG Cecil Archibald Grant BEd 1970

HOGG Christine McColl *MA 1970
d of James T. H. depot man., CA Inl Rev and Jessie M. Garlick secy; b Edin 8.11.47
teacher Engl: Cumbernauld h s 1971–73, Banff acad 1973–75
m Aber 21.8.70 Bruce K. Gardner MA 1971 teacher s of Alexander M. G. scient instrum maker/res asst nat phil Aberd

HOGG John *MA 1966
s of Alexander H. bldr and Margaret M. MacGillivray; b Nairn 8.5.42
teacher Engl Perth h s from 1967
m Aber 15.5.65 Jessie Campbell MA 1964 *qv*

HOGG Kathleen Louise MA 1969
d of William W. H. baker and Christina Gillan; b Aber 11.1.48
teacher Engl: St Mary's acad Bathgate 1970–72, Morgan acad Dun from 1972

HOGG Nigel Robert Laurence MA 1970
s of Peter L. H. chartered shipbroker and Elizabeth W. Humble; b W Hartlepool 6.1.49
F Inst Chartered Shipbrokers 1976
asst ag man. with loc shipbrokers Hull 1970–71; tanker chartering asst short sea chartering Göteborg Sweden 1971–72; Hartlepool: man. timber ag dept with loc shipbrokers 1972–74, comp secy, dir shipbrokers and fwdg ag from 1974
m Gifford 16.9.72 Elizabeth R. S. Taylor MA 1970 *qv*

HOGG William Murray *MA 1966
s of Gavin M. H. draper and Rose Davie; b Brechin 20.1.18
teacher mod lang Brechin h s from 1967
m Liv 15.11.41 Grace W. Fairlie d of W. S. F. Brechin

HOLBOURN Frances Moira *BSc 1966

HOLBOURN Sheila Catharine *BSc 1964
d Athelstan H. M. H. MA(Edin) lect phys Aberd and Joyce H. Brown BSc(Oxon); b Oxford 9.3.42
crofter Foula from 1964
m Scalloway 9.9.64 James R. Gear fisherman/crofter s of David M. G. Foula

HOLDER Valerie Elinor MA 1966 Dip Ed 1967

HOLDSWORTH Lily Florence Jane MA 1960
d of Cyril H. ship's cook and Frances A. Woolverton factory worker; b Bo'ness 5.7.18
teacher: Peterhead 1961–67, spec s Orpington from 1967
m Bo'ness 11.4.44 Frederick Birks civ serv s of George F. B. Falkirk

HOLDSWORTH Patricia Dorothy MA 1963
d of Douglas H. and Ethel F. Hunter; b Aber 18.12.42
teacher maths: High s for girls Aber 1964–65, Carolan g s Belfast 1965–68, Sir Wilfrid Laurier h s London, Ontario 1969–70, Bankhead acad 1970–74; asst prin maths Kincorth acad Aber 1974–75, prin guid Harlaw acad from 1975
m Aber 14.7.65 Niall A. Young BSc 1964 *qv*; marr diss 29.5.80

HOLLER Zeb North PhD 1967
s of Zeb N. H. BA(Davidson coll NC USA) teacher, bus. man and Mary V. Harrison mus teacher; b Atlanta Georgia USA 2.8.28
AB(Davidson coll NC) BD(Richmond Va)
assoc pastor central presb ch Atlanta 1967–68; univ minister NC state univ Raleigh NC 1968–72; gen pastor Orange presb PCUS Durham NC 1972–75; pastor: Fort Hill presb ch Clemson SC 1975–79, presb ch of the

Covenant Greensboro NC from 1979
m Pensacola Fla USA 22.8.53 Charlene Levey BS(Richmond) teacher d of Charles H. L. Pensacola

HOLLIDAY Richard Durden BSc(eng) 1962
s of Harry A. H. elect. eng comp dir and Kathleen Thomas teacher; b Watford 22.5.39
Lond: elect. eng 1962–67, reinsur broker 1967–73, insur underwriter Lloyds' from 1973
m Sevenoaks 10.6.67 Diana G. Reid secy, governess d of Nevile R. BA(Oxon) Kildary

HOLLOWAY Colin William PhD 1967
BSc(Wales)

HOLLOWAY John Stevenson BSc(for) 1969
s of John T. H. MSc(Otago) for. ecol, res admin and Una S. Stevenson Dip Home Sc(Otago); b Dunedin NZ 13.8.44
BSc(Otago) 1966
NZ for. serv: Gisborne 1969–71, dist for. Tampanui 1972–74, sen for. Dunedin from 1975
m Rangiora NZ 30.5.70 Linda J. Brown MB ChB 1964 *qv*

HOLLOWAY May Norma Duff MA 1968
d of Norman W. H. civ serv and May D. Mallows; b Lond 20.10.46
Dip Ed(Dund) 1969
teacher Engl Harris acad Dun 1969–74; working in France 1974–75; teacher Engl/hist Newtyle s from 1975

HOLM Isabel MA 1967
d of Evan M. H. farm. and Annie Ferguson farm.; b Resolis 13.6.46
teacher Avoch s 1968–72
m Dingwall 29.7.72 D. George Ross farm. s of John A. R. Fearn

HOLMES David *BSc 1969

HOLMES Hazel Brown MA 1969
d of Thomas B. H. farm. and Agnes A. Mitchell; b Edin 4.4.48
teacher Fr: Craigshill h s Livingston 1970–71, Douglas acad Milngavie 1971–72
m Currie 10.8.71 Robert Lamont farm. s of John L. Dumgoyne Glasg

HOLMES Paul Robin *BSc 1970

HOLMES Sheila MA 1970
m Aber 3.4.72 Stewart B. Telfer MSc 1969 *qv*

HOLMES William Alexander MB ChB 1962

HONEYMAN Ian MA 1962
s of John H. min of relig and Helen D. S. Aitchison; b Falkirk 12.1.42
div stud. licensed by C of S 1965; asst to regist univ Botswana, Lesotho and Swaziland 1965–66; asst min Aber 1966–67; admin asst Sus 1967–69; clerk to sc s Strath 1969–71; chief admin off. coll of tech Glasg 1971–73; plan. off. univ of S Pacific Fiji from 1973
m Lerwick 25.7.67 Eleanor J. Leask d of Laurence L. Lerwick

HONIGMANN Frederick John Reinhard *MEd 1962
s of Hans D. H. PhD(Heidelberg) zool and Ursula M. Heilborn res tech zool; b Breslau Silesia 9.8.26
MA(St And) 1951 Dip Ed(St And) 1952 ABPsS 1965
teacher Aber acad 1962; educ psych ch guid serv Edin 1962–66; lect Craigie coll of educ Ayr from 1966
m Aber 9.7.55 Margaret M. L. Matheson BA(OU) d of John M. Aber

HOOD Charles Murray MA 1970
s of William E. H. bank man. and Isobel M. Marr; b Edin 2.4.49
Assoc Chart. Inst Sec. 1974
admin asst W Lothian c c Linlithgow 1970–71; admin trainee Midlothian c c 1971–73, admin asst 1973–75; committee clerk Lothian reg c from 1975
m Edin 23.7.76 Catherine F. Wilkinson BSc(Edin)

HOOD Ellis *BSc(eng) 1970

HOOD James Wilkie *MA 1964

HOOD Margaret Elizabeth BSc 1960
m Goudie

HOOD Virginia Agnes MA 1970
d of Francis C. H. MA(Edin) univ prof and Muriel Dodds MA(Cantab) univ lect; b Newcastle-u-Tyne 29.3.48
secy: dept of Greek Edin 1971–73, part-time Strath 1974–75
m Durham 26.4.73 Gordon M. Thomson LL B 1969 *qv*

HOPKIN Duncan James *BSc 1965 MSc 1970

HOPKIN Pamela Mary BSc 1966
m Davidson

HORN Irene Elizabeth MA 1969
d of Douglas J. L. H. civ eng and Agnes M. Tawse; b Kintore 6.11.47
teacher: Poole 1970–72, Glenrothes from 1972
m Aber 11.8.72 Alexander W. MacFarlane BSc 1970 *qv*

HORN Jennifer Rattray MA 1965
d of Charles G. H. farm. and Barbara Simpson; b Fyvie 29.9.44
Dip Ed(Edin) 1966
teacher: Edin 1967–69, Sydney, Aust 1971–73, Gvarv, Norway from 1973; secy Oslo 1970–71
m Fyvie 29.9.69 Rein D. Follestad potter s of Einar F. Oslo

HORNBY Windham Brownrigg *MA 1968 MEd 1979
stepson of John D. Brebner and s of Helen S. M. Lockhart; b Glas 7.4.46
teacher Malvern 1969–75; lect econ RGIT Aber from 1975
m Oxford 24.8.68 Allison J. Horncastle MA 1968 *qv*

HORNCASTLE Allison Jean *MA 1968 Dip Ed 1969
d of Charles L. H. loc govt off. and Elizabeth D. Rae secy; b Grays 12.6.46
teacher Engl Malvern 1969–71; Engl tut. 'A' level Worcester 1971–73; evening class tut. Higher Engl Aber 1977–79
m Oxford 24.8.68 Windham B. Hornby MA 1968 *qv*

HORNE Alexander Robert *BSc(agr) 1966

HORNE Helen Edith *BSc 1963
m John R. L. Howitt BSc 1962 *qv*

HORNE Jeanette Barbara MA 1962
d of William A. H. garage man. and Jane H. Webster; b Edin 17.11.41
teacher maths: Annan acad 1963–64, Lossiemouth h s 1964–67; remed/adjustment teacher Elgin East End s

1967–68; staff man. Marks & Spencer 1968–71; teacher maths: Circencester Deer Park s 1971–72, Cliftonville s Northampton 1972, St Mary's s Northampton 1972–73, Annan acad from 1973
m Elgin 22.8.70 Nicholas J. Smith garage man., BL area superv s of William H. S. Bristol

HORNE Margaret Helen *BSc 1967
d of Alexander H. shopkeeper and Ruth Yule shopkeeper; b New Deer 22.10.44
teacher geog: Marist s Manc 1967–70, head dept 1969–70, evening classes Falkirk from 1975
m Aber 6.4.68 Thomas N. Bowden BSc 1965 *qv*

HORNE Norman John *MA 1960
s of James H. bus driver and Helen Riddoch; b Turriff 10.12.37
teacher classics Hamilton acad 1961–66; prin classics: Nicolson inst Stornoway 1966–71, Royal acad Inv 1971–72; asst head h s Inv 1972–77; rector Milne's h s Fochabers from 1977
m Aber 6.12.61 Ann Gavin shorthand typist d of Robert G. Aber

HORNE Ralph Ross *BSc 1962
s of Ralph A. H. MB ChB 1934 *qv*; b Aber 5.9.40
PhD(Birm) 1967 Polar medal 1971
geol: Brit antarctic surv Antarctica, Birm 1962–69, geol surv Ireland Dublin from 1969
m Leek 10.7.70 Margaret A. Horner nurse

HORROCKS Rodger BSc 1968
s of Sidney H. MB ChB(Liv) g p and Marjory C. Conners; b Derby 18.5.45
teacher biol Mackie acad Stonehaven 1969–73, prin biol from 1973
m Aber 11.5.66 Sandra J. Norrie BSc 1968 *qv*

HORSFALL George Lister MB ChB 1957
s of George A. C. H. master jeweller and Mabel Feavers tailoress; b Halifax 20.5.28
DA 1961
h o ARI 1957–58; sen h o anaest spec hosps Aber 1958–61; regist anaest S Teesside hosps Middlesbrough 1961–64; g p/anaest Thornaby-on-Tees from 1964
m Aber 22.5.61 Edna M. Fraser RGN d of James F. Bucksburn

HORSMAN Eileen Lesley MB ChB 1968
d of Squire R. H. teacher and Marjorie Plummer teacher; b Scarborough 2.3.44
FFARCS 1975
h o Aber 1968–69; sen h o: Jamaica 1969–70, Birm 1972–74; regist Birm 1974–75; sen regist Manc 1975–79; consult. Manc from 1979

HOSIE Linda Elizabeth Amy MA 1969
d of Manson B. H. elect. contr and Elizabeth Davidson; b Inverurie 12.9.48
teacher Aber from 1970
m Inverurie 16.8.69 Frank D. Davidson acct s of David D. Inverurie

HOSKISON Felicity Margaret *MA 1969

HOSSACK John James Grieve *MA 1969

HOUGHTON Thomas MB ChB 1964
s of Thomas H. insur man. and Kathleen Hargreaves; b Brighton 17.12.39
sen h o obst/gyn UCH Jamaica 1965–66; trainee g p Hatton and Cruden Bay 1966–67; sen h o anaest ARI 1967–68; g p Jersey from 1968

HOUSE Frank Raymond MSc 1968
Dip Tech(Lond)

HOUSE Judith Isa MA 1958
d of George H. A. H. superv Shell-Mex and Dorothy E. Ibbotson teacher; b Hedon 15.3.37
Dip Soc St(Leeds) 1959
Birm: soc case worker Council of Soc Serv 1959–60, youth leader The Settlement 1960–61; teacher county inf s Horncastle from 1966
m Hedon 19.4.60 Gerald B. Gorst div youth off. s of Gerald E. G. Preston

HOUSTON Neil Campbell MSc 1969
s of David H. red leader, welder and Nellie Campbell SRN; b Troon 1.12.40
BSc(Glas) 1963 FRMS 1974 MIBiol 1977
Torry res stat Aber: asst exper off., higher scient off. bact/electron microscopy from 1963
m Giffnock 3.6.66 Irene H. A. Dod data process. oper d of Credric N. D. BEng(Liv) Giffnock

HOUSTON Raymond MB ChB 1962

HOUSTON William Bernard MB ChB 1961

HOWARD Christopher Bernard *BSc 1966 MSc 1970 PhD 1976
s of Bernard H. H. BSc(Manc) prof biochem and Molly Rackett; b Stockport 9.3.44
Aberd: res asst 1966–73, res off. chem from 1973
m Aber 3.1.69 Isobel M. Greensmith BSc 1968 *qv*

HOWARD Geoffrey BSc 1964
s of Frank H. quantity surv and Margaret Baron; b Leeds 29.2.44
MSc(Lond) 1971
res asst Huntingdon res centre 1964–65; teacher: head biol dept Alleyns s Lond; lect: Trent coll Nott 1971–72, Park Lane coll Leeds 1972–77, sen lect from 1977
m Lond 20.10.69 Janet E. Franklin secy d of Harold F. Belvedere

HOWARD Patricia Anne *MA 1968
d of Harold G. H. head teacher and Violet E. Kelly; b Ayr 20.4.46
plan. off. town and county plan. dept Lancs c c 1968–73
m Aber 27.10.69 Richard M. Galloway BSc 1967 *qv*

HOWAT John Morrey BSc(for) 1958
b Edin 1.6.36
for. off, conserv for. E Nigeria 1958–67; teacher biol Perth 1968–71; conserv off. Countryside Comm for Scot. from 1971, media advis off. from 1975

HOWELL Joan Christine MA 1970
m Green

HOWELL John Bede Joseph BSc(for) 1962
s of Alfred J. H. wing comdr RAF and Mary A. Trinham; b Moasca Egypt 21.8.35
woodman France 1962–63; Worcs: jun consult. 1963–67; ptnr in firm of for. consult. from 1967
m Chelsea 11.9.65 Elizabeth M. Hungerford BSc(Belf) child nutrit d of Richard H. Dublin

HOWIE David Neville MA 1965 LLB 1967
s of Thomas W. H. MA(Glas) C of S min and Alexanderina McLennan; b Glenluce 28.1.43
Aber: law app 1967–69, leg. asst 1969–70, ptnr John Laurie & Co solic from 1970
m Aber 23.12.68 Aileen J. M. Henderson MA 1965 *qv*

HOWIE Ian Harrison *BSc 1966 MSc 1967 PhD 1977

HOWIE John Mackintosh *MA 1958 DSc 1970
s of David Y. H. MA(Glas) C of S min Ruthrieston S ch Aber and Janet M. Mackintosh; b Chryston 23.5.36
DPhil(Oxon) 1961 FRSE 1971
asst dept maths Aberd 1958–59; asst, lect maths Glas 1961–67; visiting asst prof Tulane univ New Orleans USA 1964–65; sen lect maths Stir 1967–70; regius prof maths St And from 1970
m Aber 5.8.60 Dorothy J. M. Miller MA 1956 *qv*

HOWIE Kathleen Allison MA 1964
m McCaig

HOWIE Margaret McLennan MA 1964

HOWIE Robert *MA 1958
s of Robert R. H. cloth finisher and Mary N. Allison; b Aber 21.11.36
LRAM 1960
teacher mus: Torry acad 1959–60, Aber acad 1960–64; lect mus Aber coll of educ from 1964
m Aber 3.8.62 Helen M. Smith secy d of William S. Aber

HOWIE William MA 1960 BD 1963 CASS 1972
s of Robert R. H. cloth finisher and Mary N. Allison; b Aber 29.2.40
STM(NY) 1964
Aber: asst min Northfield par ch 1964–67; Aber assoc of soc serv: dev off. 1967–70, asst secy 1972–73, secy from 1974
m Aber 19.7.63 Elizabeth A. Gill MA 1963 *qv*

HOWIESON James Stephen Paterson BSc 1963

HOWIESON Margaret Paterson MA 1963

HOWITT Angus Philip *MA 1956

HOWITT David Scott BEd 1969

HOWITT John Robert Lewis BSc 1962
s of John H. bonus clerk and Annie S. McLellan; b Aber 21.8.42
teacher Fraserburgh 1963–65; educ off.: N Nigeria 1965–69; RAEC Harrogate 1970–73, Herford W Ger from 1973
m Aber 22.12.64 Helen E. Horne BSc 1963 *qv*

HÖYERALL Hans Martin MB ChB 1963
b Oslo 13.5.36
Dr Med(Oslo) 1976
pre-reg posts Stavanger, Sortland Norway 1964–65; m o h Skellefteå Sweden 1965–66; asst lege (g p) in clin paediat: Umeå Sweden 1966–67, Bergen Norway 1967–70; res worker in clin immunology and rheumat Oslo 1970–74; asst lege in rheumat 1974–76, neurology 1976–77, internal med from 1977
m Fredrikstad 27.7.63 Solveig E. Löken

HUCKVALE Eric Lindsay *BSc(agr) 1970
s of Edward F. H. eng and Ella Urquhart; b Warwick 1.10.46
teacher: Sudbury g s 1970–71, Bransholme h s Hull from 1972
m York 12.7.72 Bertha F. Stirling BMedBiol 1969 *qv*

HUGGAN Robert Elliot *MA 1964
no longer on GC reg

HUGHES Janice Butters *MA 1970
d of James H. master baker/caterer and Elizabeth Murray; b Aber 23.8.47
teacher: Fr Lond 1970–71, Fr/Ger Lewes 1971–73
m Aber 31.7.70 Ian M. Randall MA 1968 *qv*

HUGHSON Charles Bernard *MA 1968

HUGHSON Robert Martin *MA 1967

HULL Thomas Glenn *BSc(agr) 1970
s of Robert H. steelworks foreman, linesman and Dorothy Bradley; b Newcastle-u-Tyne 24.4.47
Newcastle: hosp porter 1970–72, insur ag 1972–73; exec off. civ serv Lond, Newcastle 1973–76, higher exec off. Newcastle from 1976
m Boldon Colliery Mary Coyme midwife d of William C. Boldon Colliery

HUMES Walter Malcolm *MA 1967 PhD 1972
s of David H. farm lab. and Agnes Graham; b Newton Mearns 10.12.45
MEd(Glas) 1976
teacher Engl: Kingsdale s Lond 1968–69, Eastwood h s Renfrewsh 1972–74; lect: Engl Notre Dame coll of educ Glasg 1974–76, educ Glas from 1976

HUMPHREY Margaret *MA 1964 Dip Ed 1965
d of Robert S. H. rly clerk and Margaret I. Cooper governess; b Wick 4.5.42
teacher: geog Thurso 1965–66, asst, prin geog Hussey coll Warri Nigeria 1966–67; temp asst head Hussey model s 1968; temp head CDC school Tiko Cameroons 1970; secy Pentland geophys Wokingham from 1972
m Aber 6.4.66 Alistair M. Souter BSc 1964 *qv*

HUMPHREYS Douglas Eric Robin BSc 1968

HUMPHRIES Wilfred Reynold *MA 1969

HUMPHRIS Peter Maurice BSc(eng) 1969

HUNG Wai Mun MB ChB 1970

HUNT Andrew LLB 1969
s of Frank H. H. H. civ serv and Nancy M. Smart; b Edgeware 18.8.46
Perth: law app 1969–71, leg. asst 1971–73, ptnr solic from 1973

HUNT Barbara Jean MB ChB 1956

HUNT Jennifer MA 1969 CASS 1971
m Wright

HUNT Stewart Marshall Sanderson *MA 1970

HUNTER Alexander Freeland Cairns MA 1960 LLB 1962

HUNTER Andrew Robb *MA 1967
b Glasg 15.1.40
PhD(Stir) 1976
lect H-W from 1970

HUNTER Archibald Stewart MB ChB 1960
s of Archibald M. H. MA(Glas) prof biblical crit Aberd/Master Christ's coll Aber and Margaret W. Swanson; b Comrie 7.3.36
DCH(Glas) 1962 MRCPGlas 1966 MRCPE 1966
h o, regist Aber hosps 1960–66; paediat cardiol: regist Gr Ormond St London 1966–67, sen regist RHSC Edin

1967–69; sen res assoc dept ch health Newcastle 1969–72, res fell. Penn State univ USA 1972–73, consult. univ hosps Newcastle-u-Tyne/lect ch health N'cle from 1973
m Aber 9.12.60 Valerie M. Ewing bus. exec d of Andrew M. E. Aber

HUNTER Beatrice Josephine Nicholls BSc 1962
d of Gordon W. H. farm. and Beatrice E. Taylor; b Banchory 4.11.39
computer progr Glas 1962–69
m Aber Frank F. D. Stott comp dir s of Frank W. S. Tayport

HUNTER Edward Bryce BSc 1966
s of Edward H. butcher and Dorothy E. C. Davidson; b Aber 3.10.45
work study eng Lanarksh 1966–70; work study sect. leader/sen eng Dun 1970–73; sen man. consult. Nova Scotia from 1973
m Aber 17.9.66 Doreen H. Miller d of Norman M. Aber

HUNTER Elinor Isobel MA 1970
m Forbes

HUNTER Elizabeth *MA 1966
d of John H. farm./comp dir and Isabel J. Wallace; b Hitchin 23.4.44
teacher geog: Blyth s Norwich 1967–71, Dunstable s 1971–73; decorative arts course V & A museum Lond 1973–74; asst oriental art gallery 1974–75; lib/lect art hist polytech Stoke-on-Trent from 1975

HUNTER Fiona Mary MA 1959
d of Archibald M. H. MA(Glas) prof biblical crit Aberd/Master Christ's coll Aber and Margaret W. Swanson; b Oxford 14.2.39
teacher Aber 1960–61; ch guid serv Glasg from 1969
m Aber 5.7.61 John L. Harper BSc(eng) 1958 *qv*

HUNTER Graham Cran MA 1958 LLB 1960
s of John R. H. MA 1925 *qv*(II, III) and Janet D. Cran MA 1925 *qv*; b Huntly 4.10.36
law app Aber 1960–61; leg. asst Stornoway 1961–62, Inv 1962–63; leg. asst, ptnr Edmonds & Ledingham advoc Aber from 1963, joint clerk to Seven Incorporated Trades of Aber from 1976
m Aber 17.7.61 Janet C. Matheson MA 1959 *qv*

HUNTER Heather MA 1959
d of John G. H. asst dir of educ and Jane B. Watt; b Lerwick 25.1.38
teacher: Aber 1960–62, Lerwick from 1974
m Aber 11.7.62 George A. Smith MB ChB 1962 *qv*

HUNTER Iain Hamilton BSc 1969

HUNTER James Fraser *MA 1966 Dip Ed 1967
s of William H. joiner and Jane S. Fraser secy; b Aber 25.2.43
Dip Soc Work (Stir) 1975
tut./house parent Murree Christian s W Pakistan 1967–71; soc worker Aberdeensh 1971–73: soc worker Grampian reg from 1975
m Aber 17.8. 67 Alison M. Craig nurse d of John C. Aber

HUNTER James Kirton MA 1963
s of Andrew H. comp dir and Hilda Clark; b Peterhead 3.9.35
Edin: trainee 1963–67, stockbroker from 1967
m Aber 17.3.65 Vivien M. D. Alcock d of Thomas B. A. Keith

HUNTER James More MB ChB 1961
s of James M. H. FRAS insur broker and Elsie A. Shirran; b Aber 10.8.30
g p Edin from 1965
m Aber 17.7.61 Margaret E. Ramsay d of Alexander C. R. Aber

HUNTER James Wood MB ChB 1959

HUNTER Sheena Gordon *MA 1964
d of Gordon H. salesman and Edith M. Law; b Aber 25.2.42
teaching asst univ of Alta, Canada 1964–66; ch psych Bancroft s New Jersey USA 1966–68; psych educ spec Sacred Heart Village Toronto 1968–71
m Aber 3.8.66 James B. Campbell BSc 1962 *qv*

HUNTER Thomas George BSc(eng) 1958
s of James J. H. and Minnie F. Clark; b Victoria BC Canada 28.8.34
asst eng city eng's dept Aber 1958–61; Lerwick: eng Zetland county surv 1961–68, area eng N of S water board 1968–75, prin eng Shetland Is council from 1975
m Aber 22.7.60 Erica A. Laidlaw MA 1958 *qv*

HUNTER William Fiddes *MA 1964
s of William H. joiner and Jeannie S. Fraser; b Aber 6.3.41
PhD(Cantab) 1972
lect Span.: Aberd 1964–65, Exe from 1968
m Aber 12.8.67 Marilyn W. Beattie MA 1964 *qv*

HURRY Anne Campbell MA 1962
m Daniel

HURRY Patricia *MA 1970

HUTCHEON Alexander Austin Clark Barnacle BSc 1962 MSc 1967

HUTCHEON Andrew William MB ChB 1968 MD 1977
s of George Hutcheon grocer and Elsie S. Murrison nurse; b Aber 21.5.43
MRCP 1971
h o ARI, Balfour hosp Kirkwall 1968–69; sen h o Woodend hosp Aber 1969–70; regist WI Glasg 1970–73; res fell. Glas 1973–75; lect med WI Glasg from 1975
m Kirkwall 14.7.66 Christine G. Cusiter teacher d of Francis G. C. Kirkwall

HUTCHEON Elizabeth Margaret *MA 1970 Dip Ed 1971
d of George C. H. estate overseer and Matilda M. H. Fraser MA 1927 *qv*; b Inv 13.9.48
MEd(Glas) 1976
teacher Engl Bearsden acad 1971–73, Cathkin h s from 1973
m Aber 26.9.75 James G. Bell MB ChB(Glas) g p s of David G. B. Stepps

HUTCHEON Jean Gordon McKenzie BSc 1958 *1959
d of James H. MB ChB 1924 *qv*; b Aber 26.5.37
teacher sc Aber h s for girls 1960–63
m Aber Hamish S. MacRae MA 1951 *qv*

HUTCHEON Muriel MA 1960
m Wilson

HUTCHEON William Vincent *BSc(agr) 1968
s of Andrew W. H. farm. and Lily Murison; b Aber 8.5.45
lect Aberd 1968–69; agr res Tafo Ghana 1969–78; lect NOSCA Aber from 1978

HUTCHESON Carole Jean *BSc 1959
d of John M. H. farm. and Esther A. W. Munro; b Inv 25.12.37
MSc(Adel) 1962
univ dem Adel Aust 1959–62; asst warden Orielton field centre Pembroke 1964–65; teacher biol Southend 1966; tech off. in hosp lab Sunderland 1967–70
m Inv 7.4.69 John Bainbridge BSc(Leeds) teacher s of John G. B. Ossett

HUTCHESON Christine Anne MA 1964
d of John H. gen merch and Margaret A. Maclean sub-postmistress; b N Kessock 17.2.43
teacher Engl: Dingwall acad 1965–66, Summerhill acad Aber 1966–70; lect Engl/commun Aber coll of commerce from 1977
m Muir of Ord 1.4.66 William A. Milne med rep s of William J. M. Aber

HUTCHESON Lilian Mary BSc(agr) 1956
d of John M. H. farm. and Esther A. W. Munro; b Petty Invsh 3.8.34
MSA(Tor) 1963 PhD(NSW Aust) 1968
res asst: Huntingdon res centre 1956–58, 1959–60, Ontario agr coll 1958–59, 1960–64; res fell. univ of NSW Aust 1964–68; clin biochem Canada: Vancouver gen hosp 1968–72, royal Columbian hosp from 1973
m Guelph Ontario 27.6.64 Alistair Ewen

HUTCHESON Moira Mary BSc 1969
d of James H. civ eng and Mary Marshall saleswoman; b Stirling 21.5.48
teacher biol: Slough 1969–71, Newcastle-u-Tyne 1972–73, Blackburn Lancs from 1973
m Tullibody 9.8.72 Peter C. Johnson sports complex man. s of Robert J. Lond

HUTCHESON Rosemary Joan Fraser MA 1970
d of John H. clerk and Margaret A. MacLean shopkeeper/postmistress; b Inv 6.7.48
teacher Bonnyrigg from 1971
m Knockbain 1971 Andrew S. Barker BSc(Coventry) civ serv, computer progr s of Kenneth S. B. Filey

HUTCHISON Alexander Howieson *LLB 1966
s of Alexander S. H. min of relig and Grace M. Ferguson; b Renton 12.4.44
AHA 1970
nat admin trainee NHSO SE Scotland 1966–69; hosp secy Edin Royal Victoria hosp 1969–70, Simpson mem mat. pavilion 1970–72; Lond: hosp secy Lewisham hosp 1972–74, gen admin Lewisham health dist from 1974

HUTCHISON Alexander Norman *MA 1966
s of Gordon H. MB ChB 1930 *qv*; b Buckie 20.10.43
PhD(NW univ USA) 1975
lect Engl Vic BC Canada from 1966; Canada council doct fell. 1968–70
m Victoria BC 28.12.71 Nora S. Seaborne BA(Vic BC) univ lect d of Kenneth S. Victoria

HUTCHISON Charles MA 1969

HUTCHISON Iain George Campbell *MA 1967

HUTCHISON Kathleen Liston PhD 1970
BSc(Glas)
m Cartwright

HUTCHISON William Watt *BSc 1957
PhD(Tor) 1962
pres Geol Assoc of Canada 1973, secy gen Int Union of Geol Sciences, dir gen Geol Survey of Canada from 1981

HUTH Herbert Erich BEd 1969

HUTT Patricia Augusta BSc 1963

HUTTON David George BSc 1967
s of Kenneth B. H. MA(Oxon) and Barbara A. Britton BA(Oxon); b Winchester 12.10.46
teacher: Uganda 1968, Basildon 1969–73, Gt Missenden 1973–75, Aylesbury 1975–76, Wigmore from 1977
m Harrogate 26.8.72 Janet M. Hambly BA(Exe) teacher

HUTTON Eleanor Jean MA 1961 Dip Ed 1962
d of James G. H. rly investigating clerk and Ann H. W. Keith clerkess; b Aber 21.5.40
teacher maths Aber from 1962
m Aboyne 22.10.76 Michael D. Watson BSc 1971 drilling fluids eng s of Douglas C. W. Aber

HUTTON Elizabeth Mary MA 1956
d of Alexander H. wholesale draper and Mary G. Melvin secy; b Aber 18.1.36
information scient Mullard radio valve co Mitcham junction 1956–59; teacher Engl Abbots Bromley 1970 information scient RARDE Halstead Sevenoaks from 1973
m Aber 31.7.59 Grahame V. J. Weston army off. s of Victor J. W.

HUTTON Lisella Margaret *BSc 1970
d of Hugh H. LRCPE g p and Mary D. Donald nurse; b Carlisle 27.6.49
DipLA(Edin) 1972 AILA 1974
asst landscape arch.: Stonehouse and E. Kilbride dev corp 1972–73, William Gillespie & Ptnrs Glasg from 1973

HUTTON Ray Forbes MA 1969
m Hamilton

I'ANSON Annette Elizabeth MA 1963 Dip Ed 1964
d of Leonard I'A. boiler attendant and Jeannie C. Donaldson; b Aber 19.2.42
teacher Aber: Abbotswell p s 1964–68, King St p s from 1968
m Aber 21.11.59 Kenneth C. R. Hepburn civ serv s of George H. Aber; marr diss 1972

IBBOTSON Bernard Ross *BSc(for) 1961

IBELL Robert Leslie BSc(eng) 1967
s of William E. I. head teacher and Freda E. Hopwood head teacher; b Woodford 11.1.46
MICE 1973
civ eng, site man. Taylor Woodrow construct. UK from 1967
m Middlesbrough 25.10.69 Patricia I. Wilkie MA 1967 *qv*

IBIAM Tolulope Idam Ngbo MB ChB 1970

IBRAHIM Hassan Suliman MSc 1968
BSc(agr)(Khart)

IKENWIWE Lawrence Ifeayin-Chukwu BSc(eng) 1965

ILLINGWORTH William John BSc(eng) 1961

ILLSLEY Raymond PhD 1956
s of James I. potter's asst and Harriet Chamberlain

kitchenmaid; b Woodville 6.7.19
BA(Oxon) 1948
econ asst commonwealth econ comm Lond 1948–49; soc & econ res off. Crawley New Town 1949–51; Aberd: sociol MRC 1951–64, prof sociol 1964–75, prof med sociol from 1975; hon dir MRC med sociol unit from 1965
m Oxford 15.6.48 Jean M. Harrison BA(Oxon) teacher d of Arthur J. H. Oxford

ILOKA Lazarus Obidigeo BSc(eng) 1965
s of Ugonna O. I. and Nwalie Ezeodili; b Abatete Nigeria 30.10.39
MSc(Loughborough) 1966 MBA(Loughborough) 1967 Dip Gen Man.(Turin) 1974 Dip Proj Appraisal(Milwaukee) 1976
dev eng BCC Wembley 1967–68; sen evaluation eng Honeywell controls Glasg 1968–72; Nigeria: proj eng Shell BP 1972–73, man. consult. centre for man. dev 1973–74, area man. dev bank from 1975
m Loughborough 1.10.66 Helen Okoye secy d of Francis O. Abatete

IMAM Abubakar MB ChB 1956
s of Alkali Jafaru, chief Alkali of Kano and Hajiya H. Yarshirayi; b Kano 13.7.31
MRCOG(Lond) 1963 FCS(W Af) 1964 FMCOG (Nigeria) 1970 FRCOG 1977 OON (Off. of the Order of the Niger) 1978
Kano Nigeria: m o 1957–64, consult. obst/gyn 1964–68, sen consult. obst/gyn 1968, chief m o 1968–75, dir health serv 1975–76, chief consult. 1974–76; voluntarily retd govt serv 1977; med dir Mustapha mem hosp from 1977

IMAM Alkali Ja'Afaru Kalli Goni BSc(for) 1957
s of Goni Imam area court judge and Amina S. Imam Hamsami; b Maiduguri 2.3.28
asst conserv for. N Nigeria 1957–59; Nigeria: prin for. s Jos 1960–61, conserv, chief conserv for. Kaduna 1961–68; perm secy: min of agr and nat resources Maiduguri NE state 1968–75, min of health 1975–76, Brino state min of finance/econ plan. from 1976
m Maiduguri 19.12.65 Hamra Mohammed BA (Ahmadu Bello) asst regist univ of Maiduguri d of Mohammed Shuwa Maiduguri

IMLACH Alexander Reid McLean MA 1956
s of James I. fisherman and Mary McLean; b Aber 27.1.36
Dip Soc Ad(Glas) 1969
teacher Engl Torry acad Aber 1959–60; teacher/housemaster Oakbank list D s Aber 1960–65; Rossie list D s Montrose: third i/c 1965–69, dep head from 1969
m Montrose 28.3.64 Grace M. W. Amps teacher d of William A. Fraserburgh

IMLACH James Alexander BSc 1961 *1966 MSc 1967 PhD 1972

IMRAY Bryan Charles BSc 1958
s of Charles I. master grocer and Gladys Ingram; b Aber 9.2.36
MEd(univ of Montana USA) 1974
geol govt surv Ghana 1958–62; educ off. Dar-es-Salaam Tanzania 1963–68; teacher Grande Prairie Alberta 1968–72; prin Peace River h s Alberta from 1972
marr diss
m(2) Peace River 21.4.73 Jennifer E. Gray Dip Ed(N'cle) d of James G. Ingleton

IMRAY James McGregor MB ChB 1957
s of William I. farm. and Barbara M. McGregor secy; b Inv 24.9.33
DA 1962 FFARCS 1969
h o ARI 1957–58; regist: surg Hobart Tasmania 1958–61, anaest ARI 1961–62; part-time farm. Abdnsh/anaest ARI 1962–71; consult. anaest ARI from 1971
m Strathdon 20.8.65 Lucy C. Anderson SRN d of James A. Strathdon

IMRAY John MA 1958
s of Robert C. I. docker and Elizabeth Stevenson; b Edin 2.7.13
FEIS 1977
Aber: teacher Kirkhill p s 1958–66, dep head Victoria Road p s from 1966
m Aber 22.7.36 Mildred Allathan teacher d of Alexander A. Culter

IMRAY Mildred Marion MA 1958
m Davis

IMRIE Janet Yvonne *BSc 1970
m Henderson

INALSINGH Calvin Holmes Rajpat MB ChB 1963
s of Cyril H. I. chief clerk, crown solic's off. and Charlotte S. Dookransingh prop.; b Trinidad 16.8.36
Trinidad: h o Port of Spain hosp 1964–65, dist m o Sangre Grande 1965–72, dist m o, regist i/c Arima hosp from 1972 and private pract from 1965
m Trinidad 8.2.68 Marina R. Persand d of Bharat P. Trinidad

INALSINGH Carol Homer Amar MB ChB 1961
s of Cyril H. I. acct and Charlotte S. Dookransingh prop; b Tunapuna Trinidad 26.10.34
DMRT(Lond) 1966
h o gen hosp Port of Spain Trinidad 1961–63; regist: Hammersmith hosp Lond 1965–66, gen hosp Port of Spain 1966–71; USA: asst prof radiol Johns Hopkins univ Maryland 1971–75, dir of radiation oncology Blake mem hosp Bradenton Florida 1975–79, Manatee mem hosp Bradenton from 1979
m Trinidad 2.9.63 Mira Naipaul BA(Leeds) teacher

INALSINGH Vanessa Savriti MA 1966
d of Cyril H. I. chief clerk, crown solic's off. and Charlotte S. Dookransingh prop.; b Trinidad 30.4.43
teacher Engl St Joseph's convent Trinidad from 1967

INGHAM Valerie MA 1964

INGLIS David Simpson Blacklaw BSc 1968

INGLIS Donald Bain Carrick MA 1963 *MEd 1968
s of William C. I. comm rep BR and Margaret A. C. Bain; b Aber 17.12.41
BD(Glas) 1975
teacher: Engl/hist Northfield s s Aber 1964, Engl/hist Ellon acad 1965–68; asst educ psych Lanarksh Hamilton 1968–71, sen educ psych 1971–72; asst min at Bathgate high ch 1975–77; educ psych Fife reg c from 1977
m Glasg 24.9.74 Yvonne M. S. Cook secy d of James D. C. San Paulo Brazil

INGLIS John Gladstone BEd 1969

INGLIS John Proven BSc 1970
s of John P. I. contr off. NCB and Margaret H. Brand; b Glasg 24.11.47
scient off. metrop police forensic labs Lond 1970–73; teacher Dartford g s 1973–74; supt PO telecomm Lond from 1975
m Aber 11.9.70 Elizabeth S. Moncrieff MA 1970 *qv*

INGLIS Julian Thomas BSc 1967
s of Thomas I. BSc(St And) teacher and Patricia J. Lake school lib; b Meikleour 29.7.46
MSc(Carleton univ Ottawa) 1975
teacher Peterhead, Toronto 1967–68; range biol Canada: Inuvik N W terr 1968–70, Arctic Is 1970–73; land man. biol and acting head land man. sect. govt of Canada Ottawa from 1973
m Glasg 5.6.70 Aileen A. Urquhart BSc 1968 *qv*

INGLIS Leslie Glennie MA 1963

INGLIS Mary Horne *BSc 1970
m Smith

INGLIS Thomas BSc(eng) 1968
s of Thomas M. I. security off. and Annie M. Patterson; b Montrose 5.3.47
hydrologist to Forth River purif board Stirling 1968–72; eng/hydrol Cheshunt: Lee conserv catchment board 1972–74, Lea div Thames water auth from 1974
m Montrose 26.10.68 Frances P. Easton sales ledger clerk d of George E. Montrose

INGLIS William Raymond *MA 1970
s of William I. instrument tech and Mabel C. McEwan receptionist; b Alloa 18.3.48
Alloa acad: teacher Engl 1971–73, asst prin guid 1973–74, prin guid 1974–76; prin guid Lornshill acad from 1976
m Sauchie 22.8.70 Lorna I. Young MA(St And)teacher d of Peter Y. Sauchie

INGOLFSSON Agnar *BSc 1961
s of Ingolfur Davidsson Mag Sc(Copenhagen) botanist and Agnes Christensen weaver; b Reykjavik 29.7.37
PhD(Mich) 1967
asst prof Mass USA 1967–71; dosent (lect) Reykjavik 1971–73, prof from 1973
m Reykjavik 25.12.72 Linda Wendel med tech d of Andres W. Reykjavik

INGRAM Alexander Lindsay BL 1957
s of Garson I. banker and Margaret N. Lindsay; b Comrie 7.2.31
AIBankers(Scot) 1953
law asst WS firm Edin 1957–61; proc fiscal dep Cupar 1961–73, proc fisc Forfar from 1973
m Cupar 3.6.67 Margaret C. E. W. Meldrum adoption off., play s supt d of Arthur G. M. Cupar

INGRAM Alex Simpson *BSc 1968 PhD 1971
s of George I. woodcutter and Margaret J. Simpson; b Huntly 5.6.45
tech off. St And univ 1971–73; res chem, plant man., team leader Fisons Loughborough 1973–77; sen chem Lancaster synthesis from 1977
m Huntly 27.3.71 Marlene McIrvine MA 1971 d of Robert I. McI. Forgue

INGRAM Anne Wilson MA 1957

INGRAM Christopher Laidlaw BSc(for) 1969
s of Lawrence I. MB BS(Durh) g p and Mary E. Laidlaw teacher; b E Bolden 11.2.46
util off. Zambian for. dept Kitwe 1969–72; asst branch man. Tilhill for.(Scot) Elgin 1973–74; reg man. Tilhill for.(marketing) at Stirling 1974–76, Elgin from 1976
m Leith 31.7.69 Jean B. K. Mathie teacher d of Edward J. M. Leith

INGRAM Greig Webster MA 1969
s of William J. I. farm. and Margaret V. Booth teacher; b Burnhervie 20.11.47
Glasg: teacher Holyrood s s 1970–72, Lourdes s s 1972–74, prin mod stud. St Margaret Mary's s s from 1974
m Glasg 28.12.77 Patricia A. Miller bank off. d of Duncan M. Glasg

INGRAM Margaret Jane *BSc 1969
d of John L. I. man. flooring and Georgina L. Addison nurs sister; b Nott 12.2.47
asst Molteno inst of biochem parasitology Cantab 1969–70
m Nott 6.12.69 Sean F. O'B. Donaghey BSc 1969 *qv*

INGRAM Roy MA 1960

INKSON Dennis Wright BSc(eng) 1969
s of James I. butcher and Violet Ledingham typist; b Aber 25.2.48
grad eng Aber city eng 1969–74; site eng 1974–75; eng Lothian reg c 1975–77; roads eng Dubai municipality UAE from 1977
m(2) Aber 26.9.75 Lesley A. S. Allan LLB 1974 d of Douglas A. Aber

INKSON James Henry Kerr *MA 1963
s of John K. I. MA 1929 *qv* and Frances Wilson MA 1928 *qv*; b Aber 13.1.42
MPhil(Lond) 1968 PhD(Otago) 1980
post grad stud. Lond 1963–65; assoc res fell. Aston Birm 1965–68: lect psych Aston 1968–70; lect indust psych univ of Otago Dunedin NZ, sen lect in indust psych from 1973
m Muir of Ord 19.8.66 Nan Tuach BSc 1965 *qv*

INKSTER David White MA 1961

INKSTER Elizabeth Mary MA 1963
d of Walter W. I. fisherman and Barbara Inkster; b Hamnavoe 21.7.42
teacher: maths/sc Wick 1964–65, sc Thurso 1965–66
m Lerwick 19.4.65 Andrew B. Bryce BSc(eng) 1958 *qv*

INKSTER Hugh BSc(eng) 1970
s of Hugh C. I. comp secy and Dorothy Taylor; b Kirkwall 2.5.47
man. trainee to prod. gen man. Keighley from 1971

INKSTER Raymond *MA 1967 BD 1970
s of John I. and Kathleen I. Paterson; b Perth 20.6.45
Baptist ch min: Gilcomston Park ch Aber from 1971
m Aber 19.7.69 Muriel M. Fowler BEd 1969 *qv*

INNES Alan John MA 1965 LLB 1967
s of John L. I. MA 1926 *qv*; b Aber 30.3.44
law app 1967–69; solic Peterkin & Duncans advoc Aber from 1969

INNES Arthur James MB ChB 1965
b Kemnay 5.6.42
DABS 1974
h o RI Perth 1965–66; USA: intern Norwalk hosp Conn 1966–67; lt, lt cdr US Navy 1967–69; surg resid Norfolk gen hosp Virginia 1969–73; private pract gen surg Springfield Oregon from 1973

INNES Brian Peter BSc 1969

INNES Doreen Cormack *MA 1962
d of John F. I. newsag and grocer and Thomasina Cormack; b Aber 26.5.40

Ireland schol 1963 Classical hon moderations(Oxon) 1964 DPhil(Oxon) 1968 MA(Oxon) 1969
stud. Somerville coll Oxon 1962–65; res fell St Hugh's coll Oxon 1963–67; lect classic stud. univ of Kent 1967–69; fell. and tut. in Literae Humaniores St Hilda's coll Oxon from 1969

INNES Eurwen Harries MB ChB 1958
d of John I. pharm and Sarah Harries; b Peterhead 12.6.34
DCH(Lond) 1960 DObstRCOG 1961 MRCP 1968 DPM 1971
h o Aber 1958–59; h o, sen h o, regist in various hosps 1959–72; consult. phys (rheumat and rehabilitation) Hastings clin area from 1972

INNES Francis Albert Shaw BSc(eng) 1968

INNES Graham Gilchrist MA 1967

INNES Isabel Cunningham *BSc 1969 MSc 1972
d of Henry I. loc govt off. and Evelyn L. Cunningham shop asst; b Aber 14.3.47
res chem Richards Aber 1969–73
m Aber 11.7.70 Ian Murray BSc 1971 agr chem s of Cecil M. Aber

INNES Jean Alexandra MA 1969
d of William A. I. farm. and Sophie Anderson; b Forres 29.2.48
ALA 1972
Aber city lib: lib asst 1969–70, asst lib 1971–72, lib i/c central lending lib from 1972
m Aber 23.9.71 Fergus R. M. Dodds MA 1972 ptnr Rainbow Enterprises (printer/publ) Aber s of John M. D. MA 1926 *qv*

INNES John Michael *MA 1963
s of John S. I.; b Aber 13.11.41
PhD(Birm) 1969 ABPsS 1970
lect: dept of sociol Birm 1963–65, dept of psych Birm 1965–73, visiting lect dept of psych univ of Michigan Ann Arbor USA 1972–73; lect dept of psych Edin from 1973
m Aber 1964

INNES Leslie Gordon *MA 1958

INNES Lorraine Hilary MA 1968
d of Cameron R. I. MB ChB 1950 *qv*; b Glasg 26.6.46
Inst Pers Man.(Dun)
exec off. PO grad appointments centre Lond 1968–70; stud. Dun coll of comm(IPM) 1978–79
m Corpach 25.4.70 Hugo Y. Shaw LLB(Dund) civ serv, app solic s of Hugh S. Fort William

INNES Margaret Annie MB ChB 1965
m Cameron

INNES Norman Lindsay *BSc(agr) 1957 PhD 1968

INNES Patricia Anne *MA 1967
m Falconer

INNES Patrick Gordon BSc(eng) 1957
s of John A. I. BSc 1913 *qv* and Elizabeth Stephen MA 1913 *qv*; b Aber 23.2.31
Guest Keen & Nettlefolds Midlands: grad app Birm 1957–58, pers asst to prod. dir 1958–60; The British Screw Co Leeds: asst works man. 1960–64, dir and joint gen man. 1964–66, man. dir 1966–72; Crompton Nettlefold Stenham Ashton-in-Makerfield: man. dir 1972–74; GKN Fastener Tools div of GKN Screws & Fasteners Birm: man dir from 1976
m Aber 15.9.56 Florence Hendry cook d of George H. MA 1922 *qv*

INNES Sheila Valaine MA 1966
d of Cameron S. I. MBE col serv and Christian D. Robb civ serv hosp admin; b Aber 9.5.23
teacher Luthermuir 1967–75
m Chapelhall 7.10.43 William J. Cantlay BSc(agr) 1943 *qv*

INNES William MA 1960 Dip Ed 1961

INNES William BSc 1961
s of William G. I. fisherman and Mary A. Mair; b Cullen 24.8.40
teacher: maths/sc Aberchirder 1962–65, maths Keith g s 1965–74, prin maths Fortrose from 1974
m Kirkwall 23.7.74 Moira L. Tait teacher d of Andrew T. Kirkwall

INNES William George MA 1962
s of Gordon D. I. gamekeeper/for. worker and Maggie Taylor; b Bucksburn 23.3.40
Powis acad Aber: teacher 1963–70, year master 1970–74, asst head from 1974
m(2) Aber 27.2.76 Abigail L. Hay MA 1967 *qv*

INNES William George MB ChB 1966

INNES William James Alexander *MA 1956
s of William J. I. insur ag and Helen M. M. Porter; b Ballater 11.10.34
RAF off. gen duties branch 1956–72; prin Home Office Lond 1972–76; asst secy N Ireland off. from 1977
m Aber 27.6.59 Carol I. Bruce MA 1958 *qv*

INNES-WILL Brian Norman *MA 1967

INNOCENT Barbara Jean *MA 1969
m Jones

IORNS David Spencer *BSc 1970
s of Edward G. I. acct and Olive Chilton; b Aber 23.10.48
Grad RIC(Hatfield poly) 1972
process eng Welwyn 1970–75; prod. dev chem Leiden Holland 1975–78; res dev man. Scarborough from 1978
m Aber 24.9.71 Alison Fraser MA 1971 d of William C. F. Banchory

IRONSIDE Graham Johnston MA 1958
s of Basil I. MA 1926 *qv*; b Aber 14.6.37
CNAA Dip Educ Tech(Jordanhill) 1979
teacher: Aber 1959–63, Singapore 1963–65, Aber 1965–66; lect: f e Aber 1966–79, sen lect educ resources Aber coll of comm from 1979
m Aber 30.3.63 Joan T. Milne teacher p e d of George M. Aber

IRUOHA Iruoha Oke MB ChB 1965

IRVIN Carolyn Anne *BSc 1959
d of Richard I. trawl owner and Florence J. Ramsden; b Peterculter 17.5.36
BA(Lond) 1968
Lond: edit. asst inst of phys 1960–62; teacher Sydenham s 1962–64; stud. Bedford coll 1965–67
m Lond 18.3.67 Reginald G. Harlow BSc(Lond) lect s of Alfred R. H. Lond

IRVIN Thomas Thoburn MB ChB 1964 PhD 1968

IRVINE Alison McLean BSc 1967 PhD 1972
d of Patrick F. B. I. stockbroker and Janette M. Johnson physioth; b Aber 28.5.47
path. dept Aberd: res asst 1967–69, Georgina McRobert fell. in cancer res 1969–72
m Aber 27.7.67 George P. M. Crawford MB ChB 1970 *qv*

IRVINE David Lawrence Morrison MA 1967

IRVINE Edward Charles Fordyce BSc(eng) 1956

IRVINE Elizabeth Marjorie MB ChB 1965

IRVINE Gladys Christine MA 1970
d of George I. farm. and Bella Dunn; b Aber 29.10.48
Dip Lib(Strath) 1972 ALA 1973
trainee lib Mitchell lib Glasg 1970–71; lib: Mitchell lib 1972–73, Paisley publ lib from 1974
m Aber 10.12.73 Alan D. Macmillan-Kelly bldg contr s of Donald M.-K. Wokingham

IRVINE James Robert Sinclair MA 1970
s of Harry I. farm. and Hannah M. Henderson teacher; b Virkie Shetland 24.3.47
teacher: Lerwick p s 1971–73, asst head 1973–77, dep head from 1977

IRVINE Joseph Andrew BSc 1966
s of Robert I. lorry driver and Jemima M. Hardy knitwear worker; b Mossbank Shetland 18.6.44
Lerwick: teacher sc 1967–68, maths from 1968
m Aber 3.4.68 Ishbel M. Cruickshank hairdresser d of John M. C. MA 1926 *qv*(III)

IRVINE Keith Robert *BSc 1968

IRVINE Margaret Anderson MA 1961

IRVINE Robert *BSc 1956

IRVINE Ronald David *MA 1967

IRVINE Veronica Mary MA 1959
d of John A. I. streets/roads insp and Jean Scollay; b Aber 18.10.38
teacher: Marchburn inf s Aber 1960–62, Sholing inf s Southampton 1963–65, Guardbridge p s, Langlands p s St And from 1974
m Aber 4.7.61 George M. Phillips MA 1960 *qv*

IRVINE William Stuart MA 1963
s of William S. I. man. fishcuring fact. and Agnes I. Paterson; b Aber 18.10.42
teacher: p s Lossiemouth 1964–65, p s Cumbernauld 1965–68; dep head p s St Ninians Stirling 1968–71; head: Shieldhill p s Falkirk 1971–75, Ellon p s from 1975
m Aber 18.12.65 Monica M. Davidson teacher d of Bertie M. D. Aber

IRVINE-FORTESCUE Margaret Ann *MA 1966
d of William G. I.-F. army off. and Kathleen S. Bennett-Jones lect Dunfermline coll of p e; b Quetta Pakistan 20.7.44
Dip Soc Admin Stud(Oxon) 1967 Dip Ed(Edin) 1968
teacher Engl/soc stud. Middx 1968–70; asst apptments off. univ of E Ang Norwich from 1970

IRVING John Ramsay *BSc(eng) 1969

ISAAC Philip Edward *BSc(eng) 1969

IUTZ Josephine MA 1962
d of Max C. F. I. man. wool export firm and Kathleen E. Davey soc worker; b Bingley 10.8.41
part time teacher f e Ilkley from 1974; post-grad stud. hist and phil of sc Leeds univ
m Aber 20.10.60 Tokefat C. Pacsoo MB ChB 1962 *qv*

IZATT Jack Birrell *BSc(eng) 1957 PhD 1959
s of William I. art lect and Winnifred Graham; b Buckhaven 13.7.35
FIEE 1974 CEng 1974
BBC res dept Kingswood Tadworth: eng aerial sect. 1960–62, sen eng receiver sect. 1962–65; Solartron Electronic Group Farnborough: team leader 1965–68, group leader 1969–71, chief eng dynamic analysis R & D 1972–75, res and dev man. syst div from 1976
m Aber 2.4.58 Katrine I. L. Macleod MA 1956 *qv*

IZATT Tom Graham MA 1959
s of William I. art lect and Winnifred Graham; b Stonehaven 21.6.37
CEng MIEE 1973 MSc(Salf) 1977
res eng BBC Kingswood 1959–69; lect Preston polytech 1969–75, sen lect from 1975
m Sutton 12.4.66 Jacqueline Belchamber teacher

IZOD Jeffrey Edward LLB 1966
s of Edward J. I. shop owner and Edith M. Esson; b Aber 17.11.43
oil marketing Lond: man. trainee 1967–68, area man. 1968–69, real estate negotiator 1969–71, sales man. 1971–74; agreements negotiator N Sea oil 1974–78; oil comp lawyer from 1978
m(2) Ashford 8.11.78 Cherry F. Hill secy d of Bertum W. H. Frimley

JACK Daniel MacPherson *MA 1969
s of Daniel R. J. drift net fisherman and Jessie MacPherson; b Hopeman 15.11.30
teacher econ: Fraserburgh acad 1970–71, Moray coll of f e from 1971

JACK David Alexander *MA 1967
s of George D. J. tel superv and Marjory Lee; b Inv 28.6.44
teacher: Portsmouth 1968–71, Lond from 1971
m Lond 10.8.74 Hilary M. Dove teacher d of Job D. Lond

JACK Edwin Alexander BSc(eng) 1963 *1964
s of Wilfred J. J. mech supt and Mearl A. Younker; b Bartica Guyana 16.5.37
M.Phil(Lond) 1971
asst city eng city eng Georgetown Guyana 1964–72; sen eng Trinto Plan. Consult. Tacarigua Trinidad from 1972
m Port of Spain 31.10.64 Barbara P. Raymond MA 1962 *qv*

JACK George Clark *BSc 1959

JACK George Wishart *BSc 1967
s of George W. J. PO eng and Willexia Gardiner; b Wick 3.12.44
PhD(Brist) 1971
post doct fell. dept bact Brist 1970–71; sen scient off. microbiol res estab Porton Down from 1971
m Aber 16.7.68 Kathleen A. Robilliard MA 1965 *qv*

JACK Ian MA 1970

JACK James Ironside *BSc 1961
s of James I. J. farm., farm man. and Dorothy C. Gibb; b New Deer 23.4.39
MIMM
geol: Cape Province S Africa 1961–64, Aber 1965–66;

teacher Aber 1967–68; chief explor geol Nimba Liberia 1968–73; sen geol Elstree 1974; explor man. Tehran from 1974
m Aber 26.6.65 Lorna W. Brown d of William W. B. Aber

JACK James Wynd *BSc 1966 PhD 1971
s of William A. J. civ serv and Margaret R. McKenzie nurse; b Portsmouth 21.7.44
MSc(Birm) 1967
Carnegie fell. Aberd 1971–72; syst eng Ferranti Edin from 1972

JACK Jeanette Isobella MA 1966
d of James K. J. journalist and Annie Bruce man.; b Aber 4.3.45
teacher: Achimota prep s Accra 1968–69; Berlin: Spandau p s 1970–72, Gatow s 1973–76; Osnabrück: Wellington s from 1976
m Aber 3.8.67 Frederick C. F. Cowie MA 1962 *qv*

JACK Lindsay MA 1967
d of Adam J. caretaker and Euphemia B. Laidlaw; b Thornton, 11.7.45
teacher Traralgon Vict Aust from 1970
m Rosewell 13.2.65 Anthony R. Griffin BSc(for) 1967 *qv*

JACK Shona Margaret MA 1969
d of Alexander F. M. J. bank acct and Evelyn Harper nurse; b Aber 19.12.46
teacher: Crown p s Inv 1970–73, Gateside s Fife 1973–74, Levenvale p s Alexandria 1974–76, Haldane p s Balloch from 1976
m Aber 19.4.73 George H. Dickie hosp eng s of George G. D. MB ChB 1936 *qv*

JACK-HINTON Colin *MA 1957
s of Harold H. indust, C of E clergyman and Elizabeth B. Jack; b Newchurch-in-Rossendale Lancs 1.1.33
PhD(ANU) 1963 MRInst Navig 1977
dist off./asst secy overseas civ serv BSIP 1957–59; res schol ANU Canberra 1960–62; lect univ of Singapore 1963–65; res fell. ANU 1965–66; sen curator W Aust museum Perth 1966–69; dir museums and art galleries of N Territory Darwin from 1970
m Aber –.4.56 Anne H. McDonald; marr diss

JACKARIA Abdool Carrim MB ChB 1961
s of Abdool S. J. merch and Fatmah T. Salehmamode; b Mauritius 2.5.35
FFARCS 1968
h o Woodend hosp Aber, ARI 1961–62; Mauritius: r m o min of health 1962–66, asst spec anaest 1968–69, spec anaest 1969–77, consult. from 1977
m Mauritius 16.8.63 Salma Ebrahim d of Abdullah E. Mauritius

JACKSON Alistair MA 1969

JACKSON Arthur David BSc 1965 MB ChB 1968
s of Herbert G. J. min of relig and Jean Martin nurs sister; b Congo 13.7.42
DObstRCOG 1970 MRCGP 1974 FPA(Cert) 1977
h o Inv RI, ARI, Aber mat. hosp, paediat RACH 1968–70; med regist/clin tut. Aber spec hosp group 1971–73; g p: Stockton-on-Tees 1973–76, Holmes Chapel from 1976

JACKSON Peter Tulloch *BSc 1962
s of Charles E. J. civ serv and Agnes H. R. Gair teacher; b Aber 3.4.40
PhD(Cantab) 1966
tech off. ICI Billingham 1966–69; tech serv eng with UOP Lond from 1969

JACKSON Philippa Judith Sagar *MA 1969
d of Harold S. J. solic and Kathleen M. M. Heap BA(Manc) teacher; b Leeds 25.4.47
psych/civ serv Lond 1969–71; market man. Thames Ditton 1971–72; free-lance market res consult. Surrey 1972–73; prop. Philippa Cowking consult. Weybridge from 1973
m Giggleswick 18.7.69 Thomas L. Cowking MA 1968 *qv*

JACKSON Ruth Lesley MSc 1967
BSc(Wales)

JACOBSON George Alexander BSc(eng) 1967
s of Andrew L. D. J. lorry driver and Joan C. Eunson; b Dunrossness Shetland 30.9.45
asst eng Duncan Logan(Construct.) Ross-shire 1967–70; eng asst Herts c c 1970–73; asst resid eng Inv c c 1973–74, resid eng from 1974

JAFFRAY Alan *BSc 1960
s of Arthur J. soldier and Ann Walker; b Aber 15.2.39
prod. dev & tech serv rep Delft Holland, Manc 1960–64; tech prod. man. PVC Grangemouth, Barry 1965–75; tech man. Manc from 1975
m Manc 25.7.64 Judith Osborne d of Leslie O. Manc

JAFFRAY Ian Alistair BSc(agr) 1960
s of Charles J. farm. and Winifred M. Rennie; b Nakuru Kenya 4.4.38
man. wheat farm Njoro Kenya 1960–65; farm man. broiler chicken comp Cape Town 1965–68, farm. own bacon pig prod. farm Pietermaritzburg S Africa from 1968
m Nakuru Rosemary S. Foster teacher d of James C. F. Wye

JAFFRAY James Robertson BSc 1963
s of James M. J. rep, bus comp owner, hotelkeeper etc and Isabella Robertson catering superv; b Aber 11.1.41
teacher: maths Forfar 1964–65, maths/sc Edzell 1965–69, maths/sc Brechin 1969–73, remed s s Brechin 1973–75; asst work stud. and methods man. Fraserburgh from 1976

JAFFREY Helen Elizabeth MA 1964 Dip Ed 1965
d of William M. K. shoemaker, retailer and Alexerina Imray dressmaker; b Insch 19.12.42
teacher Engl: Denny 1965–68, Dunfermline 1968–70
m Insch 13.7.68 Charles S. Oram BSc(H-W) indust eng s of Douglas O. Dunfermline

JAGANI Himatlal Permanand *BSc 1962
s of Permanand Sakerchand Depala clerk and Surajben P. Depala; b Aden 20.4.37
MSc(Alta) 1970
lect: tech inst Aden 1962–65, univ of Ife Nigeria 1965–77; sen lect univ of Ife from 1977
m Dhrangdra India 21.1.64 Kundanbala H. Depala d of Santilal B. D. BA(Bhavnagar) Gujrat State India

JAKOBSEN Arnt cMB ChB 1963
s of Arnt J. prof of surg univ of Oslo and Solveig Solumsmoen nurse; b Oslo 2.7.38
MD(Oslo) 1973 spec gen surg from 1977
Norway: h o Fredrikstad 1964, g p Asköy 1965, lect army med corps Oslo 1965–66, surg h o Oslo 1966–67, res fell. surg inst Rikshospitalet Oslo 1967–71, jun regist surg Rikshospitalet, Oslo 1971–73, regist Oslo city hosp 1973–77, sen regist Rikshospitalet Oslo 1977–78, transplant surg Rikshospitalet Oslo from 1978

m Aber 18.8.64 Sheila M. Michie DA textile des/lect in art d of Arthur R. M. Peterhead

JAMES Alasdair Macleod MA 1962

JAMES Alfred Timothy BSc(eng) 1963

JAMES Angela Margaret *MA 1969
d of Robert E. J. CPO writer (RN), man. (health and safety) and Agnes Watt secy Aber fed. SWRI; b Aber 20.11.47
edit. asst (Engl, mod lang school books) Macmillan 1969–70; teacher Engl Southfields s Lond from 1972
m Aber 21.8.70 John D. G. Bell MA 1969 *qv*

JAMES William PhD 1965
s of William J. eng and Cornelia James; b Johannesburg 15.8.37
BSc(eng)(Natal) 1958 Dip Hyd Eng(Delft) 1961
lect, sen lect univ of Natal 1965–71; visiting prof Queen's univ Kingston Canada 1970; prof McM univ Hamilton Canada from 1971; guest prof Lund and Lukeå univs Sweden 1977–78
m Aber 19.3.65 Evelyn M. Stephen MA 1965 *qv*

JAMIESON Andrew William *BSc 1970
s of Basil A. J. TU secy and Grace Williamson; b Yell 18.7.48
elect eng Plessey Templecombe 1970–71; glaciologist Brit antarctic surv S Georgia, Fossil Bluff Brit antarctic territory 1971–75; eng Shell UK explor and prod. from 1977

JAMIESON Christine MA 1965
d of John J. BSc(agr) 1929 *qv*; b Shetland 23.7.43
teacher: Stanley p s 1966–67, Aber 1967–68
m Shetland 16.8.67 Alfred Langmead diesel mech s of Ernest L.

JAMIESON Colin MB ChB 1968
s of John G. J. civ serv and Minnie Stewart; b Aber 23.11.43
g p: Strathdon 1969–70, Dumfries from 1970
m Aber 13.7.68 June Anderson teacher d of John A. Torphins

JAMIESON Donald Gavin ᶜMB ChB 1958
s of Thomas J. bank man. and Donella J. Sutherland teacher; b Aber 5.6.36
MRCPE 1963 MRCP(Lond) 1965 FRCPE 1974
h o Aber 1958–59; sen h o Edin 1959–60; med regist: Aber 1960–63, Smethwick 1963–65; sen med regist Dun 1965–67; consult. neurol Birm from 1967
m Aber 8.10.65 Grace K. R. MacRae MB ChB 1962 *qv*

JAMIESON Ernest BSc 1969

JAMIESON Ernest Charles MB ChB 1967
s of John J. sen insp ACT and Esther P. Andrews; b Aber 19.4.43
Dip Av Med 1972
h o ARI, Woodend hosp Aber 1967–68; RAF: jun m o Valley Wales 1968–69, m o Seletar Singapore 1969–71; m o RAF inst of aviation med Farnborough 1971–72; lect aviation med RAF aviation med training centre N Luffenham 1972–74; g p Moulton nr Spalding from 1974
m Aber 15.7.67 Diane Bell teacher d of Albert D. B. Aber

JAMIESON Ethel MA 1961
d of William J. gen merch and Constance R. Gordon shopkeeper; b 12.12.40
Dip Soc Ad(LSE) 1962
family caseworker Aber 1962–65; soc worker Kinc/Deeside dist from 1975
m Aber 17.10.64 James D. Aberdein BSc(agr) 1959 *qv*

JAMIESON Gordon MB ChB 1960

JAMIESON Hugh Gilbert John BSc(eng) 1967
s of Hugh T. J. foreman stevedore and Christina G. Robertson clerkess; b Lerwick 16.11.44
MICE MIMunE
jun eng (roads) Aber 1967–69; eng asst Ross-shire 1969–72; asst eng Stirlingsh from 1972
m Aber 1.8.69 Elizabeth A. Hewet MA 1967 *qv*

JAMIESON James Chilles PhD 1967
s of John M. J. youth organis and Margaret C. Chilles; b Aber 15.5.39
BSc(H-W) 1964 MRIC
asst lect biochem Aberd 1966–67; univ of Manit: post doct microbiol/sessional lect chem 1967–68, asst prof chem 1968–71, assoc prof chem from 1971
m Aber 19.8.67 Muriel M. Shaw MA 1966 *qv*

JAMIESON James Thomas *MA 1968
s of John J. BSc(agr) 1929 *qv* and Marjory J. Morrison MA 1931 *qv*(III); b Gluss Shetland 10.4.46
teacher Engl Elgin 1968–69; TEFL: Kaysere Turkey 1970–71, Emden Fed. Repub Ger 1971–73; teacher Engl Inv from 1973
m Inv 27.6.70 Jean S. Taylor MA(Edin) res asst d of Thomas G. T. Inv

JAMIESON, Jane Murray *MA 1968
m Darling

JAMIESON Lesley Mary MA 1967
m Peterculter 7.11.70 Malcolm D. Leiper Brechin

JAMIESON Norman *MA 1968
Dip TP

JAMIESON Peter Burnett *BSc 1963 PhD 1966
s of George J. cashier and Violet Burnett; b Aber 9.7.41
member tech staff Bell tel labs NJ USA 1966–68; res fell. chem Aberd 1968–69; res scient Ferrania-3M (Savona) Italy 1969–70; sen res scient Harlow 1970–75; res superv 3M St Paul MN USA 1975–77; res man. 3M Harlow from 1977

JAMIESON Susan Jane MA 1970 CASS 1972

JAMIESON Thomas Dean *BSc(eng) 1969
s of William J. and Helen J. Fraser; b Peterhead 30.11.23
MSc(Essex) 1970
teacher: elect. eng Inv 1970–73, sc/maths Saudi Arabia for BAC from 1974

JAMIESON Walter Nicolson *BSc(eng) 1956

JAMIESON William Stuart MB ChB 1956
s of John G. J. civ serv and Minnie Stuart; b Lerwick 23.4.32
MRCPGlas FRCP(Can)
nat serv RAMC Malaysia 1957–59; regist Gartcosh 1960–63; capt, lt-col RAMC England, Singapore 1964–70; consult. Westlock Canada from 1971
m Aber 1957 Ann Donald d of William D. Portsoy

JAMIESON Wilson *MA 1969
s of Andrew J. tailor and Emily C. Wilson; b Preston-

pans 21.12.31
Stirling: teacher St Modan's h s, spec asst, asst prin mod stud., prin mod stud. 1970–73; lect Jordanhill coll of educ Glasg from 1973
m Blantyre 8.8.59 Frances C. Milligan secy d of Hugh M. Blantyre

JAN Li Men MSc 1968
BSc(Sun Yet Sen)

JANJUA Sadiq MB ChB 1962
BSc(Panj)

JAPPY James Reid MB ChB 1961
s of George J. fisherman and Jeannie Reid; b Buckie 9.8.17
DObstRCOG 1964
h o ARI, Woodend hosp Aber 1961–62; h o obst Lond 1962–63; locum, trainee g p Bathgate, Edin 1963–64; g p Edin from 1964
m Motherwell 9.5.53 Mary E. Hamilton MB ChB(Glas) g p d of James S. H. Bellshill

JARROLD Robert Murray *BSc(for) 1967
s of William S. J. min of relig, missionary and Martha H. Cowan missionary; b Kachhwa UP India 20.10.44
PhD(Edin) 1971
asst conserv for. Kenya 1967–69; rural econ Songkhla S Thailand from 1971
m Ealing 6.8.66 Valerie M. Bate teacher d of Alan B. Ealing

JARVIS Anthony MB ChB 1966
s of Harold J. eng, tool maker and Marion Tyrer; b Leic 17.7.37
DObstRCOG 1973 MRCGP 1974 FPA cert 1974
h o med, surg Leic 1966–67; m o RAF squad. ldr UK, Sardinia, Germany 1967–73; g p Leic from 1973
m Syston 27.7.63 Josephine Shelton matron, nurs nurse d of John S. Queniborough Leics

JARVIS Raymond Hugh MA 1970
s of Alfred J. solic and Violet L. Cox; b Woodford 22.2.43
teacher: housemaster Great Walstead s Sussex 1970–76, prin geog Holmewood House s Kent 1976–78, St Michael's s Devon from 1978
m Windsor 17.4.71 Daphne Holt audiologist d of Eric H. Holbeach

JAYASINGHE Jinapriva Balachandra PhD 1958
BVSc(Ceylon)

JEEVARATNAM Jeevarajah MSc 1960 PhD 1963
BSc(Ceyl)

JEFCOATE Trevor Edward Stephen BSc(agr) 1967
s of Edward A. J. comp acct and Anne E. Page; b Chesham 23.11.45
Scott Sutherland s of arch.—farm bldgs Aber 1967–68; dev off. Stratford-u-Avon 1968–70; proj man. Selsey 1970–71; teacher biol comp s Havant 1972–74; head dept environmental and rural sc Manc 1975–77; co-ordinator of sciences Manc from 1977
m Glasg 2.8.69 Ann K. Thomson MA 1969 *qv*

JEFFERIES Frances Mary MA 1965
m(1) Dreisbach
(2) Knight

JEFFREE Christopher Edward *BSc 1969 PhD 1974
s of Edward P. H. PhD 1957 *qv*; b Aber 19.8.46

JEFFREE Edward Percival DSc 1957
s of Frank H. J. civ eng and Maud M. Le Couteur; b Woodford 23.4.08
BSc(Lond) 1930
head bee res dept NOSCA Aber 1946–60; sen lect sc Hull coll of educ 1960–63; head sc dept Avery Hill coll of educ Eltham 1963–73; assoc edit. *Annals of Applied Biology* from 1973
m Lond 9.4.42 Daphne J. Arnold asst edit., headmistress d of Arthur J. A. Leigh-on-Sea

JEFFREY James Martin BSc 1960
s of James P. J. BSc(Glas) CA and Belle E. Bain MA 1926 *qv*; b Aber 5.9.39
teacher Aber 1960–61; computer salesman: Dagenham 1961–66, IBM (UK) Edin from 1966
m Methil 21.4.73 Whilma A. Black secy d of John B. B. Methil

JEFFREY Joan Patricia *BSc 1956
phys Rolls Royce Derby 1956–62
m Aber 19.9.59 Roland J. Hill MA(Cantab) phys

JEFFREY John Peter MSc 1966
s of James P. J. BSc(Glas) CA and Belle E. Bain MA 1926 *qv*; b Aber 1.7.41
ARGIT CEng MIEE 1971 PEng(Ont) 1971
res eng Ferranti Edin 1967–69; tech eng Grampian TV Aber 1969–70; res and dev man. Littons: Toronto 1970–71, Los Angeles 1971–72; gen man. J. T. L. Parkinson Aber from 1972
m Aber 1.9.72 Judith A. Carry secy d of Joseph R. C. Aber

JEFFREY Sheena Isobel Burnett *BSc 1958
d of James P. J. BSc(Glas) CA and Belle E. Bain MA 1926 *qv*; b Aber 21.6.37
AEO with ARC unit of biometr genetics Birm 1958–60; teacher Hilton j s s Aber 1960–61; part-time scient off. govt fisheries dept Nkata Bay, Monkey Bay Malawi 1961–63; res asst Scot. dev dept river surv Pitlochry 1974; soc worker Tayside reg c from 1975
m Aber 17.9.60 Robert B. Williamson BSc 1958 *qv*

JEFFRIES Colin Edwin *BSc 1963 MSc 1964
s of George E. J. RAF mech and Jean S. Brown; b Forfar 26.11.40
teacher Hawick 1967–71; Eyemouth: prin teacher 1971–74, asst head from 1974
m Aber 17.7.65 Rosemary Ogilvie MA 1964 *qv*

JELLEY Robert Michael PhD 1961
MA(Oxon)

JEMMETT Kathleen Elizabeth MA 1970
d of Eric J. farm. and Mary M. Forbes; b Newcastle 5.2.49
teacher Engl: Stranraer acad 1971–73, Forres acad 1973–74; bank clerkess Elgin 1974–75
m Dingwall 4.10.72 Brian H. Keenan BA(Strath) teacher s of Hugh K. Glasg

JENKINS David Alwyn BSc 1969

JENKINS Eileen Morven *MA 1962
m Archer

JENNER Robert Corfield BSc 1967

JERMIESON John *MA 1961
s of Joseph F. J. baker and Norah Sutherland clerkess; b Aber 9.7.39

teacher: Engl: Broughton sen s s Edin 1962–64, RGC Aber 1964–72, prin Engl from 1972

JEROME Janet Morag Cameron MB ChB 1965
d of Brian S. J. army off. and Sara M. Cameron BSc(Glas) microbiol; b York 22.8.38
DObstRCOG 1968 DA 1972
sen h o: surg/gyn Weston-Super-Mare 1966–67, obst Cardiff 1967–68; res asst in breast cancer trial Cardiff 1968–69; g p trainee Somerset 1969–70; sen h o anaest Weston-super-Mare 1970–72; regist anaest: Edin 1972–73, Jersey 1973–75; g p Jersey from 1975

JESSOP Alexander Smethurst MA 1964 LLB 1966
s of Thomas A. J. draper and Ethel M. Robertson teacher p e; b Montrose 17.5.43
ptnr leg. pract Montrose 1966–76; dep proc fiscal Perth 1976–78; prin asst Crown office Edin from 1978
m Montrose 16.9.67 Joyce I. J. Duncan physioth d of David W. D. Montrose

JESSOP Chasser Robertson *MA 1963
s of Thomas A. J. draper and Ethel M. Robertson teacher p e; b Montrose 12.12.39
L ès L (Rennes) 1964 MA(Leeds) 1973
France: lect d'Anglais: univ of Rennes 1963–64, univ of Nancy 1964–66; lect: Fr univ of Brad 1966–70, Engl univ of Oran Algeria 1970–72; dir of govt ling. centre Abidjan Ivory Coast from 1973
m Guiseley 27.6.69 Susan M. Marshall secy d of Alwyn M. Guiseley

JEZZARD Janet Elizabeth Isobel MB ChB 1956
d of Robert J. teacher and Isobel H. H. Anderson teacher; b Lond 11.11.32
h o Aber 1956–57; cas off. Rotorua NZ 1961–66; g p Bethesda Wales 1971–72; g p Rotorua NZ from 1974
m Aber 13.9.57 Stanley D. Richardson BSc(Oxon) prof for./consult. s of George R. Culter

JOHN Malick Abdul Karim BSc(eng) 1967
s of Abdul K. J. bus. man and Mam Binta Jagne; b Banjul Gambia 16.6.43
Eng. Degree(Grenoble)
asst eng Lond trans board 1967–68; exec eng Banjul 1968–70; co-man. Gambia river basin proj Banjul, Dakar Senegal 1970–74; dir dept of hydrol and meteorol Banjul from 1974
m Banjul –.10.72 Fatou Janneh secy d of Howsoon O-S. J. Banjul

JOHN Reginald Samuel PhD 1970
BSc(agr)(Ceylon)

JOHNSON Agnes Harriet MA 1965
d of Thomas H. J. crofter and Elizabeth Ratter crofter; b Voe 4.7.44
Dip Lib(Strath) 1968 ALA 1970
lib asst Aber 1966–67; asst lib Glasg 1968–79; resid Shetland
m Lerwick 4.4.72 James M. Hannah BA(OU) teacher s of William H. Alexandria

JOHNSON Brenda BSc 1969
d of John W. J. planer, baker and Doris Carr confectioner; b Gateshead, 16.12.47
lib course RGIT Aber 1969; res tech X-ray crystallography soil sc dept Aberd 1970–73
m Aber 8.4.71 Donald M. Grant derrickman, wayleaves off., mud eng (oil comp) s of Kenneth G. Blair Drummond

JOHNSON David Charles *MA 1964
s of Sir Ronald E. C. J. MA(Cantab) head SHHD and Elizabeth G. Nuttall MA(Cantab) teacher/concert singer; b Edin 27.10.42
BA(Cantab) 1966 PhD(Cantab) 1972
freelance composer and writer on mus Edin from 1970
m Edin 12.5.73 Maureen Bagnall BSc(Edin) d of Albert B Ayr

JOHNSON Elizabeth Ann Dorothy MA 1960
d of Benjamin M. J. driver and Agnes Hay; b Voe 3.12.39
teacher: p s Firth 1961–65, Bells Brae p s Lerwick 1965–67
m Lerwick 18.7.62 Peter G. Williamson BSc 1958 *qv*

JOHNSON John Hector BSc 1958

JOHNSON Lilian Ethel MA 1968
m Dixon

JOHNSON Margaret *BSc 1957
b Darwen 31.8.34
teacher sc: High s for girls Aber 1959–60, Princes Risborough from 1966
m Aber 15.7.58 John M. Dinwoodie BSc(for) 1957 *qv*

JOHNSON Margaret Anne *MA 1960
d of Frederick A. J. RAF eng, civ eng and Alexanderina McKerron bank clerk; b Aber 12.11.36
translator of Fr air ministry Lond 1961–62; teacher Fr Brechin, Edin 1963–64
m Aber 28.8.65 William J. Ross elect. eng s of William R. Aber

JOHNSON Matthew Francis *BSc 1968
s of Sir Ronald E. C. J. MA(Cantab) head SHHD and Elizabeth G. Nuttall MA(Cantab) teacher/concert singer; b Edin 20.9.46
Edin: res eng in nuclear med comm equipment, Nuclear Enterprises 1968–71, chief exec scientology acad from 1971
m Edin 12.10.68 Ann H. MacGregor d of Archibald K. MacG. BSc(Edin) Assam

JOHNSON Richard Patrick Craig PhD 1967
s of Cecil G. J. BSc(S'ton) entomologist and Margaret U. Black; b Lond 3.3.36
BSc(Lond) 1960 MIBiol
res asst DSIR Bedford coll Lond 1960–62; bot dept Aberd: res asst DSIR 1962–64, asst lect 1964–67, lect 1967–74, sen lect from 1974
visiting res worker biol dept Mount Allison univ Sackville New Brunswick 1970
m Georgeham 19.11.60 Philippa M. Boutwood SRN d of Aubrey B.

JOHNSON Ronald George *BSc 1957
s of Thomas G. J. mech eng and Helen W. Cruickshank; b Elgin 28.10.34
grad app Manc 1957–60; flying off. RAF 1960–62; eng Motherwell 1962–64, sect. leader Manc 1964–73, res and dev man. Sidcup from 1973
m Aber 5.11.60 Sheila Y. McDonald MA 1957 *qv*

JOHNSON Roy Rowland *MA 1961

JOHNSON Sylvia Mary MA 1965 Dip Ed 1966
d of Bernard J. foreman D o E and Alice M. Yewdall; b Horsforth 20.10.43
Essex: teacher Eng/Fr Maldon g s 1966–70, Plume s Maldon from 1970
m Maldon 10.4.71 John Carpenter P.O. tech off. s of John C. Maldon

JOHNSTON Alexander McIntyre *MA 1968 MEd 1974

JOHNSTON Arthur George Leighton *BSc(agr) 1966
s of Arthur G. J. market gardener and Mary I. Henderson teacher; b Ellon 3.1.31
teacher: AGS 1968–70, prin biol Ellon acad from 1970
m Aber 16.8.69 Mary M. Hay secy d of John A. H. Aber

JOHNSTON Brenda Anne *MA 1970
m Conn

JOHNSTON Charles Stewart MA 1964
s of James J. confectioner and Carrie Davy; b Methven 29.10.27
teacher Beechwood s Aber from 1965
m Aber 21.8.53 Mildred R. Bisset clerkess d of Charles D. B.

JOHNSTON Derek William *MA 1966
s of John Johnston civ eng and Annie M. McInnes; b Langholm 1.12.43
PhD(Hull) 1970
sen res off. Oxon from 1970
m Aber 23.12.66 Mary B. Thom BSc 1966 *qv*

JOHNSTON Edith Helen *MA 1969 Dip Ed 1970
d of John H. J. asst barrack warden and Isabella J. Shipp off. worker; b Forres 23.4.47
teacher Aber 1970–73
m Aber 2.4.70 Alan W. Fraser BSc 1969 *qv*

JOHNSTON Edna *BSc 1970 Dip Ed 1971
d of Archie J. master baker and Annie M. Cruickshank; b St Cyrus 28.10.48
teacher geog Hutcheson's g s Glasg 1971–77
m St Cyrus 9.8.75 Hamish W. Cameron BSc 1969 *qv*

JOHNSTON Hugh Walker MA 1962

JOHNSTON James Grant *MA 1969

JOHNSTON James Laughton BSc 1965
s of James M. J. MB ChB(Edin) psychiat and Elizabeth Balneaves writer; b Aber 11.4.40
Shetland: teacher p s 1967–69; asst reg off. Nature Conserv Council 1969–75, teacher from 1978
m Brighton 10.9.66 Patricia M. Royces

JOHNSTON John Keith MA 1970
s of Sydney M. J. off. man. and Margaret M. McIntosh tel; b Keith 14.12.49
CA 1974

JOHNSTON Kathleen Ann MA 1961
d of George A. M. J. comp dir and Elizabeth A. Robb; b Aber 25.4.40
Dip Sec St(St Godric's coll Lond) 1961
Lond: secy leg. dept Brit fed. of master printers 1961–63, worked for exhibition organis 1963–64
m Aber 15.8.64 Charles A. Hicks indust rel exec s of George W. H. Fleet

JOHNSTON Margaret BSc 1970
d of Andrew G. J. marine arch. joiner and Williamina M. Laurenson hotel housekeeper; b Lerwick 11.2.48
teacher maths Currie h s 1971–73 and from 1978
m Aber 12.3.70 Frederick H. Tait marine elect. eng s of Laurence S. J. T. Aith

JOHNSTON Margaret Joan *BSc 1956
d of James W. J. BSc 1929 *qv*; b Aber 25.3.35
PhD(Edin) 1960
res chem ICI(fibres) Harrogate 1956–57; scient off. (agr chem) Hannah dairy res inst Ayr 1960–63
m Aber 3.6.63 David J. Green BSc(Edin) syst analyst s of Henry L. G. BA(Cantab) Salisbury

JOHNSTON Mary Isabella MA 1959
d of John H. J. soldier, civ serv and Isabella J. Shipp off. worker; b Edin 9.4.38
teacher Engl Hilton s s Aber 1961–62
m Aber 12.10.59 George Eddie MB ChB 1962 *qv*

JOHNSTON Neil Roderick MB ChB 1960
s of Herbert W. J. cable eng, exec and Elizabeth Leslie; b Rio de Janeiro 22.7.35
DObstRCOG 1962 MRCGP 1970
h o: Aber 1960–61, mat. hosp Hull 1961–62; g p: trainee Eastbourne 1962–63, Norwich 1963–64, Edin from 1964
m Aber 3.4.62 Moyra G. Coutts teacher d of Albert C. Aber

JOHNSTON Nigel McLauchlan MB ChB 1970

JOHNSTON Norman Howard *MA 1969

JOHNSTON Patricia Anne Margaret *MA 1966
m Boxall

JOHNSTON Robin Forsyth MB ChB 1962

JOHNSTON Ronald Park *MA 1970

JOHNSTON Shona Nan MA 1970
d of Ronald D. G. J. man. dir and Nancy F. Price; b Fenwick 17.3.48
hotel receptionist, secy etc: Cape Town, Johannesburg, Aust, NZ, Far East 1970–74; teacher inf 1975–77, TEFL Lond from 1978

JOHNSTON William Alan *BSc(eng) 1965
s of John J. farm. and Jessie P. M. Matthew; b Glenbuchat 2.2.43
trainee eng Jas Howden & Co Glasg 1965–66; Burroughs machines Dumbarton: prod. eng 1966–70, sen prod. eng 1970; des eng PED Babcock & Wilcox (OPS) Renfrew 1970–71; sen scient off. Torry res stat Aber DTI/MAFF from 1971
m Aber 4.4.67 Susanne L. Watson secy d of Alexander W. Gamrie

JOHNSTON William George MB ChB 1958
s of James S. J. blacksmith/agr eng and Magdalena R. Tocher; b Fintray 4.9.33
DTM & H(Lond) 1961 FRCSE 1967
h o ARI 1959–60; HM Forces RAMC trainee surg, consult. surg lt-col UK, Singapore, Nepal, Germany including Berlin, Oman, Belize from 1960
m Aber 25.7.60 Anne Ross MA 1955 *qv*

JOHNSTON William Ross MA 1960 Dip Ed 1961

JOHNSTONE Dorothy Jane MA 1966
m Hughson

JOHNSTONE Frank Dennis MB ChB 1967 cMD 1978
MRCOG

JOHNSTONE Gavin Wildridge PhD 1969
s of Arthur S. J. off. RE and Mary Wildridge; b Broughton, Peblessh 15.5.41
BSc(Brist) 1963 Dip Conserv(Lond) 1964
Melbourne: biol Antarctic div Aust Nat antarctic res

exped at Macquarie Is 1969–71, Davis, Antarctica 1972; head off. Melbourne from 1972
m Hobart 11.11.72 Kerry A. Nolan nurse d of Christopher J. N. Tasmania

JOHNSTONE Lesley *MA 1958
PhD(Cantab)

JOHNSTONE Lesley Margaret Harriet *MA 1969
d of Frank C. J. BA(Glas) lect hist Aber coll of educ and Margaret Foord teacher; b Ayr 26.2.47
Dip Soc St (Edin) 1974 Dip Ed(Edin) 1977
res fell. Aber 1969–72; soc worker Edin 1972–73, 74–76
m Aber 19.2.72 John R. Inglis BSc 1971 res stud. s of John I. Aber

JOHNSTONE Margaret Jane BEd 1970

JOHNSTONE Raymond George MA 1969

JOHNSTONE Ronald Clark Beckett MSc 1968
BSc(for) Edin

JOINER Vera Margaret MA 1958 Dip Ed 1959
d of Edward J. baker and Margaret W. Gavin psychiat nurse; b Banff 19.10.38
Dip Russian 1964
assistante anglaise Uzerche France 1959–60; teacher, spec asst Galashiels acad 1960–72; teacher Elgin acad 1972–74
m Melrose 10.8.65 John S. Tweddle chartered surv s of Alexander M. T. Melrose

JOLLY Caryl Ann Howard BSc 1970

JOLLY Ian *BSc(eng) 1959 MSc 1961

JONES Alexander Alfred Albert *BSc(eng) 1962

JONES Ann Harriet MA 1966

JONES Arthur Stanley PhD 1960
BSc(Durh)

JONES Christine Louise *MA 1968

JONES Elinor Margaret LLB 1968

JONES Elizabeth Helen BEd 1970
d of Arthur G. J. civ serv and Hilda J. Cumming MA 1939 *qv*; b Ealing 7.8.48
teacher: Fr Blackpool 1970–71, Fr/Engl Selkirk 1971–72, Congleton 1972–74
m Selkirk 1.8.72 Michael J. Godfree BSc(Sus) computer progr s of Eric F. G. Bournemouth

JONES Gavin David *MA 1962

JONES Glyn David LLB 1966
s of Clifford C. J. eng/works man. and Annie J. Murphy; b Glenboig 15.3.46
asst Robinson Rentals Bedford 1967–68; lect in law Aber coll of comm 1968–69; exec asst, man. chamber of shipping of UK Lond 1969–75; asst dir nat assoc of Brit and Irish millers Lond from 1975
m Glasg 1.4.70 Anne D. Muir teacher p e d of William A. M. Glasg

JONES Helene Marie MA 1956
d of Joseph G. J. seaman MN and Jessie A. Robertson nurse, shopkeeper; b Inverurie 15.6.34
teacher: Kinellar p s 1957–59, Insch p s 1959–64, Bucksburn p s 1964–65; temp relief teacher Aberdeensh s from 1968
m Aber 13.7.63 Alexander Gray miller, mason's lab, BR and NCL fitter s of John G. Newmachar

JONES Idwal Pryderi Vaughan MA 1966

JONES Jeffrey BSc 1967

JONES John Nicholas BSc 1967
s of John E. S. J. comp dir and Norah E. Daniel; b Wells 6.1.45
stockbroker Lond 1967–70; comp dir (animal feed) Wells from 1970
m Clayhidon 29.7.72 Pauline A. Tyrrell MB BS(Lond) med pract d of Douglas A. T. Clayhidon

JONES Keith Greig LLB 1969
s of Stanley J. BSc(eng) Manc and Sybil V. Greig; b Edin 10.9.48
law app Aber 1969–71; leg. asst Dun 1971–72; solic Stonehaven from 1972; prin solic to Kincardine & Deeside dist c

JONES Margaret Ann MB ChB 1960
d of Horace M. J. banker and Kathleen I. Burrell; b Worcester 14.4.36
MRCPath 1977
h o ARI 1960–61; sen h s City hosp Aber 1961–62; lect path. Aberd 1962–65; regist part time path. Glasg R.I.; sen regist part time Chelsea and Kensington Lond 1970–72; locum consult. path. Eastbourne and Hastings reg board 1973–75; sen regist path. Edin RI from 1976
m Aboyne 21.12.60 Angus K. McIntyre MA 1961 *qv*

JONES Marianne Elizabeth BSc 1959 *1960
d of William E. J. BA(Oxon) dean and hon canon of Brecon cath and Rachel M. Powell BA(Lond) soc worker Welsh nat gov of BBC; b Perth W Aust 15.12.36
med biochem univ coll hosp Lond 1960–62
m Brecon 1962 Bernard J. Aylett BSc(Cantab) univ teacher chair of chem Lond univ s of Francis P. A. Teddington

JONES Mary Cornelia *MA 1959
d of William I. J. BA(Cardiff) clergyman, missionary and Swantina J. de Young BA(Mich) teacher, missionary; b Chicago 13.9.37
teacher: classics Balfron 1960–61, Aber 1961–65; inf mistress Lockerbie 1965–69; inf mist./superv jun classes Linton Camp NZ 1970–71
m Palmerston N. NZ 2.1.71 Robert A. C. Stewart PhD(Massey) univ lect, prof s of Robert A. S. MA(NZ) Wellington

JONES Mary Ellis MA 1969
d of David J. J. BSc(Cardiff) m o h and Megan Jones BA(Cardiff) teacher; b Northampton 28.2.48
Dip Pers Man.(Lond) 1972
pers off.: Canadian Pacific Co Lond 1970–72, insur comp Sydney 1972–73; lect pers man. and psych Sydney poly from 1973
m Rugby John Dickie BSc(Lond) master brewer s of David D. Solihull

JONES Michael Hugh *BSc 1967

JONES Michael John PhD 1968
BSc(St And)

JONES Olwen Margaret *MA 1956
d of William I. J. MA(Cardiff) clergyman/teacher and Swantina J. de Young BA(Mich) teacher; b Aden

31.1.34
asst lib Aber publ lib 1957
m Aber 30.8.57 Paul M. Doe MA(Oxon) univ teacher s of Maurice N. D. BA(Birm) Norwich

JONES Robert Bruce *BSc 1967

JONES Shelagh Anne Lesley MA 1967

JONES Shirley MB ChB 1960
m Bremner

JONES Susan Primrose MA 1963
m (1) Pariente
(2) Addison

JORDAN Neville Arthur Joseph BSc(eng) 1964

JOSLIN Paul William Bamber MSc 1967
BSc(BCol) MA(Tor)

JOSS Alexander William Leslie *BSc 1967 PhD 1972
s of William J. and Rebecca Gilbert; b Rhynie 8.12.45
scient MRC Edin 1970–75; sen biochem Raigmore hosp Inv from 1975
m Aber 1969 Elizabeth Baird MA 1969 *qv*

JOSS Alison Margaret BSc 1970
d of Edward G. J. shipmaster and Patricia E. Carbery secy; b Aber 2.11.49
admin off. GLC educ dept ILEA Lond 1970–76
m Aber 24.10.70 Brian S. Smith MA 1970 *qv*

JOSS Gary Anthony MA 1969

JOWETT Pamela Hardy LLB 1970
d of Christopher H. J. MA(Oxon) diplomat and Mary D. Burnett-White teacher; b Falkirk 31.10.48
Aber: law app 1970–72; leg. asst Lefevre & Co advoc 1972–78
m Aber 6.7.71 William G. Gray MA 1969 *qv*

JOWETT Richard Andrew MA 1969

JUNGR Minoslav BSc 1957

JUTAGIR Torrance MB ChB 1964

KABAARA Adriel Mukatha MSc 1960
s of Reuben M. teacher/peasant and Miriam N. Muceke; b Meru Kenya 1934
BSc(Lond) 1955 PhD(Brist) 1974
soil chem: Ukiriguru Tanzania 1960–63, Namulonge Uganda 1963–65; Ruiru Kenya: soil chem 1966, dep dir (R) 1966–71, dir of res from 1971
m Meru Kenya 29.8.64 Ruth G. Mantu teacher d of Josiah M. Meru

KADIO Kisaka Robert MSc 1968
BSc(agr)(W Pak)

KAGIA James MB ChB 1965
s of Joseph M. K. and Rakeli W. M. Wangeci; b Kiambu Kenya 1931
MPH(Harv) 1977 Fell. Paediat and Statist(Harv) 1977
intern med Dumfries RI, surg Neath gen hosp, h o Bradford gen hosp 1965–67; Kenya: m o Nakuru then i/c Kapsabet hosp Nandi 1967, Karuri health centre Kiambu 1968–70; lect dept commun health univ of Nairobi 1970–79, prof from 1979
m Nairobi 21.3.70 Ruth W. Munge BA(Nairobi) teacher d of John M.

KAITIFF David Isaac MB ChB 1961

KALE Vasant Dattatraya MSc 1964 PhD 1968
BSc(Poona)

KAMALUDDIN Abul Fazal Muhammed PhD 1967
MA(Dacca)

KANDIL Mohammed Fakhry Mahmoud PhD 1966
BSc(agr) MSc(Cairo)

KARIMU Sikiru Ajani BSc(for) 1965

KARLSEN Steinar Johan MB ChB 1969
s of Oskar K. K. BSc(Trondheim) dir Voss elect board and Gunnvor Holthe; b Trondheim 4.9.44
regist surg Oslo univ hosp Lørenskog
m Voss 15.7.67 Olov G. Hallstensen radiographer d of Ola H. Fitjar Norway

KARMODY Allastair Michael MB ChB 1962 ChM 1969
FRCSE FRCS(Lond) 1967 FACS 1973
sen regist surg ARI 1969–70; Albany NY: asst prof surg 1970–75, assoc prof surg from 1975
m Aber Rhona S. Chisholm teacher home econ

KASENALLY Abu Twalib MB ChB 1969
s of Abdul R. K. headmaster and Bibi K. Beebeejaun; b Mauritius 10.8.41
FRCSE 1974
h o ARI 1969–70; lect dept path. Aberd 1970–71; sen h o gen/orthop surg Aber 1971–72; res fell. vasc surg Aberd 1973–74; regist gen surg Aber teaching hosps from 1974
m Mauritius 31.3.72 Najmabanu Abbasakoor d of Ismael A. C. A. Port Louis

KASONDE Joseph Mwenya MB ChB 1966 cMD 1976
s of Edmund K. teacher and Gertrude L. Sunkutu; b Mazabuka Zambia 30.1.38
MRCOG 1972
h o Lusaka 1966–70; h o obst/gyn Oxford 1970–72; regist obst/gyn Stirling 1972–73; res fell. Oxford from 1973
m Lond 7.11.40 Mary C. Mukandi SRN d of Enock S. M. Mbala Zambia

KAWA Mambu Alphan Barbington MB ChB 1966

KAY Catherine Helen Maxwell MA 1965
d of James B. K. bank man. and Margaret P. M. Meldrum; b Kirkcaldy 10.3.44
teacher Engl: Bridge of Don s 1966–70, Glenrothes h s 1970–71; asst prin Engl Glenrothes from 1971
m Kirkcaldy 12.10.74 Ian R. Downie BSc(Edin) teacher s of David D. Lundin Links

KAY Jennifer Ann Yule MA 1958 LLB 1965
d of Frederick R. K. LLB(Cantab) col serv and Constance M. Yule; b Aber 17.12.37
lib McG univ Montreal 1958; lect Engl Makerere night s Kampala Uganda 1961; lect Aber coll of comm 1969; restaurateur Maryculter from 1970
m(1) 4.1.58 John Lothian MA 1958 *qv*; husb *d* 13.2.62
(2) Aber 3.12.66 Iain R. Martin MA 1966 *qv*; marr diss 1975

KAY Jillian Gay Ashley MA 1966
d of Frederick R. K. MA(Cantab) col off. and Constance M. Yule; b Aber 19.5.43
m Montrose 12.9.64 Ivan C. F. Wisely MB ChB 1967 *qv*

KAY Michael PhD 1963
s of Herbert B. K. shoe retailer and Amy Griffiths; b

York 10.3.38
BSc(Leeds) 1960 ARIC 1964
prin scient off. Rowett res inst Aber from 1963
m Aber 6.4.68 Moira Murray d of William M. Bucksburn

KAYLL Albert James PhD 1964
s of Swinburne A. K. B Arch(Penn) arch. and Mary Hardy; b Vancouver 21.1.35
BSF(BC) 1959 MF(Duke) 1960
Canada: res scient Chalk River 1960–68, asst prof for./co-dir fire sc centre univ UNB Fredericton 1968–71, assoc prof 1971–77, prof and chmn dept for resources from 1977
m Chilliwack BC 12.6.62 Jennifer J. M. Wellington d of John H. W. ScD(Cantab) Johannesburg

KEATING Christine MB ChB 1970
d of James M. K. BSc(Swansea) electronic eng and Cecelia A. J. Rodda teacher; b Swansea 10.5.46
sen h o, regist, lect haemat Lond 1972–76; g p HM Forces Münster W Ger from 1976
m Eastbourne 17.1.76 Andrew Borthwick-Clarke MB BS (Lond) med pract s of Aubrey B.-C. Salisbury

KEAY David Malcolm BSc(agr) 1959

KEAY Hugh John *BSc(eng) 1962

KEAY Irene Hutchison *MA 1967
m Khan

KEAY Lorna Mary MA 1957 Dip Ed 1958
d of John K. MA 1919 *qv*; b Banchory 8.4.36
teacher: Aber 1958–59, Reading 1959–61, Welwyn Garden City 1961–62, Norwich from 1975
m Reading 1.4.61 Robert W. McTear br man. life assur comp s of Ian McT. Reading

KEAY Marjorie Kilgour MA 1961
d of James T. K. shop man. and Margaret N. Anderson; b Aber 22.2.40
teacher inf Aber 1962–63, Leic 1963–64, Exeter 1964–66
m Aber 3.7.63 Robin N. Trezise bus. exec s of Nolan T. T. Cullompton

KEAY Peter Neil *MA 1970

KEDDIE Gordon James *BSc 1966
s of David G. A. K. draughtsman/sports reporter and Norah S. Elder asst postmaster; b Edin 29.12.44
Dip Ed(Edin) MDiv(Pittsburgh PA) 1973 MIBiol 1979
teacher biol Trinity acad Edin 1967–70; min North Hills reformed presb ch Pittsburgh USA from 1974
m Beaver Falls PA 18.5.74 Jane A. McMillan BA(Beaver Falls) d of John M. McM. Marion Iowa

KEELAN John *MA 1966
s of Andrew K. fitter and Elizabeth Henry; b Glasg 15.3.26
DPA(Glas) 1954
teacher mod lang Cults 1967–70; prin mod lang: Clydebank 1970–72, Stirling from 1972
m Aber 14.7.69 Susan I. Somerville MA 1969 *qv*

KEENAN Colin Grant *MA 1970

KEENLEYSIDE Clunie Bonner MSc 1968
d of Colin B. K. farm. and Isobel Routledge teacher; b Haltwhistle 23.10.46
Agr Tripos(Cantab) 1967
asst res off. countryside comm Lond 1968–70; asst secy N Pennines rural dev board Appleby 1970–71; sen countryside asst Durham c c 1971–79; sen res off. countryside comm Newcastle-u-Tyne from 1979

KEEPING Joseph Douglas MB ChB 1970
s of Joseph C. K. patent examiner and Dorothy K. Hawkins; b Liverpool 18.2.44
MRCOG 1976 F Aust COG 1979
h o, regist Aber hosps 1970–76; sen regist Wellington NZ 1976–77; lect obst/gyn Brisbane Aust from 1978
m Aber 3.8.68 Roberta A. Nichol LLB 1968 *qv*

KEIL Cheryl Maureen MA 1970
m Wylie

KEILLAR Doreen Nan MB ChB 1969
d of John R. K. and Nan F. Mitchell; b Dun 6.1.46
h o royal Devon and Exeter hosp Exeter 1969–70; Aust: r m o base hosp Maryborough, Queensland 1971–72; g p: Alstonville NSW from 1972, Lismore psychiat admission unit from 1975
m Alstonville 2.3.73 Richard A. Bacon grazier, real estate ag s of Christopher H. B. BA(Cantab) Broughton Chester

KEIR Hamish Alexander MSc 1961
A H-W C

KEIR Rhona Mary MA 1970
d of Duncan K. farm. and Betty H. Dunbar farm.; b Aber 10.11.49
teacher maths Castle Douglas h s from 1974
m Alford 20.8.69 Marcel H. Rivard agriculturist s of Marcel R. Canada

KEITH Gordon BSc 1970

KEITH Ian Cameron MB ChB 1967

KEITH John Macpherson BSc 1970 *1973
s of Alexander M. K. MA 1931 *qv*; b Glasg 20.9.47
res asst royal coll of surg dent. res unit teratology dept Kent from 1973
m Aber 8.10.70 Alexandra A. Davidson computer oper d of Alexander D. S. Queensferry

KEITH Kathleen *MA 1965
m Ewen

KELBIE David *LLB 1967
s of Robert K. elect. linesman and Monica E. Pearn; b Inverurie 28.2.45
advoc Edin 1968–79; Sheriff of N Strathclyde at Dumbarton from 1979
m Aber 7.9.66 Helen M. Smith MA 1966 *qv*

KELLAS Alfred Gordon *MA 1969
s of Alexander K. racing motor cyclist/motor cyclist salesman and Dorothy A. Brown hair stylist; b Aber 14.12.41
sales off. man. BSA Guns Birm 1969–70; sen organis and methods analyst Scot. Widows' Fund & Life Assur Soc Edin 1970–78, sen organis and methods off. Grampian reg c from 1978
m Stonehaven 15.6.68 Joy A. Green secy d of Douglas R. G. Stonehaven

KELLAS James Grant *MA 1958
s of James F. Kellas MA 1920 *qv*; b Aber 16.5.36
PhD(Lond) 1962
tut. fell. hist Bedford coll Lond 1961–62; asst hist Aberd 1962–64; lect politics Glas 1964–73, sen lect 1973–77, reader from 1977
m Aber 8.9.62 Norma R. Craig MA 1959 *qv*

KELLAS Peter Duncan *BSc(eng) 1969
s of George D. K. MA 1930 *qv*; b Huntly 20.4.47
Grad IMechE 1970
Rolls Royce E Kilbride: grad trainee 1969–71, performance eng from 1971

KELLY Alastair Fraser MA 1966

KELLY Frances MB ChB 1967
MA(Edin)

KELLY George Watson *MA 1968

KELLY Irene MA 1968

KELLY Jane Avril MA 1966
d of Robert K. police off. and Mary A. Archibald; b Stirling 5.4.45
Dip Sec Sc(Strath) 1967
Lond: exec secy 1967–68, asst brand man. 1968–71
m Alloa 22.3.69 John B. Chesworth BSc(eng) 1974 civ eng construct. man. s of Joseph S. C. Kingsley

KELLY John *MA 1958

KELLY Winifred MA 1958
d of William C. K. tel exec and Winifred I. Toman; b Aber 26.8.38
teacher, spec asst Aber 1959–73; teacher Inv from 1973

KELMAN Alice Jane BSc 1961
m Diack

KELMAN Celia MA 1967
d of Andrew L. K. BSc(St And) indust chem and Catherine E. Robinson MA(Glas) teacher; b Newcastle-u-Tyne 21.1.46
assistante lycée Coulommiers France 1967–68; teacher: Fr Hull g s 1969–70, Engl Huelva Spain 1970–71, Engl Zaragoza, Granada Spain 1971–72; Fr/Span Queen Elizabeth g s Hexham from 1972

KELMAN Elizabeth Jane Cooper MA 1964
d of William J. K. bldg mason and Elizabeth J. Cooper nurse; b Torphins 20.11.42
teacher: Engl/remed subjs Gordon s Huntly 1965–73
m Aber 1.8.70 William T. Duffton auctioneer s of Alexander D. Huntly

KELMAN James Smith MSc 1962
s of George S. K. BL 1950 *qv*; b Aber 29.5.39
CEng MIMechE 1972
grad app AEI Manc 1962–64, performance eng 1964–67; lect RGIT Aber from 1967
m Manc 1.7.67 Dorothy M. Wilkinson SRN d of Reginald W. Blackpool

KELMAN James Tarves MA 1965
(conferred for long service of exceptional merit)
s of James K. tailor and Nellie Tarves dressmaker; b Turriff 31.8.14
ARICS 1951 FRICS 1975
Aberd: asst secy (edilis & lands) 1957–63, dep secy (edilis & lands) 1963–68, buildings off. and factor 1968–78; retd
m Aber 14.6.39 Helen Paterson jeweller's asst d of William P. Aber

KELMAN John Matheson MA 1960

KELMAN Margaret Elizabeth MA 1964
d of George O. K. elect./mech eng and Alice J. Duncan teacher; b New Deer 1.6.43
teacher: Lat/hist Brierley Hill 1965–67, hist Lasswade 1968–70, hist Dingwall 1970–76; secy at Aberd 1976–78, teacher hist/mod stud. Inv from 1978

KELMAN Maureen McKenzie *BSc 1964
d of George S. K. BL 1950 *qv*; b Torphins 11.1.42
govt serv (patent examiner) Lond from 1964

KELMAN Patricia Elspeth MA 1960
m Lenehan

KELSALL John *MA 1970
s of Lawrence K. teacher and Catherine J. Fortune; b East Retford 31.7.47
Fullerton Moir & Gray schol Aberd 1970; PhD(Glas) 1976 Member Composers' guild of G.B. 1973; Member Royal Mus Assoc 1976
teacher mus Renfrew h s 1975–77; lect mus Kingston poly from 1977; OU tut. from 1973; organist/choirmaster Christ Church, Sutton Lond from 1977
m Glasg 17.6.72 Heather J. Wilson MA(Glas) stud. advis d of William R. W. Glasg

KELTY Roger Fyfe *MA 1960

KEMP Alexander George *MA 1962

KEMP Alexander John *BSc 1961 MSc 1962
s of Albert W. K. woollen manuf/wholesale draper and Isabella D. McIntyre MA 1921 *qv*; b Aber 20.10.38
FRAS 1970 MSc(Lond) 1974
lect The City univ Lond from 1965; part time tut. astron S Havering coll adult educ from 1973
m Aber 22.7.64 Margaret J. V. Brown MA 1962 *qv*

KEMP David Alexander MA 1957

KEMP John Cumming *MA 1966

KEMP Marjorie Isabelle MB ChB 1956

KEMP Mary Lois BSc 1961
d of William K. TU off. and Mary A. Baxter; b Glasg 17.12.39
res asst biochem DRI 1961–62; Glas: tech biochem 1966–67, res asst biochem 1967–70, part time tech elect. eng dept from 1974
m Aber 16.10.61 Alexander Hobbs MA 1958 *qv*

KEMP William Charles *BSc(eng) 1964
s of William K. T U off. and Mary A. Baxter; b Glasg 11.3.41
MSc(Birm) 1966
eng Elliott Automation Rochester 1964–65; Ferranti Bracknell: des eng 1966–69, sen syst eng from 1970

KENDLE Janet Margaret MSc 1969
d of Sidney F. K. eng, shopkeeper and May R. Goldfinch; b Lond 12.6.47
BSc(Sus) 1968
res bot dept Aberd 1970–71; civ serv computer progr, syst analyst Edin 1971–77; progr analyst Lond from 1977
m Edin 20.3.72 David C. Watterson MA(Edin) Dip Ed (Aberd) 1969 teacher, admin s of Leslie C. W. Edin

KENNAWAY Nancy Gordon *BSc 1959
d of Charles G. K. MA 1922 *qv*(II, III); b Aber 20.3.37
DPhil(Oxon) 1967
exp asst Scot. nat blood transfusion assoc Edin 1960–62; scient off. MRC Oxford 1962–67; Portland USA: res assoc univ of Oregon med s 1968–69, fell. genetics univ of Oregon med s 1969–73, instr med genetics 1974–77, asst prof med genetics from 1977

KENNEDY Bryan Ross MB ChB 1960
s of William D. K. MA 1921 *qv*; b Fraserburgh 19.6.35
FFARCS
lect anat Aber 1962–63; regist, sen regist united Cardiff hosps 1964–67; lect anaest Welsh nat s of med 1967–68; consult. anaest Aber from 1968

KENNEDY Craig Daniel BSc(eng) 1959
s of Robert W. K. garage prop. and Constance A. Daniel; b Aber 14.4.36
des eng Glasg 1959–63; resid eng Edin 1963–64; field eng BC Canada 1964–66; resid eng Nova Scotia 1966–68; sen eng/assoc ptnr Glasg from 1969
m Edin 8.8.64 Irene Galbraith examiner in estate duty off. d of Alexander G. Edin

KENNEDY Duncan Meldrum MA 1965
s of John K. banker and Cathie J. A. Macdonald health visitor; b Tillycoultry 3.7.40
teacher Stirling 1965–71, asst prin teacher from 1971
m Stirling 2.8.72 Margaret A. Murdoch secy d of John M. Stirling

KENNEDY Elizabeth Ann MA 1970
d of Hamish K. gamekeeper/stalker and Elizabeth MacPherson; b Urray 14.12.49
teacher Engl/hist Kinlochleven s 1971–75; asst prin Engl Thurso h s 1975–78; asst rector Plockton h s from 1978

KENNEDY Eric *MA 1961
d 1.10.68

KENNEDY James Douglas *MA 1961
b Inv 18.3.39
m 6.7.67

KENNEDY Katherine Stuart MA 1962
d of George G. K. grocer and Jessie A. McIntyre; b Forres 9.10.41
teacher: Forres 1963–64, Peterhead 1964–65, Huntly 1967–73, Elgin 1974–76, Forres from 1976
m Forres 11.7.64 George D. Smith police sgt s of George R. S. Nairn

KENNEDY Michael Thomas MA 1967 Dip Ed 1968

KENNEDY Richard *MA 1969

KENNERLEY Peter Charles MB ChB 1969
s of Tordiff A. S. K. MB ChB(Birm) g p and Eleanor J. Reynolds; b Birm 10.8.42
DCH 1971 DObstRCOG 1972 DA 1975
h o: paediat Middx hosp Lond 1971–72, Addenbrooke's hosp Cambridge 1972–73, anaest Middx hosp 1973–76; g p Brackley from 1976
m Exeter 21.9.74 Alethea M. S. Coleridge nurse d of Anthony D. C. Newton Abbot

KENNEY John Richard *BSc(eng) 1969
s of Gordon F. K. time study eng BR and Phyllis E. Butcher; b Peterborough 29.6.47
grad asst eng Edin 1969–71; resid civ eng Dunoon, Shetland from 1971
m Dunrossness 2.9.69 Mary E. Robertson MA 1969 *qv*

KENT Anthony William David Charles BSc 1966
s of Charles A. K. RN and Isabella M. H. Fraser, admin secy; b Inv 5.2.47
Dip Aquaculture & Fishing Man.(Stir) 1977
teacher biol: Perth 1967–68, Linlithgow 1968–71, prin biol Campbeltown 1971–74; shipyard worker Campbeltown 1974–76; aquaculture stud. Israel, Scot. from 1976
m Fyfield 27.7.68 Susanna J. Leiper BSc 1968 *qv*

KENT Margaret Rena MA 1960
m Thomson

KENT Michael PhD 1967
BSc(Leic) MSc(Lond)

KERR Carolyn Margaret Landon *BSc 1965 PhD 1970
d of Robert R. K. MA(Oxon) sheriff and Mona Kerr ARCM; b Berkhamstead 8.5.43
res assoc/instr univ of Tennessee Knoxville USA 1970–72; S'ton: SRC res fell. 1972–73, Royal Society res fell. from 1973

KERR Gordon Alexander BSc(eng) 1969

KERR Janet Helen MA 1970
m Gibbons

KERR Jean Johnston MB ChB 1957
d of John N. K. seed and potato merch and Susanna T. Johnston teacher dom sc; b Aber 21.4.34
DObstRCOG 1960
h o Aber 1957–58, Lond 1958–59, Bellshill 1959–60; g p trainee Edin 1960–61; sen h o, regist dermat Glasg 1961–63, clin asst from 1970
m Aber 16.9.61 Alexander D. McNeill MB ChB (Glas) consult. surg s of Lachlan McN. Glasg

KERR Margaret Mary Orr *BSc 1970
d of William K. nurseryman and Janet B. Black; b Kilmacolm 28.7.48
teacher: Port Glasgow 1971–73, remed Greenock 1973–74, gen sc/biol Greenock 1974–77, Glasg from 1977
m Greenock 1.7.77 Martin Archibald MA(Glas) teacher s of William A. Bearsden

KERR Olive Pandora de Maillard MA 1967

KERRIGAN Herbert Aird LLB 1967 *1968
s of Herbert K. BSc(Glas) chem and Mary A. W. Hamilton; b Glasg 2.8.45
Dip Criminol(Keele) 1969 MA(Keele) 1970 Admitted to fac of advoc Edin 1970
Edin: lect crim law and criminol 1969–72, Scots Law 1972–74, tut. constit law 1972–74, advoc from 1973 and prof compar law univ of S California from 1976

KERRY Lionel Retna BSc(eng) 1970
s of Leopold P. K. civ serv and Kathleen M. Gordon b Berbice Guyana 18.11.41
AMIHE 1972
Aber dist council: grad asst eng 1970–72, asst eng 1972–73, roads dept from 1973
m Lerwick –.8.65 Agnes C. Morrison teacher d of John M. Bigton

KESHAVARZ Rahmati BSc 1964

KEY Anthony Wallace *MA 1960
s of John R. K. man. driving s and Mary M. Low; b Edin 6.3.39
DPhil(Oxon) 1963
lect phys univ of Natal 1963–66; post doct fell. univ of Toronto 1966–68, visiting scient Nat Accelerator Lab Chicago 1968–70; asst prof univ of Toronto 1970–73, assoc prof from 1973
m Oxford 10.1.63 Sandra M. D. Mills broadcaster d of Algernon S. M. Salisbury Rhodesia

KHALIL Khalil El Sayed Ahmed PhD 1965
s of Sayed A. K. LLB(Cairo) judge and Ihsan El Yamani teacher; b Mahalla Egypt 14.10.38

BSc(Cairo) 1960
lect Cairo univ 1966–72; teacher phys Cults acad Aber 1973–75; lect phys Aber tech coll from 1975
m Aber 24.1.63 Irene M. Stuart MA 1966 *qv*

KHAN Indira Sphina-a-Naz MA 1961
m Pringle

KHAN Iqbal Hussain MB ChB 1961
BSc(Kar) FRCSE
h o ARI 1961–62; lect path. Aberd 1962–63; regist surg: Ayr county hosp 1963–65, Kilmarnock I 1965–67, asst surg from 1967
m Aber 30.3.64 June L. Banks teacher

KHAN Nagib Hamed BSc(civ eng) 1966 *1968 BSc(elect. eng) 1967

KHAWAJA Jahangir Ahmed MSc 1968
MSc(Panj)

KIDD Arthur Graeme *BSc(agr) 1965
s of Arthur L. K. plumber and Margaret M. Lobban nurs sister; b Holm 23.8.42
farm man. dev off. ICI Cumberland 1965–68; res off. W Kilimanjaro, Tanzania 1968–70; ICI: farm man. rep W Yorks 1970–74, marketing off. Billingham from 1974
m Mwanza Tanzania 14.12.68 Shelagh Bland sales trainer d of Bruce B. Windermere

KIDD James *MA 1959
s of Charles S. K. farm. and Elspeth Duncan; b Drumoak 19.10.36
ALA(Glas) 1964
nat serv RHA Salop, Woolwich, Hants, Aden 1960–62; St And univ: asst lib 1963–66, sub lib (chief cataloguer) from 1966
m St And 25.7.72 Maureen S. Galbraith lib d of Maurice S. G. St And

KIDD Sheena Ann Mary MA 1968
m Agnew

KILKENNY Terence Michael *MA 1968
s of John C. K. teacher/gp capt RAF/reg dir central council for phys recreation and Gladys Booth teacher; b Nott 15.4.45
Dip Psych(WAIT) 1974
Aust: teacher educ dept W A 1969–70, school psych educ dept W A from 1971 (Albany s h s)
m Inv 31.8.68 Isabel M. Ross MA 1968 *qv*

KILLMAN John Cowling *BSc 1963

KIMBER Victor Robert MB ChB 1969
s of Robert A. K. civ serv and Mary A. Gough secy; b Manc 19.6.44
DObstRCOG 1973
h o Aber 1969–70; sen h o Aber mat. hosp 1970–71; interne Nazareth hosp Israel 1971–72; g p: trainee Aber 1972–73, Clay Cross Chesterfield 1973–74, Marple 1975, Stone from 1975
m Matlock 14.9.74 Wendy A. March secy d of William A. M. Matlock

KINCAID James MA 1957 BD 1960
s of James S. I. K. eng, shop owner and Mary A. B. Duncan; b Aber 21.2.34
C of S min: asst Aber 1960–63, Mossgreen and Crossgates 1963–70; missionary Transkei S Af 1970–76; Fintray with Keithhall with Kinellar from 1977
m Aber 1963 Valerie R. Moir missionary d of Joseph S. M. Aber

KINCAID Mary BSc 1964
d of Peter K. security off. and Isabella J. H. Hay; b Ellon 18.9.43 teacher maths: Inverurie acad 1965–68 High s for girls Aber 1968–69
m Aber 29.12.65 John A. Webster BSc(eng) 1964 *qv*

KINDNESS Agnes Johnston BSc 1958
d of Robert K. examiner BR and Agnes L. Johnston; b Aber 1.7.36
teacher maths: Aber h s for girls 1959–62, Albyn s for girls Aber 1971–74; prin maths St Margaret's s for girls Aber from 1974
m Aber 9.4.60 Alexander E. Urquhart BSc(Strath) lect RGIT Aber s of Alexander R. U. Aber

KINDNESS Eileen Moir *BSc 1966 Dip Ed 1967
d of George M. K. LDS(Edin) dent. and Helen Hutcheon; b Aber 1.4.44
teacher: Melbourne 1969–70, Vancouver from 1976
m Aber 27.12.67 John F. G. Mackay BSc 1965 *qv*

KINDNESS Lindsay Margaret *MA 1970
d of George M. K. LDS(Edin) dent. surg and Helen Hutcheon secy; b Aber 7.8.48
trainee staff man. Marks & Spencer Glasg, Preston, Blackpool 1970–73
m Aber 26.8.71 Anthony P. Haslam NDA(Lancs) agr acct s of Edward M. H. Turton

KING Alexander BSc(eng) 1965
s of Thomas R. K. trawl master and Jessie T. Kay; b Aber 26.9.43
M AssocProf Eng(Ont) 1969
struct des: Brit Reinforced Concrete co Glasg 1965–66, Guest Keen & Nettlefold Glasg 1966–67, Gen Engineering Toronto 1967–68; Albery, Pullerits, Dickson and assoc: struct eng 1968–69, resid eng of construct. Welland Tunnel Ont 1970–73, sen eng 1973–75, assoc from 1975
m Aber 23.10.64 Ellen C. Morrice secy d of Francis H. M. Aber

KING Anthony Desmond BSc 1965

KING Henry John Bell *MA 1968
s of Henry C. K. bank man. and Jane M. Dunn; b Nairn 1.9.46
MBA(Strath)
BLMC Birm: trans proj asst 1969–72, progr analyst 1972–73; progr co-ordinator, progr analyst man. 1973–74, sales progr man. from 1974
m Birm 4.3.72 Mary A. Dickson SRN d of Vincent D. Rathfriland Co Down

KING Kathleen May *MA 1962
d of Frederick T. K. trans auth employee and Margaret B. Sutherland; b Dornoch 15.10.39
teacher Paisley 1964–65 and from 1972
m Dornoch 4.9.63 John R. W. Maclaurin CA, textile merch s of John D. M. Houston Renfrewsh

KING Linda Mary MA 1966

KING Margaret Hay MA 1963
d of James K. comp dir and Elizabeth L. Robertson; b Aber 29.4.42
teacher Fr/Ger Harlaw acad Aber from 1964

KING Margaret Rosalind MA 1967

KING Melville Douglas *MA 1967
s of William M. K. MA(Edin) C of S min and Margaret I. Black; b Ballater 29.7.44

MEd(Edin) 1974
teacher Liberton s Edin 1969–72, prin geog 1973–76; asst head Tynecastle h s from 1976
m Edin 26.7.69 Alison J. Reid MA(Edin) teacher d of Donald D. R. MB ChB 1937 *qv*

KING Michael George *BSc 1965 PhD 1969
s of George T. K. power loom tuner and Margaret A. Smith clerkess; b Aber 31.7.42
FCS(Iowa) 1968 ACS 1975
post doct res fell. chem: USAEC Ames Iowa 1968–70, Aberd 1971; lect chem Fourah Bay coll Sierra Leone 1971–73; USA: instr chem Iowa State univ 1973–74, res chem ASARCO S Plainfield New Jersey from 1974
m Aber 18.9.71 Margaret A. Schaefer PhD(Iowa State) res chem d of Frank S. BA(Concordia) Waltham Minnesota

KING Roger Hatton MSc 1965
s of George H. K. sqn ldr RAF and Vera O. L. Coe; b Barry Glam 16.12.41
BSc(UW) 1963 PhD(Sask) 1969
tut. univ coll Swansea 1969–70; univ of W Ontario: asst prof 1970–76, assoc prof from 1976
m Swansea 28.8.65 Gillian M. Williams BA(Wales) d of Emlyn W. Swansea

KINGDON Doris MA 1960
d of William J. K. insur ag, teacher and Jeannie A. Stuart; b Kingston-u-Thames 24.2.40
secy to head almoner Guy's hosp Lond 1961–64; teacher Engl comm s Oporto Portugal 1964–65; clerk mail order dept Bourne & Hollingsworth Lond 1965; secy/translator/interpreter Oporto 1965–67; secy/pers man. Donside Paper comp Aber 1967–72
m Banchory-Devenick 23.12.71 Ernest Smith interior decorator s of Harry S. Aber

KINGHORN Jean Ann MA 1968
d of Alexander G. K. farm worker and Margaret A. Ewen; b Keig 23.11.47
teacher: Bathgate p s 1969–71, Inv 1971–73, Edin 1973–74, Ringshall from 1974
m Oyne 28.9.74 Geoffrey D. Moore BSc(eng) (Imp Coll Lond) civ eng s of Thomas C. M. Felixstowe

KINGHORN Peter David LLB 1970
s of James S. K. solic and Grace Nucho; b Brechin 30.3.49
law app Edin 1970–72 leg. asst, dep burgh prosec Thurso 1972–74; ptnr law firm Brechin from 1974
m Edin 17.12.71 Carol A. Sandeman BSc 1971 insur clerk d of Arthur S. Brechin

KINGSLEY Reginald Graham MSc 1970
s of William K. and Olive Pilgrim; b St John's Newfoundland 13.9.44
Dip Eng(Nfld) 1964 BEng(NSTC) (Halifax Nova Scotia) 1966
lect coll fisheries, navig, marine eng and electronics St John's Newfoundland from 1970
m St John's 15.5.68 Dianne Hoyles R.N. d of John V. H. BA (Memorial univ) St John's

KINNAIRD Anne Barclay BSc 1961
d of Thomas K. farm. and Jessie B. Ross clerkess; b Kinross 25.12.40
teacher: sc Kinross 1961–62, biol Ballingry 1963–65
m Scotlandwell 10.3.65 Charles A. MacGregor farm. s of William M. Lauder

KINNAIRD Annice Macleod *MA 1962
d of Alexander K. flesher and Catherine A. Macleod; b Stornoway 9.4.40
teacher hist Sidney Nova Scotia 1963–65; prin hist Fortrose 1965–69; teacher hist (BFES) Hamm Germany 1969–72; prin guid Gordon s Huntly from 1972
m Elgin 9.7.80 James Macleod retailer s of James M. Stornoway

KINNAIRD June *BSc 1966
m Irvine

KINNAIRD Moira Margaret MA 1958
d of William K. works man. and Annie W. Cobb; b Aber 14.12.36
teacher Aber 1959–61, Uddingston 1961–63 and from 1975
m Aber 14.7.61 Alexander E. McIlwain MA 1954 *qv*

KINNELL Anne Hoare MB ChB 1956
d of G. J. K. BD(Lond) provost St Andrew's cath Aber and Anne E. Dunford; b Aber 28.12.32
h o, sen h o, regist anaest England 1956–61; g p Danbury from 1961

KINNELL Herbert Gladstone MA 1968 MB ChB 1968

KIRK Alexander Charles MB ChB 1968
s of Alexander K. MB ChB(Glas) g p and Margaret M. C. Dickie nurs sister; b Birm 6.10.35
cas off. Aber 1968–69; Rhodesia: obst Mpilo hosp 1969–70, g p Bulawayo from 1970; major Rhodesia AMC; r m o Selous Scouts from 1976

KIRK Robert David *MA 1970
s of Robert K. decorator and Grace Pearson; b Edin 20.1.47
MPhil(Glas) 1972
commun dev off. Motherwell burgh 1972–74; soc facilities off. central Lancs dev corp 1974–75; sen policy analyst Dun dist from 1975

KIRK William Logan MTh 1969
s of Henry B. K. MB ChB(Edin) g p and Catherine S. P. Logan; b Gullane 6.6.31
MA(Edin) 1954 BD(Edin) 1957 Cert Agr(Edin) 1966
asst min St Giles Cath Edin 1957–59; farm work E Lothian 1959–66, tractorman Duns from 1968

KIRKLEY James Colin BSc 1960

KIRKMAN John Henry PhD 1965
s of Thomas P. K. BR employee and Muriel M. Neale; b Boston Lincs 29.9.38
BSc(agr)(Durh) 1960 BSc(Durh) 1961 MNZIC 1967
lect soil sc univ coll Dub 1964–66; sen lect soil sc Massey univ Palmerston North NZ from 1966
m Broxburn Dorothy A. Jones theatre sister d of William I. J. BA(Cardiff) Broxburn

KIRKPATRICK James Alexander *MA 1965

KIRKWOOD Elizabeth Watson MA 1964
d of William K. butcher and Helen G. Ferguson; b Kilmarnock 9.8.43
Dip Ed(Edin) 1965
teacher Fr/Ger: Penicuik 1965–67, Kidsgrove 1967–68, Maidenhead 1968–70
m Boat of Garten 15.4.67 David R. Davidson BSc(Edin) elect. eng s of David R. D. Grantown-on-Spey

KIRKWOOD Mary MA 1959 *MEd 1962
d of Peter K. elect. eng NSHEB and Jannetta Milne teacher; b Brighton 3.8.38

teacher Fr/Lat Aber acad 1960–64; asst youth employment off. Buckie 1964–66; Peterhead acad: teacher Fr/Ger, prin asst i/c careers 1966–71, prin guid from 1971

KIRTON Heywood Cameron MSc 1966
s of Harry H. K. farm. and Jeannie C. MacLeod; b Taree Aust 14.1.41
BSc(Syd) 1961
Sydney: biometrician NSW dept agr 1961–68, dep chief biomet from 1968
m Taree 29.9.62 Lynne G. Kidd teacher d of Andrew E. K. Taree

KITAKA Francis Xavier Saebampitako BSc 1967

KITCHIN Alison Margaret *BSc 1959 PhD 1967
d of Ian D. Kitchin MB ChB 1930 *qv*; b Lancaster 20.1.37
teacher biol coll of comm Aber 1967–72; lect agr bot Aberd from 1972
m Lancaster 8.8.62 Robert Innes TD CEng MIMechE prin lect tech educ Aber coll of educ s of George I. Nairn

KITSON Richard Frederick MA 1968
s of Norman F. K. publican and Elizabeth M. Beaton; b Aber 24.3.41
Ford Motor Co: buyer maintenance and contr Warley 1968–73, buyer truck manuf oper Romford 1973–75; chief buyer Acme Signs & Displays Enfield from 1975

KLEIN Thomas *BSc 1960

KLINE Paul *MEd 1963
s of Maurice V. K. civ serv and Ivy Simmons; b Lond 8.3.37
BA(R'dg) 1958 Dip Ed(Swansea) 1959 PhD(Manc) 1968 ABPs S 1970
res assoc dept educ Manc 1963–66; lect Exe: educ 1966–69, psych 1969–73, reader psychometrics from 1973
m Swansea 8.8.59 Frances S. Golding BA teacher d of Reginald G. Bromley

KNAPMAN Mary Louise MA 1960
d of George R. K. comp dir and Louise D. G. Brown hotel prop.; b Brixham 27.11.38
teacher: Engl Northfield acad Aber 1961–64, Engl/Fr High s Perth 1965–66
m Ballater 4.7.64 Duncan Mackenzie DA teacher art s of Duncan M. Inv

KNIGHT Diana Maud BSc 1970
d of Cecil K. comp man., comp dir and Ruby G. Parris des, man.; b St Michael Barbados 28.6.46
BSc(Lond) 1971
travel admin Lond 1971–72; food scient nutrit centre Bridgetown Barbados 1973; teacher: chem Airdrie 1976–78, chem/sc Edin from 1978
m Edin 1.6.74 David C. Arulanantham BSc(eng) 1969 *qv*

KNIGHT Donald William MSc 1966 PhD 1969
BSc ACGI(Lond)

KNIGHT Jean Elizabeth MA 1970
d of John A. K. police driver and Jean C. Smith cashier; b Aber 4.12.48
teacher Engl/liberal stud. tech coll Aber 1971–74
m Aber 21.7.71 David T. Yacamini MA 1971 teacher s of David T. Y. Perth

KNOWLES David Alexander MA 1970
s of R. B. K. acct and Christine I. Rutherford; b Edin 11.1.49
CA
app Edin 1970–74, self employed CA from 1974

KNOWLES Iain Colin Campbell *MA 1967
s of John K. teacher and Janet Campbell; b Banff 25.3.45
bus. econ Rolls Royce small eng div Watford 1967–71; fin. analyst: long range plan. Chrysler International S.A. Lond 1971–73, plan. Rank Xerox Welwyn eng dept Welwyn Garden City 1973–74; bus. analyst: plan. Rank Xerox res lab Milton Keynes 1975–76, syst Rank Xerox manuf and supply oper Uxbridge from 1977

KNOWLES James Gordon *BSc 1964 PhD 1969
s of James G. K. store man. and Margaret M. M. Forbes; b Aber 26.6.41
sen scient off. Amersham from 1967
m Aber 23.9.66 Elaine Davidson BSc 1966 *qv*

KNOWLES Kathleen Melrose *BSc 1967
m Watts

KNOWLES Maureen MA 1968
m Innes-Will

KNOWLES Peter Mitchell *MA 1969 Dip Ed 1970

KNOWLES Sheila Elizabeth MA 1969
d of Robert B. K. acct and Christine I. Rutherford; b Edin 3.9.47
teacher geog Boroughmuir s Edin 1970–75
m Edin 6.7.73 John A. L. Miller LLB 1970 *qv*

KNOX Alison Frances Ann *MA 1970
d of Francis H. K. BL 1945 *qv*(III) and Frances M. Strachan MA 1939 *qv*; b Edin 2.11.48
teacher Engl Cults Aber 1971–74
m Aber 17.7.73 William R. Fraser BSc 1966 *qv*

KNOX Ian Davidson BSc 1963 Dip Ed 1964

KNOX Patricia Campbell *BSc 1969
d of T. Marshall K. CA and Hazel Campbell; b Aber 29.6.47
MA(Sheff) 1972 MRTPI 1974
plan. asst: Aber c c 1969–70, Lancs c c Preston 1972–73; asst then prin plan. off. S Ribble Boro' c Preston from 1973

KNUTZEN Hanna Berit MB ChB 1965
d of Hans C. K. clerk/bus. man. and Kristine Larsen bus. man.; b Oslo 9.10.40
spec in anaest from 1973; member Norwegian assoc of anaest; sen h o anaest univ of Bergen 1967–68, resid regist anaest univ of Oslo 1969–70, sen regist 1970–77; consult. anaest Drammen from 1978

KOJECKÝ Roger Miroslav Francis *MA 1966
s of Miroslav K. allied air force off. and Sheila B. Watson; b Lond 29.1.43
DPhil(Oxon) 1969 George Adam Smith (D. M. Cowan) prize Aberd 1973 for book *T. S. Eliot's Social Criticism* (Faber) 1972
Brit Council lect Tokyo 1970–72; part time lect Harrow coll of f e 1973–74; bus. multinat comp from 1974; part-time lect Lond univ extra-mural dept from 1974
m Northwood 2.7.77 Marie-Christine Dieudonné d of Gilbert H. D. Saint Paul de Vence France

KOLACZ Marie Leona MA 1968

KÖNIG Ingeborg Irma *MA 1966
d of John K. joiner and Eva König; b Jaworze Poland 9.8.42
teacher mod lang: St Margaret's s for girls Aber 1967–69; Aboyne acad 1973–77
m Aber 14.7.67 Lionel J. Davis MA 1966 *qv*

KÖNIG John Charles BSc(eng) 1968

KONKAMKING Laval MB ChB 1965

KOSS Paul MA 1970
s of Pawel K. sales rep and Elsie Bruce; b Aber 27.7.47
teacher: Hawick 1971–72, Engl Chapelton Jamaica from 1972
m 24.2.68 Morag Russell teacher d of Hugh R. Shapinsay

KPEDEKPO Gottlieb Mawulor Kwasi Dip Stat 1963 PhD 1966
s of Winfried Kwami K. cocoa farm. and Aurelia Semenu; b Adaklu Abuadi Ghana 25.12.35
BSc(Lond) 1961 FRSS 1965 FIS 1976
res fell., sen res fell. univ of Ghana 1966–71; UN tech asst expert in statist with title of prof Makerere univ Kampala 1971–77, personal prof. dept econ from 1977
m Aber 10.9.65 Margaret S. Burnett secy d of George P. B. Aber

KRISS Anthony *BSc 1969

KUFAAS Torbjörn MB ChB 1962
s of Gunnar K. merch N capt, ships insp Norway and Solveig Lie; b Trondheim 17.1.34
spec gen surg Norway Med Assoc 1969 spec paediat surg Norw Med Assoc 1974
h o, m o h, g p Trondheim, Lofoten 1963–64; regist: surg, orthop Trondheim 1964–67; regist surg Sahlgrenska Sjukhuset, Gothenburg univ Göteborg Sweden 1967–68; sen regist surg Trondheim 1968–72; regist paediat surg Helsinki 1972–74, sen h o paediat surg Sheff 1975; consult. paediat surg Trondheim from 1975
m Aber 12.7.62 Jill Walker MB ChB 1962 *qv*

KUMAR Indra PhD 1957
BSc(Agra) MSc(Alld)

KUMOLU Joseph Babalola Omoyele *BSc(eng) 1959 MSc 1962
s of Solomon K. farm. and Sarah Odumlami; b Imesi-Ile Nigeria 14.10.34
GIMechE 1962 MNSE 1963
Port Harcourt Nigeria: jun eng Shell BP 1963, proj eng 1963–65, sen proj eng 1965–67; Warri: head eng serv 1967–72, chief eng 1972–75, exec dir and man. from 1975
m Manc 3.9.60 Gladys O. Olaiya nurse d of John O. Lagos

KYD David Robertson *MA 1964
s of David R. K. greengrocer and Williamina Robertson; b Echt 13.4.41
member Internat Inst for Strategic Stud. Lond; member Royal Inst of Internat Relations Brussels; news edit. overseas serv Swiss BC Berne 1964–65; NATO: comm secy Paris, Brussels, head Press Serv and spokesman from 1974
m Wald Switzerland 3.8.66 Anna E. Schraner secy d of Leo S. Wald

KYDD Douglas William Bruce *BSc 1967

KYDD Frances Ann MA 1970

KYNASTON Colin Moffat MA 1969
s of George M. K. fire safety off. and Isabella G. Moffat hosp receptionist; b Dunfermline 18.3.48
met. Brit antarctic surv Antarctica 1970–73; teacher 1973–75; roughneck Amer drilling comp ODECO on 'Ocean Kokuei' North Sea 1975–76; directional surv of bore holes with Eastman Whipstock North Sea, Gulf of Suez from 1976

KYNOCH Douglas Robert MA 1959
s of Alfred B. K. man. fishing comp and Nan Morrison chief cashier AUP; b Aber 23.8.38
teacher Engl in lang s Brunswick W Ger 1960–61; announcer and progr presenter Grampian TV Aber 1961–67; Glasg: news presenter TV BBC Scot. 1967–73; Christian work Gospel Radio 1973–74, free lance Christian work, writing and broadcasting from 1974

LA HOVARY Nicholas John MB ChB 1965
s of Christopher La H. bus. man. and Ida Mercinier painter of landscapes; b Cairo 19.8.30
BSc(agr)(Melb) 1953
h o Woodend hosp Aber 1965–66; sen h o Cornhill hosp, RACH 1966–67; h o Bellshill mat. hosp Glasg 1967–68; sen res paediat, anaest Ottawa civic hosp 1968–69; family doctor Ottawa from 1969
m Bellshill 26.8.67 Françoise Perret nurse, sister tut. d of Pierre-André P. Neuchatel Suisse

LACHOWSKI Eric Edward *BSc 1970 PhD 1977
s of Stanislaw L. sales rep and Elizabeth R. Main clerkess; b Aber 1.2.48
res asst dept chem Aberd from 1970
m Aber 7.8.70 Alison C. Gray MA 1969 *qv*

LAD Mohanlal Bhulabhai MB ChB 1963

LAIDLAW Erica Ann MA 1958
d of Archibald S. D. L. and Erica A. Heller; b Aber 23.5.37
teacher: Springhill p s Aber 1958–60, Lerwick p s 1960–65 and 1970–78, asst head Sound p s Lerwick from 1978
m Aber 22.7.60 Thomas G. Hunter BSc(eng) 1958 *qv*

LAIDLAW James Foster *MA 1970

LAING Eric Thomas *BSc 1963
s of Eric C. C. L., bank man. and Jean Bathie; b Dun 7.6.41
MSc(Edin) 1973
teacher sc Leith acad Edin 1964–66; lect phys Napier coll of sc and tech Edin 1966–71; asst dir of educ W Lothian 1971–73; asst dir of educ Edin 1973–75; asst to dir of educ Lothian reg from 1975
m Edin 28.8.67 Anne M. Napier teacher bus. stud. d of William N. Edin

LAING (Frank) Keith Anderson MB ChB 1958
s of William F. L. off. customs and excise and Joan R. Anderson; b Aber 8.4.30
DObstRCOG 1960 MRCOG 1965 FRCOG 1979
consult. gyn Caithness and Sutherland Thurso from 1966
m Aber 17.3.56 Barbara D. Nisbet MA 1957 *qv*
d Halkirk 27.6.79 *AUR* XLVIII 354

LAING Hamish *BSc 1968

LAING John Alistair BSc(eng) 1962
s of John S.L. comp dir and Isabella H. R. Blackwood; b Edin 19.11.37
AMIHE 1962 AMICE 1969 MIHE 1972 FIHE 1974 MICE 1972

site eng Fife 1960–64; sen eng, site ag Dun 1964–70; estimator Dun 1970–71; Nigeria: contr dir Lagos 1971–74, man. dir Kaduna from 1974
m Aber 13.7.61 Fay A. Muir secy d of John M. Aber

LAING John Dennis MA 1959

LAING Kenneth George *BSc(eng) 1968

LAING Lewis Alexander *MA 1968

LAING May Normana Agnes MA 1964
m McCallum

LAING Susan Mary *MA 1968
d of Andrew L. master plumber and Emily A. Adam; b Aber 4.5.46
computer progr Lond, Glasg 1970–72; syst analyst Edin 1973–75; computer advis NHS Edin from 1975

LAING Thomas George *MA 1958
s of Thomas L. MA 1925 *qv*; b Kilmarnock 27.2.37
teacher: Dun 1959–65, Invergordon 1965–67; prin hist: Portree 1967–71, Kincorth acad Aber 1971–76; asst rector Forres acad from 1976
m Dun 9.7.65 Kathleen E. MacBain teacher d of Duncan MacB. Longforgan

LAING William BSc 1960
(conferred for long service of exceptional merit)
s of William L. sawmill lab and Mary Dawson; b Aber 8.3.93
elected fell. Inst of Sc Tech 1955
Aberd: chief tech chem dept 1929–1961, trg off. (part-time) 1961–65; retd
m Aber 18.8.20 Margaret C. Mackie bookseller's shop asst d of George M. Aber
d Aber 7.9.65 *AUR* XLI III

LAIRD May Austen MA 1966
d of Ian A. L. CA comp dir and Frances M. McKinlay; b Kilmalcolm 17.7.44
exec off.: min overseas dev Lond 1966–68, F O Lond 1968–69; pers asst to chmn Brit Printing Ink Co Lond 1969–70; part time work for prisoners' wives serv from 1977
m Kilmalcolm 13.6.70 Gilbert M. Woods MA(Oxon) banker, solic s of Ellison M. W. MA(Oxon) Lond

LAIRD Norman James BSc 1970

LAKIN Francis Henry Grewar MB ChB 1960

LAKIN Kathleen Elizabeth MA 1964 Dip Ed 1965
d of Alexander M. L. marine eng and Elizabeth F. Beattie secy; b Aber 3.10.42
teacher, Lode 1965–66, Aber 1966–71
m Aber 12.8.66 David J. Northcroft MA 1964 *qv*

LAMB Charles Scott *MA 1970
s of David B. L. watchmaker and jeweller and Dorothy H. Martin; b Stirling 2.12.47
teacher Croydon from 1972

LAMB Georgina *MA 1970
d of George M. L. car park attendant and Helen A. W. Kirton; b Aber 1.10.48
teacher geog Glasg from 1972
m Aber 25.7.69 William J. G. Livingstone insur clerk s of William L. Aber

LAMB James Summers *MA 1969

LAMB MacGregor Ashley Webster MEd 1962
MA(Edin)

LAMB Norman Bruce Christieson BSc(eng) 1957

LAMB Raymond Johnston *MA 1965

LAMB Robert Esson *MA 1965

LAMB Roy Scott BSc(for) 1957
s of William G. L. eng and Winifred Scott; b Aber 21.7.31
dist for. off. Co Londonderry from 1957

LAMBERT Robert Alexander BSc 1969
s of James R. L. clerk and Anne P. Matthew; b Salford 19.2.49
geophys data processing Lond 1969–71; geophys field data analyst: Muscat Oman 1971–73, Melbourne, Alice Springs 1973–74; geophys seismologist Brisbane, Perth Aust from 1974
m Aber Priscilla Walker cler off. d of William W. Aber

LAMBERT Susan Margaret *BSc 1961
d of Norman L. BSc(Durh) HM insp factories and Doris L. Nolan b Middlesbrough 20.11.39
teacher: Birm 1961–62, High Wycombe 1962–63, Stirling 1969–72, Fife 1976–77
m Birm 4.8.62 Charles N. Henderson BSc 1961 *qv*

LAMBIE Elizabeth Anne *MA 1968
d of John S. L. MA(Glas) teacher and Ada Garden clerkess; b Glasg 17.7.46
teacher: classics Mackie acad Stonehaven 1969–74, part time Lat Aboyne acad from 1978
m Stonehaven 28.3.70 Ian O. Ritchie BSc 1968 *qv*

LAMBRAKIS Demetrios Panayotis PhD 1966
BSc(Athens) Dip Stat (Manc)

LAMOND Nelida Kathleen M Litt 1970
d of S. Erroll L. BA(S. Af) schoolmaster and Kathleen S. Carlton; b Pietermaritzburg S Af 5.6.28
BSocSc(Natal) 1966 Dip Nurs Educ(Natal) 1956
prof and head of dept of nurs univ of Natal Durban 1971–77

LAMONT Alan McGregor MA 1960
s of William A. L. MA(Glas) schoolmaster and Barbara H. McGregor; b Glasg 23.2.40
army off. RA UK, Ger 1961–64; teacher maths: Ellon acad 1965–67, Glasg acad 1967–74, Dunblane s 1974–75; prin maths Alness acad from 1975
m Aber 10.4.68 Alison F. Rae MA 1962 *qv*

LAMONT Alison Jean Katherine MA 1960
d of Alexander L. rubber planter and Alexa L. Will MA 1922 *qv*; b Aber 26.5.39
teacher: Torry j s s Aber 1961, Fr Aber acad 1961–66
m Aber 9.5.64 Charles P. Skene photogr/comp dir s of Cecil R. S. Aber

LAMONT Anne Caroline *MA 1966
d of Thomas L. printer and Jessie M. A. Hainey; b Dunfermline 29.12.43
teacher: John Neilson h s Paisley 1967–78, Renfrew h s 1969–70
m Dunfermline 12.7.67 Alan D. Carstairs DA(Dun) teacher of art(f e) s of David B. C. Cupar

LAMONT Ann Patricia MA 1958 MEd 1961
d of William E. L. master baker MN and Helen M. F.

Campbell; b Aber 28.12.37
Dip Ed(Edin) 1959
teacher St Peter's p s Aber 1959–61; asst educ psych Renfrewsh 1961–63; educ psych Dover ch guid clin from 1963
m Dover 9.11.63 Alexander S. Flint ship's capt, marine supt, port master s of Keith F. Dalmuir

LAMONT Bruce Malcolm MA 1956
s of John I. M. L. civ serv and Lillian Lynch bus. woman; b Hong Kong 12.5.34
teacher: Engl/geog Turriff 1960–66, geog Nairn from 1966

LAMONT Colin Campbell *MA 1966

LAMONT Daniel Richard *MA 1966

LAMONT Donald Alexander *MA 1970
s of Alexander L. rubber planter and Alexa L. Will MA 1922 *qv*; b Aber 13.1.47
trainee syst analyst Brit Leyland motor corp Oxford 1970–72, p a to man. dir Austin-Morris group of Brit Leyland motor corp Birm 1972–73; F & CO Lond 1974–77; first secy UK mission to IAEA and UNIDO Vienna from 1977

LAMONT Margaret Bruce BEd 1969
d of Alexander L. insur insp and Davina Bruce; b Aber 27.12.32
teacher Engl Brechin h s from 1969
m Aber 30.5.53 William F. Haining BSc 1952 *qv*

LAMONT Margaret Mary MA 1967
d of William L. grocer and Flora I. Macdonald; b Edin 21.4.46
progr: Lond 1967–68, Glasg 1968–70; analyst/progr: Aber 1971–73, Lond 1973–74, Glasg 1974–77: progr data processing Aberd from 1977
m Aber 16.7.76 John M. R. Miller data processing man. s of Robert M. Dun

LAMPERT Brigitte Anita MA 1964

LAM SHANG LEEN Kee Kwee Chun Yun BSc 1967
s of Look-Siong Ng Cheng Hin prop. shoe factory and Chun Yun Lam Shang Leen; b Mauritius 27.4.42
MSc(Lond) 1969 CChem MRIC 1974
sen tech QMC Lond 1967–69; lect Imp coll Lond 1969–72; biochem St Thomas hosp Lond 1973–74; analytical chem Parke-Davis Ontario 1974–75; res and dev ag CRIQ Quebec from 1975
m Aber 5.7.63 Man Lee Ng Wing Wye secy d of Ng Wing Wye Mauritius

LAM SHANG LEEN Yong-Kwee Chun Yun BSc 1969
s of Look-Siong Ng Cheng Hin prop. shoe factory and Chun Yun Lam Shang Leen; b Mauritius 9.6.43
BSc(Pharm)(RGIT Aber) 1975
continental tel Lond 1969–70, various posts Montreal 1971–72; man. pharm Leyland, Leicester 1976–78; prop. pharm Aber from 1978
m Aber 29.3.71 Sheila Seivewright MA 1969 *qv*

LANGLANDS Alison Agnes Graham MA 1967

LANGLANDS James Patrick PhD 1962
BSc(agr)(Lond)

LANGLANDS Marianne Margaret MA 1968
d of George N. L. master plumber and Margaret W. Hampton; b Forfar 12.7.47
Dip Secy(Dun) 1969
Nat brewery comp Lond: secy to marketing dir 1970–73, fin. analyst 1973–75
m Forfar 18.6.70 William B. Plaskett BSc 1969 *qv*

LANGLEY Susan Elsie MA 1970

LANGSTON David *MA 1968

LAPPIN Henry Cameron *MA 1963 Dip Ed 1964
s of George A. L. riveter and Bridget O'Neil; b Paisley 9.12.20
teacher: Engl Inverurie acad 1964–68, Engl/gen stud. Inv tech coll 1968–69, Engl Inv royal acad 1969–72, Engl/gen stud. Moray coll of f e Elgin from 1972
m Inverurie 4.4.56 Frances J. Donald nurse d of Robert D. Inverurie

LARDER David Frederic PhD 1968
s of Frederic R. A. L. pharm, hotelier and Lilian W. Hadfield nurse; b Lowestoft 20.2.35
BSc(Edin) 1958 BSc(Strath) 1959 FRIC 1970
Nelson B.C. Canada: dean of acad stud. 1963–69, acting pres and vice-chancellor 1969–70, prof 1970–72, vice-pres (acad) from 1972
m Montreal 27.12.61 Corrine O'Donnell hotel bus. d of Patrick O'D. Edin

LARNACH Alison Jean MA 1960
d of William L. retailer and Alice Dunnett; b Wick 26.11.40
m Aber 14.8.63 John B. Stuart tea planter, retailer s of Harry S. Aber

LARYEA Alexander William Daniel MB ChB 1966
s of William D. L. sen insp of taxes and Sophia Amah; b Accra Ghana 16.12.38
DObstRCOG 1968 MRCOG 1972
h o Hitchin, Banbury 1967–68; sen h o obst/gyn Kingston, Hitchin 1968–70; regist obst/gyn: Ipswich gen hosp 1970–72, Farnham and Frimley Park hosp 1972–74; spec obst/gyn Ghana: Mampong Ashanti mat. hosp 1974–77, Ridge hosp from 1977
m Golders Green 11.8.74 Harriet Dodoo nurs off. d of Harry A. D. Accra

LATHAM Peter Edmunds BSc 1968
s of Ronald G. L. acct and Annie C. White nurse; b Manc 23.7.45
Sen For. Cert of RFS 1976
for. Ripon from 1968
m Aber 11.12.67 Rosalind S. Hayward d of John C. U. H. Kilmacolm

LATIMER Sheila MA 1970
m Holme

LAW David Gordon BSc(eng) 1960
s of David D. L. comp dir/wholesale boot factors and Caroline Lamb; b Aber 27.4.38
MIMechE C Eng 1971
construct. eng power stat sites 1960–65, comp secy Aber 1965–68, construct. eng Dungeness 1968–70, proj man. Babcock & Wilcox, Renfrew from 1970
m Aber 12.3.66 Sandra Cromar nurse d of Alexander A. C. Aber

LAW George Rae MA 1957 *BSc 1961 MSc 1962
s of George L. grocer and Julia Rae nurse; b Aber 8.4.29
asst lect geol Aberd 1959–62; dir Site Exploration serv Aber 1962–77; geol Zaire grit explor Kinshasa from 1977

m(1) Aber 5.4.60 Elizabeth A. Abernethy BSc 1945 *qv*; marr diss 1974
(2) 1976

LAW Robert David *BSc 1960

LAW Sidney James MA 1961

LAWRENCE Anne Cruickshank MA 1966

LAWRENCE Catherine MA 1969

LAWRENCE Dorothy MA 1967
d of William L. shopkeeper and Alice M. Thorpe; b Lond 9.1.21
m Newcastle –.4.44 Robert E. Craig BSc(Edin) civ serv s of Robert M. C. BSc(St And) Edin

LAWRENCE Jean Stuart *MA 1966
m Wilson

LAWRENCE Kathleen *MA 1969
d of Alexander L. clerk and Eveline M. Menzies paper mill worker; b Ellon 5.6.47
teacher hist Inverurie acad 1971–72
m Bucksburn 4.8.71 Angus T. Smith MA 1970 *qv*

LAWRENCE Richard Keith *BSc(eng) 1967
s of Frederick E. L. salesman and Rita N. A. Harrington; b Oxon 11.2.45
AMIEE 1967 MIEE CEng 1979
BBC: grad trainee 1967–69, electronics des from 1970
m Crookham 23.6.73 Jennifer G. Mercer secy d of Henry J. M. Fleet

LAWRENCE Roger MA 1963 LLB 1965
s of Charles W. L. comm trav and Margaret Bruce; b Aber 2.3.42
law app/leg. asst Aber 1965–71, ptnr Burnett & Reid advoc Aber from 1971
m Golspie 1.7.70 E. Joan Percy teacher d of Harold S. P. Golspie

LAWRENCE William Gordon MA 1957
s of William G. L. joiner and Annie I. R. Imlah; b Turriff 20.1.34
Dip Soc/Psych of Educ(Leic) 1967
RAEC 1957–61; rep Lloyds & Scot. Fin. Aber, Leic; lect lib stud Charles Keene coll Leic 1962–64; sen lect educ Bede coll Durh 1965–71; sen soc scient (consult.) Tavistock inst of human relations Lond from 1971 and hon consult. Rosehill inst of human relations Toronto from 1975
m Leic 31.5.62 Eszter Nagy shoe manuf d of Gyula N. Budapest

LAWRIE Diane Park MB ChB 1967
d of William G. R. L. man. Patrick Thomson's Edin then owner/man. Lawries of Barnton and Mary B. Hardie; b Edin 2.6.42
m Aber 31.3.64 Maurice Q. Cramb MA 1962 *qv*

LAWRIE Eleanor Weir MA 1966
m Simpson

LAWRIE Margaret Elizabeth BEd 1970
d of Thomas L. gardener and Catherine H. Porteous; b Aber 13.6.31
teacher: Skene Square p s Aber 1970–74, Drumgarth inf s Aber 1974–76, Fintray p s 1976–78, Marchburn inf s Aber from 1979
m Aber 11.7.53 William B. Milne joiner s of David M. Aber

LAWRIE William Alistair Buchan *MA 1970

LAWRIE William George *MA 1966

LAWRIE William John Neilson BSc 1956

LAWS Dennis Walter *MA 1966

LAWS Iain McColvin MB ChB 1969
b Banchory 23.2.38
BDS(St And) 1961 FDSRCS(Eng) 1964
consult. oral surg Royal Free/Whittington hosps Lond from 1972

LAWSON Anne Elizabeth BSc 1964

LAWSON Charles Frank MA 1970
s of Frank C. L. P O tel eng and Elsie M. Low; b Inv 2.7.37
teacher maths Millburn s s Inv from 1971
m Inv 2.9.59 Rosaleen M. Stewart

LAWSON Henry Florence MA 1956

LAWSON Terence Anthony *BSc 1963

LAWTON David Maxwell *BSc 1970 PhD 1974
s of Stanley E. L. PhD(Manc) tech man. and Joyce Airey man. asst; b Grappenhall 1.5.47
post-doct fell. in ultrastructural plant cytology, bot dept univ coll Cardiff from 1974

LAYCOCK Rex Adrian Harding *BSc(eng) 1969
s of Rex E. L. surv and Frances M. Wibberley teacher; b Derby 9.7.47
MSc(agr eng)(R'dg) 1973
civ eng: contr Kitwe Zambia 1969–70, consult. Rhodesia 1970–71, Lond 1971, Kano Nigeria 1974–77; in private pract own firm consult. eng Bedford from 1978
m Perth 4.12.71 Christine M. Bonomy BSc 1969 *qv*

LEACH Joseph Henry PhD 1969
b Sturgeon Falls Ontario 20.2.31
BSA(Tor) 1954 MSc(Guelph) 1966
res scient Ontario min of nat resources Lake Erie res stat from 1969
m Huttonville Ontario 8.10.55 Mary L. Fraser BHSc(Tor) dietitian

LEAKER Margaret Dalton MA 1968
d of Dudley R. L. arch. and Mary V. James secy; b Bristol 12.1.47
teacher: VSO Fr/Engl Takoradi s s Ghana 1968–69, Engl/mus The Charlton s Wellington 1970–75
m Cumbernauld 4.4.70 Peter H. Halstead LLB 1968 *qv*

LEASK Aileen Margaret MA 1970
d of John L. MB ChB 1938 *qv*; b Inverurie 15.6.41
teacher: Edin 1971–73, Stirlingsh from 1973
m Aber 4.4.73 Alastair Masson bank clerk s of Alastair M. Evanton

LEASK Audrey Kathryn MA 1968
d of Laurence L. L. div road foreman and Kathleen J. Manson; b Shetland 1.6.47
teacher Engl Crieff 1969–71; head South Nesting p s Shetland 1971–77
m Bigton 4.4.73 Alistair W. Mulley BP AD depot superv s of Andrew W. M. Bigton

LEASK Margaret MA 1958
d of Magnus L. trans oper and Jessie Smith clerkess; b Lerwick 19.4.37

teacher Lerwick: Engl/Lat Anderson inst 1960–63, p s 1963–65, part-time p s/relief Anderson h s 1966–73, Bell's Brae p s part-time from 1973
m Aber 20.12.58 Gordon R. Silver travel ag/trans oper s of Frederick W. S. Bucksburn

LEASK Margaret Emma *MA 1964
d of Henry A. L. motor eng, man. dir and Emma M. Scott secy; b Aber 13.9.42
BA(Cantab) 1966 barrister-at-law Lincoln's Inn 1972
teacher Engl Thessaloniki Greece 1966–67; lect in law Queen Mary coll univ of Lond from 1967
m Aber 30.3.68 Peter S. Noble BA(Cantab) lect s of Peter S. N. MA 1921 *qv*

LEASK Mary Janet *MA 1967

LEASK Susanna Jean Isbister MA 1962
b Stromness 1.11.40
m Orkney 22.9.67 Ronald K. Leonard

LEATHAR Douglas Sutherland *MA 1969 PhD 1975

LEATHEM Christina Gilray MA 1966
d of James L. shopkeeper and Robina Robertson shopkeeper; b Wishaw 15.6.44
teacher: Wishaw 1966–69, Auchmuty j h s Glenrothes 1969–72
m Aber 16.4.68 Findlay M. Coutts MA 1964 *qv*

LEDINGHAM Christine Jean MA 1968
d of Robert G. L. and Christina MacMillan; b Aber 27.6.47
Secy Dip. (Lond) 1969
pers asst Lond 1969–70; W Ger: teacher Bonn 1970–71, teacher Engl Bonn-Hardtberg g s from 1972
m Ballater 8.8.70 Klaus Eichner Staats Examen (1 & 2) (Bonn) civ serv s of Wolfgang E. PhD(Bonn) Bonn

LEDINGHAM Roderic Bentley *MA 1966
s of Leslie A. L. MB ChB 1934 *qv*; b Aston-on-Trent 29.12.42
Dip Cartography(Glas) 1970 JP(Adelaide)
met. Antarctica Brit. ant. surv 1966–69; geol Aust Selection Pty Kalgoorlie 1970–76 and from 1978; off. i/c Aust Antarctic res exped Macquarie Is 1976–77

LEDINGHAM Stewart Charles BSc 1965

LEE Chong Soon MSc 1969
s of Lee Eng Teng surv and Khoo Choo Lean; b Penang 10.7.42
BAgrSc(Malaya) 1966 PhD(NCSU) 1977
Kuala Lumpur: biometrician dept of agr 1966–71; statist Malaysian agr res and dev inst from 1971
m Malaysia 12.2.70 Chang Sue Lyn nurse d of Chang Hoey Chan MB BS(Sing) Malaysia

LEE June Rose MA 1968

LEE Richard Martyn *BSc 1957 PhD 1961
s of Frederick G. L. civ eng and Beatrice M. Butler acct; b Merton Lond 22.11.34
Dip Entomology(Lond)
res biochem Wellcome foundation Berkhamsted 1960–65; sen lect vet pharm Portsmouth 1965–67; dept head parasitology SK & F Labs Welwyn Garden City 1967–74; dept head biochem SK & F Labs from 1974
m Aber 29.3.61 Arthurina R. M. Black MA 1955 *qv*

LEE Rodney Alan MA 1968

LEEGAARD Jens Michael MB ChB 1961

LEES Gordon McArthur MB ChB 1961 PhD 1968
s of Neil M. L. MB ChB(Glas) g p and Emelyn N. Laing dom sc teacher; b Dun 6.9.38
ARI: h o neurosurg, med 1961–62; Aberd: res fell. physiol 1962–66; lect: physiol 1966–68, pharm from 1968; visiting prof dept of pharm Loyola univ med center Maywood, Illinois 1970 and 1974
m Aber 14.12.63 Doris I. Manson MB ChB 1948 *qv*

LEES Joan cMB ChB 1960
d of James L. monum sculptor and Jessie C. Main; b Stonehaven 10.4.36
DCH(Lond) 1962 DPH(Tor) 1977
h o: Stracathro hosp 1960–61, Dun RI 1961–62; Carnegie s Edin 1962–63; Canada: resid Kingston gen hosp 1963–64, hosp for sick ch Toronto 1964–65; assoc m o h Borough of N York Ontario
m Tor 9.7.65 Ian McCausland BSc(Belf) prof elect. eng Tor s of Joseph McC. MA(Londonderry) Belfast

LEES Louisa Nelson Sharman Waugh MA 1962
m Fiddes

LEES Martin McArthur MB ChB 1958 MD 1971

LEES Moyra Isobel *MA 1968
d of Alexander C. L. hotelier/shopkeeper and Robina M. Ironside hotelier; b Aber 26.12.31
teacher Engl Mackie acad Stonehaven from 1969
m Aber 10.9.71 Norman J. Elder jet fuel supt s of Norman M. E. Glenelg

LEES Peter *MA 1960 MSc 1962
s of Peter L. waiter and Ann Grant; b Aber 22.6.38
AFIMA 1967
lect maths RGIT 1962–66; lect eng Aberd from 1966
m Aber 26.12.66 Gail Moir d of James M. Newmachar

LEES Ronald Forbes Barton MB ChB 1956

LEFEVRE David BSc 1969
s of Norman L. motor trade rep and Lilian Cassie; b Aber 6.3.48
MIWSP 1971
Wiggins Teape Aber: work-study asst 1969–71, work study off. 1971–73, man. acct 1973–75; John Wood Group (Aber) man. exec 1975–76; Woodacon Oils sales man. 1976–77; John Wood Group Offshore admin and dev man. 1977, gen man. from 1977
m Aber 26.7.69 Margaret McLeod cashier d of Alexander McL. Aber

LEFEVRE Frank Hartley MA 1956 LLB 1958

LEGG William Clubb Robson *BSc(eng) 1964

LEGGATT Irene Joan MA 1964

LEGGE Gordon Fraser BSc(agr) 1961
s of John A. L. pharm and optician and Jean G. Fraser; b Glasg 16.1.37
resid bot Hill farm. res organis Glensaugh Laurencekirk 1962–64; teacher sc: Arbroath h s 1965–69, Montrose acad 1969–71, prin biol from 1971
m Aber 30.3.64 Rhoda I. Ross BSc 1960 *qv*

LEGGE Joseph Smith cMB ChB 1966 MD 1972
s of Robert C. L. fisherman and Lily J. Smith; b Portessie 12.11.43
MRCP(UK) 1973

h o ARI 1966–67; res fell. dept med Aberd 1967–72; regist gen med Aber hosps 1972–73; sen regist respir med Tayside health board 1973–77; consult. thoracic med Aber from 1977, hon sen lect thoracic med Aberd
m Kirkwall 25.7.69 Sandra E. Leith nurse d of Alex L. Kirkwall

LEGGETT Stuart Ernest BSc(for) 1966 Dip Ed 1967

LEIGH Elizabeth Dowie *MA 1959

LEIPER Alan MA 1958 LLB 1960

LEIPER James George BSc(eng) 1958

LEIPER Margaret Christie *MA 1969
d of William L. fish merch and Gladys D. West; b Aber 25.6.46
MLS (univ of W Ontario Lond Canada) 1973
teacher Frederick St s s Aber 1970–71; acting lib coll of fam phys of Canada Lond Ontario 1974–75
m Aber 21.7.69 Gordon L. Dickie MB ChB 1968 *qv*

LEIPER Sandra May MA 1964
d of Thomas L. insur ag and Mabel Craigmyle; b Aber 18.12.43
Powis acad Aber: teacher maths 1965–68, 1969–71 and from 1974
m Aber 30.7.66 Ian E. Donald insur ag s of John D. Aber

LEIPER Susanna Jean BSc 1968
d of Robert C. L. BA(Oxon) solic and Janet M. Oakden; b Woodford Green Essex 27.4.46
med lab tech ERI 1968–71
m Fyfield 27.7.68 Anthony W. D. C. Kent BSc 1966 *qv*

LEIPER William MA 1968
s of William L. fish merch and Catherine J. Boddie clerkess; b Aber 17.9.46
Dip Man. St(RGIT) (Aber)
fish merch Aber from 1968
m Aber 11.9.70 Audrey G. J. Walker MA 1971 teacher d of Andrew A. W. Aber

LEISHMAN Douglas Andrew BSc(eng) 1963
s of Mathew R. L. L. bank man. and Nancy B. Watt; b Colombo Ceylon 6.8.38
MICE 1968
asst eng Glasg: sitework 1961–63, office and site 1963–67, publ health off. from 1967

LEITCH Robert Findlay MA 1965

LEITH Duncan Meldrum Thomson MA 1961

LEJEUNE Anne MB ChB 1959
d of François L. (Roman, Liège) merch and Betty Careless; b Newcastle-u-Tyne 1.9.34
m Lond 25.8.59 John P. Llewellyn BSc 1954 *qv*

LENDRUM Elizabeth Ann LLB 1966
d of John F. L. MA(Cantab) headmaster and Mary A. M. Campbell nurse; b Aden 14.5.44
market res off.: Standard Bank Lond 1966–67, Proprietary Perfumes Ashford Kent 1967–68, B A C Lancs 1968–69; teacher from 1976
m Great Chart 14.9.68 Robert M. Boddy journalist s of Robert A. B. Lytham St Annes

LENDRUM Robert Donald Currie MA 1966
s of Alan C. L. BSc(Glas) prof path. and Elizabeth B. Currie MA(Glas) almoner; b Glasg 9.4.44
MB ChB BAO(univ coll Galway NUI) 1972 MRCGP 1977
h o: surg Perth RI 1972–73, med Stracathro hosp 1973; sen h o obst Perth RI 1973–74, med Bridge of Earn from 1974
m Dun 1.9.73 Sheila Whyte MB ChB(St And) med pract d of Thomas B. W. LLB(Lond) Bromley

LENEY Fiona Margaret MSc 1970 PhD 1974
d of Alfred M. L. MA(Oxon) fruit grower and Patricia N. M. Liston physioth; b Edin 16.8.47
BSc(Brist) 1968
asst res off. Countryside Comm for Scot. Perth 1973–74; res off. Dartington amenity res Trust Devon from 1974

LENG John Edward MB ChB 1958
s of John P. Leng MA(Edin) min of relig and Emma A. Fay; b Motherwell 21.6.35
DObstRCOG 1961 Dip Theol(Lond) 1962
hosp posts Aber area, Lanarksh 1958–60; supt mission hosp W New Guinea 1963–67; g p: Motherwell 1969–73, Lenzie from 1973
m Gourock 8.9.61 Fiona E. S. Forrest nurse d of Robert F. Gourock

LENMAN Bruce Philip *MA 1960
s of Jacob P. L. fisherman, PO tel, dep dir of fin. for. comm and May Wishart PO tel; b Aber 9.4.38
MLitt(Cantab) 1964 FSAScot
lect: Commonwealth hist St And, Queen's coll Dund 1963–67, Commonwealth/Scot. hist Dund 1967–72, Scot. mod hist St And from 1972
m Perth 2.9.67 Sheila G. Wilson MB ChB(St And) g p d of William W. MB ChB(Edin) Perth

LENNON James MA 1963
s of James L. and Isobel MacGillivray wages clerk; b Nairn 23.5.41
JP
teacher Seafield p s Elgin 1964–67; dep head Applegrove p s Forres 1967–73; head: Cawdor p s Nairn 1973–75, Muirtown p s Inv from 1975
m Lossiemouth 8.10.73 Elizabeth S. Campbell secy d of James S. C. Lossiemouth

LENNOX Donald Iain *BSc 1965

LENNOX John Macdonald Williamson MA 1963

LENNOX Leslie Grant MA 1963

LEONARD Elizabeth Marjorie LLB 1969
d of John L. L. tea planter and Elizabeth T. Robb; b Shillong, India 8.9.47
law app St And 1969–71, asst solic: Dun 1971–73, Leven from 1973

LEONTIADES Leontios Ioannou BSc(for) 1958
s of Ioannis P. L. farm./secy Ashia co-op credit soc and Paraskevi Mattheou; b Ashia Cyprus 17.10.33
Member Brit Ornithologists' Union
Cyprus: asst conserv for. 1958–62, 63–66 (for. off. postgrad course Oxon 1962–63); conserv for. Class I 1966–73; seconded dir game and wildlife serv 1973–74; conserv for. Class I 1974–77; acting asst dir dept of for. from 1977
m Nicosia 21.10.61 Androula Nicolau d of Nicolaos Georghiou Nicosia

LESLIE Alan Gilbert *BSc 1969
s of Gilbert L. compositor and Isabella McIntosh; b Aber 23.9.46
tech serv eng Monsanto Chemicals Ruabon Wales 1969–71; teacher maths Fairchildes h s Croydon 1971–73;

Orpington coll of f e: lect maths 1973–77, sen lect (sciences) from 1977
m Bromley 12 7.74 Norma R. Collins BA(Birm) teacher, lect d of Bernard M. C. Lond

LESLIE Alistair Winchester BSc 1960 Dip Ed 1961
s of Charles L. upholsterer and Annie F. Winchester; b Stonehaven 11.4.27
teacher: Castle Douglas 1961–73, prin chem/biol Grangemouth from 1973
m Oldmeldrum 4.10.52 Isabel M. Cooper cook d of George C. Tarves

LESLIE Denis Falconer BSc 1969 Dip Ed 1970
s of Charles L. upholsterer and Annie F. Winchester; b Stonehaven 7.1.48
teacher maths: Arbroath 1971, Kirkcudbright 1971–72; computer progr Aber from 1972
m Elgin 26.7.74 Joan E. McGowan MA 1972 teacher d of Robert McG. Elgin

LESLIE Elizabeth Margaret McKay MB ChB 1957
d of George W. B. L. farm., factor, fisherman and Margaret M. Reid; b Shetland 31.7.33
h o Aber 1957–58; intern Stenford USA 1958–59; h o RACH 1959–60; resid anaest Chapel Hill USA 1960–61
m Aber 14.7.60 H. Thomas Frank PhD (Duke) USA prof of relig s of Dallas M. F. Newport News, Va

LESLIE George William Davidson BSc(agr) 1960
d 1972

LESLIE Ian Stewart BSc(eng) 1960

LESLIE James *BSc(eng) 1959
s of William L. shepherd/sub-postmaster and Maggie A. Flaws; b Quendale 30.5.38
MBA(McG) 1967 Abex Indust schol. 1965 1st McGill winner of Seagram bus. fell. 1966
eng Blyth & Blyth Edin Inv 1959–62; Montreal eng comp: eng 1962–65, sen superv econ and valuation div 1967–69, asst man. econ and val div 1969–71, man.: man. sciences, man. consult. div 1971–74, dir of plan. 1974–75; vice-pres plan. from 1975 also pres/dir Monenco computing serv from 1975 and dir Monenco holdings from 1975
m Inv 3.11.62 Marjorie S. Ness secy d of William M. N. Inv

LESLIE James Charles *BSc 1970
b 17.6.48
teacher Elgin from 1971

LESLIE Jean Hamilton MA 1961
b Aber 12.8.40
teacher Engl/hist: Northfield s s Aber 1962–65, Larkhall acad 1965–66; prin guid Bankhead acad Aber 1970–75; asst head Northfield acad from 1975
m Aber 10.7.63 Eric Wilson contr rep

LESLIE Jennifer Stewart *MA 1965
d of Theodore L. farm., miller and Jean R. L. Stewart; b Aber 2.11.42
teacher: mod lang Aber h s for girls 1966–69, Engl Düsseldorf W Ger 1969–70, mod lang St George's s Edin 1970–71, Engl Kiel W Ger 1971–73; prin mod lang Albyn s for girls Aber from 1974

LESLIE Joan Elizabeth Agnes *MA 1968
m Speed

LESLIE John Alexander MA 1963

LESLIE John Stewart *MA 1970
s of John A. L. BSc 1938 *qv*; b Rugby 23.3.48
teacher Engl Larnaca, Cyprus 1970–71; HM insp taxes Fulham from 1971
m Woodhouse Eaves 2.11.74 Angela M. E. Porter MA 1970 *qv*

LESLIE Lydia MA 1961
d of Ernest S. L. acct, lect and Williamina Smith shop asst, nursery s asst; b Aber 5.1.40
teacher Ferryhill p s Aber 1962–65
m Aber 5.4.63 Joseph C. Coutts tv eng s of Joseph C. India

LESLIE Norman Grant *MA 1964

LESLIE Norman William *MA 1967 Dip Ed 1968
s of William L. civ serv and Annie W. Petrie; b Aber 23.1.35
teacher Hillhead h s Glasg 1968–69; Canada: teacher Oakwood collegiate Toronto 1969–73; assoc chmn soc and phil stud. Cawthra Park s s Mississauga Ont from 1974
m Aber 13.7.68 Sheila A. Watt BSc 1968 *qv*

LESLIE Patricia Edith MA 1968
m Logan

LESLIE Roy McIntosh BSc 1970

LESLIE Stanley Macdonald MA 1963
s of George M. L. conduct. BR dining car, hotel porter and Georgina W. Cox tailoress; b Aber 29.3.41
teacher Engl Peterhead acad 1964–73, asst prin Engl from 1973
m Aber 24.7.68 Charlotte J. MacWilliams shorthand typist MA 1977 d of John P. M. RAF killed in action 1945

LESSELLS Gordon Stewart *MA 1970
s of James L. MA(Edin) teacher classics and Frances M. Taylor MA 1941 *qv*
MSc(Oxon) 1971
lect: Glas 1973–74, univ of Benin Nigeria from 1974

LETHAM Adam MA 1967
s of Robert L. L. farm. and Margaret McNeil; b Lanark 2.8.44
Masaka Uganda: teacher Kako sen s s 1968–71, asst head from 1971

LETHAM John McNeil MA 1964
s of Robert L. L. farm. and Margaret McNeil; b Carfin 5.3.43
teacher: Souillac France 1965–66, Lanark from 1966

LEVACK Hamish Hunter BSc(for) 1969
s of William L. L. MA(Glas) clergyman and Deborah A. C. Mayer; b Mauritius 25.7.44
BSc(Auck) 1967
NZ: for. Rotorua 1969–75, Wellington from 1975

LeVANN Helen Patricia MA 1967

LEVENE Lawrence Barry BSc 1966

LEVERETT James William *BSc 1962
s of Benjamin L. and Nell Lloyd; b Norfolk 11.10.22
teacher RGC Aber 1963–65, prin asst 1965–68; prin Cults acad Aber 1968–72, asst rector 1972–75, dep rector from 1975
m Dyce 27.6.47 Isobel Fearnside d of Alfred F. Dyce

LEVETT Barry Richard *BSc(eng) 1970
s of Richard E. K. L. BSc(eng)(Cantab) mech eng and

Jessie Banks; b Bognor Regis 30.8.47
MICE 1973
asst eng Crouch & Hogg Glasg 1970–72; eng Ross & Cromarty Dingwall 1972–74; resid eng Wallace, Stone & Arcubos Peterhead 1974–77; asst proj eng Halcrow Sharjah UAE from 1977
m Wick 15.8.70 Avril H. B. Banks radiogr d of Harold B. Wick

LEVIE David Stuart Craigen BL 1958
s of William E. L. MA(by ordinance) 1945 advoc in Aber/prof conveyancing and Catherine S. Craigen teacher; b Aber 5.7.33
col serv dist off. Kadavu, Fiji 1958–61; advoc in Aber ptnr Milne & Reid 1961–64, ptnr John Sergeant & Co E Kilbride 1964–71, ptnr Burnett & Reid advoc Aber from 1971
m Daviot 6.2.60 Mary M. R. Mackie MA 1958 *qv*

LEVISON Lionel Hana Lothar MB ChB 1964
BSc(econ) Lond

LEVITT Charles Samuel Alexander Wheatley MB ChB 1961
s of Charles W. L. MB ChB 1936 *qv*; b Aber 6.12.35
h o: City hosp Aber, ARI 1961–62; resid m o mat. hosp Hull 1962–63; g p Alyth, Aber from 1963
m Aber 22.12.61 Winifred C. Clark MA 1959 *qv*

LEW HO CHEUN Lew Kum Yeung MA 1966

LEWIS David Charles MB ChB 1968
s of Henry D. L. factory worker and Lilian M. Wilkinson; b Hertford 23.5.43
FRCS(C) 1974
Canada: intern Kingston 1968–69, resid med Toronto 1969–70, resid ophth Montreal 1970–73; private pract Barrie Ontario from 1973
m Owen Sound Ontario 4.10.69 Susan J. Scopis BA(Tor) comp dir d of Nicholas W. S. Owen Sound

LEWIS Geoffrey Gordon *BSc 1969 PhD 1972
s of Eric W. L. comp rep and Joyce H. Davidson; b Aber 4.12.46
res off. CEGB scient serv dept (NW reg) Manc from 1972
m Runcorn 1.4.74 Gwyneth H. Jarvis exper off. pharm div ICI d of George H. J.

LEWIS Gerald Patrick Thomas *MA 1970
s of Thomas J. L. farm. and Theresa M. Jessett; b Haverfordwest 17.3.26
Dip Soc St(Belf) 1971 Dip Soc Work(Belf) 1972 Dip counselling in educ settings (univ of Aston, Birm) 1974
pres SRC(Queen's univ Belf)—sabbatical year 1972–73
m Adare, Ireland 31.8.74 Ann C. Barry lib d of Patrick E. B. Limerick

LEWIS Karen Joan MA 1968

LEWIS Robert Alexander MA 1963

LEWIS Rosemary Ann BSc 1958
d of Robert M. L. timber merch, clerk in holy orders and Dorothy M. L. Bisset; b Milford Haven 28.8.38
teacher: Sawston village coll Cambridge 1959–60, Nott 1966; tut. dem univ and tech inst Hamilton NZ from 1970
m Ripon 30.6.59 Kenneth M. Mackay BSc 1957 *qv*

LEWIS Sheila Maude *MA 1961
d of John A. L. shipbuilder/dir and Sheila Sandison MA 1930 *qv*; b Aber 28.4.38
Dip Sec St(St Godric's coll Lond) 1962
secy: Mitchell & Muil Aber 1961–62, A. Walker fish market Aber 1962–63; geog secy John Bartholomew Edin 1963–66
m Aboyne 17.9.65 Ian A. G. Kinniburgh MA(Edin) asst lect Glas, edit man. John Bartholomew & Son Edin vice-pres Brit. Cartographic Soc s of John K.

LIDDELL Charles Richard Wilson MB ChB 1969
s of Charles M. L. MB ChB 1937 *qv* and Elsie J. Thomson MB ChB 1937 *qv*; b Aber 17.10.44
trainee g p Aber 1970–71; g p Cults/Peterculter from 1971
m Bieldside 26.3.70 Jacquelyn K. R. Anderson teacher d of William C. A. Bieldside Aber

LIDDERDALE Ian Gavin *MA 1970
s of Ian M. L. garage prop. and Grace B. Cooper; b Stafford 27.1.48
MSc(Hull) 1971
sen psych MoD(RAF) HQ RAF SC, RAF Brampton, Huntingdon from 1971
m Upper Largo 31.7.68 Pauline J. Lister MA 1969 *qv*

LIDDLE Dorothy Isabelle MA 1969
d of Robert L. BSc(Edin) customs off., teacher and Janet A. Lambert BA(Edin) teacher; b Dunfermline 1.6.48
teacher mod lang Marr coll Troon 1970–72
m Aber 1.8.69 Philip A. Galbraith BSc 1968 *qv*

LIEBNITZ William Falconer *BSc(eng) 1969 MSc 1973
s of James S. L. fisherman and Elizabeth Falconer; b Lossiemouth 2.10.47
S Queensferry: prod. eng 1971–73, prod. eng superv from 1973
m Alves 11.9.73 Judith J. Sim d of George S. Alves

LIGHT Jeremy James *BSc 1968 PhD 1977

LIGHTBOWN Raymond George *BSc 1970
s of George L. indust contr maintenance painter and Helen Hutton lect; b Blackburn Lancs 29.5.47
BPhil(Liv) 1972 ABPsS 1974
prob clin psych Liv 1970–72; basic grade clin psych Brist 1972–74, sen clin psych from 1974

LILLIE John Gordon MB ChB 1958
d 1977

LI LUI SANG Roland Serge BSc(agr) 1967

LILY Michael *MA 1969

LIND John BSc(agr) 1963
s of John M. L. farm. and Jessie P. Fell masseuse; b Methlick 24.6.41
farm. Methlick from 1963
m Fyvie 21.11.63 Doris M. Kinghorn d of James K. Rothienorman

LINDLEY David Keith *BSc(for) 1963
s of George V. L. sales rep NCB and Annie G. Griffiths nurse; b Birm 27.2.40
MSc(Mich) 1964
res stud. Aberd 1965–67; scient off. for. comm Surrey 1967–70; sen scient off. nature conserv Grange-over-Sands 1970–74; prin scient off. ITE Grange from 1974
m Essex 3.9.67 Joanna C. Bellis MB ChB 1964 *qv*

LINDQUIST Roy Philip MSc 1969
s of Vincent C. L. elect. tech and Elizabeth J. Philip

nurse; b Aber 1.4.46
BSME(Mass) 1967 MBA(Mass) 1978 Member Amer Soc of Mech Eng
1st lt/instr US army air defense s Texas 1970, tactical duty off. 38th Air defense arty Osan, Korea AFEM, NDSM (military decorations) Jan–Nov 1971; Foxboro Co Mass: prod. eng 1971–72, dev eng 1972–74, res eng 1974–77; natl secy dynamic syst and control div of ASME from 1977
m Aber 26.6.70 Wendy J. Bisset nurse d of Reginald R. B. BSc(eng) 1937 *qv*

LINDSAY Allan Home LLB 1966

LINDSAY Ann Hunter MA 1968
d of Duncan E. L. bank acct and Margaret H. Thomson BSc(Glas) teacher; b Dornoch 2.3.46
teacher Fr Cults acad 1969–73; teacher of deaf Aber s for the deaf 1973–74
m Aber 24.9.75 Joseph P. Richards ACSM mining eng s of Edward J. R. Truro

LINDSAY Anne Fettes MA 1968
d of Charles L. insp GPO and Mary S. Singer; b Aber 14.6.47
teacher Engl Northfield acad Aber 1969–71
m Aber 18.12.69 Michael A. Forsyth ARICS chartered quantity surv s of Albert F. Aber

LINDSAY David William MacDiarmid PhD 1962
s of William L. L. MA(Edin) teacher and Elizabeth MacDiarmid teacher; b Dunfermline 21.3.36
MA(Edin) 1957
asst Engl dept Aberd 1959–63; lect Engl: Queen's univ Belf 1963–66, UCNW 1966–76, sen lect from 1976
m Aber 17.10.59 Jean Forrest PhD 1962 *qv*

LINDSAY Elizabeth Mary MB ChB 1968
d of William T. L. comm RN, estate man. and Mary Duncan; b Windsor 28.8.44
fell. Amer acad of paediat 1975
h o Stracathro hosp Brechin 1968–69; Baltimore USA paediat intern 1970–71, paediat resid 1971–72, chief resid paediat 1972–73, instr paediat univ of Maryland hosp from 1973
m Aboyne 6.7.68 Peter G. Ruff BBA(Texas) importer s of Paul G. R. Midland Texas

LINDSAY Hamish William Harrower LLB 1970
s of Alexander R. L. bus. man and Isabel S. McLean; b Harrow 31.3.49
Übersetzen-Munchen Dolmetscher Inst 1973
lumberjack Sweden 1970–71; translator Germany 1971–74; Edin: law app 1974–76, solic 1976; solic Aber from 1976

LINDSAY Helen Martin MA 1967
m Boyle

LINDSAY James Gordon MA 1969

LINDSAY John Alexander BSc(agr) 1969 *1970 MSc 1977
s of Alexander C. K. L. publ serv and Helen Blain nurse; b Glasg 17.3.47
husb off. Queensland dept of primary industries from 1977

LINDSAY LeRoy Rader PhD 1965
AB BD(Kentucky)

LINDSAY Nigel Bruce *MA 1970 MLitt 1973
s of Duncan D. L. BA(Oxon) univ lect and Eunice A. Harris teacher; b Scunthorpe 27.3.48
lib party organis W Aberdeensh 1973–74; reg organis Shelter from 1975; member: Aber town council 1973–75, Aber dist c from 1977, univ court Aberd 1976–80

LINDSAY Roger *BSc(eng) 1961

LINDSAY Ronald McLean BSc 1969

LINDSAY Stanley John Edwin *MA 1965 PhD 1971
s of Stanley F. L. MB ChB 1937 *qv*; b Aber 12.9.42
res psych M o D Farnborough 1971–75; clin psych Broadmoor hosp 1975–77; lect inst of psychiat from 1977

LINKLATER Maud MA 1957 Dip Ed 1958

LINTS Alice Milne MA 1967
m Collinson

LIPP Donald MB ChB 1959
s of George R. L. MB ChB 1914 *qv*; b Sheffield 3.12.33
h o ARI, Woodend hosp Aber 1959–60; h o obst/gyn Mansfield 1960–61; g p Killamarsh, Sheff from 1961
m Aber 17.10.59 Ida I. Haeseler nurse d of Caesar H. Frankfurt-am-Main Germany

LIPSCOMB Pamela Grace MB ChB 1968
d of Ernest J. L. chart. surv and Grace A. Hamilton shop asst, clerk; b Upminster 27.2.43
m Romford 20.7.68 Victor C. Mason BSc(Glas) lect, sen scient off., res leader Copenhagen s of Harold E. M. DCM Marchwiel

LISLE Philip Neil Teasdale *BSc(eng) 1970
s of John T. L. overseas civ serv/advis to Botswana govt and Margaret I. Wilkinson; b Gosforth 16.9.47
consult. civ & struct eng Glasg: eng asst 1970–73, sect. eng, resid eng on construct. site Straiton, Ayrsh 1973–77, resid eng on construct. site Riding Mill, Northumberland from 1977

LISTER David Hugh *BSc 1965 MSc 1967
s of James T. L. BR perm. way insp and Janet W. Drummond; b Forfar 6.2.44
res asst with GR-Stein Refractories Bonnybridge 1967–71; dev chem Cape Insulation Stirling 1971–74; prod. dev man. Flexible Ducting Milngavie from 1974
m Bonnybridge 9.8.69 Ann K. Macaulay lib/typist d of James M. Cumbernauld

LISTER Doris Anne MB ChB 1970
d of Douglas L. MA(Glas) C of S min and Marion W. Read teacher mus; b Rothesay 9.9.46
h o ARI 1970–71, res fell. therap Aberd 1971–72; trainee g p Lond 1972–73; sen h o: obst DRI 1974, paediat Paddington Green ch hosp 1974–75; g p The Abbey med centre Lond from 1975
m Upper Largo 1.10.77 James A. Mackonochie newspaper man. s of James S. M. Tonbridge

LISTER Pauline Janette MA 1969
d of Douglas L. MA(Glas) C of S min and Marion W. Read; b Hamburg 16.3.48
m Upper Largo 31.7.68 Ian G. Lidderdale MA 1970 *qv*

LISTON Elizabeth Margaret MA 1970
d of William A. L. MBChB(Edin) obst and Elizabeth A. Macaulay; b Edin 7.9.48
teacher Greendykes p s Edin 1970–74
m Edin 1974 Donald A. Bremner eng s of Donald D. B. Edin

LISTON Margaret Petrie *MA 1970
d of Thomas M. B. L. quantity surv and Marjorie F. Petrie; b Glasg 10.3.48
Engl lang asst école normale d'instituteurs Paris 1970–71; teacher Eastwood sen h s from 1972
m Glas 19.12.75 Evan Mawdsley BA(Haverford Coll USA) lect Glas s of Evan M. Dorset

LITTLE Joan *MA 1958
m Dickson

LITTLE Joan Ross *BSc 1967
d of Hugh W. L. dep chmn bldg firm and Eleanor J. Cumming; b Forres 11.8.45
teacher: Dumbarton acad 1968–70, Perth acad 1970–71, St Augustine's Edin 1971–73
m Aber 18.12.71 Adebayo Olusanya MB ChB(Edin) regist surg s of Josiah A. O. Ibadan, Nigeria

LITTLE Patricia Cumming MA 1967
d of Hugh W. L. quantity surv and Eleanor J. Cumming; b Aber 7.9.46
teacher Skene St p s Aber 1968–73
m Aber 22.12.69 Robert A. Minett MA 1969 *qv*

LITTLE William MA 1966

LITTLEJOHN Alastair Lewis *BSc 1969

LITTLEJOHN Alistair George *BSc(eng) 1957
s of James D. L. comm trav and Alice M. Henry MA 1925 *qv*; b Aber 17.2.35
civ des eng, hydraulics res site eng: Knutsford 1957–59, Trawsfynydd 1959–66; sen site eng, bldg proj man. Liv 1966–71; dir Lond from 1971
m Waenfawr 16.2.63 Mairwen L. Jones air stewardess d of Henry L. J. Waenfawr

LITTLEJOHN Elizabeth Jane Wilson MA 1968 LLB 1970
d of Louis H. L. rubber planter and Anne Wilson; b Penang 1.5.47
law app, leg asst Milne & Mackinnon advoc Aber 1970–73; leg. asst Wilsone & Duffus advoc Aber 1973; hotel man. Aboyne 1973–77; leg. asst Lefevre & Co advoc Aber from 1977

LITTLEJOHN Margaret Isobel BSc 1964
d of John A. L. head gamekeeper and Isobel Lamb clerk; b Aber 5.5.43
asst exper off. Edin 1964–67; teacher biol Aber 1968–72, in 1973, 1974–75 and from 1978
m Maryculter 10.4.71 Robert J. Robertson blacksmith s of James R. Archiestown

LITTLEJOHN Robert King MA 1968
s of Robert H. L. comm clerk, shopkeeper and Doreen C. Barclay; b Aber 17.3.46
commissioned RAF educ br 1969; stat educ off. RAF Henlow 1970–74; stat educ off. and ground s educ off. No 4 flying training s RAF Valley, Wales 1974–76; stat educ off. RAF Luga Malta 1976–78; stud. Sus from 1978
m Crieff 9.11.68 Anna A. M. Devine DA(Edin) d of Daniel D. Crieff

LIVESEY Hilary Joyce *MA 1966 Dip Ed 1967
d of Herbert L. exec off. civ serv and Doris Bamber clerk; b Accrington 12.10.44
teacher Engl Haslingden g s Lancs 1967–71
m Accrington 16.5.70 Brian P. Timson quantity surv s of Philip D. T. Blackburn

LIVINGSTON Roderick George BSc 1968
s of Hugh L. MA 1927 *qv*; b Birm 10.12.44
ADPA(Exeter) 1969 ACIS 1972 FSAScot
univ admin: grad asst Aberystwyth 1969–70, admin asst 1970–72; Dund: sen admin asst 1972–75, asst secy from 1975
m Edin 23.9.74 Wilma Watt d of William W. Edin

LIVINGSTONE Andrew Hugh *BSc 1967
s of David L. ironmonger and Anne W. McClements agr advis; b Campbeltown 7.12.44
Dip Ed(Glas) 1968
teacher: Glasg 1968–70, prin maths Paisley from 1970
m Airdrie 5.7.72 Christine M. Henderson teacher d of James H. MA(Glas) Dun

LLOYD David Ellrington Burton MSc 1968
BA(Oxon)

LLOYD-LAWRENCE Adrian Hugh *BSc 1964
s of Arthur J. L-L. MA(Cantab) soil chem and Gladys M. Wilson BSc 1932 *qv*; b Harpenden 16.4.42
PhD(Lond) 1977
geol: min resources div govt of Tanzania Dodoma 1964–67, Hunting Geol & Geophysics Borehamwood 1967–69; dep chief prospector for CAST (Diamonds Ghana) Akwatia Ghana 1969–72; advis to Algerian govt from 1977
m Lond 21.8.69 Catherine E. Marshall teacher/graphic des d of Cyril F. M. Nice France

LOBBAN Dorothy Kidd BSc 1961
d of James A. L. rep and Mary M. Kidd tailoress; b Aber 21.3.40
teacher Renfrewsh 1962–63, Lenzie 1963–64, Aber from 1964
m Aber 10.8.63 James G. Shand teacher s of William J. S. Aber

LOBBAN Elizabeth Taylor BSc 1967
d of James A. L. comm trav and Mary M. Kidd tailoress; b Aber 26.8.46
systems progr: ICL: Lond 1967–70, Dalkeith 1970–72, Sus Brighton 1972–73, ICL Dalkeith 1973–74, contr progr from 1975
m Aber 6.10.71 Kenneth J. Brown BSc 1968 *qv*

LOBBAN Graeme Alexander BSc 1967

LOBBAN James George *MA 1964
s of George A. L. maintenance eng and Christina T. Calder; b Aber 9.9.42
teacher mus Inverurie acad 1965–66, prin mus from 1967

LOCHHEAD James Robert David BSc(for) 1969

LOCK Roger John *BSc 1969
s of Harold E. L. fishmonger and Enid M. Frost shop asst; b Thetford 22.9.47
teacher: Kilmarnock 1970–71, Birm 1971–73; prin biol/sc Trinity s Leamington Spa 1973–78; lect educ(biol) univ of Leeds from 1978
m Leamington Spa 22.4.74 Ann C. Lea typist/receptionist d of Christopher J. L. Birm

LOCKHART Brian Robert Watson *MA 1967
s of George W. L. nurse and Helen Rattray nurs. s teacher; b Edin 19.7.44
Dip Ed(Edin) 1968

Edin: teacher hist 1968–71, spec asst 1971–72, head hist dept George Heriot's s from 1972
m Girvan 4.4.70 Fiona A. Sheddon MA(St And) teacher d of James B. S. Girvan

LOCKHART Gordon Burgess BSc(eng) 1964 *1965 MSc 1967

LOCKIE David BSc(eng) 1964
s of David L. shepherd and Helen U. Ross; b Wick 2.4.43
Glasg: grad trainee eng 1964–66, des eng-elect. motors 1966–67, des eng-temp controls 1967–70, sen des eng 1970–77, sen proj eng DIG clocks/timers from 1977
m Patna Ayrsh 31.10.69 Elizabeth M. M. Clark nurs, theatre supt d of William R. C. Patna

LOCKIE John *BSc 1959
s of David L. shepherd and Helen U. Ross; b Bilbster 22.9.36
teacher sc AGS 1960–66, prin biol RGC Aber 1966–68; lect Craigie coll of educ Ayr from 1968
m Aber 19.7.63 Norma L. Ewen MA 1962 *qv*

LODGE Geoffrey Arthur PhD 1958
s of Arthur L. master mariner and Winifred R. Whitfield; b Newcastle-u-Tyne 18.2.30
BSc(agr)(Durh) 1951 FIBiol 1978
royal tank regt 1951–53; scient off. Rowett res inst Aber 1954–59, sen scient off. 1959–61; lect anim prod. Nott univ 1961–66, reader 1966–68; sen res scient anim res inst Ottawa 1968–74, prin res scient 1974–78; Strathcona-Fordyce prof agr Aberd and prin NOSCA Aber from 1978
m Aber 7.4.56 Thelma Calder d of William F. C. Aber

LOFTHOUSE Adam Robert BSc(eng) 1962

LOGAN Ian William LLB 1963
s of Robert L. BSc(Glas) teacher, asst dir of educ, coll prin and Agnes Coutts MA(Glas) teacher; b Glasg 19.1.41
CA 1966
Aber: app CA, qual asst Meston & Co CA 1963–68; acct, comp secy J. & J. Crombie 1968–75; fin. controller/dir Aber min water co from 1975
m Drumnadrochit 22.10.77 Margaret F. Morrison MA 1969 *qv*

LOGAN Robert Malcolm MB ChB 1960
s of Robert L. BSc(Glas) teacher, asst dir of educ, prin Aber tech coll and Agnes C. Coutts MA(Glas) teacher; b Glasg 22.2.36
h o ARI 1960–61; asst g p 1961–62, locums 1962–63; P & O ship's surg 1963–64; g p Fraserburgh from 1964
m Aber 8.8.64 Lena J. Watkins MA 1959 *qv*

LOGGIE Derek Leith *MA 1966
s of William J. L. off. man. and Margaret J. Bain driving s prop.; b Aber 13.2.44
posts in prod. control man. Glasg from 1966
m Aber 13.7.66 Christine E. Oliver BSc(Nott) dairy advis, lect d of Thomas H. O. Burton-u-Trent

LOGGIE Evelyn Joan MA 1961
m Hill

LOGGIE Ronald George Cran *BSc 1956
s of William G. L. police insp and Joan G. Riddoch; b Aber 3.1.34
scient off. Harwell 1956–57, Dounreay 1957–65; lect phys Thurso tech coll 1965–69, sen lect from 1969
m Glasg 23.12.67 Alexandra M. S. Thomson chem d of Alexander M. T. Glasg

LOGIE Alexander Wylie MB ChB 1963
s of David L. LDS(Edin) consult. orthodontist and Nancy L. Macmillan; b Aber 5.11.38
MRCP(UK) 1972 DA(Lond) 1965 DObstRCOG 1967
h o Aber hosps 1963–66; g p trainee Insch 1966–67; m o MRC The Gambia W Af 1967–69; regist med Aber hosps 1969–72; lect therap Aberd 1972–73; sen med regist Aber 1973–76; consult. phys Scot. borders from 1976
m Aber 12.7.66 Dorothy E. Caie MB ChB 1966 *qv*

LOGIE John Robert Cunningham MB ChB 1970
s of Norman J. L. MB ChB 1927 *qv* and Kathleen M. C. Neill BSc 1940 *qv*; b Aber 9.9.46
FRCSE 1974 FRCS 1975
h o ARI 1970–71; res fell. surg Aberd 1971–73; lect surg Aberd from 1973
m Aber 16.7.70 Rosemary Bates radiographer d of Victor B. Banchory

LOGIE Patricia Margaret Cunningham MA 1969
d of Norman J. L. MB ChB 1927 *qv* and Kathleen M. C. Neill BSc 1940 *qv*; b Aber 26.10.48
teacher: Causewayend p s Aber 1970–72, Grove acad Dun 1972–73, asst prin Engl Albert s s Glasg 1973–76, part time Engl Greenock h s 1978, John Neilson h s Paisley from 1978
m Aber 10.4.70 Stephen A. G. Taylor MA 1972 retail area man. (Dorothy Perkins) s of Robert T. Cowdenbeath

LOGIE Raymond Alexander BSc 1970
s of Alexander L. steward and Barbara L. Fraser; b Forres 11.6.49
Brit Aluminium Invergordon: cell tech 1971–72, prod. superv 1973–74, prod. supt 1975–76; prod. supt Kinlochleven from 1976
m Elgin 17.9.69 Janine M. E. Forteath teacher d of Ronald B. F. Elgin

LOGIE Robert John Milne BSc(agr) 1966

LOMAS Christopher James *BSc(agr) 1970
s of Ernest L. farm. and Myra H. Broadhurst; b Cheshire 20.9.41
MSc(R'dg) 1971
agr stud. Honiara Solomon Is 1971–72; agr off. Jenoi The Gambia from 1973
m Leeds 28.8.71 Susan J. Bentinck BSc 1969 *qv*

LOMAX Donald Ernest MEd 1962
s of Ernest H. L. steelworks foreman and Edith Howarth; b Bolton 21.8.34
BA(Belf) 1960 DipEd(Belf) 1961 PhD(Manc) 1969
teacher Engl Bolton g s 1962–64; prin lect educ Didsbury coll of educ Manc 1964–69; lect educ Manc from 1969
m Belfast 27.12.62 Anne F. Kirkpatrick BA(Belf) head mod lang dept g s d of William R. K. Belf

LOMAX Kathleen Susan MB ChB 1968

LONG Muriel Wood MA 1962

LONG William Frederick MSc 1967 PhD 1970
BSc(Lond)

LONGBOTTOM Molly Elizabeth MA 1966
d of William F. L. postman and Williamina Munro;

b Ullapool 5.1.46
teacher: Luanshya, Kabwe, Mongu Zambia 1967–69; bank clerk Ullapool 1970–71
m Ullapool 25.10.66 Alasdair B. Maclennan BSc(agr) 1966 *qv*

LONGMOOR Peter Morrice MA 1969
s of Alexander P. L. tea planter/eng and Helena M. Morrice MA(Edin) teacher; b Elgin 10.8.47
ARICS 1974
app, asst valuation surv Aber from 1969

LONGMORE Alexander Bryan George MA 1956 LLB 1958
s of William A. L. BSc(agr) 1920 *qv*(II); b Evanton 30.4.35
trust off. Nat Trust Co Tor 1958–60; TEFL Europ s Modena Italy 1960–61; solic Inv from 1961
m Inv 29.9.58 Leonella L. A. M. Ferrari MA 1958 *qv*

LONGMORE Isobel BSc 1962
d of George M. L. rly eng driver and Davina M. Slater; b Aber 8.11.39
teacher: maths Aber 1963–64, p s Boddam 1969–73, maths Banff from 1973
m Aber 1.4.63 George H. Gray art teacher s of James G. Aber

LONIE, Alice MA 1969
m Stout

LONIE Valerie Margaret Young MA 1969

LOPATOWSKA Danuta Eleanora MA 1970

LOPES Anthony Damian MB ChB 1964
s of Caetano M. L. and Alexandra L. b 29.9.35
MRCOG 1969 FRCS(C) 1972
h o: ARI 1964–65; sen h o, regist mat. hosp Aber 1966–71; Canada: chief resid obst/gyn Mt Sinai hosp Tor 1971–72, consult. obst/gyn Tor from 1972

LORENZONI Maria Vittoria MLitt 1969
d of Paolo L. Dottore (Padua) lawyer and Gigiola Avancini Dip(Florence) civ serv; b Trento Italy 15.7.36
Dott Ling(Venice) 1966
fell. Bozsista Venice 1970–73; teacher Engl; inst for tourism Venice 1973–74, univ of Venice from 1974
m Coredo 11.12.71 Bruno Palaja Dottore (Padua) teacher phys s of Pasquale P. Treviso Italy

LORIMER Alan Gilmour Bruce MA 1967
s of Frederick G. L. MA (St And) teacher and Helen B. Anderson MA(Edin) teacher; b Inv 8.1.45
BSc(H-W) 1975
teacher maths Loretto s Edin 1967–68; instr lt RN Portsmouth 1968–71; Edin: app CA 1971–72, teacher maths Craigroyston s 1973–74, asst prin maths St Augustine's h s 1975–77, lect maths/statist Stevenson coll from 1977

LORIMER James MB ChB 1970

LORIMER James William *MA 1964
s of James W. L. dye house operative and Elizabeth C. Clark; b Aber 4.10.41
teacher: mod lang Aber 1965–67, Engl/hist Fort Hall Kenya 1968–70, Fr/guid Aber from 1970
m Aber –.3.67 Eileen M. Reid MA 1965 *qv*

LORIMER Patricia Rose *MA 1960
m Young

LORVIK Edgar *BSc(eng) 1970
s of Paul L. carpenter and Torny M. Valset; b Malvik Norway 6.5.45
civ eng with Sir Robert McAlpine & Sons Edin from 1970
m Bearsden 25.10.71 Marjorie L. Heath MA(Glas) teacher d of Daniel H. Bearsden

LÖSETH Harald MB ChB 1968

LOTHIAN Alan Thomas *MA 1970

LOTHIAN Annona Joan MA 1969

LOTHIAN John Kermack Milne *MA 1958
s of John M. L. MA(Glas) prof Aberd and Barbara Cattanach MA(Glas) teacher/lect; b Saskatoon Canada 1.5.35
lect McG Montreal 1958–59; Shell internat Kampala/Nairobi 1959–62
m Aber 4.1.58 Jennifer A. Y. Kay MA 1958 *qv*
d in plane crash Corsica 13.2.62 *AUR* XXXIX 387

LOTT Edna Mary *MA 1969
d of Joshua L. painter/decorator and Agnes P. Donald; b Newcastle-u-Tyne 11.5.47
civ serv (syst analyst) DHSS N'cle-u-Tyne from 1969
m N'cle-u-Tyne 11.10.69 John Hinds publican s of Martin H.

LOUGHRAN Verne Elizabeth MA 1970
d of John M. L. MB ChB(Edin) HM comm for mental welfare in Scot. and Moyra E. Reid MA(Edin) teacher; b Edin 27.3.49
asst p r off. Glasg Citizens Theatre 1971–72; exec off. HMSO Norwich from 1972
m Edin 6.10.73 Peter A. Hardingham leg. exec s of Harry H. Norwich

LOUW Hendrik Andries PhD 1958
s of William A. L. farm. and Wilhelmina A. Bruyns teacher; b Paarl S Af 3.9.29
BSc(agr)(Stellenbosch) 1951 MSc(agr)(Stellenbosch) 1955
Stellenbosch S Af: sen lect microbiol 1959–61, prof microbiol 1961–73, dean of fac of agr from 1973
m Tulbagh S Af 1.4.55 Carolina J. de Kock teacher d of Frederick C. de K. Tulbagh

LOVE Edwin Dereck *BSc 1970

LOVE John Alexander *BSc 1970

LOVE Penelope Rose MA 1969
d of Hugh L. man. and Margaret Anderson art teacher; b Stockport 12.5.45
m Maryculter 1969 Andrew D. Barbour MA(Cantab) fell. of CAI s of David B. BA(Cantab) Amersham

LOVE Philip Noel MA 1961 ᶜLLB 1963
s of Thomas I. L. gen merch and Ethel V. Philip; b Aber 25.12.39
ptnr Campbell Connon & Co solic Aber 1963–74, consult from 1975; Aberd: part time lect evidence and proced 1968–74, prof conveyancing and prof pract of law from 1974
m Aber 21.8.63 Isabel L. Mearns teacher d of Innes T. M. Aber

LOVIE David Christian
see Shepherd

LOVIE John Cormack *BSc 1958 PhD 1962

LOW Aileen Jean MA 1966
m Smith

LOW Alan James *BSc(for) 1959 PhD 1963
s of Robert M. L. MA 1925 *qv* and Katherine L. Gow MA 1926 *qv*; b Elgin 18.5.37
MScF(New Brunswick) 1960
asst dept for. Aberd 1960–63; dist for. off. for. comm: Inv 1964–65, Lochgilphead 1965; dist for. off. res div for. comm Edin from 1965

LOW Alison Mary *BSc 1965
d of John N. L. lect and Annabella M. Grant; b Dun 31.12.43
Dip Cartography(Glas) 1966
tech asst dept town and reg plan. Glas 1966–69
m Dun 1969 Wilfred Cameron MA 1965 *qv*

LOW David Melvin BEd 1969

LOW Elizabeth Grant MA 1957
d of Andrew L. farm. and Elizabeth M. Grant; b Aber 15.12.36
teacher: Sunnybank s 1958–61
m Peterculter 1.11.61 Douglas M. Benton estate man. s of Joseph B. Malaya

LOW George *MA 1956
b Aber 7.11.20
McGregor prize Aber coll of educ. 1957
teacher gen stud. Ruthrieston s s Aber 1957–60; lect Engl, sen asst Engl and lib stud., head dept Engl and commun stud. Aber coll of comm from 1960
m Banff 14.12.39 Winnifred Gerrard

LOW Isobel MA 1968
d of David L. BSc 1938 *qv*; b Aber 1.6.47
jun syst analyst with nat data processing syst PO Lond 1969–71
m Aber 1.1.71 Roger L. Jagger army capt REME s of Walter L. J. Worcester Park

LOW James Alan Scott MA 1965 *LLB 1967

LOW John Royston *BSc 1967

LOW Katherine Jean MA 1961
d of Robert M. L. MA 1925 *qv* and Katherine Gow MA 1926 *qv*; b Fochabers 15.4.40
teacher Forres 1962–66
m Lossiemouth 7.10.66 Douglas J. Murray MB ChB (Edin) g p s of Iain M. M. MA(Edin) Portree

LOW Lindsay Peter *MA 1961

LOW Margaret *BSc 1965
d of David L. farm. and Annie J. Pirie teacher; b Ellon 18.3.43
PhD(Glas) 1970
res asst: Cantab 1965–67, Glas 1967–71; post doct fell. Denver Colorado from 1971

LOW Margaret *MA 1968
d of James L. joiner and Ruth McPherson typist; b Aber 5.6.45
Dip Sec St(Strath) 1969
secy to man. of IEG prod. group Ferranti Edin 1969–71; secy NATO h q Brussels from 1972

LOW Mary Fraser BSc 1967 Dip Ed 1968
d of David L. BSc 1938 *qv*; b Fraserburgh 1.12.45
teacher maths Craigroyston h s Edin 1968–72
m Edin 5.4.71 Donald R. Murray BA(OU) teacher art RGC Aber s of James M. Edin

LOW Ramsay Allan *BSc 1966
s of William J. L. MA 1937 *qv*; b Rhynie 26.6.44
indust chem ICI Nobel div Stevenston 1966–71; teacher: Kilmarnock 1972–75, asst prin chem Ayr acad from 1975
m Aber 15.8.70 Esther B. McTaggart secy d of Andrew McT. Kilbirnie

LOW Rose Margaret MA 1959
d of Peter F. L. nurse and Rose H. McDonald nurse; b Portsoy 12.11.37
Dip R Ed 1960
teacher: Aberchirder p s 1960–62, Rothiemay s s 1962–64, Milne's h s Fochabers 1964–68, Broughton p s Edin 1968–69, Grantown g s 1969–70, Milne's h s Fochabers from 1970

LOW Sheila MA 1957
d of Alexander G. L. gen merch and Annabella Laurie; b Aber 15.6.36
Aber: teacher St Margaret's epis s 1958–60, Engl Northfield acad 1960–71, prin guid from 1971

LOW Sheila Murray MA 1970
d of John M. L. shift foreman and Jane B. Johnston shop worker; b Montrose 16.1.49
Dip Soc Ad(Dund) 1971 CASS(Dund) 1973
trainee soc worker Glenrothes 1971–72; soc worker Clackmannan from 1973

LOW Thomas Alexander MA 1969

LOWE Maurice Douglas MB ChB 1960
s of William H. L. store man. and Janet B. Dick; b Aber 29.10.35
h o Stracathro hosp Brechin 1960–61; sen h o, obst h o Ayrsh hosps 1961–62; trainee g p Bruton 1963–64; g p Clive from 1964
m Aber 25.7.60 Dorothy M. Silver BSc 1956 *qv*

LOWE Rudolf BSc 1970

LOWNDES Michael Daniel *BSc(eng) 1966 MSc 1968
s of Daniel E. L. comp dir and Dorothy S. Croft; b Walsall 25.10.43
res asst Aberd 1968–72; lect RGIT Aber from 1972
m Ullapool 30.3.68 Joan M. Fleming MA 1967 *qv*

LOWNE Barbara Oliver *BSc 1963
d of Ernest W. J. L. chem eng and Dorothy B. B. Coutts bookkeeper; b Aber 1.11.40
MPhil(Lond) 1966
dem in mycology UCNW 1965–67; res asst in bot ANU 1968–72
m Rochdale 18.12.65 Michael P. Austin BSc(Lond) res asst s of Philip V. A. Hornchurch

LOWRIE Agnes Elizabeth MA 1964
d of John L. fisherman and Elizabeth B. Fairbairn; b Dun 4.2.44
teacher Engl: Powis s s Aber 1965–67, Ruthrieston s s Aber 1967–69, Inverallochy s 1969–71
m Eyemouth 6.8.66 Alexander G. R. McKay BSc 1962 *qv*

LUBICZ-NAWROCKI Andrzej Emil Piotr *MA 1969

LUBICZ-NAWROCKI Christopher George *BSc 1966

LUCAS Alison Mary MA 1967
resid Sheffield

LUCK Beverly Arline MA 1960

LUDGATE Langley Robert *MA 1966 Dip Ed 1974

LULMAN Phillip David *BSc 1969

LUMSDEN Alexander Thomson McIntosh BSc(eng) 1970
s of Alexander T. L. vehicle bldr and Edna H. McIntosh insur ag; b Aber 26.8.35
proj eng elect. eng Ayr 1970–71; elect. supt shipping comp Glasg from 1971
m Aber 31.7.72 Catherine A. Sutherland MA 1970 *qv*

LUMSDEN Duncan Stordy *MA 1967

LUMSDEN Ian McAllister MA 1967
s of Peter M. L. comp rep and Catherine M. McGilvray; b Perth 20.10.46
asst O & M analyst Shepherd Building Group York 1967–70; man. serv off. New Town Dev Corp Irvine 1970–72; O & M man. with Halifax bldg soc Halifax from 1972
m Huddersfield 29.6.68 Joan D. Parker MA 1969 *qv*

LUMSDEN June Margaret MA 1966
d of James W. L. master elect./ch off. and Marion Jamieson clerkess-typist; b Aber 21.4.45
teacher: head maths dept St Dominic's g s Harrow 1966–73; maths tut. RNO hosp s Stanmore 1970–74; maths Adeyfield comp s Hemel Hempstead 1974
m Aber Ian A. M. Grant BSc 1964 *qv*

LUNDSGAARD Anne ᶜMB ChB 1959
d of Erik L. civ eng and Else A. Engelsen; b Copenhagen 26.7.25
h o Woodend hosp Aber, ARI 1959–60; h o Frederiksberg hosp Denmark 1960; h o Aber mat. hosp 1960–61; Denmark: part-time clin asst blood bank state serum inst 1961; jun surg Copenhagen county hosp Glostrup 1961–62; jun surg Frederiksberg hosp 1962; res and clin asst bloodgrouping dept state serum inst 1962–67; assoc med dir reg blood transfusion centre Aalborg from 1967

LUNNEY David Christopher *BSc(agr) 1967
s of Alfred J. L. chief fire off. and Dorothy E. Proctor; b Stoke-on-Trent 15.2.43
labourer bldg sites and fish factory Aber 1967–69; asst farm man. NOSCA Craibstone farm Bucksburn Aber from 1969
m Aber 15.7.67 Marguerite P. Pritchard teacher d of Richard W. P. Alness

LUNNEY Dorothy Christine MB ChB 1970
d of Alfred J. L. chief fire off. AERE and Dorothy E. Proctor med secy; b Macclesfield 15.12.47
DObstRCOG 1973 MRCGP 1976
h o Aber hosps 1970–71; sen h o: Inv hosps 1971–72; Swindon 1972–73; various posts for Wilts health auth 1973; g p: British Army Germany 1973–76; Jeddah Saudi Arabia from 1977
m Aber 15.7.70 Alexander S. Benzie MB ChB 1970 *qv*

LUQMAN Hafedh Mohammed Ali MB ChB 1966
s of Mohammed A. L. LLB(Bom) barrister-at-law and Ruqaiya Nasser; b Aden 11.12.39
h o Brighton 1966–67; sen h o surg, orthop, gen med Aden 1968–74; regist med Aden 1974–75
m Aden 20.12.69 Raga Shamach of Mombasa Kenya

LWANGA Stephen Kaggwa MSc 1967
s of Benoni K. L. ch min and Victoria Manjeri; b Mukono Uganda 21.11.40
BA(Lond) 1965 FRSS 1967 MS(Harv) 1970
Makerere univ Kampala: lect 1967–69, lect. sen lect, assoc prof 1971–78; statist WHO TDRC Zambia from 1978
m Kampala 9.9.72 Peace Kivengere d of Festo K. Uganda

LYALL Alison BSc 1966
d of William L. MA 1932 *qv*; b Galashiels 7.12.44
teacher: Aber 1966–67, E Lothian from 1968
m Aber 27.2.68 Derek Cuddeford MSc 1968 *qv*

LYALL Ardyn Anne MA 1959
d of Andrew L. MA 1927 *qv* and Elizabeth H. M. Innes MA 1924 *qv*; b Newburgh Aberdeensh 3.9.38
teacher Waterlooville Hants from 1970
m Aber 15.12.59 Alastair W. S. Brown MB ChB 1958 *qv*

LYALL Francis MA 1960 ᶜLLB 1962 PhD 1973
s of Francis L. capt MN and Agnes A. Thomson MA 1930 *qv*; b Aber 24.1.40
LLM(McG) 1965
asst lect, lect law Aberd 1964–69; visiting lect law Auck NZ 1968; Aberd: lect publ law 1969–72, sen lect publ law 1972–73, prof publ law from 1974
m Aber 1.8.67 Heather F. Smith MA 1965 *qv*

LYALL George Auchmuty *MA 1968
s of George A. L. town plan. and Katherine Auchmuty; b Edin 31.7.46
MSc(Strath) 1970 MRTPI 1973
plan. asst, sen plan. asst Dun 1970–75; plan. off. Scot. dev dept Edin from 1975
m Edin 17.4.71 Pamela J. Fox secy d of John F. F. Edin

LYDON Richard John *BMedBiol 1968 MB ChB 1971
s of James A. L. printer and Ivy M. Pearshall; b Birm 23.11.46
h o Woodend hosp Aber 1971–72; res fell. pharm Aberd 1972–73; trainee g p Bucksburn Aber 1973–74; g p Tutbury from 1974
m Aber 13.12.69 Yvette H. F. Johnstone MB ChB 1972 g p d of John A. J. Aber

LYLE Ronald Cameron *MA 1970
s of John L. shipmaster and Marjory C. Wilson; b Edin 26.5.48
MSc(Birm) 1972
lect clin psych dept psychiat Edin from 1972
m Edin 10.9.75 Marilyn C. Dunn secy at Edin univ d of James D. Edin

LYLE Valerie Catherine MA 1967
m Innes

LYNCH George William PhD 1964
BSc(econ) MSc(econ)(Lond)

LYNCH Michael *MA 1969
s of Francis J. L. eng insp and Kathleen Lynch; b Aber 15.6.46
lect hist UCNW from 1971
m Lond 1971 Mary Moore MA 1970 *qv*

LYON David *BSc 1964 PhD 1968
s of James L. fisherman and Evelyn L. Noble; b Banff 13.6.42
res scient Esso Abingdon from 1967
m Oxford 17.10.70 Ferraleth A. Standing chirop d of Samuel S. Oxford

LYON John Alexander MB ChB 1956
s of Douglas L. MB ChB 1916 *qv*; b Peterborough

27.12.32
h o City hosp Aber, ARI 1956–57; g p Lond from 1957
m Aber 28.2.59 Ada M. Christie nurse d of Peter C. Aber

LYON Joyce Hilda MA 1959
d of Duncan L. farm. and Hilda L. McAra; b Kemnay 20.4.38
teacher Engl Northfield acad Aber 1960–62 and 1964
m Aber 28.7.62 James G. Cormack MN capt s of John C.

LYON Marjorie Anne *MA 1956
d of Adam J. L. hotel prop. and Marjory Baird hotel prop.; b Peterhead 7.12.33
translator commonwealth bureau of anim nutrit Bucksburn Aber 1956–58; lib asst McG univ Montreal 1958–61; teacher Ger (part-time) convent of sacred heart Aber 1969–71; teacher Fr/Ger St Margaret's s for girls Aber from 1972
m Aber 6.9.58 George D. Watt BSc(eng) 1955 *qv*

LYON Patricia Mary Harper MA 1959
m Sloan

LYON Phyllis Stewart MA 1967
d of Franklin L. fish merch and Maisie A. G. Ramsay market res; b Aber 22.2.45
market res trainee, jun res 1968–70, cler off. milk marketing board Aber 1971–72; cler work from 1973, in Canada from 1974
m Aber 17.7.72 Ian Hamilton journalist s of John M. H. Stonehouse

McALLAN Francis MA 1965

McALLAN Frank Thomson MA 1968

McALLAN Murray *MA 1962 Dip Ed 1963

McALLISTER James *MA 1963

McALLISTER Patricia Mary *MA 1968
d of Frederick G. McA. maintenance eng and Mary B. Jamieson; b Ellon 28.8.46
teacher geog Thorold sen s s Ontario 1970–75
m Aber 16.7.69 Charles G. Duncan MB ChB 1967 *qv*

MacALPINE Bridget Fiona MA 1963
d of James MacA. army capt and Deirdre P. M. Doherty; b Jerusalem 20.3.41
teacher: Maldon 1964–65, Engl Philip Morant c s Colchester 1966–72, prin Engl from 1972

McANDREW Carl Stewart Cowie BSc(eng) 1956
s of Charles S. N. McA. signwriter and Rosanna Cowie sales man.; b Aber 12.3.34
site eng Sir R. McAlpine on oil refinery Is of Sheppey 1956–58; nat serv RE Gibraltar 1958–60; asst eng city eng dept Aber 1960–61; W. A. Fairhurst & ptnrs Aber: eng 1961–77, ptnr from 1977
m Gillingham Kent 11.5.57 Irene Erridge shorthand typist d of Robert F. E. Nott

McANDREW Donald Colin MA 1970

McANDREW Gordon Miller MB ChB 1957
s of John B. McA. cert acct and Violet Coutts; b Aber 20.5.33
MRCPE 1962 MRCP(Lond) 1966 FRCPE 1975
consult. phys geriat: York 1971–73, Edin from 1973
m Aber 20.7.62 Leonora J. H. Murray MB ChB 1959 *qv*

McARA Michael James Dinnie *BSc(eng) 1969
s of Francis J. McA. BCom(Edin) CA and Florence E. Winter; b S Croydon 11.10.46
Johannesburg: jun eng des off. 1969–71, site eng 1971–72; site eng Lilongwe Malawi from 1972
m Johannesburg 4.9.71 Margaret A. Whiting secy d of Noel F. W. Johannesburg

McAREE Derek William MA 1965
s of William McA. grocery man. and Mary A. W. Taylor; b Dun 1.12.43
teacher: Aber 1966–67, Stirling 1967–73, asst prin mus Stirling from 1973
d in road accident Blairdrummond 11.6.79

McARTHUR Alison MA 1964
d of Douglas P. McA. acct and Jessie L. Beaumont clerkess; b Aber 8.2.43
teacher Abbotswell p s Aber 1965–68; supply teacher Hawkesbury Ontario 1968–69
m Aber 14.7.66 Ian M. Warrack MB ChB 1966 *qv*

MacARTHUR Allan John *BSc 1961 PhD 1965
s of Donald M. teacher and Catherine M. Martin teacher; b Ness Is of Lewis 26.11.39
Dip Polymer Sc and Tech (Brunel) 1965
res chem: Epsom 1964–68, Grangemouth from 1968
m Aber 5.8.64 Marjorie F. Cormack MA 1961 *qv*

MACARTHUR Angus MA 1962
s of Donald M. headmaster and Catherine M. Martin teacher; b Ness Is of Lewis 22.2.42
teacher Engl/geog: Kirkton h s Dun 1963–68, Perth h s 1968–70; asst prin guid Grove acad Dun 1970–75, prin guid from 1975
m Urquhart 20.7.66 Edna Douglas catering man. d of Edmund D. Urquhart

MacARTHUR Deirdre Catriona Caoirtiona MB ChB 1957
d of Archibald MacA. MA 1930 *qv*; b Tientsin N China 27.6.33
h o: Woodend hosp Aber, Bridge of Earn 1957–59; m o blood transfusion serv Glasg 1960–61; sen h o ARI 1962–63; m o Stirling c c 1967–74; cytologist Falkirk RI 1968–78, now Stirling RI
m Aber 3.4.59 Thomas G. Sprunt MB ChB(St And) consult. orthop surg s of Thomas S. MB ChB(Edin) Dun

MACARTHUR Donald BSc 1966
s of Norman M. weaver and Jessie B. MacLeod; b Carloway Is of Lewis 12.5.44
teacher: spec asst maths Inv 1967–72, part-time maths and warden of boys' hostel Inv 1972–78; prin guid Inv r acad from 1977
m Broadford Skye 3.10.69 Elizabeth M. Robertson matron of hostel d of John R. Broadford

MacARTHUR Donella Catherine MA 1965

MACARTHUR Doreen MacLeod MA 1967
d of Donald M. joiner, trades foreman and Kate A. MacLeod teacher; b Stornoway 24.10.43
Lanarksh: teacher Ridgepark spec s 1968–72, Knowetop spec s (later Firpark s) 1972–73, prin tut. from 1973
m Aber 2.7.71 Murdoch M. Smith clerk, RAF welf off., soc worker s of Murdo S. Stornoway

MacARTHUR Grace Sutherland MA 1969 *1974
d of Norman MacA. MA 1929 *qv*; b Falkirk 16.10.47
teacher Engl: Bankhead acad 1971–72, 1974–75, St Margaret's s for girls Aber 1975–76
m Aber 7.7.70 Alexander S. Mather BSc 1966 *qv*

MACARTHUR Hamish Ewart BSc 1969

MACARTHUR James BSc 1960
s of Kenneth D. M. joiner/Harris tweed weaver and Marion MacLeod; b Carloway Is of Lewis 29.11.39
Dingwall acad: teacher maths 1961–72, prin guid from 1972

McARTHUR Jean Hamilton *MA 1962
MA(Cantab)
m Oliver

MacARTHUR Mairi Catherine Ealasaid MA 1956
d of Archibald MacA. MA 1930 *qv*; b Aber 15.8.35
teacher: Errol 1957–59, Callander 1959–60, Winnipeg 1960–61, Flatbush and Fawcett Alberta from 1961
m Westlock Alberta 4.7.62 Edward M. Elgert farm. s of Darius E. Fawcett

McARTHUR Malcolm *BSc 1969

MACARTHUR Malcolm William BSc 1961
s of Malcolm M. crofter/weaver and Margaret Morrison; b Barvas Is of Lewis 28.3.40
asst exper. off. UKAEA Dounreay 1963–66; chief assayer Af Manganese Comp Nsuta-Wassaw W reg Ghana from 1966

McARTHUR Margaret Beaumont MA 1958
d of Douglas P. McA. comm acct and Jessie L. Beaumont; b Aber 28.6.37
teacher maths/relig instr: Aber 1959–60, Largs 1960–61, Kilmarnock from 1972
m Aber 5.8.60 George L. Marr MA 1957 *qv*

MACARTHUR Murdo BSc 1966
s of Donald M. crofter/weaver and Jane Morrison teacher; b Breasclete Is of Lewis 20.2.46
teacher maths/sc Tain r acad 1967–69; prin chem South-peace sen s s Dawson Creek BC Canada 1969–70; teacher: chem/phys Hazlehead acad Aber 1970–72, maths/guid Dingwall acad from 1972
m Tain 2.8.73 Ishbel M. Robertson teacher d of William R. Tain

MACARTNEY Elizabeth Morag MB ChB 1970
d of William M. MA(Edin) C of S min and Jessie H. I. Low teacher; b Glasg 2.6.46
h o RNI Inv, City hosp Aber 1970–71; doctor i/c Maasai dev centre Olooseos, Kenya 1972–74
m Hutton 28.8.71 Colin P. Crabbie farm. s of John P. C. BA(Oxon) Edin

MACARTNEY Ian Millar *BSc 1970

MACASKILL Chirsty MA 1958

MACASKILL Kenneth Finlay MA 1967

MACASKILL Margaret Ann MA 1956

MACASKILL Norman Duncan *BMedBiol 1979
MB ChB 1973
s of Donald M. MB ChB 1946 *qv*; b Stornoway 29.7.48
MRCPsych 1977
h o Woodend hosp Aber, ARI 1973–74; sen h o psychiat Kingseat hosp Newmachar 1974–75; regist: royal Cornhill hosp Aber 1975–76, Ross clinic Aber 1976–77, RACH 1977–78
m Aber 25.9.70 Ann Kelly MA 1974 d of Kenneth K.

MacASKILL Thomas MA 1963
s of Ewen MacA. crofter and Mary Campbell; b Is of Skye 20.2.40
teacher Engl/gen subjs: Annan acad 1964–66, Dunvegan s Skye 1966–69; civ serv Lond from 1969

MACAULAY Charles Garden *BSc(eng) 1970
MSc 1972
s of Charles M. M. postman and Elsie M. D. McAllan; b Midmar 8.10.48

MacAULAY Donald John MacPhail MA 1968
s of Murdo MacA. MA(Edin) min of relig and Dolina MacPhail; b Edin 21.3.47
Glasg: teacher Engl Possilpark s s 1969–70, Waverley s s 1970–73, lect Engl Anniesland coll from 1973

MACAULAY Ewen Duncan Macrae BSc 1959

MACAULAY Ian Innes MB ChB 1959
s of John L. M. MB ChB(Glas) g p and Rose W. Innes nurs sister tut.; b Lybster 19.9.32
DObstRCOG 1961
h o hosps Aber, Inv 1959–61; sen h o Maryfield hosp Dun 1961–62; regist med Stracathro hosp 1962–63; g p: Dunblane, Fortrose, Alloa 1963–68, Aber from 1968, dep police surg Aber from 1972; diving doctor Dept Energy from 1974; m o BP Dyce from 1977
m Alyth 24.3.62 Helen L. Graham nurse d of James G. G. Alyth

MACAULAY Jennifer Ann MA 1968 Dip Ed 1969
d of Duncan M. factory foreman and Ann MacLarty; b Dunoon 8.8.47
teacher Karlstad Sweden 1969–70, Summerhill acad 1970–75, prin guid 1973–75, Honiara Solomon Is 1975–78, Fraserburgh (spec unit for maladjusted) from 1979
m Taynuilt 17.7.71 John F. Kinnon MB ChB 1971 med pract s of John H. K. Inv

MACAULAY Margaret Grant MB ChB 1968
m Macdonald

McAULAY Margaret Isobel MA 1965

McAUSLANE Nancy Barr MA 1970
d of John S. McA. joiner and Elizabeth Aitken; b Glasg 11.3.49
teacher mod lang St Ninian's s Kirkintilloch from 1971
m Kirkintilloch 7.7.72 John Broom BSc 1971 med stud. Glas s of John T. B. Kirkintilloch

McAUSLIN Edith James BEd 1970
d of James McA. bank man. and Edith A. Forrester off. worker/book-keeper; b Anstruther 15.6.40
MEd(Glas) 1975
Glasg: res asst on youth proj 1970–71, commun worker 1972–73
m Anstruther 21.8.65 Robert Hamilton MA 1973 youth worker/lect poly Liv s of William C. H. Cardross

McBAIN Anne MA 1959
d of Alan McB. MA 1920 *qv*(II, III); b Aber 11.8.38
secy Conemsco Lond 1960–61; teacher: Fr Cults acad 1973–74, Fr/Ger Alford acad 1974–76, supply from 1976
m Aber 3.6.61 David K. Craik farm. s of James C. MA (St And) Alford

McBAIN Ian William Arbuthnot *MA 1962
s of William McB. and Margaret Buchan; b Peterhead 16.9.37
RAF educ off. 1963–71; teacher Engl Lossiemouth h s 1972–79; SOAF educ off. Muscat Oman from 1979
m Stonehaven 13.12.74 Sieghild Naue

MACBEAN Ann Veronica MA 1962 Dip Ed 1963
d of David A. M. marine eng and Lillias L. Davidson; b Aber 5.5.42
BLibSc(BrCol)
lib Canada till 1971; educ lib Goldsmiths coll univ Lond 1971; then asst lib i/c non-print material Brighton poly
m Brighton 24.3.79 David E. House dep lib Brighton poly

MACBETH Katharine Marion MA 1964
m Dawes

McBLANE Fiona Agnes LLB 1970
d of John McB. chief insp royal mint and Fiona M. Laing nurs. nurse; b Dunfermline 7.2.49
law app: Cupar 1970–71, Kirkcaldy 1971–72; solic Edin from 1972
m Aber 2.8.72 John D. Stephenson MA 1969 *qv*

McBOYLE Evelyn Marguerite *MA 1963
d of Joseph M. McB. bank man. and Alice E. Reid nurse; b Huntly 5.11.40
teacher geog/hist: Perth 1964–66, (temp) Bridge of Earn 1967
m Aber 27.8.66 Alexander J. Taylor BSc(agr) 1962 *qv*

McBOYLE Fredrick George BSc(eng) 1958
s of John McB. farm. and Elizabeth Dempster; b Turriff 19.1.38
MICE 1964 MIWE 1968
site eng (contractors) NE and highlands Scot. 1958–61; des off eng Snowy Mountains Aust 1962–63; asst eng water dept Aber 1964; site eng (contr) Inv, Fort William 1965–66; asst, dep, prin eng loc govt Caithness/Sutherland from 1967
m Aber 28.7.64 Elizabeth M. Harper MA 1964 *qv*

McBOYLE Geoffrey Reid *BSc 1964 PhD 1969
lect geog univ of Waikato Hamilton NZ 1966–69; univ of Waterloo Canada: asst prof geog 1969–72, assoc prof geog from 1972, assoc dean fac of environmental stud. 1974–75, chmn dept geog from 1975

McCAFFERTY John Kenneth MA 1956

McCALLION Margaret Theresa MB ChB 1960
m Gair
d 27.3.68

McCALLUM Archibald MA 1967
s of Archibald McC. fisherman and Agnes Ritchie; b Aber 6.2.45
BA(OU)
grad trainee syst analysis Birm 1967–68; teacher maths, asst prin maths Aber 1969–79; prin maths Westhill acad Skene from 1979
m Cornhill 28.12.68 Violet H. Thom teacher d of Robert T. Cornhill

McCALLUM Cornelius George MB ChB 1964

McCALLUM Forbes MA 1968
s of James McC. loc govt off. and Isabella F. Livingston; b Aber 10.6.47
Dip Pers Man.(RGIT) 1969 IPM 1969
pers off. Glaxo labs Montrose 1969–73; pers man. Richards Aber 1973–75; lect s of bus. man. stud. RGIT Aber from 1975; councillor city of Aber dist from 1977

McCALLUM Moyra MA 1957
d of Albert McC. eng and Ruby Kemp; b Fraserburgh 17.7.35
BD(St And) 1965
teacher Aber 1958–62; lect Aberd 1969–70; par. deaconess Aber 1970–71; coll tut. Edin from 1971

McCALLUM Nancy Buchanan MA 1963

MacCALLUM Patricia Mary MA 1967
d of William K. MacC. turbine driver/fitter NSHEB and Constance M. Rawson; b Inv 2.6.46
teacher nr Turriff 1968–69, Grangemouth 1969–72
m Glenmoriston 14.8.70 Robert G. Scott process oper BP refinery s of Adam G. M. S. Armadale

McCALMAN Ian Alister *MA 1964

McCALMAN Stuart *MA 1969

McCANCE Mary *BSc 1962

McCARTHY Daniel Peter Justin MB ChB 1967
s of Thomas J. McC. G.M. supt police and Margaret M. J. Bowden civ serv; b Bootle 4.7.39
T.D.
work in med Lond, member Inner Temple, Home Counties from 1969; major RAMC(V)

McCARTHY James BSc(for) 1959
s of Jacob F. McC. antique dealer and Lilybell McKenzie; b Dun 6.5.36
Churchill fell. USA 1976
Leverhulme res schol Makerere coll Univ E Af Kampala 1959–61; dist for. off. Tanzania 1961–63; Nature conserv: dep reg off. Grange-over-Sands 1963–69, reg off. Edin 1970–75; dep dir (Scot.) Nature conserv council Edin from 1975
m Kampala 30.7.60 Margaret J. Stebbings teacher d of Fred S. Romford

McCASKIE Thomas Conrad *MA 1967

McCASKILL Betty Dalziell Craig MA 1956
m Aber 23.8.58 William N. Gilchrist MA 1952 *qv*

McCAW Graeme *LLB 1968
s of Robert McC. motor factor and Dorothy Booth bookkeeper; b Aber 17.12.46
solic Lefevre & Co Aber 1969; ptnr Cohen & McCaw
m Aber 22.12.72 Teresa McHardy secy d of James McH. Aber

McCAW Patricia Joan MA 1966
b Kilmarnock 11.6.46
teacher Fr: Manc 1967–69, Derby 1969–70, E Lothian 1972–77, Cambridge from 1977
m Aber 10.8.68 John F. Smithson BSc(eng) 1967 *qv*

McCLELLAND George BSc 1970

McCLEVERTY Jon Armistice *BSc 1960
s of John F. McC. treas Aberd and Agnes E. Melrose approved s matron; b Aber 11.11.37
DIC(Imp coll Lond) 1963 PhD(ICL) 1963
res assoc MIT USA 1963–64; univ of Sheff: asst lect 1964–65, lect 1965–73, sen lect 1973–74, reader inorg chem from 1974
m Aber 29.6.63 Dianne M. Barrack MA 1961 *qv*

McCLUCKIE Peter MA 1967
s of Andrew McC. MA(Glas) teacher, lect Aber coll of educ and Marion Richmond; b Kilmarnock 6.4.41
MI Pers Man.(Liv coll of comm) 1969
pers man.: Plessey Chorley 1968–73, Yorks Imperial Metals Dun 1973–76, Distillers Co Edin from 1976

m Aber 14.1.67 Jane Paterson MA(Edin) teacher d of John P. Sauchie

McCLURG Kathleen Joyce MA 1967
m Harrison

MacCOLL Malcolm David BSc(eng) 1965

McCOMBIE Brian MB ChB 1967

McCOMBIE Charles *BSc 1967
s of George McC. and Christina Ross; b Aber 25.6.45
PhD(Brist) 1971
sen scient off. reactor phys dept UKAEA Winfrith 1970–74; Switzerland: reactor phys Swiss Fed Inst for reactor res Würenlingen 1974–79; proj leader at nat co-operative for disposal of radioactive wastes Baden from 1979
m Aber 12.7.67 Elizabeth Rennie d of James R. Aber

McCOMBIE Eric Lumsden *BSc(eng) 1967

McCOMBIE Hamish Murdoch BSc 1960
s of James G. McC. bank teller and Elizabeth J. Murdoch teacher; b Aber 30.8.38
weather forecaster Entebbe Uganda 1961–62; met. analyst Nairobi Kenya 1962–66; scient off. world met. organis Geneva 1966–73; scient off. policy plan. off. UN environment progr Nairobi 1974–76; chief Asia div world met. organis Geneva from 1976
m Nairobi 6.10.62 Barbara J. McCulloch secy, airline stewardess d of Leonard D. McC. Stanmore

McCONACHIE Elizabeth Margaret *MA 1969
d of John A. McC. MB ChB 1945 *qv* and Jean M. Macpherson MB ChB 1946 *qv*; b Aber 16.4.47
asst prin Home Office 1969–70; teacher ILEA from 1970
m Aber 28.8.70 Robin D. Reid MA 1969 *qv*

McCONDICHIE Jean McGiven MB ChB 1965
m Turner

McCONNACH Michael James BSc(agr) 1962

McCONNACHIE Gordon *BSc 1970 PhD 1974

McCONNACHIE Robin Inglis *MA 1961
s of William McC. bank man. and Christine J. Macrae; b Uig Skye 27.2.40
BA(Oxon) 1963
Lond: asst prin Inl Rev secy's off. 1963–68, prin IR secy's off. 1968–71, assoc dir Orion banking group 1971–73, prin p secy to head of civ serv from 1973
m Cruden Bay 5.10.68 Gwendoline L. Glennie MA 1967 *qv*

McCONNACHIE William Allan *MA 1967

McCONNEL John Robert BSc(agr) 1969

McCONNELL Rosalind Anne MA 1970
d of Martin J. McC. sales rep and Adele Marioni shorthand-typist; b Ellon 8.11.47
teacher: hist/mod stud. Peterhead 1971–73, hist Aber from 1973
m Aber 22.10.73 James M. Livingston BSc(Glas) civ eng s of James L. Airdrie

McCORMACK Agnes MA 1964 Dip Ed 1965

MacCORQUODALE Helen Mary Franklin MA 1968

McCRACKEN James Spowart MB ChB 1957
s of James O. McC. wool spinner and Anne Spowart; b Glasg 8.12.30
DObstRCOG 1960 MRCGP 1967 DCH RCPSGlas 1968
h o Stirling, City hosp Aber 1957–58, sen h o women's hosp Nott 1958–59; g p Nott, lect g p univ of Nott, clin asst geriatrics Sherwood hosp Nott, clin m o Notts AHA(T) from 1965
m Nott 5.12.59 Annie Richmond radiogr d of David R. Nott

McCRAE Elizabeth Murray BSc(agr) 1956
d of Robert H. B. McC. MB ChB (Glas) g p and Rhoda M. Sinclair dom sc teacher; b Wick 16.10.34
agr bact NOSCA Aber 1956–57
m Aber 15.6.57 Charles A. McCombie farm. s of Charles McC. Knock

McCRAW Ian Alexander BSc(eng) 1961
s of Alexander J. McC. insur man. and Isabelle J. Armstrong; b Perth 17.5.38
MIEE 1971 C Eng 1971
BBC Lond: proj eng 1961–77, sen eng broadcast syst from 1977
m Lacey Green 7.9.63 Margaret A. Pitcher SRN d of Douglas P. Lacey Green

McCRINDLE Dorothy Jane MA 1969
m Clark

McCRONE Michael *MA 1970
s of Alexander McC. furn salesman and Mary Robertson; b Aber 20.10.48
teacher Lond 1972–74, head of dept from 1974

MacCUISH Christine Mary MA 1968
d of Angus M. MacC. C of S min and Dolina Macarthur p o clerk, nurse; b Glasg 19.9.48
teacher Nicolson inst Stornoway from 1969

MacCUISH Dolina MEd 1970
d of Roderick MacC. lighthouse keeper and Elizabeth Macdonald; b Kenmore Rosssh 18.5.29
MA(Glas) 1950 Dip Ed(Edin) 1951
teacher Ardersier 1970, asst head Lochardil s Inv from 1970

McCULLOCH Helen Cormack *BSc 1964 Dip Ed 1965
d of Andrew R. McC. motor eng and Helen Cormack tailoress; b Aber 2.2.38
teacher: Perth 1965–70, Bathgate 1970–71, Blackburn 1972; lect Bathgate from 1973
m Aber 8.8.70 Anthony R. Dallison BD(Lond) min of relig s of Kenneth J. D. MA(Cantab) Daventry

McDERMENT John MA 1958
s of John McD. roadman and Grace E. R. Dixon teacher; b Aber 2.5.37
nurs asst as nat serv 1959–61; teacher Aber/shire 1962; employed Campbell & Sellar Aber mainly taxi driving 1962–64; civ serv MPNI Lond 1964–66; on cler staff PO tel Aber from 1967
m Paisley 8.4.72 Barbara Dickson nurse d of Robert D. Barrhead

MacDERMID Gordon Edward PhD 1967
s of Edward K. MacD. boilermaker and Katherine M. Morrison; b Sydney Nova Scotia 22.9.39
BA(Mt Allison univ New Brunswick) 1959 BD(Halifax Nova Scotia) 1961
parish min West Bay Nova Scotia 1962–65; Halifax NS

prof ch hist Pinehill div hall 1967–71, prof ch hist Atlantic s of theol 1971–74, parish min St Andrew's united ch from 1974/prof ch hist (part time) Atlantic s of theol from 1974
m Kentville NS Marjorie P. McReynolds BSc(Mt Allison) dietitian d of Kenneth McR. Dorval Quebec

MacDONAGH Brian James LLB 1970

MACDONALD Aileen Ann *MA 1970 MLitt 1972 Dip Ed 1972
d of Allan M. joiner and Jessie I. Finnie ch nurse; b Turriff 12.5.47
part time res stud. Aberd from 1972; lect Fr RGIT Aber 1973–75, asst edit. OUP from 1975

MACDONALD Alan Gordon MB ChB 1960

McDONALD Alexander Sutherland *BSc 1967

MACDONALD Alison Margaret MA 1970
d of Alistair J. M. marketing man. and Agnes B. Garden; b Kirkcaldy 2.3.48
teacher: Hollywood s Perth W Aust 1971–75, Swanley Kent 1975–77
m Aber 26.6.70 Brian D. Outlaw BSc 1971 petr geol s of Arthur L. O. Cranbrook

MACDONALD Alistair Gerould *MA 1968
s of Thomas K. M. BL 1933 *qv*; b NY 30.1.46
res stud. Aberd 1968–72; teacher mus Peterhead acad from 1972

MacDONALD Allistair Morrison BSc(agr) 1956
s of Donald MacD. BSc 1922 *qv*; b Barberton S Af 24.8.33
agr off. Brit col serv Tanganyika 1959–62; agronomist S Af sugar cane res stat 1962–64; tech off. export Murphy chem co Wheathampsted 1964–72; area man. USSR Stauffer chem co USA from 1972

MACDONALD Alys Taylor MA 1963
b Inv 17.1.43
m Inv 8.7.67 Alan D. Weir CA

MACDONALD Angela Ishbel MA 1961
d of Angus M. police serg and Mary M. Mackinnon SRN nurse; b Inv 21.11.39
Dip Secy Sc(Scot. coll of comm) 1962
statist asst SAI Edin 1962–63; f e teacher: Esk Valley coll Newton Grange 1963–65, Engl in secy coll Stockholm 1965–67, central coll of comm Glasg 1967–70
m Glasg 10.4.70 Alasdair B. Gillies BDS(Glas) dent surg s of John M. G. Glasg

McDONALD Angus *MA 1958
s of Alexander McD. carpenter/joiner and Elizabeth Watson; b Aber 4.1.36
H.M. col serv and overseas civ serv admin off. N Rhod/Zambia Lusaka 1959–71; secy to govt: Gilbert Is Tarawa 1972–78, Tuvalu Funafuti from 1979

MACDONALD Angus MA 1967
s of John M. weaver and Katie A. Macleod; b Harris 31.10.45
nat trainee hosp admin Edin 1967–69; admin asst Ninewells hosp Dun 1969–70; hosp secy: Samaritan hosp for women, W ophth hosp Lond 1970–74, St Mary's hosp Lond from 1974
m Holcombe 12.9.70 Jean Price midwife d of William P. Holcombe nr Bury

MacDONALD Angus John Alexander *MA 1969
s of Alan MacD. crofter and Morag A. MacDonald; b N Uist 6.4.47
res in Gaelic folk tales of N Uist at Aberd and s of Scot. stud. Edin 1969–72; teacher: geog Lochen s s Glasg 1973–74, Gaelic Portree h s from 1974
m Kilmore Skye 24.3.70 Mary MacDonald MA 1969 *qv*

McDONALD Ann Louise *MA 1970
m Scott

MacDONALD Barry MA 1957 Dip Ed 1962 *MEd 1963
s of John M. MacD. miner, soldier, clerk etc and Barbara Ross tailoress; b Aber 29.9.32
teacher: Coalsnaughton p s 1963–65; lect coll of educ Glasg; curriculum proj evaluator Lond 1968–70; sen lect in educ, centre for applied res in educ univ of E Anglia 1970–76, acting dir from 1976
m Aber 5.11.58 Sheila Buchan receptionist, secy d of Maxwell C. B. Aber

McDONALD Catherine Pirie MA 1961
d of James C. McD. farm. and Helen B. Pirie; b Aberchirder 6.6.39
teacher Fr: Helensburgh 1962–63, Toronto 1969–72, Northampton commun coll Pa USA 1974–77; Rutgers NJ USA: grad stud. from 1976, teaching asst from 1977
m Georgetown Guyana 2.8.63 Roger H. Hewins BSc 1962 *qv*

MACDONALD Catriona MA 1968 Dip Ed 1969
d of Allan M. MA(Glas) head teacher and Kathleen M. Harkness; b Epsom 20.11.45
Dip TEFL(R Soc Arts) 1971
TEFL Berlitz Paris 1969–70, King's s Bournemouth 1970–71; EFL teacher supervis educ centre Kuwait 1971–73, ESP teacher fac commerce Kuwait univ from 1973
m Kuwait 11.11.76 John M. S. Roberts audio vis aids off. s of Charles W. R. Shaldon nr Teignmouth

McDONALD Charles William Esson MB ChB 1966
s of William McD. master slater and Diana S. Harper draper; b Aber 27.5.43
FRCSE 1971
h o: ARI, city hosp Aber 1966–67; sen h o WI Glasg 1967–69; regist: Bridge of Earn hosp 1969–72, Greenock RI from 1972
m Glasg 1.3.69 Jennifer M. Brown nurse d of William B. Glasg

MACDONALD Christina MA 1961
d of Angus M. boarding-house prop. and Mary Macdonald; b Drinishadder Harris 9.1.40
teacher: Engl/geog Paible j s s N Uist 1962–66, Engl/hist/geog Dufferin j h s Toronto 1966–67, Engl Kingussie s s 1967–68, Eng/hist Iochdar j s s S Uist 1968–70, remed Engl Mallaig s s from 1977
m Glasg 10.7.68 Angus A. MacLean MA 1956 *qv*

MacDONALD Christina Annabella MA 1964
d of Angus MacD. sheep farm. and Annabella MacLeod; b Tierra del Fuego 1.5.44
Dip Pastoral/Soc Stud. (St And) 1974
teacher: Dunfermline 1965–67, Aber 1967–73

MacDONALD Donald MA 1960
s of Kenneth H. MacD. crofter and Malcolmina Finlayson; b Glasg 6.3.38
div stud. Free Ch coll Edin 1960–64; licensed Stornoway 1963; Free Ch min Carloway from 1964

m Inv 11.7.68 Mary E. Macleod teacher d of Duncan J. M. Carloway

MacDONALD Donald *MA 1962

MacDONALD Donald John MA 1966
s of Donald MacD. seaman and Mary MacLeod; b Stornoway 26.3.44
teacher Mount s Greenock 1967–68; asst prin teacher h s Inv from 1968
m Aber 2.8.69 Heather C. Paynter radiog d of Lionel P. Aber

MacDONALD Donald Stewart *BSc 1965

MacDONALD Donald William Buchanan *BSc 1966
s of D. W. MacD. min of relig and Isabella M. Mackenzie MA 1930 *qv*; b Torridon 1.10.44
PhD(E Ang) 1969 MA(Cantab) 1974
res stud univ of E Ang 1966–69; SRC res fell. Cambridge 1969–70; dept genetics Cambridge: univ dem 1970–75, lect from 1975
m Lower Kingswood 24.8.74 Mary V. Goddard BSc (S'ton) plant path. d of Wilfred H. G. Lower Kingswood

MACDONALD Donalda MA 1969
m Stewart

McDONALD Duncan Charles MA 1958
s of William A. M. McD. gamekeeper and Annie R. MacLeod; b Glenmoriston 5.7.37
nat serv RAF UK, Germany 1959–63; teacher Lanarksh from 1964

McDONALD Duncan Gladstone *BSc 1961
DSc(Lond)

MACDONALD Duncan William MB ChB 1966
s of William D. M. tea planter and Margaret McLean head inf s; b Inv 4.8.41
MRCPsych 1974
m o Zambia flying doctor serv Ndola 1968–69; m o Mombasa Kenya 1969–71; regist psychiat Rochford 1971–74; sen regist Lond from 1975

MacDONALD Elaine Margaret *BSc 1969 PhD 1973

McDONALD Elspeth Caldwell MA 1965
d of Alexander McD. bank man. and Sophie E. Young; b Kirkwall 20.11.43
teacher Aber 1966–71
m Aber 3.4.69 Peter W. Rockwell MA 1965 *qv*

McDONALD Eric James *BSc(eng) 1969 MSc 1971
s of James C. McD. agr eng and Mabel Smith; b Ellon 12.8.47
R & D electronics eng Ferranti Edin from 1971
m Aber 18.9.71 Hazel A. Beattie catering man. d of William B. Brechin

MACDONALD Farquhar Graham MB ChB 1957
s of John M. hotel prop. and Ann Graham; b Edinbane Skye 10.7.28
h o Inv, Aber 1957–59; sen h o Glasg 1959–60; g p Bearsden 1960–63, Glasg from 1963
m Birkenhead 24.3.62 June S. Grant MB ChB(Liv) g p d of Ross A. G. MB ChB(Glas) Birkenhead

MACDONALD Fiona Mary MA 1968
d of Colin D. J. M. MA 1929 *qv* and Elizabeth M. M. Nimmo BEd 1970 *qv*; b Peterhead 4.11.48
teacher: Inverdee inf s Aber 1969–74; Engl in Hauptschule, Aue-Wingeshausen W Ger 1974–75; post-grad secy/linguist course Aber coll of comm 1977–78

MACDONALD Flora Ann MA 1960
b Harris 17.11.40
teacher: Scalpay p s Harris 1961–68, asst prin Engl/hist Sir E. Scott s Tarbert Harris from 1971
m Inv 26.7.67 William Morrison

MACDONALD Fraser John Rigg *MA 1964

MACDONALD Gavin Grant *MA 1963
s of Donald M. shopkeeper and Elsie D. McDonald shopkeeper; b Inv 23.10.41
trainee man. dept store Manc 1966–67; computer progr: Lond 1968–73, Glasg 1973–77; shopkeeper Elgin from 1977
m Manc 24.4.71 Maureen Todd shop superv d of Hugh T. Manc

MACDONALD Hazel Jean MA 1968
m Mackenzie

McDONALD Ian *BSc 1970

McDONALD Ian Alexander MB ChB 1969

MacDONALD Ian Bradley BSc(agr) 1957
s of Donald MacD. BSc(agr) 1922 *qv* and Bessie MacBean nurse; b Barberton Transvaal 4.11.34
Dip Agr(Cantab) Dip Trop Agr(Trin)
agr off. col serv Somaliland 1959–60; comm sales man. Richardson's Fertilisers (ICI NI) Belf from 1960
m Aber 29.7.61 Kathleen F. Smith BSc 1959 *qv*

MACDONALD Ian Robert PhD 1970
s of Robert H. M. acct diplom serv and Jannetje W. Marang secy; b The Hague 4.5.39
MA(St And) 1961
lect Span. Aberd from 1965
m Bolton 20.4.62 Frances M. Alexander MA(St And) secy d of James R. A. MA(St And) Bolton

McDONALD Ian Ross *BSc 1970
s of James R. McD. painter/decorator and Elizabeth R. Massie shop asst; b Aber 27.11.47
geol Aust: Kambalda 1970–75, Townsville 1975–79, Tasmania from 1979
m Dun 5.8.70 Margaret E. Waterston BSc 1970 *qv*

MACDONALD Iris Dickson MA 1969
m Warburton

MACDONALD James Alexander BSc 1956
s of William M. fencing contr and Helen Mackay; b Balintore 28.8.32
RAF from 1956
m Amesbury 1970

MacDONALD James Cameron BSc(agr) 1969
s of Davaid MacD. elect. eng and Jessie C. Mackenzie; b Inv 12.8.45
asst lands off. DAFS Aber 1969–70, Ayr from 1970
m Glenurquhart Jean M. Girvan SRN d of David L. G. Glenurquhart

MacDONALD James Grant BSc(eng) 1958

MACDONALD James Murdo BSc(eng) 1961

MACDONALD Jane MA 1969

MACDONALD Janice MA 1969
m Blackhall

MACDONALD Jean Ronald MA 1969
d of Ronald M. M. postman/poultry keeper and Margaret M. Watson clerk; b Aber 12.10.48
shorthand typist Leeds 1970–72; showroom asst Dewsbury 1972–79; secy Mirfield from 1979
m Strachan 9.8.69 Martin J. Webster bldg contr s of Willie W. Mirfield

MACDONALD Jennifer Alison *MA 1964
d of Archibald M. master baker/horse breeder and Georgina Morrison man. dir; b Elgin 17.9.43
res asst univ coll Swansea 1964–65; teacher Engl Elgin acad 1967–69
m Aber 23.4.69 Stewart B. Dunlop BSc 1964 *qv*

MacDONALD Jessie Norma *MA 1969

MACDONALD John *BSc 1964
s of Norman M. wool mill worker and Christina Mackay; b Stornoway 9.6.43
chem Brit steel corp Motherwell from 1966
m Glasg 7.8.71 Catherine Campbell nurse d of Edward C. West Kilbride S Uist

MACDONALD John Douglas MB ChB 1956
s of Douglas R. M. MB ChB 1921 *qv*; b Nairn 11.1.33
MID 1958 DObstRCOG(Lond) 1960 MRCGP 1964
h o Aber hosps 1956–57; nat serv RAMC Cyprus 1957–59; sen h o obst Inv 1959–60; g p Nairn from 1960
m Rochdale Joy M. King teacher p e d of Robert H. K. Rochdale

MACDONALD John Gillies BSc 1970
s of Alexander M. seaman, lt RNR, crofter, millworker and Christina Gillies crofter; b Shawbost Is of Lewis 3.9.47
teacher maths Helensburgh 1971–73, asst prin maths from 1973

MACDONALD John Stuart MA 1964

McDONALD Joyce Margaret MA 1970
d of Ewan McD. MA(Glas) headmaster and Mary Rowntree MA(Glas) teacher; b Glasg 17.2.50
LLB(Edin)
Edin: examiner Estate Duty off. 1971–73, organis univ settlement 1973–74, teacher maths 1974; teacher law f e coll Kirkcaldy 1974–79; worker commun proj N'cle from 1974

MACDONALD Katherine Campbell MA 1967

MACDONALD Kathleen Montgomery MA 1965
m Rose

MACDONALD Kenneth Ian *MA 1966
s of Norman M. MA 1932 *qv* and Bella MacLeod MA 1931 *qv*; b Inv 13.8.44
BPhil(Oxon) 1968
sen res off. Nuffield coll Oxon 1968–70; lect univ of Essex Colchester 1970–72; dir SSRC surv archive 1972–74; sen lect Essex 1975–76; univ lect/fell Nuffield coll from 1976

MACDONALD Lesley Marjory MB ChB 1970
d of Walter J. M. MPS dispensing chem and Frances C. Macdonald; b Nairn 18.3.47
h o ARI, Culduthel hosp Inv 1970–71; sen h o Hull, Rochdale 1971–72; trainee g p Aber 1972–73
m Aber 14.8.69 Paul Duffty MB ChB 1970 *qv*

McDONALD Linda Gordon MA 1969
d of Donald McD. painter/decorator and Mary A. S. Gordon; b Elgin 6.4.48
teacher Engl: Elgin acad 1970–74, Whitehills s s Dennistoun Glasg 1974–75
m Aber 24.8.74 David J. Grieve tv camera man s of Herbert J. M. G. Motherwell

MacDONALD Madeline Viola MA 1966
d of William J. MacD. master mariner and Madeline Watt secy; b Macduff 11.5.45
teacher: Engl/hist/geog St Mungo's h s Falkirk 1967–69, geog Banff acad 1969–72
m Portsoy 22.7.71 Ian Flory art teacher s of Reid F. Huntly

MacDONALD Margaret Anne MA 1970
d of Alexander MacD. stalker/for. and Annabel MacLennan; b Dingwall 11.2.48
teacher Muir of Ord p s 1971–73, head Kinlochewe p s from 1973
m Inv 8.12.73 Donald J. MacLean bldg contr s of William MacL. Dundonnell

McDONALD Margaret Annie MA 1961
d of John McD. bus driver and Alice Gauld doctor's receptionist; b Aber 8.11.37
teacher Fr/Ger: Peterhead 1962–67, Inverurie 1967–68, Peterhead 1968–77, prin Ger from 1977

MACDONALD Margaret Macleod MB ChB 1968
d of Finlay M. min of relig and Margaret Anderson; b Strath Halladale 24.12.44
DPM(Lond) 1971
Liv: h o Whiston hosp Prescot, St Helen's hosp 1968–69, sen h o psychiat Sefton gen hosp 1969–71, regist psychiat 1971, asst psychiat psych day hosp 1972
m Inv 20.7.68 Alistair D. MacKay teacher s of Hector M. Lochinver

MACDONALD Margaret Rose *MA 1967
d of George M. and Rose M. Taylor; b Huntly 25.6.45
teacher Aboyne acad from 1968
m Huntly 30.7.67 Ian C. Cordiner BSc 1965 *qv*

MacDONALD Marsaili Elizabeth MA 1961 LLB 1963

MACDONALD Mary MA 1969
d of John S. M. fisherman/crofter and Agnes Murchison; b Sleat Skye 21.6.49
teacher Engl: Dalkeith h s 1970–71, part time Lochend s s 1974; dem model ag Edin 1973; teacher: Paible j s s 1977, hist Portree h s from 1977
m Kilmore Skye 24.3.70 Angus J. A. Macdonald MA 1969 *qv*

MACDONALD Mary Bell MA 1968

MACDONALD Morag Ann MA 1965
d of Allan M. crofter and Marion A. Macdonald cook; b N Uist 17.12.43
teacher: maths Paible s 1966–77, guid 1975–77, maths Hawick h s 1977–78, maths/guid Paible s from 1978
m Daliburgh S Uist 28.6.79 Allan MacIsaac bldr s of Donald A. MacI. Locheport N Uist

MACDONALD Morag Holmes *MA 1970
d of Ronald M. M. pattern maker/poultry farm./postman and Margaret G. Watson bank clerk; b Aber 12.10.48
caseworker in fam serv. unit Glasg from 1970

MACDONALD Murdina MA 1968 CASS 1970
m Maciver

MACDONALD Murdo *MA 1970

McDONALD Muriel MA 1958 Dip Ed 1959
d of Edward McD. publican, insur man. and Betsy Goodall clerkess; b Brechin 19.3.37
teacher: Errol 1959–60, Perth 1960–65, remed Kincardine from 1973
m Brechin 22.7.61 John Adams roads eng/div road surv s of Frederick A. Brechin

MACDONALD Neilalice MA 1966

MACDONALD Norma Myra *MA 1970

MACDONALD Paul MA 1968
s of John M. charge eng (power stat) and Mary E. Gardiner; b Dartford 4.7.46
Dip Career Guid (Strath) 1972
careers off. older leaver spec Glasg 1968–73; area trg advis Furniture & Timber ITB Perth 1973–76; lect psych/careers guid Hull from 1976
m Aber 4.9.70 Jennifer A. Cantlay d of William J. C. BSc(agr) 1943 *qv*

MACDONALD Ranald Roderick *BSc 1967
MSc(Stir)

McDONALD Raymond William George MA 1966
CA

MacDONALD Rhoda MA 1965
d of Norman MacD. crofter/weaver and Ina MacLennan; b Lurebost Is of Lewis 24.1.44
teacher Engl Dingwall acad 1966–72, asst prin Engl from 1972

McDONALD Ronald William MA 1970 MEd 1974
s of Ronald McD. bulldozer driver and Annie M. McIntosh; b Longside 31.5.35
FSAScot
prin teacher hist Torry acad Aber from 1971
m Aber 7.12.63 Sheena C. Jackson d of James J. Aber

MACDONALD Sandra Irene MB ChB 1965
d of Walter J. M. pharm and Frances C. Macdonald; b Nairn 13.3.41
h o: Dumfries, Aber, Inv 1965–67; sen h o Dunfermline 1967–68; regist gen med Inv 1968–70; regist geriat Oslo, Norway 1971–72, bedriftslege Namdal sykehus from 1972
m Nairn 21.4.73 Arne J. Aursnes C.Ph.(Oslo) teacher s of Ivar A. Namsos Norway

MACDONALD Sheila Mary MA 1968

McDONALD Sheila Young MA 1957
d of Alexander McD. bank man. and Sophia E. Young; b Kirkwall 28.3.36
teacher: geog Aber 1958–60, Malmesbury 1961–62, Aber 1962, high s Blantyre 1962–63
m Aber 5.11.60 Ronald G. Johnson BSc 1957 *qv*

MacDONALD Shina Ann MB ChB 1967
d of Murdo MacD. joiner and Bessie B. MacKillop teacher; b Inv 19.12.40
h o RACH, Woodend hosp Aber 1967–68; g p: Crieff 1968–69, Ontario 1970–71, Kinlochleven 1972–77; part-time work later
m Kinlochleven 29.10.77 James M. Young contr s of Archibald M. Y. Ballachulish

MacDONALD Theresa Elizabeth *MA 1963
d of Donald MacD. for. and Margaret Henaghen cook; b Glasg 18.2.42
teacher Haverhill 1963–64; part-time tut. extra-mural dept Glas from 1969
m Fort Augustus 17.8.63 John F. Ross MA 1961 *qv*

MacDONALD Vernon BSc 1966

MACDONALD William MB ChB 1959

MACDONALD William James Douglas *BSc 1967 PhD 1970
s of A. W. M., MC TD JP free lance journalist and Muriel F. Pirrie; b Aber 26.3.45
ARIC 1971 FCS 1972 ACCA 1974
lect: Makerere univ Kampala Uganda 1970–72, Cardonald coll of f e Glasg 1973–74, sen lect from 1975
m Aber 20.8.70 Patricia A. Craigen univ tech d of William A. C. Aber

McDONALD William Reid *MA 1956

McDONNELL Edwin Joseph Anthony *BSc 1967

McDOUGAL Malcolm James *MA 1968 Dip Ed 1969
s of James McD. cabinetmaker and Christina D. Edmund shop asst; b Holyoke Mass USA 5.1.32
teacher: Engl AGS 1969–70, spec asst Banchory acad 1970–72, prin Engl Alford acad 1972–77
m Aber 6.4.57 Maureen Knowles mus teacher d of George K. Aber
d Aber 1.11.77

McDOUGALL Alice Joan MA 1969
d of Kenneth McD. lab/crofter and Catherine MacLeod; b Barvas Is of Lewis 2.6.47
teacher hist/mod stud. Finnart h s Greenock 1970–74
m Crieff 5.8.72 Kenneth J. Allan BSc 1971 teacher s of John R. A. Beauly

MacDOUGALL Carol Campbell *MA 1969
d of Peter C. MacD. insur ag and Caroline D. Dallas; b Stonehaven 26.9.46
teacher Fr/Ger Edin 1970–72; Germany: teacher Engl Bottrop 1972–73, Freising 1973–75; asst prin mod lang Edin from 1976

MACDOUGALL John Davidson MB ChB 1968

McDOUGALL John Finlay *MEd 1970
s of Thomas W. McD. MA(Glas) teacher and Emily F. Marshall teacher; b Paisley 15.12.45
MA(Glas) 1967
admin asst Edin 1967–68; teacher: classics RGC Aber 1970–73, prin classics Dunoon g s from 1973

McDOUGALL Martin Andrew LLB 1969
s of Andrew C. McD. bank man. and Mary A. Fry; b Oban 24.7.48
solic Greenock from 1969
d 9.1.81

McDOWALL Judith Howie *MA 1967
d of William C. McD. BA(Oxon) high court judge (Anglo-Egypt, Sudan), chief exec Nobel explosives Co and Margery H. Wilson BA(Oxon) member of commun council, commun health council/JP; b Birm 16.2.45
VSO teacher econ Silliman univ Dumaguete City Philippines 1967–69; exec off.: P O Lond 1969–70, admin postal man. coll Rugby 1970–73; post exec 'C' finance div operations postal board h q in Scot. Edin from 1973

McDOWALL Robert John *MA 1964

McDOWELL Lindsay Anne *MA 1967
d of John C. McD., BCom(Lond) comp dir and Molly Hirst lib/teacher; b Dun 19.6.44
m Broughty Ferry 25.8.67 Roger D. Watkins MB ChB 1968 *qv*

McEWAN Brian Grant MA 1959

McEWAN Iain *MA 1962
b Perth 26.10.39
teacher hist Lenzie acad 1963–67; prin hist Arbroath acad 1967–74, Morgan acad Dun from 1974
m Edin 14.7.66 Nancy Graham MA(Edin) teacher

McEWAN Irene Barbara *BSc 1968
d of Andrew D. McE. CA and Irene M. Kinnear; b Bradford 15.8.46
Manc: des progr for Internat Computers 1968–71; syst progr reg computer centre from 1971
m Manc 9.3.73 Frederick Lawton draughtsman, computer oper man s of Frederick L. Stretford

MacEWAN James Alex Iain *MA 1969 BD 1972
s of James A. MacE. C of S min and Edith M. Culbert teacher; b Glasg 27.7.47
C of S min: asst Lochwood par ch Easterhouse Glasg 1972–74; min Stockethill par ch Aber 1974–80, Abernethy, Cromdale and Advie from 1980
m Aber 4.7.69 Aileen A. Barron MA 1968 *qv*

McEWEN Andrew Durrad BSc(for) 1968
s of Jock M. McE. LLB(NZ) and Ruth C. Durrad; b Feilding NZ 12.6.44
BSc(Well NZ) 1966 PhD (Cant. NZ) 1976
NZ for. serv.: Invercargill 1968–71, scient. for. res inst Rotorua from 1971
m Wellington NZ 17.12.66 Winifred M. Fleming BSc (Vict NZ) teacher d of Charles A. F. BA(NZ) Wellington

MacEWEN David Martin LLB 1967

McEWEN Gavin Thomas *MA 1968
b Hawick 21.10.46
MA(Kansas) 1970 DPhil(Oxon) 1980
Aberd-Kansas univ grad exch scholarship, asst instruct Lawrence Kansas 1968–70; res Bonn W Ger 1970–72; stud. Queen's coll Oxon 1972–75; Inland Revenue from 1975
m Arbroath 10.7.71 Aileen M. Petrie teacher

McEWEN James Gordon Keith MSc 1962
s of McEwen MD(West Ont) phys and Laura B. Errett; b Ekfrid Township Ontario
BSc(for)(Tor)
Canada: res scient for. Ont 1962–70; lect Lakehead univ Thunder Bay Ont from 1973
m Ottawa 16.6.45 Ruth E. Gill
d Ontario 10.1.75

McEWEN John Fraser BSc(for) 1959

MacEWEN Lawrence Traquair BSc(agr) 1964
s of William I. L. MacE. RN, farm. and Edith A. T. Nicol BA(Cantab) marine biol; b Is of Muck 24.7.41
farm. Is of Muck

McFADDEN Eleanor Thomson MA 1970
d of Jack R. McF. man. dir paint manuf and Agnes H. D. Dunlop hairdresser; b Glasg 12.5.48
computer progr dept soc med Aberd 1970–74; comp progr syst analyst Grampian health board Aber from 1974

McFADDEN Ian Andrew BSc 1964
s of Jack R. McF. comp dir/secy and Agnes H. Dunlop; b Ayr 15.11.42
Aber: trainee man. fish processing indust 1964–66, prod. man. 1966–69, gen man. 1969–76, dir 1976–77, man. dir from 1977
m Aber 3.10.66 Evelyn J. Churchard d of John C. Aber

McFADDEN John Alexander Crawford MA 1959 LLB 1962
s of John A. McF. MA(Glas) C of S min and Johanna L. D. Todd; b Dunoon 11.9.36
leg. asst, ptnr Edin 1962–68, Dumfries from 1968
m Surbiton 27.8.64 Patricia M. Thompson MB ChB 1963 *qv*

MACFARLANE Alexander BSc(eng) 1959
s of Duncan J. M. farm. and Amelia B. P. Massie; b Culsalmond 24.3.37
aircraft stress eng Warton 1959–61; aero eng repair eng Glasg 1961–62; Hamilton: tech asst aero eng dev 1962–64, sect. leader aero eng dev 1964–66, asst dev eng 1966–69; E Kilbride: dev eng aero eng 1969–73, proj man. from 1974
m Glasg 25.9.68 Anne J. Sutherland MA(Glas) teacher d of Donald S. Wishaw

MACFARLANE Alexander William *BSc 1970
s of Frederick A. M. farm. and Mary Reid farm.; b Insch 23.7.48
asst eng Plessey Co Poole 1970–72; des eng GIM Glenrothes from 1972
m Aber 11.8.72 Irene E. Horn MA 1969 *qv*

McFARLANE Barbara Lena MA 1968 LLB 1971
d of Harry A. McF. area eng g p o tel and Lena R. C. Still MA 1969 *qv*; b Aber 9.7.47
Aber: law app Paull & Williamsons advoc 1971–73, leg. asst Burnett & Reid advoc from 1973

MACFARLANE Duncan John *BSc 1963
s of Duncan J. M. farm. and Amelia B. P. Massie; b Insch 23.12.40
DIC 1964 PhD(Lond) 1969
seismologist The Hague 1968–69, Lagos 1969–73, Lond from 1974
m Lond 20.7.67 Margaret O. Conroy teacher

McFARLANE Gladys MA 1968
m Taylor

McFARLANE Hugh BSc(eng) 1965
s of William A. McF. MA(St And) C of S min and Jeanie K. Roberts MA(Edin) teacher; b Edin 24.12.43
Aber: gen asst dist eng NSHEB 1967–69, 3rd asst dist eng from 1969
m Glasg 21.7.73 Catherine S. Grant teacher d of Archibald G. Glasg

MACFARLANE Michael Watt MA 1959

MACFARLANE Mildred MA 1956
d of Francis T. M. policeman and Gladys Orr clerkess; b Port Glasg 23.2.35
teacher: Tillydrone p s Aber 1957–60, Engl Prince Rupert s Rinteln Germany from 1973
m Aber 27.12.58 John T. Coull MB ChB 1958 *qv*

MACFARLANE Murdoch MA 1962
s of Murdo M. mill foreman and Henrietta M. Mackenzie; b Is of Lewis 30.11.40
BEd(Sask)

teacher Hilton Ross-shire 1963–67; Saskatoon Sask: teacher 1967–74, vice-prin 1974–77, prin from 1977
m Sturgis Sask Caroline D. Wilgosh d of Mike W. Hazel Dell Sask

MACFARLANE Neil Archibald Arthur *BSc 1967

McFARLANE Richard Hamilton LLB 1970
s of Ian D. McF. MA(St And) prof Fr Oxon and Marjory N. Hamilton MD(St And) med pract; b Cambridge 5.5.47
law app, solic Cupar from 1971
m St And 14.4.73 Anne M. Steele nurs nurse d of Andrew R. S. St And

McFARLANE Wilma MA 1966
d of William P. McF. linotype oper and Mary Anderson; b Aber 11.7.46
exec off.: DHSS Lond 1967–69, soc sc res council Lond from 1970
m Aber 30.7.66 Roderic G. McAra marketing exec pharm s of Alistair R. McA. MA 1937 *qv*

MacFARQUHAR David MacGregor *MA 1966

MACFARQUHAR Iain Alexander MB ChB 1959
s of John M. M. MB ChB 1923 *qv*; b Kintore 27.11.36
DObstRCOG 1961
g p Elgin from 1962
m Ilford 9.3.63 Margaret O. Bell asst purser d of William T. B. Ilford

MACFARQUHAR Joan MB ChB 1957
d of John M. M. MB ChB 1924 *qv*; b Kintore 9.9.33
DA 1961
h o: Woodend hosp, mat. hosp Aber 1957–59; h o S C hosp Glasg 1959–60; sen h o anaest Inv 1959–60; regist anaest Aber 1960–62
m Aber 15.9.62 William J. Leishman MB ChB(Glas) part-time anaest Stirling R I s of James L. Condorrat

MacFARQUHAR Roderick Campbell *MA 1963

McGEOCH Gay Christine Kesteven *MA 1966

McGHIE Duncan MB ChB 1966

McGHIE Jean Grant MA 1962
d of John McG. MA(Glas) C of S min and Isabel R. Allan; b Camelon 23.9.41
syst analyst Internat Computers Nairobi from 1963

McGHIE Rhona Robertson *MA 1958
d of John McG. MA(Glas) min of relig and Isabel R. Allan; b Falkirk 5.11.36
teacher: Blairgowrie 1959–61, Aber 1961–66, Homa Bay Kenya 1966–72
m Nairobi 19.6.71 Brian C. Hurst BA(Cantab) teacher s of Robert J. H. BA(Cantab) Lond

McGIBBON Graeme MSc 1964 PhD 1967

McGILL Gordon Ramsay MA 1965

McGILL Janice Margaret MA 1969
m Burn

McGILL Robert Leiper Craig MA 1969
s of Patrick J. McG. univ hall porter, buyer elect. store and Robertina Craig hosp superv; b Aber 8.3.45
teacher hist Peterhead acad 1970–73; asst prin hist from 1973; part-time teacher f e Peterhead from 1971

m Aber 4.4.67 Margaret Beattie teacher d of John B. Cove

MacGILLIVRAY Alexander Jamieson *BSc 1958 PhD 1962
s of Adam MacG. shoemaker and Isabella Jamieson; b Insch 24.7.36
scient Imp Cancer res fund Lond 1961–67; sen scient asst Beatson Inst cancer res Glasg 1967–76; reader in biochem s of biol Sus from 1976

MacGILLIVRAY Alexander John MA 1966
s of Donald MacG. tweed merch and Effie Robertson teacher; b Benbecula 31.10.43
teacher Castletown 1967–71; head: Knock p s Is of Lewis 1971–75, Balivanich p s Is of Benbecula from 1975
m Inv 27.12.68 Annie MacLeod MA 1967 *qv*

McGILLIVRAY Rhonda Moray MA 1968
d of Donald R. McG. army major, hotel man. and Henrietta MacLennan bookkeeper, hotel man.; b Aber 19.3.47
soc worker Aber c c 1968–72
m Aber 7.9.71 John A. G. Scott occupational therap s of Alexander G. S. Aber

McGINLEY Michael Owen MA 1969 LLB 1971

McGINN Barry Charles MA 1966
s of Ronald McG. turf comm ag and Susanna Lowdon; b Inv 1.7.45
Dip Rose Bruford coll of sp and drama 1969
actor Provinces/Lond and for tv and films from 1969

McGLASSON John Christopher *MA 1964

McGOOGAN James Alexander LLB 1969
s of James M. McG. BSc(Glas) teacher and Mary J. Davies; b Coatbridge 22.6.48
Dip Criminology(Edin) 1970
soc work asst Glasg 1970–71; asst reporter to ch panel Glasg 1971–72, dep reporter Paisley 1972–73; law app Coatbridge 1973
m Aber 18.8.72 Euphemia Brand MB ChB 1973 path. d of James B. Ford

McGOWAN George Cockburn BSc(eng) 1966
s of George McG. bank man. and Annabella Cockburn; b Thurso 29.5.43
asst civ eng Marples Ridgway Aber, Port Talbot 1966–68; site ag: F. J. C. Lilley (Marine) Aber, Shetland, Glasg 1968–71, W. H. Rankin Is of Mull 1971–72, F. J. C. Lilley (Marine) Glasg, Montrose, Aber 1972–75; self-employed civ eng contr George C. McGowan (contracts) Banchory from 1975
m Aber 12.8.69 Geraldine M. Drayson BSc 1968 *qv*

McGOWAN Peter Anthony *MA 1969

McGRATH Katharine Ann *MA 1968

McGREGOR Alan Graham *BSc(agr) 1970
s of Ian G. McG. MB ChB(Edin) g p and Mary I. Allan land army, ch welfare off.; b Edin 17.6.46
ICI agr div rep Shrewsbury area Staffs/Shropsh from 1970, later marketing rep Hereford/S E Wales

MacGREGOR Alan Mackenzie *MA 1966
s of Laurence MacG. acct and Henrietta A. Mackenzie; b Inv 23.6.44
marketing exec York 1966–68; Lond: marketing man. 1968–71, man. internat fin. from 1972
m Lond –.7.77 Anne Roberts MA 1966 *qv*

MacGREGOR Alastair Scott Russell *MA 1966
s of Norman MacG. MBChB(Glas) and Mary D. R. Roddick; b Glasg 30.6.43
sales exec: Xerox Ottawa 1967–74, Rank Xerox Glasg 1974–77; br man. Nashoa Ottawa from 1977
m Vancouver 21.2.69 Janet Myles d of Gwyn D. M. Ottawa

MACGREGOR Andrew McPherson MA 1969

McGREGOR Ann Lewese *MA 1970
d of Lewis McG. PO exec eng and Maria M. Forbes secy; b Aber 1.11.47
MA(McM) 1972, BEd (K'ston, Ont) 1974
m Aber 13.12.69 Marc O. M. Abrioux MA 1971 s of Olivier M. A. PhD 1949 *qv*

MacGREGOR Campbell MB ChB 1968
s of Robert A. MacG. bank man. and Mary B. Hamilton lib; b Edin 15.8.42
h o ARI, Woodend hosp Aber, RACH, mat. hosp Aber 1968–70; g p Aber from 1970
m Coatbridge 31.10.69 Jennifer W. Scott BA(Strath) soc worker d of William T. S. Coatbridge

MACGREGOR Catherine Elizabeth MB ChB 1965
m Tucker

MacGREGOR Christina Una MA 1969

McGREGOR Colin Masson *BSc 1968 PhD 1971
b Aber 2.12.46
lect maths Glas from 1971
m Bearsden 29.6.79 C. Joyce Paterson

McGREGOR David *BSc 1967
s of Patrick D. McG. grocer and Alexandrina M. McKay; b Aber 29.11.44
res asst Unilever res lab Aber 1968–70; tech Zool soc of Lond 1970–73, res fell. 1973–76, higher scient off. MAFF lab Weymouth from 1976
m Aber 5.7.69 Sheila M. McKenzie BSc 1966 *qv*

McGREGOR Douglas Robert *BSc 1961

McGREGOR Elizabeth Margaret MA 1965

McGREGOR Forbes Clement BSc(eng) 1965
s of David T. McG. army off. and Mary R. Forbes tailoress; b Nairn 14.10.42
Canada: jun eng Northern Elect. Co Montreal 1965–67; central off. equipment eng B C tel co Vancouver 1967–68; asst master Cambrian coll Sudbury 1968–69; chief numerical control instr Sperry-Rand Montreal 1969–71; assoc master Sault coll Sault Ste Marie from 1971
m Montreal 2.9.67 Laura M. M. Demers secy d of Louis T. D. Kiosk Ontario

MacGREGOR Gelda Margaret *MA 1968
d of Ian B-K. MacG. MB ChB(Edin) g p, reg m o and Rosa F. McLaren MB ChB(Glas) g p; b Kilmarnock 5.9.46
MPhil(Edin) 1974
grad teaching asst univ of W Ont Canada 1968–69, res asst dept educ stud. Edin 1970–72; home-school relations off. 'Priority' educ proj Liv 1972–74; adult literacy organis Dun 1974–75; adult literacy co-ordinator Lothian reg. from 1975

McGREGOR Griselda Sarah MA 1969
d of Alexander D. MacG. army off. MBE MC TD and Margaret S. M. Reid MB ChB 1926 *qv*; b Aber 25.5.47
medal for journalism from American Legion 1975
travel USSR, Poland, Czechoslovakia, W Europe 1969–70; journalist D.C. Thomson's *Dundee Courier* from 1970
m Dun 18.7.75 Charles H. Main print man. s of William M. Aber

MacGREGOR, Helen Elizabeth MA 1970
m Frew

McGREGOR Ian *BSc 1968
s of Robert L. McG. eng and Ruby Forman nurse; b St Fergus 14.3.46
PhD (S Fraser) 1974
intramural superv dept recreation S Fraser univ B C Canada 1974–77, dir of recreation from 1977

MacGREGOR Ian Duncan *BSc 1957

MacGREGOR John Donald *BSc(agr) 1970
s of James J. MacG. BSc(Glas) univ lect and Elizabeth C. Millar MA(Edin); b Eynsham 12.8.46
MSc(Lond) 1971
farm man. consult. Lugg & Gould Burgess Hill 1971–74, sen consult. and area man. from 1974
m Dumfries 24.9.71 Kathleen H. Wilson MA 1970 *qv*

McGREGOR Joseph Don MA 1970
s of Alistair J. McG. elect., motor mech and Catherine J. Grant; b Braemar 6.6.49
app CA Aber 1971–75, CA with Whinney Murray & Co from 1977

McGREGOR Keith Alexander LLB 1969

McGREGOR Peter Alexander *BSc 1964

McGREGOR Sheila Nicol *BSc 1968
m Joiner

McGREGOR William Stewart Petrie MB ChB 1958
s of Robert McG. elect. eng and Margaret H. Petrie; b Fraserburgh 15.9.33
FRCSE 1967
h o Aber, Nott 1958–59; RAMC from 1959
m Aber 13.6.59 Doreen M. Macleod d of James A. M. Aber

McGRORY Eileen MA 1964
d of John McG. publican and Catherine Bain; b Fraserburgh 12.4.42
Lond: secy 1965–69, edit. asst 1969–71
m Aber 28.5.66 John H. Donald BSc 1963 *qv*

McGRORY Ian or John *MA 1963
s of John McG. publican and Catherine Bain; b Fraserburgh 25.2.40
CA 1967
acct: Adelaide S Aust 1967–77, Salisbury S Aust from 1971
m Launceston Tasmania 13.1.68 Patricia A. Paterson teacher d of Thomas M. P. Exeter Tasmania

McGRORY John Joseph *MA 1969
s of James McG. excavator driver and Mary A. Strain; b Clydebank 31.5.43
teacher Dunbartonsh from 1970
m Clydebank 5.8.72 Anne Lennon teacher d of John L. Clydebank

McHAFFIE Michael Ernest Ninian BSc 1964

McHARDY Aileen Jean MB ChB 1966
d of William J. McH. gardener and Helen J. Petrie; b Torphins 29.8.42

h o Aber 1966-67; trainee asst g p Cults 1967–68; dept m o Aberdeensh 1968–70; m o VD clin Aber from 1972
m Durris 4.9.68 Robert W. M. Downie MB ChB 1960 *qv*
husb *d* 9.5.72

McHARDY Ellen MA 1964 Dip Ed 1965
d of Archibald James McH. farm. and Margaret Smith nurse; b Buckie 29.1.44
teacher Sunnybank p s Aber 1965–69
m Aber 16.8.66 Roderick Smith MA 1964 *qv*

McHARDY Marigold Margaret Anngela Helen BEd 1969
m Gray

McHARDY William James *BSc 1958 PhD 1962
s of William J. McH. gardener and Helen J. Petrie; b Durris 28.3.36
scient off. Macaulay inst for soil res Aber from 1962
m Aber 29.5.65 Eileen E. Forbes secy d of John W. F. Aber

MACHIN David Harry *BSc(agr) 1969
s of John M. man., dir and Edna Young; b Sheffield 24.6.46
MSc(UCNW) 1972
scient off. Spillers res centre Newmarket 1969–70; lect univ of Botswana, Lesotho, Swaziland 1971–74; overseas tech exec Paulsard Whites International Ipswich 1974–76; nutrit-higher scient off. Trop prod inst Min of Overseas Dev from 1976
m Romiley 10.7.71 Janet D. Bailey BSc 1971 chem, quality controller d of Norman B. Romiley

MACHRAY Wilma Margaret *MA 1961
d of William M. and Nettie H. Youngson; b Inverurie 30.11.39
teacher: geog Aber 1962–66; prin geog: Bankhead acad 1966–70, Ellon acad 1970–72; lect Aber coll of educ from 1972
m McDonald

McILVRIDE Sandra Mary *MA 1961
d of Donald G. McI. bulb farm man. and Gladys Maxwell; b Spalding 11.11.39
teacher: Demonstration s Aber 1962–67, Inverurie acad: p s 1967–72, dep head p s 1972–75; asst head Kellands p s Inverurie 1975–76; head: Stoneywood p s 1976–79, Hazlehead p s Aber from 1979

MacINNES Lindsay Jane MA 1970 Dip Ed 1972
d of Angus MacI. acct and Jean C. Anderson secy; b Edin 4.4.50
asst in fin. off. H.-W. from 1976
marr diss

MACINNES Margaret Ella MA 1965
d of Niel G. M. insp taxes and Elizabeth L. Clunie; b Halifax 23.12.35
teacher Hayshead p s Arbroath 1957–58
m Aber 31.10.58 Ian D. Herd publican s of Douglas H. Aber

MacINNES Mary Flora MA 1965
d of John L. MacI. farm. and Euphemia MacDonald; b Tiree 28.12.43
teacher: Engl/Gaelic/soc stud. Inv 1966–68, Engl Edmonton 1968–69, prin Engl Vancouver 1969–72, Engl Hong Kong 1972–73, govt trg off. (land div) Hong Kong 1974–77
m Hong Kong 7.8.72 Alexander MacArthur police off. s of Donald MacA. Tiree

MACINTOSH Alan Archibald *MA 1965
s of Daniel M. lect maths/navig and Anne T. Murphy; b Glasg 11.8.43
teacher Engl: Wilkie h s Saskatchewan 1966–69, Stir h s 1968–69, head Engl dept Shiney Row s s Co Durh; Engl Big River Sask 1969–71, Russell Manitoba 1971–75, Yorkton Sask from 1975
m Morpeth 11.8.65 Susan P. Turner MA 1965 *qv*

MACINTOSH Alastair BSc 1966

McINTOSH Alexander Selbie MB ChB 1963

MACINTOSH Anne MA 1965
d of Donald M. model maker and Margaret Bruce; b Peterhead 6.2.45
teacher Peterhead from 1966

McINTOSH Charles MA 1963
d 27.4.64

McINTOSH Charles Mearns *MA 1956
s of William McI. rly signalman and Jeannie F. Mearns milliner; b Insch 23.12.33
FRGS
RNVR 1956–59; teacher geog Banff acad 1960–62 prin geog from 1962
m Aber 4.7.59 Maureen M. Craighead teacher d of James G. C. Aber

McINTOSH Colin Stephen MB ChB 1964
s of Alexander McI. eng and Ann Stephen; b Fraserburgh 13.12.40
MRCP 1970
h o ARI 1964–65; sen h o Woodend hosp Aber, ARI 1965–66; regist med ARI 1966–70; Lond: lect dept nephrology St Bart's hosp 1970–72, sen med regist Westminster hosp from 1972

MACINTOSH Fiona McLean *MA 1966

McINTOSH Francis George *BSc(eng) 1963 MSc 1965
s of Alexander M. McI. hotel prop. and Jean Selbie; b Inverurie 19.3.42
MIEE 1972 CEng 1972
grad app SETS Glasg 1963–64; lect electronics RGIT Aber 1965–71, sen lect from 1971
m Kemnay 2.4.64 Frances M. Morgan teacher d of Alexander M. Kemnay

McINTOSH Gordon *BSc 1960

McINTOSH Graham Henderson MB ChB 1967
s of John D. M. McI. master butcher and Mary Taylor; b Stonehaven 28.8.42
DObstRCOG 1971 MRCGP 1975
h o ARI 1967–69; sen h o anaest ARI 1969–70; g p: trainee Aber 1970–71, Stonehaven from 1972
m Aber 3.4.68 Elizabeth M. Emslie teacher p e d of William E. MA 1926 *qv*

McINTOSH Ian Alexander *MA 1969
s of Ernest McI. buyer chem indust and Mabel W. Turner teacher; b Wanstead 18.11.44
TEFL(UCNW)
teacher (Brit Council) to Finnish Brit Soc Helsinki, Turku 1969–71; lect Engl Turku/Åbo: Turku s of econ 1972–74, Åbo Akademi (Sudd univ) of Turku/Åbo from 1974

McINTOSH James *BSc 1962

McINTOSH James Robert Barclay *MA 1970 PhD 1976
s of Robert T. McI. joiner and Isobel Barclay nurse; b Banchory 5.12.46
Aber: MRC res stud. 1970–73, MRC res scient 1973–77; res fell Glas from 1977
m Southport 24.6.72 Jean B. Creswell PhD 1976 d of Barry E. C. Southport

McINTOSH James Stuart MB ChB 1958
s of James S. McI. comp dir and Bessie D. Nicol teacher; b Turriff 10.11.34
DObstRCOG 1965
h o ARI 1958–59; m o Tasmanian govt Latrobe 1960–61, m o royal women's hosp Melbourne 1961–62; g p: Maffra Aust 1962–63, Coventry from 1963
m Aber 21.7.59 Norma Welsh MA 1958 *qv*

McINTOSH John Alistair Reid *BSc 1958
s of John D. M. McI. butcher and Mary H. Taylor cashier; b Stonehaven 21.1.36
Aberd: res asst 1958–61, clin phys 1961–64, lect 1964–74; chief phys Coventry area health auth from 1974
m Aber 3.7.63 Alison Grant nurse d of Ian G. Inverugie

McINTOSH John Leslie MA 1959
s of Wilfred D. McI. confectioner and Christina A. Black confectioner; b Banff 4.1.37
FSA Scot. 1962 BA(Lond) 1975
teacher Engl Turriff acad 1960–62; Banff acad: 1962–67, spec asst 1967–72, prin guid from 1972

MACINTOSH Kathleen Macdonald MA 1962
d of Donald M. stores clerk and Joan K. C. Ross teacher; b Inv 1.1.40
Dip Pers Man.(Glasg tech) MIPM 1973
pers off.: Worthing 1963–68, Chichester, Cambridge 1971–75; tax off. higher grade Cambridge from 1976
m Cambridge 7.10.78 Peter S. Gates res chem ARIC s of Eric S. G. Hunstanton

McINTOSH Kathleen Mary MA 1965
m Carle

MacINTOSH Peter MacCallum *BSc 1966
s of Peter MacI. fatstock off. and Andrina J. G. Robertson; b Meikleour 5.5.44
computer electronics: sen eng Poole 1966–71, prin chief eng Towcaster from 1971
m Aber 27.7.68 Margaret E. Fraser BSc 1967 *qv*

McINTOSH Stewart Mellis MA 1968

McINTOSH Sylvia *BSc 1961
d of Keith N. McI. joiner and Isabel MacKenzie; b Findhorn 28.3.39
teacher maths Madras coll St And 1962–69
m Findhorn 15.7.67 William M. Cockburn LRIC indust chem s of Edwin J. C. Strathkinness
husb *d* 1.6.77

McINTOSH William Eric MA 1965 *1967 Dip Ed 1968
s of Wilfred R. D. McI. confectioner and Christina Black; b Banff 20.8.44
teacher Bankhead acad 1968–72, prin Engl Ellon acad from 1972
m Aber 28.12.68 Sandra A. Gamblin MB ChB 1968 *qv*

McINTOSH William McKenzie BSc(eng) 1967

McINTYRE Alan MA 1970
s of Henry McI. shop asst and Nora McI. Bain; b Aber 5.4.30
teacher Summerhill acad Aber 1971–74; asst prin Engl from 1974
m Aber 26.1.52 Sarah Ogston audit clerkess d of William O. Aber

McINTYRE Angus Kennedy MA 1961
s of Angus McI. marine eng and Jean H.; b Renfrewshire 30.8.36
journalist: Aber 1961–64, Glasg 1964–70, Lond 1970–75, Edin from 1975
m Aboyne 21.12.60 Margaret A. Jones MB ChB 1960 *qv*

McINTYRE Charles Clouston BSc(agr) 1958
s of James C. F. McI. BSc(agr)(Edin) agr advis and Florence M. Clouston agr advis (poultry/dairy); b Newport on Tay 10.9.36
NDA 1959
farm man. Lathrisk Fife 1959–62, farm. Lathrisk 1962–68, E Lathrisk from 1968 and chief exec Fife Growers (farm co-op) Cupar 1972–76; ptnr Kettle Produce, veg pre-packing and wholesaling from 1976
m Freuchie 19.2.68 Elizabeth McLaren RSAM mus teacher d of James McL. Cupar

MacINTYRE Donald Hutchison *MA 1961 Dip Ed 1964

McINTYRE Elizabeth Pauline MLitt 1968
BA(BrCol)
m Diamond

MacINTYRE John MB ChB 1965 PhD 1973
s of George A. MacI. french pol and Ethel B. C. Sutherland; b Inv 26.3.40
FRCSE 1971
h o Aber 1965–66; res fell. surg Aberd 1966–69; regist surg ARI 1969–73; lect surg King's coll hosp med s Lond 1973–75, sen lect 1975–78; consult. surg Perth RI from 1978
m Inv 10.7.65 Anne MacFarquhar teacher

McINTYRE Patricia Joan MA 1960
d of Peter J. McI. CA and Caroline W. Lipp teacher home econ; b Broughty Ferry 18.10.39
teacher maths St Andrews 1961–64; syst analyst Toronto 1964–65; computer progr Vancouver 1965–67
m Vancouver 1.4.67 Rudolph E. North B Com(Br Col) invest. counsellor s of Albert E. N. Vancouver

McINTYRE Ruaraidh Wishart MB ChB 1957

McINTYRE William John *BSc 1969
s of William McI. man. and Marion S. G. Whyte; b Inv 22.6.45
Lic Inst Biol 1971
teacher: Gracemount s Edin 1970–74, Greenhall h s Gorebridge from 1974
m Stirling 19.10.73 Margaret S. Hill MA 1972 d of David H. Stirling

McIVER Charles John Esslemont MA 1962 LLB 1964
s of C Gordon E. McI. MA 1949 *qv* and Doris L. Shiach MA 1951 *qv*; b Turriff 14.1.43
NP 1971
leg. asst Clark & Wallace advoc Aber 1965–67, ptnr from 1967
m(1) Aber 2.6.66 Rosalind I. Hanson MA 1965 *qv*
(2) Aber 5.7.75 Janise M. Barron

MACIVER Donald John Morrison *MA 1967
s of Norman M. teacher and Annie Morrison; b Is of

Lewis 12.11.42
teacher Gaelic Nicolson Inst Stornoway 1968–73, prin Gaelic from 1973
m Stornoway 9.7.69 Alice MacLeod teacher d of Alexander MacL. Stornoway

MACIVER Donald Norman *MA 1963

MacIVER Iain Davidson MA 1963
s of Thomas MacI. MA(Glas) teacher, f e off. and Ann C. Davidson cordon bleu; b Inv 18.8.42
organis Moray & Nairn liberal assoc 1963–64; stud s of librarianship coll of comm Glasg 1964–65; trav lib Herefordsh c lib 1965–67; mobile lib Lanarksh c lib 1967–74; dep br lib Lanark dist lib from 1974
m Hamilton 13.7.74 Jennifer Meers secy, soc work asst d of Thomas P. M. Hamilton

MACIVER Iain Finlay *MA 1965
s of John A. M. MA(Glas) head teacher and Marion M. Maclean MA(Glas) teacher; b Stornoway 12.11.43
MLitt(Edin) 1977
asst keeper dept mss nat lib of Scot. Edin from 1968
m Edin 17.7.71 Lesley M. Stewart lib asst d of Archibald G. S. Edin

MACIVER Iain MacDonald *MA 1969 *MEd 1973

MACIVER John MA 1968
s of Angus M. tech off. and Mary M. MacLeod; b Stornoway 24.1.45
off. customs & excise 1968–70; teacher Stornoway from 1971
m Stornoway 29.9.73 Janet A. Burrough clerkess, typist d of Hubert P. B. Mordialloc Victoria Aust

MACIVER Kenneth Maclean LLB 1969

MACIVER Norma Euphemia MA 1967 CASS 1969
d of Norman M. headmaster and Annie Morrison clerk; b Uig Is of Lewis 5.7.44
soc worker Aber 1969–72; prin soc worker Is of Lewis 1972–75; dep dir soc work W Isles 1975–78, dir soc work from 1978
m Aber 8.7.65 Finlay MacLeod MA 1965 *qv*

MACIVER Norman *MA 1967

McIVOR Colin McKenzie BSc(eng) 1956

McKAY Alan Campbell *BSc 1970
s of George B. McK. shopkeeper and Jean M. Campbell sub-postmistress; b Inv 29.10.48
barman Kingshouse hotel Argyll 1971–72; teacher: geog/sc Lochaber h s Fort William 1972, geog Inv h s from 1973

MACKAY Alasdair MA 1966

McKAY Alexander Gordon Reid *BSc 1962
s of Alexander W. McK. trans driver and Elsie R. Gordon; b Lossiemouth 10.2.40
quality control chem paint factory 1963–68; works chem canning factory from 1968
m Eyemouth 6.8.66 Agnes E. Lowrie MA 1964 *qv*

MACKAY Alexander James Mackenzie BSc(agr) 1965
s of Andrew M. crofter and Janet Sutherland; b Bonar Bridge 29.8.42
agr consult.: Fife 1965–68, Angus from 1968
m Aber 12.8.66 Elizabeth A. Cargill teacher d of Robert C. Ruthvenfield Perth

MACKAY Alexander John Ramsay LLB 1970

McKAY Alison *MA 1970
d of James McK. bank man. and Vera G. Frary; b Fraserburgh 23.4.47
teacher: f e Aber 1971–72, asst prin classics Edin from 1972

McKAY Alison Bruce MA 1968
d of John F. McK. pharm and Hannah B. Walker; b Aber 22.8.47
Dip Pers Man.(Strath) 1969
market. asst advt ag Lond 1969–73; market res exec in res ag Lond 1973–76; sen res psych in res ag Lond 1977–78; assoc dir in res ag from 1978
m Aber 19.9.73 Nicolas B. Palmer BSc(Lond) bank man. s of Cyril P. Brighton

McKAY Alistair Paterson MA 1956
s of Alexander P. McK. and Elsie J. Gardiner; b Cullen 6.3.35
teacher Buckie p s 1957–59; teacher, head Deskford p s 1959–62; teacher: Portgordon s s 1962–64, prin Ger Buckie from 1965

McKAY Andrea *MA 1967 Dip Ed 1968
d of Andrew McK. painter and Annie G. McKenzie; b Aber 12.2.45
teacher maths St Margaret's s for girls Aber 1968–70; educ psych Aber c c 1971–73
m Aber 8.7.66 Edwin B. Grant fireman s of John G. Aber

McKAY Betty Jane *BSc 1964
d of John McK. for./estate man. and Betsy Duncan; b Craigellachie 5.5.42
Edin: marine biol 1964–69, vet immunologist 1969–71
m Aber 12.2.68 Alistair E. Philip MA 1961 *qv*

MACKAY Cairine Duncan MA 1961
d of William D. M. law clerk and Elizabeth Robertson; b Aber 9.10.40
journalist D.C. Thomson Dun 1961–62; teacher Engl Dun from 1963
m Aber 3.4.65 Donald W. Smith comm artist/teacher s of Peter S. Dun

MACKAY Calum MB ChB 1960
s of John M. headmaster, min of relig and Mary Macdonald teacher; b N Uist 3.5.32
h o, sen h o ARI, Woodend hosp Aber 1960–62; g p: West Riding Yorks 1962–64, Thurso from 1964
m Aber 18.12.57 Norna Pottinger MB ChB 1958 *qv*

MACKAY Catherine MA 1970
d of Peter M. crofter/driver and Flora Nicolson; b Uig Is of Skye 19.1.49
teacher: Inv 1971–73, Garelochhead p s 1973; exec off.: dept for nat savings Glasg 1974–75, customs and excise Greenock from 1975

MACKAY Christina Orr MA 1968
d of George K. M. CA and Daisy D. Orr; b Dornoch 15.7.47
teacher Fr: Langholm 1969–70, Annan 1970–72
m Dornoch 23.12.69 James Black acct s of William B. Annan

MACKAY Christine MacDonald BSc 1967
d of Neil M. fishing skipper and Mary B. Sutherland; b Helmsdale 1.3.46
teacher maths: Golspie 1968–73, Helmsdale from 1974
m Helmsdale 10.7.70 David Cowie fishing skipper s of David C. Helmsdale

MACKAY David John *BSc 1963

MACKAY David William *BSc(agr) 1969
s of William M. farm. and Harriet E. Moir; b Turriff 8.1.46
farm man. rep Durham 1969–75;-prod. man. Billingham from 1975
m Aber 6.1.73 Mary R. Brown BA(Stir) d of Charles W. B. MA 1942 *qv*

McKAY David Wood *BSc 1968

MacKAY Donald Iain *MA 1959
s of William MacK. banker and Rhona Couper teacher; b Kobe Japan 27.2.37
Council R Econ Soc from 1976 Council Scot. Econ Soc from 1977
syst analyst, cost controller Bradford 1959–62; asst lect, lect pol econ Aberd 1962–66; lect, sen lect applied econ Glas 1966–71; prof pol econ Aberd 1971–76; prof econ H-W Edin from 1976; visiting prof Cornell univ Ithaca USA 1974–75
m Aber 31.7.61 Diana M. Raffan MA 1961 *qv*

MacKAY Donald James MA 1967
s of James S. MacK. factory process worker and Agnes K. D. Binnie MA(Glas) teacher; b Stirling 14.6.44
teacher Lat Allan Glen's s Glasg from 1968

MACKAY Donald John Norman MA 1965

MACKAY Duncan Roderick MA ChB 1959

MACKAY Eleanor Margery Sinclair MA 1968
d of William R. M. BSc 1934 *qv*; b Edin 10.8.47
ALA 1974
res bibliog univ of Guelph Canada 1969–70; asst Westminster city libs Lond 1971–73; sen asst Dund lib 1974–77; asst lib med section N'cle univ from 1977
m Aber John D. C. Harte BA(Cantab) barrister/lect s of John D. H. MB BS(Lond) Bedford

McKAY Evan Alexander *BSc 1970
s of Peter A. McK. foreman joiner and Helen A. Dick; b Inv 26.11.48
Dip Ed(Edin) 1971
teacher chem Elgin acad 1971–74; preacher of gospel from 1974

MACKAY Fiona Currie *MA 1969
d of Alexander M. motor mech and Christina Cumming; b Glasg 7.3.47
lib asst marine lab Oban 1970–71; teacher p s St Combs from 1972
m Aber 28.12.68 John W. B. Stephen fisherman

MACKAY Fiona Susanne MA 1969
d of Gordon M. quantity surv and Margaret M. Macpherson teacher; b Aber 5.1.49
Dip Grad Secy(Aber coll of comm) 1971
pers secy: Lond 1971–72, Glasg 1972–74, Brussels from 1974
m Hugh F. O'Toole

MACKAY Harry Allan *MA 1959
PhD(Kingston)

McKAY Helen Fiona Boyes BSc 1970
d of John R. McK. MRCVS(Glas) vet surg/farm. and Agnes C. Hunter; b Manc 9.9.49
teacher: Kitwe Zambia 1971–75, Lond from 1976
m Wigtown 3.7.71 Trevor M. B. Abell BSc(for) 1968 *qv*

MACKAY Isabella Tulloch *MA 1970
m Bolton

McKAY James *MA 1968 *MEd 1971
s of Adam F. McK. grocer and Elsie E. Kemp; b Aber 21.10.46
teacher Aber: Engl Northfield acad 1969–76, asst prin Engl Torry acad from 1976
m Aber 12.4.75 Linda J. Robb

MACKAY James Gordon *MA 1964
s of John K. M. bank clerk and Edith Bolton nurse; b Aber 18.12.38
MEcon(Adel) 1974
tut. econ univ of Adelaide 1964–67; lect: Queen's univ Belf 1967–69, RGIT Aber from 1967
m Aber 17.7.64 Hilda C. Davie SRN d of George H. D. Newmachar

MACKAY James Murray *MA 1967
s of James M. M. C of S min and Elizabeth Stewart; b Inv 14.5.45
teacher: Aber 1968–70, Nassau 1970–73, Lond from 1973
m Lond 10.8.74 Monica Sibson teacher, pers asst d of Alan W. S. Banbury

MACKAY Jane Margaret Mackenzie MA 1969
d of John S. M. M. timekeeper and Waltrena M. Mackenzie man./owner drapery bus.; b Cromarty 5.12.48
youth employ. off. Aber 1969–71; searcher (soc secur off.) Inv 1971; teacher Inv tech coll 1971–72; educ dept staffing clerk Dingwall 1972–73
m Cromarty 7.5.71 Lewis Patience skipper/share owner MV s of George P. Avoch

MACKAY Joan Morrison MA 1969 Dip Ed 1970
d of John M. MA(Glas) min of relig and Jean L. Morrison teacher; b Glasg 5.9.47
teacher Engl Perth h s 1970–72, Linlithgow acad 1972–73
m Munlochy 15.7.72 Andrew A. Cox MA 1972 teacher s of Thomas L. C. Pershore

MacKAY John Angus MA 1969
s of Alexander MacK. weaver and Mary Macdonald; b Stornoway 24.6.48
circulation rep D.C. Thomson Aber 1970–71; Glasg: teacher Engl N Kelvinside s s 1972–75, asst prin Engl Colston s s; commun co-operative field off. for HIDB Lewis from 1977
m Skye 25.3.70 Joan Martin MA 1971 teacher d of Malcolm M. Portree

MACKAY John Francis Graham *BSc 1965 PhD 1968
s of Alexander N. C. M. admin asst and Muriel J. Smith; b Aber 9.4.43
res asst (for. products): Melbourne 1968–73, Vancouver from 1973
m Aber 27.12.67 Eileen M. Kindness BSc 1966 *qv*

McKAY John William MA 1962
s of James S. McK. eng and Mary Noble MA 1969 *qv*; b Burma 7.3.41
BA(Oxon) 1964 PhD(Cantab) 1969
teacher classics Ayr 1964–66; lect theol Hull 1969–74; asst curate St Mary's Cottingham from 1970
m Aber 14.8.64 Elsie M. Sim MA 1964 *qv*

MACKAY Jonathan Angus MB ChB 1970

MACKAY Judith Ann MA 1968

MACKAY Kenneth MA 1958

MACKAY Kenneth Cameron MA 1969
s of Donald M. MA 1922 *qv*; b Is of Lewis 26.7.33
teacher Engl Tain royal acad from 1970
m Aber 13.9.68 Christina Maclean nurse d of Murdo M. MB ChB(Glas) Dunvegan

MACKAY Kenneth James MA 1966 BD 1970
s of Kenneth A. M. lorry driver/storeman and Marion C. Burgess; b Inv 14.9.41
C of S min Dun from 1970
m Birstall Leic 1972 Janet Rogers BA(Hull) soc worker d of Arthur N. R. Birstall

MACKAY Kenneth Malcolm *BSc 1957
s of John K. M. bank teller and Edith Bolton nurse; b Aber 22.2.35
PhD(Cantab) 1960
asst lect Nott 1960–62, lect 1962–70; reader univ of Waikato Hamilton NZ from 1970
m Thornton Watlass 30.6.59 Rosemary A. Lewis BSc 1958 *qv*

McKAY Leslie George MA 1956
s of Alexander McK. fisherman and Maggie Hay; b Sandend 17.8.35
Cert Pers Man.(Glasg) 1957
teacher Aberchirder s s 1957–67, dep head Inverurie acad 1967–72, head Kemnay s s from 1972
m Rothiemay 15.7.60 Helen Adam teacher d of Alexander A. Huntly

MACKAY Margaret MB ChB 1969
d of John D. M. army off., teacher and Winifred H. Potterton SRN; b Norwich 25.3.45
h o: Bruntsfield hosp Edin 1969–70; g p: Edin 1970–71, Leith from 1971
m Kincardine O'Neil 20.9.69 David M. Chambers BPharm(Lond) lect pharm Edin s of Reginald H. D. Brighton

MACKAY Margaret Collie MA 1959
d of George K. M. CA and Daisy D. Orr; b Salford 7.2.39
teacher: Perth 1960–61, Dornoch 1961–62, Laurieston from 1962
m Dornoch 20.7.62 John Macpherson chem eng, teacher, life assur off. s of John M. Bonar Bridge

McKAY Margaret Helen MA 1964
d of James D. McK. wireless oper and Ella Shirreffs shopkeeper; b Aber 7.3.28
teacher Aber from 1965
d Aber 9.5.81 *AUR* XLIX 139

MACKAY Marianne Elizabeth Houston MA 1964
d of George A. M. M. comp dir and Margaret Houston; b Thurso 16.12.43
Dip St Godric's Secy Coll Lond 1965
Aber: private secy 1965–66, teacher from 1967
m(1) diss
(2) Aber 11.7.73 Iain J. Inkson BSc(eng) 1972 dev eng s of James I. Aber

MACKAY Marlene Anne MA 1968
d of Donald M. M. Harris tweed weaver and Annie M. Morrison; b Stornoway 30.4.47
teacher: Innerleithen p s 1969–73, Dunkeld p s from 1973

McKAY Mary Beatrice *MA 1967
m Maclennan

MACKAY Moira Eleanor MA 1970
d of Hugh M. M. shepherd, crofter and Margaret R. H. Ross; b Dingwall 29.9.49
teacher maths Dingwall acad 1971–73, Gledfield p s Ardgay 1973–77
m Ardgay 21.7.73 William R. Cameron shepherd s of Roderick C. Alness

MACKAY Norman Harold MA 1958
s of Donald M. MA 1922 *qv*; b Barvas Is of Lewis 27.6.36
teacher: Peterhead acad 1959–62, Bankhead acad 1962–68, Nicolson inst Stornoway from 1968
m Stornoway 20.7.67 Johanna Morrison teacher d of Angus M. Laxdale Is of Lewis

McKAY Ralph Alexander BSc 1965 Dip Ed 1966
s of Alexander McK. and Jessie R. Potter; b Elgin 30.7.44
EdB(Winnipeg) 1970
teacher maths: Aber 1966–69, Winnipeg from 1969
m Winnipeg 15.7.72 Claudette Berard teacher

MACKAY Roberta Duncan *MA 1962
d of Stewart M. prison off. and Mary A. Alcorn compositor; b Edin 25.1.40
teacher classics Aber 1964–70; prin classics: St Margaret's s Aber 1970–73, Harlaw acad 1973–78; remed teacher Aber from 1978
m Aber –.7.66 George J. Stephen MA 1960 *qv*

MACKAY Ronald MA 1957
s of John M. headmaster, min of relig and Mary M. Macdonald teacher; b Berneray Harris 13.7.36
teacher: Killin s 1960–64, girls' h s Kitwe Zambia 1964–67, Thurso h s 1967–68; head: Lieurary s Caithness 1968–74, Park s Oban 1974–78, Banchory p s from 1978
m Aber 23.12.74 Alison M. Craig MA 1958 *qv*

MACKAY (Smith) Ronald George *MA 1967

MacKAY Ronald Graham *MA 1968

MACKAY Ronald Ross *MA 1963
s of William M. banker and Rhona Couper teacher; b Delhi 25.11.40
Dip Royal Econ Soc 1973
res asst Strath 1963–65; lect econ N'cle 1965–79; sen lect econ/dir inst econ res Bangor from 1979
m Whitley Bay 17.12.66 Christine M. Wood secy d of Edgar W. BSc(Imp Coll Lond) Whitley Bay

MacKAY Sheena Patricia MA 1960
m Packham

MACKAY Sheila MA 1967
d of Duncan M. stationmaster and Lily Reid; b Inv 17.2.45
teacher: Inv p s 1968–70, geog Inv from 1970

McKAY Shona Elizabeth MA 1964
m Grant

MACKAY Thomasina ᶜLLB 1970
d of George C. M. farm man. and Isabella Henderson: b Evanton 29.10.27
app, leg. asst Aber 1970–73; leg. asst Inv 1973–75, ptnr from 1975

MACKAY William David *MB ChB 1959

McKEAN Donald Campbell DSc 1967
s of James McK. BSc(Lond) eng and Winifred M.

Gardner; b Sanderstead 6.5.28
MA(Oxon) 1953 D Phil(Oxon) 1953
Aberd: lect chem 1955–67, sen lect 1967–73, reader from 1973
m Guestwick 28.7.54 Lucy M. H. Thorpe BA(Lond) min of relig d of Archibald F. T. MA(Cantab) Guestwick

MACKEAN Elspeth Mary *MA 1968
d of Andrew N. M. MA(Glas) C of S min and Janet E. Milne MA 1939 *qv*; b Port of Spain Trinidad 3.10.46
spec proof reader OUP 1968–70; teacher Dublin from 1974
m Wallasey 7.8.70 Michael J. Haren BA(NUI) civ serv s of James J. H. Fivemiletown Co Tyrone

McKEAND John Shorland MA 1969

McKEANE Patricia Mary *MA 1969
accidentally killed Baldock Herts 2.2.70 *AUR* XLIII 447

McKECHNIE Alasdair Alner MB ChB 1960 MD 1978
s of Alexander J. McK. semi-skilled lab at factory for disabled and Margaret A. Parker teacher; b Inv 17.10.36
DPM 1966 MRCPsych 1971
h o Aber hosps 1960–66; sen res assoc dept psych med N'cle; consult. psychiat Bangor vill hosp W Lothian 1970–72, phys supt/consult. psychiat from 1973
m Aber 22.7.61 Sheila Smith teacher d of Arthur J. S. Aber

MacKEITH Neil James *BSc 1968
s of Walter B. MacK. civ serv and Isobel Sutherland off. man.; b Aber 29.8.46
seismologist M East, Africa 1968–72; teacher sc Alford 1973–74; geophys Johannesburg from 1974
m Aber 16.4.74 June M. Moir MA 1965 *qv*

MACKELLAR Margaret Chesser MA 1970
d of Archibald M. clerk and Mary Bruce postwoman; b Campbeltown 8.2.49
teacher Hounslow 1971–74, Bolton 1974–75, Chorley from 1975
m Tarbert Argyll 19.9.70 Graham Jackson BSc 1971 scient civ serv s of William J. Liv

McKENDRICK Archibald Stewart *BSc 1970
s of William A. T. McK. MB ChB(Edin) med pract and Mary J. Stewart; b Bedford 18.6.48
teacher: biol Inverurie acad 1971–74, prin biol: Balfron h s 1974–77, Park Mains h s Erskine from 1977

McKENDRICK Barbara Vivian MA 1969

McKENDRICK Sheila Ann Elizabeth *BSc(agr) 1966
d of Robert E. McK. farm. and Mary G. Telfer; b Windygates 9.4.44
agr econ, sen agr econ Belfast from 1966
m Perth 9.5.70 Patrick J. Magee MSc(Edin) arch., town plan. s of Daniel M. Downpatrick NI

McKENNA John Alan *BSc 1970

McKENZIE Alan *BSc 1970

MACKENZIE Alan *BSc 1970 MSc 1972
s of William A. M. gen lab and Christina Forbes; b Forres 4.10.48
teacher chem Peterhead from 1972
m Forres 26.8.72 Sandra L. Fraser shorthand typist d of Hugh M. F. Forres

MACKENZIE Alan *MA 1963

McKENZIE Alastair John *BSc 1963

MACKENZIE Alexander *MA 1956

MACKENZIE Alexander Archibald MA 1958
s of Alexander G. M. hotel man. and Christina M. Macdonald; b Ullapool 23.11.36
CA 1963
ptnr Macdowall & Co CA Dingwall 1964–74; practice on own account A. A. Mackenzie & Co Dingwall from 1974
m Inv 29.7.60 Isobel M. Macdonald secy d of John M. killed in action 1940

MACKENZIE Alexander Miller BSc(eng) 1956
b Beauly 6.8.35

MACKENZIE Alexander Stewart ᶜMB ChB 1959
s of James S. M. master draper and Elizabeth M. Robertson; b Grantown-on-Spey 1.12.34
FRSM 1971
h o ARI 1959–60; g p Auchenblae, Rhynie 1960–62; h o Aber mat. hosp 1961–62; g p Banff from 1962
m Aber 16.7.59 Margaret J. D. Forbes teacher d of Alfred H. F. Forres

MacKENZIE Alisdair Grant *MA 1969

MacKENZIE Alistair Donald BSc(eng) 1959

McKENZIE Alastair George Stuart *BSc 1966
s of Alexander McK. MA 1933 *qv*; b Lossiemouth 31.8.44
teacher N'cle 1967–68; res and dev phys Morganite Resistors N'cle 1968–71; teacher: N'cle 1968–71, Aber 1973–76; Bible coll 1976–78; teacher Cambridge 1978–79; lect Uxbridge from 1980
m Chelmsford 10.12.77 Jennifer White

McKENZIE Ann Jean BEd 1970
d of James McK. relief foreman Dun corp trans and Eira C. Hood shorthand typist; b Dun 26.5.49
teacher Engl: Kirkton h s Dun 1970–73, Harris acad Dun 1973–74
m Dun 16.10.71 Robert R. Ballantine MA(Dund) tut. asst, soc worker s of Alexander P. B. Markinch

MACKENZIE Anna Vass BSc 1970

MacKENZIE Annabelle MA 1963
d of Angus MacK. tech teacher and Catherine M. MacPherson; b N Uist 27.6.43
teacher Engl: Hamilton 1964–69, part time Fochabers 1974–77 and from 1979
m Glasg 31.3.66 James Barnett BSc 1966 *qv*

MACKENZIE Anne MA 1958

MACKENZIE Anne Margaret MB ChB 1965
d of Colin M. MB ChB(Glas) g p and Margaret M. Robertson MB ChB 1937 *qv*; b Inv 12.3.41
FPA cert 1971
h o ARI, royal northern I Inv 1965–66; sen h o Ross clin Aber 1967–71; f p assoc m o Liv 1971–74; clin asst psychiat Leighton hosp Crewe from 1974
m Tain 19.9.66 George B. Rawsthorne MB ChB 1965 *qv*

MACKENZIE Catherine MA 1966
d of John M. fisherman and Annie MacArthur; b Isle of Lewis 8.5.45
teacher Engl Woodside s s Glasg 1967–68; curric asst lib Ont inst for stud. in educ 1968–71; teacher Engl Stirling h s 1971–72

m Aber 15.7.68 Kenneth T. Kennedy BA(Strath) educ admin, res fell. s of Robert K. Glasg

MACKENZIE Catherine Joan *MA 1963
d of Donald M. motor driver and Louise W. Campbell; b Ullapool 18.1.41
teacher: Hermitage acad Helensburgh 1964–67; Singapore: RAF g s Changi 1967–69, sen mistress RAF s s Seletar 1969–71; head of house/geog Denbigh s Bletchley 1971–73; sen mistress John Bunyan s Bedford 1973–75, dep head from 1975
m Bolton 16.7.71 Keith Cowcill des eng s of Stanley C. Bolton

MACKENZIE Catriona BSc 1968
d of John D. M. MA(Glas) teacher and Chirstie Mackay nurse; b Stornoway 4.5.45
teacher biol Rosa Bassett s Inner Lond 1969–70; lect sc Queen Margaret coll Edin from 1970

MACKENZIE Christina MA 1962

MACKENZIE Christine Craig *MA 1968
d of Alexander A. M. furn des and Annie L. Craig leg. acct; b 28.1.47
Dip Lib(Lond) 1970 ALA 1979
lib Dartford from 1977
m St Leonards-on-Sea 1970 James D. Johnston BA(Durh) organist s of James H. J. BD(Edin) St Leonards-on-Sea

MacKENZIE Christopher MA 1963 *1965
s of Angus MacK. crofter/joiner and Catherine MacPherson cook; b N Uist 24.3.40
teacher: Engl Powis j s s Aber, prin Gaelic Plockton from 1967
m Aber 29.6.62 Elizabeth M. K. Ely MA 1962 *qv*

MACKENZIE Colin Campbell Bannerman *MA 1970
s of Colin M. acct and Isabella W. Brown; b Aber 23.8.36
teacher Powis acad Aber 1971–73, prin hist from 1973
m Aber 26.7.69 Jean A. Birse d of John B. Aber

MACKENZIE Colin Ferguson MB ChB 1968
s of Lewis M. LRCPE g p and Janet S. Ferguson physioth; b Sheffield 16.3.42
FFARCS 1973
h o ARI 1968–69; m o Zambia flying doctor serv Ndola 1969–70; sen h o anaest, paediat univ hosp WI Kingston Jamaica 1970–71; sen h o anaest Middx hosp Lond 1972–73; regist anaest Royal Free hosp Lond 1973–74; sen regist anaest St Thomas's hosp Lond 1974–75; asst prof anaest univ of Maryland hosp Baltimore USA from 1975

MACKENZIE Colin Norman Paterson BSc(eng) 1961

MacKENZIE Colin Robert MA 1967
s of Daniel L. MacK. cabinetmaker and Irene Davie; b Glasg 11.11.35
Dip Educ Tech(Lond) 1974
lect Glenrothes tech coll 1968–70; sen lect educ tech Stevenson coll of f e Edin 1970–77; prin lect i/c continuing educ Portsmouth coll of art, des and f e from 1977
m Aber 25.9.65 Yvonne G. Mennie MA 1964 *qv*

MACKENZIE David George MA 1966

MACKENZIE David Shaw MA 1969 Dip Ed 1970

MacKENZIE Deirdre Catherine Ruby MA 1969
d of Alaister I. MacK. MA(Edin) C of S min and Deirdre Grenville (formerly Christine MacKenzie); b Kirkcaldy 29.8.47
teacher: Aber 1970–72, Airdrie 1973
m Aber 5.7.71 Charles McLaughlin MA 1972 insur broker/man. s of Charles McL. Glasg

MACKENZIE Derek MA 1958 Dip Ed 1959

MACKENZIE Donald BSc 1961 Dip Ed 1967
s of Alexander M. plumb. contr and Mary Macdonald teacher; b Plockton 12.11.40
teacher sc Portlethen s s 1962–69, Mackie acad Stonehaven 1969–76; prin sc Mearns acad from 1976; superv f e centre Mackie acad from 1973
m Aber 24.7.63 Sheila Walker teacher homecraft, lect Aber coll of educ d of John W. Turriff

MACKENZIE Donald *MA 1970
s of Roderick M. MA(Glas) teacher and Mary A. Mackenzie teacher; b Stornoway 3.1.49
res stud. Cantab 1970–73; lect Engl lit. Glas from 1973

MacKENZIE Donald Bothwell MA 1967 MEd 1970
s of Murdo J. MacK. MB ChB 1939 *qv* and Ethel Bothwell nurse; b Aber 14.7.46
ABPsS 1975
teacher Engl/psych N Lond h s 1968–70; educ psych: Lindsey c c 1970–74, Lincs c c 1974–78; dir Toynton Hall f e centre for handicapped school leavers (Linkage commun trust) Toynton from 1979
m Aber 8.8.69 Eileen M. Thow catering superv d of William T. Aber

McKENZIE Donald Seaton *BSc 1964
s of Donald A. McK. BSc(Glas) dir of stud. s of agr Aber and Sarah W. Seaton teacher home econ; b Tadcaster 2.8.42
PhD(Lond) 1967
post doct stud. univ Illinois Champagne-Urbana USA 1968–70; lect Queen Eliz coll Lond from 1971
m Urbana 13.2.70 Sati Parameswaran BSc(Delhi) res asst

McKENZIE Doris Irene MA 1970
m Beedie

McKENZIE Dorothy Jane MB ChB 1968
d of Alexander E. McK. iron driller, school jan and Lily W. Gavin cashier; b Aber 18.3.45
h o Hairmyres hosp Renfrewsh 1968–69, g p: Glasg 1969–71, part time Surbiton 1974–75, New Malden 1975–76, Long Ditton from 1976
m Aber 20.7.68 John A. MacKintosh BSc(agr) 1967 *qv*

McKENZIE Douglas MA 1963
s of Peter McK. hairdresser and Annie B. Daniel bookkeeper; b Peterhead 5.7.39
teacher maths Northfield acad Aber 1964–73, asst prin maths from 1974
m Aber 1.8.68 Beryl Booth teacher d of Alexander B. Aber

McKENZIE Douglas Andrew John *MA 1969

MACKENZIE Eona Flora MA 1960
d of John M. bus driver and Florence E. Maclennan clerkess; b Inv 31.12.39
teacher: Engl/Lat/geog Inv 1961–63, Rothes 1963–66, Lossiemouth 1966–70, geog Huntingdon from 1971
m Forres –.12.68 Christopher J. Lawless RAF s of Christopher J. L. Dublin

McKENZIE Francis Neil MB ChB 1968 ᶜMD 1973
s of Donald A. McK. BSc(Glas) dir of stud. s of agr Aber and Sarah W. Seaton teacher home econ; b Wetherby 13.6.44
FRCSE 1973
h o ARI 1969, regist; lect Aberd
m Rattvik Sweden 26.6.71 Anette M. Wallenstål lab tech d of Gősta W. Uppsala

McKENZIE George Rodney *BSc 1970
s of George McK. civ serv and Agnes Conlin; b Edin 7.9.46
genetics dept Aberd: res asst on ARC grant 1970–74, res off. from 1974
m Edin 4.9.68 Marian E. Stewart dom bursar, cler off.

McKENZIE Gerald Wood BSc 1964

MACKENZIE Gordon Ross BSc(agr) 1969
s of Alexander M. gardener/estate worker and Freda G. Johnston shop asst; b Nairn 8.1.48
BD(Glas) 1975
agr advis off. Benbecula 1969–72; C of S min Kirkmichael and Tomintoul par ch from 1977

MACKENZIE Grace Margaret BSc 1970
d of John H. M. boatbuilder and Mary A. Bunyan; b Buckie 6.5.44
m Fochabers 2.3.68 Derek C. Bain BSc 1966 *qv*

McKENZIE Hamish Stewart BSc 1958

McKENZIE Hazel BSc 1970

McKENZIE Heather Budge MA 1969 Dip Ed 1970
d of Sinclair McK. deep sea diver, tobacconist and Catherine W. Budge; b Thurso 22.3.48
Thurso h s: teacher Engl 1970–72, asst prin Engl 1972–76, prin Engl from 1976

MacKENZIE Hector Ralph *MA 1956
b Edin 8.8.34
FRGS 1962
lect geog Craigie coll of educ Ayr from 1965
m Aber 9.7.63 Leonora Garden BSc 1962 *qv*

MACKENZIE Helen Sey MA 1962
m Grant

MACKENZIE Helen Steedsman MA 1965
d of William M. shop owner and Helen Herd civ serv; b Dun 1.7.44
teacher: Johnstone 1966–68, Glengarnock 1971–74, in spec unit for ment handicapped Ballingry from 1974
m Aber 2.7.66 David Glover shop owner s of Douglas G. BD(Aber) 1971

MACKENZIE Hugh Niven MB ChB 1957
s of Herbert M. M. watchmaker and Leila M. Dunn teacher; b St Margaret's Hope Orkney 9.6.33
DObstRCOG 1964
h o Aber hosps 1957–58; m o RN UK, overseas 1958–63; h o obst Inv 1963–64; Canada: Nupawin Sask 1964–69; resid anaest Vancouver 1969–70, g p/anaest Powell River BC from 1970
m Croy –.10.64 Helen E. Glennie nurse d of William C. G. Gollanfield

MACKENZIE Iain MA 1964 BD 1967
s of Andrew H. M. carpenter, C of S min and Annie B. Barbour; b Clydebank 30.5.38
asst min Northfield ch Aber 1967–68; C of S min Blochairn ch Glasg 1968–73, St Martin's ch Port Glasg from 1973
m Glasg 10.6.61 Anna D. Rennie d of George R. Glasg

MACKENZIE Iain(John) Douglas BSc 1968

MacKENZIE Iain Grant *BSc 1967
s of Alastair G. MacK. MA 1930 *qv*; b Aber 27.2.45
MSc(Lond) 1971
dyn eng H.S.D. Stevenage 1967–69; math/statist R.C.A. Sunbury 1969–70; syst eng Elliott Bros Frimley 1970–71; lect maths RGIT Aber from 1972

MacKENZIE Ian Campbell MA 1966 BD 1969
s of John MacK. joiner and Jessie Dunsmore cashier; b Inv 11.2.45
C of S min: asst then ordained asst St James' (Pollock) ch Glasg 1969–70, min Gairbraid par ch Glasg from 1971
m Glasg 28.4.73 Mary J. Thomson secy d of James H. T. Glasg

McKENZIE Ian McLennan *MA 1964 MEd 1972

MACKENZIE James Alexander *MA 1970
s of James M. gamekeeper and Nancy Baikie; b Lairg 13.4.48
progr, syst des Logica Lond 1970–73; market. rep for computer syst Burroughs Wolverhampton 1973–77, market. man. from 1977

MacKENZIE (Hannah) Joan MA 1966
d of Angus Mack. carpenter/seaman and Mary M. MacLennan; b Aultbea 24.1.45
teacher: Fauldhouse s s 1967–70, backward pupils Dingwall acad 1970–72
m Inv 31.7.69 Douglas J. W. Milne MA 1967 *qv*

MACKENZIE Joan Margaret MA 1967 Dip Ed 1968
d of Murdo A. M. haulage contr and Margaret Macaulay teacher; b Ullapool 10.9.46
teacher: Lornshill acad Alloa 1968–69, Nicolson inst Stornoway 1969–71, Ullapool j s s 1971–74, Tain r acad from 1974
m Ullapool 18.10.77 Roderick P. Smith BSc(Edin) teacher s of Roderick S. Penicuik

MACKENZIE John MA 1958

McKENZIE John Neil MA 1970

MacKENZIE Kenneth MA 1965

MACKENZIE Kenneth *MA 1966
s of Daniel B. M. clerk and Emily S. Duthie; b Aber 27.6.44
Lond: econ Courtaulds 1966–68, dir's asst 1968–70; comp dir Hunter Barr & Co. Glasg 1970–72; dir Wilkinson Riddell & Larkins Birm 1972–76, man. dir from 1976 and chmn I. R. Morley from 1977
m Aber 15.10.66 Marjorie C. Thomson d of Edwin J. T. Aber

MacKENZIE Kenneth Angus Duncan *BSc 1969 PhD 1977

MACKENZIE Kenneth Donald BSc 1956 Dip Ed 1957
s of Kenneth J. M. civ serv and Louisa Mackenzie; b Stornoway 20.5.30
FBCS 1969
teacher Aber 1957–60; exper off. AWRE 1960–63; computer man. Atlas Computing Serv Lond 1963–68; asst dir univ of Lond computing centre from 1968

m Aber 4.7.58 Margaret J. McDonald teacher dom sc d of William M. McD. Cults

McKENZIE Kenneth John BSc(eng) 1967, 1968

MACKENZIE Lilian BSc 1970

MACKENZIE Malcolm Cumming BSc 1964
s of John M. plumber and Mary B. Cumming; b Tain 28.2.37
teacher: maths/sc Aberfoyle 1965–69, sc Inv h s 1969–72, prin biol from 1972
m Tain 23.4.57 Helen Macgregor hairdresser d of Alister M. Tain

MacKENZIE Malcolm Kenneth MA 1958
s of Kenneth M. MacK. and Emily Bryson; b Stornoway 9.7.37
BA(Lond) 1968 MA res (univ of E Af, Makerere Kampala) 1971 PhD(Lond) 1978
teacher Engl. hist, mod stud.: Fraserburgh acad 1959–61, Kemnay s s 1961–64; head Engl/geog St Joseph's coll Arua Uganda 1964–68; head geog Kololo sen s s Kampala 1968–71; teacher: Auchterderran j h s Glenrothes h s in 1968 and 1971; lect geog Notre Dame coll of educ Bearsden from 1971
m Aber 2.4.63 Mary S. Gardner nurse d of Hutton A. G. Kirkcaldy

MACKENZIE Margaret Miller Marwick MA 1970

McKENZIE Margaret Wood BSc 1959
d of George D. McK. MM marine engineman and Maggie A. D. Wood; b Aber 22.10.36
teacher maths: Aber acad 1960–65, part time Albyn s for girls Aber from 1972
m Aber 20.7.62 George D. Matthew BSc(eng) 1952 *qv*

MacKENZIE Marsali MA 1970

MACKENZIE Mary Isabel *BSc 1964 PhD 1967
d of Donald J. M. gen merch and Janet M. MacCulloch SRN; b Torridon 2.11.42
res asst potato market. board NOSCA Aber 1967–70
m Inv 21.9.68 William G. W. Paterson BSc(agr)(Glas) s of Hugh D. P. Hamilton

MACKENZIE Mary Macfarlane MA 1968 CASS 1970
b Applecross 3.5.47
soc worker Dunbartonsh from 1970

MACKENZIE Moira *MA 1968
d of Roderick A. M. area man. BR and Margaret Cowper; b Perth 8.5.46
freelance translator: Oss, Holland 1969–71, Lond from 1971
m Aber 18.7.69 Michael J. Dower BSc 1968 *qv*

MACKENZIE Mona Forbes MA 1967
m Paterson

MACKENZIE Morag MA 1961

McKENZIE Morag Anne MA 1965
d of James McK. master bldr/slater and Annie Stewart; b Aber 15.8.44
teacher: Engl/hist Aber 1966–68, Engl Elgin acad 1968–69, Engl/woman advis Keith g s 1969–71, asst rector from 1971
m Aber 2.8.68 Grant Munro acct s of Alexander B. M. Cornhill

MACKENZIE Myra MA 1962

MacKENZIE Nancy Baikie BSc 1964
m Reid

McKENZIE Richard Holder BSc(eng) 1968
s of John J. McK. fisherman and Doris E. Holder; b Lossiemouth 3.12.46
MICE 1973
Edin: site eng 1968–71, asst des eng from 1971
m Brora Isobel A. Fraser teacher d of Edward W. F. Brora

McKENZIE Robin Charles MA 1966
s of Robert T. McK. gen man. and Edith R. Kidd secy; b Castle Donnington 30.3.43
trg asst Stewarts & Lloyds (British Steel) Glasg 1966–67; pers man. Thomson reg newspapers Edin, Lond, Hemel Hempstead 1967–76; employee relations man. Weatherford/Lamb inc Aber from 1976
m Aber 26.8.67 Margaret Sinclair MA 1966 *qv*

MACKENZIE Robin Russell *MA 1961
s of George R. M. master ironmonger and Margaret K. P. Faulconbridge nurse; b Forres 8.10.39
MA(McM) 1966
Br. Council secondment Joensuu Finland 1962–63; teacher Engl Glasg 1963–65; grad teaching fell. Hamilton Canada 1965–66; Finland: dir EFL Helsinki 1966–67, univ lect Tampere 1967–70; lect Engl coll of tech Dun 1970–74; sen Engl instr King Faisal dir acad Riyadh, Saudi Arabia 1974–75; dir of stud. The Basil Paterson s of EFL Edin from 1975
m Forres 12.7.67 Eva-Liisa H. Hukari lib d of Erkki T. J. H. Viiala Finland

MACKENZIE Rosemary *MA 1965
d of Muriel J. M. farm man.; b Glasg 9.2.43
teacher Engl/hist RGC Aber 1966–69
m Aber 15.7.66 John R. Souter BSc 1963 *qv*

MacKENZIE Sheila BSc 1970
d of Simon M. prison off. and Nora A. Watt teacher, headmistress; b Perth 30.3.49
Dip Pers Man. (RGIT) MIPM
Marks & Spencer: trainee staff man. 1971–72, asst staff man. Lond (Kingston) 1972–73; teacher-training Perth W Aust 1974

McKENZIE Sheila Margaret BSc 1966 Dip Ed 1967
d of Allan McK. grocer and Margaret I. Watt; b Aber 22.10.45
teacher: Gordon Schools Huntly 1967–69, Powis s s Aber 1969, Inverurie acad 1969–70, Holt s Wokingham 1971–75
m Aber 5.7.69 David McGregor BSc 1967 *qv*

MacKENZIE Stuart Gregor *MA 1968

MACKENZIE Susan Patricia MA 1967

McKENZIE Swanson MA 1969
s of James McK. stone mason and Isabella Fowler; b Aber 24.2.27
teacher Aber from 1970
m Aber 10.5.50 Hilda M. Duguid MA 1969 *qv*

MACKENZIE Terry Faulconbridge *MA 1970
s of George R. M. master ironmonger and Margaret K. P. Faulconbridge nurse; b Forres 20.2.48
youth leader key youth centre E Kilbride 1972–74; museum educ off. Hamilton from 1974

m Aber 3.6.71 Patricia M. Hyslop MA 1972 d of James T. H. Huntly

McKENZIE Tessa BSc 1959
m Cowie

MACKENZIE Theodora MA 1959
d of William J. M. pre-cast cement bldr and Joanna W. Macdonald; b Alness 26.3.39
teacher: Engl/Lat Lenzie acad 1960–62, maths Netherhall, Cambridge 1962–64, head of dept 1964–66, maths/Latin Rumson country day s NJ USA 1967–68, chem Pike s Andover Mass USA from 1976
m Inv 26.7.62 John Logan BSc(Glas) dept head Bell tel labs USA s of Alexander J. L. Kildary

MacKENZIE Torquil BSc 1965

MACKENZIE Torquil Bruce MA 1961

MACKENZIE Vivianne Ross LLB 1970
d of Hugh M. master outfitter and Williamina M. Ross shopkeeper; b Inv 1.11.49
law app Tain 1970–72; leg. asst 1972–74
m Tain 19.8.72 John M. Reid asst acct s of John G. R. Aber

MACKENZIE William Donald *MA 1963
s of Matthew M. BSc(Glas) teacher and Jessie M. Campbell teacher; b Elgin 10.4.39
teacher Kirkcaldy 1964–67; sen fisheries dev off. Inv from 1967
m Aber 22.7.71 Eileen E. Bennett teacher d of John C. R. B. Aber

McKEOWN, John Robert *MA 1969
s of Robert M. O. McK. MB ChB (Belf) g p and Isabel A. Owen SRN; b Islington 23.2.46
Dip Ed(Sur) 1972 MEd(Sus) 1974
teacher ILEA Lond 1970–72; area educ psych W Sussex c c from 1974

McKERCHER Robert Barrie PhD 1966
s of James B. McK. farm. and Zelma E. Edgar; b Rosetown Sask Canada 3.1.31
BA(Sask) 1954 BSA(Sask) 1954 MSc(Sask) 1956
dept asst soil sc univ of Sask Saskatoon 1955–63; visiting res Macaulay inst for soil res Aber 1963–66; asst prof Sask 1966–71, assoc prof 1971–77, prof from 1977; visiting lect soil sc Aberd 1976–77
m Aber 26.3.65 Norma M. Mellis stenog d of Harry M. Aber

McKERLIE Marie Middleton *MA 1962
d of James McK. mech eng and Edith Middleton secy; b Aber 21.3.40
Dip Ed(Edin) 1963
teacher Engl: Aber 1963–66, Greenock 1967–68, Kilmarnock 1968–69
m Aber 22.7.66 Robert Cormack BSc(c eng) (Edin) civ eng s of William C. MRCVS Wick

McKERRELL Euan Harvey *BSc 1969
s of Robert McK. stat supt BEA Aber and Anna L. M. Harvey; b Kirkwall 25.3.45
scient Shell res Sittingbourne from 1969
m Aber 27.12.69 Sheena L. Forrest teacher d of James M. F. Aber

MacKERRON Donald Kinloch Lindsay *BSc 1966 PhD 1972

McKESSACK Ian Cecil MA 1964

MACKIE Aileen Elizabeth MB ChB 1962
d of Thomas G. M. furniture sales man. and Theresa M. Mitchell; b Aber 2.9.38
Aber: h o 1962–64, sen h o 1971–72, cas off. 1972–73, res asst genetics 1973–75, res asst med from 1975
m Aber 16.9.61 Alistair M. Flett BSc 1959 *qv*

MACKIE Alan Graham *MA 1970 MLitt 1972
s of Alan C. M. MA(Glas) teacher and Annie S. Graham MA(Glas) teacher; b Glasg 24.9.48
insp taxes Lond from 1971

MACKIE Alastair James MB ChB 1969
s of Gordon M. M. BCom 1937 *qv*; b Aber 31.7.45
MRCPsych 1975
employed by Grampian health board from 1969, spec psychiat from 1972
m Aber 2.1.70 Jennifer N. Pinnock MA 1970 *qv*

MACKIE Alexander Milne *BSc 1961 PhD 1965
s of Alexander M. joiner and Jemima Mathieson; b Aber 5.3.39
MIBiol 1972
res fell. dept chem Edin 1964–65, dept brewing and chem H-W 1965–66; res off. NERC inst of marine biochem from 1967

MACKIE Ann Elizabeth *MA 1968
d of Alan C. M. MA(Glas) teacher and Anne S. Graham MA(Glas) teacher; b Glasg 18.9.46
teacher maths Br of Don s Aber 1969–70; asst exper off. statist 1970–71, Scot. 1970–71; statist asst and market res Leyland 1971–73
m Aber 31.7.69 Kenneth G. Murdoch acct

MACKIE Brian Melvin BSc 1968
s of John A. M. civ serv and Catherine Hay secy; b Aber 24.4.47
Kingswood: actuarial stud. 1968–71; syst analyst from 1971

MACKIE Bruce George Wishart MA 1962

MACKIE Charles Christopher *BSc(eng) 1970
s of Alexander G. A. M. BSc 1932 *qv*; b Sandal 28.4.48
grad eng Freeman Fox & Ptnrs Lond 1970–76; eng Ninham Shand Cape Town from 1976
m Perth 3.3.73 Fiona J. Izatt d of Gordon W. I. Perth

MACKIE Charles Keith *BSc(agr) 1967
s of Charles T. M. eng and Mary A. Slessor; b Aber 9.9.44
agr advis Aber/Orkney 1967–71; advis off. (grassland) Aber from 1971

MACKIE David Morson *BSc 1967

MACKIE Dorothy Elizabeth MA 1958
m Hopkins

MACKIE Elizabeth Ann *MA 1969
d of Leask M. farm. and Annie Carnegie; b Ellon 4.9.46
Dip Cartog(Glas) 1970
asst cartog edit. map publ firm Lond 1971–72; asst translator and edit. Paris from 1972
m Dun 18.9.71 Ivan Sevo s of Jozo S. Trogir Yugoslavia

MACKIE Grahame John Sinclair BSc 1968
s of James M. M. shipbroker and Esther E. Sinclair teacher dress and des; b Ellon 4.9.46
teacher phys Peterhead acad 1969–70; trainee CA Aber

1970 Davidson prize acct Aber
m Aber 7.8.70 Elizabeth A. Duncan MA 1966 *qv*

MACKIE Isobel Macleod MA 1957
d of Adam G. M. bank man. and Mary A. Macaskill; b Tarbert Harris 2.1.37
teacher: royal s of Dunkeld 1958–59, Rhynie j s s 1960–61
m Aber 14.7.59 James F. Scott min of relig s of Robert S. Dalmally

MACKIE Isobel Margaret BSc 1966
d of Irvine M. farm. and Isabella G. Innes; b Rathen 21.10.44
teacher maths: Goodlyburn s s Perth 1967–71, Elgin acad 1971–74, asst prin maths from 1974

MACKIE Kathleen Isobel MA 1966
m McConkey

MACKIE Lesley Margaret Hall BSc 1970
m(1) Jamieson
(2) Anderson

MACKIE Maitland BSc(agr) 1958 *MA 1971
s of Maitland M. BSc(agr) 1932 *qv*; b Aber 21.9.37
farm. Westertown Oldmeldrum from 1958
m Norway 30.7.62 Halldis A. Ramn MB ChB 1963 *qv*

MACKIE Margaret Clubb BSc 1956
d of William A. J. M. shoemaker and Jane J. Clubb shopkeeper; b Aber 23.3.35
teacher Aber: sc Ruthrieston s s 1957–60, biol coll of comm 1967–73, sc/biol Kincorth acad from 1973
m Hatton 21.9.57 John F. Bruce arch. s of Fyvie B. Cruden Bay

MACKIE Mary Elizabeth *MA 1956
m Fraser

MACKIE Mary Mowat Ross MA 1958
d of Maitland M. BSc(agr) 1932 *qv*; b Rothienorman 15.8.36
teacher: Bankhead acad Aber 1959–60, Kadavu prov s Fiji 1960–61, Kintore 1961, Duncanrig s E Kilbride 1969–74, part-time Aboyne acad from 1974
m Daviot 6.2.60 David S. C. Levie BL 1958 *qv*

MACKIE Michael James BMedBiol 1970 MB ChB 1973
s of James F. M. MB ChB 1947 *qv*; b Aber 17.11.48
h o ARI 1973–74; lect dept med Aberd from 1974
m Aber 22.5.70 Shiona E. R. Hambrook MB ChB 1972 trainee g p d of Frederick H. Malaya

MACKIE Neil Lorimer BSc 1962

McKIE Penelope Jane *MA 1968 Dip Mediaeval St 1969
d of James M. F. McK. quantity surv and Jane G. Hendry; b Glasg 19.8.45
rare book cataloguer Lib Comp of Philadelphia USA 1970–72; asst archivist GLRO (Middx records) Lond 1973–75
m Aber 25.7.70 Colin S. Berry PhD(Lond) biochem s of Joseph G. B. Hayes

MACKIE Robert Norrie MB ChB 1960 *MD 1965
s of Robert C. M. man. dir N of S Orkney & Shetland shipping comp, Lloyds underwriter and Jessie A. Norrie; b Aber 29.7.36
Strachan bursary 1959 Venn essay prize 1959 McQuibban prize med 1960 Cash gold medal, Thursfield award 1965
h o Gilbert Bain hosp Lerwick, Woodend hosp Aber 1960–61; Aberd: Garden res fell./lect anat 1961–65, lect med 1965–66; dep dir stud. health serv Aberd; sen resid Balgownie Lodge Aber 1967–71; inaugural dir stud. health serv univ of W Aust, Perth from 1971; many locums g p and private pract UK, W Aust from 1961 and m o WA sec teachers' coll from 1976
m Aber 31.10.62 Beatrice W. Findlater teacher d of John W. F. Aber

MACKIE Ruth Anne MA 1967
m Hillen

MACKIE Sylvia Christina Winifred MA 1956
m Lewis

MACKIE Thomas David BSc 1966
s of Thomas M. elect. eng and Gladys N. Mathieson; b Aber 24.12.42
Brit Petroleum Co: supply analyst Lond 1966–71, supply asst New York 1972–73, proj analyst Lond from 1973

MACKIE William Alexander BSc(eng) 1963

McKILLIGAN Margaret Jean *BSc 1970
d of John McK. publican and Margaret Mathieson; b Aber 24.1.49
Dip Lib(Strath) 1974
res Aberd 1970–73; abstractor/lib Edin 1974–76
m Aber 14.2.76 John R. Tillson BEng(UWIST) scient, farm. s of Wilfred T. Boston Lincs

McKILLIGAN Neil Gordon *BSc 1965 Dip Ed 1966

McKILLIGAN Sheila Ann *BSc 1968 PhD 1971
d of Stanley M. McK. PO tel tech and Mary J. Gordon; b Aber 27.6.46
Harkness fell. of commonwealth fund of NY univ of Calif Berkeley 1971–73; lect maths Aberd from 1973

McKILLIGIN Gordon George BSc(agr) 1962
s of Foster F. McK. bank man. and Lizzie I. Stewart; b Ellon 20.5.37
civ serv: asst insp DAFS Thurso 1962–74, insp Ayr from 1974
m Turriff 21.3.64 Evelyn M. Stephen clerkess d of Walter S. S. Turriff

McKILLIGIN Helen Rose MB ChB 1958
d of Foster F. McK. bank man. and Lizzie I. Stewart; b Ellon 29.8.34
DCH(Glasg) 1960 DObstRCOG 1960 FRCP(C)1965 MPH(Berkeley) 1974
resid regist sick ch hosp Yorkhill Glasg 1960–64; St John's Newfoundland: paediat 1964–66, chief neonatology Grace gen hosp 1966–73, prof mat. and ch health Memorial univ from 1974
m Tor 1966 Dexter Hawkins insur adjuster s of Harry H. Mt Pearl Newfoundland

MACKILLOP, Morag Johnston *BSc 1956
m Butler

MACKINNON Adèle Francis MA 1968 (conferred for long service of exceptional merit)
d of Robert M. OBE civ serv and Georgette du Betier; b Glasg 1917
Aberd: member of staff of dept of p e from 1943 and dir of p e for women students from 1958; retd 1975

MACKINNON Catriona Jean MA 1970

McKINNON Christina Margaret MA 1962
d of Roderick McK. weaver and Mary A. Macdonald; b Lochs Is of Lewis 12.11.39
teacher: AGS 1963–65, Reading 1966–69
m Aber 22.7.65 John Slater MA 1961 *qv*

MACKINNON John Angus LLB 1968
s of Alexander M. postman and Margaret Macraild; b Skye 22.1.47
law app Edin 1968–70; Fraserburgh: asst solic 1970–74, ptnr in law firm from 1974
m Aber 2.7.71 Sandra M. Rankin MA 1969 *qv*

MACKINNON Kathleen Lamont *MA 1962
d of John C. M. master mariner and Elizabeth L. Macdonald teacher; b Inv 3.10.40
MA(Nova Scotia) 1964 Dip Psych(NUI) 1974
asst archivist St Francis Xavier univ Nova Scotia 1963–64; teacher Engl/Gaelic Bellahouston acad Glasg 1965–67; clin psych ch hosp Crumlin Dublin from 1974; part time lect psych univ coll Dublin from 1974
m Glasg 30.8.67 John M. Kennedy PhD(Lond) lect UCD s of David K. MSc(Belf) Belfast

MACKINNON Margaret Christine Macdonald MA 1964
d of Hugh M. min of relig and Annie M. Mackinnon MA(Glas) teacher; b Uig Is of Skye 4.11.41
teacher: St Andrew's p s Rothesay 1965–67, remed asst Rothesay p s from 1967

MACKINNON Neil Bruce MA 1964 *1966
s of Neil M. oil comp supt and Andrewina McKenzie; b Aber 12.1.25
teacher: Aber 1967–75, Gaelic Argyll 1975–76; indep Gaelic res Highlands and Islands/admin in oil and oil-related indust from 1976
m Aber 9.11.55 Louise Reid bus. prop. d of Robert R. Cults

MACKINNON Patricia Isabella MB ChB 1968
d of John M. textile teacher and Isabella W. Hewat; b Edin 12.1.44
LMCC 1971
h o: RNI Inv 1968–69, Whiston hosp Prescott 1969; g p Brockville Ontario from 1969
m Aber 27.12.67 Alexander Slowey MB ChB 1968 *qv*

MACKINTOSH Elizabeth Cameron
see Cameron-Mackintosh

MACKINTOSH Frances Mary *BSc 1965
d of Alexander W. P. M. textile machinery inventor and Eunice M. Moulden; b Leic 17.3.43
m Toronto 31.12.65 Alan H. Vŷse BSc(for) 1964 *qv*

MACKINTOSH Helen Campbell BSc 1963
d of Robert M. bank man. and Isobel M. J. C. Campbell; b Elgin 27.1.43
computer progr: BAC Weybridge 1963–66, Strath 1966–69, CAP 1969–72
m Dornoch 16.12.72 Philip H. Baldwin comput oper man., quality assur analyst

MACKINTOSH John Allan *BSc(agr) 1967
s of Alexander M. crofter/agr merch and Catherine M. Cameron; b Fort William 19.5.43
W of S agr coll: agr econ Glasg 1967–72, Ayr 1972–73; man. prod. econ Milk Marketing Board Thames Ditton 1973–77, sen econ from 1977
m Aber 20.7.68 Dorothy J. McKenzie MB ChB 1968 *qv*

MACKINTOSH Marguerita Graham MA 1964
d of Kenneth M. MA 1924 *qv* and Annie S. Brown MA 1927 *qv*; b Bombay 3.4.44
teacher Engl Prestonpans from 1965
m Edin —.3.75 Kenneth Mackenzie police off. s of Kenneth M. Ardersier

MACKINTOSH Peter Jones *MA 1970

McKIRDY Ian William *MA 1970
s of William McK. salesman and Margaret Murphy teacher; b Glasg 16.4.48
m Aber 25.6.70 Jennifer Wilson teacher d of William W. Yetholm

MACKLAND Sheila *BSc 1970
d of Alexander M. comm man. and Georgina K. Loveday; b Aber 1.8.48
children's lib Aber c lib 1970–75
m Aber 21.12.73 Ian Wildgoose BSc 1964 *qv*

MACKLIN Frederick Creswell *MA 1958
s of Frederick C. M. comm trav and Elizabeth G. W. Angus; b Aber 11.3.35
teacher Fr/Span: AGS 1960–66, Queen's s BAOR Rheindahlen W Ger 1966–70; prin Fr Anderson h s Lerwick 1970–72; lect mod lang Aber coll of educ from 1972
m Forres 20.7.62 Anne Paterson teacher d of William P. Forres

MACKLON Alan Edward Stephen PhD 1962
s of Charles S. M. civ serv and Olive A. Pinks GPO tel; b Dover 2.10.36
BSc(Nott) 1959
scient off. Macaulay inst for soil res Aber from 1962; res assoc Washington state univ 1966–67
m Cambridge 30.4.60 Bridget J. Carr SRN d of Oliver G. C. Cambridge

MACKNESS Jennifer Mary BSc 1968
d of Ronald A. M. BSc(Lond) dep dir gen meat & livestock comm and Mary E. Bird; b Northampton 10.8.46
res tech: vet coll Edin 1969–71, electron microscopic unit vet coll Lond 1971–75
m Radlett 17.7.71 Alan W. Downie BSc(H-W) civ eng s of David M. D. Edin

McKNIGHT Elizabeth Mary MA 1959
m Duncan

MacLACHLAN David Connor MB ChB 1966
BDS(Glas)

McLACHLAN Derek Neil BSc 1967
s of Donald McL. surv. customs & excise and Eva Blair; b Aber 21.10.46
computer progr: N'cle-under-Lyme 1967–69, Edin 1969–74; sen computer progr Edin 1971–73; syst consult. Edin 1973–74; analyst/progr Vienna from 1974
m Edin 21,7.72 Catherine P. Brown SRN d of Andrew B. B. Edin

MacLACHLAN Janet Low MA 1969
d of John L. MacL. BSc. 1955 *qv*; b Inv 27.11.47
stud. interpreter/translator Aber from 1972; qualif as interpreter/translator Aber coll of comm 1975

MacLACHLAN Joan Mairi Scott MA 1963
d of John S. MacL. MA 1937 *qv* and Ena B. S. Duguid MA 1937 *qv*; b Inv 27.5.42
teacher Aber: h s for girls 1964–69, Cornhill p s from 1969
m Aber 17.7.74 George P. Gordon MA 1968 *qv*

MacLACHLAN Robin Mathieson MB ChB 1958
s of Albert MacL. prof footballer, hotelier, club steward and Jean Mathieson; b Dumfries 8.1.34
DObst(NZ) 1961
Wanganui N Z: h s posts 1958–60, g p from 1961
m Wellington NZ Pamela A. Mirams d of L. Holden M. N Z

McLANNAHAN James Maxwell BSc(for) 1968
s of George G. McL. airline pilot, man. exec and Marjorie Maxwell; b Cairo 19.1.44
conserv Lower Swansea valley proj 1968–69; asst dir of for. Grosvenor Estates Chester 1969–71; area man. Eastern Woodlands assoc Norwich 1971–75; lect for. Cumbria coll of agr & for. Newton Rigg Penrith from 1976
m Plemstall 1.9.69 Heather M. C. Kneale D.Phil(Oxon) res scient anim behaviour d of Thomas K. BSc(eng)(Liv) Chester

McLAREN Alison Christine Muirhead MA 1969
d of Hugh C. McL. MB ChB(Glas) prof obst/gyn Birm and Lois E. J. Muirhead; b Birm 9.12.47
teacher: Fr Northfield comp s Birm 1972–73, Fr/Ger Edgbaston h s for girls 1973–74
m Birm 28.12.73 Brendan M. Coughlan MB ChB(Dub) consult. obst/gyn s of Rupert C. Dublin

MACLAREN (Archibald) Allan *MA 1964 PhD 1971
s of William M. rly eng driver and Jane Ritchie; b Brechin 3.11.33
lect: pol econ Aberd 1965–68, sociol Strath from 1968

McLAREN Brian Alfred BSc 1969

MacLAREN Donald *BSc(agr) 1966
s of Ian MacL. factor and Agnes W. Mitchell; b Douglas Lanark 1.9.42
MS(Corn) 1968 PhD(Corn) 1970
lect agr econ Aberd from 1970; visiting assoc prof univ of Gwelph Canada 1975
m Aber 28.7.66 Eileen Gordon BSc 1962 *qv*

McLAREN Elizabeth Drysdale *MA 1968
d of Hugh M. McL. MB ChB(Glas) g p and Patricia J. S. Drysdale nurse, dietitian; b Glasg 21.5.46
teacher geog: Helensburgh 1969–70, Allan Glen's s Glasg 1970–72, Cranhill s s Glasg 1972, prin geog Glasg h s for girls (later Clevedon s) 1972–74
m Aber 21.9.73 James A. Wilson BSc(eng) 1968 *qv*

McLAREN James Fergus *MA 1970 LLB 1972
s of Robert C. McL. MB ChB(Edin) g p and Elizabeth M. Ross SRN; b Edin 29.2.48
law app Brodies W.S. Edin 1972–74, solic and leg. asst 1974–75, ptnr from 1975

McLAREN Jean MA 1957
d of William McL. boilerman and Lizzie E. Gray; b Keith 8.6.36
teacher Cairnie p s 1958–59, Aberlour s s from 1971
m Keith 15.4.59 William G. Stuart draper s of William S. Keith

McLAREN Lorna Elizabeth MA 1969
d of Archibald D. McL. squad ldr RAF and Eleanor Macfarlane teacher; b Perth 27.7.48
teacher lang: Dun 1970–71, Maidstone 1971–72, Inv from 1973
m Dun 10.7.71 Allan M. Robertson BSc(Dund) civ eng s of Walter G. R. Dun

McLAREN Lyndon Edison PhD 1956
s of Uriah A. McL. farm. and Eulah L. Mitchell teacher; b St Thomas Jamaica 15.4.23
BSc(Edin) 1950 MRCVS 1950 MIBiol 1956
Min of Agr Jamaica: vet off. Montego Bay 1951–53, anim nutrit off. Old Harbour 1956–65, dir live stock res Old Harbour 1965–72, chief tech off. Kingston 1972–76, permanent secy Kingston 1976–78; reg dir Antillean Zone Inter American Inst of Agr Sciences Santo Domingo Dominican Republic from 1978
m Kingston 30.6.62 Leonie G. Perkins BA(USA) journalist/broadcaster d of Kenneth G. P. St Ann Jamaica

McLAREN Maurice Paterson Ross BSc(agr) 1967 *1968

McLAREN Morag MA 1968
d of William McL. boilerman and Lizzie E. Gray; b Keith 9.6.47
teacher: Fr/Engl Banff 1969–70, Keith from 1970
m. Keith 18.7.70 David A. Sadler elect. eng s of Jim S. Northwich

McLAREN Peter BSc(agr) 1961
s of James McL. farm. and Elizabeth W. S. Craig; b St Andrews 17.7.39
farm. Fife from 1961
m Kettle 23.7.64 Margaret M. Sangster BSc(Edin) teacher d of Harry S. BSc(agr) 1950 *qv*

McLARTY Donald Gillies MB ChB 1965 ᶜMD 1974
s of Donald McL. sea capt and Janet Duff civ serv; b Ardrishaig 22.6.40
MRCP 1971
res asst, Hall fell., res regist med W I Glasg 1966–72; lect materia medica Glas 1972–77; sen lect med univ of Dar Es Salaam from 1977
m Edin 4.7.69 Dorothy C. T. Buchanan physioth d of Thomas B. Gullane

McLAUGHLIN Robert Henry *BSc 1961

MACLEAN Alasdair *MA 1970

MACLEAN Alasdair Smith MA 1965
s of Donald M. crofter/insur ag and Mary A. Smith; b Stornoway 21.3.44
Dip. Bus. Man.(Strath) 1966
NAAFI: trainee dist man. Aden 1967–68, dist man. Lincolnsh 1968–69, Persian Gulf 1969–70, Newcastle 1970–71, Glasg 1971–72, Londonderry 1973–74, Yorks 1974–75, Düsseldorf W. Ger from 1975
m Glasg 4.1.74 Dolina McInnes hosp caterer d of Donald McI. Tong Is of Lewis

McLEAN Alastair John *BSc 1960
s of Hugh McL. comm trav and Alice A. Elliot; b Aber 19.6.39
geol/geophys Nyasaland geol surv Blantyre 1960–64; hydro geol/eng geol Ghana geol surv Kumasi 1964–65; open cast exec nat coal board/site geol Westfield Fife 1965–66; NSW Aust: coal geol Broken Hill Proprietary Co NSW and Queensland Newcastle NSW 1966–69; Clutha Dev coalmining geol and exploration Aust and N Z: geol Camden NSW 1969–71, sen geol 1971–74, chief geol from 1974
m Aber 5.9.60 Ariane Charitonowsky MA 1964 *qv*

McLEAN Albert MA 1966
s of Albert F. McL. soldier and Jane D. Farquhar; b Aber 17.5.42
teacher Aber: Holy Family p s 1967–70, Cornhill p s 1970–73, asst head Broomhill p s from 1973
m Aber 19.9.64 Christian B. McCallum secy d of George McC. Aber

MACLEAN Alexander Fitzroy MB ChB 1965
s of Donald M. master grocer and Mary M. Dickie milliner; b Helensburgh 7.8.39
DObstRCOG 1968 MRCGP 1975
h o: ARI, City hosp Aber, Aber mat. hosp 1966–67; g p Banchory from 1967
m Helensburgh 2.4.66 Margaret A. McKinlay teacher mus d of James McK. Helensburgh

MACLEAN Alice Isobel MA 1960
d of Duncan M. roadman and Margaret Maciver; b Gairloch 17.9.39
teacher: inf Dingwall acad 1961–64, Poolewe 1964–69, Gairloch from 1969
m Achnasheen 2.4.69 Roderick MacKenzie butcher s of Kenneth MacK. Gairloch

MACLEAN Alison Mary MA 1961
d of Ronald M. MB ChB 1930 *qv*; b Inv 14.3.40
teacher Engl/Fr Bridge of Don s Aber 1962–66
m Inv 27.3.65 Harold A. Bremner MB ChB 1964 *qv*

MacLEAN Alistair William *MA 1965
s of Roderick C. MacL. MA 1940 *qv* and Gladys Calder MA 1937 *qv*; b Aber 24.4.43
MA (Queen's univ Kingston Canada) 1967 PhD (Queen's univ) 1969
commonwealth school Queen's univ Kingston Canada 1965–69; res assoc/post doct fell. Edin 1969–71; asst prof psych Queen's univ Kingston 1971–75, assoc prof from 1975
m Edmonton 15.7.67 Helen E. Seth BA(Alta) ch psych/univ instr d of William E. S. Castor Alta

MacLEAN Allaster Graham *BSc(eng) 1967

MacLEAN Angus Alick MA 1956
s of Allan McL. ferryman/storeman and Marion MacDougall; b N. Uist 30.5.34
nat serv RAEC BAOR Germany 1957–59; teacher Paible j s s N Uist 1959–62; housemaster Balmacara s 1962–65; dep head Paible j s s 1965–68, head 1968–73; head Mallaig j s s from 1973
m Glasg 10.7.68 Christina Macdonald MA 1961 *qv*

MACLEAN Christeen BEd 1969
d of Jon L. MacL. driver and Hannah Macdonald book keeper; b Isle of Lewis 4.4.48
teacher: drama Aber 1969–70, Engl/head of house Lond from 1970
m Aber 17.7.70 Christopher A. Fleming BSc 1970 *qv*

MACLEAN Christina Anne MA 1965
d of Lachlan J. M. seaman and Johanna Smith; b Glasg 8.2.44
Dip. Soc Sc(Edin) 1966
ch care off. Dunbartonsh 1966–69; soc worker, area soc worker Argyll from 1968

MACLEAN Christina Joan MA 1961

McLEAN Doris Margaret MB ChB 1967 MD 1973
d of James J. McL. MA 1931 *qv*; b Aber 24.1.42
DObstRCOG MRCOG 1974
h o Aber hosps 1967–69; res fell. dept obst Aberd 1969–73; sen h o obst/gyn Aber hosps; temp lect dept obst/gyn and physiol Aberd 1974–75; lect obst/gyn and physiol Aberd from 1975
m Aber 3.8.68 Alasdair J. Campbell BSc 1963 *qv*

MacLEAN Douglas Gordon BSc 1962

MACLEAN Effie *MA 1957

McLEAN Elspeth Margaret MA 1961
d of Robert K. McL. tea planter and Helen C. McLean MA 1931 *qv*; b Assam 12.1.40
teacher Engl: Ijebu-Ode g s W Nigeria 1962–64, Duncanrig s s E Kilbride 1964–65, teacher trg coll Machakos 1969–70, Machakos boys' s Kenya 1970–71, Mumbuni s Machakos 1971–72
m Aber 24.7.62 Alasdair G. MacLure MA 1957 *qv*

MacLEAN George Frederick *MA 1970
s of Calum G. MacL. stevedore and Jessie C. MacBean clerk/shorthand typist; b Middlesbrough 17.3.48
teacher Engl: Dingwall acad 1971–74, Millburn acad Inv from 1974
m 20.7.76 Mary MacLeod MA 1969 *qv*

MacLEAN Gillian Isabel *MA 1968
d of Roderick C. MacL. MA 1940 *qv* and Gladys Calder MA 1937 *qv*; b Aber 25.7.47
Dip Lib(Strath) 1972
lib: mus dept publ lib Edin 1968–70, Wm Porteous Glasg 1970–71; contr res asst BBC Glas from 1972
m Aber 26.7.68 Iain K. Brodie MA 1966 *qv*

MACLEAN Graham Douglas MB ChB 1962
s of Frank S. M. MB ChB 1925 *qv*; b Leicester 25.5.38
MRCGP 1973
h o: Gilbert Bain hosp Lerwick, Woodend hosp Aber ARI 1962–64; resid m o Aber mat. hosp 1964; regist dermat ARI 1964–68; g p Aber from 1969
m Aber 20.7.63 Margaret M. Hepburn teacher d of Alexander J. H. MA 1930 *qv*(III)

MACLEAN Hamish *MA 1970
s of Alistair M. banker and Sandra M. Fraser; b Inv 4.10.48
teacher; Portobello h s Edin 1971–76, Bridge of Don acad Aber from 1976

MACLEAN Hugh Alexander *BSc 1970
s of Donald J. M. bldg contr and Margaret Sutherland; b Dornoch 5.12.48
teacher geog Wallace h s Stirling from 1971

MACLEAN Iain Edgar *MA 1967
s of John M. bank man. and Annie E. Hunter; b Aber 2.8.45
ABPsS
dem psych dept Strath 1967–69, lect 1969–71; lect educ stud. Callander Park coll of educ Falkirk 1971–74; lect educ psych Aber coll of educ from 1975
m Aber 2.7.69 Patricia M. Ewen MA 1967 *qv*

MACLEAN Iain Gilleasbuig *MA 1967
s of Donald A. M. MA(Glas) head teacher and Margaret J. C. Smith; b Waternish Is of Skye 1.1.45
BR: man. trainee Scot. h q Glasg 1967–69, asst area man. Irvine 1969–71, relief superv Aber 1971–72, Scot. h q asst greater Glasg trans stud. 1972–73, plan. asst Suburban serv Glasg from 1973

MACLEAN Iain Lorne *MA 1967

MACLEAN Iain Matheson MB ChB 1962
s of Murdo M. MB ChB(Glas) g p and Catherine Matheson SRN; b Dunvegan 12.2.36
DObstRCOG 1966
h o City hosp Aber, cas unit Aber 1963–64; govt m o Darwin Falkland Is 1964–65; h o obst W Gen hosp Edin, Barrow-in-Furness 1965–66; sen h o surg RI Glasg 1966–67; regist obst Glasg 1967–69; g p: Edin 1969–74, Is of Tiree from 1974

m Glasg 1968 Alexandra Macdonald SRN d of Doney C. J. M. Inv

MacLEAN Ian George Armstrong BSc(eng) 1970

MacLEAN Ian Teasdale MA 1961 LL B 1963
s of Roderick MacL. master baker and Joan Teasdale; b Stornoway 3.6.40
Aber: law app 1961–64, leg. asst J. D. Mackie & Dewar advoc from 1965
m Aber 1.8.73 Lavinia M. Symonds d of Henry A. S. Aber

MacLEAN Ian William BSc 1964
s of William MacL. slater and Isabella Ross MA 1923 *qv*; b Inv 30.1.38
teacher phys Inv from 1965

MACLEAN Ishbel Macleod MB ChB 1969
d of John M. bldg contr and Mary Macleod teacher; b Skye 18.6.46
h o: City hosp, Woodend gen hosp Aber 1969–70; m o Dun 1973–74; part-time med pract in leprosy/gen med clin Taipei Taiwan from 1975
m Aber 27.12.68 Cameron Tallach MB ChB 1968 *qv*

MACLEAN Jeannie Bishop MA 1967
d of Duncan M. M. farm. and Marion B. Learmonth; b Carlisle 11.9.45
Dip Marketing(Strath) 1968
teacher Glasg 1968–69; pers asst Yorks 1969–71; Lond: coordinator 1971–72, admin from 1972

MACLEAN Jennifer Munro MA 1968 Dip Ed 1969
d of Donald B. M. gardener, engineer and Martha Munro teacher; b Invergordon 12.6.47
teacher p s Glasg 1969–70
m Aber 7.9.70 Alexander R. Dawson LL B 1968 *qv*

McLEAN John MA 1962
s of John McL. trawl skipper and Violet Harrison factory worker; b Aber 3.11.38
BD(Edin) 1965
C of S min: asst Edin 1966–67, mission. Nagpur India 1967–70, Bathgate from 1970
m Aber 18.3.63 Iris McDonald tax off. d of William McD. Aber

MACLEAN John BSc 1970
s of Neil M. crofter/weaver and Mary Macleod; b Carloway Is of Lewis 17.12.48
MLitt(Edin) 1973
retail sales dept Procter & Gamble Glasg from 1973

McLEAN Kenneth MB ChB 1956
s of Leslie G. McL. MB ChB 1924 *qv*(II, III) and Helen I. Yuill MA 1924 *qv*; b Dun 28.4.32
Dip Soc Med(Edin) 1969 MRCGP 1972
h o ARI, Woodend hosp Aber; nat serv capt RAMC 1957–59; g p: Notts 1959–60, Dalkeith from 1960
m Edin 7.3.58 Nancy P. Cruickshank MB ChB 1957 *qv*

MACLEAN Margaret MA 1965
d of Dugald M. butcher and Isabel M. Macrae nurse; b Stornoway 26.9.42
civ serv: Lond 1965–70, Edin from 1970

McLEAN Margaret *MA 1968

McLEAN Margaret Brodie MA 1967
d of James McL. s admin asst and Mary B. McFarlane cler asst; b Paisley 16.11.46
teacher Engl Paisley 1968–73, asst prin Engl from 1973
m Glasg 15.7.71 David Arthur MA(Glas) teacher s of David A. Glasg

MACLEAN Margaret Park MA 1962 Dip Ed 1963
d of Alexander J. M. MA 1929 *qv*; b Is of Lewis 26.6.41
teacher: p s Broxburn 1963–66, Prince Rupert s BFES Wilhelmshaven, Germany 1966–67, Engl dept Fairchildes h s Croydon 1967–69
m 12.8.67 John V. O'Brien BE(Dub) chem eng s of John J. O'B. Lismore

MACLEAN Marion MA 1965
d of Angus M. fisherman and Mary Macsween; b Heswall 30.5.43
teacher Logan Ayrsh p s 1966–68, maths Hastings s s NZ 1968–71 and from 1975
m Hastings NZ 8.2.72 Winfried L. Heuser horticulturist s of Andreas H. W Ger

McLEAN Marlyn Hamilton MA 1969

MACLEAN Mary *BSc 1968
m Panko

MACLEAN Murdina *MA 1969
d of Neil M. crofter/weaver and Mary Macleod; b Carloway Is of Lewis 25.1.47
teacher: Lochside RC j s s Fort William 1970–71, Kincorth acad Aber 1971–72
m Carloway 13.8.71 James A. Skinner MB ChB 1969 *qv*

MACLEAN Murdoch William MB ChB 1961
s of Murdoch M. police off., hotelier and Lilian D. Rolles hotelier; b Lond 9.11.35
DObstRCOG 1963 MRCOG 1967 ECFMG 1970 FRCOG 1980
h o Aber 1961–63; regist sen regist Aber hosps 1963–73; consult. obst/gyn Highland health board/clin sen lect Aberd from 1973
m Aber 21.6.63 Margaret R. Anderson MB ChB 1961 *qv*

MacLEAN Norman *MA 1967
s of Dugald MacL. butcher and Isobel M. Macrae nurse; b Stornoway 22.3.45
Dip Urb & Reg St(Birm) 1969
teacher 1968; GLC tree counter 1970; hosp porter, PO clerk 1971; tv prod. 1972–74; elect. from 1975

MACLEAN Patricia MacDonald *MA 1969

McLEAN Roderick *MA 1962
s of McGregor McL. LDS dent surg and Margaret E. Forbes nurse; b Aber 12.10.40
teacher Engl Fraserburgh 1963–72; prin Engl Banchory from 1972
m Aber 29.6.63 Alice M. Stevenson pharm d of David S. Aber

McLEAN Ronald Alexander *BSc 1969

MacLEAN Ronald Deans *MA 1964

McLEAN Sheila Stewart MA 1968
d of Malcolm A. McL. publican and Lily M. McGregor; b Torphins 4.7.46
teacher hist/mod stud. Dunfermline 1969–70
m Edin 27.6.70 Ian D. Miller LL B 1967 *qv*

McLEISH Alan Watson MA 1970
s of James McL. baker and Agnes Smith; b Edin 14.2.47
teacher hist Penicuik 1971–76, asst prin guid from 1976

McLEISH David Nigel Kerr *BSc 1969

McLEISH Robert *MA 1968
s of Robert McL. clerk and Elizabeth H. Lang clerkess; b Glasg 13.12.45
BMus(Liv) 1969
teacher mus: John Hampden s High Wycombe 1969–70, RGC Aber 1971–75; prin mus Kirkcudbright acad from 1975

MacLELLAN Ailsae Mary *BSc 1969
d of Angus J. MacL. MB ChB(Glas) g p and Anne B. Martin nurs sister; b Dublin 27.3.45
Dip Plant Taxonomy(Edin) 1970
res stud. Aber 1971–74

McLELLAN Colin Currie MA 1957
s of John S. McL. baker and Catherine Currie; b Airdrie 7.8.30
teacher maths Lanarksh 1958–70; prin maths Strathclyde reg from 1970
m Glasg 4.8.61 Margaret P. Munro d of John M. Glasg

McLELLAN John Currie McKellar *MA 1956

McLEMAN Alexander Watt BSc 1968 *1971
s of James McL. postman and Rosemary Watt; b Fraserburgh 4.4.47
teacher chem: Peterhead acad 1969–70, Portobello h s 1971–73; asst prin sc Broughton h s 1973–80, prin chem Lasswade h s from 1980
m Fraserburgh 24.7.71 Elizabeth C. Buchan teacher d of James B.

McLEMAN Doreen MA 1961

McLEMAN James BSc 1970
s of James McL. lab, postman and Rosemary Watt; b Fraserburgh 15.8.48
MInstAM 1976 MMS 1978
trainee organis and method Edin 1970–73; organis and method analyst Stratford-on-Avon from 1973
m Aber 12.9.70 Dena Y. Robertson lab tech d of George B. A. R. Aber

McLEMAN Margaret Fraser MA 1967
d of George L. McL. dept foreman and Margaret F. Johnstone; b Fraserburgh 18.6.46
teacher: Fr/Lat Fraserburgh acad 1968–72, prin guid from 1972

MacLENNAN Alasdair Balfour BSc(agr) 1966
s of William B. MacL. pilot and Jeannie Logan; b Birkenhead 8.6.43
anim husb off. (seconded from ODM) Mongu Zambia 1966–69; scient off. nature conserv Edin 1969–71; res. off. Lumle agr centre Nepal 1971–73; self-employed landscape contr Ullapool from 1973; occasional consult. work for Hunting tech serv Middle East from 1973
m Ullapool 1966 Molly E. Longbottom MA 1966 *qv*

MACLENNAN Annabel Ross *BSc 1966
d of Andrew R. M. mason/crofter and Betsy Urquhart; b Inv 20.8.44
teacher maths Dingwall 1967–74, asst prin maths from 1974
m Kirkhill Invernesssh 15.8.70 George Fraser farm. s of Donald F. Kiltarlity

MACLENNAN Anne Margaret Welsh MA 1956
m Farquharson

MACLENNAN Colin Breck *BSc(eng) 1958

MacLENNAN Colin Hamilton MA 1966
s of John D. D. MacL. farm. and Rosamund M. J. Plowright artist; b Kingston-u-Thames 9.2.44
teacher Biggleswade j s from 1967/school lib from 1971/1st yr group leader from 1972
m Bedford 26.5.69 Barbara A. Crawte teacher d of Jack C. Bedford

MacLENNAN David Neall *BSc 1962

McLENNAN David Orkney *MA 1964
s of David E. McL. linotype oper and Mary J. S. Orkney; b Edin 24.8.38
teacher Aber coll of comm 1965–70; adult educ tut. organis Kirkcaldy tech coll from 1970
m Aber 15.7.67 Anne G. Gray secy d of James G. Aber

MACLENNAN Donald John MA 1956

MACLENNAN Donald John MA 1959
s of Donald J. M. crofter and Johanna Maclean; b Stornoway 14.7.37
teacher: Engl subjs Aber 1960–63, prin Engl Lionel s s Is of Lewis from 1963
m Aber 2.4.60 Rena C. Lawson teacher homecraft d of Roy C. L. Colliston Arbroath

MacLENNAN Duncan MA 1962
s of Colin MacL. carpenter/crofter/haulage contr and Ann MacDonald; b Kiltarlity 14.4.37
teacher Engl Inv, asst prin Engl from 1963
m Inv 28.7.64 Deirdre M. A. Denoon MA 1962 *qv*

MacLENNAN Elspeth Ann BSc 1965

McLENNAN George Alexander *MA 1958

MACLENNAN Helen Margaret MA 1969
m Mackie

MACLENNAN John MA 1959
s of Alexander M. merch seaman and Jessie Mackay; b Gress Is of Lewis 10.5.33
teacher Back s s Is of Lewis from 1960
m Johnshaven 12.7.61 Lily A. M. Ritchie MA 1959 *qv*

MacLENNAN Kenneth Alexander *MA 1966
s of Kenneth J. MacL. postmaster and Christian McLaren; b Dingwall 12.12.43
grad comm trainee G. Wimpey & Co Lond 1966–68; Toronto: asst sales man. 1968–72, market. man. from 1972
m 14.7.73 Maré L. Rice nurse d of Robert D. R. San Mateo Calif

MACLENNAN Kristin MA 1962
d of Christopher M. MA 1927 *qv* and Mary E. Harvey BSc MA 1933 *qv*; b Edin 27.4.42
Dip Ed(Edin) 1963
teacher: Larne and Lurgan 1963–65, mainly Hampshire 1965–68; civ serv Hants 1969–71 and from 1972–75; internat civ serv Geneva 1971–72; volunteer Dar es Salaam from 1975
m Lancaster –.8.63 William Barrett MA 1963 *qv*

MacLENNAN Lesley Davidson MA 1969

MACLENNAN Marion Harvey MB ChB 1963 MD 1971
d of Christopher M. MA 1927 *qv* and Mary E. Harvey BSc MA 1933 *qv*; b Aber 5.5.39
MRCOG 1969

Aber: h o 1963–65, sen h o 1965–66, regist 1966–69; Aberd: lect obst/gyn 1969–73, consult. from 1973
m Aber 17.2.59 Peter A. Hall BEd 1972 teacher s of Thomas T. H. N'cle-u-Tyne

McLENNAN Marion Margaret *MA 1970
m Flett

MacLENNAN Randall Davidson BSc 1968
s of Alexander MacL. motor mech and Annabel McIntosh; b Banchory 18.4.39
computer progr Lond 1968–71; teacher maths/computer stud. Aber coll of comm from 1971

MACLEOD Alexandra MA 1961
d of Murdo M. dock lab and Mary Macleod; b Stornoway 10.10.40
teacher: Nicolson p s Stornoway 1962–65, Stockbridge p s Edin 1966–67, Whitdale p s Whitburn 1970–74, Holmston p s Ayr from 1974
m Aber 3.8.65 Maurice J. Roberts BA(Durh) teacher, min s of David R. Sale

MacLEOD Alison Ann MA 1963
d of Alexander MacL. MA(Edin) teacher and Rhona C. Lawrie MA 1930 *qv*; b Stirling 7.10.41
teacher Fr/Ger: Guelph Ont 1968–71, Winnipeg 1971–75, Ottawa 1975–78, Guelph from 1978
m Bridlington D. Peter Stonehouse BSc(agr)(Guelph) agr econ s of Ronald G. S. Bridlington

MacLEOD Allan John *MA 1970
s of Kenneth MacL. crofter and Mary Smith; b Barvas Is of Lewis 8.5.48
res. off. econ Belf 1970–77; proj off. Nairn Floors Kirkcaldy from 1977

MacLEOD Allan William MA 1962
s of Allan MacL. fishcurer and Ina Smith; b Cullen 30.6.25
teacher: Barrhead h s from 1963; spec asst from 1965, housemaster from 1969, asst head from 1973
m Glasg 12.7.71 Elsa P. Brown MA(Glas) teacher d of James P. B. Glasg

MACLEOD Angus Mackenzie *MA 1965

MacLEOD Angus Norman MA 1960
s of John A. MacL. gardener and Christina MacSween; b Ardvourlie Harris 18.8.38
teacher maths/warden s hostel: Lochaber h s Fort William 1961–68, Nicolson inst Stornoway 1968–74; prin maths Plockton h s from 1974

MACLEOD Annie MA 1967
d of George M. fisherman/merch seaman and Annie MacDonald; b Stornoway 13.6.46
teacher: Castletown p s 1968–71, Stornoway p s 1971–75
m Inv 27.12.68 Alexander J. MacGillivray MA 1966 *qv*

MACLEOD Catherine MA 1960
d of Alexander J. M. MA 1938 *qv* and Dolina MacPhail BSc 1939 *qv*; b Is of Lewis 1.4.40
teacher: Kincardine 1961–66, Perth & Kinross 1967–71, Lanarksh from 1971
m Aber 4.8.65 Hamish Anderson claims supt s of George W. A. Kinellar

MacLEOD Catherine Isabel MA 1961

MACLEOD Catherine Johanna MA 1961
d of John M. road surfaceman and Mary Macleod; b Balallan Is of Lewis 1.6.38
teacher Bathgate j s s: asst Engl and gen subj 1962–64, prin Engl 1964–67; lect Engl and lib stud. Esk Valley coll Dalkeith 1967–73; prin guid Dunbar g s 1973–76, Preston Lodge h s Prestonpans from 1976

MACLEOD Catherine Marion MA 1970
m Stornoway 3.4.73 Donald K. MacLeod MA 1970 *qv*

McLEOD Charles Conchie *MA 1965
s of Charles S. McL. MA 1924 *qv* and Janet B. M. Conchie MA 1929 *qv*; b Glasg 30.5.44
MSc(Waterloo Ont) 1966 FSA 1969
actuarial asst Toronto 1966–68; Manuf Life Insur Comp: actuary Johannesburg 1969–71, group actuary Toronto 1972–74, asst vice-pres from 1974
m Thunder Bay Ontario 9.8.69 Sharon F. Lee BSc (Waterloo Ont) syst analyst d of Frederick L. Thunder Bay

MacLEOD Charlotte MA 1959
d of John MacL. s janitor, f e teacher and Charlotte McBain; b Peterhead 6.12.37
teacher Inverallochy 1960–65, Boddam p s 1965–70, Buchanhaven p s Peterhead 1970–75, Stobhill p s Gorebridge from 1975

MACLEOD Christine Mairi MA 1970
m Leathar

MACLEOD Christopher James BSc 1957
s of Christopher J. M. coal merch and Elsie M. Brimmel; b Lossiemouth 1.2.36
teacher: maths Nairn 1958–59, sc Rothes 1959–60, sc Lossiemouth 1960–63; RAF educ off. UK, Germany 1963–68, squadron ldr from 1968
m Rothes 4.10.62 Alison G. Smith lab asst d of William S. Rothes

MACLEOD Daniel Stevenson *MA 1967
s of Daniel M. MB ChB(Edin) med missionary, g p and publ health doctor and Mary M. Stevenson MA(Glas) teacher; b Kirkwall 23.10.44
MEd(Glas) 1975
teacher: Engl Dollar acad 1968–71, Stirling h s 1971–72; res. off. reading res unit Edin from 1972
m Auchterhouse 25.8.67 Morag J. Bisset MA 1967 *qv*

McLEOD David Angus MB ChB 1956

MACLEOD Dolina MA 1969
d of Roderick M. and Chirsty M. Morrison; b Isle of Skye 31.12.47
Dip Sec St(Strath) 1970
private secy Glasg 1970–72; teacher Engl Glasg 1973–76, prin remed educ Glasg 1976–79
m Inv 13.7.73 Kenneth S. Smith mech eng s of Kenneth S. Kiltarlity

MacLEOD Dolleen Ross MA 1965

MACLEOD Donald Alexander MB ChB 1962

MacLEOD Donald Angus *BSc 1958
MA PhD(Cantab)

MACLEOD Donald John MB ChB 1970
s of Alexander J. M. MA 1938 *qv* and Dolina M. MacPhail BSc 1938 *qv*; b Is of Lewis 10.10.47
DObstRCOG 1974 MRCGP 1974
h o Aber hosps 1970–71; sen h o g p vocational trg Aber hosps, Peterculter health centre 1971–74; g p Portree from 1974

m Aber 28.12.70 Marjory T. Burnett dietitian d of Alastair S. M. B. Aber

MACLEOD Donald John *BSc 1963
s of Donald M. crofter and Catherine Murray; b Ness Is of Lewis 20.7.41
teacher Fraserburgh 1964–69; prin chem: Kirriemuir 1969–72, Forfar from 1972
m Aber 19.9.66 Eileen M. Watts d of Sidney W. Aber

MacLEOD Donald John *MA 1965
s of Donald MacL. and Morag MacDonald; b Ardhasaig Harris 1.1.43
PhD(Glas) 1969
lect Glas 1965–79; dir commun educ proj Western Isles from 1979

MacLEOD Donald Kenneth MA 1970
s of Kenneth MacL. MA(Glas) headmaster and Mary A. Morrison nurse; b Ness Is of Lewis 19.11.48
lect f e Lews Castle coll Stornoway 1971–80; asst dir f e Western Isles from 1980
m Stornoway 3.4.73 Catherine M. Macleod MA 1970 *qv*

MacLEOD Donald Roderick Angus MA 1962
s of John MacL. weaver/crofter and Christina Macleod; b Carloway Is of Lewis 26.9.40
teacher Engl: Crookston Castle Glasg 1963–66, Nicolson inst Stornoway 1966–73, prin Engl and allied subjs Shawbost s s Is of Lewis from 1973
m Inv 16.10.73 Jean C. Hamilton teacher d of William M. H. Irvine

MacLEOD Duncan Charles *MA 1957

MACLEOD Effie MacPhail MA 1966
d of Alexander J. M. MA 1938 *qv* and Dolina Macphail BSc 1939 *qv*; b Bragar Lewis 29.12.45
teacher: Ayr 1967–68, Lat Tarbert Harris from 1968
m Tarbert 16.7.69 John MacSween P O asst s of Donald A. MacS. Harris

MacLEOD Finlay MA 1965 *1966 PhD 1969
s of John MacL. crofter and Catherine A. MacLeod; b Lewis 5.5.37
lect Aberd 1969–72; teacher Lewis 1972–73; p s advis W Isles 1973–78; asst dir of educ (primary) Western Isles from 1978
m Aber 8.7.65 Norma E. MacIver MA 1967 *qv*

MACLEOD Flora MB ChB 1956
d of Angus M. BSc(agr) 1911 *qv* and Clara E. Graham MA 1919 *qv*; b Stornoway 19.9.32
h o: Lewis hosp Stornoway 1956–57; gyn ARI/midwifery mat. hosp Aber 1957–58; Long Beach Calif: rotating internship Seaside hosp 1958–59, rotating and mat. internship Mem hosp 1959–61; publ health phys ch health care from 1970
m Arcadia Calif 18.10.59 Robert W. Erickson MS(Eng) (univ of S Calif) s of Arthur W. E. Wollaston Mass

MACLEOD Hugh Sime Matheson MB ChB 1964
s of Ian M. M. MB ChB(Edin) g p and Annie F. Sime; b Inv 30.7.40
h o ARI, city hosp Aber 1965–66; h o obst/gyn Irvine 1966; g p: Nairn 1966–67, Fearn from 1967
m Monimail 8.8.62 Isabel C. C. Laird teacher p e d of James M. L. Glasg

McLEOD Ian Ronald LLB 1966
s of Ronald McL. MA 1939 *qv*; b Aber 23.9.45
Aber: law app 1966–68, law asst 1968–70, ptnr Allan Buckley Allan & Co later amalgamated with Wilsone & Duffus advoc
m Banff 11.8.67 Jennifer Main teacher d of David M. Banff

MACLEOD Ian Torquil *MA 1959
s of Ian T. M. lt col/pharm rep and Isabella M. McLaren MA 1916 *qv*; b Inv 6.5.36
lect d'Anglais univ of Rennes France 1959–60; teacher Fr Inv acad 1961–68; spec asst Fr 1968–70, prin asst 1970–72; prin guid from 1972

MACLEOD Innes Fraser *MA 1959

MACLEOD Isabella Margaret MA 1969
d of James S. M. postman/crofter and Elizabeth A. Dickson cook; b Westfield Thurso 28.2.48
teacher: Cranham p s Worc 1970–75, Woodside county junior s Telford 1975–76
m Thurso 1.6.72 Michael J. Hitchings BSc 1973 lab asst/sen scient off. s of Edwin T. H. Chipping Campden

MacLEOD Jessie Christina MA 1968

MacLEOD Joan MA 1959
d of John MacL. s janitor and f e teacher and Charlotte McBain; b Peterhead 6.12.37
teacher: Cockenzie p s 1960–61, Boddam p s 1961–71, Buchanhaven p s Peterhead 1971–75, Gorebridge p s 1975–76. Loanhead p s from 1976

MACLEOD John MA 1960

MACLEOD John MA 1967
s of Macleod MA(Glas) headmaster and Peggy Macleay; b Glasg 9.7.46
teacher Engl Glasg 1969–73, prin Engl from 1973
m Glasg 1969 Erica M. Maclean Laxdale Is of Lewis

MacLEOD John MA 1969

MacLEOD John Ross MA 1963
s of Alister MacL. policeman and Kathleen Macdonald; b Isle Ornsay Skye 20.8.42
teacher: Dunbarney j s s Perth 1964–66, Njumbi h s Kenya 1967–68; prin Engl Chadiza s s Zambia 1969–72, Kagumo h s Kenya 1973–78
m Chadiza Zambia –.10.71 Susan E. Ridley MB ChB 1968 *qv*

MACLEOD John William Bartholomew MA 1970
s of Murdo D. M. prison gov/reg dir of prisons and Dolina Macleod; b Stornoway 2.5.49
teacher geog Dingwall acad from 1971
m Dingwall 25.7.74 Anne M. Maclean MA 1972 teacher d of William M. Glendale Is of Skye

MACLEOD Kathleen MA 1968
d of John M. motor mech and Margaret Macrae; b Stornoway 1.1.47
RGN 1970 SCM 1972
post grad nursing course Aber 1968–70; midwifery trg Bellshill 1971–72; nurse missionary Central India 1973–78; temp matron eventide home Glasg 1978; part time stud. Bible coll Glasg 1978–79; stud. commun health Liv s of tropical med 1980; return to India 1980

MacLEOD Katrine Isabel Lewis MA 1956 Dip Ed 1957
d of Angus MacL. MA 1927 *qv* and Helen E. Riddoch MA 1928 *qv*; b Aber 24.3.35
teacher Aber: Powis s 1957, Quarryhill 1958–59; remed C of E s Cranleigh part-time 1970–75
m Aber 2.4.58 Jack B. Izatt BSc(eng) 1957 *qv*

McLEOD Kenneth MB ChB 1966
s of Kenneth McL. grocer and Christina Simpson; b Elgin 3.7.42
FFARCS(Lond) 1970
h o Aber 1966–67; regist anaest Aber 1968–71; sen res off. N'cle 1971–75, consult. anaest from 1975
m Elgin 14.2.64 Sandra G. Grant nurse d of William G. Elgin

MACLEOD Kenneth James BSc 1960
s of Kenneth M. farm. and Anne Fraser MA(Glas); b Conon Bridge 1.3.38
FRMetS 1974
met Nairobi 1961–75, UNEP Nairobi from 1975
m Nairobi 30.6.68 Anita D. Duncan d of Ivan D. H. D. Nairobi

MacLEOD Lewis *MA 1970
s of Kenneth MacL. bldg contr and Cathleen Harris; b Stornoway 19.1.49
PhD res fell. St John's Canada 1970–73

MacLEOD Malcolm MA 1963

MacLEOD Malcolm BSc 1967

MACLEOD Malcolm MA 1968

MacLEOD Margaret MA 1964
d of Donald MacL. crofter/weaver and Christina MacLeod; b Carloway Is of Lewis 2.3.43
teacher: Plean 1965–67, Montreal 1967–72, Lond 1972–73, Denny 1973–74, Inv from 1974

McLEOD Marguerite Fiona Logan MA 1958 CASS 1971
d of Peter McL. MA(Glas) teacher and Eva Munro law stud.; b Inv. 14.5.38
Dip Secy Sc(Glasg) 1959
teacher: Croy 1960–64, Lossiemouth 1965–69; soc work Elgin from 1971

MACLEOD Marjory Barron MA 1960
m Macdonald

MACLEOD Mary *BSc 1968
d of Murdo M. merch seaman, dock lab and Mary Macleod; b Stornoway 3.12.46
MSc(Lond) 1969
planner: Rosssh 1970–75, Highland reg c from 1975
m Glasg 28.12.76 Donald H. MacDonald farm. s of Alexander A. MacD. Duncanston

MACLEOD Mary MA 1969
d of Donald J. M. weaver and Catherine A. Macarthur; b Carloway Is of Lewis 19.3.48
teacher: Nicolson inst Stornoway 1970–76, Inv r acad from 1976
m Aber 20.7.76 George F. Maclean MA 1970 *qv*

MacLEOD Mary Anne Millar MA 1966
m McCormack

MacLEOD Moragh Alison *MA 1965
d of Alexander MacL. bank man. and Sheila M. Caldwell; b Buenos Aires 21.4.43
VSO teacher Engl Amedzofe trg coll Ghana 1965–66; teacher Engl: Stockland Green bilateral s Birm 1966–67; Ghana: Kpandu s 1967–70, Tema s s 1971–75; Cameroon; presb coll Bali 1976–78, Sacred Heart coll Bamenda from 1978
m Aber 2.9.67 David T. A. Gibson BA(Dub) teacher s of Angus E. G. Lincoln

MACLEOD Murdo *MA 1958
s of George M. gamekeeper and Dolina McKinnon; b Ardhasaig Harris 24.2.31
teacher geog: Glasg 1959–65, Thornhill acad 1965–67; lect Stevenson coll of f e Edin from 1967
m Aber 13.2.65 Evelyn J. E. Carle d of William C. C. Cults

MACLEOD Murdo MA 1958 Dip Ed 1959
s of Donald M. dock lab and Mary MacIver; b Stornoway 2.12.37
teacher: Leverburgh 1959–62, Glasg 1962–69, Stornoway from 1969
m Stornoway 13.10.71 Katie M. Martin teacher d of Alexander M. Stornoway

MacLEOD Murdo Alexander MA 1963
s of Alexander MacL. min of relig and Catherine MacLeod; b Ness Is of Lewis 15.10.35
Dip Free Ch Coll Edin 1966
min Drumchapel Free ch Glasg 1966–72, Free ch Dingwall from 1972
m Glasg 24.8.66 Annie B. Nicolson MA 1962 *qv*

MACLEOD Murdo Donald MB ChB 1970
s of Murdo M. seaman/crofter/fisherman/wool carder and Isabella Macaulay fish trade worker; b Knock Is of Lewis 5.3.45
MRCGP 1977
h o royal N I Inv 1970–71; sen h o obst/gyn Raigmore hosp Inv 1971–72; sen h o paediat Bridgend hosp Glam 1972, g p trainee N Middx hosp Lond 1972–74; g p Aldershot from 1974
m Inv 5.3.71 Elizabeth G. Eunson RGN d of George J. E. Brechin

MACLEOD Nan Shepherd MA 1956
d of Mary M.; b Portnaguran Is of Lewis 7.1.35
teacher: Engl Selkirk 1957–59, Sandwick p s 1959–66, Engl Bayble from 1974
m Inv 2.8.61 John M. Macleod insur ag s of Malcolm M. Garrabost Is of Lewis

MACLEOD Neil Munro *MA 1960

MacLEOD Robert Dewar Murray MB ChB 1960
s of Robert B. M. MA(Glas) headmaster and Helen T. S. Murray MA(Glas) teacher; b Aber 17.5.37
DObstRCOG 1962 MRCPE 1965
res asst Aberd 1962–63; regist Aber hosps 1963–66; sen regist Edin hosps 1966–77; consult. phys/geriat Elgin from 1971
m Aber 15.7.61 Gwendoline C. Mair lib d of John S. S. M. Aber

MACLEOD Roderick MB ChB 1970
s of Roderick M. bldr and Chirsty M. Morrison; b Portnalong Is of Skye 14.11.45
h o Woodend hosp Aber, Bridge of Earn hosp 1970–71; regt m o 1st Bn Gordon Highlanders Inv, Ireland, Singapore 1972–75; g p m o Paderborn Sennelager garr BAOR Germany 1975–76; sen h o obst/gyn mil hosp Colchester 1976; g p Kilsyth 1976–77, Ballachulish/Duror/Glencoe and m o to Glencoe hosp from 1977

MACLEOD Roderick Alexander *MA 1970
s of Neil J. M. bldr's foreman and Alice Livingstone; b Inv 23.5.47
syst analyst Aber 1970–72; syst sales man. Carlisle 1972–75; reg sales man. 1975–77; manuf's ag UK and Middle East based Brampton from 1977
m Inv 27.2.71 Elizabeth J. A. Urquhart d of George U. Inv

MACLEOD Roderick John MA 1960
s of John M. shipwright and Jessie Macleod; b Stornoway 11.10.39
teacher: maths Nicolson inst Stornoway 1961–72, prin guid from 1972, asst rector from 1974
m Stornoway 2.4.69 Anna M. Murray staff nurse d of Alexander M. Gress Is of Lewis

MACLEOD Roderick John *MA 1960

McLEOD Ronald Erskine BSc 1963

MACLEOD Seonaid BSc 1957

MACLEOD Sheila Elizabeth Mairi BSc 1960
d of Robert B. M. OBE MA(Glas) headmaster and Helen T. Murray MA(Glas) teacher; b Aber 19.6.39
teacher sc/maths Aber 1961–64; lab asst Wash USA 1964–65; Macclesfield: teacher p s 1965–66, part-time from 1972
m Aber 12.7.63 Raymond A. Bowie BSc 1961 *qv*

MACLEOD William *BSc 1961
s of Donald M. farm. and Jessie T. Macdonald; b Strathnaver
MBA(Mass) 1976
geol: Nigerian geol surv Kaduna Nigeria 1961–67, Union Corp Springs Transvaal 1967–69; Mass: progr/syst analyst Norton Co Worcester 1969–74, Harvard bus. s Boston 1974–76
m Worcester Mass 9.11.58 Virginia L. Pierpont BA (Boston) d of Harlan T. P. Worcester

McLINTOCK Michael John *MA 1968 Dip Ed 1969
s of Robert P. McL. BSc(Edin) analyt chem and Mary E. Sim civ serv, bookkeeper; b Edin 9.6.46
publ exec Aber Journals 1969–72, sen publ exec from 1972
m Burghead 12.7.68 Marion J. Ralph MA 1966 *qv*

MacLURE Alasdair Gow MA 1957
s of John MacL. hotelier and Isabella D. Gow; b Buckie 12.6.35
teacher: Kaimhill s s Aber 1959–62, Ijebu-Ode boys' g s Nigeria 1962–64, Duncanrig sen s s East Kilbride 1965–67, Machakos boys' s Kenya 1968–72, Bankhead acad Aber from 1973
m Aber 24.7.62 Elspeth M. McLean MA 1961 *qv*

McLUSKY Donald Stewart *BSc 1966
s of Robert F. McL. tel eng and Ethel C. Fellingham teacher; b Harrogate 27.6.45
PhD(Stir) 1969 FLS MIBiol
lect Stir from 1968
m Aber 13.7.68 Ruth A. Donald BSc 1966 *qv*

McMAHON James Donald Robertson MB ChB 1966
s of James M. McM. surv customs & excise and Flora MacDonald bank clerk; b Huntly 24.9.42
h o ARI 1966–67; trainee g p Portlethen 1967–68; Ont Canada: g p Hawkesbury 1969–72, Ottawa from 1972
m Aber 12.7.68 Jessie S. Macrae MA 1966 *qv*

McMANUS Terence Charles BSc(eng) 1964

MACMILLAN Andrew MB ChB 1967
MA(Glas)
d Oxford 18.10.79 *AUR* XLVIII 354

MACMILLAN Colin Bonnar LLB 1970

McMILLAN Helen MA 1970
d of William G. McM. exec eng PO tel and Jessie M. B. McIntosh tel, teaching auxil; b Lerwick 5.11.48
teacher Crianlarich 1971–73
m Aber 6.10.72 John Sinclair foreman joiner s of Thomas S. Killin

MACMILLAN Ian Reid Anderson MA 1960 LLB 1962
s of William G. M. BSc 1925 *qv* and Doris Farquhar MA 1928 *qv*; b Buckie 16.6.39
law app Aber 1960–63; solic Peterhead 1963–68; Canada: articled stud. Winnipeg 1968–69, barr and solic from 1969
m Aber 11.5.63 Joan E. C. Sinclair BSc 1961 *qv*

MacMILLAN James Bain MA 1967

MacMILLAN James Douglas MA 1963
s of James MacM. farm., bldg contr and Jessie MacLachlan dressmaker; b Achosnich Ardnamurchan 30.9.33
stud. theol Free Ch of Scot. coll Edin 1963–66; licensed by Free Ch presb of Lorn 1966; ordained and inducted St Columba's Free Ch Aber 1966, St Vincent st Free Ch Glasg 1974
m Aber 13.9.61 Mary F. Campbell MA 1958 *qv*

MACMILLAN Janette Mary *MA 1968
d of Donald M. sea capt Burmah Oil Co and Jessie M. Groves secy; b Glasg 18.4.47
Dip Ed(Edin) 1969
teacher: Whitburn 1969–70, sec spec class Linlithgow 1970–71; Whitburn 1971–72; educ psych Aberdeensh from 1972
m Aber 21.9.72 David I. R. Fotheringham MRCVS(Glas) vet surg s of John F. Aber

McMILLAN Margaret Anne MA 1969
m McKay

MacMILLAN Margaret Flora MA 1962

McMILLAN Margaret King MA 1963
d of Duncan McM. J.P. miner and Annie S. Wilson cotton winder; b Law Carluke 2.3.36
teacher mod lang. Aber h s for girls 1964–65, Lanark 1965–66, Gloucester 1966–67, Aber 1967, Uddingston 1967–68, Bellshill 1968–70, Wishaw from 1971
m Mtwara, Tanzania 13.8.65 Peter C. Henderson supervis pipe line maintenance with Arabian Gulf Explor s of Alexander R. H. Torphins

McMILLAN Mary MB ChB 1965
d of Evan McM. BSc(Edin) teacher and Helen G. Hunter; b Elgin 29.11.41
h o: Woodend hosp Aber 1965–66, Dumfries 1966–67; regist path. Dumfries 1967–69
m Dumfries 25.11.68 Alistair B. Gavin BSc(eng)(Birm) eng, prod. man. s of Robert J. G. Royston

MACMILLAN Neil Norman MA 1968
s of John M. army off. and Joan Kennedy; b Nairn 27.3.46
educ. off. Brit Steel Corp Motherwell 1967–69; pers off. Amp of Gt Brit Port Glasgow 1969–70: dir MCS group of comp, man. dir MCS Recruitment Serv/man. dir MCS Brockies Glasg/Lond from 1970
m Hamilton 18.4.70 Ishbel B. McLellan des d of William K. McL. Hamilton

McMILLAN Ronald Edwards *MA 1969

McMILLAN Sadie Woods MA 1964
d of Duncan McM. miner and Annie S. Wilson cotton winder; b Law 15.11.33
teacher Aber: Northfield acad 1965–70, Hilton acad

1970–73, year mistress Linksfield acad from 1973
m Khartoum 16.4.56 Mohamed E. Elsarrag DKSM (Khart) med pract/consult. psychiat s of Hassan E. Omdurman; marr. diss

McMULLEN Adrian James *MA 1967
s of James McM. invest. man. and Joan E. Gilling; b N'cle-u-Tyne 24.11.45
teacher: gen subjs St Wilfrid's s m s Gateshead 1967–68, geog/maths/r e Hartlepool 1968–71; teacher reading to backward ch St Andrew's p s Blyth from 1976

McMURTRIE John MA 1959

MACNAB Francis Auchline MA 1958 PhD 1960
s of James D. M. farm. and Mary A. L. Hughes; b Aust 21.6.31
fell world acad scholars 1975 FAPsS 1975 FBPsS 1976 FACE 1977
Aust: dir Cairnmillar inst Melbourne from 1961 and min presb ch Prahran Melbourne 1961–70, Collins Street (indep) Uniting ch Melbourne from 1971
m Aber 17.7.58 Sheila B. Ewen MA 1957 *qv*

McNAB John Winton BSc 1960 *1961 MB ChB 1967 DMRD 1975
s of J. Winton McN. bank man. and Elizabeth S. Cooper; b Stranraer 17.5.36
FRCSE 1973 FFRRCSI 1977
works chem Grangemouth 1961–62; h o, sen h o ARI and Shetland hosps 1967–70; regist surg Inv hosps 1971–73; regist radio diagnosis ARI 1973–76; sen regist radio diagnosis Dun from 1976
m Aber 30.4.77 Patricia Quigley nurs. off. d of Luke Q. Clydebank

MACNAB Rachel MA 1957
d of Gilbert M. estate surv and Elizabeth H. Aird; b Bridgend Is of Islay 29.7.37
BLS(BC) 1967 ALA(RGIT) 1975
teacher Engl/hist/geog: Aber 1958–62, Montreal 1962–65; lib asst univ of BC Vancouver 1965–66, lib New Westminster publ lib Vancouver 1967–69; tut/lib Thurso tech coll from 1969
m 30.7.76 Clive E. Lovelace BSc(eng)(Lond) eng des s of Garth E. L.

McNALLY Brian Peter BEd 1969
s of Peter McN. MA(Glas) headmaster and Jeanette Gallacher; b Glasg 7.7.41
teacher Ayr acad 1969–71, spec asst 1971–73, asst prin guid from 1973
m Ayr 13.7.73 Constance A. McGuire teacher d of William C. McG Mauchline

MacNAUGHTAN Elizabeth Mary BMedBiol 1967 MB ChB 1970
d of Ian P. J. MacN. MB ChB(Edin) consult. surg and Jean Wiseman BSc(St And) bact; b Edin 1946
h o Aber 1971; g p Leuchars from 1974
m Aber 1969 Roger W. Williams MB ChB 1969 *qv*

McNAUGHTON James Leslie LL B 1965
s of William R. D. McN. advoc in Aber and Elizabeth Duncan secy; b Aber 8.12.43
law app Aber 1965–68; leg. asst Banff 1968–70; ptnr Stewart Watson solic Banff from 1970
m Aber 1.8.70 Pauline Booth teacher homecraft d of Joseph C. B. Aber

McNAUGHTON John Davidson BL 1956
s of William R. D. McN. advoc in Aber and Elizabeth Duncan secy; b Aber 17.7.35
leg. asst: Ranken & Reid SSC Edin 1959–60, Furst & Furst SSC Edin 1961–64; ptnr Patrick & James WS Edin 1964–68; dep proc fisc: Glasg 1968–69, Dunfermline 1970–75; proc fisc Dornoch from 1975
m Edin 3.10.64 Joan T. Lyall secy d of Joseph L. Kirkcaldy

McNAUGHTON William Robert Duncan BL 1957

MacNAY Gordon Roberts MA 1969
s of Gordon R. MacN. MA 1969 *qv*; b Aber 16.9.47
teacher Douglas acad Milngavie from 1970

MACNEIL Joseph *MA 1970
s of Joseph M. master mariner and Elizabeth Currie; b Blantyre 20.8.32
teacher St Patrick's h s Coatbridge 1971–73, asst prin mod lang from 1973
m Glasg 4.8.71 Rose M. O'Boyle teacher d of Thomas O'B. Glasg

McNEILL Anne Christina MA 1960
d of William M. McN. MA(Oxon) asst conserv for. Ceylon, sen lect for. Aberd and Dorothy N. Maw BSc(Lond) hosp almoner; b Aber 22.12.39
Dip Soc St(Edin) 1961 M Inst Almoners(Lond) 1962
med soc worker: St Mary's hosp Lond 1962–64, dept g p Edin 1964–66, city hosp Edin 1966–67 and occasional work from 1969
m Aber 25.3.66 Edmund R. Seiler MB ChB(Edin) med pract s of Henry E. S. MB ChB(Glas) Edin

McNEILL Bridget Margaret MB ChB 1970
d of William M. McN. MA(Oxon) sen lect for. Aberd and Dorothy N. Maw BSc(Lond) med soc worker; b Aber 22.1.46
h o: city hosp, mat. hosp Aber 1970–71, Green Lane hosp Auckland NZ 1971; m o Vaiola hosp Nuku'Alofa Tonga 1972–74; med/psychiat regist Timaru hosp NZ 1975–76; m o i/c psychiat patients Vaiola hosp from 1977
m Otane, Hawkes Bay NZ 4.12.71 Filimoto M. Taumgepeau DSM(Fiji s of med) m o govt of Tonga s of Siosifa M. T. Ha'a pai Tonga

McNEILL Francis *MA 1968

McNEILL Morag Deirdre MA 1968
d of Daniel A. McN. BL(Glas) solic and Jean I. D. Wilson; b Edin 23.1.47
secy course St Godric's coll Lond 1968–69
secy: chartered patent ag Glasg 1969–72, trade assoc Edin 1973, dir publ comp Edin 1973
m Dunblane 1.5.71 James A. Brown CA s of Frank B. Glasg

McNEILL Stuart *BSc 1964
s of Donald S. McN. mining elect. eng, newsp man., market gardener and Dorothy L. Hodges; b Letchworth 9.3.42
PhD(Lond) 1969 DIC 1969
asst lect Imp coll Lond 1967–70, lect from 1970
m Aber 10.8.67 Jean M. Sinclair BSc 1965 *qv*

MacNICOL Essel Marie MA 1967

MACNICOL Helen Joan *BSc 1969
m Brough

McNICOL Maureen Ann BL 1957
b Aber 29.7.37
employed Shell Lond
m 1958 R. Y. Birley

MacPHAIL Angus LLB 1967 MA 1969
s of William D. MacP. MA(Glas) headmaster and Elizabeth Brown; b Bonhill 15.1.47
solic: Edin 1970–75, Saudi Arabia from 1975

McPHAIL Dennis McKinnon MA 1968

MacPHAIL Douglas *MA 1970
s of Mary MacP.; b Campbeltown 20.4.46
Dip Ed(Edin) 1971
teacher mod lang royal h s Edin from 1971

MacPHAIL Evelyn Ann BSc 1960
d of Alexander MacP. hosp gov and Jessie D. Downie hosp matron; b Edin 6.6.39
teacher: maths/sc Kelso h s 1961–67, maths Mainholm Ayr 1967–68
m Tarbert 8.9.67 Robert A. Ross B Mus(Glas) lect mus s of Robert R. Kilmarnock

MacPHAIL James Brown MA 1966 LL B 1968
s of William D. MacP. MA(Glas) headmaster and Elizabeth Brown; b Bonhill 5.12.45
self-employed econ Regina, Vancouver 1968–70; law app, leg. asst Edin 1970–73; court asst leg. pract Aber 1974–75; sen solic Lothian reg c 1975–78; comm and leg. advis petro-chem industry Reading from 1978
m Ayr 14.7.73 Vivienne S. Law secy d of David L. Ayr

MACPHAIL Joan MA 1970
d of John M. haulage contr and Mary J. Scott; b Glasg 22.3.49
teacher: Engl/hist/remed Penicuik h s 1971–74, Engl Forrester h s Edin 1974–77, Engl lang Brit inst Thessaloniki Greece from 1977

MacPHAIL Kenneth Donald Weir MA 1963
s of Murdoch MacP. MA(Glas) clergyman and Georgina M. McDougall; b Balvicar 2.7.34
teacher Invsh 1964–66, Oban 1967–69, Easdale 1970–72, Glasg from 1972

MacPHAIL Lachlan BSc(eng) 1970

MacPHAIL Malcolm LLB 1957
s of Malcolm M. MacP. civ eng and Jean F. P. Wyse; b Kuala Lumpur 26.6.28
BSc(econ) (Lond) 1954
leg. asst A. C. Morrison & Richards advoc Aber 1957–58; solic Scot. Midland Guarantee Trust Edin 1958–59; leg. asst corp of city of Aber 1959–62, proc fisc dep Dun 1962–73; proc fisc Kincardine Stonehaven from 1973
m Dun 15.9.66 Moira C. Bleackley teacher d of James B. Dun

MacPHAIL Murdoch MA1960 LLB 1964
s of William D. MacP. MA(Glas) headmaster and Elizabeth Brown; b Renton 13.8.39
self-employed solic Dingwall from 1970
m Glenlyon 2.11.63 Brenda M. Martin nurse

McPHAIL Robert James Field MA 1968 LLB 1970
s of Thomas F. McP. shipowner and Marjorie M. Gunn; b Edin 10.4.47
CA 1973
CA Graham, Smart & Annan Edin 1970–74, Gill & Johnson, Deloite & Co Nairobi from 1974
m Aber 21.10.72 Kathryn M. Murray MA 1971 Brit high commission Nairobi d of John N. M.

MacPHEE Anne *MB ChB 1961
m Chew

McPHEE Christine Mary *MA 1968 Dip Ed 1969

McPHEE Kathleen Isabella MA 1970
d of William J. McP. gas fitter and Sadie McLean; b Inv 22.8.49
clerkess NSHEB 1971–78
m Inv 26.6.70 Finlay MacKintosh plumber s of Finlay MacK. Drumnadrochit

MacPHEE Kenneth John BEd 1970

MACPHERSON Beatrice Gillian MB ChB 1962
m Wood

MACPHERSON Charles Lachlan *MA 1970

McPHERSON Christina Margaret BSc 1966

McPHERSON David Ross BSc 1969
s of George McP. clerk of works and Margaret McIntosh; b Peterhead 12.11.46
MIBiol 1971
teacher sc Peterhead acad 1971–73, asst prin sc from 1973

McPHERSON Duncan James MA 1956
s of James McP. coffee exporter and Flora M. Macpherson; b Santos, Brazil 29.10.30
Dip Agr 1959
farm. Rosssh from 1959
m Aber 9.1.60 Vivian M. Wylie teacher p e d of William W. Carluke

McPHERSON Edith Joan *MA 1968
d of George McP. MA 1939 *qv* and Isabel M. Ross MA 1937 *qv*; b Liskeard Cornwall 6.11.45
ALA 1972
asst lib civ serv from 1970

MACPHERSON Elizabeth MA 1963 Dip Ed 1965
d of Ian M. 1928 *qv*(III) and Elizabeth Cameron MA 1928 *qv*; b Forres 12.5.42
teacher Engl Aber 1965–66; bank clerk Atlanta USA 1967–68
m Dunphail 12.9.64 Alister C. Baillie BSc 1963 *qv*

McPHERSON Frank Murdoch *MA 1960
s of Frank McP. shop worker and Ethel Greenlaw shop worker, seamstress; b Aber 2.9.38
Dip Clin Psych (Edin) 1962 PhD(Edin) 1968 FBPsS 1977
asst lect Edin 1960–63, lect 1963–71; sen lect Dund from 1971
m Edin 14.9.62 Karin Maria Langenheim DPhil(Kiel) lect Edin d of Konrad L. DPhil(Kiel) Kiel W Ger

McPHERSON Harry MB ChB 1959

McPHERSON Ian *BSc 1961
s of John McP. GPO worker and Matilda Hemphill; b Lairg 18.9.38
PhD(Strath) 1972
scient off. admiralty Dunfermline 1961–65; lect phys Falkirk tech coll 1965–67; res asst Strath 1967–70; lect N'cle polytech 1970–73; sen lect Glasg coll of tech from 1973
m Inv –.7.72 Rachel L. Macrae MA(Glas) teacher, GPO tel d of Donald A. N. MA(Glas) Tarbert Is of Harris

McPHERSON Ian Alexander Douglas *MA 1959
s of Alexander W. McP. solic and Kathleen N. F. Brown MA 1920 *qv*; b Macduff 12.2.36
teacher: Eastwood h s 1960–69, prin mod lang Barrhead h s 1969–73; asst head Peterhead acad from 1973

m Glasg 2.7.65 Maureen A. Fotheringham MA(Glas) teacher d of Ian S. S. F. Whitecraigs

McPHERSON Ian David MB ChB 1967
s of John G. McP. mason and Jenny Henderson nurse; b Aber 21.12.42
CCFP(Can) 1971
g p Ottawa
m Aber 1968 Margaret Walker

MACPHERSON Ian Richard *MA 1956
s of George M. clerk and Violet A. Warwick; b Aber 4.1.34
PhD(Manc) 1960
asst lect Manc 1959–60, lect univ of Wales 1960–64, lect Durh 1964–72, sen lect 1972–75, reader from 1975; visiting prof univ Wis USA 1970–71
m Cheshire 7.8.59 Sheila C. Turner BA(Manc) teacher

McPHERSON James King MA 1970

MACPHERSON Jane Eileen MA 1970

MACPHERSON Jean Elizabeth *BMedBiol 1970 MB ChB 1973
d of Ian M. MB ChB(Edin) g p and May Hails SRN; b Bradford 13.6.49
h o Bradford 1973–74, sen h o paediat 1974–75; sen h o path. Leeds 1975–76, regist from 1976
m Boddy

MacPHERSON John Fiddes MA 1959

McPHERSON Joyce Anne MA 1970 Dip Ed 1971
m Peckitt

McPHERSON Kathleen Elizabeth MB ChB 1969

MACPHERSON Mary Elizabeth Fraser MB ChB 1959
d of Donald F. M. MRCVS(Edin) vet surg and Mary Henderson MA(Edin) civ serv; b Nairobi 3.12.33
h o Victoria ch hosp Hull 1961–62
m Kingussie 26.3.60 Ian S. Robertson BSc 1955 *qv*
d Aber 6.1.78

MACPHERSON Mary Isabella *MA 1956 Dip Ed 1957
teacher geog: Inv royal acad 1957–59, Torry j s s Aber 1959–60, part time St Margaret's s for girls Aber 1967–68
m Aber 15.7.59 Frederick C. H. Nisbet BSc 1955 *qv*

McPHERSON Stephen MB ChB 1956

MacPHERSON Thomas Ian *MA 1967
s of Thomas MacP. head stalker and Mary A. C. W. Stuart; b Invercauld 14.3.42
teacher: geog Madras coll St And 1968–71, prin geog Buckie h s from 1971
m Dun 7.10.71 Margaret E. Kay BSc(St And) teacher d of William D. K. Dun

McPHERSON William James *BSc 1970
s of James McP. eng and Chrissie Cassie secy; b Fraserburgh 9.1.48
Courtaulds: res chem Coventry 1970–74, group leader (res and dev) Coventry 1974–76, sect. leader (implementation of res projects into prod.) Grimsby 1976–78, sect. leader res and dev acrylics Coventry from 1978
m Fraserburgh 6.9.69 Jean L. Watt teacher d of Owen J. W. Memsie

McPHERSON Winifred MB ChB 1962
d of Robert M. McP. bldr/hotelier and Winifred Buckner; b Inverurie 20.6.38
Aber: h o Woodend hosp 1962–63, sen h o, regist City hosp 1963–66; regist clin path. Bristol RI 1966–68; clin asst haemat Melbourne Aust 1969–71; clin asst radiol Leic/g p Leicsh 1972–76
m Aber 3.7.67 Alastair Bissett-Johnson LLB(Nott) barrister and assoc prof McG Montreal s of Edward O. B-J. Banstead

MACPHIE Anne Winning *MA 1961
m Smith

McPHIE James Langley MB ChB 1969
s of James McP. comp rep and Agnes Brown; b Denny 7.3.45
h o ARI 1969–70; terminable lect path. Aberd 1970–73, lect from 1973
m Aber 2.12.72 Margaret MacKenzie RGN nurs sister d of George MacK. Lhanbryde

McPHILLIMY William Noble *MA 1968 *MEd 1972
s of Noble McP. foreman moulder and Mary Neil knitter; b Glasg 18.2.43
teacher Engl Inverurie acad 1969–71; educ psych (child guid) Aber 1972–73; lect educ psych coll of educ from 1973
m Aber 12.11.66 Dorothy C. B. McWee MA 1968 *qv*

McQUEEN Earl Ingram *MA 1959
s of Earl I. McQ. piano tuner and Violet C. Reid; b Aber 12.4.37
BA(Cantab) 1961 MA(Cantab) 1964 MLitt(Cantab) 1966
lect classics Brist from 1964

MacQUEEN Shiona Catherine Joan *MA 1969

McQUILLAN John MA 1965
s of John McQ. foreman steel fixer and Christina Butler; b Glasg 3.7.39
teacher: Lat/Russian Dumbarton 1966–67, Lat Cheshire 1967–69, Engl Hereford 1969–73; asst head Hereford from 1973
m Sanderstead 6.8.66 Sandra J. Beckley MA 1966 *qv*

McQUISTAN Fiona Eugenie Winifred MB ChB 1964
d of John K. McQ. asst works man. and Eugenie W. Kivlichan teacher; b Glasg 27.8.39
DObstRCOG 1966 DA 1970
h o: Dumfries and Galloway RI, Woodend hosp Aber 1964–65; sen h o gyn Leeds, h o obst mat. hosp Aber 1965; sen h o: Law hosp Carluke 1965–67, Nat Women's hosp Auckland NZ 1967; regist anaest Wellington hosp NZ 1968–70; regist anaest Dumfries and Galloway RI 1970–71, part-time from 1971
m Dumfries 16.12.70 John D. C. Smith MA(Glas) solic s of Andrew C. S. MA(Glas) Glasg

MacRAE Anabel Janet MA 1969

MacRAE Catriona Flora Gillanders MB ChB 1961
d of John A. MacR. bank man. and Mary R. Nicolson nurse; b Wick 3.3.38
h o Aber 1961–62; part-time g p Cirencester 1962–63; sessional clin work (publ health) Lincoln 1967–70; part-time publ health Glos from 1970
m Aber 1960 Gordon L. Smith MBChB 1961 *qv*
husb *d* 14.2.75

McRAE Derek James *BSc(eng) 1968

MACRAE Donaldina Agnes MA 1966
d of George M. carpenter and Catherine Morrison; b Stornoway 15.1.45

teacher: Engl/allied subj Edinbarnet s s Clydebank 1967–69, Engl Kingsridge s s Glasg 1969–72, asst prin Engl 1972–73; prin Engl: City Public s s now Allan Glen's Glasg 1973–75, Garthamlock s s Glasg from 1975
m Aber 1.3.75 Thomas M. Jess insur broker s of Joseph J. Glasg

McRAE Edith MA 1968
m Stephen

MACRAE Grace Kathleen Roslyn MB ChB 1962
d of Edward G. M. man. dir and Grace C. Ross secy/cashier: b Aber 31.3.39
DPM 1967 MRCPsych 1974
h o: Aber 1962–63, Lond, Birm 1963–64; sen h o, regist Birm 1964–65; regist Dun 1965–67; regist, sen regist Birm 1967–72; consult. psychiat Birm from 1972
m Aber 8.10.65 Donald G. Jamieson MB ChB 1958 *qv*

MACRAE Helen Shepherd Blake MA 1966
b Inv. 30.6.45
teacher Engl Aber 1967–68, Stranraer 1968–71
m Inv 24.7.68 D. M. Rothwell

MacRAE Helen Sylvia MB ChB 1961
m Wilkinson

MacRAE Hugh MA 1958
s of Donald MacR. crofter and Margaret Mackinnon; b Applecross 19.11.36
teacher Aber: Frederick St s 1959–69, prin Engl 1969–72; prin guid Harlaw acad from 1972
m Aber 28.12.72 Shirley Hepburn cook d of Alexander H. Aber

MACRAE Jean Gillean Cameron MB ChB 1966
m Turner

MACRAE Jessie Salmond MA 1966
d of Farquhar M. bank teller and Jessie A. Cargill; b Inv 15.2.46
teacher Kittybrewster p s Aber 1967–68
m Aber 12.7.68 James D. R. McMahon MB ChB 1966 *qv*

MacRAE John Alexander LLB 1969

MACRAE John Alexander Cargill BSc(eng) 1965

MacRAE John Mackinnon MA 1965

MacRAE Kenneth Duncan *MA 1964 PhD 1970
s of John D. MacR. sailor and Henrietta Gunn; b Forres 27.10.42
FRSS 1970
asst lect psych Aberd 1965–67; lect: psych Belf 1967–69, med statist Belf 1969–76; sen lect statist Charing Cross hosp med s from 1976
m Belfast 5.9.69 Julie A. Thompson MSc(Belf) occup psych d of Malcolm G. T. Lond; marr diss 1976

MacRAE Madeline MA 1963
m Millar

McRAE Mairi Margaret BSc 1957
d of Hugh McR. MA(Glas) teacher, educ psych and Margaret Campbell BSc(Glas) teacher; b Bearsden 15.6.36
res asst: Macaulay inst of soil res Aber 1957–62, path. dept Swedish hosp Seattle USA 1962–64, asst, head chem Washington state lab Seattle 1964–69; various posts in NZ 1971–73
m Seattle 5.3.66 Ian M. Munro

MacRAE Mary Morrison MA 1969
m Ferguson

McRAE Moira Ida Elder BEd 1970
d of George J. McR. and Jean R. McIntosh lab tech; b Keith 29.1.47
teacher: Engl (employed by Brit centre for teachers in Germany) Augsburg 1970–73, Engl/Fr coll of f e Augsburg from 1973

McRAE Norma MA 1968
m Thomson

McRAE Stuart Gordon *BSc 1965
s of Donald McR. sales rep and Elizabeth H. Wood; b Aber 31.10.42
PhD(Lond) 1971
lect soil sc Wye coll, univ Lond from 1965
m Aber 12.8.67 Hazel M. Adam MA 1966 *qv*

MacRITCHIE Kenneth John MB ChB 1960
s of John MacR. crofter and Margaret Macleod; b Barvas Is of Lewis 21.12.32
Dip Psych Med 1960 CRCP(C) 1967 MRCPsych 1972 FRCP(C) 1973
h o ARI 1960–61; regist psychiat: Aber 1961–62, Glasg 1962–64; fell. med/psychiat Rochester USA 1964–66; sen regist psychiat Aber 1966–67; psychiat Toronto 1967–71, asst prof fac of med univ of Toronto/chief in-patient serv dept psychiat Toronto gen hosp 1971–76; dep psychiat-in-chief Tor sen hosp from 1976
m Rochester USA Rhoda McDonald d of John McD. Stockinish Is of Harris

MacRITCHIE Murray MA 1964
d Aber 8.4.74 *AUR* XLV 450

McROBBIE Margaret Ishbel MA 1958
d of Alexander McR. Hong Kong police and Violet M. Cruickshank MA 1928 *qv*; b Hong Kong 10.12.36
teacher: central s Fraserburgh 1959–67, Hythehill p s Lossiemouth 1968–69, Torphichen W Lothian 1969–70
m Aber 22.7.69 Calum McCallum lect tech coll s of Malcolm G. McC. Campbeltown

McROBERTS James Montgomery MA 1962
s of Hugh B. McR. master mariner and Annie Montgomery; b Carnlough Co Antrim 20.1.11
teacher AGS 1963–70; retd
m Kilmun 22.6.46 Ronalda D. B. Watson d of Mearns B. W. Aber
d Aber 8.9.78 *AUR* XLVIII 107

McROBERTS Milton Rudolph PhD 1961
MSc(Purdue)

McSEVENEY Elizabeth Beattie MA 1969

McSPORRAN Archibald McDonald *MA 1958

MacSWEEN Kenneth Somerled BSc(for) 1968
s of Kenneth J. MacS. bank acct and Flora J. Macdonald MA(Glas) teacher; b Lamlash 31.5.46
tech serv proj leader pulp & printing indust Fort William, Beaconsfield, Cardiff, Tillycoultry 1969–72; area for. Fountain Forestry Stirling 1972–75; sales man. Northern Nurseries 1975–77; self-employed salesman and broker consult. of nursery stock, landscape contr./for. contr from 1977
m Aber 16.3.73 Morag R. Ronald MA 1969 *qv*

McVEIGH Gerald BSc(for) 1961

McVICAR Alasdair Harkness *BSc 1967 PhD 1973
s of Donald McV. farm. and Frances Harkness nurse; b Glasg 21.5.44
res asst zool Aberd 1967–70; sen scient off. DAFS marine lab Aber from 1970
m Kirkwall 8.8.68 Elizabeth M. Thomson MA 1966 *qv*

McVIE Fiona Jean Richmond MA 1969

McWATT Peter Joseph MB ChB 1969

McWEE Dorothy Carol Bruce MA 1968
d of Ernest McW. shop man. and Mary Graham health visitor; b Glasg 19.3.46
teacher p s: Kemnay 1969–72, Rothienorman 1972–74, Hillocks Bucksburn 1974–75; head Kingswells p s from 1975
m Aber 12.11.66 William N. McPhillimy MA 1968 *qv*

McWILLIAM Alan George *BSc 1970
s of George P. McW. SPCA insp and Dorothy C. G. Riddell MA 1935 *qv*; b Edin 8.7.47
Greenock: computer progr 1970–73, syst analyst IBM (UK) 1973–75; syst analyst BMW Münich W. Ger 1975–78; syst eng IBM (UK) St Albans from 1978

McWILLIAM Alexander Davidson *BSc 1961 MSc 1963 PhD 1968
s of Adam McW. eng, trg off. and Jessie Davidson cashier; b Elgin 2.9.39
asst lect Aberd 1965–68; phys Hilger & Watts Lond 1968–70; Margate: dev man. 1970–74, prod. group man. from 1974
m Aber 26.7.68 Valerie C. Waterston civ serv d of James W. Aber

McWILLIAM Angus Anderson *BSc 1968 PhD 1974

MacWILLIAM Anne Margaret BSc 1956
d of John MacW. MA 1905 *qv*; b New Pitsligo 15.12.35
tech res asst Unilever Warrington 1956–57; teacher Hilton s s Aber 1958–60, St Margaret's Aber 1960–63, internat s Geneva 1964–68, St Margaret's Aber 1968–69, Lively h s Ontario 1969–70, Hutcheson's boys' g s Glasg 1970–74, dep prin phys Madras coll St And from 1974

McWILLIAM David Gordon MA 1970

McWILLIAM Elizabeth MA 1969 Dip Ed 1970
d of William J. McW. blacksmith and Helen M. Taylor; b Huntly 25.10.48
teacher mod lang: Perth h s 1971–73, Holly Lodge h s for girls Liv from 1973
m Huntly 4.8.73 Joseph E. Pardoe civ serv s of Joseph E. P. Huntly

McWILLIAM Helen Ann Wood MA 1961
d of William J. McW. sawmiller, warehouseman and Euphemia Wood; b Lossiemouth 5.11.40
teacher mod lang Elgin acad 1962–66
m Elgin 13.7.63 Ian McKidd chief off. merch navy s of James McK. Elgin

McWILLIAM Irene Wilson MA 1956
d of James McW. civ serv and Alexandrina Wilson; b Aber 24.8.35
teacher Westerton p s Aber 1957–60
m Aber 27.12.58 Albert Birnie sen scient off. s of Alexander B. Aber

McWILLIAM Ralph Robertson BSc(eng) 1959

McWILLIAMS Dennis *MA 1965

MADDEN Craig Alexander *MA 1969
s of Alexander L. M. insur off. and Mary S. McKenzie secy; b Aber 16.12.46
PhD(Glas) 1976
Glasg: teacher Cathkin h s 1972–74, Hutcheson's g s 1974–75, asst prin hist Shawlands acad from 1975
m Aber 13.7.71 May Simpson MA 1969 *qv*

MADELEY Charles Richard MB ChB 1961 ᶜMD 1965
s of Charles L. A. M. furn consult. and Elsie J. Mann MB ChB 1921 *qv*; b Birm 14.8.32
h o ARI 1961–62; polio fund res fell. dept of bact Liv 1962–65; lect med micrcbiol St Thomas's hosp med s Lond 1965–70; MRC res fell. inst of virology Glas 1970–72; sen lect clin virol/hon consult. virol Glas 1972–79; prof virol N'cle from 1980
m Burbage 25.7.63 Margaret A. Martin mus d of Gordon O. M. Oare Marlborough

MAGEE Carolyn Isabel *MA 1967
d of Frank M. LLD 1979 and Isobel M. Noble civ serv; b Aber 21.12.44
teacher: Engl & Fr Inv 1967–68; Fr Aber 1971–72 and from 1973
m Aber 15.7.67 Ian S. D. Begg MB ChB 1967 *qv*

MAGEE Margaret Frances MA 1961 *1968
d of Frank M. LLD 1979 and Isobel M. Noble; b Aber 24.1.40
L-ès-L(Rennes) 1969 M-ès-L(Rennes) 1970 Dip App Ling(Edin) 1971
teacher: Aber 1962–65, Hamburg 1965; lect H-W Edin from 1971
m Edin 11.8.75 Andrew M. Lang M.Phil(Edin) arch. s of Robert M. L. Spinningdale

MAGEE Penelope Jane *MA 1969
d of Frank M. LLD 1979 and Isobel M. Noble; b Aber 7.10.46
teacher: Engl Rennes France 1971–73, Fr Aber from 1973

MAHMUD Mohammed Darus Bin *BSc(for) 1962

MAIN Alan MA 1957 BD 1960 PhD 1963
s of James E. W. M. gen fish merch and Mary A. R. Black; b Aber 31.3.36
STM(NY union theol seminary) 1961
C of S min Chapel of Garioch 1963–70; presb moderator 1969–70; chap. Aberd from 1970–80; prof pract theol Christ's Coll Aber/head dept pract theol Aberd from 1980
m Aber 30.7.60 Anne L. Swanson MA 1957 *qv*

MAIN Alexander Norman *MA 1964
s of Alexander O. M. lab and Susan S. Cruickshank; b Aber 14.11.41
post grad res Aberd 1964–66; lect psych Strath 1966–73; co-ordinating off. comm of vice-chancellors and principals Lond 1973–76; advis educ methods to Strath from 1976
m Aber 17.12.66 Alison M. Walker d of Ronald P. W. MA 1931 *qv*

MAIN David *BSc 1969
s of David M. elect. and Ann H. Coull; b Buckie 28.12.45
Dip Ed(Makerere) 1970
teacher, prin chem: Njiris s s Kenya 1970–73, Sekolah Menengah Sains Kuala Lumpur 1974–75; prin sc Kgari Sechele s s Molepolole Botswana 1976–78, Naledi s s Gabórone Botswana from 1978
m Ashford Surrey 27.10.73 Clare I. Walker secy d of John C. W. Staines

MAIN Dorothy MA 1966
m Francis

MAIN Douglas Edmund Thomson *BSc 1961
s of Alexander R. M. garage attend. and Ann C. A. Thomson; b Aber 2.12.38
teacher: Inverurie acad 1962–68, Machakos boys' board. s Nairobi 1968–73, Banff acad 1973, John Forrest sen h s Perth W Aust from 1974
m Aber 25.1.64 Rona A. McCarthy med photogr

MAIN James Jennings BSc(eng) 1964

MAIN Margaret Mein MA 1956
d of David M. M. fisherman and Christine Duggie; b Nairn 12.2.34
ALA 1963
lib asst Aber publ lib 1957–63; lib Ottawa publ lib 1963–64; res off. Scot. Nat Lib 1964–65; lib Ottawa publ lib from 1965, head of adult serv from 1978

MAIN Rosemary Susan MA 1970
d of George K. M. MA(Glas) customs and excise surv and Edith M. Mole secy; b Lond 5.4.49
teacher Edin from 1972

MAIN Sandra MA 1968
d of David M. banker and Jessa R. Dallas; b Aber 14.1.47
teacher geog Elgin acad 1969–71
m Nairn 1971 John G. McConnachie police constable s of Joseph McC. Inv

MAIN William Eric BSc(eng) 1965

MAIN William Mein BSc(eng) 1956
s of Isaac M. M. fisherman and Christina Duggie; b Nairn 6.12.35
MEng(McM) 1975
civ eng: Port Talbot, Glasg, Toronto, Lond(Ont), Winnipeg 1956–59; civ eng instr tech coll Hamilton Canada from 1969

MAINLAND Margaret Miller MA 1959
d of Harold M. teacher and Margaret C. Jamieson teacher; b Kirkcaldy 5.4.37
teacher prim subjs/Lat/Fr various schools, latterly Arbroath acad from 1960
m Montrose 17.4.54 John Findlay MA 1954 *qv*

MAINLAND Thomas James BSc(eng) 1957

MAIR Alexander Stirling Fraser *BSc(eng) 1957
s of Alexander W. R. M. farm./acct and Agnes W. Stirling; b Drumblade 20.7.35
app Rolls-Royce Glasg 1957–71; tech off. RAF Lond 1960–62; man dir Caithness Glass Wick 1971–75; market dir Worcester Royal Porcelain Co 1975–76; group man. dir Caithness Glass Wick from 1977
m(1) 14.10.61 Alice A. Garrow BSc 1959 *qv* (*d* 29.12.75)
(2) Crieff 21.10.77 Mary C. Bolton d of Thomas B. Crieff

MAIR Brian Alexander MA 1968
s of Alexander M. missionary and Helen E. Gaussen missionary; b Lond 25.10.47
journalist: reporter Inv 1968–70, edit. Paris 1970–76, edit. and translator Hong Kong from 1976

MAIR Frank Fentie MB ChB 1969
s of Stuart G. M. farm. and Mary P. Bruce; b Turriff 19.5.45
h o ARI 1969–70; sen h o obst, dermat ARI 1970–71; g p Banchory from 1971
m Aber 11.7.68 Morag R. Brown clerkess d of James F. B. Turriff

MAIR George Wood MA 1961

MAIR James *MA 1958

MAIR John BSc 1958

MAIR John Miller Mitchell *MA 1959
s of Alexander W. R. M. acct and Agnes W. Stirling; b Huntly 14.5.37
Dip Psych(Lond) 1960 PhD(Lond) 1964 ABPsS
lect psych Middx hosp med s Lond 1963–67, sen lect from 1967; fell. Neths inst adv study in humanities and soc sc Wassenaar, Holland 1971–72
m Harpenden 20.1.62 Katharine J. Lindsay BA(R'dg) clin psych/writer d of Robert L. BSc(Lond)

MAIR Joyce Willetta MA 1958

MAIR Stuart Bruce BSc 1959

MAITLAND Alison Isabel *MA 1969 PhD 1972
d of James J. M. farm. and Isabella H. Monro; b Aber 17.7.47
asst to H. C. Robbins Landon, Haydn schol: Florence 1972–73, Vienna 1973–74, Aber from 1974
m Aber 31.8.74 Robert S. Shiel BSc(agr)(N'cle) horticultural advis s of Stanley H. S. Morpeth

MAITLAND Dorothy Isobel MA 1963
d of James M. insp of works and Margaret Wilson; b Aber 30.9.40
teacher: Ballater p s 1964–65, Cloverfield p s Bucksburn 1965–73, asst head from 1973
m Aber 17.8.71 George D. M. Dow DA teacher of art s of Marshall D. Aber

MAITLAND Ronald George BSc 1967

MAKIN Michael John MSc 1963
BA(Oxon)

MALCOLM Hugh MacGregor *BSc 1966
s of MacGregor M. bank man. and Christina B. B. MacFarlane; b Edin 28.5.44
STC E. Kilbride: tel exchange proj and dimensioning eng 1966–69, circuit des lab 1970–72; circuit eng for private and export Crossbar tel syst Plessey Beeston Nott 1972–74; tel traffic and syst stud. eng STC E Kilbride from 1974

MALCOLM Neil Law BSc(agr) 1961

MALCOLM Ronald Innes *MA 1960 Dip Ed 1961 MEd 1963
s of Edward C. M. chartered mech eng and Evelyn Frain secy; b Glasg 12.8.38
teacher: Laurencekirk 1961–64, Dun 1964–70, E. Kilbride 1970–72; asst dir of educ Moray & Nairn 1972–75; div educ off. Highland reg c from 1975
m Aber 30.12.64 Christine J. Williamson teacher d of Charles W. Dollar

MALCOLM Stella Margaret *BSc 1960
d of Norman L. M. eng and Winifred M. Forrest SRN nurs sister/midwife; b Lond 31.12.37
Unilever Isleworth: res chem 1960–65, sect. man. consumer stud. 1965–67

m Lond 18.1.64 Alfred J. W. Ludford gold marker s of Alfred W.L. Lond

MALINS Donald Clive PhD 1967 DSc 1976
s of Richard H. M. and Mabel M. Warner; b Lima, Peru 19.5.31
BA(Wash) 1953 BS(Wash) 1956
Seattle USA: univ prof/progr head NOAA 1967–74, also dir environmental conserv dir NOAA dept commerce from 1974
m Seattle 27.1.62 Mary L. Leiren univ stud. d of Linus L.

MALLEY Alexander Bruce MA 1965
s of Alexander M. sawmill foreman and Ann F. Bruce; b Ellon 25.8.42
teacher Kirkhill p s Aber 1966–69; head audio-vis aids dept Ardleigh Green j s Hornchurch 1969–72; head Daviot p s Inverurie from 1972
m Fraserburgh 15.8.69 Sandra J. Sim MA 1969 *qv*

MALLEY Ian MA 1963 BSc 1968
s of Alexander M. sawmill foreman and Ann F. Bruce; b Fraserburgh 6.7.40
ALA 1973
lib Maria Mercer phys lib univ of Brist 1970–77; information off. for user Educ Brit lib from 1977

MALLINSON Donald Leslie BSc(for) 1959

MALLINSON Peter David *BSc 1969 PhD 1972
s of Harry M. div secy friendly soc and Phyllis Hargreaves; b Northampton 30.6.47
FCS 1972 CChem MRIC 1972
R'dg: asst edit. *Molecular Physics* 1972–73; SRC post-doct res asst 1973–75; applications progr univ of Lond computer centre 1975–77; computer progr user serv univ of Aston Birm from 1977
m Aber 16.12.69 Margaret C. M. Mair MA 1971 d of Arthur B. M. Aber

MALLOCH Susan Margaret Jennifer *MA 1969
d of George C. M. MB ChB(Edin) g p and Eileen M. Littlewood MA(Edin) SRN; b Edin 24.2.46
Lond: p a, secy to chmn opinion res centre 1969–70, secy to gen man. Brit wool market. board 1970–71; teacher: Fr Headington s s Oxford 1972–74; TEFL Oxf 1974

MALOIY Geoffrey Moriaso Ole PhD 1968
s of Rokoi O. M. farm. and Keis E. Korio; b Ngong Kenya 10.8.39
BSc(BC) 1964 MIBiol(Lond) 1968 Scient Fell. Lond Zool Soc 1968
Kenya: head anim physiol div E.Af vet res inst Muguga 1968–71; univ of Nairobi: head dept anim physiol from 1972, prof anim physiol from 1975, dean faculty of vet med from 1976; visiting scient inst of anim physiol Cambridge 1971; sen Fulbright Hays schol and res assoc biol labs Harvard USA 1975

MALONE Brian Francis *BSc 1968 MSc 1970

MALONE Mary Elizabeth *MA 1967

MALTHOUSE Ray Edward *BSc(eng) 1969
s of Edward M. civ eng and Joyce E. Podger; b Stockport 22.7.46
MICE 1973
asst eng: Taylor Woodrow Lond 1969–70; Poole burgh council 1970–71, Warks c c 1971–74; sen eng Oxfordsh c c Oxford from 1974
m Bournemouth 12.6.71 Janet L. Freegard draughtswoman d of Ronald A. F. Poole

MALYA Meenakshi Manjeshwar MSc 1964
MA(Madras)

MANGAL Subash BSc 1965

MANGAT Sukhdev Singh BSc(eng) 1968
BA(Panj)

MANLEY Duncan John Russell MSc 1961
s of Ernest R. M. bank man. and Sarah Rees BA (Swansea) teacher; b Croydon 31.3.38
BSc(Exe) 1959
soil surv (of Eng and Wales) Devon 1961–64; scient liaison off. Rank Hovis McDougall Lond 1964–67; tech and dev man., tech and buying dir Chiltman Biscuits Lond 1967–77; food process tech Baker Perkins Peterborough from 1977
m Cheam 14.7.62 Jane M. Howell secy d of Arthur C. H. Cheam

MANN David Leask *BSc 1970
s of Stanley O. M. bact, prin scient off. and Anna M. Leask; b Aber 9.3.48
PhD(Strath) 1973
proj man. Unilever res Sharnbrook 1973–78; tech man. United Biscuits Glasg from 1978
m Aber 6.7.71 Brenda L. Green teacher d of Raymond G. Aber

MANN Maureen Elizabeth MA 1969
m Collin

MANN Thomas Leslie John BSc 1962
s of Thomas L. M. M. sales man. and Anne H. Purdy; b Norfolk 30.4.41
Dip Ed(Adel) 1975
exper off. Torry fisheries Aber 1963–64; Aust: res asst dept anim husb Sydney univ 1964–66, livestock res off. dept of agr Adelaide 1966–68, haemat off. IMVS Adelaide 1969, supt field stat CSIRO div of nutrit and biochem Adelaide 1970–72, farm man. nr Adelaide 1973–74, res off. agr Roseworthy coll S Aust from 1974
m Adelaide 28.10.67 Elizabeth A. Webb nurs sister d of Martin W. Marwell Victoria Aust

MANSI Morid Girgis MSc 1965
s of Girgis S. M. sen clerk Sudan railways Atbara and Afifa H. Toma; b Atbara 20.6.39
BSc(Alex)
Gezira res stat Sudan: agronomist 1965–67, statist 1967–69 PhD stud dept expt statist NCSU, USA 1969–72; sen statist/head of statist sect. 1973–78; prof biometrics agr res corp Wad Medani from 1978
m Alexandria Egypt 24.8.67 Nagat N. Bissada BSc(eng) (Alex) chief agr eng Sudan Gezira board d of N. B. Alexandria

MANSON David Leslie *BSc 1958
s of Frederick W. M. CA and Margaret R. McAdam; b Elgin 19.8.35
res stud. Aberd 1958–61; indust chem: Manc 1961–63, Middlesbrough 1963–70; computer analyst/progr Middlesbrough from 1970
m Aber 20.5.60 Margaret I. Robertson hostel housekeeper d of James A. R. Brechin

MANSON Donald McAllister *MA 1962
s of Donald M. M. fishmonger and Jean Wallace teacher needlework; b Aber 26.4.37
teacher: Caol 1964–65, Banff acad 1965–68; sen educ psych Cumnock ch guid centre from 1968
m Aber 6.7.63 Mary Mitchell MA 1960 *qv*

MANSON Doreen Mackenzie MA 1970 Dip Ed 1971
d of William C. M. police sergt and Margaret A. Mackenzie clerkess; b Fearn 19.6.49
teacher p s Stirlingsh 1971–75, Invsh from 1975
m Aber 4.7.77 Bruce A. Matheson s of James M. Inv

MANSON Henry John MB ChB 1970
s of James M. farm. and Mary E. Peterson; b Northmavine Shetland 9.2.46
ARI: h o 1970–71, sen h o anaest 1971–72, regist anaest from 1972
m Errol 3.4.71 Edith M. McFarlane RGN d of William P. McF. Glencarse

MANSON John George Mackay *BSc 1968
s of Francis M. insur ag and Johan Mackay; b Wick 26.1.46
teacher chem: Wick h s 1969–71; RGC Aber 1971–76; prin chem Lochaber h s Fort William from 1976
m Wick 9.7.71 Anne M. Fraser nurse d of Victor F. Wick

MANSON Marion Scott *MA 1962
d of Alexander M. and Christina Mair; b Peterhead 3.2.39
teacher
m David W. N. Stewart coll lect

MANSON Neil Bressay *BSc 1963 MSc 1966 PhD 1968
s of Frederick W. M. CA and Margaret R. MacAdam; b Elgin 17.8.40
asst prof Los Angeles 1968–70; res assoc Queen Mary coll Lond 1970–72; ANU Canberra: res fell. 1972–78, sen res fell. from 1978
m Aber 13.9.68 Patricia A. Garland secy d of Victor H. G. Aber

MANSON Roger John MB ChB 1956
d Coventry 2.3.61 *AUR* xxxix 205

MANSOUR Ali Hafez MLitt 1967
s of Hafez M. bus. man and Bahaya Mohamed; b Egypt 26.3.32
BCom(Ein Shams) 1956 PhD(St And) 1970
statist insur co Cairo 1956–59; Cairo univ: asst 1959–62, lect literature, econ 1970–75, reader from 1975
m Egypt Wedad Tulup d of Marawan T. Egypt

MANTELL Helen Diana Mary *MA 1965
d of Henry P.M. dist supt ALC Zambia and Barbara A. Lyall MA 1921 *qv*; b Zambia 4.1.44
teacher: Lond 1966–67, Lusaka 1967–69; curric dev off. Lusaka 1969–73; teacher Banffsh 1974–76; lang teacher Engl lang foundation Edin from 1976

MARCELLA Camille *MA 1969
d of Domenico M. insur salesman and Flora M. Murray sales asst; b Aber 14.6.48
Lond: proof reader market res comp 1969–70, admin asst publ 1970–72, teacher 1973–78; resid Hong Kong from 1978
m Aber 2.7.71 George W. Simpson arch. s of Norman S. Stoneywood

MARDON David Kenneth BSc 1966 MSc 1975
s of George F. F. RAF, insur ag and Edith G. Milligan PO clerk; b Retford 13.5.43
res asst zool Aberd from 1969
m Aber 12.10.72 Glenda E. Tomlin hotel caterer

MARIONI Lina Della BSc 1964
d of Luigi A M. shopkeeper and Delina Barbieri; b Ellon 13.5.43
teacher maths: Stirling 1965–69, Ellon 1970–73, prin maths from 1973

MARIONI Norma Luigina MA 1969
d of Luigi A. M. shopkeeper and Delina L. Barbieri; b Fraserburgh 18.5.48
teacher Engl: Bathgate 1970–72, Dun 1972–75, Aber from 1975

MARK Colin Brown Downie MA 1959
s of Alexander M. lorry driver, blacksmith and Mary Bruce; b Campbeltown 26.12.36
teacher p s: Turriff 1959–61, Peterhead 1961–68; head: Burnmouth 1968–72, Gourdon from 1972
m 26.7.63 Jean C. Thom nursery worker d of James T. Aber

MARKS Gillian Mary *MA 1969 Dip Ed 1970
d of Robert S. M. HMIS and Mary G. Pyne s secy; b Stirling 10.12.47
teacher Engl: Bell–Baxter h s Cupar 1970–71, Tomlinscote c s s Frimley from 1971
m Torphins 6.8.71 David I. Gould BSc(N polytech Lond) lect/syst analyst s of Francis C. G. Stokenham

MARNOCH Jennifer Jean MA 1970
d of Daniel J. M. M. head for. and Margaret S. Menzies hairdresser; b Glenalmond 15.12.49
teacher: geog Dunblane h s 1971–75, prin guid from 1975
m Perth 30.7.77 Michael S. McHale policeman s of Patrick McH. Auchterarder

MARNOCH Patricia June BSc 1960
m Currie

MARQUISS Michael *BSc 1970 PhD 1977
s of Maurice M. elect. eng and Mary Simmons bookkeeper/typist; b N'cle-u-Tyne 2.2.47
PhD stud. Aberd mtn and moorland res stat Banchory 1970–73; h s o ITE (predator res) out-posted at Dumfries from 1974
m Aber 4.8.72 Elizabeth A. Henderson physioth d of William H. Aber

MARR Douglas *MA 1969 Dip Ed 1970

MARR George Laurie MA 1957 dBD 1960
s of George C. M. wood working machinist and Margaret W. Stopper; b Aber 3.6.36
C of S min: St Adrian's ch Anstruther 1961–67, Grange ch Kilmarnock from 1967
m Aber 5.8.60 Margaret B. McArthur MA 1958 *qv*

MARR Iain Lovat *BSc 1961 MSc 1963 PhD 1966
s of Donald H. M. life assur off. and Margaret Hooson; b Aber 21.6.39
Fritz Feigl prize of Austrian microchem soc 1970
asst lect Aberd 1964–66; CIBA fell. technische hochschule Vienna 1966–67; lect chem Aberd from 1967; visiting lect univ Kuala Lumpur Malaysia 1970–71 and 1977
m Vienna 11.8.66 Eva Watzka teacher Engl d of Otto W. Vienna

MARR Ian Scott BSc 1966

MARR Kathleen Ann *MA 1970
m Malone

MARR Sheena Margaret Smith MA 1965
m Furie

MARRIOTT Richard Welton *BSc 1966
m Dorothy K. Forbes BSc 1966 *qv*

MARSH Elizabeth-Ann MB ChB 1967

MARSH Jennifer Frances *MEd 1966
d of Andrew M. comp secy and Frances Chrystal translator; b Pinner 10.11.37
MA(Cantab) 1961
teacher geog Aboyne acad from 1966

MARSHALL Adrian Gerald *BSc(agr) 1963 PhD 1969
s of C. F. M. BSc(eng)(Edin) eng and Marjorie M. K. Fry; b St And 10.10.40
MS(Calif) 1965
teaching asst UC Berkeley Calif 1963–65; lect zool Aberd from 1965; seconded lect univ of Malaya 1966–68

MARSHALL Alexandra Rose MA 1967
d of William K. M. relief stat master and Elizabeth A. Lawson; b Kingussie 16.8.46
teacher Lossiemouth p s 1967–71, asst head 1971–77; head Portknockie p s from 1977

MARSHALL Hugh Gordon Walker BSc(for) 1962

MARSHALL Keir Cleland LLB 1970
s of Thomas K. M. town clerk and Isabella Thomson; b Paisley 18.11.47
NP 1974
law app Elgin 1971; exec off. HIDB Inv 1972; law app Inv 1972–74; solic Inv from 1974
m Bishopbriggs 4.4.74 Heather E. Cousin MA(Glas) teacher d of William C. Bishopbriggs

MARSHALL Linda Joyce BSc 1968
m Lamb

MARSHALL Margaret Williamson *MA 1967
d of John M. MA(Glas) headmaster and Maria R. Williamson; b N. Berwick 5.7.44
post grad Certif Advanced Europ Stud.(econ)(Bruges) 1968
trainee Europ commun inst for univ stud. and EEC Brussels 1968–69; res asst centre for contemp Europ stud. Sus 1969–70; part-time TEFL Helsinki 1971; part-time teacher Ger f e/freelance writer and translator Cheshire 1972–74; res assoc dept soc admin and med s Manc 1974–77
m Aber 26.3.70 Richard J. Potton BSc(Sus) univ lect s of Sydney C. P. Epsom

MARSHALL Peter Michie MA 1969
s of Alexander M. grocery man. and Mary A. McLeod nurse; b Banff 29.9.46
MICA 1974
CA Edin 1969–75, Lond from 1975
m Edin 5.5.73 Margaret W. Forbes secy d of James W. F. Edin

MARSHALL Robert *MA 1967
s of Wilfred R. M. gas board employee and Margaret Duncan; b Aber 21.8.44
lect inst d'anglais univ de Strasbourg 1968–71; information off. Brit consul. gen Strasbourg from 1972
m Derby 24.7.71 Patricia Daly SRN, secy dip. serv d of William M. D. Winslow

MARSHALL Sheila Ross MA 1970
d of Robert J. M. police insp and Jean M. Ross teacher; b St And 5.9.48
banker Paisley, Glasg 1970–74
m Cupar 10.7.70 Peter W. Mills BSc(eng) 1970 *qv*

MARTIN Anne Don *MA 1968 CASS 1970
d of John M. clerk of works dept environment Aber and Alexandrina McIntyre teacher; b Glasg 24.3.46
Glasg: med soc worker Western I 1970–72, sen med soc worker Gartnavel gen hosp 1972–75, fieldwork teacher Western I 1975–77; soc worker Kingseat hosp Newmachar from 1977
m Aber 3.6.77 Alan K. Foulis BSc(Glas) med pract s of Keith F. MB ChB(Glas)

MARTIN Brian Anthony Bernard *BSc 1969
s of Edward L. M. printer and Doris M. Allen; b Lond 22.11.45
PhD(Warw) 1973
SRC res stud. Warwick univ 1969–73; wissenschaftlicher asst Max-Planck inst für biochemie Münich from 1973

MARTIN Carol June Lofthus *MA 1970
d of John M. M. foreman joiner and Ethel M. Lofthus; b Aber 24.1.49
asst teacher: Aylesbury 1971–74, Cleveland educ auth 1974–75; Cleveland educ auth: coll lect 1975–76 and from 1979
m Aber –.9.70 David K. J. Baldwin MA 1970 *qv*

MARTIN Christine MA 1964

MARTIN David Michael Weir BSc 1969
s of Gavin L. M. teaplanter, farm. and Jean I. Gavin; b Aber 27.1.43
Lond: syst analyst ICL 1969–73, Dataskil (salesman) 1973–74; Sydney: salesman NCR 1975–77, comp dir Martin Henderson from 1977
m Aber 3.7.69 Lilian U. Bald MA 1968 *qv*

MARTIN Eleanor Marie MA 1968
d of Alexander M. M. farm man. and Helen R. Thomson teacher; b Salisbury 3.7.47
trg off. installation of data prep syst and of comm computer packages for customers in computer bureau Lond 1968–77
m Lond 17.8.74 Roy K. Kunar BSc(Imp coll) consult. eng s of David P. K. AIEd(Lond) Guyana

MARTIN Elizabeth Margaret *BSc 1967
d of David M. M. crofter and Margaret I. Morrice; b Kingswells 3.3.46
MSc(Dund) 1969
teacher maths Summerhill acad, Old Aber s s 1970–75
m Aber 6.6.75 Thomas C. Kirkpatrick tel eng s of Thomas K. Lockerbie

MARTIN George McKenzie *MA 1962
s of David M. M. crofter and Margaret I. Morrice; b Aber 9.3.40
lect Ger Aberd from 1965
m Aber 22.12.73 Eleanor J. Henderson MA 1971 teacher d of Ross M. H. Aber

MARTIN Iain Robert MA 1967

MARTIN Ishbel McDonald *MA 1967
d of John M. clerk of works and Alexandrina McIntyre teacher; b Glasg 4.12.44
Engl asst Rennes univ France 1967–68; res stud. Aberd/Paris 1968–71; lect Fr: Edin 1971–72, Nott 1972–73, Manc polytech from 1973
m Cheadle 24.5.75 John M. Coy MSc(Brad) lect accounting/author s of William H. L. C. Reevesby nr Boston

MARTIN James McBride MA 1961

MARTIN James Mulholland MA 1970
BD(Dund)

MARTIN John Stuart MA 1967
s of John L. M. dir fam bus. tea/coffee merch and Bessie Ewan secy; b Sale 7.9.45
CA(Eng and Wales) 1972
Thornton Baker & Co CA Manc: articled clerk 1967–70, audit sen 1970–72; audit man. Pannel Fitzpatrick & Co CA Manc
m Accrington 4.8.71 Nancy P. Lodge teacher d of Spencer L. Accrington

MARTIN Lesley Elizabeth McLeod MA 1966
d of Stanley E. M. MA 1934 *qv*; b Aber 15.9.44
teacher: Peterhead 1967–69, 1971–72, Langholm acad from 1975, remed educ from 1976
m Peterhead 9.4.69 Alexander D. McBay ARCO mus teacher Galashiels, Langholm acad s of Alfred D. McB. Peterhead

MARTIN Mary Ann MacSween MA 1966

MARTIN Pamela May MA 1970 Dip Ed 1971
d of John M. M. joiner and Ethel M. Lofthus typist; b Aber 29.7.47
teacher Tullos p s Aber 1971–73; teacher/lib Overleigh Middle Chester 1973–75
m Aber 21.12.67 Alexander S. Robertson MA 1967 *qv*

MARTIN Ruaridh MacCuish *MEd 1969
s of John M. radio oper/tech and Catherine A. MacCuish teacher; b Stranraer 6.9.42
MA(Edin) 1964 Dip Ed(Edin) 1965
teacher maths Golspie h s 1965–68; asst educ psych Sutherland 1969–72; educ psych Western Is reg Stornoway from 1973
m Dingwall 10.7.70 Marion A. MacLeod teacher d of William MacL. Dingwall

MARTIN Scott Russell MB ChB 1964
s of James R. M. MB ChB 1932 *qv*; b Aber 11.2.38
LMCC(Can) 1973
h o ARI 1964–65; RAF med br 1965–70; g p Port Perry Canada from 1970
m(2) Port Perry 30.7.77 Susan Schwan nurse Whitby Ont
d Port Perry 9.79 car accident *AUR* XLVIII 354

MARTIN Sheila Christina MB ChB 1958
d of James N. M. papermill worker and Annabell Duncan papermill worker; b Peterculter 22.7.33
MRCOG 1963 MRCGP 1966
NHS hosp posts N Wales, Scot. 1958–67; private pract and hon work Christian hosp Quetta Pakistan from 1967
m Glasg 17.12.66 Jahansoz F. Patel BA(Punjab) elect. eng/bus. man. s of Framrose B. P. Quetta

MARTIN Sheila Smith BSc 1957
d of John A. M. motor hirer and Mary M. Mann secy; b Inv 3.9.36
FCS 1972
teacher chem: Aber h s for girls 1958–65, spec asst 1965–69, royal acad Inv from 1969

MARTIN Valerie Claire *MA 1969
d of Wilfred H. M. head attendant House of Lords and Annie E. Beddoes; b Coleraine NI 29.4.42
C Phil(Calif) 1975
exch schol univ of Kansas USA 1969–70; instr Swedish lang and lit. univ of Calif Los Angeles 1970–75; instr Swedish lang US army 1974; Calif: instr Swedish Pomona coll Claremont 1974–77, dir lang lab Pomona coll 1975–76, instr Swedish Reseda commun adult s from 1975, owner Nordic translation serv Claremont from 1977; instr Swedish lang: Chaffey coll Alta Loma from 1977, Calif state poly univ Pomona from 1978, Citrus coll Azusa from 1979, parent educ Claremont adult s from 1979, Swedish s Mar Vista from 1980
m Los Angeles 11.6.75 Robert L. Gustaveson BS(Utah) civ eng s of Robert T. G. Salt Lake City

MARWICK David Corrigall *BSc 1964
s of William C. M. MA 1937 *qv*; b Stafford 16.5.42
teacher: VSO Lusaka Zambia 1965–66, Aber 1966–68, Lerwick 1968–70; nurs auxil 1970–72, stud. nurse Aber from 1972
m 11.7.68 Jean M. H. Sandison MA 1966 *qv*

MARWICK John Sinclair *BSc 1970

MASING Jawie MB ChB 1967
s of Masing Ak Jerenang farm. and Kumang Ak Emparan farm.; b Marau Sarawak 3.3.42
DPH(Singapore) 1972
h o Hairmyres hosp Glasg 1967–68; m o Simanggang Sibu Sarawak 1968–71, sen m o 1972–74; g p Sarikei, Sarawak from 1974
m Sibu, Sarawak 28.11.70 Mary Wong P. H. clerk d of Wong P. Kwong Sibu

MASON Lesley Marie MA 1967
d of Thomas L. M. elect. and May A. McMillan cashier/bookkeeper; b Manc 15.1.45
Dip Ed(Belf) 1968
teacher Engl Belf 1968–70, prin Engl Dungannon NI 1970–72; lect Engl Portadown NI 1972–74; commun tut. for adult educ Peterborough from 1975
m Newtownards NI 4.7.70 William H. Stewart comp dir s of James S. Kircubbin

MASSEY Juliet Cathron BSc 1968
d of Humphrey L. M. CA and Catheron J. R. Formoy; b Harlow 25.4.46
jun tech, med lab tech: Oxford 1969–71, Ibadan Nigeria from 1972
m Lochgilphead 27.11.71 Donald R. Clark MB BS(Lond) med pract s of Roger H. C. Battle

MASSIE Arthur MA 1970

MASSIE Harry McKenzie MA 1968
s of Harry M. police off. and Nellie I. McKenzie hairdresser; b Turriff 31.8.46
grad trainee acct Bradford city treas 1968–71; tech asst educ. fin. Leic city treas 1971–74; audit asst Leics c c from 1974
m Arbroath 6.6.70 Christine A. Robertson nurs sister d of Donald R. Arbroath

MASSIE Helen Watson BSc 1969 MB ChB 1971
d of George M. stillman and Helen A. W. Watson; b Oldmeldrum 5.7.45
DObstRCOG 1973
h o Aber hosps 1971–72; sen h o obst/gyn Inv 1972–73; civ med pract Osnabrück Ger from 1973
m Aber 4.12.72 Roderick J. M. MacDonald MB ChB 1971 RAMC s of Duncan MacD. Conon Bridge

MASSIE Kathleen Forbes BSc 1962

MASSIE Maureen BSc 1956
d of Alexander M. bank teller and Isabella J. B. Masson; b Aber 7.5.35
teacher maths/sc: Northfield acad Aber 1957–60, part-time posts Aber 1962–70; sc Peterhead acad from 1971

m Aber 29.12.59 Alexander G. Armstrong pharm s of Allan M. A. MA 1925 *qv*

MASSIE Maureen Elizabeth Symmers MA 1969
d of James M. blacksmith and Mary M. F. Taylor psychiat nurse; b Strathdon 14.6.46
m Bucksburn 25.11.69 George M. Dorward sales rep s of Alexander G. M. D. Stirling

MASSON Aileen Justine MA 1966
m Wilson

MASSON Andrew *BSc 1970

MASSON Catherine Kelly MB ChB 1958
m Skinner

MASSON Christina *BSc 1962 MSc 1964
d of John M. fisherman and Annie Ritchie; b Inverallochy 12.3.40
lect: RGIT Aber 1963–64, H-W univ Edin 1964–65; part-time asst Aberd 1966 and 1969; temp lect RGIT 1971–73; part-time dem H-W univ Edin from 1974
m Noble

MASSON George Fraser BSc(eng) 1961
s of George M. scient instrum maker and Janet Dufton; b Aber 5.6.40
MICE
grad eng Swindon 1961–63; Lond: site eng 1963–64, asst eng 1964–67, eng 1967–69; tech rep Birm from 1969
m Swindon 5.9.64 Valerie S. Scott teacher d of Mervin J. S. Swindon

MASSON Gordon Machray MB ChB 1968 ᶜMD 1973
s of Alexander M. firemaster and Dorothy M. Davie; b Greenock 3.4.45
MRCOG 1974
h o ARI 1968–69; sen h o Gilbert Bain hosp Lerwick 1969–70; sen h o mat. hosp Aber 1970; MRC fell. obst Aberd 1970–72; regist obst/gyn Aberd 1972–74; clin instr obst/gyn med coll Wisconsin Milwaukee USA 1974–75; lect obst/gyn Aberd 1975–77; sen lect human reproduction and obst S'ton/hon consult. obst/gyn Hants area (teaching) from 1977

MASSON Margaret Dean BSc 1957 *1958
d of Alexander C. F. M. eng(telecomm) and Margaret I. Allan; b Elgin 4.5.35
teacher: Dalkeith h s 1959–62, prin geog Keith g s 1962–65, Weymouth g s 1965–71, Helston comp s 1975–76, Elgin acad 1978–81, Kincorth acad Aber from 1981
m(2) Elgin 3.7.65 Bruce E. Weightman electronics eng s of William E. W. N'cle-u-Tyne

MASSON Mary Bella Ritchie BSc 1961
m Steele

MASSON Peter Davie MB ChB 1965
d 4.4.66

MASSON Robert Alan *BSc 1968
s of Robert M. fish merch and Nellie G. T. Livingstone; b Inverallochy 7.3.46
teacher sc Peterhead acad 1969–72; app CA Inv 1972–76; CA Aber from 1976

MASSON Robert Edwin *BSc 1969 PhD 1973
s of Robert M. painter and Isabella M. Masson; b Stonehaven 20.5.47
teacher chem: Kirkcaldy h s 1973, Torry acad Aber from 1973
m Aber 27.12.72 Mary R. Taylor BSc 1970 *qv*

MASSON Sandra BSc 1968
d of Alexander S. M. merch navy and Isabella M. Morgan; b Aber 30.8.48
teacher: Alford acad 1969–70, St Mary's acad Bathgate 1970–72, Linksfield acad Aber 1972–75
m Aber 4.7.75 Andrew J. Bolsover BSc(St And) teacher s of John F. B. Stockport

MASSON Sheila Ann BEd 1970
d of Robert M. painter and Isabella M. Masson; b Stonehaven 8.5.49
teacher: mod lang Perth h s 1970–74, Engl St Matthias gym Gerolstein W. Ger 1974–76, mod lang/ housemistress Hartcliffe comp s Bristol from 1976

MASTERMAN Michael BSc(eng) 1970
s of Leonard M. mech eng foreman and Catherine Burke; b Durh 25.1.47
asst eng: Perth 1968–69, Northallerton from 1969
m Spennymoor 3.6.72 Hazel Dixon bank clerk d of William J. D. BSc(Lond) Spennymoor

MASTERMAN Veryan Loveday Serrell BSc 1970
teacher Bucks 1971–73; recorder for *The Zoological Record* Brit Museum (nat hist) from 1973

MATHER Alexander Smith *BSc 1966 PhD 1972
s of Alexander S. M. farm. and Mary M. Smith MA 1924 *qv*; b Aber 17.9.43
lect geog Aberd from 1967
m Aber 7.7.70 Grace S. MacArthur MA 1969 *qv*

MATHER Arthur Cameron Mackay *BSc 1963
s of Osmund K. M. army off. and Jean C. Allan shop man.; b Thurso 18.9.41
MSc(City univ Lond) 1977
seismic computer Bromley 1963–65; scient information off. Lond 1966–77; bookshop prop. Cowes from 1978
m Hampstead 21.3.70 Elizabeth Holdstock SRN d of Raymond P. H. Lond

MATHERS Helen Tait *MA 1966 Dip Ed 1967
d of David S. M. MA(St And) teacher and Jean K. Rutherford BSc(St And) teacher; b Campbeltown 6.2.44
teacher Engl N Berwick h s 1967–69; head p s Fetlar 1969–71
m Aber 23.7.69 Anthony R. Mainwood BSc(Brist) asst warden Fair Isle bird obs/RSPB warden Fetlar/lorry driver/teacher s of Henry R. M. OBE Whitstable

MATHERS John Shirreffs BSc(agr) 1956
s of James C. M. eng and Frances H. Findlater nurse; b Edin 5.3.31
SDA NDA(Edin & E. Scot. coll of agr)
reg admin off. Scot. agr trg board Perth from 1970
m Aber 12.6.58 Jenny Johnston nurse d of James W. J. Aberchirder

MATHERS John Walker *BSc(eng) 1966

MATHERS Kathleen Paterson BSc 1969
d of Alexander R. M. farm. and Jenny Paterson teacher; b Kintore 16.2.48
Vereeniging S Af: bact Rand Water board 1970–71, teacher from 1971
m Vereeniging 6.2.71 Logan R. G. Fitchie BSc 1969 *qv*

MATHESON Alasdair Burnett MB ChB 1964

MATHESON Catherine Ross MA 1964 Dip Ed 1966
d of James R. M. gamekeeper, crofter, s bagpipe instr and Helen C. Tough; b Kinlochewe 16.6.43
teacher: Aber 1965–66, Sutherland 1968, Aber 1973–75,

Porchester from 1975
m Aber 22.6.63 Antoine K. Ah-See MB ChB 1965 *qv*

MATHESON Catherine Ross *MA 1958

MATHESON Christina *MA 1962
d of Alexander M. MB ChB 1931 *qv*; b Inv 12.9.39
Dip Clin Psych(Edin) 1964
clin psych Stratheden hosp Fife 1964–65; part-time lect dev psych Euro section univ of Maryland Italy 1965–66; part-time res asst Strath 1967–69; part-time clin psych RHSC Glasg 1969–73; sen clin psych from 1973
m Aber 4.9.65 Bruno U. V. Del Priore arch. s of Domenico Del P. Salerno Italy

MATHESON Donald William MA 1956
s of Kenneth M. crofter and Catherine MacDonald; b Brue Is of Lewis 10.6.33
MBE 1973
serv RAEC UK, Borneo, Malaya, Hong Kong from 1957; major, sen educ off. Guards depot Pirbright
m Aber 19.1.57 Alice I. Durno d of Ferguson D. Oldmeldrum

MATHESON Iain James MA 1963
s of Donald J. M. BSc 1933 *qv*; b Conon Bridge 1.8.42
higher exec off. HM Customs & Excise from 1963
m Glasg 1.7.70 Marilyn A. Boyd mus d of Arthur T. H. B. Glasg

MATHESON Janet Catherine MA 1959 Dip Ed 1960
d of Alexander M. MB ChB 1931 *qv*; b Edin 13.9.37
teacher: Engl Northfield s Aber 1960–61, Stornoway 1962, Inv h s 1962–63
m Aber 17.7.61 Graham C. Hunter MA 1958 *qv*

MATHESON Jennifer Ruth Victoria MA 1966
m McGinn

MATHESON Margaret Norma MA 1961
d of Malcolm M. MA(Glas) schoolmaster and Winifred M. Spink teacher; b Aberfeldy 19.1.41
teacher: Engl Bridge of Earn 1962–63, Engl/hist Breadalbane acad Aberfeldy 1963–68
m Strathtay 24.7.64 John Kidd joiner s of John I. K. Strathtay

MATHESON Mhairi Lindsay MB ChB 1957
d of David M. bank man. and Mary S. S. Lindsay MA(Edin) teacher; b Kirkcaldy 9.4.33
h o: ARI 1957–58, Dumfries & Galloway RI 1958–59, mat. hosp Aber 1959; g p: Crieff 1959–60, Kyle of Lochalsh 1960–65, Falkirk also prin m o (indust) from 1965; factory doctor Falkirk 1966–72

MATHESON Norman Alistair MB ChB 1956 *ChM 1965
s of Allan J. M. and Margaret A. Mutch; b Inv 26.3.32
FRCS 1961 FRCSE 1961
h o Aber 1956–57; lect Aberd: materia medica 1957–58, anat 1958–59; surg regist Aber gen hosps 1959–61; lect surg Aberd 1961–64, sen lect from 1964 and consult. gen surg Aber gen hosps from 1967
m Aber 10.9.58 Helen I. Grant d of John G. Ballindalloch

MATHESON Stephen Charles Taylor *MA 1961

MATHESON Susan Marie MA 1968
d of Donald J. M. BSc 1933 *qv*; b Nairn 26.2.48
nurse Skye 1968–69; teacher Lossiemouth 1970–71
m Croydon 29.12.70 Roger A. Lockley pilot lt RN s of Leslie H. L. Croydon

MATHEWSON Alastair George *BSc 1962 MSc 1964 PhD 1967

MATHEWSON Iain MB ChB 1959

MATHIESON Alastair Merchant MA 1960 LLB 1962
s of Alexander M. master butcher and Constance E. Coutts cashier; b Aber 12.6.39
exch schol bus. man. univ of Kansas USA 1963–64; asst solic Aber: James & George Collie advoc 1964–65, A. C. Morrison & Richards advoc 1965–66, Paull & Williamsons advoc 1966–69, ptnr from 1969
m Aber 31.8.63 Sally A. Jack health visitor d of Frank W. J. Inverugie

MATHIESON Alexander Willox *MA 1966
s of Alexander M. plumber and Christina Bissett; b Aber 3.4.44
MInstM FRGS
fin. analyst Ford motor co Brentwood 1966–69; British Leyland (Austin Morris div) Birm: pricing supervis 1970–71, man. price and budget analysis 1971–74, marketing man. 1974–75; marketing serv man. Leyland cars from 1975
m Hampstead 23.7.66 Carol M. Critchley MA 1966 *qv*

MATHIESON George McKenzie MA 1958 LLB 1960
s of William M. M. loc govt off. and Nell A. Main; b Aber 20.3.38
MILGA 1972 AMBIM 1973
law app Aber 1958–61; leg. asst: Banff 1961–63, loc govt Inv 1963–64; dep town clerk Elgin 1964–73, town clerk 1973–75; sen leg. asst Moray dist c from 1975
m Aber 18.6.60 Roseann Dunbar shorthand typist d of Albert D. Aber

MATHIESON John Watt *BSc 1965 PhD 1969
s of John R. M. stonecutter and Mary Watt; b Aber 31.12.42
res fell. Baylor univ USA 1969–71; teacher Aber from 1971
m Aber 30.7.65 Netta Skinner teacher

MATHIESON June MA 1960
d of Harry R. M. crane driver/machineman and Alice P. Fyfe; b Aber 10.6.39
teacher Northfield acad Aber 1961–73, asst prin remed educ from 1973
m Aber 31.3.72 George A. Cruickshank teacher s of George C. Aber

MATIER Kenneth Ogilvie *MA 1963
s of William R. M. printing man. and Janet B. Pollock; b Glasg 13.6.34
BA(Cape T)
univ lect classics: Salisbury Rhodesia 1963–64, Grahamstown S Af 1965–74, sen lect from 1974
m Wolmaransstad S Af 6.1.68 Rosemary Bach BMus (Rhodes) teacher d of Marx B. Wolmaransstad

MATTHEW Andrew Murray MA 1970

MATTHEW James Andrew Davidson *BSc 1960 PhD 1964
s of James M. power stat eng and Georgina Milne typist; b Aber 22.11.38
FInst P 1974
Aberd: res stud. 1960–62, asst 1962–64; res asst Cornell univ USA 1964–65; lect York univ 1965–75, sen lect from 1975
m York 23.3.68 Kathryn A. McKenna BA(York) publ relations off. d of Michael J. McK. Nott

MATTHEW Jean Greig MA 1956
m Cheriyan

MATTHEW Myrtle Irene *MA 1964
d of Robert S. M. papermaker/watchmaker/school janitor and Myrtle I. Munro; b Aber 9.12.40
Dip Lib(Lond) 1970
lib: res asst Nat Lib of Scot. Edin 1964–65, asst Aberd 1965–73, coll of adult educ Manc 1973–75; lib asst Aberd from 1975
m Aber 24.9.73 Gordon Anderson-Smith MA 1966 *qv*

MATTHEWS Angela Rosemary *MA 1970
d of F. D. M. housing man. consult. and M. J. A. Matthews; b Welwyn Garden City 11.5.48
PO exec off. Edin 1970–71; pers off. Invergordon 1971–74; careers off. Fife from 1974

MATTHEWS Frances Smith MA 1962

MAUGHAN Evelyn Mary MA 1969
d of Francis M. eng and Elizabeth M. Smith bank clerkess; b Rhynie 18.12.47
teacher Lockerbie 1970–74
m Lockerbie 20.12.73 Roy B. Carlyle farm. s of William J. C. Moffat

MAXWELL Elsa Pricella Ann MA 1970
d of James W. M. warehouse man. and Elma M. King teacher dom sc; b Stronsay 11.11.49
teacher Dun from 1971
m Kirkwall 12.9.68 Stanley C. Nutt s of Stanley C. N. Alloa

MAXWELL Esmé MA 1967
d of Thomas B. M. farm. and Ella Johnstone; b Annan 3.4.45
lect Engl: coll of tech Rotherham 1967–71, coll of comm Hammersmith Lond 1972–73
m Aber 2.8.67 Atholl R. Forbes MB ChB 1966 *qv*

MAXWELL Phyllis Kathleen *MA 1958
d of Edwin A. M. MA 1928 *qv* and Greta L. Sykes MA 1929 *qv*; b Cambridge 24.2.35
teacher: Clitheroe g s 1959–61, Wycombe h s 1961–63; head scripture: Northwich g s 1963–67, Pennywell comp s Sunderland from 1967

MAY Andrew BSc 1956

MAY Andrew MA 1962
s of George M. M. M. fisherman and Helen Lawrence; b Fraserburgh 4.9.40
teacher: Hilton s s Aber 1963–65, Inverallochy p s 1965–68; dep head Fraserburgh cent s 1968–71; head: Inverallochy p s 1971–76, New Pitsligo and St John's s s from 1976
m Fraserburgh 15.9.62 Zena M. F. Gibb d of Thomas M. G. Sandhaven

MAY Andrew Bruce *MA 1968 Dip Ed 1969
s of John M. sea capt and Catherine R. Murray dispensing asst; b Buckie 10.3.35
teacher Engl Brechin h s 1969–73, asst prin Engl from 1973
m 29.5.62 Marchia M. Clunie d of Andrew C. Brechin

MAY Jeanne Moir BSc 1958
d of Roderick J. G. M. maintenance eng and Jane R. M. Moir; b Aber 7.3.37
teacher biol Aber acad from 1959 and year mistress from 1970

MAY Joan Bruce MA 1970
m Lawrie

MAY John MA 1963
s of John M. fisherman and Catherine R. Murray dispenser; b Buckie 2.1.42
teacher: St Peter's s Buckie 1964–65, hist/Lat Forfar acad from 1965 and prin guid from 1972; supt Forfar f e centre 1970–75
m Aber 4.10.67 Patricia M. Low teacher d of George L. MA 1956 *qv*

MAY John Mathieson BSc 1967
s of John M. restaurateur and Shiela Mathieson teacher; b Aber 5.2.46
teacher maths AGS 1968–74, prin maths Bridge of Don acad Aber from 1974
m Aber 23.5.69 Valerie A. Yeats shorthand typist d of Alexander L. Y. Aber

MAY John Robertson BSc 1969
s of George M. MB ChB 1947 *qv* and Margaret S. Hamilton MB ChB 1947 *qv*; b Edin 5.4.49
LRCP MRCS 1976 MB BS(Lond) 1976
scient off. Lond 1970–71; h o Royal Free hosp Lond 1976–77; trainee g p Bridgend Wales 1977–79; sen h o, regist anaest Sheff from 1979
m Pembrokesh 12.11.77 Janice E. Mathias physioth d of Charles E. M. Fishguard

MAY Rhoda Kathleen BSc 1969
d of Roderick J. G. M. maintainance eng and Jane R. Moir; b Aber 4.8.48
teacher geog/sc Hilton acad Aber 1970–79
m Aber 20.10.75 Gary G. Wright BSc(N'cle) soil surv s of George W. Solihull

MAY Robert Leslie BL 1956
s of Robert C. M. BL 1927 *qv*; b Aber 12.11.32
solic: Edin 1956–57, ptnr Mackenzie & Wilson advoc Aber from 1957

MAY William Stewart *BSc 1961
s of William M. marine eng MN and Elizabeth M. Stewart; b Lond 27.1.38
CChem MRIC 1976
AGS/Rubislaw acad Aber: teacher sc 1962–66, spec asst 1966–73, asst prin sc 1973–74, prin chem from 1974

MAYBANK Graham Thomas *BSc(agr) 1966
s of Thomas W. M. comp dir and Doris E. G. Bartholomew; b Bath 29.10.41
PhD(Stir) 1971
forensic biol Home Office S O Nott 1971–72; lect/head biol sect. Walsall and Staffs tech coll (now Walsall coll of tech) 1972–76, sen lect from 1976
m Stockton-on-Tees 27.7.68 Mary E. Child MA 1968 *qv*

MAYCOCK James Hewitt BSc 1968
s of Joseph M. MA(Liv) C of S min and Lilian Hewitt nurse; b Kirkcaldy 7.7.43
G Inst P(RGIT) 1977
teacher phys Harlaw acad Aber from 1969
m Aber 8.4.71 Helen R. Finlayson BEd 1969 *qv*

MAYS Enid Margaret MA 1970
d of William M. turner/eng and Eileen W. Nuttall milliner; b Coatbridge 1.6.49
MA(Texas) 1973
teaching asst Engl/stud. W. Berlin 1970–71; teacher Fr/stud. Austin Texas 1971–73; civ serv Lond from 1974

MEADOWS Martin Ivo BSc(for) 1970

MEAGER Anthony *BSc 1969
s of Donald J. M. house-bldr and Molly Birch off. worker; b Bletchley 24.10.45
PhD(Warw) 1972 Beit Mem Fell. 1972–75
post-doct res MRC Mill Hill Lond 1972–75; MRC sen res fell. Warwick univ from 1975

MEARES Patrick DSc 1959
s of Thomas P. M. civ serv and Violet E. Warne; b Croydon 1.7.23
MA(Cantab) 1947 PhD(Cantab) 1948 ScD(Cantab) 1975 FRSE
res stud. Cantab 1943–46; res fell. Lond 1946–49; Aberd: lect chem 1949–60, sen lect 1960–65, reader 1965–69, prof from 1969
m York 24.5.47 Rhoda M. Small MA(Cantab) teacher d of Horace E. S. Mexborough

MEARNS Kathleen Mary *MA 1967 Dip Ed 1968
d of John C. M. agr rep and Alice M. Taylor MA 1928 *qv*; b Aber 11.4.45
teacher Springburn p s Glasg 1968–69, Kelvinside acad 1969–74; asst educ psych Angus 1974–75; teacher Southesk p s Montrose 1975–76
m Aber 22.3.75 Peter Strachan teacher

MEARNS Yvonne *MA 1965

MEDFORD William Lisle MA 1970 CASS 1974

MEGHU Beulah Barbara MA 1960
d of Thomas M. grocer and Dolly A. Seepaul; b Trinidad 19.12.26
Trinidad: teacher Naparima girls' h s from 1951, prin from 1964

MEIKLEJOHN Dorothy MA 1968 Dip Ed 1969
m von Weymarn

MEINERTZHAGEN Ian Anthony *BSc 1966
PhD(St And) 1971
res stud. Gatty marine lab St And 1966–69; Aust nat univ: res asst dept neurobiol 1969–71, post doct fell. 1971–73; sen post doct fell. Harvard univ USA from 1973

MELDRUM Ian Greig *BSc 1961 PhD 1964
s of Robert U. M. foreman joiner and Isabella Greig; b Aber 1.3.39
res fell. Glasg 1964–69; res chem: Sunbury 1969–73, Epsom 1974–76, Sunbury from 1976
m Paisley 23.7.66 Ina F. Ritchie teacher d of William F. R. Lochwinnoch

MELDRUM Maureen Wendy MA 1967 Dip Ed 1968
d of Alexander M. baker and Ethel Dinnie; b Huntly 29.1.46
teacher: Ellon 1968–74, Inverurie from 1978
m Inverurie 27.12.68 Richard A. Cruickshank water insp s of Richard C. Newmachar

MELDRUM Moira Sutherland MB ChB 1958
d of Roy M. arch. and Gladys M. Sutherland; b Aber 16.4.34
DCH(Eng) 1961
h o Woodend hosp Aber 1958–59; sen h o: ch hosp Nott 1959–60, paediat Manc 1960–61; part-time asst m o Lancs from 1964
m Aber 29.9.61 William H. Mellor MB ChB(Manc) g p s of Hezekiah M. Manc

MELDRUM Patricia Mary MA 1967
m Nile

MELDRUM Stuart James *BSc 1966
b Forfar 8.2.44
M Inst P 1970 PhD(Lond) 1973
St Bart's hosp Lond: phys dept med electronics 1966–70, sen phys 1970–74; lect med electronics St Bart's hosp med coll 1974–76; prin phys St Bart's hosp from 1976
m Glasg 1.9.67 Claire K. Young MA 1967 *qv*

MELFORD Lilian Fleming MA 1969
d of Michael J. M. factory dept man. and Jean A. Fleming secy; b Ellon 14.6.49
teacher mod lang Peterhead acad from 1970
m Peterhead 14.4.73 Maynard C. Buchan BSc 1968 *qv*

MELLING John *MA 1962

MELLIS James Alexander *MA 1968 PhD 1977
s of Duncan M. M. employ. whisky indust and Margaret G. Rennie; b Glasg 1.6.46
Aberd: res stud. 1968–70, asst Ger dept 1969; lect Ger: Glas 1970–75, Aberd from 1976
m Aber 20.9.68 Margaret J. W. Hay MA 1968 *qv*

MELLIS Patricia Mary MA 1961
d of John R. M. drapery man. and Mary Bond; b Stonehaven 10.7.40
teacher: Eastwood s s Glasg 1962–63, Lossiemouth h s 1966–67, St Margaret's s for girls from 1973, asst head from 1975
m Aber 12.7.64 Graham C. Stalker MN off. s of George D. S. Aber

MELLOR Valerie Anne Clark *MA 1970
d of Eric D. M. civ eng and Marion Young nurse; b Middlesbrough 30.8.47
TEFL Kokkola Finland 1970–71; psychotherap with disturbed adolescents Parkside hosp Macclesfield 1971–72; teacher Fr Woodmill h s Dunfermline from 1973

MELOTTE Christopher John *MA 1970

MELVIN James Stuart *BSc 1966 PhD 1971
s of Archibald M. farm. and Annie Paul farm.; b Glasg 4.4.40
lect nat phil Aberd from 1971
m Aber 2.10.63 Elizabeth M. Thomson MA 1963 *qv*

MELVIN Jennifer Margaret Ord *BSc 1966
m Lawrie

MELVIN Marjory Catherine MA 1962
m Paget

MELVIN Ray MA 1968
d of Alexander W. M. farm. and Violet M. Cruickshank MA 1928 *qv*; b Huntly 12.3.47
res asst drug addiction stud. Toronto 1968–69; post grad course Aber coll of comm 1969–70; Düsseldorf: asst foreign advert. dept Ger newspaper 1970–71, asst to publ of comm information serv 1971, asst to dir of admin head of Ger off. of Brit manuf audio-visual teaching aids 1971–76; advt admin co-ordinator for Culligan (America) Brussels from 1976
m Kildrummy 8.9.79 Richard C. Marcus BSEE(City Coll NY) dir internat marketing s of William J. M. New York

MEMERY Kevin Stuart Rowden *MA 1965

MENCHER June *MA 1958
m McKimmie

MENDHAM Nicolette Claire *BSc 1967 MSc 1968
d of Norman V. M. BSc(Lond) teacher and Marie L. Robin BA(Lond) teacher; b Lancaster 8.5.45
rest asst to chief exec Flintsh c c Mold 1968–74, ecologist to county plan. dept Mold Clwyd 1974–75
m Ackworth 27.10.73 Michael T. Richardson BSA(Dub) tech serv man. ICI s of Thomas N. R. Sandyford Co Dublin

MENMUIR Patricia Margaret *MA 1960
d of Alexander M. BSc 1926 *qv*; b Aber 6.11.36
Dun: teacher mod lang 1961–71, woman advis 1971–72, asst rector (guid) from 1972

MENNIE Alexander Milne MA 1968

MENNIE Catherine Fraser MA 1957
d of Alexander M. insur salesman and Catherine F. Bandeen; b Aber 10.8.36
teacher: Byron Park p s Aber 1958–61, St John's RC s Perth 1961–63, Hunter's Tryst p s Edin from 1970
m Aber 29.7.61 William A. Steele chartered elect. eng NSHEB s of George S. Aber

MENNIE George Hardie MB ChB 1965
s of William P. M. police supt, farm. and Ethel A. Hardie; b Elgin 30.5.42
DObstRCOG 1967 MRCGP 1975
h o Falkirk 1966–67; g p Dumfries 1968; med and health off. S Pacific health serv Fiji 1969–71; g p Banchory from 1971
m Aber 5.4.68 Dianne R. Hepburn midwife d of Angus I. H. Stornoway

MENNIE Ian Low *BSc 1957 Dip Ed 1958
s of John H. M. insp SPCC Aber and Jean Low clerkess; b Aber 28.5.34
teacher: spec asst sc Inverurie acad 1958–65, prin phys St Margaret's s Aber 1965–68; Newfoundland: asst prof mem univ from 1968, conductor St John's symphony orch from 1969
m Aber 1962 Maureen E. Hay lib/teacher d of Alexander H. Aber

MENNIE Kathleen Sheila MA 1961

MENNIE Margaret Mary MA 1969
d of Alexander T. M. MB ChB 1949 *qv*; b Aber 26.4.48
teacher Victoria Road p s Aber 1970–72; Lanarkshire: rural schools 1972–78, head Auchengray p s from 1978
m(1) Desougi
(2) Carmichael 8.8.77 John L. Cooper farm. s of John C. Hyndford Bridge

MENNIE Yvonne Gillian MA 1964
d of James M. pharm RGIT and Rose Harris; b Aber 7.10.42
teacher: remed spec Tullos p s Aber, Carleton p s Glenrothes; lect in numeracy/literacy TOPS prep course Portsmouth coll of art des and f e from 1977
m Aber 25.9.65 Colin R. MacKenzie MA 1967 *qv*

MENZIES Anne Frances Mary MA 1962
m Cunningham

MENZIES Annie Elizabeth MA 1959

MENZIES Avril Margaret Isobel BSc 1960
d of Charles S. M. MA 1934 *qv*; b New Pitsligo 21.1.40
chem PYE Electronics 1960–62; translation edit. Pergamon Press 1965–71
m Aber 16.8.60 John M. Hay BSc 1959 *qv*

MERCER David *MA 1969 MEd 1973
s of William B. M. joiner and Ella Cooper; b Aber 4.10.46
teacher econ York 1973–76; admin off. MDC Sheffield from 1976
m Dunblane 18.8.73 Debbie A. Anderson cook d of Thomas H. A. Glasg

MERCER Roy MB ChB 1960
s of John M. credit trader and Mary M. Hector; b Lond 27.8.36
DA(Eng) 1964
h o RACH, city hosp Aber, Craigtown mat. hosp St And 1961–62; sen h o regist anaest Vict hosp Blackpool 1962–65; g p Gt Yarmouth from 1965
m Cleveleys 9.11.63 Susan M. Bond SRN d of Thomas B. Cleveleys

MERCHANT Bruce Alastair LLB 1965
s of Alastair D. M. solic and Marcia A. Bruce; b Edin 17.5.45
law app James & George Collie advoc Aber 1965–67, solic 1967–68; ptnr: Fredk A. Black & Imrie solic Inv 1968–71, South, Forrest, Mackintosh & Merchant solic Inv from 1971
m Inv 20.1.68 Joan I. S. Hamilton LLB 1967 *qv*

MERRICK John Brian *MA 1959
s of John M. iron moulder and Annie Unsworth; b Newton-le-Willows 12.1.36
Dip Man.(educ) 1976
teacher: Nantwich 1961, St Helen's 1961–64; prin lect (head of dept) coll of higher educ Manc from 1964
m Newton-le-Willows 23.7.63 Patricia F. Hankey secy d of Fred H. Newton-le-Willows

MICHAEL Ian MacRae *MA 1962
s of Robert M. bank man. and Harriet MacRae; b Lerwick 23.7.40
DPhil(Oxon) 1966
res stud.: Hertford coll Oxford 1962–64, Queen's coll Dund 1964–65, asst lect maths Queen's coll Dund1965–67; post doct fell. McM univ Canada 1969–70; lect maths Dund 1967–77 and warden Chalmers hall 1973–77; theol stud. Westcott House Cambridge 1977–79; asst curate parish of All Saints Kings Heath Birm from 1979

MICHAEL-PHILLIPS Peter John Charles MA 1968
s of Albert H. M-P. MB BS(Lond) med pract and Edna M. Thompson nurse; b Kettering 7.11.45
teacher Fr/Ger: Wisbech 1964–73, Chipping Campden from 1973
m York 1971 Fiona M. Sinclair teacher d of Jack S. York

MICHAELIDES Euripides Damianou BSc(for) 1958
s of Damianos Hj Michael farm. and Anna Samara; b Arghaki Cyprus 1.11.26
Dip Sc Indust Man. 1970 AMBIM 1971
asst dir for. Nicosia Cyprus 1958–75 (stud. for. off. course Oxon 1961–62) dir dept for. Nicosia from 1976
m Kyrenia Cyprus 24.4.61 Rena Petrides

MICHIE Alexander John *MA 1964

MICHIE Alistair Davidson MB ChB 1956
s of William A. M. master mariner and Jean Kelly secy; b Aber 5.3.32
MRCGP 1968
h o Woodend hosp Aber 1956–57; capt RAMC Malaya, Singapore 1957–60; g p Portlethen 1960–61; sen h o obst ARI; g p/clin asst psychiat Lostwithiel/Bodmin from 1962

m Aber 24.10.57 Dorothy J. Gloyer lib d of Marshall G. Aber

MICHIE Helen Gordon MB ChB 1968
d of Gordon A. M. bank man. and Jessie Currie MA 1940 *qv*; b Aber 16.11.45
MRCOG 1974
h o: City hosp, Woodend hosp Aber, EGA hosp Lond 1968–70; sen h o: Edin RI, Nott, N gen hosp, Jessop hosp Sheffield 1970–73; regist obst/gyn Dun hosps 1973–74; lect obst/gyn univ Edin 1974–75; locum regist obst/gyn Edin RI 1976; consult. obst/gyn republic of Seychelles from 1976

MICHIE Helen Kennedy MA 1958
d of Alexander M. seed warehouseman and Annie O. Rennie typist; b Aber 30.3.37
teacher: Engl/hist Mortlach s s Dufftown 1959–62, St Andrew's p s Nassau Bahamas 1962–63, Engl/hist Williams Lake h s BC Canada 1963–64, Aber: Muirfield p s 1965–73, remed Walker Rd p s from 1973

MICHIE John Charles Alexander BSc 1961

MICHIE Uisdean Macleod *BSc 1968

MICHIE William Guthrie McGregor LLB 1968
s of William M. MA 1930 *qv* and Vera C. A. Booth MB ChB 1945 *qv*; b Aber 20.12.47
CA(Edin) 1972
merch banker Lond from 1972
m West Camel Somerset 18.6.77 Susan J. Griffin d of Philip J. G. West Camel

MIDDLER Elizabeth Thomson MA 1958

MIDDLER James Ian Findlay MA 1960
s of James M. M. fireplace contr and Gladys Findlay store man.; b Aber 6.8.38
teacher: p dept RGC Aber 1961–67, Engl Kelowna s s BC Canada from 1967
m Aber 5.8.71 Caroline A. Murray teacher d of James M. (missing in action 1944)

MIDDLETON Alan James *BSc 1967

MIDDLETON Alexander Bruce BSc(eng) 1962
s of Charles G. M. bus driver and Alexandra Bruce; b Insch 4.2.41
grad trainee on SMETA course W of Scot. area 1962–64; prod. man. manuf of M/C tools Glasg from 1964
m Aber 10.10.64 Patricia A. Spalding clerkess d of Robert M. S. Inverurie

MIDDLETON Bryson Bannochie BSc(for) 1956

MIDDLETON Elizabeth Fraser MA 1960
d of Peter M. rly ganger and Mary M. Cassie; b Elgin 24.12.38
BEd(New Br) 1971
teacher Glas 1961–65; Canada: teacher Engl h s Shellbrook Sask 1965–66, Fredericton h s New Brunswick from 1967
m Strathroy Ontario 14.7.66 Walter Brereton res tech univ of New Br s of Thomas B. Liverpool

MIDDLETON Gordon George Alexander MB ChB 1958
s of George P. M. MB ChB 1926 *qv*; b Aber 11.5.33
RAMC Major army fam med Singapore, Munster W Ger 1960–65; g p MoD Sungei Patani Malaya, Camb, Hong Kong, Tidworth 1966–72, g p Aylesbury from 1972
m Chichester 7.4.62 Janet M. Bradshaw nursery nurse, med secy d of James S. B. MB ChB(Liv) Chichester

MIDDLETON Irene Mitchell MA 1958 Dip Ed 1959
d of Andrew M. M. baker and Ethel M. Rettie; b Aber 6.5.38
teacher Aber: Inchgarth p s 1959–67, RACH 1967–70, Cornhill p s 1970–74
m Aber 11.7.72 George M. Cordiner joiner s of James C. Aber

MIDDLETON Linda Mary *BSc 1970
d of Arthur M. foreman bldr and Mary F. Kemp; b Torphins 6.4.48
Dip Ed(Edin) 1971
teacher biol: Penicuik 1971–74, AGS from 1975
m Aber 24.10.74 John Price BSc(Belf) res asst dept spectrochem Edin s of agr, field investig off. dept nutrit biochem Rowett res inst Aber s of John A. P. Newtonabbey Co Antrim

MIDDLETON Marjory Stevenson *MA 1967
d of James W. M. PO overseer and Marjory C. B. Stevenson mus teacher; b Edin 10.12.44
teacher: N'castle-u-Tyne 1968–69, Fife 1969–71; asst educ psych Fife 1971–72; adult literary assessor from 1974
m Aber 14.8.68 Alexander W. Burnett MA 1966 *qv*

MIDDLETON Rose Elspet MA 1957
m Hirsch

MIDDLETON Sheila Margaret Silver MB ChB 1962
d of George P. M. MB ChB 1926 *qv*; b Aber 13.6.38
DObstRCOG 1965
h o Woodend hosp Aber, Whipps Cross hosp Lond 1962–63; trainee g p Ballater 1963–64; h s mat. hosp Aber 1964; res asst nat coronary drug proj Cleveland Ohio 1966–67; med off. FPA Cardiff 1971–72, Sheffield from 1973
m Ballater 15.5.65 Ian D. Cooke MB BS(Sydney) prof obst/gyn Sheff s of Douglas C. Sydney

MIDDLETON Stuart Auldjo *MA 1961
s of Stuart A. M. CA and Irene M. Esson; b Aber 31.5.39
trainee advert copywriter Lond 1961–71; dir Ogilvy Benson & Mather Lond from 1971; man. dir Ogilvy & Mather Malaysia Kuala Lumpur from 1975; sen dir Ogilvy Benson & Mather Lond from 1978
m Aber 3.8.63 Margaret G. Edmond MA 1960 *qv*

MIDDLETON William Cordiner BSc 1959

MIDDLETON William Craig Noble MA 1965

MIDDLETON William John MA 1960
s of John M. M. painter/decorator and Mary Henderson; b Lamlash 10.7.38
BD(Edin) 1963
C of S min: Rerrick and Auchencairn Kirkcudbright 1964–71, Carnwath Lanark from 1971
m Glasg 1963 Mary M. Kerr insur clerkess d of William K. Lochranza Is of Arran

MILBURN Christopher John BSc 1967 MB ChB 1972
s of John F. M. insur comp man. and Kathleen Wilson; b York 15.12.43
DRCOG 1977 MRCGP 1978
h o City hosp Aber, ARI 1972–73; lect path. Aberd 1973–74; sqdn ldr RAF med branch 1974–79; g p Aber from 1979

m Aber 25.3.74 Catherine M. Pirie MB ChB 1972 med pract d of Alexander A. P. MA 1891 *qv*

MILBURN John Anthony PhD 1964
s of Tom M. headmaster and Agnes M. Johnson teacher; b Carlisle 7.8.36
BSc(N'cle) 1958
agronomist Bookers sugar estate Guyana 1958–61; lect bot Glas 1964–75; overseas visiting fell. (Brit Council) India 1972; Fulbright Hays schol/res fell. (Charles Bullard) Harvard univ 1973–74; sen lect bot Glas from 1975; visiting fell. Messina univ Sicily 1979

MILES Fiona Anne MA 1970
d of Robert M. joiner and Ellen P. MacIntyre; b Osterley 12.4.49
teacher geog: Glasg 1971–72, Thurso 1972–76
m Aber 1.8.72 Hugh G. Boyd lect in agr s of John M. B. Huntly

MILES Susan Henderson MA 1967
d of Leslie A. M. RAF and Ruth B. M. Torrington; b Tunbridge Wells 19.11.43
teacher Aber: maths Kaimhill s s 1969–70, Fr Summerhill acad 1971, Hilton acad 1971–72, maths American s 1973–75, prin maths 1975–79; supply maths Grampian reg from 1979

MILESON Jill Stroud *BSc 1966

MILLAR David Gavin MB ChB 1967
s of William M. M. MB ChB(Edin) prof mental health Aberd and Catherine M. Rankin LDS(Glas) dentist; b Aber 23.4.47
MRCGP 1974
h o Aber, Inv 1967–68; sen h o: Kirkcaldy 1968–69, Aber 1969–70; lect path. Aberd 1970–71; g p Aber from 1971
m Aber 11.4.69 Judith A. Gibb MA 1967 *qv*

MILLAR Elizabeth Moyes BSc 1964
d of William M. M. MB ChB(Edin) prof psychiat Aberd and Catherine M. Rankin LDS(Glas) dentist; b Edin 14.6.43
VSO teacher Zaria Nigeria 1964–65; teacher: chem Firhill s s Edin 1966–68, maths/chem Fort Portal Uganda 1969–70, maths Powis acad Aber from 1970, prin guid from 1972
m Aber 23.6.79 Alexander J. Riddell MA 1965 *qv*

MILLAR Henry Rankin *B Med Biol 1969 MB ChB 1972
s of William M. M. MB ChB(Edin) prof psychiat Aberd and Catherine M. Rankin LDS(Glas) dentist; b Aber 23.4.47
MRCPsych 1976
h o ARI 1972–73; res fell./sen h o commun med/gen med Aber 1973–74; sen h o, regist psychiat Edin 1974–77, sen regist psychiat Dun from 1977
m Aber 30.3.70 Frances M. Lee catering man. d of Robert S.L.

MILLAR Jillian Joan *MA 1968
d of James T. G. M. men's outfitter and Irene H. Dorward teacher; b Dun 1.7.46
teacher Engl/hist Perth h s 1969–73
m Dun 3.8.71 Charles E. S. Cassie MA(Edin) teacher s of Charles E. S. C. Leith

MILLAR Margaret Malcolm MA 1969
d of William M. M. MB ChB(Edin) prof mental health Aberd and Catherine M. Rankin LDS(Glas) dentist; b Edin 19.2.49
Dip Soc Admin(Edin) 1970
soc worker soc work dept Aber 1970–74
m Aber 25.9.70 Peter R. S. Duffus MB ChB 1970 *qv*

MILLAR Peter William MA 1965
s of Gavin R. M. MA(Edin) hosp supt/g p and Mary R. Birrell; b Edin 24.5.43
BD(Edin) 1968 ThM(Princeton) 1969
teaching posts India, Aust 1969–70; asst min Crown Court ch Lond 1970–71; C of S min: Glasg 1971–77, Madras India from 1977
m Glasg 29.9.73 Dorothy A. Somerville BSc(Edin) univ lect/bact d of William C. S. BSc(Edin)

MILLAR Roslyn Jean BEd 1970

MILLARD Helen Joyce Macpherson MSc 1968 PhD 1974
d of Arthur V. M. loc govt off. and Helen M. M. Docherty; b Barrow-in-Furness 3.12.45
BSc(N'cle) 1967
res asst Dund from 1971
m Carlisle 4.9.71 Rodney A. Herbert PhD 1970 *qv*

MILLER Alistair James Mitchell MA 1958
s of Alfred J. M. MA 1926 *qv*; b Aber 27.8.38
CA 1964
app, clerk Meston & Co CA Aber 1958–64; asst Cooper Brothers & Co CA Lond 1964–65; asst comp secy Newman Hender & Co Stroud 1965–69; group comp secy Pegler–Hattersley Doncaster from 1970
m Aber 18.8.65 Barbara S. Young MA 1960 *qv*

MILLER Bruce John Fleming MSc 1970 PhD 1974
s of Robert G. M. BSc(Edin) for. and Anne F. Fleming BA(Edin) mathematician; b Ndola Zambia 16.10.45
BSc(Guelph) 1969
grad clerk dept sc Canberra Aust 1974–77; asst to pro-rector polytech Huddersfield from 1978
m Honley 6.4.74 Aileen M. Slater BSc(UCNW) teacher d of James B. S. Huddersfield

MILLER Charles Bruce BSc 1959
s of Charles B. M. mus seller and Gladys R. Stuart; b Aber 29.5.37
teacher sc Aber acad 1960–62; joined C. Bruce Miller & Co mus sellers Aber 1962, comp dir from 1965
m Aber 26.7.63 Marjory L. Bain teacher p e d of Robin D. B. Stonehaven

MILLER Christine Elizabeth MSc 1970
d of Ian M. C of S min and Jean M. Watson MA(Glas) teacher; b Edin 27.2.63
BSc(St And) 1965
lect: univ of Loughborough 1967–68, St And 1969–75; stud. deaconess TEV course St Ninian's ch of Scot. Crieff 1975–76

MILLER Donald Wares MA 1958
s of Alexander M. fisherman and Mary A. Doull; b Wick 27.7.37
teacher maths Wick h s from 1959
m Wick 11.8.61 Georgina D. Coghill clerkess d of William C. Wick

MILLER Dorothy Joyce Mitchell MA 1956
d of Alfred J. M. MA 1926 *qv*; b Aber 6.10.35
teacher Sunnybank p s Aber 1957–60
m Aber 5.8.60 John M. Howie MA 1958 *qv*

MILLER Douglas MA 1965
CA

MILLER Frank Israel *BSc 1968 MSc 1970 PhD 1973

MILLER Gordon Reginald *BSc 1957
s of Reginald E. M. cinema man. and Elizabeth A.

McIntyre secy; b Harrogate 28.9.33
PhD(N'cle) 1962
res asst agr MAFF grant to N'cle 1957–60; res scient Nature Conserv: unit grouse and moorland ecology Aber 1960–66, Banchory 1966–70; res scient ITE Banchory from 1970
m Fyvie 16.10.58 Lesley M. Sleigh BSc 1955 *qv*

MILLER Heather Margo MA 1961
m Liversedge

MILLER Hugh Graham *BSc(for) 1963 PhD 1969
s of Robert G. M. BSc(for)(Edin) for. off. and Anne Fleming MA(Edin) teacher; b Zambia 22.11.39
res scient Aberd from 1963
m Aber 4.7.66 Thelma Martin d of James M. Aber

MILLER Ian David LLB 1967
s of John M. M. bldr/civ eng, dir and Dolores McLaughlan; b Edin 13.7.48
ptnr A. & W. M. Urquhart solic Edin from 1974; Austrian consul for Edin 1974
m Edin 27.6.70 Sheila S. McLean MA 1968 *qv*

MILLER Ian James MA 1959
s of John B. M. house furn and Mary B. Herd; b Fraserburgh 21.10.38
LLB(Edin) 1962
law app Edin 1959–62; solic Dun 1963–68; sen leg. asst Inv c c 1968–70; dep county clerk, county clerk Ross & Cromarty Dingwall 1970–75; chief exec Inv dist council 1975–77; dir of law and admin Grampian reg c from 1977
m Edin 19.9.64 Sheila M. Hourston secy d of William A. M. H. Edin

MILLER Ina Margaret *MA 1966
m Hughes

MILLER Isobel *MA 1958
d of Alexander M. MA(Edin) teacher and Christina Mackie; b Elgin 3.12.35
teacher Fr/Ger: Harris acad Dun 1959–62, Turriff from 1973
m Aberlour 19.7.61 Robert Greig MA 1958 *qv*

MILLER James *BSc 1970
s of David G. M. fisherman and Janet W. Calder; b Keiss 19.2.48
MSc(McG) 1977
VSO Cebu City Philippines 1970–73; grad stud. McG univ Montreal 1973–74; awarded Max Binz burs McG univ for continuation of grad stud. 1974–75; Brit Council staff from 1975

MILLER James Gordon MB ChB 1970
s of James R. M. bank man. and Lily H. Tait; b Perth 24.7.46
MRCGP 1975
h o Aber 1970–73; g p: Hull 1973–78, Mintlaw from 1978
m Aber 16.7.70 Judith M. A. Warden MA(Edin) teacher d of William W. St Cyrus

MILLER John Ashley Laing LLB 1970
s of George W. M. pharm and Elizabeth M. Laing MB ChB 1929 *qv*; b Essex 4.8.48
Edin: law app 1970–73, solic from 1973
m Edin 7.7.73 Sheila E. Knowles MA 1969 *qv*

MILLER John Dow Booth MB ChB 1968 ChM 1978
s of John B. M. wine and spirit merch and Hilda Dow; b Aber 10.7.43
FRCSE 1974
regist surg Aber 1974–78; res fell. surg Harvard USA 1975–76; lect surg Aberd from 1978
m Aber 18.7.72 Isobel Murray teacher d of Robert M. Aber

MILLER John Robertson MB ChB 1957

MILLER Judith Gibson MA 1970

MILLER Magnus Alexander *BSc(agr) 1968
s of David B. M. farm. and Margaret G. Muir; b Methlick 5.3.34
econ with meat and livestock comm Bletchley 1968–70; tech advis Bayer UK agrochem div Kinross from 1970
m Aber 25.7.59 Doreen C. Urquhart teacher home econ d of Sinclair M. U. Aber

MILLER Norman Melvin MA 1965 Dip Ed 1966
s of George P. M. foreman shipbuilding and Isabella C. Melvin laundress; b Aber 19.9.43
teacher Engl Arbroath acad 1966–67; rly clerk Lond 1967–71; warden model lodging house Aber from 1973

MILLER Peter Edmund *MA 1963

MILLER Raymond MB ChB 1958

MILLER Robert MB ChB 1960
s of William F. M. insur off. and Ann H. Gunn; b Dunfermline 11.7.37
h o Woodend hosp Aber, Edin RI 1960–62; Inv: sen h o Raigmore hosp 1962, g p from 1962
m Edin 31.3.61 Mary C. Cowie teacher d of Joseph C. Whithorn

MILLER Stanley Scott MB ChB 1962 ChM 1976
s of Robert S. M. pharm and Mary Reid; b Whitley Bay 24.12.38
FRCS 1970 FAS 1973
h o ARI 1962–64; lect physiol Aberd 1964–68; regist surg ARI 1968–70, sen regist 1970–74; resid asst surg hosp for sick ch Gt Ormond St Lond 1974–76; consult. surg ARI from 1976
m Aber 24.7.64 Madeline E. McGown speech therap d of Charles G. McG. MA(Glas) Forres

MILLER Stuart BSc 1964

MILLER William John BSc 1957

MILLERS John BSc 1969
s of J. E. M. master mariner and E. Ozols; b N'cle 2.6.47
retail area rep Texaco oil comp 1969–72; UK wrought sales responsib Alcan aluminium comp from 1973
m Lond 15.9.73 Gundega Jankavs physioth

MILLHAM Richard Henry George MA 1960

MILLIGAN George Allan BSc(agr) 1956

MILLS Jeremy Charles Risby *BSc 1970

MILLS John Robert *BSc 1970
s of Robert M. shopkeeper and Olwen Fitz-hugh SRN; b Stockport 23.1.47
teacher Perth 1971–76; lect Dun 1976–77; asst prin teacher chem Perth from 1977
m Perth 11.7.72 Helen L. Bonomy BSc 1971 teacher d of William B. MA(Glas) Perth

MILLS Peter William BSc(eng) 1970
s of Harry M. comp dir and Laura Shaw; b Marple

29.9.47
Babcock & Wilcox Renfrew: grad app 1970–72, tech eng 1972–73; sales eng T. A. Kennedy & Co Glasg from 1973
m Cupar 10.7.70 Sheila R. Marshall MA 1970 *qv*

MILLWOOD Arthur Edward *MA 1960
s of William H. M. mech/elect. eng and Millicent R. MacKenzie; b Inv 25.1.38
sales Pilkington Bros: Glasg 1960–66, Johannesburg 1967–70; sales W. R. Grace (Africa) 1970–71; lect commun/bldg materials univ of Port Elizabeth S Africa from 1971
m Southport 1.5.72 Jean Timpany

MILNE Alan Ducat MB ChB 1964
s of George P. M. MB ChB 1934 *qv*; b Carlisle 3.8.40
MRCGP 1971 DA(Lond) 1967
h o Woodend hosp Aber, ARI 1964–65; regist anaest Aber 1965–68; g p Aber from 1968
m Aber 16.7.65 Nanette L. M. Gordon MB ChB 1965 *qv*

MILNE Alan Henry MB ChB 1967

MILNE Alexander Strachan BSc(eng) 1967
s of William M. fisherman, lab and Christina S. Strachan; b Billingham-on-Tees 27.3.45
MIEE 1972
trainee Inveresk Paper Group Aber 1967–69; elect. eng Donside paper mills 1969–70; proj eng: Bowater Paper Group Northfleet 1970–75, R. H. Cuthbertson & Ptnrs Edin from 1975
m Huntly 17.8.67 Flora A. Flory MA 1966 *qv*

MILNE Alistair Angus BSc(agr) 1961
s of William M. police off. and Margaret Angus nurse; b Aber 25.6.39
BVMS(Edin) 1965
vet res off. Stormont N Ireland 1965–69, vet pract Aber from 1969
m Aber 15.7.61 Margaret Reid d of Alexander R. Aber

MILNE Arthur Donald *BSc 1969
s of Arthur M. banker and Alice M. Main; b Forres 5.10.46
Brit petrol. co: geol Yarmouth 1969–70, Djakarta 1970–71, Yarmouth, Aber 1971–75, NZ 1975–76, Singapore from 1976

MILNE Brian MB ChB 1966
s of Joseph P. M. MB ChB 1934 *qv* and Margaret J. Strachan MA 1928 *qv*; b Elgin 9.1.42
DObstRCOG 1968 MRCOG 1972
h o Aber 1966–67; sen h o surg Orkney 1968; regist gyn/obst: Inv 1968–72, Glasg 1972–74; sen regist gyn/obst Leicester from 1974, spec from 1977
m Kildrummy 6.9.67 Mary I. B. Ellis SRN ultrasound tech d of James E. Alford

MILNE Catherine Morag BEd 1969

MILNE David James *BSc(eng) 1969
s of William C. M. eng and Flora Macdonald; b Aber 30.11.46
MICE 1974 MIHE 1976 CEng
asst eng Lond 1969–72; sect. eng Glasg 1972–74; asst resid eng Keswick northern by-pass 1974–76; proj eng Shell Expro Aber from 1976
m Aber 18.8.73 Wendy A. Wisely MA 1969 *qv*

MILNE David James *BSc 1970
s of Alexander M. MA 1933 *qv*; b Wick 1.4.47
MSc(Warw) 1972
oper res BL Birm, Liverpool 1972–75; prod. control Smith's Industries Cheltenham 1975–77, with PE Consult. Group from 1977

MILNE Donald McLean BSc(eng) 1961

MILNE Dorothy Christie BSc 1958
m Sim

MILNE Douglas James Wood *MA 1967 BD 1970
s of John A. M. MA(Edin) headmaster and Mary M. Wood; b Dun 1.1.44
ThM(Westminster theol seminary, Philadelphia) 1971
min Free Ch of Scot. Glenurquhart 1972–79, Aust from 1979
m Inv 31.7.69 (Hannah) Joan Mackenzie MA 1966 *qv*

MILNE Douglas Malcolm *MA 1962 Dip Ed 1963
d Nairn 31.3.75 *AUR* XLVI 327

MILNE Eileen MA 1963
d of Alexander M. banker and Luella Mackenzie, ch's nurse; b Forres 28.5.42
m Inv 22.8.64 William H. Burnett prod. man. s of William H. B. Inv

MILNE Elizabeth May MA 1968
d of John N. M. eng and Margaret J. Thomson secy; b Guildford 1.7.47
Cert Soc St(Glas) 1969 Dip App Soc St(Glas) 1970
soc worker: Glasg 1970–72, Paisley 1972–74, Nairobi 1975; sen soc worker Crawley from 1975
m Nairobi 2.10.74 Robert C. K. Mbugua hosp admin s of Jotham M. Kenya

MILNE Euan Cameron MA 1964

MILNE Florence MA 1969
d of George S. M. clerk and Mary Williamson; b Aber 21.11.47
teacher Byron Park p s Aber 1970–72
m Aber 31.7.70 John H. Adam quantity surv s of John H. A. Aber

MILNE George Alexander *BSc 1963 Dip Ed 1964
s of George S. M. clerk and Mary Williamson; b Aber 22.9.40
teacher biol: Gordon s Huntly 1964–65, Inverurie acad 1966–71; prin biol Arbroath h s from 1971
m Aber 7.10.72 Marjorie A. Watt or Downie BSc 1965 *qv*

MILNE Gladys Ledingham MA 1959
d of John M. M. farm. and Anne B. Ledingham; b Echt 13.2.38
teacher: Alford s 1960–62; Perth: Goodlyburn s 1962–65, St John's s 1965–66, High s 1973–74; remed: Forrester h s Edin 1974–77, Aberdeensh from 1977
m Alford 28.7.62 Archibald M. Cobban civ serv s of Archibald C. Monymusk

MILNE Gordon Graeme MB ChB 1968
s of George P. M. MB ChB 1934 *qv*; b Carlisle 4.7.43
DA 1971
h o ARI, Woodend hosp Aber 1968–69; trainee g p Peterculter 1969–70; sen h o, regist anaest ARI 1970–73; g p/part-time anaest Gray's hosp Elgin from 1973
m Aber 10.7.68 Margaret J. Milne MA 1965 *qv*

MILNE Hamish Kenneth *BSc 1970

MILNE Helen Margaret BEd 1970
d of John M. farm. and Helen D. Garden MA 1927

qv; b Aber 6.1.48
teacher infants St Stephen's RC s Blairgowrie 1970–75, Dun s Montrose 1975–76
m Fettercairn 25.7.75 David A. Ritchie master joiner s of John A. R. Fettercairn

MILNE Helen Mary MB ChB 1968
d of Albert M. policeman, secur off., safety & fire prev off. and Alice Milton secy; b Keith 16.5.41
h o RACH, St Helen's hosp Lancs 1968–69; locum sen h o Chesterfield royal hosp 1969; sen h o anaest: Chesterfield hosp group 1969–70, united Sheffield hosps 1970–71, Chesterfield hosp group 1971–72; regist anaest: Chesterfield hosp group 1972–73, N Tyneside hosp group 1973–74; trainee g p Hemsworth 1974–75; locum regist anaest S Teesside hosp group 1975; clin off. ch health and fam plan. Cleveland area health auth 1975–76; clin off. ch health Staffordsh area health auth 1976–77; g p Tamworth from 1977
m Aber 21.6.76 Terry D. Kinnis MB BS(N'cle) g p Tamworth s of John F. K. Stockton-on-Tees

MILNE Henry *BSc 1960 PhD 1964
s of William G. M. for. and Mary Robertson; b Huntly 16.9.35
Aberd: asst lect zool 1963–65, lect 1965–72, sen lect from 1972
m Aber 14.9.60 Margaret J. Machray display artist d of Alexander M.

MILNE Ian Alexander BSc(eng) 1956
s of James S. M. elect. and Helen M. Dawson; b Rothiemay 9.6.35
asst site eng hydro-elect. Loch Shin 1956–59; div hydraul eng MoW Kisumu Kenya 1959–62; des eng hydro-elect. Lond 1962–65; proj eng indust hydro proj Niagara Falls 1965–70; exec eng hydro-elect. proj Buenos Aires 1970–73; exec eng power div Buffalo USA from 1973
m Perthsh 20.3.65 Hazel M. Ross pharm d of Donald J. R. Comrie

MILNE Ian McDonald *MA 1957
s of John W. M. painter and Annie McDonald; b Aber 14.10.34
teacher: royal acad Inv 1959–61, Daniel Stewart's coll Edin 1961–66, prin mod lang Gordon s Huntly 1966–77, prin Fr AGS from 1977
m Aber 21.7.60 Katherine M. C. Allan teacher d of William D. A. Edin

MILNE Isabel Alice MA 1963
m Hutcheon

MILNE Isabella Galbraith MA 1958

MILNE Isobel Frances *MA 1965
d of Robert L. M. auctioneer/valuator and Elsie I. Mackie teacher; b Aber 1.8.42
VSO teacher Sierra Leone 1965–66; res asst FO Lond 1966–69; Sudan: s s teacher Omdurman 1969–71, Amer s Khartoum 1971–73, lect Engl fac of econ univ of Khartoum from 1973
m Aber 25.5.71 Abdel G. I. Dafa'alla orthop/optician s of Ismail M. D.

MILNE James Campbell *MA 1970

MILNE James Dawson *BSc 1959

MILNE John Alexander Barclay MA 1957
s of John A. M. MB ChB 1905 *qv*(II, III); b Aber 25.6.19
teacher: Powis acad Aber 1957–59, Banchory acad 1959–79; retd
m Easingwold 22.7.41 Jessie L. W. Leonard bank clerk d of Samuel N. L. Paisley

MILNE John Gilbert *BSc 1958

MILNE Lesley Mary *BSc 1957 Dip Ed 1958
m McIntyre

MILNE Leslie BSc 1969

MILNE Margaret Eveline BSc 1964
d of John M. comm trav and Eveline M. Blair clerkess; b Aber 5.11.43
teacher maths: Aber 1965–69, Canterbury 1969–73
m Aber 30.7.70 Roger Price BSc(Birm) univ lect s of Stanley P. Swindon

MILNE Margaret Harris MA 1958

MILNE Margaret Helen *MA 1957
d of John C. M. MA 1922 *qv* and Jane W. Shewan MA 1917 *qv*; b Aber 8.4.34
teacher: Eng/Fr Fraserburgh acad 1958–59, Springhill and Fernielea p s Aber 1959–62, Brockley jun mixed s Lond 1962–63, Engl/hist Tarves j s s from 1963

MILNE Margaret Jean MA 1965
d of George M. farm. and Helen Mair catering superv; b Skene 6.9.44
teacher Ferryhill p s Aber 1966–69; part-time lect Moray coll of f e Elgin from 1975
m Aber 10.7.68 Gordon G. Milne MB ChB 1968 *qv*
d Aber 19.7.81

MILNE Margaret Joan *BSc 1970
d of Ronald M. M. area superv Tennant Cal. Breweries and Margaret H. Reid teacher; b Forres 2.6.48
Dip Ed(Edin) 1971
teacher sc Armidale NSW Aust 1971; part-time dem bot James Cook univ N Queensland 1975–77; teacher sc Dunedin NZ 1978
m Armidale 17.7.71 Anthony P. Spenceley BSc 1970 *qv*

MILNE Margaret Joyce MA 1959
d of Joseph P. M. MB ChB 1934 *qv* and Margaret J. Strachan MA 1928 *qv*; b Aber 22.5.38
teacher: Banffsh 1960–66, N Province Zambia 1967–69; proof reader Luanshya Zambia 1969–73; teacher Elizabeth Vale S Aust from 1974
m Aber 14.7.61 William R. Sutherland MA 1963 *qv*

MILNE Marjory MA 1960
d of John I. W. M. MA 1931 *qv*; b Aber 2.9.39
teacher mod lang: Knox acad Haddington 1961–66, Stirling h s 1966–72, spec asst 1972–73, asst prin mod lang and asst prin guid from 1973

MILNE Melville Kermack MB ChB 1965
s of Alexander K. M. bank acct and Agnes Austin shop asst; b Glasg 4.4.41
FFA 1971
h o Aber 1965–66; sen h o obst/gyn Perth 1966–67; regist anaest Perth 1968–70; sen regist anaest Dun 1970–73; consult. anaest Dun from 1974
m Aber 30.3.67 Wilma J. Mortimer BSc 1962 *qv*

MILNE Michael William *BSc(eng) 1968
s of Cameron M. M. MA 1934 *qv*; b Turriff 26.12.46
Scot. elect. trg scheme 1969–70; dev eng Ferranti Edin from 1970
m Edin 22.6.74 Joan E. Muir MA 1969 *qv*

MILNE Morgan James BSc(agr) 1968
s of Arthur J. M. farm. and Mary M. Garden; b Forfar 20.9.46
MSc(N'cle)
oper trainee-oil, oil terminal superv Lancs 1971–73; asst agr eng Grimsby 1973–74; agr eng man. Grimsby from 1975
m Aber 2.5.70 Nicola M. Gearing secy d of George D. G. Udny Station

MILNE Pamels Anderson MA 1970
d of James R. M. garage prop. and Eunice R. Anderson; b Aber 5.7.49
Dip Soc Ad(Glas) 1973 Dip Soc Work(Glas) 1974
soc worker: Ruchill hosp Glasg 1971–72, Renfrew c c 1974–76
m Aber 6.2.71 Laurence A. Cheyne MA 1970 *qv*

MILNE Patrick Findlay Creighton MA 1962

MILNE Paul Stocks *MA 1964
s of William M. lect and Ada L. Laing; b Aber 27.7.42
insp of taxes 1964–65; lect econ univ of Hull from 1965

MILNE Raymond Taylor *BSc 1970 PhD 1974
s of Herbert M. fitter and Margaret S. Taylor; b Forfar 17.11.47
dev chem Billingham from 1973
m Aber 2.4.70 Irene M. Sandison teacher d of John P. S. Cullen

MILNE Rosemary Joyce MB ChB 1970
d of George P. MB ChB 1934 *qv*; b Carlisle 11.6.46
DObstRCOG(Lond) 1973
h o: gyn ARI 1970, Aber City hosp 1971; sen h o gen surg Balfour hosp Kirkwall 1971–72; sen h o obst Aber mat. hosp 1972–73; g p Bray Eire from 1974
m Aber 28.4.72 James A. W. Lee restaurateur, med stud. s of William L. Belf

MILNE Russell MA 1970
s of Albert E. M. maintenance man. and Edith A. W. Annand; b Aber 10.12.47
computer progr, analyst Manc 1969–74; sen syst analyst F. W. Woolworth Manc 1974–76; proj leader hydro-electric Aber from 1976
m Aber 26.12.69 Elizabeth A. Davis MA 1969 *qv*

MILNE Stella Dagmar MA 1959
d of Andrew M. MN home trade master and Frances G. Connon shop asst; b Aber 19.9.38
teacher Aber 1960–62
m Aber 19.7.61 Alastair F. L. Esson MN chief off., maritime pilot Aber s of Herbert W. E. MA 1951 *qv*(III)

MILNE Stephen Halkerston *MA 1970 Dip Ed 1971
s of John I. W. M. MA 1931 *qv*; b Aber 18.7.47
teacher: mod lang Alloa acad 1971–73, asst prin mod lang 1973–74, prin mod lang from 1974

MILNE Thomas Graham MA 1956 LLB 1958
s of Archibald M. MA(Glas) teacher and Helen M. Brown teacher; b Finzean 22.3.35
leg. asst: Dumfries c c 1959–61, Aber c c 1961–65; leg. asst, dep town clerk Galashiels t c 1965–68; town clerk Forfar 1968–74; dep dir of admin Tayside reg from 1974
m Aber 27.6.59 Eleanor F. Davidson MA 1956 *qv*

MILNE Valerie MA 1967
d of Alan M. despatch clerk and Nancy Smith; b Aber 11.11.44
teacher Engl/hist Torry acad Aber 1969–71
m Aber 21.8.65 Alan W. R. Brock eng, stock controller s of Charles B. Aber

MILNE Victor Gordon *BSc 1957
b Aber 1934
MA(Tor) 1958 PhD(Tor) 1962
Canada: geol geol branch Ontario dept mines Toronto 1962–72; chief geol/asst director Ontario geol surv div of mines Min of Natural Resources Toronto from 1972
m 1964 Florence M. Dore

MILNE William Burnett Proctor BSc 1960
s of William P. M. MA 1903 *qv*; b Bristol 13.8.11
MC 1943 OBE 1947
teacher sc Northfield acad Aber 1961–72; retd; resid Aber
m Aber 29.1.52 Barbara F. Souper d of Hugh R. S. MA 1908 *qv*(II, III)
d Aber 8.5.81

MILNE William Hendry *MA 1966
s of Gordon M. mason, insur ag and Jeanie Hendry dressmaker; b Aber 3.11.41
teacher hist Ellon acad 1967–71, prin hist from 1972

MILTON Aileen *MA 1964
d of Robert D. M. farm worker and Margaret Innes; b Roseisle 23.9.42
teacher VSO Rawalpindi Pakistan 1964–65; asst lib Glas 1965–68
m Glasg 1.9.68 Richard Fletcher BSc(Manc) lect s of John R. F. BSc(Birm) Abergele

MILTON Alan John Simpson *BSc 1970 PhD 1975
s of John S. M. insur ag and Mary M. Innes; b Aber 4.6.48
dev chem Wiggins Teape Stoneywood from 1973
m St And 29.6.74 Margaret E. Keracher teacher home econ d of Thomas M. K. St And

MILTON Colin *MA 1965 PhD 1974
s of Harry L. M. carpenter and Anne B. Miller; b Aber 21.8.43
lect Engl Aberd from 1967
m Aber 9.5.64 Ailsa M. Sutherland MB ChB 1969 *qv*

MINETT Robert Anthony *MA 1969 Dip Ed 1970
s of Albert M. lect automative stud. and Hilda Speed part-time s secy; b Wolverhampton 5.8.46
teacher mod lang Rubislaw acad 1970–73, asst prin mod lang 1973–74; sen lect Ger coll of comm Aber from 1975
m Aber 22.12.69 Patricia C. Little MA 1967 *qv*

MINIO-PALUELLO Maria-Luisa MLitt 1965
D in L(Venice)
m Cochran

MINTO Joan Edith *MA 1968
d of Robert W. M. eng, printer and Phoebe R. Gareh shorthand typist; b Inverurie 10.6.46
res asst Aberd 1968
m Aber 10.9.65 Gordon W. Arbuthnott BSc 1964 *qv*

MINTY Alistair Leslie MA 1968

MINTY Ian Stuart Harris MA 1970

MIRGHANI Tag El-Din MSc 1968
BSc(Khart)

MIRRILEES Christine *MA 1968
m Findlay

MISTRY Chandan MB ChB 1966
m Ward

MITCHELL Alexander Brown LLB 1970
s of George M. comp dir and Georgina Mitchell; b Hamilton 20.3.49
law app Glasg 1970–72; leg. asst Glasg 1972–73; solic John Stuart & Wilson Huntly/Keith 1973–76, ptnr from 1976
m Aber 29.7.71 Evelyn J. S. Wilson teacher home econ d of Andrew S. Wilson MA 1934 *qv*

MITCHELL Alexander Grant *MA 1962

MITCHELL Andrew Smith BSc(for) 1968

MITCHELL Anita Mary Burgess *MA 1968
d of Thomas B. M. insur sect. supt and Edith Nicol secy; b Grantown-on-Spey 4.3.46
Edin: teacher Fr/Ger Firhill s s 1969–70, Trinity acad 1970–74
m Edin 29.12.72 James D. Nolan MA(Edin) teacher s of John P. N. Dunfermline

MITCHELL Anne Clouston *MA 1968
d of Alexander D. M.. insp fisheries civ serv and Margaret B. Eddie teacher; b Aber 24.2.46
teacher: Engl Kirkcaldy 1969–71, asst prin Engl Lossiemouth 1971–74, Engl Lüdenscheid Ger 1974–75, Engl St Leonards 1975–77, prin Engl N Berwick h s from 1977

MITCHELL Anne Stewart MA 1960
d of George H. M. ship's eng and Anne S. Stewart; b Lossiemouth 26.1.39
teacher Engl Elgin 1961–63 and from 1973
m Aber 26.7.62 William Coull cereals man. Scot. Malt Distillers s of William J. S. C. Rothes

MITCHELL Barbara Anne Margaret MA 1967
d of William M. MA(Glas) teacher, HMIS and Patricia E. Duncan nurse; b Aber 22.9.46
teacher infants: Aber 1967–73, BFES Germany from 1973

MITCHELL Beryl BSc 1969
d of D. Stephen M. quantity surv, man. dir bldg comp and Isabella Shaw shorthand typist; b Aber 20.9.47
teacher maths: Aber 1970–71, Edin from 1979
m Aber 12.7.69 Stuart C. Poole MA 1971 trans plan. s of Ronald B. P. Lond

MITCHELL Charles Hendry BSc(eng) 1970
s of Henry M. grocer and Christina M. Watt; b Aber 28.12.48
eng, sect. eng, agent from 1970
m Fairlie 26.3.75 Elaine M. Archibald teacher d of Gilbert M. A. Blantyre

MITCHELL Charles James BSc(eng) 1964

MITCHELL Christopher John *MA 1967

MITCHELL Colin Henry Whiteford BSc(agr) 1965
s of Arthur N. M. farm. and Isabella M. Whiteford; b Dun 31.5.43
DFMBO 1966
farm. Leuchars from 1966
m Crieff 11.7.68 Elizabeth M. Miller teacher p e d of James R. M. BSc(Glas) Crieff

MITCHELL Colin Stephen *BSc 1964
s of William A. M. bank man. and Christina M. Stephen; b Aber 18.11.41
des eng Philips indust Croydon 1964–68; Philips elect.: tech/comm asst Lond 1968–71, prod. man. VCR equipment Lond 1971–73; prod. man. TV Lond from 1973
m Lond 7.9.68 Joyce M. Watt civ serv d of George W. W. Aber

MITCHELL Dorothy Mary MA 1965
d of James G. M. eng and Dorothy M. Geddes tel superv; b Aber 10.11.43
teacher Engl: Powis acad Aber 1966–68, Gracemount s s Edin 1968–71, prin guid from 1971
m Aber 2.8.68 Ian R. Yule teacher tech subjs s of Thomas D. Y. Mintlaw

MITCHELL Easton Anderson *MA 1967
s of John W. T. M. traffic insp ACT and Annie Christie; b Aber 22.11.43
teacher mod lang Aber h s for girls (Harlaw acad) 1968–73; asst prin mod lang Kincorth acad Aber from 1973
m 5.4.76 Alison M. Gossip MA(St And) d of William H. G. MB ChB 1931 *qv*

MITCHELL Eileen MA 1965

MITCHELL Elizabeth Margaret MA 1963
m Rattray

MITCHELL Evelyn MA 1970
d of Alexander M. farm. and Evelyn G. Wildgoose; b Aber 12.6.47
Aber: nurse 1970–72, unqual nurse tut. 1973–74, teacher from 1975

MITCHELL Frances Elizabeth *BSc 1965
m Baxter

MITCHELL George Robertson *BSc 1969
s of George A. M. farm. and Elizabeth Robertson; b Torphins 5.7.47
teacher sc: St Augustine's s Edin 1970–72, Hazlehead acad Aber 1972–75, prin chem Banchory acad from 1975

MITCHELL Gordon David *BSc(eng) 1968

MITCHELL Graham *BSc(eng) 1966

MITCHELL Hamish Lewis Mackay MA 1961 LLB 1963
s of Lewis M. M. acct and Gladys J. Martin MA 1923 *qv*; b Kuala Lumpur 2.6.40
Aber: law app Edmonds & Ledingham advoc 1963–64, leg. asst Paull & Williamsons advoc 1964–67, ptnr from 1968
m Aber 31.7.65 May M. Fraser teacher d of George B. F. Aber

MITCHELL Isabel Ross MA 1968 Dip Ed 1969
d of John E. M. master cabinetmaker and Bella Fraser; b Aber 28.9.32
teacher Aber: Kittybrewster p s 1969–70, Harlaw acad 1970–74, prin guid from 1974
m Aber 17.9.55 Joseph B. Coull marine eng s of Joseph B. C. Aber

MITCHELL Janet Campbell BEd 1970

MITCHELL Janet Elizabeth MA 1968
m Riddler

MITCHELL Jessie Davidson Falconer BSc 1958
d of Alexander M. baker and Jessie Falconer; b Aber 18.7.37
teacher Aber 1959–63

m Aber 12.8.61 James W. D. Smith MA 1973 teacher s of William S. Aber

MITCHELL John *MA 1958

MITCHELL John Ivor *MA 1966
s of Ivor M. man. serv dept Goodyear Tyre Co and Myrtle E. M. Macdonald bank clerk; b Wolverhampton 18.11.43
teacher Engl St Austell g s Cornwall 1967–71; second prin Engl royal g s High Wycombe from 1972
m St Austell 1970 Elizabeth M. Trudgian teacher d of Percival J. T. St Austell

MITCHELL John Robertson MA 1970

MITCHELL June MA 1968
d of Thomas B. M. bank man. and Margaret M. Gordon; b Keith 4.6.47
Athens: teacher Hambakis lang s 1969–74, Ambelokipi lang centre 1975–78; opened own lang s Glyfada 1978
m Athens 26.12.71 Dimitris Sachinides electronic eng s of Maralambos S. Athens

MITCHELL June Margaret Ross *MA 1959
d of Alexander J. M. travel ag and Violet Ross; b Aber 21.10.35
secy to dir of res Molins Lond 1961–74, to man. dir Concord Lighting Internat Lond 1974, to dir of eng Rank Xerox Lond from 1974
m Skovshoved Denmark 20.10.64 Jørgen A. H. Orth indust film prod. s of Frits O. LDS(Copenhagen) Klampenborg

MITCHELL Kate Fowler Falconer White MA 1966
m Legg

MITCHELL Kathleen Mary Anderson *MA 1965
d of John M. MA 1928 *qv*; b Elgin 8.2.43
res asst M o D Lond 1965–69; attaché Brit High Commission Singapore 1969–71; edit. asst Graphmitre Tavistock from 1979
m Aber 11.8.71 Robert W. Perkins lt-col Royal Marines s of Robert S.P. Surrey

MITCHELL Lewis Stuart MB ChB 1965
s of John M. bookseller/newsag and Marjory C. Stuart; b Keith 14.2.38
h o ARI, Raigmore hosp Inv 1965–67; g p: Bucksburn 1967–69, Hobart Tasmania from 1969
m Inv 29.7.64 Maragret L. J. Allison nurs sister d of William D. A. Kirkhill Invsh

MITCHELL Lilian Maud PhD 1960
MA LLB EdB(Glas)

MITCHELL Margaret Anne MA 1961
d of Alexander M. fisherman and Edith Bainbridge hairdresser; b Lossiemouth 18.9.40
teacher Lossiemouth from 1962
m Lossiemouth 7.10.67 Alexander Mackenzie shop owner

MITCHELL Margaret Henderson MA 1959
d of Alexander M. eng insp and Margaret Allison; b Crewe 10.2.39
M Libr(Wash) 1965
teacher: Bannockburn 1961–62, Ash Vale Surrey 1962; univ of Wash: lib asst 1963–65, lib 1965–68; univ of Vict BC: asst bibliographer soc sc res centre 1969–73, bibliographer from 1974
m Aber 14.8.61 David G. W. Edwards BSc 1959 *qv*

MITCHELL Marjory Gibbon MA 1966
d of Robert W. A. M. elect. and Helen D. Young shop asst; b Edin 29.4.45
teacher: Clydebank h s 1967–69, Fraserburgh acad 1969–70, Cardinal Wiseman s Greenford 1971–73
m Aber 21.11.70 Eric J. C. Brew BSc 1967 *qv*

MITCHELL Mary *MA 1960
d of Jean Edmondstone; b Aber 4.9.37
secy to edit. Lond 1961; teacher: Isle of Barra 1962–63, Glasg 1963–64, Banff 1965–66, Cumnock from 1971
m Aber 6.7.63 Donald M. Manson MA 1962 *qv*

MITCHELL Michael James *MA 1970
b Stonehaven 22.2.48
MCIT 1977
rly man. Liverpool, Wolverhampton from 1970
m Edin 4.9.71 Jillian M. Tomory MA 1970 *qv*

MITCHELL Moira Taylor MA 1964
d of John C. S. M. baker and Jeannie D. P. Wight; b Aber 30.9.42
teacher Northfield acad 1965–69, later teacher f e
m Aber 5.8.67 Joseph Leiper MA 1971 teacher s of George L. Aber

MITCHELL Patricia *MA 1969
m Ashenford

MITCHELL Patrick John Stuart *BSc 1959
s of Patrick M. MA 1924 *qv* and Gertrude H. Stuart MA 1930 *qv*; b Aber 8.1.36
post grad res Aber 1959–60; res chem: petro chem Billingham 1960–62, tobacco Bristol 1962–70; works/dev chem carbon paper Caribonum Turriff 1970–74 tech eng petroleum explor/prod. industry Dowell Schlumberger Aber from 1974
m Aber 16.2.60 Jorja M. Carnegie nurse d of George F. C. Aber

MITCHELL Roger MA 1967

MITCHELL Rose McNeill MA 1956
d of George M. saw doctor and Mary Downie; b Fraserburgh 27.10.35
teacher: Pitlochry h s 1957–59, Sunnybank s Aber from 1970
m Aber 22.8.59 George S. Hall warehouse dept man. s of Wilson H. Aber

MITCHELL Stuart John *BSc 1965 PhD 1969
s of Mark G. M. teacher and Jane H. Elder teacher; b Brentwood 16.12.43
scient off. UKAEA Aldermaston 1968–71, sen scient off. 1972–73; sen scient off. MoD 1973–76; prin scient off. MoD Lond from 1976
m Aber 7.4.66 Sheila B. Fulton radiographer d of James G. F. BL 1952 *qv*

MITCHELL Trevor Anderson *MA 1970
s of William I. C. M. BSc(agr) 1924 *qv*; b Elgin 20.9.46
teacher Ger/Engl/Fr/geog Congleton c g s for girls 1971–78; head Ger dept Wycombe h s High Wycombe from 1978
m Aber 5.7.69 Yuko Motomura MA(Waseda univ Tokyo) interpreter, translator, teacher d of Takeo M. Tokyo

MITCHELL William BSc 1968

MITCHELL William Ingram BSc(for) 1958

MITCHELL William Stuart *MA 1970 PhD 1974

MITCHELL William Stuart Gabriel *MA 1967

MITCHELL William Sutherland *BSc 1969
s of Andrew A. S. M. MA 1930 *qv*; b Wick 25.9.43
MSc(Br Col) 1973
geol from 1973
m Tacoma Wash USA 28.7.73 Courtney E. Soule MSc (Stanford)

MITTELSTEIN John Edward Cowie *MA 1969
s of Edward S. A. M. seaman and Margaret Cowie; b Skopun Faroe Is 9.8.47
trainee, shipping exec The Ben Line Steamers Edin from 1970
m Glasg 27.8.71 Kathleen Wotherspoon d of David W. Glasg

MIZERA Franz *BSc(agr) 1967
s of Franz M. machine tool indust, soldier and Wanda Marciniak; b Wyrzysk Poland 11.9.43
M Econ(ANU) 1971
Canberra: res econ bureau of agr econ dept primary indust 1967–70, sen fin. off. Commonwealth Treasury 1970–72; internat wool secretariat: res econ Lond 1972–73, econ and market res man. Brussels from 1973
m Poznan Poland 29.6.74 Bożena Jożefowicz econ (publ serv) d of Mieczylaw J. Poznan

MIZON Margaret Shaun MA 1965

MMBANDO Charles Stanislaus BSc(for) 1966

MOAR Ann Maxwell MA 1963
d of William I. M. bldr and Eileen F. Horne; b 7.11.42
teacher (VSO) Freetown Sierra Leone 1963–65; Edin: teacher Engl Ainslie Park s 1966–67, Niddrie Marischal s 1967–68
m Aber Peter A. Dean MA 1963 *qv*

MOAR Patricia Ann MA 1970
d of John P. M. civ eng and Wilhelmina M. Pottinger; b Lerwick 24.5.49
teacher Fr/Ger Lerwick from 1971
m Dunrossness Shetland 13.10.73 William B. Burgess arch. tech s of William B. Dunrossness

MOAR Peter Windwick MA 1968
s of John P. M. civ eng and Wilhelmina M. Pottinger; b Lerwick 25.9.45
teacher: Kayseri Koleji, Kayseri Turkey 1970–71, Kirkcudbrightsh 1971–74; lect: Dumfries and Galloway coll of tech 1974–79, Eng lit Basrah univ Iraq from 1979
m Aber 24.9.69 Angela M. Robertson secy d of James K. R. Aber

MOBBS Ian Gaynor *BSc 1967
s of Eric E. G. M. marine supt and Sarah Tait; b Glasg 25.2.41
MSc(McM) 1969 PhD(UWO) 1975
univ of W. Ont: grad stud. 1969–74, sen instr 1972–73, lect 1973–76; asst prof Dalhousie univ Nova Scotia from 1976

MOFFAT Alistair Gibson MA 1961

MOFFAT Sheila Patricia BSc 1963

MOFFETT Jonathan Wallace BSc(for) 1959
s of Robert W. M. wholesale draper, soldier, driver and Helen G. McCracken secy; b Belfast 30.4.37
dist for. off. Co Antrim 1959–63; itinerant 1963–67; orchardist Hastings NZ from 1967
m Hastings NZ 17.12.64 Christine R. Walker nurse d of Hector W. W. Hastings NZ

MOGGACH Gordon MA 1965
s of William C. M. farm. and Olive Ingram; b Keith 21.7.43
Dip Bus Man(Strath) 1966 ACMA 1971
Lond: budget acct Air Products 1966–70, comp acct Ingersoll Locks 1970–71; sen man. acct HIDB Inv from 1971
m Lairg 5.4.75 Elspeth D. Ross civ serv d of Andrew J. A. R. Lairg

MOHAMED Babiker Fadlalla PhD 1967
s of Fadlalla M. wholesale dealer and Nur E. El Sheikh; b Khartoum 9.7.34
MSc(Khart)
Khart: dem 1958–63, lect 1967–79, assoc prof from 1979, head bot dept from 1980
m Huntly 11.6.68 Elizabeth A. Russell staff nurse d of Alexander R. Aber

MOIR Alan Clark *MA 1970 Dip Ed 1971
s of Harry M. mill man. and Irene L. M. Clark; b Elgin 18.4.47
teacher hist Belmont acad Ayr 1971–74, asst prin hist 1974–76; prin hist Auchinleck acad from 1976
m Prestwick 28.3.75 Margaret Aird teacher home econ d of Alexander A. Prestwick

MOIR Alexander Ian *BSc 1966
s of Alexander M. foreman links and parks dept Aber and Robina Cruickshank; b Aber 3.3.44
teacher maths Inverurie acad 1968–71; prin maths Keith g s from 1971
m Aber 2.8.74 Kathryn E. McKenzie teacher d of Robert M. McK. Buckie

MOIR Annette Nicol MA 1959
m Rogerson

MOIR Arthur John Goddard *BSc 1969 PhD 1973
s of John H. M. woodworker and Ellen Scott; b Lond 25.11.46
post doct res fell. MRC Birm from 1973
m Aber 20.8.73 Anne McKenzie BSc 1971 post grad stud. Birm d of John A. McK. Gartly

MOIR David Alexander MA 1966
s of Alexander M. eng and Williamina C. Munro; b Aber 11.12.45
Dip. Bus. Stud.(Strath) 1967 AMBIM 1974
Plessey & Co. Poole: progr/analyst 1967–69, proj leader 1970–72, syst man. 1973–74; sen syst analyst Farnborough from 1974
m Aber 14.1.66 Kathleen Robertson teacher d of John B. R. Aber

MOIR Dorothy Watt *MA 1961
m Caldwell

MOIR Elizabeth Drummond MA 1968
d of David M. police sgt and Elizabeth Davidson secy; b Keith 3.2.47
Dip Sec St(Strath) 1969
coll of estate man.: secy to secy Lond 1969–72, sen admin asst to prin Lond/Reading 1972–73, controller of postal course div Reading 1973–75, dir of courses Reading from 1975

MOIR Grace Gordon MA 1956
m Morrison

MOIR Graeme Kelman *BSc 1970 PhD 1974

MOIR Hamish David Alexander BSc(eng) 1964

MOIR Ian Alexander BSc 1960
s of William A. M. M. fireman and Wilhelmina Alexander nurse; b Dun 20.11.39
phys UKAEA Dounreay 1960–63; commissioning eng Trawsfynydd 1963–65; oper eng SSEB Hunterston 1965–67; fuelling eng CEGB Wylfa 1967–74; oper eng SSEB Hunterston from 1974
m W Kilbride 17.6.66 Helen L. Davidson computer progr d of Alexander McH. D. W Kilbride

MOIR Ian Andrew MA 1956 BD 1959
s of Andrew F. M. banker and Mabelle M. Scott secy; b Aber 9.4.35
sub-warden St Ninian's trg centre Crieff 1959–61; supt Pholela inst Bulwer Natal S Af 1962–73; C of S overseas council Edin: staffing secy 1974–76, joint secy ptnrship from 1977
m Edin 25.8.61 Elizabeth M. M. Fraser teacher d of James F. Edin

MOIR James Chalmers *MA 1970
s of James G. M. grocer and Mary M. Craig; b Aber 29.12.48
salesman Manc 1970–72, area man. Edin 1972–77, dist sales man. 1977–79, nat sales man. Manc from 1979
m Carnwath 6.4.74 Margaret M. Park MA(Edin) teacher d of T. M. P. MB ChB(Glas) Carnwath

MOIR James McGrath MA 1965

MOIR Jessie Ann Hay MA 1956
d of Alexander M. and Catherine W. Baird; b Aber 22.5.31
teacher: Aberdeensh 1957–65, Singapore 1965–66, Aber from 1968
m Assam 23.4.66 Andrew M. Tracey

MOIR John Donald *MA 1962

MOIR June Milne MA 1965
d of Alfred G. M. M. bank man. and Lily Smith; b Aber 22.6.44
Dip Soc Ad(St And) 1966
teacher Aber 1967–74, remed Johannesburg from 1974
m Aber 16.4.74 Neil J. MacKeith BSc 1968 *qv*

MOIR Kathleen Munro MA 1962
d of Alexander M. eng and Williamina C. Munro; b Aber 29.6.41
teacher: maths/r e Grangemouth 1963–65, maths Ruthrieston s Aber 1965–66, maths/r e Aber h s for girls 1966–69
m Aber 11.8.65 Grahame M. Henderson BD 1972 C of S min s of David H. MA(Glas) Bieldside Aber

MOIR Maureen Catherine *BSc 1969
d of Herbert B. M. joiner and Anne G. Allen; b Aber 5.12.47
teacher chem: Royal h s Edin 1970–74, Lower Hutt NZ 1974–76, AGS 1976–77, Cults acad Aber from 1977
m Aber 27.12.79 Nigel R. M. Scott tax acct s of Malcolm P. S. Montgarrie

MOIR Michael *BSc 1969 PhD 1972
s of Benjamin M. butcher and Ina Hosie; b Huntly 21.6.47
FCS 1968 MInst Brewing 1978
res fell. Zürich 1972–73, Stirling 1973–77; sen res chem Scot. & Newcastle Breweries Edin from 1977

MOIR Michael BSc 1967
s of William M. M. butcher and Jane Robertson; b Aber 31.10.33
teacher maths Hilton acad, Harlaw acad Aber 1968–73, asst prin maths from 1974
m Aber 9.3.57 Elizabeth M. Gordon bakery asst d of Jeremiah W. G. Aber

MOIR Michael Joseph *MA 1962
s of Joseph S. M. elect. eng and Irene E. Barrett shop asst; b Aber 29.9.41
Black Prize for Latin Aberd 1962 BA(Cantab) 1964 MA(Cantab) 1968
teacher classics Peterhead acad 1965–66; lect Victoria univ of Wellington NZ: classics 1966–67, gen ling. 1968–70; prin translation div Neths min of foreign affairs The Hague 1970–73; lect ling. Engl inst univ of Amsterdam from 1973; translator The Hague dist court 1973

MOIR Patricia Margaret MA 1967
m Copland

MOIR Philip Malcolm MA 1969

MOIR William Leonard Neill MA 1962
d 1972

MOJSIEWICZ Andrzej Bruno *MA 1969

MONCRIEFF Elizabeth Sinclair *MA 1970
d of James S. M. lab and Agnes C. Ewen; b Perth 7.4.48
lib asst Bexley 1971–72; Lond: market res asst 1972, res exec with Westward TV 1972–74, higher grade tax off. Inl Rev 1944–47
m Aber 11.9.70 John P. Inglis BSc 1970 *qv*

MONCRIEFF Mitchell William *BSc 1967
s of Mitchell J. M. crofter and Eliza A. Scott; b Sandness Shetland 7.4.44
DIC 1968 PhD(Lond) 1970 FRMet Soc 1970
Imp coll Lond: post doct res fell. dept meteorology 1970–72, lect met. from 1972
m Shetland 6.9.67 Patricia M. M. Nicolson catering superv d of George M. N. Bixter

MONCUR Charles Cheyne *MA 1969

MONRO Graeme Cooper *BSc(eng) 1967

MONRO Stuart Kinnaird *BSc 1970
s of William K. M. comp dir and Williamina M. Fothergill; b Aber 3.3.47
FGS(Lond) 1972 MIGeol 1978
geol S Lowlands unit of inst of geol sc Edin from 1970
m Aber 31.7.71 Shiela D. Wallace teacher p e d of Thomas A. L. W. Aber

MONTGOMERY Catherine *MA 1960

MONTGOMERY Malcolm Nicolson *MA 1959

MONTGOMERY Neil *MA 1965
s of John M. millworker and Annie B. Macdonald; b Stornoway 6.2.43
teacher: Jordanhill coll s Glasg, Annan acad, Hillpark s s Glasg, Lourdes R C s Glasg, Nicolson inst Stornoway, Hillhead p s Glasg 1966–81 (prin geog at Annan acad and Hillpark p s)
m Glasg 11.10.69 Effie Smith nurse d of Donald S. Bragar Is of Lewis

MONTGOMERY Ronald BSc 1960

MOON Gordon Michael *BSc 1969

MOON Helen Janet MB ChB 1969
d of John M. M. mental nurse and Helen Watt teacher, nurse; b Banff 14.7.45
DCH(Glas) 1972
Aber: h o 1969–70, trainee g p 1970–71, h o paediat 1970–72, m o publ health from 1972
m Aber 15.7.69 Innes R. Stephen journalist s of Leslie P. S. Turriff

MOON Helena Margaret MA 1969
m Whitmore

MOONEY James MA 1966
s of Charles M. chef and Annie Daly shopkeeper; b Port Glasg 27.5.25
MEd(Glas) 1970
teacher: Engl Greenock 1967–69, asst prin Engl 1969–71; prin Engl Port Glasg from 1971
m Greenock 6.5.52 Maureen Keogh dressmaker d of William K. Greenock

MOORE Adam Gillespie Nichol MB ChB 1964
s of Merrill M. BA(Vanderbilt) phys/poet and Ann L. Nichol BSc(ed)(Tufts) pre-s educator; b Boston Mass 21.10.31
AB(Harvard) 1956 Struthers gold medal/prize Aberd 1959 Munday Prize Aberd 1962 Amer med assoc physician's recog award 1970–73, 1973–76, 1976–79 Dip Amer Board of fam pract 1975 Cert lib Comm of Mass dept of educ 1974
milit serv pvt to maj MSC 1951–67; Boolt mem home board & Gtr Boston adv board 1967–73; trustee rep Mass hosp assn 1970–72; L fell. Boston med lib (Tr 1975–80); prop. Boston Athenaeum from 1964;h o ARI 1964–65; Mass. USA: resid paediat Carney hosp 1965–66, asst phys UHS Harvard law s Cambridge 1968–72, private fam pract Squantum from 1968
m Aber 15.10.66 Rosamie Alexander med secy d of Robert A. LDS(St And) Aber

MOORE Brian Hendry BSc 1969

MOORE Eileen Mary Campbell MA 1961
m Rueckert

MOORE Mary *MA 1970
m Lynch

MOORE Maurice John *MA 1967

MOORE Michael Archibald MA 1956

MOORE Roderick Francis Inglis *BSc(eng) 1969

MOORHOUSE Mary Charlotte MA 1959
d of Charles R. M. maintenance eng and Mary Reekie; b Aber 16.6.38
teacher: Aber 1960–65; prin relig educ Clacton 1965–71, St Osyth 1971–72, prin r e Colchester 1972–74; sen tut. Frinton from 1974

MORAN Peter Antony *MEd 1968
s of Joseph M. MA(Glas) teacher, headmaster and Gertrude O'Callaghan MA(Glas) teacher, lect coll of educ; b Glasg 13.4.35
MA(Glas) 1963 LTCL 1974 Lic Phil(Greg) 1955
Lic S Theol(Greg) 1959
teacher classics, mus Blairs coll Aber from 1968

MOREY Colin Robert *BSc 1967
s of Charles H. M. elect. eng/civ serv and Florence G. Langdon book-keeper loc govt; b Waterlooville 10.8.44
FGS 1968 MIBG 1972 Dip Man. Stud.(Plymouth poly) 1976 MPhil(CNAA) 1980
prod geol UK 1967–68; sen tut. Slapton Ley 1969–74; dep warden Orielton Pembroke 1974–75; lect geol Brooklands tech coll Weybridge from 1976
m Epsom 28.4.79 Maureen E. F. Symons BSc(Brist) teacher d of Stanley C. S. Stamford

MORGAN Alexander MB ChB 1960
s of Andrew M. M. fisherman, naval off. RNR, tel eng and Jamesina O. Strachan fishworker, canteen server; b Peterhead 6.6.37
h o Woodend hosp Aber, ARI, Airthrey Castle Bridge of Allan 1960–62; g p Stuartfield from 1962
m Aber 15.10.60 Elizabeth M. G. Mackintosh nurse d of John G. M. MA(Edin) Cruden Bay

MORGAN Audrey Mackay MB ChB 1959
d of Albert M. tech teacher and Jeannie Inverarity; b Aber 15.6.36
DA 1963 Educ Council for Foreign Med Grad(America) 1966
h o RACH, Woodend hosp Aber, Whittington hosp Lond 1959–61; sen h o, regist King George hosp Ilford 1961–64; part-time res fell. anaest (Harvard) Mass. gen hosp Boston USA 1966–67
m Aber 19.5.62 Harold S. Winsey MB BS(Lond) consult. gen surg s of Geoffrey C. W. Beaulieu

MORGAN Brian Robert *MA 1969

MORGAN David Gordon MA 1967 LLB 1969
s of Thomas N. M. MB ChB 1931 *qv* and Roberta Gordon MA 1932 *qv*; b Aber 3.5.46
law app, leg. asst James & George Collie advoc Aber 1969–72; leg. asst Fyfe Ireland & Co WS Edin 1972–74; ptnr James & George Collie from 1974

MORGAN David Ivor *MA 1958 LLB 1961
s of Leslie P. M. off. customs & excise and Helen Fisher; b Giffnock 7.12.36
leg. asst G. H. Bower & Gibb advoc Aber 1961–62; solic Davidson & Garden advoc Aber 1962–64, ptnr from 1964
m Aber 28.4.62 Diane C. Scott MA 1958 *qv*

MORGAN Finlay McLeay MA 1959 LLB 1962
s of Finlay M. pharm and Charlotte J. Jamieson pharm; b Farnham 11.11.38
law app Aber 1962–63; leg. asst Ayr 1963–64, Edin 1964–66, Glasg 1966–67; leg. asst Dove, Lockhart, Mackay & Young WS Edin 1967–72, ptnr from 1972
m Wisbech 24.8.68 Elizabeth M. S. Scrafton teacher dom sc d of Philip R. S. Wisbech

MORGAN George Eric MA 1970
s of George M. M. wine and spirit rep and Violet Davidson; b Aber 23.1.43
FSA Scot.
teacher Engl Hilton acad Aber 1971–73; prin Engl/hist Langholm acad from 1973
m Aber 30.12.69 L. Susan Marr MA 1973 teacher d of Gordon P. M. chartered surv Aber

MORGAN John Adam BSc(eng) 1959
s of John S. M. MA 1928 *qv*; b Aber 16.8.37
post grad trainee Marconi Chelmsford 1959–61; elect. eng Honeywell Motherwell 1961–65; IBM Greenock: assoc eng 1965–69, sen assoc eng 1969–73, staff eng from 1973
m Aber 2.4.64 Marjory G. Stuart MA 1960 *qv*

MORGAN John Alexander BEd 1969

MORGAN John Francis MA 1958

MORGAN Karen BSc 1969
d of Thomas M. PO tech off. and Joan Adams publican; b Glamorgan 5.3.47
teacher Buchlyvie p s from 1977
m Gilfach Goch 26.9.68 Angus A. McWilliam PhD 1974 teacher s of Stuart W. McW. MA(Edin) Glasg

MORGAN Lois Cecily *MA 1967
d of George D. M. policeman and Eunice L. O'Neal; b Bridgetown Barbados 29.8.40
teacher: Greatfield p s Hull 1968–70, Combermere Barbados 1970–72
m Aber 22.7.64 Carl L. Ince BA(Hull) diplomat s of Leon St. C. I. St Michael Barbados

MORGAN Margaret Anne BSc 1957
d of James M. rubber planter and Kathleen L. Cormac; b Batu Gajah Malaysia 16.4.36
Dip Bact(Strath) 1959
asst scient off. nat collection of indust bact Torry res lab Aber 1959–61
m Aber 8.1.60 William M. Cooke BSc(Edin) soil chem Macaulay inst s of William P.C. Edin

MORGAN Maureen Gladys MA 1957

MORGAN Roslyn Elizabeth BSc 1968
d of Arthur M. chartered surv/land ag and Margery R. Jones; b Torquay 13.1.45
scient off. plant breeding dept of nat veg res stat Wellesbourne 1968–72
m Newton Abbot 11.4.70 David Gray BA(Oxon) sen scient off. s of Hugh G. Ogbourne St George

MORGAN Sheila Elisabeth Gordon MA 1961
d of Thomas N. M. MB ChB 1961 *qv* and Roberta Gordon MA 1932 *qv*; b Aber 12.8.40
teacher
m Aber 5.7.63 Melville F. Watson MA 1959 *qv*

MORGAN William Charles *BSc 1961 MSc 1962 PhD 1967
s of Robert M. comm trav and Elizabeth J. Mann; b Inv 30.9.39
dem geol N'cle 1964–67; temp asst geol Aberd 1967–68; res scient geol surv of Canada Ottawa from 1968
m Aber 23.12.67 Rohays A. I. Morrison BA teacher d of John A. M. Aber

MORICE George Pirie *MA 1957
s of George P. M. barman and Mary Still; b Aber 29.8.29
asst lect phil Edin 1959–62, lect 1962–77, sen lect from 1977
m Aber 28.7.55 Cecilia F. M. Innes teacher of art d of Charles I. Aber

MORLEY Michael Charles David BSc(eng) 1969
s of David M. farm man. and Margaret M. Winfield; b Swaffham 28.4.46
civ eng contr and des; Sir R. McAlpine: site eng Bristol 1969–70, Glasg 1970–71; sect. eng Michelin factory Dun 1971–73; des eng Ove Arup Dun 1973, sen sect. eng Ardyne Point (oil platforms) Argyll from 1974
m Aber 8.5.70 Marion G. McDonald millworker d of Angus McD. Kintore

MORRELL Michael *MA 1970 MEd 1974

MOREEN Alison Mary MB ChB 1961
m Graham

MORREN David BSc(eng) 1957

MORRICE Alan *MA 1965

MORRICE Alan George *BSc 1969
s of Harold M. M. insur ag and Catherine M. Cambell off. supt; b Aber 20.5.47
M Chem Soc(Lond) 1970 PhD(Illinois) 1974
univ of Illinois Urbana USA: teaching asst 1969–70, res asst 1970–72, teaching asst 1972–74; chem instr nat acad of dance Urbana/teaching asst univ of Illinois from 1974
m Chicago 16.8.74 Elaine C. Mancini BA(Illinois) stud. d of Edward A. M. Chicago

MORRICE Alexander Malcolm *BSc 1963
s of Alexander M. ocean res vessel capt and Emily McRuvie; b Aber 23.12.40
MSc(S'ton) 1974
joined RN 1963, lt-cdr 1969, commander from 1976
m Nursling 14.8.65 Sarah A. Taylor d of George T. Romsey

MORRICE Alice Isabella MA 1970
d of James M. farm. and Alice Lunan; b Mintlaw 23.7.49
teacher mod lang Fraserburgh from 1971
m Aber 24.7.73 Alexander G. Douglas farm. s of Alexander G. D. Fraserburgh

MORRICE Andrew BSc 1963

MORRICE Anne Marie MA 1963

MORRICE Edward Dolan MA 1965

MORRICE Gordon Wilson MA 1965

MORRICE Graham Durward MB ChB 1959
s of John M. eng and Gertrude Walker dressmaker; b Aber 22.2.35
DRCOG 1967 DO(Lond) 1977
RAMC capt Far East 1960–62, m o Charteris hosp Kalimpong India 1964–66, Quarriers Homes Bridge of Weir 1966–76; sen h o ophth Woodend hosp Aber 1976–77, regist ophth from 1977
m Aber 30.9.67 Sanchamaya Yonjan SRN d of Ranman Y. Darjeeling

MORRICE Graham Taylor MB ChB 1967

MORRICE Jennifer Elizabeth MA 1970

MORRICE Kenneth Ewan MA 1965 Dip Ed 1969 MEd 1978
s of Kenneth E. M. Gordon Highlanders (retd) and Williamina M. Armstrong weaver; b Aber 31.3.39
teacher Peterhead cent s 1966–70; head Udny Green p s 1970–72; asst secy St And 1972–73; head: Foveran p s 1973–75, Buchanhaven p s from 1975
m Longside 24.12.60 Elspeth W. Birnie teacher d of William B. Rora

MORRICE Margaret MA 1964
m Reid

MORRIN Catherine Mary MA 1966

MORRIS Graham MB ChB 1965

MORRIS Megan Lumley BSc 1968
d of Robert L. M. bank man. and Anne M. James LLB(Aberystwyth) solic; b Haverfordwest 6.3.47
Dip Ed(Aberystwyth) 1969
teacher: sc Bradford 1969–70, biol Rollestonon Dove, Burton-on-Trent 1970–73, i/c biol from 1973
m Cemaes 9.8.69 Simon J. Cooper BSc 1968 *qv*

MORRIS Raymond John Fowlie BSc 1969

MORRIS Robert Irvine Simpson *BSc(eng) 1965 MSc 1967

MORRIS Rona Jane Steward MA 1970 Dip Ed 1971

MORRISH Ann Loxton MA 1960
m Wong

MORRISON Agnes Anne *MA 1970
d of John C. M. farm worker, tractorman, bakery storeman and Helen Lorimer; b Fyvie 19.11.47
MA(Essex) 1971
lect pol econ Aberd 1971–74
d Aber 6.1.76 *AUR* XLVI 418

MORRISON Alastair MB ChB 1965
s of William M. seaman/crofter and Margaret MacCuish; b Locheport N Uist 7.6.41
DObstRCOG 1967 MRCGP 1977
h o Inv 1965–67; sen h o Perth 1967–69; g p Crieff from 1969
m Edin 5.8.67 Eileen E. MacPherson MB ChB(Edin) med pract d of Roderick MacP. Edin

MORRISON Alexander Ferguson BSc 1963

MORRISON Alexander George *BSc 1960

MORRISON Angus Norman MA 1967 Dip Ed 1968
s of Malcolm M. soldier, lab, min of relig and Mary A. Nicholson ch's nurse; b Kinlochewe 31.7.36
RMN 1961 Dip R E
teacher: Engl Vale of Leven acad Dunbartonsh 1968–71, prin guid: Paisley 1971–74, Greenock h s from 1974
m Glasg 12.6.67 Bella A. MacLeod teacher d of Roderick MacL. Grimsay N Uist

MORRISON Anne Isabel *BSc 1960
d of Aulay M. wholesale comp dir and Christina M. MacLeod nurse; b Stornoway 28.9.38
jun res fellow marine bact Torry res stat Aber 1960–61; res asst biochem Edin 1961–64
m Stornoway 27.12.62 Iain H. Anderson BSc 1958 *qv*

MORRISON Carolyn Ann MA 1965
d of George J. M. clerk of works and Caroline Laird; b Aber 1.8.44
teacher Engl/hist: Glasg 1966–67, Engl Inv 1967–73
m Aber 27.12.71 Pietro M. Bisset tel eng s of Alexander B. Inv

MORRISON Charles *BSc 1970

MORRISON Chrissisabell MA 1966
d of Angus M. lab and Margaret Mackinnon; b Lochs Is of Lewis 9.1.46
teacher: Engl/Gaelic Nicolson inst Stornoway 1967–74, guid 1973–74
m Inv 22.12.72 Cameron M. MacLeay BSc(Strath) teacher s of Duncan MacL. MA(Edin) Fearn

MORRISON Christina MA 1969
m Macdonald

MORRISON Christine Bews MA 1969

MORRISON David LLB 1969
s of Eric S. M. PO overseer and Ruth I. Andrews; b Aber 8.11.47
law app Campbell Connon & Co. advoc Aber 1969–72, leg. asst 1972–73, ptnr from 1974
m Aber 1.7 72 Sandra I. Barron teacher d of Alexander M. B. Aber

MORRISON Donald John *MA 1965
s of John M. MB ChB 1939 *qv*; b Edin 12.12.42
res Brasenose Coll Oxford 1965–67; lect Aberd 1967–71; teacher Aber, Fochabers from 1971
m Grantchester 8.8.66 Linda M. Grant MA 1964 *qv*

MORRISON Gordon James MA 1970

MORRISON Harvey Elmslie LLB 1969
s of Eric E. M. MA 1940 *qv*; b Aber 5.1.47
CA 1973
Williamson & Dunn CA, Aber: app 1969–73, chartered acct from 1973, ptnr from 1976
m Aber 25.7.73 Lesley E. Adam d of James W. A. Aber

MORRISON Ian *MA 1970
b Is of Lewis 28.1.35
teacher Aber from 1971
m Windermere 13.4.63 Olive Nunns

MORRISON Ian Robin *MA 1968
s of Peter C. M. farm. and Maggie E. Taylor; b Edin 14.1.45
lect Fr stud. N'cle from 1970
m N'cle-u-Tyne 26.3.71 Janet S. Burnett MA(Tor) lect politics d of James T. B. Sims N Carolina USA

MORRISON Isobel Chalmers MA 1965
d of William J. M. dairy farm. and Isobel S. Chalmers dairy farm.; b Banff 26.3.44
teacher: Bracoden p s 1966–68, Toronto 1968–70, nursery Aberchirder from 1977
m Macduff 27.12.67 Neil S. Duguid joiner s of James D. Aberchirder

MORRISON James Arthur BSc 1970
s of George M. indust chem and Marjorie E. Ingram; b Aber 16.2.49
man. trainee Norwich city c 1970–72; admin asst soc serv dept Norwich 1972–74; sen admin off. mid Suffolk dist council 1974–76, prin admin off. from 1976
m Aber 17.9.71 Margaret A. Stewart secy d of William A. H. S. Aber

MORRISON James Edward MA 1968
s of Ronald C. C. M. draughtsman and Peggy E. Maunder; b Glasg 3.8.46
teacher Engl: Summerhill j s s Aber 1969–70, The King's s Macclesfield from 1970
m Poulton-le-Fylde 29.7.72 Susan M. Holt BSc(Manc) syst analyst d of William O. H. Poulton-le-Fylde

MORRISON James Murray *BSc 1964
PhD(Glas)

MORRISON James Roger MA 1959
s of James R. M. chief marine eng and Lizzie Connon; b Aber 16.5.31
teacher: Engl/hist/geog Northfield acad Aber 1960–71, hist Cults acad 1971–76, hist/mod stud. Powis acad Aber 1976–77, Engl/hist/mod stud. AGS from 1977
m Aber 11.4.58 Rona E. M. Mackay teacher p e d of Donald M. BSc(agr) 1924 *qv* (II, III)

MORRISON James Wilson Rennie *MA 1965

MORRISON Jean Isobel MB ChB 1962

MORRISON Jessie MA 1962
d of Murdo M. crofter and Isabel Mackenzie; b High Borve Is of Lewis 17.10.40
teacher: Engl Adelphi Terr s s Glasg 1963–65, gen subj Kiltarlity 1965–70, Millburn Inv 1970–71, prin Engl Bolobo-sur-Fleure Zaïre from 1971
m Inv 16.8.74 David L. Boydell BA(Durh) teacher s of Ronald H. B. Leeds

MORRISON Jessie Mary MA 1968
d of Alexander M. warper and Duncanina Smith; b Stornoway 22.4.47
lib: Aber 1970–72, Stornoway from 1972

MORRISON John Alexander BSc 1969 *1970

MORRISON John Archie *MA 1965
s of Peter M. lobster fisherman and Flora McLean; b Lochmaddy 2.2.43
teacher: Engl Rubislaw acad Aber 1966–70, prin asst Engl 1970–72, prin Engl h s Thurso 1972–76, prin Engl Banff acad from 1976
m Aber 4.4.74 Patricia M. Cushnie BBC secy/producer's asst d of Albert P. D. C. Aber

MORRISON John Bernard MA 1969

MORRISON Joyce Campbell MA 1967
d of James C. M. lorry driver and Anne F. Cameron; b Ellon 9.8.46
market res investig Lond 1967–72; civ serv HM customs and excise Lond 1972–75; soc worker Dun from 1975
m Bond

MORRISON Kathleen Isabel BEd 1970

MORRISON Leslie Valentine MA 1960
s of George L. S. M. baker and Margaret Simpson; b Aber 14.2.39
FRAS(Lond) 1961 MSc(Sus) 1968
asst exper off., prin scient off. astronomy Royal Greenwich Observatory from 1960
m Eastbourne 2.6.65 Susan A. Bailey astronomer d of Gerald P. B. Eastbourne

MORRISON Lewis Duncan MB ChB 1960
s of James M. police off. and Louisa R. Adams; b Aber 1.12.35
h o Aber hosps 1960–61; sen h o Victoria I Glasg 1961–63; regist Inv hosps 1963–66; g p/part-time hosp posts Golspie from 1966
m Inv –.10.65 Jean M. Maxwell RGN d of Henry A. M MA(Oxon) Inv

MORRISON Madeline MB ChB 1962
d of Alexander F. M. eng driver BR and Margaret McKessock; b Aber 30.10.37
MRC Psych 1976
h o: Woodend hosp Aber 1962–63, city hosp Edin 1963; sen h o (part-time) Cornhill hosp Aber 1970–73; regist (part-time) RACH from 1973
m Aber 1.2.63 Ian R. Brown BSc(for) 1957 *qv*

MORRISON Marcelle Ritchie *BSc 1967
d of George C. M. MA 1930 *qv*; b Edin 8.8.45
PhD(Glas) 1971
post doct fell. biochem univ of Cincinnati 1971–75; asst prof dept of neurol univ of Texas health sc center Dallas from 1976

MORRISON Margaret Flora MA 1969
d of Neil M. farm./for. and Agnes Small hairdresser; b Inv 28.10.48
Dip Pers Man. (RGIT Aber) 1970 MIPM
lect Inv tech coll 1970; pers off. J & J Crombie Grandholm Aber from 1970
m Drumnadrochit 22.10.77 Ian W. Logan LLB 1963 *qv*

MORRISON Margaret Isobel MA 1967

MORRISON Margaret June MA 1968
d of James M. farm. and Mary Robertson teacher; b Pitcaple 27.6.47
Dip Pers Man.(Strath) 1970 MIPM 1975
pers asst Balfour Kilpatrick Paisley 1970–71; job evaluation off. NAAFI Lond 1972–73; asst pers off. Merton & Sutton AHA Lond 1973–75, Camden & Islington AHA Lond 1976–77
m Ilford 27.2.76 Roger Barber LLB(Lond) solic s of Richard B. Sidcup

MORRISON Margaret Leslie MA 1959
d of George C. M. MA 1930 *qv* and Marjory L. Bruce MA 1925 *qv*; b Aber 21.10.38
secy London, Auckland, Melbourne 1960–61; teacher: Adelaide 1962–63, The Hague 1963–65, Melbourne 1965–67, adult educ Baden Switzerland from 1972
m Adelaide Aust 2.3.62 Dick La Hey eng s of Jacobus H. Haarlem Holland

MORRISON Margaret Mary MA 1967

MORRISON Margaret Sheila BSc 1966
m Reid

MORRISON Marie Ewart MA 1963
d of Norman Morrison MA 1923 *qv*; b Aber 29.10.44
BDS(St And) 1967
h o Dun dent hosp 1967–68; regist Glasg dent hosp 1968–70; lect oral biology Glas from 1970
m Aber 24.7.67 Alexander Watt MA 1964

MORRISON Mary *MEd 1961
d of Murdo M. merch/sub postmaster and Annie M. Montgomery dist nurse; b Laxdale Is of Lewis 16.5.35
MA(Glas) 1956 ABPsS 1966
asst educ psych Edin 1961–63, part-time 1964–70, Midlothian part-time 1971–77, full-time sen educ psych from 1977
m Glasg 26.3.62 Donald Macaulay MA(Glas) advoc s of John M. Bragar Is of Lewis

MORRISON Mary MacLean MA 1968 Dip Ed 1969
d of Donald M. MA(Glas) teacher and Agnes MacLean occup therap; b Glasg 28.12.47
teacher Engl: Govan h s 1970–71, Elliot Lake Ontario 1975–76
m Glasg 1.8.70 Stewart J. Christine mech eng s of Stewart C. Oban

MORRISON Murdo Nicolson *BSc 1956
s of Donald M. joiner, piermaster and Mary Nicholson teacher; b Tarbert Harris 22.6.33
ARIC (1960)
trainee BP Lond, Wales, Grangemouth 1957–59; BP refinery Grangemouth: chem i/c gas analysis lab 1959–63, dev chem tech dept 1963–67, sect. head distillation area 1967–77, area controller from 1977
m Kilbarchan 2.4.60 Anne L. Dick nurse d of Robert K. D. Kilbarchan

MORRISON Neil *MA 1970 Dip Ed 1971

MORRISON Peter MA 1966

MORRISON Peter George MA 1967
s of George M. indust chem and Marjorie E. Ingram seamstress; b Wellingborough 16.9.45
trainee progr, team leader Birm 1967–70; chief progr, progr man. Bonnybridge 1970–75; software eng Cumbernauld from 1975
m Aber 27.7.68 Frances M. Barrack MA 1966 *qv*

MORRISON Roderick Murray MB ChB 1970

MORRISON Wendy Joan *MA 1965

MORRISON William MA 1964
s of William M. crofter and Catherine Gunn; b Thrumster 14.7.43
teacher: Glasg 1965–66, Wick from 1966
m Lybster 9.8.68 Diane Miller receptionist d of James M. Lybster

MORRISON William Alexander *BSc(eng) 1968
d Glasg 11.12.76

MORRISON William James MB ChB 1959
s of James C. M. milk roundsman and Caroline I. Bruce; b Turriff 22.4.36
DObstRCOG 1961
h o City hosp Aber, Gilbert Bain hosp Lerwick 1959–60; cas off. royal N infirm. Inv 1960–61; h o obst Robroyston hosp Glasg 1961; g p Insch 1961–62, Ellon from 1962
m Aber 31.3.65 Anna I. C. Robertson staff nurse d of James R. Cairnie

MORTIMER Gerald *MA 1958
s of Adam M. rlyman and Isabella McIntosh; b Glassel 27.1.36
FSAScot 1969
educ off. 1st btn Gordon Highlanders Celle Ger 1958–60; teacher hist Harris acad Dun 1961–66; prin hist Invergordon acad 1966–68; lect soc stud. Hamilton coll of educ from 1968
m Aber 27.6.60 Elizabeth J. Gibb MA 1959 *qv*

MORTIMER Sheila Williamina MA 1960
d of John M. insur br man. and Adeline S. Laing telegraphist; b Aber 15.12.39
Dip Soc St(Edin) 1961 Cert Inst of Med Soc Work(Lond) 1962
Aber: soc worker mat. hosp 1963–65, sen soc worker RACH 1965–68, mat. hosp 1968–69, Woodlands hosp from 1973
m Aber 5.4.66 Howard O. Smith BSc 1964 *qv*

MORTIMER Wilma Jean BSc 1962
d of William C. G. M. car sales man. and Jane M. Simpson; b Aboyne 1.11.41
teacher: maths/sc Summerhill acad Aber 1963–67, Perth h s 1967–70, maths Summerbank s Broughty Ferry 1975–78, maths/sc Dun from 1978
m Aber 30.3.67 Melville K. Milne MB ChB 1965 *qv*

MORTON Alan David *BSc 1968

MORTON Douglas George BSc(eng) 1960

MORTON Neil *BSc(agr) 1967
s of Norman M. B Com(Manc) passenger trans eng, trans plan. res and Florence Elliot; b Cheadle 12.8.42
MSc(Lond) 1968 DIC 1968 FRES(Lond)
Swaziland: govt res entomol 1968–71, entomol cotton res corp 1972–75; entomol ICI plant protection dir Bracknell from 1976
m Manc 5.10.68 Susan J. Thom physioth d of Alexander M. T. BSc(eng)(Glas) St Martin's Guernsey

MOSCATI Shane MA 1964
d of Clifford G. M. smallholder/mussel farmer and Jean C. Vass; b Lond 28.2.43
teacher: Aber 1965–67, Invergordon 1968, Khart 1968–71; lect Engl Omdurman 1971–74; instr Khart from 1975
m Aber 3.2.65 Hassan O. Abdelnour BSc(for) 1967 *qv*

MOSS Christine Margaret MA 1964

MOSS Robert PhD 1967
s of Leonard M. clothing manuf/des and Lore Elkan; b Leeds 30.11.41
BSc(Lond) 1963
scient off., sen scient off., prin scient off. Nature Conservancy/ITE(NERC) Banchory from 1967

MOTT Brian Leonard *MA 1969
s of Leonard M. printer and Beryl E. Cowland; b Lond 20.8.46
PhD(Barcelona) 1978
lect phonetics Engl dept: Zaragoza univ Spain 1969–72, Barcelona univ from 1972 and co-ordinator Engl dept univ lang s from 1976

MOUAT James Henry LLB 1966

MOUAT Katherine Ann MA 1960
d of John G. M. trans man. and Joan C. Smith; b Lerwick 26.2.39
teacher Engl/hist: McLaren h s Callander 1961–63, Scalloway j s s 1963–65, Dunblane s s 1965–67, Engl Mackie acad Stonehaven from 1976
m Lerwick 31.3.64 James A. G. Mathers marine eng s of James M. Port of Menteith

MOUAT Patricia MB ChB 1966
b Shetland 7.9.41

MOUNCE Robert Hayden PhD 1958
BA(Wash) BD ThM(Ful Theol Sem)

MOUNIB Mohamed Said PhD 1956
BSc MSc(Alex)

MOUSSA Mohammed Ahmed Sayed Ahmed PhD 1966
BSc(Ain-Shams)

MOWAT Alexander Parker MB ChB 1958
s of William M. trawl fisherman and Isabella P. Mair; b Cullen 5.4.35
MRCP(Lond) 1963 FRCP(Lond) 1975
nat serv RAMC Hong Kong 1959–61; h o med, paediat Aber, Lond 1961–65; res fell., assoc prof paediat Yeshiva univ NY USA 1968–69; sen regist paediat Aberd 1965–70; consult. paediat King's coll hosp/Maudsley hosp Lond from 1970
m Cullen 23.9.61 Mary A. S. Hunter civ serv d of Samuel H. Cullen

MOWAT Anne Mary MA 1965
d of Victor S. M. bank man. and Jemima B. T. McNicol lib; b Edin 7.12.44
comm asst BP Co Lond 1966–68; teacher BC Canada 1968–69
m Aber 25.3.68 George A. R. Stark BSc(Lond) econ BP Co s of Allan R.S. BSc(Glas) Sunbury-on-Thames
d Torphins 17.11.78

MOWAT Charles Donald MB ChB 1957
s of Charles D. M. fish merch and May C. Middleton; b Aber 7.1.32
h o Woodend hosp Aber 1957–58; m o RAF E Anglia 1958–61; g p: St Walburg Sask 1961–67, Barnard Castle Co Durh 1967–69, Stony Plain Edmonton Alberta from 1969
m Aber 21.7.58 Joan B. Williamson secy d of P. de L. H. W. BCom 1926 *qv*

MOWAT Colin Ralph *MA 1967 Dip Ed 1968
s of William R. M. civ serv and Margaret M. McClenaghen; b Aber 14.5.45
teacher geog: Bo'ness acad 1968–69, Kirkcaldy tech coll 1969–74; educ off. (6th form) geog Bandar Seri Begawan Sultanate of Brunei from 1975
m Aber 16.8.69 Beryl Fyfe MA 1968 *qv*

MOWAT Ian Robert Mackenzie *MA 1968
s of Robert J. B. M. banker and J. Violet Mackenzie; b Dingwall 20.4.46
MA(Sheff) 1970 BPhil(St And) 1975
asst lib: St And univ 1970–72, H-W 1972–75, asst keeper Nat Lib Scot. 1975–78, head Reader Services Glas univ lib from 1978
m Sunderland 24.8.68 Margaret L. Jackson teacher d of Victor J. Sunderland

MOWAT John *BSc(eng) 1961
b Douglas Lanark 20.5.39
trainee SETS 1961–63; eng: NSHEB Blairgowrie 1963–66, SSEB Musselburgh 1966–67, UKAEA Dounreay 1967–78, Culham from 1978

MOWAT John Stuart Simpson MB ChB 1958
s of Alexander G. M. MB ChB 1924 *qv*; b Stoke-on-Trent 31.1.30
h o med, cas Bury St Edmunds 1959–60; RN from 1960
m N'cle-u-Lyme 3.6.61 Eva-Maria V. Borel SRN d of Gustave A. B. Neuchâtel Switzerland

MOWAT Katherine Ann Mackenzie BSc 1963
m Morrison

MOWAT Malcolm David Yuille LLB 1966
s of John M. MA(Glas) min of relig and Margaret A. Howie MA(Glas); b Aber 1.10.44
CA 1969
app Williamson & Dunn CA Aber 1966–69; auditor: Price Waterhouse & Co Paris 1970–73, Lisbon 1973–75, audit man. Whinney Murray & Co Aber from 1975
m Paris 26.8.72 Susan Tunningley d of Robert T. Lond

MOWAT Norman Ashley George MB ChB 1966
s of William M. fisherman and Isabella P. Mair; b Cullen 11.4.43
MRCP 1971
h o Woodend hosp Aber, ARI 1966–67; sen h o, regist Aber hosps, clin tut. med Aberd 1968–72; lect med Aberd 1972–73; clin lect gastroenterology St Bart's hosp Lond 1973–74; consult. phys/clin sen lect Aberd from 1975
m Fordyce 23.7.66 Kathleen M. Cowie teacher d of James D. C. Fordyce

MOWAT Stanley Ian *BSc 1966 MSc 1968

MOWAT Thomas James Smith BSc(eng) 1966

MOWAT William MB ChB 1961

MOWATT Christina Cecilia MA 1970
m Thomson

MOWATT John Edward Arthur BSc 1957

MUIR Andrew BSc(agr) 1968

MUIR George Watson *MA 1968

MUIR Isabella *MA 1956 Dip Ed 1957

MUIR Joan Elizabeth MA 1969
d of James F. M. plan. eng and Katherine W. Macgregor; b Inv 10.5.48
Dip Grad Secy(Edin coll of comm) 1971
Edin: secy Ferranti 1971–73; inst of CA of Scot. Edin: secy to edit. *The Accountant's Magazine* 1973–75, edit. asst 1975–76; edit. and prod. man. 1976–77, asst edit. 1977
m Edin 22.6.74 Michael W. Milne BSc(eng) 1968 *qv*

MUIR John Geates BSc(agr) 1967
s of Stephen M. farm. and Bella L. A. Harcus; b Sanday Orkney 31.1.45
Dip FMBO 1968
DAFS: asst insp Aber 1968–77, insp Thurso from 1977
m Aber 28.7.73 Morag Ross d of Ronald R. Aber

MUIR Lisbeth *MA 1970
d of George M. M. driver (*d* 9.4.55) and Nellie Coull shopkeeper; b Millport 19.4.48
Dip YESTB
careers off. Lanarksh 1970–75; area careers off. Strathclyde reg (Ayr div) from 1975
m Millport 23.6.73 Peter J. Lamb ACA s of John L. L. Addington

MUIR Lynn *MA 1970

MUIR Neil Marshall LLB 1970

MUIR Richard Ernest *MA 1967 PhD 1970

MUIR Sarah Jane *MEd 1967
d of John I. M. BSc(Glas) headmaster and Jean C. Howgate teacher dom sc; b Grahamstown S Africa 1.9.42
MA(Edin) 1964
educ psych: N'cle-u-Tyne 1967–72, Bexley Lond from 1972
m Dalmeny –.3.72 Charles F. Morley BSc(Manc) prod. marketing man. s of Francis E. M. Manc

MUIRDEN Elaine MA 1969
d of Alexander H. M. master grocer and Mary Bruce master grocer; b Aber 7.10.48
teacher maths Crawley 1970–73
m Aber 28.8.71 William B. M. Rowlands BSc(Leeds) process eng s of William R. R. Llandovery

MUIRHEAD Ronald Archibald *BSc 1965
s of John S. M. master glazier and Martha Craig; b Glasg 15.11.35
MSc(Liv) 1974
res asst immunochem Liv 1965–67; hosp biochem Sefton gen hosp Liv from 1967
m Wolvey 10.9.66 Lorna E. Fox midwifery tut. d of Donald R. F. Nuneaton

MUKHERJEE Debangshu Bhusan PhD 1960
BSc(Agra) MSc(Alld)

MUKHI Lajpat Mangharam BSc(eng) 1957
BSc(Bom)

MUKHTAR Nuri Osman MSc 1970
s of Osman Mukhtar Hussein and Miyasa Ahmed; b Dongula Sudan 1.1.39
BSc(Khart)
m Cairo 20.11.69 Fatma I. D. Salih d of Izzel D. S. Cairo

MUKTAR Omar Mohamed Ahmed BSc 1959
s of Mohamed Ahmed teacher and Zeinab Osman; b Omdurman 21.9.31
Dip Agr(Khart) 1955 MSc(univ Wales) 1963 PhD(Texas) 1970
Sudan: agr advis serv W Sudan 1955–56; agr res div Wad Medani 1959–60, co-man. soil surv div 1964–68, dir soils dept min of agr Wad Medani from 1971
m Swansea Patricia M. Wright BA(UCW) teacher d of Edward W. Loughborough

MULHOLLAND Alastair Brodie MB ChB 1956
s of Alexander B. M. sales rep and Isabella Hamilton; b Aber 23.2.32
DA(Lond) 1960 FFARCS(Lond) 1965 Cert Anaest RCS(C) 1965 Lic Med Council(Can) 1966
h o Aber 1956–57, m o RAMC Malaya 1957–59; sen h o anaest. regist anaest Aber 1959–65; Canada: sen resid anaest Vancouver 1965–66, staff anaest Vict gen hosp 1966–71, chief dept anaest Vict 1971–74
m Elgin 2.9.61 Isabella H. Turnidge nurse d of Stafford T. Elgin

MULHOLLAND Freda Jane MB ChB 1969
m Brown

MULHOLLAND Mary Grant MA 1969
d of Joseph M. postal insp and Evelyn M. A. Jefferson; b Elgin 20.9.48
teacher: Dun 1971–73, Brit high comm Dar-es-Salaam Tanzania from 1973
m St And 27.10.72 Alexander R. Anderson customs & excise off. s of Alexander A. Alford

MULKAY Michael Joseph PhD 1970
BA(Lond) MA(S Fraser)

MULLER Emil-Roy PhD 1962
BSc(agr)(Natal)

MULVEY Charles *MA 1963
s of Charles M. shopkeeper and Mary P. Bruce; b Aber 13.2.41
Trinity coll Dublin; asst in econ 1963–64, lect econ 1964–72; econ advis to Sec of State for Scot. Edin 1972–73; sen lect econ Glas from 1973
m Dublin 28.1.66 Gerarda E. Vermeulen d of Adrianus V. Bray Co Wicklow

MUNIR Yasser Husein MSc 1970
BSc(Cairo)

MUNRO Alexander MB ChB 1967 ChM 1968
s of William G. agr contr and Jane A. McKay SRN; b Jemimaville 5.6.43
FRCSE 1972
sen h o HSC Gt Ormond St Lond 1969–70; regist ARI lect surg Aberd 1971–75; sen regist surg: Aber 1975–77, St Mary's hosp Lond 1977–78; consult. gen surg Inv hosps from 1978
m Edin 17.7.72 Maureen E. McCreath staff midwife d of James McC. CA Glasg

MUNRO Alexander Falconer *MA 1967
s of William M. civ eng and Annie E. MacDonald nurse; b Forfar 1.1.44
Glasg: man. trainee BR 1967–69, costing asst BR 1969–70; p a to man. dir Caithness Glass Wick 1970; United Glass: sales exec Bridge of Allan 1970–74, market. dev man. Staines from 1974
m Wick 17.8.68 Julia A. M. Aitkenhead pharm d of Robert C. A. Rhodesia

MUNRO Andrew *MA 1964 PhD 1971
s of Alexander M. dyer and bleacher and Janet McCracken; b Port Glasgow 1.1.36
BD(Glas) 1967 Ordained C of S min 1972
prin teacher relig educ: Banff acad 1971–72; lect theol Trinity coll Ghana 1972–76; prin teacher r e Elgin acad from 1976
m Aber 27.7.63 Sheila Smith BSc 1962 *qv*

MUNRO Angus Archibald Donald *MA 1970

MUNRO Anne Macintosh BEd 1969
d of Duncan M. head for. for. comm and Mary C. Galbraith MA(Glas) teacher; b Campbeltown 9.11.45
teacher: Engl Edin 1969–72, drama Aber from 1972

MUNRO Caroline Helen *MA 1963
d of Thomas A. M. cabinetmaker and Caroline Gordon; b Wanlockhead 21.9.41
teacher geog coll of comm Aber 1965–66; asst lib sc lib univ of W Ontario 1967–68
m Aber 17.7.65 David G. Dawson BSc 1963 *qv*

MUNRO Cathleen Anne MA 1964
d of Angus H. M. banker, farm. and Kathleen W. F. Manson hotelier; b Nairn 27.4.43
teacher: Garrowhill 1965–66, Slade Green, Bexley 1966–68, Malpas 1968–69, Ellesmere Port from 1975
m Huntly 14.7.66 Peter R. Aikman BSc 1966 *qv*

MUNRO Donald BSc 1956

MUNRO Donald *MA 1959

MUNRO Donald James *MA 1964
s of William M. civ eng and Annie E. Macdonald nurse; b Forfar 22.2.42
asst dept mss John Rylands lib Manc 1964–66; inst of hist res univ of Lond: bibliogr asst 1966–73, asst lib from 1973
m Ashton-u-Lyne 27.3.67 Beryl Swetnam teacher d of James S. Ashton-u-Lyne

MUNRO Frances Helen MA 1957

MUNRO Gillespie Donald MA 1960
s of John B. M. comm trav and Emma McCallum insur clerkess; b Aber 28.4.39
teacher: Lumphanan s s 1961–63, Ballater p s 1963–67; head Monymusk p s from 1967
m Ballater 17.10.64 Mary H. Davidson teacher d of Donald D. Ballater

MUNRO Hamish David *BSc 1964 PhD 1967
s of James S. M. pharm and Isabella Thomson; b Kilwinning 24.4.42
Chartered Patent Ag 1975 Gill Prize 1975
res fell. univ of Mainz Germany 1967–68; chem Procter & Gamble N'cle 1968–71; patent tech asst Carpmaels & Ransford Lond 1972–75; Procter & Gamble: patent ag Cincinnati Ohio 1975, man. of patents Europe Strombeek-Bever Belgium from 1976
m Aber 6.1.68 Alison B. Walker BSc 1964 *qv*
d Lond 9.2.80 *AUR* XLVIII 443

MUNRO Ian Alexander MA 1966

MUNRO Jean Margaret MA 1968
d of Frank A. M. motor mech, loc govt off. and Martha M. Anderson seamstress, shop asst; b Inv 11.1.47
Dip Sec Sc(Strath) 1969
secy: Lond 1969–71, Edin 1971–73; res asst Edin from 1973
m Edin 14.4.73 Terence Foster BSc(Edin) teacher s of George F. Birm

MUNRO John Gray BSc(eng) 1961
s of John G. M. MA(Cantab) group capt RAF and Rita M. Walkey nurs sister; b Bromley 8.4.39
GMIMechE 1962
Bristol: grad app BAC 1961–62; organis and methods asst etc United Builders Merchants 1962–72, dir UBM Group from 1972
m Wraxall 26.6.65 Elizabeth R. Scantlebury d of Eric S.

MUNRO Margaret Catherine MA 1967
d of William G. M. blacksmith and Margaret Mackay; b Brora 13.8.46
teacher: mod lang Hillhead h s Glasg 1968–72, Engl anglic mission s Nuku Alofa Tonga 1972–73, Millburn acad Inv 1975–78
m Brora 17.10.70 John E. Rae MA 1965 *qv*

MUNRO Margaret Jean Waters MA 1968
m Munro

MUNRO Margot Gunn *MA 1963
d of Robert G. M. MB ChB 1923 *qv*; b Sheff 16.1.36
ARCM 1959 LRAM 1963 Dip Lib(Sheff) 1966
trainee lib Torry res stat Aber 1964–65; asst lib St And univ from 1966

MUNRO Mary Dunbar MA 1962
d of John M. butcher and Davina Sinclair; b Thurso 2.5.41
teacher Miller acad p s Thurso 1953–65 and from 1972
m Thurso 1963 David J. Lyall nuclear chem s of John L. Duns

MUNRO Robert Alexander *MA 1968

MUNRO Robert Charles PhD 1966
s of Ralph M. manuf and Bertha L. von Melcher BS(W Reserve univ) nurse, entrepreneur; b Mansfield Ohio 25.11.38
B Foreign Serv(Calif)
proj superv B. F. Goodrich Co Akron Ohio 1966–67; superv of accts internat B. F. Goodrich Frankfurt Germany 1967–68; Jos. Schlitz Brewing Co: man. spec assignments Milwaukee Wisconsin 1968–69, asst dir sales Europe Ghlin Belgium 1969–70; man. market. plan. and res ITT world directories Brussels 1970–72, man. market. plan. dev and res Brussels 1972–76, res analyst ITT world hq NY City 1976–77; man. market dev Fundacion Chile Santiago 1977–78; ITT world hq NY City: asst man.-corporate market. 1978–79, man. market and bus. strategy 1979, man. corporate indust and employee relations from 1979
m S Juan PR 10.2.75 Maria do R. de F. M. Ribeiro-Fernandes BA(Lisbon) advis acct exec d of Joaquim d'A R-F. Portugal

MUNRO Robert James *BSc(eng) 1964

MUNRO Robert Kenneth *MA 1968
s of Donald W. M. flt lt RAF and Ethel Stoten; b Dunstable 7.4.46
teacher geog: AGS 1969–70, Whitburn acad 1970–71, prin geog Douglas Ewart h s Wigtown 1971–74; lect geog Hamilton coll of educ from 1974
m Blair Atholl 10.8.68 Janet S. Seaton teacher d of Alexander S. Blair Atholl

MUNRO Robert Lawrence *MA 1966
s of Hugh A. C. M. M. insp taxes and Elsie M. Chapman; b Cromarty 12.6.44
insp taxes: Aber 1966–68, Glasg 1968–72, Ardrossan 1972–73, Lond from 1973

MUNRO Robin Murray *MA 1969
s of Ian S. M. MA(Glas) lect and Mary M. Allan; b Bute 10.5.46
Arts Council award 1973
writer Catterline and Shetland from 1971; teacher Galloway from 1975; poetry collections: *Shetland, like the World* 1975, *The Land of the Mind* 1975

MUNRO Roderic MA 1968
s of Frederick A. M. and Annie Jessiman; b Forres 3.4.47
teacher: dep head maths dept Little Ilford comp s Lond from 1970

MUNRO Sheila Margaret MB ChB 1969
m Mathewson

MUNRO Wendy MA 1969
m Chaligne

MUNRO William Alexander BSc(eng) 1967
s of Thomas A. M. cabinetmaker and Caroline Gordon shop asst; b Glasg 7.5.40
MInstHE 1968 CEng MICE 1971
measurement eng R. J. McLeod Drumnadrochit 1967–68; Forfar: asst eng Angus c c roads dept, sen eng from 1972
m Aber Dorothy W. Neish hairdresser/man. d of Archibald C. N. Brechin

MUNSADIA Ishwarlal Dahyabhai MB ChB 1963

MURCHIE Anne MA 1959
m Morton

MURCHIE Innes Fyfe *MA 1966
s of Charles S. M. eng and Elizabeth L. Innes bookseller; b Aber 10.11.43
bank clerk Aber 1967–69; res asst Clydesdale bank Glasg from 1970
m Aber 28.6.69 Heather Cobban secy d of Charles C. Aber

MURCHIE Marjory Elizabeth *MA 1968
d of James L. M. chief supt police and Marjory Dean; b Glasg 27.3.46
teacher: Hillhead h s Glasg 1969–72, prin geog Knightswood s s Glasg from 1972
m Glasg 21.3.70 Hamish G. Reid BSc(eng) 1968 *qv*

MURCUTT Miriam Sinclair MA 1969

MURDOCH Anne Grace MA 1970
d of George M. garage serv man. and Annie G. M. Robb nurse; b Dun 18.1.49
Dip Soc Ad 1971 Dip Soc Work 1972
soc worker: royal Edin hosp 1972–73, Lancs c c 1973–76
m Monifieth 23.3.74 Bernard Strawson BSc(Lond) pers off. BL s of Bernard S. Liv

MURDOCH Elizabeth Margaret MA 1969
d of George M. M. joiner and Janet C. Aitken comptometer oper; b Glasg 9.9.48

teacher: Lat Kilmarnock acad 1970–71, p s Evanton 1971–72, Lat Invergordon acad 1972–74
m E Kilbride 7.4.71 John K. Clark MA 1969 *qv*

MURDOCH James BSc 1964

MURDOCH Keith Kinord Ian MA 1966
s of Colin C. I. M. artist/art dealer and Rosalind A. J. D. Cruickshank; b Aber 4.2.44
teacher: direct method Engl Paris 1966–69, supply Engl Brighton 1969–70, Engl Cambuslang from 1970; other non-teaching temp posts

MURDOCH Robert Bell MA 1956
s of Robert B. M. civ serv and Marguerita C. Bell newsagent; b Stonehaven 28.10.31
teacher: maths Arbroath h s 1957–58, Carnoustie p s 1958–60; dep head: p dept Carnoustie j s s 1960–67, p dept Laurencekirk s s 1967–71, Arduthie p s Stonehaven from 1971
m Stonehaven 19.9.53 Alice M. Ross pharm's asst d of William R. Aber

MURDOCH Ronald McLean MA 1968

MURDOCH William Forman MA 1964 *MEd 1966
s of William F. M. gardener and Jeannie Simpson; b Cruden 6.4.39
Kirkcudbrightsh: teacher 1966–68, educ psych 1968–70; Abdnsh: sen educ psych 1970–71, head spec s 1971–76, advis spec educ Grampian reg c from 1976
m Aber 12.7.63 Christine A. Gear BSc 1960 *qv*

MURISON Norma MA 1967
m Smith

MURPHY Arthur John *MA 1967

MURPHY Helen Margaret *BSc 1970
m Salford 25.9.70 David J. Hall BSc 1970 *qv*

MURRAY Alexander BSc(agr) 1957
s of James M. farm. and Margaret Mitchell teacher; b Cornhill 26.7.33
asst exper off. Scot. Soc for res in plant breeding Roslin 1958–60; asst agr advis NOSCA Stonehaven, Inv 1960–62; asst insp, insp DAFS Edin, Kirkwall, Dun from 1963

MURRAY Alexander Irvine BSc 1969
s of Irvine M. M. accts man. and Margaret J. Mackenzie; b Nairn 25.9.46
trainee computer progr Barrow-in-Furness 1969–70; computer progr Inv 1970–72; computer syst analyst Norwich from 1972
m Edin 4.11.72 Alys G. M. Roberts teacher of art d of Arthur R. R. Edin

MURRAY Alistair William *BSc 1958 PhD 1962

MURRAY Anne Scott MA 1968
d of Malcolm S. M. p e instr and Noel J. Corrigall; b Lossiemouth 7.6.48
Dip Pers Man(RGIT) 1970
Lond: secy, admin asst various companies 1970–74, exec off. MoD 1974–79
m Aber 30.1.71 John M. M. Dixon MA 1969 *qv*

MURRAY Bernard Marshall BSc(eng) 1969

MURRAY Bruce BSc 1960
s of George J. G. M. agr rep and Bella G. Lamb; b Aber 2.11.39
teacher maths/sc Ruthrieston s Aber 1961–65; various posts with IBM (UK) Greenock from 1965
m Aber 3.8.62 Sheila M. West RGN d of Malcolm W. Aber

MURRAY Catherine MA 1960
d of Donald M. Harris tweed millworker and Murdina Morrison; b Stornoway 24.1.39
teacher: Laurencekirk s s 1961–63, Cloverfield p s Aber 1964–67, Tough p s Dunfermline from 1975
m Aber 29.3.65 Donald Smith BSc 1961 *qv*

MURRAY Charlotte MA 1960 Dip Ed 1961
d of Charles M. cattleman and Lily R. Henderson; b Inv 12.6.39
teacher Engl/hist: Kirriemuir 1961–66, Stornoway from 1966
m Dun 1.8.69 Murdoch Macleod weaver s of George B. C. M. Tong, Is of Lewis

MURRAY Christina Margaret MA 1958
d of Donald M. and Murdina Morrison; b Stornoway 20.3.37
teacher: Inverallochy p s 1959–62, Stoneywood p s 1962–65
m Aber 17.7.63 John Anderson MA 1960 *qv*

MURRAY Christopher Hugh *MA 1969
s of William M. MBE MM for./head for. and Mary B. MacRae; b Inv 17.1.47
grad acct trainee Tannochside Viewpark 1969–72; cost acct Fochabers 1972–75; acct stud. Edin 1975–76; lect bus. stud. Elgin coll 1976–77; chief acct Fochabers from 1977
m Aber 12.9.69 Audrey F. A. Park BEd 1969 *qv*

MURRAY David Cairns *MA 1964 Dip Ed 1966
s of Robert J. M. hortic advis NOSCA and Mary McGuckian secy, teacher; b Glasg 6.8.41
teacher geog AGS 1966–68; lt RN educ off. RNAS Culdrose 1968–73, lt comm RN met. off. HMS *Daedalus* Lee-on-Solent 1973–75; sen forecaster HMS *Ark Royal* 1975–77, staff met. off. to capt i/c Hong Kong from 1977
m Westbury 9.4.69 Monica J. Grenfell SRN d of Richard C. G. Westbury

MURRAY David Findlay BSc 1969

MURRAY Donella MA 1957

MURRAY Douglas MA 1970 LLB 1972
s of John M. baker and Ida Leighton-Hall; b Perth 31.1.49
law app Edin 1972–74; leg. asst Paull & Williamsons advoc Aber 1974–80, ptnr from 1980

MURRAY Eleanor Margaret MB ChB 1961 DPH 1966
m Steiner

MURRAY Elizabeth Cooper MA 1959

MURRAY Ernest MB ChB 1965
s of Alexander M. gardener and Charlotte Coutts; b Alford 15.3.41
h p Woodend hosp, City hosp, mat hosp Aber 1965–67; g p Poole from 1967
m Aber 30.9.65 Eva I. W. Law secy d of Robert L. Keig

MURRAY George *BSc 1961 MSc 1962 PhD 1965
s of George M. trawl fisherman and Agnes Coull; b Aber 23.5.39

asst lect maths Queen's coll Dun 1964–66; lect nat phil Aberd from 1966
m Aber 2.10.72 Margaret A. Scrimgeour MA 1964 *qv*

MURRAY Gordon BSc(for) 1957
s of Alan D. M. teacher and Helen Bowick MA(St And) teacher; b Forfar 2.4.36
MSc(Purdue univ Indiana) 1969 PhD 1972
2nd lt RE 1957–59; teacher sc Kirriemuir 1959–60; exper off. Nature Conserv Monkswood 1960–66; grad res inst Purdue univ 1966–72; Lakehead univ s of for. Thunder Bay Ontario: asst 1972–77, assoc prof from 1977
m Lossiemouth 9.7.60 Laura Leask radiogr d of Robert J. L. Lossiemouth

MURRAY Hazel *MA 1958
d of John M. chef and Jean Ormiston; b N'cle-u-Tyne 22.12.36
teacher mod lang: Perth 1960–62, Elgin 1962–63; asst prin mod lang Aberlour 1967–76, prin mod lang from 1976
m Aberlour 28.4.62 William Fraser postman

MURRAY Helen Kilpatrick *MA 1970
m Matthews

MURRAY Hugh Bruce *MA 1967
s of James M. bank man. and Anne Bruce health lect; b Aber 11.5.45
Dip Ed(Glas) 1968
teacher: prin hist St Leonard's s Glasg, prin soc stud Bermuda from 1970
m Bermuda 22.7.71 Mary M. Doherty MA 1967 *qv*

MURRAY Ian BSc(eng) 1968

MURRAY Ian James BSc(eng) 1970

MURRAY Isabella Reid *MA 1970
m Macdonald

MURRAY James *BSc 1964

MURRAY James Alexander MB ChB 1957
s of James A. M. motor salesman and Robina Berry; b Aber 24.3.34
RAF 1958–61; h o Forth Park mat. hosp Fife 1961; g p Kirkcaldy from 1961
m Aber 10.4.57 Mabel M. Gavin d of William G. Aber

MURRAY James Charles *MA 1970 Dip Ed 1973
s of James M. bank man. and Annie Bruce lect; b Ayr 7.8.47
L ès L(Clermont-Ferrand) 1971
lect Engl univ of Clermont-Ferrand France 1970–71; res stud. Aberd 1971–72; lect econ Engl Paris 1973–74; teacher Fr Hazlehead acad Aber 1974–75; asst prin mod lang Cults acad Aber from 1975
m Sens France 15.7.74 Liliane C. L. Carreau L ès L (Sorbonne) teacher d of Louis A. C. Sens

MURRAY James Frederick *MA 1969
s of James G. M. pharm and Anne M. Taggart; b Aber 13.5.46
teacher St And 1970–74; lib asst Dun 1974–76; post grad ALA stud. RGIT Aber 1976–77; lib asst Aber from 1977

MURRAY James Morrison MA 1968

MURRAY Jennifer Anne MA 1965 *MEd 1968
m Reid

MURRAY John Young *MEd 1966
s of Charles M. MA(Edin) teacher, HMIS and Margaret I. Young MA(Edin) teacher; b Kirkcaldy 5.2.43
BSc(Edin) 1964
teacher chem Annan 1966–72, prin chem from 1972
m Inv 4.7.66 Barbara A. Williams teacher d of Edwin M. W. Inv

MURRAY Katharine Gale *MA 1966
d of Andrew D. M. soc statist and Joan M. St Aubin lect; b Lond 10.10.42
teacher Engl: Dunfermline 1972–74, Corsham s 1974–76
m Lond 23.7.66 David J. Curry BSc 1965 *qv*

MURRAY Laurence Oliphant Nairne MA 1964

MURRAY Leonora Janet Hunter MB ChB 1959
d of Robert H. M. bricklayer/mason and Jessie Sim hotel prop.; b Cluny 20.2.34
h o Woodend hosp Aber, ARI 1959–60; sen h o: geriat Woodend hosp, psychiat royal mental hosp Aber 1960–65; regist psycho-geriat Royal Vict hosp Edin from 1975
m Aber 20.7.62 Gordon M. McAndrew MB ChB 1957 *qv*

MURRAY Margaret Jane Irvine MA 1965
d of James D. M. mill worker and Eva M. Davidson waitress; b Aber 19.9.30
teacher Aber from 1966
m Aber 3.10.51 William P. Booth painter/decorator s of Alexander B. Aber; husb *d* 7.4.60

MURRAY Margaret Muir MA 1970 Dip Ed 1971
d of Walter M. M. dist lib and Helen R. Brown school lib; b Motherwell 26.12.49
teacher geog: Dumfries 1971–73, Lond 1973–76; educ off. HM prison Perth 1977; teacher geog Perth from 1977
m Alloa 24.12.76 Robert J. C. Watt MA 1973 lect Dund s of William S. W. MA (Glas) prof humanity Aberd

MURRAY Marjory Henderson MA 1970 Dip Ed 1971
d of William M. steelfixer/scaffolder and Loveday M. D. Mackay off. man.; b Golspie 21.11.49
au pair France 1971–72; teacher Ger/Fr Golspie 1972–73, Fr Manc 1973; exec off. civ serv Manc, Edin 1974–76
m Golspie 27.10.73 Stuart F. Carnegie BSc 1971 res scient s of James R. C. Inverarity

MURRAY Matthew Archibald Gillespie BEd 1970

MURRAY Muriel Gray Carnegie MA 1958
d of George J. G. M. agr salesman and Bella G. Lamb; b Aber 5.8.37
teacher: Crathes 1959–60, Fernielea s Aber 1961–69
m Aber 1.3.69 Ian D. Knight off. man. OPM s of James K. Meikle Wartle

MURRAY Neil MA 1959
s of James M. blacksmith/crofter and Marion MacIver; b Back Lewis 3.3.36
teacher Laxdale j s 1960–65; sen lect Lews Castle coll Lewis from 1965
m Aber 27.12.62 Catherine Graham shop asst d of Angus G. Back

MURRAY Neil Macbeth MA 1969
s of Stuart M. clerk and Christina I. McBeth; b Elgin 6.3.48
prof footballer: Edin 1969–73, Greenock 1973–74, teacher s s Greenock from 1974

MURRAY Norman MA 1967
s of Donald M. crofter/weaver and Margaret Smith; b Lewis 1.7.46
BA(Strath) 1973
Glasg: teacher hist 1968–72, asst prin guid 1972–73, prin hist from 1973

MURRAY Rhoda Violet BSc 1968
d of George J. A. M. M. head for. and Rhoda Ralph nurse; b Portskerra 9.4.45
asst scient off. Marine lab Aber 1969–72
m Tomintoul 29.7.67 James Gray BSc 1963 *qv*

MURRAY Rhona Mary MA 1969
m Mackenzie

MURRAY Ronald Gordon Ireland Clark MA 1958 Dip Ed 1959

MURRAY Rosemary Lilian *MA 1964 Dip Ed 1978
m Watson

MURRAY Roy MB ChB 1967

MURRAY Sheila Margaret *MA 1963
d of Alexander M. bank man. and Elsie F. Nicol civ serv, acct work; b Inv 4.4.42
teacher mus: Aber acad 1964–65, Thurso h s 1965–66; prin teacher mus Lerwick c s 1966–70, asst Anderson h s Lerwick from 1970
m Aber 29.7.66 James G. Bruce chief clerk banking s of Alexander G. B. MA(Edin) Thurso

MURRAY Stewart *BSc 1966
s of Robert M. MN off. and Catherine N. Stewart; b Aber 18.9.37
geol NCB: Wales 1966–69, Scot. 1969–74; lands off. W Scot. from 1974
m Aber 26.7.71 Helen M. Kean MA 1952 *qv*

MURRAY Violet MA 1968 BD 1972
d of Allan M. Br Legion car park attend. and Nellie S. Dodds; b Aber 10.8.26
teacher Peterhead from 1973

MURRAY William MA 1959
s of William K. M. joiner and Elsie Barber; b New Byth 26.8.36
teacher Fr/prin guid Moffat acad from 1960
m Rousay 17.7.58 Kathleen F. S. Grieve MA 1958 *qv*

MURRAY William John BSc(eng) 1964
s of William M. farm. and Jeanne A. Milton; b Keith 27.7.42
Dip Man.(McG) 1971
N Telecom Canada: dev eng 1964–73, dept head digital trans div from 1973
m Barbados 21.12.69 Sally J. Edghill physioth d of J. H. C. E. Christchurch Barbados

MURRAY-SMITH David James *BSc(eng) 1963 MSc 1964
s of William M-S. grain merch and Katherine B. Trail; b Aber 20.10.41
PhD(Glas) 1970
res eng Ferranti Edin 1964–65, Glas: asst 1966–67, lect 1967–77, sen lect from 1977
m Aber 9.8.66 Effie M. Smith MA 1963 *qv*

MUSA Mohammed Musa PhD 1963
BSc(agr)(Khart)

MUST Christopher John MB ChB 1957
s of John S. M. BA(Cantab) clerk in holy orders and Katrine Russell MA 1929 *qv*; b Lond 19.11.33
DO(Lond) 1961 FRCS(C) 1967
h o Aber hosps 1957–58; ophth RAF Eng, Aden 1958–63; regist ophth Carlisle 1963–66; consult. ophth Peterborough Ontario from 1966
m Aber 26.7.58 Janella H. S. Baxter leg. secy d of John B. Aber

MUST Michael James BSc 1960
s of John S. M. BA(Cantab) clerk in holy orders and Katrine Russell MA 1929 *qv*; b Wembley 18.7.38
teacher phys co-ed g s Biggleswade 1960–62; oil comp: clerk board statist Lond 1962–63, computer syst auditor Hemel Hempstead 1963–65, superv auditor 1965–70, costing unit man. Lond, computer syst audit man. PO central audit dept 1972–76; computer audit superv oil comp from 1976
m Roxton 18.4.64 Janet Bates nurs nurse, teacher d of Charles J. R. B. Roxton

MUSTAFA Muktar Ahmed MSc 1966
BSc(Khart)

MUTCH Alexander James BSc(eng) 1957
s of William K. M. clerk and Violet French; b Insch 15.6.37
des eng: Scot. gas board Aber 1957–58, city eng's dept Dunedin city council NZ 1958–62, Macdonald Wagner & Priddle consult. eng Sydney 1962–73, assoc dir from 1973
m Dunedin 18.12.59 Melva R. Milne nurse d of Anthony W. M. Aber

MUTCH Douglas Bruce MA 1969
s of Henry D. M. bus driver and Mary A. Bruce superv; b Ellon 8.11.48
teacher mod lang: Bankhead 1970–71, Arbroath 1971–74, Arran from 1974
m Aber 7.7.71 Hilary M. Rhodes MA 1969 *qv*

MUTCH George Porter *MA 1970 MLitt 1974
s of William M. cycle dealer and Elsie C. Milton law clerkess; b Keith 28.9.49
stud. Oxon 1971–73; lect: école normale supérieure Paris 1973–74, univ de Paris–III 1974–76, univ de Paris–IV–Sorbonne from 1976

MUTCH Gwendoline MA 1967
m McCaskie

MUTCH John *MA 1964 Dip Ed 1965

MUTCH John Robert Young MA 1958 LLB 1961

MUTCH Lesley Margaret Mollison MB ChB 1956
d of Henry J. M. M. rubber planter and Myra M. Watt MA 1910 *qv*; b Peterhead 17.1.34
h o RACH 1956–57; h o obst, sen h o med Antrim NI 1957–58; sen h o paediat Carshalton 1958–59; g p Bicester 1959–67; res MRC progr on foetal growth and dev Oxford 1970–74; sen clin m o Avon area health auth Bristol from 1975
m Bicester 3.7.65 David C. Smith FRS prof s of John S. N. Harrow

MUTCH Margaret Forman *BSc 1970 PhD 1980
lect anat Aberd from 1970
m Inverurie 22.8.59 James J. Bruce LLB 1972 solic

MUTCH Richard Moir *MA 1968
s of Richard A. M. mason and Elma S. Moir; b Ellon

25.3.46
journalist: Aber 1968–72, Glasg 1972–73, Aber from 1973
m Aber 16.6.69 Pauline H. Hay staff nurse d of Joseph M. H. Aber

MUTCH William Alexander Ritchie MA 1961 LLB 1963
s of William P. M. grocery storeman and Bella P. Ritchie; b Aber 22.12.40
NP 1973
solic Edin 1968–71; Bank of Scot.: asst law secy 1971–73, law secy from 1973
m Aber 29.7.66 Alison C. Rae MA 1964 *qv*

MUTURI David Symon BSc(for) 1968
s of Simeon M. farm. and Dorcas Wanjiru; b Othaya Kenya 24.4.41
Kenya: for. Maji Mazuri 1968–69, div for. off. 1969–71, for. man. plans off. h q 1971–78, conserv for. i/c insp hq from 1978
m Nyeri 21.12.78 Rahab W. Kirathe BEd(Exe) teacher d of Paul K. Othaya

NAIRN Audrey *MA 1957
d of James R. N. comm trav and Annie G. Spence; b Aber 30.11.34
Dip Lib Archive Admin(Lond) 1959
asst lib: Glas 1958–60, Leeds univ 1960–63
m Aber 2.11.63 Adrian T. Hall MA(Leeds) lib s of Arthur H. Hornsea

NAISH Peter Laurance *BSc(eng) 1967
s of Stanley J. N. insur ag and Grace E. K. Russell; b Johnstone 14.12.44
MICE 1973
site civ eng Lond from 1967
m Peterlee 30.5.70 Lesley M. Coleman secy d of Leonard E. L. C. BSc(Lond) Peterlee

NALL Andrew Redmarley BSc(for) 1964
s of Alfred K. N. comp secy and Marion Fletcher teacher; b Rochdale 28.11.41
asst to for. consult. Berwicksh 1964–65; asst contr man. Co Durh 1965–67; asst head for. Staffordsh 1967–69; asst for. off. Bucks c c 1968–74; for. off. S Oxford dist council from 1974
m Stanley 24.7.65 Carol M. Cowie MA 1964 *qv*

NALUSWA James Tucker MSc 1970
s of Stanley G. W. B. N. for. ranger and Eriosi M. Tamunoza; b Iwemba Nabirere Uganda 26.5.38
BSc(for)(Sarajevo univ Yugoslavia) 1969
Uganda: dist for. off. Toro 1970–71, grad res asst Makerere univ 1971–74, prov comm for for. Gulu 1974–76, Mbale from 1976
m Lond 22.7.67 Margaret Wampande nurs. sister d of Zadoki W. Namungalwe Uganda

NAPIER James Frederick *MA 1969
s of William N. sales man. and Vera Gregory; b Perth 10.4.47
post grad trainee Rolls Royce Bristol; teacher: hist Bristol 1970–72, sc/hist Leigh 1972–73; housemaster boys' boarding s Oakham from 1974
m Stowe 29.7.72 Rosemarie J. Salway s matron d of Austin H. S. Weston-super-Mare

NAPIER Thomas Macdonald *BSc 1962 MSc 1963
s of James K. N. MA(Glas) C of S min and Mary M. Deans MA(Glas) teacher; b Forfar 20.1.41
res asst phys dept Leeds univ 1963–67, sen exper off. 1967–70; payload eng European space technol centre Noordwijk Holland 1970–72; electronics eng health phys Cern Geneva 1972–79, dev man. Nuclear Enterprises Edin from 1979

NAPPER Adrian John MB ChB 1970
s of Percy T. R. N. off. HM customs and excise and Catherine J. Carter RGN; b Northampton 4.2.46
h o Woodend hosp Aber, ARI 1970–71; res fell., sen h o surg Aberd 1971–72; m o Nessie Knight hosp Qumbu Transkei 1972–73; sen h o: paediat Darlington 1973–74, psychiat Dun from 1974
m Aber 27.4.74 Rona M. Ferguson RGN d of Frederick F. Aber

NARAYAN Lakshmi PhD 1958
BA(Patna) MA(Calc)

NARGUNDKAR Ashok Shankar BSc(eng) 1968
BSc(Bom)

NARGUNDKAR Mukund Shankar BSc(eng) 1963
MSc(Bom)

NASH Edward John *MA 1959

NAYSMITH Elizabeth BEd 1969
d of Duncan N. master painter and Elizabeth Gammie health centre receptionist; b Insch 25.4.48
teacher geog: St David's h s Dalkeith 1969–72, Ashford c s from 1972
m Aber 14.4.72 John G. Brander MA 1969 *qv*

NDUKA Otonti Sunday Amadi *MA 1957
s of Isaiah Nduka Oludi farm. and Rosannah C. Amadi; b Rumueme Nigeria 9.5.26
Dip Ed(Lond) 1962 MPhil(Lond) 1969 PhD(Ibadan) 1979
Nigeria: educ off. insp/admin Port Harcourt 1958–62, lect phil univ Nsukka 1963–65; commonwealth schol LSE 1965–67; Nigeria: sen educ off. Lagos 1967–68, lect, sen lect educ Ibadan univ 1969–80; prof educ Port Harcourt univ from 1980
m Lond 20.1.58 Pamela E. M. Holderness educ asst d of Frederick W. H. Harrow

NEAL Andrew Graham BSc 1965

NEAVE David John Benjamin MA 1956

NEEDHAM Adrian Douglas *BSc(eng) 1969
s of Charles D. N. MD(Lond) med consult. and Margaret V. D. Roden; b Lincolnsh 2.6.47
MICE 1973 FGS 1976
Lond: asst civ eng Sir Alex Gibb & Ptnrs 1969–73, sen eng Cementation Ground Eng 1973–74, assoc Dames & Moore from 1974

NEEDHAM Michael Roy MA 1964

NEILAN Henry Thomas *MA 1958
s of Henry N. staff superv and Mary McCallum; b Hamilton 5.5.36
teacher Fr/Span: Motherwell 1959–61, Kingston Jamaica 1961–64, Aber 1964–69, Tarbes France 1969–70, Dumfries from 1970
m Aber 30.6.59 Sheila Wood MA 1958 *qv*

NEILL Patricia Mary Helen MA 1967
d of Thomas F. N. min of relig and Jane Bruce; b Lesmahagow 26.10.46
teacher: Godmanchester 1968–70, Burton-on-Trent from 1972
m Aber 16.11.67 George S. Halliday MA 1966 *qv*

NEILSON Robert Ewan *BSc(agr) 1967 PhD 1971
s of Robert B. N. tel eng and Ada Redford secy; b Forfar 4.6.44
res off. bot dept Aberd from 1970
m Ellon 29.6.68 Helen A. Sangster secy d of John S. Ellon

NEIZER Justice Amonoo BSc(eng) 1960
m Lond 2.9.75 Barbara A. Thompson MA 1952 *qv*

NELSON James Stanley PhD 1968
BA BD(Bethel Minn)

NELSON William James Adair MA 1960
(conferred for long service of exceptional merit)
b Aber 2.4.07
CA 1929
finance off. Aberd 1948–75; retd

NEOPHYTOU Joannis Polykarpou MA 1961
s of Polykarpos N. farm. and Victoria T. Rousou; b Paphos Cyprus 8.12.29
MSc(W Ont) 1965
teacher phys Nicosia Cyprus 1961–63, stud. Lond Ont 1963–65, geophys: geol surv of Cyprus Nicosia from 1965 Br Council schol seismol Edin, Camb, Imp Coll 1973
m Nicosia 14.9.62 Elpiniki N. Papadopoulou d of Nestor P. Nicosia

NERLAND Beate *MA 1970
d of Knut N. fisherman/farm. and Inger A. Kirkeslett; b Sør-Aukra Norway 10.1.26
teacher Swedish/Norwegian Harlaw acad/coll of comm Aber 1971–72, EFL/tech Engl Bergen coll of tech Norway 1972–74; teacher/edit. own work course TEFL (multi-racial classes) coll of comm/Harlaw acad Aber 1974–76, TEFL inst of foreign lang Baku USSR 1976–77; teacher Engl/Free Ch mission s Tonga S Pacific 1978–80
m Meldal Norway 5.10.46 James C. Gibson master mariner s of Robert G. St Abbs

NEVIN Brian McElroy PhD 1968
s of Samuel C. M. N. clerk and Iris L. Wheeler clerk; b Durban 3.2.32
MA(Natal) 1954
sen lect maths univ of Natal Pietermaritzburg 1969–78, prof maths from 1978
m Kloof S Af 20.7.57 Jennifer M. Robbins MSc(Natal) lect d of Colin J. J. R. Kloof

NEWBIGGING Alice Ross MA 1969
d of John G. N. factory worker and Doreen Ross shop asst; b Bucksburn 16.9.48
Dip Soc Admin(Edin) 1970 Dip Soc Work(Edin) 1973
trainee soc worker Aberdeensh 1970–72; soc worker Livingston from 1973
m Aber 30.5.75 Thomas L. G. Leckie psychiat soc worker s of James L. Falkirk

NEWLANDS Winnifred Jean MA 1967
d of John N. farm. and Jane Shand ch's nurse; b Forres 31.7.46
m Rothes 21.3.67 James Falconer Dyke

NEWMAN Briony Frances BSc 1970
d of Donald R. N. warrant off. RAF and Ella J. Walker cler off.; b Lincoln 5.1.48
res asst genetics Glas 1970–73; teacher sc/maths Aberlour from 1974

NEWMAN Christopher John Edwin BSc(eng) 1967
s of Harold E. M. N. army off. and Margaret H. Smith; b Epsom 25.8.46
site eng: George Wimpey & Co Livingston 1967–68, Shanks & McEwan (contr) Dumfries 1968–70; Aust: eng Melbourne & Metrop board of works 1970, asst eng state wheat board Toowoomba Queensland from 1970
m Dumfries 3.8.68 Patricia M. Findlay MA 1966 *qv*

NEWTON John *BSc 1968
s of William R. N. LLB(Lond) dist comm nat savings and Joyce C. M. Ives; b Llandudno 13.3.46
biochem tech vet coll Lond 1968–73; field biol pest control N Lond 1973–78; entomologist pest control from 1978

NEWTON Raymond Garbet *MEd 1967
s of Robert G. N. clerk and Alice L. Harding; b Southport 21.2.27
BSc(Lond) 1956
lect geog Aber coll of educ from 1962
m(2) Ellon 22.6.73 Gisèle Bessaguet

NEWTON Robert Ian *MA 1970
b Stranraer 21.1.49
sen clin psych Argyll & Clyde health board from 1977
m Stranraer 8.8.70 Christine Frew

NGANGA Francis BSc(for) 1968

NG CHENG HIN Raymond Louis Tsien Kwee MB ChB 1963

NG CHENG HIN Thomas BSc 1967

NG WING WYE Ng Yiow Sem MA 1970

NICHOL Peter Howard *MA 1969

NICHOL Roberta Allan LLB 1968
d of Robert S. N. army off. and Gladys Allan; b Aber 30.10.47
law app, leg. asst Aber 1968–76
m Aber 3.8.68 Joseph D. Keeping MB ChB 1970 *qv*

NICHOLS Colston Edward BSc 1965
s of Colston E. N. warden Birch Lawn Home S'ton and Helen G. Milne asst matron; b Aber 30.11.43
RAF from 1965
m Aber 25.2.67 Julie M. E. Duthie teacher d of Robert P. D. Aber

NICHOLS Judith Ann *MA 1961
d of Walter M. N. MB ChB(Glas) neuro-surg and Barbara L. Thompson SRN; b Manc 30.10.39
teacher Engl: Perth 1962–64, Glasg 1964–67
m Aber 21.12.63 Lachlan A. Cameron BA(Cantab) univ lect s of Alexander R. C. BSc(St And) St Fillans

NICHOLSON Anthony Paul MB ChB 1958
s of Wilfrid N. loc govt off. and Jessie B. Sherwood; b Tresco Is of Scilly 5.10.27
NHServ Aber from 1958
m Aber 25.9.59 Audrey Clark d of Herbert C. Aber

NICHOLSON Bertram Milton *BSc 1970

NICHOLSON Catherine Mary MA 1968
d of Andrew F. N. marine eng and Margaret D. Clark; b Kirkcaldy 12.7.47
teacher: Ger Thurso h s 1970–74, asst prin mod lang 1974–75, prin mod lang 1975–78; W Ger from 1978

NICHOLSON George MA 1967

NICHOLSON John Wallace MA 1967 Dip Ed 1968
s of Wallace B. N. MA(Edin) min of relig and Ann Macleod; b Bayhead N Uist 20.9.43
teacher maths Plockton from 1968
m Inv 18.8.67 Sarah Macmillan secy/machine oper (NCR) d of William M. Glenshiel

NICOL Alastair William *BSc 1959 PhD 1962

NICOL Alexander John BSc(agr) 1969 *1970
s of J. C. N. civ serv and Helen Hutcheon nurs sister; b Huntly 5.11.46
asst arable marketing man. R.H.M. agr Essex 1970–72; training advis Argyll 1972–74; agr advis NOSCA from 1974
m Aber 15.11.74 Catherine E. Munro nurs sister d of Murdo R. M. Conon Bridge

NICOL Andrew Dick BSc 1961 *1963 PhD 1967
s of William G. D. N. shop asst, naval petty off., insur ag and Isabel Elder shop asst; b Aber 31.5.39
Aberd: biochem clin chem 1961–62, asst lect chem path. 1963–67; sen biochem REHSC 1967–72; prin biochem royal Alexandra hosp Rhyl from 1972
m Leeds 9.10.65 Julia M. Kingham MA(Edin) res asst, OU tut. d of Frank K. Leeds

NICOL Andrew Graeme MB ChB 1958 PhD 1968
s of Andrew N. BCom 1922 *qv* (II, III); b Aber 28.1.35
MRCPE 1963 MRCPath 1967 FRCPath 1977
h o ARI, Woodend hosp Aber 1958–59; m o RAMC UK, Arabia 1959–61; lect, sen lect path. Aberd 1961–77; m o Abu Dhabi Pet. Co 1977–79; sen m o ADLO-ADMA Abu Dhabi UAE
m Aber 16.4.66 Christine F. Walker nurse, midwife d of Robert W. Motherwell

NICOL Ann Louise MA 1966

NICOL Arthur McAllan *MA 1960

NICOL Brian David *BSc 1967 MSc 1970

NICOL Donald Rose *BSc 1960

NICOL Eleanor Freda BEd 1969
d of John N. rly signalman and Elizabeth A. N. Boyne waitress; b Nairn 27.4.48
teacher Engl Forfar 1969–73, asst prin Engl from 1973
m Udny 25.7.69 Ronald Fordyce policeman s of John F. Pitmedden

NICOL George Williamson BSc 1965
s of Anderson Nicol MA(Glas) min of relig and Jane B. Williamson; b Edin 14.8.44
VSO Nigeria 1965–66; Sheffield: Unilever UCMDS trainee 1968–70, asst prod. man. 1970–73, prod. man. from 1973
m Paisley 17.8.68 Joy D. Crichton teacher d of George C. Paisley

NICOL Graeme Douglas MA 1967
s of John N. asst chief constable Aber and Margaret S. Meakin; b Aber 2.7.46
trainee off. Goodyear Tyre Rubber Co Wolverhampton 1967–70; trg advis furn and timber indust trg board E Scot. 1970–74; man. dir Kilgour & Walker (sales) Aber from 1974
m Brora 17.8.68 Isobelle M. Sutherland teacher d of Andrew S. Brora

NICOL Helen MA 1963
m Reid

NICOL Iona Agnes BSc 1959
d of Anderson N. MA(Glas) C of S min and Jean B. Williamson; b Edin 7.2.38
Dip Ed(Edin) 1960
teacher sc Ainslie Park s s Edin 1960–63; USA: res asst Harvard med s Boston 1963–64, res asst Washington univ med s St Louis 1964–66, teacher sc W Ladue j h s St Louis 1966–68; program dir/instructor Spaulding racquet ball club St Louis from 1973
m Aber 13.6.66 John W. Long Bs(Ohio State) bonder Toledo Ohio

NICOL Isobel Helen *BSc 1970
d of Alexander N. garage prop. and Mary Hay ptnr; b Aber 18.2.48
teacher: geog Thornes House s Wakefield 1971–72, geog/gen stud. Elgin tech coll from 1972
m Aber 1970 William A. Stark BSc 1969 *qv*

NICOL James BSc 1958 *1966
s of James A. W. N. master baker and Florence Hutton; b Peterhead 3.3.33
teacher: sc Peterhead acad 1959–65, geog Fraserburgh acad 1966–68; Peterhead acad: prin geog 1968–73, asst head 1973–75, dep rector 1975–79; rector Crieff h s from 1979
m Peterhead 26.12.58 Ina Thores d of Edwin T. Peterhead

NICOL Leslie McKenzie *BSc(eng) 1961

NICOL Margaret MA 1961
d of James N. herring indust board off. and Margaret Buchan; b Peterhead 26.4.33
Dip R Ed 1962
teacher St Peter's epis s Peterhead from 1962
m Aber 30.7.54 Robert Buchan eng s of Andrew S. B. Peterhead

NICOL Mary Stuart *MA 1957
m Barnes

NICOL-SMITH Colin Alexander BSc(eng) 1959
s of Alistair N.-S. jeweller and Elizabeth M. Rankin teacher, occup therap; b Aber 16.3.38
Inst of C Eng 1966 Inst of Struct Eng 1967; Assoc of Prof Eng of BC 1965
civ/struct eng: Aber, Lond, Edin 1959–64, Montreal, Vancouver 1964–72; dev eng Council of For. Industries of BC Vancouver from 1972
m Montreal 12.1.65 Judy B. Shepherd teacher d of Alan W. S. Vancouver

NICOL-SMITH Ruth Mary MA 1959
d of Alistair N.-S. comp dir and Elizabeth M. Rankin teacher art, occup therap; b Aber 14.10.39
BBC studio man. Lond 1961–65; youth employment off. Aber, Edin 1965–67; teacher Engl Woolston h s Warrington from 1975
m Lond 11.4.63 Robert A. Harrison BBC tv prod. s of Daniel H. Manc

NICOLL Edward Alexander MA 1969

NICOLL William Duncan BSc(agr) 1964
s of Andrew F. N. farm. and Sheila M. H. Hawkins nurs sister; b Nairobi 5.9.41
Rhodesia: conserv and extension off. min of agr Nyamandhlovu 1964–71, group off. Sinoia from 1971

m Bulawayo 10.12.66 Frances M. Ralph teacher d of Thomas D. M. R. Burghead

NICOLSON Annie Bella MA 1962
d of Finlay C. N. millworker and Christina Campbell; b Stornoway 5.3.41
teacher Glasg, Rosssh 1963–66
m Glasg 24.8.66 Murdo A. MacLeod MA 1963 *qv*

NICOLSON James Peter *MA 1968 Dip Ed 1969
s of Robert P. N. crofter, bldr's lab, seaman and Mary C. Ganson; b Shetland 28.7.46
teacher Aith j h s Shetland from 1969
m Sandwick 15.8.69 Lillian R. Sinclair bank clerkess d of Adam S. Levenwick

NICOLSON James Robert MA 1956 BSc 1961
s of Frank H. N. crofter, seaman, coast preventive man customs and excise and Helen B. Tait; b Aith Shetland 10.7.34
FRGS 1961 FGS(Lond) 1961
geol Marampa Mines Sierra Leone 1961–67; Shetland: fisherman/author 1967–72, geol/author from 1972
m Lerwick 6.9.65 Violet H. Sinclair nurse d of Gideon S. Scalloway

NICOLSON Peter Balfour BSc 1969
s of William H. N. man. dir and Eleanor M. Dunlop MA(Glas) teacher; b W Kilbride 26.11.41
instr p e Inverclyde nat recreation centre (Scot. sports council) Largs 1971–72; teacher geog/asst prin guid Glasg from 1972

NIDEROST Adrian Carl MSc 1963
s of Carl N. Q.C. LLB(Sask) solic and Lillian I. Crum BA(Sask) teacher of mus; b Saskatoon 9.8.39
BSc(McG) 1961 B o T Athlone scholarship 1961–63
proj eng: Domtar Montreal 1963–65; Domtar Pulp Lebel-sur-Quevillon Quebec 1965–68; process eng 1965–68, pulp mill supt 1968–70, eng supt 1970–72; pulp prod. supt Domtar Fine Papers Windsor Quebec from 1972
m Montreal 30.8.61 Heather I. Attridge BA(McG) teacher d of Walter G. A. Montreal

NIKODEM Dirk *MA 1970 MSc 1974
s of Wilhelm N. sales rep and Agnes Schilling secy; b Germany 13.9.45
progr/analyst Aber from 1972
m Aber 12.7.74 Catherine F. Cullen MA 1968 *qv*

NIMMO Elizabeth Macdonald Mackay BEd 1970
d of Andrew N. steel erector and Alison G. Mackay; b Glasg 13.2.17
teacher Engl/remed Rosehearty s from 1970
m Paisley 25.12.45 Colin D. J. Macdonald MA 1929 *qv*
d 12.7.78

NISBET Barbara Darge *MA 1957
d of James D. N. teacher, HMIS and Marjorie M. Macgregor lib asst; b Glasg 5.10.34
teacher Engl: Aber h s for girls 1958–61, Linlathen s Dun 1964–66; infants Lieurary s Caithness 1968–69, art Pennyland s Thurso 1969–73, Engl Thurso h s 1973–78; temp lect Engl univ of Maryland Thurso from 1979 and schools liaison off. Grampian TV from 1980
m Aber 17.3.56 Keith A. Laing MB ChB 1958 *qv*
husb *d* 27.6.79

NISBET James BEd 1970
s of Henry A. N. mining/civ eng and Mary B. Wyllie SRN; b Glasg 14.12.37
teacher geog/mod. stud. Kirkland h s Methil 1970–73, prin mod. stud. from 1974

NISBET Jennifer Baillie *MEd 1968
d of John N. grocer and Janet Ritchie; b Prestonpans 10.6.44
MA(Edin) 1966 PhD(Leic) 1979
res off. Joseph Rowntree higher educ res proj univ Lanc 1968–71, sen res off. 1971–73
m Lancaster 29.7.72 David H. Thompson BS(tech) (Cardiff) psych/counsellor univ of Keele appt and counselling serv s of James H. T. Bolton

NISBET Moyra Jean *MA 1963
d of James D. N. teacher, HMIS and Marjorie M. Macgregor lib asst; b Insch 23.9.41
MA(Alta) 1966
Canada: post grad stud./teaching asst Alta 1963–64, instructor Engl univ of Victoria 1964–65; USA: part-time lect Smith coll Mass. 1965–67, edit. asst Corn. NY 1967–68; part-time extra mural tut. Glas 1973–75
m Aber 2.9.65 David D. Buchan MA 1960 *qv*

NIVEN Donald Ferries *BSc 1970 PhD 1973
s of William N. and Margaret I. Donald; b Aber 5.3.47
res asst Aberd 1970–73; res fell. univ of Kent Canterbury 1973–76; res assoc Macdonald coll of McG Montreal from 1976
m Aber 22.5.65 Maureen Ferguson d of James F. Aber

NIVEN John Alexander MA 1970
s of Alexander F. N. MB ChB 1940 *qv*; b Chatham 10.8.47
stud. pilot Oxford 1970–71; airline pilot BA (Europ div) Heathrow from 1971

NIVEN Sheila Mary MA 1959

NIXON Alan John Chamberlain *BSc 1969
s of Ian A. N. meteorologist and Margaret C. MacFadyen teacher; b Stirling 16.8.47
PhD(McM)
Canada: teacher Hamilton 1976–77, post doct fell. 1977–79, res assoc 1979–80
m 4.7.75 Martha J. Oliver BMus(McM) nurs stud. d of T. Leonard J.O. Brantford Canada

NIXON Julie Anne MA 1967 Dip Ed 1968
s of Stanley N. solic and Phyllis Crowe; b Redcar 28.4.45
teacher Fr/Span Surrey, Kent 1968–70, Bucks 1970–74, prin mod lang s of St Mary and St Anne Abbots Bromley Staffs 1974–78

NIXON Karen Patricia *MA 1961
d of Robert N. eng man. and Barbara Jordan; b Gillingham 30.11.38
teaching posts grammar/upper schools 1961–74; CSE examiner and private tut. from 1975
m Market Harborough 1973 Graham B. Jones bus. man s of John H. J. Peatling Magna

NJOKU Boniface Onogbo MSc 1965
s of Njoku Anugwara farm. and Nwanyi Njoku Chikere; b Nigeria 5.2.36
BSc(Lond) 1963
res off. in agr res inst Ibadan Nigeria from 1966
m Umuabia Nigeria 2.5.70 Bernice A. Osuji BSc(Ibad) res off. d of Godson O. Owerri

NNODI Anukem Oparanozie MSc 1964
BSc(agr)(Ibad)

NOBLE Alexandra Mary MA 1965
b Edin 28.5.44

teacher: Summerhill s Aber 1966–67, Kingsdale s Lond 1967–70
m Aber 29.3.67 Alistair R. Cruickshank MA 1966 *qv*

NOBLE Andrea MA 1961

NOBLE Andrew Alexander John *MA 1963
s of Andrew M. N. insur ag and Catherine J. Duffy; b Stirling 24.2.39
DPhil(Sus) 1970
lect Engl Strath from 1966
m Drumnadrochit 22.3.68 Jennifer R. Mackay nurse d of James A. M. Drumnadrochit

NOBLE Audrey Mitchell MA 1957
d of George N. town c employee and Jean D. Noble; b Fraserburgh 3.4.36
teacher: Dunkeld 1958–62, Dar Es Salaam Tanzania 1965–66, Lushoto 1967–68, Dalbeattie from 1973
m Aber 23.7.62 Carl L. Bryant BSc(for) 1957 *qv*

NOBLE Benjamin Wiseman *MA 1958

NOBLE Charles BSc 1966

NOBLE Christina Elizabeth *MA 1969
d of Albert N. motor mech and Charlotte Paterson SRN; b St Combs 9.5.46
teacher: Fr/Ger Colston s s Glasg 1971–73, Engl with Centre for British Teachers Mädchen Gymn, Bünde Ger 1973–75, angestellte Lehrerin from 1975
m Glas 14.7.69 Gilbert Whitelaw eng s of John W. Glasg

NOBLE Elizabeth Mary *MA 1967

NOBLE Fiona Winifred MA 1970
d of John N. CA and Mae Bonnington; b Edin 28.1.49
teacher Fernielea p s Aber from 1972

NOBLE Gillian Mae *MA 1969
d of John N. CA and Mae Bonnington; b Edin 18.11.47
MSc(Lond) 1974
econ DoE Lond 1969–76, HM Treasury from 1976

NOBLE Ian *BSc 1965 Dip Ed 1966

NOBLE Irene MA 1956
m Dyer

NOBLE Irene Buchan *MA 1962 Dip Ed 1963
d of John N. insp sea fisheries and Christian T. N. Buchan; b Inverallochy 28.10.39
teacher: Aber 1963–65, Fleming Fulton s Belf from 1973
m Aber 14.8.63 William Byth MA 1962 *qv*

NOBLE Iris MA 1965
m Main

NOBLE Isabella Bruce BSc 1959
m Tandy

NOBLE John *MA 1957 MEd 1968
s of John N. fisherman and Christina Duthie; b Fraserburgh 11.2.35
teacher Larbert h s 1958–61, Fraserburgh acad 1951–63, coll of comm Aber 1964–68; asst psych Aber 1969–72; sen asst psych Aberdeensh 1972–74; prin psych E Lothian from 1974

NOBLE John Crawford BSc 1957
s of Alfred N. sailmaker and Kate McLean; b Rosehearty 7.10.33
Fraserburgh acad: teacher maths 1958–66, spec asst maths 1966–73, asst prin maths from 1973
m Sandhaven 26.12.58 Helen R. S. B. Fraser d of George P. F. Sandhaven

NOBLE John Gardiner MB ChB 1956

NOBLE Mary MA 1969
d of William N. and Beatrice M. Porter; b Aber 10.5.13
m Strichen 23.4.34 James S. McKay eng Burmah Oil Co India s of John McK.

NOBLE Robert BSc 1966

NOBLE Violet McClelland MA 1960
(conferred for long service of exceptional merit)
b Udny Station 20.6.1900
member of admin staff Aberd 1918–60

NOBLE William BSc 1961 *1962
s of Alexander N. baker, teacher p e, security guard and Dolina F. Mitchell secy; b St Combs 29.7.40
teacher biol Dun 1963–66; lect Kirkcaldy 1966–73; sen lect from 1973
m Lonmay 29.6.63 Mary I. Fyvie nurse d of Alexander C. F. Lonmay

NOKE Frederick James BSc 1968
s of Leonard C. N. fisherman and Charlotte N. S. Criggie; b Gourdon 27.1.47
asst prod. chem Schweppes (foods) Montrose 1969–70, prod. supt 1971–73; cake man. Cadbury-Schweppes (foods) Moreton Liv from 1974
m St Cyrus 5.5.73 Sandra A. Ruxton off. worker d of Alexander F. R. St Cyrus

NORBROOK Hamish Thomas Ellis *MA 1969
s of Donald H. E. N. BBC Aber, Nigeria, Singapore, Oxford and Eleanor I. M. Hutchison MA 1939 *qv*; b Lond 17.8.47
teacher: VSO Engl école secondaire de Matana Burundi 1969–71; Fr Faraday comp s E Acton Lond 1972; BBC Bush House Lond: studio man. external serv 1972–74, asst overseas dev auth scheme Engl by radio 1974–76, prod. Engl by radio from 1976
m Lond 24.7.76 Dominique J. Mandier L ès L(Lyon) teacher d of Pierre M. St Etienne France

NORFOLK Jeremy Paul MA 1970

NORMAND Anne Margaret MA 1969 Dip Ed 1970
d of George F. N. teacher and Margaret B. D. Paton; b Perth 12.9.48
teacher: Prestonpans p s 1970–72, Edin from 1972
m Perth 20.10.73 John Mowat MA(Edin) teacher s of Ian J. G. M. LDS(Edin) Dumfries

NORQUAY Margaret MA 1970

NORRIE Jean Gibb MA 1959
d of William P. N. master coach builder and Ella G. Mair typist; b Aber 27.2.38
teacher Engl/hist Aber 1960–65
m Aber 7.4.65 John McBain CA s of Alan McB. MA 1920 *qv* (II, III)

NORRIE Sandra Jane BSc 1968
d of Alexander N. outfitter and Violet E. Anderson secy; b Aber 18.11.46
m Aber 11.5.66 Rodger Horrocks BSc 1968 *qv*

NORRIE William BSc(for) 1960

NORRIS Derek John BSc 1970
s of Douglas T. N. sales rep and Amelia T. Gilmour; b Aber 6.4.49
ACA 1975
VSO Mauritius 1970–71; Thomson McLintock Lond 1972–76; Bank of America Eur M East Africa div from 1976

NORRIS John William MB ChB 1957 MD 1971

NORRIS Linda Campbell MA 1970

NORTH Richard Alan BSc 1969 MB ChB 1969 PhD 1973
s of Douglas A. N. wool merch and Constance Ramsden; b Halifax 20.5.44
h o Aber 1969–70; Marr Walker res fell. Aberd 1970–71; MRC res fell. Aberd 1971–73; res assoc univ of Loyola Chicago 1972–73; res fell. Aberd from 1974
m Aber 15.7.69 Jean V. A. Hall MA 1967 *qv*

NORTHCROFT David John *MA 1964
s of Henry J. N. customs and excise off. and Jean M. Murrell; b Cheadle 6.2.42
MLitt(Cantab) 1969
teacher Engl AGS 1967–71; lect Engl Aber coll of educ from 1971
m Aber 12.8.66 Kathleen E. Lakin MA 1964 *qv*

NORTHCROFT Janet Heather *MA 1968
d of Henry J. N. customs and excise off. and Joan M. Murrell; b West Dulwich 2.9.46
Dip Soc Ad/Soc Work(Manc) 1970
probation off. Manc prob and after-care serv from 1970
m Altrincham 4.3.72 Michael Pickering computer progr/prob off. s of James W. P. Oldham

NORTON Katherine Judith Morren MA 1966 Dip Ed 1967
d of William H. hotelier and Jean D. Montgomerie; b Ayr 16.4.44
teacher Engl Hilton acad Aber from 1967

NORTON Royan *MA 1968

NORVELL Elizabeth Diana BSc 1969

NOTTAGE Bernard Jonathan MB ChB 1969

NOWLAND John Louis MSc 1963
BA(Manc)

NWACHUKU Nathan Iheanyichuku Chukudi PhD 1970
BSc(Lond) MS(Hawaii)
m Aber 25.1.64 Oludotun M. Odugbose MB ChB 1966 *qv*

NWANKWO Lawrence BSc 1958 Dip Ed 1959
s of Anowi N. customary court judge and Angelina Dijiure; b Umulogho Nigeria 1928
Nigeria: vice-prin Okigwi 1959–64; chmn dist council Etiti 1964–66, member home defence Etiti 1966–69; prin Arugo h s Oweri from 1970
m Umulogho 1961 Rosaleen Azuogu teacher

NYLANDER Percy Palgrave Shaftesbury MB ChB 1958 *MD 1976
s of Africanus G. R. N. civ serv and Lucretia P. Thomas; b Lagos 30.1.25
MRCOG 1962 MRCPE 1964 FRCOG 1974 FRCPE 1979
h o ARI, Aber mat. hosp, sen h o Withington hosp Manc, regist Dudley Rd hosp Birm 1958–63; sen regist UCH Ibadan; univ of Ibadan: lect, sen lect 1965–70, prof obst/gyn from 1970
m Birm 1964 Carmen O. Hume nurse d of Sydney O. H. Leic

OAKLAND Gail Barker PhD 1956
s of Theodore J. O. hardware merch and Winnifred J. Barker; b Lang Sask 11.2.14
BA(Sask) 1933 MA(Minn) 1939 FRSS 1958
Ottawa: sen biometrician 1956–59, sen math advis 1959–62; prof statist univ of Mass. Amherst from 1962

OAKLEY John Stafford BSc(for) 1959

OATES James *MA 1963

OATES Leonard Francis MSc 1970
s of James H. O. MSc(Loughborough) lect aeronaut eng and Bessie Evans secy; b Loughborough 27.2.46
BSc(UCW) 1967 Dip Ed(UCW) 1968
lect chem Braintree 1970–72; Devon: bldr 1972–77, dev chem 1977–79, teacher from 1979

OBODOECHINA Francis Okechukwu *BSc(eng) 1961
s of Ojinnak O. farm. and Mary A. Azikiwe; b Onitsha Nigeria 15.10.36
grad asst, asst civ eng Crouch & Hogg Glasg 1961–63; Nigeria: exec eng MoW E Nigeria Enugu 1964–66, water eng i/c water supply Old Port Harcourt prov 1967–69; sen exec eng i/c water supply Old Abakaliki prov 1970–73; prin exec eng i/c plan. & des E.C.S. water board Enugu 1973–75; chief proj eng Enplen Group consult. eng Enugu from 1975
m Onitsha 2.1.65 Patricia N. Egbunike teacher d of Simon Muonweoku

O'BRIEN Alison Burroughs MA 1963
d of Thomas H. O'B. CA and Dora M. Burroughs; b Brocket Hall 20.6.42
Lond: res asst Engl Elect. 1963–65, res analyst W. S. Crawford 1965–66, market res exec market information serv 1966–68; freelance market res consult. Croydon 1968–71; sen market res exec Richardson Merrell Lond 1971–72; res off. States of Jersey 1972–74; freelance market res consult. from 1974
m(2) Jersey 3.3.73 Christopher S. Le Brun law clerk

O'BRIEN Eric Adam *MA 1959
s of William O'B. church off. and Annie Murray; b Alfrod 31.10.36
teacher Hawick h s 1960–62; prin geog: N Berwick h s 1962–65, Dumbarton acad 1965–67, Galashiels acad 1967–74; asst rector Galashiels acad from 1974
m Galashiels 3.10.69 Christina J. Anderson bookkeeper d of Adam A. Melrose

O'BRIEN Kathleen Jean MA 1966 Dip Ed 1967

O'CARROLL Brian William BEd 1970

O'CONNELL John Richard *MA 1961

O'CONNOR Peter John PhD 1960
s of John E. O'C. wholesale/retail tobacconist and Marjorie G. Griffin; b Ilkeston 16.5.32
BSc(Nott) 1956
teacher Oldham 1959–60; res asst Christie hosp and Holt radium inst (Paterson labs) Manc from 1960; visiting fell. dept pharm Yale univ New Haven Conn 1964–66; sen scient Paterson labs from 1966
m Oldham 8.8.59 Barbara M. Nelson BSc(Nott) teacher d of Leslie N. Oldham

O'DELL Duncan Shortreed *BSc 1961
s of Andrew C. O'D. BSc(Lond) prof geog Aberd and Queenie L. Smith BA(Lond) teacher; b Lond 6.6.40
PhD(Cantab) 1965
res stud., res worker MRC Cambridge 1961–67; post-doct fell. royal soc Europ progr Naples 1967–68; res worker MRC Lond 1968–70; lect zool univ coll Lond from 1970

O'DELL Felicity Ann *MA 1969
d of Andrew C. O'D. BSc(Lond) prof geog Aberd and Queenie L. Smith BA(Lond) teacher; b Aber 4.7.47
PhD(Birm) 1975
post grad stud. centre for Russian/E Europ stud. Birm 1969–72; teacher mod lang St Philip's RC g s for boys Birm 1972–73; part-time aux nurse Birm 1974; res asst proj on Soviet vocational educ and soc stratification Cantab 1974–76; TEFL Cambridge from 1976

O'DRISCOLL Dorothy MA 1964

ODUGBOSE Batatunde Olusegun BSc 1968

ODUGBOSE Oludotun Mofolusho MB ChB 1966
d of David O. O. headmaster and A. A. Majekoclunmi; b Ibadan Nigeria 28.4.39
m o Ghana med serv 1967–71; prin m o Nigerian rly corp Lagos from 1971
m Aber 25.1.64 Nathan I. C. Nwachuku PhD 1970 *qv*

OFFICER John Burness *MA 1959

OGENDO Reuben Benjamin *BSc 1960
s of Zechariah Aloo farm. and Mariam Abo farm.: b Nyahera Kisumu Kenya 29.7.28
PhD(Lond) 1967
prin teacher geog Maseno s s Kenya 1960–61; univ of Nairobi: lect geog 1962–68, sen lect 1968–72, assoc prof 1972–78, prof from 1978, dean fac of arts from 1978
m Maseno 24.12.51 Truphosa Anyango teacher d of Harun Adoche Yala Kenya

OGG Graeme McPherson *MA 1965
s of James O. ACT employee and Esther Paterson; b Aber 26.9.42
teacher Fr/Span. Perth acad 1968–69; translator DTI Lond from 1969

OGG Hilary Ruth MA 1970

OGG John MacMillan BSc 1964 Dip Ed 1965

OGG Lindsay Anne *MA 1969
d of Thomas O. civ serv and Amelia W. Veitch civ serv; b Aber 11.11.46
teacher: geog/humanities and dep house head Wanstead Lond 1970–73; W Ger: teacher Engl Wipperfürth 1974, Engl centre for Brit teachers in Europe Cologne 1974–75
m Aber 21.7.70 Andrew J. D. Smith CA s of James D. S. Aber

OGG Thomas Winchester MB ChB 1964
s of Thomas O. civ serv DHSS and Amelia W. Veitch civ serv; b Aber 20.6.40
DA 1968 FFARCS(Lond) 1971
h o Woodend hosp Aber, Raigmore hosp Inv 1964–65; major RAMC short serv comm; post grad course Lond 1965, cas off. Benghazi 1966–67, anaest Iserlohn, Hanover Ger 1967–69, ARI, Hanover 1969–71; ARI: regist, sen regist and clin lect anaest Aberd from 1971
m Aber 20.7.65 Monica M. Wilson MA 1963 *qv*

OGILVIE Anne Patricia *MA 1967

OGILVIE Brian BSc 1968

OGILVIE Christopher James MA 1967
s of George T. A. O. chartered land ag and Jean C. Barrett; b Ravenglass 20.4.47
Dip Pers Man.(RGIT) 1968
man. trainee BR Glasg 1968–71; store man. trainee Marks & Spencer Paisley 1971–72; Beecham pharm Irvine: asst pers off. 1973–74, pers off. from 1974
m Edin 2.8.69 Elizabeth J. Graham MA 1969 *qv*

OGILVIE David Wilson MA 1963

OGILVIE Eileen Millar MA 1961
d of George G. O. farm. and Nan Duthie secy; b Forfar 8.4.40
teacher Lond 1962–64; bus. prop./founded youth centre Perthsh 1965–71; secy to hosp matron Angus 1971–73
m –.5.74 Gilbert Rimmer ship's capt/dredging consult.

OGILVIE Elizabeth Baxter McDonald MA 1968
d of Alexander M. O. comm man. and Leonora C. Douglas; b Dun 8.1.47
teacher mod lang Kirkton h s Dun 1969–72, asst prin mod lang 1972–73; teacher mod lang Elgin acad from 1973
m Dun 8.4.72 Robert M. G. O'Brien MA(St And) organis outdoor educ Moray & Nairn s of William O'B. Woolston

OGILVIE Isobel MA 1956
d of John W. O. meal miller and Isabella Mackay; b Elgin 8.6.34
teacher Stanley 1957–61, Inv 1961–70; prim. staff tut. Inv 1970–74, prim. advis Rosssh from 1974

OGILVIE Marjory MA 1961
d of Charles O. long dist driver (BRS) and Ann Smith; b Aber 21.7.35
teacher: Smithfield p s Aber 1962–63, Coventry from 1963
m Aber 2.4.63 Brian Rattray tech rep West Midlands Gas Board s of John R. Aber

OGILVIE Rosemary *MA 1964 Dip Ed 1965
d of George T. A. O. farm., land ag and Jean S. Barrett; b Selkirksh 12.11.41
teacher Engl Aber 1965–67
m Aber 17.5.65 Colin E. Jeffries BSc 1963 *qv*

OGILVY Munro Michael *BSc 1968 PhD 1972
s of John O. fruit grower and Frances Monro; b Dun 25.11.46
res fell. univ of Warwick 1971–73, sen exper off. UMIST Manc 1973–74; res chem The Wellcome Foundation Dartford 1974–78, man. dev res from 1978

OGSTON David Dinnes MA 1966 BD 1969
s of James G. O. farm. and Mary C. Dinnes; b Ellon 25.3.45
C of S min: asst St Giles cath Edin 1969–73, parish min Balerno from 1973
m Forres 6.8.70 Margaret C. Macleod teacher d of William M. Forres

OGSTON Graeme Leslie LLB 1970
s of Harry O. MA 1936 *qv* and Iris C. Watt MA 1941 *qv*; b Aber 1.11.49
law app, solic A. C. Morrison & Richards advoc Aber 1970–73; solic Clark & Wallace advoc Aber from 1973
m Aber 26.2.72 Vivien M. P. Clark LLB 1970 *qv*

OGSTON Walter MacTavish PhD 1966
s of Walter H. O. E India merch and Josephine E. Carter; b Birkenhead 5.12.17
BA(Oxon) 1939 MA(Oxon) 1946 MS(Calif Tech) 1947 FIME 1973
Power Jets Lutterworth 1940–49; Commonwealth fell. Pasadena USA 1946–47; Eng Elect. Co Rugby 1949–56; Centrax Newton Abbot 1956–59; lect, sen lect eng Aberd from 1959
m Bilton Rugby 9.4.49 Freda Gibson soc worker d of Frederick J. G. Rugby

O'HAGAN Philip John BSc 1969

O'HANLON Anne *BSc 1964
d of Andrew H. miner and Rosa Ward; b Blackhall 27.10.39
teacher: Co Durh 1964–67, Kingston Jamaica 1967–70, Coatbridge 1971–72, prin sc Peterlee from 1972
m Blackhall 23.10.76 Robert Potts BSc(Teesside poly) mech eng

OJO Gabriel Oluwole Ayodele *BSc(for) 1965

OJO now OJO-ATERE Joseph Oluwatayo MSc 1967
BSc(Ibad)

OKAFOR Jonathan Chukwuemeka BSc(for) 1962

OKARU Paul Newton *BSc(eng) 1959
s of David O. O. bldg contr and Nkwo Ossai; b Oguta Nigeria 27.7.28
BSc(Lond) 1953 CEng MIEE 1968 MNSE 1972
grad app AEI Manc 1959–60; Nigeria: eng elect. utility Lagos 1961–62; undertaking man. Abeokuta 1962–64, dist man. Jos 1964–65; transmission eng sen control eng HQ Lagos 1965–70; head transmission rehabilitation Enugu 1970–71; Lagos: sen oper plan. eng 1972–73, man. oper 1973–74; dir oper 1975–77, gen man. oper from 1977
m Aber 31.3.59 Valentina I. Olisa Dip. Dom Sc, asst chief educ off. Lagos d of His Highness R. R. O. Onitsha Nigeria

OKEKE Raphael Ekemezie Chukwubuike BSc(for) 1961
s of Alfred I. O. civ serv and Eunice Igwego; b Amawbia Nigeria 24.6.33
Nigeria: asst conserv for. Ikom SES 1961–66, sen asst conserv for. Umuahia, Amawbia ECS 1967–75, conserv for. Amawbia/Enugu 1975–77, chief conserv for. Enugu Anambra from 1978
m Enugu Bernice Ejindu teacher d of Moses E. Onitsha

OKIGBO Lawrence Chukwuemeka BSc(for) 1960

OKOYE Humphrey Chigbo *BSc 1961
BSc(Lond)

OLAJIDE Samuel Omolayo BSc(for) 1966
s of Josiah O. farm. and Ibilola Ogundejie; b Isinbode-Ekiti Nigeria 1.12.36
Nigeria: asst conserv for. Ibadan 1967–72; asst conserv soils Oshogbo from 1973
m Isinbode-Ekiti –.12.59 Victoria I. Adeyemo

OLATUNJI Oladapo MB ChB 1967
s of Akanbi O.; b Nigeria
DTM & H(Lond) 1969 DCH(Lond) 1970 DPH(Liv) 1971 Fell. Nigerian Med Council in Public Health 1976
h p and h s Joyce Green hosp Dartford 1967–68; sen h o paediat Alder Hey ch hosp Liverpool 1969–70; sen h o infect. diseases Fazakerley hosp Liverpool 1970–71; dept m o Lancs c c 1971–72; sen m o, later acting chief m o Ahmadu Bello univ Zaria Nigeria 1972–76; med dir Mobil Nigeria Lagos from 1976
m Lond –.8.69 Olabisi Akinlabi d of O. Akinlabi

O'LEARY Michael Joseph *MA 1969
s of Joseph O'L. civ serv and Winifred C. E. Ridgley secy; b Hammersmith Lond 2.4.46
Dip Man. Stud.(Strath) 1976
Chrysler Scot. Linwood; budget analyst 1969–70, sen budget analyst 1970–71, supervis acct methods/audit. 1971–75; United Biscuits: sen audit. North from 1975
m Aber 6.12.69 Alyson M. Carter MA 1968 *qv*

OLEJNIK Henry Hugh MA 1969
s of Edward O. distillery worker and Johanna C. H. Kemp; b Beauly 9.6.47
GMIPM(RGIT) 1970
pers off. Ruislip 1970–72; salary admin/indust rel off. Harrow 1972–75; pers man. Polaroid Milngavie from 1975
m Dingwall 23.11.74 Joan J. Fowlie Europ prop. invest. co-ordinator d of William S. F. Dingwall

OLEMBO Titus Wycliffe PhD 1970
s of Nahashon O. farm. and Damary Olembo; b Wanakhale-Bunyore Kenya 28.5.37
BA(NY State)
res for. (path.), head for. div EAAFRO, sen res off., prin res off. Muguga and throughout E Africa from 1970
m Bunyore 11.9.61 Priscah Achando nurse, secy d of Patrick Kweya Maseno Kenya

OLET Erisa Dickson BSc(for) 1970
BSc(Makerere)

OLIVER David Ruskin *BSc 1968
s of Arthur R. O. MB ChB(Edin) g p and Barbara H. Rhodes; b Edin 30.12.37
teacher biol Dunoon g s 1969–71; prin biol Wick h s from 1971
m Glasg 27.12.73 Angusina C. MacLeod MA(Glas) teacher d of George MacL. Edderton

OLIVER Thomas Dalgleish BSc(agr) 1956 MSc 1973

OLIVER William Bruce *BSc 1970
s of William A. O. BSc(Lond) sqd ldr RAF and Florence I. Fitzpatrick MA(Glas) teacher; b Weston-super-Mare 3.9.46
PhD(H-W) 1975
res asst Birm 1970–71; res stud. H-W 1971–75; res scient Pauls and Sandars Ipswich from 1975
m Huddersfield 26.7.75 Heather A. Slater BSc 1973 civ serv d of James B. S. Huddersfield

OLSON Ian Alistair MB ChB 1962 MD 1969
s of Andrew G. O. BBC recording eng and Doreen Carlee midwife; b Aber 5.5.39
h o ARI 1962–63; lect anat Brist 1963–69; sen lect anat Nott 1969–75; vice-dean/prof anat Kuwait med s from 1975
m Aber 27.12.73 Elizabeth A. Hamilton MA 1962 *qv*

OMABEGHO Sonny MB ChB 1962

OMAND Donald *MA 1958
s of Donald O. rly employee and Jean Ross; b Lybster 8.1.36
MSc(Strath) FSAScot. FRSGS
teacher geog Bingley 1959–60; admin UKAEA Dounreay 1960–63; teacher Halkirk 1963–66; lect f e Thurso 1966–70; univ tut./organis extra-mural dept Aberd Elgin/Halkirk from 1970
m Stronsay 15.7.59 Emma S. Peace MA 1959 *qv*

OMAND Jean Sandra *MA 1966
d of James O. BSc(Edin) vet surg and Nettie C. Jack secy; b Ayr 16.11.42
teacher geog: Forfar acad 1967–73, Lossiemouth h s 1973–74; prin guid Lossiemouth h s from 1974

OMAR Ali MSc 1969
BSc(Makerere)

OMAR Medhat Omar Mohamed Hassan PhD 1970
MB(Cairo) MSc(Assuti)

OMER Banaga Mohamed Ahmed MSc 1967
BSc(eng)(Khart)

OMUFWOKO Henry Dickson BSc(agr) 1968
s of Jacton T. O. bus. man. and Grace Akhamuru bus. woman; b W prov Kenya 15.1.40
Kenya: agr res off. Kisi 1968–70; teacher chem Kisumu h s from 1971; later sen sc master St Mary's Yala
m Glasg 19.8.67 Alice B. Ochami teacher d of Daudi O. Maseno Kenya

O'NEALE Eugene Charles Henry MA 1967
s of Henry O'N. wine merch and Violet E. Benfell; b Lond 12.12.43
law app Haddington, Edin 1968–71; solic Edin 1971–73, ptnr leg. practice spec in court work Edin from 1973, dir comp owning hotels and mus publ
m Lond 22.4.71 Marjory Davidson hairdresser d of Archibald D. Glasg

O'NEILL John Albert MSc 1966
BSc(Belf) 1963 MSc(Belf) 1964 PhD(Belf) 1974
sen scient off.: dept of agr, fac of agr Queen's univ Belf 1965–69; man. proj res and dev Gallaher (tobacco) Belf 1969–79, factory man. from 1979
m Belf 1965 Dama Green

O'NEILL Joseph Patrick *MA 1960

ONWELUZO Bennett Samuel Kanayochuku BSc(for) 1963
s of Phillip W. A. O. teacher and Elizabeth N. Okafor; b Nnewi Nigeria 16.1.36
MSc(Ghent) 1966
Nigeria: for. res off. (soils) fed. dept of for. res Ibadan 1963–65, for. res off. Enugu (civ war in Nigeria) 1966–70, for. res off. grade 1 fed. dept of for. res Ibadan 1970–72, sen res off. 1972–76; prin res off. 1976; chief sc off. Nat Sc and Tech Dev Agency (i/c for. div) from 1976
m Onitsha E.C.S. Nigeria 16.5.70 Keziah U. Ojukwu teacher d of Daniel O. Nnewi

ONWUEGBUNA Okechukwu MA 1957
b Nibo Awka Nigeria 31.12.21
AIE(Lond) 1965
Nigeria: civ serv Enugu 1957–76, asst chief insp of educ 1976; chief and traditional ruler Nibo from 1977

OPENSHAW Keith *BSc(for) 1961 *MA 1967
s of Herbert J. M. O. teacher and Nellie Walter; b Salford 20.12.36
res asst for. dept Aberd 1961–66; for. econ FAO(UN) Tanzania, Thailand; for. consult. Aber from 1972

O'PRAY Michael *MA 1968
s of Hugh O'P. auto. eng and Elizabeth Stewart; b Ellon 13.8.46
Ford Motor Co Liv: trg off. 1968–70, pers off. from 1970
m Liv 24.8.74 Linda Roberts typist d of Robert O. R. Liv

ORANGUN Cornelius Oluwasade *BSc(eng) 1960
s of Joseph O. farm. and Felicia Obisesan; b Erin-Ijesha Nigeria 16.6.32
PhD(Leeds) 1963 MICE 1968 MASCE 1968
asst eng: William Halcrow & Ptnrs Lond 1960–61, W. V. Zinn & Assoc Lond 1963–64; lect univ of Lagos 1964–72, assoc prof 1972–74, prof from 1976; visiting prof univ of Benin 1975–76
m Lond 1.8.64 Oluyemisi Sofekun BA(Keele) educ off., admin off. d of David O. E. S. Sagamu Nigeria

ORD Michael John MA 1966
s of John O. marine eng and Mary Howes; b Aber 20.10.45
DBM(Strath) 1967 CIPFA 1976
syst analyst Glasg 1967–73; fin. analyst Coatbridge 1973–78; fin. acct Edin from 1978
m Glasg 11.7.70 Isabel M. G. Wood BSc(Strath) computer progr d of James W. Glasg

ORDOR Ihekachi Tamunonenginyeofori James BSc(eng) 1957
Nigeria: mech eng MoW Port Harcourt 1960–63; plant eng Nigerian Petroleum Refining Co Port Harcourt 1964–68, eng consult. Fed Min of Indust Lagos 1970–71, gen man. Aba textile mills 1971–72; gen man. Nigerian Petroleum Refining Co Port Harcourt 1972–75; gen man. Nigerian Nat Oil Corp Lagos 1975; man. dir/chief consult. Unitech, consult. eng Port Harcourt from 1976
m Lond 9.11.57 Mabel Ekeke nurse d of Inglis E. Aba

O'REGAN Jeremy *MA 1967
s of Terence O'R. police off. and Jane Coffin; b Oxford 20.4.43
Dip Ed(Edin) 1968
teacher Edin 1968–69; lect psych Moray House coll of educ Edin from 1969
m Aber 3.8.68 Susan Beddard MA 1967 *qv*; marr diss 1974

ORR Craig Smith MA 1957

ORR Robert John BSc 1970
s of Robert O. lect and Agnes R. Lannigan; b Bellshill 1.2.46
teacher Wishaw from 1971
m Eastwood 6.4.77 Gina J. Landles BSc(Glas) teacher d of James R. L. Glasg

ORR William McLean BSc(eng) 1962
CA

O'SHEA Gerrard Joseph LLB 1968
s of John S. O'S. manuf ag and Frances E. Hamblet teacher; b Cheadle 21.8.46
articled solic clerk Manc 1969–72; prosecuting solic Middlesbrough from 1973

O'SHEA Martin John *MA 1965
s of John S. O'S. manuf ag and Frances E. Hamblet teacher; b Cheadle 23.7.43
Engl lang asst Bédarieux France 1965–66; asst lect tech coll Lurgan NI 1966–72; lect/students' union liaison off. tech coll Darlington from 1972

OSHIKANLU John Adebayo MB ChB 1961
d Nigeria 1975

OSOBAMIRO Samuel Adewole *BSc(eng) 1957
s of James O. farm. and Odunaike Sigbeku; b Nigeria 22.8.32
MICE 1961

Lond: asst eng Sir William Halcrow & Ptnrs 1957–59; site eng Cleveland Bridge & Engr 1959–60, asst RE Mott Hay & Anderson 1960–61; Nigeria: eng, sen eng, prin eng M of W & Transport W state 1961–71, chief eng, tech dir LAO Banjoko & Co civ eng contr & bldrs Ibadan 1971–77, man. dir from 1977
m Lond 9.8.58 Omfunmilayo F. Kalejaiye BA(Dub) teacher d of E. O. K. Zaria Nigeria

OTIM Stephen Ildefonsi BSc(for) 1965

OUSLEY William Rettie MA 1967

OWEN Kathleen Ann MA 1970
d of Thomas V. O. RAF and Lilias M. Morrice clerkess; b Aber 31.1.48
teacher Brechin from 1971
m Aber 24.7.71 Dennis Hastie MA 1969 *qv*

OWENS William Leo PhD 1961
BSc(Wash) MSc(Calif)

OXFORD Karl Anthony BSc(eng) 1967

OXLEY Edward Ralph Blackett *BSc 1964

OYAPERO Samusi Aremu BSc(for) 1966

OZGA Jennifer Teresa *MA 1970 *MEd 1972

PACITTI John *MA 1958

PACITTI Stephen Anton MA 1959
s of Paolo A. P. ice cream vendor and cafe prop. and Jean M. Forrest; b Aber 14.7.38
min: Dundonell par ch 1963–72, Glencairn ch Pollokshields 1972–76; lect bib. stud. Yu Shan Theol coll Hualien Taiwan from 1977
m Aber 22.6.63 Sylvia A. Long bookkeeper/typist d of Stanley H. L. Aber

PACK Julie Macdonald MA 1961
d of George B. P. comp dir and Janet M. Watson comp dir; b Fraserburgh 8.9.40
teacher Aber 1962–63; Ottawa: teacher oral Fr 1963–66; teacher via tv 1966–68; exper proj co-ordinator IRTV 1968–70; consult./admin educ tv and audio-visual progr 1970–72; teacher oral Fr adult educ div from 1973
m Aber 17.8.63 Ian A. Dewar MA 1963 *qv*

PACSOO Tokefat Christian MB ChB 1962
s of Chia P. bus. man. and Fing K. Wong; b Mauritius 10.6.36
DMRD(Lond) 1968
h o Ayr, Leeds 1962–63; govt m o Georgetown Guyana 1963–66; training posts in radiology Glasg 1966–71; radiol Yorks from 1971
m Aber 20.10.60 Josephine Iutz MA 1962 *qv*

PADDISON Ronan PhD 1969
BA(Durh)

PADMORE Lloyd Gregory MB ChB 1963
b Trinidad WI 1.6.35
MRCOG 1969 FRCS(C) 1972
obst/gyn Toronto from 1972
m Aber 18.1.66 Johan MacSween midwife

PAGE John Graham MB ChB 1968 ChM 1977
s of George R. P. BSc(Lond) lect pharm and Lilian A. Kay pharm; b Liv 16.2.43
FRCSE 1972
h o ARI 1968–69; lect path. Aberd 1969–70; sen h o surg ARI 1970–71; regist surg ARI 1971–77; res fell. surg Harvard univ Boston 1974–75
m Aber 30.8.69 Jessie S. Hossack nurs sister d of Ebenezer G. H. Menstrie

PAGE Kenneth Robert *BSc 1966 PhD 1970
s of Robert W. P. dist man. Prudential Assur Co and Constance L. Fish; b Peterborough 17.5.37
ARIC 1972
Aberd: ICI res fell. 1969–71, lect biophys chem from 1971
m Varde Denmark 6.9.60 Ingrid von T. Sivertsen teacher d of Paul G. S. Med Lic(Copenhagen) Copenhagen

PAINTING Josephine MA 1968
d of Harold G. C. P. man. NAAFI and Mabel H. Sotherton; b Kuala Lumpur 12.2.48
teacher Chatham from 1974
m Aber 30.12.66 Kevin Murphy salesman s of Gerald M. Birkenhead

PAKIANATHAN Samuel John Wright MSc 1968
s of John M. P. acct and Emily R. David; b Kuala Lumpur 5.10.33
BSc(Adel) 1962 PhD(Lond) 1975 MIBiol
res biochem Adelaide 1962–63; rubber res inst of Malaysia: plant physiol res off. 1963–76, sect. leader, sen prin res off. from 1976
m Singapore 24.4.65 Sarojini D. Paul MB BS(Bom) med pract d of S. D. P. Singapore

PALIT Gordon Baladev MA 1958 LTh 1967
s of Kanai L. P. LRCPE med pract and Marion R. Spence nurse; b Karachi Pakistan 4.10.29
LTCL(Lond) 1977
teacher: geog, Engl r e Turriff acad 1959–61, geog, Engl Dun 1961–64, geog Glasg 1967–69, prin r e Lond 1969–72; lect lib stud. Ayr tech coll 1972–74; teacher Engl as second lang Birm Educ Auth from 1979

PALIT Stephen MA 1961
s of Kanai L. P. LRCPE med pract and Marion R. Spence; b Glasg 20.7.34
C of S min: asst St Nicholas ch Aber 1961–62; teacher Lanarksh 1962–64; min Dundonell par ch Rosssh from 1973

PALMER Christine Janet MSc 1969
BA(Oxon)

PALMER John MacDougall BSc 1968

PALMER Tessa Jane Helen Douglas MA 1968
d of Kenneth N. V. P. MA(Cantab) consult. phys and Rosemary B. de M. Douglas radiogr; b Lond 17.9.47
Dip Soc Ad(Edin) 1969 Dip App Soc Stud.(Lond) 1972
Lond: child care off. 1969–72, psychiat soc worker 1972–73, asst dir nat assoc for ment health from 1974
m Lond –.3.79 David M. D. Mills BA(Oxon) lawyer

PARDOE Kathleen Frances MA 1969 Dip Ed 1970
d of Joseph E. P. RAF P & TO and Helen M. Shand shop asst; b Huntly 7.4.48
teacher: Engl/hist Methlick j s s 1970–72, Engl Oban from 1972
m Huntly 6.8.71 David F. Whyte BSc 1971 teacher s of John W. Edin

PARIENTE David MB ChB 1967
s of Samuel R. P. comp dir and Sara Benady disp chem; b Lisbon 9.12.39
DPM(Lond) 1973 MRCPsych 1974

h o ARI, Woodend hosp Aber 1967–68; Lond: sen h o Royal Free hosp 1968–69, g p 1969–71; regist psychiat Wembley hosp 1971–72, regist psychiat Napsbury hosp 1972–74, sen regist psychiat 1974–75, hon clin asst Univ Coll hosp 1974–75, consult. psychiat Napsbury hosp from 1975
m Lond 18.8.71 Judith Katzenberg med secy d of Moshé K. BEd(Wurtzburg) Lond

PARIS Walter Walker MA 1962
CA

PARK Anne MA 1969

PARK Audrey Forbes Annand BEd 1969
d of Andrew P. ironmonger/salesman and Dorothea F. Taylor; b Newtonhill 26.5.47
teacher Tannochside p s Viewpark 1970–72
m Aber 12.9.69 Christopher H. Murray MA 1969 *qv*

PARK Frank George Stephen MA 1969
s of Frank S. P. postman and Janet A. Stephen sales asst; b Aber 15.9.48
computer progr Southampton 1969–72; computer consult. Lond from 1972
m Aber 26.12.69 Rita Eddie d of John T. E. Aber

PARK Helen Jean *MA 1961

PARK Ian Michael Scott MA 1958 LLB 1960
s of Ian M. P. BSc 1924 *qv* (II, III); b Aber 7.4.38 leg. asst Paull & Williamsons advoc Aber 1961–63, ptnr from 1963; hon sheriff Aber
m Edin 20.6.64 Elizabeth M. L. Struthers BL(Edin) solic d of Alexander M. S. BSc(Glas) Edin

PARK John Charles BSc 1969
s of Alastair H. Park MB ChB 1954 *qv* and Annie B. Will MA 1936 *qv*; b Aber 27.2.47
teacher biol Hilton acad Aber from 1970

PARK Raymond *MA 1963 LLB 1966
b Aber 24.5.41
ptnr Park & McRae advoc Aber from 1969
m Aber 18.4.69 Marie Lines nurse

PARK Roy MacLean MA 1956
s of George P. draughtsman, shopkeeper etc and Jessie MacLean for.; b Insch 12.6.35
nat serv interpreter Cyprus 1957–59; teacher: Lat/Engl subjs New Deer s 1959–62, Engl/hist Galashiels acad 1962; sen asst Lindsey county lib h q Lincoln 1965–66; cataloguer MoT lib Lond 1966–69; dep lib MoAgr central vet lab Weybridge 1969–77; lib i/c Gt Westminster ho branch lib Lond from 1977
m N'cle-u-Tyne 1.6.66 Barbara B. Ewing BA(Melb) lib d of Allan R. E. Melbourne

PARK Sheila Nan Robb MA 1956

PARK William McGillivray MB ChB 1960
s of William M.P. and Hannah N. McGillivray nurse; b Aber 6.4.36
DMRD 1964 ECFMG 1965 FFR 1969
h o Aber 1960–62; regist radiol WI Glasg 1962–64; instr radiol Yale s of med USA 1965–66; consult. radiol Oswestry from 1967
m Wellington Salop 1.7.61 Anne E. Staddon MB ChB 1959 *qv*

PARKER Brenda Mary *BSc 1961 PhD 1964
d of Ronald P. publ lighting eng and Alice M. Lovell teacher; b Aber 4.12.39
SRC res asst UMIST 1964–67; scient civ serv RAE Farnborough from 1967

PARKER Elizabeth Susan MA 1967
d of Michael E. P. papermaker, publican and Florence M. C. Duffus; b Aber 23.1.47
Dip Sec St(Strath) 1968
Lond: secy to head of corporate plan. Cerebos 1968–69, secy/res asst head of market forecasting Consolidated Gold Fields 1969–71; Purnell Books: asst edit. 1971–73, asst foreign rights 1973–76, foreign rights man. from 1976

PARKER Ian Charles *MA 1970
s of Malcolm D. B. P. civ serv/crofter and Kathleen H. Sunderland civ serv; b Bradford 27.4.49
VSO Sennar and Shendi Sudan 1970–71; teacher Lerwick from 1973

PARKER Joan Dorothy MA 1969
d of Alan C. P. eng buyer and Mary A. Cameron typeroom man.; b Aber 11.6.47
clerk in pers with area health dept Huddersfield from 1974
m Slaithwaite 29.6.68 Ian M. Lumsden MA 1967 *qv*

PARKER Timothy Robert Walker LLB 1967

PARKHILL Anne Lindsay MA 1967
d of John C. P. oil comp man. and Chryssie S. C. King secy; b Inv 8.4.46
teacher: Inv 1968–70, Edin 1970–71
m Inv 10.7.70 Allan D. Chisholm MA 1967 *qv*

PARKINSON Alexander Tough MB ChB 1961

PARKINSON David Kelly MA 1962
s of John T. L. P. comp dir and Alice M. Tough; b Aber 25.2.41
CA 1966
fin. dir J. T. L. Parkinson Aber construct. group 1966–70; farms dir R. H. Leonard E. Yorks from 1970; man. dir Amatola Hotel Aber 1978
m Aber 18.6.66 Lilian G. Rannie d of William R. Cults

PARKINSON George Leslie *MA 1957
s of George W. L. P. C of S min and Helen Leslie waitress; b Aber 7.2.35
BD(Glas) 1960
C of S min: Kirkwall 1961–71, Chapel of Garioch 1971–73; visiting teacher of mus Aberdeensh 1974–75
m Aber 23.7.60 Catherine M. Glendinning MA 1957 *qv*
d Aber 2.3.81 *AUR* XLIX 139

PARKINSON John David MB ChB 1962
s of David P. elect. contr and Margaret T. Clubb; b Aber 15.9.33
h o Aber 1962–63; sen h o paediat Inv 1963–64; g p: Ballater 1964–65, Lond from 1965
m Boat of Garten 15.6.68 Margaret H. Gibson MB ChB (Edin) med pract d of George H. G. MB ChB(Glas) Boat of Garten

PARKS Valerie Sharon MA 1967
d of Harold P. eng and Marguerite I. Chivas tax off.; b Aber 24.2.46
teacher Aber from 1974
m Aber 28.10.67 Douglas A. Jamieson staff and fin. exec PO tel s of George J. Peterculter

PARLEY Sheila MA 1960
m Craig

PARRY David John *BSc 1965 PhD 1968

PARRY Stephen Byron Dove MA 1964
b Portsmouth 15.12.43
Aber: teacher maths St Peter's RC s s 1965–68, Summerhill acad 1968–70, Rubislaw acad/AGS 1970–73, asst prin maths from 1973
m Aber 30.6.73 Barbara-Anne Munro food hyg off.

PARSLOW John Lewis LLB 1969

PARSONS Margaret MA 1968
d of Harold P. man. printing and Frances M. Webster clerk; b Croydon 31.3.27
teacher maths Aber from 1969
m Manc 19.7.50 John J. Connell BSc(Manc) asst dir res s of John E. C. Manc

PARTINGTON Naomi Anne MA 1957
d of James P. comp secy, fin. dir and Anne Williams; b Bolton 25.3.36
trainee buyer Harrod's Lond 1957–58; teacher Engl: Yew Tree comp s Manc 1958–60, Southland's girls' s Reading 1960–63, Heyward tech s Bolton 1963–64; teacher Engl/hist Umtali girls' h s Rhodesia, Gilbert Rennie s for boys Lusaka Zambia 1964–65; speed reading tut. Princeton USA reading lab 1965–66
m Bolton 7.8.65 Kenneth M. Young MA 1957 *qv*

PATCH Derek BSc(for) 1965
s of Llewellyn P. pharm/optician and Alice Crabtree BSc(Manc) teacher; b Chadderton 5.3.44
Nat Dip Agr 1972 MIFor(GB)
for. off. Cheshire 1965–69; lect arboriculture Merrist Wood agr coll Worplesdon 1970–74, course tut. arboriculture from 1974
m Aber 16.8.68 Patricia F. L. Gordon MA 1966 *qv*

PATE Jean Lesley MB ChB 1968

PATEL Arvind Rai MB ChB 1963 MD 1973
s of Dahyabhai C. P. bus. man. (automobiles) and Gangaben D. Patel; b Thika Kenya 27.2.36
MRCP 1970
h o Aber 1963–64; Glasg: regist med 1965–71, sen regist 1972–75, consult. phys from 1975

PATEL Minu Kaikhashru MSc 1960
BSc(Bom) MSc(Agra)

PATERSON Alan Burness *BSc 1969
s of Stanley B. P. insur off. and Irene M. Clayton; b Kirkcaldy 26.2.47
MSc(Aston) 1970
Bakelite Xylonite: scient off. polyethylene div Aycliffe, Grangemouth 1970–78, dev man. expanded rubber and plastics div Croydon from 1978

PATERSON Alan Keith Gordon *MA 1961
s of Albert P. MA 1923 *qv* (II, III) and Helen T. Horne MA 1923 *qv*; b Aber 8.5.38
PhD(Cantab) 1965
asst lect/lect Queen Mary coll univ of Lond from 1965
m Lund Sweden 20.7.64 Anna T. Holm Med Kan(Lund) d of Tage H. Phil Mag(Lund) Malmö

PATERSON Alan Stuart BSc 1961

PATERSON Alistair Lawrence MA 1969
s of Alexander J. P. fisherman and Frances J. Lawrence; b Banff 25.12.47
teacher Fr Banff 1970–72; prin Fr: St Columba's RC s s Perth 1972–78, St Andrew's s Nassau Bahamas from 1978

PATERSON Catherine Isabella MA 1968
d of George E. P. salesman and Catherine Smith; b Kirkwall 30.8.47
m Aber 17.5.68 Douglas J. Stewart MB ChB 1969 *qv*

PATERSON Colin BSc 1968

PATERSON David Lawrence *MA 1968

PATERSON Doreen MA 1966
m Cuthbert

PATERSON Eliza Martha MA 1968
d of Andrew P. plumber and Martha M. Harrigan; b Inv 8.11.46
teacher: East Plean 1970–71, Edin 1971–72, Stonehaven from 1978; owner private nursery s Stonehaven 1973–75
m Fort Augustus 21.9.68 Ian N. Guthrie DA teacher, lect Aber coll of educ, asst keeper Aber Art Gallery s of John G. Sandwick

PATERSON Erna Jean MA 1968
m Laing

PATERSON Geoffrey Forbes *BSc 1969

PATERSON Gordon Allan MA 1969
d Cyprus 13.10.73 *AUR* XLV 450

PATERSON Helen Margaret MA 1966
d of David P. dist man. Scot. gas board and Henrietta Blair; b Banff 25.2.45
teacher: Cumnock 1968–71, Kirkwall 1971–76.
m Aber 16.4.71 Frank T. Dry BSc 1965 *qv*

PATERSON Ian Arthur *BSc 1967

PATERSON Isobel MA 1965
d of William J. P. farm worker, millwright and Lily Ironside; b Turriff 10.4.44
teacher: Smithfield p s Aber 1966–67, Crimond p s; exec off. Inl Rev Worthing 1970–72; teacher remed Campbeltown g s, Kinloch p s 1972–73
m Campbeltown 14.4.73 Peter S. Armour BA(Strath) clerk Hudson Bay Co, exec Ford Co, comp dir s of Peter S. A. Campbeltown

PATERSON Jean Margaret Diack *MA 1969
d of Archibald P. civ eng and Margaret H. McRobert; b Glasg 13.5.48
ALA 1971
grad trainee lib Aberd 1969–70; dep lib marine lab Aber 1971–75; lib Macaulay inst for soil res Aber 1976–77
m Tighnabruaich 30.6.72 Stephen R. Alcock MB ChB 1969 *qv*

PATERSON Jeffrey Norman McCheyne *MA 1968 Dip Ed 1969

PATERSON Joan Stuart MA 1962
d of Cyril D. P. loc govt off. and Margaret Stuart; b Forres 9.7.41
teacher Applegrove p s Forres from 1963

PATERSON John Simon *BSc 1969
s of Thomas R. P. salmon fishing lessee and Mona F. Mackenzie MA 1967 *qv*; b St Andrews 21.12.47
analytical chem Enfield 1971–72; ptnr commercial sea salmon fishing bus. Strathy Thurso from 1972

PATERSON John Thomson MB ChB 1963

PATERSON Kenneth Norman BSc 1964
MEd(Glas)

PATERSON Laura Beedie MA 1964
m Levy

PATERSON Lily Jane MA 1963
d of William J. P. farm lab, painter and Lily Ironside; b Turriff 17.1.42
teacher Engl Bankhead acad from 1974
m Turriff 14.9.62 Ian A. Scott ordnance surv/tech Grampian roads dept s of Clifford S. Dewsbury

PATERSON Maureen Lilian MA 1969
m Akintewe

PATERSON Neil *BSc 1966 PhD 1970
b Forres 1944
lect chem path. Aberd from 1966

PATERSON Richard George *MA 1956

PATERSON Ronald McNeill LLB 1970

PATERSON Ronald Seaton BSc(agr) 1969
s of Colin S. P. farm. and Anna M. Smith typist; b Alyth 11.5.48
Dip FMBO(NOSCA) 1970
asst lands off. Stirling 1970–75; lands off. Lerwick from 1975
m Stirling 26.12.70 Aileen Stephen teacher d of James Stephen

PATIENCE Hugh James Mackintosh *BSc 1970
s of Hugh P. harbour pilot and Elma Maclauchlan; b Inv 3.3.48
Dip Ed(Edin) 1973 MEd(Glas) 1978
teacher Beauly j s s 1970–71; actuarial stud. Legal & Gen Assur Soc Lond 1971; teacher: Kirkton h s Dun 1971–72, high s Inv 1973–75, Allan Glen's s s Glasg 1975–76, Hillhead h s Glasg 1976–78, Harvey g s Folkestone from 1978
m Glasg 3.7.76 Edith M. Culbert teacher mus d of James A. C. Glasg

PATON John Alexander MA 1966

PATON Kathleen Scott BEd 1969
d of John P. chiropodist and Grace I. Scott; b Ellon 19.7.48
teacher mod lang Peterhead acad 1969–71; Peebles h s 1971–74
m Aber 31.7.71 Clive P. Alder BSc 1970 *qv*

PATON Keith Alan *MA 1962

PATON Thomas John Grindley MB ChB 1966
s of Thomas D. P. meat livestock controller and Isabella G. McLean; b Duns 23.8.42
h o Inv 1966–67; g p Perth 1968, Mahalapy Botswana 1969–71, Ottawa from 1971
m Aber 19.5.67 Kathleen Davidson d of Alexander D. Fyvie

PATON Wilma Ann MA 1967 CASS 1969
d of William S. P. bricklayer, foreman, site superv and Agnes J. Allan waitress; b Forres 20.9.46
soc worker/fieldwork teacher Aber 1969–76; lect in soc work RGIT Aber from 1976

PATRICK Anthony Graham *BSc 1969 MSc 1971
s of Graham M. P. civ serv and Barbara A. Worboys; b Royston 7.8.46
army maj from 1978

PATRICK Barbara Howie *MA 1969 Dip Ed 1970

PATRICK David Malcolm MA 1970
s of Thomas E. P. arch. and Dorothy B. Malcolm chirop; b Edin 20.2.47
CA 1973
Edin: acct Deloitte & Co CA, Dalgliesh & Tullo CA 1970–79; group acct Eastern Motor Co from 1979
m Aber 20.7.73 Alyson T. Greig MA 1971 teacher

PATRICK Elizabeth Boyd MLitt 1967
MA(Glas)

PATRICK George *MA 1963

PATTERSON Donald BSc(for) 1956

PATTERSON Dorothy Elizabeth BSc 1965
d of James R. P. quantity surv and Marian E. McEwan MA 1924 *qv*; b Aber 27.5.44
teacher Duddingston p s Edin from 1966
m Edin 21.10.72 John D. Rutherford motor eng s of John R. Bonnyrigg

PATTERSON Ian James *BSc 1961
s of James A. P. rlyman and Mary C. N. Darling; b Duns 30.3.39
D Phil(Oxon) 1964
res fell. zool Aberd 1964–66, lect zool 1966–77, sen lect from 1977
m Dun 28.7.62 Muriel J. Birse MA 1960 *qv*

PATTERSON Kathleen Anne *MA 1970
d of Andrew P. civ serv and Daisy F. MacDonald; b Aber 1.12.47
teacher geog/mod stud. Blairgowrie 1971–75, Aust 1975–76, Malta 1976–78, Cyprus from 1978

PATTERSON Margaret Helen MA 1958
d of James R. P. quantity surv and Marian E. McEwan MA 1924 *qv*; b Aber 2.8.37
teacher: Byron Park inf s Aber 1959–69, Royal High p s Edin 1969–72
m Edin 31.3.71 David N. Smith bank man. s of Thomas S. Edin

PATTERSON Michael Hugh *MA 1970
s of Henry B. W. P. BSc(Durh) chem eng and Constance M. Wright; b Birkenhead 30.8.47
diagnostic and remed teacher Marshfield e s n s Peterborough 1971–76; sen clin psych paediat assessment centre Chesterfield from 1976

PATTERSON Robin James Michael BSc(eng) 1964

PATTERSON Valerie Ann Newton MA 1963
m Wharton

PATTIE Ann More Williamson MA 1967
d of Robert S. P. prod./plan. eng and Margaret W. Taylor nurse; b Glasg 27.9.45
teacher Riverside s s Glasg 1968–72, prin guid 1972–74
m Inverurie 5.4.69 George Brown driver s of Douglas B. Rutherglen

PATTIE Robert BSc(eng) 1968
s of Robert S. P. engraver and Margaret Taylor; b Glasg 14.7.47
CEng MIEE

grad eng Derby 1968–70; sen tech off. Glasg 1970–75; eng asst Lond from 1975

PAUL Anil Krishna MSc 1968
s of Lal Mohan P. teacher and Kunja Kamini; b Dacca Bangla Desh 15.1.24
BSc(Dacca) 1944 MSc(Dacca) 1946 PhD(Calc) 1972
lect organ./biochem Calcutta nat med coll 1948–54; Haringhata farm W Bengal: res asst, asst res off., res off. anim nutrit directorate of anim husb 1954–67, res off. physiol chem 1969–73; physiol chem from 1973
m Calcutta 2.3.49 Bina Kundu d of S. S. K. MB(Calc)

PAUL Douglas Wyness Thomson MB ChB 1968
s of Douglas A. P. gen man. Hall Russell & Co and Margaret M. Thomson lib; b Aber 4.9.44
MRCGP 1974
h o Aber, Wick 1968–69; sen h o Thurso 1969; g p Wick from 1969
m Aber 23.7.67 Alexandra M. Lee teacher d of Robert L.

PAUL Helen Margaret Wyness MA 1970
d of Douglas A. P. naval arch./gen man. Hall Russell & Co Aber and Margaret M. Thomson lib Torry res stat; b Aber 22.2.49
teacher Aber from 1971
m Aber 24.7.70 George C. Stove BSc 1972 tut. geog dept Aberd s of George J. S. Sandwick Shetland

PAUL Parul Rani BSc 1962
d of Radha K. P. Dip Eng(Dacca) tech asst and Promode K. Dutta; b Bangladesh 7.4.37
BA(Calc) 1958
teacher Convent s Malaya 1959 and 1965–67
m Calcutta 1.5.64 Madhabendra M. Guha PhD 1951 *qv*

PAYNE Dorothy Ruth PhD 1969
d of Charles F. P. civ serv and Violet M. Denne civ serv; b Croydon 26.8.36
BSc(Lond) 1960 MIBiol(Lond)
lect physiol Aberd from 1964

PEACE Emma Smith MA 1959
d of Donald P. farm. and Margaret Chalmers; b Stronsay 29.3.38
teacher: Lat Bradford 1959–60, remed Halkirk 1965–67, p s Thurso 1967–70, p s Elgin 1970–71, f e Elgin 1973–74, prin guid/Engl Thurso from 1975
m Stronsay 15.7.59 Donald Omand MA 1958 *qv*

PEACOCK Robin Geoffrey MA 1970
s of Geoffrey P. civ serv and Irene D. Baker; b Ilford 8.7.47
Dip Man. St(RGIT Aber) 1971 Dip Marketing 1972
Kwikform Birm: export admin asst 1971–72, market res off. 1972–73; J. C. B. Rocester Uttoxeter market intell spec 1973–75; Massey Ferguson Coventry market and econ res spec 1975–77, marketing res man. Europe, Africa, Asia, Australasia—parts oper from 1977
m Edin 28.6.69 Gillian E. M. Alsop BEd 1969 *qv*

PEAD Beryl-Anne BSc 1968

PEARCE Gordon James Martin PhD 1959
s of Walter P. secy and Harriet Seager; b Lond 27.12.09
BA(Lond) 1937 MA(Birm) 1944
baptist min: Tamworth 1936–44, Bradford 1944–52, Crown Terrace Aber 1952–60; dean and tut. Oxon 1960–74
m Lond 25.1.36 Doris P. Hancock dressmaker d of Humphrey H. RN Brixton Lond
d 11.2.74

PEARCE Janet Elizabeth BSc 1970
m Haworth

PEARSON Charles Arthur *MA 1962
s of Douglas H. P. fl/lt RAF and Christina M. Campbell secy; b Tain 15.5.40
cler work Invergordon 1963–65; teacher hist Middlesbrough from 1965

PEARSON Ian Henderson MA 1967
s of Magnus H. P. master bldr and Alice M. Scott MA 1925 *qv*; b Lerwick 29.10.45
Dip Man. St 1969
Scot. gas Edin: grad trainee 1969–70, organis and methods off. from 1970
m Aber 24.7.70 Kathleen J. Yeoman MA 1968 *qv*

PEARSON Isobel Gilfillan MA 1958
d of William P. tobacconist and Isabella Mark nurse; b Keith 22.10.37
teacher Aber 1959–60
m Aber 22.7.59 Patrick A. Symon MA 1952 *qv*

PEARSON James Murray *BSc 1959 PhD 1962
s of James S. P. tobacconist and Jeannie E. Hendry; b Aber 22.11.37
post doct res fell. NY state coll of for. Syracuse NY USA 1962–64; asst lect, lect chem Aberd 1964–66; assoc lect Polymer res inst NY state coll of for. Syracuse 1966–68; man. Polymer sc area xerographic tech dept Xerox corp Rochester NY from 1968
m Aber 30.5.62 Hilary L. Buckett d of Robert B.

PEARSON Jean Robertson *BSc 1959
m Alison
d 26.3.67

PEARSON Nigel William LLB 1965

PEAT Conrad Ian BSc(for) 1961
s of Rex A. P. master butcher and Lily Barnes; b Sheff 16.5.40
Kenya: asst conserv for. Elburgon, Londiani, Thomson Falls, Nairobi 1961–66; sen work study off. papermaking indust Exeter, Lond, Fort William from 1966
m Inv 11.4.70 Margaret R. L. Richards catering man. d of Robert L. MB ChB 1932 *qv*

PEAT Elizabeth Booth MA 1967
d of Reginald A. P. MB ChB 1943 *qv*; b Jamaica 26.3.46
Dip Pers Man.(Middlesex poly)(Hendon) 1970
Lond: admin attaché dip. serv 1967–69; exec off. civ serv 1971–73, admin asst Lond 1973–74; soc worker Lond from 1975

PECK Catherine Pryde MB ChB 1968
d of George T. P. seaman/weaver and Janet R. Dickson nurse; b Strathaven 2.7.43
h o Stornoway, Stonehaven 1963–69; regist haemat Law hosp Carluke 1969–71; g p Hamilton from 1971
m Hamilton 9.4.71 John Braithwaite BA(Strath) organis and methods off./syst analyst s of William L. B. Hamilton

PEDEN Donald George MSc 1968
s of Ernest E. P. man. agr and feed supply comp and Bernice L. Swanston; b Victoria Canada 23.1.46
BSc(Vict) 1967 PhD(Colorado State Univ) 1972 PDF (Calg) 1973
res scient (ecol) Canadian wildlife serv Saskatoon from 1973

PEDERSON *BSc 1967
s of C. P. P. eng worker and Georgina L. Wilson; b Aber 9.4.34
teacher: Stonehaven 1967–73, asst prin maths Banff from 1973

PEDERSEN Roy Norman MA 1966
s of Hans N. P. supt Aber harbour board and Anne W. Black; b Ardrossan 22.11.43
teacher Stevenston 1967; exec off. min of tech Lond, DTI 1970–71; asst admin off. HIDB Inv 1971–73, freight trans off. 1973, res off. from 1974
m Lond 21.11.70 Jennifer Walpole secy d of Herman T. W. Lond

PEGG Christopher Arthur Sunley ChM 1969
s of Arthur T. P. MA(Sheff) headmaster, supt remand home and Dorothy A. Sunley matron remand home; b Norfolk 3.7.37
MB BS(Lond) 1962 FRCS 1966
h o/sen surg cas off. St Thomas's hosp Lond 1962–64; h o Worthing gen hosp 1964; sen h o Gt Ormond St HSC Lond 1964–65; regist, sen regist, hon clin lect surg ARI/Aberd 1965–73; res fell. surg Harvard univ Boston Mass 1968–69; consult. surg/hon clin teacher surg Nott univ hosp from 1973
m Cheltenham 8.2.64 Ann J. Ault MB BS(Lond) med pract d of Frederick H. A. Cheltenham

PENNIE David Alexander *MA 1969
s of Gibb N. P. MA 1930 *qv*; b Dalbeattie 19.7.46
Dip Lib Stud.(Belf) 1971 ALA 1973
trainee lib Durh 1969–70; sen lib asst S'ton 1971–76; asst lib Hull from 1976

PENNIE Rona MA 1970

PENNINGTON John Barry BSc(eng) 1966

PENNY Helen BSc 1970
d of Charles P. MB ChB 1922 *qv*; b Derby 9.3.47
secy course Oxford 1970–71; res secy Bristol 1971–72; radio secy Derby 1973; med rep Bristol from 1974
m Derby 17.6.76 Stephen B. Lyus BA(Warw) man. consult. s of Brian G. L. Marlborough

PENNY Rebecca *MA 1966
d of Charles P. MB ChB 1922; b Derby 21.3.42
Dip Ed(Edin) 1967
teacher Fr/Ger Derby 1967–69; TEFL: Cologne Ger 1969–73, Madrid from 1973

PEPPER Jean Margaret *MA 1968
d of William A. P. and Lilian M. Weetman; b Lond 28.1.46
teacher Engl Ashford 1968–69; exec off. univ of Ulster Coleraine 1969–71; temp posts Watertown Mass USA 1971–73
m Cheadle Hulme 20.7.68 Alan W. Hazel BSc 1968 *qv*

PEPPIETTE Geoffrey Charles Christopher BSc(eng) 1962

PERCIVAL Alan PhD 1960
BSc(Manc)

PERCIVAL James Sidney *MA 1963 Dip Ed 1964
b Tandjong Kassau Indonesia 12.10.25
teacher mod lang: Aber acad 1964–65, Inverurie acad 1965–68, coll of comm Aber 1968–69; asst prin mod lang Inverurie acad from 1969
m Inverurie 24.12.49 Elizabeth McRae

PERCY Graham Charles Booth *MA 1968
s of Ernest R. P. eng and Violet E. Booth lib; b Aber 2.3.46
BBC: progr oper Lond 1968–70, prod. radio Nott from 1970
m Ratcliffe-on-Trent Jennifer Meakin p a/des d of William K. M.

PEREIRA Brian Anthony *BSc(eng) 1968
s of Anthony P. comp dir and Ursula Figueira; b Guiana 7.12.45
computer eng Greenock from 1968
m Aber 14.9.68 Heather M. Petrie MB ChB 1967

PEREZALEMAN Salvador de Jesus MSc 1970
DVM(Venez)

PERFECT Martin John MA 1968
s of Ernest J. F. MA(Oxon) schoolmaster and Eleanor P. D. Denton journalist; b Oxford 23.5.47
telephonist Lond from 1968
m Aber –.10.73 Brenda J. Thompson edit. d of Benjamin C. T. Bridge of Don

PERKS Helen Marjorie MA 1956
d of Jackie P. CBE DSC capt RN and Isabel Burns; b Portsmouth 22.4.66
teacher: Bracoden j s 1957–59, Macduff h s 1959–61, drama Banffsh 1971–74, asst prin guid Banff acad from 1974
m Aber 4.8.60 James A. S. McPherson MA 1949 *qv*

PERMAN Anne MA 1966
b Kent 24.12.44
resid Buxton Derbysh
m Escritt

PEROMBELON Michel Marie Clement *BSc 1962 MSc 1963

PERRIE James Fraser *MA 1959 Dip Ed 1960
d 5.3.70

PERRIE William Thomas *BSc 1965

PERRINS Margaret Janet MB ChB 1969

PETERS David James *BSc(eng) 1967
s of David F. M. P. exec eng PO tel and Daisy Grieve hairdresser; b Aber 27.3.45
CEng 1971 MICE 1971 MSc(Strath) 1972 MIPHE 1972 Aff IWPC 1973
sect. eng Taylor Woodrow construct. Dounreay, Wylfa Anglesey, Invergordon 1967–70; asst eng Babtie Shaw & Morton consult. eng Glasg 1970–71; sen asst eng Dun city eng dept 1972–75; sen group leader WPC Tayside reg c water serv dept from 1975
m Elgin 1.8.69 Christine M. Guthrie nurs/inf teacher d of William J. R. G. Elgin

PETERS Gordon *MA 1958
s of James R. P. farm. and Nellie Reid; b Cluny 26.12.35
teacher hist/Engl: Camphill h s Paisley 1959–60, Inverurie acad 1960–64; prin hist Gordon s Huntly from 1964
m Aber 29.7.66 Edith I. Wilson MA 1956 *qv*

PETERS Gordon Grieve *BSc 1970
s of David F. M. P. exec eng PO tel and Daisy Grieve hairdresser; b Ellon 8.9.48
PhD(Edin) 1974

res asst MRC Edin 1974; res fell.: univ of Wisc Madison USA 1974–77, Imperial Cancer res fund Lond from 1977

PETERS Mary Elizabeth *MA 1963
d of Bernard F. P. plan. eng (cars) and Nellie I. Faunch; b Luton 20.7.40
commonwealth schol univ of Sri Lanka 1963; teacher Walsall 1964–66; lect: Cornwall 1967–68, coll for deaf Walton from 1979
m Luton 26.8.67 William J. Warren solic s of William J. W. Camborne

PETERSON Anne Elizabeth MA 1966

PETERSON Christina June MA 1970
d of Arthur P. lorry driver and Mary A. Robertson dom serv; b Lerwick 13.12.49
teacher Anderson h s Lerwick from 1971
m Lerwick 16.7.71 John A. E. Johnson joiner s of Sinclair J. Bixter

PETERSON Gordon Craig *BSc 1965 PhD 1974
s of William G. P. B Com 1927 *qv*; b Aber 1.2.43
scient Unilever res Port Sunlight from 1969
m Aber 1968 Helen E. Cant MA 1969 *qv*

PETERSON James Peter MA 1960
s of Alexander M. P. merch seaman and Jessie A. Pole; b Sandness Shetland 3.6.39
teacher Shetland: Hamnavoe 1961–68, Walls 1968–70, Aith 1970–75; dep dir leisure and recreation dept Shetland Is c from 1975

PETERSON Jemima Alice MA 1958
d of Alexander M. P. merch seaman and Jessie A. Pole; b Sandness Shetland 9.11.36
teacher: Aber 1959–62, Edmonton Alta 1970–72
m Shetland 4.4.60 Duncan Armstrong BSc 1958 *qv*

PETERSON John Magnus MA 1970

PETERSON Louis Keith *BSc 1957 PhD 1960
s of James P. P.; b Shetland 12.8.35
res assoc USC California 1960–62; lect City univ Lond 1962–65; assoc prof Simon Fraser univ BC Canada from 1965
m Jill J. Macdonald

PETRIE Doreen Alexandra MA 1969
d of William A. P. bus driver and Marie W. L. Haldane; b Aber 17.2.48
advt canvasser: Aber 1971–72, Edin 1972–74; pers asst Edin 1974–75, admin asst in educ Stonehaven 1975–77
m Braemar 18.9.71 Brian J. Wood BSc 1971 teacher s of Frank W. Aber

PETRIE Hazel Christine MA 1968
d of Robert E. P. man. hardware shop and Mabel Allerton cler off.; b Stoke-on-Trent 29.1.46
Dip Soc Stud.(Edin) 1969
Edin: trainee welfare off. dept health and welfare 1969–70; loc auth soc worker 1970–72; soc worker for Shelter 1972–73
m Haddington 3.10.70 George M. V. Dier syst eng s of Hubert V. S. D. BA(Oxon) Dumfries

PETRIE Heather Margaret MB ChB 1967
d of James B. P. headmaster and Margaret McDonald; b Melksham 9.8.44
h o Raigmore hosp Inv, Woodend hosp Aber 1967–68
m Aber 14.9.68 Brian A. Pereira BSc(eng) 1968 *qv*

PETRIE Helen Cattanach *BSc 1966
d of James W. H. P. MA(Edin) teacher and Janet Cattanach MA 1935 *qv*; b Elgin 9.10.44
teacher geog/maths Kaimhill s Aber 1967–68, Bankhead acad Aber 1968–70; dir Ben Reid & Co Aber from 1970
m Aber 27.7.67 John Fraser nurseryman s of Robert F. MB ChB 1935 *qv*

PETRIE James Colquhoun MB ChB 1964
s of James B. P. MA 1932 *qv* and Cairine R. MacLean MA 1940 *qv*; b Aber 18.9.41
h o ARI 1964–65; sen h o/regist Aber hosps 1965–69; lect therap Aberd 1969–71; sen lect therap Aberd/hon consult. phys Aber hosps from 1971
m Aber 16.7.64 Margaret X. P. Forbes MB ChB 1964 *qv*

PETRIE Mhorag Jean BSc 1961
m Taylor

PFISTER Maria Regina *MA 1966
d of Charles P. asst man. American Express co inc Lucerne and Margaretha Buehler clerk; b Sirnach Switzerland 9.8.40
teacher Stadtische Töchterhandelsschule Luzern, Switzerland from 1966
m Lucerene 28.4.73 Hans B. Fricker chief eng Canton of Lucerne s of Hans F. Aarau Switzerland

PHA Jean Cyril *MA 1967

PHEMISTER Elizabeth Reid *MA 1957
d of Thomas C. P. BSc(Glas) prof geol Aberd and Mary W. Reid MA(Glas) teacher; b Cambridge 8.7.34
secy to dir: Joseph Lucas (electrical) Birm 1958–62, world h q internat wool secretariat Lond 1962–65; teacher mod lang Leamington coll for girls Leamington Spa 1966–72; secy to man. dir L Maurer UK Warwick 1973–74; exec off. Midland road construct. unit DoE Leamington Spa 1974–75; dep admin off. Mid-Warwicksh coll of f e Leamington Spa from 1975
m Warwick 23.6.70 Dennis B. Matthews tooling investig eng s of Robert B. M. Lighthorne

PHILIP Alexander Schroder *BSc 1965
s of Andrew F. P. bank acct and Martha H. Schroder; b Aber 26.5.43
MIERE C Eng 1972
telecomm Liv: dev eng 1965–72, eng man. from 1972
m Aber 5.8.66 Gillian M. Crofts BSc 1965 *qv*

PHILIP Alistair Erskine *MA 1961
s of James P. dairyman and Gertrude M. Erskine; b Aber 10.7.38
PhD(Edin) 1968 Dip Clin Psych(Edin) 1963 ABPsS
prob clin psych SE(Scot.) reg hosp board Edin 1961–63; clin psych NE(Scot.) reg hosp board Aber 1963–65; scient staff MRC unit for epidemiological stud. in psychiat Edin 1964–71; prin clin psych Bangour village hosp W. Lothian from 1971
m Aber 12.2.68 Betty J. McKay BSc 1964 *qv*

PHILIP Alistair Fowlie *BSc(eng) 1968
s of John P. rubber planter and Helena M. Fowlie teacher; b Aber 9.3.46
MSc(Cranfield) 1970
helicopter pilot RAF: Odiham 1970–78, Aeroplane & Arm. Exper Est Boscombe Down from 1978

PHILIP Charles Ian BSc(eng) 1959

PHILIP George MA 1958

PHILIP Grace Cameron MA 1960
d of Richard P. master grocer and Grace E. Cameron piano teacher; b Aber 23.7.39
teacher p s RGC Aber 1961–64; part-time visiting mus spec p s Aber from 1975
m Aber 17.7.62 Philip F. Simpson gen secy Aber YMCA s of John A. M. S. Aber

PHILIP Ian MA 1966 MEd 1968
s of James P. eng and Helen N. Mitchell; b Peterhead 31.12.43
Dip Applied Ling(Edin) 1972
TEFL Mumbwa Zambia 1968–71; lect inst of tech Kitwe Zambia 1972–78; sen lect coll of tech Mumbane Swaziland 1975–78

PHILIP Margaret McKenzie MB ChB 1957
d of Peter W. MB ChB 1924 *qv* (II, III); b Huntly 20.11.33
h o RACH 1957–58; m o (ch health) Aberdeensh 1972–75; part-time regist (ment deficiency) Woodlands hosp from 1975
m Aber 16.9.57 Geoffrey M. Gill MB ChB 1953 *qv*

PHILIP Maureen Anne BSc 1963 Dip Ed 1964
d of Henry P. law acct and Janet M. Mitchell off. worker; b Aber 29.1.42
teacher maths St Margaret's s for girls Aber 1964–68; part time lect maths Aber coll of comm from 1979
m Aber 4.4.66 Thomas W. Simpson MB ChB 1964 *qv*

PHILIP Patrick Blake BSc(eng) 1957

PHILIP Robert Finlay *BSc(eng) 1960
s of Arthur P. PO eng and Christina Findlay printer's asst; b Aber 26.4.38
MIEE CEng 1970
proj eng Ferranti Edin 1960–65; lect Dund from 1965
m Aber 3.4.64 Anne F. Simpson MA 1961 *qv*

PHILIP Robert Freeland MA 1960
s of Robert P. foreman fish filleter and Christina R. Sanders dressmaker; b Aber 5.12.39
stud. Scots cong coll Edin 1960–63; attendant Gogarburn ment hosp Edin 1963–64; untrained teacher Crossgates s Fife 1964; min: Forsyth mem cong ch Glasg 1964–70, Mastrick cong ch Aber 1970–78, Avonbridge cong with cong wing Grahamston United ch Falkirk from 1978
m Berwick-u-Tweed 1.8.64 Yvonne Ingles MA(Edin) teacher of deaf d of John A. W. I. Berwick-u-Tweed

PHILIP Suzanne *MA 1959
d of Peter W. P. MB ChB 1924 *qv*; b Huntly 18.3.36
teacher: Fr/Ger High s for girls Aber 1960–61, Bridge of Don 1962–63, The Gordon s Huntly from 1963
m Aber 28.9.61 Gordon C. Shirreffs MB ChB 1957 *qv*

PHILIP Wilma MA 1964

PHILLIP Sheena Mary MA 1960 Dip Ed 1961
d of William C. P. MA(St And) teacher and Mary D. Flight shorthand typist; b Dun 10.4.39
teacher Engl/hist: Mackie acad Stonehaven 1961–66, Old Aber s 1966
m Aber 10.4.65 Clement A. Stewart MA 1962 *qv*

PHILLIPS Alexander BSc 1969
s of John P. slater and Louisa Hendry; b Aber 7.11.47
various posts in computing Dunstable 1969–76; sen syst analyst Edin from 1976
m Aber 1.7.69 Margaret P. Gibson d of Douglas G.

PHILLIPS Anne Clemency Sarah ᶜMB ChB 1961
d of Ernest B. P. MTh(Lond) min of relig/lect Biblical lang and theol and Alice Gordon artist; b Rugby 26.5.36
h o ARI, RACH 1961–62; m o Empress Zauditu mem hosp Addis Ababa 1962–63; sen h o Fulbourn hosp Cambridge 1964; g p Binfield from 1972
m Binfield 30.12.63 Colin W. Mitchell PhD(Cantab) lect geog s of Arthur C. M. Chelsea

PHILLIPS George McArtney *MA 1960 MSc 1961
s of George P. dent mech and Elizabeth McArtney; b Aber 30.7.38
PhD(St And) 1969
asst maths Aberd 1961–62; teacher Allhallows s Devon 1962–63; lect: maths S'ton 1963–67, St And 1967–73, sen lect from 1973
m Aber 4.7.61 Veronica M. Irvine MA 1959 *qv*

PHILLIPS Ian George Knox BEd 1969

PHILLIPS James Dawson *MA 1959

PHILLIPS Michael William BSc(eng) 1967

PHILLIPS Roger John MA 1970

PHILLIPSON John Tobin *BSc(eng) 1962

PHILLIPSON Nicholas Tindal *MA 1958
s of Andrew T. P. BA(Cantab) prof Cantab and Rachel M. Young; b Aber 15.8.37
BA(Cantab) 1962 PhD(Cantab) 1967
nat serv RAF Norfolk 1958–60; lect hist Edin from 1965; visiting fell. Davis centre Princeton univ USA 1970–71, visiting lect Yale univ USA 1977

PHILP Arthur Andrew Kinninmonth *BSc 1970
s of Robert P. trans man. and Miriam L. F. Kinninmonth; b Dunfermline 7.5.48
trainee computer spec Lond 1970–73; Perth: computer progr 1973–74, computer progr proj leader 1974–75, syst analyst 1975–77, asst computer oper supt from 1977
m Aber 19.9.70 Joan Watson secy d of James W. Aber

PHILP Bruce *BSc 1970
s of James T. P. hotelier and Dorothy King hotelier; b Crieff 12.10.47
res asst Ibadan Nigeria 1970–71; teacher biol Portree from 1972

PHILP Richard Paul *BSc 1968

PICKARD James Roy MLitt 1969
s of Reginald J. P. PhD(Sheff) headmaster and Eileen M. Alexander; b Lindrick 20.8.42
BA(Lond) 1964
asst lib Aberd from 1965

PICKARD Joyce Isobel Helen MA 1970
m Petrie

PICKEN Hilda Hamilton MA 1966

PICKFORD Douglas Thomson BSc 1961

PICKLES Ian Munro *MA 1967
s of John W. P. MB ChB 1932 *qv*; b East London S Af 3.6.44
Master Town & Country Planning (Syd) 1977 Member Royal Aust Plan. Inst
teacher Lond 1967–68; supermarket warehouse man. Lond 1968–69; Aust: town plan. asst Sydney, Melbourne

1970–72, asst town plan. N Sydney munic council 1973–77, dep town plan. Waverley munic council Bondi Sydney from 1977
m Sydney 28.12.71 Kathleen A. Littler BA(Syd) teacher d of John E. L. BA(Syd) Sydney

PIERCY John David BSc(eng) 1970
s of Frederick J. P. LDS dent. surg and Rebecca F. Maugham; b Wimbledon 2.10.47
trg RAF Cranwell, Oakington, Thorney Is 1970–73; co-pilot *Hercules* Lyneham from 1973
m Aber 31.3.73 Mary L. Marshall LLB 1972 articled clerk d of Alexander M. Aber
d flying accident –.9.78 *AUR* XLVIII 107

PIGGINS James Milne *BSc 1969
s of James M. P. shipowner/shipbroker and Mary Milne; b Aber 2.12.47
PhD(Cantab) 1975
res stud. radio astron Cambridge 1969–72; hosp phys Inv 1972–74; non-destructive testing Babcock & Wilcox Renfrew 1975–78; res fell. med phys Edin from 1978

PIGOTT Colin Peter BSc(eng) 1967
s of Kenneth P. P. comp dir and Dora Goodman comp dir; b Maghull nr Liv 29.5.45
piling eng 1967–71; proj man. 1971–74; estimator Ormskirk from 1974
m Aber 23.11.68 Ray B. Watson LLB 1965 *qv*

PIKE James Adam BSc(eng) 1970
s of John T. P. fisherman and Catherine Clark; b Aber 19.6.47
Brinsley: grad app Plessey trg centre 1970–72, asst eng electro-mech syst Plessey Crossbar syst lab 1972–73, eng-electronic des 1973–75, sen eng 1975–77, prin eng advanced SWG div from 1978

PIKE Malcolm Cecil PhD 1963
BSc(Rand) Dip Math Stat(Cantab)

PILGRIM Roy Malcolm BSc 1970
s of Leslie P. steelworks foundry insp and Mary A. Simmerson stock control clerk; b Sheff 15.3.48
MICA 1974
Sheff: articled clerk CA 1970–74, man. acct Edgar Allen Tools 1974; group chief acct High Mead Eng Holdings

PINNOCK (Baird) Jennifer Naomi MA 1970
d of Malcolm R. P. MB ChB 1950 *qv* and Ethel Melville dispenser; b Aber 14.4.49
teacher: Aber 1971–75, Inverurie from 1976
m Aber 2.1.70 Alastair J. Mackie MB ChB 1969 *qv*

PINSENT Elizabeth Margaret *BSc 1967
d of Robert J. F. H. P. MB ChB(Cantab) med pract and Ruth M. Morrison MA(St And) civ serv; b St And 2.11.44
PhD(Edin) 1973
res assoc Edin 1967–71; lect biol sc Napier coll of sc & tech from 1971
m Birmingham 3.4.72 George M. Alder MA(Cantab) lect s of George V. A. BSc(Brist) Bristol

PINSENT Robert Hugh *BSc 1968
s of Robert J. F. H. P. MD(Cantab) med pract and Ruth M. Morrison MA(St And); b St And 10.3.46
MSc(Alta) 1971 PhD(Durh) 1974
explor geol Vancouver 1971–72; res stud. Durh 1972–76, econ geol Winnipeg 1976–79; explor geol Vancouver from 1979

PIRIE Alexander Flett *BSc 1957

PIRIE Edna Louise *MA 1956

PIRIE Gordon Douglas *BSc 1964 PhD 1968

PIRIE Harold Rothnie MA 1966
s of James P. master shoemaker and Mary S. C. Clyne shop asst; b Insch 28.11.44
teacher: Engl/geog/hist Cumnock 1967–68, Engl/geog/mod stud. New Deer j s s 1968–69, Engl Inverurie acad 1969–71, gen subj Entoto s Addis Ababa Ethiopia 1971–72, Engl Bankhead acad 1972–75; prin guid Tarbert s from 1976
m Hopeman 21.7.73 Evelyn A. Jack staff nurse d of John J. Hopeman

PIRIE Isobel MA 1960
d of James P. garage propr and Margaret I. Pittendreigh; b Kemnay 21.1.39
teacher: Aber 1961–63, Knopi Finland 1963–64, Aber 1964–65, Rio de Janeiro Brazil 1965–67, Aber 1972–73, Perth W Aust from 1977
m Aber 4.3.67 Ian M. Ramsay MA 1962 *qv*

PIRIE James *BSc 1966

PIRIE James Gordon BSc 1968

PIRIE John Alexander MA 1962

PIRIE John Douglas *BSc 1961 MSc 1963 PhD 1965
s of Alexander A. P. MA 1891 *qv*; b Oldmeldrum 1.9.39
lect nat phil Aberd from 1965

PIRIE Michael Douglas MA 1968

PIRIE Sandra Isabel MA 1969

PIRIE Sheila Margaret MB ChB 1965
d of Richard T. P. BSc(eng) 1949 *qv*; b Aber 29.3.40
LMCC(C) 1967
h o: ARI 1965–66, Perth RI 1966; g p and Queensway gen hosp Toronto from 1966
m(1) Lyon—marr diss
(2) Toronto 24.12.76 William Zatelny MD(Tor) phys/surg s of Casimirus Z. Portage la Prairie Canada

PITTENDREIGH David William MA 1969
s of David P. eng and Elizabeth M. Porter; b Aber 5.3.48
Aber coll of educ 1969–70; RAEC: educ off. Rhyl 1970–73, Belf 1973–74, Paderborn W Ger 1974–75, inst army educ Lond 1976–77; RAEC centre Beaconsfield from 1977

PLASKETT William Baskerville BSc 1969
s of Vincent C. P. min of relig and Margery Baskerville; b Nott 14.5.45
med rep Lond 1970–73, prod. man. Guildford 1973–78; publisher from 1978
m Forfar 18.6.70 Marianne M. Langlands MA 1968 *qv*

PLOWMAN Michael BSc 1964
s of William P. comm vehicle salesman/eng and Barbara A. Smith; b Aber 9.2.42
teacher maths Northfield acad Aber from 1965
m Aber 25.3.67 Carol A. M. Dale d of John F. D. Aber

PLUCINSKA Teresa *BSc 1969
m Dorcey

PLUMMER Rachel Mary *MA 1968 Dip Ed 1969
d of Mark M. P. MA(Oxon) fam bus. man. and Margaret Rhodes MA(Oxon); b Guernsey 7.12.45
teacher Engl Hove g s Sussex 1969–73; external examiner for Lond 1972–74; AEB, Middx & Metropolitan from 1974
m Guernsey 11.7.67 Malcolm K. Redford MEd 1969 *qv*

PLUMMER Richard Henry BSc(eng) 1963

PLUMMER Susan Jane MA 1965
d of Alfred P. comp dir and Dilys M. Jenkins; b Tredegar 29.5.44
syst analyst IBM Lond 1965–69
m Oxford 30.9.67 John C. Brierley LLB 1964 *qv*

POCKLINGTON Trevor MSc 1967 PhD 1969
s of Ernest F. P. fitter and Edna M. Senior; b Hull 8.7.44
BSc(N'cle) 1966
res asst med phys Aberd from 1971
m Aber 5.2.73 Priscilla E. Buchan lab tech d of David G. B. Aber

POGUE Hilary Margaret *MA 1969
d of Victor C. P. BA(Dub) par min/Baird res fell. and Emmeline Houston BA(Dub) teacher; b Kirkwall 26.10.47
MPhil(Warw) 1973
trainee lib Dub univ (SCONUL) 1969–70; teacher Engl: Musselburgh 1973, Inverkeithing from 1973
m Cumnock 13.10.73 Michael D. Attfield BSc(Wales) med statist s of Leonard P. A. Barnet

POLE Francis George *BSc 1969
s of Peter P. merch seaman and Margaret H. Frazer; b Shetland 25.5.47
serving off. RAF from 1969
m Lorna C. Davidson MA 1971

POLLARD Janet Evelyn *BSc 1967

POLLARD John Henry PhD 1961
BSc(Brist)

POLLET John Eugene BMedBiol 1969 MB ChB 1972
s of Maurice P. DLitt(Paris) prof Engl lit and Myrtle F. Roberts BSc(R'dg) lect Engl stud.; b Woolwich 14.2.47
h o Aber 1972–73; lect path. Dund 1973–74; sen h o surg Aber 1974–76; regist surg Aber from 1976
m Oldmeldrum Sheena M. Blench BMedBiol 1969 *qv*

POLLITT Alastair Buchan *BSc 1970 MEd 1975
s of Arthur G. P. comm man./polit ag and Lesley S. Buchan MA 1935 *qv*; b Aber 20.10.48
VSO teacher chem Berbice h s Guyana 1970–72; teacher chem Auchmuty h s 1974–75; res assoc Godfrey Thomson unit for acad assessment Edin from 1975

POLLOCK John Gordon MB ChB 1964

POLLOCK Nigel James LLB 1970
s of George A. P. MB ChB(Glas) consult. orthop and Nora E. Ogilvie; b 12.2.48
Edin: law app 1970–72; qualif asst solic from 1972

POLSON Donald MA 1970

POLSON Hugh Alistair Edwin MA 1968
s of Hugh P. customs & excise off. and Roma St C. Wakelin; b Birm 27.6.46
dept man. Marks & Spencer Aber 1968–69; asst brand man. Baxter's of Speyside Fochabers 1969–71; market. serv exec Stats (MR) Birm 1971–72; prod man.: Mettoy Northampton 1972–74, Cadbury Schweppes Birm from 1974
m Macduff 8.8.70 Brenda Wood hairdresser d of Charles W. Macduff

POLSON Janet BEd 1970

POLSON Walter Angus BSc 1970

PONT Alice *BSc 1959
d of Henry B. P. eng and Alice Cowie; b Aber 7.5.37
teacher: Aber acad 1960–64, Marlborough girls' coll Blenheim NZ 1965–67; prin phys Lockerbie acad 1968–73; asst rector Arbroath h s from 1973

PONT Henry Barnett *BSc 1960 *MEd 1963
b 3.5.38
ABPsS
teacher sc Ellon acad 1961–63; educ psych Midlothian 1963–65; res assoc Edin/Manc 1965–69; lect educ Leeds 1969–72; lect psych Strath from 1972
m Aber 1964 Helen A. Hall

POOLE Freda Joan MA 1967
d of William F. P. prop. bus. equipment comp and Winifred M. Gill; b Aber 13.2.46
teacher Engl: Whitburn 1969–71, N Kelvinside s Glasg 1971–75; West Park s for deaf Crosshouse from 1979
m Glasg 1978 George Gardner BA(OU) distrib serv man./prod. man. s of George G.

PORTEOUS William Gunn *BSc 1969 PhD 1974

PORTER Angela Margaret Elizabeth *MA 1970
d of Thomas P. dist man. SW gas (Bath) and Pearl I. Allen BA(Brist) teacher; b Cinderford 13.3.48
TEFL Larnaca Cyprus 1970–71; trg off. with Caltex (UK) Lond from 1971
m Woodhouse Eaves 2.11.74 John S. Leslie MA 1970 *qv*

PORTER Jessie Pirrie *MA 1960

PORTER John Frederick PhD 1969
s of Frederick A. P. eng and Edith M. Rhodes; b Dunstable 22.2.41
BSc(St And) 1964 MIBiol 1970
post doct res fell. Aberd 1969–71; biomed res secy internat plan. parenthood fed. Lond from 1971

PORTER Robert Duguid BSc(eng) 1960
s of Robert P. grocer and Elizabeth Duguid; b Insch 14.9.39
asst civ eng publ works Argyll 1960–66; sen asst eng (water supply): Cirencester 1966–69, Chesterfield 1969–74; supply eng Chesterfield from 1974
m Aber 4.7.61 Frances H. Burnett MA 1960 *qv*

PORTER Ronald Wayne PhD 1970
BA(Mt All) BD MTH(Pine Hill)

PORTER William Henderson MA 1970

PORTFORS Ernest Andrew MSc 1963
BSc(Alta)

POTRATZ Gisela Barbara *MA 1968
d of Erich P. bank man. and Elisabeth Hartung acct; b Greifswald W Ger 18.12.43
teacher Aber 1969–71
m Düsseldorf 16.12.66 Robert M. Cumming BSc(Edin) lect s of Ian C. Edin

POTTER Eva-Maria ***MA 1970**
d of David S. P. FCO and Maria Hadner; b Klagenfurt Austria 23.9.46
teacher: Lond 1972–73, Colwyn Bay from 1974

POTTER Kenneth Evan Duke BSc(eng) 1958

POTTINGER Norma MB ChB 1958
d of Thomas B. P. farm. and Annie P. Tait teacher; b Stronsay Orkney 22.5.32
h o Woodend hosp Aber, ARI 1959 and 1961–62; j h m o ARI 1962; locums Yorks, Caithness 1963–66; g p Thurso from 1966
m Aber 18.12.57 Calum Mackay MB ChB 1960 *qv*

POULET Roger John ***BSc 1967**
s of Maurice V. P. diplomat and Edith M. Stober teacher; b Lond 18.7.42
PhD(Cantab) 1970
Lond: scient civ serv DoE 1970–72, man. consult. Peat Marwick Mitchell 1972–74, man. consult./dir Reid & Timpson Assoc from 1974
m Knightsbridge 18.9.71 Rebecca M. Grant barrister d of John W. H. G. E Twickenham

POWELL Roderick Walter Morrison MA 1969

POWELL Wilfred ***BSc 1970 PhD 1973**
s of Wilfred V. P. machine oper glass indust and Jessie Critchley; b St Helen's 25.8.47
res asst for. dept Aberd from 1973
m St Helen's 4.7.70 Anne Farnen MA 1972 psych d of Kenneth J. F. Eccleston Park

PRAGNELL Frederick Anthony ***MA 1970 MEd 1972**
s of Laurence H. P. civ serv and Mary Bowens; b Lond 31.1.47
MA(Lond) 1975
teacher: Fr/Lat Lond 1972–76, Engl with BAC Saudi Arabia from 1976

PRATHIPASEN Ratchani MA 1960
BA(Bangkok)

PRATT George Michael ***MA 1968**
s of George A. P. solic/clerk to magistr and Jessie Booth teacher; b Oswaldtwistle 7.1.45
VSO teacher Bo Sierra Leone 1968–70; sales exec for Africa Longmans Group (publ) Harlow 1970–71; teacher Blackpool collegiate g s from 1972
m Bolton 22.6.68 Philippa S. Bellis radiogr d of Thomas B. B. Bolton

PRATT Michael Alexander MB ChB 1967
s of Alexander P. BSc(St And) lect and Mary R. V. Wilson; b Cupar 20.5.44
MRCP 1972
h o, sen h o ARI 1967–69; med regist ARI 1969–71; g p Aber from 1971
m Aber 4.11.71 Norma E. Hodder SRN d of A. Norman H. Aber

PREMPEH Thomas Bonsu MB ChB 1966

PRENTICE Ian Miller LLB 1969
s of John D. P. secy and Elizabeth Miller secy; b Stirling 15.1.44
Edin; CA app 1969–73, acct from 1973
m Alloa 11.9.70 Shelagh A. Gordon MA 1967 *qv*

PRESHAW Colin Taylor MB ChB 1967

PRESHAW Roy McFarlane MB ChB 1959 MD 1965

PRESLY Alexander Hadden ***BSc 1970**
s of Alexander C. P. master butcher and Jeanette K. Hadden; b Aber 3.11.48
Dip(Imp coll Lond) 1971 MSc(Lond) 1971 PhD(Birm) 1978
scient off. plant path. nat veg res stat Wellesbourne from 1971
m Sedgefield 19.4.76 Lorna Gray BSc(Trent-poly) tech microbiol Lanchester poly Coventry d of William G. Stockton-on-Tees

PRESLY Allan Smith ***MA 1963**
PhD(Edin)

PRESLY Graham Charles BSc(eng) 1968

PRESLY James Gordon ***BSc 1970 Dip Ed 1971**

PRESTON Stanley David **ᶜMB ChB 1960**

PRICE Wilfred John MA 1964 Dip Ed 1965
s of Jesse P. bldr and Alice M. Bevan; b Crickadarn 18.8.23
teacher maths Aber acad/Hazlehead acad Aber 1965–72, yearmaster from 1972
m Aber 18.9.48 Hazel Mitchell clerkess d of John M. Aber

PRIMROSE Mary Marr MB ChB 1970
d of William S. P. works man. Brit Steel Corp and Marjory M. Marr; b Glasg 2.4.46
m o publ health dept Nassau Bahamas 1970–71; fam practice Dartmouth NS Canada from 1973
m Biggar 23.8.71 Hugh A. J. Roddis BSc(Lond) proj man. eng Hermes Electronics s of John W. R. BSc(Lond) St John's Newfoundland

PRIMROSE Robert Chalmers ***MA 1956**

PRINGLE Alexander Ferguson MB ChB 1960
s of Alexander F. P. MB ChB 1924 *qv*; b Aber 21.5.35
g p: Aber 1961–68, Lower Largo from 1968
m Anstruther 21.2.70 Margaret Williamson secy d of James W. Glasg

PRINGLE Duncan Macmillan ***BSc 1970**
s of Alexander J. P. clerk of works and Christina Macmillan shopkeeper; b Tarbert 24.4.47
teacher geog Perth h s 1971–73, asst prin guid 1973–77; prin guid Perth acad from 1977
m Fraserburgh 24.7.71 Jean Gibb MA 1970 *qv*

PRINGLE James Craighead BL 1957
s of William E. P. woollen manuf and Beatrice M. Craighead secy; b Inv 29.5.35
CA 1960
Inv: acct James Pringle woollen manuf 1960–61; asst John C. Frame & Co CA, ptnr from 1962 (firm now Frame, Kennedy & Forrest CA); sole pract James C. Pringle & Co CA from 1977
m Aber 22.7.60 Maureen M. Taylor MA 1958 *qv*

PRINGLE Katherine Gibson ***MA 1969**
d of Alexander K. P. BSc(Glas) field geol, univ lect, prof and Janet R. Templeton MA(Glas) teacher; b Aber 20.3.48
Dip Educ Psych(Glas) 1971
educ psych Glasg corp ch guid serv from 1971
m Glasg 19.7.72 Alexander H. Adam MB ChB(Glas) med pract s of Alexander Y. A. MB ChB(Edin) Galashiels

PRINGLE Robert Macaulay MB ChB 1964

PRIOR Colin James BSc(eng) 1965
s of Frederick J. P. prod. eng and Elizabeth C. Reeves; b Watford 8.9.43
MICE C Eng 1969
grad eng Babtie Shaw & Morton Workington, Glasg 1965–68; resid eng Leonard & Ptnrs Huddersfield 1968–69; sen des eng, estimator Taylor Woodrow internat: posts in Romania, Aust, Oman, now Lond from 1969
m 1976

PROCTOR David Wilson cMB ChB 1961
s of Sydney S. P. MB ChB 1922 *qv* and Margaret J. Rennet MB ChB 1923 *qv*; b Chester 6.9.34
DRCOG 1969 FFARCS 1968
h o ARI, Raigmore hosp Inv, Perth RI, RHSC Glasg 1961–64; ARI: regist med 1964–66, regist anaest 1966–69; sen regist anaest WI Glasg 1969–71; consult. anaest WI Glasg from 1971
m Hexham 20.10.73 Jennifer Coulson MB BS(Lond) anaest d of Joseph R. C. Whitley Bay

PROCTOR Patricia Lawson MA 1956
m Davidson
d 27.4.62

PROSSER Alan James BSc 1970
s of James W. P. civ serv and Barbara Mitchell; b Aber 8.1.49
teacher maths Hilton acad Aber 1971–77; asst prin maths Kincorth acad Aber from 1977
m 28.7.73 Dorothy E. Foote receptionist d of Eric C. F. Peterborough

PROUD Ian Philip Saxby *MA 1967

PROUDFOOT James MB ChB 1958
s of James L. P. rep and Margaret G. Lawson; b Dun 3.8.34
MRCGP 1974
h o ARI 1958–59; m o RAF UK/Germany 1959–64; med advis Roche pharm Basle Switzerland 1964–65; g p Kirby Maxloe from 1965
m Anstruther 21.1.59 Catherine A. Fowler d of Thomas F. Anstruther

PROUDFOOT Winifred MB ChB 1959
d of Frederick J. P. comp dir and Winifred Crawford; b Carlisle 22.6.34
m Carlisle 19.8.61 Peter J. T. Tait BSc 1956 *qv*

PROUT Lesley Jean Margaret Honor MB ChB 1970
m McMillan

PULLICINO Mark *BSc(eng) 1969
s of Philip P. MBE diplomat, ambassador and Laura Cavarra; b Malta 23.3.46
Dip BA(Edin) 1971 AMBIM 1974 MICE 1975 MEd(Mich) 1975
grad asst civ eng Valetta Malta 1969–70; civ eng/arch. Berlin 1971–72, prof eng/arch. from 1972
m 1977 Katherine Mackenzie, Tain

PUNI Michael Kwaku Tufuor MB ChB 1967
s of Nana K. Y. P. cocoa farm. and Margaret Adade; b Ntronang Ghana 24.5.35
h o Queen Mary hosp Sidcup 1967–68; Ghana: m o Effia Nkwanta hosp Sekondi 1969, m o i/c health centre, central prisons, boys' remand home Essikado, Sekondi, Esipon 1969–70; m o i/c govt hosp/dist m o Tarkwa 1970–72; trainee Hammersmith s of hyg & trop med Lond 1973–76; phys spec Cape Coast hosp 1976–78; med dir Kwame Tufuor mem hosp Oda Ghana from 1978
m Accra 20.12.69 Agnes V. Ntiful teacher d of Paul N. Akrofuom Ghana

PUNK Jozsef BSc 1960

PURANG Iswurdut MA 1960
s of Ramdutti P. trader and Savitri Ramphul; b Port Louis Mauritius 22.4.36
Dip Soc Ad(LSE)
Port Louis: admin asst 1961–63; asst secy 1963–70, prin asst secy 1970–71, prin p secy to prime min 1971–75; perm secy from 1975
m Curepipe Mauritius 5.2.64 Yassoda Ramtohul teacher d of Jaymohunt R. Curepipe

PURCELL Giles Barclay MA 1965

PURITCH George Sydney PhD 1969
s of George W. P. auto mech and Isabella Lamond; b Perth 5.9.43
BSc(Vic BC) MSc(Mass) 1966
res scient DoE Can. for. serv Victoria BC from 1969
m Victoria BC –.5.67 Elaine L. Downey teacher d of Clair D. Sidney BC

PURSELL Patricia Ann MA 1957
d of Wilfred A. P. shopkeeper and Ann Macleod; b Lond 1.4.36
Is of Lewis: teacher: p s Leurbost j s 1958–62, s s Laxdale j s 1965–66; spec class: Aird 1968–71, Nicolson inst Stornoway 1971–73; remed reading Leurbost and other p s from 1973
m Stornoway 31.3.60 Donald Macleod joiner s of Colin M. Leurbost

PYATT David Graham *BSc(for) 1961 PhD 1978
s of David S. P. teacher and Constance N. Basford teacher; b Cheadle 30.3.39
dist off. for. comm (soil surv): Alice Holt Lodge Farnham 1961–65; Edin 1965–68; dist off. soils res for. comm northern res stat Roslin 1968–74, head of site stud. res 1974–77, sen scient off. from 1977
m Aber 17.7.65 Rosalind A. Hay MB ChB 1965 *qv*

PYLE David MA 1968 Dip Ed 1969
s of Robert M. P. plumbers' warehouseman and Kathleen McHattie; b Aber 18.8.47
educ off. Kigezi h s Uganda 1969–71; teacher dep head Engl Hereford s Grimsby from 1972
m Aber 11.9.65 Irene H. Chester teleph/secy d of Edward H. C. Aber

PYLE Ronald Leslie MB ChB 1958
s of Thomas D. P. MB ChB(Glas) med pract and Mary A. Leslie poultry advis; b Hamilton 29.11.34
DObstRCOG 1960
h o: city hosp Aber, Bridge of Earn hosp, RI Perth 1958–60; short serv comm RAMC 1960–65; g p Blairgowrie from 1965
m Annan 25.11.66 Morna G. C. Vivers teacher dom sc d of Robert C. V. Annan

PYLE William Dryden MB ChB 1958
s of Thomas D. P. MB ChB(Glas) g p and Mary A. Leslie poultry advis; b Hamilton 29.11.34
DObstRCOG 1964 MRCGP 1968
h o Inv, City hosp Aber 1958–59; regt m o 13/18 R Hussars Malaya, Germany 1959–61; h o: Aber mat. hosp 1961–62, RHSC Glasg, Kirkwall 1963–66; g p: Camborne 1966–74, Canisbay from 1974
m Kirkwall 31.3.66 Jacqueline I. T. Turfus SRN d of John T.

PYPER Joy Patricia MA 1970
m Aber 8.8.80 Norman J. Dunbar

PYPER Robert Ferguson *BSc 1969

QAYUM Abdul MLitt 1969
MA(Panj)

QUINN Kevin BSc 1968

QURASHI Afzal Ahmad MB ChB 1963
s of Mohammed Rafique supt GIP rly Jhansi India and Bano Begum; b Jhansi 10.4.37
BSc(Sind Kar)
h o Woodend hosp Aber, ARI, Bellshill mat. hosp 1964–65; sen h o Kingseat hosp Aber 1965–66; m o City hosp Kano Nigeria 1966–69; prin in g p Witham from 1969
m Inv 19.2.66 Maureen Smart

RADCLIFFE Elaine Barbara *MA 1967
d of Percy R. farm. member House of Keys (Manx parl) and Barbara F. Crowe; b Ramsey I of M 2.4.43
part-time lect tech coll Carlisle 1968–69, stud. lib Napier coll Edin from 1975
m Sulby I of M 12.8.67 Michael W. Cartney BSc(eng) 1966 *qv*

RADDON David John *MA 1970

RAE Alison Christine MA 1964
d of Alan G. R. oil well eng and Aileen M. Henderson MA 1925 *qv*; b Digboi Assam India 14.5.43
teacher Edin 1965–69
m Aber 29.7.66 William A. R. Mutch MA 1963 *qv*

RAE Alison Fay MA 1962
d of Bennett B. R. MA 1926 *qv*; b Aber 27.7.41
asste Lycée St Jean d'Angély, France 1962–63; teacher: Montreal h s 1964–66, Ellon acad 1966–67, Cranhill s s Glasg 1967–70
m Aber 10.4.68 Alan M. Lamont MA 1960 *qv*

RAE Angus Chisholm BSc(agr) 1960 MSc 1962
s of Donald J. R. grain merch and Annie Adam; b Perth 10.7.38
grass breeder min of agr (NI) Loughgall 1962–63; plant breeder with Sinclair McGill Ayr from 1963
m Perth 2.5.64 Alison M. Brooke MA(Edin) teacher d of Peter T. B. Perth

RAE Annetta MA 1966
d of Charles S. R. elect. welder and Margaret McGinley ch nurse; b Glasg 31.3.45
teacher: Summerhill acad 1967–69, Wainwright h s Alberta Canada from 1969
m Aber 15.8.69 Donald M. Mackee BEd(Alta) teacher s of John J. M. Dornoch

RAE Beverley Anne BEd 1970
d of Arthur C. R. BSc(BC) corp vice-pres and Joy V. Robinson; b Paterson NJ USA 22.10.48
teacher Engl Kapuskasing h s Ont Canada from 1972
m Kapuskasing 22.6.73 Gérard Lalonde BEd(Montr) teacher

RAE Doreen Anne MA 1968 Dip Ed 1969
d of George M. W. R. contr and Annie M. Laird; b Insch 1.11.47
Aber: qual control asst 1969–70, teacher 1970, exec off. civ serv (supp benefits) 1970–76
m Aber 14.4.72 David J. Cameron BSc 1973 lect RGIT s of Thomas J. D. C. Aber

RAE Gordon *MEd 1969
s of John R. insur ag and Marion Dow nurse; b Rutherglen 21.7.45
BSc(Glas) 1967
teacher phys Aber 1969–71; lect educ psych Aber coll of educ from 1971

RAE Gordon Hogarth *BSc 1970
s of Robert R. comp dir and Margaret N. Gordon; b Huntly 10.4.47
fish farm. res: exper ecologist Unilever Lochailort from 1971

RAE Ian Livingstone *BSc 1968
s of William H. R. customs and excise off. and Irene B. Bowler; b Birkenhead 30.11.46
MSc(Strath) 1971
res asst Strath 1969–70; geol Noranda Kerr Portmadoc 1971–72; stud. teacher Glasg 1972; teacher: geog Glasg 1972–75, head of soc stud. Morant Bay Jamaica 1975–77, geog Stirling from 1977
m Blairlogie 9.12.78 Jane C. McLearie teacher d of James McG. McL. Clydebank

RAE John Edward MA 1965
s of William M. R. MA(Glas) asst chief constable and Grace B. Hutchison secy; b Glasg 24.5.44
CA 1970
CA Arthur Young McLelland Moores & Co Glasg 1970–72; govt audit. of Tonga Nuko'Alofa 1972–74; man. Thomson McLintock & Co CA Inv 1974–79; ptnr Morris & Young CA Perth from 1980
m Brora 17.10.70 Margaret C. Munro MA 1967 *qv*

RAE Maureen MA 1959
d of Douglas H. S. R. master baker and Jessie Guyan; b Aber 11.12.37
MEd(Exe) 1978
teacher: Engl/hist East Kilbride 1964–66, Glasg 1966–67; lect Leic 1967–68; head Engl dept Slough 1968–70; lect Engl Rolle coll Exmouth 1970–74, sen lect from 1974
m Largs 2.7.60 Sean Oliver (later called Lalor) liaison off. Dartmoor nat park s of John Oliver

RAE Norman John BSc 1967
s of Francis J. R. foreman stonemason and Mary B. K. Morrison shop asst; b Kintore 18.1.46
teacher maths/sc Kintore 1968–73; statist. Grampian police Aber from 1973

RAE Patricia MA 1970
d of Alexander R. wholesale egg merch and Myra Webster bookkeeper; b Aber 27.12.48
teacher geog Aber from 1971
m Aber 3.4.71 Alexander C. Wilson fish merch s of Alexander W. Aber

RAE Richard Bennet *BSc 1969
s of Bennet B. R. MA 1926 *qv*; b Aber 12.11.46
scient off. MoD (PE) AWRE Aldermaston from 1969

RAE Richard Gordon *MA 1964
s of Richard S. R. grocer and Mary A. Jamieson nurse; b Aber 23.11.32
LTCL 1960
teacher geog: Turriff acad 1965–67, Wallace Hall acad Dumfriessh 1967–73, Lawside RC acad Dun 1973–77, Menzieshill h s Dun from 1977
m Aber 10.9.68 Margaret M. Fraser civ serv d of William M. F. Aber

RAE Spence MA 1960

RAE William Philip MA 1970
s of William N. M. R. foreman eng and Audrey Philip clerkess; b Aber 7.12.48
teacher geog/hist/mod stud. Torry acad Aber from 1971
m Aber 16.10.71 Eileen M. Andrews secy d of Frederick M. S. A. Aber

RAFFAN Diana Marjory MA 1961
d of George A. R. men's outfitter and Betty K. Lamb; b Aber 20.12.40
teacher Bradford 1961–62, Aber 1962–64
m Aber 31.7.61 Donald I. MacKay MA 1959 *qv*

RAFFAN Jennifer Twort MA 1967
d of Alfred W. R. MB ChB 1938 *qv* and Jean C. Twort MB ChB 1939 *qv*; b Aber 10.11.45
Dip Secy St(Strath) 1968
secy: FCO Lond 1968–70, Brit emb Vienna 1970–72, centre for indust consult. and liaison univ of Edin 1973–74
m Aber 22.9.72 Anthony G. D. Johnston BA(Oxon) CA s of Hon Lord Douglas H. J. MA(Oxon) Edin

RAFFAN Rosemary Frances MA 1970
m Norfolk

RAHMAN Quazi Abu Taher Muhammad Habibur PhD 1965
s of Quazi S. Ahmed marr regist and Saleha Khatun; b Jhalakati Bangladesh 16.7.36
BSc(Dacca) 1958 MSc(Dacca) 1959 F Zool Soc Bangladesh 1974
Bangladesh: asst prof zool govt coll Sylhet 1965–68, Titumir coll Dacca 1969, Jagannath coll Dacca 1970–74; assoc prof zool Jagannath univ coll from 1975
m Dacca 27.10.68 Sufia Rahman d of Muhammad A. W. MSc(agr)(Calc) India

RAITT David Gordon MB ChB 1969
s of William J. R. MB ChB 1924 *qv*; b Aber 28.3.46
DA 1973
h o Aber 1969–70; m o RAF: Ballykelly NI 1970–71, Masirah Oman 1971–72; anaest RAF Ely Cambs from 1972
m Aber 1969 Elizabeth S. Davies MA 1969 *qv*

RAITT Douglas Ferrier Stewart *BSc 1957 PhD 1967
d Rome 27.11.76 *AUR* XLVII 215

RAITT John Stewart *BSc 1962
s of William J. R. MBChB 1925 *qv*; b Aber 13.6.39
Aust: geophys bureau of min resources Melbourne, Canberra 1962–65, Continental Oil Co Sydney 1965–68; Conoco: geophys Lond 1968–70, staff geophys Princeton USA 1970–72, area geophys Stamford USA 1972–74, man. geophys Cairo Egypt from 1974

RAKHA Ahmed Mohamed Hassan PhD 1965
BVSc(Cairo) FRVCS(Stockholm)

RALPH Alan John BSc 1970
s of Issac R. fisherman and Marion Snook; b Somerset 13.2.49
acct Edin from 1970
m Elgin 14.7.72 Susan M. Grant teacher d of Donald G. Elgin

RALPH Alison Joyce MA 1966
d of Thomas D. M. R. fisherman and Jessie S. Main nurse; b Elgin 28.8.45
teacher Fr/Engl Grantown g s 1967–68
m Burghead 19.7.68 Harry M. Ross BVMS(Edin) vet surg s of Alexander M. R. MA(Edin) Bonnyrigg

RALPH Marion Jean MA 1966
d of Isaac R. fisherman and Marion W. J. Snook retail asst/WRNS; b Butleigh 23.11.45
teacher Fr Peterhead acad from 1967
m Burghead 12.7.68 Michael J. McLintock MA 1968 *qv*

RAMADAN Isfendiar BSc 1960

RAMANATHAN Manickavasagar MB ChB 1961

RAMANATHAN Markandu MB ChB 1963

RAMANATHAN Perumal Chetty MSc 1964
BSc(agr)(Madras)

RAMCHARAN Conrad MB ChB 1966

RAMM Halldis Aslaug MB ChB 1963
d of Finn Kielland R. capt and Aslaug Ekeland; b Bergen Norway 1.10.37
DCH(Glas) 1969 DRCOG 1977
h o ARI, RACH 1963–64; g p: Fyvie 1965–66, Insch 1966–76; sen h o obst/gyn Raigmore hosp Inv 1976–77; g p Insch from 1977
m Fana Norway 25.7.61 Maitland Mackie BSc(agr) 1958 *qv*

RAMNAUTH Coomar Surendra *BSc(eng) 1969
s of Jai R. priest and Bhanmatie Sungh; b Guyana 5.11.44
eng MoW and commun Georgetown, Guyana from 1969
m Guyana 17.12.72 Sattie Sankar d of Kayman S. Essequibo Guyana

RAMSAY Andrew Douglas Kirk *MA 1970 Dip Ed 1973
s of William N. M. R. BSc(Edin) univ lect and Janet D. K. MacKendrick hosp sister; b Edin 5.7.47
MA(Manit) 1974 MEd(Tor) 1974
head warden Fetlar nature reserve Shetland 1972; teacher Edin, Lochaber h s Fort William, Kirkwall g s from 1975

RAMSAY Iain McRobert MSc 1970
s of John C. R. foreman joiner and Katherine J. McRobert nurs. sister; b Aber 18.2.44
Dip Arch.(RGIT) 1968 RIBA 1974 ARIAS 1975
lect arch. RGIT Aber 1970–73; arch./plan. Baxter, Clark & Paul Aber 1973–74; lect arch. RGIT from 1974
m Aber 27.8.71 Sandra A. Reid school matron, hotel housekeeper, shop man. d of Alexander R. Aber

RAMSAY Ian McKay MA 1962
s of William R. R. wine & spirit merch and Agnes S. Hill; b Dun 14.6.26
teacher hist AGS 1963–72, asst head 1972–74; sen master educ dept W Aust Perth; prin Carmel s Perth WA from 1976
m Aber 4.3.67 Isobel Pirie MA 1960 *qv*

RAMSAY Keith Michael Moynihan *MA 1958
s of Andrew M. R. MA 1923 *qv*; b Molleno Cape Province S. Af 5.12.33
LRAM(Sp and Drama) 1973
teacher Engl Finchley 1959–62; Surrey: head Engl/drama Frenshaw Heights 1962–73, artistic dir W Surrey youth theatre 1957–73, drama dir Dolmetsch festival 1973–74; lect drama Bishop Grosseteste coll of educ Lincoln from 1973
m West Wittering 13.7.57 Isabella M. O. Richards MA 1958 *qv*

RAMSAY Roderick Alan Macgregor *MA 1964

RAMSAY William Alexander *MA 1956
d 29.6.69

RANDALL Ian Maurice MA 1968 *1970
s of Leslie R. evangelist and Jeannie Ewen; b Wick 9.1.48
telecommun man. Lond 1970–72; admin elect. Brighton from 1972
m Aber 31.7.70 Janice B. Hughes MA 1970 *qv*

RANDALL Richard Frank *BSc(eng) 1967
s of Rex C. R. chartered surv/eng and Ethel Price; b Luton 28.2.45
MICE 1973
asst eng Sidcup 1967–69; site eng Mombasa Kenya 1969–71; des eng Lond 1971–73; sect. eng Potter's Bar Lond from 1973
m Harpenden 15.7.72 Charmian L. Houslander-Green BSc(S'ton) admin off. d of Derrick G. G. Kingswear

RANKIN Beryl Margaret Morton MA 1963
m McKay

RANKIN Bryan John MA 1966
s of Gerald M. R. pedigree cattle breeder/farm./comp dir and Sheena M. Brown; b Dumfries 14.7.45
CA 1969
Robertson & Maxtone Graham CA Edin: app CA 1966–69, qualif asst 1969–70, asst man. 1970–71, man. 1971–73, ptnr from 1973
m Aber 10.7.65 Kathleen E. Savage MA 1965 *qv*

RANKIN James MA 1965

RANKIN Sandra Mary MA 1969
d of Alexander I. R. fish salesman and Mary J. Craig shop asst; b Stonehaven 16.11.47
teacher maths: Peterhead acad 1970–72, Fraserburgh acad 1972–75
m Aber 2.7.71 John A. MacKinnon LLB 1968 *qv*

RAO Hebbule Venkola Gundu PhD 1963
MSc(Mysore)

RAPP Sandra Louise MA 1968

RATTRAY George Cheyne BSc(eng) 1960
s of George C. R. confectioner and Arthurina (Effie) Strachan clerkess; b Fraserburgh 6.2.39
MICE 1966
asst eng: Sir M. MacDonald & Ptnrs Norfolk 1960–61, Wm Tawse Banff/Aber 1961–62, Scot. dev dept Edin, Fort William 1962–65; asst resid eng Notts c c Cromwell 1965; Reid, Carter & Wilson: eng i/c Perth, Edin, Amersham from 1965, ptnr from 1969
m Denver 25.8.65 Ann Watson teacher d of Leslie R. W. Denver Norfolk

RATTRAY Graham Alexander Lindsay BSc(eng) 1968

RATTRAY Jennifer Elizabeth MA 1962
d of John B. R. pharm and Jessie D. George; b Elgin 27.5.41
Cert Secy Sc(Strath) 1963
Edin: secy/edit. asst *Accountants' Magazine* 1963–65, secy to sen ptnr Brodie, Cuthbertson & Watson WS 1965–68; Lond: secy to mineral broker 1968–71, pers asst to G. L. Bourne FRCS FRCOG Harley Street from 1971
m Russell

RAVEN John *BSc 1959

RAVEN Norman MA 1969 LLB 1971
s of Norman R. eng and Helen Buchan shop asst; b Fraserburgh 8.8.48
law app Fraserburgh 1971–73; solic Blairgowrie 1973–74; govt solic Edin from 1974
m Lonmay 17.10.75 Margaret B. Duthie MA 1969 *qv*

RAWSTHORNE George Brian MB ChB 1965
s of Joseph L. R. bldg contr and Caroline D. Ball; b Woolton Liv 5.5.37
FRCSE 1968 FRCS 1973
h o, sen h o Aber 1965–68; surg regist, sen surg regist Liv 1968–73; consult. surg Crewe from 1973
m Tain 10.9.66 Anne M. Mackenzie MB ChB 1965 *qv*

RAYMOND Barbara Pearl MA 1962
d of Emmanuel C. R. plant supt and Violet E. R. Gloudon; b Labrea Trinidad 27.5.37
teacher St Francois girls' s Port of Spain Trinidad 1962–64, Georgetown Guyana: teacher St Rose's h s 1964–65, St Joseph's h s 1965–67, Tutorial h s 1968–69; clerical asst Trinidad Tobago high comm 1971–72; teacher Providence girls' h s Port of Spain 1973–75, acting vice-prin from 1975
m Port of Spain 31.10.64 Edwin A. Jack BSc 1963 *qv*

REA Alan Michael *BSc 1970

READ Margaret MA 1968 Dip Ed 1969
d of Jack R. publ man. and Doris E. Cooper; b Richmond 1.12.43
teacher Aber: head mod lang dept Rosemount s s 1969–72, year mistress Summerhill acad 1972–73; teacher Fr Amer s Singapore 1974–76, Bundaberg Queensland Aust 1976
m Wokingham 31.8.68 Errol H. Gomes BSc 1967 *qv*

REAMSBOTTOM Stanley Baily *BSc 1968

REAPER Leslie James BSc(eng) 1970

REARY James Brown *BSc 1967 PhD 1970
s of James B. R. insur supt and Margaret R. Walker; b Fraserburgh 2.5.44
res fell.: univ of Virginia USA 1970–71, univ of Exeter 1971–73; sen residue analyst Fisons, Chesterford Park res stat from 1973
m Galashiels 25.7.70 Lilias T. Amos BEd 1969 *qv*

REASON Janet Mary BSc 1964
d of Eric F. R. insur dir and Violet E. Walker; b Worthing 19.11.42
asst clin path. ARI 1964–65; asst biochem Fisons Holmes Chapel Cheshire, Loughborough 1966–71
m Lond 12.10.68 Peter G. Killingback MSc(Manc) MPS res biol s of Ernest K. BSc(Lond) Enfield

REDFERN Derek Briddon *BSc(for) 1963

REDFORD Malcolm Kenneth *MEd 1970
s of Leonard K. R. BA(S'ton) dir educ and Mary Gardner; b S'ton 29.12.44
BSc(econ)(Hull) 1967 M Psych Soc 1970
teacher econ Hove g s from 1969; external examiner AEB from 1973, Oxford from 1976
m Guernsey 11.7.67 Rachel M. Plummer MA 1968 *qv*

REDSHAW Edward Stephen *BSc 1958
s of George E. R. livestock off. Jamaica and Mary V. Thomson; b Jamaica 24.9.35
M Agr(C Rica) 1965 PhD(Alta) 1968
agr off. govt Jamaica 1958–63; farms supt Reynold

Jamaica mines 1968–70; Canada: res assoc Alta 1970–73; head plant sect. soil and feed testing lab govt of Alberta from 1973
m Kingston 2.9.59 Marguerite A. Silvera hair stylist d of Chandos J. S. Jamaica

REECE Anne Pauline *MA 1969

REED Alexander Cheyne *MA 1957

REEKIE Gladys *MA 1956
d of Richard M. R. travel courier, shipping clerk and Vera I. Faulkner shorthand typist; b Aber 25.3.34
Aber: lib asst 1956–57, spec tech reader to printer AUP from 1957
m Aber 29.3.63 George S. Menhinick civ serv

REES Wendy Anne MSc 1966
BSc(Lond)

REEVES Thomas Joseph PhD 1966
BA(S Carolina) BD(Columb)

REIACH Maureen Annand MA 1961
m Johnston

REID Alan MA 1967
s of William R. bank man. and Ellen S. Dunnett; b Edin 21.5.46
Dip Pers Man.(RGIT) 1968
pers off.: Manc 1968–73, Balloch 1973; reg pers off./training man. Glasg from 1973
m Manc 10.10.70 Linda Slater secy d of Harry K. S. Stretford Manc

REID Alan Robert MB ChB 1966
s of Robert R. comm trav and Catherine M. Craigmile; b Aber 22.11.43
h o Aber hosps 1966–67; g p: Aber 1967–68, Wick 1968–75, Cumbernauld 1975–76; indust m o Middlesbrough from 1977
m Aber 29.12.65 Mary R. Halley MA 1963 *qv*

REID Alice Margaret Chree MA 1957
d of Charles J. R. farm. and Mary Cockburn MA 1929 *qv*; b Stonehaven 8.10.36
teacher Kincardinesh 1958–62; secy SCSS Islay 1971–73; teacher Perth from 1978
m Aber 8.10.59 Alexander S. Collie MA 1954 *qv*

REID Alison Alexandra Margaret *MA 1969
d of William R. civ serv and Margaret B. Smith nurse; b Irvine 26.8.47
LRAM 1970
teacher mus: Banff 1970–71, Elgin 1971–74; asst mus organis Moray and Nairn 1974–76; teacher mus Elgin 1976–77
m Elgin 26.7.75 William G. Knox marine eng s of William C. K. New Elgin

REID Alison Anne MA 1970
d of Alexander R. gen merch and Christabel M. Stuart secy; b Aber 30.1.49
teacher Engl/relig educ Bankhead acad 1971–72
m Aber 31.8.70 William A. McWhirr MA 1971 teacher bus. stud. s of Peter F. McW. Banff

REID Atholl *BSc(eng) 1964

REID Christina Legge MA 1956
d of Thomas R. farm. and Eleanor A. McIntosh; b Rathven 22.5.36
teacher: Portessie j s s 1957–60, Lhanbryde j s s 1961–62, asst head Heathery Knowe p s from 1963
m Buckie 12.4.60 Donald S. Miller caterer s of William M. Wick

REID David Douglas MB ChB 1957
s of Douglas R. rly clerk and Janet W. Stephen nurse; b Huntly 28.4.33
FRCGP 1968
h o: ARI, RACH 1957–58, Latrobe Tasmania 1959–61; g p Alford 1961–64; Tasmania: dist m o Maydena 1964–65, g p Wynyard from 1965
m Cooee Tasmania 3.4.61 Anne Turnidge teacher d of Leonard E. T. Burnie Tasmania

REID David Jackson MA 1969
s of Eric W. R. BMus(Edin) teacher and Isobel S. Jackson BMus(Edin) teacher; b Edin 12.3.48
CA 1975
acct Edin from 1969
m Edin 7.10.72 Inez G. Henderson SRN d of James H. Runcorn

REID Dennis MB ChB 1967

REID Derek Donald MA 1967

REID Doreen Violet *MA 1964
m Presly

REID Dorothea Lesley Thomson MA 1969
d of John R. acct and Maria A. Smith teacher; b Peterhead 27.8.48
Dip Sec(City of Lond poly); MInst Health Serv Admin
Lond: secy: to chmn/man. dir Astor Petrochem 1970–71; to head of man. dev Brit inst of man. 1971–72; gen admin asst Hammersmith hosp 1972–75; dep sector admin St Mary's hosp from 1975

REID Dorothy Joan *MA 1970 Dip Ed 1971
d of Albert G. R. asst distill man. and Harriet Simpson; b Rhynie 15.6.48
teacher maths Inverurie acad 1971–74
m Kennethmont 14.7.73 Ian D. Pirie farm. s of Ian D. P. Turriff

REID Duncan Harman BSc(agr) 1957
s of Walter A. R. farm. and Christine N. Harman; b Brechin 4.9.35
nat serv UK, Christmas Is 1957–59; anim nutrit dept (farms) J. Bibby & Sons Liv 1960–65; poultry farm. Perth 1965–71, poultry and gen farm. Brechin from 1971
m Southport 17.8.62 Brenda M. Hughes BA(Liv) teacher d of Frederick H. Southport

REID Eileen Mary *MA 1965
d of Joseph R. and Elsie M. McKenzie; b Ellon 6.5.44
teacher geog/Engl Bankhead acad 1966–67; head geog dept Murang'a s s Kenya 1968–69; acting prin teacher geog Northfield acad Aber 1971–72; teacher remed maths Summerhill acad from 1973
m Aber 23.3.67 James W. Lorimer MA 1964 *qv*

REID Eric James MA 1957 PhD 1961
d 20.8.70 *AUR* XLIV 112

REID Euphemia Mitchell MA 1968
d of William M. R. range oper MoD and Jessie B. McLean; b Rosehearty 3.4.47
teacher: Rosehearty p s 1969–70, Scotstown p s Aber from 1970
m Aber 5.9.68 James Taylor DA teacher sculpture/ceramics s of James T. Rosehearty

REID Gavin Clydesdale *MA 1969

REID George Gordon *MA 1968
s of George R. burgh surv and Gertrude P. Scott; b Forfar 20.11.46
Dip Pers Man.(RGIT) 1970
labourer Aber 1968–69; naval off. from 1970

REID George Greig Forbes *MA 1961 MEd 1965

REID George Guilland *BSc(eng) 1969
s of George T. H. R. DD 1969 *qv*; b Edin 25.11.46
MSc(UCNW) 1970 MIEE C Eng 1975
des eng indust dev unit UCNW Bangor 1970–72; consult. marine consults. YARD Glasg from 1972

REID George William *MA 1967
s of William R. papermaking machineman and Ethel Young; b Aber 15.7.44
PhD stud. King's coll Lond 1967–69; lect phil univ of IFE, Ile-Ife Nigeria 1969–72; asst rep Brit Council Maseru, Lesotho from 1972
m Blackburn Aberdeensh 24.6.67 Sheila E. Sim MA 1967

REID Gordon Findlay MB ChB 1968
s of Alfred R. bank man. and Emil Catherine Findlay; b Aber 6.8.45
FRCSE 1972
h o, sen h o ARI 1968–72; regist surg: N'cle hosps 1972–73, ARI 1973–76; regist urology N'cle 1976–78; res fell. Inst of Urology Lond from 1979

REID Hamish George *BSc(eng) 1968
s of James W. R. chief clerk of works Aber c and Isabella C. Kennedy leg. secy; b Aber 3.2.46
asst civ eng: Scott Wilson Kirkpatrick & Ptnrs Lond 1968–69, Glasg corp 1969–76, sen civ eng Strath reg c from 1976
m Glasg 21.3.70 Marjory E. Murchie MA 1968 *qv*

REID Hamish Peter BSc(agr) 1959

REID Ian Maitland BSc(agr) 1963
s of Adam M. R. man. dir and Catherine C. Walker; b Aber 5.11.41
Master Nutrit Sc(Corn) 1965 PhD(Corn) 1967
res asst Cornell univ 1963–67; post doct fell. Pittsburg s of med 1967–70; exper path. ARC Newbury from 1970
m Aber 20.8.66 Sally M. Paterson nurse d of George A. P. Aber

REID Ian Stewart MA 1966 *1968

REID Ida Engel MA 1970
(conferred for long service of exceptional merit)
d of Ernest V. Tetzner and Barbara Henderson; b Aber 11.7.05
member of admin staff Aberd 1929–70

REID Ivan William *BSc 1969

REID James Bruce BSc(eng) 1969

REID James Bryce *MA 1967
s of Gavin B. R. bank cashier and Emily E. Graham; b Glasg 12.4.41
MSc(H-W) 1969
town plan. asst Scot. dev off. Edin 1969–71; asst town plan. Glasg 1971–74; developer Nairobi from 1974
m Edin 29.3.70 Mary Magrys secy

REID James Dures *MA 1969
s of James T. R. BL(Glas) solic and Ann Dures; b Aber 9.4.47
NCB: admin asst 1969–71; Harrow: acct-opencast exec 1971–74, head contr sect.-opencast exec 1974–78; purchasing and contr man. Lond from 1978

REID James Milroy BSc 1967 *MEd 1972
s of David R. clerk and Mary Milroy; b Glasg 23.3.46
teacher Torry acad 1968–73; educ psych: Aber ch guid centre 1973–74, Suffolk s psych serv Bury St Edmunds from 1974
m Aber –.11.68 Moira K. Farquharson MA 1971 d of John F. Aber; marr diss 1974

REID Joan Heather *MA 1957

REID Joan McKenzie MA 1963
d of Joseph R. woollen mill worker and Elsie A. A. McKenzie; b Ellon 16.1.42
teacher Aber: Engl Summerhill acad 1964–70, prin guid Summerhill acad 1970–71, prin remed Northfield acad from 1979
m Aber 15.7.64 Alexander J. Sadler MA 1961 *qv*

REID John MB ChB 1959 MD 1967
s of Stanley R. comp dir and Hilda Wood; b Leeds 15.3.33
h o Woodend hosp Aber, Nott city hosp 1959–60; lt, capt RAMC Cyprus 1960–63; regist dermat Bradford RI 1963–65; Squibb res fell. skin hosp Manc 1965–67; g p/dermat Jersey CI from 1967
m Cyprus 18.2.60 Alice P. A. Chua d of Kai Hai C. Singapore

REID (Iain) John Cowie Dunlop *BSc 1967 MSc 1970
s of John D. R.; b Buckie 10.11.44
asst tech man. Harlow from 1974

REID John Geddes *MA 1966
s of John R. joiner and Mary Geddes; b Buckie 13.9.44
teacher geog: Powis s s Aber, Tertowie resid s 1967–68, Aberlour s s, Mortlach s s 1968–69, A. N. Myer s s Niagara Falls Can 1969–71, Maxwellton h s 1971–73, Kirkcaldy h s, Balwearie h s from 1973
m Inv 4.4.69 Anne M. Barton BEd 1969 *qv*

REID John MacBean *MA 1961
s of John R. acct and Maria A. Smith teacher; b Peterhead 3.11.38
Rowntree Mackintosh: market asst 1961–65, brand man. 1965–69, prod. group man. 1969–77, market dir from 1977
m York 17.10.64 Norma F. Kendall clerk d of Joseph K. York

REID John Mackay MSc 1964
A H-W C

REID John Paul *BSc 1968 MSc 1970

REID John Sinclair *BSc 1964 PhD 1970
s of Norman S. R. CA and Mildred E. Watkis; b Rickmansworth 9.5.42
lect nat phil Aberd from 1968
m Aber 24.9.70 Aenea J. Nicol PhD 1974 progr advis d of Anderson N. MA(Glas)

REID John Spence Grant *BSc 1964 PhD 1967
s of John G. R. painter/decorator and Helen Spence; b Huntly 27.3.42
Royal Society European progr fell. univ of Fribourg Switzerland 1967–69; asst lect biochem Nott 1967–69, chef de travaux (lect) inst de Biologie Végétale univ of

Fribourg 1970–73; lect biochem Stir from 1974
m Aber 24.7.64 Maureen Donald BSc 1966 *qv*

REID Katharine Isabella MA 1956
m MacLennan

REID Kathleen Ann *MA 1969
d of John C. N. R. fish merch and Frances K. Horne teacher; b Aber 12.10.46
Dip Soc Admin(Liv) 1970 Dip App Soc Stud.(Dund) 1971
med soc worker: Stracathro hosp Brechin, ARI 1971–72, part-time ARI from 1974
m Aber 14.4.71 Colin D. Sinclair MB ChB 1971 g p s of David C. S. MB ChB(St And) Perth W Aust

REID Kenneth Bannerman Milne *BSc 1965 PhD 1968
s of John R. acct and Maria A. Smith teacher; b Peterhead 22.9.43
scient off. fisheries biochem res unit Aber 1968–69; ICI res fell. biochem Oxon 1969–71; MRC immunochem unit dept biochem Oxon: member MRC scient staff from 1971
m Aber 10.9.69 Margery R. Gilmour lab tech d of Thomas G. Aber

REID Lorna Anne MA 1965 Dip Ed 1966
m Brown

REID Margaret Elspeth *MA 1970
d of Norman S. R. CA and Mildred E. Watkis secy; b Watford 28.9.46
res asst Aberd 1970–71; post grad stud. Edin 1971–73; lect med sociol Glas from 1973
m Glasg David F. Hamilton BSc(Edin) lect s of David A. H. BA(Lond) Bury St Edmunds

REID Marjory Blair *MA 1969
m Dooley

REID Mary Catherine *MA 1957
d of Charles A. R. gardener and Elspeth R. Jaffray; b Insch 19.12.35
teacher Walsall 1959–61
m Aber 7.10.61 William M. Broomfield BSc(eng) 1959 *qv*

REID Maureen MA 1970
d of Walter Reid sen insp and Dorothy W. Thomson; b Aber 30.5.49
teacher Engl Karlshamn Sweden 1971–73; civ serv/receptionist PER 1974; typist (Swedish and Spanish) mod lang dept Aberd 1974–75, sen secy from 1975
m Aber 1.7.70 Stig Z. Fritzon chem eng s of Valter K. F. Karlshamn

REID Norman Haydn LLB 1969
s of Harry R. civ serv and Marjory G. Christie; b Aber 16.3.48
CA 1973
fin. acct Kleinerts of Europe Perth 1973–74; man. acct Scotsman publ Edin 1974–76; asst acct St Cuthbert's Co-op Assoc 1976–78; chief acct Northern Co-op Soc Aber from 1979
m Aber 28.7.71 Patricia C. Robertson MA 1970 *qv*

REID Robert Leslie PhD 1957
BSc BAgr(Belf)

REID Robert Thomas Fraser *MA 1969

REID Robin Davidson *MA 1969
s of Robert R. eng and Jessie E. Davidson MA 1928 *qv*; b Cairo 22.11.46
MA(Lond) 1973
teacher hist: Pollards Hill h s Mitcham 1970–74, Kingsdale s Dulwich Lond from 1974
m Aber 28.8.70 Elizabeth M. McConachie MA 1969 *qv*

REID Stella Frances MA 1970
d of Alexander W. R. tea planting advis and Mary E. Simpson teacher; b S India 21.9.49
teacher: drama Edin 1971–73, Engl Örebro Sweden 1973–74; drama Edin from 1974
m Aber 5.8.74 Colin J. Youngson MA 1970 *qv*

REID Stewart *MA 1966 Dip Ed 1967
s of Stewart R. eng and Jeannie Skakle; b Aber 8.11.42
teacher AGS 1967–72; prin mod lang Linksfield acad from 1972
m Elgin 1.8.69 Jennifer A. Masson teacher d of William A. M. Spey Bay

REID Thomas Myles Sutherland *BMedBiol 1969 MB ChB 1972
s of George R. MA 1939 *qv*; b Aber 31.7.48
h o ARI 1972–73; lect bact Aberd 1973–78; consult. bact City hosp Aber from 1978
m Perth 5.9.75 Marjory H. Robertson

REID Veronica BEd 1969
d of William R. farm. and Helen D. Morrison MA (Edin) teacher; b Meikleour Perthsh 3.10.47
teacher Fr: Dun 1969, Essex 1970; lib asst Essex 1970–73; admin asst: Oxford 1973, Hertford from 1973

REID William Gordon BSc(agr) 1968
s of William F. R. BSc(agr) 1935 *qv*; b Dun Montrose 25.12.46
BSc(Dund) 1979
farm. Montrose 1968–76; stud. Dund 1976–79; res microbiol Brist from 1979
m Montrose 17.2.73 Alison H. Rae MA(Edin) market. co-ordinator d of William R. Lond

REID William Macpherson MA 1959 LLB 1962
s of William A. R. master butcher and Mabel McLeod; b New Elgin 6.4.38
admitted advoc 1963; sheriff: Lothian & Borders July 1978, Glasg & Strathkelvin Oct 1978
m Geneva 18.9.71 Vivien A. Eddy d of Thomas B. D. E. FRICS Wisbech

REID William Mitchell *BSc(eng) 1967

REID William Thomas LLB 1965
s of Thomas H. R. BSc(St And) teacher and Annabella McIntosh MA 1930 *qv*; b Inv 5.12.44
law app Aber 1965–67; leg. asst: Aber 1967–69, Ellon 1969–70, Edin 1970–72; ptnr Edin from 1972
m Dun 24.7.71 Catriona M. Houston asst dom supt Edin RI d of John G. H. Dun

REILLY John Francis MA 1967

REILLY Patricia *MA 1968
d of John R. tile fixer and Catherine McKinlay; b Glasg 14.6.47
Dip Ed(Glas) 1969
teacher Engl: Glasg 1969–74, Alva 1974–76; prin Engl Alloa from 1976
m Glasg 28.6.74 James Rafferty BA(Stir) draughtsman, teacher, man. s of George R. Glasg

REITH Edna Harrison MA 1963
d of Harrison R. baker and Jessie Stables; b Keith 6.9.42

teacher Prestonpans 1964–67; lib Montreal 1967; journalist Lond from 1967

REITH Margaret Elizabeth *MA 1962
d of Harrison R. baker and Jessie Stables; b Keith 11.9.40
teacher Newmarket 1962–66; part-time work in adult illiteracy progr Reading from 1975
m Cambridge 28.3.64 Colin H. Walker MSc 1961 *qv*

RENDALL Ian Alexander *BSc(eng) 1970
s of Alexander R. grocer and Elizabeth J. Macdonald; b Wick 9.7.48
eng Aber from 1970
m Aber 14.12.70 Johan Simpson teacher d of James S. Thurso

RENDALL Margaret MA 1967
s of David J. R. farm. and Mary C. Clyne; b Deerness Kirkwall 23.4.46
m Kirkwall 19.7.68 John C. Garden lorry driver s of James G. New Deer

RENDALL Ruth MA 1969 Dip Ed 1970
d of John R. farm. and Anne E. Harvey nurse; b Kirkwall 19.12.48
teacher Stromness 1970–75
m Finstown 19.12.73 Maxwell C. St C. Tait farm. s of Eric St C. T. Dounby

RENNEY Ian Telford MB ChB 1965

RENNIE Alistair MA 1968
s of George R. shipyard worker and Edith R. Connon; b Aber 10.3.39
Rolls-Royce Derby: O & M off. 1968–69, expenditure plan. off. 1970–73, prod. support acct from 1973
m Aber 8.10.66 Sheila A. Ewen secy d of James E. Aber

RENNIE Clifford Alfred John *MA 1969 *BD 1972
s of Charles R. chief stoker and Margaret W. Rosser; b Aber 15.7.43
C of S min: asst Garthdee Aber 1972–74, Altnaharra and Farr Sutherland from 1974
m Aber 2.7.74 Fiona M. Sheach nurs sister d of James M. S. Dufftown

RENNIE Donald Gordon MA 1968 LLB 1970
s of Gordon R. bldr and Flora MacLeod; b Aber 25.4.47
Edin: law app 1970–72, leg. asst Bonar, Mackenzie & Kermack WS 1972–73, ptnr 1973–75; ptnr Connell & Connell WS from 1977
m Glasg 10.9.71 Brenda L. Dewar LLB 1969 *qv*

RENNIE Graeme William John *MA 1970
s of Francis J. R. area eng PO(tel) and Joan Davie nurse; b Aber 3.6.39
MA(Cantab) 1975
res asst hist Aberd 1970–72; admin off. Cantab from 1972
m Aber 30.3.63 Audrey M. E. Thomson secy d of James H. T. Dunphail

RENNIE Ian *MA 1969

RENNIE James BSc 1962

RENNIE Morag Flora *MA 1966
m Duncan

RENNIE Morna Mabel Wilson BEd 1970
d of William J. R. blacksmith/welder and Mabel B. Wilson; b Aber 27.11.46
teacher p s Peterhead 1970–74
m Dyce 22.12.73 Alistair A. Clarke elect. eng s of Thomas C. Aber

RENNIE Pamela Margaret MA 1965
d of John H. M. R. shoe shop prop. and Frances D. Ingram; b Ellon 2.3.44
teacher Fr Aber acad 1966–68; peripatetic teacher prim. Fr Aber 1968–69
m Aber 15.8.67 Owen Rowlands MA 1967 *qv*

RENNIE Thomas George LLB 1968

RENNIE William McKenzie BSc 1965 Dip Ed 1966
s of William H. R. shopkeeper and Alexandrina McKenzie shopkeeper; b Aber 8.7.27
teacher phys Bankhead acad 1966–68, spec asst phys RGC 1968–72, prin phys Keith g s from 1972
m Elgin 26.12.76 Mabel Coggs MA(Edin) teacher d of John M. C. Nairn

RENTON Ross Langlands MB ChB 1958
s of David R. R. pharm and Margaret C. Black; b Berwick-on-Tweed 28.11.33
DIH 1963
h o Woodend hosp Aber, N Ormesby hosp Middlesbrough 1959–60; govt m o Barakin Laki N. Nigeria 1960–62; asst indust m o Slough indust health serv 1963–65; Nicholas res lab Slough: med advis 1965–72, dir med serv UK 1972–74, dir group med serv 1974–76; g p from 1976
m(1) Aber 6.8.56 Kathleen Ironside
(2) Beaconsfield 4.3.78 Jennifer Smith

RENUCCI Luigi Sileno *MA 1968

REPPER Dorothy Aileen MA 1956
d of William R. shipbroker and Alice W. Alcock secy; b Aber 28.1.35
teacher Inchgarth p s Aber 1957–63
m Aber 25.7.62 Alasdair D. Campbell scient civ serv s of George I. D. C. Banchory

REPPER Margaret Alcock MA 1959
d of William R. shipbroker and Alice W. Alcock secy; b Aber 17.10.38
Dip Soc St(Edin) 1960 AMIMSW 1961
med soc worker Glasg RI 1961–69
m Aber 12.10.68 Richard C. Hill BSc(Glas) sen lect acct coll of tech Glasg s of Richard T. W. H. Bearsden

RETTIE Charles Young Stuart MB ChB 1958

RETTIE Doreen Lilian MB ChB 1965
m Aitken

RETTIE Marlene Elspeth MA 1959

RETTIE Sheila Mitchell MA 1970
b Aber 1949
admin asst Legal & Gen Insur Co Lond 1970–71; teacher: Lond 1971, Victoria educ dept Euroa Aust 1972–74

REVEL Karl Jarvey Thomson BEd 1970
s of William T. R. MA(Glas) C of S min and Lilian M. A. Cluness; b Lonmay 19.8.46
teacher Peterhead 1970–73; head: Maud p s 1973–77, Pitfour p s Mintlaw from 1977
m Rathen 6.7.71 Mabel Buchan MA 1969 *qv*

REVERON Ruido Angel Esteban MSc 1968 PhD 1971
DMB(Venez)

RHEAD Celia Margaret BSc 1968
d 13.7.68

RHIND Eileen Margaret BEd 1969
d of John M. R. surv Customs & Excise and Beatrice Leigh; b Glasg 30.11.47
p s teacher: Methil 1969–70, Sheffield 1970–71, Inv 1971–72
m Inv 11.8.70 Richard J. Ardern BSc 1969 *qv*

RHIND Gordon Baird MB ChB 1965
s of Gordon R. publican and Williamina M. Baird; b Huntly 30.8.38
h o ARI 1965–66; g p Cults, Aber from 1966
m Aber 12.8.66 Doreen A. Walker fashion buyer d of George A. C. W. Aber

RHODES Hilary Margaret MA 1969
d of Albert S. R. comp secy/bursar and Helen M. Leach; b Shipley 6.6.48
teacher Fr/Span Brechin h s 1970–74
m Aber 7.7.71 Douglas B. Mutch MA 1969 *qv*

RIACH Alan Bryson BSc(eng) 1968
s of William J. R. farm. and Isobel Tough; b Botriphnie 18.10.45
des internat harvester comp Doncaster 1968–70; des, sect. leader, des eng Scammell lorries Watford 1970–73; des eng Leyland motors Lancs 1973–77; eng man. Leyland vehicles Bathgate from 1977
m Watford 26.5.73 Cynthia I. Tingle teacher d of Trevor H. Walterstone

RIACH Alison-Mary *BSc 1963
d of Joseph T. R. civ eng and Alison K. Christie clerkess/pa; b Aber 14.9.41
MIBiol 1975
teacher sc Currie h s Midlothian 1964–67; first asst biol Benwell s N'cle-u-Tyne 1967–69; prin biol Hylton Red House comp s Sunderland 1970–72, head sciences from 1972
m Aber 3.4.67 Hedworth F. Oliver eng, ski instructor, ski s and sports man. s of Hedworth O. Sunderland

RIACH Doreen Mary MA 1966
d of George R. bank man. and Eveline M. S. Tulloch teacher; b St Andrews 20.10.45
Froebel Cert 1968 Madeline McIver schol 1968
Marchburn inf s Aber: teacher 1968–69, i/c nursery class 1969–70; teacher i/c nursery Milton House Edin 1970–71
m Aber 27.12.70 Robert W. Black MA 1969 *qv*

RIACH Douglas Cameron *MA 1968
s of Ronald A. C. Riach grocer and Margaret Douglas; b Crail 8.8.46
MLitt(Edin) 1970 PhD(Edin) 1976
visiting sen schol Amer council of learned societies 1972; lect Jyväskylä Finland 1973–76; res fell. Charles Warren Center Harvard 1976–77
m Aber 29.12.71 Anne F. Donaldson MA 1969 *qv*

RICE Alison Findlay *MA 1969
d of James I. R. MB ChB 1939 *qv* and Jane M. F. Scroggie MA 1936 *qv*; b Stafford 19.11.47
BPhil(Oxon) 1971
lib asst Oxford 1971–73; teacher Harris 1974–77
m Aber 24.8.73 Andrew J. D. Johnson BA(Cantab) teacher, now hotel prop.

RICE Charles Duncan *MA 1964
s of James I. R. MB ChB 1939 *qv* and Jane M. F. Scroggie MA 1936 *qv*; b Aber 20.10.42
PhD(Edin) 1969
Henry fell. Harvard USA 1965–66; lect hist Aberd 1967–69; Yale USA: fell. Amer council of learned societies 1969–70, asst prof hist 1970–75, dean Saybrook coll 1972–74, 1975–77, Morse fell. 1974–75, assoc prof hist from 1975
m Providence Rhode Is USA 2.7.67 Susan I. Wunsch MLitt 1970 *qv*

RICE William Patrick BSc(agr) 1960
s of William J. R. MRCVS(Glas) vet surg; b Montrose
sugar agronomist Booker's sugar comp Blairmont Guyana 1960–62; agr advis/reg cattle advis Scot. and N Eng J. Bibby & Sons 1962–68; agr off. Bahamas Govt Nassau 1968–73; gen man. Caledonian farms Grand Cayman, Cayman Is BWI from 1973
m Chester 3.4.65 Dorothy Sharp d of John S. Abergele N Wales

RICHARDS David William Lawson MB ChB 1965
s of Robert L. R. MB ChB 1932 *qv* and Margaret B. Howieson MA 1933 *qv*; b Mount Vernon 18.5.41
DObstRCOG 1967 MRCGP 1975
h o Aber hosps 1965–67; sen h o City hosp Aber 1967–68; regist Aber hosps 1968; g p Cults 1968–9, Cults/Culter from 1969
m Aber 23.9.66 Margaret R. Esslemont nurs sister d of J. Bryce E. BL 1928 *qv*

RICHARDS Isabella Margaret Olivier MA 1958
d of William A. R. MB ChB(Lond) surg regist/g p and Noel Olivier MB ChB consult. phys/paediat; b Lond 4.5.33
m West Wittering 13.7.57 Keith M. M. Ramsay MA 1958 *qv*

RICHARDS Maureen Elizabeth MA 1970
d of Frederick J. R. police serg and Elizabeth H. Davidson hosp receptionist; b Fraserburgh 7.6.49
teacher Fr/Engl Milne's h s Fochabers 1971–74
m Keith 7.7.72 George C. Newlands stone mason DoE s of George N. Lumsden

RICHARDS Peter Robin *BSc 1970
s of Ronald R. supt regist and Olive C. Slater; b Brist 10.1.47
PhD(CNAA) 1977 FZS 1976 FLS 1976

RICHARDS Susan Jane *MA 1970

RICHARDSON Colin Geoffrey BSc 1967

RICHARDSON Fraser MB ChB 1968
s of Frank R. exec off. HM customs and excise and Isobel A. Fraser secy; b Lynchmere 9.6.44
ARI: h o, sen h o 1968–70, regist gen med 1970–74; g p Aber from 1974
m Aber 20.11.71 Cynthia Ford nurse d of Sydney W. J. F. Dunfermline

RICHARDSON Ian Milne PhD 1956
s of William A. R. solic and Elizabeth C. Milne; b Edin 4.3.22
MB ChB(Edin) DPH(Glas) 1948 MD(Edin) 1953 FRCPE 1956 JP 1960 FRCGP 1973
Aberd: sen lect group med 1956–68, reader gen pract 1968–70, James MacKenzie prof gen pract from 1970
m Glasg 12.10.46 Mary S. C. Gibb teacher d of William W. G. Wishaw

RICHARDSON William Henry *MA 1967 MEd 1973

RICHES Kenneth Maurice PhD 1962
s of Maurice W. R. compositor and Ivy Livermore; b Lond 29.10.36
CChem MRIC 1959
res chem: Shell plastics lab Manc 1961–65, Deutsche Shell Bonn Ger 1965–66, Shell agr res centre Kent 1966–71, Shell res Thornton Chester from 1971
m Manc 21.12.63 Jean Stewart d of James S. Manc

RICHMOND Eileen Elizabeth Hope MA 1965
d of John H. R. publican and Helen M. J. Mitchell shopkeeper; b Aber 13.12.42
teacher maths/sc Summerhill acad Aber 1966–71
m Aber 19.12.69 John Martin coxswain/mech s of John G. M. Aber

RICHMOND Helen Morag Hope MA 1969 Dip Ed 1970
m Cults 1.9.80 Charles J. Croydon s of John C. Ipswich

RICHMOND William *BSc 1965
s of James W. R. MRCS LRCP(Lond) g p and Joan Brander BA(Lond) teacher, lect tech coll, magistrate; b Peterborough 6.12.41
Dip Indust Man. 1966
agr zool, tech market. asst Lond 1966–71; teacher Croydon 1971–75; fin. admin Lond from 1975

RICHMOND-WATSON Marilyn Olivia MA 1967

RICKETTS John Anthony LLB 1966

RIDDELL Alexander Gall MA 1956
d 18.6.71

RIDDELL Alexander John MA 1965 Dip Ed 1966
s of John M. R. blacksmith and Elizabeth S. L. Gray; b Aber 4.1.44
teacher: Engl/hist Middle s s Aber 1966–68, hist Powis acad from 1968, prin guid from 1973
m Aber 23.6.79 Elizabeth M. Millar BSc 1964 *qv*

RIDDELL Andrew Alexander MA 1967
s of George A. R. BCom 1929 *qv*; b Lond 15.3.44
MA(E Ang) 1975
trainee lib Birkbeck coll Lond 1967–68; bookseller Cologne, tech translator Paris 1968–69; teacher: Hillingdon educ auth 1970–72, Engl g s centre for Brit teachers in Europe Braunschweig W Ger 1972–74, Engl g s centre for Brit teachers in Europe Rheinberg W Ger 1975–76; trainee interpreter, asst interpreter EEC Comm Brussels from 1976
m Lond 20.7.74 Carol A. Ross BA(Tor) teacher d of Clancy A. R. Toronto

RIDDELL George Steedman *BMedBiol 1970 MB ChB 1973
s of George S. R. MD 1949 *qv*; b Aber 27.2.48
h o: Dumfries 1973–74, Aber 1974; Aber: sen h o anaest 1974–75, regist anaest 1975–78; sen regist anaest Cardiff from 1978

RIDDELL Joan Harriet MA 1966 Dip Ed 1967
d of Robert R. bank man. BA(OU) and Janet G. Sutherland; b Inv 30.6.45
teacher: Helmsdale p s 1967–71; relief Fr/Engl/prim. and remed subj Sutherland from 1971
m Kirkmichael 26.7.69 George T. H. Murray joiner/woodwork instr f e centre

RIDDELL Linda Elizabeth MA 1968
d of John M. R. blacksmith and Elizabeth S. L. Gray tailoress/shop asst; b Aber 19.4.47
teacher: Menstrie 1969–74, Grangemouth from 1974

RIDDELL Margaret Isobel *MA 1965 Dip Ed 1966

RIDDELL Patricia Ann BSc 1962
m Daniels

RIDDELL Robert Gordon *BSc 1968
s of Albert R. poultry farm. and Anne Drummond poultry farm.; b Glasg 9.5.46
paper-coating tech: Cardiff 1968–72, Blackburn from 1972
m Weston-s-Mare 13.3.71 Kay Reeks nurse d of Eric W. R. Calcutta

RIDDELL Ronald MA 1957
s of Frederick G. R. monumental mason/blacksmith's hammerman and Violet Urquhart sales asst; b Aber 24.3.35
2/lt RAEC garrison educ off. SAAA Manorbier Wales 1958–60; teacher: Middlefield p s Aber 1960–62, spec in relig educ Bell–Baxter h s Cupar 1962–64, prin asst relig educ Aber acad 1964–68; lect relig educ Jordanhill coll of educ Glasg 1968–74; advis in relig educ Aber educ comm 1974–75; Gramp reg councillor from 1975
m Aber 26.7.63 Agnes Webster MA 1978 lab asst d of Alexander W. Aber

RIDDLE Michael MA 1968
s of William R. dairyman and Jean M. Campbell; b Nairn 8.4.47
BA(OU) 1978
teacher hist/mod stud. St Columba's h s Dunfermline 1969–78, prin guid 1970–78; asst head (guid) Speyside h s from 1978
m Nairn 21.9.68 Elizabeth I. Campbell teacher d of Peter C. Nairn

RIDDLER Alexander Marryatt Hay BSc 1959
s of Marryatt G. R. tech off. DAFS and Helen D. Hay; b Aber 25.4.36
Dip Integrated Surveying ITC–Unesco centre Enschede The Neths 1973
teacher maths Inverurie acad 1959–60; soil surv NSW DA Sydney from 1960
m Sydney NSW 31.8.63 Laurel J. Thompson paymistress d of William R. T. Port Stephens NSW

RIDDLER Gordon Peterkin *BSc 1967

RIDDOCH Ella Falconer MA 1966
d of Henry J. R. farm. and Agnes Jamieson; b Huntly 30.5.45
teacher: Engl Glasg 1967–69, maths 1969–71, prin maths 1971–72, maths Aber 1972–73, asst prin maths Glasg from 1973
m Drumblade 10.8.73 Francis W. Lawrence bank clerk s of John L. Fraserburgh

RIDDOCH Hilda Ellen MA 1970
m Armour

RIDDOCH James Skene BSc(eng) 1970
s of Walter S. R. driving instruct. and Isabella H. Skene; b Dufftown 1.10.39
bus. man
m Dufftown 11.7.65 Anne E. W. Niven d of John N. Aber

RIDDOLLS Anthea MSc 1969
BSc(St And)

RIDLEY Susan Elizabeth MB ChB 1968
d of Ernest F. R. MB ChB(St And) g p and Catherine

M. Malcolm MB ChB(St And) g p; b Glasg 20.6.44
DObstRCOG 1972
h o Aber 1968–69; rotating intern Edmonton Alberta 1969–71; consult. m o Nyeri hosp Kenya 1972–78
m Zambia 2.10.71 John R. Macleod MA 1963 *qv*

RILEY Alasdair James MA 1968
s of James F. R. MB ChB(Edin) g p and Marina E. Fraser; b Perth 31.1.46
journalist: *Kent Messenger* 1968–71, *Evening Standard* Lond 1971–76, Scottish TV Glasg 1976–78, *The Sun* Lond from 1978

RILLEY Charles MA 1963

RILLEY Elizabeth Jean MA 1956
d of Norman S. R. insur acct and Sophie M. Work; b Aber 9.3.35
LTCL(Lond) 1969
teacher Portlethen p s from 1957

RINGE James Peter PhD 1956
BSc(Lond) ARIC

RINGSLEBEN Mary Ruth Elizabeth PhD 1956
d of William C. R. MSc(Queen's Ont) mining eng and R. Dorothy Sharp BA(Queen's Ont); b Timmins Ontario 30.7.28
BA(Tor) 1950 Dip Archives Admin(Liv) 1957
admin asst Leeds from 1957

RITCHIE Alan Alexander BSc(eng) 1970

RITCHIE Alison Mary MA 1967
m Monro

RITCHIE David Alexander *BSc(eng) 1970
s of David S. R. nurs off. and Margaret F. Wood nurs sister; b Banff 30.6.49
MIEE 1978
eng ICI Ardeer 1970–73; gen man. Motherwell Bridge Electrical Motherwell 1973–79; elect. eng Roche Prod. Dalry from 1979
m Banff 12.4.68 Margaret I. Falconer MA 1971 teacher d of George F. Banff

RITCHIE David Andrew *BSc 1970
s of David R. eng and Henrietta R. Mair; b Philippine Is 21.10.47
Lond: tech rep 1970–73, sen sales exec from 1973
m St Albans 23.9.72 Kathleen W. McDonagh SRN d of John T. McD. St Albans

RITCHIE Doris Jean MB ChB 1957
d of Gordon R. millwright and Jeanie Law; b Huntly 23.9.33
h o RACH 1957–58; g p: asst Stonehaven, Hayes 1958–63, ptnr Aber from 1974
m Aber 17.10.59 George D. Dalgarno higher exec off. Customs & Excise s of George H. D. Aber

RITCHIE Ethel Margaret MA 1959
d of Kenneth R. motor mech, shopkeeper and Annie C. Allardyce shop asst; b Peterculter 27.6.39
teacher: maths/geog Aboyne acad 1960–62, sc Peterhead acad 1963; Blackhills p s 1966–74, acting head 1974–75, Anna Ritchie spec s Peterhead from 1975
m Peterculter 30.6.62 James R. Cruickshanks plumber, prison off. s of James C. Banchory

RITCHIE Ian Ogilvie *BSc 1968
s of Charles O. R. baker and Isabel M. Simpson; b Johnshaven 13.5.46
res stud. Aberd 1968–70; teacher: AGS 1971–72, Stonehaven 1973–77, Aboyne from 1977
m Stonehaven 28.3.70 Elizabeth A. Lambie MA 1968 *qv*

RITCHIE Irene Allardyce MA 1964
d of Kenneth R. shopkeeper and Annie C. Allardyce; b Peterculter 7.4.42
teacher: maths Banchory acad 1967–70, p s Banchory acad 1970–72, maths St Columba's RC s Perth 1973–75, maths Perth acad from 1975
m Banchory 12.10.60 Robert W. Singer gen man. s of George S. Banchory

RITCHIE Irene Mary MA 1969
d of James A. R. machine oper and Georgina H. M. Raeper; b Aber 5.12.47
teacher: Aber 1970–72, Linlithgow 1972–76
m Aber 21.7.72 Oswald C. Finnie MA 1969 *qv*

RITCHIE Jean McCurrach MB ChB 1958
d of George F. T. R. rly guard and Mary McCurrach nurs sister; b Aber 13.6.34
DA(Eng) 1960
Glasg: h o sick ch hosp Yorkhill, Stobhill hosp 1958–59, sen h o anaest Stobhill hosp, RI 1959–63; g p Brighton
m Aber 27.2.63 John M. Howat MB ChB(Glas) paediat surg s of Robert H. Irvine

RITCHIE John BSc(eng) 1970

RITCHIE John Miller MA 1968

RITCHIE John Russell BSc(eng) 1964
b Fraserburgh 29.3.42
MIEE 1972 AMBIM 1974
elect. eng NSHEB from 1964
m Aber 26.7.67 Mary M. Davidson

RITCHIE John Winter *BSc(eng) 1964

RITCHIE Kenneth Brian MB ChB 1967
s of Kenneth R. newsagent and Annie C. Allardyce; b Stonehaven 31.12.43
h o Dumfries 1967–68; obst Falkirk 1969; paediat Ayr 1969; g p: Dalry 1970–72, Inverkeithing from 1972
m Aber 17.12.66 Maureen Kelly civ serv d John K. Aber

RITCHIE Lily Ann McBay MA 1959 Dip Ed 1960
d of Charles O. R. master baker and Isabel M. Simpson; b Gourdon 2.1.39
teacher: Mackie acad Stonehaven 1960–61, mod lang Nicolson inst Stornoway 1968–73, Fr Back s/Leurbost s Is of Lewis from 1973
m Johnshaven 12.7.61 John Maclennan MA 1959 *qv*

RITCHIE Margaret Janet MA 1967
b Aber 11.6.46
teacher Aber from 1968
m Aber 25.7.74 John M. Elsom MSc(E Ang) res asst

RITCHIE Margaret Murray MA 1969
d of David R. haulage contr/farm worker and Jean R. Macleman SRN; b Inv 4.1.48
teacher Crown p s Inv 1970–72
m Cromarty 24.7.71 James M. Scott ptnr fam garage/motor mech s of Hugh S. Conon Bridge

RITCHIE Margrit Rose *MA 1965
d of Alfred A. R. banker and Anna-Margarethe Kull nurse; b Aber 26.7.42
teacher: Fr/Ger Aber 1966–67, Cambridge 1967–69
m Aber 12.8.67 Don W. Cruickshank MA 1965 *qv*

RITCHIE Patricia MA 1966 Dip Ed 1967
d of Joseph R. postman and Robina S. Galbraith clerk; b Aber 11.12.44
teacher: Aber 1967–72, Brisbane Aust 1974–75
m Aber 27.7.66 Adam H. Findlay MA 1970 *qv*

RIVIERE Marc Serge *MA 1970

RIXON Frank Gerald *LLB 1967

ROAF Jane Isobel *MA 1966
m Stubbes

ROBB Catherine Roberta Steele MA 1969
m Haggart

ROBB Christian Mackenzie Thomson MB ChB 1959 DPH 1963
d of James A. T. R. marine eng and Christian R. Norrie pers secy; b Ilford 11.6.36
MFCM 1972
h o, sen h o Woodend hosp Aber 1959–61; rotating internship Vancouver gen hosp 1961–62; m o, sen m o health dept Aber 1963–74; commun med spec Grampian health board Aber from 1974

ROBB Colin Collie MA 1963 LLB 1965
s of Stanley L. R. soldier, checkweighman and Ena Collie; b Aber 9.3.42
Aber: law app 1965–67, solic 1967–75; Grampian reg c: asst dir law & admin 1975–79, dep dir from 1979

ROBB David Strachan *MA 1969
s of Erland S. B. R. civ serv and Margaret M. Strachan; b Aber 6.1.47
asst instr in lit State univ NY New Paltz NY USA 1969–70; lect Engl Dund from 1973

ROBB Eileen May *MA 1969
m Halborg

ROBB George Alan *MA 1964
s of George R. solic and Phyllis M. Allan; b Aber 20.5.42
LLB(Edin) 1966 WS 1968
law app Davidson & Syme WS Edin 1966–68; leg. asst Edmonds & Ledingham advoc Aber 1969–71; lect publ law Aberd 1970–73; leg. asst Brander & Cruickshank WS Aber 1971–72, ptnr from 1973
m Aber 3.8.73 Moira A. Clark teacher d of Sydney M. C. Aber

ROBB John Bertram Leslie Macdonald MB ChB 1960
s of Bertram G. R. rep and Anne M. Peters MA 1930 *qv*; b Edin 23.2.36
regist psychiat Bangour Midlothian 1964–69; g p Fauldhouse from 1970
m Morebattle 12.10.63 Pauline E. Yearnshire midwife d of William Y. Alnmouth

ROBB Margaret Niven Davidson *MA 1968
m Buchan

ROBB Norah Mary Steele MA 1969

ROBB Ronald Reith *MA 1961

ROBBIE Alice Mary MA 1962
m Curley

ROBBIE Angus Abercrombie MA 1958
s of James R. horticulturist and Margaret J. Abercrombie; b Aber 28.5.37
Dip Voc Guid 1966 gen serv medal 1960
educ off. RAEC/1st batt RHF Aden 1958–60; youth employ. off. Edin 1960–63; careers off. Birm 1963–67; careers off. Aberd from 1967
m Cambridge 7.7.62 Patricia G. Pollock med secy

ROBBIE John Forsyth BSc(eng) 1958 *1965
s of John D. R. for. and Jane M. Souter MA 1917 *qv*; b Alves 25.3.35
eng: Freeman Fox & ptnrs N Wales 1958–60, James Williamson & ptnrs Glasg 1960–64; lect Aberd 1965–72, sen lect from 1972
m Aber 2.5.59 Sheila M. Inkster radiogr d of Andrew R. I. Banchory

ROBBIE Sheila Catherine MA 1960
d of John G. R. gen man. dept store and Catherine Craigmyle; b Aber 25.8.39
interpreter/translator Fr/Engl Noumea New Caledonia 1970–71; teacher Engl at Fr s Bucharest Rumania from 1973
m Noumea 21.2.61 Marcel L. Ropert L-ès-L(Rennes) univ lect Melb, diplomat Tokyo, Bucharest s of Marcel M. R. Saint Brieuc France

ROBBINS Alan Marcus James *BSc(for) 1970
s of Eric R. J. R. farm. and Margery Bryant; b Osterley 7.3.47
MSc(Oxon) 1971
for. res asst Commonwealth for. inst Oxford 1971–72; for. res ODM tech aid Matagalpa Nicaragua from 1972

ROBERTS Anne *MA 1966 Dip Ed 1967
d of Llewelyn L. R. univ admin and Marjorie Wear; b Aberystwyth 26.10.42
cler off. civ serv Leic 1967–68; trainee careers off. Leic 1968–69, Kent 1969–70, careers off. Leic 1970–71, sen careers off. 1971–77
m(2) Lond 20.7.77 Alan M. MacGregor MA 1966 *qv*

ROBERTS Celia Frances MA 1967
m Reid

ROBERTS Joyce Cameron MB ChB 1970
d of Robert C. R. off. fire brigade and Eleanor D. Cameron; b Aber 24.1.47
FFARACS
h o Aber 1970–71; Brisbane Aust: sen resid 1971–72, regist anaest 1972–74; regist anaest Middx Lond from 1975
m Brisbane –.10.72 Ralph G. Cobcroft MB BS(Queensland) phys s of Athol J. C. Redcliffe Queensland

ROBERTSON Aileen BEd 1969
d of Hugh R. MA 1950 *qv*; b Aber 28.9.47
teacher: Fochabers 1969–71, Kinloss 1971–73, Glasg East 1973–76, Glasg West 1976–77
m Forres 13.10.73 Donald M. Davidson BA(Strath) CA s of Thomas S. D. Inv

ROBERTSON Alan Mackenzie BSc(agr) 1961
s of Ian R. joiner and Elsie R. Pope; b Banchory 29.1.37
exper off. ARC farm bldg unit Silsoe 1961–64; farm bldg advis PIDA and MLC Bush estate Edin 1964–69; investigator SFB IU NOSCA Craibstone, Bucksburn from 1969
m Tarland 2.6.62 Margaret Walker civ serv d of Allan W. Tarland

ROBERTSON Alastair Ogston LLB 1967
s of Ian R. clerk of works and Edith V. Silver teacher;

b Aber 13.7.46
Aber: law app Clark & Wallace advoc 1967–69, solic, ptnr Burnett & Reid advoc from 1969
m Cullen 3.8.68 Catherine E. Robertson MA 1967 *qv*

ROBERTSON Alastair Thomson LLB 1969

ROBERTSON Alexander MA 1960
s of Alexander R. fish merch and Helen R. Robb; b Aber 13.8.39
Dip Soc St(Edin) 1961 PhD(Edin) 1974
trainee psychiat soc worker N'cle-u-Tyne 1961–62; res asst Leic 1962–64; res off. Essex 1964–66; lect Ipswich civ coll 1966–68; res off. MRC unit for epidemiological soc stud. Edin 1968–72; lect soc admin Edin from 1972
m Leic 26.9.64 Elaine Walden soc worker d of Henry G. F. W. Sanderstead

ROBERTSON Alexander Stewart *MA 1967 *MEd 1972
s of Alexander J. R. MA 1925 *qv*; b Forfar 17.10.45
teacher RGC Aber 1967–73; head Engl/communications/related stud. fac Castell Alun h s Hope Wales 1973–78; dep head Yogol Bryn Elian, Colwyn Bay from 1978
m Aber 21.12.67 Pamela M. Martin MA 1970 *qv*

ROBERTSON Alison Kinloch MA 1966
m Smith

ROBERTSON Alistair Charles MB ChB 1968
s of George P. R. R. R. soldier, woodman and Annie S. Smith shop asst; b Huntly 18.4.44
h o Aber, Dumfries 1968–69; asst g p Annan 1969–70; sen h o Lancaster 1970–72; g p: Arbroath 1972–73, Hessle N Humberside from 1973
m Aber 20.7.70 Susan M. Gallantry teacher d of Tom G. Aber

ROBERTSON Andrew *MA 1958 *MEd 1960
s of John R. trawlmate/fish market porter and Williamina D. M. Barnie; b Aber 28.8.36
teacher: Culter 1959–60, New Deer 1960–61; lecteur Rennes univ France 1961–62; teacher/spec asst Banchory acad 1962–68, prin Fr Kaimhill s s Aber 1968–71, prin Fr/asst head/dep head Kincorth acad from 1971
m Aber 14.7.60 Edna M. Sangster lab tech/dispensing asst d of Norman F. S. Aber

ROBERTSON Anne Christine MB ChB 1968
m Napier

ROBERTSON Anne Wilson MA 1966 Dip Ed 1967
d of Charles W. R. MA 1934 *qv*; b Dumfries 11.2.46
teacher Thornhill p s Dumfries 1967–76
m Belhelvie 7.7.72 James Boyle master painter/decorator s of Robert H. B. Thornhill

ROBERTSON Annette Walker BSc 1957
d of Robert W. R. gen merchant, clerk and Emma S. Stevenson tailoress; b Aber 19.11.34
electron microscopist: Surrey 1957–59, Hampshire 1959–61; sub-postmistress from 1974
m Aber 1958 Michael B. Bagley brewery sales man. s of Walter E. W. B. Portsmouth

ROBERTSON Barbara Reid MA 1960
d of Thomas F. R. grocery br man. and Barbara C. Reid; b Aber 6.6.39
teacher inf Aber 1961–67
m Aber 31.7.65 Ian G. Morrice CA s of Alexander T. M. Aber

ROBERTSON Brian Kellock *BSc 1970 Dip Ed 1971

ROBERTSON Catherine Edith MA 1967
d of George A. R. retail outfitter and Catherine E. Clark nurse; b Aber 17.8.46
teacher Engl/Fr Bankhead acad 1968–70
m Cullen 3.8.68 Alastair O. Robertson LLB 1967 *qv*

ROBERTSON Christian Scott MA 1967
m Tait

ROBERTSON David MA 1966
s of Edwin J. R. wireless mech/radio tv shop prop. and Fanny T. Moir prop. hi-fi tv radio bus.; b Aber 23.2.38
prop. hi-fi tv radio bus. Aber/Fraserburgh from 1966
m Aber 27.3.68 Norma C. Simpson MA 1969 *qv*

ROBERTSON David Alasdair MB ChB 1959

ROBERTSON David Lewis *BSc 1958
s of David R. BSc 1924 *qv* and Margaret W. Lewis MA 1929 *qv*; b Bieldside 2.2.37
grad app Ericsson Telephones Beeston 1958–60; electronics dev eng: Ferranti Bracknell 1960–64, Elliott Automation Camberley 1964–72; man.: Quality Assurance, Marconi Space and Defence Systems Camberley from 1972
m Oxford 19.12.59 Winifred G. Macgillivray d of Alexander M. Oxford

ROBERTSON David Stewart Malcolm MA 1958
s of William H. R. civ serv and Isabella B. Malcolm; b Glasg 1.6.28
teacher: Engl/allied subj Rothiemay s s 1959–61, Engl Nairn acad 1961–74, prin Engl Glenurquhart s s from 1974
m Streatham 29.4.50 Eileen M. Adams d of William F. A. Streatham

ROBERTSON Edwin BSc(eng) 1958

ROBERTSON Eleanor Margaret BSc 1968
d of Ogston R. farm. and Rosaline B. Adams secy; b Stonehaven 9.8.47
teacher: maths/geog Montrose acad 1969–71, maths/sc Tarves s 1971–73
m Aber 4.8.71 John S. Law farm. s of William S. L. Fyvie

ROBERTSON Elizabeth Ann MA 1959
d of John R. CEng F I Mun E county road surv and Margaret G. Wright; b Inv 26.6.38
teacher Engl Hilton j s s Aber 1960–63
m Kirkwall 21.5.63 Robert G. Bain farm. s of Robert G. B. Tankerness Orkney

ROBERTSON George Ewen *MA 1970 *MEd 1972
s of Donald E. R. asst gen man. dept store and Heather G. Sutherland; b Aber 21.4.47
teacher Fr/Ger Mackie acad Stonehaven 1972–75; asst prin Fr/Ger Bankhead acad 1975–78; prin Ger Inverurie acad from 1978
m Aber 17.7.70 Sheila M. Grant MA 1966 *qv*

ROBERTSON George Lindsay MB ChB 1967

ROBERTSON George Malcolm MacNeill BSc 1968
s of George A. R. man. dir and Morag D. Wark; b Aber 21.7.47
med rep: Wellcome Foundation central Scot. 1969–73, ICI Aber from 1973
m Aber 19.12.70 Irene P. Henderson teacher d of Alexander S. H. Aber

ROBERTSON George Ross MA 1961

ROBERTSON George Slessor MB ChB 1958 MD 1973
s of John B. R. garage prop. and Alice J. S. Clyne teacher; b Peterhead 31.12.33
Struthers gold medal 1963 FFARCS 1964
h o Aber, Lond 1958–61; lect anat Aberd 1961–63; sen h o anaest, regist, sen regist anaest Aber 1963–67; asst anaest Winnipeg Canada 1967–68, consult. anaest/hon sen lect anaest Aberd from 1969
m Aber 21.9.60 Audrey E. McDonald med res asst d of Hector McD. Aber

ROBERTSON Gillian Gibbs MA 1966
d of Thomas G. R. MA 1926 *qv*; b Elgin 17.12.43
teacher mod lang: Whitburn acad 1967–70, Edin 1970–71, Ellon 1971, Harlaw acad Aber 1971–73 latterly asst prin mod lang
m Aber 6.4.71 Kenneth J. Chew BSc 1968 *qv*

ROBERTSON Gordon Watson *BSc(agr) 1969

ROBERTSON Graeme William BSc 1969
s of William R. bank man. and Marjory J. Thain PO civ serv; b Aber 30.1.47
higher scient off. Macaulay inst for soil res Aber from 1971

ROBERTSON Hamish Thomson MA 1970

ROBERTSON Helen Lawrence MA 1956
BEd(Manit)
m Caswell

ROBERTSON or Johnston, Helen Mary MB ChB 1962
b Aber 21.3.38
m Sumner

ROBERTSON Ian *BSc(eng) 1966
s of Robert C. R. grocer and Daisy A. M. B. Masson nurse; b Cardenden 12.12.44
MICE 1971 MEng(Glas) 1972
eng: Aber 1966–67, Longannet 1967–68, Stirling 1968–71; sub-ag Erskine 1971–73; ag Coulport from 1973
m Aber 28.10.67 Muriel E. R. Leiper computer oper d of Alexander W. L. Aber

ROBERTSON Ian *MA 1967
s of John R. bank man. and Alice R. Walton; b Lond 17.1.45
Dip Ed(Cantab) 1968
teacher Engl Fettes coll Edin 1968–72; BBC sports broadcaster/rugby commentator Lond from 1972

ROBERTSON Ian Graeme *BSc 1964

ROBERTSON Irene Adams MA 1965
d of William R. farm. and Katherine P. Adams teacher; b Aber 23.12.43
Dip Soc St(Edin) 1966
fam case worker Aber assoc soc serv 1966–68
m Marykirk 11.8.66 Stuart H. W. Duncan MB ChB 1965 *qv*

ROBERTSON Isobel Margaret MA 1961
d of James G. R. farm. and Jane S. Cruickshank; b Insch 1.1.38
teacher of blind Dorton House s for the blind Seal Sevenoaks from 1963
m Aber 23.12.63 Charles B. Yule tv tech s of Charles N. D. Y. Huntly

ROBERTSON James Albert *BSc 1961
s of James S. R. farm. and Anne Gillanders; b Boyndlie Fraserburgh 17.12.38
teacher: Galston 1962–63, chem Dumfries acad 1963–71, prin chem Wallace Hall acad from 1971
m Aber 10.8.66 Sheana McGregor teacher

ROBERTSON James Alexander *BSc 1956
s of Robert R. R. MA(Edin) C of S min and Jessie G. S. McCready MA(Edin) teacher; b Edin 3.3.35
Kilgour sen schol(Aberd) 1956–58 R S McLaughlin resid fell. Queen's univ (Kingston Ont) 1956–57 MSc(Ont) 1960
Ont Canada: summer geol asst 1954–56, field party leader 1956–60, geol Ont dept mines 1960–72, chief mineral deposits geol Ont div of mines Min of nat resources Toronto from 1972
m Toronto 20.1.68 Reima M. Bogle secy d of Leslie P. B. Toronto

ROBERTSON James Edwin *BSc 1967

ROBERTSON James Forsyth BSc(eng) 1961

ROBERTSON James Youngson MA 1961
s of James R. grocer and Eileen G. Nicol cashier; b Aber 21.9.40
teacher: Inverkeithing p s 1962–64, Townhill, Dunfermline p s 1964–65, Bridge of Don, Scotstown p s Aber 1965–70; head O'Neil Corse p s from 1970

ROBERTSON Jane Petrie MA 1967
d of John C. R. RN police and Joan W. Petrie dressmaker; b Perth 8.6.45
teacher geog: Lond 1968–69, Windsor 1969–73, head geog 1973–75
m Aber 8.8.69 Iain G. N. Harris MA 1968 *qv*

ROBERTSON Janet Gibson MA 1962
m Maclaren

ROBERTSON John Gordon MB ChB 1959

ROBERTSON John Grant *BSc(eng) 1967
s of John M. R. sales man. and Betty C. Edmonstone; b Edin 3.1.44
MEng(Glas) 1971 MICE 1973
des eng/site RE Edin 1967–72; des eng Lagos Nigeria 1972–75; sen des eng Edin 1975–76; sen designer/loc off. man. Kuwait from 1976
m Arbroath 5.4.68 Elma C. Bishop teacher d of Richard S. B. BD(Edin) Arbroath

ROBERTSON John Hamish *MA 1969
s of Eric D. R. BSc(for) 1934 *qv*; b Delhi 18.3.45
edit. coins, medals and currency weekly Indep Mags Lond 1969–72; radio journalist Aust broadcasting commission publ affairs sect. Sydney/Brisbane from 1972

ROBERTSON John Macdonald *BSc 1969
s of Wilfred R. mill worker and Jane L. Rothnie; b Ellon 29.1.47
Dip Genetics(Edin) PhD(Edin) 1973
m Portobello 28.11.70 Moira S. M. McKenzie BSc(Edin) 1967 tech off. d of John R. McK. Edin

ROBERTSON John Watt MB ChB 1959
s of William R. fishing skipper and Maggie J. Watt dressmaker; b Gardenstown 3.10.23
DRCOG 1962 MRCGP 1965
h o Aber 1959–60; trainee g p Aber 1960–61; h o Inv 1961–62; g p: Aber 1962–70, Tarbert Harris from 1970
m Kirkintilloch 27.7.57 Alexandrina Gillies SRN d of Donald G. Kirkintilloch

ROBERTSON Kathleen Jean MA 1968
m Edmiston

ROBERTSON Kathleen Mary *MA 1959
resid Glasg

ROBERTSON Kenneth George *MA 1963 Dip Ed 1964

ROBERTSON Kenneth Gordon *MA 1970
s of Norman M. R. off. man. and Jane H. Gordon; b Aber 14.3.47
PhD(R'dg) 1980
lect sociol R'dg from 1972
m New York 9.4.78 Ellen F. Greenberg BA(NY) market res Metal Box corp d of William G. Rockaway Beach

ROBERTSON Laurna Mary Scott MA 1965

ROBERTSON Leonora Wood MA 1957 Dip Ed 1958

ROBERTSON Lindsay BSc 1963

ROBERTSON Lorraine Irvine MA 1970
d of George R. bookbinder and Helen L. Wilson ptnr in fam bus. (Geo Jolly); b Aber 29.3.48
teacher Engl: Summerhill acad Aber 1972–74, Kincorth acad Aber 1974–76; signwriter (own bus.) Orkney from 1976
m Aber 22.4.77 David H. Bichan BSc 1976 shipping ag s of Howard B. Deerness

ROBERTSON Margaret Cormack MA 1969 Dip Ed 1970
d of Henry S. R. fish merch and Isabella M. Baxter; b Aber 27.7.48
teacher St Margaret's s for girls Aber 1970–73
m Aber 21.12.70 John F. Hendry LLB 1968 *qv*

ROBERTSON Margaret Hamilton Stewart MA 1967
d of Stanley G. R. BSc(Glas) sen scient papermaking and Margaret B. Stewart; b Hamilton 19.1.46
teacher: Catrine 1968–69, Stranraer 1969–71
m Aber 5.8.67 John G. Davidson BSc 1967 *qv*

ROBERTSON Marion Isabel BSc 1956
d of Mark R. master joiner/cabinetmaker and Marie C. C. Reilley secy; b Aber 23.11.34
BA(OU) 1979
aircraft des Brist 1956–57; teacher maths Aber: High s for girls 1958–63, Kincorth acad 1970–74, Torry acad from 1974, prin guid from 1975
m Aber 4.4.60 Edward D. Turner teacher s of Harry T.

ROBERTSON Marjorie Anne MA 1969
m Mitchell

ROBERTSON Marjory Elizabeth *MA 1970 Dip Ed 1971
d of William R. bank man. and Marjory J. Thain; b Aber 30.1.47
teacher Fr/Ger Perth h s from 1971
m Aber 27.7.76 John Lewis BSc(Sheff) teacher s of Sydney L. Cardiff

ROBERTSON Mary Elizabeth MA 1969
d of Adam A. R. merch seaman/weaver and Tina M. Mouat; b Lerwick 14.7.48
asst soc worker Edin 1970–72; soc worker Argyll 1972–73; p o tel Lerwick from 1973
m Dunrossness 2.9.69 John R. Kenney BSc 1969 *qv*

ROBERTSON Michael Lawrance MA 1967
s of William V. R. eng man. and Christina F. Smith hairdresser; b Aber 22.2.44
trg off. Bolton 1968–69; man. consult. Bolton 1969–72; prod. dir Londonderry 1972–75; man. consult Belf from 1975
m Aber 28.10.67 Marjorie J. Gilbert tel d of George G. Aber

ROBERTSON Michael Mundie *BSc 1958 PhD 1962

ROBERTSON Myrtle Emslie BSc 1965
m Watson

ROBERTSON Neil MA 1966 LLB 1968
s of George R. bank man. and Margaret R. Stephen teacher; b Dufftown 24.12.45
law app Aber 1969–71; admin asst: loc auth Inv 1972–73, secy's off. Aberd from 1973
m Aber 22.12.71 Sylvia J. Yeats secy d of Alexander C. Y. Aber

ROBERTSON Neil BSc(eng) 1967
s of William F. R. insur area man. and Daisy Sutherland ch's nurse; b Aber 4.12.42
MICE 1974 MIMunE 1975
asst eng Rosyth 1967–69; asst eng then sect. leader Glasg 1970–72; asst eng Aber 1972–75; sen eng Stonehaven from 1975
m Aber 18.10.68 Brenda A. Christie MA 1965 *qv*

ROBERTSON Ouaine Mitchell MA 1962
m Bain

ROBERTSON Patricia Clare MA 1970
d of William J. R. granite merch and Clare Hodge teacher; b Aber 21.7.49
post grad stud. nurse Aber 1971–72
m Aber 28.7.71 Norman H. Reid LLB 1969 *qv*

ROBERTSON Patricia Mary *MA 1957
d of Peter D. R. bookseller and newsagent and Mary H. R. Rhind; b Insch 30.9.35
Lond: export/import bi-ling secy 1958–59, embassy translator/secy 1960–62, bi-ling confidential secy (statist) 1962; bi-ling p a: invest comp 1963, eng 1963–65, comm radio 1965–66; teacher mod lang 1971–75; secy (architects) 1975–76; secy (univ) from 1977
m Chelsea 18.5.63 Christopher P. Downey elect. distrib eng s of Michael J. D. Lond

ROBERTSON Robert BSc 1965

ROBERTSON Robert Elrick MB ChB 1962

ROBERTSON Robert John MB ChB 1958
s of Lindsay R. tourist information off. and Joan C. Johnson; b Aber 4.3.32
trainee g p Lerwick 1959–60; g p: Unst 1960–78, Voe from 1978
m Lerwick 1.3.59 Marion E. Gamble midwife d of James G. Cardonagh Co Donegal

ROBERTSON Ronald Charles Ramsay *BSc 1970
s of James B. R. marine eng and Elizabeth L. Ramsay ch's nurse; b Glasg 20.3.44
grad stud. McM univ Hamilton Ont 1970–71; explor geol Eire 1971; grad stud. Queen's univ Kingston Ont 1972–79; explor geol: Peru and Bolivia 1977 and 1978, Alaska from 1979
m Kingston Ontario 18.1.75 Maria del Pilar Rosario Belon BEd(Catolica Santa Maria) teacher d of Miguel B. Arequipa Peru

ROBERTSON Sandra Mary Stewart *MA 1965
m Morrison

ROBERTSON Sheena MB ChB 1963
d of John W. R. fisherman and Christina McLeman; b Fraserburgh 4.12.38
h o ARI, Addenbrookes hosp Camb 1963–65; asst m o Caernarvon 1965–73; g p Stirling 1973–75; regist virol W I G Glasg 1975–78; temp lect Middx med s Lond from 1978
m Aber 1.8.64 Stewart R. Sutherland MA 1963 *qv*

ROBERTSON Sheila MA 1966
d of George R. farm serv and Agnes Duncan; b Longside 30.1.45
teacher Seaton p s Aber 1967–69
m Aber 21.7.67 Gordon J. Fraser police serg s of James F. Ellon

ROBERTSON Sheila Margaret MA 1969 Dip Ed 1970
d of James A. R. farm. and Mabel Cameron nurse; b Huntly 12.8.48
Lond: trainee computer progr 1970–71, progr 1971–72, sen progr 1972–73, analyst/progr from 1973
m Huntly 10.6.72 Steven R. Johnson ACA s of Kenneth C. J. BSc(eng)(Leeds) Sheffield

ROBERTSON Shonaid Elizabeth MA 1960
m Barr

ROBERTSON Stuart Forrest MB ChB 1964
s of James A. R. sales man. and Alice S. Forrest nurse; b Aber 24.7.40
h o: Woodend hosp Aber 1964–65, Bridge of Earn hosp 1965–66; sen h o Manc royal eye hosp 1966–68; lect anat Aberd 1968–71; asst m o h Kincardine c c 1971–74; clin m o commun health div Grampian health board(south dist) Aber from 1974
m Aber 7.2.72 Morag Macleod RGN d of Kenneth M. Melbost Borve Is of Lewis

ROBERTSON Susan Florence MA 1969
d of John S. R. fish merch and Dorothy L. Bittiner secy; b Aber 9.3.48
Düsseldorf Ger: bi-ling secy 1970–73, acct exec in advertising ag 1973–77
m Düsseldorf 22.6.76 Gerhard H. Hermenau prod. (tech serv dept) in advertising agency s of Bruno H. H. Ahrensburg W Ger

ROBERTSON Thomas Wilson BSc(agr) 1969
s of John R. farm. and Mary F. Wilson; b Keith 23.2.47
MSc(N'cle) 1971
farm worker nr N'cle-u-Tyne 1971–72; jun res assoc N'cle 1972–74; mechanisation advis NOSCA Aber from 1974
m Aber 18.8.70 Linda G. Coletta journalist d of Guido C. Aber

ROBERTSON Vincent Charles *BSc 1961
s of Alexander S. R. janitor and Helen F. Buckle; b Elgin 31.8.39
De Havilland aerobatics trophy winner 1972
RAF: trainee pilot South Cerney, Weeming, Valley 1961–63, Vulcan pilot Scampton 1963–66, Canberra pilot/flt comm Laarbruch Ger 1966–69, qualified flying instr Bristol 1969–72; central flying s instr Little Rissington 1972–73; comm off./sqdn ldr Queen's univ air squadron Belf 1973–76; Brit Commanders in Chief Mission to Soviet forces in Ger (Berlin) from 1976
m Aber 10.12.60 Christine F. Owen civ serv d of Robert S. O. Aber

ROBERTSON Violet *MA 1961

ROBERTSON William *BSc(eng) 1967 MSc 1969

ROBERTSON Winifred Helen Joyce *MA 1963
d of Alexander S. R. janitor and Helen F. Buckle; b Elgin 22.8.41
teacher: Kirkton h s Dun 1964–67, Elgin acad 1967–68, Aber acad (Hazlehead acad) 1968–73, Cardinal Manning Boys' s Lond 1973–74, Hazlehead acad from 1974
m Elgin 23.7.68 Donald T. Graham tut/prin s of radiography s of John G. Is of Raasay

ROBILLIARD Kathleen Anne MA 1965 Dip Ed 1966
d of Henry S. R. bldr and decorator and Lilian le Gallez; b Hyde 12.10.43
teacher Fr/Engl: Northfield acad Aber 1966–68, Kingswood boys' s Bristol 1968–70; employ. off. (civ serv) Salisbury 1971–74
m Aber 16.7.68 George W. Jack BSc 1967 *qv*

ROBIN Sara Veronica BSc 1970 *1971
d of Angus H. R. BA(Cantab) admin and Katharine V. Harvey; b Edin 21.9.49
Dip Ed(Syd) 1977
teacher VSO Kamuli Uganda 1971–72; Brit Council admin Lond 1973–74; Oxfam/youth organis Glasg 1974–76
m Balfron 29.8.75 Hugh MacPherson BSc(eng) 1971 civ eng s of Duncan H. MacP. BSc(eng)(Edin) Edin

ROBINSON Iain Robert MA 1970
s of Douglas R. R. farm./agr merch and Isabel M. W. Nicol; b Hutton 10.5.49
app acct Glasg 1970–73; farm man. trainee Whauphill Newton Stewart from 1973

ROBINSON Keith PhD 1966
BSc(Leeds)

ROBINSON Patricia Joan Martin MA 1966
d of Wilfred M. R. MB ChB(Glas) g p and Joan B. S. Davie MA(St And); b Glasg 19.10.45
passenger ag Air Canada Vancouver 1966–67; staff man. Marks & Spencer Oxford 1968–69; secy Glasg 1970–71
m Kilmacolm 4.6.71 George M. Morton MA(Glas) solic s of John M. Paisley

ROBISON Douglas *BSc 1964
s of George D. R. plumber/gas meter collector and Madeline P. Harris dressmaker; b Aber 28.9.41
Dip Ed(Makerere coll univ of E Af) 1965
teacher: head maths KNCU s s Moshi Tanzania 1965–67, head maths Robinson Rd h s Nassau Bahamas 1967–70, maths Ainslie Park comp s Edin 1970–73, maths Ingiliz Linesi Istanbul 1973–74, head maths from 1974

ROBSON Donald Selby BSc 1963

ROBSON Edith MA 1962

ROBSON Fraser McPherson *BSc(eng) 1970 MSc 1972
s of William L. M. R. comp dir and Muriel M. A. Fraser; b Elgin 22.1.48
civ eng Binnie & ptnrs Lond from 1972

ROBSON Primrose Christine *BSc 1969
m Brown

ROCKWELL Peter MA 1967
s of Lloyd W. R. BSc(Harvard) oil broker and Grace M. Sutton; b Tunbridge Wells 30.7.18
teacher mod lang Powis acad Aber from 1968
m Aber 12.8.42 Wilma G. Philip d of William P. OBE MC TD Aber

ROCKWELL Peter William MA 1965 LLB 1967
s of Peter R. MA 1967 *qv*; b Aber 16.11.43
solic Aber from 1967; ptnr Adam Thomson & Ross (now Adam Cochran & Co) advoc Aber; secy Law Soc of Scot. Aber and NE leg. aid committee
m Aber 3.4.69 Elspeth C. McDonald MA 1965 *qv*

RODDIS Linda Judith Ann MB ChB 1970
s of John W. R. BSc(Lond) lect elect. eng and Muriel E. R. Chard teacher comm subjs; b Plymouth 21.11.45
h o Aber, Dumfries 1970–71; Newfoundland Canada: resid St John's 1971–72, St Anthony 1972–73; g p Wimbledon 1973–76; part-time g p Halifax Nova Scotia from 1977
m Aber 26.4.71 Alan D. Thomson MB ChB 1971 phys s of Angus M. T. MB ChB(Glas) N'cle-u-Tyne

RODGER George David *BSc 1962
s of George A. R. farm. and Annie I. Kidd; b Bridge of Cally 5.8.40
teacher sc: Kintore 1963–67, Alford from 1967

RODGERS Patricia Elaine Joan *MA 1970
d of Kenneth V. A. R. MB ChB(Edin) phys/surg and Anatol C. Reeves MA(Atlanta) headmistress; b Nassau Bahamas 13.7.48
Dip Internat Relations(Grad Inst Internat Rel Univ of W Indies) 1972 PhD(Geneva) 1977
Min External Affairs Nassau: admin cadet 1970–71, asst secy 1972–73, member of Bahamas delegation to 3rd UN conference on the law of the sea in Caracas 1974 and 1975, 1st asst secy 1977–78; counsellor Bahamas emb Washington from 1978 and chargé d'affaires ad interim Aug 1979 to March 1980

RODGERS William Alan MSc 1966
BSc(Lond)

ROE Isabelle Marie MB ChB 1958
d of Frederick C. R. MA(Birm) prof French Hull, Aberd and Claire A. Frebault L es L(Lyons) teacher/writer Fr text books; b Aber 25.11.33
Aber: trainee asst g p 1959–60, sen h o paediat City hosp 1960–61, med asst radio therap ARI 1962–69; sen h o, regist psycho-geriat Murray royal hosp Perth from 1970
m Aber 4.4.61 George F. J. Donald MA 1957 *qv*

ROGER Anne Young BSc 1966

ROGER Brian Mitchell MA 1967

ROGERS Howard Clive MA 1969
s of David R. consult. comp pension scheme and Gladys I. Goddard; b Ealing 22.7.48
Croydon: export man. sales trainee 1969–71, computer input clerk 1971–72; teacher Fr: Tividale comp s Warley 1972–74, St Michael's h s Sandwell from 1974

ROGERS John Simon Blackford MA 1970

ROGERS Teresa Anne MA 1965
d of William B. L. R. teacher, army capt, trainee RC priest and Dora M. Carnelly soc worker; b Folkestone 5.11.35
BA(Lond) 1972 Dip Lib(Aberystwyth) 1969
asst lib Lond: Tower Hamlets 1965–67, Wandsworth 1969–71; edit. asst OUP Lond 1972–73; Orion insur clerk Folkestone 1976–77; recept/tel Inter-city Tours Folkestone 1977–78; lib asst Lond 1978–79

ROLAND Philip Godfrey BSc 1969
s of Egbert R. headmaster and Joan R. Severs valuation off. loc govt; b Exeter 9.11.47
AMICE 1970 AMIStructE 1970
civ eng Lond 1969–72; gen man. Seven Seas Dredging Weybridge from 1976
m Eltham 5.8.72 Lindsey J. Perkins teacher d of Leslie G. F. P. Eltham

ROLBIN Cecil MB ChB 1956

ROLLAND Fiona Mary BSc 1970
d of Charles F. R. MB(Cantab) g p Edin and Venetia G. Payne nurse; b Edin 22.11.48
air stewardess BEA 1970–72; Lond; sub-edit. *Brit Journal of hosp med* 1972–73, sub-edit. *Over 21* mag. from 1973
m Cox

ROLLASON John David LLB 1969
s of William N. R. MB ChB(Birm) consult. anaest and Margaret Rowbotham dietitian; b Scunthorpe 27.9.48
Lond: consult. fin. serv 1969–74, insur broker from 1975
m Lond 6.10.73 Sarah P. Lunn SRN d of Eric J. A. L. France

ROLLO Elizabeth Anne MA 1969
d of George R. mason and Lizzie McKnight; b Fraserburgh 7.8.47
for. lang secy Freiburg W Ger 1970–72
m New Pitsligo 7.8.69 Klaus Jordan (staatsexamen Freiburg 1969) teacher s of Günter J. Bohringen W Ger

ROLLO Sheila Noble BSc 1966
d of Robert N. R. farm. and Evelyn R. Bisset; b Crimond 31.1.45
teacher maths: Peterhead acad 1967–71, Fraserburgh acad 1971–73
m Crimond 31.7.65 Alexander J. Miller baker s of Alexander M. Blackford

ROLTON Hilary Ann *BSc 1968 PhD 1972
d of Grahame W. R. des eng and Ann Riley; b Melton 12.6.46
res fell.: Max Planck inst Berlin 1972–73, Beatson inst for cancer res Glasg 1973–76; biochem Monklands dist council hosp Airdrie from 1976
m Edin 28.12.74 Robert K. S. Gray BSc(Edin) teacher s of Robert K. S. G. Edin

RONALD Alison LLB 1970
m Carruthers

RONALD Guinevere *MA 1968
b Aber 28.10.44
teacher Aber 1969–77; prin Ger AGS from 1977
m Aber 3.8.64 Jürgen K. A. Thomaneck MEd 1970 *qv*

RONALDSON John Blues *MA 1957 Dip Ed 1958
s of Traill S. R. contr and Christina L. Blues; b Brough Caithness 5.8.35
MEd(St And) 1968
asst école normale d'instituteurs Arras France 1958–59; teacher mod lang Anstruther 1959–67; educ psych ch guid clin Kirkcaldy 1967–69; staff tut. psych of adolescence N'cle 1969–73; lect applied psych N'cle from 1973
m St And 6.7.63 Juliet E. Corden d of William C. Cambridge

ROOK David Anderson BSc(for) 1957 *1958 PhD 1963
s of John I. R.; b Bukoba Tanzania 27.6.36
MSc(NY state coll of for.) 1960

asst lect for. Aberd 1960–64; scient in for. res inst Rotorua NZ from 1964
m Aber 19.7.61 Dorothy M. Pirie

ROPER Philip John BSc(for) 1968

RORIE Neil Iain George *MA 1967 *MEd 1969
s of James H. K. R. acct and Gertrude Yeaman; b Dun 29.5.44
teacher Dun h s 1969–71; head hist/sen housemaster Wombwell h s Yorks 1971–75; dep head Frogmore s from 1975
m Dun 4.4.70 Susan H. Gibson MA(St And) teacher d of Alexander G. Dun

ROSE Alwyn Lionel Edgar MB ChB 1968
BSc(How Wash)

ROSE Christopher John BSc(for) 1969
s of Charles R. painter/decorator and Ruby M. E. Frost asst matron; b Scunthorpe 9.11.47
for. Lincs 1969–70; trainee man. Civic Trees Nationwide 1970–71; for. Lincs; asst for. off. Milton Keynes dist council 1973–74, for. off. from 1974
m Folkestone 12.8.72 Judith B. Winspear teacher d of Terence W. Folkestone

ROSE George Charles Robert *BSc(eng) 1967

ROSE Isla Margaret BSc 1959
d of John R. BSc(agr) 1911 *qv*(II, III); b Port Charlotte Islay 1.9.37
eng White Waltham 1959–60; computer progr: Chelmsford 1960–64, Dounreay 1964–69; teacher maths Thurso from 1970
m Inv 24.9.66 David Thom asst man. fast reactor fuel reprocessing s of David T. Dun

ROSE James Hendry BSc 1959
s of James R. works eng and Barbara Hendry; b Aber 22.5.38
nat serv (RE) Germany 1959–61; teacher: maths/sc Oldmeldrum 1963–68, maths Bankhead acad from 1968
m Aber 2.6.62 Sheila C. Anderson secy d of Alfred J. S. A. Aber

ROSE John MA 1964
s of William R. clerk and Margaret Stronach; b Keith 20.1.44
teacher: Fr Bankhead acad Aber 1965–72, prin Fr Ellon acad from 1972

ROSE John Laurence *BSc(eng) 1966
s of John R. BSc(agr) 1911 *qv*(II, III); b Rodel Is of Harris 17.1.40
MICE 1970
Glasg: grad eng Sir Wm Halcrow & ptnrs 1966–67, asst eng Cowan & Linn 1967–70, sen eng 1970–74, sen proj eng 1974–76; head of struct dept James Williamson & ptnrs from 1976
m Dunbeath 30.8.63 Elizabeth M. Sutherland BSc(Glas) teacher d of James E. P. S. Thurso

ROSE Norman *MA 1970

ROSS Aileen Mary MA 1962
d of George H. R. mason and Mary Davidson off. worker; b Inverurie 10.6.41
teacher: Foxbar p s Paisley 1962–63, Inverurie acad 1965–68; housemistress/dep head Limuru girls' s Kenya 1969–73; teacher/housemistress Harrogate coll 1973–74; teacher/year mistress Powis acad Aber from 1974

ROSS Alexander Hugh MA 1956
d Caputh 24.1.74 *AUR* XLV 450

ROSS Alison Clark MA 1962
d of John A. R. banker and Elspet M. Clark; b Aber 22.1.41
Dip Soc St(Edin) 1967
Engl asst Schleswig Ger 1963–64; teacher mod lang: Turriff 1964–66, Kelvinside acad Glasg 1967–71
m Aber 6.8.70 Ian B. McKellar MA(Glas) lect hist Jordanhill coll of educ s of Donald McK. Dalmuir

ROSS Andrew Alexander *MA 1963
s of George R. BCom(Edin) acct clerk Unilever and Elspet I. Milne nurse, hosp matron; b N Cheam 27.9.41
man. trainee, jun man. steelworks Consett Iron Co Durh 1964–66; teacher: prin geog/sen housemaster Old Moshi African boys' resid s s Moshi Tanzania 1966–69, geog Boroughmuir s s Edin 1969–71, John Street s s Glasg 1971–73, asst prin geog Duncanrig s s E Kilbride 1973–75, prin geog Doon h s Dalmellington from 1975
m Glasg 10.7.71 Patricia A. Tait MA(Glas) teacher d of Alexander W. T. Glasg

ROSS Angus Roderick BSc 1969

ROSS Avril Elizabeth MA 1965
d of Donald C. R. pharm and Elizabeth Macleod; b Lairg 26.4.44
teacher Fr Inv royal acad 1966–69
m Cromarty 21.12.68 Robert G. Ritchie CPO RN s of Archibald G. R. Chessington

ROSS Barbara Adams Fenton *BSc 1966
m McKenzie

ROSS Barbara Bruce MA 1959

ROSS Catherine MA 1966
d of James R. fireman NEFB and Johana N. Livingstone shopkeeper; b Lochgilphead 21.5.45
teacher: Willowpark inf s Aber 1967–72, 1974–77; nursery Drumgarth inf s from 1977
m Aber 9.8.68 Roderick F. Cameron MA 1966 *qv*

ROSS Catherine Anne BEd 1969

ROSS Catherine Frances Hay MA 1968
d of John H. R. off. man. and Kathleen M. R. Hay comptometer oper; b Aber 29.8.47
teacher Engl Aber 1969–73
m Aber 4.4.70 Neil Cromar LLB 1966 *qv*

ROSS Catherine Lindsay MA 1961
d of James R. R. gen merch and Jessie S. MacPherson teacher; b Helmsdale 18.4.40
teacher dem p s Aber 1962–63; Norway: lib Molde 1974–75, Tromsø from 1975
m Aber 3.10.60 Sigurd B. Wisløff MB ChB 1963 *qv*

ROSS Charles Melville Brown *MA 1958
s of Charles R. haulage contr and Christy M. MacAskill teacher; b Inv 12.12.36
teacher classics Stirling h s 1959–66 (spec asst 1965–66); prin classics: Turriff acad 1967–71, Banff acad from 1971
m Falkirk 26.12.59 Elizabeth C. Henderson clerkess/typist d of John W. H. Falkirk

ROSS Christine Donaldson BSc 1967
d of Murdo A. R. salesman and Janet G. Donaldson typist; b Inv 7.4.47
computer syst eng Edin 1967–72

m Nairn 25.9.71 Howard W. Corfield BSc(Strath) computer eng s of Howard L. C. Clydebank

ROSS Claude Marie Louise MA 1960
d of R. H. R. man. dir and Germaine Lery L ès L(Paris); b Paris 24.6.23
m Edin 31.10.44 Norman S. Whitehead man. dir s of Frank W. Aber

ROSS David MA 1969
s of Robert R. lab. and Hughina McPherson; b Nairn 27.3.48
Dip Youth Commun Work(Edin) 1974
teacher Aber: Bankhead acad 1970–73, Harlaw acad 1974–77, Summerhill acad 1977–78, Bankhead acad from 1978

ROSS David Alexander *MA 1962
s of David R. bldr and Lena N. Davidson nurse; b Forres 23.4.40
PhD(Lond) 1967
lect Fourah Bay coll univ of Sierra Leone Freetown 1965–68; assoc prof hist Simon Fraser univ Burnaby BC Canada from 1968

ROSS David Sinclair *BSc 1967 MSc 1969 *BD 1977
s of William F. S. R. plasterer and Elspeth Black; b Aber 24.7.45
PhD(Glas) 1971
res chem with Philips Aachen W Ger 1971–74; min C of S Peterhead from 1978
m Aber 6.7.68 Heather G. Watt BSc 1970 *qv*

ROSS Donald Forrester MA 1963
s of Edward S. R. MA 1923 *qv*; b Aber 14.6.42
CA 1967
CA app G & J McBain Aber 1963–67; audit asst Thomson McLintock & Co Glasg 1967–69; C of S asst treas Edin 1969–75, dep treas from 1975
m Glasg 25.6.70 Dorothy R. Nelson teacher d of Jack N. Glasg

ROSS Donald George MB ChB 1967
s of John R. civ serv customs & excise and Barbara Cruickshank teacher; b Lonmay 6.6.44
FFARCS 1973
h o, sen h o Queen Mary's hosp Sidcup 1967–69; ARI: sen h o, regist, sen regist anaest 1969–77; consult. anaest from 1977
m Aber 12.12.69 Doreen A. Garvin radiogr d of Thomas G. Coleraine NI

ROSS Donald Hugh *MA 1964
s of John R. MA 1930 *qv* and Elizabeth Fraser MA 1930 *qv*; b Balintore 8.3.42
sub-edit. *Scotsman* Edin 1964–69; Lond: polit edit. gallup poll 1969–71, edit. *Labour Weekly* from 1971
m Glasg 29.8.70 Anne Macleod BA(OU) 1977 teacher d of Angus M. Shawbost Is of Lewis

ROSS Dorothy Susan Aitken MA 1967 CASS 1969

ROSS Douglas Fraser MA 1961
s of Simon D. R. BSc 1930 *qv* and Lilias M. Garland MA 1932 *qv*; b Pretoria S Af 25.11.40
CA
acct/comp secy: J. T. L. Parkinson–Twaddle Glasg 1969–70, J. T. L. Parkinson Aber 1970–71; acct inter-city transport Cumbernauld 1971–74; gen man. John Russell (Grangemouth) Grangemouth from 1974
m Glasg 6.7.68 Marjorie A. McNaught exec off. BoT d of Arthur B. McN. MA(Glas) Glasg

ROSS Edward Forrester *MA 1960
s of Edward S. R. MA 1923 *qv*; b Aber 13.6.37
teacher: coll de Geneva Geneva 1961–62, St Albans 1962–63, Bremen Ger 1963–66; head upper s Gilberd s Colchester from 1966
m Bremen 1966 Rosemarie Balzereit

ROSS Flora Munro *MA 1961
d of Angus W. R. farm. and Emily J. Hill clerkess; b Invergordon 1.12.39
BLitt(Oxon) 1968
post-grad stud. Oxon 1961; lect in Engl Liv 1963; Aber 1965
m Aber 8.9.70 John H. Alexander DPhil(Oxon) univ lect s of John A. Bath

ROSS Frank Leslie *BSc 1962 PhD 1965

ROSS Freda Mary MA 1964
m Binns

ROSS Gemmell Bowman MA 1970
s of Charles W. R. printer and Winifred C. Rennie secy; b Aber 6.6.49
RAF pilot flying Harriers No 3(F) sqdr Wildenrath W Ger (rank flt lt) from 1970
m Aber 20.12.73 Maureen L. Mathison MA 1973 pers secy d of George D. M. Aber

ROSS George MA 1960 dLLB 1962
s of George R. master baker and Ruby Nicol shop-keeper; b Aber 6.3.37
leg. asst Stephen & Smith advoc Aber 1962–65, ptnr from 1965; Aberd: part-time asst Scots Law 1962–70, part-time lect Scots Law/Private Law from 1970
m Aber 5.9.62 Anne Bruce hosp secy d of Alexander B. Aber

ROSS Glen Stewart Adam BSc 1964
s of Archibald R. master elect./plumber and Patricia Stewart (*d* 1943); b Aber 31.1.43
Cert Radiation Safety(Manc) 1975
teacher maths Bervie s s 1965–67; prin phys/area exams secy Lango coll Lira Uganda 1968–72; teacher phys/sc Lossiemouth h s 1972–76; prin sc/phys Speyside h s from 1976
m Aber 20.6.70 Isabella A. Russell teacher (*d* 1975) d of John D. R. MA(Glas) Rosemarkie

ROSS Graham Garland *BSc 1966

ROSS Gwyneth MA 1962
d of George W. R. MA 1928 *qv*; b Aber 7.8.41
Dip Sec Sc(Strath) 1963
m Edin 8.7.67 Raymond A. McCabe MA(Glas) fin. dir s of James O. McC. BA(Edmonton) Glasg

ROSS Hamish Fordyce *BSc 1959

ROSS Helen MA 1956
d of Stanley A. N. R. telecomm mech and Elizabeth B. Cocker tailoress; b Aber 23.7.36
teacher Renfrewsh 1957–61, Kent 1961–62
m Inv 29.12.62 Leslie P. Best

ROSS Helen Margaret MA 1969
m Antcliffe

ROSS Hilary Anne *MA 1967
d of John R. assur dist man. and Annabella C. Milne; b Ellon 9.12.44
DEP(Glas) 1969

asst educ psych Notre Dame child guid clin Glasg 1969–70; teacher Long Eaton p s Derbysh 1970–71; biometrician med dept Ciba–Geigy Basel from 1971
m Manc 31.5.69 M. Jamil Chaudri BSc(Salf) mathematician s of M. Khalil C. Toronto

ROSS Iain Paul BSc 1965 PhD 1970
s of John R. customs off. and Barbara Cruickshank teacher; b Lonmay 28.1.43
res stud. med s Aber 1965–70; clin biochem W gen hosp Edin 1970–73; lab scient univ hosp Edmonton Alberta 1974; truck driver Edmonton 1974–75; civ serv Alberta prov govt from 1975

ROSS Iain Sutherland MB ChB 1964 PhD 1970
s of William S. R. man. dir farm comp and Ruby Clark; b Enfield 18.9.38
sen lect chem path. Aberd from 1973
m Aber 12.2.66 Joan A. Bell d of James M. B. Bearsden

ROSS Isabel MacDonald *MA 1968
d of John Ross MA 1930 *qv* and Elizabeth Fraser MA 1930 *qv*; b Dingwall 4.10.46
Dip Psych(WAIT) 1974
W Aust: teacher soc stud. Armadale h s 1969–70; res asst Melbourne 1970; teacher Engl Balcatta h s 1971–72; guid off. Loreto convent Claremont 1974; tut. psych to external WAIT stud. Albany 1975; school psych Albany 1976–77
m Inv 31.8.68 Terence M. Kilkenny MA 1968 *qv*

ROSS James MA 1964 BD 1967
s of David R. fisherman and Elizabeth Johnston; b Port Seton 26.4.33
C of S min: Kilsyth from 1968
m Tranent 1.9.55 Mary C. Somerville typist d of Robert S. Port Seton

ROSS James BSc(eng) 1970
s of John R. maintenance worker process ind and Andrewina M. Crawford; b Fraserburgh 13.4.43
instrumentation eng dev Glasg 1970–72; Cambuslang: process dev eng 1972–73, asst works eng from 1973
m Aber 5.8.71 Elaine M. Duncan MA 1968 *qv*

ROSS James MacLean MA 1963

ROSS John *BSc 1964

ROSS John BSc 1961 PhD 1964

ROSS John Alexander *MA 1970
s of Samuel T. R. comm clerk and Helen M. Christie hotel receptionist; b Aber 1.2.38
Dip Lib(Strath) 1973
Esso petr comp: market. trainee Lond 1970–71, oper superv N Shields 1971–72; lib Lanark c c E Kilbride 1973–74, dep lib Bishopbriggs dist lib from 1974

ROSS John Fraser *MA 1961
s of John R. MA 1930 *qv* and Elizabeth Fraser MA 1930 *qv*; b Inv 27.6.40
MA(Alta) 1962
lect Glas from 1964
m Fort Augustus 17.8.63 Theresa E. MacDonald MA 1963 *qv*

ROSS Kathleen Anne MA 1969
d of Frederick G. R. pharm and Lily H. Munro; b Ellon 11.7.48
stud. YESTB Manc poly 1970–71; careers off. Bolton corp 1970–72
m Stonehaven William A. Wright sub edit. *Daily Mail* Manc s of William W. Didsbury

ROSS Lorna Alison Ishbel MA 1968

ROSS Margaret Isobelle Fraser MA 1968 Dip Ed 1969
d of John A. R. mech, traffic warden and Margaret C. Fraser; b Maryburgh 8.6.47
Edin: teacher mod lang Tynecastle h s 1969–73, asst housemistress 1972–73, prin Fr from 1973

ROSS Marion Catherine MA 1965
m Robb

ROSS Marjory Millikin MA 1962
b Peterhead 18.12.40
Perth h s: teacher Engl 1963–70, spec asst 1970–72, asst prin Engl from 1972

ROSS Mary Jane Storey MA 1958

ROSS Maureen Vallely MA 1966
m Watts

ROSS Patricia Frances Bernadette MA 1968
d of John R. MB ChB 1937; b Fraserburgh 22.3.47
Lond: marketing asst 1969–70, proj admin 1970–71, pers asst 1971–76
m Aber 30.8.71 Richard G. L. Stileman BSc 1968 *qv*

ROSS Philip Wesley MB ChB 1960 ᶜMD 1970
s of George W. R. MA 1928 *qv*; b Aber 6.6.36
MIBiol 1970 FLS 1973 TD 1974
lect bact: Aberd 1961–64, Edin 1964–73; sen lect bact/hon consult. bact Edin RI from 1973; sen warden outward halls and student houses Edin from 1972
m Aber 12.8.60 Stella J. Shand MA 1958 *qv*

ROSS Rhoda Isabella *BSc 1960
d of David R. clerk and Christina S. Allan photog asst; b Aber 26.3.38
res stud. dept bot Aberd 1960–61; teacher Montrose 1962–68
m Aber 30.3.64 Gordon F. Legge BSc(agr) 1961 *qv*

ROSS Sheila Margaret Craig MA 1970
d of William G. R. market gardener and Isabella H. C. McHarg; b Laurencekirk 3.3.49
teacher Fr/Ger Arbroath acad from 1971

ROSS Simon Fraser Robertson *MA 1965
s of Finlay R. R. welding eng and Mary V. Fraser secy; b Inv 24.6.40
jun, middle, sen man. posts Indust & Comm Fin. corp Lond, Leic, Lond 1965–70; Edin: Scot. rep Williams Glyn & Co 1970–73, man. dir Royal Bank Dev 1973–76, man. dir Monross Investments from 1976
m Dingwall 26.9.70 Patricia M. Longmoor MA(Edin) soc worker d of Alexander P. L. Kincraig

ROSS Susan Christine *MA 1968
m Tinch

ROSS Susan Janet Ferguson MB ChB 1970
m Morrison

ROSS Valerie Anne MA 1962
m Begg

ROSS William Alexander MA 1968
s of William R. ironmonger and Annie M. Knox nurse; b Forfar 7.4.46

teacher: Arbroath 1969–70, Aber from 1970
m Arbroath 1.8.70 Marjory E. H. Drever teacher d of Samuel D. MA(St And) Arbroath

ROSS William James *BSc 1964

ROSS Wilson MA 1968

ROTHIN David John *MA 1969
s of Arthur R. carpet fitter and Ethel Moore; b Wolverhampton 17.4.47
computer progr: GPO Lond 1969–71, Morrison's assoc comps Glasg 1971–74; computer analyst/progr Lanarksh c c Hamilton from 1974
m Motherwell 20.4.73 Aileen M. Sinclair MA 1972 teacher d of John S. Inv

ROTHNIE Douglas William MB ChB 1957
s of Alexander R. farm worker and Barbara Duguid; b Fyvie 6.11.30
h o royal ment hosp, City hosp Aber, ARI 1957–58; m o RAF UK, Aden, Persian Gulf 1959–62; sen h o: cas Woolmanhill Aber 1962–63, Risedale mat. hosp Barrow-in-Furness 1963–64; g p Barrow-in-Furness from 1964
m Denmark 8.5.60 Edel H. Henriksen nurse d of Peder H. Staellands Odde

ROWELL Michael John MSc 1969
s of Basil W. R. marine eng and Claire D. Heather; b Lond 6.1.46
BSc(Hull) 1967 PhD(Sask) 1974
Canada: sessional lect soil microbiol Saskatoon 1972–73, post doct fell. Edmonton 1974, sess lect 1974–75

ROWLANDS Brian MacLean *MA 1968
s of Arthur W. R. banker and Helen C. S. MacLean MB ChB 1936 *qv*; b Aber 3.7.46
Dip Ed Psych(Lond) 1969
teacher Greenwich (ILEA) 1969–71; educ psych Bradford from 1971
m Greenwich 2.10.70 Valerie Burton teacher d of Samuel H. B. MA(Cantab) Dulverton

ROWLANDS Owen *MA 1967
s of William M. R. teacher and Gladys Hunt teacher; b Wolverhampton 19.1.44
teacher Fr/Ger RGC Aber 1968–70; prin mod lang: Earlston 1970–72, Galashiels acad from 1972
m Aber 15.8.67 Pamela M. Rennie MA 1965 *qv*

ROWLING Christopher Lewis *BSc(eng) 1968
s of Gerald A. R. bank off. and Edna Pearman; b Croydon 17.12.45
Lond: tv elect. circuit des eng IBA 1969–72, oper broadcast eng 1972–73, broadcast eng Capital Radio from 1973
m Bitteswell 29.6.74 Janis L. Moignard loc govt off. d of C. George M. Bitteswell

ROWORTH Colin Campbell *BSc 1970
s of William L. R. ARIBA arch. and Mary O. S. Campbell nurse; b Edin 17.1.49
proj leader (res and dev) papermakers Wiggins Teape Beaconsfield 1970–72; res and dev tech Tullis Russell & Co Glenrothes 1972–76; group leader (chem tech serv) Tullis Russell from 1976
m Beaconsfield 14.10.72 Susan Lockhart teacher d of Clement L. Beaconsfield

ROY Bharatendu Narayan PhD 1957
MSc(Calc)

ROYLE Trevor Bridge *MA 1967
s of Kenneth B. R. army off. and Kathleen B. Page; b Mysore India 26.1.45
Edin: edit. William Blackwood 1968–70, lit. dir Scot. arts council from 1971
m(1) Shrivenham 26.8.67 Jane B. Sibbald MA 1968 *qv*; marr diss 1.2.73
(2) Edin 27.4.73 Hannah M. Rathbone MB ChB(Edin)

RUBBI Saiyid Fazl-I PhD 1964
MSc(Dacca)

RUBIN Freda *MA 1967

RUDDIMAN Kenneth Wilson *MA 1962
m Helene A. Stewart MA 1962 *qv*

RUFF Lynda *BSc 1965 PhD 1968
d of Wilfred S. R. dir eng firm and Laurel W. Dexter secy; b Radlett 27.9.41
asst res path. Denbigh 1968–69
m Rickmansworth 4.5.68 Christopher J. Flemming MB ChB 1968 *qv*

RUKUBA Martin BSc(for) 1959

RULE Frank *BSc 1962
s of George W. R. rly guard and Winifred Gray; b Cambridge 29.7.24
teacher biol Blairgowrie 1963–65, prin biol 1965–69; lect coll of educ Aber from 1969
m Lusaka Zambia 5.11.49 Margaret Keith nurs sister d of William K. Mintlaw stat

RUNCIE Moira Anne Gardiner *MA 1969
d of William R. pharm/optic and Margaret Tait teacher; b Aber 6.6.47
lect Engl univ of Malawi Blantyre 1969–70, Zomba from 1976
m Blantyre Malawi 23.8.69 Patrick D. Hardcastle BSc(for) 1968 *qv*

RUNOLFSSON Sveinn BSc(agr) 1970
s of Runolfur Sveinsson BSc(Copenhagen) dir soil conserv serv and Valgeröur Halldrösdóttir; b Hvanneyri Iceland 28.4.46
MSc(Corn) 1972
Gunnarsholt Iceland: asst soil conserv 1970–72, dir soil conserv serv from 1972
m Iceland 27.12.73 Oddný Saemundsdóttir nurse d of Saemundur Jónsson

RUSH Christopher *MA 1968

RUSHTON Sarah Ruth *MA 1970
d of Edwin P. K. R. MB ChB(Birm) med pract and Joyce W. Newman nurse; b Bristol 14.2.49
asst solic Northampton 1974–79
m Leeds 10.7.70 Anthony P. Sturdee BSc 1968 *qv*

RUSHWORTH Alison Louise MA 1970
d of William R. R. BA(Lond) teacher and Dorothea A. Gladstone headmistress; b Wimbledon 24.4.49
BA(Lond) 1973
teacher Engl to adults in Volkhochschule: Stuttgart Ger 1973–74, Heidelberg from 1975

RUSK Isabel Henderson *MA 1956
d of William M. R. R. MA(Glas) lect r e and Constance A. Henderson; b Glasg 3.4.35
Cert Soc St(Edin) 1957
ch care off. Aber 1958–62
m Aber 24.2.62 William J. Farquhar MA 1958 *qv*

RUSSELL Agnes Jean MLitt 1968
BA(Lond)
m Short

RUSSELL Alan Gordon MA 1963

RUSSELL Alison Margaret Joan BSc 1969 *MEd 1973
d of James K. R. hotel man. and Ivy J. Hill; b Aber 9.7.48
teacher maths: Kingussie 1970–72, internat s Geneva 1973–75
m Aber 15.4.74 David J. Ryan teacher s of John J. R. Weymouth

RUSSELL Andrew BSc 1970
s of James R. telecomm supt and Joan A. Finch BBC receptionist; b Huddersfield 20.8.49

RUSSELL Brian Montgomery *BSc(eng) 1970
s of Andrew M. R. MA(Glas) C of S min and E. Pauline Allan nurse; b Arbroath 19.10.48
des progr 1970–73; team leader progr 1973–77; sen eng LSI Exploitation ICL Manc from 1977
m Pudsey 19.8.72 J. Margaret Kingman BSc(Leeds) progr d of Reginald K. Pudsey

RUSSELL Dorothy May *MA 1962
m Ellis

RUSSELL George MB ChB 1959
s of George R. merch/farm. and Elizabeth M. Law teacher; b Insch 2.7.36
MRCP(Lond) 1964 FRCP 1977
h o, sen h o, regist Aber 1959–65; res fell. univ Colorado med center Denver USA 1965–67; lect ch health Aberd 1967–68; consult. paediat Grampian health board Aber from 1969; prof paediat univ of Riyadh, Saudi Arabia 1977–78 (leave of absence)
m Aber 20.8.62 Gillian D. Simpson radiogr d of Douglas B. S. Kirriemuir

RUSSELL Helen May *BSc 1965
d of George S. R. baker and Catherine Buchan teacher; b Inv 9.12.43
town plan. asst Aber 1965–67
m Aber 17.9.66 Ian P. Souter MA 1964 *qv*

RUSSELL Ian Farquhar *BMedBiol 1970 MB ChB 1973
s of Alexander R. gamekeeper and Kathleen M. Baxter nurse, bookkeeper; b Insch 11.11.48
FFARCS 1977
resid m o Latrobe Tasmania 1973–74; sen resid m o Sir Charles Gairdner hosp Perth Aust 1975–76; regist anaest ARI 1976–77; spec paediat anaest Janeway hosp Newfoundland 1978; sen regist anaest ARI from 1977
m Aber 15.7.72 Helen S. Campbell BSc 1973 tut. histology d of Thomas G. M. C. Aber

RUSSELL James *BSc 1958 PhD 1963
s of James R. foreman shoe repairer and Jane W. Youngson; b Aber 24.11.35
FCIPA 1970 European Patent Attorney
patent off. min of aviation Lond 1961–64; patent off. liaison with US govt Brit emb Washington DC 1964–67; sen patent off. RAE Farnborough 1967–78; prin pat. off. MoD Lond from 1978
m Aber 19.12.60 Elspeth R. Geggie teacher p e d of Thomas W. G. Glasg

RUSSELL James Gordon MB ChB 1966
s of Alexander R. butcher and Eileen J. Emslie; b Fyvie 11.4.42
DObstRCOG 1968 MRCGP 1972 DPharm Med 1977
h o ARI 1966–67; sen h o: obst Northampton gen hosp 1967, med Killearn hosp 1968, paediat Alder Hey ch's hosp Liv 1968–69; ship's surg royal fleet auxil MoD 1969; g p Bucksburn 1969–75; med advis Ciba–Geigy (UK) from 1975
m Aber 6.5.72 Jennifer M. Renton occup therap d of David R. R. Aber

RUSSELL Jennifer Mary MA 1968
d of Archibald R. R. man./comp dir and Irene Rowlings; b Falkirk 14.9.47
Dip Ed(Glas) 1969
teacher: geog Dalry h s 1969–70, geog/mod stud. Garnock acad Kilbirnie 1970–72, asst prin guid 1972–74; prin guid Auchenharvie acad Stevenston 1974–76
m Largs 11.7.75 Crawford W. Logan BSc(Paisley tech coll) gen man. s of James W. L. MB ChB(Glas) Largs

RUSSELL John Grant BSc(eng) 1969

RUSSELL Kathleen BSc 1962
d of George S. R. baker and Catherine Buchan teacher; b Inv 17.3.41
teacher maths: Inv 1963–65, Aber 1965–66, Lond from 1973
m Aber 13.7.65 Bryan Hickson MB ChB 1965 *qv*

RUSSELL Leslie MA 1962
s of William R. baker and Mary Leslie shop asst; b Aber 1.6.41
Higher Dip R Ed(Aber) 1963
teacher relig educ: Falkirk h s 1963–68, Aber acad/ Hazlehead acad 1969–73, asst prin r e 1973–75, prin r e from 1975
m Aber 10.4.65 Anne W. S. Douglas shorthand typist d of Alexander D. Aber

RUSSELL Mhairi Ballantyne MB ChB 1966
d of Robert S. B. R. LDS(Glasg) dent. and Mabel E. Duthie; b Torphins 28.4.43
Aber: h o City hosp, RACH, mat. hosp 1966–68; trainee g p Elgin 1968–69, part-time g p Cullen/Portsoy from 1969
m Aber 25.8.69 Iain D. Legge agr insp Dept Agr(Scot.) s of John A. L. Invergordon

RUSSELL William *BSc 1964
s of James R. foreman shoe repairer and Jane W. Youngson; b Aber 4.2.41
Cert Computer Sc(Brunel) 1972
VSO lect Guyana s of agr corp 1964–65; Lond: scient off. police scient dev branch Home Office 1965–68, sen scient off. 1968–71, prin scient off. civ serv dept 1971–77, sen prin scient off. 1977–79; dep town clerk/chief exec Aber from 1979
m Aber 1.7.67 Sandra Ross civ serv d of Alexander I. R. Aber

RUST Mary Wilson MA 1957 Dip Ed 1965
d of James H. R. MA(Edin) C of S min and Mary Wilson mission.; b Moukden China 26.11.36
teacher Dumfries 1959–64 and from 1970; head Dunsyre p s 1965–70

RUTHERFORD Andrew Adams PhD 1963
s of James S. R. MA(Royal Univ Ireland) presb min and Bertha C. Robb; b Warrenpoint Co Down 3.1.25
B Agr(Belf) 1951 M Agr(Belf) 1957 FRSS 1959
off. i/c field exper Loughry agr coll Cookstown Co Tyrone; post grad stud. statist Aberd 1954–56; off. i/c field exper Macaulay inst for soil res Aber 1956–57; scient off., prin scient off., consult. statist ARC unit of

statist Aberd; dept agr NI/head agr biometrics Belf 1964–76; head statist dept East Malling res inst from 1976
m Rostrevor Co Down Harriet M. Clarke receptionist stud. health centre d of William C. Newry

RUTHERFORD Barbara Anne MA 1962
d of John R. flt lt RAF eng fitter/farm. and Mary C. I. Collingwood shop asst; b Aber 9.12.40
teacher Engl: to for. stud. Kent 1964–65, Brit council scheme Halden Bodø Norway 1965–67, Willington Co Durh from 1968

RYAN Pamela *MA 1970 MLitt 1972
d of Angus C. R. HGV driving instr and Euphemia Mundie; b Glasg 31.3.49
teacher: Brittons s Essex 1972–74, Walthamstow girls' h s Waltham Forest from 1974
m Helensburgh 12.8.72 Graham H. Munn MA(Glas) civ serv s of Thomas M. Cardross

RYDER Carol Ann *BSc 1969

SAAD Zakaria Abdalla Mohamed BSc(for) 1969
BSc(Khart) MSc(Khart)

SAAKWA-MANTE Kwaafo MSc 1964
s of Saakwa-Mante merch and Korkoi Mensan; b Accra Ghana 17.2.24
MB ChB(Leeds) 1952 DTM&H(Lond) 1954 DPH 1956 MFCM 1974
sen m o Accra 1964–68; chief med statist centre for health statist Ghana from 1968
m Crewe 8.6.54 Nora Clegg d of Thomas C. Rochdale

SABRI AL-OZAIRI Sudad PhD 1968 *ChM 1972
MB ChB(Bagh)

SACHS Monica Trevor MA 1966

SADLER Alexander James MA 1961
s of George S. area man. petr comp and Mary Cruickshank; b Lairg 7.12.40
BA(OU) 1977
teacher maths Aber: Hilton s s 1962–70, coll of comm 1970–73, prin maths Torry acad from 1973
m Aber 15.7.64 Joan M. Reid MA 1963 *qv*

SADLER Glenn Edward PhD 1967
AB(Ill) MA(Calif)

SADLER Michael George LLB 1967 *MA 1970
s of William R. S. LRCPGlas med pract and Margaret T. Marshall MA(Glas) teacher; b Stranraer 25.2.47
ACCA 1972
acct manuf indust N'cle-u-Tyne 1970–73; plant acct man. Manc 1973–75; Melton Mowbray: fin. acct man. manuf indust 1975–77, fin. controller from 1977
m Edin 10.8.70 Susan W. Stewart MA 1969 *qv*

SADLER Robin Mischa *BSc(for) 1964
s of John S. teacher and Eveline M. Sanders artist; b Macclesfield 8.10.41
Brit Council schol inst for Skogskjøtsel Vollebekk Norway Bergen, Vollebekk 1964; teacher: Congleton s mod s Congleton 1965, biol King's s Macclesfield 1965–79; sheep farmer Laxey I o M from 1979
m Laxey 30.7.66 Margaret H. Clague textile des d of Robert Q. C. Laxey

SADLER Rodney Grayston BSc(eng) 1958
s of Frederick W. S. sales rep and Ellen M. Annison; b Aber 11.7.36
CEng MICE 1964
engineer: asst Wimpey 1958–61, exec with water supplies div of Govt West Nigeria 1961–63, section Taylor Woodrow 1964, section to proj man. Costain Civil 1964–74, reg man. Wales Shellabear Price contr 1975–76, div man. SE England Bovis Civil 1977–80, comm dir Protern des bldg Wales from 1980
m Aber 11.9.59 Elizabeth A. S. Metcalfe comptometer oper, cler asst d of George M. Aber

SAID Abdullah Babiker Mohamed MSc 1967
s of Babiker Mohamed S. and Elhassan El Sania Fatima; b 1.1.39
BSc(agr)(Beirut)
Sudan: land use off. Elfasher Darfur prov 1967–68, Elobeid Kordofan prov 1968–69; co-man. Savanna dev proj Khartoum 1969–73; asst dir proj: rural dev dept 1973–75, soil conserv and land use dept from 1975
m Omdurman Sudan Abdel Halim Ahmed Fathia secy d of Abdel Halim Ahmed Omdurman

SAINT Christine MA 1969
m McLaren

SAINT Lorna Sinclair MA 1956
d of Ernest S. police off. and Anne G. Sinclair; b Aber 21.12.35
admin secy Internat Airadio Lond 1957–58; teacher Engl govt s for boys Bo Sierra Leone 1958–59
m Bo Sierra Leone 23.6.58 William D. Carslake BSc(for) 1955 *qv*

SALARDINI Ali Akbar MSc 1962 PhD 1965
BSc(agr)(Teheran)

SALIH Fathi Mohamed BSc(for) 1967

SALIH Hussein BSc(for) 1964

SALVIN Janice Lillian MA 1968
m Reid

SAMA Daniel Sundima MB ChB 1963
s of Thomas S. farm. and Marie S. Ndomahina; b Njala Sierra Leone 24.12.30
DTM & H 1965 FRSocTM & H
Sierra Leone: m o 1965–68, m o Njala Un Coll 1968–70; regist psychiat Haddington 1970–73; s m o Njala Un Coll from 1973
m Aber 30.11.60 Olivia T. Caulker d of Alphoso C. Shenge Sierra Leone

SAMPSON Alan John BSc(for) 1961
s of Ronald D. S. heating eng and Dorothy M. Jarman; b Milton Regis 7.4.37
physiol asst, sen agronomist Shell biosciences lab Kent from 1961
m Sittingbourne 5.9.59 Geraldine Gutsole

SAMPSON Enid Elizabeth MSc 1970
d of John H. S. marine eng and Eleanor M. Douglass teacher; b Middsx 1918
BSc Sp(Ext) (Lond) 1942
asst to rural plan. consult 1970–72
m Cambridge 1943 John S. D. Bacon ScD(Cantab) res scient and univ teacher s of Charles H. B. BSc(Lond) Lond

SAMUELS Digby John LLB 1970

SANANIKONE Prasong BSc(agr) 1969

SANANIKORN Prida *BSc(agr) 1965
s of Thao Peng Sananikorn banker/politician and Boonthan bus. woman; b Vientiane Laos 4.8.40
Thailand: sen man. (marketing) Bangkok 1965–68, sen exec (advt) 1968–71, chief sales div Construct. Material Marketing Comp Bangkok from 1971
m Aber 14.4.65 Avril R. Clarke MA 1965 *qv*

SANDERS Penelope Jane *MA 1969
d of Brian G. S. ophth optician and Edith M. Holt; b Walsall 7.4.47
Dip Clin Psych(Br Psych Soc) 1976
secy: FCO Lond 1970, Royal Free hosp Lond 1970–71, Price Waterhouse Assoc Lond 1971–72, Brit dom appliances Peterborough 1972–73; prob clin psych: Peterborough dist hosp 1972–73, Norfolk area health auth Norwich 1974–76; clin psych Broadmoor hosp 1976–77
m Coleshill 15.7.72 John E. Spinks LLB(Lond) retail exec s of Ronald L. S. King's Lynn

SANDERSON John Graham *BSc(eng) 1968

SANDISON Alan George *MA 1958
s of William A. S. farm. and Bella J. Meston; b Ballater 13.11.32
PhD(Cantab) 1963
asst Engl Aberd 1960–62; lect Engl: Exe 1963–71, Durh 1971–74; prof Engl Strath from 1974

SANDISON Derek James BSc 1966
s of James S. S. clerk (retd) and Margaret H. Burnett; b Ellon 17.9.45
aerodynamics eng BAC Brist 1966–68; sen scient computer analyst de Havilland aircraft Toronto 1968–78; syst man. HG Engineering Toronto from 1978

SANDISON Jean Mary Harrison MA 1966
d of Arthur M. S. crofter/road lab. and Peterina Brown clerkess; b Heylor Shetland 15.1.45
teacher Anderson inst Lerwick 1967–71
m 11.7.68 David C. Marwick BSc 1964 *qv*

SANDRINGHAM Peter Rankin LLB 1966

SANDS David Clifford MB ChB 1969

SANDS Jeremy Nicol *MA 1958
s of Harvey T. N. and Alice R. E. Benzie; b Glasg 18.1.37
resid California USA

SANDSTRAND Ivar Peter Kaare MB ChB 1963

SANGSTER Alan John *BSc(eng) 1963 MSc 1964 PhD 1967
s of William J. S. postal worker and Edna M. Walker teacher; b Aber 21.11.40
CEng MIEE 1971
res eng Ferranti Edin 1964–69; sen eng, prin eng, group leader Plessey Radar Is of Wight 1969–72; lect H-W Edin from 1972
m Aber 12.4.69 Barbara M. Wilkie staff nurse d of James W. Aber

SANGSTER Alistair Scott MA 1970

SANGSTER Barrie MB ChB 1968
s of Joseph S. bank man. and Mary A. McPherson; b Elgin 16.9.45
h o: ARI, Law hosp Carluke 1968–70, Stirling hosp, RACH 1970–72; g p Leeton NSW Aust from 1972
m Fyvie 14.8.70 Mary A. K. Hosie d of Alexander H. Fyvie

SANGSTER Christopher Leslie Gordon BEd 1969
s of James H. S. MA 1930 *qv* and Mary A. Stewart MA 1929 *qv*; b Elgin 20.5.47
teacher Perthsh 1969–73; lect educ tech S Thames Coll Lond 1973–74; advis educ tech SCET Glasg 1974–75; organis i/c teachers' resource centre Portsmouth 1975–78; trg consult. Guardian BS Lond from 1978
m Broughty Ferry 18.7.70 Gillean H. B. Thomson

SANGSTER Gillian Mary MB ChB 1962
d of James H. S. MA 1930 *qv* and Mary A. Stewart MA 1929 *qv*; b Elgin 10.8.39
h o RAHC, ARI, Woodend hosp Aber 1962–64; trainee g p Mells Frome 1964–65
m Aber 14.4.65 Alastair M. Suttie MB ChB 1961 *qv*

SANGSTER Harry Maxwell *BSc(agr) 1964
s of Harry S. BSc(agr) 1950 *qv*; b Perth 6.2.42
agr dev off. Edin, Lanarksh from 1964
m Methven 4.8.66 Sheena M. Wann chirop d of John W. Methven

SANGSTER Lorna Mary BSc 1966
d of Edwin H. S. sales rep and Daisy H. Youngson; b Aber 3.1.45
teacher maths: St Peter's s Aber 1967–68, Powis acad Aber 1968–70, Fleetwood s Chessington 1970, Darroch s Edin 1970–71, Kincorth acad Aber 1972
m Aber 20.7.69 Willson D. Taylor MB ChB 1969 *qv*

SANGSTER Michael James Lyon *BSc 1964
s of James H. S. MA 1930 *qv* and Mary A. Stewart MA 1929 *qv*; b Elgin 14.9.42
PhD(R'dg) 1968
lect R'dg from 1968; res fell. Frankfurt/Munich 1968–69
m Bootle 4.8.73 Mary C. McTegart BSc(Liv) teacher d of Charles W. McT. J.P. Bootle

SANGSTER Moira Helen MA 1967
d of George T. S. joiner and Helen Moir; b Aber 2.9.46
teacher Cults, Dyce p s from 1968

SANGSTER Rosemary MA 1962
m Logan

SANGSTER Valerie Joan *BSc 1970 PhD 1974
d of William M. S. and Joan M. M. Davis; b Aber 2.4.48
post doct res asst s of agr Nott 1974–76, res fell. from 1976
m Aber 15.12.73 Colin R. Black BSc 1971 lect

SANN Alan BSc 1967 Dip Ed 1975

SANTOS Francis Olayimika BSc(eng) 1957 *1958
s of Stephen O. S. pharm and Christiana A. Onasanya bus. woman; b Nigeria 22.4.33
MICE 1963 F Nigerian Soc Eng 1979
eng: jun C. S. Allots & ptnrs Manc 1957, asst Aber city c 1958, asst F. A. Macdonald & ptnrs Kirkcaldy 1958, Ove Arup & ptnrs Edin 1960–61, exec Western Nigeria dev corp Ibadan 1961–63, chief Obi Obembe & assoc Lagos 1963–71, ptnr Olaniyan Omotoso Santos & assoc Lagos from 1971
m Manc 5.10.57 Grace A. Johnson nurse, journalist d of Iubueabeokun J. Benin City Nigeria

SAPRA Parkash Chander BSc(eng) 1959

SARELIUS Sonja Marie MSc 1969
MA(Well)
m McKinlay

SARGENT Alice Anne *BSc 1968
m Smith

SARGENT John Reid *BSc 1958 PhD 1961
s of Alexander C. S. fisherman and Annie Reid; b Buckie 12.10.56
Bond gold medal of Amer oil chemists soc 1977
res fell. Courtauld inst Lond 1961–64; lect biochem Aberd 1964–70; prin scient off. NERC inst marine biochem Aber 1970–77, merit sen prin scient off. from 1977
m Aber 21.12.61 Elizabeth J. Buchan BSc 1961 *qv*

SARSON David Michael MA 1966 Dip Ed 1969
s of Ronald H. S. man. dye works and Marjory E. Whalley; b Leic 17.10.43
teacher Powis acad Aber 1967–69; dep prin maths Ashfield s Kirby-in-Ashfield 1967–71, dep prin maths, prin maths Kirkley h s Lowestoft from 1971, later also sen master
m Aber 10.9.66 Patricia Morrison staff nurse d of William S. M. Keith

SAUNDERS Jennifer Jane BSc 1966

SAVAGE Kathleen Elaine MA 1965
d of William S. BA(Lond) teacher, civ serv and Florence M. Barclay civ serv; b Aber 21.11.42
teacher p s St George's s for girls Edin 1969–71
m Aber 10.7.65 Bryan J. Rankin MA 1966 *qv*

SAVAGE Robert Henry MSc 1962
BSc(eng)(Alta)

SAVEGE Jill Margaret MB ChB 1967
d of David S. CA and Colinda Geddes; b Arbroath 28.3.44
DPM 1970 MRCPsych 1972 LGSM(Lond) 1970 LTCL (Lond) 1971 FTCL(Lond) 1972 Cert Adult Psych 1976 Child Psych 1977 (Amer Board Psychiat & Neurol)
h o Woodend gen hosp Aber 1967–68; sen h o Ross Clinic Aber 1968–69; regist Dingleton hosp Melrose 1969–70; regist, sen regist commun psychiat royal Edin hosp 1970–72, sen regist gen psychiat 1972–73; sen regist adolescent psychiat Tavistock clin Lond, Hillend hosp St Albans 1973–74; fell. adolescent/fam psychiat George Washington univ DC USA 1974–75; fell. ch psychiat ch's hosp DC USA 1975–76, part-time private pract from 1976
m Bethesda 12.10.75 David E. Scharff MD(Harv) psychoanalyst and child psychiat s of Nicholas S. St Louis USA

SAVIDGE Malcolm Kemp *MA 1970

SAVIN Anne *MA 1966
m Knowles

SAVORY Christopher John *BSc 1967 PhD 1974

SAW Choo Ban MSc 1967 PhD 1974
s of Seng H. S. shop keeper and Geck K. Tan; b Penang 27.1.40
BSc(Peking) 1963
struct eng: Penang 1963–64, Lond 1964–66; res stud. Aber 1966–69; asst lect eng Aber 1969–70, lect from 1970
m Lond 3.6.67 Koon Tee Lim midwife d of Lan K. L. Penang

SAWYER Madlene Marina BSc 1967 MB ChB 1972
d of John N. S. and Doris H. Brooks; b Nassau Bahamas 25.9.44
h o: St James' hosp Leeds 1972–73, Law hosp Lanarksh 1973; m o paediat Princess Margaret hosp Bahamas 1973–74, regist obst/gyn from 1974

SAYLE Timothy George BSc(eng) 1966

SAYLES Elisabeth Anne BSc 1965
d of Henry S. S. BA(Cantab) chem mech eng and Betty A. Allen secy; b Middleton St George 2.12.43
teacher: sc Goodlyburn j s Perth 1966–67, biol Morgan acad Dun 1967–69, part-time biol Kirkton h s Dun from 1972
m Largs 8.7.67 John W. Vigrow MA 1965 *qv*

SAYLES Hilary Margaret Jean MA 1961
d of George O. S. MA(Glas) historian and Agnes J. Sutherland; b Glasg 30.6.40
cataloguing rare continentals Folger lib Wash DC USA 1961–63; teacher Bedales, Petersfield 1965–66; indexing emblem books Art Hist inst Utrecht from 1966

SAYLES Michael George Alexander BSc 1959
s of George O. S. MA(Glas) prof hist Aberd and Agnes J. Sutherland; b Glasg 30.5.37
Member Inst Trg Dev 1979
RAF off. (sqn ldr) Cyprus 1960, UK 1963–71, Arabian Gulf 1971–72, UK and RAF staff coll Bracknell from 1972
m Church Fenton 20.6.64 Jacqueline V. S. Beaumont d of Lesley S. B. Yorks

SCACE Robert Chaston *MA 1964
s of Norman C. S. actor and Isobel Robertson dental nurse; b Aber 20.10.42
MA(Calg) 1968 PhD(Calg) 1972
Canada: grad asst, instr univ of Calg 1964–72; lect Red Deer coll 1968, Mt Royal coll 1971–74; pres Scace & Assoc environmental consult. Calgary 1971–78; geogr Reid Crowther & Ptnrs consult. eng and plan. Calgary from 1978
m Sylvan Lake Alberta 9.6.73 Margaret E. Wright biochem res tech d of Kenneth A. W. Three Hills Alberta

SCARGALL Isabel Anne *MA 1966

SCARGILL Sally Penelope *MA 1969

SCARLETT Stewart McLaren MA 1961
s of Stewart L. S. bricklayer, mason, bldg contr, BR employee and Margaret Wisely; b Aber 3.4.38
teacher: asst Ayr 1962–65, prin Engl Singapore 1965–71, dep head Ayr 1971–74, dir guid United World coll SE Asia Singapore from 1974
m Maybole 16.10.64 Hazel Rodgers teacher d of James R. Maybole

SCHARF Eric Manfred BSc(eng) 1970
s of Erich F. A. S. indust des and Ida M. G. Scheffel; b Brist 5.10.47
MSc(Wales) 1971 PhD(Sur) 1977
res Sur Guildford from 1971

SCHIRMER Lise MB ChB 1967
d of Helge S. bank off. and Gunvor Drangsholt; b Aber 22.10.38
Norway: h o Narvik 1968–69, g p Finnmark 1969, jun regist Vadsø 1969–71; g p Gøtene Sweden 1971; regist: Porsgrunn Norway 1971–76, Uyo Nigeria 1972, univ clin Bergen from 1976

SCHOOREL Pauline Marie BSc 1960
m Shand

SCHWARZ Pamela Margaret MA 1968
d of Edward S. BSc(Lond) head teacher and Kathleen R. Ratcliffe secy, teacher, lib; b Burgess Hill 17.4.47
Dip Housing Man. Member Inst Housing 1975
teacher maths: Sussex 1968–69, Internat Vol Serv Mbabane Swaziland 1970–71, temp work Sussex 1972; Mosscare Housing Manchester: trainee housing man. 1973–74, asst housing man. 1975–76, housing man. 1977–78, sen housing man. from 1979

SCLATER John Bingham BSc(for) 1957
b Dun 3.2.31
for. off. Perth Aust 1957–69 and from 1972; sen for. Lau-Aust Reforestation Proj Vientiane Laos 1969–72; for. off. W Aust 1972–74

SCOALES Robert Alexander MA 1959

SCOBBIE Valerie Ann MA 1970
d of William R. S. security consult. and Vivien M. Pirie; b Aber 7.6.49
cler asst educ dept Aber 1970–73
m Aber 25.7.70 Samuel D. Sinclair police serg LLB 1975 s of John G. S. Dornoch

SCORGIE Anne Moyra *MA 1959
d of William S. nurse and Sarah A. McFarquhar; b Daviot Aberdeensh 23.2.36
admin asst Manc 1959–61; teacher Engl Graeme h s Falkirk from 1972
m Aber 23.8.61 Graeme M. Bruce MA 1958 *qv*

SCOTLAND Colin George Emmerson LLB 1969
s of James S. MA(Glas) prin Aber Coll Educ and Jean Cowan MA(Glas); b Glasg 27.7.48
CA 1973
app CA Aber 1969–73; merch banker Lond: invest. exec 1973–75, man. 1975–78, assoc 1978–79, dir from 1979
m Aber 14.6.72 Sheila M. Fraser MA 1970 *qv*; separated 1978

SCOTT Alexander John BSc 1970 CASS 1976
s of Charles A. N. S. MA 1933 *qv* and Isabella G. McDonald MB ChB 1944 *qv*; b Elgin 6.8.48
teacher Edin 1972–73; trainee soc worker Aber 1973–74; commun worker Aber 1976–79; fieldwork teacher (commun work) Aber from 1979
m Aber 25.3.75 Alison M. M. Smith MA 1972 teacher d of Malcolm S. Dingwall

SCOTT Alison Hunter MLitt 1968
d of Harold S. MB ChB(St And) g p and Phyllis M. P. Baird; b Glasg 23.2.45
MA(St And) 1966
m Brackley 23.7.73 Duncan S. James

SCOTT Alison Mary MA 1965
m Clark

SCOTT Allan David BSc(eng) 1966

SCOTT David Baillie Crichton *BSc 1957
s of John S. comp dir and Helen M. A. Crichton nurse; b Calcutta 4.8.34
PhD(Glas) 1963
res asst, asst lect Glas 1958–63; seconded: tropical fish culture res inst Malacca Malaya 1960, E Af freshwater fisheries res organis Jinja Uganda 1962–63; lect zool St And from 1963
m Glasg 1961 Sybil G. Ward BSc(Leic) d of Peter A. W.

SCOTT Dennis PhD 1964
BSc(Durh)

SCOTT Derek Alexander *BSc 1958

SCOTT Diana Hendry BEd 1970
d of Charles S. BSc 1934 *qv*; b Aber 25.1.48
teacher mus: Pitmedden area Aberdeensh 1970–71, Turriff acad from 1972
m Montgomery

SCOTT Diane Cowperthwaite *MA 1958
d of James S. shoemaker instr and Hannah Laing milliner; b Aber 12.2.36
BA(Cantab) 1961
lect Engl Dalhousie univ Halifax Canada 1958–59, part-time lect RGIT Aber; journalism from 1968 founder/edit. *Leopard* mag. Aber
m Aber 28.4.62 David I. Morgan MA 1958 *qv*

SCOTT Eleanor Mary *BSc 1961
d of Charles W. S. BSc(Glas) for. off. and Isobel G. M. Stewart; b Aber 27.3.38
tech asst haemat dept med s Cantab 1961–65
m Aber 16.8.61 Roger H. Fairclough MA(Cantab) map lib s of James F. Carnforth

SCOTT Elizabeth Mora Joan MB ChB 1968
d of Gordon I. S. MB ChB(Edin) surg and Mora J. Craig MB ChB 1940 *qv*; b Aber 21.5.44
h o Bridge of Earn hosp, East Ham mem hosp Lond 1968–69; h o, sen h o City of Lond mat. hosp, royal northern hosp Lond 1969–71; g p Woking from 1972
m Elgin 8.1.72 David K. Wilson CA s of Peter R. W. Inverkeilor

SCOTT Elspeth Susan MA 1969
d of Arthur S. bank off. and Agnes I. M. Hutcheson teacher dom sc; b Edin 11.12.48
CA 1975
hotel waitress S Queensferry 1969–70; trainee computer oper NCB Edin 1970; app CA 1970–75; CA T. Hunter Thomson & Co Edin
m Queensferry 15.10.77 Alexander W. W. Munro CA app, salesman, driver s of Alexander F. M. Dalkeith

SCOTT Frederick MA 1969
s of Robert S. papermaker and Elizabeth K. Adams; b Aber 10.6.25
teacher Fyvie from 1970
m Aber 20.6.64 Barbara J. Lewis BSc N(Lond Ont) nurse, superv of nurs d of Frederick C. L. Sudbury Canada

SCOTT Helen Massie *MA 1969
m Edwards

SCOTT Hugh Lawrence *BSc(eng) 1963 MSc 1965
s of John S. master baker and Ethel Urquhart master baker; b Aber 3.7.41
res eng Eng Elect. Whetstone 1965–68, sect. leader 1968–70; tech eng Simon-Carver Stockport 1970–72; self employed gen merch 1972–78; constr insp man. Hunt Co Int Iran from 1978
m Aber 15.12.64 Margaret S. Whitton nurse d of David M. W. Arbroath

SCOTT Ian Malcolm *MA 1958 PhD 1980

SCOTT James Norman Gallie BSc(eng) 1970
s of Charles W. S. BSc(Glas) for. and Isobel G. M.

Stewart; b Oxford 30.12.46
dev eng Ferranti Edin 1970–78, Littet W Ger from 1978
m Banbury 6.4.74 Joy L. Barratt MA 1971 careers off. d of Albert G. B. Adderbury

SCOTT Joan Frances MA 1968
d of Frank A. S. draper and Robertha J. Ollason; b Lerwick 8.2.47
teacher Scalloway j h s Shetland 1969–72
m Lerwick 9.7.69 David W. Pottinger draper s of David S. P. Burra Isle Shetland

SCOTT Kathleen Charleston MA 1970
d of George A. S. MA 1930 *qv*; b Banff 14.6.49
asst staff man. Marks & Spencer Glasg 1971–73; pers dept HIB Inv 1973–74; teacher from 1976
m Aber 12.7.73 Roderick M. Manson MA 1971 teacher s of Anderson M. BSc(agr) 1933 *qv*

SCOTT Kathleen Mary Winifred MA 1967
d of Albert S. T. S. crofter and Catherine B. Tulloch; b N Ronaldsay 11.9.45
teacher: Mintlaw 1968–71, Linlathen h s Dun; seconded from Dun educ auth for cert in youth/commun work 1974–75; prin guid Linlathen h s Dun from 1976

SCOTT Linda Kathryn MA 1969
d 15.10.71

SCOTT Margaret MA 1964
d of Alexander R. S. chief display advt clerk Aber Journals and Alexis Smith; b Aber 3.2.43
Cert Soc St(Glas) 1965
ch care off. Lanark c c 1965–67
m Aber 6.3.67 Kenneth R. Young asst hotel man./teacher catering s of Lachlan B. Y. MA(Glas) Perth

SCOTT Michael Lennox BSc(eng) 1960
s of John S. S. tea planter and Irene Bird-Wilson lect, man.; b Calcutta 11.11.38
M Eng Sc(NSW) 1965 CEng(Aust) MIHE(Lond)
civ eng dept main roads NSW Aust 1960–66; sen asst eng traffic Kingston-u-Thames 1966–68; civ eng dept main roads NSW 1968–70; hwy eng Vallentine Laurie & Davies Bangkok, Kuala Lumpur 1970–71; resid eng N. D. Lea & Assoc Bangkok 1971–73; proj eng Ibadan Nigeria 1973; resid eng, sen hwy eng Ibadan, Kano 1973–74
m Cairns Queensland Aust Penelope J. Watsford teacher d of Stephen D. W. MD, BS(Melb) Yorkey's Knob Queensland

SCOTT Michael McGillivray MB ChB 1967
s of George A. S. MA 1930 *qv*; b Banff 4.10.43
DObstRCOG 1971 FRCSE 1975
h o, sen h o Aber gen hosps 1967–69; m o flying doctor serv Ndola Zambia 1969–70; sen h o Aber gen hosps 1970–71; surg sen h o Derbysh RI 1972–73; regist surg univ of W Manc Salford 1973–75; sen regist orthop and clin lect United Birm hosps from 1975

SCOTT Norman Marshall PhD 1967
s of Charles S. farm. and Williamina C. Marshall; b Aber 2.7.24
FRIC 1976
prin scient off. Macaulay inst Aber from 1967
m Aber 18.12.55 Margaret McFarlane d of Robert McF. Aber

SCOTT Owen Rae *MA 1969
s of James R. S. cler worker insur comp and Euphemia B. Jones wages clerk insur comp; b Dunoon 24.7.46
Ford Motor Co. Essex: job eval off., organis analyst 1969–72, pers policies analyst 1972–73; staff advis Brit Leyland Preston from 1973

SCOTT Patrick William BSc 1959
s of William S. civ serv and Mary L. Gray; b Huntly 10.10.37
teacher maths AGS from 1961, prin guid from 1972

SCOTT Peter Allardyce *MA 1970

SCOTT Robert James *MA 1970

SCOTT Robin Douglas Murray MB ChB 1964
s of Ian M. S. MB ChB(Edin) med pract and Liebe B. Rankine; b Carlisle 2.2.41
MRCPE 1968 MRCP(Lond) 1968
h o, sen h o Aber 1964–66; regist med Aber 1966–71; res fell. Washington univ s med St Louis USA 1969–70; lect med Edin 1971–75; consult. phys Windsor from 1975
m Aber 14.7.64 Alexandria Shearer secy d of Alexander S. Aber

SCOTT Robin Ford cMB ChB 1966
s of Laurence F. S. master mariner and Barbara H. Wilson loc govt off.; b S Shields 8.9.42
MRCGP
h o RACH, ARI 1966–67; terminable lect path. Aberd 1967; trainee g p 1970; g p Grays, Dun from 1970 and asst tut. dept g p Dund from 1972
m Aber 24.7.68 Sheila M. Fraser MA 1966 *qv*

SCOTT Ronald LLB 1970
s of William S. and Christina M. Finnie; b Turriff 19.10.48
law app John Laurie & Co Aber 1970–72; law app, leg. asst corp of City of Aber from 1972
m New Byth 24.7.71 Edna Imray teacher d of Gordon J. I. New Byth

SCOTT Rosemary MA 1969
d of James S. for. and Helen Turner; b Kelso 26.6.48
teacher maths Galashiels acad 1970–78
m Duns 8.7.77 Roger H. Wardman B Tech(Brad) lect s of Ernest W. Otley

SCOTT Sinclair Tulloch BSc(eng) 1960
s of Albert S. T. S. crofter and Catherine B. Tulloch; b Kirkwall 19.1.37
nat serv 1960–62; Ranco Motors: grad app Tantallon 1962–64, res dev Uddingston Glasg 1964–66; des eng Montreal 1966–68; crofter N Ronaldsay from 1968
m Glasg 29.3.65 Catherine Marquis d of Alexander M. Glasg

SCOTT William Forbes *MA 1968
s of William S. MA 1936 *qv*; b Aber 12.11.46
PhD(Dund) 1971 FFA 1974
temp lect maths Glas 1970–71; lect actuarial maths/statist H-W from 1971
m Aber 5.8.70 June Leys teacher d of Alexander M. L. Portsoy

SCOTT William John *BSc 1961
s of William S. plumber and Hannah M. Rutherford; b Perth 19.11.39
asst exper off. Macaulay inst Aber 1961–63; teacher: Govan h s Glasg 1964–66, Douglas Ewart h s Newton Stewart asst prin guid, prin guid from 1966
m Glasg 27.3.67 Wendy E. Pearson nurse d of Kenneth B. P. Glasg

SCOTT William Oliver BSc(agr) 1957

SCOTT-BROWN Alastair William MB ChB 1958 Dip Psychother 1972
s of Sir William Scott-Brown MA 1912 *qv*; b Madura S India 12.11.34
DPM(Lond) 1965 MRCPsych 1971
h o Woodend hosp Aber 1958–59; RN UK and Far East surg lieut 1959–63, training in psychiat and spec posts 1963–74; surg comm RN consult psychiat and clin tut. Royal Victoria hosp Netley Southampton from 1974
m Aber 15.12.59 Ardyn A. Lyall MA 1959 *qv*

SCOTT-BROWN Ronald MA 1958 LLB 1960
s of Sir William Scott-Brown MA 1912 *qv*; b Madras 14.2.37
solic and invest. man. 1961–66; ptnr Brander & Cruickshank advoc Aber from 1966; dir East of Scot. Invest. Man. from 1973
m Aber 8.9.66 Jean L. Booth lect Aber s of dom sc d of Albert B. Aber

SCRIMGEOUR Margaret Aitken *MA 1964
b Forfar 5.7.41
teacher Fr: Perth 1965–68, Banchory from 1968
m Aber 2.10.72 George Murray BSc 1961 *qv*

SCROGGIE Brian Charles *MA 1968

SEATON John Gow BSc(eng) 1969
s of Alexander S. gen merch and Janet Gow MA(Edin) teacher; b Aberfeldy 16.6.47
asst eng; D. Logan Invsh 1969–70, Tarmac constr Forres 1970–71; des eng Fairhurst & Ptnrs Aber 1971–72; sect. eng Tarmac constr Forres 1972–73, ag from 1973
m Kintore 13.9.69 Patricia E. Davidson d of Alexander D. Kintore

SEATTER Kathleen *MA 1965
d of William Y. S. blacksmith, male nurse and Margaret Sim laundry worker; b Aber 28.5.42
teacher: High s for girls Aber 1967–70, Cults acad Aber from 1970
m Aber 20.12.68 Arun K. Naha BSc(Calc) syst dev eng govt serv s of Jogendra C. N. Calcutta

SEDDON Thomas Michael MB ChB 1962
s of Thomas S. cotton manuf and Edith Houghton; b Rochdale 30.10.33
h o Blackpool 1962–63; sen h o Kendal, Blackpool 1963–64; lect anat Aberd 1964–65; g p Slyne-with-Hest from 1965
m Rawtenstall 3.1.59 June Coleman d of Frederick C. Rawtenstall

SEED Carol Irene MA 1965
m Lockhart

SEIVEWRIGHT Sheila MA 1969
d of Charles E. S. shoemaker and Martha Lowe; b Lancs 1.8.47
continental tel Lond 1970–71; various posts Montreal 1971–72
m Aber 29.3.71 Yong-Kwee Lam Shang Leen BSc 1969 *qv*

SELAND Johan Harald cMB ChB 1965
s of Harald S. S. BSc(pharm)(Oslo) pharm and Rachel Sunde; b Stavanger 7.6.41
Cand Med(Oslo) 1965
Norway: h o county hosp Kristiansund 1966–67, asst dist doct Meløy 1967, indust doct Glomfjord 1967–68, m o Norw air force Sola air base 1968–69, h o ophth univ hosp Bergen 1969–71, res fell. ophth univ of Bergen from 1971
m Stavanger 18.12.65 Kari M. Galta nurse d of Daniel G. Sørbø Norway

SELF Michael Barnard BSc(for) 1966
s of Peter B. S. BSc(Lond) teacher and Beryl Y. Wood; b Brist 25.2.45
for. off. Munda Solomon Is 1967–72; timber contr Brist 1972–73; for. off. Honiara Solomon Is 1973–77; harvesting and marketing man. Tilhill For. Farnham from 1977
m Aber 31.7.67 Elizabeth A. Brooks BSc 1966 *qv*

SEMEONOFF Irina *MA 1964
d of Boris S. MA(Edin) univ lect and Catherine I. Davie MA(Edin) teacher; b Edin 9.2.43
stud. occup psych Birkbeck coll Lond 1964–67; part-time quality control eng Rochester 1968
m Lond 4.12.65 Alfred J. Alexander eng s of Alfred A. Laurencekirk

SERWANGA Edward Kiddugavu BSc(for) 1962

SESHADRI Holavanhalli Srinivasaiyengar PhD 1963
s of Srinivasaiyengar S. MA(Madras) supt of police and Laxamma Laxamma; b KGF India 30.1.27
BSc(Bangalore) 1948 MSc(Bangalore) 1959
India: lect chem Mysore 1948–59, lect biochem univ of Mysore 1959–71, reader biochem from 1971
m 29.5.49 Narayanachar Anandam d of Narayanachar, Hindupur

SHACKLES Charles John Dalglish *BSc(agr) 1964
s of Derek H. S. CBE solic. and Lella D. Kirkland; b Edin 20.10.39
MIBiol(Nott) 1968
asst reg off. nature conserv council E Anglia from 1970

SHAH Rajnikant Prabhulal MB ChB 1962

SHAHID Khalil Akhtar MSc 1969 PhD 1971
MSc(Panj)

SHAKSPEARE Anthony Evan MA 1967

SHAND Aeneas John *BSc 1959 PhD 1962
s of John S. S. cashier Elgin burgh council and Elspeth T. Robertson; b Elgin 6.9.37
FCS 1957 FRIC 1976 CChem 1976
group ldr Miles lab Stoke Poges 1962–65; lect organ. chem Middx polytech: Enfield 1965–66, Hendon 1966–70; sen lect organ. chem Napier coll of comm and tech Edin from 1970
m Bridgend 6.4.63 Margaret W. Dickson shop asst d of Henry D. Tweedmouth

SHAND Eden Lennox Arthur *BSc(for) 1963

SHAND Edward MA 1970
s of Edward S. painter/decorator and Mary Mackintosh; b Aber 10.9.49
teacher: Hilton acad Aber 1971–73, Banff acad from 1973
m Aber 4.12.70 Linda J. Greig MA 1970 *qv*

SHAND James Sim MB ChB 1964
s of Herbert D. S. fire off. and Marjory G. Wilson; b Aber 27.10.39
h o Woodend hosp, City hosp Aber 1964–65; g p Aber from 1965
m Aber 17.7.64 Valerie H. Stewart insur clerkess d of Hugh S. Aber

SHAND John Fordyce *BSc 1967
b Ellon 12.2.45

SHAND John Herbert *BSc 1970 PhD 1977

SHAND Margaret Moncrieff *MA 1961
d of Hector S. man. dir and Isabella Leishman; b Perth 27.9.36
teacher: Turriff 1962–63, Glasg 1963–65, 1969–70, Aber 1970–72; Aber: prin teacher guid 1972–74; asst head teacher from 1974
m Aber 1961 Charles A. Barron MA 1958 *qv*

SHAND Michael Robertson BSc 1966
s of John S. S. cashier and Jean Stevens; b Elgin 13.2.45
syst progr Plessey Co Liv 1966–69; diagnostic progr/analyst NCR Dun 1970–74; syst progr ICL Dalkeith 1974–76; teacher maths/computer stud. Elgin from 1977
m Dun –.7.73 Mary Lynch teacher d of James L. Errol

SHAND Rory Alexander BSc 1970

SHAND Roy Cooper BSc(eng) 1960

SHAND Stella Joyce MA 1958
d of Joseph S. head for. and Marie Sargent secy; b Methlick 17.9.36
teacher: Culter s 1959–62, Peffermill from 1976
m Aber 12.8.60 Philip W. Ross MB ChB 1960 *qv*

SHAND William Alexander *BSc 1961 MSc 1962 PhD 1965
s of James A. S. MA 1936 *qv*; b 30.4.40
lect nat phil Aberd 1965–68; govt serv Christchurch 1969–79, Malvern from 1979
m Keith 28.8.65 Moyra E. King d of Alfred J. F. K. Keith

SHAND William Fraser *BSc 1963

SHANKS Gordon William MA 1967
s of William A. S. banker and Muriel H. Boyd tracer; b Arbroath 10.12.45
teacher maths Stranraer h s 1968–70; asst prin maths Shoeburyness comp s 1970; prin maths/sc Pilton s and comm coll Barnstaple 1971–74; asst head Logie s s Dun from 1974
m Stonehaven 23.9.67 Margaret E. Carr d of James C. Stonehaven

SHANKS Michael Fraser BMedBiol 1968

SHANNON Jean Greig *BSc 1966
d of William G. S. waterguard supt HM customs and excise and Maud D. Hamilton; b Glasg 20.10.44
PhD(Lond) 1969
Lond: res asst St Mary's hosp 1966–69; lect 1969–70; dem/lect Edin 1970–72; OU tut. Camberley from 1975
m Aber 31.8.68 Gordon P. Ebbon BSc 1965 *qv*

SHARP David Williamson *BSc 1969 PhD 1972

SHARP Evelyn Mary MA 1959
d of George M. S. farm. and Mary C. F. Wood cashier; b Cookney 10.10.38
teacher: Mackie acad Stonehaven 1960–62, New Byth 1962–64, Angus, Kincardine 1972–75, Fettercairn from 1976
m Cookney 1.8.62 Stuart Riddell farm worker s of Joseph R. Alford

SHARP Margaret Rothnie *MA 1970 MLitt 1975
m Michael G. A. Christie MA 1966 *qv*

SHARP Neil Wood *MA 1970
s of James H. W. S. PO tel eng, head of plan. N of Scot. PO telecom board and Finlayson W. M. Neil lib, cler off. Inl Rev; b Glasg 14.8.47
MA(Lanc) 1972
lect in sociol: Bournemouth and Poole coll of f e Poole 1972–79, i/c soc sciences coll of arts and tech N'cle-u-Tyne from 1979
m N'cle-u-Tyne 14.9.68 Ann E. Bettridge BSc 1969 *qv*

SHARP Ronald James *MA 1970

SHARP Rosemary Elaine Christine *BSc 1968

SHAW Alexander Martin *MA 1963 LLB 1965

SHAW Cecilia Helen MB ChB 1961
d of John C. Shaw teacher and Agnes C. Page; b Alyth 20.9.36
h o RACH, Ipswich and E Suffolk hosp 1961–62; sen h o anaest Ipswich and E Suffolk hosp 1962–63; regist anaest Law hosp Carluke 1963–64; resid anaest Ottawa 1975–77
m Pitlochry 20.9.63 Colin T. Downie BSc(H-W) phys s of Alistair D. Blairgowrie

SHAW Christopher Patrick James BSc 1968

SHAW Edwin Louis *BSc 1970
s of Noel S. eng and Elizabeth Sievewright; b Perivale 15.11.47
FCS 1972 CEng MIProd.E 1979
res stud. Aberd 1970–73; sect. man. Internat Sports Co Horbury 1973–74, dept man. 1974–75; sect. leader work study Tower Housewares Wombourne 1975–77; chief work study eng T.I. Sunhouse Walsall 1977–78, indust eng man. from 1978

SHAW Josephine May MA 1968 Dip Ed 1970

SHAW Milton William PhD 1965
s of William S. clerk to urban dist council and Margaret Brown; b Colne 21.9.24
BSc(agr)(Leeds) 1944 MSc(Leeds) 1953 FR Ent Soc (Lond) 1959
asst entomol: Harper Adams agr coll Newport Shropsh 1945–46, MAFF Tettenhall 1946–50; asst advis entomol NOSCA Aber 1950–63, advis entomol from 1963
m Edgmond Newport 3.5.49 Iris Bolas secy d of Samuel G. B. Edgmond

SHAW Muriel Margaret MA 1966 Dip Ed 1967
d of John G. S. reader Aber journals and Muriel Norrie clerkess; b Aber 18.12.44
teacher Engl h s Winnipeg from 1967
m Aber 19.8.67 James C. Jamieson PhD 1967 *qv*

SHAW Robert *MA 1958
s of Robert S. grocery asst and Violet H. Scorgie; b Aber 2.5.36
BPhil(Oxon) 1960
asst lect econ Keele 1960–62; lect pol econ Aberd 1962–70, sen lect from 1970
m Aber 24.9.60 Valerie Hunter occup therap d of Frederick A. H. LDS(Edin) Stonehaven

SHAW William Peterkin Gordon *BSc 1963

SHEACH Gordon Chisholm BSc(eng) 1969
s of Alexander S. master bldr and Emily H. Watt; b Dufftown 7.4.48
site eng Lond 1970–73, site eng and sub ag Tayside

1973–77, estimator Lond from 1978
m Ilford 26.8.72 Barbara J. Gorman teacher d of John H. G. Cardiff

SHEARER Blanche Anne MA 1967
d of Raymond P. S. joiner and Blanche S. Wilson s canteen attendant; b Cornhill 21.9.46
teacher maths Banff acad 1968–74
m Cornhill 17.7.70 Ronald G. L. Sim BDS(Glas) dent surg s of George S. S. Cornhill

SHEARER Charles Anthony BSc 1970

SHEARER Elsa Margaret LLB 1968
d of Ernest J. M. S. BSc(Edin) path./bact and Helen M. Lenman MB ChB(Edin); b Edin 4.6.47
Edin: law app 1968–70; teacher Tollcross p s 1971–72
m Laurencekirk 20.12.69 David Christie BA(Strath) lect econ/author s of William C. Menstrie

SHEARER John Robertson cMB ChB 1966 PhD 1975
s of John A. S. MB ChB 1934 *qv*; b Aber 29.8.42
FRCSE 1971
h o ARI 1966–67; res fell. Aberd 1967–69; MRC jun res fell. Aberd 1969–70; regist surg Aber 1970–72; sen orthop regist 1972–74; lect orthop surg Oxon 1975–76; prof orthop S'ton from 1976
m Leven 18.10.68 Gloria A. Lemon physioth d of William L. MA(Strath) Leven

SHEARER John William *MA 1966

SHEARER Kathryn Isobel MA 1968
d of William S. butcher and Catherine D. A. Findlay; b Saskatoon 11.5.47
teacher Engl: Elgin acad 1969–75, Buckie h s from 1975
m Aber 3.8.66 Charles Boyle swimming pool man. s of Charles B. Glasg

SHEARER Margaret-Ann Milne MA 1966
m Kaloo

SHEARER Peter John *MA 1967

SHEARER Phyllis Jean MA 1957 Dip Ed 1958
d of Mary S.; b Glasg 28.1.37
teacher: Slains p s 1958–60, Eday p s Orkney 1965–72, remed Grampian ch guid Huntly area from 1975
m Rothiemay 12.8.58 Thomas Goodall MA 1961 *qv*

SHEARMAN Duncan Ward BSc 1970
s of John R. S. clerk and Vera M. Knowles; b Preston 20.9.48
Cannock: progr (computer) 1970–72, computer syst analyst from 1972
m Deerness Orkney Jennifer M. Bichan MA 1971 d of James H. B. Deerness

SHEDDEN Alfred Charles MA 1966 LLB 1967
s of Alfred H. W. S. bookkeeper and Jane M. Kay; b Edin 30.6.44
law app Arbroath 1967–68, Glasg 1968–69; leg. asst Glasg 1969–70; ptnr McGrigor, Donald & Co Glasg from 1971
m(1) E Kilbride 3.8.68 Rosalyn E. M. Terris MA 1967 *qv*; marr diss 19.7.79
(2) Glasg 6.12.79 Irene Munro

SHEDDON Dorothy Joanna BSc 1968
d of Alexander C. S. town clerk/burgh chamberlain and Josephine M. Johnston; b Dunfermline 6.7.45
Dip Ed(univ of E Af) 1969
teacher maths, head dept Tororo girls' s Uganda 1969–74; teacher maths Westfield s Watford from 1974

SHEEHAN William MSc 1968
s of William S. blacksmith and Margaret R. Mahoney; b Farranfoxe Co Kerry 27.7.32
BSc(Cork) 1961 PhD(Dub) 1976
prin res off. agr inst Creagh Ballinrobe

SHENNAN Andrew Theodore MB ChB 1967
s of Edward T. S. MB ChB 1939 *qv*; b Aber 22.3.43
MRCP 1972 LMCC 1974
h o RACH 1967–68; sen h o paediat Musgrove park hosp Taunton 1968–69; lect ch health Aberd 1969–71; regist paediat RACH 1971–73; Coutts clin fell. in neonatology sick ch hosp Toronto from 1974
m Aber 20.1.68 Anne Stewart MA 1965 *qv*

SHENNAN Jean Lindsay *BSc 1959
d of Theodore S. MB ChB(Edin) med pract and Ann L. Thomson MB ChB 1930 *qv*; b Aber 5.4.36
PhD(Glas) 1973
schol (May & Baker) post-grad res W of Scot. agr coll 1959–63; microbiol BP Proteins Grangemouth 1964–78; microbiol BP Co res centre Sunbury-on-Thames from 1978

SHEPHERD Allan Nicol BSc(eng) 1970
s of George S. farm. and Jessie I. Wilson clerkess; b Stonehaven 27.7.48
site eng (contr) Loch Duich 1970–71; grad eng Dumbarton 1971–73; sen asst eng (consult.) Glasg from 1973

SHEPHERD Brian *BSc 1970

SHEPHERD Charles Henderson *BSc 1969
s of Charles A. S. dev insp and Agnes M. Henderson; b Aber 30.12.46
MSc(Sheff) 1970 PhD(Salf) 1976
res fell. Salf 1974–79; nuclear phys Nuclear Power Comp Whetstone from 1979
m Leeds 25.8.79 Jill E. Thirsk BSc(Salf) d of Harold E. T. Knottingley

SHEPHERD David Christian MB ChB 1965
s of James G. L. caretaker and Christina D. Main; b Birse 29.12.37
DObstRCOG 1968
h o ARI, city hosp Aber, RACH, mat. hosp Aber 1965–67; sen h o Ross clin Cornhill Aber 1967–68; g p Chatham from 1968
m Ballater 4.8.62 Kathleen M. Shepherd d of William J. S. Ballater

SHEPHERD David Ian MB ChB 1968 *MD 1976 (Thursfield Award)
s of James I. R. S. comp secy and Mary M. Baird MA 1933 *qv*; b Aber 4.10.44
MRCP(UK) 1973
h o ARI, Dumfries RI 1968–69; sen h o ARI 1969–70; Sir Ashley Mackintosh res fell. dept med Aberd 1970–71; regist gen med Aber 1972–74; sen regist neurol: Aber 1976, S'ton from 1976
m Aber 15.5.70 Hilary J. Sharp RGN d of Thomas V. S.

SHEPHERD George Wilson *BSc(agr) 1965
s of George S. farm. and Jessie I. Wilson secy; b Cookney 5.4.42
agr dev off. Cambridge 1965–69; agr consult. Cleveland 1970–73; asst fertiliser marketing man. Edin 1974–75, area sales man. Guildford from 1977
m Cambridge 12.7.69 Diane M. Maskell secy d of Claude C. M. Cambridge

SHEPHERD Ian *MA 1968
s of John S. MA(St And) teacher; b Dun 12.3.44
res stud. Belf 1968–70; lect geog ABU Nigeria 1970–73; teacher Dun coll of comm from 1973

SHEPHERD James BSc(eng) 1956

SHEPHERD Malcolm Gaul MA 1958 LLB 1960
s of Frederick M. S. police supt and Maggie B. M. Simpson; b Banchory 14.1.37
leg. asst A. C. Morrison & Richards advoc Aber 1960–62, ptnr from 1962
m Aber 9.2.63 Edna M. McKenzie tel oper d of George D. McK. Aber

SHEPHERD Margaret MA 1958
d of Andrew C. S. master plasterer and Jessie J. Mackintosh; b Nairn 20.5.37
teacher: p s Hawick 1959–60, Fr/Ger Brora 1962–70, Fr/Ger Inv from 1970
m Edin 12.12.59 John M. McFeat MA(St And) teacher s of James McF. Auchterarder

SHEPHERD Marion PhD 1968
d of Hector S. insur man. and Mary Pope; b Dun 25.11.29
BSc(St And) 1950
hon fell. Aberd 1968–70
m St Andrews 18.3.52 Samuel C. Frazer MB ChB(Glas) prof chem path. Aberd s of John K. F. Airdrie

SHEPHERD Patricia Joanna MA 1959

SHEPHERD Roger Edward *BSc 1968

SHEPHERD Ronald *BSc(agr) 1956
s of John J. S. farm. and Catherine C. Cruickshank; b Rafford Moray 4.4.34
Malaysia: res off. Prang Besar estate Kajang 1957–65, dir of res Prang Besar res stat Kajang 1966–75; dir res Harrisons & Crosfield Malaysia from 1975
m Aber 4.4.68 Elsie M. Main MA 1954 *qv*

SHEPHERD Ronald Shearer Gordon MB ChB 1961

SHEPPARD David Dawbarn MA 1970

SHERAN John Duncan *MA 1968
d 26.6.72 *AUR* XLV 128

SHERET Brian Sydney *MA 1966 *BD 1969
s of Sydney G. S. chief clerk and Ruth Park; b Aber 9.6.44
DPhil(Oxon) 1972
C of S min: asst Corstorphine Old ch Edin 1972–73; locum Northfield Aber 1973–74, St Columba's Kilbirnie 1974–75, Aber 1975–77, John Knox Ch Gerrard St Aber from 1977

SHERWOOD Robert Tom BSc(for) 1956
s of Gerald B. S. civ serv and Margaret E. Harper teacher; b Epsom 2.11.30
dist for. off. Co Down from 1956
m Newcastle Co Down 9.8.58 Shirley C. Wheeler teacher dom sc d of Charles C. W. Newcastle Co Down

SHEVELS Terence *BSc 1970

SHEWAN Doreen Baxter MB ChB 1970

SHEWAN Frederick David Fitzgerald MA 1966 BD 1969
s of Albert S. farm./sheep dealer and Mary J. Fitzgerald nurse; b Whiterashes 24.3.42
C of S min: asst Glenrothes 1969–70, Northesk par ch Musselburgh from 1970
m Rayne 25.12.65 Iris P. Barrack MA 1966 *qv*

SHIACH Donald McGregor *MA 1960

SHIACH Gordon McGregor MA 1965 *MEd 1968
head Donaldson's School for the Deaf Edin
d Edin 24.4.77 *AUR* XLVII 215

SHIELS David Anthony MA 1962
MEd(Glas)

SHIELS Murray Brett *MA 1963 Dip Ed 1966

SHIMMINS James George *BSc 1960

SHIPMAN Nigel Christopher Leslie *MA 1967
s of Leslie H. S. bank man. and Violet Dawson fashion buyer; b Louth 1.9.44
asst prin civ serv Edin 1967–72, prin from 1972

SHIPP John McKenzie BSc 1957

SHIRAZI Rahmati Keshavarz BSc 1964

SHIRRAN Margaret Anne *BSc 1969
d of Andrew G. S. banker and Winifred M. Falconer secy; b Elgin 26.10.47
Dip Cartog(Glas) 1970
cartographic edit. Glasg 1970–75
m Elgin 11.9.70 Cameron A. Ewen BSc(eng) 1967 *qv*

SHIRRAN William Alexander Andrew *BSc(eng) 1967
s of Andrew G. S. banker and Winifred M. Falconer secy; b Elgin 15.4.45
MICE 1972
asst eng Glasg, Evanton, Peterhead 1967–75, eng with Highland reg (Evanton) from 1975
m Aber 1.8.68 Lorna M. Campbell teacher d of Ephraim C. MA 1933 *qv*

SHIRREFFS Gordon Chisholm MB ChB 1957
s of William S. banker and Tomina F. Gordon; b Cochin S India 26.3.34
DA(Lond) 1962
h o ARI 1957–58; surg lt royal Aust navy 1958–60; sen h o anaest ARI 1961–62; g p Huntly from 1962
m Aber 28.9.61 Suzanne Philip MA 1959 *qv*

SHIRREFFS Marjorie Anne MA 1970
d of Andrew G. S. CA and Georgiana (Nan) C. Kelman MA 1940 *qv*; b Aber 15.2.50
teacher classics Inverurie acad 1971–72
m Aber 5.4.72 John W. Graham comp dir s of Charles F. G. Aber

SHIRREFFS Murdoch John MB ChB 1970
s of John S. bank acct and Isobel Campbell; b Aber 25.5.47
DObstRCOG 1973 MRCGP 1974
h o ARI 1970–71; trainee g p Aber 1971–74; g p prin Bucksburn from 1974
m Aber 17.7.71 Jennifer A. McLeod BSc 1976 d of James A. McL. Aber

SHIRREFFS Richard Cameron MA 1968 ᵈLLB 1970
s of Andrew G. S. CA and Nan C. Kelman MA 1940 *qv*; b Aber 25.2.47
law app 1970–72; solic/ptnr Mackie & Dewar advoc Aber from 1973; secy AU Alumnus Assoc from 1973

m Aber 18.4.73 Gillian M. Fisher MA 1972 med soc worker d of John W. F. MA(Cantab) Oxford

SHIRREFFS Wallace BSc(eng) 1960
s of William W. W. R. S. ship's rigger and Margaret E. Warrender; b Aber 21.5.38
MIHE 1962 MICE 1967
dept main roads NSW Aust Sydney 1960–61; grad eng: city eng's dept Aber 1961–63, chief eng's dept Cumbernauld 1963–64; highway des eng Scott Wilson Kirkpatrick & Ptnrs Glasg 1964–66; des eng Cowan & Linn consult. eng Glasg 1966–67; superv eng Lanarksh c c Hamilton 1967–72; group leader Inv c c 1972–74; dep county road surv Kincardine c c Stonehaven 1974, asst div road surv Kincardine–Deeside div Grampian reg c from 1975
m Rutherglen Glasg 9.9.67 Rose G. Murphy teacher d of John M. MA(Glas) Rutherglen

SHIRRIFFS George Geddes cMB ChB 1963
s of William S. S. master painter and Mary A. Geddes MA 1926 *qv*; b Aber 10.2.40
h o ARI 1963–64; Aberd: Garden res fell. 1964–66, dept res fell. therap 1966–68; g p Aber from 1969
m Aber 12.3.65 June V. Sinclair nurs sister d of John S. Aber

SHODERU Rasheed Omokayode BSc(eng) 1967

SHORT John Robert Thomas DSc 1957
s of Victor A. S. army off. and Marion D. von Langen; b Perth W Aust 26.6.24
BSc(Univ W Aust) 1946 DPhil(Oxon) 1950
lect, sen lect agr zool Aberd 1952–65; ANU Canberra: sen lect zool and warden Garran Hall 1966–73, later reader zool from 1973
m Cambridge 6.8.52 Elizabeth Y. Campbell MA(Edin) lib, res asst d of John Y. C. DD(Edin) Cambridge

SHORT Lesley Margaret MA 1968
d of Frank S. acct and Margaret Hill secy/typist; b Manc 1.8.46
Dip Ed(N'cle) 1970
teacher Fr/Ger Perth W Aust 1972–73, part-time Fr 1975–77, part-time remed Engl from 1977
m Wilmslow 26.8.68 Colin Heinzman BSc 1968 *qv*

SHRUBSOLE Martin Richard *MA 1970
s of Stanley A. H. S. loc govt off. and Margery Hutt lib; b Maidstone 29.7.47
BR Scot. reg: traffic man. trainee 1970–72, asst stat man. Waverley stat Edin 1972–73, freight comm intelligence asst Glasg 1973–75, asst area man. Partickhill 1975–77; area man. BR Grantham from 1977
m Maidstone 14.8.71 Wendy E. Lawson BA(Bangor) teacher d of Walter G.A.L. Maidstone

SHUTTLEWORTH Graham Rex *BSc 1963
s of Norman H. S. eng (aeronautical) and Mabel L. French; b Wolverhampton 16.5.41
MSc(Birm) 1966
hosp biochem: Birm 1963–73, Bournemouth from 1974
m Wolverhampton 21.3.64 Susan M. Jenkins teacher d of Trevor I. J. BSc(Swansea) Claverley nr Wolverhampton

SIAFA Salu Franklin MB ChB 1963

SIBBALD Jane Bonnie *MA 1968
d of John S. soldier, teacher and Rita M. Hall; b Farnborough 31.12.44
Edin: asst antique shop 1968–69, MoT cler asst 1970–71; exec off. SED 1971–73; admin trainee MoD Lond 1974–76, higher exec off. (admin) 1977, prin 1978
m Shrivenham 26.8.67 Trevor B. Royle MA 1967 *qv*; marr diss 1973

SIBLEY Graham Hugh Milne BSc(agr) 1967

SIEVEWRIGHT David Campbell BL 1957
s of James A. D. S. loc govt off. and Ann G. Campbell; b Aber 16.8.37
leg. asst: Aber c c 1960–64. Lanark c c Hamilton 1964–65; private pract Hamilton from 1965
m Aber 18.9.61 Hazel M. Wilson pharm d of James W. Aber

SIEVEWRIGHT Joan LLB 1966
d of James A. D. S. treas Aber c c and Ann G. Campbell; b Aber 30.4.46
Aber: law app 1966–68; solic 1968–70, part-time from 1970
m Aber 14.7.67 Graeme R. D. Catto MB ChB 1969 *qv*

SILVER Dorothy Mary BSc 1956
d of James S. insp taxes and Isabel R. McLaren; b Selby 19.4.35
teacher Aber 1957–60
m Aber 25.7.60 Maurice D. Lowe MB ChB 1960 *qv*

SILVER Patricia Cameron BSc 1957 *1958
m Reid

SILVER Sheila Allison MB ChB 1961

SILVER William Allan MSc 1970
s of Harold A. M. S. farm. and Mary B. Watson teacher; b Oxbow Sask Canada 3.10.32
BA(Sask) 1953 BSc(Sask) 1954 MD CM(McG) 1956 FRCS(C) 1967
med res fell. Sask 1968–69; McLaughlin trav fell. Aberd 1969–70; asst prof surg (orthop) Sask from 1970
m Hudson Bay Sask 6.8.54 Eunice S. Black BA(Sask) asst lib d of John A. B. Sask

SILVERSTONE Peter Isaac MB ChB 1968
s of Michael S. locksmith and Ada Oland secy; b Hampton Court 27.5.41
DObstRCOG 1970 MRCOG 1974
h o geriat/gyn Aber 1968–69; sen h o: Carlisle 1969–71, N'cle-u-Tyne 1971–73; regist obst/gyn N'cle-u-Tyne 1971–73; res fell. obst N'cle-u-Tyne 1973–75, sen regist 1975–77; consult. obst/gyn Gateshead hosps from 1977
m Lond 14.2.71 Beryl Lux BA(Lond) teacher

SIM Alan James *BSc(eng) 1970
s of James H. S. shopkeeper and Anne McWilliam; b Aber 13.12.47
MICE 1973
eng city eng's dept Aber 1970–73; Aber: des eng W. A. Fairhurst & Ptnrs from 1973
m Aber 3.10.70 Nancy Ramsay secy d of George H. R. Aber

SIM Alan William Paterson MA 1966

SIM Betty May *MA 1961
d of Robert L. S. mason and Christina R. Hay MA 1928 *qv*; b Ellon 21.8.39
teacher Thurso: geog 1962–63, geog/Engl from 1973
m Aber 2.8.63 Derek Bradstreet physicist s of James B. Norfolk

SIM Catherine Mary MB ChB 1970
m Legg

SIM David Morrice MB ChB 1963

SIM Denis O'Brien MA 1967
s of John S. police off. and Ruth O'Brien MA 1930 *qv*; b Huntly 27.8.46
teacher: Dumbarton 1968–69, New Pitsligo 1969–71; exec off.: Metrop Police Civil Comm Lond 1971–73, Scot. Home and Health Dept Edin 1973–78, higher exec off. SED Edin from 1978
m Edin 27.10.73 Anne P. Broderick dept man. John Lewis d of Joseph B. Dublin

SIM Dorothy BSc 1960
d of William R. S. joiner and Mary Low; b Aber 25.3.39
teacher: Perth 1961–64, Montreal 1964–67, Edin from 1967
m Low

SIM Elsie Marguerite MA 1962
d of Alexander A. S. quarry man. and Marguerite B. Low; b Old Deer 15.11.40
teacher: Fr/Engl/hist Hopeman s s 1963–64, Fr/Engl Auchinleck 1964–65, Lat/Fr/Engl Drumley House, Ayr 1965–66, Ely h s Cambridge 1966–67
m Aber 14.8.64 John W. McKay MA 1962 *qv*

SIM George Hugh Bremner *BSc 1960
b Aber 28.5.37
comp dir
m Aber Dorothy C. Milne BSc 1959 *qv*

SIM Johann Christine MA 1960
m Bowen

SIM John McBain BSc(eng) 1963

SIM John Robert MA 1968
s of William S. sales rep and Margaret M. Harcus clerkess, nurse; b Kirkwall 9.12.46
merch seaman 1969–70; teacher: Engl Dunfermline 1970–72, Engl/hist Kirkwall from 1972
m Westray Orkney 12.7.72 Thora H. Drever hosp dom d of Stewart B. D. Westray

SIM John Wilson MB ChB 1964
s of John J. W. S. elect. and Isabella K. Beattie; b Aber 16.1.37
h o ARI, Perth, Irvine 1965–66; g p Yorks from 1966
m Aber 15.7.64 Muriel Buchan MA 1958 *qv*

SIM Lesley Beatrix MA 1959
m Milligan

SIM Marta (Martha) Gorrod *MA 1957
d of George G. S. plasterer and Nelly W. Sim; b Aber 10.1.35
teacher mod lang: Morrison's acad Crieff 1958–60, Aber acad 1960–63, spec asst 1963–69; prin mod lang Rosemead s Littlehampton 1969–73; acad tut. from 1973
m Aber 9.4.69 Alexander G. Watt mushroom grower s of George W. Littlehampton

SIM Morag Kathleen O'Brien MA 1961
d of John S. police serg and Ruth S. O'Brien MA 1930 *qv*; b Ellon 15.11.40
teacher maths: Bankhead acad 1962; part-time Aber coll of comm 1968–71, Inverurie acad 1971–75, asst prin maths Bankhead acad 1975–76
m(1) Fraserburgh 4.8.62 William G. Innes MA 1962 *qv*; marr diss
(2) Fraserburgh 13.8.76 Andrew J. Cooper master printer s of Dennis R. C. Fraserburgh

SIM Sandra Jean *MA 1969
d of Alexander S. security off. and Helen W. Ritchie kitchen asst; b Aber 10.5.47
clin psych: Warley hosp Brentwood 1969–72, Royal Cornhill hosp Aber 1972–75
m Fraserburgh 15.8.69 Alexander B. Malley MA 1965 *qv*

SIM Sheila Elizabeth *MA 1967
d of John S. electric pylon erector and Elizabeth Harvey; b Aber 31.3.46
teacher: Engl/hist Lond 1967–69, Engl Ife Nigeria 1970–72; curric dev, Engl and edit. Distance Teaching Maseru Lesotho 1973–76; teacher Engl Lond 1977–79; PGCE in Engl as foreign lang at Inst of Educ Univ London from 1979
m Kinellar 24.6.67 George W. Reid MA 1967 *qv*

SIMISON Aileen Margaret MA 1963

SIMMERS Gillian Jean MA 1968
d of William S. farm. and Jeannie R. Morrison MA 1937 *qv*; b Fraserburgh 22.5.47
teacher: geog Bannockburn 1969–70, geog/remed Nairn acad 1970–74, remed Forfar acad 1974–77
m Aber 16.7.75 Robert A. Gall BSc(St And) teacher s of Robert G.

SIMMONDS John Stewart MA 1969
s of Wilfrid T. S. clerk and Margaret Campbell; b Elgin 17.1.47
teacher hist/mod stud. Forres acad 1970–73; capt RAEC Pirbright 1973–74; comm Sandhurst 1974
m Lossiemouth 1.4.72 Anne Campbell civ serv d of John C. Lossiemouth

SIMMONS Thomas Caithness BSc(for) 1960

SIMMS Ian Howard MA 1968
s of Louis S. BSc(Lond) headmaster and Edna J. Joseph vice-prin coll of adult educ; b Lond 15.7.46
salesman Lond 1968–69; area man. (sales/admin) Brist 1969–73; man. dir of own comp Brist from 1973

SIMPSON Alan BSc 1970
s of Kenneth S. and Edith M. Cruickshank; b Aber 19.11.49
Sterling Winthrop Group Surbiton: computer progr, syst analyst 1970–74, unit man. from 1974
m Ashford Middx 21.9.74 Marion Walker export clerk d of Edward W. E Molesey

SIMPSON Alexander *MA 1965 *MEd 1978
s of William B. S. cinema man. and Jane E. S. Goldsmith; b Aber 22.7.35
Dip Ed(Lond) 1971
Aber: lect geog coll of comm 1966–72, prin teacher geog Northfield acad 1972–78, lect psych coll of comm from 1978
m Aber 22.3.58 Hilda D. Brown teacher d of Alexander B. Aber

SIMPSON Alexander BSc 1969
s of James S. farm., tech off. dept of agr and Colina MacLellan shopkeeper; b Campbeltown 27.5.48
scient off. (field geol) inst of geol sc Lond 1969–73; teacher geog Falkirk from 1974

SIMPSON Alexander *MA 1968
s of Alexander S. fisherman and Mary M. Sutherland; b Lossiemouth 10.8.43
MSc(Strath) 1975
teacher Lond 1969–71; computer progr civ serv Lond 1971–72; teacher Airdrie 1972–73

m Nairn 22.3.67 Jean H. Munro civ serv d of James A. M. Nairn

SIMPSON Alexander Milne BSc 1957
s of Alexander M. S. process oper and Maggie A. Easton; b Lonmay 28.3.36
UK AEA Dounreay 1958–62; asst exper off. Winfrith Heath Dorset 1962–65; tech off. ICI organics div Stevenston from 1965
m Aber 12.8.57 Margaret I. Adie med lab tech d of Norman J. A. Aber

SIMPSON Ann *MA 1961
d of W. Douglas S. MA 1919 univ lib Aberd and E. Dorothy Mason bank employee; b Aber 25.4.38
secy stud. Lond 1961–62; translator Paris 1962–66; Lond: cler off. Central Bureau for educ visits and exchanges 1966–67, admin asst Council for Brit Archaeology 1967–68, various posts MRC 1968–78, sen admin asst (internat relations) NALGO from 1978

SIMPSON Anne Frazer MA 1961 Dip Ed 1962
d of George S. detect. insp/regist man. for trawl fishermen and Margaret Frazer lab tech/chem; b Aber 9.3.40
teacher: Engl/hist/geog Torry s s Aber 1962–64, Engl Firrhill s s Edin 1964–65; part-time lect Engl f e College of Art Dun
m Aber 3.4.64 Robert F. Philip BSc(eng) 1960 *qv*

SIMPSON Bernard Alan MA 1965 Dip Ed 1966

SIMPSON Brian Dalgleish BSc 1966
s of James M. S. tweed indust man. and Kate Little; b Aber 12.10.44
teacher phys: Cults acad 1967–72, RGC Aber 1972–74; asst prin phys RGC from 1974

SIMPSON Catherine Mary MA 1957
d of Douglas J. S. elect. eng and Catherine R. Reid; b Aber 17.3.37
Dip Ed(Hong Kong) 1969
teacher Engl Diocesan girls' s Kowloon Hong Kong 1969–72, sen Engl mistress from 1972
m Brit Solomon Is Protectorate 28.9.57 Robin R. Mason BSc(Lond) agr scient s of Alfred H. M. Ashby-de-la-Zouche

SIMPSON David Clark *MA 1966
b Johnshaven 20.11.35
teacher Engl/hist Bervie 1967–69; Mackie acad Stonehaven: teacher hist/year master 1970–72, teacher hist/prin guid 1972–73, prin hist from 1973

SIMPSON Dorothy Anna BSc 1959 *1960
m Williams

SIMPSON Douglas John *BSc(eng) 1956

SIMPSON Duncan Simmie BSc(eng) 1962

SIMPSON Eileen Mary MA 1967
d of James D. G. S. blacksmith and Mary A. Cowie milliner; b Aber 20.11.46
teacher: Engl/hist Whitburn 1968–73, prin Engl/hist Tranent from 1973

SIMPSON Elizabeth Ann Brand *MA 1959
m Dare
d 27.4.66

SIMPSON Elma Watt MA 1967
d of James W. S. farm. and Mabel J. Watt; b Fraserburgh 22.6.46
teacher mod lang: Camphill h s Paisley 1968–71, Woodfarm h s Renfrewsh 1971–73; asst prin mod lang Castlehead h s Paisley from 1973
m Rosehearty 29.7.72 Ian L. H. Cummings MA(Glas) teacher s of Robert M. C. Paisley

SIMPSON Frank BSc 1965

SIMPSON George MA 1961

SIMPSON George Henry *MA 1956
s of Joseph H. S. master cabinetmaker and Janet M. Henderson; b Leeds 6.12.14
Higher Dip RE (Aber coll of educ) 1957
teacher: Engl Viewforth s s Kirkcaldy 1957–59, Aber Tech coll: teacher lib stud. 1959–63, head gen stud./man. dept from 1963
m Aber 11.6.48 Frances T. Wilson d of Robert M. W. Aber

SIMPSON Hamish Milne BSc 1969
s of Thomas S. distill man. and Margaret A. Milne; b Rothes 6.6.48
jun geol Geosurv of Aust Adelaide 1969–70; geol: Rockfall Co Barrhead 1970–73, Foundation Eng Lond from 1973
m Ilford 26.7.75 Christine M. Tomlinson teacher d of James T. Ilford

SIMPSON Helen Joyce MA 1965

SIMPSON Ian Grahame MB ChB 1966
s of John W. S. licensed grocer and Hilda Milne; b Aber 2.7.42
Dip Soc Med(Edin) 1970
h o Aber 1966–67; trainee g p Aber 1967–68; regist med Aber 1968–69; fell. in med admin Aber, Edin 1969–72; asst sen m o NERHB Aber 1972–74; spec commun med Aber 1974–75; dist m o Aber 1975–78; asst secy med def union Lond from 1978
m Aber 20.7.68 Heather W. McLaughlin BA lib d of William R. D. McL. Portlethen

SIMPSON Jacqueline Margaret *BSc 1969
d of Alexander S. BSc(Lond) prin navig coll and Yvonne M. White typist; b Glasg 1.11.46
PhD(Lond) 1973
m Lond 27.6.70 Martin Gordon BSc 1969 *qv*

SIMPSON Janis Mary MA 1970
d of Charles D. S. elect. eng and Mary S. Forsyth; b Aber 9.4.49
teacher: Engl/hist Lossiemouth h s 1971–73, remed Northfield acad Aber from 1973

SIMPSON John Cruer *MB ChB 1965 PhD 1975
s of Alexander N. S. acct and Isabella Noble; b Toronto 15.5.41
MRCPath 1973
h o ARI 1965–66; Aberd: Garden res fell. dept med 1966–67, MRC fell. dep med 1967–68, lect path. 1968–75; visiting prof Mich univ 1975–77; sen lect path. Aberd from 1978

SIMPSON Leonard McPherson BSc(for) 1959

SIMPSON Lilian Janet Weir MA 1961
d of George S. grocery vanman and Lily M. Menzies cook; b Rothes 7.12.39
teacher Struy p s 1962–64, Beauly j s 1964–67; head Struy p s 1967–71; part-time remed Inv 1974–78; teacher

Knockbain p s from 1978
m Strathpeffer 20.7.63 John Gordon carpenter, contr s of Hugh G. Struy

SIMPSON Margaret Elizabeth *MA 1963
d of Robert S. cashier and Elizabeth C. Rennie bookkeeper; b Aber 19.4.41
teacher Aber acad 1964–66
m Aber 3.8.63 William D. Hardie MA 1953 *qv*

SIMPSON Marnel MA 1961
d of Johnston O. S. and Dorothy Bremner; b Peterhead 20.6.40
asst lib univ of Edin from 1963
m Peterhead 6.8.66 Valnor Powell BA(Bangor) univ lib

SIMPSON May *MA 1969
d of Philip S. joiner and Elsie Beattie nurse; b Tarves 15.5.47
teacher classics Hutcheson's girls' g s Glasg 1970–74
m Aber 13.7.71 Craig A. Madden MA 1969 *qv*

SIMPSON Moreen Anne *MA 1970
d of Alexander D. S. audit asst and Kathleen Beedie uphol sewer; b Aber 22.2.48
journalist Aber from 1970
m Aber 8.4.74 Douglas M. Cameron BSc 1970 *qv*

SIMPSON Neil Alasdair *BSc 1966

SIMPSON Neil Alexander *MA 1962
b Blairgowrie 20.2.40
ALA 1966
lib asst Fulwood 1962–63; asst lib Guildhall lib Lond 1964–68, various posts Manc publ lib 1968–74; prin asst (pers) cultural serv dept Manc 1974; asst chief lib (oper serv) Tameside 1974–77; asst dir (culture) Stockport from 1978
m Aber 18.9.63 Sheila A. Brown MA 1962 *qv*

SIMPSON Neil Norman *MA 1968
s of Neil M. S. motor mech, gardener and Ann W. G. W. Webster; b Aber 24.3.37
teacher hist Aber acad (later Hazlehead acad) 1969–73; prin hist/mod stud. Bridge of Don acad Aber from 1974
m Aber 6.6.61 Sheila Main teacher d of William M. Aber

SIMPSON Norma Craigmile *MA 1967 PhD 1971
d of Alexander C. S. flower/fruit shop prop. and Isabella H. Allan shorthand typist; b Aber 12.6.45
Aberd: res asst mental health dept 1967–69, res fell. from 1969
m Robertson

SIMPSON Norman Stanley Riach *MA 1962

SIMPSON Patricia Marion *MA 1968
d of Robert G. E. S. dental tech, licensed victualler and Mary W. Edgar MA(Glas) teacher, physioth; b Glasg 4.7.47
Dip Lib(Strath) 1970 ALA 1972
trainee lib Milngavie 1968–69, asst bibliographer J. Whitaker & Sons Lond 1970–71; sen asst lib Basingstoke from 1971
m Lond 20.4.71 Donald H. N. Ferguson BSc 1968 *qv*

SIMPSON Robert MA 1966

SIMPSON Robert William *MA 1963
s of William T. S. sheet metal worker and Annie C. Mearns; b Aber 30.7.41
B Phil(Oxon) 1965
lect moral phil Aberd from 1965
m Aber 27.9.63 Gladys D. Murison teacher d of Robert M. Aber

SIMPSON Sandra Mary MA 1969

SIMPSON Sheena Grant *MA 1958
d of Walter S. S. and Harriet H. Wills; b Peterhead 22.1.38
Engl lang asst Beauvais France 1958–59; teacher Fr/Ger Aber 1960–64, Fortrose from 1972
m Aber 30.3.63 Graham Munro MA(Edin) teacher s of William D. M. Dingwall

SIMPSON Sheila Margaret MA 1965
d of George S. and Nan Hay; b Huntly 23.9.44
teacher geog/hist Keith g s 1966–68, spec asst 1968–73; prin geog Abbott's coll Cape Town S Af from 1974
m Elgin 19.7.72 Edward S. R. McAllister navig off. MN s of Alexander S. McA. Tomintoul

SIMPSON Sybil Elizabeth Gray MB ChB 1959
d of Thomas S. stationmaster BR and Thomasina D. Redpath ch's nurse; b Edin 12.4.34
DObstRCOG 1963
h o, sen h o Woodend hosp Aber, Perth, Bridge of Earn 1960–62; Perth: trainee g p 1962–63, sen h o regist anaest 1963–67, med asst anaest from 1967

SIMPSON Thomas William MB ChB 1964
s of Thomas F. S. civ serv and Sarah V. McDade secy; b Aber 23.2.39
DA 1968
h o: Dumfries RI 1964–65, Woodend hosp Aber 1965–66; regist anaest ARI 1966–68; g p Aber from 1968
m Aber 4.4.66 Maureen A. Philip BSc 1963 *qv*

SIMPSON Vera Fraser *MA 1966
d of William S. police serg, gen merch and Margaret J. A. Milne gen merch; b Aber 16.5.44
Dip Engl as second lang(Leeds) 1968
VSO teaching fell. Njala univ coll Sierra Leone 1966–67; Bradford: teacher Engl to immigrant children 1968–70 and 1972–74; res asst computer based learning proj Leeds univ 1970–72; teacher Engl Chosen Hill s Churchdown from 1974
m Aber 6.9.68 Robert W. Clouston BSc 1968 *qv*

SIMPSON Vincent Leslie BSc(eng) 1960
s of Vincent J. A. S. paper mill worker and Florence Leslie; b Peterculter 1938
asst eng Argyll c c Strachur 1960–63; asst eng/sub ag Wm Tawse Aber: Strachur, Mull, Clacton 1963–66; Argyll: ag/civ eng man. W. H. Rankin Sandbank 1966–73, ptnr/dir Bonnar construct. co civ eng contr Kilmun from 1973

SIMPSON William Barber *BSc 1959 PhD 1962
s of William S. baker and Margaret Barber; b Aber 31.5.36
res fell. Nott 1962–64; lect: Trinity coll Dublin 1964–68, RGIT Aber from 1968
m Aber 7.6.61 Hazel M. Grant civ serv d of Robert G. Aber

SINCLAIR Alan George *BSc 1957 PhD 1960
s of Samuel S. weaver/crofter/grocer's asst and Anne S. Johnston; b Sandwick Shetland 7.7.35
Lincs: indust chem 1960–65, lect coll of tech 1965–69; scient agr res Mosgiel NZ from 1969
m Aber 8.8.58 Isabella M. Bruce indust radiogr, saleswoman d of John B. Aber

SINCLAIR Ann Gordon MA 1968
d of Duncan T. R. S. bank insp and Charlotte G. Hay postal worker; b Aber 1.3.47
teacher lang Perth W Aust 1970–72
m Aber 1.9.69 John A. Bunting BSc 1969 *qv*

SINCLAIR Anne MA 1966
d of George S. S. man. herring trade and Johan R. Strachan; b Peterhead 12.1.44
teacher: St Peter's R C s Aber 1967–68, Dingwall acad 1968–70, Invernesssh from 1972
m Aber 29.8.66 John J. A. Dodds BSc 1965 *qv*

SINCLAIR Catherine Croy *MA 1957

SINCLAIR Christina Sandra MA 1969
d of John S. farm man. and Elizabeth L. W. Tait; b Peebles 31.7.49
computer syst progr throughout UK from 1969
m Banchory 3.6.72 Callum Fraser BSc 1968 *qv*

SINCLAIR Douglas Walker BSc 1964

SINCLAIR Duncan Alexander MA 1961

SINCLAIR Duncan John *MA 1958

SINCLAIR Elizabeth Burness MA 1967
d of David B. S. estate worker and Lizzie K. Rutherford; b Perth 26.4.41
teacher: Kaimhill s s Aber 1968–69, Milnes h s Fochabers 1969–71, Porchester s s 1973–75
m Elgin 1.8.70 Raymond V. Bennett off. RN s of Arthur B. Dawlish

SINCLAIR Elizabeth Katherine MA 1960
m Dawson

SINCLAIR Ernelyn Jean MA 1968

SINCLAIR Janet Anne MA 1965 Dip Ed 1966
d of Robert S. crofter and Mary M. MacRae teacher; b Inv 17.1.44
teacher: Croy 1966–70, Inv 1970–73; staff tut. Inv educ auth from 1973
m Fraser

SINCLAIR Jean Milne BSc 1965
d of Farquhar C. S. joiner and Jessie Paterson; b Aber 7.1.44
teacher girls' g s Newbury 1966–69
m Aber 10.8.67 Stuart McNeill BSc 1963 *qv*

SINCLAIR Joan Elisabeth Cumming BSc 1961
d of Ian J. S. indust consult. and Janet F. Ross teacher dom sc; b Lossiemouth 26.10.40
res asst biol Aberd 1961–64; relief teacher Peterhead acad 1965
m Aber 11.5.63 Ian R. A. Macmillan MA 1960 *qv*

SINCLAIR John *BSc 1956
s of Arthur J. S. farm. and Frances A. Anderson; b Lhanbryde 17.11.31
AMBIM 1972
process supt SAI: Leith 1956–57, Aber 1957–61; Ilford photogr materials manuf Cheshire: dept man. 1961–71, dep works man. 1971–76; pers man. Inveresk Paper Co (coated papers) Macclesfield from 1976
m Macclesfield 20.10.70 E. Doreen Lytton soc worker and estate ag sales d of Robert J. L. Timperley

SINCLAIR John *BSc(eng) 1967
s of Alexander H. S. eng and Elizabeth McPherson; b Findochty 29.5.46
MICE MIWES
grad eng Sunbury 1967–68; asst eng Lond 1968–71; eng: Bristol 1971–74, Piuca Peru 1974–76, Ankara Turkey 1976–78, Najran Saudi Arabia 1978–79
m Elgin 20.6.70 Frances S. Taylor d of James M. T. Elgin

SINCLAIR Joyce Elaine MA 1964
m Mawson

SINCLAIR Margaret MA 1966
d of Alister J. S. tech teacher and Isobel Rilley dem; b Aber 5.4.45
computer syst progr Edin 1966–70
m Aber 26.8.67 Robin C. McKenzie MA 1966 *qv*

SINCLAIR Margaret Florence MA 1968
d of Harold S. draper and Blanche Rossetter; b Golspie 18.12.46
teacher Fr Creighton s Lond 1969–75
m Lond 28.8.73 Bernard Whiting civ serv s of William G. W. Robertsbridge

SINCLAIR Morag Anne Stuart MA 1963
d of Ernest J. S. farm. and Ivy J. L. Hourston subpostmistress; b Orkney 18.6.42
Orkney: teacher Finstown p s 1964–66, remed Birsay p s 1973–74, remed Rendall 1977–78
m Orkney 22.7.66 James M. Rendall farm. s of Alexander S. R. Stromness

SINCLAIR Morag Margaret MA 1968
d of William P. S. photogr man. and Margaret White; b Aber 24.2.46
teacher Fr/Ger Newbattle h s Dalkeith 1969–73, Craigroyston s s Edin from 1973
m Aber 13.7.73 James H. Robertson MA(Edin) C of S min s of James R. Stirling

SINCLAIR Neil Thomson *MA 1967
s of Duncan S. bank man. and Doris M. Thomson LDS(Glas) dentist; b York 20.6.44
Assoc Museum Ass. 1973
trainee museum asst Cheltenham 1967–72; sen asst museum curator Sunderland 1972–75; curator: Monkwearmouth Station Museum 1975–77, Sunderland Museums from 1977

SINCLAIR Norma Murray *MA 1968 Dip Ed 1969
d of Benjamin M. S. auctioneer and Ann B. Mackenzie teacher; b Wick 28.5.46
teacher phys Wick from 1969

SINCLAIR Peter Rayment *MA 1969
PhD(Edin)

SINCLAIR Robert Andrew *BSc 1960 MSc 1962 PhD 1965
s of Robert S. merch seaman and Jemima A. Peterson; b Trondavoe Shetland 18.3.38
FCS 1960 Fulbright schol(S Calif) 1965–67
asst lect Lond 1963–64; post doct fell.: S Calif Los Angeles 1965–67, Lond 1967–68; sen scient: 3M Co Harlow 1968–73, 3M St Paul USA from 1973
m Lossiemouth 18.7.63 Jean R. Smith BSc 1961 *qv*

SINCLAIR Robert Forbes BSc(eng) 1963
s of Alfred M. S. turner and Christina C. Ritchie; b Aber 10.10.41
AMIEE 1963
trainee eng Glasg 1963–65, 4th asst eng Bathgate 1965–66; 3rd asst eng: Ardrossan 1966–67, Kilmarnock 1967–74, 2nd eng Glasg from 1974

SINCLAIR Wilma MA 1960
d of William J. H. S. RNVR and trawl skipper and Christina Slater: b Aber 25.5.39
teacher Errol 1961–63, Toronto 1965–67
m Aber 24.8.63 Carl W. Groskorth RCAF fighter pilot, capt Air Canada s of Carl L. G. Parry Sound Ontario

SINGER Derek Alexander LLB 1964
s of Alexander S. sqdn leader RAF and Marjory W. Pullar; b Forfar 2.7.43
BA(Cantab) 1968
law app Edin 1964–66; solic, called to bar 1966–69; Lond: trainee merch bank. 1969, leg. asst F. A. R. Bennion barrister 1969–71; leg. draftsman min of fin. Jamaica, Kingston 1971–74; gen counsel to merch bank Kingston from 1974
m St Andrew Jamaica 25.12.72 Sandra A. G. Abrahams BMus(Kentucky) off. man. d of William V. A. St Andrew

SINGER Linda Mary Coutts MA 1970
d of James C. S. CA and Helen S. Niven; b Fyvie 12.4.49
teacher: Fife 1972–73, Musselburgh 1973–75, Prudhoe 1976–78
m Kintore 8.8.75 Roland W. J. McKinney BSc(St And) biochem s of Robert McK. Galashiels

SINGER Wilma Wallace *MA 1970
d of William S. tyre serv rep and Dora Ewen accts clerkess; b Aber 28.8.49
teacher hist Lanarksh 1971–72; Lond: actuarial dept life assur comp 1972–73, trainee fin. planner 1973–74, life and pensions plan. consult. from 1974
m Aber 20.12.75 Duncan D. Simpson-Fraser BSc(Glas) elect eng, comp dir s of S. S-F. Lochwinnoch

SINGH Kesar MB ChB 1964

SINGH Kulbir Kartar *BSc(eng) 1963 MSc 1965

SINGH Kulrajmohinder MB ChB 1968
s of Kartar S.; b Tanga Tanzania 13.4.42
h o: Lond 1968–69, paediat Aber 1970–71, Nuneaton 1971–72, anaest Burnley 1972–73; g p Fillmore Sask Canada from 1973
m Nairobi 23.8.70 Tejinder K. Jabbal

SINGH Madan Mohan MB ChB 1965

SINGH Manik PhD 1960
s of Shri P. S. farm. and Shrimati Pasinda Kuer; b Patna India 1.10.21
BSc(B.H.U. India) 1940 MB BS(Patna) 1946
lect anat Aberd 1960–61; prof/head dept anat P.W. med coll Patna from 1962
m Bihar India 11.5.46 Shakuntala Singh PhD 1962 *qv*

SINGH Neville Bharat BSc(eng) 1966
s of Udho S. farm./bus. man. and Meghbati Singh bus. woman; b Georgetown Guyana 14.9.38
MICE 1972 MSc(Ohio) 1973
Guyana: resid eng Mackenzie highway Demerara 1966–68; proj eng Corentyne Highway E Berbice 1968–69; spec eng: structures roads div MoW/hydraulics 1969–70, maintenance, hydraulics & supply 1970–72, plan. Central Transport plan. unit Min of econ dev from 1973
m Aber 26.2.66 Aileen S. Forbes teacher d of H. M. C. F. Aber

SINGH Shakuntala PhD 1962
d of Sarju P. S. LLB(Patna) judge and Moti Singh; b Brahampur Bihar India 10.6.31
BA(Patna) 1947 MA(Patna) 1949 MEd(Patna) 1954
lect Hindi MM coll Patna univ from 1957
m Bihar 11.5.46 Manik Singh PhD 1960 *qv*

SIOU Leon Ange Pierre Mee *BSc(eng) 1969
s of Leon L. M. A. S. land surv and Lucia C. K. Hong hairdresser; b Port Louis Mauritius 31.5.44
asst eng LCC 1969–70; Toronto: field eng for contr 1970–71, proj eng/estimator/proj man. for contr 1971–74, VP/gen man. from 1974
m Toronto 3.12.71 Brenda V. Cannon med secy d of Alfred C. Enfield

SIYO Wells Jones *MEd 1966
BA Dip Ed(SA) BEd(Natal)

SKARDHAMAR Torfinn *BSc 1958
s of Odmar S. comm attaché for Faroese trade affairs and Ingeborg Poulsen; b Tórshavn Faroe Is 25.8.35
MSc(Birm) 1960
phys: inst for atomenergi Kjeller Norway 1959–61, AB atomenergi Stockholm 1962–68; phys/proj leader Kjeller 1968–75, sen phys/group leader Kjeller from 1976; also sen consult. Scandpower A/S Norway
m Horten Norway 17.10.70 Anne-Karí Raaen Cand. Philol.(Oslo) teacher

SKEETE Maureen Valeria Harford MB ChB 1969
d of Lee H. S. MA(Durh) teacher, headmaster and Myra M. A. Nicholls teacher; b Barbados 18.1.44
Dip Dermat(Lond) 1974
h o Queen Elizabeth hosp Barbados 1969–70; sen h o univ hosp of WI Jamaica 1970–71; chief med asst, regist univ of WI 1971–72; m o Wandsworth Lond 1973; sen h o dermat, res fell. St John's hosp Lond 1974–77; sen regist dermat univ hosp of WI 1977; asst consult. (Queen Eliz hosp Barbados)/assoc lect dermat univ of WI from 1978
m Barbados 9.5.70 Henry S. Fraser MB BS(univ of WI) s of Robert S. F. Barbados

SKENE Alfred MA 1969

SKENE Donald Scott *BSc 1959
s of Kenneth C. S. S. MD(Lond) g p and Margaret P. Paterson; b Lond 16.7.36
PhD(Lond)
Blackman stud. E Malling res stat 1959–63; res off. CSIRO Melbourne Aust 1963–68; Cabot found. fell. Harvard univ USA 1968–70; res sc E Malling res stat from 1970
m Grantham 12.3.63 Ella J. Basker BSc(Nott) horticulturist

SKENE Elizabeth Ann *MA 1969
d of William R. R. S. insp BR and Jessie B. Taylor teacher home econ; b Insch 19.3.47
teacher Bankhead acad 1970–71
m Peterculter 25.7.70 Stephen R. Duthie wholesale grocer s of Walter S. D. Cults Aber

SKENE John Robert MB ChB 1962
s of Kenneth C. S. S. med pract and Margaret P. Paterson secy; b Willesden 8.3.33
DObstRCOG
h o surg/med/obst Aber 1962–64; sen h o gyn Aber 1964–65; g p Taunton from 1966
m Bournemouth 3.7.65 Wendy H. Taylor RGN d of Ian H. T. MB ChB(Glas) Bournemouth

SKENE Richard Mackie LLB 1969

SKENE William George cMB ChB 1962

SKINNER Alexander Cumming *BSc 1968
s of Alexander S. bldr and Jessie Cumming; b Dingwall 24.11.47
FGS(Lond) 1972
geol: Brit antarctic surv Stonington Base E Antarctica, Birm 1968–72, overseas div inst of geol sc Lond, Shan States Burma, Lond, Lobatse Botswana from 1972
m Tain 10.7.71 Catherine M. Corbett BSc 1967 *qv*

SKINNER Alexander Morrison MA 1963
s of James B. S. MA 1934 *qv*; b Aber 23.9.42
FFA 1969 F Pensions Man. Inst 1977
trainee actuary, actuary Edin 1963–70; asst group actuary Montreal 1970–71; actuarial/pensions advis Kingston Jamaica 1971–72; pensions (sales) man. Edin from 1972
m Aber 16.7.66 Gay H. Brown teacher home econ d of William B. Aber

SKINNER Annie Mackenzie MA 1959
d of David A. S. merch seaman and Christian E. Harkus; b S Shields 12.6.38
teacher: Inv 1960–65, Helmsdale 1965–66, Golspie from 1969
m Balintore 3.4.65 Allan C. Barclay BSc(Glas) teacher/asst rector s of John B. B. Inv

SKINNER Craig *MB ChB 1965
s of James S. acct and Jane A. Craig; b Stonehaven 1.10.40
MRCP(Lond) 1970
h o ARI 1965–66; lect path. Aberd 1966–67; sen h o, regist, sen regist med Aber gen hosps 1967–74; sen regist respir med Sheffield from 1974
m Lond 15.11.61 Beryl Findlater teacher d of James F. Aber

SKINNER George BSc(eng) 1961
s of George S. fisherman and Barbara Allan; b Balintore 28.9.40
MICE
Montreal eng co Calgary Alberta in 1974
m Tain Margaret Vass teacher d of Kenneth V. Tain

SKINNER Ian Ross MA 1968

SKINNER James Allan MB ChB 1969
s of George S. fisherman and Barbara Allen; b Balintore 12.9.46
h o RACH, Woodend hosp Aber, Inv 1969–70; sen h o obst Bellshill 1971; g p Aber 1971–72, Fearn from 1972
m Carloway Is of Lewis 13.8.71 Murdina Maclean MA 1969 *qv*

SKINNER Martha Helen MA 1969
m Lennox

SKINNER May Elizabeth MA 1967
d of George C. S. farm. and Marguerite C. Reid teacher; b Aber 15.5.42
m Aber 1.9.65 Satya S. Amar MB ChB 1966 *qv*

SKINNER Michael John *BSc 1970

SKINNER Morna Logan LLB 1967
m Hinch

SKINNER Peter Jackson MA 1967

SKINNER Tom Anthony *BSc(eng) 1965
s of David A. S. seaman and Christian Harkus; b Balintore 20.11.42
MEng(Carleton) 1972
eng: Ferranti Edin 1965–66, Canadian gen elect. 1966–67; res eng (scient staff) Bell Northern res Ottawa 1967–73; sen eng Telesat Canada, Ottawa 1973–74; prin Miller commun Ottawa 1974–76; pres Kantel Ottawa from 1976
m Balintore 22.7.66 Angela R. Thompson teacher d of Alexander T. Tain

SKOYLES Douglas *BSc 1968 PhD 1971

SLACK Margaret Mary MB ChB 1963

SLATER Francis William *BSc 1970

SLATER John PhD 1956
ARIC

SLATER John *MA 1961 MSc 1962 PhD 1969
s of David J. S. fish salesman and Martha Summers clerkess; b Fraserburgh 23.9.39
asst lect, lect R'dg 1964–68; syst eng IBM Lond 1968–69; ass prof computer sc Calgary univ Alberta 1969–72, assoc prof from 1972
m Aber 22.7.65 Christine M. McKinnon MA 1962 *qv*

SLATER Peter Anderson ᶜMB ChB 1966
s of William S. MB ChB 1941 *qv*; b Aber 6.9.41
FRCSE 1972
h o ARI 1966–67; lect path. Aberd 1967–68; sen h o ARI: surg 1968–69, orthop 1969–70; regist: surg Middlesbrough gen hosp Teesside 1970–72, orthop Selly Oak Birm accident hosps 1973–75; sen regist orthop surg ARI 1975–78; consult. orthop surg Stracathro hosp from 1978
m Aber 21.7.67 Isobel M. Craig MB ChB 1966 *qv*

SLATER Rosalyn Jane *MA 1970
s of William S. MB ChB 1940 *qv*; b Nairobi 2.9.46
res asst med sociol Aberd 1971–72
m Aber 20.8.70 David Stephen civ serv (Scot. off. audit unit) s of John S. J. S. Aber

SLEIGH or Kennedy, Allison Margaret MB ChB 1960
d of F. R. S. MB ChB 1923 *qv*; b Hampton Hill 28.4.36
h o Aber: RACH, Woodend hosp 1960–62; FPA/MRC Cardiff 1966–68; BTS Aber 1968–70
m(2) Aber 1.12.73 Iain Fraser BL(Glas) advoc in Aber s of Donald F. Glasg

SLEIGH Elizabeth Anne MA 1969

SLESSOR Eva Margaret BSc 1962
d of William M. K. S. teacher and Eva J. K. Ross teacher; b Aber 23.10.39
teacher: Torry acad 1963–65, Sheerwater s s Woking 1965–68, Holme j s Headley from 1975
m Aber 31.7.65 Robert Falconer MA 1963 *qv*

SLESSOR Ian Munro MB ChB 1956
s of John S. costing clerk and Helen B. Milne cashier; b Aber 19.5.32
MRCGP 1967 MSc 1978
h o Aber gen hosps 1956–58; dem anat dept Queen's coll Dund 1958–60; regist surg Aber gen hosps 1960–62; g p Aber 1962–69; med advis Astra Chemicals Watford from 1969

SLESSOR William Ross BSc 1964 Dip Ed 1965
s of William M. K. S. teacher and Eva Ross teacher; b Aber 12.3.41
teacher sc Torry s s Aber 1965–68; injured in climbing accident 1968

SLETTEN Jorgen MB ChB 1964
s of Andreas S. man. elect. works and Helga Kviteng; b Mo Norway 18.4.37
FRCGP 1972
h o Stornoway 1964–65; Norway: g p Ardal 1965–66, g p/loc m o h Laerdal 1966–70; g p trainee Bangour (Scot.) gen hosp 1970–72; g p/distriktslege (m o h) Løten Norway from 1972
m Aber 3.4.64 Annabel J. Bain teacher, med secy d of James B. St Fergus

SLORACH Ronald George BSc 1960

SLOWEY Alexander MB ChB 1968
s of Frank S. publ works contr and Margaret More; b Burghead 2.2.42
LMCC 1970
h o Inv, Liv 1968–69; g p Brockville Ontario from 1969
m Aber 27.12.67 Patricia J. Mackinnon MB ChB 1968 *qv*

SMALL Alan *MA 1959
s of Frank S. eng and Alice M. Carnie; b Westminster Lond 25.8.37
FSAScot. FSA(Lond)
asst lect, lect geog Aberd 1961–68; sen lect, reader geog Dund from 1969
m Oslo 30.8.68 Sigrun Holdhus Cand Real(Oslo) res worker/teacher d of Sigurd H. Oslo

SMALL Basil Oscar Samuel MSc 1962
BSc(New Br)

SMALL Olwen Margaret Henderson MA 1970

SMALLWOOD Michael John BSc 1969 *1975 MSc 1976
s of John S. and Kathleen Dixon; b Bradford 3.11.44
teacher Aber 1969–70; asst trans man. Lond 1970–72

SMART Allan Gordon *MA 1956 MEd 1973

SMART Ernest Ross Duncan MA 1958 LLB 1961
s of Percy C. S. buying man. and Abigail Tawse; b Aber 19.3.37
BD(Glas) 1978
law app Aber 1958–61; admin asst Lond 1961–63; stud. Christ's coll Aber 1963–66; C of S min: asst Motherwell 1966–67, Carluke 1967–74, Merrylea Glasg from 1974
m Aber 9.4.65 Rosemary C. D. Carmichael MA 1962 *qv*

SMART Frances Mary MA 1964
d of George S. maintenance eng and Isabella A. Robertson; b Aber 22.2.44
m Kemnay 4.8.64 John A. Glennie MB ChB 1962 *qv*

SMART Hazel MA 1962
d of Charles R. S. foreman textile waterproofer and Mabel C. D. Kemp; b Aber 24.10.41
teacher: Middle s, Powis s Aber 1963–65; part-time Aber coll of comm 1968–70
m Aber 27.7.63 James F. Reaper scient off. s of Robert W. R. Aber

SMART James Alexander MA 1966

SMART Jane Frances BSc 1969
d of George G. J. S. MA(Cantab) dir salmon fishings and Frances B. McFadyean; b Montrose 20.1.48
secy Lond zool gardens 1969–70; temp secy etc Aust 1971–73; curator biol sc museum of NT Darwin Aust 1973–74; secy 1974–77
m Melbourne Aust 26.4.74 David C. Tucker BSc(James Cook univ) geol s of Horace F. T. MB BS(Melbourne) Sandringham Vic Aust

SMART John Kirkton BSc(for) 1958
s of John K. S. manuf's ag and Margaret C. Cathro; b Aber 20.6.34
prof off. W Aust govt for. serv Perth W Aust from 1958
m Aber 27.4.57 Margaret I. Smith potter d of Andrew S. Aber

SMART Judith Mary *MA 1970
d of Gordon A. S. arch. and Mary Anderson MB ChB 1938 *qv*; b Lond 4.6.48
teacher, secy for Finnish, Brit soc Jyväskylä Finland 1970–71; Lond: sub edit. med dept Butterworths, house edit. Bailliére Tindall, med publ 1972–75; sub edit. John Wright med publ Bristol
m Aber 28.4.73 Alan Watt jun man. life assur off. s of Charles N. W. Edin

SMART Lynne Watkins MA 1965 LLB 1967
d of James S. soc worker and Beryl M. Watkins; b Hertford 9.3.44
law app town clerk's dept Aber 1967–69; leg. asst Burnett & Reid advoc Aber 1970–71
m Aber 22.12.69 Dennis J. Williams comp chmn s of Percival J. W. BSc(eng) Lond

SMART Marjory Ann *MA 1968
d of Alexander W. S. rly clerk and Christina Taylor shop asst; b Aber 15.9.45
Lond: stud. secy duties City of Westminster coll 1968–69, private secy to dir of import/export comp 1969–72
m Aber 12.9.70 Roy R. Dover cler off. BR s of Thomas R. D. Lond

SMART Norman Alexander MA 1964

SMART Peter Alexander Fordyce BSc 1964
s of Douglas G. S. rubber estate man. and Annie W. Porter; b Malang Indonesia 10.7.42
Dip App Ling.(Edin) 1973
various posts Scot. 1964–67; TEFL: Sweden, Saudi Arabia, W Ger 1967–72, Poland, Saudi Arabia, W Ger 1973–78; teacher Colchester from 1978
m Kirkcaldy 6.9.74 Jean Ford MA(St And) d of James F. Kirkcaldy

SMELLIE Isabel Ann MA 1961
m Johnston

SMITH Aileen Andrea MA 1970

SMITH Aileen Campbell MA 1970

SMITH Alan Howard *BSc 1969

SMITH Alan Wilson BSc(for) 1956
b Middlesbrough 1.9.35
reg man. Flintshire Woodlands; resid Shrewsbury

SMITH Alastair Davidson MA 1966

SMITH Alexander Adams MA 1970

SMITH Alexander Gordon *BSc 1956
s of James W. S. BSc(agr) 1929 *qv*; b Inv 18.8.34
PhD(Lond) 1961
geol, geol surv dept Lusaka Zambia 1959–65; site geol Consol. Gold Fields Strontian 1965; patent examiner DTI Lond from 1966
m Bushey 5.5.73 Mary V. Glanville SRN d of Arthur V. G. Bushey

SMITH Alexander John *MA 1966 Dip Ed 1967
s of Alexander G. S. bank acct and Jessie R. Kistler; b Edin 25.8.43
Edin: teacher Engl Boroughmuir s s 1967–70, Craigmount s s 1970–73 and asst housemaster 1972–73, prin guid Trinity acad from 1973
m Berwick-u-Tweed 29.12.67 Shona F. Geggie teacher d of Peter G. G. Berwick-u-Tweed

SMITH Alexander Low *MA 1969 Dip Ed 1970
s of Alexander L. S. baker and Jeannie Lindsay; b Forfar 7.3.47
teacher: geog Forfar acad 1970–73, prin geog Forres acad from 1973

SMITH Alistair Joseph Watt *MA 1962

SMITH Angus Thomson *MA 1970
s of Leslie S. S. BR rly clerk and Nellie Thomson; b Aber 30.5.27
teacher hist Keith g s from 1971
m Bucksburn 4.8.71 Kathleen Lawrence MA 1969 *qv*

SMITH Ann MA 1960 Dip Ed 1961

SMITH Anne Josephine MA 1968

SMITH Basil Forbes Lowden BSc 1956
s of James S. bank man. and Eva McIntosh; b Insch 4.5.34
radar fitter RAF UK, Malaya 1957–59; analytical chem SSO Macaulay Inst Aber from 1959
m Ansley Nuneaton 10.9.66 Mary E. Woodward BSc (Birm) statist d of Aubrey F. W. Atherstone

SMITH Ben *MA 1966
s of Benjamin S. and Mildred W. Stephen MA 1935 *qv*; b Woking 17.1.44
ANU Canberra: res schol 1966–68, sen tut. 1968–71; lect Strath from 1972
m Stonehaven 21.9.66 Elizabeth Synge BSc 1966 *qv*

SMITH Brian Stuart *MA 1970
s of Reginald J. S. wireworks gen man. and Irene Bowles attend. blood transfusion serv; b Aber 13.1.48
Ford Motor Co 1970–76; sales progr and distribut man. Leyland Vehicles Leyland 1976–80; man. dir Leyland Vehicles (Ireland) from 1980
m Aber 24.10.70 Alison M. Joss BSc 1970 *qv*

SMITH Brian William Wright *BSc 1969

SMITH Callum Ian MA 1968
s of Malcolm S. shopkeeper/crofter and Allanina Martin; b Leurbost Is of Lewis 18.7.46
teacher maths Oban h s from 1969

SMITH Campbell David MA 1970
s of David S. headmaster and E. Sylvia East; b Ellon 14.4.49
RAF off. UK, Cyprus from 1970
m Tankerness Orkney 10.4.71 Isobel Robertson BEd 1971 teacher d of George R. Kirkwall

SMITH Charles Crombie BSc(eng) 1961
b Huntly 19.1.40
MI Mun E 1963 M Inst HE 1964
city eng dept Aber: grad asst 1961–63, asst eng 1963–69, prin eng from 1969

SMITH Charles Graham *BSc 1965

SMITH Christopher David MA 1966 *1968 PhD 1978
s of Richard E. S. schoolmaster and Doris Lowry; b Wolverhampton 3.3.46
lect, sen lect psych Harris coll Preston, Preston polytech from 1971
m(1) Dun 26.8.72 Patricia A. Boyack MA 1967 *qv*; marr diss
(2) Hereford 29.12.78 Rhiannon Phillips Powell BA (Durh) res fell. Strath d of Charles P. P. MA(Oxon)

SMITH Colin James Webb MA 1969
s of Auckland R. S. baker and Elspeth M. Carnie; b Aberchirder 26.5.47
teacher hist Earlston from 1970
m Earlston 20.7.74 Shirley H. Paterson stud. d of William D. P. Earlston

SMITH Colin Peter BSc 1969

SMITH Conal Robertson Cumming *MA 1969

SMITH Craigie Alexander Donald BL 1959

SMITH David Allan Addison MA 1965

SMITH David Balfour *BSc(eng) 1967 MSc 1969 PhD 1978
MIEE 1974 CEng

SMITH David Christopher MSc 1968 PhD 1976
s of Bertram T. H. S. warden hall of resid Leic poly and Florence M. Drage asst warden; b Leic 29.5.46
BA(Cantab) 1967 MA(Cantab) 1971
lect geol N Lond poly 1972–74; geochemist geol surv Trondheim Norway 1974–77; res fell. Edin 1977–80; dep dir mineralogy dept nat hist museum Paris from 1980
m Bois-Guillaume France 7.7.77 Elisabeth Delaunay documentation eng d of Henri D. Bois-Guillaume

SMITH Dennis *MA 1967
s of Winifred M. J. Smith clerkess; b Aber 7.3.45
post-grad stud. Queen's coll Oxon 1967–70; res asst Nat Lib of Scot. Edin from 1970

SMITH Derek Stewart Hunter *BSc 1969 PhD 1973

SMITH Diana Margaret BSc 1970
d of Dennis N. R. S. res scient and Hilda H. Williams nurse; b High Wycombe 3.11.48
sen tech in plant path. lab RHM res centre from 1970
m High Wycombe 1.9.74 Douglas W. Taylor MA(Glas) records off., information off. s of Ian G. T. Prestwick

SMITH Donald BSc 1961 *MEd 1968
s of Roderick S. weaver and Normina Macphail; b Bragar Is of Lewis 28.7.39
teacher Aberdeensh 1962–68; lect Aber coll of comm 1968–70; prin teacher maths Woodmill h s Dunfermline 1970–77; asst rector Inverkeithing h s from 1977
m Aber 29.3.65 Catherine Murray MA 1960 *qv*

SMITH Donald Robert MA 1962
CA

SMITH Doreen MA 1964
m Gilmour

SMITH Douglas McKinnon *MA 1968
s of Alexander D. S. insur ag and Annie McKinnon; b Aber 27.9.46
MBA(Strath) 1969
Lond: marketg exec Rank Hovis McDougall 1969–74, marketg man. RHM Foods from 1974

SMITH Edward Alistair *MA 1961 PhD 1967
s of Archibald S. bank man. and Jean M. Johnston; b Aber 16.1.39
asst lect geog Aberd 1963–67, lect from 1967

SMITH Edward Gordon *BSc 1962
s of Frank G. S. textile worker and Isabel Anderson; b Fochabers 10.11.39
Dip Ed(Glas) FCS
teacher: Lira Uganda 1963–65, Kisumu Kenya 1967–69, Glasg from 1970
m Isel Cumberland 6.7.66 Annie Sutton BA(Nott) soc worker d of Sydney S. Blindcrake

SMITH Effie Macphail MA 1963
d of Roderick S. crofter/weaver and Normina Macphail; b Stornoway 9.4.43
teacher: Fife 1964–66, Dunbartonsh 1966–68 and 1975–76; trainee computer progr. from 1976
m Aber 9.8.66 David J. Murray-Smith BSc 1963 *qv*

SMITH Elaine Grace MA 1967
m Niven

SMITH Elizabeth Ann *MA 1968

SMITH Elizabeth Ann Scott MA 1962
d of Wilson H. S. MA 1926 *qv*; b Aber 24.1.42
Dip Secy Pract(Glasg)
secy to dir Mugiemoss Mill Bucksburn 1963–64
m Aber 4.10.63 Keith W. Ferguson MA 1953 *qv*

SMITH Elizabeth Mary BSc 1966

SMITH Eric Leslie MB ChB 1959
s of William R. S. licensed grocer and Martha D. Lees; b Aber 3.2.35
MRCPE 1964 FRCP 1978
regist dermat venereology ARI 1959–63; sen regist and tut. Middx hosp and St John's hosp for diseases of the skin Lond 1964–66; head dermat and vd dept Mowasat hosp Kuwait 1967–68; prin in pract consult. dermat Camberley dist gen hosp 1969–74; head dermat and vd dept cent hosp United Arab Emirates from 1975
m Aber 6.8.64 Ethne I. Cook d of Andrew C.

SMITH Esmé Agnes MA 1957
m Reid

SMITH Esther Margaret BEd 1970
d of William W. S. farm. and Esther M. Lowe; b Cardenden Fife 7.1.49
teacher geog/mod stud. Lesmahagow 1970–73
m Dun 28.7.70 John C. Bicket farm. man. asst s of David B. Kirriemuir

SMITH Eva Roberta *MA 1957
m Foote

SMITH Fay Whyte MA 1965
m Simpson
d 9.10.71 *AUR* XLIV 322

SMITH Francis William MB ChB 1970 DMRD 1975
s of William S. BSc 1934 *qv*; b Colchester 8.1.43
ARI: h o, sen h o 1970–72, regist nephrol 1972–73, regist radiodiagnosis from 1973
m Newcastle-u-Tyne 5.12.70 Pamela A. Cox SRN nurs sister d of James C. Whitley Bay

SMITH Geddes MA 1957 *MEd 1977

SMITH George MB ChB 1970
s of Benjamin S. ship's eng and Edith M. S. Bond; b Banff 13.6.47
DA(Lond) 1973 DObstRCOG 1973 FFARCS 1977
med off. RAF med br 1970–78; sen regist anaest Derbyshire RI, Groby Road hosp Leic and Nott City hosp from 1978
m St And 17.7.70 Fay R. Marshall dom sc teacher d of John R. M. St And

SMITH George MA 1969
s of George A. S. elect. eng and Mary C. D. Murray; b Portlethen 15.3.48
pilot RAF Leuchars from 1969
d air crash Canary Islands 26.5.78

SMITH George Alexander MB ChB 1962
Lerwick: g p from 1965, anaest from 1970
m Aber 11.7.62 Heather Hunter MA 1959 *qv*

SMITH George Bruce Pirie ᶜLLB 1967
s of William S. master coach painter and Anna Pirie; b Aber 15.6.47
law app, leg. asst James & George Collie advoc Aber 1967–70; leg. asst Paull & Williamsons advoc Aber 1970–72, ptnr from 1972

SMITH George Cowie MA 1969

SMITH George Nicholson *MA 1969
s of George N. S. turbine driver and Isabella D. Begg; b Aber 15.6.47
MSc(Oxon) 1974
res asst dept psych Dund 1969–70; dept man. Marks & Spencer Kirkcaldy 1970–72; dep supt boys' remand home Grimsby 1972; soc worker Oxon soc serv Abingdon from 1974

SMITH Gerald Sutherland MA 1967

SMITH Gladys Jane Hogarth MA 1965
d of Robert S. farm./driver and Gladys G. Bisset civ serv; b Buckie 15.3.44
teacher Broomhill p s Aber from 1966
m Aber 30.7.71 Richard Little civ serv (ordnance surv) s of John J. E. S. L. Leith

SMITH Gordon *BSc 1963 PhD 1968
s of Allan S. and Margaret S. Willocks; b Aberfeldy 6.11.41
lect bot univ of Malaya Kuala Lumpur from 1968

SMITH Gordon Anderson
see Anderson-Smith

SMITH Gordon Ansell Morrison MA 1957
s of James M. S. MB ChB 1924 *qv*; b York 27.11.35
teacher Engl Northfield acad Aber from 1960
m Antrim NI 27.7.61 Ethel E. Marquess teacher home econ d of Harold F. M. Muckamore Co Antrim

SMITH Gordon Laird *MA 1968 MSc 1973
s of William E. S. g p and Elsie G. Chisholm; b Glasg 20.4.47
FRSS 1969
res fell. dept statist Aberd 1968–71; Torry res stat Aber: scient off. DTI 1971–72, MAFF 1972–73, higher scient off. MAFF 1974–77, sen scient off. MAFF from 1978

SMITH Gordon Lamont MB ChB 1961
s of Howard L. S. civ eng and Doris Sharples; b Aber 12.4.34
D Av Med 1974

m Aber 1960 Catriona F. G. MacRae MB ChB 1961 *qv*
d Farnborough 14.2.75 *AUR* XLVI 240

SMITH Grace Neilson MA 1956
d of John R. S. insur ag and Mary R. Neilson; b Aber 24.6.36
teacher Tillydrone p s, Braeside p s Aber from 1957
m Aber 5.8.60 Michael E. Welsh admin off. Aberd s of Eric St C. W. Aber

SMITH Graham Francis *MA 1960
b Lond 30.5.33
PhD(Cantab) 1963
asst prof Calif Los Angeles 1963–65; lect univ of Wales Swansea 1965–70; sen lect Stir from 1970
m 18.7.64 Angela M. BA(Birm) univ lect

SMITH Hamish George *BSc(eng) 1970

SMITH Hance Duncan *BSc 1968 PhD 1973
s of Hance S. ferry boat owner/oper and Emmie J. Duncan; b Lerwick 12.11.45
post-grad res, tut. stud. geog Aberd 1968–72; lect geog: Aber coll of educ 1972–74, N'cle-u-Tyne poly 1974–76, univ of Wales inst sc and tech from 1977

SMITH Hazel *MA 1967

SMITH Heather Fiona Cameron *MA 1965
d of James L. S. comm trav and Mary W. Robertson shop asst; b Glasg 12.5.43
Dip Cartog(Glas) 1966
grad cartog Aberd 1966–70; Brit council exchange fell. univ of Budapest Hungary 1967; visiting lect geog Auck univ NZ 1968
m Aber 1.8.67 Francis Lyall MA 1960 *qv*

SMITH Helen Ann MA 1961
d of John N. S. Harris tweed mill worker and Christina MacMillan; b Stornoway 2.7.40
teacher: Bathgate j s s 1962–64, Uphall W Lothian 1964–66, Dun 1966, Edin 1966–67
m Dun 1.10.66 Ian Ferguson electronics eng s of Donald F. Lochmaddy N Uist

SMITH Helen Isobel MA 1960
m Reid

SMITH Helen Mary MA 1966
d of William R. S. farm. and Helen M. Paterson teacher; b Aber 15.12.45
teacher: Engl Whitburn s s 1967–68, Linlithgow p s 1968–72
m Aber 7.9.66 David Kelbie LLB 1967 *qv*

SMITH Howard Ogilvie *BSc 1964
s of George O. S. elect. eng and Dora Dickson; b Aber 7.7.42
RGC Aber: teacher 1965–69, housemaster Sillerton house 1969–73, prin geog from 1973
m Aber 5.4.66 Sheila W. Mortimer MA 1960 *qv*

SMITH Humphrey Graham MSc 1968
b Farnworth 6.6.45
BSc(Edin) 1967 PhD(Edin) 1973
biol Brit antarctic surv: Signy Antarctica 1968–71, Edin 1971–74; lect ecology Lanchester poly Coventry 1974–77, sen lect from 1977

SMITH Iain Graham LLB 1970
s of Donald S. civ serv and Margaret Urquhart; b Glasg 14.4.49
man. trainee Hayes 1970–71; law app Aber 1971–73, solic from 1973
m Glasg 26.6.71 Anna D. Wilson MA 1973 ground hostess Air Anglia d of Hugh T. W. Dallas Moray

SMITH Ian MB ChB 1961
b Chapel of Garioch 29.6.37
DObstRCOG 1963 FFARCS 1969
h o Aber, Dun, Inv 1961–63; sen h o, regist, sen regist anaest Aber 1964–72; staff anaest Toronto 1972–73; consult. anaest Aber from 1974
m Aber 6.8.66 Mary Donald

SMITH Ian *MA 1969

SMITH Ian Barclay *BSc 1962 PhD 1965
s of James B. S. process engraver overseer and Margaret A. Drunsfield; b Aber 3.10.39
CChem MRIC 1970
post doct fell. Atlantic reg lab NRC(Can) Halifax Nova Scotia 1965–67; assoc res off. NRC(Can) 1967–72; sect. leader cement phys sect. res lab Blue Circle Industries 1972–76, dep man. basic res dept from 1976
m Aber 5.9.64 Elizabeth M. E. Hay d of William Hay MB ChB 1933 *qv*

SMITH Ian Beveridge BSc(eng) 1960

SMITH Ian James BSc 1970 *1971
s of John S. plumber and Jeannie Cowling; b Aber 1.7.46
teacher sc Northfield acad Aber 1972–74 asst prin sc from 1974
m Aber 24.9.66 Elizabeth Benzies teacher d of Charles F. B. Aber

SMITH Ian Slessor BSc 1956 BL 1959
s of George F. S. wholesale fruiterer and Anne Shaw; b Inv 4.2.35
solic Munro & Noble Inv from 1961
m Edin 9.7.60 Jennifer A. Casson MA(Edin) law app

SMITH Jacqueline East MA 1965 Dip Ed 1967
d of David S. schoolmaster and Evelyn S. East; b Grimsby 6.5.45
VSO El Obeid Sudan 1965–66; teacher Engl Finnish/Brit soc Imatra Finland 1967–68; lect Engl at Finnish lang inst trg translators and interpreters Turku Finland from 1972
m Imatra 3.7.68 Ismo J. Lento syst analyst s of Kaarlo L. Salo Finland

SMITH James *BSc 1956 PhD 1959
s of Andrew S. fisherman and Jeannie Murray; b Buckie 12.11.35
ARIC 1963 FRIC 1973
asst lect Aberd 1958–63; DSIR sen res fell. NATO univ of Zürich 1960–61; lect, sen lect, prin lect chem Slough coll of higher educ from 1963
m Huntly 20.8.60 Mary A. Featch teacher d of Alexander F. Huntly

SMITH James BSc 1966
s of Alexander S. fisherman and Katie Smith; b Edin 26.4.44
teacher maths Whitburn 1967–69, Lossiemouth 1969–72; prin maths Lendrickmuir from 1972
m Lossiemouth 5.4.68 Margaret E. Riddell teleph, nurse d of Douglas B. R. Lossiemouth

SMITH James David Blackhall *BSc 1962 PhD 1965
s of James S. master butcher and Marion MacQueen; b Peterhead 25.4.40

FCS 1963 ARIC 1965 ACS 1968 MIEEE 1976
Fulbright res fell. Syracuse univ NY USA 1965–66; sen scient Laporte Indust Luton 1967–68; fell. scient Westinghouse elect. corp res center Pittsburgh Pa USA from 1968

SMITH Jean Reid BSc 1961
d of John S. shopowner and Grace Souter; b Edin 23.8.39
teacher maths: Hopeman 1962–63, Lond 1963–64, Los Angeles USA 1965–66
m Lossiemouth 18.7.63 Robert A. Sinclair BSc 1960 *qv*

SMITH Jennifer Margaret MA 1968
d of William L. S. market gardener and Margaret A. Bell shorthand typist; b Torphins 2.2.48
teacher Aber 1969–71
m Skene 11.7.69 Alexander D. Leys chef s of Alexander L. Sauchen

SMITH Jennifer May MA 1962
b Aber 13.2.42
teacher Quarryhill p s Aber 1962–64; res off. educ dept Aberd from 1964
m Welsh

SMITH Jenny Ford MA 1969

SMITH Joan Doreen *MA 1959 PhD 1964
m Taylor

SMITH John BSc 1963
s of John D. S. baker and Helen Gordon; b Aber 27.11.19
teacher: phys AGS 1964–66, maths Aber coll of comm 1966–70; sen teacher computer stud. Aber coll of comm from 1970
m Aber 4.8.71 Constance Paterson bakery man. d of Alexander P. Aber

SMITH John MB ChB 1968
s of Finlay S. haulage contr and Catherine MacIver; b Breasclete Is of Lewis 28.1.45
MRCGP 1975
h o Belford hosp Fort William, city hosp Aber 1968–69; sen h o mat. hosp Middlesbrough 1969–70; g p Portree 1970, Stornoway from 1970
m Inv 10.4.70 Muriel K. MacDonald nurse d of Roderick MacD. Lochs Is of Lewis

SMITH John Angus MB ChB 1962 MD 1966
s of John S. blacksmith and Henrietta MacKay; b Shader Is of Lewis 6.8.36
FRCP(C) 1971
h o Aber 1962–63; asst lect bact Aberd 1963–64; lect microbiol Monash univ Melbourne 1964–67; lect infect. diseases Glas 1967–69; assoc prof med/med microbiol Tor. Canada 1969–77; assoc prof path./assoc in med univ of Br Col from 1977
m Aber 2.10.63 Elizabeth Thomson nurse d of George F. T. Aboyne

SMITH John Hay *BSc 1966 PhD 1969
s of John S. fisherman and Mary Hay; b Sandend 23.1.46
res and dev chem ICI Grangemouth from 1969
m Grangemouth 30.10.71 Dorothy Mentiply secy d of James A. C. M. Grangemouth

SMITH John Lane MA 1968

SMITH John Smart *MA 1963 PhD 1969
s of John A. R. S. civ eng and Vera M. H. Campbell; b Aber 14.2.41
FSAScot.
asst lect geog Aberd 1965–68, lect 1968–74, sen lect from 1974
m Aber 23.3.67 Gillian A. Campbell MA 1965 *qv*

SMITH June Ellison MA 1967 Dip Ed 1968
d of Charles C. S. merch N and Frances E. Skene; b Aber 12.6.40
teacher Engl/r e: Bankhead acad 1968–69; journalist Hemel Hempstead from 1971
m Nairn 8.8.70 John Z. Chisholm supermarket man. s of James C. Nairn

SMITH Karl Alworth MB ChB 1960 cMD 1977
b St Ann Jamaica 3.3.29
WHO fell. 1964–65; Milbank fac fell. 1966–71; Ford found. grant Yale 1967–68
MPH(Yale) 1965 DrPH(Yale) 1971 MFCM 1973
h o ARI 1960–61, h o/jun regist univ hosp WI Jamaica 1961–62; spec m o/MRC epidemiol res unit UWI MoH Jamaica Lawrence Tavern 1962–66; dept soc and preventive med UWI Jamaica: lect, sen lect 1968–77; dir fam plan./epidemiol unit 1972–74; visiting assoc prof dept h care & epidemiol UBC Canada 1975–76; h sciences rep Internat Dev Res Centre reg off. E & Cent Africa from 1978

SMITH Kathleen Forbes BSc 1959
d of Campbell G. S. civ serv and Catherine H. Pointer; b Aber 16.7.38
teacher Aber and NI 1960–76; head sc dept Forthill girls' s Lisburn NI from 1976
m Aber 29.7.61 Ian B. MacDonald BSc(agr) 1957 *qv*

SMITH Kathleen Jessie BSc 1957
d of James W. S. BSc(agr) 1929 *qv*; b Inv 18.9.36
chem Esso petr co Southampton 1956–57; Canada: lab tech NB hosp Frederickton 1957–58; res tech NRC Ottawa 1958–61; chem Calopet Foods Oakland Ca USA 1961–72
m Frederickton 15.2.58 William L. M. McKillop BSc(for) 1954 *qv*

SMITH Linda MA 1969
b Scone 20.1.48
teacher Engl Livingston 1970–74
m Aber 1.8.67 Denis Cheyne BSc 1970 *qv*

SMITH Lindsay Scott *BSc 1964
s of Daniel S. S. motor mech and Margaret A. Irvine; b Lerwick 17.9.39
asst seismologist Sultanate of Muscat of Oman 1964–66; seismol Onitsha Biafra 1967–68; sen seismol: Donala Cameroons 1968–70, Asaba Nigeria 1970–72; dep dev off. Lerwick 1972–74; asst man. (Ocean Inchcape) Lerwick 1974–76; oper man. (Norscot Serv) Lerwick from 1976
m Lerwick 3.10.63 Agnes G. Williamson d of William T. W. Yell Shetland

SMITH Lorna Anne *MA 1970 MLitt 1972 PhD 1980
m Stewart

SMITH Lorraine Josephine Jeannie MA 1970
m Donnelly

SMITH Louis Mark *MA 1969
s of George W. S. eng and Genevieve Kenny; b Sheffield 7.8.44
oil rig catering N Sea in 1974
m Gt Yarmouth 27.6.70 Elspeth J. A. Gow MA 1970 *qv*

SMITH Lynda Kaye Storm BSc 1963
m McDowall

SMITH Malcolm Murdo MA 1965
d 3.2.68

SMITH Margaret Scott MA 1969
d of Edward S. lab and Mary Scott; b Buckie 31.12.47
lect maths/statist Aber coll of comm 1969–70; computer progr UKAEA Thurso 1970–71; part-time lect Thurso tech coll 1972–77
m Buckie 27.9.69 Alexander Bruce elect. eng s of Alexander B. Findochty

SMITH Marjorie Young MA 1969
d of James Y. S. comp dir, agr seedsman and Margaret A. S. Russell; b Ayr 17.11.48
teacher: Havering 1970–72, Hatfield Peverel 1972–74, Darlington 1974–75
m Ayr 21.8.70 Iain F. Gilmour MA 1969 *qv*

SMITH Mary Frances BSc 1967 Dip Ed 1968
d of Edward S. crane driver, lab, storekeeper and Mary Scott; b Buckie 15.5.46
teacher maths: Ellon acad 1968–69, Buckie h s 1969–74, asst prin maths from 1972
m Buckie 7.8.71 Langley C. Forbes photogr s of John C. F. Buckie

SMITH Mary Reid MB ChB 1970
d of Maurice W. S. farm. and Ann R. Mutch clerkess; b Huntly 6.12.46
DObstRCOG 1972 FPA certif 1974
h o: Woodend hosp, City hosp Aber, Yorkhill hosp Glasg, mat. hosp Aber; sen h o Gray's hosp Elgin; res regist mat. hosp Aber; clin m o (fam plan.) GGHB
m Aber 3.5.74 Thomas M. Scott MB ChB(Glas) s of Thomas S. MB ChB(Glas) Inv

SMITH Maureen Rose MA 1961
m Paterson

SMITH Michael *MA 1966

SMITH Muriel Glenda MA 1959

SMITH Neil Gordon BSc(agr) 1958

SMITH Patricia Anne MA 1968
d of James B. S. process engraver overseer and Margaret A. Drunsfield; b Aber 29.4.47
Canada: soc worker Halifax 1969–70, caseworker Ottawa 1971–74; Engl tut. Würzburg W Ger 1974–76; clerk Ottawa 1976–77
m Ottawa 22.10.70 Gregory S. Bezanson PhD(Carleton) microbiol s of Gerald E. B. Nova Scotia

SMITH Patrick Fleming *MA 1965 MSc 1967

SMITH Peter MA 1969

SMITH Peter McGregor *BSc 1966 PhD 1974

SMITH Reginald George PhD 1962
BSc(Edin)

SMITH Robert Allan MA 1970 BSc 1973

SMITH Robin Bailey
see Bailey-Smith

SMITH Roderick MA 1964 Dip Ed 1968
s of William S. gen merch and Alexina Macleod postmistress; b Keose Is of Lewis 9.2.40
lect RAEC Scot. infantry depot Br of Don Aber from 1965
m Aber 16.8.66 Ellen McHardy MA 1964 *qv*

SMITH Roderick John MA 1969
s of Malcolm S. crofter and Allanina Martin; b Leurbost Is of Lewis 16.11.47
teacher maths Western Is from 1970
m Stornoway 31.3.72 Annie Campbell d of Norman C. Sandwick

SMITH Ronald George
see Mackay (Smith) Ronald George

SMITH Ronald Ian Lewis *BSc 1964 PhD 1968
s of Ian L. S. BSc(eng) 1935 *qv*; b Aber 29.1.42
bot Brit antarctic surv S Orkney Is Antarctica 1964–67, Aber 1967–69, South Georgia Subantarctica 1969–71; head B.A.S. bot sect. Birm from 1971
m Stronsay Orkney 1.7.70 Elinor M. M. Groat staff nurse d of John G. Stronsay

SMITH Rosalind Ailsa Hamilton *BSc 1968

SMITH Rosemary MA 1965

SMITH Rosemary Anne *MA 1963 Dip Ed 1964
d of Reginald D. W. S. quality control insp and Megan Whitely; b Welwyn 1940
lect coll of educ Hitchin 1964–66; head Engl dept The Bishop Perowne s Worcester 1966–71
m Hitchin 1965 John A. Cattanach area/branch sales man. computers s of Alexander B. C. BSc 1931 *qv*

SMITH Sandra *MA 1968
m Campbell

SMITH Sandra Whyte MA 1965
d of Robert W. B. S. BOAC navig, oper off. BAA and Margaret H. Whyte home help organis; b Airth 30.12.42
Penguin books: i/c sale of foreign rights contr dept Harmondsworth 1965–67; asst book edit. univ of Lond Press 1967–71; freelance book edit. royal coll of nurs/ULP from 1971
m Burnham 4.1.69 Hugh M. R. Dawson journalist/chief sub edit. *Daily Mail* s of William D.

SMITH Sheila Murdoch *BSc 1962
d of Charles H. I. S. acct and Janet R. Ross lab asst; b Edin 11.11.40
teacher Ruthrieston j s s Aber 1963–64
m Aber 27.7.63 Andrew Munro MA 1964 *qv*

SMITH Sheila Taylor MA 1968

SMITH Sheila Thomson MA 1967
d of George T. S. serv eng and Annie G. McKnight; b Banff 4.10.46
teacher: Perth 1968–71, Glenrothes 1971–72, Aber from 1972
m Aberchirder –.7.71 Edward F. McLerie draughtsman s of John F. McL. Newburgh Fife

SMITH Simon Fleming *BSc 1958 Dip Ed 1960
s of William R. S. marine eng and Winifred M. Fleming; b Singapore 18.3.37
teacher maths AGS 1959–65; prin maths: Banchory acad 1965–66, Cults acad Aber from 1966
m Aber 21.7.61 Irene M. Rannie teacher d of William S. R. Milltimber Aber

SMITH Stanley Leith *MA 1960 Dip Ed 1962
s of Stanley L. S. comp dir and Alice Johnston; b Aber 17.12.35
ACCA 1976
trainee man. Peterhead 1960–61; teacher geog Arbroath acad 1962–65, prin geog N Berwick 1966–70; comp secy/dir New Pitsligo Aber 1970–76, comp acct from 1976
m Aber 15.7.66 Jessie Bremner nurs sister

SMITH Stella Rankine MA 1968
d of David S. farm. and Muriel C. Smith secy; b Stonehaven 1.6.47
Dip Secy 1969
secy Leeds 1969–70; teacher: Engl govt h s Nassau Bahamas 1970–73, Fr/Engl Monks Hill h s Croydon 1973–74; TEFL St George's s Montreux Switzerland 1974–75; part-time tut. Fr Walker tech coll Wellington, Telford from 1976
m Aber 4.7.70 Godfrey P. Davis MA 1969 *qv*

SMITH Stewart Mitchell MA 1966
s of Gordon S. S. policeman and Barbara A. Mitchell; b Aber 23.12.31
teacher Fr/guid Linksfield acad Aber from 1967
m Aber 1.8.59 Heather G. Douglas

SMITH Stuart Lauchlan MA 1964 *BSc(eng) 1967 MSc 1970
s of James C. S. elect. eng and Jean Stuart; b Kilmarnock 24.4.44
plant eng chem indust ICI Wilton 1969–75, proj eng chem indust from 1975
m Hexham 6.9.69 Rachel C. Davidson BSc 1969 *qv*

SMITH Trefor Leslie *MA 1970
s of Leslie J. S. MA 1931 *qv*; b Aber 4.7.48
BMus(Liv) 1971 Assoc R Manc Coll Mus 1973
Diplomprüfung (piano) Hamburg 1977
pianist Hamburg from 1973

SMITH Vivien Evelyn Mark MB ChB 1962
d of Louis A. S. bank man. and Evelyn K. Mark; b Aber 19.2.36
DCH(Lond) 1964
h o: RACH 1962–63; Whipps Cross hosp, Qu Eliz hosp for ch Lond 1963–65; regist psychiat Aber 1965–71; instr psychiat Temple univ Philadelphia 1971–72; regist psychiat royal Cornhill hosp Aber from 1972
m Aber 16.7.65 Neil Edward MB ChB 1961 *qv*

SMITH Walter John Scott BSc 1963
s of William B. S. cabinetmaker/stone polisher and Mary A. Beattie; b Aber 31.1.26
Aber acad: teacher 1964–65, i/c careers 1966–70, year teacher (later Hazlehead acad) from 1970
m Aber 24.3.51 Hannah Webster d of John A. W. Aber

SMITH Wendy Anne *BSc 1966
m Ratcliffe

SMITH William *MA 1970
s of Alexander S. S. elect. eng and Margaret E. L. Aitken; b Glasg 22.2.46
MSc(McG) 1972
univ lect geog: Christchurch NZ 1972–76, McG Montreal from 1976

SMITH William BSc 1968

SMITH William Gordon BSc 1966 *1972

SMITH William Holmes Macfarlane *BSc 1967
s of Alexander M. S. OBE gen man./eng Dun harbour trust and Catherine P. Macfarlane; b N'cle-u-Tyne 23.4.42
MIBiol 1970 PhD(R'dg) 1976
res dem genetics dept agr bot R'dg 1967–71; res fell. genetics dept biol sc Dund 1971–72; barley breeder/tech man. Rothwell plant breeders Lincs 1972–78; admin head brassica dept Scot. Plant Breeding Stat from 1978
m Sandford St Martin 18.4.70 Daphne Henderson BSc (R'dg) res asst d of Frank H. Enstone

SMITH William Merson MB ChB 1969
s of William S. farm./bus. man. and Daisy Merson; b Rathven 18.2.44
h o Aber 1969–70; m o RAF 1970–72; lect aviation med/physiol RAF from 1972
m Belf 5.5.71 Roberta A. Stevenson RGN d of Howard M. S. MB ChB(Belf) Ballylesson

SMITHSON John Franklin BSc(eng) 1967
b Adlington 30.4.45
CEng MICE MIWES
asst eng Manc 1966–69; asst resid eng Derby 1969–70; resid eng Haddington 1970–74; civ eng Edin 1974–77; sen eng Cambridge from 1977
m Aber 10.8.68 Patricia J. McCaw MA 1966 *qv*

SMYTH Elizabeth Anne *MA 1968
d of Sidney G. C. S. bus. man. and Vivian A. Donn BA(Lond) teacher; b E London S Af 28.11.44
member of authors' soc 1979 MA(Essex) 1980
studio man. BBC Lond 1968–71; VSO teacher univ of Indonesia 1971–73; univ lect Saudi Arabia 1974–77; ELT advis Brit Council Lond 1977–79

SNAITH Sybil Mary PhD 1968
BSc(Lond) 1965
res biochem Rowett inst Aber 1968–76
m Birm 29.3.74 W. R. McAleese dir teaching centre Aberd

SNEDDEN James Leishman BSc 1960
s of George F. S. teacher and Elizabeth S. Ruthven; b Glasg 30.11.38
teacher sc Kirriemuir s s 1961–63; spec asst, prin asst, prin teacher Brechin h s from 1963
m Aber 12.7.62 Jean McLeod teacher d of James McL. Lerwick

SNEDDEN Marion Elspeth MA 1957 *EdB 1960
d of Andrew S. gamekeeper and Christina Morrison teacher; b Forres 4.8.36
teacher Torry s s Aber 1958–60; asst educ psych Perth 1961–62, educ psych St Francis esn s Birm 1962–64
m Dyke Forres 20.10.62 Arthur G. Fraser BSc 1959 *qv*

SNOW Thomas D'Oyley *MA 1969
s of George D. S. BA(Oxon) headmaster, bishop and Joan M. Way piano teacher; b Godalming 8.2.45
area off. nat union of public employees Kent from 1969

SNOWIE Anne Fowlie MA 1967
d of George B. S. farmer and Anne W. Fowlie; b Echt 9.4.45
teacher: Echt s 1968–69, Kinellar s 1969–71
m Echt 6.8.68 Douglas J. Burnett farm./haulage contr s of James B. Echt

SOBACZEWSKA Marysia Bernadine MA 1967

SOBEY Douglas George MSc 1970 PhD 1976
s of George A. S. mech and Rowena A. Lockhart secy/stenog; b Summerside Prince Edward Is Canada 10.6.47

BSc(Mt All) 1969
teaching asst bot Belf 1973–74; lect Stranmillis coll Belf from 1974

SOHAIL Mahmood Ali MSc 1970
BSc(AH)(Panj) Dip TVM(Edin)

SOKOLOWSKI James *BSc(eng) 1967
s of Antoni S. maintenance eng and Elizabeth Lowson; b Glasg 2.1.45
MICE 1972
asst site eng Balfour Beatty & Co Brist 1967–69; asst des eng EPDC Sidcup 1969–70; asst resid eng Sir M. MacDonald & Ptnrs Baghdad Iraq 1970–72; sect. eng, asst construct. man. Reed & Mallik Brist from 1972
m Brist 4.10.69 Lesley L. Bailey tracer/draughtswoman d of H. W. F. B. Brist

SOLIMAN Mohamed Hassan Mohamed PhD 1967
s of Hassan M. S. merch and Saida Hegazy; b Alexandria 16.4.33
BSc(Alex) 1958 MSc(Cairo) 1962 MA Clin Bioch 1965
Alexandria: lect 1958–74, asst prof 1974–80, prof biochem med res inst from 1980
m Alexandria 1965 Nahed E. El-din BA(Alex) teacher Engl d of Joseph E. E. Alexandria

SOLSTAD Karl Jan MLitt 1970
Cand Mag(Berg) Mag Art(Oslo)

SOMERVILLE David Henry Norman *MA 1963 *MEd 1965
s of David H. P. S. mining eng and Christian T. Flannery; b Edin 11.6.40
teacher Fr/Lat Kelvinside acad Glasg 1965–68; lect psych: coll of educ Hamilton 1968–70, Liv univ 1971–72, Craigie coll of educ Ayr from 1972

SOMERVILLE Susan Isabel *MA 1969
d of James L. S. ARIBA(Edin) arch. and Marjory S. Prophet; b Aber 22.12.46
teacher mod lang Clydebank 1970–72
m Aber 14.7.69 John Keelan MA 1966 *qv*

SOPER Frederick Robert Charles MB ChB 1957
s of Frederick C. S. comm man. and Evelyn Fiddes; b Aber 31.10.32
h o ARI 1957–59; g p: Porth S Wales 1959–69, New Deer from 1969
m Merthyr Maur Glam 4.1.58 Maureen Lewis BSc (Cardiff) d of Robin L. Nantmoel

SOPPITT Alastair Ian MA 1963
s of John A. W. S. clerk and Eliza J. McWilliam; b Aber 16.6.42
LHA 1971
admin asst NERHB 1963–65; sen admin asst board of man. Aber gen hosps 1965–69; prin admin asst NERHB 1969–71, asst secy 1971–74; dist admin southern dist Highlands health board Inv from 1974
m Aber 27.6.64 Elizabeth A. Sim statist asst d of Henry M. S. Aber

SORLEY Alison Mary MA 1957
m Morrice

SORRIE George Strath MB ChB 1957
s of Alexander S. baker and Florence Strath secy; b Lynn Mass USA 19.5.33
DPH(Lond) 1963
asst m o h Reading 1962–65; lect statist Lond s of hyg/trop med 1965–67; g p: Rhynie 1967–73, Aber 1973–75; employment med advis for NE Scot. Aber from 1975
m Aber 22.9.59 Gabrielle A. Baird MB ChB 1959 *qv*

SORRIE James Maclean BSc 1960

SOUDEN Carol Elizabeth MA 1970
d of Robert S. trans insp and Mary H. Paul auxil nurse; b Aber 1948
m Aber 29.12.70 Lesley Wiseman MA 1971 fin. consult. s of Bertram W. Aber

SOULSBY John Allan *MA 1959
s of Sydney H. S. BSc(N'cle) marine eng and Alice M. Allan; b Grosmont Whitby 18.1.35
MA(Dub) 1964 PhD(Dub) 1970
res asst Leeds 1959–61; lect geog: Trinity coll Dub 1961–64, St And from 1964; visiting prof univ of Missouri Columbia USA 1968–69; visiting lect W Washington state coll Bellingham USA 1969; prof Earth Sc univ Malawi Zomba 1976–79 on secondment
m Aber 3.8.61 Evelyn M. Coutts MA 1959 *qv*

SOUTAR Lynda Margaret Hay MA 1967
d of William H. S. bank. man. and Joan M. Biltcliffe; b Ellon 22.6.46
teacher Galashiels acad: Engl/r e 1968–70, esn class 1970–72; maladjusted class Kingsway h s Chester 1972–73, esn class Dee Point Middle s Chester 1973–74; Careers/Engl Stanney c s Ellesmere Port from 1974

SOUTAR Marjorie Elizabeth *MA 1969 PhD 1972
d of Alexander A. S. advis mus Dun and Lisbeth A. B. Anderson; b Arbroath 19.11.46
MA(St And) 1967 LRAM ARCM 1967
teacher mus Dollar acad 1973–75; lect mus Glas from 1975
m Glasg 17.8.76 David S. Rycroft BSc(Lond) res fell. chem Glas s of Kenneth R. Clitheroe

SOUTER Alan Cunningham *BSc 1965

SOUTER Alistair McMillan *BSc 1964
s of George S. lighthouse keeper/handyman and Maude S. McMillan ch nurse; b Montrose 7.8.42
asst seismologist Seismograph Serv UK, Denmark 1964–66; seismol UK, Nigeria 1966–67; party chief various seismic crews Nigeria, Cameroons 1968–72; consult. geophys own comp Pentland Geophysical Lond from 1972
m Aber 6.4.66 Margaret Humphrey MA 1964 *qv*

SOUTER Christina Imlach MA 1961 Dip Ed 1963
d of Alexander S. fisherman and Christina A. Murray; b Buckie 9.5.41
teacher: Fr Kaimhill s s Aber 1962–64, Fr/Lat Aber acad 1964–66, Fr/Ger Elgin acad 1966–71
m Aber 31.7.70 Ian S. Suttie BSc 1964 *qv*

SOUTER Elizabeth Margaret MA 1970
d of Roy S. skipper/owner/inshore fisherman and Lizzie M. H. Ritchie; b Stonehaven 14.3.50
teacher: geog Kirkcaldy h s 1971–73, Engl Wick h s 1973–76
m Aber 11.7.73 Iain Johnston MB ChB 1973 g p s of Douglas J. Lochore Lochgelly

SOUTER George Robert Fraser MA 1968

SOUTER Graham William BSc 1969

SOUTER Ian Alexander BSc(eng) 1970

SOUTER Ian Patrick MA 1964
s of Maitland E. S. clerk and Annie M. Burr nurse/teacher parentcraft; b Aber 15.3.43
CA 1967
app CA Aber 1964–67; audit sen, man. Lond 1967–75; ptnr Whinney Murray & Co Aber from 1975
m Aber 17.9.66 Helen M. Russell BSc 1965 *qv*

SOUTER Isobel Gove MB ChB 1964
d of John G. S. self-employed and Elisabeth Stephen; b Gourdon 4.5.39
DMRD 1972 MR Aust Coll Radiol 1978
h s: ARI 1964, St James' hosp Leeds 1965; res asst surg univ of Wales 1968–70; regist radiol: univ hosp of Wales Cardiff 1970–72, Western I Glasg 1972–73; sen regist radiol RI Glasg; radiol and dir of radiol Mater hosp Brisbane Aust 1976–78; radiol in private practice Brisbane from 1978
m Aber 21.7.64 Colin M. Furnival MB ChB 1964 *qv*

SOUTER John Randell *MA 1966
s of Andrew W. S. MA(McG) and Florence M. Randell; b Johnshaven 5.2.44
edit. asst Collins & Co Glasg 1966–67; teacher Almonte h s Ontario from 1968
m Smith's Falls Ontario 26.5.73 Mary L. Murphy BA (Carleton Ottawa) lit critic d of W. Ormond M. MD CM(Queen's univ Kingston Ont) Smith's Falls

SOUTER John Reginald *BSc(eng) 1963 MSc 1967

SOUTHWICK Christopher Alexander Patrick *BSc 1970

SPATE Gordon Robert MA 1966
s of Leslie E. S. dept store man. and Isabel M. Craig stenogr; b W Kilbride 18.10.41
RAF off. (helicopter pilot) from 1967

SPEAKMAN Kenneth PhD 1965
s of Frank S. eng and Irene Graham; b Middlesbrough 3.2.38
FRIC 1972
Watford: res scient bldg res stat 1965–73; scient UK DoE from 1973
m Teesside 19.3.60 Pauline Reed d of Aaron R.

SPEED Robert Malcolm MSc 1970
BSc(Wales)

SPEIRS Margaret Gray BSc 1967

SPEIRS Ronald Cowan *MA 1969
s of Andrew C. S. civ serv and Joyce Aird nurse; b Inv 15.8.43
PhD(Stir) 1974
lect Ger Birm from 1971
m Aber 29.8.69 Susan W. Elder MA 1969 *qv*

SPELLS Angela Kathleen *MA 1969
b Watford 7.1.45

SPENCE Andrew BSc 1970
s of John C. S. lab and Williamina M. Sutherland; b Unst Shetland 27.2.49
teacher: maths Anderson h s Lerwick 1971–78, asst prin guid from 1973
m Unst 11.8.71 Williamina Laurenson typist d of James W. L. Unst

SPENCE Charles BSc 1965
s of John C. S. lab/crofter and Williamina M. Sutherland; b Unst Shetland 21.11.42
teacher: Lerwick 1966–67, Alloa 1967–71, Stromness 1971–72, Unst from 1972
m Unst 3.4.68 Mary J. Laurenson clerkess d of James W. L. Haroldswick Unst

SPENCE Edith Lochrie MA 1970
s of William D. S. civ serv and Isabella Percy nurse; b Lennoxtown 2.4.49
teacher Port Glasg 1971–74; prin mod lang Greenock 1974–75; prin Ger Largs from 1975
m Gourock 1.8.73 James M. Leckie BSc(Strath) teacher s of William L. Greenock

SPENCE Elizabeth Ann MA 1961

SPENCE Elizabeth Catherine *MA 1965
m Young

SPENCE Graham Cruickshank *MA 1969
s of James C. C. S. GPO overseer and Elsie M. Wilson; b Inv 27.6.47
teacher hist Inv 1970–73; prin hist Portree 1973–77; asst head Alness from 1977
m Inv 29.8.69 Helen M. McIntyre d of Duncan McI. Inv

SPENCE Ian William *BSc 1968

SPENCELEY Anthony Philip *BSc 1970
s of Kenneth du G. S. teacher and Dulcie V. Cowan teacher; b Ilford 21.8.47
grad res stud. univ New England Aust 1971–73; tut. geog James Cook univ of N Queensland Aust 1973–77; asst lect geog univ Otago NZ 1977–78; lect geog univ Papua N Guinea from 1978
m Armidale NSW Aust 17.7.71 Margaret J. Milne BSc 1970 *qv*

SPENCER Joan Margaret MA 1965

SPENCER Peter Frederick BSc(for) 1962 *1963

SPENCER Ruth Elizabeth BMedBiol 1969
d of Harold S. PhD(Edin) prof oriental stud. and Hilda Nunn BA(Durban) secy, lib; b Hyderabad India 27.3.48
MB ChB(Birm) 1972
h o: Worc RI 1972–73, Mpilo hosp Bulawayo Rhodesia 1973, Ronkswood hosp Worc 1973–74; g p Halesowen 1974–75; clin asst: Nott ch's hosp 1975–79, haemat Royal Liv hosp from 1980
m Edin 12.1.74 Roger Ferguson MB ChB(Birm) consult. phys s of Alan H. F. BA(Oxon) Lincoln

SPENNING Per MB ChB 1965
s of Knut L. S. MA(Oslo) rector and Signe Eilifsen MA(Oslo) teacher; b Bergen 6.1.40
ECFMG 1965
Norway: Vadsø/Tana 1965–66, m o h Tana 1966–69, private practice Askim 1969–77, soc med Fredrikstad from 1977
m Aber 17.2.62 Muriel B. Cruickshank MA 1962 *qv*

SPERRING Peter *BSc(eng) 1970
s of Frank S. headmaster and Margaret Reynolds teacher; b Ruislip 10.8.48
civ eng Kitwe Zambia from 1970

SPICER Hugh Joseph Michael MB ChB 1958
s of Elvon L. S. prop. and Irene P. Woodroffe; b Trinidad 3.5.33

h o Port of Spain gen hosp Trinidad 1959–60; private pract Port of Spain from 1960
m Barbados WI 16.10.71 Ann G. Kerr man. reservations Air Canada d of William K. MB ChB(Edin) Bridgetown Barbados

SPILSBURY Sarah Vivienne MLitt 1969 PhD 1973
d of Charles A. S. outfitter and Gladys Britton; b Bristol 19.5.41
BA(Brist) 1965
lect French Aberd from 1970

SPITTAL Robin Mackay *MA 1967

SPRAGINS Conway Fitzhugh PhD 1965
s of John D. S. MA(Davidson univ) presb min and Mary M. Fitzhugh BA(Arkansas) teacher; b Little Rock Arkansas 4.9.35
BA(Arkansas) 1957 BD(Union Theol Seminary Richmond Va) 1963 MDiv 1971
prof of religion Arkansas coll Batesville from 1965
m Batesville 25.8.60 Ann Westmoreland BA(Arkansas) teacher d of Weldon O. W. Batesville

SPROUL Edna Winifred MA 1964
d of Munro D. S. carpenter and Barrie M. Crichton; b Kintore 26.1.43
teacher: Gordon s Huntly 1965–66, Irlam s s Lancs 1966–68, Murrayburn p s Edin 1968–69
m Aber 2.7.66 David M. Wildgoose MA 1964 *qv*

SQUIRES James Finlay Robertson MA 1957
s of Alfred G. S. comm trav and Isabella Cairncross; b Glasg 21.2.32
BD(Glas) 1960
post-grad Peter Marshall bursar Princeton USA 1960–61; Brown-Downie fell. Marburg 1961–62; teacher Riverside s s Glasg 1961–62; lect: syst theol Glas 1962–65, r e Aber coll of educ 1965–66, prin lect from 1966
m Glasg 9.9.60 Catherine Hamilton nurse d of Alexander D. H. Glasg

STABLES Ronald Alexander BSc 1969
s of Alexander S. joiner and Freda Hopkins; b Aber 29.5.47
teacher Nassau Bahamas 1970–73; stud. UCNW 1973–74; teacher Grampian reg from 1974

STADDON Anne Elizabeth MB ChB 1959
d of Frederick W. S. horticulturist and Edith Clegg teacher; b Wellington Salop 25.6.34
DObstRCOG 1961
h o Woodend hosp Aber, ARI 1959–60; h o obst Aber mat. hosp 1960–61; trainee g p Church Stretton Salop 1961–62; sen h o med Barrow-in-Furness 1962; s m o Salop c c 1968–72; g p Oswestry from 1972
m Wellington 1.7.61 William M. Park MB ChB 1960 *qv*

STAFFORD David Kenneth Bryce *MEd 1970
MA(Edin)

STALKER Anne Elizabeth Richards MA 1968 Dip Ed 1969
d of Alexander L. S. MB ChB 1943 *qv* and Mary E. C. McLean MB ChB 1943 *qv*; b Aber 7.9.47
teacher: prin geog Slough 1969–73, Engl lang Helsinki Finland 1973–74, prin geog Lond from 1974

STALKER Heather Leith MA 1970
m Begg

STALKER William MA 1967

STAMPER Christopher Paul *BSc 1969
s of Frank S. superv plastics div ICI and Eva Griffiths; b Blackpool 29.4.47
scient off. soil surv Engl and Wales Wolverhampton 1969–70; teacher: goeg Ash Green h s, joint prin adult educ centre Coventry 1970–73, Sixth Form coll Darlington from 1973, head geog dept from 1978
m Aber 28.11.69 Shiona R. Cantlay teacher d of William J. Cantlay BSc(agr) 1943 *qv*

STANBRIDGE Catherine Clark *MA 1969
d of Elias S. factory worker and Gladys W. Singer; b Aber 28.6.47
secy/typist Aberd 1970–73; teacher Banchory p s from 1974
m Aber 7.7.78 George M. McA. Slater herring curer s of William G. S. Aber

STANGER Ian Leslie MA 1962

STANLEY Terence Eric *BSc 1965
s of Eric W. S. civ serv and Winifred M. Longman; b Watford 11.1.43
MSc(N'cle) 1966 PhD(Lond) 1970
lect maths The City univ Lond 1968–78; sen lect from 1978
m Burton-u-Stather 5.8.72 Margaret R. Armstrong secy d of Rev Wilfred T. A. OBE MA(Oxon) Scunthorpe

STARK Ronald David cMB ChB 1965 PhD 1969
s of John S. comm trav and Williamina Chalmers secy; b Edin 12.6.41
MD(Birm) 1973 MRCP 1973
h o Aber gen hosps 1965–66; Garden res fell. physiol Aberd 1966–68; Canadian MRC fell./lect pharm Manit 1968–70; clin res fell. med Birm 1970–74; clin physiol ICI pharm Macclesfield from 1974
m Aber 22.7.66 Alexandra M. Gray nurse d of Alexander G. Kirriemuir

STARK William Alexander BSc 1969
s of William B. S. mill man. and Margaret Kidd; b Perth 15.1.47
Assoc Member Textile Inst 1973
trainee man. Darlington 1969–72; asst mill man. Keith from 1972
m Aber 1.9.70 Isobel H. Nicol BSc 1970 *qv*

STARKS Richard Gordon *BSc 1968 MSc 1970
s of John F. S. naval arch. and Violet L. Veazey authoress; b Portsmouth 30.3.47
tech edit. *Canadian Pulp and Paper Industry Magazine* Toronto 1970–72; asst edit. *The Financial Post* Toronto from 1973

STAUNTON Irene Anne MA 1969

STAVE Rolv Elias MB ChB 1965

STEELE Donald Hamish *MA 1966
s of James S. headmaster and Elsie J. Gordon teacher; b Inv 28.7.44
Dip Ed(Edin) 1967
teacher geog George Heriot's Edin 1967–70, prin geog Bathgate acad 1971–76; asst rector Royal h s Edin 1976–78, seconded as asst to Dir of Educ Lothian reg
m Aber 27.12.68 Moira J. L. Welsh MA 1966 *qv*

STEELE Dorothy Robertson MA 1963
m Mein

STEELE Grace Mitchell Fairley MA 1969
d of Robert B. D. S. BSc(St And) schoolmaster and

Helen D. Jamieson MA(St And); b Perth 6.1.49
teacher r e Galashiels acad 1970–78; asst prin guid Breadalbane acad Aberfeldy from 1978

STEELE John Douglas LLB 1969
s of Andrew R. S. teacher and Janet O. Y. Dalgleish; b St And 21.2.48
law app Dun 1969–71; solic Glasg from 1971

STEELE Joyce Mary MA 1956
d of Archibald S. wholesale confectioner/grocer and Georgina A. Yule; b Aber 16.11.35
teacher Engl/geog Angus 1957–59
m Aber 11.9.59 Brian K. Crookshanks MA 1949 *qv*

STEELE Patricia Marr *MA 1970
m Bedford

STEER Margaret Rose MA 1964
d of John M. S. power loom tuner, lab, inventor and Violet J. Ross millworker; b Aber 5.5.42
teacher: Nairobi, Johannesburg 1964–66, Bishopbriggs, Knightswood Glasg 1967–70; artist/printmaker Chewoyet Kenya 1970–72; teacher Stirling, Glasg 1972–75
m(2) Nairobi 7.2.72 Gideon S. Annand MA 1962 *qv*

STEEVES Martin Paul Taylor *MA 1964

STEIGERWALT Mary Susan PhD 1967
AB(Calif)

STEINER Mark Rudie LLB 1968

STENHOUSE Donald cMB ChB 1961

STENHOUSE Robert James BSc(agr) 1964
s of Robert J. S. farm. and Rebecca Pyper; b Stonehaven 2.8.40
DAFS: tech asst Edin 1964–66, asst insp Perth 1966–74, insp Perth from 1974
m Kinneff 4.8.64 Glenda L. Duncan d of Alexander D. Catterline

STEPHEN Alison Margaret MA 1958
m Sibbald

STEPHEN Allan Grant MA 1968
s of Mary Findlater; b Turriff 14.12.45
teacher Engl: Auchterarder s s 1969–70, Turriff acad from 1970
m Aber 10.4.73 Joan M. Gorman teacher d of John N. G. Balmedie

STEPHEN Anne MA 1969
d of James S. BR train guard and Mary R. Garvock; b Aber 3.5.48
Dip Soc St(Glas) 1970 CASS(Dund) 1973
soc worker Dun from 1970
m Miller

STEPHEN Charles Gordon BSc(eng) 1963
s of Charles S. fisherman/clerk and Gordon Noble; b Cairnbulg 23.4.28
prod. eng Burrough Machines Cumbernauld 1963–67; dev eng: Rolls Royce Hamilton, E Kilbride 1967–71, manuf of counting devices Veeder Root Dun 1971–75; teacher tech educ from 1976
m Stirling 5.4.68 Christian C. Taylor boarding s matron d of Hugh T. Auchnagatt

STEPHEN David James LLB 1969

STEPHEN David Sheriff *MEd 1967
BSc(St And)

STEPHEN Dennis Duncan *BSc(eng) 1966
s of Samuel S. agr worker and Anne McKandie; b Banff 27.1.44
electronic eng Chelmsford 1966–70; prod. man. (computers) Kidsgrove from 1970
m Nantwich 26.6.71 Bridget M. Smith midwifery sister d of Thomas E. S. Kells Co Meath Eire

STEPHEN Dorothy *BSc 1961

STEPHEN Evelyn Mary MA 1965
d of Robert S. banker and Vera S. Smith; b Aber 23.1.44
Dip Ed(Natal) 1967 PhD(Natal) 1971
m Aber 19.3.65 William James PhD 1965 *qv*

STEPHEN Frank Graham BEd 1970
s of Frank S. master farrier/blacksmith and Helen E. Paterson; b Brechin 6.6.42
teacher Southesk p s Montrose from 1971

STEPHEN George MB ChB 1970
s of George S. depot man. and Eileen E. Garrett; b Fraserburgh 11.5.46
h o, sen h o ARI, RACH 1970–73; g p Portlethen from 1973
m Rothiemay 28.8.71 Norma G. Birnie nurse d of William B. Rothiemay

STEPHEN George John *MA 1960

STEPHEN George Willson MB ChB 1961
s of Alexander S. MA 1918 *qv*; b Aber 12.2.37
DObstRCOG(Lond) 1963 DA(Lond) 1972
h o ARI 1961–62; sen h o: obst, anaest Middlesbrough 1963–64; ship's surg Royal Fleet auxil serv Far East 1964–66; g p Thornaby from 1966; clin asst anaest S Teesside from 1970
m Hong Kong 6.8.65 Patricia McAlpine teacher d of Douglas McA. Whitley Bay

STEPHEN George Wilson MB ChB 1956
s of George S. fish salesman and Margaret Duthie; b Mallaig 9.10.31
FFARCSI 1962 FFARCS 1963
h o Stockton, Aber 1956–57; sen h o anaest Dun, Liv 1958–60; regist anaest Derby 1961–64; res asst anaest Philadelphia USA 1964–66; lect anaest Edin 1967–70; consult. anaest Lond from 1970

STEPHEN Ian Berneaud *MA 1962 Dip Ed 1963

STEPHEN Isobel Marion *BSc 1966

STEPHEN James Flockhart MA 1965
s of James F. S. eng and Sophie E. Mutch midwife; b Aber 31.3.26
teacher: maths Cults acad 1966–71, spec asst maths/careers 1971–72; maths/prin guid Cults acad Aber from 1972
m Aber 7.3.53 Frances M. Allan oper theatre sister d of Francis A. Aber

STEPHEN James Gordon BSc(agr) 1958

STEPHEN John *BSc 1956 PhD 1960
s of Thomas S. fisherman and Jeannie M. Smith; b St Monance 15.11.34
scient off. Rowett res inst Aber 1956–62; sen res fell. microbiol res estab Porton 1962–65; lect Birm 1965–74,

sen lect from 1974
m Peterhead 21.6.58 Elizabeth F. Buchan teacher d of George B. Peterhead

STEPHEN John Matthew *MA 1965
s of George M. S. comm trav and Christina F. Matthew; b Aber 25.3.43
radio journalist Swiss shortwave serv Bern 1965–68, asst edit. news dept 1968–69; chief sub-edit. BBC external serv news dept Lond from 1969
m Aber –.8.66 Diane K. McAra d of Alastair R. McA. MA 1937 *qv*

STEPHEN Kenneth James *MA 1964
s of William S. S. clerk and Annie M. Sim; b Fraserburgh 13.3.42
teacher Engl: Inverurie acad 1965–68, Blairgowrie h s 1968–72, asst prin Engl 1972–74; prin Engl Lossiemouth h s from 1974
m Fyvie 16.7.69 Margaret C. Cowie DA teacher of art d of Peter C. Oldmeldrum

STEPHEN Lorna Margaret MA 1962
d of Andrew D. S. clerk/f-lt RAF and Helen M. Byers nurse; b Glasg 2.8.42
secy mod lang sect. school broadc dept BBC Lond 1963–71
m Grantown-on-Spey 30.8.69 Adrian Banks ophth optic s of Reginald F. B. Orpington

STEPHEN Margaret Elizabeth MB ChB 1967
s of William D. S. pharm asst and Jessie Bell pharm; b Aber 11.7.43
h o Woodend hosp Aber, Bangour gen hosp Broxburn 1967–68; trainee g p Edin 1968–69; g p Armadale from 1969
m Edin 23.9.72 Smith Tennant comm clerk s of Smith T. Bathgate

STEPHEN Mary Lindsey MA 1965

STEPHEN Maureen Youngson *MA 1962
m Morrison

STEPHEN Richard Leslie MA 1969

STEPHEN Robert Brown Sangster *MA 1962
s of Robert A. S. fisherman and Sophia Cordiner self-employed shopkeeper; b Boddam 6.11.38
Glasg: teacher geog Crookston Castle s s 1963–67; prin geog Grange s s 1967–71, Queen's Park s s 1971–74; asst head Cathkin h s Cambuslang from 1974
m Motherwell 11.7.64 Emily J. Campbell nurse d of John C. Motherwell

STEPHEN Thomas George BSc(agr) 1956 MSc 1976
s of Leslie S. teacher and Christina E. A. Soutar teacher; b Nuneaton 14.5.33
agr off. HM overseas civ serv Kumasi Ghana 1956–60; agr advis: BOCM Inv 1960–64, PIDA Aber 1964–68; dev off. meat and livestock comm Aber 1968–76; lect Clinterty agr coll 1976–77, NOSCA from 1977
m Aber 9.1.58 Margaret H. B. Gray teacher d of James G. C. Bucksburn

STEPHEN William *MA 1956
s of James S. fisherman and Harriet Noble dressmaker; b Fraserburgh 29.10.33
nat serv 1956–58; teacher Musselburgh g s 1959; Aber coll of comm: teacher 1959–61, sen econ 1961–63, head of prof stud. 1963–70, second dep prin from 1970
m Aber 15.9.56 Eleanor Goodrum typist d of James G. Aber

STEPHEN William Strachan *MA 1958
s of James S. eng and Andretta W. Noble; b Fraserburgh 21.11.34
teacher Engl: Arbroath h s 1959–61, Buckhaven h s 1961–65, Aber acad 1965–70, prin guid 1970–73, asst head Hazlehead acad from 1973
m Aber 27.12.60 Anita M. Young teacher d of George Y. Aber

STEPHENSON Christopher Stanley BSc 1967
s of Stanley R. S. newsagent/stationer and Kathleen M. Irwin bookkeeper; b N'cle-u-Tyne 28.5.44
fisherman 1967–68; man. retail newsagency Morpeth 1968–70; self-employed fisherman Oban from 1970
m Derby 7.9.68 Marion M. Martin teacher dressmaking/millinery d of Gideon M. M. Derby

STEPHENSON Gillian MB ChB 1957
m Craig

STEPHENSON Joan MB ChB 1959

STEPHENSON John David *MA 1969 Dip Ed 1970
s of Ernest S. clerk and Ada Clunie teacher; b N'cle-u-Tyne 4.2.45
teacher Daniel Stewart's and Melville coll Edin 1970–73, housemaster from 1973
m Aber 2.8.72 Fiona A. McBlane LLB 1970 *qv*

STEVEN Robert Lewis Tocher *BSc 1961 MSc 1963

STEVENSON David William Stewart MA 1969

STEVENSON Ian McLeod BEd 1970

STEVENSON James Alexander Stewart MA 1969

STEVENSON John Campbell MA 1966
s of Alexander N. S. lab and Jean M. Campbell; b Johannesburg 27.1.45
bank clerk Clydesdale Bank 1967–68; teacher Engl/hist Aboyne acad 1968–71; head Towie p s from 1971
m Dinnet 18.12.71 Seonaid E. Grant stud. d of James I. S. G. Dinnet

STEVENSON John Thomas MacSween *BSc 1967 MSc 1969
s of William A. S. farm. and Mary S. Firth postmistress; b Stromness 21.11.46
dev eng Ferranti Dalkeith 1968–74, res fell. Edin from 1974
m Glenesk 9.10.68 Winifred M. Sanderson milk and food hyg off. d of Allan A. S. Arbroath

STEVENSON Margaret Paplay MA 1969
d of Henry S. joiner and Maggie Paplay MA 1932 *qv*; b Kirkwall 12.12.48
Cardiff: teacher kindergarten Elm Tree House s 1972–73, Engl Bryn Hafren comp s 1973–74; secy to firm John Jolly Kirkwall 1975–76
m Stromness 31.7.71 James W. Spence BSc(Wales) naval off. s of James W.S. Stromness

STEVENSON William BSc(eng) 1960

STEVENSON William *MA 1963
s of Raymond W. H. S. BA(Oxon) prof phys and Stephanie B. Roberts MA(Rhodes); b Charlottetown PEI Canada 27.5.41
FRCO 1963
teacher Edin 1964–69; prin mus Morgan acad Dun from 1969
m 16.7.66 Lorna Murray teacher d of David M. Aber

STEWART Alan Duff *BSc 1961 MSc 1962 PhD 1965
s of John D. S. MA 1924 *qv*; b Aber 29.11.38
lect phys Dund from 1965
m Aber 18.3.66 Frances G. Pirie teacher d of Thomas P. Aber

STEWART Alexander *BSc 1967
b Elgin 22.11.45
MIEE C Eng
dev eng: Marconi Radar Syst Chelmsford 1969–72, Ferranti Edin from 1972

STEWART Alison BSc 1965
d of John S. MA 1926 *qv*(III); b Aber 6.6.45
m Aber 21.10.66 John A. Simpson fisherman s of William S. Whalsay

STEWART Andrew MA 1966
s of George S. crofter and Catherine Graham; b Back Is of Lewis 3.7.43
RAF off. from 1966
m Lond 13.12.69 Patricia A. Malloy MA(St And) med soc worker d of Joseph H. M. MB ChB(Dund/St And) Abbotts Bromley

STEWART Andrew Macmillan *MA 1965
s of Howard M. S. BSc(Lond) consult. civ eng and Sybil D. Thornton ballet dancer/teacher; b Esher 9.8.42
MBPsS Foreign Affiliate Amer Psych Assoc Assoc RC Psych FSS
res stud. Aberd 1965–67; asst lect Surrey univ 1967–69; pers man. IBM(UK) 1969–74; sen fell. (seconded 1972–74) inst of manpower stud. Sus 1972–77; ptnr Macmillan Stewart & Ptnrs, dir Macmillan Stewart from 1978
m(2) Guildford 8.5.72 Valerie G. Haycock PhD(Sheff) indust psych d of Alec T. H. Coalville

STEWART Anne MA 1965
d of Harvey S. bank man. and Annie Gray teacher; b Ellon 25.7.42
teacher Engl Gordon s Huntly 1966–68
m Aber 20.1.68 Andrew T. Shennan MB ChB 1967 *qv*

STEWART Audrey Fraser MB ChB 1960
m Gunn

STEWART Brian Richard *BSc(eng) 1969
s of Richard S. elect. eng and Edith M. Wallaker; b Aber 7.4.47
CEng MICE 1973
site eng Birm 1969–70; asst eng Edin from 1970
m Aber 10.10.69 Margaret W. Speirs clerkess/typist d of Joseph S. S. Aber

STEWART Catherine Anne MA 1970 CASS 1972
d of James S. MRCVS(Edin) vet surg and Ella Dunse; b Kendal 1.9.49
soc worker Perth 1972–74; Harpenden: part-time youth worker 1977–79, soc worker sessional from 1979
m Aber 4.7.72 Edward Pattison

STEWART Charlotte Forbes MA 1967
m Duncan

STEWART Clement Allan MA 1962 *MEd 1970
s of Henry T. S. MA(St And) teacher and Evelyn Ogilvie teacher; b Strichen 9.1.41
teacher: maths AGS 1963–69, spec asst maths 1969–70; prin maths Dunoon g s 1970–72, asst rector 1972–74, dep rector 1974–77; head Lochgilphead h s from 1977
m Aber 10.4.65 Sheena M. Phillip MA 1960 *qv*

STEWART Donald Herbert MA 1968 MEd 1970

STEWART Donald Robert *MA 1963
s of Alexander B. S. MA 1925 *qv* and Alice F. Bowman MA 1921 *qv*; b Aber 21.9.40
res stud. Aberd 1963–66; lect Ger UCNW 1966–72; asst secy St And univ from 1972

STEWART Donald William Hugh BSc 1960 MA 1962
s of Alexander M. S. farm. and Elizabeth I. Macleod; b Inv 17.11.32
teacher Invsh 1963–64; scient information off. Aber from 1964
m Aber 16.9.66 Catherine H. Bisset BSc 1962 *qv*

STEWART Donella Kinmond MA 1970
m Cooper

STEWART Douglas James MB ChB 1969
s of Douglas G. S. CA and Anne Dunbar; b Aber 30.6.46
FRCSE 1973
h o ARI 1969–70; Anderson and Thomson fell. path. Aberd 1970–71; sen h o surg ARI 1971–72; regist surg Aber teaching hosps 1972–76; sen regist surg ERI from 1976
m Aber 17.5.68 Catherine I. Paterson MA 1968 *qv*

STEWART Douglas Lunan BSc(eng) 1959
s of James D. S. MA 1931 *qv*; b Aber 19.2.38
Dip H&TEng 1972
asst eng: Sir William Halcrow & Ptnrs Inv 1959–60, W. A. Fairhurst & Ptnrs Aber, Dun 1960–66; asst eng to traffic eng Aber c c 1966–75; prin eng Grampian reg c 1975–79; self-employed Aber from 1979
m Aber 1.4.66 Lesley J. Watt MB ChB 1968 *qv*

STEWART Evelyn MB ChB 1961

STEWART Evelyn Ogilvie BSc 1962 ᶜMB ChB 1964
d of Henry T. S. MA(St And) headmaster and Evelyn Ogilvie teacher; b Fraserburgh 26.10.39
h o ARI, RACH 1964–65; Garden res fell. Aberd 1965–66; res asst anaest Glasg RI from 1973
m Aber 25.7.64 Geoffrey D. Parbrook MB ChB(Birm) anaest s of George H. P. Torquay

STEWART Frances Lindsay *MA 1969
d of James D. S. MA 1931 *qv*; b Aber 17.4.46
MSc(N'cle) 1974
teacher: Brentwood p s 1969–70, ESN(M) Sheff 1970–71, ESN(S) Sheff 1971–72; educ psych N'cle-u-Tyne 1974–76; advis pre-s handicapped ch N'cle from 1976
m Aber 9.4.79 Keith A. Humphreys BEd(Lond) teacher, lect s of Joseph H. Barrow-in-Furness

STEWART George James Lionel BSc(eng) 1967

STEWART George Macleod MB ChB 1959 DPH 1969
s of James G. S. marine eng and Mary D. Stephen nurs sister; b Singapore 1935
DTM&H(Lond) 1964 DIH(Lond) 1970 MFCM 1972
h o ARI, Woodend hosp Aber 1959–60; gen duty m o RAMC Singapore, Malaya, N Borneo 1960–63; r m o 1st Bn Grenadier Guards BAOR & UNFICYP Ger, Cyprus 1964–65; dem army health RAM coll Lond 1966; instr s of army health Ashvale Aldershot 1966–68; dep asst dir army health Brisbane Aust 1970–72; dep asst dir army health and res MoD Lond 1972–74, asst dir from 1974
m Aber 4.8.60 Audrey W. Young MB ChB 1959 *qv*

STEWART Gordon Grant *MA 1957
resid Perth

STEWART Hélène Annette MA 1962
m Kenneth W. Ruddiman MA 1962 *qv*

STEWART Hugh McKenzie MA 1957

STEWART Ian Malcolm Alexander *MA 1962

STEWART Ian Murdoch *BSc 1956
s of William S. MA 1913 *qv* and Jessie K. Davie MA 1913 *qv*; b Aber 17.4.33
Stafford: res tech Nelson res lab Eng Elect. Co. 1956–64, head phys metall sect. 1964–70; man. Electron Optics Group Walter C. McCrone Assoc Inc Chicago USA from 1970
m Aber 14.6.56 Shirley M. Kelman BSc 1955 *qv*

STEWART Ilene Robertson MA 1969 Dip Ed 1970
d of Ian D. S. hairdresser and Sarah D. Bradley; b Meikleour 1.2.48
teacher maths: f e Aber 1970–74, Driffield from 1974
m Auchterarder 18.7.70 Michael A. Hall MB ChB 1974 h o Hull RI s of Antony H. Rushden

STEWART Iris MA 1956
b Nairn 28.2.36
resid Edin

STEWART Isabella Davidson MA 1956

STEWART James Harvey *MA 1962
s of Harvey S. banker and Anne Gray teacher; b Ellon 15.8.39
Dip Adv St (Soc Admin)(Manc) 1964
hosp admin Edin 1965–67; prin admin asst hosp man. York 1967–68, dep group secy York 1968–73; area admin Northumberland area health auth Morpeth from 1973
m Aber 24.4.65 Fiona M. M. Reid teacher d of John R. Peterhead

STEWART James John BSc 1958
s of William S. fisherman and Agnes H. Murray; b Lossiemouth 23.1.37
HM forces intellig corps 1958–61; Wiggins Teape: prod. trainee Stoneywood 1961–65, paper mill foreman Scot. pulp and paper mills Corpach 1965–68; chief papermaker Empire Paper Mills Kent 1968–71; paper mill supt Bowater Scott Corp Barrow-in-Furness 1971–74; tissue mill supt Harir Pars Co Haft Tappen Khuzestan Iran 1975–77; comm supt Sulzer Bros Basrah Iraq 1977–78; consult. paper tech from 1978
m Aber 18.11.61 Christina A. Stephen asst pharm d of William J. S. Aber

STEWART James Keith MA 1969

STEWART Jamesina Sinclair MA 1963
m Milne

STEWART Joan Helen MA 1963

STEWART John MA 1966 LTh 1969
s of Alexander S. gen merch and Annabella Cameron; b Glasg 6.11.31
MTh(Lond) 1971
C of S min Bowmore Islay 1970; min United Reform ch (St Andrews) Canterbury from 1971; dist chmn 1972–73; on univ court of univ of Kent at Canterbury from 1974
m Glasg 11.12.57 Joyce B. Woods d of Alfred G. W.

STEWART John Macfarlane *BSc 1960 PhD 1966
s of James M. S. master grocer and Mary Keillor; b Dun 29.4.39
MRC schol zool Aberd 1960–63; Georgina McRobert res fell. cancer dept path. Aberd 1964–67; lect biol Stir from 1967; biol inst (Carlsberg foundation) Copenhagen 1974–75
m Dun 4.4.62 Kamala M. Saggar MA(St And) teacher d of Jainti D. S. MB ChB(St And) Dun

STEWART John Marsh *MA 1970
s of John M. S. dir/gen man. Ulster Steamship Co and Anne Thompson; b Belf 20.7.47
econ Courtaulds Lond from 1970

STEWART John McLeod BSc 1959 Dip Ed 1961

STEWART Joseph *BSc 1969 PhD 1973
b Elgin 16.2.47
teacher Perth acad 1972–76, Whitfield h s Dun from 1976
m Fochabers 12.9.70 Lorna A. Smith MA 1970 *qv*

STEWART Kathleen Anne MA 1957

STEWART Kathleen Mairi MA 1970
d of Allan S. farm. and Ella M. L. Harman; b Cromarty 11.4.49
teacher: Carfin p s 1971–72, South Park p s 1972–73
m Inv 10.7.71 Archibald K. Fraser BSc 1968 *qv*

STEWART Kathleen Ross *MA 1963
m Macpherson

STEWART Kenneth George *BSc(eng) 1970

STEWART Laspic Gilchrist LLB 1966

STEWART Magnus *BSc 1962
s of John S. MA 1926 *qv*; b Aber 2.11.40
teacher: maths/sc Banchory acad 1963–64, chem AGS 1964–73, prin chem Northfield acad Aber from 1973
m Aber 12.6.64 Norah Hogg nurse d of Charles H. Aber

STEWART Margaret Ollason MA 1962 Dip Ed 1963
d of Douglas L. S. MA 1934 *qv* and Christina M. Laurenson MA 1936 *qv*; b Lerwick 20.10.41
teacher: p s Bonnyrigg 1963–66, partially deaf Sydney Aust 1966–69, remed Bedford 1971–73, p s Macduff from 1974
m Aber 3.3.66 Henry J. L. Mantell arch. s of Henry P. M. Macduff

STEWART Mary Edmar *BSc 1960
d of Edwin S. storeman and Elizabeth A. B. Macdonald civ serv; b Aber 16.2.38
steroid biochem: St Mary's hosp Lond 1960–62, res unit Aber 1962–65
m Aber 19.8.62 Ronald W. Caie MA 1960 *qv*

STEWART Mary McBeth MA 1966
d of James S. rly worker and Mary McBeth; b Oban 16.1.45
teacher: Oban h s 1967–69, hist Kirkton h s Dun 1971–74, prin hist from 1974
m Dun 12.8.67 Henry G. Cameron MA 1966 *qv*

STEWART Mary Smith MA 1958

STEWART Morna Grace MA 1968
d of William R. S. BSc(St And) man. dir and Irene E. G. Henderson MA(St And) teacher; b Dun 11.8.46
teacher Engl/hist Belf 1970–72; TEFL: Aber 1972–73, Cambridge from 1973

STEWART Murdina MA 1968
d of John S. crofter and Peggy Campbell; b Skye

17.4.46
teacher Gaelic: Badenoch 1969–73, Nova Scotia 1973–78, bilingual educ proj Skye from 1978

STEWART Murray Lessels *MA 1959

STEWART Neil BSc(eng) 1962

STEWART Neil MA 1964
s of Archibald S. farm. and Catherine Buchanan; b Isle of Skye 1.12.34
stud. divinity at Free ch coll Edin 1964–67; min of Free C of S Conon Bridge

STEWART Patricia Louise MA 1957
d of John H. S. bank man. and Ada C. L. Paterson BCom(Edin) secy Amer consular serv; b Aber 5.2.36
Cert for Teachers of Deaf(Manc) 1958
teacher of deaf: Woodford Green 1959, Edin 1959–60, Herts 1967–68, Edin from 1969
m Aber 10.10.59 James E. Fraser MA 1953 *qv*

STEWART Peter James Neilson *MA 1967
s of William N. S. granite merch and Dorothy Chalmers BSc 1926 *qv*; b Aber 11.1.45
reporter *Highland News* Inv 1967–68; edit. *Caithness Courier* Thurso 1968–69; sub-edit. *Evening Echo* Hemel Hempstead 1969–71; Hong Kong: dep chief sub-edit./features edit. *China Mail* 1971–73, asst to edit. *Sunday Standard* 1973–74, news edit. and fin. edit. *Hong Kong Standard* 1974–76, chief edit. Rediffusion (Hong Kong) TV 1976–78
d Hong Kong 26.5.78

STEWART Ralph Robertson Ferguson *MA 1964
MA(Sask)

STEWART Ronald Ramsay MA 1960 *1962
s of William S. salesman and Lavinia Macdonald jute weaver; b Dun 5.5.39
teacher Engl Hozier s s Lanarksh 1962–63; prob clin psych Lancs 1963–65; res assoc N'cle 1965–67, res fell. Liv 1967–72; lect educ psych Liv from 1972

STEWART Susan Winifred MA 1969
d of James G. S. acct and Winifred E. Hooker; b Glasg 7.7.48
teacher Fr: Harpurhey h s Manc 1970–71, Shiremoor mid s Northumberland, Balliol mid s Longbenton N'cle, Seaton Sluice mid s Northumberland, N Manc h s for girls 1971–74
m Edin 10.8.70 Michael G. Sadler LLB 1967 *qv*

STEWART William Brodie MA 1965 Dip Ed 1966

STEWART Winifred Margaret MA 1964

STEWART Winthrop Rodney PhD 1965
s of Winthrop F. S. industrialist and Martha Rediger; b Hollywood Ca USA 31.12.33
BA BD(Calif)
Arizona USA: pastor Hope Baptist ch Phoenix 1965–72; exec dir Esperança Inc from 1972
m Norwalk CA 4.2.56 Regina Bullinger nurse

STEYN John Hofmeyr PhD 1967
s of Johannes S. S. MD(Groningham) ophth surg and Blanka Hablutzel; b Johannesburg 3.10.29
MB ChB(Cape Town) 1952 FRCS(Eng) 1957 FRCSE 1973
consult. urologist ARI/Aberd 1967–69; consult. in admin charge dept urology Aber from 1969
m Johannesburg 6.4.53 Daphne M. Nelson BA(Witwatersrand) d of Bernard N. LLB(Witwatersrand) Johannesburg

STILEMAN Richard Graham Learmonth *BSc 1968
s of Peter L. S. insur exec and Rhoda E. C. Garrick; b Reigate 20.12.44
Chapman & Hall book publ Lond: edit. 1969–75, man. dir from 1975
m Aber 30.8.71 Patricia F. B. Ross MA 1968 *qv*

STILL Alexander William BSc(eng) 1961
s of Alexander I. S. gardener and Helen A. Jamieson; b Redhill 2.4.39
consult. eng Glasg 1961–63; site eng Yorks 1964–67; sen civ eng Aber 1967–70; chief estimator/comm. man. Lond from 1970
m Aber 9.3.63 Isobel R. Coull MA 1961 *qv*

STILL Elaine Lily MA 1967
d of Albert E. S. cashier and Lily Frain; b Aber 25.6.46
teacher: Walker Dam inf s Aber 1968–70, Oxford p s Münster Germany 1970–73, Catcott County p s nr Bridgwater from 1974
m Morpeth 29.7.72 Philip Gosling army off. s of Christopher F. J. G. Gateshead

STILL Joan MA 1961
d of Johnstone S. master butcher and Jean Milne shop asst; b Aber 27.6.41
teacher Engl/hist Powis s s Aber 1962–68
m Aber 28.3.67 Ronald G. Walker auctioneer and valuator s of Alfred W. Rothienorman

STILL John Mackenzie MA 1963
CA

STILL Lena Robson Cooper MA 1969
b Aber 3.2.21
Aber: teacher maths coll of comm 1970–73, St Margaret's s for girls from 1973
m Aber 3.8.44 Harry A. McFarlane area eng GPO tel

STILL Ronald David *BSc(eng) 1969

STIRLING Bertha Fiona BMedBiol 1969 MB ChB 1972
d of Charles S. res eng and Bertha M. Wescott nurse; b Darlington 12.8.47
Hull: h o med/surg 1972–73, surg clin asst 1973–74
m Haxby 12.7.72 Eric L. Huckvale BSc(agr) 1970 *qv*

STIRLING Hamish MA 1959 LLB 1961
s of James S. BSc(St And) univ lect and Ann W. Black teacher; b Liv 9.7.38
law app Jameson, McGhie & Munro solic Elgin 1961–62; proc fisc dep: Dun 1963–70, Duns/Hawick/Jedburgh/Selkirk 1970–74, Glasg 1974–75; admitted fac of advoc 1976
m Aber 15.8.63 Margaret D. Bottomley nurse d of Harry B. MA(Oxon) Milltimber

STIRRAT Helen Margaret Rosemary MB ChB 1967
d of Hugh S. BSc(Lond) lect econ RGIT and Helen M. Oakes civ serv; b Enfield 6.1.43
DPM(Lond) 1973
h o Lond, Tor 1967–68; g p trainee Lond 1969–70; sen h o, regist psych Ilford, Epsom 1970–73; m o fam plan. assoc Woking 1970–73; res fell. inst of psych Tor from 1973
m Aber 15.7.67 Peter F. Meier solic s of Frederick J. M. Diessenhofen Switzerland

ST LOUIS Patrick Joseph *BSc 1967 PhD 1971

STOCKAN Kathleen Irida Harcus MA 1967
d of James D. S. farm. and Agnes W. Harcus; b Orkney 25.3.46
ALA 1972
Aber publ lib: lib asst 1968–69, asst lib from 1970
m Aber 18.7.69 John M. Corall teacher s of Thomas M. C. Aber

STOCKDALE Christopher Leo *BSc 1969 MSc 1971

STODDART David Michael *BSc 1965 PhD 1968
s of James H. S. BSc(Glas) prin examiner HM patent off. and Elizabeth M. McCutcheon; b Lanark 19.4.43
post doct fell. natural environm res Council Oxford 1968–69; lect zool King's coll Lond from 1969
m Aston Clinton 27.12.69 Lydia B. Treutler teacher d of Hermann H. W. T. Aylesbury

STOESSEL Horace Edward PhD 1962
AB(K Coll, Tenn) BD ThM(UTS NY)

STOESSL Michelle Madeline BSc(eng) 1969
d of Edmund S. acct/comp dir and Alice H. Schweitzer; b Lond 26.11.48
m Amersham 3.8.68 Richard K. D. Cook BSc(eng) 1969 *qv*

STOKER Roger *BSc 1965 PhD 1968

STONE Beryl Margaret MB ChB 1959
d of Archibald C. S. ironmonger and Ruth L. Dodsworth SRN; b High Wycombe 15.6.23
BSc(Lond) 1953 Affiliate RCPsych 1962
h o Royal Halifax I, Crumpsall hosp Manc 1959–60; sen h o Barony hosp Nantwich 1960–61; regist: Herrison hosp Dorchester 1961–62, St George's hosp Morpeth 1962–65; asst psychiat Lawn hosp Lincoln 1965–73
m Aber 14.4.61 John McN. White MB BS(Lond) asst psychiat Lawn hosp s of William L. A. W. Hornchurch
d Charleville-Mézieres Ardennes France 26.4.73 *AUR* XLV 321

STONE Gordon Victor MB ChB 1969
s of Victor J. S. bookkeeper/cashier and Madeleine O. Imlach secy dept chem Aberd; b Lond 4.10.45
DCM(Edin) 1976 MFCM 1977
h o Aber 1969–70; unit m o RAF: Anglesey 1970–71, Laarbruch Ger 1971–74; sen m o RAF Gloucester 1974–75; Scot. Health Serv Fell. in commun med 1975; spec in commun med Grampian health board from 1978
m Aber 16.7.69 Aileen S. Wilson BSc 1969 *qv*

STONE Michael Terence MA 1967

STONES William Clark BSc(for) 1956
s of John G. S. farm. and Ada J. Tiplady teacher; b Richmond Yorks 6.7.34
nat serv 1956–58; for. comm surv Argyll 1959–60; farm. N Yorks from 1960
m Crook Greta Nicholson bank clerk d of Joseph S. N. Crook

STONEY David Thomas William BSc 1968

STONEY Margaret Marshall MA 1961
d of John A. S. banker and Margaret M. Fullerton secy; b Glasg 5.4.41
teacher: Aberdeensh 1961–62, Oxfordsh 1962–63, part-time Midlothian 1972–76, full-time 1976, prin remed dept Penicuik h s from 1977
m Aber 25.8.62 David J. Fletcher MA 1960 *qv*

STOPPER Irene May MA 1968
m Sinclair

STORM Isabella MA 1958
d of George S. fisherman and Christina Campbell; b Nairn 11.1.37
teacher: Kinloss p s 1958–62, Dalneigh p s Inv 1962–68, Fort William p s from 1978
m Nairn 1.8.62 Alexander McIntosh policeman s of Robert McI. Nairn

STORRY John Edgar PhD 1960
s of Ernest R. S. textile ag and Norah M. Burchell teacher; b Nott 14.5.35
BSc(Nott) 1957
post grad schol physiol min of agr Rowett res inst Aber 1957–60; scient off., sen scient off., prin scient off. chem dept Nat Inst Res Dairying Reading from 1960
m Edin 9.7.60 Catherine I. Dickson chem d of William D. Portobello

STOTT Eileen May MA 1965
d of John W. S. farm. and Georgina G. Cumming; b Aber 25.7.44
teacher: Bankfoot p s Perthsh 1966–69, Albyn s for girls Aber from 1969

STOTT James Joseph MA 1960
s of James S. eng, hotelier, farm. and Oslena E. Prosser secy; b Aber 7.6.37
BD(Edin) 1963
C of S min: asst Broughton Pl par ch Edin 1963–65, Denbeath par ch Buckhaven 1965–70; independent evangelist Aberdeensh from 1973
m Aber 5.9.64 Anne R. Esslemont MA 1960 *qv*

STOTT John LLB 1970
s of John S. elect. board off. and Doreen Davidson; b Aber 6.5.49
tourist (6 mths) India 1970; law app, leg. asst Paull & Williamsons advoc Aber 1971–75; leg. asst Wilsone & Duffus Aber from 1975
m Sutton-cum-Lound 19.8.72 Elizabeth M. Morton BSc 1972 teacher d of Alexander F. M. BA(Oxon) Retford

STOTT Mary Louise MA 1966
m Tait

STOTT Peter LLB 1967
s of F. Floyd S. stockbroker and B. Marjorie Henderson; b Aber 13.9.45
law app Aber 1967–69; solic: Glasg 1970–71, Aber 1972; ptnr Paull & Williamsons advoc Aber 1973; corporate lawyer Westburne Internat Indust Calgary Alberta from 1974
m St And 25.5.74 Priscilla M. Cook secy d of David C. Cook MA(Edin) Elie

STOTT Roderic Michael *BSc(eng) 1964

STOUT William MA 1965

STOW Philip Roger *BSc(eng) 1970
s of Cedric A. S. man. timber merch and Doris Leeming; b Keighley 21.5.48
MICE 1978
Sir Alfred McAlpine: temp works des eng Wirral 1970–71, site eng: Runcorn 1971–72, Ince 1972–74; plan. eng Dowsett Engineering Harrogate 1975–78; temp works & plan. eng Robert McGregor Manc from 1978
m Keighley 27.9.69 Susan E. Cook nurse d of Willie C. Keighley

STRACHAN Alexander BSc 1970

STRACHAN Arnold BSc 1970
s of Norman W. farm. and Annie Brodie; b Aber 12.1.49
teacher geog Eastwood h s Newton Mearns from 1972
m Aber 26.12.73 Mary Jarvie hair stylist d of John J. Aber

STRACHAN Benjamin BSc 1959
s of Benjamin S. fisherman and Jane S. Ritchie; b Inverallochy 30.5.38
teacher sc Northfield acad Aber 1960–69, prin asst teacher 1969–73, prin phys from 1973
m Aber 5.4.61 Catherine Third d of Andrew T. Inverallochy

STRACHAN Bruce Cordiner BSc 1968

STRACHAN Christina Helen MA 1970
d of John R. S. farm. and Helen B. Anderson; b Huntly 12.2.49
teacher Paisley from 1971
m Aber 18.8.71 Peter H. Cowie BSc(eng)(Strath) mech eng s of Alfred H.C. Inverurie

STRACHAN Daphne Mary Andrea MA 1956
d of Andrew A. S. BSc(St And) dir telecomm Fed. Malay States and Mary L. McIntosh; b Malaysia 4.3.35
asst to Lond rep univ of Ife Ibadan Nigeria 1965–72; Lond rep univ of Ife 1972–78; prin asst secy nat univ comm (Nigeria) Lond from 1978

STRACHAN David Gillan BSc 1970
s of George S. foreman joiner and Annie Maitland; b Aber 2.12.48
work stud. off.: Philips Hamilton 1970–71, Pye Airdrie 1971–73, Aber c c from 1974
m Aber 19.9.70 Moira Jamieson MA(Glas) teacher d of George J. Aber

STRACHAN Diana MA 1970
d of Roy S. news ag and Gladys Dinnie; b Insch 1.8.49
lib asst King's coll lib Aberd 1971–73
m Aber 21.7.71 Keith Nicol sales rep s of William N. Kintore

STRACHAN Dugald James John *MA 1965
s of William J. S. bank man. and Mary S. McDonald; b Elgin 15.4.43
NERC grant dept geog Aberd 1965–66; teacher geog: Aber acad 1967–68, Elgin acad 1968–70, prin geog from 1970
m Elgin 24.7.68 Jennifer A. Barclay teacher d of Herbert A. B. Elgin

STRACHAN Eileen Mary MA 1956
d of William S. and Isabella M. MacIntosh; b Peterhead 20.2.35
Dip Secy St(Glasg) 1957
secy officers' assoc Glasg 1957–58; Bankhead acad: teacher classics 1959–64, spec asst 1964–66; prin teacher classics Denny h s 1966–67, asst prin teacher classics Ellon acad 1976
m Aber 20.7.66 Robert J. Burr MA 1956 *qv*

STRACHAN Euan Simpson *BSc(eng) 1960
s of George M. S. bank man. and Mary A. Mutch; b Aber 9.2.38
MIEE
elect. eng: Ferranti Edin 1961–65, Rolls Royce & Assoc Derby from 1965
m Kincardine O'Neil 5.5.62 Helen A. Smith teacher d of James S. Glassel

STRACHAN Fiona Katherine MA 1965
m Peacock

STRACHAN Graham MA 1958 LLB 1961
s of John S. law acct and Annie I. Sutherland; b Fraserburgh 14.4.36
law app Davidson & Garden advoc Aber 1961–62, ptnr from 1962
m Breda Neths 8.1.66 Elizabeth M. G. B. de Koning soc worker d of Jacobus de K. Breda

STRACHAN Helen Scott MA 1963
m Bell

STRACHAN Ian Munro MA 1965
s of Joseph M. S. elect. eng and Sophia Munro; b Keith 20.11.42
teacher Glenwood j h s Glenrothes 1966–67; TEFL Benghazi Libya 1967–69; head O'Neil Corse p s 1969–71; lect Engl Gulf tech coll Bahrain from 1971
m Aber 12.8.65 Isobel M. Bisset teacher d of James A. B. Keithhall

STRACHAN James Wood LLB 1966
s of James D. S. PO eng and Edith Wood; b Aber 26.10.45
law app Aber 1966–68; solic Montrose from 1968
m Aber 7.5.71 Christine M. Ayrton clerkess d of Tom A. Aber

STRACHAN Jeannie MA 1957
d of William D. S. fisherman and Jeannie Mair; b Peterhead 6.5.37
Dip Sec Sc(Strath) 1958
educ off. Stewart & Lloyds Glasg 1958–59; secy to asst man. dir Reed Paper Group Lond 1959–60; teacher Engl/hist Lond 1960–61; admin asst Aust nat univ Canberra 1962–65; personnel off. (leg. off.) Edin 1966–67; teacher Alloa 1968–73
m Aber 6.1.62 David R. Anderson MA 1958 *qv*

STRACHAN Marlene MA 1965
d of Robert S. butcher and Christian B. W. Murison armature winder; b Fraserburgh 30.9.44
teacher: Cultercullen s Aberdeensh 1966–67, Bucksburn s 1967–69, Scalloway s 1969–71
m Aber 9.8.67 William Y. Doverty customs off. s of John D. D. Aber

STRACHAN Mary Catherine *MA 1967
m Hardie

STRACHAN Peter *MA 1968 Dip Ed 1969

STRACHAN Robert MA 1959
s of John W. S. harbour pilot and Elizabeth J. Strachan fishworker; b Fraserburgh 25.12.38
nat serv Hildesheim Ger 1960–62; teacher: Govan 1963–65, Jedburgh from 1965
m Old Deer 10.7.68 Maureen Ritchie secy d of Henry R. Mintlaw

STRACHAN Robert Alexander MB ChB 1966

STRACHAN Robert George MB ChB 1957
s of Robert G. S. fisherman and Agnes Buchan; b Peterhead 13.8.33
DObstRCOG 1959 DCH(Lond) 1972 MRCGP 1974
Dip Ven 1977

h o Aber, Glasg, Aber 1957–59; ship's surg Canada 1959–60; g p Pudsey from 1960
m Leeds 28.5.60 Muriel Hopkins nurse/midwife d of Reginald H. Leeds

STRACHAN William BSc 1957

STRACHAN William Reith *BSc 1959
s of Ian W. S. farm. and Isobel S. Reith; b Aber 18.5.37
soil surv Macaulay inst Aber 1959–62; agr sales rep Aberdeensh 1962–64; farm. West Balquhain from 1964
m Aber 2.8.62 Irene R. Ferguson MA 1960 *qv*

STRACHAN William Watson *BSc 1969 MSc 1971
s of William S. fatstock off. DAFS and Georgina Esslemont; b Aber 22.11.46
MRTPI 1976
plan. asst Salop c c 1971–73; sen plan. asst Inv c c 1973–74; prin plan. off. Tewkesbury borough council 1974–77, asst borough plan. off. from 1978
m Peterculter 3.8.68 Christine F. Bambrick teacher home econ d of Martin F. B. Peterculter

STRANG Ian William MB ChB 1967
s of Gavin S. farm. and Katherine I. Lawson; b Dinnet 12.5.41
FCM 1972 Dip Soc Med 1973 MFCM 1977
virologist Burroughs Wellcome Lond 1969; lect bio eng Strath 1970; dep med supt Glasg northern hosps 1972; sen regist commun med 1973; consult. epidemiologist to Scot. Head Injury Study 1977; CMS Argyll and Clyde Health Board 1977

STRATFOLD Anthony Leslie John BSc(eng) 1967

STRATTON Thomas Mackie BSc(eng) 1958

STRAW Jennifer Ann MA 1965
d of Leonard S. sales rep and Edna M. Aldred clerk; b Nott 6.10.44
teacher: Birm 1967–71, Mitcham 1971–73; exec off. MAFF Lond from 1973

STRONACH Andrew Fraser *BSc(eng) 1968
s of Andrew S. brewer and Elizabeth I. Webster; b Elgin 18.8.46
res stud. Aberd 1968–69; lect Aberd from 1969
m Aber 20.7.68 Marilyn J. L. Dunn MA 1965 *qv*

STRONACH Charles George *MA 1965 Dip Ed 1966

STRONACH Ian Macdonald *MA 1967
s of Peter D. S. bank acct and Louie Moir teacher; b Aber 16.3.45
MEd(Brist) 1978
teacher: Huntly 1968–69, Zambia 1969–72, Peterhead 1972–74, Zambia 1974–77; educ res Glasg from 1978
m Banff 21.6.69 Kathleen M. Falconer nurse d of Stanley F. Banff

STRONACH Patrick Moir *BSc(eng) 1966
s of Peter D. S. bank acct and Louie E. Moir teacher; b Aber 7.10.43
CEng MICE 1973
Aber: civ eng 1966–77, resid eng 1977–78, sen eng from 1978
m Aber 4.3.67 Margaret J. Forbes nurse d of Alexander F. Fordoun

STRONG Paul James Henry BSc(agr) 1970
s of Kenneth S. BSc(R'dg) farm. and Phyllis Drane; b Norfolk 16.1.47
Dip Milk Prod./Processing (Seale Hayne agr coll) 1971
farm man. consult. (consultancy comp mainly in undev countries) from 1971
m Winchester 8.7.72 Helena R. Franks farm secy d of Colin B. F. Basingstoke

STROUD Marjory BSc 1968
d Edin 6.8.75

STRUDWICK Christine Mary MA 1968
d of Leon A. S. civ serv and Ethel M. Stephenson teacher; b Richmond Yorks 3.4.48
teacher: Crawley 1969–73, Barrhead from 1973

STRUDWICK Michael John *BSc 1969
s of Leon A. S. civ serv and Ethel M. Stephenson teacher; b Richmond Yorks 3.4.48
teacher chem Harlaw acad Aber from 1970
m Aber 4.8.73 Alison J. Troup occup therap d of George T. Perth

STRUTHERS Eileen *MA 1966
m Ferguson

STRZALKOWSKA Wanda Christina MB ChB 1969

STUART Alison MA 1966
d of William S. farm. and Agnes F. Oliphant secy; b Ellon 20.7.45
secy to dir *Encounter* mag Lond 1967–68; information off., sen information off. with consumers' assoc publ of *Which?* Lond 1968–72; teacher Lond from 1973
m Lond 17.9.71 Colin P. Loxley comp dir/wine importer s of John L. L. Ashtead

STUART Ann Grant MA 1970
d of John S. mech eng REME and Marion N. G. Paterson MA(Edin) teacher; b Grantown-on-Spey 6.3.50
Dip Soc Ad(Edin) 1973
VSO teacher mod lang/dep head Sagamu Nigeria 1970–72; Orangeville Canada: ch care worker 1973–74, teacher arts/crafts from 1974

STUART Brian Sansom MB ChB 1969

STUART Charles Alexander *BSc 1967

STUART Charles James MA 1969
s of Charles S. prod. man. woollen mill and Barbara E. Angus; b Keith 17.1.49
teacher asst prin guid Speyside h s Aberlour from 1970
m Aberchirder 13.10.73 Lorna A. Stephen d of George S. Aberchirder

STUART Christina Carol MA 1970

STUART Irene Margaret MA 1966 Dip Ed 1968
d of John M. S. tel eng and Gladys W. Johnston; b Insch 13.9.43
MA(TEFL)(Cairo) 1971
teacher Engl Amer univ Cairo 1969–72; prin guid Inverurie acad from 1972
m Aber 21.1.63 Khalil E. A. Khalil PhD 1965 *qv*

STUART James Campbell BSc(agr) 1969
s of James D. S. MRCVS(Edin) vet surg and Marjorie E. Campbell; b Inv 14.9.46
MSc(N'cle) 1971
farm. Conon Bridge from 1971
m Leeds 12.1.74 Mary M. Travers MRCVS(Edin) d of Thomas T. Leeds

STUART John Thomson MA 1965
s of John T. S. soldier, civ serv, clerk and Elen H. Petrie; b Aber 4.12.28
chaplain: Highland Brig depot Aber 1965–66; 1st batt Scots Guards Malaya 1966–67, Scots Guards Edin, Pirbright 1967–69, Scot. Infantry depot Aber 1969–71, St Andrew's ch Aldershot 1971–74, St Andrew's ch Tidworth 1974–76, Scot. Infantry depot Glencorse 1976–78; minister Bedrule, Denholm and Minto from 1978
m(1) 1.5.57 Audrey Thomson nurse d of James E. D. T. Aber; wife *d* 17.6.73
(2) 23.3.78 Elsie M. Ogilvie catering off. d of John W. O. Pluscarden

STUART Judith Helen MA 1967
d of Alexander G. S. pharm and Dolly C. Scott; b Aber 21.11.46
Aber: computer oper 1968–69, cler asst 1970–71
m Aber 25.6.69 Robert Donald LLB 1968 *qv*

STUART Margaret Mary MA 1968
d of John S. and Marion Paterson MA(Edin) teacher; b Grantown-on-Spey 3.5.47
Dip Sec St(Strath)
secy WCC Geneva 1969–70; secy translator: Battelle inst Geneva 1971, UNESCO Paris from 1971

STUART Marjory Grace MA 1960
d of George S. mech eng and Marjory A. D. Grant; b Aber 8.4.38
teacher Muirfield p s Aber 1962–64
m Aber 2.4.64 John A. Morgan BSc 1959 *qv*

STUART Michael John *BSc 1969
s of John A. S. master painter and Gladys M. Penny PO clerk; b Fraserburgh 24.11.46
teacher: geog Fraserburgh 1970–71, Glasg 1971–72; prin geog Irvine from 1972
m Aber 5.7.71 Danièle M. Bathier teacher d of Marcel U. B. Clermont-Ferrand France

STUART Norman BSc 1970 Dip Ed 1971
s of Hugh H. C. S. process worker and Jessie A. Copland; b Banff 10.12.46
teacher maths Queen Anne h s Dunfermline 1971–73, asst prin maths from 1974
m Renfrew 30.6.73 Rosaleen M. Miller soc worker d of William M. MA(Glas) Renfrew

STUART Roderick *MA 1970

STUART Sheila Mary Amelia MA 1967

STUART Thelma Lorraine MA 1969
m Dickie

STUART Valerie Madeleine Garrick MA 1966
d of Thomas S. master joiner and Eliza Stuart teacher; b Tomintoul 2.4.46
teacher Fr: Alford acad 1967–70, Invergordon acad 1970–72
m Tombae Glenlivet 9.10.71 John A. Hill elect. s of Joseph H. Cullen

STURDEE Anthony Peter *BSc 1968
s of E. P. L. S. farm., acct and Pilar C. Fuller arch. asst; b Gerrards Cross 3.3.45
PhD(Leeds) 1972
res asst anat Leeds 1969–72; lect developmental biol Wolverhampton poly 1972–75; sen lect cell biol Coventry poly from 1975
m Leeds 10.7.70 Sarah R. Rushton MA 1970 *qv*

STURDY Robin Geoffrey MSc 1966
BA(Cantab)

STURM Maxwell Graeme de L'Isle BSc 1961
s of Maxwell G. de L. S. MB ChB 1927 *qv*; b Darlington 6.12.35
MSc(Lond) 1969 PhD(Univ of West Indies) 1975
teacher LCC 1962–64; res off. fisheries dept of game and fisheries min of nat resources Zambia 1965–68; res dem univ of WI Trinidad 1970–75; lect zool Bayevo univ Kano Nigeria from 1977

STURROCK Isabel Anne MA 1962
m Oxley

STURROCK Jane Traquair *MA 1968
d of Alexander P. S. MA(St And) journalist and Chrissie M. Traquair MA(St And) secy; b Glasg 13.4.46
staff man. Marks & Spencer Doncaster, Huddersfield 1968–69; secy univ of Edin 1969–74; secy ICFC Edin from 1974
m Edin 1.4.72 Michael Williamson marketing man. s of Henry R. W. ARIBA(Edin) Musselburgh

SUBIOTTO Arrigo Victor PhD 1969
MA(Lond)

SUDWEEKS Anthony William *MA 1961

SUE-A-QUAN Cerise Delphinium *BSc 1970
d of Kelvin S-A-Q and Edna E. Lee; b 8.12.47
m Aber 30.6.70 Jerry Sue-Chue-Lam MB ChB 1971 post-grad stud. surg s of Frank S-C-L. Toronto

SUMMERS Andrew MA 1957
s of Andrew S. fisherman and Elsie Bruce; b Peterhead 13.6.35
teacher Sauchie 1961–64; dep head Tullibody 1964–65; head Maryculter 1965–68; lect Dun from 1968
m Peterhead 1961 Helen M. Stephen des tweed mill d of William M. S. Peterhead

SUMMERS Patricia *BSc 1960 MSc 1961
d of Peter R. S. fishing skipper and Maggie Goodbrand; b Fraserburgh 8.8.38
biochem: Rowett inst Aber 1961–62, city hosp Aber 1962–64; teacher chem Fraserburgh acad from 1973
m Aber 22.12.61 Oddstein Uri MB ChB 1964 *qv*; marr diss 1975

SUMMERS Ronald Watson *BSc 1970 PhD 1974
s of Ronald S. MB ChB(St And) med pract and Doris Bulloch; b Dun 26.6.47
post doct res asst univ of Cape Town S Af 1974–77; employed by ODM to work for Grasslands Trial Unit Falkland Islands
m Aber 16.5.74 Judith A. Dunnet secy d of George M. D. BSc 1949 *qv*

SURAPHIBUL Kannica PhD 1968
BSc(B'kok)

SURGEONER James Hamilton LLB 1967

SUTHERLAND Aileen Mackenzie *MA 1963
d of Alexander W. S. gen merch and Elizabeth M. McKenzie nurse; b Mulben 10.3.42
careers off. educ auth Edin 1964–66; town plan. asst: Stirling 1966–67, N'cle 1967–70; careers off. Aberd from 1970

SUTHERLAND Ailsa Margaret MB ChB 1969
d of James H. S. elect. eng/farm. and Eleanor E.

Walton; b Frimley 9.5.43
Aber: h o 1969–70, g p trainee 1970–71, psychiat regist 1971–73, part-time from 1974
m Aber 9.5.64 Colin Milton MA 1965 *qv*

SUTHERLAND Alexander Dermot MA 1967

SUTHERLAND Anne Elizabeth *MA 1959 *MEd 1963

SUTHERLAND Astrid Elizabeth MA 1969

SUTHERLAND Barbara Elizabeth MA 1960 *1962
d of William S. farm. and Barbara M. Taylor; b Lancaster 12.11.38
teacher geog: Grove acad Dun 1963–66, Liberton s s Edin 1966–68
m Aber –.7.66 Norman G. Robb BSc(H-W) electronics eng/sen computer progr s of William C. R. MA(Glas) Hawick

SUTHERLAND Catherine Ann *MA 1970
d of George S. MA(Edin) miss., C of S min and Margot Davidson MA(St And) teacher; b Edin 22.12.47
teacher Engl: Smithycroft s s Glasg 1971–73, Stirling 1973–75, Hermitage acad Helensburgh from 1976
m Alexander T. M. Lumsden BSc(eng) 1970 *qv*

SUTHERLAND Colin Robert BSc(eng) 1963
s of Robert S. MA 1922 *qv*; b Aber 1.4.42
CEng MICE 1969
eng Sir Robert McAlpine & Sons UK, Bahamas from 1963
m Scunthorpe 12.8.67 Margery Foster lect in art, teacher d of Lawrence F. Scunthorpe

SUTHERLAND David George *MA 1962
s of David A. P. S. eng, s janitor and Flora George shop asst; b Aber 28.9.40
DPhil(Oxon) 1966
Cern fell. Geneva 1966–67; lect phys Glas from 1967

SUTHERLAND David Ivor Macpherson *MA 1960 *MEd 1962
s of David S. MA 1932 *qv*; b Wick 22.1.38
teacher mod lang AGS 1962–66; lect: educ Stranmillis coll Belf 1966–69, psych Craigie coll Ayr 1969–72; asst dir of educ Sutherland c c 1972–75; div educ off. Inv 1975–79; dep dir of educ Highland reg c from 1979
m Aber 16.7.64 Janet H. Webster teacher d of Alexander S. W. Aber

SUTHERLAND Denis Ian MA 1961 BD 1963
s of James S. master grocer and Jessie K. Balfour; b Aber 5.1.39
C of S min: asst Aber 1963–64, evangelist to Scotland's travelling families Perth 1964–70; co-ordinator of socio-educ proj to travelling families Perth 1970–73; parish min Glasg from 1973
m Aber 1.9.62 Norma M. Carroll nurse, health visitor d of Charles C. Aber

SUTHERLAND Donald Fraser *MA 1965

SUTHERLAND Gerald Murray BSc(eng) 1968
s of William G. M. S. road haulage contr and Eleanor M. Milne secy; b Forres 2.8.47
MICE 1978
eng asst, asst eng Banff c c 1968–75; eng Grampian reg c Elgin 1975–79; sub ag Morrison constr Elgin from 1979
m Banff 14.8.70 Catherine H. Smith clerkess d of James A. M. S. Banff

SUTHERLAND Iain Alexander MB ChB 1967

SUTHERLAND Ian Raffan BSc 1968
s of James R. S. banker, gen merch and Mary Mitchell leg. secy, gen merch; b Fraserburgh 18.9.45
applications eng in refrig (indust) Dartford 1968–72; acct Aber from 1972
m Fraserburgh 12.8.67 Sylvia C. Park teacher d of John S. P. Fraserburgh

SUTHERLAND Inga Maxine MA 1961
d of Andrew S. postman and Ivy E. E. Sutherland sub-postmistress; b Orkney 28.9.40
teacher: Kirkwall g s 1962–63, Bell-Baxter h s Cupar 1963–65, supply Orkney from 1965
m Orkney 10.3.66 George S. G. Rosie coxswain/marine oper s of James R. S. Ronaldsay

SUTHERLAND Jane Mitchell MA 1958
d of William J. S. banker and Jane H. Mitchell; b Colombo Ceylon 15.12.37
edit. asst AEI Lond 1959–61
m Lond 5.3.61 Alexander Hamilton BA(Cantab) civ eng s of John H. Bolton

SUTHERLAND Joan More *BSc(agr) 1967
d of John S. farm. and Alice A. Bremner; b Latheron
MSc(Carleton univ Ottawa) 1976
plant path. agr res stat Tanzania 1967–69; res asst: Carleton univ 1971–76, biol sc Dund 1976–79, fell. from 1979; PhD stud. from 1976

SUTHERLAND John Graham Martin BSc(eng) 1960
s of John G. G. M. S. man. iron foundry and Elizabeth S. S. Forbes cashier; b Aber 1938
CEng 1966 MICE 1966 MIMunE 1969 MIHE 1970
eng Sir Robert McAlpine & Sons Port Talbot, Gloucester, Lond 1960–62; civ eng consult. Flint & Neill Lond, Cambridge 1962–64; asst eng Aber c c 1964–66; prin asst eng, group leader (roads) Aber 1966–76; sen civ eng Sir Frederick Snow & Ptnrs Scot. 1977; asst proj dir Arab Union Contr Co Libya, Syria, Egypt 1978
m Aber 30.6.67 Kathleen A. T. Ellington MA 1966 *qv*

SUTHERLAND John Matheson MA 1961
s of Robert S. boat bldr/hirer and Mary A. Matheson teacher; b Portree 23.9.30
teacher sc Old Aber s s 1962–66; dep head Cornhill p s Aber 1966–75; head Hanover St p s Aber from 1975
m Aber 15.9.61 Jean MacDonald cler asst d of James MacD. Aber

SUTHERLAND John William MA 1970

SUTHERLAND Kathleen Mitchell MA 1960
d of James R. S. banker, gen merch and Mary Mitchell leg. secy; b Fraserburgh 13.9.39
man. gen merch bus./sub p o Rathen from 1961

SUTHERLAND Keith Farquhar *MA 1970 *MEd 1976

SUTHERLAND Laurence Anderson *BSc(eng) 1962 MSc 1963
s of John D. S. farm. and Eliza I. Williamson MA 1925 *qv*; b Orkney 8.1.41
res asst Aberd 1963–66; scient off. nat eng lab E Kilbride 1966–69; lect Napier coll of sc/tech Edin from 1969
m Aber 1965 Angela M. Tinsley teacher d of Joseph T. BSc(R'dg) Aber

SUTHERLAND Mackenzie Stewart MB ChB 1962 Dip Psychother 1971
b Carluke 31.3.33
MRCPsych 1972

SUTHERLAND Margaret Shepherd MA 1968 Dip Ed 1969
d of William J. S. elect. and Mary A. Macleod; b Brora 7.5.47
teacher: Bathgate 1969–71, Bournemouth from 1971
m Glasg 22.7.71 Hugh F. Walding PhD 1968 *qv*

SUTHERLAND Marian Will MA 1965
d of James R. S. banker, gen merch and Mary Mitchell leg. secy; b Fraserburgh 1.3.43
teacher Fr/Ger Glasg 1966–67; lib asst Aber from 1967
m Aber 23.3.73 Alastair C. Beaton journalist s of Robert A. B. Stonehaven

SUTHERLAND Mary Margaret MB ChB 1960
d of John S. audit acct and Annie F. Mackay RGN; b Aber 30.9.36
DPM(Lond) 1972 MRCPsych(Lond) 1973
h o Lerwick, Aber 1961–62; regist med Peel hosp Galashiels 1962–64, Northallerton hosp 1964–66; regist geriat N'cle gen hosp 1966–70; regist royal Cornhill hosp Aber 1970–75; consult psychiat Dingleton hosp 1975–76, Bilbohall hosp Elgin from 1976
m Aber 22.8.64 Alexander I. Simpson MB BS(Durh) s of Alexander J. S. Durh

SUTHERLAND Michael Alexander Owen MA 1966
s of Donald A. S. bus. man., hotelier, confectioner and M. Jean Hackett; b Wick 31.8.42
Dip Bus. Man.(Manc) 1967
Metal Box Co: trainee, comm asst, comm man. from 1971; resid Wrexham
m Lond 27.11.67 Sally Kirkwood secy/pa d of John H. K. Vict Aust

SUTHERLAND Nan Elizabeth MA 1959
m Martin

SUTHERLAND Ray Duncan *MA 1969
d of William G. S. master baker and Margaret E. Rae; b Aber 17.9.46
Dip Ed(Dund) 1971 LLB(Dund) 1974
law app Dun 1974–76; solic Dun 1976–77, Glasg from 1977
m Aber 28.12.70 Stanley L. Mann MB ChB(St And) radiol s of Allan S. M. Arbroath

SUTHERLAND Robert *BSc 1969
s of Robert S. factory supt and Hilda Whyte; b Peterhead 15.11.46
teacher Ayr acad 1970–73; prin teacher Prestwick acad from 1973

SUTHERLAND Sandra Mackenzie MB ChB 1962
m Dymock

SUTHERLAND Stanley BSc 1961
s of James Esson shipyard painter and Selina Sutherland glove stitcher; b Aber 7.5.22
Master Mariner (foreign going) certif(Aber) 1956
lect navigation Aber 1962–64; teacher phys/maths/sc Aber from 1964
m Aber 9.2.43 Mary B. Styles d of Herbert S. Aber

SUTHERLAND Stewart Ross *MA 1963
s of George A. C. S. comm trav and Ethel Masson; b Aber 25.2.41
BA(Cantab) 1965 MA(Cantab) 1969
asst lect phil UCNW 1965–68; lect phil Stir 1968–72, sen lect 1972–76, reader 1976–77; visiting fell. humanities res centre ANU Canberra 1974; Gillespie visiting prof relig coll of Wooster Ohio USA 1975; prof hist and phil of religion King's coll univ of Lond from 1977
m Aber 1.8.64 Sheena Robertson MB ChB 1963 *qv*

SUTHERLAND Susan Mary BSc 1960
d of George S. excise off. and Catherine Rainbird; b Edin 2.5.39
teacher: maths Edin 1961–63, jun s Derby 1963–64, Beverley 1964–66
m Forres 7.9.63 Anthony C. Stewart BVM&S(Edin) vet surg s of Henry G. S. MRCVS(Glas) Binfield

SUTHERLAND Thelma Ann MA 1967

SUTHERLAND William John MA 1970

SUTHERLAND William Ross MA 1963
teacher: Banffsh 1964–67, N Province Zambia 1967–69; lect correspondence educ Zambia 1969–73; teacher S Aust from 1974
m Aber 14.7.61 Margaret J. Milne MA 1959 *qv*

SUTHERS Susan *MA 1969 Dip Ed 1970
d of George A. S. bank clerk and Doris Hargreaves; b Bury 10.5.47
teacher Engl: Bo'ness 1970–72, Edin 1972–74, Lond from 1974
m Lond 10.4.76 Vivian W. Willson BSc(Bolton) PO tel eng s of William H. J. W. Woking

SUTTIE Alastair Mackintosh MB ChB 1961
s of John S. MRCVS(Edin) vet surg and Annie S. Miller MA(Edin) teacher; b Enniskillen NI 5.4.38
DObstRCOG 1963 MRCGP 1975
h o: Woodend hosp, Ross clin Aber, Raigmore hosp Inv 1961–63; g p: locums Scot., Canada 1963–64, Hawick from 1964
m Aber 14.4.65 Gillian M. Sangster MB ChB 1962 *qv*

SUTTIE Ian Simpson *BSc 1964 Dip Ed 1965
s of John S. MRCVS(Edin) vet surg and Annie S. Miller MA(Edin) teacher; b Forres 13.2.42
teacher biol Elgin acad 1965–68, prin biol from 1968
m Aber 31.7.70 Christina I. Souter MA 1961 *qv*

SUTTIE James McDonald BSc(agr) 1956 MSc 1970
s of James M. S. gardener and Jane L. Nicoll; b Kirkmichael Perthsh 13.6.34
Dip Agr(Cantab) 1957 DTA(Trinidad) 1958
agr off. Kenya 1958–69; pasture spec FAO of UN India 1970–71, Madagascar 1971–77, Pakiston Punjab from 1977
m Nyeri Kenya 10.2.61 Elizabeth R. Andrews MA 1955 *qv*

SUTTLE Neville Frank PhD 1964
BSc(R'dg)

SUTTON Alastair Morris LLB 1966
s of Ernest E. M. S. trans man. and Nancy Venn; b Bristol 6.1.45
LLM(Lond) 1967 Dip Air and Space Law(Lond) 1967
barrister-at-law(Middle Temple) 1971
lect in laws Lond/tut. Lond inst of world affairs 1967–73; prin admin/dir gen for external relations comm of Europ communities Brussels from 1973
m Aber 2.9.68 Eileen Taylor BSc 1966 *qv*

SUTTON Anthony Hubert PhD 1964
ARIC

SVEINBJORNSSON Sveinn *BSc 1970
s of Sviensson S. capt/shipowner and Laufey Gudlaugsdottir; b Neskaupstadur Iceland 5.3.45
sen scient off. fisheries biol pelagic species Reykjavik from 1970
m Reykjavik 29.12.74 Margret Samuelsdottir clerk criminal court Reykjavik d of Samuel Kristjansson Reykjavik

SVENDSEN Johan Harald
see Seland

SVOBODA Andrew Pavel MA 1966

SWAN Thomas Clarke *MA 1969

SWANSON Anne Louise MA 1957
d of Alexander J. S. head postmaster and Georgina W. Sutherland civ serv; b Annan 30.5.37
teacher Engl Thurso h s 1958–60; NY: teacher Brick presb ch s 1960–61, St Hilda's/St Hugh's s 1961; Aber: teacher Engl Northfield s s 1961–63, remed educ Linksfield acad from 1972
m Aber 30.7.60 Alan Main MA 1957 *qv*

SWANSON James Macaulay BSc(agr) 1963

SWANSON Patricia Anne BSc 1969
d of Thomas G. S. accounts man. and Edith M. Gray secy; b Aber 11.2.47
teacher sc Harrison coll Barbados WI 1969–71; tech i/c blood transfusion dept N Devon RI from 1972
m Aber 1.2.69 Robert M. Brown MB ChB 1969 *qv*

SWANSON Ruth Agnes MA 1966
m Walker

SWIFT Margaret Jeanne BEd 1970
d of Maurice S. eng and Margaret Jaques artist; b Chorlton-cum-Hardy Manc 7.1.24
teacher Harlaw acad from 1971
m Aber 8.6.46 Ronald M. Dick plumber/insp house drainage s of Alexander D. Aber

SYME David Couper MA 1963
s of Colin R. S. civ serv and Lucy H. Richmond secy, bank clerkess; b Perthsh 22.6.42
Dip Russian Lang(Strath) 1968
teacher: mod lang Bankhead acad, Inverurie acad 1966–69, TEFL Schwerte W Ger 1969–71, mod lang Summerhill acad 1971–73; instr/off. RAEC Guards depot Pirbright from 1973
m Halstead 7.7.69 Patricia M. Wood nurse d of Nowell W. W. Halstead

SYMON Doreen MA 1956
m Grieve

SYMON Jennifer *MA 1968
d of Lindsay J. S. MB ChB 1944 *qv*; b Aber 31.5.46
teacher: inf Gt Dunmow 1969–71, spec class juniors Montrose 1971–72
m Lossiemouth 16.8.69 Robert W. Y. Martin MB BChir (Cantab) g p s of Thomas Y. M. Tottington

SYMON John Charles *MA 1957
s of Charles S. traffic supt Aber corp and May Devlin typist; b Aber 19.1.30
LTh(Greg) 1953
teacher hist Blairs coll Aber 1957–61; lect phil/theol St Andrew's coll Melrose 1961–72; parish priest Aber 1972–74; teacher r e Edin 1974–77; parish priest Thurso from 1977

SYMON Robert John Charles MA 1960 LLB 1965

SYMON Sheena Margaret *MA 1958
m Crozier

SYMONS Gordon Leonard *MA 1966

SYNGE Elizabeth *BSc 1966
d of Richard L. M. S. BA(Cantab) res biochem and Ann Stephen MB B Chir(Cantab) doctor, teacher; b St Albans 3.5.44
PhD(ANU Canberra) 1970
Aust nat univ Canberra: res schol 1966–70, res asst 1970–71; Glas part-time: dem 1972–74, res asst from 1974
m Stonehaven 21.9.66 Ben Smith MA 1966 *qv*

SYNGE Jane *MA 1964
d of Richard L. M. S. MA(Cantab) res biochem and Ann Stephen BA(Cantab) doctor, teacher; b Leeds 11.4.43
PhD(LSE) 1971
asst prof sociol: univ of Illinois Urbana USA 1970–72, McM univ Hamilton Ontario from 1972
m Philadelphia 1.1.70 Bunli Yang BA(Harv) trans analyst s of T. Yang MA(Harv) Villanova Penn

SYPULA Pauline Zofia MA 1969
m Lane

TAGGART William John BSc(agr) 1956
s of John A. T. granite merch and Annie W. Ross; b Aber 9.9.34
PhD(Edin) 1972
farm. Kincardine 1956–61; agr advis NOSCA Aber 1961–65; res fell. agr dept Edin 1965–67; lect agr Edin 1967–69; agr bus. consult. Cumberland 1969–74; agr advis to Clydesdale Bank Glasg from 1974
m Aber 2.7.58 Ann C. Falconer teacher d of James D. F. Aber

TAILOR Thakorbhai Jinabha *BSc 1963

TAIT Andrew MA 1963
s of Andrew D. T. fisherman and Maria L. McKenzie; b Fraserburgh 3.4.41
teacher AGS 1964–69; dep head Culter p s 1969–71; head: Crimond p s 1971–73, Hillocks p s Bucksburn 1973–76, Mill O' Forest p s Stonehaven from 1976
m Fraserburgh 10.8.63 Rosemary Green teacher d of Joseph G. Fraserburgh

TAIT Brian Copeland MA 1967

TAIT Catherine Joyce MA 1967
d of John O. T. wholesale fruit/potato merch and Muriel Chubb; b Perth 7.9.46
teacher: Uddingston 1968–70, Whitburn 1970–72, asst prin Fr from 1972

TAIT Douglas John BSc(eng) 1962

TAIT Elspeth Muriel MA 1958

TAIT George Henry *BSc 1958
s of Henry J. T. shipmaster and Margaret J. Barron; b Aber 27.12.36
PhD(Lond) 1961

St Mary's hosp med s Lond: res fell. 1961–64, asst lect 1964–65, lect 1965–70, sen lect from 1970
m Edin 6.9.62 Deirdre E. Ross med lab tech

TAIT Helen Stewart MA 1964
d of Walter S. C. T. loco eng and Harriet Mackie; b Aber 3.4.42
teacher: p s AGS 1967–68, Engl Hazlehead acad Aber 1974, Summerhill acad Aber from 1975
m Aber 28.10.61 Henry Barber eng/chief tech nat phil dept Aberd s of John B. Aber

TAIT Ian Sim MA 1965
s of Alexander D. T. store man. and Jean N. Sim; b Fraserburgh 15.10.42
BA 1979
teacher: asst prin maths Fraserburgh acad 1966–74; lect computer educ Aber coll of educ from 1974

TAIT John *BSc 1960
s of Andrew T. farm. and Jemima A. J. Dalziel nurse; b Aith Shetland 20.12.38
teacher: prin maths Lerwick s s 1961–66; comp dir Whalsay Shetland from 1966
m Whalsay 20.12.63 Charlotte H. Sutherland dom worker d of Hugh S. Whalsay

TAIT John Mervyn *BSc 1969 PhD 1973
s of John T. bus driver and Enid Annal hotelier; b Kirkwall 30.3.47
electron microscopist Macaulay inst for soil res Aber from 1972
m Kirkwall 3.4.70 Heather A. Tullock midwifery sister d of Robert T. T. Kirkwall

TAIT Katherine McAdie BEd 1968
d of John T.; b Wick 13.5.44
teacher Wick h s 1968–71; grad asst Stir 1971–77, asst dir p e Stir from 1977

TAIT Peter John Thomas *BSc 1956 PhD 1959
s of John T. fisherman and Elizabeth Tulloch; b Lerwick 22.10.34
Ramsey mem fell. Aberd 1959–61; sen lect chem UMIST Manc from 1961
m Carlisle 19.8.61 Winifred Proudfoot MB ChB 1959 *qv*

TALLACH Cameron MB ChB 1968
s of James A. T. min of relig and Elizabeth D. Fraser shopkeeper; b Kames 5.12.43
h o Aber gen hosps 1968–69; temp lect physiol Aberd 1969–70; sen h o surg Aber gen hosps 1970–72; m o Dun publ health serv 1972–74; med missionary Taipei Taiwan 1974–77, Taichung Taiwan from 1977
m Aber 27.12.68 Ishbel M. Maclean MB ChB 1969 *qv*

TALLACH James Ross MB ChB 1967

TAMBER Einar Rolf MB ChB 1970
s of Ragnvald A. T. DSC admiral royal Norwegian navy and Nini M. Aas; b Edin 16.11.43
Norway: resid path. Norwegian radium hosp Oslo 1970; h o Lillehammer 1971; asst m o Skjervøy Troms 1972; lt (med br) royal Norwegian navy (ship's surg on frigate) Bergen 1972–73; cas off. Bergen 1973; m o Namdalseid from 1974
m Sandvika Norway 31.7.71 Daisy S. H. Wong MB ChB 1970 *qv*

TAMLYN Lynda Kay MA 1969
d of Charles W. C. T. chain store man. and Olive E. Meecham; b Cardiff 8.7.48
Bristol: soc worker 1969–70, prin nurs s 1970–74, stud. Redland teacher trg coll 1974

TARBAT Lorna Mary MA 1963
d of Henry T. civ serv and Violet Scrimgeour clerkess; b Aber 1942
teacher
m Aber –.7.65 Ian F. Hall lithographic artist s of John H. Edin
d Edin 7.2.74

TASIE Godwin Ohyemaechi Mgbechi PhD 1969
BA(Nig)

TASKER Helen Anne MA 1969
d of Norman H. T. elect. welder and Elizabeth H. Thomson shop asst; b Aber 24.11.47
teacher Engl: Powis acad Aber 1970–71, Dumbarton acad from 1971
m Aber 6.8.71 Bruno R. Dimambro civ serv s of Rossato D. Aber

TAUSJØ Johan Elling MB ChB 1970
s of Johan T. M. T. MD(Oslo) surg and Aasta Mjaaland mus teacher; b Haugesund Norway 24.5.44
Spec in Oncology & Radiotherapy(Norway) 1980
h o Stavanger 1970–71; milit serv (lt, capt) Oslo 1971–72; regist radium hosp Oslo 1972–74; fell. oncology univ hosp Madison Wisc USA 1974–76; sen regist radium hosp Oslo from 1976
m Madison 10.8.69 Janet L. Ficken MA(Wisc) teacher d of Robert F. BA(Wisc) Wisconsin

TAVADIA Hosie Byram MB ChB 1964
s of Byram C. T. stock exch broker and Gool S. Patel; b Canton China 24.2.37
DObstRCOG 1966 MRCPath 1971
grant from leukaemia res fund 1974–75
h o Raigmore hosp (RI Inv) 1964–65; sen h o Perth RI, Ayrsh gen hosp Irvine 1965–66; regist lab med southern gen hosp Glasg 1966–70; lect path. Glas hon sen regist path. Glasg RI from 1970; consult. histopathologist Forth Valley health board from 1975
m Aber 19.7.65 Catherine W. M. Ross teacher d of Menzies M. R. Invergordon

TAVADIA Phiroza MB ChB 1961
d of Byram C. T. stock exch broker and Gool S. Patel; b Hong Kong 5.2.34
h o RACH, ARI 1961–62; Lond: sen h o Prince of Wales hosp 1962, h o Elizabeth Garrett Anderson hosp 1963–64; g p 1964–69; clin asst gyn Elizabeth Garrett Anderson hosp 1972–75; g p Hong Kong from 1975

TAVENDALE Bruce *BSc 1960

TAWSE Euan William *MA 1969

TAWSE Peter Alexander Lagrange *BSc 1968
s of Peter C. T. council lab and Edith M. H. Walker MA 1929 *qv*; b Insch 14.1.46
res stud. Aberd 1968–71; Banff acad: teacher geog 1972–73, asst prin guid 1973–74; lect geog Trinity & All Saints' colleges Leeds from 1974
m Peel IOM 2.8.73 Bernadette M. McHugh MB ChB 1972 g p d of Hubert McH. Peel

TAYLOR Alan Murray *BSc 1969
s of Henry G. T. MA(Edin) priv secy (lit) and Mary W. Hughson MA(Edin) teacher; b Lerwick 29.3.47
man. trainee Brit Ropes Doncaster 1969–71; pilot RAF flt/lt from 1972

m Conisbrough 30.9.72 Sheila Ross secy d of Samuel R. Southend

TAYLOR Alec Stuart BSc 1967

TAYLOR Alexander John BSc(agr) 1962
s of Alexander T. farm. and Elsie McKinnon; b Longside 13.7.40
agr advis NOSCA Perth from 1962
m Aber 27.8.66 Evelyn M. McBoyle MA 1963 *qv*

TAYLOR Alexander Kinnear BSc 1970

TAYLOR Alison Cursiter BSc 1958

TAYLOR Andrew Thomas *BSc 1965
s of Thomas M. T. MA 1920 *qv* and Helen M. Jardine MB ChB 1920 *qv*; b Aber 20.11.43
M Inst P 1969
instrum man. ICI Teesside from 1965
m Redcar Margaret S. Coyle secy d of Joseph H. C. Redcar

TAYLOR Anne Vaughan MA 1969

TAYLOR Annette Mollison MA 1964
d of George S. T. foreman maintenance eng and Annie M. Proctor tailor's cutter; b Forfar 8.1.43
teacher mod lang Montrose acad 1965–69; part-time lect Engl lang Angus tech coll Arbroath from 1976
m Montrose 23.7.66 James A. Thomson plan. eng, app instr, trg man., comp man. s of James A. T. Montrose

TAYLOR Arthur MA 1968

TAYLOR Catherine Margaret *MA 1970
adopted d of Henry W. T. millwright and his sister Margaret Taylor; b Aber 6.2.49
Aber: lib asst 1971–73, stud. lib RGIT 1973–74, trainee publ lib 1974–75; asst ref lib Aber city dist lib from 1975

TAYLOR Charles Cormack Greig *MA 1970 Dip Ed 1971

TAYLOR Christina Chirrey Smith MA 1957
m Macdonald

TAYLOR Christopher Martin *BSc 1968

TAYLOR Colin Ross MB ChB 1964
s of Colin F. T. MA 1932 *qv* and Edith I. Dargie MA 1930 *qv*; b Inv 7.12.40
DCH(Glas) 1966 ECFMG(USA) 1974 MD(Connecticut) 1977
h o Stracathro hosp, RACH 1964–65; sen h o paediat Stobhill hosp Glasg 1965–67; sen h o, regist Stobhill hosp Glasg 1967–70; assoc, sen assoc dir clin res Pfizer Inc Connecticut USA from 1970, also on med staff of Lawrence hosp New Lond Conn; holder of USA patents in electocardiography and drug treatment; co-chmn American coll of cardiology annual meeting 1978
m Buckie 11.7.64 Helen M. Calder artist d of James C. Buckie

TAYLOR David *MA 1965

TAYLOR David McKinlay *MA 1967 Dip Ed 1968
s of Colin F. T. MA 1932 *qv* and Edith I. Dargie MA 1930 *qv*; b Madderty 27.7.45
MEd(Glas) 1975
teacher hist Dunfermline h s 1968–71; prin hist Garnock acad Kilbirnie 1971–77, asst rector from 1977
m Glasg 1.8.68 Jacqueline M. Thomson MA 1967 *qv*

TAYLOR Denys Anthony Walton BSc(agr) 1970
s of Denys R. W. T. comp dir and Margaret M. Forster; b Durh 16.6.44
trainee man. Lond 1971–72; teacher: sc Lond 1972–73, biol Surrey from 1974

TAYLOR Dianna Louise MA 1965

TAYLOR Duncan McKay *BSc 1963

TAYLOR Edward Thomson *MA 1970
s of Edward E. T. civ serv and Jemima Yule; b Dun 22.5.35
export man. Peterhead 1970–71; lect coll of comm Aber from 1971
m Trier Ger 17.4.66 Ursula D. Spring teacher d of Arthur S. Eng(Bingen W Ger) Trier

TAYLOR Eileen BSc 1966
d of Nelson T. teacher and Vaunda E. Murray clerk; b Dunfermline 16.10.45
computer progr NCB Cannock 1966–68; software progr internat bus. machines Lond 1968–70
m Aber 7.9.68 Alastair M. Sutton LLB 1966 *qv*

TAYLOR Elizabeth Buchan *MA 1966
d of Alexander W. T. toolmaker and Elizabeth M. Buchan; b Fraserburgh 13.2.44
res asst educ tech Sur 1974–75; teacher Godalming coll Surrey from 1975
m Aber 17.10.64 Donald G. Cruickshank MA 1963 *qv*

TAYLOR Elizabeth Royda Sinclair MA 1970
d of William T. textile des and Elizabeth R. Hargreaves; b Edin 14.12.49
Secy/Ling Dip(City of Westminster coll) 1971
p a to publ Lond 1971–72; secy to arch. Edin 1972–73; secy to man. chem comp Hartlepool 1973–74; p a gen man. Mineral Grinding Co Hartlepool 1974–76
m Gifford 16.9.72 Nigel R. L. Hogg MA 1970 *qv*

TAYLOR Elizabeth Wilson BSc 1967 Dip Ed 1968
d of Alexander T. farm. and Agnes E. L. Maxwell farm.; b Elgin 18.12.46
teacher: sc Lossiemouth acad 1969–72, p e Laurencekirk 1972–74, p e and guid Laurencekirk 1975; purser/watchkeeper on STS *Robert Gordon* RGIT Aber from 1975

TAYLOR Ethel Ann MA 1966 Dip Ed 1967
d of Alexander T. supermarket owner and Ethel Garden off. man.; b Aber 30.12.45
teacher Bexley Heath 1967–72; home teacher Hillingdon 1974–75
m Aber 17.8.68 James A. M. Gilmour man. bldg soc s of James G. Helmsdale

TAYLOR George Abel MB ChB 1958
s of Alexander T. farm. and Margaret J. Abel receptionist; b Home Hill Queensland Aust 11.8.33
MRCGP 1972
h o Woodend gen hosp Aber, ARI 1958–59; sen h o Woodend hosp 1959; nat serv m o (army) Edin, Glasg, W Isles 1960–62; g p Aber from 1962
m Aber 3.10.64 Margaret E. Willox BSc 1959 *qv*

TAYLOR Graeme Charles Stuart LLB 1970

TAYLOR Iain James Gray *MA 1970
s of Charles G. S. T. MA 1921 *qv*; b Stornoway 8.3.48
Dip Town Reg Plan.(Glas) 1972
teacher: Victoria Dr s s Glasg 1973–74, Oban h s 1974–

75, Nicolson inst Stornoway 1975–76; lib asst Dingwall from 1976

TAYLOR James Mann *BSc 1958

TAYLOR John MB ChB 1958
s of John T. credit draper/salesman and Margaret S. Hamilton factory process worker; b Saltcoats 29.9.34
MRCGP 1972
h o Woodend hosp Aber, Kilmarnock I 1958–59; m o Colchester milit hosp 1959–61; h o Forth Park mat. hosp Kirkcaldy 1961–62; g p: Kilwinning 1962–64, Greenock from 1964
m Stevenston 15.7.59 Alison G. Cameron teacher d of William O. C. Stevenston

TAYLOR John *MA 1967

TAYLOR John Murray *MA 1964 Dip Ed 1965
s of John M. T. MA 1931 *qv*; b Aber 18.7.42
teacher classics: Dunfermline h s 1965–68, spec asst classics 1968–70; prin classics: Kirkcudbright acad 1970–74, Liberton h s Edin 1974–76, McLaren h s Callander 1976–78; asst dir of educ Central reg from 1978

TAYLOR John Randolph PhD 1956
s of H. Kerr T. BD(Richmond Va USA) clergyman and Fanny B. Graham missionary; b Taichow Kiangsu Province China 12.1.29
AB(Davidson coll NC) 1951 BD(Richmond) 1954 DD(Oglethorpe Atlanta Ga) 1974
pastor: ch of the pilgrims Washington DC 1956–67, central presb ch Atlanta 1967–76, Myers Park presb ch Charlotte NC from 1976
m Shreveport La 1.6.51 Arline Johnson BA(Centenary coll) d of William M. J. Shreveport

TAYLOR Judith MA 1969
m Salkeld

TAYLOR Kathleen Anne BSc 1963

TAYLOR Keith *MA 1961
s of James T. warehouseman and Leslie Clubb; b Aber 3.11.38
teacher Engl Mackie acad Stonehaven from 1962, year master from 1972

TAYLOR Lesley Jane *BSc 1965
m Dickson

TAYLOR Linden Estelle MA 1970

TAYLOR Margaret Watt BSc(agr) 1956
d of Alexander W. T. farm. and Helen M. Crichton teacher; b Aber 4.4.35
asst exper off. Torry res stat Aber 1956–57; area organis Scot. Assoc of Young Farmers' Clubs 1957–60
m Aber 1.7.60 William Anderson farm. s of Ronald A. MB ChB 1923 *qv*

TAYLOR Mary Ross *BSc 1970 PhD 1975
d of William S. T. pharm and Winifred M. Ross MB ChB(St And) med pract; b Aber 25.2.48
res asst dept chem Aberd 1970–72, res off. from 1972
m Aber 27.12.72 Robert E. Masson BSc 1969 *qv*

TAYLOR Maureen McGrotty MA 1958
d of George G. T. civ serv and Frances H. S. McGrotty teacher; b Aber 29.1.38
teacher: Kirkhill p s Aber 1959–60, Hilton p s Inv 1961–63; pers secy Inv from 1973
m Aber 22.7.60 James C. Pringle BL 1957 *qv*

TAYLOR Michael James LLB 1969

TAYLOR Michael William BSc 1970 MB ChB 1975
s of James A. T. comp dir and Doris M. R. Webster; b Aber 19.7.48
MRCP 1977
Aber hosps, Grampian health board: h o, sen h o 1975–77, med regist from 1977
m Aber 28.4.75 Anne M. Skinner SRN d of Henry G. S. MB ChB 1938 *qv*

TAYLOR Patricia Mary MA 1964
d of John G. T. head janitor Ellon acad and Mary C. Taylor; b Ellon 29.7.43
Marks & Spencer: head pers dept Leeds, Oxford, Liverpool 1964–68, selector/merchandiser head off. Lond 1969–71
m Ellon 1.5.71 Michael J. Turner man. dir internat merch bank in Hong Kong s of Alfred T. Taunton

TAYLOR Pauline MA 1967
d of George M. T. munic off. and Amy Jackson; b Sheffield 5.2.46
Somerset: teacher Churchill 1968–71, Huish epis s 1971–73, dir first yr stud. 1973–74, head lower s from 1974
m Bridgwater 30.5.73 John A. S. Clarke schoolmaster s of Frank E. S. C. Fordingbridge

TAYLOR Peter Bruce MB ChB 1967
s of George H. C. T. MB ChB 1940 *qv*; b N'cle-u-Tyne 30.6.44
FFARCS 1972
h o Raigmore hosp Inv 1967–68; stat m o RAF Leeming, Sharjah, Muharraq (Trucial Oman States), N Luffenham 1968–72; sen h o, clin asst anaest St Thomas hosp Lond 1972; spec anaest RAF hosp Halton 1972–74; regist anaest ARI from 1974
m Scalloway Shetland 8.8.69 Jamesina M. Robertson midwife d of Thomas J. R. Scalloway

TAYLOR Rachel Thomson Brown MA 1965
d of Albert G. T. farm man. and Janet R. Morrison; b Carnwath 21.5.44
teacher Edin 1966–69
m Aber 16.5.69 William J. Barclay BSc 1966 *qv*

TAYLOR Robert Smart *MA 1963

TAYLOR Robin Dempster *BSc 1970 PhD 1974

TAYLOR Ross Jenkins MB ChB 1966
s of Neil T. clergyman and Mary E. Livingstone MA (Edin) teacher; b Bearsden 16.4.43
DCH 1970 MRCGP 1972
m o/spec phys RAF sqn ldr 1966–73; lect g p Aberd 1973–78, sen lect from 1978
m Thurso 7.9.65 Armida M. Craig nurse d of Donald A. C. Thurso

TAYLOR Stewart McConachie BSc 1958

TAYLOR Thomas Gilchrist MB ChB 1965
s of Thomas G. T. supt works Inv c c and Catherine S. Cross; b Hamilton 18.2.40
MRCPath 1974
h o Woodend hosp Aber, RNI Inv 1966–67; sen h o: Inv, St George's hosp Lond 1967–68; regist: path. W Middx hosp 1968–70, haemat St Mary's hosp Lond 1970–71; sen regist haemat Kingston hosp Surrey, St Thomas' hosp Lond 1971–75; consult. blood transfus/haemat Highland health board Inv from 1976
m Lond 27.12.67 Jean E. Cumming MB ChB 1965 *qv*

TAYLOR Timothy John *BSc 1967

TAYLOR William Alexander MA 1961
s of Colin F. T. MA 1932 *qv* and Edith I. Dargie MA 1930 *qv*; b Aber 22.5.39
BA(Lond) 1970 FSA Scot. 1973
teacher Summerhill acad Aber 1962–67, spec asst 1967–73, asst prin 1973–76; prin hist Linksfield acad from 1976
m Aber 30.6.62 Margaret J. Allan teacher d of Robert F. A. Aber

TAYLOR William Hay *MA 1957 *MEd 1959
s of Walter F. T. cooper and Jessie R. Maclennan nurse; b Findochty 30.8.35
MSc(Kansas) 1960
teacher Engl/hist Hyndland acad Glasg 1960–62; lect: Falkirk tech coll Stirling 1962–64, St Luke's coll of educ Exeter 1964–78, Exe from 1978
m Buckie 9.7.61 Odile G. M-L. Saunier L ès L(Caen) teacher d of Bernard S. Etretat, Seine Maritime France

TAYLOR William James *MA 1966 LLB 1969
s of Cecil T. clerk and Ellen Daubney clerkess; b Nairn 13.9.44
law app Aber, Edin 1969–71; Scot. bar Edin from 1971; councillor Edin corp, Lothian reg council from 1973
m Aberlemno 31.7.71 Margaret U. Russell MA(St And) admin d of A. Colin R. CMG MA(Oxon) Aberlemno

TAYLOR Willson Davidson MB ChB 1969
s of Williamson A. T. newsag and Margaret M. J. T. Davidson shop asst; b Aber 25.11.45
MRCP 1974
h o Woodend hosp Aber 1969–70; m o Queen's Own Highlanders Edin, BAOR 1970–72; phys milit hosp Catterick 1972–74; regist dermat N'cle-u-Tyne 1974–75; sen spec dermat Brit milit hosp Hong Kong 1975–78; sen regist dermat RVI N'cle-u-Tyne from 1978
m Aber 18.7.69 Lorna M. Sangster BSc 1966 *qv*

TELFER Alison Shaw MA 1969
d of John H. T. man. dir spinning mill and Alice Shaw; b Hawick 20.10.48
Dip Soc Work(Glas) 1975
asst ch's home Edzell Lodge Edin 1969–70; nurs asst royal Edin hosp 1970–71; trainee soc worker Crichton royal hosp Dumfries 1971–73; stud. Glas 1973–75

TELFER Stewart Bryson MSc 1969
s of Thomas B. T. MBE chartered quantity surv and Isabella M. Young; b Edin 15.11.45
BSc(Glas)
lect anim physiol & nutrit univ of Leeds from 1971
m Aber 3.4.72 Sheila Holmes MA 1970 *qv*

TELLING Geoffrey Morgan MSc 1965
s of Robert E. T. master carpenter and Elsie G. Morgan; b Newport 10.2.32
Grad RIC 1960 MChemA 1969 CChem FRIC 1970
res chem Unilever res Sharnbrook from 1964
m Alford 19.9.64 Margaret S. Baxter MA 1961 *qv*

TEMPLETON Alexander Allan MB ChB 1969
s of Richard T. and Minnie Whitfield; b Glasg 28.6.46
MRCOG 1974
Aber: h o 1969–73, res fell. dept obst 1973–74, regist obst/gyn from 1974

TEMPLETON Helen Margaret MA 1969 Dip Ed 1970
d of George M. T. LDS(Glas) dent. surg and Margaret J. Coutts; b Turriff 28.8.48
teacher Plaistow Lond 1970–71, Harringey Lond 1971–72, Cheshunt 1972
m Turriff 12.8.72 Malcolm McMillan MA(St And) syst analyst s of Donald McM. Northwood

TEMPLETON Margaret Barbour MA 1958

TEMPLETON Richard *BSc 1959 PhD 1963

TENGEY James Gbeze Kofi MLitt 1969 PhD 1973
BA(Ghana)

TENNANT Charles MA 1958 Dip Ed 1959
b Aber 23.11.36
teacher: Engl Northfield s s Aber 1959–64, Engl/commun Aber coll of comm from 1964
m Aber 4.8.61 Loretta A. M. Pole

TENNANT John Milton MA 1965
s of John T. MA 1937 *qv*; b Gartly 22.11.29
C of S min St Andrew's ch Lochgelly from 1968
m Dun 31.3.56 Jean McMillan teacher d of Martin P. E. McM. Dun

TENNANT Maurice Henderson MA 1968

TENNENT Justine Rose MA 1969
d of William T. comp dir and Justine Clark mus; b Glasg 18.10.48
Dip Pers Man. (RGIT) 1970
pers man.: Fine Fare superstore Aber 1970–72, Skean Dhu hotel Dyce Airport 1973–76; lect Aber coll of comm from 1976
m Aber 1.6.70 Donald K. McIntosh prod. group man. s of Milton McI. Burton-u-Trent

TENNENT Ruth Margaret Goodwin MA 1962
m Ndakala

TERRIS Rosalyn Elizabeth Marlin MA 1967
d of John M. T. MBChB(Edin) med pract and Edith H. D. Robertson secy, teacher; b Newtongrange 2.3.47
teacher Glasg: asst Woodside nurs s 1969–71, head Mile End nurs s 1971–72, head Ayr St nurs s 1972–73, asst Anderson St nurs s 1976–77, asst Kelso nurs s 1977–79
m(1) E Kilbride 3.8.68 Alfred C. Shedden MA 1966 *qv*; marr diss
(2) Glasg 17.8.79 Douglas D. Faulds quantity surv

TETHER John Gordon Gurney *BSc 1965
s of Cyril H. G. T. fin. journalist and Marjorie L. Gurney; b Hatfield 28.7.42
geol surv off.: Moroto Soroti Uganda 1967–73, Lusaka Zambia from 1974
m Aber 6.4.66 June E. Ballantyne teacher d of Samuel B. MA(Glas) Aber

TEWNION Alexander *BSc 1961 Dip Ed 1962
s of John T. master bldr and Alice G. Cran; b Auchnagatt 8.9.20
teacher sc Dollar acad 1962–65, prin biol from 1965
m Aber 21.9.51 Agnes D. Richards BSc 1944 *qv*

THAIN Alexander Buchan MB ChB 1959
s of James T. fisherman and Margaret Buchan; b Peterhead 25.2.35
DObstRCOG 1966 CIH(Dund) 1974
h o, sen h o psychiat Montrose 1959–61; trainee g p/hosp Inv 1961–63; regist dermat Inv 1963–64; sen h o obst Stirling 1964; g p Invergordon 1964–65; regist med Inv 1965–66; g p: Fort William 1966–71, Ardersier/Nairn from 1971
m Aber 28.2.64 Helen K. Simpson RGN d of John S. Inv

THAIN John Forrest *BSc 1961 PhD 1964
s of John F. T. metal turner and Margaret A. M. Moir envelope maker; b Aber 20.10.39
univ of E Ang Norwich: sen res assoc biophys 1964–67, lect biol from 1967
m Hemel Hempstead 22.10.66 Vivien M. Pratt BSc(Brist) teacher d of Charles E. P. Hemel Hempstead

THAIN Linda Mary *MA 1969
d of Harold B. T. civ serv and Alice McKimmie secy, admin asst; b Aber 5.7.47
teacher Aber: Engl Summerhill acad 1970–71, Powis acad 1971–72; part-time r e St Margaret's s for girls from 1973
m Wolviston 18.7.69 David Henderson police constable s of Dawson H. Methlick

THAIN Rita Frances MA 1970
d of Henry F. T. Aber c c worker (amenities dept) and Rosetta L. Black; b Alford 8.3.49
teacher Engl Dumfries h s 1971–72; exec off. Customs & Excise Aber 1972–74, Dun 1974–79
m Aber 9.8.73 Graham R. I. Milton MA 1974 careers off. s of John S. M. Aber

THAIN William MSc 1964 PhD 1967
ARGTC

THAKUR Vikram Chandra MSc 1967
BSc MSc(Panj I)

THINN Anne Buyers MA 1963
m Sinclair

THIRD David *BSc 1963
s of Hugh B. T. eng and Annie A. Whyte; b Peterhead 23.6.41
MSc(S'ton) 1972 C Eng MIEE 1976
teacher chem Ellon acad 1964–66; lect phys RAF Cosford Wolverhampton 1966–70; teacher Engl RAF Upwood Huntingdon 1970–71; lect electronic eng RAF coll Cranwell 1971–77; trg consult. M o D(TSS) from 1977
m Aber 7.8.64 Sandra E. T. Young teacher d of Adam H. Y. Aber

THIRD George Thomas BEd 1970 MEd 1972
s of Taylor M. T. hotelier/farm. and Annie Matthew; b St Fergus 30.4.45
teacher Scotstown s Aber 1972–73, Balgownie s 1973–74; educ psych: Aber 1974–76, city div Grampian reg from 1976
m Aber 2.8.68 Eileen M. Macleman teacher d of Alexander MacL.

THIRD Marion Jessica MA 1966

THIRD Robert Taylor *MA 1966
s of Taylor M. T. farm./publican and Annie Matthew; b St Fergus 27.7.43
publ man. Aberdeen Journals 1967–69; creative serv superv *North Eastern Evening Gazette* Middlesbrough 1969–73, man. Keyhead hotel St Fergus 1973–78
m Aberfeldy 23.10.71 Beryl Chadwick MA 1968 *qv*

THOM Alan Mackay *MA 1969 Dip Ed 1970

THOM Anne Shirley *BSc 1964
d of Robert J. T. MA 1934 *qv*; b W Cults Aber 2.3.41
VSO Malawi 1964–65; ICL Lond 1965–70 and from 1973

THOM Florence Margaret MA 1958

THOM Ian Alexander James MA 1965

THOM James Alistair MB ChB 1960
s of Neil T. bus. consult. and Susan H. Johnston; b Cargill 21.2.36
DTM & H 1965 MSc(Lond) 1973 DIH 1973
h o Aber, Glasg 1960–62; m o RN med serv 1962–78; sen lect environ mental health univ Sydney from 1978
m Aber 23.3.61 Agnes M. Smith polit ag d of Ogilvie M. S. Whitestripes Bridge of Don

THOM Mary Beatrice (Marie) *BSc 1966
d of George J. T. lorry driver and Mary Morrison; b Aber 6.7.44
PhD(Hull) 1970 Dip Clin Psych(Brit Psych Soc) 1977
res off. Kingswood approved s 1968–71, Oxon 1971–77; lect clin psych Royal Free hosp s of med Lond univ from 1977
m Aber 23.12.66 Derek W. Johnston MA 1966 *qv*

THOM Peter McGregor MB ChB 1970
s of Alexander M. T. BSc(eng)(Glas) and Jane S. Robertson; b India 30.6.43
h o Woodend hosp Aber, RACH 1970–71; vocational trg scheme g p Wessex reg hosp board Bournemouth, Poole 1971–74
m Aber 17.7.71 Margaret E. Peebles teacher d of David S. P. Aber

THOMANECK Jürgen Karl Albert *MEd 1970
b Stettin 12.6.41
DPhil(Kiel) 1969
lect Ger dept Aberd from 1969
m Aber 3.8.64 Guinevere Ronald MA 1968 *qv*

THOMAS David Hugh MSc 1967
BSc(Sheff)

THOMAS David Kashope BSc 1967
s of David A. T. govt printer Sierra Leone and Kezia A. Sawyerr; b Freetown Sierra Leone 5.2.36
M Assoc Clin Biochem 1968 Dip Clin Biochem(Sur) 1971 MSc(Sur) 1971 PhD(Ibad) 1978 MIBiol 1979
clin biochem govt of Sierra Leone, Connaught hosp Freetown 1967–78; lect clin biochem univ Ife Nigeria from 1978

THOMAS Elizabeth Mair Trefor *MA 1967
m Hope

THOMAS Oswald Augustus PhD 1966
BSc(agr)(Corn) MNS(Corn)

THOMAS Richard Howard *MA 1968
s of Alan T. publ/bookseller/off. man. and Linda Barnes secy; b Preston 24.9.44
asst man. mail order publ/retail gift store Preston 1968–70; asst edit. dictionaires Collins publ Glasg 1970–74, sen edit. 1974–78, publ man. from 1978
m Paisley 4.4.77 Mary S. Balderston BSc 1966 *qv*

THOMIS Helen Rosemary *MA 1966
m Macdonald

THOMPSON David Squire *BSc(eng) 1970
s of Squire T. garage prop. and Elsie Eden; b Sunderland 20.2.48
self-employed motor trader Sunderland from 1970
m New Silksworth 19.6.71 Karen M. Sanderson nurse d of William G. S. Vancouver

THOMPSON Derek MA 1959
s of Henry E. T. fruiterer/confectioner and Vida I. Garthwaite; b Hartlepool 17.6.37
Dip PE(Leeds)

teacher p e Middlesbrough 1960–62; Hartlepool: head of p e 1962–73, head of year from 1973
m Hartlepool 1960 Sylvia M. Robson d of Frederick R. Hartlepool

THOMPSON Diana Mary BSc 1970
d of George D. T. teacher and Sylvia F. Franklin teacher; b Sleaford 7.3.49
univ tech lung function ARI 1971–73; tech respir dept royal post grad med s Hammersmith Lond from 1974
m Dun 31.7.71 Ian R. Hunter MA 1972 supplies off. NHS Northwick Park hosp Harrow s of Jim H. Dun

THOMPSON Diana Ruth Brodie *MA 1960

THOMPSON Ethel Dorothy Barbara PhD 1965
d of Fred T. civ eng and Helen Bolton teacher; b Stretford 15.8.21
BA(Manc) 1946 Dip Soc St(Manc) 1947 AIMSW 1948 fell. Eugenic Soc 1967
sociologist: MRC obst med unit Aber 1951–65, MRC med soc unit from 1965; seconded MRC labs Gambia W Af 1961–64

THOMPSON Francis BEd 1969

THOMPSON Joseph Kell PhD 1968
s of William K. T. farm. and Elizabeth Milliken teacher; b Mallusk Co Antrim 2.7.29
BSc(Belf) 1950 BAgr(Belf) 1951 MS(Purdue univ Indiana) USA 1955
asst lect NOSCA Aber 1951–67; nutrit advis NOSCA/ recognised teacher Aberd from 1967
m Aber 22.7.60 Margaret R. Summers teacher d of John B. S. Cairnbulg

THOMPSON Margaret Mary *MA 1958
d of Alexander G. T. tea planter, sub-postmaster and Lizzie E. J. Davidson sub-postmistress; b Fordyce 13.4.37
teacher maths: Banff 1959–61, part-time St Peter's s Buckie 1965–66, Buckie h s from 1966
m Fordyce 12.7.61 Alexander Wilson farm. s of John W. Buckie

THOMPSON Mary Belle Elizabeth MA 1969
d of Gilbert T. T. tel eng and Elizabeth F. Bain; b Lerwick 21.1.47
teacher Engl Lasswade 1970–71; relief teacher Engl Grampian reg from 1972
m Lerwick 10.7.70 John E. Inglis civ eng s of George L. I. Aber

THOMPSON Patricia Mary MB ChB 1963
d of Charles H. T. PhD(Manc) archivist and Norah M. Cann headmistress; b Plymouth 3.10.38
h o: paediat, gen med Aber, rheumat Edin 1963–65; g p: Edin 1966–67, part-time Dumfries 1969–75, ptnrship g p from 1975
m Surbiton 27.8.64 John A. C. McFadden MA 1959 *qv*

THOMPSON William Gilbert *MA 1962
s of Gilbert S. T. merch seaman, PO linesman and Robertha A. Thomason nurse; b Edin 10.4.39
PhD(Strath) 1970
teacher Glasg 1963–66; asst lect econ hist Wigan tech coll 1969–70; lect hist Glasg coll of tech from 1971
m Aber 3.4.63 Noreen I. Butler MA 1962 *qv*

THOMPSON William John *MA 1965

THOMSEN John Kenneth *BSc(eng) 1968

THOMSON Alan James *BSc(agr) 1963 PhD 1966
s of Alexander T. dent. tech and Jane N. Adams; b Aber 3.3.40
scient off. plant breeding inst Cambridge from 1966
m Aber 27.7.65 Elizabeth A. Coutts BSc 1962 *qv*

THOMSON Allan McLean MB ChB 1957

THOMSON Angus William *BSc 1970 PhD 1975
s of Angus T. housing insp and Jessie Macdonald; b Inv 13.2.48
MSc(Birm) 1971
MRC res stud. Birm 1970–71; Aberd: SRC res stud. 1971–74, Marr Walker res fell. 1974–75, lect immunology from 1975; sub-warden Johnston Hall 1977

THOMSON Ann Kilpatrick MA 1969
d of John T. taxi driver and Ann D. Troup; b Glasg 27.10.47
tut. McLenan proj Kirklands Selsey 1971–73; teacher: St Luke's s Portsmouth 1972, Havant g s Hants 1972–74; head econ dept Havant Sixth form coll 1974
m Glasg 2.8.69 Trevor E. S. Jefcoate BSc(agr) 1968 *qv*

THOMSON Anne Macdonald Collie *BSc 1969
d of William T. sales rep and Georgina Collie cloth examiner; b Aber 7.2.47
teacher: Ruthrieston s Aber 1970–73, Ellon acad from 1973
m Aber 10.8.72 Clifford Brown med lab tech s of James B. Aber

THOMSON Austin Mathers LLB 1966
s of Matthew O. T. dent. surg and Ann S. Mathers; b Ellon 20.9.45
Edin: law app Shepherd & Wedderburn WS 1966–68, leg. asst Brodies WS 1968–71; ptnr A. C. White, Silver, Young & Cosh solic Ayr from 1971
m Edin 6.10.69 Felicity A. Vaughan d of Mansel C. M. V. RAF Ger

THOMSON Barbara Ann MA 1969
d of John T. and Veronica Ironside admin asst Aberd; b Haslemere 26.6.48
teacher: Sunnybank p s Aber 1970–72, Beechwood s Aber 1972–75, Inverurie acad 1975–77
m Aber 29.7.72 Colin D. Adamson MA 1973 teacher, roustabout s of David L. A. Aber

THOMSON Christina Philip Gillanders MA 1968
d of James T. RN and Elizabeth S. Gillanders tailoress; b Aber 22.4.29
BEM
teacher Torry acad Aber 1969–72, asst prin geog from 1972

THOMSON Colin Barron BSc(eng) 1964

THOMSON David Bryan BSc(agr) 1962

THOMSON David Sinclair *MA 1965
s of David S. T. merch seaman and Wilhelmina Cooper; b Aber 13.3.43
Dip Ed(Makerere) 1966
teacher: Manjasi h s Tororo Uganda 1966–68, Engl Birm 1968–74, St George's j s Birm from 1974

THOMSON Dereck *MA 1962 Dip Ed 1963

THOMSON Diane Nicolson MA 1964
d of John T. fisherman and Margaret I. Ritchie; b Whitehills 9.6.43
Dip Soc St(Edin) 1965

fam casework Sheffield 1965–67; Edin: ch care off. 1967–68, play group superv 1968–70
m Whitehills 30.3.68 Paul W. Williams MA(Edin) lect s of Peter D. W. Salt River, Cape, S Af

THOMSON Donald Maclean MB ChB 1968
s of Donald T. MA 1929 *qv*; b Oban 1.6.43
g p: Aber 1968–70, Ontario from 1970
m Aber 8.6.66 Mary M. Shepherd secy d of John S. Alford

THOMSON Dorothy Anne MA 1969
d of Robert P. T. eng and Millicent F. Mayers; b Aber 5.11.48
teacher Musselburgh g s 1970–71
m Aber 19.9.69 Ivor J. A. Moir CA s of Joseph M. Aber

THOMSON Douglas MA 1963
s of George C. T. lab and Helen Baxter fishworker; b Aber 6.4.29
teacher: Powis acad Aber 1964–67, prin hist Old Aber s s 1967–74, also dep head 1970–74; dep head Summerhill acad Aber from 1974
m Aber 2.4.54 Mary A. Dempster d of George D. Aber

THOMSON Douglas Gavin MB ChB 1964

THOMSON Douglas King BSc 1967
s of William J. T. crofter, postman, lorry driver and Henrietta M. McBeath soc work care asst; b 12.10.45
teacher maths: Peterhead acad 1968–74, also housemaster Banff acad from 1975

THOMSON Elizabeth MA 1970
d of James T. master butcher and Catherine B. Henderson teacher; b Longside 28.2.36
m Aber 8.8.60 George R. Duguid BSc 1966 *qv*

THOMSON Elizabeth May MA 1963
d of Douglas T. shop man./ch off. and Isabella C. Grant; b Insch 24.5.42
teacher: maths Aber h s for girls 1964–66, part-time maths/sc Aber tech coll from 1966
m Aber 2.10.63 James S. Melvin BSc 1966 *qv*

THOMSON Elizabeth Mowat MA 1966 Dip Ed 1967
d of William R. G. T. grocer and Robina S. Mowat nurse auxil; b Kirkwall 22.6.45
teacher Skene 1967–71
m Kirkwall 8.8.68 Alasdair H. McVicar BSc 1967 *qv*

THOMSON Geoffrey Riddell MA 1969
s of Edward R. T. MA 1938 *qv*; b Kintore 21.7.48
Dip Cartog(Glas) 1970
cartogr geog dept univ of Winnipeg from 1970
m Winnipeg 26.10.74 Erlinda A. Elefante BSc(Manila) d of Miguel E. Manila

THOMSON Gordon Matthew LLB 1969
s of Matthew O. T. LDS(Glas) dent. surg and Ann S. Mathers; b Girvan 22.1.48
law app Edin 1969–71; Glasg: leg. asst, solic 1972–78, ptnr MacRobert Son & Hutchison from 1978
m Durh 26.4.73 Virginia A. Hood MA 1970 *qv*

THOMSON Helen Laing MB ChB 1956
b Uddingston 21.5.32
DA(Lond) 1958 FFARCS 1964
sen h o anaest Aber 1957–59; regist anaest Liv 1959–66; clin asst anaest Carlisle from 1968
m Aber 5.12.64 Brian J. Spencer BA(Dub) med pract

THOMSON Iain Urquhart MA 1967 BD 1970
s of Charles M. T. ironmonger, bus. rep and Ann L. Urquhart; b Dun 13.12.45
C of S min: Ayr 1970–72, par ch Skene from 1972
m(1) Inv 11.8.72 Shona G. Kinnon MB ChB 1973 d of John K. Inv; wife *d* 15.10.73
(2) Aber 30.7.75 Christine S. Freeland secy d of Patrick F. Aber

THOMSON Ian *BSc 1964

THOMSON Ian Sim MA 1969
s of John M. T. postman and Annie Sim; b Aber 20.7.44
teacher Aber from 1970
m Aber 5.7.73 Jennifer A. Yule teacher p e d of Davie Y. Aber

THOMSON Irene Edna *MA 1965
d of Michael T. fish merch and Edna M. Kinloch; b Aber 7.11.41
asst edit. Thos Nelson publ Lond 1965–66; edit. William Collins publ Glasg 1966; teacher geog Keith g s 1968–70; lect geog Aber coll of comm 1970–79
m Lond 9.8.75 Peter J. Bates tech s of John H. B. Lond

THOMSON Jacqueline Margaret MA 1967 Dip Ed 1968
d of James H. T. lt RSF, insp Glasg city police and Jane I. Scott MA(Glas) soc worker, bookshop asst; b Glasg 9.5.46
teacher Engl/geog: Queen Anne h s Dunfermline 1968–71, Garnock acad Kilbirnie 1971–72; temp Kilbirnie from 1973
m Glasg 1.8.68 David M. Taylor MA 1967 *qv*

THOMSON James Alan *MA 1967

THOMSON Janette Davis MA 1967
d of Robert D. T. baker, stillman and Phyllis E. C. Watt canteen asst, newsp reporter; b Grantown-on-Spey 4.6.46
RSA Dip TEFL 1979
teacher Engl: Glasg 1968–74, asst prin Engl Glasg 1974–75; peripatetic teacher immigrant pupils Dunbartonsh from 1978
m Grantown-on-Spey 16.8.69 Peter J. Robertson packag tech, postman s of Peter R. Clydebank

THOMSON Jean Ann BSc 1970
d of Allan S. T. watchmaker/instrum repairer and Jane Simpson; b Torphins 15.7.49
civ serv Lond from 1971

THOMSON John *MA 1968
s of John T. fisherman and Isobel M. Ritchie lib; b Whitehills 28.1.46
area salesman Procter & Gamble E Anglia from 1974
m Belfast 25.10.71 Mary B. Hopkirk teacher d of Frederick J. H. Belfast

THOMSON John Campbell BSc 1958 *1959
s of John C. T. fisherman and Elsie Farquhar; b Lossiemouth 15.9.37
MSc(Wales) 1974
teacher Elgin acad 1960–62; RN instr/meteorol and oceanographic duties Portsmouth, Arbroath, Singapore, Northwood, Plymouth, Lossiemouth, Oslo, Antarctica, Helston 1962–77; gen man. Ocean Routes (UK) Aber from 1977
m Arbroath 13.4.63 Anne H. Farmer teacher d of George W. F. Southampton

THOMSON John Edward Fraser LLB 1965
s of John E. T. wholesale stationer, hotel prop. and Helen S. Johnston prop.; b Aber 5.4.44
Aber: law app 1966–68, leg. asst 1969–70, ptnr Stronachs advoc Aber from 1970
m Aber 16.8.67 Patricia I. Johnston secy d of George J. Aber

THOMSON John McEwan *MA 1967

THOMSON Kenneth James *MA 1967
s of Angus M. T. MB ChB(Glas) med res scient and Alice A. C. Lyon MA 1936 *qv*; b Aber 30.9.45
MSc(Lond) DIC(Lond) 1968 MS(Iowa) 1972
stud.: Imp coll Lond 1967–68, Edin 1968–69; res assoc dept agr econ N'cle 1970–71; res Iowa state univ 1971–72; lect agr econ N'cle from 1972

THOMSON Lorna Kathleen MA 1962
m Paterson

THOMSON Mary Helen MA 1967
d of John T. farm. and Lizzie H. Robbie MA 1931 *qv*; b Torphins 24.5.43
teacher: Kirkhill p s Aber 1968–69, Middlefield p s Aber 1969–70, supply Kincardine/Deeside 1977–79, Mill o' Forest p s Stonehaven from 1979
m Aber 8.2.68 Kenneth G. Stuart sales exec s of John S. Inverurie

THOMSON Michael John Duthie *MA 1968
s of Henry T. civ serv and Jean Duthie; b Fraserburgh 29.10.46
MSc(Dund) 1973
oper res: British Steel Corp Corby 1970–73, United Biscuits Liv 1973–78; stock man. United Biscuits Lond from 1978
m Liv 18.8.75 Joanna C. Deane clerk d of Antony D. Liv

THOMSON Nichol Gilbert *MA 1969

THOMSON Robert Nairn *BSc(eng) 1958

THOMSON Rosemary Doreen *MA 1969
d of David T. MA(Glas) schoolmaster and Doreen S. Rose secy; b Johnstone 11.4.47
PhD(Cantab) 1975
res stud. Newham coll Cambridge 1969–73; lect Engl: Birm 1973–74, univ coll Lond from 1974
m Cambridge 7.8.71 Gerard Ashton BA(Cantab) univ lect s of Gerard A. Hindley Green Wigan

THOMSON Sarah MA 1967

THOMSON Stella Helen Campbell *MA 1961
m Donaldson

THOMSON William Farquhar *BSc 1957 Dip Ed 1958
s of John C. T. and Elsie Farquhar; b Lossiemouth 17.10.35
teacher: Nairn acad 1958–62, Elgin acad from 1962
m Aber 4.4.61 Elizabeth H. Donald d of William D. Aber

THORAT Padmakar Laxman MSc 1967 PhD 1969
MSc(Agra)

THORBURN Ailsa Catriona *MA 1967
d of Adam T. MA(Edin) univ lect and Mary M. Christie sculptress; b Haddington 8.5.43
lang asst Lycee d'Anthony Paris 1967–68; teacher: Fr St Frideswides s Didcot 1969–70, Fr/Ger Falkirk h s 1970–71, Fr/Ger St Modan's h s Stirling 1971–75
m Aber 22.8.67 Alastair B. Duncan MA 1966 *qv*

THORBURN Dorothy Margaret MA 1963
d of William T. banker and Isabella K. Forsyth; b Turriff 21.3.40
teacher: Glasg 1965–68; teacher Engl Arabic s Abu Dhabi
m Aber 26.7.63 Costas C. Constantinides MB ChB 1956 *qv*

THORBURN Richard Thomas MA 1967 LLB 1969
s of David R. T. MA(Glas) teacher and Mary G. Sutherland; b Aber 12.8.47
law app Edin 1969–72; stud. D.A.A.D. course—Ger law Düsseldorf and Freiburg W Ger 1972–73; barrister at Middle Temple Lond 1973–76; solic: Edin 1976–77; ptnr McGoogan Thorburn & Co solic Coatbridge

THORES Orison Alistair MB ChB 1960

THORNTON David Conrad *BSc 1970 MSc 1972
s of Frank W. A. T. ladies'/gentlemen's outfitter and Jane R. Webster ladies' outfitter; b Arbroath 1.1.48
Aberd: res stud. nat phil 1970–73, res asst from 1973

THORNTON Douglas *MA 1970
s of Douglas S. T. and Mary L. McWilliam; b Fraserburgh 11.9.47
Dip LD(N'cle) 1972
landscape arch. Tyne and Wear c c plan. dept N'cle-u-Tyne from 1974
m Lily N. Watt

THORNTON Patricia Anne *MA 1970 PhD 1980
d of Edwin P. G. T. man. dir BICC (cables div) and Joyce I. Partridge; b Manc 15.1.48
res fell. inst of soc/econ res St John's Newfoundland Canada 1970–73; res Aberd from 1973

THORNTON Roger Vincent BSc(for) 1965
s of James W. T. master butcher and Ethel Clarkson; b Leeds 26.4.44
prod. man. Aber 1965–69; timber buyer Bowaters Cheshire 1969–72; purchasing dir STP Cowie 1972–77; man. Scotland Taylor Maxwell Timber from 1977
m Aber 27.7.67 Norma Reid teacher d of George R. Macduff

THORP Carole Jean Strathdee MA 1968
d of Leonard M. T. comp dir and Gertrude K. M. Strathdee; b Aber 10.2.47
Lond: secy: to dir Weidenfeld & Nicholson publ 1969–70, Gordon Harbord theatr and lit. ag 1970–71; Ottershaw s Chertsey from 1971
m Aber 12.6.71 Philip G. Hogarth-Gaute insur loss adjuster s of Joseph H. H. G. Woking

THORPE Hugh Rankin PhD 1963
s of Fred T. market gardener and Isobel J. McCaw deaconess; b Otaki NZ 30.9.36
ME BSc(Canterubry NZ) 1960
NZ: asst eng MWD Wellington 1964–65, eng i/c MWD central labs. Lower Hutt 1965–69; Colombo plan. advis univ of Khon Kaen Thailand 1970–72; sen eng MWD water/soil div Wellington 1973–77; scient MWD water/soil div Christchurch from 1978
m Lauriston Canterbury NZ 19.12.59 Rhona M. Scarth BA(Canterbury NZ) teacher d of George W. S. Lauriston and Mary A. Anderson MA 1926 *qv*

THORPE William BSc(agr) 1968 *1969
s of Sidney W. T. farm. and Joan M. Feary; b Wisbech

4.3.46
VSO with Oxfam, rural dev team Chizera Zambia 1969–70; res stud. anim breeding res organis Edin from 1970

THORSTEINSSON Vilhjálmur BSc 1970
s of Thorsteinn Loftsson and Vilhelmina Tymstra BSc(Amster); b Iceland 9.9.43
teacher Reykjavik Iceland 1970–74; scient off. Icelandic marine lab. Húsavik N Iceland from 1974
m Reykjavik 8.3.74 Stefania Juliusdottir BA(Iceland) teacher d of Július Júliusson Kópavogi Iceland

THOW John BSc(eng) 1957

TIETJEN Rodney Stephen MA 1968
s of Albert T. draughtsman and Brenda Schofield; b St Helens 6.5.46
tech selection off. Lond 1968–69; teacher Whiston 1969–70, prin Engl from 1970
m Lond 31.3.69 Stella M. Thompson teacher d of Walter T. St Helens

TIKU Moti Lal PhD 1964
s of Mahishwar N. T. eng and Tarawati Pandit; b Kashmir India 10.1.36
BA(Kashmir) 1955 MA(Panj) 1957 MA(Patna) 1960
lect applied statist R'dg 1964–68; Canada: assoc prof maths Guelph univ 1968–69, assoc prof statist McM univ 1969–74, prof statist McM from 1974
m Kashmir 17.1.57 Govri Dhar BA(Kashmir)

TIMMIS Roger *BSc(for) 1966
s of William T. maintenance mech and Barbara Davies shorthand typist; b Altrincham 21.7.44
PhD(Br Col) 1973
VSO asst conserv for. N Nigeria Lokoja 1967–68; grad stud. B.C. Vancouver 1968–72; post doct fell. B.C. for. serv res div Victoria Canada 1973–74; for. regeneration physiol Weyerhaeuser Comp Centralia Washington state USA from 1974

TIMMONS James BSc 1968
s of Andrew T. coal miner and Helen O'Hear; b Chapelhall 14.8.26
MIBiol 1971
teacher: Lanarksh 1969–71, prin biol Coatbridge from 1971
m Glasg 27.8.55 Janet Shields teacher d of Henry S. Glasg

TIMOTHY Robin Reginald Warren *BSc 1969
s of George A. T. RAF off., schoolmaster and Daisy K. Frary; b Hunstanton 5.3.47
computer syst eng IBM: Lond 1969–70, Birm 1970–73; computer salesman IBM Birm from 1974

TIMPERLEY David John MA 1964
s of Robert T. and Edith E. H. Dickinson; b Burnley 19.1.42
articled clerk Blackburn 1964–67; acct Oswaldtwistle from 1967
m Whalley 9.5.71 Patricia M. Nutter secy d of Kenneth N. Whalley

TINCH Robert Templeton *BSc 1968 MSc 1970

TINCH William Robson BSc(eng) 1965 MSc 1968 PhD 1973
s of William T. comp chmn, chartered surv and Martha Templeton; b Barrhead 4.10.42
Aberd: asst lect 1968–69, lect eng 1969–72; contr man. A. Hall & Sons (Bldrs) Edin 1972–77; prod. man. J. Fyfe Aber 1977–78; man. dir Autospeed Cars Aber from 1979
m Dalkeith 10.5.80 Carol J. Reid d of James R. Dalkeith

TINKLIN Richard PhD 1966
s of Ernest S. G. T. clerk and Phyllis S. Parry; b Bristol 19.9.40
BSc(Brist) 1963
asst lect agr botany Wye coll univ Lond 1966–68; lect biol Norwich city coll 1969–71; sen lect microbiol Hull coll of tech 1972–76, sen lect biol Hull coll of higher ed from 1976
m Wye 31.8.67 Irene G. Cozens BSc(Lond) d of William J. C. BSc(Edin) Watford

TINSTON David James *BSc 1969
s of Sydney J. T. progress chaser and Margaret H. Jardine; b Stockport 14.4.44
respiratory physiol central toxicology labs (ICI) Macclesfield from 1970

TINTO James Ferguson *MA 1962
s of James F. T. MA(Glas) univ lect and Isabella Calder; b Carluke 4.12.15
teacher Engl: Aber acad 1963–68, Rubislaw acad (AGS) 1968–73, asst prin Engl from 1973
m Aber 21.5.53 Ethel J. J. Gerrie soc worker d of George D. G. Aber

TISDALL Jeremy Peter *BSc(eng) 1963

TITTENSOR Andrew Malcolm *BSc 1966
b Wolverhampton 31.4.44
PhD(Edin) 1970
sen scient off. min of agr Worplesdon from 1970
m Edin 4.9.68 Ruth M. White MA(Oxon) free-lance ecologist

TOCHER Alison Margaret MA 1961

TOCHER Frances Mary *MA 1969
m Bell

TOCHER Kathleen Anne MB ChB 1967
d of Wilfred I. M. T. MA 1945 *qv*; b Aber 24.4.43
LMCC 1969
Canada: rotating intern Saskatoon 1967–68; private pract Port Coquitlam 1968–75; asst m o Vancouver health dept from 1976
m New Westminster 4.10.69 David G. W. Carter commun tech s of Francis B. C. Surrey Canada

TOD Anne Stuart MA 1969
d of Alexander A. T. pharm and Mary-Jane Stuart nurse; b Fyvie 3.6.48
AIL(Lond)
teacher Fr: Craigroyston s Edin 1970–72, Whitney inst Smith's Bermuda 1972–75
m Roberts

TODD James Martin PhD 1968
s of James T. LDS(Leeds) dent. surg and Elsie Hey teacher; b Kingston-u-Hull 24.6.33
LRCP(Lond) 1958 MRCS 1958 DPM(Leeds) 1963 MRCPsych
h o, sen h o: Leeds, Lancaster 1958–61; regist psychiat Hull 1961–63; sen regist psychiat Ross clin Aber/clin tut. ment health Aberd 1963–66; dep phys, supt, consult. psychiat Dingleton hosp Melrose 1966–67, dir day center Soundview/Throgs Neck ment health center/clin asst prof Albert Einstein coll of med, consult. psychiat Bronx State hosp NY USA 1968–69; staff psychiat/med dir Rutland ment health serv Rutland Vermont USA 1969–71;

private pract psychiat Rutland 1972–74; staff psychiat Brattleboro Retreat Vermont from 1974/clin asst prof psychiat univ of Vermont Burlington USA 1969–75; asst prof psychiat Dartmouth med s Hanover NH USA from 1975
m Leeds 30.11.56 June A. Kirkcaldy nurse d of Donald K. Bradford

TODD Ronald MA 1965

TOMASSON Thorsteinn *BSc(agr) 1970
s of Thomas Tryggvason Phil lic(Uppsala) geol and Kerstin Jancke cashier; b Uppsala Sweden 17.7.45
res off. agr inst Iceland 1970; plant-breeding stud. Uppsala univ from 1974
m Reykjavik 6.7.68 Sophie I. L. Kofoed-Hansen BSc (Boston) teacher of deaf d of Agnar K-H. Reykjavik

TOMKINS Richard George William BSc(agr) 1968
s of Charles R. T. farm./seed merch and Constance A. Dewis; b Northampton 28.11.46
Dip Farm Bus. Ad(Wye) 1972
farm man. Rutland 1969–71; farm man., farm. Northants from 1972
m Kettering 11.7.75 Penelope J. Bilson BSc(Leic) prob off., teacher d of W. Antony R. B. Kettering

TOMLINSON Christopher Malcolm BSc(eng) 1968
s of Norman T. machine tool merch and Joan E. Taylor; b Manc 4.1.47
site eng civ eng contr: Birm, Warrington 1968–72, Lond 1972–73; machine tool merch Manc from 1973
m Ollerton Knutsford 26.10.74 Janet A. Stirling teacher d of Alexander F. S. Ollerton

TOMLINSON Sheila Mary BSc(agr) 1966
d of Henry T. bank man. and Wyn Milne ptnr/asst stock and share broker; b Rochdale 29.5.44
sen res asst Unilever Bedford from 1962
m Chadderton 11.5.68 Tom Irvine, Udny

TOMORY Jillian Mary *MA 1970
d of Kenneth A. M. T. MB ChB(Edin) RAMC and Evelyn F. McGuinness teacher; b Dublin 6.2.48
Dip Lib(UCW) 1971 ALA 1974
Liverpool: secy/p a 1972, asst lib 1972–75; branch lib Wirral 1975–77
m Edin 4.9.71 Michael J. R. Mitchell MA 1970 *qv*

TOOLAN Paul MA 1965

TORRIE Stephen Milne *BSc 1961 Dip Ed 1962

TOSH Agnes MA 1961
d of John T. civ serv and Constance Stevenson; b Aber 11.3.40
teacher Kaimhill s s Aber 1962; lektor Engl Folkuniversitet Maricstad, Ludköping Sweden 1962–64; TEFL Bexhill 1964–70; teacher: hist Blackfen s for girls Sidcup 1970–73, Engl/hist Lyndon s Solihull from 1974
m Aber –.12.64 Cornelis M. Groeneveld tech eng s of Cornelis M. G. Amsterdam

TOSH Victor Lamont MB ChB 1958
s of William A. T. salesman and Jessie Lamont; b Bankhead 1.12.32
DObstRCOG 1961
h o, sen h o: Woodend hosp, Ballochmyle hosp, Forth Park mat. hosp Kirkcaldy 1959–60; RAMC: sen h o Princess Louise Margaret hosp Aldershot 1960–61, gen duties m o Brit milit hosp Kingston Jamaica 1961–62, BAOR Hohue W Ger 1962–63; g p Fraserburgh from 1963
m Aber 19.7.58 Eva M. Smith teacher d of Alfred F. S. Aber

TOUCH Peter Gerald *BSc 1967
s of Arthur G. T. CMG MA(Oxon) phys/civ serv, chief scient min of supply, M o D, FO and Phyllis Wallbank MA(Oxon) teacher; b Washington DC, USA 21.2.44
Beecham labs Brockham Park: dev chem 1967–68, pharm regist off. 1968–70, head of regulatory affairs unit from 1970
m Dorking 2.8.69 Frances A. Weatherhead teacher d of Christopher S. W. BA(Cantab) Dorking

TOUGH Alexander Henry Furneaux *MA 1962

TOUGH Elizabeth Agnes MA 1970 Dip Ed 1971
d of Alexander T. works foreman and Elsie M. Furneaux; b Aber 9.7.49
teacher Engl Kincorth acad from 1971
m Aber 24.7.70 Colin R. Russell policeman s of Andrew M. R. MA(Glas) Aber

TOUGH Harry Gordon MB ChB 1956

TOUGH John Richard BSc 1968
s of Robert J. S. T. distillery man. and May G. Munro; b Knockando 22.11.47
SSEB Glasg: trainee computer progr, progr, sen progr, sen analyst progr from 1968
m Turriff 24.4.70 Marian J. Connon MPS hosp pharm d of Alexander W. C. Turriff

TOUGH Laurence Michael *LLB 1970
s of Alfred T. teacher and Margaret Milne; b Aber 10.7.47
law app Stewart & Murray advoc Aber 1970–72, solic from 1972
m Edin 30.3.74 Sandra E. C. Shaw d of Norman M. S. Edin

TOUGH Michael Cameron *BSc(eng) 1970
s of George T. distillery worker and Edith M. Cameron; b Dufftown 31.7.48
asst civ eng: Glasg 1970–72, Helensburgh 1972–73; resid eng: Craignure Mull 1973, Stromness 1973–75, Peterhead power stat site from 1975

TOUGH Ronald Brebner MA 1957

TOUGH Sheila Violet *MA 1961 Dip Ed 1962
b Clatt 26.6.38
teacher Greenhall h s Midlothian from 1969

TOWELL Richard John *MA 1969

TOWERS George Alexander MA 1969
s of William J. T. instrum mech and Violet Ward; b Dunfermline 11.3.46
budget accts man. Glasg 1970–71; prin teacher geog Kelvinside acad Glasg from 1972
m Bearsden 21.8.71 Moira E. Connell med secy d of Stewart J. C. Dunoon

TOWNS Alan Thomas LLB 1969
s of Thomas C. T. off. man. and Helen McPherson; b Aber 8.3.49
law app John & W. G. Craigen advoc in Aber 1969–71; leg. asst: John & W. G. Craigen 1971–73, corp of city of Aber 1973–75, prin leg. asst city of Aber dist council from 1975

TOWNSEND Alan Brian *MA 1968

TOWNSEND Helen McGregor MA 1967

TOWNSON John Michael PhD 1967
s of Allan T. cashier and Edith M. Hird teacher; b Silsden 19.7.36
BSc(eng)(Lond) 1957 Assoc City & Guilds Inst 1957 MICE 1961
lect Aberd 1962–68; prin lect Teesside polytech 1968–70; sen lect Strath from 1970
m Helensburgh 28.7.62 Judith M. Peel teacher home econ d of Robert A. P. Helensburgh

TOWNSON Lorna Mary Stephen *MA 1969
d of Edward B. T. army off., insur ag and Amelia J. McLean secy; b Crieff 21.1.47
teacher Old Aber s s 1970–71; freelance work with Times Ed Supp, BBC and ante-natal teacher trg with National Childbirth Trust 1971–73; asst head Engl dept Musselburgh g s from 1973
m Aber 30.7.69 James A. T. Dyer MB ChB 1970 *qv*

TOWSE John Beckwith MSc 1970
s of David B. T. comp dir and Margaret B. Watson teacher; b Leighton Buzzard 20.5.44
BSc(Lond) 1969 GRIC 1969
post grad res: Aberd 1970–72, Brittany 1972–73; marketing radio chem centre 1973–74; marketing (export) High Wycombe from 1974

TOYE Michael Ian Andrew BSc(eng) 1963

TOYER Elizabeth Anne MA 1965 Dip Ed 1966
d of Harvey C. A. T. papermaker and Doreen Skinner; b Worksop 27.12.43
teacher: prin hist/Engl Mintlaw j s s 1966–67, hist Bagshot s mod s 1967–68, Engl the Convent Banjul The Gambia 1968–69, Engl Chilanga s Zambia 1971–73, Amer s Dacca Bangladesh from 1977
m Sunderland 16.8.67 Paul S. Hindmarsh BSc(agr) 1967 *qv*

TOZER Ralph Arthur MB ChB 1958
BA(Brist)

TRAIL Marjorie Webster *MA 1970

TRAILL Alister Barron *BSc 1970

TRAILL Carol Irene MA 1970
d of Francis P. M. T. shopkeeper and Edith E. M. Daws civ serv; b Helmsdale 29.9.49
teacher: Fr/Ger Invergordon 1972–73, Fr Golspie 1973–76; TEFL St Gym Wermelskirchen Ger 1976–78; teacher Fr/Ger Galashiels 1978–79, Lossiemouth from 1979

TRANTOR Moira Rosalind MB ChB 1970
m Milne

TREDINNICK Beatrice Anne *MA 1966
m Pollard

TREVELYAN John Francis BSc(for) 1958
s of Charles W. T. MA(Oxon) teacher and Maud D. Dixey; b Wokingham 5.2.34
NZ: for. Tokoroa 1959–64, teacher Te Puke 1964–76, orchardist Te Puke from 1976
m Weston-super-Mare 1.11.58 Elizabeth M. Brockenshaw BSc(Brist) microbiol d of Harvey B. Weston-super-Mare

TREVENA Iain Christopher *BSc 1966 PhD 1970

TRICKER Edward Forbes MA 1967 MEd 1972
s of Edgar H. T. naval off. RN, hotel prop. and Helen Forbes waitress, hotel prop.; b Gillingham 4.10.37
HNC(naval arch.) 1959
ship's draughtsman 1953–59, 1961–64; des draughtsman Ford Motor Co 1959–61; teacher maths AGS 1968–72; prin guid Powis acad Aber 1972–79; asst head Ellon acad from 1979
m Aber 19.3.60 Robina Annand tracer d of Robert A. Aber

TRIGGS Peter Ronald *MA 1969

TROUP Annette *BSc 1962
d of Ronald C. T. market gardener and Mary Farquhar cook; b Ellon 26.9.39
teacher Summerhill s s Aber 1963–66; headmistress Kampala Uganda 1967
m Belhelvie 6.4.63 Colin P. Neave CA s of David J. N. Aber

TROUP Norma MA 1964
d 19.4.68

TROUP Richard Forbes LLB 1968
s of Arthur D. T. MA 1925 *qv*; b Peterhead 16.9.47
Edin: law app 1968–70, solic from 1970
m Edin 10.2.73 Sandra E. Sinclair secy d of Alastair S. Edin
d Edin 3.7.75

TRUSLER Gillian Anne *MA 1970
d of Donald C. T. solic's clerk and Ann L. Argo sewing machinist; b Lond 31.7.48
teacher mus: Ruthrieston s s Aber 1971–73, Harlaw acad Aber 1973–76, AGS from 1976

TUACH Ann Ishbel MA 1967 Dip Ed 1968
d of Kenneth D. T. farm worker/bldg lab and Jessie Finlayson; b Fearn 13.7.46
teacher: Falkirk 1968–70, Lond 1970–71, Leeds 1971–72, Wetherby from 1972
m Aber 28.8.71 Roger J. K. Tibbett sales ag s of James D. K. T.

TUACH Helen *MA 1965
d of Kenneth D. T. farm worker/bldg lab and Jessie Finlayson; b Fearn 20.6.43
teacher W-central Scot. 1966–71; lect infant work Callendar Park coll of educ Falkirk 1971–72
m Aber 4.9.65 William H. Fraser MA 1963 *qv*

TUACH Nan BSc 1965
d of James A. T. fencer and Hannah Mackenzie; b Muir of Ord 21.3.44
teacher sc: Duddeston Manor bilat. s Birm 1966–69, Kaikorai Valley h s Dunedin NZ 1971–72
m Muir of Ord 19.8.66 James H. K. Inkson MA 1963 *qv*

TUCKLEY Catharine Mary MB ChB 1962
d of Laurence T. clerk in holy orders and Mary A. Hill; b Stafford 19.6.33
h o: ARI, Woodend hosp Aber, city hosp Derby 1962–64; g p Derby from 1964

TULEY Graham *BSc(for) 1970
m 1969 Margot Bell MA 1970 *qv*

TULLETT Adam MB ChB 1956

TULLO Alan William *BSc 1970
s of William S. T. shopkeeper and Janet E. Milne

SRN; b Elgin 7.2.48
PhD(Stir) 1974
lect maths Edin 1973–74; oper res scient Brit Steel (Teesside) from 1974

TULLOCH Andrew Thomas Hawick BSc(eng) 1956
s of John T. bus. man and Elizabeth M. Hawick teacher; b Shetland 11.1.36
jun eng Sir Robert McAlpine & Sons Kent 1956–58; county surv dept Zetland c c Shetland 1958–63; dir knitwear manuf comp Shetland from 1963
m Bedford –.9.60 Wilhelmina V. Scott d of John S. Lerwick

TULLOCH Ian BSc(eng) 1964

TULLOCH John William *MA 1958

TULLOCH Marian Isabella BSc 1961 PhD 1966
d of Margaret I. T. hosp cook; b North Ronaldsay 8.5.40
Aberd med s: res asst med phys 1961–67, res fell. therap 1967–74
m Aber 17.5.68 John K. Chesters BA(Cantab) biochem s of John H. C. BSc(Sheff) Sheffield

TULLOCH Ragna MA 1970
d of Robert G. T. BSc 1941 *qv*; b Elgin 8.5.49
teacher maths/sc: Stornoway 1971–72, Fochabers 1973, Stornoway 1973–74, Elgin 1974–75, São Paulo Brazil 1975–77, Bexley 1977–78; woman police constable Lond from 1978

TUNNARD Christopher Timothy LLB 1970
s of Thomas N. T. MA(Oxon) teacher/organist, HMIS and Noreen M. Petherick; b Kidlington 3.8.48
solic's articled clerk/law stud. Birm 1971–74; asst solic: Birm 1975–76, Tadcaster from 1976

TÜRKER Hilmi MSc 1969 PhD 1971
BSc(Ankara)

TURNBULL Andrew Robert *MA 1967 PhD 1973

TURNBULL David Alexander LLB 1959
BA(Oxon)

TURNBULL Ian William BSc 1969
s of William S. T. man. dir and Nora S. Henderson; b Glasg 5.8.48
CA 1974
app CA Glasg 1969–74; CA Arthur Young McClelland Moores 1974–77; dir/comp secy Grays of Fetterangus (1972) from 1977

TURNER Charles Cason PhD 1956
AB(Davidson Coll) BD(Union Theol Sem Va)

TURNER George Alexander MA 1963

TURNER Gordon Hepburn MA 1958
d of Percy J. T. rly off. and Evelyn Hepburn; b Lincoln 13.9.36
MEd(Manc) 1976
teacher Fr/Ger: Gordon s Huntly 1959–61, Aber coll of comm 1962–67; prin Fr Aber coll of comm from 1967
m Aber 5.8.61 Barbara A. Brebner MA 1957 *qv*

TURNER Grace Constance MB ChB 1958 cMD 1963
d of Edward T. civ serv and Christina A. Paterson; b Aber 22.8.34
h o RACH 1958–59; g p trainee Auchinblae 1959–60; lect bact Aberd 1960–63; regist bact city hosp Aber 1963–64; part-time lect bact Aberd 1971–72; part-time g p Bucksburn from 1978
m Aber 4.8.62 Robert A. Chalmers DSc 1968 *qv*

TURNER Janet Lesley MA 1968 Dip Ed 1969
d of Cyril G. T. publ consult. and Katharine S. Elder MA 1930 *qv*; b Colchester 14.9.46
teacher Fr/Ger: Edin 1969–71, Alva 1971–74
m Dedham 24.7.71 Thomas G. Harvie BSc(eng) 1970 *qv*

TURNER Juliet Wilson MA 1962
d of Harry E. T. BSc(Manc) teacher, C of S min and Jean Wilson; b Dumfries 5.7.40
Dip Theol(Lond) 1967 Dip Bible-training Inst Glasg 1967
teacher Engl/hist: Cumnock acad 1963–67, Hampton Park s S'ton 1967–68; part-time teacher needlework St Judes s Islington Lond 1974–76
m Peebles 10.8.68 Brian K. Mann teacher s of Vernal K. M. Loughborough

TURNER Paul Barrie BSc(for) 1968
s of Harold F. T. gardener and Doris Irvin bookkeeper; b Birkenhead 28.2.44
man. trainee Thames Board Mills (Unilever) Warrington 1969–72; tech sales rep Milchem inc Houston Texas from 1973

TURNER Susan Patricia MA 1965
d of James F. T. RAF, gen merch and Jean Lackie; b Cheltenham 21.1.45
Canada: teacher Russell Manitoba 1971–74, freelance journalist/columnist for weekly newspaper Yorkton Sask from 1975
m Morpeth 11.8.65 Alan A. Macintosh MA 1965 *qv*

TURNER William Robert Clyne MB ChB 1960
s of Edward Turner civ serv and Christina A. Paterson secy; b Peterhead 1.11.37
DObstRCOG 1963
h o: Stracathro hosp Brechin, Falkirk RI, ARI 1960–62; lect anat Aberd 1962; g p: Aber, Purley, Lincoln 1965–67 and clin asst Linc 1967; private pract Banff Alta Canada 1967–77; pres med staff Mineral Springs hosp Banff Canada 1973–74 (active staff 1967–77); g p Tunbridge Wells Kent 1977–78; private pract Calgary/courtesy staff Rockyview and Holy Cross hosps from 1978
m Aber 22.6.63 Patricia E. Kelly RGN d of Christopher K. Falkirk

TURPIE Derek McDonald MA 1969
s of Alexander M. T. wagon repairer, park ranger and Mary J. Mackie midwife; b Aber 19.7.48
teacher geog Whitburn from 1970
m Aber 27.6.70 Jeanette C. Duncan MA 1969 *qv*

TURRIFF William *MA 1968 *MEd 1972
s of William T. postman and Mary S. McDonald; b Peterhead 6.9.45
DEP(Glas) 1970
teacher Causewayend p s Aber 1970–72; educ psych Exeter 1972–74; sen educ psych Stonehaven from 1974
m Aber 2.8.68 Geraldine O. Smith teacher d of John S. USA

TURTON John Neville *MA 1969 *MEd 1975

TURTON John Samuel PhD 1966
s of Colin T. civ serv and Annie G. Brown; b Sale 28.12.29
BSc(eng)(Lond) 1955 MSc(eng)(Lond) 1959 C Eng MIMechE(Lond) 1961

lect mech eng Sus univ from 1966
m Battersea 1957 Margaret D. Stockley teacher d of Ernest W. S. London

TUTTLE Albert Austin MA 1969
s of Albert T. eng and Margaret H. Ballingall; b Forfar 27.9.47
MEd(Ottawa) 1975
teacher: Motherwell 1970–71, Ottawa from 1971
m Aber 29.12.70 Sheena Gow MB ChB 1965 *qv*

TUTTLE Angus Swanson MB ChB 1968

TUTTLE Irene Margaret MB ChB 1970
d of Albert A. T. eng and Margaret H. Ballingall; b Dun 9.10.45
DObstRCOG 1972
h o Aber 1970–71; g p Pembroke Ont Canada 1970–72 and from 1973; sen h o obst Stirling 1972–73
m Pembroke Ont 13.1.78 Floyd D. Skuce pres Dalmar Paving s of Lloyd S.

TWATT John William BSc(agr) 1970
s of Stephen M. T. farm. and Brenda Tait; b Kirkwall 24.11.47
temp posts Canada 1970–73; asst insp DAFS Aber, Oban 1973–78; insp DAFS Orkney from 1978

TWEEDIE Quentin William BSc(eng) 1967

TWIGGS Arthur Ronald *BSc 1969
s of Sydney T. RAF off. and Frances G. Cumming; b Lincs 18.3.48
field geol/mine geol NT Aust 1969–71; field geol W Aust 1971–72; sen geol (eng) Lond based from 1973

TYRRELL Marcus Alexander BSc(for) 1959

TYSON Robert Donald Grigor MA 1966

TYTLER Peter *BSc 1964 PhD 1968
s of Peter T. MB ChB 1940 *qv*; b Stirling 11.9.42
Stir: NERC res fell. 1967–69, res lect attached to SMBA Oban 1969–72, lect biol 1972–78; asst prof univ of Kuwait 1978–80
m Stirling 9.4.70 Stephanie Flaherty prin's secy Stir d of Stephen F. Stirling

U'REN William Graham *BSc 1970
s of Henry G. U. MA 1976 (by ordin) and Catherine C. Graham; b Glasg 28.12.46
Dip TP(Strath) 1974 MRTPI 1974
town plan. asst: Clacks c c 1970–72 Lanark c c 1972–75; prin plan., chief plan. off. Lanark dist c from 1975
m Glasg 15.10.70 Wendy M. Hogarth

UDDOH John Adewa *BSc(eng) 1960
s of Samuel M. U. and Ugioro Ogiefa; b Agbani Nigeria 22.4.32
Dip Civ Eng(Yaba tech inst) 1953 AF Inst Pet 1964 Regd Eng(Coren, Nig) 1973
exec eng (roads) M o W Umuahia Nigeria 1960–61; BP Nig: oper eng Lagos 1961–63, dist oper eng Kano, Jos, div eng Port Harcourt Benin 1964–70, gen man. Gwato Nig Benin (road constr comp) 1970–73, man. dir Progress Eng comp Benin from 1973
m Lond 15.8.59 Patricia M. Mudahy nurse d of J. M. Kingston Jamaica

ULLMANN Liselotte Ludovicka PhD 1957
MA(Oxon)
m De Kock

UMAR Mohammad PhD 1968
s of Haji C. Din bus. man and Wazir Begum; b Lahore Pakistan 6.9.36
BSc(Punj) 1958 MSc(Punj) 1964
sen res off. PCSIR Lahore 1968–70; lect analyt chem Punjab univ Lahore 1970–74, asst prof from 1974
m Lahore 7.1.62 Hamida Shafi d of Haji M. S. Lahore

UNDERWOOD Ian Richard MB ChB 1968

URE James Murray BSc(for) 1957

URI Oddstein MB ChB 1964
s of Jonas U. farm. and Halldis Brekke; b Valldal Norway 30.12.34
Spec Pediat(Bergen) 1971
Norway: intern Flekkefjord 1965; jun regist Tromsø 1966–68, Voss 1969–70, Bergen 1970–72; private pract Tønsberg 1973–77; chief m o Ibb, Yemen 1977–78; private pract Tønsberg from 1978
m(1) Aber 22.12.61 Patricia Summers BSc 1960 *qv*; marr diss 14.2.75
(2) Tønsberg 24.2.75 Turid Lutnes physioth d of Magne L. Rena Norway

URQUHART Aileen Alexander *BSc 1968
d of George F. U. BSc(Strath) civ eng/comp dir and Elizabeth E. Stiller secy; b Glasg 20.9.45
res asst plant biol Bangor univ coll N. Wales; Canada: tech med biochem Ottawa univ 1971–74, grad stud. PhD plant physiol Carleton univ Ottawa from 1974
m Glasg 5.6.70 Julian T. Inglis BSc 1967 *qv*

URQUHART Alastair Alfred MA 1961
s of Alfred U. comm trav and Violet Duncan; b Turriff 13.1.40
teacher: Turriff acad 1962–73, Toronto from 1974

URQUHART Alison Anne Mairi MA 1964
d of Alexander U. MA(Glas) teacher and Annie B. Scott MA 1925 *qv*; b Inv 11.5.43
teacher: Mosspark p s Renfrew 1965–69, Portessie p s 1969–74, Stornoway p s from 1974

URQUHART Barrie Stephen LLB 1966
s of Stephen U. dent. tech and Gladys Barrie; b Aber 12.5.45
law app 1967–69 Greenock; solic Greenock, Hamilton 1969; solic Aber from 1969
m Glasg 25.4.70 Irene F. Harvey bank clerkess d of David L. H. Glasg

URQUHART Gillian Rose MA 1967 Dip Ed 1968
d of George S. U. gen grocer and Mavis O. Davis: b Lucknow India 1.11.45
teacher Engl/Amer hist Philadelphia dance acad USA 1968–69; teacher: Engl/hist Kinning Park Glasg 1969–71, asst prin Engl Barrhead h s 1971–72, Engl Verdin comp s stud. induction course for spec educ Hartford 1974; teacher p h s Winsford from 1975
m Hatfield Alan E. Howes loc govt off. s of Eric H. H. Hatfield; marr diss

URQUHART Gordon Alexander *MA 1959 MSc 1964

URQUHART Gordon Greig BSc(eng) 1963

URQUHART Helma Muriel MA 1957
d of James L. U. civ serv and Wilhelmina Forsyth; b Stornoway 18.4.36
tech lib Aber/Beaconsfield Cambs 1961–67; lib tapes for blind stud. Lond from 1967

URQUHART Jean McDonald BSc 1967

URQUHART Robert George Inglefield BSc(eng) 1963
s of Colin U. grocer and Agnes I. Mitchell; b Portsoy 18.9.42
MICE 1968 MIHE 1967
grad asst eng Aber c c 1963–65; asst eng Banff c c 1965–68; sen eng: SE roads conserv unit Maidstone 1968–72, Perth c c 1972–74; supt eng defence dept Muscat Sultanate of Oman from 1974
m Grangemouth 22.7.67 Rosalind W. Jeffreys computer oper d of William J. Grangemouth

URQUHART Ronald John *MA 1959

UYANWAH Philomena Obiageliuwah MB ChB 1964 MD 1978
m Akpom

VADLAMUDI Babu Pitchi PhD 1968
BSc(Andhra) MSc(Saugar)

VALENTINE John Murray BSc(for) 1967
s of J. Stuart V. BA(Vict Well NZ) teacher and Nancy P. Rutherford; b Wellington NZ 8.4.43
BSc(Well) 1965 PhD(Wash) 1975
NZ for. serv: for. Tuatapere 1967–69, scient Rotorua 1969–78, prin for. Wellington from 1978

VALENTINE Maurice Keith BSc 1970
s of William W. V. regist of births, deaths, marriages and Elsie Rowe; b Dun 10.11.49
syst analyst: Babcock & Wilcox (Ops) Renfrew 1970–74, Renfrew c c Paisley 1974–75, Strathclyde reg c Glasg from 1975, proj leader
m Aber 4.8.72 Kathleen Bruce MA 1972 teacher d of Colin S. B. Aber

VALENTINE Ranald John Harben *BSc 1959

VALENTINE Wyn Patricia *BSc 1966
d of Henry W. V. MA 1931 *qv* and Winifred Stoddart MA 1931 *qv*; b Aber 1.8.44
computer progr Lond 1966–67; teacher Longniddry p s from 1977
m Aber 28.1.67 Andrew J. Williamson MA 1966 *qv*

van der KAMP Bart John PhD 1967
s of Walter van der K. headmaster and Derkje van Dyk; b Kampen Neths 30.12.41
BSF(Br Col) 1964
univ of Br Col Vancouver Canada: asst p a 1967–74, assoc p a from 1974
m Capelle a. d. Yssel Holland 22.12.64 Adriana Schippers d of Hendrik S. a. d. Yssel

van der TOORREN Vivien Lois MA 1967 Dip Ed 1968
d of Jan van der T. airline pilot and Lorna R. Murray; b Londonderry NI 9.6.45
teacher: VSO Freetown Sierra Leone 1966–67, Brent Lond 1968–69; publ Longmans Harwell 1968–69; teacher Reading 1969–73
m Aber 29.11.69 William J. Attenborough BSc(R'dg) farms man. s of William A. East Carlton

VANN Janet Petronella *BSc 1966
d of C. Roland V. schoolmaster and Eileen M. Norris head teacher; b Mansfield 25.7.43
teacher geog Royal Masonic s Herts 1966–68; Procter & Gamble: sales prom dept 1968–72, brand man. 1972–76; Braun AG, W Ger: group prod. superv 1976–78, internat marketing man. *Hair Care* 1978–79, prod. line dir *Oral Care* from 1980

VARGAS CUBIDES Esperanza MSc 1968
Chem(Nat Univ Coll)

VARRIE Melvyn Keith *MA 1969
s of George A. W. V. painter/decorator and Elsie Jacques; b Dumfries 26.1.47
Dip Ed(Edin) 1971
teacher Dumfries 1969–70, post-grad stud.: UCW 1970–71, Edin 1971–72; teacher: Dun 1972–75, Irvine from 1975

VASS Evelyn Rosemary *MA 1966
d of John V. MA 1937 *qv*; b Aberfeldy 5.12.44
MSC(Lond) 1967 PhD(Lond) 1973
Lond: clin psych 1967–70; sen psych Guy's hosp 1970–74, prin psych from 1974
m Lond 7.10.66 David F. Hendry MA 1966 *qv*

VASS Mary McIntosh Forbes MA 1958
d of Alexander V. works man. and Isabella Forbes; b Fraserburgh 30.8.36
admin asst Strath 1965–69; asst secy Jordanhill coll of educ Glas 1969–72
m Glasg 17.12.71 Campbell B. Burns MA(Glas) prof of bus. law s of James B. Glasg

VAUGHAN Gordon Henry MB ChB 1957
s of Henry E. V. caterer and Nellie B. Yoxall; b Aber 19.3.33
FRACGP 1973
h o Woodend hosp Aber 1957–58; capt RAMC(NS) Tidworth 1958–60; phys Stanvac Sumatra Indonesia 1960–62; med supt KI gen hosp S Aust; med pract Turramurra NSW Aust from 1965
m Glasg 14.7.55 Anne L. Gibson BSc(Glas) teacher d of William G.

VAUGHAN Ian MA 1965

VAUGHAN Ludlow Murcot MA 1963
s of Aaron T. V. clerk and Albertha Robinson; b Montego Bay Jamaica WI 20.5.25
Dip Ed(Glas) 1966
teacher Edinbarnet s s Faifley Clydebank 1964–69; dep head Dalreoch p s Dumbarton 1969–72; head Edinbarnet p s Faifley from 1972
m Glasg 15.5.48 Archibaldina M. Rough d of Archibald R. Glasg

VAZ PORTUGAL Apolinário José Barbosa da Cruz PhD 1964
s of Apolinario P. Ms Chem(Coimbra) chem and Celeste da C Vaz prof; b Murtosa Portugal 9.11.30
Dip Nutrit Physiol(Sorbonne) 1959 D Vet Sc(Lisbon) 1967
res fell min of agr Lisbon 1967; head of biochem/anim nutrit dept of inst of anim prod. Vale de Santarem, Portugal 1967–69, dir of inst prod. res from 1973; prof anim prod. fac of vet sc Lisbon from 1969; secy of state for agrarian dev from 1978
m Portugal 3.10.69 Ana M. G. Correia d of Manuel da Silva C.

VEITCH Angela Georgette *BSc 1967
d of George B. W. V. teacher of art and Margaret M. Gordon; b Inv 9.4.44
biochem Raigmore hosp Inv from 1967

VELAYUTHAM Mariappan PhD 1968
MSc(Madras)

VELLACOTT Terence Charles Frederick Bishop *MA 1967
s of Jack F. B. V. elect. eng and Elsie M. Pedder; b

Romford 27.11.42
teacher: Engl Eton coll 1968–69, Engl/Lat St Paul's cath choir s 1969–76; prin classics Montpelier prep s Paignton from 1976

VERMOUTH Paul Clinton *MA 1969
s of Paul C. V. bus. man and Shirley L. Johannis; b Keene NH USA 6.10.46
MA(Lond) 1970
grad stud. Af stud. Lond 1969–70; fell. Af stud. center Boston univ Mass 1971–73, also sen teaching fell. from 1973

VICCA Mario Luigi MA 1959 LLB 1961
s of Peter V. restaurateur and Elvira Zumpani; b Aber 22.10.37
NP 1978
ptnr Storie, Cruden & Simpson advoc Aber from 1963
m Glasg 21.5.63 Joan M. Carroll teacher p e d of William C. Glasg

VICKERS Ivan George BSc(agr) 1966 *1967
s of George D. V. and Violet G. Maplestone; b Lincoln 23.8.43
BA(Cantab) 1974 Vet MB MRCVS 1977
livestock husb advis min of agr ADAS Chelmsford 1967–72; stud. vet med Churchill coll univ of Cambridge 1972–77; min of agr vet off. Bury St Edmunds from 1977

VIGROW John Will *MA 1965
s of John W. V. engraver and Florence Clarkson; b Aber 24.8.32
Morgan acad Dun: teacher geog 1966–68, spec asst 1968–70, prin asst 1970–72, prin guid from 1972
m Largs 8.7.67 Elisabeth A. Sayles BSc 1965 *qv*

VIGROW Mary Louisa Mitchell *MA 1963
d of George W. V. factory worker and Jessie Lakin photographer; b Newhills 12.2.24
teacher Engl Bankhead acad from 1964
m Bucksburn 12.8.46 Frederick Crade master upholsterer and coach trimmer s of Samuel C. London

VINCENT Clifford BSc 1970
b Aber 4.5.49
teacher maths Powis acad Aber 1971–73, asst prin maths 1973–75; prin guid Bankhead acad from 1975

VINYCOMB Dorothea Harden MA 1968
d of Godfrey B. V. BA(Cantab) eng and Christina J. Glendinning; b Belfast 29.8.47
ch care off. Norwich 1968–69; med soc worker Liv 1969–70; teacher Engl Mitundu s s Malawi 1974–76
m Monifieth 31.5.69 Robert K. M. Hay BSc 1967 *qv*

VIPOND Peter Wilfred *BSc 1966 PhD 1969

VIRGO Keith James MSc 1965
s of Alfred J. V. wholesale grocery/comp dir and Doris M. Portwine; b Woking 9.4.41
BSc(agr)(Lond) 1962 Dip Agr Eng(NCAE) 1976)
soil surv/pedologist: Hunting tech serv Sudan, Middle East 1964–67, dept agr Canada 1967–68; sen soil surv/land classifier Hunting tech serv Thailand, Niger, Côte d'Ivoire, Ethiopia, Swaziland, Somalia, Bahrain from 1968
m Sandown I of W 6.4.68 Sandra G. Martin cartogr d of Stanley A. M. Sandown

VIVEKANANDAN Kandavanam PhD 1970
s of Kanapathipillai K. and Sinnathamby Sinnammah; b Ceylon 6.9.36
BSc(Ceylon) 1961 MIBiol 1970
res off. for. dept Colombo Ceylon from 1970
m Ceylon 26.1.72 Arulmanidevi Thambirajan d of Ponniah T. Batticaloa, Ceylon (Sri Lanka)

Von KUENSSBERG Verity Constance Evelyn MA 1968
m Duncan

VORHAUS David Glyn BSc 1966

VYSE Alan Horsley *BSc(for) 1964
s of Adam V. fish merch and Joan H. Horsley teacher; b Tynemouth 31.8.42
MScF(Tor) 1971
for. econ Canadian for. serv Victoria BC 1966–73; res for. BC for. serv Williams Lake from 1974
m Toronto 31.12.65 Frances M. Mackintosh BSc 1965 *qv*

WADDELL Sheila Buchanan MA 1969
d of Roy W. bus. man. and Maureen C. Buchanan teacher dom sc, nurse; b Glasg 24.4.48
Assoc I P R 1975
leader writer *Glasgow Herald* 1969–70; teacher Engl Douglas acad Milngavie 1972; information asst (p r off.) Babtie Shaw & Morton consult. civ & struct eng Glasg 1972–74, teacher: Engl/hist Barrenjoey h s NSW Aust 1975, Engl Bishopbriggs h s Glasg from 1976

WADDS Geoffrey Alan *BSc 1966 PhD 1970
s of Edward A. W. aircraft insp and Joan Dilley civ serv; b Oxford 20.6.43
res analyst Lankro chem Eccles 1969–72; analyst/biochem Beecham pharm Harlow 1972–78; head analytical dept Anstead Billericay from 1978
m Cheadle 28.12.68 Linda P. Will nurse d of Thomas W.

WADSWORTH Ronald Stuart [d]LLB 1968
s of Arnold W. woollen textile spinner and Margaret S. Chree; b Huntly 3.11.47
law app, qualif asst, ptnr Mackie & Dewar advoc Aber 1968–73; ptnr Philip & Wadsworth advoc Aber from 1973; part time asst private law Aberd from 1968
m Luton 29.3.69 Margaret Clarke SRN d of Thomas S. C. Luton

WADSWORTH Sheila LLB 1967
d of Stanley W. CA and Eva Whitworth; b Middleton 17.8.46
qualif solic Aston, Manc 1968; articled clerk Epsom c 1968–71; lect in law tech coll Ewell from 1971
m Rochdale 12.6.71 James H. Surgeoner LLB 1967 *qv*

WAITE James Howard Raymond LLB 1969
s of Ralph R. W. and Margaret E. H. Pearson BSc(Lond); b Gloucester 7.4.48
solic Guildford from 1973

WAITER Sheila MA 1956
d of Hugh G. W. fish merch and Julia M. Imrie clerkess; b Inverbervie 1.4.35
m Inverbervie 6.7.57 Alexander D. Mathieson farm., conservative ag s of Andrew M. Laurencekirk

WAKELIN Derek Raymond *BSc 1970 PhD 1974
s of Bernard W. fitter and Lillian Holdsworth; b Rugby 20.10.46
lect: Aberd 1973–74, N'cle poly 1974–79, sen lect from 1979

WAKEMAN Norman Henry *MA 1959
s of Henry E. W. soldier/painter and Elizabeth Cooper; b Hartlepool 30.10.36
sergeant instr RAEC 1959–61; Hartlepool: teacher 1961–

63, careers and exam. master 1963–73, head careers dept from 1973
m Hartlepool 9.9.60 Jean C. Fraser SRN/midwife d of Alexander E. F. Hartlepool

WALDING Hugh Frederick PhD 1968
s of Frederick E. W. off. at Law Soc and Lilian E. Bridge secy; b Norbury 24.7.43
MA(Oxon) 1965
res asst agr Glas 1968–71; lect Bournemouth coll of tech from 1971
m Glasg 22.7.71 Margaret S. Sutherland MA 1968 *qv*

WALDON Geoffrey MB ChB 1961

WALKER Aileen Isobel Anne MA 1968 Dip Ed 1969

WALKER Aileen Margaret MA 1961
d of William B. W. fisherman and Annie Parley waitress; b Aber 28.3.41
Aber: teacher Mile End s 1962–66; visiting teacher of mus prim. schools 1969–71; teacher Kintore s from 1974
m Aber 20.7.63 Robin M. Dyer MA 1961 *qv*

WALKER Alastair Alexander Wallace *MA 1965

WALKER Alexander Davidson Ross BSc 1961 *1963

WALKER Alexander Lyell BSc 1962
s of Alexander W. teacher and Jean R. Cook teacher; b Hamilton 30.7.41
Dip Ed(Glas) 1963
teacher: Glasg 1963–66, Western Samoa 1966–68; prin teacher RGC Aber 1969–72, Kincorth acad Aber from 1972
m Aber 19.12.64 Ann O. Anderson MA 1963 *qv*

WALKER Alison Barclay BSc 1964
d of Edward W. insur off. and Christina Barclay shorthand typist; b Aber 16.5.43
teacher maths Arbroath h s 1965–67
m Aber 6.1.68 Hamish D. Munro BSc 1964 *qv*

WALKER Andrew BL 1957
s of Thomas W. trawl owner and Margaret L. Mitchell; b Aber 29.2.36
Aber: trawl owner 1957–60, fish merch 1960–78, fish broker from 1978
m Aber 17.8.60 Christina M. Clark d of James G. C Aber

WALKER Anne MA 1970 *MEd 1977
d of Alfred W. W. cabinetmaker and Marion Esslemont secy; b Aber 28.11.48
teacher: Engl Torry acad Aber 1971–75, asst prin Engl Powis acad Aber from 1975
m Aber 8.8.70 Russell R. Orchard data control clerk s of Anthony R. O. Lond

WALKER Arthur Wellesley *BSc 1962 Ph D 1966

WALKER Brian James *BSc 1968

WALKER Christopher Howard *MA 1966
s of Harold W. min of relig and Kathleen Ushaw; b Birm 1.4.44
Dip Soc Admin(Manc) 1968
nat trg scheme for hosp admin Aber, Manc 1966–68; dept of soc admin univ of Hull: res asst 1968–69, asst lect 1969–71, lect from 1971
m Shere 10.4.71 Sarah J. Thompson BA(Hull) teacher d of Graham B. T. Dorking

WALKER Christopher Royston BSc 1969
s of Stanley W. clerk and Muriel N. Brown; b Norton Malton 30.7.48
computer progr: Nat West. bank Lond 1969–78, team leader corp of Lloyds insurers Chatham from 1978
m Cullen 29.5.71 Jane A. N. Woollam MA 1969 *qv*

WALKER Colin Harold MSc 1961
s of Harold H. W. prop. mus shop and Eleanor M. Bashford; b Thornton Heath 28.4.36
BSc(R'dg) 1959
scient. off., sen scient off. The Nature Conservancy, Abbots Ripton 1962–67; lect physiol/biochem R'dg from 1967
m Cambridge 28.3.64 Margaret E. Reith MA 1962 *qv*

WALKER Colin Nairn *BSc 1968

WALKER Daniel Graham *BSc 1961
s of Daniel G. W. insur ag and Thomasina Mahaffey; b Aber 22.6.38
teacher NZ: maths/sc New Plymouth 1961–64, Bay of Islands coll from 1965
m New Plymouth 19.4.62 Carol E. Evans d of Idris L. E. Brit army Singapore

WALKER Doreen Isobel MB ChB 1966
d of Ian W. man. and Doris I. Stewart hairdresser; b Aber 6.5.42
h o gyn, med ARI 1966–68; sen h o psychiat Ross clin Aber 1968; part-time m o publ health Dun 1970–73; commun m o (sessional) Glenrothes and Leslie from 1973
m Aber 1.9.64 Thomas P. Reid sen process eng in electronics s of Thomas P. R. Aber

WALKER Edith Harriet MA 1963
m Beanan

WALKER George Stuart BSc(eng) 1962

WALKER Ian Cossar BSc 1967

WALKER Ivy Ada MA 1967 Dip Ed 1968
d of Alfred W. gen merch/grocer and Christina Duguid; b Rothienorman 30.10.46
teacher: Engl/hist Northfield acad Aber 1968–74, Turriff acad 1974–76
m Aber 12.4.73 William Cruickshank farm. s of William M. C. Rothienorman

WALKER James Findlay MB ChB 1967
s of John W. fish merch and Annie Findlay; b Aber 3.9.43
DObstRCOG 1971
h o: Perth RI, Victoria I Kirkcaldy 1967–69; g p Edin 1970–73; dir of res: Merrell nat labs Cincinnati Ohio 1973–76, Merek, Sharp & Dohme Philadelphia from 1976
m Aber 22.7.67 Yvonne E. Souter secy d of Robert S. Aber

WALKER James Stewart *BSc 1959

WALKER Jean Middleton *MA 1965
m Riach

WALKER Jill MB ChB 1962
d of Thomas W. trawl owner and Margaret L. Mitchell teacher; b Aber 19.7.38
m Aber 12.7.62 Torbjørn Kufaas MB ChB 1962 *qv*

WALKER John Anderson BSc 1970 Dip Ed 1971
s of Robert W. tech instr. and Muriel W. Webster; b Aber 11.12.47

teacher sc Haddington 1971–74, prin chem Eyemouth from 1974
m Aber 19.7.72 Patricia A. Kelman nurs nurse d of John C. K. Aber

WALKER John Marshall MB ChB 1966
s of Alexander C. W., BSc(H-W) eng consult. and Jane Ross; b Aber 27.2.43
FFARCS 1972
h o: ARI, Tasmania 1966–68; g p/anaest Perth Aust 1968–70; anaest/regist: Inv 1970–72, Edin 1973–74; anaest Diaconessenhuis Heemstede Neths from 1974
m Nairn 11.7.66 Elisabeth Ker d of John K. Nairn

WALKER John Murray MA 1969
s of John A. W. grocer and Jane Y. Murray grocer; b Keith 1.7.48
teacher p s Lossiemouth h s 1970–73; dep head Speyside h s Aberlour 1973–76; head Cullen p s from 1977

WALKER Katharine Alice MA 1962 (conferred for long service of exceptional merit)
d of George W. MA(Edin) clergyman DD 1922 *qv*(II) and Isabella Strong; b Aber 21.4.1900
asst lib Aberd 1922–65

WALKER Margaret Ann MEd 1967
d of John C. W. BA(Cantab) civ serv and Mollie Wallwork civ serv, teacher; b Bamford 18.3.43
MA(St And) 1964
VSO teacher Magburaka Sierra Leone 1964–65; lect Engl lang Ahmadu Bello univ Zaria Nigeria from 1973
m Hertford Heath –.4.63 Michael J. Jones PhD 1968 *qv*

WALKER Marget Blackwood MA 1960

WALKER Margaret Helen MA 1961 Dip Ed 1962

WALKER Michael George Russell *BSc 1969

WALKER Michael Grant MB ChB 1964 ChM 1976

WALKER Norma Ann BSc 1960
d of Alfred W. gen merch and Christina Duguid; b Rothienorman 12.2.39
teacher biol: Blairgowrie 1961–63, Inverurie 1963–64, Huntly 1965–67
m Aber 25.11.64 James J. F. Fawns farm. s. of James F. Huntly

WALKER Patricia Eveline *MA 1968
d of William G. W. mech eng and Grace Cobban; b Aber 8.3.46
teacher Fr: Marple Hall g s Cheshire from 1969
m Aber 16.8.68 Gordon M. Coull quantity surv s of William C. Aber

WALKER Patrick John MA 1962
s of John W. carpenter and Isabella Barron; b Aber 20.12.39
teacher: Powis s 1963–65, New Deer p s 1965–68; head: Tough p s 1968–71, Hatton (Cruden) p s 1971–75, Kellands p s Inverurie from 1975
m Aber 20.8.65 Phyllis Wyness d of Philip W. Kintore

WALKER Peter Anthony MB ChB 1965
s of Richard J. W. MB ChB 1937 *qv*; b Aber 19.10.41
FRCSE 1970 MRCPath 1977
h o: ARI, Woodend hosp Aber 1965–66; terminable lect path. 1966–67 and 1969–70; sen h o: ARI, Glasg Western hosp 1967–69; lect path. Aberd 1972–81; Fife health board: consult. histopathologist Victoria hosp Kirkcaldy from 1981
m Aber 27.7.72 Gillian U. Price nurs sister d of John A. P. MA(Glas) Kintore

WALKER Thomas PhD 1966
BSc(Dunelm)

WALKER William *BSc 1966
s of William W. farm. and Isabella Legge; b Banff 11.12.43
teacher AGS 1967–73; prin phys Inv royal acad from 1972

WALKER William Brimlow BSc(for) 1965
s of John M. T. W. furniture manuf and Mary K. Brimlow; b Glas 9.4.43
MIFor(GB) 1968
conserv lower Swansea valley proj (univ res proj) 1965–67; sen for. off. Norfolk c c Norwich 1967–69; for. man. Midlands private for. comp Shrewsbury 1969–72; reg man. S Scot. private for. comp Moffat from 1972
m Devizes 2.9.67 Diane R. Hiscox d of Stanley G. H. Devizes

WALKER William Thomson MA 1965

WALLACE Bruce MA 1966 BD 1969

WALLACE Elizabeth Ann Hay MB ChB 1965
d of George E. E. surv of customs and excise and Margaret E. Hay teacher; b Elgin 6.8.32
MA(Edin) 1955 DPH(Glas) 1970
h o: Raigmore hosp Inv, Bridge of Earn, Craig Dunain Inv 1966–67; sen h o geriat Ashludie Dun 1967–68; asst m o Banffsh 1968–74, Grampian health board from 1974

WALLACE George Noble *MA 1966
s of George H. W. eng and Mary S. Trail; b Fraserburgh 11.4.44
teacher Engl: Peebles 1967–68, Turin 1968–75, Dun 1975–76, and interpreter/translator Alba Italy from 1976

WALLACE Glenis Winifred MA 1963
m Humphreys

WALLACE Ian Grant MA 1957
s of Alexander R. B. W. hosp porter and Jane T. Innes; b Aber 1.12.34
BPhil(Oxon) 1959 Dip Ed(Edin) 1960 MEd(Glas) 1966 PhD(Glas) 1971
lect Glas: logic 1960–66, psych from 1966
m Banchory 9.7.59 Elva J. F. Durward teacher d of Alexander F. D. Banchory

WALLACE Irene Isobel *MA 1966
m Hughson

WALLACE Janice Clare MA 1968
d of Alexander F. W. arch. and Jeannette MacDougall; b Strathblane 22.6.47
secy: admin Wolsey Hall Oxford 1969–70, cognition proj psych Edin 1970–71; teacher: Easthall p s Easterhouse Glasg 1972–73, Harestones p s Kirkintilloch from 1973

WALLACE Judith Carol *MA 1968

WALLACE Margaret Alison *MA 1966
d of Alexander B. W. MB ChB(Edin) surg and Marguerite I. Burke nurse; b Edin 24.2.44
Edin: secy/edit. asst cartographic bus. 1967–68, edit. publ firm 1968–69
m Ceres 17.1.70 Alan J. Masson BSc(Edin) lect(Kodak) s of Hamish M. MA(Edin) Edin

WALLACE Martha Walker MA 1967

WALLACE Michael Kennedy BSc 1969
s of Ian H. W. plumber and Irene Kennedy clerkess; b Aber 17.11.47
teacher sc Kaimhill j s s Aber 1970–71; exec off. M o D Lond from 1971

WALLACE William BSc(eng) 1970

WALLIS Richard Godfrey *MA 1958
s of Richard H. W. customs & excise off. and Grace Godfrey; b Aber 15.2.35
teacher mod lang Dunfermline h s 1959–63, spec asst 1963–65; prin mod lang Peterhead acad 1965–67; prin Fr Dunfermline h s 1967–72; rector Bridge of Don acad Aber from 1972
m Kirkpatrick-Fleming 30.3.64 Mary Beattie BSc(Edin) teacher d of Thomas L. B. Kirkpatrick-Fleming

WALMSLEY Rosanne Mary MA 1967

WALSH Alan Robertson BSc 1970

WALSH Kieran James *BSc 1969
s of James W. headmaster and Winefride M. Little teacher; b Wrexham 21.9.43
teacher Summerhill acad Aber 1970–73; asst prin guid 1973–74, prin guid from 1974

WALTERS Jacqueline Mary MB ChB 1963
m Bressan

WALTERSON Laurence Imlach MB ChB 1957
s of Peter W. policeman and Jessie M. Imlach nurse; b Lossiemouth 7.6.33
h o Woodend hosp Aber 1957–58, ARI 1958–59, Woolmanhill Aber 1959; ship's surg 1959–60; sen h o Woolmanhill 1960–62; g p Aber from 1962
m Aber 19.6.64 Jean Anderson MA 1955 *qv*

WALTON Michael John Stewart MA 1967
s of John K. W. oil merch and Ruth G. Stewart; b Alyth 22.10.44
NCR: spec assignments Dun 1967–68; oil merch J. Walton & Son Newtyle from 1968
m Perth 13.6.66 Penelope J. Rogers MA(St And) d of John R. MB ChB(Glas) Dun

WALUDA Jerzy Marian BSc(eng) 1969
s of John W. quarry chargehand and Maria Zon; b Lancaster 2.8.47
asst eng highways/bridges Carlisle 1969–74; resid eng Greta Bridge Co Durham from 1974
m Hawes 13.9.69 Marjorie Whitehead stud. nurse d of Jason W. Gayle

WANG Stanley Way Shien MB ChB 1969

WANN Kenneth Taylor *BSc 1970 PhD 1975

WARBURTON David Hart BSc(for) 1969

WARD John PhD 1969
MAgrSc(R'dg)

WARD John Neve MA 1968
s of Albert E. W. shop man. and Marget D. Finlayson shop asst; b Nairn 24.1.48
indust dev off. HIDB Inv from 1968
m Fort William 26.10.74 Georgina R. Walker dent. nurse d of Alexander I.M.W. Inverlochy

WARD John William BSc 1966

WARD Nuala Clare MA 1965
d of James J. W. MA(Glas) teacher/headmaster and Catherine J. Goulding hairdresser, for. worker; b Lond 26.1.43
MA(St And) MRTPI 1973
plan. asst: Lanarksh 1965–67, Perth 1967–68; res asst, res off. Perth 1968–74, plan. off. from 1974

WARD Stephen David PhD 1968
BSc(Wales)

WARDELL Heather Lucy MA 1968

WARDLAW Don Mark PhD 1959
BA(Columbia univ NY) BD(Union Theol Seminary, Richmond Va)

WARDLE Clement Shreen *BSc 1962 PhD 1973
s of Arthur C. W. eng, teacher and Frances T. Schensinger MA(Oxon) lect; b Mere 1.10.39
dev comm fisheries stud. Lowestoft 1962–64; Aber: jun res fell. Torry res 1964–66, sen res fell. marine lab 1966–70, sen scient off. marine lab 1970–72, prin scient off. from 1972
m Birm 17.7.62 Penelope A. Stripp teacher d of H.A.S. Dar-es-Salaam Tanganyika

WARDLE Penelope Margaret MA 1964

WARES Roy *BSc 1964 MSc 1979
s of James W. and Mary D. Taylor; b Aber 16.8.42
MSc(Kingston Ont) 1971
Canada: field geol Ont 1964–68, proj evaluation geol Vancouver 1968–74, sen geol Vancouver 1974–77; plan. Grampian reg c Aber 1979–80; res geol Squamish Canada from 1980

WARNOCK John Fraser BSc 1969
s of John C. W., BSc(Glas) civ serv and Flora M. Fraser teacher; b Glas 18.2.47
CA 1974
app acct Turner, Hutton & Lawson Glasg 1969–74

WARNOCK Shaw William *MA 1967
s of Samuel S. W. freight man. and Marion I. Burns; b Stirling 24.3.45
M Litt(Cantab) 1973
stockbroker's clerk (res dept) London from 1970

WARRACK Ian McArthur MB ChB 1966
s of John W. MB ChB 1932 *qv*; b Doncaster 26.12.41
CCFP 1973
h o Woodend hosp Aber, ARI 1966–67; trainee g p Culter 1967–68; Canada: fam phys Hawkesbury Ontario 1968–74, Ottawa 1974–77, lect family med univ of Ottawa from 1977
m Aber 14.7.66 Alison McArthur MA 1964 *qv*

WARREN Andrew *BSc 1959
s of Thomas W. MA(St And) teacher and Janet S. McPhail teacher; b Kalimpong N Bengal 27.10.37
PhD(Cantab) 1967
soil surv Hunting tech serv UK, W Pakistan 1960–61; lect univ coll Lond from 1964; fell. ACLS Lincoln Nebraska USA 1967–68
m Aldringham 19.8.67 Inga M. Kerridge occup therap d of Peter K. Ongar

WARREN Geoffrey Austin Richard BSc 1966

WARREN Janet Gwyneth *MA 1961
d of Thomas W. MA(St And) teacher and Janet S. Macphail teacher; b St And 25.11.39

part time lect Farnborough tech coll 1967–70; TEFL Engl lang coll Bielefeld, W Ger 1970–72; Farnborough: teacher comp s 1973–75, part time lect tech coll from 1975
m Aber 10.7.62 Richard H. Hardie MB ChB 1963 *qv*

WARREN Susan Elizabeth BSc 1968
d of Harold J. M. W. elect. eng and Phyllis Todd; b Grays 26.9.47
teacher sc Hilton s Aber 1969–71
m Aber 8.10.70 Douglas J. Grimes drilling fluid eng s of Harold C. G. Aber

WARRENDER, Jean MA 1964
m Morris

WARRINGTON Brenda Elizabeth MA 1969
d of Clifford W. head warehouseman and Margaret C. Johnston saleswoman; b Inv 13.1.48
exec off.: SED Edin 1969–72, dept for nat savings Glasg from 1972
m Inv 17.6.72 Norman Fawcett asst landscape off. s of John F. Workington

WARRINGTON Sandra BSc 1966
d of Clement E. W. vicar and Euphemia M. Mackenzie; b Glasg 20.8.44
Dip Dietetics(Glasg) 1976
scient information off. Commonwealth Bureau of Nutrition Rowett res inst Aber 1966–73; dietitian Manc area health auth Manc RI 1976; sen dietitian Rochdale area health auth Birch Hill hosp 1976–78, area dietitian from 1978

WARWOOD Alasdair Iain MA 1968
s of Kenneth A. I. W. hotelier and Helen I. N. Turnbull; b Newbury 17.7.48
syst analyst Burroughs Machines Birm 1968–72; dep computer serv man. BSG Birm 1972–74; syst analyst delegacy of loc exams. Oxford 1975–76; asst secy Finance Houses Assoc Lond from 1977

WASHINGTON Angela Mary *BSc 1967
d of Noel W. MA(Cantab) teacher and Pauline M. Jarvis; b Rotherham 7.10.45
teacher geog Gloucester h s for girls 1968–72; lect geog/geol Gloucester City coll of tech from 1972

WATERFIELD Angela Alice *BSc 1969 PhD 1973
d of Thomas W. prod. man. and Margaret Murphy; b Leigh 25.7.45
Aberd: res asst 1969–73, res fell. from 1973

WATERHOUSE Sheena Mary Alexandra *MA 1965

WATERS Robert Pearse BSc(for) 1960
insp of taxes from 1961

WATERSTON Margaret Elizabeth *BSc 1970
d of William H. W. MA(Dund) assay clerk and Margaret Bore clerkess; b Dun 14.2.48
geol Kambalda Aust 1970–75
m Dun 5.8.70 Ian R. McDonald BSc 1970 *qv*

WATERSTON William George LLB 1970
s of George W. LLD(Dund) ornithol and Nancy G. Ritchie; b Edin 2.2.49
Edin: WS ptnr Pearson, Robertson & Maconochie WS from 1974
m St Andrews Andrea L. Bennett SRN d of Peter H. B. BA(Oxon) Ottawa

WATKINS Lena Joan *MA 1959
d of George A. W. man. dir light eng comp and Elizabeth M. Smith teacher; b Bexley 1.4.37
teacher Aber h s for girls 1960–64
m Aber 8.8.64 Robert M. Logan MB ChB 1960 *qv*

WATKINS Roger Dexter MB ChB 1968
s of Dudley D. W. cartoonist/illustrator and Doris E. Taylor; b Dun 21.7.43
MRCGP 1977
h o Inv 1968–70; g p Helensburgh from 1970
m Broughty Ferry 25.8.67 Lindsay A. McDowell MA 1967 *qv*

WATSON Alan Edward *BSc(eng) 1970
s of Edward B. W. papermaking foreman and Muriel Forrester; b Fyvie 3.9.48
grad asst civ eng: Bucks c c Aylesbury 1970–72, Aber city eng dept 1972–74, Grampian reg water serv from 1974

WATSON Ann *BSc 1966
d of James W. BSc 1932 *qv*; b Aber 25.5.45
res asst Exe 1967–70; computer progr: Bristol univ 1970–72, Birkbeck coll Lond 1972–75, Bristol univ from 1975
m Aber 18.2.65 Christopher N. French BSc 1966 *qv*; marr diss 1975

WATSON Anna Galbraith MA 1961
d of Melville E. W. livestock auctioneer and Kate A. Forsyth; b Aber 29.11.40
market res investig Lond 1961–62; N'cle-u-Tyne: market res plan. 1962–65, asst pers superv for women 1965–69
m Aber 23.3.68 Peter R. Pearks BSc(chem eng)(Swansea) process dev eng s of Eric J. P. Torquay

WATSON Arthur *BSc(eng) 1964 MSc 1965

WATSON Arthur Vincent Reid MB ChB 1958
s of Vincent M. M. W. MB ChB 1921 *qv*; b Aber 18.2.30
DObstRCOG 1961 MRCGP 1971
g p Birmingham 1960–67, Torphins from 1967
m Arbroath 10.6.61 Linda M. G. McMaster d of Thomas McM. Arbroath

WATSON Brian MacDonald *MA 1970

WATSON David Beresford BSc 1961

WATSON Derek *MA 1965
s of James W. man. dir and Elizabeth Wilson; b Aber 14.12.42
Lond: computer progr 1966–68; syst analyst 1968–74; lect computer stud. coll of tech Dun from 1974
m Wimbledon Lond 7.9.68 Beryl Johnson computer consult. d of Albert J. Wimbledon

WATSON Edith *MA 1966
d of George W. farm. and Edith M. Morison MA 1939 *qv*; b Aber 5.1.44
Dip Ed(Edin) 1967
teacher geog Edin 1968–71; lect geog Craiglockhart coll of educ Edin 1971–76
m Aber 19.4.73 Robert A. Sykes BSc(eng)(Strath) civ eng s of Hubert S. Kirkmahoe Dumfries

WATSON Eleanor McLeod Munro *MA 1963
d of William H. W. clerk and Helen M. M. Boyd piano teacher; b Aberlady 4.4.42
teacher geog E. Kilbride 1964–65
m E. Kilbride 10.7.64 David Butters min of relig s of Joseph B. Lochgelly

WATSON Gillian Mary MA 1963
d of Philip E. W. comp dir and Mary E. Burton; b Aber 2.4.43
Dip Soc Sc(Edin) 1964, MIMSW(Lond) 1965
med soc worker ERI 1965–66
m Aber 9.10.65 Dennis A. Carswell BSc lect geol s of Dennis L. C. Howwood

WATSON Graham MA 1962

WATSON Helen Margaret MB ChB 1970
d of George W. farm. and Edith M. Morison MA 1939 *qv*; b Aber 27.2.46
h o Aber 1970–71
m New Pitsligo 20.7.70 Alexander P. Fowler MB ChB 1969 *qv*

WATSON Iain Scott Michie *MA 1967
s of John S. W. MB ChB 1936 *qv* and Elizabeth Michie MA 1936 *qv*; b Aber 21.6.45
joint man. dir Northern Jewellers (Scot.) Aber from 1968
m Aber 4.5.70 Marilyn Smith comp dir

WATSON Ian Rees BSc(agr) 1970
s of John F. W. carpenter/joiner and Mary M. Rees; b Croesgoch Haverfordwest 16.7.46
MSc (UCW) 1974
res asst UCW Aberystwyth till 1973; commercial diver from 1974

WATSON Irene Abercromby MB ChB 1959
d of William H. W. MA 1929 *qv* and Dorothy J. M. Smith MA 1929 *qv*; b Loudon Malawi 9.8.34
m o city hosp Aber, RACH Aber 1959–61; part-time govt m o: Mwenzo/Isoka Zambia 1961–74; private pract Lusaka 1974–76
m Aber 15.7.59 James L. Wilkie MA 1956 *qv*

WATSON James Sinclair MA 1967
s of James G. W. san insp and Mary M. Sinclair clerkess; b Glasg 12.5.45
BA(OU) 1976
teacher maths Kelso h s 1968–74, asst prin maths from 1974
m Gordon 5.4.74 Muriel H. Ford d of James R. F. Gordon

WATSON John Richard PhD 1970
b Otley Yorks 2.5.46
BSc(Durh) Grad Dip Rec(WA) ARIC
res fell. soil sc univ of Western Australia 1970–76; environmental off. dept conserv and environment Perth 1976–78

WATSON Kathleen MA 1970
d of James W. warehouse foreman and Kathleen Wallace; b Aber 18.12.48
cler asst city assessors Aber 1971–72 cler off. customs & excise Edin from 1972
m Aber 12.1.74 Robin G. M. Mutch quantity surv s of Eric G. M. Hayes

WATSON Ken Murray BSc(agr) 1965
s of Robert P. W. farm. and Valerie L. Wood teacher p e; b St And 25.6.43
Dip FM(NOSCA) 1966
agr advis: Inverurie 1967–68, Orkney 1969, farm man. Fife from 1969
m St And 19.6.70 Pamela B. Millar nurse d of Tom B. M. St And

WATSON Melville Forsyth MA 1959 LLB 1961
s of Melville E. W. livestock off. and Kate A. Forsyth; b Edin 30.8.38
law app, leg. asst Aber 1959–64; ptnr Storie, Cruden & Simpson advoc Aber from 1964; chmn nat insur appeal tribunal Aber from 1972
m Aber 5.7.63 Sheila E. G. Morgan MA 1961 *qv*

WATSON Michael John BSc(eng) 1968
s of Daniel S. W. BSc(eng) 1932 *qv*; b Portsmouth 9.8.45
eng Rolls Royce Derby 1968–71; instr RN 1971–77; teacher Woodbridge s 1977–80; RAF from 1980
m Aber Josee A. Lentz d of Emile E. L. Lond

WATSON Nancy Hunter MA 1966

WATSON Nigel John Fairley *MA 1970

WATSON Ray Buchanan LLB 1965
d of William W. oil comp exec and Elizabeth J. Rae; b Aber 11.7.44
leg. app Aber 1965–67, solic Aber from 1967
m Aber 23.11.68 Colin P. Pigott BSc(eng) 1967 *qv*

WATSON Robert Haldane BSc(for) 1956

WATSON Roderick Bruce *MA 1965
s of Mearns B. W. BSc 1933 *qv*; b Aber 12.5.43
PhD(Cantab) 1971
lect Engl lit univ of Vict BC Canada 1965–66; res stud. Cambridge, Edin 1966–70; Arts Council grant for own poetry 1970–71; lect Engl lit Stir from 1971
m Aber 14.7.66 Celia H. Mackie d of Stanley M. Aber

WATSON Rosemary Anne MA 1959
d of Philip E. W. man. dir and Mary E. Burton secy; b Aber 20.6.38
secy to prod. overseas talks and features BBC 1960; pers secy to dir Rowett res inst Aber 1960–65
m Aber 29.12.65 James N. Hay BSc(Glas) univ lect s of John H. Alloa

WATSON Stanley James *MA 1969 Dip Ed 1970
s of William H. W. MA 1929 *qv* and Dorothy J. M. Smith MA 1929 *qv*; b Aber 25.11.38
teacher Engl AGS 1970–72, prin guid Ellon acad from 1972
m Aber 4.7.66 Elizabeth M. Jones teacher d of Frederick J. J. Colwyn Bay

WATSON Valerie MA 1969
d of Henry M. W. bus. man. elect./radio/tv and Gertrude A. Milne; b Banff 8.12.37
teacher: Quarryhill p s Aber 1960–64, St Christopher's ch s Manama Bahrain, RAF s Muharraq Bahrain 1965–66
m Aber 1963 Frederick D. Routledge pilot/mooring master s of Frederick S. R. Elgin

WATT Aileen Elizabeth Clare BEd 1969
d of Archibald W. MA 1936 *qv*; b Machyllneth N Wales 20.11.46
teacher Fr Portobello h s 1969–73; asst prin mod lang Craigmount h s Edin from 1974
m Aber 20.1.73 Matthew M. Little BSc(Edin) teacher, insur clerk s of Arthur L. Langholm

WATT Alan Charles MB ChB 1958
s of Charles W. asst postmaster and Charlotte McGregor nurs sister; b Keith 5.1.34
LMCC 1976
h o Woodend gen hosp Aber, Perth RI 1958–59; m o colony of N Borneo Beaufort and Keningaw now Sabah Malaysia 1959–62; h o mat. hosp Aber 1963; termin lect anat Aberd 1963–64; med pract Westlock Alta Canada from 1965

m Aber 29.7.59 Margaret O. Willox RGN d of Alexander W. Cuminestown

WATT Alan Stewart Mitchell *BSc 1970

WATT Alastair BSc(eng) 1970

WATT Alastair Douglas BSc(eng) 1966
s of James W. eng and Isabella S. Ferguson; b Aber 25.7.44
jun, intermed eng Racal Bracknell 1966–68; sen eng, proj man. RDL (EMI) Camberley 1968–71; sole prop. Hillhouse Systems Camberley from 1971
m Weybridge 28.9.65 Veronica S. Handy d of Dennis J. H. Walton on Thames

WATT Alexander *MA 1964 PhD 1967
s of Alexander M. W. farm. and Elma Taylor; b Ellon 24.11.41
asst lect nat phil Aberd 1967–68, lect Glas from 1969
m Aber 24.7.67 Marie E. Morrison MA 1963 *qv*

WATT Alexander *BSc 1967
s of James C. W. fisherman and Helen A. Watt; b Crovie 2.9.37
teacher: sc Bankhead acad 1968–74, chem Aber tech coll from 1974
m Fraserburgh 2.1.62 Christine Murray d of John M. Gardenstown

WATT Alexander John MB ChB 1956
s of Adam N. S. W. MB ChB 1925 *qv* and Margaret A. Mackay MB ChB 1926 *qv*(III); b Dagenham 3.7.33
h o ARI, Raigmore hosp Inv 1957–58; g p: Grimsby 1958–67, Perth from 1967; CAA authorised examinr Perth/part time m o Perth aerodrome from 1968
m Whitekirk 24.3.62 Elizabeth A. Brash BSc(Edin) teacher d of George M. B. BSc(Edin) Edin

WATT Alexandra Adam *MA 1964
m West

WATT Andrew John *BSc 1963 PhD 1966

WATT Andrew Robin LLB 1970
s of Andrew W. CBE BA(for)(Oxon) comm of for. and Helen M. McGuffog; b Edin 31.3.49
law app Edin 1970–72, solic from 1972

WATT Ann Elizabeth MA 1963
m(1) Hendry
(2) Seymour

WATT Ann Marie MA 1957
d of Charles W. W. man. draper's shop, clerk and Ellie H. Hutcheon; b Aber 9.11.35
teacher Aber: Muirfield s 1958–64, RGC 1964–68
m Aber 27.12.68 William I. Campbell eng draughtsman, tech coll lect s of Hugh C. North Shields

WATT Avril Martin *MA 1966

WATT Catherine Allardyce MA 1963
d of William A. W. long dist driver, trans foreman and Elisabeth B. Cross waitress, superv; b Aber 4.8.42
part time teacher mod lang coll of comm Aber from 1964
m Aber 14.10.63 Michael R. Hewitt BSc(eng) 1962 *qv*

WATT Charles Cameron *BSc(agr) 1969
s of Walter W. police/ch's panel and Jean R. Wood; b Haddington 20.11.46
lands off. DAFS Oban 1970–73; reg tech advis Atcost Scot./N Eng 1973–74; lands off. DAFS Glasg, Orkney, Stirling from 1974
m Tranent 26.8.70 Margaret Hart teacher dom sc d of William H. Elphinstone

WATT Chrissy MA 1956
d of Charles W. acct and Williamina Fraser; b Aber 9.7.36
teacher Pitmedden p s 1957–68; teacher/housemistress Albyn s for girls Aber 1968–74; teacher Balgownie p s 1974–77; asst head Cults p s Aber from 1977

WATT David Alexander *BSc(for) 1969
s of Alexander S. W. oil refinery superv and Doris G. Paine; b Lond 26.6.48
landscape asst (for.): Kent c c estates dept Maidstone 1970–74, Islington (Lond) plan. dept 1974–78, arboricultural off. parks dept from 1978

WATT David Alexander Fraser *MA 1964

WATT Donald Alexander [e]LLB 1966
s of James W. civ serv and Jamesina McLennan; b Spey Bay 27.2.45
law app Dun 1966–68; solic: Clydebank 1968–69; Kirkcaldy 1969–73; solic/town clerk Burntisland 1973–75; dep dir of admin Kirkcaldy from 1975
m Hamilton 6.12.69 Yvonne R. Jennings nurse d of Patrick J. Middlesbrough

WATT Donald William Clement MB ChB 1962
s of James C. W. fisherman and Mary Macdonald nurse; b Macduff 21.1.37
DMRD(Lond) 1965 CRCP(C) 1969
h o, sen h o ARI 1963–65; regist RI Glasg 1965–67, sen regist Victoria I Glasg; consult. radiol, dir radiol Holy Cross hosp Calgary Canada from 1968
m Glasg 10.9.60 Elizabeth Lambert secy d of James L. Glasg

WATT Elspeth Murray Richards BSc 1970
d of Harold M. R. W. MA 1942 *qv* and Elizabeth F. C. Richards MA 1941 *qv*; b Aber 26.4.49
teacher: Elphinstone p s Tranent 1971–72, Speke, Liv 1972–73; insur clerk Guardian Royal Exchange Insur Co Preston 1973–76
m Aber 22.9.72 Alastair S. Leaver BSc 1971 brewer s of Harry L. Largs

WATT Eric *MA 1961
s of James W. W. fisherman and Charlotte Johnston; b Banff 25.3.39
brand man. York 1961–66; asst marketing man. Peterborough 1966–68; marketing man. Birm 1968–72; Lond: European man. 1972–76, marketing controller 1976–78, comp dir from 1978
m Camberley 14.9.63 Diana M. White BA(R'dg) psych, teacher d of Richard H. W. Camberley

WATT Forbes *MA 1967
s of Joseph W. tailor, fisherman and Rose Forbes gen merch; b Pennan 13.9.25
Cert Master Mariner 1960
teacher: geog Fraserburgh acad 1968–70; Buchan tech coll Fraserburgh: teacher soc/gen stud. 1970–71, lect navigation 1971–72, head dept naut stud. from 1972
m Gardenstown 17.3.56 Mary W. Robertson nurse/sister d of William R. Gardenstown

WATT Francis *BSc(eng) 1967
s of George A. W. fisherman and Jamesina Smith; b Aber 1.1.44
Canada: lubrication eng Saskatoon 1967–68, petr eng Edmonton 1968–70; pilot RAF UK, Cyprus from 1970

m Aber 30.7.66 Sylvia E. Reeve teacher d of Terence C. R. RN

WATT Francis Austen MA 1966
s of Francis W. BSc 1933 *qv*; b Kelso 26.2.44
Chrysler UK (purchasing): fin. analyst, office man. Coventry 1966–70; Internat Computers (ICL) sales exec Harrow, Glasg, Manc 1971–75; acct Finnie, Ross, Allfields CA Lond 1976–79; fin. controller P & O Consultancy & Computer serv Watford from 1980
m Stoke-on-Trent 3.4.71 Ursula M. Regan teacher; wife *d* 1.10.72

WATT Francis James MB ChB 1965
s of James W. eng and Isabella Ferguson; b Aber 5.4.40
DA 1967 DObstRCOG 1968 FRCP(C)Anaes 1977 FACA 1978
h o Aber 1965–66, sen h o Sheffield, Irvine 1966–68; g p Cinderford, Keswick 1968–72; resid anaest Toronto 1972–75; consult. anaest Newmarket Ontario from 1975
m Perth 29.4.66 Adena Thomson nurse/midwife d of George T. Perth

WATT Gavin William BSc 1970
s of William N. W. toolmaker and Violet Cockburn teacher; b Aber 13.5.46
teacher Paignton 1970–71; res chem Nott 1971–77; PGCE Nott univ 1977–78; teacher Hawick from 1978
m Aber 29.8.70 Christine A. Davidson clerkess d of Alexander D. Fraserburgh

WATT Gordon Alastair James *MA 1965

WATT Graham Gordon *BSc 1967

WATT Guy Ridley *BSc(for) 1969
s of Alexander J. W. and Audrey Z. D. Ridley; b Surrey 3.10.45
BLitt(Oxon) 1971
Min Overseas Dev Lond 1971–72; consult. FAO Rome 1972; asst conserv for. Honiara Solomon Is 1972–74; consult. Min Overseas Dev Lond 1974–75; for. res inst Rotorua NZ from 1975
m Newick 26.2.72 Rosemarie J. Jenkins d of Neville C. J. Farnborough

WATT Heather Güldmar BSc 1970
d of William G. W. teacher, min of relig and Thelma G. Taylor secy, teacher; b Aber 4.5.47
res asst pharm Strath 1968–69; teacher sc in NATO s Brunssum Holland 1972–73; trainee acct: Aber 1977–78, Peterhead from 1978
m Aber 6.7.68 David S. Ross BSc 1967 *qv*

WATT Ian Joseph MA 1967 MEd 1972
s of Joseph W. fisherman and Christina W. Duncan; b Lerwick 25.8.40
teacher Lerwick 1968–71
m Lerwick 25.9.67 Eleanor J. Paton d of James J. P. Lerwick

WATT James Currie MB ChB 1969

WATT James Dennis MacPherson *MA 1967
d Bristol 8.3.69 *AUR* XLIII 218

WATT James Norman Mackenzie *MA 1968 Dip Ed 1971

WATT Janet Farquhar *BSc 1956
m Stollery

WATT Jill Emerson *MA 1969
m Crofts

WATT John Alexander MB ChB 1962
s of William J. W. farm. and Marjory McRobb farm.; b Rothes 19.8.38
DPM 1966 CRCP(C) 1968 MRCPsych 1972 FRCP(C) 1972
h o, sen h o ARI 1962–63; Garden res fell. bact Aberd 1963–64; lect Aberd 1964; regist psychiat Ross clin Aber 1965–66; regist Kingseat hosp Newmachar 1966–67; visiting clin instr psychiat Strong mem hosp univ of Rochester NYS, USA 1967–68; staff psychiat: Clarke inst Toronto 1968–71, Homewood sanatorium Guelph Ont 1971–72, med dir from 1972
m Whithorn 2.7.62 Olga Petrucci teacher d of Italo P. Whithorn

WATT John Alexander Menmuir BSc(agr) 1956
s of William B. S. W. farm. and Margaret E. Menmuir teacher; b Stonehaven 1.3.35
farm. NSW Aust 1956–57; nat serv 1957–59; reg advis R. Silcock & Sons Midlands 1959–68; W & J Pye NW England: tech advis 1968–78, tech & market. man. from 1978, also dir Nutrition Control Services Lancaster
m Southport 16.12.61 Elizabeth A. Wollaston nurse d of Geoffrey G. W. Southport

WATT John Ritchie MA 1969

WATT John Simpson MB ChB 1956
d Edmonton 14.11.68 *AUR* XLIII 86

WATT Joyce Stephen MA 1957 *MEd 1965 PhD 1980
d of William M. W. circuit man. oil comp and Josephine M. Stephen; b Aber 28.5.37
teacher St Margaret's s for girls Aber 1958–65; lect Dun coll of educ 1966–72, Aberd from 1972

WATT Lesley Jane MB ChB 1968
m Stewart

WATT Linda May MA 1970
d of William W. surv and Doris E. McLeod teacher; b Aber 9.5.49
governess Algeria 1971–72; teacher Royal h s Edin 1972
m Edin 29.8.72 Michael Naismith-Beeley naval off. s of Bruce N-B. Irvine

WATT Margaret MA 1958
m Lyall

WATT Margaret MA 1969

WATT Margaret Ann BSc 1967
m Chalmers

WATT Marjorie Anne BSc 1965
d of John W. man. and Annie S. Henderson secy; b Aber 2.5.44
teacher maths: Inverurie acad 1966–68, Grove acad Dun 1968–69, Bridge of Don s Aber 1970–72
m(1) Downie
(2) Aber 7.10.72 George A. Milne BSc 1963 *qv*

WATT Mirren Adams MA 1958
d of Walter A. W. acct and Margaret C. I. Coulter teacher; b Aber 12.3.37
teacher Engl Northfield acad 1959–70, prin asst Engl/guid/careers 1965–70
m Aber 21.12.68 Joseph Watson branch man. s of Joseph W. Aust

WATT Morag Elizabeth MA 1962
m Tamisari

WATT Nicol Lumsden BSc 1956 *1958
s of George W. san insp and Mary W. S. Lumsden; b Turriff 6.8.35
MInstP 1967 CEng MIEE 1968
phys: Assoc Elect. Indust Manc 1958–63, Hammersmith hosp Lond 1963–67, Patent off. Lond 1968–69, univ of Manitoba Winnipeg 1969–71, poultry res centre Edin from 1972
m Bonn 12.6.70 Sigrid M. G. Stegert nurse Marburg

WATT Pearl Wiseman BSc 1970
m Noble

WATT Sheila Anne BSc 1968
d of Douglas A. W. cashier and Anne B. Stewart; b Aber 25.2.47
BEd(Tor) 1970
res proj Glasg RI 1968–69; Tor: teacher maths Winston Churchill coll inst 1970–73, L'Amoreaux coll inst 1973–75, asst head maths from 1975
m Aber 13.7.68 Norman W. Leslie MA 1967 *qv*

WATTIE James Alistair MB ChB 1960
m Aber 17.12.65 Joanna M. Garrioch MB ChB 1966 *qv*

WATTS-RUSSELL Grayling Jessica Pepita MA 1968
d of David R. W. R. W-R. landowner and Gina S. Baker BA(Rome); b Hamburg 5.10.47
Dip Vocat Guid(R'dg) 1973
TEFL: Vientiane Laos 1968–70, Cambridge 1970–71; careers off. Surrey c c 1972–74
m Reading 10.2.73 Andrew M. Wright BA(Cantab) med pract s of John W. W. BSc(Cantab) Effingham

WEATHERLEY Jill Margaret *MA 1967 Dip Ed 1980
d of Paul E. W. BA(Oxon) univ prof Aberd and Margaret L. Pirie poultry man.; b Kampala Uganda 13.9.45
m Irvine

WEAVER Ian Robert Sidney *BSc(eng) 1960
s of Sidney W. dir of amenities Aber c c and Grace T. MacGregor; b Winchester 14.7.39
MICE 1966
asst eng: Angus c c 1960–61, Midlothian c c Edin 1961–64; eng asst R. H. Cuthbertson & Assoc Edin 1965–66; teacher sc: Bearsden 1968–71, Montrose 1971–72; sen asst eng, resid eng Forfar, Brechin from 1972
m Forfar 9.10.71 Sheila E. Blair MA(St And) teacher d of William B. Forfar

WEAVER Rhoda Jean MA 1964
m Murdoch

WEBB Alastair Richard John MA 1970
s of Richard J. W. environmental health off. and Margaret M. Johnston; b Glasg 29.5.48
teacher: geog/Engl Glasg 1971–73, geog Perth 1973–75, geog/guid from 1975
m Glasg 5.4.72 Helen W. Moffat art teacher d of David M.

WEBB Ian Scott *BSc 1969 PhD 1976
s of Kenneth R. W. solic and Gwen L. Scott artist; b Berkhamsted 13.10.46
soil scient with land resource surv team Honiara Solomon Is 1969–70; post grad stud. soil sc dept Aberd 1971–73; sen scient off. min of agr Auki, Honiara 1973–77; res scient (ODM) Rothmansted exper stat 1977–78; soil scient/plan. Electrowatt Eng Serv (Lond) Lond, worldwide from 1978
m Aber 4.4.72 Linda A. McKay MA 1971 teacher d of William D. McK Winchester

WEBB John MacLeod BSc 1966
s of Arthur B. W. eng and Margaret MacLeod nurse; b Barnet 11.1.45
Lond: computer progr, syst des 1966–71, syst/progr man. 1971–73, syst exec 1973–74; data base man. Tehran Iran 1975–77; proj man. Bath, Reading from 1977
m Aber 19.3.66 Pamela N. Pollock LLB 1971 computer syst analyst d of Capt K. P. Poole

WEBB Michael John MSc 1966
s of Harry F. W. optical eng and Dorothy A. M. Butler; b Birm 8.5.44
BSc(N'cle) 1964
res stud. Lanc 1966–69; scient, sen scient Shell Res(agr chem) Sittingbourne from 1969
m N'cle-u-Tyne 25.5.68 Judith Greenwood BSc(N'cle) d of Maurice G. N'cle-u-Tyne

WEBB Moraig Anne MacLeod MA 1961
d of Arthur B. W. eng and Margaret MacLeod nurse; b Barnet 8.7.40
teacher: Engl/hist Macduff 1962–67, Engl/Latin Elgin 1967–68
m Nairn 11.7.64 George M. Gray farm. s of Robert G. Banff

WEBER Ursula Hilde MB ChB 1965

WEBSTER Alexander David BSc 1956 *1957 Dip Ed 1958
s of David A. W. licensed grocer and Jemima Hutchison; b Brechin 30.1.35
teacher chem Perth acad 1958–64; prin chem Nairn acad from 1964
m Brechin 5.8.64 Donna J. Robertson d of George S. R. Brechin

WEBSTER Alistair Kellas MB ChB 1964
d Hereford 31.7.70 *AUR* XLIV 112

WEBSTER Brydon MB ChB 1961
d 26.1.63 *AUR* XL 208

WEBSTER Charlotte Hutchison MB ChB 1956
d of David A. W. lic grocer and Jemima Hutchison; b Brechin 24.5.32
h o Strachathro hosp Brechin 1956–57; sen h o ARI 1957–58; chest phys royal Ottawa sanatorium 1958–60; Leeds: lect path. 1961–64, m o FPA from 1969
m Brechin 4.9.57 Denis Greig PhD 1958 *qv*

WEBSTER Colin James *BSc 1964 PhD 1967
s of James W. lorry driver and Coleena McIntosh; b Aber 29.7.42
post doct res Tor Canada 1967–68; scient ICI organics div Stevenston 1968–77, asst oper man. Manc from 1977
m Aber 3.9.65 Margaret Harper med secy d of Hugh M. H Aber

WEBSTER Elizabeth Ann MB ChB 1970
d of Harold V. W. postman and Vera B. Reed; b Lond 28.8.47
h o: ARI 1970–71, Lond 1971–72; sen h o Ilford 1972–74; g p Ilford from 1974
m Ilford 14.8.71 John B. Houston bank clerk s of Joseph H. MA(Dub) Glengarnock

WEBSTER Elizabeth Joan MA 1964
d of John W. farm. and Elizabeth Thomson; b Turriff 30.3.43

remed teacher sec dept; Rosehearty and Turriff 1965–74; prin guid and remed teacher Turriff acad from 1974
m Turriff 16.7.66 David R. Christie farm. s of James C. Fordoun

WEBSTER Ewan Burgess *BSc 1969
s of William W. bank man. and Mary H. Burgess SRN; b Keith 12.9.47
scient off., sen scient off. AEA Dounreay from 1969

WEBSTER Gordon Johnstone MA 1959 Dip Ed 1960

WEBSTER James MB ChB 1969
s of James G. W. soldier and Kathleen M. Cowie; b Aber 16.9.30
h o Woodend hosp Aber 1969–70; g p: Aber 1970–71, Oldmeldrum/Fyvie, Aber from 1971
m Fyvie 24.7.71 Caroline J. Mair physioth d of Scott M. M. Aber

WEBSTER John BMedBiol 1970 MB ChB 1973
s of William J. W. fisherman and Emma Watt; b Aber 17.3.48
MRCP 1975
h o ARI 1973–74; temp lect therapeutics/clin pharm Aberd 1974–75; sen h o med Woodend gen hosp Aber 1975; lect therap/clin pharm Aberd from 1975
m Fraserburgh 20.5.76 Mary G. Simpson midwife d of William J. C. S. Maud

WEBSTER John Alexander *BSc(eng) 1964 MSc 1965 PhD 1968
s of John A. W. man. dir bldg/civ eng contr and Lilias W. Wilson; b Aber 12.2.43
Aberd: asst lect eng 1965–66; lect eng maths 1966–69; res scient CSIRO Canberra Aust 1969–72; res eng MWD Wellington NZ 1972–75; sen lect arch. Well from 1975
m Aber 29.12.65 Mary Kincaid BSc 1964 *qv*

WEBSTER Michael Joseph BSc 1968
s of Francis W. dir textile comp and Nancy K. Elsmie; b 25.4.46
Dip Acct(Strath) 1974 CA 1978
man. trainee Arbroath 1968–73, app CA Aber 1974–77, acct Arbroath from 1977

WEBSTER Nicol Ewen *MA 1968

WEBSTER William Gordon MSc 1964
s of Gordon W. W. BSc(Alta) chem eng and Ena Youngblood nurse; b Calgary Alta 24.5.39
BSc(elect.eng)(Alta) 1961
Athlone fell. BoT UK 1962–64; Canada: res eng trans eng CN Rail from 1964
m Edmonton Alta 9.7.62 Phyllis G. Roos BSc(Alta) nurse d of Val K. Roos BEd(Alta) Edmonton

WEDDELL Ann *BSc 1968

WEDDLE Richard Braid *BSc 1969
s of Hugh E. W. BSc(Durh) solic's clerk and Margaret A. Braid solic's clerk; b 13.2.47
res asst (food tech/biochem) Unilever res Aber from 1969

WEIGHTON David Michael *BSc(agr) 1966
s of David W. storekeeper and Betsy W. Hardie; b Forfar 24.12.42
MSc(UCNW) 1967
Boots Co: tech off. insecticide dev Nott 1967–69, tech off. Sydney Aust 1969–71, sen tech off. insecticides/fungicides res Nott 1971–76, sen dev off. from 1976

WEIR Elizabeth McDonald MA 1970
d of John D. M. W. teacher tech subjs and Agnes D. Irvine piano accompan dance in schools; b Aber 19.2.49
Dip Grad Sec(Edin coll of comm) 1971
secy; Alex Hall & Son (bldrs) Aber 1971–72, Aber Construction Group 1972; secy/pa Colin Wood Antiques Aber 1972–74; secy/typist fac of Arts Aberd 1975–78, sen secy/typist mod lang from 1978

WEIR Iain Thomson MA 1968

WEIR James Alexander BSc 1961
s of James W. farm. and Louisa Farquhar; b Portnockie 13.3.39
teacher sc Powis acad Aber 1962–71; prin sc Old Aberdeen j s s 1971–73; prin phys Powis acad from 1973
m Aber 8.8.67 Mary M. Tod teacher d of David J. T. Kirkcaldy

WEIR James William Henderson Cameron BSc(agr) 1961
s of John N. C. W. BSc(agr)(Glas) agriculturalist and Jessie F. Henderson nurs sister; b Aber 24.1.39
BVMS(Glas) 1966
asst vet surg Aber 1966–69; ptnr vet surg Aber 1969–75, prin from 1975
m Aber 29.3.68 Yvonne D. C. Carle teacher dom sc d of Robert C. Aber

WEIR Jane Gibb *MA 1969
d of John S. W. RAF, postman and Evelyn Moir shop asst; b Abingdon 24.4.47
m Aber 20.12.68 Roderick H. Cameron eng draughtsman s of Roderick C. Greenock

WEIR John Grant Colin BSc(agr) 1966
s of John N. C. W. BSc(agr)(Glas) agriculturalist and Jessie F. Henderson nurs sister; b Aber 31.1.42
Dip FM(Aber) 1970
agr advis NOSCA: Benbecula 1966–69, Dingwall 1970–72; farm man. NOSCA farm Aldroughty Elgin 1972–74
m Nairn 30.7.70 Elspeth G. M. Fraser MA 1963 *qv*
d Elgin 22.3.74 *AUR* XLV 450

WEIR Marion Preston BSc 1959
d 23.10.66

WEIR Robert James BSc 1962
s of Robert W. textile des and Jessie A. Tough mill worker; b Keith 3.6.41
teacher: maths/sc Edzell j s s 1963–65, chem Mackie acad Stonehaven 1965–73; prin chem Bankhead acad from 1973
m Aber 14.8.65 Sheila M. Adam sen lab tech d of Walter A. Aber

WELCH Linda May MA 1969

WELFORD John George BSc(for) 1958
d 19.1.64

WELFORD Peter Alexander Rex BSc 1970
s of Peter G. W. MA(Oxon) teacher and Enid D. Blackmore teacher; b Weymouth 22.6.48
lab Is of Skye 1971–72; teacher: Edin 1972–77, New York 1977–78, Edin 1978–79; Is of Skye: bldg contr 1979–80, mus from 1980

WELLS Janet MB ChB 1968
d of John A. N. W. eng and Joan Broadman secy; b Clacton 13.6.45
Aber: h o ARI 1968–69; Aberd res fell. dept path. 1969–

71; trainee g p Torphins 1972–73; med co-ordinater NE Scot. reg hosp board 1973–74; m o Bexley and Greenwich area health auth 1974–75; m o Kent area health auth 1975–79; regist commun med SE Thames area health auth from 1977
m Sidcup 25.7.64 David J. Hall MSc 1967 *qv*

WELLS Judith Angela MA 1959
d of Joseph N. W. fish merch and Thirza Robertson; b Grimsby 3.11.37
Secy-Dip Bi-lingual(Ealing tech coll) 1960
bi-ling secy Dow-Unquinesa SA Bilbao Spain 1960–61
m Aber 9.9.61 Jose L. Gervas BEcon(Bilbao) capt SpMN s of Victor G. Sestao-Vizcaya Spain

WELLS Michael *BSc 1957 PhD 1968
s of Stanley R. W. clerk and Jessie P. Featherstone cashier; b Norwich 25.4.34
teacher sc Ellon acad 1958–60; asst exper off. DAFS Perth 1960–62; res asst dep mat. med-therapeutics Aberd 1962–68; lect biol sc H-W Edin from 1968
m Aber 28.12.59 Elizabeth M. Gloyer shorthand typist d of Marshall H. G. Aber

WELLS Russell Emerson PhD 1970
s of Emerson H. W. farm. and Vera E. Wheatland; b Unity Sask Canada 2.6.33
BSc(agr)(Sask) 1956 MSc(Alta) 1961
Can. dept agr soil surv Edmonton 1956–62; organis of Amer states soil surv Chile 1962–63; Can. land inventory (soil surv and land classif) Newfoundland 1963–67; Can. for. serv (environmental surv): Newfoundland 1967–73, Quebec from 1973
m St John's Newfoundland 28.12.67 Elizabeth R. Carter d of John C. St. John's

WELSH Elizabeth Katherine Cochrane MA 1965
d of Graham C. W. MA 1937 *qv*(III) and Bessie King; b Edin 4.1.45
Dip Secy Sc(Strath) 1966
secy ag work Edin 1965–66; staff secy Kennet comp s Thatcham from 1977
m Edin 23.7.66 Gareth J. Rowlands MA(Cantab) statist s of Vernon W. R. BA(Bangor) Liv

WELSH Jane Alexandra Cochrane MA 1968

WELSH Jean Saddler BSc 1970
d of William P. W. joiner, teacher and Esther Saddler; b Fraserburgh 2.12.48
computer progr Aber c c 1971–72
m Aber 18.2.72 John G. Smith BSc 1972 scient off. s of James S. Fraserburgh

WELSH Margaret Cramond MB ChB 1968
m Underwood

WELSH Moira Jean Lennox *MA 1966
d of Martin W. mech eng and Helen R. Hislop clerkess; b Edin 26.6.44
Dip Ed(Edin) 1967
teacher Silverknowes p s Edin 1967–70; educ psych Edin 1970–73
m Aber 27.12.68 Donald H. Steele MA 1966 *qv*

WELSH Norma MA 1956
d of Norman G. M. W. vanman/gen store owner and Mary W. Watson; b Inverurie 31.3.35
teacher: Johnstone 1957–58, Aber 1958–59
m Aber 21.7.59 James S. McIntosh MB ChB 1958 *qv*

WEMYSS Robert Duncan *MA 1970
s of Duncan W. male nurse and Duncanina McKinnon; b Inv 28.3.48
MSc(H-W) 1972 MRTPI 1974
town plan. asst Ayr burgh 1972–75; asst dir (plan.) Cumnock and Doon valley dist c from 1975
m Inv 12.9.70 Marilyn H. Lobban clerkess d of George I. L. Inv

WEMYSS Thomas MA 1969
s of James A. W. factory foreman and Margaret G. McKay filleter; b Fraserburgh 2.6.46
teacher sp/drama: Aber corp 1970–72, Aber coll of comm from 1972
m Aber 14.9.68 Margaret V. Hamilton MA 1969 *qv*

WENHAM Martin William PhD 1966
BSc(Wales)

WERNHAM Archibald Garden LLB 1967

WESSEL Ivar MB ChB 1968

WEST Alexander William MA 1963
s of Alexander W. W. and Rose N. Davidson; b Stonehaven 14.11.39
teacher Aber 1964–76; prin geog Linksfield acad Aber from 1976; leader Sandy West's Jazzmen band
m Aber 23.5.72 Edith S. Crabb

WEST Carole Margaret MA 1965
d of Stephen W. MA 1930 *qv* and Mary C. Scroggie MA 1933 *qv*; b Huntly 16.12.44
assistante d'Anglais Riom France 1966–67; teacher Cuminestown 1967–68; civ serv Winchester 1968–74; free-lance computer progr from 1975
m 4.8.71 Anthony W. Cox tech asst s of Sidney C. Winchester

WEST Edna MA 1962
d of Francis W. fisherman, comp dir and Emily West; b Gardenstown 15.6.41
teacher maths Rosyth 1963–68; Malawi: teacher maths Blantyre 1969–70, maths and gen subj Limbe 1970–71; computer progr Limbe 1971–72, secy-wages clerk Lilongwe 1972–73
m(1) Grant
(2) Lilongwe 26.8.72 Roger Kennington owner steel work comp s of Jack H. K. BSc Embangweni S Africa

WEST James Scott MA 1959
s of Forbes W. fisherman and Barbara J. Watt; b Macduff 1.12.36
teacher Portsoy, Banff from 1960
m Macduff 17.7.63 Elizabeth M. Thain teacher d of Robert T. Macduff

WEST Katharine Jane Mitchell *MA 1964
d of George W. bank clerk and Jane Mitchell; b Inv 8.1.42
asst lib Aberd 1965–68
m Aber 7.8.67 William J. Burnett MA 1961 *qv*

WEST Margaret Munro BSc 1956
d of Gordon R. W. banker and Mary A. Aird nurse; b Rangoon Burma 8.11.33
teacher sc Aber 1957–60, Lower Hutt NZ 1970–71; sc tech Lower Hutt from 1973
m Aber 30.7.58 John E. C. Flux BSc 1957 *qv*

WESTWATER Gary David MA 1970

WESTWOOD Carole MA 1967
d of Clifford J. W. scrap metal dealer and Ethel M. Crosby; b Middlesbrough 8.10.44

teacher Fr Bertram Ramsey comp s Middlesbrough 1967; cler off. DHSS Middlesbrough 1968–69; clerk Brit passport off. Kampala Uganda 1969–71
m Middlesbrough 5.8.67 David Watkins PO telecom eng s of Walter W. Middlesbrough

WESTWOOD William Dickson *BSc 1959 PhD 1962

WETHERLY Vivien Joyce Erskine MA 1964
d of William R. W. elect./mech eng, insur underwriter and Isabella MacKintosh; b Aber 25.11.46
Dip Sec St(Strath) 1965
res asst, secy to Prof Charles Wilson, Jesus coll Camb, writing hist of Unilever, Lond and Camb 1965–66; res asst/secy external serv BBC African serv Lond 1966–67; teacher Addison p s Lond 1968–70 and from 1972
m Lond 4.11.67 Mihalaki Fotiadis BSc(eng)(Istanbul) civ eng dir civ eng comp s of Yani F. Istanbul

WHALLEY Margaret Joyce BSc 1965
d of Geoffrey W. man. and Edith M. Brueton; b Aber 14.3.44
computer progr Internatl Computers Kidsgrove 1965–70
m Aber 24.2.68 Samuel A. Alcock BA(OU) prod. control man. s of Samuel A. Stoke-on-Trent

WHEATLEY James Alexander McIntosh *BSc(eng) 1962

WHELCHEL Michael Anthony PhD 1966
BA(Belhaven) BD(Columbia Theol Sem Georgia)

WHIGHT Evelyn Ann PhD 1970
d of Thomas B. W. BA(Queensland) teacher, headmaster, sen tut. maths Macq univ and Nellie E. L. Williams secy; b Chatswood NSW Aust 10.9.38
BSc(Syd) 1959 MSc(Syd) 1961
Aust: lect maths/statist univ of Syd 1968–72, Macq from 1973
m Blockley Glos 2.1.65 Roger W. Eyland PhD(Cantab) univ lect s of Thomas W. E. Sylvania Waters NSW

WHINN Marjorie *BSc 1967

WHITAKER Ian Michael BMedBiol 1969

WHITAKER Margaret Anne MA 1968

WHITCOMBE Kenneth Barry *MA 1968
s of Douglas H. W. trans man. and Gwendoline I. French; b Nantwich 17.7.46
teacher geog Cults acad 1969–71; prin geog Cowdenbeath from 1971

WHITE Alexander Robert MB ChB 1960

WHITE Anthony MB ChB 1966
s of Cyril W. miner and Florence M. Dicks; b Warsop nr Mansfield 11.11.39
h o 1966–68; g p: trainee Aber 1968–69, Glasg from 1970
m Glasg 30.9.72 Margaret A. Christison SRN d of David C. MB ChB(Glas) Glasg

WHITE David Alexander *MA 1969
s of Peter M. W. shop prop. and Catherine P. Peters; b Kilwinning 12.12.46
teacher Kings Rise s s Birm 1969–72, prim. supply East End Lond 1972–73; lect psych & commun Falkirk coll of tech from 1973; examiner in child educ for Scot. nursery nurse exam. board from 1978
m Largs 20.4.76 Janette Williamson teacher p e d of James W. Largs

WHITE Edward James Milner *BSc 1967
s of Leslie M. W. landscape arch. and Mary N. Muir; b Woking 28.4.45
PhD(Lond) 1971
res asst as Leverhulme fell. muscular dystrophy Guy's hosp Lond 1967–71; lect biochem Glas from 1971

WHITE Frances Geraldine LLB 1967
d of Harold G. W. civ serv and Margaret McInally civ serv; b Perth 30.3.45
Lond: solic's articled clerk 1967–70; solic: N Thames gas board 1970–72, CEGB from 1972
m Cookham 20.5.78 Noël C. O. Mizen eng s of Dennis G. M. Cookham

WHITE George Baird MB ChB 1968
s of George D. W. joiner and Dorothy M. Triptree; b Aboyne 9.10.42
h o ARI, Maryfield hosp Dun 1968–69; trainee g p Aber 1969–70; sen h o Aber mat. hosp, ARI 1970–71; g p Congleton 1971–72, Mold Clwyd N Wales 1972, Chester from 1972
m Banchory 5.8.67 Carole W. H. Tincker secy d of Maurice A. H. T. MA(Cantab) Banchory

WHITE Graham Robert BEd 1969
s of Robert W. welf off. loc auth and Isobel L. C. Veitch lib; b Aber 23.3.46
teacher: Hazlehead p s Aber 1969–71, Scotstown p s Aber 1971–73; dep head Cults p s 1973–75; lect Jordanhill coll Glasg from 1975
m Aber 10.7.71 Alison C. McKenzie teacher d of Alexander McK. Aber

WHITE Ian Hendry *BSc 1970 PhD 1977
s of John G. W. baker, fisherman and Bessie Joiner; b Banff 29.6.48
res asst: dept of chem path. Aberd 1970–74, dept of biochem Liv 1974–76; lect dept of chem path. Aberd from 1976
m Portsoy 9.10.71 Isobel M. Cooper HCO Scot. telecom d of James C. Portsoy

WHITE Isobel Anne MA 1967 Dip Ed 1968
d of William W. blacksmith and Maria Lindsay; b Aber 14.6.44
teacher Fr-Ger Aber h s for girls 1968–73, asst prin mod lang Summerhill acad 1973–75
m Aber 23.12.69 John W. Malcolm MA(Glas) journalist, teacher, lect s of Andrew R. M. Glasg

WHITE Janet Elizabeth MA 1967
d of Reginald W. works man., pers man. and Annie L. Mercer secy; b Wakefield 11.6.47
teacher: Ossett g s 1968–70, Summerhill acad Aber 1970–71, Hilton acad Aber 1971, Douglas acad 1971–76, part-time Cleveden s from 1979
m Wakefield 30.3.70 Frederick D. Yule MA 1968 *qv*

WHITE Michael George MA 1967
s of Frederick G. W. grocer and Dora J. Smith; b Wolverhampton 21.11.46
AMBIM 1976 AIPM 1978
exec off. PO Birm 1967–69; Lond: asst postal controller 1969–71, higher exec off. PO 1971–77, head of group PO from 1977

WHITEFIELD Elizabeth McCombe BEd 1970
d of James P. W. comp dir and Mary F. Thom; b Glasg 28.8.47
teacher mus/Engl Airdrie 1970–76
m Glasg 6.8.71 James Noble BSc(Glas) surg s of John R. N. Glasg

WHITEFORD Elizabeth Sim *MB ChB 1967
d of John W. BSc(Glas) and Elizabeth Strachan MA 1927 *qv*; b Forres 12.4.44
MRCPath 1976
h o ARI 1967–68; lect path. Aberd from 1968
m Aber 7.7.69 Laurence Gray MA 1966 *qv*

WHITEFORD Michael Hugh McLeod *BSc(eng) 1966
d 11.2.67

WHITEHEAD Paul Bryant *BSc(eng) 1967
s of Jack W. sales man. and Peggy Calligan; b Huddersfield 2.5.44
MICE 1974
sect. eng Edmund Nuttal civ eng contr 1967–69; civ constr eng ICI 1969–73; sen eng Edmund Nuttal 1973–75; proj man. Christiani & Nielsen civ eng contr from 1975
m Aber 22.7.66 Wilma E. Barrack d of William J. B. Aber

WHITEHEAD Peter John BSc 1968
s of John W. loc govt off. and Alice Richardson; b Liv 25.3.46
dev off. Birds Eye foods Liv 1968–71, asst prod. man. 1972–73; teacher sc Kincorth acad Aber 1974–78, Cults acad from 1978; also part-time farm. from 1974
m Fetternear 22.8.69 Frances A. Wilson teacher d of Robert W. Kemnay

WHITEHOUSE Alan John MA 1961 LLB 1965

WHITELAW Francis George PhD 1962
s of Francis G. W. and Hannah M. Taig; b Ardrossan 29.5.35
BSc(agr)(Glas) 1958
res scient Rowett inst Aber from 1958
m Aber 26.3.63 Anthea W. W. Bickford BSc(UCW) res scient, teacher d of Humphrey A. B. Malaya

WHITELEY David *BSc(for) 1965
s of Sidney W. BSc(Manc) res chem and Margaret E. Simon; b Hatch End 16.2.43
MSc(ANU) 1974
various posts/schol. Sweden 1965–66; Canberra Aust: for. off. logging res for./timber bureau 1966–73; clerk for. policy sect. Aust dept of agr 1973–75; asst div for. off. WA dept of for. Manjimup Aust from 1975

WHITELEY Fleur St Clair *MA 1965
d of Archibald W. M. W. MA 1929 *qv*; b Aber 22.2.43
Dip D'Etudes Francaises(Sorbonne)1963 B Litt(Oxon 1971
res stud. Oxon 1965–68; teacher Fr Manc g s 1968–69; asst lect Belf 1969–70; lect Manc 1970–71
m Oxford 11.7.70 Walter J. Houston MA(Cantab) min of relig s of Henry H. MA(Penn) Stockport

WHITELOCK Cecil Elizabeth MB ChB 1968
m Macdougall

WHITLEY Michael William MB ChB 1970

WHITTAKER Edith *BSc 1957 PhD 1960
d of James E. W. BSc(eng)(Lond) elect. eng area man. NSHEB and Edith Hopkinson; b Bradford 28.7.35
res fell. dept bot Aberd 1960–63
m Aber 1.9.60 Richard M. Cormack PhD 1961 *qv*

WHITTINGHAM Thomas Anthony MSc 1967
BSc(Lond)

WHYTE Alastair Graham Donald *BSc(for) 1960 PhD 1964
s of Alistair G. D. W. MA 1927 *qv* and Eveline S. Mackie MA 1927 *qv*; b Aber 8.2.39
Dip For.(Oxon) 1964 MIFor(NZ) 1970
NZ: res scient Rotorua 1964–69; lect Christchurch univ from 1969
m Rotorua 14.12.69 Rosemary E. Harris teacher d of John M. H. MSc(Well) Rotorua

WHYTE Alistair John *MA 1962

WHYTE Angela Jean Graham BSc 1969
d of James S. W. MA 1933 *qv* and Janet R. Graham MA 1934 *qv*; b Kirkcaldy 17.6.48
Wolverhampton: teacher maths girls' h s 1970–73, The Regis s Tettenhall from 1973
m Aber 25.7.70 Timothy Hodges MA 1967 *qv*

WHYTE Brenda Agnes *BSc 1959
m Lenssen

WHYTE Colin Graham BSc(eng) 1965
s of James S. W. MA 1933 *qv* and Janet R. Graham MA 1934 *qv*; b Aber 2.7.44
post-grad trainee Brechin 1965–67; market res eng Brechin 1967–68; market. eng Coventry 1968–69; Brechin: sales market. eng 1969–70, commercial sales man. 1970–76, sales dir 1976–79, sales & market. dir from 1979
m Tannadice 12.12.70 Margaret S. Bell secy, hotel receptionist d of George B. MA(Edin) Montrose

WHYTE George Garden MB ChB 1960

WHYTE Johan Geddes *MA 1968
d of Gilbert W. painter and Johan Geddes bonus clerk; b Peterhead 2.3.46
teacher Stow-on-the-Wold from 1972
m Aber 24.12.68 Robert H. C. Davidson MA 1968 *qv*

WHYTE Kathleen Anderson MA 1965
m Winter

WHYTE Roderick James *BSc 1960
s of Roderick W. tradesman and Helen Taggart; b Inv 8.11.38
MSc(RS of Mines) 1973 DIC 1973 MIMM 1974
explor geol: Malawi 1960–63, Ghana 1963–65, UK 1965–66; Zambia: chief mining geol Chibuluma 1966–72, asst geol supt 1974–75; geotech eng Maidenhead 1975–77, proj eng Johannesburg from 1977
m Inv 29.2.64 Diana I. A. Sutherland nurs sister d of John S. Kilmarnock

WHYTE Roger William *MA 1970

WIEBE Paul Arthur MSc 1963
b Winnipeg Manitoba 11.2.38
BASc(Br Col) 1960 Athlone fell. 1962–64 DIC(Lond) 1964
jun civ eng Vancouver BC 1960–62, sen hydraulic eng Niagara Falls Ont 1964–69; spec advis to Epwapda on hydraulics & hydrology Dacca E Pakistan (now Bangladesh) 1969–71; head water resources div Montreal from 1971
m Vancouver 1962 Joanne W. Rosene BA(Br Col) teacher

WIGHT James Reid *MA 1960 *MEd 1964
s of James M. W. bakery van salesman and Alice Reid; b Inverurie 6.9.36
teacher Aber 1961–64; asst dir of educ Fife 1965–69; lect educ man./admin Moray House coll of educ Edin from 1969
m Aber 12.8.64 Madeleine A. Burnett MA 1960 *qv*

WIGHT Wendy Jean *MA 1960

WILD Valerie Frances *MEd 1969
d of Barton R. W. man. English Elect. subsid and Flora F. C. Lewis BSc(Lond) teacher; b Preston 20.8.46
MA(Oxon) 1967 Dip Ed 1968
Aber: res asst psych Aberd 1969–70, lect coll of comm 1970–71, lect coll of educ 1971–75; teacher Barthol Chapel 1975–79; head Cairnorrie p s from 1979
m Oxford 26.8.67 David A. Smart MA(Oxon) forensic biol s of George A. K. S. Glossop

WILDGOOSE David Middleton MA 1964
s of Alexander M. W. civ serv and Alice H. R. Milne; b Aber 5.10.43
Dip Pers Man.(Strath) 1965 MSc(Strath) 1976
trg off. AEI Manc 1965–68; pers off. Thomson Organis Edin 1968–70; pers man. Collins publ Glasg 1970–76; lect Dun coll of tech from 1976
m Aber 2.7.66 Edna W. Sproul MA 1964 *qv*

WILDGOOSE Ian BSc 1964
s of Robert W. W. farm. and Mary H. Stewart; b Urquhart 22.9.43
teacher chem: Lossiemouth h s 1965–73, Bankhead acad from 1973
m Aber 21.12.73 Sheila Mackland BSc 1970 *qv*

WILKEN Ronald *MA 1959

WILKENS Thomas Gene PhD 1968
BA BD(Luther USA)

WILKIE Brenda MA 1968
d of William J. W. eng and Jessie A. Milne teacher; b Batu Gajah Malaysia 24.2.49
teacher Engl: Forrester s s Edin 1969–71, Eastbank acad Glasg 1971–74, Perth acad 1974–76
m Glasg 18.7.74 Melvin C. Cooper adv plumber s of Charles W. C. Bridge of Alford

WILKIE Charles Alexander Spark MA 1970
d Aber 13.1.74

WILKIE David Sharp *BSc 1970

WILKIE Iain James MA 1967
s of John W. salmon fisher, factory worker and Annie D. Robertson secy; b Perth 17.11.46
police constable Aber 1967–73, sgt from 1973
m Aber 4.6.71 Esmé E. McDerment health visitor d of John McD. Aber

WILKIE James *MA 1963 M Litt 1974
s of George R. W. blacksmith and Jane M. Poustie; b Dun 1.2.38
teacher hist Perth 1964–67; prin hist Golspie 1967–71; lect coll of educ Aber from 1971
m Aber 8.6.63 Agnes McLennan nurse d of William A. McL. Findochty

WILKIE James Lindsay *MA 1956 BD 1959
s of James L. W. comm trav/news ag and tobacconist and Annie Hamilton teacher; b Dunfermline 30.1.34
C of S min: asst St Machar's cath Aber 1959–60; Zambia: missionary min of ch of Central Africa in Rhodesia, Mwenzo 1961–65, miss. min of united ch of Zambia Isoka 1965–69, synod treas of UCZ Lusaka 1970–71, Christian Council chaplain to stud. in univ of Zambia 1971–76; exec secy (Africa) Brit Council of Churches from 1976
m Aber 15.7.59 Irene A. Watson MB ChB 1959 *qv*

WILKIE Patricia Isabel MA 1967
d of Peter W. P O eng and Isabella M. Craig french polisher; b Aber 8.7.46
off. Nat West Bank Lond, Middlesbrough, Shepperton 1969–73
m Middlesbrough 25.10.69 Robert L. Ibell BSc(eng) 1967 *qv*

WILKIE Victor Macfarlane BSc 1966 Dip Ed 1967
s of William W. joiner, clerk of works and Margaret Pirie; b Elgin 1945
MI Gas E 1973 C Eng 1973
eng (Scot. gas) Edin, Aber, Uddingston from 1967
m Crook of Devon Kinross 19.3.74 Barbara Whitson nurse d of Donald W.

WILKIN Jennifer MA 1967
d of John A. W. mech eng and Williamina Tait; b Aber 20.1.46
teacher: Skene Sq p s Aber 1968–69, Cornhill p s Aber from 1969

WILKINS Brian *BSc 1969
s of William S. W. headmaster and Elizabeth A. Cordiner; b Cruden Bay 12.12.46
MSc(Sus) 1970 DPhil(Sus) 1973
teacher chem Crawley from 1973
m High Wycombe 12.8.72 Hazel J. Shapter BSc(Sus) teacher d of Ronald F. S. High Wycombe

WILKINS Roberta *MA 1970

WILKINSON David MB ChB 1956
s of Ernest W. MA(Cantab) HM insp taxes and Muriel M. Wyatt; b Derby 13.2.32
h o Stracathro hosp Brechin 1957–58; m o RAF fl lt Wilmslow, Upavon 1958–61; g p Potton 1961–62; h o obst Farnham 1962; g p S Elmshall from 1962
m Aber 10.6.57 Katharine P. Carter RGN d of Charles C. OBE BSc(Leeds) Aber

WILKINSON Martin Arthur BSc(for) 1970
s of Arthur W. teacher and Agnes G. Harrison; b Leigh 9.10.48
private for. man. comp: for. asst, asst br man. Lhanbryde 1970–72, asst br man. Jedburgh 1972–73, br man. Ludlow from 1973
m Jedburgh –.7.74 Alison A. Ritch teacher d of Leslie S. S. R. Jedburgh

WILKINSON Norma Jean Ross MA 1964

WILKS Jocelyn PhD 1963
BA(Brist)

WILKS Robin John PhD 1967
BSc(Brist)

WILL Alexander James BSc(eng) 1959

WILL Alexander Ogilvie MA 1962
s of Alexander O. W. butcher and Annie B. Milne; b Peterhead 17.8.41
teacher Peterhead cent s 1963–68; head: Rothienorman p s 1968–75, South Park p s Fraserburgh from 1975
m Peterhead 25.7.64 Eileen F. Milne teacher d of Joseph M. Peterhead

WILL Diana Beatrice Robertson *MA 1959
d of Hunter M. Will MA 1928 *qv*; b Aber 27.5.37
teacher: geog Edin 1960–65, Lugton s Dalkeith from 1975
m Aber 7.4.62 John M. Legge arch. s of Andrew L. Aber

WILL Duncan BSc 1956
s of Sydney W. master stevedore and Helen Watt; b Fraserburgh 23.4.35
Grad Inst Phys(Paisley coll of sc and tech) 1969

teacher: maths/sc Fraserburgh acad 1957–63, phys Berwicksh h s 1963–65; prin sc Forebraes s Alloa 1965–69; prin phys Lornshill acad Alloa from 1969
m Inverallochy 30.3.63 Grace B. Crawford clerkess d of John W. C. Inverallochy

WILL Frank BSc(eng) 1970
s of Elizabeth M. Will; b Ellon 2.11.49
grad asst eng Perth and Kinross c c Perth 1970–75; prof grade asst Tayside reg c from 1975
m Aber 15.7.72 Diane H. Mackie MA 1972 computer progr d of George M. Aber

WILL Hunter Alexander Bonnar *BSc(eng) 1966
s of Hunter M. W. MA 1928 *qv*; b Aber 12.12.44
CE MICE 1971
des eng: Aber 1966–67, Glasg 1967–68; eng asst Aber 1968–77, prin eng from 1977

WILL Patricia MA 1959

WILL Peter Milne *BSc(eng) 1958 PhD 1960
s of James W. cooper and Margaret Milne; b Peterhead 2.11.35
res scient: AEI Manc 1960–61, AMF Sonning Common Reading 1961–64, AMF Springdale Conn USA 1964–65; res staff member IBM T. J. Watson res centre Yorktown Hts NY from 1965; also lect univ of Conn Stamford Branch grad s in elect. eng 1966–71
m Aber 21.3.59 Angela H. Giulianotti

WILL Sylvia Jennifer *MA 1965
m Fulton

WILLCOX Graham *MA 1962

WILLETS Lynn Denise *BSc(agr) 1970
d of Harold W. gen man. textile firm and Bertha Ramsden; b Farnworth 13.8.47
res stud. Tillycorthie farm Udny 1970–72
m Aber 23.6.72 John Gilbert HGV driving instr s of John G. Kintore

WILLETTS Patricia Mary MA 1970

WILLIAMS Angela Catherine *MA 1965
m David S. Hewitt PhD 1969 *qv*

WILLIAMS Frances Ann MA 1967
d of John A. W. and Charlotte K. Morrison; b Huntly 1.8.46
Dip Pers Man.(Strath) 1968
tech sales corresp Edin 1968–70
m Aber –.2.70 David G. M. Carpenter mar. eng s of Albert G. C. Tarbet

WILLIAMS Gaynor Myfanwy MA 1965 Dip Ed 1966
m(1) Sinclair-Gieben
(2) Hamilton

WILLIAMS Geraldine Mary BSc 1970
d of Arthur W. aircraft eng and Dorothy M. J. Lee secy; b Gainsborough 26.3.49
teacher: p s Sydney Aust 1971–72, Sheppey Kent from 1972

WILLIAMS Jacqueline Ann *MA 1969

WILLIAMS Paul MA 1968

WILLIAMS Richard Peter BSc 1967
s of William R. W. supt marine eng and May Deakin; b Bristol 17.6.46
quality controller food indust Grimsby 1967–68, entomologist Arusha Tanganyika 1968–70; quantity controller food Cleethorpes 1971–72; teacher: Gt Coates 1974–77, Jamaica, El Salvador (cent Amer) from 1977

WILLIAMS Roger Walford MB ChB 1969
s of John E. W. comp rep and Elsie J. S. Evans teacher; b Shrewsbury 12.5.45
h o Aber hosps, Airdrie and Coatbridge hosps 1969–71; g p Fife 1971–72; sen h o Dunfermline hosps 1972–73; g p Fife from 1973
m Aber 1969 Elizabeth M. Macnaughtan B Med Biol 1967 *qv*

WILLIAMSON Alastair Mitchell BSc 1964 *MA 1966

WILLIAMSON Andrew John *MA 1966 Dip Ed 1967
s of Arthur S. W. fisherman/cooper and Mary Anderson; b Whalsay 31.5.44
teacher Alloa acad 1967–70, prin geog: N Berwick h s 1970–71, Musselburgh g s 1972–74; asst head Dalkeith h s from 1974
m Aber 28.1.67 Wyn P. Valentine BSc 1966 *qv*

WILLIAMSON Anne Margaret *MA 1958
d of George J. W. farm. and Janet Walker; b Inverurie 17.9.36
teacher: Perth h s 1959–62, exchange Indianopolis USA 1962–63
m Indianopolis 3.8.63 Gale M. Helft AB(Indiana) teacher s of Nathan H. Indianopolis

WILLIAMSON Brian PhD 1969
s of Ronald W. T. W. BA(Lond) teacher and Jean Walsh; b Rossendale 6.4.44
BSc(UCW) 1965 MSc(Nott) 1966
NATO post doct res fell. biol Woolwich polytech, med fac Mem univ of Newfoundland St John's Canada 1970–72; post doct res asst for. NERC Aberd 1972–73; plant path. Scot. hortic res inst Invergowrie from 1973
m Ringwood 1971 Janet M. Saunders radiogr d of Alan S. St Leonards nr Ringwood

WILLIAMSON Elliot Allen MB ChB 1961
s of Alexander A. W. bldg contr and Jane J. Martin; b Aber 10.8.38
DObstRCOG 1965
h o: paediat Inv 1962, obst/gyn Irvine 1963; g p Balloch; h o anaest Perth 1965–66; g p Oakville Ont Canada from 1966; pres med staff Oakville hosp from 1975
m Dunbar 1963 Helen E. Bruce teacher p e d of Archibald B. Dunbar

WILLIAMSON Frances Olwen MA 1962
d of Alexander A. W. bldg contr and Jane J. Martin; b Aber 18.3.42
teacher: Aber 1962–67, Dun 1967–68, Aber 1968–71
m Aber 19.8.67 Gordon W. Cook MA 1961 *qv*

WILLIAMSON Grace Agnes MA 1963 Dip Ed 1964

WILLIAMSON James MSc 1963 PhD 1965
s of Thomas W. supt marine eng and Kathleen Simpson; b Liv 5.4.39
BSc(Nott) 1967
Imp Coll Lond: res fell. metall 1965–70, lect metall/materials sc from 1970
m Aber 16.7.66 Aldon T. Baxter MA 1966 *qv*

WILLIAMSON John MA 1970 Dip Ed 1971
s of Robert J. W. chef and Edith M. Crofts; b Aber 11.3.39
teacher geog Glenrothes 1971–74, asst prin mod. stud.

from 1974
m Aber 3.8.63 Maureen Yeoman acct machine oper d of Douglas E. Y. Aber

WILLIAMSON Kenneth Harry *BSc 1970
s of Thomas L. W. clerk of works (loc govt) and Harriet E. Anderson; b Lerwick 8.2.48
PhD(Lond) 1975
sen scient off. hydrogeology unit inst geol sc Lond (work concerns geothermal explor proj overseas) from 1975

WILLIAMSON Laurence Angus Leslie BSc(eng) 1956
s of William T. H. W. BSc 1910 *qv*; b Cairo 17.10.34
De Havilland Eng Co Edgware: app 1956–58, tech asst rocket tech office 1958–60; tech sales, power plant dept George Cohen Machinery Lond; assoc edit. *Machine Design Engineering* Rowse Muir publ./Mercury Ho publ Lond 1965–68; p r o Rolls Royce Derby 1968–71; press off. eng div Tube Investments Lond 1971–77; publicity man. machine div Tube Investments Coventry from 1977
m Aber 29.3.61 Diana J. Findlay occup therap d of Frank A. F. Kingswells

WILLIAMSON Marjory Johan Duncan MA 1960

WILLIAMSON Mary McIntosh McConnell MA 1970
d of Archibald W. comm trav and Jean H. McIntosh shop asst; b Glasg 27.9.40
ALA 1973
loc hist lib NE Scot. lib serv Aber from 1972

WILLIAMSON Peter Garrick *BSc 1958
s of Robert W. seaman/crofter and Ursula M. Garrick sub postmistress; b Ollaberry Shetland 30.1.36
teacher sc Anderson h s Lerwick from 1960
m Lerwick 18.7.62 Elizabeth A. D. Johnson MA 1960 *qv*

WILLIAMSON Robert Buchanan *BSc 1958
s of Archibald M. M. W. MA 1920 *qv*(II, III); b Edin 12.4.35
fishery res trg grant fisheries lab Pitlochry 1958–60; Malawi: govt fisheries res off. Nkhata Bay, Monkey Bay 1960–65, govt chief fisheries off. Zomba 1966–70; Freshwater Fisheries lab Pitlochry: sen scient off. 1970–76, prin scient off. from 1976
m Aber 17.9.60 Sheena I. B. Jeffrey BSc 1968 *qv*

WILLIAMSON Sheila Mary MA 1970
m Russell

WILLIS Douglas Peter *MA 1965 MLitt 1967
b Methlick 19.7.43
tut./stud. geog Aberd 1965–67; prin teacher geog: Cults acad 1968–75, Fortrose acad from 1975
m Ullapool 2.4.68 Catherine M. Campbell MA 1965 *qv*

WILLOX Alexander *BSc(eng) 1962

WILLOX John Brand MA 1963
s of Sydney M. W. pharm and Elizabeth M. Brand; b Aber 14.4.40
ITA teacher fell. Glas 1969 Churchill fell. Scandinavia 1970
teacher: Ellon 1964–65, Peterhead 1965–66; head: Laggan p s 1966–67, Knockando p s 1967–70, Dufftown p s 1970–72; p s advis Caithness 1972–76; asst dir BFES from 1976
m Peterhead 22.7.64 Sheena F. Grant teacher d of Charles G. Peterhead

WILLOX Margaret Elizabeth BSc 1959
d of James W. man. dir Aber hide skin & tallow comp and Elizabeth Mitchell secy; b Aber 19.9.38
AEO biochem/microbiol Torry res stat. Aber 1959–66
m Aber 3.10.64 George A. Taylor MB ChB 1958 *qv*

WILLS Leslie Charles MB ChB 1966
s of Charles L. W. draper and Anne E. Wright; b Aber 21.2.40
FRCSE 1972
h o Aber hosps 1966–67; sen h o ARI 1967–68; lect anat Aberd 1969–71; regist ENT ARI/tut. Aberd 1971–72; sen regist ENT ARI/lect Aberd 1972–75; sen regist/lect prof unit royal nat nose throat ear hosp Lond 1975; consult ENT surg ARI/sen lect surg Aberd from 1975
m Aber 19.6.67 Frances C. Gove teacher d of David G. Cults

WILSON Aileen Susanna *BSc 1969 MSc 1971
d of James M. W. wholesale grocer and Christina F. Livingstone; b Aber 20.10.47
res asst computer dept Aberd 1970–71; oper res. analyst Düsseldorf W. Ger 1971–72; res fell. computing centre Aberd 1978
m Aber 16.7.69 Gordon V. Stone MB ChB 1969 *qv*

WILSON Alan Chaney *BSc 1968 PhD 1972
s of William A. W. MD(Lond) med statist and Mary L. Harvey; b Kampala Uganda 30.7.45
trav fell. Boehringer Mannheim corp 1971 held in univ of Bari Italy; res assoc biochem Baylor coll of med Houston Texas USA 1971–76; res fell. biochem univ of Ottawa 1976–77; NRC visiting fell. Ottawa res stat agr Canada from 1977

WILSON Alexander BSc(for) 1964

WILSON Alexander Bruce *BSc(eng) 1962 MSc 1964
s of Alexander W. MA 1925 *qv* and Jessie C. Bruce MA 1922 *qv*; b Kirkcaldy 8.8.40
turbine des Manc 1964–67; refrig des Dun 1967–75; res eng Renfrew from 1975
m Aber 14.7.64 Marjory M. Cameron MA 1961 *qv*

WILSON Alexander Dey *BSc(eng) 1963
s of Alexander D. W. MA 1936 *qv* and Mary C. Anderson BSc 1938 *qv*; b Stromness 7.4.41
grad trainee Scot. elect. trg scheme 1963–65; asst eng NSHEB: Keith 1965–67, Huntly 1967–68, Peterhead 1968–69; ICI: elect. eng (plastics div) Wilton works Cleveland 1970–76, sen elect. des eng (paints div NW) Hyde 1976–78, works elect. instrument eng (paints div) Newton Works Hyde from 1978
m Aber 27.7.66 Eleanor M. Coutts teacher d of William C. MA 1925 *qv*

WILSON Alexander George *MA 1969
s of Joseph S. W. lab attendant and Adeline H. Crockett; b Aber 25.2.47
LTCL 1965 LRAM 1970
res stud. St John's Cambridge 1969–73; violinist Bergen S O Norway from 1973
d Norway –.6.75 *AUR* XLVI 328

WILSON Alexander John MA 1969
s of Alexander J. W. master stove enameller and Anne Milne; b Aber 15.10.46
trainee admin man. Aber 1969–70; Glasg: asst admin man. 1970–71, admin controller 1971–77, admin man. Poole branch Marley Tile Co from 1977
m Kirkintilloch 7.7.73 Sheena E. Turnbull teacher d of James T. Lenzie

WILSON Alexander Shand BSc(agr) 1964
s of James O. W. farm. and Mary S. Shand nurse; b Banff 15.8.41

farm. Banff from 1964
m Banff 24.5.69 Mary G. Duff bank clerk d of George D. Banff

WILSON Anthony James *MA 1970
s of James T. W. admin and Elsie A. Merrick; b Aber 1947
res stud. Oxford univ 1970–72; lect Paisley from 1972

WILSON Barbara Helen *MA 1966
d of Henry J. S. W. BA(Cantab) headmaster and Marjorie L. Cruden horticulturalist; b Market Harborough 11.3.43
Dip Ed(Edin) 1967 ALA 1969
asst lib: Street 1967–68, Liv 1970; tut. lib Kirkby coll of f e Liv 1970–72, chief lib N Warks coll of tech and art Nuneaton from 1972
m Sheffield 14.7.68 Stuart L. Heaton BA (Warw) draughtsman/lect s of Jack H. Bridgwater

WILSON Brian LLB 1969
s of George C. W. BL(Glas) solic and Margaret I. Lavers nurs sister; b Perth 20.2.46
law app Banff c c 1969–71, leg. asst 1971–72; sen leg. asst Inv c c 1972–73; dep county clerk Banff c c 1973–75; dir of admin and leg. serv Banff and Buchan dist council Banff 1974–78; chief exec Inv dist c from 1978
m Buckie 9.4.69 Isobel Esson teacher d of John E. Buckie

WILSON Catherine Martin MA 1964
d of Hubert M. W. MA(Cantab) dir of educ Shropsh and Ida M. Samuel BA(Cantab) county organis Shrops WRNS, member Telford dev corp; b Shrewsbury 11.11.42
trainee, buyer D. H. Evans 1964–67; boutique buyer Swan & Edgar 1967–72; opened own shop for young fashion in Pinner 1972
m Lond 15.2.69 David A. Aubrey buyer BHS s of Geoffrey E. A. Lond

WILSON Cynthia Dolores BSc 1956
d of Archibald W. fisherman and Mabel Gault nurse; b Aber 27.11.33
analytical chem Peterhead 1957–65; teacher: Peterhead acad 1966–67, Summerhill acad 1967–70, prin guid 1970–73; prin guid Linksfield acad from 1973
m Aber 10.10.59 Archibald McRaw MA(Glas) lect bus. man. RGIT s of James McR. MA 1908 *qv*(II, III)

WILSON Denis Maclean *MA 1960 MSc 1961
s of George S. W. silver engraver and Jean S. Maclean lib; b Elgin 6.8.37
asst lect maths Aberd 1961–63; syst progr IBM UK labs Hursley 1963–64; lect computing sc Aberd from 1964

WILSON Donald Fraser *MA 1964

WILSON Dorothy Lawrence *MA 1965
d of James W. W. bank man. and Anne L. Stewart nurs sister; b Aber 10.3.43
teacher mod lang: Albyn s for girls Aber 1966–68, King's s Gütersloh Germany 1968–74
m Aber 19.8.71 Philip G. Snell BSc(Brist) teacher s of Gerald T. S. Umberleigh

WILSON Edith Isabel MA 1956
d of Alexander W. MA 1925 *qv* and Jessie C. Bruce MA 1922 *qv*; b Kirkcaldy 6.4.35
teacher maths: Brechin h s 1957–59, Inverurie acad 1959–63; spec asst maths Inverurie acad 1963–66, Gordon s Huntly 1966–72, prin guid Gordon s Huntly from 1972
m Aber 29.7.66 Gordon Peters MA 1958 *qv*

WILSON Elizabeth Whyte MA 1965
m Thom

WILSON Erlend Ramsay *MA 1957

WILSON Gavin Bruce MA 1962 ᵉLLB 1964
d 3.10.69

WILSON Gladys MA 1958
d of George G. W. carpenter and Maggie A. Paterson; b Macduff 10.10.36
teacher: Aber 1959–61, part time Banffsh and Grampian reg from 1974
m Aber 12.7.61 Reginald L. Henderson MA 1956 *qv*

WILSON Gladys Helen MA 1960
d of George P. W. bldr and Elspeth J. Law; b 3.12.39
m Aber 30.7.65 Charles E. Simpson arch.

WILSON Gladys Maclean Watt MA 1956
m Srivastava

WILSON Hamish Robert McHattie *MA 1967
s of James W. teacher and Margaret A. P. McHattie; b Aber 19.1.46
BA(Cantab) 1969 MA(Cantab) 1973 PLD(Cantab) 1976
Croom Robertson res fell. Emmanuel coll Cambridge 1969–72; health serv admin Aber from 1972
m Aber 18.6.70 Ann M. V. Shewan RGN d of James M. S. BSc 1931 *qv*

WILSON Harold MEd 1966
s of Albert W. trade union off. and Ann Reay; b Stanley Co Durh 11.9.42
BSc(Manc) 1964 ABPsS 1972
teacher maths: Peterhead 1966–67, Stonehaven 1967–68; educ psych Lanarksh 1968–71; prin psych: Clackmannan 1971–75, Central reg from 1975
m Stonehaven 23.12.68 Dorothy T. Campbell teacher d of John C. C. MA(Edin) Glenrothes

WILSON Helen Irene *MA 1966
d of John W. trawl skipper and Elizabeth Gardiner; b Aber 5.10.44
teacher Fr: Aber h s for girls 1967–70, private tuition Frodsham 1970–73, part-time Helsby county g s for girls from 1973
m Cullen 12.9.70 Humphrey C. Bowen MA(Oxon) res man. ICI s of Edward A. B. MA(Oxon) Oxford

WILSON Ian Alexander BSc(eng) 1966

WILSON Isabel Ann MA 1956
m Middleton

WILSON James Anthony *BSc(eng) 1968 MSc 1970
s of Alexander D. W. MA 1936 *qv* and Mary C. Anderson BSc 1938 *qv*; b Aber 25.7.46
asst consult. eng: Glasg 1970–72, Helensburgh 1972–73; sen consult. eng Glasg 1973–75; proj eng from 1975
m Aber 21.9.73 Elizabeth D. McLaren MA 1968 *qv*

WILSON James George
***BSc(eng) 1961 MSc 1963 MA 1966**
s of James W. marine eng and J. Farquhar; b Buckie 29.11.30
BA(OU) 1974
teacher maths AGS 1967; lect maths Aber tech coll from 1967
m 1960 Moira Wood BA(OU) d of Angus M. W.

WILSON James Moir *BSc 1960 MLitt 1975
s of William G. W. fisherman and Alexanderina McKay; b Whitehills 20.4.38
M Inst P
teacher: phys AGS 1961–64, prin phys Nairn acad 1964–

70, Inv royal acad 1970–71; Aber coll of educ: lect phys sc 1972–77, sen lect i/c phys sc dept from 1977
m Aber 21.7.66 Jean G. Duncan secy d of George L. D. Aber

WILSON Jean MA 1965
d of George W. seaman and Alice Wilson; b Turriff 6.1.44
teacher: Engl Friern Barnet g s 1966–68, nat soc for ment handicapped ch Lond 1968–70, Edin 1970–72, asst prin Engl Craigroyston s Edin from 1972

WILSON John Allan *BSc 1969
s of George P. D. W. elect. and Isobella W. Allan; b Forfar 24.1.48
res stud. Imp coll 1969–73; res assoc Birm from 1973

WILSON John Dewar PhD 1969
s of Stuart W. exec eng GPO telecom and Jenny R. Jamieson shop asst; b Edin 27.5.39
MA(Edin) 1960 Dip Ed(Edin) 1961 MEd(Glas) 1964
lect educ Aberd 1969–70; prin lect educ Moray House coll of educ from 1971
m Glasg 27.7.65 Margaret A. Miller teacher d of Robert M. M. Glasg

WILSON John Haldane BSc(eng) 1963

WILSON John Smith *MA 1970
s of John W. bldg contr and Mary H. Smith; b Lossiemouth 30.3.25
teacher Engl AGS 1971–75; asst prin Engl Kincorth acad Aber from 1976
m Lossiemouth 17.11.50 Irene Smith teacher d of James A. S. Lossiemouth

WILSON Kathleen Helen MA 1970
d of Alexander W. farm. and Kathleen M. Ling nurse; b Dumfries 13.1.49
soc worker: Kent c c Canterbury 1970–71, Brighton soc serv 1972–73
m Dumfries 24.9.71 John D. Macgregor BSc 1970 *qv*

WILSON Keith William *BSc 1967 PhD 1974
s of James G. H. W. farm lab and Isobel E. Cound; b Shrewsbury 29.9.44
scient civ serv sen scient off: MAFF Burnham-on-Crouch 1970–77, NW water auth Warrington from 1977
m Aber 13.9.69 Linda F. Hall MA 1970 *qv*

WILSON Lorna Murray MA 1957 Dip Ed 1958
d of Gordon D. W. papermaker and Annie T. Murray; b Bucksburn 11.3.36
teacher: maths Tarbert Is of Harris 1958–62, high s for girls Glasg 1962; mathematician UKAEA Windscale 1962–64
m Aber 17.10.63 Philip R. Stanwix BSc(Glas) res chem s of William P. S. Darlington

WILSON Margaret Anderson MA 1968
m Mikulsiti

WILSON Margaret Elizabeth BSc 1962
d of Frank J. W. foreman maltman and Isabella Younie; b Rafford 9.3.41
teacher: sc Goodlyburn s s Perth 1963–65, spec asst 1965–66, maths St Stephen's h s Port Glasgow 1974–76, High Tunstall comp s Hartlepool from 1976
m Rafford 10.7.65 Hamish A. Copland radar tech RAF, electronic test eng IBM s of Robert S. C. Abernethy

WILSON Margaret Hill MA 1970
s of David D. W. painter/decorator and Helen Hill; b Stirling 25.5.48
journalist *Weekly News* Glasg from 1970

WILSON Moira MA 1969
d of Alexander W. orthop tech and Mary H. Sangster lib, stock superv; b Perth 6.8.47
Inv: temp sales asst, temp clerkess Inv t c 1969; asst collector of taxes Inl Rev from 1970

WILSON Monica Mary MA 1963
d of James O. W. farm. and Mary Shand nurs sister; b Banff 11.10.42
teacher: p s Stonehaven 1964–65, Amer s s Benghazi Libya 1966
m Aber 20.7.65 Thomas W. Ogg MB ChB 1964 *qv*

WILSON Muriel MA 1967
m Greig

WILSON Neil *BSc 1957

WILSON Peter Richard BSc(for) 1962

WILSON Philip Melvin MB ChB 1969

WILSON Robert Charles Duncan MB ChB 1956
s of Charles D. W. MB ChB 1924 *qv*(II, III) and Margaret T. Munro MA 1925 *qv*; b Darlington 19.7.32
ECFMG(USA) 1962 LMCC 1962 CCFP(C) 1970
h o Aber 1956–58; internship Calgary Alta 1958–59; h o Westminster hosp Lond Ont 1959–60; clin lect fam med univ of W Ont Canada from 1967; g p Lond Ont from 1962
m Lond Ont 1.2.74 Maureen A. Gregory d of George E. G. Gravesend

WILSON Robert Keith BSc 1967
s of Robert W. farm. and Frances Gray teacher; b Aber 4.5.44
advt exec J. Walter Thompson Co Lond 1967–70; asst advt man. Scottish & N'cle Breweries Edin 1970–72; advt exec Roche Prod. Lond 1972; sen acct superv McCann Erickson Lond from 1973

WILSON Robert Murray BSc(eng) 1966
s of Peter M. W. chmn/man. dir and Agnes B. Calder teacher elocution; b Bearsden 30.3.43
Montreal: boiler des eng 1966–67, sales eng 1967–68; Clydebank: sales eng 1969–75, sales and marketing dir from 1975

WILSON Robin George MA 1969

WILSON Roger Victor *MA 1966
s of Robert W. W. tech auth, pers off. and Ada S. Rickwood; b Lond 30.6.44
ABPsS 1969 MPhil(Lond) 1972
psych, sen psych MoD Farnborough 1966–72; univ careers advis Leeds from 1973

WILSON Ronald George MB ChB 1961
FRCSE 1970
lect surg Nott

WILSON Stewart Roger Devine *MA 1966

WILSON Susan Margaret MA 1965

WILSON Wendy Scott MLitt 1970
d of John D. W. comp pres and Shirley J. Mansfield; b Litchfield Illinois 21.1.46
BA(Wells) 1968
USA: teaching fell. Northeastern univ Mass. 1970–71, teacher Lexington s Mass. from 1971, lect Northeastern

univ from 1972, writer Prentice-Hall publ from 1980
m Weston Mass. 24.11.71 Lloyd M. Thompson BA(Northeastern) teacher s of Lloyd M. T. Scituate Mass.

WILSON William Alan MB ChB 1968
s of William C. W. MB ChB(Edin) emeritus prof surg Aberd and Ivy M. Allan; b Aber 13.1.42
MRCGP 1974
h o ARI, RACH 1968–69; g p Aber from 1969, med asst ARI from 1975
m Aber 26.12.63 Eileen M. Machray teacher d of John W. M. Lyne of Skene

WILSON William Stewart *BSc 1960
s of Robert S. W. civ serv and Elizabeth K. K. Hamilton; b Aber 15.5.37
teacher AGS 1961–66; prin maths Banchory acad 1966–72, dep rector 1972–78, rector from 1978
m Aber 3.8.66 Elizabeth A. Gorrod bank teller d of George G. Aber

WILSON Wilma Elizabeth Bruce MA 1963
m Hunter

WINCHESTER Alexander MA 1957

WINCKWORTH William Haydn LLB 1968 *1969
s of Wilfrid H. W. highways eng and Joan F. Thurlow; b S'ton 8.6.47
admitted solic Eng 1972
articled clerk, asst solic Lancs c c Preston 1970–73; sen solic Telford dev corp Salop 1973–78; solic Lond & Manc Assur Co Exeter from 1978
m Aber 3.4.71 Jean Middleton teacher d of William M. Aber

WINGFIELD Nigel Richard Haydon MA 1970

WINNING Timothy John MB ChB 1970

WINPENNY Alexander Rae *MA 1963

WINTON Douglas BSc 1957

WINTON Peter Garden BSc 1966

WIRK Harwant Kaur MB ChB 1968

WISELY Dorothy Constance MA 1966
d of Norman F. W. haulage contr/farm. and G. Constance Robertson; b Aber 18.12.45
teacher p s Cults acad Aber 1967–69
m Aber 19.7.68 Douglas R. Harper BSc 1962 *qv*

WISELY Ivan Charles Fraser MB ChB 1967
s of John A. K. W. teacher and Elizabeth A. M. Fraser MA 1927 *qv*; b Aber 28.1.43
DA 1971
h o, sen h o, regist anaest ARI 1967–73; g p: Aber 1973–74, Dyce/Bucksburn from 1974
m Montrose 12.9.64 Jillian G. A. Kay MA 1966 *qv*

WISELY Kathleen MA 1965 *MEd 1970
teacher: Engl/hist Northfield acad Aber 1966–74, prin guid Kincorth acad Aber from 1974

WISELY May *MA 1969

WISELY Norman Robertson *BSc(eng) 1969
s of Norman F. W. haulage contr/farm. and G. Constance Robertson; b Aber 4.1.48
Dip Man. St(Strath) 1974
prod. dev eng Gen Motors Scot. Newhouse 1969–73; sales dev eng Baker Perkins Jaxons Glasg from 1973
m Aber 5.8.72 Margaret A. Sinclair MA 1972 teacher d of Iain A. M. S. Aber

WISELY Wendy Adie *MA 1969 Dip Ed 1970
d of Albert J. W. salesman and Jane Aitken; b Aber 23.3.47
MSc(Strath) 1973
teacher p s Lond 1970–72; educ psych Dunbartonsh 1974; teacher: i/c tut. centre Workington 1974–75; p s Arlecdon 1975–76
m Aber 18.8.73 David J. Milne BSc(eng) 1969 *qv*

WISEMAN Alasdair BSc(agr) 1963
s of Alexander W. gen merch and Elizabeth A. Shaw teacher; b St Fergus 29.12.40
BVMS(Glas) 1967 PhD(Glas) 1978 MRCVS
dept vet med Glas vet s: asst lect 1967–70, lect 1970–77, sen lect from 1977
m Culsalmond 24.12.69 Patricia A. Duncan hairdresser d of William D. Insch

WISEMAN Alexander Sutherland MB ChB 1958

WISEMAN Carl McQueen MB ChB 1961
s of Alfred R. M. W. hairdresser and Isobel McQueen nurse; b Banff 16.4.37
CRCP(C) 1971 FRCP(C) 1972
h o Norwich 1961–62; g p Essex 1962–63; sen h o, regist psychiat Norwich 1963–65; Canada: staff phys Brandon Manit 1965–68, resid psychiat St Boniface 1968–69, staff phys/clin dir Brandon, private pract (psychiat) Brandon from 1972
m Dovercourt 1961 Patricia A. McCurry teacher d of Patrick McC. Dovercourt

WISEMAN David MB ChB 1959
s of Joseph G. W. fisherman and Barbara Wiseman; b Gardenstown 28.2.35
DObstRCOG 1968
h o Woodend hosp Aber, Stracathro hosp Brechin 1959–60; sen h o Royal Vict hosp Blackpool 1960–61; regist anaest royal Salop hosp Shrewsbury 1961–62; g p: Kirkwall 1962–67; Withernsea 1967, Auchenblae from 1967
m Aber 16.1.60 Hazel Anderson nurse d of James D. B. A. Kirkwall

WISEMAN Graham Richmond *MA 1956
b Aber 30.10.32
teacher mus AGS 1957–58, Aber acad 1957–61; prin mus Inverurie acad 1961–67; county mus organis Moray and Nairn 1967–75; advis in mus Grampian reg from 1975
m Aber 11.7.62 Winifred R. Emslie shorthand-typist

WISEMAN Margaret Macdonald MA 1967
d of Henri R. W. plumber and Jessie S. Birss; b Inv 28.7.47
part-time teacher Engl, mod lang, r e Wick h s 1970–77; asst regist Wick from 1978
m Dufftown 5.8.67 Kenneth G. Wood MA 1966 *qv*

WISEMAN Raymond MB ChB 1964
s of Joseph G. W. fisherman and Barbara Wiseman; b Gardenstown 4.1.41
MRCPath 1970 Dip Bact(Lond) 1970
h o Woodend, City hosp Aber 1964–65; terminable lect bact Aberd 1965–69; asst, sen bact Luton 1969–72; consult. bact Bangour from 1972
m Aber 3.4.65 Esther H. Wood teacher d of Alexander W. Aber

WISEMAN Robert Lindsay *BSc 1963 PhD 1967
s of James C. W. MA 1930 *qv* and Winifred A. I. Melvin MA 1930 *qv*; b Elgin 18.12.40
USA: post doct fell./res staff Yale 1968–72, res assoc publ health res inst NY from 1973
m NY 15.9.73 Anca M. Vasiliu MA(Bucharest) teacher d of Constantin V. MSc(Bucharest) Tuckahoe NY

WISLEY Ada May MA 1968
m Bain

WISLØFF Sigurd Brun MB ChB 1963
s of Carl F. W. DD(Oslo) prof ch hist and Ingrid Brun; b Oslo Norway 13.3.36
Norway: h o Stavanger 1964–65, m o h/g p Bratvaag/Haram 1965–69; regist: soc med Molde 1969–70, psychiat Molde 1970–73, consult. psychiat Molde 1974, chief consult Åsgård sykehus univ psychiat hosp Tromsø
m Aber 3.10.60 Catherine L. Ross MA 1961 *qv*

WITO James Alexander BEd 1969
b Arbroath 19.1.42
teacher Arbroath 1969–70; prin Fr Kinross 1970–73; asst prin mod lang Dunfermline 1973–75; prin mod lang Ballingry from 1976
m Aber 11.11.67 Moira A. Harrison BEd 1969 *qv*

WITTE Elizabeth Mary *MA 1970 PhD 1980
d of William W. PhD 1935 *qv* and Edith M. S. Melvin MA 1932 *qv*; b Aber 13.12.47
teacher mod lang Harlaw acad Aber 1971–74; stud. PhD Aberd from 1974
m Aber 17.7.70 Bryan A. Dargie MA 1963 *qv*

WONG Cheong Ngan BSc 1970

WONG Daisy Sai Hui MB ChB 1970
d of Ngiong H. W. bus. man and Chung I. Chong; b Sarikei Sarawak 30.5.42
h o: Aber, Kirkwall 1970–71; asst radiol Bergen Norway 1972–73
m Sandvika Norway 31.7.71 Einar R. Tamber MB ChB 1970 *qv*

WONG David Kwok Hung MB ChB 1968

WONG Shing Lai Alexis BSc(eng) 1969
s of Wong Kam merch and Sui Ping Leung; b Hong Kong 3.7.45
Hong Kong: jun site eng 1969–70, grad eng 1970–71, asst resid eng 1971–73, asst eng 1972–73, des eng 1973–77, proj man. from 1978
m Hong Kong 12.10.74 Florence Foon Hang Chan secy d of Chan Chik Yuen, Hong Kong

WOOD Alastair James *MA 1956

WOOD Alexander Stewart *BSc 1968

WOOD Alfred Wallace *MA 1959

WOOD Ann Veronica *MA 1963
d of William W. MA 1930 *qv* and Margaret S. Geddes MA 1932 *qv*; b Dufftown 4.8.40
Cert Soc Work(Exe) 1964
ch care off. Hertford c c Hemel Hempstead 1965–67; soc worker Edin 1967–71; lect soc work Goldsmiths Lond univ from 1971

WOOD Anne Elizabeth Harthill BSc 1965 Dip Ed 1966
m McDonald

WOOD Annie Mary MA 1962

WOOD Catherine Margaret MA 1964
m Craig

WOOD Douglas Simpson *MA 1958
s of George T. N. W. master plumber and Dorothy M. Simpson; b Aber 25.12.36
nat serv UK, Germany 1958–60; market res exec: Lond 1960–64, Hull 1964–65; market res man. Lagos 1965–67, Kuala Lumpur 1967–68, Singapore 1968–71; Lond: market res ag dir 1971–73, proj dir Soc Res inst from 1973
m Borehamwood 11.7.64 Elizabeth P. J. Hooton secy d of Gordon H. Borehamwood

WOOD Ella BSc 1970
m Smith

WOOD Fiona MB ChB 1968
DObstRCOG 1970
m Aber 1968 Ian G. C. Coutts BSc 1960 *qv*

WOOD Frank BSc 1960

WOOD Geoffrey Edward *MA 1967
s of Edward W. coach painter and Ellen Ross; b Aber 19.8.47
lect univ of Warwick 1968–71 and from 1973; res econ Bank of England (on leave from Warwick univ) 1971–73
m Aber 8.4.69 Lesley A. Henry BA(Lond) teacher d of George H. Mansfield

WOOD Ian Clark *BSc 1964
s of John W. comp dir and Margaret Clark; b Aber 21.7.42
man. dir John Wood Group (Abdn) Aber from 1964
m Aber 25.9.70 Helen MacRae d of Murdo MacR. Inv

WOOD James Falconer MB ChB 1960

WOOD Jane Anne McLeod MA 1968
d of William W. plasterer and Lilian Walters; b Mansfield 26.11.46
BA(Strath) 1978
teacher Engl Glasg from 1971

WOOD John *BSc 1965
s of John W. sea capt and Isabella Slater; b Portknockie 28.3.43
MSc(W Ont) 1970
Canada: field geol Toronto 1965–68, exploration geol NW Territories 1969–70, Alberta 1970–71; Precambrian surveys geol Ontario from 1971
m Norwich Ontario 1969 Janet J. Pollard BA(W Ont) teacher d of James I. P. Norwich Ont

WOOD John Bruce Murray LLB 1970
s of Arthur E. S. W. MB ChB(Edin) g p and Robina Bruce; b Edin 30.6.49
Edin: asst examiner 1970–73, executry asst 1973–74, cler off. Lothian reg c 1977–78, cler off. Lothian reg trans 1978

WOOD John Keith MA 1968 Dip Ed 1969
s of Alfred J. W. farm. and Mary C. Keith dist nurse; b Kirkwall 10.10.47
teacher Engl: Forfar 1970–71, Stromness 1971–77; asst head Stromness from 1977
m Kirkwall 14.8.69 Fiona C. Groundwater bank clerkess d of Alexander G. Kirkwall

WOOD Kenneth George MA 1966
s of Albert G. W. indust civ serv MoD and Amy B. Sandoe; b Queenborough 10.7.44
teacher mod lang Eastwood h s 1967–70; Wick h s: asst

prin mod lang 1970–78, asst prin guid from 1978
m Dufftown 5.8.67 Margaret W. Wiseman MA 1967 *qv*

WOOD Kenneth McDonald LLB 1968
s of Gordon W. slater, night superv and Edna M. Falcon; b Aber 21.1.48
invest analyst: Philips & Drew stockbrokers Lond 1968–69, Gilbert Eliott & Co stockbrokers Lond from 1969
m Lond 19.12.70 Diane B. Freedman stockbroker's clerk d of Philip F. Leyton Lond

WOOD Margaret Ann MA 1963 Dip Ed 1964

WOOD Margaret Ann MA 1969
d of Robert S. R. W. eng and Anna Reid florist; b Fraserburgh 2.2.48
Dip Biling Secy (Aber coll of comm) 1973
teacher Fr Grimshaw Alberta 1970–72; Peace River Alberta: stenog dept indust, trade & comm 1973–74, teacher p s 1974–76, Fr 1977–78, p s from 1979
m Fraserburgh 29.6.73 Michael A. S Arnold BEd(Alta) vice-prin elem s s of Stanley A.S.A. Lond

WOOD Margaret Buchanan MA 1970
d of James S. L. W. MA 1929 *qv*; b Newtonmore 5.1.49
tut./translator Ger/stud. medieval Ger Munich 1972–73
m Torphins 18.8.73 Gerhard Weber Dip Biochem(Munich) s of Gerhard W. Niederbayern

WOOD Margaret Mair MA 1960
d of William M. W. lt-comm RNR, fishing skipper-owner and Williamina Campbell; b Rothesay 21.10.40
teacher Engl/hist Macduff h s 1961–62, Portknockie j s s 1962–69
m Findochty 22.12.62 James G. King lect p e s of Archibald W. W. K. Keith

WOOD Maureen Jessie *BSc 1968
d of Joseph W. manuf's ag and Jessie Burton; b Cartmel 8.2.46
PhD(Belf) 1975
Belf: post grad stud. 1968–71, teaching asst 1971–72; post doct res asst King's coll Lond 1972–74; teacher biol Sunbury-on-Thames 1975; cryobiol MRC lab ans centre Carshalton from 1975

WOOD Michael *BSc 1963
s of James S. L. W. MA 1929 *qv*; b Insch 25.6.41
Dip Cartog(Glas) 1964
Glas: res asst 1964–66, asst lect 1966–69; lect geog Aberd from 1969
m Aber 6.8.66 Margaret R. L. Barr MA(Glas) teacher d of James C. B. Stevenston

WOOD Moira Jean Campbell MA 1965
d of William M. W. fisherman and Williamina Campbell; b Findochty 30.10.45
teacher: geog Kintore 1966–68, Engl Cambridge 1968–69, Engl Welwyn Garden City 1969–72
m Findochty 4.4.70 John M. Knapman MA(Cantab) computer syst eng s of Gordon A. K. Lond

WOOD Sheila MA 1958
d of Edwin W. marine eng and Josephina Smith; b Aber 25.7.37
teacher: Carfin 1959–61, Fr The Priory s Kingston Jamaica 1963–64; lect mod lang Galloway coll of tech Dumfries from 1978
m Aber 30.6.59 Henry Neilan MA 1958 *qv*

WOOD Stanley *BSc 1957

WOOD Susan Elizabeth MB ChB 1967
d of Gordon W. MA(Edin) solic and Agnes E. Stephens physioth; b Walton-on-Thames 16.5.43
DCH(Lond) 1970
h o Inv, Aber, Maidstone 1967–68; sen h o paediat Luton, Kingston 1969–70; regist paediat Chelmsford 1971–72; clin m o commun med Kingston from 1972
m Aber 14.4.72 Gordon P. R. Antonio electronics eng s of Oscar R. A. Bangalore India

WOOD Sydney Arthur Rankin BSc 1967

WOOD Thelma MA 1966 *MEd 1970
d of John W. master mariner and Fanny C. McKenzie; b Stonehaven 14.3.45
teacher mod lang Linlithgow 1967–69; asst educ psych Edin 1970–72; sen educ psych Forfar 1972–74
m Stonehaven 19.9.70 George F. Ritchie BSc(H-W) electronics eng s of George F. R. Stonehaven

WOOD William Rae *MA 1959
s of Alexander C. W. taxi driver and Ethel Rae bakery worker; b Aber 30.11.36
Dip Ed(Lond) 1960
educ off. N Nigeria 1960–71; teacher hist Bellahouston acad Glasg 1971–73, prin hist Whitehill s s Glasg from 1973
marr diss

WOOD Willina Ross MA 1957
d of William W. trawlmaster and Williamina R. Wood; b Aber 13.11.36
Lond: trainee life dept Royal Insur Co 1958–60, off. superv Paterson Eng Co 1960–62, priv secy Peter Lind & Co 1962–63
m Aber 17.6.61 Iain H. Muir bank trust off. s of John C. M. Glasg

WOODBURN Winifred Margaret MA 1969

WOODFORD Helen MA 1969
d of Leonard A. W. postman, farm., ambul driver and Eileen M. Baker dist nurse, midwife; b Crawley 7.6.47
Dip Ed-TEFL(Manc) 1972
Brit council teacher Engl Kokkola Finland 1969–70; TEFL Padworth coll Reading 1970–77; Brit council teacher Engl Vientiane Laos 1972–75

WOODHEAD William David BSc(for) 1958 *1959

WOODHOUSE Sylvia BEd 1969
d of Denis K. W. arch. and Rosa M. S. Barclay governess; b Toronto 9.9.17
teacher: Blackburn Lancs 1969–70, Rishton 1970–76
m Aber 22.9.51 William T. Main linotype oper, prod. man. s of William M. Aber

WOODROW James Dow MA 1963

WOODS Ian Cecil Cordner *MA 1970

WOODS William John Francis LLB 1970

WOOE-CHUNG Rudolph Theodore MA 1959

WOOLFENDEN David BSc(for) 1956
s of Edward W. hat manuf and Muriel Gill teacher; b Denton 12.4.32
for. off.: NI 1956–66, Kasama Zambia 1966–69, NI 1969–74, Roseau Dominica WI from 1974
m Enniskillen NI 9.7.66 Gillian M. West teacher d of James W. Ballycassidy Co Fermanagh

WOOLLAM Jane Anne Nelson MA 1969
d of Frederick W. master grocer and Phyllis Nelson hairdresser; b Banff 7.10.48
teacher hist/Engl Lond 1970–71, accts asst *Daily Express* Lond 1971–72; supply teacher (home tuition dept) Gillingham Kent from 1978
m Cullen 29.5.71 Christopher R. Walker BSc 1969 *qv*

WOOLLARD Maureen Lydia MA 1959
b Aber 5.1.37
secy in Aberd 1960; teacher: Aber 1962–65, Wallasey 1966–68
m Aber 15.7.64 Hamish A. Anderson BSc 1962 *qv*

WOOLVERTON Peter Roy *MA 1970
s of Michael W. estate surv and Isabella Smith; b Edin 17.10.47
Liberton h s Edin: teacher geog from 1971, later asst prin outdoor educ

WORLING Michael James BSc 1966

WORRELL Joy Irma Cecil MA 1968

WRAY Aileen Isabel Mackie MA 1958
d of Vincent L. W. man. nat carriers Aber and Edith Walker MA 1925 *qv*; b York 6.6.37
teacher mod lang: W Midlands 1958–65, Notts from 1972
m Aber 18.8.60 Peter B Knott teacher s of Harold A. K. Reading

WRIGHT Alan Beattie BL 1960
s of John M. W. MA 1929 *qv* and Jane H. Beattie MA 1930 *qv*; b Aber 2.5.39
CA 1962
acct Lond 1962–66; chief acct/comp secy Kampala Uganda 1966–69; proj auditor Teheran Iran 1969–72; divisional acct Sale 1972–75; gen man. Dun 1975–79; acct in profession Dun from 1979
m Banff 28.5.66 Isabel G. Wood teacher d of John J. W. Banff

WRIGHT Alexander Neill PhD 1958
BA(Oxon)
resid Faversham

WRIGHT Constance Clarice Mathieson *MA 1963
d of Thomas M. W. basketmaker and Clarice Brett french polisher; b Aber 24.5.41
BD(Lond) 1978
teacher Engl: Hermitage acad, Helensburgh 1964–68, Aber acad 1968–74; stud. Birm Bible Inst 1974–78; teacher r e/Engl/hist Lea Mason C of E s Birm from 1978

WRIGHT David Gerard *MA 1966

WRIGHT David Glover *BSc(eng) 1969

WRIGHT Dorothy Gillian *MA 1967

WRIGHT Genefer Gail Finlayson MA 1966
d of William C. W. BL 1939 *qv*; b Inv 28.5.45
FSA Scot 1974
teacher Leeds 1967–68; interviewer for govt soc serv 1968–69
m Dornoch 26.8.67 David R. Clark BSc 1965 *qv*

WRIGHT Grace Elberta *MA 1961

WRIGHT Ian James *BSc 1968 PhD 1971

WRIGHT Jacqueline Elizabeth Margaret MA 1965
d of John W. elect. and Agnes A. Watt; b Aber 19.12.44
m St Albans 23.7.66 Anthony B. Harbour MA 1966 *qv*

WRIGHT Jean Anne MB ChB 1958
m Cameron
d Watford 8.2.66 *AUR* XLII 91

WRIGHT John David Maitland *MA 1964
s of Edward M. W. BSc(Lond) princ Aberd 1962–76 and Elizabeth P. Harris; b Aber 20.5.42
Simpson Prize, De Gurbs Schol
DPhil(Oxon) 1967 FRSE 1978
lect Christ Church Oxford 1965–68; fell./tut. St Catherine's coll Oxford 1968–70; prof pure maths R'dg from 1971
m Aber 17.9.65 Helen Butler

WRIGHT John Richard BSc(eng) 1970
s of Herbert W. police off., civ def off., law off. and Kathleen Rogers; b Wallasey 18.12.48
Brit Aerospace: flight test instrumentation dev eng Warton Lancs 1970–73, sen FTI calibration eng from 1973
m Aber 18.3.72 Sandra M. Marr bank clerk, secy d of Walter A. M. Aber

WRIGHT Norman John Duncan MA 1969
s of William C. W. BL 1939 *qv*; b Inv 4.4.48
LLB(Edin) 1971
post grad res sociol of law Edin 1971–73; law app Dornoch 1973–75; leg. asst Arthur & Carmichael, Dornoch 1975–77, ptnr from 1977
m Inv 27.7.73 Susan Abbott MA 1969 *qv*

WRIGHT Susan Margaret BSc 1970
d of John N. W. MA 1951 *qv*; b Lond 12.7.48.
lab asst; psych dept Aberd 1970–74, med lab Wis Madison USA from 1974
m Aber 3.7.70 Ronald N. Buick BSc 1970 *qv*

WRIGHT William George *BSc 1956
s of Frank W. textile worker and Margaret I. Ellis shopkeeper; b Garmouth 27.12.33
jun tech RAF UK, Germany 1956–58; res chem Birm 1959–62; sen scient off. (textiles) Dun 1962–71, post-grad res work Dund 1971–73; tech man. (textiles) Dun 1973–76; chem (distilling indust) Tormore from 1977
m Urquhart 31.10.59 Isabella B. Farquhar shorthand typist d of Alexander F. Garmouth

WU San San MB ChB 1965
d of Shu H. W. BA(China) bus. man and Siok H. Ng; b Sarawak 11.8.35
DPH(Singapore) 1972 MFCM 1974
Singapore: m o Kerdang Kerbau mat. hosp and paediat unit gen hosp 1967–68; health off. mat. and ch serv 1968–70, trg and health educ unit min of health 1970–72, sen regist mat. and ch health serv from 1973

WUNSCH Susan Ilene M Litt 1970
d of Samuel W. bus. owner and Etta H. Waldman; b Providence Rhode Is USA 7.3.46
BA(Wellesley coll USA) 1967
Yale USA: electron microscopist 1969–73, asst dir undergrad admissions 1973–74, dean Saybrook coll 1974–75, 1978–79; asst dean Yale coll 1977–78
m Providence 2.7.67 Charles D. Rice MA 1964 *qv*

WYCHERLEY Gwyneth MA 1957
m Henderson

WYLIE Alastair Graham PhD 1965
s of Hance G. W. police off. and Isabella P. Neilson; b Glasg 26.4.36
BSc(Strath) 1961
ICI Cheshire: res chem 1965–66, res and dev chem 1966–72, res and dev group man. from 1972

m Cheadle-Hulme 12.9.68 Norma Atkinson med lab tech d of Joseph A. Cheadle-Hulme

WYLIE Brian Gilfillan MA 1969

WYLIE Ralph Clark *BSc 1970
m Banff 1.4.72 Jane P. Eaton BSc 1970 *qv*

WYLIE Roslyn MA 1968
d of Drummond W. bank man. and Doris Lancashire; b Dunfermline 2.10.47
Dip Soc Ad(Edin) 1969 CASS(Brist) 1971
trainee soc worker Edin 1969–70; asst psychiat soc worker Murray royal hosp Perth 1971; soc worker/commun worker Roxburghsh Hawick 1972–73
m Scone 30.10.71 Alan Anderson LLB(Edin) solic s of Andrew A. Coldstream

WYLIE-RITCHIE John Young MA 1969

WYLLIE Andrew David Hamilton BSc 1964 *MB ChB 1967 PhD 1975
s of Andrew M. W. MB ChB(Glas) phys supt Royal Cornhill hosp Aber and Marjorie H. Maxwell BSc 1930 *qv*; b Aber 24.1.44
MRCP 1970 MRC Path 1975
h o ARI 1968–69; termin lect path. Aberd 1969–70; MRC jun res fell. Lond 1970–72; lect path. Edin 1972–75; res fell. cancer res campaign Cambridge 1976–77; sen lect path. Edin from 1977
m Leic 18.9.71 Hilary Walder

WYLLIE Anne Margaret *MB ChB 1960
d of Andrew M. W. MB ChB(Glas) phys supt Royal Cornhill hosp Aber and Marjorie H. Maxwell BSc 1930 *qv*; b Dumfries 8.7.38
Dip Ophth(Lond) 1963 Fell. Ophth(Edin) 1966
h o Perth, Aber 1960–62; sen h o Glasg 1962–63; regist Aber 1963–65; sen regist 1965–70; consult. Portsmouth 1970–77, Lanarksh from 1977

WYLLIE Marjorie Rose *BSc 1957
d of Andrew M. W. MB ChB(Glas) phys supt Royal Cornhill hosp Aber and Marjorie H. Maxwell BSc 1930 *qv*; b Dumfries 17.6.35
PhD(Glas) 1961
grad dem zool Glas 1957–60; Glas: asst lect 1960–61, part-time res asst/dem 1961–64; temp lect zool Jordanhill coll of educ 1964–65
m Aber 17.9.60 John B. Wilson MA(Glas) electronics eng, forecasting man., man. consult. s of Frank B. W. Glasg

WYNESS Helen Pirie MB ChB 1965
d of Gordon W. and Betty M. Pirie teacher homecraft; b Aber 11.10.43
Dip Av Med 1967 Dip Hyperbaric Physiol(Calif) 1975
m o RAF Halton, Wroughton, Kinloss, Farnborough 1966–69; g p Cardiff 1971; cas off. St Davids Cardiff 1972–73; m o publ health Aber 1973–75; m o oceaneering internat diving comp from 1975; med advis royal Omani army Muscat
m(1) Lee-Mason
(2) Aber 11.2.76 Austin Tobin

WYNESS Phyllis Jane MB ChB 1969

WYNN Michael MB ChB 1964
s of Michael J. W. comp dir and Mary A. McDonald; b Elgin 20.11.38
h o: ARI, Bridge of Earn 1965–66; sen h o: Bellshill mat. hosp, anaest Preston RI 1966; g p Glasg 1966–67, Buckie from 1967
m Falkirk 16.6.69 Jennifer D. Bruce nurs sister d of Andrew D. B. Falkirk

WYNNE Rosalind Clare *MA 1964
m Gow

WYNTER Roderick Anthony MB ChB 1958
s of Hugh H. W. and Clare Oritinaire; b Jamaica 12.6.30
DCH(Lond) 1964
h o: Woodend hosp Aber, Kingston publ hosp Jamaica 1958–59; g p Antigua WI/dist m o 1959–62; rotating regist univ of WI 1963; SC hosp Toronto: sen asst resid/fell. cardiol/assoc resid 1964–66; Sunnybrook hosp Toronto jun asst resid med 1966; SC hosp Toronto teaching fell./post grad med course/fell. nephrol 1967–68; g p Toronto 1968–72; clin teaching fam pract Wellesley hosp univ of Toronto/courtesy staff Toronto W hosp/staff fam phys Wellesley hosp from 1972, lect fam/commun med/courtesy staff Women's coll hosp

XENOPHONTOS Constantinos BSc 1966 *1967
s of Xenophon Polycarpou farm. and Styliani Constantinou; b Nicosia 24.3.40
MSc(eng)(Queen's univ) Kingston Ont 1972 F Geol Soc Greece Fulbright schol PhD(Calif)
geol grade II with geol surv Cyprus 1968–70; commonwealth s Queen's univ Canada 1970–72; geol grade I Cyprus 1972–75
m Nicosia 22.7.68 Rosalind M. Mitchell MA(St And) teacher d of Andrew F. M. Dun

YACKIMINIE Ann Bona *MA 1961 Dip Ed 1962
d of Alexander Y. eng and Barbara Shivas; b Aber 26.8.39
teacher: Hong Kong 1963–66, Sutherland 1966–70, Cyprus 1970–73
m Aber 10.8.62 Stewart Simpson civ serv s of George S. Aber

YASSIN Tag Elsir MSc 1968
BSc(agr)(Khart)

YEATS Ian Martin *MA 1963
s of Alfred Y. MA 1929 *qv*; b Aber 14.2.41
BA(Oxon) 1965 BCL(Oxon) 1966 MA(Oxon) 1970
barrister (Inner Temple) 1972
lect law Q Mary coll Lond from 1966; visiting lect univ of Adelaide Aust 1974

YEATS Katherine Hilda MA 1969
d of James C. R. Y. lib and Mary Barclay; b Bristol 10.6.48
au pair Paris, Berlin 1969–70; temp clerkess Lond, Aber 1970–71; lib asst Aber publ lib 1972–73; lib trainee RGIT Aber 1973–74; lib asst Aberd 1974–77; temp clerkess from 1978
m Aber 21.7.75 Peter S. C. Smith ARICS quantity surv s of William C. B. S. Lochgoilhead

YEE Chee Pong BSc(eng) 1963

YEOMAN Hilda McLean BSc 1962
d of Charles Y. painter/decorator and Mabel D. Edwards; b Stonehaven 25.4.41
teacher maths/sc Laurencekirk s s (Mearns acad from 1977) 1963–72, asst prin guid 1972–75, prin guid from 1975

YEOMAN Joyce Elizabeth *MA 1970
d of William S. Y. proj eng and Jessie McKenzie; b Aber 27.7.48
computer progr Baric Glasg 1970–73
m Aber 13.5.72 Joseph T. McAdie lorry driver s of Alexander J. McA. Ardgarten by Arrochar

YEOMAN Kathleen Janice MA 1968
d of James Y. hosp audiology tech and Daisy M. Cook; b Aber 8.7.47
teacher: Aber 1969–70 Midlothian 1970–72
m Aber 24.7.70 Ian H. Pearson MA 1967 *qv*

YING David Andrew *MA 1969

YORKE Douglas McKenzie *LLB 1968
s of Guy U. Y. MB ChB 1964 *qv*; b Aber 6.1.46
LLM(Penn) 1969
lect law Glas 1969–73; sen lect Glasg coll of tech from 1973
m Old Kilpatrick 17.3.73 Izella C. Dunbar secy d of James D. Old Kilpatrick

YORKE Guy Ultan MB ChB 1964
s of Harold L. Y. shipping comp clerk and Onra L. Powell; b Christchurch NZ 5.11.24
BSc(Canterbury NZ) 1953
h o, sen h o royal northern hosp, W Fife hosp Dunfermline, Balfour hosp Orkney 1965–66; g p Aber, Inv, Tokanui and Mataura, Runanga NZ 1966–69; cas off. Southland hosp NZ 1970; supt Riverton hosp/g p NZ 1971–74; port health off./indust m o Ocean Beach/g p Bluff NZ from 1974
m Aber Margaret T. Mackenzie shop man. d of William McK. Aber

YOUNG Alan John Ward MA 1966
CA

YOUNG Alastair Cushnie MB ChB 1964
s of Robert Y. rly signalman and Helen R. T. Gillespie secy; b Comrie 28.2.41
MRCP 1970
h o Aber hosps 1964–65; h o, sen h o neurol/neurosurg Killearn hosp 1965–66; regist Aber hosps 1966–71; regist neurol inst of neurol sc Glasg 1971–73; sen regist neurol Oxford from 1973
m Kilbirnie 5.7.69 Myra R. Rabey teacher d of Robert R. R. Kilbirnie

YOUNG Alexander Douglas BSc(agr) 1957

YOUNG Ann Lesley *MA 1966
d of Alexander Y. insur exec and Annie Muir; b Edin 8.6.44
teacher geog: Perth h s 1967–68, Powis s s Aber 1968–70
m Aber 12.7.68 Neil G. Meldrum teacher of mus s of William J. S. M. Aber

YOUNG Anne Elizabeth MA 1965
d of John Y. and Marjory F. James admin asst corp of Aber; b Aber 11.3.44
Dip Soc St.(Edin) 1966 Dip App Soc St.(Harris coll Preston) 1971
soc worker Angus from 1966
m Aber 11.4.74 Gerald L. Crighton DA arch. s of Leslie C. Aber

YOUNG Antony Richard *BSc 1970
MSc(Lond) 1972 PhD(Lond) 1980
Lond: teacher 1972–76, res asst 1976–79, res assoc from 1979

YOUNG Audrey Winifred MB ChB 1959
m Aber 4.8.60 George M. Stewart MB ChB 1959 *qv*

YOUNG Barbara Shand MA 1960 *BSc 1963
d of John Y. MA 1929 *qv*; b Singapore 2.12.39
teacher: Ladies' Coll Cheltenham 1964–68, York Coll for girls from 1977
m Aber 18.8.65 Alistair J. M. Miller MA 1958 *qv*

YOUNG Christina Jean Taylor MA 1969
d of Alexander F. T. Y. MA(Glas) C of S min and Phyllis M. R. Chisholm MA(St And) teacher; b Dumfries 3.10.47
teacher geog Shoreditch comp s Lond 1970–73, prin geog from 1973
m Edin 15.8.75 James A. Fadden BSc(Lond) teacher s of Thomas J. F. Liverpool

YOUNG Claire Keir *MA 1967
b Glasg 14.6.45
teach Engl: cent foundation girls' s Lond 1968–71, Queensbury s Dunstable 1971–75; res asst Hatfield poly 1976–78
m Glasg 1.9.67 Stuart J. Meldrum BSc 1966 *qv*

YOUNG Colin McIntyre PhD 1964
s of Archibald Y. Y. farm., soldier, civ serv and Florence Stirling; b Kelvington Sask Canada 27.7.36
BSA(Tor) 1961
Canada: post doct fell. univ of Guelph 1964–65, sessional lect 1965–66, asst prof Laurentian univ 1966–68, assoc prof from 1968

YOUNG David Paterson *MA 1960
s of James P. Y. steel worker, shopkeeper and Elizabeth J. Rugg shopkeeper; b Rutherglen 30.11.37
FRGS 1961
teacher: Cumnock acad 1961–64, prin geog 1964–70; dep rector Grange acad Kilmarnock 1970–77; rector Kilwinning acad from 1977
m Edin 30.11.68 Jean M. Brown lect d of John B. Edin

YOUNG Donald Stirling MB ChB 1957
s of John S. Y. BSc(Glas) prof path. Aberd and Ruth M. Whipple BA(Cantab) econ; b Belfast 17.12.33
PhD(Lond) 1962
lect materia medica Aberd 1958–59; regist post grad med s Lond 1962–64; USA: visiting scient nat inst of health Bethesda 1965–66, chief clin chem sect. nat inst of health 1966–67, head sect. clin chem Mayo clin Rochester from 1977
m Rockville MD USA 1972 Silja Meret BS(Vassar)

YOUNG Douglas *MA 1961 PhD 1969
s of James Y. gasfitter and Isabella Brand; b Aber 15.6.40
instruct. univ of Victoria Canada 1962–64; teacher Engl Aber acad 1964–67; lect Engl Aber coll of educ from 1969
m Auldearn 18.7.64 Margaret Forbes teacher d of Kenneth F. Auldearn

YOUNG Eileen Margaret *MA 1958
d of Alexander L. Y. CBE MA(Glas) teacher and then dir educ Aberdeensh and Ellen O. Duffy MA(Glas) teacher; b Glasg 23.7.37
LRAM 1954 MA(Oxon) 1964 LLM(Harvard) 1961
barrister-at-law (Lincoln's Inn 1963); asst lect law Brist 1961–63; asst leg. advis, leg. counsellor FCO from 1963
m Lond 8.10.66 John Denza MA 1956(Cantab) FCA s of Luigi C. F. D. Lond

YOUNG Francis BSc 1956 Dip Ed 1957
s of Fanny B. Young; b Logie Pert 19.12.34
teacher sc Perth acad 1957–61; prin sc Tain royal acad 1961–63; prin phys: Vale of Leven acad 1963–65, RGC Aber 1965–71; sen lect phys Kingsway tech coll Dun from 1971
m Perth 16.4.60 Victoria F. Davie BSc 1956 *qv*

YOUNG George BEd 1970

YOUNG Gordon *MA 1964

YOUNG Gordon Anthony BSc 1967
s of Albert T. Y. sales rep and Eileen E. Eden shopkeeper; b Nantwich 8.11.45
BVMS MRCVS(Edin) 1972
tech asst (MRC grant) psych Aberd 1967–68; vet g p Sevenoaks 1972–73, Etwall from 1973
m Edin 14.7.72 Dorothy A. Hogg d of James E. H. Edin

YOUNG Hazel Mitson MA 1968
d of Norman W. Y. MA(Glas) and Margaret Mitson cler off.; b Torphins 21.8.47
m Aboyne 17.8.68 Robert D. Knorr arch. tech, plan. tech s of Lawrence E. K. Aboyne

YOUNG James Alexander Taylor *BSc 1962
s of Alexander F. T. Y. MA(Glas) clergyman and Phyllis M. R. Chisholm MA(St And) teacher; b Peebles 4.4.40
PhD(Edin) 1966
univ dem Edin 1962–66; lect Edin from 1966; visiting lect Nairobi 1975
m Sheff 16.7.66 Gillian M. Randall MA(Edin) teacher d of John A. R. Sheff

YOUNG John BEd 1970 MEd 1973
s of James Y. joiner and Janette R. Y. Halkerston; b Perth 15.2.43
teacher Engl/hist Stonehaven 1970–73: educ psych Edin 1973–76; sen educ psych from 1976
m Jedburgh 14.7.71 Valerie A. J. Bennett teacher of art d of John B. FRCO Jedburgh

YOUNG John Charles MA 1965 LLB 1975
s of John Y. lorry driver and Marjory F. James secy; b Aber 11.3.44
MITransport 1969
various post road trans indust Aber, Newport (Mon), Livingston, Dun 1965–72; law app, leg. asst Glasg; solic Stornoway

YOUNG Johnstone Oliphant *BSc 1960
s of Johnstone O. Y. and Winifred C. Morrison; b Huntly 15.3.38
PhD(UCNW) 1963
asst lect zool Leic 1963–64; lect zool Liv 1964–77; sen lect from 1977; visiting lect zool univ of Nairobi 1971–72
m Bangor 31.8.63 Beryl M. Randall BA d of Ernest F. R. Bangor

YOUNG Kenneth Moir *MA 1957
s of John S. Y., BSc(Glas) prof path. Aberd and Ruth M. Whipple BA(Cantab) econ; b Belf 13.12.35
PhD(Princeton) 1969
stud. app AEI Manc 1957–59; res scient AEI Aldermaston 1959–63; grad stud. res staff member plasma phys lab Princeton univ NJ 1963–70; lect phys UMIST 1970–74; res phys plasma phys lab Princeton univ from 1974
m Bolton 7.8.65 Naomi A. Partington MA 1957 *qv*

YOUNG Marilyn Elizabeth MA 1968
m Douglas

YOUNG Niall Andrew *BSc 1964 MSc 1966
s of Andrew Young loc govt off. and Marion M. Watt; b Glasg 16.6.43
PhD(Belf) 1968
res fell. Lond Canada 1968–70; lect computing sc Aberd from 1970
m Aber 14.7.65 Patricia D. Holdsworth MA 1963 *qv*

YOUNG Oswald Courtenay BSc 1963
s of Urias M. Y. bookkeeper and Mabel E. Kong; b Trinidad WI 5.4.29
med/clin biochem gen hosp Port of Spain Trinidad from 1963
m Port of Spain 19.3.50 Rita C. Affonso d of Silvano A. Port of Spain

YOUNG Pamela Anne *MA 1968
m Morris

YOUNG Prudence Ann *MA 1960
d of Archibald G. B. Y. MB ChB 1937 *qv* and Annie S. Bain MB ChB 1931 *qv*; b Aber 6.5.38
m Aber 23.7.60 John A. King BSc(eng) 1952 *qv*

YOUNG Robert Macfie Douglas LLB 1970
s of Robert M. Y. MA(Edin) solic and Margaret A. MacCaig; b Inv 23.10.48
NP 1973
law app Edin 1970–73; solic: Edin 1973, Inv from 1973

YOUNG Ronald Noble *BSc 1960 PhD 1963
s of Charles E. Y. shop man. and Mary S. Noble; b Aber 15.5.38
res fell.: Akron univ Ohio USA 1963–64, Hull univ 1964–65; lect chem Sheff from 1963; visiting prof: Syracuse univ NY USA 1973, Akron univ 1972 1976 1978
m Aber 2.6.62 Mally Tompkins

YOUNG Susan Margaret MA 1967
d of John D. Y. ship broker and Isabel Macdonald physioth; b Cardiff 11.10.45
civ serv Lond 1967–71; E Sussex c c Lewes: traffic eng 1971–79, pers off. indust relations from 1979
m Bromley 11.4.70 Arthur J. M. Hammond BA(Birm) civ serv s of Arthur H. Bisley

YOUNG Sylvia Jean *MA 1962
d of R. H. Y. and Jane H. Webster; b Forfar 7.8.40
m Aber 1963 Alistair J. W. Smith MA 1962 *qv*; marr diss 1971

YOUNG Thomas Ogilvie *BSc 1956
s of James D. Y. piano tuner and Elizabeth S. Carr; b Aber 11.6.34
scient off., sen scient off. MoD AWRE Aldermaston 1956–76; prin insp health & safety exec Lond from 1976
m Aber 24.7.57 Kathleen M. Grant BSc 1956 *qv*

YOUNG Valerie May MA 1958 Dip Ed 1959
d of James A. Y. pharm and Rachel Cowling private secy; b Aber 13.1.38
teacher maths Aber 1959–69 and from 1974
m Aber 22.7.64 Dennis Kelly comp dir s of Bruce K. Cults

YOUNG William Fisher MA 1969 *BSc 1972 MSc 1973
s of Charles G. Y. civ serv Inl Rev and Frances O. Fisher teacher; b Inv 24.4.47
scient off. sub div of soil sc, ITE, natural environment res c, based at Banchory res stat

YOUNG William James MA 1958
s of Alexander C. Y. quarry man. and Annie Shand; b Garmouth 25.12.37
teacher: Kaimhill s s Aber 1960–62, prin geog Gambia h s Bathurst The Gambia W Af 1962–66; asst head Elgin East End p s 1967–71; head: Logie p s 1971–75, Burghead p s from 1975
m Aber 15.3.62 Joyce H. A. Murray d of Stewart M. Aber

YOUNG William McDonald ***BSc 1960 MSc 1961 PhD 1964**
s of Robert Y. salmon fisher and Jessie A. McDonald; b Inverbervie 23.4.39
res stud. nat phil Aberd 1960–63, asst 1963–64, lect phys Dund from 1964

YOUNGSON Alan Falconer ***BSc 1970**

YOUNGSON Alexander Hovell **MA 1961**

YOUNGSON Colin James ***MA 1970 Dip Ed 1971**
s of James A. Y. man. multiple tailors and Flora J. MacOwan head Causewayend p s Aber; b Aber 27.10.47
teacher Engl Kelvinside acad Glasg 1971–73; TEFL Örebro Sweden 1973–74; teacher Engl Craigmount h s Edin from 1974
m Aber 5.8.74 Stella F. Reid MA 1970 *qv*

YOUNGSON James Andrews Robert **MA 1957**

YOUNGSON Linda Clare ***MA 1968**
d of William C. Y. arch. and Muriel Windsor; b Milngavie 1.4.46
Dip Lib(Strath) 1970
grad trainee Stir univ lib 1968–69; asst lib Stirling c lib 1970–72; sen lib asst Stir univ from 1972

YOUNGSON Marika Elizabeth **MA 1969**
d of John A. Y. MSHAA consult. audiologist and Rita E. Milonopoulou; b Aber 17.6.48
computer progr Lond 1969–70; asst to sen progr Perth 1970–73
m Aber 31.8.68 Denis I. Squire ARICS bldg surv s of Ronald A. S. Aber

YOUNGSON Richard Windsor ***BSc(for) 1964**
s of William C. Y. arch. and Muriel Windsor; b Milngavie 19.5.42
exper off. Nature Conserv red deer res Scot. 1964–69; res off. Unilever salmonid cultivation Lochailort 1969–75; field off. Red Deer Comm red deer man. from 1975
m Nairn 17.7.75 Margaret F. Macnaughton d of Charles C. M. Lochailort

YOUNIE Peter George Hugh **BL 1956**
s of John Y. MA(Edin) judge ICS and Dorothy Mitchell MB ChB 1921 *qv*; b Aber 12.8.31
WS 1959 TD 1967
law app Watt & Cumine Aber 1953–56, Edin 1956–58; solic Hunter Harvey Webster & Will WS Edin 1958–60, ptnr from 1960
m Edin 3.3.61 Morag A. Tod MA(Edin) 1959 admin secy d of John L. T. Lasswade

YOUNIE Richard David **BSc(eng) 1964**

YOUSOF Abdul Mohsin **MB ChB 1961**
s of Alabdul R. Y. bus. man and Noon Yousof; b Singapore 27.10.34
MRCPGlas 1966 PhD(Prague) 1973 FRCPGlas 1976
h o Aber 1961–62; h o, regist Kuwait 1962–64; visiting regist Aber 1964–65; Kuwait: regist 1965–67, sen regist 1967–68, consult. cardiol 1968–74, prof med & founding Dean of s of med from 1974
m Kuwait 8.5.64 Shuaa Al Sumait d of Jassem H. A. S. Kuwait

YSART Adèle Louise **MA 1970**
d of Paul M. Y. glassmaker and Margaret Irvine; b Perth 30.9.47
man. Mackays hotel Wick 1970–76; exec secy Dubai colour tv Dubai UAE from 1976
m Dubai 28.2.80 Lewis M. Robertson BSc(Belf) electronics eng s of Duncan McR. R. Aber

YSEBAERT Marie-Josée Margherita **MA 1962**
d of Sylvain Y. factory owner and Elodie Loeys bus. ptnr; b Moldegem Belgium 17.4.25
teacher: Fr Aber 1962–68, Fr/Engl Manitoba 1968–69, Fr/Engl Kettwig Germany from 1969
m Belgium 27.3.47 Fraser

YUILL Robert Alexander **[e]MB ChB 1959**
s of William Y. master baker and Jeannie Raffan; b Aber 2.11.34
DObstRCOG 1962 MRCGP 1976
h o Woodend hosp Aber, ARI, Perth RI, Bridge of Earn hosp 1959–62; g p: Auchterarder, Perth 1962–65, Aber from 1966
m Aber 25.7.59 Mary M. Hunter secy d of James W. H. Aber

YULE David Kenneth ***MA 1969**
s of Kenneth R. J. Y. sales man. SAI/farms man. and Jane Johnston; b Aber 14.5.47
post grad stud.: computing centre Aberd 1969–70, pers man. RGIT Aber 1970–71; Aberd: admin asst tech trg 1971–74, clerk to faculty of med from 1974
m Aber 28.12.70 Janet M. G. Forsyth MA 1969 *qv*

YULE Denis Noble **LLB 1970**
s of James F. Y. des eng and Phyllis M. Noble secy; b Aber 7.6.48
law app Aber 1970–72; leg. asst Aber 1972–73; ptnr L. Mackinnon & Son advoc Aber from 1973
m Aber 30.7.70 Yvonne I. Smith teacher d of John W. S. Aber

YULE Frederick Duncan ***MA 1968**
s of Alasdair B. Y. baker, shopkeeper and Margaret McNeil hairdresser, shopkeeper; b Peterhead 8.3.46
res stud. Aberd 1968–71; lect Glasg coll of tech from 1971
m Wakefield 30.3.70 Janet E. White MA 1967 *qv*

YULE Roy ***MA 1966**

YULE Sheila Kathleen **MA 1957**
m Lenthall

YULE William ***MA 1962**
s of Peter C. Y. fam grocer and Mary A. Moir mental nurse; b Aber 20.6.40
Dip Psych(Lond) 1963
res off. MRC soc psych res unit Lond 1963–64; res off., lect ch dev inst of educ Lond 1964–69; lect psych inst of psychiat Lond 1969–73, sen lect from 1973
m Sudbury 6.3.72 Bridget A. Osborn BSc(econ)(Lond) res worker ch psychiat d of Mark G. O. Hartest

YULL Leonard Louis **BSc(for) 1957**
s of Louis A. Y. tree felling/land clearing contr and Fanny H. M. Holloway secy; b Lond 21.10.35
nat serv RE UK, Cyprus 1957–59; Tanganyika: dist for. off. Rondo, for. man. off. Dar es Salaam 1960–69; promotions off. Edon For. Kendal Cumbria 1969–73; dir Econ For.(Northern) Kendal from 1973
m Glasg 26.9.69 Elizabeth C. Martin teacher p e, secy d of David P. M. Glasg

ZAFAR Mukhtar Muhammad **PhD 1968**
BSc MSc(Punj)

ZANRE Michael Luigi Peter **LLB 1969**
s of Joseph D. Z. publican and Linda M. Ostacchini; b

Lond 2.10.47
CA 1975
Aber: app CA 1969–73, asst to group acct Davidson Radcliffe 1973–74, chief acct PSF offshore (Scot.) 1974–76, fin. controller Wm Hay & Sons from 1976
m Aber 15.1.72 Annabella B. Ritchie asst scient off. Rowett inst Aber d of George S. R. Fraserburgh

ZELUFF James Daniel PhD 1964
s of Ulrich C. Z. BS(Mich) off. US treasury dept and Ruth I. Yeats; b Tampa Florida 28.4.30
BS(Florida) 1953 M Div(Union Theol Seminary Richmond Va) 1956
USA: assoc prof Queen's coll Charlotte NC 1964–68, assoc dir of Interpreter's House Lake Junnluska NC and clin psych Asheville Psychiat Assoc 1968–77, pres Zeluff & Assoc Asheville NC (stress and time man. consult.) from 1978; author *There's Algae in the Baptismal Font* 1978
m Staunton Va 28.5.55 Elizabeth Sheffer pres Snelling & Snelling Asheville

ZIEDAN Ibrahim Elsayed Mohammed MSc 1964 PhD 1967
BSc(eng)(Cairo)

ZORAB Richard Arthur *BSc 1970
s of Edward C. Z. MBBS(Lond) ophth surg and Janet K. Baillie nurs sister; b Tomsey Hants 28.2.46
outdoor activities instruct. Aviemore 1970–71, Europe 1971–72; edit: Wm Collins publ Glasg 1972–73, Churchill Livingstone Edin from 1973

MARRIED WOMEN GRADUATES 1956–1970 WITH HUSBANDS' NAMES IN ALPHABETICAL ORDER

An asterisk (*) indicates an Aberdeen University graduate.
The year of graduation follows the name if there is another graduate of the same name or if, in the case of a husband, he graduated outwith the 1956–1970 period.

Husband	Wife
Abbott John R P	Blackie Sheila M
*Abdelnour Hassan O	Moscati Shane
Abel Charles	Campbell Mary A
*Abell Trevor M B	McKay Helen F B
Aberdein Harvey J	Douglass Lesley H
*Aberdein James D	Jamieson Ethel
Abernethy Kenneth R	Alexander Gwynyth M
*Abrioux Marc O M (1971)	McGregor Ann L
Adam	Clarkson Susan T
Adam Alexander H	Pringle Katherine G
Adam Alexander N	Hendry June R
*Adam John	Cheyne Lorna R
Adam John H	Milne Florence
*Adams Christopher J	Birrell Elizabeth F
*Adams James A	Elliot Elizabeth M
Adams James R R	Craig Amber M
*Adams James T W	Baker Rosemary C
Adams John	McDonald Muriel
*Adamson Colin D (1973)	Thomson Barbara A
Addison	Jones Susan P
Agnew	Kidd Sheena A M
*Ah-See Antoine K	Matheson Catherine R
*Aikman Peter R	Munro Cathleen A
Ait-Hocine	Forbes Patricia
*Aitken Donald A	Clarke Muriel
*Aitken Gordon G	Rettie Doreen L
Akinsete	Browne Felicia I
Akintewe	Paterson Maureen L
Akpom	Uyanwah Philomena O
Alcock Samuel A	Whalley Margaret J
*Alcock Stephen R	Paterson Jean M D
*Alder Clive P	Paton Kathleen S
Alder George M	Pinsent Elizabeth M
Alexander Alfred J	Semeonoff Irina
*Alexander Ian K	Frith Susan A
Alexander John H	Ross Flora M
*Ali Zaffar	Fachie Moira A R
Alison	Pearson Jean R
Allan Archibald B	Dix Helen M
Allan Douglas I	George Kathleen M
*Allan Duncan S	Allan Valerie P
Allan Fergie	Doughty Flora M S
Allan John C E	Fraser Alison
*Allan Kenneth J (1971)	McDougall Alice J
Allan Lawrence D R	Henderson Margaret
Allanach	Campbell Grace S
*Allison Stuart N	Davie Marguareta M F
Amaechi	Hall Wendy M A
*Amar Satya S	Skinner May E
Anderson	Gibb Jennifer R
Anderson	Mackie Lesley M H
Anderson Alan	Wylie Roslyn
Anderson Alexander R	Mulholland Mary G
*Anderson Brian A	Flockhart Mary R
*Anderson Brian A	Mackay Marianne E H
Anderson Charles W	Anderson Sheila M
*Anderson David J B	Dick Eleanore St V
*Anderson David R	Strachan Jean
Anderson Hamish	Macleod Catherine
*Anderson Hamish A	Woollard Maureen L
*Anderson Iain H	Morrison Anne I
*Anderson John	Murray Christina M
*Anderson Robert M L (1962)	Gavin Mary T
*Anderson Roderick S	Cook Jennifer V
Anderson William	Taylor Margaret W
*Anderson William A	Allan Anne M
*Anderson-Smith Gordon	Matthew Myrtle I
Angus Graham P	Auld Alison M
*Annand Gideon S	Steer Margaret R
Antcliffe	Ross Helen M
Antonio Gordon P R	Wood Susan E
*Arbuthnott Gordon W	Minto Joan E
Archbold	Findlay Alice D
Archer	Jenkins Eileen M
Archibald Martin	Kerr Margaret M O
*Ardern Richard J	Rhind Eileen M
Armour	Riddoch Hilda E
Armour Peter S	Paterson Isobel
Armstrong Alexander G	Massie Maureen
Armstrong Duncan	Peterson Jemima A
Arnold Michael A S	Wood Margaret A
Arnott Sidney J	Edward Alison J E
Arpino Vincent A	Frost Yvonne M
Arthur David	McLean Margaret B
*Arulanantham David C	Knight Diana M
Ashenford	Mitchell Patricia
Ashton Gerard	Thomson Rosemary D
*Ashton Robert W	Barclay Helen M

ATHAWES	FELL Margaret E
*ATKINSON Adrian P C	JONES Christine L
ATTENBOROUGH William J	VAN DER TOORREN Vivien L
ATTFIELD Michael D	POGUE Hilary M
AUBREY David A	WILSON Catherine M
AULD Edward G	DURNO Joyce
AURSNES Arne J	MACDONALD Sandra I
AUSTIN Michael P	LOWNE Barbara O
*AYERST John M	COBB Alice M
AYLETT Bernard J	JONES Marianne E
BACON John S D	SAMPSON Enid E
BACON Richard A	KEILLAR Doreen N
BAGLEY Michael B	ROBERTSON Annette W
BAGNALL	ENGLAND Carol S
*BAILLIE Alister C	MACPHERSON Elizabeth
BAILLIE Hugh D	CROOKSHANKS Noreen M
BAIN	ROBERTSON Ouaine M
BAIN	WISLEY Ada M
*BAIN Derek C	MACKENZIE Grace M
*BAIN Ian A (1971)	BEATTIE Maureen J
BAIN Robert G	ROBERTSON Elizabeth A
BAINBRIDGE John	HUTCHESON Carole J
*BALDWIN David K J	MARTIN Carol J L
BALDWIN Malcolm B	ELLIS Janet E
BALDWIN Philip H	MACKINTOSH Helen C
BALFOUR William J	GRAY Isobel S
BALLANTINE Robert R	MCKENZIE Ann J
BANCROFT	ADDISON Barbara
BANKS Adrian	STEPHEN Lorna M
BARBER Henry	TAIT Helen S
BARBER Roger	MORRISON Margaret J
BARBOUR Andrew D	LOVE Penelope R
BARCLAY Allan C	SKINNER Annie M
*BARCLAY David J C	BRYCE Jennifer A
*BARCLAY David S	BENZIE Sheila
*BARCLAY Gordon	GORDON Meriel
BARCLAY Lionel G D	CRAWFORD Sarah H
*BARCLAY William J	TAYLOR Rachel T B
BARKER Andrew S	HUTCHESON Rosemary J F
BARLOW Roger W	FRASER Angela
BARNES	NICOL Mary S
BARNES Patrick H	GILL Angela
*BARNETT James	MACKENZIE Annabelle
BARR	ROBERTSON Shonaid E
*BARR Peter	HOBBIN Maureen E
*BARRACK James W	HARDIE Betty T
*BARRETT William	MACLENNAN Kristin
*BARRON Charles A	SHAND Margaret M
BASTIEN	CHRISTIAN Glenda A
BATES Peter J	THOMSON Irene E
BATH George M	CRUICKSHANK Isobel
BAUMANN Walter	ADAM Margaret E
BAXTER	MITCHELL Frances E
BAXTER Leslie M	HENDERSON Mabel C
BEANAN	WALKER Edith H
*BEAR Keith P	GRAY Jean E
*BEATTIE Alan R (1955)	BOA Donalda F
BEDFORD	STEELE Patricia M
BEEDIE	MCKENZIE Doris I
BEGG	ROSS Valerie A
BEGG	STALKER Heather L
*BEGG Ian S D	MAGEE Carolyn I
BELL	STRACHAN Helen S
BELL	TOCHER Frances M
BELL Charles J	BRUCE Dorothy E
BELL James G	HUTCHEON Elizabeth M
BELL James P S	BICKERTON Judith C
*BELL John D G	JAMES Angela M
BENNETT Archibald	CAMERON Jean N
*BENNETT James R	EUNSON Barbara M
*BENNETT Norman B	ADEY Gillian D
*BENNETT Peter J	GILL Rhoda C
*BENNETT Peter N	BROCKLEHURST Jennifer M
BENNETT Raymond V	SINCLAIR Elizabeth B
BENTON Douglas M	LOW Elizabeth G
*BENZIE Alexander S	LUNNEY Dorothy C
BERRY Colin G	BOOTH Catherine M
BERRY Colin S	MCKIE Penelope J
BEST Leslie P	ROSS Helen
BEVAN-BAKER John S	FINDLAY June M
BEZANSON Gregory S	SMITH Patricia A
*BICHAN David H (1976)	ROBERTSON Lorraine I
BICKET John C	SMITH Esther M
BINNS	ROSS Freda M
BIRKS Frederick	HOLDSWORTH Lily F J
BIRLEY R Y	MCNICOL Maureen A
BIRNIE Albert	MCWILLIAM Irene W
BISHOP Alan R	FELL Rosaleen M
BISSET Pietro M	MORRISON Carolyn A
BISSETT-JOHNSON Alastair	MCPHERSON Winifred
*BLACK Colin R (1971)	SANGSTER Valerie J
BLACK James	MACKAY Christina O
BLACK John E	CARNEGIE-SMITH Kaetrin
BLACK Norman A	ABBOTT Elizabeth M
*BLACK Robert W	RIACH Doreen M
BLACKHALL	MACDONALD Janice
BLADON Frederick A	DUDMESH Yvonne M
BLAKEMAN John P	DAVISON Elizabeth A
BLANCHARD David D	AIKEN Laura J
BLAXTER Kenneth L	HALL Mildred L
BLYTH Alistair H	DONALD Ethel M
BODDY	MACPHERSON Jean E
BODDY Robert M	LENDRUM Elizabeth A
BOLSOVER Andrew J	MASSON Sandra
*BOLTON Alan	MACKAY Isabella T
BOND Peter J	MORRISON Joyce C
BOOTH	FORSYTH Margaret E
BOOTH William P	MURRAY Margaret J I
BORTHWICK-CLARKE Andrew	KEATING Christine
*BOWDEN Thomas N	HORNE Margaret H
BOWEN	SIM Johann C
BOWEN Humphrey C	WILSON Helen I
*BOWIE Raymond A	MACLEOD Sheila E M
*BOWLING Dudley J F	DAUN Sheila M
*BOWMAN Iain B R	BARRON Patricia
BOX Anthony G	FLETT Hazel M G
BOXALL	JOHNSTON Patricia A M
BOYD Hugh G	MILES Fiona A
*BOYD Peter D A	FOX Evelyn Y
BOYDELL David L	MORRISON Jessie
BOYLE	LINDSAY Helen M
BOYLE Charles	SHEARER Kathryn I
BOYLE James	ROBERTSON Anne W
*BRADLEY Peter M (1971)	FLEMING Rosslyn M
BRADSTREET Derek	SIM Betty M
BRAITHWAITE John	PECK Catherine P
*BRANDER John G	NAYSMITH Elizabeth
*BREBNER John M T	FAWKES Mary J
BREBNER John T	GRANT Lilian A

*Brechin Derek M	Brunnen Rosemary A
Breckenridge John R T	Bruce Audrey B
Bremner	Liston Elizabeth M
*Bremner Alan	Jones Shirley
*Bremner David M	Gibson Alice S
*Bremner Harold A	Maclean Alison M
Brereton Walter	Middleton Elizabeth F
Bressan	Walters Jacqueline M
*Brew Eric J C	Mitchell Marjory G
*Brierley John C	Plummer Susan J
*Bristow Christopher D	Blakemore Marie
Brock Alan W R	Milne Valerie
*Brockie Colin G F	Gordon Barbara K
*Brodie Iain K	MacLean Gillian I
Brodie Ian T	Chalmers Margaret M
*Broom John (1971)	McAuslane Nancy B
*Broomfield William M	Reid Mary C
Brough	MacNicol Helen J
Brown	Dalgarno Loraine M
Brown	Mulholland Freda J
Brown	Reid Lorna A
Brown	Robson Primrose C
Brown Andrew N	Dewar Anne A
*Brown Charles	Downie Margaret R
Brown Clifford	Thomson Anne M C
Brown Colin A	Craven Linda J M
Brown Frederick B	Fraser Moira
Brown George	Pattie Ann M W
*Brown Ian R	Morrison Madeline
Brown James	Henderson Antoinette M
Brown James A	McNeill Morag D
*Brown John	Bremner Catherine M
*Brown Kenneth J	Lobban Elizabeth T
Brown Richard G	Davidson Alicia R
Brown Robert M	Craven Janet M
*Brown Robert M	Swanson Patricia A
*Bruce James J (1972)	Mutch Margaret F
Bruce Alexander	Smith Margaret S
*Bruce Graeme M	Scorgie Anne M
Bruce James G	Murray Sheila M
Bruce John F	Mackie Margaret C
*Bruce Robert G	Christie Moira M
*Bryant Carl L	Noble Audrey M
Bryce	Duncan Jean D
*Bryce Andrew B	Inkster Elizabeth M
Brydone John	Barclay Margaret
*Buchan Alexander	Cutt Jennifer A
Buchan Alexander S	Robb Margaret N D
*Buchan Charles C	Buchan Georgina S
*Buchan David D	Nisbet Moyra J
*Buchan Maynard C	Melford Lilian F
Buchan Robert	Nicol Margaret
*Buick Ronald N	Wright Susan M
Bull Gordon C B	Brown Aileen
Bullen J B	Green Anne M
Bulmer	Abbey Heather D
*Bunting John A	Sinclair Ann G
Burgess Gethyn	Birkbeck Helen M A
Burgess William B	Moar Patricia A
Burke Martin C P	Davies Dorothy V A
Burn	McGill Janice M
Burness	Christie Moyra M
Burnett	Eddie Fiona E
*Burnett Alexander W	Middleton Marjory S
Burnett Douglas J	Snowie Anne F
*Burnett Gordon B	Bell Wendy E W
Burnett William H	Milne Eileen
*Burnett William J	West Katharine J M
*Burns Alasdair M	Garvie Sheila M
Burns Campbell B	Vass Mary M F
*Burr Robert J	Strachan Eileen M
Butler Ian J	Gordon Patricia M
Butters David	Watson Eleanor M M
Byrom David	Davies June A
Byth	Glennie Janet M
*Byth William	Noble Irene B
*Caie Graham D	Abbott Ann P
*Caie Ronald W	Stewart Mary E
Calder Graeme S M	Heath Margaret G
Caldwell	Moir Dorothy W
Callander Ian	Eddie Valerie A
Cameron	Innes Margaret A
Cameron	Wright Jean A
*Cameron David J (1973)	Rae Doreen A
*Cameron Douglas M	Simpson Moreen A
*Cameron Hamish W	Johnston Edna
*Cameron Henry G	Stewart Mary M
*Cameron Henry O	Grant Fiona C
*Cameron Ian K M	Annells Jane-Ann W
*Cameron John F	Douglas Diana M
Cameron Lachlan A	Nichols Judith A
*Cameron Roderick F	Ross Catherine
Cameron Roderick H	Weir Jane G
*Cameron Wilfred	Low Alison M
Cameron William R	Mackay Moira E
Campbell	Smith Sandra
Campbell Alasdair D	Repper Dorothy A
*Campbell Alasdair J	McLean Doris M
Campbell Anthony S	Gonnella Frances
*Campbell James B	Hunter Sheena G
Campbell Marcus M	Bannerman Emily
*Campbell Neil A	Alexander Elizabeth M
Campbell Neil S	Gray Monica M
Campbell Thomas B S	Donald Alice M
Campbell William I	Watt Ann M
Campion Alan J	Fowler Ruth K
Cannings	Bishop Marigold R
*Cantlay Kenneth G	Copland Valerie A
*Cantlay William J (1943)	Innes Sheila V
*Cantlay William S	Greig Rosemary J
Carey Sidney J	Graham Christine
Carifio James M	Hilton Susan N
Carle	McIntosh Kathleen M (1965)
*Carle Alexander R	Findlay Judith M
Carlyle Roy B	Maughan Evelyn M
Carmichael	Cunningham Elizabeth M
Carmichael	Ferguson Kathryn A
*Carnegie Stuart F (1971)	Murray Marjory H
Carpenter David G M	Williams Frances A
Carpenter John	Johnson Sylvia M
Carr Stephen J	Farquhar Freda J
*Carruthers David R	Ronald Alison
*Carslake William D	Saint Lorna S
Carstairs Alan D	Lamont Anne C
Carswell Dennis A	Watson Gillian M
Carter Clive S	Bradford Ann P
Carter David G W	Tocher Kathleen A
Cartmell John	Cobb Judith M
*Cartney Michael W	Radcliffe Elaine B

CARTSHORE	DUNCAN Anne L
CARTWRIGHT	HUTCHISON Kathleen L
CASON	ADAM Helen M
CASSIE Charles E S	MILLAR Jillian J
CASTELL Keith S	BOWEN Jennifer E
CASWELL	ROBERTSON Helen L
CATTANACH John A	SMITH Rosemary A
*CATTO Graeme R D	SIEVEWRIGHT Joan
CAVALLO Marcello	DAVIS Betsy M A A
*CAWTHORN Nigel G	FLORENCE Mary I
CAWTHORN Richard G	BURNETT Patricia A
CHALIGNE	MUNRO Wendy
CHALMERS	BLAIRS Margaret C
CHALMERS	WATT Margaret A
*CHALMERS Robert A	TURNER Grace C
*CHAMBERLAIN Brian R	GILMOUR Helen S
CHAMBERS David M	MACKAY Margaret
CHANDLER	BENNET Anne M
CHAUDRI Mohammed J	ROSS Hilary A
CHERIYAN	MATTHEW Jean G
CHESTERS John Knight	TULLOCH Marian I
*CHESWORTH John B (1974)	KELLY Jane A
CHEW	MACPHEE Anne
*CHEW Kenneth J	ROBERTSON Gillian G
*CHEYNE Denis	SMITH Linda
*CHEYNE John A L	BUTLER Eileen A
*CHEYNE Laurence A	MILNE Pamela A
*CHISHOLM Allan D	PARKHILL Anne L
*CHISHOLM Duncan D	DOYLE Rosemary G
*CHISHOLM James A	DUNCAN Ruebena A
CHISHOLM John Z	SMITH June E
CHRISTIE Brian T	FORBES Hilda M
CHRISTIE David	SHEARER Elsa M
CHRISTIE David R	WEBSTER Elizabeth J
CHRISTIE James H	GASKIN Celeste E
*CHRISTIE Malcolm A B	FRASER Christian D
*CHRISTIE Michael G A	SHARP Margaret R
CHRISTIE Ronald H	DUNBAR Patricia M
CHRISTINE Stewart J	MORRISON Mary M
CLARK	McCRINDLE Dorothy J
CLARK	SCOTT Alison M
*CLARK David R	WRIGHT Genefer G F
CLARK Donald R	MASSEY Juliet C
CLARK Harry P	GREIG Norma A M
*CLARK John K	MURDOCH Elizabeth M
CLARKE	DUFFUS Anne
CLARKE Alistair A	RENNIE Morna M W
*CLARKE Ian A (1911)	ADAM SMITH Margaret E
CLARKE John A S	TAYLOR Pauline
CLAYTON David B	EVANS Ruth E M
*CLEGG Ian A	BUTLER Joyce E
CLEGHORN William T M	DAWSON Elizabeth H
CLELAND John	BUCHAN Jennifer R
*CLOUSTON Robert W	SIMPSON Vera F
COBBAN Archibald M	MILNE Gladys L
COBCROFT Ralph C	ROBERTS Joyce C
COCHRAN	MINIO-PALUELLO Maria-Luisa
COCKBURN William M	McINTOSH Sylvia
*COLLIE Alexander S (1954)	REID Alice M C
*COLLIE George S	GALL Barbara
COLLIN	MANN Maureen E
COLLINS	GRANT Ruth M
COLLINSON	LINTS Alice M
*CONDIE Roy G	CRUICKSHANK Wilma M P
CONN	JOHNSTON Brenda A
CONNELL John J	PARSONS Margaret
*CONSTANTINIDES Costas C	THORBURN Dorothy M
COOK	GREIG Isobel E
*COOK Gordon W	WILLIAMSON Frances O
*COOK Richard K D	STOESSL Michelle M
COOKE	GRANT Elspeth A
COOKE Ian D	MIDDLETON Sheila M S
COOMBES Philip J	DEMPSTER Elaine A
COOPER	CATTANACH Helen B
COOPER	STEWART Donella K
COOPER Alexander G	DAVIDSON Margarita M
COOPER Andrew J	SIM Morag K O'B
COOPER John L	MENNIE Margaret M
COOPER Melvin C	WILKIE Brenda
*COOPER Michael	ANGUS Jennifer A
*COOPER Simon J	MORRIS Megan L
COOPER Sydney M	DOW Marion B A
COPLAND	MOIR Patricia M
COPLAND Hamish A	WILSON Margaret E
CORALL John M	STOCKAN Kathleen I H
CORDINER George M	MIDDLETON Irene M
*CORDINER Ian C	MACDONALD Margaret R
CORFIELD Howard W	ROSS Christina D
CORKE	APPLIN Josephine M
CORMACK	GAVIN Irene S
CORMACK James G	LYON Joyce H
*CORMACK Richard M	WHITTAKER Edith
CORMACK Robert	McKERLIE Marie M
*COTCHING Ian G (1971)	CHARLES Gaynor B
COUGHLAN Brendan M	McLAREN Alison C M
COULL Gordon M	WALKER Patricia E
*COULL John T	MACFARLANE Mildred
COULL Joseph B	MITCHELL Isabel R
COULL William	MITCHELL Anne S
*COUTTS David	ANGUS Margaret G
*COUTTS Findlay M	LEATHEM Christina G
*COUTTS Ian G C	WOOD Fiona
COUTTS Joseph C	LESLIE Lydia
COWCILL Keith	MACKENZIE Catherine J
COWIE	EDMOND Carol M
COWIE	MACKENZIE Tessa
COWIE Christopher F	EWBANK Corinna V
COWIE David	MACKAY Christine M
*COWIE Frederick C F	JACK Jeanette I
*COWIE James	BACKETT Anne L
COWIE Peter H	STRACHAN Christina H
*COWKING Thomas L	JACKSON Philippa J S
COX	ROLLAND Fiona M
*COX Andrew A (1972)	MACKAY Joan M
COX Anthony W	WEST Carole M
COX Harry	COWELL Susan E
COY John M	MARTIN Ishbel M
CRABBIE Colin P	MACARTNEY Elizabeth M
CRADE Frederick	VIGROW Mary L M
CRAIG	GAVIN Pamela E
CRAIG	PARLEY Sheila
CRAIG	WOOD Catherine M
*CRAIG Alexander S	CARNIE Dorothy F
*CRAIG David M (1954)	STEPHENSON Gillian
*Craig Peter M	GALL Marjory A
CRAIG Robert E	LAWRENCE Dorothy
CRAIK David K	McBAIN Anne
CRAIN John L	AUCHINACHIE Isobel M T
*CRAMB Maurice Q	LAWRIE Diane P
*CRAWFORD Derick A	DONALD Elizabeth L

Husband	Wife
*Crawford Frederick	Bishop Frances M
*Crawford George P M	Irvine Allison M
Craze John L	Duncan Hazel
Crighton Gerald L	Young Anne E
Crofts	Watt Jill E
*Croll Neil M	Hill Veronica M
*Cromar Neil	Ross Catherine F H
Crook Alan R	Boyes Pamela A M
Crooke William M	Morgan Margaret A
*Crookshanks Brian K (1949)	Steele Joyce M
Crossland John R	Gregory Angela C
Croydon Charles E J	Richmond Helen M H
Crozier	Symon Sheena M
*Cruickshank Alistair R	Noble Alexandra M
*Cruickshank Don W	Ritchie Margrit R
*Cruickshank Donald G	Taylor Elizabeth B
Cruickshank George A	Mathieson June
Cruickshank Gordon W	Colleran Ethel M
Cruickshank James R	Ritchie Ethel M
*Cruickshank Leonard G	Brown Anne G
Cruickshank Richard A	Meldrum Maureen W
Cruickshank William	Walker Ivy A
*Cubitt Ian R (1971)	Blair Mary S
*Cuddeford Derek	Lyall Alison
Cumming	Calder Joan C
Cumming Robert M	Potratz Gisela B
Cummings Ian L H	Simpson Elma W
Cunningham	Menzies Anne F M
Curley	Robbie Alice M
Currie	Marnoch Patricia J
Currie Andrew M	Blackie Ruth V
*Curry David J	Murray Katharine G
Cuthbert	Paterson Doreen
*Cuthbert John A M	Frazer Kirsty M
Dafa'alla Abdel G I	Milne Isobel F
*Dahl Peter H	Goldie Dorothy M
Dalgarno George D	Ritchie Doris J
*Dalgarno William A	Brennan Patricia A
Dallison Anthony R	McCulloch Helen C
Daniel	Hurry Anne C
Daniels	Riddell Patricia A
*Dargie Bryan A	Witte Elizabeth M
Darling	Jamieson Jane M
Davey Nigel M G W	Buchanan Jane A M
Davidson	Brown Caroline E
Davidson	Glass Lesley R
Davidson	Gordon Catherine D
Davidson	Hopkin Pamela M
Davidson	Proctor Patricia L
Davidson David R	Kirkwood Elizabeth W
Davidson Donald M	Robertson Aileen
Davidson Frank D	Hosie Linda E A
*Davidson John Gordon	Robertson Margaret H S
Davidson Robert	Barr Kirsten H
*Davidson Robert H C	Whyte Johan G
*Davidson-Lamb Richard W	Flockhart Nanette J
Davies	Griffith Margaret A
*Davies Christopher J	Burt Susan H H
Davis	Imray Mildred M
*Davis Godfrey P	Smith Stella R
*Davis Lionel J	König Ingeborg I
Dawes	Macbeth Katherine M
Dawson	Sinclair Elizabeth K
*Dawson Alexander R	Maclean Jennifer M

Husband	Wife
*Dawson David G	Munro Caroline H
Dawson Hugh M R	Smith Sandra W
Day	Davidson Kathleen
*Dean Peter A	Moar Ann M
Deans	Bruce Rosaleen A
Deans	Guyan Alice M
Dekock	Ullman Liselotte L
DelPriore Bruno U V	Matheson Christina
*Denoon Brian D J	Campbell Sheila M
Denza John	Young Eileen M
Desougi	Mennie Margaret M
de Quincey John E C	Cameron Marion B
de Silva	Hector Moira E M
*Dewar Ian A	Pack Julie M
Diack	Kelman Alice J
*Diamond Antony W	McIntyre Elizabeth P
Dick Ronald M	Swift Margaret J
Dickie	Stuart Thelma L
Dickie George H	Jack Shona M
*Dickie Gordon L	Leiper Margaret C
Dickie John	Jones Mary E
Dickson	Little Joan
Dickson	Taylor Lesley J
Dickson John A	Fethney Moira
Dier George M V	Petrie Hazel C
*Dillon Geoffrey	Grieve Helen F B
Dimambro Bruno R	Tasker Helen A
*Dinwoodie John M W	Johnson Margaret
Dixon	Burt Cynthia K
Dixon	Johnson Lilian E
Dixon James M	Grimes Katherine M V
*Dixon John M M	Murray Anne S
Dodds Allan G	Dunn Elizabeth A
*Dodds Fergus R M	Innes Jean A
Dodds Iain L N	Fraser Christine M
*Dodds John J A	Sinclair Anne
*Dodds John K M	Cormack Ingrid A J
Doe Paul M	Jones Olwen M
*Donaghey Sean F O'B	Ingram Margaret J
*Donald George F J	Roe Isabelle M
Donald Ian E	Leiper Sandra M
Donald James F	Gerrie Anne
*Donald John H	McGrory Eileen
Donald Norman A	Donald Sylvia M B
*Donald Robert	Stuart Judith H
Donaldson	Thomson Stella H C
*Donaldson William	Challis-Sowerby Loraine
Donnelly	Smith Lorraine J J
Dooley	Reid Marjory B
*d'Orban Paul T	Ho-A-Shu Laura S J
Dorcey	Plucinska Teresa
Dorward George M	Massie Maureen E S
Douglas	Young Marilyn E
Douglas Alexander G	Morrice Alice I
Dover Roy R	Smart Marjory A
Doverty William Y	Strachan Marlene
Dow George D M	Maitland Dorothy I
*Dow Robin J	Gaffron Wendy J
*Dower Michael J	Mackenzie Moira
Dower Nigel	Beyts Diane M
Downey Christopher P	Robertson Patricia M
Downie	Gerrard Erica M
Downie Alan W	Mackness Jennifer M
Downie Colin T	Shaw Cecilia H
Downie Ian R	Kay Catherine H M

*Downie Robert W M	McHardy Aileen J
*Downie William T	Cardno Edith C J
Dreisbach	Jefferies Frances M
*Dry Frank T	Paterson Helen M
Dryden Myles M	Cargill Margaret M
Duffton William T	Kelman Elizabeth J C
*Duffty Paul	Macdonald Lesley M
*Duffus Peter R S	Millar Margaret M
*Duguid George R	Thomson Elizabeth
Duguid Neil S	Morrison Isobel C
Dukes	Dodd Sara M
*Dunbar Richard N F	Davie Margaret H
Duncan	Findlay Angela B
Duncan	Rennie Morag F
Duncan	Stewart Charlotte F
Duncan	Vonkuenssberg Verity C E
*Duncan Alastair B	Thorburn Ailsa C
*Duncan Alistair (1971)	Duffus Evelyn E
Duncan Arthur V	Abel Patricia Margaret
*Duncan Charles G	McAllister Patricia Mary
*Duncan David A	Rennie Morag F
*Duncan Stewart H W	Robertson Irene A
Duncan-Austwick	Duncan Helen P
*Dunlop Stewart B	Macdonald Jennifer A
Durand Andrew	Ewen Jane H E
Duthie John L C	Downie Sheena E
Duthie Stephen R	Skene Elizabeth A
*Dye Malcolm (1976)	Barron Anne A
Dyer	Noble Irene
*Dyer James A T	Townson Lorna M S
Dyer Philip	Flett Joan
*Dyer Robin M	Walker Aileen M
Dymock	Sutherland Sandra M
*Earl Charles R A (1971)	Ashton Shirley E
*Ebbon Gordon P	Shannon Jean G
*Eddie George	Johnson Mary I
Edmiston	Robertson Kathleen J
*Edward Neil	Smith Vivien E M
Edwards	Scott Helen M
*Edwards David G W	Mitchell Margaret H
Eichner Klaus	Ledingham Christine J
Elder Norman M	Lees Moyra I
*Eleftheriou Anastasius	Craib Margaret
Elgert Edward M	MacArthur Mairi C E
Ellis	Russell Dorothy M
Elrick	Grant Mavis
Elsarrag Mohamed E	McMillan Sadie W
Elsom John M	Ritchie Margaret J
Erickson Robert W	Macleod Flora
Escritt	Perman Anne
Esson Alastair F L	Milne Stella D
*Evans Thomas R	Fraser Wendy P
Evison	Hepworth Joan S
Ewen	Grant Moira B
Ewen	Keith Kathleen
Ewen Alistair	Hutcheson Lilian M
*Ewen Cameron A	Shirran Margaret A
Ewins David M	Frydman Anna
Ewles Douglas J	Clark Margaret J
Eyland Roger W	Whight Evelyn A
Fadden James A	Young Christina J T
Fairclough Roger H	Scott Eleanor M
Falconer	Innes Patricia Anne
Falconer James	Newlands Winnifred J
*Falconer Robert	Slessor Eva M
*Farquhar Eric	Fraser Audrey
*Farquhar William J	Rust Isabel H
Farquharson	Maclennan Anne M W
Faulds Douglas D	Terris Rosalyn E M
Fawcett Norman	Warrington Brenda E
Fawns James J F	Walker Norma A
Ferguson	Crombie Margaret H
Ferguson	MacRae Mary M
Ferguson	Struthers Eileen
*Ferguson Donald H N	Simpson Patricia M
Ferguson George A W	Grant Helen I
Ferguson Ian	Smith Helen A
*Ferguson Keith W (1953)	Smith Elizabeth A S
*Ferguson Kenneth M	Bertram Julia S
Ferguson Roger	Spencer Ruth E
*Ferguson Sinclair B	Allan Dorothy M
Fergusson Kenneth A B	Dworzak Antoinette E
*Fettes Peter H	Bell Mary R
Fiddes	Lees Louisa N S W
Findlay	Mirrilees Christine
*Findlay Adam H	Ritchie Patricia
*Findlay John (1954)	Mainland Margaret M
*Findlay John W A	Hey Jean M
*Findlay Leonard M	Downie Isobel M
Finnie	Donald Margaret J
*Finnie Oswald C	Ritchie Irene M
Firth Rodney A	Babbe Jean E M
Fisher	Fowlie Jean
Fisher Eric H	Duthie Anne E
Fisher Michael S	Crockett Isobel M
Fisher Peter R	Brodie Isobel F
*Fitchie Logan R G	Mathers Kathleen P
Fitzpatrick James	Gray Sheenagh M
Flavill	Davies Eileen J A
Flaws Andrew L B	Black Elizabeth M D
*Fleming Christopher A	Maclean Christeen
Fleming Ian	Hodgart Susan W
*Fleming Kenneth	Duthie Pamela A
*Flemming Christopher J	Ruff Lynda
Fletcher David C	Espley Sally M
*Fletcher David J	Stoney Margaret M
Fletcher Hugo J	Beck Thelma C
Fletcher Peter D	Campbell Ruth M
Fletcher Richard	Milton Aileen
Flett	McLennan Marion M
*Flett Alistair M	Mackie Aileen E
Flett John	Henderson Rosalind L
Flint Alexander S	Lamont Ann P
Florence Alexander F	Esslemont Marjory E H
Flory Ian	MacDonald Madeline V
Floyer John N	Dunlop Sally M D
*Flux John E C	West Margaret M
*Fogg Arnold G	Carson Joyce M
Follestad Rein D	Horn Jennifer R
Foote	Smith Eva R
Forbes	Hunter Elinor I
*Forbes Atholl R	Maxwell Esmé
Forbes Charles J	Hendry Alison M
Forbes Langley C	Smith Mary F
Fordyce Ronald	Nicol Eleanor F
Forsyth Leo V M	Cannon Dorothy M S
Forsyth Michael A	Lindsay Anne F
Foster Terence	Munro Jean M

Fothergill John E	Gilmore Linda A
Fotheringham David I R	MacMillan Janette M
Fotiadis Mihalaki	Wetherley Vivien J E
*Foubister Alan J	Cutbush Elizabeth A
Foulis Alan K	Martin Anne D
*Fowler Alexander P	Watson Helen M
*Fowlie Douglas G	Donaldson Marjory A R
Francis	Main Dorothy
Frank H Thomas	Leslie Elizabeth M McK
Frankish Karl D	Barclay Sheena M
Franks David R	Bailey Mary J G
Fraser	Mackie Mary E
Fraser	Sinclair Janet A
Fraser	Ysebaert Marie-Josée M
*Fraser Alan W	Johnston Edith H
*Fraser Archibald K	Stewart Kathleen M
*Fraser Arthur G	Snedden Marion E
*Fraser Callum	Sinclair Christina S
*Fraser Douglas M	Connon Rhoda A E
Fraser Francis I J	Clark Moira G
Fraser George	Maclennan Annabel R
*Fraser George L	Gordon Frances C
Fraser Gordon J	Robertson Sheila
Fraser Henry S	Skeete Maureen V H
Fraser Iain	Sleigh Allison M
Fraser Iain D	Anderson Isabella A
*Fraser James E (1953)	Stewart Patricia L
Fraser John	Grant Ishbel S
Fraser John	Petrie Helen C
Fraser Kenneth J	Fraser Sylvia R
Fraser Robert J M	Bain Priscilla A
Fraser William	Murray Hazel
*Fraser William H	Tuach Helen
*Fraser William R	Knox Alison F A
Frazer Samuel C	Shepherd Marion
French Christopher N	Watson Ann
Frew	MacGregor Helen E
Fricker Hans B	Pfister Maria R
Fritzon Stig Z	Reid Maureen
Fry Kenyon G	Blackhall Margaret I
*Fullerton Hance	Cowie Jeannie R
Fulton	Will Sylvia J
Furie	Marr Sheena M S
*Furnival Colin M	Souter Isobel G
*Galbraith Philip A	Liddle Dorothy I
Galilee George D S	Duncan Isobel M
Gall Robert A	Simmers Gillian J
Gallacher Alexander R	Harper Lillian H
*Galloway Richard M	Howard Patricia A
Gammie	Henderson Elisabeth A R
Garden John C	Rendall Margaret
Gardiner John A	Elwick Susan A
*Gardiner Robert H B	Coote Audrey E
*Gardner Bruce K (1971)	Hogg Christine M
Gardner George	Poole Freda J
*Garrow Alexander G	Fraser Margaret
Gates Peter S	Macintosh Kathleen M
Gault	Garden Isabel S
Gavin Alistair B	McMillan Mary
Gear James R	Holbourn Sheila C
Gemmell Ian R	Davidson Aileen E
*George Robert W	Clark Moira
*German Gordon A	de Silva Angela R
Gervas Jose L	Wells Judith A
Gibb	Forsyth Audrey T
Gibb Michael G H	Esslemont Elizabeth M
Gibbons	Kerr Janet H
Gibson Charles B S	Bell Eileen J
Gibson David T A	MacLeod Moragh A
Gibson James C	Nerland Beate
Gibson Robert R	Grant Morag H K
Giffin Patrick	Hall Alison M
Gilbert	Gifford Rosalind M
Gilbert John	Willets Lynn D
*Gilchrist William N (1952)	McCaskill Betty D C
Giles Peter B	Coombs Janet
*Gill Geoffrey M (1953)	Philip Margaret M
*Gill William P (1953)	Davidson Dorothy H
Gillies Alasdair B	MacDonald Angela I
Gilmour	Smith Doreen
*Gilmour Iain F	Smith Marjorie Y
Gilmour James A M	Taylor Ethel A
*Gladstone Patrick J	Gunn Margaret M
Glass	Fraser Margaret M
*Glasser Fredric P	Dent Lesley S
*Glennie John A	Smart Frances M
Glover David	Mackenzie Helen S
*Gloyer Robert I	Fethney Hilary A
Goda David F	Greig Marion G
Godfree Michael J	Jones Elizabeth H
Golbourn	Davies Lesley C
*Gomes Errol H	Read Margaret
*Goodall Thomas	Shearer Phyllis J
*Goodlad James A	Buchan Margaret E
*Gordon George P	MacLachlan Joan M S
*Gordon Hugh M	Davidson Elsie P J
Gordon James	Elder Lilian M
Gordon John	Simpson Lilian J W
*Gordon Martin	Simpson Jacqueline M
*Gordon Peter J (1971)	French Elspeth M
Gordon Roger	Geddes Margaret E
*Gorie	Dutch Eileen W
Gorst Gerald B	House Judith I
Gorvett Denis	Duguid Margaret G
Gosling Philip	Still Elaine L
Gossip Christopher J	Davidson Jean C
Goudie	Hood Margaret E
Gould David I	Marks Gillian M
Gow	Wynne Rosalind C
Graham	Morren Alison M
Graham Donald T	Robertson Winifred H J
Graham John	Graham Alexina
Graham John W	Shirreffs Marjorie A
Grainger Peter N	Cassie Elizabeth A
Grant	Buie Christine M
Grant	Govan Eileen T
Grant	Mackay Shona E
Grant	Mackenzie Helen S
*Grant Alan B	Cooney Eileen
Grant Charles M	Burnett Janet C
Grant Donald McA	Johnson Brenda
Grant Edwin B	McKay Andrea
*Grant Ian A M	Lumsden June M
Grant James A	Baird Margaret D
*Grant Neil F	Douglas Louise M
Gray	Barnes Mavis
Gray	McHardy Marigold M A H
Gray Alexander	Jones Helene M
Gray David	Morgan Roslyn E

GRAY George H LONGMORE Isobel
GRAY George M WEBB Moraig A M
GRAY Gilbert FRASER Lorna K
*GRAY James MURRAY Rhoda V
GRAY James H W GRAY Elsie M
*GRAY John D (1971) BRACEWELL Margaret J
*GRAY Laurence WHITEFORD Elizabeth S
GRAY Robert K S ROLTON Hilary A
*GRAY Roger W EHRHARDT Johanna E U W
*GRAY William G JOWETT Pamela H
GREARSON Quentin D COLVILLE Penelope M
GREEN HOWELL Joan C
GREEN David J JOHNSTON Margaret J
*GREENHALGH James F D GEE Isoline
GREIG BOOTHBY Patricia M
GREIG WILSON Muriel
*GREIG Denis WEBSTER Charlotte H
*GREIG Robert MILLER Isobel
GRIEVE SYMON Doreen
GRIEVE David G MCDONALD Linda G
GRIEW Paul V BROWNLIE Kathleen A
*GRIFFIN Anthony R JACK Lindsay
GRIMES Douglas J WARREN Susan E
GROCOTT John A HENDRY Kathleen A
GROENEVELD Cornelis M TOSH Agnes
GROSKORTH Carl W SINCLAIR Wilma
*GROSSERT Ian G COLVILLE Penelope M
GUEST David H COPLAND Alison A
*GUHA Madhabendra M (1951) PAUL Parul R
GUNN STEWART Audrey F
*GUNN Hamish I (1955) BENZIE Heather A
*GUNN Lewis A FINDLAY May F
*GUNN Robert M AVENT Yvonne G
GUSTAVESON Robert L MARTIN Valerie C
GUTHRIE Ian N PATERSON Eliza M

HADDOCK BAKER Susan J
HADDOCK George H ARNOT Katharine A K
HAGGART ROBB Catherine R S
*HAGGART David B HALL Gwendolen M
*HAINING William F (1952) LAMONT Margaret B
HALBORG ROBB Eileen M
HALL AIKEN Marigold H
HALL DAVIDSON Elizabeth W
HALL MACLENNAN Marion H
HALL Adrian T NAIRN Audrey
*HALL Colin D GORDON Valerie
*HALL David J (1967) WELLS Janet
*HALL David J (1970) MURPHY Helen M
HALL George S MITCHELL Rose McN
HALL Ian F TARBAT Lorna M
*HALL Michael A (1974) STEWART Ilene R
*HALL Peter A (1972) MACLENNAN Marion H
HALLIDAY Alexander CROALL Margaret M
*HALLIDAY Donald C BAKIE Elspet M
*HALLIDAY George S NEILL Patricia M H
*HALSTEAD Peter H LEAKER Margaret D
HAMILTON CARMICHAEL Barbara M
HAMILTON HUTTON Ray F
HAMILTON WILLIAMS Gaynor M
HAMILTON Alexander SUTHERLAND Jane M
HAMILTON David F REID Margaret E
HAMILTON Ian LYON Phyllis S
*HAMILTON Peter G (1972) FORBES Emily C
*HAMILTON Robert (1973) MCAUSLIN Edith J

*HAMILTON Stewart M HALL Pamela M
HAMMOND Arthur J M YOUNG Susan M
HANNAH James M JOHNSON Agnes H
HANNANT David J BARRON Norma M
HANSON Geoffrey BURNS Sheila A V
*HARBOUR Anthony B WRIGHT Jacqueline E M
*HARDCASTLE Patrick D RUNCIE Moira A G
HARDIE STRACHAN Mary C
HARDIE George M FORBES Elspeth A
*HARDIE Myles D G GRAY Marjory
*HARDIE Richard H WARREN Janet G
*HARDIE William D (1953) SIMPSON Margaret E
HARDING CAMPBELL Joan G
HARDINGHAM Peter A LOUGHRAN Verne E
HARDY Christopher R C ALEXANDER Muriel E
HAREN Michael J MACKEAN Elspeth M
HARGRAVE CHRISTIE Linda S M
HARLOW Reginald G IRVIN Carolyn A
*HARMAN Brian S R ELLWAY Judith M
*HARPER Douglas R WISELY Dorothy C
*HARPER John L HUNTER Fiona M
*HARRIS Iain G N ROBERTSON Jane P
HARRISON DUNCAN Sheila
HARRISON MCCLURG Kathleen J
HARRISON Robert A NICOL-SMITH Ruth M
HARRY CURRIE Kathleen I
HART BISSET Gladys M
*HART John R (1971) BROWN Pamela M
HARTE John D C MACKAY Eleanor M S
*HARVIE Thomas G TURNER Janet L
HASLAM Anthony P KINDNESS Lindsay M
*HASTIE Dennis OWEN Kathleen A
HAWKINS Dexter MCKILLIGIN Helen R
HAWORTH PEARCE Janet E
*HAY Alan J BISHOP Janet M
HAY David W GRAY Isabel A
HAY Herbert D FLORENCE Elizabeth M
*HAY Ian S DEAR Elizabeth M A
HAY James N WATSON Rosemary A
*HAY John M MENZIES Avril M I
*HAY John Y L ANDERSON Elizabeth M B
*HAY Robert K M VINYCOMB Dorothea H
HAYES Gregory P HAY Kathleen M
HAYTON William B ALEXANDER Anita J
*HAZEL Alan W PEPPER Jean M
HEATON Stuart L WILSON Barbara H
*HEGGS Glenville W HENDERSON Jeanette
*HEINZMAN Colin SHORT Lesley M
HELFT Gale M WILLIAMSON Anne M
HELLMAN Knut CASELEY Jane R
HENDERSON FRASER Carole
HENDERSON IMRIE Janet Y
HENDERSON Brian W ENGLAND Esther M R
*HENDERSON Charles N LAMBERT Susan M
HENDERSON David THAIN Linda M
*HENDERSON Grahame M (1972) MOIR Kathleen M
*HENDERSON Hamish (1971) FIELDING Jacqueline A
HENDERSON Peter C MCMILLAN Margaret K
HENDERSON Peter R BRUCE Margaret A M
*HENDERSON Reginald L WILSON Gladys
*HENDRY David F VASS Evelyn R
*HENDRY John F ROBERTSON Margaret C
HENRY Antony F H ARGO Frances E
HEPBURN EDWARD Janice E
HEPBURN Kenneth C R I'ANSON Annette E

*Herbert Rodney A	Millard Helen J M
Herd	Gerrard Margaret E
Herd Ian D	MacInnes Margaret E
Hermenau Gerhard H	Robertson Susan F
Heuser Winfried L	MacLean Marion
*Hewins Roger H	McDonald Catherine P
*Hewitt David S	Williams Angela C
*Hewitt Michael R	Watt Catherine A
*Hickie John F	Hings Rosemary
Hicks Charles A	Johnston Kathleen A
*Hickson Bryan	Russell Kathleen
Hill	Loggie Evelyn J
Hill John A	Stuart Valerie M G
Hill Richard C	Repper Margaret A
Hill Roland J	Jeffrey Joan P
Hillen	Mackie Ruth A
Hinch	Skinner Morna L
Hindley Neil W	Flett Joan R
*Hindmarsh Paul S	Toyer Elizabeth A
Hinds John	Lott Edna M
Hirsch	Middleton Rose E
*Hitchings Michael J (1973)	MacLeod Isabella M
*Hobbs Alexander	Kemp Mary L
*Hodges Timothy	Whyte Angela J G
Hogarth-Gaute Philip G	Thorp Carole J S
*Hogg John	Campbell Jessie
*Hogg Nigel R L	Taylor Elizabeth R S
Holden Frank D	Brander Heather
Holland Dennis	Anderson Frances M
Hollands Richard D	Cameron Seonaid E
*Holloway John S	Brown Linda J
Holme	Latimer Sheila
Hope	Thomas Elizabeth M T
Hopkins	Mackie Dorothy E
*Hornby Windham B	Horncastle Allison J
*Horrocks Rodger	Norrie Sandra J
Hosain Iftikhar	Bhatti Perveen A
House David E	MacBean Ann V
Houston John B	Webster Elizabeth A
Houston Walter J	Whiteley Fleur St C
*Howard Christopher B	Greensmith Isobel M
Howat John M	Ritchie Jean M
Howes Alal E	Urquhart Gillian R
*Howie David N	Henderson Aileen J M
*Howie John M	Miller Dorothy J M
*Howie William	Gill Elizabeth A
Howieson Maurice M	Alexander Dianne M
Howitt	Gray Elma
*Howitt John R L	Horne Helen E
*Huckvale Eric L	Stirling Bertha F
Hudson Stewart	Davidson Jennifer
Hughes	Miller Ina M
Hughes Barry O	Gray Helen
Hughson	Johnstone Dorothy J
Hughson	Wallace Irene I
Humphreys	Wallace Glenis W
Humphreys Keith A	Stewart Frances L
Hunt Leslie	Carmichael Flora C C
Hunter	Bray Beverley J
Hunter	Wilson Wilma E B
*Hunter Graham H	Matheson Janet C
*Hunter Ian R (1972)	Thompson Diana M
Hunter Thomas G	Laidlaw Erica A
*Hunter William F	Beattie Marilyn W
Hurst Brian C	McGhie Rhona R
Husband	Brack Margaret H
Hutcheon	Milne Isabel A
Hutcheon Kenneth M	Gall Kathleen M
Hutcheson John	Fraser Doreen C
Hutton Leslie	Barron Joan L
*Ibell Robert L	Wilkie Patricia I
Imlach	Brydon Brenda V
Imray	Allan Helen A
Ince Carl L	Morgan Lois C
Inglis John E	Thompson Mary B E
*Inglis John P	Moncrieff Elizabeth S
*Inglis John R (1971)	Johnstone Lesley M H
*Inglis Julian T	Urquhart Aileen A
Ingram Malcolm D	Hardman Lorna
*Inkson Iain J (1972)	Mackay Marianne E H
*Inkson James H K	Tuach Nan
*Inkster Raymond	Fowler Muriel M
Innes	Farquhar Marjory N
Innes	Lyle Valerie C
Innes Robert	Kitchin Alison M
*Innes William G	Hay Abigail L
*Innes William G	Sim Morag K O'B
*Innes William J A	Bruce Carol I
Innes-Will	Knowles Maureen
Irvine	Kinnaird June
Irvine	Weatherley Jill M
Irvine Tom	Tomlinson Sheila
Isherwood Stanley T J	Fletcher Jane M
*Izatt Jack B	MacLeod Katrine I L
*Jack David (1954)	Cowie Isabell C
*Jack Edwin A	Raymond Barbara P
*Jack George W	Robilliard Kathleen A
Jackson Christopher D	Brown Josie
*Jackson Graham (1971)	MacKellar Margaret C
Jackson Robert	Colleran Nan P D
Jacobs	Campbell Myra A
Jagger Roger L	Low Isobel
James Duncan S	Scott Alison H
*James William	Stephen Evelyn M
Jamieson	Mackie Lesley M H
*Jamieson Donald G	MacRae Grace K R
Jamieson Douglas A	Parks Valerie S
*Jamieson Hugh G J	Hewet Elizabeth A
*Jamieson James C	Shaw Muriel M
*Jefcoate Trevor E S	Thomson Ann K
*Jeffries Colin E	Ogilvie Rosemary
Jess Thomas M	MacRae Donaldina A
Jewitt	Higgins Katharine
Johnson Allan	Couper Laureen M
Johnson Andrew J D	Rice Alison F
Johnson John A E	Peterson Christina J
Johnson Peter C	Hutcheson Moira M
*Johnson Ronald G	McDonald Sheila Y
Johnson Roy M	Duncan Allison I
Johnson Steven R	Robertson Sheila M
Johnston	Bannerman Roslyn
Johnston	Reiach Maureen A
Johnston	Smellie Isabel A
Johnston Anthony G D	Raffan Jennifer T
*Johnston Derek W	Thom Mary B
*Johnston Iain (1973)	Souter Elizabeth M
Johnston James D	MacKenzie Christine C
Johnstone	Gordon Elizabeth

JOINER	McGREGOR Sheila N
JONES	INNOCENT Barbara J
JONES Graham B	NIXON Karen P
*JONES Michael J	WALKER Margaret A
JONES Winston G	BROOKS Marjorie
JORDAN Klaus	ROLLO Elizabeth A
*JOSS Alexander W L	BAIRD Elizabeth
KALOO	SHEARER Margaret-Ann M
*KEELAN John	SOMERVILLE Susan I
KEENAN Brian H	JEMMETT Kathleen E
*KEEPING Joseph D	NICHOL Roberta A
*KELBIE David	SMITH Helen M
*KELLAS James G	CRAIG Norma R
KELLY Dennis	YOUNG Valerie M
KELMAN	HALL Sandra
KELSO	CHRISTIE Dorothy L
*KEMP Alexander J	BROWN Margaret J V
*KENNEDY Duncan M	BAXTER Margaret M
KENNEDY John M	MACKINNON Kathleen L
KENNEDY Kenneth T	MACKENZIE Catherine
KENNEDY William M	FERRARIS Mary
*KENNEY John R	ROBERTSON Mary E
KENNINGTON Roger	WEST Edna
KENRICK Trevor L	ELDER Elizabeth F
*KENT Anthony W D C	LEIPER Susanna J
KERSHAW	FORMAN Jennifer C
*KHALIL Khalil E S	STUART Irene M
KHAN	KEAY Irene H
KIDD John	MATHESON Margaret N
*KILKENNY Terence M	ROSS Isabel M
KILLINGBACK Peter G	REASON Janet M
KING James G	WOOD Margaret M
*KING John A (1952)	YOUNG Prudence A
KING John M	GRANT Elaine M
KINNIBURGH Ian A G	LEWIS Sheila M
KINNIS Terry D	MILNE Helen M
*KINNON John F (1971)	MACAULAY Jennifer A
KIOSSOGLOU Kosmas A	ADAMS Angela C
KIRKPATRICK Ian G	FULTON Anne B G
KIRKPATRICK Thomas C	MARTIN Elizabeth M
KNAPMAN John M	WOOD Moira J C
KNIGHT	JEFFERIES Frances M
KNIGHT Ian D	MURRAY Muriel G C
KNORR Robert D	YOUNG Hazel M
KNOTT Peter B	WRAY Aileen I M
*KNOWLES James G	DAVIDSON Elaine
KNOX William G	REID Alison A M
*KUFAAS Torbjörn	WALKER Jill
KUNAR Roy R	MARTIN Eleanor M
LACEY Harris J	DUNCAN Eleanor M C
*LACHOWSKI Eric E	GRAY Alison C
LA HEY Dick	MORRISON Margaret L
LAING	PATERSON Erna J
*LAING Frank K A	NISBET Barbara D
LALONDE Gérard	RAE Beverley A
LALOR Sean O	RAE Maureen
LAMB	MARSHALL Linda J
LAMB Peter J	MUIR Lisbeth
LAMBOURNE Archie	ELLEN Judith L
*LAMONT Alan M	RAE Alison F
LAMONT Robert	HOLMES Hazel B
*LAM SHANG LEEN Yong-Kwee C Y	SEIVEWRIGHT Sheila

LAND Derek G	BALLARD Sylvia T
LANE	SYPULA Pauline Z
LANG Andrew M	MAGEE Margaret F
LANGMEAD Alfred	JAMIESON Christine
LANGTON Francis G	FARQUHAR Marian D
LANHINGLIT	CHUNG Pin Yong
LAW John S	ROBERTSON Eleanor M
LAWLESS Christopher J	MACKENZIE Eona F
LAWRENCE Francis W	RIDDOCH Ella F
LAWRIE	MAY Joan B
LAWRIE	MELVIN Jennifer M O
LAWTON Frederick	McEWAN Irene B
*LAYCOCK Rex A H	BONOMY Christine M
LEATHAR	MACLEOD Christine M
*LEAVER Alastair S (1971)	WATT Elspeth M R
LeBRUN Christopher S	O'BRIEN Alison B
LECKIE James M	SPENCE Edith L
LECKIE Thomas L G	NEWBIGGING Alice R
LEDGARD	GAMMIE Eileen M C
LEE James A W	MILNE Rosemary J
LEGG	MITCHELL Kate F F W
LEGG	SIM Catherine M
*LEGGE Gordon F	ROSS Rhoda I
LEGGE Iain D	RUSSELL Mhairi B
LEGGE John D	WILL Diana B R
*LEIPER Joseph (1971)	MITCHELL Moira T
LEIPER Malcolm D	JAMIESON Lesley M
LEISHMAN William J	MACFARQUHAR Joan
LENEHAN	KELMAN Patricia E
LENNOX	SKINNER Martha H
LENSSEN	WHYTE Brenda A
LENTHALL	YULE Sheila K
LENTO Ismo J	SMITH Jacqueline E
LEONARD Ronald K	LEASK Susanna J I
LESLIE	BIRSE Sheila M
*LESLIE John S	PORTER Angela M E
*LESLIE Norman W	WATT Sheila A
*LEVIE David S C	MACKIE Mary M R
*LEVITT Charles S A W	CLARK Winifred C
LEVY	PATERSON Laura B
LEWIS	MACKIE Sylvia C W
LEWIS John	ROBERTSON Marjory E
LEYS Alexander D	SMITH Jennifer M
*LIDDERDALE Ian G	LISTER Pauline J
LIEW Meng Leong	AU NYUK CHENG Dorothy
*LINDLEY David K	BELLIS Joanna C
LINDSAY David W M	FORREST Jean
LINDSAY Peter J	BULLOUGH Frances S
LINGARD	DAVIDSON Elizabeth J
LINKLATER Karl A	GIBB Margaret C
LITTLE Matthew M	WATT Aileen E C
LITTLE Richard	SMITH Gladys J H
LITTLEJOHN Andrew G	FRASER Leila A
LIVERSEDGE	MILLER Heather M
LIVINGSTON James M	McCONNELL Rosalind A
LIVINGSTONE Duncan	BERTRAM Barbara C
LIVINGSTONE William J G	LAMB Georgina
*LLEWELLYN John P (1954)	LEJEUNE Anne
*LOCKIE John	EWEN Norma L
LOCKLEY Roger A	MATHESON Susan M
LODGE John C	FAIRLIE Isobel A
LOGAN	LESLIE Patricia E
LOGAN	SANGSTER Rosemary
LOGAN Crawford W	RUSSELL Jennifer M
*LOGAN Ian W	MORRISON Margaret F

LOGAN John	MACKENZIE Theodora
*LOGAN Robert M	WATKINS Lena J
LOGGIE John M	BEATON Mary
*LOGIE Alexander W	CAIE Dorothy E
*LOMAS Christopher J	BENTINCK Susan J
LONG	COSTELLO Heather P M
LONG John W	NICOL Iona A
*LONGMORE Alexander B G	FERRARI Leonella L A M
LOOI Albert C K	CHUA Dorothy P L
LORIMER	HALL Maureen Y
*LORIMER James W	REID Eileen M
*LOTHIAN John	KAY Jennifer A Y
LOVELACE Clive E	MACNAB Rachel
LOW	SIM Dorothy
LOWDON James G	GIBB Marilyn R
*LOWE Maurice D	SILVER Dorothy M
*LOWNDES Michael D	FLEMING Joan M
LOXLEY Colin P	STUART Alison
LUDFORD Alfred W L	MALCOLM Stella M
LUKE	FLANAGAN Elizabeth
*LUMSDEN Alexander T M	SUTHERLAND Catherine A
*LUMSDEN Ian M	PARKER Joan D
LYALL	WATT Margaret
LYALL David J	MUNRO Mary D
*LYALL Francis	SMITH Heather F C
*LYNCH Frederick P (1955)	BIRNIE Alison F H
*LYNCH Michael	MOORE Mary
*LYON DEAN Charles W (1971)	GRANT Margaret H
LYUS Stephen B	PENNY Helen
MACADIE James	FRASER Julia M
MCADIE Joseph T	YEOMAN Joyce E
MCALEESE W R	SNAITH Sybil M
MCALLISTER Edward S R	SIMPSON Sheila M
MCANDREW	FRASER Rosemary A
*MCANDREW Gordon M	MURRAY Leonora J H
MCARA Roderic G	MCFARLANE Wilma
MACARTHUR Alexander	MACINNES Mary F
*MACARTHUR Allan J	CORMACK Marjorie F
MACAULAY Donald	MORRISON Mary
MCBAIN John	NORRIE Jean G
MCBOYLE	CRUICKSHANK Edith E
*MCBOYLE Frederick G	HARPER Elizabeth M
MCCABE Raymond A	ROSS Gwyneth
MCCAIG	HOWIE Kathleen A
MACCALLUM	DEMPSEY Mary H
MCCALLUM Archibald M	LAING May N A
MCCALLUM Calum	MCROBBIE Margaret I
MCCASKIE	MUTCH Gwendoline
MCCAUSLAND Ian	LEES Joan
*MCCLEVERTY Jon A	BARRACK Dianne M
MCCOMBIE Charles A	MCCRAE Elizabeth M
MCCONACHIE George J	BEATTIE Sheena M
MCCONKEY	MACKIE Kathleen I
MCCONNACHIE John G	MAIN Sandra
*MCCONNACHIE Robin I	GLENNIE Gwendoline L
MCCORMACK	MACLEOD Mary A M
MACDONALD	CRUDEN Norma J M
MACDONALD	MACAULAY Margaret G
MACDONALD	MACLEOD Marjory B
MACDONALD	MORRISON Christina
MACDONALD	MURRAY Isabella R
MACDONALD	TAYLOR Christina C S
MACDONALD	THOMIS Helen R
MCDONALD	WOOD Anne E H
*MACDONALD Angus J A	MACDONALD Mary
*MACDONALD Colin D J (1929)	NIMMO Elizabeth M M
MACDONALD Donald H	MACLEOD Mary
*MACDONALD Ian B	SMITH Kathleen F
*MCDONALD Ian R	WATERSTON Margaret E
MACDONALD Raymond C	BRUCE Irene M J
*MACDONALD Roderick J M (1971)	MASSIE Helen W
MACDONALD William A	FRASER Cristabel
MACDONALD William S	HASTIE Isobel G
MACDOUGALL	WHITELOCK Cecil E
MCDOWALL	SMITH Lynda K S
*MACEWAN James A I	BARRON Aileen A
*MCFADDEN John A C	THOMPSON Patricia M
*MACFARLANE Alexander W	HORN Irene W
MCFARLANE Harry A	STILL Lena R C
MCFEAT James	SHEPHERD Margaret
*MACGILLIVRAY Alexander J	MACLEOD Annie
MCGINN	MATHESON Jennifer R V
*MCGOWAN George C	DRAYSON Geraldine M
MCGREGOR	BIRNIE Myrtle E
*MACGREGOR Alan M	ROBERTS Anne
MACGREGOR Charles A	KINNAIRD Anne B
*MCGREGOR David	MCKENZIE Sheila M
*MACGREGOR John D	WILSON Kathleen H
MCHALE Michael S	MARNOCH Jennifer J
*MCILWAIN Alexander E (1954)	KINNAIRD Moira M
MCILWAINE Ronald J	DUFFUS Gillian M
*MACINTOSH Alan A	TURNER Susan P
MCINTOSH Alexander	STORM Isabella
MCINTOSH Donald K	TENNENT Justine R
MCINTOSH Harry D	FORBES Margaret I S
*MCINTOSH James S	WELSH Norma
MCINTOSH John R	DUNCAN Nicolas A
*MACINTOSH Peter M	FRASER Margaret E
*MCINTOSH William E	GAMBLIN Sandra A
MCINTYRE	MILNE Lesley M
*MCINTYRE Angus K	JONES Margaret A
MACISAAC Allan	MACDONALD Morag A
MACIVER	MACDONALD Murdina
MACIVER Anthony D D	GRAY Catherine J
*MCIVER Charles J E	HANSON Rosalind I
MCKAY	MCMILLAN Margaret A
MCKAY	RANKIN Beryl M M
*MCKAY Alexander G R	LOWRIE Agnes E
MACKAY Alistair D	MACDONALD Margaret M
*MACKAY Calum	POTTINGER Norna
*MACKAY Donald I	RAFFAN Diana M
MACKAY Ian S	DAVIE Isobel M
MCKAY James S	NOBLE Mary
MACKAY James W	GARDEN Margaret A F
*MACKAY John F G	KINDNESS Eileen M
*MCKAY John W	SIM Elsie M
*MACKAY Kenneth M	LEWIS Rosemary A
*MACKAY Ronald	CRAIG Alison M
MACKEE Donald M	RAE Annetta
*MACKEITH Neil J	MOIR June M
MCKELLAR Ian B	ROSS Alison C
MACKENZIE	BURNS Marilyn R
MACKENZIE	GRAHAM Ann E
MACKENZIE	MACDONALD Hazel J
MACKENZIE	MURRAY Rhona M
MCKENZIE	ROSS Barbara A F
MACKENZIE Alan G	ANGUS Jeanette A
MACKENZIE Alexander	MITCHELL Margaret A

*MacKenzie Christopher	Ely Elizabeth M K
*MacKenzie Colin R	Mennie Yvonne G
MacKenzie Duncan	Knapman Mary L
*MacKenzie Hector R	Garden Leonora
MacKenzie Ian V	Ellen Sigma A M
MacKenzie Kenneth	Mackintosh Marguerita G
MacKenzie Kenneth P	Campbell Norma
*McKenzie Robin C	Sinclair Margaret
MacKenzie Roderick	MacLean Alice I
*McKenzie Swanson	Duguid Hilda M
McKidd Ian	McWilliam Helen A W
Mackie	MacLennan Helen M
*Mackie Alastair J	Pinnock Jennifer N
*Mackie Grahame J S	Duncan Elizabeth A
*Mackie Maitland	Ramn Halldis A
Mackie Richard E	Buchan Kathleen I M
*McKillop William L M (1954)	Smith Kathleen J
McKinney Roland W J	Singer Linda M C
*MacKinnon John A	Rankin Sandra M
MacKintosh Finlay	McPhee Kathleen I
*Mackintosh John A	McKenzie Dorothy J
Mackonochie James A	Lister Doris A
MacLaren	Robertson Janet G
McLaren	Saint Christine
*MacLaren Donald	Gordon Eileen
McLaren John H	Crighton Barbara A M
*McLaughlin Charles (1972)	MacKenzie Deirdre C R
Maclaurin John R W	King Kathleen M
McLean	Bisset Katrine M
McLean Alastair J	Charitonowsky Ariane
McLean Alexander C	Bremner Joan A
*MacLean Angus A	MacDonald Christina
MacLean Donald	Downie Mary C
MacLean Donald J	MacDonald Margaret A
*MacLean George F	MacLeod Mary
*MacLean Iain E	Ewen Patricia M
MacLean John A	Graham Margaret
MacLean John K L	Begg Wilma A C
*McLean Kenneth	Cruickshank Nancy P
*MacLean Murdoch W	Anderson Margaret R
MacLeay Cameron M	Morrison Chrissisabell
MacLennan	McKay Mary B
MacLennan	Reid Katharine I
*MacLennan Alasdair B	Longbottom Molly E
*MacLennan Duncan	Denoon Deirdre M A
*MacLennan John	Ritchie Lily A M
MacLeod	Davies Joan M
*MacLeod Daniel S	Bisset Morag J
MacLeod Donald	Pursell Patricia A
*MacLeod Donald K	MacLeod Catherine M
*MacLeod Finlay	McIver Norma E
MacLeod John M	MacLeod Nan S
*MacLeod John R	Ridley Susan E
*MacLeod Murdo A	Nicolson Annie B
MacLeod Murdoch	Murray Charlotte
McLerie Edward F	Smith Sheila T
*McLintock Michael J	Ralph Marion J
*MacLure Alasdair G	McLean Elspeth M
*McLusky Donald S	Donald Ruth A
*McMahon James D R	MacRae Jessie S
McMillan	Prout Lesley J M H
*MacMillan Ian R A	Sinclair Joan E C
*MacMillan James D	Campbell Mary F
McMillan Malcolm	Templeton Helen M
MacMillan-Kelly Alan D	Irvine Gladys C
*MacNab Francis A	Ewen Sheila B
MacNamara	Heslop Jane S
McNeill Alexander D	Kerr Jean J
*MacNeill Angus	Gordon Jennifer M
*McNeill Stuart	Sinclair Jean M
MacPherson	Stewart Kathleen R
*MacPherson Hugh (1971)	Robin Sara V
MacPherson Ian	Bruce Jane I
*McPherson James A S (1949)	Perks Helen M
McPherson John	Mackay Margaret C
*McPhillimy William N	McWee Dorothy C B
*McQuillan John	Beckley Sandra J
McQuitty George L	Drummond Sheelagh M
MacRae	Heard Sheila M
*MacRae Hamish S (1951)	Hutcheon Jean G M
MacRae Norman M	Beaton Margaret H
*McRae Stuart G	Adam Hazel M
McRaw Archibald	Wilson Cynthia D
McRobert William R	Docherty Margaret I
MacSween John	MacLeod Effie M
McSween John N	Caie Christina
*MacSween Kenneth S	Donald Morag R
McTear Robert W	Keay Lorna M
*McVicar Alasdair H	Thomson Elizabeth M
*McWhirr William A (1971)	Reid Alison A
*McWilliam Angus A (1974)	Morgan Karen
Macki Salim H	Florence Margaret M
*Madden Craig A	Simpson May
Magee Patrick J	McKendrick Sheila A E
Main	Bigwood Winifred K
Main	Noble Iris
*Main Alan	Swanson Anne L
Main Charles H	McGregor Griselda S
Main William T	Woodhouse Sylvia
Mainwood Anthony R	Mathers Helen T
*Mair Alexander S F	Garrow Alice A
Malcolm John W	White Isobel A
*Malley Alexander B	Sim Sandra J
Malone	Marr Kathleen A
Manjra Mohammed Y	Campbell Frances B
Mann	Farquhar Doreen M
Mann Brian K	Turner Juliet W
Mann Stanley L	Sutherland Ray D
*Manson Donald M	Mitchell Mary
*Manson Roderick M (1971)	Scott Kathleen C
Mantell Henry J L	Stewart Margaret O
Marr Forbes	Christie Kathleen H
*Marr George L	McArthur Margaret B
*Marriott Richard W	Forbes Dorothy K
Marshall	Elrick Margaret R
Martin	Sutherland Nan E
Martin	Brown Irene
*Martin David M W	Bald Lilian V
Martin George I M	Campbell Jean M
*Martin Iain R	Kay Jennifer A Y
Martin John	Richmond Eileen E H
Martin Norman W	Gillespie Margaret B D
Martin Robert W Y	Symon Jennifer
*Marwick David C	Sandison Jean M H
Mason Robin R	Simpson Catherine M (1957)
Mason Thomas L	Anderson Catherine M (1969)
Mason Victor C	Lipscomb Pamela G
Masson Alan J	Wallace Margaret A
Masson Alastair	Leask Aileen M
*Masson Robert A	Campbell Dorothy M

*Masson Robert E	Taylor Mary R
*Mather Alexander S	MacArthur Grace S
Mathers James A G	Mouat Katherine A
Matheson Alexander	Davidson Irene M
Matheson Allistair G	Black Margaret C
Matheson Bruce A	Manson Doreen M
Mathewson	Munro Sheila M
Mathieson Alexander D	Waiter Sheila
*Mathieson Alexander W	Critchley Carol M
Mathieson Ian A	Grant Moira E
*Matthew George D (1952)	McKenzie Margaret W
Matthews	Murray Hellen K
Matthews Dennis B	Phemister Elizabeth R
Mawdsley Evan	Liston Margaret P
Mawson	Sinclair Joyce E
*Maybank Graham T	Child Mary E
Maybin James M	Gordon Margaret A
*Maycock James H	Finlayson Helen R
Mbugua Robert C K	Milne Elizabeth M
Mearns Alan R	Guthrie Janet M
Meier Peter F	Stirrat Helen M R
Mein	Steele Dorothy R
Meldrum Neil G	Young Ann L
*Meldrum Stuart J	Young Claire K
Mellanby	Dickson Fiona J
*Mellis James A	Hay Margaret J W
Mellor William H	Meldrum Moira S
*Melvin James S	Thomson Elizabeth M
Menhinick George S	Reekie Gladys
*Merchant Bruce A	Hamilton Joan I S
Michie	Copeman Mary E
Michie	Gordon Rosemary E
Middleton	Cantlay Valaine I
Middleton	Wilson Isabel A
*Middleton Stuart A	Edmond Margaret G
Mikulsiti	Wilson Margaret A
Millar	MacRae Madeline
*Millar David G	Gibb Judith A
Miller	Drummond Elizabeth M
Miller	Stephen Anne
Miller Alexander J	Rollo Sheila N
*Miller Alistair J M	Young Barbara S
Miller Donald S	Reid Christina L
*Miller Ian D	McLean Sheila S
*Miller John A L	Knowles Sheila E
Miller John M R	Lamont Margaret M
Miller Thomas H	Stephen Anne
Milligan	Sim Lesley B
Mills David M D	Palmer Tessa J H D
*Mills Peter W	Marshall Sheila R
Miln Barnaby K G	Barber Elizabeth A
Milne	Stewart Jamesina S
Milne	Trantor Moira R
*Milne Alan D	Gordon Nanette L M
*Milne Alexander S	Flory Flora A
*Milne David J	Wisely Wendy A
*Milne Douglas J W	MacKenzie Joan
*Milne George A	Watt Marjorie A
*Milne Gordon G	Milne Margaret J
*Milne Melville K	Mortimer Wilma J
*Milne Michael W	Muir Joan E
Milne Russell	Davis Elizabeth A
*Milne Thomas G	Davidson Eleanor F
Milne William A	Hutcheson Christine A
Milne William B	Lawrie Margaret E
*Milton Colin	Sutherland Ailsa M
*Milton Graham R I (1974)	Thain Rita F
*Minett Robert A	Little Patricia C
Mitchell	Binnie Lorna
Mitchell	Robertson Marjorie A
*Mitchell Alexander I (1972)	Fyfe Lindsay A
Mitchell Colin W	Phillips Anne C S
*Mitchell Michael J R	Tomory Jillian M
Mitchell Peter A	Hay Audrey M W
Mitchell William	Birnie Mae L
Mitchell Wilson S	Finlayson Brenda E
Mizen Noël C O	White Frances G
Moir	Coull Dorothy C
Moir	Dey Elizabeth M
Moir	Fleming Fiona M
Moir Ivor J A	Thomson Dorothy A
Moni Giustino	Giuliana Maria A
Monro	Ritchie Alison M
Montgomery Kenneth M	Scott Diana H
Moore Geoffrey D	Kinghorn Jean A
Morales	Durnin Monica M
*Morgan David I	Scott Diane C
*Morgan John A	Stuart Marjory G
Morley Charles F	Muir Sarah J
Morrice	Sorley Alison M
Morrice Ian G	Robertson Barbara R
Morris	Fraser Julie
Morris	Warrender Jean
Morris	Young Pamela A
Morrison	Moir Grace G
Morrison	Mowat Katherine A M
Morrison	Robertson Sandra M S
Morrison	Ross Susan J F
Morrison	Stephen Maureen Y
*Morrison Donald J	Grant Linda M
Morrison Neil D	Henderson Mary F
*Morrison Peter G	Barrack Frances M
Morrison William	Macdonald Flora A
Morrow	Grainger Maureen C
Mortimer Anthony A	Bruce Kate M
*Mortimer Gerald	Gibb Elizabeth J
Morton	Murchie Anne
Morton George M	Robinson Patricia J M
Moss Robin C	Halley Jean
Mowat	Graham Marjory H
*Mowat Colin R	Fyfe Beryl
Mowat John	Normand Anne M
Muir Alan S	Greenshields Irene
Muir Iain H	Wood Willina R
Mullay Alistair W	Leask Audrey K
Munn Graham H	Ryan Pamela
Munro	Munro Margaret J W
Munro Alexander W W	Scott Elspeth S
*Munro Andrew	Smith Sheila Murdoch
Munro Graham	Simpson Sheena G
Munro Grant	McKenzie Morag A
*Munro Hamish D	Walker Alison B
Munro Ian M	McRae Mairi M
Murdoch	Weaver Rhoda J
*Murdoch Charles A (1972)	Cantlay Jean L
*Murdoch James K (1971)	Armstrong Alison M
Murdoch Kenneth G	Mackie Ann E
*Murdoch William F	Gear Christine A
Murison Derek J	Gray Margaret R R
Murison Thomas	Bruce Annie

Murphy Kevin	Painting Josephine
Murray	French Catherine M
Murray	Hird Marilyn
Murray Alexander D	Anderson Aileen A
*Murray Christopher H	Park Audrey F A
Murray Donald A K	Goldie Muriel J
Murray Donald R	Low Mary F
Murray Douglas J	Low Katherine J
*Murray George	Scrimgeour Margaret A
Murray George T H	Riddell Joan H
*Murray Hugh B	Doherty Mary M
*Murray Ian (1971)	Innes Isabel C
*Murray James (1971)	Cowie Maureen M
Murray Malcolm S	Cumming Ann P
Murray Roderick A C	Grant Elizabeth H
*Murray William	Grieve Kathleen F S
*Murray-Smith David J	Smith Effie M
Mutch	Davidson June R S
*Mutch Douglas B	Rhodes Hilary M
Mutch Robin G M	Watson Kathleen
*Mutch William A R	Rae Alison C
Naha Arun K	Seatter Kathleen
Naismith-Beeley Michael	Watt Linda M
*Nall Andrew R	Cowie Carol Mary
Napier	Robertson Anne C
Ndakala	Tennent Ruth M G
Neave Colin P	Troup Annette
Needler Roger M	Allan Christine S
*Neilan Henry T	Wood Sheila
Newlands George C	Richards Maureen E
*Newman Christopher J E	Findlay Patricia M
Nicol	Cheyne Muriel M
Nicol Keith	Strachan Diana
Nicoletti Enrico G R	Gibson Joan S B
Nightingale Peter R	Buxton Rosalind C C
*Nikodem Dirk	Cullen Catherine F
Nile	Meldrum Patricia M
*Nisbet Frederick C H (1955)	Macpherson Mary I
Niven	Smith Elaine G
Noble	Buchan Patricia A B
Noble	Duncan Anne
Noble	Masson Christina
Noble	Watt Pearl W
Noble James	Whitefield Elizabeth M
Noble Peter S	Leask Margaret E
Nolan James D	Mitchell Anita M B
Norfolk	Raffan Rosemary F
Normand	Alexander Anne E
*North Richard A	Hall Jean V A
North Rudolph E	McIntyre Patricia J
*Northcroft David J	Lakin Kathleen E
Nutt Stanley C	Maxwell Elsa P A
*Nwachuku Nathan I C	Odugbose Oludotun M
O'Brien John V	Maclean Margaret P
O'Brien Robert M G	Ogilvie Elizabeth B M
O'Grady	Baker Penelope A
O'Hagan	Hannay Margaret K
*O'Leary Michael J	Carter Alyson M
O'Neill	Allan Helen A
*O'Regan Jeremy	Beddard Susan R
O'Toole Hugh F	MacKay Fiona S
*Ogg Thomas W	Wilson Monica M
*Ogilvie Christopher J	Graham Elizabeth J

*Ogston Derek (1952)	Clark Cecilia M
*Ogston Graeme L	Clark Vivien M P
Oldman	Forrest Irene J
Oliver	McArthur Jean H
Oliver Hedworth F	Riach Alison M
*Olson Ian A	Hamilton Elizabeth A
Olusanya Adebayo	Little Joan R
Olusanya Bandele A	Brebner Eileen
*Omand Donald	Peace Emma S
Oram Charles S	Jaffrey Helen E
Orchard Russell R	Walker Anne
*Orr Robin M (1971)	Crane Nicola H F
Orth Jørgen A H	Mitchell June M R
Osborough William N	Clark Margaret E
*Outlaw Brian D (1971)	Macdonald Alison M
Oxley	Sturrock Isabel A
Packham	MacKay Sheena P
*Pacsoo Tokefat C	Iutz Josephine
Paget	Melvin Marjory C
Palaǰa Bruno	Lorenzoni Maria V
Palmer Nicolas B	McKay Alison B
Panko	Maclean Mary
Parbrook Geoffrey D	Stewart Evelyn O
Pardoe Joseph E	McWilliam Elizabeth
Pariente	Jones Susan P
*Park William M	Staddon Anne E
*Parkinson George L	Glendenning Catherine M
*Patch Derek	Gordon Patricia F L
Patel Jahansoz F	Martin Sheila C
Paterson	Begg Lorna M
Paterson	Davie Anne
Paterson	Mackenzie Mona F
Paterson	Smith Maureen R
Paterson	Thomson Lorna K
Paterson Robert	Clark Eileen M
Paterson William G W	Mackenzie Mary I
Patience Lewis	Mackay Jane M M
*Patterson Ian J	Birse Muriel J
Patterson Nicol P	Hepburn Sheila D
Pattison Edward	Stewart Catherine A
Peacock	Strachan Fiona K
*Peacock Robin G	Alsop Gillian E M
Pearks Peter R	Watson Anna G
*Pearson Ian H	Yeoman Kathleen J
Peebles Kenneth M	Clark Margaret S
Peckitt	McPherson Joyce A
Pennington	Deans Isabella M
*Pereira Brian A	Petrie Heather M
Perkins Robert W	Mitchell Kathleen M A
*Peters Gordon	Wilson Edith I
*Peterson Gordon C	Cant Helen E
Petrie	Brooks Elizabeth C
Petrie	Pickard Joyce I H
*Petrie James C	Forbes Margaret X P
*Pha Jean C	Gill Anna B
*Philip Alexander S	Crofts Gillian M
*Philip Alistair E	McKay Betty J
Philip Andrew M	Dunbar Mary
Philip George G	Burnett Irene M
Philip Gordon M	Charleson Euphemia B
*Philip Robert F	Simpson Anne F
*Phillips George M	Irvine Veronica M
Phillips Ivor W	Hay Jean M
Pickering Michael	Northcroft Janet H

*Pigott Colin P	Watson Ray B
Pirie Ian D	Reid Dorothy J
*Plaskett William B	Langlands Marianne M
Pollard	Tredinnick Beatrice A
*Pollet John E	Blench Sheena M
*Pollock Nigel J	Clure Anne E
Pollock-Smith Russell D J	Cumming Elsie J
*Poole Stuart C (1971)	Mitchell Beryl
Popineau Jean-Luc J	Bourner Sybil A
Porter George D	Ferguson Fiona M
*Porter Robert D	Burnett Frances H
Pottinger David W	Scott Joan F
Potton Richard J	Marshall Margaret W
Potts Robert	O'Hanlon Anne
Powell Valnor	Simpson Marnel
*Prentice Ian M	Gordon Shelagh A O
*Preshaw Colin T	Bruce Carole
Presly	Reid Doreen V
Price John	Middleton Linda M
Price Roger	Milne Margaret E
Primmer Brian A S	Burgess Anna M
Pringle	Khan Indira S
*Pringle Duncan M	Gibb Jean
*Pringle James C	Taylor Maureen M
Pritchard Dorian J	Herford Penelope J
*Pyatt David G	Hay Rosalind A
Rae	Alexander Patricia A
*Rae John E	Munro Margaret C
Rafferty Alan	Buchan Joan C
Rafferty James	Reilly Patricia
*Raitt David G	Davies Elisabeth S
Ramsay	Hendry Sylvia M
*Ramsay Ian M	Pirrie Isobel
*Ramsay Keith M M	Richards Isabella M O
*Randall Ian M	Hughes Janice B
*Rankin Bryan J	Savage Kathleen E
Ratcliffe	Smith Wendy A
Rattray	Mitchell Elizabeth M
Rattray Brian	Ogilvie Marjory
*Raven Norman	Duthie Margaret
*Rawsthorne George B	Mackenzie Anne M
Rayner Richard R	Duncan Catherine R
Reaper James F	Smart Hazel
*Reary James B	Amos Lilias T
*Redford Malcolm K	Plummer Rachel M
Reid	Brand Winifred C D
Reid	Corsie Mary
Reid	Mackenzie Nancy B
Reid	Morrice Margaret
Reid	Morrison Margaret S
Reid	Nicol Helen
Reid	Roberts Celia F
Reid	Salvin Janice L
Reid	Silver Patricia C
Reid	Smith Esme A
Reid	Smith Helen I
*Reid Alan R	Halley Mary R
Reid Albert McK	Forsyth Kathleen M
*Reid George W	Sim Sheila E
*Reid Hamish G	Murchie Marjory E
*Reid John G	Barton Anne M
Reid John M	Mackenzie Vivianne R
*Reid John S G	Donald Maureen
*Reid Norman H	Robertson Patricia C

*Reid Robin D	McConachie Elizabeth M
Reid Thomas P	Walker Doreen I
Reinhardt	Boa Mary I
Rendall James M	Sinclair Morag A S
*Rennie Donald G	Dewar Brenda L
*Revel Karl J T	Buchan Mabel
Riach	Walker Jean M
*Riach Douglas C	Donaldson Anne F
*Rice Charles D	Wunsch Susan I
Richards	Strzalowska Wanda C
Richards Joseph P	Lindsay Ann H
Richardson Michael T	Mendham Nicolette C
Richardson Stanley D	Jezzard Janet E I
*Riddell Alexander J	Millar Elizabeth M
Riddell Stuart	Sharp Evelyn M
Riddler	Mitchell Janet E
Rimmer Gilbert	Ogilvie Eileen M
Ritchie David A	Milne Helen M
Ritchie George	Benzie Carmen H E
Ritchie George F	Wood Thelma
*Ritchie Ian O	Lambie Elizabeth A
*Ritchie John W	Gray Patricia
Ritchie Robert G	Ross Avril E
Rivard Marcel H	Keir Rhona M
Riviere	Christie Dorothy
Robb	Ross Marion C
Robb Norman G	Sutherland Barbara E
Roberts	Tod Anne S
*Roberts Alasdair G (1975)	Cobban Marion M
Roberts David S	Durward Wilma A M
Roberts David T	Fordyce Jane E
Roberts Ernest F	Edmond Carol M
Roberts John M S	Macdonald Catriona
Roberts Maurice J	Macleod Alexandra
Robertson	Alvis Patricia A
*Robertson Alastair O	Robertson Catherine E
*Robertson Alexander S	Martin Pamela M
Robertson Allan M	McLaren Lorna E
*Robertson George E	Grant Sheila M
*Robertson Ian S (1955)	Macpherson Mary E F
Robertson Ian S	Hall Hilda R
Robertson James H	Sinclair Morag M
Robertson James P	Barron Veronica M
Robertson John L	Farquhar Mary E
*Robertson Neil (1967)	Christie Brenda A
Robertson Neil M	Cusa Rosalind J
Robertson Peter J	Thomson Janette D
Robertson Robert J	Littlejohn Margaret I
Robinson Michael J	Cook Josephine A H
Robinson Nigel S	Bell Kathleen T
*Rockwell Peter W	McDonald Elspeth C
Roddis Hugh A J	Primrose Mary M
Rogerson	Moir Annette N
Ropert Marcel L	Robbie Sheila C
Rose	Charlton Maureen
Rose	Fraser Irene
Rose	Macdonald Kathleen M
*Rose John I (1952)	Esslemont Marjory E H
Roser Bruce J	Ellis Susan T
Rosie George S G	Sutherland Inga M
Ross	Bremner Williamina
Ross	Gallacher Jane M
*Ross David S	Watt Heather G
Ross Donald G	Holm Isabel
Ross Eoin M	Gibbons June E K

Ross Harry M	Ralph Alison J
*Ross James	Duncan Elaine M
*Ross John F	MacDonald Theresa E
*Ross Philip W	Shand Stella J
Ross Robert A	MacPhail Evelyn A
Ross William J	Johnson Margaret A
Ross-Browne Michael	Biggar Susan M
Rothwell D M	Macrae Helen S B
Routledge Frederick D	Watson Valerie
Rowlands Gareth J	Welsh Elizabeth K C
*Rowlands Owen	Rennie Pamela M
Rowlands William B M	Muirden Elaine
*Royle Trevor B	Sibbald Jane B
*Ruddiman Kenneth W	Stewart Helene A
Rueckert	Moore Eileen M C
Ruff Peter G	Lindsay Elizabeth M
Russell	Carnie Ann
Russell	Fraser Sheila M
Russell	Williamson Sheila M
Russell Colin R	Tough Elizabeth A
Russell Hugh B L	Duncan Erica B A W
Russell Norman G F	Dawson Margaret J
Rust James D	Hamilton Elizabeth M J
Rutherford John D	Patterson Dorothy E
Ryan David J	Russell Alison M J
Rycroft David S	Soutar Marjorie E
Sachinides Dimitris	Mitchell June
*Sadler Alexander J	Reid Joan M
Sadler David A	McLaren Morag
*Sadler Michael G	Stewart Susan W
Salkeld	Taylor Judith
Salmon Ian D	Gordon Pamela J
*Samuel Alan D M B (1971)	Brown Rosalind A
*Sananikorn Prida	Clarke Avril R
Sands Jeremy Nigel	Campbell Margaret C
*Sargent John R	Buchan Elizabeth J
Saunders Jeremy C L	Coutts Penelope A
*Savage Peter G (1972)	Cormack Elizabeth A
Sawyer	Frater Susan E
Scharff David E	Savege Jill M
*Scotland Colin G E	Fraser Sheila M (1970)
Scott	Bradford Helen M
Scott	Craig Evelyn R
Scott	McDonald Ann L
Scott David J G	Banks Dorothy A
Scott Ian A	Paterson Lily J
Scott James M	Ritchie Margaret M
Scott John A G	McGillivray Rhonda M
Scott John F	Mackie Isobel M
Scott Nigel R M	Moir Maureen C
Scott Robert G	MacCallum Patricia M
*Scott Robin F	Fraser Sheila M (1966)
Scott Thomas M	Smith Mary R
Scott Victor J	Affleck Georgina S
*Scott-Brown Alastair W	Lyall Ardyn A
Scott-Pillow Henry T	Dean Helen M
Seager John	Feather Elizabeth A
Seiler Edmund R	McNeill Anne C
Selbekk Reidar	Hammerstad Bodil
*Self Michael B	Brooks Elizabeth A
Senior	Barron Margaret
Sevo Ivan	Mackie Elizabeth A
Seymour	Watt Ann E
*Shand Edward	Greig Linda J

Shand James G	Lobban Dorothy K
Shanks Ronald S C	Green Dorothy
*Sharp Neil W	Bettridge Ann E
Shaw George A M	Cameron Elizabeth
Shaw Hugh Y	Innes Lorraine H
Shea	Brown Patricia H
Shearer	Forbes Isabel C
Shearer	Groundwater Myra C
*Shedden Alfred C	Terris Rosalyn E M
*Shennan Andrew T	Stewart Anne
Shepherd Hugh M	Cowie Carol A C
Shepherd John F	Davidson Catherine M
*Shewan Frederick D F	Barrack Iris P
Shiach Robert J	Cooper Kathleen S
Shiel Robert S	Maitland Alison I
*Shields Michael A (1954)	Birkbeck Valerie E R
Shirreffs Gordon C	Philip Suzanne
Sibbald	Stephen Alison M
Sills John A	Forsyth Hope G M
Silver Gordon R	Leask Margaret
*Sim George H B	Milne Dorothy C
*Sim John W	Buchan Muriel
Sim Ronald G L	Shearer Blanche A
Simpson	Hendry Jacqueline A
Simpson	Lawrie Eleanor W
Simpson Alexander I	Sutherland Mary M
Simpson Charles E	Wilson Gladys H
Simpson John A	Stewart Alison
*Simpson Neil A	Brown Sheila A
Simpson Norman	Marcella Camille
Simpson Philip F	Philip Grace C
Simpson Stewart	Yackiminie Ann B
*Simpson Thomas W	Philip Maureen A
Simpson-Fraser	Singer Wilma W
Sinclair	Stopper Irene M
Sinclair	Thinn Anne B
*Sinclair Colin D (1971)	Reid Kathleen A
Sinclair John	McMillan Helen
*Sinclair Robert A	Smith Jean R
*Sinclair Samuel D (1975)	Scobbie Valerie A
Sinclair-Gieben	Williams Gaynor M
Singer Robert W	Ritchie Irene A
*Singh Manik	Singh Shakuntala
Skea Ian W	Budge Rosemary K
Skelsey	Calder Charlotte N
Skene Charles P	Lamont Alison J K
Skinner	Masson Catherine K
*Skinner Alexander C	Corbett Catherine M
*Skinner James A	Maclean Murdina
*Skinner James M	Barclay Hazel D E
Skuce	Tuttle Irene M
Slater George M McA	Stanbridge Catherine C
*Slater John	McKinnon Christina M
*Slater John N (1971)	George Sheila C
*Slater Peter A	Craig Isobel M
Sloan	Lyon Patricia M H
*Slowey Alexander	Mackinnnon Patricia I
Smart	Coull Sandra M
Smart David A	Wild Valerie F
*Smart Ernest R D	Carmichael Rosemary C D
Smith	Anderson Rosemary
Smith	Crighton Maureen R
Smith	Fraser Jean E E
Smith	Inglis Mary H
Smith	Low Aileen J

Smith	MacPhie Anne W
Smith	MacRae Catriona F G
Smith	Murison Norma
Smith	Robertson Alison K
Smith	Wood Ella
*Smith Alistair J W	Young Sylvia J
Smith Andrew J D	Ogg Lindsay A
*Smith Angus T	Lawrence Kathleen
*Smith Ben	Synge Elizabeth
*Smith Brian S	Joss Alison M
*Smith Christopher D	Boyack Patricia A
Smith David C	Mutch Lesley M M
Smith David N	Patterson Margaret H
*Smith Donald	Murray Catherine
Smith Donald W	Mackay Cairine D
Smith Ernest	Kingdon Doris
Smith Frederick G	Douglas Lois E
*Smith George A	Hunter Heather
Smith George D	Kennedy Katherine S
*Smith Howard O	Mortimer Sheila W
Smith Hugh M	Cowie Alison K
*Smith James W D (1973)	Mitchell Jessie D F
Smith John D C	McQuistan Fiona E W
*Smith John F (Lord Kirkhill) 1974	Clark Frances Mary
*Smith John G (1972)	Welsh Jean S
*Smith John S	Campbell Gillian A
Smith Kenneth S	Macleod Dolina
*Smith Louis M	Gow Elspeth J A
Smith Martin S	Cameron Margaret E M
Smith Murdoch M	Macarthur Doreen M
Smith Nicholas J	Horne Jeanette B
Smith Peter S C	Yeats Katherine H
*Smith Roderick	McHardy Ellen
Smith Roderick P	Mackenzie Joan M
*Smith Stuart L	Davidson Rachel C
*Smithson John F	McCaw Patricia J
Snell Philip G	Wilson Dorothy L
Somerville	Annand Patricia R
Somerville Robert H C	Cruickshank Sheila
*Sorrie George S	Baird Gabrielle A
*Soulsby John A	Coutts Evelyn M
Souter	Campbell Colinne
*Souter Alistair M	Humphrey Margaret
*Souter Ian P	Russell Helen M
*Souter John R	Mackenzie Rosemary
Speed	Leslie Joan E A
*Speirs Ronald C	Elder Susan W
Spence James W	Stevenson Margaret P
*Spenceley Anthony P	Milne Margaret J
Spencer Brian J	Thomson Helen L
*Spenning Per	Cruickshank Muriel B
Spinks John E	Sanders Penelope J
Spring Michael S	Beddard Susan R
Sprunt Thomas G	MacArthur Deirdre C C
Squire Denis I	Youngson Marika E
Srivastava	Wilson Gladys M W
Stalker	Cooper Elaine H
Stalker Brian A	Cumming Anne D
Stalker Graham C	Mellis Patricia M
Stalker James H	Carlisle Eleanor M
Stanwix Philip R	Wilson Lorna M
Stark George A R	Mowat Anne M
*Stark William A	Nicol Isobel H
Steele	Masson Mary B R
*Steele Donald H	Welsh Moira J L
Steele Thomas A	Clark Denise F
Steele William A	Mennie Catherine F
*Steele William M (1971)	Crighton Joan B
*Stein (Walter) Peter G (1955)	Chamberlain Janet M
Steiner	Murray Eleanor M
Stephen	McRae Edith
Stephen David	Slater Rosalyn J
*Stephen George J	Mackay Roberta D
Stephen Innes R	Moon Helen J
Stephen John W B	Mackay Fiona C
Stephen Michael J R	Gordon Joan E
*Stephenson John D	McBlane Fiona A
Steven	Duncan Jennifer E
Stevenson James P	Carson Graham M G
Stevenson John D	Gardner Elizabeth C J
Stevenson Robert	Dick Elizabeth M
Stewart	Macdonald Donalda
Stewart	Smith Lorna A
*Stewart Andrew M	Fyson Mary J
*Stewart Clement A	Phillip Sheena M
*Stewart David W (1973)	Colville Christine P
Stewart David W N	Manson Marion S
*Stewart Donald W H	Bisset Catherine H
*Stewart Douglas J	Paterson Catherine I
Stewart Douglas L	Henderson Jennifer J
*Stewart Douglas L	Watt Lesley J
*Stewart George M	Young Audrey W
*Stewart Joseph	Smith Lorna A
Stewart Norman M	Campbell Mary S
Stewart Robert A C	Jones Mary C
Stewart William H	Mason Lesley M
*Stileman Richard G L	Ross Patricia F B
*Still Alexander W	Coull Isobel R
Stoker	Buchanan Maria T
Stollery	Watt Janet F
*Stone Gordon V	Wilson Aileen S
Stonehouse D Peter	MacLeod Alison A
Stott Frank F D	Hunter Beatrice J N
*Stott James J	Esslemont Anne R
Stout	Lonie Alice
*Stove George C (1972)	Paul Helen M W
Strachan	Grant Doris M
Strachan George	Gammie Agnes D D
Strachan Peter	Mearns Kathleen M
*Strachan William R	Ferguson Irene R
Strathdee Robert G	Barclay Win F M
Strawson Bernard	Murdoch Anne G
*Stronach Andrew F	Dunn Marilyn J L
Stuart	Ferguson Elizabeth S
Stuart James F	MacQueen Shiona C J
Stuart John B	Larnach Alison J
Stuart Kenneth G	Thomson Mary H
Stuart William G	McLaren Jean
Stubbes	Roaf Jane I
Stubbins William H	Garriock Kathleen W M
*Sturdee Anthony P	Rushton Sarah R
*Sue-Chue-Lam Jerry	Sue-A-Quan Cerise D
Summers Robert S S	Buchan Ann
Sumner	Robertson Helen M
*Surgeoner James H	Wadsworth Sheila
Sutherland Donald M	Allan Barbara G
Sutherland John D	Bone Jessie M
Sutherland John G	Henderson Margaret E
*Sutherland John G M	Ellington Kathleen A T
Sutherland Malcolm	Davidson Ruth I

*SUTHERLAND Stewart R	ROBERTSON Sheena
*SUTHERLAND William R	MILNE Margaret J
*SUTTIE Alastair M	SANGSTER Gillian M
*SUTTIE Ian S	SOUTER Christina I
*SUTTON Alastair M	TAYLOR Eileen
SWOGGER John H	COWIE Marion P
SYKES	CORDINER Stella
*SYMON Patrick A (1952)	PEARSON Isobel G
TAGART	GAMMIE Eileen M C
TAIT	ROBERTSON Christian S
TAIT	STOTT Mary L
TAIT Frederick H	JOHNSTON Margaret
TAIT Maxwell C St C	RENDALL Ruth
*TAIT Peter J T	PROUDFOOT Winifred
TAIT Ronald E	COOPER Ingrid M J
*TALLACH Cameron	MACLEAN Ishbel M
TAMBER Einar R	WONG Daisy S H
TAMISARI	WATT Morag E
TANDY	NOBLE Isabella B
TAUMGEPEAU Filimoto M	MCNEILL Bridget M
TAYLOR	ALLARDYCE Janette H
TAYLOR	BRUNTON Jennifer M
TAYLOR	HAMBLIN Caroline A
TAYLOR	MCFARLANE Gladys
TAYLOR	PETRIE Mhorag J
TAYLOR	SMITH Joan D
*TAYLOR Alexander J	MCBOYLE Evelyn M
*TAYLOR David M	THOMSON Jacqueline M
TAYLOR Douglas W	SMITH Diana M
*TAYLOR George A	WILLOX Margaret E
*TAYLOR James (1971)	HAY Morag C
TAYLOR James	REID Euphemia M
TAYLOR James G	DALGETTY Yvonne A
*TAYLOR Stephen A G (1972)	LOGIE Patricia M C
TAYLOR Thomas F	CORDINER Sheila E W
*TAYLOR Thomas G	CUMMING Jean E
*TAYLOR Willson D	SANGSTER Lorna M
*TELFER Stewart B	HOLMES Sheila
*TELLING Geoffrey M	BAXTER Margaret S
TEMPLETON Phillip K	GORDON Sheila E
TENNANT Smith	STEPHEN Margaret E
THAYER	BRUCE Christine F H
*THIRD Robert T	CHADWICK Beryl
THOM	DUTHIE Ruth
THOM	WILSON Elizabeth W
THOM David	ROSE Isla M
*THOMANECK Jürgen K A	RONALD Guinevere
THOMAS	BUCHAN Barbara B
*THOMAS Richard H	BALDERSTON Mary S
THOMAS Richard S	HIND Angela J
THOMPSON	EDGE Rosemary A
THOMPSON David H	NISBET Jennifer B
THOMPSON Hennessey A S	GRAY Laurina G E
THOMPSON Lloyd M	WILSON Wendy S
THOMPSON Raymond H	ALLEN Hilary
*THOMPSON William G	BUTLER Noreen I
THOMSON	BOOTH Kathleen M D
THOMSON	HARVIE Winifred A
THOMSON	KENT Margaret R
THOMSON	MCRAE Norma
THOMSON	MOWATT Christina C
*THOMSON Alan D (1971)	RODDIS Linda J A
*THOMSON Alan J	COUTTS Elizabeth A
*THOMSON Allan M	BRUCE Charlotte
*THOMSON Douglas A (1973)	BAIN Elizabeth W
*THOMSON Gordon M	HOOD Virginia A
THOMSON James A	TAYLOR Annette M
THOMSON Nichol	BURNETT Lorna M
THOMSON Robert G	BRUCE Patricia H
THOMSON Ronald K	ALLISON Margaret M
TIBBETT Roger J K	TUACH Ann I
TIFFANY Alan	COOK Irene B
TILLSON John R	MCKILLIGAN Margaret J
TIMSON Brian P	LIVESEY Hilary J
*TINCH Robert T	ROSS Susan C
TOBIN Austin	WYNESS Helen P
TOPP William D	FRASER Evelyn M
TRACEY Andrew M	MOIR Jessie A H
TREVENA	DEY Elizabeth W
TREZISE Robin N	KEAY Marjorie K
TUCKER	MACGREGOR Catherine E
TUCKER David C	SMART Jane F
*TULEY Graham	BELL Margot
*TULLIS Douglas K	ATKINSON Alison M
TURNER	MCCONDICHIE Jean M
TURNER	MACRAE Jean G C
TURNER Edward D	ROBERTSON Marion I
*TURNER Gordon H	BREBNER Barbara A
TURNER Michael J	TAYLOR Patricia M
*TURPIE Derek M	DUNCAN Jeanette C
*TUTTLE Albert A	GOW Sheena
TWEDDLE John S	JOINER Vera M
TYRER	HARTNOLL Gillian P
UNDERWOOD	WELSH Margaret C
*URI Oddstein	SUMMERS Patricia
URQUHART Alexander E	KINDNESS Agnes J
VALTONEN Mauri	ATTIN Kathleen M
VAUGHAN	GRIGGS Daphne E
*VIGRON John W	SAYLES Elisabeth A
VIPOND	BISHOP Prudence M
VON WEYMARN	MEIKLEJOHN Dorothy
*VYSE Alan H	MACKINTOSH Frances M
*WALDING Hugh F	SUTHERLAND Margaret S
WALEN Tore	DAVIE Kathleen F
WALKER	SWANSON Ruth A
*WALKER Alexander L	ANDERSON Ann O
WALKER Christopher R	WOOLLAM Jane A N
*WALKER Colin H	REITH Margaret E
WALKER John K	FYDA Janina C Z
WALKER Ronald G	STILL Joan
WALLACE	EMSLIE Helen G
WALLACE Edward B	GUNN Nancy S
WALLACE Harry C H	GONNELLA Frances
WALTON James W	ELLIS Dorothy J M
WARBURTON	MACDONALD Iris D
WARD	MISTRY Chandan
WARD Errol S	GORDON Margaret J
WARD John	GORDON Sheila E
WARDMAN Roger H	SCOTT Rosemary
*WARRACK Ian M	MCARTHUR Alison
WARREN William J	PETERS Mary E
WATKINS David	WESTWOOD Carole
WATKINS David A	BARRON Kathleen E
WATKINS John M	BABBÉ Jean E M
*WATKINS Roger D	MCDOWELL Lindsay A

WATSON	BUTLER Marilyn
WATSON	MURRAY Rosemary L
WATSON	ROBERTSON Myrtle E
WATSON Joseph	WATT Mirren A
*WATSON Melville F	MORGAN Sheila E G
*WATSON Michael D (1971)	HUTTON Eleanor J
*WATSON Steven E	FERGUSON Joanne A L
WATT	ANDERSON Gladys M
WATT Alan	SMART Judith M
WATT Alexander	GEDDES Jean Munro
*WATT Alexander	MORRISON Marie E
WATT Alexander G	SIM Mart(h)a G
*WATT Andrew P (1955)	CLUNESS Anne M
*WATT George D (1955)	LYON Marjorie A
WATT James F	ANGUS Elizabeth R
*WATT Robert J C (1973)	MURRAY Margaret M
WATTERSON David C	KENDLE Janet M
*WATTIE James A	GARRIOCH Joanna M
WATTS	KNOWLES Kathleen M
WATTS	ROSS Maureen V
WEBB Jack R	CARNIE Patricia A
WEBER Gerhard	WOOD Margaret B
WEBSTER	HARROWER Margaret E M
*WEBSTER John A	KINCAID Mary
WEBSTER Martin J	MACDONALD Jean R
WEIGHTMAN Bruce E	MASSON Margaret D
WEIR Alan D	MACDONALD Alys T
*WEIR John G C	FRASER Elspeth G M
WEIR Norman R	DUGUID Eleanor J
WELCH Bruce T	GALL Elsie M
WELHAM	BENZIE Helen
WELSBY	DONALD Sheila E
WELSH	SMITH Jennifer M
WELSH Michael E	SMITH Grace N
*WEMYSS Thomas	HAMILTON Margaret V
WEST	WATT Alexandra A
WESTERN Charles F	FOWLIE Sylvia M
WESTGARTH Terry	COLLERAN Ethel M
WESTON Grahame V J	HUTTON Elizabeth M
WHARTON	PATTERSON Valerie A N
WHEELER	HARRISON Jacqueline M
WHITE David H	BARR Margaret
WHITE John H M	STONE Beryl M
WHITEHEAD Norman S	ROSS Claude M L
WHITELAW Gilbert	NOBLE Christina E
WHITING Bernard	SINCLAIR Margaret F
WHITMORE	MOON Helena M
*WHYTE David F (1971)	PARDOE Kathleen F
WHYTE Gordon T	BIRNIE Mary J
WIGHT	ANGUS Zena J
*WIGHT James R	BURNETT Madeleine A
*WILDGOOSE David M	SPROUL Edna W
*WILDGOOSE Ian	MACKLAND Sheila
WILKIE	CAMERON Ruth E
*WILKIE James L	WATSON Irene A
WILKIE Thomas J	CAMPBELL Sherry E
WILKIE William D	GREIG Evelyn M
WILKINSON	MACRAE Helen S
WILL Roy	CLYNE Isobel A
WILLIAMS	SIMPSON Dorothy A
WILLIAMS David P G	BURNS Rosalind A
WILLIAMS Dennis J	SMART Lynne W
WILLIAMS Paul W	THOMSON Diane N
*WILLIAMS Roger W	MACNAUGHTAN Elizabeth M
*WILLIAMSON Andrew J	VALENTINE Wyn P

*WILLIAMSON James	BAXTER Aldon T
WILLIAMSON Michael	STURROCK Jane T
*WILLIAMSON Peter G	JOHNSON Elizabeth A D
*WILLIAMSON Robert B	JEFFREY Sheena I B
*WILLIS Douglas P	CAMPBELL Catherine M
WILLSON Vivian W	SUTHERS Susan
WILSON	ADEN Sandra
WILSON	HUTCHEON Muriel
WILSON	LAWRENCE Jean S
WILSON Alexander	COMLOQUOY Sheena
WILSON Alexander	THOMPSON Margaret M
*WILSON Alexander B	CAMERON Marjory M
WILSON Alexander C	RAE Patricia
WILSON David K	SCOTT Elizabeth M J
WILSON Eric	LESLIE Jean H
*WILSON James A	MCLAREN Elizabeth D
WILSON James L	CHRISTOPHER Moira A
WILSON John B	WYLLIE Marjorie R
*WILSON Keith W	HALL Linda F
WINSEY Harold S	MORGAN Audrey M
WINTER	WHYTE Kathleen A
*WISELY Ivan C F	KAY Jillian G A
WISEMAN	BRANDS Sheila J C
WISEMAN Andrew W	ALLAN Patricia M I
*WISEMAN Lesley (1971)	SOUDEN Carol E
*WISLOFF Sigurd B	ROSS Catherine L
*WITO James Alexander	HARRISON Moira A
WITTS David E	DUTHIE Jennifer M
WOLK	ASHFORD Anne M
WONG	MORRISH Ann L
WOOD	EDDIE Jean L
WOOD	MACPHERSON Beatrice G
*WOOD Brian J (1971)	PETRIE Doreen A
*WOOD Kenneth G	WISEMAN Margaret W
WOODS Gilbert M	LAIRD May A
WOODWARD Ralph J	GRANT Margaret I
WRIGHT	COOPER Stephanie
WRIGHT	HUNT Jennifer
WRIGHT Andrew M	WATTS-RUSSELL Grayling J P
WRIGHT Gary G	MAY Rhoda K
*WRIGHT Norman J D	ABBOTT Susan
WRIGHT William A	ROSS Kathleen A
WYLIE	KEIL Cheryl M
*WYLIE Ralph C	EATON Jane P
WYLLIE William A S	FARQUHAR Fiona M
YACAMINI David T (1971)	KNIGHT Jean E
YANG Bunli	SYNGE Jane
YOUNG	LORIMER Patricia R
YOUNG	SPENCE Elizabeth C
*YOUNG Francis	DAVIE Victoria F
*YOUNG John A (1973)	DOAK Noreen M H
*YOUNG Kenneth M	PARTINGTON Naomi A
YOUNG Kenneth R	SCOTT Margaret
*YOUNG Niall A	HOLDSWORTH Patricia D
*YOUNG Thomas D	GRANT Kathleen M
YOUNGSON	BUDGE Margaret
*YOUNGSON Colin J	REID Stella F
YULE Charles B	ROBERTSON Isobel M
*YULE David K	FORSYTH Janet M G
*YULE Frederick D	WHITE Janet E
YULE Ian R	MITCHELL Dorothy M
YUSUF	BUTCHART Dorothy A G
ZATELNY William	PIRIE Sheila M

HONORARY GRADUATES 1956–1970

The designations are as at the time of laureation.
The first *AUR* reference is to the laureation address. Where available some later information has been added.
An asterisk (*) is prefixed to the names of those who hold, or have held, degrees of Aberdeen University other than honorary degrees and further information about these may be found in the appropriate Section(s) of this volume and earlier volumes of the Roll of Graduates.

ADAM SMITH or Carleton, Janet Buchanan LL D 1962
author and journalist; literary edit. *New Statesman and Nation* 1952–60; *AUR* XXXIX 346

AITKEN Robert Stevenson (Sir) LL D 1960
MD (NZ) DPhil(Oxon) LL D (Dalh, Melb, Panj, McG, Penn) DSc(Syd) FRCP (Lond, Edin) FRACP
vice chancellor Birm univ; chmn comm of vice chancellors and principals; *AUR* XXXIX 40

ALEXANDER Charles LL D 1968
businessman and farmer; *AUR* XLII 308

ALEXANDER Peter LL D 1966
CBE FBA
regius prof Engl lit. Glas univ 1935–63; *AUR* XLI 307
d 18.6.69

ALLEN George Vance (Sir) LL D 1963
d 2.10.70

ANDERSON Colin Skelton (Sir) LL D 1963
Hon ARIBA Hon Des RCA Officer of the Order of Orange-Nassau
chmn Trustees of the Tate Gallery; chmn joint deptmental comm on grants for students 1958–60; *AUR* XL 174
d -.10.80

ANDREWES Christopher Howard (Sir) LL D 1963
MD(Lond) FRS
dep dir National Institute for Medical Research 1952–61; *AUR* XL 171

ANGUS William Stephenson LL D 1969
MA LL B
secy and factor Aberd 1952–67; *AUR* XLIII 186

ASHBY Eric (Sir) LL D 1958
DSc(Lond) ScD(Dub) LL D(St And)
pres and vice chancellor Queen's univ Belfast from 1950; *AUR* XXXVII 393

ASHMOLE Bernard LL D 1968
CBE MC MA BLitt(Oxon) Hon ARIBA FBA
Lincoln prof classical archaeology Oxford univ 1956–61; Geddes Harrower prof Greek Art and archaeology Aberd 1961–63; visiting prof archaeology Yale univ 1964; *AUR* XLII 313

ATHOLL His Grace the Duke of
nominated for the award of LL D degree but *d* 8.5.57 before the day of graduation

ATTLEE Clement Richard, The Rt Hon Earl LL D 1956
AUR XXXVI 414
d 8.10.67

AULD Alan Talbert LL D 1970
secy of the Aberdeen Association of Social Service from 1945; member of the Scottish Council of Social Service; *AUR* XLIV 91

BAIRD Dugald (Sir) LL D 1966
MD(Glas) FRCOG LL D(Glas) DSc(Manc)
regius prof obst/gyn Aberd 1937–65; *AUR* XLI 313

BAIRD May Deans (Lady) LL D 1960
BSc MBChB(Glas)
chmn N E Reg. Hosp Board, Scot.; *AUR* XXXVIII 553; nat governor BBC in Scot. 1965–70

BANNERMAN John Macdonald LL D 1958
OBE MA BSc(Glas)
rector Aberd 1957–60 *AUR* XXXVIII 175; Life Peerage 1967 Lord Bannerman
d 10.5.69 *AUR* XLIII 332

***BARTLETT Henry Matthew DD 1963**
MA(Aberd) 1923 BD(Aberd) 1926
min par of Logie from 1928 and clerk to Dundee presb; *AUR* XL 168
d 21.12.80 *AUR* XLIX 136

BERKHOF Hendrik DD 1965
ThD
prof systematic theol Leiden univ; *AUR* XLI 123

BETJEMAN John LL D 1965
CBE Hon DLitt(R'dg, Birm) Hon ARIBA
poet and author; *AUR* XLI 116; Kt 1969; Poet Laureate from 1972

BILSLAND The Rt Hon Alexander Steven (Lord) LL D 1956
AUR XXXVI 414
d 10.12.70

***BODONHELYI Jozsef DD 1960 (in absentia)**
PhD(Aberd) 1926 DD(Debrecen)
vice dean of Theol seminary of the Hungarian Reformed Church, Budapest; *AUR* XXXVIII 552
d Budapest 1966 *AUR* XLI 341

BOEGNER Marc DD 1960
DTheol(Paris)
pres French Academy of Moral and Political Sciences; *AUR* XXXIX 39
d 1972

***BROWN William Scott (Sir) LL D 1956**
KCIE CSI MA(Aberd) 1912
rector's assessor on univ court Aberd from 1951; *AUR* XXXVII 82
d Aber 17.5.68 *AUR* XLII 350

***BRUCE Frederick Fyvie DD 1957**
MA(Aberd 1932, Cantab)
prof biblical hist and literature Sheff univ from 1955; *AUR* XXXVII 176

BRUFORD Walter Horace LL D 1958
MA(Cantab)
Schroder prof Ger in Cambridge univ from 1951; fell. St John's Coll, Cambridge; corresponding member of The Deutsche Akademie, Munich; *AUR* XXXVII 395

***BURNS Hendry Stuart Mackenzie LL D 1956**
BA(Cantab) MA(Aberd) 1921 BSc(Aberd) 1922
pres Shell Oil Company Inc USA; *AUR* XXXVII 82
d 28.10.71 *AUR* XLIV 319

CADMAN William Healey DD 1956
MA BLitt(Oxon) BD(Lond) DTheol(Stras)
prof biblical stud. Mansfield Coll Oxon from 1944; *AUR* XXXVII 82
d. 12.9.65

CAIRD George Bradford DD 1966
DPhil DD(Oxon)
prof O T lang and lit Alta univ 1946–50; prof N T lang and lit McG univ 1950–59; sen tut. Mansfield Coll Oxford from 1959 and Grinfield lect in The Septuagint at Oxford from 1961; *AUR* XLI 315; prin Mansfield Coll from 1970

***CALDER John DD 1957**
MA(Aberd) 1900
min emeritus of St Peter's Church North Sydney Aust; *AUR* XXXVII 177
d Sydney Aust 19.10.62 *AUR* XL 74

***CAMERON George Gordon DD 1962**
MA(Aberd) 1925 STM (NY)
min Glenburn Paisley; *AUR* XXXIX 344

CAMPBELL Archibald Hunter LL D 1963
regius prof public law Edin univ from 1945; dean of fac of law from 1958; *AUR* XL 175

CAMPBELL David (Sir) LL D 1960
MC MA BSc MD(Glas) LL D(Glas, Dub, Liv) DCL (Durh) FRFPSGlas FRCP(Lond) FRSE
regius prof materia medica Aberd 1930–58; *AUR* XXXVIII 554
d Aber 30.5.78

CLAPHAM Arthur Roy LL D 1970
CBE PhD(Cantab) FRS FLS
prof bot Sheff univ 1944–69; member successively of the Nature Conservancy and the Natural Environment Research Council from 1956; chmn Brit nat comm for the International Biological Programme; *AUR* XLIV 93

CLYDE The Rt Hon Lord (James Latham McDiarmid Clyde) LL D 1960
PC BA(Oxon) LL B(Edin) LL D(Edin, St And)
Lord Justice-General of Scotland; *AUR* XXXIX 41
d –.6.75

COATS The Rt Hon Thomas, The Lord Glentanar LL D 1966
member of the governing bodies of the Rowett Research Inst and of NOSCA; chmn Advisory Council for Scotland of the Air Training Corps; chief of the Boy Scout Association in Scotland; *AUR* XLI 262
d 28.6.71

COGGAN Frederick Donald DD 1963
DD
the Most Reverend and Rt Honourable Archbishop of York; *AUR* XL 169; Archbishop of Canterbury 1975–80; created Baron of Canterbury and Sissinghurst in the county of Kent 1980

COING Helmut LL D 1968
Dr Juris(Gott) Dr(hc) (Lyons, Montpellier, Vienna)
prof law and former rector of Frankfurt-am-Main univ; dir the Max Planck Inst of European Legal History; *AUR* XLII 310

COURVOISIER Jaques DD 1956
prof church hist Geneva univ; some time dir ecumenical commission for P o W's set up by the World Council of Churches; *AUR* XXXVII 82

***CRAIG Albert DD 1967**
MA(Aberd) 1932 MB ChB(Aberd) 1936 DTM(Calc)
C of S med missionary Charteris hosp Kalimpong from 1937; *AUR* XLII 160

***CRAIG John LL D 1964**
MB ChB(Aberd) 1921 FRCPE
prof ch health Aberd 1948–63; *AUR* XL 378
d Aber 19.4.77 *AUR* XLVII 211

***CRAMB Maurice LL D 1966**
MA(Aberd) 1932 LL B(Aberd) 1934
member of the bus. comm of the General Council Aberd from 1949 and vice convener from 1963; member univ court Aberd from 1960; *AUR* XLI 308

***CROMBIE James Ian Cormack (Sir) LL D 1957**
KCB KBE CMG MA(Aberd) 1925
chmn Board of Customs and Excise from 1955; *AUR* XXXVII 178, 205
d Lond 22.5.69 *AUR* XLIII 214

CROSS Frank Leslie DD 1959
BSc(Lond) MA DPhil DD(Oxon)
Lady Margaret prof divinity and Canon of Christ Church Oxford from 1944; *AUR* XXXVIII 173
d 30.12.68

***CRUICKSHANK Ernest William Henderson LL D 1959**
MD(Aberd) DSc(Lond) PhD(Cantab) MRCP FRSE
regius prof physiol Aberd 1936–58; *AUR* XXXVIII 176
d 29.12.64 *AUR* XLI 109

***CRUICKSHANK Robert LL D 1968**
CBE MD(Aberd) 1925 FRCP(Lond, Edin) FRSE
prof bact Edin univ 1958–66; prof soc and preventive med univ of the West Indies from 1966; *AUR* XLII 311
d Edin 16.8.74 *AUR* XLV 108

CURSITER Stanley LL D 1959
CBE RSW RSA FRSE
Her Majesty's painter and limner in Scotland from 1948; *AUR* XXXVIII 176
d 22.4.76

de VALOIS Ninette (Dame) LL D 1958
DBE Mus Doc(Lond) DLitt(R'dg) DMus(Sheff) Chev. Leg. d'H
dir Sadler's Wells Ballet, the Sadler's Wells Theatre Ballet and Sadler's Wells Theatre; founder of the Sadler's Wells School of Ballet and of the National School of Ballet Turkey; *AUR* XXXVII 395

de VAUX Pere Roland LL D 1964
Dr Theol
superior of l'Ecole Biblique de St Etienne, Jerusalem and dir of the French School of Archaeology in Jerusalem from 1945; dir of the Palestine Archaeological Museum; *AUR* XL 377
d –.9.71

de VISSCHER Fernand LL D 1961
Dr-en-Droit(Ghent) Dr h.c. (Grenoble, Strasbourg, Paris, Rennes, Lille)
member of the Belgium Royal Academy; member of the Italian National Academy; prof law Louvain univ 1936–59; pres International Society for the History of the Laws of Antiquity; *AUR* XXXIX 175
deceased

***DIACK Peter DD 1957**
MA(Aberd) 1912
min of the Park Church Glasgow; *AUR* XXXVII 177
d Edin 4.5.67 *AUR* XLII 181

***DICKSON John Abernethy LL D 1969**
MA(Aberd) 1936 BSc(for)(Aberd) 1938
successively dist off., divisional off. and conserv and from 1968 dir-general of the Forestry Commission; *AUR* XLIII 192

***DIKE Kenneth Onwuka LL D 1961**
BA(Durh) MA(Aberd) 1947 PhD(Lond)
prin and prof of hist in univ coll Ibadan Nigeria; *AUR* XXXIX 176

DINWIDDIE Melville DD 1959
CBE DSO MC
controller in Scot. of BBC 1933–57; *AUR* XXXVIII 174
d Edin 12.6.75

DOUGLAS-HOME The Rt Hon Sir Alexander Frederick LL D 1966
Prime Minister and First Lord of the Treasury 1963–64; *AUR* XLI 261

***DOWNIE Allan Watt LL D 1957**
MB ChB(Aberd) 1923 MD(Aberd) 1929 DSc(Aberd) 1938
prof bact Liverpool univ from 1943; *AUR* XXXVII 179

DURNO James LL D 1960
CBE
farmer and stockbreeder; *AUR* XXXVIII 555
d Aber 7.1.71 *AUR* XLIV 216

ELDJÁRN Kristján LL D 1969
MA PhD
curator and head of the National Museum of Iceland 1947–68; pres of the Republic of Iceland from 1968; *AUR* XLIII 187

***FALCONER Ronald Hugh Wilson DD 1960**
MA(Aberd) 1934 BD(Aberd) 1937
organiser of religious broadcasting for Scotland; *AUR* XXXIX 40
d Glasg 20.5.77 *AUR* XLVII 213

FISON Joseph Edward DD 1958
MA BD(Oxon)
Canon of Truro, Cornwall; *AUR* XXXVII 392
d. 2.7.72

FOHRER Georg DD 1969
DTheol
prof O T studies Erlangen univ from 1962; *AUR* XLIII 194

FORBES-LEITH Robert Ian Algernon Bt (Sir) LL D 1967
MBE JP
Lord Lieut of the county of Aberdeen from 1959; *AUR* XLII 154
d 17.3.73

GARDNER Helen Louise (Dame) LL D 1967
DBE DLitt FBA FRSL
fell. of Lady Margaret Hall and Merton prof Engl Oxford univ from 1966; *AUR* XLII 155

***GEDDES Alexander Ebenezer McLean LL D 1956**
OBE MA(Aberd) 1906 DSc(Aberd) 1915 FRSE FRMetS
member of the staff of dept nat phil Aberd from 1909 and reader until retirement in 1955; *AUR* XXXVII 82
d 26.12.70 *AUR* XLIV 145

GIBB Andrew Dewar LL D 1957
MBE QC MA LL B(Glas)
advoc and barrister at law, regius prof of law Glas univ from 1934; *AUR* XXXVII 179
d 24.1.74

GIBSON Alexander LL D 1968
CBE FRCM
mus dir of Sadler's Wells Opera 1957–59; prin conductor and mus dir of Scottish National Orchestra from 1959; artistic dir of the Scottish Opera Company from 1962; *AUR* XLII 312; Kt 1977

GOLLWITZER Helmut DD 1966
DTheol DD
ordinarious prof theol univ of Bonn 1950–57; ordinarious prof theol Free univ of Berlin from 1957; *AUR* XLI 316

GORDON (née Boissier) Beatrice Mary June (Countess of Haddo) LL D 1968
FRCM
conductor of the Haddo House Choral Society; *AUR* XLII 308; Marchioness of Aberdeen

GRAHAM John Macdonald LL D 1964
CBE DL JP DD
Lord Provost of the city of Aberdeen 1952–55 and 1961–64; prof systematic theol Aberd from 1937; *AUR* XL 380; retd; resid Comrie

***GRANT Joseph DD 1958**
MC MA(Aberd) 1925
C of S min Cromdale Grantown-on-Spey; *AUR* XXXVII 392

GUTHRIE (William) Tyrone (Sir) LL D 1965
administrator of the Od Vic and Sadler's Wells Theatres 1939–45; chancellor of Queen's univ Belfast
d 15.5.71

HALL John Fiddes LL D 1965
CBE
convener Aberdeen Education Committee 1950–52; chmn governors of Robert Gordon's Colleges 1952–63; *AUR* XLI 117
d 17.12.68

HARDY Alister Clavering (Sir) LL D 1962
MA DSc(Oxon) FRS FLS FZS
regius prof natural history Aberd 1942–45; fell. Merton Coll and Linacre prof zoology and comparative anatomy Oxford univ 1945–61; *AUR* XXXIX 347

HARROD Roy Forbes LL D 1956
MA(Oxon) FBA
Nuffield reader in internat economics in Oxford univ and joint edit. of the *Economic Journal*; *AUR* XXXVII 82; Kt 1959
d –.3.78

HEPBURNE-SCOTT The Rt Hon Henry Alexander the Lord Polwarth LL D 1966
chancellor Aberd 1966; *AUR* XLI 258; governor Bank of Scotland 1966–72; chmn then pres Scottish Council (Development and Industry) 1955–72

HETHERINGTON Hector James Wright (Sir) LL D 1961
KBE DL MA(Glas) LL D(Glas, Liv, St And, Sheff, Wales, Prin, Cantab, London, Edin, Belf, Tufts(USA), Br Col) DLitt(McG) D-es-L(Laval) LHD (Wooster, Ohio) Hon ARIBA Hon FRFPSGlas FKC Hon FEIS
vice chancellor and prin Glas univ from 1936; *AUR* XXXIX 177
d 15.1.65

HEUGHAN William LL D 1964
agent and chief trustee of the MacRobert Estates, Tarland; *AUR* XL 381
d 15.8.65 *AUR* XLI 155

HIRST Edmund Langley LL D 1960
CBE MA BSc PhD LL D(St And) DSc(Birm) MSc (Manc) FRIC FRS FRSE
Forbes prof of organic chem Edin univ and pres of the Royal Society of Edinburgh; *AUR* XXXIX 42
d 29.10.75

HOGG Norman LL D 1967
JP
Lord Provost of the City of Aberdeen and ex-officio member of univ court Aberd 1964–67; *AUR* XLII 152
d 25.6.75

***HOWIE James William (Sir) LL D 1969**
MB ChB(Aberd) 1930 MD(Aberd) 1937 FRCP FCPath
head of dept of path. and bact in The Rowett Research Inst Aber 1946–51; prof bact Glas univ 1951–63; dir of Public Health Laboratory Service from 1963; pres of Coll of Pathologists from 1966; pres BMA 1969–70; *AUR* XLIII 236

HUDDLESTON Ernest Urban Trevor DD 1956
MA(Oxon)
member of the Community of the Resurrection from 1941 and lately Provincial of that Order in S Af; *AUR* XXXVII 82; Suffragan Bishop of Stepney 1968–78; Bishop of Mauritius from 1978

HUGGINS Charles LL D 1966
MD DSc MS FRCS FRCSE FACS
dir Ben May Lab for cancer res in univ of Chicago from 1951; *AUR* XLI 310; dir Ben May Lab 1951–69; chancellor Acadia univ 1972

***IRVINE Archibald Clive DD 1958**
MA(Aberd) 1913 MD(Aberd) 1925
head of Chogoria hosp and sen missionary of the C of S mission in Kenya; *AUR* XXXVII 392
d Nairobi 7.6.74 *AUR* XLVI 107 & 235

JACKSON Willis (Sir) LL D 1960
DSc(Manc, Brist) DPhil(Oxon) Dr Sc Tech(Zur) FRS MIEE MIMechE FInstP
pres of Institution of Electrical Engineers; *AUR* XXXVIII 555
d 17.2.70

***JARDINE or Taylor, Helen Margaret (Lady) LL D 1966**
MB ChB(Aberd) 1920 MD(Aberd) 1937
member of Board of Directors of ARI 1944–48; member NE Scotland Regional Hospital Board 1948–58; chmn NE Scotland Regional Nurse Training Committee from 1952; member of the Academic Advisory Committee of St And univ; *AUR* XLI 309

***KEITH Alexander LL D 1967**
MA(Aberd) 1916
farmer and writer; *AUR* XLII 155
d Stonehaven 5.10.78 *AUR* XLVIII 103 & 61

KENNEDY Archibald Cowan LL D 1963
DD
regius prof Hebrew and semitic lang Aberd 1932–62; *AUR* XL 170
d 1.3.66

KLOSTER Robert LL D 1962
Kt of Order of St Olav MA PhD(Oslo)
dir of the Vestlandske Kunstindustrimuseum Bergen from 1949; *AUR* XXXIX 348
d 7.2.79

KNEALE William Calvert LL D 1960
MA(Oxon) FBA
fell. and tut. in philosophy at Exeter Coll Oxford; *AUR* XXXVIII 556

LARSEN Carl Syrach LL D 1966
MF Dr Agr PhD
dir of the Arboretum of the Royal Veterinary and Agricultural College at Horshølm Denmark from 1937; *AUR* XLI 311
deceased

LASCELLES The Rt Hon George Henry Hubert the Earl of Harewood LL D 1966
artistic dir of the Edinburgh International Festival of music and drama 1961–65; *AUR* XLI 263

LAUTERPACHT Hersch (Sir) LL D 1959
QC MA LL D(Cantab) Dr Jur Dr Sc Pol(Vienna) FBA
judge of the International Court of Justice at the Hague; *AUR* XXXVIII 177
d 8.5.60

***LAWRENCE Philip Douglas DD 1966**
MA(Aberd) 1919
minister of Rubislaw church Aber from 1940; *AUR* XLI 314
d Aber 1.6.67 *AUR* XLII 184

LEAVIS Frank Raymond LL D 1970
PhD Hon Litt D(Leeds, York)
reader in Engl Cambridge univ 1959–62; fell. Downing coll 1936–62; edit. *Scrutiny* 1932–53; *AUR* XLIV 95
d –.4.78 *AUR* XLVII 361

LEDERER Edgar LL D 1968
DrPhil(Vienna) Dr-ès-Sc Phys(Paris)
prof biol chem univ of Paris at Orsay 1959; dir of the Institute for the Chemistry of Natural Substances at Gif-sur-Yvette (Central National de la Recherche Scientifique) from 1960; *AUR* XLII 317

***LEITCH Isabella LL D 1965**
OBE MA(Aberd) 1911 DSc(Aberd) 1919
dir of the Commonwealth Bureau of Animal Nutrition 1946–60; *AUR* XLI 118
d Aust 21.7.80 *AUR* XLIX 66

LENNOX Robert Smith LL D 1970
JP
Lord Provost of the City of Aberdeen and ex-officio member univ court Aberd 1967–70; *AUR* XLIV 92

***LILLIE John Adam LL D 1967**
QC MA(Aberd) 1906 LL B(Edin)
sheriff of the counties of Fife and Kinross from 1941 and Convener of the Sheriffs 1960–65; *AUR* XLII 153

***LOCKHART Robert Douglas LL D 1965**
MB ChB(Aberd) 1918 ChM(Aberd) MD(Birm)
prof anat Birm univ 1931–38; regius prof anat Aberd 1938–64; *AUR* XLI 119

***MacDONALD Donald DD 1961**
MA(Aberd) 1913 BD(Aberd) 1920
chap. on the Indian Ecclesiastical Establishment 1924–46; min of Well Road ch Moffat 1946–58; *AUR* XXXIX 173

***MACDONALD Donald John LL D 1957**
MA(Aberd) 1923
rector Inverness r acad from 1944; *AUR* XXXVII 182

***McHARDY William Duff DD 1958**
MA(Aberd) 1932 BD(Aberd) 1935 MA(Edin) DPhil (Oxon)
Samuel Davidson prof O T stud. London univ from 1948; *AUR* XXXVII 393

***McINTOSH Ian Donald LL D 1962**
MA(Aberd) 1930 MA(Cantab)
head George Watson's coll Edin 1953–58; head Fettes coll Edin from 1958; *AUR* XXXIX 349
d Edin 18.1.75 *AUR* XLVI 238

MACIVER Robert Morrison LL D 1969 (in absentia)
MA DPhil Hon Litt D Hon DSc Hon LHD Hon LLD
lect political sc Aberd 1907–15; prof political sc univ Toronto 1915–27; prof at Barnard coll USA 1927–29; prof sociology Columbia univ 1929–50; *AUR* XLIII 189
d 16.6.70 *AUR* XLIII 189 & XLIV 112

MACKIE James Alexander LL D 1958
CBE JP FCIS
magistrate and member Aberdeen town council from 1940; governor of Robert Gordon's Colleges Aber from 1938; *AUR* XXXVII 397
d Aber 9.11.63

MACKIE Maitland LL D 1957
OBE
chmn Board of Governors of NOSCA 1947–56; *AUR* XXXVII 180
d Tarves 30.7.75

MacKINNON Donald MacKenzie DD 1961
MA(Oxon)
regius prof moral phil Aberd 1947–60; Norris-Hulse prof of divinity Cambridge univ from 1960; *AUR* XXXIX 174

McMILLAN William LL D 1957
CVO RA RBS
Sculptor; *AUR* XXXVII 183

MARWICK Hugh LL D 1956
OBE MA DLitt(Edin) Chevalier of the Royal Norwegian Order of St Olaf
hon sheriff substitute of Orkney from 1936; dir of educ for Orkney 1929–46; *AUR* XXXVII 82
d Orkney 21.5.65 *AUR* XLI 155

MATTHEWS James Robert LL D 1960
CBE MA(Edin) FLS FRSE
regius prof bot Aberd 1934–59; *AUR* XXXVIII 557
d Banchory 12.4.78

MAYNEORD William Valentine LL D 1969
CBE DSc FRS FInstP
prof of physics as applied to med Lond univ 1940–64; trustee of the National Gallery from 1966; *AUR* XLIII 193

MELVILLE Harry Work LL D 1957
PhD(Edin, Cantab) DSc(Edin) MSc(Birm) FRS
prof chem Aberd 1943–48; secy DSIR from 1956; *AUR* XXXVII 181

***MILNE John Nelson LL D 1960**
BCom(Aberd) 1922 MA(Aberd) 1946 LL B(Aberd) 1947
convener of the bus. comm of the General Council Aberd; *AUR* XXXIX 43

MITTON Charles Leslie DD 1964
MTh PhD
prin Handsworth (Methodist) coll Birmingham from 1955; *AUR* XL 382

***NEILL Robert Macfarlane LL D 1965**
MC MA(Glas) DSc(Aberd) 1941 FRSE
successively asst lect and reader in dept of natural hist Aberd 1920–64; *AUR* XLI 120
d 30.7.69

NEUBERGER Albert LL D 1967
CBE MD PhD FRS FRIC
prof chem path. St Mary's hosp Lond univ from 1955; *AUR* XLII 156

NICHOLSON Edward Max LL D 1964
CB
dir general of The Nature Conservancy from 1952; *AUR* XL 378

***NICOL Thomas James Trail DD 1968**
MBE MC MA(Aberd) 1938
asst chap. general to the Forces; *AUR* XLII 314

NISSIOTIS Nikos DD 1967
DD
prof theol Athens univ; prof theol and, from August 1966, dean of the Graduate School and dir at the Ecumenical Inst at Bossey; *AUR* XLII 161

***NOBLE Thomas Alexander Fraser LL D 1968**
MBE MA(Aberd) 1938
vice chancellor Leic univ from 1962; *AUR* XLIII 70

PERY Edmund Colquhoun 5th Earl of Limerick LL D 1961
GBE KCB DSO TD
Lieutenant of the City of London; chmn of the Medical Research Council 1952–60; *AUR* XXXIX 178
d 4.8.67

PITT Harry Raymond LL D 1970
PhD FRS
lect maths Aberd 1939–42; prof maths Queen's univ Belfast 1945–50; prof pure maths Nott univ 1950–64; vice chancellor R'dg univ from 1964; *AUR* XLIV 94

PLEYDELL-BOUVERIE William, Seventh Earl of Radnor LL D 1959
KCVO
chmn Forestry Commission from 1952; *AUR* XXXVIII 177
d 23.11.68 *AUR* XLIII 86

POLANYI Michael LL D 1959
DSc(Princ, Leeds) MD PhD (Budapest) MSc(Manc) FRS
prof soc stud. Victoria univ Manc 1948–58; *AUR* XXXVIII 178

***RAE Francis William DD 1965**
MA(Aberd) 1931 BD(Aberd) 1924 STM
min par of Cardonald in Glasg presb from 1948; *AUR* XLI 124

***RAE James DD 1956**
MA(Aberd) 1910 BD(Aberd) 1914
lately moderator of the General Assembly of the Presbyterian Church of England; *AUR* XXXVII 82
d Lond 4.5.60 *AUR* XXXVIII 589

RAILTON Ruth LL D 1960
OBE FRAM FRMCM
founder of the National Youth Orchestra of Great Britain; *AUR* XXXVIII 557

REID George Thomson Henderson DD 1969
MC MA BD(Edin)
min W Church of St Andrew Aber from 1955; *AUR* XLIII 195

RENGSTORF Karl Heinrich DD 1962
ordinary prof N T theology and exegesis in the Westfälische Wilhelms Universität Münster from 1948; *AUR* XXXIX 345

RIEGER Clarence Oscar Ferroro (Sir) LL D 1969
CBE MB BS FRCSE
hon consult. surg at Adelaide Children's hosp; past pres of the Blue Cross Association of Australia; pres of the Australian Medical Association from 1967 and immediate past pres of the BMC; *AUR* XLIII 238

***ROBERTSON Alexander LL D 1958**
MA(Aberd) 1919 BSc PhD(Glas) FRS
Heath Harrison prof chem Liv univ 1933–57; member of the University Grants Committee; *AUR* XXXVII 397
d Grantham 9.2.70 *AUR* XLIII 444

ROBERTSON James Jackson LL D 1956
OBE MA(Glas) BD(Lond) FRSE FEIS JP
rector Aberdeen Grammar School from 1942; *AUR* XXXVII 82
d 9.6.70 *AUR* XLIV 112

ROE Frederick Charles LL D 1958
MA(Birm) L-es-L(Lyons) D de l'univ (Paris, Rennes, Cler Ferr) Chev Leg d'H Laur Fr acad
prof French Aberd 1932–57; *AUR* XXXVII 398
d 6.12.58 *AUR* XXXVIII 12

ROSS Frank Mackenzie (The Honourable) LL D 1961
CMG MC KStJ LL D(Br Col)
Lieut Governor of the province of British Columbia 1955–60; *AUR* XXXIX 178
d 11.12.71

RUPP Ernest Gordon DD 1962
MA DD(Cantab)
prof ecclesiastical hist Manc univ from 1956; *AUR* XXXIX 346

SCOTT Peter Markham LL D 1963
CBE DSC
rector Aberd 1960–63; *AUR* XL 176

SCOTT Robert Balgarnie Young DD 1968
MA BD PhD DD(Tor)
prof religion Princeton univ from 1955; *AUR* XLII 314

SHAW Charles James Dalrymple, The Honourable Lord Kilbrandon LL D 1965
QC BA LL B
senator of the College of Justice in Scotland and Lord of Session from 1959; chmn Scottish Law Commission; *AUR* XLI 117

***SHEPHERD Anna (Nan) LL D 1964**
MA(Aberd) 1915
lect Engl at Aberdeen Training Centre for Teachers 1915–56; *AUR* XL 382
d Aber 27.2.81 *AUR* XLIX 136

***SIMPSON William Douglas LL D 1960**
OBE MA(Aberd) 1919 DLitt(Aberd) 1924 FSA FSAScot
lib Aberd and regist of the General Council; *AUR* XXXIX 44
d Aber 9.10.68 *AUR* XLIII 24, 27

SKYDSGAARD Kristen Ejner DD 1968
DTheol
prof dogmatics and N T exegesis in Copenhagen univ and dir of the Ecumenical Institute, Copenhagen; *AUR* XLIII 71

***SMITH John LL D 1965**
MBChB(Aberd) 1915 MD DSc(Aberd)
chief bacteriologist in the City Hospital Aber 1920–58; *AUR* XLI 121
d Aber 19.6.76

SMITH Thomas Broun LL D 1969
QC MA DCL LL D FBA
prof Scots law Aberd 1949–58; prof civil law Edin univ 1958–68 then prof Scots law there; *AUR* XLIII 188

SOUCEK Josef Bobuslav DD 1969
Hon D Theol
prof of N T in Prague univ and dean of the Comenius Faculty of Protestant Theol in the univ from 1966; member of the Ecumenical Council of Churches in Czechoslovakia; *AUR* XLIII 197
d –.9.72

***STEEL David DD 1964**
MA(Aberd) 1932 BD(Aberd) 1935
min par of St Michael's Linlithgow from 1959; *AUR* XL 383

STEPHEN George LL D 1959
Lord Provost of the City of Aberdeen and ex-officio member of the univ court Aberd from 1955; *AUR* XXXVIII 178
d Aber 18.1.72

STEVEN Henry Marshall LL D 1964
CBE PhD FRSE
prof for. Aberd 1938–63; *AUR* XL 379
d 15.2.69

STEVEN William DD 1960
min Queen's Park West Church Glasg; *AUR* XXXVIII 553
d 31.8.64 *AUR* XLI 61

STRÖMBACK Dag Alvar LL D 1958
Fil Dr(Uppsala)
prof Scandinavian and Comparative Folklore Uppsala univ from 1948; *AUR* XXXVII 399
d 1.12.78

SUNDKLER Bengt Gustaf Malcolm DD 1967
D Th
prof church history Uppsala univ from 1949; dir of the Swedish Institute for Missionary Research from 1951; bishop of Bukoba Tanzania 1962–65; *AUR* XLII 162

SUTHERLAND Joan (Mrs Richard Bonynge) LL D 1968
CBE
prima donna of the Royal Opera House Covent Garden from 1952; *AUR* XLII 309

SWANN Michael Meredith LL D 1967
MA PhD FRS FRSE
prof natural hist Edin univ 1952–65; prin and vice chancellor from 1965; *AUR* XLII 157; Kt 1972; chmn BBC from 1973

***SWAPP George LL D 1961**
DCM MM JP C St J MB ChB(Aberd) 1924
g p in the city of Aberdeen; *AUR* XXXIX 179
d Aber 24.5.69 *AUR* XLIII 213

***TAYLOR William LL D 1962**
CB MA(Aberd) 1913
under secretary at Min of Labour 1946–52; chancellor's assessor to the univ court Aberd from 1955; *AUR* XXXIX 349

***THOMSON Arthur Landsborough (Sir) LL D 1956**
CB OBE MA(Aberd) 1911 DSc(Aberd) 1920
second secy to the MRC from 1949; *AUR* XXXVII 82
d 9.6.77 *AUR* XLVII 286

THURIAN Pere Max DD 1964
dep prior to the community of Taize; *AUR* XL 384

TOOTHILL John Norman (Sir) LL D 1966
published the *Toothill Report on the Scottish Economy* 1961; *AUR* XLI 264

VON ALLMEN Jean-Jacques DD 1970
Dr Theol
prof practical theology in Neuchatel univ; *AUR* XLIV 96

WADDINGTON Conrad Hal LL D 1966
CBE ScD DSc FRS
Buchanan prof anim genetics Edin univ from 1947; *AUR* XLI 312
d Edin 29.9.75

***WALKER Horace DD 1967**
MA(Aberd) 1932 BD(Aberd) 1935
secy depute of the Home Board of the Ch of Scot. 1948–57; secy from 1957; *AUR* XLII158

WALKER Norman Thomson LL D 1966
OBE PhD
successively lect and reader in education and head of the dept of educ Aberd 1925–60; dir of extra mural stud. Aberd 1955–65; *AUR* XLI 310
d 20.4.75 *AUR* XLVI 327

***WATSON William Hay DD 1964**
MA(Aberd) 1929
missionary of the C of S in Livingstonia and Blantyre from 1933; *AUR* XL 385

***WATT Archibald DD 1959**
MA(Aberd) 1923 STM
min of Edzell par ch and convener of the social service comm of the General Assembly of C of S; *AUR* XXXVIII 175
d Aber 1.1.81 *AUR* XLIX 137

WATT William Montgomery DD 1966
MA BLitt PhD
lect, then reader and from 1964 prof of Arabic in Edin univ; *AUR* XLI 316

WILSON William Combe LL D 1963
FRCSE
regius prof surg Aberd 1939–62; *AUR* XL 172
d 12.3.74 *AUR* XLV 451

WOOTON Barbara Frances (Baroness Wooton of Abinger) LL D 1969
MA Hon LHD Hon LL D Hon DSc
prin Morley coll for Working Men and Women 1926–27; dir of stud. in adult educ Lond univ 1927–44; reader, later prof in soc stud. London univ 1944–52; *AUR* XLIII 190

YOUNG Frank George LL D 1965
FRS FRIC DSc PhD MA
prof biochem Cambridge univ from 1949 and master of Darwin coll; *AUR* XLI 122

YOUNG John Stirling LL D 1963
MC MD FRSE
regius prof path Aberd 1937–62; *AUR* XL 173
d Aber –.10.71

SECTION II

SUPPLEMENT
TO ROLL OF GRADUATES 1860–1955

ABD-EL-ALL Mostafa Shukri Abd-el-Halim PhD 1955

ABEL or Falconer, Catherine Florence MA 1935
d 29.12.71

ABERCROMBY Ann McLean Riddell MA 1917
d Aber 21.3.70 *AUR* XLIII 442

ABERCROMBY Edward George BSc(eng) 1931
FICE MIWE
dep new works eng from 1959: King Geo VI reservoir Staines, Qu Eliz II reservoir Walton-on-Thames, filtrat works Ashford Common, Thames–Lee Tunnel main; retd 1.4.68

ABERCROMBY Norman Jackson *MA 1923
officier de l'ordre des Palmes Académiques 1970; head of Fr dept George Heriot's s Edin 1940–63; retd

ABERDEEN Jennie Watson *MA 1919 PhD 1934
lect Engl and dep prin Avery Hill coll Lond 1934–58; retd; resid Aber

ABERNETHY Barclay Chivas MB ChB 1949
b Aber 18.1.28
FRCSE 1958 FRCS 1959
sen surg regist E Fife hosp 1960–66; consult surg E Fife hosp based at Vict Hosp Kirkcaldy from 1966

ABERNETHY David Forbes BSc(agr) 1955
farmer Rosehearty from 1958
m Rosehearty 16.7.66 Mary Duncan teacher d of George S. D. Rosehearty

ABERNETHY Elizabeth Anna BSc 1945 *1947 MB ChB 1958
sen h o dermat and vd Aber 1960–61; asst clin chem dept Aber 1961–62; res asst dept mental health Aber 1968–72; regist mental deficiency Woodlands hosp Aber 1972–75; consult mental deficiency Ladysbridge hosp Banff from 1975
m Aber 5.4.60 George R. Law MA 1957 *qv*; marr. diss 1974

ABERNETHY or Anderson, Hilda Mary MA 1949

ABERNETHY James BSc(eng) 1951
d Cupar 17.9.68 *AUR* XLIII 86

ABERNETHY James Smart MA 1929 LLB 1931
d Kingston Moray 25.5.76

ABRIOUX Olivier Marie PhD 1949

ADAM Alexander MB ChB 1942
clin lect surg Aberd 1962–70, clin sen lect from 1970

ADAM Ann Ida MA 1931
LRAM 1933
teacher: Badenscoth 1949, Inverurie 1953; retd 1971
m 1934 George D. Rowe
d Inverurie 17.5.75

ADAM Anne Grigor MA 1935

ADAM Catherine Kennedy MB ChB 1951
FFARCS 1960
regist anaest: Southampton 1957–59, Mt Vernon hosp Northwood 1959–60, sen regist anaest Sheffield 1960–61, consult. anaest Kirkcaldy from 1961

ADAM David Thain BSc(agr) 1923
member of tc Royal Burgh Forfar from May 1961
wife *d* 1.9.55

ADAM or Cameron, Eliza Smith MA 1942
d 2.5.75

ADAM George BSc 1910
no longer on GC reg

ADAM Gertrude Bryce MA 1935
teacher Mile End s from 1937

ADAM Hugh Grant MA 1912

ADAM James Horatius George MA 1929

ADAM Jane MA 1935

ADAM or Falconer, Janet Scott MA 1922
no longer on GC reg

ADAM John MB ChB 1926
no longer on GC reg

ADAM John Law MB ChB 1890

ADAM or Lawson, Olive Bessie *BSc 1946 PhD 1960
univ of Melbourne: sen dem bot 1960–73, prin tut. from 1973

ADAM Peter *MA 1936
d 9.9.65 *AUR* XLI 250

ADAM William MA 1902 *BD 1908
d Milnathort 13.7.61 *AUR* XXXIX 270

ADAM William MA 1947 BSc(agr) 1949
farm. Banchory

ADAM William James MB ChB 1922
d Eastbourne 24.7.67 *AUR* XLII 359

ADAMS or Dawson, Anne Elizabeth MA 1928
resid Fingask Fraserburgh

ADAMS Arthur Richard MB ChB 1949
FRCPE 1972 RD
Western Aust: phys in charge chest unit repatriation gen hosp Hollywood 1964–68, Sir Charles Gairdner hosp Shenton Park, clin lect Univ of W Aust from 1968
surg comm RANR

ADAMS or Sim, Christina Margaret MA 1948

ADAMS Eleanor Mary MB ChB 1954 [c]MD 1960
g p Derby: asst 1961–62, prin from 1962
d Derby 14.7.79 *AUR* XLVIII 354

ADAMS George MB ChB 1951
g p: Seahouses 1961–69, Spennymoor from 1972

ADAMS James Henderson BSc 1947
MIPlantE 1961 CEng 1972 FInstF 1974
NCB East Midlands: fuel tech 1959–64, area fuel tech 1964–68; Midlands Sales reg area fuel tech from 1968

ADAMS John Charles MA 1927
d Natal S Af 31.7.76

ADAMS John Jackson *MA 1954 MEd 1956
asst dir of educ Dun 1961–62, Lanarksh 1962–66; dep dir of educ Glasg 1966–71, sen dep dir of educ from 1972
d Plymouth 1.6.74 *AUR* XLVI 111

ADAMS or Anderson, Lily Christine Gray *MA 1920
d Forres 21.10.72

ADAMS or Alexander, Margaret Ross *BSc 1931
resid Banchory

ADAMS or Ritchie, Marjory Mabel MA 1954

ADAMS William MB ChB 1924
g p Leeds; retd 1970

ADAMS William BSc(agr) 1941
farm. Anguston Peterculter

ADAMS William Main BSc 1949 BSc(eng) 1953

ADAMSON or Petrie, Elma MA 1949

ADAN Harold George Wickham *BSc 1897
d Aber 20.12.65 *AUR* XLI 236

ADDIE Annie Frances MA 1933
teacher Oakbank s Aber; retd 1964

ADDIE or Pickard, Margaret Sybil MA 1925
resid Lond

ADDISON Alexander MB ChB 1954
DObstRCOG 1960 MRCGP 1966
h o Woodend hosp Aber 1954–55; capt RAMC jun med spec 1955–58; h o Bellshill mat. hosp Lanarksh 1958–59; g p Douglas, Lanarksh from 1959
m Aber 24.8.55 Joan Wood RGN d of John W. Bucksburn

ADDISON George Munro MA 1931
d Botriphnie 24.9.69 *AUR* XLIII 331

ADDISON John BSc(eng) 1945
d 1981

ADDISON Rodney Murison BL 1949
ABSI 1963 FIA 1967 OBE 1976
staff solic and loans man. Malaya Borneo Bldg Soc Kuala Lumpur 1957–63; ptnr Wilsone & Duffus advoc Aber from 1964; tech asst expert ODM 1963, 1967, 1969; chmn Scot. group bldg soc inst 1969–71; secy City of Aber savings comm 1963–70, chmn from 1970; chmn Grampian reg sav comm and vice chmn Nat sav comm for Scot. from 1975; hon secy Aber branch RNLI 1965–74, chmn from 1974; member exec comm Scot. Life Boat council from 1965; secy treas Victoria model lodging house Aber 1966–75

ADDISON William MA 1908 BSc 1909
d Banff 9.4.62 *AUR* XXXIV 376

ADDISON William Eric PhD 1953
BSc(Glas) 1948
sen lect inorg chem Nott from 1964; dep regist UMIST from 1967

ADEL Emanuel Paul MB ChB 1934

ADIE Albert Reith MA 1936
headmaster Braemar s

ADIE Margaret *MA 1933
teacher Engl Aber until 1975; retd

AGASSIZ Cuthbert Delaval Shafto MB ChB 1908 DPH 1910 *MD 1912
d 16.11.72

AHMED Mohammed Abdel Maged MA 1955

AIKEN or Brebner, Doris Margaret MA 1944 Dip Ed 1953
Kingston Canada: fac admin off. Queen's univ 1967–75; asst regist from 1976
m(2) Kingston 1.8.73 Bruce K. Laughton MA(Oxon) univ prof s of Norman B. L. MB(Edin) Fordingbridge

AIKEN Edith Elizabeth Smith MA 1938
teacher Aber until 1944

AIKEN or Reid, Gladys MA 1952

AIKMAN Thomson Smith BCom 1928
retd 1973
d Aber 8.4.74 *AUR* XLV 448 and XLVI 109

AIRD Robert MA 1897 MB ChB 1901
d 1.3.64

AIRLIE William Higgins MA 1948
b Glasg 26.10.20
prin teacher Engl/maths Kintore s from 1960

AITKEN or Clunie, Agnes Smith BSc 1924
d 4.12.68

AITKEN Albert Stuart MA 1953 LLB 1955
TD
ptnr A. C. Morrison & Richards advoc Aber from 1959 major RASC/RCT(TA) 2 1/C 153 Regt RCT Dunf from 1967

AITKEN Angus *BSc 1950 PhD 1954
sen scient off. MAFF exper factory Aber 1959–61; sen scient off./prin scient off. Torry res stat Aber from 1961
m Aber 30.9.61 Wilma W. Smith BSc 1954 *qv*

AITKEN Arthur Jeffrey Hood MB ChB 1944
d Clacton 9.2.63

AITKEN Donald Andrew ᶜMB ChB 1954

AITKEN Dorothy Ritchie MA 1954
teacher: Beauly 1960–61, Inzievar s Oakley 1961–62, Blacklaw s Dunfermline 1962, St Leonards, Dunfermline 1968–70, Lat Dunfermline h s from 1970
m Dunf 24.10.60 Allan Hempseed surv s of Henry H. Rosyth
d 15.2.74

AITKEN or Bradley, Elizabeth Handley MA 1945
teacher: Magwa Asian j s s Jinja Uganda 1960–62, Victoria Nile s Jinja 1963–64, Arusha s Tanzania 1964–71, Victoria Nile s 1971–72, Jinja sen s s 1972; ptnr/prop. with husb gen store/sub PO Skegness from 1973

AITKEN or Hancock, Elizabeth Mary BSc 1954

AITKEN or Reid, Ella Taylor MA 1916
d 1972

AITKEN Elsie Mary MA 1925

AITKEN Henry MB ChB 1928
FRCSE 1938
consult. surg oto-rhino laryngology Royal Victoria hosp, Ulster hosp Belfast; retd 1972

AITKEN Hilda MB ChB 1947 DPH 1965
dept m o health dept city of Aber now dept commun med Grampian health board from 1965

AITKEN or Gilmore, Isobel MA 1951
teacher: Victoria Rd p s Aber until 1960, temp teaching Scone and Perth 1975–77, Robert Douglass mem s Perth from 1977

AITKEN John BSc(for) 1922
retd 1964

AITKEN or Griffith, Leslie Mercy Veronica MB ChB 1948
clin asst Hurstwood Park hosp Haywards Heath 1968–70; g p (ptnr) Worcester from 1971

AITKEN Margaret Ferrier BSc 1920
d 1962

AITKEN or Chalmers, Margaret Stuart MA 1945
teacher Camberley from 1970

AITKEN Robin Christopher BSc(eng) 1945

AITKEN Thomas *MA 1949

ÅKERBERG Blenda Clarice MA 1949
teacher: Walker Rd p s Aber from 1972
d Aber 30.10.75

ALEXANDER Alexandra Duncan MA 1916
d Nairn 15.6.74 *AUR* XLVI 107

ALEXANDER or Dale, Audrey Jean MA 1944
Aber: teacher Kaimhill s 1955–60, part-time pre-nursing coll, coll of comm 1960–77

ALEXANDER Doreen Wood *MA 1950

ALEXANDER or Taggart, Doris Elizabeth MA 1948

ALEXANDER or Storm, Elizabeth Ann Murison *MA 1915

ALEXANDER Eric Archie BSc(eng) 1945
tech Derby from 1949
m Derby 2.6.62 Jean M. Toms d of Arthur T. Derby

ALEXANDER George Sim MA 1930
d Kemnay 4.9.62 *AUR* XL 93

ALEXANDER Harry William MA 1921
teacher: dep head Victoria Rd s Aber; retd 1966
d 14.1.81

ALEXANDER or Caird, Helen Catherine Elizabeth MA 1953

ALEXANDER Henry Gavin MA 1944
MA(Oxon) 1954
commonwealth fell. Univ of Minnesota 1956–57; teacher: Maidstone g s 1960–65; head Guisborough g s 1966–69, Hampton s Mddx from 1970
m Kew 31.3.64 Barbara A. Richards BA(Oxon) 1961 teacher d of Sydney R. Manchester

ALEXANDER Herbert Alexander Darg MA 1915
d 2.1.81 *AUR* XLIX 135

ALEXANDER Isobel Bisset MB ChB 1949
DPH(Leeds) 1965 MFCM 1972
sen dep m o West Riding c c Harrogate and dep m o h Knaresborough 1965–74; sen m o h Harrogate N Yorks AHA from 1944

ALEXANDER James BSc(eng) 1931
Hong Kong: asst dir of publ works 1961–64, govt civ eng 1964–68, retd from col serv 1968

ALEXANDER John *MA 1898 BSc 1906
d Aber 23.2.68 *AUR* XLII 345

ALEXANDER Joseph MB ChB 1918
no longer on GC reg

ALEXANDER Mary MA 1935
sen exper off. DSIR Lond 1938–53; tech asst to sc attaché Br embassy Washington DC 1953–58; exec vice-pres Herner & Co from 1958
m Washington 7.8.54 Saul Herner BS(Wisc) pres Herner & Co

ALEXANDER or Miller, Mary Ramsay MB ChB 1942
N'cle: sen res assoc gyn dept 1961–63, Nuffield res assoc midwif dept 1966–67, fam plan. from 1964 and from 1971, loc auth Newcastle and Northumb 1971–75; sen m o (child health) N Tyneside from 1975

ALEXANDER or Macaree, Mary Watson MA 1943

ALEXANDER or Moffat, Maud Kilgan MA 1933

ALEXANDER Stella Margaret BSc 1936
Aber: prin teacher sc Rosemount s until 1972, Kincorth acad 1972–73; retd

ALEXANDER William MA 1912
d Aber 14.4.66 *AUR* XLII 83

ALEXANDER William MA 1951 LLB 1954

ALEXANDER William Johnstone BSc(eng) 1945
MSc(Leeds) 1973
chief eng ITT Bell & Gossett Letchworth 1961–66; grad certif in educ Leeds 1967; lect eng Bradford tech coll 1967–75, sen lect from 1975

ALISON Crichton MB ChB 1915
no longer on GC reg

ALLAN Alexander MA 1931
d Aber 31.12.73

ALLAN Alice Mary MA 1928

ALLAN Alice Williamina MA 1929
retd 1971

ALLAN Charles Baird MA 1948 LLB 1950

ALLAN Charles Davidson MB ChB 1921 DPH 1941
d Edin 4.12.74 *AUR* XLVI 236

ALLAN Cuthbert Alastair *MB ChB 1921
g p Dun
d Dun –.6.67

ALLAN Donald McKay MA 1939
d Midhurst 1973

ALLAN Douglas John Innes MA 1936
FEIS 1972 JP 1975
head Prestonpans p s from 1957

ALLAN Eva Mary MA 1928
SCM 1933
Nurs trg ARI, ERI 1929–33; midwifery trg Mother's hosp Hackney 1933–34; Queen's nurse E Barnet 1935–40; asst supt Queen's trg home Hackney 1940–43; supt midwives/health visitors Aber 1943–45; asst supt nurses E Suffolk 1945–48; Queen's nurse/asst supt Aber 1948–66; retd

ALLAN Frances MB ChB 1953
DPM(Lond) 1970 MRCPsych(Lond) 1973
asst m o h Inverness-sh 1962–66; psychiat regist Rainhall hosp Liverpool 1966–69; sen m o (mental health) Stirling cc; sen regist Lea Castle hosp Kidderminster 1970–72; consult. psychiat Royal Scot. Nat hosp Larbert from 1972

ALLAN George James MA 1923 MB ChB 1927
d 29.6.65

ALLAN George William[s] MB ChB 1901
no longer on GC reg

ALLAN Gertrude Alice Bisset MA 1932
teacher Ashley Rd s Aber from 1947; retd 1975

ALLAN or Adie, Hazel Elizabeth MA 1950
teacher until 1955

ALLAN or Palmer, Helen Margaret BSc 1942
teacher sc Bo, govt s Sierra Leone 1946–47
resid Bexhill-on-Sea

ALLAN Hellen Anderson *MA 1929
teacher mod lang; retd 1970; resid Dufftown

ALLAN Isabella May Ogg MA 1924 MB ChB 1928 DPH 1938
d Aber 3.7.72 *AUR* XLV 127

ALLAN James Gray MA 1954
teacher: first asst Sanday s 1958–62, prin Engl Jedburgh g s 1962–68 also dep rector 1968–76; head Moray middle s Grangemouth from 1976

ALLAN James Sunley MB ChB 1954
DPH(Lond) 1960 DIH(Lond) 1973 FRSM
post grad stud. Lond s of hyg & trop med 1959–60; m o Unilever Lond 1960–74; sen m o UML (Unilever) Port Sunlight from 1974
m Glasg 1959 Mary M. Tannahill MB ChB(Glas) 1957 consult. psychiat d of Andrew R. T. Glasg
d 14.6.79 *AUR* XLVIII 354

ALLAN or Robinson, Jessie Roberta Forgan *MA 1928

ALLAN John MA 1889

ALLAN John Birnie MA 1931 BD 1934
MBE 1963
retd 1974; resid Rochester

ALLAN John Black MA 1926 BD 1928
m Myra T. Duncan MA 1926 *qv*
resid Edin

ALLAN John Mearns MA 1904
d –.1.62

ALLAN John Murray MA 1922

ALLAN John Robertson *MA 1928
writer; resid Methlick, then Lincoln

ALLAN Leslie Christie MB ChB 1938
m o h Calgary 1960–73; dep m o h Edmonton from 1973

ALLAN Lindsay Hay MB ChB 1939
g p Barrow-in-Furness from 1946

ALLAN or Stewart, Maggie MA 1923

ALLAN or Donaldson, Margaret MA 1952

ALLAN or Henderson, Margaret Manson Oman MA 1943

ALLAN or Kernoff, Margaret Pirie MB ChB 1938
part time m o fam plan clin LCC 1948–73

ALLAN or Ritchie, Margaret Stephen MA 1917
Lady Ritchie 1941
d Banchory 2.6.76 *AUR* XLVII 102

ALLAN Marjorie Jane Gordon MB ChB 1945
res asst Royal Marsden hosp Lond from 1963

ALLAN Marjory Fyfe MA 1927
d Montrose 4.2.73

ALLAN or MacLeod, Mary Anderson MA 1943
teacher: Mortlach 1961–71, Keith p s from 1971
husb *d* 27.5.72

ALLAN Mary Davidson MA 1927 *MEd 1946
Zambian Distinguished Service Medal 1979
prin psych M o D (air) Lond 1946–65; dir of tech aid in occup psych Zambia 1965–67; dir of occup assessment for govt of Zambia from 1967–73
d –.9.81

ALLAN Moira Margaret MA 1942
teacher Rothes s from 1949

ALLAN Norman Duncan MB ChB 1930
retd from g p and St John ambul brig 1973
d 7.9.80 *AUR* XLIX 68

ALLAN Richard George Gordon MB ChB 1951
g p Scunthorpe

ALLAN Robert MA 1948
Dip Deaf (Chaplain) 1973
min St Andrew's North Church Kilmarnock 1961–73; chap. to the deaf Ayrsh from 1972

ALLAN Robert Milne MB ChB 1942
d Kilmarnock 8.1.78

ALLAN Robin Thomas Phillips BSc(agr) 1949
ICI: agr dev off. Yorks & Co Durham 1954–65; tech rep agr Isle of Man from 1965

ALLAN Theodore Martin MB ChB 1941
asst dir N E Scot. blood transfusion serv from 1956
m Conon Bridge 1953 Isabel M. Sellar LLB(Edin) d of Rev. John S. MA(Edin)

ALLAN William MB ChB 1909 DPH 1912
d 30.12.66

ALLAN William Garland Leith MB ChB 1946 MD 1980

ALLARDYCE Alexander MA 1904 *BL 1907
no longer on GC reg

ALLARDYCE or Cameron, Jean Garden MA 1945
soc work for handicapped and deprived ch Portugal, Turkey, Philippines, Uruguay, Austria from 1952

ALLARDYCE Marian Jane *MA 1912
d Pagnell 8.1.65 *AUR* XLI 55

ALLARDYCE William Frank Gray BSc(eng) 1953
MICE 1959 MIWE 1964
Angus c c eng dept: asst 1956–58, sen asst 1958–64, chief asst 1964–74, dep county eng 1974–75; asst dir (new works-des) water serv dept Tayside reg c from 1975

ALLAWAY Ernest Edward MB ChB 1907
no longer on GC reg

ALLCROFT William Miller Ord BSc(agr) 1930 PhD 1934
retd from min of agr 1965; settled in NZ 1968

ALLENBY or Hughson, Myrra Hutcheon Sewell *MA 1939 BD 1951
teacher Aber 1972–76; retd

ALLISON Brian Johnstone BSc(for) 1951

ALLISON Ernest Russell BSc 1921 MB ChB 1928
d Aber 10.7.66 *AUR* XLI 338

ALLISON Robert Whitelaw MA 1922
no longer on GC reg

ALLISON Thomas Philip Gray MB ChB 1950
g p Aber

AMONOO Kofi Alfred *BSc 1952
d Accra –.8.58 *AUR* XLIII 86

ANDERSON Adam Connan BSc(agr) 1955
asst advis NOSCA Keith, Inverurie 1957–62; tech advis N E Farmers Aber 1962–67; farms man. Strutt & Parker Elgin 1967–71; g p farm man. (own bus.) Forres from 1971
m Boat of Garten 24.7.58 Shona G. MacDougall teacher d of James M. Grantown-on-Spey

ANDERSON or Hepburn, Agnes Forbes *MA 1953
ARCM(violin teaching) 1968
mus critic *Press & Journal* Aber 1956–58; free lance violinist (from 1964) e.g. for Scot. Opera; Edin: private teacher violin from 1969, teacher violin George Watson's coll 1968–72

ANDERSON Alan Gauld *MA 1955
BOCM Co: market res man. Scot. 1958–62, asst chief cattle advis Lond 1962–66, Tomkinsons GMBH: gen man. Hanover 1966–68, export man. Kidderminster 1968–74; man. dir Anderson Exports from 1974

ANDERSON Alexander MB ChB 1932 MD 1946
FRSM 1960
chief m o BP 1963–69; retd
d Glasg 16.9.75 *AUR* XLV 417

ANDERSON Alexander Donald Stewart MA 1927
d Lond 5.6.62 *AUR* xxxix 383

ANDERSON Alexander George BSc(eng) 1945
dir Aberdeen Construction Group 1969–72; chmn/joint man. dir William Tawse Aber from 1972

ANDERSON Alexander Greig
MA 1905 *MB ChB 1909 *MD 1914 LLD 1949
d Aber 21.5.61 *AUR* xxxix 200

ANDERSON Alexander Wilson BSc 1913

ANDERSON Alred Lyall Smith MB ChB 1941
g p Holmfirth from 1950

ANDERSON or Lawrence, Amanda Margaret MA 1949

ANDERSON Andrew Black *MA 1923
d 22.1.63

ANDERSON or Watson, Angelica *MA 1914 *BSc 1914
d 9.3.62 *AUR* xxxix 380

ANDERSON or Esslemont, Annabel Margaret MA 1947
head teacher: Aldbar by Brechin 1964–73, Careston by Brechin from 1973

ANDERSON or Ferguson, Annie MB ChB 1919

ANDERSON Annie MB ChB 1920
MBE 1970
g p Oldmeldrum from 1947

ANDERSON or Hill, Annie Cecilia Stewart MA 1935

ANDERSON or Christie, Annie Isabella MA 1927
teacher Sunderland 1929–32

ANDERSON Annie Jane MA 1919 BSc 1922

ANDERSON Archibald Stirling Kennedy
MA 1909 *MB ChB 1914 DPH 1921
d –.3.72

ANDERSON Audrey Lucy MA 1949

ANDERSON or Bourne, Barbara Eileen MB ChB 1945
part time clin m o Barnet AHA from 1974

ANDERSON Beatrice Margaret MA 1946

ANDERSON Betty Ann Forbes MA 1949
teacher: BFES s Sennelager Germany 1958–61, Highgate h s Kuala Lumpur 1961–64, Buckie h s (p dept) 1965–67, head Inveravon p s Ballindalloch from 1967

ANDERSON Caroline Mary MA 1929
teacher Methlick; retd 1970

ANDERSON or Macdonald, Catherine MA 1944

ANDERSON Catherine Gifford Isbister MA 1927

ANDERSON Charles MB ChB 1926
g p Burnley 1937–62; retd
deceased

ANDERSON Charles Ernest BSc(eng) 1952
contr eng (elect.) Bowater Paper Corp North Fleet 1952–70; retd

ANDERSON Charles James Barton MB ChB 1940
surg Arbroath from 1957

ANDERSON David *BSc 1952 MEd 1954
d 16.10.77

ANDERSON David Bruce *BSc 1955 PhD 1959

ANDERSON Davidson Wallace BSc 1948
asst head/prin maths Moray s s Grangemouth 1961–68; rector: Camelon h s Falkirk 1968–74, Woodlands h s Falkirk from 1974

ANDERSON or Taylor, Dora *MA 1922
head teacher Engl Mortlach s s Dufftown 1923–25; tut. asst Engl univ of Cape Town 1927; lect in children's lit Buxton Nursery School Training Centre Claremont Cape 1938–40; secy to jun lit soc Cape Town 1942–62; writer of articles on S Af lit for '*Trek*' Cape Town 1942–48
d Hemel Hempstead 12.10.76

ANDERSON Edith Kathrine MA 1934
teacher until 1950

ANDERSON Edward MB ChB 1946
MRCGP 1968 JP
g p Glenlivet from 1965

ANDERSON Edward James BSc 1946
NCB: reg opencast man. (dev) W. Midlands 1964–68; reg opencast man. (dev) Central 1968–74; reg opencast geol Central E from 1974
m 15.3.52

ANDERSON Edwin MB ChB 1942
b 20.8.1918
g p Gillingham from 1947
m Gillingham 7.5.60 Rosalind M. L. Darby LRCP g p d of Frederic M. D. Warrington

ANDERSON Elizabeth Margaret MA 1954

ANDERSON Elizabeth Margaret Davidson MA 1926

ANDERSON Elizabeth Mary Stewart MA 1951
teacher Engl: Ballater s 1956–67, Cults acad from 1967

ANDERSON or Twatt, Elizabeth Norman MA 1933

ANDERSON or Nesbitt, Ella MA 1931
teacher kindergarten Albyn s for girls Aber 1960–71; retd; resid Oldmeldrum

ANDERSON or Pirie, Ella Edith MA 1904

ANDERSON Eric Alexander MA 1949 Dip Ed 1956

ANDERSON Ernest Arthur BSc(for) 1942

ANDERSON Ethel Margaret MA 1930
teacher geog Ellon acad 1947–70
d Aber 17.9.74

ANDERSON Francis MB ChB 1904
no longer on GC reg

ANDERSON George Menzies MB ChB 1923
g p Manchester from 1926

ANDERSON George Stevenson MB ChB 1938
consult. surg Inv from 1964

ANDERSON George Walter MA 1955 MEd 1957
DEP(Glasg) 1965
psych Glasg 1963–68; head Nerston resid s E Kilbride 1968–70; dep prin psych Fife from 1970
m Aber 14.4.62 Lilian M. Brockie

ANDERSON George Walter Fraser MA 1928 MB ChB 1933
Tangier from 1934

ANDERSON George William MA 1953 *MEd 1968

ANDERSON Gordon Rae *MA 1949
MA(Cantab) 1966
asst secy Aberd 1963–65; Cambridge: asst registrary 1965–70, sen asst registrary from 1970

ANDERSON Hazel Leith *MA 1944
prin teacher classics Aber h s for girls 1964–73; asst head Harlaw acad Aber from 1973

ANDERSON or Geddes, Helen Isobel MA 1914
d Aber 20.8.71 *AUR* XLIV 316

ANDERSON Henry Francis BSc(eng) 1939

ANDERSON Ian Alfred BSc 1929 *1930 *MB ChB 1933 *MD 1950
FRCPath
retd 1970
m Aber 31.10.36 Kathleen I. W. Duthie d of David H. D. MA 1893 *qv*(I, II)

ANDERSON Ian Hall MB ChB 1952
MIH (Harv) 1960 Certificate Military Medicine (Air) (Canadian Forces Med Council) 1968 FAMA 1970
RCAF: 1 Air Div Zweibrucken Germany 1960–65; inst of aviat med Toronto 1965–71; sen consult. civ aviation med–fed govt Ottawa from 1971

ANDERSON Ian Vernon MB ChB 1955

ANDERSON Irene Rosalind *MA 1950
teacher Engl Vigo, Spain 1960; free-lance translating of books etc., abstracting scient papers, edit., mss, original writing from 1963
m(2) Pitlochry 12.6.79 Garth Logan

ANDERSON or Child, Isabel Cruden MA 1938

ANDERSON or Ritchie, Isabel Innes MA 1938
teacher Engl Old Aber s from 1959; retd

ANDERSON or Manley, Isabella Lamont MA 1935
d Aber 18.1.62

ANDERSON or Mackworth, Isabella Largie MA 1903
d 13.7.67 *AUR* XLIV 178

ANDERSON or Way, Isobel Margaret MA 1938

ANDERSON James MA 1890

ANDERSON James MA 1912
no longer on GC reg

ANDERSON James BSc(agr) 1938

ANDERSON James Adams MB ChB 1951
g p Skegness from 1957

ANDERSON James Bruce MA 1910 MB ChB 1910

ANDERSON James Reid *BSc 1921
d Montrose 12.8.71 *AUR* XLIV 319

ANDERSON James Stirling MA 1914 *1919 *MB ChB 1921 *MD 1923
retd 1956; resid Barrington

ANDERSON Jane Barbara Carrie MA 1925 BSc 1925 *1926
retd 1962

ANDERSON Janet Watson MB ChB 1945
m o (mat. & ch health) Nairobi 1965–71
m Nairobi 1966 James O'Gorman agr eng

ANDERSON Jean MA 1955
resid Aber
m Aber 19.6.64 Laurence I. Walterson MB ChB 1957 *qv*

ANDERSON or Ferguson, Jean Stuart MA 1948
resid Glenrothes

ANDERSON or Geddes, Joan Grant MA 1954
teacher: asst prin biol Banff acad from 1969

ANDERSON John MB ChB 1916

ANDERSON John MB ChB 1938
g p Shaftesbury, Stockton and Seaham Harbour from 1947

ANDERSON John Christie MB ChB 1904
deceased

ANDERSON John James Hall MB ChB 1921
d Jersey –.9.64 *AUR* XL 399

ANDERSON John Leonard BSc(agr) 1954

ANDERSON John Rognvald MB ChB 1943
g p: Scourie 1963–65, Gloucester from 1965

ANDERSON or Hall, Katherine Evelyn MA 1933

ANDERSON or Gare, Margaret Ann Taylor MA 1941

ANDERSON Margaret Brown MA 1935
teacher Hanover St s Aber 1936–73; retd

ANDERSON or Angus, Margaret Collie *MA 1941
admin asst St. Andrew's House Edin 1941–42; war service in ATS 1942–43; various teaching posts Roxburgh from 1964; cler asst SSEB Galashiels from 1975

ANDERSON or James, Margaret Constance MA 1952
teacher Melbourne from 1973

ANDERSON or Gill, Margaret Elsie MA 1919
teacher Aber 1941–65; retd
d Aber 28.11.78

ANDERSON Margaret Jane MB ChB 1923
asst bact S Af inst of med res Johannesburg seconded to publ health dept municipality of Johannesburg to initiate immunisation serv
m Cape Town 9.11.35 George Park eng s of George P. Strichen

ANDERSON or Stephen, Margaret Jane MA 1929
farm. 1960–79; resid Nairn
husb *d* 26.9.60

ANDERSON or Pardy, Marie Hogg BSc 1924 *1925
resid Aber from 1957
d Aber 1.10.79

ANDERSON or Duguid, Marie Louise MB ChB 1941
h o RACH 1941–42; g p: Elgin 1942–44, Coventry 1944–47

ANDERSON Mary (May) *MA 1915
d Edin 27.4.61 *AUR* XXXIX 202

ANDERSON or Smart, Mary MB ChB 1938 DPH 1942
resid Aber

ANDERSON Mary Ann MA 1925
teacher NSW Aust: maths Bowral h s 1929–30, Hay h s 1930–34, Katoomba 1934, Sydney girls' h s 1935, Hay h s 1936
m Christchurch NZ 12.9.36 George W. Scarth farm. s of James S.

ANDERSON or Wilson, Mary Craigie BSc 1938
teacher maths Elgin acad 1967–74; retd

ANDERSON or Dewar, Mary Sinclair MA 1926
resid Edin

ANDERSON or Wilson, Mary Still MA 1905

ANDERSON Patrick Hector Roberts BSc(agr) 1922 MB ChB 1934 MD 1954
div m o h Surrey c c Epsom 1946–65; m o h borough of Epsom and E. Ewell 1965–67; retd

ANDERSON Robert BSc(eng) 1949
sen asst eng Edin from 1960

ANDERSON Robert *MA 1951
sen lect Fr univ of Durh from 1967

ANDERSON Robert John MB ChB 1943
JP parish of Rosemarkie 1972
g p Fortrose from 1947
d Fortrose 14.2.80 *AUR* XLVIII 443

ANDERSON Robert Leslie BSc 1952
teacher maths Dalkeith from 1958

ANDERSON Robert Moir Lechmere MB ChB 1910
d 1969

ANDERSON Robert Moir Lechmere MB ChB 1942
g p Stainforth and Hatfield, Doncaster from 1946

ANDERSON Ronald MB ChB 1923
d Chelmsford 26.1.68 *AUR* XLII 360

ANDERSON Ronald Elrick BSc 1953

ANDERSON Sarah Tulloch MA 1929
d Inv 31.3.74

ANDERSON or Liston, Shona Isobel MA 1950

ANDERSON or Sheldon, Sophie MA 1930

ANDERSON Sylvester Campbell MB ChB 1938

ANDERSON Thomas Edge *MB ChB 1926 *MD 1930
FRCPE 1962 Member Brit Assoc of Dermatology from 1938 (President 1967–68); retd 1968
d Aber 21.9.73 *AUR* XLV, 319

ANDERSON Thomas Gordon Greig BSc 1955 Dip Ed 1958
teacher sc Oban h s from 1962

ANDERSON Thomas Kennedy BSc(agr) 1925 *1927 *BSc 1926
d Aber 19.1.65 *AUR* XLI 58

ANDERSON Una MA 1954

ANDERSON or Robson, Valerie Elizabeth MA 1949 MB ChB 1954
resid Potton

ANDERSON or Hossack, Vera Isobel BSc 1945
part-time teacher chem and archae Vancouver from 1968

ANDERSON Wardlaw MB ChB 1940

ANDERSON William MB ChB 1915
no longer on GC reg

ANDERSON William MB ChB 1919
d 19.3.73

ANDERSON William Ainslie MB ChB 1947
consult. gen surg Derbysh RI from 1961

ANDERSON William Alexander BSc 1940
SAI 1945–75; retd

ANDERSON William Archibald MA 1951
MC TD

ANDERSON William George MA 1938
head Peterhead c s from 1970

ANDERSON William John *MA 1940
lib and teacher Engl sixth form coll Brockenhurst from 1962

ANDERSON William John Moir MA 1931
retd 1972; resid Boddam

ANDERSON William John Ronald MB ChB 1946
consult. obst/gyn Coventry from 1961

ANDREW or Buchan, Ella Mary MA 1945
teacher Aber until 1953

ANDREW Herbert Francis *BSc 1952

ANDREW Robert Alexander MB ChB 1951
g p: Mansefield 1955–63, Leven Yorks from 1967

ANDREW or Fraser, Shirley Margaret MA 1955

ANDREWS Elizabeth Ross MA 1955
teacher: BFES Malacca, Malaya 1959–60, Hospital Hill s Nairobi 1968–70
m Nyeri Kenya 10.2.61 James M. Suttie BSc(agr) 1956 *qv*

ANDREWS or Anderson, Margaret Walker MA 1952
resid Dun

ANGELO or McKellar, Paula Marjorie MB ChB 1954

ANGUS Douglas John *BSc(eng) 1950
Trent poly Nott sen lect 1966–73; prin lect from 1973

ANGUS Hamish Thomas Ingram MA 1930
teacher Peeblesh; retd
d 5.4.80

ANGUS Ian Alexander MB ChB 1939
MRCPsych 1972
HM Prisons: sen m o Winchester 1960–63, Birmingham 1963–67; prin m o Home Office prison dept Manchester 1967–75
d 11.12.77 *AUR* XLVII 360

ANGUS or Craig, Jeannie Gertrude MB ChB 1923
retd from g p 1967
d Aber 9.4.77 *AUR* XLVII 212

ANGUS Magnus Miller *MA 1951
teacher Newmachar p s from 1969

ANGUS or Bell, Margaret Isabella Rennie *MA 1942
civ serv until marriage; resid Edin

ANGUS Margaret Jean MA 1941

ANGUS or Sibley, Margaret Mitchell MA 1930

ANGUS Ronald George *MA 1947 Dip Ed 1948
lect RGIT Aber from 1949

ANGUS William BSc(agr) 1900
no longer on GC reg

ANGUS William George Stewart BSc(agr) 1931
d Sandiacre 4.1.72

ANGUS William Rogie MA 1924 BSc 1926 *1927 DSc 1940
sen lect in phys chem UCNW Bangor; retd 1970

ANGUS William Stephen MB ChB 1908
d Aber 18.5.64 *AUR* XL 395

ANNAND Dudley Nicolson MA 1954 LLB 1957
ptnr Esslemont & Cameron advoc Aber from 1961

ANNAND Duncan Matheson MA 1936
d Aber 24.6.71 *AUR* XLIV 321

ANNAND James Mitchell MA 1952 BD 1955
min Dryfesdale church Lockerbie from 1966

ANNAND John Carmichael MA 1932 MB ChB 1937
g p Broughty Ferry from 1945
m Aber 27.7.40 Elizabeth D. McEwan d of David McE. Aber

ANNAND Pearl Jane MA 1941

ANNANDALE James Scott MB ChB 1910
d Stonehaven 19.5.64 *AUR* XL 397

ANTON Alexander Elder MA 1946 LLB 1949
CBE FBA 1972
member of Scot. Law Comm: part time 1966–73, full time from 1973; resigned chair of juris Glasg 1973

ANTON Charles Edward MA 1955 LLB 1957
ptnr Adam Thomson & Ross advoc Aber from 1961

ANTON Henry Craigen MB ChB 1946
DMRD(Edin) 1957 FFR 1961
consult. radiol Stobhill hosp Glasg from 1963

ANTON Ian Robert MA 1949
no longer on GC reg

ANTON John Bernard MA 1953
solic Lond and W. Aust 1962–68; stipendiary magistrate: Kalgoorlie W Aust 1968–72, Midland W Aust from 1972

ANTON or Donald, Lucy Margaret *MA 1948
JP 1966
resid Aboyne
m Blairs 20.2.56 James R. Donald, Aber

ARCHDALE Arthur Joseph MA 1950
head York House s Rickmansworth from 1963

ARCHIBALD Alexander *MA 1890 MB CM 1894
deceased

ARCHIBALD Alexander Spring MA 1926
retd from Crawford Church 1972
wife *d* 27.3.66

ARCHIBALD Charles MA 1902
no longer on GC reg

ARCHIBALD John Ingram BSc 1948

ARGO or Price, Isobel Mary MA 1944
comp secy with T. Norman Price (Dudley), Dudley from 1966

ARGO or Collins, Jean MA 1947
teacher Exeter from 1970

ARGO John Duncan MA 1933
teacher Aboyne and Torphins 1935–45 (not 1941); head Canberra p s East Kilbride 1963–74; retd

ARKHURST Frederick Siegfried *MA 1952

ARKLAY James Taylor BSc 1934
d Forfar 6.1.80 *AUR* XLVIII 442

ARKLIE Eileen Agnes Stuart MA 1948
head Balgay s Dun 1960–61; teacher Aber 1961–63, lect soc stud. RGIT Aber from 1963

ARMSTRONG Alexander William *BSc 1925
no longer on GC reg

ARMSTRONG Allan MacLeod MA 1925
retd from teaching 1968; resid Dyke

ARMSTRONG or Gray, Dorothy MB ChB 1950
g p New Cross Lond from 1952

ARMSTRONG James Muir *MA 1936
Arbroath h s: prin asst 1968–71; asst prin Engl 1971–77; retd

ARMSTRONG John Bruce Ormiston MB ChB 1953
g p Croydon from 1956

ARMSTRONG Peter Charles BSc 1948
s of Philip G. A. sales rep and Doris A. Matthews; b Glasg 23.12.26
tobacco chem Bristol, Glasg 1950–57, tech & prod. man. Salisbury Rhodesia 1957–65; tech & dev man. Belf 1965–70; prod. dir Lurgan, Andover 1970–75; dev man. Lond, Jos Nigeria from 1976
m Bristol 19.9.53 Betty P. Merchant d of Stanley V. M. Bristol

ARNAUD Frederick Cooper BSc(eng) 1939

ARNAUD John Charles Stanley *MA 1948 Dip Ed 1949
JP for Banffshire 1972
prin teacher Engl Keith g s from 1960

ARNAUD Stanley William BSc(eng) 1950

ARTHUR George Gordon *MA 1950
teacher mod lang: Aberlour h s 1960–65, Aber coll of comm 1965–68; asst prin mod lang RGC Aber from 1968

ARTHUR Helen Elizabeth MA 1936

ARTHUR John Hay MB ChB 1924
MBE
d Eccleston 4.4.78 *AUR* XLVII 356

ARTHUR William Hay MB ChB 1929
g p Bridlington and member of staff of Lloyd hosp Bridlington from 1930; retd 1963
d 9.5.80

ASHBY Arthur Sinckler MB ChB 1937
visiting surg gen hosp Barbados from 1948

ASHER William Alexander MA 1919
no longer on GC reg

ASHWORTH Michael Raymond Frederick PhD 1941

ATKINSON James Leslie *MA 1952
staff man. Ford Motor Co 1959–67; personnel man. Celanese Corp 1967–69; manpower man. Plessey Co 1969–71; organis and pers planning man. British Leyland from 1971

ATKINSON Thomas Henry *BSc 1953
tech off. (chem) Billingham from 1953

ATTISHA Paul Elias MB ChB 1930
g p Basrah Iraq 1946–71; retd

ATTYGALLÉ John Wilhelmus Samuel **MB ChB 1897**
deceased

AUCHINACHIE Douglas William **MA 1924 BSc 1926 *1927 PhD 1931**
d Wakefield 1.2.61 *AUR* XXXIX 203

AUCHINACHIE or Nugent, Elizabeth Eleanor **MA 1915**
d 25.2.64

AULD Mary Innes Ruxton **MB ChB 1951 DPH 1956**
asst m o h Kincardine 1958–74; clin m o Grampian health board from 1974

AULD or Hardie, Phyllis Amy Isobel **MA 1934**
teacher: relief work St Margaret's s for girls Aber 1955–63, part time Bristol 1966–68; resid Cromarty

AULD William Harry Ruxton **MB ChB 1944 *MD 1954**
FRCPath 1968 FRCPGlas 1975
consult. chem path. group lab St Mary Abbot's hosp London 1956–61; consult. med biochem Ballochmyle hosp from 1961

AUTY or Duncan-Brown, Eunice Mary **MB ChB 1941**
g p Greenock from 1947

AYMER Alexander Lindsay **MB ChB 1913**
no longer on GC reg

AYMER Charles Alastair **MB ChB 1921**
g p Lond 1931–76; retd

AYMER or Gordon, Frances **MA 1909**
no longer on GC reg

AYRTON or Jones, Elsie Elizabeth **MA 1926**
retd 1966; resid Lond

BADDON or Wardlaw, Catherine Ann **MA 1926**

BADENOCH Agnes Margarete **MA 1923**
d 20.9.73 *AUR* XLV 318

BADENOCH Alexander Guthrie **MA 1919 *MB ChB 1923 *MD DPH 1934**
d Edin 5.12.63

BADENOCH Alexander William **MA 1923 MB ChB 1927 MD 1929 ChM 1944**
Lond: visiting urol Royal Masonic hosp till 1970, civ consult. urol RAF, consult. surg St. Peter's hosp for Stone and St. Bart's hosp; consult. urol Samaritan hosp for women till 1959; pres: Hunterian Soc 1959, urol sect. Royal society of Med 1958, British Assoc urol surg 1968–69; awarded St. Peter's medal 1974; joint-edit. *European Urology*

BADENOCH David Sutherland **MB ChB 1912**
d Lichfield 1.8.69 *AUR* XLIII 328

BADENOCH Emily Mary **MB ChB 1920 DPH 1921**
d Aber 1.3.72 *AUR* XLIV 429

BADENOCH George **MA 1897**
no longer on GC reg

BADENOCH or Third, Hilda Jean **MB ChB 1923**
g p Nelson 1923–66
resid Skipton

BADENOCH Jessie **MA 1904**
d 15.2.64

BADENOCH Mary **MA 1926**
retd 1965; resid Buckie

BADENOCH or Davidson, Nancy **MB ChB 1955**
LMCC (Ott) 1973
part time m o publ health serv Glasg 1958–64; Toronto: school health serv 1966–68, m o rehab centre 1970–74; g p Dundas Ontario from 1974

BADENOCH Sarah Graham **MA 1922**
no longer on GC reg

BAGGLEY Charles Arthur **MB ChB 1944**

BAGGLEY or Sidery, Margaret Evelyn **MA 1935**
resid Burgess Hill

BAIKIE or Lennie, Lucy May **MA 1907**
resid Beauly
d 23.9.80 *AUR* XLIX 66

BAILEY Gordon Raymond **BSc 1952**
PhD (Br Col)

BAILEY Henry Patrick ***BSc(eng) 1936**
Vickers (ship-bldg group) Barrow-in-Furness: elect eng i/c nuclear proj des team 1957–67, man. spec serv dept 1967–72; man. spec proj elect. dept from 1972

BAILEY-THOMSON or Dillon, Joyce Doreen **MB ChB 1938**
g p Nott from 1938

BAILLIE Alexander Main **MB ChB 1915**
d Torquay 10.1.74

BAILLIE Angus William **BSc(agr) 1954**
agr advis in E Perthsh and East of Scot. coll of agr from 1954

BAILLIE David Main **MB ChB 1909 MD 1912**
d 6.2.71

BAILLIE Donald John **MA BSc 1937 MEd 1949**
dir educ Kirkcudbrightsh
d Dumfries 28.2.75 *AUR* XLVI 239

BAILLIE Elizabeth Crosse **BSc 1926**
retd 1966; resid Nairn

BAILLIE George Roderick Bannerman MA 1930 BSc 1932
d New Pitsligo 24.2.70 *AUR* XLIII 446

BAILLIE James MA 1903
no longer on GC reg

BAILLIE James Francis MA 1929
DBEA
v-pres Edin Esperanto Soc; resid Auldearn

BAILLIE or Laird, Margaret Bell BSc 1941
teacher sc/biol Sittingbourne 1957–70; resid Elgin

BAIN Alexander Adam Ness MB ChB 1936
d Inv 26.8.66 *AUR* XLI 341

BAIN or Young, Annie Simpson MB ChB 1931
g p Aber from 1939

BAIN or Brown, Annie Wilson MA 1930
teacher: Bradfield 1931–38, Ipswich 1952–63, prin maths Leicester 1963–68; retd; resid Woodbridge

BAIN or Gibson, Barbara Cheyne MA 1932
teacher Edin 1960–68; resid Edin

BAIN or Jeffrey, Belle Emslie MA 1926
teacher: Tillydrone s Aber 1958–71; retd; resid Bieldside Aber

BAIN Catherine Brown Wilson MA 1930

BAIN Charles Stewart MA 1927

BAIN Ewen Grant MA 1935
head Logie Durno s 1958–75

BAIN Flora Elizabeth MA 1946

BAIN George Munro MA 1908
d 4.1.63

BAIN Ian McPherson *MA 1910
BA(Oxon)
resid Broughty Ferry
d Dun 9.8.81

BAIN or Christie, Isabel Grant *MA 1923
d Aber 8.9.72

BAIN James Andrew BSc 1954 *BSc 1956
Lond: mineralogist min resources div overseas geol surveys 1960–67, prin scient off. mineralogy unit Inst Geol Sc from 1967

BAIN John Alexander *MA 1938
asst edit. *The Iraq Times* Baghdad 1946–50; edit: *The Singapore Free Press* 1960–63, *The Malay Mail* Kuala Lumpur 1963–67; sen sub edit. *The West Australian* Perth W Aust from 1967
m Leeds 20.9.63 D'Orise Timmins teacher d of William T. Cape Town

BAIN John William Laing MB ChB 1936
d Aber 24.10.78 *AUR* XLVIII 106 and 232

BAIN Lawrence Weir MB ChB 1913
no longer on GC reg

BAIN Logie Samuel MB ChB 1937
D Phys Med (Lond) 1953 DL MRCPGlas 1975
resid Aber

BAIN Margaret Amelia MA 1908
d 4.1.67

BAIN Margaret Isobel *MA 1923
Dip Univ Paris 1931
Prin Edge Hill trg coll Ormskirk 1947–64
resid Edin

BAIN or Horne, Marjorie MA 1927
teacher Abdnsh: Lyne of Skene s 1956–59, Cluny s 1959–70

BAIN or Craig, Marjorie Simmonds MB ChB 1942
resid Glenbuchat

BAIN or Wrigglesworth, May Murray MA 1931

BAIN Robert MA 1902
d 12.6.64

BAIN Robert *BSc(eng) 1948

BAIN Roderic MB ChB 1944
g p Stainland Yorks from 1946
d Stainland –.10.80 *AUR* XLIX 135

BAIN Roderick McLean MB ChB 1947 DPH 1951
MFCM 1972
sen clin m o Wigan from 1961

BAIN William BSc(agr) 1949
teacher sc Bridge of Don s from 1952

BAIN William Alexander *MA 1904
d Dunlop Ayrsh 28.7.68 *AUR* XLIII 77

BAIN William Cranna MA 1942 *BSc 1948 PhD 1951
sen prin scient off. Appleton Lab Slough from 1964

BAINES Doreen *MA 1949
m Dawson

BAIRD Agnes Alexandra MA 1931

BAIRD Anna Frances MA 1928

BAIRD or Graham, Annie Frances MA 1925

BAIRD Eba Crichton MB ChB 1943 DPH 1948
MFCM 1972
m o h Burgh of Hamilton from 1970

BAIRD Edward George *MA 1925 MB ChB 1932
d 25.1.67

BAIRD or Gimingham, Elizabeth Caroline MA 1945 Dip Ed 1946
Aber: lib Harlaw acad 1967–72, asst lib Bankhead acad from 1973

BAIRD James Alexander *BSc 1932 MA 1934
DipEd (Lond) 1962 JP 1969
head New Pitsligo and St. John's s Aberdeensh from 1965

BAIRD Jessie Elizabeth Crichton MB ChB 1939
FRCOG 1976
consult. gyn/obst Royal Samaritan hosp for women and Rutherglen mat. hosp Glasg

BAIRD John Wilson *MA 1950

BAIRD or Penman Splitt, Joyce Deans MA 1949 MB ChB 1954
MRCPE 1973
Edin: res fell. and clin asst dept therap univ and R.I. 1957–64; MRC res fell. and clin asst dept med univ and W Gen hosp 1965–68; m o Scot. Home and Health dept St. Andrews House 1969–70; lect med univ and W Gen hosp from 1971; sen lect med univ and consult. phys W Gen hosp from 1976

BAIRD or Shepherd, Mary Margaret MA 1934
resid Milltimber Aber

BAIRD William Scott *MA 1937
head Elgin West End s 1954–76; retd

BAKER Joseph John BCom 1931
retd J. W. Baker Aber 1971

BAKER Sheila Marian MB ChB 1943
consult. diag radiol East Dorset dist Wessex RHA from 1959

BAKHSHI Rewati Raman MB ChB 1926

BALCH or Taylor, Dorothy Janet MA 1946
resid Dunedin NZ

BALCH Douglas Freeman BSc 1933
retd teaching 1971; resid Aber

BALCH Hubert William MB ChB 1937
consult phys med and rheumat Grampian reg hosp board from 1963 sen clin lect rheumat Aberd from 1966

BALFOUR or Dufton, Eleanor Youl *MA 1921
resid Huntly

BALFOUR Jean MA 1945

BALL Hayward Percy MA 1901
no longer on GC reg

BALLANTYNE Thomas Arnott MA 1950 LL B 1953
solic: Mayer & Fraser Keith 1956–58, Brown & McRae Fraserburgh 1958–61, Wight & Aitken Aber 1964–70; man. dir Marcliffe hotel Aber 1961–70; retd; resid Edin

BAND Robert William Ingram MA 1929

BANISTER or Sutherland, Anne Elizabeth BSc 1951
Hobart Tasmania: teacher biol Friends' s 1966–71, sen Fahan Presb girls' coll from 1971

BANKS Charlotte MA 1910 *1912
no longer on GC reg

BANKS Francis Sinclair *MA 1932 BD 1935
min Strachur and Strathlachlan par ch Argyll from 1965
d 29.1.79

BANKS Janet *MA 1935
resid Forres

BANKS Mary Margaret Mitchell MA 1948
teacher Inchgarth s Aber from 1949

BANNERMAN Agnes Winifred *MA 1928
retd teaching 1968; resid Sherborne

BANNERMAN or Fleming, Lizzie (Elizabeth) MA 1915
no longer on GC reg

BANNERMAN Mary Macleod MA 1951
teacher George Watson's Ladies' coll Edin from 1962

BANNERMAN Norman George BSc(eng) 1954

BANNERMAN Robert Chalmers *MA 1928
retd 1967
d Coldwaltham Pulborough 15.8.75

BANNOCHIE or Godward, Dorothy Mary MA 1920
resid Milltimber Aber

BAPTY Leonard MB ChB 1936
FRCS(C) 1972
Victoria BC Canada: on active staff Victoria gen hosp, on visiting staff Royal Jubilee hosp from 1972

BARBER Allan *MA 1953

BARCLAY Alexina McConnachie MA 1926
no longer on GC reg

BARCLAY Ann Freeman Stewart MA 1954

BARCLAY or Rowe, Annie McConnachie MA 1927
d Banff 17.8.76

BARCLAY Annie Taylor MA 1933
teacher: Dem s Aber 1935–38, Woodside s 1938–50, Rhenish g h s Stellenbosch Cape Province SA 1950–51, Davidson's Mains p s Edin 1951–68, mistress i/c p dept James Gillespie's h s for g Edin 1968–73, head James Gillespie's p s 1973–76

BARCLAY or Duncan, Bessie Isabella *MA 1924
resid Bieldside Aber

BARCLAY David MB ChB 1936 DPH 1939
JP
Provost Stonehaven 1972–75

BARCLAY or Argo, Edith MA 1944
resid Laurencekirk

BARCLAY or Paterson, Elizabeth MA 1921
d 15.2.72

BARCLAY or Main, Emily Margaret MA 1947
Dip Spec Educ(Glasg) 1976
teacher Merkland spec s Kirkintilloch 1970–75 and from 1976

BARCLAY or Fraser, Ethel MA 1914
no longer on GC reg

BARCLAY or Christie, Flora MA 1942
resid Banchory

BARCLAY George Copland *MA 1950
teacher: sp asst Engl Hawick 1951–64, prin Engl Scunthorpe 1964–66, asst prin Engl Hawick from 1966

BARCLAY Gordon Powell MB ChB 1936
d Glensford 21.1.62 *AUR* XXXIX 385

BARCLAY Hector Summers MA 1949
Hamnavoe Shetland: teacher maths/sc 1958–65, head from 1965

BARCLAY Ian Campbell BCom 1926
resid Aboyne

BARCLAY James Alexander
MA 1930 BSc 1933 MB ChB 1937
physiol dept med s Birm: retd

BARCLAY Jane Scott MA 1930
secy Brander & Cruickshank advoc Aber 1954–68; retd 1968

BARCLAY Jeanie Gordon *MA 1938
asst Hilton nurs s Aber from 1968; retd 1974

BARCLAY or Stephen, Jeannie Margaret
***MA *BSc 1914**
d Aber 18.6.71 *AUR* XLIV 317

BARCLAY John Wood MA 1954
d Aber 6.1.75

BARCLAY Louise MA 1927

BARCLAY Mary Dorothy MA 1949
teacher maths: Govan s s 1955–58, 1959–66; Gladstone h s Vancouver BC (on exchange) 1958–59
m Aber 18.9.65 Norman Maclean radio off. M N s of Alexander M. Glasg

BARCLAY or Kemp, Nora Burgess MA 1951
teacher Aber: Middlefield s 1952–58, Deeview s 1969–74, Greenfern s 1974–75; asst head (early stages) Hanover St s from 1975

BARCLAY or Mavor, Sheena Watson MA 1932
resid N'cle-u-Tyne

BARDSLEY Raymond Alan Peter BSc(agr) 1951
served RA (field branch) U.K., Burma, India 1943–47, final rank capt; Lancashire: field off. pig indust dev auth 1963–68, dev off. meat and livestock comm 1968–73; spec at h q Bletchley from 1973

BARKER Horace Armstrong MB ChB 1925
d 12.4.77

BARKER Noël Camilla Berners MA 1948
m Peel

BARKER or Peel, Rosalind Cordelia MA 1944

BARKLEY or Landsberg, Sylvia Yuille PhD 1955
resid Southampton

BARLOW or Girvan, Florence MA 1926
resid Kirkcaldy

BARLOW or Gray, Juliet MA 1923
d Airdrie 13.11.77

BARNET John Brebner MB ChB 1941
g p Dun from 1948
d 27.4.76 *AUR* XLVI 418 and XLVII 106

BARNETT or Glasson, Adeline Elizabeth MA 1924
no longer on GC reg

BARNETT Christopher Charles MA 1925 BD 1927
d 18.9.63

BARNETT Eleanora Mary MA 1910
retd 1954; resid Wishaw

BARNETT Elizabeth MA 1917 ᵈLLB 1921
sen ptnr A. C. Morrison & Richards advoc Aber until retd 1966; only woman member Soc of Advoc Aber until 1973

BARNETT Euphemia Cowan BSc 1918 DSc 1940
d Aber 12.3.79 *AUR* XLIII 442

BARNETT George BSc 1950
flying off. RAF 1950–52; Canada BC Hydro Vancouver: distrib des 1954–56, indust rep 1956–62, rates analyst 1963–65, cost of serv superv 1965–68, man. rates/cost dept from 1968
m Abbotsford BC 2.5.59 Patricia J. O'Neill home econ d of Peter O'N. Co Cork

BARNETT James Grubb MB ChB 1953
resid Iver Bucks
d Iver 24.10.80 *AUR* XLIX 70

BARNETT James William MB ChB 1907
d Farnham 31.5.65 *AUR* XLI 145

BARR James MB ChB 1945
d 19.3.80

BARR John Edwin BSc(eng) 1936

BARR John Hamilton BSc(agr) 1953

BARR or Kidd, Margaret Miller MA 1938
res Christchurch NZ

BARR-SIM Albert Edward MB ChB 1916
d Inverurie 31.1.68 *AUR* XLII 354

BARRACK or Andrew, Mary Frances MA 1953
resid Kingswells Aber

BARRACK or Rutherford, Robina Robertson MA 1941
teacher Kincardine O'Neil p s from 1968

BARRACLOUGH Ronald MB ChB 1935
col late RAMC, late hon surg HM The Queen; resid Gyfelia Wrexham 1976

BARRETT William *MA 1909
d Guisborough 6.12.60 *AUR* XXXIX 101

BARRIE James Alexander *BSc 1949 PhD 1952
Brit rayon sen res fell: Aber 1952–54, Lond 1954–55; lect Imp Coll Lond 1955–67; visiting prof MIT Boston USA 1961–62, sen lect Imp Coll Lond from 1967
m Lond 3.4.61 Maureen M. Wantstall secy d of Robert W. Lond

BARRIE or Anderson, Margaret Bowman MA 1930
resid Fordoun

BARRON Alfred Saunders MA 1912 BD 1915
d Crieff 20.11.73 *AUR* XLV 317 and 446

BARRON Annie *MA 1926
teacher classics: Madras coll St And 1927–43, Morgan acad Dun 1943–64
m St And 14.7.45 William Ramsay security off. s of James R. Armadale

BARRON or Mackay, Annie Knight MA 1910
d Turriff 2.12.60 *AUR* XXXIX 201

BARRON Arthur Morison *MB ChB 1924 MD 1932
d Poole 10.10.79 *AUR* XLVIII 353

BARRON Bruce Morison MB ChB 1951
g p Poole from 1959

BARRON Catherine Ann MA 1948
teacher Aberdeensh: Rosehearty 1961–62, Inverurie 1963–70, Oldmeldrum 1973–76
m Oldmeldrum 21.7.76 Alfred J. Burns, Billingham

BARRON Charles Leith MB ChB 1931
d Dunblane 1.12.72 *AUR* XLV 128

BARRON or Robertson, Dorothy Elizabeth MB ChB 1947
g p Aber from 1955

BARRON Eliza Christina Margaret MA 1900
d 13.5.70 *AUR* XLIII 440

BARRON Elizabeth Walker MA 1928
teacher Aber 1954–60, Drumgarth inf s Aber 1960–72; retd 1972
resid Aber

BARRON or Routledge, Elsie MA 1939
teacher Derbysh: Cromford 1960–63, Bakewell 1969–73

BARRON or Dickson, Enid May MA 1952
resid Prestwick

BARRON James Smith MA 1914
no longer on GC reg

BARRON Jane Gray *MA 1917
d Stracathro 23.3.74

BARRON or Anderson, Jane McGee BSc 1950

BARRON Jeannie Helen Mary MA 1926
teacher: St Clement St s Aber 1927–37, Linksfield s Aber 1944–47, Oxgangs s Edin 1948–66
m Aber 4.3.38 Herbert Rae master mariner

BARRON or Marshall, Jessie Eliza Coutts MA 1928
d 29.5.75

BARRON John MB ChB 1949
MRCPsych 1971
consult. psychiat E Surrey and W Sussex from 1971

BARRON John McKay BSc 1949
head: Rayne N s Aberdeensh 1962–65, Melrose g s from 1965

BARRON or Mackay, Lucy Maud MA 1907
d 24.8.77

BARRON Marjory Henderson MA 1936
teacher Aber: Middlefield p s from 1943; retd 1976

BARRON Robert Mackay MB ChB 1930
Police surg retd 1960; chmn Dudley Worcs exec council from 1961, med off. Dudley coll of educ from 1944

BARRON or Duggie, Seonaid Margaret MA 1953

BARRON William Douglas MA 1909
d Edin 1.5.70 *AUR* XLIII 440

BARRON William James MA 1924
d Aberlour 9.2.73 *AUR* XLV 225

BARRON Williamina Agnes *MA 1918 BSc 1920
no longer on GC reg

BARTLET James Eric Alexander MB ChB 1939 MD 1947

BARTLET Leslie Bow MB ChB 1951
DCH 1959 MRCPsych 1972
sen psychiat regist Herts C G Clin 1957–60; consult child psychiat Hampshire ch guid serv 1960–65; consult ch psychiat S'ton hosps/clin teacher med faculty S'ton
m Lond 23.4.60 Suzanne M. Brilliant BSc(LSE) stud. counsellor S'ton d of Charles B. Wembley Park

BARTLET Margaret Taylor MA 1919
MBE 1966
head Tynepark approved s for girls Haddington till retd 1966; resid Edin

BARTLETT Henry Matthew MA 1923 BD 1926 DD 1963
part time chaplain DRI 1955–69; awarded City of Orleans medal 1963; clerk Synod of Angus and Mearns 1967; dir City of Dundee educ trust; retd as min of Logie 1969; retd as clerk to presb Dun 1972
d 21.12.80 *AUR* LXIX 136

BARTON George Edward Colledge MA 1929
head jun s Robert Gordon's coll Aber from 1933; housemaster 1937–64; retd

BATE Phillip Argall Turner *BSc 1931

BATTEN Ronald Mortimer MA 1947

BATTISBY Christina MA 1921
teacher: retd from Frederick St s Aber 1962

BATTISBY or Barber, Keturah Mary Connon *MA 1930
teacher Edin: Norton Park s s 1957–61, Boroughmuir s s 1961–64; lady advis David Kilpatrick s s 1964–72; retd
d West Calder 1.4.80

BAUER David BSc 1948
deceased

BAXTER or McAllister, Alexandra MA 1927
inf teacher Paisley: Carsbrook St s 1956–62, Williamsburgh 1962–69
d Paisley 30.5.76

BAXTER Archibald Green *MA 1932

BAXTER or Coutts Milne, Catherine Hannah MB ChB 1925 DPH 1927
resid Farnham

BAXTER Flora Leslie MB ChB 1927
m (2) Amersham Bucks 14.2.70 Hugh W. Broatch AIB banker s of Richard B. J.P. Lochmaben

BAXTER Helen Robertson *MA 1902
no longer on GC reg

BAXTER Ian Francis George MA 1936 LLB 1938
prof law Tor from 1966; dir Fam Law Study for Ont Law Reform Comm 1965–68; co-dir Vanier res proj on fam support 1967–70; dir Leg. Res Proj for Canadian Pharm Assoc 1970; co-ordinator Connaught Progr on Fam Law and Soc Welfare 1976–78; NATO prof univ of Louvain Belgium 1967; visiting prof Brist 1975–76

BAXTER or Eccles, Isabella Anne MB ChB 1922

BAXTER James Houston BD 1920
d St And 1.4.73 *AUR* XLV 224

BAXTER William MB ChB 1913
no longer on GC reg

BAXTER William Gordon *BSc 1941
OBE 1970
W. A. Baxter & Sons Fochabers: prod dir 1946–49, man. dir 1949–69, chmn from 1969; chmn Best of Scotland Fochabers from 1970; loc dir Bank of Scotland Aber from 1972

BAYER Jacob Max MB ChB 1923
no longer on GC reg

BAYER Philip MB ChB 1925

BAYNHAM John William *BSc 1952 PhD 1955

BEAN or Chileen, Elizabeth Helen MA 1910
no longer on GC reg

BEANGE Margaret Helen *MA 1931
teacher mod lang Turriff acad Abdnsh 1967–73
m Boddam 14.11.63 James Cummine farmer s of James C. Turriff

BEARSLEY Eleanor Emma *MA 1916
resid Edin

BEATON Arnold BSc(for) 1952

BEATON James MA 1929
d 1965

BEATON Lily MA 1936
teacher Edin; retd

BEATON Mabel Margaret MA 1931
no longer on GC reg

BEATON or Wyness, Millicent MA 1927
resid Bramhall

BEATTIE Alan Gordon MB ChB 1951
g p Poole from 1954
m Aber 2.4.53 Isabel Coutts teacher d of Andrew C. Aber

BEATTIE Alan Rae *BSc 1955 PhD 1959
res staff Texas Instruments Inc Dallas USA 1959–63; univ coll Cardiff: lect applied maths 1963–68, sen lect from 1968; visiting lect Nairobi univ 1974–75

BEATTIE Alexander Gordon MB ChB 1939 DPH 1958
FRCGP 1972
g p Aber from 1945

BEATTIE Alexander William MA 1936

BEATTIE Arthur James *MA 1935
prof Greek Edin from 1951

BEATTIE George Fisher *BSc 1940
res chem Manchester from 1943; retd

BEATTIE or Wright, Jane Hastings MA 1930
resid Aber

BEATTIE John MA 1941
head dept Sheerness tech s 1966–70; div tut. Sheppey s from 1970

BEATTIE Katrina *BSc 1954
m Kolizeras

BEATTIE Margaret Carroll *MA 1924
teacher maths head dept Oakdene Beaconsfield 1953–71
d Banchory 22.8.76

BEATTIE or Wisely, Margaret Watson MA 1927
resid New Pitsligo

BEATTIE Nellie (Helen) MA 1901
no longer on GC reg

BEATTIE Peter Henry MB ChB 1936 MD 1949
Ophth regist Addenbrooke's hosp Cambridge 1946; consult ophth Norfolk and Norwich hosp from 1947; retd 1974

BEATTIE or Gruer, Rosamund *MB ChB 1950
Dip Soc Med(Edin) 1968
g p Kemnay 1964–67; dept soc med Edin: res fell. 1968–73, sen res fell. from 1973

BEATTIE or Hay, Violet MA 1928
d Auchterless

BEATTIE Walter Gordon MA 1953 BD 1956
min W Parish ch Fraserburgh from 1962

BEATTIE William Forbes MB ChB 1912
deceased

BEAUMONT or Forbes, Maggie Porter *MA 1922
d Aber 18.6.70 *AUR* XLIV 110

BECK-SLINN Kathleen MA 1931
MBE 1972
retd Torry Res Stat 1972

BEDDIE Alastair James MB ChB 1934
retd 1974; resid Kelowna BC Canada

BEDDIE Lewis Beaton MA 1888
d Aber 23.1.65 *AUR* XLI 34

BEEDIE or Hogg, Hazel Gill MA 1948
resid Tawa NZ

BEEDIE James MA 1942
prin teacher Engl: Arbroath acad 1962–68, Powis acad Aber 1968; asst head Powis acad from 1973

BEEDIE William MB ChB 1904 MD 1914
no longer on GC reg

BEER Keith Edward *BSc 1949
CEng FIMM 1975
prin geol SW Eng unit Inst of Geol Sc Exeter from 1963; part time lect Exe 1969–74

BEGG Alan Duncan *MA 1954

BEGG Albert Tulloch *MA 1923
d Aber 8.3.65 *AUR* XLI 57

BEGG Andrew Macdonald MA 1952
ptnr with father and wife in Andrew Begg & Son Elgin and Buckie; also ptnr with wife in Andrew Begg, Forres from 1973; town councillor Elgin from 1960, Dean of Guild then Bailie/JP from 1967

BEGG Charles Michael Macintyre MA 1939 *BSc 1942
FRS(Edin)
reader zool Aberd
m(1) wife died
(2) 1966 Lavender Miller d of Donald M. Aber

BEGG Donald Leslie Bartlett *MA 1938
teacher: Hilton acad Aber from 1947, prin hist from 1965
d Aber 2.1.80 *AUR* XLVIII 443

BEGG Francis William MB ChB 1903
d 12.6.61 *AUR* XXXIX 271

BEGG Ian Forbes MA 1931 DD 1971
Aber: priest i/c St. Ninian's Seaton till 1973; canon St. Andrew's Cath 1965; dean diocese Aber and Orkney 1969; bishop Aber and Orkney from 1973

BEGG John Hudson MB ChB 1939
LAIHA (New South Wales) 1958 FACMA 1968
med supt: Queen Victoria hosp Adelaide S Aust 1950–60, Ballarat base hosp Victoria Aust 1961–71; S Aust dept publ health Adelaide from 1971

BEGG or Ross, Muriel Jean MA 1925
d 6.5.73

BEGG Thomas Leslie MB ChB 1947 DPH 1950
prin m o (mental health) lect (admin mental health serv) Liv from 1952; retd 1974

BEGG William MB ChB 1906 DPH 1908

BELL Aluinn Neil *MA 1955
teacher geog
m Cults, Fife 21.7.60 David S. Petrie MA(Glas) teacher classics/dep head

BELL Andrew Farm Hamilton MA 1930 dLLB(c) 1932
Assoc Aust Soc Acct 1964

asst solic: Aber, Glasg 1932–39, 1945–51; Sydney Aust: asst acct 1952–72, internal auditor 1972–79; retd

BELL Archibald Brown Ross BSc(agr) 1954
farm. Ardormie from 1963

BELL Clement Wood *MA 1942
BA(Lond)
dep prin Daniel Stewart's & Melville coll Edin from 1966

BELL Elizabeth Andrew MA 1949
Glasg: teacher classics: Albert s s till 1963, Allan Glen's 1964–68; prin teacher guid: Riverside s s 1968–72, Albert s s 1972–74; asst head Grange s s from 1974

BELL or Turnbull, Elizabeth Paterson Nicol MB ChB 1950 MD 1954
resid Oxford

BELL Harry McAra *MA 1924
MA(Cantab) 1927 M.Ed(Glas) 1932
rector Dollar acad till 1960; hon res fell. St. And from 1972
m Glasg 9.10.33 Sophia M. Fulton d of Alexander B. F. Glasg

BELL James Clark MB ChB 1929
g p East Ham from 1934

BELL John Hamilton MB ChB 1924
d Lond 4.1.69 *AUR* XLIII 213

BELL Kenneth Hamilton LLB 1935
admitted solic of Supreme Court NSW Aust 1960
held 4 positions in law off. Sydney 1959–69, Queensland 1969–71; retd; resid Manly NSW

BELL Kenneth Mackenzie MB ChB 1939
MRCGP 1954
g p Harrow; chmn Harrow and Hillington BMA 1969

BELL Michael William BSc(Eng) 1951

BELL or Strath, Rhoda Duncan *MA 1951
Aber: teacher lang part-time High s for girls 1960–62, Albyn s for girls 1968–74, Cults acad from 1974

BENNET James Anderson PhD 1953
sen lect elect. eng Dund from 1964
wife *d* 1963
m(2) Edin 1964 Anne T. B. Fraser civ serv d of James F. Edin

BENNET Robert Alasdair MB ChB 1955 MD 1967
b Glasg 27.10.30
h o ARI and Manor hosp Nuneaton 1956–57; m o RAMC 1957–61; res fell. orthop dept Edin 1961–64; lect path. dept Dund from 1964

BENNETT Harold Stanley MB ChB 1945
consult. radiol Royal Cornwall hosps Truro from 1954

BENNETT Margaret Edith *MA 1936
head Lansdowne House s Edin till 1974; retd

BENNETT or Blank, Miriam MB ChB 1950
Fell. Amer Board Fam Practice 1976
g p Bridgeport Conn USA from 1951

BENNETT or Smith, Violet Jane MA 1910
d Aber 8.5.73 *AUR* XLV 316

BENSON or Fraser, Kathleen Elizabeth MA 1944
resid Edin

BENSON or Lachman, Mary Isobel Falconer MA 1940
JP 1969
teacher Colne: head lang Park County s s 1958–68, sen lang Grammar s 1968–78

BENTON or Duthie, Alexandra Hay MB ChB 1924 DPH 1934
resid Chichester

BENTON James Lipp Brown BSc 1941 *1947

BENZIE or Duguid, Agnes Mildred Emslie MB ChB 1922 DPH 1925
d near Aber 13.1.73 *AUR* XLV 225

BENZIE Alexander Swan MB ChB 1923
g p retd; resid Pamber Heath nr Basingstoke 1976

BENZIE Annie Ronald MA 1926
resid Fraserburgh

BENZIE or Gordon, Helen Watt MA 1930
teacher: temp relief Kennethmont, Gartly 1957–61, Rhynie 1962–69, Gordon Schools Huntly 1969–74

BENZIE Jeannie MB ChB 1924
resid Fraserburgh

BENZIE Robert James *MA 1940
d 2.1.72

BENZIE Sheila Allan MA 1952
m Aber 1.6.63 John Tanner
resid Buckhurst Hill

BENZIE William MA 1953 *1955 MEd 1957 PhD 1967
lect Engl Vic BC Canada from 1958

BERGER Michael Jona *MA 1950
M Jur (Hier) 1965 admitted Israel Bar 1968
sen dir of control State comptroller's off. Jerusalem 1962–73; dep leg. counsel Securities Authority of Israel from 1973

BERKLEY Arnold Ber (BERKOWITZ Abraham Ber) MB ChB 1923
no longer on GC reg

BERLINGUET Lorne Francis Caven MB ChB 1935
gen surg St Joseph Hosp Three Rivers Canada

from 1939 geriat spec Cooke hosp Three Rivers Canada from 1960
m(2) –.11.74 Frances Keating

BERNARD George Reid MB ChB 1939
RAF 1941–46; g p Ipswich from 1946

BERNARD Robert McFarlane MB ChB 1940

BERRY Alexander Ian MA 1940

BERRY Douglas Austen Oldfield *MA 1951

BERRY Douglas Wales MB ChB 1915 DPH 1922 *MD 1923
d East Fortune 13.6.73 *AUR* XLV 317

BERRY or Duncan, Elsie Janet Isobel MA 1916
d Aboyne 27.7.80 *AUR* XLIX 66

BERRY Harriet Ann Ford MA 1908
d Basle Switzerland 5.1.70 *AUR* XLIII 440

BERRY Janet Clerihew MA 1926
d Aber 27.7.62 *AUR* XL 92

BETENSON William Francis Whitaker MB ChB 1917

BETHUNE or Kerr, Anna Macleod MA 1926
d Rosskeen, Invergordon 15.4.62 *AUR* XXXIX 383

BETHUNE or Sangster, Barbara Una Doull MA 1932
resid Edin

BETTSON Denis John BSc(agr) 1949

BEVERIDGE or Notholt, Agnes Arnot MA 1949
teacher Breakspear s Ickenham Lond boro Hillingdon 1957–59 and from 1969

BEVERIDGE Evelyn Eleanor MA 1950
teacher Kingswells p s Abdnsh from 1952
m Aber 8.8.67 Douglas Shirran printer

BEVERIDGE John Walker MB ChB 1954
g p Great Harwood 1962–63; Tasmania Aust d m o Flinders Island 1963–65, g p Launceston 1965 and from 1969, d m o Evandale 1965–69; capt RAAMC army reserve from 1969

BEVERIDGE Margaret Edith MB ChB 1955
FFARCS 1967
regist anaest hosp for sick children Gt. Ormond St Lond 1966–67; consult. anaest Aber gen hosps from 1969

BEVERIDGE Robert Noel *BSc(eng) 1950
ICI: plant eng metals div Liv 1955–57, sen des eng Nobel div Glasg 1957–60, proj eng plastics div Welwyn Garden City 1960–63, sect. man. plastics div Darwen 1963–65, head off. Millbank Lond 1965–68; plastics div Welwyn Garden City: tech co-ordinator 1968–70, head admin from 1970

BEVERLEY or Clarke, Gladys Margaret Watt MA 1938

BEWGLASS Mary Melven Law BSc 1937

BEWS or Orr, Barbara Jessie *MA 1941

BEWS or Cheyne, Jean Fyfe MA 1952
resid Br of Don

BEWS John William Simpson MA 1926
d Aber 2.6.68 *AUR* XLIII 84

BHANDARI Kodlamogati Lakkana BSc(agr) 1924
coffee planter: man. coffee estates Coorg India 1928–61
m Mangalore India 29.5.28 Sarsa Saraswathi land owner d of B. Mahabaleshwara Shetty, Brahmavar, S Kanara, India

BICHAN Isabella Hepburn MA 1905
no longer on GC reg

BICHAN Patrick Isbister BSc(agr) 1951
b 22.11.25
BOCM: farms man. Yorks 1953–59, farms dir Yorks and Leicester 1959–65; cattle husb advis Eng/Scot. 1965–72; man. dir Farm Ptnrs Lincs from 1972

BICKERSTETH Jean Elfride *MA 1945
Cert Ed (Lond) 1971
Hull: tut. Kingston-u-Hull coll of educ 1967–71, univ lect theol and warden Lambert Hall from 1972

BICKERSTETH Ursula Mary *MA 1950
teacher: head classics Wimbledon h s 1976

BIEDA Kazimierz *MA 1948
asst lect econ Singapore 1949–51; lect econ Auckland NZ 1951–57; sen lect econ: Kumasi Ghana 1957–59, Armidale Aust 1959–66; reader econ Brisbane from 1966

BILLE Ian Robertson MA 1955
b 1.8.21
teacher Aber from 1956

BINNS William Osborne *BSc(for) 1955

BIRD Dorothy Mary MA 1944

BIRKETT Nichol Thomson MA 1948 *MEd 1950
visiting prof educ nat inst educ univ of Delhi/consult spec educ to Nat Council Educ Res and Trg, Govt of India 1963–65; sen lect dept spec and remed educ Jordanhill coll of educ Glasg 1965–75, prin lect from 1975; hon lect psych Glas 1976

BIRKS Colin Alastair MB ChB 1940
g p Sleaford from 1949

BIRNIE or Ross, Ada Mary MA 1952
teacher Mile End s Aber from 1973

BIRNIE Alexander BSc(agr) 1926

BIRNIE Alexander Brodie *MA 1933
chmn traffic comm Scot. traffic area Edin from 1965

BIRNIE Alexander John Milne MB ChB 1954
FRCSE 1968
orthop: m o Stracathro hosp 1960–61, regist Ipswich and E Suffolk hosp 1961–64, Royal South Hants hosp S'ton 1964–65, Queen Mary's hosp for children 1965–66; regist gen surg Newcastle gen hosp 1966–68; sen regist orthop Middlesbro gen hosp 1968–71; consult. orthop surg Dryburn hosp Durh, orthop and accident hosp Sunderland, from 1971
m(1) diss –.2.67
(2) Newcastle-u-Tyne 18.3.67 Audrey J. Fairservice SRN d of B. W. F. Mitcham

BIRNIE Bella Garden MA 1931
teacher Engl/hist Banff acad 1947–69; retd

BIRNIE Charles John MA 1949
teacher Engl/allied subj orphanage Aberlour 1961–63; relief teacher Banffsh 1963–67; div course Aber 1967–69; C of S min Annbank from 1969

BIRNIE Edith Bennett BSc 1946
Banffsh: teacher maths/sc Portessie 1969–72; maths Buckie h s from 1972

BIRNIE Ian Malcolm BSc(eng) 1942
turbine eng CEGB NW reg from 1975

BIRNIE James Arthur MA 1927 MB ChB 1931
MBE 1972 FRCGP 1973
g p Aber from 1948

BIRNIE or Clarke, Jeannie Morrison MB ChB 1921
d Malmesbury 8.6.79

BIRNIE Mary Morrison MA 1929

BIRNIE Norman MA 1932
min Bannockburn 1936–42, Guyana 1943–50, Monquhitter 1951–54, Stockton-on-Tees 1955–60, Cardiff 1960–71; mod. gen assembly Presb C of E 1969–70; min St. George's ch Bexhill-on-Sea from 1971

BIRNIE William MB ChB 1936
g p Garelochhead till 1964; Kingseat hosp Newmachar: locum regist Apr–Aug 1965; med asst psychiat August 1965–75; retd 1975

BIRSE or Cameron, Emma Leslie MB ChB 1951 MD 1956
DPM(Lond) 1970 MRCPsych 1975
asst m o h Fife c c 1963–67; sen asst m o h Dun 1967–68; med asst: Strathmartine hosp Dun 1968–70, Stratheden hosp Cupar 1970–72; psychiat Weston Day hosp Cupar from 1972

BIRSE Eric Leslie *BSc 1950
soil scient Macaulay inst for soil res Aber from 1953

BIRSE or Dunlop, Margaret Williams MA 1927
no longer on GC reg

BIRSE William Milne *MA 1910 *BSc 1911
d Ontario 3.9.67 *AUR* XLII 180

BIRSS or Munro, Ann Grace Fulton BSc 1954
resid Edin

BIRSS John Gordon Michie MA 1946

BIRSS Ronald MA 1937

BISHOP David McLean *MA 1942
sect. man. control eng ICI petro chem div Teesside from 1963: vice pres Inst Measurement and Control 1971–74, pres 1974–75

BISSET Alexander MB ChB 1900
d 1968

BISSET Alexander Andrew MB ChB 1908 MD 1910
no longer on GC reg

BISSET or Hall, Alice Joyce *MA 1940
resid Guildford

BISSET Anna Black *MA 1941
CRK(Lond) 1966
teacher mod lang Selhurst g s for girls Croydon 1954–60; head Fr dept later dep head Farrington s s for girls Chislehurst 1961–70; teacher Engl Karnataka theol coll Mangalore S India 1971–76; pers secy *Christians Abroad* Lond from 1976

BISSET or Fyvie, Anne McRae MA 1952
LLB(Edin) 1955 Dip Ed(Edin) 1955
teacher Sutton from 1964

BISSET Arthur James MA 1938 LLB 1946
ptnr Connon, McRobert & Bisset solic Stonehaven from 1947

BISSET or Dawson, Catharine *MA 1909
d Haddington 29.8.62 *AUR* XL 78

BISSET Charles Barron MA BSc 1923
d Edin 16.6.66 *AUR* XLI 339

BISSET Charles Bruce MA 1940
Aber: last head Rosemount s s 1969–72; dep head Harlaw acad from 1973

BISSET David Gove MB ChB 1941

BISSET David Robert BSc(agr) 1943
sen agr advis Kincardinesh from 1968

BISSET or Rogers, Doris Isobel MB ChB 1948
resid Moffat

BISSET Eleanor *MA 1914
d Torphins 18.4.71 *AUR* XLIV 209

BISSET or Ritchie, Frances Margaret MA 1944
teacher Haddington p s from 1965

BISSET George Bruce BSc(agr) 1924
MS(Corn) 1924
sen lect R'dg univ until 1965; retd

BISSET or Spackman, Georgina *MA 1919
resid Blackburn

BISSET or Lyall, Iva Isabella MA 1913
d Ashton-under-Lyne 20.8.69 *AUR* XLIII 329

BISSET John Davidson MA 1919
rector St Modoc's Doune and St Mary's Aberfoyle till 1966; retd; canon St Ninian's Cath Perth 1965–66; hon canon from 1967

BISSET May Simpson MB ChB 1946
sen regist anaest Middlesex hosp 1954–57; part time anaest Boston Mass USA 1957–58; consult. anaest: Queen Mary's hosp Carshalton 1960–62, Mt Vernon hosp and Harefield hosp Northwood Lond 1962–72; private anaest practice nursing homes in loc area and Lond from 1972
m Aber 3.4.56 Gerald P. Blanshard BA(Cantab) consult. phys s of William B. Doncaster

BISSET Rita MA 1924
teacher Buckie h s till 1963; retd

BISSET Reginald Rust BSc(civ eng) 1937 BSc(elect eng) 1938
Elgin: man. dir David Forsyth & Co civ eng contr 1972–78, consult. civ eng i/c northern off. Cowan & Linn consult. civ/struct eng Glasg from 1978

BISSET Ruth Johnstone MA 1941
teacher Aber: Central s s, Aber acad, Hazlehead acad 1950–78
d Aber 24.5.78

BISSET or Findlay, Sheila Stodart BSc 1924
resid Fochabers

BISSET Walter Davidson MA 1921
resid Herne Bay
d Herne Bay 3.10.80 *AUR* XLIX 67

BISSET William John George BL 1929

BITTINER John Bruce MB ChB 1943
TD 1965
consult. Nott from 1963; clin teacher Nott from 1973

BLACK Agnes *MA 1912 *BSc 1913
no longer on GC reg

BLACK Alfred Alexander MA 1895
d Aber 11.8.65 *AUR* XLI 236

BLACK Arthurina Rosemary Margaret MA 1955
teacher: Lyne of Skene 1960–61, Berkhamsted 1961–66; part time: Waterlooville 1966–68, Hitchin from 1968
m Aber 29.3.61 Richard M. Lee BSc 1957 *qv*

BLACK or Bain, Catherine Helen MA 1933
teacher Abdnsh: Logie Durno 1961–67, Chapel of Garioch 1968–72

BLACK Flora Weir *BSc 1940
scient civ serv Building Res Stat D o E from 1951

BLACK Gertrude May MA 1924 BSc 1926 *1927
woman advis Nicolson Inst Stornoway till 1968; retd

BLACK Isabella MA 1910
head Ardmiddle s Turriff 1945–54; retd

BLACK or Christie, Isabella MA 1917
no longer on GC reg

BLACK or Henderson, Isabella Ferguson MA 1902
no longer on GC reg

BLACK Jane MA 1912
teacher various posts Scot. 1913–17; spec qualif Ger 1918; teacher mod lang Huddersfield Greenhead h s for girls 1925–45; various posts Caithness 1947–51
d 5.12.81

BLACK or Atkins, J. Marguerite *MA 1932
BA(Oxon) 1937
prin and prof Engl Maharani univ coll for women Mysore India 1937–40; member HM diplom serv 1966–72; tut. in tut. coll from 1972

BLACK John Gordon MB ChB 1929
DDMS: (BR) corps NW Europe 1958–60, h q TPS Malta 1960–61; retd as brig. 1961; civ m o RNAS Lossiemouth 1962–72; retd

BLACK or Petrie, Kathleen Jean MA 1933
teacher classics/Fr St John Rigby g s later 6th form coll Wigan from 1965

BLACK or Neville, Margaret BSc 1954
part time lab asst nat rubber prod. res assoc Welwyn Garden City 1970–73; part time teacher maths Verulam s St Albans from 1974

BLACK or Gray, Margaret Carmichael MA 1929
teacher Scalloway j s Shetland till 1966; retd

BLACK Marjorie Macadie MB ChB 1944 DPH 1949
MFCM 1972
sen clin m o Dun from 1970

BLACK Morrice Alexander MA 1886
no longer on GC reg

BLACK or Siviter, Nancy Mary Briscoe *MA 1930
resid Kingswood Surrey

BLACK or MacVicar, Nellie Maria MA 1919
resid Dunbar
d 16.2.81

BLACK Robert Alexander Ross *BSc 1948

BLACK Russell *BSc 1950 PhD 1958

BLACK Stanley Alfred Briscoe MB ChB 1931 DPH 1933 MD 1944
wife *d* 1963
dep sen admin m o NE reg hosp board Aber from 1963; retd 1974

BLACK Thomas Muir BSc(for) 1953 *1954 PhD 1957
d 2.11.72

BLACK William George *MA 1928
retd Beverley 1972
d Lond –.11.78

BLACK Winifred Constance Robertson *MA 1922
teacher: spec asst mod lang High s for girls Aber till 1965; retd

BLACKADDER or Evans, Isabelle Rosemary *MA 1941

BLACKBURN Raymond Forrester MB ChB 1951 DPH 1958
DObstRCOG 1957 MFCM 1972 MBIM 1975
2 i/c 23 para fd amb 1963–66; c o 23 para fd amb/s m o AB forces 1967–70; c o BMH Hong Kong 1970–72; ADMS Eastern dist Colchester 1973–74; dep cmdt RAMC TC 1974–75, ADG MoD 1975–76; ADMS SE dist Aldershot from 1976
m(2) Farnborough 4.6.66 Ann D. Hubbard d of William G. H. Richmond Surrey

BLACKHALL or Carlyle, Agnes Ethel Sharp MA 1941
teacher Barassie p s Troon 1970–73; asst head Bank St s Irvine from 1973

BLACKHALL Alexander BSc 1949 *1950 PhD 1953
res chem ICI: dyestuffs div 1956–62, petro chem and polymer lab Rincorn 1962–65, dyestuffs div Blackley Manc 1965–71, sen res scient fibres div Harrogate 1971–76; lab admin ICI Fibres Harrogate from 1976

BLACKHALL or Robertson, Isabella Ewan MA 1913
no longer on GC reg

BLACKHALL John Anderson *BSc 1951
indust chem ICI Manc from 1955
m Manc 12.7.58 Sheelagh M. M. McKay secy d of Charles S. McK. Middleton

BLACKIE Mary Jane Garden MA 1915

BLACKLAWS Hector Ross MA 1924 BCom 1926
S Africa from 1933: dir wool marketing comp Adolf Mossenthal Port Elizabeth, secy civ serv club Cape Town
d Cape Town 21.3.79

BLACKLAWS or Steele, Joan Mathieson MA 1951
teacher Aber: part time pre nurs coll 1960–62 and 1964–74, Northfield acad 1974–75, prin guid Powis acad from 1975

BLACKLAWS Peter Campbell *MA 1951
Dip Ed(ESN)(Lond) 1966
Lond: teacher spec s 1962–66, head remed dept 1966–69; remed advis borough of Waltham Forest 1969–73; Wales: sen tut. Caerleon coll of educ Mon 1973–75, dir of stud. Gwent coll of higher educ from 1975
m Lond 20.8.65 Ann M. Evans Glam

BLACKWELL Alistair Macleod MB ChB 1950
Derby: clin asst psychiat Pastures hosp Mickleover from 1964, ptnr in group pract from 1971

BLAIR Edith MA 1908
no longer on GC reg

BLAIR or MacNeill, Gwendolyn Ann *BSc 1955

BLAIR or Leyland, Margaret Johnstone Grieve MA 1952

BLAKE or Donald, Adelaide Victoria BSc 1925
no longer on GC reg

BLAKE Isabella Downie *MA 1924
resid Aber

BLANCE George William MA 1927
JP 1966
head Central p s Lerwick till 1966; retd
d Lerwick 11.3.77

BLANCE or Barclay, Laura Margaret MA 1951
teacher Hamnavoe Shetland from 1965

BLANCE Thelma *MA 1953 PhD 1956
Glasg corp plan. dept 1957–73; Aber NESJPAC sen plan. 1973–75; Grampian reg c: dep dir phys plan. from 1975
TA: Aberd OTC 1952–57; signals regiments Glasg (capt, sqdn cmdr) 1957–69

BLUES Ernest Thompson *BSc 1953
PhD(R'dg)

BLUES Roy Gibb MB ChB 19848
g p Lochgelly from 1959

BLYTH John MA 1910

BLYTH Norman Macgregor Downie MB ChB 1948
FRCOG 1973
regist obst/gyn St Mary Abbots hosp Lond 1960–62; locum consult. obst/gyn Welsh hosp board 1962–64; consult. obst/gyn E Glamorgan gen hosp Wales from 1964

BOCHEL Alexander Main BSc(eng) 1949
sen asst W. A. Fairhurst & Ptnrs (formerly F. A. Macdonald & Ptnrs) consult. eng Glasg from 1954

BODDIE or Laing, Margaret Sim MA 1943
teacher Springhill p s 1962–72; Powis acad: remed teacher from 1972, also year mistress from 1973

BODENSTEIN Nicholas Combrink *MB ChB 1921
d S Africa 29.9.74

BODIE Samuel Murphy Walford MB ChB 1940
d Aber 1.1.74 *AUR* XLV 449

BODONHELYI Joseph PhD 1936 DD 1960
d Budapest 1966 *AUR* XLI 341

BOGGIE Robert *BSc 1953 PhD 1956
Macaulay Inst for soil research Aber from 1956

BOND or Connon, Margaret Donaldson MA 1946
teacher Weymouth: div educ comm 1963–70, sen mistress Engl dept Convent of the Sacred Heart from 1970

BONNAR Beatrice Dunnett MA 1926 BD 1937
min EU Congr church Langholm 1941–66; retd Langholm

BONNER or Garden, Davidina Barclay *MA 1931
teacher Engl High s for girls Aber; retd

BONNEY Henry Claude MB ChB 1925

BOOKER Patrick Kilgour *MA 1949
OBE 1968
Aden: asst chief secy 1961–63, sen then prin advis Br High Comm 1963–67; seconded as dev secy Fed of S Arabia 1965–66 then perm secy Min of Finance Fed of S Arabia 1966–67; retd from HM overseas civ serv 1968; contr admin Rolls Royce 1968–69; Aberd: sen admin asst 1969–70, asst secy from 1970

BOOKER Robert Kilgour MA 1950 [d]LLB 1950
sen ptnr Allen & Gledhill advoc and solic Singapore from 1960; advoc and solic of the High Court of Singapore and Malaysia; solic Scot. and Eng, n p, comm of oaths; dir of numerous publ and private comps Far East from 1960; chmn Brit Assoc of Singapore; gov of United World Coll of SE Asia; member Internat Council of United World colleges; chmn or pres of several charitable organis Singapore
m Singapore 8.10.58 Hazel E. Nathan d of J. S. N. BA(Cantab) Singapore

BOON-LONG Twee Swasdi BCom 1926

BOOTH Alan James MB ChB 1948
FFARCS 1958
sen anaest regist Liv 1958–60; consult. anaest: Liv 1960–62, Inv from 1962

BOOTH Alexander MA 1900
d Kingston, Jamaica 15.8.61 *AUR* XXXIX 268

BOOTH Alexander Graham MB ChB 1929
d Bedford 28.3.74 *AUR* XLVI 109

BOOTH Herbert Watt MB ChB 1941
d Aber 31.10.64 *AUR* XLI 60

BOOTH Ian Farquhar *MA 1932
rector Maxwelltown h s Dumfries 1970–74; retd

BOOTH James
BSc 1924 *1925 PhD 1929 MB ChB 1938
d Aber 4.9.75 *AUR* XLVI 322

BOOTH James Graham Mackenzie
MA BL 1919 LLB 1922
d Stonehaven 4.12.69 *AUR* XLIII 444

BOOTH or Gauld, Kathleen MB ChB 1924
d Dumfries 28.9.77 *AUR* XLVII 286

BOOTH or Horne, Lorna Leslie MA 1946

BOOTH or Simpson-Craib, Moyra Louise MA 1939
resid Fochabers

BOOTH Robert George MA 1933
head Fraserburgh central s 1954 to 1974

BOOTH or Michie, Vera Constance Anne
MB ChB 1945
part-time m o casualty dept ARI from 1970
husb *d* 23.3.78

BOOTH William MB ChB 1925
d Derby 12.7.65 *AUR* XLI 150

BORTHWICK Edward Kerr *MA 1946
Edin: sen lect Greek 1967–70, reader from 1970

BORTHWICK or Yuill, Mary Murdoch *MA 1944
city/county councillor Nott 1972–77; member South Nott commun health c from 1978
marr diss 1973

BOSE Probodh Kumar PhD 1955

BOTHWELL Alexander Fairweather
MA 1915 MB ChB 1922
d Aber 13.3.78 *AUR* XLVII 356

BOTHWELL Beatrix Bennet MA 1929
retd 1968; resid Aber

BOTHWELL James BSc 1935
Peterhead acad: prin teacher phys from 1960; retd 1975

BOTHWELL James Edward MA 1927 LLB 1929
sole ptnr Macqueen & Findlater advoc Aber from 1936; Soc of Advoc Aber: lib from 1966, secy 1967–79
d Aber 14.11.80 *AUR* XLIX 68

BOTHWELL or Herbert, Jessie Anderson MA 1936

BOTHWELL Peter William
MB ChB 1946 DPH 1950 [d]MD 1961
lect epidemiology and publ health Brist till 1967; head motor cycle res unit Birm 1967–69; head bio-eng BSA/Triumph res estab Warwicksh 1969–71; consult. bio-eng to Denver res inst USA 1971–72; man. dir Caliber Design Stratford-on-Avon from 1972

BOW or Burnett, Anne Edith MA 1946
resid Edin
husb *d* 4.9.80

BOWEN Neville Arthur PhD 1949
sen lect maths: Aberd 1959–61, Leic 1961–65; prof maths Royal univ Msida Malta from 1965; dean eng, arch. and sc from 1972
m Rome 21.7.58 Jacqueline Arrighi, Licence es Lettres (Grenoble) teacher Engl Casablanca d of Jacques F. A. Rome

BOWER Haddon Graham *MA 1933 LLB 1935

BOWER or Barron, Mary MA 1933
teacher Strichen till 1972; retd

BOWICK John BSc 1955
LIBiol (Wolverhampton Poly) 1972
teacher biol Bankhead acad: asst 1967–72, prin from 1973; post-grad study plant path. s of agr Aber

BOWIE Frederick John Thomas MB ChB 1924 DPH 1927
d Aber 14.11.73 *AUR* XLV 447

BOWIE Harold Ian Cameron MB ChB 1942

BOWIE Helena Mary *MA 1920
d 21.7.75

BOWIE James Cameron MB ChB 1940
Birm: asst m o till 1970; dep m o 1970–73; phys health serv 1973–75

BOWIE Mary Taylor MA 1933
d Fochabers 17.7.68 *AUR* XLIII 85

BOWIE Sheila Mary Lumsden *MA 1951
asst prin teacher Engl Edin: Liberton s s 1961–74, Cranley from 1974

BOWIE Stanley Hay Umphray *BSc 1941 DSc 1969
silver medal RSA 1959 FMSA 1963 FRS(Edin) 1970 FIMM 1973
Lond: chief consult. geol UKAEA 1955, asst dir chief geochem Inst of Geol Sc 1968; visiting prof applied geol Strath 1968; chmn Internat comm on ore microscopy (IMA) from 1970

BOWMAN or Stewart, Alice Fisher *MA 1921
resid Aber

BOWMAN Frank James Sandison MB ChB 1933
retd g p 1973
resid Milltimber Aber

BOWMAN John Wilson MB ChB 1917
resid Southampton

BOWMAN Margaret Philip MA 1919 MB ChB 1922
g p till 1965; retd; resid Newcastle-u-Tyne

BOWMAN Robert MA 1918 LLB 1920

BOWMAN William MA BSc 1933 MB ChB 1940
lect clin chem Aberd from 1952; retd 1974
d Aber 18.3.77

BOWRING Michael John BSc(for) 1952
m Aber 1956 Margaret N. Stewart DA d of William N. S.

BOWYER Alexander Albert MA 1932 BD 1936
min of C of S North ch Aber from 1958; retd 1976; resid Stonehaven
d Aber 19.6.78 *AUR* XLVIII 104

BOXHALL John Alfred *MA 1951
overseas course B Oxon 1958–59; Tanganyika: d c Kilbondo 1959–60; treas off. Dar es Salaam 1960–62; asst master Crosfields s Reading 1962–66; asst secy s Oriental and African stud. Lond 1966–71; secy inst adv leg. stud. from 1971

BOYD Alexander Millar MA 1902
no longer on GC reg

BOYD Angus Archibald William MB ChB 1949
g p Bolton from 1970

BOYD, Annabella Constance Eva BSc 1925
d Aber 16.5.67 *AUR* XLII 365

BOYD Annie Evelyn BSc 1913
d 13.9.73 *AUR* XLV 317

BOYD Catherine Thomson MA 1935

BOYD Elizabeth Johnstone MA 1909 BSc 1910
d 6.1.68

BOYD James Rodgers MB ChB 1940
visiting phys Bannockburn I D hosp Stirling from 1958
m 16.2.42 Kathleen M. T. Black, Fyvie

BOYD Jeannie Strathdee MA 1928
d Northallerton 15.9.67 *AUR* XLII 186

BOYD Leslie George MB ChB 1936
g p Northallerton from 1946; retd 1976
d Northallerton 27.8.80 *AUR* XLIX 69

BOYD or Davidson, Mary Falconer MA 1903
no longer on GC reg

BOYD or Buchan, Olwyn *MA 1925
teacher mod lang Peterhead acad 1956–59

BOYD Percy Stuart *MA 1948 PhD 1952

BOYD Roderick MacSwan MA 1945
min C of S Amulree and Strathbrann ch Dunkeld 1961–71; retd; resid Edin
d Edin 31.8.76 *AUR* XLVII 106

BOYD William Hugh Falconer MB ChB 1941
sen anaest Bangour hosp W Lothian from 1950; retd

BOYNE Alexander William BSc 1944 *1948
FRS(Edin) 1973
head statist dept Rowett inst Aber from 1948

BOYNE James Anderson MA 1923
d Aber 4.4.71 *AUR* XLIV 211

BOYNE or Witheridge, Jean McDonald MA 1944
resid Stony Stratford
husb *d* 29.12.73

BRADLEY Hunter Witley MA 1946
teacher: head geog/geol dept John Marley s N'cle-u-Tyne from 1959

BRADY Harold Samuel MB ChB 1934
no longer on GC reg

BRAID Kenneth William BSc(agr) 1913 BSc 1914
retd; resid Skene

BRAND Hamish Douglas Ferguson MB ChB 1913
no longer on GC reg

BRAND Jane *MA 1928
teacher mod lang Perth acad till 1966; retd

BRAND Margaret Hilda MA 1924

BRAND Margaret Mary MA 1947
teacher Aber: Ferryhill s 1961–62, High s for girls 1962; secy/translator to man. dir USM (France) Paris from 1962
m Aber 19.10.62 Paul E. Darmon; marr diss 1971

BRANDER James Melvin *BSc 1953

BRANDER or Paterson, Lillian Mary BSc(agr) 1940

BRANDS Alexander Campbell MA 1930 LLB 1931
d Aber 21.1.67 *AUR* XLII 369

BRANDS John BSc 1948
FRSS 1956
plan. man. Ciba Labs Horsham from 1969

BRANNEN Ian Cameron MB ChB 1947
MFCP(Lond) 1972
dep county m o Norfolk 1963–73; dist commun phys Norwich from 1974

BRASH Robert Alexander BSc 1944

BREBNER Allan MB ChB 1929
reg m o Min of Health Lond till 1968; retd; resid Aber

BREBNER Arthur *BSc(eng) 1947 PhD 1952
prof eng Queen's univ Kingston Ont from 1957

BREBNER George Gill *MA 1948
def res staff British Emb Wash DC 1959–62; RAE Farnborough from 1962

BREBNER Hugh *MA 1905 BSc 1906
retd
d Bearsden 4.12.73 *AUR* XLV 444

BREBNER Hugh MB ChB 1943 MD 1954
FRCPGlas 1968 FRCP(Lond) 1972
consult. phys West I Glasg and hon clin lect Glas from 1955

BREBNER or Speirs, Inez Mary MB ChB 1942
part time g p 1942–63; asst m o h Stirlingsh 1963–73; m o DHSS from 1966

BREBNER James Joseph *MA 1953

BREBNER John Low *BSc 1955 PhD 1959
asst lect nat phil Aberd 1958–60; NRC post doct fell. Ottawa 1960–62; res scient CERI Geneva 1962–68; assoc prof Montr 1968–74, prof from 1974
m Geneva 24.7.69 Eva M. Pobitschka, Dip Biol (Geneva) res asst immunology d of Ernst A. P. Dip Ing(Dresden) Dormagen Germany

BREBNER Lilias White *MA 1951
Univ Leeds: warden Lupton Hall till 1960, lect Ger till 1968
m Leeds 18.4.68 Richard F. M. Byrn, BA(Dub) lect Ger univ Leeds s of Francis M. B. MB ChB(Dub) Kilmacanogue Co Wicklow

BREBNER Margaret Evelyn MA 1954 Dip Ed 1955
teacher mod lang Turriff acad 1956–65; spec asst from 1965

BRECKENRIDGE Mary Morrison MA 1949

BREEZE John MB ChB 1950
MRCOG 1958 FRSM 1968 FRCOG 1974
consult. obst/gyn Gt Yarmouth and Waveney dist from 1968

BREMNER Charles *MA 1925
d 1.2.64

BREMNER James George MB ChB 1926
no longer on GC reg

BREMNER Mary Aileen Anne MA 1944

BREMNER or Allan, Mary Christina BSc 1923 MA 1924
resid Crookston Glasg

BREMNER or Christie, Mary Flett MA 1928
husb *d* 1969
teacher Smithfield s Aber 1965–67
d Fochabers 31.8.80

BREMNER Robert Yool *MA 1904 BSc 1907
no longer on GC reg

BREMNER William MA 1907
no longer on GC reg

BREMNER William Andrew Alexander *BSc 1953

BREMNER William James MB ChB 1927
g p Hale till 1964; consult. anaest Wythenshowe & N Cheshire hosps 1964–70; retd; resid Ramsey IOM
d Sutton Coldfield 4.12.79

BREMNER William John *BSc 1952

BRÉTONIÈRE or Bamford, Marianne de la MA BCom 1936
secy trg Lond 1936–37, secy posts Lond/ARP h q Aber 1939–41; secy to dir Fraserburgh/Lond 1941–45; organis secy Scot. marr guid council Edin 1952–64; teacher: bus. stud. Edin 1965–69, prin bus. stud. from 1969

BREWSTER Gordon Watt MA 1952
head teacher Aberdeensh: Finzean 1962–66, Tarland 1966–69, Clerkhill Peterhead 1969–74, Dyce from 1974

BRIDE John William BSc(for) 1951

BRIDGES or Rae, Mary Davidson *MA 1939
resid Glasg

BRIEN Thomas Ralph *BSc 1951
head sc dept St Gregory's comp s Kirkby 1960–64; lect Jordanhill coll of educ Glasg from 1964

BRIGHT Edgar Bulmer MB ChB 1937
hon phys to H.M. the Queen 1971–72; dir of health and res (RAF) Lond 1970–71; off. comm Princess Alexandra's hosp Wroughton 1971–72

BRISTER Graham Harrold BSc(for) 1953
PhD(Wash) 1970
col for. serv till 1964; post grad course Oxon 1959–60; Wash. USA: timber eng 1964–65, teaching asst 1965–70; asst prof Georgia from 1970

BRITTAIN David Antony MA 1952 LLB 1954

BROCKIE Arthur Alexander MB ChB 1941
d Northland NZ 1.3.71

BROCKIE Edward Henry MA 1952

BROCKIE Margaret Millicent MA 1912
d Aber 29.7.77

BROCKIE or McCrea, Mary Davidson MA 1915
teacher Kirkcaldy 1916–28
resid Newark-on-Trent
d 1977 *AUR* XLVII 284

BROCKS Arthur William MA 1948
(conferred for long service of exceptional merit)
d Aber 7.4.75 *AUR* XLVI 325

BROCKS Basil Ernest MB ChB 1941
d Brentwood 14.1.79 *AUR* XLVIII 232

BRODIE or Read, Alison Garland MB ChB 1944
resid Blebo Craigs

BRODIE Douglas MacBean MB ChB 1941
d Altrincham –.11.78

BRODIE Edward Adam MA 1930 LLB 1932
sole ptnr A. and E. A. Brodie solic Banff 1933–76; then consult.
wife *d* 20.1.70

BRODIE James Hurrie MB ChB 1937
m o DHSS Blackpool from 1971
m Singapore 28.10.59 Winifred M. Hiscock DPH(Lond) med pract d of Walter G. H. PhD(Lond)

BRODIE or MacGillivray, Margaret Ann MA 1912
d Newtonmore –.1.74

BROMBERG or Jay, Helena June *MA 1949
Lond: freelance broadcaster 1955–65; market res p r asst 1965–72; organis secy/admin dir from 1972

BROMBERG Priscilla Betty MA 1952
Toronto: secy Shell Oil Co 1959–61; off. man. lib board of educ 1962–63; lib asst univ of W Ont Lond Ontario from 1963; private scholar working in field of 16th cent. Engl printing from 1970
m Tor 1.10.60 Robert W. Tracy BA(Tor) city plan.

BROOK David Whiteley PhD 1952
sen tech off. Br Titan Products Billingham 1962–66; tech serv man. Titanium Intermediates 1967–75; teacher chem Cleveland educ auth from 1976

BROOKER Ian Mackintosh MB ChB 1950
g p Shetland: Yell till 1965, Levenwick from 1965

BROOKER William Dixon BSc 1953 *1958
prin teacher geog Aberlour h s 1959, Keith g s 1960–62, 65–66; seconded King Richard s Dhekelia Cyprus 1962–65; tut. organis extra-mural stud. Aberd: Elgin 1966–69, Aber from 1969

BROOKS Alexander MB ChB 1925
major RAMC; on staff Blaina hosp Nantyglo Mon from 1955

BROOKS Helen Porter MA 1948
teacher Inverurie acad 1964–75, Kellands s Inverurie from 1975

BROUGH Esther Jones MA 1911
no longer on GC reg

BROWN Alexander MB ChB 1936
consult. anaest Hull and E Riding from 1950

BROWN Alexander Aitken Lawson *MA 1952
prin teacher classics Ellon acad 1950–76

BROWN Alexander Phimister LLB 1949
d Aber 18.6.78 *AUR* XLVIII 107

BROWN or Stewart, Alice Ann MA 1918
resid Aber
husb *d* Aber 14.7.66 *AUR* XLI 338
d Aber 25.3.80

BROWN Andrew Hunter MA 1912 BSc 1912 MB ChB 1915
d 14.9.73

BROWN or Robertson, Anna Maria Margaret MA 1937
d 6.4.67

BROWN or House, Annie MA 1942

BROWN or Mackintosh, Annie Stewart MA 1927
d Cullen 14.2.72 *AUR* XLIV 431

BROWN Augusta Elizabeth Rudmose *MA 1904
d Westbury on Trym, Bristol 13.12.66 *AUR* XLII 80

BROWN or McLachlan, Barbara Annie MA 1917
resid Aber

BROWN Beatrice Rose MA 1922
retd 1962; resid Aber
d Aber 7.1.79 *AUR* XLVIII 228

BROWN or Steen, Catherine Elizabeth MA 1950 *1951
teacher Westholme indep s Billinge End Blackburn till 1960; emig Australia 1963

BROWN or MacLaren, Catherine McKay MA 1923
teacher Aber till 1957; resid Aber
d Aber 23.10.79

BROWN Charles Alexander MA 1935 MB ChB 1939 MD 1946
consult. ophth surg Bristol Eye hosp and SW reg health auth from 1951

BROWN Charles Grant MA 1927 LLB 1929
JP
sen ptnr Burnett & Reid advoc Aber from 1943; dir publ and private comps
d Aberlour 11.8.81

BROWN Charles Wilson MA 1942
BA(OU) 1973
teacher phys: Aber tech coll 1959–77 (seconded to Ifunda tech coll Tanzania 1966), Inverurie acad from 1977

BROWN or John, Christine Beatrice Anderson MB ChB 1947
d 1.12.66 *AUR* XLII 374

BROWN Donald Duncan MB ChB 1942 MD 1946
no longer on GC reg

BROWN or Murray, Dorothea Catherine Wallace BSc 1948
relief teacher Kensaleyre s Skye 1957–73; vice-county-recorder Skye for BSBI from 1966

BROWN Douglas Alexander BSc(eng) 1950

BROWN Douglas Watson BSc(eng) 1933

BROWN Eelin Mary MA 1953

BROWN Ellen Mary MA 1931
youth and commun serv organis Aber educ comm till 1972; retd

BROWN or Gould, Florence Elisabeth McCaw *MA 1951
ABPsS 1954
Southampton: part-time teacher 1962–65; member res team surv of disturbed adolescents Wessex 1965; publ as *Stress in Youth* 1971; part-time educ psych from 1966

BROWN Frances Mary *MA 1919
no longer on GC reg

BROWN Francis Frederick MB ChB 1913
no longer on GC reg

BROWN Frederick William Campbell MB ChB 1915 DPH 1921 *MD 1922
d 22.2.71

BROWN George Taylor MA 1919
d Aber 1.5.66 *AUR* XLII 85

BROWN Georgia Ella MA 1919
d Aber 21.12.77 *AUR* XLVII 356

BROWN Helen Clow MB ChB 1954

BROWN Hilda MA 1919
no longer on GC reg

BROWN Ian Macdiarmid MB ChB 1942
consult geriat Eastbourne hosp group from 1965; BMA: member council 1968–69, and chmn group med admin 1972–76

BROWN Ian Mitchell LLB 1949

BROWN or Singer, Isabel Mary MA 1947
radon asst Aberd 1947–49; teacher: ISS Centre Awali Bahrain 1962–64, Mackie acad Stonehaven 1965–70, Lochaber h s Fort William from 1970

BROWN Isobel Campbell MB ChB 1920

BROWN Isobel Janie MA 1929
teacher Aber till 1968; retd

BROWN James BSc 1923
no longer on GC reg

BROWN James MB ChB 1944 MD 1956
FRCR
consult. radiol: Manc and Lanc from 1954

BROWN James Donald BSc(agr) 1924
CBE 1976
Orkney: DL from 1968, convener c c from 1970
d Stromness 1.5.78

BROWN James Mortimer *MA 1950
Essex: head Engl dept Torells c s Grays, head sen s Hassenbrook c s Stanford-le-Hope; head Beacon Hill s Aspatria Cumberland

BROWN or Clark, Jenny Brewster *MA 1922
retd 1958; resid Stonehaven
husb *d* 3.9.64

BROWN John MA 1953
teacher Aber: Ruthrieston s s 1961–64, 1st asst jun

s RGC 1964–73/housemaster RGC boarding house 1964–69, Kittybrewster p s 1973; asst head: Cummings Park p s 1974, Walker Rd p s from 1974

BROWN John Gatherer MB ChB 1914
d 10.12.62

BROWN or McPherson, Kathleen Nora Frances MA 1920
resid Aber
husb *d* –.6.49

BROWN or Glogan, Lesley Elizabeth Melville MA 1948
resid Hastings

BROWN or Hudson, Louise MA 1914
resid Aber

BROWN Mabel Kathleen MA 1955
teacher: Mufulira h s Zambia 1960–62, Aber coll of comm 1965–67, Oldhall s Hethersett 1967–70, Dereham h s Norfolk from 1971
m Mufulira 9.12.61 Raymond H. Rawlins sales dir s of Henry R. Newbury

BROWN Maggie MA 1948
(conferred for long service of exceptional merit)
d Aber 28.10.64 *AUR* XLI 60

BROWN Margaret MA 1929

BROWN Margaret MA 1932
d Peterhead 28.2.68 *AUR* XLII 370

BROWN or Brunnen, Margaret Christian Thomson MA 1942
Aber: part-time soc worker child guid centre 1953–55, part-time interviewer soc surv soc dept Foresterhill 1962–64, part-time case worker Assoc Soc Serv from 1964

BROWN Margaret Eliza *MA 1915
resid Aber
d Aber 10.7.76

BROWN or Macleod, Margaret Florence MA 1919
retd; resid Darlington

BROWN or Parker or Saxby, Mary Murray MA 1943
MSc(Louisville)
d 19.8.75

BROWN Patricia Margaret *BSc 1953
Aberd: res asst dept chem 1964–72, res off. from 1972

BROWN or Steventon, Rachel Mitchell MA 1913
no longer on GC reg

BROWN Richard Petrie *MA 1949

BROWN Robert *MB ChB 1905 *MD 1907
no longer on GC reg

BROWN Robert MB ChB 1951
MRCP(C) 1965 FRCP(C) 1969
Canadian Decoration and clasp
sen m o Metz France 1958–63; asst head dept psychiat nat def med centre Ottawa 1963–68 promoted lt col; chief psychiat Can. Forces hosp Kingston, Ont from 1968; now med dir reg psychiat centre (Ont) for Canadian penitentiary serv

BROWN Robert Pearson Masson MB ChB 1935
h o Hereford gen hosp 1935–36; g p: Inv 1936–37, Edzell 1937–45, W Bromwich 1945–48, Aber from 1948

BROWN Robert Walker MB ChB 1913
d Peterhead 19.3.62 *AUR* XXXIX 380

BROWN Roy Dudley MA 1935 LLB 1937
Lond: dep dir Shipbuilders & Repairers Nat Assoc and secy Shipbuilding Corp from 1938

BROWN William BL 1926
ptnr Esslemont & Cameron advoc Aber from 1944; secy Aber and N E legal aid comm 1952–70; member Council Law Soc of Scot. 1961–75; member Scot. solic discip comm from 1971; hon sheriff from 1974

BROWN William Baxter Brodie MB ChB 1925
d Aboyne 6.4.63 *AUR* XL 205

BROWN William Cairns *MA 1945

BROWN William Imray *MA 1950

BROWN William Peddie MA 1956

BROWN William Scott (Sir) *MA 1912 LLD 1956
d Aber 17.5.68 *AUR* XLII 350

BROWNE Francis James MB ChB 1906 *MD 1919
d Sydney Australia 17.8.63 *AUR* XL 300

BROWNE Magdalene Gordon MA 1928
d Aber 19.12.69 *AUR* XLIII 446

BROWNE Ronald Austin MB ChB 1953

BROWNE William BD 1911
d 19.5.69

BROWNIE William Campbell *BSc(eng) 1947 MA 1953
MIMechE 1958 CEng 1962
AEI(M/c):grp ldr 1958–68; Thurso Tech coll: lect 1968–74, sen lect from 1974

BROWNLEE Robert Wyness *MA 1925
FEIS 1950
prin teacher maths St. Modan's h s Stirling till 1969; retd
wife *d* 1966
m(2) Bridge of Allan 27.12.67 Jane M. Anderson or Dean milliner d of Charles A. Hamilton

BROWNLEE William BSc(eng) 1953

BRUCE or Lamb, Agnes MA 1926
b Peterhead 20.11.26
resid Christchurch NZ

BRUCE or Dobie, Agnes Gladys MB ChB 1922
d 3.11.63

BRUCE Alexander BCom 1924
no longer on GC reg

BRUCE Alexander *BSc 1931 MA 1932
prin teacher chem Aber g s 1962–74; retd
m Aber 29.3.69 Agnes F. Gray Aber

BRUCE Alice Margaret MA 1948

BRUCE or Pearson, Alice Mary *MA 1947

BRUCE Andrew Buchan MA 1922
d Wick 9.11.64 *AUR* XLI 57

BRUCE Andrew Watt MB ChB 1947

BRUCE Charlotte Diverall MA 1928
teacher: Pegswood 1930–33, Carlisle 1933–35, Ashington 1935–38, Windsor 1938–43, Newport (Salop) 1943–46, Chichester from 1946; retd 1965

BRUCE David MA 1951
teacher Nairn acad: 1964–73, asst prin classics from 1973
m Inverurie 24.7.64 Rosella Gall d of William G. Inverurie

BRUCE David Breckinridge *BSc 1949 PhD 1953
head chem lab Courtauld's chem eng Coventry 1958–67; tech man. Internat Paint Co Birm 1967–70; dev dir Goodlass Wall & Co Liv from 1970

BRUCE or Milne, Doris Margaret MA 1923
resid Reading

BRUCE Douglas James BSc(eng) 1945
MIMechE 1957 SA Govt Certif Mech Eng 1958, Elect Eng 1959 MIEE 1966 CEng 1966
chief eng Nat Chem Products Durban 1960–62; Atomic Power Constructions Lond: sen eng 1962–68, group eng 1969–75; Eptisa-Ghesa-TRSA Madrid: chief eng mech equip sect. from 1975

BRUCE Douglas Walter MB ChB 1909
deceased

BRUCE Duncan McKenzie MA 1949
C of S min N Parish Ch Stirling from 1963

BRUCE Edward George MA 1914 BSc(agr) 1919
resid Aber

BRUCE Elizabeth Alexandra MA 1926
teacher sc pre-nursing coll Aber till 1969; retd

BRUCE Ethel Mary *MA 1916

BRUCE or McGlashan, Frances Elizabeth MB ChB 1927
no longer on GC reg

BRUCE Frederick Fyvie MA 1932 DD 1957
MA(Manc) 1963 FBA 1973
prof bibl crit and exegesis Manc from 1959

BRUCE George MA 1908
retd 1952; resid Edzell
d Edzell 24.6.79

BRUCE George MB ChB 1948
g p: Dornoch 1952–53, Woking from 1953

BRUCE George Gordon MB ChB 1915
retd; resid Aber
wife *d* 5.11.73
d Inverurie 6.6.76 *AUR* XLVII 102

BRUCE George Macpherson MA 1936
dep rector Br of Don acad Aber from 1972

BRUCE George Robert *MA 1932
retd BBC 1970; first fell. creative writing Glas 1971–73; extra mural lect Glas 1973; USA: visiting prof Union theol seminary Richmond Virginia Jan 1974; poet in resid Orescott coll Prescott Arizona from Feb 1974; visiting prof Coll of Wooster 1976–77

BRUCE George Smith BSc(agr) 1922
d Edin 24.2.67 *AUR* XLII 360

BRUCE or Holmes, Isobel Annie MA 1927
no longer on GC reg

BRUCE James MB ChB 1954
h s mat hosp Dumfriessh 1958–62; g p Edin from 1962
m Edin 27.7.64 Patricia A. McAinsh MA(Edin) d of James McA. Edin

BRUCE or Coull, Jannetta MA 1921
resid Brentwood

BRUCE or Noble, Jean Malcolm MA 1937
resid Hamilton Ontario

BRUCE or Pirie, Jeannie Reid MA 1926
head Dunecht s till 1961; teacher maths Cults acad 1964–68
husb *d* –.9.60

BRUCE or Macpherson, Jeannie Robertson MA 1949
teacher Aber: Kittybrewster s till 1960, St Peter's RC s 1966–67; Fernielea s from 1967, sen remed teacher from 1972

BRUCE or Wilson, Jessie (Janet) Coull MA 1922
retd (teaching) 1962
d Aber 30.11.73

BRUCE John MB ChB 1941
g p Crowle from 1970

BRUCE John BSc 1944

BRUCE John Brantingham BSc(for) 1947
for. serv BC Canada from 1947

BRUCE Kenneth *MA 1916
no longer on GC reg

BRUCE or Dick, Margaret MB ChB 1946
g p: Rotherham and clin asst Sheffield and Rotherham hosp till 1965, Wakefield 1965–71; locum sen h o ERI from 1973

BRUCE or Bowman, Margaret Jamieson Hill *MA 1949
teacher Fr/Lat Aboyne acad from 1950

BRUCE Margaret Morrice MA 1924
no longer on GC reg

BRUCE Marjorie Graham *MA 1951

BRUCE or Morrison, Marjory Leslie MA 1925
teacher Ferryhill s Aber; retd 1964; resid Aber
d Aber 7.8.79 *AUR* XLVIII 441

BRUCE Mary Brown MA 1948
prop. pharm Balfron from 1969

BRUCE Mary Helen MA 1947
Lond: asst prin mental health soc worker City of Westminster 1965–70; soc work sen off DHSS Alexander Fleming House from 1970

BRUCE or Lindsay, Mary Wilson MB ChB 1944
resid Aboyne

BRUCE or Burnett, Muriel Georgina MA 1941

BRUCE Nan Helen MB ChB 1947
DA 1966
anaest: Leeds area, Hull 1957–59, Aber 1959–61, Teesside, N'castle reg from 1961

BRUCE or Davidson, Priscilla Constance BSc 1954
resid Mintlaw

BRUCE Robert *MA 1933
OBE 1962
cultural attaché Brit emb Budapest 1963–65; rep Brit council Hong Kong 1966–68; assoc prof polit sc Eastern Kentucky univ USA 1968–69; prof polit sc Prescott coll Arizona from 1969

BRUCE Robert Anderson *MA 1933
head dept gen educ Singapore polytech 1957 to retd; resid Aber

BRUCE Robert Douglas MB ChB 1928
OStJ 1963
RAF med br 1939–63; m o M o D Lond from 1963

BRUCE Robert Gauld MB ChB 1955
MRCGP 1965
sen h o: Gorleston hosp Gt Yarmouth 1958–59, West Norwich hosp 1959; g p Oulton Broad Lowestoft from 1959

BRUCE Ronald John MB ChB 1945

BRUCE Ronald Marshall *MA 1950
teacher Dun: Harris acad 1952–61, coll of comm 1961–67; prin hist Forfar acad from 1967

BRUCE Ronald Reith BSc(eng) 1947

BRUCE or Birch, Sheila MA 1950
resid Romford

BRUCE or Brown, Stella MA 1950
teacher Abdnsh: Hatton 1960–69, Boddam from 1969–74, Auchterellon from 1974

BRUCE Wilhelmina MA 1910

BRUCE William MB ChB 1925
d Inv 18.4.62 *AUR* XXXIX 383

BRUCE William Anderson MA 1951

BRUCE William Riddoch MB ChB 1950

BRUCE Winifred Mary MA 1952
teacher maths Norfolk: Westcliff h s 1964–70, head of dept King's Lynn 1970–78; head maths dept Alice Harpur s Bedford from 1978

BRUNNEN Peter Lance MB ChB 1939
FACCP 1958
consult. thoracic surg Grampian Health Board from 1952; clin sen lect thoracic surg Aberd from 1970

BRYANT Ronald William Gower *MA 1937
Canada: dev plan off. Halifax Nova Scotia 1961–62; asst prof Univ de Montréal 1962–66, assoc prof Concordia univ Montreal from 1966; consult. to Quebec prov govt and govt Canada from time to time; author of *Land, Private Property, Public Control* (Montreal 1972) and numerous papers

BUCHAN Agnes King *MA 1938
teacher Fr High s for girls Aber 1963–66; lect coll of educ Aber from 1966

BUCHAN Alexander MB ChB 1936
consult. obst/gyn E Reg hosp board from 1946

BUCHAN Alexander McIntosh *MA 1919
d St Louis USA 16.7.69 *AUR* XLIII 329

BUCHAN Alexander Presley MB ChB 1942 DPH 1947
med supt and consult. psychiat St. Margaret's hosp Birm from 1957
d Tamworth 18.5.81

BUCHAN Alexander Reid BCom 1926

BUCHAN Alexander Reid BSc(eng) 1956

BUCHAN Alfred John MB ChB 1922
d Ilford 15.12.68 *AUR* XLIII 212

BUCHAN Andrew *MA 1934
teacher Peterhead: jun instr centre 1938–40, acad 1940–41, Central s 1946–57; RA intellig corps Europe 1941–45; spec ag Prudential insur co of America Montclair 1957–79; retd
m Montclair NJ 20.7.57 Jean C. Cowe

BUCHAN Andrew Robertson MA 1946 LLB 1949
d Nassau, Bahamas 1.10.79

BUCHAN or Suckling, Anna BSc 1930 *1931 PhD 1935
d 19.7.64 *AUR* XL 400

BUCHAN Christian *MA 1946

BUCHAN or Nieuwenhuyzen, Dorothy May MA 1951

BUCHAN Edith MA 1928
d Rhyl 28.7.77

BUCHAN or Merchant, Elizabeth MA 1916
resid Torphins

BUCHAN Elsie Isabel MA 1925
teacher maths/sc Kaimhill s Aber till 1964; retd

BUCHAN Forbes MB ChB 1924

BUCHAN Ian James MB ChB 1942
g p Poole from 1947

BUCHAN Isobel Bruce *MA 1935
teacher mod lang: Gordon s Huntly 1941–48, Perth acad 1948–73; retd

BUCHAN or MacInnes, Jean Park MA 1941
remed teacher Engl Stromness acad Orkney from 1972

BUCHAN or Black, Jeanetta MA 1946

BUCHAN Jim *MA 1949 *MEd 1954
prin teacher Engl subj and dep head Culter s 1960–66; prin teacher hist and dep rector Cults acad 1966–71; dep rector 1971–75; rector Peterhead acad from 1975

BUCHAN John BSc(eng) 1953

BUCHAN John Andrew Noble MA BCom 1929

BUCHAN Joseph MA 1950

BUCHAN Joseph Forrest MA 1924
d Elgin 3.3.79 *AUR* XLVIII 228

BUCHAN Lavina Evelyn MA 1938
Northfield s Aber: woman advis 1963–72, dep head from 1972

BUCHAN or Pollitt, Lesley Smith *MA 1935
prin teacher guid Inv h s from 1972

BUCHAN or Merchant, Lizzie MA 1916
no longer on GC reg

BUCHAN or Duchovny, Margaret MA 1951

BUCHAN Margaret Mary Cordiner MA 1946
Peterhead: teacher Buchanhaven p s 1963–66, dep head 1966–76; head Meethill p s from 1976

BUCHAN or Collin, Margaret Noble MA 1928

BUCHAN or Wilkie, Martha Third MA 1926
teacher Engl/Fr/geog/hist Skene s s 1960–67; retd; resid Aber

BUCHAN or Adams, Mary MA 1919
resid Grangemouth
d Grangemouth 12.5.79

BUCHAN or Martin, Mary Simpson MB ChB 1942
school m o Birm from 1957; sen clin h o Birm

BUCHAN Ogilvie Milne Clarke *MA 1951
lect hist of polit thought univ of W.I. Jamaica 1960–63; staff tut. phil Durh from 1964
m(2) London 22.8.58 Wendy I. M. Oldridge; marr diss 1964
(3) Durham 14.10.67 Janet M. Rennie

BUCHAN Robert BSc 1954
Member Assoc Prof Eng of Ontario 1965
Ontario: field geol Sudbury 1954–61, geol/mineralogist Falconbridge Nickel Mines Thornhill from 1961
m Copper Cliff Ontario 15.12.56 Mema Nicoli secy d of Joseph N. Copper Cliff

BUCHAN Robina Smart MA 1928
Walthamstow: teacher St Mary's C of E s 1930–38, Beaconsfield s s 1938–52, dep head 1952–67; retd; resid Rosehearty

BUCHAN Samuel MA 1925 BSc 1927 *1928
works dir Wright Dental Co Dundee 1959–70; retd

BUCHAN Stevenson BSc 1929 *1930 PhD 1934
CBE 1971 FRSE 1962
dep chief scient off./asst dir spec serv geol surv 1960–67; chief geol Inst Geol Sc 1967–68; chief scient off./dep dir Inst Geol Sc 1968–71; retd 1971

BUCHAN William BSc 1931
d Aber 2.1.68 *AUR* XLII 370

BUCHAN William MA 1916 MB ChB 1918 *MD 1926
second asst to prof path. Aberd 1921–22
Aber: g p till 1958, member med board MPNI 1940–66; part-time asst reg m o N E reg board 1958–75; m o i/c limb clin ARI 1969–73

BUCHAN William Robertson MB ChB 1950
CCFP 1970
Canada: g p Whitehorse Yukon till 1972; asst prof univ BC dept fam pract Vancouver from 1975

BUCHANAN Donald MB ChB 1908 MD 1911
no longer on GC reg

BUCHANAN or Crichton, Isabel Alison *MA 1935 *MEd 1937
resid Bieldside Aber

BUCHANAN John Brownlie *BSc 1951

BUCHANAN John Robert Mungo MA 1947 Dip Ed 1949
Aber: dep head Muirfield p s 1958–66; dep head Middlefield p s 1966–70, head Springhill p s from 1970

BUCHANAN Malcolm MA 1925
retd 1972; resid Conon Bridge

BUCHANAN or Davison, Mary Alston BSc 1951
part-time teacher Dunfermline from 1965

BUCHANAN Michael Stuart *BSc 1951
geol surv Nigeria: geol 1951–61, sen geol Jos 1961–64, prin geol Ibadan 1964–65, asst dir 1965–66; lect geol Aberd from 1966

BUCHANAN Percival William *MA 1951 LLB 1954
town clerk Alloa from 1963; dir admin and leg. serv reg c from 1974
m Aber 6.6.64 Anna D. Barron shorthand typist d of John B. Aber

BUCHANAN Robert Thomson *MA 1951
PhD(Edin) 1958
lect econ Brist 1961–68; lect indust relations Strath from 1968
m Edin 7.9.69 Eunice M. Allan MA(Edin) teacher d of Ebenezer A. Arbroath

BUCHANAN-SMITH Alick Drummond MA 1922 BSc(agr) 1923
Hon DSc (H-W) 1972
vice chmn pigs indust dev auth till 1966; created Baron Balerno of Currie in the County of Midlothian; life peer 1963; chmn Court of H-W 1966–72; disting alumnus Iowa State univ 1967; pres Royal Scot. Geog Soc 1968–74; hon assoc Royal Coll of Vet Surg 1970; hon member Royal Vet Assoc 1976; treasurer Royal Soc Edin 1966–77
wife *d* 1947

BUDGE Catherine Christina MB ChB 1948
DPH(Glas) 1966
Glasg: asst m o corp health dept 1966–73, g p from 1973

BUDGE Neil MB ChB 1942

BUIE or Maclennan, Catherine Mary MA 1955
d S Africa 6.6.71

BULLEN Jennie MA 1947
teacher Dounby Orkney 1952–61
m Stromness Orkney 4.4.61 David R. Corse master mariner s of Robert W. C. Falkirk

BULLEN John Herbert BSc(eng) 1943

BULMER George Gordon MA 1921
sen master Cedarhurst prep s Solihull 1963–73; retd

BULTITUDE Frederick William *BSc 1953
PhD(Lond) 1957
prin scient off. AWRE Aldermaston from 1964
wife *d* 17.7.71

BUNDY Colin Thomas BSc(for) 1954
Nyasaland: asst conserv for. 1957–64; Zomba, Malawi: sen asst conserv for. 1964–67, man. for. indust div 1967–71; Rhodesia: asst man. prod./sales Umtali 1971–76, man. timber promotion council Salisbury from 1976
m Glasg 31.7.63 May F. McLaughlin d of David McL. Glasg

BUNTING Julia MA 1923
d Aber 26.5.61 *AUR* XXXIX 203

BURGER Roelof du Toit PhD 1955
prof soil sc univ of O.F.S. Bloemfontein S Africa from 1960

BURGESS Annabella MA 1921
d 30.11.65

BURGESS Margaret MA 1923
no longer on GC reg

BURGESS Stanley Everatt MA 1930 *EdB 1956
d Grantham -.9.62 *AUR* XL 94

BURGESS Wilson Merchant MB ChB 1937
JP 1957
g p Middlesbrough 1937–38; h s Sunderland RI 1938–39; g p Longside 1939–42 and from 1945; hon med supt Peterhead cott hosp 1962–73
d Longside 2.4.77 *AUR* XLVII 214

BURLEY Flora Macdonald *MA 1923
resid Aber
m Aber 10.10.72 Alexander C. Anderson BA(Cantab) MRCS LRCP lt col IMS (retd) s of Sir John A. MA 1877 *qv*(I, II)

BURN John Kenneth Arthur MB ChB 1941
MRCGP 1959
sen h m o anaest Grimsby, g p of hosps from 1955

BURNESS Alexander MB ChB 1936
d Sunderland 29.11.70 *AUR* XLIV 215

BURNETT Agnes Howe MA 1921
teacher Aber till 1960; retd

BURNETT Alexander Ramsay MB ChB 1948
MRCGP 1960
Thurso: g p from 1962; anaest Dunbar hosp from 1966

BURNETT Alice Mary MA 1925
teacher lang Oldmeldrum s till 1963; retd
d Aber 15.3.79 *AUR* XLVIII 228

BURNETT or Ross, Catherine Redpath MA 1926

BURNETT Charles *MB ChB 1924
d Edin 17.12.67 *AUR* XLII 361

BURNETT David *MA 1921 *BSc 1922
prof maths Rhodes univ Grahamstown S Af till 1960; high altit observatory Boulder USA 1961–64; lect Aberd 1965–69; retd

BURNETT Donald James *BSc 1951
indust chem Kodak Harrow from 1954

BURNETT or Thomas, Elspeth Helen MA 1942
resid Kingussie

BURNETT Ernest Wood MA 1931
C of S min Rothiemay from 1966; retd 1975

BURNETT or Birse, Evelyn Mary *BSc 1951
resid Aber

BURNETT George Murray *BSc 1943 PhD 1947
FRSE 1957 JP Aber 1968
Aberd: prof chem 1955–74, vice prin 1966–69; vice-chancellor and prin H-W from 1974
d Edin 4.9.80 *AUR* XLIX 70 & 139

BURNETT Gerrard *MB ChB 1921
Pontefract Yorks: g p retd 1959, m o Remploy Factory from 1948 (except 1972); retd 1976

BURNETT Hugh MB ChB 1934

BURNETT James Donald *BSc 1946 PhD 1949

BURNETT Janet Findlay Martin MA 1907 MB ChB 1923
d Swindon 11.8.62 *AUR* XL 77

BURNETT Muriel BSc 1950
Dip Ed(Sheff) 1969
indust chem Manc 1949–63; teacher Rotherham 1969–71
m Sale 5.1.57 Harold G. Glover BSc(Lond) scient s of Thomas G. Timperley

BURNETT Robert Alexander *MA 1919 *BSc 1920
d Stockport 23.1.75

BURNETT Ruby Alice MA 1945
Dip Teacher of Physioth 1962
teacher Aber hosp s of physioth from 1962

BURNETT Walter Sinclair BSc(for) 1954
for. consult. and land agent Munlochy from 1965

BURNETT William MA 1931
headmaster Boddam till 1973; retd

BURNETT William *MB ChB 1943 *ChM 1957
FRCPSGlas 1961 FRACS 1964
Brisbane: prof/head dept surg univ of Queensland and hon sen surg royal Brisbane hosp from 1963; on royal Brisbane hosp board 1973–76; sen commonwealth res fell. UK 1967
d 30.8.81

BURNETT William Ronald Barrington MA 1938
second dep city chamberlain Aber from 1967; retd 1975; later on part time basis

BURNETT or Scott, Winifred Elizabeth MA 1920
teacher Albyn s for girls: 1945–62, head jun s 1962–65; retd

BURNS Andrew Sheridan MB ChB 1924
no longer on GC reg

BURNS Arnold Marischal MA 1931
Aber: JP from 1955, member town council till 1975

BURNS Charles BSc 1938

BURNS or Macdonald, Elsie Jessie MA 1920
resid Rothes
d Aber 1.8.80

BURNS or Smith, Ethel Annie MA 1924
resid Sutton

BURNS Hendry Stuart Mackenzie *MA 1921 *BSc 1922 LLD 1956
d 28.10.71 *AUR* XLIV 319

BURNS or Munro, Hilda Elizabeth MA 1931
teacher Kirkcaldy till 1969; retd

BURNS James BSc 1923 *1924 PhD 1927
CBE 1967
North Thames Gas Lond: chief eng 1949–59, dep chmn 1959–62; chmn: Northern Gas N'cle 1962–67, Southern Gas Southampton 1967–69; retd; fell. and hon life member Inst of Gas Engineers, Pres 1958–59, fell. Inst of Fuel, pres 1960, fell. Inst Chem Eng

BURNS James Henderson PhD 1952

BURNS Malcolm McRae PhD 1936
KBE 1972 FNZIC 1943 FNZIAS 1968 FRSNZ 1963 FAAAS 1966 hon DSc(Canterbury) 1974
prin Lincoln agr coll NZ 1952–74; chmn phys environment comm 1968–70, fact-finding g p on nuclear power 1976–77; member: nat dev council 1969–74, nat museum council from 1974, beech for. council 1972–78; trustee Norman Kirk mem etc. chmn DSIR res council 1959–62; NZ rep Harkness fell. 1961–76

BURNS or Sharp, Mary Stuart *MA 1943
teacher Fr/Ger Morrison's acad Crieff from 1960

BURNS William BSc 1932 MB ChB 1935 DSc 1944
CBE 1966 FRCP 1973
prof physiol Lond (Charing Cross hosp med s) from 1947

BURNS William George MA 1915
no longer on GC reg

BURR George Paterson MB ChB 1911
d Aber 24.3.62 *AUR* XXXIX 378

BURR Graham Erskine BSc(eng) 1950

BURR Mary Gladys MA 1933
teacher Kittybrewster s Aber 1961–72; retd

BURR Patrick Dickie BSc(eng) 1935

BURRELL Joan Mary MB ChB 1945 [d]MD 1953
DCH 1955
g p Aber from 1953

BURRY Harris Sheffield BSc 1945

BURRY John Neilson MB ChB 1950
MRCPE 1964
private pract Alice Springs NT Aust 1957–60; dermat St. John's hosp Lond and Wilkinson 1961–64; dermat in private and hosp practice Adelaide S Aust from 1964; lect i/c dermat teaching univ Adel; member edit. comm of journal *Contact Dermatitis*

BUSHELL Peter John *BSc 1955
MA DPhil(Oxon) 1962
Oxon: res lect Christ Church 1959–62, lect Magdalen 1962–63, Dartmouth coll USA 1963–64, Sus 1964–75, reader Sus 75; Nairobi 1967; assoc prof Dartmouth coll USA from 1972–73; sen visiting fell. Wis Madison USA from 1973
m Oxford 1963 June Walton MA(Oxon)

BUTCHART or Bull, Catherine McKenzie MA 1935
resid Cambridge

BUTCHART Henry Jackson BL 1905 LLD 1952
OBE DSO TD
d Aber 30.8.71 *AUR* XLIV 231

BUTHLAY Alan Donald *MA 1953
teacher: spec asst Inverurie acad 1959–64, prin Engl Banchory acad 1964–68, lect Engl Aber coll of educ from 1968
d 9.10.81

BUTHLAY Eric BL 1949
ptnr Christie, Buthlay & Rutherford advoc Aber 1962–75, Raeburn Christie Buthlay & Rutherford from 1975

BUTHLAY Kenneth George *MA 1949
Dip App Linguistics (Edin) 1966
lect Scot. lit Glas from 1966, sen lect from 1975

BUTT Raymond Alexander BSc(for) 1944
HM Overseas Civ Serv (for. serv) 1944–64; for. consult. Scot. Woodland Owners Assoc Co Edin from 1964

BUXTON Robert Edward BSc(eng) 1945

BUYERS Jessie MA 1903
d Banchory 4.10.64 *AUR* XLI 53

BUYERS or Gilchrist, Winifred MA 1913
d 29.2.64

BYARS John Robbie MB ChB 1934 DPH 1938
dep county m o h Leicestersh 1949–74; retd

BYRNE Charles BCom 1937
head of war pensions DHSS (sen prin) Blackpool from 1961

BYTH Alexander Skinner MA 1928
JP 1963
wife *d* 5.5.72
headmaster Cluny s 1944–72; retd
d Aber 15.11.78 *AUR* XLVIII 104

BYTH George Lawrence MB ChB 1936
g p Liverpool from 1947

BYTH John Gordon MB ChB 1936
Ernest and Minnie Dawson Cancer Trust Prize 1959
g p: Blackpool 1947–66, Jersey 1966–72; retd
d Jersey 20.12.76

CABLE James MB ChB 1915
d Forfar 3.3.71 *AUR* XLIV 210

CADENHEAD Robert McNeil MB ChB 1937
g p Lerwick from 1950

CADGER Alexandrina MA 1946
teacher Tore s Rosssh from 1950

CAHILL Dennis Neville BSc(agr) 1951
Dip Agr Ext (Melb) 1970
asst prov conserv and extension off. Bulawayo, Rhodesia 1962–65; Victoria, Aust: soil conserv off. Heathcote 1965–67, dist soil conserv off. Heathcote 1967–68, sen conserv off. Horsham 1968–72, reg conserv off. Horsham from 1972

CAHILL John Alfred BSc(eng) 1945
AMIMechE 1953 CEng 1971
grad app GEC Witton, Erith 1947–48; jun des eng turbine des off. Fraser & Chalmers Erith 1948–49; contr eng Sturtevant Eng co Lond 1949–53; asst mech eng(dev) Steetley Magnesite Co W Hartlepool 1953–57; dev eng Chem Insulating Co Darlington 1957–61; Laporte Industries Grimsby: proj eng 1961–63, des/proj man. 1963–76, site eng man. from 1976

CAIE or Phillips, Frances Stewart MA 1929

CAIE Jane Ann *MA 1925
d Aber 30.8.62 *AUR* XL 91

CAIE John *MA 1932 MB ChB 1938
g p Warwick and Leamington Spa from 1943

CAIE Rachel MA 1927 BSc 1930
d Aber 26.4.76

CAIN Alexander Mathieson *MA 1950 PhD 1954
asst keeper Br Museum 1954–66; lib syst analyst

and assoc prof Upstate med center Syracuse NY 1966–69; rare book lib state univ of New York Buffalo 1969–71; spec collections lib and assoc prof univ of Illinois med center Chicago 1971–73; asst keeper Nat Lib of Scot. from 1973

CAIRD or Searle, Catherine Annie MA 1933
teacher Engl/hist/commerce St Margaret's s Exeter till 1974; retd; teacher Crediton prep s 1974–78; retd

CAIRD or Bailey, Margaret MacCallum MA 1935

CAIRNS or Stuart, Elizabeth Richardson MB ChB 1929

CAIRNS Robert Hill *MA 1950

CALDER Alexander BSc(agr) 1925
FRSE 1929 OBE 1953
chief marketing off. Pigs Marketing Board Lond 1935–53 and dir of pig supplies Min of Food Lond 1945–53; dir pig indust board Rhodesia 1953–63; retd; resid Denbigh
m Pwllheli N Wales 1948 Iona Williams civ serv d of John T. W. Pwllheli

CALDER Alexander Chalmers MA 1946 LLB 1949
Edin: leg. asst 1961–62, ptnr in leg. firm 1962–69, leg. asst 1969–77

CALDER Alexander John Williams MA 1906 MB ChB 1910
d Hornsea 11.6.62 *AUR* XXXIX 375

CALDER Alistair Davidson MB ChB 1952

CALDER Andrew BSc(agr) 1921
no longer on GC reg

CALDER or Logan, Annie Mary MA 1921
no longer on GC reg

CALDER Charles Cumming BSc 1908 BSc(agr) 1908
d Aber 18.4.62 *AUR* XXXIX 376

CALDER Charles Cumming MA 1936 LLB 1940
sole ptnr W. J. C. Reed & Sons solic Laurencekirk
m Aber 30.7.45 Isobel E. R. Pirie d of John W. P. Aber
d Laurencekirk 6.12.77

CALDER Edith Ellen MA 1915

CALDER Enid MB ChB 1920
d Lowestoft 4.1.63 *AUR* XL 202

CALDER or MacLean, Gladys MA 1937
Milngavie: teacher 1955–69, asst head from 1970; retd 1976

CALDER or Goodwin, Gladys MA 1955

CALDER Hew Maclaren Neville MB ChB 1925
d 16.5.75 *AUR* XLVI 322

CALDER James BSc(agr) 1934

CALDER James Black MA 1910
d 18.4.72 *AUR* XLIV 427

CALDER or Breedon, Jessie Catherine MA 1941

CALDER John MA 1900 DD 1957
d Sydney Aust 19.10.62 *AUR* XL 74

CALDER or Watson, Margaret Winifred MA 1912 *1913 MB ChB 1920
d Distington 20.1.66 *AUR* XLI 242

CALDER Mary Lawrence *MA 1944

CALDER William John MA 1906 MB ChB 1909
d Aboyne 1.6.69 *AUR* XLIII 208

CALDER William Norman MB ChB 1939
g p Aber from 1947

CALDER William Victor BSc(for) 1936

CALDWELL Ian Wingate MB ChB 1939 MD 1954
FRCP 1970
S'ton med s hosps: consult. dermat from 1962, hon lect from 1971

CALDWELL James McAuley BSc(eng) 1946
C.Eng 1967 FIEE 1967
NSHEB Edin: sen eng transmission construct. 1963–71, chief transmission and distrib eng from 1971

CALDWELL John *MA 1951
MSc (Cranfield Inst Tech)
d Macclesfield 18.3.75 *AUR* XLVI 240

CALDWELL John Stewart MB ChB 1945
MRCGP 1964
g p Aberlour from 1949

CALDWELL or Mair, Marie Isobel MB ChB 1940

CALDWELL Thomas Douglas BSc 1952
Lond: sen master Risinghill comp s 1960–65, head South Hackney comp s from 1965

CALDWELL William Mitchell Hunter MA 1945

CALLAN or Davidson, Sheila Margaret Jane MA 1932

CALLANDER David BSc(agr) 1951

CALVERT Norman Hillbrook BSc(eng) 1953
CEng MIMechE 1964
Baker Perkins Peterborough: asst proj eng 1960–64, proj eng 1964–68, sen proj eng from 1968
m Peterborough 27.2.60 Isabella M. Donn teacher d of Robert C. D. Glasg

CALVERT Rhoda Margaret MA 1942 *MEd 1944
prin educ psych Dunbartonsh from 1949

CAMPBELL or Hobsley, Jane Fairlie MB ChB 1945
clin m o Enfield Lond from 1967

CAMERON Albert James *BSc 1931 *1932
d Kingston Surrey 20.7.69 *AUR* XLIII 331

CAMERON Alistair Simpson MB ChB 1937
g p Brighton S Aust from 1958

CAMERON Allan *MA 1908
d 2.5.64 *AUR* XL 395

CAMERON Allan Ross *BSc(eng) 1948
MInstMC 1957 FIEE 1962 FIMechE 1969 MBNES Lond: res eng and dep chief eng nuclear div Elliott Brothers (Lond) 1948–57; chief control and instrumentation eng/chief elect. eng Atomic Power Construct. 1957–70; chief elect. eng (Sutton) then chief eng KoRi proj Brit. Nuclear Des and Construct. 1970–76; chief eng Roject dept Assoc Nuclear Serv from 1976
m Edin 22.6.51 Sheila M. C. Dovey d of Rev Archibald C. D. MA(Edin)

CAMERON or Campbell, Anna Magdalen MA 1949
teacher Kemnay from 1968

CAMERON or McCaskie, Annie Maria Grace MA 1911
d Elgin 31.10.75 *AUR* XLVI 320

CAMERON or McKay, Annie May MA 1925
no longer on GC reg

CAMERON Charles William Morrison MB ChB 1923
d 25.8.71

CAMERON Colin *MA 1952

CAMERON or Macpherson or Bremner, Elizabeth *MA 1928
freelance journalist from 1929
resid Nethybridge

CAMERON Eva Margaret *MA 1927
since retirement in 1960 relieving posts in Engl depts Elgin acad and Lossiemouth

CAMERON Frances MA 1932 BCom 1934
MBE 1963
trg coll and s s teacher SE Nigeria with Presb Ch 1938–68; teacher Banchory acad 1968–71; retd

CAMERON Francis MA 1922
head teacher: Skene Street s Aber 1948–57, Sunnybank s Aber 1957–62; retd
d 17.11.81

CAMERON George Gordon MA 1925 DD 1962
C of S min: Glenburn ch Paisley 1958–69, assoc min St Columba's, Pont St Lond 1970–75
d Edin 20.11.80 *AUR* XLIX 67

CAMERON Hugh Fraser MB CM 1890
no longer on GC reg

CAMERON Iain Angus BSc(agr) 1951
chief agr off. Lusaka, Zambia 1966–69; proj co-ordinator HIDB Inv from 1969

CAMERON Ian *MA 1952
asst c clerk Selkirk 1968–70, town clerk Linlithgow 1970–75; dep dir admin Stirling dist c from 1975
m Edin 3.4.65 Kathleen A. Beevers insur clerkess d of John C. B. Edin

CAMERON Iona McDonald *MA 1955

CAMERON or Milton, Isabel Jean BSc(agr) 1953
resid Deskford

CAMERON or Grant, Isabella Mary *MA 1944
teacher Fr Inv acad from 1969

CAMERON James BSc(eng) 1945
Dip Internat Man. (NW Univ USA) 1968
Rugby: commercial man. Power Generation group Eng Elect. Co 1966–68, contr dir GEC Turbine Generators 1968–77; reg dir GEC Turbine Generators Seoul S Korea from 1977

CAMERON James *BSc 1939 DSc 1957
FIMM 1972
tech advis uranium resources (field expert) of IAE Agency of UN, Turkey, Philippines, Uruguay, Egypt, Ecuador, Somalia 1962–68; tech advis uranium resources HQ for IAEA Vienna from 1968
d Vienna 2.4.80

CAMERON James McKilligan MA 1949 Dip Ed 1950
head Fraserburgh N p s from 1969

CAMERON or Mitchell, Jane Thomasina MA 1927
resid Banff

CAMERON or Hobbes, Janet Seaton MB ChB 1922
retd; resid Birm

CAMERON Jean Bremner *MA 1930

CAMERON or Stokes, Jeannie Rose-Innes MA 1915
d Sutton 19.1.77

CAMERON Jessie Mortimer MA 1933 BSc 1934
teacher maths/sc h s for girls Aber till 1972; retd; resid Peterculter

CAMERON or Ross, Joan Duncan BSc(agr) 1950
teacher: sc Auchmuty 1959–61, biol Invergordon 1973–74, asst prin guid 1974–75, prin guid from 1975

CAMERON John MA 1939
teacher Dingwall acad from 1971
d Inv 22.7.73

CAMERON John Andrew MB ChB 1933
g p New Pitsligo till 1966
resid Grantown-on-Spey

CAMERON John Brunton *MA 1932 BD 1935
C of S min Flowerhill ch Airdrie 1956–76; resid Aber
d Aber 23.6.78 *AUR* XLVIII 105

CAMERON John Macphail MA 1909
d 29.7.68

CAMERON John Mowat BSc 1956

CAMERON John William Gillanders MA 1909
d Aber 9.11.65 *AUR* XLII 82

CAMERON Kenneth MA 1900
no longer on GC reg

CAMERON Kenneth Sutherland MB ChB 1951
FFARCSI 1964
consult. anaest NW Durh group hosps from 1964

CAMERON Lewis Legertwood Legg BSc(agr) 1920 DD 1953
d Edin 19.3.73 *AUR* XLV 225

CAMERON or Harvey, Lilias Margaret MA 1938
retd ill health 1958; resid Aber

CAMERON or MacLeod, Lily McKenzie MA 1912
d 1963

CAMERON Margaret Dickson MB ChB 1937

CAMERON or Baker, Margaret Robertson MA 1947
d Boston Lincs 9.4.72

CAMERON Norman Austin *MA 1929

CAMERON Patrick Stephen Gerrard MB ChB 1918
d N Shields 13.4.70 *AUR* XLIII 443

CAMERON Scott MB ChB 1941
g p Manc till 1964; Lond: m o Treasury med serv 1964–68, dept m o borough of Waltham Forest from 1968; retd

CAMERON Sheila Smith BSc 1951

CAMERON Thomas William Ferguson MB ChB 1929
g p Chatham till 1967; retd; resid Iver Heath
d 28.3.77 *AUR* XLVII 212

CAMERON or McCracken, Una Margaret Isabel MA 1925
resid Barnes, London
d 30.7.78

CAMERON William MB ChB 1901
d Bromley 7.4.66 *AUR* XLI 236

CAMERON William James MB ChB 1935
g p: Luddendenfoot till 1966, New Mills, Fife 1966–68, Halifax from 1969

CAMERON William John MA 1907
d Dunfermline 31.8.67 *AUR* XLII 179

CAMERON or Hoyte, Wilma Emelda Mary MB ChB 1953

CAMPBELL Alan Newton DSc 1929
Manit, Winnipeg: retd head chem dept 1966, retd teaching staff 1969, emeritus prof 1969

CAMPBELL Alexander Elmslie MA 1911 *BSc 1912 *MB ChB 1914
no longer on GC reg

CAMPBELL Alexander George MA 1910
d Saskatoon Canada 22.6.73

CAMPBELL Alexander Gibson *MA 1939
ABPsS 1964 MEd(Edin) 1966 FSA Scot 1968
Edin: educ psych/careers counsellor George Heriot's s 1956–64; lect Scots law corp f e serv 1964–67; sen lect leg. stud. Napier coll of sc and tech 1967–74; head dept law Napier coll of comm and tech from 1974

CAMPBELL Alistair Matheson *MA 1927
Montreal: pres Sun Life Assce Co of Canada 1962–70, chmn from 1970

CAMPBELL Angus Murdo MA 1950
head Fidigary s Lewis from 1969

CAMPBELL or MacLean, Anne Thomson MA 1929
teacher: Portsoy 1959–60, Milne's h s Fochabers 1960–69; resid Stromness
husb *d* 5.7.77

CAMPBELL or Greig, Christina Mitchell MA 1930

CAMPBELL Colin William *MA 1954

CAMPBELL Constance Gill MA 1947
BEd(Sask) 1970 MS(Syracuse NY) 1971
educ consult. publ s board of educ Saskatoon Canada from 1972

CAMPBELL or Mackay, Constance Maud *MA 1942
resid Aber
husb *d* 28.2.77

CAMPBELL David BSc 1921
d Aber 15.3.62 *AUR* XXXIX 382

CAMPBELL David Davidson BSc(mech eng) 1955 BSc(civ eng) 1956
eng asst Kincardine c c 1961–67; eng McAdam contr Aber from 1967

CAMPBELL Donald MB ChB 1922
g p Poole 1935–63; retd

CAMPBELL Donald MA 1929
C of S min Bervie from 1958
wife *d* 29.3.47

CAMPBELL Donella MA 1950
d Hamilton NZ 13.3.71 *AUR* XLIV 216

CAMPBELL or Duthie, Dorothy Frances MA 1941
resid Purley

CAMPBELL Duncan Ian *MA 1938
prin Brummana h s Lebanon till 1962; teacher gen subj comp s Lond 1962–64; lect dept educ stud. Edin 1964–73, sen lect from 1973

CAMPBELL Edward Arthur Dudley MB ChB 1937
no longer on GC reg

CAMPBELL or Macmurray, Elizabeth Hyde *MA 1915
husb deceased
stud. painting Lond, writer of fiction from 1930

CAMPBELL or Marsh, Elizabeth McCutcheon *BSc 1938

CAMPBELL or Fitzwilliam, Elizabeth Mary *MA 1947
resid Esher

CAMPBELL Ephraim MA 1933 *BSc 1936
Elgin acad: spec asst sc 1962–72; asst prin teacher guid from 1972; retd 1975

CAMPBELL or Garry, Flora MacDonald *MA 1922
Arts Council Award (*Bennygoak and Other Poems* publ 1974); resid Comrie

CAMPBELL George William Douglas MB ChB 1943
d Kingston Jamaica 30.11.78

CAMPBELL or Bowers, Grace Alexandra MA 1955
resid Tokoroa NZ

CAMPBELL Gregor Mackenzie BSc 1931 *1933
head Drumsmittal p s 1958–67
d North Kessock 25.3.67 *AUR* XLII 186

CAMPBELL or Thomson, Helen Donaldson *MA 1940
teacher maths Glasg from 1956

CAMPBELL or Chalmers, Helen Morris MA 1929
resid Aber

CAMPBELL or Tonge, Helenora Seymour MA 1910
d Thurso 28.6.66 *AUR* XLI 336

CAMPBELL or Peuschel, Ishbel Patricia MA 1951

CAMPBELL James MA 1910
d 15.4.66

CAMPBELL James Duthie BSc 1947

CAMPBELL or Burgess, Jane Wilhelma Burgess *MA 1912
temp work civ serv Edin 1956–60; retd

CAMPBELL or Smith, Jean Johnstone MA 1907
d Lerwick 9.5.68 *AUR* XLII 345

CAMPBELL Jean Menzies MA 1951
teacher Engl Dunbar g s from 1956
m Edin 12.7.63 John S. McKie MA(St And) teacher

CAMPBELL or Falconer, Jessie Catherine *MA 1947
resid Auldearn

CAMPBELL or Hall, Jessie Mackintosh MA 1946
teacher: Kinloss 1965–69, Forres from 1969

CAMPBELL John MA 1902 BL 1905
no longer on GC reg

CAMPBELL John Duthie MB ChB 1951
cas off. St Tydfil's hosp Glamorgan 1958–64; g p Luton from 1964

CAMPBELL Kenneth MA 1948

CAMPBELL Lilias Ann Turnbull MA 1909
no longer on GC reg

CAMPBELL or MacGregor, Margaret Christina MA 1913
no longer on GC reg

CAMPBELL or Maguire, Margaret Frances MA 1939

CAMPBELL or Ross, Margaret Gault *MA 1943

CAMPBELL or Watt, Margaret Jemima MA 1954
teacher Barnehurst s Kent from 1969

CAMPBELL Margaret McKay MA 1919
no longer on GC reg

CAMPBELL Marie Dorothy MA 1942
lect soc stud. RGIT Aber 1968–74; lect soc work Monash univ Melbourne Aust from 1974

CAMPBELL or Morrison, Marion Pitt *MA 1932
teacher Lat Wallace Hall acad 1941–42; teacher Fr: Benedictine convent 1942–44, Dumfries acad 1958–70

CAMPBELL or Glen, Mary Grant MA 1943
teacher: Bretby House New Malden from 1971

CAMPBELL or Crotty, Mary Sinclair MA 1942
MA(Dub) 1961
dir practical trg dept soc stud. Dub from 1959
m(2) Patrick Lynch MA(NUI) prof econ univ coll Dub(NUI) s of Daniel L. Dublin

CAMPBELL Murdo MA 1951
JP Invernesssh 1966
head: Croy s Inv 1965, Merkinch s Inv from 1975

CAMPBELL Nancy Allan MA 1952

CAMPBELL Neil MA 1952
Inv: head: Inchmore p s Kirkhill 1968–71, Tomnacross p s Kiltarlity from 1971

m Glasg 4.7.62 Janet Macleod teacher d of Norman M. Leverburgh Harris

CAMPBELL Peter MA 1910
d Forres 8.6.67 *AUR* XLII 180

CAMPBELL Robert Clark MB ChB 1955
FRCSE 1963 FRCS 1963
regist: surg ARI 1960–64, plastic surg Norwich 1964–66; sen regist plastic surg Leeds 1966–68; Robert W. Johnson fell. plastic surg univ of Miami USA 1968; consult. plastic surg Cantab from 1971

CAMPBELL Robert Mackenzie BSc 1952
dep head Helmsdale s from 1966

CAMPBELL Roderick George MA 1933
d Dingwall 20.5.80 *AUR* XLIX 68

CAMPBELL Roderick Macrae MA 1929 *MB ChB 1933
OBE 1972 FFCM 1972
Inv: dep sen admin m o 1950–62, sen admin m o North reg hosp board 1962–73

CAMPBELL Rosa Margaret BSc 1934
sen exper off. Rowett Inst Aber from 1951; resid Bieldside Aber

CAMPBELL Rosemary Elizabeth MA 1955
teacher army s Hong Kong from 1958
m Aber 10.9.60 John E. Flowers army off. s of Charles E. F. Lond

CAMPBELL Tormaid MA 1930
d –.6.66

CAMPBELL or Winter, Violet Mary BSc(agr) 1949

CAMPBELL William Beaton MA 1905
d Inverurie 30.9.71 *AUR* XLIV 316

CAMPBELL William Henry McKay BSc(agr) 1950
area agr advis NOSCA

CAMPBELL William Robert Hugh *MA 1933
prin teacher classics Fortrose acad from 1964; retd 1965

CANT or Young, Mary McPherson MA 1944
MA(Alta) 1968 PhD(Alta) 1974
asst prof depts anthrop and relig stud. Alta Edmonton

CANT Ronald Fraser MB ChB 1948
consult. radiol Isle of Thanet group of hosps from 1958

CANTLAY Alexander MA 1931

CANTLAY or Mutch, Isabella Christian MA 1947

CANTLAY or Bartlet, Isabella Margaret MA 1917

CANTLAY Violet May MA 1922
retd 1961; resid Blackpool

CANTLAY William John BSc(agr) 1943
teacher: Northfield s Aber 1960–67, Laurencekirk s 1967
d 29.11.77

CANTLIE James MB ChB 1942
g p Christchurch Dorset from 1954
m Bournemouth 22.6.71 Eva von Hofmann secy d of Rolf von H. BSc(Berlin) Esslingen-Nechar W Ger

CANTLIE Keith *MA 1908
Kt
d Lond 29.4.77

CANTLIE Neil *MB ChB 1914
d Lond 16.5.75 *AUR* XLVI 321

CARCARY Mary McLeod *MA 1945

CARDNO George Watt MB ChB 1951
g p Howe of Fife from 1956
m Kilmacolm 14.9.63 Kathleen Calder MB ChB(Glas) d of Rev Alastair S. C. TD MA(Edin) Kilmacolm

CARDNO Harry Spark BSc 1942
d Aber 13.10.80

CARDNO Ian Robertson MA 1931
head Culter s Peterculter from 1966; retd 1974

CARDNO James Alexander *MA 1938
MA(Cantab) 1946 FBPsS 1962 FAPsS 1966 FAPA 1972
assoc prof psych univ Tasmania 1961–65, prof from 1965

CARDNO James Halliday MA 1912 BSc 1915
d Peterhead 3.6.67 *AUR* XLII 181

CARDNO James Stuart MA 1930
asst dir educ Kincardinesh 1963–70, dep dir from 1970

CARDNO John Alexander MB ChB 1931 ᶜMD 1938
retd 1973; resid Kinross

CARDNO Rachel MA 1943
teacher: Winnipeg and New Westminster, Canada 1959–60, Knox acad Haddington 1960–67, Dunnikier s Kirkcaldy from 1967

CARGILL William McHardy MA 1930
teacher maths: Fyvie 1958–66, Turriff acad 1966–72; retd

CARLE Annie Cook MA 1930
teacher: spec asst Fr Harlaw acad Aber from 1962

CARLE or Weir, Jeanie Strath MA 1918

CARLE John Leslie MB ChB 1932
d Southend-on-Sea 5.7.63 *AUR* XL 303

CARLISLE Alan PhD 1954
sen res off. Imper Forest Inst Oxford 1956–58;

prin scient off. Nature Conserv Merlewood res stat Grange-over-Sands 1958–68; progr man. Canadian For. Serv Petawawa for. exper stat Chalk River Ontario from 1968

CARMICHAEL Dennis Dickinson MB ChB 1950
univ of NC Chapel Hill NC USA: resid in psychiat 1958–61, fell. in child psychiat 1961–63, asst clin prof psychiat from 1966; Charlotte NC: child psychiat mental health center 1963–66, private pract child psychiat from 1964

CARMICHAEL John Harald *MA 1929 BSc 1931
retd 1973; resid Badenscoth

CARMICHAEL Norman Bayne MA 1930 MB ChB 1941
g p Derby from 1947
d Derby 22.2.78 *AUR* XLVII 358

CARMICHAEL William BSc(for) 1948
FLS 1965
Tanzania: reg for. off. Mwanza 1960–62, Tabora 1963–64, Mwanza 1964–65, conserv for. Arusha 1965–69; Edin: stud. New coll 1962–63, 1967 and 1970, C of S asst min Holy Trin ch 1970–71, min Restalrig ch from 1971

CARNEGIE Agnes Crighton *MA 1934
High s for girls Aber (Harlaw acad from 1971): prin teacher Engl 1957–64, dep head 1964–72; lect univ of Sacred Heart Tokyo 1973–75; retd

CARNEGIE Austen Ogston *MA 1951
teacher: Northfield s Aber 1956–60; Auchterderran j h s Cardenden: prin Engl 1960–70, dep head from 1970

CARNEGIE Charles BSc 1914
d Perth 13.7.73 *AUR* XLV 317

CARNEGIE Isabel Margaret MA 1937

CARNEGIE James MA 1935

CARNEGIE Leslie Thompson BL 1941
county clerk and other posts Dumfries from 1954; clerk: SW Scotland Water Board from 1960, SW Scotland dev auth from 1972; chief exec Dumfries and Galloway reg c from 1974

CARNEGIE-SMITH George BSc(eng) 1933
Bedford: sen eng MOT 1964–70; dept environment: sen eng 1970–72, prin prof and tech off. from 1972; retd 1974
d Bedford 10.9.77

CARNIE Frank Alexander *BSc 1935
rector Banchory acad 1967–77; retd

CARNIE or Dawson, Margaret Isabel MA 1929

CARNIE Mary Helen MA 1920
Dun: teacher 1921–37, sc 1940–59, retd; resid Kintore
m Dun 1.7.37 George Campbell MA(Edin) teacher s of Hugh C. Melvich

CARNIE or Fullerton, Maud Mary Adams BSc 1937
resid Trail BC Canada

CARR or Elder, Agnes Lawson Stewart MA 1943
resid Aber

CARR Thomas Lauder MB ChB 1942 ChM 1956
consult. orthop surg ARI from 1954

CARRIE Alistair Ramsay BSc(eng) 1951

CARRIE James MB ChB 1924
d 25.5.64 *AUR* XL 399

CARRIE William Wilson BL 1940
d Aber 23.9.80 *AUR* XLIX 70

CARSLAKE William Dodd BSc(for) 1955
FBCS 1972
asst conserv for. Bo Sierra Leone 1957–61; IBM Lond from 1961

CARSWELL Robert Finlayson BSc(eng) 1945

CARTER Andrew McKenzie MA 1951

CARVER Evelyn Beckett Faber MA 1924
no longer on GC reg

CARVER John George Campbell MA 1926
head Sandhead s Wigtown till 1970; retd; wife *d* 1966
m(2) Glasg 12.7.69 Jessie B. M. Stevenson or Buchanan BSc(Glas) teacher d of Archibald M. S. Paisley

CASEBY Joy Murray Rodger *MA 1948

CASSIE Alexander MA 1937

CASSIE Alexander Whyte MA 1897 MB ChB 1901
d 29.6.63 *AUR* XL 198

CASSIE or Walker, Barbara Bathea MA 1927
resid Bexhill

CASSIE or Routledge, Elizabeth Mary MA 1951

CASSIE Francis George Monro BSc(eng) 1947
d Aber 6.3.76

CASSIE George MB ChB 1952 DPH 1957
MFCM 1973
Lanarksh: asst sen m o 1960–66, sen m o from 1966; commun med spec Greater Glasgow health board 1974

CASSIE Gordon Fordyce MB ChB 1944 ChM 1958
Gorham-Peters res fell. Harvard med s USA 1957–58; consult. surg Queen Eliz II hosp Welwyn Garden City from 1962

CASSIE or Henderson, Joyce MA 1947
teacher: Kent till 1957, Bexley from 1969

CASSIE Margaret MA 1934
teacher Walker Road p s Aber 1936–76; retd

CASSIE or Johnston, Margaret Duff BSc 1943
resid Richmond Surrey

CASTLE or Hay, Margaret Anne MA 1948
Dip. in Reading Dev (OU) 1977
teacher: Turriff p s, Bredalbane p s 1962–65, Banff acad 1965–72, remed Banff p s from 1972

CASTLE or Kilgour, Frances Christina MA 1931
resid Banchory

CATO George Christopher *MA 1931 BD 1938
sen lect phys univ of Natal, Durban from 1963; retd 1975

CATTANACH Alexander Belmont Leslie BSc 1930

CATTANACH or Tough, Edith Julienne *MA 1954
teacher Fr Oakhill s Stoke on Trent 1971–75

CATTANACH or Petrie, Janet *MA 1935
teacher Gordonstoun till 1969; resid Elgin

CATTANACH Ronald Gibson BL 1951
advoc in Aber

CATTANACH or Milne, Sandra Isobel Don MA 1955
teacher Burnside s Aber 1956–62
m Aber 4.4.61 Thornton G. Milne chartered surv s of George S. M. New York

CATTERALL Sydney MB ChB 1940 MD 1954
Assoc MBPS 1960 FRCPsych 1973
psychiat Edmonton 1963–67, consult. psychiat Liff hosp Dun from 1968

CATTO Alexander Godsman MA 1905 BD 1908
d Edin 21.5.67 *AUR* XLII 345

CATTO Anne *MA 1921
retd teaching Maxwellton s Dumfries 1966; resid Aber
d 4.6.77

CATTO David *MA 1926
teacher Engl, prin Engl, dep head Frederick Street s s Aber 1927–64; retd
m Aber 29.6.40 Annie J. Connon d of James C. Dufftown

CATTO Forbes Shepherd MB ChB 1923
d 15.2.76 *AUR* XLVI 416

CATTO Gavin Anderson BSc(agr) 1939
JP(Perthsh) 1967 OBE 1968 FRAgrS 1969 (found. fell.)
prov dir E of Scot. coll of agr Edin from 1967
d Bridge of Earn 19.4.75 *AUR* XLVI 240

CATTO Gordon Duffus BSc(eng) 1951
CEng MIMechE 1966
proj eng Scottish & Newcastle Breweries Edin 1961–67; sen mech eng Andrews-Weatherfoil (Scot.) Paisley from 1968
m Edin 10.9.60 Agnes J. W. Marshall secy d of James M. Hamilton

CATTO Henry Gray BL 1938
Aber c c: solic 1960–72, dep c clerk 1972–75; clerk NE Scot River Purif Bd from 1975

CATTO or Cormack, Isabella Ogg MA 1932
d Aber 11.1.68 *AUR* XLII 371

CATTO James Alexander BCom 1923
d 20.3.71

CATTO James Rankine Wilson MB ChB 1942
g p Coventry from 1947

CATTO John BL 1947
d Edin 22.2.67 *AUR* XLII 373

CATTO Laura Deas MB ChB 1924

CATTO William Dawson MB ChB 1939
MRCGP—founder member
g p Aber from 1946
wife *d* –.7.78

CAY David Robert Bellamy MA 1949 LLB 1952
advoc Scot. from 1954

CAY Edward MB ChB 1934
d Edin 8.12.74

CESSFORD Edward Allan Macpherson MA 1940 *MEd 1944
AMBPsS 1960
dep prin psych Ayrsh from 1973

CHADWICK John Peter MB ChB 1950
m o Brit Alum. Comp Awaso, Ghana from 1952

CHALMERS Adeline Knox BSc 1933
d Sittingbourne 7.4.78

CHALMERS Alan Ferguson *BSc(eng) 1953
AFRAeS 1960
b Dunblane 12.10.31
aerodynamicist to asst chief stressman Hayes 1953–62; sen progr to div man. Boreham Wood 1962–73, marketing exec from 1973

CHALMERS Alexander *MA 1930
teacher Loughborough coll 1946–68; retd

CHALMERS Alexander MB ChB 1931
MRCGP 1952 C St J 1968
g p Sittingbourne

CHALMERS Alice Lesley *MA 1931
retd 1970; resid Stevenage

CHALMERS Audrey Miller BSc(agr) 1949
agr econ NOSCA till 1969
m Broughty Ferry 12.8.69 Lachlan G. Low-Mitchell

CHALMERS Davena Annie *MA 1947
prin teacher mod lang: Bridgwater girls' g s Somerset 1962–68, Hamilton acad 1968–76; prin teacher French Peterhead acad from 1976

CHALMERS Derek MB ChB 1954
regist ARI 1958–59; Edin RI: regist 1960, sen regist 1961–63; dir med affairs E. R. Squibb & Sons Twickenham from 1964; dermat Gt Ormond St hosp from 1969

CHALMERS or Stewart, Dorothy BSc 1925 *1926
resid Cults

CHALMERS Edmund MA 1912

CHALMERS Frederick Grant Duncan MA 1916
no longer on GC reg

CHALMERS George Quinton MA 1919
no longer on GC reg

CHALMERS or Reid, Isobel Mary Smart MB ChB 1942
d nr Thirsk 31.7.67 *AUR* XLII 186

CHALMERS James Alastair MB ChB 1945
g p Westcliff-on-Sea from 1951

CHALMERS James Durno MB ChB 1945
MRCGP 1963
g p Insch from 1952

CHALMERS or Stewart, Jeannie Ann Gordon Fenton MA 1924
no longer on GC reg

CHALMERS John Taylor MA 1930
head Hatton Fintray s from 1951; retd

CHALMERS or Fraser, Maggie MA 1926
resid Oldmeldrum

CHALMERS or Spira, Margaret MA 1922

CHALMERS or MacKay, Margaret MA 1944

CHALMERS Margaret Irvin PhD 1951
biochem Rowett res inst Aber from 1946

CHALMERS or Nairn, Margaret Johnstone MA 1938
resid East Sheen, Lond

CHALMERS or Ainscow, Mary Ann MA 1912 MB ChB 1916
d Cumberland 9.5.69 *AUR* XLII 328

CHALMERS or Fraser, Mary Ewen MB ChB 1943
med asst dept obst and gyn Aberd from 1964, clin lect cervical cytology

CHALMERS or Gray, Norah Ellis MA 1944
resid Cape Town

CHALMERS or Inglis, Norma MA 1928
resid Portsoy

CHALMERS Robert Westland MB ChB 1909
no longer on GC reg

CHALMERS Theodore MB ChB 1906
d Inv 1.2.73 *AUR* XLV 223

CHALMERS William Gordon BL 1948
Edin: sen proc-fiscal dep 1959–63; sen leg. asst in Crown Office 1963–67; dep Crown Ag 1967–74, Crown Ag from 1974

CHAMBERLAIN Charles Deryck BSc 1944
DipEd(Oxon) 1965
teacher maths the Priory s for boys Shrewsbury from 1965

CHAMBERS Graham Peter *MA 1950

CHAMBERS Henry Daniel MB ChB 1932 ᶜMD 1938

CHANCE Robert Maxwell MB ChB (1910 *MD 1912
no longer on GC reg

CHANNON Anthony Guy *BSc 1952

CHANOCK Leon MB ChB 1925
lect surg anat univ of Cape Town from 1940

CHAPMAN or Esslemont, Isobel Barbara MA 1946
teacher Fyvie from 1963

CHAPMAN or Gibbs, Mabel Scott MA 1919
no longer on GC reg

CHAPMAN Wallace Milne MB ChB 1936
g p Shaftesbury 1938–73; retd
d 1981

CHAPMAN William MB ChB 1909
d S Af 16.7.62 *AUR* XL 78

CHAPMAN William Gordon *MA 1950
d Oxford 9.2.68 *AUR* XLII 374

CHARLES Audrey Elsie MA 1950
head teacher Aber: Cairncry inf s 1967–69, Braeside inf s from 1969

CHATTERJI or Ghosh or Sutherland, Leila (Savoja) MB ChB 1922

CHEN Foong Kong MA 1917 MB ChB 1921

CHEN Chung PhD 1944

CHESSAR Lilias Robina MA 1910
retd headmistress; resid Turriff

CHESSOR George Clinton MB ChB 1943
g p Alloa from 1955

CHEYNE Agnes Christina MA 1923
teacher Engl Ellon acad 1959–61; retd; resid Inverurie

CHEYNE Alexander *MA 1912
d 23.3.76 *AUR* XLVII 286

CHEYNE Alexander Ian MB ChB 1954
DPM 1966 MRCPsych 1972
g p: Littleport 1958–64, Dalkeith 1964–65; regist Crichton royal hosp Dumfries 1965–67; psychiat Hillcrest hosp Adelaide S Aust 1967–68; Gartnavel royal hosp Glas: sen regist 1968–70, consult. psychiat from 1971

CHEYNE Alexander Ingram MB ChB 1923 MD 1940
d Leamington Spa 23.4.72 *AUR* XLV 126

CHEYNE Alfred William Harper MB ChB 1914 DPH 1920

CHEYNE Douglas Gordon MB ChB 1910 MD 1914 DPH 1914
d Lond 26.6.66 *AUR* XLI 336

CHEYNE Eleanor Rose Lornie MA 1926
no longer on GC reg

CHEYNE George Collie MA 1907 BSc(agr) 1909
d Maud 6.1.65 *AUR* XLI 54

CHEYNE George Duguid MA 1927
SSC
ptnr W H Mill, McLeod & Rose WS Edin from 1931

CHEYNE Janet Forbes MA 1911
no longer on GC reg

CHEYNE or Leslie, Lorna Birnie MA 1941

CHEYNE Margaret Annetta Boon *MA 1921
no longer on GC reg

CHEYNE William George MB ChB 1921
d Cosham Portsmouth 24.12.73 *AUR* XLV 447

CHINN Gertrude Annie MA 1912
d Aber 21.3.65 *AUR* XLI 148

CHINNIAH Samuel Ernest Nalla-nayagam MB ChB 1928

CHISHOLM Alexander Gordon MB ChB 1952
DPM(Leeds) 1962 MRCPsych 1971
sen h m o De La Pole hosp 1963–71; consult. ch psychiat dept ch and fam psychiat N Tees gen hosp Stockton-on-Tees from 1971
m Hull 1962 Margaret W. Jenkins MA 1955 *qv*

CHISHOLM or McDermott, Christina Isobel MA 1946
teacher geog St David's h s Dalkeith from 1970

CHISHOLM Donald MA 1949

CHISHOLM Fanny Bisset BSc 1926
d 7.2.78

CHISHOLM Georgina MA 1920
no longer on GC reg

CHISHOLM or Innes, Margaret Ann Jamieson MA 1933

CHISHOLM Ronald Harry Eddie *MA 1949
Edin: head mod langs Melville coll 1960–72, head Ger/Russian dept Daniel Stewart's and Melville coll from 1972

CHITTY Edward Charles *MB ChB 1924
FBOA(Emeritus) 1966
consult. surg St Stephen's hosp Lond 1948–60; retd

CHRISTIE Albert MA 1932 MB ChB 1936
consult. anaest Glasg from 1939; retd 1977
m Glasg 9.12.39 Eva E. Walker d of Robert W. Aber

CHRISTIE or Conacher, Alexa Margaret Davidson MA 1952
teacher Aber 1958–62 and from 1971
husb *d* 8.10.76

CHRISTIE Alexander BSc 1953

CHRISTIE Alexander Wesley *MA 1920
d Huntly 4.3.75

CHRISTIE Alexander William *MA 1948
prin scient off. trans and road res lab D Tp Crowthorne from 1955

CHRISTIE Alexandrina Margaret *MA 1932
head Engl dept Nairn acad 1943–71; retd

CHRISTIE Andrew MA LLB 1951
solic Aber
m Aber 16.10.59 Hazel L. Souter chirop d of Charles M. S. Aber

CHRISTIE Andrew Barnett MA 1930 MB ChB 1935 ᶜMD 1939
DCH 1948 FRCP 1972 FFCM 1972
head dept infect diseases Liv 1946–74; prof infect diseases Benghazi from 1975

CHRISTIE or McDonald, Betty Margaret MA 1953
Nairn: teacher Millbank s 1967–73, remed 1973–77, remed Rosebank s from 1977

CHRISTIE Charles Mowat *BSc(eng) 1954
MInstMC 1975
Wiggins Teape Stoneywood paper mill: head spec investig sect. tech dept 1960–62, head paper dev tech dept 1962–65; instrument man. ICI paints div Hyde group Cheshire from 1965

CHRISTIE or Ure, Dorothy Margaret Jane MA 1944 *1964
res asst Aberd 1964–66; educ psych: Aberdeensh educ dept 1967–71, Aber city educ dept from 1972

CHRISTIE Elizabeth MA 1923
teacher: Alves s s 1944–54, Lhanbryde j s s 1954–56, East End p s Elgin 1956–66; retd

CHRISTIE Elizabeth MA 1926
JP 1970
teacher: Dunnottar s Stonehaven 1940–67; retd

CHRISTIE Forbes Grant BCom 1926
no longer on GC reg

CHRISTIE Frances Rumgay MB ChB 1945 DPH 1963
FMFCM 1972
dept m o: Banff c c 1963–66, Aber c c 1966–69, sen m o child health Grampian health board from 1969

CHRISTIE George Alexander Geddes BSc(agr) 1952
farm. Fordyce from 1952

CHRISTIE George Davidson BCom 1924
no longer on GC reg

CHRISTIE Gwendoline MA 1955

CHRISTIE Harcourt Lawrence MA 1925
d Aber 16.2.69 *AUR* XLIII 214

CHRISTIE Harry Donald MB ChB 1926
g p Lond retd; resid Stonehaven

CHRISTIE or Thomson, Isabella Mary MA 1935
teacher part-time Kirkhill s Aber 1969–71

CHRISTIE James Gray MB ChB 1908
no longer on GC reg

CHRISTIE James McDonald MB ChB 1936
g p Leeds from 1941

CHRISTIE James Walker Melvin MB ChB 1931
retd 1971; resid Betwys-y-Coed N Wales

CHRISTIE John Duncan *MA 1932
teacher maths Wallace Hall acad Dumfriessh 1967–71; retd

CHRISTIE Joseph Dryden MA 1938
BA(Lond) 1972
RN 1948–64, teacher Dun: Grove acad 1964–65, Kingsway tech coll from 1965
d Dun 1975 *AUR* XLIV 417

CHRISTIE Lyall Lees BCom 1923
MCIT
retd 1962; resid Herne Bay

CHRISTIE or Dalgleish, Mabel Alexandra MA 1929

CHRISTIE or Cooke, Margaret Anderson MA 1948
resid Lossiemouth

CHRISTIE or Duncan, Mary MA 1924
d 23.11.66

CHRISTIE or Brown, Mary Burnett MA 1939
teacher Findochty 1940–42, Loreburn St John's Dumfries 1942–46, Cogrieburn Dumfriessh 1946–50; NZ: clerk soc security dept Auckland 1952, teacher Gisborne 1953, part time Te Anau and Manapouri from 1953
m Otorohanga North Is NZ 21.8.54 John A. B. Brown bushman, carpenter and hotel man. (now deceased) s of John A. B. B. Riverton Southland NZ

CHRISTIE or MacKellaig, Mary Jane MA 1924
teacher Nethybridge 1930–31; resid Fort William

CHRISTIE Reginald Cecil MA 1946 LLB 1949
advoc Aber from 1949
d Aber 13.4.80

CHRISTIE Robert Alexander MB ChB 1951
d Manitoba 11.2.62 *AUR* XXXIX 386

CHRISTIE or Henderson, Sheila Isobel *MA 1928
resid Oxford

CHRISTIE Thomas John MA 1947
shoe retail bus. from 1947; resid Petworth

CHRISTIE William MA 1921
d Aber 26.1.66 *AUR* XLII 85

CHRISTIE William *MA 1925
PhD(St And) 1968
HMIS: western div 1946–54, north eastern div 1954–63; retd; resid Dun
d 27.9.79

CHRISTIE William *MA 1929 LLB 1976
JP
head Summerhill s s Aber 1961–67; retd; law app Aber from 1976

CHRISTIE William BSc 1952
chief works chem Whakatane board mills, NZ 1966–73; prod. supt from 1973

CHRISTIE William Sam George MB ChB 1924
retd 1963; resid Aber

CHRYSTALL Dorothy Mitchell MB ChB 1935
g p Ladywell med centre Edin from 1971

CHRYSTALL or McGregor, Margaret McGregor MB ChB 1949
MRCGP 1960
g p Turriff from 1966

CLAMP or McHardy, Gertrude PhD 1932
resid Pulborough

CLAPPERTON or Lock, Marian Nichol *MA 1930
teacher: QASM Moascar garrison Egypt 1951,

Aber 1952, Nairobi 1957–59, Surrey 1963–67; resid Wimbledon

CLAPPERTON Mary Frederica MA 1904
no longer on GC reg

CLAPPERTON Thomas MB ChB 1907
d 10.12.69

CLARK or Reid, Agnes Mary MA 1925
d in Australia

CLARK Alexander John MA 1954

CLARK Alexander John Ogilvie MA 1946

CLARK Alexander Mackenzie BSc 1945
res eng (electronics) Ferranti Edin from 1948

CLARK Alexander William *MA 1924
head Darvel h g s Ayrsh 1947–68; retd; part time tut. double bass Ayr c c 1968

CLARK Andrew MA 1906
no longer on GC reg

CLARK Ann MA 1906
no longer on GC reg

CLARK or McDonald, Anna Bella MA 1933
teacher Dun from 1959; retd; resid Dun

CLARK Anne Elizabeth MA 1937

CLARK or Cooper, Anne Paterson MA 1948
teacher Broomhill p s Aber from 1968
husb *d* 6.10.69

CLARK Annie MA 1933
teacher Aber h s for girls 1944–71; retd
d Aber 7.10.77

CLARK Annie Simpson MB ChB 1924
g p Leyton Lond from 1935; retd; resid Aber

CLARK or Brennan, Catherine Johana MB ChB 1923 DPH 1924
g p Dowlais Glam; clin asst Merthyr and Cynon Valley Mid Glam; retd 1961

CLARK Charles MB ChB 1943
barrister-at-law Middle Temple 1957: HM coroner county of Essex from 1960

CLARK Charles Alexander *MA 1941
prin teacher hist Kirkwall 1956–62; lect econ RGIT Aber 1962–67; head econ dept Dun coll of commerce from 1967
m Aber 24.7.56 Norah C. Milne teacher

CLARK Charles Grant ᶜMB ChB 1953 MD 1960 *ChM 1966
sen lect surg Aberd 1961–64; reader surg Leeds 1964–67; prof surg univ coll hosp Lond from 1967

CLARK or Crabb, Christianna Amy MA 1911
d Aber 7.5.73 *AUR* XLV 224

CLARK David Findlay *MA 1951 PhD 1975
FBPsS 1969
prin clin psych Leicester area psych serv 1960–66; consult. clin psych Grampian HB for mentally handicapped Ladysbridge hosp Banff and clin sen lect dept ment health Aberd from 1966

CLARK or Watt, Dorothy Cameron MA 1946
resid Alford

CLARK or Stawart, Elma Hay *MA 1941
resid Berwick-on-Tweed

CLARK or Dean, Elspet Forrest MA 1929
resid Aber

CLARK Francis MB ChB 1949

CLARK George Norman *MB ChB 1927
Alberta: g p Coal Valley 1954–58, Morinville from 1958; retd 1970
coroner Province Alberta from 1970

CLARK George Ogilvie *MA 1915 *BSc 1920
d Aber 24.10.66 *AUR* XLII 84

CLARK George Ogilvie MB ChB 1946
consult. surg Wolverhampton & Dudley group of hosps from 1957

CLARK Hannah Hendry MA 1936
teacher inf: Sandhaven p s 1937–40, Aber: King St p s 1941–68, Ashley Rd p s 1968–79; retd

CLARK Helen Smith MA 1954

CLARK Ian Jardine *MA 1937
prin teacher mod lang Hilton acad Aber 1968–79; retd 1979
wife *d* 1963
m(2) Aber 5.8.75 Katherine M. Keith or Nicol nurs nurse d of James K. Clola

CLARK Isabella MA 1933
dep head p dept Banchory acad from 1965

CLARK Isabella Ewen MA 1927
no longer on GC reg

CLARK James MB ChB 1904 *MD 1907
d 13.12.71 *AUR* XLIV 426

CLARK James MA 1917 BSc 1920
rector Invergordon acad 1939–59; retd; resid Aber

CLARK James BL 1925
proc-fiscal Dun 1946–64; retd; resid Jedburgh
d 19.10.80

CLARK James *MA 1950
Ontario civ serv comm: sen staff dev off. 1963–72, policy dev off. 1972–76, chief exec dev from 1977

CLARK James Alexander Macdonald MB ChB 1907 MD 1913
resid Holsworthy
d 19.2.74 *AUR* XLV 446

CLARK James George *MA 1930
d 27.4.67

CLARK James McKillican MB ChB 1906
no longer on GC reg

CLARK James Reid *MEd 1947
CBE 1966 FEIS 1967
dir educ city of Aber 1957–75; retd

CLARK Jean Marion Findlay MA 1927

CLARK or MacIntyre, Jenette Annabelle Graham MA 1924

CLARK or Bisset, Jessie Ann MA 1922

CLARK John *MA 1923 *BSc 1924

CLARK John BSc(agr) 1925
d Aber 31.7.75 *AUR* XLVI 322

CLARK John Gordon BSc 1949

CLARK Leah MA 1917
no longer on GC reg

CLARK or Stewart, Lillias Jean Fowlie MA 1923
resid Aber

CLARK Lillie Dunbar MA 1945
teacher Aber: High s for girls till 1966; inf mistress: Seaton p s 1966–70, asst head Mile End p s from 1970

CLARK or Dey, Magdalene MA 1945 Dip Ed 1958
teacher St. Margaret's s for girls Aber 1964–69; lect Engl Speech and Drama coll of educ Aber from 1969

CLARK or Abel, Margaret Rutherford MB ChB 1937
retd; resid Norwich

CLARK or Aitken, Mary Ann MA 1928
teacher Dun coll of comm 1968–70; retd 1970

CLARK Mary Anton MA 1912
resid Blairgowrie

CLARK or Hutcheon, Moira MA 1954
Inv: lect Engl/soc stud. tech coll 1963–66, asst head Cent s from 1970, head teacher Cent p s from 1976

CLARK Muriel Mary MA 1948
teacher maths Turriff acad from 1949

CLARK Norman Stuart BSc 1933 MB ChB 1936 *MD 1955
FRCP 1964
reader ch health Aberd from 1964

CLARK Norman Walker McNicol MA 1933
d Edin –.8.73 *AUR* XLV 449

CLARK Robert James MB ChB 1916 DPH 1929
d Grappenhall –.12.70 *AUR* XLIV 210

CLARK Robert Towers MA 1922 BCom 1924
Fell. Inst Admin/Comm of S Af 1935
retd prin tech coll E London S Af 1964; lect: Natal tech coll 1965–74, univ of Durban-Westville from 1975
d Durban S Af 5.3.80

CLARK or Gibson, Rona Williamina McLennan MA 1936
teacher: p dept Turriff acad 1962–69, dep head from 1969; retd 1975

CLARK Victoria Elizabeth *MA 1915

CLARK William Duncan BCom 1924
no longer on GC reg

CLARKE Agnes Dorothea Barr MA 1940
secy in Aberd from 1948, admin asst Aberd from 1974

CLARKE Alison MB ChB 1941
MRCGP 1953 FRCGP 1970
m o (part time) stud. health serv Glas till 1971; m o (part time) reg m o SHHD Glasg; clin tut. undergrad med educ Glas from 1972

CLARKE or Niven, Barbara Dorothy Theresa MA 1951

CLARKE Christine Lyon MA 1917
d Aber 15.9.69 *AUR* XLIII 329

CLARKE Edward Colin BSc(for) 1950

CLARKE Ian Anderson MA 1911 BSc(agr) 1912
d 1939

CLARKE John MB ChB 1923
hon surg Porth & dist hosp from 1928

CLARKE John Innes *MA 1950 PhD 1956
FRGS
prof geog univ coll Sierra Leone 1963–65; reader geog Durh 1965–68; visiting prof univ of Wisconsin USA 1967; prof geog Durh from 1968

CLARKE William Alexander MB ChB 1931

CLARKSON Alexander MA 1928 BCom 1929
d Aber 13.9.70 *AUR* XLIV 110

CLARKSON or Hynes, Marion Mackay Petrie MB ChB 1937
d 9.1.69

CLAY Arthur John Mackenzie BSc(for) 1953
for. off. London Yorksh motorway 1957–60; land-

scape consult. 1960–65; Canberra: arboriculturist with parks and gardens 1966–73, landscape des and consult. horticulturist from 1973

CLAY Austin Cuthbert MB ChB 1940 MD 1942
g p Aber from 1945; retd
d 22.12.81

CLEGHORN Robert Allen DSc 1932
FRCP(Can) 1965 FRCPsych 1972
dem dept med Toronto 1933–46; major RCAMC No. 1 res lab Italy, NW Europe 1943–45; dir lab exper therap and asst to prof psychiat Allan mem inst Montreal 1946–64; dir Allan mem inst, chmn dept psychiat McG univ Montreal 1964–70; hon consult. McG univ from 1971; emeritus prof
m Aber 2.4.32 Sheena M. Marnoch BA(Oxon) d of Sir John M. MA 1888 *qv*(I, II, III)

CLIFFORD Margaret MA 1951
d 30.5.73

CLIFFORD Sydney Charles MB ChB 1950
g p Royston Barnsley from 1956

CLOUSTON John Herbert Thomas MA 1936
d Orkney 29.11.75

CLOUSTON or Jones, Sheila MB ChB 1955
part time locum health and welfare dept Aber 1959–73; retd
m Aber 4.7.53 Rodney Jones BSc(Liv) marine biol s of Henry J. Cheltenham

CLOW Archibald
MA BSc 1929 *1931 PhD 1934 DSc 1940
scient and tech historian sen consult. BBC/OU from 1970

CLOW or Tulloch, Enid Matilda Murray
MB ChB 1937 DPH 1942
Bristol: asst s m o 1965–70, sen dept m o from 1970
husb *d* 4.1.65

CLUBB Alexander William MB ChB 1955
MRCOG 1964 FRCOG 1977
capt RAMC 1958–61; regist obst and gyn City gen hosp Sheffield 1961–64; sen regist united Birm and reg hosps 1964–66; consult. obst and gyn N Staffordsh hosp centre from 1966

CLUBB or Leatherby, Ethel Forbes MA 1950
secy pers asst. High Wycombe from 1957

CLUNAS or Fraser, Dorothy Isobel MA 1945

CLUNIE James Gourlay PhD 1952
no longer on GC reg

CLUNIE Thomas MB ChB 1924

CLYNE Andrew Christopher MB ChB 1944
no longer on GC reg

CLYNE Henry MA 1920 MB ChB 1924

COBBAN Andrew Christopher MB ChB 1944
g p Aber 1952–54; Alberta: Barrhead 1954–56, Westlock from 1956

COBBY John England BSc(for) 1944
conserv for. Nairobi 1960–64; dist for. off. Cape Town 1964–74; reg dir for. King Williams Town S Af.
wife *d* Cape Town 22.11.70
m(2) Cape Town 15.9.73 June E. Morecroft or Chisholm travel consult. d of Herbert T. M. Hoylake

COBURN Alexander Milne Wilson MB ChB 1941
g p Seaton Devon from 1946 and div surg St John ambul brig.

COCCALIS Nicholas *MA 1952
MEd(Alta) 1968 PhD(Alta) 1970
Canada: teacher Calgary publ sen h schools 1959–66, Alta 1966–70; McG univ: asst prof 1970–76, assoc prof from 1976

COCHAR William Smith MB ChB 1921
retd 1959; resid Ashton-u-Lyne
m Manc 6.4.33 Eleanor J. Wallace teacher d of Alexander W. MRCS Ashton-u-Lyne

COCHRAN David Gordon LLB 1925
d Aber 3.1.72 *AUR* XLIV 430

COCHRAN Duncan Scott MB ChB 1931
o c: milit hosp Catterick 1960–64, royal Herbert hosp Woolwich 1964–66; retd col late RAMC; m o army careers information off. Birmingham from 1966
d Dun 8.8.81

COCHRAN Ian McIntosh MB ChB 1949
d Glasg 12.3.69 *AUR* XLIII 218

COCHRAN William MB ChB 1949
consult. paediat surg Ulster hosp and royal Belfast hosp for sick ch from 1962

COCHRANE Helen Bain Tainsh MA 1952
asst head Gracemount p s Edin from 1968
m Edin 29.10.70 John E. King MA(Cantab) schoolmaster s of Herbert A. K. MA(Cantab) Holt Norfolk

COCHRANE or Dishington, Mary Margaret Campbell
BSc 1950

COCK Gilbert Henry BSc(agr) 1923

COCKBURN Arthur George BSc(eng) 1943
TD 1964 CEng 1951 FIWE 1969 FICE 1972 FRSH 1972 MBIM 1973
chief eng (water) Perth c c 1965–68; dep eng (oper) east of Scot. water board Invergowrie by Dun 1968–75; sen dep dir water services Tayside reg c Invergowrie from 1975

COCKBURN Charles MA 1929 MB ChB 1933
consult i/c ophth depts Aber hosps from 1960: pres Scot. ophth club 1972; retd

COCKBURN George Rae *MA 1923
head Hilton s s Aber 1955–65; retd

COCKBURN Lucy MA 1912
d Market Drayton 24.11.69 *AUR* XLII 328

COCKBURN Mary MA 1929
m Aber 30.11.34 Charles J. Reid farm. s of Alexander R. Slains; resid Johnshaven

COCKBURN William MB ChB 1938
d 14.8.71 *AUR* XLIV 321

COCKBURN William Charles MB ChB 1936 MD 1963
FRCP 1971
dir central publ health lab Colindale 1958–60; m o virus diseases WHO Geneva 1961–74; dir div communicable diseases from 1974

COCKER Francis MA 1939

COCKER Phyllis Margaret MB ChB 1955
h o obst and gyn Dunfermline mat. hosp 1958–59; sen h o cas and orthop Raigmore hosp Inv 1959–60
m Inv 29.4.61 Kenneth J. Macdonald MB ChB 1954 *qv*

COCKIE Bruce Mavor MA 1951
teacher: spec asst Engl/geog Bervie j s s 1965–69; Mackie acad Stonehaven: spec asst Engl/geog 1969–70, prin asst coordinator Brunton stud. 1970–72, asst prin guid from 1972

COGHILL John George Jamieson MB ChB 1922
d 14.3.71

COLDWELL or Williams, Joan Margaret *MA 1938

COLE Emmanuel Latundi *MA 1952

COLE Enid MA 1955 Dip Ed 1956 MLitt 1973

COLEMAN Andrew Leslie Edmund Filmer MB ChB 1907 MD 1912
d 25.1.64

COLLIE Alexander Shepherd MA 1954
head: Johnshaven p s Kincardinesh 1964–69, Port Ellen p s Islay 1969–72, Stanley p s Perthsh from 1973

COLLIE Benjamin *BSc 1931
ICI prod. plan. man. (leathercloth div) 1962–71; retd; resid Wilmslow

COLLIE Donald Cumming *BSc(agr) 1951

COLLIE George Francis BL 1933
CBE (civil) 1964
ptnr James & George Collie Aber from 1934; vice-chmn board of man. for Aber spec hosps 1952–60, chmn 1960–68; hon col 51st (H) div RASC(TA) then hon col 153 highland regt RCT(V) 1964–71; dir then chmn Aber univ press from 1953; pres soc of advoc Aber 1974–76

COLLIE or Stephen, Hester Margaret MA BSc 1928
teacher: human biol with BFES Hamm W Ger 1961–63, anat and physiol pre-nursing stud. Littlehampton from 1963

COLLIE Ian *MA 1955 Dip Ed 1956
MEd(Glasg) 1966 MBIM 1971 FSA(Scot) 1975
teacher: Eastwood s Clarkston 1958–64, Langside coll Glasg 1964–66; asst dir of educ Stirlingsh 1966–69; dep dir educ: Dunbarton 1969–72, Stirlingsh 1972–74; dir educ Central reg from 1974; hon lect dept Educ Stir 1977
m Clarkston 3.7.64 Helen S. Meikle MA(Glas) teacher d of Robert M. Clarkston

COLLIE John BSc(eng) 1935

COLLIE Joyce Philip *MA 1951 PhD 1954

COLLIER or Durbin, Joyce *MA 1915
d 10.9.78 *AUR* XLVIII 227

COLLIER Mary MA 1923
teacher Banff acad till 1961; retd

COLLINGWOOD Margaret Walker Hill MA 1926
retd 1975; resid Montreal

COLLINGWOOD or Thomson, Marian Stancliffe BSc 1924
resid Montreal
husb *d* Quebec 20.10.64 *AUR* XLI 56

COLLINS Henry Duckworth MB ChB 1933

COLLINS Herbert Davidson MB ChB 1941
d Aber 17.3.74 *AUR* XLV 449

COLLINS Kenneth Thomas *BSc 1952 Dip Ed 1955 *MEd 1957
Exeter: head educ dept and dean of stud. St Luke's coll 1973–77, dep prin from 1977

COLLINS or Finlayson, Margaret Mackie MA 1927
teacher maths Leith acad 1940–66; retd; resid Edin

COLLINS Mitchell MA 1950

COLLINS Thomas MA 1950
prin teacher relig knowledge RGC Aber from 1955

COLT Joan Margaret Roper *MA 1953 MB ChB 1959
h o Lond 1959–60; sen h o: Ashford Middx 1960–61, S'ton 1961–62; asst ship's surg Brit India SN Co Lond 1963–64; part-time asst m o BBC Lond 1964–65; part-time m o Bromley A H A from 1976
m Lond 3.10.64 John M. Campbell BA(Cantab) pers man. s of Arthur J. C. Lyme Regis

COLVIN Robert Cowan MA 1914 BSc(agr) 1914

COLWELL Jeffrey David PhD 1955
BA(ANU) 1966
Aust: analyst NSW dep agr Sydney 1950–52; res fell Macaulay inst Aber 1952–55; Aust: res off. dept agr

Wagga Wagga NSW 1955–60, res scient Commonwealth scient and indust res organis Canberra from 1960

CONACHER Gilbert Stewart MA 1955
teacher Aber: 1956–60, maths Kincorth acad 1960–76
d Aber 8.10.76 *AUR* XLVII 106

CONCHIE or McLeod, Janet Borrowman MA 1929
resid Claygate Surrey

CONCHIE or Dorrell, Julia Grant Wilson MA 1938 BSc 1940
Dip Soc Sc (Glas) 1941
pers man. Newcastle, Lond 1941–44, scient admin (gas indust) Lond 1944–47; salesman, waitress etc USA 1947–50; scient admin (coal indust) Lond from 1950
m Lond 14.10.55 Peter G. Dorrell BSc(Lond) lect archaeology

CONN George Keith Thurburn *MA 1933
OBE FInstP FRAS
dir Norman Lockyer Observatory Sidmouth from 1961
d 4.6.75 *AUR* XLVI 325

CONNOCHIE Charles Cumming MB ChB 1926
d Lochaber 18.4.75 *AUR* XLVI 323

CONNON Campbell MA 1941 LLB 1949
d Cairngorms 18.12.63 *AUR* XL 303

CONNON Edwin William BSc(eng) 1929

CONNON Frank Clark MA LLB 1951
Aber: leg. asst Burnett & Reid till 1961; own practice 1961–63; sen ptnr Campbell Connon & Co solic from 1963

CONNON George Leslie BSc(eng) 1947
scient MoD Portland: exper off. till 1959, sen scient off. 1959–66, prin scient off. from 1966

CONNON William Catto BL 1949
town clerk and chamberlain Dufftown 1955–71; part time town clerk and chamberlain Aberlour 1960–73; town clerk Grantown-on-Spey 1971–73; disposed of solic bus. Dufftown 1973; sen solic East Kilbride and Stonehouse dev corp 1973–77; prin solic Dumbarton dist c 1977

CONNON William Lewis BL 1949
ptnr Mackenzie & Wilson solic Aber from 1954

CONOCHIE Douglas Alexander Ferguson BSc 1949 MA 1951 MEd 1958
FBPsS
educ psych Cambridge 1961–65; prin educ psych counties of Aberdeen and Kincardine 1965–75; dep reg educ psych Grampian from 1975
wife deceased
m(2) Aber 11.10.80 Cairine R. McLean or Petrie MA 1940 *qv*

CONOCHIE Jean Barbara *MA 1955 Dip Ed 1956
b Lerwick 14.4.33
sen clin psych child psychiat serv Cambridge 1961–63; part-time sen clin psych royal hosp for sick children Edin from 1971 and part-time res psych dept ch life and health Edin from 1972
m Cambridge 3.12.60 Frank Bechhofer MA(Cantab) reader in sociol Edin s of Ernest B. Nottingham

COOK Allan Montague MB ChB 1950
MRCPsych 1971
Ladysbridge hosp Banff: consult. and psychiat 1962–64

COOK Bertram John MA 1905
no longer on GC reg

COOK David Kay MA 1910
d Ballater 2.7.62 *AUR* XL 79

COOK David Lamb *BSc 1950
Canadian Pratt & Whitney Aircraft Montreal: chief of perf & control 1963–70, chief proj eng turbofans 1970–79, proj man. PTT turboprop from 1979

COOK Ethel MA 1915
teacher Fife: Kelty s 1915–20, West Wemyss s 1920–45, West j s s Kirkcaldy 1945–56; retd; resid Strichen
d Fraserburgh 2.3.79

COOK Henry Burness MB ChB 1921 MD 1929
d Cults 25.3.74 *AUR* XLV 447

COOK Iain Anderson MB ChB 1949 *MD 1959
b Glasg 26.9.26
FRCPath 1972
consult. haemat and reg dir N of S blood transfusion serv Inv from 1960

COOK John *MA 1912
part-time teacher Herefordsh/Yorks 1953–65 publ *The Strad and Other Poems* (Lond) 1967
d Inv 21.2.74 *AUR* XLV 447

COOK or Duncan, Linda Ritch *BSc 1955
asst lect biochem dept Aberd 1956–58
resid Elgin

COOK or Laidlaw, Margaret Morgan *MA 1937
teacher mod lang Keith g s 1939–40, prin mod lang Mortlach s s 1940

COOK or Harris, Mary Jane Smith *MA 1908
resid Minehead
d Minehead 17.2.79

COOK Michael *MA 1954

COOK Nicholas *MA 1923
retd 1970; resid Buenos Aires

COOMBE Robert Gorton BSc(agr) 1923
no longer on GC reg

COOPER Alexander MA 1917 MB ChB 1921
d Dundee 27.6.73

COOPER Alfred *MA 1948
man. family bus. millwrights and joiners Strichen from 1954

COOPER Alfred William Howden MA 1919

COOPER or Christie, Anna Jessie Durno MA 1939
resid Grange

COOPER Constance Stewart MA 1931
Dun: transferred to St Mary's 1967, released from community of St Peter to work in Dun 1972, Rev Mother Superior St Mary's sisterhood from 1973

COOPER Douglas Alexander BSc(agr) 1954
Edmonton Alberta: man. mill oper N Alberta 1958–71, gen man. seed oper for prov of Alta and Brit Col from 1971

COOPER Geoffrey MA 1955
prin teacher Engl/hist Alford s 1961–62; head Tullynessle p s 1962–65, Rayne North p s 1965–69, Newtonhill p s from 1969

COOPER George MB ChB 1906
g p Lond 1907–61; retd; farm. Insch from 1925

COOPER George BSc 1952
prin teacher: maths/sc Culter s s 1960–66, sc Cults acad 1966–68, sc Bridge of Don acad from 1968–76, phys from 1977
d 23.8.80

COOPER Hamish Rae *BSc 1946 PhD 1950
prin res off. Shirley Inst from 1961

COOPER or Carle, Harriet Thomson MA 1928
resid Aber

COOPER Herbert George MA 1908
no longer on GC reg

COOPER Isabel BSc(agr) 1950
resid Bourtie Inverurie

COOPER James MB ChB 1924
g p Birm 1928–62; retd; resid Aber
d Worcestersh 6.6.77 *AUR* XLVII 286

COOPER James Young *BSc 1950 PhD 1954

COOPER Jessie MA 1936
d Aber –.4.68 *AUR* XLII 371

COOPER John BSc(agr) 1915
no longer on GC reg

COOPER John George BSc(eng) 1949
sect eng GEC–Elliott Process Automation Leicester from 1966

COOPER or Sanderson, Margaret BSc 1953
resid Inverurie

COOPER Margaret Jessie Corrigall MA 1935

COOPER Patrick Ashley (Sir) LLB 1912
d at sea 24.3.61 *AUR* XXXIX 202

COOPER William Davidson *MA 1925 *BD 1927
hon canon St Andrew's cath Aber from 1962; retd 1977
d Peebles 27.2.78 *AUR* XLVII 356

COPELAND or MacLean, Lily Rennie MA 1922
resid Aber
husb *d* Aber 26.3.77

COPEMAN Graeme James Frank BSc(agr) 1948
head dept of grassland husb NOSCA Aber from 1956; pres Brit Grass Soc 1976–77

COPLAND George Alistair BSc 1954
scient Inveresk res labs Weybridge 1960–61; Jointine Prod. comp (paper converters) N Hykeham: chief chem 1961–74, man. tech serv from 1974
m Aber 24.6.61 Aileen Melvin clerk d of Alexander M. Stoneywood

COPLAND Helen Ellis MA 1906
d Aber 16.1.69 *AUR* XLIII 208

COPLAND or Stephens, Helen Margaret MA 1935
teacher: Crookedholme Ayrsh 1946–49; teacher Engl: Frederick St s Aber 1949–52, Glasg 1957–60, Aboyne 1962–68; resid Ballater
m Aber 28.12.45 Alexander Stephens, Kilmarnock

COPLAND or Barry, Janet Ellis Webster MB ChB 1944
resid Cork, Eire 1976

COPLAND Myra Frances BSc 1941
FBCS 1968
computer progr DH Propellers/Hawker Siddely Dynamics Hatfield 1952–64; computing man. CI Data Centre Aldershot from 1964

COPLAND William Alexander MB ChB 1946
FFR 1956 FRCSE 1975 FRCR 1976 VRD
member clin teaching staff Edin univ from 1962 consult. radiol Lothian health board; QHP 1972–73; retd (surg capt) RNR 1973

CORALL John Mitchell MB ChB 1936
DMR(Lond) 1947
consult. radiol Medway and Gravesend and mid-Kent group of hosps from 1950

CORBETT Donald Cameron MacRae *BSc 1953

CORBETT or Davies, Evelina Isabella MB ChB 1922 DPH 1923
resid Bosbury

CORBETT or Hansford, Lizzie Marjory MA 1914
d 1978

CORDICE Gideon John MB ChB 1950

CORDINER Adelaide Russell Balfour MA 1916
d 24.2.62 *AUR* XXXIX 380

CORDINER or Ritchie, Jean Mowat MA 1940
resid Peterhead

CORDINER John Hutchison MA 1935
JP 1975
teacher Ellon acad 1935–72; retd; RAF 1940–45; provost Ellon 1958–65

CORDINER John Noble MA 1924
d Stirling 16.8.78

CORDINER Robert William MA 1948
teacher Peterhead N s 1949–55, dep head 1955–77; retd

CORMACK Alexander BSc(eng) 1951
CEng MIMechE 1959 OBE 1980
works man. AEI turbine generator works Glasg 1964–65; N Ireland: gen man. GEC turbine generator works Larne 1965–73, man. dir Everton engineering Newton Abbey from 1973, pres N Ireland engineering employers assoc Belfast from 1973

CORMACK Alexander Allan *MA 1913
author of various publications and of numerous articles to *AUR* etc; orig member/chmn of Aber county rent appeal committee 1955–73
d Aber 9.6.76 *AUR* XLVII 101

CORMACK Alexander Cumming *MA 1950 Dip Ed 1959 MEd 1962
head dept remed and spec educ coll of educ Aber from 1975
marr. diss 1973
m (2) Aber 22.6.73 Margaret Ritchie or Waite lect coll of educ Aber d of Alfred R. BSc 1926 *qv*

CORMACK or Bond, Barbara Stevenson MA 1955
resid Gidea Park

CORMACK Edwin James BL 1954
leg. asst firm of patent ag Salisbury Rhodesia 1955–58; ptnr Fisher Cormack and Botha patent and trade mark ag Salisbury, Lusaka, Blantyre 1959–79; man. patent ag dept Spoor and Fisher patent attorneys Pretoria from 1979
m Salisbury Rhodesia –.4.66 Kathleen M. A. Gale teacher d of William D. G. Salisbury

CORMACK or Berrie, Ella MA 1904
no longer on GC reg

CORMACK or Simpson, Elsie Stott Pickering MA 1941
teacher: Orpington 1957–67, Upper Poppleton York from 1968

CORMACK George MB ChB 1939
g p Cambo from 1944
marr. diss 1968

CORMACK Gertrude Elizabeth MB ChB 1920
retd

CORMACK James Maxwell Ross *MA 1932
regius prof Greek Aberd from 1965
wife *d* 1968
m(2) Reading 14.8.68 Sybil P. Dadley BA(R'dg) teacher d of Harry G. D. Reading
d Aber 4.6.75 *AUR* XLVI 324

CORMACK or Murray, Janet Isabella MA 1941
resid Aber

CORMACK John William *MA 1912
d Glasg 16.11.69 *AUR* XLIII 328 and 441

CORMACK Robert MA 1912
no longer on GC reg

CORMIE James Ernest Dingwall BL 1951
dep town clerk Perth from 1966

CORMIE or Tough, Robina Andrew BSc 1948
scient ICI dyestuffs div 1948–71; organics div from 1971; resid Rochdale

CORNER Harold Hartmann BSc(agr) 1919
agr advis Roxburgh till 1961; retd
wife *d* 1968
d 16.2.79

CORNER Malcolm Manford MA 1922 BD 1925
C of S min West Church Grangemouth 1960–69; retd; resid Edin

CORNER William *MB ChB 1916 *MD 1924
DTM & H (Lond) 1925
g p Hove from 1930
wife *d* 1971
d Hove 15.8.81

COROON John MA 1949
d Lond 3.4.75

CORRIGAL Donald MA 1904
d Rothiemay 24.5.66 *AUR* XLI 335

CORSER James Ronald MA 1928
head Findhorn p s 1963–66; dep head Kinloss p s 1966–70; retd; resid Elgin

COSTIE Isaac MA 1933 *MEd 1936

COTTERILL Leonard MB ChB 1899
no longer on GC reg

COULL Alexander *BSc(eng) 1953 PhD 1961
FRSE 1971 FICE 1973 FIStructE 1973
lect: eng Aberd 1957–62, civ eng univ of S'ton 1962–66; prof struct eng Strath from 1966–76; regius prof civil eng Glas from 1977
m Aber 22.12.62 Frances B. Moir teacher d of Francis T. C. M. Aber

COULL or Atkins, Catherine Mary MB ChB 1943
MFCM 1972
sen m o county borough Southampton 1967, prin m o 1971–74; spec commun med Dorset A H A 1974

COULL David Carnegie MB ChB 1940
ophth surg Aber from 1947

COULL George Morrison BCom 1923
prin Weybridge tech coll 1958–63; retd; resid Bognor Regis

COULL James BSc 1924

COULL James Riddell *MA 1933
no longer on GC reg

COULL John BSc 1955

COULSON Thomas William Gibson BSc(for) 1950
dist off. For. Comm from 1952; resid Campbeltown

COULSON William James BSc 1947 *1948
MRIC 1963 C Chem 1976
teacher sc Galashiels acad 1957–60, Kelso h s 1960–62, Graeme h s Falkirk 1962–69; teacher chem Paisley: Oakshaw p s 1969–74, St Mirin's and St Margaret's comp h s from 1974

COULTHARD James William *MEd 1952
lect educ/psych Moray House Edin 1953–65; visiting Fulbright prof univ of Toledo Ohio USA 1965–66; Moray House: sen lect psych 1966–72, prin lect/head dept psych from 1972

COUPER John Mill *MA 1935 PhD 1948
Sydney: lect Engl univ of NSW 1959–72; assoc prof Engl Macquarie univ from 1972

COUPER Robert Scott *MA 1942
rector Forres acad from 1968

COURT Helen Elizabeth *MA 1927
no longer on GC reg

COUTTS or Donald, Bertha Mary MA 1955
resid Milltimber Aber

COUTTS Catherine Elizabeth BSc 1949

COUTTS David *MA 1910
no longer on GC reg

COUTTS or Birss, Dorothea Harper MA 1932
teacher Aber: King St s 1956–62, Summerhill s 1962–69, Middle/Frederick St s 1969–72; retd

COUTTS Elizabeth Milne MA 1906 BSc 1917
d 4.3.79 *AUR* XLVIII 226

COUTTS George MA 1949
JP Aber 1971
Aber: dep head King St s 1962–66; head: Tillydrone p s 1966–73, Mile-End p s from 1973

COUTTS or Patterson, Helen MA 1941
resid Montrose

COUTTS or Sexton, Helena Martha Lumsden MA 1925

COUTTS Isabella Leys MA 1908
d Aber 8.2.61 *AUR* XXXIX 201

COUTTS James MB ChB 1926
dep med supt S Wales sanat Talgarth 1947–69; retd; resid Cardigan
d 28.6.78

COUTTS or Butt, Janet Grant MA 1947
resid Edin

COUTTS or Macdonald, Jessie Milne MA 1927
d 30.8.76

COUTTS or Harris, Margaret Constance MA 1913
no longer on GC reg

COUTTS or Murray, Margaret Janet MB ChB 1922
d Aber 30.6.75 *AUR* XLVI 322

COUTTS or Monkhouse, Marion Charlotte MA 1914
retd 1949; resid Harrogate

COUTTS or Anderson, Mary MB ChB 1924
resid Banstead

COUTTS or McKerrigan, Mary Jane MA 1907
d Leeds 22.7.70 *AUR* XLIV 107

COUTTS or Price, Patricia Jane MacLeod MA 1925
d W Kilbride 4.4.74 *AUR* XLV 448

COUTTS Thomas Gordon *MA 1955 [c]LLB 1957
QC 1973

COUTTS Vera Cecile MB ChB 1953
b Glenfarg 27.6.28
DPM(St And) 1959 MFCM 1972
asst m o h: Perth & Kinross c c 1959–62, Fife c c 1962–65; sen asst m o h Fife c c from 1965; sen clin m o Fife health board

COUTTS William MA 1925
d Portgordon 27.6.63 *AUR* XL 205

COUTTS William Ernest MA MB ChB 1937
g p Cardiff from 1946

COUTTS William Shivas MB ChB 1924
d Leeds 15.9.68 *AUR* XLIII 84

COW Alexander Strachan Miller *MA 1927
teacher maths Kelso h s 1928–67; retd; resid Matlock

COW Catherine Mair MA 1947
teacher Peterhead acad from 1948; resigned 1969
m 30.7.80 Hurry

COWAN Ian Campbell BSc 1936 MB ChB 1943 MD 1952
dir phys med (consult. status) Sunderland area from 1952

COWAN James *MA 1918
no longer on GC reg

COWAN Nigel Smart BSc(eng) 1933
retd army brig 1960; admin Nat Trust Waddesdon Manor Aylesbury 1960–70; ag Waddesdon estate from 1969
d 2.4.80

COWE Alexander May *BSc 1953 MB ChB 1958
h s mat. hosp Aber 1961–63; g p Ilkeston from 1963

COWIE Alexander Carnegie BSc 1955
BVMS(Glas) 1961 MRCVS(Glas) 1961
DVSM(Edin) 1967
vet surg Stonehaven 1961–64 and from 1964; vet off. min of Agr Cornwall 1964–76; div vet off. anim health div Min of Agr Tolworth from 1974
m Aber 27.9.61 Muriel M. Black teacher d of Alexander L. B. Aber

COWIE Alexander Smith MA 1907

COWIE Alfred MB ChB 1933
g p Leeds 1951–73: retd; resid Cults

COWIE Catherine Mary MA 1920

COWIE or Murison, Christian Ewen MA 1915
d 7.6.72 *AUR* XLV 125

COWIE Clement Alexander MB ChB 1923
g p Warwicksh till 1958; retd to Dalkeith W Aust
d Felixstowe 14.12.79

COWIE Douglas George BSc(eng) 1953
eng Traction proj dept Metro Vickers Elect. Co Manc later AEI 1955–65; elect. des eng ICI Fibres Harrogate 1965–67; elect. maintenance eng Wilton 1967–70; mech plant eng petro chem div ICI 1970–77; eng supervis Chevron Petroleum (UK) Aber from 1977
m Barton Lancs 16.7.60 Patricia R. Taylor teacher d of William E. T. Glazebrook Warrington

COWIE or Kinghorn, Elizabeth Jane MA 1947

COWIE Frank Philip MA 1952
DipEd(Dund) 1970 *MEd(Dund) 1971
prin teacher maths: Goodlyburn s s Perth 1964–69; Perth g s 1971–73; asst rector Perth g s from 1973
m Clunie 2.4.60 Lorna C. Allardice RGN nurse d of James M. A. Blairgowrie

COWIE George *MA 1931
rector Alva s 1958–70; retd; resid Elgin

COWIE George MB ChB 1955
DObstRCOG 1960
h o gyn and obst gen hosp Northampton 1958; g p Ashington 1958–59, Great Barr Birmingham 1959–61, Grimethorpe Barnsley 1961–66, Stockport from 1966
m Birmingham –.7.65 Joyce P. Wright secy d of Arthur W. Birm

COWIE George Alexander *MA 1927
d Montrose 14.12.73 *AUR* XLV 448

COWIE George Robert *MA 1933 dLLB 1935
OBE 1977 LLD(Belf) 1980
secy Queen's univ Belf 1948–77; retd
wife *d* 28.5.72

COWIE or Johnston, Gladys May MA 1917
d Norway 11.12.70 *AUR* XLIV 210

COWIE Gordon Strachan *MA 1955 LLB 1958
nat serv 2nd lieut RPC 1958–60; lect internat and compar law Queen's Coll Dundee, St And 1960–67; sen lect publ law Glas 1967; prof publ law Glas from 1973; dean fac law Glas from 1977; admitted to fac of advoc 1962
m Dusseldorf 11.8.61 Angela M. Whelband d of Rowland G. W. BAOR

COWIE or Hutchison, Helen Alice Creswell MA 1944

COWIE Howard Elphinstone BSc(agr) 1923

COWIE Isabel Proctor *MA 1933
teacher Fr/Ger: Keith g s 1944–62, spec asst Gordon Schools Huntly 1962–72; retd

COWIE Isabella Sutherland MA 1952
teacher: Strichen 1953–60, Perth acad 1960–61, San Fernando Trinidad 1961–63; resid Mbabane, Swaziland
m Port of Spain Trinidad 13.8.60 John C. Philip bank man. s of William P. Strichen

COWIE James Hay *MA 1948
prin teacher mod lang Morgan acad Dun from 1963
m Newcastle Staffs 29.6.68 Vera Porter secy d of George P. Madeley nr Crewe

COWIE James Macrae MB ChB 1898 DPH 1900 *MD 1903
d Burton on Trent 9.3.61 *AUR* XXXIX 198

COWIE James Strachan *MA 1952
dist off. N Rhodesia 1953–66; asst regist univ of Kent at Canterbury from 1966
m Aber 13.9.52 Sheila Mackay

COWIE Jane MA 1923
d Portsoy 10.10.69 *AUR* XLIII 330

COWIE Jessie Geddes MA 1955
teacher: Findochty 1956–60, Middlefield s Aber 1960–62; Inverallochy 1962–65 and from 1974; resid Fraserburgh
m Buckie 24.12.60 Gordon Clark eng s of Peter C. Aber

COWIE John MB ChB 1946
d Lond 24.6.70 *AUR* XLIV 111

COWIE John Lawless MA 1947
C of S min Rosyth parish Dunfermline 1960–70; exper team min Richmond Craigmillar Edin 1970–77; Christian Fellowship of Healing Edin from 1977

COWIE Lillis Marion MA 1924
teacher Engl: Arbroath till 1960, Brechin h s 1960–63; retd

COWIE or Clark, Mabel Margaret MA 1920
d 19.10.75 *AUR* XLVI 322

COWIE Nellie Durno MA 1914
no longer on GC reg

COWIE William *MA 1951

COWIE William Archibald Douglas MA 1923
retd 1968; resid Cummertrees Annan
d Cummertrees 8.3.76

COWIE William Bagrie MA 1930 BCom 1932 LLB 1934
d 1.11.71 *AUR* XLIV 432

COWIE William George *MA 1934
Jordanhill coll of educ Glasg: lect econ/mod. stud. 1973–77; retd; lect adult educ (WEA) Strathclyde from 1977

COWIE William John Gavin *MA 1951
lect fac of agr N'cle from 1963

COX George Frederick *MA 1910
d N Berwick 7.12.64 *AUR* XLI 55

COX or Glascodine, Margaret Elizabeth MA 1953
temp teacher Lennoxtown p s 1962–68; teacher Engl Townhead j s s 1968–71; asst prin Engl Kirkintilloch h s from 1972

COX Reginald Tom MB ChB 1915
d 15.7.80

COX Richard *MA 1946
prin teacher maths Forrester s Edin 1959–65; head Sutherland tech s Golspie 1965–68; head W Calder h s from 1968

CRABB or Fraser, Catherine Amy *MA 1938
teacher Colliston Angus from 1956
marr diss 1961
m(2) Guthrie 18.9.63 John Strachan MBE eng s of George M. S. Guthrie

CRAGGS Joyce MA 1950
Graz Austria: exchange teacher 1966–68; Lehrbeauftragte univ Graz 1967–68; teacher g s from 1968
m Graz 10.7.69 Franz Scherz gymnasiat prof Mag Phil(Graz) s of Franz S. Graz

CRAIB David Andrew MB ChB 1939
g p Eastbourne from 1947

CRAIB Kathleen MA 1953 MEd 1958
educ psych Glasg ch guid serv 1962–65; sen clin pysch Douglas Inch clin for psychiat Glasg 1965–70; tut. organis ch panel trg, dept extra-mural and adult educ Glas
m Aber 14.9.62 Robert I. Murray farm. s of Sir Robert A. M. Glasg

CRAIB William BSc(agr) 1929
CBE
d Edin 30.10.72

CRAICK William BSc(eng) 1942

CRAIG or Thomson, Agnes McCulloch *MA 1955
sen psych clin NERHB 1961–69; lect psych Aberd from 1970

CRAIG or Cooper, Ailsa BSc 1953
teacher sc Hilton acad Aber from 1967

CRAIG Alan Gordon MB ChB 1951
St Louis Missouri: res psychiat Wash univ 1963–66, chief resid psychiat 1966–67, instr psychiat 1967–68, asst prof from 1968; pres med staff St Vincent's hosp from 1975

CRAIG Albert MA 1932 MB ChB 1936 DD 1967
ordained presb Glasg 1947; C of S min St Andrew's ch Peebles from 1967

CRAIG Alexander Henderson MB ChB 1916
d Lichfield 26.5.61 *AUR* XXXIX 203

CRAIG Andrew MA 1932 LLB 1934
b Aber 16.6.11
town clerk Peterhead 1946–75, harbour clerk Peterhead 1946–76; retd

CRAIG Andrew Hugh *MA 1952
teacher mod lang Alloa acad 1956–67; prin teacher Lornshill acad Alloa from 1967
m Aber 7.8.63 Grace R. M. Henderson florist d of William H. Udny

CRAIG or Barron, Ann MA 1926
teacher Mile-end p s Aber 1942–46
husb *d* 4.5.65

CRAIG Annie MA 1935
retd 1973; resid Aber

CRAIG David Main *MA 1954
lect Engl univ Ceylon 1959–61; organis tut. WEA North Yorks 1961–64; univ Lanc: lect and sen lect Engl 1964–72, sen lect without dept duties from 1972

CRAIG David Ogilvie MB ChB 1946

CRAIG Doris Agnes MA 1925
no longer on GC reg

CRAIG Elma Cruickshank MA 1953 Dip Ed 1966
Dip Ed of Deaf (Manc) 1958
teacher of deaf: Ohio s USA 1962–64, Aber s 1964–66; lect educ of deaf univ Lond inst of educ 1966–70; res fell. R'dg 1970–73, hon lect N'cle schol educ 1973–76; lect City Lit Inst London from 1976
m McMillan

CRAIG Eric MA 1955
BD(Edin) 1960
C of S min Chalmers-Lauriston ch Edin from 1966

CRAIG Eric John Dickson MB ChB 1946
clin asst radio therap Essex county hosp Colchester from 1957

CRAIG Ernest Duncan MA 1911
no longer on GC reg

CRAIG Esther Mary *MA 1955
mus mistress King's Norton g s for girls Birm 1958–62; sen mus mistress North Kesteven g s Lincolnsh 1962–64
m Aber 12.12.64 Reginald Barrett-Ayres BMus(Edin) reader in music Aberd s of Frederick G. B-A. Aviemore

CRAIG George Alexander Barclay MA 1942
HMIS Edin from 1964

CRAIG Ian George Logan MB ChB 1942
g p Stanford-le-Hope from 1953

CRAIG Isla MB ChB 1955 MD 1963
MRCPath 1965 FRCPath 1977
regist clin path. Sunderland RI 1960–63; sen regist path. Manchester teaching hosps 1963–65; consult. path. Selly Oak hosp Birm from 1965

CRAIG James MA LLB 1937
OBE 1970
sole ptnr R. Addison-Smith & Co WS Edin; now in ptnrship with son James L. J. C.

CRAIG James Alexander MA 1932 BD 1939

CRAIG James Wood MB ChB 1924
d Stirling 8.6.68 *AUR* XLIII 84

CRAIG or Still, Jane Douglas MA 1915
resid Aber
d 1.2.79

CRAIG or Melville, Jean Forrest MA 1934
d of James C. MA 1902 *qv*(II, III)
teacher Aber: Porthill p s, Seaton, King St, Hanover St 1936–42; Rugby: New Bilton c s 1942–43, Hillmorton Paddox j s 1943–47
m Rugby 25.7.42 William S. Melville BSc(eng) 1938 *qv*

CRAIG John *MA 1906
declined CBE 1939, elected member Athenaeum 1943; resid Hazlemere
d Wimbledon 9.6.81

CRAIG John *MB ChB 1921 LLD 1964
Hon FAAP 1958
prof ch health Aberd 1947–63; retd
d Aber 19.4.77 *AUR* XLVII 211

CRAIG John McLennan MB ChB 1950
FACOG(Lond) FRCS(C) FRCOG
Calgary: consult. gyn and obst Holy Cross hosp, Calgary gen hosp 1962–73; consult i/c foetal monitoring chief dep obst and gyn Holy Cross Hospital Calgary Alberta
m Farnham 9.3.57 Elisabeth Schuler

CRAIG John Peter *MA 1927
head Ballater s 1943–67; retd
d Aber 22.7.77 *AUR* XLVII 286

CRAIG Joseph *BSc(eng) 1942
b Aber 29.9.21
dir Craig Stores Aber from 1951

CRAIG Mackenzie Melville MB ChB 1943

CRAIG or Daniel, Margaret Forrest BSc 1955
teacher: Beath h s Cowdenbeath 1960–62, Northfield acad Aber 1970–75, Sunnybank p s Aber from 1975

CRAIG or Gibson, Mary MA 1935

CRAIG Mary Ann MA 1919

CRAIG Mary Ann MA 1931
teacher: Fordoun s 1938–70; retd; resid Auchenblae

CRAIG or Macdonald, Mary Jessie *MA 1917
d 1.3.65 *AUR* XLI 56

CRAIG or Scott, Mora Joan MB ChB 1940
g p Elgin from 1941
husb *d* –.12.71

CRAIG Norah Alison MA 1925
d Aber 25.4.71 *AUR* XLIV 211

CRAIG Norman James *MA 1930 MB ChB 1935
d 9.6.65

CRAIG Ronald Anderson BL 1936
consult. MacDiarmid & Craig solic Aber from 1976

CRAIG Sheila Phillips MA 1953
teacher Inverurie acad from 1954

CRAIG or Blackburn, Sheila Wood MB ChB 1951

CRAIG Theodore Watson BSc(agr) 1921
d Kirkhill Invernesssh 4.8.54

CRAIG Victor MA LLB 1952
solic Glasg 1952–57 and from 1960; pers off. Paisley 1957–60
m Glasg 24.6.54 Catherine M. McEwen comptometer oper/typist d of William McE. Glasg

CRAIG William *MA 1907 *BD 1913
d Nairn 15.1.67 *AUR* XLII 346

CRAIG William MA 1931
CA

CRAIG William Elliot BSc(agr) 1938
area man. SW Scot Chem Bldg Prod. Lond from 1950, man. Scot. off from 1976; ROC 1947–77; bar to long serv medal 1970

CRAIG or David, Winifred Anne MA 1950
resid Aber

CRAIGEN or Beedie, Patricia Young MA 1944

CRAIGEN William Gordon Cameron MB ChB 1945
d 14.2.69 *AUR* XLIII 217

CRAIGHEAD Edward Alexander *MA 1948
prin Quinte s s Belleville Ontario from 1969

CRAIGHEAD Robert BSc 1930

CRAIGHEAD William MA 1922
d Grangemouth 5.6.67 *AUR* XLII 185

CRAIGIE Betty MA 1952
teacher: Inverallochy 1962–69, Fraserburgh inf s from 1969

CRAIGIE John Dustan *BSc 1933
sc master/dep rector Sanquhar acad; retd 1971

CRAIGMYLE Alexander Donald *MA 1907
retd; resid Newburgh Aberdeensh
d Newburgh 7.1.78 *AUR* XLVII 355

CRAIK David MA 1907

CRAMB Finlay Ross *MA 1912
d Aber 4.2.62 *AUR* XXXIX 378

CRAMB Maurice MA 1932 LLB 1934 LLD 1966
head dept Rom Law 1947–51; convener bus. comm of General Council Aberd 1971–79; General Council assessor 1960–63 then (to 1979) Chancellor's assessor univ court Aberd; executive trustee Carnegie Trust

CRAMOND David Stephen MB ChB 1945

CRAMOND James MB ChB 1941 DPH 1947
Lond: g p Knightsbridge 1945–59, advis occup health to various organis from 1955–69; Northern reg hosp board (Scot.) Inv 1969–71; g p Kent 1971–73, Lond Kensington and Farnham Surrey from 1973; consult. aviation med

CRAMOND Tom BSc(agr) 1951
MBE 1973
prin teacher agr and rural subj Stranraer acad from 1965

CRAMOND William Alexander MB ChB 1947 ᶜMD 1954
FANZCP 1969 FRCPsych 1971 FRACP 1973
S Aust: dir mental health 1961–65, prof mental health Adel 1963–71; prin m o mental health Scot. home and health dept Edin 1971–72; dean of fac of med and prof mental health Leic 1972–75; prin and vice-chancellor univ Stir 1975–79

CRAN Brennan Scott *MB ChB 1928 *MD 1931
consult. surg and urologist Tees-side hosps from 1945; retd

CRAN Doris Kellas MA 1929
head Craigellachie p s 1948–73; retd; resid Lower Cabrach

CRAN Douglas MB ChB 1915
retd army col; resid Kilmacolm

CRAN or Jamieson, Edith MB ChB 1924

CRAN Edward Gray BSc(eng) 1950
eng insp Scot dev dept Edin from 1971
m Aber 18.8.61 Wendy I. M. Diack

CRAN Eva Margaret MA 1931 MB ChB 1936
acting div m o Division I LCC 1964–65; dep m o Lond bor of Hammersmith 1965–69; retd full time, working on sessional basis Hammersmith from 1969

CRAN or Bruce, Helen Jean Geddes MA 1934
resid Keith

CRAN or Blair, Helen Johnston BSc 1927
resid Milltimber, Aber

CRAN Ian Mitchell MB ChB 1947
consult. surg Queen Alexandra milit hosp Lond 1966–69; joint prof milit surg RCS England and royal army med coll Lond 1969–70; retd army 1970; g p Taree NSW Aust 1970–72; consult. surg Manning River dist hosp Taree from 1973

CRAN James MB ChB 1941
g p Wellingborough from 1953

CRAN James Hunter *MA 1947
rector Falkirk h s from 1962
d Carronshore 27.1.71 *AUR* XLIV 215

CRAN or Hunter, Janet Davidson *MA 1925
teacher Gordon s Huntly: inf dept 1938–50, asst then spec asst mod lang 1950–68; retd
husb *d* 1.2.38

CRAN or Graham, Jean Jamieson MA 1954
resid Troon

CRAN John BCom 1927
no longer on GC reg

CRAN Victor Alexander MB ChB 1938
g p Tilbury from 1949

CRANNA or Robbie, Ella MA 1930
teacher Tarves from 1963

CRANNA or Farquhar, Helen Jane Christian Park MA 1915
no longer on GC reg

CRANSTON or Mann, Chrissie Coutts MA 1923
d Forres 3.12.73 *AUR* XLV 447

CRANSTON Margaret Isabella MA 1908
resid Forres
d 26.12.77

CRANSTON Thomas MA 1912
d Edin 30.8.66 *AUR* XLI 337, XLII 83

CRANSTON William Ian ***MB ChB 1949 MD 1957**
MA(Oxon) 1962 FRCP 1965
first asst RPM dept Oxon 1960–64; prof med St Thomas' hosp med s Lond from 1964

CRAWFORD or Holland, Anna Margaret **MA 1935**

CRAWFORD David Chalmers
MA 1901 BSc(agr) 1906 BSc 1909
no longer on GC reg

CRAWFORD Douglas Murray **BSc(agr) 1952**

CRAWFORD or Macdonald, Elizabeth **MA 1934**

CRAWFORD Ian Milne Cay **MA 1948**

CRAWFORD John Henry Forbes **MB ChB 1951**
LM(Dub) 1955 MRCGP 1961
ship's surg: M.S. *Meteor* 1969–71, Royal Fleet Auxiliary from 1974

CRAWFORD Kenneth Stewart **MB ChB 1938**
consult. anaest Nottingham groups of hosps from 1946

CRAZE Margaret Catherine **MA 1939**
vice-prin h s Montreal 1964–69; co-ordinator of curric Prot school board of Greater Montreal 1969–70; asst supt PSBGM 1970–76; reg dir PSBGM from 1976

CRAZE Mary Betty **MA 1943**
teacher Montreal 1958–63; head maths dept Lachine h s from 1963

CREIGHTON Barbara Helen ***MA 1915**
no longer on GC reg

CREIGHTON Mary Anne Findlay **MA 1912**
d Aber 15.4.73 *AUR* XLV 224

CRERAR Archibald **MB ChB 1935**
JP 1949
g p Millport from 1953

CRICHTON Alexander **MB ChB 1940**
d Wellington 30.7.75 *AUR* XLVI 325

CRICHTON Alexander McKerrow ***MA 1932**
McLaren h s Callander: prin teacher classics 1947–59, also dep rector 1959–72; dep rector from 1972; retd 1975
wife *d* 2.9.72

CRICHTON Arthur **MA 1914 BSc(agr) 1920**
TD
d Brechin 12.1.72 *AUR* XLIV 428

CRICHTON or Kellas, Isobel Margaret **MA 1939**
resid Ballater
husb *d* 17.2.68

CRICHTON John Andrew **MA BSc(agr) 1922**
dep dir Rowett Inst Aber 1963–64; agr res consult. Havana Cuba 1964–66; retd; resid Aber

CRICHTON William McKerrow ***MA 1934**
OBE 1968
head Ntare sen s s Mbarara, Uganda 1955–72; retd; resid Bieldside Aber

CRICHTON William Paterson **BSc(eng) 1953**

CRICHTON or Bremner, Jemima Findlay **MA 1925**
teacher E. Lothian 1964–70; retd; resid Prestonpans

CRICHTON or Petrie, Jessie Allan **MA 1926**
teacher Peterhead cent s 1953–64; retd

CRICHTON Margaret Murray
MA 1953 Dip Ed 1956
teacher: Aber 1956–64, W Lothian 1964, Edin 1964–65, Glasg 1965–73, asst prin teacher from 1973

CRICHTON William George **BSc(agr) 1942**
vet pract New Deer 1950–70; vet off. Lawson's Dyce from 1970 and vet dir Aber and dist MMB cattle breeding div from 1973

CROCKART or Jolly, Margaret Clementina
MA 1910
d 11.9.74

CROCKETT Alexander Stewart **BSc(eng) 1942**
FIStructE 1958 FIMunE 1958 FICE 1970
borough eng and surv Chesterfield 1960–65, sen dep city eng Edin 1965–74; city eng Edin 1974–75; dir of highways Lothian reg c from 1975

CROCKETT Charles Stephen **MB ChB 1955**
MRCGP 1968
g p: New Pitsligo from 1956, Oakville Ontario 1969
m(2) Glasg 13.4.78 Carol I. Cross BEd(Glasg) secy BBC d of John C. Glasg

CROCKETT Joseph **MA 1950 LLB 1953**
LLM(Lond) 1968
sen admin asst nat superan scheme Lond 1957–60; asst secy Cocoa Choc & Confect Alliance Lond 1960–62; lect/sen lect Hatfield polytech 1962–69; prin lect law polytech Newcastle-u-Tyne 1969–71; head of dept leg. stud. polytech Wolverhampton from 1971

CROLL or Paterson, Eirene Victoria **MB ChB 1924**
d 14.1.61

CROLL Jean Flett **MB ChB 1935**
asst county m o h Northants from 1953; retd 1975
m Cheltenham 26.8.64 Thomas Woolfenden clerk in holy orders s of Thomas W. Kettering

CROLL John MacArthur **MB ChB 1929 DPH 1931**
FRCPath 1963
retd 1971; resid Lincoln
d Derby –.6.81

CROMAR Alexander **MA 1953 *MEd 1965**
prin teacher maths Torry s s Aber from 1964; asst head Torry acad 1973, dep head from 1974

CROMAR Arthur Clement **MA 1935 LLB 1937**
law app Cochran & Macpherson advoc Aber

1934–37; leg. asst Hogart & Burn Murdoch WS Edin 1938–39, Cochran & Macpherson advoc Aber 1939–40; RAF wireless oper/intell off./flt lt 1940–46; leg. asst Merchant Co Edin/secy & solic Scottish YH assoc Edin/Stirling 1946–68; dep town clerk Stirling 1968–75; asst dir admin & leg. serv Cent reg c 1957–78; retd
m Edin 22.9.64 Elizabeth C. F. Smith MA(Edin) teacher d of William S. MA(Edin) JP Edin
d Comrie –.8.81

CROMAR Colin Douglas Leslie MB ChB 1932
FRCS(USA) 1973 Assoc Fell. Amer Proctological Soc 1959
resid North Jackson Mississippi 1961–62; surg pract Pasadena and Houston Texas from 1962
marr diss

CROMAR Peter Law MA 1952 MEd 1962
ABPsS 1965
asst educ psych child guid serv Edin 1962–66; Moray & Nairn joint c c: educ psych Elgin 1966–71, prin educ psych from 1971

CROMBIE Alan Alexander Cran BSc(eng) 1945

CROMBIE George Edmond *MA 1930
counsellor H M Emb Dublin 1961–65; Brit High Comm Bathurst, The Gambia 1965–67; retd 1968
d Aber 9.12.73 *A UR* XLV 226

CROMBIE Hugh Mackenzie MB ChB 1925
d Aber 23.4.61 *A UR* XXXIX 204

CROMBIE Irene Helen MA 1932
JP 1964
secy to Lord Provost Aber 1951–72; retd; resid Aber
d Middlesbrough 22.11.76

CROMBIE James Ian Cormack (Sir) *MA 1925 LLD 1957
d Lond 22.5.69 *A UR* XLIII 214

CROMBIE or Brown, Katherine Isabel MA 1928
m Aber 26.8.43 James Brown
resid Aust 1944–77
d Ashford Middx 3.11.77

CROMBIE or Parker, Kathleen Mary *MA 1935
resid Middlesbrough

CROMBIE or Croll or Finlayson, Margaret Mary MA 1926
d 16.4.71

CROMBIE Peter *MA 1933
d Aber 1.11.75

CRONE or Bruce, Anna Hunter *BSc 1945
resid Liverpool

CROOKE Myles PhD 1950
for. entomol (for. comm) Farnham 1951–60; lect Aberd from 1960

CROOKSHANKS Allan Stephen MA 1927
d Dumfries 19.3.71 *A UR* XLIV 211

CROOKSHANKS Brian Kerrington MA 1949 [d]LLB 1952
TD 1967
Aber: asst solic Cormack, Cramb & Gibb 1966–75, dep proc fiscal from 1975; comm serv 51(H) signal regt TA 1955–67

CROOKSHANKS George Coutts MA 1923
d Aber 8.3.70 *A UR* XLIII 445

CROSBIE Alexander John *MA 1952
FRGS 1956 PhD(Edin) 1965
lect univ Edin 1964–72, sen lect from 1972
wife *d* 19.12.62
m(2) Logie 2.6.65 Nicola J. Watson MA(Edin) d of A. J. S. W. Bridge of Allan

CROSBIE or Donald, Jane MA 1915
resid Aber

CROSSLING Frank Turner MB ChB 1949
FRCSGlas 1970
consult. surg Stobhill hosp Glasg 1964–67 and from 1968; sen lect surg Nairobi Kenya 1967–68

CROUCHER Barbara Margaret MA 1942
head PNEU s Harlow 1961–64; Lond: sen mistress Jewish s Manor House 1964–67, sen mistress Garden House s Sloane Square 1967–71; teacher in ILEA schools from 1971, in Falconbrook j m s Wandsworth from 1973

CROW Henry James MA MB ChB 1949 [c]MD 1964
MRCPsych 1971 FRCPsych 1977
clin dir Burden neurol hosp and inst Bristol from 1956

CROW Robert Stewart MB ChB 1945 [c]MD 1958
FRCP 1971
consult. phys Torquay from 1962

CROW William Conacher MA 1934

CROWLEY Eamon BSc(eng) 1940
RAF 1940–46; des eng Ont hydro Toronto 1947–57; Canada: dir of eng BC power comm Victoria BC 1957–61, gen. man. internat power eng consult. (IPEC) Vancouver/pres Canadian eng consult. Ottawa 1961–73, vice-pres IPEC/man. syst des & construct. BC hydro and power auth Vancouver from 1973
m London Ont 11.12.48 Marion W. Neil nurse

CROWLEY Gerald Patrick BSc 1935
d Bury 13.2.78 *A UR* XLVII 359

CROWLEY Thomas Michael MA 1940

CROWLEY Timothy John MB ChB 1952
g p Woodchurch and part time anaest Wirral group hosps 1960–66; then surg Royal Fleet Aux. Serv MoD Lond from 1966
d 6.6.75

CROZIER Theodore James MA 1950

CRUDEN or Hacket, Christina Melville MA 1949

CRUDEN James McNab BSc(eng) 1950
resid Canada

CRUICKSHANK Alan Hamilton *MB ChB 1936 *MD 1942
MRCPath 1963
reader path. Liv from 1966

CRUICKSHANK Alexander MB ChB 1922 *MD 1934
m o min of health Lond 1951–65; med advis Tenovus Cancer information centre Cardiff 1965–70; retd; resid Crail

CRUICKSHANK Alexander MA 1922 MB ChB 1925
d Walton-on-Thames 6.8.80 *AUR* XLIX 67

CRUICKSHANK or Davidson, Alice Lawrie MA 1947
resid Forres

CRUICKSHANK or Semple, Alison Ballenden *MB ChB 1939
med asst (part-time) E of Scot. blood transfusion serv from 1955; resid Dun

CRUICKSHANK Alistair BSc(agr) 1953
conserv and extension off. Filabusi S Rhod 1953–61; farm. Fyvie 1961–77

CRUICKSHANK Andrew MA 1899
d Bearsden Glas 10.10.64 *AUR* XLI 52

CRUICKSHANK Andrew Whyte MA 1949
head: Holytown p s Lanarksh 1967–71, Petersburn p s Airdrie from 1971

CRUICKSHANK or McGillivray, Anne Calder MA 1925
resid Helmsdale
husb *d* 24.2.72

CRUICKSHANK Annie MA 1928
teacher maths NSW Aust 1929–37; head Rogart p s 1941–68; retd
m Grantown-on-Spey 3.12.37 Mackay Mackay MA *qv*
husb *d* 5.3.67

CRUICKSHANK or Davidson, Annie Wilson Corrie MA 1933
resid Nairn

CRUICKSHANK Arthur Lewis *BSc 1928
chief telecomm supt Bedford 1953–69: retd; resid Ringwood

CRUICKSHANK or Watt, Caroline Margaret MA 1918
d Inv 31.3.78

CRUICKSHANK Charles Burr MA 1893
no longer on GC reg

CRUICKSHANK Charles Greig *MA 1936
FRHistS 1971
exec secy Commonwealth econ comm 1964–66; dir commodities div Commonwealth secretariat 1967–68; BoT (reg export div London and SE) 1969–71; Channel Is occupation official historian 1970–71; insp FCO 1971–72; asst secy civ aviation auth Lond 1971–72; asst secy DTI Lond 1972–73; retd; resid Lond

CRUICKSHANK Charles Ian Thomas MB ChB 1953
MRCGP 1961
g p: Gairloch W Ross 1960–64, Kintore 1964–67 and in group practice Inverurie from 1967

CRUICKSHANK Cyril Edgar BSc(eng) 1932 *1933
AMICE 1939 AMIWE 1945 FIWE 1969
eng asst Westminster 1935; chief asst Aber c c 1959–68; area eng cent area NE of Scot water board from 1968; retd 1973

CRUICKSHANK Daniel MA 1942 LLB 1949
ptnr leg. firm Dun from 1955

CRUICKSHANK Donald Campbell *MA 1933
dep rector Banff acad on closure of Fordyce acad 1964; retd 1971; resid Fochabers

CRUICKSHANK or Macdonald, Dorothy Mary *MA 1925
resid Aber

CRUICKSHANK Douglas Scott BCom 1926
CA
no longer on GC reg

CRUICKSHANK Douglas William MA 1927
sen met. off. and lect climatology RAF Thorney Is; retd 1970; resid Aber
d Aber 1.7.81

CRUICKSHANK or Doig, Elizabeth MA 1949

CRUICKSHANK Elizabeth Scott MA 1921
d Aber 5.8.71 *AUR* XLIV 319

CRUICKSHANK or Jolly, Elizabeth Walker MA 1946
Glasg: teacher handicapped (m h and p h) children 1960–69; dep head Kennyhill s for m h children 1969–73; head Rottenrow (later Abercorn) s for m h children from 1973

CRUICKSHANK Elsie Margaret MA 1940
teacher Smithfield s Aber 1965–66; clerkess Aber from 1967

CRUICKSHANK or McGee, Elsie Margaret MA 1950
resid Aber

CRUICKSHANK Eric Hugh *BSc 1953 PhD 1956

CRUICKSHANK Eric Kennedy *MB ChB 1937 *MD 1948
OBE 1960 FACP 1970 FRCPGlas 1972
dean post grad med and prof post grad med educ Glas from 1972
marr. diss

m (2) Kingston Jamaica 6.11.69 Josephine W. Williams nurse d of Theodore R. W. CMG MA(Oxon) Jamaica

CRUICKSHANK Ernest William Henderson MB ChB 1910 *MD 1920 LLD 1959
d 29.12.64 *AUR* XLI 109

CRUICKSHANK Ethel Margaret BSc 1923 PhD 1926
MA(Cantab) 1965
res under MRC Dunn nutrit lab Cambridge 1940–73; retd; resid Cambridge

CRUICKSHANK or Sayce, Ethel Margaret Lindsay *MA 1930
resid East Kilbride

CRUICKSHANK George *MA 1913 *BSc 1920
OBE BA(Cantab)
d Weybridge 11.9.72 *AUR* XLV 124

CRUICKSHANK George Alexander MA 1931 BSc(agr) 1933
SAI Edin from 1945

CRUICKSHANK George Grant MA 1953
teacher Dyce s from 1969

CRUICKSHANK George Watt MB ChB 1951
g p Lond from 1959

CRUICKSHANK Gordon BSc(eng) 1944

CRUICKSHANK Hector MA 1932 BSc(for) 1934
d Aber 11.3.63 *AUR* XL 206

CRUICKSHANK Helen Margaret BSc 1944
teacher sc Keith g s from 1949; resid Lhanbryde

CRUICKSHANK or Smith, Helen Taylor *MA 1952
on edit. staff Canadian Med Assoc Journal 1956–62; resid Oakville, Ontario

CRUICKSHANK Isobel Watt MA 1912
no longer on GC reg

CRUICKSHANK Jack Naughton *BSc 1941
prin scient off. MoD from 1959
m Birm 11.5.51 Joan Corbett

CRUICKSHANK James BSc 1922
no longer on GC reg

CRUICKSHANK James Henry *BSc 1933 PhD 1936
asst gen man. ICI Europa Brussels 1968–72; retd; resid Stockport

CRUICKSHANK James Robert Leslie MA 1925 LLB 1928
WS 1937
Edin: leg. asst 1927–36; ptnr Menzies & White, WS later Menzies, Dougal & Milligan, WS from 1936
m Edin 5.9.35 Norah Burke d of Matthew J. B. Middletown Armagh N Ireland

CRUICKSHANK James Stephen MB ChB 1936
d Sheffield 20.12.72 *AUR* XLV 227

CRUICKSHANK James William *BSc 1951

CRUICKSHANK Jeannie Ann *MA 1920
retd 1960; resid Inv

CRUICKSHANK John Alexander MA 1937
teacher Engl/hist/geog Aber/Aberdeensh 1939–40; war serv RAF N. Af/Italy 1940–45; various teaching posts 1945–47; teacher Aber: Engl/hist/geog Frederick St s, prin hist/geog/mod stud. Linksfield acad 1947–76; retd

CRUICKSHANK John Benton MB ChB 1937
d Glasg 1.4.69 *AUR* XLIII 216

CRUICKSHANK or Downie, Katherine MA 1932
resid Salcombe

CRUICKSHANK Katie Isabella MA 1911
no longer on GC reg

CRUICKSHANK Leslie Duffus MB ChB 1955
Aber: h s (obst) mat. hosp 1959, trainee asst 1960; g p Forfar from 1960; (locum tenens Parry Sound Ontario July Aug 1972)

CRUICKSHANK Leslie Valentine *MA 1931
OBE
sqn ldr RAF; retd
d Shaftesbury 26.3.81 *AUR* XLIX 138

CRUICKSHANK Lorna Collie *MA 1950
Edin: teacher mod lang St. Denis s 1963–70, head of dept from 1970; Goetheschule Hanover (centre for Brit teachers) 1975–77

CRUICKSHANK Maggie Bell MA 1924
spec asst teacher maths Airdrie acad; retd 1966

CRUICKSHANK or Clark, Margaret Stewart MA 1935
teacher Turriff acad from 1967

CRUICKSHANK Martin Melvin BSc 1911 MB ChB 1912 *MD 1925 ChM 1927
d 19.10.64 *AUR* XLI 32

CRUICKSHANK Mary MA 1922
teacher Hilton s s Aber 1932–61; retd

CRUICKSHANK or Campbell, Mary Barbara *MA 1930
d Lausanne Switzerland 29.3.47

CRUICKSHANK or Lawson, Mary Elizabeth MA 1923
resid Inv

CRUICKSHANK Peter BSc(eng) 1955

CRUICKSHANK Peter Bruce BSc(for) 1950
NE reg man. Bowaters Forest Products Fordoun from 1968

CRUICKSHANK Robert *MB ChB 1922 *MD 1925 LLD 1968
FRSE 1957 FRCPE 1962 CBE 1966
prof soc and preventive med univ of WI, Kingston Jamaica 1966–68
d Edin 16.8.74 *AUR* XLV 108

CRUICKSHANK or Houston, Thelma Cromarty MB ChB 1943
clin med off. Camden and Islington A H A from 1972

CRUICKSHANK or McRobbie or Melvin, Violet Mary MA 1928
resid Huntly
husb (A. W. Melvin) *d* 1965

CRUICKSHANK William Durward MB ChB 1915
d Rustington 10.10.61 *AUR* XXXIX 278

CRUICKSHANK William Leslie BSc(eng) 1940

CRUICKSHANK William Walker *MA 1901 *BD 1915
d 6.4.69 *AUR* XLIII 208

CRUICKSHANK or MacKay, Williamina MB ChB 1925
g p; retd 1939; resid Bexhill-on-Sea

CRUICKSHANK or Milne, Williamina Hay MB ChB 1938
Royal Cornhill hosp Aber 1968–72; part time g p from 1972

CRUICKSHANKS John MA 1937
dep dir educ Moray and Nairn 1967–75; div educ off. Moray div Grampian reg c from 1975

CRUSE Clara *MA 1921 BSc 1922
teacher maths Lemington g s Northumberland 1926–59; retd; resid N'cle-u-Tyne

CULLEN or Isles, Alice May MA 1946

CUMMING Alexander Farquharson BSc(agr) 1906
no longer on GC reg

CUMMING Alexander George MA 1938
FEIS 1963
head Portknockie s s from 1961; retd 1977
d 10.10.80

CUMMING Alexander (R.) *MA 1901
no longer on GC reg

CUMMING Alexander Robertson Ritchie MB ChB 1935 MD 1940
d Cottingham 31.5.66 *AUR* XLI 341

CUMMING or Graham, Alexandrina Wilson MA 1922
no longer on GC reg

CUMMING Annie Ogilvie MA 1931

CUMMING or Bisset, Catherine Munro BSc 1925 *1926
d Lond 9.11.61 *AUR* XXXIX 282

CUMMING Douglas BSc(agr) 1954
DAFS: asst insp Aber 1958–71, insp Ayr 1971–78, insp Aber from 1978

CUMMING or Schofield, Ella *MA 1909

CUMMING George MA 1904
no longer on GC reg

CUMMING George Ingram MA 1929

CUMMING or Jones, Hilda Jamieson *MA 1939
teacher: Engl Galashiels acad 1963, Selkirk h s 1963–77; retd 1977

CUMMING or Gray, Ida Jean MA 1934
resid Aber

CUMMING or Young, Isobel McRae MA 1927
resid Insch

CUMMING James Collie *MA 1929

CUMMING James Munro *MA 1930
d Tain 30.11.67 *AUR* XLII 369

CUMMING John *MA 1936
HMIS 1950; HM(dist)IS from 1962
d 5.4.78 *AUR* XLVIII 106

CUMMING Joyce Edith MA 1953
resid Menorca Balearic Is Spain
m Mahon Menorca 4.4.73 Juan Cardona maker of costume jewellery s of Antonio C.

CUMMING Mary BSc(agr) 1948
farm. Newburgh Aberdeensh

CUMMING Mary *MA 1952
teacher Fr: Insch 1958–60, Bankhead acad from 1960

CUMMING Patricia May MB ChB 1955
DPH 1961
Banff c c: asst m o h 1961–64, dep m o h 1964–65, clin m o h Glasg from 1973
m Craigellachie 23.7.65 Neil M. Jack DA(Edin) arch. s of Donald D. J. FRIBA

CUMMING Patrick MA 1928 LLB 1930
joint clerk univ court St And and secy Council Queen's Coll Dundee 1954–63; ptnr Gray, Robertson & Wilkie solic Dun 1963–67; town clerk Banff 1967–70; retd 1970

CUMMING Robert Alexander MB ChB 1933
FRCPath 1964 (founder fell.) FRCPE 1970 FRCSE 1971
reg dir SE Scot. blood transfusion serv from 1947; retd 1974
hon con phys (Blood Transf) ERI

CUMMING Ronald Anderson MB ChB 1925
retd 1961; resid Banchory
d Aber 12.2.79 *AUR* XLVIII 229

CUMMING Ronald Patrick MB ChB 1945
consult. surg to Shetland hosps from 1957

CUMMING or Cunningham, Rosa Mary Gordon MA 1914
d 12.8.65

CUMMING William James MB ChB 1928

CUMMINS Gordon Theodore Martineau MB ChB 1948

CUNNINGHAM Donald Cameron *MA 1955 MEd 1957
Aber: teacher Engl Hilton s 1960–61, Aber acad 1961–63, RGC 1963–66; lect coll of educ from 1966

CUNNINGHAM Henry Campbell MA 1915
no longer on GC reg

CUNNINGHAM Ira James PhD 1931
d NZ 29.8.71

CUNNINGHAM Shirley Margaret *MA 1952 *MEd 1967
journalist 1952–65; Aber: teacher hist/Engl 1967–69; lect educ coll of educ from 1969

CURR Alexander Ian MB ChB 1921
d Poole 7.11.69 *AUR* XLIII 329

CURRID John Gilbert *MA 1919 MB ChB 1924
d Chadwell Heath 31.5.70 *AUR* XLIV 109

CURRID Patrick Grant MA 1920 MB ChB 1923
d Lond 22.5.68 *AUR* XLII 358

CURRIE Alan BSc(eng) 1945

CURRIE Andrew MB ChB 1941
MFCM 1971
N Nigeria: sen m o hosps admin M of H Kaduna 1959–61; sen m o admin Kano med div 1961–62; Scot.: dept med supt Inv hosps 1963–65, med supt Inv hosps 1965–73, dep sen admin m o Northern reg hosp board 1973–74; c m s Highland health board 1974–75; c m s Argyll and Clyde health board from 1975

CURRIE Annie Watson MA 1915
d Keith 9.8.72

CURRIE George Alexander *BSc(agr) 1923 DSc 1936 LLD 1948
LLD (Dalhousie Can) 1958 LLD (NZ) 1961
LLD (univ of Papua and New Guinea) 1976
vice-chanc univ of NZ 1952–61; chmn comm on educ in NZ 1960–62; chmn comm on higher educ Papua and New Guinea; resid Canberra

CURRIE Helen Littlejohn MA 1950
Ellon acad: prin teacher mus 1959–72, prin teacher guid 1972–73; Aber: year mistress Harlaw acad from 1973; organist and choir mistress Ferryhill N church Aber from 1971

CURRIE James BSc 1951
Aber: prin teacher maths Powis acad 1963–73; asst head Harlaw acad from 1973

CURRIE James Glen BSc(agr) 1955

CURRIE or Michie, Jessie MA 1940
teacher Engl Ijebu-ode g s W Nigeria 1949–56; Zaria N Nigeria: lect Engl coll of arts sc and tech 1958–61; head Ahmadu Bello staff s 1963–66; Viewlands p s Perth: teacher 1970–74, asst head from 1974

CURRIE Norman Lamont MA 1928 BCom 1930
head Bonhill p s Dunbartonsh 1965–72; retd; resid Dumbarton
d Dumbarton 2.8.76

CURRIE Robert MA 1949
C of S min Dowanhill ch Glasg from 1969

CURSITER William Nisbet *BSc(eng) 1951
FIStructE MICE
chief eng Dorman Long & Amalgamated Eng Lagos 1961–62; asst to export dir Dorman Long & Co Lond 1962–67; contr man. (export) Redpath Dorman Long Glasg 1967–75; contr man. Redpath Dorman Long Glasg from 1975

CUSHNIE or Robertson, Agnes Jean Carswell MA 1941
teacher Rosebank s Nairn from 1966

CUSITER Douglass James MB ChB 1937
m o h and div m o West Riding c c: Mexborough, Conisbrough and Dearne 1961–72, Rotherham, Kiveton Park and Maltby from 1972
d Scarborough 27.5.74 *AUR* XLVI 110

CUSITER Hilda *MA 1932
Fairfield h s Manc: sen classics mistress 1950–58, dep head from 1958; retd 1975

CUTHBERT or Young, Jean Spiers *BSc 1955

CUTHBERT Mary McLaren Gordon MA 1956

CUTHBERTSON Iain *MA 1952 LLD 1978
gen dir of prod. Citizens' Theatre Glasg 1961–64; asst dir Royal Court Theatre Lond 1965–67; dir Perth Theatre from 1967: Rector Aberd 1975–78
m Glas 6.1.64 Anne C. K. Biles actress d of Reginald N. B. Glasg

CUTHBERTSON Lilias Margaret MA 1953
m Aber 15.10.60 William E. Strachan MB ChB 1954 *qv*
resid Plymouth

CUTHILL James Caithness BSc 1941

CUTLER James Raymond *BSc 1954
civ serv Fed Govt of Nigeria, Kano 1955–59; stored prod. entomologist/pesticides DAFS Edin from 1959

CUTT James Ritch MA 1925
Aber: head Cornhill s 1951–63, Sunnybank s 1963–65, Mile End s 1965–69; retd

CUTTS John Raymond *MA 1953

DAKERS John BSc 1923 *1924
prin teacher chem Portobello s s 1962–68; retd

DALE Alexander Robb MA 1949
FEIS 1972 RNVR lt (A) (O) 1942–46
Aber coll of comm: teacher 1959–63, sen teacher 1963–73, acting head of dept 1973, later head of dept

DALE Brian Bozier MB ChB 1953
MLCO 1969 MFHom 1976
dir stud. Lond coll of osteopathy and at Harley House Marylebone Rd from 1967

DALGARNO Charles William BSc(eng) 1950
civ eng Wm Tawse Aber from 1954
d Aber 10.5.78

DALGARNO Christian Edith MA 1939

DALGARNO or Reid, Ethel Margaret MA 1907
d S Af

DALGARNO Helen Ruth MA 1927
retd 1955; resid Edin

DALGARNO John BSc(eng) 1955

DALGARNO Myra Theresa *MA 1948
teacher mod lang Tunbridge Wells 1960–71; head of dept from 1971

DALGARNO Wilfred Tait MA 1928 BSc(agr) 1930
teacher: Old Rayne 1960–61, Bucksburn 1961–72; retd; resid Princes Risborough

DALGLEISH George Robert White BSc(eng) 1948
Peterhead: asst civ eng Admiralty 1948–50, resid eng harbour improvement work 1950–53; civ eng Sir Alex Gibb Ptnrs Edin 1953–54; plan. ag contr man. Holland & Honnen & Cubitts (Scot.) Edin and N'cle 1954–61; contr man. Richard Costain Construct. N'cle and Leeds 1961–66; Higgins Hill Northern Leeds: contr man. 1966–68, reg. man. 1968–72, dir from 1970

DALGLEISH James White MA 1937 LLB 1939
Cardiff: dir C H Bailey 1962; dir Allseas Shipping Services and subsids 1965; dep chmn C H Bailey from 1970

DALGLEISH or Leyton, Sheila Robertson MB ChB 1943
Eng: g h m o Powick hosp 1960–62, clin asst path. Bromsgrove gen hosp 1962–63; Horsham Aust: private psychiat 1968–71, school m o from 1973

DALLAS Marjorie Gordon MA 1908
no longer on GC reg

DALLAS Robert Duncan MA 1933
teacher Banchory acad from 1947

DALTON Alfred Hyam *MA 1948
CB 1976
Inland rev: dep chmn from 1973

DALY Robert MA 1948
JP Perth 1967
C of S min: Inchture and Kinnaird ch linked with Longforgan ch from 1963; mod Dun presb from 1973

DALZIEL or Wetherly, Agnes Johnston MA 1946
teacher: Commercial Rd p s Sunderland 1964–66, Hillview p s Sunderland 1966–68, asst head St Margaret's s for girls Aber 1968–75, asst head Cults p s 1975–77; head Greenbrae p s Bridge of Don Aber from 1977
husb *d* 1963

DANIEL Leslie Morren BSc(agr) 1952

DANIEL Renwick St. Clair Calder *MA 1951
ACMA 1962 FCMA 1966
area cost dev off. NCB Fife area, Dysart 1961–66; lect man. acct RGIT Aber from 1966

DANSON James Gordon MB ChB 1908 MD 1922
d Bath 18.6.69 *AUR* XLIII 327

D'ARCY Rosina Cannon MA 1952

DARGIE or Taylor, Edith Isabella MA 1930
remed teacher Ferryhill s Aber 1966–72; retd
husb *d* 12.1.66
d Aber 13.2.80

DARK Victor Marshall BSc(eng) 1951
CEng MICE 1957 MIWES 1959
eng with various consult. on water supply, harbour and bldg proj in UK, Libya, Saudi Arabia, Brunei 1965–78; Moxley Jenner & Ptnrs Swindon from 1979

DARLING James Grahame BSc 1908
no longer on GC reg

DARNLEY Ernest Marshall MB ChB 1934

DARNLEY William Russell MB ChB 1935
no longer on GC reg

DAS Nadella Vinkata BSc(agr) 1924
no longer on GC reg

DASTOOR Jamshed Khorsted MB ChB 1915
no longer on GC reg

DASTUR Ratan Edulji MB ChB 1912
no longer on GC reg

DAVID Ian Ainsley Fearon BSc(eng) 1943 MA 1949
FSA Scot 1970
retd; resid Aber

DAVIDSON Adrian Cyril BSc(eng) 1945
supt Central Thermal Serv Ontario hydro Toronto from 1972

DAVIDSON Alastair Grant MB ChB 1948
g p Helmsdale from 1957

DAVIDSON Alexander Dyce MA 1929 MB ChB 1933
g p Steyning from 1945
d W Chiltington 20.2.77 *AUR* XLVII 212

DAVIDSON Alexander Masson MB ChB 1937
Lond: consult. ch welfare Borough of St Pancras 1946–48; clin asst St Mary's hosp for women and children Plaistow 1950–62; patron soc of portrait sculptors from 1962; retd from med pract 1971; resid Oxford
d Oxford 2.11.80

DAVIDSON Alexander Munro BL 1951
ptnr C & P H Chalmers advoc Aber from 1952
m Hampstead Lond 23.5.59 Anne P. Hayes
d Cults Aber 23.4.78 *AUR* XLVII 360

DAVIDSON Alexander Robert *MA 1922
d Kilmarnock 15.9.69 *AUR* XLIII 330

DAVIDSON Alfred MA 1949
teacher: Townhill Dunfermline 1952–54. Gordon Schools Huntly 1954–60; Huntly: head Largue s 1960–66; Gordon Schools Huntly: dep head (prim) 1966–72, head from 1972
m Huntly 15.8.56 Elizabeth M. McIrvine teacher d of John McI. Glass

DAVIDSON Alfred Harry BSc 1923
FEIS 1962
retd
d Leicester 10.9.76 *AUR* XLVII 105

DAVIDSON or Innes, Amelia Shaw Ethel MA 1949
resid Huntly

DAVIDSON or Lobban, Annabella Lobban MA 1903

DAVIDSON or Bruce, Annie Bertha MA 1932
resid Buxton

DAVIDSON or Jones, Annie Dawson MA 1941
teacher St Luke's Brighton 1964–66, post of spec responsibility for mus from 1966

DAVIDSON or Hutchinson, Annie Margaret McKessar MA 1936 *BSc 1938
resid Poole

DAVIDSON Annie Milne MA 1920
no longer on GC reg

DAVIDSON or McNab, Bessie MA 1915
teacher: maths/Fr Anderson inst Lerwick 1916–17, maths Fraserburgh acad 1917–56, spec asst 1956–62; retd
d Fraserburgh 12.12.76

DAVIDSON Charles Ingram BSc(eng) 1951
d Aber 14.2.60 *AUR* XXXVIII 600

DAVIDSON Constance Annie MA 1924
teacher: Inverurie acad 1925–28
d Aber 24.11.74

DAVIDSON Donald MA 1926
d Edin 26.8.65 *AUR* XLI 246

DAVIDSON Donald Arbuthnot BL 1923
ptnr Wilsone & Duffus advoc Aber 1936–73; retd

DAVIDSON Donald Falconer BSc(for) 1938

DAVIDSON Douglas Steel BL 1951
d Edin 15.3.72 *AUR* XLIV 433

DAVIDSON or Skene, Edith Anne MA 1907
d Aber 18.4.66 *AUR* XLII 82

DAVIDSON Edith Margaret *MA 1945
teacher: second master Engl Dundee h s 1965–73; prin guid Grove acad Broughty Ferry from 1973

DAVIDSON Edwin Maxwell Murray BD 1913
C of S min: retd from Markinch 1960; resid Perth
d 29.3.77

DAVIDSON or Fyvie, Eleanor M. MA 1941
teacher Fyvie from 1969

DAVIDSON or Harper, Elizabeth Cruickshank MA 1924
teacher Fyvie s till 1967; retd
d 22.9.76

DAVIDSON or Gray, Elizabeth Mary BSc 1945
teacher maths: Airdrie acad 1971–73, Woodmill h s Dunfermline from 1973; in spec class unit Ballingry jun h s from 1976

DAVIDSON or Abbas, Elma Rutherford MB ChB 1946
doctor i/c trg Internat Planned Parenthood Fed reg off. Nairobi from 1971

DAVIDSON Ethel Margaret May MA 1929
d Brechin 28.8.61 *AUR* XXXIX 282

DAVIDSON or Mathie, Ethel Mary Falconer MA 1930

DAVIDSON Flora Mary *BSc 1954 PhD 1957
biochem: Lond chest hosp 1959–73, Willesden gen hosp from 1973

DAVIDSON Frank George Shepherd MA 1932 BL 1934
advoc in Aber

DAVIDSON Frank Norrie BSc(eng) 1942
MICE 1951 ERD 1965
dep dir roads Tayside reg c from 1975

DAVIDSON George MB ChB 1908 DPH 1909
retd 1965; resid Bedford 1965–70, Aber from 1970
d Aber 6.11.76 *AUR* XLVII 211

DAVIDSON George Chessor BSc(eng) 1945
FIEE
NSHEB: area eng Elgin from 1966

DAVIDSON George Ian MB ChB 1935
d Aber 9.3.74 *AUR* XLV 449

DAVIDSON or Dickie, Georgina Christian MA 1925
matron Tertowie resid s Kinellar 1945–60; teacher Aber 1960–73; retd
husb *d* 27.3.60

DAVIDSON Gilbert MA 1934
FEIS 1972
head St. Ronan's s s Inverleithen from 1945

DAVIDSON Graham MacGregor MB ChB 1949
g p Bradford from 1954

DAVIDSON Hector BSc(agr) 1952

DAVIDSON or Sleigh, Helena Margaret MA 1920 MB ChB 1923 DPH 1924
Lond: organis of courses Women's Corona soc 1958–63; overseas med advis Save the Children Fund 1963–73; resid Tunbridge Wells
d 13.7.81

DAVIDSON Henry William MA 1899
no longer on GC reg

DAVIDSON Iain Francis William Knowles *MA 1954 EdB 1956
teacher St. Peter's RC s Gloucester 1960–63; educ psych Bexley 1964–67; Ontario inst for stud in educ Toronto: res assoc 1967–69, PhD stud. 1969–71; lect dept of spec educ from 1972
m Aber 19.8.67 Barbara A. Marshall teacher d of Joseph M. East Sheen Lond

DAVIDSON Ian *BSc(eng) 1952
lect eng Queen's coll univ St. And/Dund univ from 1967

DAVIDSON Ian Mackenzie BSc 1951
teacher maths/sc Alford 1956–61; relief teacher maths/sc/prim. subjs various schools Aber/Aberdeensh 1961–73

DAVIDSON Ian Winsted BSc 1929

DAVIDSON or Chalmers, Ida Helen MA 1916
no longer on GC reg

DAVIDSON Irene Girdlestone MA 1940
teacher: Colegio Internacional Arequipa Peru till 1961; Aber: teacher prim. relief staff 1962, geog/mod stud/scripture Aber h s for girls—Harlaw acad—1961–75, geog from 1975

DAVIDSON James MB ChB 1902
no longer on GC reg

DAVIDSON James Johnston *MA 1924
d Hythe Kent 5.6.71 *AUR* XLIV 320 & 430

DAVIDSON James Meldrum MA 1942
C of S min: Dalziel h ch Motherwell 1960–67, St. Andrew's ch Inverurie from 1967; town councillor 1969–75

DAVIDSON James Smart *MA 1926
FEIS
d 3.10.75

DAVIDSON James Watt MB ChB 1944
g p Clevedon Avon from 1960

DAVIDSON James Watt [c]MB ChB 1953 MD 1969
MRCP & SGlas 1963 FRCP(C) 1972
regist med N'cle reg hosp board 1960–61; sen regist radiol: DRI 1962–63, Western Inf Glasg 1963–65; Canada: staff radiol Toronto gen hosp 1965–71, assoc prof radiol univ of Toronto 1971–74; dir radiol Chedoke hosps Hamilton and assoc clin prof radiol McM univ Hamilton 1974, dir radiol Henderson gen hosp Hamilton Ont 1977

DAVIDSON or Gibson, Jane Isabella *MB ChB 1940
FRCPath 1965
lect path. Aberd from 1970

DAVIDSON or Thomson, Janet Anderson MA 1947
resid Towthorpe York

DAVIDSON or Milne, Janet Dorothy MB ChB 1954
med asst dept of venereology Bristol RI; sen m o fam plan. clin from 1977

DAVIDSON or Jackson, Jean Lawrie MB ChB 1949
m Edin 11.1.52
resid North Bay Ontario

DAVIDSON or Taylor, Jean Margaret MA 1947
resid Dyke Forres

DAVIDSON or Reid, Jessie Elizabeth MA 1928
resid Aber

DAVIDSON John BSc 1948
d 4.10.64

DAVIDSON John BSc 1951 *1952

DAVIDSON John PhD 1953
CChem FRIC 1962
head dept chem and phys analysis Rowett res inst Aber from 1970

DAVIDSON John Bruce BSc(eng) 1949

DAVIDSON John Farquhar MB ChB 1922 DPH 1926
d 20.7.79 *AUR* XLVIII 351

DAVIDSON John Fergus Chalmers MA 1955
MBKS 1971
teacher: Mile-End p s Aber 1956–62, Aber g s 1962–63; lect audio-visual media Aber coll of educ 1963–66; asst dir Scot Film Council Glasg 1966–70; head educ film div Encyclopaedia Brit Lond from 1970–73; elected vice-pres internat council for educ media Stockholm 1969; man dir educ and trg div Transmedia (W H Smith group) 1974; formed own co Fergus Davidson Associates to distribute film television audio and video materials 1975, chmn and man dir

DAVIDSON John Forsyth MA 1923
JP FRES
d Banchory 25.2.76

DAVIDSON John Maxwell MB ChB 1925
no longer on GC reg

DAVIDSON or Davidson, Julia Forgie MB ChB 1946
Aberd: res asst dept soc med 1968–73; part time res asst dept commun med from 1973

DAVIDSON Lawson Douglas MB ChB 1945
O St J 1971
consult. anaest NE reg board (Scot.) from 1963; hon med supt St. John nursing home Aber

DAVIDSON Lily Robertson MA 1923

DAVIDSON or Walker, Margaret Elizabeth McKenzie MA 1943 Dip Ed 1957
m(2) Surrey 6.8.60 Francis E. Benwell army off. s of Frederick B. Johannesburg
resid Bushey

DAVIDSON or Massie, Margaret Elizabeth Meta MA 1925
no longer on GC reg

DAVIDSON Margaret Isobel MB ChB 1955
g p Aber from 1957

DAVIDSON or Hunter, Marion MA 1916
no longer on GC reg

DAVIDSON Marjory Stuart MA 1920 BSc 1923
d Bournemouth –.9.72

DAVIDSON or Hay, Mary Gordon MA 1955
resid Aber

DAVIDSON or Murray, Mary Maxwell MA 1946
resid The Hague, Holland

DAVIDSON or Dinnes, Nancy Rosemary Chalmers MA 1949
asst town clerk Cupar 1959–64; secy: Scot. Boatowners Mutual Insur Assoc Buckie 1965–70, Peterkin & Duncans advoc Aber 1970–73, Brander & Cruickshanks advoc Aber from 1974

DAVIDSON Norman James Hunter MB ChB 1938
FRCPath 1963
path. All Saints hosp Chatham from 1956

DAVIDSON Patricia McKenzie MA 1951

DAVIDSON Peter McLaren BSc 1924
retd from Pilkington Bros 1967; resid Eccleston St. Helens

DAVIDSON or Slessor, Phyllis Eileen MB ChB 1939
resid Edin

DAVIDSON Rachel Mary MA 1926
retd; resid Aber

DAVIDSON Rena Mayor Simpson MA 1923
teacher: Culloden s 1942–45, Canonmills s Edin 1945–55, Carrick Knowe s Edin 1955–64; retd

DAVIDSON Richard Charles BSc(eng) 1950

DAVIDSON Robert MB ChB 1923

DAVIDSON Robert BSc(agr) 1947

DAVIDSON Robert MA 1949 *MEd 1952
teacher Aber and Banffsh 1950–54; asst dir of educ Kincardinesh 1954–63; dep head Ferryhill p s Aber from 1963

DAVIDSON Robert MB ChB 1951
MRCPsych 1971
Glasg: sen m o Woodilee hosp 1957–65; consult. psychiat: Hartwood hosp 1965–67, Woodilee hosp from 1967

DAVIDSON Robert Andrew Welsford BCom 1923
no longer on GC reg

DAVIDSON Robert Murray MB ChB 1955
g p Atherstone Warks from 1966

DAVIDSON Stephen *BSc 1951 PhD 1954
lect nat phil Aberd from 1958

DAVIDSON Sydney Gordon MA 1920 MB ChB 1924 LLD 1975
surg ARI; retd 1965
d Aber 22.3.80 *AUR* XLVIII 440

DAVIDSON or Preece, Sylvia Hendry Miller MA 1955

DAVIDSON Thomas Bendelow MB ChB 1940
g p Aber from 1947

DAVIDSON Thomas John MB ChB 1922 DPH 1923
DTM & H 1929
IMS 1923–48; retd col; resid Bridport
m Loughborough 1951 Ethel I. Harvey

DAVIDSON or Shewan, Vera Eileen Jeannie MA 1931
resid Aber

DAVIDSON William BSc(eng) 1952

DAVIDSON William Campbell *MB ChB 1928 MD 1934 DPH 1938
retd 1966; resid Matua Tauranga NZ

DAVIDSON William Gordon MB ChB 1931
d Grimsby 31.8.64 *AUR* XL 400

DAVIDSON William Mackay MB ChB 1934 *MD 1957
FRCPath 1963 FRSE 1964
prof haemat King's coll hosp med s Lond from 1959: emeritus prof Lond univ from 1974

DAVIDSON William Sharp MB ChB 1931
DPH 1948 FACMA 1968 CBE 1980
RN surg lt 1932–35; IMS 1938–48 retd with hon rank of lt col; dep commissioner of publ health and dep prin m o of West Aust 1949–62, comm publ health and prin m o WA 1963–74

DAVIDSON-LAMB William MB ChB 1938

DAVIE Alexander MA 1910
d Insch 1961 *AUR* XXXIX 273

DAVIE Alexander Brodie MB ChB 1936
g p fam doctor unit health centre Hounslow from 1970
d 7.2.78 *AUR* XLVIII 232

DAVIE or Oughtred, Armorel Margaret *MA 1950
resid Ottawa

DAVIE Christian Stephen MA 1929
retd 1969; resid Hatton

DAVIE Doris Helen Gordon MA 1933

DAVIE or Robertson, Elaine Agnes MA 1944

DAVIE Frederick *BSc 1948

DAVIE George Forbes BSc 1927
d 9.4.64

DAVIE Hilda Stephen MA 1939
teacher: year mistress Hazlehead acad Aber from 1970

DAVIE James Ferguson BCom 1932
teacher Ruthrieston s s 1940–73, Harlaw acad from 1973; retd

DAVIE Jean Keith MA 1949
teacher Aber: various schools 1949–50, maths/sc Kaimhill s s 1950–71, maths Kincorth s s 1971–74, asst prin (admin) Kincorth s s from 1974

DAVIE or Butterworth, Jessie Henderson MA 1927
retd 1967; resid Aber
d Aber 5.7.80

DAVIE or Stewart, Jessie Keith MA 1913
d 25.7.66 *AUR* XLI 338

DAVIE Louis Helen Gordon MA 1933
no longer on GC reg

DAVIE or Fyfe, Margaret Ann Birnie BSc 1949
teacher sc Torry acad and Cults acad Aber from 1970
husb *d* 1.2.68

DAVIE Violet Cameron *MA 1914
retd; resid Banff

DAVIE or Barbour, Wendy Jean Alison MB ChB 1948

DAVIE William Alexander James *BSc 1953
FBCS 1959 MInstP 1971 MSc(eng) (Cranfield Inst Tech) 1955
tech man. Elliott Bros Birchamwood 1966; Welwyn Garden City: man. dir Direct Data 1966–74, man. dir Automated Lib Syst from 1974
marr diss 1978

DAVIE William George *MA 1924
teacher maths Boroughmuir s s Edin 1956–68; retd

DAVIES Edwin Braithwaite PhD 1937

DAVIES Rupert Meredith BSc 1924

DAVIS Arthur Joseph MA 1940 Dip Ed 1947
awarded papal Benemerenti medal for serv to church and commun 1979 retd head Corpus Christi s Wilford Nott when amalgamated with indep g s to form Becket comp s 1975; counsellor Becket comp s 1975–79; retd

DAVIS Brian Noel Kittredge BSc 1955
PhD(Nott)

DAVIS or Anderson, Eileen MB ChB 1950
dental anaest Derby from 1961

DAVIS or MacTaggart, June Mary MB ChB 1948
MFCM 1973
sen m o Torbay county borough 1968–74; spec commun med Devon A H A from 1974

DAVISON John Landfear *MA 1952
prin teacher Engl Wallace Hall acad Dumfriessh from 1969
m Dumfries 17.7.59 Barbara A. Douglas teacher d of George D. Dumfries

DAWSON Alexander MB ChB 1905
resid Aber
d Aber 21.6.80 *AUR* XLIX 66

DAWSON Allan Alexander BSc(agr) 1927 PhD 1930

DAWSON Andrew Erskine BSc(agr) 1952

DAWSON or Duncan, Annie Alexandra MA 1924
resid Aberlour

DAWSON Daniel Sutherland BSc 1909
no longer on GC reg

DAWSON or Steven, Dorothy MA 1927
no longer on GC reg

DAWSON or McWilliam, Eileen Vanora MA 1909
no longer on GC reg

DAWSON Emma MA 1912
no longer on GC reg

DAWSON Ernest Vincent Coutts MB ChB 1944
MRCGP 1959 FRCPE 1971
g p Elgin from 1952

DAWSON George Forbes MA 1903 MB ChB 1906
d Musselburgh 20.6.66 *AUR* XLI 335

DAWSON George Gardiner MA 1910
d Elgin 12.2.71 *AUR* XLIV 209

DAWSON Gladys MA 1935
d Aber 7.4.71 *AUR* XLIV 212

DAWSON or Gibson, Helen Mary MA 1925
d Falkirk 20.1.73

DAWSON Henry James
MA 1916 MB ChB 1921 DPH 1931
d Aber 10.3.69 *AUR* XLIII 211

DAWSON James Gordon
***BSc(mech eng) 1937 *BSc(elect eng) 1938**
Zenith Carburetter Co Lond: man. dir 1970–76, chmn from 1976

DAWSON James Norman BSc 1955

DAWSON or Sobecki, Jean MA 1949 Dip Ed 1950
teacher Edin: Liberton p s 1959–62, Bruntsfield p s from 1967

DAWSON or Stewart, Jenny Naomi MA 1920
resid Alloway

DAWSON John Alexander
MA 1915 *MB ChB 1918 MD 1933
d Aber 24.1.72 *AUR* XLIV 428

DAWSON or Dunbar, Kathleen Mary
MB ChB 1949
school m o Forth Valley from 1970

DAWSON Leslie Knight MB ChB 1945
MRCGP 1965
g p Skene from 1966

DAWSON Margaret Elizabeth MA 1939
d 1950

DAWSON or Trubshaw, Margaret Isobel MA 1926
no longer on GC reg

DAWSON or Coburn, Mary Lindsay MA 1942

DAWSON Philip MA 1940 LLB 1949
ptnr James & George Collie advoc in Aber from 1952

DAWSON Reginald David BSc 1914

DAWSON Robert MA 1914 MB ChB 1921 MD 1932
g p Middleton-in-Teesdale from 1921; retd 1963

DAWSON Robert Ernest BSc(eng) 1939

DAWSON Robert George BSc(eng) 1929
MIEE 1962
farm. Phingask Fraserburgh from 1945

DAWSON or Purchase, Sheila Marshall
MB ChB 1951
JP(Hove)
g p Brighton from 1954

DAY Stephen Lunan MA 1938
dep head Middlefield p s Aber from 1970
d 29.11.81

DEAN Agnes Mary MA 1930

DEAN Alan Charles Barclay MB ChB 1954 ChM 1970
res asst, lect surg King's coll hosp med s Lond 1959–65; sen lect surg Edin from 1965; hon secy Royal coll of surg Edin from 1978
m Lond 14.9.60 Fidelity J. Montagu-Pollock d of Sir William M-P. BA(Cantab) Copenhagen

DEAN or Mackenzie Stuart, Amy Margaret
***MA 1918**
chmn John Reid and Robert Nicol Trusts, Aber
d Aber 13.10.78

DEAN Charles Alfred MB ChB 1925
d Brechin 22.2.72 *AUR* XLIV 430

DEAN or Bryce, Constance Elsie MA 1929
retd 1970; resid Sunderland

DEAN Douglas MB ChB 1923
d Crosby Liverpool –.2.68 *AUR* XLII 360

DEAN or Manson, Elma Fraser MA 1929

DEAN or Borowiak, Helen MA 1922
no longer on GC reg

DEAN Ian MA 1953 LLB 1956

DEAN Isabella MA 1917
teacher: inf mistress Ferryhill p s Aber till 1961; retd

DEAN or Grant, Isabella Lyon *MA 1917
d 26.6.1977 *AUR* XLV 120

DEAN Jessie Clara MA 1924
d Aber 24.4.76

DEAN or Macfadyen, Laura Margaret Isobel BSc 1924 *1925
no longer on GC reg

DEAN Myra BSc 1948

DEAN William John Lyon MB ChB 1933
g p Lossiemouth 1945–66; chmn joint c c Moray and Nairn 1962–71; member white fish auth from 1953; chmn herring industry board from 1971; resid Edin

DEANS or Milligan, Ethel *MA 1931
resid Aber

DEANS Hilda Agnes MB ChB 1944 DPH 1954
MFCM 1972
sen asst commun med Dun from 1968

DEANS Maxwell Duncan MA 1928 LLB 1931
retd; resid Edin

DEANS Winifred Margaret *MA 1922 *BSc 1923
retd; resid Aber

DEMPSTER Douglas George BSc 1938 BSc(agr) 1939
sen lect agr Aberd superv univ farms from 1954

DEMPSTER Mary Rae *MA 1952
Dip Man St(RGIT) 1975
teacher Harlaw acad Aber 1960–74; admin/pers asst Comex Diving Aber 1976–77
m 30.3.77 George G. Niven CA

DENHAM Robert Henry George Hector MB ChB 1923 DPH 1928 MD 1933
FRSH 1964 MFCM 1974
member NE Somerset hosp man. comm 1948–68; secy W of Eng branch soc of m o h 1947–63; member council soc of m o h 1947–63; publ health rep Bath div BMA 1950–64; retd; resid Bath

DENNEHY Moira Whitley PhD 1935

DENOON David MA 1925
d 19.3.64

DENOON Marjory MA 1937
teacher Newmachar p s 1964–76; retd

DENOON or Thomson, Mary McKenzie MA 1930
resid Aber

DENTON Eric James PhD 1952
ScD(Cantab) 1964 FRS 1964 FIBiol 1964 Fell. univ coll Lond 1965
physiol Plymouth 1956–64; res prof Royal Society Bristol from 1964

DERIDDER Johannes MB ChB 1923

DESAI Anand Devarao PhD 1939
Hyderabad India: agr dem 1931–33, chem asst 1933–40, agr chem 1940–46; retd; resid Karnatak state

DESSON Robert Gregor *BSc 1941

DEVENISH Walter John MA 1947

DE VILLIERS Isaac Bernhardi MB ChB 1905 *ChM 1906
no longer on GC reg

DEVLIN or Downham, Elizabeth Stirling MA 1935
Sunderland: lect maths Monkwearmouth coll f e 1963–64; teacher maths St Anthony's g s 1965–75

DEVLIN or Hay, Winifred Marguerite MA 1946

DEWAR Eric BSc(eng) 1955

DEWAR James MA 1887
d 31.1.62 *AUR* XXXIX 369

DEWAR Ranald Somerled MB ChB 1939
g p Queensland Aust
m(2) Brisbane 15.1.76 Ursula E. Prestwood nurse d of William P. W Aust

DEWARS Jane Laing *MA 1923
retd 1966; resid Brechin

DEY Annie MA 1907
no longer on GC reg

DEY Dorothy Margaret MA 1933
teacher Skene Square s Aber 1939–74

DEY George Alexander BSc(for) 1950
dist off. for. comm: Kincardine/Angus 1950–54, Argyll 1954–64, Glamorgan 1964–70, Aberdeensh/Banff 1970–73; acquisitions/plan. off. Aber 1973–76, Wester Ross dist from 1976
m Auchenblae 27.3.54 Mary B. G. Watson clerkess d of Barclay W. Auchenblae

DEY James Alexander MA 1949
teacher Knox acad Haddington 1950–74; prin Preston Lodge h s from 1974

DEY James Riddoch MA 1926
d Aber 20.9.70 *AUR* XLIV 110

DEY Jenny Louise Riddoch MA 1953
teacher mod lang: Aber h s for girls 1961–63, Banchory acad 1963–68, Hazlehead acad Aber from 1968

DEY Walter Lewis MA 1940
teacher: prin phys Torry acad Aber from 1962

DEY William Harley BSc(eng) 1947
civ eng Sir Robert McAlpine & Sons Lincolnshire from 1949

DEZSO Ladislas PhD 1930
pastor Debrechen 'Great Church' Reformed Church from 1953; member gen synod of Hungarian Reformed Church

DIACK Alan George BSc(eng) 1955
RAF sqdn ldr from 1974

DIACK Hugh MA 1951
teacher: Glasg acad 1967–68, A G S/Rubislaw acad from 1968

DIACK Hunter *MA 1930
sen lect educ Nott from 1964
d Nottingham 12.12.74 *AUR* XLVI 237

DIACK or Cown, Isobel Wyness MA 1933
d 16.9.72

DIACK James Ian Donald MB ChB 1951
j h m o orthop ARI 1959–60; trainee g p Southborough 1960–61; g p Littlehampton from 1961, clin asst orthop Bognor Regis war mem hosp from 1963

DIACK or Morrison, Lillias Mary Helen MA 1952
teacher Oxgangs p s Edin from 1966

DIACK Mary Margaret MA 1948
teacher geog and remed Peterhead acad from 1968
m Aber 31.3.65 Alexander H. Aird depot eng

DIACK or Brown, Nellie Shaw MB ChB 1921

DIACK Peter MA 1912 DD 1957
d Edin 4.5.67 *AUR* XLII 181

DIACK Peter MA 1948
C of S min Elgin S par ch from 1956

DICK Andrew James Mennie *MA 1928

DICK George Robert Farney *BSc 1939
asst head The Gordon Schools Huntly from 1974

DICK Janet Young *MA 1932
retd 1972; resid Aber

DICKIE Alexander Ironside *MA 1934
OBE 1969
retd 1972; resid Muckhart Dollar
d Stirling 25.4.80 *AUR* XLVIII 442

DICKIE David Bannerman Wood MA 1930
head Broomhill p s Aber 1960–69; retd

DICKIE George Green MB ChB 1936 DPH 1938
d Aber 19.7.73 *AUR* XLV 321

DICKIE James Lindsay Tocher MB ChB 1942 DPH 1947
g p Crimond from 1952
d Crimond 6.1.79 *AUR* XLVIII 233

DICKIE or Armstrong, Jessie Ann *MA 1920
d S Af 22.9.77

DICKIE John Mackinlay *MA 1915
edit. Chambers's *Twentieth Century Dictionary* 1957–58; retd: publications: *Great Angling Stories* (anthology 1941; reprints 1941, 1947, 1955); *How to Catch Trout* (1963); resid Edin

DICKIE Marie Louise MA 1925
retd 1962; resid Aber

DICKIE or Collie, Myra Catherine *MA 1931
resid Wilmslow

DICKIE or Whitmarsh, Phyllis Margaret MA 1939
resid Aber

DICKIE William Macfarlane *MA 1918 PhD 1926
FLA 1930
Aberd: asst logic and metaphysics 1918–22
retd 1961; resid Dun

DICKIE William Wood *MA 1927
retd 1966; member 1st GTC for Scot 1970–71, 2nd GTC from 1971: resid Aber

DICKIE-CLARK William Findlay MB ChB 1939
ENT surg Cape Town and Groote Schuur hosp Cape Town from 1947

DICKINSON Ada MA 1924
no longer on GC reg

DICKSON Alexander BSc(for) 1953

DICKSON Alice *MA 1942
Lond: admin asst Uganda dev corp 1954–62; asst secy inst of health sen admin from 1962

DICKSON Andrew MB ChB 1928
g p Old Deer 1936–62; asst dermat ARI 1962–68; asst photobiol unit Dund from 1968; retd
d 16.8.79

DICKSON or Simmons, Barbara Macdonald MA 1943
resid Lethbridge Alberta

DICKSON Dugald Macdonald MB ChB 1946
g p Bristol from 1951

DICKSON or Currie, Elizabeth Helen MA 1941
resid Deskford

DICKSON George Fortune BL 1928
Huntly: solic from 1929, man. British Linen Bank from 1940, burgh prosecutor from 1929

DICKSON Iain Alexander BSc(agr) 1951
MAgric (Purdue univ Indiana USA) 1959
spec anim husb W of S agr coll from 1963; seconded to Min Overseas Dev member of team reporting agr indust in Falkland Is 1969–70

DICKSON Jessie Isabella MA 1925
retd 1967; resid Aber

DICKSON John Abernethy MA 1936 BSc(for) 1938 LLD 1969
CB 1970 FBIM 1975
dir Scot. for. comm Edin 1963–65; Lond: comm (harvesting and marketing) 1965–68; dep chmn and dir gen 1968–76; chmn standing comm on Commonwealth Forestry 1968–76; chmn Commonwealth Forestry Assoc 1972–75, vice-pres 1975–76: retd 1976

DICKSON John Chisholm MA 1950
C of S min St Fittick's ch Aber from 1957; chap: Craiginches prison Aber 1959–69, army cadet force from 1951; moderator presb of Aber from 1976

DICKSON Kathleen MA 1946
teacher: remed work infants/juniors Smannell Hants 1970, Vernham Dean 1971–73, Weyhill 1974–76
m Andover 28.10.61 Andrew K. Briant BA(Cantab) late dir agr Zanzibar s of Alfred B. Newbury
husb *d* 1966

DICKSON Margaret Laing MA 1930
resid Fraserburgh
m Aber 20.9.41 William A. P. Reid master baker s of William A. R. Dinnet
husb *d* 1969

DIKE Kenneth Onwuka *MA 1947 LLD 1961
Hon DLitt: (Boston Mass) 1962, (Birm) 1964, (Ahmadu Bello) 1965, (Ibadan) 1979;
Hon DSc (Moscow) 1963
vice chancellor Ibadan univ 1960–67; chmn Assoc of Commonwealth univs 1965–66; Andrew W. Mellon prof Afr Hist Harvard from 1973

DINGLEY or Brown, Vera Mary BSc 1944
teacher phys Badminton s Brist from 1967

DINGWALL Hilda Anderson *MA 1922 BSc 1923
teacher Aber acad 1944–64; retd; resid Fetterangus

DINGWALL Ian Macdonald MB ChB 1951
med supt Texaco Trinidad Inc W Indies from 1955

DINGWALL or Sorley, Jessie Ross Grant MB ChB 1925 DPH 1927
d Aber 15.11.76 *AUR* XLVII 287

DINGWALL Robert Crichton Macdonald MB ChB 1943

DINNES or McKenzie, Agnes Ferguson MA 1905
d 18.2.71 *AUR* XLIV 208

DINNIE Doreen Audrey MA 1954
kindergarten teacher Newark Delaware USA from 1975 (completed pre-s curric & child dev courses univ of Delaware 1976, 1977)
m Aber 19.7.68 Robert Rayne mech des eng s of Andrew R. Philadelphia

DOBBIE or Thom, Hazel *BSc 1950 PhD 1953
lect dept ch health Aberd from 1958; resid Aber

DOBSON James Samuel MA 1950
d 29.3.64

DOCKAR Alexander Watt MB ChB 1924
Birm: g p 1924–62, dep m o HM prison 1937–61; retd; resid Droitwich

DODDS Edwin Mathieson *MA 1923 DSc 1937
d Minehead 30.7.74 *AUR* XLVI 108

DODDS James George *BSc 1950 PhD 1956
lect bot Edin from 1954

DODDS John Mathieson *MA 1926 BSc 1926 *BSc(eng) 1928
res dir AEI Manc 1961–70; retd; resid Strathdon

DODS or Laing, Julian Ursula MB ChB 1945
resid Oxted

DODSWORTH Thomas Little PhD 1951
JP Aberdeenshire 1961 FRAgrS 1973
Head anim husb dept NOSCA and lect dept of agr Aberd from 1947

DOIG Barbara Mary MA 1952
teacher: Aber 1953–55, Reading 1962–64; Somerset: dep head Backwell 1964–72; Surrey: head Compton 1973–75, Shere from 1975
m Aber 26.6.54 Michael J. Hannagan BSc(agr) 1953 *qv*

DON Alexander Victor Reid MB ChB 1920 ChM 1922
retd 1971
d Ashford 5.11.76 *AUR* XLVII 103

DON Charles Sydney Douglas *MB ChB 1925 ᶜMD 1928
d 7.9.73 *AUR* XLV 319

DON Eric George *MB ChB 1922 ᶜMD 1929

DONALD Agnes MA 1938
teacher Portlethen p s 1946–76; retd

DONALD Alexander MA 1924
d 31.12.63

DONALD Alexander MA 1942
no longer on GC reg

DONALD Alexander Bothwell MB ChB 1933 MD 1937
retd 1970; resid Edin

DONALD or Radcliffe, Alexandra Margaret MA 1936

DONALD Amy MA 1905
no longer on GC reg

DONALD Annie Isabella MA 1921 BSc 1924
resid Fleet
d Fleet 9.5.80 *AUR* XLVIII 440

DONALD Charles *BSc 1932 PhD 1936
ICI (organics) man. tech dev dept Grangemouth 1965–72; retd

DONALD or McKay, Christobel MB ChB 1953
g p Whitehaven from 1958

DONALD Daniel Barker BCom 1923
d Paris 11.2.33

DONALD David *MA 1927
retd 1971; resid Aber

DONALD David Mitchell Cooke BL 1935
Lond: man. dir Robert Fleming & Co merch bankers from 1960; chmn: Invest Trust Corp and London and Holyrood Trust from 1972

DONALD Derek George Mansell BSc(for) 1952
MSc(for) (Stellenbosch) 1964
DSc (Stellenbosch) 1968
S Af: sen lect silviculture Stellenbosch univ 1960–75; prof Merensky Chair of Silviculture from 1975

DONALD or Rayne, Elizabeth *MA 1921
no longer on GC reg

DONALD or Barrie, Elizabeth Florence MA 1937
deceased

DONALD or McIntyre, Elizabeth Walker MA 1925
no longer on GC reg

DONALD Ella MA 1950
head woman asst Peterhead cent s 1970
m Peterhead 28.6.69 John H. Sheran trans man. Crosse & Blackwell s of William S. Peterhead

DONALD Francis Cantlie MA 1905
resid Nairn
d Inv 18.1.74 *AUR* XLV 446

DONALD Frederick John BSc(for) 1950

DONALD George BSc(agr) 1919
d Oxford 18.1.62 *AUR* XXXIX 280

DONALD George McIntyre BSc(agr) 1922
no longer on GC reg

DONALD Heather Margaret *MA 1949
retd joint intell bureau 1961; publ *The Life of Lord Mount Stephen* Vol I 1965, Vol II 1977; occasional hist articles for learned journals; wrote quarterly econ reviews for Economist intell unit 1963–66, articles on Maghreb for *Annual Register*
m Lond 2.7.60 Ian G. Gilbert MA(Edin) civ serv, asst secy DHSS s of Alexander G. G. DCM Kenya

DONALD Ian MB ChB 1954
g p Aber and attachment ARI from 1959

DONALD or Shepherd, Isabel MA 1939
teacher: sen mistress Greenhead Sixth Form coll Huddersfield from 1973

DONALD James *MA 1930
d Arisaig 30.7.75

DONALD James Alexander *MA 1938
CBE 1962
man. dir: Borneo Co Lond from 1962, Inchcape (WA) Pty Perth West Aust 1968, Jaxon Construction Pty Perth WA from 1975
m Singapore 24.1.48 Joan L. McLean d of Frank A. McL. West Perth WA

DONALD James Booth *MA 1938

DONALD James Crosbie MB ChB 1954
Cert Competence in Pediat Surg RCS(C) 1976
surg resid Seattle 1963–68; consult. surg Royal Jubilee hosp Victoria BC Canada from 1968
m Victoria BC 26.5.62 Ann M. Clarke nurse d of Hugh E. C. Victoria BC

DONALD James Knight MB ChB 1924
d Fleet 31.12.71 *AUR* XLIV 430

DONALD Jessie MA 1925
retd 1966; resid Fleet

DONALD or Smith, Joan Grant MA 1948

DONALD John George MB ChB 1951
OBE 1971 DTM & H(Edin) 1964 (Greig medal in trop med) MRCGP 1971 MFCM 1972 FRCGP 1977
sen m o RAF Waddington 1960–64; stud. RAF staff coll Bracknell 1965; sen m o HQ AFCENT Fountainbleau France 1956–68; dep dir med pers MoD Lond 1968–72; comm off. RAF hosp Akrotiri Cyprus 1972–76, RAF hosp Ely 1976–78, prin m o HQ Germany from 1978

DONALD Laurence BSc(eng) 1953

DONALD or Sargison, Mabel MA 1926
retd 1960; resid Majorca

DONALD MacKenzie Munro MA 1903
no longer on GC reg

DONALD Margaret MA 1931
retd 1969; resid Aber

DONALD or Thomson, Margaret Patricia *MA 1942
lect Sus 1964–66; visiting prof State univ of NY at Buffalo USA 1966–67; reader Sus from 1967
m(2) Brighton 20.5.66 Maurice Evans PhD(Cantab) univ prof Exe

DONALD Margaret Smith Mowat MA 1950 Dip Ed 1958 *MEd 1960
asst educ psych ch guid serv Aberdeensh and Kincardine 1966–75, Grampian reg c from 1975

DONALD or Merrifield, Margaret Wason MA 1909
resid Acme, Alberta
husb *d* 20.1.73

DONALD or Robson, Marion Gordon MA 1910
resid Edin

DONALD or Jobson, Mary MA 1917
no longer on GC reg

DONALD or Rodger, Mary Ann MA 1951

DONALD Norman BSc 1947
dep head Insch s from 1966; elected member Gordon dist council 1974–80

DONALD Norman Frederick *MA 1927
retd 1970; resid St And
wife *d* 29.6.76

DONALD Priscilla Thomson MA 1922

DONALD Robert Turner MB ChB 1951
MRCGP 1961 DPM 1979
g p Lenham Kent 1956–76; clin asst psychiat Oakwood hosp Maidstone 1970–76; g p Montrose from 1976/hosp pract psychiat from 1980

DONALD Thomas Hunter MA 1902
no longer on GC reg

DONALD Walter *MA 1933
d Blairgowrie 24.3.68 *AUR* XLII 371

DONALD William John BSc(agr) 1953

DONALD Winifred Wilson *MA 1939
prin teacher Engl Lansdowne House s Edin from 1959; educ publ Collins 1963–65

DONALDSON Alan Malcolm MB ChB 1948
MRCGP 1968 DIH (soc of apothecaries) 1972
g p Lincoln 1959–74; reg m o DHSS Lincoln from 1974

DONALDSON Alistair BSc(eng) 1955
FIHE 1957 DipTE 1963 MAPLE 1966 FIMunE 1969 MBIM 1972 FIPHE 1974 MILGA 1974 FICE 1975
sen asst (roads) Peebles c c 1959–62; Cumberland c c: sen eng 1962–65, asst surv 1965–71; county surv Fife c c 1971–75; county surv Clwyd c c from 1975

DONALDSON or Shaw, Catherine MA 1918
d 10.7.65

DONALDSON or Runcie, Christina MA 1942
Grantham: teacher Engl/drama girls' central s 1963–65; head Engl dept Walton girls' s from 1965

DONALDSON Elizabeth *MA 1914
resid Stirling

DONALDSON Elsie MA 1928
teacher maths Portknockie 1969–70; retd; resid Portknockie

DONALDSON George Gregor MB ChB 1940
consult. anaest Gateshead hosp group 1949–74; retd

DONALDSON Hector Alexander MA 1927 BSc 1929 *1930
d Aber 30.4.68 *AUR* XLII 367

DONALDSON Helen MA 1916
retd 1968; resid Peterhead

DONALDSON John Edward *MA 1928
d Wick 23.2.67 *AUR* XLII 368

DONALDSON Robert Fyfe BCom 1923
no longer on GC reg

DONALDSON Sheina Margaret MA 1954
teacher: Linlithgow 1959–62, Darlington 1962–64; resid Keyworth
m Edin 27.7.62 Roy Francis Weston BSc(eng)(Lond) civ eng

DONALDSON William John *MEd 1948
FRIC 1950
sen lect Aber coll of educ 1963–75; retd

DORIAN or Dewar, Emily Prout MA 1936
teacher Glasg 1970–75

DORIAN or Douglas, Sheila MA 1949
resid Leatherhead

DORIAN Thomas Charles *MA 1924
head Albert sen s s Glasg 1960–67; retd

DORNHORST Hubert Karl Wilhelm Haartsz MB ChB 1906
no longer on GC reg

DORNLEY Ernest Marshall MB ChB 1934

DOSS Paul Thangasami Jesu MB ChB 1927
no longer on GC reg

DOUGALL or Walsh, Jean Barr Marshall MA 1945
resid Pointe Claire Quebec

DOUGHERTY Charles *MA 1933
no longer on GC reg

DOUGHERTY or Bishop, Margaret *MA 1928
teacher i/c Craigielea reception and assessment centre Aber 1957–67
d Aber 4.11.75

DOUGLAS Andrew Morrison MA 1954
C of S min: Bon-Accord St Paul's ch Aber 1963–72, Gardner Mem with West and St Columba's ch Brechin from 1972

DOUGLAS Arthur Wallace Murison MB ChB 1924
resid Braishfield
d 28.1.78

DOUGLAS Edward Annand MA 1906
no longer on GC reg

DOUGLAS Hugh Brown MA 1950
Lond: p r staff Brit hotels & restaurants assoc 1960–74, BR from 1974
m Belf 4.4.62 Sheelagh S. Knox BA(Belf) teacher d of Albert E. K. Limavady

DOUGLAS Ida Constance MA 1927
resid Banchory

DOUGLAS or Halton, Isobel Jean *MA 1938

DOUGLAS James Murray MA 1945
Lond: Treasury 1960–63, asst secy min of housing and loc govt 1964–66, secy royal comm on loc govt in England and Wales 1966–69, secy gen county landowners assoc from 1970

DOUGLAS or Kamsley, Janet Evelyn MA 1939

DOUGLAS or Wilkinson, Margaret Helen Keith MA 1942

DOUGLAS or Murphie, Margaret Isabel *MA 1920
Fort William: provost till 1959, made freeman of burgh 1967

DOUGLAS or Deans, Marjory Cumming Sutherland *MA 1944

DOUGLAS Muriel Mary Ogilvie *MA 1923
d 2.5.71

DOUGLAS Vivienne Mary *MA 1955
teacher Engl and relig educ Albyn s for g Aber 1956–67; resid Brunei 1976
m Aber 9.7.66 Sherlock S L Chin MB ChB 1965 *qv*

DOVE Ian Mayor MB ChB 1923
d 12.4.72

DOVERTY or Laird, Lilian Helen MA 1951
teacher Edin 1956–65

DOW Alexander Rattray MB ChB 1952
Sunderland: g p 1954–73, consult. A/E unit RI from 1973

DOW or MacLennan, Alison Agnes Smith MA 1934
husb *d* 14.4.75
d Aber 22.6.77

DOW or Cooper, Dorothy Janet MA 1919 MB ChB 1922
no longer on GC reg

DOW or Cox, Elizabeth May MA 1918 MB ChB 1919
asst anat dept Aberd 1919–20; h o Nottingham: ch hosp 1920–22, gen hosp 1922–25
resid Nott

DOW Herbert MA 1955

DOW James MB ChB 1937 DPH 1957
MFCM 1972
retd surg cdr RN 1964; asst m o h/sen m o West Lothian 1964–68; Midlothian and Peebles: sen m o 1968–71, dep m o h 1971–72; resid Edin
d Edin 27.12.79 *AUR* XLIX 69

DOW or Fraser, Margaret Mary Maclaren MA 1928 BSc 1929
teacher Harris acad Dun 1962–72; retd
husb *d* 15.7.62

DOW or Cooper, Marjorie Johanna Macpherson MB ChB 1925 DPH 1929
resid Dun
husb *d* 27.6.73

DOW Ronald *MA 1952
Preston: head organis and methods Engl Elect. Co 1959–62, BAC 1962–65; Ashridge man. coll Berkhamsted: lect 1965–69, progr dir from 1969

DOW Thomas McLaren BSc(for) 1948

DOWNIE Allan Watson MB ChB 1946
FRCP 1972
asst/assoc prof neurol univ of N Carolina 1958–65; sen lect med and hon consult. neurol Aberd and NE reg hosp board from 1965

DOWNIE Allan Watt *MB ChB 1923 *MD 1929 DSc 1938 LLD 1957
FRCPath
retd prof bact Liv 1966; visiting prof paediat univ of Denver Colorado 1966–69; res work on MRC grant 1969–72, part-time consult. path. Sefton gen hosp from 1973

DOWNIE Balfour *MA 1909
d Aber 25.2.68 *AUR* XLII 348

DOWNIE Dorothy McIver MA 1928
d Aber 30.1.79

DOWNIE George *BSc 1954
lect geol Aberd from 1960

DOWNIE John George MA 1926
retd 1970; resid Culsalmond

DOWNIE or McIntosh, June MA 1954

DOWNIE Richard Duthie *MB ChB 1923
OBE 1966 MRCGP (founder member)
g p Sheffield 1923–66; locum work since retirement; resid Salcombe
d Southport 27.8.78 *AUR* XLVIII 104

DOWNIE William Spence MA 1922 BSc 1924
Aber: head Ruthrieston f e centre 1956–58, dep head Sunnybank p s 1939–62; retd

DOYLE George Mitchel BSc 1948 *1949

DOYLE Thomas *MEd 1955
d Bridgend Wales 3.11.75

DRAPER William MA 1952

DREVER or Rutter, Daisy Don MA 1916
no longer on GC reg

DREWERY James *MA 1952

DRON Kenneth Walker *MA 1951 Dip Ed 1954
dep rector Falkirk h s 1966–69; rector Brechin h s from 1969

DRON William Douglas Duff BSc(agr) 1949

DRUMMOND Edith Margaret MA 1938
DBE 1966
dir WRNS Lond 1964–67; retd; resid Holt Norfolk

DRUMMOND James Gilmour *MA 1907 DD 1951
d Glasg 20.2.63 *AUR* XL 199

DRUMMOND John Alexander BSc(for) 1947

DUCAT Eric Francis MB ChB 1945
g p Bath from 1948

DUCAT or Webster, Helena Mary Lawson *MA 1934
resid N Berwick

DUCKWORTH Ronald Barrett PhD 1952
FIFST 1968
sen scient off. MAFF Aber 1955–56; lect food sc Strath 1956–66, sen lect 1966–70, reader from 1970
m Aber 22.2.55 Margaret C. Johnston teacher d of James W. J. Aberchirder

DUFF Agnes Helen MA 1908
d Edin 16.3.78 *AUR* XLVII 355

DUFF Alexander Dewar MB ChB 1927
d 10.6.77 *AUR* XLVII 287

DUFF Alistair Duncan Stewart *BSc(agr) 1950

DUFF Caroline Stevenson MB ChB 1951
g p Dover from 1954

DUFF or Fish, Dora Grant MA 1931
d Camberley –.8.67

DUFF or Ritchie, Elizabeth Helen *MA 1913
chief escort to 500 evacuee ch by sea to Canada 1940; resid Edin

DUFF Harold Bissett BSc(eng) 1932
civ eng Ford Motor Co Dagenham 1947–65
d Streatham 19.11.77

DUFF Rachel Tolmie *MA 1911
d Paisley 15.5.68 *AUR* XLII 350

DUFF Stewart MB ChB 1939
g p Grimsby from 1949

DUFFTON Robert Alexander Lawson BL 1937
retd 1978; resid Cheltenham

DUFFUS Adrian Michael Campbell MB ChB 1948
MRACP 1961 FRACP 1972
clin res dir Roche Products Welwyn Garden City from 1962

DUFFUS Alan Alexander MB ChB 1920 DPH 1922
Watford: m o and surg/med supt Shrodells hosp 1931–45, g p till 1961; resid Fernhurst Haslemere

DUFFUS Alexander James BL 1950
ptnr Wilsone & Duffus advoc Aber from 1953

DUFFUS Beatrice MA 1940
resid Fraserburgh

DUFFUS George Macnaughton Rae MB ChB 1931
g p Aber 1936–39 and from 1952
d Aber 27.1.81 *AUR* XLIX 138

DUFFUS Helen Mary Isabella MA 1942
d 1971

DUFFUS James Catto MA 1912 [d]LLB 1914
d 17.8.62 *AUR* XL 80

DUFFUS Janet Rennie MA 1925
resid Aber
d Aber 16.8.81

DUFFUS or Penman, Jeannie McKenzie MA 1936
teacher N'cle-u-Tyne from 1960; retd

DUFFUS Stanley Herbert MA 1949
teacher Galashiels acad from 1950

DUFTON Alexina Margaret MA 1955

DUFTON or Smith, Margaret Johnston MB ChB 1918

DUGAN Alexander Mathieson MB ChB 1918 DPH 1921
Manchester educ comm 1926–59; retd
d Aber 29.8.75 *AUR* XLVI 322

DUGAN or Sommerville, Alice Henrietta MA 1931 BSc 1934
keeper of herbarium dept of bot Aberd 1954–77; retd

DUGAN or Burnett, Dorothy Jane Elizabeth BSc 1922
resid Aber

DUGAN or Emslie, Elizabeth Madeline MA 1926 BSc 1929
resid Banchory
husb *d* 14.5.72

DUGGIE or Gordon, Christina Baillie Main MA 1940
resid Huntly

DUGGIE David Main BSc(for) 1948

DUGUID Alexander George *MA 1949
Wing Cmdr

DUGUID Annabelle Murdina MA 1948 MB ChB 1953
regist anaest UCH Kingston Jamaica 1956–57; sen h o anaest Edin 1959–61; anaest Medicine Hat Alberta 1963–64; med asst anaest Wrexham Wales
m Kingston, Jamaica 16.6.56 Jan F. Bras MB (Amsterdam) ophth surg s of Johannes B. Indonesia

DUGUID David Shepherd *MA 1914
d Aber 1.3.68 *AUR* XLII 352

DUGUID or Pirrie, Ellie Forbes MA 1908
husb *d* 1956
resid Keith
d 11.7.78

DUGUID or MacLachlan, Ena Bauchope Sutherland MA 1937
teacher: h s for girls Aber 1966–68, speech and drama dept Aber 1968–74, Smithfield p s 1974
husb *d* 7.9.71

DUGUID or Oldershaw, Frances Marjory MB ChB 1921
no longer on GC reg

DUGUID Francis Massie BSc 1947 *1948
prin teacher sc Ellon acad from 1957

DUGUID Helen Leslie Duff MB ChB 1944 MD 1951
FRCPath 1971
consult. path. i/c cytology and assoc histopath RI Dun from 1963
m Helensburgh 23.9.63 Alistair S. L. Rae MB ChB(Edin) consult. psychiat s of Alexander R. Edin

DUGUID Ian McIver MB ChB 1948 MD 1959
FRCS 1961 PhD(Lond) 1962
Lond: consult. ophth surg Lond hosp 1962–63, ophth surg Moorfield eye hosp from 1963, ophth surg Westminster hosp from 1964

DUGUID John MB ChB 1939
d 2.1.73

DUGUID John Bright MB ChB 1920 *MD 1925
d 21.12.80 *AUR* XLIX 136

DUGUID or Lamont, Margaret Sinclair MB ChB 1942
m o Sunnyside psychiat hosp Christchurch NZ from 1972

DUGUID Raymond Maurice MB ChB 1942
g p Coventry from 1946
d 7.10.76

DUGUID Robert Hutton BCom 1926
retd bus. admin Prot s board of Greater Montreal 1962; Aber: acct Middletons (Aber) 1965–72; asst acct James Blake 1974–77; retd

DUGUID William MB ChB 1909
d 21.8.76

DUNBAR Alexina MA 1929
d 23.4.72

DUNBAR David Milne MB ChB 1942

DUNBAR or Gray, Elizabeth Alexina MB ChB 1923
resid Portsoy
husb *d* 1.2.72

DUNBAR Elsie Williamina MA 1914
no longer on GC reg

DUNBAR Helen MA 1905
d Cullen 19.4.77

DUNBAR or Ponting, Helen Milne Cooper MA 1942
head teacher Bexley Lond from 1967

DUNBAR James MA 1925 MB ChB 1929
MRCGP 1967
g p Gillingham Kent from 1933

DUNBAR Jane *MA 1913
d Cullen 8.6.71 *AUR* XLIV 316

DUNBAR Jessie Isabella *MA 1930
retd 1969; resid Bearsden

DUNBAR Joan Gordon Thain MB ChB 1927
d of Duncan D. shepherd; b Fordyce 20.12.1900
resid Cullen

DUNBAR Joseph MA 1955
dep head Meldrum s 1966–72; asst prin teacher Bankhead acad responsible for school/industry liaison career work from 1972

DUNBAR Leslie MB ChB 1948
g p Dunblane from 1951

DUNBAR or Simpson, Lorna Margaret *MA 1950 Dip Ed 1951
lect educ psych coll of educ Aber from 1966

DUNBAR Margaret Stewart MA 1907
d Buckie 11.9.72 *AUR* XLV 123

DUNBAR or Innes, Mary Jessie MA 1911
d Hull 2.11.75 *AUR* XLVI 320

DUNBAR or Foster, Norah May Esson MB ChB 1929
retd; resid Cullen

DUNCAN or Philip, Adeline Myron *MA 1925
resid Elgin

DUNCAN Albert Tait MB ChB 1925
g p Banff 1925–30; Falkirk 1930–31, Portsoy 1931–35; Dun 1935–67; retd; resid Banff
d Banff 14.9.77 *AUR* XLVII 287

DUNCAN Alexander BL 1950

DUNCAN Alexander Stuart BSc(for) 1932
estate man.: Argyll 1959–62, E Anglian estates 1962–73; retd; resid Elgin

DUNCAN Alfred George Brown *MB ChB 1915 [c]MD 1919 DPH 1920
retd 1960; resid Aboyne

DUNCAN Alfred Henry MB ChB 1948
g p Blackburn Lancs from 1951
m Manc 6.1.68 Ruth Thompson nurs sister d of George R. T. Manc

DUNCAN or MacLeod, Alice Lindsay MA 1953
teacher hist Arbroath h s from 1967

DUNCAN or Pullar, Amy Rose MA 1929
b Lhanbryde 24.12.06
teacher maths/hist Forres acad 1964–68; retd; resid Lossiemouth

DUNCAN Angus MA 1923 BD 1926
d Edin 19.9.71 *AUR* XLIV 429

DUNCAN Anne MA 1943
Aber: teacher Rosemount s 1948–72, woman advis from 1959; Harlaw acad teacher and careers mistress from 1972

DUNCAN or Esslemont, Anne Elizabeth *MA 1923 [d]LLB 1925
d Wick 20.9.72 *AUR* XLV 126

DUNCAN or Fleming, Betty Fraser MA 1930
resid Keith

DUNCAN Charles MA 1944 LLB 1949

DUNCAN or Munro, Christian Brown Smart MA 1932 LLB 1935
d 31.1.66

DUNCAN Cyril Gordon McKenzie BSc(agr) 1955 *1966
asst insp DAFS Edin 1960–64; farm. Elgin from 1964

DUNCAN David MB ChB 1924 DPH 1929 MD 1934

DUNCAN Donald *MA 1950
computer progr Crosse & Blackwell Lond 1961–64; trg off. Distillers Co Epsom 1964–66; Unilever Merseyside Port Sunlight: head man. trg centre 1966–70, company pers man. from 1970

DUNCAN Douglas Mackenzie BCom 1930

DUNCAN Douglas Stanley *MA 1937 BSc 1938
FEIS 1965
dep head Northfield acad Aber from 1967

DUNCAN or Purdie, Edith *MA 1935
resid Gatehouse of Fleet

DUNCAN Edith Mackenzie MA 1928

DUNCAN or Ogston, Edith Margaret MA 1944
resid Elgin

DUNCAN or Shewan, Elizabeth Christina MA 1924
resid Lochearnhead

DUNCAN or Bruce, Elizabeth Craven MA 1929
resid Edin

DUNCAN Elizabeth Deans MA 1930
m Smith

DUNCAN Elizabeth Eleanor MA 1953
private secy J & J Crombie Grandholm works Aber 1955–61
m Aber 18.12.61 George F. Howie CA s of William H. Aber

DUNCAN or Carlisle, Elsie Mary BL 1936
resid West Huntingtower Perth

DUNCAN Eric Henry Weir MB ChB 1931 DPH 1949
g p Culter from 1953

DUNCAN Eric Marr *MA 1929 BD 1934
retd 1972; resid Stirling

DUNCAN Ethel Helen Laing *MA 1931 BSc 1933

DUNCAN Ethel Mary Maudaline MA 1936
retd 1975; resid Peterhead

DUNCAN Forbes MA 1930
head Camdean s Rosyth 1953–72; retd; resid Dunfermline

DUNCAN or Wood, Freda Campbell MA 1945

DUNCAN George BCom 1928
d 1980

DUNCAN George Douglas MB ChB 1948 DPH 1952
FFCM 1972
sen admin m o E Anglia reg hosp board 1968–73; reg m o E Anglia reg health auth from 1973

DUNCAN George Gordon MB ChB 1950 DPH 1955
g p Rothes from 1959
m Wilmslow 2.3.57 Hilary J. Piggin nurs sister d of Edward P. Weston Crewe

DUNCAN Helen Margaret Eveline *MA 1930
volunt soc worker Red Cross from 1945; resid Aber

DUNCAN Henry Charles BSc(agr) 1946
NOSCA: hort advis Aberdeensh/Banffsh 1962–73, head hort div from 1973
d 8.10.77

DUNCAN James MB ChB 1923
d Frinton-on-Sea 4.12.72 *AUR* XLV 127

DUNCAN James BSc(eng) 1947
comp dir Methlick from 1957
wife *d* 11.8.71

DUNCAN James George MB ChB 1945
FRCSE 1967 MRCPGlas 1971 FRCPGlas 1975 FRCR 1975
visiting prof univ of Rochester USA 1969; consult. radiol in admin charge Glasg RI and assoc hosps from 1969

DUNCAN James Hugh *BSc 1954
FICeram 1972
geologist fed of Malaya 1954–60; min/ceramist English Elect. Co Stafford 1960–69; sen prin scient off. BR board r & d div Derby from 1969

DUNCAN James Robertson MA 1932
head Strathdon s 1947–61; Melbourne Aust: teacher Princess Hill h s 1962–63, Camberwell s 1963–64; sen asst (post of responsib) Box Hill h s from 1965; retd 1975

DUNCAN Janet Campbell MA 1947 MB ChB 1951
C of S missionary Charteris and leprosy hosp Kalimpong India 1955–69; Wick: part-time g p 1969, part-time h s Bignold hosp 1973; C of S missionary rural health progr Kalimpong from 1973
d Wick 10.9.78 *AUR* XLVIII 107

DUNCAN or Smith, Jessie Edgell MA 1907

DUNCAN John MA 1927
head Udny Green s Aberdeensh 1960–70; retd; resid Aber

DUNCAN John McWilliam MB ChB 1936
g p Worcester from 1947

DUNCAN or Sproat, Kathleen Watson MA 1955
resid Kirkcudbright

DUNCAN or Torrance, Lorna Lawrence MB ChB 1942
JP (Leicestersh) 1962
g p Leicester from 1946

DUNCAN Maggie Ann (Madge) MA 1917
d Lond 30.1.64 *AUR* XL 398

DUNCAN Margaret Garden MA 1945
DipEd(Oxon) 1946
resid Kirkcaldy
m Buckie 16.9.59 David J. L. Innes BA(Oxon) textile manuf s of John L. I. LLB(Edin) Kirkcaldy

DUNCAN Margaret Simpson MA 1909
d Aber 29.6.70 *AUR* XLIV 107

DUNCAN or Talbert, Marjorie Ada *MA 1952

DUNCAN or Hunter, Mary MA 1915
d 17.11.72 *AUR* XLV 224

DUNCAN Mary Ann MA 1909

DUNCAN or Butterworth, Mary Elizabeth MA 1916 *1917

DUNCAN Mary Elizabeth MB ChB 1953

DUNCAN or Atkinson, Mary Hattle *MA 1944

DUNCAN Mary Lawson Philip *MA 1926
d Aber 1.3.56 *AUR* XXXVI 436

DUNCAN Mary Patricia *MA 1946

DUNCAN or Davis, Moira Manton *BSc 1948
resid Harrogate

DUNCAN or Allan, Myra Thomson *MA 1926
resid Edin

DUNCAN Norman Alistair MB ChB 1912
no longer on GC reg

DUNCAN Norman James BSc(eng) 1955

DUNCAN Peter MB ChB 1940
d 10.1.79

DUNCAN Robert Alexander Low BSc(agr) 1933
d Fraserburgh 15.11.71 *AUR* XLIV 321

DUNCAN Robert Erskine Burt *BSc 1951 PhD 1954
FRIC 1964
man. Glenochil res stat Distillers Co Menstrie from 1974

DUNCAN Robert Hendry MB ChB 1951
USA: clin dir High Point hosp Portchester NY 1960–63; dir mental health serv NE New Mexico 1963–65; dir Courts' clinic Rochester NY 1965–69; consult Rochester City school dist NY from 1965; dir mental health serv Livingston and Wyoming countries NY from 1969

DUNCAN Robert Morris Turner MA 1950 Dip Ed 1954

DUNCAN Robert Reid MB ChB 1905 DPH 1910
no longer on GC reg

DUNCAN or Watson, Sheila Margaret MA 1945
husb *d* 1968
Cert Soc Work (RGIT) 1974
soc worker Aber from 1973

DUNCAN or Wood-Smith, Sybil Mary Anderson MA 1929

DUNCAN Thomas MB ChB 1938
psychiat i/c Essex Hall, royal E Counties hosp Colchester 1966–68; clin dir King's County hosp Waterville Nova Scotia 1968–73; consult. in Bury St Edmund's health dist from 1974

DUNCAN Thomas McPetrie MA 1924 BD 1928
d Bishopbriggs 9.8.71 *AUR* XLIV 320

DUNCAN Thomas Strachan *MA 1938
prin maths teacher Peterhead acad from 1961

DUNCAN Walter *MA 1929
d Aber 23.5.68 *AUR* XLII 368

DUNCAN William MB ChB 1954
FFR(Lond) 1962 FRCPE 1972 FRCSE 1977
consult radiotherap Christie hosp and Holt radium inst Manc 1964–71; prof radiotherapy Edin from 1971

DUNCAN William Alexander James MA 1954

DUNCAN William Gavin BCom 1928
d Newport 5.11.68 *AUR* XLIII 84

DUNLOP or Carmichael, Alexandrina Gladys MA 1932
teacher: spec asst Fyvie 1966–74; retd; resid Badenscoth

DUNLOP Charles Moir MB ChB 1946
MRCGP 1968
g p Eastbourne from 1950

DUNLOP Harry Young BSc(agr) 1954
agr advis NOSCA from 1966; resid Dinnet
d Dinnet 4.7.81

DUNN Alexander Simpson *BSc 1949

DUNN Edward BSc 1934 *1935

DUNN George Alexander Farquhar MA 1951
asst prin teacher maths Peterhead acad from 1973
m Aber 29.7.61 Jean A. Harris teacher bus. stud. d of Andrew H. Aber

DUNN Helen Ann MA 1924
no longer on GC reg

DUNN or Coull, Irene Jean MA 1945
prin teacher: Engl Rosemount s s Aber 1969–72, guid Harlaw acad from 1972

DUNN or George, Jessie Addison MA 1930
d Hillside 5.3.66 *AUR* XLII 88

DUNN or Clements, Margaret Jane Heron MA 1919

DUNNE Eileen Carmel Kober MA 1944 *1948
asst head Sacred Heart h s Paisley from 1971
m Old Kilpatrick 2.7.60 Lawrence Peacock mech eng/teacher s of William P. Dumbarton

DUNNE Jane Ann MA 1926
dep head St Mary's RC s Aber 1959, St Joseph's 1960–64

DUNNE Joseph Peter MB ChB 1940
supt m o 1942–50; regist to med psychiat units 1950–60; j h m o psychiat Pastures hosp Meikleover Derby 1960–66; med asst psychiat Moorhaven hosp Ivybridge from 1966

DUNNET Charles William MA 1920
d 14.10.71

DUNNET George Mackenzie *BSc 1949 PhD 1952
FRSE 1970 FIBiol 1974
Aberd: sen lect nat hist 1966–71; prof zoology 1971–74 regius prof nat hist from 1974

DUNNET William Nicholson MB ChB 1944 MD 1961
MFCM 1974 FFCM 1978
DHSS HQ Lond: m o epidemiological sect. 1963–65, sen m o 1965–77, prin m o head of div of communicable diseases from 1977

DUNNETT Arthur Hugh MB ChB 1941
DPH(St And) 1961 FACMA 1967
m o Norfolk Is 1961–63; commonwealth dept of health Canberra Aust from 1963

DUNNETT May MA 1930
no longer on GC reg

du PREEZ James John MB ChB 1910
no longer on GC reg

DURIE Frederick Lewis *BSc(eng) 1933

DURIE or Dugan, Isobel Forbes MA 1926
resid Aber

DURNIN John Valentine George Andrew MA 1942 MB ChB 1946
DSc(Glas) 1961 MRCPGlas 1963 FRCPGlas 1969 FRSE 1976
prof physiol Glas 1973

DURNIN Joseph John *MA 1930
head Holy Family RC s Aber 1959–72; retd; resid Aber

DURNO Charles *MA 1903
d Aber 9.1.67 *AUR* XLII 345

DURNO John Fyvie MB ChB 1924
g p Lond 1956–63; blood transf Sutton 1963–66; retd
d Glasg 29.8.75 *AUR* XLVI 322

DURNO or Leyden, Mary Bannerman BSc 1953
resid Pitlochry

DURNO Mary Margaret Grant Mearns MA 1909
d Aber 7.8.61 *AUR* XXXIX 273

DURNO Robert BSc(eng) 1944 BSc(civ eng) 1948
d Dun 8.5.72

DURNO Sydney Elmslie BSc 1949 PhD 1967
MIBiol 1951
Macaulay inst for soil res Aber from 1949

DURWARD James *MA 1919
d 2.12.71

DURWARD James Mortimer *BSc(eng) 1940
MBE 1957
Lagos Nigeria: sen eng in fed min of works 1957–70, chief eng from 1970

DUTCH John Henry MA 1947 BD 1949
d Helensburgh 10.11.68 *AUR* XLIII 86

DUTCH Ralph Douglas *MA 1951 *MEd 1953
prin lect educ psych Aber coll of educ from 1963

DUTHIE or Finniecome, Alice Mary MA 1910
no longer on GC reg

DUTHIE Andrew May MA 1920 *MB ChB 1924 MD 1929
retd: resid Newtonhill
d 14.10.81

DUTHIE Andrew Ritchie MB ChB 1954
trainee asst Inverurie 1957–58; g p Turriff from 1958

DUTHIE Austin Leslie Smith MB ChB 1950
d Leeds 15.4.76 *AUR* XLVI 418

DUTHIE Birnie Winchester MB ChB 1949
MRCGP 1973
g p Aber from 1954

DUTHIE Charles Sim *MA 1932 BD 1935 DD 1952
prin New College Lond 1964–77; pres: Cong Union of Scot. 1952–53, Cong Ch in England and Wales 1971–72
d Edin 11.1.81

DUTHIE Clifford Raymond BSc(eng) 1948
FInstPet. 1962 CE 1958 MIMechE 1958
refinery supt eng Mina-al-Ahmadi Kuwait 1961–67; construct. supt Stone & Webster Eng 1967–73; mech eng consult. London Bridge Eng from 1973

DUTHIE Douglas Watt MA 1925 *BSc 1927 PhD 1935
d Keynsham nr Bristol 20.6.69 *AUR* XLIII 330

DUTHIE Edwin MA 1932
retd 1965; resid Aber

DUTHIE Edwin William MB ChB 1931
d 2.1.70

DUTHIE Effie Mitchell MB ChB 1924
g p and m o Hulme s s for girls Chadderton Oldham 1931–69; g p and dental anaest (schools) 1969–72; retd nat health practice 1969; contd private practice till 1973 and s m o Hulme g s for girls Oldham till 1972; retd

DUTHIE or Cameron, Eileen Marischal MB ChB 1942
m o in dept Waltham Forest, Lond from 1966; m o Salop AHA from 1976

DUTHIE or Miller, Elsie Cowie BSc 1926
resid Aber

DUTHIE Eric Edmonston *MA 1926
d Thorndon Cross Devon 22.10.74 *AUR* XLVI 109 & 236

DUTHIE or Gill, Eveline Elizabeth MA 1935
resid Edin

DUTHIE Frank BCom 1922
d 10.3.65

DUTHIE Frederick Mitchell MB ChB 1931
retd surg cdr RN from 1953; med exam. off. RN/RM Manc from 1958; resid Oldham
d 10.4.78

DUTHIE George Stewart BSc 1949
Aber: prin teacher maths/sc Old Aber s s 1961–66; dep head Torry acad 1966–74, head Torry acad from 1974

DUTHIE or Ross, Gladys Belle MA 1931
rural head teacher Aberdeensh

DUTHIE Ian Wilson *BSc(eng) 1930
3 awards for inventions
res scient with RN Admir HQ Lond till 1966; QAD insp and res plastics Haslemere from 1966

DUTHIE James Leask *BSc 1952
W. J. Emmons award 1972 (AAPT)
geophys Brit petr co: UK, Senegal, Iran 1955–63; bituminous materials eng BP res centre 1963–74; BP southern Africa 1974–76

DUTHIE Joan Noble MA 1929

DUTHIE John MB ChB 1948

DUTHIE John BSc(eng) 1954
MICE 1962
site eng Mitchell construct co Invernesssh 1959–60; des eng James Williamson & Ptnrs Glasg 1960–61; superv eng Montreal eng co 1962–69, sen superv eng from 1969

DUTHIE John James Reid MB ChB 1935
Edin: reader dept of med 1964–68, prof med (rheumat) from 1968
m Edin 4.4.73 Kathleen W. Beaton area off. soc work dept Edin d of John M. B. Edin

DUTHIE John Milne MA 1929 BSc 1931
JP
head Skene j s s 1947–69; retd
d Aber 4.3.72 *AUR* XLIV 432

DUTHIE John Stephen MA 1939
NCB London 1959–63; Blue Circle Group: chmn Malayan Cement 1963–68, man dir Assoc Pan Malaysia Cement group Kuala Lumpur and Singapore 1967–68, dir Assoc International Cement Lond 1970, dir Blue Circle Group 1975, chief exec Blue Circle Cement UK 1977

DUTHIE Louis Herbert MB ChB 1937
surg capt RN 1964–72; retd; civilian m o RN coll Greenwich from 1972

DUTHIE Louisa MA 1915
no longer on GC reg

DUTHIE Margaret Alexander BSc 1924
retd 1958
no longer on GC reg

DUTHIE or Traill, Margaret Stephen BSc 1927
no longer on GC reg

DUTHIE Maureen Benton BSc 1949 MB ChB 1954
Christie hosp and Holt radium inst Manc: sen regist 1963, asst radiotherap (s h m o) 1963–66, consult. radiotherap from 1966

DUTHIE Phyllis MA 1919
no longer on GC reg

DUTHIE Robert *MA 1949

DUTHIE Robert James MB ChB 1922 *MD 1924
d Chichester 4.1.71 *AUR* XLIV 210

DUTHIE Stephen *MA 1931 BSc 1932
prin teacher sc h s Inv 1951–72; retd

DUTHIE or Bruce, Winifred Margaret *MA 1928
teacher Fr/Ger Aber h s for g 1938–45; Fr Hamilton Park s Glasg 1956–59; head Fr dept Broomlea s Whitecraigs Glasg 1959–62; asst Fr/Ger Hutchesons' girls' g s Glasg 1964–68; resid Callander

DUTHIE or Skinner, Winifred Rose Margaret MA 1925
resid Cambridge

DYKER or Gauld, Janet McCallum *MA 1947
resid Vancouver

EADY George Edward *MA 1953
sen dep prin Aber coll of comm from 1962

EAGER Richard MB ChB 1905
no longer on GC reg

EAGGER Arthur Austin MB ChB 1922
med dir Slough indust health serv 1947–63, retd, consult. from 1963; resid Exeter

EAGGER Mary Thomson MA 1914
d Aber 22.12.62 *AUR* XL 82

EASSON William McAlpine *MB ChB 1954 ᶜMD 1967
Dip Gen Psychiat 1963 Dip Ch Psychiat 1966 MRCPsych 1972
inst psychiat univ of Sask 1959–61; USA: fell. ch psychiat Menninger Clin Topeka 1961–63, consult. 1963–67; prof and chmn dept of psychiat Med Coll of Ohio, Toledo 1967–72, prof univ of Minnesota Minneapolis 1972–74, prof and head of dept of psychiat Louisiana State Univ med s New Orleans from 1974

EASTON James David MA 1911
d Daviot Abersh 6.3.65 *AUR* XLI 55

EASTON Robert Morrison MA 1907 MB ChB 1911
d Erith Kent 23.10.69 *AUR* XLIII 327

EASTWOOD Wilfred PhD 1949
FIStructE 1959 FICE 1963
pres inst of struct eng 1976–77; Univ of Sheffield: prof civ eng 1964–70, consult. eng from 1970

EATON David BSc 1906
d Stonehaven 6.11.70 *AUR* XLIV 208

EDDEY Leslie George MB ChB 1938
d Salisbury Rhodesia 22.10.67 *AUR* XLII 372

EDDIE Alfred Alexander Pratt MA 1913
d Aber 2.1.71 *AUR* XLIV 209

EDDIE or Badenoch, Christina Snowie *MA 1923
resid Clifford Yorks

EDDIE or Cameron, Elizabeth Watt BSc 1940
Dip Spec Educ (Jordanhill coll Glasg) 1963
teacher: St Andrews s Inverurie 1963–71, Dingwall acad 1971–73, Brimmond assessment centre Aber 1973–75, Woodlands hosp s Aber from 1975
husb *d* 22.7.73

EDDIE or Mitchell, Irene MA 1950
resid Aber

EDDIE or Saunders, Mabel MA 1953

EDDIE Robert William MB ChB 1909
d Aber 22.10.62 *AUR* XL 79

EDDIE Vernon James MA 1927 BCom 1929
d Lond 15.3.69 *AUR* XLIII 215

EDDISON John Michael *BSc(eng) 1952
MIStruct E 1961 MEIC 1966 FICE 1974
FASCE 1975
Scott Wilson Kirkpatrick and Ptnrs Lond: Lond off. 1963–66; res eng dept of trans Vancouver 1966–67; res eng Belize Br Honduras 1967–68; res eng Brunei 1969–73; off. Hong Kong 1973–74; res eng Sabah 1974–77; proj eng (airports) Asian Dev Bank Manila from 1977

EDIE Charles Benjamin *MA 1937
C of S min ch of the Holy Rude Stirling from 1955

EDIE or Mackie, Katharine Mary MA 1939
resid Edin

EDMOND James Taylor *MA 1940
FInstP 1967
RN scient serv Baldock 1948–59; res off. CEGB Leatherhead 1959–67; sen lect Dund from 1967
m Sutton 5.10.63 Judith M. E. Vincent secy d of Albert V. Sutton Surrey

EDMOND John Stephen MA 1955
b 28.5.33
teacher: Bankhead acad 1959–66, prin geog Northfield acad Aber 1966–71, Hillpark s s Glasg 1972–73, prin geog John St s s Glasg from 1973
m Aber 2.4.62 Dorothy A. Thomson BSc 1953 *qv*

EDMOND Neil Lennox MB ChB 1953 DA 1957
g p Rochdale from 1960

EDMONDS Donald Thomas *BSc 1955
res fell. Oxon 1957–61; on staff univ of California 1960–61; fell. Wadham coll Oxon from 1962, lect Oxon 1965–67; Yale univ USA 1967–73; sen tut. Wadham Coll Oxon 1973–76

EDWARD or Buchan, Evelyn May MA 1933

EDWARD Henry BSc(for) 1931
civ serv min of trans from 1958; retd 1975

EDWARD Ian David MA 1927
d 6.2.66

EDWARD James Falconer BSc 1932

EDWARD Margaret Duguid *MA 1947
Aber acad: spec asst maths 1956–65, prin asst maths 1965–70, year mistress Hazlehead acad Aber from 1970

EDWARD Mary *MA 1928
retd 1968; resid Stonehaven

EDWARDS Alan Tawse MB ChB 1950
FRCPath 1972
consult. path. Halifax area hosps from 1959

EDWARDS Albert Gray BSc(eng) 1945

EDWARDS Alexander Fraser *MA 1948
prin teacher mod lang Douglas-Ewart h s Newton Stewart from 1956

EDWARDS Alfred *MA 1923
retd 1962; resid Aber
d Glasg 23.11.80 *AUR* XLIX 67

EDWARDS Alfred John Meldrum MA 1924 BCom 1927
head Skene Square p s Aber 1958–63; part-time teacher Robert Gordon's coll Aber 1963–77; retd

EDWARDS Daniel BSc 1949 *1950
head pharm s RGIT Aber from 1959

EDWARDS David (Sir) MA 1912 ᵈLLB 1914
d Lond 28.2.66 *AUR* XLI 242

EDWARDS or Jamieson, Elizabeth Mary MB ChB 1912
venereologist Arcoats hosp Manc 1941–48; retd
d Hemel Hempstead 7.2.77 *AUR* XLVII 211

EDWARDS or Wood, Ezel Anna Bella MA 1936

EDWARDS Farquhar Duncan MB ChB 1947
g p Brechin from 1951

EDWARDS Harold George *BSc 1951
housemaster Tonbridge s from 1965

EDWARDS Henry William McGregor MB ChB 1948
med off. NCB S Midlands from 1972
d Nuneaton 11.7.79

EDWARDS Herbert John BL 1922 MA LLB 1923
retd 1973; resid Aber

EDWARDS James Gordon Hastings LLB 1948
d Cults Aber 9.3.72 *AUR* XLIV 433

EDWARDS Jane Lucy MA 1952
dep head approved s Warrington 1959–61; area off. ch's dept Lancs c c 1961–66; lodging & welfare off. Birm 1966–69; insp ch's dept Home Office Birm 1969–71; soc work serv off. DHSS Birm from 1971
m Birm 22.9.73 Farhang Bakhtar BSc(Birm) univ lect s of Mostafa B. Iran

EDWARDS Jean McGregor MA 1940 MB ChB 1950 DPH 1956
sen m o (clin) Wigan AHA from 1956
m Bolton 9.2.63 Edward J. Desmond MB ChB(Cork) sen m o (occup health) Greater Manc council s of Jeremiah F. D. Cork

EDWARDS Lindsay Duncan BSc 1955
teacher: Glasg 1958–59; maths/sc Douglas Ewart h s Newton Stewart 1959–70; comm educ branch RAF from 1970
m Edin 19.7.58 Margaret A. C. C. Teese teacher d of Thomas K. T. Glasg

EDWARDS Phyllis Allan MA 1948
teacher Engl Elgin acad 1960–61; ch guid serv Aber from 1971
m Lossiemouth 30.7.60 William A. Taylor ACII insur insp s of Hector M. T. New Elgin

EDWARDS or Simmons, Phyllis Mary MA 1939
teacher: head Engl dept Sholing g s S'ton from 1959

ELDER Charles Gordon *MA 1910 MB ChB 1940
d Aber 23.10.69 *AUR* XLIII 328

ELDER George William MB ChB 1915
no longer on GC reg

ELDER Ian *MA 1949 Dip Ed 1950 MEd 1965
Aber: asst dir educ 1967–72, dep dir from 1972

ELDER James Bremner MB ChB 1902
no longer on GC reg

ELDER James Evan MA 1904
d 1.1.67

ELDER John George MB ChB 1912
no longer on GC reg

ELDER John Rawson ***MA 1902 DLitt 1914 LLD 1943**
d Dunedin NZ 12.4.62 *AUR* XXXIX 373

ELDER or Turner, Katharine Silver MA 1930
resid Colchester

ELDER Norma McDonald MA 1920
no longer on GC reg

EL HADIDI Moustafa Saleh PhD 1953
dean higher inst of agr Kafi El Sheikh Egypt 1958–68; visiting prof Baghdad univ Iraq 1969–73; head/prof bot fac of agr: Kafi El Sheikh 1973–74, Mansoura Egypt from 1974

ELLIN or Booker, Catherine Scott *MA 1952
resid Banchory

ELLINGER Gabrielle Marianne PhD 1951
res biochem Rowett res inst Aber from 1946

ELLIOT Elizabeth Patterson *MA 1949
prin teacher mod lang Mackie acad Stonehaven from 1968

ELLIOT Isabella Craig MA 1923
retd 1961; resid Aber

ELLIS Alexander Gordon Glennie BSc(agr) 1911
d Elgin 21.9.62 *AUR* XL 80

ELLIS Clarence Isidore MB CM 1896 MD 1901
d 19.11.61

ELLIS or Dickson, Eleanor MA 1929
resid Aber
d Hayle 7.7.81

ELLIS Elizabeth Helen MA 1947

ELLIS or Sutcliffe, Ethel MA 1916
d Nairobi 21.1.77

ELLIS Frederic Stuart BSc(eng) 1949
FBCS 1968
educ serv man. Systems Reliability Luton from 1975

ELLIS John BSc(agr) 1922
farm. from 1947; resid Alford; retd

ELLIS John Alexander Gordon BSc(for) 1949
acting conserv of for. Kumasi Ghana 1959–60; retd from HM overseas for. serv 1960; teacher: sc Elgin acad 1961–64; biol Kirkcaldy tech coll 1964–65; prin teacher biol Glenrothes 1965–74; dep rect Milne's h s Fochabers from 1974

ELLIS Richard Tunstall MA 1939 LLB 1948
OBE 1970 DL
ptnr Paull & Williamsons advoc Aber from 1949; chmn board of gov Dunfermline coll of phys educ 1964–67; chmn Scottish area TSB assoc 1967–76; memb TSB cent board from 1976

ELMSLIE or Garden, Eleanora Johnston **MA 1948 MB ChB 1953**
g p Timaru NZ from 1965

ELMSLIE Elizabeth Esther MA 1910
d Balmedie 8.7.66 *AUR* XLI 337

ELMSLIE Gordon Sinclair BSc(eng) 1951
FInstHE 1956 MICE 1958 MAmer Soc CE 1963
constr supt/asst chief eng Reynolds Jamaica Mines Jamaica 1959–65; contr man. (overseas) Middle East/reg man. Sydney Green & Sons (Contractors) Henley-on-Thames 1965–71, resid eng Sandford Fawcett Wilton & Bell consult. eng Lond 1971–72; group ldr Inv c c Isle of Skye 1972–73; sen eng Blyth & Blyth consult. eng Inv from 1973

ELMSLIE John Alexander Grant MB ChB 1951
g p Halifax from 1957

ELMSLIE John Grant MB ChB 1920
d Aber 3.1.67 *AUR* XLII 358

ELPHINSTONE John Joseph **MB ChB 1932 MD 1946**
Perth W Aust: dept publ health 1958–68; g p from 1968

ELRICK or Hatvany, Doris Margaret *MA 1946

ELRICK Joan Davidson MA 1915
no longer on GC reg

El Shazly Khaled PhD 1951
nat res award agr sc 1961, 1969
univ of Alexandria: lect dept anim prod. 1951–58, asst prof 1958–65; prof 1965–70, head of anim prod. dept 1970–74; nutrit off FAO Rome 1974–76; Dep Min of Agr 1976; prof anim nutrit 1977

ELWELL Harry Willmott MB ChB 1902
no longer on GC reg

EMMANUEL Antoine Fathallah MB ChB 1927
m o various govt hosps and clins from 1927 to 1958; private practice in afternoons; retd 1968
d Baghdad 16.10.75

EMSLIE Alfred George *MA 1928
PhD(Corn)

EMSLIE Alfred George ***MB ChB 1929 ᶜMD & DPH 1933**
FRCP(Lond) 1969
hon consult. phys Eastbourne group of hosp from 1972

EMSLIE Alfred William *MA 1950

EMSLIE Alice MA 1937
teacher Engl and remed Harlaw acad Aber from 1971

EMSLIE Arthur Raymond Gordon DSc 1934
d Ontario 27.9.65 *AUR* XLII 89

EMSLIE Calthorpe MA 1950
teacher Penicuik from 1965

EMSLIE or Angus, Charlotte Sylvia Smith MA 1949
resid Radcliffe-on-Trent

EMSLIE Dorothy Margaret Jane MB ChB 1919
retd 1964; resid Lond

EMSLIE Ethel Richmond
MB ChB 1922 DPH 1927 MD 1932
retd 1960; resid Ballater

EMSLIE Harold George MA 1950
Aber: dep head Craighill s 1964–70, Fernielea s 1970–75, Mile End s from 1975
m Peterculter 5.8.64 Olive A. Jamieson teacher d of William J. Peterculter

EMSLIE John BSc(agr) 1923
head Slains s 1937–65
d Ellon 4.4.76

EMSLIE John Alexander Simpson MB ChB 1922
MRCGP 1964
g p Eastbourne from 1946

EMSLIE John William BSc(agr) 1922
d Troon 1.6.73 *AUR* XLV 318

EMSLIE Michael John ᶜMB ChB 1954
MRCGP 1972
g p Eastbourne from 1957
m Lond 14.11.59 Jill Smyth d of Stanley C. S. Kensington

EMSLIE or Attisha, Victoria Clare
MB ChB 1926 DPH 1929
g p Basrah Iraq 1934–71; retd
d Calgary 13.12.79 *AUR* XLVIII 441

EMSLIE William MA 1926 LLB 1928
d Banchory 14.5.72 *AUR* XLV 127

EMSLIE William Harold Lees MB ChB 1927
phys homoeopathic hosp out patients Glasg from 1945

EMSLIE William Ingram MB ChB 1936
g p Kirkwall 1939–63; ARI: sen h o anaest 1963–65; regist anaest 1965–68; med asst anaest from 1968
wife *d* 1973
m(2) Stromness 31.8.74 Edith S. Horrie med secy/matron eventide home d of Thomas R. H. Firth Orkney

EMSLIE-SMITH Alan Hugh
MB ChB 1937 ᶜMD 1958

EMSLIE-SMITH Donald MB ChB 1945 *MD 1957
FRCPE 1965 FRCP(Lond) 1968
sen regist and tut. royal post grad med s of Lond and Hammersmith hosp 1958–61; sen lect med St And and hon consult. phys DRI 1961–67; Dund: sen lect med and hon consult. phys DRI 1967–71; reader med and hon consult. phys DRI and Ninewells hosp from 1971
m Lond 19.9.59 Ann E. Milne d of Col Thomas M. CB DSO Milford-on-Sea

ENDEAN Frank BSc(for) 1954 *1955
asst conserv for. Kitwe, Zambia 1956–67; res scient Canadian for. serv Edmonton 1967–73; consult. for. Forestal Internat Vancouver from 1973

ENGLISH or Bain, Elizabeth Barbara MA 1953
resid Aber

ENGSTROM Victor Ralph Whitcomb BCom 1930

ENTWISTLE Jessie MA 1920
d 18.2.71

ERSKINE or Stronach, Janet MA 1948
vol serv organis board of man. for Moray hosps from 1973; resid Elgin

ERSKINE or Innes, Marguerite Norah Laidlaw
MB ChB 1941
locum tenens Aber 1948–54

ESCOFFERY William Henry MB ChB 1941

ESCOFFERY William Ignatius MB ChB 1913

ESPLIN or Lord, Elizabeth Grant MA 1944

ESSLEMONT Alexander Gordon BCom 1923
retd 1967; resid Harrow
m(2) Harrow 12.5.79 Winifred D. G. Wheeler d of James T. Leach Sheerness

ESSLEMONT Donald Alexander Logie *MA 1951
prin teacher classics Inverurie acad from 1958

ESSLEMONT Elizabeth MA 1914

ESSLEMONT George Beedie
MA 1925 BCom 1927 LLB 1930
city chamberlain Glasgow 1943–70
d Glasgow 21.11.75 *AUR* XLVI 416

ESSLEMONT James Bryce BL 1928
ptnr Wilsone & Duffus advoc Aber 1936–75; retd; consult. Wilsone and Duffus

ESSLEMONT John Connon BCom 1925
man. dir John E. Esslemont Aber 1961–74; retd

ESSLEMONT Margaret Christina Taylor MA 1942

ESSLEMONT or Williamson, Marianne Rollo
MA 1936

ESSLEMONT Mary
BSc 1914 MA 1915 MB ChB 1923 LLD 1954
founder member RCGP FRCGP FBMA Vice-pres BMA
member univ court Aberd 1946–74; retd 1962; resid Aber

ESSLEMONT or Scott or Clay, Mary Gerrie MB ChB 1940
resid Aber

ESSON Alexander George Duncan MA 1915

ESSON George Alexander Cockburn MB ChB 1936
retd; resid Elgin

ESSON or Walker or Warren, Mary Bella MA 1910
d Portsoy 18.12.70 *AUR* XLIV 209

ESSON Norman Watson MA 1952
teacher sc Bawating s Sault Ste Marie Ontario from 1967

ESSON Walter Louis MA 1920 MB ChB 1924
O St J 1970
member, chmn war pensions and indust boards Manc 1952–70
m Aber 9.12.27 Elizabeth Reid d of William R. Johannesburg
d Manchester 29.2.80 *AUR* XLVIII 440

ETOE Owen Mansell *MA 1951

ETTLES or Fraser, Ann MA 1940
resid Forres

ETTLES William Alexander *MA 1941
clasp to VRD 1967 JP
lt cdr RNR retd
teacher Engl Keith g s Banffsh 1962–69; prin teacher Engl Buckie h s from 1969

ETTMAN Irving Kelsey MB ChB 1934
FACR 1964
clin prof radiol univ of Tennessee Memphis from 1970

EUNSON Leonard Harvey MB ChB 1924

EVANS Gwynfryn Pugh *MEd 1947

EWAN or MacLean, Alice May MA 1906
retd; resid Inv

EWAN James MA 1951

EWAN John Muir *MA 1955

EWAN Mary Strachan *MA 1930
prin lect maths Crewe coll of educ 1959–73; retd; resid Aber
d Aber 30.9.79 *AUR* XLVIII 353

EWAN Matilda Annie (Ramsay) *MA 1912
resid Aber
d Aber 18.9.78 *AUR* XLVIII 102

EWAN William Alexander BSc(eng) 1950

EWAN William John Strachan MB ChB 1936
FRCP(Lond)
consult. phys Haroldwood hosp and Rush Green hosp Essex

EWART Hugh James PhD 1936

EWEN Alan Burness MA 1941

EWEN Alastair Hamilton MA 1923
retd; resid Ellon

EWEN Douglas Richard *MA 1949
assoc prof Laurentian univ Canada 1965–66; sen lect univ of WI Trinidad 1968–70; chmn Engl dept York univ Toronto from 1973

EWEN or Murray, Elsie May MA 1918
d 21.12.70

EWEN James Barclay MB ChB 1927 ᶜMD 1933 DPH 1934
d Royston 20.3.71 *AUR* XLIV 211

EWEN or Inkson, Jane MA 1914
d Aber 31.1.61 *AUR* XXXIX 202

EWEN or Farquhar, Jeannie May MA 1919
d 19.5.71

EWEN Robert MA 1902
no longer on GC reg

EWEN William MA 1910 BD 1914
d Banff 16.2.71 *AUR* XLIV 209

EWEN William Alexander MA 1928
head Demonstration s Aber 1964–70; retd

EWING or White, Isabella Helen *MA 1907
d 18.5.74

EWING James MA 1910 BSc 1911 DSc 1916
no longer on GC reg

EWING Maggie Anderson MA 1916

EWING or Macdonald, Mary Angus MA 1921
no longer on GC reg

FAIRBAIRN Nellie MA 1916

FAIRLEY or Macpherson, Aileen Margaret Crichton MA 1949
resid Trumpington

FAIRLIE Andrew Lindsay BSc(agr) 1945

FAIRWEATHER or Cruickshank, Joan Isobel MA 1953
resid Fyvie

FAIRWEATHER or Watt, Kathleen Adela MA 1910
d 25.7.71 *AUR* XLIV 427

FALCONER Alfred *MA 1925
retd 1968
d Aber 23.2.78 *AUR* XLVII 356

FALCONER Bernard Paul Anthony *MA 1954

FALCONER Catherine Jean BSc(agr) 1955
m McCorkindale

FALCONER or Dawson, Dolina Barbara *MA 1926
no longer on GC reg

FALCONER or Barbour, Eva Farquharson MA 1950
teacher: Middlefield s Aber from 1968

FALCONER Ian McLeod BSc(eng) 1953
MICE 1961
des eng Sir Wm Halcrow & ptnrs consult. eng Lond 1959–60; sen eng, at A. A. Stuart Aigas of Kilmorack hydro schemes Invsh 1960–64; Crudens bldg and civ eng contr: proj eng Ninewells hosp Dun 1964–71, proj man. phase III Dun coll of art 1971–73, Dun coll of tech 1973–76; contr man. Taylor Woodrow Glasg 1976–79; bldgs off. Dund from 1979

FALCONER James *MA 1906
d Perth 3.11.70 *AUR* XLIV 167

FALCONER James Duncan *BSc 1952 PhD 1955
tech marketing superv Ruabon Wrexham from 1972

FALCONER John *MA 1920
no longer on GC reg

FALCONER or Cowan, Kathleen MA 1915
no longer on GC reg

FALCONER Margaret Sim MA 1911
no longer on GC reg

FALCONER Neil Douglas *MA 1954
comm asst ICI till 1962; Scot Adhesives Co Glasg from 1963, latterly dir
m Glasg 7.1.63 Roseanne S. M. Anderson BA(Dub) d of Samuel A. BSc(Glas) Glasg

FALCONER or Smith, Rachel MA 1948
teacher: Crieff 1965–73, maths Crieff s s from 1973

FALCONER or Macdonald, Rona Morven MA 1945

FALCONER Ronald Hugh Wilson MA 1934 BD 1937 DD 1960
William Thyne schol of ESU for first visit of Scotsman to Aust and NZ branches of ESU 1970
OBE 1971
retd BBC 1971; advis on relig TV: to NZ broadcasting corp 1971–72, to S. Afr. churches from 1972; consult. radio and TV World Assoc for Christian Commun from 1971; convener C of S dept of publ and publication from 1971; retd; resid Glasg
d Glasg 20.5.77 *AUR* XLVII 213

FALLOWFIELD or Mackay, Patricia Mackay *MA 1947
m(2) Wilson

FALLOWFIELD Thomas Leslie MB ChB 1955
MSc(Birm) 1960
RN(perm serv) from 1956

FARKAS Paul Lapislas PhD 1931

FARMAN or Crozier, Gertrude Elizabeth MA 1933

FARMER Victor Colin PhD 1947
FRIC 1964
sen prin sc off. Macaulay Inst for soil res Aber from 1968

FARQUHAR Alexander Proven MA 1950
teacher Aber: 1951–63, first asst RGC 1963–66; dep head Cults s 1966–73, head Milltimber s from 1973

FARQUHAR Alice Margaret Mary *MA 1946
woman advis St Peters RC s Aber from 1965

FARQUHAR or Collie, Barbara MA 1924
retd; resid Crimond

FARQUHAR or Rankin, Barbara Drummond MA 1915
resid Invercargill NZ

FARQUHAR or MacMillan, Doris MA 1928
d 4.3.71 *AUR* XLIV 212

FARQUHAR George Greig MB ChB 1900
d Darlington 12.8.63 *AUR* XL 299

FARQUHAR Ian Ewen *BSc 1954 PhD 1957
lect maths Queen Mary coll Lond 1961–68; res fell. theoret phys Norges Tekniske Høgskole Trondheim, Norway 1966–67; lect/sen lect theoret phys St And from 1968

FARQUHAR or Temple, Irene Elizabeth MA 1952
teacher Engl: Aber h s for girls 1965–70, Beath sen h s Cowdenbeath from 1970

FARQUHAR or Baxter, Isobel Reid MA 1949

FARQUHAR or Grant, Isobel Rust MA 1924
retd 1965; resid Aber
husb *d* 7.5.81

FARQUHAR James Alexander MA 1900
d 22.5.64 *AUR* XL 394

FARQUHAR or Stobbs, Jean Floyd MB ChB 1923
resid Hartlepool
husb *d* 1965

FARQUHAR or Simpson, Jessie Margaret MA 1941

FARQUHAR John BSc(for) 1947

FARQUHAR John David BSc(for) 1944

FARQUHAR or Sellar, Mary Morison MB ChB 1925 DPH 1951
resid Aber

FARQUHAR Moira BSc 1953
analytical chem ICI Ardeer, Stevenston 1953–61

m Aber 6.5.61 Norman S. Wallace BSc(Glas) res chem s of Norman G. W. Falkirk

FARQUHAR Oswald Cornell PhD 1951

FARQUHAR Robert Forbes BSc(eng) 1950

FARQUHAR Robert Warrender BSc(agr) 1925 MB ChB 1937 DPH 1947
d Lancaster 15.2.68 *AUR* XLII 365

FARQUHAR or Hamilton, Stella MA 1931
resid Fraserburgh

FARQUHARSON Charlotte Simpson BSc 1932

FARQUHARSON Edward MB ChB 1930 MD 1934
d Bournemouth 26.1.61 *AUR* XXXIX 283

FARQUHARSON or Locke, Eva Grant MA 1928
d 15.2.74

FARQUHARSON Gordon Booth MB ChB 1950
MRCGP 1970
g p Inv from 1963

FARQUHARSON or Gardiner, Grace Helen Gordon MA 1945
teacher Aboyne p s from 1965

FARQUHARSON Henry MA 1936 LLB 1937
life insur indust, spec in estate plan. Toronto from 1954

FARQUHARSON Horace BSc 1954
med rep G. D. Searle & Co., Aber 1960–64; Scot div man. Searle lab pharm div Scot. 1964–74; reg sales man. from 1974

FARQUHARSON Ian Glennie *MA 1950
prin teacher classics Kirkcaldy h s 1966–75; dep rector Blairgowrie h s from 1975

FARQUHARSON or Harper, Isobel MA 1908
d Aber 19.4.73

FARQUHARSON James Kennedy BSc(for) 1932 MB ChB 1937
retd 1973; resid Ellon
d 14.11.81

FARQUHARSON John BSc 1926 *1927 PhD 1930 DSc 1939
d Surrey 22.8.64 *AUR* XL 399, XLI 247

FARQUHARSON John Ogilvie MA 1940 [d]LLB 1949
ptnr Brander & Cruickshank advoc Aber from 1952

FARQUHARSON or Elphinstone, Kathleen Rhoda BSc 1949

FARQUHARSON or Corlette, Margaret MB ChB 1948
resid Sydney Aust

FARQUHARSON or Irvine, Margaret Elizabeth Ann MA 1954
teacher mod lang Arundel s Salisbury Rhod 1960–63

FARQUHARSON Myrtle MB ChB 1954
DA(Lond) 1957 D Obst RCOG(Lond) 1963 DPH(Glas) 1964
jun h m o chest diseases Ruchill hosp Glasg 1959–60; sen h o obst Kirkcaldy 1963; s m o Glasg 1963–66; m h o Peace River Area BC Canada 1966–68, g p White Rock BC from 1968

FARQUHARSON William Cowie MA 1923
secy Scot. Bible Soc Edin from 1966
retd 1968; resid Edin

FARRANT John Frederick Ames MA 1951 BD 1958 MTh 1980
rector: Holy Trinity epis ch Motherwell 1965–70, All Souls' Anglican ch Lae, Papua New Guinea 1970–74, St Bride's epis ch Glasg 1974–77, canon St Mary's cath Glasg from 1977

FARRELL Edna Bessie MA 1955
teacher Aber: Cummings Park p s 1956–70, Broomhill p s from 1970

FARRELL James Malcolm MB ChB 1951
g p Fochabers from 1966

FASKIN Annie MA 1920
no longer on GC reg

FAULKNER Roy BSc(for) 1948
for. comm res div: asst geneticist Edin 1959–62, prin geneticist Roslin from 1962

FEARNLEY Doris Ethel MA 1931
teacher Engl Harrogate 1938–71; retd; resid Harrogate

FEARNLEY or Clark, Gladys *MA 1935
resid Harrogate
husb *d* 1966

FEARNLEY Joseph Eric *BSc 1928
retd 1966; resid Harrogate

FEINSTEIN Samuel MB ChB 1922
no longer on GC reg

FELL William Ian Andrew MB ChB 1930
d Thurso 29.3.62 *AUR* XXXIX 384

FENTON Alexander *MA 1951
dep keeper Nat Museum of Antiquities of Scot. i/c Scot. country life sect. Edin from 1959; hon fell. s of Scot. stud. Edin from 1969

FENTON Edward Wyllie MA 1912 BSc 1913 DSc 1936
d 16.9.62 *AUR* XL 81

FERGUSON Allan William George BSc(eng) 1955

FERGUSON or Cowie, Beatrice Doreen MA 1944
resid Aber

FERGUSON or Rahman, Doreen MB ChB 1954
m o: packages factory Lahore 1961–63, outpatients' dept Holy Family hosp Rawalpindi 1966–67; resid Benghazi Libya

FERGUSON Elizabeth Margaret Graham MA 1950
Weston Park s Southampton: head geog dept 1958–66, dep head 1966–74; dep head Harlaw acad Aber from 1974

FERGUSON Elizabeth Mowat MA 1925
retd; resid Edin

FERGUSON or Smith, Evelyn MA 1915
no longer on GC reg

FERGUSON Fergus Graeme *BSc(eng) 1940
MIWE 1973
eng Sir Alexander Gibb & Ptners Reading from 1949

FERGUSON or Drummond, Hilda MA 1947

FERGUSON or Jack, Jean Alexandra MB ChB 1939
resid Carlops Penicuik
husb *d* 16.5.64

FERGUSON John BSc(agr) 1947
FRICS 1969 BA(OU) 1973
sen lands off. dept agr for Scot: Thurso 1968–71, Inv 1971–75; tech dev off. DAFS Edin from 1975

FERGUSON Keith MA 1948 dLLB 1952
DPA(Lond) 1973
town clerk Buckhaven and Methil 1959–62; secy and leg. advis Glenrothes dev corp from 1962

FERGUSON Keith Webster MA 1953 LLB 1955
leg. asst L. Mackinnon & Son advoc Aber 1958–62, ptnr from 1962
m Aber 4.10.63 Elizabeth A. S. Smith MA 1962 *qv*

FERGUSON Malcolm MA 1953
prod.: schools dept BBC Edin 1962–71, audio-visual unit Strath 1971–76; dir television 1976–77; dir audio-visual serv Glas univ from 1977

FERGUSON or Cattell-Jones, Margaret Kidd *MA 1922
d 1972

FERGUSON or Fraser, Margaret Redman Gibson *MA 1938
resid Kingswells, Aber

FERGUSON Mary Ann Hay *MA 1924
d Edin 19.2.66 *AUR* XLI 340

FERGUSON Vivian Leslie MB ChB 1920
d 17.11.69

FERGUSSON or Macfarlane, Marian Melville MB ChB 1939
resid Montrose

FERRES Gordon Kemp dMB ChB 1928
retd 1963; resid Banchory
m(2) Chichester 6.10.58 Sheila E. Bennett physioth d of Stephen B. Guildford

FERRIER or Gammie, Anne Taylor MA 1950

FERRIER William Roderick BL 1948
Clydesdale Bank: trust. off. Aber 1960–65, asst man. trust. dept 1965–69; man. trust. dept Lond 1969–71; dep trust. man. head off. Glasg 1971–72, trust. man. 1972–76; asst gen man. from 1976

FERRIES Catherine Anderson MA 1951
teacher: Fr/Lat Aboyne j s s 1953–62, maths/remed subj Gordon s Huntly from 1968
m Aber 15.8.62 George Stephen farm. s of George S. Rothienorman
husb *d* 8.10.76

FERRIES or Donald, Elizabeth Williamina MA 1941

FERRIES or Stewart, Evelyn Mary MA 1949
resid Chilliwack BC Canada

FERRIES George William *MA 1951
lect applied psych univ of Aston Birm from 1963

FERRIES Harvey BL 1950
sole ptnr Carle Duthie & Ferries advoc Aber from 1961

FERRIES John Morrison MB ChB 1948
consult. North Vancouver gen hosp from 1957

FERRIES Magdalene MA 1946 Dip Ed 1969
Dip Educ Deaf (Edin) 1970
teacher: Aber s for deaf 1968–71, Gateside centre for educ of deaf Paisley 1972–74; Aber s for deaf from 1976

FETTES Frances MA 1910
d Aber 1.10.74

FETTES William MB ChB 1928 DPH 1931
retd 1970; resid Lytham St Annes

FETTES William Youngson MB ChB 1938
retd 1971
d Ardersier 10.11.73 *AUR* XLV 449

FIDDES Christopher MA 1932
retd 1971; resid Edin

FIDDES Douglas Alexander BSc 1947
d Salisbury Rhodesia 29.4.75 *AUR* XLVI 325

FIDDES John MB ChB 1919 *MD 1926

FIDDES John Douglas MA 1905 *BSc 1907 MB ChB 1909
d Billericay Essex 24.6.66 *AUR* XLI 335

FIDDES Mary Elizabeth *MA 1930
teacher: prin Fr/Ger Aberlour h s 1944–59, asst Fr/Ger Elgin acad 1960–61, spec asst Keith g s 1962–69; retd; resid Keith

FIDDES William Ogilvie BCom 1923
d 8.5.78

FIDLER Mysie (Jemima) MA 1911
d Berwick 26.2.65 *AUR* XLI 147

FIELD or Cowie, Valerie Aileen ᶜMB ChB 1948 ᶜMD 1951
PhD(Lond) 1967 FRCPsych 1971
asst dir MRC psychiat genetics res unit London 1959–69; consult. psychiat Fountain and Carshalton group hosps Surrey 1961–67; USA visiting scient nat inst of health Bethesda and res assoc in neurol ch hosp dist of Columbia Washington 1968–69; hon consult. psychiat: Maudsley and Bethlem royal hosps Lond 1967–68, Mayday hosp Croydon 1968–75; hon consult. St George's hosp from 1975; chmn ment defic sect Royal Coll Psychiat from 1975
husb *d* 1970

FINDLATER Alexander George Craig MB ChB 1945
DA(Lond) 1967
g p Launceston, Tasmania from 1969
d 6.11.78

FINDLATER or Cairns, Helen *MA 1944
dep head: Wood Green s Lond 1964–67, Haringey s 1967–69; head High Cross s Haringey from 1969

FINDLATER William Thompson BSc(agr) 1953
vis aids off. s of agr Aberd from 1971

FINDLAY Adam Fyfe *MA 1889 DD 1923 LLD 1948
d Aber 19.1.62 *AUR* XXXIX 268

FINDLAY Alexander *MA 1895 *BSc 1897 DSc 1902 LLD 1944
d 14.9.66 *AUR* XLI 286

FINDLAY Alexander MB ChB 1923
retd; resid Chigwell

FINDLATER Alexander John MA 1907 BSc(agr) 1909
chief agr advis col serv S Nigeria; retd 1954
d Aboyne 26.12.76

FINDLAY or Kitz, Alice Duff MB ChB 1939
d Halifax Nova Scotia 20.5.69 *AUR* XLIII 216

FINDLAY Annie MA 1912
no longer on GC reg

FINDLAY or Strang, Bella MA 1934

FINDLAY Charles Bruce MB ChB 1936
insp of aliens port of Folkestone 1956–64; med advis Carter Wallace pharm Folkestone from 1964

FINDLAY or Cox, Diana Avril *MA 1953

FINDLAY Francis *BSc 1941
no longer on GC reg

FINDLAY Garden Whyte MA 1951
DTI from 1961

FINDLAY George Alexander MB ChB 1943
g p Chryston, Glasg from 1950

FINDLAY George Daniel BSc(agr) 1951

FINDLAY George Ian Garrioch MB ChB 1931
d Askerwells 23.12.76 *AUR* XLVII 213

FINDLAY Graham MB ChB 1953
g p Ilford from 1954

FINDLAY Harry David MA 1924 MB ChB 1928
g p Marlow-on-Thames from 1969

FINDLAY Henry Ritchie MB ChB 1939
g p Huddersfield from 1949

FINDLAY Ian Douglas MB ChB 1946
DPH(Tor) 1960 Cert Publ Health(Can) 1961
BC Canada: m o h S central health unit Kamloops 1959–69; g p Irving clin Kamloops from 1969

FINDLAY Ian James MA 1931 BSc 1935
d 23.7.75

FINDLAY James MA 1954
teacher Portsoy s s 1960–64; Buckie: dep head h s 1964–69; head p s from 1969
m Dingwall 16.7.60 Jessica M. Young teacher d of John Y. Dingwall

FINDLAY James BL 1954
town clerk dep Aber 1972–75; dep dir law and admin Grampian reg c from 1975
m Aber 2.3.63 Wilma A. Anderson secy/police off. d of William A. A. Aber

FINDLAY James George MA 1952
head teacher: Fintry, Turriff 1965–67, Monquhitter 1971–75, Turriff p s from 1975

FINDLAY or Robertson, Jean *MA 1939

FINDLAY or Duthie, Jeannie MA 1951
teacher Wester Langlee p s Galashiels 1964–68, asst head from 1968

FINDLAY John MA 1954 Dip Ed 1955
teacher mod lang: Laurencekirk j s 1958–62, dep head Sanday j s s Orkney 1962–67, Stranraer h s 1967–68; dep head Park p s Stranraer 1968–71; head: transition s Macduff 1971–76, Ladyloan p s Arbroath from 1976

FINDLAY John Angus MB ChB 1955 MD 1973
h o ARI 1958–60; lect anat Aberd 1960–61; univ coll S Wales and Mon, Cardiff: lect anat 1961–72,

serv lect from 1972
m Grantown-on-Spey 1.5.59 Elisabeth Allan Durh

FINDLAY John Gray BSc 1924
no longer on GC reg

FINDLAY Leslie MA 1915
no longer on GC reg

FINDLAY or Ennals, Margaret Buyers MA 1930
d Camberley 1.1.73 *AUR* XLV 226

FINDLAY or Cumming, Mary MA 1909
no longer on GC reg

FINDLAY or Stuart, Mary Isabella MA 1942

FINDLAY or Gall, Rhoda Gertrude MB ChB 1924 DPH 1926
retd 1963; resid Aber

FINE Samuel Harry MB ChB 1925
no longer on GC reg

FINLAYSON Bruce MA 1954 MEd 1956
teacher Engl AGS 1960–67, prin asst Engl 1967–71; prin Engl Kincorth acad Aber from 1971

FINLAYSON Eric Cameron MA 1926
CA Aber from 1932; retd 1976

FINLAYSON Horace Courtenay Forbes *MA 1907
d St Leonards-on-Sea 3.12.69 *AUR* XLIII 440

FINLAYSON Isobel Eleanor Mary MA 1911
no longer on GC reg

FINLAYSON James Kerr *BSc(eng) 1943 *MB ChB 1954
FRCP(Lond) 1973
instr and fell. in med Rochester NY 1958–60; ARI: sen regist med 1960–64, consult. phys from 1964

FINLAYSON John Dugald MA 1904
no longer on GC reg

FINLAYSON Kenneth Macdonald MB ChB 1928
no longer on GC reg

FINLAYSON or Shupe, Lily Helen MA 1939
teacher BC Canada: Mission City 1958–60, Fort St John 1961–63, Salmon Arm 1966–74; retd

FINLAYSON Margaret Scotland MA 1931
teacher Edzell 1948–73; retd

FINLAYSON Margaret Watt MA 1941
teacher Walker Rd p s Aber from 1949

FINLAYSON Roderick Alexander MA 1919
retd 1966; resid Edin

FINLAYSON Sidney Knight MA 1913
d Orpington –.7.69 *AUR* XLIII 329

FINLAYSON William MA 1910
d 1.2.71

FINNIE Alison Murray MA 1915
no longer on GC reg

FINNIE Andrew Scott MA 1938
MICA(Scot)
Aberd: part-time lect acct 1960–66, head of dept from inception in 1966 to 1973; ptnr Whinney Murray & Co
m(2) Peterculter 5.6.64 Johne S. Balmain CA d of Kenneth F. B. Edin

FINNIE or Gray, Davina Milne MA 1955
teacher: Portknockie p s 1965–66, Portsoy p s 1966–68, remed Banff acad 1968–71; head Botriphnie p s from 1971

FINNIE Isabella MA 1925
retd 1968; resid Edin

FINNIE James Sadler MB ChB 1946 MD 1959
g p Aber from 1951

FINNIE Margaret Maud Keith MA 1927
teacher Cults s 1935–68; retd; resid Aber
d 22.10.81

FINNIE or Kant, Rosemary Stewart MA 1951
secy phys dept Portland state univ Oregon USA 1968–70; teacher Dumfriessh 1970–72; pers secy to man. dir Century Aluminium Co Sanquhar 1972–75; Jordanhill coll of educ 1975–76; sec cert Lat/Engl teacher Glasg from 1976

FINNIE Williamson Jackson BSc 1935 MB ChB 1938
consult. anaest Bradford hosp group from 1947; retd

FIRTH Ian George Macdonald MB ChB 1915
no longer on GC reg

FIRTH James Stevenson MB ChB 1928
retd 1969; resid Rousay

FIRTH Norman John MA 1929
head Tankerness s Orkney
m 1931 Helen Hendry teacher
d Tankerness 21.10.52

FITZPATRICK Ewart Adsil PhD 1951
sen lect dept of soil sc Aberd from 1969

FLAWS Muriel MA 1925
no longer on GC reg

FLEMING or Robinson, Anne Elsie MA 1929
resid Belfast

FLEMING Eric James MA 1949

FLEMING Stanley David BSc(agr) 1955

FLEMING Thomas Aitchison BSc(for) 1949

FLETCHER David Livingstone MB ChB 1938
g p Pickering from 1945

FLETCHER Edith Eleanor MA 1934
teacher Woodside s Aber from 1943; retd 1975

FLETCHER Grace MA 1955

FLETCHER Harold Roy PhD 1933
hon DSc(Edin) 1971 hon DSc(St And) 1972
regius keeper Roy Bot Gdn Edin 1958–70; pres Bot Soc of Edin 1959–60; vice-pres Royal Soc Edin 1961–65; pres internat assoc of bot gardens 1964–69; HM botanist in Scot. from 1966; hon prof bot Edin from 1968
d 27.8.78

FLETCHER John Robert BSc(for) 1950
for. comm: for. off. Chester 1953–58, Bakewell 1958–67, Kendal 1967–72, Thetford 1972–76, Edin from 1976
m Adel Leeds 2.11.57 Maureen Hobson

FLETT Alexander Campbell BSc 1955 PhD 1958

FLETT Alexander Smith MA 1948
d Aber 1.2.75 *AUR* XLVI 240

FLETT or Howie, Constance Florence MA 1923
resid Aber
husb *d* 2.12.76
d Aber 13.2.81

FLETT George BSc 1928 MA 1930
head Inverallochy 1962–71; retd; resid Torphins

FLETT George BSc 1949
teacher Dunbartonsh: guid post Bradfield s from 1972

FLETT George Reid BSc(for) 1933 BSc 1935
teacher: Blackburn p s W Lothian 1936–37, Lindsay h s Bathgate 1937–40; educ off. RAF 1940–45; head Longridge p s 1945–46; head of sc: Russel s E Croydon 1946–54, John Newnham s E Croydon 1954–56; asst head internat s Geneva 1956–64; exchange teacher Chadwick s Los Angeles 1964–66; Lossiemouth h s 1966–75; retd; resid San Diego Calif

FLETT Helen Jane MA 1905
no longer on GC reg

FLETT Ian Stark *MA 1943 *MEd 1948
dep educ off. Kingston-u-Hull 1963–66; dir educ Fife 1966–75; dir educ Fife reg c from 1975

FLETT or Hughes, Isabella MA 1924
d Aber 16.4.71 *AUR* XLIV 211

FLETT John Alexander *MA 1946
teacher maths AGS from 1950
m Macduff 2.7.55 Jean P. Thomson health visitor d of George T. Macduff

FLETT John Alexander MA 1949

FLETT or Reid, Margaret MA 1946

FLETT or Tarlton, Nelly MA 1920 MB ChB 1924
d Bristol 22.11.65 *AUR* XLII 85

FLETT or Stone-Wigg, Sheelagh Mairi BSc 1954
Kericho p s Kenya: teacher 1967–70, head from 1970

FLETT or Elder, Sheila Margaret MA 1949
Malaya: head Engl dept Bentong h s Pahang 1964–65, Uplands s Penang 1965–66; teacher Causewayend p s Aber 1968–75, asst head from 1975

FLETT William MA 1911
no longer on GC reg

FLETT or Kilpatrick, Williamina Smith BSc 1944 *1946
MEd(Tor) 1976
Toronto: teacher St Clement's s for girls 1960–63, Don Mills C I 1963–69, asst head maths G. S. Henry s s from 1969

FLOCKHART David BSc 1936

FLOCKHART Helen Rattray BCom 1929
d 17.12.65

FLORENCE Alexander Leslie MB ChB 1950
g p Tawa, Wellington NZ from 1966

FLORENCE Elsie Mary MA 1932
teacher Aberdeensh from 1933: Buchanhaven s, Chapel of Garioch s

FLORENCE Janet Leslie MA 1911 *1912
retd 1954
d Stirling 4.2.77

FLORENCE or Chalmers, Patricia Barbara MA 1951

FLORY Janet MA 1952
retd; resid Ellon
d Ellon 31.1.79 *AUR* XLVIII 233

FLOWERDEW Richard Edward MB ChB 1908
d Nairobi 9.12.71 *AUR* XLIV 427

FORBES or Robb, Agnes Kate MB ChB 1932
part time school m o Leicester from 1965

FORBES Alexander MA 1928
head Ferryhill p s Aber 1964–67; retd; resid Tarland
d 8.8.81

FORBES Alexander *MA 1948
dep rector Fraserburgh acad from 1969

FORBES Alexander Riach MB ChB 1919
retd: resid Tadworth

FORBES Allan Massie BSc(agr) 1951
nutrit advis Farm Feed Formulators Northallerton from 1970

FORBES Andrew MB ChB 1932
d 3.12.73 *AUR* XLV 448

FORBES or McDonald, Annabella Allan *MA 1942
prin teacher maths Hamilton g s Lanarksh from 1970

FORBES or Robertson, Annie MA 1907

FORBES or Paul, Barbara Anderson *MA 1947
Cambridge electron accelerator Harvard univ 1956–62; teacher Fr Lexington publ s Mass USA 1964–66, 68–71

FORBES Charles Brown MA 1922
retd 1964; dir Aber FC from 1936
d Aber 15.4.80 *AUR* XLVIII 441

FORBES Charlotte Clark *MA 1913
retd 1952
d Daviot Abdnsh 11.1.80

FORBES or Fraser, Christina MA 1924
resid Beauly

FORBES or Angus, Christina Findlay MA 1951
d 2.8.77

FORBES David Albert MB ChB 1943
d Chesterfield 18.10.70 *AUR* XLIV 111

FORBES Donald Fraser Christopher BSc(for) 1952
m Innerleithen 11.7.64 Agnes H. Dodds civ serv d of James W. D. Peebles

FORBES Eleanor Margaret MA 1924
secy posts mainly with ICI Lond 1924–36
m Aber 23.7.36 James P. Norrie BSc(eng)(Glas) consult. mining eng RST Rhodesia s of William N. Cape Town
husb *d* Cape Town 1978

FORBES or Rendle, Elizabeth Ann MA 1928
resid Okehampton

FORBES Elsie McKenzie MA 1916
no longer on GC reg

FORBES Etta Broughton MA 1914
resid Tunbridge Wells
d 31.3.78

FORBES The Hon Sir Ewan MB ChB 1944
Bart JP
resid Brux Alford

FORBES Ewen Maitland MA 1955

FORBES Francis Dawson MB ChB 1938
d Hartford Huntingdon 29.6.62 *AUR* XXXIX 386

FORBES Frank Mathieson MA 1947 LLB 1949
solicr; retd 1975

FORBES Frederick Alastair MB ChB 1939
g p Aber from 1946; retd

FORBES Frederick Stanley Arnot MB ChB 1941 DPH 1947
JP 1971 O St J(Wales) 1973
g p Chepstow from 1949

FORBES George MA 1905
d Peterhead 15.8.68 *AUR* XLIII 77

FORBES George Barnet MB ChB 1937 MD 1951
FRCPath 1963
consult. path. Kent & Canterbury hosp Canterbury from 1948

FORBES George Wilson MB ChB 1942
g p Watton-at-Stone from 1952

FORBES Gordon BCom 1923
resid Tunbridge Wells
d 28.3.76

FORBES or Pratt, Grace Christina MA 1948
Aber: teacher maths Hilton acad 1970–73, year mistress Northfield acad from 1973

FORBES Ian MA 1951
Aber: teacher 1952–73, asst head guid from 1973

FORBES Ian Mackenzie MA 1948
PhD(Glas) 1977
C of S min Dalziel par ch Motherwell 1966–77, Kemnay par ch from 1977

FORBES Isabelle Mary *MA 1946
Glasg: sen teacher mod lang Langside coll 1964–70, head lang dept Cardonald coll from 1970

FORBES Isobel Munro MA 1947
asst head/guid The Gordon Schools Huntly from 1971

FORBES or Adamson, Jane *MA 1923
resid Cullen

FORBES Jane Mearns Mackie MA 1935
Birm: teacher 1954–58, dep head 1958–60; Stonehaven: mus asst Mackie acad 1961–62, teacher Fetteresso and Arduthie p s till 1973; retd
m Stonehaven 30.3.46 Douglas C. W. Stewart pol constable s of Agnes S. Shrewsbury; marr diss

FORBES or Campbell, Janet Jane MA 1935
teacher: head maths dept Bulstrode g s Hounslow 1955–68, head Green House Hounslow Manor s GLC 1968–74

FORBES or Kay, Janet Syme MA 1949
teacher North s Kirkcaldy from 1964

FORBES Jessie Margaret MA 1925
teacher James Clark s s Edin 1943–69; retd
d 7.6.77

FORBES John MB ChB 1900
no longer on GC reg

FORBES John MB ChB 1954
DA 1960
asst anaest Teesside from 1965
m Stockton-on-Tees 5.10.63 Winifred Peacock SRN d of Alfred M. P. Stockton-on-Tees

FORBES John Alexander MA 1947 MB ChB 1951 MD 1963
MRCGP 1962 FRCGP 1971
Southampton med s: sen lect commun med 1969–72, prof primary med care from 1972

FORBES John Clark MB ChB 1924
retd 1958; resid Aber
d Aber 29.6.79 *AUR* XLVIII 351

FORBES John Edward MA LLB 1952
solic John Wilson and Turnbull Falkirk from 1961

FORBES Lesley Lumsden Wilson MA 1939
teacher Aber from 1941

FORBES Lyla Catherine MB ChB 1922
d 19.1.71

FORBES or Innes, Margaret MB ChB 1936

FORBES or Burnett, Margaret Elizabeth Alexandria BSc 1920
d Stockport 31.3.73

FORBES or Orr, Margaret Jane MA 1921
d Rothesay 9.8.75 *AUR* XLVI 322

FORBES or Graham, Margaret Jean MA 1949
resid Glasg

FORBES or Gray, Margaret Shepherd MA 1928
retd 1969; resid Aber

FORBES or Millar, Margaret Thomson *MA 1949
teacher: Aber acad 1955–57, Elgin acad 1957–58, Nairn acad 1960–62, Perth acad 1963–65, Rothesay acad 1966–68, asst prin mod lang Dunfermline h s from 1969

FORBES Margaret Valentine MA 1936
Aber: teacher Woodside p s from 1941

FORBES Mary Isabella MA 1913
no longer on GC reg

FORBES or Middleton, Mary Isobel MB ChB 1937
resid Broughty Ferry

FORBES or Shiach, Mildred MA 1935
d Dumfries 16.2.63

FORBES Patricia Rose MA 1951
teacher Inv r acad from 1954

FORBES Robert Fraser MA 1913
no longer on GC reg

FORBES or Brittain, Rosa Jean MA 1931
resid Calne

FORBES Stanley *MA 1950
Oakbank s Aber: asst head 1961–66, dep head from 1966

FORBES William *MA 1922
d Aber 21.12.69 *AUR* XLIII 444

FORBES William Henry Brough BSc(for) 1951

FORBES William Skene MA 1952
no longer on GC reg

FORBES or Sim, Willma Coutts MA 1953
Inf Mist. endorsement 1969 Inst of Ling Exam Ger Grade II 1973 Intermed Grade Pts I and II 1974
Aber: teacher Mile-End s 1967–73, Fr and Ger in prim. schools from 1973

FORD William MA 1946
d Elba –.7.73 *AUR* XLV 321

FORDYCE or Donovon, Elizabeth Jane *MA 1933
OBE 1968
retd 1972; resid Verwood
husb *d* 1976

FORDYCE Gordon Esslemont MB ChB 1932
consult. surg N'cle-u-Tyne reg hosp board from 1952; retd 1975

FORGAN or Findlay, Margaret Rose MA 1909 MB ChB 1912
retd 1957; resid Leven

FORGAN Robert MA 1911 MB ChB 1915 *MD 1924
retd 1971
d Brentwood 8.1.76 *AUR* XLVI 414

FORGIE Alexander Davidson MB ChB 1927 MD 1945
d Lond 11.6.64 *AUR* XL 400

FORGIE or Walker, Jane Ross MB ChB 1934
resid Edin

FORMAN Bruce *BSc 1949 PhD 1956
FRSA 1971
The Nature Conservancy: reg off. E. Anglia Norwich 1961–66, spec scient advis Lond 1966–67, conserv off. (England) Lond 1967–74, dep dir England from 1974

FORMAN Frank *MB ChB 1922 *MD 1932
d Israel 9.3.80 *AUR* XLIX 67

FORRAI Gabriel Louis MB ChB 1955
g p: Crook, Durh 1960–63, Ilford, Barking, Dagenham from 1963

FORREST or Austin, Aileen *BSc 1949
resid Sheffield

FORREST Alastair William Fordyce MA 1950
Aber: dep head Cummings Park p s 1965–67, Abbotswell p s 1967–69; head Causewayend p s 1969–71, Abbotswell p s from 1971

FORREST Alistair William *MB ChB 1927
FRCGP 1972
g p Aber 1954–74; retd
m(2) Aber 8.9.60 Agnes E. Whitter MB ChB 1951 *qv*

FORREST Elsie Marjorie MA 1940
teacher Fernielea p s Aber from 1961
m Aber 18.3.72 John M. Telfer MA(Edin) army/MN s of Thomas M. T. Edin

FORREST James *MA 1899
no longer on GC reg

FORREST James Sim MA LLB 1950
employed Union Castle Mail Steamship Co Lond and Capetown 1950–72; off. man. housing dept Edin 1972–75, chief asst admin from 1975

FORREST or Cowie, Jean Ailsa MA 1948
resid Edin

FORREST John *MA 1948
deceased

FORREST John Berry MA LLB 1950
ptnr Adam Thomson & Ross advoc Aber from 1954

FORREST Robert Andrew Dermod *MA 1914
d –.1.77 *AUR* XLVII 211

FORREST Stanley MA 1920 MB ChB 1924
coronation medal 1937 KPR medal 1963
hon m o Kenya police reserve 1949–63; retd; resid Kenya
d Nairobi 17.5.81

FORRESTER Robert Smith MB ChB 1947
DCP(Lond) 1956 MRCPath 1963
DMJ(Path)(Lond) 1967 FRCPath 1974
surg cmdr RN retd; late consult. path. RN; c m o HMS *Raleigh* Cornwall
m Stanwell 27.10.48 Elizabeth C. Wright nurse d of Francis W. W. Aber

FORRESTER Thomas Martin *BSc 1949 ᶜMB ChB 1957
d Aber 17.3.71 *AUR* XLIV 216

FORSTER Dorothy BSc 1925 EdB 1945

FORSTER Frank Northman MB ChB 1944
g p Kemnay from 1970; retd 1977

FORSTER George Robert *BSc 1949
Plymouth marine lab: on scient staff dept sc and indust res from 1951
m Plymouth 8.8.61 Alison M. Livingstone d of Duncan L. Plymouth

FORSTER Margaret Gena MA 1927 BSc 1929 *1930
retd 1972; resid Aber

FORSTER Reginald Arthur MB ChB 1905

FORSYTH Alexander BSc 1935
BA(OU) 1979
man. dir group of chem firms formed by T. & H. Smith (latterly joined to Glaxo group) 1957–70; full time member HIDB Inv 1970–75; OU stud. 1975–80; retd

FORSYTH Archibald Goodall BSc(agr) 1949
d Edin 15.3.63 *AUR* XL 207

FORSYTH Barbara *MA 1922
retd 1962; resid Fortrose

FORSYTH Douglas Charles Tetley *BSc 1954
sen scient off. inst for marine environmental res Edin from 1954; retd 1977

FORSYTH Gordon *MA 1948
war serv Scots Guards, 6th Gurkha Rifles India, Middle East, Italy 1940–46; teacher Aberdeensh 1949–57; overseas civ serv educ off. Port of Spain Trinidad 1958–69; lect coll of comm Aber from 1969
m(2) 14.2.58 Mairi W. Stewart d of James S. S. MB ChB 1913 *qv*

FORSYTH Gordon *BSc 1949
ICI tech serv dept plastics div from 1965

FORSYTH John BSc 1951 *1952
lect agr entomology univ of Ghana 1959–62; entomologist royal horticultural soc Wisley, Surrey 1963–66; lect nat hist dept of extra-mural stud. Queen's univ Belf 1966–76, sen lect from 1976

FORSYTH John Alexander MA 1946
teacher: Engl/Lat Bracoden j s 1947–51, Lat/geog Fordyce acad 1951–64; county drama advis from 1964

FORSYTH Robert McCallum BSc 1953
teacher: sc Portsoy j s s 1962–68, phys Banff acad from 1968
m Aber 11.7.61 Velta Piksis MA 1953 *qv*

FORSYTH Stanley *MA 1939

FORSYTH Theodore *MA 1933
d Dumfries 21.8.74 *AUR* XLVI 109

FORSYTH William George Cameron PhD 1946
United Brands Co hq New York: i/c corporate res and dev

FORTH Dorothy Mary Margaret MB ChB 1942
MRCGP
g p Cromarty 1962–76; m o Kingseat hosp Aber from 1976

FORTUNE Ronald Denis *BSc 1951
DSc(Gen)

FORTUNE William James MA 1908 *1910
Dip(Caen) 1907 Dip Phonetics(Marburg) 1908
retd 1951; resid Crieff
m(2) Crieff 21.11.68 Sybil J. E. Mackintosh MA(St

And) d of William F. M. Dun
d Crieff 15.1.81

FOSTER Margaret Stoddart MA 1934
teacher: Cullen s s 1962–69, Whitehills 1969, Engl Banff acad from 1969

FOSTER or Watson, Winifred Mary MB ChB 1922 DPH 1927
d Willington 21.8.68 *AUR* XLIII 80

FOTHERINGHAM or Thomson, Euphemia Mary MA 1929
resid Comrie

FOTHERINGHAM Ian King *BSc(eng) 1948

FOTHERINGHAM Ian Murray *BSc 1952

FOTHERINGHAM Thomas BCom 1923
no longer on GC reg

FOTHERINGHAM William Milne MB ChB 1931
part time indust m o BTR from 1942

FOUBISTER Donald MacDonald BSc 1924
no longer on GC reg

FOUBISTER John Bichan MA 1901 BSc 1904 MB ChB 1914
d Aber 15.12.68 *AUR* XLIII 208

FOUBISTER Thomas Benjamin MA 1936 MB ChB 1941
g p Echt from 1955

FOUBISTER William James BSc(eng) 1949
MICE 1951 MIWE 1955 FIMunE 1973
civ eng: Paisley corp 1949–51, Aber c c 1951–62; div road surv Aber c c 1962–75; area road surv Grampian reg c from 1975

FOUIN Francois Louis Pierre MB ChB 1954
MRCGP 1966
g p Cults/Culter dist from 1959

FOWLER Alexander Burn BSc(agr) 1928

FOWLER or Lewes, Alice Lyon MA 1908
d 28.6.61 *AUR* XXXIX 273

FOWLER Andrew MB ChB 1916
d Aber 18.11.71 *AUR* XLIV 317

FOWLER or Hardie, Catherine Jane MA 1925
resid Aber

FOWLER Edna Violet Moir *MA 1949
teacher Inverurie acad from 1959

FOWLER Elijah MB ChB 1939
g p Stockport from 1946

FOWLER Elizabeth Fordyce MA 1921
d Aber 25.11.71 *AUR* XLIV 319

FOWLER James Archibald MB ChB 1953
g p Victoria BC Canada from 1959

FOWLER James John *MA 1923
d 11.10.65 *AUR* XLII 86

FOWLER Joanna Aitken MA 1915
no longer on GC reg

FOWLER or Smith, Mary Jean MA 1933 *MEd 1948
sen educ psych Dun 1960–72; retd
m Aber 8.7.50 Stewart F. Smith civ serv

FOWLER Thomas Mair MB ChB 1936
promoted col RAMC 1964; retd 1971; resid Ellon

FOWLIE or Finlayson, Anna Beatrice MA 1935
resid Hawick

FOWLIE George Gordon BSc 1941 *1947
MInst P
Nobel's Explosives Co Stevenston Ayrsh: sen plant man. 1970–73, comp safety dept man. from 1973

FOWLIE Hugh MA 1920 BSc(agr) 1921
d 1941

FOWLIE or Sparke, Gertrude Elizabeth MA 1930
resid Aber

FOWLIE or Watmough, Jessie Robertson MA 1933
teacher: Cleethorpes 1951–70; retd; resid Humberston Grimsby

FOWLIE John MA 1926
d Aber 6.3.70 *AUR* XLIII 445

FOWLIE Mary Susan MA 1910
d Aber 24.11.77

FOWLIE Spencer Stephen MA 1912
retd 1956; resid Buckie
d Elgin 17.2.79 *AUR* XLVIII 226

FOX Andrew Fraser MA 1939
Broughton, Peeblessh: head cent p s from 1952

FOX Edgar Alexander MB ChB 1949
g p Bishop Auckland from 1951

FRAIN or Grant, Elizabeth Rae *MA 1922
resid Aber

FRAIN Ian Miller MA 1951
head Laurencekirk s s from 1965; provost burgh Laurencekirk from 1960; chmn Kincardine Deeside dist c from 1974

FRANCE Ronald Spalding MA 1946
chmn and man. dir J. Haighton & Sons Nantwich; gen comm of Inland Revenue Crewe from 1961

FRANCIS Jacqueline Olive Priscilla McKay MA 1947

FRANÇOIS Charles Arthur MB ChB 1928

FRANKLIN Montague MB ChB 1938
g p Glasg from 1948

FRASER Alan John MA 1928

FRASER Alan Norman BSc(eng) 1932

FRASER Alastair Hugh BSc(agr) 1955

FRASER Albert Grant MB ChB 1943
DObstRCOG 1961 FRCGP 1973
g p Aber from 1948

FRASER Alexander MA 1951

FRASER Alexander Birnie MB ChB 1949
no longer on GC reg

FRASER Alexander Mackenzie MB ChB 1924 DPH MD 1929
d Inv 27.7.61 *AUR* XXXIX 281

FRASER Alexander Skinner MA 1930
d Aber 18.2.67 *AUR* XLII 369

FRASER Alfred BSc(agr) 1921
d 7.9.69

FRASER Alistair Mearns *BSc 1950

FRASER Allan BSc(for) 1950

FRASER Allan Henry Hector BSc 1925 MB ChB 1928 *MD 1929 DSc 1953
d Aber 12.7.79 *AUR* XLVIII 351

FRASER or Murray, Anita Garden BSc 1947
resid Currie

FRASER Annie MA 1936
d Aber 1.11.76

FRASER or Jamieson, Annie *MA 1939

FRASER Archibald Stewart *BSc 1955
lect geog: univ of Auckland NZ 1961–65, later univ of W Aust, Perth; sen lect Flinders univ of S Aust Bedford Park from 1967
m Beverley W Aust 20.5.63 Sarah M. Barrett-Lennard farm./banker d of Geoffrey B.-L. Beverley

FRASER Arthur MA 1906
no longer on GC reg

FRASER or Walker, Bessie MA 1934
resid Haddington

FRASER Campbell Victor MB ChB 1953
g p Bedford from 1954

FRASER Catherine Margaret MA 1944
teacher Quarryhill p s Aber from 1954

FRASER Charles George BSc(eng) 1953

FRASER or Goodbody, Charlotte Mary *BSc 1951
part-time dem zool dept univ of W.I. Kingston Jamaica from 1956

FRASER Christine Grace MA 1954 LLB 1956
solic Inv: ptnr MacArthur & Co from 1967
m Killearnan 30.10.76 Daniel MacWilliam

FRASER or Sutherland, Constance Elizabeth Anderson MA 1947 LLB 1950
lect in law s of bus. man. stud RGIT Aber from 1967
marr diss

FRASER David Edward MB ChB 1949
FRCGP 1973
g p Bucksburn from 1955

FRASER Donald BSc(agr) 1922
no longer on GC reg

FRASER Donald MB ChB 1929
retd 1971; resid Winchester

FRASER Donald Edward Kerr BSc(eng) 1955
MICE 1968
D. Logan: asst civ eng Gartcosh Strip mill 1959–62, sub ag Dunbar cement works 1962–63, sub ag Tay road bridge 1963–66; W A Fairhurst & Ptnrs Dun: asst civ eng 1966–68, sen civ eng from 1968
m Invergordon 5.9.62 Marguerite C. G. Mackenzie Queen's nurse d of Thomas A. M. Invergordon

FRASER Donald Robertson *MA 1937 BD 1942
C of S min Balquhidder par ch from 1973

FRASER Donald William MA 1955

FRASER or Simpson, Dorothy Mary *BSc 1952 PhD 1955
MRC fell. Birm 1956–58
resid Hartlepool

FRASER Douglas James MB ChB 1934

FRASER Douglas McLaren MB ChB 1949
g p Swallowfield from 1959

FRASER Douglas Morrison Milne MA 1913 MB ChB 1916
d 17.3.63

FRASER Duncan *BSc 1933 PhD 1951
secy for Asia and Aust overseas council Edin 1965–71; retd; resid Kiltarlity

FRASER or Ross, Elizabeth MA 1930
resid Fearn

FRASER or Wisely, Elizabeth Ann Mutch MA 1927
teacher: spec asst maths Albyn s for girls Aber from 1948; retd
d Aber 15.11.77

FRASER or Macdonald, Elizabeth Clark **MB ChB 1936**
part-time g p/PH and Treasury med serv 1942–68; resid Brisbane

FRASER Elizabeth Donaldina **MA 1941 *EdB 1943 PhD 1955**
Aberd: sen lect psych 1963–64, Anderson prof psych from 1964; dean fac Arts and Soc sciences 1976–79

FRASER or Quarman, Emily **MA 1931**
resid Balham Lond

FRASER or Lyall, Fiona Jane **MB ChB 1954 DPH 1958**
Grampian reg councillor Mearns 1974; g p Laurencekirk and the Mearns

FRASER Forbes John **MA 1949**
teacher Longside s 1950–69; farm. Longside from 1969

FRASER Francis Stewart Gordon ***MA 1925**
d Monifieth 15.7.62 *AUR* XL 91

FRASER George **MA 1917**
retd 1953; resid Aber

FRASER George Angus Paterson **MB ChB 1927**
retd 1965; resid Bourne
d Lond 5.2.79

FRASER George Knowles **MA 1911 BSc 1912 BSc(for) 1919**
no longer on GC reg

FRASER George Paterson ***BSc 1949 PhD 1952**

FRASER Georgina Fowler **MA 1911**
no longer on GC reg

FRASER Hector Alexander ***MA 1932**
Edin: group man. Standard Life Assur co 1961–69, asst gen man. 1969–72; retd 1972
hon secy Faculty of Actuaries 1968–70
wife *d* 21.8.66
m(2) 7.4.67 Christine E. Walker

FRASER or Wilson, Helen **MA 1910**
no longer on GC reg

FRASER or Wilkie, Helen **MA 1924**
no longer on GC reg

FRASER or McLean or Macdonald, Helen Cumming **MA 1931**
teacher: Bridge of Don 1945–68, Scotstown 1968–69
resid Fintray Aberdeensh

FRASER or Sutherland, Helen Elizabeth **BSc 1952**
resid Cults

FRASER Helen Mackenzie **MA 1944**
teacher: Milne's h s Fochabers 1950–60, Mortlach s s Dufftown 1960–67, Hopeman s s 1967–70; resid Dufftown
m Aber 12.12.70 Alan D. Bennett civ serv

FRASER or Clarke, Helen Susanna **MB ChB 1942**
resid Lond

FRASER Henry **MA 1927**
head Inchgarth p s Aber 1965–70; retd; resid Aber

FRASER Hugh Simon **MB ChB 1936 MD 1938**
chest phys Wessex reg hosp board 1948–73; retd; resid Llandrindod Wells Wales

FRASER Iain Alexander **MB ChB 1943**

FRASER Ian Charles **MB ChB 1954**
DTM & H(Lond) 1963 DPH(Lond) 1964
DIH(Lond) 1965 MFCM 1972
m o 2nd Bn Royal Tank regt Libya, Germany, UK 1959–60; RAMC: army health spec 1961–68, sen spec in army health; lt-col from 1968; retd 1973; univ m o Leeds from 1973
m Montrose 31.5.58 Lancetta D. Archibald secy d of Lancelot A. Montrose

FRASER Ian Ross ***MA 1953 MEd 1955**
prin teacher geog Elgin acad 1960–66; rector Waid acad Anstruther 1966–71, Inv r acad from 1971

FRASER or Gill, Isabel Mary **MA 1947**
teacher: Boddam 1963–64, Peterhead cent s 1964–65, Kinnoul s Perth 1966–69, Quarryhill p s Aber from 1974; resid Milltimber Aber

FRASER or Wood, Isabella Macdonald **MA 1948**
resid Brora

FRASER or Hvistendahl, Isabella Milne **MA 1917**
resid Tonsberg Norway
husb *d* 1972

FRASER Isabella Murray **MA 1927**
no longer on GC reg

FRASER James **MB ChB 1914**
d France 5.4.63 *AUR* XL 201

FRASER James **MA 1919**
d Alness 18.9.62 *AUR* XL 85

FRASER James **MA 1928**
teacher: Dingwall acad 1951–69; retd; resid Inv

FRASER James **MA 1929**
Petrol Indust serv; retd 1974; resid S Croydon

FRASER James Cobban **MA 1929 MB ChB 1939**
g p Aber 1948–67; retd; resid Inverurie

FRASER James Edward ***MA 1953**
Scot. office: p secy to perm. under-secy of state 1960–62, p secy to parl under secy of state 1962; prin Home and Health dept 1962–64, Cabinet office 1964–66, HM Treasury 1966–68, SHHD 1968–69; asst secy

SHHD 1970–76; under secy Scottish off. (Fin. Div) from 1976

FRASER James Fowler MA 1914 *MB ChB 1922
retd; resid Aber
d Aber 23.2.79 *AUR* XLVIII 226

FRASER James George Davidson BSc(eng) 1937

FRASER James Henry *MA 1899

FRASER Jamesina Rose MA 1911
d 4.8.72 *AUR* XLV 124

FRASER Jane Ellen *MA 1910
d Aber 9.1.76 *AUR* XLVI 414

FRASER or Kestner, Jean Grace Sutherland *MA 1941
scient information off. Commonwealth Bureau of agr econ Oxford from 1965

FRASER or Hunt, Jeannie Drummond MA 1911
no longer on GC reg

FRASER or Maclean, Jemima MA 1922
teacher: Kinross j s s 1946–65: town councillor 1956–59; retd; resid Aber

FRASER Jessie Elspet MA 1937
teacher Grantown g s from 1948; retd 1977

FRASER or Florence, Joan Mary MA 1936
teacher: Ross-shire 1938–40, Aber 1941–47 and from 1958; retd 1975

FRASER John MA 1914 BD 1919
d Aber 9.8.63 *AUR* XL 302

FRASER John MB ChB 1937 MD 1954
med supt Astlie hosp Edin 1949–76

FRASER John Annand MA 1919 DD 1951
Chaplain to HM The Queen 1952–64, extra Chaplain from 1964
C of S min Aberdalgie & Dupplin 1960–70; conv bus. comm of Gen Ass. 1962–67; conv gen admin comm of Gen Ass. 1962–67; chmn judicial comm of Gen Ass. 1962–66; chmn C of S Trust 1962–66; member Broadcasting Council for Scot. 1963–67; retd 1970; resid Perth

FRASER John Milner Ross MA 1949
teacher: Mile End p s Aber 1950–69, Tulliallan p s Fife from 1973

FRASER John Stuart MB ChB 1953
g p East Bridgford from 1959

FRASER Kenneth MA 1921
no longer on GC reg

FRASER Kenneth Boyd MB ChB 1940 *MD 1950 DSc 1961
FRSE 1961
res fell. (Nuffield award) Walter and Eliza Hall inst Aust 1951–52; res fell. (NIHA award) dept genetics Glas 1959–61; sen lect inst virol Glas 1961–66; prof microbiol Queen's univ Belf from 1966

FRASER or Fraser, Leslie Winifred MB ChB 1942
part-time dem bact dept Melb univ Aust 1951–52; resid Belfast

FRASER Malcolm BSc(agr) 1955
estate man. Lovat Estates from 1973
m Inv 12.8.62 Juliana S. Ferguson d of Hugh F. Muir of Ord

FRASER Margaret Ann MA 1920
d Inv 30.5.66 *AUR* XLI 338

FRASER or Ramsay, Margaret Elizabeth MA 1946
teacher Aber 1947–53; resid Bieldside Aber

FRASER Margaret Fowlie MA 1917 MB ChB 1921 DPH 1930
resid Milltimber Aber

FRASER Margaret Helen MA 1939
teacher Grantown g s from 1961; retd 1977

FRASER Margaret Lilias Ross BSc 1923
retd 1963
d 14.2.75

FRASER Margaret Rose *MA 1916
no longer on GC reg

FRASER Mary MA 1911
d Forres 24.1.74 *AUR* XLVI 446

FRASER or Grigor, Mary Ann MA 1941

FRASER or Brown, Mary Bella MA 1933
teacher: Cults p s 1959–66, Cults acad 1966–74, Cults new p s from 1974; retd 1975

FRASER or Chivas, Mary Gault MA 1942

FRASER or Hutcheon, Matilda Margaret MA 1927
no longer on GC reg

FRASER or Jones, Murdina Isabella MA 1911
retd 1952; resid Tain
d Tain 26.2.75 *AUR* XLVI 320

FRASER or Mathieson, Muriel Alice MA 1943
teacher Aber: King St p s 1958–60, high s for girls 1960–70, Muirfield p s from 1970

FRASER Muriel Gordon MA 1940

FRASER or Gray, Muriel Winifred MA 1938
d Banchory 20.7.78
husb *d* 24.1.69

FRASER Norman Grant MB ChB 1950
MRCPsych 1973
res fell. psychiat univ of Pittsburgh USA 1959–60;

consult. psychiat and dep phys supt Woodilee hosp Lenzie, Glasg from 1961
m Aber 30.12.61 Daphne Inglis d of William H. I. Aber

FRASER Ogilvie Murray MB ChB 1927
RAF: civ m o Felixstowe 1959–62, dep pres med board off. and aircrew selection centre Biggin Hill 1962–76; resid Bath

FRASER Olive *MA 1931
Chancellor's Medal for Poetry (Cantab) 1935
d Aber 9.12.77 *AUR* XLVII 359

FRASER Ranald Lamont MA 1917
d 1965

FRASER Robert
MB ChB 1935 DPH 1937 MD 1946
chest phys NE reg hosp board from 1948; retd 1977

FRASER Robert James Alexander MB ChB 1939
clin sen lect neuro-surg Aberd from 1958

FRASER Robert Sherriffs MA 1925
teacher: maths/sc Girvan h s 1926–43, maths Central s s Aber 1943–49; prin maths: Old Aber s s 1949–51, Hilton s s Aber 1951–66; retd; resid Cults Aber
m Stonehaven 21.8.48 Kathleen M. B. Smith teacher d of William F. S. Stonehaven
d Cults 5.5.78 *AUR* XLVII 356

FRASER Ronald George Juta *BSc 1924 PhD 1926
exec secy internat council of scient unions 1949–63; retd; resid Lower Hutt NZ

FRASER Ronald McWilliam MB ChB 1954
LMCC 1970 CCFP(Can) 1973
g p Clarkston 1958–62, Fochabers 1962–66, Hinton, Alberta from 1966

FRASER or Stellman, Rose Margaret MB ChB 1939
MFCM 1972
sen m o London boro' of Bexley health dept 1970–74; prin m o child health Bexley health dist from 1974

FRASER or Gray, Sheila MA 1929
resid Inverurie

FRASER or Campbell, Sheila MA 1944
resid Ardrossan

FRASER or Spensley, Sheila Ross MA 1953 EdB 1955

FRASER Simon John Coulter
MB ChB 1893 MD 1903
d 30.5.67

FRASER Thomas BSc 1923 *1924
retd 1966; resid Inv

FRASER Thomas Alexander
MB ChB 1929 MD 1934
d 7.12.65 *AUR* XLI 249

FRASER Thomas Donald Noble MA 1926
no longer on GC reg

FRASER or Scott, Violet Muriel BSc 1923
no longer on GC reg

FRASER Walter Allan MA 1906
d Findhorn 18.7.61 *AUR* XXXIX 273

FRASER William BSc(eng) 1936

FRASER William Augustus Carr DSc 1931

FRASER William Donald BSc(agr) 1942

FRASER William Elrick
MA 1935 BSc 1936 *1938 PhD 1957
Aberd: sen lect geol and mineralogy 1963–70, reader from 1970

FRASER William Gordon *MA 1914
d 5.1.66

FRASER William Jack *BSc 1955

FRASER William Thompson MA LLB 1952
various leg. posts 1952–70; founder/ptnr Fraser & Mulligan advoc Aber from 1970; part-time member Rent Assessment panel for Scot. from 1975; part-time lect agr law Aberd from 1976

FRASER or Masson, Winifred Margaret MA 1946
teacher Lusaka Girls' s Zambia from 1964

FRATER Clifford Sydney Horler BSc(eng) 1947
reg army off. col home and overseas from 1948; resid Farnham
m Andover 21.4.51 Grace P. M. Curtis

FRAZER Allan Cameron *MA 1934 LLB 1937
Chevalier in the Order of Orange Nassau 1972
sen ptnr Hagart & Burn-Murdoch WS Edin from 1948; hon consul for Neths in Edin from 1965; rector's assessor Edin 1967–68; dean consular corps Edin–Leith 1976–77; pres Edin Sir Walter Scott Club 1975

FRAZER Fred Young BSc(eng) 1928
d Aber 20.12.63 *AUR* XL 302

FREELAND Alexena Walker MA 1948
teacher Aber from 1963

FREELAND or Morrice, Helen MA 1950

FRENCH or Ferguson, Christina Moir MA 1925
no longer on GC reg

FRENCH Isobel *MA 1942
prin teacher hist Elgin acad from 1969

FRENCH William George MB ChB 1942
g p Stonehaven from 1951

FREW or Robertson, Christina Rose MA 1902
no longer on GC reg

FRIEDLAND Garson MB ChB 1926

FRIEDLÄNDER or Young, Ernestine Hannah MA 1950

FRITH Anthony Charles Gauvain BSc(for) 1945

FUGLESTVED Per Bengt MA 1951

FULLERTON or Caldwell, Enid MB ChB 1951
Founder Member R C Psych 1971: Member Brit Psycho-Analytical Soc 1976
consult. psychiat Lansdowne clin Glasg 1963–66; assoc psychiat McLean hosp Belmont Mass from 1966

FULLERTON Harold Williams MA 1925 *MB ChB 1931 MD 1937
d 14.7.70 *AUR* XLIV 28

FULLERTON or Bothwell, Isobel MA 1946
resid Stratford-on-Avon

FULLERTON John MA 1938
min United ch of Canada Trail BC from 1972

FULLERTON Robert Gerrard BSc 1924 *MA 1925 PhD 1932 MB ChB 1938
g p Aber 1939–66; boarding m o min of soc security Aber from 1966
d Aber 12.4.79 *AUR* XLVIII 228

FULLERTON Thomas Anderson MA 1901
no longer on GC reg

FULTON Graeme Lascelles *BSc 1946

FULTON James Graham BL 1952
OBE FCIS
ptnr Brander & Cruickshank advoc Aber from 1952; dir: Aber Univ Press from 1959, East of Scot. Trust from 1963, Scot. Fishermen's Organis from 1973, East of Scot. Investments Managers from 1975; chmn Scot. Herring Producers' Assoc from 1957

FYFE Albert BSc 1948
lect Enfield coll of tech 1961–74, sen lect Middx polytech Enfield from 1974
m Barnet 5.8.61 Georgina R. Smith secy d of Arthur S. Lond

FYFE Edwin Reginald MB ChB 1951
g p Culross from 1962
d Dunfermline 1.2.68 *AUR* XLII 375

FYFE Forest William MA 1933 MB ChB 1937
prof anat Dalhousie univ Nova Scotia 1964–78; retd

FYFE George MA 1930

FYFE Grace Cameron MA 1938
teacher: Castleton and Catterline p s Kincardine 1939–47, Pitlochry h s 1959–64, maths Breadalbane acad Aberfeldy 1964–72, Perth g s from 1972
m Dunnottar 27.9.47 William J. Duguid (*d* 1972)

FYFE or Boyle, Isabella Stuart Chalmers MA 1910
no longer on GC reg

FYFE Malcolm Hewer Durke Findlay BSc(agr) 1953 MSc 1965
dir agr S Cameroons 1960–63; MMB res fell. Aberd 1963–65; agr econ NOSCA 1965–69, sen agr econ 1969–75; dir studies from 1975
m Buea, S Cameroons 12.5.61 Avril A. Pitcher d of Raymond P. P. Cape Town

FYFE or McAusland, Sheila Glennie MA 1941 LLB 1947
d 13.11.81

FYFE William Stuart Fraser BSc(agr) 1954

FYFFE or McCutcheon, Joan MA 1948

FYVIE or Campbell, Agnes MA 1933
teacher: Newhall p s Ross & Cromarty 1958–63, Drumsmittal p s from 1963
husb *d* 1967

FYVIE Elizabeth Mary *MA 1937

FYVIE or Raven, Elizabeth Milne *MA 1938
resid Aber

FYVIE Norman Gammie MB ChB 1954
d 17.7.75

GADSBY James Burnet MB ChB 1944
g p Burnley from 1952

GADSBY Norman Burnet MB ChB 1919
d Aber 8.6.69 *AUR* XLIII 211

GADSBY or Main, Sheila Mary *MA 1950
teacher Engl Penicuik 1952–53, Eskisehir coll Turkey 1956–58, Portobello h s from 1966

GAFFRON David John MA 1948
teacher Ashley Road p s Aber 1949–74; retd

GAFFRON Sonia Anne MA 1955
Assoc Memb Market Res Soc 1965
A C Nielsen Co. Oxford 1960–64, Lond: market res Monsanto 1964–66, United Biscs 1966–70; teacher maths ILEA from 1970

GAGE Albert MB ChB 1951
MRCPsych 1971 MA(Cantab) 1977
consult. ch psychiat: Manc 1961–63, Cambridge from 1963

GAIR Charles Ian Mackenzie BSc(agr) 1945
dir Royal Highland and Agr Soc of Scot. Edin 1966–73; chmn nat dairy exam board Lond 1969–71; member north of Scot. milk marketing board Inv from 1967; chmn Scot. Milk Records Assoc Paisley 1977–79

GAIR or Doig, Janette Jane Elizabeth Henrietta MA 1913

GAIR or Roberts, Margaret Milne MB ChB 1925
resid Craigellachie

GAIT James MA 1929
rector St Palladius' ch Drumtochty, St Andrew's ch Fasque and St Laurence's ch Laurencekirk from 1954

GAITER John Alexander MB ChB 1924
d 12.12.70

GALBRAITH or Brameld, Edith Minnie Staveley MA 1903
no longer on GC reg

GALBRAITH Frederic Winbolt Staveley MA 1904
no longer on GC reg

GALBRAITH or Wilson, Jean MA 1954
teacher: Woodside p s 1957–59, Goodlyburn j s s Perth 1960–64; resid Crieff

GALL Annie Catto MA 1934
d Aber 12.1.68 *AUR* XLII 371

GALL Christian Jane Wedderburn BSc(agr) 1933
d 12.8.77

GALL or Rintoul, Eliza MA 1923
teacher Kennoway Fife 1924–27
resid Abergavenny

GALL or Brown, Elizabeth MA 1928
resid Edin

GALL Frederick BSc(eng) 1945

GALL or Mackay, Harrietta MA 1950

GALL Henderson Alexander *MA 1952
with Reuters in S Af and the Congo 1960–63; foreign correspondent ITN worldwide incl Vietnam 1965–75; newscaster/for. corr ITN from 1970; publ *Gold Scoop* 1976; rector Aberd from 1978

GALL John Reid MA 1912
d Aber 22.8.66 *AUR* XLI 337

GALL or Elmslie, Lilian Fyfe MB ChB 1921
d Aber 15.1.76 *AUR* XLVI 415

GALL or Harvey, Margaret Joan MA 1925
no longer on GC reg

GALLIE John MacLean MA 1932
rector of St Machar's ch Bucksburn 1950–67; canon St Andrew's cath Aber from 1967
d Aber 12.12.77 *AUR* XLVII 359

GALLOWAY Alexander MA 1921 MB ChB 1925
d Alresford 24.9.66 *AUR* XLI 244

GALLOWAY Alexander Ogilvy MA 1907
d Tasmania 10.6.65 *AUR* XLI 239

GALLOWAY Ethel Lawrence Rutherford MB ChB 1924
d Mansfield 30.6.62 *AUR* XL 90

GALLOWAY Ian Charles Robert *MA 1952 Dip Ed 1955

GALLOWAY or Thompson, Jane Henderson MA 1919 MB ChB 1922 MD 1959
MRCPsych 1973
consult. psychiat and dep med supt Northgate and dist mental deficiency hosp Morpeth 1952–67; hon med dir and consult. psychiat to Newcastle and dist counselling centre from 1965

GALLOWAY Margaret de Villeneuve *MA 1930
d Aber 1975

GALLOWAY Maurice Edgar Emslie BSc(agr) 1924
retd; resid Banff

GALLOWAY Rudolph William MB ChB 1914
d 22.3.76 *AUR* XLVI 415

GALT George Gordon *MA 1925
retd 1967; resid Banchory

GAMMIE Alastair James *MA 1951 MEd 1956
Aberd: asst lect educ 1960–62, lect 1962–72, sen lect from 1972

GAMMIE Alexander Edward *MB ChB 1919
d 27.12.70

GAMMIE Douglas Strachan *MA 1930

GAMMIE James *BSc(eng) 1944
supervis Bell tel labs N Andover Mass USA from 1956
m Providence Rhode Is Emily P. Stickney BFA (Rhode Is s of Design) advt man. d of Charles A. S. BA(Dartmouth) Lancaster Mass

GAMMIE John Wilson MB ChB 1941
DA 1958
g p Elgin from 1946; spec anaest Elgin from 1967

GAMMIE Robert Petrie MB ChB 1923 MD 1930
OBE 1967 MRCGP
retd 1966; resid Cambridge
wife *d* 24.6.71

GAPPER William Frederick MB ChB 1930 DPH 1935
d 11.12.60

GARCIA-PINEDA Maria Dolores PhD 1954
USA: biochem dept NYU 1961–62; investigator junta de energia nuclear Madrid from 1962

GARDEN Alexander *BSc 1934
HMIS: Ayrsh 1948–59, Edin 1959–64, Orkney, Caithness, Sutherland from 1964
resid Lossiemouth

GARDEN Alexander Davidson MB ChB 1924
private med pract and res Lond 1925–28; private study econ Battle 1929–34; private aeronaut res (patients) Lond 1935–39; war serv major RAMC Gloucester 1940–43; g p and med/aeronaut res (patients) 1943–63; retd; resid Westcliff-on-Sea
d Westcliffe-on-Sea –.6.75

GARDEN Alexander Murray MA 1909
d Toronto 11.7.66

GARDEN Allan *BSc 1952

GARDEN David William MA 1922 BSc 1924
prin teacher maths/sc Macduff h s till 1960; retd; resid Macduff

GARDEN Edwin MB ChB 1924
d Leytonstone 18.12.70 *AUR* XLIV 211

GARDEN Edwin Laurie MA 1940
d Aber 16.5.66 *AUR* XLI 342

GARDEN George BSc 1945

GARDEN or Milne, Helen Davidson MA 1927
resid Fettercairn

GARDEN James BL 1939
ptnr Alexander George & Co solic (formerly George, Riddell & McPherson) Macduff from 1950

GARDEN James David MB ChB 1953
g p Timaru NZ from 1965

GARDEN James Taylor BSc(agr) 1922
retd 1959; resid Inverugie Peterhead

GARDEN James Waddell MB ChB 1944
anaest Stracathro hosp from 1953

GARDEN John Flett *BSc 1953 PhD 1956
FRIC 1964
sen lect Slough coll of tech 1962–63; dep head chem dept Portsmouth poly from 1963

GARDEN Lewis Beattie *MA 1936
C of S Edin: secy dep comm on soc serv 1961–66; dir soc serv from 1966
d Edin 6.10.80 *AUR* XLIX 69

GARDEN or Bruce, Linda Agnes
***BSc 1951 PhD 1954**

GARDEN Margaret Helen MA 1931
teacher Auchmuty h s Glenrothes 1961–69; resid Edin
m Edin 10.12.60 William G. R. Bodie arch. and plan. s of John M. B. Aber

GARDEN Margaret Isabella MA 1937
resid Lossiemouth

GARDEN Ralph BSc(eng) 1947
prin teacher phys Perth acad from 1972

GARDEN Richard Ramsay
MA 1914 *MB ChB 1917 DPH 1920
d Bristol 11.4.66 *AUR* XLI 243

GARDEN Robert Symon MB ChB 1934
FRCS 1969
hon consult. orthop surg Preston R I from 1975

GARDEN Ronald Jamieson Beattie
***MA 1930 M Litt 1977**
Aber: head Rosemount s s 1965–66, head Ruthrieston s s 1966–72; retd

GARDEN Ruth Jane Morgan MA 1930 *MEd 1949
d 5.1.67 *AUR* XLII 370

GARDEN or Shaw, Vera Margaret MA 1938
no longer on GC reg

GARDEN William John MA 1922
no longer on GC reg

GARDEN William Sim MB ChB 1902 MD 1908
no longer on GC reg

GARDINER Alexander MA 1954 Dip Ed 1955
prin teacher navigation Buckie h s from 1967
m Cullen 4.4.63 Isabella J. Mair bank clerkess d of John W. M. Cullen

GARDINER Alexander James MB ChB 1927
g p Coventry 1931–64; retd; resid Brixham

GARDINER Audrey Isabel MA 1949

GARDINER James Aitken *MA 1949

GARDINER James Martin BCom 1926
OBE 1967
retd; resid Bieldside Aber
m Buckie 3.3.34 Nell Sutherland

GARDINER James Stewart
MB ChB 1946 MD 1972
MRCGP 1959 DIH 1973
g p Falkirk 1952–66; Grangemouth: part time works m o ICI 1959–66, full time 1966–74; div m o pharm div Alderley Park 1974–76, organics div Blackley from 1976; hon lect dep soc and occup med Dund from 1973

GARDINER Joseph MB ChB 1943

GARDINER or Wells, Margaret Findlay
MB ChB 1929
resid Totnes

GARDINER Margaret Hay MA 1950

GARDINER or Rae, Mary Wilson MA 1943
teacher Engl Styles s s Gt Yarmouth 1967–73; soc worker Gt Yarmouth from 1974

GARDINER Robert MB ChB 1951
MFCM(RCP) 1972

sen asst m o Fife County health dept 1966–67, sen m o 1967–74; spec commun med Fife health board from 1974

GARDNER Alastair *BSc 1951

GARDNER Alfred Gordon MA 1937
asst clerk Middx c c 1964–65; GLC: prin solic 1965–69; dep solic and parliamentary off. 1970–74; dir leg. serv 1974–76; retd

GARLAND or Mitchell, Irene Stevenson *MA 1936
part time teacher Fr/Lat Rosebery g s Epsom 1962–78; retd

GARLAND or Ross, Lilias May *MA 1932
resid Aber
husb *d* 16.5.65

GARNER Mildred Maxine PhD 1952
fell. Amer Inst of Indian stud. Poona India 1962–63; Wallace Eugene Rollins prof of relig Sweet Briar coll, Virginia USA from 1969

GARRIOCH or Begg, Isabel Mary Taylor MA 1953
ptnr A. Begg & Son Elgin and Buckie from 1957; man. ptnr A. Begg Forres from 1973

GARROW Duncan Smith MA 1910
d Inverurie 8.12.74

GARROW Frederick Campbell MA 1926 BSc 1928 *1930 MB ChB 1940
d Canso Nova Scotia 27.5.63 *AUR* XL 205

GARROW George BSc 1950
head Thornhill p s Stirling from 1963

GARROW or Macleod, Isabel Mary *MA 1935
head Raigbeg s Tomatin Invshire from 1968
husb *d* –.6.68

GARROW or Hart, Jane *MA 1909
resid Edin

GARROW Robert Philip MB ChB 1907 *MD 1911
d Strathkinness 1.3.71 *AUR* XLIV 208

GARSON Magnus Sinclair *BSc 1949
PhD(Leeds) 1961 FIMM 1973
sen geol Zomba, Malawi govt 1962–64, prin geol 1964–66 (independence medal); prin scient off. inst geol sciences 1967–77 (gold medal of consolidated goldfields); seconded as proj man. UNDP Cairo 1972–74

GARSON Mary (Sister) MA 1942
charitable foundations for destitute India, Sri Lanka; resid Worth Abbey Crawley

GARSON Ronald David MB ChB 1953
Dip Board of Life Insur Med 1973
Canada: g p Port Arthur 1962–69; assoc med dir Metropolitan Life insur comp Ottawa from 1969; addiction res foundation Ottawa from 1969

GARVIE Denis Scott BSc(eng) 1935
OBE

GARVIE Donald William BSc(eng) 1933

GATHERER Alexander MB ChB 1951 [c]MD 1960
FFCM 1973
dep county m o h Northamptonsh 1962–65; m o h Reading from 1965

GATHERER or Coutts, Margery MA 1948
resid Aber

GATHERER William Alexander *MA 1948
HMIS Glasg 1961–73; head educ advis serv Edin from 1973

GATT or Bonsell, Williamina Forbes MA 1946

GAUL or Norrie, Jean Margaret MA 1951
resid Turriff

GAULD or Elder, Alice Mary *MA 1946
asst teacher W. Kirby g s for girls Lea, Wirral from 1976

GAULD Charles Edward BSc(agr) 1925
d Glen Tanar 17.8.62 *AUR* XL 92

GAULD Charlotte Mary MA 1944
lect tech coll Aber 1972–78, sen lect from 1978

GAULD Edgar Norman MB ChB 1937
FRCP(Can) 1972
chief dept of med Chedoke gen hosp Hamilton, Ontario 1960–70; consult. phys Hamilton Civic hosps from 1972

GAULD Edgar Reuben MB ChB 1928
m o BR (S region) from 1954

GAULD Elspeth Jean MA 1947
Aber: teacher Seaton p s 1964–70, Hazlehead p s 1970–71; dep head Walker Road p s 1972–74, asst head Springhill p s from 1974

GAULD Forbes Fraser BSc(mech eng) 1947 *BSc(civ eng) 1948
Canada: struct eng BLM Regina 1960–64; div eng Wright Engineers Vancouver 1964–67; sen eng Acres consult. serv Vancouver from 1967

GAULD or Struthers, Frances Charlotte MA 1936
teacher: Engl/Fr/RI Paignton girls' s s Torbay 1965–69, Fr Hatton s s Sevenoaks 1969–71
widowed 1964
m(2) Torquay 5.4.69 John J. G. H. Harbord army off. (capt) (PSC)/educ off. s of John J. H. Gillingham

GAULD or Thompson, Isobel Margaret MA 1943
teacher St Denis s for girls Edin from 1969

GAULD James MB ChB 1939
FRCGP 1971
g p Aber from 1947

GAULD Jessie Ann MA 1928

GAULD or Wallace, Katharine Winifred MA 1926
Dip univ Poitiers 1926
teacher Watford 1962–67
m(2) Harrow 29.3.67 John Wagner JP retd bank man. s of William F. W. Harrow

GAULD Lawson MA 1950
RAF air crew WO 1941–46 India/Burma; head King Edward p s from 1961

GAULD Mary Begg *MA 1950 Dip Ed 1951
lect hist Aber coll of educ 1966–67, prin lect from 1967

GAULD Patricia Mary BSc 1952

GAULD William Gordon James BSc 1950
prin teacher maths/sc Kemnay s s from 1959

GAULD William Robertson MB ChB 1935 MD 1938
FRCP 1962
reader clin med Aberd from 1975; retd

GAULD William Wallace *MA 1943
under-secy DAFS Edin from 1972

GAULD or Greenaway, Winifred Ogston MA 1942
Devon: teacher Mount Radford s Exeter 1957–67; dir Dartmouth Potteries from 1969

GAVIN Alexander Cram MB ChB 1901
no longer on GC reg

GAVIN or Ashcraft, Catherine Irvine *MA 1928 PhD 1931
awarded Medal of Honour Helsinki univ Finland 1970
chief publications: non fict *Liberated France* 1955; fict *Madeleine* 1957, *The Cactus and the Crown* 1961, *The Fortress* 1964, *The Moon into Blood* 1966, *The Devil in Harbour* 1968, *The House of War* 1970, *Give Me the Daggers* 1972, *The Snow Mountain* 1973, *Traitors' Gate* 1976
resid San Francisco

GAVIN or Calder, Doreen Mary Alexander MA 1939
teacher Crumpsall Lanc inf s Manc from 1946; retd

GAVIN Evelyn Edith *MA 1953
PhD(Strath) 1969
lect in law Strath 1964–70, sen lect from 1970
m Glasg 16.4.63 Christopher Iain MacDonald

GAVIN Hamish Crilley Reid BSc(for) 1952
DPA(Vic BC)
for. BC for. serv Canada 1953–64; insp BC Lands serv 1964–66; govt of Canada: Manitoba: plan. nat parks serv 1966–71, dev off. dept of reg econ expansion 1971–72, man. environmental protection serv from 1972

GAVIN John Abernethy MB ChB 1945
reg m o DHSS Lond from 1975

GAVIN Lewis *MA 1912
d Strichen 26.4.65 *AUR* XLI 149

GAVIN Lewis Den Munro MB ChB 1939 MD 1947
FRSTrop Med & Hyg 1943 MRCGP 1968 Memb Soc Occup Med
exam med off. DHSS 1955–74; chief med off. Southern Elect. Board from 1974

GAVIN Robert MA 1926 LLB 1928
chief ILO mission to Congo 1960–61; chief off. relations and conference serv and secy governing body 1961–66; retd 1966; indust relations consult. Ford Foundation India 1967–68; resid St Etienne du Grès, France

GAVIN William MB ChB 1925
h o mat. hosp Aber, RACH RAHSC 1925–26; g p Yorks 1927–28; h o Park hosp Davyhulme, Manc 1929–30; locum g p Lancs 1930–32; g p Horwich, Bolton 1932–66 (RAMC Europe and M. East 1939–45); retd; resid Muchalls
m Penistone 7.7.39 Phyllis A. Lawrence SRN d of George A. L. Dunford Bridge

GAWN Ernest King MB CM 1895 MD 1904
no longer on GC reg

GEALS James *MA 1929
teacher classics RGC Aber 1933–70; retd; resid Cults Aber

GEARY Malcolm Walker MA 1937
teacher Rosemount s s Aber till 1969

GEDDES Alexa Margaret Brownie MA 1936
asst lib Lancs county lib Preston 1938–45; lib Macaulay inst soil res Aber from 1945

GEDDES Alexander MB ChB 1955
g p firm of Geddes, Gray and Davies Clacton-on-Sea from 1957

GEDDES Alexander Ebenezer McLean *MA 1906 *BSc 1907 DSc 1915 LLD 1956
d 26.12.70 *AUR* XLIV 145

GEDDES Alexander Marr MB ChB 1909 MD 1928
d Aber 10.1.73 *AUR* XLV 223

GEDDES Alexander Slater MA 1938 BD 1941
C of S min: Huntly par ch 1961–67, St Mary's par ch Banff from 1967

GEDDES Charles John McWilliam MB ChB 1930
MRCGP 1953
g p New Eltham and clin asst Eltham hosp from 1948

GEDDES or MacTaggart, Christina Carnegie BSc(eng) 1947
resid Maidenhead

GEDDES Edith Elsa *MA 1947
d Aber 14.1.72 *AUR* XLIV 433

GEDDES or Dawson, Elizabeth Taylor MA 1921 *BSc 1924
resid Grantown-on-Spey

GEDDES or Milton, Emma Margaret MA 1926
resid Aber

GEDDES George MB ChB 1932
g p Lancaster from 1935

GEDDES George Barclay *MA 1946
teacher: Inverurie acad 1957–67, prin mod lang Bankhead acad Aber from 1968

GEDDES Godfrey Power *MA 1915
d Aber 27.6.64 *AUR* XL 398

GEDDES or Davidson, Helen Alisoun MB ChB 1954
part time work in publ health clin from 1956; resid Broughty Ferry

GEDDES or Feggetter, Helen Winchester MB ChB 1939
resid Keswick

GEDDES James MA *BSc 1927
d Stirling 13.12.74 *AUR* XLVI 236

GEDDES or Law or Watson, Jean MA 1938

GEDDES Jeannie MA 1908
no longer on GC reg

GEDDES Jeannie *MA 1920
resid Aber

GEDDES or Bradley, Jessie Watson MA 1913
no longer on GC reg

GEDDES John *BSc 1933
FRIC 1954
rector Peterhead acad 1964–75; retd

GEDDES John BSc(agr) 1940
agr insp: Aber 1946–56, Edin from 1956
m Nott 28.10.50 Doris S. Daft

GEDDES John Fowlie MA 1925
d Drumoak 24.1.70 *AUR* XLIII 445

GEDDES or Bain, Margaret MA 1923
woman advis Inverurie acad 1950–66; retd

GEDDES Margaret Calder MA 1948
Mackie acad Stonehaven: teacher 1958–69, asst prin guid 1969–72, prin guid from 1972

GEDDES or Wood, Margaret Simpson *MA 1932
resid Aberlour
d Elgin 29.4.80

GEDDES Marjory Inglis *MA 1910
d Murtle Aber 24.12.60 *AUR* XXXIX 102

GEDDES Mary MA 1936
d Fordyce 3.11.74

GEDDES or Shirriffs, Mary Allan MA 1926
d 2.5.64

GEDDES Mary Thomson MA 1925
retd; resid Drumoak

GEDDES Walter BL 1949
Civ Def long serv medal 1966 Dip Scot. Council Health Educ 1972
county clerk Peeblesh 1955–75; chmn Scot. council of health from 1973; chmn Borders loc health council from 1975

GEDDES Walter MB ChB 1953
DPH(St And) 1966 MFCM 1974
g p Thurso 1958–67; publ health Aber from 1967
d 13.11.81

GEDDES William MA 1909
no longer on GC reg

GEDDIE Colin More MB ChB 1914
no longer on GC reg

GEDDIE John Moncrieff MB ChB 1938
g p Aber from 1945

GEDDIE Marie Murdoch Cameron MA 1924
retd 1963; resid Dufftown

GEERSHON or Chanock, Dorothy Florence MB ChB 1928
resid Cape Town

GEILS James *MA 1938 ᶜLLB 1940
solic Davidson & Garden Aber 1946–48; lawyer Shell leg. dept Lond 1948–63, dep head 1963–73; secy The Shell Transport & Trading Co Lond from 1966
m Pentir Caerns, N. Wales 19.7.47 Heather N. MacLeod 3rd off. WRNS d of Donald MacL. Pentir Caerns

GEILS Mary Milne MA 1942

GELLATLY or Duncan, Joyce Mary MB ChB 1954
resid Edin

GEORGE Charles BSc 1939 *1940
teacher r g s N'cle-u-Tyne from 1950
d Gosforth N'cle-u-Tyne 25.1.78 *AUR* XLVII 359

GEORGE Charles Mathieson MA 1930 BSc 1930 *1932

GEORGE Ernest Alan BSc(agr) 1955

GEORGE Gordon Young MA 1951
prin teacher Engl Sanquhar acad Dumfriessh 1966–69; asst head Kinross h s from 1969

GEORGE or Tavener, Katharine Jameson MA 1919
resid Aber

GEORGE Rosemary Violet MA 1923
teacher: jun s RGC Aber 1928–64; retd; resid Aber
d Aber 18.8.80

GEORGE Walter Henry BSc 1936

GEORGESON Alice Margaret *MA 1933
teacher classics Holmwood prep s for boys Formby 1940–61; retd; resid Aber

GEORGESON or Shaw, Charlotte Gordon *MA 1929
resid St Lucia Queensland Aust

GEORGESON William Wares *MA 1927
retd; resid Thames Ditton

GERARD William Wilson *BSc 1955
man. dir Eli Lilly & Co, 1963–71; man. dir and chief exec Berk pharmaceuticals from 1972

GERRAND Waistel Gordon BSc 1951
BVMS(Glas) 1959 MRCVS 1959 DVSM(Edin) 1965
vet pract Montrose 1959–61; vet off. Beverley 1961–71; div vet off. min of agr Lond from 1971
m Rutherglen Elizabeth E. Hamilton med lab tech/teacher d of William M. H. Rutherglen

GERRARD or Emslie, Evelyn Winifred MA 1950
teacher Applegrove s Forres from 1965

GERRARD James Dennis MA 1953
teacher: prin Engl Stranraer acad 1963–70, asst prin Engl Stranraer acad (comp) 1970–73; prin Engl Drummond s s Edin from 1973
m Stranraer 15.7.67 Dorothy C. Graham med secy d of Alexander J. G. Stranraer

GERRIE or Menzies, Grace Stewart MA 1947

GERRIE Mary Hannah MA 1904
no longer on GC reg

GERRIE Norman *MA 1951 Dip Ed 1958

GERRY Harold Joseph Cruickshank *MA 1949
FIL 1969
tech translator Lond 1952–71; freelance tech translator St. Albans from 1971

GIBB Alan George MB ChB 1941
sen ENT consult. Tayside area Dun 1960–69; hon sen lect otolaryngology Dund from 1969
m Invergowrie 6.9.66 Elisabeth A. Addison nurse d of George A. Invergowrie

GIBB Alexander MA 1945 LLB 1950
ptnr Stewart & Watson solic Turriff from 1953

GIBB Alexander John Brown MB ChB 1948

GIBB Dorothy Constance BSc 1931 PhD 1935
employed by H. Tempest Nott from 1953

GIBB or MacFarlane, Isobel Margaret MA 1934
teacher inf: Walker Rd s Aber 1936, AGS 1936–39, St Martin's, Lincoln 1941–44; part-time AGS 1957–66, Kingswood s Aber from 1966; retd 1974

GIBB Jean Ford MA 1954

GIBB John MA 1943 BD 1947
d Selkirk 19.9.74 *AUR* XLVI 236

GIBB or Leslie, Margaret MA 1954
resid Alford

GIBB Margaret Winifred *BSc 1936 MB ChB 1945
g p Aber from 1950

GIBB or Malcolm, Mary Robertson MA 1936

GIBB Maxwell Grant *MB ChB 1928
MRCGP 1958
retd; resid Aber

GIBB Muriel Elizabeth MA 1932
sen hosp m o ENT: Lanarksh 1960–61, Ayrsh 1962–63; consult. ENT Ayrsh from 1965

GIBB Robert MB ChB 1942
hon memb sociedade Brasileira de Radiologia 1966 FRCR 1975
dep dir radiotherapy Christie hosp Manc 1964–66; lect radiotherapy Manc from 1966; hon treas RCR 1973

GIBB Robert Alexander Stephen MB ChB 1941
g p Salford from 1947

GIBB Thomas BL 1937
retd 1975; appted hon sheriff Aber 10.10.72
d Aber 2.11.80 *AUR* XLIX 69

GIBB William Scott MA 1943
FSCA 1974
joint controlling interest as dir in G. L. Gibb & Co timber merch Aber 1958–76

GIBB or Macdonald, Winifred Inglis Buchanan MB ChB 1931
resid Budleigh Salterton

GIBBON or Coulter, Dorothy Isobel McKay MA 1913
no longer on GC reg

GIBSON Charles Anderson *MA 1931
d Australia 1973

GIBSON David Hall *BSc(eng) 1955 PhD 1958
MICE 1963 FIOB 1971
eng J. Mowlem, Hunterston 1958–61; des eng C. S. Allot Manc 1961–63; man./man. dir F. J. Gibson (bld) Wilmslow from 1963; member council Keele univ from 1969
m Wilmslow –.9.64 Angela C. Heslop BSc(Manc) pharm d of John P. H. Wilmslow

GIBSON or Stuart, Eileen MA 1933
teacher: Ellon acad 1935–41, 1944–60, maths Hilton acad 1960–71, prin guid 1971–77; retd

GIBSON George MA 1924
d Aber 19.2.74 *AUR* XLV 448

GIBSON Harrison Raymond MB ChB 1955
BSc(Otago) 1949
g p Silverdale NZ 1966–75; Ruakaka Northland NZ from 1975

GIBSON Ivor *MA 1954
C of S min Kelty 1959–65; tut. organis adult educ Fife 1965–69; res St And 1967–69; teacher re Glenrothes 1970–74, Edin from 1974
m Kelty 6.8.60 Margaret T. B. Gillespie teacher d of William G. Kelty

GIBSON Jane *MA 1921
retd 1958; resid Edin
m Robert W. Urquhart MA 1920 *qv*

GIBSON John Stalker BSc(eng) 1952
CEng MIMechE
lt-col REME
War Office equipment sponsorship 1963–66; min of tech proj off. with Canadair in Montreal 1966–69; Quality Assur and equipment support plan. appts with REME tech group Lond 1969–79

GIBSON or Dutch, Mary Kerr *MA 1952 Dip Ed 1953
teacher Engl Aber coll of comm 1969–71; lect Aber coll of educ 1971–73; teacher Engl Banchory acad 1973–74; year mistress Rubislaw acad Aber from 1974

GIBSON William Cameron *MA 1934
capt (signals intelligence) Burma 1940–45; prin teacher/dep rector Galashiels acad 1965–72; dep rector 1972–75; retd; resid Aber
d Aber 29.4.79 *AUR* XLVIII 232

GIBSON William Naldrett BSc(for) 1932
FIF(GB)
dist for: Inv/Edin/Dumfries 1935–51; asst conserv for. Dumfries 1951–66; branch man. Filhill Forestry Stirling 1966–69; reg man. Econ Forestry from 1969
m Inv 11.6.52 Janet M. Stewart secy d of Angus S. Fort William

GILBERT or Allen, Elspet Frances MA 1944

GILCHRIST Robert Niven *MA 1909 *1910
d Aber 21.1.72 *AUR* XLIV 427

GILCHRIST William Niven MB ChB 1934
g p Barnes, Lond till 1971; sessional work DHSS Lond 1971–75; retd

GILCHRIST William Normandale *MA 1952

GILCHRIST William Scott BL 1950
teacher Aber 1964–73; retd

GILES Alexander Rennie BSc(agr) 1933
farm. Tarves from 1945, also Moss-side of Gight, Fyvie from 1965
d St Katherines 25.5.79

GILES Andrew Milne Mitchell MA 1927
retd 1967; resid Carnoustie
d 12.9.81

GILES Archibald William MA 1926
MBE 1946
CA Aber 1930; Lond: acct (ca) 1930–39; RAF sq/ldr accts dept 1939–46, banker/man. dir Baring Bros & Co 1947–68, comp dir from 1968
m Lond Alison F. Z. Judd MB BS MD(Lond) med pract d of Harold G. J. CA Hampstead

GILES or Duncan, Catherine Margaret MA 1943

GILES Florence May MA 1944
teacher Aber: Muirfield p s 1957–62 and from 1966, Sunnybank p s 1963–66

GILES George Marr MA 1903
no longer on GC reg

GILFILLAN or McLachlan, Helen Urquhart MA 1939

GILL Alexander John BSc(agr) 1949
lect Ont agr coll Guelph till 1959; farm. Macduff from 1959

GILL Alexander McIntosh BSc(eng) 1952
MICE 1960
Aber: civ eng Wm Tawse contr 1960–71; man. dir Bon-Accord Construction struct eng from 1972

GILL Bella *MA 1912
resid Aber

GILL David James MB ChB 1947
FRCP(C) 1974
man. dir James Gill & Sons Aber 1962–68; Canada: resid psychiat univ of Alta 1968–72, phys (psychiat) Alberta hosp Edmonton from 1972

GILL or Buchan, Doreen Clark MA 1946

GILL Geoffrey Munro MB ChB 1953
MRCGP 1963
g p Inverurie from 1957

GILL or Ebsworth, Gladys Mary Badenoch MB ChB 1945
g p Farnborough from 1957

GILL Helen Mitchell MA 1927
teacher: Cults p s till 1968; retd; resid Aber

GILL or Bruce, (Isobel) Dorothea *MA 1951
resid Bourne End

GILL James Cruickshank BSc(agr) 1948
asst farm man. Rowett res inst Aber 1963–72, sen scient off. from 1972

GILL James Munro Christie MB ChB 1927
FBMA 1966 founder member RCGP, elected FRCGP 1970
g p Inverurie till 1967; retd

GILL John Frederic *MB ChB 1906
no longer on GC reg

GILL John Murray Dunlop MB ChB 1955
regist obst/gyn: Creigton hosp Fife, Irvine cent hosp 1957–61; private pract Kingston Jamaica 1961–63; resid radiol Princess Margaret hosp Toronto 1964–65; fam plan. admin univ of Michigan 1966; med advis fam plan. progr govt of Kenya 1966–69; private pract Toronto 1970; WHO consult. Philippines 1970; assoc dir health sc internat dev res centre Ottawa 1971–75, dir from 1975

GILL John Paterson Beveridge MA 1929 MB ChB 1935
m o dist of Canisbay (incl Is of Stroma) Caithness till 1968; retd; resid Peterculter

GILL or Payne, Margaret *MA 1949
resid Lytham St Anne's

GILL Margaret Macgillivray MA 1931

GILL Norman MB ChB 1935
d Preston 18.12.76

GILL Norman MB ChB 1936
g p Wakefield from 1946

GILL Robert Douglas *MA 1949
prin teacher: mod lang Peterhead acad 1962–65, Ger Perth acad 1965–68; prin examiner mod lang for SCE exam board 1966–69; rector Beath sen h s Cowdenbeath 1969–72; head Rubislaw acad (AGS) from 1973

GILL Wallace John MB ChB 1923
d Sonning-on-Thames 15.2.72 *AUR* XLIV 429

GILL William MacGregor *MA 1946
head hist dept: Stranraer h s 1962–70, Stranraer acad from 1970

GILL William Proctor MA 1953 BL 1955
acct Spicers paper makers and merch Lond 1960–62 and Sawston Cambridge 1962–64; Lond: asst secy Reed Paper Group Lond 1964–69, fin. controller Charterhouse Indust later Charterhouse Group Lond 1969–76; fin. dir Alenco (internat) fittings manuf Henley-on-Thames from 1976
m Aber 11.9.65 Dorothy H. Davidson MA 1956 *qv*

GILLAN Alexander Stuart *MA 1930
d Kirkcaldy 30.3.70 *AUR* XLIII 446

GILLAN Archibald Wedderburn BL 1930
d Dun 19.11.76

GILLAN Ian Thomson *MA 1937 BD 1940
curate Musselburgh 1970–72, par priest Jedburgh 1972–73; received into Anglican Communion by Bishop of Moray Inv 1973, licensed to serve as priest in Epis ch (Scot.); asst priest St Andrew's cath, Aber 1973; precentor St Andrew's cath Inv 1974; priest in charge St Clement's ch Mastrick Aber from 1976

GILLAN John Thomson Clifford *MA 1950 LLB 1953
ptnr: Alexander & Gillan advoc Aber 1963–75, Wilsone & Duffus advoc Aber from 1975
m Aber 15.3.65 Isobel M. Wood MA 1948 *qv*

GILLAN Percival Milne *MA 1926
d 15.9.78 *AUR* XLVIII 104

GILLAN Robert Urquhart MA 1920 MB ChB 1924
DOMS(Lond) 1934
hosp ophth serv Lond 1948–63, gen ophth serv Lond from 1963

GILLAN William George *MA 1935
prin teacher classics Elgin acad 1961–77; retd; resid Elgin

GILLANDERS Anne Cruickshank BSc 1932
sen haemat tech Sorrento mat. hosp Birm till 1970; retd; resid Aber

GILLANDERS or Scott, Helen Georgia MA 1954
teacher Middlefield p s Aber from 1970

GILLESPIE or Swapp, Anne Margaret MA 1952
LTCL 1963
teacher Aber 1960–64; resid Aber

GILLESPIE or Smart, Hilda Annie Mary MA 1933
resid Dunecht

GILLESPIE James Ross MB ChB 1954
g p Hull from 1956

GILLIES Angus John MA 1942
MA(Windsor) 1964
Canada: head Engl dept W. D. Lowe tech s Windsor, Ont 1960–64; head Engl dept A. B. Lucas s s London, Ont 1964–67; Windsor board of educ: asst supt of schools 1967–73, supt of progr from 1973
m Windsor Ont 21.12.63 Merle L. Worthy secy

GILLIES Daisy MA 1910
no longer on GC reg

GILLIES Hugh Donald Mackay MB ChB 1944
g p Stornoway from 1947
d Inv 29.3.77 *AUR* XLVII 214

GILLIES John MacDonald MA 1918
C of S min S. Knapsdale till 1964; retd; resid Lochgilphead

GILLIES Kenneth MA 1922
C of S min Gardner St ch Glasg from 1924
d Glasg 26.7.76

GILLIES Neil Radasi MB ChB 1954
g p Stornoway from 1957

GILLILAND Susan Mary MA 1950
publ relations exec Lond 1958–60; teacher Engl Tormead s Guildford from 1972
m Lond 6.12.58 Michael Milliken MA(Oxon) man. consult. s of E. Kenneth M. MA(Oxon) Tunbridge Wells

GILLIS Allan Webster BSc 1949

GILMORE Elizabeth Duthie MA 1910
no longer on GC reg

GILMOUR John BSc 1948
spec asst maths Aber acad 1966–73, asst prin maths (now Hazlehead acad) from 1973

GIMINGHAM Charles Henry PhD 1948
FRSE 1961 FI Biol 1967
Aberd: sen lect bot 1961–64, reader 1964–69; pers chair 1969–72, second chair 1972

GIULIANI Raffaello Giuseppe *MA 1948 Dip Ed 1949
teacher Engl Natick Mass USA (chmn Engl) 1964–65
m Castelfiorentino, Florence 20.7.68 Maria Innocenti secy d of Nino I. Castelfiorentino

GLASCODINE John Kenneth BSc(eng) 1952
C Eng MIMech Eng FInstF MCIBS
man. nat indust fuel efficiency serv Glasg from 1971

GLASHAN Alexander James BSc 1944 *1948
rector Turriff acad 1961–64, Elgin acad from 1964

GLASHAN Sheila Esslemont MA 1948 Dip Ed 1969
teacher Aber: Walker Rd p s till 1959, Rosemount s s 1960–71, year mistress Kincorth acad 1971–73, dep head from 1973

GLASS Alexander Gibb MA 1899
no longer on GC reg

GLASS Cecil Bentley-Innes PhD 1952
civ serv: prin scient off. 1961–72, sen prin scient off. (head of oper res group govt comm hq Cheltenham) 1972; dep chief scient off. 1977 (head of electronics res and dev div govt comm hq Cheltenham)

GLASS Charles Alexander MB ChB 1930
g p Manchester till 1968; retd

GLASS Charles Stanley MB ChB 1911
d 21.4.66

GLASS Isabella Adeline MA 1923
spec asst Engl/lib Brandon h s Motherwell 1960–65; retd; resid Aber

GLASS James Gerald MA 1926 BSc 1927
head New Byth s till 1968; retd; resid Fochabers
wife *d* 29.12.72

GLASSMAN Charles MB ChB 1934
b 29.8.1903
g p Brooklyn NY USA 1934–73; retd; resid Jamaica NY

GLASSMAN Max Samuel BSc 1934 MB ChB 1937
d New York 9.1.78

GLEGG or McRae, Agnes Alice BSc 1947 *1949

GLEN Archibald BSc 1950
Isaac Spencer Aber: tech serv man. 1960–64, man. paints div 1964–70, dir paints div 1970–75, man. dir from 1975

GLEN Marjory Ann Duncan MA 1908
no longer on GC reg

GLEN-CAMPBELL Edward Arthur Dudley MB ChB 1937

GLEN-CAMPBELL Maynard Joscelyne MB ChB 1940

GLENNIE Agnes Elisabeth BSc 1926
DSIR Cambridge/Lond till 1963; retd; resid Lond

GLENNIE or Clarke, Cicily Margaret *MB ChB 1936
MFCM 1972 (founder member)
asst res med psych Cambridge till 1963; sessional m o Merton/Richmond-u-Thames 1967–68; sen m o commun care Richmond 1969–74; area spec commun med (soc serv) Kingston/Richmond AHA from 1974

GLENNIE or Cameron, Ethel Wilma Whyte MA 1948
teacher Arnage p s 1958–61; resid Fraserburgh

GLENNIE or Tanner, Evelyn Winifred MB ChB 1935
locum anaest apptments under S W reg hosp board at various hosps; asst F P clin univ coll hosp Lond from 1967

GLENNIE Harry Philip MA 1928
man. dir J. A. Prestwich Indust from 1958

GLENNIE Henry Hay Ian MB ChB 1936
surg P & O steam navig comp/NZ shipping co 1959–62; g p Hamilton NZ from 1962

GLENNIE Herbert Charles *MA 1925
rector Linlithgow acad till 1967; retd; resid Edin

GLENNIE James Cruickshank *MA 1931
C of S min Mauchline old ch from 1948
d 13.1.80

GLENNIE James Stephen MB ChB 1940

GLENNIE John Acton Sinclair MA 1928 LLB 1930

GLENNIE Nora Frances *MA 1924
prin maths Albyn s for girls Aber from 1953; retd 1967
d Aber 6.12.75 *AUR* XLVII 212

GLENNIE or Grant, Norma Grant Hay MA 1931 ᵈLLB 1933
resid Lossiemouth

GLENNIE Ronald Edward MB ChB 1933 MD 1951
d Cambridge 18.7.70 *AUR* XLIV 111

GLENTWORTH Robert PhD 1941
head soil surv of Scot. Macaulay inst of soil res Aber from 1946; retd 1976

GLEW Denis Richard BSc(for) 1949

GLOVER Ian BSc(eng) 1930
no longer on GC reg

GLOVER William Edward MB ChB 1911
no longer on GC reg

GODDEN Wilfred John MB ChB 1936

GODFREY Elizabeth Robertson MA 1906 *1907
d Aber 20.9.62 *AUR* XL 77

GODSMAN or Watt, Lilian BSc 1928
teacher Stoneywood p s 1929–32; resid Bieldside
husb *d* Bieldside Aber 7.1.77

GOLDIE or Brown, Evelyn MB ChB 1926
g p Lond from 1930

GOLDIE William MA 1927 MB ChB 1932
d Leeds 13.2.70 *AUR* XLIII 445

GOODALL or Scott, Catherine Jane MA 1941
resid Glasg

GOODALL or Troup, Ethel Dolly Allan MA 1949
temp teacher Winchester Virginia USA from 1970

GOODALL Isabella Cooper MA 1932
teacher: spec asst maths Keith g s 1943–73; retd

GOODALL John *MA 1929
prin teacher sc: Fortrose acad till 1965, Tain royal acad 1965–66; retd; resid Fortrose

GOODALL or Wilson, Murial Olive MA 1944
resid Bucksburn

GOODALL or McGregor, Shirley Cameron MA 1954

GOODBODY Ivan Miles PhD 1954
Jamaica: sen lect zool univ of W.I. 1962–64, prof from 1964

GOODBRAND Alan Reid BSc(eng) 1942

GOODBRAND Stephen MB ChB 1908
d Banchory 16.1.68 *AUR* XLII 348

GOODBRAND Stephen MA 1949
moderator: synod of Merse and Teviotdale 1961–62, presb of Jedburgh 1972–73; min Southdown par ch linked with Hobkirk from 1973

GOODLAD John Fordyce Robertson MA 1930 MB ChB 1934
d Lincoln 18.3.76 *AUR* XLVI 417

GOODSPEED Morley James *BSc 1949
CSIRO div of land res Canberra, Aust from 1962
wife *d* 1963
m(2) Melbourne 7.7.65 Marie P. F. Murphy d of John M. Mt Martha Vict Aust

GOODWIN John Francis BSc(for) 1945
chief educ trg off. for. comm from 1970; resid Basingstoke
m Cinderford 31.12.52 Edith Usherwood

GORDON Agnes MA 1925

GORDON Agnes May MA 1928
d Aber 31.1.69 *AUR* XLIII 215

GORDON Alice MA 1910
no longer on GC reg

GORDON Alistair James BSc(eng) 1950

GORDON Andrew MA 1913
d Dun 30.7.75 *AUR* XLVI 321

GORDON or Macpherson, Annie MA 1927
no longer on GC reg

GORDON Annie Isabella BSc 1933 MA 1934 BD 1945
min presb C of E Rankin mem ch Liv 1961–66; tut. St Andrew's Hall Selly Oak Birm 1966–68; retd; resid Edin

GORDON Charles Eddie Talbot MB ChB 1946
g p Fraserburgh from 1949

GORDON Charles Harold *MA 1929
FEIS 1963
rector Dunfermline h s till 1968; retd; dir. time-tabling advis serv Scot. Moray House coll of educ from 1968 and for dept of educ in Eire from 1972

GORDON or Georgeson, Charlotte Helen MA 1901
d Aber 25.9.65 *AUR* XLII 80

GORDON Christie Wilson MB ChB 1938
FRCP 1971 FFCM 1972
reg m o W. Midlands reg health auth Birm 1976
d Birmingham 9.8.79 *AUR* XLVIII 353

GORDON Christina Scott MA 1928
retd 1967; resid Macduff

GORDON or Hamilton, Christine Jean BSc(agr) 1940
resid West Calder

GORDON or Dixon, Clara MA 1912
no longer on GC reg

GORDON Coral Ogilvie MB ChB 1919
no longer on GC reg

GORDON Daniel George John MA 1921 MB ChB 1924
FBMA 1958 FRCGP 1971
g p Ellon till 1961; retd; resid Inverurie

GORDON Diana Mary MA 1954 MB ChB 1965
SRN(Lond) 1958
h o Longmore hosp Edin 1965–66, ARI 1968; part-time m o Lindsey c c Lincs 1968–72; part-time g p Lincoln 1971–72; resid Swaziland; m o i/c St Teresa's clin Manzini
m Shirebrook 15.4.63 William J. Reeves BS(Lond) s of Ernest R. Clapton-on-the-Hill

GORDON Donald Hugh McKay *MA 1945
gen man. Tootal Licensing Manc from 1947

GORDON Donald McDonald *MA 1944
CMG 1970
HMFO: first secy Rangoon 1960–62, counsellor S Af 1962–66, Imperial def coll Lond 1966–67, counsellor and consul-gen Saigon 1967–70; FO 1970–72, dep high comm Kuala Lumpur 1972–75; Brit High Commissioner Cyprus from 1975

GORDON Donald Roderick BSc(agr) 1954
field off. min of agr Lincoln 1958–60; lands off. DAFS Thurso from 1960
m Inv 5.6.65 Helen W. Shepherd cler off. civ serv d of Alexander R. S. Inv

GORDON Dorothy Belle MA 1937
Aber: prin asst teacher Engl High s for girls 1965–73 (now Harlaw acad); asst prin teacher 1973–75; retd
d Aber 13.5.80

GORDON Douglas McKenzie MA 1937
min cong ch Montrose from 1947; chmn Cong union of Scot. 1965–68

GORDON Douglas Thomson MB ChB 1950 DPH 1954 ᶜMD 1962
res asst phys Ham Green hosp Bristol till 1960; Plymouth: sen h m o Scott hosp 1960–67; g p from 1967

GORDON Duncan MA 1954
teacher Engl: Inv h s 1955–60, Lachine h s Montreal 1960–65, Inv h s 1965–66; spec asst Engl Fortrose acad Rosssh 1966–72; prin Engl Millburn s s Inv 1972–75; Fortrose acad from 75
m Inv 2.4.60 Margaret E. Sinclair teacher p e d of James M. S. Inv

GORDON or Beveridge, Elizabeth Anderson MA 1947
resid Glasg

GORDON or Jones, Elizabeth Annie Watts MA 1933

GORDON Elizabeth Helen MA 1941

GORDON or Simpson, Elizabeth McVicar MA 1914
d Edin 18.3.74 *AUR* XLV 447

GORDON Eric Christie MB ChB 1923
d Cornwall 12.5.73

GORDON or Morrison, Ethel Mary BSc 1923
no longer on GC reg

GORDON Evelyn Mary *MA 1945
spec asst mod lang Fraserburgh acad 1951–62; Aust: teacher mod lang Bendigo h s 1962–70, sen mistress from 1970

GORDON Frederick William *MA 1919 MB ChB 1922 ᶜMD 1935
d 16.3.71

GORDON George Alexander Connell MB ChB 1914 DPH 1920
d 18.10.75 *AUR* XLVI 415

GORDON George Hector Miller MB ChB 1951

GORDON George Norrie BSc 1925 BL 1931

GORDON or Black, Georgina Berry MA 1937

GORDON Grace Forbes MA 1928
retd 1964; resid Aber

GORDON or Harrison, Grace Thomson MA 1947
teacher biol Bartholomew s Eynsham Oxford from 1967

GORDON Harold Cowie MA 1948 *BSc 1951
teacher: AGS 1952–56, London area 1956–58, Aske's Hatcham boys' s Lond 1958–67; lect Britannia RN coll Dartmouth from 1967

GORDON or Robson, Hazel MA 1952
teacher Rothes 1958–65, Aberlour 1966–73, prin guid 1973–76, prin guid Speyside high commun s from 1976

GORDON or Abercrombie, Helen MA 1920
no longer on GC reg

GORDON Helen Elizabeth MB ChB 1943
DA 1947 FFARCS 1954 FFARCSI 1955
consult. anaest N W Durh hosp group 1955–74; retd
m Shotley Bridge Co Durh 6.3.71 Kenneth G. F. Mackenzie MB BChir(Cantab) consult. surg s of John M. MA 1896 *qv*(I, II, III, IV)

GORDON Henry Gray McKerron MA 1948 PhD 1952
d St And 7.6.63 *AUR* XL 207

GORDON Ian BSc 1929 MB ChB 1932
hon clin reader med Aberd from 1948

GORDON Ian Alastair BSc(agr) 1951
tech off. SAI till 1969; reg sales man. (Scot.) Rumenco from 1969

GORDON Ian Stuart BSc(for) 1935

GORDON Ian James MB ChB 1946
FRACS 1961
Aust: hon surg Bendigo N dist base hosp from 1961, hon urologist from 1969

GORDON Ian Lionel Victor Lumsden MB ChB 1923

GORDON Isabella *BSc 1922 DSc 1928
Commonwealth Fund Fellowship 1926–28
OBE 1963 FLS 1931 FZS 1932 FInstBiol 1964
member edit. board of *Crustaceana* from inception, publd in Holland 1959–66; retd; resid Lond

GORDON James MB ChB 1924
g p Hull 1929–75; retd; resid Cottingham E Yorks
m(2) Hull 18.7.41 Elsie Hatfield d of Walter H. Hull
d Cottingham Yorks 24.9.79 *AUR* XLVIII 351

GORDON James Alexander MA 1922 MB ChB 1925
d Aber 27.4.76 *AUR* XLVI 416

GORDON James Alexander *BSc 1928
d 14.9.63

GORDON James Bremner MB ChB 1942
d Peterhead 29.10.74 *AUR* XLVI 240

GORDON James Burgess BSc(eng) 1947

GORDON James Gray BSc 1925
no longer on GC reg

GORDON James Lawrie *BSc(eng) 1952
MASCE MEIC MCEA MCSCE regist prof eng in Quebec & Alta
Montreal Eng Co: asst man. hydro div 1964–72, chief hydraulic eng from 1971

GORDON James William BSc 1955

GORDON or Felgate, Jamesina MB ChB 1937
d Leeds 28.10.75

GORDON (Jane) Margaret Cockburn MA 1930
retd from teaching 1967; resid Aber
d Aber 12.7.81

GORDON or Hay, Jean Innes MB ChB 1940 DPH 1965
h o RACH 1940–41; sen h o Maidenhead hosp 1941; flt lt med res RAF 1941–46; j h m o Bellsdyke mental hosp Larbert 1956–58; m o ch health Aber health dept/Grampian N area health board from 1962
m Aber –.6.46 Spottiswood R. Hay farm. s of Thomas R. H. Edin

GORDON or Mackay, Jean Morrison MA 1950
teacher: Lat Alexandra g s Singapore 1960–62; remed reading Bannockburn from 1969

GORDON Jeannie Wallace MA 1929
d Stornoway 30.10.66 *AUR* XLII 86

GORDON or Smith, Jessie MA 1950
teacher Canada: Lester Pearson sen s s New Westminster 1961–62, Alberni dist s s Port Alberni BC 1962–66, Gold River s s BC from 1967

GORDON Jessie Ann MA 1926
d Stornoway 30.10.66 *AUR* XLVI 86

GORDON or Stewart, Joan Cameron MA 1938
teacher: temp Alford area 1960–62, Engl Alford acad from 1963

GORDON or Reid, Johan Aiken MA 1953 Dip Ed 1954
teacher Aber High s for girls till 1962; resid Bieldside Aber

GORDON John BSc(for) 1940

GORDON John Alexander *MB ChB 1928
d Lond 14.7.73 *AUR* XLV 320

GORDON John Duncan MB ChB 1925
d Aber 30.1.69 *AUR* XLIII 215

GORDON John Grant BSc(agr) 1948 PhD 1955
JP 1969
prin scient off. Rowett inst Aber from 1965

GORDON John Robert *MA 1954
Canada: plan. res dir metro Tor plan. board 1957–68; h s teacher geog Borough North York, Tor from 1968

GORDON John Younie BSc 1954
Aber: prin teacher chem RGC 1966–71, asst head from 1972
m Aber 30.3.61 Anna R. Bremner teacher homecraft d of William T. B. Aber

GORDON Joseph Evans BSc(agr) BSc(for) 1920
dep prin E of S coll of agr/sen lect agr Edin till 1961; retd; resid Longniddry
d Haddington 14.9.77

GORDON or Middleton, Margaret Augusta *MA 1936

GORDON or Gordon, Margaret Grant MA 1919
no longer on GC reg

GORDON Margaret Sinclair MA 1945
prin speech therap Caithness c c from 1973

GORDON Mary MA 1914
resid Aber
d Aber 23.2.79

GORDON Mary Paton MA 1912
d 10.6.66

GORDON or Greenshields, Muriel Glenesk MA 1951

GORDON or Snartt, Netta Terras *MA 1905
Charing vicarage Kent 1955–59; retd Gander Newfoundland 1959–63; resid London 1963–79, resid

Victoria BC from 1979
husb *d* London 1976

GORDON Peter Mitchell *MA 1952 BD 1957
C of S min Brechin cath from 1965
m Edin 21.10.61 Fiona S. McDonald MA(St And) deaconess/teacher d of Thomas P. McD. MA LLB(Edin) Edin

GORDON Robert MA 1909
d Aber 2.4.65 *AUR* XLI 146

GORDON Robert Fraser BSc 1930 DSc 1947
CBE 1972 FRCVS 1970 hon DVSc(Liv) 1970
dir poultry res stat Houghton, Huntingdon; chmn and non-scientific dir The Animal Health Trust Lond; edit. *The World's Poultry Science Journal*
d –.2.81 *AUR* XLIX 137

GORDON or Morgan, Roberta *MA 1932
resid Aber
husb *d* 4.5.69

GORDON Ronald Macgregor BSc(eng) 1954
civ eng corp of Trinity House Lond 1961–64; man. construct. dept MB Dredging Co Erith 1964–66; Lond: sect leader Rendel Pelmex & Tritton 1966–68, HM civ eng insp of factories from 1968

GORDON Ronald Murray MB ChB 1937 DPH 1939
MFCM 1974
sen m o SHHD Edin 1955–75; retd
wife *d* –.4.68
m(2) Edin 31.12.69 Doris M. Imrie BA(Oxon) d of William C. I. Dun
d 21.8.81

GORDON or Cowan, Rosemary MA 1951

GORDON Thomas Barclay MB ChB 1936
g p Littleport from 1941; retd 1974
d Peterborough 29.9.79 *AUR* XLVIII 353

GORDON Thomas Robert MB ChB 1925
retd; resid Canada 1977–79, Bexhill from 1979
wife *d* Vancouver 15.11.78

GORDON Walter Mitchell *MA 1954
market res exec and man. posts Lond 1954–66; asst secy univ apptments board Liv 1966–70; sen counsellor OU NW reg England from 1970
m Lond 29.6.60 Anne P. Woods secy d of John W. Beckenham

GORDON William MA 1898
no longer on GC reg

GORDON William James MA 1933
s of William J. G. hosp gov; b Kirkcudbright 24.4.12
dep head King St p s Aber 1958–62, head from 1962; retd

GORDON William Johnston MA 1905
d Ratcliffe-on-Trent 15.12.64 *AUR* XLI 53

GORDON William Law *MA 1919
retd; resid Sunningdale

GORDON William Leslie MB ChB 1938
d –.9.66

GORDON William Lindsay Drummond BSc(agr) 1935

GORDON William Morrison MA 1953 LLB 1955 PhD 1963
Glas: sen lect private law 1965–69, Douglas prof civ law from 1969

GORDON William Thomson MB ChB 1935

GORDON-RUSSELL James Bertrand MB ChB 1943
MRCP(Lond) 1948 DPM 1950 FRCPsych 1971 FRCP(Lond) 1973
sen reg psychiat SW metro reg hosp board 1950–52; consult. psychiat S Somerset clin area 1953–57; consult. psychiat and phys supt Roundway hosp Wiltshire/consult. psychiat Swindon hosp group 1957–64; dep chmn Melbourne mental health auth State of Victoria, Aust 1964–66; consult. psychiat Bristol clin area/clin tut. and reg tut. post grad psychiat Brist/reg advis Royal Coll of psychiat/chmn vocat trg sub-comm SW reg/visiting consult. psychiat BRHSC/consult. psychiat Bristol ch and fam guid serv from 1967
m 28.6.50 Margaret M. O'Byrne

GORDON-RUSSELL William Colin MB ChB 1937

GORROD Charles Elgar MB ChB 1936 DPH 1939
m Aber 25.12.45 Margery Aspinall

GORROD or Crookshanks, Jean Soutar BCom 1925
resid Aber
d 18.12.81

GORROD William Cowie MB ChB 1924
g p Sheffield 1927–73; retd

GORTON or Ford, Isabel Mary Simpson MA 1946

GOSSIP Margaret Elizabeth *MA 1925
MA(Oxon)
dep head N. Lond Collegiate s till 1962; retd; resid Edgware

GOSSIP Robin Arthur John *MA 1927
d Edin 21.2.62 *AUR* XXXIX 384

GOSSIP William Henderson MB ChB 1931
MRCGP 1961
g p Dun till 1973; retd
d Dun 5.6.80 *AUR* XLIX 68

GOURLAY Alice Edith MA 1948
teacher maths Kirkton h s Dun 1963–74
resid St Cyrus

GOVE Daisy Dugid *MA 1951
teacher Luanshya h s N Rhodesia 1962–74,

Randfontein h s Transvaal from 1974
m Luanshya 12.12.59 Lawrence J. Greeff eng s of Johan C. G. Springs Transvaal

GOVE or Anderson, Doreen May Mowatt MB ChB 1949
JP 1971
dept m o Wakefield AHA from 1966; staff surg to W Yorks police from 1965

GOVE James George MA 1945
HM for. serv: FCO 1946–73; Berlin, Paris, Lond 1958–73; retd; now with Gallaher group

GOVE or Ironside, Mary Jack MB ChB 1947

GOVE Reginald Bisset MB ChB 1949 MD 1967
MRCP(Lond) 1955
phys MoH Cent. Af Fed. 1960–63; sen spec phys dept health Zambia 1964–76; phys Wenela spec hosp Johannesburg from 1976
resid Johannesburg S Af republic

GOVE Robert Morrison *BSc(eng) 1947

GOW Alistair Ian Stuart BSc(eng) 1953

GOW Edward MA 1935

GOW Edward James MB ChB 1947
med asst psychiat Craig Dunain hosp Inv from 1963

GOW Florence Helena MA 1902
no longer on GC reg

GOW James John BL 1947 PhD 1952 LLD 1964
member Fac of Advoc from 1952

GOW Jenny MA 1924
no longer on GC reg

GOW John *MA 1913
no longer on GC reg

GOW or Low, Katherine MA 1926
resid Lossiemouth

GOW Katherine Mary MA 1947
teacher Aber: Springhill p s 1961–68, Woodside p s from 1968

GOW or MacDonald, Mary MA 1916
no longer on GC reg

GRAFTON Mabel BCom 1930
Lond: bookkeeper Stonehouse & Ptnrs insur brokers 1932–33; secy work Charles Packer & Co 1933–34; resid Twickenham
m Aber 7.4.34 Thomas C. Young CA s of Archibald Y. MA(Glas) Aber

GRAHAM Alexander John MB ChB 1951
MRCPE 1961 FRCPGlas 1974
sen hosp m o Woodilee hosp Lenzie 1959–62; consult. psychiat Hartwood hosp Lanarksh 1962–69, phys supt from 1969

GRAHAM Amelia Lillie MA 1932
teacher Aber from 1936

GRAHAM or Macleod, Clara Eliza MA 1919
d Stornoway 1.8.68 *AUR* XLIII 80

GRAHAM David Alan *MA 1954

GRAHAM David Spence *MA 1950 Dip Ed 1953
lect Moray House coll of educ Edin 1961–65; HMIS Glasg 1965–72; HM dist insp Aber 1972–75, HMCIS West of Scot. from 1975

GRAHAM Duncan John Macfarlane BSc(for) 1953
teacher geog Stanstead coll Quebec from 1958; consult. Inst for World Order NY from 1971; pres Global Citizens Assoc from 1975

GRAHAM or Thomson, Elizabeth Ann Frances MA 1951
teacher: Rayne N 1960–62, Brackens s Dun 1967–74, Dyce nursery s 1974–76, Beechwood s Aber from 1976

GRAHAM Frederick Duncan BSc 1926
FEIS 1955
retd 1969; resid Dun

GRAHAM or Whyte, Janet Russell *MA 1934
teacher maths St Margaret's s for girls Aber 1961–72

GRAHAM Marion *MA 1924
retd 1967; resid Aber

GRAHAM Robert Henry BSc(for) 1952

GRAHAM Walter MB ChB 1925 MD 1928
g p St John's Wood Lond from 1928

GRAINGER or Gordon, Emily MA 1925
d Lond 14.7.65 *AUR* XLI 150

GRANT or Poole, Agnes Strachan MA 1929
resid Winchmore Hill Lond

GRANT Alan MA 1929 MB ChB 1933 *MD 1938
MRCP(Lond) 1949 FRCPath
sen lect forensic serology Guy's hosp med s Lond/hon consult. forensic serologist Guy's hosp

GRANT Alan John *MA 1926
awarded Coll of Educ gold medal for distinguished serv to educ
head Jeppe h s for boys Johannesburg 1943–62; retd; lect maths Johannesburg coll of educ 1962–76
m Johannesburg 28.6.32 Catherine R. Barclay d of John B. Aber

GRANT Alastair Burness MA 1948
d in Nigeria 27.3.77

GRANT Alastair Neish BSc(eng) 1947

GRANT Alastair Patrick BSc(agr) 1937

GRANT Alastair Robertson MB ChB 1913 MD 1924
retd; resid Goosnargh, Preston

GRANT Alexander BCom 1922
d Dun 29.2.72 *AUR* XLIV 429

GRANT Alexander BSc(agr) 1948
Dip Agr Econ(Oxon) 1949 ACMA 1953 BSc(econ) (Lond) 1965
agr econ NOSCA Aber 1949–66; lect: Galashiels coll of f e 1967–69, Scot. coll of textiles Galashiels 1969–73; sen lect Falkirk tech coll from 1973

GRANT Alexander Christie BSc 1949 *1950
ICI dyestuffs sales man. Scot. Glasg from 1969

GRANT Alexander Dow BSc(for) 1934

GRANT Alexander Flett MA 1955
teacher maths Aber: St Peter's RC s 1956–67, Kaimhill s s 1967–71; spec asst maths Kincorth acad 1971–73; prin teacher maths Hilton acad from 1973
m Aber 7.7.69 Patricia A. Milne teacher d of James D. M. Aber

GRANT Alexander Rae *MA 1920 BD 1922
retd; resid Aber

GRANT Alexandra Mariel MA BSc 1926
teacher maths/biol and woman advis Grantown g s 1957–67; retd

GRANT Alison Marion MA 1914
d Milltimber Aber 15.4.77

GRANT or Innes, Anna Helen MA 1930

GRANT Anna Thomson *MA 1922
retd 1962; resid Aber

GRANT Anne MA 1927 BCom 1928
pers off. in industry till 1939; squad off. WAAF 1939–45
m Lond 8.1.44 Arthur B. W. Greenhough (capt) MBE MC FRSA arch. s of Edward G. MA(Cantab) Eardisland
husb *d* 22.9.74

GRANT or Miller, Annie Mary Jane MA 1926
teacher mod lang: Hyndland s s Glasg 1961–62, Fortrose acad 1962–68; retd

GRANT or Speight, Annie Mabel MA 1908
d Hanover New Hampshire USA 4.10.66 *AUR* XLII 82

GRANT Bertie James *MA 1922
d Aber 23.7.71 *AUR* XLIV 320

GRANT Charles MB ChB 1943
MRCGP 1968
asst g p Insch 1944–45; g p Crail from 1950

GRANT Charles Murdoch MA 1937

GRANT Charles Murdoch Stronach BSc(agr) 1931

GRANT Christina Bruce MA 1915
d Golspie 20.6.70 *AUR* XLIV 109

GRANT or Youngson, Daphne Margaret MA 1949
lect Engl Nanyang univ Singapore 1967–69; resid Hong Kong

GRANT Donald Austin MB ChB 1940
g p Brechin from 1946

GRANT Donald Cumming *MA 1951 Dip Ed 1952
prin teacher geog: Aberlour h s 1960–67, Dunbar g s 1967–72; asst head Dunbar from 1972
m Aber 22.12.62 Margaret M. Campbell MA(St And) teacher d of Alexander D. C. Montrose

GRANT Donald Stewart *MA 1952

GRANT Donella MA 1953
teacher/stud. Canterbury NZ 1953–55; teacher Glasg 1957–59, Invsh 1959–62, Fort Augustus from 1974
m Edin 22.12.62 Patrick D. C. L. MacDonald garage owner

GRANT Edith MA 1918
no longer on GC reg

GRANT or Craig, Edna Jane Fordyce MA 1951

GRANT Edward BSc(eng) 1953
MICE 1959 MIMunE 1962 MSc(N'cle) 1968 FIHE 1969
city eng dept latterly prin eng(traffic) Aber 1957–75; chief asst eng Aber div dept of roads Grampian reg c from 1975
m Aber Patricia R. Glennie tech d of George G. Bicester

GRANT or Baird, Elizabeth Innes *MA 1911
d Wishaw 23.1.68 *AUR* XLII 350

GRANT Eric Donaldson *MA 1951

GRANT Ethel Stewart MA 1917
d Buckie 25.11.70 *AUR* XLIV 210

GRANT or Noble, Ethel Stewart MA 1938
teacher Aberdeensh: Birkenhills s 1957–64, Ardallie s 1965–67, Ellon p s 1967–70; resid Aber

GRANT or Kellock, Evelyn Marjory Forbes MA 1944
teacher Caol s from 1967

GRANT Florence Liddell MA 1930
LCP 1935
retd 1966; resid Bath

GRANT George Lockhart MB ChB 1946 DPH 1961
DIH(Dun) 1968 MFCM 1972
commun med spec Dun from 1974

GRANT Gordon Couper BSc(for) 1922
retd 1969; resid Peterculter

GRANT Hamish Brown MA 1933 LLB 1935
CBE 1975
Scot. secy Federation of Brit Indust 1953–65

GRANT Henry Frederick Lyall MA 1898
no longer on GC reg

GRANT or Mackie, Isabella MA 1906
d Banff 23.3.54

GRANT Isabella MA 1923
d Fochabers 23.5.65 *AUR* XLI 50

GRANT James BSc(agr) 1931
d Pitlochry –.12.75

GRANT James BSc(eng) 1951
prin dev eng GEC Commun Coventry 1962–70, superv eng from 1970

GRANT James Forgan MB ChB 1906
d Bexhill 24.12.66 *AUR* XLII 82 & 346

GRANT Janet Macpherson MA 1912
resid Lossiemouth
d Elgin 5.9.78

GRANT or Anderson, Jessie MA 1924
resid Aber

GRANT Jessie MA 1925
teacher and chief prim. asst Hopeman s 1935–69; retd; resid Fochabers

GRANT or Hepburn, Jessie Margaret *MA 1940
resid Dunkeld

GRANT John MA 1915
d 25.11.65

GRANT John MB ChB 1921
d Orpington 30.3.61 *AUR* XXXIX 203

GRANT John George MB ChB 1929
d –.4.67

GRANT John King MB ChB 1924
d Brechin 22.3.76

GRANT John Philip BL 1953
prof acct Arthur Young McClelland Moores & Co Aber from 1970

GRANT John William MA 1919 BSc(agr) 1921

GRANT John William BSc(agr) 1937
NDD(Glasg) 1937
reg dir NOSCA Aber from 1947
m(2) Caddonfoot 30.8.63 Meave M. MacLeod cler asst d of Alasdair MacL. Beauly

GRANT Joseph MA 1925 DD 1958
C of S min Cromdale and Advie 1959–71; retd; resid Grantown-on-Spey; chmn Moray and Nairn educ comm 1958–60

GRANT Lawrence Barron MA 1924 *BSc 1925
retd 1976; resid Glasg

GRANT Lesley Dunbar MA 1954
teacher Crossroads s Durris 1963–73, head from 1973
member Banchory t c from 1971, Dean of Guild from 1971; hon treasurer until 1975; member selection comm for Scot. women's golf 1976

GRANT Lewis Neish *MA 1950

GRANT or Speight, Mabel MA 1908
no longer on GC reg

GRANT or McArthur, Maggie Irvine MA 1908
no longer on GC reg

GRANT or Burton, Margaret Isabella MA 1910
d Victoria BC 6.3.80

GRANT Margaret Janet MA 1910
resid Forres

GRANT or Melvin, Margaret Macpherson MA 1918
farm. Brechin; resid Brechin

GRANT or Craig, Margaret Paterson MA 1928
no longer on GC reg

GRANT or Bremner, Margaret Shand MA 1931
resid Forres

GRANT Marjory Jean MA 1954
teacher: Alford s 1960–66, Insch s 1967–69, Keith g s from 1969

GRANT or Wilson, Mary Philip BSc 1944
teacher maths Ruthrieston s s (later Harlaw acad) Aber 1964–77; retd

GRANT or Thomson, Moira MA 1955 Dip Ed 1956
head Fetternear p s 1963–68; asst prin teacher Inverurie acad 1968–71, Stoneywood p s Aber from 1971
husb *d* 5.10.64

GRANT or Whittaker, Moyreen MA 1955
resid Aber

GRANT Murdo Macdonald MA 1952 *1954 Dip Ed 1955
prin teacher Engl Golspie h s 1964–68, head Kingussie h s from 1968

GRANT Muriel Catherine MA 1941
High School Asst Cert(Tor) 1959 Dip Lib Sc 1968
teacher Moray and Nairn 1942–44; teacher/lib Port Elgin, Ont from 1959
m Lossiemouth 1944 W. James Meikle stained glass artist s of William M. Toronto

GRANT or Hedges, Nora Christina MA 1936

GRANT Norma Cissy MA 1948

GRANT Patrick Thomas *BSc 1951
FRSE 1969 FIBiol 1970 OBE 1980
reader biochem Aberd and dir fisheries biochem res unit 1963–70; dir inst of marine biochem and hon lect marine biochem Aberd from 1970

GRANT Quentin Alexander Frain Rae *MB ChB 1951
Foundation FRCPsych 1972
USA; asst dir ch psychiat Johns Hopkins univ, Baltimore 1960–61, dir ment health St Louis county Missouri 1962–64, chief soc psychiat NIMH Washington DC 1966–68; Canada: psychiat-in-chief hosp for sick ch Tor and prof child psychiat Tor from 1968

GRANT Robert MA 1946 *BSc 1949
sen prin scient off. and head of soil surv of Scot. Macaulay inst for soil res Aber from 1950

GRANT Robert Charles MA 1893
no longer on GC reg

GRANT Ronald Kirkham MB ChB 1921

GRANT or Farquhar, Sheila Leonard MA 1950 dLLB 1953
resid Radlett

GRANT Stuart Cowie BSc(eng) 1944
d –.1.62

GRANT William MA 1915
d Monifieth 28.6.70

GRANT William Gordon MB CM 1895 MD 1898
d Dunbar –.11.60 *AUR* XXXIX 95

GRANT William Ligertwood Main MA 1905
no longer on GC reg

GRANT William Morton MA 1919 BD 1922 PhD 1928
C of S min Falkirk W ch 1927–67; retd

GRANT William Sutherland *MA 1926
d 9.8.65 *AUR* XLI 246

GRASSICK Donald McCombie BSc(eng) 1944
d 2.10.71

GRASSICK John Robertson MA 1949
teacher Engl Selkirk h s
d Galashiels 17.10.78

GRASSICK William James MA 1919
d 1.10.63

GRASSIE Dorothy Isobel BL 1952

GRASSIE or Hibbard, Elizabeth Donald MB ChB 1951 MD 1963
lect dept of obst and gyn Liv 1963–73; stud counsellor Welsh nat s med from 1974

GRASSIE James Campbell DSc 1948
Aberd: reader dept of eng till 1963
d Glasg 14.5.76 *AUR* XLVII 106

GRASSIE John Taylor MB ChB 1934
g p Cheltenham from 1935; anaest Cheltenham gen hosp 1937–62

GRASSIE Norman *BSc 1945 PhD 1948
DSc(Glas)

GRATE Robert Alexander MA 1932
d 6.3.66

GRATTIDGE Alan Edwin Thomas BSc(eng) 1950
FIMechE 1969
Aber: tech dir John M. Henderson & Co from 1965; dir C. F. Wilson (1932) & Co from 1973

GRATTIDGE Isobel Riddell MB ChB 1942
g p Nott from 1949

GRAY Adam MB ChB 1909 MD 1912
d 13.2.70 *AUR* XLIII 440

GRAY or Graham, Aileen Jean MA 1952
resid Bieldside, Aber

GRAY Alan Taylor MA 1953
head maths dept Castle s Taunton 1966–71; dep head Barnoldswick s West Riding, 1971–74; head La Mare de Carteret s Guernsey from 1974

GRAY Albert Henry *MA 1928
asst actuary Sun Life Assur Co of Canada from 1954

GRAY Alexander MA 1909
d Stonehaven 17.6.68 *AUR* XLIII 78

GRAY Alexander MA 1911
d Portsoy 1.2.72 *AUR* XLIV 427

GRAY Alexander MA 1925 LLB 1927
ptnr Gray & Kellas advoc Aber from 1930
d 10.10.81

GRAY Alexander BSc(eng) 1947
Banff c c: chief asst eng 1965–67, dep county surv from 1967

GRAY Alexander James MB ChB 1953
Tasmania: dist m o Cygnet 1967–69, Evandale from 1969; also m o to tuberculosis div Launceston from 1969

GRAY Alexander Pirie MB ChB 1924
retd 1964; resid Durh
m Wheatley Hill, Durh 1962 Ann Gribbens

GRAY Alexander Robertson MA 1921 LLB 1922
d 6.11.76 *AUR* XLVII 105

GRAY Alexander Thomson *BSc(eng) 1948

GRAY Andrew Latto Craig MA 1951
min Pinelands presb ch Cape Town from 1959

GRAY Andrew Paton MB ChB 1912
d 19.11.63

GRAY Barbara Mary Young *MA 1933
d –.10.71

GRAY or Ross, Bella Rainy MA 1909
d 4.11.76

GRAY Brian Scott *BSc 1953 PhD 1970
MIBiol 1968
dir of res Harrison & Crosfield Malaysia 1960–70; on staff World Bank Jakarta, Indonesia 1970–75, Washington DC from 1975
m Kuala Lumpur 24.8.68 Adèle M. Surin bus. woman d of Herbert P. S. Ipoh Malaysia

GRAY Charles Duncan Stewart *MA 1940
asst man. periodicals advt dept *The Times* Lond 1961–65; man. *The Times* Edin off. and advt man. *The Times Educational Supplement Scotland*
m Aber 11.11.66 Barbara B. Smith
d Edin 15.6.74 *AUR* XLVI 110

GRAY Charles Hugh MA 1900
no longer on GC reg

GRAY Daniel BL 1959
d Aber 11.6.61 *AUR* XXXIX 205

GRAY David George MB ChB 1955
FRCP(C) 1966
Canada: phys royal Ottawa sanatorium 1957–62, resid Ottawa gen hosp 1962–66, radiol Ottawa gen hosp/assoc prof univ of Ottawa med s 1966–76, chief dept of radiol Queensway-Carleton hosp Ottawa from 1976

GRAY or Spence, Diana Norma MA 1949

GRAY or Hartgerink, Dorothy *MA 1944
ALA(Aust) 1972
part time lib in arch. and univ lib Sydney Aust from 1967

GRAY Douglas MA 1944 *1949
man. dir and founder Park Film Studios Glasg from 1959; man. dir Campbell Harper Films Edin from 1972

GRAY Douglas Alexander Gordon BSc(eng) 1953
d Sutton Coldfield 4.11.70 *AUR* XLIV 216

GRAY or Stuart, Elizabeth MB ChB 1915
d 11.1.71

GRAY Eric *MA 1951
prin teacher mod lang: Lasswade h s 1960–65, Mary Erskine s Edin 1965–70; Airdrie acad: head upper s 1970–71, dep rector 1971–73; rector Beath sen h s Cowdenbeath from 1973

GRAY Eric Duff MA 1919 MB ChB 1922 MD 1933
retd 1965; resid Manchester
wife *d* 2.7.53
m(2) Manc 26.9.59 Helen P. Hampson almoner d of Francis C. H. Bramhall

GRAY Ethel Elizabeth Maitland MB ChB 1921 DPH 1923
d Aber 19.11.68 *AUR* XLIII 80

GRAY or Shirreffs, Eva Cecile Gordon MB ChB 1945
clin asst Leic RI from 1957

GRAY or Smylie, Evelyn Allan MA 1949
part-time remed teacher RACH 1968–72, full-time from 1972

GRAY Francis Gillespie MA 1922
d Edin 11.2.73

GRAY George *MA 1946
asst lib univ St And from 1946

GRAY George Milne MA 1916 MB ChB 1920
d Lamarsh 6.8.62 *AUR* XL 84

GRAY Hamish William *MA 1949
schoolmaster Lond from 1954

GRAY Harry MB ChB 1951

GRAY Hector Mulholland MB ChB 1928
med pract Johannesburg from 1930; retd
m(2) Johannesburg Grace Pease d of John P. Illinois USA

GRAY Helen Mackay MA 1909 BSc 1911 MB ChB 1915
d Lond 1.9.70 *AUR* XLIV 107

GRAY Isobel Margaret MA 1942

GRAY James MA 1946

GRAY James Garden MA 1892
no longer on GC reg

GRAY James Smith MA 1901 MB ChB 1904
d 21.1.61 *AUR* XXXIX 98

GRAY or Watt, Jane Henderson MA 1925
d 19.5.65

GRAY or Ironside, Jeannie Moir MA 1913
d 15.2.70

GRAY John MA 1930
Shetland: head Scalloway j s s till 1966; retd

GRAY John MB ChB 1942
g p Thornley from 1948

GRAY John Alexander *BSc 1942
chem res and dev dept Bakelite Birm from 1959

GRAY John Gordon MA 1914
retd; resid Aber

GRAY John Hector MA 1932 ᶜLLB 1939
ptnr Gray & Kellas advoc Aber from 1946

GRAY John William Reid *MA 1949 LLB 1952
resid magistrate Uganda till 1962; temp proc-fiscal dep Glasg 1962–63; Dund: lect private law from 1964; warden Airlie Hall 1966–75

GRAY or Gray, Lilian Elizabeth MA 1926
resid Kenilworth Cape Town
husb *d* 14.1.62

GRAY Malcolm *MA 1939
Aberd: sen lect econ hist dept of pol econ 1962–66, reader econ hist 1966–69; reader econ hist dept of econ hist from 1969

GRAY or Comfort, Margaret Ann MA 1942
teacher Lat/Engl Alford acad from 1943

GRAY or Hector, Mary Forrest MB ChB 1945
g p Maseru Lesotho 1960–66; part time lect dept of path. Aberd 1967–75, res asst dept genetics 1977–80

GRAY or Allan, Priscilla Elizabeth MA 1948
resid Scunthorpe

GRAY Robert *BSc 1951
asst rector Mackie acad Stonehaven from 1972
m Aber 27.3.59 Edith Smith

GRAY Robert Alexander Harper MA 1901
no longer on GC reg

GRAY Ronald MB ChB 1955
h o St James hosp Tredegar 1959–61; g p: Cwmbran 1961–72, Birm from 1972
m(2) Merthyr Tydfil 25.10.69 Nina Davis midwife d of Sidney D. Merthyr Tydfil

GRAY Stuart Thomas Gordon MB ChB 1935 DPH 1937
O St J 1963 C St J 1971 FFCM 1972
C MoH and prin school m o E. Suffolk 1952–74; retd
wife *d* 11.11.75
m(2) Eye 29.12.77 Lucille B. Stables or Swinney d of William S. Aber

GRAY Theodore Grant MB ChB 1906
d Wellington NZ 8.9.64 *AUR* XL 394

GRAY Trevor BSc(mech eng) 1936 BSc(elect eng) 1937

GRAY or Gordon, Vera MA 1937
resid Edin

GRAY William Cowan MB ChB 1901
d Jersey 2.6.67 *AUR* XLII 345

GRAY William Hedley *MA 1949

GRAY Williamina MA 1910
retd; resid Aber
d Aber 1977

GRAY Winniefred Margaret MA 1910 MB ChB 1913 DPH 1914
d Perth 9.11.72 *AUR* XLV 124

GREEN or Brown, Annie Bella MA 1912
d 25.4.66 *AUR* XLII 84

GREEN or Fyfe, Annie Fraser MA 1911
d Aber 29.9.73

GREEN Elizabeth Aimée MB ChB 1951
DPM MRCPsych
Cell Barnes hosp St Albans: sen regist 1962–67, consult. psychiat from 1967

GREEN George Dunbar BSc 1933 MA 1938
lect maths Thurso tech coll 1967–77; retd

GREEN James *MA 1929
d Aber 11.9.73

GREEN Mabel MA 1953
Dip Phonetics (Edin) 1963
sen lect speech unit Engl dept Moray House coll of educ Edin from 1971

GREEN Marion Winifred *MA 1936
retd 1970; resid Aber

GREEN or Crook, Nancie Hilda *MA 1936

GREEN Patrick John MA 1901
d Aber 24.2.66 *AUR* XLII 80

GREEN Peter BL 1938

GREENE or Biezanek, Anne Campbell BSc 1947 MB ChB 1951
g p Wallasey Cheshire from 1963
marr diss July 1972
m(2) Wallasey 9.11.72 Frank Le R. Perrée retd soc worker High Wycombe

GREENHORNE Marcus Fernando Hillarion BSc(eng) 1931
d Aber 27.3.71 *AUR* XLIV 212

GREENLAW Karl Stewart Guthrie MA 1937
d Edin 15.1.75 *AUR* XLVI 239

GREENSMITH Leonard Alexander *MA 1928
teacher maths Stirling h s 1960–68; retd; resid Aber
d Aber 12.8.79

GREESON Clarence Edward MB ChB 1910 MD 1913
d 10.6.79 *AUR* XLVIII 350

GREGOR or Berry, Emily Isabella MA 1931

GREGOR Ewen William BSc(for) 1955

GREGOR Robert MA 1912
retd 1949; resid Edin

GREGOR Walter MB ChB 1922
d Bridge of Earn 21.9.71 *AUR* XLIV 320

GREGOR or Murdoch, Winifred Montgomery MA 1950

GREIG or Irvine, Alice Mary Geddes MA 1910
d 12.8.62 *AUR* XL 80

GREIG or Cheetham, Clara MA 1944
teacher: King's House Calcutta 1955–60, Bishopbriggs Glasg 1961–62, Engl Lenzie acad Glasg 1962–65; form mistress/teacher Engl Foundation of King Edward VI Macclesfield 1965–67; head: Maryton s Montrose 1967–70, Sandford s Strathaven from 1970

GREIG or Gardiner, Georgina Imray MA 1929
resid Brixham

GREIG Hazel Williamina MA 1941
lect in craft Aber coll of educ 1962–65
m Aber 17.12.65 Leslie Wilson comp dir s of Thomas W. Cleckheaton

GREIG John *MA 1949
FSAScot 1971
col off. Devonshire Ho Lond 1950–51; col admin serv Nyasaland 1951–55; asst prin col off. Lond 1955–57; sen lab off. Blantyre, Nyasaland 1957–60; asst comm of lab Aden 1960–64; teacher hist Bell-Baxter h s Cupar from 1969

GREIG John Lyall BSc(agr) 1924 BSc 1926
OBE 1956
schol: Oxon/Imp coll of trop agr Trinidad 1926–28; dept agr Malaya 1928–50; dir agr N. Borneo 1950–56; advis (World Bank) govt of Iran 1957–61; chief of mission FAO of UN to Ethiopia 1962–67; resid Guildford

GREIG or Crabb, Kathleen Ogilvy Lindsay MA 1949

GREIG or Maclagan, Laura Mary Hutcheon *MA 1930

GREIG or Macaulay or Dodd, Margaret Helen Ingram BSc 1942 *1943
St And: Nuffield res fell. 1951–57; res fell. 1957–60; MRC res fell. Leeds 1963–68; SRC res fell. Bangor Wales from 1970

GREIG Thomas Paton BSc(eng) 1949

GREIG William James BSc(eng) 1948
civ eng Cementation Co UK, Iraq, India, Israel, Spain, USA 1949–71; man. dir Carbeth construct. co Airdrie 1972–76; construct. man. Mass transit rly corp Hong Kong from 1976
m Bearsden 22.6.74 Catherine Morrison MA 1955 *qv*

GREY Robert MB ChB 1914
no longer on GC reg

GRIBBLE James George MA 1954

GRIEVE Donald McLeod BSc(agr) 1941
farm. Dumfriessh 1941–50; col agr serv Nigeria 1950–60; chartered land ag Dumfries 1960–65; ptnr Bell–Ingram chartered survs Perth from 1965
m Eckford, Roxburgh 23.7.58 Ann E. Scott d of George S. Kelso

GRIEVE Edwin MA 1953 LLB 1955
ptnr: Donaldson & Henderson solic Nairn 1958–68, Rollo, Steven & Bond solic Dun 1968–70, A. C. Morrison & Richards advoc Aber from 1970

GRIEVE Elizabeth Anderson MA 1908
d –.4.61

GRIEVE or Mitchell, Elizabeth Napier MB ChB 1953
resid Aber

GRIEVE George McKenzie Denny *MA 1941 BD 1944

GRIEVE James MA 1918 MB ChB 1922
retd 1961; resid Ferring

GRIFFIN Mona MB ChB 1943 DPH 1948
g p Aber from 1954

GRIFFITH Frank MB ChB 1913
no longer on GC reg

GRIFFITH or Wardell, Sheila Munro *BSc 1954
Chelmsford: school lab tech 1969–73; res eng Marconi wireless tel comp from 1973

GRIFFITHS David Ronald BSc(eng) 1946

GRIFFITHS George Ian MA 1939 BD 1942
C of S min Chalmers ch Wishaw 1950–76, High Cross ch Melrose from 1976

GRIFFITHS or McLeod, Margaret Evans MA 1928
teacher maths/Engl RGC Aber 1966–73
husb *d* Port Harcourt Nigeria 8.3.66

GRIGOR James BSc 1931 *1933
d Forres 30.1.74 *AUR* XLV 448

GROENEWALD Pieter Fourie MB ChB 1933

GROUNDWATER Randolph Cumming MA 1949
d Ontario Canada 15.3.72

GRUBB Anthony James MA 1933
C of S min Deer from 1954

GRUBB Craig McIrvine *BSc(eng) 1953

GRUER Edith Mary *MA 1910
d Edin 30.12.66 *AUR* XLII 82

GRUER Kenneth Terence MB ChB 1950
g p Kemnay 1953–67; Scot home & health dept Edin: reg m o 1967–70, sen m o from 1970

GUILD Alexander Eddie BSc(eng) 1930
FIWE 1951 FICE 1968 OBE 1973
President IWE 1969–70
eng and man. Newport: Newport & S Mon water board 1960–70, Gwent water board 1970–74, Welsh water auth to retirement 1974

GULLETT or MacDonald, Adeline Isabel MA 1936
head Walker Dam inf s Aber from 1967

GUNN Alasdair James Manson BSc(agr) 1955

GUNN Alastair James MA 1924
insp of schools Europ educ dept N Rhodesia 1953–55; retd; part-time teaching posts: NZ 1955–57, boys' g s Eng 1957–66; resid Downderry nr Torpoint

GUNN Alexander MA 1925
head Castletown j s s Caithness from 1938
deceased

GUNN Alexanderina MA 1950

GUNN Benjamin Williamson MA 1928 ᶜLLB 1931
retd 1968; resid Fochabers
d Buckie 12.6.81

GUNN Christina Alexandra MB ChB 1936
retd 1972; resid Bognor Regis

GUNN Colin Fraser MA 1907
no longer on GC reg

GUNN Flora McKenzie MA 1955
d 31.7.65 *AUR* XLI 252

GUNN Hamish Iain BSc 1955
asst head Halkirk 1962–67; Thurso h s: teacher sc 1967–72, prin guid 1972–74 and asst head from 1974

GUNN John Alexander MA 1915
C of S min: St Fittick's ch Aber till 1956; chaplain H.M. Prison Craiginches, Aber 1943–58; resid Bridge of Weir
d Bridge of Weir 18.1.80 *AUR* XLVIII 440

GUNN or McVay, Marie McKenzie MA 1924
no longer on GC reg

GUNN or Beardmore, Marion Ellen Maggie MA 1906
d 18.7.69 *AUR* XLIII 327

GUNN Murdo MacKenzie MB ChB 1923
no longer on GC reg

GUNN or Tait, Norma Mary MA 1953

GUNN William MA 1919 *MB ChB 1924
d Wick 18.1.68 *AUR* XLII 357

GWYNN Arthur Montague MB ChB 1942
MA(Dub) 1967
dep edit. *Medical Journal of Australia* Sydney 1960–77, edit. from 1977

GYLE John McGregor BSc(agr) 1950
farm. Esslemont, Ellon from 1950
m Dun 25.10.52 Doreen G. Paterson d of Donald F. P. Dun

HAASE or Rosowsky, Erika Ernestine MA 1944
resid North Hill Lond

HACKET or Johnstone, Dorothy Christian Liddle *MA 1935 *1937
Gwilym Gibbon res fell. Nuffield coll Oxon 1973–74 comm of customs and excise 1964–76; excise advis BAT Lond 1976–77
d 24.2.81 *AUR* XLIX 138

HADDEN Charles Strachan MA 1912
no longer on GC reg

HADDEN George Campbell MB ChB 1944
g p Blackheath Birm from 1950
m Sedgley 25.6.60 Patricia Baker MB ChB(Birm) med pract d of Henry B. B. Sedgley

HADDEN Helen Elizabeth MA 1915
no longer on GC reg

HADDEN Jeannie MA 1936
teacher King St s Aber from 1950

HADDEN Jeannie Chalmers MA 1931
retd 1970; resid Aber

HADDEN Jessie Harper *MA 1919
retd 1959; resid Inverurie

HADDEN or Gould, Winifred Reith MA 1925
resid Bo'ness

HADDOCK William *MA 1954
MInstP 1963 MRInst Navig 1964
prin eng Marconi Space and Defence Syst (Combined GEC, Engl Elec Co, AEI) Stanmore from 1968

HAINING Kenneth Anderson BSc 1949
RAF serv in Korea, Cyprus, Philippines, Brunei, Aden, UK; retd 1965; teacher Nott: Eastwood s mod s 1965–72, head sc Eastwood comp l s from 1972
m Kegworth 14.2.68 Rosalie I. Swann comp dir d of Henry S. Liv

HAINING William Fulton BSc 1952
teacher maths/sc Hatton 1961–63; head Kinneff p s from 1963

HALCROW Marjory Elizabeth Agnes MA 1943
resid Aber

HALDANE William Duncan BSc(for) 1933
retd 1970; resid Crockey Hill York

HALKETT or Brebner, Evelyn *MA 1928
resid Turriff

HALL or Saxby, Agnes Milne MA 1929
resid Leighton Buzzard

HALL Agnes Taylor Cameron MA 1930
head Kirkhill p s Aber 1957–61; retd
m Aber 8.4.61 Alexander Keir MA 1905 *qv*
husb *d* 3.1.71

HALL Alan Stirling *MA 1954
FSA(Lond) 1973
lect classics Keele 1961–72; sen lect from 1972; visiting lect dept classical stud. univ Pennsylvania Philadelphia 1968–69; hon secy Brit inst of archae Ankara 1973
m Cambridge 7.7.63 Gillian M. Carver BA(Keele) ch care off. d of Ralph C. Sawston

HALL Alfred Petrie MB ChB 1906
d Aberfeldy 31.3.63 *AUR* XL 198

HALL David MB ChB 1955
g p Milton Keynes

HALL Eric George
BSc(elect eng) 1944 BSc(civ eng) 1948
FICE 1973
Edin: dep res eng James Williamson & Ptnrs 1953–66; dir Mitchell construct comp (Scot.) 1966–73, gen man. Farrans 1973–74; associate James Williamson & Ptnrs from 1974

HALL Frederick *MA 1952
col educ serv: prin coll in Kenya 1953–66; univ of Malawi 1966–68; dep head educ Doncaster coll of educ from 1968
marr diss

HALL George William Hutchison BCom 1926
no longer on GC reg

HALL James Christian MB ChB 1920
d Stowmarket 17.10.66 *AUR* XLII 85

HALL John Alexander BSc 1950
retd 1973; resid Alness
d 5.3.77

HALL Leonard Duncan BSc(eng) 1951
SAI: prod. controller Edin 1961–69, works eng Aber 1969–73, eng sen man. from 1973

HALL or Gates, Mary Jane Cruickshank MA 1940

HALL or Rugg, Vera Winifred Duguid
MB ChB 1941 DPH 1948
dep m o h Caithness from 1963

HALLIDAY Alastair George Brand *MA 1937
trained for Presb min Westminster coll Cambridge 1969–71; asst Trinity presb C of E Harrow 1971–72; ordained and inducted Trinity presb C of E Streatham Lond 1972

HALLIDAY George BSc(for) 1922
no longer on GC reg

HALLIDAY or Jope, Henrietta Margaret *BSc 1937
hon res fell. geobiochem Belf from 1965

HALLIDAY John Alexander *MA 1927
retd 1970; resid Perth

HAMILTON Daniel Currie BSc(agr) 1949
Edin: man. dir SAI (horticulture) 1964–70, consult. from 1970

HAMILTON David Anderson MB ChB 1936
d Montrose 2.3.62 *AUR* XXXIX 386

HAMILTON Elizabeth Findlay MB ChB 1954
ophth inst Glasg: sen regist 1960–62; sen h m o (part time) 1962–71, med asst from 1971

HAMILTON Gilbert Frewin
BSc 1933 MB ChB 1938
visiting prof Marquette univ Milwaukee USA 1961
d Aber 10.6.74 *AUR* XLVI 110

HAMILTON John BSc(eng) 1945

HAMILTON Joseph Stewart
MB ChB 1939 DPH 1947
founder FFCM 1971 FRSH 1961
area m o Staffs from 1964

HAMILTON Malcolm Thomas Henderson
***MA 1952**
asst rector Blairgowrie h s from 1972

HAMILTON or Newton, Margaret Macfarlane
MA 1949
resid Wells

HAMILTON or May, Margaret Steedman
MB ChB 1947
BA 1978
g p Bolsover from 1961

HAMILTON Ronald Thomas BSc(eng) 1953
CEng MICE 1959
dir Mitchell Construction Co: Stockton-on-Tees 1961–73, Stamford from 1973

HAMILTON Thomas Graham MB ChB 1954

HAMILTON William Aitken Brown *MA 1931
dir pers/under secy-gen of UN NY 1959–62; asst under secy of state F C O Lond 1962–68; retd; resid Tunbridge Wells

HAMILTON-BELL Patrick MB ChB 1937
g p Richmond Surrey from 1950

HAMILTON-PEARSON Edgar Alan
MB ChB 1912
d Alderney 23.5.61 *AUR* XXXIX 274

HAMLEY Kenneth Norman MA 1952

HAMPTON Myron Grant *BSc 1953
tech off. SAI Edin 1958–67; head eng R & D div Brooke Bond Liebig Reading from 1967
m South Weald 9.9.61 Virginia M. Davis SRN d of Edward D. South Weald

HANNAGAN Michael John BSc(agr) 1953
Dip Agr (Cantab) 1954 DTA(Trin) 1955
agr off. col serv Tanganyika 1955–61; agr advis Spillers S Eng and S Wales 1961–71; formulations man. Spillers farm feeds Lond from 1971
m Aber 26.6.54 Barbara M. Doig MA 1952 *qv*

HARBRON Patrick *MA 1953
Uttoxeter: sixth form master Alleyne's g s 1964–74, head sixth form/sen teacher from 1974
m Pontesbury 17.4.63 Blanche Malcolm BA(Nott) teacher d of Lewelyn-Bar M. Pontesbury

HARDCASTLE Edward John Brierly BSc(for) 1950
TD
man. dir Engl for. assoc Reading 1958–67; major: 4th KOSB(TA) till 1960, 4/6th Royal Berks regt (TA) 1960–66; dir Engl Woodlands Uckfield from 1968

HARDIE Alexander Merrie
MA 1931 *BSc(elect eng) 1933 *BSc(mech eng) 1934 PhD 1959
MRWEA 1970
vice-prin Bristol coll adv tech 1963–66; prof phys univ of Bath from 1966 and pro-vice-chancellor 1966–71

HARDIE Alexander Waldie MB ChB 1937
consult. anaest royal Surrey county hosp Guildford from 1947

HARDIE or Johnston, Annie MA 1910
no longer on GC reg

HARDIE or Sussex, Elizabeth *MA 1953
Lond: contrib to Brit film inst publ from 1962, edit. asst *Sight and Sound*, asst edit. *Monthly Film Bulletin* 1964–66, freelance writer and res from 1966; publ works: *Lindsay Anderson* (Studio Vista) 1969; autobiog novel under pseudonym 1971; prod. and directed docum film *Can Horses Sing?* 1971; *The Rise and Fall of British Documentary* (Univ of Calif Press) 1975
m Aber 15.6.59 Alan Sussex BA(Oxon); husb *d* 1965

HARDIE Ethel Louisa MA 1921

HARDIE Frances Irene MA 1952
teacher Glasg from 1961

HARDIE Frederick William MA 1909
d 8.4.68 *AUR* XLII 348

HARDIE or Bruce, Helen Glennie Yule MA 1954
dept econ dev Victoria BC Canada from 1965

HARDIE Hugh Grant Macpherson PhD 1948
retd 1972; resid Cults Aber

HARDIE James Leslie MB ChB 1950
g p: Southland NZ 1967–70, York from 1970

HARDIE Peter MA 1926 BCom 1929
retd; resid Aber

HARDIE Raymond Ledingham *BSc 1954 PhD 1957

HARDIE William Dunbar *MA 1953
FHA 1970
asst secy: NE reg hosp board Aber 1963–76, Grampian health board from 1976
m Aber 3.8.63 Margaret E. Simpson MA 1963 *qv*

HARDING Albert William *MA 1952
MEd(St And) 1962 PhD(Dund) 1976
lect hist Dun coll of educ from 1962

HARDY Eric Gordon *MB ChB 1940 MD 1954
first asst dept surg Durh from 1954; consult. surg Chester R. I. from 1959

HARE Christopher Leighton PhD 1941

HARGREAVES Claude Christian MB ChB 1915
retd; resid Brighouse

HARGREAVES Herbert MB ChB 1909
no longer on GC reg

HARKER Alan Brook BSc(agr) 1951
farm man. N Walsham 1951–56; BOCM: advis Suffolk 1956–60, prod. man. Erith 1960–62, advis Glasg 1962–68, p r and training man. Basingstoke 1968–73; sales man. Boe & Silcock Shrewsbury 1973–75; agr advis Glasg from 1975
m Leic 10.5.52 Sheila M. V. Boddy BSc(agr)(Lond) res asst d of James A. V. B. Leic

HARKINS or Simpson, Anne MA 1948
farm. Karoi, Rhodesia
m(2) Salisbury Rhodesia 26.2.64 John P. Adams farm. s of John W. A. MB ChB(Lond) E Lond S. Afr

HARKINS Denis MB ChB 1937
d Derby 20.5.75 *AUR* XLVI 325

HARKINS or Gammie, Helen Davidson
MB ChB 1941
g p Elgin from 1961

HARKINS William *MA 1926 MB ChB 1931
retd 1972; resid Strichen

HARLEY Robert Chalmers BSc(agr) 1952
insp DAFS from 1953; resid Keith

HARPER Alfred Alexander
MA 1929 MB ChB 1932 *MD 1947
N'cle: prof physiol 1963–72, emeritus from 1972

HARPER Alister Donald *MA 1942
Brit Council: asst rep Buenos Aires 1961–65, overseas "A" div 1965–73, home div from 1973; retd 1981

HARPER or Rhind, Charlotte Cockburn MA 1950
teacher: Huntly 1960–70, Scotstown 1970–73, Cults Aber from 1973

HARPER or Wallace, Daisy Isabel Margaret
MA 1931
d Inverurie 27.11.79

HARPER Douglas MA 1902 *BL 1905
no longer on GC reg

HARPER Elizabeth MA 1911 BSc 1915
d Manchester 20.6.67 *AUR* XLII 181

HARPER Eric Imlay MA 1933 MB ChB 1938
g p Swindon from 1946; retd 1978

HARPER Francis Gordon BSc(for) 1931
owner and man. Glebe farm and nursery Aboyne from 1958

HARPER James Hall McPherson BSc 1941

HARPER John Stuart MB ChB 1924
d Trowbridge 9.9.77 *AUR* XLVII 286

HARPER or McKay, Mary Scott MA 1928
resid Banff

HARPER Peter Charles BSc 1948 *1949

HARPER William Francis MA 1904
no longer on GC reg

HARRINGTON Albert Blair MB ChB 1938 MD 1944
FMFCM 1972
chief med advis civ serv dept from 1976

HARRIS or Allan, Barbara Munro MA 1950

HARRIS or Gordon, Dorothy Morton MB ChB 1925
g p Goodmayes 1926–63
d Vancouver 15.11.78

HARRIS Herbert Reginald MB ChB 1927
d Ipswich 12.10.69 *AUR* XLIII 330

HARRIS Matthew Hughs MB ChB 1903
no longer on GC reg

HARRISON John Clive BSc(for) 1949
dist off. for. comm: E England 1950–54, New Forest 1954–62; Kent 1962–73, Malvern from 1973
m Southampton –.9.56 Marie J. Murray d of William M. Southampton

HARROW John Alexander MB ChB 1941
g p Keswick from 1947

HARROW Mary Elizabeth MA 1930 MB ChB 1934 DPH 1938

HART Alis MA 1932
retd 1966; resid Stonehaven

HARVEY Charles Alexander MB ChB 1917 DPH 1921
d Bedfordsh 12.9.76 *AUR* XLVII 102

HARVEY Derek John *MA 1954

HARVEY Douglas MA 1923 BSc 1924 PhD 1927
commonwealth bureau of anim nutrit Rowett inst Aber: scient asst 1952–56, asst dir 1956–60, dir 1960–66; retd

HARVEY Helen Margaret MA 1920
no longer on GC reg

HARVEY Ina Berry MA 1926
d –.12.62

HARVEY Jeanie MA 1928
teacher: Logie Durno 1942–47, Old Rayne 1947–66
m Insch 28.1.30 Charles W. Ross farm. s of Alexander R. Insch

HARVEY or Sutherland, Margaret Mary MA 1932
d Kirkcaldy 16.12.78

HARVEY Mary Elizabeth MA 1928
retd 1971; resid Aber

HARVEY or Maclennan, Mary Elizabeth BSc MA 1933
teacher maths/sc Perthsh 1955–70; resid Blairgowrie

HARVEY Peter MB ChB 1952
d Leeds 27.12.69 *AUR* XLIII 447

HARVEY William Alexander BCom 1935
retd 1969; resid Market Harborough
d 4.10.76

HASSAN Ali MB ChB 1929

HASSAN Hassan Mohamed MA 1955

HASSAN Kamal PhD 1947

HASTINGS Alexander Gordon MB ChB 1926
no longer on GC reg

HASTINGS or Page, Ann Wilson MA 1915 *1916
d London 23.3.75 *AUR* XLVI 236

HASTINGS Edward *MA 1913 DD 1950
joint-edit. *The Expository Times* 1922–64; edit. and published *The Speaker's Bible* in 36 vol; other publications
d Aber 31.7.80 *AUR* XLIX 66

HATT or Forbes, Mabel MA 1923
resid Auckland NZ

HAUGHS Margaret Agnes BSc(agr) 1949
NOSCA: agr econ 1955–71, sen agr econ from 1971

HAWES Arthur Joseph MB ChB 1916
d 27.11.74 *AUR* XLVI 236

HAY or Begg, Alice MA 1938
head Glenlyon s Aberfeldy from 1968

HAY or Auchnie, Alice MA 1947
resid Keithhall Inverurie

HAY Andrew Bertram MB ChB 1936

HAY Andrew Leslie MA 1925 [d]LLB 1927
sen ptnr Cooper & Hay advoc Aber; part-time lect Aberd: evid and proced 1945–64, tax. law 1961–77

HAY Arthur Colson MA 1937
MB ChB(St And) 1943
g p Wallasey from 1949

HAY or Mitchell or Dunn, Barbara Helen Douglas MA 1952

HAY or Gillies, Camilla Hill *MA 1934
asst lect Fr/Lat univ of Leeds from 1945; asst examiner JMB Lond, Oxon, Cantab from 1940
d Harrogate 20.6.78 *AUR* XLVIII 105

HAY Charles Albert MB ChB 1920
d Aber 7.11.76

HAY or Sim, Christina Riddell MA 1928
m Aberdeensh Robert Lumsden Sim
d –.5.58

HAY David MA 1951
head Rainford h s St Helen's from 1961

HAY David Sinclair BL 1932

HAY David Stuart BSc(agr) 1952
ICI agr div: dep chmn 1977
m Hitchin 20.8.60 Patricia K. Jespersen BA(Lond) teacher/pers off. d of Svend A. J.

HAY Francis Walker Christie MA 1947 *1949
teacher: prin hist/mod stud. Aberfeldy h s 1962–65, prin hist Banff acad 1965–70, asst rector from 1970 national convener R. Brit Legion (Scot.) from 1967

HAY George BSc(eng) 1945
control construct. eng: 1958–70, proj. man. Lond and Renfrew from 1970

HAY George Gordon Wallace MB ChB 1921
d 23.10.69

HAY Gladys Ann Campbell MA 1941
teacher: Whitehills 1942–44, Dufftown 1944–46, Charleston USA 1946–47, Dufftown 1947–52, Chilliwack BC Canada 1952–53, Elgin 1954–78; retd

HAY Gladys Rose MA 1948
Aber: year mistress Summerhill acad 1970–72, dep head Hilton acad from 1972

HAY Hamish Gordon *BSc 1948
teacher-missionary meth coll Uzuakoli E Nigeria 1958–62; head phys Matthew Murray s Leeds 1962–70; head sc Tong comp s Bradford from 1970

HAY Harold Mills BSc(eng) 1947

HAY or McDougall, Helen Jane MA 1916
d Tribune Sask 4.8.75

HAY or Fairley, Helen Mary MA 1910
d Lanark 9.7.77

HAY Ian Kennedy MB ChB 1941
FACMA 1968
Aust: m o h NSW 1960–67, metrop m o h Sydney 1967–72, prin m o h health comm NSW Sydney from 1972
d Sydney 13.5.77

HAY James Robert William MB ChB 1926 DPH 1928 *MD 1930
m o h Kirkcaldy 1937–64; retd; resid Kinnoull Perth

HAY Jane Laing MA 1931
retd 1970; resid Fortrose

HAY or Webster, Janet (Jessie) MA 1913
husb *d* 1957
d Aber 21.2.80

HAY Janet Guthrie MA 1943
teacher Engl/hist Rothes s s 1963–68
m Elgin 14.9.68 Norman Burns chief supt police s of James D. B. Kincardine o' Neil

HAY or Brown, Jean Cameron MB ChB 1951
dept m o Herts c c 1968–75; m o Rudolph Steiner curative schools from 1975

HAY Jessie Helen MA 1925 BSc 1925 *1926
retd 1967; resid Elgin

HAY John McKay BSc(eng) 1952

HAY John Rae BSc(agr) 1927
no longer on GC reg

HAY John Sutherland *MA 1945
prin teacher classics James Gillespie's h s Edin from 1966

HAY or Birch, Lorna May *MA 1936
d Lond 23.8.69 *AUR* XLIII 331

HAY Margaret Ann MB ChB 1936
retd 1974; resid Lond

HAY or Cowan, Margaret Geddes MB ChB 1948
asst m o Edinburgh corp from 1969; clin m o Lothian health board
husb *d* 1967

HAY Mildred Barnett MA 1944
higher exec off. govt commun hq from 1965

HAY Robert Gall *MA 1939
rector Arbroath h s from 1962

HAY Ronald John *BSc 1945 PhD 1948
ICI Fibres: chem eng Harrogate 1959–64, tech asst indust market res from 1964

HAY or Summers, Ruth Watson *MA 1941
resid Portknockie
d 14.11.79

HAY William MB ChB 1933
g p Aber from 1947

HAY William BSc(agr) 1938

HAYES Norman Frank *BSc 1952 PhD 1955
res chem Allen & Hanbury's Ware from 1958

HAYMAN Ann Elizabeth MA 1950
teacher: sc Fort William 1967–68, maths Laurencekirk from 1977
m Fort William 20.6.60 Robert S. Hunter

HAYMAN Edward William BL 1954
sen leg. asst Ayr c c 1961–69, chief leg. asst 1969–75; asst dir admin Strathclyde reg c from 1975

HAYWOOD Laurence MA 1951 Dip Ed 1952
Aber: dep head: Tillydrone p s 1965–67, Muirfield p s 1967–70; head Quarryhill p s from 1970

HAZELWOOD James Scott MA 1925
no longer on GC reg

HEAD Malcolm John PhD 1950
visiting reader anim nutrit Sur, Guildford; consult. anim nutrit

HEALD Peter Joseph PhD 1952
DSc(Manc) 1962 FRSE 1967
head dept anim biochem Twyford Lab 1961–66; prof biochem Strath from 1966

HEARD or Peet, Helen Asher MA 1929
no longer on GC reg

HEARNE Arthur Ambrose MB ChB 1916 MD 1925
d –.5.67

HECTOR George Pittendrigh
***MA 1901 BSc 1906 DSc 1922**
d Aber 12.11.62 *AUR* XL 74

HECTOR or Fowler, Irene BSc 1951
teacher: Scotland, England, Canada till 1957
m 16.7.53 James A. Fowler MB ChB 1953 *qv*
d Victoria BC 12.7.80

HECTOR or Bradfield, Joyce Marguerite BSc 1951
resid Aber

HECTOR Ralph Melville MB ChB 1937
CBE 1963
consult. radiol military hosp: Catterick 1957–60, Accra 1961–63 and sen m o Brit joint serv trg team; consult. radiol Cambridge milit hosp Aldershot 1963–74; retd

HECTOR William Litster *MB ChB 1922
d Brighton 2.9.72 *AUR* XLV 125

HEDDLE Christine Louise MA 1953

HEDDLE Harald Scott MB ChB 1945
g p Benbecula and S Uist from 1955

HEDDLE Inga Pirie MA 1949
teacher: Arusha Tanganyika 1958–61, St Andrew's private s Maraval, Trinidad 1962–76; resid Burnley
m Port of Spain 31.1.74 John E. Pritchard textile tech

HEGGIE David John Gordon BSc(agr) 1947
dairy farm. Wigtownsh from 1953

HEGGS Thomas Barrett MB ChB 1902 MD 1904
no longer on GC reg

HELMRICH or Clow, Nan Louise
***BSc 1931 MA 1934**
scient historian
d Welwyn Garden City 10.2.73

HEMS John Macqueen PhD 1954
tut. Engl/soc stud. Langside coll Glasg 1959–66; Canada: prof phil Carleton univ 1966–67 (Canada council grant 1968), assoc prof phil univ of Guelph 1967–69, prof phil from 1969 (Fr govt grant 1970)

HENDERSON or Rae, Aileen Margaret MA 1925
resid Dollar

HENDERSON Alastair Gordon BSc 1951 *1952
teacher: sc Stonehaven 1953–64, prin sc Alford 1964–65, sen teacher Aber from 1965

HENDERSON Alastair Wingate
MB ChB 1927 MD 1934
retd g p 1969; part time m o Bicester Ordnance Oxon and part time assessor MHSS from 1969

HENDERSON Alexander Davidson
***MA 1950 MSc 1969**
statist NE reg hosp board Scot. Aber from 1967, Grampian health board from 1974

HENDERSON Alexandra MA 1909
retd; resid Heswall
d 1977

HENDERSON Alistair Mitchell BSc(agr) 1925
no longer on GC reg

HENDERSON or Millington, Arabella Victoria
MA 1909
resid Seaview Is of Wight
d Is of Wight 28.1.80

HENDERSON Arthur Graeme BSc(eng) 1950
FInstPet MSPERIM & Mech eng Professional eng Trinidad
Trinidad: dist petr eng for. reserve 1960–63, dist supt Barrackpore 1963–66, consult. petr eng 1966–68; man. Singapore 1968–69: SE Asia man. Jakarta 1969–73; spec proj man. Santa Flora Trinidad from 1973

HENDERSON Caroline Lamond MA 1910
d 23.10.71

HENDERSON Charles Shaw *MA 1930
retd 1969; resid Scone

HENDERSON Christina Dickson MA 1927 BSc 1930
retd 1967; resid Aber
d Newmachar 10.5.81 *AUR* XLIX 137

HENDERSON David BSc(for) 1950

HENDERSON David MA 1951 Dip Ed 1952
Dunfermline: teacher Engl/gen stud. Lauder tech coll 1960–64, sen asst i/c dept Engl/gen stud. from 1964

HENDERSON David *BSc 1952

HENDERSON Denys Hartley MA 1953 LLB 1955
ICI: various posts/dir i/c fertilisers agr div Billingham from 1957
m Aber Doreen M. Glashan d of Robert C. G. Aber

HENDERSON or MacKenzie, Dorothy Catherine *MA 1926
d Falkirk 27.8.62 *AUR* XL 92

HENDERSON or Esson, Dorothy Johanna Margaret MA 1932
teacher Ellon 1940: resid Huntly

HENDERSON or Thomson, Dorothy May MA 1931
d Lond –.8.42

HENDERSON or Turner, Edith Mary *MA 1935
resid Forfar

HENDERSON Elizabeth Harriet Mitchell MA 1944
teacher Burnside inf s Aber from 1954

HENDERSON or Forrest, Elizabeth Mary MA 1918
resid Bromley

HENDERSON Ellen Mary *MA 1924
acting prin hist Central s s Aber 1943–49; prin Engl/hist Banchory acad 1949–64; retd; resid Banchory

HENDERSON Eric Douglas BSc 1950

HENDERSON Esther Williamina MA 1929

HENDERSON Forbes Wilson MB ChB 1943
g p Sheffield from 1948

HENDERSON George David Smith *MA 1953
MA PhD (Cantab) 1961 FSA
Graham Robertson res fell. Downing coll Cantab 1960–63; lect dept hist of art Manc 1962–65; lect dept fine art Edin 1966–71, reader 1971–73; lect and head of dept hist of art Cantab from 1974

HENDERSON George Richard BSc(agr) 1946

HENDERSON Gordon Harvey MA 1937 LLB 1939
d Aber 20.3.70 *AUR* XLIII 446

HENDERSON Gordon Nicol BSc(eng) 1949
FICE 1972
sen ptnr A. Henderson & Ptnrs Aber from 1972

HENDERSON Hector McBain MB ChB 1934
d 25.5.81

HENDERSON or Leslie, Helen McIntosh MA 1942
resid Cleadon village Nr Sunderland

HENDERSON Henry *MA 1931
resid Inv

HENDERSON Henry Laurence MA BCom 1925
retd 1965; resid Musselburgh

HENDERSON Isabella Barclay MA 1926
resid Edin

HENDERSON James MB ChB 1924
d Scarborough 14.7.73 *AUR* XLV 319

HENDERSON James BSc(for) 1951
Aberd: lect for. 1964–72, sen lect from 1972; lieut cdr RNR Aberd RN unit from 1968

HENDERSON James Gordon ᶜMB ChB 1949 MD 1970
FRCPsych 1971
consult. psychiat Grampian area health board from 1959 and clin sen lect mental health dept Aberd

HENDERSON or Lund, Jane Dalrymple MA 1913

HENDERSON or Haddock, Jane Reid *MA 1920
resid Inverurie

HENDERSON Jean *MA 1926
prin teacher Ger Aber acad 1960–69; retd; resid Garlogie Skene

HENDERSON Jeannie Elizabeth MA 1912
no longer on GC reg

HENDERSON Jessie Jane MA 1934
teacher Gordon s Huntly from 1954

HENDERSON John MA 1910
d 9.3.61

HENDERSON John Dunlop MB ChB 1904
no longer on GC reg

HENDERSON John Hope MB ChB 1954
DPM 1960 FRCPsych 1971 MFCM 1972 FACP 1973
sen m o Woodend hosp Aber 1960–61; consult. psychiat/phys supt Dr Gray's and Bilbohall hosps Elgin 1962–69; Edin: consult. psychiat/phys supt Bangour village hosp and Western gen hosp 1969–72,

prin m o/consult. psychiat SHHD 1972–76; advis on mental health WHO from 1977

HENDERSON John Murdoch MA 1926
d Aber 10.11.72 *AUR* XLV 127

HENDERSON John Peter BSc(eng) 1947

HENDERSON John Wishart MA 1904 BL 1906
no longer on GC reg

HENDERSON Kenneth Douglas
***MA 1952 Dip Ed 1953**
spec asst Engl AGS 1957–65; lect Engl Aber coll of educ from 1966; co-edit. *Education in the North*; recog teacher for BEd degree Aberd 1972

HENDERSON Laurence Peter MA BSc(agr) 1923
d 16.12.69

HENDERSON or Fraczek, Louise Buchanan
MA 1942
d Barnes 5.7.79

HENDERSON or Murtock, Mabel Adams
MB ChB 1938
resid Sunderland

HENDERSON or Millar, Margaret Elizabeth
MA 1955

HENDERSON or McCreadie, Marjorie Muriel
MA 1940
resid Mequon Wisconsin USA

HENDERSON or Williams, Mary Margaret
MA 1944

HENDERSON or Macrae, Mary Simpson MA 1952
Dip Nursery Educ(Aber) 1972
inf teacher Cloverfield s Bucksburn 1960–72, nursery teacher i/c Oldmeldrum 1973–76, asst head Marchburn inf s Aber from 1976

HENDERSON Moira Elizabeth Keill
***BSc 1952 PhD 1955**
scient off. microbiol dept Macaulay inst for soil research Aber 1952–64
m Aber 26.10.63 Alexander R. Wilcox man. s of Thomas H. W. Aber

HENDERSON or Lemerle, Muriel Osbourne
MB ChB 1942
g p Southborough Tunbridge Wells from 1944
husb *d* 1969

HENDERSON or Stephen, Nancy Falconer
MA 1930
resid E. Grinstead

HENDERSON Peter MB ChB 1929 MD 1931
CB 1965
sen prin m o dept educ and sc 1964–69; retd; hon phys HM Queen 1964–67; short term consult. WHO SE Asia and Middle East 1969–74; resid Guildford

HENDERSON or McCallum, Rica BSc 1924
resid Edin

HENDERSON Richard Bruce *MB ChB 1924
DTM & H 1929 LM (Dub) 1935
RAMC hon rank capt 1945
resid Bexley Heath

HENDERSON Robert Dalrymple
MA 1927 MB ChB 1931
FRSM 1946
retd 1972; resid Epping
d 29.5.79

HENDERSON Robert Gregory
MB ChB 1929 DPH 1931 MD 1933
consult. phys and med supt Southern hosp Dartford 1939–59; resid Brenchley Tonbridge
m Brenchley 18.11.60 Josephine E. Merricks or Beeney d of Walter M. Icklesham

HENDERSON Robert Thomas Smith
MB ChB 1950

HENDERSON Thomas George *MA 1927
dir educ Argyll 1946–71; retd; resid Dunoon

HENDERSON or Conn, Violet Lindsay MA 1937

HENDERSON William MB ChB 1912
d 16.11.67

HENDERSON William Gordon MB ChB 1944

HENDERSON William Lewis BSc(agr) 1939
d Aber 8.8.66 *AUR* XLI 342

HENDRIE or Duffus, Elizabeth Catherine
MB ChB 1947
resid Aber

HENDRY Alexander William
MB ChB 1914 MD 1918
d Aber 22.7.72 *AUR* XLV 124

HENDRY Amy *MA 1916
no longer on GC reg

HENDRY or Hay, Annie Mary Hay MA 1913
d 17.9.69

HENDRY Anthony Morrice *MB ChB 1924
d Birmingham 10.9.67 *AUR* XLII 185 & 362

HENDRY Arnold William
***BSc(eng) 1941 PhD 1946 DSc 1954**
prof bldg sc Liv 1957–63; prof civ eng Edin from 1964
wife *d* 1966
m(2) Edin 1968 Elizabeth L. A. Inglis admin asst d of Harry R. G. I. Edin

HENDRY or Addison, Charlotte Patricia MA 1914
no longer on GC reg

HENDRY or Jones, Charlotte Souttar ***MB ChB 1923 DPH 1924**

HENDRY Elizabeth ***MA 1925**
no longer on GC reg

HENDRY Eric Grassick **MB ChB 1940**
g p Buckie from 1946

HENDRY or Welbourn, Esther **MB ChB 1936 ᶜMD 1939**
MA(Cantab) 1964
Cambridge: clin asst dermat Addenbrooke's hosp from 1963; dir stud. in med sc New Hall from 1964; fell./lect anat New Hall from 1966

HENDRY Frederick William Firman **BSc 1923**
no longer on GC reg

HENDRY George **MA 1903**
no longer on GC reg

HENDRY George **MA 1922**
d Stratheden Fife 22.3.66 *AUR* XLII 85

HENDRY George Alexander **BSc 1935 MB ChB 1938**
d N'cle-upon-Tyne 13.7.71 *AUR* XLIV 321

HENDRY George Alexander **MB ChB 1948 MD 1971**
d Leigh-on-Sea 2.5.76

HENDRY George Stuart ***MA 1924 DD 1949**
pres Amer theol soc 1971; prof emeritus Princeton theol soc NJ 1973

HENDRY Gordon Frederick ***MA 1942**
Scot. office Edin: econ advis 1965–67; asst secy from 1967

HENDRY or Fyfe, Gwendoline McKenzie **MA 1940**

HENDRY Harold Gordon **BSc(eng) 1953**
MIHE 1955 AMBIM 1976 FICE 1976
eng prov roads dept Pietermaritzburg 1953–60; Burmah Oil Co: supt eng Calcutta 1960–63, proj man. Lahore 1963–73, consult. Adelaide 1973–74; BP (North Sea oil dev) 1974–76; consult. Nairobi from 1976
marr diss

HENDRY Helen **MA 1909**
no longer on GC reg

HENDRY Ian Murdo ***MA 1948**
rector: Dunoon g s 1969–75, Dollar acad from 1975

HENDRY Innes Craig ***BSc 1951**
MInstP 1969 FInstPet 1975
lect/res fell. Stir 1968–72; lect RGIT Aber from 1972

HENDRY James **MB ChB 1947 DPH 1953**
Cert Path(Can) 1960 FRCPath(Can) 1972
path. Brandon gen hosp Manitoba from 1957

HENDRY or Cumming, Jessie Elizabeth **MA 1930**
resid Inverurie

HENDRY Jessie Tait **MA 1927**
retd 1966; resid Aber

HENDRY John ***MA 1929**

HENDRY John Smith **BSc 1953**
Dornoch acad: teacher maths 1962–67, prin maths 1967–72; prin guid Cults acad from 1972

HENDRY Joseph **MA 1952**
prin teacher geog Grantown g s Grantown-on-Spey from 1956

HENDRY or Gardiner, Mabel Blaikie **MA 1914**
d Edin 27.11.71

HENDRY or Gerard, Margaret Edith **MA 1955**
resid Kingsworthy

HENDRY or Black, Margaret Garden **MA 1950**
teacher Hightae Dumfriessh from 1974
husb *d* 1972

HENDRY Neil Geddes Clarkson **MB ChB 1939**
CBE 1976
clin sen lect orthop Aberd from 1968

HENDRY Robert William **MB ChB 1926**
retd 1970; resid Halifax

HENDRY or Paterson, Ruth Davidson **MA 1928**
resid Edin

HENDRY Thomas Begg Tawse **MA 1922 BCom 1924**
no longer on GC reg

HENDRY William Ewart **BSc 1935 *1936**
head Inverarity s Angus from 1952
wife *d* 1963
m(2) Inverarity 1.7.67 Catherine L. B. Mills SRN theatre sister d of Charles M. Tealing

HENDRY William Garden **MB ChB 1936**
consult. surg Highlands gen hosp Lond from 1946

HENDRY William Gordon **MA 1940 LLB 1947**

HENDRY William Thomson **MB ChB 1944**
g p Aber from 1951; lect forensic med Aberd from 1957; police surg Aber from 1956

HENEKE Paul Michael **MB ChB 1942**
g p Cape Town from 1946

HENFIELD Marie Adelaide Gordon **MA 1933**

HENRIQUES Stella Grace Alice **MB ChB 1923**
retd 1964; resid Stamford

HENRY Alexander Falconer **MB ChB 1950**
CCFP 1977

g p Ottawa Ont 1956–72; chief emerg dept Ottawa civic hosp from 1972
m 1.7.54 Christina H. Mitchell d of John M. Stornoway

HENRY or Littlejohn, Alice Mary MA 1925
resid Aber

HENRY Annie MA 1925
dept head prim. dept Laurencekirk s s 1965–67; retd

HENRY or Gillis, Daisy MA 1942
teacher Fr Northwich girls' g s Cheshire from 1965

HENRY John Alexander BSc(agr) 1949

HENRY or Hall, Kathleen Margaret Ross MA 1946
d 31.7.68

HENRY Kathleen Mary PhD 1933
retd 1965; resid Glenageary Co Dublin

HENRY or Norrie, Margaret Ogston MA 1923
Aber: teacher Engl Albyn s for girls 1942–46; temp post asst teacher s for deaf 1954–63; retd

HENRY Norman Fordyce McKerron *MA 1931 *BSc 1934
Cantab: lect mineral.-petrology from 1947; fell. St. John's coll 1960

HENRY or Hunter, Phyllis Roberta MA 1928
retd 1967; resid Scalloway
d Shetland 4.2.78

HENRY Robert *MA 1929
retd 1969; resid Macduff

HENRY Sheena Landsborough MA 1950

HENRY or Spark, Sophia Ogston *MA 1924
resid Ringwood
husb *d* 8.4.69

HENRY William Millar MA 1903
d Lond 20.12.61 *AUR* XXXIX 271

HENSON Ronald *MA 1930
d Aber 11.10.68 *AUR* XLIII 84

HEPBURN Alfred *BSc 1954

HEPBURN Athol Noble MB ChB 1954
DPH(Lond) 1961 surg cdr RNR(Lond) RD 1971
m o BOAC Lond 1961–69; sen m o RAF Farnborough 1969–72; dir civ med serv procurement exec MoD Lond from 1972
m Lond 26.10.63 Julia E. B. Smith SRN d of Leonard B. S. Llangoedmor Cardigan

HEPBURN or Sants, Elsie Ann Watt MA 1943 *MEd 1948
Bangor N Wales: educ psych ch guid clin 1961–63, part-time sen lect St Mary's coll 1963–66: miscellaneous lect/res Sus from 1966

HEPBURN or Stokoe, Helen Rose MA 1925
d Lond 6.2.61 *AUR* XXXIX 105

HEPBURN John MB ChB 1954
MRCGP
g p: Barnhill 1962–63, Skelmorlie from 1963

HEPBURN Mark Ireland MB ChB 1941

HEPBURN Ronald William *MA 1951 PhD 1955
prof phil Edin from 1964

HERBERT Ellenor *MA 1916
d Aber 14.4.76

HERBERT George Leslie MB ChB 1942
g p Kexborough nr Barnsley from 1948

HERBERT Norman MEd 1950
d Banchory 18.1.71 *AUR* XLIV 216

HERBERT William MB ChB 1937

HERD or Galt, Bethia Cooper Rodger MA 1928
resid Aber

HERD George McLeman MA 1954
teacher: Kaimhill s Aber 1964–65, Cent s Fraserburgh 1965–69; head New Byth s from 1969

HERD or Ferguson, Isabella Flett MA 1925
resid Aber

HERD James MB ChB 1944 DPH 1948
g p Banchory from 1948

HERD or Catto, Mary MA 1937

HERON Ernest Mercer *MA 1927
d Edin 23.7.69 *AUR* XLIII 330

HERRIOT Alexander MB ChB 1951
FRCOG 1972
sen regist obst and gyn: Leeds RHB 1961–63, Southern gen hosp Glasg 1964–66; consult. obst and gyn E Fife hosps from 1967

HERVEI Geyza Joseph *MA 1928
d 25.1.71 *AUR* XLIV 431

HEUCHAN or Thomson, Mary Jane MA 1902
no longer on GC reg

HEWET Alexander Ross *MA 1936
lect maths Aber coll of educ 1962–68, sen lect from 1968

HEWETT or Edwards, Alison Hayward MB ChB 1952
m 1.7.50
resid Tonbridge

HILL Alexander Campbell MA 1916 MB ChB 1918
d Hove 15.11.67 *AUR* XLII 352

HILL Alfred BSc 1909 BSc(agr) 1911
d Auckland NZ 3.1.61 *AUR* XXXIX 101

HILL Amelia MA 1952
teacher: Iraq petr comp Dukhan Qatar 1959–62; Brechin from 1972
m Brechin 9.6.62 Dudley Waller garage prop. s of Edwin H. W. Streatham

HILL Ethel Massie MA 1932
teacher AGS from 1950; retd 1974

HILL John Kingsley BSc(eng) 1945

HILL Robert Dougan MB ChB 1951 MD 1976
g p Isle of Barra from 1963

HILL Ronald Johnstone *MA 1949
Chevalier des Palmes Academiques 1970
prin teacher mod lang Liberton Edin 1960–62; advis mod lang Edin corp from 1970

HILLS or Thorpe, Frances Elizabeth BL 1940
resid Lond

HILSON Norman James Macfarlane MA 1919
resid Aber

HILTON Raymond Walwork BSc(for) 1933 MB ChB 1950
d Oswestry 24.8.75 *AUR* XLVI 325

HINDS Lesley PhD 1952
ICI plastics div Welwyn Garden City from 1952

HINGSTON Alfred Alwyne MB ChB 1900
no longer on GC reg

HIRD Alexander MB ChB 1949
asst g p Ashington 1951–56, g p Aber 1957–77; resid Aber

HIRD Gordon MB ChB 1947

HIRST Herbert Alexander BSc(eng) 1938
d 1.10.63

HOARE or de Navarro, Agnes Dorothea Mackenzie *MA 1923
PhD(Cantab) 1929
pres assoc of Newnham coll 1958–63; memb par council Broadway from 1967; founder memb Broadway Trust (regd with Civic Trust), secy 1963–72, chmn 1972–76, vice pres from 1976

HOARE Florence Margaret MA 1909
no longer on GC reg

HOARE Janette Mary *MA 1913
d 1967

HOARE or MacTavish, Margaret Wilma MA 1925

HOARE Samuel *MA 1919
d Cheltenham 31.3.76 *AUR* XLVI 415

HOBART Nettie MA 1906

HOBBIN Gordon Marnoch BCom 1931 MB ChB 1936
d Burnham Bucks 15.8.69 *AUR* XLIII 331

HOBBIN Ruby Gordon MA 1929
no longer on GC reg

HOBSON Bruce Morris *BSc 1948
Edin: sen lect obst & gyn 1959–66; reader from 1966

HODGE or Shea, Isabella *MA 1906
d –.6.70

HODGE John Brian Symons BSc(for) 1948
timber trade from 1952; resid Surbiton

HOGAN Elsie MA 1910
no longer on GC reg

HOGG Alexander Adam McDougall *MA 1952
Aber coll of educ: lect geog 1964–69, sen lect from 1969
m Arbroath 30.9.61 Moira MacKenzie hotel man. d of Duncan MacK. Aviemore

HOGG Cecil Berisford MB ChB 1914
no longer on GC reg

HOGG Charles Gordon MA 1932 LLB 1933
proc-fiscal: Cupar 1961–68, Dun from 1968

HOGG or Champion, Margaret Mary MA 1939

HOGGARTH Frank Evans MA 1928
d Lond 12.4.74

HOGGARTH Marion Duncan *MA 1927
retd; resid Aber

HOLDEN George Walker BSc(agr) 1955

HOLIDAY John Edward MB ChB 1955
DA(Lond) 1969
g p Rowlands Gill Tyne & Wear 1960–65; clin asst anaest Gateshead hosp group from 1965

HOLLANDS Edwin James MA 1931
rector: St George w St Barnabas Manc 1958–60, St Congan Turriff 1960–74; elected canon of St Andrew's cath Aber 1969; retd; resid Poulton-le-Fylde

HOLLOWAY Christopher John DLitt 1955
LittD(Cantab) 1970
Cantab: reader Mod Engl 1966–72, prof from 1972

HOLM Davina *MA 1938
teacher: asst prin mod lang Invergordon acad 1961–71; prin Ger Dingwall acad from 1971

HOLM or McLeod, Isabella Deas MA 1930
d Tain –.6.55

HOLM or Campbell, Isabella Fraser Mackenzie MA 1939
head Killen s Rosssh from 1961

HOLM or Riddell, Peploe Campbell MA 1934
Edin: teacher inf mistress Prestonfield s 1960–64; James Gillespie's h s 1964–69; asst head inf S Morningside s from 1969
marr diss 1954

HOLMAN Howard Henry PhD 1937

HOLMES or Carpenter, Daphne Elizabeth *MA 1953

HOLMES Dorothy Mildred MB ChB 1920
no longer on GC reg

HOOD or McAllan, Alison MA 1955
secy Victoria League in Scot. from 1956; resid Wick

HOOD or Macpherson, Ena *MA 1927
resid Dunfermline

HOPKIN Vincent David *MA 1954
prin psych and head psych sect RAF inst of aviation med Farnborough from 1965

HOPKINS Herbert Desmond BSc(eng) 1935
dir Lyds & Scot. fin. Nott 1963–68; man. dir Internat Factors Brighton 1968–71; dir pers and admin Lyds & Scot. fin. Edin from 1971

HOPKINS Herbert Owen *MA 1924
d 1974

HOPKINS Ronald Isaac BSc(eng) 1951

HOPKINSON Andrew Douglas BSc(agr) 1911
d 8.10.69

HOPPER Albert St Clair BSc(eng) 1942

HOPPER Noel Brian MB ChB 1950
MRCGP 1954
g p Stonehaven from 1951
wife *d* 13.3.63
m(2) Stonehaven 30.12.75 Carolyn S. M. French staff nurse d of David M. F. Newburgh Fife

HORÁNSZKY DE HORA Ladislaus PhD 1927
no longer on GC reg

HORN Alexander MB ChB 1907

HORN Annie Keir *MA 1919
retd 1964; resid Buckie
d Aber 13.3.80

HORN David MB ChB 1934

HORN Eleanor Jean *MA 1949 Dip Ed 1950

HORN Ian Ross MB ChB 1934
no longer on GC reg

HORNE Dorothy Louisa May MA 1947
teacher Northfield acad Aber from 1963

HORNE Elizabeth MA 1944

HORNE or Paterson, Helen Taylor *MA 1923
no longer on GC reg

HORNE Henry James MB ChB 1922
d Blackpool 22.9.65

HORNE Henry Murray MB ChB 1951
Tasmania: g p Latrobe 1966–76, Devonport from 1976

HORNE Ralph Alexander MB ChB 1934
g p Portlethen 1937–73; retd; resid Portmahomack

HORNE William Donald *MA 1919
no longer on GC reg

HORNE William Ian MB ChB 1950 ᶜMD 1963
FRCPath 1972 FRCP(Can) 1972
path. Hotel-Dieu hosp Windsor Ontario from 1963

HORROX Fred MA 1911
d 1.2.77

HOSIE Stewart MacGregor BSc 1953
ptnr site explor serv 1956–72; geol with C. H. Dobbie & Ptnrs consult. eng Lond 1972–76
m (2) 3.9.66 Janet Hodgkinson teacher
d Aber 2.3.78

HOSSACK Christina Ross Forbes MA 1914
resid Coupar-Angus

HOSSACK William Strachan MB ChB 1953
g p Banff from 1958
m Aber 27.8.60 Catherine R. Sellar cashier d of James S. S. MacDuff

HOUGHTON William Nusum MB ChB 1900
no longer on GC reg

HOUSTON Bradford George *BSc(agr) 1952
sen res off. Tengeru Tanzania 1964–68; Aber: teacher biol AGS 1968–72, prin biol Northfield acad from 1972

HOUSTON John Anderson MB ChB 1939

HOUSTOUN George Provan *MA 1952
prin teacher Queen Anne h s Dunfermline 1962–65: Dun: dep head Rockwell s s 1965–72, rector Rockwell h s from 1971
d 31.10.81

HOWARD Stewart Carlisle MB ChB 1906 *MD 1908
no longer on GC reg

HOWELL Frances Helen Kemp *MA 1954 Dip Ed 1955
prin teacher hist Craigholme s Glasg from 1960

HOWIE or Hopkins, Cecil Don BSc 1927

HOWIE David Porter MA 1909
d Kilmarnock 5.7.73 *AUR* XLV 316

HOWIE George *MA 1937 *MEd 1939
PhD(Leeds) 1961
assoc prof educ univ of Sydney Aust from 1965
d Sydney 16.5.80 *AUR* XLIX 69

HOWIE or Ross, Helen Doris BL 1948

HOWIE James William *MB ChB 1930 *MD 1937 LLD 1969
HM hon phys 1965–68 Kt 1969 FRCPGlas 1958 FRCP 1963 hon fell. Path. Soc (GB and Ireland) 1977 hon fell. Assoc Clin Path. 1977 hon assoc RCVS 1977 Pres: BMA 1969, RCPath 1966–69, assoc clin path. 1972–73; prof bact Glas 1951–63, dir publ health lab serv Eng and Wales 1963–73; retd resid Newtonmore

HOWIE or Peterson, Jean Nicol MB ChB 1926 DPH 1928 MD 1933
med asst venereology dept RI Edin from 1967

HOWIE Robert George Porter MA 1914
d 19.9.64 *AUR* XL 398

HOWIE Thomas Wilson BD 1941

HOWIESON or Richards, Margaret Beattie MA 1933
d Inv 24.8.69 *AUR* XLIII 331

HOWISON James William *BSc 1954 PhD 1957
member Aust pulp & paper Indust tech assoc 1968 Wiggins Teape (Stoneywood): chief chem Aber/ Nowra NSW Aust 1962–67, chem Shoalhaven Mill Nowra NSW 1968–77; paper tech Allied Colloids (Aust) Pty Sydney from 1977
m Sydney 25.3.72 Robyn L. Pattrick d of Eric P. Shellharbour NSW

HOWITT Kelvin Stewart *MA 1946
d 20.9.62

HOWITT Lewis Finnigan MB ChB 1951 DPH 1955
MFCM 1972
Edin: asst m o h 1960–61, sen asst m o h 1962–63; dep m o h Midlothian and Peebles 1963–68, s m o SHHD Edin from 1968
m Dalkeith 23.7.55 Sheila H. E. Burns MA(Edin) teacher d of William B. Linlithgow

HOYLE Nancy Jean Campbell *MA 1948
teacher: Engl Findochty 1952–54, rural Greysteele, NI, Engl/hist Bridlington 1960–61
m Buckie 1.9.54 Jack Austin air signaller FAR s of Albert E. A. Leeds

HUGHES Albert Lewis MB ChB 1939
g p Wellington NZ 1965–67, Forestburg Alberta 1968, Torryburn Fife 1968–69, Pudsey 1969–76
m NZ 16.9.65 Maureen E. Chapman d of James G. C.
d 23.11.76

HUGHES John Stanley BL 1934

HUGHSON or Rennie, Christina Peterson MA 1929
d Aber 17.1.67 *AUR* XLII 368

HUGHSON or Gear, Wilma Anne MA 1955
teacher Mid Yell j h s Shetland from 1956

HULSE Norman Laing MB ChB 1938
FMRCGP
g p Blackley Northants from 1948

HUMBLE Henry MA BSc 1922
OBE 1970
rector Elgin acad 1950–64; retd
d Elgin 23.12.81

HUMBLE or Rae, Katherine Izobel *MA 1913 BSc 1914
d 1.7.77

HUMBLE or Phimister, Margaret MA 1942 MB ChB 1948
d Aber 20.7.78

HUMBLE or Taylor, Renée Myles BSc 1949 *1950
Inverurie acad: teacher chem 1962–66, woman advis 1966–72, asst head guid from 1972

HUME or Cope, Isobel Dorothy MA 1915
d Lond 16.12.62 *AUR* XL 83

HUME or Harper, Joan Winifred MA 1924
resid Glasg

HUME William John MA 1927
no longer on GC reg

HUMPHREY John MB ChB 1913
no longer on GC reg

HUMPHREY or Niven, Kathleen Jane BCom 1928

HUMPHREY Reginald Alexander Milne MB ChB 1926
d Geelong NSW –.6.73 *AUR* XLV 318

HUMPHREY Stanley Frank Walker MA 1925
semi-retired; resid Rivonia Transvaal
m Kalk Bay Cape Province S Af 17.7.43 Una K. Fowler d of Hugh C. F. St James Cape Province

HUMPHRIES James Ernest DSc 1926
d Aber 25.2.79 *AUR* XLVIII 229

HUMPHRIES Walter Robson *MA 1928
d Aber 11.3.80 *AUR* XLVIII 442

HUNT David Laurence BSc(elect eng) 1951 BSc(mech eng) 1952
MIEE
GEC Rugby: chief eng mining and spec drives elect. proj 1969–71, div chief eng Elliott indust controls 1971–76, div man. mining elect. proj from 1976

HUNTER Alexander MB ChB 1939
FRCOG(Lond) 1966
obst & gyn Smith clin Hawkesbury Ont from 1952

HUNTER Alexander MB ChB 1947
g p Middlesbrough from 1952

HUNTER Allan BSc 1947 *1948

HUNTER Allan Thomson *MA 1926
prin teacher Engl and dep head Old Aber s s 1948–70; head f e centre Aber 1949–70
d Aber 15.10.76 *AUR* XLVII 105

HUNTER David Ian MB ChB 1954
g p: Aber from 1963

HUNTER Douglas Alexander *MB ChB 1921 MD 1941
d Lond 10.12.69 *AUR* XLIII 444

HUNTER or Cowley, Eilean Annand MB ChB 1942
resid Hartfield

HUNTER or McCoss, Ellen Jane Martin MA 1912
d Aber 10.12.72 *AUR* XLV 224

HUNTER or Trendell, Ethel Clementina Margaret *MA 1917
d 10.10.77

HUNTER Florence Muriel MA 1925
resid Aber

HUNTER Gillies Connan BSc 1947 *1948
agr res council grantee Edin 1948–50; biol res worker Rowett res inst Aber from 1950

HUNTER Grace Beverley *MA 1948
secy/lib centre of African stud. Edin from 1962

HUNTER Graham William Galloway MB ChB 1955
DPH(Edin) 1961 DTM & H(Lond) 1963
m o fed. health serv Aden 1959–67; g p Cumnock from 1968
m Wallington 31.8.63 Fiona M. S. McNairn art teacher d of Edward S. McN. MA(Glas) Wallington

HUNTER or Bruce, Helen Elizabeth MA 1935
resid Kildrummy

HUNTER or Barrack, Isobel Mary MA 1947
resid Amersham

HUNTER James Douglas MB ChB 1949
FFARCS 1964
regist anaest county hosp Lincoln 1955–59; gen hosp Newcastle-u-Tyne: sen regist anaest 1960–64, consult. anaest from 1964

HUNTER James Greig MB ChB 1942

HUNTER or McBoyle, Madaleine Jean MA 1951
cler asst Linden centre Huntly from 1971

HUNTER Robert Ferguson BSc(agr) 1949

HUNTER Stanley Beveridge *MA 1942

HUNTER Thomas MB ChB 1941
consult. orthop surg Barking and Havering from 1957

HUNTER William Drummond MA 1912
C of S min: Middle ch Perth 1926–63; clerk to presb of Perth 1948–70
d 12.7.79

HURST Roger Trevellian BSc(for) 1955
for. comm: asst dist off. Mansfield 1958–59, Helmsley 1959–61; dist off. Wakefield 1961–64, Kendal 1964–68, Aberfoyle 1968–72; conserv and recreation off. W Scot. from 1972
m Windermere 20.1.73 Denise M. Panton SRN nurs sister d of D. P. Windermere

HUSBAND Valentine Margaret MB ChB 1943
FRCOG 1971
Lond: sen regist W Middx hosp 1958–62; consult. gyn Italian hosp 1963–69; consult. obst/gyn NE Thames AHA from 1966
m Craig

HUTCHEON Archibald MA 1900
BL(Edin)
no longer on GC reg

HUTCHEON Gladys Gladstone MA 1925
no longer on GC reg

HUTCHEON Harry MB ChB 1936
d Kingswells 21.11.67 *AUR* XLII 371

HUTCHEON Isabel *MA 1921
resid Dun

HUTCHEON James MB ChB 1924
d Aber 19.6.68 *AUR* XLIII 84

HUTCHEON James Eddie Harper *MA 1955
teacher: Inv 1958, prin Engl Inv acad from 1968

HUTCHEON Mary MA 1924
no longer on GC reg

HUTCHEON Mary Hosie MB ChB 1944
FRCOG 1976
sen regist obst & gyn univ coll hosp Jamaica 1959–60; Hammersmith hosp: sen regist obst & gyn 1963–65; Harrogate & dist hosp: consult. obst & gyn from 1965

HUTCHESON Herbert Cecil MA 1929
head: Westerton p s Aber 1966–69, Mile End p s Aber 1969–73; retd

HUTCHINSON Ralph Thomas MA 1948

HUTCHISON Alexander Cantlay MA 1936 *BSc 1938 PhD 1945
tech man. ICI HQ Lond 1960–62; Ardeer: gen

man. silicones dept 1962–69, plan. man. Nobel div 1969–71; man. dir BOH Chemicals Poole from 1971

HUTCHISON Charles Alexander *MA 1922
no longer on GC reg

HUTCHISON Charles Strachan *BSc 1955
PhD(Malaya) 1966 FGS FIMM
oilfield geol Fyzabad Trinidad 1955–57; univ of Malaya: asst lect Singapore 1957–58, lect Kuala Lumpur 1958–67, asst prof Kuala Lumpur 1967–77; prof univ of Kansas USA 1970–71; prof applied geol univ of Malaya Kuala Lumpur from 1977
m Kuala Lumpur 5.7.60 Ann Chan d of Chan Poh, Negri Sembilan Malaysia

HUTCHISON or Ogilvie, Edith Mary MA 1935
teacher: Liv 1959–63, Aber 1963–70; retd; resid Weymouth

HUTCHISON or Norbrook, Eleanor Isobel Margaret *MA 1939
teacher Nigeria 1957–59
resid Bletchingdon

HUTCHISON Gordon MB ChB 1930
d Kintyre 13.5.71

HUTCHISON Laura Ann MA 1939
teacher Ashley Rd s Aber from 1952

HUTCHISON or Chater, Margaret BSc 1928 *1929
resid Aberystwyth

HUTCHISON Robert Nicholson MA 1954 Dip Ed 1955
d Scalloway 2.2.62 *AUR* XXXIX 386

HUTCHISON Thomas Mundie BSc(eng) 1936
CEng FIMechEng 1939 FIAgrEng 1948
MBIM 1950 FIMC 1960
Urwick, Orr & Ptnrs: India, NZ, Malawi, Turkey, Nigeria, Ceylon, Kenya 1967–76; private practice from 1976

HUTTON Agnes Forbes *MA 1934
teacher Notre Dame h s Battersea 1961–75; retd; resid Abergavenny

HUTTON Marjorie Smith MA 1928

HUTTON Stewart William Reid MB ChB 1944
DA 1966
g p: Walsall 1949–66, Ramsgate from 1967

HYND or Davidson, Margaret Elizabeth MA 1933
resid Huntly

HYND or Baird, Nora MA 1940
head Kinnoir s Huntly from 1953

HYTTEN Frank Eyvind PhD 1954
MD(Sydney) 1962 FRCOG 1970
pers prof human reprod physiol N'cle from 1971

IGGO Ainsley PhD 1954
FRSE 1962 DSc(Edin) 1963
Locke res fell. Royal Society 1960–62
prof vet physiol Edin from 1962; visiting prof Kyoto univ Japan 1970, guest prof Heidelberg 1972; dean vet fac Edin 1974–77

IHSANULLAH Mohammed BSc(agr) 1923

ILLINGWORTH Keith BSc(for) 1953 *1954

IMLACH Alexander Robert BSc(eng) 1944
FIEE 1965 CEng 1965
sub lieut RN 1944–46; various eng posts elect. generating boards SW England 1946–56; reactor eng man. AEA Thurso from 1956
m Dartmouth 1.9.46 Audrey E. Le Blanc

IMLACH or Reid, Jeannie Murray MA 1947
teacher Bervie s Inverbervie from 1960

IMLAH Gertrude MA 1930

IMLAH Keith Cameron BL 1949
Lond: leg. asst 1955–67, asst leg. advis 1967–73, sen asst leg. advis 1973–77, comp secy/leg. advis from 1977
m Lond 21.12.63 Marjorie Harrington 2nd off. WRNS d of William C. H.

IMLAY or Agrell, Jean Elspeth *BSc 1933
mineralogist Tube Investments res inst Hinxton, near Cambridge 1955–60, res asst dept min petr Cantab 1969–76; Russian translator

IMLAY or Muirhead, Joan Betty *BSc 1933 PhD 1938
resid Grahamstown S. Af

IMLAY Joice Margaret MB ChB 1944
g p Manc

IMPER Albert David BSc(agr) 1924 PhD 1928
d Edin 18.5.71 *AUR* XLIV 320

IMPER or Gordon, Lilian Clara MA 1949
prin teacher Renfrew; resid Milngavie

IMPEY Cecil Vernon MB ChB 1906

IMRAY Herbert Alexander MB ChB 1954
g p Portree/Callander 1958–62; m o Fiji and Gilbert and Ellice Is 1962–71; regist psych Craig Dunain hosp Inv 1972–75, med asst psych from 1975

INGERSENT Kenneth Arthur BSc(agr) 1949
lect econ Nott from 1970
m Allestree Derby 31.8.60 Elizabeth M. Sadler BA(Oxon) d of Wilfred J. S. Derby

INGLIS Alexander MA 1926
d Banff 12.9.73 *AUR* XLV 319

INGLIS Douglas Johnstone BSc(eng) 1949 *1950
man. AST div Nat Welding comp Montreal 1957–

61; man. pollution control div Stenberg-Flygt AB Montreal/Stamford USA 1961–71; lect eng Aberd from 1971

INGLIS or Muller, Jean Elizabeth Winton MB ChB 1938
FFACS 1954
m o i/c nurs staff Groote Schur hosp Capetown 1958–70, part time m o from 1970

INGLIS or Muir, Jean Milne MA 1955
teacher: maths Banff acad 1956–58, maths Jedburgh g s from 1970 and asst prin guid from 1977

INGLIS Margaret Rose MB ChB 1948
MRCPsych 1972
consult. psychiat Ailsa hosp Ayr from 1964

INGLIS William Grant *BSc 1953 DSc 1965
Adelaide, Aust: dir S Aust museum 1968–70, dir environ & conserv 1972–76, permanent head D o E 1976

INGRAM Agnes Matheson MA 1926

INGRAM Anne MA 1952 Dip Ed 1953
teacher Colegio San Silvestre Lima, Peru 1958–62 and from 1969
m Lima 22.12.61 Alfons Buck photogr bus. s of Ludwig B. Stuttgart Ger

INGRAM Bruce Millar MA 1953

INGRAM Charles Greig MB ChB 1951

INGRAM Edward Alexander MB ChB 1942
sen regist surg ARI 1959–63; g p Lerwick from 1963

INGRAM or Gilchrist, Elizabeth Evelyne *MA 1933
resid Barnes Lond

INGRAM George Alexander *BSc 1950
prin scient off. sc civ serv from 1964
m Aber 8.10.63 Margaret H. Youngson catering man. d of James Youngson MA 1921 *qv*

INGRAM George Bremner BSc(agr) 1948
teacher rural sc Llandrindod h s from 1972

INGRAM or Constable, Harriet Gordon MA 1900
no longer on GC reg

INGRAM Helen Smith *MA 1926
retd 1966; resid Aber

INGRAM Ian William MA 1946
teacher indep s till 1971; rep NFU Nott 1971–73; sales exec Lonsdale & Bartholomew printers Nott from 1973
d 1.2.81

INGRAM James Brown MA 1950 BD 1953
teachers' coll Bulawayo, Rhodesia: head div dept 1962–65, acting then asst vice-prin 1964–65; lect inst of educ UC Rhodesia, Salisbury 1965–70; lect City of Leeds & Carnegie coll of educ Leeds 1970–72; prin lect curric stud. Margaret McMillan coll of educ Bradford from 1972

INGRAM Katherine BSc 1940
resid Keith

INGRAM Lilias Jean *MA 1932
scient work MoD from 1939
d 13.1.76

INGRAM or Patterson, Margaret Angus MB ChB 1944
MBE 1962
med supt: Dooars & Darjeeling tea assoc hosp & surg to hosp 1957–61; surg i/c surg unit Tung Wah hosp Hong Kong 1964–73; consult. in neuro-electric therap Lond from 1972

INGRAM Peter Willoughby MB ChB 1934
FRCS 1960
retd 1969; resid Maidenhead

INGRAM William Fasken MB ChB 1925
d 28.2.64

INGRAM William Wilson MB ChB1912 *MD1919
FRACP 1938
retd; resid Sydney

INKSON or Slater, Elsie Lilian Blackhall BSc 1944
resid Manc

INKSON John Kerr *MA 1929
prin teacher mod lang Dingwall acad 1946–68; retd
d Inv 16.4.79

INKSON Robert Henry Ewen *BSc 1948
FRSS 1949 FIStat 1969
Macaulay inst for soil res Aber: prin scient off. 1963–68, head dept statist from 1968

INKSTER Davina MA 1916
own s at Peterculter 1940–61; interim work in small schools in Perthsh 1962–68; retd; resid Peterculter

INKSTER John MB ChB 1909 *MD 1913

INKSTER John Scott MB ChB 1946
Lond: member council assoc of anaest 1971–73, examiner final FFARCS examination from 1973; resid Gosforth N'cle-u-Tyne

INKSTER Mary MA 1909
d Poole 20.2.78

INKSTER or McMenemey, Robina MB ChB 1920 MD 1928

INNES Alexander Henry MB ChB 1952
Royal Cornhill hosp Aber: med asst 1964–74, consult. forensic psychiat from 1974

INNES or Jenkinson, Alice Mabel Lee MBChB1920
resid Towcester

INNES Annie MA 1922
retd 1967; resid Fraserburgh

INNES Cameron Roy MB ChB 1950
JP 1965
g p: Foyers 1963–67, Fort William from 1967
d Fort William 1.6.77 *AUR* XLVIII 107

INNES or Fischer, Catherine Donaldson MA 1951
resid Luseland Saskatchewan

INNES Charles John Alexander MA 1949
Cong ch min: Saughtonhall ch Edin 1960–69, Coatdyke ch Airdrie from 1969

INNES or Cockburn, Christine Rose MA 1934
lect LSE (Lond) 1943–66; soc affairs off. UN Geneva 1966–68; res off. internat soc security assoc ILO Geneva 1968–74, dir res and documentation sect. from 1975

INNES David BSc(agr) 1959
mech advis NAAS Silsoe 1965–68; farm. Fordoun from 1968

INNES or Farquharson, Elizabeth Ann Forbes MA 1945
resid Fyvie

INNES or Lyall, Elizabeth Hughina McDonald MA 1924
teacher Newburgh Aberdeensh 1943–64; retd

INNES or Mitchell, Elizabeth Jane MB ChB 1908
d Aber 19.8.74 *AUR* XLVI 107

INNES Eric Milner BSc 1935 MB ChB 1940
d Edin 7.11.78 *AUR* XLVIII 106

INNES Francis Lumsden Farquharson MB ChB 1941
consult. plastic surg Norwich from 1959

INNES George MB ChB 1950 DPH 1957 MD 1959
MRCPsych 1971 MFCM 1972
sen res fell. dept mental health Aberd 1959–64, lect 1964–68; sen lect dept commun med Aberd 1968–76, reader from 1976

INNES George Smith BSc 1930 *1931
OBE 1971
retd 1970; resid Esher

INNES Gordon *MA 1950
PhD(Lond) 1961
lect s of Oriental & African stud. Lond 1953–74, reader from 1974; visiting prof of ling Indiana univ Bloomington USA 1966–67

INNES Helen MA 1908
no longer on GC reg

INNES or Will, Helen Reid BSc 1913
resid Coventry

INNES Helen Watt MA 1933
no longer on GC reg

INNES Ian Adam BSc(mech eng) 1945 BSc(civ eng) 1948
proj man. UN surv geotherm resources in N Chile Santiago from 1967

INNES Ian Dunbar MB ChB 1943
VRD 1959 FRCGP 1970
g p Hull/part-time clin asst in dermat Hull RI from 1948; RNVR and RNR 1949–64; final rank surg lt cdr
d Hull 8.2.78 *AUR* XLVII 360

INNES Ian George MA 1911 BSc 1912 BSc(agr) 1913 MB ChB 1918 ᶜMD 1928
d 18.2.65 *AUR* XLI 147

INNES Ian Rome MB ChB 1937 *MD 1955
Manit: assoc prof dept pharm & therap 1960–64, prof from 1964/head of dept from 1967

INNES James MA 1898
no longer on GC reg

INNES James MA 1920 MB ChB 1924
g p: Hull 1928–39, Bournemouth 1939–60 (war serv RAF 1942–45); retd 1960; resid Farnham Common

INNES James Gilchrist MA LLB 1949
ptnr Wilsone & Duffus advoc in Aber from 1952

INNES James Thomson BSc(eng) 1945

INNES or MacDonald, Jane Helen MA 1932
teacher cent. s Peterhead 1948–59; resid Deskford
husb *d* Inverboyndie Banff 21.5.73

INNES or Bruce, Jane Lunan MA 1940

INNES or Law, Joanna Kean MA 1911
d Toronto 8.11.64 *AUR* XLI 55

INNES John *MB ChB 1924 DPH 1927 ᶜMD 1930
d 8.9.72 *AUR* XLV 127

INNES John BSc(eng) 1928 MB ChB 1937
d 23.12.72 *AUR* XLV 226

INNES John Lyall MA 1926 LLB 1933
d Lond 2.8.69 *AUR* XLIII 330

INNES John Robert Stephen MB ChB 1940
g p Aber from 1946 and m o Aber prison from 1949

INNES John William MA 1910 MB ChB 1915 *DPH 1919
FRSH 1951
retd; resid Thornhill
wife *d* 1972

INNES or Ross, Lizzie Paul MA 1911
d 10.3.65

INNES or Macpherson, Maggie Robertson MA 1909
d 22.8.64

INNES Margaret Eleanor MA 1931
retd 1974; resid Aber

INNES of Macpherson, Margaret Howat Pagan MA 1923
d Edin 2.5.79

INNES Margaret Jane MA 1928
retd 1968; resid Peterculter

INNES or Steel, Mary Margaret Shaw MA 1918
no longer on GC reg

INNES Maxwell BSc(eng) 1951

INNES Maxwell Alexander Allan MA 1952

INNES Norman Duncan MB ChB 1952
g p Aber from 1952

INNES or Chitty, Penuel Mary MB ChB 1924
resid Beckenham

INNES Robert *BSc 1953 PhD 1957

INNES Robert Alexander BSc(for) 1947
MRSFS 1950 MIFor(GB) 1951
for. comm Inv: div for. off. 1956–65, asst conserv 1965–70, conserv of for. from 1970

INNES Stephen George Begg MA 1946 *MB ChB 1951

INNES Thomas Christie MB ChB 1904
d N'cle-u-Tyne 15.8.64 *AUR* XL 394

INNES Thomas Christie MA 1931

INNES William MA 1940
JP 1972
dep rector Dunblane h s from 1962

INNES William BSc(agr) 1949
farm Kincardinesh from 1949

INSCH Audrey Gordon *MA 1955
PhD(Durh) 1958
teacher: Aber acad 1959–61, head Engl Grey Coat hosp Lond 1961–68; sen lect Stockwell coll Bromley from 1968

INSCH Herbert Saunders BCom 1926
gen man. (Scot.) Bowmaker Stirling 1962–68; retd; resid Gatehouse of Fleet

IRELAND Alfred James MB ChB 1914
no longer on GC reg

IRONS William MA 1919 BSc(agr) 1919
no longer on GC reg

IRONSIDE Alastair Grant MB ChB 1953
FRCPE 1976
sen regist thoracic med united Oxford hosps 1963–64; sen lect clin epidemiology Glas 1964–66; consult. phys infect. diseases Monsall hosp Manc/part time lect commun med Manc; smallpox consult. DHSS from 1966
d Marple 24.8.80 *AUR* XLIX 70

IRONSIDE Basil MA 1926
d Aber 8.9.69 *AUR* XLIII 330

IRONSIDE Charles Edward MA 1919
D Phil
d Florida –.4.80

IRONSIDE David George BSc(agr) 1922
d 16.10.62 *AUR* XL 86

IRONSIDE Eva Constance MA 1913 MB ChB 1916
d Torbay 8.3.72 *AUR* XLIV 428

IRONSIDE or Shepherd, Jane Ann Sherrin MA 1913
d Forfar 12.11.76

IRONSIDE or Rixon, Margaret MA 1950
Grays Essex: teacher Little Thurrock p s 1961–64; head mus Deneholm p s 1966–73; remed teacher E Tilbury from 1974

IRONSIDE Marjory MA 1925
retd 1967; resid Glasg

IRONSIDE or Cox, Nellie Burns MA 1906
no longer on GC reg

IRONSIDE Redvers Nowell *MB ChB 1922
d Eastbourne 18.7.68 *AUR* XLIII 81

IRONSIDE or Merkley, Rosemary Elizabeth MA 1944

IRONSIDE Wallace MB ChB 1940 MD 1954
FRANZCP 1964 FRCPsych 1971 FRACP 1971
univ of Rochester NY: Fulbright res schol 1959, sen Buswell fell. 1959, fell. found. fund for res in psychiat 1960; Leverhulme res fell. All India inst of med sc India 1971 asst prof psychiat univ of Rochester NY 1959–61, found. prof psych med: univ of Otago NZ 1962–69, Monash univ Aust from 1969

IRONSIDE William Bickerstaff BSc(agr) 1953
farm. near Wick from 1954
m(2) Inv 5.10.63 M. A. Moir NDD

IRONSIDE William McIntosh Sinclair MB ChB 1945
consult. ENT Huddersfield from 1959

IRVINE Alastair Munro BSc(eng) 1952
MIEE 1960 AMBIM 1965
sen eng (constr) NSHEB Aber area from 1962

IRVINE Archibald Clive MA 1913 MB ChB 1917 MD 1925 DD 1958
d Nairobi 7.6.74 *AUR* XLVI 107 & 235

IRVINE Charles Ross *BSc 1930 MA 1931
retd 1971; resid Basingstoke
d 21.1.79 *AUR* XLVIII 231

IRVINE Elizabeth Fergusson MA 1916
study and writing 1946–63; author of *A pioneer of the New Psychology* publ 1963; resid Suffolk

IRVINE George Bruce BSc(eng) 1945
dep head Sandwick jun h s Shetland from 1974
m Bigton Shetland 29.12.59 Catherine M. S. Manson teacher d of Thomas M. Maywick

IRVINE James Geddes Greig *MA 1946

IRVINE Jane Elizabeth MA 1947
teacher: Prince Rupert s BFES Wilhelmshaven W Ger 1960–63, asst prin Engl Northfield acad Aber from 1963

IRVINE John Locke MA 1915
d 8.6.69

IRVINE or Newman, Lilian Lloyd *MA 1924
d Cambridge 13.5.73 *AUR* XLV 225 & 322

IRVINE or Barrie, Margaret Elizabeth Mary MA 1948

IRVINE Mary Edith MA 1930
retd; resid Portknockie

IRVINE Sidney Herbert *MA 1954 MEd 1956
PhD(Lond) 1964 Fell. Eugenics Soc 1968
FBPsS 1974
lect educ: univ coll Rhodesia 1959–64, Brist 1964–67; visiting schol. educ testing serv Princeton NJ USA 1967–68; assoc prof educ/psych univ W Ont 1968–71; Brock univ Ont 1971: prof/dean coll of educ 1971–76, prof educ res from 1976

IRVINE William Alexander MB ChB 1955
d Inv 22.4.77 *AUR* XLVII 360

IRVINE-FORTESCUE James William *MA 1937
CA 1948 JP 1957 DL (Kincardine) 1975
Kt Order of St Lazarus of Jerusalem 1975
councillor Kincardine c c/chmn Lower Deeside dist council 1964–73

IRWIN William Knox MB ChB 1908 MD 1913
d 18.7.73

ISBISTER Samuel BSc(agr) 1934
dep chief insp DAFS 1960–71; retd; resid Culbokie
wife *d* 1960
m(2) Edin 21.4.62 Mary M. M. Anderson teacher
d Culbokie 9.12.79 *AUR* XLVIII 442

IZATT or Miller, Annie Milne MA 1925
resid Carluke

IZATT or Troup, Ella Shand MA 1922
teacher Greenock 1949–67
husb *d* 1.8.48

JACK or McBain, Annie May MB ChB 1922
husb *d* 1964
resid Inv
d –.2.79

JACK David BSc(agr) 1954
farm. Jackstown,Rothienorman from 1963; also joint man. dir Jacks drapers/outfitters Peterhead
m Aber 1.9.62 Isabell C. Cowie MA 1960 *qv*

JACK Dorothy Elizabeth *MA 1930
retd 1968; resid Stonehaven

JACK or Christie, Elizabeth Turner MA 1926
d Glasg 12.9.80

JACK Ernest Munro MB ChB 1945
MRCGP 1962
g p Bolton from 1948; serving brother St John from 1967

JACK George MA 1890
no longer on GC reg

JACK George Polson MA 1936
d Edin 16.5.64 *AUR* XL 401

JACK or Falconer, Georgina Sutherland MA 1941
teacher Elgin acad: Fr 1960–72, prin guid from 1972

JACK Helen Margaret MA 1923
no longer on GC reg

JACK or Fraser, Jean Elizabeth MA 1935

JACK or Griffith, Jessie Munro *MA 1921
teacher part-time St Margaret's s Aber 1944–49; resid Aber

JACK John Argo *MA 1926
no longer on GC reg

JACK Margaret Helen Bruce MA 1936
retd 1979; resid Grantown-on-Spey

JACK Marjorie MA 1955
m Cairns

JACK or Miller, Millicent Isobel MA 1923
resid Mosstodloch Fochabers

JACK William Begg MA 1923
d 27.11.71 *AUR* XLIV 320

JACKSON James BSc(agr) 1951
farm. Brechin from 1951
m Colliston Angus 26.10.66 Maureen Geddes

JACKSON James Archie Donaldson BSc(for) 1947
MBE 1964
conserv of for. N Nigeria 1959–70, for. advis (Brit tech aid) Ethiopia from 1971

JACKSON Jessie Elizabeth Catherine MA 1944
secy loc govt Inv from 1952

JACKSON John Harrison MA 1928 BSc 1930

JACKSON or Norrie, Mary Baird MA 1926

JACKSON Philip Mott MB ChB 1940
JP St Andrew Jamaica 1972
m o and police surg Kingston Jamaica 1962–64; retd col med serv 1964; private pract St Andrew Jamaica from 1965

JACKSON Robert Hay BSc(eng) 1953
d Sabah Borneo 28.12.73 *AUR* XLV 450

JACKSON Tom Forbes *MA 1915
d 27.3.70

JACKSON William Welsby PhD 1933

JACZYNSKA Alexandra *MA 1953

JAFFRAY or Morrison, Agnes Baxter MA 1929
resid Aber

JAFFRAY Alastair Blackburn MB ChB 1932
d Rayton 21.6.60 *AUR* XXXVIII 598

JAFFRAY Annie Ada MA 1908
no longer on GC reg

JAFFRAY David Mitchell *MA 1939
d Lond 1976 *AUR* XLVI 417

JAFFRAY or Eyre-Smith, Fanny Ewerdine MA 1918
no longer on GC reg

JAFFRAY Isabella MA 1911
d Glasg 26.10.71 *AUR* XLIV 316

JAFFRAY or Pollock, Jessie Isobella MA 1916
no longer on GC reg

JAFFRAY Kathleen Mary MA 1924
d 20.2.72

JAFFRAY Reginald Andrew Baxter MB ChB 1926
retd; resid Bromley

JAFFRAY Victor Wallace MA 1940
LLB(Edin)
d 8.7.77

JAFFREY Leslie James BSc 1949 *1950
MICE 1963
prin scient off. Hydraulics res stat Wallingford from 1961

JAMES Alexander Souter *BSc(eng) 1954
consult. Lond 1958–60; man. UK branch site investig comp Aust 1960–63; prin A. S. James Pty geotech eng Melbourne from 1963

JAMES Catherine Masson MA 1938
teacher Forres acad 1956–77; retd

JAMES or Shivas, Catherine Philip MA 1930
resid Peterculter

JAMES Edward MB ChB 1923 [c]MD 1928
consult. phys to Romford and Chelmsford hosps till 1970; p/t consult. in infect. diseases Chelmsford 1954–70; retd; resid West Mersea

JAMES John Courtenay BD 1907
no longer on GC reg

JAMESON Alexander Pringle *BSc 1911 DSc 1920

JAMESON William Wilson MA 1905 *MB ChB 1909 *MD 1912 LLD 1940
d Lond 18.10 62 *AUR* XL 75

JAMIE Elizabeth Davidson MB ChB 1955
DMJ(Lond) 1965 Member Inner Temple 1971 LLB(Lond) 1972
Lond: ophth Clerkenwell med mission Haxton group of hosps and clin, clin asst eye dept Westminster, Great Ormond St. and Royal eye hosps from 1959

JAMIESON Alan *BSc 1952
prin res fell. MAFF fisheries lab Lowestoft 1965–69, prin scient off. 1969–74, individual merit award graded sen prin scient off. from 1974

JAMIESON Alexander MB ChB 1937
DPH(Edin) 1962 MFCM 1972
Edin corp: asst m o p h dept 1962–66, sen m o 1966–74, sen m o and designated m o Lothian health board commun health dept from 1974

JAMIESON Alexander Slessor *MA 1926
retd 1970; resid Edin
m –.7.31

JAMIESON or Thompson, Elizabeth BSc 1934
teacher phys Ardrossan acad 1968–72; resid W Kilbride

JAMIESON Frederick *BSc 1950

JAMIESON George Grant *MA 1920
d Nairn 9.9.73

JAMIESON George Stuart MA 1920

JAMIESON or Warrander, Irene Patricia MA 1953
teacher maths Aber: Middle s 1963–66, Powis acad from 1966

JAMIESON John MA 1923
d Edin 2.3.67 *AUR* XLII 185

JAMIESON John BSc(agr) 1929
retd 1972; resid Ollaberry Shetland

JAMIESON John Robert MA 1901 BSc 1907
no longer on GC reg

JAMIESON Julia Ann BSc 1924
retd 1962; resid Stonehaven
d Stonehaven 18.7.80

JAMIESON or Stephen, May Keith *MA 1941
form mistress Blairmore prep s for boys Glass from 1959

JAMIESON Michael Sutherland *MA 1953
lect Engl: Keele 1960–62, Sus from 1962; warden Falmer House Sus 1962–72; fell. Salzburg Seminar in Amer stud. 1965; visiting prof Facolta di Magistero univ of Rome 1969; res Berg collection NY 1973

JAMIESON Ruth Campbell *MA 1917
retd 1960; resid Banchory

JAMIESON Samuel PhD 1949

JAMIESON or Brylowskie, Violet *MA 1942

JAMIESON William George MA 1921
no longer on GC reg

JAMIESON-CRAIG Catherine Isabella Anderson MA 1915 MB ChB 1927 MD 1934
d 27.3.60

JAPPY or Mitchell, Jeannie MA 1941

JAPPY John Flett BSc(eng) 1943

JARDINE or Taylor, Helen Margaret (Lady) MB ChB 1920 MD 1937 LLD 1966
JP Aber
chmn NE Scot. reg nurse trg comm 1952–72; resid Edin
husb, Sir Thomas M. Taylor, Principal Aberd, *d* 1962

JARVIE Elizabeth Ellis MA 1941

JEANS Henry Williams MB ChB 1904
no longer on GC reg

JEFFREY David Sinclair BSc(for) 1953

JEFFREY Florence Winifred MA 1922
no longer on GC reg

JEFFREY John Colin Somerville MB ChB 1949
MBE 1945
g p Lochgilphead from 1959

JENKINS Annie *MA 1922

JENKINS Margaret Wilson MA 1955
m Chisholm

JENKINS May Chalmers MA 1940
journalist Aber Journals from 1968

JENKINS William Leyshon *BSc 1952

JERMEY Kevin Gerard *MEd 1952
MIM 1962
asst to gen man. Tracy petr comp Kirkuk Iraq 1958–59; comm man. of subsid Darlington Chem 1959–64; Lond: MSL consult. 1965–67, Rank Organis exec apptments advis 1967–70, assoc dir Canny Bowen & Associates 1971–73, dir Berndtson Internat from 1973

JESSAMINE Alexander Gordon MB ChB 1948
Ottawa: sen phys royal Ottawa san 1959, head dept med 1961–68; phys i/c Ottawa reg tuberculosis prevn serv Ontario M o H from 1968

JESSAMINE Austin Steele MB ChB 1939
MRCGP
g p Aber from 1939
d Aber 15.3.81

JESSIMAN James Brown MB ChB 1922 MD 1933
retd; resid Bromley
d Bromley 27.2.79 *AUR* XLVIII 228

JESSIMAN or Ward, Janetta Mary Gray MA 1915
no longer on GC reg

JEWERS John Milne Everett MB ChB 1941
consult. surg W Dorset group of hosps from 1965

JOCKEL Charles Marshall MB ChB 1946
g p Bolton 1949–65, Tawa NZ from 1965

JOHNSON Allan BD 1952
no longer on GC reg

JOHNSON or Semple, Dorothy MA 1951

JOHNSON Edward MB ChB 1908
d 3.6.63

JOHNSON Francis Hernaman- MB ChB 1904
no longer on GC reg

JOHNSON James Charles Manson *MA 1929
no longer on GC reg

JOHNSON Joan Mortimer MA 1949
m Chopin

JOHNSON Laurence Leask BSc 1922
resid Lerwick

JOHNSON Louis MA 1955
Shetland: relief teacher Lerwick, Fetlar, Yell 1956–57; teacher j s s Urafirth 1957–62; head North Roe p s from 1962
m Lerwick 6.4.59 Lilias M. Hawkins teacher d of Reginald C. H. Sandness Shetland

JOHNSON or Ensor, Mary Kinross MB ChB 1945
FPA Bishop's Stortford from 1952; clin asst venereol Lond from 1974

JOHNSON Maurice Buchan MB ChB 1903
no longer on GC reg

JOHNSON Rosemary Agnes *MA 1955
teacher Engl Torry s s Aber 1957–61
m Aber 27.12.60 William P. Baxter DA(Edin) artist/teacher s of George B. Aber

JOHNSTON Adam MB ChB 1906
d Aber 5.3.66 *AUR* XLII 82

JOHNSTON or Reid, Adiell Durward *MA 1923
resid Strathdon

JOHNSTON Alexander MA 1925
pres Retd Teachers' Assoc (Scot.) 1977–79
retd 1965; resid Dumfries

JOHNSTON or Mowat, Aline Cameron MA 1949
teacher Wick: p s 1966–70, mus s s 1970–78; full time mus spec for four prim. s in Wick from 1978

JOHNSTON Anthony BSc 1942 *1943
FIBiol 1970
Kew: asst dir commonwealth mycological inst 1965–68, dir from 1968

JOHNSTON David William Douglas MA 1948
C o S min Auldearn and Ardclach 1963–76; moderator Inv presb 1973–74; county c Nairnsh from 1969
d Auldearn 28.11.76

JOHNSTON or Rice, Dorothy Margaret MA 1926
d Doncaster 28.9.69 *AUR* XLIII 330

JOHNSTON Edward Alexander MA 1923 MB ChB 1927 DPH 1931
retd 1967; resid Inv

JOHNSTON Edwin *MA 1923
d Lond 28.1.69 *AUR* XLIII 212

JOHNSTON or Höy, Elizabeth Marguerite Angela MA 1944
Norway: translator Kristiansand from 1955, lect tech Engl Air Force tech coll from 1965

JOHNSTON Elizabeth Russell BSc 1940

JOHNSTON Elizabeth Whyte MA 1948

JOHNSTON or Michie, Ellenina Catherine MA 1952
teacher Kirkcaldy 1959–60; resid Aber from 1967

JOHNSTON George Andrew MA 1912
d 13.8.66 *AUR* XLI 337

JOHNSTON or Manson, Helen MA 1940
resid Peterhead

JOHNSTON Henry Watt MA 1911
d Bishop Auckland 15.1.74 *AUR* XLVI 107

JOHNSTON or Thompson, Isabella MA 1935
teacher Aber 1940–46, 1957–74; retd
husb *d* 1969

JOHNSTON Isabella Ivy *MA 1928
prin teacher Fr/Ger and woman advis Banchory acad; retd 1966; resid Insch

JOHNSTON James Bruce MB ChB 1947
d Eastbourne 24.4.79 *AUR* XLVIII 233, XLIX 70

JOHNSTON James Cooper MA 1911
no longer on GC reg

JOHNSTON James Douglas MB ChB 1953
d –.11.66

JOHNSTON James Weston BSc 1950

JOHNSTON James William BSc(agr) 1929
farm. Fintray Dyce from 1948

JOHNSTON or Marr, Janet MB ChB 1925
d Lond 13.5.73 *AUR* XLV 319

JOHNSTON Janetta Maria MA 1933
teacher Keith g s 1957–68; retd

JOHNSTON or Hedges, Janey Alison Donald *MA 1948 *EdB 1951
resid Didcot

JOHNSTON John MB ChB 1909
d Aber 31.12.62 *AUR* XL 79

JOHNSTON John Edward MA 1922 *1923
no longer on GC reg

JOHNSTON or Grieve, Kathleen Zia BSc 1941
BBC tech staff Aber 1941–44; nat pres C of S Woman's Guild 1966–69; organis BBC's Scot. telephone referral centre for adult literacy from 1975

JOHNSTON Margaret Cadger MA 1933
retd 1971; resid Fraserburgh

JOHNSTON Margaret Helen MA 1955
m Stuart

JOHNSTON or Potts, Margaret Taylor BSc 1955
resid Caton

JOHNSTON or Reid, Mary *MA 1939
resid Inv

JOHNSTON or Murray, Mary Elizabeth MA 1924
resid Aber

JOHNSTON or Esslemont, Mary Gray MA 1952
teacher; Aber 1953–56; Keithhall from 1956

JOHNSTON or Grover, Mary Ross MA 1936
teacher Hanover St p s Aber 1938–74; retd
husb *d* 1966
m(2) Aber 30.3.66 Harold J. Boorer headmaster s of Walter J. B. Wolverhampton

JOHNSTON or Birss, May MA 1941

JOHNSTON Neil Campbell MA 1944 *MEd 1948
prin teacher mod lang Bankhead acad Aber 1961–67; advis mod lang Aber educ comm 1967–75; asst dir educ Grampian reg from 1975

JOHNSTON Robert Neilson ***MB ChB 1943 MD 1953**
FRCPE 1963 FRCP 1972
hon sen lect respir diseases Dund from 1965
m(2) Aber 14.5.64 Elizabeth M. Semple capt WRAC d of Robert Semple MB ChB 1910 *qv*

JOHNSTON Thomas BSc(agr) 1954

JOHNSTON Violet Elspet Lawson MA 1933
retd 1970; resid Fraserburgh

JOHNSTON William Forsyth MA 1930
head Portgordon j s s 1963–71; retd; resid Buckie

JOHNSTONE Albert James *MA 1936
Inverurie acad: prin teacher maths from 1962, asst head from 1972; retd 1977

JOHNSTONE Alexander **MA 1914 MB ChB 1916 DPH 1920**
no longer on GC reg

JOHNSTONE Alexander Fordyce MB ChB 1947
FRCPsych 1974
consult. psychiat Craig Dunain hosp Inv from 1957

JOHNSTONE Charles George MA 1934
head Buchanhaven p s Aberdeensh from 1958; retd 1975

JOHNSTONE George Erskine MB ChB 1939

JOHNSTONE or Ogilvie, Helen Macleod MA 1916
d Liverpool 31.8.74 *AUR* XLVI 107

JOHNSTONE or Williams, Irene Constance **MA 1934**

JOHNSTONE James George MB ChB 1913
no longer on GC reg

JOHNSTONE James Hugh *MA 1950
Inv royal acad: prin teacher geog 1960–71, dep rector from 1971

JOINER Henry MA 1904
d Meigle 17.4.66 *AUR* XLII 82

JOINER John Herschel MA BSc 1925
CA firm Glasg 1925–34; Lond: statist 1934–41, CA asst 1941–46, ptnr 1946–73, sole ptnr from 1973

JOLLY or McKinnon, Elsie McKenzie MA 1933

JOLLY Eric James MB ChB 1923
d Huntingdon 12.1.68 *AUR* XLII 360

JOLLY Flora Jessie MA 1931
retd 1967; resid Aber

JOLLY George Mann BSc 1942 *1947
market gardening Skye 1958–61; statist (prin scient off. grade) ARC unit of statist: Aberd 1961–66, Edin from 1966

JOLLY Robert Alexander *MA 1931
d Bampton 21.3.74

JOLLY William Crockart *MA 1946
teacher maths Mackie acad Stonehaven from 1955
m Aber 11.8.66 Elizabeth J. Goddard secy d of James S. G. Aber

JONES Benjamin Wignall MB ChB 1917
no longer on GC reg

JONES Bronwen Jean *MA 1935
teacher Craig-y-nos prep s Swansea 1936–38; Cardiff: pers man. Gripoly Mills 1939–41, caseworker fam welfare assoc 1961–66, soc worker educ dept 1966–73; retd
m Cardiff 18.10.40 Herbert S. W. Jones chartered marine and mech eng s of William M. J. Resolven

JONES David Arthen PhD 1951
d Aber 11.11.75

JONES Joan Mary Glyn *MA 1955

JONES John Gareth Watkin PhD 1955
prin scient off. Grassland Res Inst Hurley Maidenhead 1965–70; sen res fell. dept agr R'dg 1970–75; sen lect dept agr R'dg from 1975
m Dolgellau Merioneth 30.6.73 Hilary A. Evans MA(Edin) lib d of William G. E., MBBS(Lond), Dolgellau

JONES Mair Lewys MB ChB 1951
g p Aberdulais 1957–59; resid Hamilton Mass USA
m 24.9.59 Gwyn Walters BA BD PhD(Edin) prof theol Mass USA

JONES or Humphrys, Margaret Irvine MA 1946

JONES Marion Gwyneth Cornwall MA 1920
retd 1957; resid Ilkley
d Ilkley 10.5.77

JONES or Hatch, Megan Owen Ceiron MA 1942

JONES or Watkins or Le Moine, Menna Owen Ceiron **MB ChB 1940**
FACCP
phys Oxford reg centre Woodstock Ontario 1960–77; retd

JONES or Buchanan, Nina Roberta Ceiron **MA 1951**

JONES Thomas BSc 1950
d Aber 25.8.65 *AUR* XLI 251

JONES William Park MA 1926
d Aber 26.1.63 *AUR* XL 205

JORDAAN William Petrus MB ChB 1921

JORDAN David Alma BSc(for) 1953
MIFor 1956 MA(Cantab) 1961 AIWSc 1963
Hull: dir Riplington Estates from 1951; dir Anlaby

Estates from 1963; dir Ferriby Construction Co from 1964; bldg surv for Alma Jordan 1959–73; dir South Hunsley Marketing Combine from 1973; man. dir Alma Jordan (Builders) from 1976 and (Farms) from 1975; dir Shawland Vegetable Growers from 1976
m Kirkella 2.6.36 Sheila J. Clark bank cashier d of Donald C. Hull

JOSLIN Anthony BSc(for) 1955
Dean Glos: asst educ off. 1963–68, dist off. from 1968
m Weston-under-Penyard 3.9.70 Barbara M. Bevan d of Francis J. B. Ross-on-Wye

JOSS or Brister, Alison Patricia MA 1953

JOSS or Cunningham, Dorothy Mackintosh MA 1950

JOSS George Smith MB ChB 1950
FRCSE 1960 FRSM member: Brit Assoc of Plastic Surg, Fr Soc Plastic et Reconstn Surg, Europ Assoc of Maxillo-Facial surg
sen regist plastic surg Middx hosp/Mt Vernon centre 1960–64 plastic surg: consult. United Norwich hosps Ipswich and E. Suffolk gen hosp from 1964, hon consult. Addenbroke's hosp Cambridge 1964–69, hon consult. US Air Force in Britain from 1965

JOSS or Lawrence, Margaret Robertson MA 1933
no longer on GC reg

JOSS William Taylor Barron MB ChB 1923
retd 1960; resid Edwalton
d –.2.73

JOYNER Charles MA 1915
no longer on GC reg

JOYNT Geoffrey Henry MEd 1951

JUNOR or Mackenzie, Mary Paterson MA 1930

JUPP or Wilson, Alice Marion MA 1923
no longer on GC reg

KABATA Zbigniew BSc 1955 PhD 1959 DSc 1966
parasitology: marine lab DAFS Aber 1955–67, dept environ fisheries and marine serv Nanaimo BC Canada from 1967

KAINAN (Ibrahim) Sasson Yacov BSc(eng) 1949
sen prod. eng on A/C hydraulic components Israel A/C Indust from 1969
m Israel 5.2.59 Evette Ben-Shlomo teacher d of Obadia B-S Kiriat Ono Israel

KANE or Collier, Mary Anne MA 1933

KANGA Burjorji Sorabji MB ChB 1916 MD 1919
FRIPHH(Lond) 1929
resid Bombay

KAY Margaret Horne MA 1909
d Elgin 24.1.72 *AUR* XLIV 427

KAY or Williams, Valerie Margaret Mary MA 1950 ᶜMB ChB 1955
m o cytology unit path. dept Aber

KAY William Hunter MB ChB 1915

KEAN Helen Margaret MA 1952
teacher: Muirfield p s Aber 1959–62, Sunnybank p s Aber 1963–66, maths Llywn-y-Bryn girls' g s Swansea 1967–69, phys Lanark g s from 1969
m Aber 26.7.61 Stewart Murray BSc 1966 *qv*

KEAY John *MA 1919
d 4.4.76

KEAY Margaret Elizabeth MA 1949 MB ChB 1955
g p: Birm 1961–72, Gloucester from 1972
m Sutton Coldfield 23.10.60 Chris P. Van Zyl BSc (O F State) lect Birm s of Christian V. Z. Bloemfontein

KEIR Alexander MA 1905
m(2) Aber 8.4.61 Agnes T. C. Hall MA 1930 *qv*
d Aber 3.1.71 *AUR* XLIV 208

KEIR or Phelan, Isabella Bruce MA 1925
no longer on GC reg

KEIR James MA 1904
no longer on GC reg

KEIR Robert Macdougal Stewart MB ChB 1940
sen consult. anaest Dumfries and Galloway R. I. from 1951

KEIR Walter Alexander Stewart *MA 1947
sen lect Engl Aberd from 1971

KEITH Alexander *MA 1916 LLD 1967
farm. 1944–71; author *A Thousand Years of Aberdeen* 1972; resid Stonehaven
d Stonehaven 5.10.78 *AUR* XLVIII 103 & 61

KEITH Alexander McPherson MA 1931 MB ChB 1935
d Paisley 30.7.75 *AUR* XLV 324

KEITH David Tully *MA 1951
teacher Boddam p s 1964–67; head: Logie Coldstone p s 1967–71, Whitehills from 1971
m Lond 15.4.62 Winifred H. Hopgood shop man. d of Albert H. Muswell Hill

KEITH Donald Ritchie *MA 1938 *MEd 1945
teacher Powis acad, Torry acad 1966–79; retd

KEITH Elizabeth Margaret Jeannie MA 1928
retd 1968; resid Peterculter

KEITH Elizabeth Meston MA 1949
teacher Mearns acad Laurencekirk 1953–61 and from 1971
m Stonehaven 11.10.58 Alexander J. D. Nicoll consult. eng

KEITH Frederick Leonard MB ChB 1904 MD 1918
d Aboyne 23.3.70

KEITH or Cameron, Grace MA 1955

KEITH Ian Fyvie BSc(agr) 1948

KEITH James Duncan Lindsay *BSc(mech eng) 1935 BSc(elect eng) 1936
sen mech eng Merz & McLellan consult. eng from 1945
m Northwich 11.5.44 Edith M. P. Tharme army, lab asst d of Alfred C. T. Stourton

KEITH Marshall William MB ChB 1930 DPH 1932

KEITH or Hood, Mary Jane MA 1918
teacher sc/maths Glenrothes 1954–65; retd; resid Leslie

KEITH Nelson *MA 1926
d Abernethy 14.4.66 *AUR* XLII 88

KEITH William Brooks MB ChB 1906 MD 1914
d 13.5.63

KELBIE Emmanuel Buckland BSc(eng) 1955

KELLAS Arthur Roy Handasyde *MA 1936
counsellor HM Emb Tehran 1958–62; Imperial Defence Coll Lond 1963; counsellor HM Emb: Tel Aviv 1964–66, Kathmandu 1966–70, Aden 1970–72; High Commissioner Dar-es-Salaam 1973–75

KELLAS Derek Mario Mitchell BSc(for) 1938
d 17.2.68 *AUR* XLII 373

KELLAS George Duncan MA 1930 LLB 1932
solic and notary: war serv RAF 1941–45; commissioned Malta 1942; town clerk Inverurie/clerk to Garioch dist council 1946–75

KELLAS Henry Ronald MB ChB 1936
g p Swindon from 1948

KELLAS or Legge, Isabella Dey McDonald MA 1930

KELLAS James Forrest *MA 1920 *BD 1923
C o S min Durris 1958–66; moderator Synod of Aber 1964–65; retd
d Aber 9.1.77

KELLAS or Brand, Janetta Margaret MA 1929
retd 1972; resid Benwick

KELLAS John MA 1920 *1921 DD 1950
d Edin 12.11.67 *AUR* XLII 358

KELLAS Lorna Mary BSc 1943 *1947
resid Cambus o' May

KELLAS Robert MB ChB 1910
d Lismore NSW 1.1.66 *AUR* XLII 83

KELLAS Robert Lloyd MA 1947
head Arrochar p s Dunbartonsh from 1968

KELLOCK Alexander Moir MB ChB 1932
d 27.11.73

KELLY Francis Charles *BSc 1923 PhD 1926
FRSM 1937
commander of the Chilean Order of Merit 1969
retd 1971; resid Lond

KELLY George Carmichael *BSc 1923 MB ChB 1926 *MD 1930
CBE 1959 hon MA(Brist) 1964
sen admin m o SW reg hosp board 1947–65
resid Clevedon
d Clevedon 25.7.77

KELLY Mary Carmichael MA 1916
d Edin 15.2.76

KELLY Terence O'Neil Fraser MB ChB 1942

KELLY William MB ChB 1925
d Bexhill-on-Sea 23.5.75 *AUR* XLVI 323

KELMAN Emily Thom *MA 1933

KELMAN George Smith BL 1950
joint man. dir mech supplies Aber from 1969
d 3.10.81

KELMAN or Ray, Jane Thain MA 1936
teacher: Kittybrewster p s Aber 1937–45, Horley Surrey 1955–78

KELMAN John MA 1909 BSc 1911
no longer on GC reg

KELMAN or Macleod, Muriel Hay MA 1947
resid Oban

KELMAN or Shirreffs, Nan Cameron MA 1940
resid Aber

KELMAN Richard Cameron MA 1930
MIQ 1975
chmn and man. dir of companies in extractive indust including Shirman enterprises (Aber), Craigenlow Quarries, Road Seal associated with Tarmac Roadstone

KELMAN or Stewart, Shirley May BSc 1955
resid Downers Grove Illinois USA

KELSEY Vernon BSc 1953
res chem Coalite & Chem Prod. Chesterfield from 1956

KELSO Arthur Allardyce BSc(eng) 1948

KELSO Olga MA 1934
retd 1971; resid Stonehaven

KELTY Arthur BSc 1910
no longer on GC reg

KEMP or Macleod, Agnes Helen *MA 1943
Herts: head mod lang St Francis coll Letchworth 1964–72, dep head St Angelo's s Stevenage from 1973; dept chmn N Herts bench from 1973

KEMP Alastair BSc(eng) 1954

KEMP Alastair Taylor MA 1951
d Aber 26.2.76 *AUR* XLVII 215

KEMP or Huffam, Alice Rae BSc 1932 *1933
resid Cottingham

KEMP or McLaren, Alison McIntyre MA 1954

KEMP Annie MA 1905
no longer on GC reg

KEMP or Forbes, Charlotte Davidson MA 1923
teacher Engl Peterhead North j s s 1945–67
d Dunedin NZ 30.5.76

KEMP or Buckland, Ethel Elizabeth Mary MA 1942
resid Winchester

KEMP or Howell, Ethel Hope *MA 1913
d Aber 19.6.62 *AUR* XLI 55

KEMP or Alexander, Mabel MA 1929
resid Shrewsbury

KEMP or Rutherford, Margaret Cooper MB ChB 1942
part-time asst m o with Aber burgh publ health dept from 1964; retd

KEMP Margaret Ellen MA 1908
d Letchworth –.11.73

KEMP Marion Davina Sutherland *MA 1917
d Dufftown 24.9.72 *AUR* XLV 125

KEMP or Brodie-Browne, Marjorie Paterson *MA 1937
Leamington Spa: teacher Fr/Ger Leamington coll for girls, head mod lang dept from 1966–76; retd

KEMP or Stark, Mary Ann MA 1920
resid Whitburn

KEMP Moyra Strachan Mortimer MB ChB 1947
lect anat Aberd from 1966
m Aber 14.8.62 George W. Anderson

KEMP Nellie MA 1929

KEMP Robert *MA 1929
d Edin 25.11.67 *AUR* XLII 368

KEMP or Smith, Rose MA 1913
d Aber 19.3.69 *AUR* XLIII 210

KEMP Thomas Ian MB ChB 1952
g p Enfield from 1959

KENDALL Richard Haddon BSc(for) 1949

KENNEDY Agnes MA 1935
d Aber 23.9.65 *AUR* XLI 250

KENNEDY Alan Campbell BL 1954
Aber: prin leg. asst Town clerk's dept 1962–69, burgh proc fisc 1969–75; chief exec Gordon dist c from 1975

KENNEDY Margaret Chalmers MA 1938

KENNEDY or Grant, Margaret Jane *MA 1903 *1904
teacher Mortlach s s 1904–08
d Dufftown 9.10.75

KENNEDY or Kemp, Mary Elizabeth *MA 1911
d Aber 24.2.77

KENNEDY William Birnie MB ChB 1948
DPH(Edin) 1964
RAF dep s m o 18 group Pitreavie 1961–63; s m o: Persian Gulf Bahrein 1964–66, Manby 1966–69, Hockering 1969–73; member med board OASC Biggin Hill from 1975

KENNEDY William Duff *MA 1921
retd 1962; resid Fraserburgh

KENNEDY William John BSc(eng) 1952

KENNER Lionel *MA 1953

KENWORTHY Brian John PhD 1952
sen lect Ger Aberd from 1968

KEPPIE Joseph Lockhart *BSc(agr) 1953

KER or Gray, Audrey Isabella MA 1933 LLB 1934
d Ipswich 11.11.75

KERMACK William Ogilvie *MA *BSc 1918 DSc 1925
d 20.7.70 *AUR* XLIV 25

KERR or Anderson, Agnes Wishart *BSc 1940
teacher Aber h s for girls from 1965

KERR or Campbell, Alexandra Jean Robson *BSc 1930 PhD 1936
resid Winnipeg

KERR Cecilia Elizabeth Sommerville *MA 1940
teacher girls' g s Tunbridge from 1952

KERR or Deall, Christina Ferguson MB ChB 1923
d Nott 11.8.73 *AUR* XLV 318

KERR Colin Mackay MA 1903
no longer on GC reg

KERR Elizabeth MA 1922
retd 1962; resid Retford

KERR Fergus Gordon Thomson *MA 1953
ordained priest 1962; prior of Blackfriars Oxford from 1969

KERR George Robert England MB ChB 1933
d Inv 7.5.72 *AUR* XLV 128

KERR Ian McDougall MB ChB 1938
FRCP(C) 1975
NY, USA: dir St Lawrence county mental health serv Potsdam 1959–72; dep dir clin St Lawrence state hosp Ogdensburg 1972–76; retd
d New York 29.11.78

KERR or Nicol, Margaret Isobel Goldie MA 1940
resid Aber

KERR or Rae, Mary High MA 1942

KERRIN Albert Eric MA 1951
Stranraer: part time priest i/c St John's Stranraer with St Ninian's Portpatrick from 1970; asst teacher Lochan's p s 1970–71, dep head Park p s from 1971

KERRIN Daniel *MA 1921
teacher Engl Newton acad Ayr 1957–61; retd; resid Johannesburg

KERRIN John Charles MB ChB 1922 DPH 1925 *MD 1930
d Cheadle 29.6.68 *AUR* XLIII 83

KERRIN Richard Elual MA 1920
retd 1969; resid Kemnay

KESTNER Friedrich Julius Theodor *BSc(eng) 1939
FRGS 1970
prin scient off. hydraulics res stat DSIR Wallingford from 1958

KEYS or Harkins, Annie Elizabeth Martin MA 1925
resid Aber

KEYT Frederic Dudley Ross MB ChB 1920 DPH 1921
d 5.10.67

KIDD Andrew *MA 1925
retd BBC Lond 1964; lit edit. *Evening Argus* Brighton from 1964

KIDD Dorothy Rose MA BSc 1939
retd 1976; resid Milltimber Aber
member univ court Aberd from 1978

KIDD Douglas Alexander *MA 1934
prof classics univ of Canterbury Christchurch NZ from 1957; retd 1979

KIDD Francis Tosh MA 1928

KIDD James MA 1922
d Glasg 2.11.71 *AUR* XLIV 320

KIDD Neil Malcolm Lee BSc(agr) 1954
farm man.: Lincs 1957–58, Kincardinesh 1959–63, Fife 1963–70; farm. Angus from 1970
m Careston 14.7.61 Mary H. Falconer MA(Edin) teacher d of John M. F. Finavon

KIDD or Brown, Sheila Joan MA 1948
teacher: Steward st inf s Birm 1959–60, Ferryhill p s Aber from 1965

KIDD William Gordon *MA 1951

KILGOUR James Gray MA 1923
woollen manuf Aber from 1926

KILGOUR John Lowell MB ChB 1947
psc(Camberley) 1959 jssc(Latimer) 1964
MRCGP 1961 MFCM 1973
gen staff coll Camberley 1959–60 ADMS GHQ Farilf Singapore 1960–63; joint serv staff coll Latimer 1964–68; sen m o DHSS London; head internat health div DHSS from 1971/chief med advis FCO overseas dev admin from 1973

KILGOUR or Gill, Lilian Elsie MA 1924
teacher Engl/hist Methlick j s 1960–70; retd; resid Ellon
husb *d* 13.11.68
d Aber 30.6.78 *AUR* XLVIII 104

KILLAH James BSc 1949
AInstP 1969
Gordon s Huntly: spec asst 1959–73, prin teacher phys/chem from 1973

KILLOH Ronald Bruce MB ChB 1940 DPH 1947
smo Croydon 1958–64, Bournemouth 1964–67; NSW Aust: d m o h 1967–77; retd

KILOH James Robertson *MA 1951
prin teacher mod lang: Graeme h s Falkirk 1961–64, Trinity acad Edin 1964–73, asst head from 1973

KINDNESS or MacLean-Bryant, Elizabeth Brodie MacLean MA 1929

KINDNESS or Hutchison, Gladys MA 1926
resid Kirkcaldy

KINDNESS Jane *MA 1925
educ off. Sierra Leone 1944–45; head mod lang dept St Leonard's s St And 1959–66
m Lond 12.9.45 Geoffrey L. Jobling barrister/law off. col leg. serv/judge col judic serv s of Robert J. Celebes

KINDNESS Mary Allan MA 1930
teacher Ashley Rd s Aber 1956–68; retd

KINDNESS or Steel, Winifred Mary Allan MA 1914 MB ChB 1918 DPH 1921
retd 1972; resid Lond

KINEL Zofia Krystyna Wanda MB ChB 1950
m Laszewski

KING Andrew Palfrey BSc 1945

KING or Johns, Jessie Forrester BCom 1929

KING John Abercromby BSc(eng) 1952
m Aber 23.7.60 Prudence A. Young MA 1960 *qv*

KING John Alexander Hay BCom 1929
no longer on GC reg

KING or Lory, Mary Merrily MA 1948
resid Charlwood Horley Surrey

KING Norman William *MA 1949 Dip Ed 1953

KING Oswin James Albert BSc(eng) 1940
MICE 1948
vice-pres Eng Alcan Jamaica Mandeville 1956–75; proj dir Construction Alumina Plant Madrid 1975–78; ptnr/rep Alumina Co of Canada/Royal Dutch Shell Anaconda USA/Construction Alumina Plant Limerick from 1979
m Leicester 23.9.48 Margaret E. Skene

KINGHORN Alexander Manson MA 1947 *1950 PhD 1953
Kingston Jamaica: lect Engl univ coll of W I 1960–63, sen lect 1963–67, reader from 1967

KINGHORN Doris Elizabeth Catherine MA 1948
Peterhead acad: teacher 1951–66, spec asst 1966–72, prin guid/spec asst mod lang from 1972

KINGHORN John Mackie MA 1921
d 10.1.64

KINGSTON Brian BSc(for) 1955
Uganda: asst conserv. for. 1958–66, working plans off. Entebbe 1966–69, sen working plans off. 1969–74; FAO proj Turkey 1975–77, consult. in Thailand for FAO 1978

KINMOND David MA 1951 Dip Ed 1952
teacher: prin Engl Powis s s Aber 1966–68, dep head 1968, latterly head Summerhill acad Aber
d Aber 11.8.76 *AUR* XLVII 106

KINNAIRD Frank Ferguson MB ChB 1949
DObstRCOG 1953 DIH(Eng) 1970
DHSS: m o Yorks and Humberside reg 1968–73, sen m o Norcross Blackpool 1973–74, sen m o/secy (med attendance allowance board) HQ Lond from 1974

KINNELL John Dunford MB ChB 1954
regist anaest Southend gen hosp 1958–60; sen regist Leeds gen I 1961–65; Burroughs Wellcome fell. Calif L A 1963–64; consult. anaest York hosp from 1965
m Wetherby 18.8.65 Christine Demain physioth d of John C. D. Wetherby

KINSELLA William Peter MA 1952

KIRBY Oswald *MA 1896 BSc 1901
no longer on GC reg

KIRBY Percival Robson MA 1910
d Grahamstown SA 7.2.70 *AUR* XLIII 441

KIRK Dudley Walter MB ChB 1924
no longer on GC reg

KIRK or Barron, Gertrude Mary MA 1947
d Inverurie 29.3.65 *AUR* XLI 60

KIRK John Fraser MA 1951 BD 1955 PhD 1979
C of S min: St James' par ch Forfar 1962–70, publ *St James' Forfar* 1965, Morningside par ch Edin from 1970; sen county chaplain ACF Fife 1959–77, awarded Cadet Forces Medal and clasp

KIRKBY Norman Stephen BSc(eng) 1954

KIRKNESS Marion Hamilton MA 1911
d 21.4.64

KIRKWOOD John BSc(agr) 1926
retd; resid Lanark

KIRSNER Morris Harold MB ChB 1934
MD(NY)
d New York –.1.73

KIRTON Harry Morrison *BSc 1938

KIRTON Ian Wilkison BSc(for) 1951
teacher biol: Berwicksh h s Duns 1960–71, St Mungo's acad Alloa from 1971

KIRTON John MA 1911 MB ChB 1914 *MD 1921
d 12.5.64 *AUR* XL 397

KIRTON Ronald Alexander MB ChB 1951
g p Saundersfoot from 1968

KITCHIN Ian Douglas MB ChB 1930
d Westmorland 3.9.76 *AUR* XLVII 105

KLOKOW or Jamieson, Edna MA 1947

KNIGHT Colin Robert *MA 1931
sen Engl master The Latymer School Lond 1966–75; gentleman H.M. Chapels royal St James's Palace Lond 1946–68; retd

KNIGHT Kenneth William *MA 1952

KNOWLES or MacPhail, Elizabeta BSc 1947
teacher maths/sc Forrester s s Edin 1968–72

KNOWLES or Lawrie, Ella May MA 1954

KNOWLES James MB ChB 1949
LMCC(Can) 1958
g p Aurora Ontario from 1959; member nucleus comm on ethics CMA 1967–70; past pres: York County hosp Newmarket Ont, York County med soc

KNOWLES Mary BSc 1914
retd 1945; resid Edin

KNOWLES William Henderson BSc 1923
no longer on GC reg

KNOX Alexander Campbell White MB ChB 1913
d Lond 13.11.61 *AUR* XXX 275

KNOX Alexander Cruden *MA 1907
d Lond 20.6.64 *AUR* XL 345

KNOX Alexander Mavor MB ChB 1945
g p Kelso from 1953

KNOX Edward Wilson MA 1925
d Innellan 12.3.62 *AUR* XXXIX 383

KNOX George Boddie MB ChB 1954
g p: Glasg 1958–62, Beauly 1962–65, Isle of Lewis 1965–66, Braemar 1966–67, Vale of Leven from 1967
m Glasg 18.6.66 Catriona Mackay d of Charles M. Isle of Barra

KNOX or Shepherd, Harriet Doreen MA 1938

KNOX Joseph *BSc 1900 DSc 1907
d Glasg 14.9.66 *AUR* XLII 80

KNOX or Hill, Kathleen Mary MB ChB 1943
resid Lond

KNOX Robert Strachan *MA 1910
d Toronto 12.2.75

KOPERSKA or O'Dwyer, Janina Elizabeta Maria MB ChB 1950
regist cas off. Ballinasloe Galway 1962–65; g p Edin 1965–67; asst psychiat Gogarburn hosp from 1967
m(2) Edin 2.4.66 Kazimierz P. Durkacz MD (Edin) dentist s of Jan D. Przemysl Poland

KOSTERLITZ Hans Walter PhD 1936 DSc 1944 LLD 1979
FRSE 1951
Aberd: prof pharm from 1968; emeritus prof and dir of unit for res on addictive drugs from 1973

KRAMER Alexander Eric BSc(civ eng) 1950 BSc(elect eng) 1952
SM(MIT) 1962 PhD(Aston) 1972
sect eng Hydro Quebec, Montreal 1959–61; res asst MIT Cambridge USA 1961–62; res eng Hydro Quebec, Montreal 1963–64; lect fluids Aston Birm from 1965
m Birm 21.3.68 Pauline A. Taylor d of Sidney T. Birm

KRAMER or Medhurst, Mary Rose MB ChB 1951
g p Bracknell from 1960

KROGH Grace MB ChB 1929

KWO Chia-wei MA 1921

KYNOCH James Davidson MB ChB 1937
MRCGP 1958
g p Aber

KYNOCH Joseph Bonniman BCom 1927
CA
d 20.4.77

KYNOCH or Paterson, Mary Thomson MA 1924
teacher Rosehearty 1955–65; retd; resid Cults

LAIDLAW Andrew Alec BSc(for) 1933

LAIDLAW Hilda Lucy MA 1915 *MB ChB 1919
resid Forfar

LAIDLAW Jean Johnstone MA 1936

LAIDLAW William Brittain Rutherford DSc 1932

LAIDLAW William Young MB ChB 1942

LAING Alexander *MA 1936 *MEd 1938
life fell. univ of Leeds 1979
univ of Leeds: part time advis to overseas stud. 1956–72, sen lect in educ/educ psych 1961–79; retd

LAING Alexander Walker MB ChB 1905
d 1970

LAING Alexander Wood MB ChB 1950
d Lerwick 13.6.71 *AUR* XLIV 322

LAING Alice Fyvie MEd 1954
PhD(Wales) 1972
lect in educ univ coll of Swansea 1968–73, sen lect from 1973

LAING or Phease, Amelia Henderson *MA 1914
resid Worthing Sussex
husb *d* 1958

LAING Annabella Petrie MA 1925
retd 1969; resid Aber

LAING Annie *MA 1930
retd 1968; resid Scone

LAING Arthur Gordon MB ChB 1948
MRCGP 1962 JP 1970
g p Tarves from 1956

LAING Christina Ross MA 1919 MB ChB 1923 DPH 1925
retd 1958; resid Cults Aber

LAING or Irvine, Christine Doig MA 1950
remed teacher Broomhill p s Aber from 1964

LAING David Burnett MB ChB 1925
d Sheffield 10.1.79 *AUR* XLVIII 229

LAING Donald BSc 1947 *1948
sen scient off. dept soil surv Macaulay inst Aber from 1954

LAING Elizabeth MA 1948
teacher in Angus from 1949

LAING Elizabeth Campbell MB ChB 1946 DPH 1951 MD 1952
asst m o h Aber from 1955

LAING or Miller, Elizabeth Margaret MB ChB 1929
doctor in out-patient hosp Harari, Salisbury, Rhodesia 1962; resid Saffron Walden

LAING Ellen Macgregor Ross MA 1930
Aber: head Inverdee inf s 1966–72, mus in infant s 1972–77; retd

LAING Frederick MA 1912 *BSc 1913
d Putney 10.12.65 *AUR* XLI 242

LAING George BL 1940
d 5.9.72

LAING George Duncan MB ChB 1953
g p Eston 1956–66, New Deer 1966–69; reg m o DHSS Newcastle-u-Tyne from 1969

LAING George Innes *MA 1924
teacher Banffsh: classics Banff acad 1925–27, prin classics Fordyce acad 1927–30, prin classics Keith g s 1930–68/dep rector 1950–68; head f e centre Keith 1944–56
m Enzie 23.6.56 Mary T. Gray MA(Glas) teacher

LAING or Robertson, Gertrude Moir MA 1945

LAING Gordon Smith BSc(eng) 1936

LAING Harry Gordon MB ChB 1941

LAING Iain Morrison Ross MB ChB 1951

LAING Ian Watson *MB ChB 1923
d 8.4.66 *AUR* XLI 245 & 399

LAING or Hall, Isabel Margaret MacDonald BSc 1944
resid Alness
husb *d* 5.3.77

LAING or Baird, Isabella *MA 1946
teacher Engl Invergordon acad 1963–70; asst lib Gordon s Huntly 1970–72; teacher Engl Keith g s from 1972

LAING James Allan MA 1939
C of S min: Duddingston par ch Edin 1947–62, St Andrew's Lhanbryde par ch Elgin 1962–75; moderator: Elgin presb 1972–73, Synod of Moray 1973–74; retd; resid Elgin

LAING or Walls, Jean MA 1951
teacher Buckie area p s from 1971

LAING or Thomson, Jean Ramsay Henry MA 1941
resid Victoria BC Canada

LAING John Gordon *MA 1898
no longer on GC reg

LAING Kenneth Macrae *MA 1928
retd 1972, resid Inv

LAING Leslie Gordon MB ChB 1955
h o mat. hosp Aber 1959; g p Aber 1959–60, Peterborough 1960–62, Loughborough 1962–69, Brampton Ontario/active staff Peel mem hosp from 1969

LAING or Sabiston, Margaret MA 1942
sen teacher maths Blurton h s Stoke-on-Trent from 1967
husb *d* Stoke-on-Trent 11.8.79

LAING Margaretta Lilias MA 1943 MB ChB 1954
g p Saltaire med centre Shipley from 1965

LAING Marshall George MA 1946 LLB 1949
leg. asst J. L. Anderson & Co solic Cupar 1960–62, ptnr Craig & Geddes solic Dumfries 1962–75, ptnr Symons & Macdonald solic Dumfries from 1975
m Hong Kong 25.4.56 Hikmat Talhouk d of Amin T. Beirut

LAING Nancy MB ChB 1943
g p Inverurie 1944–77; retd

LAING Peter Duncan *BSc(eng) 1951
CEng MIMechE 1959 Dip Man. St.(Glasg) 1962 AMInst Refrig 1964
Howden Compressors Glasg: dev eng 1955–60, head dev sect 1960–65, eng man. 1965–69, gen factory man. 1969–74 and dir from 1971

LAING or Harper, Rhoda MA 1944
d 8.1.66

LAING Thomas *MA 1925
prin teacher classics and dep rector Kilmarnock acad 1960–68; retd
d Nairn 13.8.77

LAING Thomas James *MA 1928
retd 1972, resid Dinnet

LAING William *BSc 1951 PhD 1954
s of William L. BSc(by ordinance) 1960 *qv*
ICI Stevenston: Nobel div res chem 1954–60; prod. man. Indian Explosives Bihar India 1960–63; ICI Stevenston: prod. man. 1963–66, petr-chem div prod. pers man. from 1966

LAIRD Alistair Noble MB ChB 1955
milit serv Cowglen hosp Glasg 1958–60; g p Penkridge 1960–61, Coventry from 1961

LAIRD Bowman Stiven BSc(eng) 1947
MICE M(A)ICE
eng min of works Benmore and Wellington NZ 1968–73
d Wellington NZ 3.8.73

LAIRD or Laird, Clara MA 1933
Kirkwall g s: teacher maths/lady advis 1965–73, prin guid 1973; retd

LAIRD George Stephen MB ChB 1950
RD 1972 JP 1975
g p Ashton-under-Lyne 1957–73; serv in RN reserve from 1954

LAIRD John Alexander Grant BSc(eng) 1949
contr man. Marples Ridgway (constructors) Edin 1965–68; chief eng Nairn Floors Kirkcaldy from 1968
m Aber 23.12.50 Morag S. Smith dom sc supt hosps d of Murdo S. Benbecula

LAIRD William MA 1950 LLB 1953
ptnr Allan McDougall & Co SSC Edin from 1961

LAKIE John Annand MA 1949
prin teacher Engl Linlathen h s Dun from 1959

LAMB Annie Elizabeth MA 1926
d 5.2.72

LAMB George Fairbairn MA 1908
d 4.2.69

LAMB or Law, Isabella Rebecca MA 1919
resid Edin

LAMB or McKenzie, Isabella Thom MA 1947

LAMB John Garden MA 1913 BSc(agr) 1914
FRMetS 1916
resid Prestwick
d Ayr 14.12.78 *AUR* XLVIII 226

LAMB Kenneth Beldon *BSc 1952

LAMB Kenneth Malcolm BSc(for) 1950
b Turriff 27.11.24
conserv of for. Buea S Cameroons 1960–61; teacher sc Aber 1963–66; for. NZFS Christchurch NZ 1966–72, sen for. from 1972

LAMB Theodore Mitchell George MA 1922
d Tor-na-dee Aber 30.1.66 *AUR* XLII 85

LAMB William Andrew *MA 1951
Aber coll of comm: teacher gen stud. 1961–65, sen teacher hist 1965–75, sen lect publ admin and soc stud. from 1975

LAMBERT John Lewis Mackenzie *BSc 1951

LAMBIE Hugh Rodger MB ChB 1922

LAMONT Angela MA 1933
d Perth 26.1.79

LAMONT Dugald Lennox Daniel MB ChB 1929
g p St Albans 1939–73; retd; resid Holt Norfolk

LANCASTER Margaret Stephen *MA 1951
teacher geog Aber acad 1959–69
m Birse 1.7.68 Francis M. Synge BA(Dub) geol s of Victor M. S. MB(Dub) Dublin

LANDELS John Gray *MA 1951
MA(Cantab) 1953 PhD(Hull) 1961
lect classics R'dg 1960–77, sen lect from 1977

LANDGREBE Frank Walter DSc 1941
prof materia medica univ of Wales 1952–77; now emeritus prof

LANE Peter Hamilton *MA 1952
flt-lt RAF educ branch 1964–72, sqr ldr admin (educ) from 1972
m Valerie M. Butts BA(Lond)

LARG Ann Henderson *MA 1915
Dip de Langue et Litterature Francaises (Rennes) 1922
resid Rothesay

LARG David Glass MA 1915
no longer on GC reg

LASCELLES Clarence Felix MB ChB 1944
MRCPsych 1971 FRCPsych 1974
consult. psychiat Cherry Knowle hosp Sunderland 1956–68; clin tut. univ N'cle from 1968

LASCELLES or Beaux, Gladys Mary *MA 1947
husb *d* 1961
m(2) Lyon France 13.6.63 Jacques Reynaud DL(Lyon) bus. dir s of Pierre R. DL(Lyon)

LASCELLES Raymond George *MB ChB 1955 MD 1964
FRSocMed 1960 DipPsychMed(Lond) 1961
FRCP(Lond) 1974
Lond: regist neurol St Thomas' hosp; sen regist neurol nat hosp Queen Sq 1962–65, sen regist neurol Guy's hosp 1965–70; consult. neurol and lect neurol MRI and univ Manc from 1970
m Lyon France 1966 Martine Reynaud d of Paul R. St Didier au Mont d'or Rhône France

LASDON Albert Harold MB ChB 1934

LAUDER Helen Mary MA 1933
asst head Banff p s 1965–72; retd

LAURENSON Angus Scollay BSc 1948 *1949
prin teacher sc Anderson h s Lerwick 1960–69, prin chem 1969–73, teacher sc Aboyne acad from 1973
d 23.11.75

LAURENSON or Stewart, Christina Margaret MA 1936
teacher Insch 1965–78; retd

LAURENSON Rae Duncan MB ChB 1953 MD 1963
in Edmonton Canada

LAURIE Gavin BSc(agr) 1938
d 22.5.64

LAW Anthony Charles *MA 1925
no longer on GC reg

LAW Beatrix Bennett MA 1920 MB ChB 1923 *MD 1928
sen ophth surg NE reg hosp board 1946–61; part time lect ophth Aberd 1946–61; retd

LAW or Jenkins, Edith Ann McPherson MA 1911
no longer on GC reg

LAW Eleanora Margaret Patricia MA 1918 *MB ChB 1921
retd 1958; resid Dinnet and Aber
d Aber 11.12.79 *AUR* XLVIII 440, XLIX 67

LAW Elizabeth Alexandra *MA 1925
no longer on GC reg

LAW or Stewart, Frances Mary MA 1928
woman advis Carnoustie h s 1966–72; retd

LAW Frederick William MA BSc(agr) 1912
d Stoke-on-Trent 29.6.70 *AUR* XLIV 109

LAW George *MA 1912
d Girvan 25.5.61 *AUR* XXXIX 202

LAW Ian McConachie *BSc 1924
retd 1962; resid Huntly
d –.7.81

LAW or Henderson, Isabel Alice *MA 1926
resid Oldmeldrum

LAW James Gordon BSc(eng) 1947
eng ag firm of quarry masters Glasg from 1960

LAW or McDonald, Jean Innes *MA 1924
resid Oldmeldrum

LAW John Dickson BSc(eng) 1954
MICE 1961 FICE 1972 MASCE 1972
resid eng Sir M. MacDonald & Ptners Lower Diyala irrig proj Iraq 1961–64; area eng Balfour Beatty & Co Kainji hydro elect. proj Nigeria 1964–68; claims eng ECI Denver Colorado USA Athens 1968–69; area eng Balfour Beatty & Co Lynemouth smelter proj Northumberland 1969–70; asst resid eng TAMS Int Corp NY Tarbela H-E proj Pakistan 1971–73; resid man. Agrar- und Hydrotechnik Emb H Essen W Ger, Semper Dam & Irrigation Proj Central Java 1974–76; eng rep Bahrain (John Taylor & Sons) 1976–77; dep constr man. Shiroro HE proj Nigeria Chas. T. Main Int Inc Boston Mass USA 1978
m New Brighton Cheshire 8.10.60 Barbara England SRN nurs sister d of Clem E. MB ChB(Sheff) Wallasey

LAW or Fraser, Margaret Nellie Stuart MA 1931
resid Aboyne

LAW Noel Pottinger MA 1951

LAW Sheila MA 1951
head Finzean s from 1970
m Aber 27.12.61 Alexander R. Harper teacher s of Alexander H. Inverurie

LAW William George MA 1952
Aber: prin teacher geog Ruthrieston s s 1965–73; co-prin teacher geog Harlaw acad from 1973
m Aber 3.8.62 Norah M. MacLeod cler off. d of Donald MacL. Lochganich Isle of Lewis

LAW William Proctor *MA 1912 BSc 1915
d Aber 27.2.73 *AUR* XLV 224

LAWIE Alexander MA 1952

LAWIE William MB ChB 1922
d Colchester 9.6.67 *AUR* XLII 185

LAWRANCE or McLeod, Ida Walker MA 1939
resid Collieston

LAWRENCE or Richards, Agnes McKillop MA 1908
d 17.2.64

LAWRENCE Albert Alexander MB ChB 1953
g p Buckie from 1957
m Aber 2.3.61 Edith M. Adam d of Herbert D. A. Inverurie

LAWRENCE or Forbes, Annie MA 1910

LAWRENCE Doreen Ross MA 1929
retd 1967; resid Aber
d Aber 7.2.80

LAWRENCE or Anton, Doris May MA 1942
lib catalog asst Edin city lib; resid Edin

LAWRENCE Emily Ann Spence MA 1926
teacher Fr Summerhill s s Aber 1962–65; retd

LAWRENCE George Morton *MA 1936 LLB 1939
ptnr James & George Collie advoc Aber from 1949

LAWRENCE George Smith MA 1910 MB ChB 1916
d 14.8.71 *AUR* XLIV 316

LAWRENCE or Jaffray, Isobel Mary *MA 1940

LAWRENCE James MB ChB 1953
g p Aberlour from 1958

LAWRENCE Margaret Helen MA 1913
resid Cullen
d Buckie 26.10.78

LAWRENCE or Black, Marjory Irene MB ChB 1934
d Aber 2.6.63 *AUR* XL 206

LAWRENCE Philip Douglas MA 1919 DD 1966
d Aber 1.6.67 *AUR* XLII 184

LAWRENCE Robert Daniel MA 1912 *MB ChB 1916 MD 1922
d Lond 29.8.68 *AUR* XLIII 78

LAWRENCE William Calder Macphail MB ChB 1953 DPH 1969
MFCM 1973
dep m o Banff c c 1966–74; spec commun med Forth Valley health board from 1974

LAWRENCE-SMITH, Alexander Maxwell MB ChB 1929
m o Port of Lond auth 1947–50, prin m o from 1950

LAWRIE Charles James Reid BSc(eng) 1950

LAWRIE George Walker MA 1937

LAWRIE Helen Margaret BSc 1950

LAWRIE John Samuel MB ChB 1928
no longer on GC reg

LAWRIE or MacLeod, Rhona Cameron MA 1930
d 27.3.63

LAWRIE Thomas Ruthven MB ChB 1951
Cert Diag Radiology(Can) 1962 FRCP(C) 1972
Canada: serv in RCN 1956–67; radiol ch hosp/Grace mat. hosp Halifax; asst prof radiol Dalhousie univ Halifax from 1967
marr diss

LAWRIE Thomas Scott MA 1948
prin teacher geog Hilton acad Aber from 1965
m Aber 3.4.58 Janet E. Cunningham teacher d of David C. Aber

LAWRIE Una MB ChB 1947 DPH 1952
sen asst m o h Notts 1957–60
m Aber 1960 John T. Cockburn BSc(Glas) teacher s of John T. C. Lanark

LAWSON or Cowie, Ann Chapman *MA 1941
Herefordsh: teacher Engl/hist and asst lib Bluecoat s s 1960–66, head hist dept Cannon Frome s s 1966–69, hist tut. The Grange Bredenbury 1969–72

LAWSON or Geddes, Annie Mary MA 1924
no longer on GC reg

LAWSON Donald Boyd Cameron MB ChB 1925
d Sheringham 26.11.69 *AUR* XLIII 445

LAWSON Gordon Cecil MA 1907 *BSc 1909 DSc 1920
d Hereford 8.3.76

LAWSON or Kennedy, Helen Cecilia MB ChB 1950
med missionary: Senegal 1954–68, Abidjan Ivory Coast 1968–75; part time clin m o Hillingdon AHA from 1975

LAWSON Ian Richard MB ChB 1954 MD 1958
MRCPE 1960 FACP 1970 FRCPE 1971
consult. phys Aber gen hosps 1961–66, dept med Christian med coll Ludhuana India 1967–68; USA: med dir Hebrew home for aged 1970–76; assoc clin prof univ of Connecticut med s from 1972; vice pres for med affairs Danbury hosp Connecticut from 1976

LAWSON Janet McFiggans MA 1948
m Hatch

LAWSON John Dempster PhD 1951
Mast. Eng(Melb) 1963 MASCE 1963
FIE(Aust) 1973
prof civ eng univ of Melbourne Aust from 1970

LAWSON John Simpson MA 1935 BCom 1937
prin teacher bus. stud. Aber acad/Hazlehead acad 1960–73; advis in bus. stud. Aber educ dept 1973–75; advis bus. stud. Grampian reg 1975–76; retd

LAWSON Mabel Gordon MA 1916 MB ChB 1918
d Folkestone 8.8.72 *AUR* XLV 125

LAWSON or West, Margaret Officer MA 1949
teacher maths: Middle s Aber 1950–52; Birm: King's Norton g s 1952–54, Selly Park s mod s 1960–61, Harrison Borrows g s 1961–63; Croydon: Ashburton s s 1970–73, Coloma g s 1973–75; resid Aber

LAWSON William Graham BCom 1924
no longer on GC reg

LAWSON William Wilfred James MB ChB 1904
d 23.12.63

LEACH Gweneth Rose *MA 1953
m Parker

LEAHY or Mulcahy, Patricia MA 1951
B Soc Work(W Aust) 1976
W Aust: soc worker mental health serv Perth 1977–78, sen soc worker commun ch health serv from 1978

LEARMONTH or Fleming, Barbara Drever BSc 1953
resid Greenlaw

LEASK Caroline Martha Mackenzie *MA 1928

LEASK James Christopher MB ChB 1941
Zambia: m o Zambian govt Livingstone 1970–73, sen m o Anglo-Amer Corp Lusaka 1973–77; m o Livingstone hosp Port Elizabeth SA from 1977

LEASK John MB ChB 1938
g p Inverurie 1948–74; retd; resid Ballindalloch

LEASK or Cameron, Margaret MA 1952

LEASK Mary Isabel Milne MA 1926
teacher: Insch, Woodside Aber, Kintore, Kent, Inverurie 1958–65
m Aber 7.8.48 Robert Jezzard teacher s of Edward J. Sandwich

LEASK Millicent Florence MA 1940

LEASK Peter MA 1903
no longer on GC reg

LEATHAM or Smiles, May Morris MA 1910
d Aber 31.10.64 *AUR* XLI 55

LEDINGHAM Alexander MA 1952
ptnr Edmonds & Ledingham advoc Aber from 1958
m Aber 26.1.63 S. Rosemary Mackintosh teacher p e d of Harvey G. M. LDS(Edin) Durris

LEDINGHAM Isabella Culbert Chessar BSc 1919
resid Gillingham Kent

LEDINGHAM James MB ChB 1933
g p N Hykeham from 1947

LEDINGHAM James George MB ChB 1953
g p Edin from 1956

LEDINGHAM John *MB ChB 1922
d Lond 23.6.70 *AUR* XLIV 110

LEDINGHAM Leslie Andrews MB ChB 1934
d Inv 25.7.73 *AUR* XLV 321

LEDINGHAM or Cox, Louisa Lemmon BCom 1939
exec clerk J Lyons & Co Lond 1940–45; Victoria BC Canada: secy to asst judge advoc Canadian armed forces 1958–59; secy to admin asst min of highways 1959–65

LEDINGHAM Robert Mackay MA 1913 LLB 1920
d Aber 27.2.69 *AUR* XLIII 210

LEDINGHAM William Lemmon Stewart MB ChB 1937
g p Tunbridge Wells from 1946

LEDINGHAM William Marshall MB ChB 1923
d 1.7.73

LEDINGHAM William Wilson MA 1950
BA(Lond) 1964
dep rector Alford acad from 1966

LEDINGHAM or Stopper, Winifred Ewen *MA 1948
Aber: teacher Engl AGS/Ruthrieston s s 1949–50, Rosemount s s 1950–57, St Margaret's s for girls 1959–72; prin Engl St Margaret's s from 1972

LEE or Stevenson, Beryl Agnes *MA 1943
teacher Dumfriessh from 1954

LEE John MA 1941 BD 1944
d 17.4.80

LEE Margaret Helen MB ChB 1946
g p Chesterfield from 1950

LEEFE John Dixon BSc(for) 1951
for. comm: dist off. Brecon Wales 1962–63, Grantham 1963–67; proj off. Linsey (Lincs) proj for. improvement of environment Lincoln 1967–70; HQ man. trg off. with for. comm Basingstoke 1970–73; prin for. coll (Brit tech assistance) Prodromos Cyprus from 1973

LEES Frank Jamieson MB ChB 1928
g p Banff from 1930

LEES John *MA 1950 PhD 1953
FInstP 1968
res phys/sen scient off. National Eng Lab E Kilbride 1958–61; phys/res man. Standard Telecomm Labs Harlow from 1961
m 6.12.58 Sheila M. Reilly

LEES John Drennan MB ChB 1933
d 21.10.65 *AUR* XLI 250

LEES William MA 1932 BD 1943
d Aber 4.7.75 *AUR* XLVI 325

LE FANU George Ernest Hugh MB CM 1901
no longer on GC reg

LEFEVRE Isabel Margaret Murray *MA 1934
prin teacher Engl St Margaret's s for girls 1959–72; retd

LEGG George Alexander Hendry BSc(eng) 1949

LEGGAT George MB ChB 1911 DPH 1913
d Grange-over-Sands 24.1.72 *AUR* XLIV 427

LEGGAT Peter Ogilvie MB ChB 1941 MD 1951
FRCP 1968
clin lect dept of med N'cle from 1965

LEGGE James Roger *MA 1922
d 24.9.64

LEIGHTON John Crichton BSc(eng) 1950
Frederick Snare Corp NY: field eng Miragoave, Haiti 1956–57, constr eng NY 1958–59, constr man. Vallenar Chile 1960–64; Kaiser Eng Calif proj man.: Renukoot India 1965–67, Melbourne 1968–72; exec vice pres Milder-Kaiser Sao Paulo 1973–75, vice pres Latin Amer oper from 1975
m Vallenar Chile 26.5.62 Anita Del C Miranda teacher d of Gregorio M. Atacama Chile

LEIGHTON Kenneth Macrae MB ChB 1947
FRCP(C) (Br Col) 1967
Vancouver: resid dept anaest Vancouver gen hosp 1963–67; asst prof dept anaest 1968–75, assoc prof from 1975; recipient BC heart foundation grant from 1968; examiner Royal Coll Physicians and Surgeons of Canada from 1972

LEIGHTON or Forbes, Mary MA 1947
pers man. J & P Coats Anchor Mills Paisley 1948–51; youth employment off. Aber educ auth 1951–53; part time med soc worker: Queen Mother's hosp Glasg 1965–67, Law hosp Carluke 1967–76, tut. soc work Motherwell tech coll; med soc worker ARI 1977

LEIPER Doreen Florence BSc 1952
teacher maths/sc/chem Aber acad 1961–70, year mistress from 1970 (later Hazlehead acad)

LEIPER or Keith, Dorothy *MA 1950

LEIPER Edwin James Reid MA 1925 *MB ChB 1930 *MD 1937
FRCP(Lond) 1969
retd 1972; resid Bishops Stortford

LEIPER John MB ChB 1927 MD 1937 DPH 1938
MBE 1964 JP 1961
retd 1968; resid Aber
m(1) Aber 10.7.31 Robina Wood Aber
(2) Aber 14.10.59 Mabel Robertson Aber

LEIPER or Ashforth, Margaret Vera *MA 1952
Edin: part-time teacher maths Princess Margaret Rose hosp s from 1976

LEITCH Isabella *MA 1911 BSc 1914 DSc 1919 LLD 1965
OBE 1949
dir (Imperial) Commonwealth Bureau of anim nutrit Rowett res inst Aber 1946–60, contd in service of Bureau preparing syst for coding and retrieval of information on nutrit and part time appointment to staff of Agr Res Council 1960–74 to prepare (with A. W. Boyne) report on composition of Brit feeding stuffs published 1976
d Aust 21.7.80 *AUR* XLIX 66

LEITCH Madelina Alison MA 1908
d 15.2.76

LEITH Elizabeth Jean MA 1944
teacher Middlefield p s Aber from 1945

LEITH or Grant, Helen Simmil MA 1948
head Armiddle s Aberdeensh 1962–76; head Monquhitter s from 1976
husb *d* 1962
m(2) Aber 3.4.69 James Pennie radio and elect. off. Merch N

LEITH James Alexander MA 1954 LLB 1956

LENCZ Sandor (Alexander) Geza PhD 1933

LENDRUM or Hale, Dorothy Mary MA 1922
resid Lond

LENDRUM or Rennie, Gertrude Helen *MB ChB 1920
retd 1958; resid Aber

LENG or Shewan, Audrey Ashill MA 1952
teacher: Tulloch p s Perth 1972–78, Perth h s from 1978

LENNON or Sorrie, Evelyn Mary MA 1952
resid Middlesbrough

LENNON George Gordon MB ChB 1934 *ChM 1945
Hon Fell. Gyn Soc 1956
prof obst and gyn Brist 1951–67; visiting prof: Istanbul/Ankara 1956, Durban, Johannesburg, Pretoria, Kampala 1958, Teheran 1965; dean fac of med univ of W Aust from 1967

LEONARD or Russell, Christina MA 1923
d 1974

LEONARD-SMITH or Garten, Anne Leslie Armstrong *MA 1945
lect Maria Grey coll of educ Twickenham 1967–70, sen lect from 1970

LE PIVERT John Alfred *BSc(eng) 1947
FICE FIArbitrators FPWI CEng
ptnr Livesey & Henderson Lond 1962–71; proj dir GEC Elliott Automation Borehamwood Herts from 1972
freeman of City of Lond

LERCHS Armin BSc(eng) 1954
Bureau Ingeco Gombert: man. consult. tech dir Cairo, Alexandria 1957–59, dir Lisbon 1959–66; Ingeco Gombert Portuguesa: chmn board of dir Lisbon, Luanda, Lourenco Marques, Rio de Janeiro from 1966
m Alexandria Egypt 20.3.59 Alice B. Djanian d of Sarkis D.

LE ROUX or Brodie, Katherine McEwen MB ChB 1949
g p trainee Lochwinnoch 1963–64, locums in Beith, Lochwinnoch and Johnstone 1964–68; g p Beith from 1969

LESLIE or Riley, Agnes Kidd MB ChB 1942
anaest Radcliffe I Oxford, Stoke Mandeville hosp Aylesbury; h s Warneford hosp Leamington Spa

LESLIE Annie MA 1935
work study Scot. & N'cle Breweries Newcastle 1968–75; retd; resid Huntly

LESLIE Charles McKay BSc(eng) 1949 *1952
MIEE 1966 Dip Man. St(Strath) 1970
MIProdE 1969 AMBIM 1970
temp controls group Honeywell Newhouse Lanark: chief eng 1964–66, chief prod. eng 1966–71, prod. eng man. Bellshill 1971–74, des eng man. from 1974

LESLIE David Alexander MA 1955

LESLIE Donald Alexander MB ChB 1944
FRCPath 1963
consult path. Sunderland from 1952

LESLIE Douglas MB ChB 1953
g p Oakville Ont Canada from 1959

LESLIE Douglas Macbeth BSc(eng) 1945

LESLIE George Christie BL 1954
ptnr McVey & Murricane solic Glasg from 1963

LESLIE George Erskine *BSc 1951

LESLIE or McLaughlin, Gladys Irvine MA 1937

LESLIE Gordon James Booth MB ChB 1955
Dip Ophth RCS 1961
sen h o eye dept ARI 1959–60; regist ophth Glasg eye I 1960–63, ophth spec Sarawak Malaysia 1963–68; clin asst ophth inst Glasg from 1968; regt m o 71st Roy Eng regt Yorkhill Glasg from 1973
m(2) Bearsden 22.8.75 Kirsten L. Plehn d of Villy S. P. Odense Denmark

LESLIE Ian BSc 1942
d Lond 8.6.67 *AUR* XLII 186

LESLIE James Campbell MA 1921 BSc(agr) 1922
d –.7.74

LESLIE Jane MA 1910
no longer on GC reg

LESLIE John Angus BSc(eng) 1938
d Loughborough 12.11.80

LESLIE John Erskine BSc(for) 1950

LESLIE or McCallum, Lizzie MA 1910
d Richmond Yorks 7.1.71 *AUR* XLIV 209

LESLIE Mansfield Alastair *MA 1948
prin teacher Engl Waid acad Anstruther from 1958

LESLIE Margaret Ethel MA 1953
teacher Aber: Mile End p s 1971–73, asst head Sunnybank p s from 1973
m Aber 27.7.62 William M. Currie s of James C. Aber

LESLIE or Rose, Mary Horn *MA 1903
d 4.6.67

LESLIE Muriel Roy MA 1932
no longer on GC reg

LESLIE Norman Hector MB ChB 1922
dep anaest Royal Victoria Inf N'cle-u-Tyne 1943–45
d N'cle-u-Tyne 9.7.74 *AUR* XLVI 108

LESLIE Phyllis Davidson MB ChB 1937
retd; resid Aboyne

LESLIE William MA 1910 MB ChB 1915
no longer on GC reg

LESLIE William [d]LLB 1953
WS/ptnr J C Brodie Cuthbertson & Watson WS (now Brodies) Edin 1955–76; a chmn industrial tribunals (Scot.) from 1976
m(2) Dalton 29.11.69 Elizabeth J. Bowden-Smith d of Ralph P. B-S. Ecclefechan

LESLIE William Allan [d]BL 1926
ptnr Frame & Macdonald solic Glasg from 1936; prov grand secy A F & A Masons Glasg from 1954

LESLIE William Norman MA 1898
no longer on GC reg

LESLIE Wilson Summers MA 1915 BD 1918
d Aber 25.12.70 *AUR* XLIV 210

LESSEL Elizabeth Isabella *MA 1917
retd 1955; resid Aber
d 15.12.81

LETHBRIDGE William MB ChB 1895
no longer on GC reg

LEVACK David Proudfoot *MB ChB 1924
retd; resid Drumoak
d Aber 26.2.79 *AUR* XLVIII 228

LEVACK John William MB ChB 1931
d Aber 1.9.73 *AUR* XLV 320

LEVACK or Aitken, Mary Robertson MA 1920 MB ChB 1924
retd 1957
d Maidstone 30.4.74

LEVITT Charles Wheatley MB ChB 1936
d 16.6.78

LEWIS or Knight, Annie Walker MA 1929

LEWIS Anthony Vincent MA 1954

LEWIS Cecil Arthur *MA 1915
no longer on GC reg

LEWIS George Alfred MB ChB 1946
FRCOG 1973
regist/sen regist obst & gyn Westminster hosp Lond 1961–69; consult. obst & gyn Gloucester from 1969

LEWIS Ivor Howells MB ChB 1949
MFCM 1974
m o, asst sen m o Manc reg hosp board 1962–64; asst sen m o, prin asst sen m o Leeds reg hosp board 1964–74; spec commun med Yorks reg health auth from 1974

LEWIS James Howells MB ChB 1952
m o commonwealth dept of health Melbourne 1959–62; g p: various UK locums 1962–77, Falkirk from 1978
m(2) Middlesbrough 29.11.68 Winifred A. Small teacher d of John W. S. Skelton

LEWIS or Robertson, Margaret Walker MA 1929
resid Bieldside Aber

LEWIS or Graham, Mary Patricia Havard MB ChB 1949
DPH(Manc) 1962 MFCM 1975
m o LHA Warrington 1955–68; sen m o Warrington dist Cheshire AHA from 1968

LEWIS Mercedes Louisa MA 1949

LEY Francis James *BSc 1953

LEYS George Murray MA 1919 *MEd 1921
d 4.5.67 *AUR* XLII 358

LEYS Thomas *BSc 1954

LIANG Lone MA 1917 LLB 1918 LLD 1945
d Yonkers NY State 12.6.67 *AUR* XLII 355

LIANG Shih-Chen PhD 1948

LIDDELL Charles Mitchell MB ChB 1937
d Milltimber Aber 15.6.74 *AUR* XLVI 110

LIDDELL Leslie Carse MB ChB 1938
g p Pennycraig Glam from 1947

LIGERTWOOD John Catto *MA 1925
retd 1968; resid Bridge of Allan

LIGHTBODY Alexander *BSc(mech eng) 1938 *BSc(elect eng) 1939
OBE 1967
tech exec naval weapons div Hawker Siddeley Dynamics Hatfield from 1963
d Herts 9.2.74

LIGHTBODY John Cumming MB ChB 1942
d 25.6.77 *AUR* XLVIII 287

LILLIE or Garrett, Helen MA 1910 MB ChB 1914 MD 1920
C of S Missionary in Punjab 1920–46; lib asst Glas univ 1948–63
d 22.1.77

LILLIE Isobel Milne MA BSc 1913
d Caithness 31.3.73 *AUR* XLV 224

LILLIE James Pickford MB ChB 1923
d 1966

LILLIE John Adam MA 1906 LLD 1967
KC 1931; sheriff of Fife and Kinross 1941–71; dep chmn and leg. comm of gen board of control for Scot. 1944–60; retd; resid Edin

LILLIE Mary Purves *MA 1915
resid Lybster

LILLIE William *MA 1921 DD 1948
lect Bibl stud. Aberd 1953–69; retd

LIND William Charles Morrison MA 1936
d Kildary 23.9.70 *AUR* XLIV 111

LINDSAY Albert George MA 1932
retd; resid Aber

LINDSAY Angus William BSc(eng) 1949
Gulf Oil Corp: chief eng E & W dist Venezuela 1959–66, proj man. Bantry Bay Ireland 1966–69, consult. Kuwait, Okinawa, Canada 1969–70, exec Venezuela 1970–73; Gulf Oil/Texaco: supt Ecuador, Quito 1973–74, feasibility stud. Paraguay and N Sea Scot. 1974–75; co-ord of transport Gull Is. hydro elect. proj Labrador from 1975

LINDSAY David Grant MB ChB 1944
NSW Aust: m o dept of publ health Sydney 1961–65, med supt Peat Is. hosp Brooklyn from 1965

LINDSAY Gordon Forbes MB ChB 1944
g p Aboyne from 1948

LINDSAY James Martin *MA 1945 PhD 1950
prof Ger univ W Aust Perth from 1969

LINDSAY or Wood, Jean Elizabeth MA 1947

LINDSAY or Thompson, Johan Dunlop BSc 1918
d Sydney Aust 1959

LINDSAY John Grant MB ChB 1930

LINDSAY or Strachan, Marjorie Gertrude Helen *MA 1933
resid Ealing Lond

LINDSAY or Pounder, Mary Grant MA 1929
no longer on GC reg

LINDSAY Sheila Taylor BSc 1927
d Edin 13.12.68 *AUR* XLIII 215

LINDSAY Stanley Frederick MB ChB 1937
d Banchory 11.8.71 *AUR* XLIV 321

LINKLATER Eric Robert Russell *MA 1925 LLD 1946
d Aber 7.11.74 *AUR* XLVI 10

LINKLATER James Reith BCom 1922

LINKLATER John Roy MA 1938 *MEd 1940
admin off. Edin div Lothian reg c 1975–79; retd

LINTS William Alexander BL 1940
sen ptnr Cornillon Craig & Co WS Edin

LIPP or Flett, Dorothy BSc 1925
resid Edin

LIPP George Robertson *MB ChB 1914
d 24.6.62

LIPP or Spence, Isobel *MA 1925
no longer on GC reg

LIPP Kenneth Lewis MB ChB 1952
asst g p: Thurso 1953–54, Willington Co Durham 1954–56; sen h o orthop ARI 1956–57; g p: Aber 1957–66, Oban and police surg/anaest Oban hosps from 1966

LIPP or Castle, Margaret MA 1917 MB ChB 1921
S Af med corps 1939–45; resid Dartington

LIPP Robert James Grant MA 1910 BSc(agr) 1911
d 21.8.65

LIPP Samuel *MA 1912 BSc 1913 BSc(agr) 1914
d Newport-on-Tay 11.9.69 *AUR* XLIII 328

LISTER George MA 1903
no longer on GC reg

LISTON John PhD 1955

LITTLE Edwin *BSc 1952

LITTLE Frank Bamford BSc(agr) 1947

LITTLE James Robertson *MA 1926
acting rector Leith acad 1969–70; retd; resid Edin

LITTLE Jean Webster MA 1938
Edin: edit. Thomas Nelson & Sons 1952–64, publ Oliver & Boyd 1964–76

LITTLE or Copland, Margaret McNeill MA 1931 MB ChB 1935
DPH(N'cle) 1960 MFCM 1970
Sunderland: sen m o 1967–70, dep m o h from 1970

LITTLE Robert *MA 1926
d –.3.65

LITTLE Robert Davidson MB ChB 1953
FRCS(Can) 1973
Canada: g p/surg spec Edmonton 1960–73, surg spec Immaculata hosp Westlock Alta from 1973
wife *d* 1967
m(2) Edmonton 9.10.68 Margaret H. McKay nurse d of William McK. MD(McG) Edmonton

LITTLEJOHN Alastair Ironside MB ChB 1955

LITTLEJOHN David *MA 1951

LITTLEJOHN George Sandison BSc 1952
FRSH 1961 FIFST 1964
res man. Metal Box Co of India Calcutta 1960–72; head overseas res serv div Metal Box Co Overseas Lond from 1972

LITTLEJOHN James George MA 1923
retd 1965; resid Ayr
d Ayr 7.5.80

LITTLEJOHN or Hopes, Margaret Primrose MA 1920
resid Torphins

LITTLEJOHN or Flavel, Mary Victoria MB ChB 1919

LITTLEJOHN Michael Peter BSc(eng) 1951

LITTLEJOHN Robert Cruickshank *MA 1925
retd 1966; resid Torphins
wife *d* Glasg –.4.60
d Torphins 21.4.79 *AUR* XLVIII 229

LIVINGSTON David Fettes MB ChB 1944
g p Sheffield from 1953
d Glasg 5.2.80

LIVINGSTON David Munro Sheldon BSc(agr) 1954 *1955 PhD 1959
FIFST 1971
Aber: sen scient off. dept applied nutrit Rowett res inst 1961–66, head dept of nutrit sc RGIT 1966–71, head s of nutrit sc RGIT from 1971

LIVINGSTON Hugh MA 1927 MB ChB 1931 ᶜMD 1935
retd 1974; resid Sutton Coldfield
d 25.10.81

LIVINGSTON Hugh Gibson BSc(agr) 1950
res off. Rift Valley prov Nakuru Kenya 1957–60; EAAFRO (East Af high command) SSO anim husb dept Kikuyu Kenya, Uganda, Tanganyika 1960–62; dir advis serv Colborn Vita Feeds Canterbury Kent 1962–67; sales dir/nutrit Burgess Feeds Thornton-le-Dale 1967–71; marketing man. Trouw & Co (G.B.) Cambridge; group tech dir Farm Feed Formulators Northallerton from 1972

LIVINGSTON or Ross, Nancy MA 1942
ACTL 1941
teacher Aber from 1942

LIVINGSTONE Cyril Joseph MB ChB 1938

LIVINGSTONE Mary MA 1918
d Aber 16.7.71 *AUR* XLIV 317

LLEWELLYN John Patrick *BSc 1954 PhD 1958
s of John M. W. L. stockbroker and Mary K. Horsey; b Bishop's Stortford 14.1.33
asst lect nat phil Aberd 1957–58; lect phys univ coll of N. Wales Bangor from 1958
m London 1959 Anne Lejeune MB ChB 1959 *qv*

LOBBAN Agnes MA 1914
d Aber 24.8.76

LOBBAN Alfred William Clark MB ChB 1940
DPH 1967 RCP & S 1967 MFCM 1972
g p Gamlingay Beds 1946–65; asst c m o Beds 1965–67; m o h N Beds dist 1967–69; sen m o Kingston-on-Thames 1969–70; 2nd dep c m o h and p s m o Beds c c 1971–72; m o h and p s m o Luton 1972–74; dist commun phys Beds AHA from 1974
wife *d* 1968
m(2) Lond 4.1.69 Ivy M. Sandover SRN d of William S. MA(Oxon) Richmond Surrey

LOBBAN or Blackmore, Catherine Margaret MA 1927
d Exeter 27.3.68 *AUR* XLII 367

LOBBAN Hilda Cook MA 1927
retd; resid Glasg

LOBBAN James Wilson MA 1924 MB ChB 1927 DPH 1929 ᶜMD 1930
retd 1969; resid Birkenhead

LOBBAN Lina Ross *MA 1931
retd 1959; resid Huntly

LOBBAN or Dott, Sybil Margaret Gray MA 1924

LOBBAN William George BSc(eng) 1949

LOCKE Alton William BCom 1926

LOCKE Donald Erskine MA 1936 [d]LLB 1938
Lond: prin dept of econ affairs 1965–67, prin nat board for prices and incomes 1967–70, prin DTI 1970–74; retd

LOCKHART Robert Douglas MB ChB 1918 ChM 1924 LLD 1965
FSA Scot 1951 FRSE 1954
retd 1965; hon curator Aberd anthrop museum from 1939

LOCKHART William BSc(for) 1922
no longer on GC reg

LODGE John Blakestone *MA 1950
chief press off. O U 1970–72; reporter *Evening Express* Aber from 1972

LOGAN or Simpson, Annie Welsh *MA 1930
BD(Edin) 1975
teacher: Engl Esdail s Ayton 1946–47, Edin acad 1947, Engl La Martinière for girls Calcutta 1947–50; relief teacher Lanarksh 1953–70

LOGAN Charles *BSc 1953

LOGAN Donald Macpherson BSc(agr) 1948
teacher chem/bot/zool Fortrose acad from 1966

LOGAN John Black MA 1927 BD 1930
Order of St Mark 1970 (conferred by patriarch of Alexandria); retd 1970; resid Crieff; Lee lect 1977

LOGAN or MacIntyre, Katherine Jean MB ChB 1947
resid Kuwait

LOGAN or Raffan, Marie Margaret MA 1937
resid Bridgend Glam

LOGG Matthew Hannah MB ChB 1921
no longer on GC reg

LOGGIE George Alexander MA 1951
prin teacher: Engl Kaimhill s s Aber 1966–73, guid Hazlehead acad from 1973

LOGGIE William John MA 1955
Aber: teacher maths Northfield s s 1961–66, prin maths Old Aberdeen s s 1966–71, year master Kincorth acad 1971–73, asst head from 1973

LOGIE Norman John [d]MB ChB 1927
retd 1969
d Aber 15.3.72 *AUR* XLIV 431

LOHR Alexander George MA 1921 BCom 1924

LOMAX-SIMPSON Josephine Mary MB ChB 1948
MRCPsych 1973
med asst Wimbledon hosp 1962–77; consult. E Grinstead fam consult. clin 1963–77; founder Messenger House Trust 1970 for unsupported young mothers, Hutchinson settlement 1977 for students

LONG John Dennis BSc(for) 1945

LONG Michael BSc(for) 1936

LONG Richard Arthur Kingslow BSc(eng) 1950 *1951 PhD 1954

LONGBOTTOM Keith Illingworth BSc(for) 1953
no longer on GC reg

LONGMORE Herbert John Alexander MB ChB 1954
MRCGP 1966
Surg regist ARI 1959–61; g p Lochmaben from 1961

LONGMORE William Andrew Dip Agr 1915 BSc(agr) 1920
no longer on GC reg

LORIMER Alan MB ChB 1949
LMCC 1961 FASCP 1967 Canadian Centennial Medal 1967 MASC 1972 FRCPath 1973 FRCP(C) 1973
lect path. Aberd 1957–59; path.: Salford royal hosp 1959–61; dept of health New Brunswick Canada from 1961
m Bolton 1956 Helen M. Greenhalgh teacher d of Frank G. Manc

LORIMER Archibald Harkness MB ChB 1948

LORIMER Garth MB ChB 1950
g p Singapore 1952–76; Aust from 1976

LORIMER John Alexander BSc 1941
no longer on GC reg

LORIMER Peter MA 1916
retd; resid Peterculter

LORIMER William Robert Wells BSc(eng) 1945
eng N E reg hosp board Aber from 1967

LOTHIAN or Watt, Marion Isabel MA BSc 1911
d Tunbridge Wells 12.2.72 *AUR* XLIV 427

LOTHIAN (William) Arthur Cunningham (Sir) MA 1908 BSc 1909 LLD 1950
d Lond 16.11.62 *AUR* XL 77

LOUDON John Russell *BSc 1953
PhD(Tor) 1960 MIMM(Can) FGeolAssoc(Canada) MGeolSoc(S Af)
Vancouver: geol Amer Metal Climax 1960–65, dist geol Texas Gulf Sulphur Inc 1965–69; reg man. Southern Africa Texas Gulf Inc Johannesburg 1970–75; man. dir Pandora Mining (Johannesburg) from 1976

LOUTTIT or Ross, Mary Sandison MA 1944
resid Alness

LOVIBOND Catherine Betty Jerrard BSc 1933 *1934

LOVIE Margaret Isabella MA 1933
no longer on GC reg

LOVIE Peter MA 1926
d Kilsyth 5.2.66 *AUR* XLII 88

LOVIE Susan Milne MA 1932
retd 1970; resid Banff

LOW or Thom, Adamina Middleton MA 1921
no longer on GC reg

LOW or King, Agnes Mary MA 1946

LOW Alistair *BSc 1952
plant breeder Etton res corp Serere Uganda 1961–65; CSIRO 1965–77; prin res scient plant breeding in oil seeds sunflower and safflower CSIRO Griffith Aust from 1976

LOW or Fraser, Betty Gordon BSc 1948 *1949 PhD 1953
lect phys Dun coll of tech 1965–67; vice-prin Trevelyan coll Durh 1967–70; asst secy Ox & Camb s exam board Cambridge from 1970

LOW Charles MB ChB 1939
MBE 1973
g p Tomintoul 1956–75; retd; resid Kessock

LOW Charles Alexander MA 1929
no longer on GC reg

LOW David *BSc 1938
Ellon acad: prin teacher of maths from 1947 and dep rector from 1956

LOW Edward Oliphant MB ChB 1931
d Tynemouth 4.10.68 *AUR* XLIII 85

LOW Ethel Isobel BSc 1952

LOW James Alexander MA 1936 LLB 1938
d Aber 2.11.76

LOW or Vannet, Jean Farquhar MA 1938
teacher Engl: Kirton h s Dun 1963–68, Grove acad Broughty Ferry 1968–76

LOW or Robertson, Jeannie Anne MA 1915
d Maud 22.2.81

LOW John *BSc(mech eng) 1933 BSc(elect eng) 1934

LOW John Alexander *BSc 1941
prin teacher phys: Golspie 1958–65, Perth from 1965

LOW John Robertson *MA BSc 1924
d 21.12.70

LOW Margaret Ross MA 1945
teacher Hilton acad Aber from 1948

LOW or Mackintosh, Muriel Agnes *MA 1933
resid Nairn

LOW Norma MA 1953
secy/translator: Glasg 1954–56; Internal Air Trans Assoc Geneva from 1975
m Aber 10.2.56 Robert C. McIntosh CA Europ controller s of Alexander McI. Aber

LOW Robert Milne *MA 1925
retd 1963; resid Lossiemouth

LOW or Bremner, Ruby Cameron MA 1949

LOW William James MA 1937
head: Hatton (Cruden) s 1961–70, Kintore s 1970–76; retd; resid Banchory

LOW William Robin Milne *MA 1954
Honiara Br Solomon Is: admin off. class 'A' from 1972, secy for soc serv 1972–73

LOW William Smith MA 1926
retd 1967; resid St And

LOW William Stewart BSc 1948
teacher: spec asst sc Mearns acad Laurencekirk from 1949

LOWE Anne Margaret MA 1951
teacher: Banff p s 1962–67, Engl/hist Banff acad from 1967

LOWE Donald Neil MA 1912
d 10.7.70

LOWE Florence Lyall MA 1914
d 30.3.65

LOWIT Ian Michael MB ChB 1953
MRCPE 1959 MRCPsych 1973
sen regist Kingseat hosp and Ross Clin Aber 1959–61; consult. dept ch and fam psychiat RACH from 1961

LOWSON David Sturrock BSc(for) 1950

LOWSON or Ross, Marion Catherine MA 1922
resid Leabrook S Aust

LUCKHOO Maurice Stanley MB ChB 1955
regist N Cambs hosp Wisbech 1957–58; clin off. RAMC (nat serv) BMH Singapore 1958–60; N Cambs hosp Wisbech: regist 1960–67, asst phys from 1967

LUDWIG Brian *MA 1950
d Aber 11.1.73 *AUR* XLV 228

LUKE or Strachan, Iris Winifred MA 1949
resid Montrose

LUMSDEN Alexander Gow *MB ChB 1917
d Lond 23.4.75 *AUR* XLVI 236

LUMSDEN Andrew Anderson BL 1922
d Aber 8.2.66 *AUR* XLII 86

LUMSDEN Charles Edward MB ChB 1936 *MD 1948
d 23.6.74 *AUR* XLVI 110

LUMSDEN Charles Gordon MA 1915 LLB 1922

LUMSDEN Charles Ian BSc(agr) 1950

LUMSDEN or McLean, Edith Ross *MA 1916
d Haddington 21.6.64 *AUR* XL 398

LUMSDEN George Henry Charles *MB ChB 1907
d 15.2.61 *AUR* XXXIX 273

LUMSDEN George Innes MB ChB 1946
g p Peterhead
d 25.10.81

LUMSDEN George Innes *BSc 1949
FRSE 1967
dist geol inst of geol sc Edin from 1970

LUMSDEN William BCom 1928 MB ChB 1938
g p Aber from 1947

LUNAN or McLaren, Ivy Scott BSc 1927
resid Wilmslow
d Wilmslow 4.4.79 *AUR* XLVIII 229

LUNAN Netty Margaret *MA 1918
d Aber 22.3.68 *AUR* XLII 356

LUNAN or Catto, Ruth Anderson MA 1947
lib MRC 1969–71

LUNDIE John Ernest MA 1921
d Aber 18.6.73 *AUR* XLV 318

LUNN James Glover Thomson MB ChB 1937
d Blackpool 8.11.65 *AUR* XLI 250

LUTTRELL Arthur Brocklehurst
see Munro-Ferguson

LYALL or Sleigh, Ada Shirley MA 1954
Stirling: teacher St Ninian's p s 1962–73, asst head Braehead p s from 1973

LYALL Alan Richards MB ChB 1951
DObstRCOG(Lond) 1957 MRCGP 1963
g p Laurencekirk from 1956

LYALL Alexander
MA 1920 *MB ChB 1923 *MD 1926 LLD 1971
d Aber 11.5.74 *AUR* XLV 341

LYALL Alexander David MB ChB 1950
accidentally drowned Shetland 22.7.65

LYALL André BSc 1943

LYALL Andrew MA 1927
head Newburgh Mathers s 1935–64; retd; resid Newburgh Aberdeensh

LYALL Anne-Marie MA 1945

LYALL or Mantell, Barbara Ann MA 1921
retd 1965; resid Macduff

LYALL Barbara Clarke *MA 1952
b 19.7.30
teacher maths Perth acad 1961–73, asst prin maths from 1973

LYALL Constance Edina *MA 1915
d Crieff 21.11.74 *AUR* XLVI 236

LYALL Douglas Jolly MB ChB 1945
d Edin 5.6.63 *AUR* XL 207

LYALL or Lowe, Florence MA 1914
d 30.3.65

LYALL Gordon MA 1907
d Lond 16.3.68 *AUR* XLII 347

LYALL Ian Hodge BSc 1955
d 30.5.64 *AUR* XL 401

LYALL Joseph Watt MB ChB 1927

LYALL Maggie *MA 1922 BSc 1923
retd 1962; resid Scone Perth

LYALL Malcolm George MA 1951 MB ChB 1956
FRCS 1970
sen h m o Aber hosps 1961–72; consult. ophth surg Essex from 1972

LYALL Ronald Alexander MA 1949 LLB 1952
ptnr: Kinnear & Falconer solic Stonehaven 1960–64, Walter Gerrard & Co. Solic MacDuff from 1964

LYALL Thomas MB ChB 1936 MD 1954
consult. venereologist Stockport, Macclesfield, Crewe from 1961

LYALL William *MA 1932
teacher phys: Edin 1933–39, Dunfermline 1939–40: RAF(S/L) Cranwell 1940–46; teacher phys Edin 1946–73; retd; resid Gifford
m Edin 25.11.39 Jane Mann teacher d of Donald M. Fortrose

LYNCH Frederick Passmore MB ChB 1955
DObstRCOG 1962 MRCGP 1966
Aber: h o mat. hosp 1958–59; g p from 1959

LYNCH Robert MB ChB 1953
g p Kilwinning from 1958

LYNN Harry Belford MA 1948
prof Engl San Antonio coll Texas from 1973

LYON Alexander MB ChB 1951
h o City hosp Aber 1951; m o RAF 1951–56; g p Inv 1956–58, Golspie 1958–60, Doncaster from 1960; clin asst anaest Doncaster RI from 1968
m Aber 6.2.54 Joan I. Paterson nurse d of William P. Aber

LYON or Thomson, Alice Anne Cowan MA 1936

LYON Christina Helen MA 1927
retd 1968; resid Alford

LYON Dorothea Mary Anton MA 1921
retd 1938; resid Aber
d 4.2.78 *AUR* XLVIII 227

LYON Douglas MB ChB 1916 DPH 1921
d –.3.67

LYON Katherine Elizabeth MA 1946

LYON Louis Carlyle MB ChB 1927
d 30.1.70 *AUR* XLIII 446

LYON Mabel Margaret Annand MA 1927
resid Aber

LYON Mary MA 1910
d Aber 11.6.65

LYONS James Michael *BSc 1949 PhD 1952
MChemInst(Can) MCIC
dir continuing educ Lachute Quebec 1967–69; Montreal: chmn chem dept Dawson coll 1969–71; chmn sc and tech John Abbott coll from 1971

MACALDOWIE John BL 1947
trustee man. Clydesdale Bank 1950–72; retd; resid Glasg

McALLAN or Emslie, Betty MB ChB 1951
asst m o h Midlothian 1961–68; g p Oldham from 1968

MacALLAN James Brown MB ChB 1908
no longer on GC reg

McALLAN James Lewis MA 1937 LLB 1939
dep county clerk Aberdeensh 1954–75; dir law and admin Grampian reg c 1975–77; retd

McALLAN James Watt MB ChB 1944

McALLAN James William Mackie MA 1895
d Aber 13.1.66 *AUR* XLII 79

McALLAN John Gilbert BSc 1944
dev eng Standard Telephones & Cables from 1944
m Golders Green 27.1.51 Margaret Bickford-Smith d of Alan B-S. Liss

McANDREW Albert Grassick Cumming BSc(eng) 1951
sen prof tech ML Aviation Co. White Waltham 1967–75; proj man. from 1975

McANDREW or Munro, Isabella Margaret MA 1943
head Ae p s Dumfries from 1958

MACANDREW Margaret Cameron *MA 1942
resid Bramhall

MACANDREW or Anscombe, Maureen Maxwell MB ChB 1944
clin asst St Mary's hosp Manc from 1965

MACANDREW Ronald Maxwell DLitt 1929
d 20.4.62 *AUR* XXXIX 384

MACANDREW Ronald William MB ChB 1954
g p Aber from 1956

McARA Alastair Ross MA 1937
d Aber 1.4.73 *AUR* XLV 227

MACARA or Barnett-Smith, Margaret Elizabeth *MA 1948

McARTHUR Alexander Allan PhD 1952
C of S min: Peterhead old par ch 1952–56, Pollokshields-Titwood par ch Glasg 1956–65, St Mary's par ch Edin from 1965
publ *The Evolution of the Christian Year* 1953, *The Christian Year and Lectionary Reform* 1958

MacARTHUR Allan Alexander MA 1912
no longer on GC reg

MacARTHUR Archibald MA 1930
retd 1968; resid Milltimber Aber
d Stirling 18.6.78 *AUR* XLVIII 104 & 353

MACARTHUR Effie Kate MA 1925
teacher Laxdale j s s 1958–64
m Edin 1.5.65 Angus Macleod retd headmaster s of Malcolm M. Carloway Is of Lewis

McARTHUR Gordon *MA 1952
PGCE(Lond) 1961
bank off.: Chartered Bank Singapore 1953–55, Indonesia 1956–57; educ off.: Sabah, Malaysia 1961–67, Hong Kong 1968–72; sen govt trg off. Hong Kong 1972–73; prin lect polytech Hong Kong from 1973
m Sabah 21.11.69 Glynis Wong Chew Ngoh teacher d of Wong Wai Chek Singapore

McARTHUR Ian BSc(for) 1937
no longer on GC reg

MACARTHUR John MB ChB 1925
d Worthing 28.10.74

MACARTHUR John MA 1939
dep head Stornoway p s 1964–74, head from 1974

MACARTHUR John Gordon *MB ChB 1937
FRCPGlas 1964 FRCPE 1969
sen lect materia medica Glas and consult. phys Stobhill gen hosp Glasg and 1950
wife *d* 13.1.74

McARTHUR Julia MA 1929
retd; resid Edin

MACARTHUR or Clarkson, Kathleen Daisy MA 1947
teacher: h s Dun 1967–71, Gillburn s Dun from 1971

MACARTHUR or Mackenzie, Mary Alexandra MB ChB 1944
part time asst m o h Kidderminster from 1970

MacARTHUR Norman MA 1929
JP Ross and Cromarty 1960
retd 1971; resid Inv

MacARTHUR William Gordon MB ChB 1908
d Yorksh –.1.71

MacASKILL Alexander John *MA 1948
prin teacher Gaelic Nicolson inst Stornoway 1960–66; head Portree h s 1966–71; rector McLaren h s Callander from 1971

MACASKILL Angus MA 1923
C of S min London Road ch Edin 1947–64; officiating chaplain RAF Turnhouse Edin 1947–64; C of S min Cults and Kettle, presb of Cupar Fife 1964–69; retd; resid Bridge of Earn
m Arbroath 23.11.32 Maureen R. Anderson d of Norman B. A. Arbroath

MACASKILL Donald MB ChB 1946
JP Ross and Cromarty
h o St Luke's hosp Bradford 1947; locum tenens Borve 1947–49; g p: Wolverhampton 1949–51, Galson Is of Lewis from 1952

MACASKILL or Vince, Margaret MA 1928

MACAULAY Alexander MA 1922
d –.9.63

MACAULAY Allan John MA 1947
head Crathie s from 1961
d Crathie 18.4.77 *AUR* XLVII 214

MACAULAY Callum Alexander *MA 1952
pers man.: Burmah–Shell refinery Bombay 1958–63, Brunei Shell Co Seria, Borneo 1963–69; pers asst Shell Internat Lond 1969–70; pers man. Shell Malaysia Kuala Lumpur 1970–72; pers sen man. Saudi Arabian airlines Jeddah 1973–74; pers admin Southeastern Drilling Serv Aber 1974–75; head of personnel Total Oil Marine from 1976
m(2) Bombay 11.10.58 Jillian R. Anderson d of Kenneth H. A. Johannesburg

MACAULAY Donald *MA 1953
lect: dept of Engl lang Edin 1957–60; dept of Irish Trinity coll Dublin 1960–63; dept of applied ling Edin 1963–67; head dept of Celtic Aberd from 1967

MACAULAY Donald Campbell *MA 1951
prin teacher mod lang Summerhill acad Aber 1967–74, prin teacher Fr Hazlehead acad Aber from 1974

MACAULAY Donald Roderick MB ChB 1938
sen dept m o Ross and Cromarty from 1970, sen m o Western Isles health board

MACAULAY Joyce Alexander BSc 1951 *1952

MACAULAY Malcolm MA 1921 BSc 1923
no longer on GC reg

MACAULAY or Pringle, May Isabella MA 1925
resid Perth
d Perth 17.9.79

MACAULAY Murdina MA 1947
Aber: teacher Rosehill inf s 1948–62, Cornhill p s 1962–65, asst head Cornhill s from 1965
m Aber 1961 David K. Cowie
d Aber 17.8.78 *AUR* XLVIII 107

MACAULAY William BSc(agr) 1936

McAUSLANE Stella Maxwell MA 1955
teacher Gordon s Huntly from 1961

McBAIN Alexander Cruden MA 1929
Lond: dir team man. consult. 1964–73, dir interscope man. serv from 1973
no longer on GC reg

McBAIN Alexander Walker MB ChB 1940 DPH 1947
d Aber 30.11.70 *AUR* XLIV 215

McBAIN Archibald Patrick MB ChB 1953

McBAIN Charles Stewart BSc 1950
AMIGasE 1955
chem eng Menstrie 1960–63; asst distillery man. Girvan 1963–69; oper man. Keith from 1969
marr diss
m(2) Fraserburgh 1.7.72 Kathleen M. Innes teacher

McBAIN Douglas MB ChB 1939
DMJ 1962
g p Aber from 1948; sen police surg Aber from 1957
m(2) Strathdon 16.10.76 Mildred M. Fraser

McBAIN or Sim, Elizabeth Stephen MA 1927
teacher comm subjs Hilton acad Aber 1953–68; retd but contd part-time till 1972

McBAIN or Sadler, Flora Munro *MA 1934

McBAIN William BSc 1949
BA(OU) 1973
dep head Laurencekirk s s from 1961

MacBEAN Alexander Fraser BSc 1934 MB ChB 1938
reg m o h from 1957; resid Exeter

MacBEAN Coila Christina MA 1933
d 30.12.63

McBEAN Donald Henderson BSc(agr) 1950
farm. Balblair from 1951
m Inv 4.4.61 Charlotte G. Holm secy d of Thomas H. Balblair

MacBEAN or Coles, Dorothea Fraser BSc 1935 MB ChB 1938
off./sister order of St John from 1960; commander/

sister order of St John from 1964; med advis joint commission St John and Red Cross Cyprus in 1964

MACBEAN Innes Black *MA 1938
teacher Fr Ampleforth coll York from 1956

MACBEAN John BSc(agr) 1937
prin: Kersewell agr coll Carnwath 1953–60, Balmacara agr s Kyle Rosssh 1961–65, Lawmuir agr coll E. Kilbride 1965–74; retd

MacBEAN Robert John Laing MB ChB 1937
d Dunbeath 11.1.69 *AUR* XLIII 216

MacBEATH John BCom 1922 *BL 1923
d 15.4.66

McBEATH or Wilson, Margaret Allan MA 1931
head partially-sighted dept Claremont OAS Salford 1960–68; teacher Leuchars p s 1968–74; retd; resid Mintlaw

MacBEATH Ronald Angus BSc 1950
housemaster Wingate coll Addis Ababa 1953–56; Sudan govt off. (educ) Khartoum, Port Sudan 1956–60; (Brit council) sen housemaster cadet coll Chittagong Bangladesh 1960–64; teaching posts in Scot. 1964–69; head Temple p s M'Lothian 1969–74; head Whitecraig p s Musselburgh from 1974
m Inv 21.8.52 Ann-Mairie Macleod secy d of John M. Nairobi

McBEY William George BSc 1949 *1950

McBOYLE or Gordon, Helen Maggie MA 1910
resid Hamilton NZ
d NZ 17.9.77

McBOYLE John Rae MB ChB 1938
TD 1960 MRCGP 1971
g p Sheffield 1946–62; reg m o from 1962

McBOYLE Patrick George MB ChB 1943
JP 1958
g p Huntly from 1947

McCALL Andrew MA BSc 1950
teacher maths Tain acad 1958–61; head Lochinver s s from 1961
m 4.8.62 Sheena L. Conway civ serv; wife *d* 2.4.77

McCALLUM Aenea Janet *MA 1940
duties in War Office (MI6) Richmond Surrey 1940–45; Lond: in advt 1946–49; edit. asst Royal Inst of Internat Affairs 1949–51; edit. secy of Oriental & Af stud. univ of Lond 1951–55
m Cambridge 11.8.55 W. Sidney Allen MA(Cantab) prof compar philol univ of Cambridge s of William P. A.

McCALLUM or Duff, Bethea Janet MA 1950
teacher: geog/Engl 1963–65, commerce 1965–71 West Calder h s Midlothian; lect commerce Steventon coll of f e Edin from 1971
marr diss 1961

McCALLUM Eoin Leslie Richardson MB ChB 1944
d Richmond Yorks 28.11.71 *AUR* XLIV 433

McCALLUM Isabella MA 1925
teacher Johannesburg 1950–66; resid Cape, S Af
m Grange Banffsh 8.4.39 Daniel S. Crichton CA s of Robert C. Errol Perthsh

McCALLUM Jennie Whitelaw PhD 1929
retd 1961; resid Edin

McCALLUM or MacLaren, Margaret Jane MA 1920
resid Edin

MacCALLUM or Henderson, Margaret Paxton *MA 1924
resid Aber

McCALLUM Mary Kennedy MA 1904
d Edin 2.6.71 *AUR* XLIV 316

McCALLUM Norman Hugh Ross MB ChB 1933
d 10.2.69

McCALLUM Robert Francis Gordon *MA 1923
head Queen's Park s Glasg; retd
d Edin 24.4.76

McCALLUM Thomas Watson MA 1904
no longer on GC reg

McCANN or Mitchell, Marjory Grace MA 1952
USA: volunteer teacher reading Schenectady 1968–70; grad stud. in s of soc work 1972
marr diss 1974

McCANN or Cahill, Mary Walker BSc 1954

McCASKIE or Macaulay, Gertrude Rhodes MA 1922
no longer on GC reg

McCLELLAN or Rybka, Hester Nicholas *MA 1951
MA(Oxon) 1966 Outstanding educators of America award 1974
Palmer jun coll Davenport Iowa: instr 1966–71, head dept Engl/phil from 1971; Nat Endowment for The Humanities fell. in resid univ of Calif at Santa Cruz 1977–78

McCLELLAN John Forrest *MA 1954
civ serv: p s to perm under-secy of state for Scot. Edin/Lond 1959–60, asst secy S.E.D. Edin 1969–77; asst under-Secy of State Scot. off. Lond/Edin from 1977

McCLURG Hamish Greig MA 1954 LLB 1957
solic Carrington & Sealy, Bridgetown Barbados from 1958

McCOMBIE Arthur Leiper *MA 1950
prin teacher hist AGS/Rubislaw acad 1961–73; dep head Rubislaw acad 1973–77, dep rector AGS from 1977

m Aber 25.7.61 Vaila M. J. MacLeod teacher p e d of Donald MacL. Nairn

McCOMBIE Charles William *MA 1948 PhD 1951
FRSE 1970
sen lect Aberd 1963–64; prof phys R'dg from 1964; visiting prof univ of Illinois USA 1972

McCOMBIE Donald Johnson MB ChB 1943

McCOMBIE or Gleeson, Effie MA 1902
no longer on GC reg

McCOMBIE Elizabeth Winton MA 1955
Aber: infant mistress Smithfield s 1969–74, head Rosewood inf s from 1974

McCOMBIE George Henry MA 1932 LLB 1936
Huntly: ptnr John Dickson & Son solic 1965–70; solic on own account from 1970

McCOMBIE Hamilton MA 1900
d 31.5.62 *AUR* XXXIX 372

McCOMBIE Harry Duncan MA 1948
teacher accounting/computer progr/law/Fr h s Listowel Ontario from 1968

McCOMBIE or Shepherd, Hazel MA 1950
d –.10.72

McCOMBIE Isabella MA 1909
d Glasg 11.2.66 *AUR* XLI 241

McCOMBIE James Daniel BL 1927
d Aber 10.11.74 *AUR* XLVI 237

McCOMBIE John MA 1888 BD 1891
d Dumfries 10.10.47

McCOMBIE Kathleen MB ChB 1947
g p; retd 1964
m Aber 5.12.64 Edward G. C. Rhind MB ChB 1935 *qv*

McCOMBIE Meta *MA 1902
no longer on GC reg

McCONACHIE Allan Milne MB ChB 1953
g p Luton from 1955

McCONACHIE Bert Stewart BSc 1944
Ontario: electronics eng Canadian Westinghouse Hamilton 1952–57; man. radar eng Raytheon Canada Waterloo 1957–74; man. Tactical Data Syst Litton Syst Rexdale from 1974
m Hamilton Ont 1957 Hannah P. L. Robinson path. secy/newsp proof reader d of John L. R. Burlington Ont

McCONACHIE or Sprunt, Elizabeth Mary MB ChB 1955
vocational trg 1974–78; locum work Dun from 1978
husb *d* 1971

McCONACHIE George William MA 1924
head Dunnottar p s Stonehaven 1954–67; retd; resid Stonehaven
d Stonehaven 6.5.81

McCONACHIE or McGregor, Helen Isabel *MA 1943
resid Banavie, by Fort William

McCONACHIE Isabella MA 1935
teacher Kinloss p s 1959–76; retd

McCONACHIE John Alexander MB ChB 1944
g p Lossiemouth from 1951

McCONACHIE or Englefield, Margaret Lipp MA 1913
no longer on GC reg

McCONNACH Bruce *MA 1955
Lond: acct exec Young & Rubicam 1960–64; advt man. *L'Oreal of Paris* 1964–65, head of sales and subscriptions consumers' assoc *Which?* 1965–70; mag sales man. *Reader's Digest* 1970–72, head of marketing consumers' assoc *Which?* from 1972

McCONNACH or Haywood, Jean Morag BSc 1951
resid Aber

McCONNACHIE or Forbes, Anne Gray MA 1926
resid Pitmedden

McCONNACHIE Catherine Elizabeth MA 1926 BD 1959

McCONNACHIE Duncan Campbell MA 1934 LLB 1936

McCONNACHIE George William Ritchie BSc(agr) 1920
no longer on GC reg

McCONNACHIE Helen MA 1934

McCONNACHIE Helen Isobel MA 1941

McCONNACHIE or Stevenson, Isabella Kemp *MA 1908
d Aber 9.6.68 *AUR* XLIII 78

McCONNACHIE James Lock BSc(eng) 1950
M Inst Eng(Aust) 1954
plant and supply eng Melb metro Board of Works Melbourne from 1968

McCONNACHIE James Stewart BSc 1935 *MB ChB 1938
consult. surg Welsh reg hosp board from 1949

McCONNACHIE or Hughes, Jeanie Simpson *MA 1913
resid Bearsden

McCONNACHIE or Donaldson, Jeannie Anne MA 1922
resid Grantown-on-Spey

McCONNACHIE or Johnson, Mary Walker **MA 1924**
resid Te Aroha NZ

McCONNACHIE Ronald William MB ChB 1946

McCOSS or Scott, Evelyn MA 1925
retd 1968; resid Galashiels

McCOWAN Daniel BSc(agr) 1953
sen scient off.: Nature Conservancy Edin 1964–72, ITE Banchory from 1974
m(2) Glasg 15.6.73 Catriona F. Finlayson MA(Edin) teacher d of Kenneth F. MA(Glas) Glasg

McCRAE Marion (Mona) MA 1941

McCRAE Stuart Rice BSc(eng) 1950

McCREADIE Samuel Robert McNay **ᶜMB ChB 1951**
Dip Amer Board of Path. 1958 Fell Amer Acad Paediat 1961
dir path. ch hosp Milwaukee Wisconsin USA/assoc prof path. med coll of Wisconsin (formerly Marquette univ) from 1960

McCREADY Margaret Scott PhD 1947
dean Macdonald inst univ of Guelph Ontario 1964–69; head home sc dept fac of agr univ of Ghana, Legon near Accra 1969–71; retd; resid Toronto

McCREATH Helen Margaret Ross MA 1942
secy Shipbuilding Conference (called Shipbuilders and Repairers National Association from 1967) 1946–77; gen secy Nat Council of Women (GB) 1977

MacCRIMMON Padruig René BSc(agr) 1953
ICI plant protection div HMOCS Nigeria 1954–63; dev off. Europe from 1963

MacCUISH Alexander John BSc 1932
d Fortrose 29.8.78 *AUR* XLVIII 105

MacCUISH Catherine MA 1924
d 28.6.66

MacCUISH Donald MA 1926

MacCUISH Donald John MA 1931
member crofters' comm Inv from 1975

MacCUISH or McDonald, Hannah Margaret **MA 1942**
resid Mapperley

MacCUISH Roderick Kenneth MB ChB 1942
FRCP
consult. phys Bradford hosps from 1958

McCULLOCH David James MB ChB 1950
d Bulawayo Rhodesia 3.2.70 *AUR* XLIII 446

McCULLOCH Gordon Louis MB ChB 1922
FRCGP 1968
provost, E Anglia fac royal coll g p's 1963; author *Man Alive* Aldus books 1967

McCULLOCH or Hutchinson, Margaret Wedderburn **MA 1913**
no longer on GC reg

McCULLOCH William Edward **MB ChB 1923 ᶜMD 1929**
no longer on GC reg

McCULLOCH Winifred Sophia MA 1912
retd 1950; resid Glasg
d Glasg 8.4.80

McCURRACH Margaret Davidson MA 1933
teacher: Frederick St s s Aber 1948–69, Bridge of Don acad from 1969

McCURRACH or Watt, Mary Smith MA 1936
resid Croydon

McCURRACH William George MA 1938
d Aber 4.7.78 *AUR* XLVIII 106

McCURRIE Janet Grierson MA 1955 LLB 1958

McCUTCHEON George Buchanan MB ChB 1952
Aust: m o spec hosp Toowoomba 1958–68, med supt Ipswich from 1968
marr diss
m(2) Toowoomba 13.2.68 Helga Waschier nurse educator d of Hans W. Karnten Austria

MacDIARMID or Hatrick, Christine Bannerman **BL 1939**
d Aber 31.8.75

MacDIARMID James Breadalbane MB ChB 1905
practised in NZ: Auckland, Tauranga
d NZ

MacDIARMID or Cormack, Moira Noel Jean **MA 1941**
teacher Engl Aber 1956–72; off. i/c Richmondhill House (Aber mother and baby home) from 1972
marr diss 1973

MACDONALD Agnes MA 1954 LLB 1956
leg. asst J & F Anderson WS Edin 1957–60; asst solic: Scot. spec housing assoc Edin 1968–73, Cuthbert Marchbank Paterson & Salmon SSC Edin from 1973
m Edin 25.7.58 Finlay Mackenzie res and dev eng/prod. market. man. (electronics)

MACDONALD Alastair Alexander *MA 1948
mem univ of Newfoundland: assoc prof Engl 1961–69, prof from 1969; contributor to magazines, reviews etc in UK Canada and USA; poetry publ *Between Something and Something* (1970), *Shape Enduring Mind* (1974), *A Different Lens* (1981)

MACDONALD Alexander *MA 1925
DD(St And)
vicar: St Augustine's Tonge Moor Bolton 1933–40,

All Souls Leeds 1940–46; sen chaplain Leeds I 1940–45; rector All Saints St Andrews from 1946; retd 1976
d -.6.80 *AUR* XLIX 67

MACDONALD Alexander MA 1929

MACDONALD Alexander *MA 1931 *MB ChB 1937 *MD 1943
retd 1978; emeritus prof; resid Aber

McDONALD Alexander *MA 1931
joiner Portsoy from 1931
d Portsoy 7.9.79 *AUR* XLVIII 354

MACDONALD Alexander Henry MA 1932
teacher Fraserburgh from 1940

MACDONALD Alexander Hugh BSc(agr) 1923
Argentine: ranch asst Las Petocas 1925–28, ranch under-man. 1929–34, frigorifico buyer Buenos Aires 1934–36, ranch under-man. Las Petocas 1937–42, 1946–57, ranch admin San Luis 1958–65
m Santa Fé 31.1.48 Gwendoline S. Smith d of Walter B. S. prov of Cordoba, Argentine

MACDONALD Alexandrina MA 1910
d Conon Bridge 13.3.68 *AUR* XLII 348

MACDONALD Alfred Emerson MA 1929 *MB ChB 1932

MACDONALD Alison Margaret Graham BSc 1951
lect chem Birm 1962–72, sen lect from 1972

MACDONALD Alistair *BSc 1949

MacDONALD Alistair Cameron MA 1913 *MB ChB 1916
d Elgin 12.1.71 *AUR* XLIV 209

MacDONALD Alistair Cameron MB ChB 1948
MRCGP 1974
g p Norton, Stockton-on-Tees from 1963

MACDONALD Alistair David MB ChB 1930 MD 1934
asst m o h King's Lynn, Norfolk c c 1960–66; asst m o h Inv c c 1966–69; retd
m(3) Kendal -.4.68 Margery M. Bridges d of Donald B. King's Lynn

MACDONALD Alistair Philip MB ChB 1934
g p Newark 1935–40 and from 1945; retd 1974

McDONALD Alistair Phinn BSc 1949
mill chem C. Davidson & Sons Bucksburn 1950–51; prod. man.: Umtali Board and Paper Mills S. Rhodesia 1951–55, C. Davidson & Sons/group tech off. Davidson Redcliffe from 1955
m Glasg 4.2.47 Mary W. Stewart

MACDONALD Allan *MEd 1953
asst psych Edin 1953–57; educ psych Berksh 1957–62, sen educ psych Glos from 1962

MACDONALD Allan Duncan MB ChB 1947
DPH(Edin) DIH(Lond) 1961
Unilever fell. indust med Lond/Gloucester/Warrington 1961–62; reg m o T. Wall & Son Gloucester 1962–64; area m o BR southern reg E Croydon from 1964
m Cirencester 20.3.65 Ann D. M. Bullock BBC secy/antique dealer d of Humphry B. CIE OBE FRHS FRGenS Cirencester

MACDONALD Andrew MA 1929
no longer on GC reg

MACDONALD Angus Lewis MA 1903
no longer on GC reg

MACDONALD Angus William Bertram BSc 1935 MB ChB 1938 MD 1951
consult. chest phys Dudley and Stourbridge group of hosps from 1952
m Helen R. Chignell

McDONALD or Dodds, Anna Low MA 1934
resid Strathdon

MacDONALD Annie **MA 1915 and 1916
d 3.9.78 *AUR* XLVIII 102

MACDONALD or Campbell, Annie MA 1932
d 1.4.61

MACDONALD Anson BSc(agr) 1950
sen lands off. Thurso from 1971

MacDONALD Archibald James BSc(agr) 1925
no longer on GC reg

MacDONALD Betsy MA 1954
m Howieson

MACDONALD Catherine MA 1912
resid Hamilton Ont Canada 1961–71; retd 1971; resid Glasg
m Stirling 24.8.60 James McKenzie hydro employee Ont s of James McK. Keiss

MACDONALD Catherine MA 1955
teacher: Hilton p s Inv 1957–65, Engl Mimir s of lang Reykjavik Iceland 1965–71, Cowdenbeath p s from 1979
m Stornoway 12.9.67 Sven Bjarnason, Cand Theol (Reykjavik) C of S min s of Bjarni B. Reykjavik

MACDONALD Catherine Isobel MA 1930
teacher: Lond 1931–51, Inv 1951–69, Drumnadrochit 1967–69; retd; resid Drumnadrochit

MacDONALD or Heriot, Catherine Jane *MA 1914
no longer on GC reg

MACDONALD Charles John MA 1930

McDONALD or Duthie, Christian Milne MA 1918
d Daviot 1.3.73

MACDONALD Christina Fraser MA 1921
teacher Glenurquhart s s s 1930–62; retd; resid Drumnadrochit

MacDONALD Christopher MB ChB 1935

MACDONALD Colin David John MA 1929 BSc(for) 1932
head Maud s 1965–73; retd; resid New Aberdour

McDONALD David *MA 1950
MBE 1974
sen classics master Opoku Ware s Kumasi, Ghana 1958–63; commissioned educ branch RAF (sqn/ldr 1966) 1963; Durh univ and Mecas, Lebanon (Arabic interpreter) 1968–70; GC HQ 1970–73; Engl lang instr Kuwait milit acad from 1974
m Coatbridge 29.7.58 Margaret M. Gillespie teacher d of Charles E. G. Coatbridge

McDONALD David Sandeman MB ChB 1951
DGM(Melb) 1977
m o Dr Gray's hosp Elgin 1952; g p Kirkoswald Cambs 1952–53, New Pitsligo 1953–56; Aust: sen m o base hosp Mildura, Victoria, Aust 1957–58, g p Red Cliffs 1958–71, Merimbula 1971–73; geriat m o Beechworth Aust from 1973
m Aber 22.8.52 Elizabeth M. Thomson secy d of John S. B. T. Inv

MACDONALD Donald MA 1913
d Kilmun 17.10.75

MacDONALD Donald MA 1913 BD 1920 DD 1961
retd; resid Montrose

MACDONALD Donald MA 1914
d Stornoway 29.10.61 *AUR* XXXIX 275

MACDONALD Donald BSc(agr) 1922
d 6.5.60

MACDONALD Donald MA 1928 BCom 1930

MACDONALD Donald *MA 1937
prin teacher Fr/Ger Fort William s s s later Lochaber h s from 1947
d 12.5.76

MACDONALD Donald MB ChB 1942
deceased

MacDONALD Donald MA 1948
JP 1969
head Aberdour s New Aberdour Aberdeensh from 1969

MacDONALD Donald Alexander MB ChB 1931
d 18.7.67

MacDONALD Donald Douglas MA 1928

MACDONALD Donald Farquhar *MA 1930
FRHistS 1967
emeritus prof mod soc and econ hist Dund 1976

MACDONALD Donald John *MA 1923 LLD 1957
retd 1962; chmn N reg hosp board 1965–71
wife *d* 1961

MacDONALD Donald John *MA 1955

McDONALD or Sim, Doreen Ellen MA 1942

MACDONALD Douglas Reginald *MB ChB 1921
d Nairn 12.1.77

MACDONALD Douglas Stephen *MA 1922 MB ChB 1931
d Budleigh Salterton 2.2.78 *AUR* XLVIII 103

MacDONALD Duncan BCom 1924
retd 1968; resid Drumnadrochit
m Chicago 25.4.28 Marion MacDonald d of Murdo MacD.

McDONALD or Edwards, Edith Mary Hutcheon MA 1942
head Fryern j s Chandler's Ford from 1963

MACDONALD or Humphreys, Eleanor MA 1914
no longer on GC reg

MacDONALD or Snowden, Elizabeth Ann MA 1940
resid Abingdon

MacDONALD or Godden, Elizabeth Frances BSc 1932
resid Guildford

MACDONALD or Somerville, Elizabeth Mary MB ChB 1948
resid Edin

MACDONALD or Taylor, Ella MB ChB 1946
g p Bradford from 1967

MACDONALD or Robertson, Elsa Milne *MA 1954
teacher: mod lang Aber h s for girls 1958–69, prin Ger 1969–75, Engl/Ger at French s Aber from 1975

MACDONALD or Elliott, Elsie Souter MA 1942
supply teacher Kent c c 1960–61; sen clin psych: (part-time) St Augustine's hosp Canterbury 1961–69, Little High Wood, Brentwood 1970–78, m h Medway commun health serv from 1978

MACDONALD Eric Alexander Mackay MA 1905
no longer on GC reg

MACDONALD Flora Helen Grant MB ChB 1924
g p Bradford-on-Avon 1940–66; retd; resid Aber

McDONALD Frank Edward *MA 1948

MACDONALD George Alexander *MA 1949
FIL 1966
Colvilles Glasg: export sales admin 1955–64, staff translator 1964–67; staff translator Br steel corp, gen steels div Motherwell from 1967

McDONALD George Alexander MB ChB 1954 ᶜMD 1960
MRCPath 1963 MRCPGlas 1968 FRCPGlas 1972 FRCPath 1976
sen regist haemat Glas RI and assoc hosps 1962–64, consult. haemat in admin charge from 1964; hon lect haemat Glas, hon consult. W Scot. blood transfusion serv

MACDONALD George Grant BSc(agr) 1909
d Cambridge 18.7.60 *AUR* XXXIX 102

McDONALD or Davidson, Gertrude Chessor MA 1922
resid Aber

McDONALD Gladys Elsie MA 1939
teacher Frederick St s s Aber, later Linksfield acad from 1947

MCDONALD or Duthie, Gladys Margaret MA 1946
teacher Rosehearty 1947–50, Stoneywood 1950–51, Aber 1964–66, Beechwood s Aber from 1966

MACDONALD Hannah Margaret MA 1922
teacher Engl/hist Ruthrieston j s s Aber 1943–62; retd

McDONALD or Bohdanowicz, Harriet *MA 1933

MACDONALD Hector MA 1951
teacher: Fyvie s 1958–63, Culter s 1963–66, Cults acad 1966–68, prin geog Summerhill acad Aber from 1968

MACDONALD or Exton, Helen Cantlie MA 1926
resid Port Erin, Is of Man
husb *d* 1969

McDONALD Herman Ewart Theodore MB ChB 1931
retd 1970; resid Mexico
wife *d* 1977

MacDONALD Hester May MA 1935
d Aber 12.4.71 *AUR* XLIV 212

MACDONALD Hugh MA 1944

MacDONALD Iain Alasdair *MA 1931
HMIS 1951–69; retd

MACDONALD Ian *MA 1926
no longer on GC reg

McDONALD Ian Arthur BSc 1951
JP
Aber: prin teacher sc Summerhill s s 1961–67, dep head Summerhill acad 1967–71, head Old Aber and Middle and Frederick St s 1971–73, head Linksfield acad from 1973

MACDONALD Ian David *MA 1954
DSc(Manc) 1970 LGSM 1977
res fell. Aust nat univ Canberra 1961–64; prof maths: univ coll Newcastle NSW 1964–67; reader in maths univ of Queensland 1967–68; visiting lect in maths Dund 1969; sen lect maths univ of E. Anglia 1969–70; sen lect maths Stir from 1970
m(1) Tintagel 20.12.65 Sheila Oates BA(Oxon) mathematician; marr diss 1972
(2) Alloa 24.2.73 Ann B. C. Fleming d of James F. Alloa

MacDONALD Ian Robert *BSc 1952 PhD 1955
sen Fulbright travel award 1960
res plant physiol univ Calif Los Angeles 1960–61; prin scient off. dept soil org chem Macaulay inst Aber from 1974

MacDONALD Ian Robert *BSc(agr) 1954
insp DAFS from 1959

MacDONALD Isabella MA 1917
resid Inv
d 7.6.77

MACDONALD Isabella Craig MA 1933
dep head The Park s for Girls Glasg 1972–76; retd

McDONALD or Scott, Isabella Gardner MB ChB 1944
asst m o h Moray and Nairn 1963–74; sen clin m o W Grampian dist from 1974

MacDONALD or MacDougall, Isabella MacGillivray MA 1914
ptnr guest house Kensington 1954–63; retd; resid Elgin

McDONALD or Paul, Isobel Mary MA 1923
d –.11.38

MACDONALD Isobel Mary MA 1928

McDONALD James MA 1901
d Aber 1.11.60 *AUR* XXXIX 99

MACDONALD James David BSc(for) 1930 BSc 1932
FRSE 1962
retd 1968; resid Brisbane

McDONALD James Hector MB ChB 1925
Argyll: g p Is of Colonsay 1951–59, Appin 1959–62; retd; resid Port Appin

MACDONALD James Mearns MB ChB 1906
no longer on GC reg

MACDONALD Jamesina MA 1946
teacher Engl/Lat Barrhead h s Renfrewsh from 1962

McDONALD Jane MA 1928

MACDONALD or Crombie, Janet MA 1925

MACDONALD or Mackenzie, Janet Bisset Wotherspoon MA 1925

MACDONALD or Howie, Janet McPherson MA 1937
resid Edin

McDONALD Janet Mary MA 1924
no longer on GC reg

McDONALD Janetta Mary *BSc 1938
sen res fell. dept agr biochem Aberd 1960–63; biol testing pharm prod. Liv from 1963; retd

McDONALD or Taylor, Jessie Ann Anderson MA 1933
resid Torphins
d 10.9.74

MACDONALD John MA 1902
d Cults 7.6.61 *AUR* XXXIX 199

MACDONALD John MA 1907
d Callander 9.5.72

MACDONALD John *MA 1909
d Nairn 17.12.70 *AUR* XLIV 208

MACDONALD John MA 1915
no longer on GC reg

MACDONALD John MA 1919
d 30.3.67

MACDONALD John MA 1920
d Aber 6.9.66 *AUR* XLI 338

MACDONALD John MA 1922
C of S min: Kilmuir-Easter Rosssh 1948–60, Lochcarron 1960–66; retd; resid Torridon

MACDONALD John MB ChB 1924

MACDONALD John *MA 1926
no longer on GC reg

MacDONALD John MB ChB 1938
hon phys to H.M. the Queen 1963
NZ: surg capt RNZN 1963, dir naval med serv RNZN 1963–70; dir med serv armed forces northern reg from 1970

MACDONALD John MA 1948
Air Efficiency Award
C of S min Lochee old par ch (formerly St Ninian's) Dun from 1949

McDONALD John *MA 1954
teacher geog: Elgin acad 1958–60, spec asst Nairn acad 1960–63, prin 1963; Inverness h s: prin teacher 1963–70, dep head from 1970

MacDONALD John Bruce MB ChB 1955

MACDONALD John Charles Mackie MB ChB 1942
g p and anaest Elgin
author *The Wolf* 1977; *Blood of the Wolf* 1978

MacDONALD John Donald Graham MB ChB 1940
d Inv 10.5.73 *AUR* XLV 321

MACDONALD John Grant *MA 1935
no longer on GC reg

MacDONALD John Norman MA 1937
d 15.6.62

MACDONALD John Stewart MA 1897
no longer on GC reg

MacDONALD or Mackinnon, Kathleen Jean Povo MA 1949

MACDONALD Kenneth James MB ChB 1954
g p: Invergordon 1959–60, Forres 1960–62, Bonar Bridge from 1962; m o Migdale geriat hosp and loc. Treasury m o
m Inv 29.4.61 Phyllis M. Cocker MB ChB 1955 *qv*

McDONALD Lizzie MA 1934
teacher Aber from 1936
d Aber 21.9.76

MACDONALD Malcolm *MA 1926
deceased

McDONALD Malcolm Edward MB ChB 1951
CCFP 1970 FRSTM & H
Newfoundland, Canada: m o i/c Brookfield hosp 1962–67, chief dept of g p Sa Grace Gen hosp St John's 1969–75, clin instr dept of fam med Memorial univ of Nfld St John's 1970–74, clin asst prof fac of med from 1974

MACDONALD Margaret MA 1912
resid Inv
d 26.8.77

MACDONALD Margaret MA 1919
resid Inv
d Inv 10.6.81

MACDONALD or Hogarth, Margaret Cameron MB ChB 1907
resid Lond

MacDONALD or Fowler, Margaret Jane BSc(agr) 1937
teacher: rural sc Colne Valley h s Huddersfield 1959–61, biol Ongar s s Essex 1961–66, p s Stapleford Abbotts 1966–75, dep head from 1975
husb *d* –.12.69

McDONALD Marie Wyness MA 1953
scient information off. Commonwealth Bureau of Nutrition Bucksburn Aber from 1960
m Aber 26.3.73 Alexander Walker asst man.

McDONALD Marjory Elizabeth MA 1925
no longer on GC reg

McDONALD or Woodcraft, Mary MA 1945
resid Loughton

MACDONALD or Reid, Mary MA 1922
resid Inv

McDONALD Mary Graham MB ChB 1943 DPH 1954
MFCM 1972
asst m o Inv c c 1961–70, sen m o from 1970
m Longniddry 18.9.71 James Campbell civ eng s of George C. Glasg

McDONALD or Catto, Mary Isabella Philip MA 1932

MACDONALD Mary Isobel MA 1945
teacher Conon p s Ross and Cromarty from 1951

MACDONALD Mary Jane Watt MA 1927
retd 1969; resid Nairn

McDONALD Mona Margaret Cruickshank MA 1950
member diplom serv 1951–70; teacher Engl in home for emotionally disturbed ch Biesfeld W Ger

McDONALD Moraig Mary MA 1952

MACDONALD or Scott, Morna Catherine MB ChB 1941
g p Alyth from 1947

MACDONALD Murdo BSc 1951
B Ed/M Ed(Winnipeg) 1961/1972
teacher Winnipeg from 1958

MACDONALD Neil MA 1931
dep head Mallaig j s 1963–70; teacher Engl/hist Inv h s 1970–73; retd
d Inv 6.4.79

MACDONALD Norma *MA 1955
M Litt(Edin) 1971
teacher: Brit inst s Madrid 1957–60, Oban h s 1960–65, f e Edin 1966–69, Jordanhill coll Glasg 1969–70; res work ch lang dev Jordanhill coll 1972–73
m Edin 28.12.68 Leslie Dickinson BA(Keele) lect univ/coll of educ

MacDONALD Norman MA 1929
retd 1970; resid Inv

MACDONALD Norman MA 1932 *BD 1938
retd 1970; resid Conon Bridge

MACDONALD Patrick David Alexander MB ChB 1925
d Lond 6.2.68 *AUR* XLII 366

MACDONALD Patrick Thomson Tulloch *MA 1903
d 1972

MACDONALD Peter Chalmers *MA 1936

MACDONALD Ranald BSc(agr) 1919
d 1962

MACDONALD Ranald Roderick *MA 1921 BSc 1922
d 10.7.63

McDONALD Robert MB ChB 1937 DPH 1947
FRCPsych 1973
retd 1979; resid Ilkley

MACDONALD Robert Fraser *MB ChB 1937 *MD 1940 DPH 1941
m o W reg hosp board 1948, later commun med spec Greater Glasg health board

MACDONALD Robert Gordon MA 1907 DD 1954
d 17.12.70

MACDONALD Roderick BSc(for) 1947
no longer on GC reg

MACDONALD Roderick BSc(agr) 1952
lands off. DAFS Thurso 1964–67; head land dev div HIDB Inv 1967–72; sen lands off. DAFS Edin 1972–75; div agr off. Edin from 1975
m Inv 27.4.62 Elizabeth Macleod SRN d of Norman J. M. MA 1926 *qv*

MACDONALD Roderick Scott *BSc 1954
teacher sc Elgin acad 1957–60, spec asst chem Nairn acad 1960–63, prin sc Tain royal acad 1963–66, head sc/prin chem Wishaw h s 1966–70, prin chem Fraserburgh acad 1970–73, asst head Fraserburgh acad from 1973

MACDONALD or Archdale, Sheena Margaret MA 1947
admin and teaching in husband's prep s Rickmansworth from 1963

McDONALD or Buchan, Sheila MA 1949
resid Peterhead

MACDONALD or McLennan, Sheila Mary MA 1943
resid Fraserburgh

MACDONALD Simon BSc(eng) 1952

McDONALD Stella Leslie *MA 1948
woman advis Milne's h s Fochabers 1956–72; asst rector from 1972

MacDONALD Thomas James Chalmers MB ChB 1924 ᶜMD 1928
d 12.10.66 *AUR* XLII 86

MACDONALD Thomas Kyd BL 1937
ptnr J. D. Mackie & Dewar advoc Aber from 1948

MACDONALD William Bass MA 1922
teacher: first asst Newmilns j s s Ayrsh and supt f e centre 1931–61; retd; resid Kilmarnock
m Kilmarnock 25.12.31 Janet W. Highet

MacDONALD William David Elder MA 1929

MACDONALD William George MB ChB 1908
no longer on GC reg

MACDONALD William George MB ChB 1950
g p Elgin from 1957

MACDONALD William Nevins MA 1901
d Aber 30.1.61 *AUR* XXXIX 199

MacDONALD William Smith MA 1923
MBE 1968
head Inchgarth s Aber 1949–65; retd; group commandant No 29 group ROC Aber 1963–68; edit. vol IV *Roll of Graduates* from Jan 1981

MACDONALD or Hides, Williamina Fletcher MA 1923 BSc 1925
teacher Musselburgh g s 1946–69; retd; resid Edin
husb *d* –.3.37

MacDONALD or Overton, Wilma McKimmie BSc 1951

McDONALD or Lumsden, Winifred Wright MB ChB 1950
m o publ health Fife 1961–68; sen m o commun med Angus dist from 1969

MacDONELL or MacPhail, Christina Rose MA 1949 DipEd 1950

MacDONELL Eileen Emma Mary MA 1942

McDOUGALL Christina Henry MA 1941
prod. progr organis radio and tv, talks and publ affairs CBC Toronto 1957–68; spec proj off. (communications) UN inst for trg and res (Unitair) NY from 1968

McDOUGALL Edith Jean PhD 1934

MACDOUGALL Hugh BCom 1938
MICA(Scot) 1946
ptnr Lond firm c a 1946–65, fin. consult. from 1965
marr diss 1960
m(2) Dunning 4.4.62 Christina H. MacNab priv secy d of William MacN. Inverkeithing

MacDOUGALL or Gale, Janet Isabel MA 1950
resid Lond

MacDOUGALL or Carter, Martha Park MA 1949
resid Windsor

McDOUGALL May Currie MA 1941

McDOWALL Alan Robert *MA 1952
FRSSoc 1954
Shell Internat: Lond 1960–65, and from 1971; Shell Eastern Singapore 1965–71

MacECHERN Christian Victor Aeneas MA 1907
C of S min Kirkmabreck ch Kirkcudbrightsh 1938–65; retd moderator presb of Wigtown
d 20.10.77 *AUR* XLVII 355

McEWAN George Lamb MB ChB 1940
g p Coventry from 1953; retd 1977

MacEWAN Ian *MA 1932
d Inv 29.12.67 *AUR* XLII 371

McEWAN or Patterson, Marian Elizabeth MA 1924

McEWEN Margaret Melrose *MA 1932
clerkess Aber c c NE counties valuation comm from 1957; retd

McFARLAND Henry Stewart Noel *MA 1946
d Durh 4.11.73 *AUR* XLV 450

McFARLANE Angus Alexander MA 1952
MInstP 1980
UK AEA (indust group): asst exper off., exper off. reactor materials lab Culcheth, higher scient off. nat centre for tribology Cheshire 1971–78, sen scient off. from 1978 RNL Risley
m(1) Dun 28.3.59 Jessie M. C. Cuthbert; marr diss –.2.77
(2) Leeds 26.8.77 Sandra A. Ingham BSc(Nott)

MacFARLANE Donald Alexander MA 1910
min of relig F P ch Dingwall and Beauly 1930–73; retd; resid Inv
m Dingwall 8.5.57 Isabella Finlayson teacher homecraft d of Angus F. Dingwall
d 25.10.79

McFARLANE Isabel Jean MA 1935
soc worker LCC 1938–65; prin soc worker health dept Westminster city council Lond 1965–75; retd

MACFARLANE James Matthew *MA 1948
sen admin off. Edin univ from 1957
d 10.9.80 *AUR* XLIX 139

MACFARLANE John Brownlie MB ChB 1931
army rank in 1961 Brigadier
d Edin 6.12.72

MACFARLANE John Clarkson MB ChB 1925
Derby: g p 1931–70; retd
obst Nightingale mat. hosp 1937–61; retd; locum g p surgeries 1971–74; m o occup health clin cent and S Derbysh hosp 1973–78

McFARLANE Robert Forbes BCom 1929

MacFARQUHAR Alexander (Sir) *MA 1925 LLD 1980
Internat Co-operation medal 1965
USA: spec advis to UN secy-gen for civ affairs in Congo NY 1960–61; under-secy (dir of pers) UN NY 1962–67; retd; resid Kingston-on-Thames

MACFARQUHAR John Mackenzie MB ChB 1924
d Fochabers 1.7.74 *AUR* XLVI 108

McGEACHIE or Saunders, Janie Gardiner MA 1951

McGEE James Ivor *MA 1951 DipEd 1955
teacher Engl: AGS 1958–63; sen teacher coll of comm Aber from 1963

McGEE William MA 1955

McGHEE Thomas Wilson *MA 1953

McGILL Alexander David MA 1934 MB ChB 1939
d Penarth 14.1.75 *AUR* XLVI 239

McGILL or Smith, Edith Kathleen Finlayson BSc(agr) 1950

McGILL Jane Craig MA 1948

McGILLIVARY Peter Walker MA 1925
d Stonehaven 20.11.77

McGILLIVRAY Alexander Shaw MA 1933

McGILLIVRAY Elaine *MA 1950
teacher mod lang Havergal coll Toronto 1960–67, head mod lang from 1967

McGILLIVRAY Eric Laing *MA 1931 BCom 1933
Lanarksh: prin teacher maths Gateside j s s 1961–70, Stonelaw h s from 1970

McGILLIVRAY George Mortimer MB ChB 1912
d Aboyne 19.4.67 *AUR* XLII 350

MacGILLIVRAY Ian BSc 1950

MacGILLIVRAY Ian Brodie BSc(agr) 1954
man. Cluny estate Newtonmore from 1958
m Kingussie 20.6.58 Joan M. Mackay teacher d of Kenneth A. M. MB ChB(Glas) Laggan

McGILLIVRAY William Harrison Jamieson MB ChB 1924

McGILLIVRAY William Harthill MB ChB 1942
consult. ENT surg Lanark county area from 1954

McGLASHAN Agnes Margaret MA 1949 MB ChB 1954
consult. psychiat and med dir: Watford ch and fam psychiat clin 1964–77; dir outpatient serv Thistletown reg cent for ch and adolescents Toronto Canada from 1977; asst prof ch psychiat Tor univ from 1977
m Lond 26.8.60 Ronald M. Gabriel LRCPE psychiat s of William G. G. Hove

McGLASHAN or Mason, Dorothy MA 1905
d 28.10.70

McGLASHAN or Napier, Frances MA 1954 DipEd 1955
resid Tain

McGLASHAN George MA 1932
d Aber 27.12.64 *AUR* XL 59

McGLASHAN or Runciman, Helen MB ChB 1904
no longer on GC reg

McGOWAN Christina Jessie MA 1936
teacher Aber 1938–45, Forfar from 1960
m Elgin 22.7.42 Andrew MacKay dir eng firm s of Charles MacK. Glasg

McGOWAN or Catto, Rowla MB ChB 1938
resid Wolfhill by Perth
husb *d* 1975

McGOWAN William Barber MB ChB 1942
Rhodesia: govt m o Filabusi 1956–66; med supt Gatooma 1966–67, med supt Umtali from 1967

McGRATH Margaret Mary MA 1927
no longer on GC reg

McGREGOR Alexander MA 1904
d Maud 24.3.72 *AUR* XLIV 426

MACGREGOR Alickina MA 1920
d Rosemarkie 25.11.73

McGREGOR Archibald MB ChB 1949
MRCGP 1960
g p Turriff from 1966

MACGREGOR or Laird, Christina MA 1945

MACGREGOR Duncan Ronald *MA 1948

MACGREGOR or Spark, Elizabeth MA 1923

MacGREGOR Elizabeth Bennett *MA 1921 BSc 1922
no longer on GC reg

MacGREGOR George William Gordon BSc 1955
Alyth h s: prin maths 1964–71, rector from 1971

McGREGOR Helen *MA 1927
d of Alexander M. quarryman; b Newhills 10.2.05
retd 1963; resid Aber

McGREGOR Henrietta Hay MA 1925
d Elgin 10.1.76

MacGREGOR Ian Wyness MB ChB 1923
retd; resid Hereford
m Brompton, Lond 17.12.42 Violet M. Rose-Richards d of Thomas P. R-R. Laugharne

McGREGOR James MA 1901
no longer on GC reg

McGREGOR James Anderson MB ChB 1949
MRCGP 1963
g p: Auchenblae 1962–67, Edin from 1967

McGREGOR James Morrison MA 1930
JP 1958–74
teacher: Louth 1931–37, teacher/dep head Walker Rd p s Aber 1937–52, dep head Woodside p s Aber 1952–56, head Muirfield p s Aber 1956–68; retd

MACGREGOR James Murdoch *MA 1947
free-lance writer short stories, novels, film scripts, radio scripts, books on photog., wine making etc from 1952

m Aber –.7.60 Margaret Murray d of RQMS Alexander M.

McGREGOR Jean Anderson MA 1952
teacher: Gwelo, Rhodesia 1957–59, Middlesex 1960–63, Torphins 1964–68, Fr/Ger Inverurie acad 1968–74, prin guid Cults acad Aber from 1974

McGREGOR or Macdonald, Jean Campbell MA 1943
teacher: Fr Ellis Guilford s Nott 1964–68, Fr/Italian Rushcliffe s Notts 1968–72, Fr/Lat Rawlins upper s Quorn from 1972

MacGREGOR or Aitken, Joan MA 1927
head Blarich p s Sutherland 1937–68; retd; resid Rogart

McGREGOR John Clark MB ChB 1934
MRCGP 1957 JP(Caithness) 1965 DL(Caithness) 1977
g p Thurso from 1946; member Scot. med practices comm Edin from 1968; retd 1976

McGREGOR John George *MA 1934

McGREGOR John Grant MB ChB 1906
no longer on GC reg

MacGREGOR Kenneth Stuart Hall MB ChB 1948
g p Sutton-in-Ashfield from 1954

MacGREGOR Malcolm *MA 1924
no longer on GC reg

MacGREGOR or Fry, Margaret Una Cameron *MA 1923
resid Weymouth

MacGREGOR or Hogg, Mary Emily Watt MA 1917
resid Edin
d Edin 25.3.80

McGREGOR Norah MA 1934
teacher Mile End p s Aber 1948–75; retd

MACGREGOR Rosabel Elizabeth *MA 1929
teacher: prin Lat/Ital Beacon s for girls Bridge of Allan 1957–73; retd; resid Alloa

McGREGOR or Hamilton, Yvonne Margaret Hogg MB ChB 1949
m o Dunfermline from 1972

MacGRUER or Noble, Christina Anne MA 1912
no longer on GC reg

McHAFFIE Alexander Taylor MA 1951

McHAFFIE Margaret Allan *MA 1947 PhD 1954
sen lect Ger Glas from 1967

McHARDY Alexander Smith *MA 1923
retd; resid Banff
d Banff 9.12.77 *AUR* XLVII 356

McHARDY or Slesser, Alice Mary MA BSc 1909
no longer on GC reg

McHARDY Barbara Jean MA 1933

McHARDY Elizabeth MA 1906
d 30.10.65 *AUR* XLI 239

McHARDY or Finegan, Elizabeth MB ChB 1909
resid Hayward's Heath Sussex

McHARDY Francis MA 1925
no longer on GC reg

MacHARDY Hamish Chisholm *MA 1950
teacher: head of mod stud. Viewforth h s Kirkcaldy 1960–65, head hist Tain royal acad from 1965

McHARDY or Anderson, Isabella Murray MA 1930
missionary: W and NW China 1936–51, Bihar NW India 1953–54, Saiburi S Thailand 1954–68; resid Denny

McHARDY James Brown MA 1954

McHARDY John MA 1903
d –.12.69 *AUR* XLIII 440

McHARDY or Hendry, Margaret Jean MB ChB 1943
resid Aber

McHARDY or Milne, Margaret Munro MA 1951
d Glasg 18.5.77

McHARDY or Muir, Marjory Ann MA 1933
lib Blenheim Ontario from 1959

McHARDY or Markham, Mary Elizabeth Garden MA 1925
retd 1966; resid Clarkston Glasg

McHARDY or Dawson, Mary Robertson MA 1927
teacher maths Kemnay 1967–69; retd

McHARDY William Duff MA 1932 BD 1935 DD 1958
prof OT stud. Lond 1948–60; regius prof Hebrew and student of Christ Church Oxon from 1960

McHARDY or Reid, Winifred Clara MA 1926
resid Nairn
d Nairn 23.7.77

McHATTIE or Williams, Annie Jane *MA 1935
resid Exeter

McHATTIE Robert MA 1938
Aber: teacher Engl Torry s s 1949–62, Old Aber s s 1962–70, prin Engl 1970–75; asst prin Engl Linksfield acad from 1975

McILWAIN Alexander Edward MA 1954 LLB 1956
pres SRC Aberd 1956–57
leg asst: Gray & Kellas Aber 1960–61, John Y.

Robertson solic Hamilton 1961–63; ptnr Teague, Leonard & Muirhead (later Leonards) Hamilton from 1963; notary publ SSC 1966, county secy Scout Assoc Lanarksh from 1967; burgh prosec Hamilton 1967–75; dist prosec Hamilton dist c 1975–76; member council of Law Soc of Scot. from 1972
m Aber 14.7.61 Moira M. Kinnaird MA 1958 *qv*

McILWRAITH or Worrell, Joyce Duddingston BSc 1950

MacINNES Angus MB ChB 1951

MacINNES Donald MA 1930

McINNES Hector John BSc(agr) 1954

MACINNES or Smith, Jean Armour MA 1946
teacher Dingwall p s from 1968

McINNES Kenneth Guthrie BSc 1949

MacINNES Marion Margaret MA 1939
teacher Engl Millburn s s Inv 1961–72, also prin guid from 1972; retd 1977

MACINNES Niel Iain *MA 1953
Lloyds Bank Lond: sect. man. overseas dept 1969–73, dep man. city, overseas br 1973–77, asst man. docum div overseas dept from 1977

McINTOSH Alastair Donald BCom 1934
teacher bus. stud. Peterhead acad 1966–69, prin bus. stud. from 1969

McINTOSH Alexander *BSc 1950

McINTOSH Alexander Wilson MB ChB 1950 DPH 1956 MD 1962
MFCM 1972
sen asst m o h Aber 1963–64; dep county m o and dep prin school m o N Riding Yorks c c Northallerton 1965–74; dist commun phys York health dist from 1974

MacINTOSH Alistair Eoin MB ChB 1943
FRCP(Can) 1972
g p Georgetown Ont from 1967

McINTOSH Annie Bell MA 1930
teacher: Helmsdale 1932–40, Airdrie 1950–52; head Ballindalloch s 1953–60; teacher Aberlour 1960–61, Grantown g s 1961–70
m Lairg 3.4.40 Thomas H. Reid BSc(St And) teacher s of Andrew D. R. Dun

McINTOSH Annie Greig *MA 1901
d Aber 7.10.63 *AUR* XL 300

McINTOSH Donald MB ChB 1947
consult. phys i/c Hounslow chest clin, Ealing Hammersmith and Hounslow AHA and W Middx hosps from 1972

MACINTOSH Donald MB ChB 1953

McINTOSH Edward *MA 1915
d Exmouth 23.3.70 *AUR* XLIII 442

McINTOSH or Burness, Frances Rae MA 1931 MB ChB 1936

McINTOSH or Scrimgeour, Helen Dalziel MA 1930
resid Frittenden
husb *d* 1974

McINTOSH or Cowie, Helen Geddes MA 1943
resid Insch

McINTOSH Iain Alexander MB ChB 1948
DPH(Lond) 1959 DIH 1960 MFCM 1972
RAF med branch from 1949
d Halton 5.2.78 *AUR* XLVIII 107

McINTOSH Ian Donald *MA 1930 LLD 1962
d Edin 18.1.75 *AUR* XLVI 238

McINTOSH Irene Margaret MA 1946
teacher Engl: Kincardine 1947–51, Aber 1952–61; supply teaching 1962–73; teacher Engl Cults acad from 1973
m(1) Aber 29.9.51 Alfred J. Marr shop man. s of Alfred J. M. Aber; husb *d* 1974
(2) 3.7.78 Ian G. M. Petrie BSc(St And) teacher

McINTOSH or Macinnes, Isobel Margaret *MA 1948

MacINTOSH James Archibald BD 1904
no longer on GC reg

McINTOSH James McInroy Dalziel MB ChB 1935
retd g p 1972; part-time ACMO health dept Hertfordsh c c from 1972

McINTOSH or Ross, Jessie (Janet) MA 1932
resid Bo'ness

McINTOSH John MB ChB 1938
m o DHSS Edin from 1966
d 19.11.81

MacINTOSH John Leitch MA 1949
no longer on GC reg

McINTOSH John Taylor *MA 1950
head: Towie s 1962–69, New Deer s from 1969

McINTOSH or Harte, Lilian MA 1937
resid W Bridgford

McINTOSH or Ferris, Margaret MA 1942

McINTOSH Murdoch BL 1939
d –.1.72

McINTOSH or Campbell, Nancy Rebecca MA 1949
d Glasg 25.1.74

MacINTOSH or Forbes, Rena Crum BSc 1950
teacher maths/sc Aber from 1951

McINTOSH Robert Fyfe BSc(eng) 1953

McINTOSH William MA 1951 *MEd 1953
d Leamington Spa 4.7.76

McINTOSH William Craib MA 1923 MB ChB 1927
retd; resid Northam, Bideford
wife *d* 1968
m(2) Bideford 22.11.69 Jeannetta P. Way or Mortimer d of Stanley W. Bideford

McINTOSH or Sutherland, Williamina MA 1912
no longer on GC reg

MACINTYRE Donald Gordon MA 1955 MEd 1957

McINTYRE Ian Sinclair MA 1950
teacher Lumphanan 1950–59; head: Berefold s 1959–65, Slains s from 1965

McINTYRE or Kemp, Isabella Downie MA 1921
teacher Fr/Engl Westlands h s Rugby 1961–67; retd

McINTYRE Peter Farnworth BSc(for) 1949
d Banchory 24.9.70 *AUR* XLIV 111

MACINTYRE or Palmer, Ruby Crombie MA 1929

McINTYRE William MB ChB 1950

MACINTYRE William Campbell MA 1950 *MEd 1954

MACIVER Alexander MA 1955
teacher City Publ s s Glasg 1962–64; head: Poolewe p s Wester Ross 1964–70, Carloway p s Is of Lewis 1970–75, Knock p s Is of Lewis from 1975
m Glasg 30.12.64 Mary A. Campbell d of Kenneth C. Point Is of Lewis

MacIVER Angus Stuart MA 1931
retd 1970; resid Westerdale Halkirk

McIVER or MacBean, Barbara Campbell MA 1911
no longer on GC reg

McIVER Charles Gordon Esslemont MA 1949
dir Lawson Turnbull & Co Aber from 1954

McIVER Colin John *MA 1907
d Aber 31.10.69 *AUR* XLIII 327

McIVER or Murray, Dorothy Coutts *MA 1923
resid Knaresborough
husb *d* 1967

MacIVER Ian Frederick BSc(for) 1949
dist off. for. comm: Malvern 1950–64, N Devon 1964–68, S Cowal 1968–72, Stirling from 1972

McIVER Ian Ronald *MA 1931
teacher: asst prin mod lang Banff acad 1964–72; retd

MacIVER John MA 1919
retd; resid Braco

MacIVER John Angus MA 1950
head Hopeman p s from 1970

McIVER Kenneth Esslemont MB ChB 1945
g p Staveley from 1949

MacIVER Kenneth Ian BSc(agr) 1954
area superv potato market. board for Fife, Kinross, Clackmannan at Cupar from 1957
d Cupar 26.5.80 *AUR* XLIX 70

MacIVER Kennethina Macpherson MA 1946
teacher Kelvindale p s Glasg from 1976

MacIVER Madeline MA 1940 *MEd 1966
d Stornoway 29.10.66 *AUR* XLII 89

MACIVER Malcolm MA 1929
headmaster Knock 1952–64; retd; resid Breasclete Is of Lewis
m(2) Glasg 2.2.74 Annie S. Macleod P O clerk d of Roderick J. M. Balallan Is of Lewis

MACIVER Malcolm Morrison MA 1922
d 1973

MacIVER or Crawford, Margaret Barbara *MA 1936
d Inv 24.7.78 *AUR* XLVIII 106

MacIVER Mary MB ChB 1951

MacIVER Murdo BSc(eng) 1948
MBE
dist man. NSHEB Western Isles Stornoway from 1968
d Stornoway 8.4.75 *AUR* XLVI 326

MacIVER Ranald Murdo BSc(agr) 1949
Dip Animal Genetics(Edin) 1950
scient off. poultry res centre Edin 1950–53; lect dept of agr Edin 1953–60; geneticist Dale Turkeys Ludlow 1960–64; lect UCNW Bangor from 1964

McIVOR William Benjamin MA 1955
head: Thrumster p s 1960–70, Miller acad Thurso from 1970
m Wick 28.3.59 Margaret E. Sutherland med receptionist d of James S. Wick

McKAIN William Thomas BSc(eng) 1952

McKAY or Kelly, Agnes Jessie MA 1923
retd 1962; resid Aber
d Aber 30.4.80

MACKAY Alexander MB ChB 1921
g p Thornaby-on-Tees 1922–58; retd; resid Northallerton

McKAY Alexander Duncan Den *MA 1919
d Dun 10.4.70 *AUR* XLVI 444

MACKAY Alexander Henderson MB ChB 1924
no longer on GC reg

MACKAY Alexander Murray MB ChB 1947
g p Edin from 1969

MACKAY Alexander Taylor *MA 1950
teacher: mod lang Ellon acad 1955–66, Schiller coll Germany 1966–71, acad dean 1970–71; prin mod lang Torry acad from 1971
m Edin 16.7.71 Dorothy L. A. Craig teacher d of William C. Edin

MACKAY Alexandrina MA 1903
d Golspie 22.11.63 *AUR* XL 300

MACKAY Angus Sim *BSc(eng) 1934

MACKAY or Morrison, Ann MA 1945
part-time teacher Laxdale p s from 1972

MACKAY Anne MA 1944
no longer on GC reg

MACKAY Annie MA 1902
no longer on GC reg

MACKAY or Smillie, Catherine Elizabeth MA 1949

MACKAY or Darby, Catherine Yvonne MA 1938
teacher maths/sc Goodall Rd s mod s Leyton 1948–55; prin maths Leyton Manor Co sec girls 1958–60; teacher: human biol/maths Ruckholt Manor Co s s Waltham Forest 1961–72, maths Woodford Co h s girls Essex 1972–73, Caterham h s Ilford 1973–77; retd

MACKAY Charles BSc(agr) 1947
MSc(Kentucky) 1960 W. K. Kellogg found. fell. 1959–60
insp DAFS Aber 1954–64, sen insp Ayr 1964–70; Edin: tech dev off. DAFS 1970–73, dept chief agr off. 1973–75, chief agr off. from 1975

MACKAY Charles Kenneth BSc 1954 MEd 1960 PhD 1978
teacher Aber 1958–60; county educ psych Bedford 1961–64; lect Aberd 1964–72, sen lect from 1972

MACKAY Christina MA 1904
d Aber 15.3.63 *AUR* XL 198

MACKAY or Macleod, Christina MA 1933

MACKAY Christina Mary MA 1953
teacher: remed Nicolson inst Stornoway from 1969
m Aber 4.4.60 Allan D. Whiteford MA 1954 *qv*

MacKAY Christine Ann MA 1953
woman advis Inv h s from 1964, asst head from 1972

MACKAY Coinneach Ian BSc(eng) 1951

MACKAY David Nicol *MA 1951

MACKAY Dennis *BSc 1954 PhD 1958
SKF res fell. Queen's coll Dund 1958–61; lect pharm Leeds univ 1961–65; US publ health fell. pharm Los Angeles 1965–66; sen lect pharm Leeds univ from 1973
m Forres 23.3.68 Moira McLennan clerkess d of John A. McL. Forres

MacKAY Donald MA 1915
d Dunfermline 15.5.1973 *AUR* XLV 318

MACKAY Donald MA 1922
asst teacher Nicolson Inst Stornoway 1922–25; head Tarradale j s s Muir of Ord till 1961; retd

MACKAY Donald *BSc 1954 PhD 1957
asst prof univ of Waterloo Canada 1960–62; Oxon: NATO res fell. 1962–63; DSIR res fell. 1963–64; assoc prof univ of Waterloo from 1964

MACKAY Donald George MA 1938 MB ChB 1943
med statist gen reg off. Somerset House 1951–56; dep med supt Inv hosp group 1956–58; med statist off. N reg hosp board (Scot.) 1958–66; sen med off. (commun med) SE Thames reg health auth from 1966

MACKAY Donald John MA 1953
highlands off. Scot. Agr Organis Serv Edin 1958–61; man. trg off. UK AEA Dounreay 1961–64; training/pers off. Brit Alum. Co Kinlochleven/Fort William 1964–65; dir An Comunn Gaidhealach Inv 1965–70; pers man. Brit alum. Co Invergordon from 1971

MACKAY Donald Ross BSc(agr) 1954
overseas col serv agr dept Lusaka Zambia 1964–69; gen man.: Tobacco Board of Zambia Lusaka 1969–72, General Farming Co Lilongwe Malawi 1972–73; tech advis Overseas Dev Admin Windward Is from 1974
m Lundazi Zambia 1962 Maureen J. Whitaker nurse Derby

MACKAY Doris Badenoch MA 1947
teacher Milne's h s Fochabers from 1948

MACKAY or Leeson, Dorothy Jean MB ChB 1942

McKAY Douglas Charles *MA 1951
head Tillycoultry s 1963–67; rector: Alva acad 1967–71, Leith acad from 1971; chmn Port of Leith housing assoc

MacKAY Duncan MA 1901
no longer on GC reg

MacKAY Duncan William MB ChB 1917
no longer on GC reg

MACKAY or Clarkson, Elizabeth MA 1907
no longer on GC reg

McKAY or Rendall, Elsie Sutherland MA 1938
teacher Pierowall j s s Westray Orkney from 1950; retd 1977

McKAY Eric *MB ChB 1948 ᶜMD 1965
FRCPE 1971 MRCPsych 1971

res fell. paediat Tor 1960–61; Aberd: lect ch health 1961–69, consult. dev paediat from 1975

MACKAY Eric Beattie MA 1948
edit. *The Scotsman* Edin from 1972

MACKAY Ethel Elizabeth Lauder *MA 1919
retd 1960; resid Edin
d Edin 22.11.79

McKAY or Fraser, Ethel Mary MA 1923
retd 1963; resid Shaftesbury

McKAY or Birnie, Félicité Rolland *MA 1934
teacher: Grangefield gr s for girls Stockton-on-Tees 1956–60, Howell's s Llandaff Cardiff 1963–71, Charters Towers s Bexhill-on-Sea from 1973

McKAY or Begg, Fiona Hunter MA 1955
teacher: maths King's Rd s Rosyth 1959–61, McLean p s Dunfermline 1965–66, remed Pathhead s Kirkcaldy 1966–69, relig educ Kirkcaldy h s from 1969

MacKAY Flora Mary MA 1939
teacher: Galloway House s Garlieston 1966–67, Ferryhill p s Aber from 1967; retd 1977

MACKAY George Patrick Gordon *MA 1937
CBE 1962 Kt 1966
gen man. E. Af Rlys & Harbours 1961–64; World Bank: 1965–78 (dep dir 1974–75, dir Saudi Arabia 1975–77); retd; resid Haslemere

McKAY George Shiach MA 1898 MB ChB 1902
no longer on GC reg

MACKAY George William MacBeath MA 1920 MB ChB 1924
retd 1964; resid Farnham
d Hampton 29.9.77 *AUR* XLVIII 103

McKAY Gilbert Watt *MA 1950
D Litt (Schiller coll Germany) 1965
sen dean St Peter's coll Oxon from 1970
m 7.12.60 Elizabeth M. Norman D Phil(Oxon) mus. and musicologist d of Sir Edward J. N. Dorking

MACKAY Hugh MA 1913
retd 1954; resid Connel

MacKAY Hugh BSc(eng) 1931

MACKAY Ian MB ChB 1950
d 13.7.73

MACKAY Ian BSc(eng) 1952
Stornoway: div road surv 1956–71; asst county surv 1972–75, dir engineering from 1975

MACKAY Ian Anderson *BSc 1936
d Birkenhead 27.4.63 *AUR* XL 206

MACKAY Ian James Hendry BSc 1951
JP 1971
area off. White Fish auth from 1953
councillor: city of Aber 1966–74, reg seat Hazlehead in Grampian reg from 1974
d Aber 28.2.77 *AUR* XLVII 215

McKAY or Ironside, Iona Margaret BSc(agr) 1952

MACKAY or McIntyre, Iris Fowler *MA 1953 DipEd 1954
Canada: pres sec assoc teachers of Engl BC 1970–71, pres BC Engl teachers' assoc 1971, pres elect Canadian council of teachers of Engl 1973–74

MACKAY or Williams, Isabel MA 1946

MACKAY Isabel Scott *MA 1927
d Elgin 30.4.75 *AUR* XLVI 323

MACKAY or Fenelon, Isabella Gray MA 1953

MACKAY Ivor Macdonald BSc(eng) 1952
CEng MIEE 1961
head elect. eng and sc coll of f e Barrow-in-Furness from 1962
d 7.10.77

McKAY James MB ChB 1950
g p Richmond Va USA from 1959

MACKAY James Finlayson MB ChB 1937
consult. venereol N Lancs/S Westmorland from 1950

McKAY James MacGregor MB ChB 1942
consult. radiol Morriston hosp Swansea/Swansea gen hosp/Llanelly hosp from 1956

MACKAY James Ross *BSc 1955
head biol dept Inverurie acad from 1963
m Alford 21.10.61 Mary B. Brown clerkess/typist d of Frederick W. B. Alford

MACKAY James Slater MA 1938
d Lossiemouth 31.3.73 *AUR* XLV 227

MACKAY or Brown, Jane Laughton MA 1901
no longer on GC reg

MacKAY or Sharp, Jean Grant MA 1949
resid Aber

MacKAY or Cruickshank, Jean Murrion Finlayson *MA 1924
retail staff man. Scotch wool shops h q London/Greenock 1959–61; consult. retail trades educ council h q Lond 1961–63; resid Yarm-on-Tees
marr diss 1966

MACKAY or Husband, Jean Reay *MA 1951

McKAY or Cross, Jean Weir MA 1927

McKAY Jeannie Anderson MA 1927
teacher Peterhead cent s 1929–37, Inverallochy s 1937–48, North s Fraserburgh 1948–69; retd

MACKAY Jessie Margaret MA 1932

MACKAY John MA 1893
d Yarm-on-Tees 14.2.66 *AUR* XLII 79

MACKAY John Alexander *MA 1912 DD 1939
retd 1959; resid Washington DC 1959–69, Hightstown NJ USA from 1969

MacKAY John Bruce MB ChB 1925
g p Bromley-by-Bow, Lond 1925–64; retd; resid Bexhill-on-Sea

MACKAY John Henry BSc(for) 1924

McKAY John Hutchison BSc(eng) 1944
MIEE 1966
sect head Kent c c supplies dept Maidstone from 1971

MACKAY John Kinnear MB ChB 1939
g p Middlesbrough from 1946

McKAY John Mair MA 1942

MACKAY John Simpson Bain MA 1926 MB ChB 1931 DPH 1933
retd 1968; resid Bury

MACKAY John Swinton MB ChB 1935
surg spec RAMC 1942–46; consult. surg Victoria I Glasg 1948–72; retd; resid Blairgowrie
m(2) Newton Abbot 17.11.46 Margaret H. Selby-Smith nurse d of Ronald S-S. Newton Abbot

MACKAY Kenneth BSc(eng) 1948
rep Procter & Gamble (formerly Thomas Hedley & Co) Redcar from 1957

MACKAY Kenneth James MB ChB 1954

MACKAY Kenneth William Peter BSc(agr) 1940
d Mauchline 2.1.77

MACKAY Lena *MA 1953
teacher: hist/Engl Dunbar 1968–77, prin guid and leisure from 1977
m Inv 30.7.60 James R. Glass loc govt. off. s of Alexander G. Dunbar

MACKAY Mackay MA 1928
d Rogart 5.3.67 *AUR* XLII 186

MACKAY Margaret Marr Esslemont MA 1928
no longer on GC reg

MACKAY Marion Elizabeth MB ChB 1953
MRCP 1965 Dip Psych Med(Manc) 1968 MRCPsych 1971
consult. psychiat Bolton from 1971

McKAY or Barron, Marjorie Kate Mabel MA 1931
resid Skene

MACKAY or Fraser, Mary Anna MA 1920

MACKAY Mary Elizabeth MA 1943

MACKAY or Button, Mary Ross *MA 1917

MacKAY Mary Ross MA 1917
retd 1961; teacher sc Invergowrie Perthsh 1963–64

MACKAY Matthew BSc(eng) 1952

MACKAY Moira Gunn MA 1953
teacher classics Nicolson Inst Stornoway from 1966

MACKAY Mona Elspeth *MA 1930
teacher Fr/Engl Grantown g s 1961–70; retd; resid Advie

McKAY Mona Isobel MA 1950
lib/tut. Loughborough coll of educ 1965–77; sub lib Loughborough univ of tech from 1977

MacKAY Murdo John BSc 1936

MACKAY Murdoch MB ChB 1950
d Staffordsh 11.5.73 *AUR* XLV 321

MACKAY Murdoch Macbeth MA 1937
chaplain royal Cornhill hosp Aber from 1961; hon lect mental health Aberd from 1973

MACKAY Muriel Helen *BSc 1944 PhD 1948
resid Didsbury

MACKAY Neil Melvin BSc(eng) 1951
FICE 1966 MIWE 1972
prov eng min of works Kenya, Nyeri 1962–63; resid civ eng Ratcliffe Power stat Nott 1964–67; resid eng M6 motorway Killington/Tebay 1967–70; proj eng Kenya coast water supply augmentation Nairobi 1971–74; proj eng Renfrew motorway from 1974

MACKAY Robert John *MA 1911 LLB 1918
d 24.11.67

MACKAY Robert Watt *BSc 1950
retd 1977; resid Middlesbrough

MacKAY Roderick MA 1901 MB ChB 1904
no longer on GC reg

MACKAY Roderick MB ChB 1924 DPH 1931 ᶜMD 1934
d 7.9.66

MACKAY Roderick Duncan BSc(eng) 1951

MACKAY Ronald MA 1950
JP Midlothian 1972
Midlothian: head Pumpherston p s 1965–73, Harrysmuir p s from 1973

MACKAY Roy Stuart MA 1950 DipEd 1951
teacher Lat: Queen's s Rheindalen Germany 1962–65, St Modan's s Stirling 1965–67; careers off. Stirling from 1967

MACKAY William Bremner *BSc 1952

McKAY William Graham MB ChB 1951
g p Whitehaven Cumbria from 1958

McKAY William Macgilvary PhD 1939
Academician (Bologna univ) Italy 1969 FIBiol Lond 1971
agr scient co-ordinator for Europe, Lederle labs 1957–65; consult. from 1965

MACKAY William Roderick BSc 1934
JP County of Inv 1962
chaplain Inv hosps from 1961

McKEE Catherine Dora MA 1949
civ serv; resid Lond

McKEE John Low MA 1949 DipEd 1950

MACKEGGIO George Alexander MA 1911 BD 1914
retd; resid Prestwick

McKELLAR Kenneth BSc(for) 1947
FRSA 1969
dir Radio Clyde Glasg from 1973

McKENDRICK Anderson Gray DSc 1927
no longer on GC reg

MACKENZIE Alan Theodore Louis BSc(eng) 1935
asst gen man. Keymer Bagshawe & Co Calcutta 1948–52; dir Barrow Hepburn & Gale (machinery) Leeds 1953–70; man. dir Mackenzie eng Keighley from 1970
m Lerwick 4.5.55 Thelma K. Lennie

MACKENZIE Alasdair Urquhart MA 1942
head: Munlochy j s 1956–68, Bridgend Alness from 1968

MACKENZIE Alastair Chisholm *MA 1924
d Falkirk 27.8.62 *AUR* XL 90

McKENZIE Alastair Grant MA 1930
d Aber 16.5.78 *AUR* XLVII 359

McKENZIE Alastair Still *MA 1950
prin teacher classics James Gillespie's p s Edin 1961–66; exam. off. SCE exam. board Edin; dep rector Stirling h s from 1971, rector Tain r acad from 1975

MACKENZIE Alexander *MA 1914 *BD 1919
d Glasg 16.3.70 *AUR* XLIII 441

McKENZIE Alexander *MA 1933
prin teacher mod lang Elgin acad 1957–75; retd

MACKENZIE Alexander William Riddoch MB ChB 1928

MACKENZIE or Paterson, Alexandrina Morag MA 1944

MACKENZIE Alice MB ChB 1940
g p Aber from 1962

McKENZIE Andrew Stuart *MA 1951 *MEd 1953
Fife: prin teacher Engl Balwearie s s 1962–65, dep head 1965–67; head King's Rd s s 1967–72; rector Inverkeithing h s from 1972

MACKENZIE Angus BSc(agr) 1926
no longer on GC reg

MACKENZIE or Bowie, Anne *MA 1937
teacher Sellypark s Birm 1956–75

MACKENZIE Annie BSc 1928 *1929
retd Keith 1966; resid Elgin

MacKENZIE or Slater, Annie Johanna MA 1940
d Aber 18.12.71 *AUR* XLIV 433

MACKENZIE or Murray, Annie Macleod *MA 1945 PhD 1955

McKENZIE Archibald BSc(for) 1934
tea planter N Bengal 1934–40 and 1946–48; war serv 8th Gurkha Rifles 1941–46; Windsor Ontario: self-employed 1948–56, budget analyst Chrysler Canada 1956–72; retd 1973
m Ealing 21.6.45 Ivy F. Alliband d of William A. Lond

MACKENZIE Barbara BSc 1954
biochem Stirlingsh from 1959
m Glasg 7.4.61 Stuart O. Kermack BA(Oxon) advoc/sheriff Forfar s of Stuart G. K. MA(Edin) Connell

McKENZIE Betty MA 1954
teacher: army s Famagusta Cyprus 1960–63, Mile End s Aber 1963–64, Farley j s Luton 1964–69, Engl s Addis Ababa Ethiopia 1969–74, Fraserburgh inf s from 1974

MACKENZIE or Gordon, Catherine Cowan MA 1946
teacher: Victoria Rd s Aber 1947–49, Madras coll St And 1955–72, asst head Canongate s St And from 1972
husb *d* 7.6.63

McKENZIE or Cameron, Catherine Hay MA 1933
d Perthsh 16.10.74

MacKENZIE or Stratford, Cecilia Mary *MA 1932

McKENZIE Charles BSc(eng) 1954
sen eng AEI Automation Knutsford 1960–64; sect. eng GEC-Elliott Process Automation Leic 1964–69; chief eng GEC elect. proj Rugby from 1969
m Oldham 20.2.59 Margaret N. Oates SRN

MacKENZIE Charles Duncan PhD 1935
no longer on GC reg

McKENZIE Christina Frances MA 1920
no longer on GC reg

MACKENZIE Colin MB ChB 1954
g p Stockton-on-Tees from 1959

MACKENZIE David Hart MB ChB 1923
d 7.9.67 *AUR* XLII 185

MACKENZIE Donald MB ChB 1928

McKENZIE Donald BSc(agr) 1922
no longer on GC reg

MACKENZIE Donald MA 1930
d 23.4.70

MacKENZIE Donald Kenneth Munro MA 1954

MACKENZIE Donaldina MA 1928
teacher Gravir p s Isle of Lewis 1929–42, Fr/Maths Nicolson inst Stornoway 1942–67, spec asst 1967–69; retd; resid Laxdale

McKENZIE Douglas Christie MA 1924 BCom 1925

MACKENZIE Duncan Murdo MA 1939
C of S min West par ch Kinross from 1962

McKENZIE Edith Middleton *MA 1944

McKENZIE or Maclean, Eileen Mary MA 1944

MACKENZIE or Cowell, Elizabeth Graham MA 1925
resid Findochty

MACKENZIE Elizabeth Margaret Fraser MA 1946
sen exec off. MRC Lond till 1970
m Buckie 17.10.70 George C. Wilson BL(Glas) solic s of George C. W. Coatbridge

McKENZIE or Cocker, Ethel Middleton MA 1944

MACKENZIE Evan Alexander MB ChB 1914 DPH 1920
d 24.8.68

MacKENZIE or MacLeod, Flora Elizabeth MA 1909
d Edin 18.9.76

MACKENZIE Forbes Alexander MB ChB 1954
g p Eccles Lancs from 1955

MACKENZIE or Fraser, Frances Mary Clara *MA 1949 *MEd 1951

MacKENZIE Francis Fiddes MA 1901
no longer on GC reg

McKENZIE George Clark *BSc 1949
prin teacher maths Elgin acad 1961–66; rector Buckie h s from 1966

MACKENZIE George Doughty MB ChB 1924
d Inv 30.1.61 *AUR* XXXIX 204

MacKENZIE George Anderson *MA 1950
prin teacher mod lang: Bishopbriggs p s 1965–70, Cathkin h s Cambuslang 1970–71; head upper s Cathkin h s 1971–73, dep rector from 1973 - c[illegible] 30/7/95

McKENZIE George Duncan MB ChB 1930 DPH 1933
d Heaton, Bolton 13.12.74 *AUR* XLVI 238

MacKENZIE George Grant BSc(agr) 1926
d Inv 30.8.73

McKENZIE George Horatius *MA 1917 *BSc 1918
retd 1957; resid Saltcoats

MACKENZIE George Ironside BSc(for) 1932
conserv for.: Cardiff 1960–64, Aber 1964–69; retd; resid Lochcarron

MacKENZIE George Stephen MA 1910
no longer on GC reg

MACKENZIE Grace *BSc 1926
no longer on GC reg

MacKENZIE Hector Lyle *MA 1929

McKENZIE or Newman, Helen Mackay MA BSc 1930
res chem Brit indust sand Redhill 1950–72; retd; resid Purley

MacKENZIE or Garden, Henrietta MA 1921

MacKENZIE Hugh BSc(agr) 1938
nat agr advis serv 1946–72; retd; tech rep Weston pharm Spalding from 1972

McKENZIE Hugh Pearce *MA 1951

MACKENZIE Hugh Skinner *MA 1899 BD 1904
d Edin 28.2.60 *AUR* XXXVIII 584

MACKENZIE Ian BSc(eng) 1953
group leader eng Inv c c from 1974

MACKENZIE Ian Alexander Ross MB ChB 1939
g p Tutbury Burton-on-Trent from 1947; pres Derby med soc 1974–75; retd 1976; resid Norfolk

McKENZIE Ian Kindness *MA 1951

MACKENZIE Ian Lorimer BSc(agr) 1939
DAFS: sen insp (GD) N area Thurso 1959–66, NE area Aber 1966–71; div agr off. St Andrew's Ho Edin from 1971

MacKENZIE or Mills, Iris Susan MA 1935
resid Inv

MacKENZIE Isabel *MA 1911
no longer on GC reg

MACKENZIE or James, Isabel Elizabeth MB ChB 1940 DPH 1957
resid Bieldside Aber

MacKENZIE or Milne, Isabella Flora MB ChB 1922
retd; resid Sutton Coldfield
husb *d* 9.9.71

MACKENZIE or Macdonald, Isabella MacIntosh MA 1930
d Skye 29.1.80 road accident

McKENZIE James MB ChB 1924
d Lumsden 5.10.67 *AUR* XLII 363

McKENZIE James MB ChB 1944
FRCS(Eng) 1961 FRSM 1962
ENT regist Manc R I 1957–61; sen ENT regist royal hosp Wolverhampton 1961–62; consult. ENT surg Wolverhampton and Dudley/Stourbridge group of hosps from 1962

McKENZIE James Alexander MB ChB 1937
retd 1971; resid Bibury Cirencester

MacKENZIE James Ross MB ChB 1906 *MD 1912
d Aber 24.9.63 *AUR* XL 301

MACKENZIE James Ross MB ChB 1946

MacKENZIE James Strath MA 1939
ptnr Brander & Cruickshank advoc Aber from 1954

MACKENZIE Jane *MA 1925
retd; resid Stornoway

MACKENZIE or Holt, Jane MA 1936
d 20.4.71

McKENZIE Janie MA 1909
d 22.10.69

MACKENZIE or Dunlop, Jean Gordon MA 1945
resid Eastbourne

MACKENZIE or Smeeton, Jeanette Campbell MA 1949

McKENZIE or Reid, Jessie MA 1929
teacher Engl: Blackwell s mod s Headstone Harrow 1949–56; Heath Park girls' s Romford 1956–68; retd; resid Peterculter

McKENZIE or Harvey-Williams, Jessie Agnes MA 1932
teacher Brecon Wales from 1964
husb *d* –.10.64

McKENZIE or Hudson, Jessie Marian MB ChB 1937
d Lond 3.1.68 *AUR* XLII 371

MACKENZIE Jessie Marie Ursula *MA 1931
d Aber 1.1.80

MACKENZIE John MA 1896 MB ChB 1900
d 2.11.70 *AUR* XLIV 107

McKENZIE John BSc 1931
head Crimond s from 1956; retd 1971; resid Stonehaven

MACKENZIE John MA 1939
no longer on GC reg

McKENZIE John MB ChB 1944 MD 1957
Aberd: sen lect embryol 1955–63, reader 1963–69, reader and head of dept of dev biol from 1969

McKENZIE John *BSc(agr) 1951
no longer on GC reg

MacKENZIE John Angus MA 1912
no longer on GC reg

McKENZIE John Grant MA 1910 BD 1912 DD 1939
d Edin 17.5.63 *AUR* XL 199

MacKENZIE John Mearns MA 1949

MacKENZIE John Moir MA 1911 MB ChB 1915
d Aber 25.12.71 *AUR* XLIV 428

McKENZIE John Robbie MA 1909
d Aber 24.3.69 *AUR* XLIII 209

McKENZIE John Ross MA 1918
no longer on GC reg

McKENZIE Joseph Morrison MB ChB 1923
g p Dewsbury 1923–26, Newport E Yorks from 1926

MacKENZIE Kenneth MA 1922
d Inv 1.1.65 *AUR* XLI 57

MACKENZIE Kenneth PhD 1931

MacKENZIE Kenneth MA 1940
d Edin 18.2.71 *AUR* XLIV 215

MACKENZIE Kenneth Campbell MB ChB 1925
g p Kent; retd; emigrated to NZ 1976

MacKENZIE Kenneth Pirie MA 1910 MB ChB 1914
d Inv 7.3.68 *AUR* XLII 348

MACKENZIE or Wishart, Lilian *MA 1929
resid Bromley

MacKENZIE or Clark, Lilias Stuart Fraser *MA 1932
resid Juniper Green, Midlothian

MACKENZIE Maimie Margaret *MA 1952
asst youth employ. off. Maidenhead 1964–65, lect Engl E Berks coll of f e 1965–68; resid Reading
m Maidenhead 28.10.67 Arthur E. Tucker acct/bursar Birkbeck coll Lond s of Frederick T. Muddiford nr Barnstaple

MACKENZIE or Gow, Mairi MB ChB 1951
assist psychiat Craig Dunain hosp Inv from 1967

MACKENZIE Margaret Elizabeth Fraser MB ChB 1946
hosp apptments Scot., Canada, England to 1955; g p: Beauly 1955–60, Inv from 1960

MACKENZIE or Craig, Margaret Findlay Brown MA 1942
teacher: Engl/maths W Byfleet c s s Surrey 1957–64, Engl Robert May's s Odiham 1964–69, maths St Nicholas indep s Fleet from 1969

MACKENZIE Margaret Jean MA 1941
head Lochcarron p s from 1966

MACKENZIE Margaret Rankin *MA 1913
resid Beauly
d Inv 9.3.78

McKENZIE or Laws, Margaret Ross MA 1934 MB ChB 1939
g p Hetton le Hole Co Durham (Tyne & Wear) 1954–70, ptnr in Hetton group pract from 1970

MACKENZIE Margaret Troup MA 1913 dBL 1921 dLLB 1922
d Golspie 11.2.71 *AUR* XLIV 209

MacKENZIE Mary MA 1937

MacKENZIE or Murchison, Mary Flora MA 1943
teacher classics Plockton sen s s from 1947
husb *d* 20.7.69

McKENZIE or Cook, Mary Gillieson MA 1941
b 6.2.21
pers man. Brit Indust Plastics Oldbury, Warley, W Midlands from 1942
husb *d* 20.8.74

MacKENZIE or Walker, Mary Mollison MA 1915
d 30.3.81

MACKENZIE May Orme MA 1904
no longer on GC reg

MacKENZIE or Rundle, Moira Elizabeth Grace MA 1951
resid Crieff

MacKENZIE Murdo MA 1915
no longer on GC reg

MACKENZIE Murdoch Roderick *MA 1951
asst prin teacher Engl Kirkcaldy h s 1959–68; prin Engl Broxburn acad W Lothian 1968–70, Perth acad from 1970

MACKENZIE Myra Aileen MA 1954
m Gill

McKENZIE Nellie Baring MA 1945
teacher: Markinch 1945–48, Muir of Ord 1948–51, Blantyre Malawi 1951–52, Tokoroa NZ 1952–60, Ullapool from 1964
m Blantyre Malawi 9.6.51 Louis O. Vernon bus. man. s of René L. V. Beja, Tunisia

MACKENZIE Niven St Clair *MA 1932
retd 1974; resid Aber

MACKENZIE Norman BSc 1949 *1950 PhD 1953
indust liaison off. RGIT Aber from 1963

MACKENZIE Rhoda Jane MA 1931
teacher Rosssh: Munlochy 1939–48, Fodderty from 1948

MACKENZIE Robert Fraser *MA 1931
prin teacher Engl Templehall j s Kirkcaldy 1952–57; head: Braehead j s Buckhaven 1957–68, Summerhill acad Aber 1968–74; retd
m Kingston-on-Thames 5.2.45 Diana C. Lister d of Harold S. L.
publ: *A Question of Living, Escape from the Classroom, The Sins of the Children, State School, The Unloved Head*

McKENZIE Roderick Eddison MB ChB 1938

MacKENZIE or Paterson, Rosabelle MA 1935
resid Crieff

MACKENZIE Roy John MB ChB 1928

MacKENZIE or Hunter, Sandra Ishbel MA 1951
teacher Fr/Ger Nairn acad 1961–70, prin Fr/Ger 1970–73; prin teacher mod lang Millburn acad Inv from 1974
m(2) Nairn 5.10.73 Daniel B. Grant MA(Edin) prin teacher geog s of Daniel A. S. G. Inv

MACKENZIE or Lawn, Sheila Isabelle MA 1946

McKENZIE or Sinclair, Sheila Kennedy MA 1951
resid Aber

MACKENZIE Somerled Macdonald MB ChB 1954
d Aber 9.6.76 *AUR* XLVII 106

MACKENZIE Thomas MA 1926
min health & local govt Lond: chief exec off. 1958–65; retd; higher exec off. 1965–70; temp serv: with Road trans and gen insur comp Putney 1970–71, with Leach Bright & Co CA Richmond 1971–72; retd; resid E Sheen

MacKENZIE William Alexander BSc 1949 *1950 MEd 1976
ARIC 1962
prin teacher sc Peterhead acad 1962–68; lect chem coll of educ from 1968
m Aber 4.7.60 Dorothea M. Still bank clerk d of James S. Aber

MacKENZIE William Henry MA 1948

McKENZIE William Thomas Daniel MB ChB 1948
MRCGP 1952
g p Thornhill Dumfriessh and clin asst Thornhill hosp from 1961; assoc advis g p

MACKENZIE or Camps, Winifred Mary Ross MB ChB 1936
d Lond 15.4.75

McKERLIE Alan MB ChB 1937

McKERRON Robert Gordon *MA 1922
d Cape Town 14.4.72 *AUR* XLV 225

McKERRON Charles MB ChB 1910
no longer on GC reg

McKERROW William Alexander Hogg *MB ChB 1906
d 9.3.72

McKESSACK Peter BSc 1892 MB ChB 1896
no longer on GC reg

MACKESSACK Robert John MA 1899
d 9.3.70 *AUR* XLIII 440

McKIDDIE John Macdonald MB ChB 1937
FRCOG 1965
consult. obst/gyn Wakefield from 1950

MACKIE Adam Argo MB ChB 1942
d Maryfield, Sask 14.9.69 *AUR* XLIII 331

MACKIE Alastair Webster *MA 1950
teacher Engl: spec asst Ward acad Anstruther from 1974

MACKIE Alexander George Angus *BSc(eng) 1932
MInstCE 1939
RE (supp reserve) 1935–41; final rank capt; civ eng Holloway Bros (Lond) 1941–59; man. dir Beechdale Eng from 1959
m Sandal 10.10.42 Joan Froggart d of Frank F. Sandal

MACKIE or Sim, Annie MA 1931
head Cookney p s Stonehaven till closed 1969; teacher Newtonhill p s from 1969

MACKIE or Aitken, Catherine Hay MB ChB 1945
part-time clin m o Enfield & Harringey AHA 1970–72; part-time g p Hornsey 1972–77; clin asst dermat Whittington hosp from 1977

MACKIE or Shepherd, Elizabeth Reid MA 1940
resid Newburgh Aberdeensh

MACKIE or Horne, Elsie MB ChB 1921
no longer on GC reg

MACKIE or Whyte, Eveline MA 1927
resid Peterhead

MACKIE Evelyn Mary MA 1950

MACKIE or Birkett, Gertrude Joan MA 1948

MACKIE Gordon Moggach BCom 1937
prin teacher comm subj Peterhead acad 1939–70; retd
m Aber 19.7.41 Winifred G. McGibbon d of Robert McG. Edin

MACKIE or MacDonald, Helen MA 1913
d Lond 18.5.60 *AUR* XXXVIII 590

MACKIE Ian Alexander MB ChB 1954

MACKIE Isabella Farquhar MA 1917
teacher: Monymusk p s 1939–40, maths St Margaret's s for girls Aber 1944; retd; resid Monymusk
d 4.9.81

MACKIE James Farquharson MB ChB 1947
MRCGP 1958
g p Walthamstow from 1950
wife *d* 1967
m(2) Lond 10.10.68 Marjorie Eaves d of George E. Worksop

MACKIE James Robertson Monro MB ChB 1932 *MD 1934
FRCP(Lond) 1970 FRCPsych 1972
consult. psychiat Leeds & Bradford area 1950–71; retd; resid Lumphanan

MACKIE James Sinclair *BSc 1951 PhD 1956
Canada: post grad fell. NRC Ottawa 1954–56; res chem Can. indust lab McMasterville and Kingston Ont 1957–69; tech man. Chancell Montreal from 1969
m Montreal 6.5.60 Jeanine Enos

MACKIE or Allan, Jean *MA 1929
dir St Nicholas s Aber/Aberdeensh 1949–72
resid Methlick and Lincoln

MACKIE Jean Grant MA 1915
d 19.7.64 *AUR* XL 398

MACKIE Jessie Christina MA 1929
teacher Broomhill p s Aber 1961–70; retd

MACKIE Lewis MB ChB 1944
MRCGP 1965
g p Oldmeldrum from 1959

MACKIE Maitland BSc(agr) 1932 LLD 1976
JP 1964 CBE 1965 FEIS 1971 FR(Ag)S 1973 KtOStJ 1977
Lord lieut Aberdeensh from 1975; convener Aber county council 1970–75; chmn Aber and dist milk market. board from 1960; vice chmn NOSCA 1975
wife *d* Rothienorman 1960
m(2) Texas 19.10.63 Pauline M. McCalip BSc(Baylor Texas) d of Edwin L. McC. MD(Vanderbilt) Weslaco Texas

MACKIE Margaret MA 1920
no longer on GC reg

MACKIE Margaret Isobel *MA 1936
MVO 4th class 1958; Officer of the Order of Orange Nassau 1958; 1st secy dip serv
d Auchencairn 13.6.71

MACKIE or Large, Mary BCom 1935 MA 1936
farmer: memb BBC agr advis comm; chmn Kesteven coll of educ
husb *d* 19.9.73

MACKIE or Johnston, Mary MA 1955

MACKIE or Mucha, Muriel Jean MB ChB 1950
d Dumfries 18.1.67 *AUR* XLII 374

MACKIE Ninian *MA 1945
solic Arthur Hunt & Hunt Lond
d Lond 20.11.69 *AUR* XLIII 446

MACKIE William MB ChB 1931 DPH 1948
dep sen admin m o SE reg hosp board Edin 1963–69; retd from NHS 1969; consult. to Johnson & Johnson Slough and to Smith & Nephew Welwyn 1970–71; retd; resid Chudleigh

MACKIE William Souter *MA 1906
MA(Oxon) 1970
resid Cape Town
wife *d* 1965
d Cape Town 17.6.80 *AUR* XLIX 66

MACKIE Williamina Stephen MA 1924

McKILLIGAN Robert Falconer MA 1910

MacKILLIGAN Winifred MA 1915
no longer on GC reg

McKILLIGIN or Banyard, Eileen Mary *MA 1929
resid Dorchester

McKILLOP Annie Buchanan Erskine MA 1950
teacher: Craighill p s Aber 1966–71, remed Tullos p s Aber from 1971

MACKILLOP or Donald, Elizabeth Mary MA 1951
resid Stellenbosch S Af

McKILLOP William Lawie Mitchell BSc(for) 1954 *1957
MSc(for) (univ of New Brunswick Can) 1959 PhD/MA (Berkeley Calif USA) 1965
for. off. Can dept for. Ottawa 1958–61; USA: asst prof univ of Calif Berkeley 1964–69, assoc prof from 1969

McKIM Mary Agnes Gardner MA 1908
d Glasg 9.12.72

McKIM Roberta Jane MA 1912
d Paisley 2.11.67 *AUR* XLII 350

McKIMMIE Michael McKerrow *MA 1952

McKINLAY or Sheale, Margaret MA 1941 *MEd 1943
educ psych Ealing from 1966

MACKINNON or Cummins, Agnes Evelyn MA 1949
supply teacher: Currie 1966–68, Edin 1968–70; teacher Blackhall Edin from 1970

MACKINNON Alan *BSc 1911 *MA 1924
d Belfast 28.3.71 *AUR* XLIV 209

MACKINNON or Beedie, Christina Margaret MA 1942
year mistress Hilton acad Aber from 1971

MacKINNON Donald Norman MB ChB 1925
d Wigan –.8.71

MACKINNON Douglas Nelson MA 1937 MB ChB 1943
OBStJ 1968 MRCGP 1969
g p Bolton from 1947

MACKINNON Edgar Charles MA 1949

MACKINNON or Cochran, Elizabeth Agnes MA 1934
various posts since leaving Kenya 1968; resid Ballitoville, Natal

MacKINNON Fiona Rose *MA 1955
teacher Falkirk h s 1956, later actg prin Woodlands h s Falkirk

MACKINNON George Duff Gordon MA LLB 1949
Chevalier De L'Ordre National Du Mérite France 1974
ptnr L Mackinnon & Son advoc Aber from 1949; relinquished comm 51(H) div signal regt TA 1960; chief signal off. Highland dist with rank of col 1960–64

MACKINNON or Greig, Helen MA 1947
d Sedgefield 22.4.72 *AUR* XLV 128

MACKINNON or Spicer, Jane Gordon *MA 1950
on staff of *Queen* mag from 1954; resid Putney Lond

MacKINNON Kenneth MB ChB 1905

MACKINNON Lachlan MA 1906 [d]BL 1908 LLB 1910
d Aber 10.8.73 *AUR* XLV 316

MACKINNON Neil Ormiston MB ChB 1924
d Lond 22.10.65 *AUR* XLII 86

McKINNON Norman BSc(for) 1923

MACKINNON Roderick MA 1928
jubilee medal 1935
C of S min: Contin 1960–70, Is of Barra from 1970
m Nigg Rosssh 22.8.42 Eileen G. Mackay d of Norman D. M. Nigg

MACKINNON Ronald Lee BL 1951
ptnr Milne & Mackinnon advoc Aber from 1969

MACKINNON Walter Grieve BSc 1923 *MB ChB 1935
g p Derby from 1936
d Derby 17.4.78 *AUR* XLVII 356

MACKINNON William Calthorpe MA 1913 MB ChB 1917
d Aber 22.5.73 *AUR* XLV 317

MACKINNON William Lunan *MA 1911 *1912
no longer on GC reg

MACKINTOSH Alexanderina MA 1919
teacher maths Inv h s 1922–63; retd
d Inv 15.1.81

MACKINTOSH Angus MB ChB 1911
no longer on GC reg

MACKINTOSH or Cramond, Bertine Janet Cameron MB ChB 1947
psychiat m o Adelaide S Aust 1962–71; regist dept psych med RHSC Edin 1971–72; asst ch psychiat Leics ch guid clin and adolescent unit 1972–75; part time regist, sen regist dept ch and adolescent psychiat RI Stirling from 1976 and at RHSC Glasg

MACKINTOSH Christina Mary MA 1917

MACKINTOSH or Garrett, Elizabeth *MA 1953

MACKINTOSH or Raithby, Elizabeth Ashen MA 1914

MACKINTOSH or Chisholm, Fanny Bissett *BSc 1926
retd 1969; resid Strathpeffer
d 7.2.78 *AUR* XLVIII 104

MACKINTOSH Finlay George MB ChB 1937

MACKINTOSH Herbert MA 1921
no longer on GC reg

MACKINTOSH Hugh Stewart PhD 1941
FEIS 1958 LLD(Glas) 1969
dir of educ Glasg 1944–68; retd

MACKINTOSH Ian MB ChB 1927
part time indust m o Kodak 1954–64; chief m o Shell-Mex and BP Lond from 1964

MACKINTOSH or Park, Isabella Jean Robertson BSc MA 1935
resid Aber
husb *d* Aber 3.12.76

MACKINTOSH James MA 1929
d Inv 22.12.61 *AUR* XXXIX 282

MACKINTOSH James Maclean BSc(agr) 1950

MACKINTOSH John MA 1916 *1919
edit. vol III *Roll of Graduates* published 1960
d Aber 11.12.67 *AUR* XLII 354

MACKINTOSH Kenneth MA 1924
clergyman/teacher Milne's h s Fochabers 1951–68; retd; resid Cullen
wife *d* 14.2.72

MacKINTOSH Lily Fraser MA 1931
no longer on GC reg

MACKINTOSH or Brooker, Mabel Wilson MA 1920
resid Aber
d Ballater 25.2.81

MACKINTOSH or Stewart, Nini Isabel MA 1928
teacher Seremban convent s Malaya 1952–65; retd; resid Nairn

MACKINTOSH Robert MA 1910 DD 1950
d Edin 1.1.62 *AUR* XXXIX 273

MACKINTOSH Thomas BSc(agr) 1921
no longer on GC reg

McKINTY Henry Bernard BL 1922 BCom 1922
d Aber 13.10.68 *AUR* XLIII 83

MACKNIGHT James Russell Chalmers BSc 1952
farms man. Aberdeensh 1952–57; crop husb advis Dept Agr Malta 1958–60; agr advis Fisons NI/Scot. 1962–73; dep secy Royal Highland & Agr Soc Ingliston Edin from 1973
d 2.8.81

MACKWORTH Norman Humphrey MB ChB 1939

McLACHLAN Douglas Gordon BSc(agr) 1950
RD 1969
asst lands off. DAFS: Thurso 1964–68; lands off. Inv 1968–75; sen lands off. Oban from 1975
RNR from 1956 lt comm
marr diss 1964
m(2) Oban 7.4.64 Mary F. Hunter teacher

MacLACHLAN John Low BSc 1955 DipEd 1956

MACLACHLAN John Scott MA 1935 LLB 1937
d Aber 7.9.71 *AUR* XLIV 321

McLAGGAN John Douglas MA 1914 *MB ChB 1920
d 1.1.67 *AUR* XLII 182

McLAREN Alexander *BSc 1941 PhD 1948

MACLAREN Atholl Hutchison MB ChB 1942
MRCGP 1960
Nott: g p from 1948, clin asst phys med city hosp from 1961; chmn Notts loc med comm; vice chmn Notts fam pract comm; pres elect Nott Medico Chirurgical Soc

MACLAREN David Martin *MA 1950
MRCPE 1963 MD(Lond) 1967 FRCPath 1977
David Bruce labs Wiltshire 1960–61; lect bact Guy's hosp Lond 1961–64; consult. group path. Stockport Cheshire 1964–74; prof clin bact Amsterdam from 1974

McLAREN George Neil MB ChB 1925
g p Darlington 1935–61; retd; resid Dalbeattie
d Kippford 16.5.77

MACLAREN Hugh McCallum *MA 1954
prin teacher sc West Calder h s 1960–63; prin phys Stirling h s 1963–69; HMIS North div from 1969; resid Bieldside, Aber

McLAREN or Macleod, Isabella Morrison MA 1916
d Inv 9.10.66 *AUR* XLII 85

McLAREN John MA 1897
no longer on GC reg

MacLAREN Mary Jane Mowat MB ChB 1918
d 21.5.76

McLAREN Robert Gordon Alexander MB ChB 1927 MD 1938
retd 1968; resid Maidstone

McLAREN or Hutchings, Shelagh Isobel MA 1947
appliance off. ARI from 1959

McLAREN Agnes MA 1916
d Fraserburgh 4.3.70 *AUR* XLIII 442

MacLEAN or Wedderspoon, Agnes King Johnston MA 1953

McLEAN Alexander *MA 1919
d Alloa 16.5.64 *AUR* XL 399

MACLEAN Alexander MA 1939
bldg contr Sydney/Bathurst Aust from 1949

MACLEAN Alexander John MA 1929
retd 1971; resid Isle of Lewis

MACLEAN or Macaulay, Alexandra Campbell MA 1930
d 6.7.73

MACLEAN Allan James *MA 1931
prin teacher phys Dunfermline h s from 1944; retd 1974

MACLEAN Andrew Iain MB ChB 1943
g p Hull from 1947

McLEAN Andrew Lewis BSc(agr) 1951

MACLEAN Angus MA 1922
d Kingussie 27.2.69 *AUR* XLIII 212

MACLEAN Angus MA 1929

MACLEAN Anne Matheson MA 1928
teacher Nicolson inst Stornoway/Stornoway p s 1959–72; retd; resid Tong Isle of Lewis

MACLEAN or Brakebill, Annie (Nan) MA 1941

MACLEAN or Petrie, Cairine Ross *MA 1940 *MEd 1954
ABPsS
teacher Ruthrieston s Aber 1958–68; sen educ psych Aber c c 1968–75; prin psych NE List 'D' schools Scotland from 1975
publ: *Backward or Maladjusted Children in Secondary School* (Ward Lock) 1970; *Child Guidance* with D. A. F. Conochie (Macmillan) 1975
husb *d* 1966
m(2) Aber 11.10.80 Douglas A. F. Conochie BSc 1949 *qv*

MacLEAN Colin George *MA 1950
sub edit. *Daily Telegraph* Lond 1960–61; asst edit. letters to edit. *The Times* Lond 1961–65; edit. *Times Educational Supp* Scot. Edin 1965–77; gen and educ edit. W. & R. Chambers Edin 1977–79; publ dir AUP from 1979

MACLEAN Donald *MA 1902
d Edin 4.1.62 *AUR* XXXIX 270

McLEAN Donald Patrick *MA 1940
dir admin Fife reg; retd

McLEAN or Henderson, Dorothy Elizabeth MA 1930
teacher Rosehill s amalgamated with Cornhill s Aber 1962–70; retd
marr diss 1947

McLEAN Douglas Gordon MA 1920
retd 1963; resid Longniddry

MACLEAN Duncan MA 1949
head Barvas s Is of Lewis from 1961

McLEAN or Clark, Eileen Mary MA 1946
resid Wolverhampton

MACLEAN Ewen MA 1906
no longer on GC reg

McLEAN Frank Summers MB ChB 1925

McLEAN or Smith, Helen MA 1910
d Aber 13.4.66 *AUR* XLII 83

MACLEAN or Rowlands, Helen Campbell Smith MB ChB 1935
d Aber 3.1.71 *AUR* XLIV 212

MACLEAN Henry Ross Colquhoun MB ChB 1944
g p Brentford from 1954

McLEAN Ian Cook MB ChB 1953
g p: Corinda Brisbane Aust from 1963

MACLEAN Isabel Grant Morrice MA 1943 LLB 1949
resid Aber

McLEAN James Alexander Forbes *MB ChB 1937 DPH 1941
MRCPath 1964 FRCPath 1965
consult. bact Mile End hosp Lond from 1964

McLEAN James Johnston MA 1931
d Aber 24.4.67 *AUR* XLII 370

McLEAN Janetta Christian MA 1926
retd 1964; resid Glasg

McLEAN or Murray, Jessie Fraser MA 1919
d Aber 20.1.75

MACLEAN John *MA 1909 BSc 1910
d 5.10.64

MacLEAN John BSc(agr) 1923
retd 1966
d Aber 26.3.77

MACLEAN John Alexander MA 1925 LLB 1930 PhD 1939
CBE 1968
dir educ Invernesssh 1943–68; retd 1968; chmn N reg hosp board from 1971; resid Inv

MACLEAN John Stewart *MA 1940
FEIS 1967
prin teacher Engl Buckie h s 1960–69; rector Stromness acad from 1969
d 5.7.77 *AUR* XLVIII 106

MACLEAN Kenneth John MB ChB 1950
DPH(Lond) 1965
surg cmdr RN 1959–68
d N'cle-u-Tyne 17.8.69

McLEAN Maitland Naisby BSc 1944 *1949
res/dev tech Kodak Harrow 1950–62; dev man./dir Salford 1962–66; man. staff Kodak Harrow from 1966

McLEAN Margaret Elizabeth Bennet MA 1938
part time teacher mus Banffsh s from 1972

MACLEAN or Stalker, Mary Elizabeth Carmichael MB ChB 1942
g p Aber 1967–77; resid Banchory

McLEAN Muriel Margaret MB ChB 1942 ᶜMD 1955
consult. paediat Clwyd AHA from 1957

MACLEAN Neil MA 1949

McLEAN Nigel Hugh BSc(eng) 1950

MACLEAN Nigel Ross MA 1937 BD 1940
C of S min St Paul's ch Perth from 1954

MACLEAN Roderick Charles *MA 1940 *MEd 1948
dir tv Glas univ 1965–69; dir audio-visual serv Glas and Strath 1969–76; head centre for educ pract Strath from 1976

MACLEAN Ronald MB ChB 1930
d Inv 28.10.68 *AUR* XLIII 85

MACLEAN William Gordon BD 1912
min emeritus First Presb ch Winnipeg; moderator Presb ch in Canada 1946–47
d 29.2.80

McLEAY Ella MA 1935
retd 1972; resid Auchenblae

McLELLAN Duncan Morison ᶜMB ChB 1950 DPH 1958
MFCM 1971
asst sen admin m o N reg hosp board 1961–65; dep s a m o E reg hosp board 1965–68; group med supt Ninewells and assoc hosps Dun 1968–71; m o/acting dir Scot. hosp centre Edin from 1971

McLELLAN John Hugh Crawford MA 1906
d Crieff 10.1.75 *AUR* XLVI 234

McLEMAN Daniel MB ChB 1955

McLEMAN Malcolm *BSc 1951

McLEMAN William John Murdoch BSc(eng) 1954
MICE 1960
des off. Sir William Halcrow & ptnrs Lond 1959–60; dir Smokeless Heating Bromley 1960–67; dir J. McLeman Heating Chislehurst Kent from 1967
m Aber 2.3.61 Mary B. Mann d of Robert M. Aber

MacLENNAN Alastair MB ChB 1934
col staff appts Germany/Egypt/UK 1952–64; insp trg army med serv M o D Lond 1964–66; DDMS h q 1st (Br) Corps Germany 1966–67; promoted to brig DDMS h q southern command Hounslow/DD gen army med serv Lond 1967–69; curator RAMC hist museum Aldershot from 1969; rank of maj-gen as retd off.
m Lond 4.7.40 Constance A. M. Cook d of Ambrose C. Rowlands Castle

MACLENNAN Alexander Bain BSc(eng) 1950

MACLENNAN or Mackenzie, Ann MA 1913
no longer on GC reg

MACLENNAN or Gallagher, Anne Gordon Innes MB ChB 1925
worked for Nat Blood Transfusion Serv and Pension Boards for Min of Pensions and locums Weymouth 1958–73
husb *d* 1956

MacLENNAN or Morrison, Catherine Mary MA 1923
resid Croy

MacLENNAN Christopher *MA 1927
retd 1967; resid Blairgowrie

MacLENNAN Donald MB ChB 1924
Wales: consult. surg Llanelli hosp/Glamorgan hosp/Carmarthen Inf 1934–68; retd
m Lond 18.7.38 Margaret Evans

MacLENNAN Donald Alexander MA 1955

MacLENNAN Donald McKay MA 1953

McLENNAN Douglas George BSc(eng) 1945
Assoc Brit Inst Radio Eng 1947

GEC Glasg branch: various appts from 1951
resid Crieff

MacLENNAN Duncan Anderson Macgregor MB ChB 1934
d Dufftown 14.4.75 *AUR* XLVI 325

MACLENNAN or Young, Flora MA 1906
d Yorkshire 7.11.75

MACLENNAN George William Grant MA 1926 BSc 1928 *1929
no longer on GC reg

MacLENNAN Harrie MA 1924
retd 1969; resid Inv

MacLENNAN or Mackenzie, Janet BSc 1920

MacLENNAN or Mackenzie, Joanna MA 1924
teacher Sanquhar acad Dumfriessh 1926–71; retd

MacLENNAN John MB CM 1895 MD 1925
d Nairn 8.5.61 *AUR* XXXIX 198

McLENNAN John Duncan MB ChB 1934 *MD 1939
d Washington DC 4.6.62 *AUR* XXXIX 385

MacLENNAN J. Munro MA 1923 BSc 1925
scient edit. Canberra Aust 1958–61; freelance Russian–Engl translator Britain, Eire, Spain, Portugal, Canada from 1961
d Ottawa 4.12.75 *AUR* XLVI 416

MacLENNAN Kenneth BSc(agr) 1912
no longer on GC reg

McLENNAN Kenneth MA 1896 BD 1903
no longer on GC reg

McLENNAN or King, Lydia Mary MA 1951
teacher Hythehill p s Lossiemouth 1965–74, head from 1974

MACLENNAN Norman Macpherson MB ChB 1921 DPH 1923 MD 1924
d 8.3.67

MacLENNAN Robert Cran MB ChB 1920
d –.12.65

MacLENNAN Robert William MA 1902
no longer on GC reg

MacLENNAN Roderick George Squair *BSc 1955
field and mining geol S Africa 1955–63; mining geol: Nchanga Zambia 1963–66, Welkom OFS S Afr 1966–67; chief geol Vaal Reefs E & M Co S Af from 1967
wife *d* 6.6.71
m(2) Queenstown S Af 8.12.72 Gillian A. May d of Harry W. M. Queenstown

MacLENNAN William George Duncan *MA 1922
retd 1966; resid Edin
d –.2.81

MACLEOD Agnes Percy *MA 1933

MACLEOD Alasdair Macgillivray MA 1910
no longer on GC reg

MACLEOD Alexander MA 1920
no longer on GC reg

McLEOD Alexander MA 1951
head Caol p s Fort William from 1963

MACLEOD Alexander Crichton BSc 1954 PhD 1958
DIC 1958
scient off. AWRE 1958–60; sen scient Morganite res and dev Lond 1960–67; sen lect metallurgy Strath from 1967
m Lond 11.3.61 Muriel O. Smith BSc(Swansea) res phys chem/admin Stir d of James S. Bridgend Glam

McLEOD Alexander Grant MA 1909
no longer on GC reg

MACLEOD Alexander John MA 1938
teacher Gaelic Sir E. Scott s s Tarbert Harris 1955–74, dep head from 1974

McLEOD Alexander Luias MB ChB 1924
no longer on GC reg

MACLEOD Alice MacLennan MA 1954

MACLEOD Alick John MA 1949
teacher Oban h s from 1953

MACLEOD Alister Ian MB ChB 1945
reg m o DHSS Manc from 1966

MACLEOD Allan John MB ChB 1910
no longer on GC reg

MACLEOD Angus BSc(agr) 1911
tech off. DAOS Stornoway 1958–62; retd; resid Stornoway
wife *d* 1.8.68

MacLEOD Angus MA 1927
d Fordoun 22.7.64 *AUR* XL 400

MACLEOD Angus MA 1929
d 17.6.67

MACLEOD Angus Maclennan MB ChB 1952
g p: Arisaig 1958–65, Mallaig 1965–68, Fort William 1968–69, Strachur Argyll 1969–75, Dunoon from 1975

MACLEOD Anne Stewart MA 1954
DipEd(Edin) 1963
teacher Bathgate: j s s 1963–65, tech coll 1965–67; Canada: teacher Merritt h s B C 1967–68, L V Rogers h s Nelson B C 1968–70; teacher Clackmannan coll of f e Alloa from 1970
m Muckhart Perthsh 28.12.73 William G. Sanderson BSc(H-W) mining eng

McLEOD or Clarke, Barbara Louie MA 1952

MACLEOD or Macdonald, Bella MA 1931
resid Conon Bridge

MACLEOD Calum Alexander MA 1955 LLB 1957
comm RAEC Belfast/Manc 1958–60; ptnr Paull & Williamsons advoc Aber from 1964; chancellor's assessor Aberd from 1979
m Inv 21.7.62 Elizabeth M. Davidson teacher d of David D. Inv

MacLEOD Calum Murray MA 1952 LLB 1964
teacher Bervie j s Inverbervie 1961–63; leg app and solic 1964–70; solic: Dun 1970–73, on own account Broughty Ferry 1973–77; acquired law firm T. & J. W Laverock Dun 1977

MacLEOD or MacLure, Catherine MA 1950

McLEOD Charles MB ChB 1946
short serv comm RN 1957–61; g p: Ripley 1961–67, Elgin from 1967
m Lond 1959 Margaret E. Redman SRN d of Christopher E. R. Southwold

McLEOD Charles Stewart *MA 1924
OBE 1961 FCIT C St J
BR from 1948: chief indust relations off. 1962–68; retd. Author *All Change* Rly indust relations in the Sixties publ Gower Press 1970

MACLEOD Christina MA 1911
d Inv 25.9.71 *AUR* XLIV 316

MacLEOD or Mackay, Christina Margaret *MA 1941

MACLEOD or Reid, Christine Soldan *MA 1938
head mod lang dept Lady Eleanor Holles s Hampton from 1966; retd 1975
husb *d* 26.3.77

MACLEOD David Macgregor BSc 1949 *1950 PhD 1953

MACLEOD Donald MA 1932
d Bettyhill 14.5.77

MACLEOD Donald MA 1936
JP
d 10.12.71

MACLEOD Donald MA 1950
teacher W. Calder h s Midlothian 1960–63; prin maths Tarbert s s from 1963
m Dennyloanhead 7.4.66 Janet C. W. Thomson teacher dom subj d of William T. Banknock by Bonnybridge

MACLEOD Donald John MA 1947
dep head Shawbost j s s 1949–65; head Valtos s Uig 1965–74; asst head Stornoway p s from 1974
m Glasg 15.7.65 Alexina Macdonald teacher d of Donald M. Shawbost

MACLEOD Donald John MA 1954
d 1972

MACLEOD Donald Norman MA 1947

MacLEOD Donovan Hutcheson MB ChB 1953
d Essex 23.2.72 *AUR* XLIV 434

MacLEOD Douglas Haig *BSc(agr) 1941

MACLEOD Duncan MB ChB 1924
d Stornoway 17.10.60 *AUR* XXXIX 204

MACLEOD Duncan MA 1927
d Aber 11.3.65 *AUR* XLI 151

MacLEOD Duncan MA 1934
head Gairloch j s s Ross from 1949; retd

MACLEOD Elizabeth Jane MA 1952
teacher Engl Fortrose acad 1973–74; asst prin Engl from 1974

MACLEOD or Catto, Elizabeth Kate MA 1917
d Stracathro 15.2.79 *AUR* XLVIII 227

MACLEOD Eric Campbell MB ChB 1954
DPM 1960 LMCC 1965 MRCPsych 1973 FRCP(Can) 1973
sen regist dept psych med Glas 1961–64; Canada: dir psychiat unit Sudbury gen hosp Ont/consult. psychiat Sudbury mem hosp and Sudbury Algoma sanatorium from 1964

MACLEOD George MA 1948
JP
d 10.5.69 *AUR* XLIII 217

McLEOD George Johnston *MA 1932
prin teacher classics Montrose acad 1952–71; retd

MACLEOD Hughina Aird MA 1912
no longer on GC reg

MACLEOD Ian MB ChB 1948
g p Kilwinning from 1968

MacLEOD Ian Ingram Scott [d]BD 1952
C of S min St Andrew's ch Arbroath from 1959

MACLEOD Isabella MA 1910
no longer on GC reg

MACLEOD James MA 1939
dep head Aber 1957–64; head Skene Square s Aber from 1964

MacLEOD James William BSc(eng) 1935

MACLEOD or Cumming, Jean MA 1954
teacher Contin from 1968

MACLEOD or Lawrie, Johanna Annabella MA 1950
teacher Inv h s 1963–70; head Aldourie p s Inv from 1971

MACLEOD John MA 1908
no longer on GC reg

MACLEOD John MA 1936

McLEOD John Alexander BSc(agr) 1951

MACLEOD John Angus MA 1910
retd 1950; resid Sunderland

McLEOD John Bryce *MA 1950
DPhil(Oxon) 1958 Whittaker Prize Edin math soc 1965 FRSE 1974
fell./lect Wadham coll Oxon from 1960; jun proctor 1963–64; visiting prof univ of Wisconsin Madison USA 1964–65, 1970–71; visiting prof univ of Minnesota Minneapolis 1977–78

MACLEOD John Morrison MA 1948
JP
head Dalneigh p s Inv 1961–68; Invernesssh: county advis for prim. educ 1968–73; asst dir of educ 1973–75; dep dir educ Highland reg c from 1975

MacLEOD John Murdo MA 1923

MACLEOD John William *BSc 1949

MACLEOD Kenneth MA 1929
d Lochaber –.5.63

MacLEOD Kenneth MA 1951

MACLEOD Lachlan MA 1921
d Inv 30.3.66 *AUR* XLII 85

McLEOD Laura Stewart *MA 1914
no longer on GC reg

McLEOD or MacDonald, Lilian Mary MA 1945
retd 1971; resid New Elgin; resumed teaching Elgin acad 1976
husb deceased

MACLEOD Mairi Elizabeth MB ChB 1949
g p Somercotes from 1964
m Derbysh 9.5.64 George R. M. Sterland farm. s of George M. S. Pentrich

MACLEOD Mairi Matheson MA 1954

MACLEOD Malcolm MB ChB 1939 MD 1960

MACLEOD Malcolm *MA 1950
teacher classics/hostel warden Nicolson Inst Stornoway 1970–74; asst prin relig educ from 1974; prin classics from 1975

MACLEOD Malcolm Donald *BSc(eng) 1950
prof eng Shell-Mex & BP Lond 1962–63; reg eng Shell & BP Scot. Glasg 1963–75; Shell UK Oil: aviations oper man. Lond 1975–76, reg oper man. Glasg 1976–79, man. plant & admin dept Lond from 1979
m Glasg 26.4.62 Anne MacDonald secy d of Angus MacD. Glasg

MACLEOD Malcolm Murdo MA 1950

MACLEOD Malcolmina MA 1935

MACLEOD Margaret Jean MA 1931

MacLEOD Margaret MacLennan MA 1950
teacher: Crimond s 1951–67, Strichen s from 1967
m Inv 28.12.60 Stanley J. Buchan farm. s of Patrick B. B. Philorth Fraserburgh

McLEOD or Beveridge, Margaret Patricia MA 1925
resid St And

MacLEOD or O'Gorman, Marie Eaton *BSc 1941

MACLEOD Marion MB ChB 1938
no longer on GC reg

MACLEOD or MacAskill, Marion Macaulay MA 1930
d 22.11.68

MACLEOD or Caie, Mary MA 1901
d 22.2.69

McLEOD or Burton, Morag Grace *BSc 1955
resid Warrington

MacLEOD Murdo MA 1922
d 25.4.64 *AUR* XL 399

MACLEOD Murdo MA 1928
JP 1953
teacher Shawbost s Ross & Cromarty 1936–43, head 1943–53; head Bayble j s s 1953–71; retd; resid Brue, Barvas Is of Lewis
m Aber 2.8.44 Isabella Morrison nurse d of Alexander M. Upper Barvas

MACLEOD Murdo *MA 1950
HMIS from 1969
m Inv 4.4.63 Catherine Fraser RGN d of Alexander F. MA(Edin) Inv

MACLEOD or Clark, Muriel Rhoda MA 1947
resid Botswana
m Drumnadrochit 16.12.52 Alexander J. F. Clark

MacLEOD Neil MA 1927

MACLEOD Norman MA 1933
retd 1968; resid Aber

MACLEOD Norman ᶜMB ChB 1951

MacLEOD Norman John MA 1926
d 24.3.66

McLEOD Patricia Ann Moir MA 1923
retd 1966; resid Aber

MACLEOD Roderick MA 1927
head Rothiemurchus s 1952–68
d Inv 1.6.68

MACLEOD Roderick Forbes *MA 1953
prin teacher Engl Grove acad Dun 1967–73; dep rector Webster's h s Kirriemuir from 1973

MACLEOD Roderick Macrae MA 1925
no longer on GC reg

MacLEOD Roderick Torquil BSc(for) 1955
assoc B C reg for.
Canada: asst for. Kamloops for. dist Br Col for. serv—silviculturist and gen management—1960–66; dist silviculturist and gen timber admin Prince Rupert for. dist 1966–72; dist appraisal off. and for. i/c East Kootenay zone Nelson for. dist from 1972

McLEOD Ronald *MA 1939
prin teacher classics AGS from 1964; sqn ldr RAFVR 1961–77

MACLEOD or Lawrence, Sheila MA 1951
teacher Buckie p s from 1966

McLEOD Susie Milne MA 1922
head kindergarten dept RGC Aber 1947–54; retd; resid Aber

MacLEOD Thomas Finlay Bidgood MA 1949
JP
d Dufftown 27.5.72 *AUR* XLV 128

MACLEOD William *MA 1932
d 24.1.66

MACLEOD William Ferrans MB ChB 1943
g p Cowdenbeath from 1947

McLUSKEY or Davidson, Margaret Beedie MA 1929

MACMAHON Antoinette Margaret Helen MB ChB 1943
MRCPE 1962
med regist paediat Northern group of hosps Edin 1961–63; sen regist paediat S Warks hosps 1964–66; asst paediat Dumfries & Galloway Inf 1966–68; med missionary Serabu hosp via Bo Sierra Leone from 1969

MacMAHON Charles Grant MB ChB 1904
no longer on GC reg

MacMAHON or Burnett, Joan Elizabeth MA 1942

McMAHON John Robertson MA 1954

McMAHON Sheila MA 1947

MacMAHON or Christie, Teresa Mary MA 1949
resid Aber
d 4.3.81

MACMILLAN Alexander MA 1898
d Liverpool 2.1.61 *AUR* XXXIX 98

MACMILLAN Alexander *MA 1910
d 11.6.65

McMILLAN or MacDougall, Alice Malcolm *MA 1933 BSc 1935 *1936
teacher Cornaigmore j s s Is of Tiree 1939–70; retd

McMILLAN or Dawson, Bethia Ross MA 1947
teacher: maths/sc Inverurie acad 1955–58, maths Milne's h s Fochabers 1963–72; maths and asst prin guid Milne's h s from 1972

MACMILLAN Duncan MA 1955
teacher Uddingston g s 1958–61; spec asst Whitehill s s Glasg/teacher Russian 1961–71; teacher Fr/asst prin guid Bishopbriggs h s 1971–73, prin guid from 1973
m Glasg 10.7.63 Margaret M. Shaw market res interviewer d of John J. S. Kildonan Is of Arran

McMILLAN Duncan Stewart *MA 1930
d Lond 19.7.69 *AUR* XLIII 331

MACMILLAN Elizabeth MA 1952

MACMILLAN James MA 1932
CA 1936
fin. dir John Summers & Sons Shotton Chester 1963–68, Holst & Co Watford 1968–72 chmn from 1969, Norwest Holst Bootle 1972–75

MACMILLAN John Murdo MA 1938
OBE 1972
head Back s s Is of Lewis from 1969

MacMILLAN or Watt, Lilias MacGregor MA 1915

MACMILLAN or Shepherd, Margaret Wallace MA 1930
resid Grimsby

McMILLAN or Winchester, Mary *MA 1945

MACMILLAN Matthew *MA 1950
OBE 1976
assoc prof Engl univ coll of Cape Coast Ghana 1962–64; prof Engl univ of Khartoum 1965–70; Engl teaching div Brit Council Lond 1970–74; 1st secy educ Brit high comm New Delhi from 1974

McMILLAN Neil BSc 1952 *1953

MACMILLAN William Boyd Robertson MA 1951 [d]BD 1954
C of S min: Fyvie par ch 1960–67, Bearsden S ch 1967–78; St Mary's par ch Dun from 1978
m Aber 22.8.62 Mary A. B. Murray MB Chb 1955 *qv*

MACMILLAN William George BSc 1925 *1926 PhD 1930
d Andreas Isle of Man 16.5.77

McMURTRIE or Tessier, Beatrice Somerville Brodie *MA 1948
France: Bronze medal, Salon d'Erquy 1972, lauréate Salon des Femmes Peintres de l'Ouest 1976, Prix de la Peinture à l'Eau Salon de Baugé 1978
one-man shows Nantes, Angers, St Brieuc, group

exhibitions Aber, Paris, La Baule, St Nazaire, Breton painters' group, Musée de Nantes etc 1968–79

McMURTRIE or Gardner, Isobel Jean BSc 1951
resid Curepipe, Mauritius

McNAB or Macalister, Annabella Johnstone MA 1937
teacher: Nethybridge p s 1953–54, Westerton p s Aber from 1965

McNAB Ian Stephen BSc 1950 *1951
MICE 1958
asst chief estimator Crudens Musselburgh 1964–71; sen contr man. Wm London & Son Bothwell 1971–74; contr man. Murdoch Mackenzie from 1974

McNAB James MB ChB 1953
resid Halifax Nova Scotia
m 1954 Hazel G. MacLean man. dir

McNAB Mary Davidson MA 1948
d Fraserburgh 24.9.69 *AUR* XLIII 331

McNAB or Geddes, Muriel Lesley MA 1952
teacher Fr: Auchmuty s Glenrothes 1965–66; Madras coll St And from 1968

McNAIR Gordon Peter [c]MB ChB 1948
consult. surg RAF UK/Germany/Bahrain/Aden, retd 1969; coll m o RAF Cranwell 1969–70; g p Rhayader Wales from 1972

McNAIR James Jamieson MB ChB 1941
DTM & H(Liv) 1960 FFCM 1973 C St J
Ceylon: sen m o AHQ and CO RAF hosp 1957–59; o c RAF inst of hyg Freckleton 1959–62; DGMS staff RAF Lond 1962–65; o c RAF hosp Changi Singapore 1965–67; p m o fighter comm RAF Bentley Priory; o c joint serv med rehabit unit Chessington 1968–71; M o D Lond: dir health and res RAF 1971–73, dep dir gen med serv RAF 1974–77; retd
m Valetta Malta 5.9.45 Zobell Pyper nurse; wife *d* 20.1.77

McNAUGHT Duncan Arthur Hutchison MB ChB 1940
sen h m o Bangour hosp W Lothian 1962–69; consult. anaest Peel hosp Galashiels from 1969

MACNAUGHTON or Watt, Agnes *MA 1922
resid Comrie

McNAUGHTON Alastair Ronald MB ChB 1951

McNAUGHTON or Thomson, Jean Herron Love *MA 1925
resid Banchory

McNAUGHTON John Love MA 191.
d Buckie 2.11.64 *AUR* XLI 55

MacNEILL Donald MB ChB 1951
g p: Crieff 1959–60, Montrose from 1960; Stracathro hosp: clin asst (orthop) 1960–77, g p hosp pract (orthop) from 1977

McNICOL Alexander Stuart BL 1928
proc fiscal Aber 1960–69; retd; resid Arbroath

McNICOL Duncan MB ChB 1950
MRCGP 1969
g p Glasg from 1954; part time tut. in g p Glas from 1973

MACNIVEN Catherine Jane MA 1921

McNUTT Margaret Rosemary MA 1942 Dip Ed 1957
Aber: teacher Powis s s 1958–63, lect coll of comm 1963–67; leg. asst A C Morrison & Richards advoc Aber 1967–69; lect coll of comm Aber 1969–70, sen lect from 1970

MACONACHIE Gordon William MB ChB 1903

McOUAT Alexander MA 1907
no longer on GC reg

MacOWAN Kenneth Duncan Simpson BSc 1932
CBE 1960
anim health advis Min of overseas dev 1963–68; retd; resid Ramsey I of Man

MacOWAN or Cunningham, Marion Margaret MA 1928 BSc 1929 PhD 1932
NZ: teacher sc Chilton St James s Lower Hutt 1950–55, head sc girls' h s Palmerston North 1961–71
husb *d* 29.8.71

McPETRIE James Duncan MA 1895
no longer on GC reg

McPETRIE James Stuart *BSc 1924 PhD 1934 DSc 1939
CB
dir gen electronics res and dev min of aviation Lond 1958–62; dir Racal Electronics Bracknell 1962–66; dir Mac Farms Slapton Devon 1966–68

MacPHAIL Angus MB ChB 1924
no longer on GC reg

MacPHAIL or Macleod, Dolina BSc 1939
resid Tarbert, Is of Harris

MACPHAIL Hugh Norman MB ChB 1950
g p Edin from 1952

MACPHAIL Ian *MA 1949

MACPHAIL Jessie Ann MA 1909
no longer on GC reg

MacPHAIL John Critchfield MA 1930
d Portpatrick 3.5.68 *AUR* XLII 370

MACPHAIL or Macleod, Mary MA 1940
inf mistress Contin s 1962–68; relief teacher Easter Ross from 1974

MacPHAIL Norman MB ChB 1912
d Carloway Lewis 31.1.61 *AUR* XXXIX 202

McPHERSON Barbara MA 1952
teacher Millbank p s Nairn from 1956

MacPHERSON or McLean, Catherine Mary BSc 1944
asst dev and des (electronics) Hayes 1945–46; publisher's tech sub-edit. Lond 1946–57; bldg soc br man. Chorkywood from 1975

McPHERSON Charles Ronaldson MA 1924
head Tarves s 1943–65; retd; resid Milltimber

McPHERSON Charlotte Anderson MA 1926

McPHERSON Christine Catherine Mary MA 1955
teacher Forres from 1964

MACPHERSON Colin Campbell Reith *MA 1952 dBD 1955
C of S min St Margaret par ch Dunfermline from 1966

McPHERSON David BSc 1940 MA 1943

MACPHERSON Ewen Donald *MA 1950
prin teacher hist Aber acad 1959–66; lect hist Aber coll of comm from 1966

McPHERSON George MA 1939 *BSc 1947
sen exper off. marine lab Aber from 1957

MacPHERSON George Milne MA 1955
retd 1972
d Aber 24.1.78 *AUR* XLVII 360

MacPHERSON George Robert MB ChB 1944
g p Inv from 1955

McPHERSON Hamish Grant MB ChB 1927
retd 1970; resid Hastings NZ

MACPHERSON Harry Gordon *BSc 1952

MACPHERSON Ian William MA 1943 *1948
member HM diplom serv: Ankara 1958–59, Geneva 1959–60, Budapest 1963–66, Athens 1972–75

MACPHERSON Ishbel Eliza MA 1930
d Huntly 14.12.75

MACPHERSON or Reid, Isobel Margaret MA 1946
teacher Broomhill p s Aber from 1969

McPHERSON James *MA 1904
no longer on GC reg

McPHERSON James Alexander Strachan MA 1949 dBL 1952 LLB 1952
ptnr Alexander George & Co solic Macduff from 1955; member Macduff t c and Banff c c 1958–75; provost Macduff 1972–75; chmn Banffsh educ comm 1967–70; convener Banff c c 1970–75; member Grampian reg c and chmn Public Protection Comm from 1974; hon Sheriff Grampian, Highlands and Is from 1972; member Grampian health board from 1974; member of the Post Office Users' Council for Scotland; DL Banffsh
m Aber 1960 Helen M. Perks MA 1956 *qv*

MACPHERSON James Cluny BSc 1952

McPHERSON James Ritchie MB ChB 1945

MacPHERSON James Stewart *MA 1937

MACPHERSON or McConachie, Jean Margaret MB ChB 1946
g p Lossiemouth; m o Gordonstoun school

MACPHERSON John MA 1905 BSc(agr) 1906
no longer on GC reg

McPHERSON John MB ChB 1909

MACPHERSON John MB ChB 1940
FRGOG 1964
sen consult. obst/gen Torbay dist hosps from 1954

MACPHERSON Kenneth Manchip *MA 1955

MACPHERSON Malcolm BSc(for) 1949
for. comm: dist off. Fochabers 1966–71, Craven Arms Salop from 1971

McPHERSON Margaret Ann *MA 1942
Edin: chief exec off. Scot. dev dept 1965–70; Scot. off. superann div: chief exec off. 1970–71, prin 1971–74; asst secy from 1974

McPHERSON or Russell, Margaret Murray MA 1928
DipDomSc(Birm) 1959
trainee dom sc Radbrook coll Shrewsbury 1958–59; teacher dom sc Glanford s s Brigg 1959–63

MACPHERSON Mary Jean Grant MA 1952 BSc 1954

McPHERSON Mary Margaret Mackenzie *MA 1938

MACPHERSON or Taylor, Mary Tait MA 1931
resid Laurencekirk

MACPHERSON Norman Letham MA 1924 BSc 1927 *1928 PhD 1931
d Quebec 7.2.72 *AUR* XLIV 430

MACPHERSON Robert William MB ChB 1906 DPH 1911 MD 1913
no longer on GC reg

MACPHERSON Ronald Taylor MB ChB 1950
FRCPath 1971
path. McKellor hosp Thunder Bay Ont from 1971

MACPHERSON or Burnett, Rosina Margaret Mill MA 1946

MACPHERSON William John *MA 1950
tut. Cai Cantab 1960–70, sen tut. 1964–65, coll lect from 1964

MACPHERSON William Noel John MA 1952

McQUEEN Andrew Milroy BSc(eng) 1953

McQUEEN David James BD 1907
d Edin 8.4.62 *AUR* XXIX 375

McQUEEN Elizabeth Milroy *MA 1901
d Aber 5.3.63 *AUR* XL 198

McQUEEN James Milroy MA 1903 *BSc 1906 *MB ChB 1907
d Aber 1963

MACQUEEN John MA 1914
d Inv 14.3.60 *AUR* XXXVIII 591

McQUISTAN Robert Ian BSc(agr) 1954
farm. Montrose from 1963

MacQUOID Margaret Kathleen MA 1920
retd 1962; resid Newport Fife
d 7.6.79

MacQUOID Peter Craik MA 1919
C of S min Turriff St Ninian's par ch 1927–66; retd

McRAE or Mackie, Agnes Irvine MA 1916
no longer on GC reg

MACRAE Alastair Douglas MB ChB 1940 *MD 1950
MRCPath 1964 FRCPath 1969
dir virus reference lab Colindale Lond 1961–70; consult. virologist reg virus lab city hosp Edin 1970–74; consult. virol/sen lect dept microbiol and publ health lab univ hosp Nott from 1974

MACRAE Alexander Duncan MA 1939

MacRAE Alick John MA 1949
teacher Engl Methlick s s 1950–53 head Badcall Inchard s Sutherland 1953–58, Bualnaluib s Ross and Cromarty 1958–67, Drumsmittal s from 1967
m Aber 26.12.53 Margaret J. Shand d of Alexander S. Methlick

McRAE Alister Murray *MA 1928
d 7.10.65

MACRAE or Smith, Ann MA 1913
d 6.5.78

MACRAE or Macfarlane, Anne Ishbel MA 1945
teacher: Engl/hist Whitehills j s s 1963–69, Engl Banff acad from 1969

MACRAE Anne Margaret Smith MB ChB 1939
Bradford: h o ch's hosp 1940–41, g p 1941–46; med asst (geriat) Southport Lancs from 1963
m Bradford 20.6.40 George M. C. Smith MB ChB 1939 *qv*

MACRAE Archibald Campbell MB ChB 1912
d 19.9.61

MACRAE Calum Og MB ChB 1953
nat serv RAF 1955–57; g p Uig Skye 1957–75; group pract Portree from 1975
m Inv 28.1.61 Sarah MacRae teacher dom sc d of Archibald MacR. Inv

MACRAE Christina Catherine MA 1906
d Inv 22.7.74 *AUR* XLVI 106

MACRAE or MacDougall, Christine MB ChB 1924
private pract Ruislip from 1948
husb *d* 1959

MACRAE Christopher BSc(for) 1954

MACRAE Christopher Donald MB ChB 1923
g p Huddersfield; retd
d 29.10.80 *AUR* XLIX 136

MACRAE Donald Kenneth *MA 1909 BSc 1910
d 19.6.64 *AUR* XL 396

MACRAE Donald Robert BSc(agr) 1924
vet surg Banff 1935–68; retd

MacRAE Donald Roderick BSc 1951

MACRAE Duncan MA 1895
no longer on GC reg

MACRAE Duncan James MB ChB 1903
d Kyle 27.5.62 *AUR* XXXIX 373

MacRAE Duncan Keith MA 1950 LLB 1953
ptnr Jenkins & Jardine solic Stirling from 1963

MACRAE or Montgomery, Duncina MA 1927
resid Kyle of Lochalsh

MACRAE or Macrae, Edith Mary MA 1919 MB ChB 1922 BSc 1925
resid Portsoy
husb *d* Portsoy 22.7.63

MACRAE Elizabeth Robertson Smathers MA 1931

MACRAE Finlay Milne BSc(for) 1951
for. off.: Inv 1951–53, Fort William 1953–63, Dingwall from 1963

MacRAE Hamish Simpson *MA 1951

MACRAE Herbert Alexander MA 1909
d Aber 12.12.67 *AUR* XLII 348

MACRAE Hugh Ross BSc(agr) 1924
no longer on GC reg

MACRAE or Taylor, Isabella *MA 1925
resid Alvesford
d 16.6.77

McRAE Ishbel MA 1926
teacher Kinloss p s 1966–71; retd; resid Findhorn

MACRAE Ishbel Margaret MB ChB 1943
spec accreditation RCOG 1974
clin asst Univ Coll hosp, Queen Charlotte's and Chelsea hosps Lond 1966–77; sen spec obst/gyn Benghazi Libya 1968–69; clin advis in fam plan. York from 1977
m Kingston-u-Thames 29.11.62 Edward J. Monks MBE lt col

MACRAE or Soutter, Johann MA 1923
d Dunfermline 15.6.72 *AUR* XLV 127

MACRAE John MA 1906
d Stornoway 7.5.54

MACRAE John Duncan MA 1913
no longer on GC reg

MACRAE John Smith MA 1929 MB ChB 1934
g p Bradford
d 2.1.80 *AUR* XLIX 68

MACRAE John William MB ChB 1921
d Portsoy 22.7.63

MACRAE or Shields, Julia Macdougall MA 1903
no longer on GC reg

MacRAE or Duval, Katreen Ismay Ferguson *MA 1953
resid Paris

MacRAE Lachlan *MA 1909
d 11.5.62 *AUR* XL 79

MACRAE Margaret MA 1917
no longer on GC reg

McRAE Mary Rose MA 1919
no longer on GC reg

MACRAE Robina Ann MA 1926
no longer on GC reg

MACRAE Roderick MA 1907
retd 1947
d Cheltenham 3.4.77

MACRAE Roderick MA 1911
no longer on GC reg

MacRAE Roderick Alexander *MA 1937
no longer on GC reg

MACRAE Ronald Duncan MB ChB 1929 DPH 1931
m o BAOR Rheindahlen Germany and München Gladbach 1964–69; cas off. Catterick milit hosp 1969–72; retd; resid Portsoy

MACRAE or Yorston, Sheila MA 1949
teacher Balmedie s from 1972

MACRAE William John MB ChB 1954
asst g p Ullapool 1957–58; sen h o med Belvidere hosp Glasg 1959–60; g p: Glasg 1960–62, Dalmally from 1962
m Inv 3.12.58 Isabel B. Macdonald

MACRAE or Graham, Williamina MA 1927
no longer on GC reg

McRITCHIE or Harrison, Bella Jane MA 1904
no longer on GC reg

McRITCHIE Douglas *MA 1908 *1909 BD 1913
no longer on GC reg

MacRITCHIE Farquhar MA 1925 LLB 1929
LLD(Edin) 1965 CBE 1968
prof conveyancing Aberd 1946–74; retd

MACRITCHIE John Donald BSc(agr) 1954

McROBB or Farquharson, Annie Masson MA 1925
d Sutton 15.9.73 *AUR* XLV 319

McROBB Keith McLeod *MA 1937
TD 1965
C of S min Balshagray par ch Glasg 1960–74, Dalserf par ch Lanarksh from 1974; chaplain TA forces 1948–67

McROBB Moira Helen MA 1954 *1956
d of Farquharson McR. indust packing case manuf and Sarah J. Hughson; b Aber 25.12.32
teacher: Fisherie 1956–57, Georgetown Guyana 1962–65, Aber tech coll 1967–68; piano teacher Harlaw acad/Broomhill s Aber from 1972
m 23.12.57 Karl A. L. Brown MA 1956 *qv*

McROBB Neil Farquharson BSc(elect eng) 1955 BSc(mech eng) 1956
Ferranti Edin: dev eng 1956–62, prod. support eng 1963–66, sen prod. supp eng 1967–71, syst eng group leader prod. supp dept from 1972
m Penicuik 16.6.61 Jean H. Keiller SRN d of William T. L. K. Penicuik

McROBBIE Alexander MB ChB 1904 DPH 1905
no longer on GC reg

McROBERT George Reid *MB ChB 1917 *MD 1923
hon FRCPE 1970
med advis to Secy of State for commonwealth relations Whitehall Lond 1958–62; pres RSTM & H Lond 1961–63 nominated governor of publ bodies by Secy of State for CR including board of man. royal post grad med s 1958–71
d Nayland 6.6.76 *AUR* XLVII 102

McROBIE or Wagstaff, Dorothy Margaret MA 1916
part-time dem phys Durh 1942–46; resid Leeds
d Leeds 17.3.80

McROBIE or Swapp, Frances Elizabeth MA 1926
d Stonehaven 29.8.75 *AUR* XLVI 323

McRONALD Angus Duncan *BSc 1950
ME(Calif) 1969 PhD(Calif) 1974
sen res off. AAEC Sydney Aust 1962–64; prin scient off. NPL Teddington UK 1964–65; member tech staff JPL Pasadena USA from 1965

MACSWEEN John MA 1922
no longer on GC reg

MACSWEEN John MA 1928
head Broadford j s s Skye 1944–69; retd; resid Breakish
d 7.12.78

MACSWEEN Murdo MA 1929

MacSWEEN Murdo MA 1949 DipEd 1950
teacher Engl/soc stud Aber trades coll 1950–59; head gen stud. dept Aber coll of comm 1959–64; third i/c Oakbank approved s Aber 1964–70; dep head Kerelaw approved s from 1970

MacTAGGART Douglas Keith *MA 1944 MB ChB 1949
MFCM 1973
m o h and dir soc serv Torbay county borough 1967–74; dist commun phys Torbay health dist from 1974

MACTAGGART William Keith BSc(eng) 1948
CEng 1966 FIMechE 1973 FRAeS 1974
RAF: C O eng squadron Tengah Singapore 1960–63; Lond: M o D intell off. 1963–65, syst analyst def oper analysis/estab 1965–67, wg/cdr des and introduction of Air Force maintenance computer syst M o D 1967–71; gp capt/C O RAF stat Newton 1971–73; dep mech eng RAF strike command 1973: air cdre/dir of air armament M o D(PE) Lond from 1973

McTAVISH or Davidson, Katrina MA 1949
Inv: teacher Merkinch s 1958–66, remed work Bishop Eden's s 1971–72, Dalneigh p s from 1972

McVEAN or Wood, Isobel Christie MA 1926
resid Bournemouth

McVICAR or MacBean, Barbara Campbell MA 1911
no longer on GC reg

MacVICAR Donald MA 1916 BSc 1922
teacher sc/geog and dep head g s 1931–60; retd

McVICKER John Louis Armitage MB ChB 1943
MRCGP 1952 DIH 1969 FRSM 1972
g p Coventry 1948–66; W Bromwich: indust med practice 1966–69, med dir W Midlands indust health serv from 1969

McWILLIAM Charles Keith MA 1919 BD 1920
clerk: synod Clydesdale 1952–66, presb Hamilton 1938–67; retd
wife *d* 14.12.72
d Cleland 11.5.76

MacWILLIAM Elizabeth Bethune MA 1942
teacher Forres acad from 1943

McWILLIAM or Hendry, Elizabeth Jean MA 1946
resid Bearsden

McWILLIAM or Berry, Elizabeth Mae MA 1953

McWILLIAM Euphemia Jemima BSc 1923
teacher maths/sc Banchory acad 1941–55; Bankhead acad Aber: teacher sc 1955–61, prin sc 1961–65; retd; resid Aber

MacWILLIAM George *MA 1906 *BD 1909
d Edin 3.4.61 *AUR* XXXIX 200

McWILLIAM George Porteous MA 1915

McWILLIAM or Donald, Helen Margaret MA 1949
resid Stonehaven
husb *d* 1.4.68

MacWILLIAM Jean Hepburn MA 1936

MacWILLIAM John *MA 1905 *BD 1908
d Aber 10.2.61 *AUR* XXXIX 200

McWILLIAM or Fraser, Margaret MA 1910
d 20.8.72

McWILLIAM or Chalmers, Margaret MA 1949

McWILLIAM or Hunter, Margaret Shewan MA 1932

MAGEE Hugh Edward DSc 1924
d 4.3.63 *AUR* XL 204

MAGUIRE Michael Finnbarr PhD 1953

MAIN Arthur William Alexander *MA 1949 BD 1953
C of S min: Douglas and Angus par. ch Dun 1955–64, St David's mem par ch Kirkintilloch 1964–70; stud. Jordanhill coll of educ Glasg 1970–71; teacher classics/relig educ Douglas acad Milngavie 1971–75, prin r e from 1975

MAIN David George Ewen MA 1920
d Aber 29.1.62 *AUR* XXXIX 382

MAIN David McDowall Gordon MA 1904
d 1.5.64

MAIN or Shiach, Doreen Elizabeth MA 1949
head Balgownie p s Aber from 1975

MAIN or Rees, Elizabeth Margaret BSc 1952
teacher chem Farrington girls' s Chislehurst Kent from 1968

MAIN Elsie Margaret MA 1954 BSc 1956
teacher sc Bankhead acad 1962–68
m Aber 4.4.68 Ronald Shepherd BSc 1956 *qv*

MAIN Ernest *MA 1912
d North Berwick 25.2.66 *AUR* XLII 84

MAIN George Walker *MA 1950
teacher: Engl Niddrie Marischal s s 1959–63, Fr, asst prin Fr Portobello h s from 1963
prod./actor Fr plays Fr inst from 1953

MAIN James Mein *BSc(eng) 1950

MAIN James Mein BSc(eng) 1955

MAIN or Inglis, Jane MA 1936
teacher Aber: King St p s 1937–38, Skene St p s 1964–77

MAIN Joseph MB ChB 1953

MAIN Kenneth Ritchie BSc(eng) 1950

MAIN or Hendry, Margaret Wallace BSc 1950
teacher infants: Dunbar 1964–70, Banff from 1971

MAIN Peter Tester MB ChB 1948 MD 1963
ERD 1957 FRSocMed 1957
lt col RAMC reserve (Suez) Egypt 1956–57; Boots Co Nott: asst dir of res 1964–68, dir of res 1968–73, dir main board 1973–77, chief exec indust div from 1977

MAIN Roland Gemmell MB ChB 1939
m o Roan Consolidated Copper Mines Mufulira Zambia from 1964

MAINLAND Malcolm Smythe BSc 1922
d 28.1.70

MAIR Alexander *BSc 1930
d 9.10.72

MAIR Alexander BSc(eng) 1931

MAIR Alexander
MB ChB 1942 DPH 1947 MD 1950
FRCP 1967 FFCM 1974
prof/head of dept publ health and soc med St And, later Dund, from 1955

MAIR Catherine Elizabeth *MA 1936

MAIR or Davidson, Charlotte Geddes *MA 1935
resid Dun

MAIR or Imlah, Elizabeth MA 1945
teacher Peterhead acad from 1966

MAIR Elizabeth Georgina MA 1932
d N'cle-u-Tyne 1.11.73 *AUR* XLV 321

MAIR Elsie Reid MA 1929
no longer on GC reg

MAIR or Laing, Ethel MA 1939
teacher: St Peter's s s Buckie 1960–69; Aboyne acad 1973–75; retd; resid Dinnet

MAIR Georgina MA 1925
d 31.5.76

MAIR or Kerr, Grace MA 1928
resid Aber
d Inv 2.1.79

MAIR Greta MA 1937
teacher Fraserburgh cent s 1959–77; retd

MAIR Ian Geddes *BSc 1952
prin teacher sc Keith g s from 1960

MAIR James Campbell BSc(eng) 1951

MAIR or Hutcheson, Jane Eliza MA 1925
resid Aber

MAIR John Alexander Paterson *MA 1926
retd 1964; resid Aber

MAIR John Magnus MB ChB 1937
MFCM
Edin: part time lect soc med 1959–75; sen dep m o h 1964–69; dir soc work from 1969

MAIR Joseph *BSc(eng) 1951
MIEE 1969
head elect. group assoc eng group res and dev Rugby 1965–69; head phys and elect. eng Clayton Dewandre Co Lincoln from 1969

MAIR or Boyd, Lily Gardiner MA 1945

MAIR or Scott, Margaret BSc 1951

MAIR Margaret Helen MA 1923
retd 1962; resid Kirk Ella, Yorks

MAIR Mary Elizabeth *MA 1928
retd 1967; resid Banff

MAIR Mary Hay MA 1941
asst prin teacher Fr Torry acad Aber from 1972

MAIR or Thom, Mary Jane MA 1942

MAIR Robert MB ChB 1954
Dip Psych(Edin) 1963 LMCC 1977 ECFMG 1977
consult. psychiat Bellevue hosp Kingston, Jamaica 1965–68; govt psychiat Zomba, Malawi 1969–73; psychiat Sudbury Algoma sanatorium Ont 1974–76

MAIR Robert George MB ChB 1947

MAIR Stanley David MA 1935
d Glasg 1.8.76

MAIR Thomas James Anderson
***MA 1938 *MEd 1940**
RAF educ br Cranwell/Far East 1949–71; group capt RAF (retd) 1971; resid Aboyne

MAIR Victoria Helen Anne MA 1916
no longer on GC reg

MAIR Vida MA 1934
teacher: spec asst Portsoy j s s 1965–69, Engl Buckie h s 1969–72, asst prin guid Buckie h s from 1972

MAIR William George MA 1905
d Peterhead 16.6.61 *AUR* XXXIX 200

MAIR William George Parker MB ChB 1936 MD 1956
MRCPath 1963 FRCPath 1968
consult. neuropathologist Nat Hosp for nervous diseases Lond 1958–78, hon consult. from 1979/hon consult. neuropath Northwick Park Harrow from 1979

MAITLAND or Brzostowski, Dorothy *MA 1949
asst dir Internat Hosp Federation Lond from 1969

MAITLAND Gladys Lucy *MA 1935
teacher: Edin 1940–44, Dyce 1950–53, Coatbridge 1954–59, Dun 1961–74
m Peterhead 12.8.41 Thomas I. Mackay min of relig

MAITLAND Helen Donaldson MA 1917
retd 1959
d Aber 20.1.77 *AUR* XLVII 211

MAITLAND Helen Mary MB ChB 1953
MRCGP 1968
g p: Peebles 1961–62, Aber from 1962

MAITLAND or Selbie, Margaret Helen *MA 1934
resid Huddersfield

MALCOLM or Harper, Eliza Morris MA 1918
no longer on GC reg

MALCOLM Ernest William MB ChB 1927
no longer on GC reg

MALCOLM Florence Johnston MB ChB 1923 DPH 1926
d Invercargill NZ 7.6.64 *AUR* XL 399

MALCOLM Ian *MA 1948 PhD 1952
teacher RGC Aber: spec asst 1963–67, prin asst 1967–71, prin maths from 1971

MALCOLM Robert Mackinnon BSc(for) 1947
Canada: timber appraiser BC govt Victoria 1960–72, consult. for. in private pract from 1973

MALCOLM William *MA 1950
Aber coll of comm: teacher 1959–63, sen hist 1963–64; head gen stud. 1964–73; retd
d Aber 13.10.78

MALLOCH Christina Muir MA 1922
no longer on GC reg

MANN Charles MA 1911 [d]LLB 1914
d 6.11.72 *AUR* XLV 124

MANN or Smith, Elizabeth Helen MA 1919
resid Richmond Surrey

MANN or Madeley, Elsie Jane *MB ChB 1921
FRSocMed 1925–65
retd 1966; resid Lond
d Lond 7.1.79 *AUR* XLVIII 227

MANN George Donald MA 1922
d Lond 10.1.80 *AUR* XLVIII 441

MANN James Alexander BSc(agr) 1923
no longer on GC reg

MANN James Angus MA 1913
d Inv 28.4.72 *AUR* XLV 124

MANN James Wallace MA 1916 MB ChB 1918
no longer on GC reg

MANN William Thomson MA 1930
no longer on GC reg

MANSON Anderson BSc(agr) 1933
retd 1968; resid N. Kessock

MANSON Ann Elizabeth MA 1913
d Aber 1.12.69 *AUR* XLIII 441

MANSON Cecil George Russell MA 1951

MANSON Charles Stewart BSc(eng) 1947

MANSON Doris Irene MB ChB 1948
lect dept med Aberd 1949–63
m Aber 14.12.63 Gordon M. Lees MB ChB 1961 *qv*

MANSON or Elder, Edna Burness Inglis BSc 1944
resid Kirriemuir

MANSON George Inglis MB ChB 1944
OBE 1974
Peterhead: g p from 1948, m o HM prison from 1955

MANSON or Cameron, Jean Margaret MA 1948
temp relief teaching Lusaka, Zambia 1958–69; resid Inv

MANSON or Leland, Katherine Mabel BSc 1946

MANSON Margaret Frances MA 1945
teacher Woodside p s Aber 1946–49; Portree h s inf 1949–52, Engl 1963–72, prin guid from 1972
m Portree Is of Skye 23.11.51 Norman N. Mackinnon postman

MANSON or Jones, Margaret Mimie *BSc 1943
resid Scarborough

MANSON William George Campbell MB ChB 1949
JP Gordon dist Grampian reg 1963
g p Alford from 1956

MANSON William Isbister BSc(eng) 1947
res eng BBC from 1947; resid Tadworth

MANT Forbes Allan MA 1952

MANTELL Ruth Margaret MA 1942
head Ramsay/Boyndie spec s Banff from 1969

MARDON Austin MA 1948

MARGACH Alastair James BSc(agr) 1927
d Uganda 4.5.62

MARIONI Giovanni Emilio Lorenzo BSc 1942
d Aber 28.10.68 *AUR* XLIII 85

MARIONI Peter MB ChB 1947
FRCSE 1963 FRCS 1964 Cert gen surg Canada 1964 FRCS(Aust) 1967
h o thoracic surg gen hosp Vancouver 1959–60; regist thoracic surg Broadgreen Liv 1960–61; lect physiol Liv univ 1961–62; regist gen surg Warrington gen hosp 1962–63; chief resid gen surg Edmonton Royal Alexandra hosp 1964–65; consult. gen surg Ashburton gen hosp NZ; private pract Windsor Ont from 1967

MARK or Davidson-Innes, Alexandrina Margaret MA 1927
no longer on GC reg

MARKS George Maurice MA 1948
d 15.3.67

MARMION John BSc(eng) 1948

MARNIE Ronald James Rattray BSc(for) 1954

MARNOCH Derek George BSc(eng) 1955
ACMA 1975
Claben Aber: prod. man. 1970–75, gen man. from 1976
m Aber 23.8.63 Kathleen Howard

MARNOCH or Burnley, Mary Fowler Ritchie MA 1927
resid Kirkcaldy
d –.2.80

MARNOCH Sheila Middleton MA 1940
teacher inf Aber from 1942

MARR Alexander John MA 1913
d Datchworth 28.12.62 *AUR* XL 81

MARR David Murdoch MB ChB 1914 MD 1919
d Inv 9.11.70 *AUR* XLIV 109

MARR Douglas John MB ChB 1906
d 27.3.64

MARR Douglas Stuart Sandeman MA 1936 LLB 1939
d 28.3.61 *AUR* XXXIX 283

MARR Elizabeth Stewart MA 1913
d Inv 17.10.66 *AUR* XLII 84

MARR or Clowes, Isobel Margaret *MA 1946
lib asst from 1948
resid Horton-cum-Studley, Oxford

MARR James William Slesser MA BSc 1925 DSc 1963
d Surrey 29.4.65 *AUR* XLI 150

MARR or Esson, Mabel Agnes MA 1942
resid Slains Ellon

MARR Neil George MB ChB 1927
d 15.10.72 *AUR* XLV 226

MARR Thomas Deans *MB ChB 1924
g p retd 1959; retd reg med c 1969; resid Lond
d 5.5.78 *AUR* XLVIII 104

MARRIOTT Francis Henry Charles PhD 1951
lect biomaths Oxon from 1965; fell. Wolfson coll Oxon from 1969
m Edin 19.12.64 Catherine F. Broadfoot SRN/tut. Glasg

MARRIOTT John Draper Middleton MA 1950
Aber: dep head Seaton p s 1962–65, dep head Middlefield p s 1965–66, head Tullos p s from 1966

MARSDEN or Marsden, Elizabeth Abernethy MB ChB 1931
asst m o and asst s m o Merthyr Tydfil from 1948; resid Aberdare

MARSH Charles Arnold PhD 1953
sen lect univ of NSW Aust 1965–72, assoc prof from 1972

MARSH Dane Ernest Marshall BSc(for) 1949
JP gazetted Nigeria 1961
dist for. off. and prin for. s Ho Togoland Tarkwa and Sunyuni Gold Coast 1950–55; asst lect Mander coll of f e Bedford 1956–58; Nigeria: prov for. off. Ikom 1959–61, reg res off. E reg Enugu 1961–63, for. advis Niger delta dev board Port Harcourt 1963–66; dir Launderettes (Bedford) from 1968 and also antique dealer Sharnbrook Beds from 1970
m Chippenham 15.10.61 Dorothy Campbell d of Archibald C. NZ

MARSHALL Doreen Gilchrist MA 1953
teacher Culter j s s till 1961; resid Aber
m Aber 4.4.60 Antony D. Cameron eng consult. s of James D. C. Carshalton

MARSHALL or Smith, Evelyn Duncan MA 1952

MARSHALL or MacDonagh, Gillian Rosemary Struan MB ChB 1948
consult. accident and emergency dept royal Portsmouth hosp from 1965
husb *d* 1965

MARSHALL or Milne, Helen Mary MA 1913

MARSHALL Ian Alexander Robert Burns BSc(for) 1945
Brit for. comm in Eng from 1946; resid York

MARSHALL Ian Howard *MA 1955 BD 1959 PhD 1963
asst tut. Didsbury coll Bristol 1960–62; methodist min Darlington 1962–64; lect NT exegesis Aberd from 1964; pers sen lect Aberd 1970–77, reader 1977–79, prof from 1979
m Carlisle 25.3.61 Joyce E. Proudfoot MA(Edin) ch care off. d of Frederick J. P. Carlisle

MARSHALL Norman MB ChB 1950 DPH 1958
g p Manly NSW Aust from 1965

MARSHALL Wilfred MA 1922 *MB ChB 1927 *MD BSc 1928

MARTIN Agnes Clark BL 1930
retd 1976; resid Peterhead

MARTIN Alasdair Peter MA 1955
head Fort William RC s from 1964

MARTIN Andrew BSc(agr) 1947
NOSCA: county agr advis Moray and Nairn 1960–67, supervis and sen lect Craibstone 1960–71; dep prin s of agr Aber from 1971

MARTIN Basil William MB ChB 1908
no longer on GC reg

MARTIN Derek Walker MA 1955 LLB 1957
leg. and admin posts c clerk's dept Inv 1960–62; leg. asst W. & J. S. Gordon solic Forfar 1962–64, ptnr 1964–67; asst c clerk Sutherland c c Golspie 1967–69, dep c clerk from 1969
m Aber 11.2.61 Lydia A. W. Howard asst city chamberlain's dept Aber d of John A. H. Aber

MARTIN Douglas *MA 1935
retd 1973; resid Kirn, Dunoon

MARTIN or Collie, Elizabeth MB ChB 1935
retd 1971; resid Brechin

MARTIN Elizabeth Ferguson MA 1925
d 18.3.66 *AUR* XLII 86

MARTIN Ellen Margaret MA 1926
no longer on GC reg

MARTIN or Mitchell, Gladys Jeannie MA 1923
retd 1965; resid Aber

MARTIN or Cameron, Gladys Mary Elizabeth MB ChB 1926
d Chatham 21.6.66 *AUR* XLI 340

MARTIN Hamish William Thomson MB ChB 1932

MARTIN or Stevenson, Helen Catherine Halley *MA 1943
teacher mod lang: The Westbourne s for girls Glasg 1964–71, spec asst from 1971

MARTIN Hugh Thomson BL 1947
solic Montrose from 1947

MARTIN James Ramsay MB ChB 1933
retd 1969; resid Ellon
d 1.11.81

MARTIN John MA 1920 BD 1922
retd 1958; resid Cardonald Glasg
d 29.8.76

MARTIN Kenneth Gavin BSc(agr) 1952
farm. 1952–73; lect agr Oatridge agr coll from 1974
m Aber 20.10.73 Moira G. Monteath secy d of William A. M. Glasg

MARTIN or Hunter, Mary Margaret MB ChB 1936 DPH 1947
dept m o h Aber corp. 1947–71; retd; resid Aber

MARTIN or Davis, Maureen Joan MA 1949

MARTIN or Steel, Sheila Eunice Nanette *MA 1935
resid Edin

MARTIN Stanley Ephraim *MA 1934
head St Peter's s Peterhead from 1939

MARTIN Victor David Randall MB ChB 1942
MFCM 1972
m o h Doncaster from 1960

MARTYN Robert Godfrey MB ChB 1912
no longer on GC reg

MARWICK David Gibson *BSc(agr) 1936
d 30.10.73

MARWICK Robert Craigie MA 1949

MARWICK William Corrigal MA 1937
d Nairn 8.1.76 *AUR* XLVI 417

MASON Ethelwyn Margaret DSc 1938

MASOR Philip Leon MB ChB 1935
USA: assoc attending surg (ophth) NY Eye and Ear inf from 1946

MASSEY Allan MB ChB 1908
no longer on GC reg

MASSEY John Edwyn BSc(for) 1950

MASSIE Francis Edward MB ChB 1928
g p Thornton Heath from 1933

MASSIE George Campbell MA 1942
head Bucksburn s from 1969

MASSIE or Allen, Gladys *MA 1954 Dip Ed 1955
teacher maths Boroughmuir s Edin from 1971

MASSIE Leslie Alexander MA 1935 LLB 1936
solic-gen (hon QC) Malaya 1959–60; advoc Scot. Bar from 1961
resid Edin

MASSIE or Watson, Letitia MA 1925
resid Whitehills Banff

MASSIE or Wallace, Louise Christian MA 1911
d Bradford 17.1.78 *AUR* XLVII 356

MASSIE or Sutherland, Margaret Elizabeth MA 1923
resid Christchurch NZ

MASSIE or Hendry, Margaret Mary Strachan MA 1947
resid Aber

MASSIE or Hogg, Mary MA 1917
resid Aber; freelance writer of verse
husb *d* 1967

MASSON or Jackson, Anne Madeline MA 1936

MASSON Charles Robb BSc 1943 PhD 1948
nat res council of Can: assoc res off. 1955–59, sen res off. 1959–65, prin res off. from 1965; resid Halifax Nova Scotia

MASSON Charles Will BSc 1950
head: Inchture p s Perthsh 1961–66, Doune p s Perthsh from 1966

MASSON David Norman MA 1912 BD 1917
d Aber 13.4.66 *AUR* XLII 84

MASSON or Todd, Frances Anne *MA 1939
resid Crieff

MASSON Gordon Baxter MA 1955 LLB 1957
advoc in Aber; ptnr W. Kirkwood & Smith Aber from 1960

MASSON or Milne, Isabella Margaret BSc 1949
teacher biol Elgin acad from 1961, also asst prin guid 1973–77, prin guid from 1977

MASSON James Leiper BSc(for) 1949
conserv of for. Kano Nigeria 1959–62; for. expert FAO: Sudan 1962–63, Thailand 1964–67, Malaysia 1967–69, Rome 1969–70, Cuba 1970–74, Peru from 1974

MASSON John Richard *MA 1951
MBE 1962 OBE 1970
asst fin. secy UK high comm off. S Africa 1961–63; Swaziland: acting secy fin. 1964–68, secy for fin. 1968–72; retd from publ serv 1972, dir of companies from 1972

MASSON or White, Katharine Isobel Mary *MA 1943
resid Edin

MASSON or Rogers, Marion Gibbins MA 1946

MASSON or Dobson, Marjorie Jean BSc 1948
resid Etna NY USA

MASSON William David MB ChB 1955
DTM & H(Lond) 1963 DCH(Glas) 1964 MRCPE 1969
lt col RAMC; g p Acharacle Argyll from 1977

MASSON William Peterkin MA 1914
resid Nethy Bridge

MATHER George Strathdee MB ChB 1916
Durham: m o h Stockton RDC 1923–58; chmn hosp man. comm Hartlepool 1955–59; retd; resid Penrith

MATHER Stuart Smith BSc 1952
LRAM (pianoforte) 1967
head Strathmartin s by Dun from 1963

MATHERS Cecil George BSc 1941 *1947
sen exper off. AEA Chem II UKAEA, DERE Dounreay from 1958

MATHERS Eleanor Anderson MA 1948

MATHESON Alexander MB ChB 1931
MRCGP
g p Stornoway/visiting phys Lewis hosp 1933–48
d Stornoway 19.12.78 *AUR* XLVIII 232

MATHESON Alexander John MA 1934

MATHESON or Beattie, Catherine Fiona MA 1954
teacher Fraserburgh inf s 1966–77; remed Warddykes s Arbroath from 1978

MATHESON Colin MA 1918 BSc 1921
d 1980

MATHESON Donald MA 1924 *BSc 1927 PhD 1932
OBE 1965
Lond: HM chem insp of factories 1938–57, HM dep sen chem insp 1957–60, HM sen chem insp/head of chem branch 1960–68; retd; internat lab off. Geneva 1969
m Luddendenfoot 12.7.39 Hilda Spencer nurse d of William S. Luddendenfoot

MATHESON Donald *MB ChB 1937
col RAMC 1961–70; retd; civ med pract milit corrective training centre Colchester from 1970

MATHESON Donald MB ChB 1938
anaest Vancouver gen hosp from 1955

MATHESON Donald MA 1948

MATHESON Donald John BSc(agr) 1933
retd 1964
d Inv 29.1.76

MATHESON Donald William BSc(eng) 1945

MATHESON Ellen MA 1928
teacher: Mackie acad Stonehaven 1958–61, Summerhill acad Aber 1961–67, retd; resid Aber

MATHESON George Philip BSc(agr) 1932
farm. Marykirk/potato merch Montrose 1955–80; retd; resid Montrose
d Aber 1.7.80

MATHESON Harry Ririe *BSc 1950

MATHESON or Waudby, Hectorina MB ChB 1951
Hong Kong relief doctor in Leprosarium Hay Ling Chau 1960–75; g p: Peace clin Kowloon 1965–66, locum for tuberculosis m o Haven of Hope Sanatorium 1966; part-time asst gyn and inf welfare clin Nethersole hosp 1968; part-time asst res Leprosy Study Centre Lond from 1976; m o Leprosy Mission Lond from 1978

MATHESON James Alexander *MA 1909
d Inv 6.6.61 *AUR* XXXIX 201

MATHESON James Roderick BSc 1919
resid Ullapool
d Inv 17.5.81

MATHESON or MacPhail, Jemima Muriel MA 1914
resid Carloway Is of Lewis
husb *d* 31.1.61

MATHESON John Gunn MB ChB 1941
consult. anaest Shotley Bridge gen hosp Co Durh and N'cle gen hosp from 1952

MATHESON Katherine Dunlop *MA 1934
d Ayr 24.12.48

MATHESON Knut Cecil Cyril *MA 1925
no longer on GC reg

MATHESON or Sweeney, Margaret MA 1931

MATHESON or Bowdler, Margaret Mary MA 1948

MATHESON Mary Grace MA 1920
no longer on GC reg

MATHESON Mary Helen MA 1931

MATHESON Murdo MA 1930
head Kiltearn p s Ross and Cromarty 1963–72; retd; resid Evanton

MATHESON Norman Allan *BSc 1950 PhD 1954
sen scient off. Rowett res inst Aber 1961–65, prin scient off. from 1965

MATHESON Peter MB ChB 1937
JP Ross and Cromarty 1968
m o West Uig Lewis from 1945

MATHEWSON or Wilson, Annie Allardyce MA 1921
resid Kintore
d Jedburgh 12.7.78 *AUR* XLVIII 103

MATHEWSON Annie Clugston MA 1915
d 26.1.73

MATHEWSON or MacLean, Elizabeth Swanson MA 1928
resid Edin

MATHEWSON or Ratcliff, Ishbel Margaret MA 1932
d Lond 25.7.71 *AUR* XLIV 321

MATHEWSON James MA 1939
farm. Tarves from 1945

MATHEWSON John George BL 1932
d Aber 9.1.75 *AUR* XLVI 239

MATHEWSON or Wilson, Mary Elizabeth MA 1919
teacher Greenness p s, Cuminestown p s 1941–42; head: Largie p s 1942–51, Craigdam 1951–63
d Aber 21.6.79

MATHEWSON William Gray BSc(agr) 1949 MSc 1974
sen agr off. Mbeya Tanzania 1951–65; asst secy NFU of Scot. Edin 1965–68; assoc prof Nova Scotia agr coll Truro Nova Scotia from 1968
m Calgary Alberta 15.3.58 Greta M. L. Ekstrand reg nurse d of Daniel E. Calgary

MATHIESON or Thomson, Ada Isobel MA 1925

MATHIESON Agnes Duguid Ferrier MA 1935
d 5.12.64

MATHIESON or Lawson, Agnes Margaret MA 1931
teacher Kittybrewster p s Aber 1951–56; head Birse p s 1956–60; teacher: Tarland s s 1960–63, maths Aboyne acad 1963–75; retd
husb *d* 9.2.69

MATHIESON Alexander McLeod BSc 1941 *1942
Fell. Aust Acad of Sc 1967
chief res scient chem phys div CSIRO Melbourne from 1965

MATHIESON or Smith, Catherine MA 1915
d Ballater 12.3.73 *AUR* XLV 318

MATHIESON Charles Edward MB ChB 1925
retd 1972; resid Leeds
wife *d* 28.11.58
d Leeds 1.7.80 *AUR* XLIX 67

MATHIESON Constance Mina MA 1947 *MEd 1949
sen clin then prin psych NE reg hosp board now Grampian area health board from 1960; also Aberd: clin lect mental health dept 1966–73, hon sen clin lect from 1973
m 18.11.63 Alexander M. Cordiner tea planter, fish merch

MATHIESON David Wyllie MB ChB 1943
med pract N Vancouver from 1960

MATHIESON or Mackay, Elsie Craig Durward MA 1927
resid Bury, Lancs (metrop county of Manc)

MATHIESON or Macdonald, Evelyn Margaret Helen MA 1940
resid Wellington NZ

MATHIESON Gordon MB ChB 1949
MSc(McG) 1960 FRCP(C) 1968
Montreal: asst prof McG univ 1957–63, assoc prof from 1963; also neuropath Montreal Neurol Inst from 1957; hon res fell. dept path. Aberd 1973–74
m Montreal 22.8.70 Julia C. Parker reg nurse Quebec province d of Herbert H. P. Montreal

MATHIESON or Walmsley, Isabel Mary MB ChB 1937
resid St And

MATHIESON James Moir MB ChB 1907
no longer on GC reg

MATHIESON or Goldie, Marie Agnes *MA 1933
resid Leeds
husb *d* Leeds 13.2.70

MATHIESON Marjory Winifred *MA 1945
resid Aber

MATHIESON Sheila MA 1950
teacher Stoneywood j s from 1954

MATTHEW George Douglas *BSc(eng) 1952 PhD 1961
MICE 1959
Aberd: sen lect eng 1967–70, reader from 1970
m Aber 20.7.62 Margaret W. McKenzie BSc 1959 *qv*

MATTHEW Hilda Cruickshank MA 1934
teacher; retd 1975

MATTHEW Ian *MA 1952
teacher: geog Aber acad 1958–67, prin geog Douglas acad Milngavie 1967–71; asst rector Douglas acad from 1971
m Aber 7.4.65 Miriam E. Buchan teacher Peterhead

MATTHEW or Williams, Jessie Donald MA 1944 *1947
Salisbury: teacher maths/geog St Edmunds s for girls 1965; maths La Retraite Convent s (formerly Leehurst) from 1965
husb *d* 17.10.64

MATTHEW John Low MB ChB 1954
g p Kirkby-in-Ashfield from 1961

MATTHEW Keith Ronald Thomson MB ChB 1929
g p Glasg from 1929

MATTHEWS Annie Peill *MA 1902
d Aber 19.8.67 *AUR* XLII 178

MATTHEWS or Matthews, Elizabeth Agnes MA 1927
teacher Fr/Ger Bankhead acad 1963–68; retd; resid Aber
husb *d* 15.11.62

MATTHEWS George Irvine MA 1945 LLB 1948

MATTHEWS Ian McPherson *BSc 1953

MATTHEWS John Drake BSc(for) 1948
FRSE 1964 FIFor 1966 FIBiol 1968
prof for. Aberd from 1963

MATTHEWS Keith Morton Lille BSc(agr) 1953

MATTHEWS Robert Begbie BSc(eng) 1952
sen dev eng GEC Coventry 1959–60; Enfield coll of tech: asst lect 1960–61, lect 1961–66, sen lect 1966–72; sen lect Middx polytech from 1973

MAVOR George Edward MA 1939 *MB ChB 1944 ChM 1953
d Aber 4.12.73 *AUR* XLV 449

MAVOR or Knox, Janet *MA 1908
d Stonehaven 5.1.73 *AUR* XLV 223

MAVOR William Ferrier *MA 1934
FRSA 1968
admin asst s of phys N'cle 1968 and counsellor (Humanities) O U northern reg from 1972

MAXWELL Edwin Arthur *MA 1928
FIMA
fell. Queens' coll Cantab till retd 1974; thereafter life fell.; keeper of records 1946–72; sen bursar 1958–65; hon secy internat comm math instr 1970–74

MAXWELL or Wyllie, Marjorie Hamilton BSc 1929 MA 1930
resid Glasg
husb *d* Oyne 8.1.76

MAXWELL-JOYNER Charles MA 1915 MB ChB 1921
MCPS(Alta) 1932 St John's medal
private pract Nassau Bahamas 1958–70; life member: British red cross; Amer med soc Vienna; co-founder Bahamas cancer soc

MAY Alexander MA 1929 BD 1935
C of S min Innerleven E ch Methil from 1949
d Leven 23.8.81

MAY George MB ChB 1947
g p Bolsover from 1950

MAY James MA 1887
no longer on GC reg

MAY James Robertson BSc(eng) 1952
MICE FIStructE
bridge eng Invsh 1959–60; Scot. dev dept Edin: bridge eng 1960–66, sen bridge eng from 1966

MAY or Good, Phyllis MA 1931
resid Southport Merseyside

MAY Robert Crouch BL 1927
ptnr Mackenzie & Wilson advoc Aber from 1937

MAY William *MA 1933
dep rector Dornoch acad 1965–68, rector from 1968

MEADOWS or Todd, Elza Harris MB ChB 1942
MFCM 1972
Surrey: asst m o h Mitcham 1961–63, dep m o h Richmond and Barnes 1963–65, sen m o Sutton; Merton (Lond borough): dep m o h 1968–72, m o h 1972–74; dist commun phys Roehampton dist 1974–78; dir occup health Charing Cross hosp from 1978
husb *d* 25.4.61

MEARNS Henry Balfour MA 1919
no longer on GC reg

MEARNS Ian Andrew MA 1954 LLB 1957
leg. asst Moray & Nairn joint c c Elgin 1968–70, chief leg. asst 1970–73; town clerk Girvan 1973–75; dep dir admin Kyle and Carrick dist c Ayr from 1975
m Elgin 28.4.62 Elizabeth A. M. Sutherland med secy d of Allan S. Elgin

MEARNS or Towers, Isobel Margaret *MA 1934
teacher: remed classes Fraserburgh North s 1958–61, Engl Fraserburgh acad 1961–72; retd

MEARNS James Godsman BSc(agr) 1923
rubber planter man. Selangor Malaysia 1923–41, 1947–48 interned Singapore 1941–45/6; retd; resid Banchory
m Aber 5.12.46 Marguerite M. Dean indust nurse d of George M. D. Ellon
d 13.2.80

MEARNS James Michie *MA 1952

MEARNS William Anderson
MA 1899 MB ChB 1903 DPH 1913

MEARNS William Ramsay MA 1954 LLB 1956
post grad stud. bus. admin Harvard bus. s 1956–57; pers/indust relations positions Massey-Ferguson: Tor (Can) Detroit, Des Moines, Racine (USA), Coventry, Vereeniging (S. Af) 1957–72; dir pers/indust relations Perkins eng co (subsid of Massey-Ferguson) Peterborough from 1972

MEE or Stephen, Annie Margaret MB ChB 1940
g p Fochabers from 1961

MELDRUM Andrew McGregor MA 1892
no longer on GC reg

MELDRUM or Moir, Annie MA 1915
no longer on GC reg

MELDRUM or McGillivray, Doreen
MB ChB 1948 DPH 1951
g p Aber 1950; later resid Cambuslang

MELDRUM or Kynoch, Elsie Jane Gillanders
MA 1928

MELDRUM Frederick James MA 1947
Aber: asst man. Barton Abrasives 1947–55; man. dir John Lawrie & Co from 1961; dir Barton & Sons Dudley from 1977

MELDRUM Helen MA 1923
retd 1963; resid Ballindalloch

MELDRUM Margaret Ann MA 1922
d Aberlour 12.3.66 *AUR* XLII 86

MELDRUM or Irvine, Margaret Catherine
MA 1942
Aber: visiting teacher p s languages from 1969

MELDRUM or Wade, Mary Elizabeth Helen
MA 1951

MELDRUM or Corser, Mona MA 1928
resid Elgin

MELDRUM Neil Ian Wilson MA 1940 LLB 1947

MELDRUM Walter James MB ChB 1921
d Norwich 31.10.71 *AUR* XLIV 429

MELDRUM William James Gillan MB ChB 1941

MELROSE John Kidd Ramsay BSc(agr) 1950
sen insp DAFS S.W. area Ayr from 1970

MELVILLE or Rae, Gladys Evelyn *MA 1945
resid Aber

MELVILLE John Douglas Scott MB ChB 1944
d Inv 12.1.79 *AUR* XLVIII 233

MELVILLE Mattie Fraser MA 1929
retd 1971; resid Bearsden

MELVILLE or Flett, Vivien Mary MA 1947
resid Bearsden

MELVILLE William Gordon MA 1950
BA(Lond) 1967
Aber: teacher Cummings Park p s 1951–64; dep head Hanover St p s 1964–66, dep head Sunnybank p s from 1966

MELVILLE William Simm BSc(eng) 1938
FIEE 1951 OBE 1963
BTH Co Rugby: grad app 1938–40, res eng 1940–50, eng man. (radar); gen man. (radar & defence) AEI, Leicester; proj man. GEC-Marconi, Chelmsford from 1968
m Rugby 25.7.42 Jean F. Craig MA 1934 *qv*

MELVIN Alfred MA 1902 *BL 1904
no longer on GC reg

MELVIN Andrew George *MA 1929
dep rector Tain acad 1968–70; retd

MELVIN Anne MA 1951 MB ChB 1956
DA 1959
regist anaest S Manc hosp group 1960–63; asst anaest Preston RI from 1964; anaest Lancs c c from 1968
m Leeds 22.9.61 James P. Lythgoe MB B Chir(Cantab) consult. surg s of Sir James L. MA(Manc) Wilmslow

MELVIN or Cruickshank, Annie *MA 1929
retd 1967; resid Kemnay
d Kemnay 31.7.75

MELVIN or MacKay, Annie Elizabeth MB ChB 1920
g p Northampton and Thornaby-on-Tees 1920–23 and 1939–46; retd; resid Northallerton

MELVIN or Witte, Edith Mary Stenhouse *MA 1932
asst Ger dept Aberd 1944–47; teacher Ger part time Aber h s for girls 1963–70
d Daviot Aberdeensh 19.1.79 *AUR* XLVIII 232

MELVIN James MB ChB 1915
d East London S Afr 29.4.72 *AUR* XLIV 429

MELVIN John Middleton MA 1950 LLB 1952
ptnr A. C. Morrison & Richards advoc Aber from 1957; clerk of the peace county of Aber 1970–75

MELVIN or Durcan, Katherine Jessie Walker *MA 1942
resid Baldrine Is of Man

MELVIN Kenneth Stewart MB ChB 1903
no longer on GC reg

MELVIN Kenneth Thomson *MA 1955 Dip Ed 1956

MELVIN or Morrison, Marion Gertrude *MA 1936
teacher Ger: various schools 1954–75, Clifton h s for girls from 1975

MELVIN Redvers George MA 1920 MB ChB 1924
d 14.3.64 *AUR* XL 399

MELVIN Robert William McIntosh BSc(eng) 1928
FICE
pres Brit waterworks assoc 1972–73; dir Brit waterworks comp; dir Bristol & West bldg soc

MELVIN or Wiseman, Winifred Anne Isobel MA 1930
resid Aber

MENMUIR Alexander MA 1926
d Aber 16.2.73 *AUR* XLV 226

MENNIE Alexander Thomson MB ChB 1949

MENNIE or Thompson, Annie Isabella Beaton *MA 1917
d Brechin 15.11.70 *AUR* XLIV 208

MENNIE Douglas MA 1942 MEd 1957
resources dev off. Grampian reg from 1975
wife *d* 5.9.77

MENNIE Duncan Mackenzie *MA 1929
prof Ger/Scandavian stud. N'cle 1959–74; emeritus prof from 1974

MENNIE Elma Rae *MA 1938
head Laurel Bank s Glasg 1963–68; headmistress' fell. Ger dept univ coll S Wales Cardiff 1968; dep head Walbottle g s N'cle-u-Tyne from 1968 (Walbottle h s from 1972); retd 1977

MENNIE or Henderson, Gertrude Mary MB ChB 1945
clin asst chest clin and mass radiography RI Sheffield from 1964

MENNIE Gordon MA 1939

MENNIE or Shire, Helena Mary *MA 1933
Cantab: assoc lect Engl King's coll/asst dir of stud. in Engl Fitzwilliam coll from 1964; member acad council and lect to Brit and Europ stud. group Lond from 1972; foundation fell. Robinson coll Cantab from 1974

MENNIE John MA 1948 *MEd 1953
d Aber 20.9.66 *AUR* XLI 342

MENNIE Robert Alexander Esslemont *MA 1942
F Inst Pet
BP: Lond 1943–48, oper man. Zürich 1948–55, asst to man. dir Hamburg 1955–57, various assignments Lond 1957–63, shareholders' rep Hamburg 1964–67, asst gen man. supply Lond 1968–76; dir publ affairs (Scot.) from 1977
m Belfast 8.12.41 Dorothy S. A. Moat B Com Sc(Belf)

MENZIES Angus MB ChB 1937

MENZIES Charles Sparke MA 1934
JP Aberdeensh 1961
retd 1974; resid Aber
d 1.9.81

MENZIES Elizabeth Ross MA 1931

MENZIES Graeme Mitchell Mill MB ChB 1925
d Aber 5.6.72 *AUR* XLV 127

MENZIES Joan Isobel MA 1947
teacher Engl Edin/Aber 1948–68; lady advis Niddrie Marischal s s Edin 1968–72, asst head 1972–74, dep head Castlebrae h s from 1974
m Currie 31.7.68 Thomas A. Miller DFC teacher p e s of Robert P. M. Hamilton

MENZIES Kenneth John MA 1947
head Stoneywood p s 1965–76; retd; resid Dyce

MENZIES Mathilda Fisher MB ChB 1920 DPH 1921 *MD 1928
retd 1958; resid Lond

MENZIES Norman MB ChB 1940
g p Acton and Chiswick Lond from 1948

MENZIES Robert Forbes MB ChB 1941
lect bact Aberd from 1946
wife *d* 13.10.66

MENZIES Thomas MB ChB 1915
d Dun 17.10.69 *AUR* XLIII 329

MENZIES Thomas MB ChB 1945
FRCS(Eng) 1962 FRCS RCPSGlas 1973
consult. surg Glasg RI and hon clin lect surg Glas from 1966

MENZIES Walter Neil *MA 1936
asst lib: Edin univ 1959–62, Aberd 1962–65; sub lib Aberd 1965–76, sen lib asst Aberd from 1976

MENZIES William MB ChB 1925
d 13.1.73 *AUR* XLV 226

MERCHANT Ethel MA 1928

MERCHANT James Murray BSc 1947 *1948

MERCHANT Janet Mitchell MA 1946
teacher: Stockethill S p s Aber 1947–61, Northfield acad Aber 1961–74, Cloverfield p s Bucksburn from 1974

MERCHANT Margaret Elizabeth Strachan *MA 1945
Alford acad: prin teacher Engl/hist from 1965, woman advis from 1966, asst head from 1973
m Lumphanan 25.7.64 John A. Cooper s of James C. Alford

MERCHANT William John Shaw BSc(agr) 1941
county advis Caithness 1948–49; Dingwall: agr advis Rosssh 1949–72, sen agr advis Ross/Sutherland from 1972

MERRIMAN Jemima Mary Phillips MA 1932
retd; resid Stromness

MERSON Alan Edmond BSc(agr) 1951
dir S. T. Law Aber from 1968

MERSON or Bonner, Dorothy Mary MA 1915
d Aber 31.3.61 *AUR* XXXIX 202

MERSON George Polson MB ChB 1933
DPH(Lond) 1953 MFCM 1974
m o Zanzibar 1940–50, sen m o Tanganyika 1950–62; m o h Gravesend 1962–76; port m o Denton Gravesend 1976–79; retd; resid Dartford

MERSON William *MA 1932

MESTON Alexander Marshall *BSc 1949 PhD 1952
ICI Stevenston: sen scient Nobel div 1969–71, dep man. NSM dept organics div from 1971
d Bury 25.12.78 *AUR* XLVIII 233

MESTON Gertrude MA 1913
d Aber 21.6.73

MESTON Michael Charles *MA 1954 LLB 1957
JD(Chicago) 1959 hon sheriff City of Aber 1972
Aberd: sen lect compar law 1964–68, prof juris 1968–71, prof Scots law from 1971

MESTON William *MA 1910 BSc 1912
d Aber 26.9.65 *AUR* XLI 241

METCALFE or Whyte, Joan Anne *MA 1937
resid Kenilworth

MICHAEL James MA 1903
no longer on GC reg

MICHELSEN or Larg, Isabella Beaton *MA 1915
no longer on GC reg

MICHELSON Everett Gladstone MB ChB 1921

MICHIE Alexander McGregor MB ChB 1933 DPH 1935
FFCM 1972
med supt Aber gen hosps 1948–71; PASMO NE reg hosp board from 1971

MICHIE Arthur Cumming *BSc 1900 DSc 1906
d Corbridge 17.5.74 *AUR* XLVI 234

MICHIE Charles MB ChB 1940
m o pneumoconiosis med panel DHSS Sheffield 1963–74; retd; now part time appt: m o pneumoconiosis med panel DHSS Glasg, indust injuries and war pensions med records DHSS Glasg and clin asst cytology dept Glasg RI

MICHIE Charles Watt *MA 1929
OBE 1943 Defence Medal 1945 Coronation Medal 1953 GMG 1960
m Edin 1933 Janet L. G. Kinloch MA(Edin) teacher d of David K. Kirkcaldy

MICHIE or Rose, Dorothy May *MA 1952 Dip Ed 1953
d Aber 3.4.63

MICHIE or Watson, Elizabeth MA 1936

MICHIE Elizabeth Woodrow MB ChB 1955

MICHIE Eric Raymond MA 1951

MICHIE Ernest James Stewart BSc(for) 1955
dist off. for. comm: Carlisle 1958–63, Fort Augustus 1963–67, Inv 1967–75, Dornoch from 1975

MICHIE Ethel Lilian MA 1941
teacher Scotstown p s Aber 1969–72
m Aber 9.7.71 Daniel J. Stephen artist

MICHIE Francis William *MA 1894
d Aber 18.3.62 *AUR* XXXIX 370

MICHIE Hellenor Ramsay Watson Thomson *MA 1907
d Ballater 4.10.69 *AUR* XLIII 327

MICHIE James Alexander *MA 1947 D Litt 1961
sen lect Engl univ of Hull from 1966

MICHIE James Alexander Davidson *MA 1951 MEd 1958
sen dep dir of educ Dun 1965–67; sen dep dir of educ Aberdeensh 1967–68, dir of educ 1968–74; dir educ Grampian reg from 1974

MICHIE James Ernest BSc(agr) 1945
prin teacher sc Kaimhill s s Aber 1961–69, dep head from 1969

MICHIE or Smith, Jean Christian MA 1952
resid Brighton

MICHIE John BSc 1933
head Longside p s 1966–73; retd
d Longside 23.5.81

MICHIE Robert Cook BSc(eng) 1941
hon Sheriff Fort William from 1972
man. dir Highland Lime Co Fort William 1952–77, man. from 1977

MICHIE Victor Gordon BSc(eng) 1948
MCIT
man. dir Charles W. Michie haulage contr Aber from 1970 and man. dir Boyne Bay Lime Co Aber from 1977

MICHIE William MA 1930 MB ChB 1935
b 27.1.11
consult. surg ARI from 1947; councillor Royal coll of surg Edin from 1971; pres assoc of surg of GB & Ireland 1972; elected member of James IV assoc of surg (internat) 1972; member of UK specialist advis comm in gen surg from 1973
d Aber 23.3.78 *AUR* XLVII 359

MICHIE William David *MA 1952
Dip Ed(Lond) 1968
insp of s Salisbury Rhodesia from 1971

MICHIE Winifred Margaret Ross MA 1944
teacher Meldrum s from 1946

MICKLEBURGH Walter Edward BSc 1949 MB ChB 1953
DPM(Melbourne) 1964 MANZCP 1965
MRCPsych 1973
Aust: psychiat mental health serv Adelaide 1964–73, dir of mental health Aust Capital Territory Canberra from 1973

MIDDLER Dorothy Findlay MA 1954
m West Vancouver 7.9.68 David E. W. Thomas comp dir s of William J. T. Hove

MIDDLETON or Brebner, Agnes Ann MA 1915
resid Bearsden
husb *d* 4.12.73
d Stirling 27.2.79

MIDDLETON or Durno, Alfreda Gordon MA 1938

MIDDLETON or Kinnes, Alice MA 1901
no longer on GC reg

MIDDLETON or Johnston, Cecilia Douglas BSc 1934 MB ChB 1940
Aber: locum tenens g p until 1974, co-ordination SAFUR from 1974; resid Longside

MIDDLETON David MB ChB 1932
g p Sunderland from 1935; chmn Sunderland div BMA 1955; member Sunderland hosp man. comm from 1967; member Sunderland AHA (N reg health auth) from 1973; retd 1977

MIDDLETON David Austin MB ChB 1954
FRSM 1965
g p: Bucksburn 1959–61, Aber 1961–65; med advis in pharm indust: Isleworth 1965–69, Ingelheim, Germany from 1969
m Frankfurt/Main Germany –.4.61 Angelika Ankele teacher d of Heinrich A. MD(Giessen) Frankfurt

MIDDLETON or Florence, Dorothea Watson MA 1950
resid Tawa, Wellington NZ 1976

MIDDLETON Douglas George Lawson BSc(eng) 1944

MIDDLETON or Cunningham, Emma *MA 1955
teacher Engl New Deer s 1957–59; resid Aber

MIDDLETON George Proctor MB ChB 1926
KCVO 1962
retd from g p Ballater and from surg apothecary HM household at Balmoral 1973
wife *d* 24.11.64

MIDDLETON Isabella Annie *MA 1944
teacher mod lang Aber h s for girls (later Harlaw acad) from 1951, prin Fr from 1966

MIDDLETON or Reid, Isabella Annie Alexandra MA 1946
resid Grantown-on-Spey

MIDDLETON or Gow, Janie Emslie MA 1923
resid Newbury

MIDDLETON John MA 1929
retd 1971; resid Lond

MIDDLETON Lewis BSc(eng) 1936
dir: Aber Construct. Group 1967–72, Hunter Construct. (Aber) from 1972

MIDDLETON or Hill, Muriel Agnes *MA 1947
teacher mod lang: Buckhaven h s 1950–58, St Thomas of Aquinas s s Edin 1971–76, Broughton h s Edin from 1976

MIDDLETON Richard Stevenson Will MB ChB 1949
MRCPGlas 1966 fell. Council of Europe 1973
assoc consult. phys Oxford 1967; consult. phys geriat

med Swindon/Cirencester 1967–70; sen consult. phys/sen clin lect dept geriat med St James's univ hosp Leeds from 1970

MILLAR Andrew Gerrie *MA 1948
prin teacher Fr Perth acad 1962–65; rector Rothesay acad Bute 1965–68; rector Dunfermline h s from 1968

MILLAR or Boyne, Janet Cuthbertson *MA 1947
teacher Engl/hist h s for girls (Harlaw acad) Aber from 1964

MILLAR or Yorston, Jessie Campbell MB ChB 1953 ᶜMD 1956
sen clin m o commun health Southampton and Winchester from 1967

MILLAR Josephine Beatrice MA 1929

MILLAR Joyce Margaret MB ChB 1951
MFHom 1960 LLCO 1962
h o: gyn royal Lond hom hosp 1954–55, S'ton 1955–56; g p Addlestone 1956–58; clin asst Lond royal Lond hom hosp; osteopath phys 1960–62; private pract from 1962; clin asst royal Lond hom hosp from 1967

MILLAR or Rudram, Mary Davies *BSc 1940
analyst with Wessex water auth Somerset rivers div Bridgwater Somerset from 1970

MILLAR William Davidson BSc(eng) 1949 *1950
lect civ eng RGIT Aber from 1960

MILLER Alexander Loudon *MA 1955 Dip Ed 1958
d 23.5.77

MILLER Alfred James MA 1926 LLB 1937 LLD 1975
MBE 1961 OBE 1969 Hon FSBI 1965
retd 1972; resid Aber
d Aber 7.5.80 *AUR* XLVIII 441

MILLER Allan Douglas Stewart BSc(for) 1949

MILLER or Mackenzie, Annie Alexina MA 1918
resid Inverurie
d 8.5.77

MILLER Charles MB ChB 1949

MILLER Charles Wilmar MA 1949
C of S min: Munro ch Rutherglen Glasg 1959–65, Cruden par ch 1965–73, Anstruther ch from 1973; Scot. council member inst of adv motorists, pres Scot. groups assoc

MILLER or Richardson, Daveen Elizabeth MA 1949
teacher: Ware 1964–69, Broxbourne 1973–76

MILLER Donald John *BSc(eng) 1947
app eng/eng: metro Vickers Manc 1947–53, Brit elect. auth Kingston-on-Thames 1953–55, Preece Cardew & Rider consult. eng Lond 1955–66; chief eng NSHEB Edin 1966–74; dir eng SSEB 1974–78, gen man. from 1978
m Edin 19.4.73 Fay Herriot MA(St And) teacher d of James H. LLB(Edin) Duns

MILLER Duncan MB ChB 1911
no longer on GC reg

MILLER Ernest *MA 1952 LLB 1955
NP 1964
exec asst Glasg 1956–57; court asst Hamilton 1957–60; proc fisc dep Glasg 1963; part time burgh prosec Rutherglen 1965–75; part time chmn DHSS tribunal Motherwell from 1966; sen ptnr John Y. Robertson & Co Hamilton and Giffnock Glasg 1963
m Glasg 30.3.59 Renee Kay leg. secy

MILLER Florence Mary MA 1922
no longer on GC reg

MILLER George MA 1950
head: Fetterangus p s 1960–65, Rhynie p s 1965–75; Insch from 1975

MILLER George Norman MB ChB 1937
g p Leigh-on-Sea from 1939

MILLER Ian BSc(agr) 1950

MILLER James BSc(agr) 1936

MILLER James Webster MB ChB 1903
no longer on GC reg

MILLER or Kennedy, Jessie Nicol MA 1906
no longer on GC reg

MILLER or Mills or Paul, Joan Mary *MA 1946

MILLER John BSc(agr) 1916
no longer on GC reg

MILLER John Lawrence *BSc(eng) 1945

MILLER John Whyte MB ChB 1942
s m o Longbenton and Killingworth, Northumberland from 1973

MILLER Mackenzie MA 1951

MILLER or Buchan, Margaret MA 1951
m(2) Duchovny

MILLER Nancy Hamilton *MA 1942
lect Engl Padgate coll of educ Lancs 1960–61; prin teacher Engl Mary Erskine s Edin from 1961

MILLER or Stewart, Patricia Scott MA 1955

MILLER Peter MA 1923
no longer on GC reg

MILLER Robert Candlish BSc 1951
CEng MIERE AMBIM MIMC
staff apptment war off. Lond 1958–63; cmdr REME

wing s of artillery Larkhill (lt col) 1963–66; dept commandant s of elect. eng REME Arborfield (lt col) 1966–69; man. consult. Harold Whitehead & Ptners Lond 1969–72; man. dir Avonmouth Eng Bristol 1972–74; man. consult. Whitehead Consult. from 1974

MILLER Stephen James Hamilton MB ChB 1937 MD 1953
surg-oculist HM household 1965–69; dep hospitaller St John's hosp Jerusalem from 1968; edit. *British Journal of Ophthalmology* from 1973; surg-oculist to HM The Queen from 1974

MILLER Thomas Balfour *BSc 1949 PhD 1952
d Aber 10.12.76 *AUR* XLVII 214

MILLER Walter Taylor MB ChB 1946

MILLIGAN Frederick Patterson MA 1890
d Edin 17.5.61 *AUR* XXXIX 198

MILLIGAN James Cameron *MEd 1950
retd; resid Aber

MILLIGAN or Mackenzie, Margaret Cranston MA 1951

MILLS or Mills, Margaret Mary MB ChB 1922
DA RCSI 1949 FFARCSI 1962
consult. anaest St Michael's hosp Dunlaore, Ireland from 1948
m 29.5.39 Joseph E. Mills BE(UCD) Co Dublin; husb *d* –.7.64

MILNE Adam BSc 1934 MB ChB 1937
d Hailsham 19.3.75 *AUR* XLVI 239

MILNE Alastair MA 1951 *MEd 1953
lect, prin lect psych Dun coll of educ 1961–69; HMIS SED from 1970
wife *d* Glasg 18.5.77

MILNE Alexander MA 1932 *BSc 1934 PhD 1938 DSc 1950
FIBiol 1963
hon member staff King's coll Durh (later univ of N'cle) and off. agr res council N'cle 1943–67; sen prin scient off. agr res council N'cle 1963–67; prof/head of dept agr zool N'cle 1967–75; emeritus prof from 1975
wife *d* 27.10.70

MILNE Alexander *MA 1933
dep rector Wick h s 1964–73; retd

MILNE Alexander MA 1936 LLB 1939
d Aber 31.1.75 *AUR* XLVI 239

MILNE Alexander BL 1937
d Aber 27.10.79 *AUR* XLVIII 354

MILNE Alexander Andrew Philip *MA 1935

MILNE Alexander Berkeley *MA 1946
OBE 1968
first secy Brit emb Brussels 1961–64; Brit residual mission Salisbury Rhodesia 1966–67; Brit emb Jedda 1968–71; counsellor Brit FMB Tehran 1974–77; FCO Lond from 1977

MILNE Alexander George MB ChB 1948
g p Portland from 1951

MILNE Alexander John Buchan MA 1922
retd 1960; resid Aber
d 18.12.78

MILNE Alexander Minty *MA 1924
no longer on GC reg

MILNE Alexander Robert MA 1926
d 2.12.65 *AUR* XLI 246

MILNE Alfred Pyper MA 1924 BCom 1926 BSc(agr) 1932
no longer on GC reg

MILNE or Caie, Alice Jane *MA 1932
resid Warwick
d Leamington 13.8.81

MILNE Andrew *MA 1913
d S Af 11.7.72 *AUR* XLV 124

MILNE Andrew Maitland MB ChB 1955
FDSRCS(Edin) 1966
RADC became major, sen spec dent. surg UK/Germany 1959–69; lect oral path. Welsh Nat s 1970–72; reg dent. off. Yorks DHSS Leeds from 1972

MILNE Andrew Noble BSc 1946 MB ChB 1953
sen accident and emergency off. Grimsby gen hosp from 1964

MILNE Angela Alica *BSc 1948 PhD 1952
MSc(Melb) 1967
prin univ women's coll Melbourne 1960–67; teacher Henley g s 1970–71; sen exper off. univ R'dg from 1971
m Melbourne 24.5.62 Lloyd H. P. Jones BAgrSc(Melb) sen prin res scient CSIRO Aust

MILNE or Duthie, Anne MB ChB 1946
h o RACH 1946–47; Birm accident hosp 1947–48; Lond: dem anatomy Charing Cross 1948–49, regist obst/gyn St Mary's hosp 1949–51; g p Leeds from 1951
husb *d* 15.4.76

MILNE Annie Watt MA 1912
d Aber 15.4.72 *AUR* XLIV 428

MILNE Archibald Cousland MB ChB 1946
Edin: sen anaest city hosp/consult. anaest RI from 1965

MILNE Arthur Hay MA 1934
war serv capt RA 1940–46; head Hobkirk p s Roxburghsh 1946–55; lect Aber tech coll from 1955
m Sunbury-on-Thames Elma A. Brown pers secy d of William E. B. Wanstead Lond

MILNE Arthur John MB ChB 1901 DPH 1903
no longer on GC reg

MILNE Arthur Young MB ChB 1917
d Willesborough Ashford Kent 11.4.62
AUR XXXIX 381

MILNE or Dickson, Barbara MA 1916
d 20.2.63 *AUR* XL 201

MILNE Bryan Coutts MA 1953 LLB 1955

MILNE Cameron McPherson MA 1934
head Kennethmont p s from 1955

MILNE or Smith, Catherine Mathers MA 1930
teacher Kintore p s 1958–70

MILNE Charles BSc(agr) 1916
d Aber 20.12.67 *AUR* XLII 355

MILNE Charles Buchan *MA 1949
Aber: dep head Frederick St s s 1966–73, Hilton acad from 1973

MILNE Charles Gordon Shaw MA 1914 MB ChB 1917 MD 1929
retd lt col RAMC(India) 1935 ED(Efficiency Decor. India) 1934
Fell. Brit Orthop Assoc 1975
sen orthop surg; retd 1967

MILNE Christian Park Newlands MA 1914
teacher; retd 1954
d Aber 21.5.78

MILNE or Ingram, Christina Jane MA 1917
d 2.11.60 *AUR* XXXIX 280

MILNE Comyn BL 1954
FRSA 1962
ptnr Wink & Mackenzie solic Elgin from 1961; TA (Seaforth, 3 Queen's own Highlanders, 51 Highland volunteers) attaining rank of major 1962–72; dir Sun Alliance Assur (local); clerk to county Income Tax for Moray

MILNE David Coutts *MA 1931
supt Carnoustie f e centre 1945–59; spec asst Arbroath h s 1969–73; retd; resid Carnoustie
d 25.11.77

MILNE David Dean MB ChB 1955
FRCSE 1963
regist surg: Aber 1957–59, Falkirk 1959–66; surg spec: Sandakan Borneo 1966–69, Tripoli Libya 1969–72; consult. surg N'cle-u-Tyne from 1972
m Banff 30.7.60 Elizabeth A. Kerr nurs sister d of George G. K. Banff

MILNE Derek Allardyce MB ChB 1941
resid Woking

MILNE Dorothy Reid *MA 1934
lect relig educ Neville's Cross coll Durh 1960–63; sen lect r e W. Midlands coll of educ Walsall 1963–74; lect r e City of Birmingham coll of educ and City of Birmingham poly 1974–77

MILNE Douglas Graeme MB ChB 1942 DPH 1952
FFCM 1973 QHS 1974
dep dir gen army med serv, rank major gen from 1975

MILNE Douglas Mearns MB ChB 1940
sen consult. thoracic surg SW reg hosp board from 1951; resid Bristol

MILNE Duncan MB ChB 1951
DPH(Dund) 1969
m o in dept Dun 1968–73, Angus from 1973
m Montrose 27.10.72 Davena Reid RGN SCM HV; wife *d* 1973

MILNE Duncan *MA 1951
sqn ldr: head ling. br HQ Air Force s Naples 1964–66; pers serv sqn RAF Locking Weston-super-Mare 1966–68; syst analyst/progr RAF pers man. centre Glos 1968–72; milit asst to comm NATO defence coll Rome 1973–78; c o RAF High Wycombe from 1978

MILNE Elizabeth Honor MB ChB 1943
g p Harrow from 1964

MILNE Elizabeth Jane *MA 1927
retd 1968; resid Aber

MILNE or McCabe, Elizabeth Mary Isabella *MB ChB 1944
S Af; s m o Frere hosp East London 1973–78; s m o dept of fam health H F Verwoerd hosp Pretoria from 1978
husb *d* 24.5.72

MILNE Ella Jean MA 1921
no longer on GC reg

MILNE or Mackay, Elspet Wilkie BSc 1927 DSc 1934
resid Edin

MILNE or Cameron, Elspeth Margaret *MA 1929
resid Stirling

MILNE Eric MB ChB 1939
MRACGP 1971 FRACGP 1975
regist surg Preston 1958–59; Mount Isa Aust: m o 1960–62, med pract from 1962
m Auckland NZ 15.12.78 Gladys L. Welbourne nurse d of Ernest W.

MILNE or Marnoch, Euphemia Jane MA 1945
teacher Tarves p s 1946–60, part time 1960–72, full time from 1972

MILNE Evander Mackay McFarquhar *MA 1948
lect univ coll Gold Coast till 1952; edit. Thomas Nelson and Sons (Edin & Lond) from 1952

MILNE Frances Forbes MB ChB 1949
DObstRCOG 1958 DPM 1964 MRCPsych 1973

C of S med missionary Rajputana India 1952–61; sen h o Goodmayes hosp Ilford 1961–62; regist Cell Barnes hosp St Albans 1962–64; regist/sen regist ch guid trg centre Hampstead Lond 1964–71; consult. psychiat ch guid clin Luton from 1971

MILNE Frank Marr MB ChB 1946
g p Coupar Angus from 1952

MILNE Frederick Alexander BSc(agr) 1934
farm./man. dir Montrose Auction Co from 1942; panel arbiter DAFS from 1947

MILNE Gavin MA LLB 1950
asst gen secy NFU of Scot. Edin from 1956

MILNE George MB ChB 1905 *MD 1908
g p Streatham 1974
d Streatham 1.2.75 *AUR* XLVI 234

MILNE George MA 1911
d St Andrews 26.3.75 *AUR* XLVI 234

MILNE George MB ChB 1927
d Pietermaritzburg Natal 21.9.69 *AUR* XLIII 330

MILNE George Alexander MA 1935
min Pacific City and Nestucca presb churches Cloverdale and Pacific City Oregon USA from 1971

MILNE George Graham BSc(agr) 1952
prin teacher biol Belmont acad Ayr from 1974

MILNE George James *MA 1905
d Aber 3.2.73 *AUR* XLV 223

MILNE George Panton MB ChB 1934
clin reader obst/gyn Aberd 1972–76; retd
member univ court Aberd from 1980
wife *d* 29.6.73
m(2) Melrose 3.11.75 Mary A. Watt teacher d of James W.

MILNE or Astle, Gladys MA 1945

MILNE Harold Samuel BSc(eng) 1928
retd 1964; resid Aber

MILNE Helen MA 1924 *1926
d Daviot Inverurie 29.7.71 *AUR* XLIV 320

MILNE Herbert John Mansfield *MA 1909
d 11.2.65 *AUR* XLI 54

MILNE Herbert Stewart MB ChB 1909 DPH 1912
retd col; resid Lymington

MILNE Hugh Fraser MA 1949
head: Dunecht p s 1961–70, Milltimber 1970–73, Scotstown Aber from 1973

MILNE Ian BL 1949
sole ptnr Mayer & Fraser solic Keith 1955–76; retd
m 22.6.68 Jeannie C. W. Stevenson
d Keith 16.2.80

MILNE Irene MB ChB 1948
DObstRCOG 1971
private g p Mt Isa Queensland Aust from 1963

MILNE or Ingram, Irene MA 1950
resid Llandrindod Wells Powys

MILNE or Grant, Isabella MA 1930

MILNE Isobel Goring BL 1939
retd; resid Aber

MILNE James *MA 1934
M o T (D o E): fin. div Blackpool/Lond 1940–52, Lond: bridges eng div/lect trg branch 1954–58, parl estimates clerk 1958–67, dep chief regist 1967–73; retd; resid Catford, Lond
m Inverurie 1.9.37 Adelaide Joss

MILNE James *MA 1951
teacher classics Morgan acad Dun 1954–63; spec asst classics Kirkcaldy h s 1963–68; prin classics: Airdrie acad 1968–72, Albyn s for girls Aber from 1972

MILNE James Bate MA 1930
head Braes p s Perthsh 1947–52, Longforgan from 1952
m 1938 Anna M. Henderson

MILNE James Pratt BSc(eng) 1945

MILNE James Scott MA 1940
no longer on GC reg

MILNE or MacKean, Janet Elizabeth *MA 1939
resid Wallasey

MILNE or Edmond, Jeannie MA 1949

MILNE Joan Margaret MB ChB 1948
h s Aber 1949–52; regist Nuffield dept surg Oxford 1952–54; regist ch dept Newcastle 1954; resid Vict, Aust
m Braemar 1955 Joseph H. Scudamore MB ChB(Brist) obst/gyn s of William E. S. Usk Mon

MILNE John MA 1919 BSc(agr) 1921

MILNE John MA 1930
d Aber 30.3.74 *AUR* XLV 448

MILNE John *MA 1934
teacher: prin mod lang Dollar acad from 1938, acting dep rector 1960–62; retd 1977

MILNE John Bruce *BSc(eng) 1947

MILNE John Clark *MA 1922
d Aber 3.12.62 *AUR* XL 86

MILNE John Coutts MB ChB 1923 DPH 1925
m o h Farnborough, Fleet & Hartley Wintney 1959–68, part time m o Surrey c c from 1968

MILNE John George MB ChB 1946
g p Yorks from 1955

MILNE John Irvine Wallace *MA 1931
prin teacher classics Dunbar g s from 1946

MILNE John Maxwell MA 1949
man. dir James G. Bisset univ bookseller Aber from 1953

MILNE John Nelson BCom 1922 *MA 1946 LLB 1947 LLD 1960
retd 1970
Aberd: member univ court 1949–70; member bus. comm of Gen Council 1930–70, convener 1944–70

MILNE Joseph Peter MB ChB 1934
g p Keith from 1935

MILNE or Dobbs, June Ishbel MB ChB 1951
dir ch dev center ch hosp Milwaukee, Wisconsin USA/assoc prof paediat med coll of Wisconsin from 1965

MILNE Kenneth Grant Sim MB ChB 1951
g p Edin from 1956

MILNE Kenneth Panton MB ChB 1946
brig/advis ophth M o D Lond from 1973

MILNE Lawrence Walker MA LLB 1950

MILNE Leonard McDonald Emslie MB ChB 1937
g p; retd; resid Wales

MILNE Leslie MA 1951
head Tullynessle p s from 1966
m Deskford 24.7.65 Isobel J. Currie bank clerkess d of William C. MBE Deskford

MILNE or Cant, Lizzie Fowlie Bruce MA 1924
d Aber 23.12.69 *AUR* XLIII 445

MILNE Lorna Christian MB ChB 1947
Dip Psychiat(McG) 1954 CRCP(C) 1968 FRCP(C) 1973
asst psychiat Montreal ch hosp 1954–55; USA: instr clin psychiat univ of Vermont coll of med Burlington 1961–67, psychiat/consult. ch health State of Vermont 1965–67; Kingston Ontario: ch psychiat reg ch centre from 1968, asst prof psychiat Queen's univ from 1972
m Kingston Ontario 1.7.50 Thomas J. Boag MB ChB(Liv) dean fac of med Queen's univ Kingston s of John H. B. Liv

MILNE or Jamieson, Mabel MA 1924
resid Edin
husb *d* Edin 2.3.67

MILNE or Mitchell, Mabel Davidson MA 1915
resid Sanderstead

MILNE Malcolm Ross *MB ChB 1943
FFARCS 1960 FFARACS 1961
dist m o Broome W. Aust 1947–50; dep dir dept of anaest royal Perth hosp W. Aust from 1962

MILNE or Summers, Margaret MA 1936
teacher Ruthrieston s s Aber from 1950

MILNE or Ribton-Turner, Margaret Mirren MA 1934
resid Whetstone Lond

MILNE Marian Byrne *MA 1929 MB ChB 1937
d Aber 15.4.72 *AUR* XLV 128

MILNE Marjorie Isabel *MA 1932
AIL 1967
teacher Beechwood s Aber 1958–73; stud. Italian Aber coll of comm/univ centre of culture for foreigners Florence Dip(Adv) 1966

MILNE Marjorie Mary MA 1916 *MB ChB 1920 DPH 1922
d Edin 30.11.75

MILNE Mary Ann MA 1911
no longer on GC reg

MILNE Mary Ann Urquhart MA 1917
d 9.7.63

MILNE Mary Cheyne BSc 1927
no longer on GC reg

MILNE or Stephen, Mary Evelyn BSc 1932 MA 1933
resid Groombridge

MILNE or Allman, Mary Gordon MA 1917 MB ChB 1921

MILNE Mary Isabella *MA 1924 BSc 1924
retd 1960; resid Bieldside Aber

MILNE or Barrie, Mary Stronach MA 1937
resid Stonehaven

MILNE or Hampson, Marybell Grant BSc 1949
Cert Dip Acct & Finance 1977
teacher sc N Manc g s for girls 1961–71; comp secy/dir Becketts bakery eng Heywood Lancs from 1971

MILNE Maurice *BSc(eng) 1936
FIMunE 1953 FICE 1954 FIWE 1956 FIStruct 1968 FRTPI 1968 FIHE 1968
dep dir gen highways D o E Lond 1970–76; pres Permanent International Assoc of Road Congresses Paris from 1977

MILNE Moira Agnes MA 1931
retd 1973; resid Stonehaven

MILNE Murdoch McIntyre MB ChB 1928 ᶜMD 1936
d Hawick 15.2.64 *AUR* XL 400

MILNE Norman BSc(eng) 1951 *1952
elect. eng AEI 1952–63; lect eng Aberd from 1963

MILNE Peter MB ChB 1941

MILNE Peter Weir MA 1925 LLB 1929 BCom 1930
resid Peterhead
d 16.4.81

MILNE Robert Alfred Charles MA 1949

MILNE Robert Blair MA 1902
no longer on GC reg

MILNE Ronald Douglas *BSc(eng) 1952
PhD(Lond) 1962 FIMA 1965 FRAeS 1970
MSc 1971
reader aeronaut. eng Lond (QMC) 1964–71; prof eng maths Brist from 1971

MILNE Ronald George MB ChB 1946
consult. anaest NE reg hosp board Aber from 1963

MILNE Rosalind Margaret Paul MB ChB 1934
consult. anaest NE reg hosp area Aber from 1948

MILNE Royston John *MA 1934 LLB 1937

MILNE or Cruickshank, Sheila Craig *BSc 1942

MILNE Sheila Isabel Duguid BL 1949
d Aber 25.3.68 *AUR* XLII 374

MILNE Stephen George *BSc 1936

MILNE Thomas *MA 1947

MILNE Thomas Beattie BSc(eng) 1938
d Calgary Canada 12.3.75 *AUR* XLVI 240

MILNE Thomas Charles Craighead *MA 1950

MILNE Valerie MacAra MB ChB 1950
g p
resid Bridgend Glam

MILNE Victor Edmond MB ChB 1921 DPH 1923
d Sutton Coldfield 9.9.71 *AUR* XLIV 319

MILNE William MA 1903
d 5.10.63

MILNE William MA 1951

MILNE William BSc(eng) 1952

MILNE William Alexander BCom 1929 *BSc 1931

MILNE William Francis Jamieson BSc 1936 *1937

MILNE William Guthrie MA 1935 LLB 1939
solic Milne & Reid advoc Aber from 1948

MILNE William James BSc 1952 *1953

MILNE William Mitchell BSc(agr) 1923
no longer on GC reg

MILNE William Proctor
MA 1903 DSc 1910 LLD 1946
d Glack 3.9.67 *AUR* XLII 178

MILNE William Shirreffs MB ChB 1939
consult. ophth NE reg hosp board and asst in ophth Aberd 1948–77; retd

MILNER George Algernon Webb MB ChB 1949
FACS 1960
consult. surg univ hosp of W. Indies from 1959

MILNER Robert Webb MB ChB 1949
DA(Dub) 1953 FFARCS(Lond) 1954
m o Kingston Jamaica 1949–53; spec in anaest: Kingston Jamaica 1954–56, St Boniface hosp Winnipeg 1956–68; chief of anaest Victoria gen hosp Winnipeg from 1968

MILNER or Kidson, Ruth MA 1937
resid Aberystwyth

MILNER Thomas Gordon BSc(eng) 1947

MILTON Alexander Gordon *MA 1924
retd 1970; resid Glasg
d 21.7.77

MILTON or Faulds, Andrena Dorothy Margaret
MA 1932
d Aber 24.2.72 *AUR* XLIV 433

MILTON George John Geddes *BSc 1934
rector Invergordon acad 1959–75; retd; resid Portgordon
d England –.9.80 (on holiday) *AUR* XLIX 68

MILTON James Sutherland MA 1915
d 26.10.64

MILTON John Alexander BSc(agr) 1928
MA(Dub) 1965
private vet pract Rutland 1960–61; lect anim husb vet s Trinity coll Dublin 1962–77; retd

MINDE Max MB ChB 1921

MINTO Alfred MB ChB 1951
DPM(Lond) 1960 MRCPsych 1972
FRCPsych 1975
Nott: sen hosp m o 1959–60, consult. psychiat from 1960

MINTO Charles Nicholson MB ChB 1944 DPH 1949
MFCM 1972
county m o h and dist hosps off. for Caithness 1953–74; dist m o Northern dist Highland health board from 1974
m Horsham 6.2.68 Elizabeth Bremner

MINTO William Henry Peter
MB ChB 1941 DPH 1947 MD 1955
d 24.10.63 *AUR* XL 303

MINTY Agnes Mavor MA 1930
teacher Northfield acad Aber from 1956

MINTY Eliza MA 1915
d Newmachar 8.4.78

MINTY Gladys *MA 1927
retd 1968; resid Fraserburgh

MINTY Herbert MA 1931
i/c Af dept J. P. Coats Glasg 1960–71
d Glasg 15.1.74

MINTY Jessie *MA 1930
teacher Fr Aber acad 1950–60, 1966–69; retd; resid Fraserburgh

MINTY or Templeton, Mary Bisset MA 1943
deceased

MINTY Schona Margaret MA 1953

MIRRLEES Stewart Turnbull Alexander *MA 1914
d Aber 27.1.70 *AUR* XLIII 441

MIRRLEES William Minto MA 1920 BCom 1922
d Liverpool 1.5.63 *AUR* XL 202

MIRTLE William Pirrie BSc(eng) 1952
CEng 1960
English Elect. co: div prod. man. MRI div Stafford 1958–61, asst gen man. Madras 1961–70; consult. dept of employ. Glasg 1970–73; gen man. Control panels Glasg from 1973, dir 1974

MITCHELL or Porter, Agnes Henderson MA 1922

MITCHELL or Norwell, Ailsa Janette Isabel MA 1934
resid Aber
husb *d* 1976

MITCHELL Alan Ogston BSc(eng) 1954
MICE 1961
asst civ eng Halcrow Lond 1959–63; sen civ eng: Balfour Beatty & Co water eng and power dev consult. London/Sidcup 1963–73; man. eng Rendel, Palmer & Tritton Lond from 1973
m Wimbledon 14.7.62 Caroline D. Waters secy d of Frederick G. W. Eastbourne

MITCHELL Alastair James Lendrum BSc(for) 1949

MITCHELL Alexander MB ChB 1910 MD 1925
no longer on GC reg

MITCHELL Alexander Lessel Stephen BL 1931
theatrical prod. Lond from 1937
wife *d* Lond 27.7.57

MITCHELL Alexander Mennie MA 1895 MB ChB 1899
no longer on GC reg

MITCHELL Alfred William Coutts *MA 1909
no longer on GC reg

MITCHELL Andrew Alexander Smith MA 1930
retd 1972; resid Bonnyrigg

MITCHELL Andrew Henry MB ChB 1916
retd 1966; resid Cardiff
m(2) Cardiff 6.5.69 Beatrice M. Clode d of Sidney H. C. Cardiff

MITCHELL Ann Christine MA 1955
teacher Ellon p s from 1961

MITCHELL or Reid, Anne Margaret MB ChB 1954
g p Hinton Alberta from 1956

MITCHELL or Florence, Annie Gray Adams MA 1931
resid Cults Aber
d 22.12.81

MITCHELL or Morgan, Betty MB ChB 1924
retd 1966; resid Cothal Dyce

MITCHELL Brian Redman *MA 1952
Cantab: res off. dept applied econ 1960–65; sen res off. 1966–67; lect econ/fell. Trinity coll from 1967
marr diss
m(2) Lymington Hants 11.9.68 Ann L. Birney SRN d of David L. B. BA(Cantab) Rusper

MITCHELL or Guy, Catherine Hutcheon MB ChB 1945
FRCOG 1973 FAGO 1974 BA 1978
retd 1974; resid Canberra Aust

MITCHELL Charles Duncan BSc 1942 *1948
Birm: prod. man. Polymers Dunlop chem div 1958–68, market res man. Dunlop chem prod. div 1968–72, quality control man. Dunlop Semtex 1972–79, tech proj man. Dunlop Semtex from 1979

MITCHELL Charles Gordon *MA 1911 *BSc 1913
d Inv 12.5.65 *AUR* XLI 149

MITCHELL Charlesina Jessie MA 1947
asst head New Elgin p s 1972–77, head Greenwards p s Elgin from 1977

MITCHELL or Gibb, Christian MA 1925
d Ealing –.12.80

MITCHELL Colin George MB ChB 1953
g p Aber from 1956

MITCHELL David MA 1929
head St Mungo p s Lockerbie 1962–70; retd; resid Langholm
m 14.7.33 Mary Douglas d of David D. Langholm

MITCHELL or Younie, Dorothy MB ChB 1921 [c]MD 1929
sen asst m o h Aber corp 1953–63; res fell. dept of ment health Aberd 1968–72; retd; resid Dyce

MITCHELL or McIntosh, Dorothy Margaret MA 1934
secy/int decorator; resid Hemel Hempstead

MITCHELL Edith Lawrence *MA 1924
d Aber 3.7.66 *AUR* XLI 340

MITCHELL or Brebner, Eileen Jean *MA 1954

MITCHELL or Duce, Eleanor Kerr *MA 1932
resid Norwich

MITCHELL or Bown, Elizabeth Milne BSc 1954

MITCHELL Elspeth Madge MA 1936
resid Aber

MITCHELL Ernest Renan *MA 1933
teacher Engl: Charters Towers East Grinstead 1936, Buckingham coll Harrow 1937, Internat s Yokohama 1937–39, Cath boys' s Shanghai 1940–43; interned by Japanese at Shanghai 1943–45; teacher Engl: Aberdeensh 1946, Whitwood tech coll Castleford 1946, Lamlash s 1946–48, Peterhead acad 1948–50, Dunfermline h s 1950–56, George Watson's coll Edin 1956–72, asst prin Engl 1972–74; retd

MITCHELL Ethel Margaret *MA 1926
teacher: prin mod lang Witney g s later Henry Box comp Oxford 1961–66, spec asst mod lang Aber h s for girls later Harlaw acad 1966–68; retd; resid Edin

MITCHELL Evelyn Jean MA 1952
BEd(Br. Col) 1958
Canada: teacher Fr Queen Elizabeth h s Surrey 1960–61, Engl/Fr Belmont h s 1961–63, substitute teacher Inuvik NWT 1966–67; part-time Parkland elem s Coquitlam 1972–75; learning assistance Langdale p s Gibsons BC from 1977
m Huntly 25.8.62 Robert J. Wetmore B Ed(Vict) teacher/prin s of James A. M. W. Vict BC

MITCHELL or Rose, Evelyn May MA 1921
head Brae p s Stonehaven 1931–62; retd; resid Aber
d Aber 31.7.80

MITCHELL Florence Mary MA 1929
retd 1969; resid Aber

MITCHELL or Stott, Frances Maureen MA 1954
resid Goring-on-Thames

MITCHELL George Archibald Grant
***MB ChB 1929 [c]ChM 1933 DSc 1950**
FRCS 1968
prof anat Manc univ 1946–74; dean Manc univ med s 1955–60, pro vice-chancellor Manc univ 1959–63
author of many books and articles and contributor of sections or chapters to *Encyclopaedia Britannica* and other encyclopaedias and books

MITCHELL George Mutch MB ChB 1951
FPS 1942 off. brother O St J 1974
sen lect materia medica/pharmacology WNSM Cardiff from 1965; hon consult. clin pharmacology and toxicology from 1969

MITCHELL George Patrick MB ChB 1940
lect orthop surg Edin from 1957; nat delegate UK to SICOT from 1972; UK repres monospecialist sect. UEMS orthop surg from 1973

MITCHELL Gladys Muriel *MA 1919 [d]LLB 1921
retd 1957; resid Aber

MITCHELL Hannah Isabel Elizabeth MA 1937

MITCHELL Hannah King *MA 1923
teacher Fordyce acad Banffsh 1924–64; retd; resid Cullen

MITCHELL or Smith, Helen Elizabeth MA 1936
d Aber 8.2.69 *AUR* XLIII 216

MITCHELL Helen Milne MA 1925
teacher Fordyce acad Banffsh 1926–63; retd; resid Cullen

MITCHELL or Thomson, Hilda MA 1935

MITCHELL Hunter Diack BSc(eng) 1951
resid St Albans

MITCHELL Ian Falconer BCom 1932
no longer on GC reg

MITCHELL Ian Harper *MA 1939

MITCHELL Ian James BSc(eng) 1945

MITCHELL Ian McRae MA LLB 1952
prin leg. asst corp of city of Aber 1969–75, sen solic to city of Aber from 1975

MITCHELL or Macdonald, Irene Elsie Helen MA 1954
teacher: AGS 1960–61, Airyhall p s 1966–68

MITCHELL or Simmonds, Irene Margaret MA 1953
teacher Engl Aber: Ruthrieston s s 1964–67; part time coll of comm 1969–73, Harlaw acad 1973–78, Cults acad from 1978

MITCHELL James BSc(agr) 1923
d Edin 7.8.69 *AUR* XLIII 330

MITCHELL James *BSc 1955

MITCHELL James Durno BSc(eng) 1946

MITCHELL James Elmsly MB ChB 1907 *MD 1910
d Hartlepool 25.5.67 *AUR* XLII 347

MITCHELL James Frederick MB ChB 1931
g p Northampton from 1946

MITCHELL James Gault
***BSc 1952 Dip Ed 1955 PhD 1978**
FRAS 1957 M Inst P 1958 MIElectronics 1972
teacher sc Aber acad 1953–56; res scient AEI Aldermaston 1956–62; res phys SRNE (instrumentation) Hayes 1962–67; lect med phys dept Aberd from 1967
m Aber 1.7.55 Jean C. Illingworth d of William I. Ballater

MITCHELL James Mitchell MB ChB 1915
d 3.8.61 *AUR* XXXIX 279

MITCHELL James Wilkie MB ChB 1927
d Luton 6.1.71 *AUR* XLIV 211

MITCHELL John MA 1928 LLB 1930
d 2.12.72

MITCHELL John Alexander MA 1952
head Marybank p s Urray Muir of Ord from 1962

MITCHELL John Charles MB ChB 1948 ᶜMD 1956
sen consult. path. Rush Green hosp Romford from 1962

MITCHELL John Marsters MB ChB 1911
d Edin –.1.75

MITCHELL John Phimister MB ChB 1907 MD 1911
d Cults Aber 1.4.62 *AUR* XXXIX 375

MITCHELL John Souter *MA 1921 BSc(agr) 1922
d Aber 8.6.69 *AUR* XLIII 329

MITCHELL or Whyte, Maggie MA 1911
d Stonehaven 27.10.68 *AUR* XLIII 78

MITCHELL Malcolm James MB ChB 1953
g p Crieff from 1956

MITCHELL Margaret *MA 1948
head moderns dept Dr F. J. Donevan Collegiate Oshawa Canada 1958–59; teacher Fr Whitby Canada from 1974
m Toronto 11.10.58 Rex E. Hopkins acct s of William H. Bristol

MITCHELL or Williamson, Margaret Amy MA 1952

MITCHELL or Gordon, Margaret MacGregor Gordon MA 1930
resid Inv

MITCHELL or Duncan, Margaret Reid MA 1929
resid Aber

MITCHELL or Smith, Margaret Rowan MA 1952
Aber: teacher Ferryhill s 1953–61, remed Tullos p s from 1975

MITCHELL or Macdonald, Mary MA 1949
part time teacher: Engl Farr s Bettyhill 1964–65, remed 1969–73; resid Brora

MITCHELL Muriel Craig *MA 1947
conference secy Royal Soc of med Lond

MITCHELL Nellie MA 1932
m Crawford
d 1970

MITCHELL Norma Constance MA 1943

MITCHELL or Mair, Patricia Mary Reid MA 1927

MITCHELL Patrick MA 1924 BSc 1926 *1927
d Aber 14.8.71 *AUR* XLIV 320

MITCHELL Patrick Charles MB ChB 1937
consult. dermat Cumberland and North Westmorland Carlisle from 1961
marr diss 1973
m(2) Carlisle 1.11.75 Alison E. S. Burnett farm. d of John G. B. of Powis MA(Oxon) Old Aber

MITCHELL Patrick Malcolm MA LLB 1951
ptnr Craigens, Glennie & Whyte advoc Aber from 1958 (amalg John & W. G. Craigen and Glennie & Whyte)

MITCHELL Peter Edward Gordon MB ChB 1953 MD 1960
T.D. 1969 MRCPath 1964 FRCPath 1976
lect path. Aberd 1956–66; consult./hon sen lect Dund from 1966
m Aber 26.10.62 Bessie T. Fulton d of Robert M. F. Aber

MITCHELL Philip Rene MB ChB 1936
d Galmpton 8.1.73 *AUR* XLV 227

MITCHELL Robert Alexander MB ChB 1950
LMCC 1959 DABPsych & Neurol 1961
Clin MITAA 1972 Teaching MITAA 1973
USA: fell. commun psychiat Albany med coll NY 1960–61, private pract psychiat Shenectady NY from 1961; clin dir upstate NY transactional analysis seminar from 1972

MITCHELL Robert Hartley Ogilvie *BSc(eng) 1950
MICE 1956
eng asst Motherwell 1950–55; 2nd lt RE (nat serv) Hants 1952–54; contractor's site eng Shetland Is/Lond/Glasgow area 1955–59; sen asst eng Argyll c c 1959–63; sen eng Stirling 1963–68; dep county surv Aber 1968–75; div road surv Grampian reg c from 1975
m Motherwell 6.4.56 Isabella M. Coutts teacher d of William A. C. Motherwell

MITCHELL Robert Lumsden BSc 1930 *1931 PhD 1934
d Aber 13.12.72 *AUR* XLV 227

MITCHELL Robert Lyell PhD 1934
head dept spectrochem Macaulay inst for soil res Aber until 1968, dir until 1975

MITCHELL Robert Wilson Downie BSc 1954
prin teacher maths/sc Stanley s Perthsh 1959–63; head Brechin h s annexe 1963–66; head Portmoak s Kinross 1966–70, Muthill Perthsh from 1971

MITCHELL or Ashby, Sheila Mary MA 1944

MITCHELL Stanley Matthew BSc(for) 1950
prin Kersewell coll Lanarksh 1961–69; head Bovington mod s Dorset from 1969

MITCHELL Thomas Chalmers BSc(for) 1948

MITCHELL Walter Alexander MA 1955 LLB 1957
ptnr A. C. Morrison & Richards advoc Aber from 1962

m Aber 17.9.64 Freda A. Butt millinery asst d of Frederick W. B. Aber

MITCHELL William *MA 1902
no longer on GC reg

MITCHELL William BCom 1922
no longer on GC reg

MITCHELL William MA 1924
retd 1964; resid Foveran

MITCHELL William Anderson *BSc 1947
d Aber 15.5.70 *AUR* XLIV 111

MITCHELL William Cameron MB ChB 1926
g p N'cle-u-Tyne 1934–67; med referee DHSS 1947–74; retd; resid Canonbie, Dumfriessh
m(2) N'cle 18.2.67 Ida Scott acct d of William E. S. Manc
d 7.9.79

MITCHELL William George Drummond MA 1930
d Aber 24.1.76

MITCHELL William Ian Cameron BSc(agr) 1924
man. Sungei Arak estate Perak Malaya 1929–30; rep: Sun Life assur comp of Canada Aberdeensh, SAI 1931–36; acting man. rubber estates (Harrison & Crossfield) Malaya 1937–41; served with FMSVF, captivity in Singapore 1942–45; man. Cluny estate Perak Malaya 1947–49; in bus. Forres 1951–61; curator MacRobert Trusts Tarland from 1962
m Penang 11.5.39 Penelope Ogston d of Thomas O. Elgin
d Tarland 9.12.80

MITCHELL William Smith PhD 1951
lib univ of N'cle 1963–73, lib fell. 1973–74; retd
wife *d* 1972
m(2) N'cle-u-Tyne 9.6.73 Christina B. Denniston or Crawford loc govt off. d of James D. Trinidad

MITCHELL William Thom MA 1950
teacher Engl/dep head St Paul's s São Paulo Brazil from 1969

MITCHELL or Morfey, Winifred Isobel Leslie MA 1930
d 26.1.81

MOAR John William Hunter *MA 1951
higher exec off. GCHQ Cheltenham from 1963

MOFFAT or Wallace, Elizabeth Jean *MA 1930
Clarkston Glasg: part-time teacher Fr Radleigh private s 1956–62, teacher Fr/Ger Eastwood s 1962–65
d Glasg 27.2.78 *AUR* XLVII 359

MOFFAT or Kaye, Margaret MA 1928
resid Tayinloan Tarbert Argyll

MOIR or Taylor, Agnes MA 1937
prop. ironmongery shop Turriff from 1963

MOIR Beatrice Milne MA 1928
head Tipperty s 1962–74; retd; resid Sauchen

MOIR or Hale, Catherine Watt Baird MA 1946
teacher Port Vale j s Hertford 1960–63; resid Solihull

MOIR Donald Meldrum MB ChB 1950
d –.8.67

MOIR Douglas Lennox BSc(eng) 1948

MOIR Duncan Wilson *MA 1954
sen lect Span S'ton from 1972
publ: *The Golden Age: Drama 1492–1700* Lond and New York and Spanish lang edit. 1971 and 1974 with prof E. M. Wilson; scholarly introductions to facsimile edit. of emblem books
m Monimail Fife 18.12.63 Adelyn L. Ross MA(St And) univ lect d of David R. MB ChB(Glas) Cupar

MOIR Eva MA 1922
retd 1960; resid Kinellar

MOIR George Alexander BSc(agr) 1932 PhD 1935
d 30.9.77

MOIR George Lumsden BSc(eng) 1937

MOIR George Wellington BCom 1931
no longer on GC reg

MOIR Harry BSc 1949

MOIR Ian Alexander *MA 1936 BD 1939
lect Christian origins (NT) Edin 1961–74, sen lect from 1974, acting head of NT dept 1974–75

MOIR or Birnie, Isabel MA 1948
teacher: Melness Sutherland 1959–61, Aberchirder j s s 1963–66, Findochty j s s 1966–69; resid Annbank Ayr

MOIR James Glegg MB ChB 1939
g p Ballater 1947–77; retd

MOIR John MA 1912 MB ChB 1915
d 9.4.67 *AUR* XLII 350

MOIR John McInnes MA 1952 BD 1955
teacher Aber 1958–61; C of S min Glenelg 1961–66; teacher: Kasama trg coll Zambia 1966–68, Aber from 1968

MOIR John Reid MB ChB MA 1927
retd 1966; resid Grange-over Sands

MOIR Leonard James MB ChB 1913

MOIR Leonard James BSc(agr) 1946
estate man. Perak Malaysia 1947–62; self-employed oyster farm. from 1962; resid Lochgilphead

MOIR Lesley MA 1942

MOIR Maureen Agnes MA 1954
Sydney Aust: teacher Engl 1968–73, head Engl/humanities NSW dept tech and f e from 1973
m Sydney 15.6.68 Winston A. Kraal

MOIR Murdo Logan *BSc 1939
d 8.11.65

MOIR or Cormie, Stella Anne MA 1955
DipEd(Dund) 1971
teacher: Cummings Park p s Aber 1956–61, adjustment ch guid centre Perth 1968–70, remed reading from 1970

MOIR Sylvia Margaret MA 1954
m Jones

MOIR William Keith BSc(agr) 1924 MA 1925
d Stracathro 23.10.67 *AUR* XLII 363

MOLLIÈRE Frédéric Herman MB ChB 1921

MOLLISON George BSc(eng) 1948
advis tech educ (Brit govt) Middle East countries Beirut, Lebanon from 1965

MOLLISON James Bain MA 1926
d 3.9.64

MOLLISON or Brind, Janet Elizabeth BSc 1937 *1938 PhD 1941
resid Harpenden

MONCRIEFF or Watson, Winifred Mary MB ChB 1947
med asst dermat Shrewsbury group hosps and Staffs central inf from 1965
m Chelsea 1950

MONCRIEFF or Fitzgerald, Zina Eveline MA 1934 MB ChB 1938
FRCP 1970
head dept paediat Royal free hosp Lond from 1971; examiner in DCH Lond from 1973

MONCUR or Taylor, Helen Ramsay MA 1934
teacher St Combs p s Fraserburgh 1956–72; head Craigo p s Montrose 1973–76; retd; resid Montrose

MONIES Thomas Harold BSc(for) 1922
d Leeds 3.8.71 *AUR* XLIV 320

MONRO Hector MA 1915
d Aber 29.10.61 *AUR* XXXIX 279

MONRO James Scott Campbell BSc 1937 MB ChB 1940
aural surg Darlington mem hosp from 1947

MONRO or Booth, Jeannie MA 1912
no longer on GC reg

MONRO or Hamilton, Margaret Webster *MA 1934
teacher Ger: Aber High s for girls 1963–70, Aber p s 1970–78
husb *d* 10.6.74

MONRO May MA 1941 MB ChB 1956 MD 1965

MONTEITH or Milne, Margaret Duncan MA 1939
teacher: Skene s s 1957–69, Bankhead acad from 1969

MONTEITH Robert Dugald MB ChB 1937
g p Chaddesley Corbett Kidderminster from 1966
d Luton 21.5.80

MONTGOMERY Donald MA 1928
retd 1968; resid Aber

MONTGOMERY George Morison MA 1928
d –.5.62

MONTGOMERY Ian Fife MA 1925
retd 1970; resid Kyle of Lochalsh
d 6.11.81

MONTGOMERY John Aitken BSc(eng) 1949
sect. head works lab Mullard Blackburn from 1969
d 15.4.80

MONTGOMERY Murdo MA 1921 BSc 1923
d 20.8.69

MOODIE James Stanley Ross BSc(agr) 1951
Balloan farm Lairg 1952–58; Rogart: Rovie farm from 1956, dairying until 1974; acquired Auchnabuach sheep farm 1967; beef and sheep from 1974

MOODIE or Shewan, Jean Isobel MA 1922
d Aber 6.2.70 *AUR* XLIII 444

MOODY or Gill, Ivy Rae MB ChB 1955
DPH(Tor) 1965 Dip Psychiat(Tor) 1970
Cert Psych 1971 Fell. Psych 1972
publ health off.: Kingston Jamaica 1962–64; Canada: north York Toronto 1965–67, resid psychiat U M Tor 1967–70; psychiat: Lakeshore psychiat hosp 1970–72, Scarborough gen hosp from 1974

MOODY Robert George Neasham *BSc 1941
teacher biol Bishop Wordsworth s Salisbury 1967–73; retd
d 1981

MOONIE or Ley, Alexandrina Jessie MA 1953

MOORE Walter BSc 1923 BSc(agr) 1924 *1925 DSc 1942
d Aber 15.4.69 *AUR* XLIII 212

MOORHOUSE or Geddes, Doris May MB ChB 1955
formerly sen m o Essex; now g p Clacton-on-Sea from 1976

MORDAUNT or Fraser, Frances Galloway *MA 1919 *1920
d 1.2.74

MORE Charles George Robb MB ChB 1943 DPH 1948
F Amer Publ Health Assoc 1964 FRSH 1965
MFCM 1973
m o h Red Deer Alberta from 1948

MORE David MA 1908
d Lond 21.6.74 *AUR* XLVI 107

MORE Isabella Main MA 1926
retd 1972; resid Aber

MORE or Weir, Katharine Ishbel Davidson MA 1943
resid Harrow-on-the-Hill

MORE William *MA 1925
d 17.1.72 *AUR* XLIV 430

MORETTI or Howitt, Lina Armida Cilinda MA 1937
resid Macduff

MORGAN Alan Douglas MA 1931 MB ChB 1935 *MD 1955
FRCPath 1964
prof path. Westminster hosp Lond from 1962

MORGAN Boyd Hepburn MA 1927 BSc 1930
JP 1959
head Dunbarney j s s Perthsh 1960–71; retd; resid Burghmuir Perth; chmn Scot. Caravan Club 1967–69, pres 1975–77

MORGAN George Roderick MB ChB 1924
d Aber 2.4.67 *AUR* XLII 363

MORGAN Henry Wright BCom 1923
MBE 1943
sen asst Harrisons & Crosfield Kuala Lumpur 1924–36; secy chamber of commerce: Kanpur UP India 1937–48, Chittagong E. Pakistan/Bangladesh 1949–55, Forth Valley Falkirk 1956–58, Canadian London England 1958–63; retd; resid Sutton
m Kanpur 24.1.48 Lorna D. Pryce d of Ernest J. P., Simla India
d 4.7.79

MORGAN James BSc(eng) 1938

MORGAN Jessie Mackenzie MA 1938
head Bramble Brae p s Aber from 1969

MORGAN John Smith *MA 1929
retd 1971; resid Aber

MORGAN Lewis MB ChB 1925
no longer on GC reg

MORGAN Mary MA 1934
secy Ladysbridge hosp Banff 1934–37; asst publ assistance off. New Pitsligo 1937–48; Scot. organis Barnardo's helpers' league 1948–58; resid Cullen

MORGAN or Taylor, Muriel Reid MA 1931
resid New Deer

MORGAN Robin Milne *MA 1952
teacher hist George Watson's coll Edin 1960–70; head Campbell coll Belf 1970–76; prin Daniel Stewart's & Melville coll & The Mary Erskine School for girls Edin from 1976

MORGAN Thomas Newall *MB ChB 1931 *MD 1934
FRCPE 1966
hon reader in med Aberd from 1959
d Aber 4.5.69 *AUR* XLIII 215 & 242

MORGAN William James BSc(eng) 1955

MORISON or Watson, Edith Minnie MA 1939
d New Pitsligo 10.4.69 *AUR* XLIII 216

MORISON Isabella MA 1930
retd 1969; resid Fraserburgh

MORISON Robert Ainslie MA 1913 LLB 1915
no longer on GC reg

MORREN William Leith MA 1908
d 31.12.63 *AUR* XLI 54

MORRICE Alexander MA 1926
retd 1968; resid Dollar

MORRICE Alexander Mackay MB ChB 1924
no longer on GC reg

MORRICE Charles Smith *MA 1954 [d]BD 1957 PhD 1959
C of S min Newarthill ch Motherwell 1959–71, St Andrew's Scots Presb ch Buenos Aires 1971–76, Mauchline from 1976

MORRICE or Davidson, Elizabeth Castle Burnett MA 1927

MORRICE George MB ChB 1936
g p Salford; retd 1973

MORRICE Helen Imlach BSc 1929 MA 1930
d Aber 18.8.75 *AUR* XLVI 323

MORRICE James Kenneth Watt MB ChB 1946 MD 1954
FRCPsych 1972
consult. Fort Logan Mental health center Denver USA 1966–67; consult. psychiat Ross clin Aber/clin sen lect Aberd from 1968

MORRICE James Wilson BL 1947
farm. Torphins 1966–78; retd

MORRICE John MB ChB 1930
retd 1973; resid Salford

MORRICE Maggie Jane MA 1923
d 6.2.63

MORRICE or Carswell, Margaret Christian MA 1924
resid Edin
d Edin 17.9.77

MORRICE Margaret Christina MA 1947
no longer on GC reg

MORRICE William MA 1920 BD 1921
d Motherwell 13.1.71 *AUR* XLIV 210

MORRICE William Gorman *MA 1951 BD 1954 PhD 1957
C of S min: Auchterarder 1957–65, Motherwell 1965–70; NT advis Brit and foreign Bible soc Lond from 1970; NT lect New coll Lond from 1972; NT tut. and lib. St Jns coll Durham from 1975

MORRIS Alexander George BSc 1953
ptnr pharm Colchester 1963–69; pharm prop. Colchester and West Mersea from 1969
m 16.9.61 Moira T. Peacock pharm dispenser d of Andrew R. P. Farnborough

MORRIS Andrew Bernard MB ChB 1903
no longer on GC reg

MORRIS Brian Taylor Jordan BSc(eng) 1954
MIEE C Eng 1971 MIWES 1975
applications eng AEI Trafford Park Manc 1958–61; sen tendering eng (contr) dept Harland eng Alloa 1961–66; sen proj and contr eng James Howden & Co Glasg 1967–73; elect./mech eng Lanarksh water board Hamilton 1973–75; div mech/elect. eng Strathclyde reg c water dept lower Clyde div from 1975

MORRIS James Pressley *MA 1954

MORRIS William Drummond MA 1891
no longer on GC reg

MORRIS William James MA 1923
FEIS 1960
retd 1965; resid Aber

MORRISON Adeline Isobel BCom 1935
retd; resid Lond
d Stonehaven 30.9.77

MORRISON or Allan, Agnes Whitelaw MB ChB 1942
resid Cheltenham

MORRISON Alexander *MA 1899 *BSc 1899
no longer on GC reg

MORRISON Alexander MA 1912
no longer on GC reg

MORRISON Alexander BSc(for) 1951

MORRISON Alexander James *MA 1909 DD 1955
d 29.1.64 *AUR* XL 396

MORRISON or Donald, Alice Barbara MA 1927
retd 1970; resid Aber
d Aber 30.8.79

MORRISON or Law, Alice Jean MA 1943
d Stevenston 5.1.76

MORRISON or Gibson, Ann MA 1917
teacher maths Golspie s s 1951–63; retd
d Golspie 13.4.81

MORRISON or Currier, Ann *BSc 1927
retd 1966; resid Inv

MORRISON or Morrison, Annie MA 1945

MORRISON Archibald MB ChB 1952
h o ARI 1952–53; nat serv RAMC 1953–55; regist: psychiat Oldham 1955–57, ARI 1957–58; sen regist psychiat de la Pole hosp Willerby, E Yorks 1958–62; consult. psychiat Fife from 1962
m Gatley 12.6.58 Ruth Goodier MB ChB(Manc) med pract/regist paediat d of James W. G. Cheadle

MORRISON Audrey Elizabeth MA 1948
teacher Surrey: Engl commonwealth girls' s Purley 1963–66, prin Engl Court Lodge s s Horley 1966–73, Engl Sutton Common h s Sutton 1973–76, prin Engl Sutton Common h s from 1976

MORRISON Catherine MA 1955 Dip Ed 1956 *MEd 1967
educ psych Aber 1967–71; lect educ psych Callendar Park coll of educ Falkirk 1972–76; part time lect psych univ Hong Kong from 1977
m Bearsden 22.6.74 William J. Greig BSc 1948 *qv*

MORRISON or Grant, Catherine Mary MA 1933
teacher Fr Rubislaw acad/AGS from 1967
d Aber 21.11.80 *AUR* XLIX 68

MORRISON Charles Albert *MA 1950
MA(Oxon) 1965
asst lect laws S'ton 1953–54; asst lect/sen lect/sub-dean of fac of laws King's coll Lond 1954–68; dean of fac Inns of Court s of law Council of Leg. Educ Lond from 1968; QC 1977
m Calverton 19.12.59 Elizabeth A. Coales catering man. d of Reginald C. Timaru NZ

MORRISON Colin George MA 1935
Dumfries h s: prin teacher maths 1964–72, asst head 1972–73, dep head from 1973

MORRISON Donald MA 1916
retd 1964; resid Croy Invsh
d Croy 24.5.79

MORRISON Douglas BSc(agr) 1944
head crop husb dept s of agr Aber/part time lect Aberd 1968–71; chmn crop prod. group s of agr Aber/part time sen lect Aberd from 1972

MORRISON Douglas Bannerman BSc 1927 MA 1928
d Chapel-en-le-Frith Manc 10.5.73 *AUR* XLV 320

MORRISON Edith Jane Douglas *MA 1909
d Bath 16.7.64 *AUR* XL 396

MORRISON or Little, Elizabeth Ann MB ChB 1944
dept m o Redbridge Lond from 1965

MORRISON Eric Elmslie *MA 1940
FIMA 1967
Aberd: sen lect maths from 1969; edit. *AUR* from 1969; member univ court 1968–79; convener bus. comm General Council from 1979

MORRISON Eric Keir *MA 1936
FIL 1951
reg army off. 1940–60; prin lect Ger Bristol polytech 1960–78; retd

MORRISON or Davidson, Ethel MA 1943
Aber: teacher Lat h s for girls 1965–73, prin classics St. Margaret's s for girls from 1973
m diss 1976

MORRISON Frank Tregear BSc(for) 1948
d 17.6.67

MORRISON George Clark MA 1930
retd HMIS 1972; reg commun dev off. Grampian reg Scot. council of soc serv Edin from 1973
wife *d* 17.6.81

MORRISON George Will MB ChB 1945
MRCGP 1957
g p Inverbervie from 1951

MORRISON or Henderson, Helen Shepherd MA 1929
resid Maryculter

MORRISON Henry Philip MA 1912
FCBA 1914 FSA 1926
resid Illinois USA

MORRISON Ian Middleton MB ChB 1944
consult. thoracic surg Liv from 1958

MORRISON or Finlayson, Isabella MA 1934
teacher N Tolsta p s Is of Lewis 1958–72; retd; resid Stornoway

MORRISON Isobel Milne MA 1925 *BSc 1925
retd 1967; resid Juniper Green Edin

MORRISON James BSc(agr) 1924
OBE 1963
prof crop/anim husb Belf and dir agr res inst of N Ireland Hillsborough Co Down 1945–65; retd

MORRISON James Alexander MA 1905
d Aber 20.4.63 *AUR* XL 198

MORRISON James Dey MA 1939
TD 1966 JP Aber 1971
comm 51(H) div regt RCT(TA) h q Perth 1963–67; brevet col on relinquishing comm of reg 1967; head Walker Rd p s from 1967; dist comm Dee dist city of Aber scout assoc 1967–73; retd

MORRISON James Gilbert MA 1937
chap. to the Forces 1942–70; min of the Community ch Nicosia Cyprus 1971–72; min of the Scots ch Rotterdam Neths from 1972

MORRISON James Macdonald MB ChB 1917
d 5.9.68 *AUR* XLIII 79

MORRISON or Thomson, Jane Ann MA 1935

MORRISON or Mackie, Jean Bruce MA 1928
resid N. Berwick

MORRISON or Simmers, Jean Robertson MA 1937
teacher Kintore 1962–77; retd

MORRISON or Brockie, Jeanette *MA 1941
d Northland NZ 17.3.63
husb *d* Northland NZ 1.3.71

MORRISON Jeannie Marr MA 1927
d Aberdeensh 27.11.68 *AUR* XLIII 84

MORRISON Jessie Ann MA 1930
teacher: Engl/hist/geog Ordiquhill j s s Banff 1932–47, geog/woman advis Macduff h s 1947–69, geog house mistress Banff acad 1969–73; retd; resid Macduff

MORRISON or Macleod, Jessie Mary MA 1911
d 25.12.70

MORRISON John MA 1915 MB ChB 1918 DPH 1921 MD 1932
d Shrewsbury 8.2.68 *AUR* XLII 354

MORRISON John *MA 1936
teacher Aber Lond Glasg
killed in road accident 7.7.53

MORRISON John MB ChB 1939
g p Portree from 1952; med supt Portree hosp from 1965

MORRISON John Alexander *BSc(eng) 1940
civ eng contr ag Aber from 1940
m Glasg 11.4.62 Mary C. J. Graham MA(Glas) teacher d of Thomas L. G. Glasg

MORRISON John Edgar BSc 1955
food tech Rothamsted res stat 1958–64; dir res and quality assur Quaker Aust from 1964

MORRISON John James Todd MB ChB 1937 DPH 1939 MD 1947
d 15.8.73

MORRISON John Peter *BSc 1948
FInstP 1966
div man. Aircraft Marine Prod. (GB) Parkstone Dorset 1960–68; man. dir Cochrane & Johnson Paisley 1968–72, consult. from 1972

MORRISON or Morrice, Katharine Jean MA 1954
resid Mill Hill Lond

MORRISON or Kennedy, Kathleen Montgomery MA 1955

MORRISON or Hadden, Kathleen Murray MB ChB 1945
g p Aber from 1957

MORRISON Kenneth James BSc(eng) 1942
elect. supt BICC Wrexham N Wales from 1968

MORRISON or Jennings, Leona Adolphus MA 1927
teacher: Coventry 1953–55, Aber 1955–57, asst

head Middlefield p s Aber 1957–59, Aber 1959–66, retd; resid Aber
d 23.10.81

MORRISON Lewis BSc(agr) 1921
d 25.3.68

MORRISON Margaret MA 1937

MORRISON Margaret MA 1942

MORRISON Margaret MA 1953 LLB 1955
leg. asst: Paull & Williamsons advoc Aber/Dundas & Wilson solic Edin 1958–65; resid Saxilby
m Aber 15.2.65 David M. Shewan BA(Cantab) med pract s of Henry A. S. MA 1928 *qv*

MORRISON or Innes, Margaret Barbara BSc(agr) 1943
resid Aber

MORRISON or Thomson, Margaret Garden MB ChB 1944
Founder Fell. Brit Soc Med & Dent Hypnosis FRSM
g p Cullen 1948–58, Southport Lancs 1963–64; locum cas off. Westmorland and N Lancs 1964–67; asst m o coll of educ Aber from 1967
m Southport 14.12.62 Thomas W. Quigley

MORRISON Margaret Hall MA 1939
teacher Newmachar p s from 1957

MORRISON or Simpson, Margaret Jane MA 1953

MORRISON or MacKintosh, Margaret Jane Barclay MA 1934
teacher: St Peter's epis s Fraserburgh 1959–61, Fraserburgh North s 1961–64; spec s Fraserburgh 1964–69, Denend p s Cardenden 1969–77; retd; resid Glenrothes

MORRISON Margaret Leith MA 1953
teacher geog/Engl Inverurie acad 1961–64; credit advis Hudson Bay Co, Victoria BC Canada 1964–66; writer of ch's books
m Victoria BC –.11.65 Robert J. Minter supervis of construct. for Greater Victoria s board s of Francis R. M. Victoria BC

MORRISON or Williams, Margaret McLean Macfarlane MB ChB 1933
lect anat univ of Wales (Univ Coll Cardiff) 1963–76, sen lect from 1976

MORRISON Marion MA 1925
retd 1964; resid Bath

MORRISON or Watson, Marjorie Elizabeth BSc 1946
resid Shrewsbury

MORRISON Marjory Watson MA 1942

MORRISON or Brownlee, Mary Dempster BSc 1953

MORRISON Mary Gordon *MA 1935
sen lect Fr univ Brist from 1963; retd 1977

MORRISON Mary Macleod MA 1953
teacher Stornoway from 1960
m Aber 31.3.62 David D. MacKenzie draper s of Donald G. MacK. Stornoway

MORRISON Murdo MA 1901
d Troon 11.4.75 *AUR* XLVI 320

MORRISON or Whitelaw, Nettie MA 1951

MORRISON Norman *MA 1923
d Kirkcaldy 17.1.71 *AUR* XLIV 211

MORRISON Roy BSc(agr) 1953
Belf: sales man. BOCM 1965–70, man. dir Assoc Agr Merchants 1970–75; Cambridge: reg man. United Agr Merchants from 1975

MORRISON Sheila Catherine MA 1953
teacher: Walker Rd p s Aber from 1954

MORRISON Stephen Duncan MA 1948
dep head: Woodside p s Aber 1961–66, Springhill p s Aber from 1966

MORRISON Susan Hay MA 1925
prin teacher Engl/lady supt Bankhead acad 1961–68; retd; resid Turriff

MORRISON Thomas Affleck MA BSc(agr) 1923 MB ChB 1931
retd 1967; resid Brighton
wife *d* 17.10.67

MORRISON Thomas Ian BSc 1950 *1951
MSc(Glas) 1973 FRIC 1968 TD 1969
lect chem Jordanhill coll of educ Glasg 1963–70; asst rector Brechin h s 1971–74; advis sec educ Angus div Tayside reg from 1974
major 2 i/c 153(H) regt royal corps of transport, T and AVR, Dunfermline; rtd brevet lieut colonel 1971
pres Scot. Hockey Assoc 1974–76
m Stirling 16.4.73 Isabel C. Forgan MA(St And) lect Jordanhill coll of educ d of Robert F. Stirling

MORRISON or Reith, Violet Margaret MA 1938

MORRISON William MA 1939
leading seaman RN 1939–46; teacher: Chiltern St Boys' s Hull 1946–52; Hornsea s Yorks: head Engl dept/housemaster 1952–58, sen housemaster 1969–75, head of middle s from 1975
m Hull 10.2.44 Phyllis M. Hutchinson SRN d of Frederick A. H. Hull

MORTIMER or Forbes, Dorothy Elizabeth MA 1953
teacher: Brit army s Singapore 1959–60, Naracoorte S Aust 1962–66, Oak Farm p s Hillingdon Mddsx 1966–68; Melb Aust: emergency teacher/volunteer crippled ch kindergarten from 1973; resid Melb Aust

MORTIMER or McConnachie, Dorothy Isabel MB ChB 1938
med asst psychiat Penyval hosp Monmouthsh from 1969

MORTIMER or Ironside, Dorothy Norris MB ChB 1953 DPH 1956
MFCM 1973
h o RACH/Halifax hosp 1953–54; sen h o Southmead hosp Bristol 1954–56; j h m o Slade hosp for infect. diseases 1956–60; dep m o h Thanet 1960–64; sen clin m o and dep m o h Tunbridge Wells from 1964

MORTIMER Douglas MB ChB 1948

MORTIMER or Troup, Elizabeth Campbell MA 1898
d Aber 28.12.73 *AUR* XLV 444

MORTIMER Gordon William James MA 1948 *BSc 1951 BD 1960
C of S min Thurso W parish ch 1961–64; spec teacher relig educ Brechin h s from 1965
m Careston 6.10.73 Catherine M. Sefton BSc(St And) teacher d of George A. S. MA 1921 *qv*

MORTIMER Hector MB ChB 1914

MORTIMER John Burnett *MA 1950
d 18.6.62

MORTIMER Margaret Forbes MA 1912
retd; resid Peterhead

MORTIMER or Allan, Margaret McWilliam Milne MA 1946

MORTIMER or Mackie, Mary Pirie MA 1924
retd 1964; resid Edin

MORTIMER or Brown, Muriel Margaret MA 1946
teacher: Aboyne till 1960, Turriff p s from 1972

MORTIMER William *MA 1941
chief acct Standard Life Assur Co Edin from 1970

MORTON or Demaine, Barbara Reid Alexander MB ChB 1922
d Wigan 1.3.70 *AUR* XLIV 110

MORTON (formerly di Veri) Charles Bertie *MA 1920
retd 1971; resid Ladysmith, Natal

MORTON Richard Grenfell *MEd 1951
lect hist dept extra-mural stud. Queen's univ Belf from 1967

MOSS Francis John BSc 1953

MOUAT or Scott, Joanna Mary Isobel MA 1927
no longer on GC reg

MOUAT John Stephen Veitch MB ChB 1950
d 21.12.67

MOUAT Stephen James Veitch MB ChB 1926
d Dumfries 14.3.75 *AUR* XLVI 236

MOULI Kalluri Chandra BSc(agr) 1924

MOWAT Alexander Goodsir MB ChB 1924
retd 1965; resid Ashton-u-Hill, nr Evesham

MOWAT Brenda *MA 1947
teacher: prin mod lang Kirkwall g s from 1955

MOWAT Donald Arthur Edward MB ChB 1953
MRCGP 1970
g p: Newtyle 1963–65, Montrose from 1965

MOWAT or Ross, Esther Margaret MA 1928
Alloa: temp teaching posts various s then Lornshill acad Grange sect./Forebraes 1950–70; retd; resid Aber
husb *d* 7.11.64

MOWAT or Leslie, Esther Mary MA 1946
teacher: Anstruther Wester s 1963–69, Cellardyke 1969–72; teacher Engl Waid acad from 1972

MOWAT George MB ChB 1898
d Bolton 22.1.61 *AUR* XXXIX 198

MOWAT George Nicol Garson MA 1928
retd 1968; resid Mansfield

MOWAT James Lawson *MA 1922 PhD 1927
chief admin div ILO Geneva 1960–64; retd; resid Geneva

MOWAT or Philip, Jane Fowler Sim MA 1950
teacher Kineff p s 1951–53, Portlethen p s 1953–54, Gatehouse p s Kirkcudbright 1954, Crossford p s Fife 1959–62, Edin 1962–64, Glasg 1964–68, Edin from 1968

MOWAT John *MB ChB 1942
d Dun 10.1.72 *AUR* XLIV 433

MOWAT John BSc 1952
d Aber 19.4.66 *AUR* XLII 90

MOWAT Lesley Anderson MA 1938 LLB 1941

MOWAT or Stirling, Marion Elizabeth MB ChB 1921
d Edin 27.10.73

MOWAT or Munro, Mora Jean MA 1950
teacher Kiltearn p s Evanton 1967–73

MOWAT Robert Philip MA 1934 BCom 1936
prin teacher econ/bus. stud. RGC Aber from 1944; retd 1978

MOWAT Ronald Rae MB ChB 1950 MD 1959
DPM(Lond) 1956
consult. psychiat Brighton & Hove SE metrop reg hosp board Royal Sussex County hosp Brighton/Lady Chichester hosp Hove and E. Sussex ch's dept from 1960
author *Morbid Jealousy and Murder* 1966

MOWAT William Paton *BSc 1954

MOWATT Thomas Douglas *MA 1927 *MEd 1929
teacher Engl/hist Glenluce s s 1952–65; retd; resid Newton Stewart
d Dumfries –.9.80 *AUR* XLIX 68

MUIR Agnes Gibson MA 1954

MUIR or Maclean, Annie Elizabeth MA 1930

MUIR Charles Mackenzie BCom 1923

MUIR Colin *BSc 1955 PhD 1959
lect nat hist dept St And

MUIR Duncan McNicol MA 1948
Aber: dep head Kittybrewster p s 1962–67, head Seaton p s from 1967
wife *d* Jan. 1970
m (2) Inverurie 6.8.71 Elizabeth M. Cook ward sister d of Alexander C. Kemnay
d Aber 18.8.79 *AUR* XLVIII 354

MUIRDEN John Robert MA 1937
d Rosskeen Alness 21.8.68 *AUR* XLIII 85

MULCAHY Maurice Joseph BSc(for) 1949
scient off. Macaulay inst soil res Aber 1949–53; Australia res scient CSIRO: Adelaide 1953–54, Perth from 1954

MULHOLLAND William Hamilton BSc(for) 1949

MULLER Ernst Robert BSc(eng) 1940
MICE 1971 MIMH 1971 F Inst Pet 1972
prop. bakery eng firm from 1947; now gen eng and oil field eng from 1972

MULLICK Dwijendra Nath PhD 1939

MULLIGAN Hugh Waddell MB ChB 1923 *MD 1930 DSc 1934
CMG 1954
dir Wellcome res lab Beckenham 1960–66; visiting lect univ of Salford 1967–76

MULLIGAN James Anderson MB ChB 1925
g p Inverbervie 1928–67; retd; resid Cadnam Southampton

MULLIGAN John Henry *MB ChB 1920
lect histology and neurology St And 1949–60; retd; resid Edzell

MULLIGAN or McManus, Kathleen Marie MA 1955
resid Dun

MULLIGAN Malachi Finn-Barr MA 1949 LLB 1952

MULLIGAN William Percival *MB ChB 1913

MUNDAY Kenneth Albert PhD 1949

MUNDIE John Harold *BSc 1949

MUNDIE Sheila Margaret *MA 1950

MUNN James Marshall MB ChB 1954
g p Stirling from 1966
m Stepps 26.5.67 Fiona M. Anderson comm artist d of John M. A. Stepps

MUNRO Alexander Fraser BSc 1934 *1935 PhD 1941

MUNRO Alexander John MA 1953
teacher: prin Engl Auchterarder 1966–68; head: Stanley p s 1968–73, Robert Douglas mem s Scone from 1973

MUNRO or Skarda, Annabelle Farquharson MA 1924
teacher: Edin 1949–56, York 1961–67, Aber 1968–73; retd

MUNRO Anne Morrison *MA 1921
retd 1961; resid Edin

MUNRO Annie Stark MA 1930

MUNRO or Booth, Charlotte Annie MA 1931
resid Dumfries

MUNRO Christine McCulloch MA 1926

MUNRO Colin Ross MA 1910
d Castlecary 28.3.61 *AUR* XXXIX 201

MUNRO Donald MA 1907
retd 1949; resid Lochmaben
d 9.1.78

MUNRO Donald MA 1922 LLB 1924
retd 1968; resid Purley

MUNRO Donald George BSc(agr) 1915
d Tain 13.5.74

MUNRO Donald Gunn MA 1912 BSc 1913
d Brora –.3.71 *AUR* XLIV 209

MUNRO Donald Sinclair MB ChB 1947 ᶜMD 1957
FRCP(Lond)
univ of Sheffield: reader clin endocrinology 1963–67, prof clin endocrinology 1967–73, Sir Arthur Hall prof of med from 1973

MUNRO or Meston, Dorothea *MA 1953
teacher mod lang Queen's Park s s Glasg 1959–60, Powis acad Aber from 1976

MUNRO Dorothy Margaret MA 1915
deceased

MUNRO or Mitchell, Elizabeth Gray BL 1934
d Torquay 22.3.73 *AUR* XLV 227

MUNRO or Cowie, Eva Jean MA 1951
teacher: Engl Powis j s s Aber 1951–58, Engl Kaimhill j s s Aber 1959–60, Fr Aber acad 1968–69, Rubislaw acad Aber from 1969
m 29.3.58 Gordon F. G. Cowie MA 1972 teacher s of James B. C. Aldershot

MUNRO or Mitchell, Evelyn Jane Morrison MA 1928
resid Cults Aber

MUNRO George Francis MA 1897
no longer on GC reg

MUNRO George Gauld BSc(eng) 1945

MUNRO Harry William MA 1926 BSc 1929
retd 1969; resid Kinghorn

MUNRO or MacLean, Hilda Margaret Lind BSc 1929
resid Inv

MUNRO Hugh MA 1924
resid supervis Craibstone coll Aber NOSCA 1960–67; retd; resid Montrose

MUNRO Hugh David Ross MB ChB 1955
MRCOG 1972
g p Crosshills 1962–67, g p hosp practitioner (obst/gyn) conjoint appt Livingston New Town and Bangour gen hosp from 1967

MUNRO Ian Mackenzie MB ChB 1929
resid Lond SW15

MUNRO Irene MA 1954 Dip Ed 1955
teacher Engl: Perth h s 1955–60, Dunbarney j s s 1960–62, Kinross s s from 1969
m Aber 16.7.60 Iain A. Robertson MA(Dund) teacher f e s of George R. Perth

MUNRO James MA 1948
teacher various schools Aber 1949–77; retd from prin maths Linksfield acad

MUNRO James John MB ChB 1924
no longer on GC reg

MUNRO James Scott Gray BL 1939
MBE 1964
ptnr Stephen & Smith advoc Aber from 1946; DL for County of City of Aber from 1964; DL for County of Aber from 1973

MUNRO Jessie Barbara MA 1931

MUNRO Jessie May MA 1930
inf mistress Elgin W End s 1959–72, asst head from 1972

MUNRO Joan BSc(agr) 1950 PhD 1954
sen scient off. Hill Farming Organis 1959–61
m Inv 8.6.61 Michael T. Fotheringham farm. s of Alfred F. Laurencekirk

MUNRO John George MB ChB 1938
FRCGP 1972
g p Beauly from 1946

MUNRO John George Clarke *BSc 1947 MB ChB 1954
g p Nambour Queensland Aust 1963–76; sen lect commun pract univ Queensland med s from 1976

MUNRO or Cran, Margaret Campbell MA 1947
resid Falkirk
husb *d* 27.1.71

MUNRO or Cox, Margaret Isabel BSc 1951
exper off. MAFF 1951–59; physiol Epsom dist hosp Surrey from 1973

MUNRO or Wilson, Margaret Tennant MA 1925
Canada: teacher Athlone boys' s Vancouver 1963–64, remed for London (Ont) board of educ 1964–70; retd
husb *d* 7.11.54

MUNRO or Keith, Mary Bella MA 1929

MUNRO Murray MA 1944

MUNRO Neil BCom 1931
free-lance journalist *Daily Express/Evening Standard/Daily Mail* Lond 1958–65; tax. off. Inl Rev and free-lance journalist *Evening Standard* Shoreham-by-Sea from 1965; retd from civ serv 1977; secy/treas Royal Brit Legion Shoreham
m Lond 20.6.49 Andree G. J. Taylor d of Herbert T. major RASC

MUNRO Norman Morrison MB ChB 1925 ᶜMD 1931
retd 1972; resid Luton
d Luton 27.12.77 *AUR* XLVII 356

MUNRO or McGregor, Rachel Catherine MA 1916
d 16.4.69

MUNRO Robert MB ChB 1915
no longer on GC reg

MUNRO or Ross, Robina MA 1918
d 9.4.79

MUNRO Roderick Alexander MA 1948 *MEd 1951
FEIS 1971
Aber: dep head Kirkhill p s 1960–65, head Victoria Rd p s from 1965

MUNRO Ronald MA 1929
no longer on GC reg

MUNRO Stewart Sinclair Fowler MB ChB 1945
consult. ophth surg to Herefordsh and Radnor group of hosps from 1960

MUNRO or Adan or Matheson, Winifred Davidson MA 1926
d Aber 22.2.73

MUNRO-FERGUSON Arthur Brocklehurst Luttrell BSc(for) 1951
resid Evanton

MURCHISON or Blues, Catherine MA 1924
teacher Inv 1925–28; resid Dalkeith

MURDOCH or Day, Elizabeth Helen McRobert MA 1944
resid Stockport

MURDOCH Eric BSc(eng) 1954
MICE 1960
sen asst eng: Inv c c 1966–67, Aber c c 1967–71; chief asst eng Aber c c 1971–75, chief asst eng Grampian reg c from 1975
m Inv 29.9.61 Mary A. M. Gillies asst matron d of Donald G. Portree

MURDOCH George Clark *MA 1952
dist off. Tanganyika 1955–61; teacher: Dollar acad 1962–64, Daniel Stewart's coll Edin 1964–68; prin mod lang Fraserburgh acad 1968–76; asst rector Elgin acad from 1976

MURDOCH or Semmence, Henrietta Scorgie MA 1919
d Galashiels 7.2.77

MURDOCH Ian Martin Calder BSc 1951
1978 Brit patent no 1507899
teacher maths/sc Methlick j s s 1961–64; retd

MURDOCH or Alderson, Jessie Elliott MA 1904
d 1977 *AUR* XLVII 286

MURDOCH John Henry MB ChB 1944
g p Vancouver from 1951

MURDOCH or Simpson, Lizzie Jane MA 1919
d Colchester 10.6.68 *AUR* XLIII 80

MURDOCH or Henderson, Marguerita Bridgeford MA 1953
teacher: supply Kincardine 1967–74, Arduthie p s Stonehaven from 1974

MURDOCH or Simmons, Marjorie Henry MA 1946
inf teacher Lothian reg Edin from 1974

MURDOCH or Imlach, Moyra Isobel MA 1947
sub-post mistress Lintmill Cullen 1964–65; teacher Portsoy from 1965

MURDOCH Sophie Allardyce Farquharson MA 1907
d Banff 30.4.76 *AUR* XLVI 414

MURDOCH Thomas Henderson MA 1930
spec in spoken Engl Roxburghsh s 1962–72; head of div for English as an acquired lang Engl-speaking board from 1972; resid Hants

MURISON Alfred Ross *MA 1912 *1914 *1919 LLD 1951
d Glasg 21.2.68 *AUR* XLII 351

MURISON Charles Alexander *MA 1929
F Inst P 1944
sen lect med physics Edin 1968–72; retd
wife *d* 18.2.75

MURISON Charles Fraser MB ChB 1939
d St Anne's on Sea 19.12.70 *AUR* XLIV 215

MURISON David Donald *MA 1933
resid Fraserburgh

MURISON or Taylor, Dorothy MA 1955
resid Peterhead

MURISON Helen Ross MA 1943
teacher: p s Aberdeensh 1945–55, Roxburghsh 1955–57, Toronto 1958–61; study in France 1961–63; teacher Fr: Lyng Hall Coventry 1963–65, Sutherland House s Cromer Norfolk 1965–71; retd; secy

MURISON James Fraser BSc(eng) 1945
sen stressman Hunting Aircraft (Airframes) 1960–61; stress off. airborne radar div EMI Hayes from 1961

MURPHY Helen Burgess MA 1933

MURPHY Peter Alexander *MA 1955 MEd 1958
prin teacher Engl Summerhill acad Aber 1965–71; head Logie s s Dun 1971–75; rector Whitfield h s Dun from 1976
m Aber 7.8.61 Margaret J. Christie chem d of John C. Keig

MURPHY Vincent John MB ChB 1953

MURPHY William Turnbull *BSc 1954

MURRAY or Ogilvie, Agnes Davidson MA 1924
no longer on GC reg

MURRAY Alexander James MA 1949
M of H 1949–59; dept chem Surr 1963–68; microbiol dept nutrit and food sc Westminster tech coll from 1968; resid Sutton

MURRAY Alexander John Robertson *BSc 1943 PhD 1949
ICI plastics div Thornton Lancs: plant man. 1961–64, sect. man. 1964–69, asst works man. 1969–71; dep gen man. plastics div ICI Europa Brussels 1971–77; works oper man. ICI Holland BV from 1977

MURRAY Alexander McPherson *BSc 1953 PhD 1956

MURRAY Alfred Edward BSc(eng) 1933

MURRAY or Mackenzie, Alice Annand *MA 1905 *BSc 1906
no longer on GC reg

MURRAY or Hugo, Alison Elisabeth BSc 1946
teacher: Kitwe N Rhodesia later Zambia, 1950–68, s s Aber from 1968

MURRAY Andrew John MB ChB 1922
d Littlehampton 26.7.60 *AUR* XXXIX 105

MURRAY Angus McKay MA 1907
no longer on GC reg

MURRAY Angus Sutherland MA 1948
d Aber 26.2.81

MURRAY Arthur Farquhar MB ChB 1937
no longer on GC reg

MURRAY Campbell MB ChB 1955
MRCPE 1965 MRCGP 1966
m o stud. health serv Aberd 1960–67, chief m o 1967–74, reg m o SHHD from 1974

MURRAY Charles Mitchell Macquibban MB ChB 1931
prof orthop surg Ahmadu Bello univ Kano Nigeria 1971–74; retd; resid Hayling Is, Hants

MURRAY Charles Peter MB ChB 1924
d 14.4.67 *AUR* XLII 363

MURRAY or Duff, Chrissy Isobel MA 1920
retd 1964; resid Torphins

MURRAY Donald Roderick MB ChB 1950

MURRAY Douglas Dalgarno BSc(eng) 1933

MURRAY Duncan MB ChB 1954
LMCC 1970 Cert Coll Fam Pract 1971
g p Hinton Alberta from 1957

MURRAY Edward George Morrison MA 1914
d 8.11.64 *AUR* XLI 56

MURRAY Ellis Edward Paul BSc 1934 *MB ChB 1937
consult: surg Portsmouth group hosps 1951–71; retd; resid Eastbourne
d Eastbourne 7.4.81 *AUR* XLIX 138

MURRAY Eric Taylor MB ChB 1944
consult. gen surg Basildon and Orsett hosps from 1960; resid Brentwood

MURRAY Ethel Macgregor *MA 1915
d 26.4.72

MURRAY Frank MB ChB 1938

MURRAY George *MA 1931
d Haddington 31.5.69 *AUR* XLIII 215

MURRAY George *MA 1936

MURRAY George Alexander MA 1910
d Aber 14.4.61 *AUR* XXXIX 201

MURRAY George Alexander MA 1930
no longer on GC reg

MURRAY Gordon Souter BSc(eng) 1945
MIME 1979
reg marine market. man. indust and marine div Rolls Royce Coventry from 1970

MURRAY Helen Taylor Kippen BSc 1926
retd 1970; resid Laurencekirk

MURRAY Hugh Alexander *MA 1929
d Wellington NZ 17.10.73 *AUR* XLV 448

MURRAY or Reid, Irene Brown MA 1944

MURRAY or Henderson, Isabel Bisset *MA 1955
MA PhD(Cantab) 1963 FSA Scot
asst keeper nat lib of Scot. 1966–74, asst lib off. Camb univ lib from 1975

MURRAY or Budge, Isabella Marion Hodgson MB ChB 1921
resid Towcester

MURRAY Isobel Alice *MA 1934
BA(Lond) 1967 Dip St Colm's Missionary Coll, Edin
teacher Fr/Lat Lossiemouth 1935–36; sen classics mistress Albyn s for girls Aber 1936–37; i/c s for C of S Poona/Madras/Arkonam India 1938–44; sen classics mistress Cranley s Edin 1945–47; tut. Paterson's coll Edin 1947–49; sen classics mistress: Ackworth s Yorks/Stratford s Lond/Skinners Company's s Lond 1949–67; teacher Fr/Russian Aber h s for girls 1967–73; retd

MURRAY James *MA 1926
C of S min St Brides Newtonmore 1962–75; retd; resid Whiterashes

MURRAY James Durno *MB ChB 1923
d Hamilton NZ 14.7.64 *AUR* XLI 57

MURRAY James Greig MB ChB 1942 ChM 1961
FRCS(Eng) 1966
prof surg Lond/hon consult. surg King's coll hosp Lond from 1964; member Senate Univ of Lond; member SE Thames reg health auth

MURRAY James John Christie MA 1934 Dip Ed 1961
head: Woodlands p s Durris 1962–68, Midmar s 1968–73; retd; resid Banchory

MURRAY James Robbie Duncan MA 1935 LLB 1938
secy White Fish Auth Edin from 1973
d Kinross 28.12.79 *AUR* XLVIII 442

MURRAY James Robertson MB ChB 1911 *MD 1914 DPH 1919
d Lond 19.6.72 *AUR* XLV 124

MURRAY James Stannard BSc(for) 1949
FIF
Aberd: sen lect for. 1961–73, reader from 1973

MURRAY Jane Elizabeth BSc 1926
teacher prin maths Lond 1926–28; temp head Glenfoudland p s Aberdeensh 1928–31; teacher maths/sc Montrose 1942–45, 1948–52, 1957–58; head: Clochcan p s Aberdeensh 1945–48, Inch p s/Cookney p s Kincardine 1952–57, Whittinghame E. Lothian 1958–64; retd; resid Haddington
m Huntly 21.6.31 John W. Mackie farm./estate off. s of Alexander M. Glenfoudland

MURRAY Jean MA 1918
d Edin 1.11.73 *AUR* XLV 447

MURRAY Jessie MA 1901
d 9.7.69

MURRAY John *MA 1900 LLD 1930
d Lond 28.12.64 *AUR* XLI 53

MURRAY John MB ChB 1907

MURRAY John MA 1922
no longer on GC reg

MURRAY John MA 1939

MURRAY John MA 1951
Is of Lewis: dep head Bayble j s s 1960–71, head Tolsta p s from 1971

MURRAY John Kerr *MA 1924
retd 1962; resid Nottingham

MURRAY John Paton MA 1919
no longer on GC reg

MURRAY John William *MA 1923
retd 1957
d Knaresborough 7.1.67 *AUR* XLII 360

MURRAY or Smith, Kathleen Marjory Fletcher MB ChB 1945
d 30.10.76 *AUR* XLVII 214

MURRAY Kathleen Taylor Finnie *MA 1936

MURRAY Kenneth Alexander George *MA 1938 *MEd 1949
civ serv selection board: chief psych 1951–63, dir from 1963; resid Leatherhead
m Aber 4.4.42 Elizabeth W. Simpson soc worker d of Arthur S. Aber

MURRAY Malcolm Gordon MB ChB 1931
g p unit Queen Elizabeth II hosp Welwyn Garden City

MURRAY Malcolm Murdo MA 1929
retd 1971; resid Stornoway

MURRAY or Banka, Margaret Harvey MA 1932
d Regina Canada 18.9.70 *AUR* XLIV 110

MURRAY or Fraser, Margaret Helen Sim MA 1943
resid Aber

MURRAY Margaret Isabell *MA 1918
resid Laggan Newtonmore

MURRAY or Horne, Margaret Jamieson MA 1923
resid Blackpool
husb *d* –.9.65

MURRAY or Gardiner, Mary *MA 1948

MURRAY Mary Adams Bisset MB ChB 1955
regist anaest: Lambeth hosp Lond 1959–62, Aber 1962–67; med asst anaest Royal Alexandra Inf Paisley 1967–79; asst anaest Perth RI from 1979
m Aber 22.8.62 William B. R. Macmillan MA 1951 *qv*

MURRAY or MacIver, Mary Sutherland MA 1923

MURRAY May Forbes MA 1929
Aber: inf mistress St Margaret's epis p s 1953–59, Hanover St p s 1960–65, Walker Rd p s 1965–71; retd
d Aber 15.3.78

MURRAY Moira MA 1948
teacher Tarves p s from 1949
m Aber 4.4.60 James Massie market gardener s of George M. Tarves

MURRAY Murdo MA 1913
d Strathpeffer 30.5.64

MURRAY Nathaniel Munro MA 1905
no longer on GC reg

MURRAY Norman MB ChB 1949
g p Stornoway from 1959

MURRAY Robert Garden MB ChB 1941 DPH 1947
MFCM 1972
m o h/prin s m o Rochdale from 1963

MURRAY Robert MacKay *BSc 1950
teacher sc Portree h s 1955–76; retd

MURRAY Robert Walker *MA 1948

MURRAY or MacDonald, Roberta Elspeth MA 1930
teacher Engl/hist Ardersier j s 1956–70; retd; resid Inv

MURRAY Sheila *MA 1931
b 21.8.08
retd 1968; resid Fochabers
m Aber 15.7.69 William J. McGeorge retd

MURRAY Sheila MA 1941
teacher Skene Square p s Aber 1946–79; retd

MURRAY or Fawcett, Sheila Jean *MA 1951

MURRAY or Gray, Stella Watt MA 1953
teacher maths Inverbervie 1954–58; resid Laurencekirk

MURRAY Thomas Patrick Edward MA 1921 LLB 1923
DL county and city of Aber from 1964
ptnr Stewart & Murray advoc Aber from 1927; clerk/treasurer Deeside dist c 1944–73

MURRAY William MA 1891
no longer on GC reg

MURRAY William George MB ChB 1921
d Aber 15.3.61 *AUR* XXXIX 203

MURRAY William George Duncan MB ChB 1947 MD 1958
FRSM 1958 DIH(RCS) 1961 FRIPHH 1968
occup health Lond 1958–71; asst secy Med Protect. Soc Lond from 1972; resid West Malling

MURRAY William Nicoll MA 1927 MB ChB 1932
retd 1971; resid Fochabers

MURRAY William Robert MA 1937
Mackie acad Stonehaven: spec asst Engl 1967–72, asst prin Engl 1972–76; retd

MURRAY or McAulay, Williamina Sinclair MA 1943
lived W Cameroon 1950–68; teacher: Benedict p s Mitcham 1969–71, Canterbury Rd p s Morden from 1971
husb *d* 10.10.69

MURRISON or Milne, Annie Mary MA 1928
resid Aber

MURSELL or Sinclair, Margaret Fraser BSc(agr) 1926
no longer on GC reg

MUSTARD or Capper, Catherine Ella MA 1942
resid Huyton-with-Roby, nr Liverpool

MUSTARD Donald Kennedy BSc 1952

MUSTARD or Graham, Elizabeth Grant BSc(agr) 1945
publ health apptment (milk and food hyg) Fife c c 1973–75, Dunfermline dist c from 1975

MUSTARD James BSc 1948 *1956
Aber: teacher sc Rosemount s s 1949–67, lect chem coll of comm from 1967

MUTCH Alexander *MA 1929
no longer on GC reg

MUTCH Andrew Mollison MA 1927 LLB 1928
no longer on GC reg

MUTCH or Durnin, Elizabeth Anne MA 1952
teacher: Aber 1953–64, Galashiels 1964–65, Dumfries from 1965

MUTCH Forbes Robertson MB ChB 1923
d Nottingham 3.5.68 *AUR* XLII 361

MUTCH George *MA 1927
retd 1968; resid Helensburgh

MUTCH Harry *MA 1951 PhD 1962
lect nat phil Aberd 1962–68; head of maths s RGIT Aber from 1968; member of BA comm (seismological investigation) 1966
m Aber 15.5.59 Susan Edgar d of John A. E. Inv

MUTCH or Johnston, Isabel Margaret *BSc 1946
resigned Macaulay inst for soil res Aber 1960

MUTCH or Zamoyski, Isobel Margaret (Countess) MA 1951

MUTCH or Bisset, Isobel Stephen BSc 1944
teacher: sc/maths Keith g s 1965–69, sc Mackie acad Stonehaven from 1969

MUTCH John MA 1913
d Aber 9.11.66 *AUR* XLII 84

MUTCH John Bernard MB ChB 1917
no longer on GC reg

MUTCH John Simpson MA 1913 BD 1915
retd 1960
d Cleveleys 14.7.77 *AUR* XLVIII 226

MUTCH or Milne, Leila Davidson MA 1923
resid Laurencekirk

MUTCH Robert James BSc 1931
head Mintlaw s s 1961–71; retd

MUTCH Sheena Doris MA 1954

MUTCH or Pitty, Sophia Anderson MA 1930
d of William F. farm.; b Crimond 27.7.07
teacher: St Combs 1932–37, supply Hyde educ div Cheshire 1950–57, girls' s s Hyde 1959–66; retd; resid Bridlington
m Aber 20.7.37 Harold E. Pitty teacher/headmaster s of Frank P. Manc

MUTCH William Alexander MA 1911
no longer on GC reg

MUTERER James George MB ChB 1908 DPH 1912
no longer on GC reg

MYERS Algernon Edgar Cyril MB ChB 1907
no longer on GC reg

MYERS John Wade *MA 1954

MYLES Robert Boulton MB ChB 1915
d 12.8.72 *AUR* XLV 125

MYLROI Derek *MA 1952
DipEd(Durh) 1953
head hist dept Faraday Hall s Billingham 1961–65; dep head St Francis RC g s Hartlepool 1965–69; head St Bede's RC comp s Peterlee from 1969

MYRON or Ross, Agnes Warwick MA 1949
resid Cults Aber

MYRON or van Niekerk, Margaret Sutherland MA 1945
resid Mandini Natal

NAPIER George *BSc 1920
no longer on GC reg

NAPIER George *MA 1923

NAPIER or McAuslan, Mary Elizabeth MA 1925
no longer on GC reg

NAPIER or Wilkie, Sheila Ruth *MA 1948
Adult Educ Cert Russian Lang (Leeds) 1967
teacher Ger Lawnswood h s Leeds 1972–73; tut. Engl for overseas stud. Swarthmore educ centre Leeds 1977

NAPIER William Ross *MA 1952 Dip Ed 1955
prin teacher classics Tain royal acad 1968–72, asst rector from 1972

NARAHARI Kosarazu BSc(agr) 1923
no longer on GC reg

NASH Charles Anthony Mariott BSc(for) 1949
d Honiara BSIP 25.8.71 *AUR* XLV 128

NASR Hamed Nasr Mohamed PhD 1950

NAUGHTIE Alexander MA 1930
d Aber 5.3.73 *AUR* XLV 227

NAUGHTON or Alexander, Margaret MA 1948

NAUGHTY Alexander Wilson *MA 1926

NAYLOR or Youngson (Brown), Elizabeth Gisborne *MA 1948
lib univ Edin 1970–74; resid Canberra, Aust

NAYLOR Roy Stewart BSc(eng) 1950
no longer on GC reg

NEATE Harry Lingwood *MA 1914
d 3.8.76

NEILL Freda Katherine *MA 1942
teacher classics: head Lat dept Selkirk h s 1943–46, Mary Erskine s for girls Edin 1946–49; educ edit. Blackie & Son Glasg 1949–55; head Lat dept Baston s for girls Bromley Kent 1959–64; edit. ch's books Blackie Lond 1965–67; head classics dept Hill House s for boys Doncaster from 1974
m Bridge of Allan 7.1.55 John Kemsley BSc(Lond) C.Eng NCB Doncaster
d Italy 30.8.78 *AUR* XLVIII 107

NEILL or Logie, Kathleen Margaret Cameron BSc 1940
resid Aber
husb *d* 15.3.72

NEILL Robert Macfarlane DSc 1941 LLD 1965
d 30.7.69

NEILSON Christina McLeod (Lynda) MA 1941
teacher: Dunure s Ayrsh 1961–70, Russel St s Ayr 1970–71, Alloway s Ayr 1971–77; retd

NEILSON or Petters, Eleanor *MA 1954

NEILSON Gladys Brock MA 1938

NEILSON Matthew Welsh PhD 1928
retd 1958; resid Ayr
d Ardrossan 12.5.81 *AUR* XLIX 137

NEILSON or Burns, Winifred MA 1930
resid Bieldside Aber

NEISH Ian Douglas MB ChB 1954
MRCGP 1969
g p Stockton-on-Tees from 1958

NEISH Isobel Kennedy MA 1955

NEISH William John Pirie *BSc 1943

NELSON or McDonald, Elizabeth Margaret MA 1926
resid Port Appin, Argyll

NELSON or Duthie, Marion Bell *MA 1926
retd; resid Okehampton
husb *d* –.10.74
d 26.10.77

NELSON Mary Masson MA 1939 BL 1948

NEMETH Alexander *MA 1954
Cert City & Guilds RTEM Aber 1978; naturalized Brit citizen 1978
photographer Aber from 1960
m Aber 15.4.63 Margaret M. Archibald nurse, photogr asst d of William J. A. Aber

NESS Thomas Dick MB ChB 1948
hon orthop surg Prince Henry hosp and Prince of Wales hosp Sydney/clin teacher orthop dept univ of NSW from 1961

NEUSTEIN Stephen Andreas BSc(for) 1952
for. comm: silviculturist (North) Edin 1961–74, asst conserv Chester from 1974

NEVILLE Hugh Henry MA 1943 *BSc 1946
prin scient off. bldg res estab Watford from 1962

NEWLANDS Annie MA 1938
teacher Culter 1953–76; resid Kintore
m Edin 7.8.76 Alexander Singer sqn ldr RAF (retd) s of Alexander S. St Katherine's Aberdeensh

NEWLANDS Constance Jean MA 1955

NEWLANDS Janet Roy MA 1914
resid Aber

NEWLANDS or McVean, Mary Isabella MA 1942
teacher Rothes p s from 1946

NEWLANDS William MB ChB 1937
g p Aber; retd
d Majorca 12.6.74 *AUR* XLVI 110

NEWTON or Dowie, Frances Elena MA 1914
d Putney 13.11.71 *AUR* XLIV 317

NEWTON John Philip BSc(for) 1950
man. dir Fountain Forestry Wells later Cheddar Somerset 1960–75; vice chmn Fountain Forestry from 1975 and dir Matthews Wrightson Land from 1971

NICHOL Edith Margaret MA 1930
teacher maths Findochty j s s till 1968; retd
d 12.7.74

NICHOLLS Thomas Burtonshaw MB ChB 1908
no longer on GC reg

NICHOLSON Andrew Broadfoot BSc(agr) 1954
member Stock Exchange Edin; ptnr Macgregor, Walker & Co from 1962, merged to become Bell, Lawrie Macgregor & Co from 1975
m Lond 11.4.73 Joanna M. Bechely-Crundall d of Noel B.-C. Ramsbury

NICHOLSON or Milne, Annie MA 1905
d Streatham Lond 19.1.72 *AUR* XLIV 427

NICHOLSON or Fielding, Doreen BSc(agr) 1948
resid Forres

NICHOLSON or Nicol, Eva MacIntosh MA 1923
d Forres 4.12.78

NICHOLSON George Duncan BSc(eng) 1945
dep resid eng Mangla dam proj Preece Cardew & Rider W Pakistan 1963–70; proj man. Kehan and Gokcekaya transmission proj Ankara and Istanbul from 1970

NICHOLSON or Lyon, Helen MA 1910
d 25.8.64

NICHOLSON John Archibald MB ChB 1916
no longer on GC reg

NICHOLSON William Dallas MB ChB 1949
g p Sale Cheshire from 1960

NICOL or Jackson, Agnes MB ChB 1945
MFCP 1972
dep m o h Ross & Cromarty (mainland) 1970–74; sen m o Highland health board (Ross & Cromarty) from 1974

NICOL Aileen Annette MB ChB 1926 DPH 1928
retd 1963; resid Inverurie

NICOL Albert Reid *MA 1924
d 2.1.67

NICOL Alexander *MA 1915
d Lymington 19.10.62 *AUR* XL 84

NICOL Alexander *MA 1927
retd 1966; resid Nairn
d 8.12.81

NICOL Alexander MB ChB 1949 ᶜMD 1962
MRCPath(Lond) 1964 FRMS 1972
FRCPath(Lond) 1976
sen regist clin path RI Manc 1962–64, dir area lab Glos royal hosp Gloucester from 1964

NICOL Alexander Adam McIntosh MB ChB 1922 MD 1926
member hosp man. comm/advis in med N'cle-u-Tyne reg hosp board/assoc clin teacher med King's coll N'cle 1948–65; retd; resid Whitburn Sunderland

NICOL Alexander Corskie MB ChB 1926
d 25.11.70

NICOL Alice Ann MA 1910
sen mistress Stanley g s Co Durham till 1947; retd; resid Insch

NICOL or Markwick, Amy Taylor MA 1930
fell./tut./lect classics Girton coll Cantab 1961–67; retd; resid Lymington
husb *d* 1946

NICOL Bruce Milligan MB ChB 1935
Coronation Medal 1953
advis nutrit UNICEF for FAO New York 1960–62; Rome: asst to dir for nutrit div FAO 1962–63, dep dir nutrit div FAO 1963–73; consult. for FAO to govt of Malaysia Kuala Lumpur 1974–75; consult. for FAO to govt of Indonesia Djakarta 1974; retd from FAO 1973; still doing consult. work for overseas govts

NICOL Cameron Macdonald MA 1911 MB ChB 1915 MD 1919
d Welwyn 19.2.65 *AUR* XLI 31

NICOL or Walker, Charlotte Jane Donald BSc 1942
head Netherley p s Stonehaven from 1947

NICOL Duncan MA 1933
head Drumblade p s Huntly from 1957

NICOL or Bell, Elizabeth Andrew MA 1918
d Glasg 9.1.77

NICOL Ethel Lumsden MA 1931
retd; resid Aber

NICOL Harvey MB ChB 1951
MRCGP 1974
g p Fraserburgh from 1956
wife *d* 3.12.76

NICOL or Brown, Helen Hendry MA 1919
husb *d* 1972
resid Portpatrick
d Stranraer 2.11.79

NICOL James Lendrum MB ChB 1928
MRCGP 1964 MNZCGP
retd 1974; resid Christchurch NZ

NICOL James Rae *MA 1937
d Lond 13.3.69 *AUR* XLIII 216

NICOL or Simpson, Janet Cruickshank MA 1917 *MB ChB 1921
d Lymington 26.9.68 *AUR* XLIII 79

NICOL Margaret Melville MA 1904
d Aber 28.4.68 *AUR* XLII 345

NICOL or Robson, Marjory Helen *MA 1952

NICOL or Geater, Mona MA 1926
no longer on GC reg

NICOL Nancy Jane MA 1929
d 11.12.73

NICOL Norman Thomas MB ChB 1950
FFR(Lond) 1959 TD 1963
consult. radiotherap Leic RI 1960–64; consult. radioth i/c radioth dept Leic RI/assoc consult. radioth centre Sheffield from 1964

NICOL Patrick Blaikie MB ChB 1938 DPH 1953
MRCPath 1965
regular navy 1939–71; QHP 1969–71; sen m o Rolls-Royce (1971) Derby

NICOL Peter Lyon MA 1935
head Port Elphinstone p s from 1950; town councillor Inverurie from 1970; chmn commun serv panel Garioch from 1966; convener swim. pool Inverurie from 1971; retd 1975; pres Inverurie Bowling Club 1978

NICOL Robert MA 1903
d Crieff 10.10.71 *AUR* XLII 316

NICOL Thomas James Trail MA 1938 DD 1968
dep asst chaplain-gen BAOR Germany 1963–67; asst chaplain-gen Edin 1967–72; min Crathie church 1972–77; domestic chaplain to Queen in Scot. from 1972; resid St Fillans

NICOL William Bernard de Bear *MA 1938

NICOLL Alfred BSc(eng) 1945

NICOLL or Watson, Annie *MA 1934
d 12.1.75 *AUR* XLVI 239

NICOLL David Ross MA 1951

NICOLSON or MacIntyre, Helen MA 1923
head Corgarff p s 1957–63; retd; resid Elgin

NICOLSON Jessie Ann MA 1930
teacher p s Kinlochiel/Eigg/Barra 1932–35; head: Southlaggan p s 1935–38, Tomacharrich Fort William 1938–72; retd

NICOLSON Thomas Henry *BSc(agr) 1950
lect/sen lect bot Queen's coll Dund 1961–69; reader biol sc Dund from 1969

NIDDRIE James MA 1954
p s teacher Aber: Stockethill 1959–61, Cornhill 1961, Fernielea 1961–67; lower s master AGS 1967–70; dep head Westerton p s 1970–74; head Craighill p s from 1974
m Aber 4.4.60 Hazel C. McIntosh teacher d of James C. McI. Aber

NISBET Alexander *MA 1950 Dip Ed 1952
dist insp Dumfries and Galloway 1969–70; HMIS (higher grade) 1970; dist insp Ayr Bute Dumfries and Galloway 1972–77; Lothian reg from 1977

NISBET Alister MacGregor MB ChB 1954
DObstRCOG 1959
g p Bridlington from 1961

NISBET Frederick Cawthorne Hutchinson *BSc(eng) 1955
FICE FIStruct E
consult. civ eng/ptnr W. A. Fairhurst & Ptnrs Aber from 1966

NISBET John Donald PhD 1952
prof educ Aberd from 1963

NISH or Chapman, Anna Aileen McInnes MA 1934

NIVEN Alan Fowler *MA 1951 LLB 1960
d Torphins 4.7.71 *AUR* XLIV 322

NIVEN Alexander Francis MB ChB 1940
g p Chatham from 1947

NIVEN Charles David *MA *BSc 1918

NIVEN or Graham, Jean Margaret *MA 1939
resid Glasg

NIVEN John Scott MA 1901
no longer on GC reg

NIVEN or Sorley, Marjorie Davidson *MA 1913 *1914
d Leura NSW 5.4.74 *AUR* XLV 447 & XLVI 107

NIVEN William MB ChB 1924
consult. radiol; chmn Huddersfield hosp comm 1964–68; retd
no longer on GC reg

NIVEN William Dickie *MA 1900 DD 1928
d Glasg 26.2.65 *AUR* XLI 145

NOBLE Alexander MB ChB 1906 DPH 1908
no longer on GC reg

NOBLE Andrew MB ChB 1940
g p Montrose from 1946

NOBLE Benjamin BSc 1946 DSc 1962

NOBLE or Griffith, Christina MA 1925
retd 1965; resid Kirby Underdale York

NOBLE Donald Haddow Macrae BSc(agr) 1954

NOBLE Douglas Oswald MA 1939
rector: St Michael and All Angels Helensburgh 1959–71, St Columba's Largs from 1971; canon of St Mary's cath Glasg from 1971

NOBLE Elizabeth Duthie MA 1929

NOBLE Isabel Mary MB ChB 1954

NOBLE John MA 1952
dep head Oakbank s Aber 1962–66; B.C. Canada: supt Brannan Lake s 1966–73, exec dir soc serv 1973–76, dep min. ministry of human resources from 1976

NOBLE or Porter, Lilian McLean MA 1952

NOBLE or Emslie, Margaret MA 1922
d Glasg 24.9.68 *AUR* XLIII 83

NOBLE or McGill, Mary MA 1929

NOBLE Mary Jane MA 1950
teacher Sandhaven till 1977; peripatetic remed teacher Grampian reg c from 1977
m Aber 31.3.67 Charles M. Watt eng s of Alexander D. W. Fraserburgh

NOBLE Mary Mearns MA 1949

NOBLE or Russell, Patricia MA 1945
teacher Crimond j s s 1961–74; head Crimond p s from 1974

NOBLE Peter Scott *MA 1921 LLD 1955
Kt 1966
vice-chancellor Lond univ 1961–64; retd; resid Edin

NOBLE Robert William Smith *MA 1938
head Newburgh Mathers p s nr Ellon 1964–78; retd; resid Aber

NOBLE Sheila Mary Grant MA 1942
Aber: teacher Fr/Engl Middle s, Frederick St s s 1970–75, Linksfield acad from 1975

NOBLE Thomas Alexander Fraser *MA 1938 *1940 LLD 1968
Kt 1971 LLD(Leic) 1976
Secy/treas Carnegie Trust 1957–62; vice-chancellor and principal: Leic 1962–76, Aberd 1976–81; retd; resid Nairn
chmn UK comm vice-chancellors and principals 1970–72

NOLTIE Henry Robert *MA 1925 BSc 1927 *1931
retd 1968; resid Broughty Ferry

NORBY Douglas Morton *MA 1952

NORQUAY or Laird, Margaret Helen MB ChB 1951
radiol Wellington publ hosp NZ from 1966
husb *d* 3.8.73

NORRIE George Beaton BSc(agr) 1945

NORRIE John BSc 1906
no longer on GC reg

NORRIE or Roberts, Mary Bedford MA 1928
teacher: Zambia/Swaziland/S. Africa; retd from Wesley s s Salt River Cape Town 1974
m Ndola Zambia 23.6.34 Horace E. Roberts asst postmaster-gen N. Rhod s of Sidney R. Evesham

NORRIE Mary Helen *MA 1914
resid Aber from 1944
d Aber 5.12.78

NORRIS Forbes James Anderson MB ChB 1935
no longer on GC reg

NORTH Alastair Macarthur *BSc 1954 PhD 1957 DSc 1965
FRSE 1971 FRIC 1971
Burmah prof physical chem Strath from 1967

NOTHOLT Arthur John George *BSc 1951
FGS 1954 MIMM 1963
employed mineral resources div overseas geol surv inst of geol sciences Lond from 1956

NOTTINGHAM Peter Maxwell PhD 1952

NOUR Ibrahim Mohamed MA 1954
MEd(Harv) 1960
prin tech inst Khartoum 1964–65, UNESCO expert: Riyad Saudi Arabia 1966–70, Baghdad Iraq 1970–73; dir higher educ Khartoum from 1973

NUTTEN Albert John *BSc 1948

NUTTEN Horace Edward MB ChB 1951 DPH 1955
MFCM 1971
m o h NW Derbyshire Buxton from 1965; m o stud. health serv: Buxton from 1968, Matlock from 1970; m o gen c of British Shipping 1974

NUTTEN Robert Edward Page MB ChB 1943
g p Aber from 1947

OAG John Alexander BSc(agr) 1922
no longer on GC reg

O'BRIEN Kevin MB ChB 1941
g p Birm; prin from 1954

O'BRIEN or Sim, Ruth *MA 1930
Fraserburgh acad: teacher Engl 1956–60, spec asst Fr/Ger 1960–72

O'CONNOR Christine Greig *MA 1915
d 5.10.65 *AUR* XLI 244

O'CONNOR William John MB ChB 1922
d 8.2.76

OFFICER Alice Edith MA 1927
no longer on GC reg

OFFICER Henry Sylvester BSc(agr) 1947

OGG George
***MA 1912 BD 1919 *BSc 1919 DD 1951**
d 18.1.73 *AUR* XLV 224

OGG Lindsay Robert Arbuthnott MB ChB 1931
d 22.12.63

OGG William Gammie
MA 1912 BSc(agr) 1913 *BSc 1914 LLD 1951
retd; resid Edzell
d Edzell 25.9.79 *AUR* XLVIII 350

OGILVIE Alexander MA 1902
d 15.12.66

OGILVIE Allan MA 1913
d Laurencekirk 24.9.68 *AUR* XLII 352

OGILVIE Helen MA 1916
d Aber 11.3.68 *AUR* XLII 355

OGILVIE Hugh Alexander *MA 1937

OGILVIE James MA 1933
teacher Banff acad 1969–73; retd; resid Macduff

OGILVIE Lawrence MA *BSc 1921
retd 1964; resid Dundry Bristol
wife *d* 1965
d Bristol 16.4.80 *AUR* XLVIII 440

OGILVIE or Craig, Mary Cowie MA 1947

OGILVIE Roberta MA 1914
resid Edin

OGILVIE Walter Johnston
MA 1919 MB ChB 1923

OGSTON Alexander MA 1912

OGSTON Derek
MA 1952 *MB ChB 1957 PhD 1962 *MD 1969 DSc 1975
MRCPE 1963 MRCP(Lond) 1967 FRCPE 1972 FRCP(Lond) 1977
lect med Aberd 1962–69, sen lect 1969, reader 1975, regius prof physiol from 1977
m Aber 19.7.63 Cecilia M. Clark MB ChB 1962 *qv*

OGSTON or Nicol, Elizabeth Marion Ross
***MA 1937**

OGSTON or Townroe or Bullimore, Helen Charlotte Elizabeth Douglas *BSc 1906
no longer on GC reg

OGSTON Henry MA 1936 ᵈLLB 1938
ptnr Clark & Wallace advoc Aber from 1949
d Aber 7.1.80 *AUR* XLVIII 442

OGSTON Isabella Sophia MA 1928
sen asst teacher Cornhill p s Aber 1951–69; retd

OGSTON John BCom 1924
d Aber 10.4.70 *AUR* XLIII 445

OGSTON or Ingram, Lillias MA 1947
resid Wishaw

OGSTON William Duncan MB ChB 1955
sen lect dept mental health Aberd 1968–77; chief of psychiat Martinez VA hosp and vice chmn univ of Calif, Davis from 1977

OGSTON William Leslie MA 1927

OLDMAN Ella Geddes MA 1954

O'LEARY Anne Rose *MA 1954
teacher Engl St Augustine's Priory Ealing 1958–62

OLIPHANT or Geddes, Elsie Mary MA 1945
teacher: Turriff 1955–68, Peterculter from 1968

OLIVER Francis William Anderson
BSc(for) 1922 BSc 1923
H.M. for. comm: div off. Dumfries 1938–46; conserv E Scot. Aber 1947–64; retd; resid Skene

OLIVER or Abrahamsson, June Marie
MB ChB 1951
Swedish med regist 1959
consult. anaest: (locum) Stockholm 1968, Ekmanska hosp Gothenburg from 1969 (formerly Elmanska hosp, later Östra hosp)

OLIVER or Robb, Wilma Margaret MA 1949
Kelso h s: teacher part time 1960–70; maths asst from 1970

OLSON James William MA 1915
resid Clarkston, Glasg
d Glasg 12.3.78

OMINDE Simeon Hongo *MA 1954

OMOND or Burn, Agnes MA 1906
no longer on GC reg

O'NEIL or Sharp, Eleanor Mary MA 1928
resid Whittlesford Cambridge
husb *d* 23.12.66

ORAM Alan Kenneth BSc(for) 1952

ORCHARDSON Ian Quiller BSc 1904
no longer on GC reg

ORD Arthur Frederic Trotter MB ChB 1934
d 21.1.71

ORD or Mackie, Mary Bremner MA 1910
d Aber 2.4.77

ORE or Beatty, Margaret Isobel BSc(agr) 1949
resid Loanhead

ORKIN Philip Alexander PhD 1951
sen lect zool Aberd 1963–79; retd

ORMISTON Margaret MB ChB 1944 DPH 1948
MFCM 1973
Aber: asst m o h 1952–58, sen asst m o h 1958–63; Leeds: sen m o 1963–69, prin m o (ch health) 1969–74; spec in commun med (ch health) Leeds area health auth (teaching) from 1974

ORR or Barton, Elizabeth Joan Boyd MB ChB 1939
intermittent g p m o Stracathro hosp Angus 1956–73

OSBORNE James Bourke BSc(agr) 1950
FRICS 1966
chartered land ag Taunton and Beds from 1960
m Great Horkesley nr Colchester 2.7.60 Susan K. Skinner teacher d of Edgar L. S. BA(Oxon) Great Horkesley

OTTY Eric Horsfield *MA 1929 *MEd 1934
FEIS 1970
prin The David Dale coll Glasg from 1949; retd 1974

OTTY Helena Horsfield *MA 1926
retd 1965; resid Gateshead

OTTY John Horsfield MA 1925 MB ChB 1927
d Bradford 10.5.74 *AUR* XLVI 109

OUTRAM Marjorie Isabella MB ChB 1923 DPH 1924
retd 1974; resid Tenterden

OVERELL Philip Alexander Wyrill BSc(for) 1951
H.M. for. comm: conserv E Eng 1962–68, NW Eng from 1968

OWEN Edwin Cecil PhD 1940

OWLER or Watt, Heather McDonald Anderson MA 1936
resid Edin
d Edin 4.10.78

OWUSU-AFRIYIE Abraham Kwabena BSc(for) 1953
MF (CSU Colo. USA) 1959
Ghana: asst conserv for. 1954–57, sen asst 1957–59, conserv for. 1959–61; dep chief conserv for. 1961–62, chief conserv for. 1962–70; dir Volta Lines (shipping co) Accra from 1970
m Lond 16.11.63 Emma Oppong hotelier d of Christian O. Dormaa-Ahenkro Ghana

PACE Eda Mary MA 1954

PACKMAN or Honigmann, Elsie McConnachie *BSc 1951 PhD 1954
OU tut. 1977

PACKMAN or Carter, Hazel MA 1951

PAISLEY Duncan Herbert MA 1955

PAISLEY William Duncan BSc 1951

PAL Dewan Har Charan Das BSc(agr) 1924

PALIT or Martin, Marion Nasmyth Clifton MA 1953
teacher: Engl lycée Cayenne Fr Guyana 1968–70, Nuffield spec Fr course Airyhall, Craighill and Hazlehead p s Aber from 1972
husb *d* 25.7.72

PALMER George MA 1932
teacher phys Preston Lodge h s Prestonpans 1968–76; retd

PALMER James Hugh MB ChB 1953
d Cults, Aber 18.9.67 *AUR* XLII 186 & 375

PALMER Kenneth John Raymond BSc 1948
man. dir Legal and General Volkskas Assur (S Af comp) Johannesburg from 1980

PALMER Ronald Mills BSc(for) 1942
chief conserv for. 1960–61; cler off. D o E Hastings from 1961

PANTON John Stuart MA 1931 *BSc(agr) 1933
d Aber 10.2.73 *AUR* XLV 227

PANTON Robert Watt MA ChB 1939
g p Croxteth Liv from 1953

PAPLEY or Stevenson, Margaret MA 1932
resid Stromness

PARDOE John George MB CM 1892
no longer on GC reg

PARDY Alexander Angus BSc 1924 BSc(for) 1926
asst bot dept Aberd 1957–72; retd

PARK Alastair Henry MB ChB 1954
d Penarth 16.8.65 *AUR* XLI 153, 252

PARK Alexander William Chrystal MA 1919
no longer on GC reg

PARK Alexandra Jane MA 1944

PARK Catherine Hazel MB ChB 1954

PARK or Murray, Cecilia Mitchell MB ChB 1942
clin m o Lond borough of Lewisham from 1966

PARK George Thomson Booth BSc(eng) 1953
AM(SA)ICE 1954 MICE 1959 Pr. Eng 1965
civ eng: Natal roads dept Pietermaritzburg S Africa, John Miles & Ptnrs Bulawayo S. Rhodesia 1957–60; Johannesburg: O Grinaker (Pty) 1960–68, McAlpine (Pty) 1968–70, Union Constr Co 1970–72, AECI from 1972

PARK or Townshend, Gillian Mitchell *MA 1950
resid Upper Langford

PARK or Milne, Helen Margaret *MA 1922
resid Dun

PARK Herbert Foster MB ChB 1933
g p Norham-on-Tweed from 1936
d 21.6.76

PARK Ian *MA 1949 Dip Ed 1950

PARK James Robert MA 1910 *LLB 1911
no longer on GC reg

PARK [James] Vincent *MA 1949
d Binghampton New York 10.1.74 *AUR* XLV 450

PARK John Mitchell MB ChB 1945
g p Hong Kong from 1948

PARK Leonora Willox MA 1933

PARK Louisa Benton *MB ChB 1923
g p Pendleton, Salford

PARK Mary Ella Gordon MA 1936

PARK Wilson Henry Gordon MA 1919 MB ChB 1923
d Aber 14.8.71 *AUR* XLIV 317

PARKER Gilbert MB ChB 1934
orthop surg Teesside from 1948

PARKINSON John Thompson Low BSc(eng) 1954
MIME 1969 MIEE 1969 MIHVE 1970 MRSH 1970 Aber: eng J. T. L. Parkinson 1959–63, dir J. T. L. Parkinson 1963–68, man. dir 1968–71; also man. dir J. T. L. Parkinson-Twaddle Glasg 1969–71; dir Aber Construction Group Aber/dir M & E div incorporating the two comps 1971–75; man. dir reconstructed fam bus. group including Parkinson and Parkinson-Twaddle from 1975; member Grampian reg c 1977 and 1978

PARTHASARATHY Dasika PhD 1952

PATERSON or Wells, Agnes MA 1912
no longer on GC reg

PATERSON Albert John Horne MA 1950 LLB 1953

PATERSON Alexander MB ChB 1926
d 7.1.66

PATERSON Alexander Cardno MA 1911
d 19.1.73

PATERSON Alexander James MA 1930 BL 1936
d Kyoto Japan 28.9.67 *AUR* XLII 186

PATERSON or McDonald, Anne Innes MA 1926
resid Ballater

PATERSON or Mackenzie, Annie Christie Dickson *MA 1940
asst prin teacher mod lang Golspie h s 1974–76; retd

PATERSON Duncan BSc 1926
retd 1965; resid Cults

PATERSON Duncan BSc(agr) 1940

PATERSON Edward Alexander MB ChB 1926
g p Hastings 1938–73; retd; resid St Leonards-on-Sea

PATERSON or Beal, Elizabeth McPherson MA 1929

PATERSON or Clunas, Emmaline Scott MA 1940

PATERSON George Wood MA 1937
Glasg: dir Thermotank 1963, fin. controller Hall-Thermotank Internat 1967–75; internal audit. Strathclyde reg c Paisley from 1975

PATERSON Hamish Barron MA 1954

PATERSON or Hardie, Helena Mackie MA 1907
no longer on GC reg

PATERSON Henry Knox MB ChB 1938

PATERSON or Weatherston, Isabella MA 1924
teacher maths St Denis Edin 1955–68; retd

PATERSON James Alexander Rogerson *MB ChB 1925
no longer on GC reg

PATERSON Jean MA 1936

PATERSON Jean Forbes MA 1949
teacher infants Peterhead 1958–61
m Aber 28.3.62 James P. Gray farm. s of James W. G. Oldmeldrum

PATERSON Jeannie Hardy MA 1930
retd 1968; resid Aber

PATERSON Joseph Middleton MB ChB 1928 DPH 1931
m o Castleford and Normanton 1947–70
d 12.7.77

PATERSON or Holm, Leila Gordon MA 1939
teacher: Engl/Lat Gordon s Huntly 1958–60, Engl/geog Inv royal acad 1960–63, Engl/geog h s Inv 1963–70, Engl Dingwall acad 1970–71, Engl/geog Fortrose acad from 1971, also prin guid from 1972

PATERSON Maggie Ann Lyall MA 1927
retd 1965; resid Macduff

PATERSON or Hunter, Margaret Davidson [c]MB ChB 1948
part time g p Hawick from 1960

PATERSON or Lumsden, Mary Stuart BSc 1924
prin sc Albyn s for girls Aber 1943–66 and second mistress 1953–66; retd
m(2) Lond 15.4.70 Alexander L. Sandison progress eng Monsanto (Chemicals) Internat s of Alexander L. S. Inv

PATERSON Robert Edward Mitchell MB ChB 1938
g p Burton-on-Trent from 1940; retd 1978

PATERSON or Wright, Sarah Rose MA 1931

PATERSON Thomas Maver *MA 1922
no longer on GC reg

PATEY Thomas Walton MB ChB 1955
d Durness 25.5.70 *AUR* XLIV 111

PATIENCE or Stalker, Annie Brodie MA 1944
resid Toronto

PATIENCE Elizabeth MA 1941
teacher Avoch p s Rosssh from 1962

PATIENCE James *MA 1947

PATON Andrew Watts BSc(eng) 1955

PATON Annie Findlay MA 1948

PATON Cumming BSc 1955 PhD 1959

PATON or Rae, Elsie Mary MA 1920
teacher: sc Inverurie acad 1940–42, sc/maths Kintore j s s 1959–63; retd; resid Rothienorman
m Aber 12.12.35 John N. Rae farm. s of David R. Maud
d Banchory 22.12.77

PATON Ethel Anne Scott BSc 1952
Assoc FIMA 1964 FBCS 1969
nat eng lab E. Kilbride: exper off. 1960–67, sen exper off. 1967–72, sen scient off. from 1972

PATON John MA 1948
teacher maths/sc Rubislaw acad from 1973

PATON John Alexander *MA 1949
FIL 1964
head mod lang coll of comm Aber from 1964

PATON Robert Charles MA 1953
d Cloppenburg Germany 14.7.77

PATRICK or Smith, Doris Neil *MA 1949
d Manchester 4.1.80 *AUR* XLVIII 443

PATTERSON or Baxter, Constance Rose MA 1953
Aber: teacher Powis acad 1954–69, Cummings Park p s from 1970

PATTERSON David McDonald BSc(eng) 1952

PATTERSON Douglas Gordon BL 1949
ptnr Watt & Cumine advoc Aber 1950–76, Stronachs advoc from 1976

PATTERSON Iain Alexander Miller BSc(agr) 1954

PATTERSON Janet Bothwell MB ChB 1939
semi retd 1974; resid Middlesbrough

PATTERSON Kenneth Harper *MA 1938
VRD 1960
teacher Edin till 1960; instr lt cdr RNVR/sen instr off. Forth div RNVR till 1960; dir acad stud. metrop police from 1960

PATTERSON or Massie, Lavina Cowie BSc 1954
part-time asst exper off.: endocrinology Torry res stat Aber 1965–66/marine lab DAFS Aber 1966–68, prod. sect. marine lab DAFS Aber 1968–70, exper off./higher scient off. from 1970

PATTERSON Robert Shanks BSc(eng) 1931
d 22.11.65

PATTILLO Alan Hutchison *MA 1951
employed film indust Lond from 1955

PATTILLO John Alexander MB ChB 1953
g p Shrewton Salisbury from 1966

PATTISON David Dickie MA 1907
d 1972

PATTISON Iain Henry BSc(agr) 1937
FRCVS 1965
dep dir agr res council inst for res on anim diseases Compton nr Newbury Berks 1967–76; retd

PATTULLO Jean MB ChB 1944 DPH 1949

PATTULLO William Ogilvy MA dLLB 1948
sen lect mercantile law Aberd 1959–61; prof commercial law Khartoum 1961; advoc Edin 1961–62; sheriff Lanarksh 1962–74
d Thorntonhall 1.11.75 *AUR* XLVI 418

PAUL Douglas Lamont BL 1949

PAUL Elizabeth Hay *MA 1913
resid Dufftown
d Dufftown 20.6.78

PAUL or Annand, Elizabeth Helen MA 1955
teacher p s St Margaret's s for girls Aber 1967–73

PAUL Ian Alexander *MA 1953
civ serv M o D (navy) 1953–75
m W Calder 1960; marr diss 1977
resid Dufftown

PAUL John Milne MA 1924
d Elgin 22.8.77

PAUL William *MA 1946 PhD 1951
AM(hon)(Harv) 1960
Gordon McKay prof of applied phys Harvard USA from 1963; prof associé faculté des sciences univ de Paris 1966–67; fell Clare Hall Camb 1974–75; assoc Clare Hall from 1975

PEACE Sydney MB ChB 1951
DObstRCOG 1964
h o obst Raigmore hosp Inv 1963; g p Kirkwall/obst and med apptments Balfour hosp from 1963

PEARCE or Latter or Shaw, Jessie (Janette) MA 1947

PEARCE Peter Anthony BSc(for) 1953

PEARCE Terrance Arthur Albert MB ChB 1950
DPM(Lond) 1960 MRANZCP 1964 FACMA 1968 MRCPsych 1972
regist psychiat NW Glasg reg hosp board Woodilee hosp Lenzie 1960–62; Victoria Aust: consult. psychiat mental hyg dept Sunbury hosp 1962–63, consult. psychiat 1960, dep psychiat supt mental hyg dept Mont Park hosp 1963–66, psychiat supt 1966–76, supt commun ment health centre Chatsworth House clin Frankston from 1976

PEARSON Edgar Alan [Hamilton-]
see Hamilton-Pearson

PEARSON Gavin Duffus *BSc 1937

PEARSON or Cruickshank, Margaret Duffus *MA 1940
teacher Aber: sc/maths Middle j s s 1941–42, sc Central s s 1942–51, High s for girls 1962–65, mus Torry s s 1966–69, sc pre-nursing coll 1969–71, phys St Margaret's s for girls from 1971

PEARSON or Arnett, Mary Helen BSc 1929

PEARSON Robert Graham MA 1951 LLB 1954

PEARSON William Ellis MA 1924
retd 1955; resid Trimley

PEAT Alfred Augustus MB ChB 1931
m o Research Unit Rockefeller Foundation Trelawny Jamaica 1933–34, m o h St Catherine Ja 1935–42, ADMS Jamaica 1943–48, DMS Trinidad 1948–56, CMO Jamaica 1956–64, Ag MOH St Thomas Ja 1966–77; retd

PEAT or Stewart, Catherine MB ChB 1926
med pract Mulanje Malawi 1930–72; retd; resid Edin
d Edin 18.4.81

PEAT Reginald Albert MB ChB 1943
m o: publ gen hosp Kingston Jamaica 1945–46, Port Royal 1946, Georgetown Cayman Is 1946–48, Malvern and ag MOH St Elizabeth Jamaica 1948–55, Highgate Jamaica 1955–58; med practice Highgate from 1968

PEDDIE John Cameron MA 1910
d 14.1.68 *AUR* XLII 349

PEDERSEN Christian Peter BSc 1955
AMIMM 1960 AMAIMM 1973
dist geol Chartered Explor (AAC) Lusaka Zambia 1960–65; div geol (Charter Consolidated) Jos Nigeria/Whitby Yorks/Akjoujt Mauretania 1965–69; Aust: sen geol John Taylor & Sons NSW WA NT Papua New Guinea 1969–71, sen geol Noranda Aust Koongarra uranium proj NT 1972–75, man. South Alligator Joint Venture 1975–77

PEEBLES or Lewis, Catherine Grimmond Robertson MB ChB 1941
d Aldershot 12.5.77

PELLY Frank Le Quesne MB ChB 1903
no longer on GC reg

PENNIE Donald Durance MB ChB 1942
MRCGP 1958
g p Forfar from 1948

PENNIE or Taylor, Elisabeth Dewar *MA 1954

PENNIE Gibb Niven *MA 1930 [d]BD 1944
rector St John's ch Greenock 1957–61, canon St Mary's cath Glasg from 1961; retd 1977; hon canon 1977

PENNIE Helen Skene MA 1929

PENNIE Ian Durance MB ChB 1939 MSc 1967
g p Golspie 1952–66; ARO Nature Conserv Sutherland 1967–68; g p W Lothian 1969–70, Edrachillis Sutherland from 1970
wife *d* 1971
m(2) Dornoch 10.8.72 Edith M. Wilkinson MB BS(Durh) anaest d of William W. N'cle-u-Tyne

PENNIE James Hamilton MA 1935
d Elgin 28.2.75 *AUR* XLVI 239

PENNY Alan Bruce MA 1953 Dip Ed 1954
teacher classics Montreal 1958–60; prin classics Port Credit Ontario 1961–63; prin lang Glenrothes 1964–72; grocer Hatton from 1972
m Aber 2.8.60 Cecilia Rennie MA 1953 *qv*

PENNY Alexander BSc(agr) 1949
Rothamsted exper stat Harpenden: exper off. 1958–65, sen exper off. 1965–71, sen scient off. 1971–76, prin scient off. from 1976
m Luton 24.9.60 Katherine C. Graham lab asst d of James T. H. G. LRCPGlas Luton

PENNY Alfred Alexander BSc 1933 *1934
d 23.8.71 *AUR* XLIV 321

PENNY Charles MB ChB 1922
d Derby 21.9.66 *AUR* XLI 339

PENNY or Sabiston, Emma BSc 1926
resid Longside

PENNY Ian Francis *BSc 1953 PhD 1956
sen scient off. low temperature res stat Cambridge 1961–67; prin scient off. meat res inst Langford from 1967

PENNY James Chalmers BSc(eng) 1953
d 22.12.61 *AUR* XXXIX 284

PEREIRA Denis Joseph Viegas MB ChB 1917
no longer on GC reg

PERTor Baxter, Wilma Watt MA 1951
teacher Engl/Fr Montrose acad from 1972

PETER James Clark BSc(agr) 1955

PETER Jean Elizabeth MA 1952
teacher Southesk s Montrose till 1960
m Montrose 5.3.60 William Thomson farm. s of William T. St Cyrus

PETERKIN Charles Duncan MA 1908 LLB 1911
d Aber 8.5.62 *AUR* XXXIX 377

PETERKIN Constance Elizabeth MA 1907
d Lond 15.7.66 *AUR* XLI 336

PETERKIN or Black, Elizabeth *MA 1905
d Lond 12.6.65 *AUR* XLI 145, 238

PETERKIN or MacIver, Ethel Marion MA 1907

PETERKIN Frank Gellie Tennant MB ChB 1903
no longer on GC reg

PETERKIN Gilbert Burgher BSc(agr) 1929

PETERKIN Janet Smith MA 1923
retd; resid Portsoy
d Portsoy 18.8.77

PETERKIN or Cowie, Millie BSc 1933
resid Oldmeldrum

PETERKIN Reginald Carnie BCom 1922
no longer on GC reg

PETERS or Robb, Anne Macdonald *MA 1930
Aber acad: spec asst Engl 1958–60, woman advis 1960–79; retd; resid Braemar

PETERS David Cargill *MA 1955

PETERS James Henderson MB ChB 1923
d 12.7.63

PETERS Janet Hunter *MA 1924
Aber acad: spec asst Fr 1956–65, prin asst Fr 1965–66; retd; resid Braemar
d Braemar 7.8.79

PETERS Martha McLaren MA 1908
no longer on GC reg

PETERS William *MA 1910 *1911
d Romsey 5.3.64 *AUR* XL 397

PETERS William *MA 1951

PETERS Willy Ernst MA 1907 *1908

PETERSON or Milne, Emily O'Hanlon MA 1930
d 27.10.70

PETERSON George Peter Scott MA 1955
Shetland: teacher Bridgend p s Burra Isle 1958–59, Hamnavoe j s s Burra Isle 1959–61; teacher Engl Brae j s s 1961–66, Engl/geog Aith j s s 1966–69, Engl/geog Brae j h s from 1969, dep head from 1971
m Lerwick 9.8.65 Frances A. Doull knitter d of Adam D. Brae

PETERSON James McInnes BSc(agr) 1922 BSc 1925 DSc 1933
prof physiol univ of Wales 1947–66; chmn edit. board *Journal of Physiology* 1947–66; retd; resid Edin

PETERSON James Magnus BSc(eng) 1954
test eng Rolls-Royce Derby 1961–63; tech sales eng Serck Radiators Birm 1963–65; S Aust: maintenance eng Eng & Water Supply dept 1966–67, des eng Woods & Forests dept 1967–68; maintenance eng Railways dept NSW Aust 1968–72; proj eng Serck Heat Transfer B'ham from 1972

PETERSON Magnus Fraser BCom 1924
prod. eng *Manchester Guardian* 1928–37; prod. dev eng Fairey Aviation Co. Stockport 1938–65; retd; resid Christchurch
m Manc 1928 Evelyn S. Bakewell teacher d of William B. Aber

PETERSON Peter Hewitt MB ChB 1940
g p Bixter Zetland 1963–73; retd (except for s dental anaest); resid Whiteness Zetland

PETERSON William Gordon BCom 1927 MA 1930
retd 1963; resid Aber
d Aber 4.9.78

PETRIE Adeline Frances MB ChB 1937

PETRIE Alexander *MA 1903
retd; resid Pietermaritzburg
d Johannesburg 1.12.79 *AUR* XLVIII 350

PETRIE Annie Jane MA 1904
no longer on GC reg

PETRIE Beryl Gertrude MB ChB 1937
m o Westminster c c from 1964

PETRIE Charles William MB ChB 1939
d Wigan 8.2.70 *AUR* XLIII 446

PETRIE David MA 1900
d Sidmouth 7.8.61 *AUR* XXXIX 268

PETRIE or Baird, Elizabeth Mary MA 1936
exec off. MAFF 1949–76; retd; resid Lond
m(2) Lond 1.9.51 Telesfor M. Kuzminski (*d* 13.1.76) s of Kazimierz K. Skolimow Poland

PETRIE Gordon *MA 1952
lect geog Glas 1958–64, sen lect from 1964; Carnegie res fell. internat trg centre for aerial surv Delft, Neths 1969–70, prof from 1977

PETRIE Ian Clark MA 1948
teacher Manc 1949–51; Wigan: teacher 1951–55, graded post 1955–58, head Engl dept 1958–60, dep head from 1960
m Wigan 28.7.54 Eunice A. Ashurst beauty consult./ hosp receptionist d of John A. Wigan

PETRIE James Beattie MA 1932 *MB ChB 1936 DPH 1939
d Lond 3.6.66 *AUR* XLI 340

PETRIE James William Gorrod BSc(eng) 1948
MICE 1951 FICE 1966
Port of Lond auth: asst eng 1951–62, div eng new works 1962–64, div eng (plans & proj man.) 1964–67, asst chief eng (proj) 1967–71, chief eng Upper Docks 1971–72, chief eng PLA from 1972

PETRIE Robert John MA 1950

PETTIGREW or Brown, Ellen Elizabeth MA 1950

PHEMISTER or Munro, Helen Reid MB ChB 1949
Dip Med Radiother(Lond) 1973
regist radiotherap Sheff from 1974

PHILIP Alexander Gunn BL 1951

PHILIP Alexander James *BSc 1922
d Sherbrooke Quebec 20.2.67 *AUR* XLII 185

PHILIP or McGregor, Alice Mary MA 1916
no longer on GC reg

PHILIP Alice Mary MA 1921 BSc 1923
d Aber 18.4.75

PHILIP Andrew William BSc(agr) 1949
lect NOSCA from 1960

PHILIP or Glass, Annie Jane Isabel MA 1919
d Aber 25.7.63 *AUR* XL 302

PHILIP Audrey MA 1954
teacher geog Airdrie from 1968
m Edin 24.3.59 Robert F. Shirra des draughtsman

PHILIP Catherine MA 1935
Peterhead acad: woman advis 1969–75, asst head 1972–75; retd

PHILIP Cecil Sleigh MB ChB 1928
retd 1966; resid Elgin

PHILIP Charles Robert MB ChB 1921 ᶜMD 1929
d 17.9.69 *AUR* XLIII 329

PHILIP Elizabeth MA 1908
d Aber –.9.69 *AUR* XLIII 327

PHILIP Flora MA 1935

PHILIP George Mackenzie MA 1951
C of S min: Sandyford-Henderson mem ch Glasg from 1956
m Glasg 26.4.61 Patricia J. Morrison MA(Edin) teacher d of Donald J. M. MB ChB(Edin) Edin

PHILIP Hardy MA 1896 BL 1898
no longer on GC reg

PHILIP or Robertson, Helen Jane MA 1937
resid Montrose
d 31.7.78

PHILIP Henry Leslie *MA 1950
HMIS Edin/Renfrew 1962–69; head Liberton s s Edin from 1969

PHILIP Isabel Mary *MA 1952

PHILIP James MA 1942
C of S min: Holyrood Abbey Edin from 1958
m Aber 19.11.60 Mary F. Moffat MB ChB(Edin) h o d of Unwin J. M. BSc(agr)(Glas) Broken Hill Zambia

PHILIP James Fiddes MB ChB 1933 *ChM 1937
clin prof oncology Aberd from 1975; clin dir Roxburghe House Tor-Na-Dee hosp Aber from 1977

PHILIP Jessie Stuart *MA 1926
retd 1964; resid Aber

PHILIP John MA 1930
warden Tertowie resid s 1960–70; retd; resid Kintore

PHILIP John George Walker BL 1954 MA LLB 1956
ptnr Philip & Wadsworth advoc Aber from 1973

PHILIP Kathleen *MEd 1950

PHILIP or Stokeld, Kathleen May Colvine MA 1945
resid N. Berwick

PHILIP or Hendry, Margaret Isabella MA 1932
teacher Kittybrewster p s Aber 1940–72; retd
husb *d* 15.8.73

PHILIP or Startup, Marjorie Ellson MA 1926
no longer on GC reg

PHILIP Richard Lewis BCom 1923

PHILIP Robert Alexander David *BSc(eng) 1950

PHILIP or Campbell, Una Jessie *BSc 1935
teacher maths: St Margaret's s for girls Aber 1936–39, Cambridge county h s for girls 1942–44, Mary Erskine s for girls Edin 1944–48; head Queen Margaret coll Wellington NZ 1949–52; lect maths Homerton coll Cambridge 1957–59; head The Royal Masonic s for girls Rickmansworth 1959–72; retd; resid Cambridge

PHILLIPS Calbert Inglis MB ChB 1946 ᶜMD 1957
PhD(Brist) 1961 MSc(Manc) 1969 FRCSE 1972 Hon F BoA 1975
consult. ophth surg St George's hosp Lond 1963–65;

prof ophth Manc/hon consult. surg Manc royal eye hosp; prof ophth Edin/hon consult. ophth surg ERI from 1972
m Edin 29.12.62 Christina A. Fulton MB ChB(Edin) ophth d of Angus A. F. BSc(eng)(St And) Edin

PHILLIPS Ernest Johnston BSc 1930
statist: col off. Lond 1960–62, central statist off. Lond 1962–71; retd; resid Ditchling

PHILLIPS James MB ChB 1936
g p: Grange-over-Sands Lancs 1946–47, Sale Cheshire from 1948

PHILLIPS John Charles Lewis BSc(for) 1951

PHILP Alexander George BSc 1949 MB ChB 1954
MRCGP 1963
g p Brentford from 1956
m Lond 3.12.60 Margaret F. Hutchinson MA(Lond) teacher d of Humphrey H. OBE BSc(Durh) S. Hetton Co Durh

PHILP Ronald Richard *MA 1950
teacher: Lossiemouth 1961, prin geog Forres acad 1961–72, asst rector from 1972

PHIMISTER George BSc 1948
analyst Colombo Comm Co Ceylon 1948–70; teacher Aber from 1971

PHIMISTER Ronald McLean MA 1947
head Dunecht p s from 1973

PICKFORD or Milne, Mabel Mary MA 1948

PICKLES John William MB ChB 1932 DPH 1940
Commander St John amb organis 1966
retd 1966; locum tenens apptments tuberculosis hosps/clin Cape Province S. Af 1966–76; emigrated to NSW Aust 1976; locum tenens apptments g p, immunological clin Mittagong shire c NSW

PICKUP Eric PhD 1940

PIKSIS Velta MA 1953
teacher Aberchirder j s s 1954–62
m Aber 11.7.61 Robert M. Forsyth BSc 1953 *qv*

PIMLEY Kenneth Gordon MB ChB 1946

PIMLEY Terence Franklin Philip MB ChB 1950
Kingseat hosp Newmachar: h o 1951–52, regist 1953–56, jun hosp m o 1956–65, asst in psychiat 1965–66; Bilbohall hosp Elgin: asst in psychiat 1966–74, consult. psychiat from 1974
m Aber 29.11.63 Sheila K. Chalmers MB ChB(St And) med asst in psychiat d of Malcolm C. MA(Glas) Broughty Ferry

PINNOCK Malcolm Raymond MB ChB 1950
g p Feckenham and Astwood Bank from 1956

PIRIE Alexander Anderson MA 1891
d Oldmeldrum 20.8.72 aged 104 *AUR* XLV 123

PIRIE Alexander Irvine
***MA 1902 BD 1907 DD 1952**
d Edin 10.9.62 *AUR* XL 74

PIRIE Alexander James *MA 1948
teacher prin hist: Blairgowrie h s 1961–65, Elgin acad 1965–69; head Craigshill h s Livingston W. Lothian from 1969

PIRIE Alexander Maxwell MA 1948

PIRIE Alfred James MB ChB 1907
no longer on GC reg

PIRIE or Adams, Annie Roger MA 1941
resid Anguston Peterculter

PIRIE Bruce Geddes MB ChB 1951
FFARCS(Lond) 1961
regist anaest Addenbrookes hosp Cambridge 1958–62; sen regist anaest Norfolk and Norwich hosp 1962–65; consult. anaest Queen Elizabeth II hosp Welwyn Garden City from 1965
m Pattishall 4.2.61 Diana J. Collins MA(Oxon) med pract

PIRIE Ella Elizabeth Philip MA 1928
resid Edin

PIRIE or Douglas, Elma MA 1947
teacher Fernielea p s Aber from 1964

PIRIE Frances MA 1930

PIRIE George MB ChB 1913
no longer on GC reg

PIRIE George Jamieson MB ChB 1898 DPH 1905
d 27.12.64

PIRIE or Pirie, Helen Calder MA 1949
teacher Engl: Middle s s Aber 1950–59, Old Aber s s 1968–75, Linksfield acad from 1975

PIRIE or Egerton, Isobel Jean MA 1944
resid Milltimber Aber

PIRIE James Elphinstone MA 1921 BD 1923
C of S min: chaplain RN Malta/UK 1932–53; Kinellar 1953–56, Heriot Midlothian 1956–59; retd; resid Edin
wife *d* Edin 9.11.72

PIRIE John Riddell Knight BSc 1931 BL 1936
edit. NEL newsletter 1964–68; retd; pres Glasg branch of Aberd Alumnus Assoc 1967; founded E coast branch of Aberd Alum. Assoc, secy & treasurer 1968; resid Scone

PIRIE Margaret Christian *MA 1944
prin teacher mod lang St Margaret's s for girls Aber from 1963

PIRIE Nora Mary BSc 1922
d Huntly 19.6.77

PIRIE Norman James *MA 1929
d 31.1.69

PIRIE Rhoda Ellen MA 1950

PIRIE Richard Thomas BSc(eng) 1949 *1950
Cia Shell de Venezuela: head of transportation Maracaibo 1959–61; Shell Int Petr: head of trans The Hague 1961–67; Shell BP Nigeria: supplies & services man. Port Harcourt 1967, man. mid west Warri 1967–69; Basrah Petr Coy gen man. Basrah Iraq 1970–72; Assoc Octel Coy: man. supply/plan. Lond 1972–73, man. pers/man. serv Ellesmere Port from 1973

PIRIE Robert William MA 1947
Aber: prin teacher sc St Peter's RC s s 1962–66, prin sc/phys Summerhill acad from 1966, asst head from 1973

PIRIE or Graham, Vivien Winifred *BSc 1950 PhD 1955
resid Carluke

PIRIE William MA 1953
head Tillydrone p s Aber from 1973

PIRRIE Margaret Jane MA 1945
teacher Rothiemay p s from 1949

PITHIE or Askew, Alice MA 1918
no longer on GC reg

PITHIE Mary MA 1910
no longer on GC reg

PITTENDRIGH Agnes Margaret BSc 1926
volunt soc worker Aber from 1946
d Aber 20.4.78 *AUR* XLVIII 357

PLANT Donald BSc(for) 1953
Methwold h s: prin maths/sc 1957–77, sen tut. from 1978; retd 1.4.80

PLEASANCE or Ogilvy, Sybil Emily Knox MA 1916
no longer on GC reg

POLE or Yule, Constance Margaret MB ChB 1949
g p Maryport Cumbria from 1966

POLE James Denham MB ChB 1921
d Australia

POLE or Morrison, Kathleen St Clair Montford MA 1954
teacher: various p s 1955–62, 1967–73; head Port Erroll p s Aberdeensh from 1974

POLLOCK George Tullo MB ChB 1953 DPH 1957
MFCM 1972
m o h/prin s m o Coventry 1972–74; area m o Coventry AHA from 1974

POLLOCK William Patrick BSc(for) 1924
no longer on GC reg

POLLOCK William Stott MB ChB 1932
retd 1973; resid Alford

POLYCARPOU Andrew BSc(for) 1952
dir dept of for. Nicosia Cyprus 1960–66; progr co-ordination off. for. div FAO Rome 1966–68; dir dept of for. Nicosia 1968–70; gen man. Cyprus For. Indust Nicosia 1970–71; sen agr advis/FAO country rep Cairo 1972–73; chief for. conserv and wild life br for. dept FAO Rome 1974–76; asst to ADG for. dept FAO Rome from 1977

PONTING Frederick William PhD 1953
FIMA 1964
sen lect maths Aberd 1961–70, reader from 1970

POPE James Albert *MA 1948
FRSS 1949
head statist and computing team Marine Lab DAFS Torry Aber from 1950

POPPLEWELL Newman MA 1908 BD 1911
d 1961 *AUR* XXXIX 273

PORTEOUS James Duncan BSc(eng) 1945
CEng 1965
asst chief eng John Brown Land Boilers Clydebank 1965–66; Foster Wheeler John Brown Boilers: eng man. Whitecrook Clydebank 1966–67, proj man. Aberthaw Lond 1967–68; eng and contr man. Diamond Power Specialty Dumbarton from 1968

PORTEOUS or Melvin, Margaret MB ChB 1919

PORTER Dorothy May MB ChB 1955
h o obst Edgware gen hosp 1959; g p Newmarket 1960–69; sen m o health dept Bury St Edmunds 1969; g p: Cuminestown 1975–76, Leighton Buzzard from 1977
m Aber 28.12.64 Colin H. Walker MB BS(Lond) g p s of Wilfrid E. W. Chingford; marr diss 1974

PORTER or Bell, Edith Barnett MA 1952
teacher: Lanarksh 1969–76, Dr Barnardo's Coltness 1976–77; lect Motherwell tech coll from 1977

PORTER Elma BSc 1950
Glaxo labs: analytical chem Montrose 1952–59, tech 1959–70, head of correspondence sect. Greenford 1970–78, tech exec, tech dir Lond from 1978

PORTER Helene Sievewright MA 1946
teacher p dept RGC Aber from 1958

PORTER or Morrison, Isabel Murray BSc 1952
Cambridge: part time lect Cambridgeshire coll arts and tech from 1976

PORTER or Ellis, Jean Bruce Maitland BSc 1940 MB ChB 1946
member Gen Nursing Council Scot. from 1970, member Grampian health board from 1974, chmn Royal Cornhill and assoc hosp board of man. 1971–74

PORTER or Diack, Laura MA 1943
resid Torphins

PORTER Richard Reginald Maitland MA 1908 *MB ChB 1912
Kt order of St John 1972
resid Aber
d Aber 24.7.79 *AUR* XLVIII 350

POTTER or Alexander, Eva Augusta MA 1930
d Aber 12.12.75

POTTINGER or Sutherland, Jessie Maggie MA 1911
d 19.1.68

POZZI Joseph MA 1893 MB ChB 1897
d St Fillans 23.3.62 *AUR* XXXIX 370

PRATT Audrey MA 1955

PRATT Donald Reginald MA 1949 MB ChB 1954
DObstRCOG 1958
g p Bournemouth from 1958
m Lytchett Matravers 16.6.62 Pamela J. Sheppard SRN d of Douglas H. S. Lytchett Matravers

PRATT James Barrie BSc(agr) 1923 BSc 1926
resid Nairn

PRATT James Davidson *MA 1912 [d]BSc 1913
joint edit. *Chemical Industry* series of monographs for Pergamon Press 1965–72; retd; resid Ightham
d Ightham 26.7.78 *AUR* XLVIII 102

PRATT or Williams, Lora Young MA 1949 MB ChB 1954
g p Leeds from 1975

PRATT Margaret Ann MA 1936
no longer on GC reg

PRATT or McCullough, Mary Christina BSc(agr) 1922 MA 1923

PRATT or Palmer, Moira Kathleen Margaret MB ChB 1951
part time g p Caloundra Aust from 1960 and m o h from 1976

PRATT or Pennycuick, Susanna Andrew Calder *MA 1938

PRATT Sydney Alexander Milne *MA 1951

PRATT William Reginald MB ChB 1924
d Bournemouth 28.12.61 *AUR* XXXIX 382

PREDDY Adeline Jane MA 1915
d Aber 3.1.70 *AUR* XLIII 442

PRESLY or Smith, Helen Mackenzie MA 1945
resid Keith

PRESSLY Isabella Pearson MA 1902
d 21.10.68

PRESTON Charles Desmond MB ChB 1931
d 7.1.75 *AUR* XLVI 238

PRICE John William MB ChB 1949
LDS RCS(Eng) 1960
sen hosp dent. off. Staffs 1961–65; g p Stoke-on-Trent 1965–66; sen dent. off. Staffs c c from 1966

PRICE or Pougiales, Mary Lomas MB ChB 1947
ophth Olmsted med group Rochester Minnesota USA from 1955

PRICE or Yule, Mona Margaret MA 1941 LLB 1947
ptnr John S. Yule & Son solic Aber from 1966

PRIEST or Hewitt, Anna Ross MA 1924
retd 1965; resid Bedford

PRIEST Elizabeth Anne Forbes MB ChB 1950
med asst diabetic serv ARI from 1972
m Aber 21.11.62 James J. Dickie LLB(Dunedin) barrister-at-law s of John Dickie MA 1895 *qv*(I, II, III)
husb *d* 13.3.67

PRIEST or Cox, May Wilson MA 1924
MBE 1945
teacher Hants 1948–51; retd; resid Farnborough
d 22.12.78

PRIEST or Turner, Mina Wilson MA 1930
retd 1968; resid Farnborough

PRIESTLEY or Reid, Phyllis Jane Holden MB ChB 1938
g p Auchterarder from 1939

PRINGLE Alexander Ferguson MB ChB 1904 *MD 1916
d Aber 10.9.62 *AUR* XL 91

PRINGLE Ivan Terence MA 1909
no longer on GC reg

PRINGLE or Hunter, Joyce BSc(agr) 1949 PhD 1953
lect soil phys dept soil sc N'cle from 1963

PRINGLE or Cooper, Norna MB ChB 1948 DPH 1955
departmental m o Aberdeensh 1963–70; clin m o Cupar 1970–76; sen clin m o NE Fife from 1976

PRISE Edward *BSc(eng) 1955
W. A. Fairhurst & ptnrs Aber: eng 1957–72, assoc 1973–77, ptnr from 1977

PRITCHARD Donald Forsyth Buchanan BSc 1927
d 22.8.79

PRITCHARD or McDonald, Margaret MA 1953
teacher Swanland E Yorks from 1973

PROCTOR David Maxwell MB ChB 1944
OBE

PROCTOR George Rennet *BSc 1952 PhD 1956
visiting fell. univ of Zurich 1960; Royal Soc visiting fell. Yale univ New Haven USA 1963; lect chem

Strath 1964–70, sen lect from 1970; visiting expert Nat Cancer Inst Bethesda Md USA

PROFEIT or Watson, Mary Helena *MA 1909
no longer on GC reg

PROFEIT Robert Alexander MA 1889
no longer on GC reg

PROSSER Dorothy Claire MA 1920
no longer on GC reg

PROSSER Douglas *MA 1947 Dip Ed 1948
dep rector Inverurie acad 1971–75; head Hazlehead acad Aber from 1975
wife *d* –.2.78

PROSSER Oswald George MB ChB 1925
d Hull 20.12.67 *AUR* XLII 366

PRYOR Graeme Derek MA 1955

PUCCI Peter Vincent MB ChB 1940
g p Chesterfield 1950–69; Edzell: commun med 1969–80

PUDDY Claude Austin PhD 1934

PURCHASE Arthur Richard BSc 1953

PURDY Henry David MA 1894
no longer on GC reg

PURVES John Elder Bootland MA 1936 *BSc 1939

PYCROFT or Baillie, Norma Cotesworth MA 1947

PYKA William Swienczyk BL 1955
CA 1960 Assoc Member Institute of Taxation 1964 Polish Gold Cross of Merit 1967 Polish Home Army Cross 1970
ptnr Cooper & Hay advoc Aber 1961–68; lect RGIT Aber 1968–70, sen lect from 1970; private advoc & NP/CA from 1968

PYLE Douglas MA 1930

PYPER or Stewart, Catherine Mary MA 1925
no longer on GC reg

PYPER or Hillelson, Ida Burton *MA 1909
d 26.8.63

PYPER Ida Malcolm Birnie *MA 1932
retd 1968; resid Peterhead

PYPER or Thomson, Mary Milne MA 1918 *MB ChB 1921
g p Kei Mouth S Af 1923–61; semi-retd; resid Kei Mouth Cape Province

PYPER William Esplin MB ChB 1936
retd; resid Tamworth

QUINE John Waddington *MA 1952
econ intell asst Pontypool 1954–58; econ Brit Nylon Spinners Lond 1958–65; econ ICI Fibres Harrogate from 1965

QUINLAN Audrey MA 1953
Aber: teacher Inchgarth p s 1966–73, Craighill p s from 1973

RAE or Bain, Anne Bruce Lumsden MA 1910
d Perth 11.5.72 *AUR* XLV 224

RAE Beatrix MA 1916 BSc 1920
d 16.11.70

RAE Bennet Birnie MA 1926 *BSc 1929 PhD 1938
FRSE 1961
Buckland prof (lect various fishing ports) 1958; sen prin scient off./asst dir Marine lab DAFS Aber 1959–71; retd

RAE Cornelius Thomson MA 1910 BD 1913
d 12.12.74 *AUR* XLVI 235

RAE or White, Elizabeth MA 1913
d 2.3.74

RAE or Thom, Elizabeth MA 1926

RAE Francis William MA 1931 BD 1934 DD 1965
C of S min: Cardonald par ch Glasg 1948–70, Dairsie and Kemback, Fife from 1970; convener home mission comm home board 1964–68, moderator Glasg presb 1968–69, convener joint home and deaconess board comm 1970–74; moderator Cupar presb 1973–75; retd; resid St Andrews

RAE Frederick Sutherland MB ChB 1937
MRCGP 1956
g p Aber from 1947

RAE George Cornelius MB ChB 1937
DPM 1940
h o Kettering hosp Northants 1938–39; asst m o Bexley mental hosp Kent 1939–41; war serv m o RAF 1941–46; asst m o Bexley mental hosp 1946–48; sen m o Banstead mental hosp Surrey 1948–56, St Andrew's mental hosp Norfolk 1956–69; retd; resid Norwich
m Norfolk 5.12.70 Barbara J. Eagling d of William A. E.

RAE Gordon *MA 1934
FEIS 1976
prin lect geog Jordanhill coll of educ Glasg 1947–76

RAE or Chakko, Grace Jane Hurry MA 1933

RAE or Hutcheson, Isabella Jessie MA 1915
no longer on GC reg

RAE or Mathers, Isabelle Josephine *MA 1934

RAE or Margetts, Isobel Watson MB ChB 1944
g p: Beeston Notts 1950–70, Elgin from 1970; also part time m o Bilbohall hosp Elgin
husb *d* 29.2.68

RAE James MA 1910 BD 1914 DD 1956
d Lond 4.5.60 *AUR* XXXVIII 589

RAE James William MB ChB 1939
d 25.12.66

RAE John James BSc(agr) 1954

RAE or Clark, Mary Janetta MA 1921
resid Aber

RAE Nancy Margaret MA 1954
teacher remed reading Craigbank p s Sauchie Alloa from 1975
m Aber 22.8.59 John A. R. Colman BSc(Glas) petr geol s of Ernest C. Gatehouse-of-Fleet

RAE William MA 1903 dBL 1906
d Victoria BC 11.11.73 *AUR* XLV 444

RAE William MA 1949
head St Boswells p s from 1958

RAE William *MA 1951

RAE William Duff BSc 1941 PhD 1946
AIRI 1967
group chief chem Silentbloc Holdings Surbiton from 1971

RAE William Jack Watson MB ChB 1950 DPH 1957 MD 1962
MFCM 1972
Aber: sen asst m o h 1959–63, jun dep m o h 1963–68, asst sen m o NE reg hosp board 1968–71, prin asst sen m o 1971–74; spec commun med Grampian health board 1974–78; retd

RAE William James *MA 1950

RAEBURN George Ferguson LLB 1938
ptnr Raeburn, Christie, Buthlay & Rutherford advoc Aber/solic Ellon from 1947; town clerk Ellon till 1975

RAFFAN Alfred William MB ChB 1938
anaest NE reg hosp board from 1948; member NE reg hosp board Scot. from 1971; member bus. comm General Council Aberd from 1971; retd hosp serv 1977
wife *d* Aber 1.9.75
m(2) 23.12.76 Hellen P. Ledingham or Gilchrist

RAFFAN Hamish McLennan MB ChB 1943 cMD 1948
FRCP(C) 1972
internal med Guelph Ontario from 1953

RAFFAN Helen Mary *MA 1917
retd; resid Edin
d Edin 27.4.80

RAFFAN Ian Duffus BSc 1955
teacher sc: St Andrew's s s Lhanbryde 1958–61, Rothes s s 1962–63, Lossiemouth h s 1963–65, spec asst 1965–69; sp asst sc Milne's h s Fochabers 1969–73, asst prin guid from 1973
m Elgin 8.7.64 Margaret A. McArthur cook d of James H. McA. Garmouth

RAFFAN John Buie MB ChB 1939
path. mid Glam AHA from 1949

RAFFAN Stanley James MA 1947
C of S min: Martyr's and North ch Greenock 1956–62, Ellon par ch 1962–73, Ellon and Slains par ch 1973–77; chaplain Crichton Royal & Nithbank hosps Dumfries from 1977

RAINNIE George Fraser *MA 1949
univ of Leeds: sen lect 1964–78, chmn of econ stud. from 1978

RAIT Robert Bain MB ChB 1935
h o Darlington 1935–36; g p Ilford 1936–41; RAMC 1941–44; g p Ilford 1944–72; retd; resid Ringwood

RAIT Williamina Alice MA 1910
d –.12.72

RAITT John Stewart BSc 1947 *1949 PhD 1953

RAITT or Fallowfield, Kathleen Mary *BSc 1953
head sc dept St Bride's s Helensburgh from 1971

RAITT Norah Patricia MB ChB 1951
part-time cytologist Raigmore hosp Inv
m Aber 26.8.61 John R. G. Watters MB ChB(Edin) g p Ullapool

RAITT William John MB ChB 1925
d Aber 3.7.61 *AUR* XXXIX 205

RAITT William Lindsay *BSc 1955

RALPH Ian Fraser MB ChB 1953

RALPH or Neill, Maggie *MA 1928
d Glasg 9.12.60 *AUR* XXXIX 105

RAMKISSOON Ramdath MB ChB 1954

RAMSAY Andrew Melvin MA 1923 MB ChB 1926 MD 1939
consult. phys infectious diseases unit Royal Free hosp Hampstead from 1948

RAMSAY or Duncan, Charlotte Edna MA 1944
teacher Drumgarth s Aber from 1961

RAMSAY Doris MB ChB 1945
g p: Shapinsay Orkney 1963–72, Thurso from 1972

RAMSAY or Dalrymple, Isobel Stuart Wyness MB ChB 1931
d Aber 1.12.76

RAMSAY Mary Paton MA 1908
d Edin 5.7.67 *AUR* XLII 179

RAMSAY Rowellyn BCom 1923
minister emeritus presb ch of Aust 1966; hon chaplain presb homes for the blind Brisbane Queensland from 1967
d 1981

RAMSAY William Leslie MB ChB 1926
retd 1970; resid Shorne Kent

RANKIN Alexander Douglas MB ChB 1925 DPH 1927
no longer on GC reg

RANKIN Andrew MA 1922
retd 1966; resid Inv
d Inv 21.9.80 *AUR* XLIX 67

RANKIN Andrew Logan MA 1954

RANKIN or Chalmers, Anita Joyce Graham MA 1947
resid St Albans

RANKIN or Junor, Margaret Elizabeth MA 1920 MB ChB 1923
resid Grahamstown S Africa

RANKIN Wilfred PhD 1929

RANKIN William James MA 1935
major TARO
retd
wife *d* 1966
d Aber 30.9.80 *AUR* XLIX 69

RANKINE Annie Anderson Primrose BSc 1937 *1938
asst head Fraserburgh acad; retd 1976; resid Gullane

RANKINE Henry William BSc 1938
MICE 1945 MIStructE 1945
county surv E Lothian c c Haddington 1962–75; consult. to Mason & ptnrs consult. eng Edin 1975–78; retd; resid Gullane

RANKINE or Binns, Janet MA 1912
d Jedburgh 3.10.70 *AUR* XLIV 109

RANKINE Rachel Levie MA 1910
resid Aber
d Aber 7.4.79 *AUR* XLVIII 226

RANNIE James MB ChB 1921 MD 1924
d Beckenham 14.7.77

RANNIE Melville Elliot McAlpine BL 1948
secy/treas: board of man. Aber spec hosps 1963–71, hon secy/treas assoc of Scot. hosp boards of man. 1965–69; secy/treas board of man. Foresterhill and assoc hosps Aber 1971–74; private leg. practice Crieff 1974–77

RAO Gargestwari Narayana Subba
see Subba Rao

RATTRAY Arthur Smith BSc 1942
d Sutton Coldfield 12.9.74 *AUR* XLVI 110

RATTRAY William MA 1899
d 2.1.71

RAWCLIFFE Gordon Hindle DSc 1944
FIEE 1946 FIEEE 1970 FRS 1972
prof elect. eng Brist 1944–75; retd
d 3.9.79

RAY Santosh Chandrah PhD 1938

RAYNER or Bain, Kathleen *BSc 1951
teacher phys St David's s Ashford Middx from 1969

REAICH or Ewing, Maggie Jane Cowie MA 1923
resid Cults Aber
d Aber 11.7.78

REAICH or Brooks, Williamina MA 1925
teacher Abbotswell p s Aber 1953–66; retd

REAPER Alexander MA 1909
d Aber 2.2.66 *AUR* XLII 82

REAY or Jason, Aileen Anne Elizabeth *MA 1952
resid Cults Aber

REAY George Adam MA 1921 *BSc 1923
d Aber 20.1.71 *AUR* XLIV 210

REAY John Sinclair Shewan *BSc 1953
SAI Edin 1958–67; Warren Spring lab DTI Stevenage: head intelligence sect. 1968–71, head air pollution div 1972–77; DTI: head prospectives unit from 1977

REDDING or Munro, Mary Elizabeth MA 1941
resid Edin

REDINGTON George DSc 1929
no longer on GC reg

REEKIE Andrew George MB ChB 1917
resid Edin

REES David Cooper MA 1911
d 5.1.63

REES Lovat Victor Charles *BSc 1950 PhD 1953 DSc 1977
sen lect chem Imperial coll Lond from 1970

REGAN Nils Albert MB ChB 1949
Lond: prin g p from 1957; clin asst hosp pract grade venereology/fam plan. Westminster hosp from 1964, St Stephen's hosp from 1977

REID Alastair David *MA 1950
teacher Engl/liberal stud. Aber coll of comm from 1960

REID Alexander MA 1921
d Edin 28.8.65 *AUR* XLII 85

REID Alexander BSc 1923
d Peterhead 29.6.62 *AUR* XL 88

REID Alexander MB ChB 1924
no longer on GC reg

REID Alexander MB ChB 1924
d Manc 2.5.72 *AUR* XLIV 430

REID Alexander MA 1925 BSc 1927
d Australia

REID Alexander *BSc 1949
d Inv 1.7.74 *AUR* XLVI 110

REID Alexander Edwin MB ChB 1921 DPH 1923
retd 1969, resid Towcester

REID Alexander Gordon MA 1954 LLB 1956

REID or Crossman, Alice MB ChB 1922
d Cheddar 17.12.69 *AUR* XLIII 445

REID Alister Ure BSc(eng) 1954
MICE 1960 MSc(Lond) 1965 DIC 1965
CEng: Lond c c 1960–65, GLC from 1965
m Dunfermline 14.10.61 Sheila C. M. Cumming d of David O. C. Dunfermline

REID or Buchan, Ann Buchan MA 1914
d 2.5.50

REID Anne Isabella MA 1952
Dip Sec Stud.(Glasg) 1953
teacher comm subj Aber coll of comm 1970–72, sen lect from 1972
m Inverurie –.4.60 Clayton B. W. Angus sen asst registrar Aber s of John A. Aber
husb *d* 1977

REID Annie MA 1914
d Aber 22.3.65 *AUR* XLI 149

REID or Allan, Annie Elsie MA 1926
resid Alvah, Banff

REID or Allan, Annie Isabella MA 1942
d Aber 11.4.61

REID Archibald Charles MB ChB 1925
no longer on GC reg

REID Arthur George *MB ChB 1916 *MD 1919
d Aber 21.5.62 *AUR* XXXIX 381

REID Arthur George MB ChB 1938
FRCGP 1970 MBE 1977
g p Auchterarder from 1940; clin asst Scot, g p res support unit (attached dept g p Dund) 1971–74

REID or Dixon, Beatrice Rae MA 1925
resid Grantown-on-Spey

REID Catherine Williamine MA 1928
teacher maths Inverurie acad 1935–67; retd

REID Charles MA 1909
d Lond 24.1.69 *AUR* XLIII 209

REID Charles
***MA 1914 *BSc 1916 *MB ChB 1917 *MD 1926 DSc 1927**
d 24.10.61 *AUR* XXXIX 276

REID Charles MA 1914 MB ChB 1921
d Craigellachie 7.9.72 *AUR* XLV 124

REID or McMillan, Charlotte Helen Mary MA 1933
resid Elgin

REID Donald Darnley MB ChB 1937 ᶜMD 1946
FRCP(Lond) 1965
prof epidemiology/dir dept med statist and epidemiology London s of hyg & trop med from 1959
d Hampton Middx 26.3.77 *AUR* XLVII 214

REID Donald Eric MA 1907
no longer on GC reg

REID or Mutch, Edith Grace MA 1931
resid Mintlaw

REID Edmund Lewis MB ChB 1910
surg ENT Sellyoak hosp Birm 1938–39; ADMS Orkney & Shetland Defences; consult. nat health hosp serv ENT Liv 1948–54; retd; resid Bicester
m Newport Mon 12.3.22 Flora M. Green physioth d of James G. Newport

REID Edward Alexander MA 1951 MEd 1958
ABPsS 1961
educ psych/advis Banffsh 1965–68; dep prin educ psych Fife 1968–70; lect/sen lect educ psych Callendar Park coll of educ Falkirk 1970–71, prin lect from 1972

REID Ella Taylor MA 1916
d 13.7.72

REID Eric *BSc 1943
Univ Sur: reader biochem from 1965; also dir of Wolfson bioanalytical centre from 1969

REID George MA 1920
d Aber 9.4.77

REID George MA 1939 LLB 1942
ptnr Alexander & Gillan advoc Aber from 1963

REID George Alexander BSc(eng) 1947

REID George Arthur *MB ChB 1916 *MD 1919
d Aber 21.5.62 *AUR* XXXIX 381

REID George Merson MB ChB 1942 DPH 1947
g p Sydney Aust from 1951

REID or Green, Grace Hendry MA 1955
teacher: Alves 1959–60, Halifax Canada 1968–69; secy Parry Sound Canada 1978–79

REID Harry Campbell MA 1937 LLB 1938
ptnr James Milne & Co CA Aber 1951–62; member exam board inst of CA Scot, 1955–63; man. indust work therap unit royal Cornhill hosp Aber 1964–68;

acct Mackenzie & Wilson advoc Aber 1968–77, ptnr from 1977

REID Helen Margaret MA 1940
Aber: teacher Sunnybank p s 1945–65, Mile End p s 1965–66, dep head Tullos p s 1966–73; head Kirkhill p s from 1973

REID or Keir, Helen Winifred MA 1949
teacher Skene p s 1966–68; asst head (qualif in early educ) Culter s from 1969

REID or Bennett, Hilda Jean *MA 1944

REID Ian Wilson Carlyle MB ChB 1954
Canada: dist med examiner Hinton Alberta from 1957, indust m o Cardinal River Coals Hinton from 1974

REID or Sharp, Isobel Ellen *MA 1939
county pres Brit Red Cross Soc Scot. Branch Banff 1967–75, pres Moray branch incorporating Banffsh from 1975; resid Keith

REID James MA 1934
TD 1961
br man. Standard Life Assur Co Manc 1964–72; retd; resid Balerno

REID James Leckie MA 1901
d Dun 24.3.70 *AUR* XLIII 440

REID James Vessman MA 1930
resid Aber

REID or Russell, Jean MA 1940
resid Elgin

REID or Couper, Jean Alison MA 1942
teacher: North s Kirkcaldy 1960–68, Kinloss s Moray 1969–75, Applegrove s Forres from 1975

REID or McGlashan, Jean Margaret *MA 1917
resid Regina Canada
husb *d* 31.5.66

REID or Still, Jean Milne Brebner MA 1950
teacher Aboyne acad 1952–59

REID Jessie MA 1929
teacher Fraserburgh cent s 1939–69; retd

REID or Ewart, Jessie MA 1945

REID Jessie Sandison MA 1935

REID or Morton, Joan Ririe MA 1929

REID John MA 1936 BD 1938
C of S min Arbroath Knox's from 1950

REID John *MA 1944
TD 1965
prin teacher mod lang RGC Aber from 1963; CO Aberd OTC 1957–65

REID John Cameron MB ChB 1945
MRCGP 1953 FRCGP 1975 JP Abdnsh 1964
g p Strathdon from 1948

REID John Carlyle MA 1927
no longer on GC reg

REID John Henderson *BSc 1932
d 8.10.81

REID John Low Thomson BSc(agr) 1952
farm. Ellon from 1952

REID John Madden *MA 1951

REID John Mortimer *BSc(eng) 1951
MIWES 1964 FICE 1970
resid eng Howard Humphreys & Sons Trinidad/Kenya/Libya 1955–64, prin eng Ethiopia, Seychelles, Ghana, Sierra Leone 1964–69; man. dir Pietrangeli & Humphreys SPA Rome 1969–73; assoc ptnr Howard Humphreys England 1974–78, Howard Humphreys Jordan (resid Amman) from 1978—all work associated with water supplies and irrigation

REID John Ure BL 1949
retd police serv 1960; Wiggins Teape Basingstoke: group safety trg advis

REID Kathleen Murray MA 1924
no longer on GC reg

REID Laurence Milne BSc(eng) 1955
MIEE 1965
hydro-elec sect. AEI heavy plant div Rugby 1961–62; J. Sykes & Ptnrs consult. eng Sheffield 1962–64; AEI electronic apparatus div which became GEC/Elliot process automation: head of power, mining and GPO sales Leicester 1964–70; careers advis univ of Brist from 1970
m Wolvercote 27.8.66 Jennifer A. Wolfe BA(Cantab) teacher d of Robert W. Oxford

REID Lydia Chisholm *MA 1950
d 9.5.81

REID Margaret Anne MB ChB 1919
no longer on GC reg

REID Margaret Elspeth Jaffray MA 1951

REID or Stacey, Margaret Farquharson Garrow MB ChB 1928
asst venereologist (locum) Sheff hosps 1960–63, g p Bakewell Derbysh 1963–65; retd; resid Sheffield

REID Margaret Jane Cornfute *MA 1910 PhD 1937
no longer on GC reg

REID or Clay, Margaret Pamela Birnie [c]MB ChB 1948
JP Reigate 1968
part time asst m o SE Surrey from 1963
d Redhill 5.6.80 *AUR* XLIX 70

REID or McGregor, Margaret Sarah Milne MB ChB 1926 MD 1932 DPH 1932
retd 1969; resid Dyce

REID Marshall Findlay BCom 1922
no longer on GC reg

REID Martha MA 1946
teacher: Aberchirder j s s 1947, Newhall 1948–56, Golborne 1956–58, Slough 1958–66, Inv 1966–72
m Nairn 9.12.72 John T. Graham comp dir s of Thomas G. Chryston

REID or Williams, Mary Ann Margaret MA 1934
teacher Fr/Engl Buckie h s 1968–73; retd; resid Portsoy

REID or Kellas, Mary Buchan Ponting MA 1947
teacher Arrochar p s Dunbartonsh from 1968

REID or MacArthur, Mary Helen MB ChB 1939
d Edin 23.2.59 *AUR* XXXVIII 218

REID or Moxley, Mary Loughran MA 1950

REID or Mair, Mary Morrison MA 1941
resid Aboyne

REID or Cartledge, Mildred Jean MA 1951
teacher: Birm 1955–61, Warks from 1961

REID Peter MB ChB 1911 DPH 1927
d Buckie 3.1.69 *AUR* XLIII 209

REID Robert Barron BSc(agr) 1938
dep dir agr Lusaka N Rhodesia 1959–65; retd; sen agr econ NOSCA Inv from 1965

REID Robert Stephen MA 1925
no longer on GC reg

REID Robert Watson MB ChB 1901
no longer on GC reg

REID or Ezles, Robina MA 1927
no longer on GC reg

REID or Gray, Sheena Edward MA 1954
teacher Fr gr s for girls Guernsey from 1975

REID or Fawcett, Sheila Macdonald MA 1939
W Aust: lib asst Scarborough publ lib 1960–62, br lib Canning Bridge, Melville, lib geol surv mines dept of W Aust, Perth 1966–78

REID or Simpson, Sheila Margaret MB ChB 1947 DPH 1952
resid Newbury

REID Stanley McRae MA 1934 MB ChB 1938
d Banstead 26.1.80 *AUR* XLVIII 442

REID or Nutten, Thomasina MA 1925
resid Inv

REID or Bowie, Victoria Henrietta BSc 1921
asst dept bot and zool NOSCA 1921–27
resid Aber

REID William MA 1912
TD
d 23.6.64 *AUR* XL 397

REID William Brebner BSc 1949
rector Earlston h s from 1965

REID William Clark BSc 1951
prin teacher maths Eyemouth from 1963

REID William Ewen MB ChB 1905
no longer on GC reg

REID William Ferris BSc(agr) 1935
farm./cattle breeding; retd dir RH & A soc; resid Montrose

REID William Innes MB ChB 1947
d Hopeman 27.2.75 *AUR* XLVI 240

REID William James MA 1906 BSc 1908 *MB ChB 1910 *MD 1914
no longer on GC reg

REID William John Walker BSc(eng) 1944
MICE 1951 MIWPC 1955 FIPHE 1967
county drainage eng Aber c c 1968–75; retd; with Hunter Construction (Aberdeen) from 1975

REITH or Oliphant, Adeline *MA 1934
teacher Engl/hist Ruthrieston s Aber 1952–70; retd

REITH Arthur MB ChB 1933
d Manc 22.9.69 *AUR* XLIII 331

REITH Douglas MA 1938 LLB 1945
QC from 1957; NHS commissioner from 1960; standing jun counsel in Scot. to customs and excise 1949–51; advoc-dep Crown Off. Scot. 1953–57; pres Pensions Appeal Tribunal (Scot.) 1958–64; chmn NHS tribunal (Scot.) 1963–65

REITH Hellen Lind MB ChB 1938
FRCOG 1971
consult. obst/gyn Paisley; retd

REITH James William Strachan *BSc(agr) 1943 PhD 1950
FRIC 1967
sen prin scient off. Macaulay inst Aber from 1977

REITH Margaret *MA 1931
retd 1970
m Inv 18.9.70 Donald Macpherson wholesale area man. s of Donald M. Uplawmoor Renfrewsh

REITH Ronald John BSc(agr) 1932
d Lond 14.2.67 *AUR* XLII 371

RENDALL James Alexander MA 1935
d Aber 19.8.62 *AUR* XL 93

RENNET David Lindsay MA 1929 LLB 1932
ptnr Butchart & Rennet advoc Aber 1935–75; retd; resid Bristow Norfolk

RENNET or Proctor, Margaret Joyce MB ChB 1923
retd 1966; resid Aber
d 24.11.81

RENNET or Stewart, Nita Isobel BSc 1923
resid Abinger Common Surrey

RENNIE or Bain, Agnes Craigen MA 1933

RENNIE Alexander James *BSc(mech eng) 1947 *BSc(civ eng) 1948
FICE 1968
Merz & McLellan consult. eng N'cle-u-Tyne: chief civ eng 1968, assoc 1969–74, ptnr from 1974

RENNIE Alexander Milne *MB ChB 1933
consult. orthop surg to army in Scot. 1960–76; prof clin orthop surg Aberd 1972–76; retd; resid Kinellar

RENNIE Cecilia MA 1953
oral Fr superv in Oakville area Ontario 1961–63; teacher remed: Methil 1968–72, Ellon area 1972–76, spec unit for sec maladjusted ch in Fraserburgh teachers' centre from 1976
m Aber 2.8.60 Alan B. Penny MA 1953 *qv*

RENNIE Duncan BSc(eng) 1945

RENNIE or Smith, Ethel Margaret MA 1928
teacher: Chapel of Garioch 1930–35, Canongate nursery s Edin 1940–45, Trefoil s Gogar Edin 1956–72; retd; resid Ellon

RENNIE George Nicholson *MA 1934
JP FEIS
d Aber 12.3.74 *A UR* XLV 449

RENNIE Gordon Grant MB ChB 1953
regist anaest: Edin 1960–63, Greenock 1963; locum consult. anaest: Greenock 1963, Glasgow/Lanarksh 1964–69; Lanarksh: med asst anaest 1969–70, consult. anaest from 1970
m Largs 2.4.67 Morag L. Davis MB ChB(Glas) d of Thomas J. D. Largs

RENNIE James Benjamin MA 1955
C of S min Blackford ch Auchterarder from 1967
m Inverurie 6.6.59 Margaret G. Pirie s secy d of George P. Inverurie

RENNIE James Fyfe *MA 1922 BD 1925
d Hamilton NZ 20.3.80 *A UR* XVLIII 441

RENNIE or Beddie, Jane Christie MA 1927
teacher Peterhead cent s 1930–63; retd
husb *d* 1968

RENNIE or Gavin, Jeannie Stephen MA 1919
resid Fraserburgh

RENNIE Joan Elise MA 1929
d 29.11.78

RENNIE John MB ChB 1908 *MD 1912
no longer on GC reg

RENNIE John Milne BSc(agr) 1922

RENNIE Lottie MA 1937
teacher Hilton acad Aber from 1942

RENNIE or Wilkinson, Margaret Louisa *MA 1930
d 1952

RENNIE Peter *MA 1951
diplomatic serv off. FCO Lond 1961–71; 2nd secy Brit Emb Belgrade 1971–74; FCO Lond from 1974

RENNIE Stephen BSc(agr) 1923
d York 12.3.69 *A UR* XLIII 213

RENNIE Thomas Fyfe MB ChB 1953 DPH 1958
FACMA 1968 Dip Health Admin (NSW) 1972
NSW Aust: m o h Western health dist 1961–67, m o h Parramatta 1967–72, dir commun health serv health comm from 1973

RENNIE Violet Falconer MA 1949 Dip Ed 1963
lect prin methods Aber coll of educ 1966–67; head Auchentoshan s for handicapped Dalmuir Dumbartonsh 1967–72, asst advis spec educ Glasg 1972–78; advis spec educ Renfrew div Strathclyde reg c from 1978

RENNIE William John BSc 1955

REPPER Edwin Norman Duncan MB ChB 1921 MD 1929
no longer on GC reg

RETIEF François Petrus Steyn (Frank) MB ChB 1924

RETTIE Hugh Leith MB ChB 1925
d 1962 *A UR* XXXIX 383

RETTIE Ian Hazelwood *MA 1953
Assoc FRAeS 1967
chief aero dynamicist BAC Brist div 1966–73; chief eng aerodyn staff Boeing comm aeroplane co Renton Washington USA from 1973

REYNARD or Greenhorn, Catherine Grainger MA 1930
resid Cupar Fife

REYNARD James Grainger BSc(agr) 1924
no longer on GC reg

REYNARD Marion Grainger *MA 1932
teacher Engl Bell-Baxter s Cupar Fife 1949–74; retd

RHIND or Walker, Alison Thackrah *MA 1936
Red Cross Badge of Honour 1978
teacher Fr h s for girls Wolverhampton 1960; o/c BRCS Wolverhampton from 1967; Red Cross rep at Consulate-gen in Lyon France to assist Brit casualties 1965; member commun health council Wolverhampton from 1976

RHIND Douglas Haig MB ChB 1939
g p Derby from 1946

RHIND Edward Gregson Grant *MB ChB 1935
FRCP 1964
consult. phys Sheffield gen hosp 1946–77; retd
wife *d* 1960
m(2) Aber 5.12.64 Kathleen McCombie MB ChB 1947 *qv*

RHIND Gordon *MA 1925
no longer on GC reg

RHIND Mary Elder BSc 1941
C of S deaconess Glasg 1960–65; w c c schol William Temple coll Rugby 1965–66; commun liaison off. Corby from 1966

RHIND Robert Gordon *MA 1931
prin teacher maths Br of Don acad Aber 1962–74; retd

RHIND William *MA 1928 BSc 1930
retd 1970; resid Lerwick

RHYNAS Ethel Isobel MA 1927
FSA(Scot) 1973
retd teaching 1962; hon curator Elgin museum 1967–71

RIACH or McMorland, Amy Forbes MA 1952
teacher: Edzell p s 1960–65, temp in Angus s from 1965

RIACH David Alexander MA 1953 *1955

RIACH William Alastair Drage MA 1937
MA(Kansas) 1970 PhD(Edin) 1978
asst prof educ Mem univ Newfoundland 1962–70, assoc prof from 1970

RIBTON-TURNER Humphrey BSc(for) 1934
security investig off. M o D royal milit acad Woolwich from 1965

RICE Agnes Walker MA 1932

RICE Denis James *MA 1955
Post Grad Cert Ed(Lond) 1960
Dip Soc St(Edin) 1960
Member Br Assoc Soc Workers 1970
educ off. RAF 1956–60; fam case worker Aber assoc of soc serv 1961–62; warden Vaughan coll univ Leic from 1962, sen lect from 1974

RICE James Inglis *MB ChB 1939
d Corgarff 3.9.72 *AUR* XLV 128

RICE Maureen Agnes MA 1948
dep head Corpus Christi RC s s Nott 1958–67
m Montrose 29.8.66 Peter W. Baxter jeweller s of George W. B. Nott

RICE Thomas Inglis MA 1928
no longer on GC reg

RICHARDS or Tewnion, Agnes Doreen BSc 1944
teacher chem Dollar acad from 1971

RICHARDS or Watt, Elizabeth Ferguson Carmichael MA 1941
resid Cults Aber

RICHARDS Ernest Glenesk BSc(for) 1938
FIFor(GB) 1958
dir for. comm h q Lond from 1974

RICHARDS John Charles Shenstone *BSc 1947 PhD 1953
reader nat phil dept Aberd from 1965
m(2) Aber 12.4.73 Alexandra G. Murdoch mus

RICHARDS or Mortimer, Louisa Ravenscroft MA 1940
resid Edin

RICHARDS Marion Brock *MA 1907 *BSc 1909 DSc 1916
d 19.6.64 *AUR* XL 395

RICHARDS Robert MA 1907 *MB ChB 1910 *DPH 1913 [c]MD 1917
d Aber 18.11.65 *AUR* XLI 239

RICHARDS Robert Lawrence *MB ChB 1939 MD 1944
FRCPGlas 1964
consult. phys Glasg Western/Gartnavel hosps; also clin lect Glas from 1963

RICHARDS Robert Lawson MB ChB 1932
d Inv 2.3.74 *AUR* XLV 448

RICHARDS William Leslie MA 1938 [d]LLB 1940
retd 1970; resid Somerset

RICHARDS William Powell Earle MB ChB 1925
d 27.9.61 *AUR* XXXIX 282

RICHARDSON or McKenzie, Edith Smith MA 1923
deceased

RICHARDSON George Barclay BSc 1944
CBE 1978
fell. St John's coll Oxon from 1951; member monopolies comm 1969–74; member royal comm environmental pollution 1973–74; secy to delegates and chief exec OUP from 1974

RICHARDSON or Mackintosh, Kathleen Campbell MA 1945

RICHARDSON Walter Dudley *BSc 1951
MSc(Lond) 1966
lect bot Imp coll Trop Agr, Trinidad 1956–62; lect/sen lect bot SW Essex tech coll 1963–66; Goldsmith's coll Lond: sen lect bot 1966–73, head biol sc dept from 1973

RICHES John Haddon PhD 1936
no longer on GC reg

RICHMOND Archibald Johnston Roddan MA 1941

RICHMOND Hendry Gilmour MB ChB 1948 *MD 1958
FRCPath 1970
consult. path. Highland health board Inv from 1960

RICHMOND Robert Hill MA 1947
C of S min Stonehaven South ch Stonehaven from 1967

RICHMOND Robert Leo BSc(eng) 1949

RICHMOND Roland Denis MB ChB 1953
anesthesia: g p Jamaica

RIDDEL or Thomas, Barbara Elizabeth MA 1938
Whitmore Park j s Coventry: teacher 1962, teacher-tut. for probationary and stud. teachers 1972–77; retd

RIDDEL Donald Olson MB ChB 1912
d Aber 7.5.63 *AUR* XL 201

RIDDEL George William MB ChB 1914 DPH 1919
d Norwich 5.2.70 *AUR* XLIII 442

RIDDEL or Forbes, Isabella Malcolm MA 1902
no longer on GC reg

RIDDEL Margaret Gertrude Black BSc 1927
no longer on GC reg

RIDDELL or Riddell, Alison Mary MB ChB 1946
resid Papatoetoe RD Auckland NZ

RIDDELL Clarence Eric MB ChB 1922
h o/locums/asst Wrexham, London, Bolton 1923–30; g p Point Kingston Jamaica 1930–41; locum/asst Lond 1941–72; retd
d 2.3.79

RIDDELL or McWilliam, Dorothy Christina Gordon MA 1935
teacher Bishopmill p s Elgin 1959–77; retd

RIDDELL George Alexander BCom 1929
Lond: secy/acct D. Napier & Son 1933–47; comptroller Engl Elect. Co 1947–62, man. dir 1962–69; dep man. dir/exec dir GEC 1969–73; retd

RIDDELL George Steedman *MB ChB 1939 DPH 1947 MD 1949
commun med spec Fife health board

RIDDELL or Gettliffe, Gladys May MB ChB 1953
W Va USA: internship 1972–73, resid paediat 1975–76; hon fell. oncology S Carolina 1976–77; paediat: Ponape TTPI 1977–78, Guam from 1979

RIDDELL John Scott MB ChB 1937
retd 1973; resid Auldearn
wife *d* 3.9.63
m(2) Stockton-on-Tees –.7.64 Winifred Hemsley asst matron mat. hosp d of Thomas H. S Shields

RIDDELL Sylvia Aileen *MA 1955
sen clin psych: Banstead hosp Surrey 1960–62, Mental h c Burnaby BC Canada 1962–66, McGill ch learning clin Montreal from 1966

RIDDELL William Shewan *MA 1913
resid Norwich

RIDDLER Munro BSc(eng) 1950
MICE 1960 FFB 1971
asst civ eng: Perthsh 1952–56, Inv 1956–60; sen civ eng Dun 1960–62; comm man. Glasg 1962–70; assoc consult. eng Glasg from 1970

RIDDOCH Anne Lillias MA 1919
d Athens 1979

RIDDOCH or Sawyer, Emily Caroline MA 1899
d 28.5.62 *AUR* XL 74

RIDDOCH or MacLeod, Helen Eliza MA 1928
resid Stonehaven
husb *d* 22.7.64

RIDDOCH Jean Walker MA 1933
retd 1966; resid Aber

RIDDOCH Mary BSc 1924 MB ChB 1927 MD 1934
d 4.3.66 *AUR* XLII 363

RIDDOCH Wyness David BCom 1924
d Rothiemay 16.1.69 *AUR* XLIII 213

RIGG or Kerr, Caroline Wilson MA 1926
JP Ayr 1965
resid Girvan

RIOCH Charles Turner MA 1947
pers man. Dunfermline 1948–50; retail man. Callander 1950–60; teacher Stranraer 1960–69; head Hoy s Orkney from 1969

RIOCH Margaret *MA 1923
d Stirling 12.5.69 *AUR* XLIII 213

RITCHIE Adam Alexander MA 1912
d 11.2.74 *AUR* XLV 447 & XLVI 107

RITCHIE or Mathieson, Agnes Duguid Ferrier *MA 1935
d 5.12.64

RITCHIE or Cordiner, Agnes Walker *MA 1924
resid Aber
d Aber 5.1.80

RITCHIE Agnes Walker MA 1937
retd 1974; resid Aber

RITCHIE Alfred BSc 1926 PhD 1936
prin scient off. Scot. home dept from 1950; resid Aber
d Aber 24.8.79

RITCHIE or Dickie, Alma Christina MB ChB 1942 DPH 1947
g p Crimond in ptnrship with husb from 1953

RITCHIE Annetta Duthie MA 1935
teacher Fraserburgh cent s from 1957

RITCHIE or Meldrum, Annie Miller MA 1931

RITCHIE Anthony Elliot MA 1933 BSc 1936
FCSP 1970 DSc(St And) 1972
secy/treas Carnegie Trust for univs of Scot. from 1969

RITCHIE Catherine MA 1940
teacher Buckie h s from 1946

RITCHIE or Barker, Charlotte Mitchell MA 1915
no longer on GC reg

RITCHIE David Alfred Rattray MB ChB 1946
consult. radiol Perth/Perthsh group of hosps from 1962

RITCHIE Duncan Ferries MB ChB 1938
retd; resid Elgin

RITCHIE Elizabeth MA 1913
retd; resid Port Elphinstone, Inverurie

RITCHIE or Rutherford, Elizabeth MA 1913
no longer on GC reg

RITCHIE Elsie BCom 1927
d Fraserburgh 6.5.65 *AUR* XLI 151

RITCHIE or Kellas, Eveline Margaret *MA 1920
resid Edin
husb *d* 12.11.67

RITCHIE or Munro, Frances Isabel MacCallum MA 1928

RITCHIE or Graham, Frances Selma MA 1945 MB ChB 1950
asst reg dir blood transfusion serv Dun till 1959; resid Broughty Ferry

RITCHIE Frederick MB ChB 1913 DPH 1922
retd Oct 1959
d Nov 1959

RITCHIE George Lee MB ChB 1914
d Aber 29.7.73

RITCHIE George Lee May MB ChB 1937 DPH 1939

RITCHIE Gordon Law MB ChB 1947
FRCSE 1958 DMRT(Edin) 1960 FFR(Lond) 1963
surg regist: Law hosp Carluke 1953–57, ARI 1957–58; regist/sen regist radiotherap Edin RI 1958–64; consult. radiotherap West Gen hosp Edin from 1964

RITCHIE Herbert MB ChB 1921
d Cowes I o W 24.7.74 *AUR* XLVI 108

RITCHIE Ian *BSc 1954
geol explor dept California Standard Edmonton 1958–61; geol in res proj Calif res corp La Habra Calif 1961–62; teacher Bankhead acad Aber 1963–64: geol in explor and prod. Chevron standard Calgary 1964–69, dist geol 1969–75, geophys 1975–76, staff geophys 1976–78

RITCHIE or Kinnear, Irene Lang MA 1950
resid Lower Fargo, Fife

RITCHIE Isabella MA 1945
teacher: Strichen j s s 1958–67, Lossiemouth h s 1967–68, Fraserburgh N s 1968–76, New Pitsligo 1977–78

RITCHIE James MA 1911
d Kirriemuir 26.5.74 *AUR* XLVI 107

RITCHIE James MA 1926
head: W Kirkton p s Dun 1949–51, Wallacetown p s 1951–62, Liff Road p s 1962–64, Fintry p s 1964–67; retd
m Dun 6.8.32 Elsie J. Gorrie

RITCHIE James Cunningham *BSc 1951 DSc 1962
Canada: assoc prof Manit 1960–65, prof biol Trent univ 1965–68, Dalhousie univ 1968–70, prof/chmn life sc Scarborough coll Tor from 1970

RITCHIE James Hunter BSc(for) 1932

RITCHIE James MacPherson *MA 1951
sen lect/assoc prof N'cle univ NSW Aust 1961–65; sen lect/warden of Grant Hall Hull univ 1965–69; prof/head dept Germanic stud. Sheff from 1969; pro vice chancellor
m Glasg 8.9.58 Sheena M. C. Watson MA(Glas) univ lib/teacher d of William W. BSc(Glas), Strathaven Lanarksh

RITCHIE James Simpson MB ChB 1945
OBE 1968 surg capt 1967 FCM 1973
sen ENT spec RN hosp Chatham 1958–61; joint services staff coll, Latimer Bucks 1961; sen m o HMS *Blake* Medit/WI 1961–63; sen ENT spec/sen m o (surg) RN hosp Plymouth 1963–72; sen m o HMS *Bulwark* UK/Far East 1966–67; m o i/c RN hosp Gibraltar 1972–77; retd from RN; m o DHSS Gosforth N'cle-u-Tyne from 1977

RITCHIE Jeanie Helen MB ChB 1923
resid Aberdeensh

RITCHIE or Coull, Jessie MA 1929
resid Aber

RITCHIE Jessie Ann MA 1931

RITCHIE John MB ChB 1910 MD DPH 1913
d Aber 10.9.66 *AUR* XLI 337

RITCHIE John Edwin *MA 1913 *BSc 1914
retd; resid Aber

RITCHIE John Hall MA 1912 BSc(agr) 1913
d 1976

RITCHIE John Miller MB ChB 1930
retd g p 1966; member/chmn m o p & i i boards Middlesbrough 1948–73

RITCHIE John Milne MB ChB 1925
no longer on GC reg

RITCHIE John Murdoch *MA 1925
d 3.8.70

RITCHIE Joseph BSc 1933
chief chem Carnegie Chemicals 1947–58; res chem Riker 3M 1958–73; retd; resid Rosehearty

RITCHIE Joseph Murdoch BSc 1944
DSc(Lond) 1960 MA(Yale) 1968 FRS 1976
USA: prof pharm Albert Einstein coll of med NY 1963–68; Eugene Higgins prof pharm Yale univ Conn from 1968

RITCHIE Lewis William MB ChB 1940
d 22.11.70 *AUR* XLIV 215

RITCHIE Macdonald Frey MA 1893 BL 1896
no longer on GC reg

RITCHIE or Waters, Margaret Buchan BSc 1941

RITCHIE Margaret Doreen MA 1933
teacher Engl subj Cullen/Portknockie 1969–71; retd; resid Buckie

RITCHIE or Annand, Margaret Duncan MA 1936
resid Aber
husb *d* 24.6.71

RITCHIE Mary Jane MA 1939
retd 1979; resid Rosehearty

RITCHIE May MA 1914
d Lonmay 4.6.67 *AUR* XLII 184

RITCHIE Michael Balfour Hutchison MB ChB 1904
d 11.2.69

RITCHIE Robert Stephen MB ChB 1948

RITCHIE or Konstam, Sheila Thompson MB ChB 1943
sessions in clin path. Orkney hosps from 1963

RITCHIE or Johnston, Stella Bremner MA 1945
teacher maths Our Lady's Convent Abingdon 1964–70, head of maths dept from 1970, first sen mistress from 1976

RITCHIE Thora Garden MA 1937

RITCHIE William MB ChB 1945
d 1.12.69

RITCHIE William Duncan MB ChB 1899
d Bovey Tracy 19.1.61

RITCHIE William Forbes *MA 1930
prin teacher classics Arbroath h s from 1950 and dep rector 1959–74; retd; memb Scottish Classics Group

RITCHIE William Geddes MA 1938
FRMetS 1968

RITCHIE William Miller MB ChB 1924
no longer on GC reg

RITCHIE William Murray MB ChB 1937

RITSON Joyce Manson MA 1944

RITSON Roy Barker MA 1949
MIPM 1962
asst head indust relations Texas Oil Co Bogota, Columbia 1959–60; pers off. Imp. Smelting Co Brist 1960–63; pers/trg off. Bookers (Zambia) Ndola Zambia 1963–69, group pers off. from 1969

RIXON David Dobson *MA 1951
pers off./staff pers man. Thames Board Mills Purfleet Essex from 1961

RIXON Peter Ernest MB ChB 1949
MRCPsych 1971
consult. psychiat: St George's hosp Morpeth 1960–63, St Audrys hosp Melton Woodbridge from 1963
m(2) Woodbridge 16.8.79 Dawn M. Tredre med soc worker d of Jack Norman Newmarket

ROBB Alexander Lawrence MB ChB 1913
d Aboyne 12.5.64 *AUR* XL 398

ROBB or Mair, Catherine MA 1946
teacher: Monquhitter s 1960–62, West Barns s E Lothian 1963–64, Damacre s Brechin 1964–66, Cults acad 1967–73; asst head Cults p s 1973–77, head Crombie p s Westhill Aber from 1977

ROBB David Bannerman MB ChB 1929
retd 1971; part time m o Dept of Health E Midlands div from 1971; resid Leicester

ROBB Douglas Alexander BCom 1927
Scott Peden & Co CA Edin from 1960, ptnr 1969–72; retd

ROBB Douglas George MA 1905
d Southsea 1.1.68

ROBB Edwin Douglas MB ChB 1932
Nott: sen m o DHSS 1963–73 retd; part time med referee DHSS from 1973

ROBB Elizabeth Agnes *MA 1918
no longer on GC reg

ROBB George Cameron *MA 1953 MEd 1957

ROBB George Mitchell McLeod MB ChB 1953
FRCS(Can) 1965 Cert Spec Gen Surg RCP&S(Can) temp lect biol chem Aberd 1960–62; resid surg Canada: resid surg Vancouver/gen surg Royal Columbian hosp/St Mary's hosp New Westminster Surrey mem hosp, Burnaby gen hosp BC from 1965

ROBB Harold Phillips MB ChB 1951

ROBB or Peers, Helen Margaret Taylor MA 1926
no longer on GC reg

ROBB or McCulloch, Isabella Esslemont MA 1920
resid Aber
husb *d* 28.8.62
d Banchory 9.9.78

ROBB James BSc(agr) 1920
no longer on GC reg

ROBB James Christie *BSc 1945 PhD 1948
prof phys chem Birm from 1957

ROBB James Philip BSc 1927 *1928 MA 1927
retd 1968; resid Aber

ROBB Jane Winifred MA 1904
retd; resid Banchory

ROBB or Elliot, Jean Anne MA 1941
Renfrewsh: teacher maths Giffnock j s s 1957–62, woman advis Woodfarm h s 1962–69, asst head from 1969

ROBB Jean Campbell MA 1925
d Banchory 27.1.70 *AUR* XLIII 445

ROBB John Walker *MA 1951

ROBB or Laidlaw, Mary Brebner MB ChB 1942

ROBB Nora MA 1946
teacher Turriff acad from 1953

ROBB Peter Yeats BSc(eng) 1949

ROBB Sheila McDonald BSc 1947 *1948
lect biol sciences Exe from 1968

ROBB William Brebner BSc 1952

ROBBIE Douglas Stewart ᶜMB ChB 1954
DA(Lond) 1958 FFARCS 1960
Lond: s r Westminster hosp group/Brompton hosp 1958–63, consult. anaest and i/c pain clin Royal Marsden hosp from 1963, consult. anaest (pain) St Christopher's hospice 1968–77

ROBBIE James Andrew *BSc 1933
d Edin 19.5.77 *AUR* XLVII 213

ROBBIE or Thomson, Lizzie Helen MA 1931
teacher Gartly 1932–39; head Cushnie p s 1939–42, Oldhamstocks p s 1959–65; teacher Earlston 1965–68, Kinnesswood 1968–72; retd; resid Kirkcaldy
husb *d* Alyth –.10.75
now Mrs. Weir

ROBBIE Thomas Alexander BSc(for) 1935
retd 1973; resid Glasg

ROBERTS Alexander MA 1931

ROBERTS or Lanning, Helen Elizabeth MA 1948

ROBERTSON Adrian Alfred Gibb *MA 1942
head mod lang Wyke manor s Bradford 1962–65; head lower s Maltby g s nr Rotherham Yorks 1966–72; sen master Maltby comp s from 1973; member council Cyrenians from 1971

ROBERTSON Alan Ogilvie MA 1949 BD 1952
JP Aber 1968
Aberd: warden Crombie Hall 1964–66, warden Crombie/Johnston Halls 1966–68, sen warden and warden Hillhead Halls from 1968

ROBERTSON Albert John *MA 1951

ROBERTSON Alexander MB ChB 1908
no longer on GC reg

ROBERTSON Alexander MA 1919 LLD 1958
d Grantham 9.2.70 *AUR* XLIII 444

ROBERTSON Alexander MA 1929 BSc 1930 LLD 1971
CBE 1963 Kt 1970 FRSE 1945 FRIC 1946
FRSH 1950 FRCVS 1970 DVSc(Melb) 1973
Edin: prof anim health 1964–70, dean fac vet med 1964–70, prof tropical anim health/dir centre tropical vet med 1970–78

ROBERTSON Alexander Duffus *MA 1912
retd 1954; resid Carluke
d Carluke 27.5.79

ROBERTSON Alexander Findlay *MA 1936

ROBERTSON Alexander John MA 1925
retd 1968; resid Montrose

ROBERTSON Alexander Kay *MA 1947 Dip Ed 1953
FO, CO and dept tech co-operation 1953–64, Min of overseas dev Lond from 1964
m Kirkliston W. Lothian 2.4.65 Pamela Miller civ serv d of George S. M. Kirkliston

ROBERTSON Alexander McQueen MB ChB 1947
DTM & H(Edin) 1956 DPH(Lond) 1960
DIH(Lond) 1965
m o Sudan 1952–56; prin health off. N. Nigeria 1956–65; sen lect Liv s of tropical med 1966–71; sen m o Esso Libya 1971–73; m o NCB N'cle 1974–77; dir occup health serv Grampian health board Aber from 1978

ROBERTSON Alexander Rollo MA 1935 LLB 1937
d Sheffield 2.11.79

ROBERTSON Alfred Malcolm *BSc 1953

ROBERTSON Andrew Forbes *MA 1932
head Newmachar p s 1962–70; retd; resid Alyth

ROBERTSON Andrew Slora *MA 1950 *MEd 1956
Aber: teacher p s 1956–59, asst mod lang AGS 1959–62, RGC from 1962, careers master from 1967, prin guid from 1972

ROBERTSON Angus Graham *BSc 1947

ROBERTSON or Russell, Anna MA 1932
resid Insch

ROBERTSON or Finlayson, Anna Isabella MB ChB 1955 DPH 1972
sen m o commun med Grampian health board
resid Cults, Aber

ROBERTSON or McDonald, Annie MA 1921
d 23.1.66

ROBERTSON Arthur Kay MA 1951
teacher Anderson h s Lerwick from 1957, asst head from 1974
m Lerwick 27.3.64 Catherine D. Kerr nurs sister d of Duncan K. Kingennie by Dun

ROBERTSON or Troup, Bessie MA 1930
d nr Greenloaning 19.4.68 *AUR* XLII 370

ROBERTSON Bruce BD 1951
resid Dunbar

ROBERTSON Castella Margaret MA 1928
retd 1968; resid Kintore

ROBERTSON Charles BCom 1928
no longer on GC reg

ROBERTSON Charles William MB ChB 1930
resid Lee Green Lond

ROBERTSON Charles Wilson MA 1934
teacher sc: Eastriggs, Eaglesfield, Ecclefechan 1937–39, Annan acad 1939–40, 1946–47; head: Dalton s Lockerbie 1947–54, Balmedie s 1954–76; retd
wife *d* 1964

ROBERTSON Christina Speed BSc 1925
no longer on GC reg

ROBERTSON David BSc(agr) 1924 PhD 1927 DSc 1937
retd 1968; resid Bieldside Aber
d Bieldside 10.12.80 *AUR* XLIX 137

ROBERTSON David BSc(for) 1945
Dip. Man. Stud.(Edin coll of comm) 1971
man. Alex Cowan & Sons papermakers Penicuik 1961–68; lect man. Edin coll of comm 1968–72; lect man. stud. Queen Margaret coll Edin 1972–73, sen lect from 1973

ROBERTSON David John Clark *BSc(mech eng) 1932 (elect. eng) 1933
CEng FIMechE MIEE
admin staff Birm poly 1971–76; retd

ROBERTSON Dawson Cameron MB ChB 1909
d Burgess Hill 14.1.63 *AUR* XL 199

ROBERTSON Donald Angus BL 1929
d 17.1.64 *AUR* XL 400

ROBERTSON or Fraser, Doreen Grant MA 1953
teacher: Hinton, Alberta 1969–70

ROBERTSON or Simpson, Dorothy Mary MA 1934
retd 1973; resid Peterhead

ROBERTSON Duncan Carmichael BSc(eng) 1944

ROBERTSON Edward Macallan MA 1949

ROBERTSON Elbert Louis Stevenson MB ChB 1944

ROBERTSON Elizabeth *MA 1948
asst rector: Banff acad 1972–73, Kirkwall g s from 1973

ROBERTSON or Michie, Elizabeth Woodrow MB ChB 1955
resid Cottingham

ROBERTSON Ella Bruce MA 1928
retd 1969
d Aber 17.5.75 *AUR* XLVI 323

ROBERTSON or Smith, Ellen Dorothy MA 1942
resid Farnham

ROBERTSON or Farquharson, Elma Jessie *MA 1950
resid Blairgowrie

ROBERTSON Elsie MA 1930
m Craig

ROBERTSON Eric Desmond BSc(for) 1934 BSc 1936
OBE 1964
BBC Lond: asst controller/controller overseas serv 1964–73, controller Engl serv/dep man. dir external broadcasting from 1973

ROBERTSON Ethel Elizabeth MA 1932
FRCPsych 1971
retd 1971; resid Edin

ROBERTSON Forbes William *BSc 1941
FIBiol 1969 FRSE 1972
sen prin scient off. ARC unit of anim genetics Edin univ 1968–70, prof genetics Aberd from 1970
m Edin 5.6.48 Katherine L. H. Brown MA(Edin) WRNS/secy d of Henry H. B. MB ChB(Edin) Edin

ROBERTSON Frederick *MA 1949
visiting prof Penn state univ USA 1968–69; sen lect

classics R'dg from 1969 and warden Windsor Hall R'dg from 1974, head classics dept R'dg from 1975

ROBERTSON Frederick Albert BSc 1944
Marconi, Chelmsford: man. tech lab 1966–70, joint progr man. Marconi radar syst 1970–72, comp quality man. from 1972

ROBERTSON Frederick John BSc(agr) 1954
Dip Agr(Cantab) 1956 DTA(Trinidad, Cornell USA) DVMS and MRCVS(Edin) 1965
agr. off. Transvaal S. Af 1957–60; g p vet med Falmouth Cornwall 1965–67; vet investigation off. Aber from 1967
m Elgin 4.10.69 Valerie A. W. Alexander MA(Edin) res physiol d of Thomas G. A. Fochabers

ROBERTSON George Booth MA 1951 BD 1954 PhD 1971

ROBERTSON George Taylor MB ChB 1938
g p Alness from 1947
d Alness 29.8.78 *AUR* XLVIII 106

ROBERTSON George Webster BSc(eng) 1949

ROBERTSON or Killah, Georgina Mary MA 1948
JP 1968
Cairney s: teacher 1961–67, head from 1967

ROBERTSON or Downie, Gertrude Isabel Buchan MA 1915

ROBERTSON Gilbert William BSc 1944
prin teacher phys Forfar acad from 1967

ROBERTSON Grace MA 1946
teacher: Engl/Lat Hopeman s s 1961–64, Elgin acad 1964–68, Engl Buckie h s 1968–70, Engl/Lat Keith g s 1970–73, prin classics Buckie h s from 1973

ROBERTSON Grigor Charles Allan BSc(agr) 1913 MA 1914
d 27.6.70

ROBERTSON Hamish *MA 1952
MBE 1966
HM overseas civ serv Nyasaland/Malawi 1955–67; UK civ serv (Scot. off.) from 1967

ROBERTSON Harry BSc 1928 MA 1929
retd 1966; resid Aber

ROBERTSON or Walker, Henrietta Lord MA 1941
resid Nelson NZ

ROBERTSON Henry Downie *MA 1952

ROBERTSON or Conn, Hilda Helen MA 1934
resid Huntly
d Huntly 14.3.78

ROBERTSON Hugh *MA 1950
Forres: prin teacher hist 1960–70, asst rector 1971–77, dep rector from 1977

ROBERTSON Hugh Sinclair *MA 1906 BSc 1908
no longer on GC reg

ROBERTSON Ian Alexander Donald *BSc 1952

ROBERTSON Ian (John) Barr MA 1939 LLB 1949
ptnr Cunningham & Robertson solic Stonehaven from 1949, later prin; town clerk Stonehaven 1964–75; reg councillor Stonehaven/Kinneff from 1974

ROBERTSON Ian Graeme BSc(eng) 1954

ROBERTSON Ian Stewart *BSc 1955 PhD 1959
lect nat phil Aberd from 1969
wife *d* 6.1.78

ROBERTSON Ida MA 1920
d Banchory 22.7.68 *AUR* XLIII 80

ROBERTSON Irene Eliza MA 1949

ROBERTSON or Waite, Isabella MA 1906
d Gartly 4.5.78

ROBERTSON Isabella Ledingham *MA 1929
teacher Broughton s s Edin 1944–68; retd; Cavaliere dell' Ordine al Merito della Repubblica Italiana 1976

ROBERTSON Isabella Leslie *MA 1918
no longer on GC reg

ROBERTSON or Gray, Isobel Agnes MA 1941
teacher hist Shotton Hall s s Peterlee Co Durh from 1963

ROBERTSON James MA 1903 MB ChB 1907
d 28.9.65

ROBERTSON James MB ChB 1925

ROBERTSON James *MA 1954 Dip Ed 1958

ROBERTSON James Dewar MB ChB 1910
d Swansea 29.12.60 *AUR* XXXIX 102 & 201

ROBERTSON James Kennedy *MA 1923
d Elgin 22.2.73 *AUR* XLV 225

ROBERTSON James Kinnaird BSc(agr) 1927
asst insp DAFS from 1957

ROBERTSON James Matheson BL 1952
law app/solic/advoc in Aber Burnett & Reid advoc Aber 1958–61; leg. asst Stronachs advoc Aber 1962–63, ptnr from 1963

ROBERTSON James Stuart MB ChB 1928 DPH 1931 [c]MD 1935
retd 1968; resid Bournemouth

ROBERTSON or Pickford, Janet Mary (Sheena) MA 1945

ROBERTSON or Anderson, Janet Watson *MA 1910
resid Aber
husb *d* 1953

ROBERTSON or Bremner, Jean Hosie MA 1930
teacher Portsoy 1958–71; retd
d 25.9.81

ROBERTSON or Gibb, Jeanie MA 1901
d Salford 23.12.61 *AUR* XXXIX 270

ROBERTSON John BSc(agr) 1936
teacher agr Elmwood coll Cupar 1958–75; retd; resid St Andrews

ROBERTSON John Archibald MA 1949 BD 1952
C of S min: John Knox ch Mounthooly Aber 1962–67, Parkdale presb ch Toronto 1967–77, par of Strath Is of Skye from 1977

ROBERTSON Lawrence Don MB ChB 1923
d 24.1.73 *AUR* XLV 225

ROBERTSON Lewis Stevens MB ChB 1919
m o S Af chamber of mines Johannesburg 1936–70; pres: S Af Red Cross soc 1950–51, med assoc of S Af 1963–64 (gold medal), nat cancer assoc of S Af 1952–75 (Oettle gold medal); retd; resid Johannesburg

ROBERTSON or Willans, Lillie Don MA 1924
d 8.8.76

ROBERTSON or Smart, Margaret Alexandrina MA 1908
d 31.3.72

ROBERTSON or Perry, Margaret Alice *MA 1943
resid Perth

ROBERTSON Margaret Helen MA 1912
no longer on GC reg

ROBERTSON or McDonald, Margaret Jessie *BSc 1949
teacher maths Bankhead acad from 1976

ROBERTSON or Melvin, Margaret Leslie *MA 1947
resid Aber

ROBERTSON or Horne, Margaret Marian MB ChB 1937
resid Tain

ROBERTSON Margaret Mitchell *MA 1910
resid Banff

ROBERTSON Marian Downie MA 1926
teacher Westhill Aber 1962–64; retd; resid Clinterty

ROBERTSON Mark Macdonald MA 1953 PhD 1959

ROBERTSON Martha Ethelwyn Young MA 1909
d Edin 9.2.67 *AUR* XLII 179

ROBERTSON Mary Constance MA 1932
med secy Aber gen hosps 1955–66; retd

ROBERTSON Mary Isabella MA 1944
teacher Cummings Park p s Aber from 1973

ROBERTSON or Simpson, Mary Williamina Urquhart *MA 1911
d 29.5.70 *AUR* XLIV 107

ROBERTSON Maurice Charles Gordon MB ChB 1925
g p Leeds

ROBERTSON Nellie Ann MA 1925
teacher maths/geog Kintore j s s 1962–65; retd

ROBERTSON Norman BSc 1944 *MA 1950
sen tut. fac of urban and reg stud. univ R'dg from 1974

ROBERTSON Norman Dale BSc 1946 *MA 1952

ROBERTSON or Fyfe, Patricia Stewart MA 1951
teacher inf Calder St s s Glasg 1961–63, supply Gilburn p s Dun 1964–66, home-teaching/part time work/St Nicholas C of E p s Newbury from 1966
marr diss 1975

ROBERTSON Patrick Dugan MB ChB 1954

ROBERTSON or Reay, Rhoda Donald BSc 1953 *1954
resid Welwyn

ROBERTSON Richard Ross MA 1922 BD 1925
d Aber 11.12.69 *AUR* XLIII 445

ROBERTSON Robert *MA 1927
retd 1964; resid Bellshill

ROBERTSON Roderick George MA 1934
head: Tullos p s Aber 1959–66, Hazlehead p s Aber from 1966; retd
m Aber 12.8.58 Alice Douglas d of John D. Aber

ROBERTSON or Brown, Roma Learmonth MA 1946

ROBERTSON Ronald MA 1935 BD 1938
C of S min Old Parish ch Scone from 1949
chap. to Lord High Commissioner Lord Mansfield 1961, 1962

ROBERTSON Ronald Graham BSc(for) 1954
retd Ghana for. dept 1961; asst conserv for. N Nigeria for. dept 1962–65; dept lands and for. Truro Nova Scotia: for. 1966–69, man. silviculture dept from 1969
m Keith 30.6.62 Isobel J. Riddoch

ROBERTSON or Thomson, Sheila Mairi Jean MB ChB 1946
s m o Aber from 1966

ROBERTSON Sibylla Georgia MA 1955

ROBERTSON Stephen Andrew Cormack MA 1954 LLB 1957
1960 various posts Lond; leg. asst Aber c c 1961–62; admin asst NE reg hosp board 1962–63; solic: Burnett & Reid advoc Aber 1963–64, Allan Buckley Allan & Co advoc Aber 1964–66, ptnr 1966–73; amalgamated with and ptnr of Wilsone & Duffus advoc Aber from 1974

ROBERTSON Thomas *MA 1897
d Aber 3.3.63 *AUR* XL 197

ROBERTSON Thomas George MA 1926
retd head St Margaret's s Aberlour 1967; resid Tower Villa Aberlour Farms Bruntlands etc Knockando from 1967

ROBERTSON Walter BSc 1931
teacher Forfar 1933–38, head Logie Pert s Angus 1938–47; war serv R Sigs 1941–46; head: Tannadice 1947–66, Newtyle 1966–72; retd; resid Whitehills Forfar
m Tannadice 28.2.38 Constance B. Reid d of Alexander R. Tannadice

ROBERTSON William *MA 1941
prin teacher classics Portobello s s from 1961

ROBERTSON William Allan *MA 1902
d 25.5.62 *AUR* XXXIX 373

ROBERTSON William George *MA 1951
teacher Engl Aber acad/Hazlehead acad from 1960

ROBERTSON William Leslie MA 1934
H.M. civ serv customs and excise dept from 1934; retd; resid Montrose

ROBERTSON William Rae BSc(agr) 1951 MSc 1969
Dip App Econ(univ coll of Rhodesia and Nyasaland) 1966 PhD(Lond) 1974 ARICS 1976
Salisbury Rhodesia: sen agronomist 1967–69, sen farm man. spec dept of conserv and extension 1969–74, chief of crop prod. dept conserv and extension 1974–75; world bank secondment staff serving as head of agr proj evaluation and plan. unit fed govt Nigeria from 1975

ROBERTSON William Stuart Justice BSc(eng) 1953
MEd(R'dg) 1972
lect f e eng subjs/maths/phys The College Swindon from 1960

ROBERTSON Williamina Charlotte MA 1910
d Inverurie 9.11.75

ROBINS Alfred Brian PhD 1952

ROBINSON or Maxwell, Grace Margaret MB ChB 1925 DPH 1927
resid Edin

ROBINSON Margaret Alice Jocelyn *MA 1953

ROBISON Walter *MA 1931
prin maths Turriff acad from 1947, dep rector from 1970

ROBLEY John Alfred Watson BSc(for) 1954
asst conserv for. Bamenda, S Cameroons 1960–61; for. util off. Blantyre, Nyasaland 1961–64; W Aust: div for. off. 1964–70, insp for. Harvey 1970–72, state bush fire control off. Perth from 1972
m Inv 27.5.58 Sheila M. Sweeney BSc 1954 *qv*

ROBSON Alexander BSc(eng) 1938

ROBSON Arthur MA 1927
retd from Windsor Place ch Portobello 1971
d 29.11.74

ROBSON or Laing, Evelyn Margaret MA 1954
LTCL (teacher's dip in Engl as second lang) 1971

ROBSON James MA 1946
C of S min St John's ch Camelon Falkirk from 1957

ROBSON John Douglas MB ChB 1953
g p Potton from 1956
d 4.4.81 *AUR* XLIX 139

ROBSON or Robertson, Margaret MB ChB 1950
part-time publ health and g p Perth Aust from 1971

ROBSON Mary Hastings Edwards MA 1951
m Crawford

ROBSON Norman Keith BSc(agr) 1922
d Aber 10.2.63 *AUR* XL 204

ROBSON Norman Keith Bonner *BSc 1951
FLS 1958
Lond: sen scient off. extra-Europ flowering plants dept of bot Brit Museum (nat hist) 1962–67, prin scient off. from 1967
m Folkestone Kent 3.9.60 Eve B. Reynolds d of Donald H. B. R. MA(Cantab) Folkestone

ROBSON Thomas Falconer MA 1934
ptnr Williamson & Dunn CA Aber from 1946

ROCHE Susan Mary Blair (Sr Véronique) MA 1949
France: religious work in serv of old ladies of every station and creed, mostly of peasant origin Sens Yonne 1951–59, Cahors Lot 1959–68, Vence Alpes Maritimes 1968–70, Rodez Aveyron from 1970

RODE or Castledine, Margaret Joyce *MA 1942
d Nott 30.11.67 *AUR* XLII 373

RODE Robert Moir *MA 1945
d –.11.63

RODEN Keith Serjeant MB ChB 1919
d 1972

RODGER Jessie Roy MA 1935

RODGERS Albert Nathaniel Ewing MB ChB 1906
no longer on GC reg

ROE Charles Francis MB ChB 1955
MD(NY) 1964 FACS 1969
USA: res fell. surg Harvard univ Boston 1961–63 (Harvey Cushing award 1963–69); instr surg Columbia univ NY city (member NY acad of sc); asst prof surg Yale univ/consult. veterans admin hosps New Haven Conn 1969–73; chief surg Lawrence mem hosp New Lond Conn from 1973 (member internat soc surg)
m NY city 31.7.69 Anita M. Bruckner MA(Corn) d of Paul B. PhD(Prague) Vienna

ROE Maurice Robert André *MA 1949
PMD(Harvard bus. s Cambridge Mass USA) 1962 man. consult. GB and France, pres Integrated Business Systems Issy-les-Moulineaux
m Neuilly-sur-Seine France 30.12.71 Monique A. M. Roca d of Santiago R. Barcelona Spain

ROGER Barbara MA 1905
d Peterhead 30.7.72 *AUR* XLV 123

ROGER Henry MA 1913 MB ChB 1917
retd; resid Banff
d Memsie 24.9.76 *AUR* XLVII 102

ROGER John Grant *BSc 1937

ROGERS or Stanislas, Adeline Mary Kate MA 1910

ROGERS Eric BSc(eng) 1950
sen eng/ag Brit contr 1958–62; dep chief resid eng Binnie & Ptnrs Mangla dam proj W Pakistan 1962–69; repres World Bank Boké proj Guinea W Af 1969–72; contr man. dir William Tawse Aber from 1973

ROGERS James William BSc(eng) 1950
CEng MICE 1959
gen man. Sierra Leone dev co 1967–70; asst man. dir Williams Mills Staffs 1970–73, man. dir from 1973

ROGERS Thomas *BSc 1951
eng Barr & Stroud Glasg from 1956

ROGIE or Crawford, Mary MA 1920
d Alford 6.2.71 *AUR* XLIV 210

ROLL Richard Clipperton MB ChB 1951
MRCGP 1962
g p Nelson Lancs from 1954

ROLLO Ian McIntosh BSc 1945
PhD(Manit) 1968
Canada: prof dept pharm and therap fac of med univ Manit, Winnipeg from 1961

ROLLO James Cowie MA 1953
teacher: Engl/hist/geog Old Deer j s s 1955–61, Mintlaw s 1961–65; head Fetterangus p s 1965–69, New Machar p s from 1970

RONALD or Gray, Winifred Jean *MA 1931
resid Victoria BC Canada

ROSE Alexander Macgregor MB ChB 1899 DPH 1901
d Cults 2.12.62 *AUR* XL 74

ROSE Beatrice Mary *MA 1912 LLD 1953
retd; resid Guildford

ROSE Harry Baxter BL 1954
teacher Powis s s Aber 1956–60; lect Aber coll of comm from 1960

ROSE James MB ChB 1949
MRCGP 1971 FRCGP 1977
g p Dun from 1956

ROSE Jessie Ann MA 1915
d 30.9.67

ROSE or Marshall, Jessie Fraser MA 1919
resid Kilsyth

ROSE John BSc(agr) 1911
d 4.7.71

ROSE John Alexander Gilbert Fiddes MB ChB 1927
consult. radiol AEA Winforth Dorset from 1960; retd consult. radiol W Dorset hosp group 1971, elected hon consult.; resid Dorchester

ROSE John Ingram *MA 1952 Dip Ed 1953 MEd 1966
lect educ psych Aber coll of educ 1966–74, lect remed and spec educ Aber coll of educ 1974–76, sen lect from 1976
wife *d* 3.4.63
m(2) Aber 12.8.65 Marjory E. H. Esslemont MA 1959 *qv*

ROSE or Hunter, Lydia Jane MB ChB 1953

ROSE Margaret Elizabeth MA 1950

ROSE Nancy Masson MA BSc 1921
retd 1964; resid Aber
d Banchory 28.10.79

ROSEDALE John Lewis DSc 1923
d 12.11.68

ROSS or Willox, Adeline Elsie Philip MA 1927
war serv C of S ladywarden: Sullom Voe Shetland 1943; hostel Tel Aviv Israel 1945–46; teacher: Lanark c c 1947–54, Carstairs s 1954–66; part time tut. hosp Carstairs 1966–71; retd; resid Helensburgh

ROSS Alexander MA 1909 BD 1913
d 26.5.65

ROSS Alexander Brown MA 1905
no longer on GC reg

ROSS Alexander Fraser BSc(for) 1930 MB ChB 1942
retd 1970; resid Fairlie Ayrsh

ROSS Alexander James BSc 1949 *1950
Bahrain: group head-prod. quality investigations 1966–80; chief chem from 1980

ROSS Alexander Wilson MA 1910
d 25.9.65 *AUR* XLII 83

ROSS or Mazur, Anabella Mackenzie *MA 1942

ROSS Andrew Cormack MB ChB 1944 DPH 1949
m o h Blaby/Lutterworth and asst m o h Leic from 1955

ROSS or Main, Anna Leila MA 1953
resid Barnhill Dun

ROSS Angus Alexander MA 1912
no longer on GC reg

ROSS Anne MA 1955
teacher Fr Alexandra s Singapore 1961–62; hosp teacher Berlin 1975–76
m Aber 25.7.60 William G. Johnston MB ChB 1958 *qv*

ROSS Anne Christina MA 1928
retd 1970; resid Stornoway

ROSS Annie Cameron MA 1911
no longer on GC reg

ROSS or Hindle, Caroline Frances MA 1925
no longer on GC reg

ROSS Carson Abbot Ainscough MA 1921 BSc 1923
d 1963

ROSS or Griffiths, Catherine Eliza *MA 1952
teacher: ESN Red Lodge Southampton 1971–72, remed Danemark s Winchester 1973–74, mus at Glen Eyre s S'ton from 1975

ROSS Catherine Ishbel MacKenzie MB ChB 1949
m Lee

ROSS or Rzechorzek, Catherine Jane Helen Smith Wallace MA 1945
Mackie acad Stonehaven: teacher mod lang/Engl 1962–68, woman advis 1968–72, asst rector from 1972

ROSS or Davie, Cecilia Durward *MA 1934
secy prisoners of war assoc Aber 1942–45; resid Glassel

ROSS or Burnett, Charlotte Bell MA 1930
resid Elgin

ROSS Christina Shearer MA 1923

ROSS Cormac Craig MB ChB 1927
no longer on GC reg

ROSS David Forbes MB ChB 1940

ROSS David George MA 1908
d Dumfries 1.11.62 *AUR* XL 78

ROSS David Warnock *MA 1953

ROSS David William MA 1935 BD 1938
d Dun 24.12.74 *AUR* XLVI 239

ROSS or Kerr, Davina MA 1924
resid Haddington
husb *d* 25.1.72
d 6.7.79

ROSS Donald MB ChB 1950
DPM 1965 MRCPsych 1971
h o psychiat Inv 1957–64; Greenock: regist psychiat 1964–65, med asst psychiat 1965–68; sen regist ch psychiat Dumfries/Glasgow 1968–71; consult. ch psychiat Lancaster from 1971
m Prestwick 8.7.65 Esther S. Paton MB ChB(Glas) med pract d of James D. P. Prestwick

ROSS Donald Ian MB ChB 1955
sen h o anaest Glasg WI 1960–62; RAMC from 1962
m Edin 8.10.60 Jean C. McCulloch nurse/midwife d of Robert McC. Northolt

ROSS or Grant, Edith Mary MA 1925

ROSS Edward Sim MA 1923
d Aber 15.11.64 *AUR* XLI 58

ROSS or McNaughton, Elizabeth MA 1913

ROSS or Davis, Elizabeth Irene Murray MA 1947 Dip Ed 1952
no longer on GC reg

ROSS or Glennie, Elizabeth Mary Aird MB ChB 1942
s m o dept health NZ from 1954; resid Christchurch NZ

ROSS George BSc(agr) 1922
FEIS 1960 JP 1935–70
retd 1962; resid Aber

ROSS George MB ChB 1947
g p Ilkeston from 1951/anaest Ilkeston gen hosp

ROSS George Alexander MB ChB 1926
retd; resid Bridport

ROSS George Cruickshank BSc(eng) 1953

ROSS George Innes Macdonald MB ChB 1942
FRCPath 1966
consult. path. Ashford hosp Middx from 1957; resid Weybridge

ROSS George Wesley MA 1928
retd 1973; resid Aber

ROSS George William *BSc 1946 PhD 1950
ICI plastics div from 1956; resid Welwyn Garden City

ROSS Gray Ernest Donald BSc(eng) 1952

ROSS Gregor Mackay MA 1935
retd 1973; resid Fearn

ROSS Harold James MB ChB 1932

ROSS or Davies, Helen Mary MA 1930

ROSS Henrietta Mary Isabella MA 1925
retd Kaimhill s s Aber 1970; teacher Fr Northfield acad 1971–72; divinity stud. Aberd from 1973

ROSS Ian BSc(agr) 1951
teacher agr: Bell Baxter h s Cupar Fife 1957–62; Barony farm s Dumfries 1962–65, prin Balmacara farm s Kyle 1965–73; teacher biol Invergordon acad from 1973

ROSS Ian MB ChB 1955
sen h o orthop ARI 1960–61; g p Aber from 1961

ROSS or Reid, Irene Philip *MA 1948
teacher maths Queen Anne's s Caversham from 1965

ROSS Isabel Georgina Temple *MA 1931
retd 1969; resid Aber

ROSS or McPherson, Isabel Mhairi MA 1937
resid Aber

ROSS or MacLean, Isabella MA 1923
d Kiltarlity 24.2.72

ROSS or Garner, Isabella *MA 1927
teacher Kent 1928–48; resid Folkestone

ROSS or MacRitchie, Isobel Margaret MA 1928
resid Aber

ROSS James BCom 1923
d 6.10.58

ROSS James BSc(for) 1936

ROSS James Alexander *MA 1907
no longer on GC reg

ROSS James Alexander *BSc 1948
staff off. M o D 1961–63; lt-col head of s branch inst of army educ 1963–66; retd army 1967; bldg/civ eng group Edin: educ and trg off. 1967–69, group pers man. from 1969

ROSS James Cameron MA 1908
no longer on GC reg

ROSS James Harper BSc 1928
d Inv 13.8.62 *AUR* XL 93

ROSS James Matthews *MA 1947

ROSS James Rae *MA 1931
d Guernsey 21.3.64 *AUR* XL 400

ROSS James Wiseman BSc 1928
d Alloa 7.11.64 *AUR* XLI 59

ROSS or Douglas, Jean Mary MA 1924
retd 1964; resid Elgin

ROSS or McLachlan, Jeannie MA 1914 BSc 1917
d Aber 13.10.75

ROSS or Napier, Johan *MA 1929
teacher Engl Dumfries h s 1961–67; retd

ROSS John MB ChB 1911
d Sydney Aust –.1.61 *AUR* XXXIX 202

ROSS John MA 1927
d 1972

ROSS John *MA 1930
dep rector Invergordon acad 1962–72; retd; resid Fearn

ROSS John MB ChB 1937
g p Fraserburgh from 1946

ROSS John Hugh Gunn *MA 1935 BD 1938
C of S min Dundurn parish ch St Fillans from 1973

ROSS John Maclennan BSc(for) 1932

ROSS John Marshall MB ChB 1930
d Beckenham 30.9.72 *AUR* XLV 128

ROSS John Munro MB ChB 1953
FCCFP 1971
Newfoundland Canada: sen m o Bonne Bay 1958–60, Placentia 1960–70, Channel 1970–71; assoc prof/chmn g p mem univ St John's 1971–75, dir residency progr in fam med 1971–78
m Deer Lake Newfoundland Doreen Janes nurse d of Sydney J. Lond

ROSS John Wilfrid Gwinnett BSc(for) 1933

ROSS Kenneth Aird MB ChB 1942
sen cas off. Addington hosp S Af 1967–73; retd Tunbridge Wells
wife *d* 29.7.73
d Tunbridge Wells 31.8.75

ROSS Lewis Davidson MA 1929
d 27.11.72

ROSS Lizzie MA 1921
retd 1961; resid Aber

ROSS Lydia MA 1926
teacher Inv 1958–71; inf mistress Dalneigh p s 1971; retd; resid Inv

ROSS or Deans, Madeline MB ChB 1951 DPH 1954

ROSS or Thomson, Margaret *MA 1917
resid Lond
husb *d* 14.9.55

ROSS or Macmillan, Margaret MA 1932
retd; resid Aber

ROSS Margaret Cumming MA 1907
d 11.8.64 *AUR* XL 395

ROSS Margaret Helen MA 1904
no longer on GC reg

ROSS or Knox, Margaret Hellen MA 1938
d 13.12.65

ROSS or Wiseman, Margaret Stewart MA 1905
no longer on GC reg

ROSS or Bain, Mary Ann MA 1910
d Stonehaven 4.1.71 *AUR* XLIV 209

ROSS or MacKillop, Mary Ann MA 1929
teacher Lat/Engl Sir E. Scott's j s s Harris 1960–68, p dept 1969–73; retd

ROSS or Milne, Mary Eleanor MA 1913
d Bloemfontein S Af 20.4.74 *AUR* XLVI 107

ROSS Mitchell Cumming BSc 1925
d Aber 21.7.70 *AUR* XLIV 110

ROSS Murdo BSc(eng) 1944

ROSS or McBain, Muriel Mary MA 1932

ROSS Norman Alfred MB ChB 1936 DPH 1939
d Ketton 2.5.78 *AUR* XLVIII 106

ROSS Norman Cruickshank BSc 1955 *1957 PhD 1960

ROSS Patricia Anne *MA 1951
civ serv dip. wireless serv Lond 1951–55; Royal Dutch Shell translator/edit. The Hague/Amsterdam 1955–61; bldg res stat D o E Garston: higher scient off./tech information off. from 1965; resid St Albans

ROSS Percival MB ChB 1922
d Shrewsbury 5.9.65 *AUR* XLII 86

ROSS Robert Forsyth BSc(for) 1940

ROSS Robert Henry *MA 1950

ROSS Robert James Ferguson *MA 1951

ROSS Robert Lewis MA 1940 LLB 1949

ROSS Robert Matthew Bruce MA 1932
prin teacher geog Bo'ness acad from 1951

ROSS Ronald Gavin MB ChB 1949
FRSM
d Orpington 31.1.74 *AUR* XLV 450

ROSS Ronald McLeod Stewart BSc(eng) 1948

ROSS Simon Douglas BSc(agr) 1930
d Inverurie 16.5.65 *AUR* XLI 152

ROSS Stewart BL 1950

ROSS Sydney Duthie *BSc 1941
teacher: papermaking Glenrothes tech coll 1968–72, chem Ballingry j h s Fife 1972–74; teacher/tech. sc dept Kirkcaldy tech coll from 1974

ROSS William Alexander *MA 1897
d Elgin 29.1.67 *AUR* XLII 79 & 345

ROSS William Andrew MB ChB 1949
g p Laurencekirk 1959–77; m o DHSS from 1977

ROSS William Wilson Michie *MA 1928 BL 1930
date of marriage: 4.3.36
retd 1969; resid Lochailort Invsh

ROSS Williamina Ann MA 1921
d Inv 11.10.75

ROSS Winifred MA 1937

ROSS-KEYT Frederic Dudley
see Keyt

ROSSOUW James Petronellus Johannes *MB ChB 1921
no longer on GC reg

ROTH Paul Bernard MB ChB 1905
d Richmond Surrey 29.12.62 *AUR* XL 76

ROTHNEY or Deming, Flora Elspeth *MA 1918

ROTHNIE Douglas Auchterlonie MA 1896 DD 1952
d Kingston Jamaica 22.11.62 *AUR* XL 73

ROTHNIE George *MA 1931
d Edin 6.11.70 *AUR* XLIV 110

ROTHNIE James Henry MA 1955
head: Bogmoor p s Moray 1960–63, Fornighty p s Nairn 1963–67; teacher Tullos p s Aber 1967–71, head St Cyrus p s from 1971

ROULSTON Thomas Love MA 1951 MEd 1955
prin Belmont House spec s Londonderry from 1961

ROWE Joseph Bevil Wrathall MB ChB 1928
chief m o Kodak Harrow from 1936
m Bromley 14.10.63 Agnes A. Boddie d of Ronald C. B. CVO DSO, Bromley

ROWLAND Roy MacDonald MB ChB 1954
surg lt RN hosp Chatham 1958–62; h s obst/gyn Hillingdon hosp Middx 1962; ptnr g p Wolverhampton from 1962

ROY Alistair Anderson MA 1948 BD 1952
C of S min Bridge St ch Wick from 1955
m Banff 10.9.68 Jean M. McIntosh teacher d of Fred McI. Banff

ROY Arnold George Rennie MA 1944 *1948
prin teacher classics Blairgowrie h s from 1956

ROY Eric James BSc(eng) 1929
no longer on GC reg

ROY Ian Leslie MB ChB 1942
g p Carlisle from 1953

ROY John James *MA 1914
retd 1956; temp teaching Engl subj Elgin acad, Lossiemouth h s, temp head Lhanbryde j s s 1956–73

ROY Peter Rennie MA 1924
no longer on GC reg

ROY or Stuart, Rosella Gladys MA 1926
resid Aber
husb *d* Oyne 8.5.68

ROYSTON Elsie Henriette BSc 1931

RUDDIMAN David MB ChB 1952

RULE Alexander MA 1920 BSc(for) 1921
tech asst to dir gen for. and timber bureau Canberra, Aust 1957–60; retd; compiled *Forests of Australia* publ Angus & Robertson Sydney 1964–66

RUMBLES Eleanor Lorimer MA 1924
retd 1964; resid Arbroath

RUMBLES Francis MA 1914
d Eastriggs Annan –.9.62 *AUR* XL 83

RUNCIE George Deans *MA 1937
BBC chief asst (tv Scot.); retd 1974; resid Gartmore Stirling

RUNDLE Leslie John BSc 1952 *1953
CChem MRIC 1973 FCS 1973
ICI: chem Grangemouth 1953–58, plant man. 1958–63, proj sponsor Calcutta 1963–69, area man. Grangemouth from 1969

RUSACK Louis Seton MB ChB 1942
g p Haddington from 1950

RUSHTON Henry Glen *BSc 1953
Regd Prof Eng(Ont) 1958
Regd Prof Geol(Alta) 1968 FGAC 1965 MCIMM 1968
Canada: geol Frobisher Tor 1956–58, Ventures Noranda Quebec 1958–63; sen geol nickel Falconbridge Val d'Or Quebec/Sudbury Ont 1963–66; sen geol/chief geol Calgary 1966–71; man. explor Fording Coal 1971–77; man. dev and explor Fording Coal from 1977

RUSSELL Alexander Wilson BSc(agr) 1925
Ceylon: tea planter 1925–40, 1946–49; army 1940–46; retd 1949–51; farm. Insch from 1951
m Insch 26.3.53 Winifred Reid

RUSSELL Aubrey Ronald Laselve MB ChB 1952
Fell Rosae Cross(Rosicrucian Order)(Calif) 1970
Cert Fam Plan.(Fertility Control)(Johns Hopkins) 1973
Jamaica: g p: Malvern 1957–63, part-time Kingston 1963–73, m o part-time Kingston publ hosp 1963–64, dep m o part-time gen penitentiary Kingston 1964–70, m o part-time Bellvue psychiat hosp from 1964, m o part-time fam plan. clin Kingston from 1964
marr diss March 1973
m(2) Kingston 17.8.73 Phyllis C. Macpherson BA(Lond) lect/res fell. WI univ d of J. A. M. Kingston

RUSSELL or Walker, Audrey Mary Brodie MA 1952

RUSSELL Bruce Arnold MB ChB 1924
no longer on GC reg

RUSSELL or Bernard, Christina MB ChB 1924
dep m o h Finchley 1948–61; retd; resid Insch

RUSSELL David Campbell BSc(eng) 1934

RUSSELL or Stirling, Eileen Catherine Smart MA 1951

RUSSELL Helen Mary Margaret MA 1944
teacher Broomhill p s Aber from 1965

RUSSELL James Alexander *BSc 1951

RUSSELL James Knox MB ChB 1942 MD 1954
N'cle: post-grad dean med s from 1968, consult. WHO human reprod from 1965, hon obst MRC unit on reprod/growth from 1966

RUSSELL or Must, Katrine MA 1929
teacher: St Matthew's s Westminster Lond 1946–48, RAF school Amman Jordan 1951–52, Westlands p s Nairobi 1952–54
m Lond 6.12.32 John S. Must BA(Cantab) clerk in holy orders s of Rev Henry M. Barnsbury Lond

RUSSELL Mildred Margaret Gray MB ChB 1922
retd 1948; resid Budleigh Salterton

RUSSELL Rognvald Gordon MB ChB 1931
OBE 1969 FRCGP 1970
g p Wingate, Blackhall, Castle Eden Co Durham from 1931; chmn Durh exec council 1962–76; memb Hartlepool hosp man. comm from 1949, chmn 1959–74

RUSSELL Stewart Innes MA 1922
d 20.4.63

RUSSELL William Affleck *MA 1897
d 10.11.66

RUSSELL William Frederick MB ChB 1939 MD 1949
g p Chaddesden, Derby from 1948/asst skin dept Derbysh RI from 1955

RUSSELL William Smith MB ChB 1931
g p Leic from 1933

RUST Margaret Philip MA 1933 LLB 1935
archivist Town Clerk's dept Aber 1955–72; retd; resid Durris

RUST Robert Alexander *BSc 1954
tech off. (chem) ICI (Dyestuffs) Huddersfield 1956–60, Fleetwood 1961–64, Teesside from 1964
m Huddersfield 17.6.61 Margaret E. Bolton

RUTHERFORD Hamish MA 1926
tut. mod. stud. Stowe s 1945–66; retd; resid Wicken, Milton Keynes
d Wicken 28.4.80 *AUR* XLVIII 441

RUTHERFORD Hubert Watson MB ChB 1942 DPH 1948
consult. venereologist NE reg hosp board/clin sen lect venereal diseases Aberd from 1966

RUTHERFORD William Armstrong *MA 1929
d Golspie 30.1.73 *AUR* XLV 226

RUTHERFORD William Hay MA 1936 LLB 1938
hon sheriff Aber, Kincardine & Banff from 1974
ptnr: Christie, Buthlay & Rutherford advoc Aber 1962–78, Raeburn, Christie & Co advoc from 1978; pres Royal Northern Agr Soc 1980

RUXTON or Watson, Annie Ellen MA 1913
d Warminster 27.2.76

RUXTON or Lee, Ethel Lewis MA 1912
d St And 24.1.78 *AUR* XLVIII 102

RUXTON Herbert William Black MB ChB 1904 DPH 1905
d St And 12.3.64 *AUR* XL 394

RUXTON Irene Tomina Joan MB ChB 1919
d Newport Gwent 9.5.78 *AUR* XLVIII 103

RUXTON or Auld, Mary Margaret MA 1907
d Aber 17.6.76 *AUR* XLVII 101

RYAN Daniel James *MA 1953 *MEd 1958
teacher Engl AGS 1962–66; sen lect educ Avery Hill coll Lond 1966–72, head of grad dept 1972
m Aber 2.4.63 Rosalie Macdonald nurse
d Eltham 14.9.72

RYDER or Spiller, Elma Pirie MA 1930
resid Stirling
husb *d* 5.3.66

RYDER Mary Elizabeth MA 1924
d 10.2.62 *AUR* XL 91

SABISTON Gordon Harvey BSc 1953
petrographer Arvida Canada 1953–56; field geol Boké Guinea W Af 1956–57; group leader Arvida 1957–68, sect. head 1968–74; supt min res Mandeville Jamaica 1974–76, chief geol from 1976
m Aber 20.8.53 Alison W. Robb

SABISTON James MA 1936
teacher Keith g s from 1955
d Keith 16.8.75

SABISTON Louis *BSc 1948
d Stoke-on-Trent 11.8.79

SACKS Ephraim MB ChB 1925

SACKS Israel MB ChB 1922 MD 1941
d Bloemfontein 11.4.64

SACKS Neville Zigmund MB ChB 1950
FRCPE 1973
Bloemfontein S Af: consult. phys Pelonomi hosp 1960–73, part-time lect in med from 1973
m Bloemfontein 15.6.58 Julie Abrahamson B Soc Sci (Cape Town) soc sc worker

SAINT Dorothy MA 1951
teacher Woodside Aber 1952–59; later at Hazlehead acad
m(1) Aber 16.5.59 Roger Mullard RAF; husb *d* 2.3.60
(2) Aber 26.7.77 John Gilmour BSc 1948 *qv*

SALISBURY or Ellis, Elizabeth Anne MA 1948

SALMOND Robert Williamson Asher *MB ChB 1907 DPH 1908 ChM 1910 *MD 1911
no longer on GC reg

SALT or Durkin, Sheila Margaret MB ChB 1944 DPH 1948
MFCM 1973 FRSH
m o Is of Man 1971–73, prin s m o 1973–75; m o/dir Sturgeon health unit Alberta Canada from 1975

SALTER or Baird, Isabella MA 1939
Elgin: teacher pre-nursing coll, asst 1955–58, head 1958–71; stud. advis tech coll from 1971

SAMMON David Campbell *BSc 1951 PhD 1954
on staff UKAEA Harwell from 1954

SAMMON Paul Matthew MB ChB 1950 DPH 1953
MFCM 1972
asst, sen asst div m o Lancs 1953–66, div m o W Riding c c, m o h urban districts Colne Valley Yorks 1966–71; div m o Lancs c c and m o h districts c Accrington area 1971–74; dis commun phys Ormskirk dist Lancs health auth from 1974

SAMSON Harry Philip MB ChB 1923
g p Eccles Manc from 1929

SAMSON James Beahan MB ChB 1922 MD 1931
retd 1960; resid Eastbourne

SANDERSON or Cochrane, Janet Andrews MA 1935
civ serv/asst lib microbiol res estab Porton Wilts 1966–72; retd; resid Salisbury Wilts

SANDFORD Cyril James MB ChB 1924
d –.3.70

SANDISON or Simpson, Charlotte MA 1931
resid Banff
husb *d* 26.7.74

SANDISON Isobel Fleming *MA 1943
teacher mod lang Buckie h s 1964–72, prin Fr from 1972

SANDISON John Forbes William MB ChB 1914
d Bournemouth 4.4.69 *AUR* XLIII 210

SANDISON John Henry *BSc 1952
agr div ICI Middlesbrough 1964–75; seconded to Price Comm Lond from 1975
m Stockton-on-Tees 5.9.59 Carol Howitt clerk d of Robert F. H. Doncaster

SANDISON or Smith, Mary Wilhelmina MA 1936
Shetland: head Eshaness p s till closure 1968; occasional relief teacher from 1968

SANDISON or Lewis, Sheila MA 1930
resid Aber

SANDLER Hyman MB ChB 1926
no longer on GC reg

SANDS or Wilkie, Mary Gavin MA 1918
no longer on GC reg

SANG Charles George BSc(eng) 1936

SANG Elma Mair MA 1935
dep head Torry acad Aber 1972–76; retd

SANG or Eddie, Isabel Margaret MA 1930

SANG James Henderson BSc 1934 *1936
FRSE 1959
asst dir poultry res centre Edin 1958–65; prof genetics Sus Brighton from 1965, dean of s of biol sc from 1972

SANGSTER or Buchanan, Alexandra Adam MA 1948
resid Aber

SANGSTER Charles Low BSc(eng) 1933 *1934
FIEE 1959 FIMechE 1960 OBE 1963
Crown Agents Lond: asst chief insp eng 1966–67, chief insp eng 1967–69, chief elect. eng 1969–70, dir 1970–73; dir (non-exec) Tradewinds Airways 1970–73; retd

SANGSTER or Bolland, Edith Mary MA 1943
resid Brussels

SANGSTER or Leslie, Elizabeth Anderson MA 1942
teacher Hampstead Garden Suburb s Lond from 1967
husb *d* 8.6.67

SANGSTER or Macaulay, Ella Murray MA 1953
resid Peterculter

SANGSTER Eric Garden BL 1942
Lond: dep dir paintmakers assoc 1963–65, dir fed. of painting contr 1965–72, dir nat fed. paint/decorating contr from 1972

SANGSTER Ernest George *MA 1954 BD 1957
chaplain St And 1961–65; C of S min: Beechgrove ch Aber 1965–76, Blackhall St Columba ch Edin from 1976
m St And 23.8.63 Alison M. Runcie MA(St And) d of Alexander M. R. MB ChB(Edin) Kirkcaldy

SANGSTER George MB ChB 1937 [c]MD 1949
FRCPE 1976
consult. phys city hosp Edin from 1961

SANGSTER George Brown Cameron MA 1945 BD 1948
C of S min: Murrayfield par ch Edin from 1964

SANGSTER Harry BSc(agr) 1950
farm. Ladybank Fife from 1954

SANGSTER James Hay *MA 1930
FEIS 1970
retd 1972; resid Edin

SANGSTER John MB ChB 1905
no longer on GC reg

SANGSTER John Ramage Marshall MB ChB 1934
d Lond 1969

SANGSTER or Macleod, Margaret Ingram MA 1909
d 9.12.70

SANGSTER Robert Gray BSc(for) 1933
CBE 1966
secy Scot. Woodland Owners Assoc Edin 1966–78

SANGSTER Robert John BSc(agr) 1949
on staff of DAFS Dun from 1950

SANGSTER or McPherson, Violet MA 1954
teacher Hopeman p s from 1969

SANGUINETTI John Fitzalan Burgoyne MB ChB 1936

SARGISON Charles William MA 1927
retd 1960; resid Majorca

SARGISON Kenneth Duthie MB ChB 1955
FRCSE 1963
regist surg ARI 1960–63; regist orthop Agnes Hunt and Robert Jones hosp Oswestry 1963–65; sen regist orthop WI Glasg 1965–67; consult. orthop surg RI Hull from 1967

SAUL Donald MA 1951

SAUNDERS Campbell Milne MA 1949 BD 1952
C of S min St Leonard's ch Ayr from 1962

SAUNDERS or Davis, Ellen Jeanie MB ChB 1919
no longer on GC reg

SAUNDERS Harold Gordon MB ChB 1950
consult. in admin charge dept anaest N & S Teesside hosp groups 1973–75, South Tees health dist from 1975

m Ferryhill Co Durh 23.6.61 Thelma Wright SRN theatre sister d of Harry W. Ferryhill
d Martin-in-Cleveland 13.12.79 *AUR* XLVIII 443

SAUNDERS John Herbert *BSc 1951

SAUNDERS Maxwell James MB ChB 1934 DPH 1936
g p Bournemouth from 1946
d –.4.80

SAUNDERS William Munro Hutchison PhD 1953
leader soil fertility Ruakura agr res centre Hamilton NZ from 1966

SAVEGE Arthur Charles Mears MB ChB 1912
d Arbroath 11.12.66 *AUR* XLII 351

SAVEGE James Maxwell MA 1913 MB ChB 1917
retd col RAMC 1958; resid Harrogate
d 6.4.74

SAVEGE Ronald Maclure MB ChB 1921
retd 1966; resid Richmond-on-Thames

SAVIDGE Cecil Arthur Grant MA 1927
MBE
dir Brit nat comm internat Chamber of Commerce 1954–73; retd; resid Gt Missenden
d 9.12.75

SAVILLE Alan BSc 1944 *1946
FRSE 1976
sen prin scient off. marine lab Aber from 1968

SAVY Jacques MB ChB 1947
g p Kingston-on-Thames from 1958

SAYLE Anthony Cashen BSc(for) 1954
for.: Br Col: inventory div BC for. serv 1957–63, for. valuation Min of Fin. 1963–73, co-ordinator timber appraisal BC assessment auth from 1973
m Victoria BC 22.10.60 Anna M. Schmidt teacher d of John H. S. Middle Lake Sask

SCATTERTY or Beaton, Margaret Smith MA 1931

SCENCZI (formerly Schmidt) Nicholas Joseph *MA 1928
d Budapest 10.7.77 *AUR* XLVII 357

SCHARENGUIVEL James Arthur MB ChB 1906
no longer on GC reg

SCHNEE or Cohen, Isadore Murray MB ChB 1934

SCHOFIELD or Kirby, Margaret Ellerker MB ChB 1946
teaching fell. anaest Jefferson med coll Philadelphia USA from 1960

SCOLLAY John Thomas Gilbert BSc(agr) 1921
organis f e Shetland 1951–53; stud. div Edin 1953–55; C of S min: Lanarksh 1955–61, Greenock 1961–66, Waterside Ayr 1966–71; retd; resid Edin

SCORGIE or Neilson, Catherine Mitchell Johnston MA 1929
resid Montrose
d Montrose 15.11.80

SCORGIE Dorothy Margaret MA 1941

SCORGIE or Mackenzie, Elsie Johnston MB ChB 1921
d 4.6.75 *AUR* XLVI 322

SCORGIE Frank *MA 1914 BSc 1921
d Aber 7.11.61 *AUR* XXXIX 277

SCORGIE or Purdie, Jean Smart MA 1932
d Edin 5.6.66 *AUR* XLI 341

SCORGIE John MA 1916
d 7.4.74

SCORGIE John MB ChB 1939
d 20.6.60 *AUR* XXXVIII 598

SCORGIE or Carr, Margaret Olga MA 1939
secy: Engl Elect. Co Rugby 1958–59, Gussen & Wolff Northampton 1959–63, various posts Aber from 1963

SCORGIE Penelope Dey MA 1938
on staff M o T Aber from 1958
d Aber 14.11.79

SCOTCHER Lilian Mary MB ChB 1951
dept m o s health serv Kent c c Maidstone from 1967
m Southborough 1.10.64 Gerald W. T. Norton bus. exec s of John H. C. C. Tunbridge Wells

SCOTT or Allan, Agnes Mary Walker MA 1926
teacher Engl/maths Rochester 1949–66, head dept Engl from 1958

SCOTT Alexander *BSc 1954 PhD 1958
lect zool Belf 1960–68; lect biol Strath 1968–73, sen lect from 1973

SCOTT Alexander Daniel Jamieson *MA 1928
TD 1946 OBE 1960
army off. (lt-col) SEAC/India 1939–46; educ off./sen educ off. Sierra Leone 1947–56; perm secy min of educ/soc welfare 1956–60; perm secy/chief of protocol PM's off. 1961–62; teacher/master i/c jun s Boroughmuir s s Edin 1962–72
m Glasg 13.3.37 Helen P. Galbraith secy d of Robert G. Dunfermline

SCOTT Alexander Mackie *MA 1947
Scot. Arts Council award 1968
Glas: sen lect Scot. lit. 1963–71, head dept from 1971, reader from 1976

SCOTT Alexander Robb *MA 1953 Dip Ed 1956
sen Engl master the Publ s Hyderabad W. Pakistan 1962–65; teacher Engl overseas Patoomwan teacher trg coll Bangkok Thailand 1965–68; asst dept Engl/commun coll of comm Aber from 1968

SCOTT or Pearson, Alice May MA 1925
deceased

SCOTT or Adam, Alice Moir *MA 1948
teacher Fr: Aber acad 1961–70, prin asst Hazlehead acad from 1970

SCOTT or Dobb, Alison Jean Anderson *MA 1951
resid Cambridge

SCOTT Allan Harper *BSc(eng) 1952

SCOTT Andrew George MB ChB 1942 DPH 1947
b 20.6.19
MFCM 1972
Dept of Health NZ from 1974

SCOTT Andrew Maxwell BSc(eng) 1939
Assoc Fell. Can. Aero/Space Inst 1962
test supt Rolls Royce Glasg 1939–50; chief test eng/sales and serv man./chief eng Rolls Royce of Canada Montreal 1950–62; sales and serv man. Rolls Royce Glasg 1962–68; comm man. Rolls Royce (1971) Derby 1968–77, asst comm dir from 1978
m Glasg 1943 Helen McCallum secy d of John R. McC. Glasg

SCOTT or Ashmore, Anne Elizabeth *MA 1938
part-time examining/teaching from 1944; resid Manc

SCOTT or Urquhart, Annie Bella MA 1925
teacher Lat/Greek Nicolson inst Stornoway 1956–66; resid Stornoway

SCOTT Charles BSc 1934
FEIS 1963
head: Pitmedden p s 1941–71, Mintlaw s from 1971
wife *d* 27.5.71
m(2) Aber 23.10.73 Lena M. Innes
d Aber 1.8.79

SCOTT Charles Alexander Nelson *MA 1933
Forres acad: prin teacher mod lang 1938–73, dep rector from 1960; retd 1976

SCOTT Charles Cameron MB ChB 1954
d Dun 2.7.73 *AUR* XLV 321

SCOTT Charles Doig BSc(agr) 1950
farm. Newburgh Aberdeensh from 1950

SCOTT Christian Austine MA 1930
retd 1969; resid Edin

SCOTT David BSc 1950

SCOTT Desmond Rodway BSc(eng) 1938

SCOTT Donald *BSc 1949
sen lect zool univ of Otago NZ 1967–71, assoc prof from 1971

SCOTT Douglas Somerville MB ChB 1916
d –.4.66

SCOTT Edith MB ChB 1938
DPH(Edin) 1958
resid Goring-by-Sea
m Edin 20.5.58 Albert J. Phillips pharm s of William P.

SCOTT or Roy, Elsie Ann Margaret *MA 1947
resid Blairgowrie

SCOTT or Alexander, Ethel Adamson MA 1941
lived in Hong Kong 1957–67; teacher Aber/Aberdeensh 1968–76

SCOTT Euphemia Ashley MA 1930
teacher Dyce p s 1962–74; retd; resid Aber

SCOTT Frederick James *MA 1929
Edin: part-time univ lect Greek from 1954; teacher classics Royal h s 1947–60, prin classics 1960–71; retd

SCOTT Geoffrey Burnett MB ChB 1955
MRCPath 1964 FRCPath 1976
sen lect path. Aberd from 1969; hon consult. path. NE Scot. reg hosp board from 1969

SCOTT George Alexander *MA 1930
retd 1969; resid Banff

SCOTT George Brebner MB ChB 1896 MD 1900
d Reigate 6.3.65 *AUR* XL 197

SCOTT George Smith *MA 1951

SCOTT Gordon MA 1938
CA

SCOTT Helen MA 1907
no longer on GC reg

SCOTT or Roll, Helen Camilla de Clèry MB ChB 1950
g p Nelson Lancs from 1958

SCOTT Helen Gordon MA 1929
retd 1967; resid Rosemarkie

SCOTT Henry Norman *MA 1928
retd 1965; resid Sauchen

SCOTT Herbert James BSc(agr) 1921
no longer on GC reg

SCOTT James MB ChB 1941
g p Alyth from 1947

SCOTT James Alexander MA 1899
d Cincinnati Ohio 16.10.63 *AUR* XL 299

SCOTT James Henry MA 1929 MB ChB 1939
g p Blackpool from 1947

SCOTT James Reid BSc(eng) 1933

SCOTT Jean Gordon *MA 1916
d Elgin 30.5.71 *AUR* XLIV 317

SCOTT or Bottomley, Jean Innes ***BSc 1950 PhD 1953**

SCOTT Jean Macdonald ***MA 1939**
m Scott

SCOTT John **MA 1907**
d Kilmarnock 13.11.60 *AUR* XXXIX 100

SCOTT John ***MA 1936**
retd 1978; resid Buckie

SCOTT John Adam **MB ChB 1932**
g p Kingston-u-Thames from 1945
m Wick 8.3.37 Sylvia D. Fitzlanders

SCOTT John Shields **BSc(for) 1954**

SCOTT Joseph ***MA 1901 *BSc 1909**
no longer on GC reg

SCOTT Kerry Owen **BSc(eng) 1951**
MICE 1958 MNZIE 1963
NZ: with hydro-elect. proj investigations and construct. from 1956

SCOTT Lorna Stephen **BSc 1951**

SCOTT or Skinner, Mabel **MA 1925**
resid Aber

SCOTT or Henderson, Maggie **MA 1919 BSc 1922**

SCOTT or Bright, Margaret **MA 1935**
resid Chippenham

SCOTT Margaret McKenzie **MA 1921**
d Port Edward S Af 12.6.77

SCOTT Marguerite McDonald **MB ChB 1943 MD 1960**
h o Highgate hosp Lond 1943–44; bact: Manc 1944–46, publ health lab Salisbury 1953–57; sen bact/consult. Virus Ref Lab Colindale Lond 1957–70; dir Virus Ref Lab from 1970; co-dir WHO Collab. centre ref and res on influenza from 1975
m Lond 1946 Helio G. Pereira D Med(Rio de Janeiro) head div virology nat inst for med res Lond s of Raul P.

SCOTT Mary Anne **BSc 1909**
no longer on GC reg

SCOTT or Meek, Mary Elizabeth **MA 1905**
no longer on GC reg

SCOTT or Hendry, Mary Elizabeth ***MA 1943**
teacher mod lang: St Leonard's s St And 1956–57, Madras coll St And 1962–69

SCOTT May **MA 1946**

SCOTT Neil **BSc(eng) 1949**

SCOTT Robert Gordon **MA 1938**

SCOTT Robert James **BSc 1926 BSc(agr) 1928**
OBE 1964
retd 1971; resid Dumfries
d 28.9.79

SCOTT Robert McDonald **MB ChB 1951**
g p Portsoy from 1953
d Aber 18.2.78 *AUR* XLVII 360

SCOTT Robert Orr **PhD 1942**
ARCST(Glas) 1939 ARIC 1939 FRIC 1973
Aber: res chem dept spectrochem Macaulay inst 1939–69, head of dept from 1969
m Aber 14.6.44 Mary R. Davidson d of William D.

SCOTT or Wynne-Edwards, Stella Julia **MA 1955**
instr dept Fr Queen's univ Kingston Canada 1966–70, admin asst dept Engl from 1970
m(2) Gartland

SCOTT or Gray, Susan ***MA 1939**
resid Lumsden 1976

SCOTT or Annand, Wilhelmina Elliot **MA 1932**
resid Perth

SCOTT William ***MA 1936**
dep head Keith g s from 1970

SCOTT William Alexander **MA 1921**
retd 1965; resid Aber
d Aber 2.4.80 *AUR* XLVIII 441

SCOTT William Antony McDonald **MB ChB 1937**
FRSM 1947
S Af: sen visiting phys Addington hosp Durban from 1967, spec phys Durban from 1967
m(2) Durban 13.11.72 Rosemary A. Gardner SRN d of George C. G. Dorking

SCOTT William Dawson **MA 1903**
d Inverurie 17.6.62 *AUR* XXXIX 373

SCOTT William McQueen **MA 1950**
JP 1970
prin teacher Engl Kinross s s 1959–69; dep head Kinross p s 1969–73, head from 1973

SCOTT William Russell **MB ChB 1931**
MRCGP
d Weymouth 10.10.74 *AUR* XLVI 239

SCOTT or Coutts, Winifred Katherine **MA 1955**
MA(Edin) 1969
resid Edin

SCRIMGEOUR Annie Somerville **BSc 1943**
exper off. Nat Eng Lab East Kilbride 1954–63; prin teacher maths Kilgraston s Bridge of Earn from 1964

SCRIMGEOUR Arthur Martin **MA 1930**
d Kent 29.4.74 *AUR* XLVI 109

SCROGGIE or Carnie, Anne Johnstone Stewart MA 1935
teacher Aber 1956–75
resid Banchory

SCROGGIE or Tait, Dorothy Findlay MA 1945
asst teacher Quarryhill p s Aber from 1964

SCROGGIE George MA 1952

SCROGGIE or Rice, Jane Meauras Findlay MA 1936
husb *d* 3.9.72

SCROGGIE or Hay, Margaret Ruth MA 1936
resid Wallasey

SCROGGIE or West, Mary Chalmers MA 1933
retd 1970; resid Fochabers

SCROGIE Ishbel Margaret MA 1911
resid Peterhead

SEAL David Trevor BSc(for) 1950

SEATH James William MA 1920
d 11.4.69

SECTOR Mary Margaret MA 1931
teacher: St Paul St s Aber 1937–60, Springhill p s Aber 1960–70; retd

SEED John MB ChB 1930
consult. geriat med E Riding Yorks/Scarborough HMCs 1963–72; retd; resid Bridlington

SEFTON Alexander Monro *MA 1911
d 13.2.67

SEFTON George Arthur MA 1921 BD 1924
C of S min: Fern and Careston 1937–66; clerk presb of Brechin and Fordoun 1945–60; retd; resid Brechin

SEGGIE or Jenner, Griselda Margaret MB ChB 1945
Dun: clin asst cytology unit Maryfield hosp 1963–78, fam plan. clin doctor 1968–78; g p Brechin from 1969

SEGGIE or Allison, Rosalind Mary MA 1948
resid Pitfodels Aber

SEIVEWRIGHT Robert Taylor MA 1909
retd 1972; resid Melton Mowbray

SEIVWRIGHT Elizabeth Ross *MA 1922
d Ellon 28.10.61 *AUR* XXXIX 281

SELBIE Gordon Stewart MB ChB 1949
g p Huddersfield from 1953

SELBIE Hector MA 1932

SELBIE James Chalmers BSc 1928 *1929
d Upminster 9.5.74 *AUR* XLVI 109

SELBIE John Stewart BSc 1926
retd 1968; resid Gourdon

SELBIE William MB ChB 1937
g p Moldgreen Huddersfield from 1939; retd

SELBIE William Philip *MA 1910
d Bath 7.4.67 *AUR* XLII 349

SELKIRK Robert Andrew BSc(for) 1934
d Perth 25.10.68 *AUR* XLIII 85

SELLAR Beatrice Mary MB ChB 1922
retd 1961; resid Aberlour

SELLAR Forbes Keith BL 1953

SELLAR James MA 1894 [d]BL 1897
no longer on GC reg

SELLAR James Alexander MB ChB 1915 DPH 1921
d Perth 25.12.71 *AUR* XLIV 429

SELLAR James Alexander BSc 1937 *BSc(eng) 1938

SELLAR Jean Henderson Graham MA 1955

SELLAR Patrick James BSc(eng) 1950
MIEE CEng
elect. eng British Gas (SE reg) Croydon from 1969

SELLAR Ronald Marischal *MA 1952
retail sales man. Lond 1962–64; sales trg man. Slough 1964–66, marketing man. 1966–68; reg man. Manc 1968–74, nat sales man. Slough from 1974

SEMMENCE Adrian George MA 1922
d 3.1.62 *AUR* XXXIX 281

SEMMENCE Adrian Murdoch MB ChB 1953 MD 1957
MSc 1972 FRCGP 1972 DIH(England) 1972
p m o civ serv dept from 1976

SEMMENCE Henry Rattray BSc(eng) 1947

SEMPLE Agnes Loudon *MB ChB 1918 DPH 1921
d Alexandria Dunbartonsh 22.2.63 *AUR* XL 202

SEMPLE John Ferguson BSc(mech eng) 1944 BSc(civ eng) 1948
man. consult. Aberdour Fife 1960–62; man. dir Kinord Associates Aber from 1962

SEMPLE Mary Clark *MA 1913
d Helensburgh 28.4.69 *AUR* XLIII 210

SEMPLE Robert *MB ChB 1910 MD 1915
d Aber 1.1.70 *AUR* XLIII 441

SEMPLE Robert *MB ChB 1939 [c]MD 1952
FRCP(Lond) 1964
lect clin med Queen's coll Dund 1954–64; consult. phys Ninewells and assoc hosps Dun from 1974 and sen lect clin med Dund

SEMPLE Roderick Ferguson BSc(eng) 1941
MBE 1961
Brit army staff Washington USA 1961–64; c o 131 parachute eng regt TA Lond 1964–66; army instr RAF staff coll Bracknell 1966–68; comm Spec Air Service group Lond 1969–72; retd; dir gen defence admin Muscat Sultanate of Oman from 1973

SENGUPTA Samaras Ranjan PhD 1949

SERAPHIM George Michael BSc(for) 1953
asst dir Cyprus for. dept 1961–71, dir from 1971

SHAHID Ismail Ahmad BSc 1949

SHAHWAN Aziz Ȧli Ismail PhD 1953
FASCE(USA) 1967
asst prof Baghdad univ Iraq 1958–59; dept tech advis major proj admin Damascus Syria 1959–61; prof of hydraulics Cairo univ from 1965; consult. eng Bank du Cairo from 1968

SHAND Bessie Lindsay MA 1910
d 23.4.70

SHAND or Taylor, Dorothy MA 1923
no longer on GC reg

SHAND Frederick John Michael *BSc 1953

SHAND George BSc 1937 BSc(eng) 1939
Manc: chief eng rly signals AEI 1964–67, chief eng Manc group AEI gen signals 1967–69; tech author Technivision serv 1970–78; retd

SHAND George Ernest MB ChB 1909 *MD 1914
no longer on GC reg

SHAND or Macdonald, Grace Ann MA 1942

SHAND Harry Edward MA 1913 BSc(agr) 1914
no longer on GC reg

SHAND James Allan MA 1936
FEIS 1971
head Aberchirder s s 1962–76; retd

SHAND or Fleming, Jeannie MA 1920
no longer on GC reg

SHAND John MA 1927

SHAND or Davidson, Margaret Milne MA 1933
teacher maths Morgan acad Dun 1959–73; retd; resid Broughty Ferry

SHAND or Harrower, Mary Geddes MA 1953
teacher Dunfermline from 1954

SHAND or Durno, Matilda Jean MA 1913
d 1.7.67

SHAND William MA 1897
d Dun 1.3.62 *AUR* XXXIX 376

SHAND William John MA 1934
d Australia 5.10.80

SHANKS John Alexander MB ChB 1948
MRCOG 1962 FRCS(C) 1964 FACOG 1972 FRCOG 1974
lect Aberd: dept path. 1960–62, dept obst/gyn 1962–64; consult. obst/gyn private pract Brockville Ontario from 1965

SHANKS Peter Lindsay BSc(agr) 1927

SHAPIRO Charles MB ChB 1921
d Israel 13.8.74

SHARKEY John Austin MB ChB 1927
retd 1969; resid Shipton Green Itchenor W Sussex
m(2) Kingston Surrey 11.9.63 Margaret E. Baker d of Henry B. Folkestone

SHARP Christabel Noel MA 1905
d Aber 24.2.66 *AUR* XLII 82

SHARP David *MA 1932
d 18.4.66

SHARP David Easton BSc 1911
d 1.6.75

SHARP George Alexander MB ChB 1930
retd g p 1972; sen ship surg P & O Brit India educ cruise div 1972–76; retd

SHARP James Garden MA *BSc 1930 PhD 1935
d Cambridge 23.12.66 *AUR* XLII 88

SHARP or Mackie, Lindsay Lyall MA 1946
husb made life peer 1974—Lord Mackie of Benshie in the County of Angus
resid Kirriemuir

SHARP or Dickinson, Margaret Isabel Anne *MA 1931
resid Malta
m(2) Baron van Weesel

SHARP Michael Storie MA 1947 LLB 1949
ptnr Davidson & Garden advoc Aber from 1955

SHARP Neil Carter MB ChB 1940
MBE 1975
member Grampian health board from 1977

SHARP Peter Ogston MA 1946 MB ChB 1951
g p Banff from 1954

SHARP Richard Lyall *MA 1937
CB
i d c (served on staff Imp Def Coll)
prin Home Civ Serv 1946; Imp Def Coll 1961; under-secy: Prices and Incomes 1966–68, HM Treasury 1968–76; ceremonial off. civ serv dept from 1977

SHAW Alastair MA 1949
teacher: St Peter's RC s Aber 1958–60, Aber coll of comm from 1960

SHAW Ian Kirk *MA 1952
Leeds: reg secy RIBA Yorks reg 1968–72, Yorks/NW/Northern reg from 1972

SHAW or McLean, Jessie Cormack MA 1917
resid Longniddry

SHAW or Crombie, Jessie Tyson *MA 1931
resid Dingwall

SHAW John MB ChB 1912
no longer on GC reg

SHAW or Naughton, Mary Ann MA 1950

SHAW Thomas BSc(for) 1955

SHEACH Jean Mackenzie MB ChB 1937 MD 1952
consult. Exeter clin area Devon from 1958

SHEACH or Dubreuil, Margaret Helen *MA 1940
MA(Vermont) 1970
Canada: asst prof Engl Macdonald coll 1961–70, assoc prof Engl McG univ 1970–77
m(2) Montreal 12.5.72 Rodney Bruce BSc(Queen's univ Kingston Ontario) engineer

SHEACH Mary Ann MA 1918
prin teacher Engl/Fr Kinross 1924–60; retd 1960; resid Aber
d Aber 15.2.76

SHEARER or Falconer, Evelyn Murray MA 1923
loc exec secy Brit assoc: Aber 1962–63, Southampton 1963–64, Leeds 1966–67, Dun 1967–68, Exeter 1968–69; head secy duties dept Queensway secy coll Nairobi 1970–74; prin Pioneer comm coll Mombasa 1975–77; retd

SHEARER Janet *MA 1947

SHEARER John Alexander MB ChB 1934
FRCGP 1971
g p Bucksburn 1938–74; retd; resid Tarves

SHEARER John Craigen BSc(eng) 1950

SHEARER Lewis George MB ChB 1930

SHEARER Margaret Ferguson Plowman MA 1917
d 1942

SHEARER William *BSc 1953

SHEARER William Fraser MB ChB 1922
no longer on GC reg

SHECHNER Isadore MB ChB 1934

SHEED or Riddell, Annie Rennie MA 1928
resid Aber

SHEED Jessie Smith MA 1926
d 21.11.65

SHENNAN David John George *BSc(eng) 1929
FICE 1959 FI Arb 1974
Sir Wm Arrol, J. Mowlem & E. Nuttall: eng/ag 1930–42, contr co-ordinator 1956–74; R E 1943–46; consult. and arbitrator from 1974

SHENNAN Edward Theodore MB ChB 1939 DPH 1947
DIH 1970 MFCM 1972
Jamaica WI: m o h parish of St Mary 1964–67, sen m o h min of health Kingston from 1967

SHEPHERD Anna MA 1915 LLD 1964
edit. *AUR* 1957–64; author *The Living Mountain* publ 1977
d Aber 27.2.81 *AUR* XLIX 136

SHEPHERD Arnold Frederick *BSc 1946

SHEPHERD David Ramsay BSc 1952

SHEPHERD or Reaper, Elizabeth Nicol MA 1917
no longer on GC reg

SHEPHERD Ella Christine MA 1943

SHEPHERD Francis George Graham [c]MB ChB 1948
MRCGP 1967
g p Aber from 1952

SHEPHERD George Alexander *MB ChB 1919
retd 1961; resid Estepona, Malaga, Spain

SHEPHERD Helen *MA 1939
JP 1969
teacher: prin mod lang/housemistress Huyton coll 1953–59, prin mod lang Congleton g s 1959–61; head: March h s Cambs 1961–69, Hereward comp s March Cambs 1969–73; sen advis teacher mod lang Cambs 1973–76; retd

SHEPHERD Ian Leslie MB ChB 1944
g p: Nott 1954–66, Burlington Ontario from 1966

SHEPHERD James Alexander MA 1904
no longer on GC reg

SHEPHERD James Forrest MB ChB 1922
d Farnham Surrey 21.10.72 *AUR* XLV 126

SHEPHERD James William Thomson MB ChB 1950

SHEPHERD Kathleen Mary *MA 1947
prin teacher mod lang: Banchory acad 1966–70, Nairn acad 1970–71; prin Ger Inv royal acad from 1971

SHEPHERD Norman BSc 1954 *1956

SHEPHERD Norman Alexander MA 1949 [d]LLB 1952
QC 1978
Canada: br leg. off. indust dev bank London Ontario

1961–63, reg leg. off. indust dev bank Toronto 1963–65; ptnr Crawford, Shepherd & Hill Wingham 1965–69, sen ptnr Shepherd & Laschuk Kincardine from 1969; pres Bruce Law Assoc from 1976

SHEPHERD Norman James Brander MA 1937 LLB 1941
MBE
d Aber 1.7.71 *AUR* XLIV 321

SHEPHERD Robert Robertson BSc(agr) 1952

SHEPHERD William Gray Aitken *MA 1948
PhD(Edin) 1962
prin teacher lang Leith acad Edin 1961–65; head Broughton s s later h s Edin from 1965

SHEPPARD Herbert Playford MB ChB 1900
no longer on GC reg

SHERRIFFS or Burn, Helen MA 1914
d Methlick 12.12.72 *AUR* XLV 224

SHERRIFFS or Gordon, Mary Ironside MA 1911
resid Bendigo Vict Aust
d Bendigo Australia 10.5.79

SHERRIFFS William Rae MA 1903 BSc 1911 DSc 1919
d Surrey 7.10.64 *AUR* XLI 53

SHEWAN or Robertson, Agnes BSc 1953
teacher sc Fyvie s s 1967–73; asst head Fyvie s from 1974

SHEWAN Alexander BSc(agr) 1922
no longer on GC reg

SHEWAN Frederick George Davidson MA 1925 dLLB 1927
retd 1975; resid Aber
wife *d* 18.8.76

SHEWAN Frederick Robert MA 1952 Dip Ed 1955
teacher Ruthrieston s s Aber 1961–62; head Tough p s 1962–67, Cove p s 1967–71, Kinnoull p s 1971–77, North Muirton p s Perth from 1977

SHEWAN Henry Alexander *MA 1928 dLLB 1932
OBE(mil) 1946 CB 1974
dep commissioner nat insur Edin 1955–66, commissioner from 1966
wife *d* 7.8.77

SHEWAN James Mackay BSc 1931 *1932 PhD 1935 DSc 1969
FRSE 1960 FIBiol 1960 FIFST 1965
retd 1975; resid Aber

SHEWAN or Milne, Jane Will *MA 1917
resid Pitmedden
husb *d* 3.12.62

SHEWAN John MA 1920
d Aber 25.4.68 *AUR* XLII 358

SHIACH or McIver, Doris Lorimer *MA 1941
resid Westhill Skene

SHIACH George Alexander MA 1932

SHIACH George Alexander Morrison *MA 1936
Castle Douglas h s: teacher classics 1962–73, asst prin guid from 1973; retd 1978
wife *d* 1963
m(2) Bearsden 24.12.66 Margaret M. R. Davidson Dip Mus teacher d of Joseph J. D. Bearsden

SHIACH or Cowie, Helen Emily MA 1954
teacher: Toronto 1958–64, York county s Ontario 1964–75; vice-prin York county s from 1975

SHIACH Hendry MA 1933
head St Peter's s Galashiels 1951–72; retd

SHIACH or Diack, Irene McLeod MA 1953
resid Germany

SHIACH James George BSc(eng) 1945 BSc(agr) 1950
F Inst Agr E JP 1969
part-time sen lect agr Aberd from 1969; chmn eng/farm bldgs group Aber s of Agr from 1969

SHIACH William Geddes MB ChB 1943
Cook hosp Gisborne NZ: surg supt from 1958, visiting surg from 1963

SHIACH William Lorimer MA 1911
d Aber 12.4.61 *AUR* XXXIX 202

SHIACH Wilma Janet MA 1944
teacher Tillydrone p s Aber from 1954

SHIELDS Michael Anthony MB ChB 1954
g p: Inverurie 1958–60, Bucksburn 1960–61, Wrexham Denbighsh from 1961
m Aber 9.9.60 Valerie E. R. Birkbeck MA 1956 *qv*

SHILLAND John Kirkcaldy Murray BSc(agr) 1952
farm. nr Dun from 1954

SHILLINGFORD Dorian Cleophas MB ChB 1954

SHINNIE Andrew James MB ChB 1908 cMD 1912
d Twickenham –.5.63 *AUR* XL 199

SHINNIE or Shaw, Ann MA 1909
d Minehead 9.1.62 *AUR* XXXIX 377

SHIRRAS Joan MA 1918
resid Sevenoaks
d 1981

SHIRRAS or Philip, Kathleen Janet MA 1943
resid Eaglesham Glasg

SHIRRAS or Gray, Ruth Georgina Patricia MA 1942
resid Glasg

SHIRREFFS Helen Catherine MA 1955 LLB 1957
leg asst Guild & Guild WS Edin 1966–68; part time

man. Chamber of Commerce Dorval Quebec 1972–75
m Aber 29.7.60 Robert Bain BSc 1956 *qv*

SHIRREFFS James Gordon MB ChB 1945
g p Barrow-on-Soar nr Loughborough from 1948

SHIRREFFS or Campbell, Mary Annella MB ChB 1947
gp/anaest Loughborough from 1952

SHIRREFFS Percy Charles Brand MB ChB 1931
comp dir from 1945; resid Lodsworth nr Petworth

SHIVAS Alice MA 1927
retd 1968; resid Aber

SHIVAS Andrew Armitage MB ChB 1944 DPH 1947 *MD 1955
TD 1965 FRCSE 1970 FRCPath 1971
sen lect Edin from 1959

SHIVAS Isobel Blanche Armitage MB ChB 1951
regist anaest Edin 1962–63 REHSC 1963–67; part-time anaest Scot. borders hosps Melrose from 1967
m Aber 20.4.63 Stuart C. L. Barber BSc(for)(Edin) for. consult. s of Arthur L. B. Heckmondwike Yorks

SHIVAS or Walker, Mary Grant BSc 1949 *1950
resid Benton N'cle-u-Tyne

SHORTT Henry Edward MB ChB 1910 ᶜMD 1936 DSc 1937 LLD 1952

SHRIMPTON Derek Howard PhD 1954

SHU Hou Jen (Suvoong Cornelius Agnew) MA 1900 MB ChB 1903 DPH 1904 MD 1908
d –.10.51

SIBBALD James Gray MA 1950 LLB 1953
prin solic Livingston dev corp from 1966

SILBERGH Alexander Edward MA 1949 MB ChB 1956
g p Buckie from 1961
m Aber 17.8.62 Anne B. Hutchison midwife d of Gordon Hutchison MB ChB 1927 *qv*

SILBERGH Michael BSc(eng) 1944 *1947

SILLARS Alexander MB ChB 1950
sen ptnr Sillars Crane & Brummitt Malmesbury from 1972

SILVER Cyril John MB ChB 1935 DPH 1939
deceased

SILVER Douglas *MA 1933
teacher: prin mod lang Aboyne acad 1968–74; retd councillor Mid Deeside Commun Council 1977, chmn 1978

SILVER Gerald Bain MA 1929

SILVER or Shivas, Isabel Margaret MA 1953

SILVER Kathleen Mary MA 1946
deceased

SILVER Rona McLaren MA 1954
teacher Edin

SIM Alfred Gall MA 1910
no longer on GC reg

SIM Arthur Henri BSc(agr) 1923 BSc 1925
no longer on GC reg

SIM or Penwarden, Dora Penny MA 1946

SIM Douglas BSc(for) 1945 Dip Ed 1964
retd Ghana 1962; for. off. UN FAO advis on for. educ Nyabyeya, Uganda 1964–72; proj man. UN Dev Progr for. coll proj Malaysia, Kepong, Selangor 1972–76; consult. for. educ Orgut-Swed Forest Consortium Ethiopia from 1976

SIM Elizabeth Shand MA 1908
no longer on GC reg

SIM George BSc(mech eng) 1944; BSc(civ eng) 1948
MICE 1970
various apptmts UK/abroad with eng consult.
sen resid eng on construct. of new chem plant in Libya from 1977
m Villablino León Spain 11.10.61 Aurora R. Alonso MIL(Lond) lang teacher

SIM George BSc 1952 *1953
teacher sc/spec asst chem Fraserburgh acad 1957–72; prin chem Lochaber h s Fort William from 1973
m Aber 4.4.61 Margaret M. Pennie radiogr d of Alfred G. P. Aber

SIM John Wood *MA 1947
prin teacher Engl Fraserburgh acad from 1964

SIM John Wyness *MA 1932
MSc(Lond) 1967
C.O. RAF s of educ Uxbridge 1960–63; chief instr basic stud. RAF tech coll Henlow 1963–64
m Mary J. Disbrey; wife *d* 19.1.79

SIM or Waugh, Marjorie Elizabeth MA 1937

SIM or Fraser, Mary Badenoch MA 1936
resid Glasg
husb *d* 23.8.67
m(2) Paisley 24.8.76 William D. Buchanan comp dir s of John S. B. Mauchline

SIM or Edwards, Mary Jane Forbes BSc 1944
resid Brechin

SIM or Littlejohn, Phyllis Margaret MA 1949
resid Ealing Lond

SIM Robert Stephen *MA 1953
prin teacher hist: Thurso h s 1961–66, Inverurie acad 1966–74; advis hist Aber city 1974–75, Grampian reg from 1975

SIM Stuart Anderson MA 1919 BSc 1921
retd 1962; resid Wolverhampton
d 26.3.74

SIMMERS Forbes MB ChB 1916
d 11.11.62

SIMMERS John Sandison MB ChB 1935
g p Keith 1946–76; retd

SIMMERS or Bulkley, Williamina Isabella BSc 1933
d Douglas I of M 27.12.75 *AUR* XLVI 417

SIMMINS or Slater, Mary Chalmers MA 1938
lib s of nurs Royal Masonic hosp Lond 1966–75; visitor Anchor Housing Assoc from 1975

SIMMONDS Trevor Henry MA 1949
LTCL(TEFL) 1971
lect TEFL coll of comm Aber from 1963

SIMON John Hood MA 1952 LLB 1956
nat serv Lond 1956–58; solic: Aber 1958–61, Inv 1961–67; asst secy (leg.) Aberd from 1967
m St And 23.6.67 Vida A. Skinner MB ChB(St And) med pract d of David S. Wormit-on-Tay

SIMPSON Agnes Teresa MA 1913
no longer on GC reg

SIMPSON Alan Walter MB ChB 1953
FRCP(C) 1973
Canada: h o anaest gen hosp St John's Newfoundland 1958–59, McG univ hosps Montreal 1959–61; staff anaest Kitchener-Waterloo St Mary's hosps Kitchener Ontario from 1961 and chief of anaest St Mary's hosp Kitchener 1972–76
m Montreal 20.5.60 Elizabeth S. Stewart RGN d of John S. Law Lanarksh

SIMPSON Albert Allan MB ChB 1925
Canada: g p Midland Ont 1961–64, Lower Sackville Nova Scotia 1964–72
d Digley Nova Scotia 20.9.75 *AUR* XLVI 323

SIMPSON Alexander BSc(agr) 1923

SIMPSON Alexander Bruce MA 1954 *BSc 1957
PhD
Johannesburg: mine geol 1959–61, temp lect geol univ Witwatersrand 1961, res worker econ geol res unit 1962–65, min nat inst metallurgy 1965–70 (study tour univs etc Aust/USA/Europe 1966–67), chief min Brick corp of S. Af. 1970–72; Cape Town: meteorite res off./PhD stud. univ of Cape Town from 1972

SIMPSON Alexander George BCom 1923
d Aber 3.11.66 *AUR* XLII 86

SIMPSON, Alexander Malcolm MA 1929
retd 1973; resid Selkirk
wife *d* 7.7.73

SIMPSON or Houghton, Anne
MB ChB 1918 DPH 1920
d Banchory 5.1.64 *AUR* XL 399

SIMPSON or Payne, Annie *MA 1913
d Fochabers 12.9.77

SIMPSON Beatrice Weir MA 1913 *BSc 1917
resid Aber
d 14.2.81 *AUR* XLIX 135

SIMPSON Brian BSc 1955
prin teacher maths: Kaimhill s s Aber 1966–71, Kincorth acad 1971–74; asst head Northfield acad Aber 1974–79, dep rector Westhill acad Skene from 1979
m Bieldside 28.12.68 Alice S. T. Watson law off. cashier d of Thomas W. Aber

SIMPSON Charles Gregor MA 1929 LLB 1931
NCB: dir gen staff 1957–67, pers consult. 1967–71; retd; member nat staff comm of NHS 1967–70; member chmn's panel civ serv selection board 1970–77; resid Moreton-in-Marsh

SIMPSON Charles Harvey *MA 1914
retd 1956; resid Edin 1956–74, Cheltenham from 1974
wife *d* 18.3.74
d Cheltenham 14.12.79

SIMPSON Colin Finlayson MA 1906 *MB ChB 1910
d Aber 2.6.64 *AUR* XL 394, XLI 145

SIMPSON David MA 1910 BSc(agr) 1912
d Jersey 19.1.76 *AUR* XLVI 414

SIMPSON Douglas Alexander Dunningham
MA 1930
d 18.1.73

SIMPSON Elizabeth Margaret Murray
MB ChB 1937
retd 1973; resid Carlisle

SIMPSON or McKenzie, Elma Moira MB ChB 1948
med asst Craig Phadrig hosp for m/ph patients Inv from 1969

SIMPSON Eric John *MA 1952 Dip Ed 1953
prin teacher hist Hawick h s 1962–66; lect hist Moray House coll of educ Edin from 1966

SIMPSON Ernest BSc(eng) 1939
d 1960

SIMPSON Frank Douglas MA 1890
d 24.5.62 *AUR* XL 73

SIMPSON George MA 1949
branch man. Aber savings bank from 1972

SIMPSON George Donald BSc(agr) 1938
MBE 1970
DAFS from 1939; resid Keith

SIMPSON Graham Robertson *MA 1955

SIMPSON or Mullan, Helen Macdonald *MA 1941

SIMPSON Henry Stewart MA 1927
d Garmouth 3.5.67 *AUR* XLII 367

SIMPSON Ian Catto MB ChB 1936

SIMPSON Ian James
***MA 1920 MEd 1922 PhD 1942**
retd 1962; resid Edin
wife *d* 3.5.68
d Edin 11.1.81

SIMPSON Ian Laing MA 1954
prin sc teacher Kinross h s from 1964

SIMPSON James Morrison MA 1927
OBE 1960
solic Stewart & Watson Banff from 1965
d Banff 26.7.74 *AUR* XLVI 109

SIMPSON Jeffrey Randal PhD 1955

SIMPSON or Brittain, Jenny Hay Anderson
MB ChB 1921
d Oldmeldrum 7.2.64 *AUR* XL 399

SIMPSON Jessie Mary *MA 1911
d Edin 10.12.67 *AUR* XLII 350

SIMPSON John BSc(eng) 1945
teacher sc/maths Gordon s Huntly 1962–65; prin sc Lossiemouth h s 1965–73, dep rector from 1973
d Lossiemouth 21.2.76

SIMPSON John Alexander *MA 1913
retd; resid Edin
d 1978

SIMPSON Joseph William MA 1947 Dip Ed 1948
head: Stonehaven p s 1968–71, Arduthie p s Stonehaven from 1971

SIMPSON or Kiddie, Lilias Innes Anderson
MA 1916 BSc 1920
resid Dun

SIMPSON Lizzie Helen Barbara MA 1907
d Aber 30.5.65 *AUR* XLI 146

SIMPSON or Simpson, Muriel Dohm *MA 1920
d Oxford 3.5.68 *AUR* XLII 359

SIMPSON Norman Charles
MB ChB 1921 *MD 1927
d Edin 12.12.67 *AUR* XLII 359

SIMPSON Peter McGregor *MA 1935
head Torphins p s 1967–76; retd; resid Old Meldrum

SIMPSON Robert Hamilton McColm BSc(eng) 1947

SIMPSON Ronald George MB ChB 1943 *MD 1949
FRCPE 1969 FRCP(Lond) 1975
lect geriatric med Dund from 1954

SIMPSON Ronald Ian *MA 1948

SIMPSON Sheila May MA 1955
teacher Skene Sq p s Aber 1963–74, asst head Ashley Road p s Aber from 1974

SIMPSON or Low, Vera Catherine MA 1949
teacher Engl: Queen Anne's s Dunfermline 1950–51, Larkhall acad 1951–52; Griffith NSW Aust: teacher Fr/head of lang dept cath h s 1965–75, i/c teaching Engl as second lang to migrant ch cath h s 1976; retd

SIMPSON Walter Murray *BSc(eng) 1953
oper eng commissioning dept EE Co Hinkley Point 'A' power stat 1961–64; dep chief comm eng comm dept NDC Sizewell power stat 1964–67; chief comm eng: BNDC Wylfa power stat 1967–73, chief comm eng NPC Hartlepool AGR power stat from 1973

SIMPSON William Douglas
***MA 1919 DLitt 1924 LLD 1960**
d Aber 9.10.68 *AUR* XLIII 24, 27

SIMPSON William John BSc 1952

SIMPSON William Nightingale MB ChB 1924
retd 1964; resid Melrose

SINCLAIR Alexander *MA 1933
prin teacher classics Milne's h s Fochabers 1936–74, dep rector from 1961; retd 1974

SINCLAIR Alistair MB ChB 1955
DIH(Soc of Apoth) 1962
m o United Steel Co., Sheffield 1960–66; sen m o Brit Steel Corp Ebbwvale 1967–73, group sen m o BSC Scunthorpe from 1974

SINCLAIR Andrew David MB ChB 1926
d 1974

SINCLAIR or Noble, Barbara Anne Mabel (Lady)
MA 1937
resid Nairn

SINCLAIR or Low, Catherine MA 1925
no longer on GC reg

SINCLAIR David BSc(agr) 1926
JP 1942
farm. Nigg Aber from 1967; retd; resid Aber

SINCLAIR or Mitchell, Ellen Carey MA 1913
no longer on GC reg

SINCLAIR Frances Mary Grace MB ChB 1921
d Walsall 29.5.66 *AUR* XLI 339

SINCLAIR George Alexander *MA 1949 *MEd 1952
FEIS 1975
prin teacher Engl/hist/geog Powis acad Aber 1961–65; dep head Northfield acad Aber 1965–67; head Powis acad from 1967

SINCLAIR George Murdoch MB ChB 1942
part-time consult. radiol Tunbridge Wells hosp man. comm from 1953

SINCLAIR or Robertson, Helen Slater MA 1951

SINCLAIR Henry Macgregor MB ChB 1930
retd 1969

SINCLAIR Ian Hunter BSc 1954
teacher maths Aber coll of comm from 1962
m Aber 8.8.62 Violet M. Stockan teacher d of John W. S. Aber

SINCLAIR Ian Wayman MB ChB 1947
MFCM 1972
sen m o East Riding Yorks and Humberside from 1969

SINCLAIR or Goodlad, Isabel MA 1928
d –.8.64

SINCLAIR Isobel Russell MA 1927
retd 1968; resid Elgin

SINCLAIR or Lowe, Jean MA 1930
d –.5.40

SINCLAIR or Robertson, Jean Boyes Wilson *MA 1931
retd 1969; resid Limuru Kenya
husb *d* 1974

SINCLAIR or McConnachie, Jessie MA 1930

SINCLAIR Joan May *MA 1951
teacher geog Peterhead acad from 1960

SINCLAIR John Henry MA 1955 Dip Ed 1956
teacher Laurencekirk s s from 1959

SINCLAIR Magnus *BSc 1954
teacher Hawick h s from 1967

SINCLAIR Margaret Macpherson MA 1917 BSc 1925
d Aber 30.9.61 *AUR* XXXIX 280

SINCLAIR or Noble, Mary Bella MA 1937

SINCLAIR Mary Elizabeth BSc 1921
Dingwall acad: prin teacher biol 1962–63, woman advis 1955–63; retd
d Inv 16.5.78 *AUR* XLVII 356

SINCLAIR or Babcock, Nita (Yuanita) Mary *MA 1928
retd 1971; resid NY

SINCLAIR or Wilson, Norah Boyes *MA 1933
resid South Ascot

SINCLAIR Robert David PhD 1932
no longer on GC reg

SINCLAIR Ronald McKerron MB ChB 1949

SINCLAIR Wilfred George MA 1935
d Aber 20.8.77

SINCLAIR William Dawson MB ChB 1943 DPH 1953
sen m o health dept Nott 1965–70; med asst Glenfrith hosp Leic from 1970
m Ashford Kent 17.11.56 Lucy J. Moryson MEd (Loughborough) lect d of Richard M. Wesel Germany

SINCLAIR William James BSc(agr) 1921
no longer on GC reg

SINCLAIR William Roy *MA 1934

SINGER Dennis Lewis BSc 1947 *1948
teacher: asst head Lochaber h s Fort William from 1972

SINGER Roland Charles *MA 1932
Dunoon g s: respons asst mod lang/i/c Ger dept from 1958, dep rector from 1963
d Dunoon 13.7.75

SINGH-SONDHI Gurcharan BSc(for) 1927
no longer on GC reg

SINGLETON Alfred Cahoon Bruce MB ChB 1939
d Vancouver 30.12.75

SINGLETON or Basil, Neith Lucy Bruce MB ChB 1941
m(2) Coats

SINTON Eric John MB ChB 1951
FRCS(C) 1972
Alberta Canada: ophth surg Red Deer/active staff Red Deer reg hosp centre, chief of staff Red Deer reg hosp centre; pres Ophthalmological Society of Alberta

SIVELL or Stowell, Elspeth Dolores *MA 1948

SIVEWRIGHT Mary MA 1914
d Aber 27.7.62 *AUR* XL 83

SIVEWRIGHT Robert Troup MA 1902
no longer on GC reg

SKAKLE George Scott MA 1942
C of S min Powis parish ch Aber from 1947
m Aber 15.4.67 Kathleen Duncan med secy d of George D. Aber

SKEA Andrew James BSc(agr) 1932

SKEA Edith Margaret MB ChB 1948
resid m o House of Daviot Inverurie from 1950
m Aber 26.4.68 James D. Conway marine eng/SRN s of James B. C. Coatbridge

SKELTON or Tosh, Eileen Joan BSc 1949

SKENE or Grant or Williams, Annie Pirie MA 1935

SKENE George BSc(eng) 1948
CEng FIMechE
chief proj eng Foster Wheeler Reading from 1955

SKENE Macgregor *BSc 1909 DSc 1914
d 8.8.73 *AUR* XLV 316

SKENE Norman Hay BL 1951

SKENE Ronald Fraser MA 1930
JP(Aber) 1961
permanent EEC exec delegate for Federation of British Port Wholesale Fish Merchants' Associations
d Aber 26.3.74 *AUR* XLV 448

SKENE William John BSc(eng) 1949

SKINNER Adam Gordon MA 1924 BCom 1925
OBE 1965
retd HMIS 1946; cler educ advis off. Edin 1967–70; retd; resid Aber

SKINNER Alexander Hugh MA 1903 *MB ChB 1907 *MD 1909
d Auckland NZ 21.10.62 *AUR* XL 75

SKINNER Alfred BSc 1952
sen lect maths Aber tech coll 1965–69, head of maths dept from 1969
m(2) Aber 23.6.72 Diane A. D. Wilmot lect gen stud. dept Aber tech coll d of Thomas E. W. BSc(Glas) Strathaven

SKINNER Anne MA 1926
retd 1971; resid Fordyce

SKINNER David MB ChB 1924
d Burnley 22.8.67 *AUR* XLII 185 & 364

SKINNER Henry Gray MB ChB 1938
DIH 1963 O(brother) St J 1969
DADAH hq Rhine dist Germany 1954–56; dem army health RAM coll 1957; DADAH hq BFAP Aden 1957–58; DADAH War Office Lond 1958–61; asst prof army health RAM coll 1961–63; consult. army health 1964; ADAH Malaya 1964–66; prof army health RAM coll 1966–70; DDAH Army Strategic Comm 1970–72; retd rank of col; resid Conon Bridge

SKINNER James Beattie *MA 1934
OBE 1960 FEIS 1966
head Dalkeith h s 1961–74

SKINNER James Mackintosh *MA 1955
PhD(Kent) 1972
asst prof Brandon univ Canada 1965–73, asst prof from 1973
m Aber 5.7.61 Hazel D. E. Barclay BSc 1960 *qv*

SKINNER James Sutherland *MA 1936

SKINNER Jean MA 1916
d 18.11.72

SKINNER John MA 1914 MB ChB 1919 DPH 1920
d Jarrow 2.12.61 *AUR* XXXIX 278

SKINNER Julia MA 1909
no longer on GC reg

SKINNER Leslie Clark MB ChB 1950

SKINNER or Elliot, Margaret MA 1928
d 27.11.60

SKINNER Mary Louisa MA 1925
d 4.7.66

SKINNER Rowland Gordon Chalmers BSc(eng) 1942

SKINNER Silvester MA 1938
C of S min: Gardenstown 1961–72, Lumphanan from 1972; retd; resid Banchory

SKROCZYNSKI or Szamocki, Jamna Zofia Maria MB ChB 1950

SLATER Alice Lawtie MA 1923
retd 1964; resid Portknockie

SLATER or Merson, Ann Cowie MA 1953
teacher Christian Brothers' coll Springs S Af 1966–67; resid Buckie

SLATER August Henry Klie *MA 1939
on staff DTI Lond from 1964; Egypt explor soc: hon treas from 1962, governor GB/E Europe centre 1968–78

SLATER David *BSc 1955
PhD(Leeds) 1965
res schol inst of Af geol Leeds 1961–65; geol Hunting Geol/Geophysics Elstree 1965–66; sen scient off. inst of geol sciences Lond 1966–69, prin scient off. 1969–75, sen prin scient off. from 1975
m Manc 9.3.63 Margaret Morrell teacher d of Harold M. Manc

SLATER Fife MB ChB 1904
d Germiston Transvaal 16.7.65 *AUR* XLI 237

SLATER George Phimister *BSc 1954
PhD(Belf) 1961
Saskatoon Canada: post-doct fell. chem dept univ Sask 1961–62, res off. Prairie reg lab, nat res council from 1962

SLATER Helen Pirie MA 1948
teacher geog Buckie h s from 1962

SLATER Ira George BSc(eng) 1945

SLATER Jeannie MA 1936
d Buckie 7.6.68 *AUR* XLIII 85

SLATER or Mearns, Jessie MA 1925
d 26.5.77

SLATER John MB ChB 1941
g p Middlesbrough from 1946
d Yarm Cleveland 15.4.79 *AUR* XLVIII 353

SLATER John BSc 1954 *MA 1956
marketing res Vancouver 1963–74; Policy Legis-

lation and Plan. Branch Min of Consumer and Corporate Affairs Victoria BC from 1975

SLATER John Cormack *MA 1912 *BSc 1913
no longer on GC reg

SLATER Margaret *MA 1953
secy/res asst to Sir Harold Mitchell Bt Geneva 1960–62
m Aber 30.4.62 Matthias H. Luchsinger textile eng s of Hermann L. Zürich

SLATER William *MA 1936
d 13.3.73

SLATER William MB ChB 1940
g p Nott from 1967

SLEIGH or Gillies, Agnes Mary MB ChB 1945
d 1973

SLEIGH Frederick Roberts MB ChB 1923
retd 1960; resid Biggar
d Biggar 5.7.79 *AUR* XLVIII 351

SLEIGH Gordon Fraser MA 1947

SLEIGH James Charles MB ChB 1918 DPH 1931
d Harpenden 17.6.65 *AUR* XLI 149

SLEIGH John MB ChB 1940
m o h S Herefordsh from 1968; resid Ross-on-Wye

SLEIGH or Miller, Lesley Margaret BSc 1955 *1956
resid Banchory

SLEIGH Rona MA 1947

SLESSOR Donald Munro MB ChB 1950
g p Aber from 1956

SLESSOR or Nutten, Dorothy MA 1944
resid Aber

SLESSOR Isabel Mary *MA 1929
retd 1971; resid Bridge of Allan
d Milnathort 25.1.81

SLESSOR James George MA 1899
d 25.7.66 *AUR* XLI 335

SLESSOR Robert Stewart MB ChB 1935

SLORACH Albert Robert MA 1938
MBE 1976
head Kinloss p s from 1946; retd 1978
wife *d* 26.8.76

SLORACH or McLachlan, Elizabeth MA 1923
retd 1967; resid Helensburgh

SLORACH John BSc 1929 MB ChB 1937
consult. psychiat Carlton Hayes hosp Leic 1951–72; member mental health review tribunal 1960–72; consult. psychiat emeritus Leic from 1972

SMAILES or Alp, Grace Elizabeth *MA 1940
head lang Wanganui girls' coll NZ from 1965

SMALL or McCrea, Catherine Isabella *MA 1918
deceased

SMART Alexander MA 1918 PhD 1938 DD 1954
d Prestwick 8.7.65 *AUR* XLI 150

SMART Annie Margaret MA 1930
head Engl dept Hammersmith polytech Wilts 1939–45; res for M of Educ Wilts 1945–47; sen mistress Bath coll of tech 1947–54; head Peckham s Lond 1954–68; retd; resid Dulwich

SMART Christina Mary MA 1930

SMART David Gordon BL 1903

SMART Evelyn *MA 1924
retd 1961; resid Langholm

SMART James Duncan BCom 1924
d 18.10.70 *AUR* XLIV 211

SMART or Clay, Margaret Caldwell Cathro MA 1953
teacher: Northside inf s Canberra 1966–72, mistress i/c Canberra gr inf s from 1973

SMART Mary Edith MA 1955
teacher: Blairgowrie 1956–59, Nairn 1959–60, Bankfoot 1960–61, Toronto from 1970
m Nairn 4.7.60 Ivan Haggart pres construct. comp s of James C. H. Stanley Perthsh

SMART Robert Arthur MB ChB 1936
MRCP(Lond) 1965 FRCP 1977
dep chief m o Supreme HQ Allied Powers Europe 1960–62; dep dir army health BAOR 1962–64; dir army health M o D 1964–68; dir med serv: Far East Land Forces 1968–70, BAOR 1970–71; retd maj gen 1972; Esso Petr Co: sen m o 1972–75, chief m o from 1975; retd 1979
m Lond 6.12.47

SMART Robert Milne MA 1914 BSc 1921
no longer on GC reg

SMART William Gerald MB ChB 1942
Tanganyika: malaria lab Amani 1951–52; dist m o Shinyanga Tabora Mbulu 1952–61, sen m o W Lake Province 1961–63; Perth W Aust: Commonwealth dept health 1963–68, sen m o dept health 1968–72; sen m o dept soc secur from 1972; med counsellor dept health 1978
m Tranent 18.3.43 Alice M. Bannerman

SMIT Henry MB ChB 1906
no longer on GC reg

SMITH Agnes Macdonald BSc 1924 *BSc 1925
d West Wickham 28.1.66 *AUR* XLI 245

SMITH Agnes Mary MA 1908
d Turriff 30.8.73 *AUR* XLV 316

SMITH Alan BL 1931
d Aber 13.2.65 *AUR* XLI 152

SMITH Alasdair McIntyre MB ChB 1920
(foundation) MRCGP
retd 1973; resid Camborne Cornwall
d Camborne 5.11.79 *AUR* XLVIII 351

SMITH Alex John *MA 1952
sec British Ports Assoc Lond from 1969

SMITH Alexander MA 1902
no longer on GC reg

SMITH Alexander MB ChB 1911

SMITH Alexander MA 1929
retd 1968; resid Aber

SMITH Alexander Edmond *MA 1926
d Dunoon 8.2.73 *AUR* XLV 226

SMITH Alexander James MA 1936
SSC Edin 1961; ptnr Lindsay Duncan & Black WS Edin from 1961
d Edin 18.10.78

SMITH Alexander James MB ChB 1953
g p Brighton from 1958

SMITH Alexander John MA 1943

SMITH Alexander John Vincent MA 1905
d 16.1.70 *AUR* XLIII 440

SMITH Alexander Johnstone Cameron MA 1929
acct Aber 1929–40, Lond 1940–74; retd 1974; resid Cobham

SMITH Alexander Mair MA 1944 *1948 PhD 1952
KB 1975
Rolls Royce Derby: head adv res 1959–67, dir/chief scient 1967–69; dir Manc polytech from 1969

SMITH Alexander Souter BL 1946

SMITH Alexander Will Hampton MA 1954

SMITH Alexandra Gordon MB ChB 1954

SMITH Alfred James *MA 1905 DLitt 1919
d Aber 15.2.62 *AUR* XXXIX 374

SMITH Alfred Nicoll *MA 1938
d 28.10.75

SMITH Alick Drummond Buchanan
see Buchanan-Smith

SMITH Alison Elizabeth MA 1951

SMITH Allan Keppie BSc(eng) 1953
CEng 1963 FIMechE 1975 FIWeldE 1975
Dip Man. St(Strath) 1966
Babcock & Wilcox Renfrew: facilities eng 1963–66, indust eng man. 1966–74; prod. dir 1974–77, man. dir from 1977
m Paisley 2.9.65 Mary B. Love typist d of James L. Paisley

SMITH Andrew Ross BSc(eng) 1952
gen man. A. Hall & Son (concrete) Aber 1965–67; man. dir A. Hall & Son/George W. Bruce Aber 1967–69; man. dir Aber Concrete Co from 1969
wife *d* –.10.72

SMITH or Frain, Annabella *MA 1932

SMITH Anne-Leslie Armstrong Leonard
see Leonard-Smith

SMITH or Allan, Anne Mary MB ChB 1930

SMITH Archibald MA 1955
dep head Ashley Road s Aber from 1972
m Aber 24.12.59 Sheila Benzies nurs nurse d of Harry B. Aber

SMITH Archibald James *BSc(eng) 1943

SMITH Arthur Forbes MA 1919
d 21.9.66 *AUR* XLI 338

SMITH Audrey Fraser BSc 1955 *1956
teacher sc Aber h s for girls/Harlaw acad from 1958

SMITH Benjamin Butler *MA 1936
dir of educ Kincardinesh 1961–75; retd; teaching Engl in Italy 1975–78

SMITH Bernard Hooper *MB ChB 1940 *MD 1956
FRCP(Lond) 1965 FRCP(C) 1972 FRCPsych 1973
prof neurol State univ of NY at Buffalo s of med NY from 1953

SMITH Bryan Taylor MA 1939
head Airyhall p s Aber 1964–80; retd

SMITH Charles *BSc(agr) 1955
DSc(Edin) 1976
anim breeding res organis(ARC) Edin 1958–68 and from 1974; dept human genetics Edin 1968–74

SMITH Christina MA 1929
spec asst maths Nicolson inst Stornoway 1942–68; retd

SMITH or Lister, Christina Wilson MA 1927
no longer on GC reg

SMITH Cyril Moore *MB ChB 1904
no longer on GC reg

SMITH David BSc(agr) 1952
farm. Arbroath from 1956

SMITH David Drummond MA 1904
no longer on GC reg

SMITH David Flett MB ChB 1935
FRCOG 1961
assoc lect obst/gyn N'cle from 1971

SMITH David Taiwan MA 1900
d 23.10.62

SMITH or Arnaud, Dena Isabella MA 1943 *MEd 1951
teacher Perth, Alyth 1952–54; asst educ psych Banffsh from 1972

SMITH Donald MA 1942

SMITH Donald MA 1949
head Airidhantuim s Shader Is of Lewis from 1965

SMITH Donald Sinclair MB ChB 1929 MD 1957
no longer on GC reg

SMITH or Reid, Dorothea Thomson MA 1929
farm. Peterhead from 1947
husb *d* 29.6.62

SMITH Dorothy Aiken MA 1926
no longer on GC reg

SMITH or Watson, Dorothy Jane Moir MA 1929
teacher: Engl/maths/hist Mzuza s s Nyasaland 1960–62, Engl Blantyre comm coll 1962–64; Engl/maths/hist/relig educ Aberfoyle s s 1965–70; resid Salisbury Rhod

SMITH or Farquharson, Dorothy Margaret MA 1926
d 7.4.75

SMITH Douglas Edward *MA 1927 *MEd 1950
dep dir of educ Banffsh 1965–71; retd; resid Keith

SMITH Douglas William Cumming MB ChB 1947
OBE 1972 TD 1966
g p Grays Essex from 1950; lt col City of Lond field ambul 1964–67

SMITH Duncan Kenneth *BSc 1952
asst dir Ont res foundation Mississauga Ontario from 1976

SMITH or Galloway, Edith Annie MA 1904
d Vancouver Is BC 6.3.53 *AUR* XXXIX 100

SMITH Edna May MA 1940
Aber: dep head Summerhill acad 1970–73, dep head Harlaw acad 1973; head Hilton acad 1974–80; retd

SMITH Edward Alexander *MA 1924
BA(Lond) 1940
teacher classics: Bellshill acad 1925–28, Hamilton acad 1928–38, AGS 1938–41; prin classics Dumfries acad 1941–56; edit: printing firm Alva 1959–62, Oliver & Boyd Edin 1962–70; retd
m Cults 2.8.44 Isabella L. Innes comm artist d of John I. Aberlour

SMITH Elizabeth Helen MA 1932

SMITH or Joss, Elizabeth Lillie Lindsay MB ChB 1923
retd 1960; resid Edwalton

SMITH or Henderson, Elizabeth Margaret *MA 1953
teacher Engl Dunfermline h s 1968–72; asst prin Engl from 1972

SMITH or Law, Elizabeth Mary MA 1930
retd 1967; resid Barnsley

SMITH Elizabeth Mary Geddes MB ChB 1944
Canada: Indian health serv Edmonton 1955–59; assoc path. Edmonton gen hosp 1963–71; private med lab pract Edmonton from 1971

SMITH or Emslie, Elizabeth Pollock MA 1912
d 4.10.72

SMITH or Brown, Elsie Coral *MA 1940
teacher Elgin from 1950

SMITH or Duthie, Emily Rose Sinclair MA 1929
teacher: Skene j s s 1953–55, part-time on relief work 1955–69; retd; resid Aber
husb *d* 4.3.72

SMITH Emily Stevenson MB ChB 1942

SMITH Eric Burnett MB ChB 1942

SMITH Ethel Violet Guinevere MB ChB 1921
d 29.1.71

SMITH or Elliott, Florence MA 1914
resid Manitoba
d circa 1979

SMITH Frances Mildred Dorothy *MA 1927
teacher: Kinellar 1945–54, Culter s 1954–65; retd; resid Aber

SMITH or McLean, Frances Moira MA 1945
teacher: Meiklerigg Crescent p s Glasg 1951–55, Bromley Kent 1964–65; nursery teacher Edin 1966–68; free-lance writer from 1965; council member The Natl Children's Bureau from 1975

SMITH Francis Godfrey BSc(for) 1949 DSc 1956
col serv/HM Overseas civ serv agr/for. dept Tabora/Arusha Tanganyika 1949–62; W Aust dept agr i/c apiculture and veg mapping Perth Aust 1962–74; dir Nat Parks W Aust from 1974

SMITH Francis Taylor MA 1955
C of S min: St Paul's ch Dunfermline from 1964; moderator presb Dunfermline and Kinross 1973–74

SMITH George MA 1893
no longer on GC reg

SMITH George *MA 1929
retd; resid Methil

SMITH George MA 1950
teacher Littleport Cambs 1961–66; head dept Hemel Hempstead 1966–69, dep head 1969–72; head Radlett 1972–78; head Garston from 1978
m Portgordon Banffsh 27.12.58 Patricia Innes

SMITH George Cameron MA 1925
no longer on GC reg

SMITH George Carnegie
see Carnegie-Smith

SMITH George Murray Cowie MB ChB 1939
m Bradford 20.6.40 Anne M. S. MacRae MB ChB 1939 *qv*

SMITH Gertrude Anne *MA 1920
retd 1961; resid Turriff

SMITH Harold *MA 1951

SMITH Helen MA 1929

SMITH or Murison, Helen MA 1930
d Edin 18.2.75

SMITH or Adam, Helen Ann MB ChB 1939
g p Sheffield from 1963

SMITH or Wood, Helen Maggie MA 1940
Banff acad: teacher Engl 1961–69 housemistress/asst prin guid/teacher Engl 1969–74, prin guid/Engl from 1974

SMITH or Mackechnie, Helen May MA 1940

SMITH or Matheson, Helen Wilson MA 1927
teacher inf: Annan acad 1929–32, Aber 1932–35, Glasg 1948–55; inf mistress Glasg 1955–70; retd

SMITH Helena BSc 1926
retd 1968; resid Fraserburgh

SMITH Henry *BSc(agr) 1952 PhD 1956
Cyanamid of G.B. Gosport: sen scient advis anim prod. 1956–69, tech man. agr prod. from 1969
m Kemnay 11.7.59 Elizabeth M. Downie teacher d of James D. Kemnay

SMITH Herbert Irving Gordon BSc(eng) 1928
CEng MIMechE 1970
lect Glasg coll of tech 1969–75; retd

SMITH Hugh Gordon Tennant MB ChB 1923
hon sheriff from 1964; retd 1966; resid Banff
d 15.10.80 *AUR* XLIX 67 & 136

SMITH Iain *MA 1949
FRLS 1974 8 Arts Council awards
Oban: asst prin teacher Engl 1955–77, full time writer under name Iain Crichton Smith from 1977
m Perth 16.7.77 Donalda Logan school nurse d of Peter L. Oban

SMITH Ian Alexander BSc 1949
teacher maths/sc: Daliburgh S Uist 1960–63, Dundee s s 1963–65, E Kilbride s s 1965–69; head dept maths/sc/phys Brisbane Aust from 1969

SMITH Ian Fyvie BSc 1942 *1943

SMITH Ian Lewis BSc(eng) 1935
MInstR 1960
chmn/man. dir Spark's of Aber from 1955

SMITH Ian Mackenzie *MA 1955
housemaster Forest Hill s Lond 1964–68; dir of stud. Sir Henry Cooper h s Hull 1968–77; vice prin SE Essex Sixth Form Coll Benfleet from 1977

SMITH Ian MacLean MA 1931
JP(Aberdeensh)
retd 1974; resid Aber

SMITH Ian Macrae *MA 1953
head geog dept Dartford h s for boys from 1962

SMITH or Campbell, Irene MA 1947

SMITH or Johnson, Isabel Copland MB ChB 1903
no longer on GC reg

SMITH Isabella MA 1926
retd 1965; resid Banff

SMITH or Bisson, Isabella Jane MA 1917
no longer on GC reg

SMITH Isobel Marjorie *MA 1945

SMITH Ivor Mitchell MA 1950

SMITH James *MA 1913 *BD 1916
d Elgin 16.7.70 *AUR* XLIV 109

SMITH James MA 1923
d Portessie 10.4.67 *AUR* XLII 361

SMITH James Alexander MB ChB 1929
g p Bolton from 1935

SMITH James David Maxwell MA 1920
d Edin 5.3.69 *AUR* XLIII 211

SMITH James Donald *MA 1939 BD 1957 DD 1978
C of S min: Cults East ch 1966–73, Auchtergaven Perthsh from 1973
Author *And All the Trumpets* 1954

SMITH James Douglas BSc(for) 1953
Glasg: apptd to exec comm Home Timber Merch Assoc Scot. 1967, dir Robinson Dunn & Co from 1968, dir Temple Builders Market from 1972

SMITH James Edward BSc 1926 PhD 1933
retd 1963; resid Sutton

SMITH James Gauld MA 1946 *MEd 1949
Management Selection: dir Glasg from 1965; man. dir Lond from 1967; chmn MSL advertising serv Lond from 1970

SMITH James Grieve Murray BSc 1949
Torry res stat Aber: higher scient off. civ serv 1958–72, sen scient off. from 1972

SMITH James Ian MB ChB 1926
g p S Shields from 1926; resid E Bordon Co Durh

SMITH James Ross *MA 1920
retd 1965; resid Airdrie

SMITH James William BSc(agr) 1929
retd 1964; resid Glenrothes

SMITH Jane Cruickshank *MA 1914
d Turriff 30.12.74 *AUR* XLVI 235

SMITH Janet Leslie MA 1915
no longer on GC reg

SMITH or Downie, Jean Murray BSc 1951
LTCL 1952
Aber: teacher sc Middle s 1958–63, prin sc Convent of the Sacred Heart 1963–71; Rubislaw acad: teacher phys 1971–73, asst head AGS from 1973

SMITH or Presly, Jeannie Grassie MA 1927

SMITH Jessie Ann MA 1926
retd 1966; resid Stonehaven

SMITH or Wattie, Jessie Beattie MA 1942
teacher Engl Forrester s s Edin from 1963

SMITH or Cormack, Jessie Gordon MA 1930
retd 1969; resid Newmachar

SMITH or Marsh, Joan Elizabeth MB ChB 1949
LMCC 1955 Dip Psy(McG) 1968 CRCP(psy) 1968 FRCP(Can) 1972
Canada: fl/lt RCAF Aylmer 1952–55, h o psychiat Lond 1955–57, McG Montreal 1964–68, consult. psychiat veterans' affairs dept of nat defence RCMP Winnipeg from 1969
m Lond, Ont 24.7.54 Bernard C. Marsh commercial pilot

SMITH John MA 1895
d 29.2.64

SMITH John MB ChB 1915 DPH 1919 *MD 1922 DSc 1927 LLD 1965
d Aber 19.6.76

SMITH John MA 1920

SMITH John *MA 1930

SMITH John Anthony McCredie MB ChB 1943 ᶜMD 1950
FRCOG 1960
consult. Burnley hosps from 1959
d 11.9.79 *AUR* XLVIII 353

SMITH John Charles MA 1905
no longer on GC reg

SMITH John Couper MB ChB 1928

SMITH John Geddes MA 1916 *MB ChB 1918
d Aber 24.7.62 *AUR* XL 85

SMITH John Lansley *MA 1927 BSc(eng) 1929
d Aber 9.4.65 *AUR* XLI 151

SMITH John Leslie Sidney MA 1926
d Greenock 31.8.74 *AUR* XLVI 109

SMITH John Robertson *MA 1952
prin mod lang/dep rector Grantown-on-Spey g s from 1965

SMITH Joseph Meston BCom 1922
d 21.12.77

SMITH or Macpherson, Joyce Isabella MA 1951
Canada: teacher Fr/Engl St John New Brunswick 1966–69, head mod lang dept Millidgeville N h s St John 1969–71, oral Fr dept Thunder Bay Ontario from 1971

SMITH or Blackie, Katharine Ironside MA 1915
no longer on GC reg

SMITH or Tocher, Kathleen Mann MA 1953
teacher Dalkeith h s 1959–63; resid Aber

SMITH or Hamilton, Kathleen Norah Ross MA 1948
resid Wellington NZ

SMITH Kenneth MA 1928
retd 1968; resid Back Is of Lewis

SMITH Kenneth MB ChB 1939

SMITH Kenneth Donald MA 1951
prod./organis Gaelic s broadcast unit Highland area (in assoc with BBC) Stornoway
m Inv 4.8.59 Rosemary Cowan hotel man. d of Douglas S. C. Rugeley

SMITH Kenneth Prahm BSc 1949

SMITH Leslie Barnet BSc(eng) 1952
teacher Baltasound Shetland from 1956

SMITH Leslie Johnston MA 1931 LLB 1933
ptnr Clark & Wallace advoc Aber 1945–71; retd 1976; resid Anglesey
d 9.12.80 *AUR* XLIX 138

SMITH or Drew, Lilian Mary Buchanan MA 1916
d St. Louis USA 16.10.80 *AUR* XLIX 66

SMITH Lorna MA 1955
teacher 1960–70
m Aber 2.10.70 Charles B. Riddoch bus driver/insp

SMITH Lyndesay Raymond Duncan MB ChB 1925
no longer on GC reg

SMITH Malcolm John Rognvald BSc(eng) 1955
on res eng staff Livishie Works Glenmoriston 1959–61; Taylor Woodrow Construction Lond: contr eng atomic power dept 1961–62, chief eng Euston stat reconstr 1962–65, sen contr eng atomic power dept 1965–71; Rendel Palmer & Tritton Lond chief plan. eng Thames barrier proj from 1971
m Derby 23.4.60 Elizabeth M. Wallace BA(Oxon) advert copywriter, publ edit. d of Andrew M. W. Derby

SMITH or Slorach, Mara Heraughty MA 1936
d Forres 26.8.76

SMITH or Currie, Margaret MA 1916 *BSc 1917
resid Canberra

SMITH or Mathieson, Margaret MA 1941

SMITH or Angus, Margaret Ann MA 1925
resid Fintray Aberdeensh
husb *d* Aber 2.11.76

SMITH or Johnston, Margaret Baron MA 1933
Enzie p s: teacher till 1963, head 1963–65; teacher Portgordon p s 1965–71; retd; resid Enzie

SMITH Margaret Campbell Gordon MA 1942
advis primary educ Aberdeensh 1967–75, Grampian reg c from 1975

SMITH Margaret Elizabeth MA 1932

SMITH or Gauld, Margaret Elizabeth *MA 1948 Dip Ed 1949
JP
teacher Fintry p s Turriff Aberdeensh 1962–63, Turriff acad: Engl 1963–71, prin Engl from 1971

SMITH Margaret Flett MA 1927
retd 1966; resid Lerwick

SMITH or Hogarth, Margaret Isobel MA 1928
teacher Sanquhar acad 1956–69
d Sanquhar 9.2.77

SMITH or Greig, Margaret Isobel MA 1944

SMITH Margaret Mary BSc 1945 MEd 1972
lect sc coll of dom sc Aber 1963–68; lect phys RGIT Aber from 1968

SMITH or Terris, Margaret Rodger MA 1955

SMITH or Smith, Marguerette Thomson MA 1947

SMITH Marion Coghill MA 1929

SMITH Marshall Alexander Hosie MA 1950 *MEd 1952
ABPsS 1961
sen educ psych Far East milit command Singapore/Hong Kong 1968–71; consult. psych United World coll S.E. Asia Singapore from 1971

SMITH or Langtry, Mary MA 1913
d Canada 26.10.73 *AUR* XLVI 107

SMITH or Trann, Mary *MA 1922

SMITH Mary Bella *MA 1919
no longer on GC reg

SMITH Mary Helen MA 1943
m Nicholls

SMITH or Robertson, Mary Jane MA 1908
no longer on GC reg

SMITH Mary Janet MA 1928
teacher Nicolson p s Stornoway 1961–67; retd

SMITH Mary Lucy MA 1928
FSA Scot.
retd 1969; resid Dun

SMITH Mary Milne MA 1924
teacher Maud j s s 1956–60, Culter j s s 1960–64; retd; resid Aber
m Aber 29.7.42 Alexander S. Mather farm. s of Alexander M. Stuartfield

SMITH or Balfour, Olive Elizabeth Duthie MA 1929
retd 1968; resid Aber

SMITH or Eady, Peggy Mairi MA 1942
lect Engl Leicester coll of comm 1958–62; resid Aber

SMITH Peter MA 1953
teacher Gordon s Huntly from 1957

SMITH Richard Williams MB ChB 1948

SMITH Robert Adam MA 1923
d Kilmarnock 27.5.68 *AUR* XLII 361

SMITH Robert Anderson MB ChB 1949
g p Burslem from 1941; Treasury m o Burslem/Admiralty surg Stoke-on-Trent from 1944
wife *d* –.4.69
m(2) Leek 30.3.72 June Proctor comp dir d of Frederick G. P. Tunstall

SMITH Robert John MB ChB 1916
no longer on GC reg

SMITH Ronald Alexander William Cochrane MB ChB 1952

SMITH Ronald Gordon Christie BSc(agr) 1946
chief off. (Scot.) meat and livestock commission Perth from 1970

SMITH or Macdonald, Sadie Mary BSc(agr) 1940

SMITH Sheena MA 1953
journalist *Evening Citizen* Glasg 1960–61; teacher Engl Kirkintilloch h s from 1972
m Aber 23.9.61 John C. Gray acct s of John R. G. Philadelphia USA

SMITH or Duncan, Sheila MA 1954
d Thurso 14.11.67 *AUR* XLII 375

SMITH or Presly, Sophie Caroline MA 1941
resid Methlick

SMITH Stanley George *MA 1936 BD 1941
spec in r e Beath h s Cowdenbeath 1956–70, prin r e h s Peebles from 1970
d Peebles 21.7.77

SMITH Stephen Reed Naisby MB ChB 1934
d –.6.72

SMITH or Walker, Sydney Eleanor MB ChB 1929
g p Manc 1932–67; retd
husb *d* 21.8.69

SMITH Sydney Robertson BSc(eng) 1933

SMITH Thomas James MA 1926
MBE 1974
head Peterhead cent. s; retd 1970; Peterhead: provost from 1971, chmn harbour trustees/chmn feuars from 1971; resid Aber 1978

SMITH Trevor Alexander Howard MB ChB 1919
d 27.10.62

SMITH Trevor George MA 1948 Dip Ed 1949

SMITH or Roger, Violet Margery Gatford *MB ChB 1919 DPH 1924
d Banff 7.9.70 *AUR* XLIV 109

SMITH Violet Mary *BSc 1930
retd 1966; resid Glassel

SMITH William MA 1907 BSc(agr) 1914
no longer on GC reg

SMITH William MB ChB 1910

SMITH William *MA 1912
d Wick 6.12.65 *AUR* XLII 84

SMITH William BSc 1934 MB ChB 1937
d –.3.77

SMITH William Alexander BSc(eng) 1950

SMITH William Gordon *MB ChB 1948 *MD 1957
d Perth Aust 29.10.69 *AUR* XLIII 331

SMITH William James *MA 1952
asst prin mod lang Hampton g s Middx 1962–66; lect i/c lang Merton tech coll Wimbledon 1967–75, prin mod lang Alford acad from 1975

SMITH William Kenneth BSc(agr) 1923
emeritus prof genetics agronomy univ Wisc retd 1965; resid Madison Wisconsin USA

SMITH William Murison MB ChB 1928
retd 1967; resid Harrogate
d 23.3.81 *AUR* XLIX 137

SMITH William Rennie BSc(eng) 1951

SMITH Wilma West *BSc 1954 PhD 1958
LTCL 1960
scient off./sen scient off. Macaulay inst for soil res Aber 1954–64; part-time curator dept geol/mineralogy Aberd from 1973
m Aber 30.9.61 Angus Aitken BSc 1950 *qv*

SMITH Wilson Hird MA 1926 LLB 1929
retd 1969; resid Aber

SMYLIE Henry Gordon MB ChB 1954 *MD 1960
MRCPath 1963
sen lect Aberd hon consult. bact to NERHB from 1964

SMYLIE William Cecil Beveridge BSc(eng) 1947
Sir Robert McAlpine: eng to ag 1949–64; Geo Wimpey & John Laing Constr: sen ag 1964–70; Simon Eng(Simonbuild) contr man. Manc from 1970
m Newton Mearns Ernestine A. Gaminek ch's nurse, phlebotomist d of Josef G. W Ger

SNOOK Laurence Cecil DSc 1939
anim prod. advis FAO Burma/Costa Rica 1963–69; consult. FAO Latin America/Asia 1970–75; farm. Bramley W. Aust from 1976

SNOW Charles Edward Francis Owen MB ChB 1894
no longer on GC reg

SNOWIE Robert Simpson MB ChB 1913
d Ilkley 19.9.71 *AUR* XLIV 316

SOMERS Ernest Archibald *BSc 1953

SOMERVILLE David Keltie PhD 1943
rector Bathgate acad from 1954
d Edin 1.11.80

SOPER Thomas Pitt PhD 1954
MA(Oxon) 1961
dir of stud. overseas dev inst Lond 1964–70; advis Barclays Bank Lond from 1970
m(2) Lond 13.4.64 June E. Brown d of J. B. B. Oxford

SORLEY Anne Christina Niven MA 1948

SORLEY or Thom, Helen Allan MA 1917
d Aust 5.8.65 *AUR* XLI 244

SORLEY Herbert Tower *MA 1914 DLitt 1939
d Salisbury Rhodesia 7.8.68 *AUR* XLII 353, XLV 447, XLVI 107

SORLEY John Tower MA 1921 MB ChB 1925
d Aber 1.4.79 *AUR* XLVIII 228

SORLEY John Tower MB ChB 1955
d Aber 6.5.65 *AUR* XLI 154

SORRIE Alexander James Strath *BSc 1951 PhD 1954
sect man. ICI petrochem div Teesside
date of marr 9.8.58

SORRIE or Skinner, Mary Ann MA 1906
d 1969

SOUTAR Alastair James MB ChB 1944
g p Downton Wilts from 1951

SOUTAR Charles Lewis Colby MA LLB 1950
solic in loc govt Ayr, Perth, Dun 1966–75; chief solic (conveyancing) Tayside reg c Dun from 1975

SOUTAR or Andrew, Ella Ann MA 1941

SOUTAR Patricia Frances MA 1952
supply teacher royal nat orthop hosp s Stanmore Middx 1968–72; private tut. to dyslexic pupils Northwood from 1975
m Dun 1.6.61 Douglas D. Scott sen exec eng PO telecom s of Robert W. S. Dun

SOUTAR Thomas MA 1948
head Strichen s from 1962

SOUTER Alexander Wilson *MB ChB 1937
g p Kirkland Lake Ontario from 1947
wife *d* –.12.67
m(2) Matheson Ont 20.9.71 Marlene A. McCabe nurse d of Gerald McC. Kirkland Lake

SOUTER or Ritchie, Caroline Margaret BSc 1938 *1940
d Elgin 4.6.74 *AUR* XLVI 110

SOUTER Edward Simpson MA 1931 BCom 1933
FEIS 1971
prin teacher comm subj Perth acad 1949–73; retd

SOUTER or Broadhead, Elcy Cruickshank *BSc 1942
part-time dem zool univ Leeds from 1954

SOUTER Eliza Hay MA 1911
no longer on GC reg

SOUTER or Morgan, Evelyn Ashley MB ChB 1945
g p Perth W. Aust from 1950

SOUTER Isabella MA 1913
teacher math Forres acad 1933–62; retd; resid Alves

SOUTER James MA 1898 MB ChB 1902
no longer on GC reg

SOUTER James Callaghan MB ChB 1921
d 3.5.61 *AUR* XXXIX 203

SOUTER James Lownie MA 1954

SOUTER or Robbie, Jane Margaret MA 1917
resid Aber
d Aber 27.1.80

SOUTER or Davidson, Kathleen May MA 1926
resid Matua Tauranga NZ

SOUTER Leslie Morrison MA 1929
teacher g tech s for boys S. Shields 1963–72; retd; resid Whitley Bay

SOUTER or Middleton, Marjorie Mary Meredith Gordon MA 1933
resid Sunderland

SOUTER or Grimwood, Tresta Stephen *MA 1937
retd from teaching in Kent 1974; resid N'cle-u-Tyne
husb *d* 1973

SOUTHERAN Margaret MA 1954
teacher: Overdale j s Leic 1961–66, part-time Devon from 1966
m Chesterfield 27.12.63 Alan L. Bentley headmaster s of Harry B. Leic

SOUTHGATE Bernard Alfred PhD 1929 DSc 1936
d 3.9.75 *AUR* XLVI 324

SOUTTER or Evans, Helen Mary MB ChB 1948
d 29.3.74

SOUTTER James Tindal MA 1910
no longer on GC reg

SOUTTER or Wernham, Rosemary Margaret MA 1943
teacher Aber 1949; volunteer/teacher Ottawa assoc for ment retarded 1968–69

SOUTTER William MB ChB 1951
g p Aber 1964–74; CMP(REME) M o D from 1974

SOUTTER William Roberts MB ChB 1925
retd 1963; resid Dunfermline
wife *d* 15.6.72

SPALDING or Holms, Florence Graham MA 1941
resid Glasg

SPARK or Reive, Barbara Wilhelmina MB ChB 1925
resid Cheadle Cheshire

SPARK Cecil Vivian MB ChB 1923
d Mancetter 8.4.69 *AUR* XLIII 213

SPARK or Standeven, Elizabeth Mabel MB ChB 1948
d 3.10.77

SPARK Gladys Agnes MB ChB 1924
no longer on GC reg

SPARK Ian Denis MB ChB 1951

SPARK Ian Fowlie MA 1949

SPARK Ian Robert *MB ChB 1921
d Nott 2.10.74 *AUR* XLVI 236

SPARK Isabella Margaret MA 1938

SPARK Robert Arthur MB ChB 1951

SPEARING Antony Gustavus Byron MA 1950
Cert Proficiency Radio-phys(Lond) 1942
Lond: asst edit. *Process Control and Automation* Colliery Guardian 1961–67, *Sheet Metal Journal* Industrial Newspapers 1967–68, asst to information eng Electrical Dev Assoc 1967–71; freelance edit., edit. *Proceedings Institute of Mechanical Engineers* 1971–73, asst edit. II British Standards Inst 1973
m Morden 4.4.62 Maria A. R. da Costa ch nurse/teacher's aide d of Ernesto R. da C. Lisbon Portugal

SPEED Isobel MA 1950
Cert Soc Stud.(Glas) 1952
Sec Teacher's Cert(Vict) 1970
asst ch's off.: Dunfermline 1954–58, ch's off. Perth 1958–63; sen asst/dep ch's off. Aber 1963–65; Aust: soc worker Vict soc welfare dept Melbourne 1965–66, res asst Monash univ 1966–68; teacher Frankston tech s Vict 1969–73, SW educ dept from 1973
m Frankston Vict Aust 10.3.69 Kevin Connolly

SPEIGHT Harold Edwin Balme MA 1908 *1909
d Victoria BC 9.8.75 *AUR* XLVI 320

SPEIRS Alexander Logan MB ChB 1943 ᶜMD 1954
FRCP(Lond) 1971 FRCPGlas 1971
consult. paediat Stirling RI/Falkirk RI/RHSC Glasg from 1954

SPEIRS John Hastie *MA 1928
reader Engl lit Exe 1966–71; author *Poetry Towards Novel*; retd; resid Lond
d Lond 22.3.79 *AUR* XLVIII 229

SPENCE Alexander James MB ChB 1943
FRCSE 1968
consult. orthop surg E/W Fife from 1962

SPENCE Alexander Stewart MB ChB 1938
m o Leanchoil hosp Forres from 1944

SPENCE Charles Clouston BSc 1951

SPENCE Douglas Roy BSc(eng) 1949
d Birm 8.7.77 *AUR* XLVII 287

SPENCE or Leese, Eileen Margaret MB ChB 1949
sen med regist Royal Free hosp group Lond 1956–62, clin asst from 1962

SPENCE or Christie, Elizabeth Sylvia *MA 1954
secy DSIR psych res unit Aber 1961–63

SPENCE or Gray, Ida Lillian MA 1905
d Aber 15.10.61 *AUR* XXXIX 272

SPENCE James Alexander MA 1950

SPENCE Johanna MA 1906
d Aber 3.8.68 *AUR* XLIII 78

SPENCE or Caseley, Katherine Carruthers MB ChB 1922 ᶜMD 1928
Singapore 1929; RAMC Malaya till 1942; retd; resid Devon

SPENCE or King, Mary Laughton MA 1933
teacher Hope j s s St Margaret's Hope Orkney 1958–72; retd; resid Kirkwall

SPENCE William Stewart BSc(eng) 1929

SPIBY Thomas Dickson MA 1939
head Cummings Park p s Aber from 1968

SPILLER Cecil Gordon *MA 1927
d Kilmarnock 5.11.62 *AUR* XL 93

SPILLER Gerald Bernard *MA 1930 LLB 1933
d Edin 5.3.66

SPILLER Thomas Reuben MA 1912 *1913
d Aber 1.3.65 *AUR* XLI 149

SPRING Douglas Martin MB ChB 1909
no longer on GC reg

STABLES Rosabel *MA 1922
no longer on GC reg

STABLES William James MA 1954

STALKER Alexander MB ChB 1924
d Portugal 19.5.67 *AUR* XLII 186 & 365

STALKER Alexander Logie *MB ChB 1942 *MD 1961
FRCPath 1970 DL county of city of Aber from 1967
Aberd: reader path. 1965–69, prof path. 1969–72, regius prof from 1972; hon surg to HM the Queen 1963–65

STALKER or Mitchell, Ella McGregor *MA 1918
from 1939: youth serv club man. YWCA Nuneaton Warks, hostel man. Northumberland/E. Sussex; stud. hostel warden Lond; retd; resid Aber

STALKER James Stephen MA 1912
d Perthsh 6.1.61 *AUR* XXXIX 103

STALKER John Alexander BSc(eng) 1945

STALKER Robert MB ChB 1951
DPH(Leeds) 1961 MFCM(Leeds) 1971
div m o W Riding Yorks 1967–74; spec commun med (soc serv) Doncaster AHA from 1974

STARK Walter John Kirkpatrick MA 1908
d 6.9.70

STARTUP Collingwood William BSc 1927 PhD 1935
no longer on GC reg

STEADMAN John MA 1950 Dip Ed 1951
dep head Langlaw p s Dalkeith 1960–66; head: Temple p s Midlothian 1966–69, Cornbank St James p s Penicuik from 1969

STEDMAN Oliver Hall MA 1949

STEDMOND John Mitchell PhD 1953
FRSC 1971
Queen's univ Kingston Ont: assoc prof 1960–63, prof 1963–68, head dept of Engl 1968–77
wife *d* 1969

STEEL David MA 1932 BD 1935 DD 1964
C of S min St Michael's ch Linlithgow from 1959
mod Gen Assembly of Ch of Scot. 1974–75

STEEL Eric Wilson BSc 1952
teacher maths Bankhead acad Aber 1963–74; asst prin maths Torry acad Aber from 1974

STEELE Archibald *MA 1950
prin teacher Engl Ruthrieston s s Aber 1965–71, dep head 1971–73, asst head Harlaw acad Aber from 1973

STEELE or Pimm, Constance Sophia MB ChB 1923
retd 1961; resid S. Oakleigh Vict Aust

STEEN James Cameron MB ChB 1954
g p: Blackburn Lancs 1956–63, Murrayville Vict Aust 1963–67, Birregurra Vict from 1967

STEEN Margaret Lawson MA 1927
no longer on GC reg

STEIN (Walter) Peter Gonville PhD 1955
FBA 1974
dean fac of law Aberd 1961–64; regius prof civil law/fell. Queen's coll Cantab from 1968; member UGC 1971–75

STEINBACH Gustav Maxim MB ChB 1933

STENHOUSE Andrew Strachan BSc 1925 BSc(agr) 1927
d 26.4.72

STEPHEN Alexander MA 1918 MB ChB 1922
d Aber 15.2.73 *AUR* XLV 224

STEPHEN Alexander MB ChB 1941
FPsych RCP & S Can 1972
dir ch psychiat province of Sask Canada from 1970
d Saskatoon 18.5.79

STEPHEN Alexander Charles *BSc 1919 DSc 1934
d Edin 3.6.66 *AUR* XLI 338

STEPHEN Alexander Hutchison *MA 1939
retd 1972; resid Kirkwall

STEPHEN Alexander Kynoch MB ChB 1951
g p Redcar Yorks from 1956

STEPHEN Andrew MB ChB 1928
s of Alexander S. farm.
Knighted 1972
g p Sheffield from 1930; chmn FA England 1967–76
d Sheffield 25.2.80 *AUR* XLVIII 442 & XLIX 68

STEPHEN Andrew William Phillips BSc(elect. eng) 1935 (mech eng) 1936

STEPHEN Anne Margaret MA 1953
tech asst Scot. Gas from 1953; resid Bucksburn

STEPHEN or Robertson, Annie MA 1907
d 22.7.66

STEPHEN or Tait, Annie MA 1945
resid Inverallochy

STEPHEN Bruce Smith MB ChB 1951

STEPHEN David Bishop MB ChB 1937
d Enfield 16.6.67 *AUR* XLII 186 & 371

STEPHEN Doris Leonora MB ChB 1949
m o blood transfusion centre N'cle-u-Tyne from 1959

STEPHEN Douglas Alan BSc 1948 *1949

STEPHEN Eleanor Elizabeth Lauder MA 1923
teacher Finnart p s Greenock 1925–41; resid Cornhill Banffsh

STEPHEN or Innes, Elizabeth MA 1913 MB ChB 1915
d Aber 9.6.69 *AUR* XLIII 210

STEPHEN or Hartopp, Elizabeth Annie *MA 1927
d Alford 26.3.71 *AUR* XLIV 211

STEPHEN or Raffan, Elizabeth Mary MA 1944
resid Forgue

STEPHEN Ella Mary Salmond MA 1923
teacher St Stephen's coll Folkestone and Broadstairs 1932–62; retd; resid Aber

STEPHEN Ernest John BSc(eng) 1943

STEPHEN or Johnston, Esther MB ChB 1915
d Glasg 27.11.75

STEPHEN Florence MB ChB 1937
g p Aber 1938–78; retd

STEPHEN George Allardyce MB ChB 1937
d Enfield –.2.63 *AUR* XL 207

STEPHEN or McLeod, Helen Marr MA 1929
teacher Fraserburgh cent s 1956–69; retd

STEPHEN Ian Trail *MA 1946
teacher maths/asst head AGS from 1974

STEPHEN James Leiper *MA 1952

STEPHEN James Lindsay MA 1931

STEPHEN James Souter
***MA 1934 PhD 1936 BD 1943**
C of S min Banffsh: Mortlach 1942–62, Botriphnie from 1962 and Boharm from 1971

STEPHEN or Clark, Janet Ann MA 1950
teacher: Leicester 1963–66, Banff 1966–72; asst head Banff from 1972

STEPHEN Jean Thomson MA 1944
infants' mistress Ashley Rd p s Aber from 1968

STEPHEN or Youngson, Jessie Kerr MA 1909
d Aber 14.10.71 *AUR* XLIV 316

STEPHEN John MA 1902
no longer on GC reg

STEPHEN John BSc(agr) 1922
no longer on GC reg

STEPHEN John Hector *BSc 1900 *MB ChB 1902
d 24.6.63

STEPHEN John Herbert MB ChB 1905 DPH 1920
d Aber 15.5.62 *AUR* XXXIX 373

STEPHEN (formerly Zamory) John Joachim
MA 1948 *MEd 1958
Rossshire: sole educ psych 1963–66, prin educ psych 1966–75; reg prin educ psych Highland reg from 1975

STEPHEN John Low
MA 1931 MB ChB 1935 ᶜChM 1945
FRCS(Eng) 1968 FRSoc Med (vice-pres surg sect. from 1971)
Lond: surg St Mary's hosp from 1958/teacher in surg St Mary's hosp med s from 1950

STEPHEN John Ronald MA 1944
teacher Elgin East End s 1954–57; some relief teaching from 1957
m Urquhart 4.3.72 Alice Petrie clerkess/typist d of James C. P. Urquhart

STEPHEN John Traill *MA 1912
d Buckie 15.7.67 *AUR* XLII 182

STEPHEN or Skinner, Margaret MA 1932
d 18.5.77

STEPHEN Margaret Agnes MA 1938
King's coll lib Aberd: res asst 1961–71, sen lib asst 1971–77/mss and archives sect. 1969–77; retd

STEPHEN or Pirrie, Margaret Eleanor BSc 1945
resid Turriff

STEPHEN or Noble, Mary (Lady) *MA 1921
resid Edin

STEPHEN Mary Janet MA 1925
no longer on GC reg

STEPHEN Mary Jean BSc 1953
teacher sc: Inverurie acad 1959–65, Aber h s for girls (Harlaw acad) from 1965, spec asst from 1969

STEPHEN Mildred Wilken MA 1935
Lond: secy 1936–40
m Lond 1940 Ben Smith

STEPHEN Moira Anne MA 1951
asst dist lib N Angus from 1975

STEPHEN Norah Turner MA 1942
Dip R Ed(Lond) 1964
teacher Wolston Coventry 1960–65, Arbroath 1965; Aber: Summerhill acad 1965–70, Harlaw acad 1971, Old Aber/Frederick St/Middle s from 1971

STEPHEN or Bain, Olive Margaret MA 1930
resid Cults Aber

STEPHEN Robert Alexander
MB ChB 1930 MD 1933 ChM 1960
FRCS 1947 QHS 1960–67
dir surg/consult. surg to army 1959–64; substant col 1957, brig 1958, maj gen 1961; dir surg/consult. surg M o D(army) 1964–67; consult. surg Royal hosp Chelsea 1960–67; off. St John 1964, CB 1965
wife *d* 1972
m(2) 1977

STEPHEN Robert Alexander Nicol *BSc 1949
teacher: phys Albyn s for girls 1961–66, prin phys Aber h s for girls (later Harlaw acad) from 1966

STEPHEN Robert John MB ChB 1924
d Bristol 30.9.69 *AUR* XLIII 330

STEPHEN Ronald John MA 1944
no longer on GC reg

STEPHEN Roy Cameron *BSc 1950 PhD 1956

STEPHEN Sheila Tyas *MA 1946 *1947
Board of Inl Rev: spec work Somerset House from 1959; sen insp of Taxes dist insp Tunbridge Wells from 1978
m Wimbledon 2.2.71 Harry H. Leedale CBE control. Surtax Board of Inl Rev s of John L. New Malden

STEPHEN Susan MA 1931
retd 1972; resid Rothienorman
m Aber 26.6.74 George Simpson

STEPHEN Walter Glennie MA 1936
head Kingswells p s from 1953; retd 1975
d Aber 31.8.78 *AUR* XLVIII 106

STEPHEN William MB ChB 1942
MRCPsych 1971
sen m o HM prison med serv 1965–70, prin m o from 1970; resid Birm
wife *d* –.3.75
m(2) –.5.78 Caroline V. Cambridge

STEPHEN William Galloway Donaldson
BSc(agr) 1950

STEPHEN William Hendry MB ChB 1923
d 18.12.73

STEPHEN William Irvine *BSc 1950 DSc 1970
FRIC 1964 CChem 1970
Birm: sen lect chem 1966–71, reader analytical chem from 1971

STEPHEN William McLauchlan MA 1931 BSc 1934
JP 1969
farm. Duffus Moray from 1938

STEPHEN William Robert MB ChB 1940
g p Fochabers from 1946

STEPHEN or Sole, Williamina MB ChB 1925
locum work Chester 1957–63; retd; resid Bieldside

STEPHEN (formerly Zamory) Wolfgang BSc(eng) 1946

STEPHENSON Ian *BSc(eng) 1940
eng surv off. Aber c c from 1948

STERRY John Roland BSc(agr) 1954

STEVEN Andrew Marshall Macdonald MA 1954 LLB 1955
Dip Ed(Belf) 1974
Queen's univ Belf: sen asst secy 1968–71, sen asst secy (pers)/head of pers dept 1971–73; lect humanities dept Castlereagh coll f e Belfast from 1968; area organis adult literacy proj from 1965; voluntary youth and community work in Belfast

STEVEN John BSc(agr) 1936
asst insp DAFS from 1955; resid Watten

STEVEN Ranald Fyfe Findlay MB ChB 1949
g p Aber from 1952

STEVEN Robert Clement *MA 1947 LLB 1950
WS 1953 TD 1962 F Corp Insur Brokers 1970
Lond: on staff of Price Forbes & Co 1963–69, dir 1970–72; asst man. dir Sedgwick Forbes UK 1973; dep chmn Claverhouse Invest Trust 1974–77, chmn from 1977
m Lond 30.1.65 Judith C. Locker teacher d of James W. D. L. Madras India

STEVENS David Alan John *MA 1936

STEVENS Helen Mary *MA 1931
retd 1969; resid Uppingham

STEVENS Philip Theodore PhD 1939
lect classics Cape Town 1938–41; war serv S Af milit intelligence 1941–45; lect Lat Liv 1945–50; prof Greek Bedford coll Lond 1950–74; emeritus prof Greek Lond 1974

STEVENSON Alexander *MA 1938
internat bank for reconstruction and dev Washington DC from 1947

STEVENSON Douglas Ogilvie MB ChB 1935
retd 1978; emeritus consult. venereologist S Lincs
d Penwortham Preston 15.1.81

STEVENSON Elsie Mary MA 1929
no longer on GC reg

STEVENSON or Volpich, Hilda MA 1925
teacher p s Dumbarton 1942–66

STEVENSON John Meikle BSc(agr) 1953
founder/man. dir food manuf comp Bo'ness from 1962

STEVENSON Raymond William Henry PhD 1953
sen lect nat phil Aberd 1965–69; prof phys univ of Rhodesia Salisbury from 1969

STEVENSON Walter Freeman BL 1949
hon sheriff 1971
solic Thornhill from 1954

STEWART or Kerr, Agnes Mary MA 1936
resid Laurencekirk

STEWART Aileen Keith MA 1947
head: Torridon p s 1964–66, Raemoir p s 1966–68, Maryculter E p s from 1968

STEWART Albert James *MA 1930 BSc 1931
dep dir of educ Argyll 1961–73; retd; resid Dunoon
d 21.6.78

STEWART Alexander MA 1913
d Aber 1.12.61 *AUR* XXXIX 275

STEWART Alexander MB ChB 1946
g p Chapel-en-le-Frith from 1954

STEWART Alexander Boyd MA 1925 BSc 1927 *1928 PhD 1932 LLD 1971
CBE 1962
retd 1968; resid Aber
d Aber 27.2.81 *AUR* XLIX 137

STEWART Alexander Graham *MB ChB 1907
no longer on GC reg

STEWART Alexander Morrice Leighton BSc(eng) 1955
d Edin 9.12.71 *AUR* XLIV 434

STEWART or Garrow, Alice Watson BSc 1928 *1929
teacher chem Harlaw acad Aber 1964–74; retd
husb *d* 27.5.63

STEWART or Paton, Alison Georgina *MA 1942
JP Gloucester 1971
resid Gloucester

STEWART or Armstrong, Annie Kemp MA 1918
no longer on GC reg

STEWART Augustus George
MA 1905 MB ChB 1909 *MD 1912
d Durban S Af 15.5.68 *AUR* XLII 346 & XLIII 77

STEWART or Bentley, Cecily Jean Macrae
MB ChB 1948
DPH(Glas) 1973 MFCM 1977
s m o Glasg 1972–74; c m s Forth Valley 1978

STEWART Charles Murray MA 1951
C of S min Viewforth St Oswald's par ch Edin 1960–72; dir youth/commun serv Scot. nat council of YMCA; nat gen secy Scot. Nat Council of YMCAs 1975; resid Edin

STEWART Charles Nelson MA 1920
d Aber 7.11.71 *AUR* XLIV 319

STEWART or Fletcher, Charlotte Simpson MA 1931
resid Lewes

STEWART Christina MA 1919
d Dufftown 1.12.69 *AUR* XLIII 444

STEWART Clyne Garden MA 1921

STEWART Clyne Robert Bruce MB ChB 1947
g p Shifnal from 1955

STEWART Colina May MA 1915
no longer on GC reg

STEWART or Coulson, Constance Philippa
MA 1954
teacher: Burgh p s Galashiels 1957–60, Kelso p s 1960–62, Victoria p s Falkirk 1962–69, Bridge of Weir p s from 1974

STEWART David BSc(agr) 1928
FISP(Inc Soc Planters) 1952
AMN(Malaysian govt) 1958
PJK(Negri Sembilan govt) 1958
planting advis Seafield Amalgamated Rubber Co 1960–65; retd; resid Nairn

STEWART David Lamb *MA 1930
d Laurencekirk 2.2.68 *AUR* XLII 370

STEWART Dolina MA 1950
teacher: Lat/geog and supt boarding house Fort Victoria s Rhodesia 1959–70, part-time Coventry 1970–74, full-time (jun s) from 1974
m Salisbury Rhodesia 31.8.60 Bernard W. Lawson elect. eng s of William E. L. Catford Lond

STEWART Donald MA 1916
no longer on GC reg

STEWART Donald BSc 1953
MSc(Manc) 1965
metall BP chem Grangemouth 1965–68; indust liaison off. Strath from 1968

STEWART Donald Mackenzie BSc 1941 *1948

STEWART Donald MacRae
MA 1918 *MB ChB 1922
d Ayr 23.12.70 *AUR* XLIV 210

STEWART Donald Sinclair
MA 1921 *MB ChB 1925
MRCGP 1952
retd g p/indust m o 1966; part-time med referee Dept of Health Surrey 1966–74; resid Abinger Common

STEWART or Prentice, Doris Harvey
BSc 1944 *1947
teacher maths Harlaw acad Aber 1966–74, Albyn s Aber from 1974

STEWART or Macphail, Dorothy Jean *MA 1926
resid Edin
d Edin 31.3.80 *AUR* XLVIII 442

STEWART or Thomson, Dorothy Margaret
BCom 1940
resid Penarth

STEWART Douglas Lawrence
***MA 1934 MB ChB 1939**
g p Insch 1946–78; retd

STEWART Edith Gordon MB ChB 1951
g p central Ottawa from 1957

STEWART Elizabeth Helen MA 1940
teacher Engl Malvern girls' coll Worcs 1967–76, sen tut. from 1976

STEWART or Fyfe, Elizabeth Mary Arthur
***BSc 1940**
resid Halifax Nova Scotia

STEWART or Pirie, Ethel Mackenzie MA 1922
d Edin 9.12.72

STEWART or Mirrlees, Evelyn Marian MA 1917
d Aber 22.5.62 *AUR* XXXIX 381

STEWART or Cronin, Evelyn Mary MA 1915
resid Carnegie, Aust

STEWART Flora MA 1915
retd 1958; resid Kyle

STEWART Florence MA 1930 MB ChB 1941
g p Aber from 1949

STEWART or Watt, Freda Florence MA 1941
resid Bramhall

STEWART Frederick Henry *BSc 1937 DSc 1975
FRS 1964 Kt 1974 DSc(Leic) 1977
prof geol Edin from 1957; chmn nat environment res council Lond 1971–73, chmn advis board for res councils Lond from 1973

STEWART George MA 1929
sen asst dept soc stud. Kingsway tech coll Dun 1962–72; retd

STEWART George MA 1947
d Lond –.3.64 *AUR* XL 401

STEWART George Alexander Murdoch MA 1953 Dip Ed 1957
Aber: teacher sc Summerhill s s 1962–68, Tullos p s 1968–69, sc Ruthrieston s s/Harlaw acad 1969–74, asst prin sc Torry acad 1974; teacher sc Dumfries h s from 1975
m Aber 2.8.66 Wilma Lawson pharm d of William A. L. Inverurie

STEWART George Macdonald BSc 1938

STEWART Georgina MA 1924

STEWART Gordon Gray MA 1908
d Ottawa 18.5.66 *AUR* XLI 336

STEWART or Hardy, Grace Henderson *BSc 1940
resid Dun
d Dun 19.5.80

STEWART Helen MA 1939
retd 1971; resid Buckie
m Buckie 24.6.68 William J. Low motor eng s of James A. L.

STEWART or Merchant, Helen MA 1944
teacher Cornhill p s Aber from 1957

STEWART or Mitchell, Hester Elizabeth MA 1936
resid Edin

STEWART Hubert James BSc 1919 BSc(for) 1921
retd AEI Richmond 1960; resid Aber
d Aber 7.7.81

STEWART Ian Edward *MA 1954
Brit Steel Corp: group sales man. Scunthorpe 1967–70, div comm man. Teesside 1970–72, asst div export man. Lond from 1972

STEWART Ian Jackson BSc(for) 1937
temp asst dept for. Aberd 1937–38; dist off. for. comm E and W conservancies Scot. 1938–70; retd; resid Arbroath

STEWART Ian Martin Steel MB ChB 1944 DPH 1953
Order St J. serv brother 1962, off. brother 1966, comm brother 1972
Order St J. Knight of Grace 1978
m o workers' compensation board Alberta Edmonton from 1958

STEWART or Kemp, Isabella MA 1935

STEWART or Dring, Isabella Cameron *MA 1947

STEWART Isobel MA 1924
retd Elgin acad 1964

STEWART James BSc(agr) 1922
no longer on GC reg

STEWART James *MA 1932
FSAScot 1961
head: Old Aber s s 1960–65, Hilton acad 1965–74; retd

STEWART James Alexander Elder MB ChB 1942
d Coventry 29.10.69 *AUR* XLIII 446

STEWART James Charles BL 1930

STEWART James Douglas *MA 1931
prin teacher classics Aber acad, Hazlehead acad 1966–73; retd

STEWART James Gordon MB ChB 1924
OBE 1967
retd; resid Royton

STEWART James Guthrie BSc(agr) 1902 MA 1903
d 3.3.68

STEWART James Harvey MB ChB 1938
g p Hatton 1946–78; retd

STEWART James Smith MB ChB 1913
d Aber 14.7.66 *AUR* XLI 338

STEWART Jane MA 1920
retd 1961; resid Aber
d Aber 26.12.79 *AUR* XLVIII 440

STEWART Jemima Ann MA 1936
town chamberlain and burgh collector Buckie 1960–75; retd

STEWART Jemina MA 1942
teacher Lochcarron p s from 1970

STEWART Jessie Rae MA 1912

STEWART Jessie Robertson MA 1905
d Aber 8.4.73 *AUR* XLV 223

STEWART John MA 1901
no longer on GC reg

STEWART John MA 1926
teacher Aber: Middle s 1927–42, dep head Seaton p s 1942–47, dep head Skene Square p s 1947–70
d Aber 22.2.77 *AUR* XLVII 212

STEWART John Duff *MA 1924 PhD 1948
dep dir and head school of maths RGIT 1964–68
m Milngavie 31.3.66 Elizabeth Summerville McBride
d Benidorm Spain 3.6.74 *AUR* XLVI 108

STEWART John Gordon *MA 1946 ᶜMB ChB 1950
d Manc 22.3.77 *AUR* XLVII 214

STEWART John Russell MA 1901
no longer on GC reg

STEWART, John Sidney MA 1948 Dip Ed 1962
FIL(Lond) 1964
teacher: Fr/Ger Aber g s 1962–67; prin mod lang Chilliwack BC Canada 1968–78; resid Chilliwack

STEWART Johnstone Macpherson MA 1936

STEWART Joseph Robert BSc 1944 *1949
teacher sc Kirkcaldy 1950–55; prin sc: Peebles 1955–59, Dun 1959–65; dir Scot. schools sc equipment res centre Edin from 1965
d 29.6.81

STEWART or Donald, Leonora Frances MA 1927
resid St And
d Edin 29.6.76

STEWART Margaret Anne MA 1951
teacher: Lossiemouth j s s 1952–53, Forres acad 1953–56, Heathcote j s s Essex 1956–58, Hope s s Hope BC Canada 1958–60; studio potter/sculptor from 1962
m Hope 1.9.60 George B. F. Gibson BA(BC) teacher

STEWART Margaret Fleming MA 1910
for. travel NZ, Aust, Europe, Can, USA; resid Lond
d Derby 6.11.79

STEWART Margaret Jameson MA 1938
teacher Symbister House j h s Whalsay Shetland 1967–75; retd

STEWART or Gardner, Margaret Mary Hain MA 1947
resid Musselburgh
husb deceased

STEWART or Brown, Margaret Maud MA 1954
resid Oban

STEWART or Fraser, Margaret Taylor MA 1930
resid Inv
husb *d* 27.7.61

STEWART Marjorie Cameron *MA 1933
d 19.8.69

STEWART Marjorie Mitchell *MA 1920
resid Aber

STEWART Marjory Jane MA 1931
teacher p s: Johnshaven/Inverbervie 1934–52, Montrose 1952–71; retd

STEWART or Buchan, Mary MA 1930
resid Carnoustie

STEWART or Sangster, Mary Adamson MA 1929
retd 1971; resid Edin

STEWART or Nicol, Mary Ann MA 1914

STEWART or Naylor, Mary Ann Forbes MA 1908
d Stracathro 15.6.71 *AUR* XLIV 316

STEWART or Gurrey, Mary Dobie Gilmour MA 1945
teacher inf Tadcaster s Yorks 1960–69; resid Collingham nr Newark

STEWART or Vick, Mary Macfarlane BSc(agr) 1928 PhD 1931
resid Welwyn Garden City

STEWART or Hercus, Mary Macpherson MA 1929
teacher prin Fr Elphinstone s s BC Canada 1964–73; retd; resid Gibsons BC

STEWART Neil Findlay MB ChB 1953
g p Burton-on-Trent from 1959

STEWART Norman Geddes *MA 1937

STEWART Peter BSc(eng) 1954

STEWART Robert MA 1905
no longer on GC reg

STEWART Robert Douglas MB ChB 1927 DPH 1932 MD 1933 DSc 1943
d Abdnsh 5.5.68 *AUR* XLII 367

STEWART Robert Weir Gilmour MB ChB 1953
d Hamilton Ont 27.8.70 *AUR* XLIV 111

STEWART Ronald *BSc 1951

STEWART Theodore MA 1920
d Edin 21.3.64

STEWART Victor Innes *BSc 1954 PhD 1958
sen lect i/c soil sc unit dept biochem/agr biochem univ Wales Aberystwyth from 1971
m Aber 6.1.62 Shirley M. Robertson occup therap d of James R. Aber

STEWART Walter MB ChB 1934
off. St J 1963 MFCM 1973
asst dir gen army med serv (army med dept pers br) War Office Lond 1961–64; dep dir army health E. Command Hounslow 1964–67; retd col 1968; dep m o h Gt Yarmouth 1968–74; s m o Norfolk AHA 1974–78; retd
wife *d* –.3.65
m(2) Norwich 24.5.75 Elizabeth G. Ridgway Cordon Bleu d of Leopold P. R. Dublin

STEWART Walter Allan MA BSc(agr) 1913
retd 1958; resid Little Brington Northants

STEWART William MA 1913
resid Aber
d Aber 20.12.79 *AUR* XLVIII 440

STEWART William MB ChB 1929 DPH 1931
retd 1971; resid Welwyn Garden City

STEWART William MB ChB 1940

STEWART William BSc(eng) 1950

STEWART William Alistair MB ChB 1954
DPM(Dublin) 1963 MRCPsych 1972
psychiat and hon clin lect mental health Ross clin day hosp and Royal Cornhill hosp Aber from 1972

STEWART William James Morrison MB ChB 1952 DPH 1955
g p Huntly from 1956

STEWART Williamina MA 1917
d 3.2.69

STICKLER William Harvey *BSc 1951
asst dir of res John G. Stein & Co Bonnybridge 1959–65; United Fireclay Products Armadale: tech dir 1965–71, works dir 1971–75, man. dir 1975–79; man. dir Darngavil Minerals Larkhall from 1979
m Bonnybridge 19.5.61 Muriel M. Napier lab analyst d of George G. N. Gosforth

STILL Athole Tosh MA 1954
freelance journalist/broadcaster and external opera stud. Morley coll, Guildhall Lond 1964–69; prin tenor Scot. Opera, Glyndebourne Opera etc. 1969–76; study in Naples 1972–73; freelance broadcaster/journalist, swimming correspondent *Sunday Times*/ITV; ptnr: Athole Still Assoc from 1978, Rawstron-Still (internat opera man.) from 1980
m Aber 12.4.63 Isobel J. Cordiner tv prod. asst d of John C. Lond

STILL or Watson, Edith Mary Simpson MA 1948
teacher: Sunnybank s Aber 1959–63, Keephatch s Wokingham Berks 1964–65; dep head Whiteknights c p s Berks 1965–67; head Loddon inf s Berks from 1968

STILL Katherine Littlejohn MA 1913
no longer on GC reg

STILL or Fletcher, Olive Adamson MA 1916
Rhodesia: teacher Chaplin h s Gwelo 1940–43, Queen Elizabeth s Salisbury 1944–48, govt correspondence s 1952–68
husb *d* Salisbury Rhod –.11.71

STILL Robert *MA 1931
prin maths/dep head Aboyne s s 1966–68; dep rector/prin maths Aboyne acad 1968–73

STILL Robert BSc(eng) 1944 *1948

STILL Sydney Cardno MA 1915
resid Aber
d Balmedie 16.6.79

STILL William James Sangster MB ChB 1951 ᶜMD 1960
FRCPath 1964
sen lect path. R Free hosp Lond 1962–65; prof path. med coll of Virginia Richmond Va USA from 1965

STIRLING or Verschelde, Barbara McKenzie MA 1927 BCom 1929
no longer on GC reg

STIRLING George Scott MB ChB 1949
FRCPsych 1977
consult. psychiat Crichton r hosp Dumfries from 1960

STIRLING Henry William BSc(agr) 1945
NE Farms Aber: tech advis 1967–72, sales dev man. 1972–77, tech man. from 1977

STIRLING Kenneth William *MA 1950
prin mod lang Beath h s Cowdenbeath 1962–72; asst head Grove acad Dun from 1972
marr diss
m(2) Edin 10.7.73 June Noble teacher home econ

ST LEGER Robert Geoffrey Tunstall *MA 1952
OBE 1965 FRES 1973
E. Nigeria: dist off. 1953–60, sen asst secy 1960–61, prin asst secy 1961–68; retd admin off. class I; prin asst secy Lesotho 1968–70; econ plan. Louis Berger Inc Uganda/Nigeria from 1970
m Enugu Nigeria 5.9.63 Priscilla A. Egiga nurse/midwife d of Jonah L. E. Ikom Nigeria

STOBIE or Lawson, Bertha Mary MA 1928

STODDART or Fletcher, Elizabeth MA 1939
d Lockerbie 29.4.66 *AUR* XLI 342

STODDART or Valentine, Winifred MA 1931
resid Haddington

STONE Eric Vaughan BSc(for) 1948

STORMONTH Georgina Walker MA 1917
retd 1961; resid Aber

STOTT Alexander Norman Barron MB ChB 1954
Fell. Fac Occup Med 1979
chief m o UKAEA Harwell from 1965

STOTT Marion Mary MA 1946
teacher Aber: Tillydrone s 1950–53; Middlefield s 1954–55; Cummings Park s 1956–57; Quarryhill s 1957–60; Springhill s from 1961
m Aber 23.3.51 Gordon D. Cruickshank MA 1969 *qv*

STOTT or Espley, Marion Mayo Josephine MA 1925
resid Bromley

STOUT or Russell, Mary Barbara MA 1933
head remed dept Gosford Hill comp s Kidlington Oxford 1965–76; retd

STOVE Magnus James MA 1936
JP Zetland
head Mid Yell j s s from 1948

STOWELL John Hilton *MA 1949
PhD(Florida)

STRACHAN Alexander Bremner MB ChB 1942
g p Goole/Treasury m o from 1947

STRACHAN Alice Mary *MA 1919
d 1972

STRACHAN Arthur Allister MB ChB 1945

STRACHAN Charles *MA 1928
retd 1966; resid Stirling

STRACHAN Charles *MA 1929
Fell. Corpus Christi Coll Cambridge 1934–37
reader nat phil Aberd 1964–77; retd
wife *d* –.8.71
m(2) Aber 14.12.73 M. Agnes Cuthell or Mathieson BA(Kingston Ont) d of John C. Vict BC

STRACHAN Charles Henry MB ChB 1928
fell. BMA 1960
retd g p 1971; part-time referee DHSS Manc from 1965; resid Wilmslow

STRACHAN David Buchan MB ChB 1948
g p Bradford from 1952

STRACHAN Douglas John MB ChB 1929
d Milltimber Aber 17.7.73 *AUR* XLV 320

STRACHAN or Whiteford, Elizabeth MA 1927
retd 1968; resid Inverurie

STRACHAN or Wilkinson, Emma Elizabeth *BSc 1951 PhD 1954

STRACHAN Eric James MB ChB 1934
g p Gatley from 1948

STRACHAN Florence Agnes *MA 1925

STRACHAN or Knox, Frances Mary MA 1939
resid Inverurie
husb *d* 9.9.55

STRACHAN Freda BSc 1949 *1950

STRACHAN Georgina Thornton MA 1924
teacher: Keith g s 1926–51, Kilmichael s Glassary Argyll 1952–54, Stranraer acad 1954–58, Rephad p s Stranraer 1958–65; retd
m Inv 4.8.51 Norman C. Mackenzie

STRACHAN or Wright, Hazel Chisholm *MA 1955
asst press lib Inst of Internat Affairs Lond 1959–61; head of BBC pronunciation unit Lond 1971–78

STRACHAN Henry James *MA 1928

STRACHAN Ian Morrison MA 1955 BD 1958
missionary Ghana 1959–66; C of S min: St Paul's ch Cambuslang 1966–71, St John's ch Gourock from 1971

STRACHAN Ian Reid *BSc 1951
MBE 1963
various admin posts: Nyasaland govt (later Malawi) until 1968, Lanark c c 1968–75, Perth & Kinross dist c from 1975
m Blantyre Malawi 3.6.67 Judith Michael teacher d of Ian L. M. Blantyre

STRACHAN Ian William James MB ChB 1950
g p Aber from 1954
m Aber 30.9.61 Susan Grant exec civ serv d of James R. G. Aber

STRACHAN or Hunter, Isabel Craib MA 1946

STRACHAN or Anderson, Isobel Marjorie MA 1948
teacher ph/mh ch Beechwood s Aber from 1968

STRACHAN James *MA *BSc 1899
d Slough 20.4.62 *AUR* XXXIX 371

STRACHAN James MA BSc 1913
no longer on GC reg

STRACHAN James MB ChB 1923
retd 1970; resid Leyland Lancs
d 3.3.74 *AUR* XLV 447

STRACHAN James MB ChB 1950
g p Elland W Yorks from 1958

STRACHAN James Forbes BSc(eng) 1940
d Wembley 10.2.68 *AUR* XLII 373

STRACHAN James Milne MA 1900
d 28.8.61 *AUR* XXXIX 270

STRACHAN John BSc(eng) 1951

STRACHAN John MA 1951 LLB 1954
ptnr Davidson & Garden advoc Aber from 1958

STRACHAN Malcolm Ian *MA 1928
d Aber 17.2.75

STRACHAN or Sim, Margaret Buyers MA 1903
no longer on GC reg

STRACHAN or Peters, Margaret Elizabeth Jane (Lady) MA 1915

STRACHAN or Milne, Margaret Jane MA 1928
resid Keith

STRACHAN or McDonald or Melville, Margaret Vivien MA 1937

STRACHAN Maureen Clark MA 1955 Dip Ed 1956
teacher Cornhill p s Aber till 1962
m Aber 1.12.62 Charles J. Marshall agr machinery manuf s of Charles M. Aber

STRACHAN or Kemp, Meta *MA 1929
husb *d* Edin 25.11.67

STRACHAN Robert MA 1910
d –.7.63

STRACHAN Robert Donald *MA 1923
retd 1967; resid Aber
d Aber 21.5.79 *AUR* XLVIII 228

STRACHAN Robert Stewart BSc(for) 1948
d –.9.63

STRACHAN Ronald West MB ChB 1953
MRCPE 1961 MRCPGlas 1962 MRCP(Lond) 1964 FICA 1965 FRCPE 1972 FRCPGlas 1978
sen regist med Aber teaching hosps/clin tut. med Aberd 1961–70; res fell. cardiol Case-Western Reserve univ Cleveland Ohio USA 1967–68; consult. phys Dumfries and Galloway RI from 1970

STRACHAN or Burgess, Sheila Ruth MA 1953

STRACHAN Stanley George *MA 1950
Dip Ed(Dund) 1968
trg advis Distrib Indust Trg Board

STRACHAN Theodore Percy *MA 1933 BD 1936
min King St presb ch (latterly URC) Oldham 1964–74; clerk of Manc presb 1965–72; min Holderness Road and E Hull joint pastorate Hull(URC) 1974–78; retd

STRACHAN or Hearn, Violet *MA 1921
no longer on GC reg

STRACHAN William *MA 1935

STRACHAN William MB ChB 1955
g p Edin from 1960

STRACHAN William Ellis MB ChB 1954
FRCSE 1961
regist surg Glasg RI 1959–61; regist neuro-surg St George's hosp Lond 1961–64; sen regist neuro-surg nat hosp nerv diseases Lond; sen regist neuro-surg Edin RI; consult. neuro-surg Plymouth from 1967
m Bucksburn 15.10.60 Lilias M. Cuthbertson MA 1953 *qv*

STRACHAN or Spooner, Winifred Mary MA 1948
resid Ruislip

STRAND or Allcroft, Ruth PhD 1934
DSc(Wellington NZ) 1964
retd 1968; resid Waikanae NZ

STRANG Alastair *BSc(eng) 1955
AMIMechE 1970 MIMechE CEng 1971
acetate and synthetic lab Coventry: sect. leader 1968–70, dep head 1970–71, head eng dev dept from 1971; dir Mornington eng subsidy of Courtauld's eng Bolton from 1972

STRATH or Rebecca, Evelyn May MA 1932
teacher Holburn St, Sunnybank p s Aber from 1955

STRATHDEE Roy Brown
MA 1920 BSc 1922 *1923 LLD 1975
retd 1965
d Guernsey 19.6.76 *AUR* XLVII 103

STRATTON Dorothy Isabella Bryce MA 1943
Bankhead acad: spec asst 1965–72, prin guid/spec asst hist from 1972
m Aber 7.7.75 Alfred Tosh warehouse superv s of George T.

STREETEN (formerly Hornig) Paul Patrick
MA 1944 LLD 1980
Fell. Balliol Coll Oxford 1948–66
visiting prof/res fell. to USA 1962–63, to World Bank in 1973; dep dir gen econ plan. Min Overseas Dev Lond; prof Sus/fell. and acting dir inst of dev stud. Sussex 1966–68, dir inst of commonwealth stud./warden Queen Elizabeth House/fell. Balliol coll Oxford 1968–78; spec advis to World Bank from 1976

STRONACH Alexander Ruddiman MA 1913
d 1962

STROUD Robert Erskine Wetherly BCom 1929
d Aber 30.10.61 *AUR* XXXIX 283

STUART or Simmers, Agnes MA 1926
no longer on GC reg

STUART or MacIntosh, Aileen Grant *MA 1953
Falkirk: teacher Engl Camelon h s 1974–78, Woodlands h s from 1979

STUART Alexander *MA 1937 *MEd 1939
FRGS 1946
Canada: teacher Engl/Fr/soc stud. Hamilton Ontario 1953–54, prin classics Aylmer Ont 1954–55, teacher classics Etobicoke Ont 1955–56; Ottawa teachers' coll: master psych in educ 1956–62, chmn psych in educ from 1962
m Cairo 27.4.45 Marie Deith d of Edward D. Lond

STUART Alexander BSc 1953

STUART Alexander Mitchell MA 1933 BD 1936
C of S min Banchory-Ternan West par ch Kincardinesh from 1966

STUART Allan Ramsay MA 1948
Zaire: hosp admin inst méd évangélique Kimpese 1954–62, mission treasurer Amer baptist mission Kinshasa 1964–66, bus. man. inst Pédagogique évangelique Kimpese from 1966
m Leopoldville (Kinshasa) 1.11.57 Carrie E. Sprague MD(Phil) med pract d of Guy B. S. Corning NY USA

STUART or Middleton, Annie Winifred MA 1929
retd 1968; resid Aber

STUART Barbara Rebecca *MA 1912
d 26.12.71

STUART or Ross, Catherine MA 1923
resid Kincraig

STUART or Pape, Catherine MA 1925
retd 1958; resid Coniston Cumbria

STUART or Hargreaves, Christina
MB ChB 1922 DPH 1923
d 5.4.68 *AUR* XLII 360

STUART Douglas MB ChB 1954
g p Nott from 1960

STUART or Elton, Elizabeth Mary MA 1952

STUART Forbes Jackson MB ChB 1906
d 6.12.65

STUART George
MA 1908 *MB ChB 1912 *MD DPH 1929
d Spey Bay 3.8.72 *AUR* XLV 124

STUART George Nicolson MA 1908
no longer on GC reg

STUART or Mitchell, Gertrude Helen MA 1930
JP Aber 1957
teacher Burnside Inf s Aber 1961–78; retd
husb *d* 14.8.71

STUART Gladys Lee MA 1918 BSc 1920
d Aber 23.7.69 *AUR* XLIII 329

STUART Gordon *BSc(eng) 1945
MBIM 1960 CEng FIEE 1968 CDip AF 1973
sen lect RGIT Aber 1963–66; with Merz & McLellan consult. eng N'cle-u-Tyne from 1966, assoc 1973–76; with Motor Columbus consult. eng Baden Switzerland from 1976

STUART Gordon William MB ChB 1944
g p Ramsgate from 1949

STUART Helen MA 1944
exchange teacher Ottawa 1959–60; inf mistress Scotstown p s Bridge of Don Aber 1969–73, asst head from 1973

STUART Helena Mary MA 1931
resid Aber

STUART Ian MB ChB 1955
JP Angus 1968
g p Arbroath from 1959

STUART Isabella Cameron MA 1933
retd 1972; resid Fochabers

STUART or Gordon, Janet Jane Reid MA 1934
head Ballogie p s Aboyne 1965–72; teacher Dyce p s 1972–73; retd; resid Oldmeldrum

STUART or Menzies, Jean Elspeth MB ChB 1940
d Aber 13.10.66 *AUR* XLII 90

STUART John Charles MA 1893
no longer on GC reg

STUART John Mitchell MB ChB 1931
sen m o Vickers 1955–71; retd; resid Lyme Regis

STUART or Hinds, Joyce Angus MA 1952
resid Welwyn Garden City

STUART Lawrence Murray *BSc 1946
res chem Bakelite Birm 1946–47; works chem Expanded Rubber Co Dun 1947–62; teacher: chem Dun h s, prin chem RGC Aber from 1972

STUART or Angus, Maggie Ann MA 1927
d 24.7.77

STUART or Campbell, Margaret Gray Hitchcock *MA 1914
retd 1953; resid Moffat

STUART Mary Ann MA 1918
no longer on GC reg

STUART or McMain, Mary Emslie MA 1941
teacher: Cairncry p s Aber 1966–68, Macalpine p s Dun 1969–75, Craigie h s Dun from 1975

STUART Patricia May *MA 1939
resid Rothes

STUART Robert Douglas
MB ChB 1927 DPH 1932 ᶜMD 1933 DSc 1943
d Oyne 5.5.68 *AUR* XLII 367

STUART Roderick Allen BSc 1930 MA 1931
d Aber 12.7.70 *AUR* XLIV 110

STUART Ronald Sangster *BSc 1950 PhD 1954

STUART Sophia Keith Grant
MA 1915 MB ChB 1918

STUART William MA 1935
ptnr Bower & Smith CA Aber from 1954

STUART William Innes BSc 1954

STURM Maxwell Gerard de L'Isle MB ChB 1927
d Trinidad 17.11.68 *AUR* XLIII 215

STURROCK Robert John BSc 1930 MA 1931
d Stonehaven 12.7.73 *AUR* XLV 320

STURTON James BSc(eng) 1938

STYLES Edward Currie Castell *BSc 1951

SUBBA RAO Gargestwari Narayana PhD 1948
MSc(Mysore)
India: fish. tech Bombay 1949–50, tech food res inst Mysore 1950–53; fish. tech FAO Rome 1953–59; reg fish. off. FAO Bangkok Thailand 1959–71; proj oper off. fish. Rome from 1971
m Mysore 30.10.50 Leela Rao d of K. V. Srinivaso Rao BE(Bangalore) Bangalore

SUMITRA Svasti BSc 1926

SUMMERS or Buchan, Ella Smith MA 1952

SUMMERS George Noble
MB ChB 1944 DPH 1949

SUMMERS Gordon Jamieson MB ChB 1932

SUMMERS or Connal, Sophia Lucy Mackworth
MA 1907 BSc 1909 DSc 1929
d 17.3.64 *AUR* XL 395

SUMMERS or Brown, Williamina *MA 1923
no longer on GC reg

SUNDARA-VICHARANA Yen BSc 1927
no longer on GC reg

SURTEES Anne Dey MB ChB 1946
m Kendrick

SUTHERLAND or Dyke, Alexandrina Booth *MA 1954 PhD 1957
resid Bath

SUTHERLAND Andrew Norman BSc(agr) 1935
head Brae j h s Shetland 1950–74; retd

SUTHERLAND Annie MA 1929

SUTHERLAND Arthur Robert MA 1904
no longer on GC reg

SUTHERLAND Audrey MB ChB 1948 DPH 1964 MD 1967
FFCM 1972
Myers res fell. Aberd 1964–67; res fell. SHHD Aberd 1967–70; prin sen m o (res) Durh c c health dept 1970–74; SCM/information serv and res N reg health auth 1974; SCM/information and serv plan. Durham AHA from 1975
d N'cle-u-Tyne 15.4.81 *AUR* XLIX 139

SUTHERLAND Christina Hunter MA 1916 BSc 1918
d Gardone Riviera Italy 9.7.72 *AUR* XLV 125

SUTHERLAND David MA 1932
min St Nicholas cong ch (union Albion & St Paul's and Belmont) Aber from 1966; pres cong union of Scot. 1968–69; chmn Aber & Dist Council of ch 1973–76; retd 1978; resid Rosemarkie

SUTHERLAND David Thompson MB ChB 1947
g p Salford from 1950

SUTHERLAND Donald John Waters MB ChB 1952
g p Terrington St Clement nr King's Lynn Norfolk 1960–66; Tasmania: royal Derwent hosp New Norfolk 1966–67, repatriation gen hosp Hobart 1967–68, g p Boronia Kingston Beach from 1968

SUTHERLAND Dorothy Anne MB ChB 1950
med asst paediat Royal Alexandra hosp Rhyl

SUTHERLAND Enid May MA 1925
d Aber 19.7.74 *AUR* XLVI 109

SUTHERLAND Finlay Fraser *MA 1950

SUTHERLAND or Carle, Florence Mackenzie MA 1929

SUTHERLAND Frank Lamond MA 1922
head Springhill p s Aber 1956–66; retd

SUTHERLAND George Graham Mackay *MA 1952
FEIS 1978
prin teacher bus. stud. and econ Morrison's acad Crieff from 1954

SUTHERLAND George Kenneth MA 1909 *BSc 1911 DSc 1916
no longer on GC reg

SUTHERLAND George Pottinger MB ChB 1945
g p Maybole from 1958
m Elgin 9.8.58 Beryl D. Harper nurs sister d of Henry S. H. Mosstodloch

SUTHERLAND Gilbert MA 1929 BCom 1931
dep head coll Sydney NSW; retd 1970; resid Edin
d 4.11.75

SUTHERLAND Gordon Alexander MA 1950
Aber: teacher Kaimhill s s 1960–64, dep head Broomhill p s 1965–73, head Muirfield p s from 1973

SUTHERLAND Gordon Wymess *MA 1951

SUTHERLAND or Garson, Helen May MA 1952
b 7.8.31
resid Ottawa

SUTHERLAND Herbert BSc 1926

SUTHERLAND Iain Johnstone Macbeth MA 1948
CMG 1974
first secy/head chancery Brit emb Havana Cuba 1959–62; first secy Brit emb Washington USA 1962–65; asst Northern Dept FO Lond 1965–67; counsellor/consul gen Brit emb Djakarta Indonesia 1967–69; head S Asian dept FCO Lond 1969–73; fell. center for internat affairs Harvard univ Cambridge Mass 1973–74; min Brit emb Moscow 1974–78; asst under secy of state for European affairs FCO Lond 1976–78; HM ambassador Athens Greece from 1978

SUTHERLAND James Runcieman *MA 1921 LLD 1955

SUTHERLAND James Wilson *BSc 1953

SUTHERLAND Jane Humphrey *MA 1955
Dip Ed(Glas) 1956
teacher Engl Perth acad 1956–65; resid Romsey Hants
m Aber 29.12.64 Norman D. Thomson MA(Cantab) schoolmaster/computer progr instruct. s of Robert T. Leven

SUTHERLAND John Gairn MB ChB 1951

SUTHERLAND John Stuart MB ChB 1954
regist anaest ARI 1959–62; g p Coventry from 1963

SUTHERLAND John Wallace Milne MB ChB 1934

SUTHERLAND Kenneth Ian MB ChB 1950
MRCGP 1964
g p Udny from 1960

SUTHERLAND Maggie Alice MA 1926
no longer on GC reg

SUTHERLAND or Alexander, Margaret Adamson *MA 1917
asst edit. *The British Weekly* Lond 1942–46
resid Canterbury Kent

SUTHERLAND or Walker, Margaret Jean MA 1931
resid Haslingfield Cambridge

SUTHERLAND Marie Sherriffs MB ChB 1935 DPH 1939
asst m o h Aber from 1941; retd 1974

SUTHERLAND or Wilson, Mary MA 1928
resid Ellon

SUTHERLAND or Ross, Mary Baillie MA 1920
deceased

SUTHERLAND Mary Elizabeth *MA 1917
d 19.10.72 *AUR* XLV 125

SUTHERLAND Mary Isabel MA 1947

SUTHERLAND or Carter, Mary Simpson *MB ChB 1924
retd 1965; resid N'cle Staffs
husb *d* 1951

SUTHERLAND Robert MA 1922
d Aber 7.2.71 *AUR* XLIV 210

SUTHERLAND Robert MB ChB 1928 DPH 1931 [c]MD 1933
FRSMed 1943 FRSH 1943
F Internat Epidemiological Assoc
sen lect prev med and p h Leeds univ 1951–64; dir Br Emp cancer campaign (Yorks council) cancer surv Leeds 1954–64; retd; resid Harrogate

SUTHERLAND Robert William BCom 1923
no longer on GC reg

SUTHERLAND Ruth Gordon MA 1926
d Aber 4.12.76 *AUR* XLVII 212

SUTHERLAND Sinclair Stewart MB ChB 1955

SUTHERLAND Victor Lloyd MB ChB 1944

SUTHERLAND William [d]BL 1935
ptnr Smith & Sutherland advoc Aber from 1946

SUTHERLAND William MA 1937 LLB 1939

SUTHERLAND William Alexander MA 1912
d Aber 8.8.73 *AUR* XLV 317

SUTTAR Thomas BSc(eng) 1949
DIC 1969 FIE Aust 1973
post grad stud. Imp coll Lond 1962–63; proj des eng hydro-elect. comm Tasmania 1963–73; eng for civil investig hydro-elect. comm 1973–77, asst chief civ eng from 1977

SWAINE Dalway John PhD 1952
sen prin res scient/head geochem sect. CSIRO div of mineralogy North Ryde NSW Aust from 1959

SWAINSON Douglas Willan *BSc(eng) 1939

SWAINSON or Fulton, Grace Robertson *MA 1943
resid Blairgowrie

SWAINSON Willan MA 1945
(conferred for long service of exceptional merit)
Aberd: founder of dept music, reader at time of retirement; founder of Aberdeen Bach choir, Aberdeen Orchestral Soc and Aberdeen Chamber Music Club
d Ballater 28.9.70 *AUR* XLIV 111

SWAN Ronald BSc(eng) 1949
contr man. for J. McAdam & Sons c e contractors Aber 1954–78, sen estimator W. Tawse c e contr Aber from 1978

SWANNEY Reginald Thomas Rosson MA 1947

SWANSON Ian Reid MB ChB 1952
DObstRCOG 1959
g p: Moe Vict Aust 1960–72, Lesmurdie W Aust from 1973

SWANSON Margaret BSc 1945
teacher: Burnham Somerset 1946, Warrington Lancs 1947–48, dep head Accrington 1953–58; Crawley Suss: teacher g s 1958–70, prin maths 1971–72, comp s from 1973
m Brent Knoll Somerset 9.8.47 James H. Tucker civ serv s of Edward T. Southall

SWANSTON Thomas MA 1952 *MEd 1954 BD 1960
C of S min: asst N and E St Nicholas ch Aber 1960–61, Holytown par ch Motherwell 1962–71, West par ch Inv 1971

SWAPP or Diack, Catherine MA 1919
resid Edin
husb *d* 4.5.67

SWAPP Garden Hepburn MA 1925 MB ChB 1928
d Stonehaven 28.1.67 *AUR* XLII 367

SWAPP Garden Hepburn MB ChB 1953
DObstRCOG 1960 DCH 1960 MRCOG 1963
FRCOG 1976
g p trainee Pitlochry 1960–61; regist obst/gyn Aber hosps 1961–63; Aberd: sen lect dept obst/gyn 1966–70, consult. obst/gyn Grampian area health board/clin sen lect dept obst/gyn from 1970

SWAPP George MB ChB 1924 LLD 1961
d Aber 24.5.69 *AUR* XLIII 213

SWAPP George David *MA 1953 Dip Ed 1954
RAF stat. and s selection off. Luga Malta 1961–63;

h q trg command Brampton 1964; stud. RAF staff coll 1965; dir staff RAF staff coll; wing comm sen educ and trg off. RAF Lyneham 1969–71, dir educ serv (RAF) M o D Lond from 1971

SWEENEY Sheila May BSc(agr) 1954
Dip Agr(R'dg) 1955
jun lect W of Scot. agr coll Ayr 1956–58; teacher: zool for. s Sunyani Ghana 1959, gen sc/biol Sir Robert Armitage s s Limbe Malawi 1964
m Inv 27.5.58 John A. W. Robley BSc(for) 1954 *qv*

SWEENIE or Davidson, Dorothy Mary McIntosh MB ChB 1951
resid Lenzie Glasg

SWINNEY George Ewen *MA 1936 *MB ChB 1941
phys/supt Woodilee and Stoneyetts hosps Glasg from 1961

SWINNEY William Dixon MB ChB 1941 DPH 1947
d Eye Suffolk 11.3.77 *AUR* XLVII 214

SYED Philip Antony Ross MA 1949
antiquarian bookseller: Cornwall 1966–70, Tewkesbury from 1970

SYKES or Maxwell, Greta Louise MA 1929
resid Cambridge

SYME Peter Salmon BSc(agr) 1919
no longer on GC reg

SYMES Bertram William (Barry) BSc 1950
teacher: Aber 1960–65, spec asst 1965–68, prin asst 1968–73, year master/prin guid Kincorth acad from 1973

SYMMERS Godfrey Roy BSc(civ eng) 1929 BSc(elect. eng) 1930

SYMMONS Saida PhD 1950
lect nat hist dept Aberd from 1951

SYMON Archibald MB ChB 1932
d Elgin 11.12.70 *AUR* XLIV 212

SYMON Ian Urquhart BS(agr) 1954
with SAI from 1954; resid Berwick-on-Tweed

SYMON James Alexander MA BSc(agr) 1911
d Edin 8.10.74 *AUR* XLVI 235

SYMON Jean *MA 1949
translator Council of Europe Strasbourg France from 1961

SYMON John Walker MA 1919
no longer on GC reg

SYMON Lindsay *MB ChB 1951
Rockefeller trav fell. Wayne univ Detroit USA 1962–63; sen neurosurg regist nat hosps/Middx hosp Lond 1963–65; consult. neurosurg: nat hosps Lond 1965–78, St Thomas hosp Lond 1969–78; prof neurol surg univ Lond Inst of Neurol Lond from 1978; civ consult. neurosurg RN from 1978

SYMON Lindsay James MB ChB 1944
g p Lossiemouth from 1945

SYMON or John, Margaret Anne Cargill MB ChB 1924
h o Lond 1927, Manc 1928; m o Dar-es-Salaam Tanganyika 1939–49; m o fam plan. Manchester/Preston 1953–65; resid Somerset

SYMON or Ritch, Mary Barbara MB ChB 1954
resid Oldmeldrum

SYMON Mary Susan MA 1911
d Brechin 11.3.67 *AUR* XLII 350

SYMON Patrick Anderson MA 1952 LLB 1954
solic: ptnr John Laurie & Co Aber from 1957, ptnr in Kemp & Auchinachie (Keith, Aberlour, Dufftown) from 1955, ptnr in Alex. Elder Anton & Son Buckie from 1977; resid Aber
m Aber 22.7.59 Isobel G. Pearson MA 1958

SYMONDS James MB ChB 1948
MRCGP 1962
g p Bonnyrigg from 1955

SYMONS or Kurland, Elizabeth Fleming MA 1929

SYMONS or Balnaves, Marion McDonald *MA 1923
d Aber 11.12.72 *AUR* XLV 225

TAGGART Annie Ross *BSc 1948
sen lect nutrit and dietetics RGIT Aber from 1965

TAGGART or Townsend, Eleanor Elizabeth *MA 1933

TAGGART George Joss MA 1923
d Aber 31.3.77 *AUR* XLVII 212

TAGGART Isabella Munro MA 1924
retd 1971; resid Brechin

TAGGART James Sinclair *MA 1950

TAGGART June Margaret MA 1948
pers secy Kingseat hosp Newmachar 1960–77, pers secy med comp centre ARI from 1977

TAGGART Norman MB ChB 1924
resid Is of Wight

TAIT Alexander *MA 1933
retd 1976; resid Edin

TAIT Dorothy Fraser *MA 1908
d 10.4.71

TAIT Eric Alexander *BSc 1950
Aberd: lect geol 1961–65, sen lect 1965–70, reader 1970–72, Kilgour prof from 1972

TAIT Henry Alexander Gardner *MA 1951 BD 1964
b 27.4.29
teacher: Calabar Nigeria 1955–61, Kinross s s 1964–65; C of S min: asst Shettleston Old par ch Glasg 1965, Crieff South and Monzievaird ch Crieff from 1966

TAIT Irene Margaret Hunter MA 1945

TAIT John Gavin *MA 1918
no longer on GC reg

TAIT or Moir, Kirsteen Maie *MA 1939
part time teaching and coaching Edin from 1962

TALLACK John Aidan MB ChB 1949
med regist Addenbrooke's hosp Cambridge 1956–57; Oldchurch hosp Romford Essex: locum regist 1957–67, asst phys from 1967
m Brentwood Essex 25.4.63 Mary M. Murphy SRN d of Patrick M. farm. Cork Eire

TARREL William MA 1913
no longer on GC reg

TATE Joyce Kathleen MB ChB 1944
private pract Jamaica from 1955

TATTON Henry MB ChB 1937
d 15.4.74 *AUR* XLV 449

TAVENDALE Alexander Blease BSc(eng) 1942

TAWSE Alastair Harry BSc(eng) 1951
MICE 1959
assoc dir Wm Tawse Aber 1963–66; Shellabear Price Walton-on-Thames Surrey: contr man. 1966–70, contr dir from 1970
m(2) Enfield Middx 12.12.69 Doreen Paterson d of William D. P. Aber

TAWSE John George MA 1932
dep head Mile End p s Aber 1950–75; retd

TAWSE Malcolm Harold *BSc(eng) 1948
d Nairobi 31.12.70 *AUR* XLIV 216

TAYLOR Alan King *BSc 1951

TAYLOR Alan Neil BSc 1953

TAYLOR Alan Skinner MB ChB 1947
d Preston Ont 29.3.68 *AUR* XLII 374

TAYLOR Alexander Abel *BSc 1953
AIFST 1962 FIFST 1973
sen scient off. ARC low temp res stat Cambridge 1961–67; prin scient off. ARC meat res inst Bristol from 1967
m Aber 16.3.63 Isabel D. Hyland d of Benjamin J. H. Aber

TAYLOR Alexander James MB ChB 1950
FRCGP
g p Fyvie from 1960; lect in g p Aberd

TAYLOR Alexander James Gourlay BL 1937
d Aber 28.10.75 *AUR* XLVI 417

TAYLOR Alexander Pyper MA 1907 *BSc 1909
d 12.8.65 *AUR* XLI 240

TAYLOR Alexander Robertson MA 1937 *MB ChB 1941
PhD(Belf) 1972
consult. neurol surg NI hosp auth 1952–73; sen lect med sc inst Dund from 1974
correspondence member neuro-surg Spanish, Ger, Scandinavian societies
d Dun 9.7.78 *AUR* XLVIII 106

TAYLOR or Mearns, Alice Margaret MA 1928
teacher: inf Ashley Rd p s Aber 1961–63, Rosewood inf s Aber 1963–71; retd

TAYLOR Alistair James MB ChB 1944 MD 1957
MRACP 1970 FRCP 1976
NZ: respir phys Otago hosp board 1960–64, sen lect med Otago univ from 1964

TAYLOR or Tennant, Anna MA 1923
no longer on GC reg

TAYLOR or Clark-Hutchison, Annie Calder Robertson MA 1930

TAYLOR Annie Stewart MA 1926
retd 1966; resid Edin

TAYLOR Arthur Henry Roan MA 1950
secy NFU Scot.: Caithness area Thurso 1961–64, Dumbarton area Cardross 1964–73; Inverclyde area Cardross from 1973
d Lond 17.7.79

TAYLOR Bruce Drummond MB ChB 1936
g p Wembley; retd to Aber 1976

TAYLOR Charles *MA 1939

TAYLOR Charles George Smith *MA 1927
retd 1970; resid Strathpeffer

TAYLOR Charles Matheson MB ChB 1945
g p Harlow Essex from 1949

TAYLOR Colin Fraser MA 1932
d Aber 12.1.66 *AUR* XLII 88

TAYLOR Daniel MA 1952
prin teacher Engl/hist/geog Lossiemouth h s 1963–69; head: Port Erroll p s Cruden Bay 1969–71, Ellon p s 1971–75, Cults p s from 1975

TAYLOR David Scott *MA 1949
teacher Fr/Ger Mackie acad Stonehaven from 1953

TAYLOR Douglass William MB ChB 1946 *MD 1957
univ of Otago med s, Dunedin NZ: sen lect physiol 1962–64, assoc prof 1964–68, pers prof from 1968; asst Dean (part-time) from 1974

TAYLOR Edward Russell *MA 1921
d 23.1.69

TAYLOR Edwin William MA 1944
head Bucksburn s 1961–69; lect Aber coll of educ from 1969

TAYLOR Elizabeth Ann MA 1948
teacher King St s Aber 1955–62
m Aber 1.9.62 George A. Duthie joiner s of George D. New Pitsligo

TAYLOR Elizabeth Colville Anderson MA 1927
d Edin 7.9.75 *AUR* XLVI 323

TAYLOR Elsie Constance Coutts MA 1929
teacher Engl: Inverurie acad 1943–63, Monifieth/ Carnoustie s s 1963–68; retd; resid Monifieth

TAYLOR Elspeth Stewart MA 1936
teacher Springhill p s Aber 1959–75; retd

TAYLOR Eric Forbes MA 1950
head Sandhaven s from 1965

TAYLOR or Cutting, Flora Mysie MA 1943

TAYLOR or Lessells, Frances Mary MA BSc 1941
resid Aber

TAYLOR Gavin Beddie MB ChB 1954
MRCGP 1965
g p Peterhead from 1959
m Doncaster 26.6.61 Margaret L. Woodmansey d of Alfred B. W.

TAYLOR Gavin Catto *MB ChB 1924
d Peterhead 6.10.62 *AUR* XL 91

TAYLOR George Alexander MA 1926 BSc(eng) 1928 *1929 PhD 1949
d Tor-Na-Dee Aber 17.12.64 *AUR* XLI 58

TAYLOR George Angus MB ChB 1932
d Oldham 1961 *AUR* XXXIX 283

TAYLOR George Gordon Massie BSc(for) 1952

TAYLOR George Henry Carr MB ChB 1940

TAYLOR George James Gibson *MA 1926
part-time lect Fr Wolverhampton tech coll 1965–66; part-time teacher Fr/Ger Wolverhampton girls' h s 1966–72; Fr oral exam. Lond univ 1965–74, exam. Fr Oxf & Camb joint board from 1966
m Wolverhampton 4.7.64 Elsa A. Walker BA(Lond) teacher

TAYLOR Harriet Johnston Sutherland MB ChB 1921

TAYLOR or Aldwinckle, Helene Lovie MA 1942

TAYLOR Henry *MA 1953 Dip Ed 1954
MEd(Edin) 1972
prin teacher geog: Mortlach sen s s Dufftown 1956–60, Peterhead acad 1960–63; dep head Royal Blind s Edin 1963–65, head 1965–72; lect educ of visually handicapped ch Moray House coll of educ Edin from 1973

TAYLOR Henry Alistair MA 1950

TAYLOR Henry Mitchell BSc(eng) 1937
FRSA 1966 FIMechE 1967 CEng 1967
head dept eng tech Luton coll of higher educ from 1957

TAYLOR Ian Bryson BSc(eng) 1947
FICE 1968
Richard Costain: dep ag Barbados 1956–60, ag 1960–61; area rep Kaduna Nigeria 1962–66, asst comm man. Lond 1966–68; contr eng Lond 1969–78, sen contr eng from 1978

TAYLOR Irene Barlow MA 1945
ordained Lond as priest of Christian Commun 1960; working Lond from 1960
m Lond –.6.63 Ormond St J. Edwards BSc(Keele) printer/priest s of Alfred E. Shrewsbury

TAYLOR or Davidson, Isabel Mary Jane MA 1946
resid Ellon

TAYLOR Isabella Florence Sutherland MA 1909
no longer on GC reg

TAYLOR James *BSc 1952
MIMM 1959 CE 1965 assoc M Aust IMM 1967
geol surv of Gt Brit Lond 1952–66; Aust: explor man. United Uranium NL Darwin 1966–73, chief geol JOC min resources Sydney/Perth 1973–74; geol Internat Atomic Energy Agency UN, Afghanistan 1974–75, Uruguay 1975, Ethiopia 1976, Greece 1976–77, Nicaragua 1978, Bolivia 1978

TAYLOR James Fraser MB ChB 1954
DPH(Edin) 1965 DIH(Lond) 1965 MFOM 1978
m o Chloride Group Swinton Manc from 1965

TAYLOR James Garden *MA 1919 DSc 1966
d Hemel Hempstead 10.9.73 *AUR* XLV 318

TAYLOR James Ingram BSc(eng) 1930 *1931
MBE 1953 FIWE 1950 FICE 1955
asst city eng Durh 1930–31; dep eng Kent river board Maidstone 1932–53; major Royal Marines Burma/ India etc 1941–45; chief eng Kent river board Maidstone 1953–74
m Marden Kent 11.7.36 Joyce M. Wheeler d of Leonard W. Marden

TAYLOR James Lennel MB ChB 1935
g p Keith from 1936; retd 1977

TAYLOR James Michael MB ChB 1955
h o mat. hosp Aber 1959–60; g p Peterhead from 1960

TAYLOR James Thomson *MA 1915
d 13.5.72

TAYLOR James William MA 1929
head Stromness p s 1961–70; retd; resid Dormansland Surrey

TAYLOR James Wilson MB ChB 1940
MRCGP 1953
g p Dyce from 1947

TAYLOR Jane Stuart MA 1935

TAYLOR Janet Isabel MA 1913
d Halkirk 15.3.67 *AUR* XLII 182

TAYLOR or Nelson, Jean Clyne MB ChB 1945
FRCPE 1971 FRCP(Can) 1973
Canada: m o loc board of health Edmonton 1958–67; m o inst for delinquent adolescent girls Edmonton 1960–67; member prov royal comm to investigate juvenile delinquency Alberta 1967–68; member McGrath penology consult. stud. group Alberta 1968–69; asst dir Well Child progr univ of Alberta 1964–68; commun paediat loc board of health Edmonton 1967–74; lect dept paediat univ of Alberta from 1955; vice-pres Vanier Inst of the Family Ottawa 1973–74; dep Min of Health province of Alberta from 1975
d Edmonton 15.1.79 *AUR* XLVIII 233

TAYLOR or Stewart, Jean Mary MA 1933
teacher p s Inverurie acad 1960–72

TAYLOR John BL 1940

TAYLOR John Cuthill MB ChB 1939
g p Goudhurst Kent 1946–76, part time g p Hawkhurst from 1977
m Maidstone 3.10.67 Daphne D. Haynes riding instr d of Lewis P. H. Hawkhurst

TAYLOR John Erskine MA 1946 LLB 1949
solic in civ serv Edin from 1956

TAYLOR John Hamilton *MA 1949
teacher: Moray/Banff 1960–72, Glasg from 1972

TAYLOR John Ingram MB ChB 1925
retd 1966; resid Sheffield

TAYLOR John Maxwell
***MA 1899 MB ChB 1905 DPH 1913**
d Dun 11.2.65 *AUR* XLI 52

TAYLOR John Mitchell MA 1954
rector: St Ninian's ch Pollokshields 1964–73, St John's ch Dumfries from 1973

TAYLOR John Murray *MA 1931
d Banchory 12.1.72 *AUR* XLIV 433

TAYLOR John Stewart MB ChB 1951
g p Elgin from 1955

TAYLOR John William MA 1916
m(3) Lond 4.11.61 Joan M. Hickman d of Bernard V. H. Wolverhampton
d Lond 25.5.74 *AUR* XLVI 108

TAYLOR Keith McLean *MA 1948

TAYLOR or Turner, Louise Barbara *MA 1929
secy joint comm of Greek and Roman societies 1949–75; resid Fortrose
edit. *Aberdeen Shore Work Accounts*

TAYLOR or McKenzie, Mabel Catherine
MA 1939 BSc 1940 *1941
teacher maths: Fraserburgh acad 1960–64, spec asst 1964–71, Mackie acad Stonehaven 1971–77; retd; resid Stonehaven

TAYLOR or Heald, Margaret Bella MA 1943
insp MOH (insur dept) Nott 1943–46; regist of appeals (fam allowances dept) N'cle 1946–48; reg welfare off. MOH/soc security Leeds 1948–50; part-time teacher Leeds 1958–72; resid Wetherby

TAYLOR Margaret Buchan MA 1952

TAYLOR Margaret Jane McKenzie
MA 1947 *MEd 1961
ch guid centre Aber: educ psych 1961–67, sen asst educ psych 1967–68, prin psych 1968–75, reg psych Grampian reg from 1975

TAYLOR or Innes, Margaret Reid MA 1926

TAYLOR or Mackenzie, Marjorie Kathleen
MA 1942
Aber: teacher (temp) 1959, Muirfield p s 1960, Quarryhill p s 1961–68, Kingswood p s 1968–75

TAYLOR or Robertson, Mary MA 1904
d 1962

TAYLOR or Stephen, Mary Elizabeth MA 1936
teacher Kingswells p s from 1962

TAYLOR or Gray, Moira Margaret BSc 1950
teacher maths/sc: Burnley h s for girls 1962–66; Tasmania: Huonville h s 1967–69, Prospect h s Launceston 1969–70, Kings Meadows h s Launceston from 1971

TAYLOR Moore MB ChB 1921 MD DPH 1928
resid Nedlands W Aust

TAYLOR Patrick Hamilton BSc(eng) 1953
MICE 1961
Terresearch Middx: eng 1958–60, contr man./superv 1960–61; DAFS Edin: asst civ eng 1961–65, civ eng 1966–72; Scot. dev dept Edin: civ eng 1972–77, sen civ eng from 1977

TAYLOR Phyllis Agnes BSc 1937

TAYLOR Robert BSc(agr) 1928
no longer on GC reg

TAYLOR Robert MB ChB 1944

TAYLOR Robert Innes MA 1934
retd 1972; resid Hillside Montrose

TAYLOR Robin Burness BSc(eng) 1947

TAYLOR Ronald Gordon BSc(eng) 1944

TAYLOR Thomas Murray (Sir) *MA 1919 LLB 1922
prin and vice-chancellor Aberd 1948–62
d Aber 19.7.62 *AUR* XXXIX 291–306

TAYLOR Thornton Lewins *MA 1928
HMIS retd 1968; dealer antiques/fine art Glasg from 1968
d Glasg 10.1.79 *AUR* XLVIII 231

TAYLOR William *MA 1913 LLD 1962
m Aber 28.9.63 Mildred Hartley MA(Cantab)
d Oxford 12.2.77 *AUR* XLVII 211

TAYLOR William *MA 1953 MEd 1958
prin teacher classics John Neilson h s Paisley from 1965

TAYLOR William Alexander BSc(eng) 1947

TAYLOR William Anderson MA 1942 LLB 1949
ptnr Mackenzie & Grant solic Forres from 1960

TAYLOR William Clyne MB ChB 1945
Canada: prof paediat Edmonton from 1968; asst dir R. S. McLaughlin exam. and res centre Edmonton from 1973
m Winnipeg Manitoba 24.4.54 Susie S. Paxton nurse d of Thomas P. Oak River Manitoba

TAYLOR William Ferguson *MA 1949

TAYLOR William John MA 1931
d Lond 2.5.63 *AUR* XL 206

TELFER or McCredie, Kathrine Carmichael MA 1928

TEMPLE John Stoddart BSc(agr) 1952
insp DAFS Edin from 1970

TEMPLETON or Dent, Mary Agnes MB ChB 1945
occasional work locum g p/fam plan. clin from 1947; resid Norwich

TENNANT Edward Robert Hector MB ChB 1951
HM overseas civil serv (med dept) N Borneo Sabah 1959–66; dep m o h, dep prin schools m o Inv 1967–70; g p Ullapool 1970–77; s m o Esso Standard Libya Inc Marsa, El Brega 1977–79; m o Brit emb Warsaw from 1979
m Inv 15.8.59 Morag J. MacLeod matron ch's home

TENNANT or Russell, Ethel Law BCom 1930
d Pitmedden 21.9.76

TENNANT John MA 1937 BD 1946
C of S min Cluny par ch 1957–70; mod. presb Garioch Inverurie 1961–63, clerk presb of Garioch 1964–69; mod. synod of Aber 1968–69; retd 1970; locum tenens: par of Ardgour with Strontian 1971–72, Duneaton 1972
d Gartly Aberdeensh 16.6.76

TENNANT Vivian Lloyd MB ChB 1937
sen m o h Ksac Jamaica 1960–64; private pract 1964–73; retd; resid Kingston Jamaica
d Jamaica W Indies 18.10.74

TENNANT William Robert (Sir) *MA 1914 *1915 LLD 1953
d St And 4.5.69 *AUR* XLIII 329

TEUNON or Shiach, Clara Macandrew MA 1937
occasional relief teaching Selkirksh 1951–72; retd; resid Galashiels

TEUNON George John MacAndrew MB ChB 1924
sen hosp m o/consult. radiol Blackburn & dist group of hosps from 1955; retd 1963; resid Banchory

TEUNON or Sharma, Hilda Margaret MB ChB 1937
resid Nainital UP India

TEUNON John MA 1941

TEUNON Lilian Margaret MA 1947

THAIN or Tellwright, Annie *MB ChB 1921
resid Market Drayton

THERON Pieter Hendrick MB ChB 1941 *ChM 1947

THICKNESSE or Garrow, Katharine Joyce MB ChB 1950
resid Pinner

THIRD James Ross Sinclair MB ChB 1933
g p Aber from 1947

THIRD John *MA 1914 dBSc 1915
d 28.10.67

THIRD or Duffus, Marjorie Ann Sinclair MA 1934

THIRD or Lewis, Sheila MB ChB 1946
d Gloucester 31.10.69

THOIRS or Queen, Isobel Louise MA 1943
resid Richmond Hill Ontario

THOLT Elizabeth MA 1929

THOM Alexander Davidson MB ChB 1947
gen surg regist King Edward VII hosp Windsor 1958–61; surg CMC hosp Pendiya Cyprus 1961–64; g p Maitland NSW Aust from 1964, hon obst/assoc surg Maitland hosp from 1966

THOM Charles Denis MA 1949

THOM Charles John MA 1909
d Glasg 2.9.67 *AUR* XLII 180

THOM Elizabeth Henderson MB ChB 1948
DPH(Glas) 1954
m Ayr 14.6.51 David A. R. Lawrie stockbroker s of David L. Bearsden

THOM Isabella Scott MA 1925
no longer on GC reg

THOM James William BSc 1926
no longer on GC reg

THOM Jane Ann MA 1918
resid Oldmeldrum
d 27.6.81

THOM or Duncan, Margaret Jean MA 1949

THOM Marjory Ferguson MA 1938

THOM Robert Jamieson *MA 1933

THOM William BCom 1922
no longer on GC reg

THOM William Cumming MA 1917 BD 1920 PhD 1924 DD 1948
retd from Sydney Aust 1968; resid Aber
wife *d* 5.9.65
d Aber 25.3.79 *AUR* XLVIII 227

THOMAS David BSc 1950
HM geol surv later inst of geol sc: geol Lond 1950–52, Manc 1952–60, Leeds 1960–71, sen scient off. from 1971; member Br Caucasus exped to USSR 1958; Lond univ exped to Jan Mayen Is 1961, Imp coll exped to Jan Mayen Is 1963
m Wrexham Ruth E. Young d of Edward Y. Wrexham

THOMAS Ena Ernestine MB ChB 1954

THOMAS Isabella Elsbeth Mary Ferguson MB ChB 1950
clin m o h Carmarthen from 1970
m Caio Carmarthensh 14.6.65 Eric M. Grey BA(Lampeter) clerk in holy orders s of Thomas G. Llandybie Carmarthensh

THOMAS William (Sir) PhD 1923
CB
d 22.11.74 *AUR* XLVI 322

THOMPSON or Donald, Alice *MA 1907 *BSc 1909
d 7.7.74

THOMPSON Alice May MA 1916
d Aber 4.9.73 *AUR* XLV 318

THOMPSON Barbara Anne MA 1952
teacher: s s Aber 1959–61, Ghana 1961–67, p s Lond from 1967
m Lond 2.9.75 Justice A. Neizer BSc(eng) 1960 *qv*

THOMPSON Edward John MA 1910
no longer on GC reg

THOMPSON George Alexander BSc(eng) 1948
CEng MIEE 1969
sect. leader Laurence, Scott & Electromotors Norwich from 1973

THOMPSON Hugh Percy BSc(eng) 1947

THOMPSON James McAllan Cormack MA 1934 *BSc 1935
FRIC
retd 1972; resid W Kilbride

THOMPSON Jane Maver MA 1927
teacher Fraserburgh acad 1947–63
resid Paisley
m Aber 1964 John I. McBurnie MA(Edin) C of S min s of Walter M. McB. Loanhead Midlothian

THOMPSON John Arthur BSc(for) 1954

THOMPSON John Edward MB ChB 1909
no longer on GC reg

THOMPSON or Malcolm, Laura Blackhall Cormack MB ChB 1943
clin m o Grampian health board (N dist)

THOMPSON or Craig, Maggie Wilken MA 1929

THOMPSON Michael Scott BSc(agr) 1955
Buxted Chicken Co.: superv farms E Anglia 1961–66; res asst NIAB Cambridge 1966–68; herbicide advis CIBA-GEIGY (UK) based on Cambridge 1968–73; comp tech advis Key & Pell E Anglia/E Midlands 1973–76; trg advis man. 1976–78; trg man. agr area BASF(UK) from 1978

THOMPSON or Morrice, Norah MA 1945
resid Aber

THOMPSON Robert McLean MB ChB 1924
d Tamworth 5.2.65 *AUR* XLI 58

THOMSON Adam Edward MA 1923 [d]MB ChB 1927
retd Dagenham 1963; resid Banchory

THOMSON or Lyall, Agnes Ann MA 1930
retd 1972; resid Aber

THOMSON or Gibson, Agnes Jane *MA 1920
resid Tain

THOMSON Alan Russell *BSc 1952 PhD 1955
leader biochem group eng sc div AERE Harwell from 1969; visiting reader Wolfson bioanalytical centre Sur univ 1973–76; comm techniques group biochemical soc from 1977

THOMSON Albert Gordon MA 1931

THOMSON Alexander Baird MA 1926
retd 1968; resid Pencaitland E Lothian

THOMSON Alexander Francis *BSc 1943
Rowntree-Mackintosh York: chief analyst 1960–67, prod. dev man. and export div dir from 1967

THOMSON Alexander Louis George ***MB ChB 1921**
g p Kei Mouth S Af 1960–73; semi-retd

THOMSON Alexander Wilson MB ChB 1944
g p Cullen from 1947
marr diss
m(2) Tarves 23.1.63 Nora I. Henderson dietitian d of William H. Tarves

THOMSON or Davidson, Alexandra Margaret **BSc 1929 MA 1931**
resid Fraserburgh

THOMSON or Hendry, Alice Cushny MA 1913
d Aber 28.9.62 *AUR* XL 82

THOMSON or Martin, Alice Margaret **MA 1922 BSc 1924**
resid Aber
d Newmachar 20.3.81 *AUR* XLIX 136

THOMSON Allister McAllister BSc(eng) 1944

THOMSON or Shewan, Ann (Annie) Fraser **MA 1929**
d Edin 7.8.77 *AUR* XLVIII 287

THOMSON or Shennan, Ann Lindsay ***MB ChB 1930 *MD 1934 dDPH 1939**
MFCM 1972
sen m o Aber c c 1968–74; retd
husb *d* –.10.48
m(2) Aber 30.9.61 Alan R. Edwards OBE MA(St And) instr/comm RN
d Aber 21.1.81 *AUR* XLIX 138

THOMSON Annie Sutherland MA 1922

THOMSON Arthur Landsborough (Sir) **MA 1911 *BSc 1914 DSc 1920 LLD 1956**
Buchanan Medal of Royal Society 1962
chmn trustees Brit Museum Lond (nat hist) 1967–69
d 9.6.77 *AUR* XLVII 286

THOMSON Atholl MB ChB 1919
d Aber 5.12.69 *AUR* XLIII 444

THOMSON Beryl MA 1955
teacher: Sunnybank p s Aber 1956–66, Beaconhill p s Beaconsfield Quebec 1966–73; resid Pierrefonds Quebec
m Beaconsfield Quebec 16.6.72 Gordon R. Biggar instrum mech Air Canada s of Louis B. Florida USA

THOMSON Charles BL 1938
d Aber 7.2.79 *AUR* XLVIII 232

THOMSON Charles David MA 1950 MB ChB 1955
d Auchterarder 5.10.64 *AUR* XLI 61

THOMSON or Steele, Christina Williamina **MA 1917**
d 5.3.80

THOMSON David Landsborough **MA 1921 *BSc 1924 LLD 1952**
LLD(Sask) 1961 LLD(Manit) 1961
d Province of Quebec 20.10.64 *AUR* XLI 56

THOMSON Derick Smith *MA 1947
prof Celtic Glas from 1963; pres Scottish Gaelic Texts Soc from 1964; chmn Gaelic Books Council from 1968

THOMSON Donald MA 1915
no longer on GC reg

THOMSON Donald MA 1929
OBE 1970
dep rector Oban h s 1967–72; retd; provost Oban 1959–62, 1968–71; pres An Comunn Gaidhealach 1962–65; chmn McCaig's Trust from 1968; chief Camanachd assoc of Scot. 1971–73; member Argyll c c from 1973
d Oban 8.7.80 *AUR* XLIX 68

THOMSON Dorothy Adèle BSc 1953
analyst chem dept Aberd 1955–63; teacher maths: Aber 1972–73; Glasg from 1974
m Aber 2.4.62 John S. Edmond MA 1955 *qv*

THOMSON Dorothy Isobel Grant MA 1915
resid Galashiels
d Galashiels 26.4.80

THOMSON Douglas Stephen MA 1952 LLB 1955

THOMSON Edward BSc(eng) 1948
head dept telecomm Aber tech coll 1963–75; retd

THOMSON Edward Riddell *MA 1938
asst head (curriculum) Inverurie acad from 1974

THOMSON Edward Worley BSc 1926
FEIS 1967
retd 1968; resid Dun
d 17.6.78

THOMSON Elizabeth Forbes MA 1920
retd 1960; resid Aber

THOMSON Elizabeth Fraser *MA 1945
lib London patent off. lib (later sc ref lib) Lond from 1960

THOMSON or Liddell, Elsie Jean MB ChB 1937
g p Cults Aber from 1946
husb *d* Cults 15.6.74

THOMSON or Duncan, Ethel Elspeth Fyfe **MA 1939**
teacher Walker Rd p s Aber till 1948; resid Aber

THOMSON or Greig, Frances Isobel MA 1927
resid Guildford

THOMSON or Milne, Freda Margaret BSc 1954
lab tech: path. dept Weston-super-Mare gen hosp 1967–68, girls' g s Gloucester 1969–73

THOMSON Frederick Alexander *MA 1954
prin teacher hist: Forfar acad 1963–67, Aber acad (Hazlehead acad) 1967–73; asst head Hazlehead acad from 1973
m Paisley 28.7.62 Elizabeth M. Muir MA(Glas) teacher d of John K. M. Paisley

THOMSON George MA 1948

THOMSON or Ross, Gladys MA 1955
head Chapel of Garioch p s from 1976

THOMSON or Glass, Hilda Macdonald MA 1933
b Kirkwall 14.7.13
teacher Kincardinesh 1934–45; women's educ Omdurman, Sudan 1946–48; teacher maths Grove acad Dun 1956–73; retd
m Khartoum 14.12.46 George A. Glass chief publ health insp Sudan

THOMSON Horace Norman Michaelson MB ChB 1944 DPH 1965
asst m o Banff c c 1965–66; m o/prin lect health educ Aber coll of educ from 1966
chmn educ comm joint c c Moray & Nairn Elgin 1962–64

THOMSON Ian BSc(agr) 1951

THOMSON Ian Angus BSc(eng) 1945
MIMavE 1958 MIMechE 1970
lect mech eng Gateshead tech coll 1951–59, sen lect 1959–61; head mech eng Wearside coll of f e Sunderland Co Durh from 1961

THOMSON Ian Gordon MB ChB 1943 MD 1959
OBE 1965
m o Ndian/Pamol/Douala, Cameroons W Af from 1967; later m o gen council of British Shipping; resid Lond

THOMSON Ian Stephen BSc(eng) 1934

THOMSON Ian Stewart MA 1913 MB ChB 1921 MD 1924
retd 1958; resid York

THOMSON Isobel Margaret MA 1937
teacher Airyhall p s Aber 1968–77; retd

THOMSON or Fröhlich, Isobel Pirie MA 1946

THOMSON James MA 1909
d Aber 26.4.68 *AUR* XLII 348

THOMSON James MA 1910

THOMSON James BSc 1925
teacher sc RGC Aber from 1942; retd 1963; resid Aber

THOMSON James BSc 1926
d Aber 16.7.73 *AUR* XLV 320

THOMSON James MB ChB 1929
d 20.11.67

THOMSON James Greig MB ChB 1927 [c]MD 1937
FRCPath 1963
retd 1970; emeritus prof univ of Cape Town

THOMSON James Ian Fraser MA 1936 LLB 1938
ptnr Edmonds & Ledingham advoc Aber from 1948
m 27.9.41

THOMSON James John George *MA 1924 BSc 1925
retd 1966; resid Edin

THOMSON James Laing *MA 1900 BD 1903
d Edin 10.7.64 *AUR* XL 394

THOMSON James Laing Spalding MB ChB 1932
MRCGP 1966 FHS 1970 FRSM 1971
g p Lond from 1933

THOMSON James Macfarlane MB ChB 1935 DPH 1939
m o h Angus c c 1944–68; retd; police surg Angus constab 1945–66; secy loc med comm Angus 1950–67; resid Aber

THOMSON James Milne MB ChB 1936
d 31.12.64

THOMSON James Oliver *MA 1911
d 31.4.71

THOMSON James Simpson MA BSc 1920
d Aber 10.2.62 *AUR* XXXIX 382

THOMSON or Smitton, Jane Elizabeth Johnston MA 1920
d Wick 3.7.77

THOMSON Jane Scott BCom 1932

THOMSON or Meldrum, Janet Craig MA 1900
d Newtonmore 29.4.61 *AUR* XXXIX 199

THOMSON Janet Gladys MA 1930

THOMSON Janet McAllan MA 1925
no longer on GC reg

THOMSON Jean Shepherd MA 1916
retd 1960; resid Aber
d 20.6.81

THOMSON Jeannie Grant *MA 1903
d Aber 10.4.61 *AUR* XXXIX 199

THOMSON or Diack, Jeannie Isabella MA 1943
teacher Kemnay 1956–78

THOMSON or Wiseman, Jessie MA 1920
resid Aber

THOMSON John Adam (Sir) MA 1947
CMG 1972 KCMG 1978
HM dipl serv: first secy Washington 1960–64; FO

1964–66; acting head plan. staff FO 1966–67, head plan. staff 1967–68; chief of assessment staff Cabinet off. 1968–72; min and dep perm rep UK deleg to NATO 1972–73; asst under-secy FCO 1973–76; Brit high comm New Delhi from 1977

THOMSON John Hendry *MA 1951

THOMSON John McNaughton MB ChB 1955
RAMC 1956–59; col med serv Dar-es-Salaam/Njombe, Tanganyika 1959–62; g p Leic 1962–69; g p/part-time m o Natal prov admin Eshowe, Zululand from 1969

THOMSON John Maitland BSc(eng) 1945

THOMSON John Peters MA 1908
d Falkirk 15.3.69 *AUR* XLIII 208

THOMSON or Watt, Lily Norrie MA 1946
resid Memsie

THOMSON Maggie MA 1931
d 13.1.71

THOMSON Magnus Louttit MA 1926 MB ChB 1930 MD 1936
d Cheadle Hulme 7.6.63 *AUR* XL 205

THOMSON Margaret Dawson MB ChB 1944
m Harries

THOMSON or Brodie, Margaret Elizabeth MA 1943

THOMSON or Wilde, Margaret Helen MB ChB 1948
resid Bridgend Glam

THOMSON or Dunnet, Margaret Henderson MA 1952
teacher Engl Mintlaw s from 1971

THOMSON or Cheyne, Margaret Isabel MA 1929
d Aber 30.5.69 *AUR* XLIII 331

THOMSON or Craig, Margaret Isabella MA 1929
resid Dollar
husb *d* Kirkhill Invsh 4.8.54

THOMSON or Holiday, Margaret Ishbel Hemingway MA 1955
retd; resid Rowlands Gill Tyne and Wear
d 27.1.79

THOMSON or Edwin, Maribel MA 1916 *BSc 1919
writer; resid Dorking

THOMSON or Huber, Mary Duffus MA 1913
resid Hamburg, Cologne and then Munich
d Munich W Ger 22.7.80

THOMSON Mary Elizabeth *MA 1901
d Daviot Abdnsh 27.8.73 *AUR* XLV 315

THOMSON or Macinnes, Mary Margaret Gray MA 1948
resid Tunbridge Wells

THOMSON or Davidson, Mattie Paterson BSc 1924
d Banchory 6.10.67 *AUR* XLII 365

THOMSON Robert MB ChB 1922
retd 1969; resid Louth Lincs

THOMSON Ronald Cooper *BSc 1946
ICI: seconded as works man. to Duperial Argentina 1961–64; prod. man. petrochemicals div Teesside from 1969

THOMSON Ronald Ross *BSc 1949

THOMSON Roy Hendry *MA 1955
Thomson of Cults: dir 1960–63, man. dir from 1963; elected off. O St J 1972

THOMSON Sheila *MB ChB 1932 DPH 1935
MM(Soc Apoth. Lond) 1937 MFCM 1971
retd 1972; resid Edin

THOMSON Spence Ford BL 1952
prin leg asst Corp Aber until 1971; retd
d Trowbridge 25.2.75 *AUR* XLVI 240

THOMSON Thomas Bentley Stewart *MA 1911 BD 1914 DD 1946
d 10.8.73 *AUR* XLV 316

THOMSON Violet May MA 1949
dep head Woodside p s Aber 1967–77, head The Hillocks p s Bucksburn Aber from 1977

THOMSON Wilfred Nicolson BSc(agr) 1948

THOMSON or Sinclair, Wilhelmina Downie Flett MA 1947
relief teacher Moray from 1963

THOMSON William LLB 1934
retd 1972; resid Edin
d Edin 4.10.78

THOMSON William Eddie Spalding *MA 1936
scient edit. Blackie & Son Glasg from 1946

THOMSON William George MB ChB 1947
DIH 1967 DMJ 1969 MFOM 1978
chief m o Smith's Indust Lond from 1959

THOMSON William Norman MB ChB 1944
consult. radiol Edin N hosp group from 1953

THOMSON Williamina Netta MA 1916
d Carluke 14.10.61 *AUR* XXXIX 279

THOMSON or Gordon, Winifred MA 1946

THORN or Wilson, Annie Florence Elizabeth MA 1908
d Torphins 19.9.70 *AUR* XLIV 107

THORN Harold Leslie BSc(eng) 1950

THORNILEY Garven Nesbitt BSc(agr) 1952
no longer on GC reg

THORNTON Ronald *MA 1937

THOW Gordon MB ChB 1925
s h m o surg Elgin 1948–67; retd g p Elgin 1970
m(2) Elgin 12.1.60 Christina Davidson

THOW Henry Abernethy MA 1920
no longer on GC reg

TIBBLES Joseph Russell MB ChB 1915
no longer on GC reg

TINDALL Daisy *MA 1933
lib Reform Club Lond 1947–71; retd

TINGLE Alfred BSc 1896
no longer on GC reg

TOCHER Alexander McKenzie Innes MA 1931
head Methlick p s 1966–72; retd; resid Aber

TOCHER Forbes Scott *MA 1906 DD 1934
d 15.8.73 *AUR* XLV 316

TOCHER Francis Edward *BSc 1951 PhD 1959
sen lect dept geol/mineralogy Aberd from 1969; asst dean (advis) fac of sc Aberd from 1973

TOCHER or Milne, Hazel Allan MA 1944

TOCHER Helen Howitt MA 1939
teacher Aber: St Clement St p s 1943–58, Springhill p s 1959–72, Sunnybank p s from 1972

TOCHER James Ross MB ChB 1938
g p Arbroath from 1945
d Arbroath 14.1.79 *AUR* XLVIII 232

TOCHER Wilfred Ian McKenzie MA 1945

TODD Edward Finlay Ross MB ChB 1944
d 25.4.61

TODD Ian Douglas Hutchison MB ChB 1950
MRCP 1958 FFR 1962 FRCP 1975 FRCR 1975
consult. radiotherap Christie hosp Manc from 1963; hon lect radiotherap Manc from 1967

TODD John David BSc(for) 1949
conserv of for. Zambia from 1964

TODD John Munro *MA 1932
d Kingussie 28.4.73 *AUR* XLV 227

TODD Martha Simpson *MA 1914
d 25.4.74

TODD Peter George MB ChB 1953

TODD William George MB ChB 1943
g p Kemnay from 1967

TODD William Maxwell *BSc 1936
prin teacher chem Morrison's acad Crieff from 1966

TOGHILL Edith Mary MA 1952

TOLMIE or Mitchell or Mason, Elizabeth Mary Falconer MB ChB 1939
staff m o Harrods Lond from 1960

TOLMIE or White, Isabella Margaret MA 1913

TOLMIE James Boyd MB ChB 1937

TOLMIE John William BSc(eng) 1946
FIEE 1975 Dip Man. St(H-W) 1965
Dip Inst Marketing 1968 BA(OU) 1977
NSHEB: dist eng Dingwall 1950–55; sen asst eng (head off.) Edin 1955–69, area eng Dingwall 1969–71, area eng Dun 1971–75; asst chief pers off. (head office) from 1975

TOMORY or Werdmuller, Louise MB ChB 1919 MD 1923
d Cape Town 5.9.73 *AUR* XLV 318

TOPPING Jeanie Bayne *MA 1911
d Aber 11.12.73 *AUR* XLV 446

TOPPING or Carey, Margaret Rosamond MB ChB 1946
resid Keynsham Bristol

TOPPING or Youngson, Robina Gordon MA 1927

TOPPING William Renton MB ChB 1927 MD 1942
d Birm 30.12.77 *AUR* XLVII 357

TORRIE Alfred MA 1919 MB ChB 1924
d Richmond Surrey 21.4.72 *AUR* XLIV 429

TORVANEY Alastair William Logie *MA 1948

TORVANEY or Hemans, Janet Helen Alison MA 1944
coach Engl lang Harpenden 1962–63; teacher Engl lit/lang St Michael's convent Leigh-on-Sea 1964, part-time Steeple Bumpstead jun s 1965–68; lect: lib stud./Engl coll of tech Southend 1969, bus. Engl f e coll 1972–78, 1st yr Fr evening class Brentwood from 1974

TOSH Annie Clarke MA 1916
resid Aber

TOSH or Kendrick, Constance Stevenson *MA 1949

TOSH Gordon Cameron *BSc(eng) 1953
sen dev eng in telecommunications Lond from 1954
m Lond 11.8.56 Iris Farrer secy d of Victor S. F. Mottingham Lond

TOSH Jack Rae *MA 1950

TOSH Sheena Mary MB ChB 1939

TOTT or Bevan, Patricia Murray MA 1948

TOUGH or Brown, Aileen Taylor MA 1952
freelance journalist Aber 1960–69; teacher: Aber 1970–71, Anlaby Yorks 1972–75, Glasg from 1975

TOUGH Andrew Crawford BL 1949
ptnr Aikins MacAulay & Thorvaldson barristers and solic Winnipeg Canada

TOUGH Arthur Farquharson *MA 1953 LLB 1956
Keele univ: admin asst 1961–63, asst regist 1963–67, dep regist from 1967

TOUGH David *MA 1946
sect. man. ICI Manchester: dyestuffs div 1948–71, organics div from 1971; resid Rochdale

TOUGH or Lennie, Elizabeth Mary MA 1946
teacher maths: Powis acad Aber 1959–63, Linksfield acad Aber from 1967

TOUGH Eric Alexander BSc(eng) 1943
dir Internat Oil and Gas div PA man. consult. Lond from 1973

TOUGH George *BSc 1951

TOUGH or Shepherd, Helen Isabella MA 1924
no longer on GC reg

TOUGH or Davidson, Isabella Jane Ritchie MA 1932
resid Aber

TOUGH James Cormack BSc(eng) 1941
teacher phys Banff acad from 1969

TOUGH or Hart, Jeannie Ann Christina MA 1930

TOUGH Mary Fraser Roberts MA 1929
head p dept High s for girls Aber 1964–70; retd

TOUGH Peter Henderson MA 1911
d Daviot Abdnsh 13.6.68 *AUR* XLIII 78

TOUGH Robert BSc(agr) 1921
no longer on GC reg

TOWERS or Ashburn, Janetta MA 1946

TOWNS or Heggie, Audrey Margaret Gourlay MB ChB 1950
Newton Stewart: fam plan. clin work from 1962 and part time g p from 1966

TOWNSEND Patrick William BSc(eng) 1950

TOWNSHEND Gerald Kilvington *BSc 1949
MInst Packaging 1964
Procter & Gamble: Geneva 1959–61, Cincinnati USA 1961–62, Brussels 1962–65, N'cle-u-Tyne 1965; Bowater Packaging Gillingham Kent: dir sales 1969–71, gen man. 1971–74; Mardon Packaging Internat: man. group dev from 1975

TRAIL Hugh MB ChB 1923
consult. chest phys hosp man. comm mid Glam area from 1948; resid Radyr Cardiff

TRAIL John Downie MB ChB 1931 DPH 1933
consult. chest phys N'cle-u-Tyne RHB 1963–70; retd; resid Washington Tyne & Wear

TRAIL or Fraser, Leslie Mitchell MA 1911
resid Belf

TRAIL or Cumming, Mabel MA 1933

TRAIL Mary MA 1926
head Fraserburgh inf s 1964–69; retd

TRAIL or Thomson, Mary Moir (Lady) MA 1912
d Lond 12.1.69 *AUR* XLIII 209

TRAIL Richard Robertson *MA 1919 *MB ChB 1923 *MD 1925
d Lond 15.6.71 *AUR* XLIV 317

TRAIL Stephen Galt *MB ChB 1910
no longer on GC reg

TRAIL William *MA 1928
d Edin 5.9.73 *AUR* XLV 320

TRANTOR Alexander William Grant BSc(eng) 1934
FIME 1943
dir/gen man. BP refinery (Kent) 1960–68; dir: Cammell Laird shipbuilders Birkenhead from 1971, Oil Refinery Serv Internat Lond from 1972, Gas & Oil Acreage Lond from 1973, oil consult. to Royal Bank of Scot. Edin from 1973

TREACHER William John Floyd MA 1932 MB ChB 1937
d Pinner Middx 26.2.74

TRETHOWAN Henry Markham MB ChB 1929

TRIBE Derek Edward PhD 1949
D Agr Sci(Melb) 1966 OBE 1977
univ Melb Aust: prof anim nutrit from 1966; member Aust comm on advanced educ 1970–77

TRINGHAM Robert MB ChB 1944
g p Bedford from 1965
m(2) Bedford 21.2.70 Isabel J. H. Colegate d of Ralph C. Norwich

TROTTER Robert Maxwell MB ChB 1894
no longer on GC reg

TROUP Arthur David MA 1925 LLB 1927
d 17.8.73

TROUP or Russell, Doris Isa MA 1930
JP Castle Eden and Peterlee Durh 1961
chmn juvenile court 1971–73, dep chmn of bench from 1971

TROUP or Patterson, Isobel Robertson Stewart MB ChB 1949
m o Hants from 1966

TROUP James Bannerman MB ChB 1951
Dipl. Amer Board Orthop Surg 1963
Fell. Amer Acad Orthop Surg 1964
consult. orthop surg Winchester mem hosp Virginia USA from 1961

TROUP or Jockel, Jean Davidson MB ChB 1949
g p Tawa NZ from 1965

TROUP Margaret MacDonald BSc 1921
d St Abbs 12.11.73

TROUP Robert George MB ChB 1949
MRCGP 1965 FRCGP 1975
g p Hornchurch Essex 1956–77; reg m o DHSS from 1977

TROUP Robert Jamieson MA 1914
no longer on GC reg

TROUP or Connon, Sylvia Helen Rose *MA 1948 Dip Ed 1952
resid Cults Aber

TROUP William Alexander MA 1919
d Glasg 18.3.77

TULLOCH Alexander Guthrie MA 1916
no longer on GC reg

TULLOCH Alistair John MB ChB 1950 MD 1976
FRCGP 1975
g p Bicester Oxon from 1963; part-time res asst unit of clin epidemiology regius dept med univ of Oxford from 1969
m Birm 26.11.66 Christine Goffe BA(Nott) med soc worker d of Cyril G. Birm

TULLOCH Hector Munro BSc(agr) 1942

TULLOCH Lawrence Gardner MB ChB 1938 MD 1950
d Astley nr Manchester 4.1.65 *AUR* XLI 60

TULLOCH or Dixon, Margaret Beatrice *MA 1912
d Lerwick 11.10.74

TULLOCH or Macleod, Mary Ann MA 1923
teacher Lochmaddy p s N Uist 1957–62; retd; resid Inv

TULLOCH Mary Elizabeth MA 1945

TULLOCH Mary Gardner *MA 1931

TULLOCH or Mackay, Nina June MA 1954
res asst dept psych Strath 1973–74; res asst dept psych Aberd 1974–75; teacher adult ment h'capped Aber from 1976

TULLOCH Robert Grant BSc 1941 *1947
d 9.12.72 *AUR* XLV 228

TULLOCH William *BSc 1945
on staff inst of geol sc Edin (formerly geol surv of Gt Br) from 1945

TULLOCH William James MA 1955 Dip Ed 1956
dep head p s Montrose acad 1962–70; head East p s Montrose 1970–76, N Links p s 1976–77, Borrowfield p s from 1977

TURNBULL Alexander Cuthbert MB ChB 1947 *MD 1966
FRCOG 1966 Thursfield award Aberd 1966
MA(Oxon) 1973
sen lect obst/gyn Aberd and consult. NE reg hosp board 1961–66; prof obst/gyn Welsh nat s of med Cardiff 1966–73; Nuffield prof obst/gyn Oxford from 1973; fell. Oriel coll Oxford from 1973

TURNBULL George Harley *MA 1950 MEd 1958
PhD(Strath) 1970
sen lect educ psych Aber coll of educ 1967–75; head psych dept Craigie coll of educ Ayr from 1975

TURNBULL Graham Dudgeon MA 1952

TURNBULL James *MEd 1946
d 6.5.67

TURNBULL or Forsyth, Prudence Isobel MA 1943

TURNER Adam Annand MB ChB 1913 MD 1926
d 7.1.64 *AUR* XL 398

TURNER Alexander *MA 1955
March Group (Spain) Lond: teaboy 1957–58, cashier 1958–59, chief cashier 1959–61, comp secy 1961–64, dir from 1964
m New Barnet 17.8.63 Ann Wilkin mus

TURNER Alistair Glass MB ChB 1951
d Lond 11.3.69 *AUR* XLIII 218

TURNER Isabella Coutts MA 1955

TURNER or Donald, Louise *MA 1923 LLB 1972
Arundel s Salisbury Rhodesia: dep head 1962–64, head 1964–68; retd; edit. vol IV *Roll of Graduates* until her death
d Montrose 21.12.80 *AUR* XLIX 136

TURNER or Wright, Margaret Elizabeth MA 1930
resid New Elgin
husb *d* 2.7.71

TURNER William Tracey EdB 1947 MEd 1966
MBE 1970
teacher: maths/sc St Columba's h s Fife 1940–45, handicapped ch Frederick St s Aber 1945–47; educ psych Cumberland 1947–49; organis off. Lancs c c 1949–64; asst educ off. Lancs 1964–72; retd; resid Clayton-le-Woods nr Chorley

TURPIE John Lawson *MA 1951

TWEDDELL William MB ChB 1924
retd; resid Clent Worcs

TWEDDLE or Main, Margaret Fimister **MB ChB 1949**
JP 1976
part time m o h Nott from 1959

TWORT or Raffan, Jean Crampton **MB ChB 1939**
part time med asst diabetic dept ARI from 1962
d Aber 1.9.75 *AUR* XLVI 325

TWORT Reginald Frank **MB ChB 1908**
d 9.2.69 *AUR* XLIII 208

TWORT Reginald Joseph **MB ChB 1936 ᶜMD 1944**
d Nott 16.6.71 *AUR* XLIV 321

TYTLER Peter **MB ChB 1940**
d Lerwick 28.12.68 *AUR* XLIII 217

URE Allan McCulloch **PhD 1954**
prin scient off. Macaulay inst Aber from 1961

URE James Smith **BSc(agr) 1950**

URQUHART Angus Munro ***MA 1899**
no longer on GC reg

URQUHART or Russell, Cecilia Valentine **MB ChB 1942 ᶜMD 1946**
part-time m o mat./ch welfare N'cle-u-Tyne 1958–72

URQUHART Helen Edith **MA 1925**
nurs trg and apptments 1951–71; retd; resid Beauly

URQUHART Ian Alexander **MA 1925**
teacher: 1st asst Victoria s Falkirk, head Buchlyvie s 1956–63; retd
d Falkirk 30.12.72

URQUHART John **MA 1951**

URQUHART or Taylor, Joy Munro ***MA 1946**
teacher various schools till 1964; Lady Spencer-Churchill coll of educ Wheatley Oxford: lect 1964–71, head of educ dept from 1971; visiting lect Central Michigan univ USA summer 1975; dean fac educ stud. Oxford polytech from 1978

URQUHART or Blackman, Margaret McRobb **MB ChB 1946**
s c m o Maidstone health dist. from 1972
marr diss 1968

URQUHART Margery **BSc(agr) 1935**
OBE 1977
dir soc work Aberdeensh/Kincardine 1969–75; dep dir soc work Grampian reg 1975–76, acting dir 1976–77; retd

URQUHART Robert William (Sir) **MA 1920 LLD 1954**
CMG 1944 KBE 1950
consul FO Lond 1938–39; insp gen consular establishments; prin off. min of home security Bristol 1940–42; consul gen Tabriz Iran 1942–43, New Orleans USA 1943–44; insp gen worldwide 1945–47; minister plenipotentiary Washington USA 1947–48; consul gen Shanghai China 1948–51; amb Caracas Venezuela 1951–55; retd; chmn Crofters' Commission Inv 1955–63; resid Edin
wife *d* 25.1.75
m(2) Edin 15.10.77 Jane Gibson MA 1921 *qv*

URQUHART William Spence ***MA 1897 DLitt 1921 DD 1930**
d Torphins 16.7.64 *AUR* XL 394

UYSAL Ahmet Edip **MA 1948**
Ankara univ Turkey: assoc prof Engl 1957–65, prof Engl 1965 and from 1968; visiting prof: Engl dept univ of Cologne W Ger 1963–64, Engl dept Texas tech univ Lubbock, Texas USA 1966–68; Carnegie fell. School of Scottish Studies Edin univ 1977–78; prof Engl dept Ankara univ from 1978
m Ankara 17.12.52 Melek Genç d of Nuri G. Iskenderun Turkey

VALENTINE Alfred Buyers ***MA 1919**
d Guildford 21.2.70 *AUR* XLIII 444

VALENTINE Edward Jordan **MB ChB 1941**
Jamaica: sen m o King George V sanatorium 1960–69, prin m o M o H 1969–73; retd; consult. phys King George V sanatorium from 1973

VALENTINE Gilbert Enos **MA 1910 MB ChB 1914**
private pract Kingston Jamaica 1931–78; retd

VALENTINE Henry William ***MA 1931**
retd 1967; resid Haddington

VALENTINE Irene Mary Findlay **MA 1930**
retd 1971; resid Aber

VALENTINE John Cheyne **BSc(agr) 1954**

VALENTINE or Mackintosh, Kate Margaret **MA 1910**
no longer on GC reg

VALENTINE Leslie MacKenzie ***BSc 1946 PhD 1949**
dir res Berger Jenson & Nicholson Lond from 1968
marr diss 1972
m(2) Lond 19.8.72 Nina Flatto BSc(Lond) civ serv

VALENTINE Margaret Hunter Strachan **MA 1918**
d Lond 7.11.62 *AUR* XL 85

VALENTINE Max Gordon **MB ChB 1940 MD 1946**
MRCPsych 1971 FRCPsych 1971
consult. psychiat Bristol from 1959

VALENTINE May Fleming **MA 1925**
teacher: Portessie p s 1955–60, Buckie h p s 1960–66; retd

VAN BLOMMESTEIN Jack Henry Greite **MB ChB 1922**
member pneumonocosis compensation board

Johannesburg 1962–72; part-time med consult. western platinum mines Marikana S Af from 1972
d Transvaal S Af 9.7.78

VAN DER MÉRWE or Westhuysen, Katherina Francisia Elizabeth MB ChB 1921

VARTY Isaac William BSc(for) 1950 PhD 1954

VASS John MA 1937 BD 1940
d Aber 21.10.74 *AUR* XLVI 240

VENTERS Robert Sharpe MB ChB 1928
d Carlisle –.6.73 *AUR* XLV 320

VERE Raymond Andrew BSc 1951
FInstPet 1973
Esso res centre Abingdon Oxon: scient 1964–67, prin scient from 1967

VERGNANO or Gambi, Ornella PhD 1952
resid Firenze, Italy

VLASTO or Higham, Patience Jane Marietta *MA 1947
resid York

WADDELL Annie Fleck *MA 1924
d 9.2.75

WADDELL Robert Lindsay BSc(agr) 1950

WADDINGTON William George MA 1901
no longer on GC reg

WADE Alan Hugh MB ChB 1953

WAGREL Martin James *BSc(eng) 1953
BP: proj eng Venice/Aden 1960–62; dev eng distrib Lond 1962–66; dev eng marketing: Milan 1966–70, Lond from 1970
m(1) Venice 1961 Patricia E. Morgan; marr diss 1967 (2) Lond 1967 April B. Coats

WAINWRIGHT Richard William MA 1947
d 16.12.63

WAITER or Tulloch, Margaret Mary MA 1955
teacher: St Cyrus p s 1956–60, North Links p s Montrose 1960–64; part-time remed Montrose dist from 1973

WALKER or Taylor, Agnes MA 1943

WALKER or Thomson, Agnes Anne MA 1926
teacher p s Mintlaw 1961–71; retd; resid Longside

WALKER Alaster Charles Andrew BSc(for) 1950
d Hobart Tasmania 19.4.77

WALKER Alexander MA 1940

WALKER Alexander Adam *MA 1925
d Aber 3.11.65 *AUR* XLII 86

WALKER Alexander Camfield Slessor MA 1937
head Tyrie p s 1963–72; dep head Fraserburgh cent s from 1972

WALKER Alexander Donald *BSc 1953
prin scient off. pedology dept Macaulay Inst for soil res Aber from 1958
m Aber 29.6.62 Eleanor W. Booth

WALKER Alexander Lumsden MA 1928 BD 1932
d 27.10.63

WALKER Alexander Mackenzie *MA 1930

WALKER or Donald, Amy Stewart *MA 1921
resid Aber
husb *d* 8.7.55

WALKER Andrew MA 1932 LLB 1934 MB ChB 1942
g p Aber; retd
m Woking 25.9.54 Anne C. Paget physioth d of Lancelot P. Beattock

WALKER or Milne, Ann MA 1940
resid Whitehills

WALKER Charles Herbert MB ChB 1951 MD 1958
g p Liverpool from 1952

WALKER Charles William MA 1915 *MB ChB 1924 *MD 1926
retd 1964; resid Hereford

WALKER Cyril George MB ChB 1927 MD 1933
g p Oxted 1933–64; retd; resid Bexhill
d 24.10.78 *AUR* XLVIII 229

WALKER Doris *MA 1918
no longer on GC reg

WALKER Dorothy June MA 1952
teacher p s Culter from 1964; exchange BC Canada 1967–68

WALKER Douglas (Bremner) MA 1951

WALKER Douglas Ewen MB ChB 1943 DPH 1948
s m o reg med off. SHHD Edin from 1975

WALKER Douglas Stewart MA 1921 LLB 1923
d Hereford 18.6.63 *AUR* XL 203

WALKER or Wray, Edith MA 1925
resid Aber
d Aber 3.9.80

WALKER or Tawse, Edith Margaret Helen MA 1929

WALKER or Murphy, Elizabeth MA 1933
resid Durris

WALKER Elsie Findlay MA 1901
d 26.8.67 *AUR* XLII 178

WALKER Frances BCom 1935
retd 1972; resid Finzean

WALKER George Forbes *BSc 1938 PhD 1948 DSc 1960
d Melbourne 17.2.70 *AUR* XLIII 446

WALKER or Mennie, Gertrude Milne MA 1942
d Aber 5.9.77

WALKER Hector MacDonald MB ChB 1925
d Manchester 21.8.69 *AUR* XLIII 330

WALKER or Hayman, Helenor Rona MA 1949

WALKER Horace *MA 1932 BD 1935 DD 1967
OBE 1978
retd 1977; resid Edin

WALKER Isabella MA 1922
retd 1966; resid Cults Aber

WALKER or Walker, Isobel Helen MA 1925
resid Hereford

WALKER James MB ChB 1938
DADMS
RAMC Middle East/Italy 1940–47; g p Manchester from 1947
m Aber 4.6.41 Roberta G. Bain d of Alexander T. B., Aber

WALKER James MA 1945
PhD(Lond) 1962
scient MRC Univ Coll Lond 1947–66; sen lect epidemiology/preventive med Glas 1966–70; sen prin psych civ serv Lond from 1970
m Lond 30.12.65 Nesta J. Majeran

WALKER James Adam *MA 1950 *MEd 1955
Dollar acad: prin maths 1964–73, asst rector from 1973

WALKER James Frederick *MA 1922
d Aber 19.1.77 *AUR* XLVII 212

WALKER James Strachan MB ChB 1922 DPH 1933 MD 1937
d Aber 21.10.70 *AUR* XLIV 110

WALKER John Davidson MA 1898
no longer on GC reg

WALKER John Leiper *BSc 1952

WALKER or Simpson, Kathleen Hazel *MA 1955 Dip Ed 1956
resid Dalgety Bay by Dunfermline

WALKER or Newlands, Margaret Jessie MB ChB 1938

WALKER or Mortimer, Margaret June BSc 1952

WALKER Mary Jean *MA 1917
d Edin 15.9.76 *AUR* XLVII 103

WALKER Norman John Jamieson MA 1905 *BL 1908 LLB 1910
d 14.3.67 *AUR* XLII 178

WALKER Patricia May MA 1952
no longer on GC reg

WALKER Patrick MA 1915
d Port Elphinstone Inverurie –.8.79 *AUR* XLVIII 350

WALKER Peter Gordon PhD 1952
prof chem path. inst orthop Lond

WALKER Ralph Spence *MA 1928
emeritus prof McG 1970; resid Haslingfield Camb

WALKER Richard Jones MB ChB 1937
d Aber 5.1.72 *AUR* XLIV 433

WALKER Robert Jackson *MA 1925
d 16.4.71

WALKER Ronald Powlett *MA 1931 *MB ChB 1936
Brit Red Cross Badge of Honour
g p Tettenhall Wolverhampton from 1939; area m o Brit Red Cross Soc

WALKER Sheila Mair MA 1954
teacher Engl Torry acad Aber from 1960

WALKER Sidney James Macara MB ChB 1942
clin div indust hyg Ont Canada from 1952

WALKER William Alexander BCom 1923

WALKER William Alexander MB ChB 1942
g p Nelson NZ 1958–78; sen m o Ngawhatu psychiat hosp Nelson from 1978

WALKER William Lumsden MB ChB 1941 DPH 1947 MD 1963
FRCPsych 1972
consult. ch psychiat United Brist hosps/Avon AHA (ch/fam guid serv) from 1966; also clin lect ment health Brist from 1970; visiting consult. Kingswood spec unit Bristol from 1964

WALKER William Wood *MB ChB 1924
g p Lee 1928–72; Treasury m o Lond 1929–72; clin asst Gyre-Miller gen hosp 1928–71; retd

WALLACE Annabella *MA 1926
no longer on GC reg

WALLACE Arthur Edward MA 1922
retd 1968; resid Largs
d 3.1.80

WALLACE or Andersz, Evaline Euphemia Baxter MA 1944
teacher Port Elphinstone Inverurie from 1952

WALLACE Gordon Profeit MA 1934 MB ChB 1939
prin m o areas 3/5 Maidstone Kent 1953–74; retd; part time clin m o Kent from 1974

WALLACE James Gilbert MA 1924 LLB 1925
d Blairs Aber 26.12.72 *AUR* XLV 225

WALLACE James Lamb BSc 1952
Aber: prin teacher maths/sc Middle s 1967–69, prin sc Frederick St s 1969–71; prin maths Old Aber s 1971–73, year master Linksfield acad 1973–75; asst head Linksfield acad from 1975

WALLACE or Murray, Janet Keith *MA 1931
d Tranent 29.11.70 *AUR* XLIV 212

WALLACE Kenneth Macdonald BSc(for) 1955

WALLACE or Cruickshank, Mary Elizabeth MA 1954
teacher Hull from 1965
m Aber 3.8.57 Stanley Cruickshank MB ChB 1963 *qv*

WALLACE Patrick Crawford MB ChB 1933
g p Middleton-on-Sea Sussex from 1948

WALLACE Robert Strachan *MA 1904 LLD 1928
d Canberra 5.9.61 *AUR* XXXIX 271

WALLACE William MA 1931
d –.6.63

WALLER Patricia May MA 1952
asst edit. Thos Nelson & Sons publ (overseas dept) Edin 1959–62
m Edin 23.9.61 Alexander Heward arch. s of Frederick W. H. Milngavie

WALTERS Louis George MB ChB 1927 MD 1936
d Natal 12.4.75 *AUR* XLVI 323

WALTON Kenneth PhD 1951
d Aber 2.1.79 *AUR* XLVIII 122

WANNOP Arthur Robson BSc(agr) 1922
d Edin 11.9.72 *AUR* XLV 126

WARDLE Philip Arthur *BSc(for) 1955
HM for, comm: Forest of Dean 1958–61, Alice Holt Lodge Farnham 1961–71; FAO UN Yugoslavia/Surinam/Rome from 1971

WARE James McWilliam BSc(agr) 1932

WARES Alastair Heddle *BSc 1949

WARES or Wilson, Barbara Calder Sutherland MA 1940

WARING Horace DSc 1939
Clarke medallist Royal Soc of NSW 1952; hon DSc univ of W Aust; Britannica gold medal for sc 1970
vice-pres Aust acad of sc 1958–59; retd 1975; emeritus prof univ W Aust
d W Aust 9.8.80

WARK or Reid, Dorothy Elizabeth *MA 1921
d 1.2.71

WARK James Miller BSc(agr) 1950

WARNER Adrian Charles Irving PhD 1955

WARRACK George Clark BSc(for) 1940
MF(Michigan) 1960 FIFor(GB)
BC for. serv Victoria BC Canada: res progr superv 1960–71, dir res div from 1971

WARRACK John MB ChB 1932 DPH 1939
retd 1971; resid Ashley Heath Shropsh

WARRACK John Hyslop MB ChB 1947
g p Derby from 1953

WARREN or Beattie, Lucy MA 1941
occasional teaching posts Elgin acad 1942–45, St John the Evangelist s Manchester 1970–73

WARREN Ronald Wilfred BSc(agr) 1949

WARREN Thomas *EdB 1951
d 19.10.71

WARREN Winifred Joyce MA 1923 BSc 1925
chief chem Unigate Creamery Hemyock Devon 1930–65; retd; resid Church Stretton Salop

WATERS Margaret Fraser MA 1941
resid Aber

WATERS or Waters, Mina Hunter MA 1910
d Edin 11.2.67 *AUR* XLII 180

WATERS Russell McFarlane BSc(for) 1951
d 8.12.69

WATKINS David Fraser MA 1938
Aber: head Seaton p s 1965–67, Cornhill p s from 1967; retd 1980

WATKINS Richard Dawson PhD 1954
MIEA 1956
sen lect civ eng Sydney univ Aust from 1956

WATKINS Sidney Maurice Kynoch MB ChB 1937
RAMC 1940–45; house surg Royal hosp Chesterfield 1949; g p Dronfield 1950–73; retd; resid Bournemouth
m Dronfield 24.5.40 Isbel R. Fowler SRCN d of George H. F. BAOR Cologne

WATLER Donald Crosbie MB ChB 1949
MRCPath 1964 FRCPath 1969 MMASC 1970 FRCPE 1972
Jamaica govt med serv Kingston: consult. path. 1960–64, dir laboratory serv from 1964

WATSON Adam *BSc 1952 PhD 1956 DSc 1967
FRSE 1971
sen scient off. Aberd 1960–71, sen prin scient off. (spec merit in res) ITE Banchory from 1971

WATSON Alexander Hepburn MA 1949
BA(Lond) 1970
Inverurie acad: spec asst 1959–73, asst prin Engl from 1973

WATSON Alexander James ***MB ChB 1947 cMD 1960**
FRCPath 1973
lect path. Glas 1954–61; sen lect path N'cle 1961–70, reader from 1970

WATSON Alexander Lindsay BSc(eng) 1948
CEng MIEE 1971 Cert Ed 1974
GEC Coventry: proj leader on Admiralty receiving equipment 1955–64; proj leader mobile radio receiving eqpment 1964–68; group leader: VHF mobile radio/UHF mobile radio 1968–71; lect telecommun sect Coventry tech coll from 1971
m Coventry 29.5.66 Doreen A. Berry teacher d of Robert B. Worsley Manc

WATSON Alexander McKay Young MA 1928
d Huntly 15.4.72 *AUR* XLIV 432

WATSON Alexander William MA 1951
teacher maths Montrose acad 1961–72; prin guid Keith g s from 1972

WATSON or Husband, Alice Raeburn BSc 1929
teacher: Invsh 1930–32, sc Castlebay Is of Barra 1932–34, S Harris/S Uist 1934–35; sc tech h s Inv 1940–43, biol Durh/N'cle-u-Tyne 1943–51; educ off. Ibadan/Zaria Nigeria 1951–59; lect St Matthias coll of educ Brist 1960–72; retd; resid Bristol
m Inv 20.8.35 William A. Husband BCom(Durh) confid clerk/univ regist s of George H. N'cle-u-Tyne

WATSON Andrew Forbes *MA 1953
asst solic: Eastbourne corp 1959–61, Ipswich corp 1961–63; sen asst solic Ilford corp 1963–65; asst town clerk Kingston-u-Thames 1965–67; dep town clerk Grimsby 1967–70, Plymouth 1970–74, chief exec/town clerk from 1974
m Northwood Middx 13.4.63 Penelope J. Archer housemother maladjusted ch d of Herbert W. A. OBE Northwood

WATSON Angelica MA 1942
sen lect soc work Stir from 1972

WATSON or Gray, Annabella MA 1915

WATSON Arthur Forbes MB ChB 1942
g p Sinoia Rhodesia from 1960

WATSON Bessie Urquhart MA 1935
retd 1973; resid Aber

WATSON or Orchiston, Charlotte Barbour MA 1917
d NZ 1969

WATSON Christina Cruickshank MA 1933
d Campbeltown 28.11.78

WATSON Constance Mary Anne *MA 1924
d 7.12.81

WATSON Daniel Stewart BSc(eng) 1932 *1933
CB 1961
Admiralty: chief scient off. 1961–68; head royal naval scient serv M o D 1968–72; retd; resid Churt Farnham

WATSON David Brown MA 1928 MB ChB 1932
d 22.2.66 *AUR* XLI 248

WATSON David John BSc 1951
teacher: sc Kelso h s 1961–70, prin biol from 1970

WATSON or Whalen, Elizabeth Law MB ChB 1947
resid Shrewsbury New Jersey USA

WATSON or Adam, Elizabeth Margaret MA 1915

WATSON George Alexander BSc 1932
retd 1974; resid Luthermuir Laurencekirk

WATSON Gladys Nellie *MB ChB 1922 DPH 1924
MRCGP 1953
g p Warley from 1947

WATSON Henry MA 1948

WATSON Henry Gavin BSc(agr) 1953

WATSON Herbert Louis BSc 1911
no longer on GC reg

WATSON Hugh Glass MB ChB 1923
d Bakewell 9.2.71 *AUR* XLIV 211 & 320

WATSON James MA 1891
d Cults Aber 16.1.63 *AUR* XL 73

WATSON James BSc 1932 MA 1933
retd 1970; resid Kirriemuir

WATSON James BSc 1944 *1949
phys Alex Pirie & Sons Stoneywood 1953–58; self-employed Northampton 1958–69; phys Alex Cowan & Sons Penicuik 1969–73; teacher Stevenson coll of f e Edin 1973–74; lect Telford coll f e Edin from 1974

WATSON James Alexander *MA 1912
d 21.6.75 *AUR* XLVI 320

WATSON James Henderson BSc(eng) 1945
FIEE 1970
St Helens Lancs: works man. Fibreglass 1961–64, works man. Pilkington Bros 1964–71, chief eng from 1973

WATSON James Innes MA 1912 MB ChB 1917
d Kelso 22.9.70 *AUR* XLIV 109

WATSON or Robson, Jane (Jean) Frances MA 1919
d Aber 15.3.45

WATSON or Pickup, Jean Patricia MB ChB 1951
cytologist Royal North Shore hosp Sydney Aust from 1964

WATSON John MB ChB 1938
g p Perth W Aust from 1950

WATSON John *BSc 1952
assoc prof maths Rensselaer polytech inst USA 1965–66; lect maths univ of E Anglia from 1966

WATSON John MA 1953
no longer on GC reg

WATSON John Alexander *MA 1938 LLB 1947
resid Ardrishaig

WATSON John Scott MB ChB 1936
d Aber 28.9.65

WATSON or Stewart, Kathleen Elizabeth *MA 1944

WATSON Kenneth Charles MB ChB 1947 ᶜMD 1955
FRCPath 1968 MRCPE 1972
assoc prof microbiol univ of Natal S Af 1964–68, prof 1968–69; consult. microbiol Western gen hosp Edin from 1969
m Canterbury Kent 8.5.59 Alys M. Gardener physioth d of Edward G. A. G. MA(Cantab) Reculver

WATSON Louisa Margaret *MA 1922
no longer on GC reg

WATSON Luke Methuen MB ChB 1929

WATSON or Whiteley, Margaret Elsie MA 1941
resid Otley

WATSON or Carmichael, Margaret Stewart MB ChB 1936
resid Derby

WATSON Mearns Bruce *BSc 1933 PhD 1936
FSAScot 1972
dep dir RGIT Aber 1968–71; retd

WATSON Murray James Alexander MB ChB 1950
d Maidenhead 14.1.77 *AUR* XLVII 287

WATSON or Rae, Norma Reid MA 1950
resid Aber

WATSON Pauline Bertha MA 1919
no longer on GC reg

WATSON Stanley Wilson MB ChB 1941
d 24.12.72

WATSON Thomas Yirrell BSc(agr) 1929

WATSON Vincent Murray McAdam MB ChB 1921
d Aber 6.12.62 *AUR* XL 85

WATSON or Wilson or Axford, Violet Irene MB ChB 1945

WATSON William Ferguson *BSc 1944 PhD 1947 DSc 1952
CBE 1978
dir rubber and plastic res assoc Shrewsbury 1959–76; dir Allied Polymer Group 1976–78; dir Portex Hythe Kent

WATSON William Hay *MA 1929 DD 1964
secy/educ secy Christian council (Nyasaland) Malawi 1962–64; C of S min: asst St Machar's cath Old Aber 1964–65, St Bride's ch Callander 1965–70; team min City presb ch Salisbury Rhodesia from 1970

WATSON William Hugh BSc(agr) 1954

WATSON William Mair MA 1934

WATSON William Norman BCom 1931

WATT Adam Niddrie Shirreffs MB ChB 1925
d 18.5.66

WATT Adrian Gray MA 1935
C of S min: Baillieston Old ch 1941–48, St Michael's par ch Edin 1948–80; part-time chap. HM prison Edin from 1973
wife *d* 4.10.78

WATT Aileen *MA 1955 Dip Ed 1956
farm. Aberlour 1961–65; also teacher spec asst Engl Nairn acad 1965–69; ptnr farm. Aberlour from 1969
m Aberlour 5.7.69 James Garrow farm. s of George W. G. Aberlour

WATT Alan Crombie Robertson *MA 1946 LLB 1949
ptnr Gray & Kellas advoc Aber 1951–72; town clerk Ballater 1952–71; a chmn indust tribunals (Scot.) from 1972

WATT Alexander MB ChB 1902 DPH 1904 MA 1904
no longer on GC reg

WATT Alexander MB ChB 1935
DPM 1953 MRCPsych 1973
psychiat Worthing from 1960

WATT Alexander James Morrison *MA 1932
teacher maths/phys Gordon s Huntly 1937–52; spec asst maths Waid acad Anstruther 1952–72; retd; resid Huntly
m Huntly 17.7.39 Jean Robertson nurse d of John W. R. Huntly

WATT Alexander John Dip Agr 1915 BSc(agr) 1919
d Aber 6.10.66 *AUR* XLII 85

WATT Alexander Stuart MA 1913 BSc(agr) 1913
M Brit Soc Soil Sc 1948 M Bot Soc Brit Isles 1952 FRS 1957 Hon M Brit Ecol Soc 1961 Hon F For. Soc(GB) 1965 Gold Medal Linnean Soc 1975
lect for. bot Cantab 1934–59; visiting lect Melb Aust 1950–51; visiting lect Colorado USA 1963; visiting prof Khartoum Sudan 1965–66

WATT Alexander William Owen BSc(agr) 1951
MBE
prin insp dept of agr for Scot. NE area from 1979

WATT Alice (Alison) Jean MA 1941
admin off. secretariat ITA/IBA Lond from 1963

WATT Alice Mabel MB ChB 1922 DPH 1923
retd 1961; resid Boston Lincs

WATT Andrew Philip BSc(agr) 1955
farm. Maud from 1958

WATT Annetta Mary MA 1951

WATT or Godsman, Annie Isabella *MA 1922
head Fisherie p s Aberdeensh 1940–60; retd; resid Aber
husb *d* Aber 1973
d Aber 9.1.79

WATT Archibald MA 1923 DD 1959
moderator Gen Assembly of C of S 1965–66; retd 1969; resid Aber
d Aber 1.1.81 *AUR* XLIX 137

WATT Archibald *MA 1936 MEd 1938
JP 1970 FSAScot 1970 FEIS 1976
prin Engl/dep rector Mackie acad Stonehaven 1962–72, dep rector 1972–77; retd
m Edzell 21.12.64 Elizabeth P. White teacher d of Arthur J. W. BA(Lond) Thame Oxon

WATT Arthur Stewart MA 1910 LLB 1911
no longer on GC reg

WATT Catherine Ann MA 1937
teacher: Causewayend p s Aber 1940–50, Powis s s Aber 1951–76; retd
m Aber 24.7.43 Eric C. Wilson driver s of Alexander W. Aber

WATT Colin John George BSc(eng) 1953

WATT David Brand MB ChB 1947
no longer on GC reg

WATT David Scott MA 1939 *BSc 1947
Royal Dutch Shell Group: gen man. Shell BP & Todd oil serv Wellington NZ 1960–66, staff assignment Shell Lond 1967–68, exploration & prod. dir A/S Norske Shell Stavanger Norway 1968–74; retd; resid Pennan

WATT Donald Elmslie Robertson *MA 1950
FRHistS 1960
sen lect mediaeval hist St And 1965–77, prof from 1977, visiting prof mediaeval hist Columbia univ NY USA 1966–67

WATT or Saunders, Dorothy Margaret MA 1950
teacher Minishant Ayrsh 1963–73; head Girvan nursery s from 1974

WATT or Blackhall, Edith MA 1916
HM off. of works/WRAF; demob 1919
resid Lordswood S'ton

WATT Edward William Murray *MA 1935
secy/treas Inv hosp board of man. 1951–74; dist gen admin Highland health board 1974–78; retd
d Inv 20.11.80 *AUR* XLIX 69

WATT or Thomson, Elizabeth Garrow MA 1946
teacher maths Buckie h s from 1967

WATT or Klose, Elizabeth Mary MA 1948

WATT or McNab, Elizabeth Mowat *MA 1901
no longer on GC reg

WATT Francis BSc 1933
dep head Tayport s s 1955–67; retd; resid Newport-on-Tay

WATT George Andrew BSc(eng) 1948

WATT George Beattie MA 1912
d Johannesburg 19.3.69 *AUR* XLIII 210

WATT George Dewar BSc(eng) 1955
MICE 1963 MIWE 1964 FIWES 1977
asst eng Blyth & Blyth consult. eng Inv 1961–62; sen eng Aber c c water dept Aber 1962–68; group leader new works NE Scot. water board Aber 1968–75; asst dir resource plan. dept of water services Grampian reg c 1975–76, dep dir 1976–78, sen dep dir from 1978

WATT George Esson *MA 1951
teacher Engl Wemyss s s 1960–63; dep head Mountfleurie p s Leven 1964–67; head Arncroach p s by Pittenweem from 1968

WATT George Fordyce *MA 1924 BSc 1924
no longer on GC reg

WATT or Morrison, Gladys Petrie MA 1922
d Brighton 17.10.67

WATT Gordon BSc(agr) 1930
d 31.5.74

WATT Gordon Imray BSc(eng) 1951

WATT Gordon Lorimer MB ChB 1949
g p Alford from 1961

WATT Harold Murray Robertson *MA 1942
JP
man. dir Aber univ press from 1958; Aberd: member univ court from 1970, vice-convener bus. comm of General Council from 1971

WATT or Inkster, Helen Milne *MA 1945
resid Gosforth N'cle-u-Tyne
d N'cle-u-Tyne 20.7.81

WATT Ian Allan *MA 1950

WATT Ian Gordon *BSc 1953

WATT Ian Mackenzie BSc(eng) 1945

WATT Ian Stuart BSc(for) 1948
for. comm: dist off. Perth 1955–70, Llandovery S Wales from 1970

WATT or Greig, Irene Alice Ogilvie MA 1924
d Aber 2.3.69 *AUR* XLIII 214

WATT or Ogston, Iris Campbell MA 1941
resid Aber

WATT James MB ChB 1945 *MD 1956
MRCPath 1965 FRCPath 1977
sen lect dept path. Liv from 1965

WATT James BSc(eng) 1948 *1949

WATT James Alexander MA 1936
sen tut. and dept head London comp schools 1960–77; retd

WATT James Mackenzie MA 1929
head Old Deer p s 1961–71; retd; resid Old Deer
d Fraserburgh 7.10.78 *AUR* XLVIII 104

WATT or Gauld, Jane MA 1927
no longer on GC reg

WATT or Taylor, Jane Runciman MA 1929
resid Aston Sheffield

WATT Jeannie Isobel MA 1926
no longer on GC reg

WATT or Gatt, Jeannie Slessor MA 1954

WATT John George Moncur MA 1942
secy Scot. Marriage Guid Council from 1964

WATT John Taylor MB ChB 1913
served in Merchant Navy during 1939–45 war
d Banchory 1.6.66 *AUR* XLI 338

WATT John Valentine MB ChB 1953
g p Erith Kent from 1958

WATT or Guthrie, Kathleen Milne MB ChB 1949
d Dun 21.6.74 *AUR* XLVI 111

WATT Leslie MB ChB 1940 ᶜMD 1947
phys i/c St Luke's clin and ven dis dept united Manc hosps/reg advis VD Manc RHB/lect in ven dis Manc univ from 1966

WATT or Davey, Lily Margaret MB ChB 1923
no longer on GC reg

WATT Margaret *MA 1910
d Banchory 9.1.80 *AUR* XLVIII 440

WATT or Wesley, Margaret Crichton BSc 1945
teacher: sc Aber tech coll 1961–68, maths Currie h s from 1971

WATT or Rhodes, Margaret Downie BSc 1945
resid Shipley

WATT or McBeath, Margaret Jessie MA 1939
teacher Banffsh 1940, Aberdeensh 1944, Aberdeensh 1963–68, Angus 1972; resid Letham

WATT Marjory Isabella Katherine MB ChB 1951
regist obst/gyn Craigtoun hosp St. And 1958–60; m o Aber publ health dept/Grampian health board from 1970; s c m o commun med dept S Grampian dist
m Kincardinesh 26.5.60 Ian B. Hamilton off. RAF/CA s of Thomas H.

WATT Mary MA 1925
no longer on GC reg

WATT or Cormack, Mary MA 1930
retd 1967; resid Findochty

WATT Mary Florence MA 1928
retd 1962; resid Aber
d Aber 19.12.78

WATT or Duncan, Mary Jessie MA 1952

WATT or Roelich, Mary Webster MA 1930
Dip Soc Sc(Lond) 1953
secy Red Cross depot Solihull Warks 1939–43; welf off. WLA Winchester 1943–45; teacher Ashford Middx 1959–75; retd
d 28.8.80

WATT Matilda MA 1920
no longer on GC reg

WATT or Loots, Moyra Helen MA 1952
teacher Harrytown h s Romiley 1969, remed Stockport 1970–71, St Paul's p s Hyde from 1972

WATT or Mutch, Myra MA 1914
d Aber 19.5.74

WATT Raymond Ian Gordon *MA 1939
lect: hist Kingsway coll for f e Lond 1948–66, hist/soc stud. Brixton coll for f e Lond 1966–67, hist/econ Princeton coll Lond from 1967; councillor Borough of Hornsey 1951–65
m Lond 22.3.63 Patricia A. Charlton med secy/lect comm subj d of Leonard F. C. Mevagissey

WATT Robert John McPherson BL 1952
teacher: Springhill p s Aber 1963–65, Flotta publ s 1965–74, Cornhill p s Aber 1974–80; retd

WATT Robert Strachan *MA 1955

WATT or Masson, Sandra Ryrie MA 1949
teacher: Invergowrie p s Angus 1964–66, Callander p s 1967–68, Doune p s Perthsh from 1968

WATT William *MA 1918
d Ellon 24.6.70 *AUR* XLIV 109

WATT William MB ChB 1942 DPH 1948
Canada: dir loc health serv Manitoba 1956–67, Alberta 1967–76; retd
wife *d* 1969

WATT William Alexander MB ChB 1946
g p Cheltenham from 1951

WATT William Andrew Fraser BSc 1951
FRSS 1970 MBCS 1973
head dept maths/sc coll of comm Aber from 1961

WATT William Gordon MB ChB 1908 DPH 1909
d Aber 12.5.76

WATT or Marshall, Williamina Margaret MA 1944
resid Newton Stewart

WATTIE Annie Kinnear MA 1919 *MB ChB 1922 DPH 1928
d Tynemouth 31.8.77

WATTIE James Alexander MA 1907
no longer on GC reg

WATTIE John Nicholson MB ChB 1947
g p Romsey Hants

WATTIE or Morgan or Cope, Katharine Betty McPherson *MA 1917
examiner Engl civ serv commissioners 1934–47; reviser Engl SED 1922–57; resid Lond

WATTIE Nora Isabel MB ChB 1921
OBE 1964
retd 1964; resid Glasg

WATTY Edward Irving MB ChB 1950
OBE 1973 DTM & H FRCP(C) F Coll Amer Path.
Dominica WI: dist m o 1951–63, govt path. from 1967
m Lond 26.12.55 Winifred P. Paul cyto tech d of Ninas P. USA

WAYMOUTH Charity PhD 1944
FAAAS 1966
USA: sen staff scient The Jackson Lab, Bar Harbor Maine from 1963, asst dir (trg) 1969–72; asst dir (res) 1976–77; assoc dir (scient affairs) from 1977; hon lect univ of Maine from 1964; Rose Morgan visiting prof univ Kansas 1971; pres Tissue Culture Assoc 1960–62; edit.-in-chief Tissue Culture Assoc 1968–75; member exec council Episc ch 1967–70; vice-chmn clergy deployment board Episc ch from 1970; chmn Episc ch comm on state of the church from 1976; member Faith & Order comm Nat Council of Churches USA 1970–73

WEBSTER Alexander BSc 1917
d Aber 21.11.68 *AUR* XLIII 80

WEBSTER Alexander MA 1947 LLB 1953
d Tornaveen Torphins 24.7.64 *AUR* XL 401

WEBSTER Alexander Urquhart MA 1906 MB ChB 1909
d 23.10.75 *AUR* XLVI 414

WEBSTER Annie Strachan *MA 1898
no longer on GC reg

WEBSTER Charles Urquhart *MB ChB 1950
MA(Oxon) 1970
surg tut. univ of Oxford from 1960; consult. surg United Oxford hosps from 1963

WEBSTER or Alexander, Dolores Frances MB ChB 1950
g p Smethwick W Midlands from 1958

WEBSTER Douglas James MA 1955
teacher Middle s Aber 1956
d Cults Aber 12.4.77

WEBSTER Douglas William Lawrence MA 1947

WEBSTER or Fleming, Frances Irene MA 1950
farm. from 1969; resid Bieldside Aber
husb *d* Aber 1969

WEBSTER Francis Lindsay MB ChB 1923
no longer on GC reg

WEBSTER Frances Milne MA 1952
teacher Ballater p s from 1962

WEBSTER Fred *MA 1938

WEBSTER George Waddell MB ChB 1953
g p Margate from 1958

WEBSTER Grace Alexandra Mary MB ChB 1947
DObstRCOG 1951 DPH(Lond) 1960 MFCM 1973
spec commun med (child health) Ealing, Hammersmith and Hounslow AHA from 1976

WEBSTER or Mackenzie, Helen Urquhart MA 1914
d East Grinstead 20.5.71 *AUR* XLIV 317

WEBSTER James MB ChB 1931 DPH 1933
retd 1968; resid N Berwick

WEBSTER or Robertson, Jessie Donald MA 1955

WEBSTER John William England MB ChB 1930
g p Malvern 1946–71; retd; resid Malvern

WEBSTER Maurice Holland MB ChB 1936 DPH 1938
FRSH 1971 MFCM(RCP) 1973 BL(Rhodesia) 1975 FFCM 1977
secy for health, dir gen med serv Rhodesia 1963–74; retd; lect law univ of Rhodesia from 1976

WEBSTER Michael Charles MA 1947

WEBSTER Peter MA 1906
d Cambusbarron Stirling –.5.61 *AUR* XXXIX 200

WEBSTER Robert MA 1903
no longer on GC reg

WEBSTER Ronald George *MA 1953

WEDDERBURN or Hughes, Christobel Mary MA 1943
resid Bangor

WEE Hiap Tock MB ChB 1920

WEINER Aaron Harry MB ChB 1934

WEIR Charles Wilson MB ChB 1912
d Leeds 11.6.62 *AUR* XXXIX 379

WEIR or MacQuoid, (Margaret) Florence Smith MA 1916
resid Turriff
d Portsoy 21.4.81

WEIR George LLB 1953

WEIR James Martin *MA 1953
prin teacher Russian Aber acad (Hazlehead acad) from 1965

WEIR John MA 1909
retd; resid Hamilton

WEIR John BSc(agr) 1950
teacher sc: Glenrothes 1961–66, Gordon s Huntly from 1966

WEIR John Gordon *MA 1945 MB ChB 1952 MD 1964
DPM 1960 MRCPsych 1971 FRCPsych 1976
Lond: sen regist St Mary's hosp 1960–63; consult. psychotherap St Bernard's hosp Southall 1963; consult. psychiat: Mildmay mission hosp from 1963, St Mary's hosp from 1968, Royal Masonic hosp from 1970, St Dunstan's from 1973

WEIR John Park MB ChB 1929
re-employed (war off.) FEMO combined serv recruiting centre Bristol 1959–70
d 17.5.79

WEIR Kathleen England MA 1946

WEIR Mackenzie Craigmile MA 1932
organis p educ Kirkcaldy 1968–74; retd; resid Selkirk

WEIR Robert *MA 1912
d Dun 5.2.62 *AUR* XXXIX 380

WEIR Roy Deans MB ChB 1950 DPH 1954 MD 1962
MRCPE 1970 FFCM(Lond) 1973
sen lect soc med Aberd 1965–69; prof soc med Aberd from 1969

WEIR William MA 1911 BSc(agr) 1913
d Aber 7.11.65 *AUR* XLII 83

WELSH Frederick Hamilton MB ChB 1905
d 20.4.64

WELSH Richard William Hepburn MB ChB 1925 MD 1939
d Guildford 13.12.75 *AUR* XLVI 417

WELSH Robert Hepburn MB ChB 1891
d S Af –.12.57

WERE Guy Laurenny MB ChB 1940

WERNHAM Archibald Garden *MA 1938
prof moral phil Aberd from 1960

WERNHAM or Wilson, Bertha MA 1944
judge of Court of Appeal Ontario from 1976

WERNHAM James Chrystall Stephen *MA 1943
prof phil Carleton univ Ottawa from 1954; chmn of dept phil 1955–70; author *Two Russian Thinkers* 1968

WESLEY Andrew Marshall BSc(eng) 1945
MIEE 1955
sen asst eng NSHEB Edin from 1968

WEST Alexander Wood MB ChB 1927 DPH 1929
d 12.1.68

WEST or Duffin, Anne Thomson MB ChB 1921
resid Greenford

WEST David *MB ChB 1924

WEST David Alexander *MA 1948
prof Lat N'cle-u-Tyne from 1969; pro vice chancellor 1976–77 and 1978–81

WEST Emily MA 1952

WEST Evelyn May MA 1949
teaching for C of S mission pre marriage, and for Government post marriage, in N Rhodesia/Zambia 1958–68; part time teacher Fr/Engl and latterly EFL at coll of f e Welwyn Garden City 1968–78
m Lubwa mission 22.7.61 Peter D. Snelson MA(Cantab) dir educ and trg progr Commonwealth secretariat Lond s of Briscoe G. A. S. Cambridge

WEST George *MA 1924
no longer on GC reg

WEST or Aitken, Gladys Mary MB ChB 1922 DPH 1924
m o h Llantrisant and Llantwit Fardre rural dist council Glam 1932–36; g p 1926–62
resid Creigiau nr Cardiff

WEST or Birkett, Margaret Adamson MA 1926
resid Burton by Lincoln
husb *d* 1969

WEST Stephen MA 1930
JP 1959
retd 1971; resid Fochabers

WEST Thomas Summers *BSc 1949
DSc(Birm) 1962 Chem Soc Medallist in chem analysis and instrumentation 1976
Imperial Coll Lond: reader chem 1963–65, prof analytical chem 1965–75; dir Macaulay inst for soil res Aber from 1975

WEST William Wiseman MA 1905
d Aber 6.5.70 *AUR* XLIII 440

WESTERMAN Arthur MB ChB 1900 *MD 1904
d 8.1.63 *AUR* XL 198

WESTERN Robert Henry *MA 1934
head Warddykes p s Arbroath from 1969; retd 1975

WESTIE Kathleen MA 1952
Rhodesia: teacher Engl Gatooma 1958–59, Roosevelt h s (girls) Salisbury 1959–60, i/c hist Girl's h s Salisbury 1960–74; hist at Mount Pleasant (co-ed) s Salisbury from 1974
m(1) Salisbury Rhod 23.1.60 Geoffrey T. Eason prop. man. s of Tom E. Berks; husb *d* Salisbury –.6.69
(2) Salisbury 20.12.78 Donald L. Forbes

WESTMORELAND Winnie MA 1938

WESTOLL Thomas Stanley DSc 1941 LLD 1979
FRSE 1943 FRS 1952 Murchison medal geol soc Lond 1967 Clough medal geol soc Edin 1977 Linnean gold medal zool 1978
Alexander Agassiz visiting prof Harvard 1952–53; prof geol N'cle (Durh from 1948) 1963–77; emeritus prof 1977; Leverhulme emeritus fell. 1977–79
member of council: Royal Soc Edin 1958–60, Royal Soc 1966–68; presid geol soc of Lond 1966–68, 1972–74; presid sect. C Brit assoc for advancement of sc Durh 1970; chmn convocation N'cle from 1979

WETHERLY James Marshall Rennie MB ChB 1951
MCSP 1936
g p Aber from 1953; med asst dept phys med/ rheumatology ARI from 1959; retd 1978

WETHERLY Robert Erskine BSc 1938 MB ChB 1951
d Sunderland 16.1.63 *AUR* XL 207

WHAMOND William Duke MB ChB 1916
d 5.11.65

WHEELAN Lorna MB ChB 1948 MD 1954
AMInst Psychoanalysts 1959 FRCPsych 1971
consult. ch psychiat King's coll hosp Lond from 1954
m Lond 1962 Sir John D. N. Hill MB BS(Lond) prof psychiat s of Jack H. Orleton nr Ludlow

WHEELER Philip Theodore MA 1953

WHELAN Lawrence Andrew PhD 1936
no longer on GC reg

WHIGHAM Jack Williamson *BSc 1951
phys with Admiralty Surface Weapons Estab from 1959
m Fareham 26.4.80 Patricia T. Bergin

WHIMSTER John Rust BL 1934
admitted fac of advoc 1950; leg. asst 1960–71; leg. off. to foreign compensation comm Lond 1971–78

WHITE Adam Duncan Ferguson MB ChB 1925
deceased

WHITE Albert Arnold MB ChB 1935 MD 1951
chief m o BM corp Birm 1964–70; retd; resid Bigton Shetland
d Shetland 10.12.76 *AUR* XLVII 214

WHITE or Smith, Dorothy Mary Agnes MB ChB 1942
clin m o Hereford county hosp; resid Ledbury

WHITE or Waugh, Elizabeth Ann MB ChB 1938
g p E Kilbride from 1960

WHITE Eric Alfred Dutton PhD 1951 DSc 1967
Lond: dir crystal growth lab Imp Coll 1965–69, reader crystal growth from 1969

WHITE James George Charles *MA 1942
ptnr Baillie Gifford & Co from 1955, sen ptnr from 1975; dir: Claverhouse Invest. Trust from 1963, Winterbottom Trust from 1963, Scot. Equit Life Assur Soc from 1971, Scottish Mortgage & Trust Co from 1978

WHITE Leslie Scott BSc 1955
d Elgin 10.6.63 *AUR* XL 207

WHITE or Drosso, Lily MB ChB 1941
d 23.8.75

WHITE Michael David Ewing *MA 1939
BSc(Carleton) 1964
analyst Canada Cement Lafarge Ottawa from 1964

WHITE or Anderson, Rosemary Helen MA 1934
d of John G. W. MA 1890 *qv*(I, II, III)
teacher Fr Manc 1966–71; resid Bolton-le-Sands, Lancs

WHITE or Moss, Sheena Margaret Jean MA 1952

WHITEFORD Allan Dinnell *MA 1954
teacher Engl Inv royal acad 1960–62; prin Engl: Portree h s 1962–67, Nicolson inst Stornoway 1967–72, dep rector from 1972
m Aber 4.4.60 Christina M. Mackay MA 1953 *qv*

WHITELEY Archibald White Maconochie MA 1928 Dip Ed 1929
MBE FSA Scot
head Kemnay s s 1967–72; retd; resid Monymusk

WHITELEY Dorothy Mary MA 1922
retd 1965; resid Aber

WHITLAM John Campbell MB ChB 1946

WHITSON Gordon Stuart *MA 1934
d 21.6.79

WHITSON William Harry Michael BSc(agr) 1950

WHITTAM Thomas Vincent PhD 1952

WHITTER Agnes Elizabeth MB ChB 1951
part time: asst m o h Aber 1960–61, med asst malignant diseases unit ARI from 1969; part time g p and sessional m o Marks and Spencer Aber
m Aber 8.9.60 Alistair W. Forrest MB ChB 1927 *qv*

WHITTER Austin Fullarton MB ChB 1951
g p Perth W Aust from 1957

WHITTON or Oglethorpe, Anne Smith MA 1913
resid Hove Sussex
d Hove 24.1.81

WHYTE or Macdonald, Agnes Elizabeth MA 1955

WHYTE Alexander *MA 1945 LLB 1949

WHYTE Alistair Gordon Donald MA 1927 MB ChB 1931
FRSM 1948 FAS 1958 FSA Scot 1972
lect anat Aberd 1959–77

WHYTE Allan Taylor MA 1946
C of S min: Kirkmichael and Tomintoul ch 1960–69, Ordiquhill, Cornhill and Ord ch from 1969

WHYTE Betty Hendry *MA 1940
lib Publ Health lab serv Lond from 1948

WHYTE Catherine Isobel MA 1920
no longer on GC reg

WHYTE David Fairweather MB ChB 1938
g p Torridon 1966–74; retd; resid Kenilworth Warks

WHYTE Edward George MA 1952
head Longside p s from 1973

WHYTE Elisabeth *MA 1909
resid Lond

WHYTE Emily Park MA 1909
no longer on GC reg

WHYTE or Campbell Allen, Ethel *MA 1910
d Harrow-on-the-Hill 22.7.75 *AUR* XLVI 320

WHYTE or Tennant, Gertrude MA 1936
resid Craigellachie

WHYTE James Alexander MB ChB 1924
no longer on GC reg

WHYTE James Douglas MB ChB 1932
retd g p 1972; Northumberland: med asst psychiat St George's hosp Morpeth/Collingwood day clin Gosforth/Tynemouth Victoria Jubilee hosp from 1972, clin asst Tynemouth Vict Jub Day Psychiat hosp N Shields
m Gateshead-u-Tyne 27.6.34 Elsie Davison health visitor d of Peter D. Hetton le Hole Co Durh

WHYTE James Harvey Strachan MB ChB 1941 MD 1954
d 5.1.75 *AUR* XLVI 240

WHYTE James Smith *MA 1933
MInstP 1970
prin tech coll Aber 1968–74; retd

WHYTE John Cowie MB ChB 1947
g p Sydney NSW Aust from 1964

WHYTE or Miller, Maggie Bella MA 1942

WHYTE or Ingram, Margaret Ritchie MA 1941

WHYTE Margarita Russell MA 1915
no longer on GC reg

WHYTE or Burbidge, Muriel Louvain *MA 1941
lect Engl Camb coll of arts/tech Cambridge from 1965

WHYTE Robert Bruce *BSc 1945 PhD 1948

WHYTE Sydney MA 1949
Lib asst Sutherland county lib 1961–63; teacher Lhanbryde p s 1964–70; head Echt p s from 1970
m Methlick 19.7.73 Yvonne C. Yule teacher d of Alexander G. Y. Maud

WHYTE William John *BSc 1937

WHYTE William John Arnold *MA 1912
no longer on GC reg

WIGGINS Albert Leslie BSc(agr) 1952
MSc(Glas)

WIGHT or Miller, Elizabeth Campbell Hendry *MA 1915
teacher Engl: Gateside j s s 1954–61, Bellahouston and Shawlands acad Glasg 1962–66; retd; resid Aber

WIGHT Robert Muir BL 1937
univ of Leic: sen lect educ 1961–62, dir p e from 1962

WILDGOOSE John Middleton MA 1931
head Kittybrewster p s Aber from 1965
d road accident Berwickshire 1.5.79 *AUR* XLVIII 232

WILKIE Alfred MB ChB 1928
d 14.11.67 *AUR* XLII 368

WILKIE Beryl Alice Gordon MA 1955
teacher St Thomas's s Keith from 1956

WILKIE James BSc(agr) 1929

WILKIE James MB ChB 1948
prin g p Fraserburgh from 1960; m o Consolidated Pneumatic Tool Co from 1963; hon m o RNLI 1964–73

WILKIE John Ritchie *MA 1943
MA(Cantab) 1972
univ of Leeds: sen lect Ger 1961–72, prof/head of dept 1972–77; prof Ger Aberd from 1978

WILKIE William Roy *MA 1954
F Inst Scient Bus. 1973
Strath: res organisation theory 1962–63, lect 1963–65, sen lect 1965–66; dir J & J Denholm (MGT) 1966–67; reader/head dept of admin Strath 1967–72; personal professorship 1974

WILKINS Alan Harley BSc(eng) 1951
FEDI 1967 MITE 1970 FICE 1971 FCIT 1972
Hong Kong: chief eng 1964–69, govt eng 1969–72, dir mass transit stud. from 1972

WILKINS Arthur James Walker MB ChB 1926 DPH 1928

WILKINSON or Mitchell, Agnes Simpson BSc 1935

WILKINSON James Anderson *MA 1899
no longer on GC reg

WILL Alan Addison MB ChB 1949
g p/m o to RNAD Coulport Kilcreggan from 1967

WILL or Lamont, Alexa Lee MA 1922
resid Aber

WILL or Park, Annie Bain MA 1936
teacher: SE Glamorgan 1966–68, Aber from 1968
husb *d* 16.8.65

WILL Charles John BL 1940

WILL or Campbell, Enid Margaret Ogilvie MB ChB 1925
d 20.12.69

WILL Hunter McLeod *MA 1928
head Ruthrieston s s from 1961
d Aber 16.2.66 *AUR* XLI 249

WILL Ian BSc(agr) 1950
prin scient off. Ghana 1960–63; farm man. anim breeding res organis Roslin from 1963

WILL Ida Mitchell MA 1933 MB ChB 1938
g p Arnold Notts from 1941

WILL or Bottomley, Isabella Margaret BSc 1934 MB ChB 1937
d Carluke 23.10.77

WILL or Walker, Jean Mitchell MA 1947
teacher: Brooklands tech coll Weybridge 1958–59, St Mark's s Mbabane Swaziland S Af 1960–61, New Town h s Hobart Tasmania 1961–65, Taroona h s Tasmania from 1967
husb *d* Hobart Tasmania 19.4.77

WILL John MA 1903 BD 1909
d Edin 30.10.65 *AUR* XLII 81

WILL Margaret Oliver MB ChB 1941
Birm: j h m o St Margaret's hosp Great Barr 1958–62, All Saints hosp 1962–65; asst psychiat St Margaret's hosp Great Barr from 1965

WILL or Brown, Mary Ann MA 1932

WILL or Lyons, Mary Shewan MA 1918
no longer on GC reg

WILL William Miller MB ChB 1911
d Tunbridge Wells 6.1.63 *AUR* XL 201

WILLER Joseph *MA 1929

WILLIAMS or MacGillivray, Alice Maude MA 1941
resid Aber

WILLIAMS Anthony Herbert Michael *MA 1950
d Salisbury Wilts 17.10.64 *AUR* XLI 61

WILLIAMS David Albert MA 1936 BD 1940
C of S min: Orphir and Stenness from 1964; county councillor Firth and Stenness 1970–73; member Orkney educ comm 1973–75

WILLIAMS Edward BSc(agr) 1931
retd HM overseas civ serv 1963; sen admin off. commonwealth econ comm/chief res off. commonwealth secretariat Lond 1963–70; retd; resid Haywards Heath

WILLIAMS Elisabeth Myra MB ChB 1938
DA(RCS) 1967
various anaest apptments: Johannesburg/Cape Town 1941–51, Cheltenham/Gloucester from 1965
m(1) Aber 1941 Stanley W. Watson MB ChB 1941 *qv*
(2) Lond 1951 Gordon S. Haggie rope maker

WILLIAMS or Brooke, Florence Margaret *MA 1940
resid Keele

WILLIAMS Jean Helen MA 1939
teacher Seafield p s Elgin from 1960; retd 1976

WILLIAMS Marjorie Humphry BSc 1916
no longer on GC reg

WILLIAMS Michael James MB ChB 1954 ᶜMD 1965
sen regist ARI 1960–61; lect mat. medica/therap Aberd 1961–68; consult. phys NE reg hosp board from 1968
m Glasg 21.1.72 Mary P. McEwan MB ChB(Glas) haemat d of Patrick McE. MA(Glas) Glasg

WILLIAMS Patrick Bertram Rotheroe MB ChB 1939
TD
TA and AER 1947–65, lt col; m o Worcs c c Worcester from 1959
d Droitwich 19.3.79 *AUR* XLVIII 232

WILLIAMS Robin Vawer MB ChB 1951
d Malta 21.1.70 *AUR* XLIII 446

WILLIAMS William George *BSc 1952 Dip Ed 1955
prin teacher biol AGS from 1961

WILLIAMS William Holmes MA 1929 BSc 1930

WILLIAMSON or Verel, Agnes Cobden Miller MB ChB 1947
Sheffield: part-time g p 1959–68, sessional m o blood transfus serv 1969–72; comp m o from 1974

WILLIAMSON Alfred John MA 1905 MB ChB 1909 MD 1911
d –.12.73 *AUR* XLV 446

WILLIAMSON Andrew Ritchie BSc(eng) 1951

WILLIAMSON or Kirk, Annie Catherine MA 1939
resid Taunton

WILLIAMSON Charles MA 1889
d –.5.60

WILLIAMSON Douglas Harris *BSc 1950 PhD 1952
MCIMM 1953 FGS(Lond) 1953 MAAAS 1964 MGeolAss(Can) 1968
Canada: Sir James Dunn prof geol Sackville NB 1954–66; prof geol/dept head Laurentian univ Sudbury Ont 1966–71, also dean of sc from 1969

WILLIAMSON Douglas Macgregor MB ChB 1941

WILLIAMSON or Sutherland, Eliza Irvine MA 1925
resid Aber

WILLIAMSON Eric Arthur MA 1955
d Brunei 21.8.76

WILLIAMSON Freda MA 1933
teacher King St p s, Ruthrieston s s Aber from 1936

WILLIAMSON George BSc(agr) 1954

WILLIAMSON George Alexander (Sir) BL 1926
d Adelaide 23.6.75 *AUR* XLVI 323

WILLIAMSON James *BSc 1941

WILLIAMSON James Henderson MA 1946 MB ChB 1953
resid Roos N Humberside

WILLIAMSON Jessie Dalziel MA 1932

WILLIAMSON Jessie Tulloch MA 1905
retd 1946; resid Aber

WILLIAMSON John Bremner BSc(eng) 1948
RE Germany 1948–50; Geo Wimpey & Co UK 1950–73; jun eng, serv ag GB & NI 1973; chief tech off. Coleraine borough c from 1973
m N'cle-u-Tyne 23.2.57 Patricia Green

WILLIAMSON John Taylor MA 1936 LLB 1941

WILLIAMSON Laurence Pierre de Loriol BCom 1926
d Ashford Middx 25.12.64 *AUR* XLI 58

WILLIAMSON Maurice Robert BSc(eng) 1954
sen dev eng Solarton Farnborough, Hants 1961–63; lect M o D: s of elect. eng REME Arborfield Berks 1963–67, s for signals Blandford camp Dorset from 1967

WILLIAMSON Robert Bertram MA 1922 LLB 1924
conducted law classes in POW camp—several students while in captivity were able to pass univ degree examinations; chmn Richards of Aberdeen from 1960; dir, then chmn Lawson Turnbull & Co Aber 1956–73; dir, then chmn Cruden Bay Brick and Tile Co from 1937; dir Scot. Salmon and White Fish Co from 1965; retd as sen ptnr Paull and Williamsons advoc Aber 1971
d Aber 20.7.76 *AUR* XLVII 105

WILLIAMSON Thomas MB ChB 1932
MC

WILLIAMSON William Turner Horace BSc 1910
d Aber 26.4.68 *AUR* XLII 349

WILLIAMSON Williamina Catherine MA 1911
retd 1955; resid Aber
d Aber 28.8.78 *AUR* XLVIII 102

WILLOCK Ian Douglas MA 1951 LLB 1954
PhD(Glas) 1963
prof juris St And (now Dund) from 1965

WILLOX Alexander MA 1930
d 9.10.81

WILLOX Alexander George *MA 1910
d Kent 8.5.68 *AUR* XLII 350

WILLOX or Brown, Alice MA 1928

WILLOX Charles Finnie *MA 1922
FEIS
retd; resid Stonehaven

WILLOX Frank Gerrie *BSc 1952
FRAeS 1968 MSc(Cranfield) 1972
chief proj eng BAe Preston Lancs 1961–66; proj man. 1966, exec dir from 1976

WILLOX Henry Norman MA 1928 BD 1931
MBE 1971
C of S min Carnwath par ch/chaplain state hosp Carstairs: clerk synod Clydesdale from 1967: war serv: milit hosp Carstairs 1939–48, seconded Shetland 1943, Middle East 1945; retd; resid Helensburgh

WILLOX Marjory Matthew MA 1954
teacher: Peebles h s 1959–62, King Richard's s Dhekelia Cyprus 1962–63, Bourne s Singapore 1963–67, McLaren h s Callander from 1967

WILLOX Norma Philip MA 1953
tut./lib coll of dom sc Aber 1963–71; lib RGIT Aber from 1971

WILSON or Panton, Agnes MA 1913

WILSON Alexander MB ChB 1909 *MD 1914
d Wimbledon 8.6.62 *AUR* XXXIX 377

WILSON Alexander *MA 1925
retd 1962; resid Aber
wife *d* 3.12.73

WILSON Alexander Dey MA 1936
dir soc educ Elgin acad 1967–72, asst rector (guid) 1972–75; retd

WILSON Alexander Hogarth MB ChB 1925
MRCPsych 1971
med supt/consult. psychiat Leeds 1939–62; lect psychiat univ Leeds 1942–62; retd; resid Walton-on-Thames
m Southend-on-Sea 20.11.29 Jean M. Robertson MB ChB(Glas) m o mat. and ch welfare off.
wife *d* 29.11.62

WILSON Alexander Roger BSc(eng) 1933
retd 1973; resid Ellon

WILSON Andrew BSc(eng) 1936

WILSON Andrew Strang MA 1934 LLB 1936
ptnr Stuart & Wilson solic Huntly from 1946

WILSON or Thomson, Anne Edith Duncan BSc(agr) 1945
dir farm. comp Nether Balgillo Forfar from 1966

WILSON or Hunter, Annie Fraser *MA 1913
resid Stonehaven

WILSON Archibald Dey MA 1915
d Chester 30.5.77

WILSON Catherine Johina Jane MB ChB 1947
no longer on GC reg

WILSON Charles Stephen BSc 1930 *1932
d –.4.69

WILSON or Bridges, Charlotte Mary MA 1920 MB ChB 1925
d Lincoln 24.12.76

WILSON Christina Oliphant Binning MA 1922
MA(Queensland) 1930
Aust: teacher Somerville Ho Brisbane h s for girls 1924–66; retd; part time Somerville Ho 1967–68; retd

WILSON or Simons, Claudine Isabel *MA 1916
resid Muswell Hill Lond

WILSON or Austin, Cristina MB ChB 1905
d Lond 17.6.60 *AUR* XXXVIII 587

WILSON David Monro BSc(eng) 1939

WILSON Douglas MB ChB 1925
no longer on GC reg

WILSON Douglas MB ChB 1934
DA(Lond) 1944 FRSM 1946
retd 1969; resid Dunstable

WILSON Edith MA 1922
head Lakes s s (girls) Dukinfield 1945–61; retd
d Buckie 17.3.76 *AUR* XLVI 416

WILSON Edith Barton MA 1924
d Nairn 27.4.70 *AUR* XLIII 445

WILSON Edith Bruce MB ChB 1925
retd 1967; resid Lond

WILSON Edward Bruce MB ChB 1898
d –.11.63

WILSON or Drummond, Elizabeth Joyce BL 1955

WILSON Elizabeth Margaret Davidson *MA 1933

WILSON Eric Blackett BSc(agr) 1925 BSc 1925
no longer on GC reg

WILSON Ernest BL 1937
asst trustee man. Royal Bank of Scot. (merged with Nat Comm Bank) 1969–71; retd; resid Devon

WILSON Florence Eva BSc 1927 MA 1930

WILSON or Inkson, Frances MA 1928
teacher maths Dingwall acad 1954–67; retd

WILSON Francis Charles McKay BCom 1927
no longer on GC reg

WILSON Frank Stanley BSc(for) 1951
for. off. Attadale W Ross 1964–66; for./conservation off. Dun from 1966

WILSON George MA 1913
d Nairn 10.1.70 *AUR* XLIII 441

WILSON George Alexander MB ChB 1928
d 9.7.62

WILSON George Alexander MB ChB 1942
anaest The Rand Mutual hosp (formerly WNLA hosp) Johannesburg from 1980

WILSON George Paterson MA 1954 BSc 1957
asst biol master Perth acad 1959–66; prin teacher biol Morrison's acad for boys Crieff from 1966

WILSON or Lawrence, Gladys Mary BSc 1932 *1933
resid Harpenden

WILSON Gwendolene Jean Emslie MA 1911 MB ChB 1918
no longer on GC reg

WILSON Helen Milne MA 1924
retd 1961; resid Dingwall
d Dingwall 10.12.79 *AUR* XLVIII 441

WILSON Herbert George Macdonald MA 1907
d 1.9.67 *AUR* XLII 347

WILSON Hilda Eleanor MA BSc 1922
d Banff 21.11.68 *AUR* XLIII 84

WILSON Hugh *MA 1946
dep rector Nairn acad from 1970

WILSON Hugh Norman Blackett MA 1926
no longer on GC reg

WILSON Ian Edward BSc 1949
sen tech off. nat inst of agr bot Cambridge from 1960

WILSON Ian Turner BSc(for) 1939
d Cornwall 20.8.71 *AUR* XLIV 321

WILSON or Thomas, Irene Catherine MA 1942

WILSON Isabella MA 1917
resid Aber
d Aber 24.3.81 *AUR* XLIX 136

WILSON or Wheatley, Isabella Anne MA 1935

WILSON or Ledingham, Isabella Elder MA 1925
resid Aber
d Cults Aber 16.10.78

WILSON Isobel Mary MA 1950

WILSON James Ingram Pirie MB ChB 1907 MD 1910
resid Southgate Lond
deceased

WILSON Janet Duff *MA 1910
no longer on GC reg

WILSON John MA 1942 BD 1945
exec dir Consumers' Assoc of Canada (Ont) from 1975

WILSON John Alexander George MB ChB 1923
retd; resid Sheffield

WILSON John Cameron MB ChB 1933

WILSON John McIntosh MA 1905 MB ChB 1907
d Aberdare 18.4.67 *AUR* XLII 346

WILSON John McIntyre BL 1947
leg. asst Milne & Reid Aber 1948–60, corp of city of Aber 1960–69; second town clerk dep 1969–71, sen town clerk dep to corp of city of Aber 1972–75, dep town clerk and chief exec 1975–77, town clerk and chief exec from 1977

WILSON John McLaren MA 1910
retd 1972; resid Fyvie
d Turriff 17.9.75

WILSON John McQueen BSc(agr) 1944

WILSON John Sutherland Macintosh MB ChB 1934
g p Aberdare Mid Glam from 1936

WILSON John Warwick BSc(eng) 1953

WILSON Katharine Margaret *MA 1917
author: *The Nightingale and the Hawk* (Allen & Unwin) 1964; *Shakespeare's Sugared Sonnets* (Allen & Unwin) 1974
resid Eltham Lond

WILSON or Moir, Kathleen Isabella MA 1923
teacher Aber: Powis s s 1949–50; remed: Old Aber s s, Ashley Rd p s, Broomhill p s, Frederick St s s, St Peter's s s 1950–63; retd
d Newmachar 7.4.79

WILSON Laura Marie *MA 1927
d Durris 28.3.72 *AUR* XLIV 431

WILSON Leslie Andrew MA 1937 MB ChB 1941 MD 1954
FRCP(Lond) 1970 FRCPE 1971
consult. phys Aber gen hosps from 1955

WILSON or Gentles, Lisette Anne Macdonald MB ChB 1905
no longer on GC reg

WILSON Louisa Mary MA 1911
d Aber 7.12.74 *AUR* XLVI 235

WILSON or Taylor, Mabel MB ChB 1923 DPH 1925
no longer on GC reg

WILSON Margaret Anderson *MA 1921
retd 1961; resid Bieldside Aber

WILSON or Miller, Margaret Barbara *MA 1930
d Daviot Aberdeensh 26.4.76

WILSON Margaret Doverty MA 1930
teacher Engl/geog/hist Whitehills j s s 1948–69; retd; resid Macduff

WILSON or Scott, Margaret Elisabeth Mathewson MA 1946
resid Newburgh Aberdeensh

WILSON or Bevan, Margaret Elspet MA 1945

WILSON Mary MA 1939
Edin: asst head: Moredun p s 1958–62; Peffermill p s 1962–78

WILSON Mary Annie Susana MA 1925
retd 1965; resid Aber

WILSON Mary Helena Taylor *MA 1939

WILSON Moira Mathewson MB ChB 1955
regist obst/gyn South Lond hosp 1960–62

WILSON Muriel Isobel May BSc 1922
no longer on GC reg

WILSON Norman James MA 1921 *LLB 1923
no longer on GC reg

WILSON Robert MA 1919 BD 1921
d Aber 20.9.67 *AUR* XLII 184

WILSON Robert *MA 1926
retd 1972; resid Aber
d 1.11.81

WILSON Robert Angus *MA 1924
teacher: Cottesmore s mod s 1951–58, Southend s m s Herts 1958–63; lect: Southend coll of tech 1963–67; retd; resid St Albans

WILSON Robert Cummins *MA 1906
no longer on GC reg

WILSON or Brooks, Sarah Jane MA 1926
teacher: Macduff h s 1951–69, Banff acad 1969–70; retd; resid Macduff

WILSON Stewart *MA 1955
head arts dept Rushcliffe g s Notts 1961–63; dep head Moorside comp s Staffs 1963–66; head: Eston Grange s Yorks 1966–71, Stapylton s Teesside 1971–73, Sutton comp s/commun centre Notts from 1973

WILSON Thomas MacSkimming MB ChB 1944
g p Stoke-on-Trent 1947–64; hotelier Aber 1964–66; g p: Audley Staffs 1966–68, Bucksburn/Dyce from 1968

WILSON Warren Woodrow MB ChB 1949
FICS 1972
g p St Anns Bay Jamaica from 1952

WILSON William MA 1909
no longer on GC reg

WILSON William Donald MB ChB 1930 DPH 1938 MD 1948
d Aber 31.8.74 *AUR* XLVI 109

WILSON William Douglas ᶜMB ChB 1953
MANZCP 1963
consult. psychiat s Canterbury hosp Timaru NZ from 1963; also private psychiat pract

WILSON William Glennie MB ChB 1939
Treasury m o 1946–68; g p/police surg Salford 1958–68; g p Leuchars 1968–74; retd; resid Mintlaw
d 8.12.81

WILSON William Harvey BSc(eng) 1955

WILSON William Milne MB ChB 1927
g p Salisbury Rhodesia 1958–77; m o Rhodesian Iron & Steel Co (RISCO) Redcliff from 1977
d Rhodesia 15.12.78 *AUR* XLVIII 229

WILSON William Murray BSc(for) 1950
d Eassie, Forfar 12.10.77

WILSON William Trail MA 1926
Dun: teacher Ancrum Rd p s 1927–35, first asst Morgan acad p s 1935–41, dep head Butterburn p s 1941–43, dep head St Michael's p s 1943–47, head Grove acad p s 1947–50, head Eastern p s 1950–71; retd; resid Broughty Ferry

WILSON William Wallace MB ChB 1923
d 1.8.63

WINROW Stanley Richard BSc(for) 1952
prin teacher biol Crawshaw s Pudsey from 1960

WINTERFLOOD Eric Gordon BSc(for) 1950
for. comm: dist for. off. New Forest 1951–60, utilisation off. Chester 1960–67, dist for. off. New Forest 1967–72, asst conserv for. man. Cambridge from 1972
m Hove 22.7.50 Edna S. Burch nurse d of Sidney T. G. Brighton

WINTON or Jamieson, Helen Leslie *MA 1945
resid Galashiels

WINTON or White, Margaret MA 1929

WINTON Margaret Jane MA 1938
first asst/asst head Hill p s Blairgowrie from 1969

WINTON Robert Mitchell *MA 1941

WINTON William Cruickshank MA 1919
no longer on GC reg

WISELY Jane (Jeannie) Troup *MA 1927
prin lect Engl/head Engl dept City of Portsmouth coll of educ 1961–70; retd; resid Aber

WISEMAN Alfred James Thomas BSc(agr) 1923
d Rhynie 5.1.63 *AUR* XL 204

WISEMAN David Flett BSc(agr) 1925 MB ChB 1937
d Wanstead 28.6.70 *AUR* XLIV 110

WISEMAN Evelyn Mary MA 1908
no longer on GC reg

WISEMAN Herbert Horace Eugene MA 1907
d Edin 2.2.66 *AUR* XLI 241

WISEMAN James Charles *MA 1930 PhD 1934
rector Forres acad 1961–68; retd; resid Aber

WISEMAN or Steele, Jane Mackie MB ChB 1953
DOH(Syd) 1975
g p Sydney Aust from 1961

WISEMAN John BSc(eng) 1951
FICE 1969 FIHE 1972 M Cons E 1977
resid eng: Sir Owen Williams & Ptnrs 1963–64, city eng dept Liv 1964–66; ptnr Wallace Evans & Ptnrs, W I from 1967, assoc ptnr UK 1972 and ptnr from 1975; resid Penarth Glam

WISEMAN John Thomson *BSc 1948

WISEMAN Laermont Douglas *MA 1937
dep rector Bo'ness acad 1962–64, rector 1964–74; retd

WISEMAN Robert Lindsay MA 1928 *BSc 1931
retd 1972
d Greenford Middx 10.10.77 *AUR* XLVII 287

WISHART Agnes Gertrude (Nan) *MA 1927

WISHART Emmie Orr *MA 1936
retd 1968; resid Aber

WISHART John Christie MB ChB 1929
g p Bromley from 1935
d Bromley 23.9.77 *AUR* XLVII 358

WISHART John Strath *BSc(eng) 1938

WISHART William Philip *MA 1909 BD 1917
d Edin 2.3.62 *AUR* XXXIX 377

WITHERIDGE Edmund Alick MB ChB 1944
d Stoney Stratford Bucks 29.12.73 *AUR* XLV 449

WITHERIDGE Neil Russell MA 1948 Dip Ed 1949
teacher Engl spec asst Harlaw acad Aber from 1970

WITT Alexis John MB ChB 1941
no longer on GC reg

WITTE William PhD 1935
DLit(Lond) 1966
prof Ger Aberd 1951–77; retd

WITTET or Stewart, Veronica Mary MA 1923
resid Edin
husb *d* 26.12.55

WOOD or Wilson, Agnes McRobie MA 1910
no longer on GC reg

WOOD Alexander MB ChB 1926
d Bournemouth 30.7.70 *AUR* XLIV 110

WOOD Alexander Lawson MA 1931
serv with Moral Re-Armament Europe/Af/Asia/Amer from 1946; resid Lond

WOOD Alexander (Alistair) Ross MB ChB 1921
MRCGP 1952
g p Preston till 1967; hon m o Preston North End AFC 1946–66; dir Preston NE 1954–66; retd

WOOD or Topping, Alfreda Margaret MA 1914
d Keynsham Somerset 27.11.72 *AUR* XLVI 321

WOOD Annabel MA 1915
d 17.6.76

WOOD Bryan Ellis *BSc 1951
FRGS 1959
dep dir of educ Sutherland 1961–75; div educ off. Sutherland from 1975

WOOD Catherine Smith MA 1950
teacher p s Findochty j s s 1961–65; supply teaching Macduff/Whitehills/Bracoden 1972–76, Portnockie p s 1976–77, Findochty p s from 1977
m Aber 29.3.61 William G. Ross MN capt/harbour master s of Alexander R. Findochty

WOOD Charles Coutts MB ChB 1908
no longer on GC reg

WOOD Charles Hutchieson BCom 1922
no longer on GC reg

WOOD David BSc(eng) 1954

WOOD Donald Alexander James BSc(for) 1947

WOOD or Westoll or Will, Dorothy Cecil Isobel BSc 1939

WOOD Douglas Moir MA 1927 dLLB 1929
retd 1972
d Dun 22.7.75 *AUR* XLVI 323

WOOD Edith MA 1908
no longer on GC reg

WOOD Edward James *MA 1925
retd prof Lat Leeds 1967; part time lect Greek Leeds 1967–73

WOOD or Sked, Elsie Mackie MA 1930
resid Glenrothes

WOOD Emily Margaret Leiper MA 1950
teacher Skene Sq p s Aber from 1954

WOOD George *BSc 1955 PhD 1959

WOOD George Alexander MB ChB 1949
Edmonton Alberta from 1970

WOOD George Anderson MB ChB 1951
g p Taranaki NZ from 1957

WOOD Harry Roy MA 1951

WOOD Helen Ramsay MA 1910
deceased

WOOD Helena MA 1947
teacher Engl/hist: Brechin h s 1961–74, Kincardine 1974, Arbroath acad from 1974
m Aber 14.7.60 James R. Forbes H M off customs & excise s of James F. MRCVS(Edin) Truro Cornwall

WOOD Henry MA 1920 PhD 1933
d Aber 15.2.69 *AUR* XLIII 211

WOOD or Jefferson, Ida Elizabeth MA 1908 BSc 1911 MB ChB 1920
d 30.3.74 *AUR* XLV 446

WOOD Isabella Joss MA 1948
m Smith

WOOD Isobel Milne MA 1948 MB ChB 1953
various posts ENT dept ARI and RACH, part-time 1965–68; med asst ENT RACH from 1968
m Aber 15.3.65 John T. C. Gillan MA 1950

WOOD James Caie MB ChB 1932
d 21.4.81 *AUR* XLIX 138

WOOD James Challoner MB ChB 1944
g p Hull from 1948

WOOD James Douglas *BSc 1951 PhD 1954
head: physiol chem defence res med lab Toronto 1961–68, prof and head dept biochem univ of Saskatchewan Saskatoon from 1968

WOOD James Stewart *MA 1929 DD 1971
C of S min: South ch Aber 1953–73; advis stud. (lay missionaries) Aber 1962–68; asst pract theol dept Christ's coll Aber 1971–77; relig advis Grampian TV from 1973; lib Christ's coll from 1976

WOOD James Walker MB ChB 1914
d S Af 4.4.68 *AUR* XLIII 79

WOOD or Cruickshank, Jean Smith MB ChB 1948
resid Blairgowrie

WOOD Jeannie Margaret Stewart MA 1922
teacher: Engl/hist Stromness acad 1923–51, prim. subjs 1951–60; retd

WOOD John MA 1920
d 6.10.63

WOOD John Armour MB ChB 1955
MRCOG 1963 CRCS(C) 1966 FRCS(C) 1973
spec obst/gyn Nanaimo BC Canada
m Aber 21.7.60 Eleanor M. Allan d of James D. A. Aber

WOOD John Hay MB ChB 1942 DPH 1947
MRCGP
g p Stoke on Trent from 1949

WOOD John Ramsay MB ChB 1953
Dip Soc Med 1968
retd RAF 1969; dep med supt Edin R I from 1970; resigned 1977

WOOD Joseph *MA 1946

WOOD Kathleen MA 1928

WOOD Kathleen MA 1946
teacher Aber

WOOD Kenneth Alexander MA 1943 *1948

WOOD or Getty, Margaret *MA 1923
d Aber 16.12.70 *AUR* XLIV 211

WOOD or Shearer, Margaret MA 1914
no longer on GC reg

WOOD or Black, Margaret Caie MB ChB 1947
MFCM 1973
sen clin m o ch health Wirral from 1973

WOOD or Bain, Mary MA 1934
teacher Portsoy 1940–46; in bus. Cullen 1946–58; teacher Portessie/Findochty/Portsoy/Banff acad 1958–74; retd
d Portsoy 24.2.78

WOOD Mary Isobel *MA 1922
retd 1963; resid Cupar

WOOD or McArthur, Millicent Mary Magdalene MA 1935
part-time prin psych civ serv dept Lond from 1962; resid Bowdon Cheshire
husb *d* –.8.58
m(2) Lond 13.10.62 Henry D. Whitehouse restaurant prop. s of Henry J. W. Disley Cheshire

WOOD or MacLennan, Patricia Miles MA 1950
teacher: Inv 1965–70, Alness 1970–73, Invergordon 1973–78, Fortrose from 1978

WOOD Peter Murray *MA 1953
d Glasg 20.1.69 *AUR* XLIII 218

WOOD or Wood, Rachael Anne Milne MA 1946
teacher; girls' coll Aden 1960–62, boys' coll Aden 1964–65; Hatfield Travis s W Riding Yorks 1965–67, Sciennes s Edin 1967–78; retd

WOOD Ronald MA 1931
MBE 1971 FEIS
retd Valley p s Kirkcaldy 1972; part time asst Abbotshall teachers' centre Kirkcaldy 1972–74

WOOD Stanley Whyte BSc(eng) 1933

WOOD Thomas William Walter BSc(for) 1952
asst conserv for. Sarawak 1953–67; FAO UN: for. off. Apia, W Samoa 1967–70, proj man. Paramaribo Surinam S Amer from 1971

WOOD William MB ChB 1904 MD 1911
OBE 1966
wife *d* 1961
d Sydney Aust 22.12.74 *AUR* XLVI 234

WOOD William *MA 1930
retd 1970
d Aber 21.1.75 *AUR* XLVI 238

WOOD Williamina MA 1945
d –.1.67

WOODCOCK Henrietta MA 1908
d 16.7.73

WOODCOCK or Brander, Margaret MA 1910
resid Beaconsfield Bucks
d 20.11.81

WOOLCOTT John Foster MB ChB 1941
m o publ health dept W Aust from 1951

WOOLLEY James Bernard MB ChB 1940
d Chichester 17.12.65 *AUR* XLI 251

WORGAN Mary Eunice *MA 1934
d Aber 21.10.71 *AUR* XLIV 321

WORK or Cromarty, Isabella Budge MA 1903
d 5.11.62

WORK or Struthers, Margaret Garrioch MA 1906
teacher Castle Douglas acad 1906–10; resid Edin

WORLING or Grant or Sehrson, Euphemia Betty MA 1944

WRIGHT Alfred *MA 1897
d 25.9.62

WRIGHT Daniel Overbeck BSc 1926 BSc(agr) 1928
Malaysia: asst/man. KMS rubber plant, Kedah 1928–41, plant advis Guthrie & Co Lond/Kuala Lumpur 1946–51; farm. Lanarksh/Surrey 1951–71; retd
m Penang 27.9.39 Hannah Appleby

WRIGHT David Livingston MA 1954 BD 1957
organist/choirmaster W St Clement's ch Aber 1946–55; Chalmers mem ch Port Seton 1957–63; C of S min: Lowson mem ch Forfar 1964–70, Old par ch Hawick from 1971, linked with Teviothead from 1972
m Cockenzie 4.8.61 Margaret Brown bank teller d of Thomas S. B. Port Seton

WRIGHT or McBain, Dorothy Evelyn MA 1950
resid Maryculter

WRIGHT or Cowan Glegg, Effie Graham MA 1912
Engl mistress Hermitage s Bath 1941–45; resid Tunbridge Wells
d 23.7.76

WRIGHT Ella MA 1920
no longer on GC reg

WRIGHT George Tod MA 1913 BD 1915
retd 1955; resid Castle Douglas
d Dumfries 29.12.78

WRIGHT or Smith, Gladys May MA 1921
d Aber 6.1.75

WRIGHT Herbert John BSc(eng) 1944

WRIGHT Herbert MacPherson MB ChB 1924
g p Birm from 1958

WRIGHT Ian McKenzie BSc(eng) 1951

WRIGHT Iris Martin MA 1949
teacher: Aber: St Margaret's epis p s 1950–59, Causewayend p s 1960–68; dep head King St p s 1968–73, asst head Broomhill p s 1973–77; head King St p s from 1977

WRIGHT Jack Clifford *MA 1955
FRAS MPhilological Soc
prof Sanskrit univ of Lond from 1964 and also head dept languages and cultures of India, Pakistan and Ceylon at SOAS univ Lond from 1969

WRIGHT James MB ChB 1925
d 16.10.75 *AUR* XLVI 417

WRIGHT John Milne MA 1929
head Sunnybank p s Aber 1965–71; retd

WRIGHT John Norman MA 1951
teacher Aber 1952–53; army educ off. capt Edin 1953–56, Kenya 1956–61; major housemaster QVS Dunblane 1961–66; sen educ off. Bridge of Don barracks Aber 1966–69; asst controller service children's educ M o D Lond 1969–73; group educ off. Plymouth 1973–76; group educ off. (Scot.) from 1976
m Blackpool 26.10.47 Hilda Chadwick

WRIGHT or Birnie, Joyce MA 1951

WRIGHT Margaret Johanna *MA 1937
Dornoch acad: woman advis from 1957, prin teacher Engl from 1973, dep head from 1975

WRIGHT Maurice Richards BL 1950 PhD 1956

WRIGHT or Seller, Muriel Christine MA 1943
teacher: classics Wakefield girls' h s 1945–48, p s AGS 1949–51; head of lower s Albyn s for girls Aber from 1964

WRIGHT Ninian Blundell MA 1926 BD 1929
retd 1973; resid Comrie

WRIGHT Nora Alexandra MA 1954

WRIGHT Robert Daniel Barron MB ChB 1931
Hull: g p from 1936; final examining m o RN/med referee M o H from 1969

WRIGHT Robert Ian BSc(eng) 1952
MIMunE 1958
sen eng: Midlothian c c 1965–68; field man. CITB Scot. from 1968

WRIGHT Stanley Cooper BSc 1932 MB ChB 1937
d Kendoon Kirkcudbrightsh 19.8.76 *AUR* XLVII 106

WRIGHT Thomas William BSc(for) 1950 PhD 1953

WRIGHT Victor Oswald MB ChB 1893
no longer on GC reg

WRIGHT William PhD 1952
ScD(Dub) 1961 FICE 1964 CEng 1964 FRSE 1965 FInst Prod.E 1966 FIEI 1969
dean of fac math eng sc Dublin univ from 1969
m(2) Manc 14.7.61 Barbara Robinson BA(Dub) Chevalier de l'ordre du merit prof Fr univ Dub d of Edward Robinson Dublin

WRIGHT William Christie BL 1939
resid Dornoch

WRIGHT William Neil MA 1924
CA
no longer on GC reg

WYLIE James MB ChB 1938
g p Sheerness Kent from 1946; m o HM prison Standford Hill Eastchurch Sheerness from 1950

WYLIE Norman Richard MA 1935 LLB 1939
admitted to fac of advoc Edin 1958

resid magistrate Kampala Uganda 1955–60; magistrate/dist court judge Hong Kong 1961–68; leg. asst Scot. off. 1969–74; retd
m Aber 24.1.61 Isabella R. Donaldson

WYLLIE James McLeod *MA 1928
d Cumbria 8.4.71 *AUR* XLIV 212

WYLLIE John Hamilton BSc 1954 *MB ChB 1957 *MD 1961
FRCS 1964 FRCSE 1964 MS(Wash) 1966
surg trg posts/lect surg Aberd 1960–65; Harkness fell. commonwealth fund NY Seattle USA 1965–66; lect inst basic med sc Lond 1966–68; personal chair in surg stud. dept surg UCHMS Lond from 1976
m Aber 16.3.68 Kathleen R. Mackay MA(Edin) teacher

WYLLIE Violet McAndrew MB ChB 1955
Dip Ophth(Lond) 1968
trainee g p Edin 1958–59; civ med pract BAOR W Ger 1960–63; g p Sutton Surrey 1964–67; ophth med pract Sutton hosp/s eye serv Sutton from 1968
m Kensington Lond 4.10.58 Emanuel G. Lucas MB ChB(Edin) consult. psychiat s of Max L. MB ChB(Edin) Bedford

WYND Alexander BSc(agr) 1950
MSc(Edin) 1962 BD(Lond) 1973
agr advis Fife from 1958

WYNESS James Alexander Davidson MB ChB 1928
resid Bramhall Cheshire

WYNESS William John Robertson MB ChB 1935
MCRA 1952 FRACR 1972
Adelaide S. Aust: visiting spec radiol Royal Adelaide hosp 1960–68, repatriation gen hosp 1960–78, Aust army consult. radiol (lt-col RAAMC) 1962–73, private radiol pract from 1960
wife *d* 30.5.76
m(2) Mitcham S Aust 14.5.77 Mary L. Pitcher or Cleland d of C. K. P. Kingswood S Aust

WYNNE-EDWARDS Hugh Robert *BSc 1955
FRS(C) 1968 Regd Prof Eng Ont 1968, Br Col 1972 DSc(hon) Memorial univ St John's Nfld 1975 Spendiarov Prize internat geol congress 1972
Canada: prof Queen's univ Kingston 1959–68, prof and head 1968–72; Cominco prof and head univ of Br Col 1972–77; asst secy (univs) min of state for sc and tech Ottawa 1977–79; vice pres and chief scient off. Alcan Internat Montreal from 1979

WYNNE-EDWARDS or Sorbie, Janet MB ChB 1955 MD 1975
MSc(Queen's univ Kingston) 1969
Queen's univ Kingston Ont Canada: res asst in med 1966–75, lect fam med 1973–74, lect med 1974–75, asst prof fam med from 1977

YATES Barbara Gertrude PhD 1953
sen lect maths Royal Holloway coll Lond from 1964

YEATS Alfred MA 1929
head: Skene Sq p s Aber 1963–66, Springhill p s Aber 1966–70; retd

YEATS James Alexander MA 1937
head Invergowrie s from 1955

YEH Shao Ying MA 1918 LLB 1919
no longer on GC reg

YELL William Lyall MB ChB 1917 MD 1928
d Macduff 7.1.63 *AUR* XL 201

YEOMAN Joseph Alexander BL 1941
ptnr Paull & Williamsons advoc Aber from 1955

YEUDALL or Forbes, Agnes Gertrude MA 1927
resid Inv

YORK Roland *BSc 1951 *MEd 1954
educ psych Lothian reg from 1975
m Edin 7.8.65 Gillian M. A. McMath d of John S. McM. Edin

YORKE James Burgoyne MA 1947
d Ayr 30.4.76

YORSTON James Roderick MA 1951
teacher geog Kinross h s from 1969

YORSTON John McLeod MA 1950
dep head Scotstown s Br of Don Aber from 1967

YORSTON Malcolm Bruce MB ChB 1953
FFARCS(Eng) 1961
consult. anaest Wessex reg hosp board Southampton from 1962

YOUNG Agnes MA 1928
retd 1970; resid Turriff

YOUNG Archibald Grahame Brown MB ChB 1937
g p Aber from 1939

YOUNG Charles Allan BSc 1945 *1948
scient civ serv RRE Malvern 1948–61; Johns Hopkins univ USA: radar syst analyst applied phys lab Silver Spring Md 1962–70, William S. Parsons fell. dept of earth and planetary sc Baltimore Md 1971–72, sen staff scient applied phys lab Silver Spring, later moved to Laurel, from 1972

YOUNG or Macdonald, Charlotte Roberta Dallas *MA 1916
d 3.2.78

YOUNG Douglas Alexander *MA 1951
sen progr and logic des Elliot Automation Borehamwood 1960–63; sen scient off. GPO res stat Lond 1963–66; asst prof/dean of computer sc univ of Manitoba Winnipeg 1966–67, assoc prof from 1967; sen res fell. Europ. molecular biol organis Edin 1970–72
m Winnipeg –.6.75 Joan G. Clark or Orman

YOUNG Evelyn Crighton MA 1945
teacher Ruthrieston s 1946–70, year mistress Torry acad from 1970

YOUNG George Douglas Paton *MA 1950

YOUNG George Forbes MA 1939 LLB 1947
ptnr Watt & Cumine advoc Aber from 1953

YOUNG Hilda Margaret MA 1930
retd 1969, resid New Deer

YOUNG Hilda Sutherland MB ChB 1920
d 26.1.76 *AUR* XLVI 415

YOUNG Ian Robert BSc 1954 PhD 1958
MInstMC 1964 CEng FIEE 1969
consult. elect. eng Lond 1967–70; tech dir Evershed Power Optics Chertsey Process Peripherals Thatcham 1970–76; dept head EMI Central Research Labs Hayes from 1976

YOUNG James Findlay *BSc(agr) 1950 PhD 1958
advis off. in grassland husb NOSCA from 1958

YOUNG or Harper, Jane Ann Gray MA 1921
d Toronto 16.10.79

YOUNG Jessie Wilson MA 1929

YOUNG John MA 1909
no longer on GC reg

YOUNG John *MA 1929
retd 1973; resid York

YOUNG John Irving *BSc(eng) 1947

YOUNG or Cowie, Sheila Stewart MA 1949

YOUNG or Dee, Winifred Morrison MA 1922
no longer on GC reg

YOUNGSON (or Brown) Alexander John *MA 1947 DLitt 1953
prof pol econ Edin 1962–74; vice-prin Edin 1970–74; dir res s soc sc Canberra from 1974

YOUNGSON Alexander Patrick MA 1925 MB ChB 1929
retd 1973; resid Broughton nr Stockbridge Hants

YOUNGSON Catherine Park MA 1951

YOUNGSON Douglas Alexander Ritchie BL 1934
ptnr Hunter & Gordon and Alexander Stronach & Son now Stronachs advoc Aber from 1934
d Aber 26.10.79 *AUR* XLVIII 353

YOUNGSON George William *BSc 1941 PhD 1948
CChem FRCS
sen lect chem RGIT from 1953

YOUNGSON or McRobie, Isobel MA 1945
teacher: Aber 1945–49, 1953–57, Aberdeensh 1961–63, Glasg 1967

YOUNGSON James MA 1921
chap. gen hosp board Aber 1945–71; retd; resid Aber

YOUNGSON James Donaldson MA 1925
retd 1964; resid Perth

YOUNGSON or Robiette, Kathleen Campbell MA 1927
resid Great Missenden

YOUNGSON Robert Murdoch MB ChB 1951
DTM & H 1964 DO(RCS) 1965 OStJ 1969
ophth trainee Brit milit hosp Gibraltar 1960–64; regist ophthal ARI 1964–65; spec ophth Tidworth milit hosp 1965–66; sen spec ophth Brit milit hosp Singapore 1966–69; ophth surg St John ophth hosp Jerusalem 1969–70; sen spec ophth: Brit milit hosp Iserlohn Germany 1970–74; consult. ophth Cambridge milit hosp Aldershot 1974–77; consult. ophth Brit milit hosp Hong Kong from 1977

YOUNIE Elspet Margaret *MEd 1955
psych audience res BBC Lond 1957–62
m Aber 20.10.62 Alasdair H. Norton BA(Oxon) merch banker/dir Comalco Melbourne s of James E. N. BA(Oxon) Farnham

YOUNIE George Grant MB ChB 1948
TD 1964
g p Aber from 1952

YOUNIE John Milne *MA 1909
d Kippen 4.1.61 *AUR* XXXIX 102

YOUNIE or Wardill, Mary BSc 1949 MB ChB 1954
part-time clin with prov chest disease serv Sudbury Ontario from 1966

YOUNIE or Hamilton, Thora Dewar *MA 1951 Dip Ed 1952
Edin: lect hist coll of comm 1969–72, Stevenson coll from 1972

YUILL or McLean, Helen Isabel MA 1925
resid Gorebridge

YUILL Robert *MA 1922
deceased

YUILL William Edward *MA 1947
prof Ger Bedford coll Lond from 1975

YULE Adam Thomson *BSc 1948
indust chem Procter & Gamble Europ tech center Belgium from 1948

YULE Joseph Lockhart Downes MB ChB 1913
lt col
d 18.8.68

YULE Robert Farquhar Spence *BSc 1951
scient off. Glaxo labs Montrose from 1954
m Montrose –.5.59 Moira E. Ogilvie teacher d of William O. Grandtully

YULE Robert Mortimer MB ChB 1949
g p Silloth Cumbria from 1957

YULE William MA 1937 BD 1939
C of S min Kemnay 1964–72; retd; resid Crieff
d Perth 15.5.78 *AUR* XLVII 359

YUNNIE Clara Henrietta *MA 1926
no longer on GC reg

ZAMORY John Joachim
see Stephen

ZAMORY Wolfgang
see Stephen

ZIMMERMAN or Simms, Madeleine Berta *MA 1952
MSc 1976
Lond: edit. Fabian soc publications 1960–64; press off./gen secy Abortion Law Reform Assoc 1964–70, res fell. The Eugenics Society 1970–75; co-author *Abortion Law Reformed* 1971; sen Leverhulme stud. Bedford coll Lond 1975–77; sen res off. Inst for Social Studies in Medical Care, Lond from 1977

MARRIED WOMEN GRADUATES PRE–1956 WITH HUSBANDS' NAMES IN ALPHABETICAL ORDER

An asterisk (*) indicates an Aberdeen University graduate.
The year of graduation follows the husband's name if he graduated after 1955 and his name therefore appears in Section I of this volume.

ADAMS John P	HARKINS Anne
AIRD Alexander H	DIACK Mary M
*AITKEN Angus	SMITH Wilma W
ALLAN	HARRIS Barbara M
ALLEN William S	McCALLUM Aenea J
ANDERSON	ABERNETHY Hilda M
ANDERSON Alexander C	BURLEY Flora M
ANDERSON George W	KEMP Moyra S M
ANGUS Clayton B W	REID Anne I
ASTLE	MILNE Gladys
ATKINS Leonard B W	BLACK Jessie M
AUSTIN Jack	HOYLE Nancy J C

*BAIN Robert	SHIRREFFS Helen C
BAKHTAR Farhang	EDWARDS Jane L
BARBER Stuart C L	SHIVAS Isobel B A
BARRETT-AYRES Reginald	CRAIG Esther M
BAXTER Peter W	RICE Maureen A
BAXTER William P	JOHNSON Rosemary A
BECHHOFER Frank	CONOCHIE Jean B
BENNETT Alan D	FRASER Helen M
BENTLEY Alan L	SOUTHERAN Margaret
BENWELL Francis E	DAVIDSON Margaret E M
BIGGAR Gordon R	THOMSON Beryl
BJARNASON Bjarni B	MACDONALD Catherine
BOAG Thomas J	MILNE Lorna C
BODIE William G R	GARDEN Margaret H
BOORER Harold J	JOHNSTON Mary R
BRAS Jan F	DUGUID Annabelle M
BRIANT Andrew K	DICKSON Kathleen
BROATCH Hugh W	BAXTER Flora L
BROWN	CROMBIE Katherine I
BROWN John A B	CHRISTIE Mary B
*BROWN Karl (1956)	McROBB Moira H
BRUCE Rodney	SHEACH Margaret H
BUCHAN Stanley J	MACLEOD Margaret M
BUCHANAN William D	SIM Mary B
BUCK Alfons	INGRAM Anne
BURNS Alfred J	BARRON Catherine A
BURNS Norman	HAY Janet G
BYRN Richard F M	BREBNER Lilias W

CAIRNS	JACK Marjorie
CAMERON Antony D	MARSHALL Doreen G
CAMPBELL George	CARNIE Mary H
CAMPBELL James	McDONALD Mary G
CAMPBELL John M	COLT Joan M R
CARDONA Juan	CUMMING Joyce E
*CHIN Sherlock S L (1966)	DOUGLAS Vivienne M
*CHISHOLM Alexander G	JENKINS Margaret W
CHOPIN	JOHNSON Joan M
CLARK Gordon	COWIE Jessie G
COATS	SINGLETON Neith L B
COCKBURN John T	LAWRIE Una
COLMAN John A R	RAE Nancy M
CONNOLLY Kevin	SPEED Isobel
*CONOCHIE Douglas A F	McLEAN or PETRIE, Cairine R M
CONWAY James D	SKEA Edith M
COOPER John A	MERCHANT Margaret E S
CORDINER Alexander M	MATHIESON Constance M
CORSE David R	BULLEN Jennie
COWIE David K	MACAULAY Murdina
COWLEY	HUNTER Eilean A
COX	FINDLAY Diana A
CRAIG	HUSBAND Valentine M
CRAIG	ROBERTSON Elsie
CRAWFORD	MITCHELL Nellie
CRICHTON Daniel S	McCALLUM Isabella
CUMMINE James	BEANGE Margaret H
CURRIE William M	LESLIE Margaret E

DARMON Paul E	BRAND Margaret M
DAWSON	BAINES Doreen
DESMOND Edward J	EDWARDS Jean M
DICKIE James J	PRIEST Elizabeth A F
DICKINSON Leslie	MACDONALD Norma
*DINNES James A (1956)	DAVIDSON Nancy R C
DORRELL Peter G	CONCHIE Julia G W
DUCHOVNY	MILLER or BUCHAN, Margaret
DUGUID William J	FYFE Grace C
DURKACZ Kazimierz P	KOPERSKA Janina F M
*DURNIN Patrick J	MUTCH Elizabeth A
DUTHIE George A	TAYLOR Elizabeth A

EDMOND	MILNE Jeannie
*EDMOND John S	THOMSON Dorothy A
EDWARDS Alan R	THOMSON Ann L
EDWARDS Ormond St J	TAYLOR Irene B
EVANS Maurice	DONALD Margaret P
FLOWERS John E	CAMPBELL Rosemary E
FORBES Donald L	WESTIE Kathleen
FORBES James R	WOOD Helena
*FORREST Alistair W	WHITTER Agnes E
*FORSYTH Robert M	PIKSIS Velta
FOTHERINGHAM Michael T	MUNRO Joan
GABRIEL Ronald M	MCGLASHAN Agnes M
GARROW James	WATT Aileen
GARTLAND	SCOTT Stella J
GIBSON George B F	STEWART Margaret A
GILBERT Ian G	DONALD Heather M
GILL	MACKENZIE Myra Aileen
*GILLAN John T C	WOOD Isobel M
GILMOUR John	SAINT Dorothy
GLASS James R	MACKAY Lena
GLOVER Harold G	BURNETT Muriel
GRAHAM John J	REID Martha
*GRAHAM Thomas C	CRAN Jean J
GRANT Daniel B	MACKENZIE Sandra I
GRAY James P	PATERSON Jean F
GRAY John C	SMITH Sheena
GREEFF Lawrence J	GOVE Daisy D
*GREIG William J	MORRISON Catherine
GREY Eric M	THOMAS Isabella E M F
HAGGART Ivan	SMART Mary E
HAMILTON Ian B	WATT Marjory I K
HARBORD John J G H	STRUTHERS Frances C
HARPER Alexander	LAW Sheila
HARRIES	THOMSON Margaret D
HATCH	LAWSON Janet M
HATVANY	ELRICK Doris M
HEMPSEED Allan	AITKEN Dorothy R
HENDERSON	ALLAN Margaret M O
HERNER Saul	ALEXANDER Mary
HEWARD Alexander	WALLER Patricia M
HILL John D N	WHEELAN Lorna
HOPKINS Rex E	MITCHELL Margaret
HOWIE George F	DUNCAN Elizabeth E
HOWIESON	MACDONALD Betsy
HUNTER Robert S	HAYMAN Ann E
HURRY	COW Catherine M
INNES David J L	DUNCAN Margaret G
JACK Neil McL	CUMMING Patricia M
JEZZARD Robert	LEASK Mary I M
JOBLING Geoffrey L	KINDNESS Jane
*JOHNSTON William G (1958)	ROSS Anne
JONES	MOIR Sylvia M
JONES Lloyd H P	MILNE Angela A
*KEIR Alexander	HALL Agnes T C
KEMSLEY John	NEILL Freda K
KENDRICK	SURTEES Anne D
KENNEDY	MORRISON Kathleen M
KERMACK Stuart D	MACKENZIE Barbara
KING John E	COCHRANE Helen B T

KOLIZERAS	BEATTIE Katrina
KRAAL Winston A	MOIR Maureen A
KUZMINSKI Telesfor M	PETRIE Elizabeth M
LASZEWSKI	KINEL Zofia K W
LAUGHTON Bruce	AIKEN Doris M
*LAW George R (1957)	ABERNETHY Elizabeth A
LAWRIE David A R	THOM Elizabeth H
LAWSON Bernard W	STEWART Dolina
LEE	ROSS Catherine I M
*LEE Richard M (1957)	BLACK Arthurina R M
LEEDALE Harry H	STEPHEN Sheila T
*LEES Gordon M (1961)	MANSON Doris I
LOGAN Garth	ANDERSON Irene R
LOW William J	STEWART HELEN
LOW-MITCHELL Lachlan G	CHALMERS Audrey M
LUCAS Emanuel G	WYLLIE Violet M
LUCHSINGER Matthias H	SLATER Margaret
LYNCH Patrick	CAMPBELL Mary S
LYTHGOE James P	MELVIN Anne
MCBURNIE John I	THOMPSON Jane M
MCCORKINDALE	FALCONER Catherine J
MACDONALD Christopher I	GAVIN Evelyn E
*MACDONALD Kenneth J	COCKER Phyllis M
MACDONALD Patrick D C L	GRANT Donella
MACDONALD Peter	FRASER Helen C
MCGEORGE William J	MURRAY Sheila
MCINTOSH Robert C	LOW Norma
MACIVER	PETERKIN Ethel M
MACKAY	CRUICKSHANK Annie
MACKAY Andrew	MCGOWAN Christina J
MACKAY Thomas I	MAITLAND Gladys L
MACKENZIE	MACDONALD Janet B W
MACKENZIE David D	MORRISON Mary M
MACKENZIE Finlay	MACDONALD Agnes
MCKENZIE James	MACDONALD Catherine
MACKENZIE Kenneth G F	GORDON Helen E
MACKENZIE Norman C	STRACHAN Georgina T
MCKIE John S	CAMPBELL Jean M
MACKIE John W	MURRAY Jane E
MACKINNON Norman N	MANSON Margaret F
MACLEAN Norman	BARCLAY Mary D
MACLEOD Angus	MACARTHUR Effie K
MCMILLAN	CRAIG Elma G
*MACMILLAN William B R	MURRAY Mary A B
MACPHERSON Donald	REITH Margaret
MACWILLIAM Daniel	FRASER Christine G
MARR Alfred J	MCINTOSH Irene M
MARSHALL Charles J	STRACHAN Maureen C
MASSIE James	MURRAY Moira
MATHER Alexander S	SMITH Mary M
MATHIE	DAVIDSON Ethel M F
MEIKLE W James	GRANT Muriel C
*MELVILLE William S	CRAIG Jean F
*MILLER Gordon R (1957)	SLEIGH Lesley M
MILLER Thomas A	MENZIES Joan I
MILLS Joseph E	MILLS Margaret M
MILNE Thornton G	CATTANACH Sandra I D
MINTER Robert J	MORRISON Margaret L
MONKS Edward J	MACRAE Ishbel M
MULLARD Roger	SAINT Dorothy
MURRAY	MACKENZIE Annie M
MURRAY Robert I	CRAIB Kathleen
*MURRAY Stewart	KEAN Helen M

*Neizer Justice A (1960)	Thompson Barbara A
Nicholls	Smith Mary H
Nicoll Alexander J D	Keith Elizabeth M
Niven George G	Dempster Mary R
Norrie James P	Forbes Eleanor M
Norton Alasdair H	Younie Elspet M
Norton Gerald W T	Scotcher Lilian M
O'Gorman James	Anderson Janet W
Park George	Anderson Margaret J
Parker	Leach Gweneth R
Peacock Lawrence	Dunn Eileen C K
Peel	Barker Noël C B
Pennie James	Leith Helen S
*Penny Alan B	Rennie Cecilia
Pereira Helio G	Scott Marguerite M
Perrée Frank Le Riche	Greene Anne C
Petrie David S	Bell Aluinn N
Petrie Ian G M	McIntosh Irene M
Philip John C	Cowie Isabella S
Phillips Albert J	Scott Edith
Preece	Davidson Sylvia H M
Pritchard John E	Heddle Inga P
Quigley Thomas W	Morrison Margaret G
Rae Alistair S L	Duguid Helen L D
Rae Herbert	Barron Jeannie H M
Rae John N	Paton Elsie M
Ramsay William	Barron Annie
Rawlins Raymond H	Brown Mabel K
Rayne Robert	Dinnie Doreen A
Reeves William J	Gordon Diana M
Reid Charles J	Cockburn Mary
Reid William A P	Dickson Margaret L
Reynaud Jacques	Lascelles Gladys M
*Rhind Edward G G	McCombie Kathleen
Riddoch Charles B	Smith Lorna
Roberts Horace E	Norrie Mary B
Robertson Iain A	Munro Irene
*Robley John A W	Sweeney Sheila M
Ross Charles W	Harvey Jeanie
Ross William G	Wood Catherine S
Sanderson William G	Macleod Anne S
Sandison Alexander L	Paterson Mary S
Scarth George W	Anderson Mary A
Scherz Franz	Craggs Joyce
Scott	Scott Jean M
Scott Douglas D	Soutar Patricia F
Scudamore	Milne Joan M
Sehrson	Worling Euphemia B
*Shepherd Ronald (1956)	Main Elsie M
Sheran John H	Donald Ella
Shewan David M	Morrison Margaret
Shirra Robert F	Philip Audrey
Shirran Douglas	Beveridge Evelyn E

Simpson George	Stephen Susan
Singer Alexander	Newlands Annie
Smith	Duncan Elizabeth D
Smith	Wood Isabella J
Smith Ben	Stephen Mildred W
*Smith George M C	MacRae Anne M S
Snelson Peter D	West Evelyn M
Stephen Daniel J	Michie Ethel L
Stephen George	Ferries Catherine A
Sterland George M S	Macleod Mairi E
Stewart Douglas C W	Forbes Jane M M
Strachan John	Crabb Catherine A
*Strachan William E	Cuthbertson Lilias M
Stuart	Johnston Margaret H
*Suttie James M (1956)	Andrews Elizabeth R
Synge Francis M	Lancaster Margaret S
Tanner John	Benzie Sheila A
Taylor William A	Edwards Phyllis A
Telfer John M	Forrest Elsie M
Thomas David E W	Middler Dorothy F
Thomson	Lyon Alice A C
Thomson Norman D	Sutherland Jane H
Thomson William	Peter Jean E
Tosh Alfred	Stratton Dorothy I B
Tracy Robert W	Bromberg Priscilla B
Traill	Duthie Margaret S
Tucker Arthur E	MacKenzie Maimie M
Tucker James H	Swanson Margaret
*Urquhart Robert W	Gibson Jane
Van Zyl Chris P	Keay Margaret E
Vernon Louis O	McKenzie Nellie B
Wagner John	Gauld Katharine W
Walker Alexander	McDonald Marie W
Walker Colin H	Porter Dorothy M
Wallace Norman S	Farquhar Moira
Waller Dudley	Hill Amelia
*Walterson Laurence I (1957)	Anderson Jean
Watt Charles M	Noble Mary J
Watters John R G	Raitt Norah P
Weesel Baron van	Sharp Margaret I A
Weston Roy F	Donaldson Sheina M
Wetmore Robert J	Mitchell Evelyn J
*Whiteford Allan D	Mackay Christina M
Whitehouse Henry D	Wood Millicent M M
Wilkinson	Strachan Emma E
Williams	Skene Annie P
Willox Alexander R	Henderson Moira E K
Wilson	Fallowfield or Mackay, Patricia M
Wilson Eric C	Watt Catherine A
Wilson George C	Mackenzie Elizabeth M F
Wilson Leslie	Greig Hazel W
Winter	Campbell Violet M
Woolfenden Thomas	Croll Jean F

HONORARY GRADUATES 1926–1955

This list does not include the names of those honorary graduates of the 1926–1955 period whose deaths have already been recorded in the previous volume of the Roll of Graduates.
An asterisk (*) is prefixed to the names of those who hold, or have held, degrees of Aberdeen University other than honorary degrees. Their first Aberdeen degrees are shown here and this will enable them to be identified in the appropriate Section(s) of this volume and other volumes of the Roll of Graduates.

ABEL John Jacob LL D 1932
deceased

ABELL George Edmund Brackenbury (Sir) LL D 1947

ABERDEEN and TEMAIR George Gordon, Marquess of LL D 1954
d Aber 6.1.65

ADAM Ronald Forbes (General Sir) LL D 1945

ADAMS John Esslemont DD 1928
deceased

ALLEN Edgar Leonard DD 1946

ANDERSON John (Rt Hon Sir) LL D 1926
d 4.1.58

APPLETON Edward Victor LL D 1935
d 21.4.65

AUCHINLECK Claude John Eyre (Field Marshal Sir) LL D 1948
d 23.3.81

BAILLIE James Black LL D 1926
d 9.6.40

BAIRD Andrew Cumming LL D 1939
d 21.1.40

BALDENSPERGER Philippe Fernard LL D 1954

BARCLAY William LL D 1941

BARRON Evan Macleod LL D 1936
d Nairn 24.4.65 *AUR* XL 152

BELL Richard DD 1927
deceased

BENNET George H. (Rt Rev) LL D 1931
d 25.12.46

BENTWICH Norman LL D 1942
d 8.4.71

BERKELBACH van der SPRENKEL Simon Frederick Hendrik Jan DD 1951
d 18.1.67

BEST Maud Storr LL D 1945
d 18.1.69

BICKERSTETH Geoffrey Langdale LL D 1955
d 29.3.74

BLACK John Bennett LL D 1954
d 25.11.64

BLISS Kathleen (Mrs) DD 1949

BLOCH Olaf LL D 1937
d 19.10.44

BOHR Neils Henrik David LL D 1952
d 18.11.62

BROAD Charlie Dunbar LL D 1947
d 11.3.71

BROWN Ivor John Carnegie LL D 1950
d 22.4.74

BROWNE Buckston (Sir) LL D 1932
d 19.1.45

BUBER Martin DD 1953
d Jerusalem 13.6.65 *AUR* XLI 153

BUCHAN John Norman Stuart The Rt Hon Baron Tweedsmuir of Elsfield LL D 1949

BUCKLER William Hepburn LL D 1935
d 2.3.52

BURLEIGH John Henderson Seaforth DD 1938

BURT Cyril Lodowic LL D 1939
no longer on GC reg

***BUTCHART Henry Jackson (Lt Col) LL D 1952**
BL(Aberd) 1905
d Aber 30.8.71 *AUR* XLIV 231

BUTLER Edwin John LL D 1938
d 4.4.43

BUTTERFIELD Herbert LL D 1952
d 1979

CAITHNESS The Rt Hon The Earl of LL D 1931
d 25.3.47

CALLANDER John Graham LL D 1932
d 18.3.38

CAMERON John LL D 1950

***CAMERON Lewis Legertwood Legg DD 1953**
BSc(Aberd) 1920
d Edin 19.3.73 *AUR* XLV 225

CARGILL James Jamieson LL D 1955
d 28.6.71

CARRITT Edgar Frederick LL D 1950
d 19.6.64

CARTON DE WIART Adrian (Lt Gen Sir) LL D 1947
d 5.6.63

CHIRGWIN Arthur Mitchell DD 1943
d 29.6.66

CHURCHILL Winston Spencer LL D 1946
d 24.1.65

CLARK George Norman LL D 1936
d 6.2.79

CLARKE John LL D 1927
d 28.9.39

CLARKE Mary Gavin LL D 1943
d 12.2.76 *AUR* XLVII 106

CRUICKSHANK Alexander DD 1932
no longer on GC reg

CRUICKSHANK John LL D 1955
d Aber 10.10.66 *AUR* XLII 91

***CURRIE George Alexander (Sir) LL D 1948**
BSc(agr)Aberd 1923

DAHLBERG Gunnar LL D 1938
no longer on G C reg

DAIN Harry Guy LL D 1939
d 26.2.66

DAVIDSON Francis DD 1931
deceased

DEAN Henry Roy LL D 1950
d 13 2.61

DEANE Frederick Llewellyn (Rt Rev) DD 1931
d 12.1.52

de ZULUETA Francis LL D 1953
d 15.1.58

DODD Charles Harold DD 1930
d 1.9.73

DRIVER Godfrey Rolles DD 1946

***DRUMMOND James Gilmour DD 1951**
MA(Aberd) 1907
d Glasg 20.2.63 *AUR* XL 199

DUFF James Fitzjames LL D 1942
d 24.4.70

***DUTHIE Charles Sim DD 1952**
MA(Aberd) 1932
d Edin 11.1.81

DYSON George (Sir) LL D 1942
d 28.9.64

***ELDER John Rawson LL D 1943**
MA(Aberd) 1902
d Dunedin NZ 12.4.62 *AUR* XXXIX 373

ELLIOTT James Sands (Sir) LL D 1939
d 26.10.59

ELMSLIE William Alexander Leslie DD 1928
d 14.11.66 *AUR* XLI 312

ELPHINSTONE The Rt Hon Baron LL D 1931
d 28.11.55

***ESSLEMONT Mary LL D 1954**
BSc(Aberd) 1914

***FINDLAY Adam Fyfe LL D 1948**
MA(Aberd) 1889
d Aber 19.1.62 *AUR* XXXIX 268

***FINDLAY Alexander LL D 1944**
MA(Aberd) 1895
d 14.9.66 *AUR* XLI 286

FLEW Robert Newton DD 1942

FORSTER Edward Morgan LL D 1931
d 7.6.70

FOSTER John DD 1945
d 3.11.73

FRASER Duncan LL D 1951
d Aber 18.2.66

***FRASER John Annand DD 1951**
MA(Aberd) 1919

FYFE William Hamilton (Sir) LL D 1949
d 13.6.65

GARDINER James Bruce DD 1938
no longer on GC reg

GARROD Alfred Guy Roland (Air Marshal) LL D 1943
d 3.1.65

GARSTANG John LL D 1931
d 12.9.56

GILSON Etienne Henry LL D 1931
no longer on GC reg

GOLDSCHMIDT Victor Moritz LLD 1944

GORDON Dudley (Lord) LLD 1948
d –.4.72

GRAHAM John Anderson DD 1931
d 15.5.42

GRANT Francis James LLD 1931
d 17.2.53

GRAY Alexander (Sir) LLD 1949
d 17.2.68

GRAY James LLD 1939
d 14.12.75

HARDY William Bate (Sir) LLD 1928
d 23.1.34

***HASTINGS Edward DD 1950**
MA(Aberd) 1913
d Aber 31.7.80 *AUR* XLIX 66

HAY Malcolm Vivian LLD 1950
d Aber 27.12.60 *AUR* XL 94

HERBERT Arthur Gabriel DD 1949
deceased

***HENDRY George Stuart DD 1949**
MA(Aberd) 1924

HILL H Erskine (The Very Rev) DD 1931
d 22.4.39

HILL Leonard Erskine (Sir) LLD 1931
d 30.3.52

HNIK Frank Martin DD 1942

HØEG Carsten LLD 1948

HROMADKA Josef L DD 1949
d 26.12.69 *AUR* XLIII 446

HUNT John (Brigadier Sir) LLD 1954

IRVINE James Colquhoun (Sir) LLD 1931
d 12.6.52

***JAMESON William Wilson (Sir) LLD 1940**
MA(Aberd) 1905
d Lond 18.10.62 *AUR* XL 75

JENKINSON Hilary LLD 1949
d 5.3.51

JOHNSTON Thomas (The Rt Hon) LLD 1949
d 5.9.65

KAHLE Paul DD 1940
d 24.9.64

***KELLAS John DD 1950**
MA(Aberd) 1920
d Edin 12.11.67 *AUR* XLII 358

***KENNEDY Archibald Robert Stirling LLD 1933**
MA(Aberd) 1880
d –.10.38

KNOX Edmund Arbuthnott (The Rt Rev) DD 1932
d 16.1.37

KOO Vi Kyuin Wellington (His Excellency) LLD 1943
deceased

LAING Alexander James Louttit LLD 1944
d Ashurst 24.11.62 *AUR* XL 94

LAMB David C LLD 1934
d 7.7.51

LAMB John (Sir) LLD 1931
d 3.7.52

***LIANG Lone LLD 1945**
MA(Aberd) 1917
d Yonkers NY State 12.6.67 *AUR* XLII 335

LIGHTFOOT Robert Henry DD 1936
d 24.11.53

***LILLIE William DD 1948**
MA(Aberd) 1921

LINDEMAN Frederick Alexander LLD 1940

LINDSELL Wilfred Gordon LLD 1946
d 2.5.73

***LINKLATER Eric Robert Russell LLD 1946**
MA(Aberd) 1925
d Aber 7.11.74 *AUR* XLVI 10

LÖFSTEDT Einar LLD 1937
deceased

***LOTHIAN (William) Arthur Cunningham (Sir) LLD 1950**
MA(Aberd) 1908
d Lond 16.11.62 *AUR* XL 77

MACAULAY Thomas Bassett LLD 1930
d Montreal 3.4.42 *AUR* XXIX 248

MacARTHY Desmond LLD 1932
d 7.6.52

***MACDONALD Robert Gordon DD 1954**
MA(Aberd) 1907
d 17.12.70

***MACKAY John Alexander DD 1939**
MA(Aberd) 1912

***McKENZIE John Grant DD 1939**
MA(Aberd) 1910
d Edin 17.5.63 *AUR* XL 199

***MACKINTOSH Robert DD 1950**
MA(Aberd) 1910
d Edin 1.1.62 *AUR* XXXIX 273

McNEUR George Hunter (The Very Rev) DD 1948

MANSON Thomas Mortimer Yule LLD 1951

MARSHALL Charles Robertshaw LLD 1931
d 2.4.52

MASSEY Vincent (The Hon) LLD 1937
d 30.12.67

MAXWELL John Stirling (Sir) LL D 1935
d 30.5.56

MAYO William James LL D 1933
d 28.7.39

MEIJERS Edward Maurits LL D 1949

MERTON Thomas Ralph (Sir) LL D 1955
d 10.10.69

MEULENGRACHT Jens Einar LL D 1939
no longer on GC reg

***MILNE William Proctor LL D 1946**
MA(Aberd) 1903
d Glack 3.9.67 *AUR* XLII 178

MILON Yves LL D 1950

***MORRISON Alexander James DD 1955**
MA(Aberd) 1909
d 29.1.64 *AUR* XL 396

***MURISON Alfred Ross LL D 1951**
MA(Aberd) 1912
d Glasg 21.2.68 *AUR* XLII 351

MURISON William LL D 1928
d Culter 26.6.41 *AUR* XXIX 87

***MURRAY John LL D 1930**
MA(Aberd) 1900
d Lond 28.12.64 *AUR* XLI 53

NICHOLSON Patrick Joseph (The Rt Rev) LL D 1953

NIELSEL Wilhelm DD 1954

***NIVEN William Dickie DD 1928**
MA(Aberd) 1900
d Glasg 26.2.65 *AUR* XLI 145

***NOBLE Peter Scott (Sir) LL D 1955**
MA(Aberd) 1921

NORDAL Sigurdur LL D 1947

NORTH Christopher Richard DD 1946
d –.7.75

NYGREN Anders Theodor DD 1950

***OGG George DD 1951**
MA(Aberd) 1912
d 18.1.73 *AUR* XLV 224

***OGG William Gammie (Sir) LL D 1951**
MA(Aberd) 1912
d Edzell 25.9.79 *AUR* XLVIII 350

OLIVER Francis Wall LL D 1926
d 14.9.51

O'RAHILLY Thomas Francis LL D 1949

ORR John Boyd (Sir) LL D 1948
d 25.6.71

PHILIP James Randall (Sir) DD 1955
d 2.5.57

PIGOU Arthur Cecil LL D 1937
d 7.3.59

***PIRIE Alexander Irvine DD 1952**
MA(Aberd) 1902
d Edin 10.9.62 *AUR* XL 74

RAVEN Charles Earle DD 1946
d 8.7.64

REITH John Charles Walsham (Sir) LL D 1933
d 16.6.71

ROBINSON of Kielder Forest and of Adelaide (The Rt Hon Baron) LL D 1951
d Ottawa 6.9.52 *AUR* XXXV 104

ROBINSON Theodore Henry DD 1929
d 26.6.64

***ROSE Beatrice Mary LL D 1953**
MA(Aberd) 1912

ROSS John Alexander LL D 1941
d 16.9.67

***ROTHNIE Douglas Auchterlonie DD 1952**
MA(Aberd) 1896
d Kingston Jamaica 22.11.62 *AUR* XL 73

SELWYN Edward Gordon DD 1927
d 11.6.59

SHENNAN Theodore LL D 1937
d 21.10.48

SHEPHERD-BARRON Wilfred Philip LL D 1954
d 6.5.79

***SHORTT Henry Edward (Colonel) LL D 1952**
MB ChB(Aberd) 1910

SIEGFRIED Andre LL D 1950
d 28.3.59

SINCLAIR John Dickson LL D 1949
d Winchester 1951 *AUR* XXXIV 190

***SMART Alexander DD 1954**
MA(Aberd) 1918
d Prestwick 8.7.65 *AUR* XLI 150

SMITH Arthur Francis (General Sir) LL D 1948
d 8.8.77

SMITH Frank Edward (Sir) LL D 1931
d 1.7.70

SMITH Sidney Earle LL D 1953
d 17.3.59

SMITH William Wright (Sir) LL D 1944
d 15.12.56

SPENCER Herbert Ritchie LL D 1934
d 28.8.41

STEWART Findlater (Sir) LL D 1931
d 11.4.60

STONEHAVEN, John Lawrence Baird, Baron LL D 1931
d 20.8.41

STORRS Ronald (Sir) LL D 1938
d 1.11.55

SUTHERLAND David McBeth LL D 1953
d 20.9.73

***SUTHERLAND James Runcieman LL D 1955**
MA(Aberd) 1921

SUTHERLAND John Donald (Colonel) LL D 1927

TAYLOR Eva Germaine Rimington LL D 1949
d 5.7.66

***TENNANT William Robert (Sir) LL D 1953**
MA(Aberd) 1914
d St And 4.5.69 *AUR* XLIII 329

***THOM William Cumming DD 1948**
MA(Aberd) 1917
d Aber 25.3.79 *AUR* XLVIII 227

***THOMSON David Landsborough LL D 1952**
MA(Aberd) 1921
d Province of Quebec 20.10.64 *AUR* XLI 56

THOMSON George Paget (Sir) LL D 1948
d 10.9.75

***THOMSON Thomas Bentley Stewart DD 1946**
MA(Aberd) 1911
d 10.8.73 *AUR* XLV 316

THURNEYSEN Edward DD 1934
d 21.8.74

***TOCHER Forbes Scott DD 1934**
MA(Aberd) 1906
d 15.8.73 *AUR* XLV 316

UNDERHILL or Moore, Evelyn DD 1939
d 15.6.41

UNWIN Stanley LL D 1945
d 13.10.68

***URQUHART Robert William (Sir) LL D 1954**
MA(Aberd) 1920

***URQUHART William Spence DD 1930**
MA(Aberd) 1897
d Torphins 16.7.64 *AUR* XL 394

VISSER t'HOOFT Willem Adolf DD 1939
deceased

Von THADDEN-TRIEGLAFF Reinold DD 1953

WALEY Arthur David LL D 1938
d 27.6.66

***WALLACE Robert Strachan LL D 1928**
MA(Aberd) 1904
d Canberra 5.9.61 *AUR* XXXIX 271

WATSON David Meredith Seares LL D 1943
d 23.7.73

WATSON William DD 1929
d 24.4.72

WATT George Fiddes LL D 1955
d Aber 22.11.60 *AUR* XXXIX 106

WATT James Cromar LL D 1931
d 19.11.40

WILSON Horace John (Sir) LL D 1934
d 19.5.72

WIMBERLEY Douglas Neil (Major General) LL D 1948

WOOD Thomas Barlow LL D 1926
d 6.11.29

WYON Olive DD 1948
d Edin 1966 *AUR* XLI 342

ZIMMERN Alfred (Sir) LL D 1941
d 24.11.57

APPENDIX

DEGREES AND DIPLOMAS AWARDED FOR YEARS 1956–1970

DEGREES AND DIPLOMAS AWARDED

		HONORARY DEGREES		HIGHER DEGREES									ORDINARY AND									
		DD	LLD	D Litt	M Litt	PhD	MSc	DSc	MD	ChM	EdB(M Ed)	MTh	MA	MA(Hons)	BSc	BSc(Hons)	BSc(agr)	BSc(agr)(Hons)	BSc(eng)	BSc(eng)(Hons)	BSc(for)	BSc(for)(Hons)
1956	M	4	9	—	—	24	—	1	5	1	9	—	35	33	16	31	13	3	12	7	11	1
	W	—	—	—	—	4	—	—	2	—	—	—	64	19	12	8	4	—	—	—	—	—
1957	M	3	7	—	—	24	—	3	11	—	6	—	38	34	14	33	9	3	18	7	13	2
	W	—	—	—	—	6	—	—	—	—	—	—	59	19	12	4	—	—	—	—	—	—
1958	M	4	6	—	—	25	—	—	6	2	8	—	48	57	16	32	7	—	14	7	15	5
	W	—	1	—	—	2	—	—	—	—	2	—	70	19	13	4	1	—	—	—	—	—
1959	M	3	7	—	—	36	—	1	6	—	1	—	48	43	23	37	7	—	18	5	14	4
	W	—	—	—	—	1	—	—	1	—	—	—	73	19	15	11	—	—	—	—	—	—
1960	M	4	10	—	—	24	5	2	8	1	2	—	44	35	26	42	7	—	22	7	13	2
	W	—	2	—	—	3	—	—	2	—	2	—	71	19	21	9	—	—	—	—	—	—
1961	M	2	6	1	—	21	11	1	4	1	—	—	49	33	23	46	9	1	20	9	11	6
	W	—	—	—	—	—	1	—	—	—	3	—	92	30	14	5	—	—	—		—	—
1962	M	3	4	—	—	33	16	2	5	—	5	—	55	62	15	45	6	1	14	11	8	3
	W	—	1	—	—	2	—	—	—	—	2	—	82	27	19	9	—	—	—	—	—	—
1963	M	2	8	—	—	27	22	1	6	—	7	—	66	62	15	47	5	8	19	13	6	5
	W	—	—	—	—	1	1	—	3	—	1	—	79	24	3	5	—	—	—	—	—	—
1964	M	4	6	—	—	33	23	—	4	—	3	—	39	60	28	53	5	3	23	14	7	4
	W	—	1	—	—	2	3	—	—	—	—	—	103	31	18	10	—	—	—	—	—	—
1965	M	2	9	—	—	35	17	2	6	2	6	—	67	68	23	45	4	3	13	15	7	3
	W	—	—	—	1	1	—	—	2	—	3	—	116	39	20	16	—	—	—	—	—	—
1966	M	4	12	—	—	35	19	2	2	1	5	—	88	97	36	64	4	5	20	16	8	3
	W	—	1	—	—	1	1	—	2	—	4	—	127	55	24	20	1	1	—	—	—	—
1967	M	4	7	—	4	46	34	3	8	—	6	—	91	109	41	69	10	11	24	24	6	4
	W	—	—	—	1	7	1	—	1	—	5	—	173	52	19	21	—	1	—	—	—	—
1968	M	3	7	—	2	54	31	2	3	—	9	1	93	108	50	81	11	6	20	21	15	3
	W	—	2	—	3	8	3	—	—	—	2	—	192	89	25	25	—	—	—	—	—	—
1969	M	3	8	—	3	51	20	2	5	—	8	3	102	132	62	101	12	9	21	35	8	3
	W	—	1	—	2	6	7	—	1	—	2	—	218	103	25	29	—	—	1	—	—	—
1970	M	1	5	—	3	35	37	1	4	2	10	—	90	152	71	129	11	12	28	39	7	2
	W	—	—	—	4	4	7	—	2	—	5	—	197	91	50	25	1	1	—	—	—	—

NOTES

The degree of BEd is conferred in terms of a University Court Ordinance of 1965. To avoid confusion the degree of EdB was renamed MEd.

The figures for MD, ChM, MB ChB and BMedBiol include those with honours, commendation and distinction.

In the faculty of Law the degree of BL is no longer awarded; the LLB degree no longer requires candidates to have a previous degree.

FOR YEARS 1956–1970

HONOURS DEGREES								TOTALS (EXCLUDING HONORARY)			DIPLOMAS							
BD	BD(Hons)	BL	LLB	LLB(Hons)	MB ChB	BMedBiol	BEd	MEN	WOMEN	TOTAL	Dip Stat	Dip Medieval Studies	CASS	DipEd	DMRD	DPH	Dip Psychother	LTh
1	—	3	8	—	48	—	—	262		394	—	—	—	—	—	—	—	—
—	—	—	2	—	17	—	—		132		—	—	—	—	—	—	—	—
5	—	6	13	—	43	—	—	282		400	—	—	—	—	—	—	—	—
—	—	1	1	—	16	—	—		118		—	—	—	3	—	—	—	—
2	—	3	8	—	49	—	—	304		434	—	—	—	12	—	5	—	—
—	—	—	1	—	18	—	—		130		—	—	—	14	—	1	—	—
3	—	3	4	—	44	—	—	297		441	3	—	—	8	—	1	—	—
1	—	—	1	—	22	—	—		144		1	—	—	7	—	—	—	
5	—	1	12	—	51	—	—	309		452	—	—	—	8	—	—	—	—
—	—	—	—	—	16	—	—		143		—	—	—	7	—	—	—	—
3	—	3	14	—	43	—	—	309		473	1	—	—	16	—	2	—	—
—	—	—	—	—	19	—	—		164		—	—	—	4	—	1	—	—
—	—	1	12	—	37	—	—	331		494	2	—	—	14	—	—	—	—
—	—	—	1	—	21	—	—		163		—	—	—	9	—	—	—	—
3	—	—	8	—	34	—	—	354		485	4	—	—	16	—	—	—	—
—	—	—	3	—	11	—	—		131		—	—	—	12	—	2	—	—
3	—	—	14	2	58	—	—	376		553	—	—	—	10	—	—	—	—
—	—	—	1	—	9	—	—		177		—	—	—	10	—	1	—	—
—	1	1	15	2	43	—	—	378		608	—	—	—	20	—	1		2
—	—	—	2	—	30	—	—		230		1	—	—	13	—	2	—	—
1	—	—	25	4	54	—	—	489		740	—	—	—	22	—	2	3	—
—	—	—	4	1	10		—		251		1	—	—	18	—	2	1	—
3	—	—	23	3	55	—	—	574		883	—	—	—	26	—	—	—	5
—	—	—	6	—	21	1	—		309		—	2	—	28	—	—	—	—
2	—	—	29	7	57	6	—	611		999	—	4	1	27	—	—	3	2
—	—	—	5	—	33	—	3		388		—	2	—	32	—	—	—	—
4	1	—	38	6	57	5	18	706		1,160	—	2	1	41	2	3	2	7
—	—	—	5	1	18	4	32		454		—	1	8	41	—	—	—	—
4	1	—	39	4	39	7	17	744		1,196	—	—	—	30	2	—	2	3
—	—	—	10	1	27	1	26		452		—	1	6	37	—	—	—	—

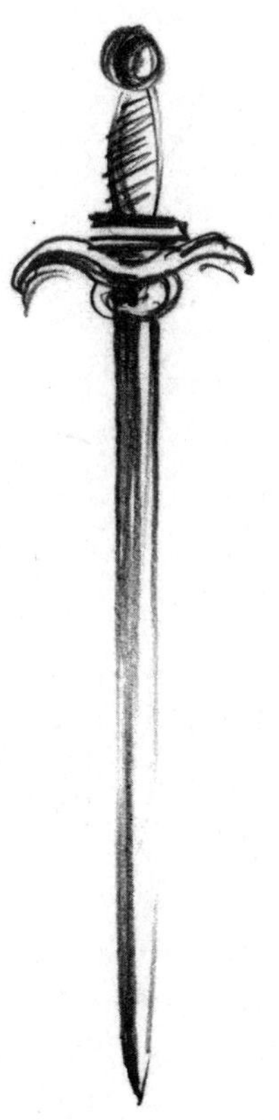

KILLING COMMENDATORE

ALSO BY HARUKI MURAKAMI

Fiction

1Q84
After Dark
After the Quake
Blind Willow, Sleeping Woman
Colorless Tsukuru Tazaki and His Years of Pilgrimage
Dance Dance Dance
The Elephant Vanishes
Hard-Boiled Wonderland and the End of the World
Kafka on the Shore
Men Without Women
Norwegian Wood
South of the Border, West of the Sun
Sputnik Sweetheart
The Strange Library
A Wild Sheep Chase
Wind/Pinball
The Wind-Up Bird Chronicle

Non-Fiction

Absolutely on Music: Conversations with Seiji Ozawa
Underground: The Tokyo Gas Attack and the Japanese Psyche
What I Talk About When I Talk About Running

HARUKI MURAKAMI

Killing Commendatore

TRANSLATED FROM THE JAPANESE BY

Philip Gabriel and Ted Goossen

Harvill *Secker*

LONDON

1 3 5 7 9 10 8 6 4 2

Harvill Secker, an imprint of Vintage,
20 Vauxhall Bridge Road,
London SW1V 2SA

Harvill Secker is part of the Penguin Random House group of companies
whose addresses can be found at global.penguinrandomhouse.com

First published by Harvill Secker in 2018
First published in Japan in two volumes titled *Kishidancho goroshi: Dai ichi-bu, Arawareru idea hen* and *Kishidancho goroshi: Dai ni-bu, Utsurou metafa hen*
in 2017 by Shinchosha Publishing Co. Ltd., Tokyo

A CIP catalogue record for this book is available from the British Library

penguin.co.uk/vintage

ISBN 9781787300194

Printed and bound in Great Britain by Clays Ltd, Elcograf S.p.A.

Penguin Random House is committed to a
sustainable future for our business, our readers
and our planet. This book is made from Forest
Stewardship Council® certified paper.

KILLING COMMENDATORE

PART 1

THE IDEA MADE VISIBLE

Prologue

Today when I awoke from a nap the faceless man was there before me. He was seated on the chair across from the sofa I'd been sleeping on, staring straight at me with a pair of imaginary eyes in a face that wasn't.

The man was tall, and he was dressed the same as when I had seen him last. His face-that-wasn't-a-face was half hidden by a wide-brimmed black hat, and he had on a long, equally dark coat.

"I came here so you could draw my portrait," the faceless man said, after he'd made sure I was fully awake. His voice was low, toneless, flat. "You promised you would. You remember?"

"Yes, I remember. But I couldn't draw it then because I didn't have any paper," I said. My voice, too, was toneless and flat. "So to make up for it I gave you a little penguin charm."

"Yes, I brought it with me," he said, and held out his right hand. In his hand—which was extremely long—he held a small plastic penguin, the kind you often see attached to a cell phone strap as a good-luck charm. He dropped it on top of the glass coffee table, where it landed with a small *clunk*.

"I'm returning this. You probably need it. This little penguin will be the charm that should protect those you love. In exchange, I want you to draw my portrait."

I was perplexed. "I get it, but I've never drawn a portrait of a person without a face."

My throat was parched.

"From what I hear, you're an outstanding portrait artist. And there's a first time for everything," the faceless man said. And then he laughed. At least, I think he did. That laugh-like voice was like the empty sound of wind blowing up from deep inside a cavern.

He took off the hat that hid half of his face. Where the face should have been, there was nothing, just the slow whirl of a fog.

I stood up and retrieved a sketchbook and a soft pencil from my studio. I sat back down on the sofa, ready to draw a portrait of the man with no face. But I had no idea where to begin, or how to get started. There was only a void, and how are you supposed to give form to something that does not exist? And the milky fog that surrounded the void was continually changing shape.

"You'd better hurry," the faceless man said. "I can't stay here for long."

My heart was beating dully inside my chest. I didn't have much time. I had to hurry. But my fingers holding the pencil just hung there in midair, immobilized. It was as though everything from my wrist down into my hand were numb. There were several people I had to protect, and all I was able to do was draw pictures. Even so, there was no way I could draw him. I stared at the whirling fog. "I'm sorry, but your time's up," the man without a face said a little while later. From his faceless mouth, he let out a deep breath, like pale fog hovering over a river.

"Please wait. If you give me just a little more time—"

The man put his black hat back on, once again hiding half of his face. "One day I'll visit you again. Maybe by then you'll be able to draw me. Until then, I'll keep this penguin charm."

Then he vanished. Like a mist suddenly blown away by a freshening breeze, he vanished into thin air. All that remained was the unoccupied chair and the glass table. The penguin charm was gone from the tabletop.

It all seemed like a short dream. But I knew very well that it wasn't.

If this was a dream, then the world I'm living in itself must all be a dream.

Maybe someday I'll be able to draw a portrait of nothingness. Just like another artist was able to complete a painting titled *Killing Commendatore*. But to do so I would need time to get to that point. I would have to have time on my side.

1

IF THE SURFACE IS FOGGED UP

From May until early the following year, I lived on top of a mountain near the entrance to a narrow valley. Deep in the valley it rained constantly in the summer, but outside the valley it was usually sunny. This was due to the southwest wind that blew off the ocean. Moist clouds carried by the wind entered the valley, bringing rain as they made their way up the slopes. The house was built right on the boundary line, so often it would be sunny out in front while heavy rain fell in back. At first I found this disconcerting, but as I got used to it, it came to seem natural.

Low patches of clouds hung over the surrounding mountains. When the wind blew, these cloud fragments, like some wandering spirits from the past, drifted uncertainly along the surface of the mountains, as if in search of lost memories. The pure white rain, like fine snow, silently swirled around on the wind. Since the wind rarely let up, I could even get by in the summer without air conditioning.

The house itself was old and small, but the garden in back was spacious. Left to its own devices it was a riot of tall green weeds, and a family of cats made its home there. When a gardener came over to trim the grass, the cat family moved elsewhere. I imagine they felt too exposed. The family consisted of a striped mother cat and her three kittens. The mother was thin, with a stern look about her, as if life had dealt her a bad hand.

The house was on top of the mountain, and when I went out on the terrace and faced southwest, I could catch a glimpse of the ocean through the woods. From there the ocean was the size of water in a washbowl, a minuscule sliver of the huge Pacific. A real estate agent I know told me that even if you can see a tiny portion of the ocean like I could here, it made all the difference in the price of the land. Not that I cared about an ocean view. From far off, that slice of ocean was nothing more than a dull lump of lead. Why people insisted on having an ocean view was beyond me. I much preferred gazing at the surrounding mountains. The mountains on the opposite side of the valley were in constant flux, transforming with the seasons and the weather, and I never grew tired of these changes.

Back then my wife and I had dissolved our marriage, the divorce papers all signed and sealed, but afterward things happened and we ended up making a go of marriage one more time.

I can't explain it. The cause and effect of how this all came about eluded even those of us directly involved, but if I were to sum it up in a word, it would come down to some overly trite phrase like "we reconciled." Though the nine-month gap before the second time we married (between the dissolution of our first marriage and the beginning of our second marriage, in other words) stood there, a mouth agape like some deep canal carved out of an isthmus.

Nine months—I had no idea if this was a long period or a short period for a separation. Looking back on it later, it sometimes seemed as though it lasted forever, but then again it passed by in an instant. My impression changed depending on the day. When people photograph an object, they often put a pack of cigarettes next to it to give the viewer a sense of the object's actual size, but the pack of cigarettes next to the images in my memory expanded and contracted, depending on my mood at the time. Like the objects and events in constant flux, or perhaps in opposition to them, what should have been a fixed yardstick inside the framework of my memory seemed instead to be in perpetual motion.

Not to imply that all my memories were haphazard, expanding and contracting at will. My life was basically placid, well adjusted, and, for the most part, rational. But those nine months were different, a period of inexplicable chaos and confusion. In all senses of the word that period was the exception, a time unlike any other in my life, as though I were a swimmer in the middle of a calm sea caught up in a mysterious whirlpool that came out of nowhere.

That may be the reason why, when I think back on that time (as you guessed, these events took place some years ago), the importance, perspective, and connections between events sometimes fluctuate, and if I take my eyes off them even for a second, the sequence I apply to them is quickly supplanted by something different. Still, here I want to do my utmost, as far as I can, to set down a systematic, logical account. Maybe it will be a wasted effort, but even so I want to cling tightly to the hypothetical yardstick I've managed to fashion. Like a helpless swimmer who snatches at a scrap of wood that floats his way.

When I moved into that house, the first thing I did was buy a cheap used car. I'd basically driven my previous car into the ground and had to scrap it, so I needed to get a new one. In a suburban town, especially living alone on top of a mountain, a car was a must in order to go shopping. I went to a used Toyota dealership outside Odawara and found a great deal on a Corolla station wagon. The salesman called it powder blue, though it reminded me more of a sick person's pale complexion. It had only twenty-two thousand miles on it, but the car had been in an accident at one point so they'd drastically reduced the sticker price. I took it for a test drive, and the brakes and tires seemed good. Since I didn't plan to drive it on the highway much, I figured it would do fine.

Masahiko Amada was the one who rented the house to me. We'd been in the same class back in art school. He was two years older, and was one of the few people I got along well with, so even after we finished college we'd occasionally get together. After we graduated he gave up on being an artist and worked for an ad agency as a graphic designer. When he heard that my wife and I had split up, and that I'd left home and had nowhere to stay, he told me the house his father owned was vacant and asked if I'd like to stay there as a kind of caretaker. His father was Tomohiko Amada, a famous painter of Japanese-style paintings. His father's house (which had a painting studio) was in the mountains outside Odawara, and after the death of his wife he'd lived there comfortably by himself for about ten years. Recently, though, he'd been diagnosed with dementia, and had been put in a high-end nursing home in Izu Kogen. As a result, the house had been empty for several months.

"It's up all by itself on top of a mountain, definitely not the most convenient location, but it's a quiet place. That I guarantee for sure," Masahiko said. "The perfect environment for painting. No distractions whatsoever."

The rent was nominal.

"If the house is vacant, it'll fall apart, and I'm worried about break-ins and fires. Just having someone there all the time will be a load off my mind. I know you wouldn't feel comfortable not paying any rent, so I'll make it cheap, on one condition: that I might have to ask you to leave on short notice."

Fine by me. Everything I owned would fit in the trunk of a small car, and if he ever asked me to clear out, I could be gone the following day.

I moved into the house in early May, right after the Golden Week holidays. The house was a one-story, Western-style home, more like a cozy cottage, but certainly big enough for one person living alone. It was on top of a midsized mountain, surrounded by woods, and even Masahiko wasn't sure how far the lot extended. There were large pine trees in the back garden, with thick branches that spread out in all directions. Here and there you'd find stepping stones, and there was a splendid banana plant next to a Japanese stone lantern.

Masahiko was right about it being a quiet place. But looking back on it now, I can't say that there were "no distractions whatsoever."

During the eight months after I broke up with my wife and lived in this valley, I slept with two other women, both of whom were married. One was younger than me, the other older. Both were students in the art class I taught.

When I sensed that the timing was right, I invited them to sleep with me (something I would normally never do, since I'm fairly timid and not at all used to that sort of thing). And they didn't turn me down. I'm not sure why, but I had few qualms about asking them to sleep with me, and it seemed to make perfect sense at the time. I felt hardly a twinge of guilt at inviting my students to have sex with me. It seemed as ordinary as asking somebody you passed on the street for the time.

The first woman I slept with was in her late twenties. She was tall with large, dark eyes, a trim waist, and small breasts. A wide forehead, beautiful straight hair, her ears on the large side for her build. Maybe not exactly a beauty, but with such distinctive features that if you were an artist you'd want to draw her. (Actually I am an artist, so I did sketch her a number of times.) She had no children. Her husband taught history at a private high school, and he beat her. Unable to lash out at school, he took his frustrations out at home. He was careful to avoid her face, but when she was naked I saw all the bruises and scars. She hated me to see them and when she took off her clothes, she insisted on turning off the lights.

She had almost no interest in sex. Her vagina was never wet and penetration was painful for her. I made sure there was plenty of foreplay, and we used lubricant gel, but nothing made it better. The pain was terrible, and it wouldn't stop. Sometimes she even screamed in agony.

Even so, she wanted to have sex with me. Or at least she wasn't averse to it. Why, I wonder? Maybe she wanted to feel pain. Or was seeking the *absence* of pleasure. Or perhaps she was after some sort of self-punishment. People seek all kinds of things in their lives. There was one thing, though, that she wasn't looking for. And that was *intimacy*.

She didn't want to come to my house, or have me come to hers, so to have sex we always drove in my car to a love hotel near the shore. We'd meet up in the large parking lot of a chain restaurant, get to the hotel a little after one p.m., and leave before three. She always wore a large pair of sunglasses, even when it was cloudy or raining. One time, though, she didn't show up, and she missed art class too. That was the end of our short, uneventful affair. We slept together four, maybe five times.

The other married woman I had an affair with had a happy home life. At least it didn't seem like her family life was lacking anything. She was forty-one then (as I recall), five years older than me. She was petite, with an attractive face, and she was always well dressed. She practiced yoga every other day at a gym and had a flat, toned stomach. She drove a red Mini Cooper, a new car she'd just purchased, and on sunny days I could spot it from a distance, glinting in the sun. She had two daughters, both of whom attended a pricey private school in upscale Shonan, which the woman was a graduate of too. Her husband ran some sort of company, but I never asked her what kind of firm it was. (Naturally I didn't want to know.)

I have no idea why she didn't flatly turn down my brazen sexual overtures. Maybe at the time I had some special magnetism about me that pulled in her spirit as if (so to speak) it were a scrap of iron. Or maybe it had nothing to do with spirit or magnetism, and she'd simply been needing physical satisfaction outside marriage and I just happened to be the closest man around.

Whatever it was, I seemed able to provide it, openly, naturally, and she commenced sleeping with me without hesitation. The physical aspect of our relationship (not that there was any other aspect) went smoothly. We performed the act in an honest, pure way, the purity almost reaching the level of the abstract. It took me by surprise when I suddenly realized this, in the midst of our affair.

But at some point she must have come to her senses, since one gloomy early-winter morning, she called me and said, "I think we shouldn't meet anymore. There's no future in it." Or something to that effect. She sounded like she was reading from a script.

And she was absolutely right. Not only was there no future in our relationship, there was no real basis for it, no *there* there.

Back when I was in art school I mainly painted abstracts. Abstract art is a hard thing to define, since it covers such a wide range of works. I'm not sure how to explain the form and subject matter, but I guess my definition would be "paintings that are nonfigurative images, done in an unrestrained, free manner." I won a few awards at small exhibitions, and was even featured in some art magazines. Some of my instructors and friends praised my work and encouraged me. Not that anyone pinned his hopes on my future, but I do think I had a fair amount of talent as an artist. Most of my oil paintings were done on very large canvases and required a lot of paint, so they were expensive to create. Needless to say, the possibility of laudable people appearing, ready to purchase an unknown artist's massive painting to hang on the wall at their home, was pretty close to zero.

Since it was impossible to make a living painting what I wanted, once I graduated, I started taking commissions for portraits to make ends meet. Paintings of so-called pillars of society—presidents of companies, influential members of various institutes, Diet members, prominent figures in various locales (there were some differences in the width of these "pillars"), all painted in a figurative way. They were looking for a realistic, dignified, staid style, totally utilitarian types of paintings to be hung on the wall in a reception area or a company president's office. In other words, my job compelled me to paint paintings that ran totally counter to my artistic aims. I could add that I did it *reluctantly,* and that still wouldn't amount to any artistic arrogance on my part.

There was a small company in Yotsuya that specialized in portrait commissions, and through an introduction by one of my art school teachers, I signed an exclusive contract with them. I wasn't paid a fixed salary, but if I turned out enough portraits, I made plenty for a young, single man to live on. It was a modest lifestyle—I was able to rent a small apartment alongside the Seibu Kokubunji railway line, usually managed to afford three meals a day, would buy a bottle of inexpensive wine from time to time, and went out on the occasional date to see a movie. Several years went by, and I decided that I'd focus on portrait painting for a fixed period, and then, once I'd made enough to live on for a while, I'd return to the kind of paintings I really wanted to do. Portraits were just meant to pay the rent. I never planned to paint them forever.

But once I got into it, I discovered that painting *typical* portraits was a pretty easy job. When I was in college I'd worked part-time for a moving company, and at a convenience store, and compared to those jobs, painting portraits was, physically and emotionally, much less of a strain. Once I got the hang of it, it was just a matter of repeating the same process again and again. Before long, I was able to finish a portrait quickly. Like flying a plane on autopilot.

After I'd been rather indifferently doing this work for about a year, I learned that my portraits were gaining some acclaim. My clients were really satisfied with my work. Obviously, if customers complain about the finished portraits, then not much work will come your way, and your contract with the agency might even get terminated. Conversely, if you have a good reputation, you get more work and your fees go up with each painting. The world of portrait painting is a fairly serious profession. I was still a beginner, but I was getting more and more commissions, and could charge higher fees with each work. The agent in charge of my portfolio was impressed, and some of my clients even glowingly commented that I had a "special touch."

I couldn't figure out why the portraits were being received so well. I was less than enthusiastic, just trudging through one assignment after another. Truthfully, I can't recall the face of a single person whose portrait I painted. Still, as my ultimate goal was to become a serious artist, once I took up my brush and faced a canvas I couldn't bring myself to paint something completely worthless, no matter what type of painting it was. To do so would tarnish my sense of artistry, and show contempt for the kind of professional I was hoping to be. Even if I painted a portrait that I didn't love, at least I never felt embarrassed about the work I'd completed. You could call it professional ethics, I suppose. For me, it was just something I felt compelled to do.

One other aspect of my portrait painting was that I insisted on following my own approach. I never used the actual person as a model. When I got a commission I would meet with the client, just the two us, to talk for an hour or so. I wouldn't do any rough sketches at all. I would ask a lot of questions, and the client would respond. When and where were you born? What kind of family did you grow up in? I asked what kind of childhood they had, what school they attended, what sort of work they did, what kind of family they had now, how they had achieved their present position. Typical questions. I'd ask about their daily life and interests, too. Most people were happy, even enthusiastic, to talk about themselves. (Most likely no one else wanted to hear those things.) Sometimes the hour interview would stretch to two, even three hours.

After this I would ask to borrow five or six casual snapshots of the person, just unposed, ordinary snapshots. And occasionally I would use my own small camera and take a few close-ups from different angles. That's it.

Most clients seemed concerned. "Aren't I supposed to sit still and pose for the portrait?" they'd ask. From the outset, they were resigned to enduring a long painting process. Artists—even if no one wore those silly berets anymore—were supposed to stand, brush in hand before the canvas, brow furrowed, as the model sat there, trying to sit up straight. Perfectly still. Clients were imagining the kind of scene they'd seen a million times in movies.

Instead of answering, I would ask them, "Do you want to do it that way? Being a painter's model is hard work if you're not used to it. You have to hold the same pose for a long time, and it's boring and your shoulders will really ache. Of course, if that's how you'd like to do it, I'd be happy to oblige."

Predictably, ninety-nine percent of my clients declined. Most all of them were busy people with busy lives, or else elderly people who had retired. They all preferred, if possible, to avoid such pointless asceticism.

"Meeting you and talking together is all I need," I would say, putting them at ease. "Whether I have a live model or not won't affect the result at all. If you find you're dissatisfied with the painting, I'll be happy to do it over again."

After this I'd spend about two weeks on the portrait (though it would take several months for the paint to fully dry). What I needed was less the actual person in front of me than my vivid memories of that person. (Having the subject present, truth be told, actually interfered with my ability to complete the portrait.) These memories were three-dimensional, and all I had to do was transfer them to canvas. I seem to have been born with that sort of powerful visual memory—a special skill, you might label it—and it was a very effective tool for me as a professional portrait artist.

It was critical to feel a sense of closeness, even just a little, toward the client. That's why during our initial one-hour meeting I tried so hard to discover, as much as I could, some aspects of the client that I could respond to. Naturally, this was easier with some people than with others. There were some I'd never want to have a personal relationship with. But as a *visitor* who was with them for only a short time, in a set place, it wasn't that hard to find one or two appealing qualities. Look deep enough into any person and you will find something shining within. My job was to uncover this and, if the surface is fogged up (which was more often the case), polish it with a cloth to make it shine again. Otherwise the darker side would naturally reveal itself in the portrait.

So, before I knew it, I had become an artist who specialized in portraits. And I became fairly known within this particular, rather narrow field. When I got married, I ended my exclusive contract with the company in Yotsuya, became independent, and—through an agency specializing in the art business—received individual commissions to do portraits for even higher fees. The agent in charge, a capable, ambitious person, was ten years older than me. He encouraged me to be independent and take my work even more seriously. After that point, I painted portraits of numerous people (mostly in the financial and political worlds, celebrities in some cases, though I'd never heard of most of them) and made a decent income. Not that I became a great authority in the field or anything. The world of portraiture is totally different from that of the *artistic* art world. And different from photography too. There are a lot of photographers specializing in portraits who are held in high esteem and whose names are well known, but you don't find that with portrait artists. Very seldom is one of our works seen in the world at large. They aren't featured in art magazines or hung in galleries. Instead they're hung in reception areas somewhere, forgotten, gathering dust. If anyone happens to look at those paintings carefully (someone with time on his hands), they still aren't about to ask about the artist's name.

Occasionally I've thought of myself as a high-priced artistic prostitute. I use all the techniques at my disposal, as conscientiously as I can, in order to satisfy my client. I possess that sort of talent. I'm a professional, but that said, it doesn't mean I mechanically follow a set procedure. I do put a certain amount of feeling into my work. My fees aren't cheap, but my clients all pay without any complaints. The sort of people I take on as clients aren't the kind to worry about price. People learned of my skill through word of mouth, and I had an unending line of clients, my appointment book always jam-packed. But inside me I felt no desire whatsoever. Not a shred.

I hadn't become that sort of artist, or that type of person, because I'd wanted to. Carried along by circumstances, I'd given up doing paintings for myself. I'd married and needed to make a stable income, but that wasn't the only reason. Honestly, I'd already lost the desire to paint for myself. I might have been using marriage as an excuse. I wasn't young anymore, and something—like a flame burning inside me—was steadily fading away. The feeling of that flame warming me from within was receding ever further.

I should have washed my hands of that person I'd become. I should have stood up and done something about it. But I kept putting it off. And before I got around to it, the one who gave up on it all was my wife. I was thirty-six at the time.

2

THEY MIGHT ALL GO TO THE MOON

"I am very sorry, but I don't think I can live with you anymore," my wife said in a quiet voice. Then she was silent for a long while.

This announcement took me by complete surprise. It was so unexpected I didn't know how to respond, and I waited for her to go on. What she'd say next wasn't going to be very upbeat—I was certain about that—but waiting for her to continue was the most I could manage.

We were seated across from each other at the kitchen table. A Sunday afternoon in the middle of March. Our sixth wedding anniversary was the middle of the following month. A cold rain had been falling since morning. The first thing I did when I heard her news was turn toward the window and check out the rain. It was a quiet, gentle rain, with hardly any wind. Still, it was the kind of rain that carried with it a chill that slowly but surely seeped into the skin. Cold like this meant that spring was still a long ways off. The orangish Tokyo Tower was visible through the misty rain. The sky was bereft of birds. All of them must have quietly sought shelter.

"I don't want you to ask me why. Can you do that?" my wife asked.

I shook my head slightly. Neither yes nor no. I had no idea what to say, and just reflexively shook my head.

She had on a thin, light purple sweater with a wide neckline. The soft strap of her white camisole was visible beside her collarbone. It looked like some special kind of pasta used in some specific recipe.

Finally, I was able to speak. "I do have one question, though," I said, gazing blankly at that strap. My voice was stiff, dry, and flat.

"I'll answer, if I can."

"Is this my fault?"

She thought this over. Then, like someone who has been underwater for a long time, she finally broke through to the surface and took a deep, slow breath.

"Not directly, no."

"Not *directly*?"

"I don't think so."

I considered the subtle tone of her voice. Like checking the weight of an egg in my palm. "Meaning that I am, *in*directly?"

She didn't answer.

"A few days ago, just before dawn, I had a dream," she said instead. "A very realistic dream, the kind where you can't distinguish between what is real and what's in your mind. And when I woke up that's what I thought. I was certain of it, I mean. That I can't live with you anymore."

"What kind of dream was it?"

She shook her head. "I'm sorry, but I can't tell you that here."

"Because dreams are personal?"

"I suppose."

"Was I in the dream?" I asked.

"No, you weren't. So in that sense, too, it's not your fault."

Just to make sure I got it all, I summarized what she'd just said. When I don't know what to say I have a habit of summarizing. (A habit that, obviously, can be really irritating.)

"So, a few days ago you had a very realistic dream. And when you woke up you were certain you can't live with me anymore. But you can't tell me what the dream was about, since dreams are personal. Did I get that right?"

She nodded. "Yes. That's about the size of it."

"But that doesn't explain a thing."

She rested her hands on the tabletop, staring down at the inside of her coffee cup, as if an oracle was floating there and she was deciphering the message. From the look in her eyes the words must have been very symbolic and ambiguous.

My wife puts great stock in dreams. She often makes decisions based on dreams she had, or changes her decisions accordingly. But no matter how crucial you think dreams can be, you can't just reduce six years of marriage to nothing because of one vivid dream, no matter how memorable.

"The dream was just a trigger, that's all," she said, as if reading my mind. "Having that dream made lots of things clear for me."

"If you pull a trigger, a bullet will come out."

"Excuse me?"

"A trigger is a critical part of a gun. 'Just a trigger' isn't the right expression."

She stared at me silently, as if she couldn't understand what I was getting at. I don't blame her. I couldn't understand it myself.

"Are you seeing someone else?" I asked.

She nodded.

"And you're sleeping with him?"

"Yes, and I feel bad about it."

Maybe I should have asked her who it was, and when it had started. But I didn't want to know. I didn't want to think about those things. So I gazed again outside the window at the falling rain. Why hadn't I noticed all this before?

"This was just one element among many," my wife said.

I looked around the room. I'd lived there a long time, and it should have been familiar, but it had now transformed into a scene from a remote, strange land.

Just one element?

What does that mean, just one? I gave it some thought. She was having sex with some man other than me. But that was "just one element." Then what were all the others?

"I'll move out in a few days," my wife said. "So you don't need to do anything. I'm responsible, so I should be the one who leaves."

"You already decided where you're going to go?"

She didn't answer, but seemed to have already decided on a place. She must have made all kinds of preparations before bringing this up with me. When I realized this, I felt helpless, as if I'd lost my footing in the darkness. Things had been steadily moving forward, and I'd been totally oblivious.

"I'll get the divorce procedures going as quickly as I can," my wife said, "and I'd like you to be responsive. I'm being selfish, I know."

I turned from the rain and gazed at her. And once again it struck me. We'd lived under the same roof for six years, yet I knew next to nothing about this woman. In the same way that people stare up at the sky to see the moon every night, yet understand next to nothing about it.

"I have one request," I ventured. "If you'll grant me this, I'll do whatever you say. And I'll sign the divorce papers."

"What is it?"

"That *I'm* the one who leaves here. And I do it today. I'd like you to stay behind."

"Today?" she asked, surprised.

"The sooner the better, right?"

She thought it over. "If that's what you want," she said.

"It is, and that's *all* I want."

Those were my honest feelings. As long as I wasn't left behind alone in this wretched, cruel place, in the cold March rain, I didn't care what happened.

"And I'll take the car with me. Are you okay with that?"

I really didn't need to ask. The car was an old, stick-shift model a friend of mine had let me have for next to nothing back before I got married. It had well over sixty thousand miles on it. And besides, my wife didn't even have a driver's license.

"I'll come back later to get my painting materials and clothes and things. Does that work for you?"

"Sure, that's fine. By 'later,' how much later do you mean?"

"I have no idea," I said. I couldn't wrap my mind around the future. There was barely any ground left under my feet. Just remaining upright was all I could manage.

"I might not stay here all that long," my wife said, sounding reluctant.

"Everyone might go to the moon," I said.

She seemed not to have caught it. "Sorry?"

"Nothing. It's not important."

. . .

By seven that evening I'd stuffed my belongings into an oversized gym bag and thrown that into the trunk of my red Peugeot 205. Some changes of clothes, toiletries, a few books and diaries. A simple camping set I had always had for hiking. Sketchbooks and a set of drawing pencils. Other than these few items, I had no idea what else to take. It's okay, I told myself, if I need anything I can buy it somewhere. While I packed the gym bag and went in and out of the apartment, she was still seated at the kitchen table. The coffee cup was still on top of the table, and she continued to stare inside it . . .

"I have a request, too," she said. "Even if we break up like this, can we still be friends?"

I couldn't grasp what she was trying to say. I'd finished tugging on my shoes, had shouldered the bag, and stood, one hand on the doorknob, to stare at her.

"Be friends?"

"I'd like to meet and talk sometimes. If possible, I mean."

I still couldn't understand what she meant. Be friends? Meet and talk sometimes? What would we talk about? It's like she'd posed a riddle. What could she be trying to convey to me? That she didn't have any bad feelings toward me? Was that it?

"I'm not sure about that," I said. I couldn't think of anything more to say. If I'd stood there a whole week, running this through my head, I doubt I'd have found anything more to add. So I opened the door and stepped outside.

When I left the apartment I hadn't given any thought to what I was wearing. If I'd had on a bathrobe over pajamas, I probably wouldn't have noticed. Later on, when I looked at myself in a full-length mirror in a restroom at a drive-in, I saw I had on a sweater that I favored while working, a gaudy orange down jacket, jeans, and work boots. And an old knit cap. There were white paint stains here and there on the frayed, green, round-neck sweater. The only new item I had on were the jeans, their bright blue too conspicuous. A random collection of clothes, but not too peculiar. My one regret was not having brought a scarf.

When I pulled the car out from the parking lot underneath the apartment building, the cold March rain was still falling. The Peugeot's wipers sounded like an old man's raspy, hoarse cough.

I had no clue where to go, so for a while I drove aimlessly around Tokyo. At the intersection at Nishi Azabu, I drove down Gaien Boulevard toward Aoyama, turned right at Aoyama Sanchome toward Akasaka, and after a few more turns found myself in Yotsuya. I stopped at a gas station and filled up the tank. I had them check the oil and tire pressure for me, and top off the windshield washer fluid. I might be in for a very long trip. For all I knew I might even go all the way to the moon.

I paid with my credit card, and headed down the road again. A rainy Sunday night, not much traffic. I switched on an FM station, but it was all pointless chatter, a cacophony of shrill voices. Sheryl Crow's first CD was in the CD player, and I listened to the first three songs and then turned it off.

I suddenly realized I was driving down Mejiro Boulevard. It took a while before I could figure out which direction I was going—from Waseda toward Nerima. The silence got to me and I turned on the CD again and listened to Sheryl Crow for a few more songs. And then switched it off again. The silence was too quiet, the music too noisy. Though silence was preferable, a little. The only thing that reached me was the scrape of the worn-out wipers, the endless hiss of the tires on the wet pavement.

In the midst of that silence I imagined my wife in the arms of another man.

I should have picked up on that, at least, a long time ago. *So how come I didn't think of it?* We hadn't had sex for months. Even when I tried to get her to, she'd come up with all kinds of reasons to turn me down. Actually, I think she'd lost interest in having sex for some time before that. But I'd figured it was just a stage. She must be tired from working every day, and wasn't feeling up to it. But now I knew she was sleeping with another man. When had that started? I searched my memory. Probably four or five months ago, would be my guess. Four or five months ago would make it October or November.

But for the life of me I couldn't recall what had happened back in

October or November. I mean, I could barely recall what had happened yesterday.

I paid attention to the road—so as not to run any red lights, or get too close to the car in front of me—and mentally reviewed what had happened last fall. I thought so hard about it that it felt like the core of my brain was going to overheat. My right hand unconsciously changed gears to adjust to the flow of traffic. My left foot stepped on the clutch in time with this. I'd never been so happy that my car was a stick shift. Besides mulling over my wife's affair, it gave me something to do to keep my hands and feet busy.

So what had happened back in October or November?

An autumn evening. I'm picturing my wife on a large bed, and some man undressing her. I thought of the straps on her white camisole. And the pink nipples that lay underneath. I didn't want to visualize all this, but once one image came to me, I couldn't stop. I sighed, and pulled into the parking lot of a drive-in restaurant. I rolled down the driver's-side window, took a deep breath of the damp air outside, and slowly got my heart rate back to normal. I stepped out of the car. With my knit cap on but no umbrella I made my way through the fine drizzle and went inside the restaurant. I sat down in a booth in the back.

The restaurant was nearly empty. A waitress came over and I ordered coffee and a ham-and-cheese sandwich. As I drank the coffee I closed my eyes and calmed down. I tried my best to erase the image of my wife and another man in bed. But the vision wouldn't leave me.

I went to the restroom, gave my hands a good scrub, and checked myself in the mirror over the sink. My eyes looked smaller than usual, and bloodshot, like a woodland animal slowly fading away from famine, gaunt and afraid. I wiped my hands and face with a thick handkerchief, then studied myself in the full-length mirror on the wall. What I saw there was an exhausted thirty-six-year-old man in a shabby, paint-spattered sweater.

As I gazed at my reflection I wondered, *Where am I headed?* Before that, though, the question was *Where have I come to?* Where *is* this place? No, before that even I needed to ask, *Who the hell* am *I?*

As I stared at myself in the mirror, I thought about what it would be like to paint my own portrait. Say I were to try, what sort of self would

I end up painting? Would I be able to find even a shred of affection for myself? Would I be able to discover even one thing shining within me?

These questions unanswered, I returned to my seat. When I finished my coffee the waitress came over and refilled my cup. I asked her for a paper bag and put the untouched sandwich in it. I should be hungry later on. But right now I didn't want to eat anything.

I left the drive-in, and drove down the road until I saw the sign for the entrance to the Kan-Etsu Expressway. I decided to get on the highway and head north. I had no idea what lay north, but somehow I got the sense that heading north was better than going south. I wanted to go somewhere cold and clean. More important than north or south, however, was getting away from this city.

I opened the glove compartment and found five or six CDs inside. One of them was a performance of Mendelssohn's Octet by I Musici. My wife liked to listen to it when we went on drives. An unusual setup with a double string quartet, but a beautiful melody. Mendelssohn was only sixteen when he composed the piece. My wife told me this. A child prodigy.

What were you doing when you were sixteen?

I called up the past. When I was sixteen I was crazy over a girl in my class.

Did you go out with her?

No, I barely said a word to her. I just looked at her from a distance. I wasn't brave enough to speak up. When I went home I used to sketch her. I did quite a few drawings.

So you've done the same thing from way back when, my wife said, laughing.

True, I've done the same thing from way back when.

True, I've done the same thing from way back when, I said, mentally repeating the words I'd spoken to her.

I took the Sheryl Crow CD out of the player and slipped in an MJQ album. *Pyramid.* I listened to Milt Jackson's pleasant, bluesy solo as I headed down the highway toward the north. I'd make the occasional stop at a service area, take a long piss, and drink a couple of cups of hot black coffee, but other than that I drove all night. I drove in the slow lane, only speeding up to pass trucks. I didn't feel sleepy, strangely enough. It felt like I'd never be sleepy again in my whole life. And just before dawn I reached the Japan Sea coast.

In Niigata I turned right and drove north along the coast, from Yamagata to Akita Prefecture, then through Aomori into Hokkaido. I didn't take any highways, and drove leisurely down back roads. In all senses of the word I was in no hurry. When night came I'd check in to a cheap business hotel or run-down Japanese inn, flop down on the narrow bed, and sleep. Thankfully I can fall asleep right away just about anywhere, in any type of bed.

On the morning of the second day, near Murakami City, I phoned my agent and told him I wouldn't be able to do any portrait painting for a while. I had a few commissions I was in the middle of, but wasn't in a place where I could do any work.

"That's a problem, since you've already accepted the commissions," the agent said, his tone harsh.

I apologized. "There's nothing I can do about it. Could you tell the clients I got in a car accident or something? There are other artists who could take over, I'm sure."

My agent was silent for a time. Up till now I'd never missed a deadline. He knew how seriously I took my work.

"Something came up, and I'll be away from Tokyo for a while. I'm sorry, but in the meantime I can't do any painting."

"How long is 'for a while'?"

I couldn't answer. I switched off the cell phone, found a nearby river, parked my car on the bridge over it, and tossed that small communication device into the water. I felt sorry toward him, but I had to get him to give up on me. Have him think I'd gone to the moon or something.

In Akita I stopped at a bank, withdrew some cash, and checked my balance. There was still a decent amount in my personal account. Credit card payments were automatically deducted . . . For the time being I had enough to continue my trip. I wasn't using that much each day. Gas money, nights in business hotels, that's about the size of it.

At an outlet store outside Hakodate I purchased a simple tent and a sleeping bag. Hokkaido in early spring was still cold, so I also bought some thermal underwear. Whenever I arrived in a place, I looked for an open campground, set up my tent, and slept there, in order to save money. Hard snow still covered the ground and the nights were cold, but because I'd been spending nights in cramped, stuffy business hotel rooms I felt relieved and free inside the tent. Hard ground below, the endless sky above. Countless stars sparkling in the sky. That and nothing else.

For the next three weeks I wandered all over Hokkaido in my Peugeot. April came, but it looked like the snow wasn't going to melt anytime soon. Still, the color of the sky visibly changed, and plants began to bud. Whenever I ran across a small town with a hot springs I'd stay in an inn there, enjoy the bath, wash my hair and shave, and have a decent meal. Even so, when I weighed myself I found I'd lost eleven pounds.

I didn't read any newspapers or watch TV. My car radio had started acting up from the time I arrived in Hokkaido, and soon I couldn't hear anything on it at all. I had no clue what was happening in the world at large, and didn't care to know. I stopped once in Tomakomai and did laundry at a laundromat. While I waited for the clothes to finish I went to a nearby barbershop and got a haircut and shave. At the shop I saw the NHK news on TV for the first time in a long while. I say "saw," but even with my eyes closed I could hear the announcer's voice, whether I wanted to or not. From start to finish, though, the news had nothing to do with me, like events happening on some other planet. Or else some fake stories somebody had cooked up for the fun of it.

The only news story that hit home was a report on a seventy-three-year-old man in Hokkaido who'd gone mushroom gathering in the mountains and been attacked and killed by a bear. When bears wake from hibernation, the announcer said, they're hungry and irritable and very dangerous. I slept in my tent sometimes, and when the mood struck me I took walks in the woods, so it wouldn't have been strange if I were the one who'd been attacked. It *just happened* to be that old man who got attacked, and not me. But even hearing that news I felt no sympathy for the old man who'd been so cruelly butchered by a bear. No empathy came to me for the pain and fear and shock he must have experienced. I felt more sympathy for the bear. No, "sympathy" isn't the right word, I thought. It's more like a feeling of complicity.

Something's wrong with me, I thought as I stared at myself in the mirror. I said this aloud, in a small voice. It's like something's messed up with my brain. *Better not get near anyone.* For the time being, at least.

Toward the latter half of April I was sick and tired of the cold, so I bid Hokkaido farewell and crossed back over to the mainland. I drove from Aomori to Iwate, from Iwate to Miyagi, along the Pacific coast. The weather got more springlike the farther south I drove. And all the while I thought about my wife. About her, and the anonymous hands caressing her this very moment in bed somewhere. I didn't want to think about it, but I couldn't think of anything else.

The first time I met my wife was just before I turned thirty. She was three years younger than me. She worked in a small architecture firm in Yotsuya, held a second-level architect certificate, and was a former high school classmate of the girl I was dating at the time. She had straight hair, wore little makeup, and had rather calm-looking features (her personality was not all that calm, but I only understood that later on). My girlfriend and I were on a date and happened to run into her at a restaurant. We were introduced, and I basically fell for her right then and there.

She wasn't exactly a standout in terms of looks. There wasn't anything at all wrong with her appearance, but neither was there anything about her that would turn any heads. She had long eyelashes, a thin nose, was on the small side, and her hair, which fell to her shoulder blades, was beautifully styled. (She was very particular about her hair.) On the right side of her full lips was a small mole, which moved in marvelous ways whenever her expression changed. It lent her a slightly sensual air, but again this was only if you paid close attention. Most people would see the girl I was going out with at the time as far more beautiful. But even so, one look was all it took for me to fall for her, like I'd been struck by lightning. Why? I wondered. It took a few weeks for me to figure out the reason. But then it suddenly hit me. She reminded me of my younger sister, who had died. Reminded me very clearly of her.

Not that they looked alike on the outside. If you were to compare photos of the two of them, most people would be hard-pressed to find any resemblance. Which is why at first I didn't see the connection either. It wasn't anything specific about her looks that made me remember my younger sister, but the way her expression changed, especially the way her eyes moved and sparkled, was amazingly like my sister's. It was like magic or something had brought back the past, right before my very eyes.

My sister had also been three years younger than me, and had a congenital heart valve problem. She'd had numerous operations when she was little, and though they were successful, there were lingering aftereffects. Her doctors had no idea if those aftereffects would get better on their own, or cause some life-threatening issues. In the end, she died when I was fifteen. She'd just entered junior high. All her short life she'd battled those genetic defects, but never failed to be anything other than positive and upbeat. Until the very end she never grumbled or complained, and always made detailed plans for the future. That she would die so young was not something she factored into her plans. She was naturally bright, always with outstanding grades (a lot better a child than I was). She had a strong will, and always stuck to whatever she decided to do, no matter what. If she and I ever quarreled—a pretty rare occurrence—I always gave in. At the end she was terribly thin and drawn, yet her eyes remained animated, and she was still full of life.

It was my wife's eyes, too, that drew me to her. *Something* I could see deep in them. When I first saw those eyes, they jolted me. Not that I was thinking that by making her mine I could restore my dead sister or anything. Even if I'd wanted to, I could imagine the only thing that would lead to was despair. What I wanted, or needed, was the spark of that positive will. That definite source of warmth needed to live. It was something I knew very well, but that was, most likely, missing in me.

I managed to get her contact info, and asked her on a date. She was surprised, of course, and hesitated. I was, after all, her friend's boyfriend. But I kept at it. I just want to see you, and talk, I told her. Just meet and talk, that's all. I'm not looking for anything else. We had dinner in a quiet restaurant, and talked about all kinds of things. Our conversation was a little nervous and awkward at first, but then became more animated. There was so much I wanted to know about her, and I had plenty to talk about. I found out that her birthday and my sister's were only three days apart.

"Do you mind if I sketch you?" I asked.

"Right here?" she asked, glancing around. We were seated at the restaurant, and had just ordered dessert.

"I'll finish before they're back with dessert," I said.

"Then I guess I don't mind," she replied doubtfully.

I took out the small sketchbook I always carried with me, and quickly sketched her face with a 2B pencil. As promised, I finished before our desserts arrived. The important part was, of course, her eyes. That's what I wanted to draw most. Back within those eyes there was a deep world, a world beyond time.

I showed her the sketch, and she seemed to like it.

"It's very full of life."

"That's because *you* are," I said.

She gazed for a long time at the sketch, apparently taken with it. As if she were seeing a self she hadn't known before.

"If you like it, I'll give it to you."

"I can have it?" she said.

"Of course. It's just a quick sketch."

"Thank you."

After this we went on more dates, and eventually became lovers. It all happened so naturally. My girlfriend, though, was shocked that her friend stole me away. She was probably thinking that we might get married. So of course she was upset (though I doubt I ever would have married her). My wife, too, was going out with someone else at the time, and their breakup wasn't easy either. There were other obstacles to overcome, but the upshot was that half a year later we were married. We had a small party with a handful of close friends to celebrate, and settled into a condo in Hiroo. Her uncle owned the condo and gave us a good deal on rent. I used one small room as my studio and focused on my portrait work. This was no longer just a temporary job. Now that I was married I needed a steady income, and other than portrait painting I had no means of earning a decent living. My wife commuted from our place by subway to the architecture firm in Yotsuya. And it sort of naturally came about that I was the one who took care of everyday housework, which I didn't mind at all. I never minded doing housework, and found it a nice break from painting. At any rate it was far more pleasant to do housework than commute every day to a job and be forced to do work behind a desk.

I think for both of us our first few years of marriage were calm and fulfilling. Before long we settled into a pleasant daily rhythm. On weekends and holidays I'd take a break from painting and we'd go out. Sometimes to an art exhibition, sometimes hiking outside the city. At other times we'd just wander around town. We had intimate talks, and for both of us it was important to regularly update each other. We spoke honestly, and openly, about what was going on in our lives, exchanging opinions, sharing feelings.

For me, though, there was one thing I never opened up about to her: the fact that her eyes reminded me so much of my sister who'd died at twelve, and that that was the main reason I'd been attracted to her. Without those eyes I probably never would have tried to win her over as eagerly as I did. But I felt it was better not to tell her that, and until the very end I didn't. That was the sole secret I kept from her. What secrets she may have kept from me—and I imagine there were some—I have no idea.

My wife's name was Yuzu, the name of the citrus fruit used in cooking. Sometimes when we were in bed I'd call her Sudachi, a similar type of fruit, as a joke. I'd whisper this in her ear. She'd always laugh, but it upset her all the same.

"I'm not Sudachi, but Yuzu. They're similar but not the same," she'd insist.

When did things start to go south for us? As I drove on, from one roadside restaurant to another, one business hotel to another, randomly moving from point A to point B, I thought about this. But I couldn't pinpoint where things had begun to go wrong. For a long time I was sure we were doing fine. Of course, like many couples, we had some issues and disagreements. Our main issue was whether or not to have children. But we still had time before we had to make a final decision. Other than that one problem (one we could postpone for the time being), we had a basically healthy marriage, on both an emotional and physical level. I was sure of that.

Why had I been so optimistic? Or so stupid? It's like I'd been born with a blind spot, and was always missing something. And what I missed was always the most important thing of all.

In the mornings, after I saw my wife off to work, I'd focus on my painting, then after lunch would take a walk around the neighborhood, do some shopping while I was at it, and then get things ready for dinner. Two or three times a week I'd go swimming in a nearby sports club. When my wife got back we'd have a beer or some wine together. If she called me saying she had to work overtime and would grab something near the office, I'd sit by myself and have a simple dinner alone. Our six years together were mostly a repeat of those kinds of days. And I was basically okay with that.

Things were busy at the architecture firm, and she often had to work overtime. I gradually had to eat dinner alone more often. Sometimes she wouldn't get back until nearly midnight. "Things have gotten so hectic at work," she'd explain. One of her colleagues suddenly changed jobs, she said, and she had to pick up the slack. The firm was reluctant to hire new staff. Whenever she came home late, she was exhausted and would just take a shower and go to sleep. So the number of times we had sex went way down. Sometimes she even had to go in on days off, too, to finish her work. Of course I believed her. There wasn't any reason not to.

But maybe she wasn't working overtime at all. While I was eating dinner alone at home, she may have been enjoying some intimate time in a hotel bed with a new lover.

My wife was outgoing. She seemed quiet and gentle but was sharp and quick-witted, and needed situations where she could be more social and gregarious. And I wasn't able to provide those. So Yuzu went out to eat a lot with women friends (she had lots of friends) and would go out drinking with work colleagues (she could hold her liquor better than me). And I never complained about her going out on her own and enjoying herself. In fact I might have encouraged it.

When I think about it, my younger sister and I had the same kind of relationship. I've always been more of a stay-at-home type, and when I got back from school I'd hole up in my room to read or draw. My sister was much more sociable and outgoing. So our everyday interests and activities didn't overlap much. But we understood each other well, and valued each other's special qualities. It might have been pretty unusual for an older brother and younger sister the ages we were, but we talked over lots of things together. Summer or winter, we'd climb up to the balcony upstairs where we hung our laundry, and talk forever. We loved to share funny stories, and often had each other in stitches.

I'm not saying that's the reason why, but I felt secure about the relationship my wife and I had. I accepted my role in our marriage—as the silent, auxiliary partner—as natural, self-evident even. But maybe Yuzu didn't. There must have been aspects of our marriage that dissatisfied her. She and my sister were, after all, different people with different personalities. And of course, I wasn't a teenage boy anymore.

By May I was getting tired of driving day after day. And sick of the same thoughts looping endlessly around in my head. The same questions spun around in my brain, with no answers in sight. Sitting all day in the driver's seat had given me a backache, as well. A Peugeot 205 is an economy car, and the seats weren't exactly high quality, the suspension noticeably worn out. All the road glare I'd stared at for hours was giving me chronic eyestrain. I realized I'd been driving pretty much nonstop for over a month and half, restlessly moving from one spot to another as if something were chasing me.

I ran across a small, rustic therapeutic hot springs in the mountains near the border between Miyagi and Iwate, and decided to take a break. An obscure hot springs tucked away deep in a valley, with a small inn that locals would stay in for days to rest and recuperate. The room rate was cheap, and there was a communal kitchen where you could cook simple meals. I enjoyed soaking in the baths and sleeping as much as I wanted. I sprawled on the tatami, read, and recovered from the exhaustion of all that driving. When I got tired of reading I'd take out my sketchbook and draw. It had been a long time since I'd felt like drawing. I started off sketching flowers and trees in the garden, then drew the rabbits they kept there. Just rough pencil sketches, but people were impressed. Some asked me to draw their portraits. Fellow lodgers, and people who worked at the inn. People just passing through my life, people I'd never see again. And if they asked, I'd give them the sketches.

Time to get back to Tokyo, I told myself. Going on like this would get me nowhere. And I wanted to paint again. Not commissioned portraits, or rough sketches, but paintings I could really concentrate on, and undertake for myself. Whether this would work out or not I had no clue, but it was time to take the first step.

I'd planned to drive my Peugeot across the Tohoku region and return to Tokyo, but just before Iwaki, along Highway 6, my car breathed its last. There was a crack in the fuel line and the car wouldn't start. I'd done hardly any maintenance on the car up till then, so I couldn't complain when it gave out. The one lucky thing was that the car gave up the ghost right near a garage where a friendly mechanic worked. It was hard to get parts for an old Peugeot in a place like that, and would take time. Even if we repair it, the mechanic told me, it's likely something else will soon go wrong. The fan belts looked sketchy, the brake pads were ready to go, and the suspension was nearly shot. "My advice? Put it out of its misery," he said. The car had been with me for a month and a half on the road, and now had nearly seventy-five thousand miles on the odometer. It was sad to say goodbye to the Peugeot, but I had to leave it behind. It felt like the car had died in my stead.

To thank him for disposing of the car for me, I gave the mechanic my tent, sleeping bag, and camping equipment. I made one last sketch of the Peugeot, and then, shouldering my gym bag, boarded the Joban Line and went back to Tokyo. From the station I called Masahiko Amada and explained my situation. My marriage fell apart and I went on a trip for a while, I told him, but now I'm back in Tokyo. Do you know of any place I could stay? I asked.

I do know of a good place, he said. It's the house my father lived in for a long time by himself. He's in a nursing home in Izu Kogen, and the house has been unoccupied for a time. It's furnished and has everything you'd need, so you don't have to get anything. It's not exactly a convenient location, but the phone works. If that sounds good, you should try it out.

That's perfect, I told him. I couldn't have asked for more.

And so my new life, in a new place, began.

3

JUST A PHYSICAL REFLECTION

A few days after I'd settled into my new mountaintop house outside Odawara, I got in touch with my wife. I had to call five times before I finally got through. Her job always kept her busy, and apparently she was still getting home late. Or maybe she was with someone. Not that that was my business anymore.

"Where are you now?" Yuzu asked me.

"I've moved into the Amadas' house in Odawara," I said. Briefly I explained how I came to live there.

"I called your cell phone many times," Yuzu said.

"I don't have the cell phone anymore," I said. That phone might have washed into the Japan Sea by then. "I'm calling because I'd like to go pick up the rest of my things. Does that work for you?"

"You still have the key?"

"I do," I said. I'd considered tossing the key into the river, too, but thought better of it since she might want it back. "But you don't mind if I go into the apartment when you're not there?"

"It's your house too. So of course it's okay," she said. "But where have you been all this time?"

Traveling, I told her. I told her how I'd been driving alone, going from one cold place to the next. How the car had finally given out.

"But you're okay, right?"

"I'm alive," I said. "The car was the one that died."

Yuzu was silent for a while. And then she spoke. "I had a dream the other day with you in it."

I didn't ask what kind of dream. I didn't really care to know about me appearing in her dream. She didn't say any more about it.

"I'll leave the key when I go," I said.

"Either way's fine with me. Just do what you like."

"I'll put it in your mailbox when I leave," I said.

There was a short pause before she spoke.

"Do you remember how you sketched my face on our first date?"

"I do."

"I take it out sometimes and look at it. It's really well done. I feel like I'm looking at my real self."

"Your real self?"

"Right."

"But don't you see your face every morning in the mirror?"

"That's different," Yuzu said. "My self in the mirror is just a physical reflection."

After I hung up I went to the bathroom and looked at my face in the mirror. I hadn't looked at myself straight on like that for ages. My self in the mirror is just a physical reflection, she'd said. But to me my face in the mirror looked like a virtual fragment of my self that had been split in two. The self there was the one I *hadn't chosen*. It wasn't even a physical reflection.

In the afternoon two days later I drove my Corolla station wagon to the apartment in Hiroo, and gathered my possessions. It had been raining since morning that day, too. The underground parking lot beneath the building had its usual rainy-day odor.

I took the elevator upstairs and unlocked the door, and when I went inside for the first time in nearly two months I felt like an intruder. I'd lived there almost six years and knew every inch of the place. But I no longer was part of this scene. Dishes were stacked up in the kitchen, all dishes she had used. Laundry was drying in the bathroom, all her clothes. Inside the fridge it was all food I'd never seen before. Most were ready-made food. The milk and orange juice were different brands from what I bought. The freezer was packed with frozen food. I never bought frozen food. A lot of changes in the two months I'd been away.

I was struck by a strong urge to wash the dishes stacked up in the sink, bring in the laundry drying and fold it (and iron it if I could), and neatly rearrange the food in the fridge. But I did none of this. This was someone else's house now. I shouldn't poke my nose in where I didn't belong.

My painting materials were the bulkiest possessions I had. I tossed my easel, canvas, brushes, and paints into a large cardboard box. Then turned to my clothes. I've never been one to need a lot of clothes. I don't mind wearing the same clothes all the time. I don't own a suit or necktie. Other than a thick winter coat, it all fit into one suitcase.

A few books I hadn't read yet, and about a dozen CDs. My favorite coffee cup. Swimsuit, and goggles, and swim cap. That was about all I felt I needed. Even those I could get along without if need be.

In the bathroom my toothbrush and shaving kit were still there, as well as my lotion, sunscreen, and hair tonic. An unopened box of condoms, too. But I didn't feel like taking all that miscellaneous stuff to my new place. She could just get rid of it.

I packed my belongings in the trunk of the car, went back to the kitchen, and boiled water in the kettle. I made tea with a tea bag, and sat at the table and drank it. I figured she wouldn't mind. The room was perfectly still. The silence lent a faint weight to the air. As though I were sitting alone, at the bottom of the sea.

All told, I was there by myself in the apartment for about a half hour. No one came to visit, and the phone didn't ring. The thermostat on the fridge turned off once, then turned back on once. In the midst of the silence I perked up my ears, probing what I sensed in the apartment, as if measuring the depths of the ocean with a sinker. No matter how you looked at it, it was an apartment occupied by a woman living alone. Someone busy at work who had next to no time to do any housework. Someone who took care of any errands on the weekends when she had free time. A quick visual sweep of the place showed that everything there was hers. No evidence of anyone else (hardly any evidence of me anymore, either). No man was stopping by here. That's the impression I got. They must have seen each other elsewhere.

I can't explain it well, but while I was in the apartment I felt like I was being watched. Like someone was observing me through a hidden camera. But that couldn't be. My wife is a major klutz when it comes to equipment. She can't even change the batteries in a remote control. No way could she do something as clever as setting up and operating a surveillance camera. It was just me, on edge.

Even so, while I was in the apartment I acted as if every single action of mine was being recorded. I did nothing extra, nothing untoward. I didn't open Yuzu's desk drawer to see what was inside. I knew that in the back of one of the drawers of her wardrobe, where she had her stockings, she kept a small diary and some important letters, but I didn't touch them. I knew the password for her laptop (assuming she hadn't changed it), but didn't even open it. None of this had anything to do with me anymore. I washed the cup I'd drunk tea in, dried it with a cloth, put it back on the shelf, and turned off the lights. I went over to the window and gazed at the falling rain for a while. The orangish Tokyo Tower loomed up faintly in the distance. Then I dropped the key in the mailbox and drove back to Odawara. The trip was only an hour and a half, but it felt like I'd taken a day trip to a far-off foreign land.

The next day I called my agent. I'm back in Tokyo, I told him, and I'm really sorry, but I don't plan to do any more portrait painting.

"You're never going to do any more portraits? Is that what you're telling me?"

"Most likely," I said.

He didn't say much. No complaints, nothing in the way of advice. He knew that once I said something, I didn't back down.

"If you ever find yourself wanting to do this work again, call me anytime," he said at the end. "I'd welcome it."

"Thank you," I said.

"Maybe it isn't my place to say this, but how are you planning to make a living?"

"I haven't decided," I admitted. "I'm by myself, so I don't need much to live on, and I've got a bit of savings."

"Will you still paint?"

"Probably. There isn't much else I know how to do."

"I hope it works out."

“Thanks,” I said once more. And tagged on a question that had just occurred to me. “Is there anything I should make sure to keep in mind?”

“Something you should make sure to keep in mind?”

“In other words—how should I put it—any advice from a pro?”

He thought it over. “You’re the type of guy who takes longer than other people to be convinced of anything. But long term, I think time is on your side.”

Like the title of an old Rolling Stones song.

“One other thing: I think you really have a special talent for portraiture. An intuitive ability to get straight to the heart of the subject. Other people can’t do that. Not using that talent would be a real shame.”

“But right now painting portraits isn’t what I want to do.”

“I get that. But someday that ability will help you again. I hope it works out.”

Hope it works out, I thought. Good if time is on your side.

On the first day I visited the house in Odawara, Masahiko Amada—the son of the owner—drove me there in his Volvo. “If you like it, you can move in today,” he said.

We took the Odawara-Atsugi Road almost to the end and, when we exited, headed toward the mountains along a narrow, paved farm road. On either side, there were fields, rows of hothouses for growing vegetables, and the occasional grove of plum trees. We saw hardly any houses, and not a single traffic signal. Finally we drove up a steep, winding slope in low gear for a long time, until we came to the end and arrived at the entrance to the house. There were two stately pillars at the entrance, but no gate. And no wall, either. It seemed the owner had planned to add a gate and wall but thought better of it. Maybe halfway through he’d realized there was no need. On one of the pillars was a magnificent nameplate with AMADA on it, almost like some business sign. The house beyond was a small Western-style cottage with a faded brick chimney sticking out of the flat roof. It was a one-story house, but the roof was unexpectedly high. In my imagination I’d been taking it for granted that a famous painter of Japanese-style paintings would live in an old Japanese-style dwelling.

We parked in a spacious covered driveway by the front door, and when we opened the car doors some screeching black birds—jays, I imagine—flew off from a nearby tree branch into the sky. They seemed none too happy about us intruding on their space. The house was pretty, surrounded by woods with a variety of trees, with only the west side of the house open to a broad view of the valley.

"What do you think? Not much here, is there?"

I stood there, gazing around me. He was right, there wasn't much there. I was impressed that his father had built a house in such isolated surroundings. He really must have wanted nothing to do with other people.

"Did you grow up here?" I asked.

"No, I've never lived here very long. Just came to stay over occasionally. Or visited on summer holidays when we were escaping the heat. I had school, and grew up in our house in Mejiro with my mother. When my father wasn't working he'd come to Tokyo and live with us. Then come back here and work by himself. I went out on my own, then ten years ago my mother died, and ever since he's been living here by himself. Like someone who's forsaken the world."

A middle-aged woman who lived nearby had been watching the house, and she came over to explain some things I needed to know. How the kitchen operated, how to order more propane and kerosene, where various items were kept, which days the trash was picked up and where to put it. The artist seemed to have led a very simple solitary existence, with very little equipment or appliances, so there wasn't much for a lecture. If there's anything else you need to know, just give me a call, the woman said (though I actually never called her, not even once).

"I'm very happy someone will be living here now," she said. "Empty houses get dilapidated, and they're unsafe. And when they know no one's at home, the wild boar and monkeys get into the yard."

"You do get the occasional wild boar or monkey around here," Masahiko said.

"Be very careful about the wild boars," the woman explained. "You see a lot of them in the spring around here when they root for bamboo shoots. Female boars with young are always jumpy, and dangerous. And you need to watch out for hornets, too. There've been people who've been stung and died. The hornets build nests in the plum groves."

The central feature of the house was a fairly large living room with an open-hearth fireplace. On the southwest side of the living room was a spacious roofed-in terrace, and on the north side was a square studio. The studio was where the master had done his painting. On the east side of the living room was a compact kitchen with dining area, and a bathroom. Then a comfortable master bedroom and a slightly smaller guest bedroom. There was a writing desk in the guest bedroom. Amada seemed to enjoy reading, as the bookshelves were stuffed with old books. He seemed to have used this room as his study. For an older house, it was fairly neat and clean, and comfortable looking, though strangely enough (or perhaps not so strangely) there was not a single painting hanging on the walls. Every wall was completely bare.

As Masahiko had said, the place had most everything I'd need—furniture, electric appliances, plates and dishes, and bedding. "You don't need to bring anything," he'd told me, and he was right. There was plenty of firewood for the fireplace stacked up under the eaves of the shed. There was no TV in the house (Masahiko's father, I was told, hated TV), though there was a wonderful stereo set in the living room. The speakers were huge Tannoy Autographs, the separate amplifier an original vacuum tube Marantz. And he had an extensive collection of vinyl records. At first glance there seemed to be a lot of boxed sets of opera.

"There's no CD player here," Masahiko told me. "He's the sort of person who hates new devices. He only trusts things from the past. And naturally there's not a trace of anything to do with the Internet. If you need to use it, the only choice is to use the Internet café in town."

"I don't have any real need for the Internet," I told him.

"If you want to know what's going on in the world, then the only choice is to listen to the news on the transistor radio on the shelf in the kitchen. Since we're in the mountains the signal isn't great, but you can at least pick up the NHK station in Shizuoka. Better than nothing, I suppose."

"I'm not that interested in what's going on in the world."

"That's fine. Sounds like you and my father would get along fine."

"Is your father a fan of opera?" I asked.

"Yes, he paints Japanese paintings, but always liked to listen to opera while he painted. He went to the opera house a lot when he was a student in Vienna. Do you listen to opera?"

"A little."

"I'm not into it at all. Way too long and boring for me. There are a lot of records, so feel free to listen to them as much as you'd like. My father has no need of them anymore and I know he'd be happy if you listened to them."

"No need of them?"

"His dementia's getting bad. Right now he doesn't know the difference between an opera and a frying pan."

"Vienna, you said? Did he study Japanese painting in Vienna?"

"Nobody's that eccentric—to go all the way to Vienna to study Japanese painting. My father originally worked on Western painting. That's why he went to study in Vienna. At the time he did very cutting-edge modern oil paintings. But after he came back to Japan he suddenly switched styles, and began painting Japanese-style. Not totally unheard of, I suppose. Going abroad awakens your own ethnic identity or something."

"And he was very successful at it."

Amada made a small shrug. "According to the public he was. But from a child's perspective, he was just a grouchy old man. All he thought about was painting, and did exactly as he pleased. No trace of that now, though."

"How old is he?"

"Ninety-two. When he was young he was apparently pretty wild. I never heard the details."

I thanked him. "Thank you for everything. I'm really grateful. This really helps me out."

"You like it here?"

"Yes, I'm really happy you're letting me stay."

"I'm glad. Though I'm hoping you and Yuzu can get back together again."

I didn't respond. Masahiko himself wasn't married. I'd heard a rumor he was bisexual, though I didn't know if it was true or not. We'd known each other for a long time, but had never spoken about it.

"Are you going to keep doing portraits?" Amada asked as we were leaving.

I explained how I'd made a clean break with portrait painting.

"Then how are you going to make a living?" Amada asked, the same thing my agent had wanted to know.

I'll cut back on expenses and get by on my savings for a while, I replied, echoing my first answer. I also wanted to try painting whatever I wanted, something I hadn't been able to do for ages.

"Sounds good," Amada said. "Do what you like for a while. But would you consider teaching art part time too? There's this arts-and-culture center near Odawara Station and they have painting classes. Most of them are for children, but they have some community art classes for adults set up as well. They teach sketching and watercolor, but not oil painting. The man who runs the school knows my father, he's not really in it for the money. And he needs a teacher. I'm sure he'd be overjoyed if you'd help out. It doesn't pay much, but you could make a little extra to live on. You'd only need to teach twice a week, and it shouldn't be too much trouble."

"But I've never taught painting, and don't know much about watercolors."

"It's simple," he said. "You're not training professionals. You just teach the basics. You'll pick it up in a day. Teaching children should be good for you, too. And if you're going to live up here all by yourself, you have to get down off the mountain a couple of times a week and be with other people, even if you don't want to, or else you'll go a little stir-crazy. Don't want you ending up like *The Shining*."

Masahiko screwed up his face like Jack Nicholson. He's always been good at impressions.

I laughed. "I'll give it a try. Whether I'll do a good job or not, I don't know."

"I'll get in touch with him and let him know," he said.

Then Masahiko drove me to the used Toyota dealership next to the highway, where I paid cash for the Corolla station wagon. My life alone on a mountaintop in Odawara began that day. I'd been on the move for nearly two months, but now I'd take up a sedentary life. It was quite a switch.

Starting the following week, I began teaching art classes on Wednesdays and Fridays at the arts-and-culture center near Odawara Station. There was a perfunctory interview beforehand, but Masahiko's introduction meant that I was as good as hired already. I was to teach two classes for adults, plus one for children on Fridays. I quickly got used to teaching the kids. I enjoyed seeing the paintings they did, and, as Masahiko said, it was a good stimulus for me as well. I quickly got to be friends with the children. All I did was go around the room, check on the paintings they did, give them a few words of technical advice, find good points about their paintings, and praise and encourage them. My approach was to have them paint the same subject matter several times, to instill in them the idea that the same object could appear quite different if viewed from a different angle. Just as people had many facets, so too did objects. The kids immediately picked up on how fascinating this could be.

Teaching adults was a bit more of a challenge. The students were either elderly retirees, or housewives whose children were grown and in school, and had time on their hands. As you might imagine, they weren't as adaptable as the kids, and when I pointed out something, they didn't easily accept my suggestions. A few of them, though, were willing to learn, and there were a couple who did some pretty appealing paintings. Whenever they asked, I gave them helpful pointers, but for the most part I let them paint however they liked. I confined myself to praising them whenever I found something nice about what they'd done. That seemed to please them. I figured it was enough for them to simply enjoy painting.

And I started sleeping with two housewives, both of whom attended the art classes and received my so-called instruction. Both my students, in other words, and incidentally both fairly decent painters. It's hard for me to tell whether that was something permissible for a teacher—even a casual teacher like me with no proper license. I basically think mutually consenting adults having sex isn't a problem, though certainly society might frown at this kind of relationship.

I'm not trying to excuse my actions, but at the time I really didn't have the mental wherewithal to decide whether I was right or wrong. I was desperately clinging to a scrap of wood that had been swept away. In pitch-black darkness, not a single star, or the moon, visible in the sky. As long as I clung to that piece of wood I wouldn't drown, but I had no clue where I was, where I was heading.

It was a couple of months after I'd moved there that I discovered Tomohiko Amada's painting *Killing Commendatore*. I couldn't know it at the time, but that one painting changed my world forever.

4

FROM A DISTANCE, MOST THINGS LOOK BEAUTIFUL

One sunny morning near the end of May I carried all my painting materials into the studio Mr. Amada had been using, and for the first time in what seemed like forever stood before a brand-new canvas. (Nothing of the master's painting materials was left in the studio. I assume that Masahiko had packed them all away somewhere.) The studio was a large, square room sixteen feet on a side, with a wood floor and white walls. The floor was bare wood, with not a single rug. There was a large open window on the north side, with simple white curtains. The window on the east side was smaller, with no curtains. As elsewhere in the house, there was nothing hanging on the walls. In one corner of the room was a large porcelain sink for washing away paint. The sink must have been in long use, for its surface was dyed with a mix of different colors. Next to the sink was an old-fashioned kerosene stove, and there was a large ceiling fan. A worktable and a round wooden stool. A compact stereo set was on a built-in shelf so he could listen to opera while painting. The wind blowing in the open window carried with it the fresh fragrance of trees. This was, without doubt, a space for an artist to focus on his work. Everything you might need was here, and not one thing extra.

Now that I had this environment to work in, the feeling of *wanting to paint something* grew stronger, like a quiet ache. And there were no limits on the amount of time I could spend for myself. No need any longer to paint things I didn't want to in order to earn a living, no more obligation to prepare dinner for my wife when she came home. (Not that I minded making dinner, though that didn't change the fact that it was an obligation.) And it wasn't just preparing meals—I had the right to stop eating altogether and starve if I felt like it. I was utterly free to do exactly what I wanted, without worrying about anybody else.

In the end, though, I couldn't paint a thing. No matter how long I stood in front of the canvas and stared at that white, blank space, not a single idea of what to paint came to me. I had no clue where to begin, how to start. Like a novelist who has lost words, or a musician who has lost his instrument, I stood there in that bare, square studio, at a complete loss.

I'd never felt that way before, not ever. Once I faced a canvas, my mind would immediately leave the horizon of the everyday, and *something* would well up in my imagination. Sometimes it would be a productive image, at other times a useless illusion. But still, something would always come to me. From there, I'd latch onto it, transfer it to the canvas, and continue to develop it, letting my intuition lead the way. If I did it that way, the work completed itself. But now I couldn't see *anything* that would provide the initial spark. You can have all the desire and ache inside you want, but what you really need is a concrete starting point.

I would get up early in the morning (I generally always wake before six), brew coffee in the kitchen, and then, mug in hand, pad off to the studio and sit on the stool in front of the canvas. And focus my feelings. Listen closely to the echoes in my heart, trying to grasp the image of something that had to be there. But this always ended in a fruitless retreat. I'd try concentrating for a while, then plunk down on the studio floor, lean back against the wall, and listen to a Puccini opera. (I'm not sure why, but all I seemed to listen to then was Puccini.) *Turandot*, *La Bohème*. I'd sit there, staring at the languidly rotating ceiling fan, waiting for an idea or motif to come to me. But nothing ever came. Just the early-summer sun that rose sluggishly in the sky.

What was the problem? Maybe it's because I'd spent so many years doing portraits for a living. Maybe that diminished any natural intuition I had. Like sand slowly washed away by the tide. Somehow the flow of my life had gone off in the wrong direction. I needed time, I thought. I had to be patient. *Make time be on my side.* Do that, and I was sure to seize the right flow. That channel would surely come back to me. Truthfully, though, I wasn't sure it ever would.

It was during this period, too, that I slept with the two married women. I think I was looking for some kind of inner breakthrough. Come what may, I wanted to break out of the rut I was in, and the only way for me to do so was to jolt my psyche, give it a prod (it didn't matter what kind). Plus I'd started to tire of being alone. And it had been a long time since I'd slept with a woman.

It occurs to me now that my days back then were pretty strange. I'd wake up early, go into that small square, white-walled studio, have no ideas for what to paint as I stared at the blank canvas, then flop down on the floor and listen to Puccini. When it came to the realm of creativity, I was basically facing a pure nothingness. When Claude Debussy had writer's block while composing an opera, he wrote, "Day after day I produce *rien*—nothingness." That summer was the same for me—day after day I took part in *producing nothingness*. Perhaps I was quite used to facing nothingness day after day—though I wouldn't go so far as to say we were intimate.

About twice a week in the afternoon, the second of the married women would drive to my place in her red Mini. We'd go straight to bed and make love. In the early afternoon we'd devour each other's flesh. What this produced was, of course, not nothingness. No doubt about it, actual flesh-and-blood bodies were involved. Bodies you could actually touch with your hands, every inch, even run your lips over them. In this way, as if I'd flipped a switch on my consciousness, I began moving between an ambiguous, vague *rien* and a vivid, living reality. The woman said her husband hadn't made love to her in nearly two years. He was ten years older than she was, and busy with work, never returning home until late at night. She tried many ways of enticing him, but nothing seemed to rouse his interest.

"I wonder why. I mean, you have such a lovely body," I said.

She gave a small shrug. "We've been married over fifteen years and have two kids. I guess I'm no longer as fresh as I used to be."

"You seem plenty fresh to me."

"Thanks. Though that makes it sound like I'm being recycled or something."

"Like recycling resources?"

"Exactly."

"It's a very precious resource, though," I said. "Contributes to society, too."

She giggled. "As long as you sort everything correctly."

A little while later, we eagerly set out to sort out resources once more.

Truthfully I wasn't all that drawn to her as a person at first. In that sense there was a different tone about our relationship than with the women I'd dated. She and I had almost nothing in common to talk about. There was hardly anything about our present lives, or our personal histories until then, that overlapped. I'm not generally a talkative person, so when we were together, she did most of the talking. She'd tell me personal things and I'd make the appropriate responses, giving my feedback, I guess you'd call it, though it was hardly a real conversation.

This was a first for me. With other women, I'd always been attracted to their personalities. Physical relationships came later, something that accompanied the initial appeal . . . That was the usual pattern. But not with her. With her the physical came first. Not that I'm complaining. When I was with her I could enjoy the act in a pure, unfettered way. And I think she could, too. She came many times as we made love, and I came many times too.

She told me this was the first time since she got married that she'd slept with another man. I had no reason to doubt her. And for me, too, this was the first time I'd slept with another woman since I got married. (No, actually there was one exception, when I shared a bed with another woman. Not that it was something I was looking for. I'll get into that later on.)

"But my friends the same age, all of them are married but most of them are having affairs," she said. "They talk about it a lot."

"Recycling," I said.

"I never imagined I'd join them."

I gazed up at the ceiling and thought about Yuzu. Was she off somewhere, in bed with somebody?

After the woman left, I felt at loose ends. The bed still showed the hollows where she had lain. I didn't feel like doing anything, so I lay out on a lounge chair on the terrace and killed time reading a book. All the books on Mr. Amada's bookshelf were old, among them a few unusual novels that would be hard to get hold of these days. Works that in the past had been pretty popular but had been forgotten, read by no one. I enjoyed reading this kind of out-of-date novel. Doing so let me share—with this old man I'd never met—the feeling of being left behind by time.

As the sun set, I opened a bottle of wine (drinking wine was my one and only luxury at the time, though of course this was inexpensive wine) and listened to some old LPs. The record collection was comprised entirely of classical music, the majority of which was opera and chamber music. All of them looked like they'd been lovingly cared for, without a single scratch. During the day I listened to opera, while at night I favored Beethoven and Schubert string quartets.

Having a relationship with that older married woman, being able to hold a real live woman in my arms regularly, brought me a certain level of calm. The soft touch of a mature woman's skin eased the pent-up emotions I'd had. At the very least, while I made love to her I was able to shelve the doubts and problems I'd been carrying around. Yet I still wasn't able to come up with an idea of what to paint. Occasionally in bed I'd do a pencil sketch of her in the nude. Most of these were pornographic. Pictures of my cock inside her, or her sucking me off. The sketches made her blush, but she enjoyed looking at them. I imagine that if these had been photos most women wouldn't have liked them, and would even have been disgusted with the man who made them, and on their guard. But I found that with rough sketches, if they were done well, women were actually happy to see them. Because they had the warmth of life in them—or, at least, they didn't have a mechanical coldness. But still, no matter how well I managed these sketches, not even a fragment of an image of what I really wanted to paint came to me.

The kind of paintings I did as a student, so-called abstracts, no longer appealed to me. My heart wasn't drawn to them anymore. Looking back on it now, I see that what I'd been wrapped up in back then was nothing more than the pursuit of form. Back when I was young, I was completely drawn to the beauty of form, and to balance. Nothing wrong with that. But in my case I didn't reach the soulful depth that should lie beyond. Now I see it very clearly, but at the time, all I could grasp was the *appeal* of shape at a superficial level. Nothing really moved me. My paintings were *smart* but nothing more.

And now I was thirty-six. Forty was just around the corner. I felt that by the time I turned forty, I'd have to secure my own unique artistic world. Forty was a sort of watershed for people. Once you get past that age, you can't keep going on as you were before. I still had four years to go, but I knew that those four years might flash by in an instant. Painting portraits for a living had taken me on a wide detour. Somehow I had to get time on my side once again.

While I lived in that house in the mountains I found myself wanting to know more about Tomohiko Amada. I'd never been interested in Japanese-style painting, and though I'd heard the name Tomohiko Amada, and he happened to be my friend's father, I had no idea what kind of person he was, or what kind of paintings he did. He might be a heavyweight in the world of Japanese painting, but he had totally stayed out of the limelight, turning his back on his worldly renown, and alone, quietly—or one might say stubbornly—focused on creating his art. This was about the extent of what I knew about him.

But as I listened to his record collection on the stereo he'd left behind, borrowed his books, slept in his bed, made meals every day in his kitchen, and used his studio, I gradually became more interested in Tomohiko Amada as a person. Something close to curiosity, you could say. The path he'd taken aroused my interest—the way he'd been focused on modernist painting, traveled all the way to Vienna to study, then after returning to Japan made a sudden return to Japanese-style painting. I didn't know the details, but in general you would think that it couldn't have been very easy for someone who'd done Western painting for so long to shift over to Japanese-style painting. You'd need to decide to abandon all the techniques you'd spent so much time and effort mastering, and begin again from zero. Despite this, Tomohiko Amada had chosen that arduous path. There must have been a compelling reason.

One day, before my art class, I went to the Odawara city library to search out collections of Tomohiko Amada's artwork. Probably because he was an artist living in the area, the library had three beautiful volumes of his work. One of them included some of the Western paintings he'd done in his twenties as reference material. What surprised me was that the series of Western-style paintings he'd done as a young man reminded me somewhat of the abstract paintings I'd done myself in the past. The style wasn't specifically the same (in the prewar period he'd been heavily influenced by Cubism), yet his stance of "greedily pursuing form" in no small way had something in common with my own approach. As you might expect from someone who went on to become a first-class artist, his paintings also had much more depth and persuasive power than mine. Technically, too, there were things about them that were, simply, astounding. I imagine they must have been highly acclaimed at the time. Still, there was *something missing*.

I sat there in the reading room at the library and carefully examined his works for a long time. So what was it that was lacking from his work? I couldn't pinpoint it. But if I had to give an opinion, I'd say they were paintings that *weren't really necessary*. The kind of paintings that, if they disappeared somewhere forever, wouldn't put anybody out. A cruel way of putting it, perhaps, but it's the truth. From the present perspective, some seventy years on, I could see that quite well.

I turned the pages and followed along, in chronological order, to see how he shifted gears to become a painter of Japanese-style art. In his early period these works were still a bit awkward, imitating the methods of previous artists, but then gradually, and undeniably, he discovered his own unique style. I could see how it progressed. A bit of trial and error at times, but no hesitation. After he took up painting Japanese-style art, his works all had something unique that only he could paint, and he himself was well aware of this. He always strode confidently toward the core of that special *something*. No more did you get the impression, as with his Western paintings, of something missing. It was less a shift and more akin to a conversion.

Like most artists of Japanese-style paintings, at first Tomohiko Amada painted realistic scenery and flowers, but eventually (and there must have been some motive for this) he began painting scenes from ancient Japan. Some were themes from the Heian and Kamakura periods, but what he was most fond of was the Asuka period at the beginning of the seventh century, specifically the period when Prince Shotoku Taishi, the legendary regent, was alive . . . On his canvases he boldly, minutely, reproduced the scenery, historical events, and lives of the people of that period. Naturally he had never witnessed those scenes in reality with his own eyes. But with his inner eye he *saw* them, clearly and vividly. Why he chose the Asuka period, I have no idea. But that became his own special period, done in an inimitable style. And with the passage of time his technique in painting Japanese-style paintings became even more refined.

If you pay close attention you can see that from a certain point on he painted exactly what he wanted to paint. From then on his brush seemed to freely leap across the canvas. The wonderful part about his paintings was the use of blank space. Paradoxically, the best part was what was *not* depicted. By not painting certain things he clearly accentuated what he *did* want to paint. This is undoubtedly one of the areas that Japanese painting excels at. At least I'd never seen such bold use of blank space in any Western paintings. Seeing this, I could somehow understand why Tomohiko Amada converted to painting Japanese art. But what I didn't understand was exactly when and how he made that daring conversion and put it into practice.

According to his brief biography at the end of the book, he was born in the mountainous Aso district in Kumamoto. His father was a great landowner, an influential local figure, and his family was quite affluent. He was always artistically talented and distinguished himself while still quite young. He graduated from the Tokyo Fine Arts School (later Tokyo University of the Arts), and with great expectations for his career studied abroad in Vienna from the end of 1936 to 1939. At the beginning of 1939, before World War Two began, he boarded a passenger ship from Bremen and returned to Japan. Hitler was in power during this time. Austria was annexed by Germany, the so-called *Anschluss* taking place in March 1938. And the young Tomohiko Amada was right there in Vienna in the midst of this turbulent period. He must have witnessed a number of historical events at that time.

So what happened to him then?

I read through a long essay in one of the collections titled "Theory of Tomohiko Amada," only to find that almost nothing was known about his time in Vienna. The essay went into great detail about his career as a painter of Japanese-style paintings after he returned to Japan, yet there was only vague, baseless speculation about the motives and details of the conversion he must have experienced during his time in Vienna. What he had done in Vienna, and what had led him to his dramatic conversion, remained a mystery.

Tomohiko Amada returned to Japan in February 1939, and settled into a rented house in Sendagi in Tokyo. By this point he had completely abandoned Western painting. But he still received an allowance every month from his family, so he wanted for nothing. His mother, in particular, doted on her son. During this period he was, apparently, studying Japanese-style painting on his own. A number of times he tried to have established painters take him under their wing, but it never worked out. Tomohiko was, from the first, not exactly the humblest of people. Maintaining calm, friendly ties with others was not his forte. Isolation from others was a leitmotif that ran through his entire life.

With the attack on Pearl Harbor in 1941, Japan entered an all-out war, and Amada left turbulent Tokyo and moved back to his parents' home in Aso. As the second son, he avoided all the problems involved in succeeding to his father's estate, and was given a small house with a maid, and lived a quiet life there pretty much isolated from the war. For better or worse, he had a congenital lung defect and thus there was no worry he would be drafted. (Though this could have been the excuse they used for the public, and his family may have worked behind the scenes to make sure he didn't have to be a soldier.) He also avoided the severe food shortages and near starvation that plagued most Japanese citizens at the time. Living deep in the mountains of rural Japan, unless some major mistake was made he could also be pretty certain that no U.S. planes would be dropping any bombs on them. So until the surrender in 1945 he lived, holed up alone, deep in the mountains of Aso. His ties with society were severed, and he devoted himself entirely to mastering the techniques of Japanese-style painting. He didn't display a single work during this time.

For Tomohiko Amada, after being in the spotlight as a promising painter of Western art, and then going to study in Vienna, it must have been a trying experience to maintain total silence for over six years, forgotten by the art world. But he was not the type to easily lose heart. When the long war was finally over, and as people struggled to recover from the chaos, a reborn Tomohiko Amada debuted again, this time as an up-and-coming painter in the Japanese style. One by one he displayed the works he'd completed during the war. This was the period when most artists, having painted stirring propaganda pieces, were forced to take responsibility for their actions and, under the watchful eye of the Occupation, were fairly compelled into retirement. Which is precisely why Tomohiko's works, revealing the possibility of a revolution in Japanese painting, garnered so much attention. The times, one could say, were his ally.

There was little to say of his career after this time. Once an artist is successful, his life is often quite boring. Of course there are some artists who, once they are successful, head straight toward a colorful downfall, but Tomohiko Amada wasn't one of them. He won countless awards over the years (though he turned down the Order of Cultural Merit award from the government, claiming it would be "distracting") and became very famous. Over the years the price for his works rose, and most were displayed in public exhibitions. There was no end to the number of commissions, and he gained a high reputation abroad, too. Smooth sailing all around. The artist himself, though, avoided center stage, and turned down any official positions. He also refused any invitations, domestic or international. Instead he stayed holed up alone in the mountaintop house in Odawara (the house I was now living in) painting whatever he liked.

Now he was ninety-two and in a nursing home in Izu Kogen, and no longer knew the difference between an opera and a frying pan.

I shut the book of paintings and returned it to the library counter.

When the weather was good I liked to lie on a lounge chair out on the terrace after dinner and enjoy a glass of white wine. And as I gazed at the twinkling stars to the south, I would consider what lessons I might draw from Tomohiko Amada's life. Naturally there should be a few lessons I should learn. The courage not to fear a change in one's lifestyle, the importance of having time on your side. And above all, discovering your own uniquely creative style and themes. Not an easy thing, of course. Though if you make a living creating things, it's something you have to accomplish no matter what. If possible, before you turn forty . . .

But what kind of experiences did Tomohiko Amada have in Vienna? What scenes did he witness? And most of all, what exactly made him decide to lay down his oil paintbrush forever? I pictured red-and-black Nazi swastika flags fluttering over a street in Vienna, a young Tomohiko Amada walking down that street. For some reason the season is winter. He has on a thick coat, a scarf, and a cloth cap pulled down low. His face isn't visible. A streetcar rounds the corner and approaches in the newly falling sleet. As he walks, he exhales white breath into the air like the very embodiment of silence. The Viennese are in warm cafés, sipping coffee with a spot of rum.

I tried visualizing his later paintings of Japanese scenes in the Asuka period overlapping with this old Viennese street scene. But my imagination was unequal to the task, and I couldn't discover any similarities between the two.

My terrace faced the narrow valley to the west, and across the way was a range of mountains about the same height as mine. And on the slopes of those mountains were a number of houses with generous space separating them, surrounded by lush greenery. To the right, diagonally across from the house I was living in, was a particularly striking modern-style house. The mountaintop house, built of white concrete and plenty of bluish tinted glass, was so elegant and luxurious the word "mansion" seemed a better term. It was built in three levels that ran along the slope. Most likely some first-rate architect had designed it. There are lots of summer homes in this area, but someone seemed to live in this house all year long, with lights on behind the windows every night. Of course it could be that the lights were on timers as a safety precaution. But I gathered otherwise, since the lights came on and turned off at different times, depending on the day. Sometimes all the lights were on at once and the windows were lit like brilliant window displays on a main street, while at other times the whole house sank back into darkness, the only light a faint glow from lanterns in the yard.

Sometimes a person would appear on the deck that faced my direction (the one that resembled the top deck of an ocean liner). At twilight I would often see the figure of whoever lived there. I couldn't tell if it was a man or a woman. The silhouette was small and usually backlit and in shadow. But from the outline of the silhouette, and the movements, my guess was that it was a man. And this person was always alone. Perhaps he didn't have any family.

What kind of person lived in a place like that? In spare moments I tried to imagine. Did this person really live all by himself on this out-of-the-way mountaintop? What sort of work did he do? No doubt his life in that chic, glass-enclosed mansion was one of luxury and ease. He couldn't be commuting every day to Tokyo from such an inconvenient spot. He must be living a life free of worries. But viewed from his perspective, looking at me from his side of the valley, I might appear to also be living a life of ease and leisure. From a distance, most things look beautiful.

That evening the figure appeared again. Like me, he sat, barely moving, in a chair out on the deck. As if he too was gazing at the twinkling stars, mulling over something. Thinking, no doubt, about things for which there was no answer, no matter how hard you thought about them. At least that's how he looked to me. Everybody has something they speculate and wonder about, no matter how blessed their circumstances. I raised my wineglass a couple of inches, a secret gesture of solidarity to this person across the valley.

Naturally at the time I never imagined that this person would soon enter my life and change its direction entirely. Without him, none of the events that happened to me would have ever taken place. At the same time, if he hadn't been there I might very well have lost my life in the darkness, with no one ever the wiser.

Our lives really *do* seem strange and mysterious when you look back on them. Filled with unbelievably bizarre coincidences and unpredictable, zigzagging developments. While they are unfolding, it's hard to see anything weird about them, no matter how closely you pay attention to your surroundings. In the midst of the everyday, these things may strike you as simply ordinary things, a matter of course. They might not be logical, but time has to pass before you can see if something is logical.

Generally speaking, whether something is logical or isn't, what's meaningful about it are the effects. Effects are there for anyone to see, and can have a real influence. But pinpointing the cause that produced the effect isn't easy. It's even harder to show people something concrete that caused it, in a "Look, see?" kind of way. Of course there is a cause somewhere. Can't be an effect without a cause. You can't make an omelet without breaking some eggs. Like falling dominoes, one domino (cause) knocks over the adjacent domino (cause), which then knocks over the domino (cause) next to it. As this sequence continues on and on, you no longer know what was the original cause. Maybe it doesn't matter. Or people don't care to know. And the story comes down to "What happened was, a lot of dominoes fell over." The story I'll be telling here may very well follow a similar route.

In any case, the first things I want to describe—the first two dominoes I have to bring up, in other words—are the mysterious neighbor who lived on the mountaintop across the valley, and the painting titled *Killing Commendatore*. I'll start with the painting.

5

HE HAS STOPPED BREATHING . . . HIS LIMBS ARE COLD

The first thing I found odd after I moved into the house was the utter lack of any paintings. Not only were none hanging on the walls, but there wasn't a single painting of any kind even stuffed away in a shed or closet. No paintings by Tomohiko Amada, but none by any other artists either. Every wall was bare, with no traces even of nails that might have once been used to hang paintings. Artists almost always had at least some paintings around them—their own paintings, or those by other artists. Before they knew what had hit them, they'd be surrounded by all kinds of paintings, like when you endlessly shovel the snow but it keeps on piling up.

Once when I called Masahiko about something else, I happened to raise the topic. How come there's not a painting of any kind in this house? Did somebody take them away, or there weren't any to begin with?

"My father didn't like keeping his own paintings around," Masahiko said. "He'd call up his art dealers when he finished a work and leave it with them. If he wasn't happy with a painting, he burned it in the incinerator in the yard. So it's not so strange that there's not a single one of his paintings there."

"He didn't own any paintings by other artists either?"

"He owned a handful. An old Matisse or Braque and the like. All of them small paintings he bought in Europe before the war. He got them from acquaintances, and they weren't so expensive at the time. Now, of course, they would bring a hefty price. When he went into the nursing home I took all those paintings to an art dealer I know and let him handle them. Can't leave them sitting there in an empty house now, can I? I imagine they're in a special air-conditioned art storage warehouse. Apart from those, I've never seen any other artists' works in the house. To tell the truth, my father didn't much like other artists. And they didn't like him either. A lone wolf, you might call him, or if we're not being nice about it, a misfit."

"Your father was in Vienna from 1936 to 1939, wasn't he?"

"Right, he was there for about two years. I don't know why he chose Vienna, since the artists he liked were mainly French."

"And then he returned to Japan and suddenly switched to Japanese-style paintings," I said. "Why do you think he made such a monumental decision? Did something unusual happen while he was abroad?"

"Hmm. It's a mystery. My father never spoke much about his time in Vienna. Occasionally he'd talk about things nobody cared about—the Vienna zoo, or food, or the opera house. But when it came to talking about himself, he was a man of few words. And I never dared to ask him. We mostly lived apart, and rarely saw each other. He was less like a father to me than an uncle who came to visit every once in a while. When I got to junior high he seemed even more annoying, and I avoided contact with him. When I went into the art institute, too, I never consulted him about it. It's not like our family was complicated, though it wasn't exactly a normal family either. You get the general idea?"

"I do."

"Anyway, my father's memories of the past are all gone now. Or have sunk away into deep mud. He won't answer you, no matter what you ask. He doesn't even know who I am. Probably doesn't even know who *he* is. Sometimes I think I should have asked all kinds of things before he got this way. Well, it's too late now."

Masahiko was silent for a time, lost in thought. "Why do you want to know that?" he finally asked. "Did something spark an interest in him?"

"Not particularly," I said. "It's just that, living in this house, I sense something like your father's shadow lurking about. I also did a little research into his life at the library."

"My father's shadow?"

"Like a reminder of his existence, maybe."

"Don't you find that a little creepy?"

Over the phone I shook my head. "No. Not at all. It's just like the presence of Tomohiko Amada is still hovering over things. Like it's in the air."

Masahiko was lost in thought again. "My father lived in that house for a long time, and did a lot of work there," he said, "so maybe his presence remains. Who knows? To tell the truth, that's why I don't want to go near the place."

I listened without comment.

"Like I said before," he went on, "to me, Tomohiko Amada was basically just a grouchy old man I knew. Always holed up in his studio, painting, with a sour look on his face. He didn't talk much, so I had no idea what was on his mind. When we were under the same roof my mom always told me, 'Don't bother your father when he's working.' I couldn't run around or yell or anything. The world saw him as a famous artist, but to a little kid, he was simply a pain. Plus when I decided to go into art myself, having him as a father was a burden. Every time I introduced myself people would ask if I was related to Tomohiko Amada. I even thought about changing my name. I realize now he wasn't such a bad person, really. I suppose he showed me affection in his own way. Though he wasn't the type to show unconditional love toward a child. But that can't be helped. Painting was always his top priority. That's what artists are like."

"I suppose so," I said.

"I could never be an artist," Masahiko said with a sigh. "That might be the only thing I learned from my father."

"Didn't you tell me before that when he was young he was pretty wild and did whatever he liked?"

"By the time I was big, he wasn't like that anymore, but when he was young he played around a lot apparently. He was tall, good-looking, a young guy from a wealthy family, and a talented painter. How could women not be drawn to him? And he was certainly fond of the ladies. Rumor is that he had some affairs that his family had to pay to clear up. But my relatives said that after he returned from his time abroad, he was a different person."

"A different person?"

"After he returned to Japan, he didn't play around anymore, and just stayed at home focusing on his painting. And he didn't socialize anymore. After he got back to Tokyo he was a bachelor for a long time, but once he could earn a good living painting, like the idea had just occurred to him, he suddenly and unexpectedly married a distant relative back home. For all the world like he was balancing the account book of his life or something. It was a late marriage for him. And then I was born. I have no clue if he ever played around with other women after he got married. Though I can say that he no longer made a show of having a good time."

"Quite a change."

"His parents were really happy, though, at how he'd changed. No more messy affairs for them to clean up. But none of our relatives could tell me what had happened to him in Vienna, or why he rejected Western painting in favor of Japanese-style art. When it came to those things my father's mouth was clamped shut, like an oyster at the bottom of the sea."

And even if you pried open that shell now, there would be nothing inside. I thanked Masahiko and hung up.

It was by total coincidence that I discovered the painting by Tomohiko Amada, the one with the unusual title, *Killing Commendatore*.

Sometimes in the middle of the night I'd hear a faint rustling sound from the attic above the bedroom. At first I thought it must be mice, or a squirrel that had found its way into the attic. But the sound was clearly not that of a rodent's feet scurrying around. Nor that of a slithering snake. It sounded more like oil paper being crumpled up. Not loud enough to keep me from sleeping, but it did concern me that there was some unknown creature in the house. I figured it might be an animal that could cause some damage.

After searching around, I located the opening to the attic in the ceiling in the back of the guest bedroom closet. I lugged over the aluminum ladder from the storage shed and, flashlight in one hand, pushed open the cover. I timidly stuck my head through and looked around. The attic was bigger than I'd thought, and dark. A small amount of sunlight filtered in through the small vent holes on either side. I shone the flashlight around but didn't see anything. At least nothing was moving. I took the plunge and hauled myself up into the attic.

The place smelled dusty, but not enough to bother me. The attic was apparently well ventilated and there wasn't much dust on the floor. Several thick beams hung low on the ceiling, but as long as I avoided them I could walk around okay. I edged forward and checked both vents. Both were covered with screens so no animals could get in, but the screen on the north vent had a gap in it. Something might have knocked against it and ripped it. Or else an animal had intentionally ripped the wire to get inside. Either way, the opening was large enough for a smallish animal to easily scramble in.

I spotted the culprit I'd been hearing at night, silently settled on top of a beam in the dark. It was a small, gray horned owl. The owl's eyes were closed and it seemed to be sleeping. I switched off my flashlight and stood away to silently observe without frightening it. I'd never seen a horned owl up close before. It looked less like an owl than like a cat with wings. It was a beautiful creature.

The owl most likely rested here during the day and then at night went out the vent hole to hunt for prey in the mountains. The sound of it going in and out must have been what woke me. No harm done. Having an owl in the attic also meant I needn't worry about mice and snakes settling in. I figured I should just leave it be. I felt close to the little owl. Both of us just happened to be borrowing this house and sharing it. It could have the run of the attic as far as I was concerned. I enjoyed observing it for a time, then tiptoed back where I'd come from. That's when I discovered the large wrapped package near the entrance.

One look told me it was a wrapped-up painting. About three feet in height and five feet in length, it was wrapped tightly in brown Japanese wrapping paper, with string tied several times around it. Nothing else was in the attic. The faint sunlight filtering in from the vent holes, the gray horned owl on top of a beam, the wrapped painting propped up against a wall. The combination felt magical, somehow, and captivated me.

I gingerly lifted the package. It wasn't heavy—the weight of a painting set in a simple frame. The wrapping paper was slightly dusty. It must have been placed here, out of anyone's sight, quite some time ago. A name tag was attached tightly with wire to the string. In blue ballpoint ink was written *Killing Commendatore*. The writing was done in a very careful hand. Most likely this was the title of the painting.

Naturally, I had no clue why that one painting would be hidden away in the attic. I considered what I should do. Obviously the correct thing to do would be to leave it where it was. This was Tomohiko Amada's house, not mine, the painting clearly his possession (presumably it was one that he himself had painted), one that, for whatever reason, he had hidden away so no one would see it. That being the case, I thought I shouldn't do anything uncalled for, and should let it continue to silently share the attic with the owl. I should just leave it be.

That made the most sense, but still I couldn't suppress the curiosity surging up inside. The words in (what appeared to be) the title—*Killing Commendatore*—grabbed me. What kind of painting could it be? And why did Tomohiko Amada have to hide away *this* painting alone in the attic?

I picked up the painting and tested to see if it could squeeze through the opening to the attic. Logic dictated that a painting that had been brought up here shouldn't have any problem being carried down. And there was no other entrance to the attic. But still I checked to see if it would squeeze through. As expected, it was a tight fit, but when I held it diagonally, it squeezed through the square opening. I imagined Tomohiko Amada carrying the painting up to the attic. He must have been by himself then, carrying around some secret inside him. I could vividly imagine the scene, as if I were actually witnessing it.

I don't think Amada would be angry if he found out I'd brought the painting down from the attic. His mind was buried now in a deep maelstrom, according to his son, "unable to distinguish an opera from a frying pan." He would never be coming back to this home. And if I left this painting in an attic with the screen over the vent hole ripped, mice and squirrels might gnaw away at it someday. Or else bugs might get to it. And if this painting really was by Tomohiko Amada, this would be a substantial loss to the art world.

I lowered the package on top of the shelf in the closet, gave a little wave to the horned owl huddled on the beam, then clambered down and quietly shut the lid to the entrance.

I didn't unwrap the painting right away. I left that brown package propped up against the wall in the studio for several days. And I sat on the floor, gazing vaguely at it. It was hard for me to decide whether I should unwrap it or not. I mean, it belonged to somebody else, and whatever positive spin you might try to put on it, I didn't have the right to unwrap it. If I wanted to, at least I should get permission from his son, Masahiko. I'm not sure why, but I didn't feel like letting Masahiko know the painting existed. I felt like it was something personal, just between me and Tomohiko Amada. I can't explain why. But that's how I felt.

I stared at the painting (my assumption, of course, that it was actually a painting)—wrapped in Japanese paper and tied tightly with string—so hard I almost burned a hole in it, and after running the next step through my mind, over and over, I finally decided to unwrap it. It was no contest: my curiosity won out over any sense of etiquette or common sense. Whether this was the professional curiosity of an artist, or simple personal curiosity, I couldn't say. Whatever, I just had to see what was inside. I don't care what anyone says, I told myself. I brought over scissors, cut the tightly bound string, and peeled away the brown wrapping paper. I took my time, and did it carefully, in case I needed to rewrap it again later on.

Underneath the layers of wrapping paper was a painting in a simple frame, wrapped in a soft white cloth like bleached cotton. I gently lifted off that cloth, as carefully as if I were removing the bandages from a burn victim.

What was revealed under the white cloth was, as expected, a Japanese-style painting. A long, rectangular painting. I stood it up on a shelf, stood back a bit, and studied it.

It was Tomohiko Amada's work, no doubt about it. Clearly done in his style and inimitable technique, with his signature bold use of space and dynamic composition. The painting depicted men and women dressed in the fashions of the Asuka period, the clothes and hairstyles of that age. But the painting startled me nonetheless. What it depicted was so violent it took my breath away.

As far as I knew, Tomohiko Amada hardly ever painted pictures that were harsh and violent. Maybe never. His paintings mostly summoned up feelings of nostalgia, gentleness, and peace. Occasionally they would take up historical events as his theme, but the people depicted in them generally faded away into the overall composition. They were shown as part of a close community in the midst of the abundant natural scenery of ancient times, esteeming harmony above all. Ego was submerged in the collective will, or absorbed into a calm fate. And the circle of life was quietly drawn closed. For Tomohiko Amada that very well may have been utopia. Over the years he continued to depict that world from all sorts of angles, all sorts of perspectives. Many called his style a "rejection of modernity" or a "return to antiquity." Of course there were some who criticized it as escapist. In any case, after he returned to Japan from studying in Vienna he abandoned modernist oil painting, and shut himself away inside that kind of serene world, without a single word of explanation or justification.

But this painting titled *Killing Commendatore* was full of blood. Realistic blood flowing all over. Two men were fighting with heavy, ancient swords, in what seemed to be a duel. One of the men fighting was young, the other old. The young man had plunged his sword deep into the old man's chest. The young man had a thin black mustache and wore tight-fitting light-greenish clothes. The old man was dressed in white and had a lush white beard. Around his neck was a necklace of beads. He had dropped his sword, which had not yet struck the ground. Blood was spewing from his chest. The tip of the sword must have pierced his aorta. The blood had soaked his white clothes, and his mouth was twisted in agony. His eyes were wide open, staring in disbelief into space. He realized he was defeated. But the real pain had yet to hit him.

For his part, the young man's eyes were cold, fixed on his opponent. Not a sign of regret in those eyes, not a hint of confusion or fear, or a trace of agitation. Totally composed, those eyes were simply watching the impending death of another, and his own unmistakable victory.

The gushing blood was nothing more than proof of that, and elicited no emotional reaction whatsoever.

Honestly, until then I had thought of Japanese-style paintings as static and formulaic, their techniques and subject matter ill-suited to the expression of strong emotion. A world that had nothing to do with me. But looking now at Tomohiko Amada's *Killing Commendatore* I realized that had been nothing but prejudice on my part. In Amada's depiction of the two men's violent duel to the death was something that shook the viewer to the core. The man who won, the man who lost. The man who stabbed and the man who was stabbed. My heart was captured by the discrepancy. There is something very special about this painting, I thought.

There were a few other figures nearby watching the duel. One was a young woman. She had on refined, pure white clothes. Her hair was done up, with a large hair ornament. She held one hand in front of her mouth, which was slightly parted. She looked like she was about to take a deep breath and let out a scream. Her lovely eyes were wide open.

And there was another young man there. His clothes were not as splendid. Dark clothes, bereft of any ornaments, the kind of outfit designed to be easy to move around in. On his feet were plain-looking zori sandals. He looked like a servant. He had no long sword, just a short sword hanging from his waist. He was short and thickset, with a scraggly beard. In his left hand he held a kind of account book, like a clipboard that a company employee nowadays might have. His right hand was reaching out in the air as if to grab something. But it couldn't grab anything. You couldn't tell from the painting if he was the servant of the old man, or of the young man, or of the woman. One thing that was clear, though, was that this duel had taken place quickly, and neither the woman nor the servant had expected it to happen. Both of their faces revealed an unmistakable shock at the sudden turn of events.

The only one of the four who wasn't surprised was the young man doing the killing. Probably nothing ever took him by surprise. He was not a born killer, and he didn't enjoy killing. But if it served his purpose he wouldn't hesitate to kill. He was young, burning with idealism (though of what kind I have no idea), a man overflowing with strength.

And he was skilled in the art of wielding a sword. Seeing an old man past his prime dying by his hand didn't surprise him. It was, in fact, a natural, rational act.

There was one other person there, an odd observer. The man was at the bottom left of the painting, much like a footnote in a text. His head was peeking out from a lid in the ground that he had partially pushed open. The lid was square, and made of boards. It reminded me of the attic cover in this house. The shape and size were identical. From there the man was watching the people on the surface.

A hole opening up to the surface? A square manhole? No way. They didn't have sewers back in the Asuka period. And the duel was taking place outdoors, in an empty vacant lot. The only thing visible in the background was a pine tree, with low-hanging branches. Why would there be a hole with a cover there, in the middle of a vacant lot? It didn't make any sense.

The man who was sticking his head out of the hole was weird looking. He had an unusually long face, like a twisted eggplant. His face was overgrown with a black beard, his hair long and tangled. He looked like some sort of vagabond or hermit who'd abandoned the world. In a way he also looked like someone who'd lost his mind. But the glint in his eyes was surprisingly sharp, insightful, even. That said, the insight there wasn't the product of reason, but rather something induced by a sort of deviance—perhaps something akin to madness. I couldn't tell the details of what he was wearing, since all that I could see was from the neck up. He, too, was watching the duel. But unlike the others, he showed no surprise at the turn of events. He was a mere observer of something that was supposed to take place, as if checking all the details of the incident, just to be sure. The young woman and the servant weren't aware of the man with the long face behind them. Their eyes were riveted on the bloody duel. No one was about to turn around.

But who *was* this person? And why was he hiding beneath the ground back in ancient times? What was Tomohiko Amada's purpose in deliberately including this uncanny, mysterious figure in one corner of the painting, and thus forcibly destroying the balance of the overall composition?

And why in the world was this painting given the title *Killing Commendatore*? True, an apparently high-ranking person was being killed in the picture. But that old man in his ancient garb certainly didn't deserve to be called a commendatore—a knight commander. That was a title clearly from the European Middle Ages or the early modern period. There was no position like that in Japanese history. But still Tomohiko Amada gave it this strange-sounding title—*Killing Commendatore*. There had to be a *reason*.

The term "commendatore" sparked a faint memory. I'd heard the word before. I followed that trace of memory, as if tugging a thin thread toward me. I'd run across the word in a novel or drama. And it was a famous work. I knew I'd seen it somewhere . . .

And then it hit me. Mozart's opera *Don Giovanni*. In the beginning of that opera was a scene, I was sure, of *Killing Commendatore*. I went over to the shelf of records in the living room, took out the boxed set of *Don Giovanni*, and read through the accompanying commentary. And sure enough, the person killed in the opening scene was the Commendatore. He didn't have a name. He was simply listed as "Commendatore."

The libretto was in Italian, and the old man killed in the beginning was called *Il Commendatore*. Whoever translated the libretto into Japanese had rendered it as *kishidancho*—literally, "the knight commander"—and that had become the standard term in Japanese. I had no clue what sort of rank or position the term "commendatore" referred to in reality. The commentary in a few other boxed sets didn't elaborate. He was merely a nameless commendatore appearing in the opera with the sole function of being stabbed to death by Don Giovanni in the opening of the opera. And in the end he transformed into an ominous statue that appeared to Don Giovanni and took him down to hell.

Pretty obvious, if you think about it, I thought. The handsome young man in this painting is the rake Don Giovanni (Don Juan in Spanish) and the older man being killed is the honored knight commander. The young woman is the Commendatore's beautiful daughter Donna Anna, the servant is Don Giovanni's man, Leporello. What he had in his hands was the detailed list of all the women Don Giovanni had seduced up until then, a lengthy catalog of names. Don Giovanni had forced himself on Donna Anna, and when her father confronted him with this violation, they had a duel, and Don Giovanni stabbed the older man to death. It's a famous scene. Why hadn't I picked up on that?

Probably because Mozart's opera and a Japanese-style painting depicting the Asuka period were so remote from each other. So of course I hadn't been able to make the connection. But once I did, everything fell into place. Tomohiko Amada had "adapted" the world of Mozart's opera into the Asuka period. A fascinating experiment, for sure. That, I recognized. But why was that adaptation *necessary*? It was so very different from his usual style of painting. And why did he tightly wrap the painting and hide it away in the attic?

And what was the significance of that figure in the bottom left, the man with the long face sticking his head out from underground? In Mozart's *Don Giovanni* no one like that appeared. There must have been a reason Tomohiko Amada had added him. Also in the opera Donna Anna didn't actually witness her father being stabbed to death. She was off asking her lover, the knight Don Ottavio, for help. By the time they got back to the scene, her father had already breathed his last. Amada had—no doubt for dramatic purposes—subtly changed the way the scene played out. But there was no way the man sticking his head out of the ground was Don Ottavio. That man's features weren't anything found in this world. It was impossible that this was the upright, righteous knight who could help Donna Anna.

Was he a demon from hell? Scouting out the situation in anticipation of dragging Don Giovanni down to hell? But he didn't look like a demon or devil. A demon wouldn't have such strangely sparkling eyes. A devil wouldn't push a square wooden lid up and peek out. The figure more resembled a trickster who had come to intervene. "Long Face" is what I called him, for lack of a better term.

For a few weeks I just silently stared at that painting. With it in front of me, I couldn't bring myself to do any painting of my own. I barely even felt like eating. I'd grab whatever vegetables were in the fridge, dip them in mayo, and chew on that, or else heat up a can of whatever I had on hand. That's about the size of it. All day long I'd sit on the floor of the studio, endlessly listening to the record of *Don Giovanni*, staring enthralled at *Killing Commendatore*. When the sun set, I'd have a glass of wine.

The painting was amazing. As far as I knew, though, it wasn't reprinted in any collection of Amada's work, which meant no one else knew it existed. If it were made public it would no doubt become one of his best-known paintings. If they held a retrospective of his art, it wouldn't be surprising if this was the painting used on the promotional poster. This wasn't simply a painting that was wonderfully done, though. The painting was brimming with an extraordinary sort of energy. Anyone with even a little knowledge of art couldn't miss that fact. There was something in this painting that appealed to the deepest part of the viewer's heart, something suggestive that enticed the imagination to another realm.

I couldn't take my eyes off the bearded Long Face on the left side of the painting. It felt like he'd opened the lid to invite me, personally, to the world underground. No one else, just *me*. I couldn't stop thinking about what sort of realm lay beneath. Where in the world had he come from? And what did he do there? Would that lid be closed up again, or would it be left open?

As I stared at the painting I listened to that scene from *Don Giovanni* over and over. Act 1, scene 3, soon after the overture. And I nearly memorized the lyrics and the lines.

DONNA ANNA: *Ah, the assassin*
has struck him down! This blood . . .
this wound . . . his face
discolored with the pallor of death . . .
He has stopped breathing . . . his limbs
are cold.
Oh father, dear father, dearest father!
I'm fainting . . . I'm dying!

6

AT THIS POINT HE'S A FACELESS CLIENT

Summer was winding down when the call came in from my agent. It had been a while since anyone had called me. The summer heat still lingered during the day, though when the sun set the air in the mountains was chilly. The noisy clamor of the summer cicadas was slowly fading away, but now a chorus of other insects had taken their place. Unlike when I lived in the city, I was surrounded by nature now and one season freely chipped away at portions of the preceding one.

We brought each other up to date, though there wasn't much to tell on my end.

"How's your painting coming along?" he asked.

"Slowly but surely," I said. This was a lie, of course. It was more than four months since I'd moved here, yet the canvas I'd prepared was still blank.

"Glad to hear it," he said. "I'd like to see how you're doing sometime. Maybe there's something I can do to help out."

"Thanks. We'll do that sometime."

Then he told me why he'd called. "I have a request. Are you sure you're not willing to do one more portrait? What do you think?"

"I told you I've given up doing portraits."

"I know. But the fee this time is unbelievable."

"Unbelievable?"

"It's amazing."

"How amazing?"

He told me the figure. I nearly let out a whistle of surprise. "There have got to be a lot of other people besides me who specialize in portraits," I replied calmly.

"There aren't all that many, really, though there are a few besides you who are fairly decent."

"Then you should ask them. With a fee like that anybody would jump at the chance."

"The thing is, the other party specifically asked for *you*. That's their condition. No one else will do."

I shifted the phone to my left hand and scratched behind my right ear.

The agent went on. "The person saw several portraits you've done and was very impressed. He felt that the vitality in your paintings can't easily be found elsewhere."

"I don't get it. How could an ordinary person have seen *several* of my portraits? It's not like I have a one-man show at a gallery every year."

"I really don't know the details," he said, sounding perplexed. "I'm just passing along what the other party told me. I told him up front that you were no longer doing portraits. I said you seemed pretty firm about it, and even if I asked you you'd most likely turn him down. But he wouldn't give up. That's when this figure came up."

I mulled over the offer. Honestly, it was a tempting amount. And I felt a bit of pride that someone saw that much value in my paintings—even if it was work I'd done half mechanically for money. But the thing was, I'd sworn I'd never paint commissioned portraits again. When my wife left me it spurred me to start over again, and I couldn't reverse my decision just because somebody was willing to shell out a pile of money.

"Why is he being so generous?" I asked.

"Even though we're in a recession, there are still people who have so much money they don't know what to do with it. There are a lot of people like that—ones who made a killing in online stock trading, or tech entrepreneurs. And getting a portrait done is something they can write off as a business expense."

"Write off?"

"In their accounts a portrait isn't included as a work of art but as office equipment."

"Talk about heartwarming," I said.

But even if they have tons of excess cash, and even if they can write it off as a business expense, I can't see entrepreneurs or people who've made a fortune trading stocks online wanting to have their portraits painted and hung on their company walls as *office equipment*. Most of these are young people decked out at work in faded jeans, sneakers, worn T-shirts, and Banana Republic jackets, proud to be drinking Starbucks from a paper cup. An imposing oil portrait didn't fit their lifestyle. But there are all kinds in the world. You can't generalize. It's not necessarily true that no one wants to be painted sipping Starbucks (or whatever) coffee (Fair Trade beans only, of course) from a paper cup.

"But there's one condition," the agent said. "The other party wants you to use the client as a live model, and paint when you're actually together. They'll make the time to do that."

"But I don't work that way."

"I know. You meet the client but don't have them model for you. That's your way of working. I told them that. They said they understood but they'd like you to make an exception and paint the client live and in person. That's the other party's condition."

"What's the purpose?"

"I don't know."

"That's a pretty odd request. Why would they insist on that? You'd think they'd be happy not to actually have to sit for the portrait."

"I agree it's unconventional. But it's hard to complain about the fee."

"I'm with you there—hard to complain about the fee," I agreed.

"It's all up to you. It's not like you're being asked to sell your soul or anything. You're a very skilled portrait painter, and they're counting on that skill."

"I feel like a retired hit man in the mob," I said. "Like I'm being asked to whack one more target."

"Though no blood's going to be shed. What do you say—will you do it?"

No blood's going to be shed, I silently repeated. The painting *Killing Commendatore* came to mind.

"What sort of person is the one I'd paint?" I asked.

"Actually, I don't know."

"You don't even know if it's a man or a woman?"

"I don't. I haven't heard a thing about the sex or age or name. At this point he's a totally faceless client. A lawyer saying he was representing the client called me. That's the 'other party' I spoke with about it."

"Do you think it's legit?"

"I don't see anything suspect about it. The lawyer works at a reputable firm and said they'll transfer an advance as soon as you accept."

Phone in hand, I sighed. "This is kind of sudden, and I don't think I can give you an answer right away. I need time to think."

"Understood. Think about it as long as you need. It's not an urgent job, the other party said."

I thanked him and hung up. I couldn't think of anything else to do so I went to the studio, turned on the light, plunked myself down on the floor, and stared vaguely at *Killing Commendatore*. After a while I started to get hungry and went to the kitchen, piled a plate with Ritz Crackers and ketchup, and went back to the studio. I dipped the crackers in the ketchup and munched them as I went back to staring at the painting. Nothing about that food tasted good. It was, if anything, pretty awful. But taste wasn't the issue. Keeping hunger at bay for a while was the priority.

That's how much the painting drew me in, from the overall composition to the small details. It truly held me captive. After a few weeks of exhaustive gazing at the painting, I ventured closer to it to inspect each detail. What most caught my attention were the expressions on each of the five people's faces. I did minute pencil sketches of each of them. From the Commendatore, to Don Giovanni, Donna Anna, Leporello, and Long Face. Just like a reader might carefully copy down in a notebook each word and phrase he liked in a book.

This was the first time I'd ever sketched figures from a Japanese-style painting, and it was far more difficult than I'd expected. Japanese painting emphasized lines, and tended to be more flat than three-dimensional. Symbolism was emphasized over reality. It's inherently impossible to transfer a painting done from that perspective into the grammar of Western painting, though after much trial and error I was able to do a fairly decent job of it. Calling it "recasting" might be a bit much, but it was necessary to interpret and translate the painting in my own way. Which necessitated grasping the intent that went into the original painting. I had to come to an understanding of Tomohiko Amada, his viewpoint as an artist, and the kind of person he was. Figuratively speaking, I had to put myself in his shoes.

After I'd done this for a while, the thought struck me: maybe doing a portrait again wasn't such a bad idea. I mean, my painting wasn't going anywhere. I couldn't even get a hint of what I should paint, or what I wanted to paint. Even if I wasn't too keen on the job, getting my hands moving again wouldn't be a bad thing. If I kept on like this, unable to draw a thing, I might find myself unable to paint ever again. *Maybe I wouldn't even be able to paint a portrait.* The fee, of course, was also pretty tempting. My living expenses at this point were minimal, but my pay from the art classes wasn't enough to cover them. I'd gone on that long trip, bought a used Corolla station wagon, and my savings were diminishing. So a sizable fee like the one I'd get from doing the portrait was, admittedly, very appealing.

I called my agent and told him that just this one time, I would take on the job. Naturally, he was happy to hear this.

"But if I have to paint the client in person, that means I need to travel to wherever he is," I said.

"No need to worry about that. The other party will come to your place in Odawara."

"To Odawara?"

"That's right."

"He knows where I'm living?"

"He apparently lives nearby. He even knows that you're living in Tomohiko Amada's place."

This left me speechless. "That's strange. Hardly anybody knows I'm living here. Especially that I'm in Amada's house."

"I didn't know that either," the agent said.

"Then how does that person know?"

"I have no idea. But you can find out just about anything from the Internet these days. For people who know their way around it, privacy is a thing of the past."

"Is it just a coincidence that that person lives near me? Or was the fact that I live nearby one of the reasons he chose me?"

"That, I couldn't say. When you meet the client, if there's something you want to know, you can ask."

"I'll do that," I said.

"So when can you start?" he asked.

"Anytime," I said.

"All right, I'll let them know, and get back to you," the agent said.

After I hung up I went out to the terrace, settled into the lounge chair, and thought about how things had turned out. The more I mulled it over, the more questions I had. First off, it bothered me that the client knew I was living here, in this house. It was like I was under surveillance, with somebody watching my every move. But why would anyone have that much interest in a person like me? Plus the whole thing sounded too good to be true. The portraits I'd done were certainly well received. And I had a certain amount of confidence in them. But these were, ultimately, the kind of portraits you could find anywhere. No way could you ever call them "works of art." And as far as the world was concerned I was a completely unknown artist. No matter how many of my paintings someone had seen and liked (not that I accepted that story at face value), would that person really shell out such an enormous fee?

A thought suddenly struck me, out of nowhere: Could the client be the husband of the woman I was having an affair with? I had no proof to go on, yet the more I thought about it the more it seemed like a real possibility. When it came to an anonymous neighbor who was interested in me, that's all I could come up with. But why would her husband go to the trouble and expense of paying a huge fee to have his wife's lover paint his own portrait? It didn't add up. Unless he was some weird pervert or something.

Fine. If that's how things are working out, then just go with the flow. If the client has some hidden agenda, just let it play out. That was a much more sensible thing to do than remaining as I was, stuck, deadlocked in the mountains. Curiosity was also a factor. What kind of person *was* this client? What did he want from me in exchange for the huge fee? I had to discover what motivated him.

Once I'd made up my mind I felt relieved. That night, for the first time in a while, I fell into a deep sleep right away, with no thoughts buzzing around in my head. At one point I felt like I heard the rustling of the horned owl in the middle of the night. But that might have just been a piece of a fragmentary dream.

7

FOR BETTER OR FOR WORSE, IT'S AN EASY NAME TO REMEMBER

My agent in Tokyo called a few more times, and we decided that I would meet our mystery client on Tuesday afternoon of the following week. (At that point the client's name was still not revealed.) I had them agree to my usual procedure, wherein, on the first day, we simply met and talked together for an hour or so, before we embarked upon a drawing.

As you might imagine, painting a portrait requires the ability to accurately grasp the special features of a person's face. But that's not all. If it were, you'd end up with a caricature. To paint a vibrant portrait you need the skill to discover what lies at the core of the person's face. A face is like reading a palm. More than the features you're born with, a face is gradually formed over the passage of time, through all the experiences a person goes through, and no two faces are alike.

On Tuesday morning I straightened up the house, picked some flowers from the garden and put them in vases, moved the *Killing Commendatore* painting out of the studio into the guest bedroom, and wrapped it up again in brown paper. I didn't want anyone else seeing it.

At five past one p.m. a car drove up the steep slope and parked in the covered driveway at the entrance. A heavy, brazen-sounding engine echoed, like some giant animal giving a satisfied purr from deep inside a cave. A high-powered engine. The engine shut off, and quiet again settled over the valley. The car was a silver Jaguar sports coupe. Sunlight from between the clouds reflected brightly off the long, brightly polished fenders. I'm not that into cars, so I don't know which model this was, but my guess was that it was the latest model, the mileage in the four digits, the price twenty times what I paid for my used Corolla station wagon. Not that this surprised me. The client was, after all, willing to pay such a huge fee to have a portrait done. If he'd appeared at my door in a massive yacht, it wouldn't have been surprising.

The person who got out of the car was a well-dressed middle-aged man. He had on dark-green sunglasses, a long-sleeved white cotton shirt (not simply white, but a pure white), and khaki chinos. His shoes were cream-colored deck shoes. He was probably a shade over five feet seven inches tall. His face had a nice, even tan. He gave off an overall fresh, clean feel. But what struck me most on this first encounter was his hair. Slightly curly and thick, it was white down to the last hair. Not gray or salt-and-pepper, but a pure white, like freshly fallen, virgin snow.

He got out of the car, closed the door (which made that special pleasant *thunk* expensive car doors make when you casually shut them), didn't lock it but put the key in his trouser pocket, and strode toward my front door—all of which I watched from a gap in the curtains. The way he walked was quite lovely. Back straight, the necessary muscles all equally in play. I figured he must work out regularly, and pretty hard training at that. I stepped away from the window, sat in a chair in the living room, and waited for the front doorbell to ring. Once it did, I slowly walked to the door and opened it.

When I opened the door the man took off his sunglasses, slipped them into the breast pocket of his shirt, and without a word held out his hand. Half reflexively I held out my hand, too. He shook it. It was a firm handshake, the way Americans do it. A little too firm for me, not that it hurt or anything.

"My name is Menshiki. It's very nice to meet you," the man said in a clear voice. The sort of tone a lecturer would make at the beginning of his talk to test the microphone and introduce himself at the same time.

"The pleasure's mine," I said. "Mr. Menshiki?"

"The *men* is written with the character in *menzeiten*—the one that means 'avoidance'—and the *shiki* is the character *iro*, for 'color.' "

"Mr. Menshiki," I repeated, lining the two characters up in my mind. A strange combination.

" 'Avoiding colors,' is what it means," the man said. "An unusual name. Other than my relatives I rarely run across anyone who shares it."

"But it's easy to remember."

"Exactly. It's an easy name to remember. For better or for worse." The man smiled. He had faint stubble from his cheeks to his chin, but I don't think he'd simply left off shaving. When he'd shaved he'd left an exact, calculated amount of stubble. Different from his hair, his beard was half black. I found it odd that only his hair was pure white.

"Please come in," I said.

Menshiki gave a small nod, removed his shoes, and stepped inside. The way he carried himself was charming, though I could sense a bit of tension. Like some large cat taken to a new place, each movement was careful and light, his eyes darting quickly around to take in his surroundings.

"A comfortable-looking place," he said after sitting down on the sofa. "Very relaxed and quiet."

"Quiet it certainly is. But kind of inconvenient when you have to go shopping."

"I would imagine for someone in your field it's an ideal environment."

I sat down in the chair across from him.

"I heard that you live nearby, Mr. Menshiki?"

"Yes, that's right. It would take a while to walk here, though as the crow flies it's actually pretty near."

"As the crow flies," I said, repeating his words. There was a somehow strange ring to the expression. "But how near is it, actually?"

"Close enough that if you wave your hand here you could see it."

"You can see your house from here?"

"Exactly."

I wasn't sure how to respond, and Menshiki asked, "Would you like to see my house?"

"If I could, yes," I said.

"Do you mind if we go out on the terrace?"

"Please, go right ahead."

Menshiki got up from the sofa and went straight from the living room to the terrace. He leaned out over the railing and pointed across the valley.

"You see that white concrete house over there? The one on top of the mountain, with the shiny windows?"

I was speechless. That was the house, that smart, elegant house I often looked at when I went out at sunset onto the terrace to enjoy a glass of wine. The large house that stood out from all the rest, diagonally to the right from mine.

"It's a little far, but if you made a big wave with your hand you could say hello," Menshiki said.

"But how did you know I was living here?" I asked, resting my hands on the railing.

He looked puzzled. He wasn't really fazed, just displaying a puzzled look. Not that his expression seemed contrived. He'd simply wanted to throw in a pause before responding.

"One aspect of my job is gathering all kinds of information," he said. "That's the sort of business I'm in."

"Is it tech related?"

"That's right. Or more precisely, that's also one aspect of my work."

"But hardly anyone knows yet that I'm living here."

Menshiki smiled. "Saying hardly anyone knows means, paradoxically, that there are some who *do*."

I looked over again at that exquisite white concrete building across the valley, and once more studied the man beside me. He was, most likely, the one who appeared almost every evening on the deck of that house. When I thought of it, his shape and movements all fit that silhouette perfectly . . . It was hard to figure out his age. That snow-white hair made me think he must be in his late fifties or early sixties, though his skin was lustrous and tight, and wrinkle free. His deep-looking eyes had the youthful twinkle of a man in his late thirties. All of which made guessing his age a tough call. I would have accepted anything between forty-five and sixty.

Menshiki went back to the sofa in the living room, and I sat down again across from him.

"Do you mind if I ask a question?" I finally ventured.

"Ask away," he said, beaming.

"Is there some connection between the fact that I live near your house and your decision to ask me to paint your portrait?"

A slight look of confusion came over him. And when he looked confused, several tiny wrinkles appeared at the corners of his eyes. Charming wrinkles. His features, viewed individually, were all quite attractive—the eyes almond shaped and slightly deep set, the forehead noble and broad, the eyebrows thick and nicely defined, the nose thin and a nice size. Eyes, eyebrows, and nose that perfectly fit his smallish face. His face was a bit small, yet too broad in a way, and from a purely aesthetic viewpoint was a little imbalanced. The vertical and horizontal were out of sync, though this disparity wasn't necessarily a defect. It's what gave his face its distinctiveness, since it was this imbalance that conversely gave the viewer a sense of calm. If his features had been too perfectly symmetrical people might have felt a bit of antipathy, or wariness, toward him. But as it was, his ever-so-slightly unbalanced features had a calming effect on anyone meeting him for the first time. They broadcast, in a friendly way, "It's all good, not to worry. I'm not a bad person. I don't plan to do anything bad to you."

The pointed, largish tips of his ears were slightly visible through his neatly trimmed hair. They conveyed a sense of freshness, of vigor, reminding me of spry little mushrooms in a forest, peeking out from among the fallen leaves on an autumn morning, just after it had rained. His mouth was broad, the thin lips neatly closed in a line, diligently prepared to, at any moment, break into a smile.

One could call him handsome. And he actually was. Yet his features rejected that sort of casual description, neatly circumventing it. His face was too lively, its movements too subtle to simply abide by that label. The expressions that rose on his features weren't calculated, but looked more like they'd arisen naturally, spontaneously. If they weren't, then he was quite the actor. But I got the impression that wasn't the case.

When I observe the face of a person I've met for the first time, from habit I sense all sorts of things. In most cases there's no tangible basis for how I feel. It's nothing more than intuition. But that's what helps me as a portrait artist—that *simple intuition*.

"The answer is yes, and no," Menshiki said. His hands on his knees were wide open, palms up. He turned them over.

I said nothing, waiting for his next words.

"I do worry about who lives in the neighborhood," Menshiki went on. "No, not worry, exactly. It's more like I'm *interested*. Especially when it's someone I see now and then across the valley."

It's a little too great a distance to say we actually *see* each other, I thought, but didn't say anything. Maybe he had high-powered binoculars and had been secretly observing me? I kept that thought to myself. I mean, what possible reason could he have to observe a person like *me*?

"And I learned that you had moved in here," Menshiki continued. "I found out you're a professional portrait artist, and that aroused my interest enough to seek out a few of your paintings. At first I saw them on the Internet. But I wasn't satisfied, so I went to see three actual paintings."

That had me puzzled. "You saw the actual paintings?"

"I went to see the people who had modeled for you and asked them to let me see the portraits. They were happy to show me them. It seems like people who sit for portraits are really pleased to show them off. I got a strange sensation when I saw the actual paintings up close and compared them to the faces of the people. It's like I couldn't tell which one was real anymore. How should I put it? There's something about your paintings that strikes the viewer's heart from an unexpected angle. At first they seem like ordinary, typical portraits, but if you look carefully you see something hidden inside them."

"Something hidden?" I asked.

"I'm not sure how to put it. Maybe the real personality?"

"Personality," I mused. "*My* personality? Or the *subject's*?"

"Both, probably. They're mixed together, so elaborately intertwined they can't be separated. It's not something you can overlook. Even if you just glance at the paintings as you pass by, you feel like you've missed something, and you can't help but come back and study them carefully. It's that indefinable *something* that drew me to them."

I was silent.

"And I had this thought: This is the person I want to paint my portrait. No matter what. I got in touch with your agent right away."

"Through an intermediary."

"Correct. I normally use an intermediary, a law office. It's not that I have a guilty conscience or anything. I just like to protect my anonymity."

"And it's an easy name to remember."

"Exactly," he said, and smiled. His mouth spread wide, the tips of his ears quivered ever so slightly. "There are times when I don't want my name to be known."

"Still, the fee is a little too much," I said.

"Price is always relative, determined by supply and demand. Those are basic market principles. If I want to buy something and you don't want to sell it, the price goes up. And in the opposite case, the price goes down."

"I understand market principles. But is it really necessary for you to go to all that length to have me paint your portrait? Maybe I shouldn't say this, but a portrait isn't something a person really *needs*."

"True enough. It's not something you need. But I'm also curious about what sort of portrait you'd do if you painted me. I want to find that out. You could think of it another way, namely that I'm putting a price on my own curiosity."

"And your curiosity doesn't come cheap."

He smiled happily. "The purer the curiosity is, the stronger it is. And the more money it takes to satisfy it."

"Would you care for some coffee?" I asked.

"That would be nice."

"I made it a little while ago in the coffee maker. Is that okay?"

"That's fine. I'll take it black, if you don't mind."

I went into the kitchen, poured coffee into two cups, and carried them back out.

"I notice you have a lot of opera recordings," Menshiki said as he drank the coffee. "You're a big opera fan?"

"Those aren't mine. The owner of this place left them. Thanks to them, though, I've listened to a lot of opera since I came here."

"By owner you mean Tomohiko Amada?"

"That's right."

"Do you have a favorite?"

I gave it some thought. "These days I've been listening to *Don Giovanni* a lot. There's a bit of a reason for that."

"What kind of reason? I'd like to hear, if you don't mind?"

"Well, it's personal. Nothing important."

"I like *Don Giovanni* too, and listen to it a lot," Menshiki said. "I heard it once in a small opera house in Prague. This was back just after the fall of the communist regime.

"I'm sure you know this," he continued, "but *Don Giovanni* was first performed in Prague. The theater was small, and so was the orchestra, and none of the singers were famous, yet it was a wonderful performance. They didn't have to sing really loud like in a big opera house, and could express their feelings in a very intimate way. Impossible at the Met or La Scala. There you need a well-known singer with a booming voice. Sometimes the arias in those big opera houses remind me of acrobatics. But what operas like Mozart's need is intimacy, like music. Don't you think so? In that sense the performance I heard in Prague was the ideal *Don Giovanni*."

He took another sip of coffee. I said nothing, observing his actions.

"I've had the opportunity to hear performances of *Don Giovanni* all over the world," he went on. "In Vienna, Rome, Milan, London, Paris, at the Met, and even in Tokyo. With Abbado, Levine, Ozawa, Maazel, and who else? . . . Georges Prêtre, I believe. But the *Don Giovanni* I heard in Prague is the one that, strangely enough, has stayed with me. The singers and conductor weren't people I'd ever heard of, but outside, after the performance, Prague was covered in a thick fog. There weren't many lights back then and the streets were pitch black at night. As I wandered down the deserted cobblestone streets I suddenly ran across a bronze statue. Whose statue, I have no idea. But he was dressed as a medieval knight. The thought struck me that I should ask him out to dinner. I didn't, of course."

He smiled again.

"Do you often go abroad?" I asked.

"Sometimes for work I do," he said. As if a thought occurred to him, he remained silent. I surmised that he didn't want to talk specifics about his job.

"So, what do you think?" Menshiki asked, looking me right in the eye. "Did I pass the test? Will you paint my portrait?"

"I'm not testing you. We're just getting together for a talk."

"But before you begin a painting you always meet and talk with the client. I heard that if you don't like the person, you won't paint his portrait."

I glanced over toward the terrace. A large crow had settled on the railing, but as if sensing my gaze, he spread his glossy wings and took off.

"I guess that's possible, but fortunately I haven't met anyone I don't like yet."

"I hope I'm not the first," Menshiki said with a smile. His eyes, though, weren't smiling. He was serious.

"Don't worry. I would be more than pleased to paint your portrait."

"That's wonderful," he said. He paused. "This is kind of selfish of me, but I have a little request myself."

I looked straight at him again. "What kind of request?"

"If possible I'd like you to paint me freely, and not worry about the usual conventions involved in doing a portrait. I mean, if you want to paint a standard portrait, that's fine. If you paint it using your usual techniques, the way you've painted till now, I'm all right with that. But if you do decide to try out a different approach, I'd welcome that."

"A different approach?"

"Whatever style you like is entirely up to you. Paint it any way you like."

"So you're saying that, like Picasso's painting during one period, I could put both eyes on one side of the face and you'd be okay with that?"

"If that's how you want to paint me, I have no objections. I leave it all up to you."

"And you'll hang that on the wall of your office."

"Right now I don't have an office per se. So I'll probably hang it in my study at home. As long as you have no objection."

Of course I had none. All walls were the same as far I was concerned. I mulled all this over before replying.

"Mr. Menshiki, I'm grateful to you for saying that, for telling me to paint in whatever style I want. But honestly nothing specific pops into my head at the moment. You have to understand, I'm merely a portrait painter. For a long time I've followed a set pattern and style. Even if

I'm told to remove any restrictions, to paint as freely as I want, the restrictions themselves are part of the technique. So I think it's likely I'll paint a *standard* portrait, the way I have up till now. I hope that's all right with you?"

Menshiki held both hands wide. "Of course. Do what you think is best. The only thing I want is for you to have a totally free hand."

"One other thing: if you're going to pose for the portrait, I'll need you to come to my studio a number of times and sit in a chair for quite a while. I'm sure your work keeps you quite busy, so do you think that'll be possible?"

"I can clear my schedule anytime. I was the one, after all, who asked that you paint me from real life. I'll come here and sit quietly in the chair as long as I can. We can have a good long talk then. You don't mind talking?"

"No, of course not. Actually, I welcome it. To me, you're a complete mystery. In order to paint you, I might need a little more information about you."

Menshiki laughed and quietly shook his head. When he did so, his pure white hair softly shook, like a winter prairie blowing in the wind.

"I think you overestimate me. There's nothing particularly mysterious about me. I don't talk much about myself because telling all the details would bore people, that's all."

He smiled, the lines at his eyes deepening. A very clean, open smile. But that can't be all, I thought. There was something hidden inside him. A secret locked away in a small box and buried deep down in the ground. Buried a long time ago, with soft green grass now growing above it. And the only person in the world who knew the location of the box was Menshiki. I couldn't help but sense, deep within his smile, a solitude that comes from a certain sort of secret.

We talked for another twenty minutes or so, deciding when he would come here to model, and how much time he could spare. On his way out, at the front door, he once more held out his hand, quite naturally, and I took it without thinking. A firm handshake at the beginning and end of an encounter seemed to be Menshiki's way of doing things. He slipped on his sunglasses, took the car keys from his pocket, boarded the silver Jaguar (which looked like some well-trained, slick, oversized animal), and gracefully eased down the slope, as I watched from the window. I went out on the terrace and gazed at the white house on the mountain he was heading back to.

What an unusual character, I thought. Friendly enough, not overly quiet. But it was as if he hadn't said a single thing about himself. The most I'd learned was that he lived in that elegant house across the valley, did work that partly involved the Internet, and frequently traveled abroad. And that he was a big fan of opera. Beyond that, though, I knew very little. Whether or not he had a family, how old he was, where he was from originally, how long he'd lived on that mountain. He hadn't even told me his first name.

And why be so insistent on me being the one to paint his portrait? I'd like to think it was because I had talent, something obvious to anyone who saw my work. Yet it was clear that this was not his sole motivation for commissioning me to do the painting. It seemed true that portraits I'd done had drawn his attention. That couldn't be a complete lie. But I wasn't naive enough to accept everything he told me at face value.

So—what did this man, Menshiki, want from me? What was his endgame? What sort of scenario had he prepared for me?

Even after we had talked, I still had no idea how to answer these questions. The mystery, in fact, had deepened. Why, for one thing, did he have such amazingly white hair? That kind of white wasn't exactly normal. I recalled an Edgar Allan Poe short story in which a fisherman gets caught up in a massive whirlpool and his hair turns white overnight. Had Menshiki experienced something just as terrifying?

After the sun set, lights came on in the white concrete mansion across the valley. Bright lights, and plenty of them. It looked like the kind of house designed by a self-assured architect unconcerned about things like the electric bill. Or perhaps the client was overly afraid of the dark and requested the architect to build a house where lights could blaze from one end to the other. Either way, viewed from afar, the house looked like a luxury liner silently crossing the ocean at night.

I sprawled out on the chair on the terrace and, sipping white wine, gazed at those lights. I was half expecting Menshiki to come out on his terrace, but that evening he didn't appear. But if he had, how should I have acted? Wave my hand in a big gesture of greeting?

I figured that, in time, my questions would be answered. That's about all I could expect.

8

A BLESSING IN DISGUISE

After my Wednesday-evening art class, when I taught an adult class for about an hour, I stopped by an Internet café near Odawara Station and did a Google search for the name Menshiki. I came up empty-handed. There were lots of online articles with the character *men* in them, as in *unten* men*kyo*—driver's license—and the *shiki* appeared in ones about partial color-blindness—shiki*jaku*. But there didn't seem to be any information out there in the world about a Mr. Menshiki. His statement that he took anonymity seriously seemed, indeed, to be the case. I was assuming, of course, that Menshiki was his real name, but my gut told me he wouldn't lie about something like that. It didn't make sense for him to tell me where he lived but not tell me his real name. And unless he had some compelling reason, it seemed to me that if he were to make up a phony name, he would choose one that was more common and didn't stand out so much.

When I got back home I called Masahiko Amada. After chatting a bit I asked if he knew anything about the man named Menshiki who lived across the valley. I described the white concrete house on the mountain. He had a vague memory of it.

"Menshiki?" Masahiko asked. "What kind of name is that?"

"It's written with the characters that mean 'avoiding colors.' "

"Sounds like a Chinese ink painting."

"But white and black are counted as colors," I pointed out.

"In theory, I suppose. . . . Menshiki? I don't think I've heard the name. I wouldn't know anything about anyone living on a mountain across the valley. I mean, I don't even know the people living on *your* side of the valley. Is there something going on between the two of you?"

"We sort of connected," I said. "And I was wondering if you knew anything about him."

"Did you check online?"

"I did a Google search but struck out."

"How about Facebook or other social media?"

"I don't know much about those."

"While you were asleep with the fish in the Dragon King's palace, like in the fairy tale, culture has forged on ahead. Not to worry—I'll check them for you. If I find anything, I'll give you a call."

"Thanks."

Masahiko was suddenly silent. On the other end of the phone it felt like he was contemplating something.

"Hold on a sec. Did you say Menshiki?" Masahiko asked.

"That's right. Menshiki. The *men* in *menzeiten*—'avoidance'—and the *shiki* in 'color'—*shikisai*."

"*Menshiki* . . . ," he said. "You know, I do remember now hearing that name before. Maybe I'm just imagining it."

"It's such an unusual name I'd think if you heard it once you wouldn't forget it."

"Agreed. Which is why maybe it's stuck in a corner of my mind. But I can't remember when I heard it, or in what context. It feels like when you have a small fishbone stuck in your throat."

If you remember, let me know, I said. Will do, Masahiko promised.

I hung up and then had a light meal. While I was eating, a call came in from the married woman I was having an affair with. Do you mind if I come to your place tomorrow afternoon? she asked. No problem, I replied.

"By the way, do you know anything about a person named Menshiki?" I asked. "He lives in the neighborhood."

"Menshiki?" she repeated. "Is that the last name?"

I explained how it was written.

"I've never heard of him," she said.

"You know that white concrete house across the valley from me? He lives there."

"I remember that house. The one you see from the terrace that really stands out."

"That's his house."

"Mr. Menshiki lives there?"

"That's right."

"So what about him?"

"Nothing, really. I just wanted to know if you knew him or not."

Her voice grew one tone darker. "Does that have something to do with me?"

"No, nothing to do with you."

She sighed, as if in relief. "Well, I'll see you tomorrow afternoon. Probably about one thirty."

"I'm looking forward to it," I said. I hung up and finished eating.

The call from Masahiko came a little while after that.

"It seems like there are a few people with the name Menshiki in Kagawa Prefecture down in Shikoku," Masahiko said. "Perhaps this Mr. Menshiki has roots in Kagawa. But I couldn't find any information anywhere on a Menshiki living now around Odawara. What's his first name?"

"He didn't tell me. I don't know what kind of work he does, either. Something tech related. If his lifestyle is any indication, he must be doing pretty well. That's all I know. I don't even know how old he is."

"I see," Masahiko said. "In that case, that might be the best you can do. Information is, after all, a product, and if you pay enough you can neatly cover your tracks. Even truer if the person knows a lot about technology."

"You mean Mr. Menshiki erased his footprints?"

"Could be. I spent a lot of time online, searching through sites, and didn't get a single hit. It's such an eye-catching name, yet there's not a thing online. Which is all pretty strange. I know you're a little naive when it comes to things like this, but for someone who is fairly active in society to completely block any information about themselves and have nothing at all get out on the web—that's no mean feat. Even information on you, and on me, is out there and available. There's information on me I didn't even know. If that's true for nobodies like us, you can imagine how much harder it is for some big shot to erase their digital presence. Like it or not, that's the world we live in. What about you? Have you checked out the information that's out there on you?"

"No, never."

"You should keep it that way."

"That's the plan," I told him.

One aspect of my job is gathering all kinds of information. That's the sort of business I'm in. Those were Menshiki's own words. If he could get hold of information that easily he could probably erase it as well.

"By the way, Mr. Menshiki said he looked me up on the Internet and saw a few of my portraits there," I said.

"And?"

"And he asked me to paint his portrait. He said he liked the portraits I've done."

"But you turned him down because you're no longer in the portrait business. Correct?"

I was silent.

"Are you telling me you didn't?" he asked.

"Actually, I didn't turn him down."

"How come? Weren't you set on not doing any more?"

"The fee is pretty hefty, that's why. I thought it might be okay to do one more portrait."

"For the money?"

"That's a big reason. I'm making hardly any money anymore, and I have to think about how I'm going to make a living. My expenses right now are minimal, but still, with one thing and another the money keeps flowing out."

"Huh. So, how much is the fee?"

I named the amount. Masahiko let out a whistle.

"Wow," he said. "That certainly makes it worth taking on. I bet you were surprised when you heard how much he'd pay?"

"Yeah, of course I was."

"Maybe I shouldn't say this, but there can't be any other odd people out there willing to pay that much for one of your paintings."

"I know."

"Don't get me wrong, I'm not saying you're not a talented artist. You do solid work, and people recognize that. I think you're about the only one of our classmates from our art school class who's managed to make a living doing oil paintings. What level of living we're talking about, I have no idea, but anyway it's admirable what you've accomplished. But honestly? You're no Rembrandt, or Delacroix. Or even Andy Warhol."

"I'm well aware of that."

"If you are, then you understand how exorbitant that fee is he's offering, right?"

"Of course I do."

"And just *by chance* he lives near you."

"Exactly."

"'By chance' is putting it mildly."

I didn't say anything.

"There might be something else to it. Didn't that cross your mind?" he asked.

"Sure, I thought about it. But what else there could be, I have no clue."

"So you accepted the job?"

"I did. I start the day after tomorrow."

"Because the fee's so good?"

"The fee's a big part of it. But that's not all. There are other reasons," I said. "Honestly, I want to see how things are going to play out. See with my own eyes why he's willing to pay so much. And if there're really other motives at work, I want to find out what they are."

"I see," Masahiko said, and paused. "Well, if there are any new developments, let me know. I'm intrigued."

Just then I recalled the horned owl.

"I forgot to mention it, but there's a horned owl living in the attic," I said. "A little gray horned owl that sleeps on a beam during the day. At night it goes out the vent hole and hunts. I don't know how long it's been here, but it seems to have roosted."

"In the attic?"

"I heard a sound from the ceiling, so I climbed up during the day to check on it."

"Really. I didn't know you could access the attic."

"There's an opening in the closet in the guest bedroom. It's a tight space, though. Smaller than what you might think of as an attic. But just the right size for an owl to roost in."

"That's a good thing, though," Masahiko said. "With an owl there, no mice or snakes will get in. I've heard it's a lucky omen to have an owl roosting in a house."

"Maybe that lucky omen brought me that high portrait fee."

"That would be nice if it did," he laughed. "You know the English expression 'a blessing in disguise'?"

"Languages aren't my strong suit."

"A camouflaged blessing. A blessing that's changed appearance. At first glance it seems unfortunate, but it turns out to bring you happiness. There are things that should be the opposite, too, of course. In theory."

In theory, I repeated to myself.

"Better keep your eyes open," he said.

"Will do," I said.

At one thirty the next day she came to see me, and as always we headed straight for bed. While we had sex we hardly said a word. It was raining that afternoon, an unusually heavy shower for autumn, more like a midsummer downpour. Heavy raindrops, carried on the wind, rapped against the window, and I think there were a few flashes of lightning, too. A thick bank of dark clouds passed over the valley, and when the rain let up, the mountains had taken on a darker hue. Flocks of birds that had taken shelter from the rain somewhere now twittered back and were busily hunting down insects. Right after rain was the perfect lunchtime for them. The sun shone from breaks in the clouds, making the raindrops on all the tree branches sparkle. While it had been raining we were deep into making love, and I had barely given the falling rain a second thought. And just as we were finishing, the rain abruptly stopped. Almost as if it were waiting for us.

We lay naked in bed, wrapped in a thin bedcover, talking. Mostly we talked about the grades her two daughters were getting in school. The older girl was good at school and had very good grades. She was a placid child who never caused any trouble. The younger daughter, in contrast, hated to study and would never settle down at her desk to do homework. But she was cheerful and upbeat, and quite good-looking as well. Self-assured, popular, good at sports. Maybe we should give up on having her do well at school, her mother said, and let her go into the entertainment field? I'm thinking of eventually putting her into one of those schools that train child entertainers, she said.

If you think about it, it was kind of strange. I was lying there next to a woman I'd known for only about three months, listening to her talk about her daughters, whom I'd never laid eyes on. She was even asking me my opinion on what sort of path they should take in life. And the two of us there, without a stitch on. Admittedly, though, not a bad feeling, to take a random peek into the lives of people I hardly knew. Brushing past the lives of people I would never have anything to do with. Their lives felt right before me, yet also far away. As she talked, the woman toyed with my now flaccid penis, which was slowly coming back to life.

"Have you been painting anything these days?" she asked.

"Not really," I answered honestly.

"No creative urge welling up?"

I hesitated. ". . . Well, tomorrow I have to start on a commission I got."

"You're going to paint on commission?"

"That's right. Have to earn some money sometimes."

"What sort of commission?"

"A portrait."

"Is it, by any chance, a portrait of that person you mentioned on the phone yesterday, Mr. Menshiki?"

"It is," I said. She was so sharp at times it took me by surprise.

"And you want to know something about this Mr. Menshiki, right?"

"At this point he's a mystery. I met him once and we talked, but I still have no idea what sort of person he is. I like to know what kind of person I'm going to paint."

"You should just ask him directly."

"He might not give me a straight answer," I said. "He might only tell me what he wants me to know."

"I could look into it for you," she said.

"You can do that?"

"I might have an idea."

"There were zero hits on him on the Internet."

"The Internet doesn't work well in the jungle," she said. "The jungle has its own communications network. Signaling with drums, tying a message around a monkey's neck."

"I don't know much about the jungle, I'm afraid."

"When civilization's devices don't operate, it's worth trying drums or a monkey."

My penis had now grown fully erect under her soft, busy fingers. She skillfully and greedily began to use her lips and tongue, and a meaningful silence descended upon us for a while. As the birds outside chirped and went about the work of making a living, the two of us began a second round of sex.

After our long second bout of lovemaking, punctuated by an intermission, we climbed out of bed, lazily gathered our clothes from the floor, and dressed. We went out to the terrace and, sipping hot herb tea, gazed across the valley at the large white concrete house there. We sat side by side on the weathered wooden deck chairs and breathed in deeply the fresh dampness of the mountain air. Through the woods to the southwest was a small patch of sparkling ocean, a mere fragment of the enormous Pacific. The mountain slopes around were already dyed with autumn colors, minute gradations of yellow and red, with an intrusion of green from the clumps of evergreens. The mix of these vivid colors made the white concrete of Menshiki's house stand out all the more. It was an almost obsessive white that looked like it would never be dirtied or treated with contempt by such things as wind, rain, dust, or even time itself. *White is a color, too*, I thought distractedly. Definitely not the lack of color. We sat there on the lounge chairs for a long time without saying a word, silence an entirely natural companion.

"Mr. Menshiki in his white mansion," she said after a while. "Sounds like the beginning of an amusing fairy tale."

But what awaited me was, of course, not some "amusing fairy tale." Or a blessing in disguise, either. But by the time that became clear to me, there was no turning back.

9

EXCHANGING FRAGMENTS WITH EACH OTHER

On Friday at one thirty Menshiki appeared in the same Jaguar. The deep roar of the engine as it climbed the steep slope grew louder as it approached, and finally came to a stop in front of the house. As before, he shut the door of the car with the same solid sound, and removed his sunglasses and slipped them into the breast pocket of his jacket. An exact repeat of the previous visit. This time, though, he wore a white polo shirt with a blue-gray cotton jacket, cream-colored chinos, and brown leather shoes. He was so impeccably dressed that he could have been a model in a magazine, though he didn't give the impression that it was all *too perfect*. It looked casual, and naturally neat. And that abundant white hair of his was, like the walls of his mansion, a pure, unadulterated white. Just as I had the first time, I watched him approach through a gap in the curtains.

The front doorbell rang and I opened it and let him in. This time he didn't hold his hand out to shake mine. He just looked me in the eye, and gave a small smile and a brief nod of greeting. I breathed a sigh of relief. I'd been a bit anxious that every time we met I'd have to go through one of his firm handshakes. Once again, I showed him into the living room and had him sit on the sofa. And brought out two cups of freshly brewed coffee from the kitchen.

"I didn't know what I should wear," he said, sounding apologetic. "Is this outfit all right?"

"It doesn't matter at this point. We can decide at the end how you should be dressed. A suit, or shorts and sandals, we can adjust the clothes later on however we want."

Or show you holding a Starbucks cup, I added to myself.

"Knowing you're going to be modeling makes you anxious. I know I won't have to take off all my clothes, but it still makes me feel like I'm being stripped down."

"You could be right. Models for paintings sometimes pose nude—in most cases actually nude, in some cases more metaphorically. The artist wants to view the model's essence, meaning he has to strip away the clothed, outer appearance. To do that, of course, takes great powers of observation and a sharp intuition."

Menshiki spread his hands on his lap and seemed to be inspecting them. He then looked up. "I heard that you don't use a live model when you paint a portrait."

"That's right. I meet the subject once and have a long talk with him, but don't have him model live for me."

"Is there a reason for that?"

"No real reason. I've just found, through experience, that things go more smoothly that way. When we first meet I concentrate as much as I can, trying to get a take on the subject's looks, expressions, quirks, and tendencies, and brand those into my memory. Once I've done that, it's just a question of reproducing them from memory."

"That's very intriguing," Menshiki said. "So, days later you take the memory you've burned into your brain, rearrange all that as an image, and reproduce it as a work of art. You must have a gift to do that—to have such extraordinary visual recall."

"I wouldn't call it a gift, exactly. More of a skill set, I'd say."

"Maybe that's why, when I saw some of the portraits you've done, I sensed something unique in them. Compared with other standard portraits—portraits done purely as commodities. The way everything's reproduced so vividly, you might say . . ."

He took a sip of coffee, took a light-cream linen handkerchief from his jacket pocket, and wiped his mouth. "But this time, unusually, you'll be using a model—with me in front of you, in other words—as you do the portrait."

"Exactly. At your request."

He nodded. "Truthfully, I was curious. About how it feels to become part of a painting, right in front of your eyes. I wanted to actually experience it. Not simply have my painting done, but to experience it as a kind of exchange."

"An exchange?"

"Between the two of us, you and me."

I was silent. The meaning of the expression "an exchange" eluded me for a moment.

"We exchange parts of us with each other," Menshiki explained. "I offer something of myself, and you offer something of yourself. It doesn't have to be something valuable. It can be simple, like a kind of sign."

"Like children exchange pretty seashells?"

"Exactly."

I thought about this. "Sounds interesting, but the problem is I don't have any nice seashells to offer you."

"You're not so comfortable doing it this way? Are you intentionally avoiding that kind of exchange? Is that why you don't use live models? If that's true, then I can—"

"No—that's not it. I don't use models because I don't need them. That's all. I'm not trying to avoid an interchange between people. I've studied painting for a long time, and have used live models more times than I can remember. If you don't mind the drudgery of sitting still in a hard chair for hours at a time, I'm totally fine with you posing for me."

"I don't mind," Menshiki said, spreading his palms up, lightly lifting them upward. "Then why don't we commence the drudgery?"

We went into the studio. I brought over a dining room chair and had Menshiki sit in that. I let him assume whatever posture he wanted. I sat on an old wooden stool facing him (no doubt the stool Tomohiko Amada used when he painted), and started sketching with a soft pencil. I needed to decide on a basic approach of how I was going to reproduce his face on canvas.

"Is it boring to sit there? If you'd like, we could listen to some music," I said.

"If it doesn't bother you, I'd love to hear some music," Menshiki said.

"Why don't you choose something from the shelf in the living room."

He spent about five minutes perusing the selection of records and returned with a four-disc boxed set of LPs of Georg Solti conducting a performance of Richard Strauss's *Der Rosenkavalier*. The orchestra was the Vienna Philharmonic, the singers Régine Crespin and Yvonne Minton.

"Do you like *Der Rosenkavalier*?" he asked me.

"I've never heard it."

"It's an unusual opera. The plot's critical, of course, like with all operas, but with this one even if you don't know the plot it's easy to give yourself over to the music and be completely enveloped by that world. The world of supreme bliss Strauss achieved at the peak of his powers. When it was first performed, people criticized it as nostalgic, unadventurous even, where in reality the music is quite progressive and uninhibited. He was influenced by Wagner, but Strauss creates his own strange, unique musical realm. Once you get into this music you can't get enough of it. I usually prefer Karajan's or Erich Kleiber's version, and have never heard Solti's. If it's all right with you, I'd like to take this opportunity to hear it."

"Of course. Let's listen to it."

He placed the record on the turntable, lowered the needle, and carefully adjusted the volume on the amp. He went back to his chair, settled into a proper pose, and concentrated on the music flowing from the speakers. I did some quick sketches in my sketchbook of his face from several angles. His face was overall nicely put together, the features distinctive enough that I didn't find it hard to capture the unique details of each. In the space of thirty minutes I completed five sketches from different angles. But when I examined them again, I was struck by an odd, helpless feeling. My sketches had accurately captured what was distinctive about his face, yet there was nothing about them beyond the sense that they were *well-done drawings*. They were all oddly shallow and superficial, devoid of depth. They were no different from caricatures drawn by some street artist. I tried doing a few more sketches, with basically the same result.

For me, this was pretty unusual. I had years of experience reconstructing people's faces in a drawing, and flattered myself that I was good at it. Whether with a pencil or a paintbrush I could almost always come up with several mental images of what I was after with no trouble. I rarely struggled to decide on the composition of a painting. But now, with Menshiki as my model, not a single image came to me.

Perhaps I was overlooking something important. I couldn't help but think that. Maybe Menshiki was adeptly hiding it from me. Or maybe it didn't exist in him to begin with.

When the B side of the first of the four records in *Der Rosenkavalier* set finished I gave up, shut my sketchbook, and laid down my pencil. I lifted the needle, took the record off the turntable, and returned it to the boxed set. I glanced at my watch and sighed.

"I'm finding it very hard to draw you," I admitted.

He looked at me in surprise. "In what way?" he asked. "Are you saying there's some pictorial issue with the way I look?"

I shook my head slightly. "No, it's not that. Of course there's nothing wrong with your face."

"Then what's making it hard?"

"I wish I could tell you. It just feels that way. Maybe we still haven't *exchanged* enough yet, as you put it. Haven't traded enough seashells."

Menshiki smiled, looking a bit perplexed. "Is there anything I can do to help?"

I stood up from the stool, went over to the window, and watched the birds flying over the woods.

"Mr. Menshiki, if it's all right with you, could you give me a little more information about yourself? I know next to nothing about you."

"Of course. I'm not trying to hide anything. No outrageous secrets or anything I'm trying to keep from you. I can tell you just about everything. What sort of information were you thinking of?"

"Well—for starters, I don't even know your full name."

"That's right!" he said, looking a bit surprised. "Now that you mention it, you're absolutely right. I was so caught up in talking I forgot to give this to you."

He took a black leather holder from a pocket of his chinos and removed a business card. He handed me the card, and I read it. The thick white card simply read:

免色　涉
WATARU MENSHIKI

On the back was an address in Kanagawa Prefecture, a phone number, and an email address. That was all. No company name or title.

"The *wataru* in my name is the character that means 'to cross a river,'" Menshiki said. "I don't know why I was given that name. I've never had much to do with water."

"The name Menshiki isn't one you see very often."

"I heard our family's roots are in Shikoku, but I have no connection to Shikoku at all. I was born and raised in Tokyo, all my schooling was in Tokyo. And I prefer soba noodles to udon, which Shikoku is famous for." Menshiki laughed.

"May I ask how old you are?"

"Of course. I turned fifty-four last month. How old do I look to you?"

I shook my head. "Honestly, I had no idea. That's why I asked."

"It must be this white hair," he said with a smile. "People often tell me they can't tell my age because of the white hair. You often hear about people whose hair turned white overnight because they were terrified. People often ask if that's what happened with me, but I never had such a traumatic experience. I just tended to have a lot of white hair, ever since I was young. By the time I was in my mid-forties it was completely white. It's weird, though, since my grandfather, father, and two older brothers are all bald. In the whole family I'm the only one who has completely white hair."

"If you don't mind me asking, what sort of work are you involved in?"

"I don't mind at all. It's just—hard to talk about."

"If you'd rather not . . ."

"It's a little embarrassing, actually," he said. "Right now I'm not working at all. Not that I'm getting unemployment insurance or anything, but officially I'm unemployed. I spend a few hours each day online in my office in stock trading and currency exchange, though we're not talking large amounts. More a hobby or to kill time. Training to keep my mind active. Like a pianist practices scales every day."

Menshiki took a quiet, deep breath and recrossed his legs. "In the past I started and ran a tech-related company, but not long ago I decided to sell all my stock and step down. The buyer was a major telecommunications company. That sale meant I have enough savings to live on for a while. I used that opportunity to sell my house in Tokyo and move here. Basically, I'm retired. My savings are divided among several overseas banks, and I move those around depending on variable exchange rates, so I make a bit of a profit that way."

"I see," I said. "Do you have a family?"

"No family. I've never been married."

"So you live in that huge house all by yourself?"

He nodded. "I do. At this point I have no household staff. I've lived by myself for a long time and am used to doing housework. But since it's such a big place, I can't clean it all myself, so I hire a cleaning service to come in once a week. Other than that, I pretty much take care of everything. What about you?"

I shook my head. "I've been on my own less than a year. Still an amateur."

Menshiki gave a slight nod, but didn't ask any questions or offer any comments. "Are you close to Tomohiko Amada?" he asked.

"No, I've never even met him. I was with his son in art school, and through that connection he asked me if I wanted to take care of the vacant house. Some things came up in my life and I didn't have any place to live then, so I decided to accept the offer. For the time being."

Menshiki gave a few more small nods. "It's not very convenient for anyone working at a regular job, but for folks like you two, I imagine it's a wonderful environment."

I gave a forced smile. "We might both be painters, but Tomohiko Amada and I are on totally different levels. It's embarrassing to even be mentioned in the same breath as him."

Menshiki raised his head and looked at me, his eyes serious. "It's too soon to say that. You might become a well-known artist someday."

There was nothing I could say to that, so I was silent.

"Sometimes people go through huge transformations," Menshiki said. "They obliterate the style they've worked in, and out of the ruins they rise up again. Tomohiko Amada was that way. When he was young he painted Western-style work. You've heard about this, I'm sure?"

"I have. Before the war he was a promising young painter of Western-style art. But after he came back from studying in Vienna he changed to being a Japanese-style artist, and after the war was amazingly successful."

"The way I see it," Menshiki said, "there's a point in everybody's life where they need a major transformation. And when that time comes you have to grab it by the tail. Grab it hard, and never let go. There are some people who are able to, and others who can't. Tomohiko Amada was one who could."

A major transformation. The words suddenly made me think of *Killing Commendatore*. And the young man stabbing the Commendatore to death.

"Do you know much about Japanese-style painting?" Menshiki asked.

I shook my head. "I'm basically a layman. I attended lectures on it when I was in art school, but that's the extent of my knowledge."

"This is a very basic question, but how is Japanese art defined, professionally?"

"It's not so easy to define. It's usually taken to mean paintings done using glue and pigment and foil leaf. And done not with a paintbrush, but with a writing brush. In other words Japanese paintings are defined mainly by the materials used to paint them. The transmission of ancient, traditional techniques is one feature, though there are lots of Japanese paintings done using avant-garde techniques, and with colors, too, there is a lot of use of new materials. So the definition has steadily become increasingly vague. But as far as Tomohiko Amada's paintings go, they're classic Japanese art. Archetypal, you might call them. They're done in a style that's recognizably his own, of course. I just mean as far as techniques are concerned."

"So you're saying that if the definition based on materials and techniques gets vague, all you're left with is the mental aspect, right?"

"Maybe so. But the mental aspect of Japanese paintings isn't easily defined. They are, from the beginning, rather eclectic."

"By eclectic you mean . . . ?"

I searched the depths of memory and recalled what I'd learned in art history class. "The Meiji Restoration took place in the latter half of the nineteenth century, and along with other aspects of Western culture Western art also was introduced into Japan, but until then the genre of 'Japanese painting' didn't actually exist. The term didn't even exist. Just like up till then the name of the country, Japan, was hardly ever used. With the appearance of Western art from abroad, the concept of Japanese art was born as a way of asserting something that could be distinguished as standing in opposition to Western art. What had existed up until then in various forms and styles was, for the sake of simplicity, lumped together under the new name of 'Japanese painting.' Of course, there were some types of painting that were excluded from that and fell into decline. Chinese ink paintings, for instance. The Meiji government established and cultivated so-called Japanese painting as a kind of national art, as part of Japanese cultural identity that could stand shoulder to shoulder with Western culture—the 'Japanese spirit' part of the popular slogan at the time—'Japanese Spirit with Western Learning.' What had been everyday designs, arts and crafts designs such as paintings on folding screens and *fusuma* sliding doors and bowls and plates, were now set in frames and featured in art exhibitions. To put it another way, items done in a natural style as part of everyday life were now accommodated to the Western system and elevated to the status of 'works of art.' "

I paused for a moment and studied Menshiki's face. He seemed to be listening closely to what I said. I went on.

"Tenshin Okakura and Ernest Fenollosa were at the forefront of this movement. What happened with art could be counted as one of the amazing success stories during this period when aspects of Japanese culture were rapidly being reconfigured. A similar process was taking place in the worlds of music, literature, and thought. It must have been a pretty hectic time for Japanese back then, since they had tons of important work they had to accomplish in a very short period of time. Looking back on it now, I'd say we did a pretty clever and skillful job of it. The merging and compartmentalizing of Western aspects and non-Western aspects took place very smoothly. Maybe Japanese are intrinsically suited to that kind of process.

"So Japanese painting wasn't clearly defined originally. You might say it was a concept based on a vague consensus. There wasn't initially a clear division, and it only came about tangentially, when external and internal pressure created one."

Menshiki seemed to be considering all this. "It might have been vague," he finally said, "but this was a consensus born of necessity, right?"

"Exactly. A consensus arising out of necessity."

"Not having a set framework was both a strength and a weakness of Japanese painting. Could we interpret it this way?"

"I think so."

"But when we look at a painting, in most cases we have the sense whether it's a Japanese painting or not. Right?"

"That's right. There's an intrinsic method used. A kind of trend, or tone. And a tacit, shared understanding. It's hard sometimes to define it, though."

Menshiki was silent for a while. "If a painting is non-Western, then does it have the form of a Japanese painting?"

"Not necessarily," I replied. "In principle there are Western paintings that have a non-Western form."

"I see," he said. He tilted his head ever so slightly. "But if it's a Japanese painting, then to some extent it will have a non-Western form about it. Would that be accurate?"

I gave it some thought. "Put that way, yes, you could say so. I hadn't thought about it that way, to tell you the truth."

"It's self-evident, but still difficult to put into words."

I nodded in agreement.

He paused for a moment, and then went on. "If you think about it, it's akin to defining yourself as compared with another person. The difference is self-evident, but still difficult to verbalize. As you said, you can perhaps only understand it as a kind of tangent produced when external and internal pressure combine to create it."

Menshiki gave a slight smile. "Fascinating," he added in a small voice, as if to himself.

What are we talking about? I suddenly thought. An intriguing topic in its own right, but what significance did this conversation hold for him? Was it mere intellectual curiosity? Or was he testing my intellect? What was the point?

"By the way, I'm left-handed," Menshiki said at one point, as if he'd just recalled this fact. "I don't know if that will be helpful, but it's another piece of information about me. If I'm told to go left or right, I always choose left. It's become a habit."

It was finally near three o'clock, and we set the date and time of our next session. He would come to my house in three days, on Monday at one p.m. As he did this day, we would spend two hours together in my studio, and I would attempt to sketch him again.

"I'm in no rush," Menshiki said. "As I said in the beginning, take as much time as you need. I have all the time in the world."

And then he left. Through the window I watched him get into his Jaguar and drive away. I picked up all the sketches I'd done of him, studied them for a time, then tossed them aside.

A terrible silence descended over the house. Now alone, it was as if the silence had become all the more weighty. I went out on the terrace and there was no wind, the air jelly-thick and chilly. It felt like it was going to rain.

I sat down on the living room sofa, reviewing the conversation Menshiki and I had had, in order. How we'd talked about posing for a portrait. About Strauss's opera *Der Rosenkavalier*. About how Menshiki had started a tech company, sold off his stock, and with the sizable profit retired young. How he lived all alone in that huge house. His first name was Wataru. Written with the character that means "to cross a river." He'd always been a bachelor, and his hair had turned white early on. He was left-handed and was now fifty-four. How Tomohiko Amada had made a bold pivot, how one should grab opportunity by the tail and never let go. The definition of Japanese painting. And finally, about the relationship between Self and Other.

What in the world did he want from me?

And why wasn't I able to do any decent sketches of him?

The answer was simple, really. *Because I had not yet grasped what lay at the core of his being.*

After talking with him I felt uneasy. Yet at the same time, my curiosity about him had grown all the stronger.

Thirty minutes later heavy drops of rain began to fall. The little birds had by then already vanished.

10

AS WE PUSH OUR WAY THROUGH THE LUSH GREEN GRASS

When I was fifteen my younger sister died. It happened very suddenly. She was twelve then, in her first year of junior high. She had been born with a congenital heart problem, but since the time she was in the upper grades of elementary school she hadn't shown any more symptoms, and our family had felt reassured, holding out the faint hope that her life would go on, without incident. But in May of that year her heartbeat became more irregular. It was especially bad when she lay down, and she suffered many sleepless nights. She underwent tests at the university hospital, but no matter how detailed the tests the doctors couldn't pinpoint any changes in her physical condition. The basic issue was supposed to have been resolved back when she'd had her operations, and the doctors were baffled.

"Avoid strenuous exercise, and follow a regular routine, and things should settle down soon," the doctor said. That was probably all he could say. And he wrote out a few prescriptions for her.

But her arrhythmia didn't settle down. As I sat across from her at the dining table I often looked at her chest and imagined the defective heart inside it. Her breasts were beginning to noticeably develop. Her heart might have problems, but her flesh continued growing nonetheless. It felt strange to see my little sister's breasts grow by the day. Up till then she'd just been a little child, but now she'd suddenly had her first period, and her breasts were slowly starting to take shape. Yet within that tiny chest, my sister's heart was defective. And even a specialist couldn't pinpoint the defect. That fact alone had my brain in constant turmoil. I spent my adolescence in a state of anxiety, fearful that, at any moment, I might lose my little sister.

My parents told me to watch over her, since her body was so delicate. While we attended the same elementary school I always kept my eye on her. If need be, I was willing to risk my life to protect her and her tiny heart. Though the opportunity never presented itself.

She was on her way home from junior high one day when she collapsed and lost consciousness while climbing the stairs at Seibu Shinjuku Station. She was rushed by ambulance to the nearest emergency room. By the time I got home and then raced to the hospital, her heart had already stopped. It all happened in the blink of an eye. That morning we'd eaten breakfast together, said goodbye to each other at the front door, me going off to high school, she to junior high. And the next time I saw her she'd stopped breathing. Her large eyes were closed forever, her mouth slightly open as if she were about to say something. Her developing breasts would never grow.

The next time I saw her she was in a coffin. She was dressed in her favorite black velvet dress, with a touch of makeup, her hair neatly combed. She had on black patent-leather shoes and lay faceup in the modestly sized coffin. The dress had a white lace collar, so white it looked unnatural.

Lying there, she appeared to be peacefully sleeping. Shake her lightly and she'd wake up, it seemed. But that was an illusion. Shake her all you want, but she would never awaken again.

I didn't want my sister's delicate little body to be stuffed into that cramped, confining box. Her body should be laid to rest on a much more spacious place. In the middle of a meadow, for instance. We would wordlessly go to visit her, pushing aside the lush green grass as we went. The wind would slowly rustle the grass, and birds and insects would call out from all around her. The raw smell of wildflowers would fill the air, pollen swirling. When night fell, the sky above her would be dotted with countless silvery stars. In the morning a new sun would make the dew on the blades of grass sparkle like jewels. But in reality she was packed away in some ridiculous coffin. The only decorations were ominous white flowers that had been snipped by scissors and stuck in vases. The narrow room had fluorescent lighting that was drained of color. From a small speaker set into the ceiling came the artificial strains of organ music.

I couldn't stand to see her be cremated. When the coffin lid was shut and locked, I couldn't take it anymore and left the cremation room. I didn't help when the family ritually placed her bones inside a vase. I went out into the crematorium courtyard and cried soundlessly by myself. During her all-too-short life, I'd never once helped my little sister, a thought that hurt me deeply.

After my sister's death, our family changed. My father became even more taciturn, my mother even more nervous and jumpy. Basically I kept on with the same life as always. I joined the mountaineering club at school, which kept me busy, and when I wasn't doing that I started oil painting. My art teacher recommended that I find a good instructor and really study painting. And when I finally did start attending art classes, my interest became serious. I think I was trying to keep myself busy so I wouldn't think about my dead sister.

For a long time, I'm not sure how many years, my parents kept her room exactly as it was. Textbooks and study guides, pens, erasers, and paper clips piled on her desk, the sheets, blankets, and pillows on her bed, her laundered and folded pajamas, her junior high school uniform hanging in the closet—all untouched. The calendar on the wall still had her schedule written in her tiny writing. It was left at the month she died, as if time had frozen solid at that point. It felt as if the door would open at any moment and she'd come inside. When no one else was at home I'd sometimes go into her room, sit down on the neatly made bed, and gaze around me. But I never touched anything. I didn't want to disturb, even a little, any of the silent little objects left behind, signs that my sister had once been among the living.

I often tried to imagine what sort of life my sister would have had if she hadn't died at twelve. Though there was no way I could know. I couldn't even picture how my own life would turn out, so I had no idea what her future would have held. But I knew that if only she hadn't had a problem with one of her heart valves, she would have grown to be a capable, attractive adult. I'm sure many men would have loved her, and held her gently in their arms. But I couldn't picture any of that in detail. For me, she was forever my little sister, three years younger, who needed my protection.

For a time after she died I drew sketches of her, over and over. Reproducing in my sketchbook, from all different angles, my memory of her face, so I wouldn't forget it. Not that I was about to forget her face. It will remain etched in my mind until the day I die. What I sought was not to forget the face I remembered at that point in time. In order to do that, I had to give form to it by drawing. I was only fifteen then, and there was so much I didn't know about memory, drawing, and the flow of time. But one thing I did know was that I needed to do something in order to hold on to an accurate record of my memory. Leave it alone, and it would disappear somewhere. No matter how vivid a memory, the power of time was stronger. I knew this instinctively.

I would sit alone in her room on her bed, drawing her, sketching her face over and over. I tried to reproduce onto the blank paper how she looked in my mind's eye. I lacked experience then, and the requisite technical skill, so it wasn't an easy process. I'd draw, rip up my effort, draw and rip up, endlessly. But now when I look at the drawings I did keep (I still treasure my sketchbook from back then), I can see that they are filled with a genuine sense of grief. They may be technically immature, but it was a sincere effort, my own soul trying to awaken my sister's. When I looked at those sketches, I couldn't help but cry. I've done countless drawings since, but never again has anything I've drawn brought me to tears.

There's one other effect my sister's death had on me—a very severe case of claustrophobia. Ever since I saw her be placed in that cramped little coffin, the lid shut and locked tight, and taken away to the crematorium, I haven't been able to go into tight, enclosed places. For a long time I couldn't take elevators. I'd stand in front of an elevator and all I could think about was it automatically shutting down in an earthquake, with me trapped inside that confined space. Just the thought of it was enough to send me into a choking sense of panic.

These symptoms didn't appear right after my sister's death. It took nearly three years for them to surface. The first time I had a panic attack was soon after I started art school, when I had a part-time job with a moving company. I was the driver's assistant in a covered truck, loading boxes and taking them out, and one time I got mistakenly locked inside the empty cargo compartment. Work was done for the day and the driver was checking to see if anything was left behind in the cargo compartment. He forgot to make sure if anyone was still inside, and locked the door from the outside.

About two and half hours passed until the door was opened and I was able to crawl out. That whole time I was locked inside a sealed, cramped, totally dark place. It wasn't a refrigerated truck or anything, so there were gaps where air could get in. If I'd thought about it calmly, I would have known I wouldn't suffocate.

But still, a terrible panic had me in its grip. There was plenty of oxygen, yet no matter how deeply I breathed in, I wasn't able to absorb it. My breathing got more and more ragged and I started hyperventilating. I felt dizzy, like I was choking, and was overwhelmed by an inexplicable panic. It's okay, calm down, I told myself. You'll be able to get out soon. It's impossible to suffocate here. But logic didn't work. The only thing in my mind was my little sister, crammed into a tiny coffin, and hauled off to the crematorium. Completely terrified, I pounded on the walls of the truck.

The truck was in the company parking lot, and all the employees, their workday done, had gone home. Nobody noticed that I wasn't around. I pounded like crazy, but no one seemed to hear. If I was unlucky I might be shut inside until morning. At the thought of that, it felt like all my muscles were about to disintegrate.

It was the night security guard, making his rounds of the parking lot, who finally heard the noise I was making and unlocked the door. When he saw how agitated and exhausted I was, he had me lie down on the bed in the company break room. And gave me a cup of hot tea. I don't know how long I lay there. But finally my breathing became normal again. Dawn was coming, so I thanked the guard and took the first train of the day back home. I slipped into my own bed and lay there, shaking like crazy for the longest time.

Ever since then, riding elevators has triggered the same panic. The incident must have awoken a fear that had been lurking within me. And I have little doubt this was set off by memories of my dead sister. And it wasn't only elevators, but any enclosed space. I couldn't even watch movies with scenes set in submarines or tanks. Just imagining myself shut inside such confined spaces—*merely* imagining it—made me unable to breathe. Often I had to get up and leave the theater. If a scene came on of someone shut away in a confined space, I couldn't stand to watch. That's why I seldom watched movies with anyone else.

One time on a trip to Hokkaido I had no choice but to stay overnight in one of those capsule hotels. My breathing became labored, and I couldn't sleep, so I went outside and spent the night inside my car. It was early spring in Hokkaido, still quite cold, and the whole night was like a nightmare.

My wife often kidded me about my panic attacks. When we had to go to a floor high up in a building she would precede me in the elevator and would wait there, enjoying me huffing and puffing my way up sixteen or so flights of stairs. But I never explained to her why I had that phobia. I just told her I've always had a fear of elevators.

"Well, it might be healthier for you to walk," she said.

I also had a feeling akin to fear about women with larger than normal breasts. I don't know if that has anything to do with my sister, or the way her breasts were just beginning to develop when she died. Still, I've always been attracted to women with more modest breasts, and every time I see them, every time I touch them, I remember my sister . . . Don't get me wrong, I wasn't sexually interested in my sister. I think I was just looking for a certain type of scene. A finite scene, lost and never to return.

On Saturday afternoon my hand was resting on the chest of my married lover. Her breasts weren't particularly small, or large. Just the right size, they fit neatly into my palm. Her nipples were still hard in my hand.

She'd never come to my house on a Saturday. She always spent the weekends with her family. But that weekend her husband was on a business trip to Mumbai and her two daughters were staying over at their cousin's house in Nasu in Tochigi. So she came to my place. And like we did on weekday afternoons, we leisurely enjoyed sex. Afterward we lay there in a lazy, indolent silence. Like always.

"Would you like to hear what the jungle grapevine turned up?" she asked.

"Jungle grapevine?" I suddenly couldn't think of what she was talking about.

"Don't tell me you forgot? The mystery man in the big white house across the valley. You asked me to look into this Mr. Menshiki the other day."

"Ah, that's right. Of course I remember."

"I found out a little bit about him. One of my housewife friends lives near him, and she could gather some info on him. Would you like to hear it?"

"Of course."

"Mr. Menshiki bought that house with the gorgeous view about three years ago. Another family was living in it before then. They're the ones who built the house, but those original owners only lived there about two years. One sunny morning they suddenly packed up all their belongings and left, and Menshiki took their place. He bought the house, which was practically brand-new. How that all came about, though, nobody knows."

"So he didn't build the house himself," I said.

"That's right. He moved into a container that was already there. Like a quick-witted hermit crab."

That was unexpected. I'd been positive he was the one who built that house. That's how closely I'd linked his image—probably corresponding to his wonderfully white hair—with that white mansion on top of the mountain.

She continued. "Nobody knows what kind of work he does. What they do know is that he never commutes to work. He stays in his house all day, probably on his computer. His study is full of those devices. Nowadays if you know what you're doing, you can find out most everything online. A man I know is a surgeon who works entirely from home. He's crazy about surfing and doesn't want to leave the ocean."

"A surgeon can work entirely from home?"

"They send him all the images and information about the patients, which he analyzes and then creates the protocols for the operations, sends these to the on-site staff, and monitors the operations remotely, sometimes giving them advice. Sometimes he uses a remote magic hand device to actually perform operations. That kind of thing."

"What an age we live in," I said. "I wouldn't like to have anyone operate on me like that."

"I wonder if Mr. Menshiki is doing something similar," she said. "No matter what kind of work he's doing, he's pulling in enough income. He lives alone most of the time in the huge house, occasionally goes on long trips. Probably trips abroad. In his house he has a home gym with lots of exercise machines, where he works out whenever he has a chance. There's not an ounce of fat on him. He mostly prefers classical music, and has a substantial listening room. A pretty luxurious life, wouldn't you say?"

"Where'd you get all these details?"

She laughed. "You seem to underestimate women's information-gathering skills."

"You could be right."

"He has four cars altogether. Two Jaguars and a Range Rover. Plus a Mini Cooper. He seems to like British cars."

"Mini Coopers are made by BMW these days, and I believe Jaguar was purchased by an Indian corporation. So it's hard to call either of them British cars."

"The Mini he drives is an older version. And whatever corporation bought Jaguar, it's still a British car."

"Did you find out anything else?"

"Hardly anybody ever comes to the house. Mr. Menshiki prefers solitude. He likes to be alone, likes to listen to classical music and read a lot. He's single and well off, yet almost never brings women home. For all appearances he lives a very simple, orderly life. Makes you think he might be gay. Though there's some evidence that points in the other direction."

"I'm thinking you must have a well-placed source of information."

"She's not there now, but until not long ago he had a maid who'd come in a few times a week. She's the one who took out the garbage, went shopping for him at the local supermarket, where there were other housewives from the neighborhood and they'd start chatting."

"I see," I said. "That's how the jungle grapevine gets formed."

"You got it. According to her, there's a kind of *forbidden chamber* in the house. He instructed her never to enter it. He made it quite clear."

"Sounds like Bluebeard's castle."

"Exactly. People often say that, right? That every house has a skeleton in the closet."

That reminded me of the painting *Killing Commendatore* hidden away in the attic. That might be a skeleton hidden in a closet too.

She went on. "The woman never did find out what was in that mystery room. It was always locked. But anyway, that maid doesn't work there anymore. Maybe she got fired for being a bit too talkative. He seems to be doing all the housework himself now."

"He told me the same thing. That aside from a once-a-week cleaning service he takes care of all the household chores himself."

"He seems very touchy about his privacy."

"Be that as it may, but isn't the fact that you and I meet like this spreading through your jungle grapevine?"

"I doubt it," she said in a quiet voice. "First of all, I'm very careful that it doesn't. And second, you're a little different from Mr. Menshiki."

"Meaning . . . ," I said, translating this into words that were easy to understand, ". . . that there are things about him that lend themselves to rumor, but not with me."

"We should be thankful for that," she said cheerily.

After my little sister died all kinds of things started to go wrong. The metalworking company my father operated went downhill, and he was so busy dealing with that he hardly ever came home. The atmosphere at home became strained. Long, heavy silences reigned over the house. It hadn't been that way when my sister was still alive. I wanted to get away from it all, and got even more absorbed in painting as a way to escape. Eventually I decided to attend art school and major in painting. My father was dead set against it. You can't earn a decent living painting, he argued. And I don't have the money to help raise an artist. The two of us argued about it. My mother intervened to smooth things over, and though somehow I was able to attend art school, my father and I never did reconcile.

If only my sister hadn't died, I sometimes thought. If she'd lived, my family would have been so much happier. Her sudden disappearance made our family fall apart. Our home became a site where people lashed out and hurt each other. I felt helpless, knowing I could never fill in the hole my sister had left behind.

I stopped drawing pictures of her. After I entered art school the things I wanted to paint were phenomena and objects that didn't have intrinsic meaning. Abstract paintings, in other words. Things in which all sorts of meanings were encoded, where new semantic meaning arose from the interweaving of one sign and another. I plunged into a world that aimed at that type of completeness, and was able to breathe normally for the first time in forever.

Creating those kinds of paintings, though, didn't lead to any decent jobs. I graduated, but as long as I stuck to abstract painting my father was right—I had no hope of earning any money. So in order to make a living (I'd already left my parents' home and needed to earn money for rent and food) I was compelled to take on portrait work. By doing a conventional job, painting those utilitarian paintings, I was somehow able to survive as an artist.

And now I was about to paint a portrait of Wataru Menshiki. The Wataru Menshiki who lived in the white mansion on top of the mountain across the way. The white-haired man the neighbors had heard all sorts of rumors about, this clearly intriguing person. He had picked me out, hired me for a huge fee to paint his portrait. But what I discovered was that at this point I *wasn't even able to paint a portrait*. Even that kind of conventional, utilitarian art was beyond me. I'd truly become hollow, an empty shell.

We should wordlessly go to visit her, pushing our way through the lush green grass. This random thought struck me. If we could, how truly wonderful that would be.

11

THE MOONLIGHT SHONE BEAUTIFULLY ON EVERYTHING

The silence woke me. That happens sometimes. A sudden sound will cut the silence, waking a person, and sometimes a sudden silence will cut through sounds, waking you.

I shot awake and glanced over at my bedside clock. The digital display read 1:45. After a moment I remembered that it was 1:45 a.m. on Saturday night, or rather early Sunday morning. Earlier that afternoon I had spent time with my married lover in this bed. She went home before evening, I'd had a simple dinner, read for a while, and gone to sleep after ten. I'm generally a sound sleeper, and don't wake up until the morning light wakes me. So having my sleep interrupted like that in the middle of the night was unusual.

I lay there in the darkness wondering why I'd awakened at this hour. It was a typical, quiet night. The nearly full moon was a huge round mirror floating in the sky. The scenery on earth was whitish, as if washed with lime. But nothing else seemed out of the ordinary. I half sat up and listened carefully. And finally realized something *was* different from usual. *It was too quiet.* The silence was too deep. It was a fall night, yet no insects were chirping. Since the house was built in the mountains, after sunset the insects invariably started their ear-splitting chirping, a chorus that went on until late at night. (It really surprised me to learn this, since until I lived here I always thought they only chirped early in the evening.) The sound was so piercing it made me think that insects had conquered the world. But this night, when I woke up, there was not a single screech or chirp. It was disconcerting.

Once awake, I found it hard to get back to sleep. I reluctantly crawled out of bed, and threw a light cardigan over my pajama top. I went to the kitchen, poured myself some Scotch, added a few ice cubes from the ice maker, and drank it. I went onto the terrace and gazed at the lights of the houses through the woods. Everyone seemed to be asleep, no lights on anywhere in any houses. All I saw was a scattering of tiny security lights. The area around Menshiki's house across the valley, too, was surrounded by darkness. And like before, there were no insects chirping. Had something happened to them?

After a while I heard a sound I wasn't used to. Or perhaps *felt* like I heard it. A very faint sound. If the insects had been chirping as loudly as usual I probably never would have caught it. But the profound silence that reigned allowed it to reach me, though barely. I held my breath and strained my ears. It wasn't the chirp of any insects. Not a naturally occurring sound. It was the sound some implement or tool might make, a kind of jingling sound. The sound a bell, or something close to it, might make.

There would be a pause, then the sound. A deep silence, then that sound ringing out a few times, then deep silence once more. As if someone were patiently sending out an encoded message. But it wasn't repeated at regular intervals. Sometimes the silence in between rings was longer, sometimes shorter. And it didn't ring the same number of times. I couldn't tell if their regularity was intentional or capricious. At any rate, it was such a faint sound that if I hadn't focused and listened hard I wouldn't have caught it. But once aware of it, in the deep silence of the middle of the night, with the moonlight so unnaturally bright, that unidentified sound irretrievably ate its way into my awareness.

I was flustered, wondering what it could be, then decided to just go outside and see. I wanted to trace the source of that mysterious sound. Someone, somewhere, was ringing *something or other*. I'm not bold. But going out into the dark night alone then didn't frighten me. Curiosity won out over my fears. And the weirdly bright moonlight might have encouraged me, too.

With an oversized flashlight in my hand, I unlocked the front door and stepped outside. A single light above the entrance threw out a yellowish tint. A swarm of flying insects was drawn to that light. I stood there, ears perked up, trying to see what direction that sound was coming from. It really did sound like a bell, but not an ordinary one. It had a deeper, dull, uneven ring. Maybe it was some special percussion instrument. But what was it, and why would someone be ringing it in the middle of the night? The only residence in the vicinity was the house I was living in. If indeed someone nearby was ringing that bell, it meant they were trespassing.

I looked around to see if anything could serve as a weapon. All I had in my hand was a long cylindrical flashlight. Better than nothing. I grasped the flashlight tightly and headed toward the sound.

I turned left from the front door, which led me to a small set of stone steps. I climbed up the seven steps and entered the woods. I walked up the gentle upward-sloping path that cut through the trees, and before long came to a clearing where there was a small shrine. Masahiko had said that the shrine had been there for a very long time. He didn't know the origins of it, but in the mid-1950s when his father had purchased the house and land from an acquaintance, the shrine already existed . . . On top of a flat stone was a sanctuary with a simple triangular roof—or, more accurately, a small wooden box made to look like a sanctuary. It was about two feet high and a foot and a half wide. It had originally been painted, though by now the color had mostly worn off, leaving one to imagine what it had once been. In the front was a small double door, and I had no idea what sort of offering was set up inside. I didn't check, but probably there wasn't anything enshrined inside. In front of the doors was an empty white ceramic pot. Rainwater had accumulated, then evaporated, over and over, leaving a number of dirty stained lines inside. Tomohiko Amada had left the shrine as it was. Not bringing his hands together in prayer as he passed it, not cleaning it, he simply let it be, swept by rain and wind. For him it must have been not a shrine, but just a plain, spare box.

"He had no interest in faith or worship or the like," his son had explained. "He didn't care a wit about things like divine punishment or retribution or anything. He said those were stupid superstitions, and looked down on them. It wasn't that he was brazen about it, it's just that he's always held to an extremely materialist view of things."

Masahiko had shown me the shrine the first time he took me to see the house. "You don't find many houses these days that come with their own shrine," he laughed, and I agreed.

"When I was a kid, though," Masahiko went on, "it creeped me out to have that kind of weird thing on our property. So when I stayed over I avoided coming near here," he said. "Even now, to tell the truth, I'd rather not go near it."

I wasn't a person who often thought in materialistic terms, but just like his father, Tomohiko Amada, having the shrine nearby didn't bother me. People in the past set up shrines in all kinds of places, much like the little Jizo and Dosojin statues you see next to roads in the countryside. This shrine blended naturally into the scenery in the woods, and when I went on walks I often passed in front of it but never gave it much thought. I never prayed to it, or made any offerings. And I didn't feel anything significant about having that sort of thing on the property where I was living. It was just part of the kind of scenery you'd find anywhere.

The bell-like sound seemed to be coming from near that shrine. Once I set foot in the woods, the tree branches above me blocked the moonlight and everything got suddenly darker. I carefully made my way forward, lighting the path with the flashlight. The wind would occasionally pick up, as if remembering to blow, rustling the thin layer of leaves on the ground. The woods at night felt totally different from walking there in the daytime. The place was operating under the principles at work at night, and those principles didn't include me. That said, I didn't feel particularly afraid. Curiosity spurred me on. I felt compelled to locate where that strange sound was coming from. I tightly gripped the heavy cylindrical flashlight, its weight calming me.

The horned owl might be in these woods somewhere, I thought. Hidden in the darkness on a branch, waiting for its prey. It would be nice if it were nearby. In a way that owl was my friend. But I didn't hear anything that sounded like the hooting of an owl. The night birds, like the insects, were keeping quiet.

As I made my way forward, the bell-like sound became ever clearer. It continued to ring out intermittently, irregularly. The sound seemed to be coming from behind the little shrine. It sounded much closer, but was still muffled, like it was filtering out from deep inside a narrow cave. The silence between each ring had grown longer, and the number of rings was decreasing. As if the person ringing the bell had grown weak, become worn out.

The area around the shrine had been cleared and the moonlight shone beautifully on everything. Stepping silently, I walked over behind the shrine. There was a tall thicket of pampas grass and, led by the sound, I pushed my way into the thicket. There I found a small mound of square stones casually piled up, a kind of ancient burial mound. Though perhaps it was too small to be called that. At any rate, I had never noticed it was there before. I'd never gone behind the shrine, and even if I had, the mound was hidden in the midst of the pampas grass. You weren't going to see it unless you had some reason to wade into the thicket.

I approached the mound and shone my flashlight directly upon it. The stones were old, but weren't in their natural form, and had clearly been chiseled into squares. They had been carried up onto the mountain and piled up behind the shrine. The stones were of different sizes, most of them covered in moss. There wasn't any visible writing or designs on them. There were twelve or thirteen stones altogether, by my count. In the past, the mound might have been taller and more orderly, but maybe an earthquake had made part of it crumble. The bell-like sound somehow seemed to be filtering out from the cracks between those stones.

I lightly rested my foot on top of the stones and searched for the source of that sound. But no matter how bright the moonlight, it was next to impossible to locate it in the dark of night. And what if I did happen to locate it? What then? I couldn't lift these heavy stones myself.

At any rate it seemed like someone below the stone mound was ringing the bell. I was sure of it. But *who*? It was at this point that an enigmatic fear began to well up inside me. Instinct told me not to get any closer to the source of that sound.

I left, and with the bell ringing behind me hurried back along the path through the woods. Moonlight filtering through the branches cast a suggestive mottled pattern on my body. I emerged from the woods, rushed down the seven stone steps, got back to the house, went inside, and locked the door. I walked to the kitchen, poured a glass of whiskey straight, no ice, no water, and gulped it down. I could finally breathe a sigh of relief. I took my glass of whiskey out to the terrace.

From the terrace I could hear the bell only faintly. If I hadn't listened carefully I wouldn't have been able to catch it. But the point was, the sound continued. The interval of silence between each ringing of the bell was definitely lengthening. I listened to that irregular repetition for some time.

What in the world lay beneath the stones of that mound? Was there a space there, and somebody locked inside who was ringing that bell, or whatever it was? Maybe it was a signal for help. But no matter how much I thought it over, I couldn't think of a single plausible explanation.

I might have thought about it for a long time. Or maybe it was but a moment. I had no idea. My sense of time had vanished. Glass of whiskey in hand, I sank back into the lounge chair, shuffling back and forth in the maze of consciousness. And then it hit me. The bell had stopped. Everything was enveloped in a profound silence.

I stood up, went into the bedroom, and looked at the digital clock. It was 2:31 a.m. I didn't know the precise time the bell had started ringing, but since it had been 1:45 when I woke up, I surmised the bell had gone on ringing for at least forty-five minutes. Soon after the mysterious sound ceased, the insects began chirping again, as if probing the new silence that had arisen. As if all the insects in the mountains had been patiently waiting for the sound of that bell to stop. Holding their breath, cautiously assessing the situation.

I went back to the kitchen, rinsed out my glass, then slipped back into bed. By this time the autumn insects were a lusty chirping chorus. I should have been too worked up to sleep, but the straight whiskey did the trick and I fell asleep as soon as my head hit the pillow. A long, deep sleep, bereft of dreams. When I woke again it was already bright outside the bedroom.

That day, before ten a.m., I walked out again to the little shrine in the woods. I couldn't hear that enigmatic sound, but I wanted to study the shrine and stone mound once more in the daylight. I found a stout oak walking stick in Tomohiko Amada's umbrella stand and took that with me. It was a sunny, pleasant morning, the clear autumn sunlight throwing the shadows of leaves across the ground. Birds with sharp bills flitted busily from one branch to another, squawking as they searched for fruit. Up above, a straight line of pitch-black crows was winging its way off somewhere.

The little shrine looked worn and shoddy in the daylight. Bathed in the bright, whitish light of the nearly full moon the shrine had looked deeply meaningful, even a bit ominous, yet now in the light of day it seemed like nothing more than a faded, seedy-looking wooden box.

I went behind the shrine, shouldered my way through the tall thicket of pampas grass, and emerged in front of the stone mound. It seemed completely transformed from the night before. What I saw before me now were merely square moss-covered stones long abandoned in the mountains. In the moonlight it had appeared like part of ancient historical ruins, covered with a mythic slime. I stood on top of the mound and perked up my ears, but couldn't hear a thing. Other than the screech of insects and the occasional bird chirp, it was silent all around.

From far away came the bang of what I took to be a shotgun. Someone might be hunting birds in the mountains. Or else it was one of those automatic devices set up by farmers to shoot blanks to scare away sparrows, monkeys, and wild boar. Either way, the sound echoed with the feeling of autumn. The sky was high, the air slightly humid, and sounds carried well. I sat down on top of the stone mound and thought about the space that might exist beneath. Was someone really under there, ringing a bell, calling out for help? Were they like me, back when I worked for the moving company and got locked inside the truck and pounded on the side panels as hard as I could, hoping someone would rescue me? The image of someone locked up in a cramped dark space put me on edge.

After a light lunch I changed into work clothes (and by that I mean things I didn't mind getting dirty), went into the studio, and once more tried my hand at Wataru Menshiki's portrait. I had to dispel the image of someone shut away in an enclosed space, hoping for help, and the chronic sense of suffocation that induced in me. I had to keep my hands busy, and painting was the only solution. This time I put aside my sketchbook and pencil. They wouldn't help, I figured. I readied my paints and paintbrushes, stood facing the canvas, and, gazing deep into that blank space, I focused on Menshiki. I stood erect, focused my concentration, and pruned away any extraneous thoughts.

A white-haired man with young-looking eyes who lived in a white mansion on a mountain. He spent most of his time at home, had what appeared to be a hidden room, and owned four British cars. How had he moved when he was here? What kind of expressions did he have on his face, what was his tone of voice, what did he look at and with what sort of look in his eyes, how did he move his hands? I recalled each and every detail. It took a while, but all the fragments started to fall into place. In my mind now, a three-dimensional, organically constructed sense of the man began to come together.

With small brushstrokes I transferred the image of Menshiki that arose from this directly onto the canvas, without the usual rough sketch. The Menshiki in my mind was facing forward, face slightly tilted to the left, his eyes looking a bit in my direction. For some reason I couldn't picture any other angle his face should be. To me, *that* was Wataru Menshiki. He had to have his face slightly tilted to the left. And had to have both eyes looking a bit in my direction. I'm in his field of vision. No other composition would accurately capture him.

I stepped away from the canvas and studied the simple composition I'd done, pretty much with a single brushstroke. It was just a temporary line drawing, but I could sense from that outline a budding, living organism. With that as the starting point, it would naturally expand from there. Something was reaching out a hand—but what was it?—and had flipped a switch inside me. A sort of vague sensation, as if an animal hibernating deep within me had finally recognized that the season had arrived, and was slowly brushing aside the cobwebs of sleep.

I washed the paint off the brush in the sink and lathered my hands with oil and soap. I was in no hurry. This was plenty for today. It was best to not rush the work. When Mr. Menshiki next came to see me, as a live model, I could then flesh out this outline. I had a premonition that this painting was going to be very different from any portrait I'd ever done before. And this painting required the flesh-and-blood Menshiki.

Which was very odd, I thought.

How had Menshiki known that?

In the middle of the night I suddenly shot awake again. The clock next to my bed read 1:46, almost exactly the same time as the night before. I sat up in bed, listening carefully in the dark. No insects chirping; it was silent all around. As if I were at the bottom of a deep sea. A repeat of the previous night. But now it was dark outside my window. That was the only difference from the night before. Thick clouds covered the sky, completely hiding the nearly full autumn moon.

Everything was in total silence. No, that wasn't entirely true. Of course it wasn't. That silence wasn't total. When I held my breath and listened carefully I could catch the faint sound of the bell wending its way past the deep silence. In the dark of night someone was ringing that bell-like object. As on the night before, it was a fragmented, intermittent sound. And now I knew exactly where the sound was coming from. From the woods, underneath that stone mound. There was no need to check it. What I didn't know, though, was *who was ringing that bell, and to what end?* I got out of bed and padded out to the terrace.

There was no wind, but a fine rain had started to fall. An invisible silent rain wetting the ground. Lights were on over in Mr. Menshiki's mansion. From over here, across the valley, I couldn't see what was going on inside his house, but he seemed to still be awake. It was unusual to see the lights on this late at night. As the fine drizzle wet me, I gazed at those lights, listening to the faint tinkling of the bell.

The rain started to pick up and I went back inside, but couldn't go back to sleep, so I sat on the sofa in the living room and turned the pages of a book I'd been reading. Not a particularly difficult book, but no matter how I focused nothing registered. I was merely tracing the words from one line to the next. Still, it was better than simply sitting there listening to the bell. I guess I could have put on some music to drown out the sound, but I didn't feel like it. I had to hear it. *Because that was a sound directed at me.* I understood that. And as long as I didn't do something about it, it would no doubt go on ringing forever. Suffocating me every night, robbing me of a good night's sleep.

I have to do something. Take some action to stop that sound. To do that, I first had to understand the meaning and purpose of that sound—of that signal that was being sent out. Why was somebody sending out from this mysterious place a signal to me every single night, and who was it? But I felt too choked, my mind too confused, for logical thought. There was no way I could handle this alone. I had to talk to somebody about it. And at this point I could only think of one person.

I went back out on the terrace and looked over at Mr. Menshiki's mansion. Now the lights were all out, with just a glimmer of outdoor lanterns in the garden.

The bell stopped ringing at 2:29 a.m., almost the same time as the night before. Soon after the bell stopped the insects' chirping returned. And as if nothing had happened, the autumn night was once more filled with the clamor of nature's chorus. Everything was a repeat of the previous night.

I went back to bed and went to sleep listening to the insects. I felt confused and anxious, but like on the night before, I soon fell asleep. Plunged into a deep, dreamless sleep.

12

LIKE THAT NAMELESS MAILMAN

Rain started falling early in the morning, and stopped before ten. Slowly, the sun began to peek out. Moist wind from the sea slowly pushed the clouds off to the north. And at one p.m., on the dot, Menshiki showed up at my place. The time signal on the radio and the front doorbell sounded at almost precisely the same moment. Many people are punctual, but seldom do you find anyone that precise. And it wasn't that he stood in front of the door, patiently waiting for the appointed time, timing his ringing of the front doorbell with the second hand on his watch. He drove up the slope, parked in his usual spot, and headed toward the front door at his usual pace and stride, and at almost the same instant he pushed the button for the front doorbell the time signal on the radio chimed. Pretty impressive.

I showed him into the studio, and had him sit on the same dining room chair as before. I put Richard Strauss's *Der Rosenkavalier* on the turntable and lowered the needle. I started at the point we'd ended up with last time. Everything was a repeat of the previous sitting. The only difference was that this time I didn't offer him a drink, and instead had him pose for me. I had him seated on the chair, facing forward, looking to the left, his eyes slightly facing toward me. That's what I wanted from him this time.

He followed my instructions exactly, but it still took a while until he got the position and pose right. The angle and look in his eyes wasn't exactly the way I wanted them. The way the light struck, too, wasn't like my mental image. I don't usually use a model, but once I do, I tend to have a lot of demands. Menshiki very patiently followed my nagging directions. He never looked put out, never complained. I pegged him as a person experienced in putting up with all sorts of trials and difficulties.

When he finally got the pose right I said, "I'm very sorry, but try to hold that pose without moving."

Menshiki said nothing, only his eyes indicating that he understood.

"I'll try to finish as quickly as I can. It might be hard, but please be patient."

Once again he nodded with his eyes. He kept his gaze still, his body unmoving, literally not moving a muscle. He did have to blink a few times, but I couldn't even tell if he was breathing. He was so still he looked like a lifelike statue. I couldn't help but be impressed. Even professional art models find it hard to get to that point.

As Menshiki endured posing, I worked on the canvas as quickly and efficiently as I could. I concentrated, eyeing his figure, and moved my brush as my intuition dictated. I was using black paint on the white canvas, and with a single fine brushstroke fleshed out the outline of his face I'd already drawn. No time even to re-grip the brush. In a limited amount of time I had to capture the various elements that made up his face and get them down on canvas. At a certain point the process switched over to something close to autopilot. It's important to bypass your conscious mind and get your eye and hand movements in sync. There's no time to consciously process every single thing your gaze takes in.

This demanded a very different type of process from me compared with the numerous portraits I'd done up till then—the countless "business items" I'd leisurely painted based solely on memory and photographs. In about fifteen minutes I'd gotten him from the chest up on canvas. It was just a rough, incomplete outline, but at least I was able to capture an image that seemed to breathe a sense of vitality, one that managed to scoop out and capture the sort of internal movement that gave birth to who this person was. If this were an anatomical drawing, though, it would be just the bones and muscles, the internal part alone boldly laid bare. It needed actual flesh and skin laid on over it.

"Thank you, you've been very patient," I said. "That's enough for today. You can take it easy now."

Menshiki smiled and relaxed his pose. He stretched his hands above him and took a deep breath. He slowly massaged his face with his fingers to loosen up the tense muscles. I stood there taking a few deep breaths. It took a while for my breathing to return to normal. I was exhausted, like a sprinter who'd just finished a race. I'd had to work speedily, with intense concentration, and with no room for compromise, something I hadn't experienced for quite some time. I'd had to flex long-dormant muscles, and though I felt tired, it also felt good.

"Like you said, sitting for a painting is a lot harder work than I'd imagined," Menshiki said. "When I think about you painting me, it feels like my insides are slowly being scraped away."

"The official view in the art world is that it's not being scraped away but rather transplanted to a different place," I said.

"Transplanted to a more permanent, lasting place?"

"Yes, if the painting is a true work of art."

"Like, for instance, the nameless mailman who lives on in Van Gogh's portrait of him?"

"Exactly."

"He probably had no idea that, well over a century later, countless people around the world would visit art museums, or look through art books, and gaze intently at his portrait."

"I'm sure he never had a clue."

"It was some odd painting done in a corner of a shabby country kitchen, painted by a man who, whichever way you look at it, was a little off."

I nodded.

"It's kind of weird," Menshiki said. "Something that, on the face of it, shouldn't be so lasting ends up having permanent value."

"Not something that happens every day."

I suddenly thought of *Killing Commendatore*. Through Tomohiko Amada's hand, was the Commendatore given permanent life, even though he was stabbed to death in the painting? And who was this Commendatore anyway?

. . .

I offered Menshiki some coffee. That would be nice, he replied, and I went to the kitchen and made a fresh pot. Menshiki remained on the chair in the studio, listening to the opera record. The coffee was ready as the B side of the record came to an end, and we went into the living room to drink it.

"So, does it look like you can do a good portrait of me?" Menshiki asked as he delicately sipped his coffee.

"I'm not sure yet," I answered honestly. "I don't know if it will turn out well. The way I've painted portraits up till now has been so different from this."

"Because you're using an actual model this time?" Menshiki asked.

"That's one reason, but only a part of it. I don't know why, but it's like I'm not able anymore to paint the sort of conventional portraits I've done up till now. I need a different method and procedure, but those are still out of reach. I'm still fumbling in the dark."

"Which means you really are changing. And I'm the catalyst for that change—wouldn't you say?"

"You may be right."

Menshiki thought for a while before speaking. "As I told you before, it's entirely up to you what style of painting you do. I'm a person who's always seeking change, always in flux. And it's not like I'm hoping you'll paint some conventional portrait. Any style, any concept is fine. What I want is for you to depict me exactly as you see me. The methods and procedure are up to you. I'm not hoping I live on like that mailman from Arles. I'm not that ambitious. I just have a healthy curiosity to see what sort of painting will emerge from this."

"I appreciate your saying that. I just have one request," I said. "If I can't come up with a satisfactory painting, then I'd like to forget the whole thing."

"You won't give me the painting then?"

I nodded. "I'll return the advance, of course."

"All right," Menshiki said. "I'll let you be the final judge. Though I must say I have a strong hunch it's not going to turn out that way."

"I hope your hunch turns out to be correct."

Menshiki looked me in the eyes. "But even if the painting's never completed, I'd be very happy if, in some way, I'm able to help you change. Truly."

"By the way, Mr. Menshiki," I said, broaching the topic a little while later, "there's something I wanted to get your advice on. Something personal, nothing to do with the painting."

"Of course. I'll be happy to help if I can."

I sighed. "It's kind of a weird story. I might not be able to tell the whole story in the right order, so it makes sense."

"Take your time, tell it in whatever order is easiest for you. And then we'll consider it together. The two of us might come up with a good idea that you couldn't come up with on your own."

So I told him the story, start to finish. How I suddenly woke up just before two a.m. and heard a weird sound in the darkness. A faint, far-off sound that I could only catch because the insects had stopped chirping. A sound like someone ringing a bell. When I tried to trace the source, it seemed to be coming from between the cracks in a stone mound in the woods behind my house. That mysterious sound continued for some forty-five minutes, intermittently, with irregular intervals of silence between. Finally it stopped completely. The same thing happened two nights in a row—two nights ago and last night. Someone might be ringing that bell-like thing from underneath the stones. Maybe sending out a distress call. But could that be possible? I was starting to doubt my own sanity a little. Was I just imagining things?

Menshiki listened to my story without comment, and remained silent even after I finished. He'd listened intently to what I'd said, and I could tell he was thinking deeply about it.

"A fascinating story," he said a little while later. He lightly cleared his throat. "As you said, it's certainly out of the ordinary. I wonder . . . if possible, I'd like to hear the sound of that bell myself, so could I come over tonight? If you don't mind?"

This took me by surprise. "Come all the way over here in the dead of night?"

"Of course. If I hear the bell too, that would prove you're not hallucinating. That's the first step. If it is an actual bell, then let's try to locate the source, the two of us. Then we can think about what to do next."

"True enough—"

"If you don't mind, I'll come over here tonight at twelve thirty. Does that work for you?"

"That's fine, but I don't want to put you out—"

A pleasant smile graced his lips. "Not to worry. If I can help you, nothing would make me happier. Plus, I'm a very curious person. What that bell in the middle of the night might mean, and if someone is ringing it, who that is—I'm dying to know. You feel the same way, don't you?"

"Of course—" I said.

"Then let's go with that. I'll see you tonight. And there's something else I thought of."

"Excuse me?"

"I'll tell you about it later. I have to make sure of something first."

Menshiki got up from the sofa and held out his right hand. I shook it. As always, a firm handshake. He looked happier than usual.

After he left I spent the rest of the afternoon in the kitchen cooking. Once a week I prepare all my meals. I put them in the fridge or freezer, then get by on these for the week. This was my meal-prep day. For dinner that evening I added macaroni to some boiled sausage and cabbage. Plus a tomato, avocado, and onion salad. In the evening I lay on the sofa as always, reading while listening to music. After a while I stopped reading and thought about Menshiki.

Why had he looked so happy when we said goodbye? Was he *really* so pleased to be able to help me out? Why? I didn't get it. I was just a poor, unknown artist. My wife of six years had left me, I didn't get along with my parents, had no set place to live, no assets, and was simply hanging out in a friend's father's house. Menshiki, in contrast (not that there was any need to make a comparison), had been successful at business at a young age, and made enough to live comfortably for the rest of his days. At least that's what he had told me. He was good-looking, owned four British cars, and lived in luxury in a huge mountaintop mansion without, apparently, doing any real work. So why would a person like that be interested in someone like me? And why would he make time in the dead of the night to help me out?

I shook my head and went back to reading. Thinking about it wasn't going to get me anywhere. It was like trying to put together a puzzle that was missing some pieces. I could think all I wanted and never arrive at any conclusion. But I couldn't help but think about it. I sighed, and put the book on the tabletop again, closed my eyes, and listened to the music. Schubert's String Quartet no. 15, played by the Vienna Konzerthaus Quartet.

Since coming here, I'd listened to classical music every day, most of it German (or Austrian), since the majority of Tomohiko Amada's record collection consisted of German classical music. His collection included the obligatory nods to Tchaikovsky, Rachmaninoff, Sibelius, Vivaldi, Debussy, and Ravel, but that's all. Since he was an opera fan there were, as you might expect, some recordings by Verdi and Puccini. But compared to the substantial lineup of German opera he didn't seem as enthusiastic about these.

I imagined Amada had intense memories of his time studying in Vienna, which may have accounted for the deep absorption in German music. Or it could have been the opposite. Maybe his love of German music had come first, and that's why he had chosen to study in Vienna instead of France. I had no way of knowing which had come first.

Either way, I was in no position to complain that German music was the preferred type in this house. I was a mere caretaker, and they were kind enough to let me listen to the records there. And I enjoyed listening to the music of Bach, Schubert, Brahms, Schumann, and Beethoven. Not forgetting Mozart, of course. Their music was deep, amazing, and gorgeous. Up to then in my life I'd never had the opportunity to really settle down and listen to that type of music. I'd always been too busy trying to make a living, and didn't have the wherewithal financially. So I decided that, as long as I'd been provided this wonderful opportunity, I'd listen to as much music here as I could.

After eleven I fell asleep for a while on the sofa listening to music. I might have slept for about twenty minutes. When I woke up the record was over, the arm back in its cradle, the turntable not moving. There were two players in the living room, one an automatic, the other an old-school manual type, but to play it safe—so I could fall asleep listening, in other words—I generally used the automatic. I slipped the Schubert record back in its jacket, and returned it to its designated spot on the record shelf. From the open window I could hear the clamor of insects. Since they were still making a racket, I wouldn't be hearing the sound of the bell quite yet.

I warmed up coffee in the kitchen and munched on a few cookies. And listened intently to the noisy insect ensemble that enveloped the mountains. A little before twelve thirty I heard the Jaguar slowly making its way up the slope. As it changed direction, the pair of yellow headlights lit up the window. The engine finally cut out, and I heard the usual solid *thunk* as the door shut. I sat on the sofa, sipping coffee, getting my breathing under control, waiting for the front doorbell to ring.

13

AT THIS POINT IT'S MERELY A HYPOTHESIS

We sat in chairs in the living room, drank our coffee, and talked, killing time until *that time* rolled around. At first we chatted about inconsequential things, but after a curtain of silence descended on us Menshiki, a bit hesitantly, yet resolutely, asked, "Do you have any children?"

The question took me by surprise. He didn't seem the type to ask that kind of question—especially of someone he didn't know well. He seemed more the I-won't-stick-my-nose-in-your-business-if-you-won't-stick-yours-in-mine type of person. At least that's the way I read him. But when I looked up and saw his serious expression, I knew it wasn't an impulsive question. He'd been thinking of asking me this for a long time.

I responded. "I was married for six years, but we didn't have any children."

"You didn't want any?"

"I was fine either way. But my wife didn't want any," I said. I didn't, though, get into the reason she gave. Even now I'm not sure that it reflected her true feelings.

Menshiki seemed hesitant, but forged ahead. "This might sound rude, but have you ever considered that there might be another woman somewhere, other than your wife, who secretly had a child of yours?"

I looked him full in the face again. What a strange question. I rummaged around, pro forma, through a few drawers of memory, but came up empty-handed. I hadn't had sex with all that many women until then, and even if something like that had taken place, I think I would have heard about it.

"I guess it's possible, in theory. But realistically—commonsensically, you might say—it's not."

"I see," Menshiki said. He quietly sipped his coffee, thinking deeply.

"Why do you ask?" I ventured.

He looked out the window, silent for a time. The moon was visible, not as weirdly bright as two days ago, but still plenty bright. Scattered clouds slowly wended their way from the sea toward the mountains.

Menshiki finally spoke up. "As I mentioned before, I've never been married. I've always been a bachelor. Work kept me busy all the time, that's one reason, but it's also because living with someone else didn't fit my personality and lifestyle. I'm sure this sounds pretty stuck-up, but I'm the type who can only live alone. I have almost no interest in lineage or relatives. I've never thought I'd like to have children. There's a personal reason for that, mostly because of my home environment when I was growing up."

He paused, took a breath, then went on.

"But a few years ago I began to think that I might actually have a child. Or I should say, I was compelled to think that way."

No comment from me.

"I find it strange myself that I'm opening up to you, about this kind of personal matter. I mean, we just met." The faintest of smiles rose to Menshiki's lips.

"I'm okay with it, as long as you are."

Ever since I was little, for some reason people have tended to open up to me about the most unexpected topics. Maybe I have an innate ability to draw out secrets from strangers. Or maybe I just seem like a good listener, I don't know. Either way, I don't remember it ever working to my advantage. After people tell me their secrets, they always regret it.

"This is the first time I've ever told anybody this," Menshiki said.

I nodded and waited for more. Everyone says the same thing.

Menshiki began his story. "This happened fifteen years ago, when I was going out with a woman. I was in my late thirties then, she was in her late twenties. She was a beautiful, attractive woman, extremely bright. I was serious about our relationship, though I'd made it clear to her there was no chance of us getting married. I don't plan to ever marry anyone, I told her. I didn't want her to have any false hopes. If she ever found someone else she wanted to marry, I would step aside without a word. She understood exactly how I felt. While we went out—for about two and half years—we got along really well. We never argued, even once. We traveled together to lots of places, and she'd often stay over at my place. She even kept a set of clothes there."

He seemed to be contemplating something, then continued his story.

"If I were a normal person, or closer to being normal, I wouldn't have hesitated to marry her. But—" He paused here and let out a small breath. "But the upshot was I chose the kind of life I have now, a quiet life all by myself, and she chose a healthier life for herself. In other words, she got married to another man who was closer to being normal than me."

Until the very end, however, she didn't disclose to him the fact that she was getting married. The last time he saw her was a week after her twenty-ninth birthday (the two of them had dined out at a restaurant in Ginza on her birthday, and later on he recalled how unusually quiet she'd been). He was working in an office in Akasaka then and she'd called him saying she wanted to see him and talk, and asked if she could see him right away. Of course, he replied. She'd never visited his workplace even once, but he hadn't thought it odd. His office was a small place, just him and a middle-aged woman secretary. So he didn't need to worry about anyone else if she stopped by. There had been a time when he'd managed a large company with lots of employees, but at this point he was developing a new network by himself. His usual approach was to work quietly by himself to develop a new business strategy; then, when he began implementing the plan, he would aggressively employ a broad range of talent.

It was just before five p.m. when his girlfriend showed up. They sat down together on his office sofa to talk. He'd had the secretary in the next room go home. It was his normal routine to continue working alone in the office after his secretary left for the day. Often he'd be so engrossed in his work that he'd stay all night. His idea was for the two of them to go to a nearby restaurant and have dinner, but she turned that down. I don't have time today, she said, I have to meet somebody in Ginza.

"You said you had something you wanted to talk about," he said.

"No, I don't have anything to really talk about," she said. "I just wanted to see you."

"I'm glad you came," he said, smiling. It had been some time since she'd spoken so openly to him. She generally spoke in a more indirect, roundabout way. He had no idea what this portended.

She moved over on the sofa and sat down in his lap. She put her arms around him and kissed him. A serious, deep kiss, tongues entwined. She reached out and undid Menshiki's belt. She took out his already erect penis, holding it in her grasp for a time. Then she leaned forward and wrapped her mouth around it. She slowly ran the tip of her long tongue around it. Her tongue was smooth and hot.

This all came out of nowhere. She was usually more passive when it came to sex—especially oral sex—and when it came to doing it, or having things done to her, he'd always felt a slight resistance on her part. But now here she was taking the lead. What's come over her? he wondered.

She suddenly stood up, tossed aside her expensive black pumps, briskly lowered her stockings and panties, again sat down on his lap, and now guided his penis inside her. Her vagina was wet, and moved smoothly, naturally, like some living being. The whole sequence had happened so quickly (and was so unlike her, since she was always so calm and deliberate). Before he realized it, he was deep inside her, that smooth wall completely enveloping his penis, squeezing him silently yet insistently.

This was unlike any sex he'd ever had with her. It was at once hot and cold, hard and soft. It was a strange, contradictory sensation, as if he were being simultaneously accepted and rejected. He had no idea what that meant. She straddled him, and like a person on a small boat being tossed around by the waves, moved violently up and down. Her black hair tossed about, supple as a willow branch in a strong wind. She lost control, her gasps growing ever louder. Menshiki wasn't sure if he had locked the office door or not. He felt he had, but also that he'd forgotten to. But this wasn't the time to go check.

"Shouldn't we use a condom or something?" he managed to ask. She was always careful about contraception.

"It's okay—today," she gasped in his ear. "Don't worry about a thing."

Everything about her was different from usual, as if a totally different personality dormant inside her had awoken and hijacked her body and soul. Menshiki imagined that today must be some sort of special day for her. There was so much that men can't fathom about women's bodies.

Her movements became increasingly frenzied. There was nothing he could do but make sure not to interfere with what she desired. They neared climax. He couldn't hold back, and ejaculated, and in time with that she let out a short screech like some foreign bird, and her womb, as if waiting for that instant, greedily absorbed his semen. A muddied image occurred to him of himself, in the darkness, being devoured by a greedy beast.

After a while she stood up, as if pushing his body aside, and silently adjusted the hem of her dress, stuffed the stockings and panties that had fallen to the floor in her handbag, and hurried off to the bathroom, bag in hand. She didn't come out for a long time. He was beginning to get worried that something had happened to her when she finally emerged. Her clothing and hair were neatly arranged now, her makeup redone. Her usual calm smile graced her lips.

She gave Menshiki a light peck on the lips, and told him she had to go, since she was already late. And she hurried out of the office, without looking back. He could still recall the click of her pumps as she left.

That was the last time he ever saw her. All contact ceased. He'd call her, and write, but never got a response. And two months later she got married. He heard about this from a mutual friend, after the fact. The friend found it odd that Menshiki was not invited to the wedding ceremony, and, in particular, that he had no idea she was getting married. He'd always thought that Menshiki and the woman were good friends (they'd always been very discreet about their relationship, and no one else had known they were lovers). Menshiki didn't know the man she married. He had never even heard his name. She hadn't told Menshiki she was planning to marry, nor even hinted at it. She just disappeared from his world without a word.

That violent embrace on the sofa at his office, Menshiki realized, must have been her final, farewell act of love. Afterward he went over those events, over and over in his mind. Even after a long time had passed, those memories remained amazingly distinct and clear. The creak of the sofa, her hair whirling around her, her hot breath in his ear—it all came back to him.

So did Menshiki regret losing her? Of course not. He wasn't the type to have regrets. He knew very well he wasn't suited to family life. No matter how much he loved someone, he still couldn't share his life with them. He needed solitary time every day to concentrate, and he couldn't stand it when someone's presence threw off his concentration. If he lived with someone he knew he would end up detesting them. Whether it was his parents, a wife, or children. He feared that above all. He wasn't afraid of loving someone. What he feared was growing to hate someone.

For all that, he had loved her very deeply. He'd never loved any other woman so deeply, and probably never would again. "Even now there's a special spot inside me just for her," Menshiki said. "A very real spot. You might even call it a shrine."

A shrine? This struck me as an odd choice of words. But for him it was likely the right way of putting it.

Menshiki ended his story there. He'd told this private tale in great detail, yet I got little sense of it being sexual. It was more like he'd read aloud from a medical report. Or maybe it really was that sort of dispassionate experience for him.

"Seven months after the wedding she gave birth to a baby girl in a hospital in Tokyo," Menshiki continued. "Thirteen years ago. I heard about this birth much later from someone."

Menshiki stared down at his now empty coffee cup, as if nostalgic for some past age when it had been full of hot coffee.

"And that child might possibly be my own," he said, seemingly forcing out the words. He looked at me, like he wanted to hear my opinion.

It took me a while to grasp what he was trying to say.

"Does the timeline fit?"

"It does. It coincides perfectly. The child was born nine months after she came to my office. She must have picked the day she was most fertile to come see me and—how should I put it?—deliberately *gathered* my sperm. That's my working hypothesis. From the beginning she wasn't expecting to marry me, but had decided to have my child. I figured that's what happened."

"But you can't confirm that," I said.

"Of course. At this point it's merely a hypothesis. But I do have a sort of basis to say this."

"That was a pretty risky experiment for her, wasn't it?" I pointed out. "If the blood types didn't match it might come out that the father was someone else. Would she risk that?"

"My blood is type A. Most Japanese are A, and I think she is too. As long as they didn't have some reason to run a full-blown DNA test, the chances are slim that the secret would come out. That much she could figure out."

"But on the other hand, unless you ran an official DNA test you wouldn't be able to determine if you're the girl's biological father or not. Right? Or else you ask her mother directly."

Menshiki shook his head. "It's no longer possible to ask the mother. She died seven years ago."

"That's terrible. She was still so young," I said.

"She was walking in the woods and was stung by hornets and died. She was allergic to them. By the time they got her to the hospital she'd stopped breathing. Nobody knew she was so allergic to their stings. Maybe she didn't even know herself. She left behind her husband and daughter. Her daughter is thirteen now."

About the same age my little sister was when she died, I thought.

"And you have some sort of basis for conjecturing that this girl is your daughter. Is that what you're saying?"

"Some time after she died I suddenly received a letter from the deceased," Menshiki said in a quiet voice.

. . .

One day a large envelope, with a return receipt, arrived at his office from a law firm he'd never heard of. Inside was a typed two-page letter (with the letterhead of the law firm) and a light pink envelope. The letter from the law firm was signed by a lawyer. The lawyer's letter read: *Ms. **** entrusted me with this letter while she was still alive. Ms. **** left instructions with me to send this letter to you in case of her death. She added a note to the effect that the letter should be for your eyes only.*

That was the gist of the lawyer's letter. The circumstances leading to her death were described simply, in a businesslike manner. Menshiki was speechless, but finally pulled himself together and snipped open the second envelope. The letter inside was handwritten in blue ink, on four sheets of stationery. The handwriting was exquisite.

Dear Mr. Menshiki,

I don't know what month or year it is now, but if you are reading this it means I am no longer among the living. I'm not sure why, but I've always had the feeling I'd depart this world at a relatively young age. Which is why I made full preparations like this for after my death. If all this ends up being wasted, of course nothing could be better—but when all is said and done since you are reading this letter it means that I've already passed away. The thought leaves me very, very sad.

The first thing I'd like to say in advance (maybe it's something I really don't need to say) is that my life has never been of much consequence. I'm well aware of that. So it seems fitting for someone like me to quietly exit the world without making a big deal of things, without any uncalled-for pronouncements. But there is one thing I need to tell you alone. My conscience is telling me that if I don't, I may forever lose the chance to treat you fairly. So I've left this letter with a lawyer I know and trust with instructions to pass it on to you.

Suddenly leaving you like that, and marrying someone else, and not saying a word to you about it beforehand—I am deeply sorry about all of it. I can imagine how shocked and upset you must have been. But you're always so calm, so maybe it didn't shock you, or bother you. At any rate, that was the only path I could follow. I won't get into details here, but I do want you to understand that. I was left with hardly any other choice.

But one choice was left to me. A choice that was condensed in one event, in one act. Do you remember the last time I saw you? That evening in early fall when I suddenly came to your office, maybe I didn't seem like it, but I was at my wit's end then, completely driven into a corner. I no longer felt like I was myself anymore. But even in that confused state of mind, the act I did was utterly intentional. And I've never, ever regretted it. This was something profoundly important in my life. Something far surpassing my own existence.

I am hoping that you will understand my intentions, and ultimately forgive me. And I pray that none of this will cause you, personally, any harm. Since I know very well how much you dislike those kinds of things.

I wish you a long and happy life. And I hope that what a truly wonderful person you were will be passed along, in all its richness, for a long time to come.

* * * *

Menshiki read the letter over so many times that he memorized it all (and he recited it to me without faltering). All sorts of emotions and suggestions played back and forth through the letter—light and dark, shadow and sunlight—creating a complex, hidden picture. Like a linguistics scholar researching an ancient language no one speaks anymore, he spent years considering the possibilities concealed in the letter's contents. Extracting each word and phrasing, recombining them, intertwining them, shifting their order. And he arrived at one conclusion alone: that the baby girl she gave birth to seven months after she got married was, he was now certain, conceived in that office, on that leather sofa, with him.

"I asked a law office I knew to investigate the daughter she left behind," Menshiki said. "Her husband was fifteen years older than she was, worked in real estate. Or, rather, he was the son of a local landowner and managed the land and properties he'd inherited from his father. He had some other real estate holdings, too, of course, but wasn't that ambitious when it came to expanding the business. He had enough assets to live on comfortably without working. The daughter's name was Mariye. The husband had not remarried after his wife's accidental death seven years ago. The husband has an unmarried younger sister who lives with them and takes care of the household. Mariye is in her first year at a local public junior high."

"And have you met this girl, Mariye?"

Menshiki was silent as he chose his words. "I've seen her from a distance many times. But never spoken with her."

"And what did you think when you saw her?"

"Did she look like me? I couldn't say. If I think there's a resemblance then everything about her resembles me, but if I don't think that way then I don't see a resemblance at all."

"Do you have a photo of her?"

Menshiki silently shook his head. "No, I don't. I could get one easily enough, but that's not what I was after. What good is carrying around a photo of her in my wallet going to do? What I'm after is—"

But nothing came after this. He was silent, the quiet buried in the lively buzz of the hordes of insects outside.

"But you told me earlier, Mr. Menshiki, that you were totally uninterested in blood relations."

"True enough. I've never cared about lineage. In fact, I've lived my life trying to avoid that as much as I could. My feelings haven't changed. But still, I find I can't take my eyes off this girl, Mariye. I simply can't stop thinking about her. There's no reason for it, but still . . ."

I couldn't find the right words to say.

Menshiki continued. "I've never had this experience before. I've always been very self-controlled, even proud of it. But sometimes now I find it painful to be alone."

I went ahead and said what was on my mind. "Mr. Menshiki, this is just a hunch on my part, but it seems like there's something you want me to do in regard to Mariye. Or am I overthinking things?"

After a pause Menshiki nodded. "I'm not sure how I should put this—"

I realized at that instant that the clamor of insects had completely stopped. I looked up at the clock on the wall. It was just past one forty. I held a finger up to my lips, and Menshiki stopped in midsentence. And the two of us listened carefully in the still of the night.

14

BUT SOMETHING THIS STRANGE IS A FIRST

Menshiki and I stopped talking, and sat still, listening carefully. The insects had stopped chirping, just like they had two days ago, and again yesterday. In the midst of that deep silence I could again make out the tinkling of the bell. It rang a few times, with uneven periods of silence in between before ringing once again. I looked over at Menshiki, seated across from me on the sofa. I could tell he was hearing the same sound. He was frowning. He lifted up his hands on his lap, his fingers moving slightly in time to the ringing of the bell. So this wasn't an auditory hallucination.

After listening intently to the bell for two or three minutes, Menshiki slowly rose from the sofa.

"Let's go where that sound's coming from," he said drily.

I picked up my flashlight. He went outside and retrieved a large flashlight from his Jaguar. We climbed the seven steps and walked into the woods. Though not as bright as two days before, the autumn moonlight clearly lit the path for us. We walked in back of the little shrine, pushing aside pampas grass as we went, and emerged in front of the stone mound. And again we perked up our ears. No doubt about it, the sound was coming from the cracks between the stones.

Menshiki slowly circled the mound, cautiously shining his flashlight into the cracks between the stones. But nothing was out of the ordinary, just a jumble of old, moss-covered stones. He looked over at me. In the moonlight his face resembled some mask from ancient times. Perhaps my face looked the same?

“When you heard the sound before, was it coming from here?” he whispered.

“The same place,” I said. “The exact same spot.”

“It sounds like someone underneath the stones is ringing a bell,” Menshiki said.

I nodded. I felt relieved to know I wasn’t crazy, but I had to admit that the unreality of the situation had now, through Menshiki, taken on a reality, creating a slight gap in the seam of the world.

“What should we do?” I asked Menshiki.

He shone his flashlight on where the sound was coming from, his lips tight as he considered the situation. In the still of the night I could almost hear the wheels turning in his mind.

“Someone might be seeking help,” Menshiki said quietly, as if to himself.

“But who could have possibly gotten under these heavy stones?”

Menshiki shook his head. He had no idea either.

“Anyway, let’s go back to the house,” he said. He lightly touched my shoulders from behind. “At least we’ve pinpointed the source of the sound. Let’s go home and talk it over.”

We cut through the woods and came out onto the empty space in front of the house. Menshiki opened the door of his Jaguar and returned the flashlight. In its place he took out a small paper bag. We went back inside the house.

“If you have any whiskey, could I have a glass?” Menshiki asked.

“Regular Scotch okay?”

“Of course. Straight, please. With a separate glass of water, no ice.”

I went into the kitchen and took a bottle of White Label from the shelf, poured some into two glasses, and took them and some mineral water out to the living room. We sat across from each other without speaking, and drank our straight whiskey. I went back to the kitchen to get the bottle of White Label and poured him a refill. He picked up the glass but didn’t drink any. In the silence of the middle of the night, the bell continued to ring out intermittently. A small sound, but with a delicate weight one couldn’t fail to hear.

"I've seen a lot of strange things in my time, but something this strange is a first," Menshiki said. "Pardon me for saying this, but when you first told me about this I only half believed you. It's hard to believe something like this could actually happen."

Something in that expression caught my attention. "What do you mean, could actually happen?"

Menshiki raised his head and looked me in the eyes.

"I read about this sort of thing in a book once," he said.

"You mean hearing a bell from somewhere in the middle of the night?"

"No, what they heard was a gong, not a bell. The kind of gong they would ring along with a drum when searching for a lost child. In the old days it was a small Buddhist altar fitting that you would hit with a wooden bell hammer. You'd strike it rhythmically as you chanted sutras. In the story someone heard that kind of gong ringing out from underground in the middle of the night."

"Was this a ghost story?"

"Closer to what's called a tale of the mysterious. Have you ever read Ueda Akinari's book *Tales of the Spring Rain*?" Menshiki asked.

I shook my head. "I read his *Tales of Moonlight and Rain* a long time ago. But I haven't read that one."

"*Tales of the Spring Rain* is a collection of stories Akinari wrote in his later years. Some forty years after he finished *Tales of Moonlight and Rain*. Compared with that book, which emphasized narrative, *Tales of the Spring Rain* was more an expression of Akinari's philosophy as a man of letters. One strange story in the collection is titled 'Fate over Two Generations.' The main character experiences something like what you're going through. He's the son of a wealthy farmer. He enjoys studying, and one night he's reading late when he hears a sound like a gong coming from underneath a rock in the corner of the garden. Thinking it odd, the next day he has people dig it up, and they find a large stone underneath. When they move that stone they find a kind of coffin with a stone lid. Inside that they discover a fleshless emaciated person, like a dried fish. With hair down to his knees. Only his hands are still moving, striking a gong with a wooden hammer. It was a Buddhist priest who long ago chose his own death in order to achieve enlightenment, and had himself buried alive in the coffin. This act was called *zenjo*. The mummified dead body was unearthed and enshrined in a temple. Another term for *zenjo* is *nyujo*, meaning a deep meditative practice. The man must have originally been quite a highly revered priest. As he had hoped, his soul reached nirvana, and the soul-less physical body alone continued to live on. The main character's family had lived on this plot of land for ten generations, and this burial must have taken place before that. In other words, several centuries before."

Menshiki ended there.

"So you're saying the same sort of thing took place around this house?" I asked.

Menshiki shook his head. "If you think about it, it's not possible. This was just a take on the supernatural written in the Edo period. Akinari knew that this tale had become part of folk legend and he adapted it and created the story 'Fate over Two Generations.' What I'm saying is, the story does have strange parallels with what we're experiencing now."

He lightly shook his glass of whiskey, the amber liquid quietly oscillating in his hand.

"So after he was unearthed, what happened?" I asked.

"The story took off in strange directions," Menshiki replied, sounding hesitant to go into it. "Ueda Akinari's worldview late in his life is deeply reflected in that story. A quite cynical view of the world, really. Akinari had a complicated background, a man who went through a lot of troubles in his life. But rather than hearing me summarize, I suggest you read the story yourself."

Menshiki took an old book out of the paper bag he'd brought inside from the car, and handed it to me. A volume from a collection of classical Japanese literature. The book contained the entire text of Akinari's two most famous books, *Tales of Moonlight and Rain* and *Tales of the Spring Rain*.

"When you told me what was going on here, right away I recalled this story. Just to be sure, I reread the copy I had on my shelves. I'll give you the book. If you'd like, please take a look. It's a short tale and doesn't take long to read."

I thanked him and accepted the book. "It's all pretty strange," I said. "Kind of unbelievable. Of course I'll read it. But apart from all that, what am I actually supposed to *do*? I don't think I can just leave things the way they are. If somebody really is buried beneath those rocks, ringing a bell or gong or whatever, sending out a call for help every night, we have to help get him out."

Menshiki frowned. "But the two of us would never be able to move that pile of stones."

"Should we report it to the police?"

Menshiki shook his head a few times. "The police won't be any help. Once you report that you're hearing a bell ringing from under stones in a woods in the middle of the night, they're not going to take you seriously. They'll just think you're crazy. It could make things worse. Better not go there."

"But if that bell keeps ringing every night, I don't think my nerves can take it. I can't get much sleep. All I can do is move out of this house. That sound is definitely trying to tell us something."

Menshiki considered this. "We'll need a professional's help to move those rocks," he said. "There's a man I know pretty well who's a local landscape designer. He's used to moving heavy rocks in landscaping. If need be, he could arrange for a small backhoe. Then it'd be easy to move the rocks and dig a hole."

"Okay, but I see two problems with that," I said. "First, I'd have to get permission to do that work from the son of the owner. I can't decide anything on my own. And second, I don't have the funds to hire someone to do that kind of job."

Menshiki smiled. "Don't worry about the money. I'll take care of that. What I mean is, that designer owes me one, and I think he'll do it at cost. Don't worry about that. As for Mr. Amada, why don't you get in touch with him? If you explain the situation, I think he'll give permission. If somebody really is shut away underneath those rocks and we just leave him to his fate, Mr. Amada will be liable for it as the property owner."

"But to ask you, an outsider, to go to all that trouble—"

Menshiki spread his hands wide on his lap, as if catching the rain. His voice was quiet.

"I mentioned this before, but I'm a very curious person. I'd like to find out how this odd story will play out. It's not something you run across every day. So, like I said, don't worry about how much it'll cost. I understand you have your own position to consider, but let me arrange everything."

I looked Menshiki in the eye. There was a keen light there I hadn't seen before. Those eyes told me that no matter what happened he was going to pursue it to the very end. If you don't understand something, then stick with it until you do—that seemed to be Menshiki's basic approach to life.

"Okay," I said. "Tomorrow I'll get in touch with Masahiko."

"And I'll contact the landscape designer," Menshiki said. He paused. "By the way, there's one thing I wanted to ask you."

"Yes?"

"Do you often have these kinds of—what should I say?—paranormal experiences?"

"No," I said. "This is a first. I'm a very ordinary person who's lived a very ordinary life. That's why I find it all so confusing. What about you, Mr. Menshiki?"

A faint smile rose to his lips. "I've had many strange experiences. I've seen things common sense can't explain. But something *this* strange is a first."

After this we sat there in silence, listening to the ringing of the bell.

As always the bell stopped completely a little after 2:30. And the mountains were again blasted with the buzz of insects.

"I'd best be going," Menshiki said. "Thank you for the whiskey. I'll get in touch soon."

Under the moonlight Menshiki got into his glossy silver Jaguar and drove off. He gave a short wave out the open window and I waved back. After the sound of his engine had faded away down the slope, I remembered that he'd had a glass of whiskey (the second glass he hadn't touched), but his face hadn't turned red at all, his speech and attitude no different than if he'd drunk water. He must be able to hold his liquor. And he wasn't driving far. It was a road that only local residents used, and at this hour there wouldn't be any cars coming the other direction, or any pedestrians.

I went back inside, rinsed out our glasses in the kitchen sink, and went to bed. I thought about people coming with heavy equipment to move the stones behind the little shrine, and digging a hole. It was hard to picture it as real. Before that happened, I needed to read the Ueda Akinari story he'd mentioned, "Fate over Two Generations." But I'd leave everything for tomorrow. Things would look different in the light of day. I switched off the bedside light, and to the background noise of buzzing insects, I fell asleep.

At ten a.m. I called Masahiko Amada's office and explained the situation. I didn't bring up Ueda Akinari, but told him how I'd had an acquaintance over to make sure that bell ringing in the middle of the night wasn't just an auditory illusion I was having.

"That is really creepy," Masahiko said. "But do you really believe there's someone underneath those stones ringing a bell?"

"I don't know. But I can't just ignore it. I hear it every single night."

"What will you do if, when you dig it all up, something weird emerges?"

"What do you mean, something weird?"

"I don't know," he said. "Some mysterious thing that's best left alone."

"You should come at night sometime and hear that sound. If you heard it yourself you'd understand why I can't just let it be."

Masahiko sighed deeply on the other end of the line. "No thanks," he said, "I'll pass. I've always been a bit of a coward. I hate scary stories, anything frightening. No thanks. I'll leave it all up to you. It's not going to bother anyone if you move those old stones and dig a hole. Do whatever you like. Just make sure not to unearth anything weird, okay?"

"I don't know how it's going to turn out, but once I know, I'll be in touch."

"If it were me, I'd just wear earplugs," Masahiko said.

After I hung up I sat in a chair in the living room and read the Ueda Akinari story. I read it first in the original classical Japanese, then in the contemporary-language version. A couple of details were different, but as Menshiki had said there was a strong resemblance between the story and what I was experiencing here. In the story the character heard the gong sounding at two o'clock in the morning, about the same time. But what I heard wasn't a gong but a bell. In the story the buzz of insects didn't stop. The protagonist hears the gong mixed in with the sound of the insects. But these small details aside, what I experienced was exactly the same as in the story. It left me dumbfounded, in fact, at how close the two were.

The unearthed mummy was completely dried up, just its hand doggedly moving, striking the gong. A terrifying vitality made the hand move almost mechanically. No doubt this priest gave up the ghost while reciting sutras and beating out a rhythm on the gong. The main character put clothes on the mummy and poured water on his lips. Before long he was able to eat some thin rice gruel and gradually put on flesh. Finally he recovered to the point where he looked like a normal human being. But you got no sense from him at all of a priest who had attained enlightenment. No intelligence or wisdom, and not a hint of dignity. And he had lost all memory of his former life. He couldn't recall, even, why he'd gone underground like that for so very long. He ate meat now, and had a considerable sexual appetite. He got married, and managed to make a living doing menial work. People nicknamed him "Nyujo no Josuke"—Josuke, the meditation guy. His pathetic figure made the villagers lose all respect for Buddhism. Is this the kind of wreck you end up as, they wondered, after all the strict ascetic training he went through, risking his life in pursuit of Buddhism? They started to despise faith, and stopped going to temple. That was Ueda's story. As Menshiki had said, the story reflected the author's cynical worldview. It's not merely some tale of the supernatural.

> *For all that, Buddhist teachings were in vain. That man must have been underground, ringing that gong, for well over a hundred years. Yet nothing miraculous came of it, and people were fed up that all that came from it were bones.*

I reread the short story "Fate over Two Generations" several times and found myself utterly confused. Say we used heavy equipment to move the stones, dug up the soil, and what emerged was a bony, pathetic mummy, then how was I supposed to handle that? Would I be responsible for resuscitating him? Was it wiser, as Masahiko had advised, to not meddle, and simply plug up my ears and leave it all alone?

But even if I wanted to do that, I couldn't simply make it go away. I would never be able to escape that sound, no matter how tightly I plugged up my ears. And say I moved somewhere else; that sound might follow me. Plus, like Menshiki, I was curious. I had to find out what lay hidden beneath those stones.

In the afternoon Menshiki called me. "Did you get Mr. Amada's permission?"

I told him pretty much everything about my conversation with Masahiko. And how he'd told me to handle it any way I wanted.

"I'm glad," Menshiki said. "I've arranged things with the landscape designer. I didn't tell him about the mysterious sound. I just asked him to move some stones out in the woods and then dig a hole there. It was a sudden request, but his schedule happened to be free, so if you don't mind, he'd like to come and look over the site this afternoon and start work tomorrow morning. Is it all right with you that he comes to check out the work site?"

"He can come over whenever he wants," I said.

"After he inspects the site, he'll arrange for the equipment he needs. The work itself should be done in a few hours. I'll be present when they're working," Menshiki said.

"I'll be there, too. When you find out what time they'll start, let me know," I said. "By the way," I added, remembering, "about what we were talking about last night, before we heard that sound . . ."

Menshiki didn't seem to follow. "I'm sorry, you mean—"

"It was about the thirteen-year-old girl, Mariye. You said she might be your real daughter. We were talking about her when we heard the bell, and that's as far as we got."

"Ah yes," said Menshiki. "Now that you mention it, we did talk about that. I'd totally forgotten. Yes, we should talk about that again sometime.

But there's no rush. We can talk about it again once we take care of the matter at hand."

After that I couldn't concentrate. I tried reading, listening to music, cooking, but all I could think of was what lay beneath those ancient stones in the woods. I couldn't shake the thought of a blackened mummy, shriveled up like a dried fish.

15

THIS IS ONLY THE BEGINNING

Menshiki called me that night to let me know that the work would begin the next morning, Wednesday, at ten.

Wednesday morning it was drizzling off and on, but not hard enough to delay the work. It was a fine rain, and a hat or raincoat with a hood was enough. No need for an umbrella. Menshiki had on an olive-green rain hat, the kind the British might use for duck hunting. The leaves of the trees, starting to turn fall colors, took on a dull color from the nearly invisible rain that soaked them.

The workers used a flatbed truck to move in a small backhoe. A very compact piece of equipment, with a tight turning radius, made to work in confined spaces. There were four workers altogether—one backhoe operator, one foreman, and two additional workers. The shovel operator and the foreman drove the truck. They all had on matching blue rainwear, jackets and trousers, and muddy thick-soled work boots, and wore protective helmets made of heavy-duty plastic. Menshiki and the foreman were apparently acquainted, and they talked for a while, the two of them beaming, next to the little shrine. I could tell, though, that the foreman remained on his best behavior toward Menshiki.

Menshiki must have had a lot of clout to arrange for this many people and equipment in such a short time. I watched this whole process half impressed, half bewildered. I had a slight sense of resignation, too, as if everything were already out of my hands. Like when I was a child and the little kids would be playing some game and bigger kids would come around and take over. I remembered that feeling.

They started the operation by using shovels and some material and boards to create a flat foothold for the backhoe to move, and then they began to actually remove the stones. The backhoe soon trampled down the thicket of pampas grass surrounding the mound. Menshiki and I stood to one side watching as they lifted the stones from the mound one by one and moved them to a spot a little ways away. There wasn't anything special about the operation. Probably the same sort of operation that takes place every day, all around the world. The workers looked ordinary too, like they were matter-of-factly following procedures they'd done a thousand times. Occasionally the backhoe operator would stop and call out in a loud voice to the foreman, but it didn't seem like there was any problem. They just exchanged a few words, and he didn't switch off the engine.

But I couldn't calmly watch the operation. Each time one of the square stones was removed, my anxiety only deepened. It was like some dark secret that I'd hidden away for years was being revealed, layer by layer, by the powerful, insistent tip of that machine. The problem lay in the fact that even I didn't know what secret I was hiding. Several times I felt I had to get them to stop the operation. Bringing in some large machinery like this backhoe couldn't be the solution. As Masahiko had told me on the phone, all "mysterious things" should be left buried. I was seized by the urge to grab Menshiki's arm and shout, "Let's stop this! Put the stones back where they were."

But of course I couldn't do that. The decision had been made and the work begun. Several other people were already involved. A not-insubstantial sum of money was changing hands (the amount was unclear, but I assumed Menshiki was footing the bill). We couldn't just stop at this point. The work continued, beyond my will.

As if he knew what I was going through, at a certain point Menshiki came over beside me and lightly patted me on the shoulder.

"There's nothing to worry about," he said in a calm voice. "It's going smoothly. It'll all be finished soon."

I nodded in silence.

Before noon all the stones had been moved. The ancient stones that had been piled in a jumble in a crumbling mound were now piled up in a neat, official-looking pyramid a little ways away. The fine drizzle silently fell on the pile. Even after removing all those stones, though, the ground hadn't appeared. Below the stones lay more stone. These stones were flat and had been methodically laid out there like a square stone flooring. The whole thing was about six feet on each side.

"I wonder why it's like that," the foreman said after coming over to where Menshiki was. "I was sure that the stones were just piled up on top of the ground. But they weren't. There seems to be an open space underneath that stone slab. I inserted a thin metal rod into a gap and it went down pretty far. Not sure yet how deep it goes, though."

Menshiki and I gingerly tried standing on top of the freshly uncovered slab. The stones were darkly wet and slippery in spots. Though they'd been artificially cut and evened up over time, the edges had become more rounded off, with gaps between the stones. The nightly sound of the bell must have filtered out through those gaps. And air could probably get in through those too. I crouched down and stared through a gap inside, but it was pitch black and I couldn't make out a thing.

"Maybe they used flagstones to cover up an ancient well. Though for a well, its diameter is a bit big," the foreman said.

"Can you remove these flagstones?" Menshiki asked.

The foreman shrugged. "I'm not sure. We hadn't planned on this. It'll make things a little complicated, but I think we can manage it. Using a crane would be our best bet, but we'd never get one in here. Each stone doesn't look that heavy. And there's a gap between them, so with a little ingenuity I think we can manage with the backhoe. We're coming up on our lunch break, so I'll work out a good plan then and we'll get to work in the afternoon."

Menshiki and I went back to the house and had a light lunch. In the kitchen I threw together some simple ham, lettuce, and pickle sandwiches and we went out on the terrace to eat as we watched the rain.

"This whole operation is delaying what we should be working on, finishing the portrait," I said.

Menshiki shook his head. "There's no rush with the portrait. Our first priority is solving this weird matter. Then you can get back to work on the painting."

Did this man *seriously* want his portrait painted? I couldn't help but wonder. This doubt had been smoldering in a corner of my mind from the very start. Did he *seriously* want me to paint his portrait? Wasn't he just using the portrait as a mere pretext, and had some other reason for getting to know me?

But what could it be? I couldn't figure it out. Was his goal unearthing what was under those stones? This didn't make sense. He hadn't known about them. That was something unforeseen that only came up after we started on the portrait. Still, he seemed overly enthusiastic about digging them up. And he was shelling out quite a bit of money for the operation, even though it had nothing to do with him.

As I was mulling over all this Menshiki asked, "Did you read the story 'Fate over Two Generations'?"

"I did," I told him.

"What did you think? A very strange tale, isn't it?" he said.

"It certainly is," I said.

Menshiki looked at me for a while, then said, "To tell the truth, that story has tugged at me for a long time. It's one of the reasons this discovery has aroused my interest."

I took a sip of coffee and wiped my mouth with a paper napkin. Two crows, cawing at each other, winged their way across the valley, undeterred by the rain. Wet by the rain, their wings would only grow a deeper black.

"I don't know much about Buddhism," I said to Menshiki, "so I don't understand all the details, but doesn't a priest doing a voluntary burial—this *nyujo*—mean he chooses to go into a coffin and die?"

"Exactly. *Nyujo* originally means 'attaining enlightenment,' so they have the term *ikinyujo*—'living *nyujo*'—to distinguish the two. They make a stone-lined underground chamber and insert a bamboo pipe to allow in air. Before a priest does *nyujo* he maintains a fruitarian diet for a set time so his body won't putrefy but will become nicely mummified."

"Fruitarian?"

"Just eating grasses and nuts and berries. They eat no cooked foods whatsoever, starting with grains. In other words, a radical elimination of all fats and moisture from the body. Changing the makeup of the body so it can easily mummify. And after purifying his body, the priest goes underground. In the darkness there the priest fasts and recites sutras, hitting a gong in time to that. Or ringing a bell. And people can hear the sound of that gong or bell through the vent hole. But at some point the sounds stop. That's the sign that he's breathed his last. And over a period of time the body gradually turns into a mummy. The custom is to unearth the body after three years and three months."

"Why would they do that?"

"So the priests could practice austerity to the point of becoming self-mummified. Doing that allows them to reach enlightenment and to arrive at a realm beyond life and death. This also connects up with mankind's salvation. So-called Nirvana. The unearthed enlightened monk, the mummy, is kept at a temple, and through praying to it people are saved."

"In reality it's a kind of suicide."

Menshiki nodded. "Which is why in the Meiji period the practice of self-burial was outlawed. People who helped in the process could be arrested for aiding and abetting suicide. The truth is, though, priests continued to follow the practice in secret. That's why there may be quite a few cases of priests being buried but never unearthed by anyone."

"Are you thinking that stone mound is the remains of a secret burial of that kind?"

Menshiki shook his head. "We won't know until we actually remove the stones. But it's possible. There's no bamboo tube there, but the way it's constructed, air could get in through the gaps, and you can hear sounds from inside too."

"And you're saying that someone is still alive underneath those stones and is ringing a gong or bell every night?"

Menshiki shook his head again. "That obviously doesn't make any sense."

"Reaching Nirvana—is that different from merely dying?"

"It is. I'm not all that familiar with Buddhist doctrine, but as far as I understand, Nirvana is found beyond life and death. You could see it as the idea that even if the flesh dies and disappears, the soul goes over to a place beyond life and death. Worldly flesh is nothing more than a temporary dwelling."

"Even if a priest were, through burial alive, to reach Nirvana, is it possible for him to rejoin his physical body?"

Menshiki said nothing and looked at me for a while. He took a bite of his ham sandwich, and a sip of coffee.

"What you're saying is—"

"I didn't hear that sound until four or five days ago," I said. "I'm certain of that. If the sound had been there I would have noticed. Even if it was small, it's not the kind of sound I would have missed. I only started hearing it a few days ago. What I mean is, even if there's somebody underneath those stones, that person hasn't been ringing the bell for a long time."

Menshiki returned his coffee cup to the saucer and studied the pattern on the cup. "Have you seen a real mummified priest?" he finally said.

I shook my head.

"I've seen several. When I was young I traveled around Yamagata Prefecture on my own and saw a few that were preserved in temples there. For some reason there are a lot of these mummified priests in the Tohoku region, especially in Yamagata. Honestly, they're not very nice to look at. Maybe it's my lack of faith, but I didn't feel very grateful when I saw them. Small, brown, all shriveled up. I probably shouldn't say this, but the color and texture reminded me of beef jerky. The physical body really is nothing more than a fleeting, empty abode. That, at least, is what these mummies teach us. We may do our utmost, but at best we end up as no more than beef jerky."

He picked up the ham sandwich he'd been eating and gazed at it intently for a moment. As if he were seeing a ham sandwich for the first time in his life.

He went on. "At any rate, let's wait till after lunch for them to move those stones. Then we'll know more, whether we want to or not."

We went back to the site in the woods just after one fifteen. The crew had finished lunch and were hard at work. The two workmen put wedge-like metal implements in the gaps between the stones, and the backhoe used a rope to pull those and raise the stones. The workmen then attached ropes to the dug-up stones, and the shovel hauled these up. It was time consuming, but one by one the stones were steadily unearthed and moved off to the side.

Menshiki and the foreman were deep in conversation about something for a while, but then he came back to join me.

"As they thought, the stones aren't all that thick. Looks like they'll be able to remove them," he explained. "There seems to be a lattice-shaped lid underneath all the stones. They don't know what it's made of, but that lid supported the stones. After they remove all the stones on top they'll need to take off that lid. They don't know yet if they can. It's impossible to guess what lies beneath that. It'll take a while for them to remove all the stones, and once they've made more progress they'll call us, so they said they'd like us to wait in the house. If you don't mind, let's do that. Standing around here isn't going to help."

We walked back home. I should have used the extra time to continue work on the portrait, but I didn't feel I'd be able to concentrate on painting. The operation out in the woods had me on edge. The six-foot-square stone flooring that had emerged from underneath the mound of crumbling old stones. The solid lattice lid. And the space that seemed to lie below it. I couldn't erase these images from my mind. Menshiki was right. Until we settled this matter we wouldn't be able to move forward on anything else.

"Do you mind if I listen to music while we wait?" Menshiki asked.

"Not at all," I said. "Play whatever record you'd like. I'll be in the kitchen preparing some food."

He chose a recording of Mozart. A sonata for piano and violin. The Tannoy Autograph speakers weren't very showy, but gave out a deep, steady sound. The perfect speakers for classical music, especially for listening to vinyl records of chamber music. As you might expect of old speakers, they were well suited to a vacuum-tube amp. The pianist was Georg Szell, the violinist Rafael Druian. Menshiki sat on the sofa, eyes closed, and gave himself over to the music. I listened to it from a little ways off, making tomato sauce. I'd bought a lot of tomatoes and had some left over and wanted to make some sauce before they went bad.

I boiled water in a large pan, parboiled the tomatoes and removed the skins, cut them with a knife, removed the seeds, crushed them, put them in a large skillet, added garlic, and simmered it all with olive oil, let it cook well. I carefully removed any scum on the surface. Back when I was married I often made sauce like this. It takes time and effort, but basically it's an easy process. While my wife was at work I'd stand alone in the kitchen, listening to music on a CD while I made it. I liked to cook while listening to old jazz. Thelonious Monk was a particular favorite. *Monk's Music* was my favorite of his albums. Coleman Hawkins and John Coltrane played on it, with amazing solos. But I have to admit that making sauce while listening to Mozart's chamber music wasn't bad either.

It was only a short while ago that I'd been cooking tomato sauce in the afternoon while enjoying Monk's unique offbeat melodies and chords (it was only half a year ago that my wife and I had dissolved our marriage), but it felt like something that had taken place ages ago. A trivial historical episode a generation ago that only a handful of people still remembered. I suddenly wondered how my wife was. Was she living with another man now? Or was she still living by herself in that apartment in Hiroo? Either way, at this time of day she would be at work at the architectural firm. For her, how much of a difference was there between her life when I was there, and her life now without me? And how much interest did she have in that difference? I was sort of half thinking about all this. Did she have the same feeling, that our days spent together seemed like something from the distant past?

The record was over, the needle making a popping sound as it spun in the final groove, and when I went to the living room I found Menshiki asleep on the sofa, arms folded, leaning over slightly to one side. I lifted the needle up from the spinning disc and switched off the turntable. Even when the steady click of the needle stopped, Menshiki continued to sleep. He must have been very tired. He was faintly snoring. I left him where he was. I returned to the kitchen, shut off the gas under the skillet, and drank a big glass of water. I still had time on my hands, so I began to fry some onions.

. . .

When the phone rang Menshiki was already awake. He was in the bathroom, washing his face with soap and gargling. The call was from the foreman at the work site, so I handed the phone to Menshiki. He said a few words, and then said that we would be right over. He handed the phone back.

"They're almost done," he said.

Outside it had stopped raining. Clouds still covered the sky, but it was lighter out now. The weather seemed to be steadily improving. We hurried up the steps and through the woods. Behind the little shrine the four men were standing around a hole, staring down into it. The backhoe's engine was off, nothing was moving, the woods strangely hushed.

The stones had been neatly removed, exposing the hole below. The square lattice lid had been taken off too, and laid to one side. It was a thick, heavy-looking wooden cover. Old, but not rotted at all. After that the circular stone-lined room below was visible. It was under six feet in diameter, about eight feet deep, and was enclosed by a stone wall. The floor seemed to be dirt. Not a single blade of grass grew there. The stone room was completely empty. No one there calling for help, no beef jerky mummy. Just a bell-like object lying on the ground. Actually less like a bell than some ancient musical instrument with a stack of tiny cymbals. A wooden handle was attached, about six inches long. The foreman shone a floodlight down on it.

"Was this all that was in there?" Menshiki asked him.

"Yes, that's it," the foreman said. "Like you asked, we left it just as we found it, after we took off the stones and lid. We haven't touched a thing."

"That's strange," Menshiki said, as if to himself. "So there really wasn't anything else at all?"

"I called you right after we lifted off the lid. I haven't been down inside. This is exactly the way it was when we uncovered it," the foreman said.

"Of course," Menshiki said, in a dry voice.

"It might have been a well originally," the foreman said. "It looks like it was filled in, leaving the hole. But it's too wide for a well, and the stone wall around it is so elaborately constructed. It couldn't have been easy to build. I suppose they must have had some important purpose in mind to construct something that took this much time and effort."

"Can I go down and check it out?" Menshiki asked the foreman.

The foreman was a little unsure. With a hard face, he said, "I think I should go down first. Just in case. If it's all clear, then you can climb on down. Does that sound good?"

"Of course," Menshiki said. "Let's do that."

One of the workmen brought over a folding metal ladder from the truck, opened it up, and lowered it down. The foreman put on his safety helmet and climbed down the eight feet to the dirt floor. He looked around him for a while. He gazed up, then shone his flashlight on the stone wall and the floor, closely checking everything. He carefully observed the bell-like object that lay on the dirt floor. He didn't touch it, though, just observed it. He rubbed the soles of his work boots a few times against the dirt floor, kicking his heel against it. He took a few deep breaths, smelling the air. He was only in the hole for about five or six minutes, then slowly clambered up the ladder to ground level.

"It doesn't seem dangerous. The air's good, and there aren't any weird bugs or anything. And the footing is solid. You can go down now if you'd like," he said.

Menshiki removed his rainwear to make it easier to move around, and in his flannel shirt and chinos, he hung his flashlight by a strap around his neck and climbed down the metal ladder. We watched in silence as he descended. The foreman shone the floodlight below Menshiki's feet. Menshiki stood still at the bottom of the hole for a while, waiting, then reached out and touched the stone wall, and crouched down to check out what the dirt floor felt like. He picked up the bell-like object on the ground, shone his flashlight on it, and gazed at it. Then he shook it a few times. When he did, it was unmistakably the same bell sound I'd heard. No doubt about it. In the middle of the night someone had been ringing it here. But that *someone* was no longer here. Only the bell was left behind. As he studied the bell Menshiki shook his head a few times, evidently puzzled. Then he carefully studied the surrounding wall again, as if looking for a secret entrance and exit. But he found nothing of the sort. He looked up at us at ground level. He seemed totally confused.

He stepped onto the ladder and held out the bell toward me. I bent over and took it from him. A dampness penetrated deep into the ancient wooden handle. As Menshiki had done, I tried shaking it a few times. It sounded louder and clearer than I'd expected. I didn't know what it was made of, but the metal portion wasn't damaged at all. It was dirty, for sure, but not at all rusted. I couldn't figure out how it had remained rust-free despite being underground in damp soil for years.

"What *is* that?" the foreman asked me. He was in his mid-forties, short but with a sturdy build. Suntanned, with a bit of stubble on his face.

"I'm not sure. Maybe some kind of Buddhist implement or something," I said. "Whatever it is, it's certainly from ancient times."

"Is this what you were looking for?" he asked.

I shook my head. "No, we were expecting something else."

"At any rate, it's a strange place," the foreman said. "I can't explain it, but there's a mysterious feeling about it. Who would make this kind of place, I wonder—and why? This was a long time ago, and it must have been quite a task to haul the stones all the way up the mountain and stack them up."

I didn't say anything.

Menshiki finally climbed up out of the hole. He called the foreman over to his side, and they talked for a long time. I stood there, bell in hand, next to the hole. I pondered climbing down into this stone-lined chamber, but then thought better of it. I wasn't as hesitant as Masahiko, but I did decide it was better not to do anything uncalled for. If things could be left alone, the smart thing might be to do so. I placed the bell, for the time being, in front of the little shrine, and wiped my palm on my pants a couple of times.

Menshiki ambled over. "We'll have them do a more thorough examination of that stone-lined chamber," he said. "At first glance it looks like just a hole, but I'll have them check it all out from one end to the other. They might discover something. Though I sort of doubt it." He looked at the bell I'd placed in front of the shrine. "It's odd that this bell's the only thing left. Since someone had to be inside there in the middle of the night ringing the bell."

"Maybe the bell was ringing by itself," I ventured.

Menshiki smiled. "An interesting theory, but I doubt it. For whatever purpose, someone was sending out a message from down inside that hole. A message to you, or maybe to us. Or to people in general. But whoever it was has vanished like smoke. Or else slipped away from there."

"Slipped away?"

"Slipped right past us."

I couldn't understand what he was getting at.

"Because the soul isn't something you can see," Menshiki said.

"You believe in the existence of the soul?"

"Do you?"

I didn't have a good answer.

"I believe that it's not necessary to believe in the soul's existence. But turn that around and you come to the belief that there's no need to *not* believe in its existence. A kind of roundabout way of putting it, but do you understand what I'm getting at?"

"Sort of," I said.

Menshiki picked up the bell from where I'd placed it in front of the shrine. He held it out and rang it several times. "A priest probably breathed his last there, underground, ringing this bell and chanting sutras. All alone, shut away in the pitch-black darkness, that heavy lid in place, in the bottom of a sealed well. And most likely all in secret. I have no idea what sort of priest he was. A respectable priest, or merely some fanatic. Either way, someone constructed a stone tumulus on top of it. I don't know what happened after that, but people then completely forgot he'd been voluntarily buried under here. Then a big earthquake occurred at some point, and the mound collapsed until it was just a pile of stones. It could have been during the Kanto earthquake of 1923, since certain areas around Odawara suffered real damage back then. And everything was swallowed up into oblivion."

"If that's true, then where did the priest who died there—the mummy, I mean—disappear to?"

Menshiki shook his head. "I don't know. Maybe at some point someone dug up the hole and took him away."

"To do that they'd have to move all these stones and then pile them up again," I said. "And then who was ringing the bell yesterday in the middle of the night?"

Menshiki shook his head again, and smiled faintly. "Good grief. We used all this equipment to move the stones and open up the chamber, and in the end all we found out for sure is that we don't know a single thing. All we managed to get was an old bell."

They examined the stone chamber thoroughly, and merely determined that there were no hidden devices anywhere. This was merely a round hole, lined with a stone wall, 8.2 feet deep with a diameter of 5.9 feet (they made precise measurements). Finally, they loaded the backhoe up onto the truck bed, and the workers collected all their tools and left. All that remained was the open hole and the metal ladder. The foreman was kind enough to leave it behind. They also laid several thick boards on top of the hole so no one would fall into it by mistake. They left some heavy stones on top to weigh the boards down so they wouldn't blow away in a strong wind. The wooden lattice cover was too heavy to lift, so they left it on the ground nearby and covered it with a plastic tarp.

Before they left, Menshiki told the foreman not to mention this operation to anyone. It had archaeological significance, and he wanted, he said, to keep it from the public until the time was right to announce the find.

"Understood," the foreman said with a serious expression. "We'll leave it all here. And I'll warn the others not to say anything about it."

After the workers and heavy machinery had left and the mountains were blanketed in their usual stillness again, the dug-up area looked like skin after a major operation, shabby and pitiful. The formerly vigorous clump of pampas grass had been trampled down beyond recognition, the ruts left by the backhoe like stitches left behind in the dark, damp soil. The rain had cleared up completely, though the sky was still covered by an unbroken layer of monotonously gray clouds.

When I looked at the pile of stones now stacked up on another piece of ground, I couldn't help but think, We should never have done this. We should have left them the way they were. On the other hand, though, the indisputable fact was that it was something we *had* to do. I couldn't go on listening to that strange sound night after night. But if I hadn't met Menshiki, I never would have had the means to dig up that hole. It was only because he had arranged for the workers, and had paid for the whole thing—I had no clue how much it cost—that the operation had been possible.

But meeting Menshiki and, as a result, having this large-scale excavation take place—was it really all just coincidence? Had it all just fallen together by chance? Weren't things just a little *too* convenient? Hadn't the scenario been all planned out in advance? With all these unanswered doubts, I went with Menshiki to the house. He carried the bell we'd unearthed. He never let go of it the whole time we were walking. As if trying to read, from the touch of it, some kind of message.

As soon as we got back inside Menshiki asked, "Where should I put this bell?"

Where indeed? I had no idea. For the time being, I decided to place it in the studio. Having that weird object under the same roof didn't sit well with me, but that said, I couldn't just toss it outside. It was, no doubt, a valuable Buddhist implement, imbued with a certain soulfulness, so I couldn't just neglect it. I decided to put it in the sort of neutral zone of the studio, which felt like a separate annex. I cleared a space on the long, narrow shelf used for painting materials and placed it there. Next to the large mug used to hold brushes, it even looked like some specialized painting tool.

"What a strange day," Menshiki said.

"I'm sorry you had to use up your entire day for this," I said.

"No, don't apologize. It's been very interesting," Menshiki said. "And this isn't the end of it, I would imagine."

Menshiki had an odd look on his face, as if gazing far away.

"Meaning something else is going to happen?" I asked.

Menshiki chose his words carefully. "I can't explain it well, but I get the feeling that this is only the beginning."

"Only the beginning?"

He held his palms upward. "I'm not sure, of course. Maybe that'll be it, and we'll just be left thinking what a strange day that was. That would probably be the best outcome. But nothing's been resolved. The same questions remain. And these are *very important* questions. That's why I have a hunch that something else is going to happen."

"Something connected to that stone-lined chamber?"

Menshiki gazed outside for a moment before he spoke. "I don't know what's going to happen. It's just a hunch."

And of course it turned out as he'd felt—or predicted—it might. Like he said, that day was only the beginning.

16

A RELATIVELY GOOD DAY

That night I had trouble sleeping. I was anxious whether the bell I'd left in the studio would start ringing in the middle of the night. If it did, then what would I do? Pull the covers up over my head and pretend not to hear anything until the next morning? Or take my flashlight and go to the studio to check it out? And what would I find there?

Unable to decide how I should react, I lay in bed reading. But even after two a.m. the bell hadn't rung. All I heard was the usual drone of insects. As I read my book I checked the clock next to my bed every five minutes. When the digital display read 2:30 I finally breathed a sigh of relief. The bell wouldn't be ringing tonight, I figured. I closed the book, turned out the bedside light, and went to sleep.

The next morning when I woke up before seven, the first thing I did was go check on the bell. It was as I'd left it the night before, on the shelf. Brilliant sunlight illuminated the mountains, and the crows were in the midst of their usual noisy morning routine. In the light of day the bell didn't look ominous at all. It was nothing more than a simple, well-used Buddhist implement from the past.

I went back to the kitchen, brewed coffee in the coffee maker, and drank it. Heated up a scone that had gotten hard in the toaster and ate it. Then went out to the terrace, breathed in the morning air, leaned against the railing, and looked over at Menshiki's house across the valley. The large tinted windows glistened in the morning sun. Probably one of the tasks included in the once-per-week cleaning service was to clean all the windows. The glass was always clean and shiny. I looked over there for a while, but Menshiki didn't appear. We still hadn't yet reached the point where we waved at each other across the valley.

At ten thirty I drove my car to the supermarket to buy groceries. I came back, put them away, and made a simple lunch, a tofu and tomato salad with a rice ball. After I ate, I had some strong green tea. Then I lay down on the sofa and listened to a Schubert string quartet. It was a beautiful piece. According to the liner notes on the jacket, when it was first performed there was quite a backlash among listeners, who felt it was "too radical." I don't know what part was radical, but something about it must have offended the old-fashioned people of that time.

As one side of the record ended I suddenly got very sleepy, so I pulled a blanket over me and slept for while on the sofa. A short but deep sleep, probably about twenty minutes. It felt like I had a few dreams, but when I woke up I couldn't remember them. Those kinds of dreams—the kind where all sorts of unrelated fragments are mixed together. Each fragment has a certain gravitas, but by intertwining they canceled each other out.

I went to the fridge and drank some cold mineral water straight from the bottle and managed to chase away the dregs of sleep that remained like scraps of clouds in the corners of my body. I felt a renewed awareness of the reality that I was living, alone, in the mountains. I lived here by myself. Some sort of fate had brought me to this special place. I remembered the bell. In the weird stone chamber deep in the woods, who in the world had been ringing that bell? And where on earth was that person now?

By the time I had changed into my painting outfit, gone into the studio, and stood looking at Menshiki's portrait, it was past two p.m. Normally I worked in the morning. From eight to noon was the time I could focus best on painting. I liked the sort of domestic quiet at those times. After moving to the mountains I'd grown fond of the brilliant and pure air that the teeming nature around me provided. Working at the same time in the same place each day has always held a special meaning for me. Repetition created a certain rhythm. But this day, partly because I hadn't slept well the night before, I spent the morning without accomplishing anything. Which is why I went to the studio in the afternoon.

I sat on my round work stool, arms folded, and from a distance of some six feet gazed at the painting I'd begun. I'd started by using a thin brush to outline Menshiki's face, then with him modeling before me for fifteen minutes also used black paint to flesh this out. This was just a rough framework at this point, though it gave rise to a productive flow. A flow that had its source in Wataru Menshiki. This was what I needed most.

As I stared hard at this black-and-white framework, an image of a color I should add came to me. The idea sprang up suddenly, all on its own. The color was like that of a tree with its green leaves dully dyed by rain. I mixed several colors together and created what I wanted on my palette. After much trial and error, I finally arrived at what I'd pictured and, without really thinking, added the color to the line drawing I'd done. I had no idea myself what sort of painting would emerge from this, though I did know that that color was going to be a vital grounding for the work. Gradually this painting was beginning to stray far afield from the format of a typical portrait. But even if it doesn't turn out as a portrait, I told myself, that was okay. As long as there was a set flow, all I could do was go with it. What I wanted now was to paint what *I* wanted to paint, the way *I* wanted to paint it (something Menshiki wanted as well). I could think about the next step later on.

I was simply following ideas that sprang up naturally inside me, with no plan or goal. Like a child, not watching his step, chasing some unusual butterfly fluttering across a field. After adding this color to the canvas I set my palette and brush down, again sat down on the stool six feet away, and studied the painting straight on. This is indeed the right color, I decided. The kind of green found in a forest wet by the rain. I nodded several times to myself. This was the kind of feeling toward a painting I hadn't experienced for ages. Yes—this was it. This was the color I'd wanted. Or maybe the color the framework itself had been seeking. With this color as the base, I mixed some peripheral, variant colors, adding variation and depth to the painting.

And as I gazed at the image I'd done, the next color leaped up at me. Orange. Not just a simple orange, but a flaming orange, a color that had both a strong vitality and also a premonition of decay. Like a fruit slowly rotting away. Creating this color was much more of a challenge than the green. It wasn't simply a color, but had to be connected with a specific emotion, an emotion entwined with fate, but in its own way firm, unfluctuating. Making a color like that was no easy task, of course, but in the end I managed. I took out a new brush and ran it over the surface of the canvas. In places I used a knife, too. *Not thinking* was the priority. I tried to turn off my mind, decisively adding this color to the composition. As I painted, details of reality almost totally vanished from my mind. The sound of the bell, that gaping stone tomb, my ex-wife sleeping with some other man, my married girlfriend, the art classes I taught, the future—I thought of none of it. I didn't even think of Menshiki. What I was painting had, of course, started out as his portrait, but by this point my mind was even clear of the thought of his face. Menshiki was nothing more than a starting point. What I was doing was painting for me, for my sake alone.

I don't remember how much time passed. By the time I looked around, the room had gotten dim. The autumn sun had disappeared behind the western mountains, yet I was so engrossed in my work I'd forgotten to switch on a light. I looked at the canvas and saw five colors there already. Color on top of color, and more color on top of that. In one section the colors were subtly mixed, in another part one color overwhelmed another and prevailed over it.

I turned on the ceiling light, sat down again on the stool, and looked at the painting. I knew the painting was incomplete. There was a wild outburst to it, a type of violence that had propelled me forward. A wildness I had not seen in some time. But something was still missing, a core element to control and quell that raw throng, an idea to bring emotion under control. But I needed more time to discover that. That torrent of color had to rest. That would be a job for tomorrow and beyond, when I could return to it under a fresh, bright light. The passage of the right amount of time would show me what was needed. I had to wait for it, like waiting patiently for the phone to ring. And in order to wait that patiently, I had to put my faith in time. I had to believe that time was on my side.

Seated on the stool, I shut my eyes and took a deep breath. In the autumn twilight I could clearly sense something within me changing. As if the structure of my body had unraveled, then was being recombined in a different way. But why *here*, and why *now*? Did meeting the enigmatic Menshiki and taking on his portrait commission result in this sort of internal transformation? Or had uncovering the weird underground chamber, and being led there by the sound of the bell, acted as a stimulus to my spirit? Or was it that I'd merely reached an unrelated turning point in my life? No matter which explanation I went with, there didn't seem to be any basis for it.

"It feels like this is just the beginning," Menshiki had said as we parted. Had I stepped into this *beginning* he'd spoken about? At any rate, I'd been so worked up by the act of painting in a way I hadn't in years, so absorbed in creating, that I'd literally forgotten the passage of time. As I stowed away my materials, my skin had a feverish flush that felt good.

As I straightened up, the bell on the shelf caught my eye. I picked it up and tried ringing it a couple of times. The familiar sound rang out clearly in the studio. The middle-of-the-night sound that made me anxious. Somehow, though, it didn't frighten me anymore. I merely wondered why such an ancient bell could still make such a clear sound. I put the bell back where it had been, switched off the light, and shut the door to the studio. Back in the kitchen, I poured myself a glass of white wine and sipped it as I prepared dinner.

Just before nine p.m. a call came in from Menshiki.

"How were things last night?" he asked. "Did you hear the bell?"

I'd stayed up until two thirty but hadn't heard the bell at all, I told him. It was a very quiet night.

"Glad to hear it. Since then has anything unusual happened around you?"

"Nothing particularly unusual, no," I replied.

"That's good. I hope it continues that way," Menshiki said. A moment later he added, "Would it be all right for me to stop by tomorrow morning? I'd really like to take another good look at the stone chamber if I could. It's a fascinating place."

"Fine by me," I said. "I have no plans for tomorrow morning."

"Then I'll see you around eleven."

"Looking forward to it," I said.

"By the way, was today a good day for you?" Menshiki asked.

Was today a good day for me? It sounded like a sentence that had been translated mechanically by computer software.

"A relatively good day," I replied, puzzled for a moment. "At least, nothing bad happened. The weather was good, overall a pleasant day. What about you, Mr. Menshiki? Was today a good day for you?"

"It was a day when one good thing happened, and so did one not-so-good thing," Menshiki replied. "The scale is still swinging, unable to decide which one was heavier—the good or the bad."

I didn't know how to respond to that, so I stayed silent.

Menshiki went on. "Sadly, I'm not an artist like you. I live in the business world. The information business, in particular. In that world the only information that has exchange value is that which can be quantified. So I have the habit of always quantifying the good and the bad. If the good outweighs the bad even by a little, that means it's a good day, even if something bad happened. At least numerically."

I still had no idea what he was getting at. So I kept my mouth closed.

"By unearthing that underground chamber like we did yesterday, we must have lost something, and gained something. What did we lose, and what did we gain? That's what concerns me."

He seemed to be waiting for me to reply.

"I don't think we gained anything you could quantify," I said after giving it some thought. "At least right now. The only thing we got was that old Buddhist bell. But that probably doesn't have any actual value. It doesn't have any provenance, and isn't some unique antique. On the other hand, what was lost can be clearly quantified. Before long, you'll be getting a bill from the landscaper, I imagine."

Menshiki chuckled. "It's not that expensive. Don't worry about it. What concerns me is that we haven't yet taken from there *the thing we need to take*."

"The thing we need to take? What's that?"

Menshiki cleared his throat. "As I said, I'm no artist. I have a certain amount of intuition, but unfortunately I don't have the means to make it concrete. No matter how keen that intuition might be, I still can't turn it into art. I don't have the talent."

I was silent, waiting for what came next.

"Which is why I've always pursued quantification as a substitute for an artistic, universal representation. In order to live properly, people need a central axis. Don't you think so? In my case, by quantifying intuition, or something like intuition, through a unique system, I've been able to enjoy a degree of worldly success. And according to my intuition . . ." he said, and was silent for a time. A very dense silence. "According to my intuition, we should have got hold of something from digging up that underground chamber."

"Like what?"

He shook his head. Or at least it seemed that way to me from the other end of the phone line. "I still don't know. But I think we have to know. We need to combine our intuition, allow it to pass through your ability to express things in concrete form, and my ability to quantify them."

I still couldn't really grasp what he was getting at. What was this man talking about?

"Let's see each other again tomorrow at eleven," Menshiki said. And quietly hung up.

Soon after he'd hung up, I got a call from my married girlfriend. I was a little surprised. It wasn't often that she'd get in touch at this time of night.

"Can I see you tomorrow around noon?" she asked.

"I'm sorry, but I have an appointment tomorrow. I made it just a little while ago."

"Not another woman, I hope?"

"No. It's with Mr. Menshiki. I'm painting his portrait."

"You're painting his portrait," she repeated. "Then the day after tomorrow?"

"The day after tomorrow's totally free."

"Great. Is early afternoon okay?"

"Of course. But it's Saturday."

"I'll manage it."

"Did something happen?" I asked.

"Why do you ask?" she said.

"You don't often call me at this time of day."

She made a small sound at the back of her throat, as if making a minor adjustment in her breathing. "I'm in my car now, by myself. I'm calling from my cell."

"What are you doing in the car all alone?"

"I just wanted to be by myself in the car, so that's where I am. Housewives sometimes do these things. Is that a problem?"

"No problem. No problem at all."

She sighed, the kind of sigh that condensed a variety of sighs into one. And then she said, "I wish you were here with me. And that we could do it from behind. I don't need any foreplay. I'm so wet you could slip right inside. I want you to pound me, hard and fast."

"Sounds good to me. But a Mini is too small inside to pound you hard like that."

"Don't expect too much."

"Let's figure out a way."

"I want you to knead my breast with your left hand and rub my clit with your right."

"What should my right foot be doing? I could manage to use it to adjust the car stereo. You don't mind a little Tony Bennett?"

"I'm not joking here. I'm totally serious."

"I know. My bad. Serious. Got it," I said. "Tell me, what are you wearing right now?"

"You want to know what clothes I'm wearing?" she asked enticingly.

"I do. My procedure might change depending on what you have on."

Over the phone she gave me a detailed rundown on the clothes she had on. It always surprised me, the variety of clothes mature women wore. Orally, she took these off, one by one.

"So, did that get you hard?" she asked.

"Like a hammer," I said.

"You could pound a nail?"

"You bet."

There are hammers in the world that need to pound in nails, and nails that need to be pounded by hammers. Now who said that? Nietzsche? Or was it Schopenhauer? Or maybe nobody said it.

Over the phone line, we entwined bodies in a way that felt so real. Phone sex was definitely a first for me, with her—or with anyone, for that matter. Her descriptions were so detailed, so arousing, that these imaginary sex acts were, in part, more sensual than what we could do with our actual bodies. Words can sometimes be so direct, sometimes so erotically suggestive. At the end of this exchange, I unexpectedly climaxed. And she seemed to have an orgasm as well.

We said nothing, catching our breath.

"I'll see you Saturday, then," she said after she seemed to have pulled herself together. "I have something to tell you about our Mr. Menshiki, too."

"You got some new information?"

"A bit of new information I gathered through the jungle grapevine. But I'll wait to see you to tell you. While we're probably doing something naughty."

"You going home now?"

"Of course," she said. "I'd better be getting back."

"Drive carefully."

"Right. I need to take care. I'm still sort of shuddering down there."

I stepped into the shower and used soap to clean my penis. I changed into pajamas, threw on a cardigan, and with a glass of cheap white wine in hand went out onto the terrace and gazed off in the direction of Menshiki's house. The lights were still on in his massive, pure-white mansion across the valley. The lights seemed to be on all over the house. What he was doing over there (most likely) all by himself, I had no idea. Seated at the computer, perhaps, engaged once more in quantifying intuition.

"A relatively good day," I said to myself.

And an odd day at that. What kind of day tomorrow would bring I had no clue. Suddenly I remembered the horned owl up in the attic. Was today a good day for it, too? Then I recalled that for horned owls, the day was now only beginning. During the day they slept in dark places. And come night, they set out to the woods in search of prey. That was a question a horned owl should be asked early in the morning. The question of "Was today a good day?"

I went to bed, read a book for a while, then turned off the light at ten thirty and went to sleep. Since I slept, without waking even once, until just before six the next morning, I imagine that the bell didn't ring during the middle of the night.

17

HOW COULD I MISS SOMETHING THAT IMPORTANT?

I never could forget the last words my wife said when I left our home: "Even if we break up like this, can we still be friends? If possible, I mean." At the time (and for a long time after), I couldn't understand what she was trying to say, what she was hoping for. I was confused, as if I'd put some totally tasteless food into my mouth. The best I could say was, "Well, who knows." And those were the last words I said to her face-to-face. Pretty pathetic, as final words go.

Even after we broke up, it felt like my wife and I were still connected by a single living tube. An invisible tube, but one that was still beating slightly, sending something like hot blood traveling back and forth between our two souls. I still had that sort of organic sensation. But before long, that tube would be severed. And if it was bound to be cut sometime, I needed to drain the life from that faint line connecting us. If the life was drained from it, and it shriveled up like a mummy, the pain of it being severed by a sharp knife would be that much more bearable. To do so, I needed to forget about Yuzu, as soon as I could, as much as I could. That's why I never tried to contact her. After I came back from my trip and went to pick up some belongings back at the apartment, I did call her once. I needed to get all my painting materials I'd left behind. That was the only conversation I had with Yuzu after we broke up, and it didn't last long.

We officially dissolved our marriage, and I couldn't contemplate the thought of us remaining friends. We'd shared so many things during our six years of marriage. A lot of time, emotions, words and silence, lots of confusion and lots of decisions, lots of promises and lots of resignation, lots of pleasure, lots of boredom. Naturally each of us must have had inner secrets, but we even managed to find a way to share the sense of having something hidden from the other. With us there was a gravitas of place that only the passage of time can nurture. We did a good job of accommodating our bodies to that sort of gravity, maintaining a delicate balance. We had our own special local rules that we lived by. And there was no way we could get rid of all that history, jettison the gravitational balance and local rules, and live simply as *good friends*.

I understood that very well. That's the conclusion I came to after thinking about it during that lengthy trip. I invariably came to the same conclusion: it was best to keep Yuzu at a distance and break off contact. That made the most sense. And that's what I did.

And for her part Yuzu didn't contact me either. Not a single phone call, not one letter. Even though she was the one who said she wanted to *remain friends*. That hurt far more than I'd expected. Or more precisely, what hurt me was actually *me*, myself. In the midst of that continuing, unsettled silence my feelings, like a heavy pendulum, a razor-sharp blade, made wide swings between one extreme to the other. That arc of emotions left fresh wounds in my skin. And I had only one way of forgetting the pain. And that was, of course, by painting.

Sunlight filtered in silently through the studio window. From time to time a gentle breeze rustled the white curtains. The room had an autumn-morning scent. After coming to live on the mountain I'd grown sensitive to the changes in smells from one season to another. Back when I lived in the city I'd hardly ever noticed those.

I sat on the stool, and gazed for a long time at the portrait of Menshiki I'd begun. This was the way I always began work, reevaluating with new eyes the work I'd done the previous day. Only then could I pick up my brush.

Not bad, I thought. Not bad at all. The colors I'd created completely enveloped the original framework of Menshiki I'd done. The outline of him in black paint was hidden now behind those colors. Though concealed, I could still make it out. I would have to once more bring that outline into relief. Transform a hint into a statement.

There was no guarantee, of course, that the painting would ever be complete. It was still inchoate, something missing. Something that should be there was appealing to the nonvalidity of absence. And that missing element was rapping on the glass window separating presence and absence. I could make out its wordless cry.

Focusing so hard on the painting had made me thirsty, so I went into the kitchen and drank a large glass of orange juice. I relaxed my shoulders, stretched both arms high above my head, took a deep breath, and exhaled. I went back to the studio and sat down on the stool and studied the painting. Refreshed, I focused again. But something was different from before. The angle I was looking at the painting from was clearly not the same as it had been a few minutes before.

I got down from the stool and checked its location. It was in a slightly different spot from when I'd left the studio earlier. The stool had clearly been moved. But how? When I'd gotten down from the stool, I hadn't moved it. That I was sure of. I'd gotten down gingerly in order not to move the stool, and when I'd come back I'd also been careful not to move it when I sat down. I remembered these details because I'm very sensitive about the position and angle I view paintings from. I have a set position and angle that I always use, and like batters who are very particular about their stance in the batter's box, it bothers me to no end if things are off, even by a fraction.

But now the stool was eighteen inches away from where it had been, the angle that much changed. All I could think was that while I'd been in the kitchen drinking orange juice and taking deep breaths, someone had moved the stool. Someone had gone into the studio, sat on the stool to look at the painting, then got down from the stool before I came back, and silently slipped out of the room. And that's when—whether intentionally or it just worked out that way—they moved the stool. But I'd been out of the studio at most five or six minutes. Who in the world would go out of their way to do something like that—and why? Or had the stool moved on its own?

My memory must be messed up. I'd moved the stool but forgotten that I had. That's all I could think. Maybe I was spending too much time alone. The order of events in my memory was getting muddled.

I left the stool in the spot where I'd found it—in other words, a spot twenty inches away from where it had been, and at a different angle. I sat down on it and studied Menshiki's portrait from that position. What I saw was a slightly different painting. It was the same painting, of course, but it looked ever so different. The way the light struck it was not the same as before, and the texture of the paint, too, looked changed. There was something decidedly animated and alive in the painting. But also something still lacking. The direction of that lack, though, wasn't the same as before.

So what was different about it? I brought my focus to bear on the painting. The difference must be speaking to me, trying to tell me something. I had to discover what was being hinted at by the difference. I took a piece of white chalk and marked the position of the three legs of the stool on the floor (location A). Then I moved the stool back twenty inches to the side to its original position (location B), and marked that, too, with chalk. I moved back and forth between the two positions, studying the one painting from the different angles.

Menshiki was still in both paintings, but I noticed that his appearance was strangely different depending on the two angles. It was as if two different personalities coexisted within him. Yet both versions of Menshiki were missing something. That shared lack unified both the A and B versions of Menshiki. I had to discover what it was, as if it were triangulated between position A, position B, and myself. What could that shared absence be? Was it something that had form, or something formless? If the latter, then how was I to give it form?

Not an easy thing to do, now is it, someone said.

I clearly heard that voice. Not a loud voice, but one that carried. Nothing vague about it. Not high, not low. And it sounded like it was right next to my ear.

I involuntarily gulped and, still seated on the stool, slowly gazed around me. I couldn't see anyone else there, of course. The clear morning light filled the floor like pools of water. The window was open, and from far off I could faintly hear the melody played by a garbage truck. It was playing "Annie Laurie" (why the garbage trucks in Odawara played a Scottish folk song was a mystery to me). Beyond that, I couldn't hear a thing.

Maybe I was just imagining things. Maybe it was my own voice I was hearing, a voice welling up from my unconscious. But what I'd heard sounded odd. *Not an easy thing to do, now, is it?* Even unconsciously, I wouldn't talk to myself like that.

I took a deep breath and from my perch on the stool again looked at the painting, focusing my attention on the work. It must have just been my imagination.

Is it not obvious? someone now said. The voice was right beside my ear.

Obvious? I asked myself. What's so obvious?

What you must discover, can you not see, is what it is about Mr. Menshiki that is not present here, someone said. As before, a clear voice. A voice with no echo, like it was recorded in an anechoic chamber. Each sound clear as crystal. And like an embodied concept, it had no natural inflection.

I looked around again. This time I got down from the stool and went to check in the living room. I checked every room, but nobody else was in the house. The only other creature there was the horned owl in the attic. The horned owl, of course, couldn't talk. And the front door was locked.

First the stool moving on its own, and now this weird voice. A voice from heaven? Or my own voice? Or the voice of some anonymous third party? Something was clearly wrong with my mind. Ever since I had started hearing that bell, I'd begun having doubts about whether my brain was functioning normally. With the bell, at least, Menshiki had been there and had heard the same sound, which proved that it wasn't an auditory hallucination. My hearing was working fine. Okay, so what could this mysterious voice be?

I sat back down on the stool and looked at the painting.

What you must discover, can you see, is what Mr. Menshiki has that is not here. Sounded like a riddle. Like a wise bird deep in the forest showing lost children the way home. *What Menshiki has that is not here*—what could that be?

It took a long time. The clock silently, regularly, ticked away the minutes, the pool of light from the small east-facing window silently shifted. Colorful, agile little birds flew onto the branches of a willow, gracefully searched for something, then flew away with a twitter. White clouds, like round slates, floated over the sky in a row. A single silver plane flew toward the sparkling sea. A four-engine propeller SDF plane, on antisubmarine patrol. Keeping their ears and eyes sharp and watchful, making the latent manifest, was their daily job. I listened as the engine drew closer and then flew away.

And finally, a single fact struck me. Literally as plain as day. Why had I forgotten this? What Menshiki had that my portrait of him did not—it was all clear to me now. *His white hair.* That beautiful white hair, as pure white as newly fallen snow. Menshiki without that white hair was unimaginable. How could I miss something that important?

I leaped up from the stool, went to my paint box and gathered up the white paint, picked a brush, and, without thinking, thickly, vigorously spread it on the canvas. I used a knife too, even my fingertip at one point. For fifteen minutes I painted, then stood back from the canvas, sat down on the stool, and checked out my work.

And there, before me, was Menshiki the person. Without a doubt, he was in the painting now. His personality—no matter what that was made up of—was integrated, manifested in the painting. I had no handle on the person named Wataru Menshiki, and knew barely a thing about him. But as an artist I had captured him on canvas, as a synthesized image, as a single, indivisible package. Alive and breathing within the painting. Even the riddles about him were present.

Still, no matter how you looked at it, this was no *portrait.* I'd succeeded (at least I felt I had) in artistically bringing the presence of Wataru Menshiki into relief on canvas. But the goal wasn't to depict his outer appearance. That wasn't the goal at all. That was the big difference between this work and a portrait. What I'd created was, at heart, a painting I'd done *for my own sake.*

I couldn't predict if Menshiki would accept this painting as his *portrait.* It might be light-years away from the kind of painting he'd been expecting. He'd told me to paint it any way I liked, and didn't have any special requests about the style it was done in. But just *possibly,* there might be some element in the painting, something negative, that he himself didn't want to recognize. Not that I could do anything about that now. Whether he liked the painting or not, it was already out of my hands, beyond my will.

Seated on the stool, I kept staring at the portrait for nearly another half hour. *I* had painted it, that much I knew, but the end product outstripped the bounds of any logic or understanding I possessed. How had I painted something like that? I couldn't even recall now. I stared dumbfounded at the painting, my feelings swinging from intimacy to total alienation. But one thing was sure—the colors and form were perfect.

Maybe I was on the verge of finding an exit, I thought. Finally able to pass through the thick wall that stood in my way. But still, things had only begun. I had only just managed to grasp a kind of clue as to how to proceed. I would have to be extremely careful. Telling myself this, I went over to the sink and methodically cleaned the paint from the brushes and painting knife. I washed my hands with oil and soap. Then I went to the kitchen and drank several glasses of water. I was parched.

All well and good, but who had moved the stool in the studio? (It had most definitely been moved.) And who had spoken in my ear in that strange voice? (I had clearly heard the voice.) And who had suggested to me what was missing from the painting? (A suggestion that had clearly been effective.)

In all likelihood it was me—I'd done this myself. I'd unconsciously moved the stool, and given myself the suggestion about how to proceed. In a strange, roundabout way I must have freely intertwined my conscious and subconscious . . . I couldn't think of any other explanation. Though of course this couldn't be the case.

At eleven, I was seated on a straight-backed chair, sipping hot tea and randomly mulling over things, when Menshiki's silver Jaguar drove up. I'd been so wrapped up in painting that the appointment we'd made the day before had completely slipped my mind. Not to mention the auditory illusion, or the voice I must have imagined.

Menshiki? Why is *he* here?

"I'd really like to take a good look at the stone chamber again if I could," Menshiki had said over the phone. As I listened to the now familiar growl of the V8 engine come to a halt, it all came back to me.

18

CURIOSITY DIDN'T JUST KILL THE CAT

I went outside to greet Menshiki. It was the first time I'd done so. I didn't have any particular reason, it just turned out that way. I wanted to get outside, stretch my legs, breathe some fresh air.

Those round slate-shaped clouds still floated in the sky. Lots of these clouds formed far off in the sea, then were slowly carried on the southwest wind, one by one, toward the mountains. Did those beautiful, perfect circles form naturally, not from any practical design? It was a mystery. For a meteorologist maybe it was no mystery at all, but it was for me. Living on this mountaintop, I found myself attracted to all sorts of natural wonders.

Menshiki had on a collared dark-red sweater, light and elegant. And well-worn jeans, so light blue they looked ready to fade away. The jeans were straight leg, made of soft material. To me (and I might be overthinking things) he always seemed to intentionally wear colors that made his white hair stand out. This dark-red sweater went very well with his white hair. His hair always was at just the right length. I had no idea how he kept it that way, but it was never any longer or shorter than it was right now.

"I'd like to go and look into the pit right away, if it's okay with you?" Menshiki asked. "See if anything's changed."

"Okay by me," I said. I hadn't been back, either, in the woods since that day. I wanted to see how things were, too.

"Sorry to bother you, but could you bring me the bell?" Menshiki asked.

I went inside, took down the ancient bell from the studio shelf, and returned.

Menshiki took a large flashlight from the trunk of his Jaguar and hung it from a strap around his neck. He set off for the woods, me tagging along. The woods seemed even a deeper color than before. In this season, every day brought changes to the mountains. Some trees were redder, others dyed a deeper yellow, and some stayed forever green. The combination was truly beautiful. Menshiki, though, didn't seem to care.

"I looked into the background of this land a little," he said while he walked. "Who owned it up till now, what it was used for, that sort of thing."

"Did you find out something?"

Menshiki shook his head. "No, next to nothing. I was expecting that it might have been some religious site, but according to what I found that wasn't the case. I couldn't find out any background as to why there would be a small shrine and stone tumulus here. It was apparently just an ordinary piece of mountainous land. Then it was partly cleared and a house was built. Tomohiko Amada purchased the land along with the house in 1955. Prior to that, a politician had used it as a mountain retreat. You probably haven't heard of him, but he held a Cabinet position back before the war. After the war he essentially lived in retirement. I couldn't trace back who owned the place before that."

"It's a little strange that a politician would go to the trouble of having a vacation home in such a remote place."

"A lot of politicians had retreats here back then. Prince Fumimaro Konoe, prime minister just before World War Two, had a summer retreat just a couple of mountains over from here. It's on the way to Hakone and Atami, and must have been a perfect spot for people to gather for secret talks. It's hard to keep it secret when VIPs get together in Tokyo."

We moved the thick boards that lay covering the hole.

"I'm going to go down inside," Menshiki said. "Would you wait for me?"

"I'll be here," I said.

Menshiki climbed down the mental ladder the contractor had left for us. The ladder creaked a bit with each step. I watched him from above.

When he got to the bottom he took the flashlight from around his neck, switched it on, and carefully checked his surroundings. He rubbed the stone wall, and pounded his fist against it.

"This wall is solidly made, and pretty intricate," Menshiki said, looking up at me. "I don't think it's just some well that's been filled in halfway. If it was a well, it would just be a lot of stones piled up on top of each other. They wouldn't have done such a meticulous job."

"You think it was built for some other purpose?"

Menshiki shook his head, indicating that he had no idea. "Anyway, the wall is made so you can't easily climb out. There aren't any spaces to get a foothold. The hole's less than nine feet deep, but scrambling to the top wouldn't be an easy feat."

"You mean it was built that way, to be hard to climb up?"

Menshiki shook his head again. He didn't know. No clue.

"I'd like you to do something for me," Menshiki said.

"What would that be?"

"Would it be an imposition for you to pull up the ladder, and put the cover on tight so no light gets in?"

That left me speechless.

"It's okay. Don't worry," Menshiki said. "I'd like to experience what it's like to be shut up here, in the bottom of the dark pit, by myself. No plans to turn into a mummy yet, though."

"How long do you plan to be down there?"

"When I want to get out, I'll ring the bell. When you hear the bell, take off the cover and lower down the ladder. If an hour passes without you hearing the bell, come and remove the cover. I don't plan to be down here over an hour. Please don't forget that I'm down here. If you did forget, I really *would* turn into a mummy."

"The mummy hunter becomes a mummy."

Menshiki laughed. "Exactly."

"There's no way I'll forget. But are you sure it's okay, doing that?"

"I'm curious. I'd like to try sitting for a while at the bottom of a dark pit. I'll give you the flashlight. And you can hand me the bell."

He climbed halfway up the ladder and held out the flashlight for me. I took it, and held out the bell. He took the bell and gave it a little shake. It rang out clearly.

"But if—just supposing—I were attacked by vicious hornets on the way and fell unconscious, or even died, then you might never be able to get out of here. You never know what's going to happen in this world."

"Curiosity always involves risk. You can't satisfy your curiosity without accepting some risk. Curiosity didn't just kill the cat."

"I'll be back in an hour," I said.

"Watch out for the hornets," Menshiki said.

"And you take care down there in the dark."

Menshiki didn't reply, and just looked up at me, as if trying to decipher some meaning in my expression as I gazed down at him. There was some kind of vagueness in his eyes, like he was straining to focus on my face, but couldn't. It was an uncertain expression, not at all like him. Then, as if reconsidering things, he sat down on the ground and leaned against the curved stone wall. He looked up and raised his hand a little. *All set*, he was telling me. I yanked up the ladder, pulled the thick boards over so they completely covered up the hole, and set some heavy stones on top of that. A small amount of light might filter in through narrow cracks between the boards, though inside the hole should be dark enough. I thought about calling out to Menshiki from on top of the cover, but thought better of it. What he wanted was solitude and silence.

I went back home, boiled water, and made tea. I sat on the sofa and picked up where I'd left off in a book. I couldn't focus on reading, though, since my ears were alert for the sound of the bell. Every five minutes I checked my watch, and imagined Menshiki, alone in the bottom of that dark hole. What an odd person, I thought. He uses his own money to hire a landscape contractor, who uses heavy equipment to move that pile of stones and open up the entrance to that hole. And now Menshiki was confined there, all by himself. Or rather, deliberately *shut away in there* at his own request.

Whatever, I thought. Whatever necessity or intentions motivated it (assuming there was some kind of necessity or intention), that was Menshiki's problem, and I could leave it all up to him. I was an unthinking actor in someone else's plan. I gave up reading the book, lay down on the sofa, closed my eyes, but of course didn't fall asleep. This was no time to be sleeping.

An hour passed without the bell ringing. Or maybe I'd somehow missed the sound. Either way, it was time to get that cover off. I got up off the sofa, slipped on my shoes, and went outside and into the woods. I was a bit apprehensive that hornets or a wild boar might appear, but neither did. Just some tiny birds, Japanese white-eyes, flitted right past me. I walked through the woods and went around behind the shrine. I removed the heavy stones and took off just one of the boards.

"Mr. Menshiki!" I called out into the gap. But there was no response. What I could see of the hole from the gap was pitch dark, and I couldn't make out his figure there.

"Mr. Menshiki!" I called again. But again no answer. I was getting worried. Maybe he'd vanished, like the mummy that should have been there had vanished. I knew it wasn't logically possible, but still I was seriously concerned.

I quickly removed another board, and then another. Finally the sunlight reached to the bottom of the pit. And I could see Menshiki's outline seated there.

"Mr. Menshiki, are you okay?" I asked, relieved.

He looked up, as if finally coming to, and gave a small nod. He covered his face with his hands, as if the light was too bright.

"I'm fine," he answered quietly. "I'd just like to stay here for a little longer. It'll take time for my eyes to adjust to the light."

"It's been exactly an hour. If you'd like to stay there longer I could put the cover on again."

Menshiki shook his head. "No, this is enough. I'm okay now. I can't stay any longer here. It might be too dangerous."

"Too dangerous?"

"I'll explain later," Menshiki said. He stroked his face hard with both hands, as if rubbing something away from his skin.

Five minutes later he slowly got to his feet and clambered up the metal ladder I'd let down. Once again at ground level he brushed the dirt off his pants and looked up at the sky with narrowed eyes. The blue autumn sky was visible through the tree branches. For a long time he gazed lovingly at the sky. We lined up the boards and covered the hole as before, so no one would accidentally fall into it. Then we put the heavy stones on top. I memorized the position of the stones, so I'd know if anyone moved them. The ladder we left inside the pit.

"I didn't hear the bell," I said as we walked along.

Menshiki shook his head. "I didn't shake it."

That's all he said, so I didn't ask anything more.

We walked out of the woods and headed home. Menshiki took the lead as we walked and I followed behind. Without a word he put the flashlight back in the trunk of the Jaguar. We then sat down in the living room and drank hot coffee. Menshiki still hadn't said a thing. He seemed preoccupied. Not that he wore a serious expression or anything, but his mind was clearly in a place far away. A place, no doubt, where only he was allowed to be. I didn't bother him, and let him be. Just like Doctor Watson used to do with Sherlock Holmes.

During this time I mentally went over my schedule. That evening I had to drive down the mountain to teach my classes at the local arts-and-culture center near Odawara Station. I'd look over paintings students had done and give them advice. This was the day when I had back-to-back children's and adults' classes. This was just about the only opportunity I had to see and speak with living people. Without those classes I'd probably live like a hermit up here in the mountains, and if I went on living all alone, I'd likely start to lose my mind, just as Masahiko said.

Which is why I should have been thankful for the chance to come in contact with the real world. But truth be told, I found it hard to feel that way. The people I met in the classroom were less living beings than mere shadows crossing my path. I smiled at each one of them, called them by name, and critiqued their paintings. No, critique isn't the right term. I just praised them. I'd find some good component to each painting—if there wasn't, I'd make up something—and praise them for a job well done.

So I had a pretty good reputation as a teacher. According to the owner of the school, many of the students liked me. I hadn't expected that. I'd never once thought I was suited to teaching. But I didn't really care. It was all the same to me whether people liked me or didn't. I just wanted things to go smoothly in the classroom, without any hitches, so I could repay Masahiko for his kindness.

I'm not saying every person felt like a shadow to me. I'd started seeing two of my students. And after starting a sexual relationship with me, the two women both dropped out of my art class. They must have found it awkward. And I did feel some responsibility for that.

Tomorrow afternoon, I'd see the second girlfriend, the older married woman. We'd hold each other in bed and make love. So she was not just a passing shadow, but an actual presence with a three-dimensional body. Or perhaps a passing shadow with a three-dimensional body. I couldn't decide which.

Menshiki called my name, and I came back to the present with a start. I'd been completely lost in thought, too.

"About the portrait," Menshiki said.

I looked at him. His usual cool expression was back on his face. A handsome face, always calm and thoughtful, the kind that relaxed others.

"If you need me to pose for you, I wouldn't mind doing it now," he said. "Continue from where we left off, maybe? I'm always ready."

I looked at him for a while. *Pose?* It finally dawned on me—he was talking about the portrait. I looked down, took a sip of the coffee, which had cooled down, and after gathering my thoughts, put the cup back on the saucer. A small, dry clatter reached my ears. I looked up, faced Menshiki, and spoke.

"I'm very sorry, but today I have to go teach at the arts-and-culture center."

"Oh, that's right," Menshiki said. He glanced at his watch. "I'd totally forgotten. You teach art at the school near Odawara Station, don't you. Do you need to leave soon?"

"I'm okay, I still have time," I said. "And there's something I need to talk with you about."

"And what would that be?"

"Truthfully, the painting is already finished. In a sense."

Menshiki frowned ever so slightly. He looked straight at me, as if checking out something deep inside my eyes.

"By painting, you mean my portrait?"

"Yes," I said.

"That's wonderful," Menshiki said. A slight smile came to his face. "Really wonderful. But what did you mean by 'in a sense'?"

"It's hard to explain. I've never been good at explaining things."

"Take your time and tell it to me the way you'd like to," Menshiki said. "I'll sit here and listen."

I brought the fingers of both of my hands together on my lap.

Silence descended as I chose my words, the kind of silence that makes you hear the passing of time. Time passed very slowly on top of the mountain.

"I got the commission from you," I said, "and did the painting with you as model. But to tell the truth, it's not a *portrait*, no matter how you look at it. All I can say is it's a *work done with you as model*. I can't say how much value it has, as an artwork, or as a commodity. All I know for sure is it's *a work I had to paint*. Beyond that I'm clueless. Truthfully, I'm pretty confused. Until things become clearer to me it might be best to keep the painting here and not give it to you. I'd like to return the advance you paid. And I am extremely sorry for having used so much of your valuable time."

"In what way is it—not a portrait?" Menshiki asked, choosing his words deliberately.

"Up till now I've made my living as a professional portrait painter. Essentially in portraits you paint the subject the way he wishes to be portrayed. The subject is the client, and if he doesn't like the finished work it's entirely possible he might tell you, 'I'm not going to pay money for this.' So I try not to depict any negative aspects of the person. I pick only the good aspects, emphasize those, and try to make the subject appear in as good a light as I can. In that sense, in most cases it's hard to call portraits works of art. Someone like Rembrandt being the exception, of course. But in this case, I didn't think about you as I painted, but only about myself. To put it another way, I prioritized the ego of the artist—myself—over you, the subject."

"Not a problem," Menshiki said, smiling. "I'm actually happy to hear it. I told you I didn't have any requests, and wanted you to paint it any way you liked."

"I know. I remember it well. What I'm concerned about is less how the painting turned out and more about *what I painted there.* I put my own desires first, so much that I might have painted something I shouldn't have. That's what I'm worried about."

Menshiki observed my face for a time, and then spoke. "You might have painted something inside me that you shouldn't have. And you're worried about that. Do I have that right?"

"That's it," I said. "Since all I thought of was myself, I loosened the restraints that should have been in place."

And maybe extracted something from inside you that I shouldn't have, I was about to say, but thought better of it. I kept those words inside.

Menshiki mulled over what I'd said.

"Interesting," he finally said, sounding like he meant it. "A very intriguing way of looking at things."

I was silent.

"I think my self-restraint is pretty strong," Menshiki said. "I have a lot of self-control, I mean."

"I know," I said.

Menshiki lightly pressed his temple with his fingers, and smiled. "So that painting is finished, you're saying? That *portrait* of me?"

I nodded. "I feel it's finished."

"That's wonderful," Menshiki said. "Can you show me the painting? After I've actually seen it, the two of us can discuss how to proceed. Does that sound all right?"

"Of course," I said.

I led Menshiki to the studio. He stood about six feet in front of the easel, arms folded, and stared at the painting. There was the portrait that he'd posed for. No, less a portrait than what you might call an *image* that formed when a mass of paint hit the canvas. The white hair was a violent burst of pure white. At first glance it didn't look like a face. What should be found in a face was hidden behind a mass of color. Yet beyond any doubt, the reality of Menshiki the person was present. Or at least I thought so.

He stood there, unmoving, gazing at the painting for the longest time. Literally not moving a muscle. I couldn't even tell if he was breathing or not. I stood a little ways away by the window, observing him. I wondered how much time passed. It seemed almost forever. As he observed the painting, his face was totally devoid of expression. His eyes were glazed, flat, clouded, like a still puddle reflecting a cloudy sky. The eyes of someone who wanted to keep others at a distance. I couldn't guess what he might be thinking, deep in his heart.

Then, like when a magician claps his hands to bring a person out of a hypnotic spell, he stood up straight and trembled slightly. His expression returned, as did the light in his eyes. He slowly walked over to me, held out his right hand, and rested it on my shoulder.

"Amazing," he said. "Truly outstanding. I don't know what to say. This is exactly the painting I was hoping for."

I could tell from his eyes that he was saying how he honestly felt. He was truly impressed, and moved, by my painting.

"The painting expresses me perfectly," Menshiki said. "This is a portrait in the real sense of the word. You didn't make any mistake. You did exactly what you should have."

His hand was still resting on my shoulder. It was just resting there, yet I could feel a special power radiating from it.

"But what did you do to discover this painting?" Menshiki asked me.

"Discover?"

"It was you who did this painting, of course. You created it through your own power. But you also discovered it. You found this image buried within you and drew it out. You *unearthed* it, in a way. Don't you think so?"

I suppose so, I thought. Of course I moved my hands, and followed my will in painting it. *I* was the one who chose the paints, the one who used brushes, knives, and fingers to paint the colors onto the canvas. But looked at from a different angle, maybe all I'd done was use Menshiki as a catalyst to locate something buried inside me and dig it up. Just like the heavy equipment that moved aside the rock mound behind the little shrine, lifted off the heavy lattice cover, and unearthed that odd stone-lined chamber. I couldn't help but see an affinity between these two similar operations that took place in tandem. Everything that had happened had started with Menshiki's appearance, and the ringing of the bell in the middle of the night.

Menshiki said, "It's like an earthquake deep under the sea. In an unseen world, a place where light doesn't reach, in the realm of the unconscious. In other words, a major transformation is taking place. It reaches the surface, where it sets off a series of reactions and eventually takes form where we can see it with our own eyes. I'm no artist, but I can grasp the basic idea behind that process. Outstanding ideas in the business world, too, emerge through a similar series of stages. The best ideas are thoughts that appear, unbidden, from out of the dark."

Menshiki once more stood before the painting and stepped closer to examine the surface. Like someone reading a detailed map, he studiously checked out each and every detail. He stepped back nine feet, and with narrowed eyes gazed at the work as a whole. His face wore an expression close to ecstasy. He reminded me of a carnivorous raptor about to latch onto its prey. But what was the prey? Was it my painting, or me myself? Or something else? I had no idea. But soon, like mist hovering over the surface of a river at dawn, that strange expression like ecstasy faded, then vanished. To be filled in by his usual affable, thoughtful expression.

He said, "Generally I avoid saying anything that smacks of self-praise, but honestly I feel kind of proud to know that I didn't misjudge things. I have no artistic talent myself, and have nothing to do with creating original works, but I do know outstanding art when I see it. At least I flatter myself that I do."

Somehow I couldn't easily accept what Menshiki was telling me, or feel happy to hear it. It may have been those sharp, raptor-like eyes that bothered me.

"So you like the painting?" I asked again to make sure.

"That goes without saying. This is truly a valuable painting. I'm overjoyed that you came up with such a powerful work using me as the model, as the motif. And of course it goes without saying that as the one who commissioned the painting, I'll take it. Assuming that's all right with you?"

"Yes. It's just that I—"

Menshiki held up a hand to cut me off. "So, if you don't mind, I'd like to invite you to my house to celebrate its completion. Would that be all right? It will be, like the old expression, a cozy little get-together. As long as this isn't any trouble for you, that is."

"None at all, but you really don't need to do this. You've done so much already—"

"But I'd really like to. I'd like the two of us to celebrate the completion of the painting. So won't you join me for dinner at my place? Nothing fancy, just a simple little dinner, just the two of us. Apart from the cook and bartender, of course."

"Cook and bartender?"

"There's a French restaurant I like near Hayakawa harbor. I'll have the cook and bartender over on their regular day off. He's a great chef. He uses the freshest fish and comes up with some very original recipes. Actually, for quite some time I've been wanting to invite you over, and have been making preparations. But with the painting done, the timing couldn't be better."

It was hard to keep the surprise from showing on my face. I had no idea how much it would cost to arrange something like that, but for Menshiki, it must be a regular occurrence. Or at least something he was accustomed to arranging . . .

Menshiki said, "How would four days from now be? Tuesday evening. If that's good for you, I'll set it up."

"I don't have any particular plans then," I said.

"Tuesday it is, then," he said. "Also, could I take the painting home with me now? I'd like to have it nicely framed and hanging on the wall by the time you come over, if that's possible."

"Mr. Menshiki, do you really see your face within this painting?" I asked again.

"Of course I do," Menshiki said, giving me a wondering look. "Of course I can see my face in the painting. Very distinctly. What else is depicted here?"

"I see," I said. What else could I say? "You're the one who commissioned the work, so if you like the painting, it's already yours. Please do what you'd like with it. The thing is, the paint isn't dry yet, so be extremely careful when you carry it. And I think it's better to wait a little longer before framing it. Best to let it dry for about two weeks before doing that."

"I understand. I'll handle it carefully. And I'll wait to have it framed."

At the front door he held out his hand and we shook hands for the first time in a while. A satisfied smile rose to his face.

"I'll see you Tuesday, then. I'll send a car over around six."

"By the way, you aren't inviting the mummy?" I asked Menshiki. I don't know why I said that. The mummy just suddenly popped into my head, and I couldn't help myself.

Menshiki looked at me searchingly. "Mummy? What do you mean?"

"The mummy that should have been in that chamber. The one that must have been ringing the bell every night, and disappeared, leaving the bell behind. The monk who practiced austerity to the point of being mummified. I was thinking maybe he wanted to be invited to your place. Like the statue of the Commendatore in *Don Giovanni*."

Menshiki thought about this, and a cheerful smile came over him as if he finally got it. "I see! Just like Don Giovanni invited the statue of the Commendatore, you're wondering how would it be if I invited the mummy to our dinner?"

"Exactly. It might be karma, too."

"Sounds good. Fine with me. It's a celebration, after all. If the mummy would care to join us, I will be happy to issue the invitation. Sounds like we'll have a pleasant evening. But what should we have for dessert?" He smiled happily. "The problem is, we can't see him. Makes it hard to invite him."

"Indeed," I said. "But the visible is not the only reality. Wouldn't you agree?"

Menshiki gingerly carried the painting outside. He took an old blanket from the trunk, laid it on the passenger seat, and placed the painting down on top so as not to smear the paint. Then he used some thin rope and two cardboard boxes to secure the painting so it wouldn't move around. It was all cleverly done. He always seemed to carry around a variety of tools and things in his trunk.

"Yes, what you said may be exactly right," Menshiki suddenly murmured as he was leaving. He rested both hands on the leather-covered steering wheel and looked straight up at me.

"What I said?"

"That sometimes in life we can't grasp the boundary between reality and unreality. That boundary always seems to be shifting. As if the border between countries shifts from one day to the next depending on their mood. We need to pay close attention to that movement, otherwise we won't know which side we're on. That's what I meant when I said it might be dangerous for me to remain inside that pit any longer."

I didn't know how to respond, and Menshiki didn't go any further. He waved to me out the window, revving the V8 engine so it rumbled pleasantly, and he and the still-not-dry portrait vanished from sight.

19

CAN YOU SEE ANYTHING BEHIND ME?

At one p.m. on Saturday afternoon my girlfriend drove over in her red Mini. I went out to greet her when she arrived. She had on green sunglasses and a light-gray jacket over a simple beige dress.

"You want to do it in the car? Or do you prefer the bed?" I asked.

"Don't be silly," she laughed.

"Doing it in the car doesn't sound so bad. Figuring out how to manage it in a cramped space."

"Someday soon."

We sat in the living room and drank tea. I told her about how I'd just managed to finish the portrait (or portrait-like painting) of Menshiki I'd been struggling with. And how it was totally different from any of the portraits I'd done professionally. Her interest seemed piqued.

"Can I see the painting?"

I shook my head. "You're a day late. I wanted to get your opinion on it, but Mr. Menshiki already took it home. The paint wasn't completely dry yet, but it seemed like he wanted to take possession as soon as he could. He seemed worried somebody else might take it away."

"So he liked it."

"He said he did, and I don't have any reason to doubt him."

"The painting's successfully completed, and the person who commissioned it likes it. So all's well that ends well?"

"I guess," I said. "And I'm happy with it. I've never done that type of painting before, and I think it's opened up some new possibilities."

"A new style of portrait?"

"I'm not sure. This time, I arrived at that method by using Mr. Menshiki as my model. But maybe it's just coincidence that it was the framework of a portrait that proved to be the entranceway to that. I don't know if the same method would be valid if I tried it again. This might have been a special case. Having Mr. Menshiki as my model may have exerted a special power. But the important thing is I'm dying to do some serious painting now."

"Well, congratulations on finishing the painting."

"Thanks," I said. "I'll also be receiving a fairly hefty payment."

"The munificent Mr. Menshiki," she said.

"And he invited me over to his place to celebrate the painting. Tuesday evening, we'll have dinner together."

I told her about the dinner that was planned. Nothing about inviting the mummy, though. A dinner for two, with a professional cook and bartender.

"So you'll finally set foot in that chalk-white mansion, won't you," she said, sounding impressed. "The mysterious mansion of the man of mystery. I'm so curious. Make sure to keep your eyes open, and observe what kind of place it is."

"As much as my eyes can take in."

"And remember exactly what sort of food was served."

"Will do," I said. "You know, the other day you mentioned getting new information about Mr. Menshiki."

"That's right. Through the jungle grapevine."

"What kind of information?"

She looked a little confused. She picked up her cup and took a sip of tea. "Let's talk about that later," she said. "There's something I'd like to do before that."

"Something you'd like to do?"

"Something I hesitate to put into words."

We moved from the living room into the bedroom. Like always.

During the six years I lived my first married life with Yuzu (my former marriage, is what it might best be called), I never had a sexual relationship with any other women, not even once. Not that the opportunity didn't present itself, but during that period I was much more interested in living a peaceful life with my wife than seeking greener pastures elsewhere. And as far as sex was concerned, regular lovemaking with Yuzu more than satisfied me.

But then at a certain point, out of the blue (to me at least) she announced that she couldn't live with me any longer. An unshakable conclusion, no room for negotiation or compromise. I was shaken, with no clue how to respond. Left speechless. But I did understand one thing: *I can't stay here anymore.*

So I threw some belongings into my old Peugeot 205 and set off on an aimless journey. For a month and a half at the beginning of spring I wandered through northern Japan—Tohoku and Hokkaido—where it was still cold. Until my car finally broke down for good. Every night on the trip I remembered Yuzu's body. Every single detail. How she'd react when I touched certain spots, what sort of cry she made. I didn't want to remember this, but I couldn't help it. Occasionally, as I traced those memories, I'd ejaculate. Another thing I didn't particularly want to do.

But during that long trip I only slept with one actual woman. A truly weird turn of events ended with me spending the night with a young woman I'd never seen before. Not that it was something I was looking for.

This was in a small town in Miyagi Prefecture along the coast. As I recall, it was near the border with Iwate, but I was on the move then and had passed through a number of towns that all blurred into one. My mind wasn't in a place where I could remember their names. I do recall that it had a big fishing harbor. Though most of the towns in that region had harbors. And I remember how everywhere I went the smell of diesel oil and fish tagged along.

On the outskirts of town, near the highway, was a chain restaurant, and I was eating dinner there by myself. It was about eight p.m. Shrimp curry and house salad. There were only a handful of other customers. I was in a table next to the window, reading a paperback book while I ate, when a young woman abruptly sat down across from me. No hesitation, no asking permission, without a word she sat down onto the vinyl-covered seat like it was the most natural thing in the world.

I looked up, surprised. Of course I didn't recognize her. It was the first time I'd ever laid eyes on her. It was all so sudden I didn't know what to think. There were any number of unoccupied tables, and no reason for her to share mine. Maybe that's how they did things in this town? I put down my fork, wiped my mouth with the paper napkin, and gazed at her, bewildered.

"Pretend like you know me," the girl said. "Like we were meeting up here." Her voice was, if anything, a bit husky. Or maybe tension made a voice temporarily hoarse. I detected a slight Tohoku accent.

I put the bookmark in my book and shut it. The woman seemed to be in her mid-twenties. She had on a white blouse with a round collar and a navy-blue cardigan. Neither one very expensive looking, or very fashionable. Ordinary clothes, like what you'd wear when you went shopping at the local supermarket. Her hair was black, cut short, with bangs falling to her forehead. She had on hardly any makeup. On her lap was a black cloth shoulder bag.

There was nothing special about her face. Pleasant enough features, but they didn't leave a strong impression. The kind of face that, if you saw her on the street, you'd forget as soon as you passed by. Her thin lips were taut, and she was breathing through her nose. Her breathing was a bit ragged, the nostrils expanding a tiny bit, then contracting. A small nose, out of balance with the size of her mouth. As if the person molding her out of clay halfway through and decided to scrape some off the nose.

"You understand? Pretend like you know me," she repeated. "Don't look so surprised."

"Okay," I answered, not knowing what was going on.

"Just keep on eating," she said. "And pretend to be talking to me like we know each other?"

"What about?"

"You're from Tokyo?"

I nodded. I picked up my fork and ate a mini tomato. Then drank some water.

"I could tell by the way you talk," the woman said. "But why are you here?"

"Just passing through," I said.

A waitress in a ginger-colored uniform came over, lugging a thick menu. The waitress had mammoth breasts, the buttons on her uniform ready to burst. The girl across from me didn't take the menu. She didn't even glance at the waitress. Staring straight at me she just said, "Coffee and cheesecake." Like she was giving me the order. The waitress nodded without a word. Still lugging the menu, she left.

"Are you in some kind of trouble?" I asked.

She didn't respond. She just stared at me, like she was evaluating my face.

"Can you see anything behind me? Is anybody there?" the woman asked.

I looked behind her. Just ordinary people eating in an ordinary way. No new customers had come in.

"Nothing. Nobody's there," I said.

"Keep an eye out for a little longer," she said. "Tell me if you see anything. Keep on talking like nothing's happened."

Our table looked out on the parking lot. I could see my decrepit, dusty little old Peugeot parked there. There were two other cars. A small silver compact, and a tall black minivan. The minivan looked new. They'd both been parked there for a while. No new cars had driven in. The woman must have walked. Or else someone gave her a ride here.

"Just passing through?" the woman asked.

"That's right."

"Are you on a trip?"

"You could say that," I said.

"What kind of book are you reading?"

I showed her the book. It was Ogai Mori's *Abe Ichizoku,* a samurai tale written over a hundred years before.

"*Abe Ichizoku,*" she intoned. She handed the book back. "How come you're reading such an old book?"

"It was in the lounge of a youth hostel I stayed at in Aomori not long ago. I leafed through it, thought it was interesting, and took it with me. In exchange, I left a couple of books I'd finished reading."

"I've never read *Abe Ichizoku.* Is it interesting?"

I'd read it once and was rereading it. The story was pretty interesting, but I couldn't figure out why, and from what sort of stance, Ogai had written it, or felt compelled to write that kind of tale. But explaining that would take too long. This wasn't a book club. And this woman was just bringing up random topics so our conversation seemed natural (or at least so that it looked that way to the people around us).

"It's worth reading," I said.

"So what sort of work?" she asked.

"You mean the novel?"

She frowned. "No. I don't care about that. I mean *you*. What kind of work do *you* do for a living?"

"I paint pictures," I said.

"You're an artist," she said.

"You could say that."

"What sort of paintings?"

"Portraits," I said.

"By portraits you mean those paintings you see hanging on the wall in the president's office in companies? The ones where big shots look all full of themselves?"

"That's right."

"That's your specialty?"

I nodded.

She said no more about painting. She might have lost interest. Most people in the world, unless they're the ones being painted, have zero interest in portraits.

Right then the automatic door at the entrance slid open and a tall, middle-aged man came in. He had on a black leather jacket and a black golf cap with a golf company's logo on it. He stood at the entrance, gave the whole diner a once-over, chose a table two over from ours, and sat down, facing us. He took off his cap, finger-combed his hair a couple of times, and carefully studied the menu the busty waitress brought over. His hair was cut short, and had some white mixed in. He was thin, with dark, suntanned skin. His forehead was lined with a series of deep, wavy wrinkles.

"A man just came in," I told her.

"What does he look like?"

I gave her a quick description.

"Can you draw him?" she asked.

"You mean a likeness?"

"Yes. You're an artist, aren't you?"

I took a memo pad from my pocket, and, using a mechanical pencil, quickly sketched the man. Even added some shading. While I drew it I didn't need to glance over at him. I have the ability to grasp the features of a person quickly and etch them into my memory. I passed the drawing across the table to her. She took it, and stared at it, eyes narrowed, for a long time, like a bank teller examining dubious handwriting on a check. Finally she laid the memo page on the table.

"You're really good at drawing," she said, looking at me. She sounded genuinely impressed.

"It's what I do," I said. "So, do you know this man?"

She didn't reply, just shook her head. Her lips tight, her expression unchanged. She folded the drawing up twice, and stuffed it away in her shoulder bag. I couldn't figure out why she would keep something like that. She should have just crumpled it up and thrown it away.

"I don't know him," she said.

"But you're being followed by him. Is that what's going on?"

She didn't reply.

The same waitress brought over her coffee and cheesecake. The woman kept quiet until the waitress had left. She sliced a bite of the cheesecake with her fork, then pushed it from side to side on the plate. Like a hockey player practicing on the ice before a game. She finally put the piece in her mouth and, expressionless, chewed slowly. Once she finished it she poured a hint of cream into her coffee and took a sip. She nudged the plate with the cheesecake to one side, as if it was no longer needed.

A white SUV had joined the cars in the parking lot. A stocky, tall car, with solid-looking tires. Apparently driven by the man who'd just come in. He'd parked the car facing in, not backing into the spot as was more usual. On the cover of the spare tire attached to the luggage compartment were the words SUBARU FORESTER. I finished my shrimp curry. The waitress came over to take away the plate, and I ordered coffee.

"Have you been traveling for a long time?" the woman asked.

"It'll be a long trip," I said.

"Is it fun to travel?"

I'm not traveling for fun, is how I should have answered. But that would have made things long and complicated.

"Sort of," I answered.

She stared at me, like studying some rare animal. "You sure are a man of few words."

It depends on who I'm talking with, is how I should have answered. But going there would have also made things long and complicated.

The coffee came, and I drank some. It tasted like coffee, but it wasn't all that good. But at least it was coffee, and piping hot. After this no other customers came in. The salt-and-pepper-haired man in the leather jacket, in a voice that carried, ordered a Salisbury steak and rice.

A string-section version of "Fool on the Hill" came over the sound system. Did John Lennon write that song, or Paul McCartney? I couldn't remember. Probably Lennon. This kind of random thought rattled around in my head. I had no idea what else I should think about.

"Did you come here by car?"

"Um."

"What kind of car?"

"A red Peugeot."

"What district is the license plate?"

"Shinagawa," I said.

Hearing that, she frowned, as if she had a bad memory associated with a red Peugeot with Shinagawa plates. She tugged down the sleeves of her cardigan and checked that the buttons on her white shirt were done all the way up. She wiped her mouth with a paper napkin. "Let's go," she suddenly said.

She drank a half glass of water and stood up. She left her coffee, only one sip taken, and cheesecake, only one bite taken, on the tabletop. Like the remains after a terrible natural disaster.

Not knowing where we were going, I stood up after her, took the bill from the table, and paid at the register. The woman's order was included, but she didn't say a word of thanks, or make a move to pay her share.

As we left, the man with the salt-and-pepper hair was eating his Salisbury steak, seemingly bored by it all. He looked up and glanced in our direction, but that was all. He looked down at his plate again and went on eating, with knife and fork, his face expressionless. The woman didn't look at him at all.

As we passed by the white Subaru Forester, a bumper sticker on it with a picture of a fish caught my eye. Probably a marlin. Of course, I had no idea why he had to have a sticker with a marlin on it on his car. Maybe he worked in the fishing industry, or was a fisherman.

The woman didn't tell me where we were going. She sat in the passenger seat and gave me clipped directions. She seemed to know the roads. She must have been from that town, or else had lived there a long time. I drove the Peugeot where she told me to go. We drove along the highway for a while out of town and came to a love hotel with a gaudy neon sign. I parked there as directed and cut the engine.

"I'm staying here tonight," she announced. "I can't go home. Come with me."

"But I'm staying in another place tonight," I said. "I've already checked in and put my luggage in the room."

"Where?"

I gave the name of a small business hotel near the railway station.

"This place is a lot better than that cheap place," she said. "Your room there must be shabby and no bigger than a closet."

Right she was. A shabby room the size of a closet was an apt description.

"And they don't like women checking in by themselves here. They're on guard against prostitutes. So come with me."

Well, at least she's not a hooker, I thought.

At the front desk I paid in advance for one night (again, no word of thanks from her) and got the key. Once in the room she filled up the bathtub, switched on the TV, and adjusted the lighting. The bathtub was spacious. It was definitely a lot more comfortable than the business hotel. She seemed to have come here—or someplace like it—many times before. She sat on the bed and took off her cardigan. Then removed her white blouse and her wraparound skirt. And took off her stockings. She had on very simple white panties. They weren't particularly new. The kind your ordinary housewife would wear when she went shopping at the neighborhood supermarket. She neatly reached behind her and unhooked her bra, folded it, and set it next to a pillow. Her breasts weren't particularly big, or particularly small.

"Come over here," she said to me. "Since we're in a place like this, let's have sex."

That was the one and only sexual experience of my whole long trip (or wanderings). Wilder sex than I'd expected. She had four orgasms in total, every single one genuine, if you can believe it. I came twice, but oddly enough didn't feel much pleasure. It was like while I was doing it with her, my mind was elsewhere.

"I'm thinking maybe it's been a long time since you had sex?" she asked me.

"Several months," I answered honestly.

"I can tell," she said. "But how come? You can't be that unpopular with women."

"There's a whole bunch of reasons."

"You poor thing," she said, and gently stroked my neck. "You poor thing."

You poor thing, I thought, repeating the words to myself. Put that way I really did feel like I was a person to be pitied. In an unknown town, in some random place, with no clue what was going on, naked in bed with a woman whose name I didn't even know.

We had a few beers from the fridge, in between rounds. It was about one a.m. when we finally slept. When I woke up the next morning she was nowhere to be seen. She left no note or anything behind. I was alone in the overly huge bed. My watch showed seven thirty, and it was light outside. I opened the curtain and saw the highway running alongside the ocean. Huge refrigerated trucks transporting fresh fish roared up and down the road. The world is full of lonely things, but not many could be lonelier than waking up alone in the morning in a love hotel.

A thought suddenly struck me, and I hurriedly checked my wallet in my pants pocket. Everything was still there. Cash, credit cards, ATM card, license, everything. I breathed a sigh of relief. If my wallet had been gone I would have freaked. These sorts of things *did* happen, and I needed to be careful.

She must have left early in the morning, while I was sound asleep. But how had she gotten back to town (or back to where she lived)? Had she walked, or called a taxi? Not that it made any difference to me. Pointless speculation.

I returned the room key at the front desk, paid for the beers we'd drunk, and drove the Peugeot back to town. I needed to get the luggage I'd left at the business hotel near the station, and pay for the one night. Along the way into town I passed by the chain restaurant I'd gone to the night before. I stopped and ate breakfast there. I was starving, and was dying for some coffee. Just before I pulled into the parking lot I saw the white Subaru Forester. Parked nose in, with that marlin bumper sticker. The same Subaru Forester from the night before. The only difference was where it was parked. Which made sense. No one spent the whole night in a place like that.

I went inside the restaurant. As before, hardly any customers. Like I expected, the same man from last night was at a table, eating breakfast. The same table as the night before, wearing the same black leather jacket. Like last night, the same black golf cap with the Yonex logo resting on the tabletop. The only difference from last night was the folded morning newspaper on top of the table. A plate of toast and scrambled eggs was in front of him. It was probably just served, steam still rising from the coffee. As I passed him, the man glanced up and looked me in the face. His eyes were even sharper and colder than the night before. There was a sense of criticism in them, or at least that's what it felt like.

I know exactly where you've been and what you've been up to, he seemed to be telling me.

That's the whole story of what happened to me in that small town along the seacoast in Miyagi. Even now I have no idea what that woman, with her petite nose and perfect teeth, wanted from me. And it was never clear to me if that middle-aged guy with the white Subaru Forester was really following her, or if she was running from him. Whatever was going on, I happened to be there, and through an odd series of events spent the night in a garish love hotel with a woman I'd just met, and had a one-night stand, the wildest sex I'd ever had. But I still can't recall the name of the town.

"Could I get a glass of water?" my married girlfriend said. She'd just woken up from a short postcoital nap.

It was early afternoon, and we were in bed. While she slept I stared at the ceiling and recalled the events in that small fishing town. It was only a half a year before, but it seemed like events from the distant past.

I went to the kitchen, poured mineral water into a large glass, and returned to bed. She drank down half of it in a single gulp.

"Now, about Mr. Menshiki," she said, placing the glass on the nightstand.

"Mr. Menshiki?"

"The new information I got about Mr. Menshiki," she said. "What I said I'd tell you later?"

"Your jungle grapevine."

"Right," she said, and drank more water. "According to my sources, your friend Mr. Menshiki spent quite a long time in Tokyo Prison."

I sat up and looked at her. "Tokyo Prison?"

"Yeah, the one in Kosuge."

"For what crime?"

"I don't know the details, but I imagine it had something to do with money. Tax evasion, money laundering, insider trading—something of that sort, or perhaps all of them. He was imprisoned six or seven years ago. Did Mr. Menshiki tell you what kind of work he does?"

"He said it was dealing with tech, and information," I said. "He started a company, and some years ago sold the stock for a high price. He's living now on the capital gains."

"'Dealing with information' is a pretty vague way of describing it. Nowadays there're hardly any jobs not connected with information."

"Who told you about him being in prison?"

"A friend of mine whose husband's in finance. But I don't know how much of that information is true. Someone heard it from someone, and passed it along to someone else. You know how it is. But from what I can make of it, it doesn't seem groundless."

“If he was in Tokyo Prison that means that he was put there by the Tokyo district prosecutor.”

“In the end they found him not guilty, is what I heard,” she said. “Still, he was in detention for a long time, and had to endure a very intense investigation. They extended his incarceration a number of times, and wouldn’t grant bail.”

“But he won in court.”

“That’s right. He was prosecuted, but wasn’t given a jail sentence. He apparently remained totally silent during the investigation.”

“My understanding is that the Tokyo district prosecutors are the cream of the crop,” I said. “A proud lot. Once they set their sights on someone, they have solid evidence before they arrest them and charge them. Their win rate in court is really high. So the investigation they did while he was in detention couldn’t have been half-baked. Most people break down under that kind of scrutiny, and sign whatever the prosecutors want them to. Ordinary people wouldn’t be able to stay silent under that kind of pressure.”

“Still, that’s what Mr. Menshiki did. He must have a strong will and a sharp mind.”

Menshiki wasn’t your average person, that was for sure . . . A strong will and a sharp mind were indeed part of his repertoire.

“There’s one thing I don’t get,” I said. “Whether it is for tax evasion or money laundering or whatever, once the Tokyo district prosecutor arrests you, it’s reported on in the newspapers. And with an unusual name like Menshiki, I would remember the case. I used to be a pretty avid reader of newspapers.”

“I don’t know about that. There’s one other thing—I mentioned it before—but he bought that mountaintop mansion three years ago. Almost forcing the owners to sell. Other people were living there then, and they had no intention at all of selling the house they’d just built. But Mr. Menshiki offered them money—or maybe pressured them in some other way—and drove them out. And then he moved in, like some mean-spirited hermit crab.”

“Hermit crabs don’t drive away what’s living in a shell. They just quietly take over the leftover shell of a dead shellfish.”

“But there must be some hermit crabs that are mean.”

"I don't get it," I said, trying to avoid a debate over the ecology of hermit crabs. "If what you're saying is true, why would Mr. Menshiki insist so strongly that it had to be *that house*? So much so that he drove the residents out and took over? That must have taken a lot of money and effort. And that mansion is really too gaudy, too conspicuous, to suit him. It's a wonderful house, for sure, but I just don't think it fits his tastes."

"Plus it's too big. He doesn't have a maid, lives alone, hardly ever has guests over. There's no need to live in such a huge place."

She drank the rest of the water.

"There must be some special reason why it had to be that house," she went on. "I have no idea why, though."

"Anyway, he's invited me over to his place on Tuesday. Once I actually visit I might learn more."

"Make sure you check out the secret locked room, the one like Bluebeard's castle."

"I'll remember to," I said.

"For the time being, things have worked out well."

"Meaning—?"

"You finished the painting, Mr. Menshiki liked it, and you got a hefty payment for it."

"I guess so," I said. "I guess it did work out. I'm relieved."

"Felicitations, maestro," she said.

It was no lie to say that I felt relieved. It was true that I'd finished the painting. And true that Menshiki had liked it. And also true that I was happy with the painting. And equally true that this resulted in a nice, healthy amount of money coming my way. For all that, though, I couldn't feel totally pleased with the way things had worked out. So much around me was still up in the air, left as is, with no clues to follow. The more I wanted to simplify my life, the more disjointed it seemed to become.

As if searching for clues, I almost unconsciously reached out to hold my girlfriend. Her body felt soft, and warm. And damp with sweat.

I know exactly where you've been and what you've been up to, the man with the white Subaru Forester said.

20

THE MOMENT WHEN EXISTENCE AND NONEXISTENCE COALESCE

The next morning I woke up at five thirty. It was Sunday morning. It was still pitch dark outside. After a simple breakfast in the kitchen I changed into work clothes and went into the studio. As the eastern sky grew brighter, I switched off the light, threw open the window, and let chilly, fresh morning air into the room. I took out a fresh canvas and set it on the easel. The chirping of birds filtered in through the open window. The rain during the night had thoroughly soaked the trees. The rain had stopped just a while before, bright gaps in the clouds showing. I sat down on the stool, and, sipping hot black coffee from a mug, stared at the empty canvas before me.

I've always enjoyed this time, early in the morning, gazing intently at a pure white canvas. "Canvas Zen" is my term for it. Nothing is painted there yet, but it's more than a simple blank space. Hidden on that white canvas is what must eventually emerge. As I look more closely, I discover various possibilities, which congeal into a perfect clue as to how to proceed. That's the moment I really enjoy. The moment when existence and nonexistence coalesce.

But on this day I knew from the beginning what I would be painting. Emerging from this canvas would be a portrait of the middle-aged man with the white Subaru Forester. Up to this moment the man had been patiently waiting, inside me, to be painted. And I had to paint his portrait not for anyone else (not by commission, not to earn a living) but for myself. Just as I had painted Menshiki's portrait, in order to make visible his reason for being—or at least the meaning it had for me—I had to paint him in my own way. I'm not sure why. But it had to be done.

I closed my eyes and called to mind the figure of the man with the white Subaru Forester. I could distinctly recall the minutest details of his features. Early that second day he'd looked straight at me from his seat in the restaurant. The morning paper on the tabletop was folded, white steam rising from his cup of coffee. The bright morning light shining in the large window, the restaurant filled with the clatter of cheap tableware. That whole scene came back in every detail. And in the midst of that scene the man's face began to show some expression.

I know exactly where you've been and what you've been up to, his eyes told me.

This time I began with a rough draft. I stood up, grabbed a stick of charcoal, and stood before the canvas. On the blank space I created the spot where the man's face would go. With no plan, without thinking, I drew in a single vertical line. A single line, the focal point from which everything else would emerge. What would emerge was the face of a thin, suntanned man, deep wrinkles on his forehead. Thin, piercing eyes. Eyes used to staring at the far-off horizon. Eyes dyed the color of the sky and sea. Hair cut short, dotted with white. My guess, a taciturn, long-suffering man.

Around that central line I used charcoal to add a few supplementary lines, so the outlines of the man's face would appear. I stepped back to look at the lines I'd done, made a few corrections, and added some new lines. What was important was believing in myself. Believing in the power of the lines, in the power of the space the lines divided. I wasn't speaking, but letting the lines and spaces speak. Once the lines and spaces began conversing, then color would finally start to speak. And the flat would gradually transform into the three-dimensional. What I had to do was encourage them all, lend them a hand. And more than anything, not get in their way.

I kept working until ten thirty. The sun had made a slow crawl to the midpoint in the sky, the gray clouds had broken into thin strands, driven away one after another beyond the mountains. No longer did water drip from the tips of the tree branches. I stepped back and examined the rough sketch I'd done from various angles. What I saw was the face of the man I'd remembered. Or rather the framework that should abide in that face. But there were a few too many lines. I needed to do some trimming. Subtraction was the order of the day. But that was for tomorrow. Best to end this day's work here.

I put down the now shorter stick of charcoal, and washed my smudged hands in the sink. As I dried my hands with a towel, my eyes came to rest on the bell on the shelf in front of me, and I picked it up. I shook it, and the sound was terribly light, dry, and outdated. I couldn't believe it was an enigmatic Buddhist implement that had been underground for ages. It sounded so different from what I'd heard in the middle of the night. No doubt the pitch black and stillness had added to the depth and clarity of the sound, and made it carry farther.

The question of who could possibly have been ringing that bell in the middle of the night remained an unsolved mystery. Though someone must have been down in the hole every night ringing it (sending out what had to be some kind of message), whoever it was had vanished. When we uncovered the hole, all that was there was this bell. The whole thing was baffling. I placed the bell back on the shelf.

After lunch I went outside and into the woods out back. I had on a thick gray hooded windbreaker, and paint-stained sweatpants. I followed the damp path to the small shrine, and walked around behind it. The thick board cover over the hole was piled with fallen leaves of different colors and shapes. Leaves soaked by last night's rain. Since Menshiki and I had visited two days before, no one else seemed to have touched the cover. I wanted to make sure of that. I sat down on the damp stones, and, listening to the calls of birds overhead, I gazed for a while at where the hole was.

In the silence of the woods it felt like I could hear the passage of time, of life passing by. One person leaves, another appears. A thought flits away and another takes its place. One image bids farewell and another one appears on the scene. As the days piled up, I wore out, too, and was remade. Nothing stayed still. And time was lost. Behind me, time became dead grains of sand, which one after another gave way and vanished. I just sat there in front of the hole, listening to the sound of time dying.

What would it feel like to sit at the bottom of that hole, all alone,

I wondered. Being shut away by oneself in a cramped dark space. Menshiki had even given up his flashlight and the ladder. Without the ladder, without someone's help (specifically *mine*) it would be nearly impossible to escape from there. Why did he have to go to the trouble of putting himself into such a predicament? Did being down in that dark hole remind him of his solitary time behind bars in Tokyo Prison? There was no way I could know that, of course. Menshiki lived his own life, in his own way.

I could say only one thing for sure. I *would never be able to do that*. Nothing scared me more than dark, confined spaces. Put me in a place like that, and I wouldn't be able to breathe, I'd be so terrified. Even so, I was drawn to that hole. Drawn *very strongly*. So much so it felt like the hole was beckoning to me.

I sat next to the hole for a good half hour. Then I stood up and walked home through the sunlight that filtered down through the trees.

After two p.m. I had a call from Masahiko Amada. He had an errand to run near Odawara and wondered if he might drop by. Of course, I told him. I hadn't seen him in a while. He drove up just before three. He brought a bottle of single-malt whiskey as a present. I thanked him. Good timing, since I'd almost run out of whiskey. As always he was stylishly dressed, neatly shaved, wearing glasses I'd seen before, with shell-rimmed frames. He looked nearly the same as he had in the past, though admittedly his hairline was beating a slow-motion retreat.

We sat in the living room and caught up. I told him how the landscapers had used heavy equipment to dig up the stone mound. How after that, a hole just under six feet in diameter had emerged. Nine feet deep, surrounded by a stone wall. A heavy lattice cover was over it, and when that was removed, all we found was an old Buddhist implement like a bell. He listened intently as I told him the story. But he didn't say he wanted to see the hole. Or the bell.

"After that I take it you didn't hear the bell at night?"

"I don't hear it anymore," I said.

"That's great," he said, sounding a bit relieved. "I can't handle those kind of spooky things. I try to avoid them at all costs."

"Let sleeping dogs lie?"

"Exactly," Masahiko said. "I leave that hole up to you. Do whatever you like."

I told him how now, for the first time in what seemed like forever, I had the urge to paint. How ever since I finished Menshiki's portrait two days ago, it was like some blockage had been removed. I felt like I was discovering a new, original style, using portraits as a motif. I'd started the painting as a portrait, but what had eventually emerged was far from a conventional likeness. Even so, it was in essence still a portrait.

Masahiko wanted to see Menshiki's portrait, but when I told him I'd already given it to him, he was disappointed.

"But the paint can't be dry yet, can it?"

"He said he'd make sure it dries properly," I said. "He seemed eager to have the painting as quickly as possible. I don't know, maybe he was worried I might change my mind and not give it to him."

"Hmm," Masahiko said, impressed. "Do you have any new work, then?"

"I started on something this morning," I said. "But it's still just a charcoal sketch, so even if you saw it, it wouldn't mean anything."

"That's okay. Would you mind showing it to me?"

I took him into the studio and showed him the sketch for *The Man with the White Subaru Forester*. It was just a rough sketch in charcoal, but Masahiko stood in front of the easel, arms folded, a hard look on his face.

"Interesting," he said a little later, squeezing the words out between his teeth.

I was silent.

"It's hard to tell how it's going to develop, but it certainly does look like someone's portrait. Like the root of a portrait. A root buried deep in the ground." He was silent for a time.

"In a very deep, dark place," he went on. "And this man—it *is* a man, right?—is angry about something? What is he blaming?"

"You got me. I haven't got that far."

"You haven't got that far," Masahiko repeated in a monotone. "But there really is a deep anger and sadness here. And he can't spit it out. The anger is swirling around inside him."

In college Masahiko was in the oil painting department, though to be blunt about it, he wasn't known as a great painter. He was skilled enough, but his work lacked depth, something he himself admitted. He was, however, blessed with the skill of being able to instantly evaluate other people's paintings. So whenever I felt stuck doing one of my own paintings, I'd ask his opinion. His advice was always accurate and impartial, as well as practical. And thankfully he had no sense of jealousy or rivalry. I guess this was part of his personality, something he was born with. I always could believe what he told me. He never minced words, but had no ulterior motives, so oddly enough even when his criticism was pretty scathing, I never felt upset.

"When you finish this painting, before you give it to anyone else, could you let me take a look at it, even just for a minute?" he asked, eyes never leaving the painting.

"Sure," I said. "No one commissioned me to do this. I'm just painting it for myself. I don't plan to turn it over to anyone."

"You want to do your *own* painting now, right?"

"Seems that way."

"It's a portrait of sorts, but not a *formal* portrait."

I nodded. "You could put it that way, I suppose."

"You might be . . . discovering a new destination for yourself."

"I'd like to think so," I said.

"I saw Yuzu the other day," Masahiko said as he was leaving. "Happened to bump into her, and we talked for a half hour or so."

I nodded but said nothing. I had no idea what I should say, or how I should react.

"She seemed fine. We didn't talk about you much. It was like we both wanted to avoid the topic. You get it, that feeling? But at the end she did ask about you. What you're doing, that kind of thing. I told her you were painting. I don't know what kind of paintings, I said, but I said you're holed up on a mountaintop and painting something."

"I'm alive, at least," I said.

Masahiko seemed to want to say something more about Yuzu but thought better of it, and clammed up. Yuzu had always liked him and had apparently gone to him for advice. Probably things that had to do with the two of us. Just like I often went to him for advice about paintings. But Masahiko didn't tell me anything. He was that kind of guy. People often sought his advice, but he kept it all inside. Like rain running down a gutter and into a rainwater tank. It doesn't leave there, doesn't spill over the sides. He probably adjusted the amount of water inside as needed.

Masahiko didn't seem to ask anyone else for advice about his own troubles. He must have had plenty, as the son of a famous artist who went to art school but wasn't blessed with much talent as an artist. There must have been things he wanted to talk over. I've known him for a long time, but I don't recall ever hearing him complain about anything, even once. That's the type of man he was.

"Yuzu had a lover, I think," I went ahead and said. "During the last part of our marriage she stopped having sex with me. I should have known something was going on."

It was the first time I'd confessed this to anyone. I had kept it all inside until this moment.

"I see," was all Masahiko said.

"But you already knew that much, didn't you?"

He didn't respond.

"Am I wrong?" I asked again.

"There are things people are better off not knowing. That's all I can say."

"But whether you know it or not, it ends up the same. Sooner or later, suddenly or not suddenly, with a loud knock or a soft one, that's the only difference."

Masahiko sighed. "Yeah. You might be right. Whether you knew about it or not, the end result is the same. But still, there are things I can't talk about."

I was silent.

"No matter how things end up, everything has both a good and bad side. I'm sure breaking up with Yuzu was hard on you. And I feel for you. I really do. But because of that you've finally begun painting what you want to paint. You've discovered your own style. A kind of silver lining, wouldn't you say?"

Maybe he was right. If I hadn't split up with Yuzu—I mean, if Yuzu hadn't left me—I'd probably still be painting run-of-the-mill portraits to make a living. But that wasn't a choice I made *myself.* That's the important point.

"Try to look on the bright side," Masahiko said as he was leaving. "This might sound like dumb advice, but if you're going to walk down a road, it's better to walk down the sunny side, right?"

"And the cup still has one-sixteenth of the water left."

Masahiko laughed. "I like your sense of humor."

I hadn't said it to be humorous, but didn't comment.

Masahiko was silent for a time, and then spoke up. "Do you still love Yuzu?"

"I know I have to forget her, but my heart's still clinging to her and won't let go. That's just the way it is."

"You don't plan to sleep with other women?"

"Even if I did, Yuzu would always come between me and the other woman."

"That's a problem," he said. He rubbed his forehead with his fingertips. He really did look perplexed.

He got in his car and prepared to drive away.

"Thanks for the whiskey," I said. It was not yet five p.m. but the sky was pretty dark. The season when the night gets longer with each passing day.

"Actually, I wanted to have a drink with you," he said, "but I'm driving. Someday soon let's go out and do some serious drinking together. It's been ages."

"We'll do it soon," I said.

There are things people are better off not knowing, Masahiko had said. Maybe so. There are probably things people are better off not hearing, as well. But they can't go forever without hearing them. When the time comes, even if they stop their ears up tight, the air will vibrate and invade a person's heart. You can't prevent it. If you don't like it, then the only solution is to live in a vacuum.

. . .

It was the middle of the night when I woke up. I fumbled for the light next to my bed and looked at the clock. The digital readout showed 1:35. I could hear the bell ringing. *That bell*, no mistake. I sat up and listened to where the sound was coming from.

The bell started ringing again. Someone was ringing it in the middle of the night—and it was much louder, much clearer than ever.

21

IT'S SMALL, BUT SHOULD YOU CUT WITH IT, BLOOD WILL CERTAINLY COME OUT

I sat upright in bed, and in the dark of night I held my breath and listened to the sound of the bell. Where could the sound be coming from? It was louder than before, and clearer. No doubt about it. And it was coming from an entirely new direction.

The bell was ringing inside this house. I could come to no other conclusion. And from a jumble of memories came the recollection that the bell had been resting on a shelf in my studio for a few days. After we uncovered that hole I'd put the bell there myself.

The sound of the bell was coming from the studio.

Absolutely no doubt.

But what should I do? I was shaken, and scared. Something truly weird was taking place inside this house, under the same roof. It was the middle of the night, in an isolated house in the mountains, and I was all alone. I couldn't help but be afraid. When I thought about it later, I think my confusion surpassed my fear at that point. The human brain is probably constructed that way. All the emotions and feelings you have are mobilized to blunt, or mitigate, fear and distress. Like at a fire, where every single container that can hold water is put to use.

I tried to gather my thoughts and figure out what to do. One choice was to pull the covers over my head and go back to sleep. The method Masahiko advocated, to ignore the inexplicable. Switch your mind off, see nothing, hear nothing. The problem was, there was no way I could go back to sleep. Even if I put my head under the covers, stopped up my ears, and switched off my mind, there was no way I could ignore the bell when it rang out this clearly. Because it was ringing inside this very house.

As always, the bell rang intermittently a few times, then came a short silence, then the bell rang out again. The silence in between was never uniform, each time a little shorter or longer than before. There was a strange human feel to that lack of uniformity. The bell wasn't ringing by itself. No device was being used to ring it. Someone was holding it and ringing it. It was sending out a message.

If I can't escape it, then all I can do is get the facts. If this keeps up, then I'll never get to sleep and my life will be totally upended. I decided to take the initiative and find out what was happening in the studio. A bit of anger was included in this—why did I have to go through this? And of course there was a dash of curiosity thrown in as well. I wanted to be certain, with my own eyes, what was going on here.

I got out of bed and threw on a cardigan over my pajamas. I grabbed a flashlight and went out to the front entrance. I grabbed the oak walking stick that Tomohiko Amada had left behind in an umbrella stand. A sturdy, heavy stick. I didn't think it would be useful, but holding something in my hand bucked up my courage. I had to be ready for anything.

Needless to say, I was scared. I was barefoot, but could barely feel the floor. My body was stiff, as if every bone in my body creaked with each step. Someone must have snuck into the house. And that someone was ringing the bell. And it must be the same person who was ringing the bell at the bottom of the hole. Who—or *what*—that was, I couldn't predict. Was it a mummy? Say I set foot in the studio and really did confront a mummy—a shriveled-up man the color of beef jerky—shaking the bell, how should I react? Smack him with Tomohiko Amada's walking stick?

No way, I thought. *I can't do that.* The mummy would have to be a Buddhist priest who'd mummified himself. We weren't talking about a zombie.

Okay, so what should I do? I was still confused. Or rather, my confusion had grown worse. If I had no good way of dealing with the situation, did that mean I'd have to resign myself to sharing the house with a mummy? Putting up with that bell at the same time every night?

I suddenly thought of Menshiki. This problem had arisen because of him. Because he'd done things he shouldn't have. Because he'd used heavy equipment to move the stone mound and uncover the mysterious hole, some unknown being had entered this house along with the bell. I thought of calling him. Despite the late hour I could picture him rushing over in his Jaguar. But I gave up the idea. I didn't have time to wait for him to get ready and drive over. I had to do something *right here, and right now*. I had to make this *my responsibility*.

I steeled myself and stepped into the living room and turned on the light. Even with the light on, the bell kept on ringing. I could clearly hear it coming from beyond the door leading into the studio. I regripped the walking stick in my right hand, tiptoed across the large living room, and put my hand on the doorknob of the studio door. I took a deep breath, made up my mind, and turned the knob. As if waiting for me to do that, the second I pushed open the door, the bell stopped cold. A deep silence descended.

The studio was pitch black, and I couldn't see a thing. I reached out to the left-hand wall, fumbled for the light switch, and snapped it on. The pendant light on the ceiling came on and the room was suddenly bathed in light. I stood, legs shoulder-width apart, walking stick in hand, ready to respond to anything, and quickly scanned the room. The tension made my throat so parched that I could hardly swallow.

No one was in the studio. No shriveled-up mummy ringing the bell. No one was there. There was the easel standing by itself in the middle of the room, with a canvas on it. In front of the easel was the old three-legged wooden stool. That was all. The studio was deserted. I couldn't hear a single insect. There was no wind. The white curtain hung down at the window, the whole scene bathed in an unearthly silence. The walking stick was shaking, I was so tense. As it shook, the tip of the stick made an irregular click against the floor.

The bell was still on the shelf. I went over and studied it carefully. I didn't pick the bell up, but I didn't see anything different about it. It was the same as when I'd picked it up in the afternoon and returned it to the shelf, with no evidence of having been moved.

I sat on the stool in front of the easel and once more scanned the room, examining every inch of it. But I still didn't see anyone. It was the same scene I was used to. The painting on the easel was the rough sketch I'd begun of *The Man with the White Subaru Forester*.

I glanced at the clock on the shelf. It was exactly 2 a.m. It was 1:35, as I recall, when the bell woke me up, so twenty-five minutes had passed. It didn't feel like that much time had passed. It felt more like five or six minutes. My sense of time was messed up. Or else the passage of time itself was messed up. One of the two.

I gave up, got down from the stool, turned off the light in the studio, went out, and shut the door. I stood in front of the closed door for a while, my ears perked up, but couldn't hear the bell anymore. I couldn't hear anything, only the silence. Hearing silence—this was no play on words. On an isolated mountaintop, silence had a sound. I stood there before the door to the studio and listened to that sound.

Just then I noticed something on the sofa in the living room I hadn't seen before. It was as big as a cushion or a doll. But I had no memory of putting it there. I looked closer and saw it was no cushion or doll. It was a small, living person, about two feet tall. That little person was wearing odd-looking white clothes. And he was squirming around, like he was uncomfortable in his outfit. I'd seen that ancient, traditional garb before. The kind a high-ranking person would have worn in ancient times in Japan. And it wasn't just the clothes—I remembered the person's face, too.

The Commendatore.

My body felt frozen. As if a fist-sized lump of ice were slowly crawling up my spine. The Commendatore from the painting *Killing Commendatore* was sitting on the sofa in my house—or, more precisely, Tomohiko Amada's house—and looking straight at me. The little man was dressed exactly like in the painting, with the same face. As if he'd escaped directly from the painting.

I tried to recall where I'd put it. That's right, I remembered, it was in the guest bedroom. Not wanting anyone visiting the house to see it, I'd wrapped it in brown washi paper and had hidden it there. If this man had escaped, then what had happened to the painting? Was it solely the Commendatore who had vanished from the canvas?

But was that possible? That a person in a picture could escape from it? Of course not. That's impossible. Obviously. No matter what anybody might think . . .

I stood there, rooted to the spot, the thread of logic lost, random thoughts racing through my head as I gazed at the Commendatore on the sofa. Time temporarily stopped moving forward, shifting back and forth as if waiting for my confusion to subside. I couldn't take my eyes off that bizarre character—all I could think was that he had somehow come from the spirit world. For his part, the Commendatore stared up at me, from the sofa. I had no words, and was silent. The shock must have done it. I was capable of nothing, other than to keep my eyes on him and breathe, my mouth slightly ajar.

The Commendatore didn't take his eyes off me either, and he didn't say a word. His lips were shut tight. On the sofa he flung his short legs out straight in front of him. He leaned back against the sofa, though his head didn't reach to the top. On his feet were oddly shaped shoes. They seemed made out of black leather, the tips pointed and curled upward. At his waist he wore a long sword with a decorated shaft. A long sword, yet of a size to fit his build, so actually nearer in length to a short sword for a normal person. But a lethal weapon all the same. Assuming it was a real sword.

"A real sword it is," the Commendatore said pleasantly, as if reading my mind. His voice carried, despite his small stature. "Affirmative! It's small, but should you cut with it, blood will certainly come out."

Even with this new information, I remained silent. No words came. My first thought was, Oh, so he can talk? My next thought was that he sure had an odd way of speaking. It was not the way ordinary people would speak. But then again, the little two-foot Commendatore was in no way ordinary. So whatever his manner of speech, it shouldn't be surprising.

"In Tomohiko Amada's *Killing Commendatore*, it is indeed me who is impaled by a sword and dies a pitiful death," the Commendatore said. "As my friends are well aware. But have I any wounds that you can see? Negative! No wounds at all. It would be a bother for me to traipse around bleeding, and it would certainly annoy my friends as well. What with blood messing up the carpet and furniture and whatnot. So I left out the stab wound. The one who took the *killing* out of *Killing Commendatore,* that's me. Affirmative! If you need a name for me, my friends can call me the Commendatore."

The way the Commendatore spoke was odd, but he wasn't a poor speaker. In fact he was actually pretty talkative. But I still couldn't get a single word out. Reality and unreality still hadn't come to a mutual understanding inside me.

"Perhaps you will put that stick down?" the Commendatore said. "It is not as though we are about to embark upon a duel . . ."

I looked at my right hand. It was still clutching Amada's walking stick tightly. I let it go . . . The oak stick made a dull *clunk* as it struck the carpet.

"It is not like I escaped from the painting," the Commendatore said, again reading my mind. "Negative! That painting—a fascinating one, by the way—remains intact. The Commendatore is still in the process of being stabbed to death. A huge amount of blood continues to flow from his heart. All I have done is borrow his shape for a while. I need some sort of shape in order to speak with my friends. So for the sake of convenience, I borrowed his form. Is that acceptable to my friends?"

Still not a peep from me.

"Not that anybody really cares. Mr. Amada has gone on to a hazy, peaceful world, and the Commendatore is not trademarked. If I had appeared as Mickey Mouse or Pocahontas, the Walt Disney Company would be only too happy to slap me with a huge lawsuit, but if I am the Commendatore, I think we are safe, my friends."

The Commendatore's shoulders shook as he laughed merrily.

"I would have been okay as a mummy, but if I'd appeared as a mummy all of a sudden in the middle of the night, I am aware that my friends might have been bothered. To see a man all shriveled up like a hunk of beef jerky, ringing a bell in the middle of the night—that would certainly give most people a heart attack."

I nodded almost automatically. True enough—a commendatore was much preferable to a mummy. If he'd been a mummy I might really *have* had a heart attack. But running across Mickey Mouse or Pocahontas ringing a bell in the dark would have been pretty creepy too. A commendatore dressed in Asuka-period costume probably was a better choice.

"Are you a kind of spirit?" I ventured to ask. My voice was hard and hoarse, like a convalescent's.

"An excellent question," the Commendatore said. He held up a tiny white index finger. "An excellent question indeed, my friends. What am I? I am now, for the time being, the Commendatore. Nothing other than the Commendatore. But this form is but temporary. I do not know what I will be next. What am I to begin with? Or I could say, what are *you*, my friends? My friends have your own appearance, but what are *you* to begin with? If you were asked that same question, my friends might indeed be confused, I imagine. It is the same thing with me."

"Can you assume any form you like?" I asked.

"No, it is not that simple. The forms I can take are quite limited. I can't take any form I want. *There is a limit to the wardrobe.* I cannot take on a form unless there is a necessity for it. And the form I could choose now was this pint-sized commendatore. I had to be this small because of the way he was painted. But this attire is highly unpleasant to wear, I am afraid."

He began squirming around in his white costume.

"To return to the pressing question that my friends have pondered—am I a spirit? No, it is nothing like that. I am no spirit. I am just an Idea. A spirit is basically supernaturally free, which I am not. I live under all sorts of restrictions."

I had plenty of questions. Or rather, I *should have had*. But for some reason I couldn't think of a single one. Why did he address me as "my friends"? But that was trivial, not worth asking about. Maybe in the world of an *Idea* there was no second-person singular.

"I have so many kinds of detailed limitations," the Commendatore said. "For instance, I can only take on form for a limited number of hours each day. I prefer the somewhat dubious middle of the night, so mostly shape-shift between one thirty and two thirty a.m. It's too tiring to do it during the day. When I don't have form I take it easy, as a formless Idea, here and there. Like the horned owl in the attic. Also, I cannot go where I am not invited. Whereas when my friends opened the pit and took out the bell for me, I was able to enter this house."

"So you were stuck at the bottom of the pit all this time?" I asked. My voice had improved, but was still a bit hoarse.

"I could not say. I do not have memory, in the exact sense of the term. Though my being stuck in the pit is a fact. I was in the pit and could not escape. But it did not feel inconvenient to me, being shut up in there. I could be stuck in a cramped dark hole for tens of thousands of years and not feel any distress. I am grateful to my friends for getting me out of there. Being free is much more interesting than not being free, needless to say. I am also grateful to that Mr. Menshiki. Without his efforts, the hole never would have been opened up."

I nodded. "That's exactly right."

"I think I must have sensed it. The possibility that the pit would be exhumed, I mean. And must have thought this: The time has come."

"So it was you who began to ring the bell in the middle of the night?"

"Precisely. And the pit was opened. And Mr. Menshiki very kindly invited me to his dinner party."

I nodded again. It was true that Menshiki had invited the Commendatore—though he'd used the word "mummy"—to dinner on Tuesday. Following the example of Don Giovanni's dinner invitation to the bronze statue of Il Commendatore. To him it was probably a bit of a joke. But this was no longer a joke.

"I never take any food," the Commendatore said. "And I do not drink, either. No digestive organs, you see. 'Tis boring if you think about it, since he has gone to the trouble of preparing such a feast. But still I went ahead and accepted. It is not often that an Idea is invited by someone for dinner."

These were the Commendatore's last words that night. He suddenly grew silent and quietly shut both eyes, as if slipping into a meditative state. With his eyes closed, the Commendatore's features took on a contemplative look. His body, too, was completely still. His whole form began to fade, the outline becoming indistinct. And a few seconds later he totally vanished. Reflexively I glanced at the clock. Two fifteen a.m. Most likely his materialization had reached its time limit.

I went over to the sofa and touched the spot where the Commendatore had sat. My hand felt nothing. No warmth, no depression. No evidence at all that anyone had sat there. Ideas most likely had no body heat or weight. That figure was a mere image and nothing more. I sat down next to where he'd been, took a deep breath, and rubbed my face hard.

It felt like it had taken place in a dream. I must have been having a long, very vivid dream. Or maybe this world now was an extension of the dream, one I was shut up inside. But I knew this was no dream. This might not be real, but it wasn't a dream either. Menshiki and I had released the Commendatore—or an Idea taking the appearance of the Commendatore—from the bottom of that strange pit. And that Commendatore—like the horned owl in the attic—had come to inhabit this house. I had no clue what that meant. Or what it would lead to.

I stood up, retrieved Tomohiko Amada's walking stick I'd dropped on the floor, turned off the light in the living room, and returned to my bedroom. It was quiet all around, not a single sound. I took off my cardigan, slipped back into my bed in my pajamas, and lay there thinking about what I should do now. The Commendatore planned to go to Menshiki's house on Tuesday, since Menshiki had invited him to dinner. And what would happen there? The more I thought about it, the more wobbly my brain became, my mind like a dining table with uneven legs.

But before long I grew overpoweringly sleepy. Like every function of my brain was mobilizing to put me to sleep, to pluck me by force from an incoherent, confused reality. And I couldn't resist. Before long I fell asleep. Just before I fell asleep, I thought of the horned owl. How was he doing?

My friends must go to sleep now. It felt like the Commendatore murmured this into my ear.

But that must have been part of a dream.

22

THE INVITATION IS STILL OPEN

The next day was Monday. When I woke up the digital clock showed 6:35. I sat up in bed, and reviewed the middle-of-the-night happenings in the studio. The bell ringing, the miniature Commendatore, the strange conversation with him. I wanted to believe it was all a dream. I'd had a very long, real dream—that's all it was. In the light of morning, that's the only way I could see it. I clearly remembered everything that had taken place, and the more I reviewed each and every detail, the more it felt like something that had happened light-years away from reality.

But no matter how hard I tried to see it all as a dream, I knew that it wasn't. *This might not have been real, but it wasn't a dream.* I didn't know what it was, but at any rate it wasn't a dream. It was something altogether different.

I got out of bed, removed the washi paper wrapping from Tomohiko Amada's *Killing Commendatore,* and carried the painting into the studio. I hung it on the wall, then sat on the stool and studied the painting. Like the Commendatore had said the previous night, nothing about the painting had changed. The Commendatore hadn't escaped from the painting into this world. Like always, the Commendatore was still there, stabbed in the chest, blood pouring out of his heart as he died. He looked up in the air, his mouth open in a grimace, groaning in agony. His hairstyle, the clothes he wore, the long sword he held, even the strange black shoes, were exactly those of the Commendatore who'd appeared here last night. No, to put it in the correct order—chronologically speaking—naturally last night's Commendatore had minutely copied the appearance of the Commendatore in the painting.

It was astounding that the fictional figure that Tomohiko Amada had painted with a Japanese paintbrush and pigment had taken on real form and appeared in reality (or something like reality), moving around under its own willpower in three-dimensional form. But as I stared at the painting, this phenomenon began to seem less and less impossible. That's how vivid and alive Tomohiko Amada's rendering was. The longer I looked at the painting, the less clear was the threshold between reality and unreality, flat and solid, substance and image. Like Van Gogh's mailman, who, the longer you looked, seemed to take on a life of his own. Same with the crows that he painted—nothing but rough black lines, but they really did seem to be soaring through the sky. As I gazed at *Killing Commendatore* I was struck once again with admiration for Amada's gift and craftsmanship as an artist. No doubt that the Commendatore (or Idea, I should say) was equally struck by how amazing and powerful the painting was, and that was why he had "borrowed" the appearance of the Commendatore. Like a hermit crab chooses the prettiest and most sturdy shell to live in.

I studied *Killing Commendatore* for some ten minutes, then went into the kitchen, brewed coffee, and, while listening to the regular news broadcast on the radio, had a simple breakfast. The news was meaningless. Or what I should say is that almost none of the news those days held any meaning for me. Still, listening to the seven a.m. news each day had become part of my routine. It might be a problem if the world was on the brink of destruction and I was the only person unaware of it.

I finished breakfast, and after confirming that that earth, despite all its various troubles, was still spinning away, I headed back to the studio, mug in hand. I drew back the curtain to let in some fresh air, then stood before the canvas and went back to work on my painting. Whether the Commendatore's appearance was real or not, whether he showed up at Menshiki's dinner or not, all I could do in the meantime was focus on the work at hand.

I called to mind the figure of the middle-aged man with the white Subaru Forester. On his table in the restaurant had been a car key with the Subaru logo, a heap of toast, scrambled eggs, and sausage on a plate.

Ketchup (red) and mustard (yellow) containers sat alongside. Knife and fork were lined up on the table. He'd yet to start eating. Morning light shone on the whole tableau. As I passed him, the man raised his suntanned face and stared at me.

I know exactly where you've been and what you've been up to, he was informing me. I recognized that heavy, dispassionate light abiding in his eyes. A light I may have seen somewhere else, though when or where I couldn't say.

I was completing that figure and that wordless message in the form of a painting. I started out using a crust of bread as an eraser to get rid of any excess lines from the charcoal framework I'd sketched the day before. After removing all that I could, I again added some lines in black to the black lines that remained. This process took an hour and a half. What emerged on the canvas was (so to speak) a mummified image of the man who drove the white Subaru Forester. The flesh pruned away, the skin dried up like beef jerky, a figure shrunken one whole size. This was depicted through the rough black charcoal lines alone. Just a preliminary sketch, but I could imagine how it linked up with the full painting to come.

"Nicely done," the Commendatore said.

I spun around. The Commendatore was seated on the shelf near the window, facing me, his silhouette distinctly backlit in the morning light. He had on the same ancient white clothes and the same long sword downsized to fit his height. *This is no dream. Of course it isn't,* I told myself.

"I am no dream, I can tell you. Negative. Of course," the Commendatore said, once again reading my thoughts. "I am closer to wakefulness than dream."

I said nothing. From my perch on the stool I gazed at his silhouette.

"I think I said this last night, but it is pretty exhausting for me to materialize when it is bright out like this," the Commendatore said. "But I wanted to watch my friends painting just this once. So I took the liberty of observing while you worked. I hope this does not offend you?"

I had no answer to this either. Whether it offended me or not, how was a real person supposed to reason with an Idea?

Not waiting for my response (or maybe taking what was in my mind as my response), the Commendatore continued. "You are quite a talented painter. Stroke by stroke, the essence of that man is coming out on that canvas."

"Do you know something about him?" I asked, surprised.

"Affirmative," the Commendatore said. "Of course I do."

"Then could you tell me something about him? What kind of person he is, what work he does, what he's doing now?"

"I wonder," the Commendatore said, slightly inclining his head, a hard look coming over his face. When he made that sort of expression he looked like a goblin. Or like Edward G. Robinson from an old gangster movie. Who knows, maybe the Commendatore had "borrowed" that expression from Edward G. Robinson. That wouldn't be impossible.

"There are things in the world my friends are better off not knowing," the Commendatore said, the Edward G. Robinson look plastered on his face.

The same thing Masahiko Amada had said the other day, I recalled. *There are things people are better off not knowing.*

"In other words, you won't tell me the things I'm better off not knowing," I said.

"Affirmative. Even if you hear it from me, the truth is that my friends *already know it*."

I was silent.

"As my friends paint that picture, you will be subjectively giving form to what my friends already comprehend. Think of Thelonious Monk. Thelonious Monk did not get those unusual chords as a result of logic or theory. He opened his eyes wide, and scooped those chords out from the darkness of his consciousness. What is important is not creating something out of nothing. What my friends need to do is discover the right thing from what is already there."

So he knew about Thelonious Monk.

"Affirmative! And of course I know Edward whatchamacallit, too," the Commendatore said, grabbing hold of my thoughts.

"No matter," the Commendatore continued. "Ah, there is one thing I must raise at this point, as a matter of courtesy. It is about your lovely girlfriend . . . Right, the married woman who drives a red car. Apologies, but I have been watching all you have been doing here. What you all enjoy doing in bed after you take off your clothes."

I stared at him without a word. *What we enjoy doing in bed . . .* To borrow her words for it, *what one hesitates to mention.*

"But you really should not mind. My apologies, but an Idea watches everything that happens. I cannot choose what I watch. But there is nothing to worry about, at all. Sex, radio exercise routines, chimney sweeping, it is all the same to me. Nothing that interesting to see. I just watch."

"There's no notion of privacy in the world of an Idea?"

"Affirmative," the Commendatore said, rather proudly. "Not a speck of that. So if my friends do not mind, then that is all we need to say. So, are you okay with it?"

I shook my head slightly again. How about it? Was it possible to focus while having sex if you knew somebody else was watching the whole time? Could you call up a healthy sexual desire if you knew you were being observed?

"I have a question for you," I said.

"I would be happy to answer if I can," the Commendatore said.

"Tomorrow, on Tuesday, I'm invited to dinner at Mr. Menshiki's. And you're invited as well. Mr. Menshiki used the expression "inviting a mummy," which actually means you. Since at that point you hadn't yet appeared as the Commendatore."

"That does not matter. If I decide to be a mummy, I can do that in a flash."

"No, stay as you are," I said hurriedly. "I would appreciate it if you stay the way you are."

"I will accompany you to Menshiki's house. You will be able to see me, but Menshiki will not. So it does not matter if I am a mummy or a commendatore. Though there is one thing I would like my friends to do."

"And what would that be?"

"My friends should call Menshiki now and make sure the invitation for Tuesday night is still open. When you do, make sure to say, 'It will not be a mummy coming with me that day, but the Commendatore.

Would that still be all right?' As I mentioned, I cannot set foot in a place unless I have been invited. The other party needs to invite me, in some form or other say 'Please, come on in.' Once I have been invited, then I can go whenever I feel like it. For this house, that bell over there acted as a substitute invitation."

"I see," I said. The one thing I couldn't have was him turning into a mummy. "I'll call Mr. Menshiki, see if the invitation is still on, and tell him I'd like him to revise the guest list from mummy to Commendatore."

"Affirmative. I would be grateful. Receiving an invitation to a dinner party is quite unexpected."

"I have another question," I said. "Weren't you originally a priest who undertook certain death austerities? A priest who voluntarily was buried underground, stopped eating and drinking, and chanted the sutras until you passed away? Didn't you die in the pit while you continued to ring the bell, and eventually turned into a mummy?"

"Hmm," the Commendatore said, and shook his head a little. "Unclear. I can't say, really. At a certain point I became a pure Idea. But I have no linear memory of what I was before that, where I was or what I did."

The Commendatore was silent, staring fixedly into space.

"Anyway, I have to disappear soon," the Commendatore said in a quiet, slightly hoarse voice. "The time during which I can materialize is nearly over. The morning is not my time. Darkness is my friend. A vacuum is my breath. I must be saying goodbye soon. So, thank you in advance for calling Mr. Menshiki."

As if meditating, the Commendatore closed his eyes. His lips were tightly sealed, his fingers locked together, as he steadily grew fainter and then disappeared. Just like the night before. Like fleeting smoke, he silently vanished in the air. In the bright morning sunshine, all that was left was me and the painting I'd started. The outline of the man with the white Subaru Forester glaring at me.

I know exactly where you've been and what you've been up to.

After noon I called Menshiki. I realized this was the first time I'd ever phoned his home. He was the one who always called me. He picked up after six rings.

"I'm glad you called," he said. "I was just about to call you. But I didn't want to bother you while you're working, so was waiting until the afternoon. I remember you mainly work in the morning."

"I just finished for the day," I said.

"Is it going well?" Menshiki asked.

"Yes, I started a new painting. Though I've barely begun."

"That's wonderful. I'm so glad to hear it. By the way, I hung the portrait you painted on the wall of my study, not yet framed. I'm letting it dry there. Even without a frame it looks wonderful."

"About tomorrow . . . ," I said.

"I'll send a car to pick you up at six," he said. "The same car will take you back. It'll just be the two of us, so you don't need to dress up, or bring a gift or anything. Please just come as you are."

"There's one thing I wanted to check with you."

"Yes?"

"The other day you said you wouldn't mind having a mummy join us for dinner, right?"

"I did say that, yes. I remember."

"Is that invitation still open?"

Menshiki considered this for a moment and then gave a cheery laugh. "Of course it is. I meant what I said. The invitation is still open."

"Something happened and the mummy won't be able to come, but instead the Commendatore says he'd like to. Is it all right to invite the Commendatore?"

"Of course," Menshiki said without hesitation. "Like Don Giovanni invited the statue to dinner, I would be pleased to have the Commendatore come to dinner in my humble abode. But unlike Don Giovanni in the opera, I haven't done anything so bad that I deserve to be thrown into hell. At least I don't think I have. After dinner I'm not going to be pulled into hell or anything, I hope?"

"That won't happen," I replied. Though honestly I wasn't all that confident. I couldn't predict anymore what was going to happen next.

"Good. I'm not ready for hell quite yet," Menshiki said cheerily. As you might expect, he was taking it all as a clever joke. "One question, though. As a dead person, Don Giovanni's Commendatore wasn't able to eat earthly food, but what about *this* Commendatore? Should I prepare food for him? Or does he not take any worldly food?"

"There's no need to prepare food for him. He doesn't eat or drink. But it wouldn't be a problem if you set a place for him."

"Because he's basically a spiritual being?"

"I believe so." An Idea and a spirit were a little different, I thought, but I didn't want to get into it.

"I'm fine with that," Menshiki said. "I'll make sure the Commendatore has his own seat at the table. It's an unexpected pleasure to be able to invite the famous Commendatore to dinner in my humble home. It's too bad, though, that he won't be able to sample the food. We'll have some delicious wine as well."

I thanked Menshiki.

"Until tomorrow, then," Menshiki said, and hung up.

That night, the bell didn't ring. The Commendatore must have been tired out from materializing during the day (and answering my questions). Or maybe he no longer felt the need to summon me to the studio. At any rate, I slept a deep, dreamless sleep until morning.

The next morning as I painted in the studio the Commendatore didn't make an appearance. So for two hours, I was able to forget everything and focus on painting. The first thing I did that day was paint over the outline, like spreading a thick slab of butter on toast.

I started with a deep red, an edgy, offbeat green, and a grayish black. These were the colors the man wanted. It took a while to mix the right colors. As I went through this process I put on the record of Mozart's *Don Giovanni*. With that music playing, it felt like the Commendatore would appear behind me at any minute, though he didn't.

That day, Tuesday, the Commendatore, like the horned owl up in the attic, maintained a deep silence. But that didn't bother me particularly. As a flesh-and-blood person, I couldn't worry about an Idea. Ideas had their own way of doing things. And I had my own life. I focused on completing *The Man with the White Subaru Forester*. Whether I was in the studio or out, standing before the canvas or not, the image of the painting was never far from my mind.

According to the radio weather report, there was supposed to be heavy rain that night in the Kanto-Tokai region. And off to the west the weather was indeed taking a turn for the worse. In southern Kyushu torrential rains had made rivers overflow, and people living in low-lying areas had had to evacuate. People in higher areas were warned to watch out for landslides.

A dinner party on a night when it's going to be pouring, I thought.

I thought of that dark hole in the middle of the woods. That weird stone-lined little chamber that Menshiki and I had exposed to the light of day when we moved the heavy rocks of the mound. I pictured myself sitting alone at the bottom of that pitch-dark hole listening to rain pounding on the wooden cover. I'm shut up inside that hole, unable to escape. The ladder's been taken away, the heavy cover shut tight right above me. And everyone in the world has completely forgotten I've been left behind. Or perhaps they think I'm long dead. But I am still alive. Lonely, but still breathing. All I can hear is the downpour. There's no light. Not a single ray reaches me. The stone wall I'm leaning against is damply cold. It's the middle of the night. All sorts of bugs might ooze their way out.

As this scene took shape in my mind, I gradually found it hard to breathe. I went out to the terrace, leaned against the railing, slowly breathed in the fresh air through my nose, and slowly exhaled through my mouth. As always, I counted the number of breaths and repeated this process at regular intervals. After repeating this for a while, I was able to breathe normally again. The twilight sky was covered in heavy, leaden clouds. The rain was getting closer.

Menshiki's white mansion appeared faintly across the valley. This evening that's where I'll be having dinner, I thought. Menshiki, me, and the famous Commendatore—three of us seated around the dining table.

Affirmative. That is real blood I'm talking about, you know, the Commendatore whispered in my ear.

23

THEY ALL REALLY EXIST

When I was thirteen and my little sister was ten, the two of us traveled by ourselves to Yamanashi Prefecture during summer vacation. Our mother's brother worked in a research lab at a university in Yamanashi and we went to stay with him. This was the first trip we kids had taken by ourselves. My sister was feeling relatively good then, so our parents gave us permission to travel alone.

Our uncle was single (and still is single, even now), and had just turned thirty, I think, at that time. He was doing gene research (and still is), was very quiet and kind of unworldly, though a very open, straightforward person. He loved reading and knew everything about nature. He enjoyed taking walks in the mountains more than anything, which, he said, was why he had taken a university job in rural, mountainous Yamanashi. My sister and I liked our uncle a lot.

Backpacks in tow, we boarded an express train at Shinjuku Station bound for Matsumoto, and got off at Kofu. Our uncle came to pick us up at Kofu Station. He was spectacularly tall, and even in the crowded station, we spotted him right away. He was renting a small house in Kofu along with a friend of his, but his roommate was abroad so we were given our own room to sleep in. We stayed in that house for one week. And almost every day we took walks with our uncle in the nearby mountains. He taught us the names of all kinds of flowers and insects. We cherished our memories of that summer.

One day we hiked a bit farther than usual and visited a wind cave near Mt. Fuji. Among the numerous wind caves around Mt. Fuji there was one in particular that was fairly large. Our uncle told us about how these holes were formed. The caves were made of basalt, so inside you heard hardly any echoes at all, he said. Even in the summer the temperature remained low inside, so in the past people would store ice they'd cut in winter inside the caves. He explained the distinction between the two types of holes: *fuketsu,* the larger ones that were big enough for people to go into, and *kaza-ana,* the smaller ones that people couldn't enter. Both terms were alternate readings of the same Chinese characters meaning "wind" and "hole." Our uncle seemed to know everything.

At the large wind hole, you paid an entrance fee and went inside. Our uncle didn't go with us. He'd been there numerous times, plus he was so tall and the ceiling of the cave so low, he'd end up with a backache. It's not dangerous, he said, so you two go on ahead. I'll stay by the entrance and read a book. At the entrance the person in charge handed us each a flashlight and put yellow plastic helmets on us. There were lights on the ceiling of the cave, but it was still pretty dark inside. The deeper we went inside the cave, the lower the ceiling got. No wonder our lanky uncle had bowed out.

My kid sister and I shone the flashlights at our feet as we went. It was midsummer outside but inside the cave it was chilly. It was ninety degrees Fahrenheit outside, but inside it was under fifty. Following our uncle's advice, we were both wearing thick windbreakers we'd brought along. My sister held my hand tightly, either wanting me to protect her, or else hoping to protect me, one or the other (or maybe she just didn't want to get separated). The whole time we were inside the cave that small, warm hand was in mine. The only other visitors were a middle-aged couple. But they soon left, and it was just the two of us.

My little sister's name was Komichi, but everyone in the family called her Komi. Her friends called her Micchi or Micchan. As far as I know, no one called her by her full name, Komichi. She was a small, slim girl. She had straight black hair, neatly cut just above her shoulders. Her eyes were big for the size of her face (with large pupils), which made her resemble a fairy. That day she wore a white T-shirt, faded jeans, and pink sneakers.

After we'd made our way deeper into the cave my sister discovered a small side cave a little ways off from the prescribed path. Its mouth was hidden in the shadows of the rocks. She was very interested in that little cave. "Don't you think it looks like Alice's rabbit hole?" she asked me.

My sister was a big fan of Lewis Carroll's *Alice in Wonderland*. I don't know how many times she had me read the book to her. Must have been at least a hundred. She had been able to read since she was little, but she liked me to read that book aloud to her. She'd memorized the story, but each time I read it, she still got excited. Her favorite part was the Lobster Quadrille. Even now I remember that part, word for word.

"No rabbit, though," I said.

"I'm going to peek inside," she said.

"Be careful," I said.

It really was a narrow hole (close to a *kaza-ana*, in my uncle's definition), but my little sister was able to slip through it with no trouble. Her upper half was inside, just the bottom half of her legs sticking out. She seemed to be shining her flashlight inside the hole. Then she slowly edged out backward.

"It gets really deep in back," she reported. "The floor drops off sharply. Just like Alice's rabbit hole. I'm going to check out the far end."

"No, don't do it. It's too dangerous," I said.

"It's okay. I'm small and I can get out okay."

She took off her windbreaker, so that she was wearing just her T-shirt, and handed the jacket to me along with her helmet. Before I could get in a word of protest, she'd wriggled into the cave, flashlight in hand. In an instant she'd vanished.

A long time passed, but she still didn't come out. I couldn't hear a sound.

"Komi," I called into the hole. "Komi! Are you okay?"

There was no answer. Without any echo my voice was sucked right up into the darkness. I was starting to get concerned. She might be stuck inside the hole, unable to more forward or back. Or maybe she had had a convulsion inside the hole and lost consciousness. If that had happened I wouldn't be able to help her. All kinds of terrible scenarios ran through my head, and I felt choked by the darkness surrounding me.

If my little sister really did disappear in the hole, never to return to this world again, how would I ever explain that to my parents? Should

I run and tell my uncle, waiting outside the entrance? Or should I sit tight and wait for her to emerge? I crouched down and peered into that hole. But the beam from my flashlight didn't reach far. It was a tiny hole, and the darkness inside was overwhelming.

"Komi," I called out again. No response. *"Komi,"* I called more loudly. Still no answer. A wave of cold chilled me to the core. I might lose my sister forever. She might have been sucked into Alice's hole and vanished. Into the world of the Mock Turtle, the Cheshire Cat, and the Queen of Hearts. A place where worldly logic didn't apply. No matter what, we never should have come here.

But finally my sister did return. She didn't back out like before, but crawled out headfirst. First her black hair appeared from the hole, then her shoulders and arms. She wriggled out her waist, and finally her pink sneakers emerged. She stood in front of me, without a word, stretched, slowly took a deep breath, and brushed the dirt off her jeans.

My heart was still pounding. I reached out and straightened her disheveled hair. I couldn't quite make it out in the weak light inside the cave, but there seemed to be dirt and dust and other debris clinging to her white T-shirt. I put the windbreaker on her. And handed back her yellow helmet.

"I didn't think you were coming back," I said, hugging her to me.

"Were you worried?"

"A lot."

She grabbed my hand tightly again. And in an excited voice she said, "I managed to squeeze through the narrow part, and then deeper in it suddenly got lower, and down from there it was like a small room. A round room, like a ball. The ceiling's round, the walls are round, and the floor too. And it was so, so silent there, like you could search the whole world and never find any place that silent. Like I was at the bottom of an ocean, in a hollow going even deeper. I turned off the flashlight and it was pitch dark, but I didn't feel scared or lonely. That room was a special place that only I'm allowed into. A room *just for me*. No one else can get there. You can't go in either."

"'Cause I'm too big."

My little sister bobbed her head. "Right. You've gotten too big to get in. And what's really amazing about that place is that it's darker than anything could ever be. So dark that when you turn off the flashlight it feels like you can grab the darkness with your hands. And when you're there in the dark by yourself, it's like your body is gradually coming apart and disappearing. But since it's dark you can't see it happen. You don't know if you still have a body or not. But even if, say, my body completely disappeared, I'd still remain there. Like the Cheshire Cat's grin remaining after he vanished. Pretty weird, huh? But when I was there I didn't think it was weird at all. I wanted to stay there forever, but I thought you'd be worried, so I came out."

"Let's get out of here," I said. She was so worked up it seemed as if she was going to go on talking forever, and I had to put a stop to that. "I can't breathe well in here."

"Are you okay?" my sister asked, worried.

"I'm okay. I just want to go outside."

Holding hands, we headed for the exit.

"Do you know?" my sister said in a small voice as we walked so no one else would hear (though there wasn't anyone else around). "Alice really existed. It wasn't made up, it was real. The March Hare, the Walrus, the Cheshire Cat, the Playing Card soldiers—they all really exist."

"Maybe so," I said.

We emerged from the wind hole, back to the bright real world. There was a thin layer of clouds in the sky that afternoon, but I remember how strong the sunlight seemed. The screech of the cicadas was overpowering, like a violent squall drowning everything out. My uncle was seated on a bench near the entrance, absorbed in a book. When he saw us, he grinned and stood up.

Two years later, my sister died. And was put in a tiny coffin and cremated. I was fifteen, and she was twelve. While she was being cremated I went off, apart from the rest of the family, sat on a bench in the courtyard of the crematorium, and remembered what had happened in that wind hole. The weight of time as I waited by that small cave for my little sister to come out, the thickness of the darkness enveloping me, the chill I felt to my core. Her black hair emerging from the hole, then her shoulders. All the random dirt and dust stuck to her white T-shirt.

At that time a thought struck me: that maybe even before the doctor at the hospital officially pronounced her dead two years later, her life had already been snatched from her while she was deep inside that cave. I was actually convinced of it. She'd already been lost within that hole, and left this world, but I, mistakenly thinking she was still alive, had put her on the train with me and taken her back to Tokyo. Holding her hand tightly. And we'd lived as brother and sister for two more years. But that was nothing more than a fleeting grace period. Two years later, death had crawled out of that cave to grab hold of my sister's soul. As if time was up, it was necessary to pay for what had been lent, and the owner had come to take back what was his.

At any rate now, at thirty-six, I realized again that what my little sister had confided to me in a quiet voice in that wind hole was indeed true. Alice really does exist in the world. The March Hare, the Walrus, the Cheshire Cat—they all *really exist*. And the Commendatore too, of course.

The weather report was off the mark and we didn't have a rainstorm. Just after five a very light rain began—so fine that you could hardly tell if it was falling or not—and continued till the next morning. Right at six p.m. a large, shiny black sedan slowly made its way up the slope. It reminded me of a hearse, but of course it wasn't one, but the limousine Menshiki had sent for me. A Nissan Infiniti. The driver, in black uniform and hat, alighted from the car and, umbrella in one hand, came over to the front door and rang the bell. I opened the door and he took off his hat and made sure of my name. I left the house and got into the car. I declined the umbrella. It wasn't raining hard enough for one. The driver opened the rear door for me. Once I was inside, he closed it with a solid *thunk* (a little different from the sound of Menshiki's Jaguar). I wore a black, light, round-necked sweater, gray herringbone jacket, dark-gray wool trousers, and black suede shoes. The most formal outfit I owned. At least it didn't have paint stains.

Even after the limo came, the Commendatore still hadn't appeared. And I hadn't heard his voice. So I had no way of making sure he'd remembered the invitation from Menshiki. But he must have. He'd been looking forward to it so much there was no way he'd forgotten.

But I worried for nothing. Soon after the car had set off, I suddenly found the Commendatore, with a nonchalant look on his face, seated beside me. He was dressed in his usual white outfit (looking like it had just come from the cleaners, without a single stain), with the jewel-encrusted long sword at his waist. He was, as always, about two feet high. The whiteness and purity of his clothes stood out even more against the black leather seats of the Infiniti. He stared straight ahead, his arms folded.

"Do not say anything to me," the Commendatore said, as if reminding me. "My friends can see me, but others cannot. My friends can hear me, but others cannot. If you talk to something that cannot be seen, people will think you are very strange. Affirmative? Nod, please, if you understand."

I nodded slightly one time. The Commendatore bobbed his head in response, and afterward sat there silently, his arms folded.

It was dark out. The crows had already withdrawn to their mountain roosts. The Infiniti slowly descended the slope, drove down the road in the valley, and came to a steep slope. It wasn't that long a distance (we were just going to the other side of a narrow valley, after all), but the road was narrow, with plenty of curves. The type of road a driver of a large sedan would not be happy to navigate. The type of road more suited to a four-wheel-drive military vehicle. But the driver's expression didn't change a bit as he calmly handled the car, and we arrived safely at Menshiki's mansion.

The mansion was surrounded by a high white wall, with a solid gate in front. Large wooden double doors painted a dark brown. Like the castle gate in an Akira Kurosawa film set in the Middle Ages. The kind that would look good with a couple of arrows embedded in it. The inside was completely hidden from view. Next to the gate was a plate with the house number, but no nameplate. Probably no need to have one. If someone was going to go to the trouble of coming all the way up to the top of this mountain, they would automatically know this was Menshiki's mansion. The area around the gate was brightly lit by mercury lamps. The driver got out, rang the bell, and spoke for a moment with someone on the intercom. Then he got back in his seat and waited for the gate to open remotely. There were two movable security cameras, one on each side of the gate.

The double doors slowly opened inward, and the driver entered, proceeding leisurely down the curving road on the grounds. The road was a gentle downward slope. I heard the doors close behind us—a heavy sound, as if informing us that there was no return to the world from which we had come. Pine trees lined both sides of the road, all neatly trimmed. The branches were beautifully arranged, like bonsai, and careful measures were obviously taken to keep them from getting any disease. Along the road was also a trim hedge of azaleas. Beyond this there were Japanese roses, and a clump of camellias. The house might be new, but the trees and plants all seemed to have been there since long ago. All of these were beautifully illuminated by garden lanterns.

The road ended in a circular asphalt-covered driveway. As soon as the driver parked, he leaped out the driver's side and opened the back door for me. I looked beside me but didn't see the Commendatore. But I wasn't particularly surprised, and didn't mind. He had his own patterns of behavior.

The taillights of the Infiniti politely and gracefully disappeared into the twilight darkness, leaving me standing there alone. Seen from the front like this, the house looked much cozier and less imposing than I'd expected. When I'd looked at it from across the valley it seemed like an overbearing, gaudy structure. Perhaps the impression changed depending on the angle. The front gate was at the highest point of the mountain, and then, descending the slope, the house was built as if to deliberately make use of the angle of inclination of the land.

On either side of the front door were two old stone statues, a pair of the *komainu* guardian dog figures found in Shinto shrines. On pedestals as well. They might actually have been real *komainu* brought over from somewhere. There were plantings of azaleas at the entrance, too. In May the place must be pretty colorful.

As I slowly walked toward the front door, it opened from inside and Menshiki appeared. He had on a dark-green cardigan over a white button-down shirt, and cream-colored chinos. His pure white hair was, as always, neatly combed and arranged naturally. It felt strange to see

Menshiki welcoming me to his own house. I'd always seen Menshiki when he roared up to my house in his Jaguar.

He invited me in and closed the front door. The entrance foyer was spacious and nearly square, with a high ceiling. A squash court could fit inside. The indirect lighting on the wall pleasantly lit the room, and on top of a large octagonal parquet table in the middle of the foyer was a large flower vase, Ming dynasty by the look of it, overflowing with a fresh flower arrangement. A mix of three different types of large flowers (I don't know much about plants so don't know the names). Probably he'd had them specially arranged just for this evening. A frugal college student could manage to live for a month on what Menshiki probably paid the florist. At least I could have, back when I was a student. There were no windows in the foyer, just a skylight in the ceiling. The floor was well-polished marble.

The living room was down three wide steps, and though not quite big enough for a soccer field was definitely large enough for a tennis court. The southeast side was all tinted glass, with a large deck outside. It was dark, so I couldn't tell if you could see the ocean from here, but I imagine you could. On the opposite wall was an open fireplace. It wasn't the cold season yet so there was no fire lit, but firewood was neatly stacked up beside it, so a fire could be started at any time. I don't know who had stacked it up, but it was placed so beautifully it looked like a work of art in itself. There was a mantelpiece above the fireplace, with a row of old Meissen figurines.

The living room floor was also marble, but covered with a variety of rugs. Antique Persian rugs, with such exquisite patterns and colors they looked less like practical objects than artistic handicrafts. I hesitated to step on them. There were several low tables and a scattering of flower vases, all full of fresh flowers. Each vase looked like a valuable antique. It was all in nice taste, and expensive. Here's hoping we don't have a big earthquake, was my thought.

The ceiling was high, the lighting subdued. Refined indirect lighting on the walls, a few floor lamps, and reading lamps on the tables. At the back of the room was a black grand piano. I'd never seen a Steinway concert grand piano in a room like this, one that made it seem smaller than it was. On top of the piano was a metronome and sheet music.

Perhaps Menshiki played. Or maybe he invited Maurizio Pollini over for dinner every once in a while.

Overall, though, the room was modestly decorated, and I felt relieved. There was nothing excessive, but it didn't have an *empty* feeling. A comfortable room, despite the size. There was a certain sense of warmth about it, you might say. Half a dozen tasteful paintings graced the walls, all modestly displayed. One of them looked like a real Léger, but I could have been mistaken.

Menshiki motioned me to a large brown leather sofa. He sat on a matching easy chair across from me. The sofa was extremely comfortable, neither too hard nor too soft. The kind of sofa that naturally adjusted to whoever sat on it. Of course if you think about it (not that it was something one had to think about), Menshiki wasn't about to put an uncomfortable sofa in his living room.

As if he'd been waiting for us to get settled, as soon as we did, a man glided in from somewhere. A stunningly handsome young man. He wasn't so tall, but was slim and had a refined bearing about him. His skin was evenly tanned, with lustrous hair done up in a ponytail. He would look good at the beach, in surfing shorts, carrying a shortboard, though today he was dressed in a clean white shirt and black bow tie. A pleasant smile played about his lips.

"Would you care for a cocktail?" he asked me. ""Please order whatever you'd like."

"I'll have a Balalaika," I said, after considering it for a few seconds. Not that I really wanted a Balalaika, but I wanted to test the young bartender to see if he really could make any kind of drink.

"I'll have the same," Menshiki said.

The young man smiled pleasantly and soundlessly withdrew.

I glanced at the spot next to me on the sofa but didn't see the Commendatore. But he had to be here somewhere in the house. He'd ridden with me in the car up to the house, and had come along with me.

"Is something the matter?" Menshiki asked me. He'd followed my glance.

"No, just admiring your gorgeous house."

"It's a little too much, don't you think?" Menshiki said, a smile rising to his face.

"No, it's much more serene than I imagined," I answered honestly. "From a distance it does look a bit luxurious. Like a luxury cruise ship on the ocean. But inside it's surprisingly relaxed. My impression's completely changed."

Menshiki listened and nodded. "I'm happy to hear that, but it took quite a lot of work to get it to that point. I bought the house already built, and when I purchased it, it was pretty gaudy. Flashy, you might say. A man who ran a big-box store built it. The extremes of bad taste of the nouveau riche, you could say, and not my style at all. So I did a huge renovation after I bought it. Which took a lot of time, effort, and money."

As if remembering all that work, Menshiki looked down and sighed. It really must not have suited his taste at all.

"Wouldn't it have been a lot cheaper to build your own house?" I asked.

Menshiki smiled, his white teeth peeking from between his lips. "You're absolutely right. That would have been the sensible thing to do. But I had my own reasons. Reasons why it had to be this house and no other."

I waited for the story to go on, but it didn't.

"Wasn't the Commendatore supposed to be with you tonight?" Menshiki asked.

"I think he'll be along later," I said. "We were together on the trip up to your house and then he suddenly vanished. I think he must be taking a tour of your house. You don't mind, do you?"

Menshiki spread his hands wide. "Of course. Of course I don't mind. He's welcome to look around as much as he likes."

The young man from before appeared, carrying two cocktails on a silver tray. The cocktail glasses were exquisitely cut crystal. Baccarat, would be my guess. They glittered in the light from the floor lamp. Next to them was a Koimari ceramic plate with slices of various cheeses and cashews. There were small monogrammed linen napkins and a set of silver knives and forks. Everything well thought out.

Menshiki and I picked up our cocktail glasses and made a toast. He toasted the completion of his portrait, and I thanked him. We lightly put our lips to the rim of the glasses. A Balalaika is made of one part each of vodka, Cointreau, and lemon juice. A simple concoction, but unless it's as bitingly freezing as the North Pole, it doesn't taste good. If somebody who doesn't have the right touch mixes it, it ends up tasting diluted, watery. This Balalaika was amazingly delicious, with an almost perfect bite to it.

"This is delicious," I said, impressed.

"He's quite good," Menshiki said lightly.

Of course he is, I thought. Menshiki wasn't about to hire a bad bartender. And of course he had Cointreau on hand, antique crystal glasses, and a Koimari serving plate.

As we sipped our cocktails and munched on some nuts, we talked about various topics. Mainly about my painting. He asked what I was working on now and I explained. I told him I was working on a portrait of a man whose name and background I knew nothing about, someone I had encountered in a distant town.

"A portrait?" Menshiki asked, sounding surprised.

"A portrait, but not a typical commercial portrait. More of an abstract-style portrait, one in which I let my imagination run free. But the motif is definitely a portrait. You might say it's the foundation of the painting."

"Like when you painted my portrait?"

"Exactly. Though this time I wasn't commissioned. It's something I decided to paint on my own."

Menshiki considered this. "Maybe my portrait inspired you to be more creative?"

"No doubt. Though I'm only at the point where my creativity is finally starting to kick in."

Menshiki took another soundless sip of his cocktail, with what I took to be a satisfied gleam deep in his eyes.

"Nothing could make me happier," he said. "The fact that I may have been of help to you, that is. If you don't mind, could I see that new painting when it's finished?"

"I'd be happy to show it to you, provided I'm happy with the result."

I looked over at the grand piano in a corner of the room. "Do you play piano, Mr. Menshiki? That's a beautiful instrument."

Menshiki nodded slightly. "I'm not good, but I do play a little. I took piano lessons as a child. Five or six years from the time I entered elementary school until I graduated. Then I got busy with schoolwork and quit taking lessons. I wish I hadn't, but the piano lessons had worn me out. So my fingers don't move the way I'd like them to, but I'm good at reading sheet music. I play some simple pieces every once in a while just for my own amusement, for a change of pace. I'm not good enough to play for other people, and I never touch the keys when other people are here."

I went ahead and asked a question I'd been wanting to ask for a long time. "Doesn't it feel a little too spacious for you, living in such a big house all by yourself?"

"No, I don't think so," Menshiki replied immediately. "Not at all. I've always preferred being by myself. Consider the cerebral cortex for a moment. Humans are provided with a wonderfully precise and efficient cerebral cortex. But normally we use, at most, less than ten percent of it. We've been divinely provided with this amazing, highly efficient organ, but sadly we haven't the ability to use it completely. You could compare it to a four-person family living in a magnificent, grand mansion but using only one small room. All the other rooms are unused and neglected. When you think that way, it's not so unnatural that I live in this house by myself."

"When you put it that way, I suppose it makes sense," I said. It was an interesting analogy.

Menshiki rolled a few cashews around in his hand for a moment and then spoke. "That highly efficient cerebral cortex might seem wasted at first, but without it we wouldn't be able to think abstract thoughts, or enter the realm of the metaphysical. Even though we use but a small part of it, the cerebral cortex has that capacity. If we could use all the rest of it, what would we be capable of, I wonder. Isn't it fascinating to consider?"

"But in exchange for that efficient brain—the price we paid for that magnificent mansion, in other words—mankind had to neglect all kinds of basic abilities. Right?"

"Exactly," Menshiki said. "Even without abstract thought or metaphysical theorizing, just standing on two legs and using clubs gave mankind more than enough skill to win the race for survival on earth. These other abilities aren't that necessary. And in exchange for our hyper-capable cerebral cortexes, of necessity we have to give up lots of other physical abilities. For example, dogs have a sense of smell several thousand times better than humans, and a sense of hearing tens of times better. But we're able to amass complex hypotheses. We're able to compare and contrast the cosmos and the microcosmos, and appreciate Van Gogh and Mozart. We can read Proust—if you want to, that is—and collect Koimari porcelain and Persian rugs. Not something a dog can do."

"Marcel Proust used a sense of smell inferior to that of a dog's to write his lengthy novel."

Menshiki laughed. "That he did. I'm just speaking in generalities."

"The question then is whether or not an idea can be treated as an autonomous entity or not, right?"

"Exactly."

Exactly, the Commendatore whispered into my ear. But following his earlier warning, I didn't look around me.

After this, Menshiki led me into his study. There were broad stairs that led out of the living room, and we took them to the floor below. Somehow these stairs seemed more than stairs, and part of the habitable space in the house. We went down the hallway past several bedrooms (I didn't count how many, but maybe one of them was the locked "Bluebeard's secret room" my girlfriend spoke of), and at the end was the study. It wasn't an especially big room, but of course, it wasn't cramped either. Built to be just the right amount of space. There were few windows in the study, just long, narrow windows like skylights near the ceiling on one wall. All that was visible from the windows were pine branches and the sky visible through the branches. (The room didn't seem to particularly require sunlight or a view.) Without many windows, the walls were that much bigger. One wall was floor-to-ceiling built-in bookcases, one section of which was for a shelf for CDs. The bookshelves were packed with books of all sizes. There was a wooden stepladder to reach the books on the upper shelves. All the books seemed to have been used at one time or another. It was clear that this was a practical collection used by a devoted reader, not decorative bookshelves.

A large office desk faced away from one wall, with two computers on top, a desktop model and a laptop. There were a couple of cups holding pens and pencils, and a neat pile of paperwork. On another wall was a beautiful, expensive-looking stereo set, and on the opposite wall, facing directly across from the desk, sat a pair of tall, narrow speakers. They were about my height (five feet eight), the cases made of high-quality mahogany. An Art Deco armchair for reading and listening to music was in the middle of the room, and next to it a stainless-steel standing lamp for reading. I imagined that Menshiki spent a large part of his days alone in this room.

My portrait of Menshiki was hanging on the wall, at about eye level, exactly between the two speakers. Bare, not yet framed. It looked like a natural part of the room, as if it had been hanging there for a long time. A painting I'd basically created in one intense sitting, yet in this study that uninhibited aspect of it felt, strangely enough, neatly contained. The unique feeling of the place comfortably stilled the painting's plunge-ahead vigor. And unmistakably concealed within that painting was Menshiki's face. To me, in fact, it looked like Menshiki himself was contained within.

I had most definitely painted that painting, but once it had left my hands and become Menshiki's possession, hanging on his study wall, it had transformed into something beyond my reach. Now it was *Menshiki's painting,* not mine. Even if I tried to comprehend something within it, like a slippery, nimble fish the painting would slip out of my hands. Like a woman who'd once been mine but was now someone else's.

"What do you think? Doesn't it fit this room perfectly?"

Menshiki was referring to the painting, of course. I nodded without a word.

"I tried putting it in lots of different rooms. But in the end I knew this was the best room and the perfect spot for it. The amount of space, the way the light hits it, the whole atmosphere is perfect. What I enjoy most is gazing at the picture from that reading chair."

"Could I give it a try?" I said, pointing to the reading chair.

"Of course. Go right ahead."

I sat down on that leather chair, leaned back into the gentle curve it inscribed, and rested my legs on the ottoman. I brought my hands together on my chest and once more gazed at the painting. As Menshiki said, this was the ideal spot from which to appreciate it. Seen from that chair (a chair so comfortable it left nothing to be desired), my painting hanging on the wall in front of me had a quiet, calm persuasiveness that took me by surprise. It looked like almost a completely different work from when it was in my studio, as if it had acquired, since coming here, its rightful life force. Or something like that. And at the same time it seemed to have severed any contact with me, its creator.

Menshiki used a remote control to turn on some music at just the right low volume. A Schubert string quartet I was familiar with. Composition D804. The sound coming out of those speakers was clear, fine-grained, refined, and elegant. Compared with the sound from the speakers in Tomohiko Amada's home, which had a simpler, unadorned tone, it seemed like different music altogether.

Suddenly the Commendatore was in the room. He was seated on the stepladder in front of the bookshelves, his arms folded, looking at my painting. When I glanced at him he shook his head slightly, signaling that I shouldn't look at him. I returned my gaze to the painting.

"Thank you very much," I said to Menshiki as I rose from the chair. "That's the perfect place to hang it."

Menshiki beamed and shook his head. "No, I should be the one thanking *you*. Now that it's found a home here, I'm liking it more and more. When I look at it, I feel like I'm standing in front of . . . a special mirror. I'm inside there, but that's not me, entirely. It's a little different me. When I stare at it for a while, a strange feeling comes over me."

As he listened to the Schubert, Menshiki again turned his attention to a silent appraisal of the painting. The Commendatore, still seated on the stepladder, likewise gazed at the painting with narrowed eyes, as if teasingly imitating him (though I doubt that was his intention).

Menshiki glanced over at the clock on the wall. "Let's go to the dining room. Dinner should be just about ready. I do hope the Commendatore shows up."

I looked at the stepladder. The Commendatore was no longer there.

“I think he’s already here,” I said.

“I’m glad,” Menshiki said, sounding relieved. He touched the remote control and stopped the Schubert. “There’s a place prepared for him, of course. It’s really a shame, though, that he won’t be able to enjoy eating the meal.”

Menshiki explained that on the floor below where we were currently seated, there was a storehouse, a laundry room, and a gym. The gym was outfitted with all sorts of workout equipment. It had a sound system so he could enjoy music while he exercised. Once a week a trainer came and led him through strength-training exercises. There was also an efficiency-sized residence for a live-in maid. It had a simple kitchen and small bathroom, though nobody was using it at present. There used to be a small indoor pool, but it wasn’t very practical and took a lot of upkeep, so he had had it filled in and made into a greenhouse. Someday he might build a two-lane twenty-five-meter lap pool, he said. If I do, he said, I’d love for you to come over and swim. That would be wonderful, I said.

We headed to the dining room.

24

MERELY GATHERING RAW DATA

The dining room was on the same floor as the study. The kitchen was in back of it. The dining room was a long room, with a large, long table in the middle. The oak table was about four inches thick, and big enough for ten people. A solid table that would look good hosting a banquet for Robin Hood and his men. But it was simply the two of us, Menshiki and myself, not a merry band of outlaws. A place was set for the Commendatore, but he wasn't there. A place mat, silverware, and an empty glass were ready for him, but they were just for show. A courtesy to indicate that was his place.

Like in the living room, one long wall was entirely glass. It looked out over the mountain range beyond the valley. Just as I could see Menshiki's house from mine, my house should be visible from his. The house I lived in, though, was nowhere as big as Menshiki's mansion, and it was a wooden building whose subdued color didn't stand out, so in the dark I couldn't make out where it was. There weren't many homes built here, but in each of the houses that dotted the mountains there were clearly lights on inside. It was dinnertime. People were with their families at the dinner table, about to enjoy a hot meal. I could sense that slight warmth in those lights.

In contrast, on the other side of the valley, Menshiki, I, and the Commendatore were seated at that large table, about to begin an eccentric, formal dinner party. Outside a fine rain continued to silently fall. But there was almost no wind, and it was a typically hushed autumn night. I looked out the window and thought again about the hole. About the lonely stone-lined chamber behind the little shrine. Even as we sat here the hole was there, dark and dank. Memories of that scene brought a special chill to me, deep inside.

"I found this table while traveling in Italy," Menshiki said after I'd complimented it. He didn't sound like he was bragging, simply stating facts. "I ran across it in a furniture store in Lucca, purchased it, and had it shipped here. It's so heavy it was quite a task to transport it."

"Do you go abroad very often?"

His lips twisted up a bit, then relaxed. "I used to. Part business, part pleasure. Not so many opportunities to do so these days. I'm doing a different sort of work now. Plus I no longer like to go out much anymore. Most of the time I'm here."

To indicate more clearly what he meant by "here," he motioned toward the house with his hand. I expected him to add more about this change in his work, but that's all he said. As always, he didn't seem eager to say much about his work, and I didn't press him about it.

"I thought we'd start with some well-chilled champagne, if that's all right with you. You don't mind?"

"Of course not," I said. "I'll leave it all up to you."

Menshiki made a faint motion, and the ponytailed young man came over and poured cold champagne into long narrow flutes. Pleasant little bubbles fizzed up in the glasses, so light and thin they seemed made of high-quality paper. We toasted each other across the table. Then Menshiki respectfully lifted his glass to the unoccupied seat for the Commendatore.

"Thank you so much for coming, Commendatore," he said.

There was, naturally, no reply from the Commendatore.

As he enjoyed the champagne, Menshiki talked about opera. About how, on a trip to Sicily, he saw a spectacular performance of Verdi's *Ernani* at the Catania opera house. The person seated next to him sang along with the performers, all the while snacking on mandarin oranges. And how he'd had some amazing champagne there.

The Commendatore finally made an appearance in the dining room, though not at the seat at the table prepared for him. Given his short stature, he would have only come up to nose level, hidden by the table. Instead he plunked himself down on a kind of display shelf diagonally behind Menshiki. He was about five feet off the floor, lightly swinging his feet clad in those oddly shaped black shoes. I raised my glass slightly to him so that Menshiki wouldn't see. As expected, the Commendatore acted as if he didn't notice.

The meal was served at this point. There was an open serving slot between the kitchen and the dining room and the bow-tied, ponytailed young man brought each dish placed there one by one to our table. For a first course, we had a beautiful dish of organic vegetables and fresh isaki fish. Accompanied by white wine. The ponytailed young man uncorked the bottle as carefully as if he were an explosives expert handling a land mine. No explanation of what kind of wine it was or where it was from, though of course it was superb. Menshiki wasn't about to serve a less-than-perfect wine.

After that we were served a salad of lotus root, calamari, and white beans. Then a sea turtle soup. The fish dish was monkfish.

"It's a bit early in the season for it, but I heard that down at the harbor they got hold of some excellent monkfish," Menshiki said. The fish was certainly fresh and amazing. Firm texture, a refined sweetness, but still a clean aftertaste. Lightly steamed, then served with (what I took to be) a tarragon sauce.

Next came thick venison steaks. There was again an explanation of the special sauce, but it was so full of specialized terms I couldn't remember half of it. At any rate, a wonderfully fragrant sauce.

The ponytailed young man poured red wine into our glasses. Menshiki explained that the bottle had been opened an hour before and decanted.

"It's breathed nicely, and it should be just the peak time to drink it."

I knew nothing about aerating wine, but it had a deep flavor. When your tongue first encountered it, then when you held it in your mouth, and finally when you drank it down, the flavor was different each time. It was like a mysterious woman whose beauty changes slightly depending on the angle and light. The wine left a pleasant aftertaste.

"It's Bordeaux," Menshiki said. "I won't sing its praises. Just know it's a Bordeaux."

"It's the kind of wine that once you started listing its good points, you'd have a long list."

Menshiki smiled. Pleasant wrinkles formed at the corners of his eyes.

"You're exactly right. It would be very long if you listed its merits. But I don't particularly like to do that with wines. I'm not good at enumerating the merits of things, no matter what they are. It's just a delicious wine—that's enough, right?"

I had no objections to that.

All this time the Commendatore watched us drinking and eating from his perch on the display shelf. He sat there, unmoving, diligently observing the scene there down to the smallest detail, but didn't seem to have any reaction to what he was seeing. Like he told me once, he merely observes. He doesn't judge, or have any partiality toward it. He's merely gathering raw data.

This might be how he observed me and my girlfriend making love in bed in the afternoons. The thought unsettled me. He'd told me that watching people have sex was for him no different from watching morning radio exercise routines or someone sweeping a chimney. And that might very well be the case. But the fact remained that it was disconcerting to think of being observed.

An hour and a half later, Menshiki and I finally arrived at dessert (a soufflé) and espresso. A long but fulfilling journey. For the first time, the chef came out of the kitchen and over to the dining table. A tall man, in a white chef's outfit. In his mid-thirties would be my guess, with a sparse black beard. He greeted me politely.

"The food was amazing," I told him. "I've hardly ever had anything so delicious."

Those were my honest feelings. I still couldn't believe that a chef who made such exquisite dishes ran a small, unknown French restaurant near the harbor in Odawara.

"Thank you very much," he said, smiling brightly. "Mr. Menshiki's always been very kind to me."

He bowed and returned to the kitchen.

"I wonder if the Commendatore was satisfied, too?" Menshiki said after the chef had left, a concerned look on his face. He didn't appear to be playacting. He seemed genuinely concerned.

"I'm sure he is," I replied with a straight face. "It's a shame, of course, that he couldn't enjoy the fabulous meal, but he must have enjoyed the atmosphere."

"I do hope so."

Of course I enjoyed it, the Commendatore whispered in my ear.

Menshiki suggested an after-dinner drink, but I declined. I was so full I really couldn't manage anything else. He had a brandy.

"There was something that I wanted to ask you," Menshiki said as he slowly swirled the brandy in the oversized glass. "It's an odd question, and I hope you're not offended."

"Feel free to ask me anything."

He took a small sip of brandy, tasting it. Then quietly laid his glass on the table.

"It's about the pit in the woods," Menshiki said. "The other day I spent about an hour in that stone chamber. No flashlight, seated alone at the bottom of the pit. The cover was on top, and rocks on top of that to hold it down. And I told you, 'Please come back in an hour and get me out of here.' Correct?"

"That's right."

"Why do you think I did that?"

"I have no idea," I answered honestly.

"I needed to do that," Menshiki said. "I can't explain it, but sometimes I need to do *that*. Be left all alone in a cramped, dark, completely silent space."

I was silent, waiting for his next words.

Menshiki continued. "Here's my question to you. During that hour did you ever find yourself, even for a moment, wanting to abandon me in that pit? Tempted to just leave me behind at the bottom of that dark hole?"

I couldn't grasp what he was getting at. "*Abandon* you?"

Menshiki touched his right temple and rubbed it, as if checking out a scar. "This is what I mean. I was at the bottom of that pit, a little less than nine feet deep and six feet across. The ladder had been pulled up. The stones in the wall were all densely laid together, and there was no way to climb up. And the cover was on tight. In mountains like these I could yell at the top of my voice or ring the bell, but no one would ever hear me—though of course *you* might. In other words, I couldn't get back to the surface on my own. If you hadn't come back, I'd have had to stay in the pit forever. Isn't that so?"

"That could be."

The fingers of his right hand were still at his temple. He'd stopped rubbing. "What I'd like to know is whether during that hour the thought ever occurred to you, even for a moment, *I'll just leave that man inside the pit. Leave him the way he is*. Tell me the truth, it won't offend me."

He took his fingers from his temple, reached for the glass of brandy, and again slowly held it up and swirled it. This time, though, he didn't take a sip. Eyes narrowed, he inhaled the aroma and put the glass back on the table.

"That thought never occurred to me," I answered honestly. "*Even for a moment.* All I thought about was that after an hour I had to take the cover off and get you out of there."

"Really?"

"One hundred percent."

"Well, if I had been in your position . . ." Menshiki said, sounding confessional. His voice was quite calm. "I'm sure I would have thought of that. I definitely would have been tempted to leave you inside that pit forever. I would have thought, This is the chance of a lifetime."

No words came to me.

Menshiki said, "Down at the bottom of the pit that's what I was thinking about the whole time. That if I was in your position I would definitely consider it. It's a strange thing. You were the one on the surface and I was the one at the bottom of the pit, but all that time I was picturing me on the surface and you at the bottom."

"But if you'd actually abandoned me in the pit I might have starved to death. I might have turned into an actual mummy, ringing a bell. You're saying you'd be okay with that?"

"It's just a fantasy. Or delusion, perhaps. *Of course* I would never actually do that. I was just imagining the scenario. Just mentally playing with the concept of death. So don't worry. What I mean is, I find it hard to fathom that you didn't feel the same temptation."

I said, "Weren't you afraid, Mr. Menshiki, being down at the bottom of that dark pit all alone? Thinking that I might be tempted to abandon you there?"

Menshiki shook his head. "No, I wasn't afraid. Deep inside me I may have actually been hoping you would."

"*Hoping* I would?" I said, surprised. "That I would leave you down in that pit?"

"Exactly."

"In other words, you were okay with being abandoned down there?"

"Don't get me wrong, it wasn't that I was okay with dying. Even I still have some attachment to this life. And starving to death or dying of lack of water aren't the ways I'd like to go. All I wanted was to *try to get closer to death,* even if just a little more. I know that boundary is a very fine line."

I thought about what he said, though I still couldn't grasp what he meant. I casually glanced over at the Commendatore, still seated on the display shelf. His face was bereft of expression.

Menshiki went on. "When you're locked up alone in a cramped, dark place, the most frightening thing isn't death. The most terrifying thought is that *I might have to live here forever.* Once you think that, the terror makes it hard to breathe. The walls close in on you and the delusion grabs you that you're going to be crushed. In order to survive, a person has to overcome that fear. Which means conquering yourself. And in order to do that, you need to get as close to death as you possibly can."

"But there's a danger to that."

"Like when Icarus flew close to the sun. It's not easy to know how close you can go, where that line is. You put your life at risk doing it."

"But if you avoid approaching it, you can't overcome fear and conquer yourself."

"Precisely. If you can't do that, you can't take yourself to the next level," Menshiki said. He seemed to be considering something. And then suddenly—at least it seemed sudden to me—he stood up, went over to the window, and looked out.

"It's still raining a little, but not so hard. Do you mind going out on the deck? There's something I want to show you."

We walked up the steps from the dining room to the living room and then out to the deck. It was a large deck, with a Mediterranean tiled floor. We went over to the wooden railing and gazed out at the valley. It was like a tourist lookout, and we were afforded a view of the entire valley. A fine rain was still falling, more like mist at this point. The lights were still on in people's homes across the valley. It was the same valley, but viewed from the opposite side like this, the scenery looked transformed.

A section of the deck was roofed over, with a chaise longue beneath it, for sunbathing or perhaps reading. Next to it was a low glass-topped table to put drinks or books on. And also a large planter with a decorative green plant, and a tall piece of equipment of some kind, covered in plastic. There was a spotlight on the wall, but it wasn't turned on. The lights in the living room were turned down low.

"I wonder which direction my house is?" I asked Menshiki.

Menshiki pointed to the right. "It's over there."

I stared hard in that direction, but with the lights out and the misty rain I couldn't locate it.

"I can't see it," I told him.

"Just a moment," Menshiki said, and walked over to where the chaise longue was. He removed the plastic cover from the piece of equipment and carried it over. It looked like a pair of binoculars on a tripod. The binoculars weren't big, but looked odd, different from normal ones. They were a drab olive green and the crude shape made it appear like some optical instrument for surveying. He placed this beside the railing, pointed it, and carefully focused.

"Here, take a look. This is where you live," he said.

I squinted through the binoculars. They had a clear field of vision, with high magnification. Not your typical binoculars that you find in a store. Through the faint vale of misty rain the far-off scenery looked close enough to touch. And it definitely was the house I was living in. The terrace was there, the lounge chair I always sat in. Beyond that was the living room, and next to it, my painting studio. With the lights off I couldn't make out the interior, though during the day you probably could. It felt strange to see (or peek into) the place where I lived.

"Don't worry," Menshiki said from behind me, as if reading my mind. "No need to be concerned. I don't encroach on your privacy. I mean, I hardly ever turn these binoculars on your house. Trust me. What I want to see is *something else*."

"What do you want to see?" I said. I took my eye from the binoculars, turned around, and looked at him. His face was cool, inscrutable as always. At night on the deck, though, his hair looked whiter than ever.

"I'll show you," Menshiki said. With a practiced hand he swung the binoculars slightly to the north and swiftly refocused. He took a step back and said, "Please take a look."

I looked through the binoculars. In the circular field of vision I saw an elegant wooden house halfway up the mountain. A two-story building also constructed to take advantage of the slope, with a terrace facing this direction. On a map it would be my nearest neighbor, but because of the topography there was no road linking us, so one would have to go down to the bottom of the mountain and ascend once more on a separate road to access it. Lights were on in the windows, but the curtains were drawn, and I couldn't see inside. If the curtains were open, though, and the lights on, you would be able to see the people inside. Very possible with binoculars this powerful.

"These are NATO-issue military binoculars. They're not sold anywhere, so it wasn't easy to get hold of them. They're bright, so you can make out images well even in the dark."

I took my eyes away from the binoculars and looked at Menshiki. "This house is *what you want to see*?"

"Correct. But don't get the wrong idea. I'm no voyeur."

He glanced through the binoculars one last time, then put them and the tripod back where they were and placed the plastic cover over them.

"Let's go inside. We don't want to catch cold," Menshiki said. We went back into the living room, and sat on the sofa and armchair. The ponytailed young man sidled over and asked if we'd like anything to drink, but both of us declined.

"Thank you very much for tonight," Menshiki said to the young man. "Feel free to go now." The young man bowed and withdrew.

The Commendatore was now seated on top of the piano. The black Steinway full grand. He looked like he preferred this spot to where he had been sitting before. The jewels on the top handle of his long sword caught the light with a proud glint.

"In that house over there," Menshiki began, "lives the girl who *may be my daughter*. I like to see her, even if it's from a distance."

For quite some time I was speechless.

"Do you remember? What I told you about the daughter my former girlfriend had, after she married another man? That she might be mine?"

"Of course. The woman who was stung by hornets and died. Her daughter would be thirteen. Right?"

Menshiki gave a short, concise nod. "She lives in *that house* with her father. In that house across the valley."

It took a while to put the myriad questions that welled up in my mind in some kind of order. Menshiki waited silently all this time, patiently waiting for my reaction.

I said, "In other words, in order to see that young girl who might be your daughter through the binoculars every day, you bought this mansion directly across the valley. You paid a lot of money and a great deal to renovate this house *for that sole purpose*. Is that what you're saying?"

Menshiki said, "Yes, that's it. This is the ideal spot to be able to observe her house. I had to get this mansion no matter what. There was no other lot around here that I could get a building permit for. And ever since, I've been looking for her across the valley through my binoculars, almost every day. Though I should say that the days I can't see her far outnumber the days I can."

"So you live alone, keeping people out as much as you can, so no one interferes with that pursuit."

Menshiki nodded again. "That's right. I don't want anyone to bother me. No one to disturb things. That's what I'm looking for. I need unlimited solitude. You're the only other person in the world who knows this secret. It wouldn't be good to confess this kind of delicate thing to people."

You got that right, I thought. And this thought occurred to me as well: Then why did you just tell *me*?

"Then why did you just tell me?" I asked Menshiki. "Is there some special reason?"

Menshiki recrossed his legs and looked straight at me. His voice was soft. "Yes, of course there's a reason. I have a special favor to ask of you."

25

HOW MUCH LONELINESS THE TRUTH CAN CAUSE

I have a special favor to ask of you," Menshiki said.

From his tone I guessed he'd been waiting for the right moment to bring this up. And that this was the real reason he had invited me (and the Commendatore) to dinner. In order to reveal his secret and bring up this request.

"If it's something I can help with, of course," I said.

Menshiki gazed into my eyes, and then spoke. "More than something you can help with, it's something only *you* can help with."

I was suddenly dying for a cigarette. When I got married I used that as the incentive to stop smoking, and in the nearly seven years since, I hadn't smoked a single cigarette. It was tough quitting—I'd been a pretty heavy smoker—but nowadays I never had the urge. But at that instant, for the first time in forever, I thought about how great it would be to have a cigarette between my lips and light it. I could hear the scratch of the match.

"What could that possibly be?" I asked. Not that I particularly wanted to know—I'd prefer to get by not knowing—but the way the conversation was going, I had to ask.

"Well, I'd like you to paint her portrait," Menshiki said.

In my head I had to dismantle the context of his words, then reassemble it all. Though it was a very simple context.

"You mean you want me to paint the portrait of this girl who *may be* your daughter."

Menshiki nodded. "Exactly. That's what I want you to do. And not from a photograph, but actually have her pose for you and paint the picture with her as the model. Have her come to your studio, like when you painted me. That's my only condition. How you paint her is up to you—do it any way you want. I promise I won't have any other requests later on."

I was at a loss for words. Several questions immediately occurred to me, and I asked the first one that came to mind. "But how can I convince the girl to do that? I might be her neighbor, but I can't very well just suggest to a young girl I don't know that *I want to paint your portrait, so would you model for me?*"

"No, of course not. That would make her suspicious for sure."

"Then do you have any good ideas?"

Menshiki looked at me for a time, then, like quietly opening a door and tiptoeing into a back room of a house, he slowly opened his mouth. "Actually, you already know her. And she knows you very well."

"I already know her?"

"You do. Her name is Mariye—Mariye Akikawa. *Aki*—the character for 'autumn'—and *kawa,* 'river.' *Mariye* is spelled out in hiragana. You do know her, right?"

Mariye Akikawa. I'd heard the name before, but it felt like some temporary obstruction was keeping me from putting name and face together. Finally the pieces fell into place.

I said, "Mariye Akikawa is in my children's art class in Odawara, isn't she?"

Menshiki nodded. "That's right. Exactly. You're her painting teacher."

Mariye Akikawa was a small, quiet thirteen-year-old girl in the children's art class I taught. The class was for elementary school children, and as a junior high student, she was the eldest, but she was so reserved she didn't stand out at all, even though she was with the younger children. She always sat in a corner, trying to stay under the radar. I remembered her because something about her reminded me of my late sister, and she was about the same age as my sister when she passed away.

Mariye Akikawa hardly ever spoke in class. If I said something to her she just nodded, with barely a word in response. When she absolutely had to say something, she spoke it in such a small voice I often had to ask her to repeat herself. She seemed tense, unable to look me straight in the eye. But she loved painting, and the expression in her eyes radically transformed whenever she held a brush and was working on a canvas. Her gaze became focused, her eyes filled with an intense gleam. And her paintings were quite appealing. Not skilled, exactly, but eye-catching. Her use of colors was especially unique. All in all, a curious sort of girl.

Her glossy black hair fell straight down, her features as lovely as a doll's. So beautiful, in fact, when you looked at her whole face, there was the sense of it being detached from reality. Her features were objectively attractive, but most people would hesitate to label her beautiful. Something—perhaps that special raw, unpolished aspect that certain young girls exude in adolescence—interfered with the flow of beauty that should have been there. But someday that blockage might be removed and she would turn into a truly lovely girl. That was still a ways off, though. Now that I thought of it, my sister's features were similar in that way. I often used to think she didn't appear as beautiful as I knew she could be.

"So Mariye Akikawa *might* be your real daughter. And she lives in the house across the valley," I said. "And I'm to paint a portrait with her as model. That's what you're asking?"

"I'd prefer to see it as a *request,* rather than that I'm *commissioning* the work. And if you're okay with it, once the painting is finished I'd like to buy it and hang it on the wall in this house. That's what I want. Or rather what I'm requesting."

Still, there was something about all this I couldn't quite swallow. I had a faint apprehension that things wouldn't simply end there.

"And that's it? That's all you want?" I asked.

Menshiki slowly inhaled and breathed out. "Honestly, there's one other thing I'd like you to do."

"Which is—?"

"A very small thing." His voice was quiet, but with a certain force behind it. "When she's sitting for the portrait, I'd like to visit you. Make it seem like I just happened to stop by. Once is enough. And it can be for just a short time, I don't mind. Just let me be in the same room as her, and breathe the same air. I won't ask for anything more. And I can assure you I won't do anything to get in your way."

I thought about it. And the more I did, the more uncomfortable I felt.

I've never been cut out to act as an intermediary. I don't enjoy getting caught up in the flow of somebody else's strong emotions—no matter what emotions they might be. The role didn't suit me. But the fact was that I also wanted to do something for Menshiki. I had to think carefully about my reply.

"We can talk about that later on," I said. "The first thing is whether or not Mariye will agree to sit for the painting. That's the first step. She's a very quiet girl, like a bashful cat. She might not want to model. Or else her parents might not give permission. They don't really know my background, so they'll be pretty wary, I would imagine."

"I know Mr. Matsushima very well, the man who runs the arts-and-culture center," Menshiki said coolly. "And I'm also, coincidentally, an investor, a financial supporter of the school. I think if Mr. Matsushima puts in a good word, things will go smoothly. You're an upright person, an artist with a solid career, and if he recommends you, I think it will assuage any concerns that her parents might have."

He's already got it all mapped out, I thought. He's already anticipated what might happen, like the opening moves of a game of go. Nothing *coincidental* about it.

Menshiki went on. "Mariye Akikawa's unmarried aunt takes care of her. Her father's younger sister. I believe I mentioned this before, but after Mariye's mother died, this aunt came to live with them and has been like a mother to Mariye. Her father is too busy with work to be very involved. So as long as the aunt is persuaded, things should work out fine. Once she agrees to have Mariye model, I would expect the aunt to accompany her to your house as her guardian. There's no way she'd allow a young girl to go by herself to the house of a man living alone."

"But will she really give permission for Mariye to model?"

"Let me handle that. As long as you agree to paint her portrait, I'll take care of any other practical issues that come up."

I had little doubt he'd be able to "take care of" any of these other "practical issues." That was his forte. But was it good for me to get so deeply involved in those problems—all these complex interpersonal relations? Didn't Menshiki have his own plans and intentions that went beyond what he was revealing to me?

"Can I be totally honest with you?" I said. "Maybe it isn't my place to say this, but I'd like you to hear me out."

"Of course. Say whatever you want."

"Isn't it better, before you put this plan into action, that you determine whether or not Mariye Akikawa really *is* your child? If you find out she isn't, then there's no need to go to all this trouble. It might not be easy, but there has to be a way. I think if anyone could discover that, you could. Even if I paint her portrait, and it's hanging next to yours, that's not going to solve anything."

Menshiki paused before replying. "If I wanted to scientifically determine if Mariye Akikawa is related by blood to me, I could. It might take some effort, but it's not impossible. The thing is—I don't want to."

"Why not?"

"Because whether she's my child or not isn't a determining factor."

I gazed at him, mouth shut. He shook his head, his abundant white hair waving, like it was fluttering in the breeze. When he spoke, his voice was calm, like he was explaining to some large, intelligent dog how to conjugate simple verbs.

"I'm not saying either way is fine. It's just that I don't feel like determining the facts. Maybe Mariye Akikawa is my biological child. And maybe she isn't. But what if I do determine that she's my real child—then what? I announce to her that I'm her real father? Try to get custody? I can't do that."

Menshiki shook his head again, rubbing his hands together on his lap like it was a cold night and he was warming himself before a fireplace. He continued.

"Mariye Akikawa is living a peaceful life in that house with her father and her aunt. Yes, her mother died, but the family—despite some issues her father has—is relatively healthy and functional. She's close to her aunt. She's made a life for herself. If I suddenly appear on the scene announcing that I'm her real father, even if I could prove it scientifically, will that solve anything? The truth will actually confuse things. And it's not going to make anyone happy. Including me."

"So you'd prefer to keep things the way they are, rather than let the truth come out."

Menshiki spread his hands on his lap. “In a word, yes. It took some time for me to arrive at that conclusion, but my feelings are firm. I plan to live the rest of my life holding on to the possibility that *Mariye Akikawa is my real child.* Watching, from a distance, as she grows up. That’s enough. Even if I knew for sure she was my child, that wouldn’t make me happy. The sense of loss would be all the more painful. And if I knew she *wasn’t* my child, that would, in a different sense, also deepen the sense of loss. Or maybe crush me. Either way there’s no happy result. Can you follow what I’m trying to say?”

“I think so. At least in theory. But if I were in your position, I’d want to know the truth. Theory aside, it’s natural for people to want to know the truth.”

Menshiki smiled. “You’re still young, so that’s why you say that. When you get to be my age, you’ll understand how I feel. How much loneliness the truth can cause sometimes.”

“So what you’re after is not to know the unmitigated truth, but to hang her portrait on your wall, gaze at it every day, and ponder the possibilities. Are you sure that’s enough?”

Menshiki nodded. “It is. Instead of a stable truth, I choose unstable possibilities. I choose to surrender myself to that instability. Do you think that’s unnatural?”

I did indeed. Or at least I didn’t see it as natural. I wouldn’t go so far as to call it unhealthy, though. But that was Menshiki’s problem, not mine.

I glanced over at the Commendatore seated on top of the Steinway. Our eyes met. He raised both index fingers upward and spread them apart, as if to say, *Let’s put that answer on hold.* Then he pointed with his right index finger to a watch on his left wrist. Of course the Commendatore wasn’t wearing a watch. He was just pointing to where one would be. And of course what that meant was, *We should be leaving soon.* The Commendatore’s advice to me, as well as a warning. I decided to heed it.

“Could I have a little time to get back to you on this? It’s a delicate matter, and I need time to consider it.”

Menshiki held up his hands from his lap. “Of course. Consider it as long as you’d like. I’m not trying to rush you. I know I may be asking too much.”

I stood up and thanked him for the dinner.

"Ah, there's one thing I forgot to tell you," Menshiki said, as if suddenly remembering. "It's about Tomohiko Amada. We talked earlier, didn't we, about how he'd studied abroad, in Austria? About how, just before World War Two broke out, he rushed back home?"

"Yes, I remember."

"I researched it a bit. I'm interested, too, in what was behind all that. It happened a long time ago, and I don't have all the facts, but there were rumors then of some sort of scandal."

"A scandal?"

"That's right. Amada was apparently caught up in an aborted assassination attempt in Vienna. It turned into a political crisis, and the Japanese embassy in Berlin got involved and secreted him back to Japan. According to certain rumors. This was right after the *Anschluss*. You know about the *Anschluss,* I assume?"

"That was when Germany annexed Austria in 1938."

"Correct. Hitler incorporated Austria into Germany. There was a lot of chaos, and the Nazis finally took over all of Austria pretty much by force, and the nation of Austria vanished. This was in March 1938. The place was in turmoil, and in the confusion of the moment a lot of people were murdered. Assassinated, or murdered and made to look like suicides. Or else sent to concentration camps. It was during this time that Tomohiko Amada studied in Vienna. Rumor had it that he fell in love with an Austrian woman and got mixed up with an underground resistance group comprised largely of college students, who plotted to assassinate a high-ranking Nazi official. Not the sort of thing either the German government or the Japanese government would condone, for they'd signed a mutual defense pact only a year and a half before this, and the relationship between the two countries was growing closer all the time. Both were dead set on avoiding anything that would hinder their pact. Though Tomohiko Amada was still young, he had already made a name for himself as an artist in Japan, and his father was a large landowner, a locally politically influential person. A person like that couldn't just be secretly blotted out."

"So Tomohiko Amada was sent back to Japan?"

"Correct. Rescued is more like it. Thanks to the political considerations of higher-ups, he narrowly escaped getting killed. If the Gestapo had gotten hold of him under suspicion of something that serious—even if they hadn't had any clear-cut evidence—that would have been the end of him."

"But the assassination didn't happen?"

"No, it was abortive. There was an informant in the group, and the plan was leaked to the Gestapo. There was a wholesale arrest of the members."

"There would have been a real uproar if they'd gone through with it."

"The strange thing is, there was no talk of it at the time," Menshiki said. "There were whispers about a scandal, but there doesn't seem to be any public record of it. For various reasons, it was covered up."

So the Commendatore in the painting *Killing Commendatore* might represent that Nazi official. The painting might be a hypothetical depiction of the assassination that never actually happened in Vienna in 1938. Amada and his lover were connected with this plot, and then it was discovered by the authorities. The two of them were torn apart, and the woman most likely killed. And after he returned to Japan Amada transferred that horrific experience in Vienna onto the very symbolic canvas of a Japanese-style painting. *Adapting* it, in other words, into a scene from the Asuka period, set over a thousand years ago. *Killing Commendatore* was a painting Tomohiko Amada painted for himself alone. He felt compelled for his own sake to paint it to preserve that awful, bloody memory from his youth. Which is precisely why he never made the painting public, why he wrapped it up tightly and hid it away in the attic.

Perhaps that incident in Vienna was one reason he made a clean break with his career as an artist of Western paintings and converted to Japanese-style painting. He might have wanted to decisively separate himself from the self he used to be.

"How did you find out about all this?" I asked.

"It didn't take a lot of effort on my part. I asked an organization run by an acquaintance to investigate it for me. But it happened such a long time ago, and they can't be held responsible for how much of it is really true. They did check with multiple sources, though, so I think the information can basically be trusted."

"Tomohiko Amada had an Austrian lover. She was a member of an underground resistance group. And he was involved in that assassination plot."

Menshiki inclined his head a bit and then spoke. "If that's true, then it's a pretty dramatic series of events. But most of the people involved are dead by now, so there's no way for us to really know what happened. Facts have a tendency to get embellished, too. At any rate, though, it's pretty melodramatic."

"No one knows how deeply he was involved in that plot?"

"No. We don't know. I've just given it my own dramatic touch. Amada was deported from Vienna, bid his lover farewell—or maybe wasn't even able to do that—was put on a ship in Bremen, and returned to Japan. During the war he remained silent, holed up in rural Aso, then debuted as a painter of Japanese-style paintings soon after the end of the war. Which took people by complete surprise. Another pretty dramatic development."

Thus ended the story of Tomohiko Amada.

The same black Infiniti I'd arrived in was quietly awaiting me in front of the house. A faint drizzle was still intermittently falling, the air wet and chilly. The season when you needed a coat was just around the corner.

"Thank you so much for coming," Menshiki said. "My thanks, too, to the Commendatore."

It is I *who should be doing the thanking*, the Commendatore murmured in my ear. His voice, of course, was only for me to hear. I thanked Menshiki once more for dinner. It was an amazing meal, I said. I couldn't be more satisfied. The Commendatore seemed grateful as well.

"I hope bringing up all of those boring details after dinner didn't spoil the evening," Menshiki said.

"Not at all. But about your request: I need some time to think about it."

"Of course."

"It takes me time to consider things."

"It's the same for me," Menshiki said. "My motto is: Thinking three times is better than two. And if time allows, thinking four times is better than three."

The driver had the rear door open, waiting. I got inside. The Commendatore should have boarded at the same time, though I didn't see him. The car started up the asphalt slope, drove out the open gate, then proceeded slowly down the mountain. Once the white mansion disappeared from view, everything that happened that night seemed like part of a dream. It was getting harder to distinguish what was normal from what was not, what was real and what was not.

What you can see is real, the Commendatore whispered in my ear. *What you need to do is open your eyes wide and look at it. You can judge it later on.*

Even with my eyes wide open, there could be many things I was overlooking, I thought. I may have actually murmured this aloud, since the chauffeur shot me a glance in the rearview mirror. I closed my eyes and leaned back against the seat. And thought this: How wonderful it would be to put off judging things forever.

I got home a little before ten p.m. I brushed my teeth in the bathroom, changed into pajamas, slid into bed, and fell right asleep. Predictably, I had a million dreams, all of them strange, disconcerting. Swastika flags flying over the streets of Vienna, a huge passenger ship easing out of Bremen harbor, a brass band playing on the pier, Bluebeard's unopened room, Menshiki playing the Steinway.

26

THE COMPOSITION COULDN'T BE IMPROVED

Two days later I got a call from my agent in Tokyo. They'd received the transfer of funds from Mr. Menshiki, the payment for the painting, and after taking the agent's fee out of it the rest had been deposited into my bank account. When I heard the total amount I was astonished. It was much higher than what I'd originally heard.

"The finished painting was better than he'd anticipated, so he added a bonus. There was a message from Mr. Menshiki requesting that you accept this as a token of his gratitude," my agent said.

I groaned faintly, but no words would come.

"I haven't seen the actual painting, though Mr. Menshiki attached a photo. From the photo, at least, it looks like an amazing work. Something that goes beyond the boundaries of portrait painting, yet remains a convincing portrait."

I thanked him and hung up.

A little while later my girlfriend called. Did I mind if she came over tomorrow morning? That would be fine, I told her. Friday was when I taught art class, but I'd have enough time to make it.

"Did you have dinner at Mr. Menshiki's place?" she asked.

"Yes, a really excellent meal."

"Did it taste good?"

"It was amazing. The wine was great, too, and the food was outstanding."

"What was the house like inside?"

"Beautiful," I said. "It'd take me half a day to describe it all."

"Could you tell me all about it when I see you?"

"Before? Or after?"

"After's good," she said simply.

After I hung up the phone, I went into the studio and looked at Tomohiko Amada's *Killing Commendatore*. I'd seen it so many times, but now, after what Menshiki told me, it took on a strangely graphic reality. This was not simply some historical picture of a past event, reproduced in an old-fashioned format. It felt—from the expressions and movements of each of the four characters (excluding Long Face)—like you could read their reactions to the situation. The young man piercing the Commendatore with his long sword was perfectly expressionless. He'd shut away his heart, hiding his emotions. In the Commendatore's face, one could read the agony as his chest was stabbed, but also a sense of pure surprise, the sense of *How could this possibly be happening?* The young woman watching this take place (in the opera, this character is Donna Anna) was torn apart by violently conflicting emotions. Her lovely face was contorted in anguish, her lovely white hand held to her mouth. The stocky man, a servant by the look of him (Leporello), was gasping for breath, gazing up at the sky. His hand was stretched out as if trying to reach something.

The organization was perfect. The composition couldn't be improved. It was a superb, polished arrangement. Each character maintained a vivid dynamism in their actions, instantaneously frozen in time. And now I saw the events of the aborted assassination that *may* have occurred in 1938 Vienna overlaying the painting. The Commendatore was dressed not in Asuka period costume but in a Nazi uniform. Maybe the black uniform of the SS. And in his chest was a saber or perhaps a dagger. *Perhaps* the one stabbing him was Tomohiko Amada himself. And who was the woman gasping nearby? Was this Amada's Austrian lover? And what was it that was rending her heart in two like that?

I sat on the stool, gazing for a long time at *Killing Commendatore*. My imagination could come up with all sorts of allegories and messages contained therein, but these were, in the final analysis, nothing more than unsubstantiated hypotheses. The background—what I took as background, that is—that Menshiki had talked about was not historical fact, but nothing more than rumor. Or else just a melodrama. Everything remained on the level of *perhaps*.

A thought suddenly struck me: I wish my sister were here.

If Komi were with me, I'd tell her everything that had happened, and she'd listen quietly, adding an occasional short question. Even with an incomprehensible, mixed-up story like this, I doubt she'd frown or show any surprise. Her calm, thoughtful expression wouldn't change. And after I finished, she'd pause, then give me some useful advice. Ever since we were little we'd had that kind of interaction. But I realized now she'd never come to *me* for advice. As far as I could recall, that had never happened. Why? Maybe she didn't have any major emotional issues? Or maybe she'd decided asking me for advice wasn't going to help? Maybe both, or half of each.

But even if she had been healthy and hadn't died at twelve, the intimate brother-sister relationship we had shared might not have lasted. Komi might have ended up marrying some boring guy, gone to live in a town far away, been run ragged by everyday life, exhausted by raising children, lost her sparkle, and no longer retained the energy to give me advice. No one could say how our lives would have worked out.

The problems my wife and I had had might have stemmed from me unconsciously wanting Yuzu to stand in for Komi. That was never my intention, of course, but now that I thought of it, ever since I lost my sister I may have been seeking, somewhere inside me, a substitute partner I could lean on whenever I was struggling. Needless to say, though, Yuzu wasn't Komi. Their positions, and roles, were vastly different. And so was the history we'd shared.

As I thought about this, I remembered the visit I'd made to Yuzu's parents' home in Kinuta in Setagaya in Tokyo, before we got married.

Yuzu's father was the branch manager of a large bank. His son—Yuzu's older brother—was also a banker, and worked for the same bank. Both were graduates of the elite economics department of Tokyo University. There seemed to be a lot of bankers in her family. I wanted to marry Yuzu (and of course she wanted to marry me, too), and the visit was for me to convey my intentions to her parents. Any way you looked at it, it was hard to call the half-hour interview I had with her father a friendly visit. I was an unknown artist who worked part-time painting portraits and didn't make what could be called a regular income. A guy with little in the way of future prospects. Not at all the sort of man a top banker like her father would view favorably. I'd anticipated this ahead of time and was dead set on not losing my cool no matter what he said, or how much criticism he heaped upon me. And I was basically the kind of person who could put up with a lot.

Yet as I listened to her father's long-winded sermon, a kind of physical revulsion welled up in me, and I lost it. I felt sick, like I was going to throw up. I stood up before he'd finished and said, I'm sorry, but I need to use the bathroom. I knelt down in front of the toilet bowl, trying to vomit up the contents of my stomach. But I couldn't vomit. Because there was hardly anything in my stomach. Even the gastric juices wouldn't come out. I took some deep breaths and calmed down. I gargled with water to get rid of the bad taste in my mouth, wiped the sweat from my face with a handkerchief, and went back to the living room.

"Are you all right?" Yuzu asked, looking concerned. I must have looked awful.

"A successful marriage is up to the people involved, but I can tell you, this one won't last long. Four, five years at the most." These were her father's parting words to me that day. (I didn't respond.) His spiteful words stayed with me, a kind of curse that remained for a long time to come.

Her parents never did agree to our marriage, but we went ahead and registered it, and officially became a married couple. By this time, I had very little contact with my own parents. Yuzu and I didn't have a wedding ceremony. Our friends rented a small place and held a simple party to celebrate, but that was it. (The person who did the most to make that happen was Masahiko, who was always good at taking care of others.) Despite the inauspicious beginning, we were happy. At least for the first few years, we were definitely happy together. For four or five years, we had no problems between us. But then, like a huge cruising ship in the middle of the ocean turning its rudder, there was a gradual change. I still don't know why. I can't even pinpoint when things began to move in a different direction. What she hoped for in marriage, and what I was looking for, must have been different, and that gap only grew more pronounced over time. And then, before I knew it, she was seeing another man. In the end our marriage only lasted some six years.

I imagine that when her father learned that our marriage had failed, he'd chuckled to himself and thought, I told you so. (Though we had stayed together a year or two beyond what he'd predicted.) It must have pleased him no end that Yuzu had left me. After we'd broken up, had Yuzu reconciled with her family? I had no way of knowing, and didn't really want to know, at that point. This was her business, not mine. But still her father's curse continued to hang over me. Even now, I sensed the vague weight of its presence. I'd been hurt, more than I cared to admit, and had bled. Like the pierced heart of the Commendatore in Tomohiko Amada's painting.

Late afternoon came on, and with it, the early-autumn twilight. The sky turned dark in the twinkling of an eye, the glossy black crows squawking their way across the valley, heading for their roosts. I went out on the terrace, leaned against the railing, and gazed over at Menshiki's house across the way. Several mercury lights were on in his garden, the whiteness of the house rising up in the dusk. I pictured Menshiki out there every night, searching through his high-powered binoculars for Mariye Akikawa. He'd purchased that white house, almost by force, for the sole purpose of doing that. Spent a huge amount of money, made a great deal of effort, all for an overly large house that didn't suit his tastes.

And strangely enough (at least to me it felt strange), I'd begun to feel a closeness to Menshiki, a closeness I'd never felt to anyone before. An affinity—no, a sense of solidarity, really. In a sense, we were very similar—that's what I thought. The two of us were motivated not by what we had got hold of, or were trying to get, but by what we'd lost, what we *did not now have*. I can't say I understood his actions. They were beyond my comprehension. But I could understand what had spurred him on.

I went to the kitchen, took the single malt that Masahiko had given me, and poured a glass on the rocks. I carried the drink out to the living room sofa and selected a record of a Schubert string quartet from

Tomohiko Amada's collection, and put it on the turntable. A piece titled "Rosamunde." The same music that had been playing in Menshiki's study. I listened to the music, occasionally clinking the ice in my glass.

The Commendatore never showed up that day. Maybe, like the horned owl, he was quietly resting up in the attic. Even Ideas needed some time off. I didn't do any painting that day, either. I needed some time off as well.

I raised my glass to the Commendatore.

27

EVEN THOUGH YOU REMEMBER EXACTLY WHAT IT LOOKED LIKE

When my girlfriend came over I told her all about the dinner party at Menshiki's. Leaving out, of course, any mention of Mariye Akikawa, the high-powered binoculars, and the Commendatore having secretly accompanied me. What I described was the dinner menu, the way the rooms were laid out in the house, the kind of furniture—safe subjects. We were in bed, completely naked, after making love for about a half hour. At first it was hard to relax, knowing that the Commendatore must be observing us, but as we got into it, I forgot all about him. If he wanted to watch, let him.

Like a rabid sports fan is dying to know how his favorite team scored in the game the night before, my girlfriend panted over every detail of the dishes we had at dinner. I painstakingly went over the details, as far as I could remember them, from the hors d'oeuvres to dessert, from the wine to the coffee. Even the tableware. I've always been blessed with great visual recall. If I focus on something, even a trivial thing, I can recall the minutest details, even after time has passed. I could reproduce the special features of every dish that was served, as if I were doing a quick sketch. She listened to my descriptions, a spellbound look in her eyes, at times actually gulping back her desire.

"Sounds amazing," she said dreamily. "Someday I'd love to have a wonderful meal like that."

"To tell the truth, though, I don't remember much of what it tasted like," I said.

"You don't remember how the food tasted? But you liked it, right?"

"Yes. It was delicious. That much I remember. But I can't recall the flavors, can't explain it in words."

"Even though you remember exactly what it looked like?"

"I could reproduce exactly what it looked like. I'm a painter—it's what I do. But I can't explain what went into it. Maybe a writer would be able to describe the flavors."

"Weird," she said. "So even when we do *this* together, you could paint a painting of it later on, but you wouldn't be able to reproduce the feeling in words?"

I gathered my thoughts. "You're talking about sexual pleasure?"

"Yes."

"Hmm. You may be right. But I think describing the flavor of a dish is harder than describing sexual pleasure."

"So what you're saying," she said, in a voice as chilly as an early-winter nightfall, "is that the taste of the dishes Mr. Menshiki served you is more exquisite, and deeper, than the sexual pleasure I provide?"

"That's not what I'm saying," I said hurriedly. "It's not a comparison of the quality of the two, but a question of the degree of difficulty of explaining them. In a technical sense."

"All right," she said. "What I give you isn't so bad, is it? In a technical sense?"

"Of course," I said. "It's amazing. In a technical sense, and all other senses, so amazing I couldn't paint it."

Truthfully the physical pleasure she provided me left nothing to be desired. Up till then I'd had sexual relationships with a number of women—not so many I could brag about it—but her vagina was more exquisite, more wondrously varied, than *any other* I'd ever known. And it was a deplorable thing that it had lain there, unused, for so many years. When I told her this, she didn't look as dissatisfied as you might have thought.

"Really?"

"Really."

She looked at me, dubiously, then seemed to take me at my word.

"So, did he show you the garage?" she asked.

"The garage?"

"His legendary garage with its four British cars."

"No, I didn't see it," I said. "It's such a huge place, and I didn't get a chance to see the garage."

"Hm," she said. "You didn't ask him if he really does own a Jaguar XK-E?"

"No. I didn't think of it. I mean, I'm not really into cars."

"You're happy with a used Corolla station wagon?"

"You got it."

"I'd love to be able to touch a Jaguar XK-E sometime. It's such a gorgeous car. I've been in love with that car ever since I saw it in a film with Audrey Hepburn and Peter O'Toole when I was a child. Peter O'Toole was driving a bright, shiny Jaguar E. Now what color was it? Yellow, as I recall."

Her thoughts drifted to that sports car she'd seen as a young girl, while what came to my mind was that Subaru Forester. The white Subaru parked in the parking lot on the edge of that tiny town along the coast in Miyagi. Not a particularly attractive vehicle. A typical small SUV, a squat little utilitarian machine. I doubt there'd be many people who would unconsciously feel like touching it. Unlike with a Jaguar XK-E.

"So you didn't get to see the greenhouse or the gym either?" she asked me. She was talking about Menshiki's house again.

"No such luck. Didn't get to see the greenhouse, the gym, or the laundry room, the maid's quarters, the kitchen, or the spacious walk-in closet, or the game room with the billiard table. He didn't show them to me."

That evening Menshiki had an important matter he had to talk with me about. He was far too preoccupied to give me a leisurely tour of the house.

"Does he really have a huge walk-in closet, and a game room with a billiard table?"

"I don't know. I'm just guessing. It wouldn't be strange if he did, though."

"He didn't show you any of the other rooms besides the study?"

"Yeah. It's not like I'm interested in interior design. What he showed me were the foyer, the living room, the study, and the dining room."

"You didn't try to spot Bluebeard's secret chamber?"

"Didn't have the chance to. And I wasn't about to ask Menshiki, 'By the way, where is the famous Bluebeard's secret chamber?'"

She shook her head a few times, clicking her tongue in frustration. "I tell you, that's what's wrong with men. Don't you have any curiosity? If it were me, I'd want to see every nook and cranny."

"The things men and women are curious about must be different."

"It seems like it," she said, resigned to it. "But that's okay. I should be happy to have gotten a lot of new info about the interior of Mr. Menshiki's house."

I was getting increasingly uneasy. "Getting information is one thing, but it wouldn't be good if this got out to others. Through your jungle grapevine . . ."

"It's all right. No need for you to worry about every little thing," she said cheerily.

She took my hand and guided it to her clitoris. In this way, our two spheres of curiosity once more significantly overlapped. I still had time before I had to go teach. At that point I thought I heard the bell in the studio faintly ringing, but I was probably just hearing things.

After she drove away in the red Mini just before three, I went into the studio, and picked up the bell from the shelf. I couldn't see anything different about it. It had just been quietly lying there. I looked around, but the Commendatore was nowhere to be seen.

I went over to the canvas, sat down on the stool, and gazed at the portrait of the man with the white Subaru Forester that I'd begun. I wanted to consider the direction I should take it in now. But here I made an unexpected discovery.

The painting was *already complete*.

Needless to say, the painting was still unfinished. I had a few ideas I planned to incorporate into it. At this point the painting was nothing more than a rough prototype of the man's face done with the three colors I'd mixed, the colors riotously slapped on over the rough charcoal sketch. In my eyes, of course, I could detect the ideal form of *The Man with the White Subaru Forester*. His face was there in the painting in a latent, trompe l'oeil type of way. But this was only visible to me. It was, at this point, only the foundation for a painting. Merely the hint and suggestion of things to come. But that man—the person I had been trying to paint from memory—was already satisfied with his taciturn form presented there. And maybe dead set against his likeness being made any clearer than it was now.

Don't you touch anything, the man was saying—or maybe commanding—from the canvas. *Don't you add a single thing more.*

The painting was complete as is, incomplete. The man actually existed, completely, in that inchoate form. A contradiction in terms, but there was no other way to describe it. And that man's hidden form looked out to me from the canvas as if signaling some hard-and-fast idea. Trying hard to get me to understand something. But I still had no idea what that was. This man is alive, I felt. Actually alive and moving.

The paint on the picture was still wet, but I took the canvas down from the easel, turned it facing away, and propped it up against the studio wall, careful not to get paint on the wall. It was harder and harder for me to stand seeing the painting. There was something ominous about it—something I shouldn't know about.

Hovering around the painting was the air of a fishing port. In that air was a mix of smells—the smell of the tide, of fish scales, of diesel engines, of fishing boats. Flocks of birds were screeching, slowly circling on the strong wind. The black golf cap of a middle-aged man who'd probably never played a round of golf in his life. The darkly tanned face, the stringy nape of the neck, the short-clipped hair mixed with gray. The well-used leather jacket. The clatter of knives and forks in the restaurant—that impersonal sound found at chain restaurants around the world. And the white Subaru Forester quietly parked in the lot out front. The sticker of a marlin on the rear bumper.

"Hit me," the woman had said in the middle of sex. Her fingernails were digging deep into my back. There was a strong smell of sweat. I did as she asked, smacking her face with an open hand.

"Not like that. Don't hold back, hit me harder," the woman said, shaking her head violently. "Harder, *much* harder. Really hit me. I don't care if there's a bruise. Hard enough so my nose bleeds."

I had no desire to hit her. I never had those kind of violent tendencies. Hardly any at all. But she was *seriously* hoping I would *seriously* hit her. What she needed was real pain. So I reluctantly hit her again, a little harder this time. Hard enough to leave a red mark on her. Every time I struck her, her flesh squeezed my penis like a vise. Like a starving animal pouncing on some food.

"Would you choke me a little?" she whispered a little while later. "Use this."

The sound seemed to be coming from another realm. She pulled out a white bathrobe belt from under her pillow. She'd had it there, ready to use.

I refused. I could never do something like that. It was too dangerous. Mess up, and she could die.

"Just pretend," she pleaded, gasping. "You don't need to really choke me, just pretend like you are. Wrap this around my neck and tighten it a little."

I couldn't refuse.

The impersonal clatter of silverware in a chain restaurant.

I shook my head, trying to drive away those memories. It was an incident I didn't care to recall, a memory I'd like to throw away and never have again. But the feel of that bathrobe belt lingered in my hands. The way her neck felt, too. For whatever reason, these stayed with me.

And this man knew. Where I'd been the night before, what I'd done. What I'd been thinking.

What should I do with this painting? Keep it here in the studio, turned toward the wall? Even turned around like that, it still made me uneasy. The only other place to keep it was the attic. The same place Tomohiko Amada had hidden away *Killing Commendatore*. The place to hide away what was in your heart.

In my mind, the words I'd spoken aloud came back to me.

I could reproduce exactly what it looked like. I'm a painter—it's what I do. But I can't explain what went into it.

All sorts of things I couldn't explain were insidiously grabbing hold of me. Tomohiko Amada's *Killing Commendatore* that I'd discovered in the attic, the strange bell left behind inside the gaping stone chamber in the woods, the Idea that appeared to me in the guise of the Commendatore, and the middle-aged man with the white Subaru Forester. And that odd white-haired person who lived across the valley. Menshiki seemed to be enlisting me into some kind of plan he had in mind.

The whirlpool swirling around me was gradually picking up speed. And there was no way for me to turn back. It was too late. That whirlpool was totally soundless. And that weird silence had me scared.

28

FRANZ KAFKA WAS QUITE FOND OF SLOPES

That evening I taught a children's art class. The assignment that day was to do rough sketches of people. The children worked in pairs, selecting the type of drawing instruments they wanted from the ones the school had prepared ahead of time (charcoal or various types of soft pencils), and took turns sketching each other in their notebooks. They were limited to fifteen minutes per drawing (I used a kitchen timer to accurately time them). They were supposed to use an eraser as little as they could, and limit themselves to one sheet of paper, if possible.

One by one the children then came to the front of the class, showed us their sketches, and got feedback from the other children. It was a small class, and the atmosphere was congenial. Afterward I went forward and taught them some simple techniques for rough sketches. I explained in general the difference between *croquis*—rough sketches—and *dessan*. A dessan is more of a blueprint for a painting, and requires a certain accuracy. Compared with that, a croquis is a free first impression. You get an impression in your mind and trace the rough outline of it before it disappears. More than accuracy, croquis require balance and speed. Many famous painters actually weren't very skilled at doing croquis. I've always prided myself on being good at drawing these kind of quick sketches.

Finally I chose one of the children to model for me and did a rough sketch of her on the blackboard in white chalk, to show them an actual example. *Wow! You're so fast! It looks just like her!* the children called out, impressed. One of a teacher's important duties is to get children to be genuinely impressed.

Next, I had them change partners and do another croquis, and the second time they were much improved. They absorbed knowledge quickly. This time, the instructor was impressed. Of course some of them were better than others, but that didn't matter. What I was teaching them was less how to draw than a way to view the world.

On this day I selected Mariye Akikawa (intentionally, of course) to serve as model when I drew an example. I did a simple sketch of her from the waist up on the blackboard. It wasn't exactly a croquis, though the elements were the same. I finished quickly, in three minutes. I wanted to use the class to test what kind of painting I could do of her. What I discovered in doing this was that, as a model for a painting, she had a lot of unique possibilities hidden away inside.

I'd never really consciously observed her before, but now, looking at her carefully as the subject of a drawing, I found her face far more intriguing than my original vague impression. It wasn't just that she had lovely features. She was, indeed, a beautiful girl, but a closer observation showed a kind of imbalance at work. And behind that unstable expression there was a latent energy, like some agile animal lurking in the tall grass.

I wanted to see if I could capture that impression, but it was next to impossible to do that in three minutes, in chalk on a blackboard. Basically impossible, I should say. I needed more time to observe her face and dissect all the elements. And I had to know more about this young girl.

I left the chalk sketch of her on the blackboard, and after the children had all left, I stayed behind, arms folded, studying the sketch. I tried to determine if there was anything of Menshiki in her features. But I couldn't decide. I could detect a resemblance in certain features, in others not so much—it could go either way. But if I had to give one feature it would be the eyes, a shared look in their eyes. The distinctive way their eyes would flash for an instant.

If you stare long enough deep into the bottom of a clear spring you discover a kind of lump that emits light. You can't see it unless you look very closely. That lump soon wavers and loses shape. The more carefully you look, the more you start to wonder if it might all be an illusion. But something there is unmistakably glowing. Having done countless portraits of people, occasionally I'll sense someone giving off that *glow*. Not many people have it. But this girl and Menshiki were among these rare few.

The middle-aged receptionist at the school came into the classroom to straighten up and stood beside me, admiring the drawing.

"That's Mariye Akikawa, isn't it," she said at first glance. "A very nice likeness. It looks like she's about to start moving. It's a waste to have to erase it."

"Thank you," I said. I got up from my desk, picked an eraser, and completely wiped the sketch away.

The Commendatore finally made an appearance the next day (Saturday). It was the first time since Tuesday night at the dinner at Menshiki's that he—to borrow his phrase—*materialized*. I was back from food shopping, in the living room reading a book, when I heard the sound of the bell tinkling from the studio. I went into the studio and found the Commendatore seated on the shelf, lightly shaking the bell next to his ear. As if making sure of the subtle sound. When he spotted me he stopped ringing the bell.

"It's been a while," I said.

"Negative. It has been nothing of the kind," the Commendatore said curtly. "An Idea travels around the world in units of hundreds, thousands of years. A day or two does not count as time."

"How did you like Mr. Menshiki's dinner party?"

"Ah, yes, an interesting dinner that was. I could not partake of the food, of course, but did feast my eyes on it. And Menshiki is a fascinating fellow. Always thinking several steps ahead. And there is much pent up inside him."

"He asked me to do a favor for him."

"Affirmative." The Commendatore gazed at the ancient bell in his hand. He did not seem interested. "I heard it all quite clearly. But it is not something that has much to do with me. It is a practical matter—a worldly matter, you could say—that is between my friends and Menshiki."

"Is it all right if I ask a question?" I said.

The Commendatore rubbed his goatee with his palm. "Affirmative. But I do not know if I will be able to answer."

"It's about Tomohiko Amada's painting *Killing Commendatore*. I assume you know the painting, since you borrowed one of the figures. The painting seems based on an incident in Vienna in 1938. Something Tomohiko Amada himself was involved in. Do you know anything about that?"

Arms folded, the Commendatore thought this over. Finally he narrowed his eyes and spoke.

"There are *plenty* of things in history that are best left in the shadows. Accurate knowledge does not improve people's lives. The objective does not necessarily surpass the subjective, you know. Reality does not necessarily extinguish fantasy."

"Generally speaking," I said, "that might be so. But that painting is calling out to anyone who sees it. I get the sense that Tomohiko Amada painted it to privately capture an event that was essential to him but that he could not share with others. He changed the characters and setting to another age, and made a metaphorical confession, using his newly acquired skills in Japanese-style painting. I even get the feeling that that was the sole reason he abandoned Western painting and converted to Japanese art."

"Cannot you just let the painting speak for itself?" the Commendatore said softly. "If that painting wants to say something, then best to let it speak. Let metaphors be metaphors, a code a code, a sieve a sieve. Is there something wrong with that?"

A sieve? But I let it go.

"No, nothing's wrong with that," I said. "I'd just like to know what made Tomohiko Amada paint it. It's clear that the painting is expecting something. The picture was, without a doubt, painted for a specific purpose."

The Commendatore continued to rub his beard with his palm as if recalling something. "Franz Kafka was quite fond of slopes," he said. "He was drawn to all sorts of slopes. He loved to gaze at homes built on the middle of a slope. He would sit by the side of the street for hours, staring at houses built like that. He never grew tired of it and would sit there, tilting his head to one side, then straightening it up again. A kind of strange fellow. Did you know this?"

Franz Kafka and slopes?

"No, I didn't," I said. I'd never heard of that.

"But does knowing that make one appreciate his works more?"

I didn't respond to his question.

"So you knew Franz Kafka, too? Personally?"

"He does not know about me personally, of course," the Commendatore said. He chuckled, as if recalling something. This might have been the first time I'd seen him laugh out loud. Was there something about Franz Kafka to make him chuckle?

His expression returned to normal and he went on.

"The truth is a symbol, and symbols are the truth. It is best to grasp symbols the way they are. There's no logic or facts, no pig's belly button or ant's balls. When people try to use a method other than the truth to follow along the path of understanding, it is like trying to use a sieve to hold water. I am telling you this for your own good. Better to give it up. Sadly, what Menshiki is doing is similar to that."

"So no matter what, it's a wasted effort?"

"No one can ever float something full of holes on water."

"So what exactly is Mr. Menshiki trying to do?"

The Commendatore lightly shrugged. Charming lines formed between his eyebrows that reminded me of a young Marlon Brando. I seriously doubted the Commendatore had ever seen Elia Kazan's *On the Waterfront,* but those lines were exactly like Marlon Brando's. Though I had no way of knowing how far he went, when it came to referencing his appearance and features.

He said, "There is very little I can explain to my friends about Tomohiko Amada's *Killing Commendatore.* That is because it is, in essence, allegory and metaphor. Allegories and metaphors are not something you should explain in words. You just grasp them and accept them."

The Commendatore scratched behind his ear with his little finger. Just like a cat will scratch behind its ear before it rains.

"I will, however, tell my friends one thing. Nothing that is enormously significant, but tomorrow night you'll get a phone call. A call from Menshiki. Think things over *very carefully* before you answer. Your answer will be the same no matter how much you think it over, but it is still best to think it over very carefully."

"And it's very important to let the other person know you're thinking things over carefully, isn't it. As a gesture."

"Affirmative. A hard-and-fast rule in business is to never accept the first offer. Remember that, and you will never go wrong." The Commendatore chuckled again. He seemed in an especially good mood today. "Changing topics, but I wondered, is it interesting to touch a clitoris?"

"I don't think you touch it because it's interesting," I said honestly.

"From the sidelines it is hard to understand."

"I don't think I get it, either," I said. So an Idea, too, doesn't necessarily understand everything.

"About time for me to disappear," the Commendatore said. "I have someplace else I need to go. Do not have much time."

And with that the Commendatore vanished. A gradual, phased disappearance, like the Cheshire Cat's. I went to the kitchen, made a simple dinner, and ate. I considered for a moment what "someplace else" an Idea would need to go to. And naturally had no clue.

Like the Commendatore had prophesized, at just past eight the following evening, I got a phone call from Menshiki.

I thanked him again for the dinner party. The food was amazing, I said. It was nothing, he replied. I want to thank *you*, Menshiki said, for letting me have such an enjoyable time. I also thanked him for the payment for the portrait, which was way more than we'd agreed to. Please don't worry about it, Menshiki said modestly. That's only to be expected, for such a wonderful painting. Once we'd finished all these polite exchanges there was a moment of silence.

"By the way, about Mariye Akikawa," Menshiki began, as casually as if discussing the weather. "You remember the other day when I asked if you would have her model for a painting?"

"Of course I remember."

"Yesterday I asked Mariye—actually Mr. Matsushima, the owner of the arts-and-culture center, asked her aunt—if it might be possible—and she agreed to model."

"I see," I said.

"So all the pieces are in place, if you'll agree to paint the portrait."

"But Mr. Menshiki, isn't Mr. Matsushima a bit suspicious that you're involved in this?"

"I've been very careful, so no need to worry. He sees me as acting as your patron of sorts. I hope you're not offended . . ."

"I don't mind," I said. "But I'm surprised Mariye Akikawa agreed. She's so quiet and docile, and strikes me as a timid girl."

"Honestly, her aunt didn't like the idea at first. She felt nothing good could come from modeling for a painting. I'm sorry if this offends you, as an artist."

"No, most people would feel that way."

"But Mariye herself seemed quite interested in modeling for the painting. She said if you'd paint her she'd be happy to pose. She's the one who persuaded her aunt to agree."

Why, I wondered? Was there some connection with the sketch of her I did on the blackboard? I didn't venture to bring this up with Menshiki.

"Things have worked out perfectly, haven't they?" Menshiki said.

I thought it over. Was this really the perfect way for things to go? Menshiki seemed to be waiting for my opinion.

"Could you tell me more about how this would unfold?"

Menshiki said, "It's very simple. You're looking for a model for a painting. And you think that Mariye Akikawa, from your art class, would be perfect. So you had the owner of the arts-and-culture center, Mr. Matsushima, sound out the girl's guardian, her aunt. That's the story. Mr. Matsushima personally recommended you. Said you have a sterling character, are an enthusiastic teacher, that you're a talented artist with a promising future. I don't appear anywhere in this. I made sure my name didn't come up. Naturally she'll be clothed when she models, and her aunt will accompany her. And you'll finish the sessions by noon. Those are the conditions they laid down. What do you think?"

Following the Commendatore's advice ("Always turn down first offers"), I put on the brakes.

"I don't have any problem with the conditions, but can I have a bit more time to think about this?"

"Of course," Menshiki said calmly. "Think about it as much as you'd like. I'm not trying to rush you. Obviously you're the one who would paint the picture, and if you don't feel like doing it, that's the end of it. I just wanted to let you know that everything's all set, as far as I'm concerned. One more thing, perhaps a little off topic, but I'm planning to pay you fully for the painting."

Things are really moving along here, I thought. Everything's evolving amazingly quickly and smoothly, like a ball rolling down a slope . . . I pictured Franz Kafka seated halfway down the slope, watching the ball roll by. I needed to be cautious.

"Can you give me two days?" I asked. "I should be able to give you an answer then."

"That's fine. I'll call you again in two days," Menshiki said.

We ended the call.

Truth be told, I really didn't need two days to give a reply. I'd already made up my mind. I was dying to paint Mariye Akikawa's portrait. Even if someone tried to stop me, I'd take on the task. The only reason for asking for two extra days was that I didn't want anyone else to dictate the pace of events. I needed to stop and take a deep breath, something instinct—and the Commendatore—had taught me.

It is like trying to use a sieve to hold water, the Commendatore said. *No one ever can float something full of holes on water.*

His words hinted at something, something to come.

29

ANY UNNATURAL ELEMENTS

I spent those two days gazing, back and forth, at the two paintings in my studio—Tomohiko Amada's *Killing Commendatore* and my own painting of the man with the white Subaru Forester. *Killing Commendatore* was hanging now on the white wall of the studio. *The Man with the White Subaru Forester* was in a corner of the studio facing the wall (only when I wanted to look at it did I return it to the easel). Other than gaze at those paintings, I killed time reading books, listening to music, cooking, cleaning, weeding the garden, taking walks nearby. I didn't feel like taking up my paintbrush. The Commendatore didn't appear, and maintained his silence.

As I hiked the mountain roads nearby, I tried to find a place from which I could view Mariye Akikawa's house. But I could never find it. When I saw it from Menshiki's house, I gathered it wasn't far from me, but the topography obstructed my view. As I hiked through the woods I unconsciously was on the lookout for hornets.

What I rediscovered, spending two days gazing at the paintings, was that my feelings were spot on. *Killing Commendatore* wanted me to break its "code," and *The Man with the White Subaru Forester* wanted the artist (namely me) to not make any more revisions. And both of these appeals were very strong—at least I felt them strongly—and I had to obey. I left *The Man with the White Subaru Forester* as it was (though I did try to fathom the basis for why it wanted to be left as is), and struggled to decipher *Killing Commendatore*. But both paintings were enveloped in an enigma, as hard as a walnut shell, and I couldn't find the means to crack the shell open.

Without the upcoming portrait of Mariye Akikawa to deal with, I might very well have spent my days, ad infinitum, gazing back and forth between these paintings. But in the evening of the second day Menshiki called, and for the time being, at least, the spell was broken.

"Did you make a decision?" Menshiki said, after we'd greeted each other. He was, of course, asking about painting Mariye Akikawa's portrait.

"I'll accept the offer," I replied. "But I do have one condition."

"Which is?"

"I can't predict what kind of painting it will turn out to be. I can't know what style I'll paint it in until Mariye is actually here and I actually begin. If no good ideas come to me, I might not finish. Or it might be finished, but I might not like it. Or you might not like it. So I'd like to do it spontaneously, not because you commissioned it, or because you suggested I do it."

A momentary pause, then Menshiki said, probingly, "In other words, if you're not satisfied with the finished painting it won't end up mine, under any circumstances. Is that what you're saying?"

"That's a possibility. Anyway, I'd like to be the one who decides what to do with the painting. That's my condition."

Menshiki gave it some thought before he spoke. "The only thing I can do, I think, is agree. If not accepting that condition means you won't paint it."

"I'm sorry about that."

"So you want to be more free artistically, not bound by the painting being on commission by me, or having any suggestions from me, is that it? Or is the financial aspect the issue?"

"A little bit of both. But what's really important is that I want to do it all more naturally."

"Naturally?"

"I want to get rid of any unnatural elements, as much as I can."

"Meaning . . . ," Menshiki said. His voice had grown a little hard. "That there's something unnatural in my asking you to paint Mariye's portrait?"

It is like trying to use a sieve to hold water, the Commendatore said. *No one can ever float something full of holes on water.*

I said, "What I mean is, with this painting I'd like to be on an equal footing with you, not in a relationship that's mixed up with questions of individual interests. I'm sorry if this sounds rude."

"No, it's not rude at all. It's only natural for people to be on an equal footing. Feel free to say anything you'd like to me."

"In other words, I'd like to paint the portrait of Mariye Akikawa as a spontaneous act, not one that you had a hand in. Unless I do that, I might not come up with any good ideas about how to paint her. That sort of thing might be a shackle, visible or otherwise."

Menshiki thought about this. "I understand completely," he finally said. "Let's forget about it being a commission. And please forget that I mentioned payment. That was me being overeager, I'm afraid. We can revisit the question of what to do with the painting once it's finished and you show it to me. Of course I'll honor your desires as the artist above all. But how about the other request I had? Do you remember?"

"About you casually stopping by my studio while Mariye is modeling for me?"

"Correct."

I thought it over. "I have no problem with that. I'm acquainted with you, you live in the neighborhood, and just happened to drop by while out for a Sunday stroll. And we just chat for a while. That strikes me as completely natural."

Menshiki seemed relieved. "I'd be very grateful if you'd arrange it. I'll make sure not to get in the way. So can I plan things so that Mariye comes over to your place this Sunday morning, and you'll paint her portrait? Actually Mr. Matsushima will act as intermediary and arrange things between you and the Akikawas."

"That would be fine. Go ahead and set it up. We'll plan on the two of them coming over on Sunday morning at ten, and Mariye will sit for the portrait. I'll be sure to finish up by twelve. It'll take several weeks to finish. Maybe five or six. That's about the size of it."

"I'll be in touch once everything's set."

We'd finished discussing all we needed to.

"Ah, yes," he said, as if suddenly remembering. "I found out a few more things about Tomohiko Amada's time in Vienna. I told you that the failed assassination attempt he was involved in took place right about the time of the *Anschluss,* but actually it was in the early fall of 1938. About half a year after the *Anschluss,* in other words. You know the facts about the *Anschluss*, right?"

"Not in much detail."

"On March 12, 1938, the Wehrmacht smashed across the border with Austria, invaded the country, and soon gained control of Vienna. They threatened President Miklas and made him designate Seyss-Inquart, head of the Austrian Nazi Party, as prime minister. Hitler came to Vienna two days later. On April tenth there was a national referendum, a vote on whether Austria should be annexed by Germany. On the surface it was a free, secret ballot, but the Nazis rigged things so any voter would have to be pretty courageous to vote *nein*. The vote was 99.75 percent *ja* for the annexation. That's how Austria as a nation vanished, reduced to being a part of Germany. Have you ever been to Vienna?"

I'd never been out of the country, let alone to Vienna. I'd never even had a passport.

"Vienna's like no other city in the world," Menshiki said. "You sense it even after being there for a short time. Vienna's different from Germany. The air's different, the people are different. Same with the food and the music. It's a special place for people to enjoy themselves, to love the arts. But back then Vienna was in total chaos, a brutal storm blowing violently through it. And it was exactly this period of upheaval in Vienna that Tomohiko Amada lived through. The Nazis behaved themselves until the national referendum, but after that they revealed their true, brutal nature. The first thing Hitler did after the *Anschluss* was build the Mauthausen concentration camp in northern Austria. It took only a few weeks to complete it. Building it was the Nazis' top priority. In a short space of time, tens of thousands of political prisoners were arrested and shipped off to the camp. Most of those sent to Mauthausen were so-called incorrigible political prisoners or antisocial elements. So their treatment was especially cruel. Lots of people were executed there, or died doing harsh physical labor in the quarries. The label "incorrigible" meant that once you were thrown into that camp, you'd never come out alive. Many anti-Nazi activists weren't sent to the camp, but were tortured and murdered during interrogation, their fate covered up. The aborted assassination attempt that Tomohiko Amada was involved in took place during this chaotic period following the *Anschluss*."

I listened to Menshiki's story without comment.

"But as I mentioned before, there's no public record at all of any abortive assassination attempt on any Nazi VIP from the summer to fall of 1938. Which is pretty strange, if you think about it. If such a plot had really existed, Hitler and Goebbels would have spread the news far and wide and used it for political purposes. Like they did with *Kristallnacht*. You know about *Kristallnacht*, right?"

"The basic facts, yes," I said. I'd seen a movie once that dealt with it. "A German embassy official in Paris was shot and killed by an anti-Nazi Jew, and the Nazis used that as an excuse for fomenting anti-Jewish riots throughout Germany. Lots of businesses run by Jews were destroyed, and quite a few people were murdered. The name comes from the way that the glass from the shattered shop windows glittered like crystals."

"Exactly. That was in November 1938. The German government announced it as spontaneous rioting, when in reality the Nazi government, with Goebbels leading the way, used the assassination to systematically plan this brutality. The assassin, Herschel Grynszpan, carried out the act to protest the cruel treatment of his family as Jews back in Germany. At first he planned to assassinate the German ambassador, but when he couldn't, he instead shot one of the embassy staff who just happened to be there. Ironically, Vom Rath, the staff member he shot, was under surveillance by authorities for anti-Nazi sympathies. At any rate, if there had been a plot at the time to assassinate a Nazi official in Vienna, a similar campaign would definitely have taken place. They would have used it as an excuse to increase the suppression of anti-Nazi forces. At least, they wouldn't have quietly covered up the incident."

"Was there some reason they didn't want it made public?"

"It seems a fact that the incident did take place. Most of the people involved were Viennese college students, and they were all arrested and either executed or murdered. To seal their lips about the plot. One theory is that one of the resistance members was the daughter of a high-ranking Nazi official, and that's why they kept it under wraps. But the facts aren't clear. After the war there was some testimony given about it, but this was all circumstantial evidence, and it's unsure whether any of it is reliable. By the way, the resistance group's name was Candela. In Latin it means a candle shining in the darkness underground. The Japanese word for lantern—*kantera*—derives from this."

"If all those involved in the plot were killed, that means the only survivor is Tomohiko Amada?"

"It does seem that way. Just before the end of the war, the Reich Main Security Office ordered that all secret documents relating to the incident be burned, and the plot was lost to the darkness of history. It would be nice if we could question Tomohiko Amada about the details of what took place, but that would be pretty difficult now."

It would, I said. Up till now Tomohiko Amada had never spoken of the incident, and his memory had now sunk deep into the thick mud of oblivion.

I thanked Menshiki and hung up.

Even while his memory was still solid, Tomohiko Amada had maintained a firm silence about the incident. He must have had some private reasons for why he couldn't talk about it. Or perhaps when he left the country the authorities had forced him to agree to never speak of it. In place of maintaining a lifelong silence, though, he'd left the painting *Killing Commendatore*. He'd entrusted that painting with the truth he was forbidden to ever speak about, and his feelings about what had occurred.

The next evening Menshiki called again. Mariye Akikawa would be coming to my house the following Sunday at ten a.m., he reported. As he'd mentioned, her aunt would be accompanying her. Menshiki wouldn't be there that first day.

"I'll come by after some time has passed, after she's gotten used to posing for you. I'm sure she'll be nervous at first, and it's better that I don't bother you," he said.

His voice was a little unsteady. That tone put me on edge as well.

"Yes, that sounds like a good idea," I replied.

"Come to think of it, though, I might be the one who's the most nervous," Menshiki said after a little hesitation, sounding as if he were revealing a secret. "I think I said this before, but I've never been near Mariye Akikawa, not even once. I've only seen her from a distance."

"But if you wanted to get close to her, you could have created an opportunity to do so."

"Yes, of course. If I'd wanted to I could have made any number of opportunities."

"But you didn't. Why not?"

Uncharacteristically, Menshiki took time to choose his words. He said, "I couldn't predict how I'd feel, or what I'd say, if I was close to her. That's why I've intentionally stayed away. I've been satisfied with being on the other side of the valley, secretly watching her from a distance with high-powered binoculars. Is that a warped way of thinking?"

"Not particularly," I said. "But I do find it a bit odd. But now you've decided to actually meet her at my house. Why?"

Menshiki was silent for a time, and then spoke. "That's because you're here, and can act as an intermediary."

"Me?" I said in surprise. "Why me? Not to be rude or anything, but you hardly know me. And I don't know you well either. We only met about a month ago. We live across the valley from each other, but our lifestyles couldn't be more different. So why did you trust me that much? And tell me your secrets? You don't seem the type to give away your inner feelings so easily."

"Exactly. Once I have a secret I lock it away in a safe and swallow the key. I don't seek advice from others or reveal things to them."

"Then how come—I'm not sure how to put this—you've confided in me?"

Menshiki was silent for a time. "It's hard to explain, but I got the feeling the first day I met you that it's all right to let my guard down. Call it intuition. And that feeling only grew stronger after I saw my portrait. I decided, *This is a trustworthy person*. Someone who would accept my way of seeing things, my way of thinking. Even if I have a slightly odd and twisted way of seeing and thinking."

A slightly odd and twisted way of seeing and thinking, I thought.

"I'm really happy you'd say that," I said. "But I don't think I understand you as a person. You go way beyond the scope of my comprehension. Frankly, many things about you simply surprise me. Sometimes I'm at a loss for words."

"But you never try to judge me. Am I right?"

That was true, now that he'd said it. I'd never tried to apply some standard to judge Menshiki's words and actions. I didn't praise them, and didn't criticize them. They simply left me, as I'd said, at a loss for words.

"You might be right," I admitted.

"And you remember when I went down to the bottom of that hole? When I was down there by myself for an hour?"

"Of course."

"It never even occurred to you to leave me there forever, in that dark, dank hole. Right?"

"True. But that sort of idea wouldn't occur to a normal person."

"Are you sure about that?"

What could I say? I couldn't imagine what lay deep in other people's minds.

"I have another request," Menshiki said.

"And what is that?"

"It's about next Sunday, when Mariye and her aunt come to your place," Menshiki said. "I'd like to watch your house then with my binoculars, if you don't mind?"

"I don't mind," I said. I mean, the Commendatore had watched my girlfriend and me, right beside us, when we'd had sex. Having someone watch my terrace from afar wasn't about to faze me now.

"I thought it'd be best to tell you in advance," Menshiki said, as if excusing himself.

I was impressed all over again how strangely honest he was. We finished talking and hung up the phone. I'd been holding the phone tightly against me, and the spot above my ear ached.

The next morning I received a certified letter. I signed the receipt the mailman held out for me, and got a large envelope. Getting it didn't exactly make me feel cheerful. My experience is that certified mail is never good news.

And as expected, the mail was from a law office in Tokyo, and inside were two sets of divorce papers. There was also a stamped, self-addressed envelope. The only thing accompanying the forms was a letter with businesslike instructions from the lawyer. It said that all I needed to do was read over the forms, check them, and, if I didn't have any objections, sign and seal one set and send it back. If there are any points that you're uncertain about, the letter said, feel free to contact the attorney in charge. I glanced through the forms, filled in the date, signed them, and affixed my seal. I didn't particularly have any *points that were uncertain*. Neither of us had any financial obligations toward the other, no estate worth dividing up, no children to fight a custody battle over. A very simple, easy-to-understand divorce. Divorce 101, you could say. Two lives had overlapped into one, and six years later had split apart again, that was it. I slipped the documents inside the return envelope and put the envelope on top of the dining room table. Tomorrow when I went to town to teach my art class all I'd need to do was toss it inside the mailbox in front of the station.

That whole afternoon I sort of half-gazed at the envelope on the table, and gradually came to feel like the entire weight of six years of married life was crammed inside that envelope. All that time—time tinged with all kinds of memories and emotions—was stuffed inside an ordinary business envelope, gradually suffocating to death. I felt a weight pressing down on my chest, and my breathing grew ragged. I picked up the envelope, took it to the studio, and placed it on the shelf, next to the dingy ancient bell. I shut the studio door, returned to the kitchen, poured a glass of the whiskey Masahiko had given me, and drank it. My rule was not to drink while it was still light out, but I figured it was okay sometimes. The kitchen was totally still and silent. No wind outside, no sound of cars. Not even any birds chirping.

I had no particular problem about getting divorced. For all intents and purposes we already were divorced. And I had no emotional hang-up about signing and sealing the official documents. If that's what she wanted, fine. It was a legal formality, nothing more.

But when it came to why, and how, things had turned out this way, the sequence of events was beyond me. I understood, of course, that over time, and as circumstances changed, a couple could grow closer, or move apart. Changes in a person's feelings aren't regulated by custom, logic, or the law. They're fluid, unstable, free to spread their wings and fly away. Like migratory birds have no concept of borders between countries.

But these were all just generalizations, and I couldn't easily grasp the individual case here—that *this woman,* Yuzu, refused to love *this man,* me, and chose instead to be loved by someone else. It felt terribly absurd, a horribly ugly way to be treated. There wasn't any anger involved (I think). I mean, what was I supposed to be angry with? What I was feeling was a fundamental numbness. The numbness your heart automatically activates to lessen the awful pain when you want somebody desperately and they reject you. A kind of emotional morphine.

I couldn't easily forget Yuzu. I still wanted her. But say she were living in a place across the valley from my house, and say I owned a pair of high-powered binoculars—would I really try to peer into her daily life through those lenses? I sincerely doubted it. What I mean is, in the first place I wouldn't pick that sort of place to live in. It would be like building a torture rack just for me.

The whiskey did its job and I went to bed before eight and fell asleep. At one thirty a.m. I woke up and couldn't get back to sleep. It was a long, lonely haul until dawn. I didn't read, didn't listen to music, just sat on the sofa in the living room blankly staring out into the empty, dark space. All sorts of thoughts swirled through my head. Most of which I shouldn't have thought about.

I wish the Commendatore were with me, I thought. I wish we could talk about something together. *Anything.* The topic didn't matter. Just hearing his voice would be enough.

But the Commendatore was nowhere to be seen. And I had no way to summon him.

30

IT REALLY DEPENDS ON THE PERSON

The next afternoon I mailed the divorce papers I'd signed and sealed. I didn't include any letter. I simply tossed the stamped return envelope with the documents into the mailbox in front of the station. Just having that envelope out of the house felt like a burden had been lifted. I had no idea what legal route these documents would take next. Not that it mattered. They could follow whatever path they liked.

And Sunday morning, just before ten, Mariye Akikawa came to my house. A bright-blue Toyota Prius climbed the slope with barely a sound and came to a stop near my front door. In the bright Sunday sunlight, the car sparkled, grandly, vibrantly. Like it was brand-new, just unwrapped. A lot of different cars had found their way to my place recently—Menshiki's silver Jaguar, my girlfriend's red Mini, the chauffeur-driven black Infiniti that Menshiki had sent for me, Masahiko's old black Volvo, and now the blue Toyota Prius that belonged to Mariye Akikawa's aunt. And of course my own Toyota Corolla station wagon (covered with dust for so long I couldn't recall what the original color had been). I imagine people have all sorts of reasons for choosing the car they drive, and of course I had no clue why Mariye's aunt had chosen a blue Toyota Prius. It looked less like a car than a giant vacuum cleaner.

The quiet Prius engine shut off, and the surroundings grew *that much* quieter. The doors opened, and Mariye Akikawa and the woman I took to be her aunt got out. The aunt looked young, though early forties would have been my guess. She had on dark sunglasses and a gray cardigan over a simple light-blue dress. She carried a shiny black handbag and had on low, dark-gray shoes. Good shoes for driving. She shut her door, removed the sunglasses, and put them in her handbag. Her hair fell to her shoulders and was neatly curled (though not with the excessive perfection of someone just emerged from a hair salon). No accessories, other than a gold brooch on her collar.

Mariye had on a black cotton sweater and a brown, knee-length wool skirt. I'd only seen her in her school uniform up till then, and she seemed different. Side by side they looked like a mother and child from a refined, elegant household. Though I knew from Menshiki that they weren't actually mother and child.

As always I observed them through a gap in the curtain. And when the bell rang I went to the entrance and opened the front door.

Mariye's aunt had a very tranquil, calm way of speaking. She had lovely features. Not the kind of beautiful woman that would turn heads, but neat, regular features. A natural, subdued smile graced her lips, like the pale moon at dawn. She was carrying a box of cookies as a present. I was the one who had asked to have Mariye model for me, so there was no reason for her to bring me anything, but she was probably the type of person who'd had it drummed into her since she was little that when you visit someone's house you always should bring along a present. So I simply thanked her and accepted it, and showed the two of them into the living room.

"Our house isn't so far from here, a stone's throw, really, but when you drive it's a roundabout road to get here," the aunt said. (Her name was Shoko Akikawa, she told me, the *sho* written with the character that meant a traditional Japanese pan flute.) "I knew of course that this was Tomohiko Amada's house, but this is the first time I've ever been up here even though we live next door."

"I've been living here, taking care of the place, since this spring," I explained.

"Yes, I heard. I'm glad it turned out we're neighbors. I look forward to getting to know you better."

Shoko bowed deeply and thanked me for teaching Mariye. "My niece really enjoys going to the school, thanks to you," she said.

"I wouldn't say I'm exactly teaching her," I said. "Basically I just enjoy drawing together with all the pupils."

"But I understand you're a very skilled instructor. I've heard many people say that."

That I found hard to believe, but I made no comment, letting these words of praise pass unremarked. Shoko was raised well, a woman who put a premium on social niceties.

Seated side by side like this, the first thing anyone would notice about Mariye Akikawa and her aunt is that their features didn't resemble each other in the slightest. From a little ways off they seemed a well-matched mother and child, but up close it was hard to find anything in common in their appearance. Mariye had lovely features, too, and Shoko Akikawa was without doubt quite attractive, but their features were poles apart. If Shoko Akikawa's features were aiming at gaining a wonderful balance, Mariye Akikawa's aimed at destroying equilibrium, demolishing a set framework. If Shoko Akikawa aimed at a gentle, overarching harmony and stability, Mariye Akikawa sought an asymmetrical friction. Still, one could sense from the mood between them that despite all this they had a warm, healthy relationship. In a sense they were more relaxed around each other than a real mother and daughter. They seemed to maintain a comfortable distance. At least that's the impression I got.

Of course I knew nothing about why a woman like Shoko, beautiful and refined, was still single, and put up with living far off in the hills like this in her older brother's home. Perhaps she'd had a lover, a mountain climber who'd perished in an attempt to reach the summit of Mt. Everest by the most arduous route, and had pledged to remain single forever, cherishing beautiful memories of her lover in her heart. Or perhaps she was having a long-term affair with a charming married man. In any event, it wasn't my business.

Shoko walked over to the windows on the west side and gazed with great interest at the view of the valley from there.

"It's the same mountain we see from our place, but this is a slightly different angle and it doesn't look the same at all," she said, sounding impressed.

Menshiki's huge white mansion glittered on top of that mountain (and he was probably over there watching my house now through his binoculars). How did that mansion appear from her house? I wanted to ask, but it seemed risky to broach that topic right off the bat. It was hard to tell what that might lead to.

Wanting to steer clear of that, I quickly led them into the studio.

"This is where I'll have Mariye model for me," I said to them.

"This must be where Tomohiko Amada did his painting," Shoko said, gazing with great interest around the studio.

"I believe so," I said.

"There's a different feeling here, even from the rest of your house. Don't you think?"

"I'm not sure. Living here day to day, I don't really get that sense."

"What do you think, Mari-chan?" Shoko asked Mariye. "Don't you find there's an unusual sort of feeling to the room?"

Mariye was busy looking around the studio and didn't reply. She probably hadn't heard her aunt's question. I wanted to hear her reply as well.

"While the two of you are working here, I'll wait in the living room, if that's all right?" Shoko asked.

"It's all up to Mariye. The most important thing is creating an environment where she can feel relaxed. Whether you stay here or not, either way is fine with me."

"I don't want Auntie to be here," Mariye said, the first time she'd opened her mouth that day. She spoke quietly, but it was a terse announcement with no room for negotiation.

"That's fine. I'll do as you'd prefer. I figured that's how it would be, so I brought a book to read," Shoko replied calmly, not bothered by her niece's stern tone. She was probably used to that sort of exchange.

Mariye completely ignored what her aunt said, and crouched down a bit, gazing steadily at Tomohiko Amada's *Killing Commendatore* hanging on the wall. The look in her eyes as she studied this rectangular Japanese painting was intense. She examined each and every detail of the painting, as if etching every element of it in her memory. Come to think of it (I thought), this might be the first time anyone else had ever laid eyes on this painting. It had totally slipped my mind to move the painting somewhere out of sight. Too late now, I thought.

"Do you like that painting?" I asked the girl.

Mariye didn't reply. She was concentrating so much on the painting that she didn't hear my voice. Or did she hear it but was just ignoring me?

"I'm sorry. She really goes her own way sometimes," Shoko said, interceding. "She focuses so hard sometimes she blocks out everything else. She's always been that way. With books and music, paintings and movies."

I don't know why, but neither Shoko nor Mariye asked whether the painting was by Tomohiko Amada, so I didn't venture to explain. And of course I didn't tell them the title, *Killing Commendatore*, either. I wasn't too worried that they'd both seen the painting. Neither one probably would notice that this was a special work not included in Amada's oeuvre. Things would be different if Menshiki or Masahiko spotted it.

I let Mariye examine *Killing Commendatore* to her heart's content. I went to the kitchen, boiled water, and made tea. I put cups and the teapot on a tray and carried it to the living room. I added the cookies Shoko had brought as a gift. Shoko and I sat on chairs in the living room and sipped tea while chatting about life in the mountains, the weather in the valley, etc. This kind of relaxed conversation was necessary before I began to work in earnest.

Mariye kept studying *Killing Commendatore* by herself for a while, then finally, like a very curious cat, slowly made her way around the studio, picking things up and checking them out along the way. Brushes, tubes of paint, a canvas, and even the old bell that had been exhumed from underground. She held the bell and shook it a few times. It made its usual light jingling sound.

"How come there's an old bell here?" Mariye, facing a blank space, didn't seem to be addressing her question to anyone in particular. She was asking me, of course.

"The bell came nearby, from out of the ground," I said. "I just happened across it. I think it's connected with Buddhism somehow. Like a priest would ring it as he recited sutras."

She rang it again next to her ear. "Kind of a strange sound," she commented.

Once more I was impressed that such a faint sound could have reached out from underground in the woods and found me in the house. Maybe there was some special way of shaking it.

"You shouldn't touch someone else's things without permission," Shoko Akikawa cautioned her niece.

"I don't mind," I said. "It's not valuable."

Mariye seemed to quickly lose interest in the bell. She returned it to the shelf, plunked down on the stool in the middle of the room, and gazed at the scenery out the window.

"If you don't mind, I was thinking of starting," I said.

"All right, then I'll stay here and read," Shoko said, an elegant smile rising to her lips. From her black bag she took out a thick paperback with a bookstore's paper cover. I left her there, went into the studio, and shut the door between it and the living room. Mariye and I were alone in the room.

I had Mariye sit in a dining room chair, one with a backrest. And I sat on my usual stool. We were about six feet apart.

"Could you sit there for a while for me? You can sit however you'd like. As long as you don't change your position too much, it's okay to move around. No need to sit completely still."

"Is it okay for me to talk while you're painting?" Mariye asked probingly.

"No problem at all," I said. "Let's talk."

"That drawing of me you did the other day was great."

"The one in chalk on the blackboard?"

"Too bad it got erased."

I laughed. "Can't keep it on the blackboard forever. But if you like that kind of thing I can do as many as you want. It's simple."

She didn't reply.

I picked up a thick pencil and used it as a kind of ruler to measure the various elements of her facial features. Different from a croquis, when drawing a dessan you need to take time and make sure you have an accurate grasp of the model's features. No matter what kind of painting it ends up being.

"I think you have a real talent for drawing," Mariye said after a period of silence, as if remembering.

"Thank you," I said. "Hearing that gives me courage."

"You need courage?"

"Sure I do. Everybody needs to have courage."

I picked up a large sketchbook and opened it.

"I'm going to sketch dessan of you today. I enjoy painting with oils directly on a blank canvas, but today I'll stick to drawing detailed dessan. That way I can gradually understand the kind of person you are."

"Understand me?"

"Drawing someone means understanding and interpreting another person. Not with words, but with lines, shapes, and colors."

"I wish I could understand myself," Mariye said.

"I feel the same way," I agreed. "I wish I could understand myself, too. But it's not easy. That's why I paint."

Using a pencil, I quickly sketched her face and figure from the waist up. How to transfer her depth to a flat medium was critical. And how to transplant her subtle movements to something static—that too was vital. A dessan sketch determines the outline of those.

"My breasts are really small, don't you think?" Mariye asked, out of nowhere.

"I wonder," I said.

"They're like bread that didn't rise."

I laughed. "You've just started junior high. I'm sure they'll get bigger. It's nothing to worry about."

"I don't even really need a bra. The other girls in my class all wear bras."

Certainly it was hard to see any development through her sweater. "If it really bothers you, you could always pad your bra," I said.

"You want me to?"

"Either way's fine with me. It's not like I'm painting you to capture your breasts. You should do whatever you like."

"But don't men like women with big breasts?"

"Not necessarily," I said. "When my younger sister was about your age, her breasts were small too. But that didn't seem to bother her."

"Maybe it bothered her, but she just didn't mention it."

"Could be," I said. But I don't think that bothered Komi. She had other things to worry about.

"Did your sister's breasts get bigger after that?"

My hand continued to move the pencil swiftly across the page. I didn't respond to her question. Mariye watched my hand glide along the paper.

"Did her breasts get bigger after that?" Mariye asked again.

"No, they didn't," I finally gave up and answered. "My sister died the year she entered junior high. She was only twelve."

Mariye didn't say anything for a while.

"Don't you think my aunt's really beautiful?" Mariye said, abruptly changing subjects.

"Yes, she's a very lovely person."

"Are you single?"

"Ah—*nearly,*" I responded. Once that envelope arrived at the law office it'd be completely.

"Would you like to go on a date with her?"

"That would be nice."

"She has big breasts, too."

"I hadn't noticed."

"And they're really nicely shaped. We bathe together sometimes, so I know."

I looked at Mariye's face again. "Do you get along well with your aunt?"

"We fight sometimes," she said.

"About what?"

"All kinds of things. When we have a difference of opinion, or when she makes me mad."

"You're an unusual girl," I said. "You're quite different from when you're in art class. I got the impression you were very quiet."

"In places where I don't want to talk, I don't," she said simply. "Am I talking too much? Would it be better if I stayed quiet?"

"No, not at all. I like talking. Feel free to talk as much as you like."

Of course I welcomed a lively conversation. I wasn't about to stay totally silent for nearly two hours and just paint.

"I can't help thinking about my breasts," Mariye said after a while. "That's all I think about, pretty much. Is that weird?"

"Not particularly," I said. "You're at that age. When I was your age all I thought about was my penis. Whether it was shaped funny, or was too small, whether it was working wrong."

"What about now?"

"You're asking what I think about my penis now?"

"Yeah."

I thought about it. "I don't give it much thought. It's pretty ordinary, I guess, and hasn't given me any problems."

"Do women admire it?"

"Occasionally there might be one who does. But that might just be flattery. Like when people praise paintings."

Mariye pondered this for a while. Finally she said, "You may be a little strange."

"Really?"

"Normal men don't talk like that. Even my father doesn't say things like that to me."

"I doubt fathers in normal families want to talk about penises with their daughters," I said. All the while my hand continued to move busily over the paper.

"At what age do nipples get bigger?" Mariye asked.

"I'm not really sure. Since I'm a guy. I'd say it really depends on the person."

"Did you have a girlfriend when you were a kid?"

"I had my first girlfriend when I was seventeen. A girl in the same class in high school."

"What high school?"

I told her the name of a public high school in Toshima, in Tokyo. Outside of people who lived in Toshima, probably no one had ever heard of it.

"Did you like school?"

I shook my head. "Not particularly."

"Did you ever see that girlfriend's nipples?"

"Yeah," I said. "She showed them to me."

"How big were they?"

I remembered the girl's nipples. "They weren't especially small, or big. Normal size, I guess."

"Did she pad her bra?"

I tried to recall the bra my girlfriend had worn back then. All I had was a very vague memory of it. What I did recall was how much trouble I had slipping my hand behind her and unhooking it. "No, I don't think she padded it."

"What's she doing now?"

What *was* she doing now? "I don't know. I haven't seen her for a long time. I imagine she's married, maybe with some children."

"How come you don't see her?"

"The last time I saw her, she said she never wanted to see me again."

Mariye frowned. "Was this because there was something wrong with you?"

"I guess," I said. Of course the problem lay with me. No room for doubt there.

Actually, I'd recently had two dreams about this high school girlfriend. In one dream we were strolling along a river on a summer's evening. I tried to kiss her, but her long black hair formed a curtain in front of her face and my lips couldn't touch hers. In the dream she was still seventeen, but I had already turned thirty-six, something I suddenly noticed. And that's when I woke up. It was such a vivid dream. I could still feel her hair on my lips. Before this, I hadn't thought about her for years.

"How much younger than you was your younger sister?" Mariye said, again suddenly changing topics.

"Three years younger."

"You said she died when she was twelve?"

"That's right."

"So that would make you fifteen then."

"Right. I was fifteen. I'd just started high school. And she'd just started junior high. Just like you."

Now that I thought about it, Komi was now twenty-four years younger than me. Since she'd died, every year the age gap only increased between us.

"I was six when my mother died," Mariye said. "She got stung by hornets. When she was walking in the mountains nearby."

"I'm very sorry," I said.

"She had an allergy to hornet stings. They took her by ambulance to the hospital but she was already in shock and went into cardiac arrest."

"Your aunt moved in with you after that?"

"Yeah," Mariye said. "She's my father's younger sister. I wish I'd had an older brother. A brother three years older."

I finished up the first dessan and began a second. I wanted to draw her from several angles. This first day I planned to devote just to sketches.

"Did you ever fight with your sister?" she asked.

"No, I don't recall ever fighting."

"So you got along well?"

"I suppose so. I never considered whether we did or not."

"What does 'nearly single' mean?" Mariye asked, again shifting subjects.

"I'll soon be officially divorced," I said. "We're in the midst of handling all the paperwork, so that's why it's 'nearly.' "

She narrowed her eyes. "I don't get *divorce*. Nobody I know has ever divorced."

"I don't get it either. I mean, it's the first time I ever got divorced."

"What does it feel like?"

"A bit bizarre, I guess. Like you're walking along as always, sure you're on the right path, when the path suddenly vanishes, and you're facing an empty space, no sense of direction, no clue where to go, and you just keep trudging along. That's what it feels like."

"How long were you married?"

"About six years."

"How old is your wife?"

"She's three years younger." Just a coincidence, but the same age difference as with my sister.

"Do you think you wasted those six years?"

I thought about it. "No, I don't think so. I don't want to think it was all for nothing. We had a lot of good times, too."

"Does your wife think so too?"

I shook my head. "I don't know. I'd hope she would, of course."

"You didn't ask her?"

"No. If I have a chance, maybe I will sometime."

Silence reigned between us for a while. I focused on the dessan, and Mariye Akikawa was lost in serious thought—thoughts about the size of nipples, perhaps, or divorce, or hornets, or maybe something else entirely. Eyes narrowed, lips tight, both hands tightly holding her knees. She'd shifted into that mode, apparently, as I was capturing her earnest expression on the white page of my sketchbook.

Every day, exactly at noon, I could hear a chime from down the mountain. Ringing from some government office, or maybe a school, to announce the time. When I heard it now, I glanced at the clock and finished drawing. I'd managed to complete three dessan during this first session. All of them pretty interesting compositions, each one hinting at something to come. Not bad for a day's work.

Mariye Akikawa had sat on the chair in the studio, posing for me, for over an hour and a half. For the first day, that was enough. For someone not used to it—especially an active, growing child—posing for a painting wasn't easy.

Shoko Akikawa had put on black-framed glasses and was seated on the living room sofa absorbed in reading her paperback. When I came in she took off the glasses and stowed the paperback in her bag. The glasses made her look quite intellectual.

"We're all finished for the day," I said. "If it's all right, could you come again the same day next week?"

"Yes, of course," Shoko said. "It feels really nice to read here. Maybe because the sofa's so comfortable?"

"You don't mind?" I asked Mariye.

Mariye nodded silently. *I don't mind*, it meant. In front of her aunt she was totally changed, and had become taciturn again. Maybe she didn't like when the three of us were together.

They got into their blue Toyota Prius and drove away. I saw them off at the front door. Shoko, sunglasses on, reached a hand out the window and gave a few short waves goodbye. A small, pale hand. I raised my hand in reply. Mariye tucked in her chin and stared straight ahead.

Once the car had disappeared from view down the slope, I went back inside. The house seemed suddenly barren. Like something that should be there wasn't anymore.

An odd pair, I thought, as I stared at the teacups still on the table. There was something peculiar about them. But what, exactly?

I remembered Menshiki. Maybe I should have taken Mariye out on the terrace so he could get a good look at her through his binoculars. But then I rethought that. Why did I have to go out of my way to do that, when he hadn't even asked me to?

Other opportunities would present themselves. No need to rush. Probably.

31

MAYBE A LITTLE TOO PERFECT

That night I got a call from Menshiki. The clock showed that it was past nine. He apologized for calling so late. Something silly came up and I couldn't get free until now, he said. I'm not going to bed for a while, I said, so don't worry about the time.

"So how did things go today? Did it work out well?" he asked.

"It did. I completed a few dessan of Mariye. The two of them will be coming over the same time next Sunday."

"I'm glad," Menshiki said. "By the way, was the aunt favorably disposed toward you?"

Favorably disposed? What a strange way of putting it.

I said, "Yes, she seems like a very nice woman. I don't know if 'favorably disposed' is the right term, but she didn't seem particularly wary."

I summed up what had taken place that morning. Menshiki listened with what seemed like bated breath, apparently trying to absorb as much detailed information as he could. Other than a couple of questions, he hardly said a word, and just listened intently. What sort of clothes the two had on, how they had arrived. How they appeared, what they'd said. And how I'd gone about sketching Mariye Akikawa. I told Menshiki all this, piece by piece. I didn't, though, delve into Mariye's obsession with the size of her breasts. That was best kept between us.

"It might be a little early, then, for me to show up next week?" Menshiki asked me.

"It's up to you. I can't say. I don't have a problem if you come over next week."

On the other end of the line Menshiki was silent. "I'll have to think about it. It's kind of delicate."

"Take your time. It's going to take a while to finish the painting, and there should be plenty of opportunities. Next week, or the week after that—either way's fine with me."

I'd never seen Menshiki so hesitant before. Quickly decisive and never wavering—that was the Menshiki I knew.

I was thinking of asking him if he'd been watching my house with his binoculars this morning. Whether he'd been able to observe Mariye and her aunt. But I thought better of it. As long as he didn't bring it up, it seemed smarter not to mention that topic. Even if the place under surveillance was the house I was living in.

Menshiki thanked me again. "I'm really sorry to ask you to go to all this trouble for me."

I said, "I'm not doing anything for your sake. I'm simply doing a painting of Mariye Akikawa. I'm painting it because I want to. I thought that's how we decided things were going to be. Both the private and public reasons for it. So there's no reason for you to thank me."

"Still, I'm very grateful," Menshiki said quietly. "In *a lot of ways*."

I didn't really understand what he meant by "a lot of ways," but didn't ask. It was getting late. We said a quick goodbye and hung up. But after I put the phone down, it suddenly occurred to me that Menshiki might be spending a long, sleepless night tonight. I could sense the tension in his voice. He probably had lots of things on his mind.

Not much happened that week. The Commendatore didn't make an appearance, and my girlfriend didn't get in touch. A very quiet week altogether. Autumn steadily deepened around me. The sky opened up, the air clear and crisp, the clouds like beautiful white brushstrokes.

I often studied the three dessan I'd done of Mariye. The different poses, the different angles. I found them fascinating, and suggestive. Though from the beginning I hadn't planned to choose one of them to use as the preliminary design for the painting. The point of doing those three sketches, as she herself had said, was so I could understand the totality of this girl. To internally assimilate her.

I looked at those three dessan over and over again, intently focusing, trying to construct a concrete picture of the girl in my mind. As I did this, I got the distinct sense of Mariye Akikawa's figure and that of my sister getting mixed into one. Was this appropriate? I couldn't say. But the spirits of these two young girls nearly the same age were already, somewhere—probably in some deep internal recesses I shouldn't access—blended and combined. I could no longer unravel those two intertwined spirits.

That Thursday I received a letter from my wife. This was the first time since I'd left home in March that she'd gotten in touch. My name and address and hers were written on the envelope in her familiar, beautiful, steady handwriting. She was still using my last name, I saw. Maybe it was more convenient, somehow, until the divorce became official, to continue to use her husband's last name.

I used scissors to neatly snip open the envelope. Inside was a postcard with a photo of a polar bear standing on top of an iceberg. On the card she'd written a simple message thanking me for signing the divorce papers and mailing them back so quickly.

> *How are you? I'm managing to get by, nothing to report. I'm still living in the same place. Thank you for mailing back the papers so quickly. I appreciate it. I'll get in touch when there's been progress in the process.*
>
> *If there's anything you left at the house you need, please let me know. I'll send it to you. At any rate, I hope both our new lives work out.*
>
> *Yuzu*

I reread the letter many times, straining to decipher the feelings hidden behind those lines. But I couldn't detect any implied emotion or intention. She just seemed to be transmitting the clearly stated message that the words conveyed.

One other thing I didn't understand was why it had taken her so long to prepare the divorce papers. It's not that much trouble to get them ready. And she must have wanted to dissolve our relationship as fast as possible. Even so, half a year had passed since I'd left our house. What had she been doing all that time? What had been going through her mind?

I gazed at the postcard with the polar bear, but couldn't read any intentions in that either. Why a polar bear from the North Pole? She probably just happened to have the polar bear card on hand and used it. Most likely that's the case, I figured. Or was she suggesting that my future was like that of the polar bear, stuck on a tiny iceberg, directionless, carried away by the whims of the current? No—that was reading too much into it.

I tossed the card into the envelope and put it inside the top drawer of my desk. Once I shut the drawer it felt like things had progressed one step forward. Like with a *click* the scale had moved one line up. Not that this was my doing. Someone, something, had prepared this new stage in my stead, and I was simply going along with the program.

I recalled how on Sunday I'd talked to Mariye Akikawa about life after divorce.

Like you're walking along as always, sure you're on the right path, when the path suddenly vanishes, and you're facing an empty space, no sense of direction, no clue where to go, and you just keep trudging along. That's what it feels like.

A directionless ocean current, a road to nowhere, it didn't matter much. They were both the same. Just metaphors. I was experiencing the real thing, and being swallowed up by reality. If I had that, who needs a metaphor?

If I could, I wanted to write a letter to Yuzu to explain the situation I found myself in now. I didn't think I could write something vague like *I'm managing to get by, nothing to report*. Far from it. My honest sense was there was *too much to report*. But if I started writing about every single thing that had happened to me since I started living here, it would spin out of control. The biggest problem was that I couldn't explain well to myself what was happening. At least I knew I couldn't find a consistent, logical context in which to *explain* it all.

So I decided not to write back to Yuzu. If I did start writing there were only two ways to go: either explain everything that had taken place (ignoring logic and consistency), or write nothing. I chose the latter. In a sense I really was the lonely polar bear left behind to drift on an iceberg. Not a single mailbox as far as the eye could see. A polar bear has no way to send a letter, now does he.

I remember very well when Yuzu and I first met, and started dating.

On our first date we had dinner, talked about all kinds of things, and she seemed to like me. She said I could see her again. From the first our minds seemed to inexplicably click. Simply put, we seemed a good match.

But it took some time before I actually became her lover. Yuzu had another man she'd been seeing for two years. Not that she was head over heels in love with him.

"He's really handsome. Though a bit boring sometimes," she said.

Very handsome but boring . . . There was no one I knew like that, so I couldn't picture that type of person. What came to mind was a dish of food that looked delicious but ended up tasting bland. Would anyone be happy with that kind of food?

"I've always had a weakness for good-looking men," she said, as if making a confession. "Whenever I meet a handsome man it's like my brain goes out the window. I know that's a problem, but I can't do anything about it. I can't get over that. That might be my biggest weakness."

"A chronic disease," I said.

She nodded. "That could be. An incurable disorder. A chronic disease."

"Not exactly great news for me," I said. Handsome features weren't my strongest selling point.

She didn't deny that, and just laughed happily. At least she didn't seem bored when we were together. She had a lot to say, and laughed a lot.

So I waited patiently for things to not work out between her and this handsome boyfriend. (He wasn't merely good-looking, but had graduated from a top university and had a high-paying job at a top corporation. I bet he and Yuzu's father got along famously.) All this time she and I talked over all sorts of things, went to all sorts of places. We got to understand each other better. We kissed, held each other, but didn't have sex. Having a physical relationship with several partners at the same time wasn't her style. "I'm a bit old-fashioned that way," she said. So all I could do was bide my time.

This went on for about half a year. For me, it felt like eternity. Sometimes I just wanted to give up. But I managed to hang in there, convinced that someday soon she would be mine.

And finally she and her handsome boyfriend broke up (at least I think they broke up—she never said a word about it, so it was conjecture on my part), and she chose me—not much to look at, not much of a breadwinner—as her lover. Soon after we decided to get married.

I remember very well the first time we made love. We'd gone to stay at a small hot-springs town in the country, and spent our first night together there. Everything went really well. Almost perfect, you could even say. Maybe a little too perfect. Her skin was soft and pale, and silky smooth. The somewhat slick hot mineral water of the hot springs bath, combined with the pale glow of the early-autumn moonlight, may have contributed to the beauty and smoothness of her skin. I held her naked body for the first time, went inside her, she moaned quietly in my ear, and dug her nails hard into my back. The autumn insects were in full chorus then, too. A cool mountain stream burbled in the background. I made a firm pledge to myself then: *Never, ever, let this woman go*. This may have been the most sublime moment of my life up till then. Finally making Yuzu mine.

After I got the short letter from Yuzu I thought about her for a long time. About when we'd first met, that autumn night when we first made love. About how my feelings for her had basically never changed, from the first moment up to the present. Even now I didn't want to lose her. That much was clear to me. I'd signed and sealed the divorce papers, but that didn't change things. No matter how I felt about it, though, the fact was that she'd suddenly left me. Gone far away—probably very far away—where even the most powerful binoculars couldn't afford me a glimpse of her.

Somewhere, while I was oblivious to it, she must have found a new, handsome lover. As always, her *brain went out the window*. I should have picked up on this when she started refusing to sleep with me. *Having a physical relationship with several partners at the same time wasn't her style.* If only I'd thought about it, I soon would have realized that.

A chronic disease, I thought. A serious illness with no prospects for a cure. A physical inclination that doesn't respond to reason.

That night (a rainy Thursday night) I had a long, dark dream.

In that small seaside town in Miyagi I was driving the white Subaru Forester (it was now my car). I had on an old black leather jacket, and a black golf cap with a Yonex logo. I was tall, deeply suntanned, my salt-and-pepper hair short and stiff. In other words, I was the man with the white Subaru Forester. I was stealthily following my wife and the small car (a red Peugeot 205) the man she was having an affair with was driving. We were on the highway that ran along the coast. I saw the two of them go into a tacky love hotel on the outskirts of town. The next day I came up behind my wife and strangled her with a narrow, white belt from a bathrobe. I was used to physical labor and had powerful arms. And as I strangled her with all my might, I screamed something. I couldn't hear what I'd yelled out—a meaningless roar of pure rage. A horrific rage I'd never experienced before had control over my mind and body. White spittle flew as I roared out.

As she desperately gasped for air, I saw my wife's temples convulse a little. I saw her pink tongue ball up and twist inside her mouth. Blue veins rose up on her skin like an invisible-ink map. I smelled my own sweat. An unpleasant smell I'd never smelled before rose up from my body like steam from a hot springs. It reminded me of the stink of some hairy beast.

Don't you dare paint me, I ordered myself. I violently thrust out an index finger at myself in the mirror on the wall. *Don't paint me anymore!*

And there I snapped awake.

I knew now what had frightened me most in bed in that love hotel in the seaside town. Deep in my heart I feared that in the last instant I really would have strangled to death that girl (the young girl whose name I didn't even know). "You can just pretend," she said. But it might not have ended with just that. It might not have ended with *just pretend*. And the reason for that lay inside me.

I wish I could understand myself, too. But it's not easy.

This is what I'd told Mariye Akikawa. I remembered this as I wiped the sweat away with a towel.

The rain let up on Friday morning, the sky turning beautifully sunny. I hadn't slept well, felt worked up, and to calm down went for an hour's walk around the neighborhood later in the morning. I went into the woods, walked behind the little shrine, and checked out the hole for the first time in a long while. It was November now and the wind was much colder than before. The ground was covered with damp, fallen leaves. The hole was, as before, tightly covered over with several boards. Many-colored leaves had piled up on the boards, and there were several heavy stones to hold the boards down. But the way the stones were lined up seemed a little different from when I'd last seen them. Nearly the same, yet ever so slightly positioned differently.

I didn't worry about it. There wouldn't be anyone else other than Menshiki and me who would tramp all the way out here. I pulled away one of the boards and peered down inside, but no one was there. The ladder was leaned up against the wall like before. Like always, that dark, stone-lined chamber lay there, deep and silent, at my feet. I put the board back on top and placed the stone back where it had been.

It didn't bother me, either, that the Commendatore hadn't appeared for a good two weeks. Like he said, an Idea has a lot of business to attend to. Business that transcended time and space.

The following Sunday finally came. A lot of things happened that day. It turned out to be a very hectic day.

32

HIS SKILLS WERE IN GREAT DEMAND

Another prisoner approached us as we talked. He was a professional painter from Warsaw, a man of medium height with a hawk nose and a very black mustache on his fair-skinned face . . . His distinctive figure stood out from afar, and his professional status (his skills were in great demand in the camp) was evident. He was certainly no one's nonentity. He often talked to me at length about his work.

"I do color paintings, portraits, for the Germans. They bring me photos of their relatives, wives, mothers and children. Everyone wants to have pictures of their closest kin. The SS describe their families to me with emotion and love—the color of their eyes, their hair. I produce family portraits from amateurish, blurry black-and-white photos. Believe me, I would rather paint black-and-white pictures of the children in the piles of corpses in the *Lazarett* than the Germans' families. Give 'em pictures of the people they murdered; let 'em take them home and hang them on the wall, the sons of bitches."

The artist was especially distraught on this occasion.

—SAMUEL WILLENBERG, *Revolt in Treblinka,* p. 96.

Lazarett was another name for the execution facility in the Treblinka concentration camp.

PART 2

THE SHIFTING METAPHOR

33

I LIKE THINGS I CAN SEE AS MUCH AS THINGS I CAN'T

Sunday was another fine clear day. No wind to speak of, and the fall colors in the valley sparkling in the sunlight. Small white-breasted birds hopped from one branch to the next, deftly pecking the red berries. I sat on the terrace, soaking it all in. Nature grants its beauty to us all, drawing no line between rich and poor. Like time—no, scratch that, time could be a different story. Money may help us buy a little extra of that.

The bright blue Toyota Prius rolled up the slope to my door at ten on the dot. Shoko Akikawa was decked out in a thin beige turtleneck and snug-fitting slacks of pale green. Around her neck, a modest gold chain gave off a muted glow. As on her past visit, her hair was perfectly done. When it swayed I could catch a glimpse of the lovely line of her neck. Today, though, she had a leather bag, not a purse, slung over her shoulder. She wore brown loafers. It was a casual outfit, yet she had clearly spent time choosing each piece. And the swell of her breasts was very attractive too. I had the inside scoop from her niece that "no padding" was involved. I felt quite drawn to those breasts—in a purely aesthetic way, of course.

Mariye was dressed in straight-cut faded blue jeans and white Converse sneakers, a 180-degree turnaround from the formality of her first visit. Her jeans had holes in them (strategically placed, of course). She had on the sort of plaid shirt a lumberjack might wear in the woods, with a thin gray windbreaker draped over her shoulders. Underneath the shirt, as before, her chest was flat. And, just as before, she had a sour expression on her face. Like a cat whose dish has been whisked away halfway through its meal.

Just as I'd done the previous week, I went into the kitchen, made a pot of tea, and brought it to the living room. Then I showed them the three dessan I had made.

Shoko seemed to like them. "They're all so full of life," she exclaimed. "So much more like Mariye than photographs."

"Can I keep them?" Mariye asked.

"Sure," I answered. "Once your portrait is finished. I may need them until then."

Her aunt looked worried. "Really? Aren't you being too— . . ."

"Not at all," I said. "They're of no use to me once the portrait's done."

"Will you use one of these dessan for your underdrawing?" Mariye asked.

"No." I shook my head. "I did them just to get a three-dimensional feel for who you are. The you who I put on canvas will be altogether different."

"Can you tell what that's going to look like?"

"No, not yet. The two of us still have to figure that one out."

"Figure out how I look three-dimensionally?" Mariye asked.

"That's right. A painting is a flat surface, but it still has to have three dimensions. Do you follow me?"

Mariye frowned. I guessed she might somehow associate the word "three-dimensional" with her flat chest. In fact, she shot a glance at the curves beneath her aunt's thin sweater before looking at me.

"How can somebody learn to draw this well?" Mariye asked.

"You mean like these dessan?"

She nodded. "Yeah, like dessan, croquis, things like that."

"It's all practice. The more you practice the better you get."

"I think there are a lot of people," she said, "who don't improve, no matter how much they practice."

She sure hit that one on the head. I had attended art school, but loads of my classmates couldn't paint their way out of a paper bag. However we thrash about, we are all thrown in one direction or another by our natural talent, or lack of it. That's a basic truth we all have to learn to live with.

"Fair enough, but you still have to practice. If you don't, any gifts or talents you do have won't emerge where people can see them."

Shoko gave an emphatic nod. Mariye looked dubious.

"You want to learn to paint well, correct?" I asked her.

Mariye nodded. "I like things I can see as much as things I can't," she said.

I looked in her eyes. A light was shining there. I wasn't sure I understood exactly what she meant. But that inner light was drawing me in.

"What a strange thing to say," Shoko said. "Like you were speaking in riddles."

Mariye didn't respond, just studied her hands. When she did look up a short while later, the light was gone. It had only been there a moment.

Mariye and I went to the studio. Shoko had already pulled out the same thick paperback—at least, it looked identical to the one she had brought the previous week—and settled down on the sofa to read. She seemed totally engrossed in the book. I was even more curious than before as to what it might be, but I didn't ask.

Mariye and I sat across from each other about six feet apart, just as we had the last time. The only difference was that now I had an easel and canvas in front of me. No paints or brush, though—my hands were empty. My eyes hopped back and forth, from Mariye to the canvas to Mariye again. All the while, the question of how best to portray her "three-dimensionally" was running through my mind. I needed a *story* of some sort to work from. It wasn't enough to just look at the person I happened to be painting. Nothing good could result from that. The portrait might be a passable likeness, but no more. To turn out a true portrait, I had to discover *the story that must be painted*. Only that could get the ball rolling.

We sat there for some time, me on the stool, Mariye on a straight-backed chair, as I studied her face. She stared back at me without blinking, never averting her eyes. She didn't look defiant so much as ready to stand her ground. Her pretty, almost doll-like, appearance sent people the wrong signal—at her core, she had a strong sense of herself, and her own unshakable way of doing things. Once she'd drawn a straight line, good luck getting her to bend it.

There was something in Mariye's eyes that reminded me of Menshiki, though I had to look closely to see it. I had felt the similarity before, but it still surprised me. Their gaze had a strange radiance—"a frozen flame" was the phrase that leapt to mind. That flame had warmth, but at the same time, it was cool and collected. Like a rare jewel whose glow came from deep within. That light expressed naked yearning when projected outside. Focused inward, it strove for completion. These two sides were equally strong, and at perpetual war with each other.

Did Menshiki's revelation that his blood might be running through Mariye's veins influence me? Perhaps that had led me to unconsciously link the two of them together.

Whatever the case, I had to transfer that glow in her eyes to the canvas, to capture how *special* it was. The core element in her expression, the thing that cut through her modulated exterior. Yet I still hadn't located the context that made such a transfer possible. If I failed, that warm light would come across as an icy jewel, nothing more. Where was the heat coming from, and where was it headed? I had to find out.

I sat there for fifteen minutes, gazing at her face, then at the canvas and back again, before finally giving up. I pushed the easel aside and took a few slow, deep breaths.

"Let's talk," I said.

"Um, sure," she answered. "What do you want to talk about?"

"I want to know more about you. If that's okay."

"Like?"

"Well, what sort of person is your father?"

Mariye gave a small smirk. "I don't know him very well."

"You don't talk?"

"We hardly see each other."

"Because he's busy with work?"

"I don't know anything about his work," Mariye said. "I don't think he cares about me that much."

"Doesn't care?"

"That's why he handed me over to my aunt to raise."

I took a pass on that one.

"How about your mother—can you remember her? You were six when she passed away, right?"

"I can only remember her in patches."

"What do you mean, in patches?"

"My mom disappeared all of a sudden. I was too little to understand what dying meant, so I didn't really know what had happened. She was there and then she just *wasn't*. Like smoke."

Mariye was quiet for a moment.

"It happened so quickly, and I couldn't understand the reason," she said at last. "That's why I can't remember much about that part of my life, like right before and after her death."

"You must have been pretty confused."

"It's like there's this high wall that divides when she was with me and when she was gone. I can't connect the two parts together." She chewed her lip for a moment. "Do you get what I mean?"

"I think so," I said. "My sister died when she was twelve. I told you that before, right?"

Mariye nodded.

"She was born with a defective valve in her heart. She had a big operation, and everything was supposed to be okay, but for some reason there was still a problem. So she lived with a time bomb ticking inside her body. As a result, everyone in our family was more or less prepared for the worst. Her death didn't hit us like a bolt from the blue, like when your mother was stung by hornets."

"A bolt . . . ?"

"A bolt from the blue," I said. "A bolt of lightning that strikes from a cloudless sky. Something sudden and unexpected."

"A bolt from the blue," she said. "What characters is it written with?"

"The 'blue' is written with characters for 'blue sky.' 'Bolt' is really complicated—I can't write it myself. In fact, I've never written it. If you're curious, you should look it up in a dictionary when you get back home."

"A bolt from the blue," she repeated. She seemed to be storing the phrase in her mental filing cabinet.

"At any rate," I went on, "we all had an idea what might happen. When it actually did, though—when she had a sudden heart attack and died, all in one day—our preparations didn't make a bit of difference. Her death paralyzed me. And not just me, my whole family."

"Did something change inside you after that?"

"Yes, completely. Both *inside* and *outside*. Time didn't pass as it had before—it flowed differently. And, like you said, I had a problem connecting how things were before her death with the way they were after."

Mariye stared at me without speaking for a full ten seconds. "Your sister meant a lot to you, didn't she?" she said at last.

"Yes," I nodded. "She did."

Mariye studied her lap for a moment. "It's because my memory is blocked," she said, looking up, "that I have trouble recalling my mom. The kind of person she was, her face, the things she said to me. My dad doesn't talk much about her either."

All I knew about Mariye's mother was the blow-by-blow account Menshiki had given me of the last time they had had sex. It had been on his office couch—the moment of Mariye's conception, perhaps—and it was violent. Not a big help at the moment.

"You must remember something, even if it's not much. After all, you lived with her till you were six."

"Just the smell."

"The smell of her body?"

"No, the smell of rain."

"Rain?"

"It was raining then. So hard I could hear the drops hit the ground. But my mother was walking outside without an umbrella. So we walked through the rain together, holding hands. I think it was summer."

"A summer shower, then?"

"I guess so. The pavement was hot from the sun, so it gave off that smell. That's what I remember. We were high in the mountains, on some kind of observation deck. And my mother was singing a song."

"What kind of song?"

"I can't remember the melody. But I do remember some of the words. They were like, 'The sun's shining on a big green field across the river, but it's been raining on this side for so long.' Have you ever heard a song like that?"

It didn't ring a bell. "No," I replied. "I don't think so."

Mariye gave a little shrug. "I've asked different people, but no one knows it. I wonder why. Do you think maybe I made it up in my head?"

"Maybe she invented it there on the spot. For you."

Mariye looked up at me and smiled. "I never thought about it like that before. If that's true—it's pretty cool."

I think it was the first time I'd seen her smile. It was as if a ray of sunlight had shot through a crack in an overcast sky to illuminate one special spot. It was that kind of smile.

"Could you recognize the place if you went there again?" I asked. "Back to that same observation deck in the mountains?"

"Maybe," Mariye said. "I'm not sure, but maybe."

"I think it's pretty cool that you carry that scene inside you."

Mariye just nodded.

After that, we just sat back and listened to the birds chirping. The autumn sky outside the window was perfectly clear. Not a wisp of cloud anywhere. We were each in our own inner world, pursuing our own random thoughts.

It was Mariye who broke the silence. "Why's that painting facing the wrong way?" she asked.

She was pointing at my oil painting (to be more precise, my attempted painting) of the man with the white Subaru Forester. The canvas was sitting on the floor, turned to the wall so that I wouldn't have to look at it.

"I'm trying to paint a certain man. It's a work in progress, but it's not progressing right now."

"Can I see it?"

"Sure. I've just started it, though. I have a long way to go."

I turned the canvas around and placed it on the easel. Mariye got up from her chair, walked over, and stood before it with her arms folded. The sharp gleam in her eyes had returned. Her lips were set in a straight line.

I had used three colors—red, green, and black—but still hadn't given the man a distinct shape. My initial charcoal sketch was now totally obscured. He refused to be fleshed out any further, to have more color added to his form. But I knew he was there. I had grasped the essence of who he was. He was like a fish caught in a net. I had been trying to pull him out of the depths, and he was fighting me at every turn. At that point in our tug of war I had set the painting aside.

"This is where you stopped?" Mariye asked.

"That's right. I couldn't find a way to push it past this stage."

"It looks pretty finished to me," she murmured.

I stood next to her and looked at the painting again from her angle. Could she really see the man lurking there in the darkness?

"You mean I don't need to add anything more?" I asked.

"Yeah, I think you should just leave it like this."

I swallowed. She was echoing what the man with the white Subaru Forester had said almost word for word. *Leave the painting alone. Don't touch it again.*

"Why do you think that?" I pressed.

Mariye didn't answer right away. Instead, she studied the painting some more. She unfolded her arms and pressed her hands to her cheeks. As if they were hot, and she was trying to cool them.

"This painting is more than powerful enough as it is," she said at last.

"More than powerful enough?"

"I think so."

"You mean a *not so good kind* of power?"

Mariye didn't answer. Her hands were still pressed to her cheeks.

"Do you know the man in the painting well?"

I shook my head. "No, to tell the truth he's a complete stranger. I ran across him a while back. In a faraway town when I was on a long trip. We never talked, so I don't know his name."

"I can't tell if the power is good or not. Maybe it could be either good or bad, depending on the situation. You know, like the way we see things changes depending on where we're standing."

"And you don't think I should let that power come to the surface, right?"

She looked me in the eye. "Suppose you did and it turned out to be a *not so good thing*, what would you do? What if it tried to grab you?"

She was right. If it turned out to be a *not so good thing*, or indeed an *evil thing*, and it reached for me, what would I do then?

I took the canvas from the easel and set it back down on the floor, facing the wall. The moment its surface was hidden, the tension in the studio released its grip. It was a tangible sensation.

Perhaps I should pack it up and shut it away in the attic, I thought. Just as Tomohiko Amada had stashed *Killing Commendatore* there, to make sure no one could see it.

"All right, so then what do you think of that painting?" I asked, pointing to *Killing Commendatore* hanging on the wall.

"I like it," Mariye said immediately. "Who did it?"

"It was painted by Tomohiko Amada, the man who owns this house."

"It's calling out to me. Like a caged bird crying to be set free. That's the feeling I get."

I looked at her. "Bird? What kind of bird?"

"I don't know what kind of bird. Or what kind of cage. Or what they look like. It's just my feeling. I think maybe this painting's a little too difficult for me."

"You're not the only one. It's too difficult for me, too. But I'm sure you're right. There is a cry in this painting, a plea that the artist desperately wanted people to hear. I react the same way you do. But for the life of me, I can't figure out what that plea is."

"Someone is murdering someone else. Out of passion."

"Exactly. The young man has plunged a knife into the older man's chest, exactly as he planned. The man being murdered can't believe what's happening. The others are in total shock at what's taking place before their eyes."

"Can there be a proper murder?"

I thought for a moment. "I'm not sure. It depends how you define 'proper' and 'improper.' Many people regard the death penalty as a proper form of murder." Or assassination, I thought.

Mariye took a moment to respond. "It's funny, a man's being killed, and his blood is flying all over the place, but it's not depressing. It's like the painting is trying to take me someplace else. Someplace where things like 'proper' and 'improper' don't matter."

. . .

I didn't pick up a brush that day. Instead, Mariye and I sat there in the bright studio talking about whatever crossed our minds. I kept a close eye on her, though, filing each expression and mannerism away in my mind. That stock of memories would become the flesh and blood of the portrait I wanted to paint.

"You didn't draw anything today," Mariye commented.

"There are days like this," I said. "Time steals some things, but it gives us back others. Making time our ally is an important part of our work."

Mariye said nothing, just studied my eyes. As if she was peering into a house, her face pressed against the window. She was contemplating the meaning of time.

When the chimes rang as always at noon, Mariye and I moved from the studio to the living room. Shoko Akikawa was sitting on the sofa, wearing her black-rimmed glasses, reading her paperback. She was so deep in the book it was hard to tell if she was breathing.

"What are you reading?" I asked, unable to bear the suspense any longer.

"If I told you what it was," she said with a smile, marking her spot and closing the book, "it would jinx it. For some reason, every time I tell someone what I'm reading, I'm unable to finish. Something unexpected happens, and I have to break off partway through. It's strange, but it's true. So I've made it my policy not to reveal the title to anyone. I'd love to tell you about the book once I'm done, though."

"No worries. I'm quite happy to wait until you're finished. I could see how much you're enjoying it, so I got curious."

"It's a fascinating book. Once I get into it I can't stop. That's why I've decided to read it only when I'm here. This way, two hours pass before I know it."

"My aunt reads tons of books," Mariye chimed in.

"I don't have that much to do these days," her aunt said. "So books are how I get by."

"Do you have a job?" I asked.

She removed her glasses and gently massaged the crease between her eyebrows. "I volunteer at our local library once a week. I used to work at a private medical college in Tokyo. I was secretary to the president there. But I gave it up when I moved here."

"That was when Mariye's mother passed away, wasn't it?"

"At the time, I thought it would just be temporary. That I would stay only until things got sorted out. But once I started living with Mariye it became hard to leave. So I've been here ever since. Of course, if my brother remarried, I would move back to the city."

"I'd go with you if that happened," Mariye said.

Shoko smiled politely but didn't say anything.

"Why don't you stay for lunch?" I asked the two of them. "I can whip up a pasta and salad in no time."

Shoko hesitated, as I knew she would, but Mariye seemed excited by the idea.

"Why not?" she told her aunt. "Dad isn't home."

"It's really no problem," I said. "I've got lots of sauce already made, so it's no more trouble to cook for three than for one."

"Are you sure?" Shoko said, looking doubtful.

"Of course. Please do stay. I eat alone all the time. Breakfast, lunch, and dinner, every day. I'd like to share a meal with others for a change."

Mariye looked at her aunt.

"Well, in that case we'll take you up on your kind invitation," Shoko said. "You're quite sure we're not imposing?"

"Not at all," I said. "Please make yourself at home."

The three of us moved to the dining area. They sat at the table, while I prepared the meal. I set the water to boil, warmed the asparagus-and-bacon sauce in a pan, and threw together a quick salad of lettuce, tomato, onion, and green peppers. When the water boiled, I tossed in the pasta and diced some parsley while it cooked. I took the iced tea from the fridge and filled three glasses. Mariye and her aunt watched me bustle about as if witnessing a rare and strange event. Shoko asked if there was something she could do. No, I replied, she should just relax—I had everything under control.

"You seem so at home in the kitchen," she said, impressed.

"That's because I do this every day."

I don't mind cooking at all. In fact, I've always liked working with my hands. Cooking, simple carpentry, bicycle repair, yard work. I'm useless when it comes to abstract, mathematical thought. Mental games like chess and puzzles are just too taxing for my simple brain.

We sat down at the table and began to eat. A carefree lunch on a sunny Sunday afternoon in autumn. And Shoko was a perfect lunchtime companion. She was gracious and witty, full of things to talk about and with a great sense of humor. Her table manners were elegant, yet there was nothing pretentious about her. I could tell she came from a good family and had attended the most expensive schools. Mariye left all the talking to her aunt and concentrated on her meal. Later, Shoko asked for my recipe for the sauce.

We had almost finished our lunch when the front doorbell gave a cheerful ring. It was no surprise to me, for just a moment earlier I thought I had heard the deep purr of a Jaguar engine. That sound—the polar opposite of the whisper of the Toyota Prius—had registered in that narrow layer between my conscious and unconscious minds. So it was hardly a "bolt from the blue" when the bell chimed.

"Excuse me for a second," I said, rising from my chair and putting my napkin down. Leaving the two of them at the table, I went to the front door. What would happen now? I didn't have a clue.

34

I COULDN'T RECALL THE LAST TIME I CHECKED MY TIRES' AIR PRESSURE

I opened the door, and there stood Menshiki.

He was wearing a white button-down shirt, a fancy wool vest with an intricate pattern, and a bluish-gray tweed jacket. His chinos were a light mustard color, his suede shoes brown. A coordinated and comfortable outfit, as always. His white hair glowed in the autumn sun. The silver Jaguar was behind him, parked next to the blue Toyota Prius. Side by side, the two cars resembled someone with crooked teeth laughing with his mouth wide open.

I gestured for him to enter. He was so tense his face looked frozen, like a plastered wall only half dry. Needless to say, I had never seen him like this before. He was always so cool, holding himself in check with his feelings packed out of sight. He had been that way even after an hour entombed in a pitch-black pit. Yet now he was as white as a sheet.

"Do you mind if I come in?" he said.

"Of course not," I answered. "We're almost through with lunch. So do come in."

"I really don't want to interrupt your meal," he said, glancing at his watch in what seemed a reflex motion. He stared at it for a long time, his face blank. As if he had a quarrel with how the second hand was moving.

"We'll be done soon," I said again. "It's a very basic meal. Let's have coffee together afterward. Please wait in the living room. I'll make the introductions there."

Menshiki shook his head. "Introductions might be premature at this stage. I stopped by assuming they'd already left. I wasn't planning to meet them. But I saw an unfamiliar car parked in front and wasn't sure what to do, so I—"

"You came at the perfect time," I said, cutting him off. "Nothing could be more natural. Just leave everything to me."

Menshiki nodded and began to take off his shoes. Yet for some reason he seemed to have forgotten how. I waited until he had struggled through the procedure and showed him into the living room. He'd been there several times before, yet he stared at the room as though it was his first visit.

"Please wait here," I said, patting him on the shoulder. "Just sit down and relax. It shouldn't take more than ten minutes."

I left Menshiki sitting there by himself—though it worried me a bit—and went back to the dining area. Shoko and Mariye had finished their meal in my absence. Their forks rested on empty plates.

"Do you have a visitor?" Shoko asked in a worried voice.

"Yes, but it's all right. Someone from the neighborhood just happened to stop by. I asked him to wait in the living room. We're on friendly terms, so there's no need for formality. I'll just finish my meal first."

I ate what remained of my lunch. Then I brewed a pot of coffee while the two women cleaned up the dishes.

"Shall we have our coffee in the living room?" I asked Shoko.

"But won't we be intruding on you and your guest?"

I shook my head no. "Not in the slightest. It's a stroke of luck—this way, I can introduce you to each other. He lives on top of the slope on the other side of the valley, so I doubt you've ever met."

"What is his name?"

"Menshiki. It's written with the characters for 'avoidance' and 'color.' 'Avoiding colors,' in other words."

"What an unusual name!" Shoko exclaimed. "I've never heard anyone mention a Mr. Menshiki before. The addresses of people across the valley are close to ours, but there's little coming and going between the two sides."

We placed the pot of coffee, four cups, and some milk and sugar on a tray and carried it out to the living room. To my surprise, Menshiki was nowhere to be seen. The room was deserted. He wasn't on the terrace, either. And I doubted he was in the bathroom.

"Where did he disappear to?" I said to no one in particular.

"Was he here earlier?" Shoko asked.

"Until a few minutes ago."

His suede shoes were gone from the entranceway. I slipped on my sandals and opened the front door. The silver Jaguar was parked exactly where he had left it. So he hadn't returned home. The sun reflecting off the Jaguar's windows made it impossible to tell if anyone was inside. I walked over to check. Menshiki was sitting in the driver's seat, rummaging around for something. I tapped on the window, and he rolled it down. He looked lost.

"What happened?" I asked.

"I want to check the air pressure in my tires, but I can't find the gauge. It should be in the glove compartment, but it's gone."

"Is there some kind of rush?"

"No, not really. I was sitting there in your living room when it started to bother me. Couldn't recall the last time I checked."

"So there's no trouble with them?"

"No, nothing in particular. They seem normal."

"Then why don't you forget about the tires for now and come back in? The coffee is made, and two people are waiting."

"Waiting for me?" he said in a hoarse voice. "Are they waiting for me?"

"Yes, I told them I'd introduce you."

"Oh dear," he said.

"Why oh dear?"

"Because I'm not ready for introductions yet. Not emotionally prepared."

He had the baffled, fearful look of someone ordered to jump from the sixteenth floor of a burning building to a net that looked the size of a drink coaster.

"You should come," I said, not mincing words. "It's really not a big deal."

Menshiki nodded and got out, closing the car door behind him. He started to lock it before realizing how unnecessary that was (what thief would stray up here?), so he stuffed the key in the pocket of his chinos.

Shoko and Mariye were waiting in the living room. They rose to greet us as we entered. My introductions were simple and straightforward. A common human courtesy.

"Mr. Menshiki has also modeled for me. I painted his portrait. He happens to live nearby, and we've been friends since we met."

"I understand you live on the other side of the valley. Have you been there long?" Shoko inquired.

Menshiki blanched at the mention of his home. "Yes, I've been living there for a few years. Let's see, how many is it now—three years perhaps? Or is it four?"

He turned to me as if for confirmation, but I didn't respond.

"Can we see your home from here?" Shoko asked.

"Yes," Menshiki said. "But it's really nothing to brag about," he added. "It's awfully out of the way."

"It's the same on this side," Shoko said affably. "Simple shopping is a major expedition. Cell phone service and radios are hit-or-miss. And the road is terribly steep. When the snow is thick, it gets so slippery I'm afraid to take the car out. Luckily, it doesn't happen that often—just once, five years ago."

"You're right," Menshiki said. "It rarely snows here. It has to do with the warmth of the wind coming off the ocean. The ocean exerts a powerful influence on our climate. You see . . ."

"In any case," I broke in, "we should be thankful it snows so rarely here." I feared he was about to launch into a lecture on the structure and effects of the warm sea currents along the coast of Japan—that's how wound up he was.

Mariye was looking back and forth at her aunt and Menshiki throughout this exchange. She seemed to have formed no opinion about Menshiki as of yet. Menshiki, for his part, acted as though Mariye wasn't there, focusing on her aunt as though bewitched.

"Mariye here is letting me paint her portrait," I said to him. "I asked her to model for me."

"I drive her here every Sunday morning," Shoko said. "It's not far as the crow flies—from your eyes to your nose, you might say—but the road twists and turns so much we have to take the car."

Menshiki finally turned to look at Mariye Akikawa. But his eyes didn't focus on any part of her face—they buzzed about nervously like a fly in winter, searching for a place to land. Yet they never seemed to find one.

"These are what I've drawn so far," I said, coming to his aid. I handed him my sketchbook. "I haven't started painting yet—we've just wrapped up the preliminary stage."

Menshiki stared at the three dessan for a long time, devouring them with his eyes. As if the drawings of Mariye somehow meant more to him than Mariye herself. This wasn't true, of course—he simply couldn't bring himself to face her. The dessan were a substitute, nothing more. It was the first time he had been close to her, and he was having a hard time controlling his feelings. Mariye, for her part, regarded the floundering Menshiki as though he were some kind of strange animal.

"They're superb," Menshiki said. He turned to Shoko. "Each is so full of life. He's really captured her!"

"I totally agree," she said, beaming.

"All the same, Mariye is a very difficult subject," I said to Menshiki. "Painting her is a challenge. Her expression is constantly changing, so it takes time to grasp what's at the core. That's why I haven't gotten around to the actual painting stage yet."

"Difficult?" Menshiki said. He looked at Mariye a second time, squinting as though dazzled by her light.

"The three dessan should show very different expressions," I said. "The slightest facial movement radically transforms the whole atmosphere. When I paint her portrait, I have to get past those superficial differences to grasp the essence of her personality. Otherwise, I'd be conveying only part of the whole."

"I see," Menshiki said, dutifully impressed. He looked back and forth between the three sketches and Mariye, comparing them. In the process, his face, which had been so pale, began to regain some of its color. Red dots popped up at first, then the dots grew to blotches the size of ping-pong balls, then baseballs, until in the end his whole face had turned rosy. Mariye watched him, fascinated, but her aunt politely turned away. I grabbed the coffee pot and poured myself another cup.

I felt I had to break the silence. "I'm thinking of starting the actual portrait next week. You know, on canvas with real paint," I said to no one in particular.

"Do you have a clear image what it will look like?" asked Shoko.

"Not yet," I said, shaking my head. "I won't know in any concrete way until I'm sitting in front of the canvas with a brush in my hand. Hopefully, the inspiration will hit me then."

"You painted Mr. Menshiki's picture as well, didn't you?" Shoko asked me.

"Yes, last month."

"It's a beautiful portrait," Menshiki said emphatically. "The paint has to dry a bit more before it can be framed, but it's hanging on the wall of my study. I'm not sure 'portrait' does it justice, though. It's a painting of me, but of something other than me, too. I don't know how to put it—I guess you could say it has *depth*. I never get tired of looking at it."

"You say it's you, yet it's not you at the same time?" Shoko asked.

"I mean it's a step beyond your typical portrait—it's deeper, more profound."

"I want to see it," Mariye said. They were the first words she had spoken since we had moved to the living room.

"But Mariye . . . you shouldn't invite yourself into someone's—"

"That's perfectly all right!" Menshiki said, cutting off her aunt's rebuke as if with a sharp hatchet. His tone was so jarring that we all—including Menshiki himself—were stunned.

"Please do come take a look," he continued after a moment's regrouping. "It's so rare for me to meet someone from the neighborhood. I live alone, so you needn't worry about disturbing anyone. Any time at all would be fine."

Menshiki's face was even redder by the time he finished. It appeared that we hadn't been the only ones shocked by the urgency in his voice.

"Do you like paintings?" Menshiki asked, this time directing his question to Mariye. His voice was back to normal.

Mariye gave a small nod.

"If it's all right with you, why don't I stop by again at this time next

Sunday?" Menshiki said. "I could escort you to my home and we could all look at the painting together."

"But we shouldn't inconvenience you—" Shoko said.

"I want to see the painting!" Mariye was firm.

In the end it was agreed that Menshiki would come to pick up the two of them the following Sunday afternoon. I was invited too, but I declined, citing an important errand. The last thing I wanted was to get sucked in any deeper. From now on, let those who were involved look after things. I would remain the outsider, however the situation turned out. I would be the mediator, nothing more—though even that had not been my intention.

Menshiki and I accompanied the beautiful aunt and her niece outside to give them a proper send-off. Shoko looked for some time at the silver Jaguar parked next to her Prius. Like a dog lover appraising another person's dog.

"This is the latest model, isn't it?" she asked Menshiki.

"Yes, this is their newest coupe on the market," he answered. "Do you like cars?"

"No, it's not that. It's just that my late father drove a Jaguar sedan. I used to sit next to him, and every so often he'd let me hold the wheel. The Jaguar hood ornament takes me back to those times. Was it an XJ6? It had four round headlights, I think. And an inline six-cylinder 4.2-liter engine."

"That is the III series, I believe. A truly beautiful model."

"My father drove that car for ages, so he must have really liked it. Although he complained about the terrible mileage. And it had one minor malfunction after the other."

"That model in particular is a real gas guzzler. And the wiring was probably faulty. The electrical system has always been the Jaguar's Achilles' heel. But if it's running smoothly, and if you don't mind shelling out for gas, you can't beat a Jaguar. For driving comfort and handling, no other car matches it—it's got a charm all its own. Most people, though, are really turned off by things like gas consumption and mechanical glitches, which is why the Toyota Prius is the one flying off the lots."

"I didn't buy this car," Shoko said, as if by way of apology, gesturing toward her Prius. "My brother bought it for me because it's safe and easy to drive, and gentle on the environment."

"The Prius is an excellent car," Menshiki said. "I've thought of buying one myself."

Was he kidding? Menshiki behind the wheel of a Toyota Prius was as hard to picture as a leopard ordering a salade Niçoise.

"This is very rude of me," Shoko said, peering into the Jaguar's interior, "but would it be all right if I sat in it for a minute? I just want to try out the driver's seat."

"Of course," Menshiki answered. He coughed lightly, as if to bring his voice under control. "Sit there as long as you like. Take it for a spin if you wish."

I was flabbergasted by how interested she was in Menshiki's Jaguar. On the surface she was so cool and poised, not my image of a car person at all. Yet her eyes were shining when she climbed into the driver's seat. She snuggled into the cream-colored leather upholstery, studied the dashboard with care, and took the steering wheel in both hands. Then she placed her left hand on the gearshift. Menshiki took the car key from his pocket and passed it to her through the window.

"Turn it on if you like."

Shoko took the key, inserted it into the ignition next to the wheel, and rotated it clockwise. Instantly, the great feline awoke. She sat there entranced for a moment, listening to the deep purr of the engine.

"I remember this sound well," she said.

"It's a 4.2-liter V8 engine. Your father's XJ6 had six cylinders, and the number of valves and the compression ratio were different too, but they may well sound alike. Both are sinful, though—they squander fossil fuel like there's no tomorrow. Jaguars haven't changed a bit on that score."

Shoko flipped on the right-turn signal. I heard a cheerful clicking sound.

"This really brings back memories."

Menshiki smiled. "Only a Jaguar's turn signal sounds like this. It's unlike that of any other automobile."

"When I was young, I secretly practiced on the XJ6 to get my driver's license," she said. "The first time I drove another car I was totally confused—the parking brake wasn't where I expected. I had no idea what to do."

"I know just what you mean," Menshiki grinned. "The Brits are fussy about the funniest things."

"I think the interior smells a bit different than my father's car, though."

"Sadly, you're right. For a variety of reasons, Jaguar can't use the exact same materials on its newer models. The smell changed after 2002, when Connolly Leather stopped supplying their upholstery. In fact, the Connolly company went out of business at that point."

"How too bad. I loved that smell. I connect it to the smell of my father."

"To tell the truth," Menshiki said hesitantly, "I own another Jaguar as well, an older model. It may well have the same odor as your father's car."

"Is it an XJ6?"

"No, it's an E type."

"Does that mean it's a convertible?"

"Correct. It's a Series 1 roadster, made back in the mid-sixties. It still runs well, though. It's also equipped with a six-cylinder 4.2-liter engine. An original two-seater. The top has been replaced, of course, so it's not exactly in mint condition."

Most of this flew over my head—I know nothing about cars—but Menshiki's words seemed to have made a deep impression on Shoko. They clearly shared an interest, and a fairly specialized interest at that, in Jaguars. That made me feel a little calmer. No longer did I have to think up topics to help them through their first meeting. Mariye's boredom was palpable, though—she seemed even less into cars than me.

Shoko got out of the Jaguar, shut the car door, and handed the key to Menshiki, who returned it to the pocket of his chinos. Then she and Mariye got in the blue Prius. Menshiki closed the door after Mariye. I was struck by the different *thunk* it made as it closed, nothing like the Jaguar. In this world, what we think of as a single sound can have so many permutations. Just as we know, from one note struck on the open string of a double bass, whether it's Charlie Mingus or Ray Brown.

"So we'll meet again next Sunday," Menshiki said.

Shoko gave Menshiki a big smile, took the steering wheel, and drove off. Menshiki and I waited until the squat rear of the Toyota Prius was out of sight before returning to the house. We sat in the living room sipping cold coffee. Neither of us spoke for some time. Menshiki looked exhausted. Like a long-distance runner who had just crossed the finish line.

"She's a beautiful girl," I said at last. "Mariye, I mean."

"You're right. She'll be even prettier when she grows up," Menshiki said. His mind seemed elsewhere.

"What did you think, seeing her up close?" I asked.

Menshiki smiled an uncomfortable smile. "I didn't get a very good look, to tell the truth. I was too nervous."

"But you must have seen something."

"Of course," he said, nodding. He paused for a long moment. "What did you think?" he asked at last, his eyes serious.

"What do you mean, what do I think?"

Menshiki's face flushed again. "Do you see any similarity between Mariye's features and mine? As an artist who has painted people's portraits for many years, I'm interested in your professional opinion."

I shook my head no. "You're right, I'm trained to take quick note of people's facial characteristics. But that doesn't mean I can tell whose child is whose. Some parents and children don't look alike at all, while total strangers can appear almost identical."

Menshiki gave a long, deep sigh. It sounded wrenched from his entire body. He rubbed his palms together.

"I'm not asking for a definitive judgment. I'm just asking for your *personal impressions*. Even the most trivial ones. I'd like to know if you noticed something, anything at all."

I thought for a moment. "As far as facial structure goes, I don't see much concrete similarity. But your eyes do have something in common. In fact, it startles me every so often."

He looked at me, his thin lips pressed together. "You're saying there's something similar in our eyes?"

"Maybe it's because they reflect your true feelings. Curiosity, enthusiasm, surprise, suspicion, reluctance—I can see those subtle emotions in both your eyes and hers. Your faces aren't all that expressive, but your eyes really are the windows to your hearts. Most people are the opposite. Their faces are expressive, but their eyes aren't nearly so lively."

Menshiki appeared surprised. "Is that how my eyes look to you?"

I nodded.

"I was never aware of that."

"You couldn't control it if you tried. Maybe it's because your feelings are on such a tight leash that your eyes are so expressive. It's not that obvious, though—you have to pay really, really close attention to read them. Most people wouldn't notice."

"But you can."

"Reading faces is my profession."

Menshiki considered that for a minute. "So she and I have that in common. But you still can't tell if we're father and daughter, right?"

"I do have certain impressions when I look at people, and I value those. But artistic impressions and objective reality are separate things. Impressions don't prove anything. They're like a butterfly in the wind—totally useless. But how about you? Did you feel anything special?"

He shook his head several times. "I couldn't tell anything in one brief meeting. I need to see her more. I have to get used to being around her first."

He shook his head again, this time more slowly. He plunged his hands into his jacket pockets as though searching for something, then pulled them out again. As though he'd forgotten what he was looking for.

"No, maybe it's not the number of times," he went on. "It could be the more we meet the more confused I'll get, the farther from any conclusion. It's *possible* she's my daughter, but then it's possible she isn't. But either way makes no difference to me. Her presence alone allows me to consider that possibility, to physically experience that hypothesis. When that happens, I feel fresh blood coursing through my body. Maybe I've never understood the true meaning of being alive until now."

I held my peace. What could I say about the feelings he was experiencing, or about his definition of being alive? Menshiki glanced at his thin, expensive-looking wristwatch and awkwardly struggled to his feet from the sofa.

"I owe you my thanks. I couldn't have done a thing if you hadn't given me a push."

With these few words he stumbled toward the door, struggled a bit to put on his shoes, and stepped outside. From the door, I watched him climb in his car and drive away. When his Jaguar was out of sight, the peaceful quiet of a Sunday afternoon enfolded me once again.

The clock said a little after two p.m. I was dead tired. I pulled an old blanket from the closet, lay on the sofa, and slept with it tucked over me. It was past three when I awoke. The angle of the sunlight in the room had shifted somewhat. What a strange day! I couldn't be sure if I had moved forward or fallen behind, or if I was just circling over the same spot. My sense of direction had gone haywire. There was Shoko and Mariye, and then there was Menshiki. Each had a special magnetism. And I had landed smack in the middle of it all. Lacking any magnetism of my own to speak of.

However exhausted I might feel, though, Sunday was far from over. The hands of the clock had only just passed three. The sun was still in the sky. Loads of time remained before a new day dawned and Sunday became a thing of the past. Yet I didn't feel like doing anything. I had taken a nap, but my head was muddled. It felt like a ball of yarn had been crammed into the back of a narrow desk drawer, and now the drawer wouldn't close properly. Maybe this was the sort of day I should check the air pressure in my tires. Anyone feeling this blah should be able to rouse himself to do that much.

Come to think of it, though, I had never checked the air pressure myself. Whenever a gas station attendant said that the air in my tires "looked a little low," I always asked him to take care of it. Which means I don't own an air pressure gauge. In fact, I don't even know what one looks like. If it fits in a glove compartment, it can't be all that big. Nor so expensive as to require monthly payments. Maybe I should buy one, just to see.

When it began to get dark, I went to the kitchen, cracked open a can of beer, and began preparing dinner. In the oven, I broiled a piece of yellowtail that I'd marinated in sake lees, then sliced pickles, made a cucumber-and-seaweed salad with vinegar, and fixed some miso soup with radishes and deep-fried tofu. Then I sat down and ate my silent meal. There was no one there to talk to, and nothing in particular I could think of to talk about. Just when I was finishing my simple, solitary dinner, the front doorbell rang. There seemed to be a conspiracy afoot to interrupt me toward the end of every meal.

So this day hasn't ended after all, I thought. I had the premonition it would be a long Sunday. I got up from the table and walked slowly to the door.

35

YOU SHOULD HAVE JUST LEFT THAT PLACE ALONE

I walked slowly to the door. Who could possibly be ringing the bell? Had a car pulled up in front without my knowledge? The dining area was toward the rear of the house, but it was a quiet night, so I should have heard the crunch of gravel and the rumble of an engine. Even the vaunted "silent" hybrid engine of a Prius. Still, my ears had picked up nothing.

No one would climb such a long, steep slope on foot at night on a lark. The road was unlit, and deserted. My house had been plopped down on top of an isolated mountain, with no neighbors close by.

For a moment, I thought it might be the Commendatore. But that didn't make much sense. I mean, he could come and go whenever he wanted, so why ring the bell?

I unlocked and opened the door without bothering to check who it was. Mariye Akikawa was standing there. She was wearing the same clothes she had worn that afternoon, only now a thin navy-blue down jacket covered her windbreaker. Naturally, it got chillier once the sun was down. She had a Cleveland Indians cap on her head (why Cleveland?) and a large flashlight in her right hand.

"Can I come in?" she asked. There was no "Good evening," no "Sorry for the surprise visit."

"Sure," I said. "Come on in." That was it. My mental desk drawer wasn't closing properly yet. That ball of yarn was still jammed in there.

I showed her into the dining room.

"I'm still eating dinner. Mind if I finish?" I said.

She nodded silently. She was free of all the tiresome social graces—they meant nothing to her.

"Want some tea?" I asked.

She nodded again. She took off her down jacket, removed her cap, and straightened her hair. I set the kettle to boil, and put some green tea in a small teapot. I wanted a cup of tea myself.

With her elbows on the table, Mariye watched me polish off the broiled yellowtail, miso soup, and salad as if she had come across something very strange. She could have been sitting on a rock in the jungle, watching a python swallow a baby badger.

"I marinated the yellowtail myself," I explained, breaking the silence. "It keeps a lot longer that way."

She didn't respond. I couldn't tell if my words had reached her or not. "Immanuel Kant was a man of punctual habits," I said. "So punctual that people set their clocks by when he passed on his strolls."

Absolutely meaningless, of course. I just wanted to see how she'd react to something so totally random. If she was really listening or not. Again, no response. The silence around us only deepened further. Immanuel Kant continued strolling through the streets of Königsberg, leading his regulated and taciturn life. His last words were "This is good" (*Es ist gut*). Some people can live like that.

I finished dinner and carried the dishes to the sink. Then I made tea. I returned with the teapot and two cups. Mariye sat there at the table watching me throughout. She was eyeballing me intently—like a historian meticulously checking the footnotes of a text.

"You didn't come by car, did you?" I asked.

At last she opened her mouth. "I walked," she said.

"All the way from your house, by yourself?"

"Uh-huh."

I waited for her to go on. But she didn't. We sat there across from each other at the table for a while without speaking. I'm pretty good at long silences, though. No accident I'm holed up by myself on top of a mountain.

"There's a secret passageway," Mariye said at last. "It's a long way by car, but not far if you take the passageway."

"I've walked all over this area but I've never seen anything like that."

"You don't know how to look," she shot back. "You really have to pay attention to find it. It's well hidden."

"You hid it, right?"

She nodded. "I've lived here since I was small. The whole mountain is my playground. I know every part of it."

"So the passageway is really well concealed."

She gave another firm nod.

"And you used it to come here."

"Uh-huh."

I sighed. "Have you had dinner?"

"I ate already."

"What did you eat?"

"My aunt isn't a very good cook," the girl said. Not a real answer to my question—it was clear she wanted to let the matter drop. Maybe she didn't want to recall what she'd eaten for dinner.

"Does your aunt know you came here by yourself?"

Mariye didn't reply. Her lips were set in a straight line. I chose to answer my own question.

"Of course she doesn't. What responsible adult would let a thirteen-year-old girl wander the mountains after dark? Right?"

There followed another period of silence.

"She's not aware of the passageway?"

Mariye shook her head several times. So her aunt didn't know.

"And you're the only one who knows about it?"

Mariye nodded several times.

"In any event," I said, "given where you live, once you left the passageway you probably went through the woods and past an old shrine to get here. Right?"

Mariye nodded again. "I know that shrine. And I know that someone used a big machine to dig up the pile of rocks behind it."

"Did you watch?"

Mariye shook her head. "I didn't see them digging. I was at school that day. But I saw the tracks. The ground was covered with them. Why did you do it?"

"I had reasons."

"What kind of reasons?"

"If I tried to explain from the beginning it would take too long," I said. So I didn't try. The last thing I wanted was for her to find out that Menshiki was involved.

"It was wrong to dig it up like that," Mariye said, abruptly.

"Why do you say that?"

She gave what looked like a shrug. "You should have just left that place alone. Everyone else did."

"Everyone else?"

"It's been there like forever, but no one touched it until now."

The girl was right, I thought. Perhaps we shouldn't have touched it. Perhaps we should have behaved like "everyone else" had. It was too late to change that now, though. The stones had been moved, the pit exposed, the Commendatore set free.

"Were you the one who removed the lid?" I asked. "Let me guess: you looked inside, then you replaced the boards and the stones that held them down. Am I right?"

Mariye raised her head and looked me straight in the eye. As if to say: How did you know?

"The rocks on the lid had been rearranged. My visual memory is pretty good, always has been. I could see the difference right away."

"Wow," she murmured, impressed.

"But the hole was empty. Nothing but darkness and damp air, right?"

"A ladder was there too."

"You didn't climb down it, did you?"

Mariye shook her head vigorously. As if to say: No way!

"And now," I said, "you've come here at this time of night for a particular reason, haven't you? I mean, this isn't just a social visit, is it."

"A social visit?"

"You know, an 'I happened to be in the neighborhood so I thought I'd stop by' kind of thing."

She thought for a moment before shaking her head. "No, it's not 'a social visit.' "

"Then what is it?" I asked. "I'm more than happy to have you visit me, but if your aunt or your father found out, it could lead to a bizarre misunderstanding."

"What kind of misunderstanding?"

"There are all sorts of misunderstandings in this world," I said. "Some go far beyond what you and I can imagine. In this case, it could make it impossible for me to paint your portrait. That would bother me a lot. Wouldn't it bother you?"

"My aunt won't find out," she said emphatically. "I go to my room after dinner and she never follows me. It's like an agreement we have. I leave through my window and no one knows. No one's ever caught on."

"So you've been walking the mountain at night for a long time?"

Mariye nodded.

"Isn't it scary all by yourself after dark?"

"Other things are a lot scarier."

"Like what, for example?"

Mariye shrugged her shoulders slightly but said nothing.

"Your aunt may not be a problem, but how about your father?"

"He's not back yet."

"Even though today's Sunday?"

Mariye didn't answer. I guessed she wanted to avoid talking about her father.

"Anyway, you don't have to worry," she said. "No one knows when I leave the house. Even if they found out I'd never give your name."

"All right then, I'll stop worrying," I said. "But why did you come here tonight of all nights?"

"Because I wanted to talk to you about something."

"Like what?"

Mariye picked up her cup and took a sip of hot tea. She looked warily around the room as if to make sure no one would overhear. Of course nobody was there but the two of us. That is, unless the Commendatore had returned and was listening in. I looked around as well. But the Commendatore wasn't there. If he was, he hadn't assumed bodily form.

"Your friend who showed up this afternoon, the guy with the pretty white hair," she said. "What was his name? It was kind of weird."

"Menshiki."

"That's right, Mr. Menshiki."

"He's not really a friend. I met him just a short while ago."

"Whatever."

"So what is it about Mr. Menshiki?"

She narrowed her eyes and looked at me. "I think," she said, lowering her voice, "that man is hiding something. In his heart."

"What sort of thing?"

"I don't know. But I don't believe he showed up this afternoon by accident, like he said. I think he came for a very specific purpose."

"What purpose is that?" I asked, a little shocked by how observant she was.

She fixed me with her gaze. "I'm not sure. Don't you know?"

"I have no idea," I lied, praying that Mariye wouldn't see through my deception. I have never been a good liar. When I lie it's written on my face. But there was no way I could tell her the truth.

"For real?"

"For real," I said. "I had no idea he would show up today."

Mariye seemed to buy my story. Menshiki had not told me he would be coming, and his sudden visit had taken me by surprise. So I wasn't really lying after all.

"His eyes are weird," Mariye said.

"Weird in what way?"

"It's like he's always *scheming* about something. Like the wolf in 'Little Red Riding Hood.' When the wolf dresses up like the grandmother and lies in bed, you can tell it's him by his eyes."

Like the wolf in "Little Red Riding Hood"?

"So you had an adverse reaction to Mr. Menshiki, right?"

"Adverse reaction?"

"A negative impression. A feeling he might harm you."

"Adverse reaction," she said. She seemed to be storing the phrase in her mental filing cabinet. Alongside "a bolt from the blue," no doubt.

"It's not like that," Mariye said. "I don't think he's planning anything bad. I just think Mr. Menshiki with the pretty white hair is hiding something."

"And you sense it, right?"

Mariye nodded. "That's why I came to see you. I thought you might be able to tell me more about him."

"Does your aunt feel the same way?" I asked, trying to deflect her question.

"No," she answered, tilting her head to one side. "That's not what she's like. She seldom has an adverse reaction to people. And I think she's interested in him. He's a bit older, but he's handsome and well dressed and I guess very rich and living all by himself . . ."

"So you think she's taken to him?"

"I guess so. She really lit up when she talked to him. Her face, and her voice—it got higher. She wasn't like usual. I bet he felt the change too."

I said nothing, just poured us both a fresh cup of tea. I took a sip.

Mariye seemed to be turning something over in her mind. "I wonder, how did he know we were going to be here today?" she asked. "Did you tell him?"

"I don't think Mr. Menshiki came planning to meet your aunt." I chose my words with care, hoping to avoid another lie. "In fact, he tried to leave when he realized the two of you were here, but I talked him into staying. He *happened* to stop by when your aunt *happened* to be here, and when he saw her he got interested. Your aunt is a very attractive woman, you know."

Mariye didn't look entirely convinced, but she didn't push the issue any further. She just sat there frowning, elbows on the table.

"In any case, the two of you are going to visit his home next Sunday," I said.

Mariye nodded. "Yes, to see your portrait of him. My aunt seems to be really looking forward to it. To paying Mr. Menshiki a visit, I mean."

"I don't blame her for getting excited," I said. "After all, she's living in the mountains with no other people around. Not like in the city, where she'd have opportunities to meet all sorts of men."

Mariye pressed her lips together for a moment.

"My aunt used to have a boyfriend," she said, as if letting me in on a big secret. "A man she saw for a really long time. When she was a secretary in Tokyo. But a lot of things happened, and in the end they broke up. It hurt her a lot. Then my mother died, and she came to look after me. She didn't tell me any of this, of course."

"I don't think she's seeing anyone now, is she?"

Mariye shook her head. "I don't think so."

"So you're a little concerned that your aunt is interested in Mr. Menshiki, and that she may be experiencing the first stirrings of something. So you came to talk to me about it. Is that right?"

"Tell me, do you think he's trying to seduce her?"

"Seduce her?"

"I mean, that he isn't serious?"

"There's no way for me to tell," I said. "I don't know Mr. Menshiki that well. They just met this afternoon, so nothing has happened between them yet. When two people's feelings are involved like this, things can change in subtle ways. What begins as a small feeling can grow into something really big, or the opposite can happen."

"But I have a kind of hunch this time," she asserted.

I sensed that I should believe her "kind of hunch," baseless though it was. For I had a similar kind of hunch.

"So you're worried something could occur that might harm your aunt psychologically," I said.

Mariye gave a quick nod. "My aunt's not a very cautious person, and she's not used to being hurt."

"It sounds like you're the one looking after her, and not the other way around," I said.

"In a way," Mariye said seriously.

"How about you, then? Are you used to being hurt?"

"I don't know," Mariye said. "At least I'm not about to fall in love."

"You will someday, though."

"But not now. Not until my chest gets a little bigger anyway."

"That may happen sooner than you expect."

Mariye made a wry face. I guessed she didn't believe me.

I felt a seed of doubt sprout in my own chest. Would Menshiki draw close to Shoko Akikawa to establish a firm connection with Mariye?

After all, he had said to me, *I couldn't tell anything in one brief meeting. I need to see her more.*

Shoko would be an important intermediary—through her, Menshiki could see Mariye on a regular basis. After all, she was the one looking after the girl. To a greater or lesser extent, therefore, Menshiki had to place Shoko under his thumb. That shouldn't be too hard for a man of Menshiki's talents. Not child's play, perhaps, but close to it. I didn't like to think that Menshiki was harboring a plan of that sort. Yet perhaps the Commendatore had been right, and he was a man who couldn't help fabricating some scheme or other. From what I had seen, however, he wasn't that cunning.

"Mr. Menshiki's house is really impressive," I said to Mariye. "You may or may not like it, but it wouldn't hurt to take a look."

"Have you been there?"

"Only once. I went there for dinner."

"It's on the other side of the valley?"

"Right across from us."

"Can you see it from here?"

I pretended to think for a moment. "Yes, but it's far away, of course."

"Show me."

I led her to the terrace and pointed out Menshiki's mansion on top of the mountain across the valley. Bathed in the light from the garden lanterns, the building floated white in the distance like an elegant ocean liner sailing the night sea. Several of the windows were also lit up. The lights burning there were small and unobtrusive.

"That enormous white house?" Mariye exclaimed in surprise. She stared at me for a moment. Then, wordlessly, she turned back to the distant mansion.

"I can see it from my house, too," she said eventually. "The angle's a bit different, though. I've always wondered who would live in a place like that."

"It does stand out, that's for sure," I said. "Anyway, that's Mr. Menshiki's home."

Mariye spent a long time leaning over the railing looking at the house. A handful of stars twinkled above its roof. There was no wind, and a small, sharp-edged cloud hung there motionless. Like a paper cutout nailed to a plywood backdrop in a play. Each time the girl moved her head, her straight black hair glittered in the moonlight.

"Does Mr. Menshiki really live there all by himself?" Mariye asked, turning to me.

"Yes, he does. All alone, in that big house."

"And he's not married?"

"He told me he has never married."

"What kind of work does he do?"

"I'm not sure. Something connected to the information business, he said. Maybe having to do with tech. He doesn't have a regular job right now, though. He lives on the money he made from selling his old business, and from stock dividends and so forth. I don't know the details."

"So he doesn't work?" Mariye said, wrinkling her forehead.

"That's what he said. Seldom leaves his home, apparently."

He might well be standing on his terrace, watching the two of us through his high-powered binoculars just as we were watching him. What would run through his mind if he saw us standing side by side like this?

"You'd better head home," I told Mariye. "It's getting late."

"Besides asking about Mr. Menshiki," she said softly, as if confiding something, "I wanted to tell you I'm really happy that you're painting my picture. I can't wait to see it."

"I hope it turns out well," I said. Her words moved me more than a little. It was strange how much this girl opened up when painting was involved.

I walked her to the door. Mariye put on her tight-fitting down jacket and crammed her Indians cap down over her head. Now she looked like a boy.

"Shall I walk with you partway?" I asked.

"I'm fine. I know the path."

"See you next Sunday, then."

But instead of leaving, she paused for a moment with her hand on the doorframe.

"One thing bothers me," she said. "It's that bell."

"The bell?"

"I thought I heard it ringing on my way here. The same kind of jingling sound that the bell in your studio made."

I was at a loss for words. Mariye's eyes were on my face.

"Where was it exactly?" I asked.

“In the woods. It came from behind the shrine.”

I listened to the dark. But I heard no bell. I heard no sound at all. Just the quiet of the night.

“Weren’t you scared?” I asked.

Mariye shook her head. “If I leave it alone, there’s nothing to be scared of.”

“Wait here just a second,” I told Mariye. I ran back to the studio. The bell was not where I had left it. It had vanished from the shelf.

36

WHAT I WANT IS NOT TO HAVE TO DISCUSS THE RULES OF THE GAME

After seeing Mariye off, I went into the studio, turned on all the lights, and combed every inch of the room. But the old bell was nowhere to be found. It had vanished from sight.

When had I last seen it? The previous Sunday, on her first visit, Mariye had taken the bell down and shaken it. Then she had returned it to the shelf. I remembered that. But had I laid eyes on the bell since? I couldn't recall. I had hardly set foot in the studio all week. Not once had I picked up my brush. *The Man with the White Subaru Forester* had stalled, and I hadn't yet started Mariye's portrait. I was what you might call "between paintings."

Then, without my knowledge, the bell had disappeared.

But Mariye had heard it ringing behind the shrine when she passed through the woods. Could someone have returned it to the pit? Should I rush there now, see if I could hear the bell with my own ears?

Yet the prospect of hurrying off into the dark woods alone didn't appeal to me. Too many surprises in one day had worn me out. Whatever one might say, I had more than filled my quota of "unforeseen events."

I went into the kitchen, pulled out the ice tray, plunked a few cubes in a glass, and doused them with whiskey. It was only eight thirty. Had Mariye safely navigated the woods and returned home through her passageway? I felt sure she had. No need for me to worry. This mountain had been her playground since she was small, she had said. And she was a lot tougher than she looked.

I took my time working my way through two glasses of Scotch, munched a few crackers, brushed my teeth, and went to bed. For all I knew, I might be roused in the middle of the night by a ringing bell. Around two a.m., as before. Nothing much I could do about that. If it happened, I would deal with it then. But nothing happened. As far as I knew, anyway. I slept like a log until half past six the next morning.

When I awoke, it was raining outside. A chilly rain, signaling the approach of winter. Quiet and persistent. It reminded me of the rain that had been falling that day in March when my wife announced that our marriage was over. I hadn't faced her as she spoke. For the most part, I had looked out the window at the rain.

After breakfast, I put on my vinyl poncho and rain hat (both purchased on my trip, at a sporting-goods store in Hakodate) and walked into the woods. I didn't take an umbrella. I circled the shrine and removed half the boards covering the pit. I made a careful search with my flashlight, but it was empty. No bell, and no sign of the Commendatore. Just to make sure, I decided to descend the metal ladder to check. I had never entered the pit before. The rungs sagged and gave an ominous creak with each step down. In the end, however, I found nothing. It was just an uninhabited hole in the ground. Perfectly round, it might have been a well were it not so wide. Had its builders intended to draw water from it, they would have made its circumference much smaller. And the construction of the wall was too intricate. It was just as the landscaper had said.

I stood in the pit for some time, lost in thought. I didn't feel trapped since I could see a cleanly severed half-moon of sky above. I flicked off my flashlight, leaned my back against the damp, dark stone wall, and closed my eyes as the rain pattered overhead. *Something* was running through my mind, but I couldn't grasp what it was. One thought would link to another, which in turn would link to still another thought. That chain was bizarre somehow, though I couldn't say exactly why. It was as if I had been swallowed by the act of thinking, if that makes sense.

The pit was thinking too, I could tell. It was alive—I could feel it breathing. My thoughts and those of the pit were like trees grown together: our roots joined in the dark, our sap intermingled. In this condition, self and other blended like the paints on my palette, their borders ever more indistinct.

At a certain point, it felt as though the walls of the pit were beginning to close in. My heart made a dry sound as it expanded and contracted in my chest. I felt I could hear its valves open and close. The sensation chilled me, as if I were approaching the realm of the dead. That world didn't strike me as altogether unpleasant, but it was not yet my time to enter.

I returned to my senses with a start. I untangled myself from my train of thought, which had run on without me, then flicked on my flashlight and looked around. The ladder was still where it had been. The sky above my head was the same. I breathed a sigh of relief. For all I knew, the sky could have vanished and the ladder disappeared. Anything could happen in this place.

With great care, I climbed from the pit one rung at a time. Only when I had emerged and was standing on the wet ground did my breathing finally return to normal. It took even longer to get my heartbeat under control. I peered down into the pit one last time. With my flashlight, I illuminated every inch of the dirt floor. But it was just a normal, everyday kind of pit. It was not breathing or thinking, nor were its walls closing in. It just sat there in silence, absorbing the chilly mid-November rain.

I moved the boards back into place and set the rocks on top. I arranged them with care, making sure that they were exactly as they had been before. That way I would know if someone moved them. Then I stuck my rain hat back on my head and walked home along the same path I had come on.

As I walked through the woods, I wondered where the Commendatore had gone. I hadn't seen him for at least two weeks. Strangely, I missed having him around. Without realizing it, I had come to feel a certain kinship with the two-foot man with the tiny sword at his side, despite his odd way of speaking, his voyeurism when my girlfriend and I were making love, and the fact that I had no clear idea what he was. I hoped nothing bad had happened to him.

When I got home, I went straight to the studio, sat down on the ancient wooden stool (the stool Tomohiko Amada must have used when he was working), and studied *Killing Commendatore* hanging there on the wall. I often did that when I wasn't sure what to do—in fact, I studied it endlessly. It was a painting I never tired of, no matter how often I looked at it. It should have been displayed in a museum as a prized example of Japanese art, but instead, it graced the wall of this small studio, and I was the only one who could enjoy it. Before me, it had been hidden in the attic, unseen by anyone.

It's calling out to me, Mariye had said. *Like a caged bird crying to be set free.*

The more I studied the painting the more I realized Mariye had hit the nail square on the head—something was desperately struggling to escape that enclosed space. It longed for a place less confined, for freedom. It was the strength of that will that gave the painting its impact. Whether we understood the meaning of the bird and the cage or not.

I felt the urge to paint something that day. Powerfully. I could feel it mounting within me. Like the evening tide coming in. It was still too early, though, to work on Mariye's portrait. That could wait until next Sunday. And I didn't feel like going back to *The Man with the White Subaru Forester* either. As Mariye had pointed out, a dangerous force lurked beneath its surface.

A new canvas sat on the easel, ready for Mariye's portrait. I sat on the stool studying it for a long time. Yet nothing came to me—no image of what to paint. The blank stayed blank. What should be my subject matter? After a while, at last, the answer rose to my mind.

I stepped away from the easel and took out my big sketchbook. Then I sat on the floor, crossed my legs, leaned back against the wall, and began to draw a chamber of stone in pencil. Not my usual soft pencil but a much harder one. It was a sketch of the strange pit we had found under the pile of rocks in the woods. I had just come from there, so it was fresh in my mind, and I rendered it in as much detail as possible. I drew the intricately fitted wall of stones. I drew the ground around the pit, and the beautiful pattern of the wet fallen leaves. The stand of pampas grass that had once hidden the pit lay flattened by the backhoe.

As I sketched, the eerie sensation that I was merging with the pit returned. It wanted me to draw it. Accurately, and in great detail. In response, my hand moved without conscious guidance. It was a pure act of creation, and it brought with it a kind of joy. When I returned to my senses, I realized that a length of time had passed (I had no idea how much), and that the page in my notebook was covered with pencil lines.

I went to the kitchen, gulped down several glasses of cold water, reheated the coffee, and carried a cup back to the studio. I placed the open sketchbook on the easel and sat down to take a second look, this time from farther away. There was the pit in the woods, in realistic detail. It looked somehow alive. Even *more* alive than the real thing. I got off the stool and examined it up close, then studied it again from a different angle. Only then did it hit me how much it looked like a woman's genitals. The clump of pampas grass flattened by the backhoe resembled her pubic hair to a T.

I shook my head and smiled a wry smile. I mean, how Freudian can you get? I imagined some egghead critic fulminating on the drawing's psychological implications: "This black, gaping hole, so reminiscent of a woman's solitary genitalia, must be understood functionally, as a symbolic representation of the artist's memories and unconscious desires." Or something of the sort. Seriously!

Yet try as I might, I couldn't get the connection between the strange circular pit in the woods and a woman's sex out of my head. So when the phone rang a short while later, I had a hunch it would be my married girlfriend.

And it was.

"Hi," she said. "Some free time just opened up, and I was wondering if I might stop by."

I glanced at my watch. "Sounds good. Let's have lunch together."

"I'll pick up something simple on the way," she said.

"Great idea. I've been working since morning, so I haven't prepared anything."

She ended the call. I made the bed, picked my clothes up off the floor, folded them, and returned them to the chest of drawers. I washed the breakfast dishes in the sink and put them away.

Then I went to the living room, placed my usual record—Richard Strauss's *Der Rosenkavalier*, conducted by Georg Solti—on the turntable, and read on the sofa while I waited for her to arrive. What kind of book was Shoko Akikawa reading, I wondered? What could have so captivated her?

My girlfriend showed up at twelve fifteen. Her red Mini pulled up in front of my house and she got out, a paper bag from the grocery store in her arms. Although a quiet rain was still falling, she carried no umbrella. Wearing a yellow vinyl raincoat with a hood, she walked quickly to my door. I met her there, took the bag, and brought it to the kitchen. She removed the raincoat, exposing the brilliant green turtleneck underneath. Beneath the sweater were two very attractive bulges. Her breasts weren't as large as Shoko's, but they suited me just fine.

"Have you been at it all morning?"

"Yeah," I said. "But it's not a commission. I felt like drawing, so I came up with something on my own, just for fun."

"Just passing the time, huh?"

"Yeah, a bit like that."

"Are you hungry?"

"Not all that much."

"That's good," she said. "Why don't we eat afterward, then?"

"Fine by me," I said.

"You were awfully passionate today. Is there a special reason?" she asked. It was afterward, and we were lying in bed.

"I wonder," I said. What I might have said was, maybe it was because I spent the whole morning madly sketching a strange six-foot-wide hole in the ground and, partway through, my mind made a connection between the hole and a woman's vagina, which must have turned me on . . . But I couldn't.

"It was because I haven't seen you for so long," I said instead.

"You're sweet," she said, tracing a line on my chest with her fingertips. "But be honest—sometimes don't you want a younger woman?"

"No, I've never thought about that."

"Really?"

"Not once," I said. I was being truthful. Our sexual relationship was pure pleasure for me, and I had no desire to seek out anyone else. (My desire for Yuzu, of course, was of a wholly different order.)

I decided not to tell her about Mariye Akikawa. If she learned that a beautiful thirteen-year-old girl was modeling for me, it would only spark her jealousy. It seemed a woman at any age—thirteen, forty-one, you name it—felt she was facing a delicate time in her life. This was one thing my modest experience with the opposite sex had taught me.

"Still," she said. "Don't you think it's strange, the way women and men hook up?"

"Strange in what way?"

"I mean, look at us. We haven't known each other that long, yet here we are lying together naked, making love like this. Completely vulnerable, with no sense of shame. Don't you think it's weird?"

"Maybe you're right," I murmured.

"Try to think of it as a game. Maybe not only that, but a kind of game all the same. Otherwise what I'm saying won't make any sense."

"Okay, I'll try," I said.

"A game has to have rules, right?"

"Yeah, you need those."

"Baseball, soccer, all the sports have a thick rule book, right, where the rules are written down to the tiniest detail, and then umpires and players have to memorize them all. Without that, the game can't take place. Isn't that so?"

"You're absolutely right."

She paused, waiting for the image to sink in.

"So what I'm trying to say is, have we ever sat down and discussed the rules of *this game* that we're playing? Have we?"

I thought for a moment. "Possibly not," I said finally.

"Yet despite that, we are playing the game by a set of hypothetical rules. Right?"

"When you put it that way, I guess you have a point."

"So this is what I think," she said. "I'm playing the game according to my set of rules. And you're playing according to yours. The two of us *instinctively* respect each other's rules. As long as the two sets don't conflict and mess things up, we can go on like this without a hitch. Don't you agree?"

I considered what she had said. "Maybe you're right. We basically respect each other's rules."

"But you know, I think there's something even more important than respect and trust. And that's etiquette."

"Etiquette?"

"Etiquette's big."

"You may be right there," I agreed.

"If all those things—trust, respect, etiquette—stop functioning, the rules clash and the game breaks down. Then we either suspend the game and come up with a new set of rules we can both follow, or we end it and leave the playing field. The big question then would be which of those two routes we decide to follow."

That was precisely what had happened to my marriage. I had called a halt to the game and walked off the field. On that cold and rainy Sunday afternoon in March.

"So are you suggesting that we should talk out the rules of our relationship?"

"You don't get what I'm saying at all," she said, shaking her head. "What I want is *not* to have to discuss the rules of the game. That's why I'm able to be naked with you like this. You don't mind, do you?"

"Not a bit," I said.

"So that leaves us with trust and respect. And most of all etiquette."

"And most of all etiquette," I repeated.

She reached down and squeezed a part of my body.

"It's getting hard again," she whispered in my ear.

"Maybe that's because today is Monday," I said.

"What does Monday have to do with it?"

"Or maybe because it's raining. Or winter is coming. Or we're starting to see migrating birds. Or there's a bumper crop of mushrooms this year. Or my cup is a sixteenth full of water. Or the shape of your breasts under your green sweater turns me on."

She giggled. My answer appeared to have done the trick.

. . .

Menshiki called that evening. He thanked me for the day before.

I had done nothing worthy of his gratitude, I replied. All I had done was introduce him to two people. What developed after that, and how, had nothing to do with me—in that sense, I was a mere outsider. And I would like to keep it that way (though I had a premonition things might not work out so conveniently).

"Actually, I'm calling about something else," Menshiki said once the pleasantries were over. "I've received some new information about Tomohiko Amada."

So he was continuing his investigation. He might not be doing it himself, but arranging for such detailed work was certainly costing him a lot. Menshiki was a man who poured money into anything he thought necessary, sparing no expense. But why, and to what degree, was tracking down Tomohiko Amada's experiences in Vienna necessary to him? I didn't have a clue.

"What we've turned up may not have a direct connection with Amada's stay in Vienna," Menshiki went on. "But it overlaps with that time, and it's clear that it had a huge personal impact on him. So I thought you would like to hear about it."

"It overlapped with that time?"

"As I told you before, Tomohiko Amada returned to Japan from Vienna in early 1939. On paper, he was deported, but in fact he was rescued by the Gestapo. Officials from the foreign ministries of Japan and Nazi Germany had met in secret, and agreed that he be extradited but not charged with any crime. The failed assassination attempt had taken place in 1938, but it was linked to two other important events of that year: the *Anschluss*—Hitler's annexation of Austria—and *Kristallnacht*. The *Anschluss* took place in March, and *Kristallnacht* in November. Once they occurred, the brutality of Hitler's plan was obvious to everyone. Austria was firmly installed as a part of the Nazi war effort. An inextricable cog in the machine. Hoping to block this flow of events, students organized an underground resistance movement, and in the same year, Tomohiko Amada was arrested for his role in the assassination plot. Get the picture?"

"In a general sort of way, yes," I said.

"Do you like history?"

"I'm no expert, but I love books that deal with history," I said.

"A number of important events were taking place in Japan that year as well. Fatal, irrevocable events, which led to eventual disaster. Does anything spring to mind?"

I dusted off my store of historical knowledge, so long untouched. What had taken place in 1938? In Europe, the Spanish Civil War had intensified. German Condor bombers had flattened Guernica. But in Japan . . . ?

"Did the Marco Polo Bridge Incident take place that year?" I asked.

"That was the year before," Menshiki said. "On July 7, 1937. With the Marco Polo Bridge Incident, the war between China and Japan went into full swing. Then in December of that year, another serious event took place."

What had happened in December of 1937?

"The fall of Nanjing?" I asked.

"That's right. What's known today as the Nanjing Massacre. After a hard-fought battle, Japanese troops occupied the city, and many people were killed. Some died in the fighting, others after the fighting ended. The Japanese army lacked the means to keep prisoners, so they killed the Chinese soldiers who surrendered as well as thousands of civilians. Historians disagree on exactly how many died, but no one can deny that a massive number of noncombatants were sucked into the conflict and lost their lives. Some say 400,000, others 100,000. But what difference is there really between 400,000 lives and 100,000?"

He had me on that one.

"So Nanjing fell in December, and many were killed. But what does that have to do with what happened to Tomohiko Amada in Vienna?" I asked.

"I'm getting to that," Menshiki said. "The Anti-Comintern Pact was signed by Japan and Germany in November of 1936, cementing their alliance, but Vienna and Nanjing were so far apart it's doubtful much news about Japan's war in China was getting through to Vienna. In fact, however, Tomohiko Amada's younger brother, Tsuguhiko, had been part of the assault on Nanjing as a private in the Japanese army. He had been drafted and assigned to one of the units fighting there. He was twenty, and a full-time student at the Tokyo Music School, now the Faculty of Music at the Tokyo University of the Arts. He studied the piano."

"That's strange," I said. "To my knowledge, full-time university students were exempt from the draft at that time."

"You're absolutely right. Full-time students were given a deferment until graduation. Yet for some reason Tsuguhiko was drafted and sent to China. In any case, he was inducted in June of 1937 and spent the next twelve months as a private second-class in the army. He was living in Tokyo, but his birth was registered in Kumamoto, so he was assigned to the 6th Division based there. That much is documented. After basic training, he was sent to China, and participated in the December assault on Nanjing. He was demobilized in June of the following year, and was expected to return to the conservatory."

I waited for Menshiki to continue.

"Not long after his discharge, however, Tsuguhiko Amada took his own life. He slit his wrists with a razor in the attic of the family home, which was where they found him. Right around the end of summer."

Slit his wrists in the attic?

"If it was toward the end of summer in 1938 . . . then Tomohiko was still an exchange student in Vienna when his brother Tsuguhiko slit his wrists, right?"

"That's correct. He didn't return home for the funeral. Commercial air travel was still in its infancy. You could only travel between Austria and Japan by rail and ship. There was no way he could have made it back in time."

"Are you suggesting that there's a connection between Tomohiko's involvement in the failed assassination and his brother's suicide? They seem to have happened almost simultaneously."

"Maybe yes, maybe no," Menshiki said. "That's in the realm of conjecture. What I'm reporting to you now are the facts our investigation was able to uncover."

"Did Tomohiko Amada have any other siblings?"

"There was an older brother. Tomohiko was the second son. Tsuguhiko was the third and last. The manner of his death was concealed, though, to protect the family's honor. Kumamoto's 6th Division was celebrated as a band of fearless warriors. If word had gotten out that their son had returned from the battlefield bathed in glory only to turn around and kill himself, they could not have faced the world. Still, as you know, rumors have a way of spreading."

I thanked Menshiki for updating me. Though what the new information meant in concrete terms escaped me.

"I'm planning to dig a bit deeper into this," he said. "I'll let you know if we turn up something more."

"Please do."

"So then I'll stop by next Sunday shortly after noon," Menshiki said. "I'll drive the Akikawas over to my place. To show them your painting. That's okay with you, right?"

"Of course. The painting is yours now. You're free to show it or not to whomever you like."

Menshiki paused. As if searching for just the right words. "To tell you the honest truth," he said. "Sometimes I'm very envious of you." There was resignation in his voice.

Envious? Of me?

What could he possibly be talking about? Why would Menshiki envy me? It made no sense. He had everything, while I had nothing to my name.

"What could you possibly be envious about?" I asked.

"I see you as the kind of person who doesn't really envy anyone. Am I right?"

I thought for a moment before replying. "You have a point. I don't think I've ever envied another person."

"That's what I'm trying to say."

All the same, I don't have Yuzu, I thought. She had left me for the arms of another man. There were times I felt abandoned at the edge of the world. Yet even then I felt no envy toward that other man. Did that make me strange?

. . .

After our phone call, I sat on the sofa and thought about Tomohiko Amada's brother slitting his wrists in the attic. It wasn't the attic of this house, that was for sure. Tomohiko had bought this place after the war. No, Tsuguhiko Amada had committed suicide in the attic of their family home. In Aso, no doubt. Nevertheless, the brother's death and the painting *Killing Commendatore* might be connected by that dark, secret room above the ceiling. Sure, it might have been pure coincidence. Or perhaps Tomohiko had his brother in mind when he hid the painting in the attic here. Still, why was Tsuguhiko compelled to take his own life so soon after returning from the front? After all, he had survived the bloody conflict in China and come home with all his limbs intact.

I picked up the phone and dialed Masahiko's number.

"Let's get together in Tokyo," I said. "I have to visit the art supply shop soon to stock up on paints. Maybe we could meet and talk then."

"Sure thing," he said, checking his schedule. Thursday just after noon was best for him, so we arranged to have lunch together.

"The art supply store in Yotsuya, correct?"

"That's the one. I've got to pick up fresh canvases, too, and I'm running out of linseed oil. It'll be quite a load, so I'll take the car."

"There's a quiet restaurant not far from my office. We could have a nice relaxed chat over lunch."

"By the way," I said, "divorce papers from Yuzu came in the mail, so I signed and returned them. It looks like our divorce will become official pretty soon."

"Is that so," Masahiko said in a subdued voice.

"What can you do? It was just a matter of time."

"Still, from where I stand it's a real shame. You guys seemed like such a good match."

"It was great as long as things were going well," I said. Just like an old-model Jaguar. A wonderful ride until the problems start.

"So what will you do now?"

"No big changes. Just keep on as I am for the time being. Can't think of what else to do."

"Are you painting?"

"Yeah, I've got a couple of paintings I'm working on. Not sure what will happen with them, but at least I'm at it."

"That's the way to go." Masahiko hesitated before adding, "I'm glad you called. There's something I want to discuss with you as well."

"Something good?"

"It's just the facts—I can't say if they're good or bad."

"Does it have to do with Yuzu?"

"It's hard to talk about over the phone."

"Okay, on Thursday then."

I ended the call and walked out to the terrace. The rain had stopped, and the cool night air was clear and bracing. I could see stars peeping from the cracks between the clouds. They looked like scattered crystals of ice. Hard crystals, millions of years old, never melting. Hard to their very core. Across the valley, Menshiki's house glimmered in the cool light of its lanterns.

As I looked at his house, I thought of trust, respect, and etiquette. Especially etiquette. As I expected, though, none of those thoughts led me to any definite conclusions.

37

EVERY CLOUD HAS A SILVER LINING

It turned out to be a long haul from my mountaintop perch on the outskirts of Odawara to downtown Tokyo. I took several wrong turns en route, which ate up a lot of time. My old used car had no navigation system or electronic pass for the highway tolls. (I guess I should have been grateful it came with a cup holder!) It took me ages to find the Odawara-Atsugi Road, and when I moved from the Tomei Expressway onto the Metropolitan Expressway it was jammed, so I opted to get off at the Shibuya exit and drive to Yotsuya via Aoyama Avenue. Even the city roads were crowded, though—just choosing the correct lane was a huge pain in the ass. Parking the car wasn't easy, either. It seems as if, year after year, the world becomes a more difficult place to live.

By the time I picked up what I needed at the art supply store, loaded it into the trunk, drove to Masahiko Amada's office in Aoyama, and found a parking spot, I was exhausted. I felt like the country mouse visiting his city cousin. When I reached his office it was past one by my watch, which meant I was more than a half hour late.

I asked the receptionist to call Masahiko. He came right down. I apologized for being so tardy.

"Don't worry about it," he laughed. "My office can adjust, and so can the restaurant."

Masahiko took me to an Italian place in the neighborhood, located in the basement of a small building. Masahiko was obviously well known there, for no sooner had they seen his face than we were guided to a private room in the back. It was very quiet: the sound of voices did not reach us and no music was playing. A quite passable landscape painting hung on the wall. It showed a white lighthouse on a green peninsula under a blue sky. Super-ordinary scene, sure, but done well enough to let the viewer think, "Hey, that place might be nice to check out."

Masahiko ordered a glass of white wine, while I asked for Perrier.

"I've got to drive back after this," I explained. "It's quite a trek."

"No kidding," said Masahiko. "Still, it's a heck of a lot better than Hayama or Zushi. I lived in Hayama once, and driving back and forth to Tokyo in the summer was awful. The whole route was jammed with people heading to the ocean from the city. A round trip was a half day's work. Compared to that, driving in from Odawara is nothing."

The menus arrived and we ordered the prix fixe lunch: prosciutto as appetizer followed by asparagus salad and spaghetti with Japanese lobster.

"So you finally decided to do some serious painting," Masahiko said.

"Well, I'm living alone now, and I don't need commissions to get by. Maybe that's why the urge to paint my own stuff hit me."

Masahiko nodded. "Everything has a bright side," he said. "The top of even the blackest, thickest cloud shines like silver."

"Yeah, but getting up there to see it is no picnic."

"I was speaking more theoretically," Masahiko said.

"I think living on top of a mountain may be affecting me too. It's the perfect spot to focus on my art."

"Yeah, when no one's there to distract you and it's that quiet, you can really concentrate. A more normal person might get a bit lonely, but I figured you're the kind of guy who can handle it."

The door opened and the appetizer was brought in. We fell quiet as the plates were laid out.

"I think the studio has a lot to do with it as well," I said once the waiter had gone. "There's something about being in that room that makes me want to paint. At times it feels like the center of the whole house."

"If the house were human, it'd be the heart, perhaps."

"Yeah, or the consciousness."

"Body and Mind," Masahiko said in English. "To tell the truth, though, it's hard for me to spend time in his studio. *His* smell has sunk in too deep. I can still feel him in the air. When I was a boy, he'd isolate

himself in that room almost all day, painting away without a word to anyone. It was his sanctum, off-limits to a kid like me. I tend to steer clear of the studio when I'm there, even now. You should be careful too."

"Be careful? Why?"

"So you don't become possessed by his spirit. It's a strong one."

"Spirit?"

"Maybe 'psychic energy' is a better term. Or 'flow of being.' His is intense enough to sweep you away. At any rate, when someone like him spends a long time in a particular place, it soaks in his aura. Like particles of smell."

"And that's what could possess me?"

"Maybe 'possessed' isn't the best way to put it. 'Absorb his influence,' perhaps? It's like he invested that room with some special *power*."

"I wonder. I'm only looking after his home, and I never met him. So maybe it won't weigh on me as much."

"You're probably right," Masahiko said. He took a sip of white wine. "Being related to him may make me more sensitive to those things. And if it turns out that his 'aura' inspires you in your work, so much the better."

"So how's he doing these days?"

"Nothing in particular is wrong with him. He's past ninety, so I can't say he's the picture of health, and his mind is confused, but he can still manage to get around with a cane, his appetite's fine, and his eyes and teeth are in good shape. You know, his teeth are better than mine—never had a cavity!"

"How bad is his memory? Can he recall anything?"

"Not a whole lot. He doesn't recognize me. He's lost the concept of family, of father and son. Even the distinction between himself and other people may have blurred. Still, maybe it's easier when those things are swept away, and you don't have to think about them anymore."

I sipped my slender glass of Perrier and nodded. So Tomohiko Amada had forgotten even his son's face. Memories of student days in Vienna must have set sail for the far shore of forgetfulness some time ago.

"All the same, what I called his 'flow of being' is still strong," Masahiko said, as if in wonder. "It's strange: he remembers almost nothing, but his will is the same as always. It's obvious when you look at him. That psychic power is what makes him who he is. I feel a bit guilty sometimes that I didn't inherit that temperament, but there's nothing I can do about it. We're all born with different abilities. Being linked to someone by blood doesn't mean you have similar gifts."

I looked in his face. It was rare to see Masahiko bare his true feelings.

"It must be awfully hard to have such a famous father," I said. "I can't even imagine what it's like. My dad was nothing special, just a small businessman."

"There are some benefits to having a famous father, but there are times that it really sucks. I think the latter are a bit more frequent, actually. You're lucky you don't have to deal with that. You're free to be who you want."

"You look like the one with a free life."

"In a sense," Masahiko said. He turned his wineglass around in his hand. "But in another sense, no."

Masahiko possessed a keen artistic sensibility of his own. He had taken a job with a medium-sized ad agency after finishing school. By now, his salary had increased, and he looked for all the world like a bachelor enjoying everything city life had to offer. I had no way of knowing if that was true, however.

"I was hoping to ask you a few things about your father," I said, broaching the reason for my visit.

"What sort of things? You know, I really don't know that much about him."

"I heard that he had a younger brother named Tsuguhiko."

"Yeah, that's true. That would be my uncle, I guess. But he died a long time ago. Before Pearl Harbor."

"I heard he committed suicide."

A shadow passed across Masahiko's face. "That's supposed to be a family secret, but it happened so long ago, and part of it's public knowledge now anyway. So I guess it's okay to tell you. He cut his wrists with a razor. He was only twenty."

"What made him do it?"

"Why do you want to know something like that?"

"I've been trying to learn more about your father. I stumbled across your uncle's story when I was looking through some documents."

"You want to learn more about my father?"

"I wanted to learn more about his paintings, but as I looked at his career I became more and more interested in his personal life. I'd like to know the kind of man he was."

Masahiko studied my face from across the table. "All right," he said. "You've taken an interest in my father's life. There may be some significance in that. Living in that house has created some sort of bond between the two of you."

He took a swallow of white wine before launching into his story.

"My uncle, Tsuguhiko Amada, was a student at the Tokyo Music School back then. A talented pianist, they say. He loved Chopin and Debussy, and high hopes were held for his future. Forgive me for sounding arrogant, but artistic talent seems to run in our family. To varying degrees, of course. However, in the midst of his studies my uncle was drafted. He should have received a student deferment, but his papers had been mishandled when he enrolled in the conservatory. If those forms had been properly filed, he could have put off military service until graduation, and probably avoided it altogether. My grandfather was a big landowner in the area, and influential in political circles. But there was a slip-up in the paperwork. It came as a great shock to my uncle. But once the system grinds into motion there's not a whole lot anyone can do to stop it. Protest was futile: the army grabbed him, gave him his basic training in Japan, and then loaded him onto a troop transport and shipped him off to Hangzhou. At the time, his elder brother Tomohiko—in other words, my father—was studying painting under a famous artist in Vienna."

I didn't say anything.

"Everyone knew that my uncle wasn't cut out for the rugged life of a soldier or the carnage of the battlefield—he was a high-strung young man, and physically weak. To make matters worse, the young men of southern Kyushu who made up the 6th Division were a rough group, known for their violence. My father agonized over the news that his brother had been drafted and sent off to war. My father was egotistic and highly competitive, a typical second son, but his younger brother was shy and retiring, the somewhat pampered baby of the family. As a pianist, he had to be careful to protect his hands. Even as a child, my father learned to look out for his little brother, who was three years younger, and shield him from the outside world. It became second nature to him—he was his brother's protector. But all he could do in faraway Vienna was sit and fret. The only information he got came in his brother's letters from the front.

"Of course those letters were strictly censored, but the two brothers were so close that the elder could read the younger's feelings between the lines. Moreover, the true meaning of those lines was skillfully camouflaged, so only he could figure it out. My uncle's regiment had fought their way from Shanghai to Nanjing, engaging in fierce battles in the towns and cities en route, and leaving a trail of murder and plunder in their wake. Those bloody events left my high-strung uncle with deep emotional scars.

"One of my uncle's letters described a beautiful pipe organ they had come across in a church in occupied Nanjing. It had survived the fighting in perfect shape. For some unfathomable reason, though, the long description of the organ that followed had been inked out. What military secrets could an organ in a Christian church possibly have compromised? The standards used by the censor attached to their regiment were impossible to fathom. As a matter of fact, it was common for him to black out the most innocuous and unthreatening passages of a letter while overlooking the parts that really might have put troops at risk. As a consequence, my father was left in the dark as to whether his brother had been able to play that organ or not.

"Uncle Tsuguhiko's year in the army ended in June of 1938," Masahiko continued. "Although he had arranged to reenter the conservatory right after his return, he went back to Kyushu instead and committed suicide in the attic of the family home. He sharpened a straight razor to a fine edge and slit his wrists. It must have taken tremendous resolve for a pianist to do that to his hands. I mean, if he had survived, he might never have been able to play again, right? They found him in a pool of blood. The fact that he had killed himself was kept a deep, dark secret.

To the world, the official cause of death was heart failure or something like that.

"In fact, though, it was clear to everyone why Uncle Tsuguhiko had taken his own life—his war experience had ruined his nerves, and wrecked him psychologically. I mean, here was a delicate young man of twenty, whose entire world was playing the piano, thrown into the bloodbath of the Nanjing campaign, surrounded by heaps of corpses. Today we talk about post-traumatic stress disorder, but that phrase—even that concept—was unknown then. In that deeply militaristic society, people like my uncle were dismissed as lacking courage, or patriotism, or strength of character. In wartime Japan, such 'weakness' was neither understood nor accepted. So the family buried what had happened, as evidence of their shame."

"Did he leave a suicide note?" I asked.

"Yes, they found a personal testament in his desk drawer. It was quite long, closer to a memoir, really. In it, Uncle Tsuguhiko recorded his war experiences in excruciating detail. The only people who saw it were his parents—my grandparents, in other words—his eldest brother, and my father. When my father returned from Vienna and read it, he burned it while the other three watched."

I waited for him to go on.

"My father kept his lips sealed about what that testament contained," Masahiko continued. "It was the family's darkest secret: to use a metaphor, it was nailed shut, weighted with heavy stones, and sent to the bottom of the ocean. However, my father did tell me the gist of what was in it once, when he was drunk. I was in grade school, and it was the first time I learned that I had an uncle who committed suicide. To this day, I have no idea whether it was the alcohol that loosened my father's lips, or if he figured that I had to hear the story at some point."

Our salad plates were cleared, replaced by the spaghetti with Japanese lobster.

Masahiko took his fork and stared at it for a moment. As if inspecting an implement used for some special task.

"Hey man," he said. "This isn't really something I want to talk about when I'm eating."

“No problem. Let’s talk about something else.”

“Like what, for example.”

“Something as far removed from your uncle’s testament as possible.”

So we talked golf as we ate our spaghetti. Of course, I had never played the game. No one around me had either. I didn’t even know the rules. Masahiko, however, had taken it up in order to play with the people he did business with. And to get back into some kind of shape after years of inactivity. He had purchased a set of clubs, and spent his weekends on the golf course.

“You may not know this,” he told me, “but golf is the oddest game you can imagine. As weird as it gets. You could say it’s a sport unto itself. Yet I’m not even sure if it can be called a true sport. The funny thing is, once you get used to its weirdness you can’t go back.”

Masahiko went on and on about the strangeness of golf, telling me one off-the-wall story after another. A great conversationalist, he made our lunch extremely entertaining. We laughed together as we hadn’t in ages.

Our plates were cleared away and coffee was brought in, although Masahiko opted for another glass of white wine.

“Anyway, back to my uncle’s suicide letter,” he said, his voice abruptly serious. “According to my father, Uncle Tsuguhiko wrote about being forced to behead a Chinese prisoner. He described it in painful detail. Of course, a common soldier like him didn’t carry a sword. In fact, he had never touched a sword up to that point. I mean, he was a pianist, right? He could read a complex musical score, but wielding an executioner’s sword was beyond him. But his commanding officer handed him one and ordered, ‘Chop off his head!’ The prisoner wasn’t in uniform and had no weapon when he was picked up. Nor was he a young man. He claimed he was a civilian, not a soldier. But the army was grabbing any likely men they could find and dragging them in to be killed. If your palms were callused, you were deemed a peasant and might be released. If they were soft, however, it was assumed that you were a soldier who’d tossed his uniform to pass as a civilian, and you were summarily executed. Arguing the sentence was a waste of breath. The method of execution was either being gutted by a bayonet or decapitated by a sword. If a machine gun unit was in the area, prisoners might be lined up in a row and shot, but there was a general reluctance to 'waste' ammunition that way—bullets were always in short supply—so bayonets and swords were used. The bodies were collected and dumped in the Yangtze River, where they fed the many catfish who lived there. I don't know if it's fact or fiction, but it was said that some grew as big as ponies on that diet.

"My uncle took the sword from the officer, a young second lieutenant who had just completed officer training school, and prepared to cut off the prisoner's head. Of course, he didn't want to do it. But it was unthinkable to refuse an order. Not something corrected by a simple reprimand. An order from an officer in Japan's Imperial Army was an order from the Emperor himself. My uncle's hands were shaking. He wasn't a strong man, and to make matters worse it was a crummy, mass-produced sword. The human neck isn't that easy to sever. His attempt failed. Blood sprayed everywhere, the prisoner thrashed about—it was gruesome."

Masahiko shook his head. I sipped my coffee.

"When it was finally over my uncle started puking. When there was nothing left he puked gastric juice, and when that was gone he puked air. His comrades ridiculed him. The officer called him a 'pitiful excuse for a soldier' and kicked him hard in the side with his army boots. No one sympathized. Instead, he was ordered to decapitate two more prisoners. This was for *practice*, to help him become *accustomed* to cutting off people's heads. A soldier's rite of passage, it was thought. Participating in such carnage made a man a 'true warrior.' But my uncle was never meant to be a warrior in the first place. He wasn't put on this earth for that. He was born to make beautiful music, to perform Chopin and Debussy. Not to chop the heads off other human beings."

"Are some people born to chop off heads?" I asked.

Masahiko shook his head again. "I can't answer that. But I do know there must be quite a few who are able to *get used to it*. People can become accustomed to almost anything, especially when they're pushed to the limit. It may become surprisingly easy then."

"Or when they're given justification for their actions."

"You're right there," Masahiko said. "In most cases, they're provided with some justification for what they do. I'm not confident that I'd be any different, to tell the truth. I might not be strong enough to stand up and say no if I were thrown into a system as violent as the military, even if I knew the order was horribly wrong or inhuman."

I thought of myself. Would I be any different if I were in his uncle's shoes? The image of the strange woman I had spent the night with in the port town in Miyagi popped into my head. The young woman who had handed me the belt of her bathrobe and asked me to strangle her in the middle of sex. I still remembered how the belt felt wrapped tight around my hands. Probably I would never forget.

"Uncle Tsuguhiko couldn't refuse his superior's order," Masahiko said. "He lacked the guts to do that. Yet later he was able to sharpen a razor and use it to kill himself. In that sense, I don't think he was weak at all. Only by taking his own life was my uncle able to recover his humanity."

"The news must have been a terrible shock to your father in Vienna."

"That hardly needs saying," Masahiko replied.

"I've heard that your father got caught up in some political events in Vienna that got him deported back to Japan. Did those have any connection to his brother's suicide?"

Masahiko folded his arms and frowned. "It's hard for me to say. You see, my father never said a word about what happened."

"What I heard was that your father fell in love with a girl who belonged to a resistance organization, and that she was involved in a failed assassination attempt."

"Yes, I know about that. Apparently she was an Austrian student at the university, and they were planning to get married. But when the plot came to light, she was arrested and sent to the concentration camp at Mauthausen. She probably died there. My father was arrested by the Gestapo and forcibly repatriated as an 'undesirable alien' in early 1939. Of course, this didn't come from my father but from someone in the family—a credible source."

"Do you think someone somewhere prevented your father from speaking about what had happened in Vienna?"

"Yeah, I'm sure that's true. I'm sure authorities on both sides—Japan and Germany—laid down the law in no uncertain terms when they arranged his deportation. He knew he had to keep his mouth shut—

that was the price he paid for saving his own neck. But I don't think he wanted to talk about those events, either. Otherwise he wouldn't have remained so close-mouthed when the war ended and the threat was gone."

Masahiko paused for a moment before continuing.

"I think it's entirely possible that Uncle Tsuguhiko's suicide played a role in my father's involvement in the anti-Nazi resistance in Vienna. The Munich Conference removed the threat of war for the time being, but it also strengthened the Berlin-Tokyo axis, and set the world moving in an even more dangerous direction. My guess is that my father was determined to try to put the brakes on that movement. He was a man who prized freedom above all else. Fascism and militarism ran against everything he believed. The death of his younger brother could only have strengthened those convictions."

"Do we know anything more?"

"My father never talked to anyone about his life. He did no interviews with the media, and left nothing written down for posterity. He was like someone who walks backward, erasing his own footsteps with a broom."

"He kept his silence as a painter too, didn't he," I said. "He exhibited none of his work from the time he returned from Vienna to the end of the war."

"Yeah, eight years in total, from 1939 until 1947. All that time, he stayed as far removed as possible from what we might call 'artistic circles.' He couldn't stand that crowd anyway, and their 'nationalist art' glorifying the war effort made him like them even less. Lucky for him, his family was well off, so he didn't have to worry about getting by. And, thankfully, he wasn't drafted to be a soldier during the war. In any case, once the postwar chaos had settled down, Tomohiko Amada reemerged, having metamorphosed into a purely Japanese-style painter. He had jettisoned his old style and adopted a totally new one."

"And thus was born a legend."

"That's right," Masahiko said. "The rest is legend." He waved his hand, as if shooing something away. As if the legend were a mote in the air, interfering with his breathing.

"As I hear you tell the story," I said, "I begin to think your father's student days in Vienna cast a shadow over his whole life. Whatever the exact circumstances may have been."

Masahiko nodded. "Yeah, I think that too. Those events changed the course of his life in a drastic way. The failure of the assassination plot must have led to a number of dreadful things. Things too horrible to speak of."

"Still, we don't know the details."

"No, we don't. I didn't know them growing up, and it's an even bigger riddle now. The man in question can't have a clue either."

Perhaps, I thought. People can forget what they should remember, and remember what by all rights and purposes they should forget. Especially when death approaches.

Masahiko polished off his second glass of white wine and glanced at his watch. He gave a slight frown.

"I've got to head back to the office," he said.

"Wasn't there something you wanted to tell me?" I asked, suddenly remembering.

He rapped his knuckles on the tabletop as if to echo my feeling. "You're right," he said. "There is something. But we spent all our time talking about my father. It'll have to be next time. It's nothing that urgent."

I looked at his face again as we were about to get up. "Why are you being so open with me?" I asked. "Showing me the skeletons in your family's closet."

He spread his hands on the table and thought for a minute. He scratched his ear.

"Let's see. For one thing, I'm getting a little tired carrying these 'family skeletons' around all by myself. Maybe I wanted to share them with someone. Someone who has nothing to gain from them, and who'll keep his mouth shut. In that sense, you're an ideal person to unburden myself to. Also, to tell the truth I'm feeling a little guilty where you're concerned, so this may be my way of trying to pay you back."

"Guilty?" I burst out. "In what way?"

Masahiko half closed his eyes. "I'd intended to tell you about that," he said. "But there's no more time today. My next appointment is one I can't miss. Let's meet again soon. Then we can talk all we want."

Masahiko paid the tab. "Don't worry," he said. "This much I can write off." I accepted with gratitude.

After that, I drove the Corolla station wagon back to Odawara. By the time I parked the dusty old heap in front of the house, the sun had almost reached the ridge of the western mountains. A large flock of cawing crows was winging across the valley, heading to their nests.

38

HE COULD NEVER BE A DOLPHIN

By the time Sunday rolled around, I had a pretty good idea how to attack the canvas I'd set aside for Mariye Akikawa's portrait. I still wasn't sure exactly what form the painting would take. But I did know *how I should begin*. Those first steps—which brush to use, what color, the direction of the first stroke—had come to me out of nowhere: they had gained a foothold in my mind and, bit by bit, taken on a tangible reality of their own. I loved this process.

It was a chilly morning. The kind of morning that heralds the coming of winter. I brewed coffee, ate a simple breakfast, went to the studio, laid out what I needed to paint, and then stood before my easel, which held the empty canvas. In front of the canvas, however, sat my sketchbook, open to the detailed pencil drawing I had done of the pit in the woods. I had tossed it off several mornings earlier without giving it much thought. I had even forgotten I had drawn it.

Nevertheless, the longer I stood there facing the drawing, the more it sucked me in. The mysterious stone chamber in the woods, the secret opening. The sodden earth, the patchwork of fallen leaves. The sunlight filtering through the branches. As my imagination filled in the penciled sketch, I began to see it as a colorful painting. I could breathe in the air of the place, smell the grass, hear the birds singing.

The pit I had drawn with such precision in my big sketchbook was beckoning me, luring me toward something—or was it somewhere? *The pit was demanding that I paint it.* I seldom thought of painting landscapes. I mean, I'd done virtually nothing but portraits for nearly ten years. But maybe a landscape painting wasn't such a bad idea.

The Pit in the Woods. This pencil sketch could be a first step in that direction.

I removed my sketchbook and closed it. The unblemished white canvas remained on the easel. The canvas that would soon be graced by my portrait of Mariye.

At a few minutes before ten, as before, the blue Toyota Prius rolled silently up the slope. The doors opened, and Mariye and her aunt Shoko stepped out. Shoko Akikawa was wearing a long, dark-gray herringbone jacket, a light-gray wool skirt, and patterned black stockings. Wrapped around her neck was a bright Missoni scarf. A chic late-fall outfit. Mariye was dressed much like before: a baggy varsity jacket, a windbreaker, jeans with holes in them, and dark-blue Converse sneakers. Her head was bare. The air was chilly, and a thin blanket of clouds covered the sky.

After a simple exchange of greetings, Shoko curled up on the sofa and, once again, immersed herself in her thick paperback. Mariye and I left her there and went into the studio. I sat on the same wooden stool, Mariye on the same simple straight-backed chair. Six feet or so separated us. Mariye took off her jacket, folded it, and laid it next to her chair. Then she removed her windbreaker. Underneath was a blue short-sleeved T-shirt and, beneath that, a gray long-sleeved T-shirt. Her chest was as flat as ever. She ran her fingers through her straight black hair.

"Aren't you cold?" I asked. There was an old-fashioned kerosene space heater in the studio, but it was unlit.

Mariye gave a slight shake of her head. As if to say *No, not particularly.*

"I'll start painting today," I said. "You don't have to do anything. It's enough if you just sit there. You can leave the rest to me."

"I can't not do anything," she said, looking me straight in the eye.

"What does that mean?" I asked, my hands on my knees.

"Like, I'm living and breathing and thinking all kinds of stuff."

"Of course," I said. "Please, breathe as much as you want and think as many thoughts as you can. All I meant was, there's nothing special you have to do. I just want you to be yourself."

Yet Mariye continued to stare straight at me. As if my explanation was too simple to swallow.

"But I want to do something," she said.

"Like what?"

"I want to help you paint."

"I appreciate that, but what do you mean exactly? Help me in what way?"

"Mentally, of course."

"I see," I said. Yet I couldn't think of anything specific she could do "mentally" to help.

"I'd like to see things as you see them," she said. "Look at myself through your eyes while you're painting me. I think I'd understand myself better if I did that. And you'd probably understand me better, too."

"I'd love that," I said.

"Really?"

"Yes, really."

"It might get pretty scary sometimes."

"Knowing more about yourself, you mean?"

Mariye nodded. "If you want to know yourself better you have to bring in something different from someplace else."

"Are you saying you can't know yourself unless you add a third-person perspective?"

"A third-person perspective?"

"In other words," I explained, "to understand the relationship between A and B you might need C, a third point of view. What we call 'triangulation.'"

Mariye thought for a moment. "Maybe," she said with a shrug.

"Are you saying that what you bring in might be scary, depending on the situation?"

Mariye nodded.

"Have you had that scary feeling before?"

Mariye didn't respond.

"If I can draw you the right way, maybe you'll be able to see yourself through my eyes," I said. "If all goes well, of course."

"That's why we need pictures."

"You're right—that's why we need pictures. Or literature, or music, or anything of that sort."

If all goes well, I said to myself.

"So let's get started," I said to Mariye. Looking at her face, I started mixing the brown for the underdrawing. Then I selected the first brush I would use on the painting.

The work progressed slowly but smoothly. The painting would show her from the waist up. She was a beautiful girl, but beauty wasn't what I was after. Instead, I had to find what was hidden beneath the surface. What underlay her personality—what allowed it to subsist. I had to find that *something* and bring it to the canvas. It didn't have to be pretty. Sometimes it might even be ugly. In either case, though, I had to know her well enough to discover what that something was. Not through words or logic, but as a singular form, a composite of light and shadow.

I concentrated on layering lines and color on the canvas. Rapidly at times, at other times with painstaking care. Mariye sat, unmoving, on the straight-backed chair, her expression never wavering. She had mustered her willpower, I sensed, and was sustaining it for as long as necessary. I could feel her strength. "I can't not do anything," she had said. And indeed, she was *doing something*. To help me, most likely. An unmistakable current of some kind was flowing between this thirteen-year-old girl and myself.

I recalled my sister's hands. She had taken my hand in hers when we entered the chilly darkness of the wind cave on Mt. Fuji. Her hand was small and warm—yet her fingers were surprisingly strong. A definite life force connected us. Each was giving something to the other, and at the same moment receiving something. It was an exchange limited to a particular time and place. It was bound to fade and disappear. But the memory remained. Memory can give warmth to time. And art can—when it goes well—give shape to that memory, even fix it in history. Much as Van Gogh inscribed the figure of a country mailman on our collective memory so well that he lives on, even today.

. . .

For the next two hours, we focused on our respective jobs without exchanging a word.

Thinning the paint with linseed oil, I began by roughing in her form in a single color. That would be the portrait's underdrawing. Mariye sat quietly in the chair, continuing to be herself. At noon, as they did every day, chimes rang in the distance, announcing that our time was up. I put down my palette and paintbrush, straightened my back, and stretched. Only then did I realize how tired I was. I took a deep breath to break my concentration, whereupon Mariye finally let her body relax.

The monochrome outline of Mariye's head and shoulders was there on the canvas before me. This was the structure upon which the portrait would be built. It was skeletal, but at its core was the source of the heat that made her who she was. That was still hidden, but if I could grasp its general location I would be able to make adjustments further down the line. Then all that would be left was fleshing out the skeleton.

Mariye didn't ask anything about what I had painted, nor did she ask to see it. I said little on my part, as well. I was just too worn out. We left the studio together and moved to the living room without a word. Shoko was still absorbed in her paperback. She marked her spot, closed the book, removed her black-rimmed reading glasses, and looked up at us. I could see that she was a bit alarmed. Our fatigue must have been written on our faces.

"Did it go all right?" she asked in a slightly worried tone.

"We're only partway through the process, but we're right on schedule."

"That's so good to hear," she said. "Would you mind if I made some nice hot tea? I've already set the water to boil. And I know where you keep the tea leaves."

Taken somewhat aback, I glanced down at her. Her lips were curved in a refined smile.

"I fear I'm being a poor host, but yes, that would be wonderful," I said. I was dying for some hot tea, but getting up and going to the kitchen to boil water was beyond me. I was exhausted. It had been ages since I'd gotten so tired painting. It felt good, though.

Shoko returned to the living room ten minutes later with three cups and a pot on a tray. We sat there quietly, each drinking our black tea. Mariye hadn't uttered a word since we left the studio. Every so often she'd reach up to push the hair back from her forehead. She had put her heavy jacket on again. As if she needed it to protect her from something.

The three of us sat there politely sipping our tea (not one of us slurped) and enjoying the lazy flow of the Sunday afternoon. No one spoke. The silence was easy and unforced, as if in accordance with the laws of nature. At a certain point, I heard a familiar sound, like waves on a distant shore, a listless and reluctant, yet somehow obligatory, lapping. Soon, however, the sound took on the unmistakable rhythm of a well-tuned engine. An eight-cylinder, 4.2-liter engine with power to spare burning (most elegantly, of course) high-octane fossil fuel. I got up from my chair, went to the window, and watched the approach of the silver car through a crack in the curtain.

Menshiki was wearing a lime-green cardigan over a cream-colored shirt. His pants were gray wool. They were clean and wrinkle-free, as if just back from the cleaners. None of his clothes appeared to be new—they all looked comfortably worn. That made them seem even cleaner. His hair, as always, was a glowing white. It seemed impervious to the seasons and the weather. I guessed that in summer or in winter, on sunny or cloudy days, its radiance would never fade. Only its tone would vary.

Menshiki got out of the car, closed the door, and looked up at the cloudy sky. He thought about the weather for a moment (at least that's how it looked to me), composed himself, and walked slowly to the front door. Then he rang the doorbell. Slowly and deliberately, like a poet selecting the precise word for a crucial passage. However you looked at it, though, it was just a common old doorbell.

I opened the door and showed Menshiki into the living room. Smiling, he greeted the two women. Shoko rose to welcome him. Mariye remained on the sofa, twirling her hair. She barely glanced his way. At my bidding, we all sat down. Would you like some tea, I asked Menshiki. Please don't bother, he replied, shaking his head several times and waving his hand in refusal.

"How is your work going?" he asked me.

Moving along as usual, I replied.

"Modeling is tiring, isn't it?" Menshiki asked Mariye. I couldn't remember him addressing her while looking her in the eye before. His tone was still a bit tense, but today at least he wasn't paling or blushing in her presence. His face looked almost normal. He was doing a good job controlling his emotions. I bet he'd been training hard to pull that off.

Mariye didn't answer. She seemed to mumble something, but it was entirely inaudible. Her hands were clasped tightly on her knees.

"You know she really looks forward to coming here Sunday mornings," Shoko remarked, breaking the silence.

"Modeling is hard work," I said, doing my humble best to back her up. "Mariye is doing a great job."

"I served as a model here for a while," Menshiki said. "I found it odd somehow. There were times it felt like my soul was being stolen from me." He laughed.

"It's not like that at all," Mariye said, in what was little more than a whisper.

The three of us turned in her direction.

Shoko looked as though she had popped something she shouldn't have into her mouth and bitten down on it. Menshiki's face registered unadulterated curiosity. I remained, as ever, the impartial observer.

"What do you mean?" asked Menshiki.

"Nothing's being stolen from me," Mariye said in a monotone. "I'm giving something, and I'm getting something in return."

"You're absolutely right," Menshiki said quietly. He seemed impressed. "I was being too simplistic. There has to be an exchange. Artistic creation can never be a one-way street."

Mariye was silent, her eyes fixed on the teapot on the table. She looked like a lone night heron motionless on the shore, glaring at the water's surface for hours on end. The teapot was simple white ceramic, the kind you can find anywhere. It was old (Tomohiko Amada had used it), and eminently practical, but apart from a small chip on the rim, nothing about it warranted close examination. Mariye just needed something to stare at right then.

The room fell silent. Like a blank, white billboard.

Artistic creation, I thought to myself. Those words had a pull to them that drew all the silence in the vicinity into a single spot. Like air filling a vacuum. No, more like a vacuum sucking up all the air.

"If you're coming to my house," Menshiki said gingerly, facing Shoko, "then perhaps we should go in my car. I'll bring you back here afterward. The backseat is a bit cramped, but the drive is so full of twists and turns—you'll find this much easier."

"Of course," Shoko said at once. "We'll ride in your car."

Mariye's eyes were still on the white teapot. She seemed deep in thought. Of course, I had no idea what was on her mind, or in her heart. I had no idea what the three of them would do for lunch, either. But Menshiki was smart. He had it all planned—there was no need for me to sweat the details.

Shoko sat in the passenger seat, while Mariye settled in the back. Adults in front, kids in back. The natural way of the world—no prior consultation necessary. I watched from my front door as the car slipped down the slope and out of sight. I went back into the house, took the teacups and teapot into the kitchen, and washed them.

When I finished, I placed Richard Strauss's *Rosenkavalier* on the turntable, stretched out on the sofa, and listened. *Der Rosenkavalier* had become my fallback when I had nothing else to do. A habit implanted in me by Menshiki. The music was somehow addictive, as he had warned. An uninterrupted stream of emotion. Musical instruments in colorful profusion. It was Strauss who boasted, "I can describe anything in music, even a common broom." Maybe he didn't say "broom"—it could have been something else. At any rate, there was something painterly about his music. Though what I was aiming for in my painting was very different.

When I opened my eyes a while later, there was the Commendatore. He was sitting in the leather easy chair across from me wearing the same Asuka-period clothing, his sword still on his hip. Perched on the chair, his two-foot frame looked quite demure.

"It's been a while," I said. My voice sounded strained and forced, as if coming from somewhere else. "How have you been?"

"As I have told my friends in the past, time is a concept foreign to

Ideas," he said in a small but clear voice. " 'A while' thus lies outside my understanding."

"It's a customary phrase. Please don't let it bother you."

"I cannot fathom 'customary' either."

Fair enough. Where there is no "time" there can be no "custom." I stood up and walked to the stereo, lifted the needle, and returned the record to its sleeve.

"As you may have surmised," the Commendatore said, reading my mind, "in a realm where time flows freely in both directions such things as customs cannot exist."

"Don't Ideas require an energy source of some kind?" I asked him. The question had been puzzling me for some time.

"It is a thorny question," the Commendatore answered, frowning dramatically. "All beings require energy—to be brought into this world and to survive. It is a principle that holds true throughout the universe."

"So what you're saying is, Ideas have to have a source of energy too. Right? In accordance with the universal principle."

"Affirmative! It is an undisputed fact. Universal law binds us one and all—there can be no exceptions. Ideas are felicitous insofar as we possess no form of our own. We materialize when others become aware of us—only then do we take shape. Though that shape is but a borrowed thing, for the sake of convenience."

"So then Ideas can't exist unless people are cognizant of them."

The Commendatore closed one eye and pointed his right index finger in the air. "And what principle can be deduced from that, my friends?"

It took a long moment to wrap my head around that one. The Commendatore waited patiently.

"This is what I think," I said at last. "Ideas take their energy from the perceptions of others."

"Affirmative!" the Commendatore said cheerfully. He nodded several times. "You have a good head on your shoulders. Ideas cannot exist outside the perceptions of others—those perceptions are our sole source of energy."

"So then if I think, 'The Commendatore doesn't exist,' you cease to exist. Right?"

"Negative! In theory, you have a point," the Commendatore said. "But only in theory. In reality, that is quite unrealistic. One is hard put to will oneself to cease thinking about a given matter. Namely, to determine to 'stop thinking' about something is itself a thought—as long as one follows that path, that something continues to exist. In the end, to stop thinking about something means to stop thinking about stopping thinking."

"In other words," I said, "it's impossible for people to escape Ideas unless they lose either their memory or their interest in Ideas."

"Truly, dolphins have that power," the Commendatore said.

"Dolphins?"

"Dolphins have the power to put the right or left half of their brain to sleep. Did my friends not know that?"

"No, I didn't."

"Affirmative! It is why dolphins have so little time for Ideas. It is why they stopped evolving, too. We Ideas tried our hardest, but I am sad to say that all of our efforts led nowhere. It was such a promising species, too. Proportionate to their size, they had the biggest brains of all the mammals until humankind reached its full development."

"So then you managed to establish a rewarding relationship with humans?"

"It is a known fact that, unlike the dolphin brain, the brain of the human species runs along a single track. Hence, an Idea that enters such a brain cannot be easily brushed aside. That allows us to draw energy therein, and thus sustain ourselves."

"Like parasites," I said.

"Nonsense!" said the Commendatore, wagging his finger like a schoolmaster scolding his wards. "When I say 'drawing energy,' I mean the tiniest amount. A shred so infinitesimal the members of my friends' species are unaware. Too small to affect health, or hinder lives in any way."

"But you told me that Ideas possess nothing like morality. Ideas are an entirely neutral concept, neither good nor bad. It all depends on how humans use them. In which case Ideas can have a beneficial effect in some cases, and a negative effect in others. Isn't that so?"

"$E = mc^2$ is neutral in itself, yet that Idea led to the creation of the atomic bomb. Then the bomb was dropped on Hiroshima and Nagasaki. In reality. Is that what you are trying to say, my friends?"

I nodded.

"My heart bleeds for you—figuratively, of course; we Ideas have no bodies, and hence no hearts. But then again, my friends, all is caveat emptor in this universe."

"What?"

"The Latin for 'buyer beware.' To wit, a vendor is not responsible for how the buyer uses his wares. Can a shopkeeper determine what manner of man will wear the suit hanging in his window?"

"That argument sounds pretty fishy to me."

"$E = mc^2$ gave birth to the atomic bomb, but by the same token it spawned a host of good things as well."

"Like what, for instance?"

The Commendatore thought about this for a moment. He seemed to be having trouble coming up with a good example, however, for he said nothing, just vigorously rubbed his face with the palms of his hands. Then again, perhaps he simply saw no point in pursuing the discussion any further.

"By the way," I asked, suddenly remembering. "Do you have any inkling where the bell in the studio disappeared to?"

"Bell?" the Commendatore asked, looking up. "What bell?"

"The old bell you were ringing at the bottom of the pit. I put it on the shelf in the studio, but when I looked the other day it was gone."

The Commendatore shook his head in an emphatic no. "Oh, that bell. Negative! I have not laid hands on it recently."

"So who do you think might have taken it?"

"How should I know?"

"Whoever it was has started ringing it somewhere."

"Hmm. It is nothing to do with me. I have no use for it anymore. The bell was never mine alone. It belongs to the place, to be shared by everyone. So if it has disappeared, there must be a reason. No need to worry—it will show up sooner or later. Just wait."

"The bell belongs to the place?" I said. "You mean it belongs to the pit?"

"By the way," he said, not answering my question. "If my friends are waiting for Shoko and Mariye's return, it will not happen soon. At least not until nightfall."

"And do you think Menshiki has something up his sleeve?" I asked my final question.

"Affirmative! Menshiki has an ulterior motive for everything. Never wastes a move, that fellow. It is the only way he knows. Using both sides of his brain, all the time. He could never be a dolphin."

The Commendatore's form faded little by little, and then, like mist on a windless midwinter morning, it thinned and spread until it was completely gone. All that sat facing me now was an old empty armchair. His absence was so absolute, so profound, I had trouble believing that, until a moment earlier, he had been there at all. Perhaps I had been sitting across from empty space, nothing more. Perhaps I had only been talking to myself.

As the Commendatore had predicted, Menshiki's silver Jaguar took a long time to show up. The two beautiful ladies seemed in no rush to leave his home. I stepped onto my terrace and looked across the valley at the white house. But I could spot no one. To kill time, I went inside and started preparing dinner. I made soup stock, parboiled the vegetables, and froze what I would not be using. I kept myself busy doing whatever I could think of, but when I finished, I still had time on my hands. I returned to the living room, put Richard Strauss's *Rosenkavalier* back on the turntable, stretched out on the sofa, and read a book.

Shoko was charmed by Menshiki. That much was certain. She looked at him differently than she looked at me. Her eyes shone. He was a most attractive middle-aged man, to say the least. A handsome and wealthy bachelor, well dressed and well mannered, a man who lived in the mountains in a huge mansion with four English automobiles stored in its garage. It was no mystery why so many women in this world might find him charming (to the same degree they might find me less than desirable). Yet it was equally certain that Mariye had a deep distrust of Menshiki. She was a girl of keen instincts. Perhaps she had intuitively divined that he was concealing the reasons for his behavior. Thus she maintained a careful distance. At least that was how it appeared to me.

What was going to happen? I was naturally curious, yet at the same time I had vague misgivings. My curiosity and those misgivings were therefore in direct opposition. Like an incoming tide meeting the outgoing current at the mouth of a river.

It was shortly after five thirty when Menshiki's Jaguar made its way back up the slope. As the Commendatore had predicted, it was already dark outside.

39

A CAMOUFLAGED CONTAINER, DESIGNED FOR A SPECIFIC PURPOSE

The Jaguar eased to a stop in front of my house, and Menshiki emerged. He walked around the car to open the door for Mariye and Shoko Akikawa, lowering the passenger seat so that Mariye could climb out of the back. The girl and the woman got into the blue Prius. Shoko rolled down the window and politely thanked Menshiki (Mariye, of course, turned the other way). Then the two drove home without stopping by to say hello. Menshiki watched them until they were out of sight, took a moment to (I assumed) recalibrate his mind and adjust his expression, and walked to my front door.

"I know it's late, but do you mind if I drop in for a few minutes?" he asked rather shyly.

"Sure, please do. I'm not busy right now," I said, showing him in.

We went to the living room; he sat on the sofa, while I sat in the easy chair that the Commendatore had just vacated. I thought I could feel the Commendatore's shrill voice still reverberating in the air.

"Thank you so much for today," Menshiki said to me. "I owe you a lot."

No thanks were necessary, I said. I really hadn't done anything.

"But if it hadn't been for your portrait—indeed, if it hadn't been for you, period—this chance would have passed me by. I would never have met Mariye face-to-face, never come this close to her. Everything has hinged on you—you're like the base of a folding fan. I'm concerned that you may not be enjoying that role, however."

"Nothing could make me happier than helping you out like this," I said. “But I must confess, it’s hard to figure out how much is accidental and how much is planned. That part of it does bother me.”

Menshiki thought for a moment. “You may not believe this,” he said, nodding, “but I didn’t plan any of this. Maybe it’s not all pure coincidence, but almost everything has unfolded quite naturally.”

“So I’m the catalyst that happened to set those events in motion? Has that been my role?” I inquired.

“Catalyst? Yes, maybe you could say that.”

“To tell the truth, though, I feel more like a Trojan horse.”

Menshiki looked up at me, as if squinting into a bright light. “What do you mean?”

“You know, the hollow wooden horse the Greeks built. They hid their warriors inside and presented it as a gift to the clueless Trojans, who dragged it inside their fortress. A camouflaged container, designed for a specific purpose.”

Menshiki took a moment to respond. “In other words,” he said, choosing his words carefully, “you think I may have exploited you, used you as a kind of Trojan horse? To get close to Mariye?”

“At the risk of offending you, I do feel a little that way.”

Menshiki narrowed his eyes, and the corners of his mouth curled in the beginnings of a smile.

“I guess that can’t be helped. But as I just said, this has been a series of unexpected coincidences. To be honest, I like you. My affection for you is personal, and very natural. I don’t find myself liking many people, so when it does happen I try to take it seriously. I would never exploit you for my sole convenience. I know I can be selfish, but I’d like to think that I’m able to draw a line between friendship and self-interest. You’re not being used as a Trojan horse—not now, not ever. So please don’t worry.”

He didn’t seem to be making this up—his words had the ring of truth.

“So did you have a chance to show them the painting?” I asked. “My portrait of you in your study?”

“Of course. That’s why they came in the first place. They loved it. Though Mariye didn’t say anything. She’s a girl of few words, as you know. But I could tell how strongly she felt. It showed in her face. She stood in front of the portrait for a very long time. Just stood there, not speaking or moving."

In fact, I couldn't remember the portrait very well, though I had finished it only a few weeks before. That was my pattern—the moment I launched into a new painting, the one I had just finished slipped from my mind. Only a vague and general image remained. I did retain a physical memory, however, of the sense of achievement I got from working on it. That palpable sensation meant more to me than the completed work.

"Their visit sure lasted a long time," I said.

Menshiki gave an embarrassed shrug. "After they'd seen your painting, I gave them a light lunch and showed them around. A tour of my house and the grounds. Shoko seemed interested, you see. The time flew by."

"I bet they were impressed."

"Shoko was, I think," Menshiki said. "Especially by my Jaguar XKE. But Mariye didn't say anything. Maybe she didn't like my house. Or maybe she's not interested in houses in general."

I guessed she probably couldn't care less.

"Did you have a chance to talk to her?" I asked.

Menshiki shook his head no. "She opened her mouth two or three times at most. And what she said was almost meaningless. She generally ignores me."

I kept quiet. I had no special thoughts on the matter, but I could picture the scene. Whenever he tried to start a conversation with Mariye, she would clam up, just mumble a word or two. Once Mariye made up her mind not to speak, trying to reach her was like ladling water onto a parched desert.

Menshiki picked up an ornament from the table, a glossy ceramic snail, and inspected it from a variety of angles. The snail had been one of the very few decorative objects left in the house. Probably a piece of Dresden china. The size of a smallish egg. Purchased long ago, perhaps, by Tomohiko Amada himself. Menshiki gingerly returned the snail to the table. Then he raised his head and looked across at me.

"I guess it will take her a while to get used to me," he said, as if addressing himself. "I mean, we've only just met. She's a quiet child to begin with, and thirteen is said to be a difficult age, the beginning of puberty. All the same, being with her in the same room, breathing the same air—it was a precious experience, priceless really."

"So then your feeling hasn't changed?"

Menshiki's eyes narrowed slightly. "What feeling do you mean?"

"That you don't care to know if Mariye is your child."

"No, that hasn't changed a bit," Menshiki said without hesitation. He chewed his lip for a moment before continuing. "It's hard to explain. But when she's near, and I look at her face and watch her move, this odd feeling comes over me. The sense that somehow my life up to now may have been wasted. That I no longer understand the purpose of my existence, the reason I'm here. As if values I'd thought were certain were turning out to be not so certain after all."

"And for you these sorts of feelings are extremely odd, am I right?" For me, they were par for the course.

"That's right. I've never experienced them before."

"And they started after spending several hours with Mariye?"

"Yes. You must think I'm some kind of idiot."

I shook my head no. "Not at all. I felt the same way when I hit puberty and met a girl I liked."

Menshiki gave a small smile. There was something rueful in it. "That's when the pointlessness of all my accomplishments and successes, and all the money I've accumulated, hit me. That I'm no more than an expedient and transitory vehicle meant to pass a set of genes on to someone else. What other function do I serve? Beyond that, I'm just a clod of earth."

"A clod of earth." I tried saying the words. They had a strange ring.

"To tell the truth, I was down in the pit when that realization hit me. Remember, that pit we uncovered behind the shrine, underneath the pile of rocks?"

"How could I forget?"

"If you'd felt like it, you could have abandoned me there. Without food and water, my body would have shriveled and returned to the soil. I would have been no more than a clod of earth in the end."

I didn't know what to say, so I remained silent.

"It's enough for me," Menshiki said, "that the *possibility* exists that Mariye and I are related by blood. I feel no compulsion to find out if it's true or not. That mere possibility has sent a beam of light into my life—now I can look at myself in a new way."

"I think I understand," I said. "Maybe not every step in your reasoning, but the way you feel. What I don't get is what you're expecting from Mariye. In concrete terms."

"It's not that I haven't given that question any thought," Menshiki said. He looked down at his hands. They were beautiful hands, with long fingers. "People devote a lot of energy to thinking about things. Whether they want to or not. Yet in the end we all just have to wait—only time can tell how events play out. The answers lie ahead."

I remained quiet. I had no clear idea what he had in mind, and no compelling desire to find out. Were I to know, my position might become even more difficult.

"I've heard Mariye is much more forthcoming with you," Menshiki said after a long pause. "That's what Shoko said, at least."

"That's probably true," I said cautiously. "We seem to be able to talk quite naturally when we're in the studio."

Of course, I didn't tell him that Mariye had come to visit me from the adjoining mountain through a hidden passageway. That was our secret.

"Do you think it's because she's gotten comfortable with you? Or because she feels some personal connection?"

"The girl is fascinated by painting, maybe artistic expression in general," I explained. "If a painting is involved, there are occasions—not always, mind you—when she's quite comfortable talking. She's not a typical child, that's for sure. When I taught her at the community center, she didn't speak much to the other kids."

"So she doesn't get along with children her own age?"

"Maybe. Her aunt says she doesn't make many friends at school."

Menshiki pondered that for a moment.

"She opens up with Shoko to some extent, I guess," he said.

"So it seems. From what I've heard, she's much closer to her aunt than she is to her father."

Menshiki merely nodded. His silence seemed charged with implication.

"What sort of man is her father?" I asked him. "Have you checked?"

Menshiki looked to the side and narrowed his eyes. "He was fifteen years older than she was," he finally said. "By 'she' I mean his late wife."

Of course, "late wife" meant Menshiki's former lover.

"I don't know how they got together, or why they married. I have no interest in those things," he said. "Whatever the case, though, it's clear he loved his wife dearly. Her death was a terrible shock. They say he was a changed man after that."

According to Menshiki, the Akikawas were a big landowning family in the area (much as Tomohiko Amada's family was in Kyushu). Although they had lost nearly half of their property in the land reform that followed World War Two, they retained many assets, enough that the family could get along comfortably on the income they produced. Yoshinobu Akikawa, Mariye's father, was the first of two children and the only son, so when his father passed away at an early age he became the head of the family. He built a house for himself at the top of the mountain they owned, and set up an office in one of their buildings in Odawara. From that office, he managed the family properties in the city and its environs: several commercial and apartment buildings, and a number of rental houses and lots. He also dabbled in real estate. In other words, while he kept the business going, he made no attempt to broaden its scale. The core of his enterprise consisted of looking after the family's assets when the need arose.

Yoshinobu married late in life. He was in his mid-forties when he tied the knot, and his daughter (Mariye) was born the following year. Then, six years later, his wife was stung to death. It was early spring, and she had been walking alone through a big plum grove they owned when she was attacked by a swarm of large hornets. Her death hit him hard. To wipe away anything that could remind him of the tragedy, as soon as the funeral was over he hired men to raze the plum trees, and yank their roots from the earth. What was left was a dreary and barren plot of land. It had been a beautiful grove, so its destruction was painful for many. Moreover, for generations those living nearby had been permitted to pick a portion of the abundant fruit to make pickled plums and plum wine. As a result, Yoshinobu Akikawa's barbaric act of retaliation deprived many local residents of one of the small pleasures they could look forward to each year. Still, it was his mountain, the plum grove was *his*, and no one could fail to understand his fury—at the hornets and the trees. As a consequence, those complaints were never voiced in public.

Yoshinobu Akikawa turned into a rather morose man after his wife's death. He hadn't been particularly social or gregarious to begin with, and now his introverted side only grew stronger. His interest in spiritual things deepened, and he became involved with a religious sect whose name was unknown to me. It is said that at one point he spent some time in India. At great personal expense, he built a grand hall for the sect's use on the outskirts of town, where he began spending much of his time. It's not clear exactly what takes place there. But it appears that a daily regimen of stringent religious "austerities" and the study of reincarnation helped him find a new purpose in life after his wife's death.

These activities reduced his involvement in the business, but his duties hadn't been all that demanding in the first place. There were three longtime employees more than capable of managing things when the boss failed to show up. His visits home became more infrequent. When he did return it was usually just to sleep. His relationship with his only daughter had, for some reason, grown more distant after his wife's death. Perhaps she reminded him of his dead wife. Or perhaps he had never really cared for children. In any case, as a result the child never really took to her father. The responsibility for looking after Mariye went to his younger sister, Shoko. She had taken leave from her job as secretary for the president of a medical college in Tokyo and moved to the house atop the mountain near Odawara on what she expected to be a temporary break to look after the child. In the end, though, the arrangement became permanent. Perhaps she came to love the girl. Or perhaps she couldn't stand idly by when her little niece needed her so much.

Having reached that point in his account, Menshiki stopped to touch his fingers to his lips.

"Do you happen to have any whiskey in the house?" he asked.

"There's about a half a bottle of single malt," I said.

"I don't want to impose, but could I have some? On the rocks."

"My pleasure. But aren't you driving?"

"I'll call a cab," he said. "No point in losing my license."

I went to the kitchen and came back with a whiskey bottle, a ceramic bowl of ice, and two glasses. In the meantime, Menshiki put the record of *Der Rosenkavalier* that I had been listening to on the turntable. We sat back and listened to the lush strains of Richard Strauss as we sipped our whiskey.

"Are you a devotee of single malt?" Menshiki asked.

"No, this was a gift. A friend brought it. Sure tastes good, though."

"I have a bottle of rare Scotch at home that a friend in Scotland sent to me. A single malt from the island of Islay. It's from a cask sealed by the Prince of Wales himself on his visit to the distillery there. I'll bring it on my next visit."

"You needn't make such a fuss on my account," I said.

"There's a small island near Islay called Jura," he said. "Have you heard of it?"

"No," I replied.

"It's practically uninhabited. More deer than people. Lots of other wildlife, too—rabbits, pheasants, seals. And one very old distillery. There's a spring of freshwater nearby, just perfect for making whiskey. If you mix the single malt with that water, the flavor is absolutely amazing. You can't find it anywhere else."

"It sounds delicious," I said.

"Jura is also known as the place where George Orwell wrote *1984*. Orwell rented a small house on the northern end of the island, really the middle of nowhere, but the winter took a terrible toll on his body. It was a primitive place, with none of the modern amenities. I guess he needed that kind of Spartan environment to write. I spent a week on that island myself. Huddled next to the fireplace each night, drinking that marvelous whiskey."

"Why did you spend a whole week in such an out-of-the-way place all by yourself?"

"Business," Menshiki said simply. He smiled.

Apparently, he wasn't going to let me in on what sort of business was involved. And I had no particular desire to find out.

"I really needed a drink today," he said. "To settle myself down. That's why I'm imposing on you like this. I'll come and pick up my car tomorrow, if that's all right with you."

"Of course, I don't mind at all."

We sat there awhile without talking.

"Do you mind if I ask something personal?" Menshiki broke the silence. "I hope you won't take offense."

"Don't worry, I'm not a guy who gets offended. I'll answer you if I can."

"You've been married, correct?"

I nodded. "Yes, I was married. As a matter of fact, I just mailed off the divorce papers, signed and sealed. So I'm not sure if I'm officially married now or not. Still, it's safe to say that I *was* married. For six years."

Menshiki was studying the ice cubes in his glass as if deep in thought.

"Sorry to pry," he said. "But do you have any regrets about the way your marriage ended?"

I took another sip of whiskey. "How does one say 'buyer beware' in Latin?" I asked.

" 'Caveat emptor,' " Menshiki said without hesitation.

"I have a hard time remembering how to say it. But I know what it means."

Menshiki laughed.

"Sure, I have regrets," I replied. "But even if I could go back and rectify one of my mistakes, I doubt it would change the outcome."

"Do you think there's something in you that's impervious to change, something that became a stumbling block in your marriage?"

"Perhaps it's my *lack* of something impervious to change that was the stumbling block."

"But you have the desire to paint. That must be closely connected to your appetite for life."

"There may be something I have to get past first before I can really get started with my painting, though. That's my feeling, anyway."

"We all have ordeals we must face," Menshiki said. "It's through them that we find a new direction in our lives. The more grueling the ordeal, the more it can help us down the road."

"As long as it doesn't grind us into the ground."

Menshiki smiled. He had finished his questions about my divorce.

I brought a jar of olives in from the kitchen to accompany our drinks. We nibbled on them while sipping our whiskey. When the record finished, Menshiki flipped it over. Georg Solti continued conducting the Vienna Philharmonic.

Menshiki has an ulterior motive for everything. Never wastes a move, that fellow. It is the only way he knows.

If the Commendatore was correct, what move was Menshiki making—or about to make—now? I hadn't a clue. Perhaps he was holding back for the moment, waiting for his opportunity. He said that he had "no intention" of exploiting me. Probably he was speaking the truth. Yet intentions were, in the end, just intentions. He was a savvy guy who had managed to survive and thrive in the most cutting-edge sector of the business world. If he was harboring an ulterior motive, even if it was dormant now, it would be next to impossible for me to avoid getting sucked in.

"You're thirty-six years old, right?" Menshiki said out of the blue.

"Yes, that's correct."

"That's the best age."

I didn't see it that way at all. But I didn't say so.

"I'm fifty-four. Too old to be fighting on the front lines in the business I was in, but still a little too young to be considered a legend. That's why you see me dawdling around like this."

"Some become legends in their youth, though."

"Sure, there are a few. But there's no great merit in that. In fact, it could be a real nightmare. Once you're considered a legend, you can only trace the pattern of your rise for the rest of your life. I can't think of anything more boring than that."

"Don't you ever get bored?"

Menshiki smiled. "I can't remember ever being bored. I've been too busy."

I could only shake my head in admiration.

"How about you?" he asked. "Have you ever been bored?"

"Of course. It happens a lot. In my case, however, boredom is an indispensable part of life."

"Don't you find it painful?"

"I guess I've gotten used to it. So it doesn't feel like pain."

"I bet that's because painting is so central to your existence. That's your core—your passion to create is born out of what you call boredom. Without that core, I'm sure you'd find boredom unendurable."

"So you're not working these days, are you?"

"That's right, I'm basically retired. I do a little computer trading on the stock markets, as I've told you, but that's not out of necessity. It's more like a game, a form of mental discipline."

"And you live in that big house all by yourself."

"Correct."

"And you still never get bored?"

Menshiki shook his head. "I have so many things to occupy my mind. Books I should read, music I should listen to. Data to gather, sort, and analyze. I'm used to staying active—it's a daily habit. I work out too, and when I need a change of pace, I practice the piano. And there's housework, of course. I haven't time to be bored."

"Don't you ever worry about growing old? About becoming a lonely old man?"

"No question, I will age," Menshiki said. "My body will decline, and I'll probably grow more and more solitary. But I'm not there yet. I have an idea what it will be like. But I'm the kind of guy who doesn't believe something until he's seen it. So I have to wait until it's sitting right in front of me. I'm not especially afraid of aging. I can't say I'm looking forward to it, but I am a little curious."

Menshiki slowly swirled the whiskey in his glass.

"How about you?" he asked, looking me in the eye. "Are you afraid of getting old?"

"I was married for six years, and it didn't turn out so well. I didn't paint a single painting for myself during all that time. I guess people would say I squandered those years. After all, I was turning out one painting after another of a sort I don't especially like. Yet, in a way, maybe I was fortunate to have gone through that. That's how I feel these days."

"I think I understand what you're trying to say. That there's a time in life when you have to discard your ego. Is that it?"

Perhaps, I thought. But maybe in my case it simply took me that long to discover what I'd been lugging around all that time. Had I dragged Yuzu along on that pointless, roundabout journey?

Am I afraid of growing old? I wondered to myself. Did I dread the advent of old age?

"I still have a hard time imagining it," I said. "It may sound foolish for a man in his mid-thirties to say this, but I feel as if my life is just beginning."

"That's not foolish at all," Menshiki said, smiling. "You're probably right—you're just getting started."

"You mentioned genes a few minutes ago," I said. "That you felt you're just a vehicle receiving a set of genes from one generation and transmitting it to the next. And beyond that duty, you're no more than a clod of earth. Right?"

Menshiki nodded. "That's what I said."

"But you don't find being a clod of earth particularly frightening, do you?"

"I may be a clod of earth," Menshiki said, laughing, "but as clods go I'm pretty good. It may sound conceited, but I think I may even be a superior clod. I've been blessed with certain abilities. Those have limits, I know, but they're abilities nonetheless. That's why I go all out in whatever I do. I want to stretch myself as far as I can, to see what I'm capable of. I have no time to be bored. That's the best way I know of keeping fear and emptiness at arm's length."

We drank until almost eight o'clock, at which point the bottle ran out. Menshiki stood up to leave.

"I should be on my way," he said. "I've imposed on you for too long."

I called for a taxi. "Tomohiko Amada's house" was all it took to identify our location. He was a famous man. The dispatcher said it would be fifteen minutes. I thanked him and hung up.

Menshiki used that time to tell me something.

"I told you earlier that Mariye's father had become deeply involved in a religious sect, didn't I?" he began.

I nodded.

"Well, it turns out that it's one of the new religions, and a shady one at that. I checked online and found out they've got a really bad track record. A number of civil suits have been filed against them. Their so-called doctrine is a pile of rubbish unworthy of the name 'religion.' Of course, Mr. Akikawa is free to subscribe to whatever beliefs he likes. That goes without saying. But he has sunk quite a lot of money into this group. His money, company money. He had considerable wealth in the beginning, was able to manage on the monthly rents he collected. But there was a clear limit to how much he could withdraw without selling property and other assets. Now he's way past that limit—he's sold a lot of those. Clearly, an unhealthy situation. Like an octopus trying to survive by devouring its own legs."

"Are you saying he's being preyed on by that cult?"

"Exactly. He's a real pigeon. When a group like that squeezes you, they take everything they can get. Right down to the last drop. Forgive me for saying so, but Mr. Akikawa's privileged upbringing may make him more vulnerable to that kind of thing."

"So you're concerned about this situation."

Menshiki sighed. "It's Mr. Akikawa's responsibility how he ends up. He's a mature adult, aware of his actions. It's not so simple for his family, though—they have no idea what's going on. Not that my worrying about them will make a bit of difference."

"The study of reincarnation," I said.

"It's a fascinating hypothesis," Menshiki said. He quietly shook his head.

The taxi finally arrived. Before getting in, he offered a most courteous thanks. His complexion and his decorum were a constant, no matter how much he drank.

40

I COULD NOT MISTAKE THE FACE

After Menshiki left, I brushed my teeth, climbed into bed, and fell asleep immediately. I drop off in no time at all under normal circumstances, and whiskey only accentuates that tendency.

In the middle of the night, however, a loud sound jolted me awake. I think the sound was real. Possibly, though, it took place in my dream. Its source could have been my own unconscious. Whatever its origins, it was a huge crash, as though an earthquake had struck. The impact lifted me into the air. That part was real, for sure, not a dream or a product of my imagination. I had been fast asleep, and now, an instant later, I was on the verge of tumbling from my bed, my mind on high alert.

According to the clock on the bedside table, it was past two. The time of night when the bell had usually rung. But I could not hear a bell. With winter approaching, there were no insect voices. A deep hush had fallen over the house. Outside, thick, dark clouds covered the sky. If I listened hard enough, I could hear the wind.

I felt for the lamp, switched it on, and slipped a sweater over my pajamas. I would take a quick look around the house. Something very strange had happened, or so it seemed. Had a wild boar crashed through one of the windows? Or had a small meteorite hit the roof? Probably not, but it was still a good idea to make sure. I was, after all, the caretaker of the house. And I would have a hard time falling back to sleep if I didn't find out. The crash had left me wide awake, my heart pounding.

I walked through the house flicking on lights, checking room by room. As far as I could tell, nothing was out of place. All was in order.

It wasn't a big house, so I would have noticed if something was amiss. When I finished my inspection, I headed to the studio. I stepped through the door connecting it to the living room and reached for the wall switch. But some thing stopped me. *Don't turn on the light*, the thing whispered in my ear. In a small but clear voice. *Better to leave it dark.* Following its instructions, I removed my hand from the switch and closed the door behind me without a sound. Quieting my own breathing, I peered into the darkened studio.

As my eyes adjusted to the light, I became aware that someone else was in the room. The signs were unmistakable. And that someone was sitting on the wooden stool that I used when I was painting. At first, I thought it was the Commendatore. That he had materialized and returned. But this person was much bigger. The silhouette looming in the dark was that of a tall, gaunt man. The Commendatore was two feet tall, if that, but this man was close to six feet in height. He was sitting somewhat hunched over, as tall people often do. And not moving at all.

I didn't move either as I stood there looking at his back, with my own back pressed against the doorframe and my left hand near the light switch, just in case. There in the dark, in the middle of the night, we were frozen, like two statues. For some reason, I wasn't scared. My breathing was shallow and the sound of my heartbeat was hard and dry. But I felt no fear. Someone I had never seen before had come barging into my house in the middle of the night. For all I knew, it could have been a burglar. Or perhaps a ghost. Either should have frightened me. Yet for some reason, I felt neither danger nor dread.

Perhaps all the strange happenings I had been experiencing—starting with the appearance of the Commendatore—had made me immune to such weirdness. Yet there was more to it than that. What was the mysterious intruder doing there in the studio so late at night? My curiosity trumped my fear. He seemed to be lost in thought. Or maybe he was staring hard at something. The intensity of his focus was obvious, even to an observer. He had no idea that I had entered the room. Or, perhaps, my presence was beneath his notice.

I tried to quiet my breathing and control the pounding of my heart against my ribs as I waited for my eyes to adjust to the dark. After a while, I began to realize what he was regarding with such ferocity. It was something hanging on the opposite wall. Which meant it had to be Tomohiko Amada's painting *Killing Commendatore*. He was sitting stock-still on the wooden stool, bent slightly forward, staring at that painting. His hands were on his knees.

At last the dark clouds covering the sky began to part, and a shaft of moonlight entered the room. It was as if an ancient tombstone had been bathed in pure, silent water, baring the secrets carved on its surface. Then the darkness returned. But only for a short time. The clouds parted again, and a pale blue light filled the room for a full ten seconds. Now, at last, I could determine the identity of the person on the stool.

His white hair fell to his shoulders. It had been uncombed for some time, for wisps jutted in every direction. Judging from his bearing, he was quite old. And withered, like a dead tree. Once, he must have had a powerful and manly physique. But now he was skeletal, wasted by age and possibly illness. That much I could tell.

His face was so emaciated it took me a while to figure out who he was. But there, in the hushed moonlight, I finally realized. I had seen only a few photographs, yet I could not mistake the face. The profile of his aquiline nose and the powerful physical aura were undeniable proof. Though the night was cold, sweat streamed from my armpits. My heart pounded even faster and harder. It seemed impossible to believe, but there was no room for doubt.

The old man was Tomohiko Amada, the artist who had created the painting. Tomohiko Amada had returned to his studio.

41

ONLY AS LONG AS I DIDN'T TURN AROUND

It couldn't be the flesh-and-blood Tomohiko Amada. That "real" Tomohiko Amada was confined to a nursing home in Izu Kogen. He suffered from advanced dementia and seldom left his bed. There was no way he could have come that far under his own steam. What I was looking at, therefore, could only be his ghost. Yet as far as I knew, Amada was still alive. Which meant I was looking at his "living spirit." Of course, he could have drawn his last breath just moments earlier. In which case, this would indeed be his ghost.

Whichever the case, this was no hallucination. It was far too real, too dense, for that. It projected an unmistakable humanity and the workings of a conscious mind. Tomohiko Amada had, through some special agency, returned to *his* studio, and was sitting on *his* stool regarding *his* painting *Killing Commendatore*. He was staring straight at it—his eyes seemed to cut through the dark. He was indifferent to my presence. I doubt he even realized I was in the room.

As the clouds rolled by, the moonlight through the window came and went, allowing me brief glimpses of his silhouette. He was sitting so I could see his profile, and wearing what could have been an old bathrobe or nightgown. His feet were bare. No stockings, no slippers. Disheveled white hair, jaw covered with a white grizzle. A haggard face, but clear and penetrating eyes.

I wasn't afraid so much as bewildered. The scene before me defied common sense. My hand hovered near the light switch on the wall. I had no intention of turning it on—I was just frozen in that posture. I didn't want to disturb Tomohiko Amada—be he ghost or phantasm—in any way. This studio was his proper place. Where he *truly belonged*. I was the intruder, with no right to interfere in whatever he wanted to do.

I waited until my breath calmed down and my body relaxed, then quietly backed out of the studio. I eased the door shut. Tomohiko Amada remained motionless on his stool throughout. Had I tripped over the table and sent the vase crashing to the floor, though, I doubt he would have noticed. His concentration was that fierce. The moon had broken through the clouds again, illuminating his skeletal frame. That last image engraved itself in my mind—embraced by the delicate shadows of night, that silhouette seemed to distill his entire life. *You must never forget this*, I told myself. I had to preserve in my memory what my eyes had seen, in all its detail.

I sat at the dining room table and drank glass after glass of mineral water. I really wanted a shot of whiskey, but the bottle was empty. Menshiki and I had drained it the previous evening. No other liquor was left in the house. There were a few bottles of beer in the fridge, but they wouldn't do the trick.

It was past four a.m. when sleep finally came calling. Until then, I just sat at the table while one thought after another passed through my head. I was too keyed up to be capable of any kind of action. All I could do was close my eyes and let my mind wander. Nothing cohered. For several hours, I followed those fragmented, meandering thoughts. Like a kitten chasing its tail.

When I grew tired, I mentally called up the image of Tomohiko Amada that I had seen mere hours before. To ensure its accuracy, I sketched it in my mind. I opened my imaginary sketchbook, pulled out my imaginary pencil, and drew the old man's silhouette. This was something I often did when I had time to spare. Actual paper and pencil weren't necessary. In fact, it was easier without them. Mathematicians go through a similar process, I imagine, when they picture a formula on an imaginary blackboard. Someday I might commit what I had seen to canvas.

I didn't really want to check the studio again. Of course, I was curious. Was Tomohiko Amada—or, more likely, his double—still there? Still sitting on his stool with his eyes riveted on *Killing Commendatore*? Sure, the possibility intrigued me. I had encountered a most rare and precious event, had seen it with my own eyes. Might it provide the key—several keys, actually—to help unravel the secrets of Tomohiko Amada's life?

All the same, I didn't want to interfere with what he was doing. He had come so far, transcending space and reason, to reexamine his *Killing Commendatore,* poring over it to find—what? He had to have sacrificed much of his dwindling store of energy just to make it here. Drained his life force. Yet something had compelled him to return to the painting one last time, at whatever cost. To study it to his heart's content.

When I opened my eyes it was already past ten o'clock. Rare for an early bird like me. I washed my face, brewed coffee, and ate breakfast. For some reason, I was famished. I ate nearly double my usual amount. Three slices of toast, two boiled eggs, and a tomato salad. Not to mention two big cups of coffee.

I checked the studio after breakfast just to be sure, but of course Tomohiko Amada was gone. What remained was the empty, silent room in the morning. An easel with a canvas (my painting of Mariye Akikawa), a round stool in front of it, and the straight-backed chair Mariye used when she posed for me. *Killing Commendatore* hanging on the wall. The bell still missing from the shelf. The sky over the valley blue, the air cold and crystal clear. The piercing calls of birds, awaiting winter's arrival.

I picked up the phone and called Masahiko's office. His voice was sleepy, though it was almost noon. A clear case of the Monday-morning blahs. After our hellos, I casually inquired about his father. I wanted to know if he had died, and if the apparition I had seen was his ghost. If Tomohiko Amada had passed away the night before, surely his son would have been notified.

"How's your father?" I asked.

"I went to see him a few days ago. His mind has passed the point of no return, I'm afraid, but he's all right physically, I guess. At least he doesn't look like he's at death's door."

So Tomohiko Amada was still alive. What I had seen wasn't a ghost. It was the fleeting embodiment of a living person's will.

"It's a strange question, I know, but have you noticed anything unusual about your father recently?"

"My father?"

"Yeah."

"Why do you want to know that all of a sudden?"

I followed the script I had prepared. "To tell the truth, I had this weird dream last night where your father visited this place. I bumped into him while he was here. It felt very real. Real enough to make me jump out of bed. That's why I wondered if something had happened to him."

"Wow," he said. "That's wild. What was my father doing while he was there?"

"He just sat on the stool in the studio."

"That's all?"

"That's it. Nothing but that."

"By stool you mean that old three-legged chair, the round one?"

"Yeah, that's the one."

Masahiko thought for a moment.

"Maybe he is reaching the end," he said in a flat voice. "They say that in our last hours, our spirit returns to where we feel we've left something undone. From what I know of my father, that would be the studio."

"But from what you've told me, he has no memory left."

"Yes, memory in the conventional sense, anyway. But his spirit's still there. His brain just can't access it any longer. The circuit's broken—his mind isn't connected. But his spirit remains, behind the scenes. It's probably the same as ever."

"That makes sense," I said.

"Weren't you scared?"

"By the dream?"

"Yeah. I mean it sounds awfully real."

"No, I wasn't afraid. But it did feel very strange. Like the man himself was right there."

"Maybe it really was him," Masahiko said.

I didn't say anything. I couldn't let on that Tomohiko Amada had likely returned specifically to view *Killing Commendatore* (actually, *I* might have invited him—had I not unwrapped the painting, he might not have shown up). If I told his son, I would have had to explain the whole story, from the moment I stumbled across the painting in the attic to when I opened it without permission and, even more blatantly, chose to hang it on the studio wall. I knew I would have to let Masahiko know eventually, but I didn't want to raise the issue at this juncture.

"Anyway," he said, "last time we met I mentioned there was a matter I needed to talk to you about? But we didn't have enough time then. Remember?"

"Yeah."

"So why don't I stop by one of these days and fill you in. Okay?"

"This house is yours, you know. Come whenever you like."

"How about this weekend? I'm thinking of visiting my father in Izu Kogen, so I could stop by on my trip back. It's right on the way."

I told him he was welcome anytime except Wednesday and Friday nights and Sunday morning. My art class was on Wednesday and Friday and Mariye's sitting was on Sunday.

He figured he'd be able to make it Saturday night. "I'll let you know beforehand," he said.

After our phone call, I went into the studio and sat on the stool. The wooden stool that Tomohiko Amada had occupied the night before. As soon as I sat down, it hit me—this stool was no longer *mine*. No, the long years Tomohiko Amada had spent sitting on it painting made it *his,* now and forever. To the uninformed, it looked like no more than an old dinged-up, three-legged chair, but it was infused with his will. I had borrowed it without permission, that was all.

I sat there and studied *Killing Commendatore* on the wall, as I had done countless times before. It rewarded multiple viewings—its depth allowed for so many different ways of looking at it. This time, though, I felt I wanted to inspect it from an entirely new angle. What was there that had made Tomohiko Amada return to it at the end of his life, to see it one last time?

I spent a long time sitting there, just studying the painting. I chose the same position, the same angle, even adopted the same posture that Tomohiko Amada's living spirit or alter ego had taken the night before, and tried to focus on it with the same intense concentration. Yet I couldn't find that *something* I had previously missed.

. . .

When I grew tired of thinking, I went outside. Menshiki's silver Jaguar was still parked in front of my house, at a slight remove from my Toyota Corolla station wagon. It had been sitting there all night, waiting quietly for its master's return, like an intelligent, well-trained pet.

I strolled on past the house, musing about *Killing Commendatore* in a vague sort of way. Walking the little path through the woods, I had the distinct impression that someone was spying on me from behind. As if Long Face had pushed up the square lid of his hole and was secretly observing me from the corner of the painting. I whipped around and looked back. But nothing was to be seen. No hole in the ground, no Long Face. Just a deserted leaf-strewn path wending through the quiet woods. This pattern repeated itself a number of times. But each time I spun around no one was there.

Then again, it might well be that the hole and Long Face were there *only as long as I didn't turn around*. Perhaps they could tell when I was about to look back, and hid themselves at that moment. Like a child playing a game.

I passed through the woods to the very end of the path, the first time I'd gone that far. I figured the entrance to Mariye's secret passageway had to be nearby. Yet I couldn't locate it. "You really have to pay attention to find it," she had said, and it did seem to be well camouflaged. In any case, she had taken the passageway after dark to reach my place from the adjoining mountain, alone and on foot. Past the thickets and through the woods.

The path came to an abrupt end at a small, circular clearing. The overhanging trees thinned out, so I could see pieces of sky. I found a flat stone bathed in a small pool of light, sat down, and looked through the tree trunks at the valley below. I imagined that at any minute Mariye might pop up out of her secret passageway, wherever that was. But of course no one appeared. My only companions were birds, who hopped from limb to limb and then flew off again. They moved about in pairs, each chirping loudly to let the other know where they were. I had once read an article describing how certain birds mate for life, and how when one died, the survivor spent the rest of their days alone. It goes without saying that they never had to sign and seal official divorce papers sent by certified mail from a lawyer's office.

A truck selling fresh produce passed in the distance, its driver listlessly broadcasting his wares over its loudspeaker. No sooner was his voice out of earshot than there was a loud rustle in the bushes nearby. What was it? It didn't sound human. A wild animal was more likely. For a scary second I thought it might be a wild boar (boars and hornets were the most dangerous things in the area), but then the sound abruptly stopped.

I stood up and started walking back to the house. When I passed the small shrine I checked the pit, just to make sure. The planks were in place, the stone weights neatly arranged on top. They hadn't been moved, as far as I could tell. Fallen leaves covered the boards. They had lost their bright colors and turned sodden in the rain. So young and fresh in spring, their quiet death had come now, in late autumn.

As I stared at the planks, I began to feel that Long Face might poke his elongated, eggplant-shaped head out of the pit at any minute. But the planks didn't budge. Obviously. Long Face's hole was square, not round, and was smaller and more personal in scale. Moreover, *this* hole was home to the Commendatore, not Long Face. Or at least home to the Idea that had borrowed the Commendatore's form. It had been the Commendatore that had rung the bell to call me here, and had made me open the pit.

Everything started with this pit. After Menshiki and I had pried open the lid with a backhoe, strange things had started happening one after another. Then again, it might have all begun when I had found *Killing Commendatore* in the attic and removed it from its packaging. That was the correct sequence. Or perhaps the two events acted in tandem. *Killing Commendatore* could have been what called the Idea to the house. The appearance of the Commendatore could have been my reward for liberating the painting. Try as I might, I couldn't tell what was the cause, and what was the result.

Menshiki's Jaguar was gone when I got back to the house. He had probably come by taxi to pick it up. Or else sent one of the people who worked for him to collect it. Whichever the case, my mud-spattered Toyota Corolla was left there, parked forlornly outside my front door.

Menshiki had been right—I should check the tires one of these days, though I hadn't bought an air pressure gauge and probably never would.

I went to the kitchen to start making lunch, but no sooner had I picked up a knife than I realized I was no longer ravenously hungry. Instead, I was very sleepy. I got a blanket, stretched out on the living room sofa, and promptly drifted off. I had a dream, a short one. It was clear and very vivid. But I couldn't remember anything about it. Just that it was clear and vivid. It felt as though a fragment of real life had slipped into my sleeping mind by mistake. Then the moment I awoke, it fled like a quick-footed animal, leaving no trace behind.

42

IF IT BREAKS WHEN YOU DROP IT, IT'S AN EGG

The next week flew by. I spent my mornings focused on my painting, and my afternoons reading, taking walks, and doing whatever housework needed to be done. One day blended into the next. My girlfriend showed up on Wednesday and we spent the afternoon making love. The constant creaking of my old bed really cracked her up.

"It's going to fall to pieces before long," she predicted during a pause in our exertions. "There'll be nothing left but splinters—we won't be able to tell if they're wood or pretzel sticks."

"Maybe we should try to make love more quietly."

"Maybe Captain Ahab should have hunted sardines," she said.

I thought about that for a moment. "Are you saying some things in this world can't be changed?"

"Kind of."

A short time later, we were back on the rolling seas, in pursuit of the great white whale. Some things really can't be changed so easily.

Each day, I worked a little on Mariye Akikawa's portrait. My initial sketch had established the skeleton, and now I was filling it out. I tried combining various colors to come up with the right tone for the background. Her face had to sit naturally over that foundation. These tasks tided me over as I waited for her next visit to the studio on Sunday. Some parts of my job were carried out while the model was present, while other preparatory work had to be done before the model's arrival. I loved both. I could take my time mulling over the various elements, and experiment to find just the right color, just the right style. I enjoyed the hands-on nature of this work, and the challenge of creating an environment from which the subject would spring to life.

While preparing Mariye's portrait, I began working on a different canvas—a painting of the pit behind the shrine. The pit had etched itself in my mind with such force that I didn't need it in front of me. I painted the scene in minute detail. The style was purely realistic, the viewpoint objective. I avoided objective representation in my art (except, of course, the portraits that were my "day job"), but that didn't mean I couldn't do it. When I wanted to, I could paint so precisely that the result could be mistaken for a photograph. I used that hyperrealistic style occasionally to change my mood, or refresh the fundamentals of my craft. I never showed those paintings to anyone, though—they were for my private enjoyment, nothing more.

In this way, the pit in the woods began to appear before me, more vivid and alive with each passing day. A mysterious round aperture half covered by thick planks. This was the pit that had given birth to the Commendatore. There were no human figures in the painting, however, just a black hole. Fallen leaves covered the earth surrounding it. A scene of perfect tranquility. Yet it felt as if someone (or something) might come crawling out of that hole any minute. The longer I pictured the scene, the stronger that premonition grew. Looking at it made my spine tingle, although I was the one who had painted it.

I worked like this every day, spending all morning alone in the studio. Palette and brush in hand, I moved back and forth between *A Portrait of Mariye Akikawa* and *The Pit in the Woods*—two more different paintings would be hard to imagine—as the mood struck me. I applied myself to the canvases while sitting on the same stool Tomohiko Amada had occupied in the dead of night the previous Sunday. Perhaps because my focus was so great, the dense presence I had felt the next morning had at some point disappeared. The old stool was once again a mere piece of furniture, there for my use. It seemed that Tomohiko Amada had gone back to where he belonged.

There were nights that week when I opened the studio door a crack to peek inside. But no one was ever there. Not Tomohiko Amada, not the Commendatore. Just an old stool parked in front of two easels. The moon cast its dim light over the objects in the room. All was quiet. *Killing Commendatore* hung on one wall. My unfinished work, *The Man with the White Subaru Forester,* was turned around so no one could see it. The two paintings I was working on, *A Portrait of Mariye Akikawa* and *The Pit in the Woods,* sat side by side on two easels. The smell of oil paint, turpentine, and poppyseed oil hung in the air. It never left, no matter how long the windows were left open. It was a special aroma, one I breathed every day, and would probably go on breathing for the rest of my life. I inhaled the air of the studio as if to confirm its presence, then quietly closed the door.

Masahiko called Friday night to say he was coming the next afternoon. He'd buy fresh fish from the market nearby, so I needn't worry about dinner. I could look forward to a special treat.

"Anything more I should bring?" he asked. "I can pick up what you want on my way."

"Can't think of anything," I answered. Then I remembered. "Now that you mention it, I'm out of whiskey. A friend and I polished off what you brought last time. Could you pick up another bottle? Any brand is okay."

"I like Chivas myself. Would that do?"

"You bet," I said. Masahiko had always been picky about food and drink. I was a different story. I ate and drank whatever was put in front of me.

When our phone call ended, I went to the studio, took *Killing Commendatore* down from the wall, carried it to my bedroom, and covered it. It wouldn't do to have Tomohiko Amada's son see the painting his father had hidden in the attic. For the time being, at least.

Now a visitor to the studio would see only *A Portrait of Mariye Akikawa* and *The Pit in the Woods*. I stood there looking back and forth at the two works in progress, comparing them. An image rose to my mind: I could see Mariye walking behind the shrine to the pit. I had a distinct sense that *something* might begin then. The lid was half open. The darkness was calling. Was Long Face there waiting for her? Or the Commendatore?

Could these two paintings be connected in some way?

Since moving to this house, I had been painting almost nonstop. I had completed Menshiki's portrait on commission, then started *The Man with the White Subaru Forester* (brought to a halt when I had just begun to add color), and now was working on *A Portrait of Mariye Akikawa* and *The Pit in the Woods* in tandem. It struck me that the four paintings might fit together to form the beginning of a story of some kind.

Then again, perhaps I was documenting the story through my painting. That's what it felt like, anyway. Had someone given me the role or the right to be that chronicler? If so, *who*? Why was I chosen, of all people?

Masahiko's black Volvo station wagon came trundling up the slope shortly before four o'clock on Saturday afternoon. He loved the toughness and reliability of those old boxy cars. He'd driven this one seemingly forever, put a ton of miles on it, yet showed no inclination to trade it in for a new one. On this occasion, he brought along the special carving knife he used for fish. As always, it was razor sharp. In my kitchen, he used it to prepare the large, fresh sea bream he had just bought in Itoh. Masahiko had always been good with his hands, a man of many talents. Without a wasted motion, he filleted the fish, sliced the flesh into sashimi, and boiled the bones for broth. He lightly grilled the skin to nibble on with our drinks. I just stood there, enjoying the show. Who knows, he might have been a famous chef had he taken that route.

"Actually, it's best to let sashimi sit a day until the flesh softens and the flavor comes out, but what the hell," he said, deftly plying the knife. "You can handle it, right?"

"No problem—I'm not picky," I said.

"You can eat any leftovers tomorrow."

"Will do."

"Hey, do you mind if I crash here tonight?" Masahiko asked. "I'd like to stay the evening so we can hang out and drink without feeling rushed. Drinking and driving is no good, right? I can sleep on the sofa in the living room."

"Sure," I said. "It's your house, after all. Stay as long as you like."

"Are you sure some woman won't show up in the middle of the night?"

"No plans as of now," I replied, shaking my head.

"Okay, then I'll stay."

"You don't have to crash on the sofa—there's a bed in the guest room."

"No, I prefer the sofa. It's a lot more comfortable than it looks. Slept like a baby on it back in the old days."

He pulled out a bottle of Chivas Regal, cut the seal, and opened it. I brought ice from the refrigerator and two glasses. The gurgle of whiskey pouring into the glass was music to my ears. Like an old friend opening his heart to me. We sipped the whiskey as we finished preparing dinner.

"It's been a hell of a long time since you and I drank like this," Masahiko said.

"It sure feels that way. I remember us putting back a lot."

"*I* put back a lot, you mean," he said. "You never drank that much."

I laughed. "Maybe not from your point of view, but it was a lot for me."

I never got totally drunk. I always fell asleep first. But he was a different kind of drinker. Once he settled in for the long haul, he went all the way.

We sat across from each other at the table, sipping whiskey and eating the seafood. For starters, we shared the eight raw oysters he had bought with the sea bream. Then we dug into the sashimi. It was a bit too firm, as he had predicted, but it was delicious nonetheless, especially with the whiskey. By the end, we had polished it all off. We were already pretty full. The only other food was the crispy fish skin, small chunks of wasabi mixed with sake lees, and a dish of tofu. We topped off the meal with the soup he had prepared.

"I haven't had a feast like this in ages," I said.

"You can't eat like this in Tokyo," he said. "Living around here wouldn't be half bad. Fresh fish anytime."

"I bet you'd find life here boring eventually, though."

"Are you bored?"

"Am I? I guess I've never found boredom that painful. And besides, there's quite a lot going on here."

That was for sure. I had met Menshiki soon after my arrival in early summer, we had dug up the pit behind the shrine, then the Commendatore had made his appearance, and finally Mariye Akikawa and her aunt Shoko had entered my life. I had a girlfriend, a housewife in her sexual prime, who came to comfort me. Tomohiko Amada's living spirit had paid me a visit. There was hardly time to be bored.

"I might not be bored here either," Masahiko said. "Did you know I used to be into surfing? I rode the waves all up and down this coast."

That was news to me, I told him. He'd never mentioned it before.

"I've been thinking of leaving Tokyo, of going back to that kind of life. I'd check out the ocean when I woke up, then grab my board and head out if the surf was up."

The idea of that kind of life left me cold.

"What about your job?" I asked.

"I only need to go to Tokyo twice a week to take care of business. Most of my work is done on computer anyway, so it wouldn't be that hard to live outside the city. The world's changing, right?"

"I wouldn't know."

He looked at me in amazement. "This is the twenty-first century, man. Haven't you heard?"

"I've heard talk."

After dinner, we moved to the living room to continue drinking. Autumn was almost over, but it wasn't so cold that we needed to light a fire.

"So then, how's your father doing these days?" I asked.

Masahiko let out a small sigh. "Same as always. His mind is shot. Can't tell the difference between his balls and a pair of eggs."

"If it breaks when you drop it, it's an egg," I said.

He laughed. "People are strange creatures, aren't they? I mean, my father was as solid as a rock until just a few years ago. Mind as clear as the night sky in winter. To an almost disgusting degree. And now his memory is like a black hole. This dark, unfathomable hole that popped up out of nowhere in the middle of the cosmos."

Masahiko shook his head.

"Who was it that said, 'The greatest surprise in life is old age'?" he asked.

I couldn't help him with that one. I'd never heard the saying. But it was probably true. Old age must be an even bigger shock than death. Far beyond what we can imagine. The day someone tells you that you're flat-out useless, that your existence is irrelevant—biologically (and socially)—in this world.

"So tell me about this dream you had of my father," Masahiko asked me. "Was it really as lifelike as you said?"

"Yeah, so lifelike it hardly seemed a dream."

"And he was in the studio?"

I took him to the studio.

"Your father was sitting there," I said, pointing to the stool in the middle of the room.

Masahiko walked over to the stool. "Just sitting?" he asked, placing his palm on its seat.

"That's right. He wasn't doing anything."

In fact, his father had been staring at *Killing Commendatore* on the wall, but I didn't tell him that.

"My father loved this stool," he said. "It was just a common old thing, but he never got rid of it. He sat on it to paint, and to think."

"It's relaxing to sit on," I said. "You'd be surprised."

Masahiko stood there with his hand on the stool, lost in thought. But he didn't sit down. After a minute, he turned his attention to the two canvases facing it. *A Portrait of Mariye Akikawa* and *The Pit in the Woods,* my two works in progress. He examined them slowly and carefully, like a doctor looking for a trace of shadow on a patient's X-ray.

"These are great," he said. "Really interesting."

"Both of them?"

"Yes, both. When you place them side by side like this, you feel a strange kind of movement between them. Their styles are totally different, but you get a sense they're somehow linked."

I nodded. I'd been thinking the same thing for a few days, in a vague sort of way.

"It seems to me that, little by little, you're finding a new direction," he went on. "Like you've finally emerged from a deep forest. You should take this really seriously, old friend."

He raised his glass and took a swallow of whiskey. The ice cubes tinkled.

I felt an urge to show Masahiko his father's *Killing Commendatore*. What would he have to say about it? His comments might provide a valuable clue. But I suppressed the impulse. Something was holding me back.

It's still too early, it said. Still too early.

We left the studio and went back to the living room. The wind had picked up—through the window I could see thick clouds edging their way north. The moon was hidden from view.

"So about what brought me here," Masahiko said, not wasting any more time. He seemed to be steeling himself for what he was about to say.

"It sounds like something that's not easy to discuss," I said.

"You're right, it's hard. *Quite* hard, in fact."

"But it's something that I need to know."

Masahiko rubbed his hands together. Like a man preparing to lift a heavy object.

"It's about Yuzu," he said, cutting to the chase. "She and I have met up a number of times. Before you left this spring, and afterward, too. She calls me when she wants to talk, and then we meet somewhere. She asked me not to tell you. I hated hiding it from you, but, well, I promised her."

I nodded. "It's important to keep our promises."

"Yuzu and I were friends too, you know."

"I know," I said. Masahiko put great stock in friendship. It could be a weakness of his.

"She had another man. Apart from you, that is."

"I know that too. *Now,* at least."

He nodded. "It started about six months before you walked out. Their relationship, that is. It hurts me to tell you this, but the guy is someone I know. A colleague of mine at work."

I let out a small sigh. "I imagine he's really handsome, right?"

"Yeah, you got it. Classic features. An agency scouted him in high school, and he modeled part-time for a while. He's that good-looking. And, well, it seems that I was the one who introduced them."

I didn't say anything.

"At least that's how it worked out," Masahiko said.

"Yuzu always had a thing for handsome men. It was almost pathological. She knew it too."

"You're not bad-looking yourself," he said.

"Thanks, man. Now I can sleep better tonight."

We didn't speak for a time. Finally, he broke the silence.

"Anyway, he's a really good-looking guy. A nice guy, too. I know this doesn't help you very much, but he's not violent, or a womanizer, or vain about his looks. He's not that type."

"That's nice to hear," I said. My voice was tinged with sarcasm, though I hadn't meant it to sound that way.

"It all started in September a year ago," Masahiko said. "He and I were out together when we bumped into Yuzu, and since it was about noon, the three of us stopped for lunch nearby. Believe me, I had absolutely no idea things would turn out this way. He's five years younger than she is."

"So the two of them didn't waste much time."

Masahiko gave a small shrug. Things must have progressed very quickly indeed.

"The guy talked to me about what was going on," he said. "Your wife did as well. It put me in a very difficult position."

I kept quiet. Anything I said would just make me look foolish.

Masahiko was silent for a moment. Then he spoke. "The fact is, Yuzu is pregnant."

I was speechless for a moment. "Yuzu? Pregnant?"

"Yeah, seven months gone already."

"She did it on purpose?"

"I don't know," Masahiko said, shaking his head. "But she's planning to have the baby. After seven months there's not much choice, is there."

"She always told me she wasn't ready for kids."

He winced slightly. "There's no chance the child could be yours, is there?" he said, looking into his glass.

I did a quick mental calculation. "No. I don't know the legal side of it, but biologically the chances are zero. I left eight months ago, and we haven't seen each other since."

"That's good," Masahiko said. "At any rate, she asked me to tell you she's going to have a baby. And that it shouldn't cause you any problems."

"But then why tell me at all?"

He shook his head. "I guess she's informing you out of courtesy."

I said nothing. *Out of courtesy?*

"I've been waiting for the chance to apologize for all this. I knew what was going on between Yuzu and my colleague, and I kept it from you. It was inexcusable. Under any circumstances."

"Then was letting me stay in this house your way of making amends?"

"Not at all—there's no connection between that and Yuzu. My father lived and painted in this house for a great many years. I figured you could keep that tradition alive. It's not something I could have asked anybody else, not like that at all."

Again, I said nothing. He sounded sincere.

"In any case," Masahiko continued, "you signed and sealed the divorce papers you received and sent them back to Yuzu, right?"

"More precisely, to her lawyer. So our divorce should be official by now. I guess those two will choose a date for their own wedding now that's taken care of."

And go on to have a happy marriage. A tall, handsome man, a small child, and little Yuzu. The three of them strolling happily through the park on a sunny Sunday morning. Heartwarming.

Masahiko added some ice and poured us more whiskey. He took a swig from his glass.

I went out to the terrace and looked across the valley at Menshiki's white house. Lights were on in some of the windows. What was Menshiki doing at this minute? What was he thinking about?

The night air was chilly. The leafless branches quivered in the wind. I went back to the living room and sat down.

"Can you forgive me?"

"It's not like you meant to hurt me," I said, shaking my head.

"I for one am sorry it turned out this way. You and Yuzu looked so well matched, and you seemed happy together. It's sad that it fell apart."

"You drop them both—the one that breaks is the egg," I said.

Masahiko laughed weakly. "So how are things now? Is there a woman in your life?"

"Yeah, there's someone."

"But not the same as Yuzu?"

"It's different. I've been looking for the same thing in women my whole life. Whatever that is, Yuzu had it."

"And you can't find that in anyone else?"

"Not so far," I said, shaking my head again.

"You have my sympathy," Masahiko said. "So what is it exactly that you've been looking for?"

"It's hard to put into words. I feel as if I lost track of something along the way, and have been searching for it ever since. Don't you think that's how everyone falls in love?"

"I don't think you can say 'everyone,'" he said with a slight frown. "You may actually be in the minority. But if you can't find the right words, why not paint it? You are an artist, after all."

"If you can't say it, paint it. That's easy to say. Not so easy to do, though."

"But it may be important to try, don't you think?"

"And perhaps Captain Ahab should have set out after sardines."

Masahiko laughed. "Sure, from a safety standpoint. But that's not how art is born."

"Hey, give me a break. Mention art, and the conversation comes to a screeching halt."

"Looks like we need some more whiskey," he said, shaking his head. He poured us another drink.

"I can't drink too much. I've got to work tomorrow morning."

"Tomorrow is tomorrow. Today is all we have right now," Masahiko said.

I found this idea strangely compelling.

"Can I ask you a favor?" I said to Masahiko. Our conversation was wrapping up, and we were about to get ready for bed. The hands on the clock pointed to a little before eleven.

"Sure, anything at all."

"I'd like to meet your father. Could you take me with you the next time you go to Izu?"

Masahiko regarded me as he might a strange animal. "You want to meet my father?"

"If it's not too much trouble."

"It's no trouble at all. But my father's in no shape to talk to you. He's quite incoherent. His mind is chaotic—a mud swamp, really. So if you have any expectations—if you're hoping to gain some insight into the person known as Tomohiko Amada—you'll only be disappointed."

"No, I'm not expecting anything like that. I just want to take one good look at him, that's all."

"But why?"

I took a breath and looked around the room. "I've been living in this house for six months now," I said. "Sitting on the stool he sat on, painting in his studio. Eating off his dishes, listening to his records. I feel his presence all over the place. That's why I have to meet the flesh-and-blood Tomohiko Amada. Once is enough. It doesn't matter a bit if we can't talk to each other."

"Then it's all right," Masahiko said, seemingly persuaded. "He won't be thrilled to see you, but he won't be ticked off either. He can't tell one person from another, you see. So there's no problem if you come along. I plan to visit the nursing home again pretty soon. According to the doctor, he doesn't have much longer—the end could come at any time. So join me on my next visit, if you're free."

I brought a spare blanket, pillow, and futon and made up a bed on the sofa in the living room. I looked around the room to make sure the Commendatore wasn't there. If Masahiko woke up in the middle of the night and saw him—two feet tall and dressed in ancient Asuka garb—he'd freak out. He'd figure he had become a real alcoholic.

Besides the Commendatore, there was *The Man with the White Subaru Forester* to worry about. I had turned the painting around so no one could see it. Still, I had no idea what strangeness might happen without my knowledge in the middle of the night.

So I wasn't kidding when I wished Masahiko a sound sleep.

I gave him a spare pair of pajamas to wear. He and I were more or less the same size, so there was no problem with the fit. He took off his clothes, put on the pajamas, and climbed under the bedding I had laid out. The air in the room was a bit chilly, but he looked snug and warm under the covers.

"You're sure you're not angry?" he asked before I left.

"No, I'm not angry," I answered.

"It must hurt a little, though."

"Maybe a little." I had the right to be a little hurt, I thought.

"But the cup is still one-sixteenth full."

"You've got it there," I said.

I turned off the living room light and retired to my bedroom. Before long I had fallen asleep, together with my slightly wounded feelings.

43

IT COULDN'T END LIKE ANY OTHER DREAM

When I woke it was already light outside. Thin gray clouds covered the sky from end to end, but the sun's benevolent rays still quietly filtered through. It was not quite seven.

I washed my face, turned on the coffee maker, and went to check the living room. Wrapped in blankets, Masahiko was fast asleep on the sofa. He appeared unlikely to wake up any time soon. The almost empty bottle of Chivas Regal sat on the table. I managed to tidy up the bottle and glasses without disturbing him.

I must have drunk quite a lot the night before, but I wasn't a bit hungover. My mind was as sharp as it was every morning. No heartburn, either. I've never had a hangover in my life. Why, I don't know. Probably it's just the way I was born. One night's sleep and all traces of alcohol vanish from my system, however much I drink. I eat breakfast and I'm ready to go.

I toasted two slices of bread, fried two eggs, and ate them while listening to the news and weather on the radio. The stock market was fluctuating wildly, a new parliamentary scandal had been uncovered, and a terrorist bombing in the Middle East had killed and wounded many people. Nothing to brighten my day. Yet none of these events was likely to affect my immediate circumstances. For now, at least, they were limited to distant places and people I had never met. I felt bad, but there was nothing I could do. The weather forecast promised nothing new either. Not a particularly gorgeous day, but not particularly awful either. Overcast, but no rain. Maybe not, anyway. But the forecasters and media types were clever—they never used vague words like "maybe." No, they stuck with convenient terms for which no one could be held accountable, like "probability of precipitation."

When the news and weather ended, I turned off the radio and cleaned up the breakfast dishes. Then I sat down again at the table, drank a second cup of coffee, and thought. Most people would have used that time to read the Sunday paper, but I didn't subscribe. So I just sipped my coffee, looked at the magnificent willow tree outside the window, and thought.

First, I thought about my wife, who, I had been told, was about to give birth. Then it hit me—she wasn't my wife any longer. No connection between us remained. Not contractual, not personal. From where she stood, I was now in all likelihood a virtual stranger, a person of no special consequence. It felt weird. Until a few months ago we had eaten breakfast together, shared the same soap and towel, walked around naked in front of each other, slept in the same bed. Now our lives bore no relationship to each other.

As I followed this train of thought, gradually I began to feel a stranger to myself as well. I placed my hands on the table and studied them for a while. These were my hands, no doubt. Right and left a symmetrical pair. I used these hands to paint, to cook, to eat, sometimes to caress a woman's body. But this morning, for some reason, they didn't look like my hands at all. They had become a stranger's hands—the palms, the backs, the fingernails.

I quit studying my hands. And thinking about the woman who had formerly been my wife. I got up from the table and went to the bath, where I removed my pajamas and took a hot shower. I carefully washed my hair and shaved in the bathroom sink. When I finished, I thought about the baby Yuzu was about to have—the baby who was not my child—again. I didn't want to, but there was nothing I could do about it.

She was about seven months pregnant. Seven months ago had been the second half of April. Where was I then, and what was I doing? I had left home and set out on a long, solitary trip in mid-March, driving my antique Peugeot 205 more or less at random all across Hokkaido and northeastern Japan. By the time my trip ended and I returned to Tokyo it was already early May. In late April I had crossed over from Hokkaido to Aomori in northern Honshu on the ferry that ran from Hakodate to Oma on the Shimokita Peninsula.

I pulled the simple diary I had kept out of a desk drawer and checked. At that time I had been traveling in the mountains of Aomori, far from the sea. Although it was well into the second half of April, it was still cold, and snow was everywhere. Why on earth had I chosen such a cold place? I couldn't remember the precise location, but I did recall a small, almost deserted lakefront hotel where I had stayed for a few days. It was an unprepossessing old building made of concrete, where they offered simple (but not bad) meals and amazingly cheap rates. There was even a small outdoor hot springs bath in a corner of the garden that was available twenty-four hours a day. The hotel had just reopened for the spring season, and I was practically the only guest.

For some reason, my recollections of that trip were vague. All I recorded in the notebook I used as a diary were the names of the places I visited, where I stayed, what I ate, the distance I had driven, and how much I spent. It was a brief, very hit-and-miss record. I could find no mention of my thoughts and feelings, or anything else along those lines. I guess there was nothing to write about. One day just flowed into another, with no distinction between them. I had jotted down the names of the places, but couldn't remember much about any of them. Many times, even their names had been left out. Looking back, I could only recall that feeling of repetition: the same scenery day after day, the same food, the same weather ("cold" and "not so cold" were my only categories).

The little sketchbook I had carried did a better job of bringing the trip back to life. (I carried no camera, so I hadn't taken a single photograph. Instead, I had sketched.) Even so, there weren't that many sketches to look at. When I had spare time, I had just whipped off simple drawings of what was before my eyes with an old pencil or ballpoint pen. Flowers and plants on the roadside, dogs and cats, mountain peaks, things like that. Now and then I would sketch someone I met along the way, but I almost always gave those pictures to whomever I had drawn.

Beneath the diary entry for April 19 I had written the words "Dream last night." That was all. I had been staying at the small lakefront hotel on that date. The words were underlined with a thick pencil. It must have been a special kind of dream to warrant such emphasis. It took me a while to remember what the dream had been about. When the memory returned, though, it arrived all at once.

The dream had come to me shortly before dawn that day. It was vivid, and very erotic.

In the dream I was back in the apartment in Hiroo. The one Yuzu and I had shared for six years. There was a bed, and my wife was sleeping in it. I was looking down at her from the ceiling. In other words, I was hovering above her. I didn't find that at all out of the ordinary. In fact, the me in the dream found floating in the air to be perfectly normal. Nothing unnatural about it. Of course, I had no idea I was dreaming. What was happening felt totally real.

Quietly, so as not to wake Yuzu, I descended from the ceiling to stand at the foot of the bed. I was sexually aroused, powerfully so. I hadn't made love to her for ages. Bit by bit, I peeled back the quilt covering her. She was fast asleep (had she taken a sleeping pill before retiring?) and showed no signs of waking up, even when I removed the quilt. She never even twitched. This made me more daring. Taking my time, I slipped off her pajama bottoms, then her panties. Her pajamas were a pale blue, her tiny cotton panties pure white. Still she did not wake. There was no resistance, no sound.

I gently parted her legs and caressed her vagina with my finger. It was warm and wet, and opened to my touch. As if it had been waiting for me. I couldn't stand it any longer—I slipped my erect penis inside. Or, from another angle, that part of her actively swallowed my penis, immersing it in what felt like warm butter. Yuzu did not open her eyes, but she sighed and let out a small moan. As if she had been impatient for this to happen. Her nipples were as hard as cherry pits when I touched them.

She might be deep in a dream, I thought. If she was dreaming of someone, though, it was surely not me. For a long while now she had resisted sex with me. Whatever dream she might be having, though, whoever she was mistaking me for, it was too late to turn back, for I was already inside her. It could be a terrible shock if she woke up in the midst of the act and saw who it was. She might well be furious. If that were to happen, I would deal with it then. Now all I could do was take it to the limit. My desire raged like a river through a broken dam, carrying me along.

At the beginning, I moved my penis slowly, trying not to arouse her so much as to wake her up, but, naturally, the pace quickened as I went on. I could tell from the way her body welcomed me that she wanted me to be more forceful. Soon, though, I reached the moment of climax. I wanted to remain inside her, but I couldn't control myself any longer. It had been ages since we had last had sex, and, though asleep, she was responding to our lovemaking with more passion than ever before.

My ejaculation was violent, and repeated. Again and again, semen poured from me, overflowing her vagina, turning the sheets sticky. There was nothing I could do to make it stop. If it continued, I worried, I would be completely emptied out. Yuzu slept deeply through it all without making a sound, her breathing even. Her sex, though, had contracted around mine, and would not let go. As if it had an unshakable will of its own and was determined to wring every last drop from my body.

I woke up at this point. I had indeed ejaculated. My underwear was drenched in semen. I quickly slipped it off to avoid soiling the bed, carried it to the sink, and washed it. Then I went out through the hotel's back door to bathe in the hot springs. As the bath was entirely exposed to the elements, with no ceiling or walls, I was freezing by the time I reached it. Once I got in, however, the water warmed me to the core.

I soaked there alone in the predawn hush, listening to the water drip as steam melted the ice, replaying the dream over and over in my head. The memory was so vivid and physical it didn't feel like a dream at all. I had *actually* visited the Hiroo apartment and had *actually* made love to Yuzu—that was the only way I could think about it. My hands remembered the touch of her silky skin and my penis could still feel her vagina. It had clung to my penis, had embraced it with a violent passion (true, Yuzu may have mistaken me for someone else, but it was me nonetheless). She had wrung me out, taking every last drop of my semen for her own.

I could not help but feel a kind of shame for having such a dream (if dream indeed it was). After all, I had raped my own wife in my imagination. I had undressed and entered her while she was sleeping, without her consent. In the eyes of the law, a man who does that to a woman—even his wife—is guilty of sexual assault. In that sense, my conduct was far from praiseworthy. Still, objectively speaking, *it was a dream*. Something experienced in sleep. I had not created it on purpose. I had not written the script.

Yet in it I had played out my truest hopes and desires. There was no question on that score. Had I been placed in a similar situation in real life—not in a dream—I might well have acted the same. I might have stripped and forcibly entered her. I wanted Yuzu's body, longed to penetrate it. I was possessed by that desire. I had been able to realize it in exaggerated form in my dream (conversely, only in a dream could it have been realized).

As I continued on my solitary journey, this "real" erotic dream provided me with a provisional kind of happiness. You might say it buoyed me up. By recalling it, I could feel that I was a living creature organically connected to the world. Linked to my surroundings not through logical or conceptual thought, but carnally, through my body.

At the same time, though, the thought that someone else—some other man—was *actually* enjoying Yuzu as I had in my dream was agony. That someone was caressing her stiffened nipples, removing her tiny white panties, and thrusting himself into her until he came, again and again. When I imagined that, it felt as though I were torn and bleeding inside. Nothing (as far as I could remember) had ever made me feel that way before.

That was the strange dream I had experienced shortly before dawn on April 19. Noted in my diary as "Dream last night" and thickly underlined in pencil.

. . .

It was right around that time that Yuzu had conceived. Of course, the precise date could not be known. But it would not be odd if it were that day.

The similarity between my situation and the story Menshiki had told me was striking. The difference was that he had made love to a flesh-and-blood woman on his office sofa *in reality*. That had not taken place in a dream. And it had been right around then that she had conceived. Immediately thereafter she had married a man of substantial means, and had subsequently given birth to Mariye. Menshiki's belief that Mariye might be his child therefore had a basis in fact. It was a long shot, perhaps, but at least it was possible. My lovemaking with Yuzu, on the other hand, had taken place in a dream. I was in the mountains of Aomori, while Yuzu was (probably) in the heart of Tokyo. Thus her child could not possibly be mine. That was the only logical conclusion. The odds were not low, they were zero. *If, that is, one was thinking logically.*

But my dream was too vivid to be so easily dismissed on logical grounds. Moreover, the pleasure I had felt during our lovemaking was greater, and far more memorable, than at any time during our six years of marriage. When I came again and again inside her, the fuses in my brain seemed to have all blown at once, melting what had been distinct layers of reality into a single heavy, turbid mass. As in the primal chaos of the earth.

So graphic an occurrence must have consequences—it couldn't end like any other dream. I felt that strongly. It had to be connected to *something*. To have some sort of impact on the present.

Masahiko woke up shortly before nine. He padded into the dining room in his pajamas and drank a cup of hot black coffee. No breakfast, thanks, he said—just coffee, if you don't mind. There were bags under his eyes.

"Are you okay?" I asked.

"I'm fine," he said, rubbing his eyelids. "I've had much worse hangovers. This is mild."

"Why don't you stick around for a while?" I said.

"Don't you have a guest coming?"

"That's at ten. There's still time. And there's no problem if you're here when they arrive. I'll introduce you. They're both very attractive."

"Both? I thought there was just one model."

"Her aunt is her chaperone."

"Her chaperone? So they still do things the old-fashioned way in this neck of the woods? Like in a Jane Austen novel. They don't wear corsets and ride in a horse-drawn carriage, do they?"

"Not a horse-drawn carriage. A Toyota Prius. And no corsets. When I'm painting the girl, the aunt sits in the living room and reads for the whole two hours. 'Aunt' makes her sound old, though—she's pretty young."

"What sort of books is she into?"

"I don't know. I asked, but she wouldn't tell me."

"No kidding," he said. "Oh yeah, speaking of books, remember the character in Dostoevsky's *The Possessed,* the guy who shoots himself with a pistol just to prove how free he is? What's his name? I figured you might know."

"Kirillov," I said.

"That's right, Kirillov. I've been trying to remember, but it keeps slipping my mind."

"Why do you want to know?"

"No special reason," Masahiko said, shaking his head. "He popped into my head, and when I tried to recall his name, I couldn't. It's been bugging me. Like a fish bone caught in my throat. But man, those Russians. They come up with the weirdest ideas, don't they?"

"There are lots of characters in Dostoevsky who do crazy things just to prove that they are free people, unconstrained by God and society. Though looking at Russia back then, maybe they weren't so crazy after all."

"Then how about you?" Masahiko asked. "You and Yuzu are formally divorced, which means you're now a lawfully unwedded man. So what comes next? Even if it wasn't your choice, freedom is still freedom, right? Why not run out and do something crazy, now that you have the opportunity?"

I laughed. "I'm not planning anything at present. Sure, I may be free for the moment, but that doesn't mean I've got to go out and prove it to the world, does it?"

"So that's how you look at it," Masahiko said in a disappointed tone. "But hey, you're a painter, right? An artist. Artists flaunt the rules left and right—they make a great show of it. But you've always walked the straight and narrow. The path of reason, I guess. So why not let loose now, throw off the restraints and do something wild?"

"Like murdering an old moneylender with an axe?"

"Yeah, that might work."

"Or falling for a prostitute with a heart of gold?"

"Even better."

"I'll think about it," I said. "But you know, it seems to me that reality itself has a screw loose somewhere. That's why I try to keep at least myself in line as much as possible."

"Well, I guess that's one way of looking at it," Masahiko said resignedly.

It's more than just "one way of looking at it," I wanted to tell him. Indeed, it felt like everything around me was becoming unscrewed—that reality was losing its grip. If I lost my grip too, then the craziness would get completely out of hand. But I couldn't tell Masahiko the whole story at this stage of the game.

"At any rate, I've got to be going," he said. "I'd love to meet the two women, but I've got work waiting for me back in Tokyo."

Masahiko finished his coffee, got dressed, and drove off in his boxy jet-black Volvo. Baggy eyes and all. "Glad we finally had a chance to talk," were his parting words.

One thing that morning completely stumped me. Masahiko's knife, the one he'd brought to prepare the fish, had gone missing. It had been carefully washed, and neither of us remembered touching it afterward, but we searched the kitchen high and low and still couldn't find it.

"Forget it," he said. "It's probably out for a walk. Grab it for me when it comes back. I'll pick it up on my next visit—I don't use it all that often."

I'll keep looking, I told him.

. . .

I checked my watch once the Volvo was out of sight. The Akikawas would be showing up before long. I removed the bedding from the living room sofa, and flung the windows wide open to let fresh air in. The sky was still faintly overcast and gray. There was no wind.

I took *Killing Commendatore* from my bedroom and hung it back where it had been on the studio wall. Then I sat down on the stool to examine the painting one more time. Red blood still gushed from the Commendatore's chest, while Long Face's sharp eyes still glittered in the lower left-hand corner of the canvas. Nothing had changed.

Even as I studied *Killing Commendatore,* though, I couldn't erase Yuzu from my mind. It had been no dream, of that much I felt sure. *I had truly visited our apartment that night.* I was as sure of that as I was that Tomohiko Amada had visited the studio several days before. Like him, I had overcome the laws of physics by some means to make my way to our Hiroo apartment, penetrate her, and discharge my semen inside her body. People can accomplish anything, I thought, if they want it badly enough. There are channels through which reality can become unreal. Or unreality can enter the realm of the real. If we desire it that strongly. Deep in our heart. But that didn't mean that we were free. It might demonstrate quite the opposite.

If I had the chance, I wanted to ask Yuzu if *she* had experienced a similar dream in late April of this year. If she had dreamed shortly before dawn that I had come to ravish her while she was fast asleep (or else somehow deprived her of her freedom). In other words, was my dream something I alone experienced, or was it a two-way street? That's what I wanted to confirm. Yet if the dream was one we had shared, wouldn't she view me as sinister, a villain? Could such a presence exist within me? I hated to think of myself in that way.

Was I free? As far as I was concerned, the question was wholly irrelevant. What I needed now more than anything was a firm reality to hold on to. A solid foundation on which to stand. Not the sort of freedom that allowed me to rape my own wife in my dreams.

44

THE TRAITS THAT MAKE A PERSON WHO THEY ARE

Mariye didn't speak that morning. She just sat there, the perfect model, in the simple straight-backed chair, and gazed at me as if at some distant landscape. Since my stool was taller than her chair, she was looking up at a slight angle. I made no special attempt to talk to her. There was nothing I had to say, nor did I feel any particular need. So I plied my brush across the canvas in silence.

I was painting Mariye's portrait, yet I could sense elements of my dead sister Komi and my former wife Yuzu creeping into the work. This wasn't intentional—they worked their way in quite naturally. Perhaps I was searching within Mariye for reminders of those two women, so important to me, whom I had lost. I couldn't say if this was healthy or not. But that was the only way I could paint at the time. No, to say "at the time" is off the mark. When I thought about it, I had operated like this from the very beginning. Giving form to what eluded me in reality. Inscribing secret signals only I could decipher.

Whatever the case, I was able to push Mariye's portrait forward with relative ease. Step by step, it moved steadily toward completion. Like a river, it followed the contours of the land, pooling in the hollows until it overflowed the final barrier to stream unobstructed to the sea. I could feel it circulate through my body, like blood.

"Can I come visit you later," Mariye said in a small voice just before we finished our morning's work. The lack of inflection made it sound like an assertion, but it was a clear question.

"You mean through your secret passageway?"

"Yes."

"I don't mind at all, but around what time?"

"I don't know yet."

"I don't think you should come after dark," I said. "You can never tell what's in these mountains at night."

All sorts of weird things could be lurking out there: the Commendatore, Long Face, the man with the white Subaru Forester, Tomohiko Amada's living spirit. Even the incubus that was my sexual alter ego. Yes, depending on the circumstances, I might turn into one of those sinister creatures that prowled the night. The thought gave me a chill.

"I'll try to come before dark," Mariye said. "I want to talk to you about something. Just the two of us."

"I'll be waiting."

We wrapped up for the day not long after the noon-hour chimes sounded.

Shoko was sitting on the sofa, once again focused on her reading. She appeared to have almost finished the thick paperback. Taking off her glasses, she noted her place with a bookmark and looked up at us.

"We made good progress today," I told her. "One or two more sessions and we should be done. I'm sorry to be taking so much of your time."

Shoko smiled. It was a beautiful smile. "Not at all," she answered. "Mariye seems to enjoy sitting for you, and I so look forward to seeing the finished portrait. And this sofa is the perfect place to read. I'm never bored in the slightest. In fact, it's a welcome change of pace for me to come here—I always feel better afterward."

I wanted to ask her how their visit to Menshiki's house had gone the previous Sunday. Had his fine mansion impressed her? What had she thought of him as a person? But asking questions like that would have been a breach of etiquette—I had to wait for her to raise the subject first.

Once again, Shoko had dressed for the occasion. It was most definitely not what a regular person would put on to visit a neighbor on a Sunday morning. A perfectly pressed camel hair skirt, a fancy white silk blouse with a big ribbon, and a dark blue-gray jacket with a gold pin adorning the collar. The pin had a jewel embedded in it, which I took to be a real diamond. The whole outfit seemed rather too fashionable to wear behind the wheel of a Toyota Prius. But who was I to say? Toyota's director of marketing would likely have a very different opinion.

Mariye was dressed as usual. The same old varsity jacket, her hole-studded jeans, and a pair of white sneakers even dirtier than the ones she usually wore (the backs of these were stomped flat).

When they were heading out the door, Mariye looked back and gave me a wink, a secret sign that said "See you later." I flashed a quick smile in response.

When Shoko and Mariye had gone, I went to the living room, lay down on the sofa, and slept. I had no appetite, so I skipped lunch. It was a brief nap, about thirty minutes, deep and dreamless. I was grateful for that. It was more than a little scary to think what I might do in my dreams, and even scarier to think *what I might become.*

My mood that Sunday afternoon was as unfocused as the weather. It was a quiet, slightly overcast day with no wind to speak of. I read a little, listened to a little music, cooked a little, but nothing helped me work out my feelings. It promised to be one of those afternoons where nothing gets resolved. Giving up, I ran a hot bath, got in, and soaked for a long time. I tried to remember the names of the characters in Dostoevsky's *The Possessed.* I was able to come up with seven, including Kirillov. For some reason, since my high school days I've had a knack for memorizing lengthy Russian names. Maybe now was a good opportunity to go back and reread *The Possessed.* I was free, with time on my hands and nothing that had to be done. The perfect conditions for reading long Russian classics.

I thought about Yuzu some more. Her belly would probably be showing after seven months. I pictured how that would look. What would she be doing now? What would she be thinking? Was she happy? Of course, I had no way to know any of those things.

Perhaps it was as Masahiko had said. Perhaps, like a nineteenth-century Russian intellectual, I should do something out-and-out crazy just to prove I was a free man. But what? Something like . . . spend an hour shut up at the bottom of a pitch-black pit? *That* was what Menshiki had done. True, his actions might not fit the category "out-and-out crazy." But they were definitely beyond the pale, to put it mildly.

It was after four when Mariye showed up. The doorbell rang, I opened the door, and there she was. She slipped through the half-open door like a wisp of cloud and looked around warily.

"No one's here."

"Nobody's here, that's true," I said.

"Someone was here yesterday."

That was a question. "Yes, a friend of mine stayed over," I said.

"A man."

"Yes, a man. A male friend. But how did you know?"

"There was an old car I'd never seen before parked in front of your house. It looked like a black box."

That would be Masahiko's ancient Volvo station wagon, what he called his "Swedish lunch box." Convenient for hauling reindeer carcasses.

"So you came yesterday."

Mariye nodded. It appeared that she was using her passageway to come and check on the house whenever she had time. She'd probably been doing this since long before my arrival. After all, it was her playground. Or "hunting ground" might be more accurate. I was just someone who had chanced to move in. In which case, could she have come face-to-face with Tomohiko Amada at some point? I had to ask her about that sometime.

I led her into the living room. We sat down together, she on the sofa, me in the armchair. I offered her something to drink, but she said no.

"The guy who stayed over is a friend from my college days," I said.

"A good friend?"

"I think so," I said. "In fact, he may be the only person I can call a true friend."

Such a good friend that he could introduce his colleague to my wife and keep me in the dark when they started sleeping together—a situation that had led to my just concluded divorce—without casting a cloud over our relationship. To call us friends would hardly be stretching the truth.

"Do you have any good friends?" I asked her.

Mariye didn't answer. In fact, she didn't bat an eye, just acted as if she hadn't heard what I'd said. I guessed it was something I shouldn't have asked.

"Mr. Menshiki isn't a good friend of yours," she said. I knew it was a question, though her intonation was flat. *Do you mean Mr. Menshiki isn't a good friend of yours?* was what she meant.

"As I've told you," I said, "I haven't known Mr. Menshiki long enough to call him a real friend. I started talking with him after I moved here, and that was only six months ago. It takes longer than that for people to become close. Still, he strikes me as a very interesting person."

"Interesting."

"How can I explain? His disposition strikes me as a little different than the average guy. Maybe more than a little, actually. He's not an easy person to figure out."

"Disposition."

"Personality. The traits that make a person who they are."

Mariye stared at me for a while. As if selecting the exact words she ought to use.

"He can see my home from his deck—it's right across the valley."

It took me a moment to respond to that. "Yes, you're right. That's the lay of the land. But he can see my house just as clearly. Not yours alone."

"Still, I think that man is *spying on* us."

"What do you mean, spying on you?"

"He's got something like a pair of big binoculars on the terrace, though he hides them with a cover. They're on a kind of tripod. He can see us really clearly if he uses those."

So the girl found him out, I thought. Watchful, observant. Eyes that missed nothing of importance.

"So you think that Mr. Menshiki has been observing you through those binoculars?"

Mariye gave a terse nod.

I took a deep breath, then let it out. "Still, that's just a guess on your part, right? They don't necessarily mean he's peeking into your house. He could be observing the moon and stars."

Mariye's gaze didn't waver. "I've had this feeling like I'm *being watched*," she said. "For a while. But I didn't know who was watching me, or from where. But now I know. It's *that person,* for sure."

I took another long, slow breath. Mariye's supposition was on the money. Menshiki was watching her through his high-powered military binoculars on a nightly basis. Yet to my knowledge—and this was not to defend Menshiki—his motives for being a peeping Tom were far from nefarious. He just wanted to see the girl. This beautiful thirteen-year-old girl who might be his biological daughter. For that reason, and that reason alone, he had purchased the mansion on the other side of the valley. Wresting it from the family living there and booting them out. Yet I couldn't reveal that to Mariye.

"Let's say you're right," I said. "But then what's his motive? Why is he so fixated on your home?"

"I don't know. Maybe he has a crush on my aunt."

"Has a crush on your aunt?"

She gave a brief shrug of her shoulders.

Mariye couldn't imagine she was the target. She hadn't yet reached the stage where she could see herself as an object of male desire. I found it strange, yet I didn't dare call her version of events into question. If that was how she read the situation, better perhaps to let it ride.

"I think Mr. Menshiki is hiding something," Mariye said.

"What, for example?"

"My aunt is seeing Mr. Menshiki," she said, not answering my question. "They met twice this week." Her tone suggested that she was passing on highly sensitive state secrets.

"On dates?"

"I think she went to his house."

"Alone?"

"She left a little after noon and didn't return until late."

"But you can't be sure she went to Mr. Menshiki's, can you?"

"I can tell," she said.

"How can you tell?"

"My aunt doesn't leave the house that much," she said. "Sure, she'll volunteer at the library or go shopping, but then she doesn't take a long shower, or paint her nails, or put on perfume and her fanciest underwear."

"You really have sharp eyes, don't you," I said, impressed. "You see everything. But are you sure the man she's meeting is Mr. Menshiki? Couldn't it be someone else?"

Mariye narrowed her eyes at me. She gave a small shake of her head. As in, *Do you think I'm that stupid?* After all, under the circumstances it was unlikely to be anyone but Menshiki. And Mariye was anything but stupid.

"So your aunt spends quite a bit of time at Mr. Menshiki's house, just the two of them together."

Mariye nodded.

"And the two of them—how should I put this?—are engaged in what we might call a very intimate relationship."

She nodded again. "Yes, a very intimate relationship," she said, her cheeks turning a faint pink.

"But you're in school all day. Not at home. So how can you know these things?"

"I can tell. I can tell that much from a woman's face."

But I couldn't tell. Yuzu had carried on an extended affair while we were living together, and I was clueless. Looking back, I should have been able to figure out that much. How could a thirteen-year-old girl pick up on something I couldn't that quickly?

"So things really moved fast between those two, didn't they," I said.

"My aunt's no dummy—there's nothing wrong with her head. But her heart has a weak spot. And Mr. Menshiki is stronger than normal people. A lot stronger—she's no match for him."

She's probably right, I thought. Menshiki did have some special power. Once he made his move, it would be almost impossible for an average person to resist. Myself included. I doubted he would find it difficult to make a woman his, if that was his goal.

"So you're worried about your aunt, right? That Mr. Menshiki is using her for some reason."

Mariye swept her hair back with her hand, exposing her ear. It was small and white, and its shape was lovely. She nodded.

"But it's not that easy to stop a relationship of this sort once it's gotten started," I said.

Not that easy at all, I said to myself. It would move forward, crushing everything in its path, like the Hindus' great wheel of karma. There could be no turning back.

"That's why I had to talk to you," Mariye said. Then she looked me square in the eye.

When it began to get dark, I took my flashlight and walked Mariye almost as far as her passageway. She said she had to be home by dinner. They usually ate around seven.

She had come to ask me for advice. Yet I hadn't been able to offer anything useful. All I could tell her was to wait and see how things developed. I knew Menshiki and Shoko might be having sex, but they were two unmarried and consenting adults. What was I supposed to do? Sure, I had some background information, but I couldn't reveal it, not to Mariye, and not to her aunt. That meant that I couldn't give useful advice to anyone. I was like a boxer trying to fight with his best arm tied behind his back.

Mariye and I walked side by side through the woods, hardly exchanging a word. We had gone partway along the path when she reached down and took my hand. Her hand was small, but its grip was unexpectedly firm. I was surprised at first, but then I had often walked this way with my sister, so it didn't put me off. Instead, it felt normal, a kind of return to my youth.

Mariye's hand was very smooth to the touch. Warm but not at all sweaty. She must have been thinking about something, for her hand squeezed mine and relaxed, squeezed and relaxed, depending, I guess, on what she was thinking. My sister had done the same thing back in the old days.

When we reached the shrine, she let go of my hand and, without a word, circled around to the back. I followed her.

The pampas grass still bore the tread marks of the backhoe. Within lay the silent pit. Its cover was made of sturdy boards, weighted down by a row of stones. I shone my flashlight on them to confirm that they hadn't been moved. They hadn't.

"Is it okay if I look in?" Mariye asked me.

"Just look."

"Just look," Mariye said.

I set some of the stones to the side and removed one of the boards. Mariye knelt and peered through the opening. I trained the flashlight on the floor of the pit. Of course, nobody was there. Only a metal ladder leaning against the wall. If one so chose, one could use it to climb down and then back up again. It would be next to impossible to get out without the ladder, although the pit was less than nine feet deep. The walls were just too smooth and slick to be scaled.

Holding her hair back with one hand, Mariye stared inside the pit for a long time. Intently, as if searching for something in the dark. I had no idea what was down there to capture her attention.

"Who built this?" she asked, looking up at last.

"I don't know. At first I thought it might be a well, but now I'm not so sure. I mean, who would dig a well in such an out-of-the-way place? Anyway, it looks very old. And it's very well put together. It must have taken a long time to build."

Mariye looked at me steadily without saying anything.

"This area has been your playground for quite a while, hasn't it?" I said.

She nodded.

"But you didn't know this pit was behind the shrine until recently."

She shook her head. No, she hadn't known.

"You found it and opened it, didn't you?" she asked.

"That's right, I may have been the one who discovered it. I didn't know it was a pit, but I figured *something* had to be under that pile of rocks. The person who arranged for the rocks to be moved and the pit to be opened, though, was Mr. Menshiki." I wanted to let her in on this much, at least. It was better to be honest.

A bird cried in the trees. It was a sharp, piercing call, as if to warn its fellow creatures. I looked up but couldn't catch sight of it. All I could see were the layered branches of the leafless trees. And beyond those the evening sky of approaching winter, flat, expressionless, and gray.

Mariye winced slightly. But she didn't respond.

"It's hard to explain," I said. "I felt as if the pit was demanding that someone open it. And that I had been bidden to perform that task."

"Bidden?"

"Invited. Called upon to."

She looked up at me. "It wanted you to open it?"

"Yes."

"*This pit* asked you to open it?"

"It could have been anyone, perhaps. Maybe I just happened to be around."

"But it was Mr. Menshiki who actually did it."

"Yes. I brought him here. I couldn't have uncovered it without him. The rocks were too heavy to move by hand, and I didn't have the cash to bring in heavy equipment. It was a fortunate coincidence."

"Maybe you shouldn't have done it," she said after a moment's thought. "I think I told you that before."

"So you think I should have left it as it was?"

Mariye didn't answer immediately. She stood up and brushed the dirt off the knees of her jeans. Not once but several times. She and I replaced the board, and the stones that held it down. Once again, I committed their location to memory.

"Yes, I think so," she said at last, lightly rubbing her palms against each other.

"I think this place may have had some kind of religious background. There might be legends or stories connected to it."

Mariye shook her head. She didn't know of any. "Maybe my father knows something."

The whole area had been owned by her father's family since before the Meiji period. The adjoining mountain was also in their hands. He might have a good idea of what the pit and shrine meant.

"Could you ask him?"

Mariye winced slightly. "I'll try," she said in a small voice. She hesitated. "If I have a chance."

"It would be a big help if we knew who built it when, and for what purpose."

"Maybe they shut up something inside, and put heavy stones on top to make sure it didn't get out," she offered.

"So you think maybe they heaped on the stones to prevent whatever it was from escaping, and then built the little shrine to ward off its curse?"

"Maybe."

"And then we went and pried it open anyway."

Mariye gave a small shrug.

I accompanied her to where the woods ended. She'd go on from there by herself, she said. The darkness was no problem—she knew the way. She wanted no one to see the passage that led to her home. It was a shortcut that she alone should know. So I turned back, leaving her there. Only a glimmer of light remained in the sky. The cold blackness was descending.

The same bird made the same piercing call when I passed before the shrine. This time, though, I didn't look up. I headed straight home, leaving the shrine behind. As I prepared dinner I sipped a glass of Chivas Regal and water. There was only enough left in the bottle for one more drink. The night was deathly silent. As if the clouds were absorbing every living sound.

You shouldn't have opened the pit.

Perhaps Mariye was right. I should have steered clear of the pit. It seemed that everything I did these days was off the mark.

I imagined Menshiki making love to Shoko. The two of them naked, entwined on a big bed in a room somewhere in that sprawling white mansion. That event was taking place in another world, of course, one that bore no connection to me. Yet the thought of the two of them together left me bereft. As if I were standing in a station watching a long, empty train pass by.

Finally, I fell asleep and my Sunday ended. A deep dreamless sleep, undisturbed by anyone.

45

SOMETHING IS ABOUT TO HAPPEN

Of the two paintings I was working on, *The Pit in the Woods* was the one I knocked off first. It was Friday afternoon when I finished it. Paintings are strange things: as they near the end they acquire their own will, their own viewpoint, even their own powers of speech. They tell the artist when they are done (at least that's the way it works for me). A spectator to the process—if one is present—can't tell the difference between a painting in process and a completed painting, for the line is virtually invisible to the naked eye. But the artist knows. He or she can hear the painting say, *Hands off, I'm done.* The artist has only to heed that voice.

So it was with *The Pit in the Woods.* At a certain point, it announced itself finished and refused my brush. Like a sexually satisfied woman. I took the canvas from the easel and leaned it against the wall. Then I sat down on the floor and regarded it at length. My painting of a half-covered hole in the ground.

I couldn't pin down my motive for painting it, or its meaning. It had just grabbed me. I couldn't come up with anything beyond that. These things happen. When something strikes me in that way—a landscape, an object, a person—I pick up my brush and am off to the races. No meaning, no motive. I just go where my gut tells me, pure and simple.

But wait, I thought. This time was different. This wasn't mere impulse. *Something* had demanded that I paint this painting. Urgently. That was why I had finished it so quickly—whatever it was, that demand had fired me up, sent me to my easel, and propelled me forward, like a hand on my back. Or maybe the pit was the agent, pushing me to draw its portrait, leaving me to guess its motive. In the same way that Menshiki, likely in pursuit of some larger plan, had enlisted me to paint his portrait.

Judged in a fair and objective way, the painting wasn't bad. I couldn't tell whether it could be called a work of art or not. (Not to make excuses, but I hadn't begun with that goal in mind.) From the standpoint of pure technique, though, it was a success. The composition was flawless, and I had captured both the light streaming through the trees and the colors of the fallen leaves. It was realistic right down to its tiniest detail, yet, nevertheless, a mysterious, symbolic aura hovered over it.

As I sat there staring at the finished work, a feeling came over me, what might be called a *premonition of impending movement*. On the surface at least, it was just as its title said: a landscape painting of the pit in the woods. It was so accurate, in fact, that "reproduction" might be closer to the truth. As someone who had been developing his craft, however imperfectly, for so long, I had the artistic skill to reproduce an exact likeness of the scene on canvas. I had not painted the scene so much as I had *documented* it.

Nevertheless, that *premonition* was there. Something was about to take place within that landscape. The painting was telling me that. Then I realized. What I had been trying to get across, or what that *something* had been trying to get me to paint, was precisely that premonition, those signs.

Sitting there on the floor, I straightened my back and looked at the painting anew.

What was about to happen? Was someone or something about to come crawling out from the darkness that lay beneath the half-open cover? Or, conversely, was someone about to climb down into the hole? Though I looked long and hard, I couldn't guess what would take place. I only knew some sort of movement was about to occur. The strength of my premonition left no doubt.

Why did the pit so badly want me to paint it? To try to tell me something? To warn me? It was a game of riddles. So many riddles, and not a single answer. I wanted to show the painting to Mariye and hear what she had to say. Maybe she could see what I couldn't.

. . .

Friday was the day I taught drawing near Odawara Station. Mariye was one of the students, so she would be there. Perhaps I could have a word with her afterward. I hopped in my car and headed to town.

There was still plenty of time when I arrived, so I parked and went to get my customary cup of coffee. No gleaming, functional Starbucks for me—my coffee shop was untouched by time, a back-alley spot run by a man on the cusp of old age who served a jet-black, muddy brew in a cup that weighed a ton. Jazz from a former era played on the ancient speakers. Billie Holiday, Clifford Brown, and other classics. As I still had time to spare when I finished my coffee, I wandered down the shopping street. I was low on coffee filters, so I bought a pack. I found a used-record store, and browsed through their old LPs. I realized I hadn't listened to anything other than classical music for a very long time. Tomohiko Amada's shelves contained no other kinds of records. If I listened to the radio, it was only to catch the news and weather on the AM dial (my location meant almost no FM reception).

I had left my records and CDs—not that there were a lot of them—in the Hiroo apartment. It would have been painful to sort out which books and records belonged to Yuzu and which to me. Impossible, really. Who did Bob Dylan's *Nashville Skyline* belong to? How about the Doors album with "Alabama Song" on it? What difference did it make who had shelled out the money? We'd shared the same music for a period of time, lived our life together listening to it. Even if we had been able to divide the records, we could never have separated the memories attached to them. I had to leave them all behind.

I looked for *Nashville Skyline* and the first album by the Doors, but couldn't find either. They may have been available on CD, but I wanted to hear them on an old-style phonograph. There was no CD player in Tomohiko Amada's house anyway. And no cassette deck. Just a couple of record players. Tomohiko Amada likely had no interest in new technology. He'd probably never come within six feet of a microwave oven.

In the end, I bought two records. Bruce Springsteen's *The River* and a collection of duets by Roberta Flack and Donny Hathaway. Both were old favorites of mine. At some point in my life, I had given up on new music. Instead, I listened to the old stuff over and over again. Books were the same. I reread books from my past, often more than once, but ignored books that had just come out. Somewhere along the way, time seemed to have come to a screeching halt.

Perhaps time really had stopped. Then again, maybe it kept nudging forward despite the fact that evolution, or anything resembling it, had ended. Like a restaurant approaching closing time that has stopped taking orders. And I was the only one who hadn't figured it out.

The shop assistant put the two records in a bag, and I paid. Then I went to a nearby liquor store to buy some whiskey. I wasn't sure what to get, but finally settled on Chivas Regal. It was a little more expensive, but would be a big hit with Masahiko the next time he stopped by.

My starting time for class was approaching, so I stashed the records, coffee filters, and whiskey in my car and entered the building where classes were held. The kids were first, starting at five o'clock. Mariye was part of that group. But I couldn't spot her. This was a first. She was passionate about the class, had never skipped it before, as far as I knew. Her absence unsettled me. I found it somehow alarming, even threatening. Was she all right? Was she ill, or had something unexpected happened to her?

Nevertheless, I carried on as though nothing was wrong, assigning simple exercises, offering comments on each child's drawing, giving advice. When class ended, the children went home and the adult class began. It too passed without incident. I exchanged good-natured pleasantries with the people there (hardly my strong point, but I can do it when required). After that, I had a brief meeting with the workshop organizer about future plans. He had no idea why Mariye was absent. There had been no word from her family.

After work, I went to a nearby noodle shop and ate a hot bowl of tempura soba. This too was my weekly habit. Always the same shop, and always tempura soba. One of life's little pleasures. Then I drove back to my house on the mountain. It was almost nine when I arrived.

I couldn't tell if anyone had tried to contact me while I was gone, for there was no answering machine (such a "clever" device probably numbered among Tomohiko Amada's bêtes noires). I gave the simple, old-fashioned telephone a long look, but it didn't speak. It just sat there, in black silence.

I had a long soak in a hot bath. Then I poured what was left of the original bottle of Chivas Regal into a glass, added two ice cubes from the fridge, and took the drink to the living room, where I sipped it while listening to one of the records I had just bought. At first, it seemed somehow *inappropriate* to be playing anything other than classical in my mountaintop domicile. The air in the room had been conditioned to that type of music for a very long time. Still, I was playing my music, so that now, song by song, a familiarity overcame the feeling of inappropriateness. As I listened, I could feel my body start to relax. I must have been tense without being aware of it.

The A side of the Roberta Flack and Donny Hathaway record had ended and the first song on the B side ("For All We Know," a really cool performance) had just begun when the phone rang. The clock said 10:30. Who on earth would be calling me so late? I didn't want to answer. Yet the ring sounded urgent. I put down my glass, rose from the sofa, lifted the needle off the record, and picked up the phone.

"Hello?" It was Shoko Akikawa.

I greeted her.

"I'm so terribly sorry to be phoning this late," she said. I had never heard her sound so anxious. "But I needed to ask you something. Mariye didn't show up at art class today, did she?"

No, I replied, she didn't. The question was a strange one. Normally, Mariye came straight from school (the public junior high in the area) in her uniform. When class ended, her aunt picked her up in the car, and the two went home together. That pattern never varied.

"I haven't seen Mariye anywhere," Shoko said.

"Haven't seen her?"

"She's missing."

"Since what time?" I asked.

"Since this morning, when she left for school. I offered to drive her to the station, but she said she'd walk. She likes walking. Much more than riding in the car. So I give her a lift when she's running late, but otherwise she walks down the hill to the bus stop and takes the bus to the station. This morning she left the house at seven thirty, as usual."

Shoko said all this in a single breath, then stopped. I could hear her trying to control her breathing. I used the pause to put what she had just told me into some kind of order.

"Today is Friday," Shoko continued. "When school lets out on Fridays, she goes directly to art class. And then I pick her up afterward. But today Mariye said she'd take the bus home instead. So I didn't go. When she says something like that, it's pointless to argue. But she still gets back by seven or seven thirty. Then she has dinner. But tonight, it turned to eight and then eight thirty and she still hadn't returned. So I called the center and asked whether she had come to class or not. They checked and said she hadn't shown up. That's when I got really worried. Now it's ten thirty and she's still not back. I've heard nothing. That's why I'm calling you—I thought perhaps you might know something."

"I haven't a clue where she is," I said. "I was rather surprised when I showed up for class and Mariye wasn't there. She's never skipped before."

Shoko gave a deep sigh. "My brother's not back yet. I don't know when to expect him—he hasn't contacted me. I'm not sure if he'll return tonight or not. I'm here all alone, and I don't know what to do."

"She was wearing her school uniform when she left this morning, correct?"

"Yes, she left in her uniform, with a bag over her shoulder. The same as always. A blazer and skirt. I don't know if she ever made it to school, though. It's late, so there's no way to check. But I'm quite sure she got there. The school contacts us if there's an unexplained absence. She was carrying enough money for a single day's expenses, no more. I make her take a cell phone just in case, but it's been shut off all day. She doesn't like cell phones. She'll use hers to call me, but she usually keeps it off the rest of the time. I've warned her about that over and over, begged her not to turn it off, explained that we may need to reach her if something important comes up, but she doesn't—"

"Has this ever happened before? Her coming home late?"

"This is the first time, really. Mariye is very dependable. She has no close friends she hangs out with, and once she's agreed to do something, she follows through, even though she doesn't like school all that much. She won a prize for perfect attendance in elementary school. She always comes straight home after school. She never loiters along the way."

Mariye's aunt was clearly in the dark about her nighttime forays.

"Was there anything she said or did this morning that was out of the ordinary?"

"No, nothing. It was a regular morning. The same as always. She drinks a glass of warm milk, eats a slice of toast, and heads out the door. Every day is identical. I made her breakfast today as I usually do. She didn't say a great deal. But that's normal. She can talk a blue streak once she gets started, but most of the time, you can't get much out of her."

I was beginning to worry. It was almost eleven at night, and it was pitch dark outside. The moon was hiding behind the clouds. What on earth had happened to Mariye Akikawa?

"I'll wait one more hour. If Mariye still hasn't contacted me by then, I'll call the police," Shoko said.

"That's a good idea," I said. "And let me know if there's anything I can do. Any time is all right—please don't hesitate, no matter how late it is."

Shoko thanked me and hung up. I drained what was left of the whiskey and washed the glass in the sink.

After that I went to the studio. I turned on all the lights and stood there in the bright room, taking another lingering look at my unfinished *Portrait of Mariye Akikawa* on the easel. It was close to done—only a little work remained. It showed a version of what a quiet thirteen-year-old girl would ideally look like. Yet there were other elements too, aspects of her that could not be seen, that made her who she was. What I was attempting in all my painting—though not, of course, in the portraits I did on commission—was to try to capture those things which lay outside my field of vision and communicate their message in a different form. Mariye was, in that sense, a most fascinating subject. There was just so much that was hidden, like a trompe l'oeil. And now as of this morning she herself had disappeared. As if swallowed by that very trompe l'oeil.

I turned to look again at *The Pit in the Woods* leaning against the wall. I had just completed it that afternoon. I could feel that painting calling out to me too, though in another way, and from a different direction, than *A Portrait of Mariye Akikawa*.

Something is about to happen. I felt this again as I looked at the landscape. Until that afternoon it had been a premonition of sorts, but now it was encroaching on reality. *The movement was already under way.* Mariye's disappearance and the pit in the woods were linked in some way. I could sense it. By finishing the painting I had set the gears in motion. And Mariye's vanishing act was the likely result.

Yet I could tell Shoko none of this. All that would do was confuse her even more.

I went back to the kitchen and rinsed the whiskey taste from my mouth with several glasses of water. When that was done, I picked up the phone and called Menshiki. I called three times before he picked up. I detected a slight edge to his voice, as if he were waiting for an important call. That it was me on the line seemed to surprise him. It only took a second, though, for the edge to disappear and the voice to turn cool and collected, as always.

"I'm very sorry to call so late," I said.

"Not at all. I stay up late, and I've got plenty of time. I'm always happy to hear your voice."

Skipping the normal pleasantries, I gave him a brief report of Mariye's disappearance. The girl had left home for school in the morning but hadn't returned. Nor had she shown up at my painting class. The news seemed to throw Menshiki for a loop. He took a moment to reply.

"And you have no idea where she might have gone, right?" he asked me.

"None at all," I replied. "It came out of left field. How about you?"

"I have no idea either, of course. She barely says a word to me."

There was no anger or regret in his voice. He was simply relating the way she treated him.

"That's just how she is—she's like that with everybody," I said. "But Shoko is at her wit's end. Mariye's father isn't home either, so she's all alone and unsure what to do."

Menshiki paused again. It was rare to see him at a loss for words—in fact, I had never witnessed it before.

"Is there anything I can do?" he said at last.

"I know it's sudden," I said, "but is there any chance you could drop by now?"

"To your home?"

"Yes. There's something in this connection that I need to talk to you about."

Menshiki took a moment to respond. "All right," he said. "I'll leave right away."

"Are you sure you don't have to take care of a matter there first?"

"It's not big enough to call a 'matter.' It's just a trivial thing," he said. He cleared his throat. He seemed to be checking his watch. "I can be there in about fifteen minutes."

When the phone call ended, I got ready to go out. I laid out a sweater and my leather jacket, and placed the big flashlight within easy reach. Then I sat on the sofa and waited for the purr of Menshiki's Jaguar rolling up the hill.

46

PEOPLE ARE POWERLESS BEFORE A STURDY, TOWERING WALL

Menshiki arrived at eleven twenty. The moment I heard his Jaguar, I slipped on my leather jacket and headed out the door. He stepped from the car wearing a padded, dark-blue windbreaker, narrow-cut black jeans, and leather sneakers. A light scarf was draped around his neck. His mane of white hair glowed in the dark.

"If it's okay, I'd like you to come with me to check out the pit in the woods," I said.

"Of course," Menshiki said. "Do you think it's connected to Mariye's disappearance?"

"I'm not sure. But I've had a premonition for a while that something bad was going to happen. Something connected to that pit."

Menshiki asked no more questions after that. "Fine," he said. "Let's go take a look."

He opened the trunk of his Jaguar and pulled out what looked like a lantern. Then he closed the trunk and set off with me toward the woods. Neither moon nor stars were out, so it was very dark. There was no wind.

"Sorry to ask you to venture out so late," I said. "But it seemed safer to have you come along. If something went wrong, I might not be able to handle it alone."

He patted my arm. As though to encourage me. "It's no trouble at all—I'm happy to do what I can."

We picked our way through the trees, shining the flashlight and lantern on our feet to avoid tripping over the roots. The only sound was the crunch of dry leaves underfoot. Otherwise it was dead silent. I sensed the animals of the woods silently watching us from their hiding places. The dark depths of midnight give rise to illusions like that. Had someone seen us, they might have mistaken us for a pair of grave robbers on their way to ransack a tomb.

"There's just one thing I'd like to ask," Menshiki said.

"What's that?"

"Why do you think Mariye's disappearance and the pit might be connected?"

I explained that she and I had visited the pit together not long before. That she had already known about its existence. That the whole area was her playground. That nothing happened here without her knowledge. Then I told him what she had said: *You should have left the place as it was. You should never have opened it up.*

"When she stood in front of the pit she seemed to have experienced something," I said. "A special feeling . . . I guess you could call it spiritual."

"And she was drawn to it?"

"Yes. She was leery, but at the same time something about the pit was drawing her in. That's why I worry it might have played a role. That she might be down there, unable to get out."

Menshiki thought for a moment. "Did you tell her aunt this?" he asked. "Does Shoko know?"

"No, I haven't said anything yet. If I mentioned the pit to her, I'd have to go back to the beginning. To how we opened it, and why you were involved. It would turn into a very long story, and I doubt I could explain myself very well."

"Yes, it would cause her a lot of needless worry."

"It would be even more awkward if the police got involved. If they grew interested in the pit."

Menshiki looked at me. "Are they investigating already?"

"She hadn't contacted them yet when I talked to her. But she could have put in a search request by now. After all, it's getting pretty late."

Menshiki nodded several times. "Yes, it's only natural. It's almost midnight, and a thirteen-year-old girl hasn't come home. No one knows where she's gone. What can her family do but call the cops?"

I could tell from his tone that Menshiki wasn't too thrilled that the police would be entering the picture.

"Let's keep the pit between ourselves if we can," he said. "The fewer people know, the better. Otherwise we could run into problems." I agreed.

The biggest problem for me was the Commendatore. It was almost impossible to explain the significance of the pit without bringing him—as an Idea, no less—into the mix. Yes, as Menshiki said, mentioning the pit would only make things worse. (And even if I did reveal the existence of the Commendatore, who would believe me? They'd just question my sanity.)

We emerged from the trees in front of the small shrine and circled around to the back. Stepping across the clump of pampas grass, whose plumes still lay cruelly flattened by the backhoe's treads, we arrived at the pit. The first thing we did was shine our lights on the boards covering the hole and the row of stones that held them down. I checked the placement of the stones. The change was subtle, but I could tell they had been moved. Someone had come after Mariye and me, removed the stones and several boards, and then, when they left, tried to return everything to its original position. My eyes could spot that slight difference.

"Someone moved the stones," I said. "There are signs that the pit has been opened."

Menshiki glanced at me. "Do you think it was Mariye?" he asked.

"I wonder. It's not a place anyone would stumble upon, and apart from you and me, she's the only one who knows about it. So the chances are good it was Mariye."

The Commendatore knew about the pit, of course. After all, that was where he had come from. Yet in the end he was an Idea. He had no fixed shape. He wouldn't have had to move those heavy stones if he wanted to go back inside.

We removed the stones and took the boards away. Once again, the hole was exposed. It was perfectly round and not quite six feet across, but it looked bigger now, and blacker, too. I imagined that the darkness was what created the illusion.

Menshiki and I leaned over the hole and directed our lights inside. No one was there. There was nothing at all. Just that empty cylindrical space surrounded by the same stone wall. There was one difference, however. The ladder had vanished. The collapsible metal ladder that the landscaper had considerately left behind after moving the pile of boulders. I had last seen it leaning against the wall of the pit.

"Where did the ladder go?" I wondered out loud.

It didn't take us long to find it lying on its side some distance away in a stand of pampas grass that the backhoe hadn't flattened. Someone had taken it from the hole and chucked it there. It wasn't heavy, so moving it required no great strength. We returned the ladder to the hole and leaned it back against the wall.

"I'm going down to take a look," Menshiki said. "Maybe I'll find something."

"Are you sure you'll be okay?"

"Don't worry, I've been down there before."

Menshiki descended the ladder with ease, lantern in hand.

"By the way, do you know the height of the Berlin Wall?" he asked as he descended.

"No."

"Ten feet," he said looking up at me. "It varied depending on the location, but that was the standard height. A little taller than this hole is deep. It was about a hundred miles long, too. I saw it with my own eyes. When Berlin was still divided into East and West. A pitiful sight."

When Menshiki reached the bottom, he inspected the pit in the light from his lantern. Even then, though, he kept on talking to me.

"Walls were originally erected to protect people. From external enemies, storms, and floods. Sometimes, though, they were used to keep people in. People are powerless before a sturdy, towering wall. Visually and psychologically. Some walls were constructed for that specific purpose."

Menshiki broke off at that point. Holding his lantern aloft, he examined every inch of the wall and the ground. Intently and carefully, like an archaeologist poring over the inner sanctum of an Egyptian pyramid. His lantern was stronger than my flashlight, so it illuminated a much wider area. He seemed to have found something on the floor of the pit, for he knelt down and examined it closely. I couldn't make it out from above, though. Menshiki said nothing. Whatever it was, it must have been very small. He stood up, wrapped it in his handkerchief, and deposited it in the pocket of his windbreaker. He looked up at me.

"I'm coming out," he said, raising his lantern into the air.

"Did you find something?" I asked.

Menshiki didn't answer. Carefully, he ascended the ladder. Each rung gave a dull creak under his weight. I kept close watch, my flashlight trained on him. The vantage point made me realize how well his daily routine had trained his body. Not a motion was wasted. Each muscle played its role perfectly. When he was back on the ground he gave a big stretch and then brushed the dirt from his trousers with care. Not that there was much to brush off.

"You can feel how intimidating the height of those walls is from down there. You really feel powerless. I saw something similar in Palestine a while ago. Israel erected a twenty-five-foot concrete wall there, with high-voltage wires running along the top. That wall is almost three hundred miles long. I guess the Israelis figured ten feet was too low, but that's enough to do the job."

He set the lantern down. Now the ground around our feet was illuminated.

"Come to think of it, the walls of the solitary cells in Tokyo prison measure about ten feet as well," Menshiki said. "I don't know why they made them so high. All you had to look at were those blank walls, day after day. Nothing else to lay your eyes on. No pictures or anything like that, of course. Just those damned walls. You start feeling like you've been thrown into a pit."

I listened in silence.

"I did some time in that place a while back. I haven't told you about that, have I?"

"No, you haven't." My girlfriend had told me he had spent time in prison, but of course I didn't mention that.

"I figure I should be the one to tell you. You know how gossips love to twist facts to spice up their stories. So it's better if I give it to you straight. It's not pretty, but this might be a good time to tell you. In passing, so to speak. Do you mind?"

"Not at all. Tell me."

"I'm not making excuses," he said after a moment's pause, "but I've done nothing to feel guilty about. I've tried my hand at many things in my life. Borne many risks. Still, I'm not stupid, and I am cautious by nature, so I've always been careful to avoid anything illegal. I know where to draw the line. In this case, though, I happened to take on a partner who was careless. Because of him, I suffered a great deal. That experience taught me never to join forces with anyone again. To take responsibility for myself and no one else."

"What were you charged with?"

"Insider trading and tax evasion. What they call 'economic crimes.' I was indicted and tried, but in the end they found me not guilty. All the same, the investigation was grueling, and I spent a pretty long time in prison. They found one reason after another to keep me locked up. I was in there for so long that now being surrounded by walls makes me a little nostalgic. As I said, I had done nothing to warrant punishment. My hands were clean. But the prosecutors had already concocted their scenario, and in it, I was guilty as sin. They had no desire to go back and rewrite it. That's how bureaucracies work. It's practically impossible to change something once it's been decided. Going against the current means that someone, somewhere down the line, has to take responsibility. As a result, I spent a long time in solitary."

"How long?"

"Four hundred and thirty-five days," Menshiki said, as if it were nothing. "A number I'll never forget, no matter how long I live."

It wasn't hard to imagine what spending that much time in solitary meant.

"Have you ever been confined in a small space for a long time?" Menshiki asked me.

"No," I said. My experience being locked in the back of the moving van had given me a bad case of claustrophobia. Now I couldn't even ride in an elevator. I'd fall apart if I were confined as he had been.

"I learned how to endure it," Menshiki said. "I spent the days training myself. In the process, I learned several foreign languages. Spanish, Turkish, and Chinese. They limit how many books you can keep in solitary, but those restrictions don't apply to dictionaries. In that sense, it's the ideal place to study languages. I'm blessed with good powers of concentration, so when I was focused on a language I could forget the walls. There's a bright side to everything."

Even the darkest, thickest cloud shines silver when viewed from above.

Menshiki continued. "What terrified me was the thought of earthquake and fire. Trapped like that, I could never have escaped. Imagining myself crushed or burned to death in that tiny space scared me so much sometimes I couldn't breathe. That was the one fear I couldn't overcome. It woke me up some nights."

"But you got through it."

"Of course. I'd be damned if I'd let those bastards beat me. Or let their system grind me down. If I had signed the papers they laid in front of me, I could have walked out of my cell and returned to the world. But signing them would have meant my utter defeat. I would have admitted to crimes I hadn't committed. So I decided to treat the experience as an ordeal sent from above, an opportunity to test my strength."

"Did you think about your time in prison when you spent that hour alone down in the pit?"

"Yes. I need to return to that experience once in a while—it's my starting point, so to speak. Where the person I am today was formed. It's easy to get soft when life is comfortable."

What a peculiar guy, I thought again. How would another person react to treatment that harsh—wouldn't they try to forget it as soon as possible?

As if remembering, Menshiki reached into the pocket of his windbreaker and pulled out something wrapped in a handkerchief.

"I found this at the bottom of the pit," he said. He unfolded the handkerchief, took out a small plastic object, and handed it to me.

I examined it under my flashlight. It was a black-and-white penguin, barely half an inch long, with a tiny black strap attached to it. The kind of thing that schoolgirls like to attach to their cell phones and schoolbags. It was clean and looked quite new.

"It wasn't there the first time I went into the pit," Menshiki said. "I'm sure of that."

"So it must have been dropped by someone afterward, when they were down there."

"I wonder. It looks like a cell phone ornament. And the strap isn't broken. So someone had to unhook it first. Doesn't that suggest it wasn't dropped—that whoever left it did so intentionally?"

"You mean they entered the pit just to leave it there?"

"Or dropped it down from above."

"Why would anyone do that?" I asked.

Menshiki shook his head. As if he couldn't understand either. "It's possible that whoever it was left it as a charm or talisman. That's just a guess, though."

"You mean Mariye?"

"Probably. After all, it's doubtful anyone else was near the pit."

"So she left it as a kind of charm?"

Menshiki shook his head again. "I don't know," he said. "It's hard to read a thirteen-year-old girl—their minds can come up with all sorts of stuff, can't they?"

I looked again at the tiny penguin in my hand. Now it struck me as a charm or amulet of some kind. An aura of innocence clung to it.

"Then who pulled out the ladder and dragged it over there? What was the reason for that?" I said.

Menshiki shook his head again. He had no idea either.

"Anyway," I said, "let's call Shoko when we get back and find out if Mariye has a penguin charm on her cell phone. She should know one way or the other."

"You hold on to the penguin for now," Menshiki said. I nodded and put it in my trouser pocket.

We replaced the boards, leaving the ladder resting against the wall of the pit. When we put the stones back I registered their exact positions in my mind. Then we headed home through the woods along the same path we had come on. I glanced at my watch—it was already past midnight. We said nothing, just shone our lights on our feet. We were both lost in thought.

As soon as we got back, Menshiki went to his Jaguar, opened the big trunk, and placed the lantern inside. Then he shut the trunk and, as if finally allowing himself to relax, leaned against it and looked up at the sky. The black sky in which nothing was visible.

"Do you mind if I come in for a few minutes?" he said. "It'd be hard for me to relax at home."

"By all means. I don't think I can sleep yet either."

Menshiki's eyes were still fixed on the sky. He seemed lost in thought.

"I can't explain why," I said, "but I can't get rid of this feeling that something bad is happening to Mariye. And that she's nearby."

"But not in the pit, right?"

"I guess not."

"What kind of bad thing?" Menshiki asked.

"That I don't know. But I feel she's in some kind of physical danger."

"And that the danger is lurking *somewhere close to here*, right?"

"Right," I said. "Near here. And it bothers me that the ladder was removed from the pit. Who took it, and why did they hide it in the grass? What does it all mean?"

Menshiki stood up and gave me another pat on the shoulder. "You're right. I don't know either. But worrying about it won't get us anywhere. Let's go inside."

47

"IT IS NOW FRIDAY, IS IT NOT?"

The moment we walked in the house I threw off my leather jacket and called Shoko. She picked up on the third ring.

"Anything new?" I asked.

"Mariye still hasn't called." I could hear her struggling to breathe normally.

"Have you contacted the police?"

"No, not yet. It still feels too early somehow. I keep thinking she'll come wandering in the door . . ."

I described the plastic penguin we had found at the bottom of the pit. Without detailing how we'd found it, I asked if Mariye carried such an object with her.

"Yes, Mariye had a penguin attached to her cell phone. It was a penguin, I'm sure . . . yes. A penguin. Without doubt. A tiny plastic figurine. She got it in a donut shop. It came free with her order, but she treasured it. As if it were a kind of protective charm."

"And she carried her phone wherever she went, correct?"

"Yes. It was turned off most of the time, but she always had it with her, yes. She didn't receive calls, but occasionally she'd call to let me know when something came up." Shoko paused for a moment. "Did you find it somewhere?"

I struggled to come up with an answer. If I told the truth, I'd have to tell her about the pit in the woods. If the police got involved, I would have to explain it to them as well—in a way they could swallow. Since the penguin was something she carried, they would comb the pit, even search the whole woods for further evidence. I would get the third degree, and Menshiki's past would be brought into it. I couldn't see how any of that would help. As Menshiki had said, it would just complicate things.

"I found it in the studio," I said. I hated to lie, but I had to. "When I was sweeping the floor. I thought that it might be Mariye's."

"Yes, it's hers. I'm sure," said the girl's aunt. "But then what should I do? Should I call the police?"

"Have you heard from your brother—I mean, Mariye's father?"

"No, I haven't been able to reach him," she said hesitantly. "I have no idea where he is. He's not someone who follows a regular schedule—I'm never sure if he's coming home or not."

The situation sounded complicated, but now wasn't the time to worry about that. I simply told her to inform the police of Mariye's disappearance. It was after midnight, and the date had changed. It was possible that Mariye had been in some kind of accident. She said she'd call them right away.

"So Mariye still isn't answering her cell phone?"

"No, she isn't answering, though I've called her many times. It seems to be turned off. Or the batteries are dead. One or the other."

"She left this morning for school, and she's been missing ever since. Right?"

"That's right."

"Which means she should be in her school uniform, correct?"

"Yes, she should be. A navy-blue blazer and vest, a white blouse, a knee-length plaid skirt, white socks, and black loafers. Oh, and a plastic shoulder bag with the school's name and emblem on it. She wasn't wearing a coat."

"Didn't she have another bag for her art supplies?"

"She keeps that in her locker at school. She uses it when they have art class, and then takes it to your class on Fridays. She doesn't bring it from home."

That was the outfit she always wore to my class—blue jacket, white blouse, tartan plaid skirt, plastic shoulder bag, and a white canvas bag with her paints and brushes. I could picture her perfectly.

"Was she carrying anything else?"

"No, not today. So I doubt she was going very far."

"Please call me if you hear anything," I said. "Any time of the day or night."

She said she would.

I hung up the phone.

Menshiki was standing beside me throughout this conversation. Only after I put down the phone did he shed his windbreaker. Underneath was a black V-neck sweater.

"So the penguin was Mariye's after all," Menshiki said.

"Seems so."

"In which case, it's likely that she went into the pit at some point—we don't know when—and left her treasured penguin there. That's what we have so far."

"So you think she left it there on purpose, as a protective talisman."

"Probably."

"But if that's so, who or what was it protecting?"

Menshiki shook his head. "I'm not sure. But it was clearly her lucky charm. So she must have left it behind for a reason. People don't part with things they value so easily."

"Unless it's to protect something they value more than themselves."

"For example?" Menshiki said.

Neither of us could answer that one.

We sat there in silence. Slowly but surely, the hands of the clock inched ahead. Each tick pushed the world that much further forward. Outside the window stretched a vast darkness. Nothing moved there. It seemed nothing could.

I suddenly recalled what the Commendatore had said about the missing bell. "The bell was never mine alone. It belonged to the place, to be shared by everyone. So if it disappeared there must have been a reason for it."

Belonged to the place?

"Just maybe Mariye didn't leave this penguin in the pit. Couldn't the pit be connected to some other location? Perhaps it isn't a sealed-off space but a conduit of some kind. If that's the case, it might be able to summon all sorts of things."

That is what I had been thinking, but said aloud it sounded ludicrous. The Commendatore might have understood. But not anyone from *this world*.

A deep silence settled over the room.

"So what could the bottom of the pit be connected to?" Menshiki said at last, as if addressing himself. "Remember, not so long ago I spent an hour alone down there. In the dark, without a light or a ladder. I tried to use the silence to focus my mind. To extinguish my physical existence and become pure consciousness. I figured if I could do that, I could transcend those stone walls and go wherever I liked. I used to try the same sort of thing when I was in solitary. But I couldn't find a way out of the pit. In the end, those walls allowed me no escape."

Perhaps the pit chose whom it wanted, I thought. The Commendatore had come to me when he left the pit. Chosen me as his lodgings, so to speak. Mariye too might have been chosen. But the pit hadn't chosen Menshiki—for whatever reason.

"In any case," I said, "we're agreed—we won't tell the police about the pit. At *this* stage, anyway. Still, we're clearly concealing evidence if we keep our mouths shut about finding the penguin there. If they find that out, we could be in a sticky position."

Menshiki thought for a moment. "So we'll keep our lips sealed—that's all there is to it!" he said at last. "You found it on your studio floor. We'll go with that."

"Maybe one of us should be with Shoko," I said. "She's home by herself with no idea what to do. Lost and confused. She's heard nothing from Mariye's father. Doesn't she need someone there?"

Menshiki furrowed his brow. "I'm in no position to do that," he said at last, shaking his head. "Her brother and I are total strangers, so if he came back . . ."

Menshiki lapsed into silence.

I had nothing to say either.

Menshiki sat there, lightly drumming his fingers on the arm of the sofa. Whatever he was thinking brought a slight flush to his cheeks.

“Would you mind if I stayed a little longer?” he asked a while later. “Shoko may try to get in touch with us.”

“By all means, please do,” I said. “I don’t think I’ll be going to bed any time soon. Stay as long as you like. You can sleep here too. I’ll lay out some bedding for you.”

Menshiki said he might take me up on my offer.

“Shall I make coffee?” I asked.

“Sounds good,” Menshiki said.

I went to the kitchen, ground the beans, and started the coffee maker. When the coffee was ready, I took it out to the living room. Then Menshiki and I drank it together.

“I think I’ll build a fire,” I said. The room had grown markedly colder once midnight passed. It was already December. An appropriate time for the first fire of the season.

I filled the cast-iron grate in the fireplace with the small stack of firewood I had set aside in the corner of the living room. Then I inserted paper under the grate and lit a match. The wood appeared to be dry, for it caught right away. I was worried that the fireplace might back up—Masahiko had said it was set to go, but you never knew until you used it. A bird could have nested in the chimney. Fortunately, however, it worked beautifully. We moved our chairs in front of the fireplace and sat there in the warmth.

“Nothing beats a wood fire,” Menshiki said.

I thought of offering him some whiskey but changed my mind. Tonight we should stay sober. Who knows, we might have to drive somewhere. So we listened to records and watched the flames dance. Menshiki selected a Beethoven violin sonata and put it on the turntable. Georg Kulenkampff on violin, with Wilhelm Kempff on piano. Perfect music for an early-winter night before a fire. It was hard to enjoy it, though, with Mariye out there shivering in the cold.

Shoko called half an hour later. Her brother had just come home and had already contacted the police. They would be there any moment to investigate. (The Akikawas were an old and wealthy family in the area, so the possibility that it was a kidnapping was making them move quickly.) There was no word from Mariye, and calling her cell phone still didn't work. They had contacted every likely person they could think of (there weren't that many) with no luck. No one knew where Mariye had gone.

"Let's hope she's all right," I said. I asked her to let me know if there was any progress, and hung up the phone.

We sat before the fire and listened to another record. Richard Strauss's Oboe Concerto. Menshiki plucked that off the shelf as well. It was the first time I had heard it. We sat there side by side as it played, watching the fire and thinking our solitary thoughts.

At one thirty, I suddenly grew terribly sleepy. I could barely keep my eyes open. I've always been an early-to-bed, early-to-rise kind of guy, so late nights are hard on me.

"Go ahead and turn in," Menshiki said, looking directly at me. "Shoko may call again, so I'll stay up a while longer. I don't need much sleep. I can skip a night without any problem. Always been that way. So please don't worry about me. I'll keep the fire burning. I can watch it while I listen to music. Do you mind?"

Of course not, I said. I brought in another load of firewood from the shed outside the kitchen and stacked it next to the fireplace. More than enough, I thought, to last until morning.

"Well then, I'm off to bed," I said to Menshiki.

"Sleep tight," he answered. "Let's rotate. I'll probably sleep for a bit around daybreak. Could you lend me a blanket or something?"

I went and got the blanket Masahiko had used, a down duvet, and a pillow, and arranged them on the sofa. Menshiki thanked me.

"I have whiskey if you'd like some," I added.

Menshiki gave a brusque shake of his head. "No, no alcohol for me tonight. We don't know what could happen."

"If you get hungry, please help yourself to the food in the fridge. There's not much, but there's crackers and cheese at least."

"Thanks," Menshiki said.

Leaving him there, I retired to my room. I slipped under the covers, flicked off the bedside light, and tried to go to sleep. Yet sleep didn't come. I was exhausted, but a tiny bug was whirring in my brain. This happens sometimes. I gave up, switched the light back on, and got out of bed.

"What might be the problem, my friends?" the Commendatore said. "You cannot sleep?"

I looked around the room. There he was, sitting on the windowsill, clad in the same white garment. Strange pointy-toed shoes, a miniature sword by his side. His hair neatly tied back. As always, a perfect replica of the Commendatore who was stabbed to death in Tomohiko Amada's painting.

"You're right, I can't sleep," I said.

"There is indeed a great deal happening these days," said the Commendatore. "No wonder people struggle so to drift off, to no avail."

"It's been a long time, hasn't it," I said.

"I cannot attest to that. I think I told my friends before, but 'long time' is lost on us Ideas. We cannot fathom 'It's been a long time,' or 'Sorry not to have written in so long.' "

"Still, your timing is perfect. There's something I need to ask you."

"And what, then, is the question?"

"Mariye Akikawa went missing this morning, and everyone is out looking for her. Where on earth could she have gone?"

The Commendatore cocked his head to one side and thought for a moment.

"As my friends know," he said, choosing his words carefully, "the human realm is ruled by three elements: time, space, and probability. Ideas, by contrast, must remain independent of all three. I cannot, therefore, concern myself with matters of the sort that my friends have just described."

"I can't entirely follow you—is the problem that you can't foresee the outcome?"

The Commendatore didn't answer.

"Or is it that you know, but can't tell me?"

The Commendatore narrowed his eyes in thought. "I am not evading responsibility—Ideas have our own constraints."

I stiffened my back and looked him square in the face.

"Let's get things straight. I must save Mariye Akikawa. She may be in great danger, and needing my help. She has likely wandered into a place from which she cannot escape. That's the feeling I get, anyway. Still, I'm at a loss how to find her. And I think her disappearance is linked in some way to the pit in the woods. I can't give you a rational explanation, but I'm quite sure there's a connection. Now, you spent a very long time confined in that same hole. I have no idea what led you to be shut up there. Nevertheless, whatever may have been the case, Menshiki and I brought in heavy equipment, moved the pile of boulders, and opened the pit. We *set you free*. That's true, isn't it? Thanks to us, you are now able to move throughout time and space, with no restriction. Appear and disappear as you like. You can even watch me making love to my girlfriend. All this is as I say, isn't it?"

"Affirmative, my friends. Affirmative!"

"I'm not demanding that you tell me precisely how Mariye can be saved. I'm not asking the impossible—I can see that the world of Ideas has its own restrictions. But can't you give me a hint? After all I've done for you, don't you think you owe me at least that much?"

The Commendatore gave a deep sigh.

"An indirect, roundabout hint is enough. I'm not trying to accomplish anything earthshaking here, like putting a stop to ethnic cleansing or global warming, or saving the African elephant. All I'm trying to do is find one thirteen-year-old girl who's likely caught somewhere, in some small, dark place, and return her to this world."

The Commendatore sat there for a long time lost in thought, his arms folded. He seemed to be having second thoughts.

"Affirmative, my friends," he said, with resignation. "When you speak in such a fashion, there is not much I can do. I will give my friends but a single hint. Yet be warned—*several sacrifices* may be required. Are you willing nonetheless?"

"What sort of sacrifices?"

"I cannot speak much of that yet. But they will be inevitable. Metaphorically speaking, *there will be blood*. That is an inevitable fact. What sorts of sacrifices are involved should grow clearer as time passes. Someone may have to risk his life."

"I don't care. Give me the hint."

"Affirmative!" the Commendatore said. "It is now Friday, is it not?"

I checked my bedside clock. "Yes, it's still Friday. No, wait a minute, it's Saturday already."

"On Saturday morning, before noon, my friends will receive a phone call," the Commendatore said. "For an invitation somewhere. No matter the circumstances, my friends must not decline that invitation. Do you understand?"

I mechanically repeated what he had just said. "Someone will call me this morning and invite me somewhere. I must not decline."

"Hold those words close," said the Commendatore. "For it is the only hint I am able to share. It traverses the narrow line that divides 'public' and 'private' parlance."

With those final words, the Commendatore began to fade away. Before I knew it, his form had disappeared from the window ledge.

I turned off the bedside lamp and this time fell asleep with relative ease. The whir of insect wings in my head was gone. A moment before I went under, I imagined Menshiki sitting in front of the fire, absorbed in his thoughts. I guessed he would keep the fire burning all night. I had no idea what those thoughts might be, of course. He was a strange man. But it went without saying that his life was bounded by time, space, and probability. Like everyone else's in this world. None of us could escape those constraints, as long as we lived. Each of us was enclosed by sturdy walls that stretched high in the air, surrounding us on all sides. Probably.

"Someone will call me this morning and invite me somewhere. I must not decline." I parroted the Commendatore's words one more time in my head. Then I slept.

48

THE SPANIARDS SIMPLY COULDN'T NAVIGATE THE ANGRY SEAS OFF THE IRISH COAST

I woke shortly after five. It was still dark outside. I slipped a cardigan over my pajamas and went to check the living room. Menshiki was sleeping on the sofa. He hadn't been asleep for long—the fire was out but the room was still warm. The stack of firewood had shrunk. He was sleeping peacefully on his side, breathing quietly with the duvet draped over his body. Not snoring at all. His manners governed even the way he slept. The room seemed to be holding its breath so as not to disturb him.

Leaving him there, I went into the kitchen and brewed coffee. I made some toast as well. Then I carried the toast and coffee into the dining area and sat there, munching and sipping, as I read my book. It was about the Spanish Armada. About the unfolding of the brutal conflict upon which Queen Elizabeth and Philip II had staked the fortunes of their nations. Why did I feel compelled to read an account of that late-sixteenth-century sea battle off the coast of Great Britain at that particular moment? All I knew was that, once I started reading, I couldn't stop. It was an old book I had found on Tomohiko Amada's shelf.

While standard accounts claim that faulty strategy caused the Armada's decimation by the English fleet, a defeat that changed the course of history, this book argued that most of the damage was caused not by direct fire from English cannon (volleys by both sides, it appeared, missed their targets to fall harmlessly into the ocean), but by shipwreck. Accustomed to the calm waters of the Mediterranean, the Spaniards simply couldn't navigate the angry seas off the Irish coast, and thus ran vessel after vessel against the dark reefs.

As I followed the sad fate of the Spanish navy and sipped my second cup of black coffee, the sky gradually brightened in the east. It was Saturday morning.

Someone will phone you, my friends, this morning, and invite you somewhere. You must not decline.

I mentally repeated what the Commendatore had told me. Then I looked at the phone. It preserved its silence. But it would ring at some point, I was sure of that. The Commendatore was not one to lie. All I could do was be patient and wait.

I thought of Mariye. I wanted to call her aunt to find out if she was safe, but it was still too early. I should wait until seven o'clock at least. Her aunt would contact me if Mariye was found. She knew how worried I was. No word from her meant no progress. So I sat at the dining table reading about the invincible Armada and, when I tired of reading, staring at the phone. But the phone maintained its silence.

I called Shoko shortly after seven. She answered immediately. As if she had been sitting beside the phone, waiting for it to ring.

"We haven't heard from her. She's still missing," she said right away. She sounded as if she'd had little (or maybe no) sleep. Fatigue filled her voice.

"Are the police looking?" I asked.

"Yes, two officers came last night. We gave them photographs of Mariye, described what she was wearing . . . We explained that she isn't the kind of girl who would run away or stay out late partying. They spread the word, and by now I'm sure it's been broadcast to all the precincts. I've asked them not to make the search public yet, of course."

"But nothing so far, correct?"

"That's right, no leads up to this point. I'm sure they're working very hard on it, though."

I did my best to console her and asked her to let me know the moment something did turn up. She promised she would.

When our call ended, Menshiki had already risen and was scrubbing his face in the bathroom sink. After brushing his teeth with the toothbrush I had set aside for him, he sat across from me at the dining room table and drank his black coffee. I offered him toast, but he declined.

Sleeping on the sofa had mussed his luxuriant hair a bit more than usual, but then his "usual" was super neat. The man sitting there was the same coolheaded, well-groomed guy as always.

I related my conversation with Shoko. "This is just my gut feeling," he said when I finished, "but I doubt the police will be very much help."

"Why is that?"

"Mariye is no typical teenager, and her disappearance is no typical disappearance. I don't think she was kidnapped, either. That means the usual police methods are likely to hit a wall."

I didn't offer an opinion. But I figured he was right. We had been given an equation with multiple functions but almost no solid numbers. To make any progress, we had to nail down as many numbers as possible.

"Shall we go take another look at the pit?" I asked. "Who knows—there might be some change."

"Let's go," Menshiki said.

We were operating under the tacit assumption that *nothing else was to be done.* I knew that the phone could ring, and that Shoko Akikawa or the person behind the "invitation" the Commendatore had mentioned might be on the other end. But I was pretty sure neither would call this early. Call it a vague premonition on my part.

We put on our jackets and headed out. It was a sunny day. A southwesterly wind had swept away the cloud cover of the previous night, leaving behind a sky almost unnaturally high and transparent. Indeed, when I raised my eyes to the sky, I had the feeling that up and down had been reversed, and that I was peering down into a spring of clear water. I could hear the faint drone of a long train running along a faraway track. When the air was like this, you could pick up distant sounds on the wind with great clarity. That's the sort of morning it was.

Without exchanging a word, we cut through the woods and around the little shrine. The plank cover of the pit was exactly as we had left it the night before. Nor had the stones holding it down been moved. When we took off the boards, the ladder was still leaning against the wall, its position unchanged. No one was in the pit. This time, Menshiki didn't offer to go down to search the floor. The bright sunlight made that unnecessary—we could see that nothing had changed. The pit looked altogether different in the light of day than it had at night. There was nothing at all unsettling about it.

We replaced the lid and rearranged the stones that held it down. Then we walked back through the woods. In front of my house, Menshiki's spotless silver Jaguar sat reticently beside my dusty, unpretentious Toyota Corolla.

When he reached his car, Menshiki came to a halt. "I think I'll head home," he said. "I'll just be in your way if I presume on your hospitality any longer, and there's nothing I can do now anyway. Do you mind?"

"Of course not. Please go home and rest. I'll let you know right away if there's any change."

"Today is Saturday, isn't it?"

"That's right. It's Saturday."

Menshiki reached into his windbreaker pocket and pulled out his key. He stood there staring at it for a moment, thinking. Trying to make his mind up about something, perhaps. I waited for him to reach a conclusion.

"There's one thing I should probably tell you," he said at last.

I leaned on the door of my Corolla as he figured out what to say.

"It's actually quite personal, so I wasn't sure if it was appropriate, but then I thought perhaps I should, for courtesy's sake. I don't want to cause any needless misunderstandings . . . Anyway, the thing is, Shoko and I have become—what's the correct word?—quite intimately involved."

"You mean you and she are lovers?" I asked, cutting to the chase.

"Exactly," Menshiki replied after a moment's pause. I thought I saw a faint blush rise to his cheeks. "You may think it quite hasty."

"No, the speed isn't the problem."

"That's correct," Menshiki acknowledged. "The speed is not the problem."

"The problem is—" I began.

"My motives, you were going to say. Am I correct?"

I didn't respond. Yet it was clear that my silence meant yes.

"You should know," he said, "that none of this was planned from the beginning. It was an entirely natural development. In fact, it happened without me being conscious of it. You may find that hard to believe, of course."

I sighed. Then I spoke frankly. "All I know is that if you started with that plan in mind, it would have been pretty easy to carry out. I'm not being sarcastic, either."

"You're probably right," Menshiki said. "I recognize that. Easy, or at least not all that difficult. *Perhaps.* But that's not how it was."

"So are you saying that you met Shoko Akikawa for the first time and fell in love right off the bat, or something like that?"

Menshiki pursed his lips as if embarrassed. "Fell in love? No, I can't make that claim. To be honest, the last time I fell in love—I think that's probably what it was—was ages ago. I can't even remember what it was like. But I can say with confidence that I find myself powerfully attracted to Shoko, as a man is attracted to a woman."

"Leaving Mariye out of the picture?"

"That's hard to know. Mariye was the reason for our first meeting, after all. But had Mariye never existed, I think I still would have been attracted to her aunt."

I wondered about that. Would a man whose mind was as complicated as Menshiki's be so "powerfully attracted" to a woman as simple and easygoing as Shoko Akikawa? Still, I was in no position to judge. The workings of the human heart are impossible to predict. Especially when sex is involved.

"I understand," I said. "At any rate, thank you for speaking so honestly. Honesty is always best, I think."

"I hope you're right."

"To tell you the truth, Mariye already knew. That you and Shoko had begun that sort of relationship. In fact, she came to talk to me about it. A few days ago."

The news seemed to catch Menshiki by surprise.

"She's a perceptive child," he said. "We tried our best not to let her find out."

"Yes, a *very* perceptive child. But she didn't find out from you. It was the things her aunt said and did that tipped her off."

Shoko was a well-brought-up, intelligent woman, but while she could conceal her feelings to a degree, her mask was bound to slip sooner or later. Menshiki was aware of that, no question.

"If that's the case . . . do you think Mariye's disappearance is connected to her discovery of our relationship?"

I shook my head. "I can't tell for sure. But I can tell you that you and Shoko ought to talk through everything together. She's beside herself with worry, and she's confused. She must be in need of your encouragement and support. Urgently in need."

"You're right. I'll contact her the minute I get home."

Menshiki wasn't finished. Something else appeared to be on his mind.

He sighed. "To tell the truth, I don't think I've fallen in love. I'm not cut out for that. Haven't been from the beginning. I don't know why I feel as I do. Would I have been so attracted to Shoko if not for Mariye? The connection between the two of them isn't clear to me at all."

I said nothing.

"But I swear I didn't plan any of it in advance. Can you believe me?"

"Mr. Menshiki," I said. "I can't explain why, but I think you're an honest man at heart."

"Thank you," he said. The corners of his mouth edged upward. It was a somewhat uncomfortable smile, but not an altogether unhappy one.

"Can I go on being honest?" he said.

"Of course."

"Sometimes I think I'm empty," he confessed. The smile still lingered on his lips.

"Empty?"

"Hollow inside. I know it sounds arrogant, but I've always operated on the assumption that I was a lot brighter and more capable than other people. More perceptive and discerning, with greater powers of judgment. Physically stronger, too. I figured I could succeed at whatever I turned my mind to. And I did. Put my hands on whatever I wanted to possess. Being locked up in Tokyo prison was a clear setback, of course, but I considered that an exception to the rule. When I was young, I saw no limits to what I could achieve. I thought I could attain a state close to perfection. Climb and climb until I reached a height where I could gaze down on everyone else. But when I passed fifty, I looked at myself in the mirror and discovered nothing but emptiness. A zero. What T. S. Eliot called a 'straw man.'"

I couldn't think of anything to say.

"My whole life may have been a mistake up till now," Menshiki went on. "I feel that way sometimes. That I took a wrong turn somewhere. That nothing I've done has any real meaning. That's why I told you I often find myself envying you."

"Envying what, for example?"

"You have the strength to wish for what you cannot have. While I have only wished for those things I can possess."

I assumed he was talking about Mariye. She was the one thing that had evaded his grasp. Yet there wasn't much I could say about that.

Menshiki slowly got into his car. Then he rolled down the window, said goodbye, and drove off. When his car was out of sight I went back into the house. It was just past eight.

The telephone rang at shortly after ten. The call was from Masahiko.

"I know it's sudden," he said, "but I'm on my way to Izu to see my father. Would you like to come along? You mentioned the other day that you'd like to meet him."

Someone will phone my friends tomorrow morning and invite you somewhere. You must not decline.

"That's great. I'd love to go."

"I just got on the Tokyo-Nagoya Expressway. I'm at the Kohoku parking area now. I think it'll take me about an hour to reach you. I'll pick you up and we can drive to Izu Kogen."

"Did something happen to your father?"

"Yeah, the nursing home called. Seems he's taken a turn for the worse. So I'm going to check on him. I'm more or less free today anyway."

"Are you sure it's all right if I go along? Aren't times like this for family only?"

"Don't worry. It's perfectly okay. No other relatives will be there, so the more the merrier." He hung up.

I put down the phone and scanned the room. Was the Commendatore around? But he was nowhere to be seen. Prophecy dispensed, he had disappeared. Probably to a realm where the dictates of time, space, and probability did not apply. Nevertheless, there had been a morning phone call, and I had been invited somewhere. So far, at least, that prophecy had been accurate. It bothered me to leave with Mariye still unaccounted for, but I couldn't do much about that. The Commendatore had instructed me, "No matter the circumstances, my friends must not decline that invitation." I could leave Shoko in Menshiki's hands. After all, she was his responsibility, to some extent.

I sat back in the easy chair in the living room and resumed the story of the invincible Armada as I waited for Masahiko. Almost all the Spanish soldiers and seamen who had managed to escape their shipwrecked vessels and crawl onto the shores of Ireland more dead than alive were murdered by those who lived along the coast. The poverty-stricken locals had slaughtered them for their possessions. It had been the Spaniards' hope that, as fellow Catholics, the Irish might show them mercy, but they were out of luck. Religious solidarity was no match for the fear of starvation. Sadly, the Spanish ship carrying the war chest holding the gold and silver intended to buy off England's powerful nobility sank as well. No one knew where all that wealth had gone.

It was shortly before eleven in the morning when Masahiko's old black Volvo pulled up in front of my house. I was still thinking about all those gold coins lying at the bottom of the sea as I threw on my leather jacket and headed out the door.

The route Masahiko chose took us from the Hakone Turnpike to the Izu Skyline highway and then down from the Amagi highlands to Izu. He explained that this way would be faster—that the weekend meant the coastal roads would be jammed—but nevertheless our route was crowded with people out on excursions. The leaf-viewing season had not yet ended, and many of those on the road were weekenders unfamiliar with mountain driving, so the trip took a lot longer than expected.

"Is your father really in bad shape?" I asked.

"He's not long for this world, that's for sure," Masahiko said lightly. "A matter of days, to be more precise. Age has whittled him down to almost nothing. He has trouble eating, and pneumonia is a constant threat. But the patient's orders are that under no circumstances are IV lines and feeding tubes to be used. In other words, he demands that he be allowed to go quietly once he can no longer eat. He arranged this with his lawyer when he was still mentally competent, signed the forms and everything. So there will be no interventions. That means he could go at any time."

"So I guess you have to be prepared for the worst."

"That's about right."

"It must be rough."

"Hey, it's a big deal when someone dies. I can hardly complain."

The old Volvo was equipped with a tape deck, and the glove compartment was stuffed with cassettes. Masahiko stuck his hand in, grabbed one, and inserted it without checking to see what it was. It turned out to be a collection of hits from the 1980s. Duran Duran, Huey Lewis, and so on. When ABC's "The Look of Love" came on, I turned to him.

"Sure feels like time has stopped in this car," I said.

"I don't like CDs. They're too shiny—they'd scare crows away if I hung them outside my house, but they're hardly something to listen to music on. The sound is tinny and the mixing is unnatural. Having no A and B sides is a drag too. That's why I still drive this car—so I can listen to my cassettes. Newer models don't have tape decks, right? Everyone thinks I'm nuts. But I'm stuck. I have a huge collection of songs I recorded off the radio and I don't want them to go to waste."

"Man, I never thought I'd hear ABC's 'Look of Love' again in this lifetime."

"Don't you think it's amazing?" Masahiko said, casting me a quizzical glance.

We went on talking about the music of the eighties, songs we'd heard on the radio, as we tooled through the mountains of Hakone. The blue slopes of Mt. Fuji loomed around each curve.

"You and your dad are quite a pair," I said. "The father listens only to records, and the son is stuck on cassettes."

"You should talk. You're just as behind the times. Worse than us, maybe. I mean, you don't even have a cell phone. And you hardly ever go online, right? I've always got my cell phone with me, and anything I need to know, I Google. I design stuff on my Mac at work. Socially, I'm light-years ahead of you."

Bertie Higgins's rendition of "Key Largo" came on. An interesting selection indeed for a guy claiming to be socially evolved.

"Are you seeing anyone these days?" I asked, changing the subject.

"You mean, like a woman?"

"Yeah."

Masahiko gave a small shrug. "I can't say it's going all that well. As usual. And things have gotten even rockier since I made this weird breakthrough."

"What kind of breakthrough?"

"That the right and left sides of a woman's face don't match up. Did you know that?"

"People aren't perfectly symmetrical," I said. "Whether it's breasts or balls, the size and shape of the two sides are always going to be different. Every artist knows that much. That lack of symmetry is one of the things that makes the human form so interesting."

Masahiko shook his head several times without taking his eyes off the road. "Of course I know that. But what I'm saying is a little different. I'm talking about personality, not form."

I waited for him to go on.

"About two months ago, I took a photo of this woman I was seeing with a digital camera. A close-up of her face from the front. I put it on the big office computer. Then I managed to divide the screen down the middle and look at the two halves of her face separately. Removing the right half to look at the left, and vice versa . . . You get the idea, right?"

"Yeah, I get it."

"That's when I realized that her left side and her right side looked like two separate people. Like Two-Face, the bad guy in *Batman*."

"I missed that one."

"You should watch it sometime. It's pretty good. Anyway, it freaked me out a bit. I should have left things alone at that point, but I went ahead and tried reversing each side to make a composite face. That way, I could double the right side to create a complete face, and do the same with the left side. Computers make that sort of stuff easy. What I was left with was images of what could only be seen as two women with two totally distinct personalities. It shocked me. I mean, there were actually two women inside every woman I met. Have you ever looked at women that way?"

"Nope," I said.

"I tested my idea on several other women. Took head shots and created left- and right-side composites on the computer. That made it even clearer. That women literally have two faces. Once I knew that, I found I couldn't figure out women at all. For example, if I was with a woman and we were having sex, I didn't know if it was her right side or her left that I was embracing. If it was the right side, then where had the left side gone—what was it doing, and what was it thinking?—and if it was the left side, then what was the right side thinking? Once I reached that point, things got really messy. Get what I'm saying?"

"Not completely, but I can see that it must be messy."

"You bet. Really messy."

"Did you try it on men's faces?"

"Yeah, I did. But it didn't work the same way. The only drastic changes were with women's faces."

"Maybe you should go see a psychologist or therapist about this," I said.

Masahiko sighed. "You know, I've always believed myself to be a totally normal sort of guy."

"That could be a dangerous belief."

"To believe that I'm normal?"

"I think it was F. Scott Fitzgerald who wrote that one should never trust people who claim they're normal. It's in one of his novels."

Masahiko thought about that for a moment. "So even a commonplace man is irreplaceable?"

"I guess that's another way of putting it."

Masahiko thought for a while, his hands on the steering wheel.

"At any rate," he said, "could you try it just once and see?"

"You know I've been a portrait painter for a long time. So I think I'm more skilled than most when it comes to examining faces. You could even say I'm an expert at it. But I've never thought that the difference between the right and left sides reflected a disparity in personality. Not once."

"But almost all the subjects you painted were men, correct?"

Masahiko had a point. I'd never been commissioned to paint a woman. For whatever reason, my portraits were all of men. The only exception was Mariye Akikawa, and she was more child than woman. And I hadn't finished her portrait, either.

"Men and women are different," Masahiko insisted. "Completely."

"So then let me ask you," I said. "Are you claiming this personality difference on the right and left sides applies to almost all women?"

"Yeah, that's my conclusion."

"So then do you find yourself attracted to one side or the other? Or do you find you like both sides *less*?"

Masahiko pondered this question for a moment. "No," he said at last. "That's not how it works. It's not that I prefer one side to the other. That I find one side cheerful and the other gloomy, or that one side is prettier. The problem is at another level: it's simply that the two sides are *different*. It's that *sheer fact* that shakes me up. Sometimes it scares me."

"It sounds to me like a kind of obsessive-compulsive disorder," I said.

"It sounds like that to me too," Masahiko said. "Just listening to myself. But it's *the truth*. I ask you, just check it out for yourself."

I promised him I would. But I had no intention of following through. That could only add to my troubles. My life was messy enough as it was.

Then we talked about Tomohiko Amada. About Tomohiko Amada in Vienna.

"My father said he heard Richard Strauss conduct one of Beethoven's symphonies," Masahiko said. "With the Vienna Philharmonic, of course. He said it was out of this world. That's one of the few stories he told me about his days in Vienna."

"What else did he say about his time there?"

"Nothing at all remarkable. He mentioned the food, the drink, the music. Stuff like that. He really loved music, you know. That was all he talked about. He never mentioned painting or politics or things of that sort. Or women either."

Masahiko paused before continuing.

"Maybe someone should write my father's biography. It could be a really interesting book. But the reality is, no one will ever take a shot at it. Why? Because there's hardly any personal information out there. My father had no friends, his family members were virtual strangers—he just spent his time shut away by himself on a mountain, painting. His only acquaintances, if you could call them that, were a handful of art dealers. He hardly spoke to anyone. He wrote no letters. So if someone did try to write his biography, they'd have almost nothing to work with. It's not just that there are a few holes in his life story, it's that his life is riddled with them. Think of Swiss cheese with more holes than cheese."

"All he's leaving behind is his work."

"You're right, his paintings and almost nothing else. That's probably the way he wanted it."

"And you. You're a part of his legacy too," I said.

"Me?" Masahiko looked at me in surprise. Then he turned back to the road. "You're right there. If I stop to think of it, I'm part of his legacy too. Not a particularly shining part, though."

"But irreplaceable."

"True enough. Run of the mill, but nonetheless irreplaceable," Masahiko said. "You know what I think sometimes? That you should have been Tomohiko Amada's son. If that were the case, things would have gone so much more smoothly."

"Give me a break!" I said with a laugh. "No one was fit for that role!"

"Maybe not," Masahiko said. "But you might have been his spiritual successor, if you can call it that. You're a lot more qualified in that area than I am—that's my gut feeling anyway."

Killing Commendatore popped into my mind. Was that painting something I had "inherited" from Tomohiko Amada? Had he led me to that attic room to discover it? Was he using it to demand something of me?

Deborah Harry was singing "French Kissin' in the USA" on the car stereo. It was hard to think of less appropriate background music for our conversation.

"I guess it must have been tough having a father like Tomohiko Amada," I said bluntly.

"I reached a point years ago where I had to make a clean break and move on with my life," Masahiko said. "Once I had done that, it wasn't as hard on me as everyone thought. I make a living from art as well, but the scale of my father's talent and the scale of mine are so dramatically different. When the gap is that huge, it stops being a problem. My father's fame as an artist doesn't hurt anymore. What hurts is the kind of human being he was, the fact that until the very end, he never opened up to me, his own son. That he didn't pass a single bit of information about himself on to me."

"So he showed nothing of his inner world, even to you?"

"Not a glimpse. His attitude was: 'I gave you half my DNA, so what more do you want? The rest is up to you.' But a relationship is based on more than DNA. Right? I never asked him to act as my guide through life. I didn't demand that. But it still should have been possible to have something like a father-son conversation once in a while. He could have filled me in just a little on what he had experienced, what he thought. Even bits and pieces would have helped."

I listened quietly to what he had to say.

When we stopped at a long red light, Masahiko took off his dark Ray-Ban sunglasses and wiped them with his handkerchief.

"My guess," he said, turning in my direction, "is that my father is hiding heavy secrets of some kind, personal secrets he has borne entirely alone and intends to take with him when he drifts from this world. It's like there's this metal safe in his heart where he stored them. He locked them all in there, and then he either threw the key away or hid it somewhere. Now he can't remember where he stashed it."

In that case, the unsolved riddle of what had taken place in Vienna in 1938 would be buried in darkness. Then again, perhaps *Killing Commendatore* itself was the hidden key. The idea struck me all of a sudden. Were that true, it would explain why, at the end of his life, Tomohiko's living spirit had returned to his mountaintop to confirm the painting's existence.

I swiveled around to look in the backseat. Just maybe, the Commendatore was sitting there. But the seat was empty.

"Is something wrong?" Masahiko said, glancing behind him.

"No, nothing at all," I said.

When the light turned green, he stepped on the accelerator.

49

FILLED WITH JUST AS MANY DEATHS

On our way to check in on his father, we stopped at a roadside restaurant so that Masahiko could use the toilet. We were shown to a table next to the window, where we ordered coffee. As it was already noon, I ordered a roast beef sandwich, too. Masahiko asked for the same thing. Then he headed for the men's room. While he was gone I stared blankly out the window. The parking lot was packed with cars. Most had come with families. The number of minivans really stood out. All minivans look identical to me. Like cans of tasteless biscuits. There was an observation deck at the end of the lot where people were using small digital cameras and cell phones to snap photos of Mt. Fuji, which towered right in front of them. It's dumb, I know, but I've never really gotten comfortable with phones taking pictures. I'm even less cool with cameras making phone calls.

While I was sitting there looking at nothing in particular, a white Subaru Forester turned off the road and into the lot. I don't know much about cars (and the Subaru Forester is hardly distinctive), but I could tell at a glance that it was the model the man with the white Subaru Forester had been driving. It trolled up and down the rows before finally nosing into an empty space. Sure enough, the logo on the spare-tire cover read SUBARU FORESTER. It appeared to be the same model as the car I had seen in the little seaside town in Miyagi Prefecture. I couldn't make out the license plate, but the more I looked, the more I was sure it was the same car I had seen that spring. Not just the same model. I mean the *exact same car*.

My visual memory is sharper than most—and more durable. As a result, I could tell that the stains and other markings were strikingly similar to those of *that car* as I remembered it. I could hardly breathe. But just when I was straining to identify the driver as he stepped out, a large tour bus pulled into the lot and blocked my view. Unable to move past the jam of cars, it just sat there. I jumped up and hurried out of the restaurant. I rushed around the bus, which had stopped dead in its tracks, and approached the spot where the white Subaru Forester was parked. But the car was empty. Its driver had gone off somewhere. He might be in the restaurant, or perhaps was taking pictures on the observation deck. I scanned the area but couldn't spot the man with the white Subaru Forester anywhere. Of course, the driver could have been someone else.

I checked the license plate. Sure enough, it read "Miyagi Prefecture." On the rear bumper was a sticker with a picture of a marlin on it. It was the same car, no question. *That man had come here.* A chill ran down my spine. I decided to search for him. I wanted to see his face one more time. To figure out why I couldn't finish his portrait. Perhaps I had overlooked something basic about him. First, though, I memorized the license plate number. It might prove useful. Then again, it might be of no use at all.

I walked around the parking lot, keeping an eye out for someone who resembled him. I checked the observation deck. But the man with the white Subaru Forester was nowhere to be seen. A man of middle age, deeply tanned, with a salt-and-pepper crew cut. On the tall side. When last seen, wearing a battered black leather jacket and a Yonex golf cap. I had whipped off a quick sketch on my memo pad and shown it to the young woman sitting across from me. "You're really good at drawing!" she had enthused.

Once I was sure no one matching his description was outside, I looked inside the restaurant. I circled the place, but he was nowhere to be seen. The seats were almost full. Masahiko was back at our table, drinking his coffee. The sandwiches hadn't shown up yet.

"Where'd you disappear to?" he asked me.

"I thought I saw someone I knew. So I went outside to check."

"Did you find them?"

"No. Probably a case of mistaken identity," I said.

After that, I kept a close eye on the white Subaru Forester outside. Yet if the man in question did come back, what should I do? Go out and talk to him? Tell him I was sure I had bumped into him twice this past spring in a small coastal town in Miyagi? *Is that so? Well, I don't remember you,* he'd probably shoot back.

Well then, why are you following me? I would ask. *What are you talking about?* he would reply. *Why the hell would I be tailing someone I don't even know?* End of conversation.

In any event, the driver of the white Subaru Forester never went back to his car. It just sat there in the lot, short and squat, silently awaiting its owner's return. We finished our sandwiches and coffee, but he still hadn't shown.

"We'd better be going," Masahiko said, glancing at his watch. "We don't have a whole lot of time." He picked up his Ray-Bans from the table.

We stood, paid the bill, and walked out. Then we climbed into the Volvo and drove out of the jammed parking lot. I wanted to wait for the man with the white Subaru Forester to return, but meeting Masahiko's father had to be my top priority. The Commendatore had driven home that message with absolute clarity: *My friends will be invited somewhere. You must not decline that invitation.*

I was left with the fact that the man with the white Subaru Forester had shown up once again. He had known where to find me and had made it clear that *he was there*. His intent was obvious. His appearance could be no accident. Nor, of course, was the tour bus that had hidden him from view.

To reach the facility where Tomohiko Amada was being cared for, we had to leave the Izu Skyline and drive down a long, winding road. The area had recently been turned into a summer retreat for city folk: we passed stylish coffee shops, fancy inns built to resemble log cabins, stands selling local produce, and small museums aimed at passing tourists. Each time we went around a curve, I gripped the door handle and thought of the man with the white Subaru Forester. Something was blocking me from finishing his portrait. A key element, something that made him who he was, had escaped me. A missing piece of the puzzle, as it were. This was new for me. I always gathered together everything I knew I would need before I started a portrait. In the case of the man with the white Subaru Forester, though, I had not been able to do that. Probably the man himself was standing in my way. He didn't like having his portrait painted, for whatever reason. In fact, he seemed dead set against it.

At a certain point, the Volvo turned off the road and passed through a big, open steel gate. The gate was marked only by a very small sign. Someone could easily drive right by if they weren't paying attention. It appeared to be an institution that didn't feel compelled to announce its presence to the world. Masahiko stopped at the small guardhouse beside the gate and gave his name and the name of the resident he was visiting to the uniformed security guard on duty. The guard made a phone call to confirm the resident's identity. Once through the gate, we entered a dense grove of trees. Most were tall evergreens, which cast a chilly shadow. We drove up the freshly paved road to the circle set atop the rise, where cars could be parked. A bed of ornamental cabbages surrounding a circle of bright red flowers sat at the center. The flowers were being tended with care.

Masahiko drove to the far end of the circle and parked his car in one of the visitor spots. Two other cars had preceded us. A white Honda minivan and a dark blue Audi sedan. Both were sparkling new—between them his Volvo looked like an aged workhorse. Masahiko, however, didn't seem to mind a bit (his Bananarama cassette tape took clear precedence). Below, the Pacific Ocean gleamed dully in the early-winter sun. A few midsized fishing vessels were plying its waters. A small humped island sat just offshore, and beyond it the Manazuru Peninsula. The hands of my watch pointed to 1:45.

We got out of the car and walked toward the entrance. The building looked quite new. It was a clean and stylish concrete structure, yet nothing was distinctive about it. Perhaps the architect who designed it lacked imaginative oomph. Or else the client, considering its function, had demanded that the building be as simple and conservative as possible. It was three stories high, and quite square—a structure made up entirely of straight lines. The blueprints could have been drawn up with a single ruler. The ground floor was mainly glass, to create as bright an impression as possible. Jutting out from the front of the building was a large wooden balcony with about a dozen deck chairs, but it was winter, so no one would be sunbathing, however bright and pleasant the day. The cafeteria had glass walls that soared from floor to ceiling. I could see five or six people inside, all well along in years, from the look of them. Two were in wheelchairs. I couldn't tell what they were doing. Perhaps watching television on the big screen on the wall. They weren't playing leapfrog, that's for sure.

Masahiko walked through the entranceway and up to a young woman stationed at the front desk. She was round-cheeked and friendly, with beautiful long black hair. A name tag was affixed to her dark blue blazer. She seemed to know Masahiko by sight, for the two of them chatted for a few minutes. I stood a short distance away and waited for them to finish. A large vase sat in the entranceway, overflowing with a lavish assortment of fresh flowers, arranged, I assumed, by an ikebana expert. At a certain point, Masahiko signed the guest register with a pen and, consulting his watch, added the precise time. He left the desk and walked over to me, hands in pockets.

"My father's condition seems to have stabilized," he said. "Apparently, he was coughing all morning and very short of breath, so they worried that he was developing pneumonia. But they got his cough under control a short while ago, and now he's fast asleep."

"Is it really okay for me to go in with you?"

"Of course," Masahiko said. "You came all this way to see him, didn't you?"

He and I took the elevator to the third floor. The corridor there was also simple and conservative. Decoration kept to a bare minimum. The one exception, as if by way of concession, was a row of oil paintings hanging on the long, white wall. All were coastal landscapes. They seemed to be a series by a single artist, who had painted spots along the same stretch of coast from a number of angles. They weren't especially well done, but at least the artist had been generous in his use of paint, and I could applaud the way his paintings disrupted the strict minimalism of the architecture. The rubber soles of my shoes squeaked ostentatiously on the smooth linoleum floor. A little old white-haired lady in a wheelchair pushed by a male attendant passed us in the corridor. She stared straight ahead, her gaze so fixed and rigid it did not even flicker when we went by. As if she was determined not to lose sight of a crucial sign suspended in the air before her.

Tomohiko Amada was in a big room at the very end of the corridor. The name card on the door had been left blank. Most likely to protect his privacy. He was, after all, famous. The room was the size of a small hotel suite, with a basic set of living room furniture in addition to the bed. A folded wheelchair rested against the bed's foot. A large southeast-facing window looked out over the Pacific Ocean. It was a magnificent, unobstructed view. A hotel room with a view like that would cost an arm and a leg. No paintings hung on the walls. Just a mirror and a round clock. A medium-sized vase filled with purple cut flowers sat on the table. There was no odor at all. Not of a sick old person, nor of medicine, nor of flowers, nor of sun-drenched curtains. Nothing. That's what surprised me most—the room's utter lack of smell. It was so striking I thought something had happened to my nose. How could odor be erased so completely?

Tomohiko Amada was fast asleep near the window, oblivious to the view outside. He slept on his back facing the ceiling, his eyes tightly shut. Bushy white eyebrows overhung his aged eyelids like a natural canopy. Deep wrinkles furrowed his forehead. His quilt was pulled up to his neck—I couldn't tell if he was breathing or not. If he was, they were extremely shallow breaths.

I knew right away that this was the mysterious old man who had visited my studio. I had seen him for only a moment or two in the shifting moonlight, but the shape of his head and his wild, white hair left no doubt: it had been Tomohiko Amada. The fact didn't surprise me in the least. It had been clear all along.

"He's dead to the world," Masahiko said to me. "We'll just have to wait for him to wake up. *If* he wakes up, that is."

"All the same, it's a blessing that he's sleeping peacefully," I said. I glanced at the clock on the wall. It said five minutes before two. I suddenly thought of Menshiki. Had he called Shoko Akikawa? Had there been any developments in Mariye's case? Right now, however, I had to focus on Tomohiko Amada.

Masahiko and I sat across from each other on matching chairs, sipping the canned coffee we had bought from the vending machine in the corridor, while we waited for Tomohiko Amada to wake up. In the meantime, Masahiko told me a few things about Yuzu. That her pregnancy was progressing nicely. That her due date was sometime in the first half of January. That her handsome boyfriend was thrilled about becoming a father.

"The only problem—from his perspective, anyway—is that she seems to have no intention of marrying him," Masahiko said.

"Huh?" I couldn't believe what I had just heard. "You mean she plans to be a single mom?"

"Yuzu intends to have the baby. But she doesn't want to marry the father, or live with him, or share custody of the child . . . that seems to be the story. He can't figure out what's going on. He assumed they'd be properly married once the divorce was final, but she completely rejected his proposal."

I thought about that for a moment. The more I thought, though, the more confused I got.

"I can't wrap my head around it," I said. "Yuzu always said she didn't want kids. Whenever I said I thought the time was right, she said it was still too early. So why does she want a child so badly now?"

"Maybe she didn't plan on a baby, but changed her mind once she got pregnant. Women can do that, you know."

"Still, it'll be tough to look after the child all by herself. Hard to hang on to her job, for one thing. So why not marry him? He is the child's father, right?"

"Yeah, he doesn't understand either. He thought they were getting along just great. And he was happy a child was coming. That's why he's so confused. He asked me about it, but I'm stumped too."

"Have you talked to Yuzu directly?" I inquired.

Masahiko frowned. "To tell you the truth, I'm trying hard not to get too sucked in. I like Yuzu, but he's my colleague at work. And of course you and I have been friends for ages. I'm in a tough spot. The more I become involved, the less I know what to do."

I didn't say anything.

"I always enjoyed seeing the two of you together—you seemed like such a happy couple," Masahiko said, looking perplexed.

"You said that before."

"Yeah, maybe I did," Masahiko said. "But it's the truth."

After that, we sat there without speaking, looking at the clock on the wall, or the ocean outside the window. Tomohiko Amada lay on his back in a deep sleep, not moving a muscle. He was so still, in fact, that I worried whether he was alive or not. No one else seemed concerned, though, so I figured his stillness was normal.

Watching him lying there, I tried to imagine how he might have looked as a young exchange student in Vienna. But of course I couldn't. This was an old man with furrowed skin and white hair, experiencing the slow but steady annihilation of his physical existence. All of us are, without exception, born to die, and now he was face-to-face with that final stage.

"Aren't you planning to contact Yuzu?" Masahiko asked me.

"Not at present, no," I said, shaking my head.

"I think it might be a good idea for you two to get together and talk things over. Have a good heart-to-heart, so to speak."

"Our formal divorce proceedings were handled through our lawyers. That's the way Yuzu wanted it. Now she's about to give birth to another man's child. Whether she wants to marry him or not is her problem. I'm in no position to say anything about it. So what exactly are the *things* we should talk over?"

"Don't you want to know what's going on?"

I shook my head no. "I don't want to know any more than I have to. It's not like what took place didn't hurt."

"Of course," Masahiko said.

All the same, to be honest there were times I couldn't tell if I had been hurt or not. Did I really have the right? I wasn't clear enough about things to know. Of course, people can't help feeling hurt in certain situations, whether they have the right to or not.

"The guy is a colleague of mine," Masahiko said after a pause. "He's a serious guy, hard worker, good personality."

"Yeah, and handsome, too."

"True. Women love him. Only natural, I guess. Sure wish they flocked to me like that. But he has this tendency that always left us all shaking our heads."

I waited for him to go on.

"You see, we've never been able to figure out why he's chosen the women he has. I mean, he always has lots of women to pick from, and yet he comes up with these losers. I'm not talking about Yuzu, of course. She's probably the first good choice he's made. But the women before her were real disasters. I still can't figure it out."

He shook his head, remembering those women.

"He almost got married a few years back. They'd printed the invitations, reserved the venue for the ceremony, and were heading off to Fiji or someplace like that for their honeymoon. He'd gotten leave from work, bought the airplane tickets. The bride-to-be wasn't at all attractive. When he introduced us, I remember being shocked by how homely she was. Of course, you can't judge a book by its cover, but from what I could see, her personality was nothing special, either. Yet for some reason he was head over heels in love. Anyway, they seemed poorly matched. Everyone who knew them felt that way, though no one said so. Then, just before the wedding, she skipped out. In other words, it was *the woman* who split. I couldn't tell if that was good or bad for him, but all the same it blew my mind."

"Was there some kind of reason?"

"Not that I know of. I felt sorry for the guy, so I never asked. But I don't think he ever understood why she did what she did. I mean she just *ran*. Couldn't stand the thought of marrying him. Something must have bothered her."

"So what's the point of your story?"

"The point is," Masahiko said, "it still may be possible for you and Yuzu to get back together. Assuming that's what you want, of course."

"But she's about to have another man's child."

"Yeah, I can see that might be a problem."

We fell silent again.

. . .

Tomohiko Amada woke up shortly before three. His body twitched at first. Then he took a deep breath—I could see the quilt over his chest rise and fall. Masahiko stood and went to his father's bedside. He looked down on his face. The old man's eyes slowly opened. His bushy white eyebrows quivered in the air.

Masahiko took a slender glass funnel cup from the bedside table and moistened his father's lips. He mopped the corners of his mouth with a piece of what looked like gauze. His father wanted more, so he repeated the process several times. He seemed comfortable with the job—it appeared that he had done it many times before. The old man's Adam's apple bobbed up and down with each swallow. Only when I saw that movement was I sure he was still alive.

"Father," Masahiko said, pointing at me. "This is the guy who moved into the Odawara house. He's a painter who's working in your studio. He's a friend of mine from college. He's not too bright, and his beautiful wife ran out on him, but he's still a great artist."

It wasn't clear how much Masahiko's father comprehended. But he slowly turned his head in my direction as if following his son's finger. His face was blank. He seemed to be looking at something, but that *something* carried no particular meaning for him. Nevertheless, I thought I could detect a surprisingly clear and lucid light deep within those bleary eyes. That light seemed to be biding its time, waiting for that which might hold real significance. At least that was my impression.

"I doubt he understands a word I say," Masahiko said. "But his doctor instructed us to talk to him in a free and natural way, as if he was able to follow. No one knows how much he's picking up anyway. So I talk to him normally. That's easier for me too. Now you say something. The way you usually talk."

"It's nice to meet you, Mr. Amada," I said. I told him my name. "Your son has been kind enough to let me live in your home in Odawara."

Tomohiko Amada was looking at me, but his expression hadn't changed. Masahiko gestured: *Just keep talking—anything is okay.*

"I'm an oil painter," I went on. "I specialized in portraits for a long time, but I gave that up and now I paint my own stuff. I still accept occasional commissions for portraits, though. The human face fascinates me, I guess. Masahiko and I have been friends since art school."

Tomohiko Amada's eyes were still pointed in my direction. They were coated by a thin membrane, a kind of layered lace curtain hanging between life and death. What sat behind the curtain would fade from view as the layers increased, until finally the last, heavy curtain would fall.

"I love your house," I said. "My work is steadily progressing. I hope you don't mind, but I've been listening to your records. Masahiko told me that was all right. You have a great collection. I enjoy the operas especially. Oh yes, and recently I went up and looked in the attic."

I thought I saw a sparkle in his eyes when I said the word "attic." It was just a quick flash—no one would have noticed it unless they were paying attention. But I was keeping close watch. Thus I didn't miss it. Clearly, "attic" had a charge that caused some part of his memory to kick in.

"A horned owl has moved into the attic," I went on. "I kept hearing these rustling sounds at night. I thought it was a rat, so I went up to check during the day. And there the owl was, sitting under the beams. It's a beautiful bird. The screen on the air vent has a hole, so it can go in and out at will. The attic makes a perfect daytime hideout for a horned owl, don't you think?"

The eyes were still fixed on me. As if waiting to hear more.

"Horned owls don't cause any damage," Masahiko put in. "In fact, they're said to bring good luck."

"I love the bird," I added. "And the attic is a fascinating place too."

Tomohiko Amada stared at me from the bed, not moving a muscle. His breathing had turned shallow again. That thin membrane still coated his eyes, but the secret light within seemed to have brightened.

I wanted to talk more about the attic, but Masahiko was beside me, so there was no way I could bring up what I had found there. It would only prick Masahiko's curiosity. So I let the topic hang in the air while Tomohiko Amada and I stared into each other's eyes.

I chose my words with care. "The attic suits owls, but it might suit paintings too. It could be a perfect place to store them. Japanese-style paintings, especially—they're really tricky to preserve. Attics aren't damp like basements—they're well ventilated, and you don't have to worry about sunlight. Of course, there's always the danger of wind and rain getting in, but if you wrap it up carefully enough a painting should keep for quite a while up there."

"You know, I've never even looked in the attic," Masahiko said. "Dusty places creep me out."

I was watching Tomohiko Amada's face. His gaze was fixed on me as well. I felt him trying to construct a coherent line of thought. Owl, attic, stored paintings . . . these familiar words all needed to be strung together. In his current state, this was no easy thing. No easy thing *at all.* Like trying to pick through a labyrinth blindfolded. But I sensed that making those connections was important to him. *Extremely* important. I stood by quietly watching him concentrate on that urgent yet solitary task.

I considered bringing up the shrine in the woods, and the strange pit behind it. To describe to him the steps that had led to it being opened, and the shape of its interior. But I changed my mind. I shouldn't give him too much to think about at one time. His level of awareness was so diminished that even one topic placed a heavy burden on his shoulders. What little he had left hung by a single, easily severed thread.

"Would you like more water?" Masahiko asked, funnel cup in hand. But his father didn't react. It was as if he hadn't heard his son's question. Masahiko drew nearer and asked again, but when his father still didn't respond, he gave up. The son was invisible in his father's eyes.

"Dad seems to have taken a real shine to you," Masahiko marveled. "He can't stop looking at you. It's been quite a while since anyone or anything held his interest like this."

I continued to look into Tomohiko Amada's eyes.

"It's strange. When I talk to him he won't turn to me, no matter what I say, but in your case he won't turn away. His eyes are riveted on you."

I couldn't help notice a mild envy in Masahiko's voice. He wanted his father to *see* him. That had probably been a common theme in his life, ever since childhood.

"Maybe he smells paint on me," I said. "The smell may be triggering his memories."

"You're right, that could be it. Come to think of it, it's been ages since I touched actual paint."

Regret no longer tinged his words. He was back to being the same old easygoing Masahiko. Just then, his cell phone began buzzing on the table.

Masahiko looked up with a start. "Damn, I forgot to turn the thing off. Cell phones are against the rules in this place. I'll have to go outside. You don't mind, do you?"

"Of course not," I said.

Masahiko picked up the cell phone and walked to the door. "This may take a while," he said, checking the caller's name on his screen. "Please talk to my father while I'm gone."

He was already whispering into the phone as he left, closing the door quietly behind him.

Tomohiko Amada and I were now alone. His eyes remained fixed on my face. No doubt he was struggling to figure out who I was. Feeling a bit suffocated, I circled the foot of his bed and went to the southeast-facing window. Bringing my face close to the glass, I looked out at the wide expanse of ocean. The horizon seemed to be pushing up against the sky. I followed the line where the sky met the water from end to end. No human being could draw a line so beautiful, whatever ruler they might use. Below that long, straight line, countless lives were thriving. The world was filled with so many lives, and just as many deaths.

Something else had entered the room—I felt its presence. I turned around and, sure enough, Tomohiko Amada and I were no longer alone.

"Affirmative, my friends. The two of you are alone no more," said the Commendatore.

50

IT WILL INVOLVE ORDEAL AND SACRIFICE

"Affirmative, my friends. The two of you are alone no more," said the Commendatore.

The Commendatore was sitting on the same upholstered chair that Masahiko had occupied a moment earlier. He hadn't changed a bit: same getup, same hairstyle, same sword, same tiny physique. I stared at him without saying anything.

"The friend of my friends will not return anytime soon," the Commendatore said, raising his right forefinger as though to pierce the sky. "His phone call promises to be a long one. So please do not worry. Instead, converse with Tomohiko Amada for as long as you desire. There are questions that my friends would like to ask him, are there not? How many he can answer, however, is a matter for debate."

"Did you send Masahiko away?"

"Certainly not," the Commendatore said. "I fear my friends have overestimated my powers. They are of a lesser sort. But company men are always at someone's beck and call. Those poor men have no weekends."

"Have you been here the whole time? Did you come with us in the car?"

The Commendatore shook his head. "Negative. It is a dreadfully long way from Odawara, and I am prone to carsickness."

"But still you came. Though you weren't invited, correct?"

"Affirmative! I was not invited. Technically, at least. But I was needed. There is a fine line between being invited and being needed, my friends.

But leaving that aside, this time it was Tomohiko Amada who needed me. And I thought I could be of use to my friends as well."

"Of use to me?"

"Indeed. I am somewhat beholden to you, my friends. You freed me from that place beneath the ground. It was thanks to you that I was able to rejoin the world as an Idea. As my friends asserted. So it is only proper that I repay that debt. Even Ideas can fathom the import of moral obligation."

Moral obligation?

"Oh well, never mind. *Something like that*," the Commendatore said, reading my mind. "In any case, my friends wish with all your heart to track down Mariye Akikawa and bring her back from the other side. Affirmative?"

I nodded. Yes, that was true.

"Do you know where she is?" I asked.

"Indeed, I met her not long ago."

"Met her?"

"We exchanged a few words."

"Then please tell me where she is."

"I know, but cannot speak."

"You cannot say?"

"I do not have the right."

"But you just said that you came here today to help me."

"Affirmative, I said that."

"But still you can't tell me where Mariye is?"

The Commendatore shook his head. "That is not my role. I am most regretful."

"Then whose role is it?"

The Commendatore pointed his right forefinger directly at me. "It is your role, my friends. You, yourself. My friends must tell yourself where Mariye Akikawa is. It is the only path that leads to her."

"I have to tell myself?" I said. "But I haven't the faintest idea where she is."

The Commendatore gave a long sigh. "My friends know. But my friends do not yet know that they know."

"That sounds like a circular argument to me."

"Negative! It is not circular. My friends will know in due course. In a place that is not here."

Now it was my turn to let out a sigh.

"Please tell me one thing. Was Mariye kidnapped? Or did she wander off on her own?"

"That is something my friends can only know after my friends have found her and brought her back to this world."

"Is she in great danger?"

The Commendatore shook his head. "Determining what constitutes great danger is a role that humans, not Ideas, must play. If my friends truly wish to bring her back, however, my friends must find the road and move quickly."

Find the road? What road was he talking about? I looked at the Commendatore for a moment. It was as though he was playing a riddle game. Assuming his riddles had answers, that is.

"So what is it that you are offering me by way of assistance?"

"What I can do for my friends," the Commendatore said, "is to send you to a place wherein my friends encounter yourself. But that is not as easy as it may sound. It will involve considerable sacrifice, and an excruciating ordeal. More specifically, the sacrifice will be made by the Idea, while the ordeal will be endured by my friends. Do I have your approval?"

What could I say? I hadn't a clue what he was talking about.

"So what is it exactly that I have to do?"

"It is simple," the Commendatore said. "My friends must slay me."

51

NOW IS THE TIME

"It is simple," the Commendatore said. "My friends must slay me."

"Slay you?" I said.

"Slay me, as in *Killing Commendatore*—let the painting be your model."

"I should slay you with a sword—is that what you mean?"

"Precisely. As luck would have it, I happen to have a sword with me. It is the real thing—as I told my friends once before, if it cuts you, then you will bleed. It is not full-sized, but I am not full-sized either, so it should suffice."

I stood at the foot of the bed facing the Commendatore. I wanted to say something but had no idea what it should be. So I just stood there, rooted to the spot. Tomohiko Amada was staring in the Commendatore's direction too, from where he lay stretched out on the bed. Whether he could make him out or not was another story. The Commendatore was able to choose who could see him, and who couldn't.

At last I pulled myself together enough to pose a question. "If I kill you with that sword, will I learn where Mariye Akikawa is?"

"Negative. Not exactly. First, my friends must dispose of me. Wipe me off the face of this earth. A chain of events will follow that could well lead my friends to the girl's location."

I struggled to decipher what he meant.

"I'm not sure what sort of chain of events you're talking about, but can I be certain they will lead me in the direction you anticipate? Even if I kill you, there's no guarantee. In which case, yours would be a pointless death."

The Commendatore raised one eyebrow and stared at me. Now he looked like Lee Marvin in *Point Blank*. Super cool. There wasn't the ghost of a chance that the Commendatore had seen *Point Blank*, of course.

"Affirmative! It is as my friends say. Maybe the chain of events will not flow so smoothly in reality. Maybe my hypothesis is based on mere supposition and conjecture. Just maybe, there are too many maybes. But there is no alternative. There is not the luxury of choice."

"So if I kill you, will you be dead to *me*? Will you vanish from my sight forever?"

"Affirmative! As far as my friends are concerned, I shall be dead and gone. One of the countless deaths an Idea must undergo."

"Isn't there a danger that the world itself will be altered when an Idea is killed?"

"How could it be otherwise?" the Commendatore said. Again, he raised one eyebrow, Lee Marvin–style. "What would be the meaning of a world that did *not* change when an Idea was extinguished? Can an Idea be so insignificant?"

"But you think I should still kill you, even though the world would be altered as a result."

"My friends set me free. And now my friends must kill me. Should my friends fail in that task, the circle would remain open. And a circle once opened must then be closed. There are no other options."

I looked at Tomohiko Amada, lying on the bed. His eyes seemed to be trained on the chair where the Commendatore was sitting.

"Can Mr. Amada see you?"

"It is about now that he should be seeing me," the Commendatore said. "And hearing our voices too. A few moments hence, he will begin to grasp the import of our discourse. He is marshaling all his remaining strength to that end."

"What do you think he was trying to convey in *Killing Commendatore*?"

"That is not for me to say. My friends should ask the artist," the Commendatore said. "Since he is right before you."

I sat back down in my chair and drew close to the man stretched out on the bed.

"Mr. Amada, I found the painting you stored in the attic. I am quite sure you meant to hide it. You would not have wrapped it so thoroughly had you planned to show it to anyone. But I unwrapped it. I know that may displease you, but my curiosity got the better of me. And once I discovered how superb *Killing Commendatore* was, I couldn't let it out of my sight. It is a great painting. One of your best, no question. At this moment, almost no one knows of its existence. Even Masahiko hasn't seen it yet. A thirteen-year-old girl named Mariye Akikawa has, though. And she went missing yesterday."

The Commendatore raised his hand. "Please, let him rest. His brain is easily overtaxed—it cannot handle more than this at one time."

I stopped talking and studied Tomohiko Amada's face. I couldn't tell how much had sunk in. His face was still expressionless. But when I looked more closely I could see a glitter in the depths of his eyes. Like the glint of a sharp penknife at the bottom of a deep spring.

I began talking again, this time with frequent pauses. "My question is, what was your purpose in painting that picture? Its subject matter, its structure, and its style are so different from your other works. It makes me think you were using it to communicate a very personal message. What is the painting's underlying meaning? Who is killing whom? Who is the Commendatore? Who is the murderer Don Giovanni? And who is that mysterious bearded fellow with the long face poking his head out of the ground in the lower left-hand corner?"

The Commendatore raised his hand again. I drew up short.

"Enough questions," he said. "It will take a while for those to permeate."

"Will he be able to answer? Does he have enough strength left?"

"No," the Commendatore said, shaking his head. "I doubt my friends will obtain answers. He does not have the energy for that."

"Then why did you have me ask?"

"What my friends imparted were not questions, but information. That my friends had found *Killing Commendatore* in the attic, that its existence was known to my friends. It is the first step. Everything begins from there."

"Then what is the second step?"

"When my friends slay me, of course. It is the second step."

"And is there a third step?"

"There should be, of course."

"Then what is it?"

"Have you still not yet figured this out, my friends?"

"No, I haven't."

"By reenacting the allegory contained within that painting, we shall lure Long Face into the open. Into this room. By dragging him out, my friends shall win back Mariye Akikawa."

I was speechless. What world had I stepped into? There seemed no rhyme or reason to it.

"It is a hard thing, without question," the Commendatore intoned. "Yet there is no alternative. Hence my friends must dispatch me now, without further ado."

We waited for the information I had given Tomohiko Amada to complete its journey to his brain. That took some time. Meanwhile, I tried to put to rest some of my doubts by peppering the Commendatore with questions.

"Why," I asked, "did Tomohiko Amada remain silent about what had happened in Vienna even after the war had ended? I mean, no one was standing in his way at that point."

"The woman he loved was brutally executed by the Nazis," the Commendatore answered. "Slowly tortured to death. Their comrades were slain in a similar fashion. In the end, their plot was a wretched failure. Only through the offices of the Japanese and German governments did he barely escape with his life. The experience savaged him. He had been arrested and detained by the Gestapo for two months. They subjected him to extreme torture. Their violence was unspeakable, but they took care not to kill him, nor to leave any physical scars. Yet their sadism left his nerves in tatters—and as a result, something within him was extinguished. Placed under the strictest orders, he bowed to the inevitable and remained silent. Then he was forcibly repatriated to Japan."

"Not long before," I said, "Tomohiko Amada's younger brother had taken his own life, probably because of the trauma of his own war experience. He had been part of the Nanjing Massacre, and committed suicide right after his discharge from the army. Correct?"

"Affirmative. Tomohiko Amada lost many loved ones in the whirlpool of those years. He himself was sorely damaged. As a result, his anger and grief put down deep roots. The hopeless, impotent realization that, no matter what he did, he could not stand against the torrent of history. As the sole survivor, he must also have felt an immense guilt. Hence he never spoke a word of what happened in Vienna, even after the gag was removed. It is as though he was unable to speak."

I looked at Tomohiko Amada's face. But I could detect no reaction as yet. I couldn't tell if he heard us or not.

I spoke. "Then at some point—we don't know exactly when—he created *Killing Commendatore*. An allegorical painting that expressed all he could not say. He put everything into it. A brilliant tour de force."

"He took that which he had been unable to accomplish in reality," the Commendatore said, "and gave it another form. What we might call 'camouflaged expression.' Not of what had in fact happened, but of *what should have happened*."

"Nevertheless, he bundled the painting up tight and hid it in the attic, out of public view," I said. "Although he had radically transformed the events, they were still too raw to reveal. Is that what you mean?"

"Precisely. It distills the pure essence of his living spirit. Then, one day, my friends happened upon it."

"So are you saying all of this began when I brought the painting out into the light? Is that what you meant by 'opening the circle'?"

The Commendatore said nothing, just extended his hands palms up.

Not long after, we noticed Tomohiko Amada's face turning pink. (The Commendatore and I had been watching him closely for any change.) At the same time, as if in response, the small, mysterious light that had been flickering deep in his eyes began to rise slowly to the surface. Like an ascending deep-sea diver gauging the effects of the water pressure on his body. The veil covering Amada's eyes also lifted, until, finally, both were wide open. The person lying before us was no longer a frail, desiccated old man on the verge of death. Instead, he was someone whose eyes brimmed with a determination to hang on to this world as long as he could.

"He is gathering his remaining strength," the Commendatore said to me. "Recovering as much of his conscious mind as he is able. But the more he regains mentally, the greater the physical torment. His body has been secreting a special substance to blot out that pain. It is thanks to the existence of such a substance that people can die in peace, not in agony. When consciousness returns, so does the pain. Nevertheless, he is trying to recover as much as he can. This is a mission he must fulfill here and now, however great the suffering."

As if to reinforce the Commendatore's words, Tomohiko Amada's face began to contort with agony. Age and infirmity had eaten away at his body until it was ready to shut down—he could feel that now. There was no way to avoid it. The end of his allotted time was fast approaching. It was painful to watch him suffer. Instead of calling him back, I might better have let him die a peaceful, painless death in a semiconscious haze.

"But he chose this way himself," the Commendatore said, again reading my mind. "It is painful to witness, but beyond our control."

"Won't Masahiko be returning soon?" I asked the Commendatore.

"Negative. Not for some time," he said with a small shake of his head. "His call was work related, something important. He will be gone a considerable time."

Tomohiko's eyes were wide open. They had been sunk within their wrinkled sockets, but now his eyeballs protruded like a person leaning out of a window. His breathing was deeper, and more ragged. It rasped as it passed in and out of his throat. And he was staring straight at the Commendatore. There was no doubt. The Commendatore was visible to him. Amazement was written in his face. He couldn't believe what was sitting in front of him. How could a figure produced by his imagination appear before him in reality?

"Negative, that is not the case," the Commendatore said. "What he sees and what my friends see are completely different."

"You mean you don't look the same way to him?"

"My friends, keep in mind that I am an Idea. My form changes depending on the person and the situation."

"Then how do you look to Mr. Amada?"

"That is something even I do not know. I am like a mirror that reflects what is in a person's heart. Nothing more."

"But you assumed this form for me on purpose, didn't you? Choosing to appear as the Commendatore?"

"To be precise, I did not choose this form. Cause and effect are hard to separate here. Because I took the form of the Commendatore, a sequence of events was set in motion. But at the same time, my form is the necessary consequence of that very sequence. It is hard to explain using the concept of time that governs the world you live in, my friends, but it might be summed up as: *All these events have been determined beforehand*."

"If an Idea is a mirror, then is Tomohiko Amada now seeing what he wishes to see?"

"Negative! He is seeing what he *must* see," the Commendatore corrected me. "It may be excruciating. Yet he must look. Now, at the end of his life."

I examined Tomohiko Amada's face again. Mixed with the amazement, I could discern an intense loathing. And almost unendurable torment. The return to consciousness carried with it not only the agony of the flesh. It brought with it the agony of the soul.

"He is squeezing out every last ounce of strength to ascertain who I am. Despite the pain. He is striving to return to his twenties."

Tomohiko Amada's face had turned a fiery red. Hot blood coursed through his veins. His thin, dry lips trembled, he gasped violently. His long, skeletal fingers clutched at the sheets.

"Stop dithering, my friends, and kill me now, while his mind is whole," the Commendatore said. "The quicker, the better. He may not be able to hold himself together much longer."

The Commendatore drew his sword from its scabbard. It was just eight inches long, but it looked very sharp indeed. Despite its dimensions, it was a weapon capable of ending a person's life.

"Stab me with this," the Commendatore said. "We shall re-create the scene from *Killing Commendatore*. But hurry. There is no time to dawdle."

I looked back and forth from the Commendatore to Tomohiko

Amada, struggling to make up my mind. All I could be remotely sure of was that Tomohiko Amada was in desperate need, and the Commendatore's resolve was firm. I alone wallowed in indecision, caught between the two of them.

I felt the rush of owl wings, and heard a bell ring in the dark.

Everything was connected somewhere.

"Affirmative! Everything is connected somewhere," said the Commendatore. "And my friends cannot escape that connection, however my friends may try. So steel yourself, and kill me. There is no room for guilt. Tomohiko Amada needs your help. By slaying me, my friends can save him. Make happen here what should have happened in the past. Now is the time. Only my friends can grant him salvation before he breathes his last."

I rose from my chair and strode to where the Commendatore was seated. I took his unsheathed sword in hand. I was past the point of determining what was just and unjust. In a world outside space and time, all dualities—before and after, up and down—ceased to exist. In such a world, I could no longer perceive myself as myself. I and myself were being torn apart.

The instant I took the sword in hand, however, I realized its handle was too small. It was a miniature sword for a tiny hand. There was simply no way could I kill the Commendatore with it, however keen its blade. The realization brought with it a sense of relief.

"The sword is too small. I can't grip it," I said to the Commendatore.

"That is a shame," he said with a sigh. "Well, there is nothing to be done. We must use something else, although that means diverging further from the painting."

"Something else?"

The Commendatore pointed to a small chest of drawers in the corner of the room. "Look inside the top drawer."

I went to the chest and slid open the uppermost drawer.

"Within is a knife for filleting fish," the Commendatore said.

Sure enough, a knife lay atop a small stack of neatly folded washcloths. The knife that Masahiko had used to prepare the sea bream he had brought to my home. An eight-inch blade honed to a razor's edge.

Masahiko always kept his tools in perfect shape. This knife was no exception.

"Now take that knife and plunge it into my chest," said the Commendatore. "Sword or knife, what is the difference. We can still reenact the scene in *Killing Commendatore*. But we must make haste. There is little time."

I took the knife in hand. It was as heavy as stone. The tip of the blade shone cold and white in the light streaming from the window. The knife had vanished from my kitchen and come to wait for me here, in the chest of drawers. Masahiko had sharpened the blade, as it turned out, for the sake of his own father. There seemed no way to avoid my fate.

I still couldn't come to a decision. Nevertheless, I stepped behind the Commendatore's chair, gripping the knife tightly in my right hand. From his bed, Tomohiko Amada stared at us with eyes as big as saucers. As if watching history unfold before his eyes. His mouth was open, exposing his yellowed teeth and whitish tongue, a tongue that lolled in his mouth as though trying to form words. Words this world would never hear.

"My friends do not have a violent bone in your body," the Commendatore said, as if to admonish me. "It is obvious. My friends are not built to kill. But sometimes people must act against their nature, to rescue something important or for some greater purpose. Now is one of those times. So kill me! I am not big, as my friends can see, and I will not resist. I am merely an Idea. Just insert the tip of the knife into my heart. What could be more straightforward?"

The Commendatore pointed his tiny index finger at the spot where his heart was. But the thought of that heart inevitably recalled my sister's. I could remember her operation as if it were yesterday. How delicate and difficult it had been. Saving a malfunctioning heart was a formidable task. It required a team of specialists and gallons of blood. Yet destroying a heart was *so easy*.

"Such thinking will get us nowhere," the Commendatore said. "If my friends wish to save Mariye Akikawa, then do the deed. Even if my friends do not want to. Trust me. Jettison all feelings, and close your mind. But not your eyes. My friends must keep them open."

I stepped behind the Commendatore and raised the knife. But I couldn't bring it down. Sure, it might be only one of a thousand deaths for an Idea, but it was still extinguishing a life as far as I was concerned. Was this not the same order the young lieutenant had given Tsuguhiko Amada in Nanjing?

"Negative! It is not the same," said the Commendatore. "My friends are doing this at my behest. It is I who am asking my friends to kill me. So that I may be reborn. Be strong. Close the circle at once."

I closed my eyes and thought of the girl I had throttled in the love hotel in Miyagi. Of course, she and I had been pretending. I had squeezed her throat gently, so as not to kill her. I had been unable to do it long enough to satisfy her. Had I continued, I might indeed have strangled her to death. On the bed of that love hotel, I had glimpsed the deep rage within myself for the first time. It had churned in my chest like blood-soaked mud, pushing me closer and closer to real murder.

I know where you were and what you were doing, the man had said.

"All right, now bring it down," the Commendatore said. "I know my friends can do it. Remember, my friends will not be killing me. My friends will be slaying your evil father. The blood of your evil father shall soak into the earth."

My evil father?

Where did that come from?

"Who is the evil father of my friends?" the Commendatore said, reading my mind. "I believe your path crossed with his not long ago. Am I mistaken?"

Do not paint my portrait any further, the man had said. He had pointed his finger at me from within the dark mirror. It had pierced my chest like the tip of a sharp sword.

Spurred by that pain, I reflexively closed my heart and opened my eyes wide. I cleared all thought from my mind (as Don Giovanni had done in *Killing Commendatore*), buried my emotions, made my face a blank mask, and brought the knife down with all my might. The sharp blade entered the Commendatore's tiny chest precisely where he had pointed. I felt the living flesh resist. But the Commendatore himself made no attempt to fend off the blow. His fingers clutched at the air, but apart from that he did not react. Still, the body he inhabited did all that it could to avoid its looming extinction. The Commendatore was an Idea, but his body was not. An Idea may have borrowed it for its own purposes, but that body would not meekly submit to death. It possessed its own rationale. I had to overcome that resistance through brute force, severing its life at the roots. "Kill me," the Commendatore had said. But I was actually dispatching another *someone*'s body.

I wanted to drop the knife, drop everything, and run from the room. But the Commendatore's words echoed in my ears. "If my friends wish to save Mariye Akikawa, then do the deed. Even if my friends do not want to."

So I pushed the blade even farther into the Commendatore's heart. If you're stabbing someone to death, there's no halfway. The tip of the knife emerged from his back—I had run him through. His white garment was dyed crimson. My hands were drenched in blood. But the blood did not spew into the air as it did in *Killing Commendatore*. This is an illusion, I tried to convince myself. I was murdering a mere phantom. My act was purely symbolic.

Yet I knew I was fooling myself. Perhaps the act was symbolic. But it was no phantom that I was killing. Without question, my victim was made of flesh and blood. It may have been barely two feet tall, a fabrication created by Tomohiko Amada's brush, but its life force was unexpectedly strong. The point of my blade had broken the skin and several ribs on its way to the heart, then passed through to the back of the chair. No way that was an illusion.

Tomohiko Amada's eyes were open even wider now, riveted on the scene unfolding before him. My murder of the Commendatore. No, for him it must have been the murder of someone else. Who was he seeing? The Nazi official whose assassination he had helped plot in Vienna? The young lieutenant who had given his brother a Japanese sword and ordered him to behead three Chinese prisoners in Nanjing? Or that evil *something*, something more fundamental, that lay at the root of those events? I could only guess. I could not read the expression on Tomohiko Amada's face. Though his mouth gaped open, his lips were motionless. Only his tongue continued its futile quest to form words of some kind.

At last, the strength left the Commendatore's neck and arms. His whole body went slack, like a marionette whose strings had been cut. I responded by pushing the knife even farther into his heart. All movement in the room came to a standstill; the scene was now a frozen tableau. It stayed that way for a long time.

Tomohiko Amada was the first to move. Once the Commendatore had lost consciousness and collapsed, the strength to focus his mind evaporated. He sighed deeply and closed his eyes. Slowly and solemnly, like lowering the shutters. As if to confirm: *Now I have seen what I needed to see.* His mouth was still open, but his lolling tongue was tucked out of sight. Only his yellow teeth were visible, like a ramshackle fence circling an empty house. His face was free of pain. The torment had passed. He looked peaceful and relaxed. I guessed he was back in the twilight world, where thought and pain did not exist. I was happy for him.

I finally relaxed my arm and drew the blade from the Commendatore's body. Blood spewed from the wound. Exactly as in *Killing Commendatore*. The Commendatore himself spilled lifelessly into the chair. His eyes were open, his mouth contorted in agony. His ten tiny fingers clawed the air. Dark blood pooled around his feet. He was dead. How much blood had come from that tiny body!

Thus did the Commendatore—or the Idea that had taken his form—meet his end. Tomohiko Amada had sunk back into his deep sleep. Standing next to the Commendatore's body, Masahiko's bloody knife in my right hand, I was the only conscious person left in the room. My labored breathing should have been the only sound. Should have been. But something was moving. I sensed it as much as I heard it, to my alarm. *Keep your ears open*, the Commendatore had told me. I did as he had instructed.

Something is in the room. I could hear it moving. Bloody knife in hand, I stood frozen like a statue, scanning the room, searching for the source of the sound. Out of the corner of one eye, I spotted something near the far wall.

Long Face was there.

Killing the Commendatore had lured Long Face into this world.

52

THE MAN IN THE ORANGE CONE HAT

The scene in the room now matched the lower left-hand corner of Tomohiko Amada's *Killing Commendatore*. Long Face had poked his head out of a hole, and was raising its square cover with one hand as he peeked at what was taking place. His hair was long and tangled, and a thick black beard covered much of his face. His elongated head was shaped like a Japanese eggplant, narrow with a jutting chin and bulging eyes. The bridge of his nose was flat. For some reason, his lips glistened like a piece of fruit. His body was small but well proportioned, as if a normal person had been shrunk in size. Just as the Commendatore made you think of a scaled-down copy of a human being.

The big difference between the Long Face in *Killing Commendatore* and here was his expression—now he looked stunned as he stared at the lifeless body of the Commendatore. His mouth gaped in disbelief. How long had he been watching us? I had no idea. I had been so focused on snuffing out the Commendatore's life, and gauging Tomohiko Amada's reaction to his death, that I had been oblivious to the odd-looking man in the corner of the room. Yet I bet he hadn't missed a thing. After all, that was the scene in *Killing Commendatore.*

Long Face remained completely still, there in the corner of our tableau. As if assigned a fixed position. I moved slightly to see how he would respond. But Long Face didn't react. He maintained the same position he had in the painting—one hand holding up the square lid, his eyes round as he gawked at the slain Commendatore. He didn't even blink.

As the tension drained from my body, I moved from my own assigned position. I edged cautiously toward Long Face, deadening my footsteps like a cat, the bloody knife in one hand. I could not let him slip back underground. To save Mariye Akikawa, the Commendatore had given his life to re-create the scene in the painting, and drawn Long Face out into the open. I must not allow that sacrifice to be in vain.

Yet how could I wrest from Long Face what I needed to know about Mariye? I was at a loss. *Who* or *what* was Long Face? How was his presence linked to Mariye's disappearance? What the Commendatore had told me was more riddle than information. One thing was clear, though: I had to get my hands on him. I could figure the rest out later.

The lid that Long Face was holding was about two feet square, made of the same lime-green linoleum as the rest of the floor. When closed, it would blend in perfectly, perhaps even disappear altogether.

Long Face did not move a muscle as I approached. He seemed rooted to the spot. Like a cat in the headlights. Or maybe he was just fulfilling his designated role—to maintain the composition of the painting for as long as possible. Whichever, it was lucky for me. Otherwise, he would have sensed me behind him and slipped back underground for good. Once the lid had been closed, I doubted it would open again.

I crept behind him, softly laid down the knife, and snatched his collar with both hands. He was wearing drab, snug-fitting clothes. Work clothes, from the look of it. Clearly different from the fine cloth of the Commendatore's garments. These looked rough to the touch and were covered in patches.

Jolted from his trance, Long Face thrashed about, desperately attempting to flee down his hole. I held tight to his collar. There was no way I was going to let him escape. I gathered my strength and tried to yank him all the way out. He fought back, grabbing the sides of the hole with both hands. He was much stronger than I'd anticipated. He even tried to bite my arm. What could I do—I slammed his eggplant-shaped head against the corner of the opening. Then I did it again, this time more violently. The second blow knocked him out cold. I could feel his body go limp. At last I could drag him out into the light.

Long Face was a little bigger than the Commendatore. Two and a half feet tall was my guess. He was wearing what a farmer might have worn in the fields, or a manservant sweeping the yard. A stiff, rough jacket over baggy work pants cinched at the ankles. His belt was a thick piece of rope. He wore no shoes, and his soles were thickly callused and stained black with dirt. His long hair showed no sign of having been recently washed or combed. Half his face was covered by a black beard. The other half was a sickly white. Nothing about him looked clean, yet, strangely, his body had no odor.

Based on appearance, I figured the Commendatore belonged to the aristocracy of his time, while Long Face was lower-class. Perhaps he was dressed the way commoners did back then. Or maybe Tomohiko Amada had imagined, *This is how people might have dressed in the Asuka period.* Historical accuracy, however, was beside the point. What I needed to do was squeeze from this man with the strange face any information that would lead me to Mariye.

I rolled Long Face over onto his stomach and tied his hands behind him with the belt of a bathrobe hanging close by. Then I dragged his motionless body to the center of the room. Because of his size, he wasn't very heavy. About the weight of a medium-sized dog. I grabbed a curtain tie and bound one of his legs to the bed. Now he had no way to flee.

Stretched out unconscious in the bright afternoon light, Long Face just looked pitiful. Gone was the weirdness that had alarmed me when he had poked his head up out of his hole, observing events with those glittering eyes. I could find nothing sinister about him. He didn't look bright enough to be evil. Instead, he looked honest in a dull-witted sort of way. And timid, too. Not like someone who concocted plans and made decisions, but, rather, the type who meekly followed his superiors' orders.

Tomohiko Amada was still stretched out on the bed, his eyes closed. He was completely still. I couldn't tell, looking at him, if he was alive or dead. I leaned down and put my ear less than an inch from his mouth. His breathing was faint, like a distant surf. He wasn't dead yet, just sleeping on the floor of his twilight world. I felt relieved. I didn't like the idea of Masahiko returning from his phone call to find that his father had died in his absence. Tomohiko's face, as he lay on his side, looked far more peaceful and satisfied than before. Maybe witnessing the slaying of the Commendatore (or someone else he wished to see killed) had put some of his painful memories to rest.

The Commendatore was slumped in his cloth chair. His eyes were wide open, and I could see his tiny tongue curled behind his parted lips. Blood was still seeping from the wound in his chest, but the flow was weaker than before. His right hand flopped lifelessly when I took it. Although his skin retained some warmth, it felt remote and somehow detached. The kind of detachment life acquires as it moves steadily toward its own end. I felt like straightening his limbs and placing him in a proper-sized coffin, one made for a small child. I would lay the coffin in the pit behind the shrine, where no one could bother him again. But all I could do now was gently close his eyes.

I sat in the chair and watched Long Face on the floor as I waited for him to regain his senses. Outside the window, the broad Pacific sparkled. A few fishing boats were still plying the waters. I could see the sleek fuselage of an airplane shining in the sun as it slowly made its way south. A four-prop plane with an antenna jutting up from its tail—probably an antisubmarine aircraft from the Japanese Maritime Self-Defense Force base in Atsugi. Some of us were quietly going about our business on a Saturday afternoon. I, for one, was in a sunlit room in an upscale nursing home, having just slain the Commendatore and fished out and tied up Long Face in my quest to find a beautiful thirteen-year-old girl. It takes all kinds, I guess.

Long Face didn't regain consciousness for some time. I checked my watch again.

What would Masahiko think if he came back now? The Commendatore in a pool of blood, Long Face bound and unconscious on the floor. Both in the unfamiliar garb of an ancient time, neither standing even three feet tall. Tomohiko Amada comatose on the bed, a faint but satisfied smile (if that's what it was) on his lips. A square, black hole gaping in a corner of the room. How could I explain what had led to this scene?

Of course, Masahiko didn't come back. He was tied up in a work-related phone call of great importance, as the Commendatore had said. He would be dealing with it for some time yet. Everything had been arranged in advance. No one would bother us. I sat on the chair, eyeing the unconscious Long Face. I had whacked his head pretty hard on the edge of the hole, but it shouldn't take him that long to come to. He'd have a fair-sized lump on his head, that's all.

At last, Long Face woke up. He twisted and turned a bit on the floor, and uttered a few incomprehensible words. Then, slowly, he opened his eyes a crack. Like a child looking at something scary—something he didn't want to see, but must.

I went and knelt beside him.

"There's very little time," I said, looking down at him. "I need you to tell me where I can find Mariye Akikawa. If you do, I'll untie you, and you can go back."

I pointed to the square hole in the corner. The lid was still raised. I couldn't tell if he understood what I was saying or not. But I decided to keep talking. All I could do was give it a shot.

Long Face violently shook his head back and forth several times. I couldn't tell if he was saying that he didn't know anything, or that my language was foreign to him.

"If you don't tell me, I'll kill you," I said. "You saw me stab the Commendatore, I bet. Well, there's no big difference between one murder and two."

I pressed the bloody blade of my knife against his dirty throat. I thought of the fishermen and the pilot of the southbound airplane. *We all have jobs we have to do.* And this was mine. I wasn't going to kill him, of course, but the knife was real, and very sharp. Long Face quivered in fear.

"Wait!" he gasped in a husky voice. "Stay your hand."

His way of speaking was strange, but I could understand him. I eased off on the knife.

"Where is Mariye Akikawa?" I pressed him. "Come on, spit it out!"

"No, sir, I do not know. I swear it."

I studied his eyes. They were big and easy to read. He seemed to be telling the truth.

"All right then, tell me, what are you doing here?" I asked.

"I am enjoined to verify and record these events. I do only what I am told to do. You have my word."

"Why must you verify them?"

"Because I was so bidden. I know nothing beyond that."

"So what on earth are you? Another kind of Idea?"

"Goodness no! I am a Metaphor, nothing more."

"A Metaphor?"

"Yes. A mere Metaphor. Used to link two things together. So please, untie my bonds, please, I beseech you."

I was getting confused. "If you are as you say, then give me a metaphor now, off the top of your head."

"I am the most humble and lowly form of Metaphor, sir. I cannot devise anything of quality."

"A metaphor of any kind is all right—it doesn't have to be brilliant."

"He was someone who stood out," he said after a moment's pause, "like a man wearing an orange cone hat in a packed commuter train."

Not an impressive metaphor, to be sure. In fact, not really a metaphor at all.

"That's a simile, not a metaphor," I pointed out.

"A million pardons," he said, sweat pouring from his forehead. "Let me try again. 'He lived as though he were wearing an orange cone hat in a crowded train.' "

"That makes no sense. It's still not a true metaphor. Your story doesn't hold. I'll just have to kill you."

Long Face's lips trembled with fear. His beard may have been manly, but he was short on guts.

"My sincerest apologies, sir. I am yet but an apprentice. I cannot think of a witty example. Forgive me. But I assure you that I am the genuine article, a true Metaphor."

"Then who is your superior—who commands you?"

"I have no superior, per se. Well, perhaps I do, but I have never laid eyes on him. I only follow orders—acting as a link between phenomena and language. Like a helpless jellyfish adrift on the ocean. So please do not kill me. I implore you."

"I can spare your life," I said, my knife still on his throat. "But only if you agree to guide me to where you came from."

"That is something I cannot do," Long Face said in a firm voice. It was the first time he had used that tone. "The road I took to get here is the Path of Metaphor. It is different for each one who traverses it. It is not a single road. Thus I cannot guide you, sir, on your way."

"Let me get this straight. I must follow this path alone, and I must discover it for myself—is that what you're saying?"

Long Face nodded vigorously. "The Path of Metaphor is rife with perils. Should a mortal like you stray from the path even once, you could find yourself in danger. And there are Double Metaphors everywhere."

"Double Metaphors?"

Long Face shuddered with fear. "Yes, Double Metaphors lurking in the darkness. The most *vile* and dangerous of creatures."

"It's all the same to me," I said. "I'm already mixed up in a whole lot of craziness. So it's no skin off my nose if the craziness grows or shrinks. I killed the Commendatore with my own hands. I don't want his death to be in vain."

"I see I have no choice. So let me offer you a word of warning before you set out."

"What kind of warning?"

"Take a light of some kind with you. You will pass through many dark places on your way. You will come across a river. It is a metaphorical river, but the water is very real. It is cold and deep, and the current is strong. You cannot cross without a boat. You will find a boat at the ferrying spot."

"How about after I cross the river—what should I do then?"

Long Face rolled his bulging eyes. "The world that awaits you on the other side, like this one, is subject to the principle of connectivity. You will have to see for yourself."

I checked Tomohiko Amada's bedside table. Sure enough, a flashlight was there. A facility like this one was sure to store one in each room in case of fire or earthquake. I flicked it on. The light was strong. The batteries weren't dead. I slipped on my leather jacket, which I had draped over a chair, and started for the hole in the corner, flashlight in hand.

"Please, sir," Long Face begged. "Will you not loosen my bonds? I fear what may transpire should I be left in this state."

"If you're a true Metaphor, untying yourself should be easy. Aren't Concepts and Ideas and others like you able to move through space and time?"

"No, you overrate me. I am blessed with no such marvelous powers. Concepts and Ideas are Metaphors of a much higher order."

"Like those with orange cone hats?"

Long Face looked stricken. "Please do not mock me, sir. My feelings can be hurt too, you know."

After a moment's hesitation, I decided to untie his hands and feet. I had bound them so tightly they took time to undo. Now that we had talked, he didn't appear to be such a bad fellow. True, he didn't know where Mariye was, but he had volunteered other information. I doubted that he would interfere or cause me any harm if I untied him. And I certainly couldn't leave him bound and trussed where he was. Should anyone find him like that, it would only make things worse. When I finished, he sat there for a moment, rubbing his chafed wrists with his tiny hands. Then he felt his forehead. It appeared a lump had already sprouted.

"Thank you, sir. Now I can return to my world."

"Go ahead," I said, gesturing to the hole in the corner. "I'll follow later."

"I shall now make my departure. Please ensure that the lid is securely closed when you follow. Otherwise, someone might trip and fall in. Or grow curious and climb down. Then I would be held responsible."

"Understood. I will make sure it's closed."

Long Face trotted to the hole and climbed inside. Then his head and shoulders popped up again. His saucer eyes had an eerie glow. As they did in *Killing Commendatore*.

"I wish you a safe journey," Long Face said to me. "I hope you can find *What's-her-name*. Was it Komichi?"

"No, her name isn't Komichi," I said. A chill ran down my spine. My throat turned to sandpaper. I couldn't speak for a moment. "The name was Mariye Akikawa. Do you know something about Komichi?"

"No, I know nothing at all." Long Face seemed to realize that he'd let drop something he shouldn't. "The name just slipped into my clumsy metaphorical brain. A simple mistake. Forgive me, please, sir."

Long Face vanished down the hole. Like smoke in the wind.

I stood there for a moment, plastic flashlight in hand. Komichi? How could my sister's name come up here, of all places? Could she be connected to this strangeness? But I had no time to ponder that question. I switched the flashlight on and entered the hole, feetfirst. It was dark below, and there seemed to be a long path sloping downward. That was odd, too, come to think of it. The room was on the third floor, so the second floor should be directly beneath. I trained the flashlight on the path, but couldn't make out where it led. I lowered the rest of my body inside and closed the lid tight behind me. Now everything was black.

The darkness was so complete that my five senses were useless. As if the links between my body and my mind had been severed, and no information was passing between them. It was the strangest feeling. As if I were no longer myself. Nevertheless, I had to go on.

"If my friends wish to save Mariye Akikawa, then do the deed."

Those had been the Commendatore's words. He had made the sacrifice. Now it was my turn to face the ordeal. I had to push forward. With the flashlight my only ally, I stepped down into the inky blackness of the Path of Metaphor.

53

MAYBE A FIREPLACE POKER

The blackness enfolding me was so thick, so complete, it seemed to have a will of its own. It felt like walking on the ocean floor, where not even a particle of light could penetrate. Only the yellow beam of my flashlight connected me to the world, and barely, at that. The passageway descended at a steady angle. The surface beneath my feet was hard and smooth—it felt like walking down a tunnel bored into solid rock. The ceiling was so low I had to stoop to keep from hitting my head. The air was chilly and odorless, and the total lack of smell disturbed me. Perhaps even the air was different here than above ground.

How long would my flashlight hold out? Its beam was strong and steady for now, but when the batteries failed (as they would eventually) I would be stranded in the dark. And if I were to believe Long Face, dangerous Double Metaphors were lurking out there, ready to pounce.

The palm of my hand that held the flashlight was sweaty from the tension. My heartbeat was a dull, hard thump. It sounded threatening, like a drumbeat would to someone lost in the jungle. Long Face had warned me: "Take a light of some kind with you. You will pass through many dark places on your way." So not everything in this passageway was pitch black. I wished it would brighten soon. I wished too that the ceiling would rise. I had always felt panicky in dark, constricted spaces. If this continued for much longer, I would soon have trouble breathing.

To calm myself, I tried to focus on other things. I needed to find something, anything, to occupy my mind. What popped into my head was an open-faced grilled cheese sandwich. Why a grilled cheese sandwich? Go figure. That's what came up first, for whatever reason. Perfectly melted cheese on a square of beautifully browned toast. Sitting on a pure white plate. So real I could reach out and touch it. And beside it a cup of piping-hot coffee. Coffee as black as a moonless night. A window opening onto a tall willow, on whose supple branches a small flock of chirping birds perched precariously, like a troupe of tightrope walkers. Everything at an immeasurable distance from where I was now.

Then, for some reason, I thought of the opera *Der Rosenkavalier*. I would listen to it as I sipped my coffee and nibbled my grilled cheese sandwich. That jet-black vinyl disk, released by Decca Records in Great Britain. I placed the heavy record on the turntable and gently lowered the needle. Georg Solti conducting the Vienna Philharmonic. The music elegant, intricate. When Richard Strauss had boasted he could describe even a broom musically, he was in his heyday. But was it a broom? I still couldn't remember. Perhaps it was an umbrella, or then again maybe a fireplace poker. In any case, how could one describe a broom in music? Or a hot grilled cheese sandwich, or someone's callused feet, or the difference between a simile and a metaphor? Could music really depict those things?

Richard Strauss conducted the same orchestra in prewar Vienna. (Was it before the *Anschluss*? After?) The program on this given day was Beethoven's 7th, a resolute yet quiet and well-groomed symphony, squeezed between its bright, uninhibited older sister (the 6th) and its bashful and beautiful younger sister (the 8th). A youthful Tomohiko Amada was in attendance. A pretty young woman sat beside him. Most likely, he was in love with her.

I imagined the city of Vienna on that day. The waltzes, the sweet Sacher tortes, the red-and-black swastikas fluttering from the roofs.

I could feel my thoughts veering off in a pointless direction. Or, more accurately perhaps, in a directionless direction. Yet I was powerless to rein them in. They were no longer under my control. It's no simple matter to hold on to your mind in total blackness. Your thoughts become a tree of riddles whose branches trail off into the dark. (A metaphor.) Nevertheless, I had to focus on *something* to hold myself together. Any old *something* would do. Otherwise, I would start to hyperventilate.

One absurdity after another sauntered through my mind as I pushed down the endless slope. The passageway was as straight as an arrow, with no bends or forks. However far I walked, nothing changed—not the height of the ceiling, or the depth of the darkness, or the quality of the air, or the angle of the slope. My sense of time was foggy, but based on how long I had been walking, I must have been deep underground. Yet in the end, that "depth" had to be a fabrication. After all, I had entered this tunnel from the third floor of a building. The darkness too had to be fabricated. Everything was either concept or metaphor, nothing more. That's what I told myself, anyway. The problem was that the darkness enfolding me was real darkness, the depth pressing down on me real depth.

Just when my neck and back were firing off warning signals about my hunched-over posture, a dim light appeared ahead. Then came a series of twists and turns. With each, my surroundings grew a little brighter, as if the night sky was giving way to day. Now I could make out where I was. I switched off my flashlight to conserve the batteries.

It was growing light, but still I smelled nothing, heard nothing. Then, at last, the cramped passage abruptly ended, and I stepped out into the open. Yet I could see no sky above me, only what looked like a milky-white ceiling, far overheard. A pale glow covered everything, as if the world was lit by a host of luminous insects. It felt odd. Yet it was a relief to say goodbye to the darkness, and to be able to walk upright again. I could relax a bit.

Outside the tunnel, the ground was rough underfoot. There was no path, only a barren, rocky plain that stretched as far as the eye could see. The downward slope had ended, and I was walking up a gentle rise. I picked my way forward, unsure of my direction. I checked my watch, but its hands held no meaning. One glance told me that much. In fact, nothing I carried—key ring, wallet, driver's license, loose change, handkerchief—promised to be of any use at all.

The incline grew steeper and steeper. After a while, I was literally crawling up the slope on my hands and knees. If I could only reach the top, then maybe I could see where I was. I pushed on without pausing to catch my breath. The only sound was the sound I was making, and even that seemed artificial, not like real sound at all. There was nothing alive that I could see. Not a tree, not a clump of grass, not a solitary bird. Not even a puff of wind. Only I moved—all else was still. It was as if time itself had come to a halt.

I finally reached the top of the rise. I could see in all directions from there, as I had anticipated. Yet my view was limited. For there was a whitish mist that hung over everything. All I could make out was what amounted to a lifeless wasteland, a craggy, barren wilderness that stretched in every direction. There was no true sky, just that milky-white ceiling. I felt like an astronaut who had crashed, and landed on an uninhabited planet. Well, at least there was some light, and air that I could breathe. I should be grateful for those.

I could find no sign of life. Finally, though, I was able to make out a faint sound. I thought it might be a hallucination at first, or possibly coming from my own body. Yet it gradually became clear that the noise was continuous, and caused by some kind of natural phenomenon. In fact, it sounded like flowing water. Perhaps it was the river that Long Face had spoken of. Bathed in the pale light, I picked my way down the bumpy slope in the direction of the sound.

The sound of water made me terribly thirsty. Come to think of it, I had been walking a very long time with nothing to drink. Yet I had been so anxious that water had never crossed my mind. Now I craved it desperately. But was the water in that river—if that was where the sound was coming from—drinkable? It might be thick with mud, or filled with dangerous toxins. Or perhaps it was metaphorical water, which my hands could not scoop up. Oh well, I would find out when I got there.

The noise grew louder and clearer as I went along. It sounded like a fast-flowing river, tumbling through rocks. Yet I still could not see it. As I headed toward the sound, the ground on both sides of me rose until I was walking between two rock walls about thirty feet in height. The path cut between those towering cliffs, though its serpentine twists and turns made it impossible to know what lay ahead. It was not a man-made trail. Rather, it appeared to have been fashioned by the forces of nature. From what I could tell, the river lay at its end.

I hurried along the walled path. I passed no tree, no blade of grass. Not a living thing. The silent cliffs were all that I could see. A sterile, monochrome world. It was as if an artist had lost interest in painting a landscape, and had abandoned it before adding the colors. I could barely hear my own footsteps. The rocks seemed to absorb sound.

At a certain point the path, which had been flat for the most part, began to slope upward again. It took some time, but at last I reached the crest, which ran like a spine along the top of the cliffs. When I leaned forward, I could see the river. Now the rush of water was even more audible.

The river was not especially wide. Maybe fifteen or twenty feet across. But its current was swift. I couldn't tell its depth. Judging from the whitecaps it sent up here and there, boulders and other hidden obstacles lay beneath the surface. The river carved a straight line through the rocky terrain. I crossed the ridge and headed down the slope in its direction.

When I reached the river, and saw it rushing past from right to left, I felt much better. At the very least, a large quantity of water was on the move. It had originated somewhere and was flowing somewhere else, following the contours of the land. In a place where nothing stirred, and no wind blew, the sound of rushing water reverberated around me. No, this world was not wholly absent of motion. That fact alone gave me some comfort.

The moment I reached the river, I knelt on the bank and scooped up water in my cupped hands. It was pleasantly cold. The river seemed snow-fed. Its water was crystal clear and appeared pure. Of course, I couldn't tell by looking at it if it was safe to drink. It might contain a deadly poison. Or bacteria that would ravage my body.

I sniffed the water in my hands. It had no odor (that is, if my sense of smell was still functioning). I took a sip. It had no flavor (that is, if I hadn't lost my sense of taste). I braced myself and swallowed deeply. I was too thirsty to resist, whatever the consequences. The water was indeed entirely tasteless and odorless. It might be real or fabricated, but thankfully, it would quench my thirst.

I knelt there, blissfully gulping mouthful after mouthful. I was thirstier than I had realized. Yet it was strange somehow to drink water lacking in taste and odor. Cold water when we are thirsty is *delicious* more than anything else. Our body sucks it in greedily. Our cells rejoice, our muscles regain their strength. Yet drinking the water from this river brought none of those feelings. It did no more than quench my thirst at a simple, physical level.

When I had drunk my fill, I stood up and looked at my surroundings one more time. Long Face had said that there would be a boat landing somewhere along the riverbank. That one of the boats could ferry me to the other side. There I would (probably) find information relating to Mariye Akikawa's whereabouts. But I could see nothing that looked like a landing, either upstream or downstream. I would have to search for it. A boat was crucial. Fording the river unaided was too dangerous. "The water is cold and deep, and the current is strong. You cannot cross without a boat," Long Face had told me. But which way should I turn to find that boat? Upriver or downriver? I had to choose one or the other.

Then I remembered Menshiki's given name, "Wataru," written with the kanji for traversing water. "The *wataru* in my name is the character that means 'to cross a river,'" Menshiki had said, when he introduced himself. "I don't know why I was given that name. I've never had much to do with water." A short while later he had added, "By the way, I'm left-handed. If I'm told to go left or right, I always choose left. It's become a habit."

It was a random comment quite disconnected to what we were talking about—I couldn't figure out why he would blurt out something like that. Which is probably why it stuck in my mind.

Maybe his comment had no special significance. It could have been mere happenstance. Yet (according to Long Face) this was a land built upon the conjunction of phenomena and expression. I ought to be able to handle the *happenstance* of any hints that came in my direction. I stood before the river and made up my mind. I would go left. If I took the unconscious tip that "colorless" Menshiki had provided and followed the tasteless, odorless river downstream, it might provide a further hint of some sort. Then again, it might not.

As I walked along the riverbank, I wondered what, if anything, lived in the water. It didn't seem likely anything did. I couldn't confirm this, of course. Nevertheless, I could see no signs of life. What organism would live in water that had neither taste nor odor? The river appeared wholly concentrated on its own identity. "I am river," it said. "I am that which flows." Certainly it possessed the form of a river, but beyond that *state of being* there was nothing. Not a thing floated on its surface, not a twig, not a blade of grass. It was simply a great quantity of water cutting across the land.

I pushed on through that boundless, cottony mist. It gently resisted me as I moved, like a filmy curtain of white lace. After a while, my gut began to react to the water I had drunk. It didn't feel unpleasant or ominous, but neither was it cause for rejoicing. A neutral feeling, whose true nature eluded my understanding. I felt I was being somehow changed, as if I were no longer the same person. It was a strange sensation. Could the water be turning me into someone physically adapted to this world?

For some reason, though, I was able to stay calm. I thought, optimistically, that there could be no real harm. My optimism had no firm basis. Nevertheless, I had passed without mishap through the narrow pitch-black passageway. With neither map nor compass, I had crossed a rocky wilderness to find this river. I had quenched my thirst with its water. I had avoided a close encounter with a lurking Double Metaphor. Dumb luck? Or perhaps it was predetermined. Whichever the case, I was heading in a good direction. So I thought. Or at least so I tried to convince myself.

Finally, a vague shape appeared through the haze. It was not a natural object—its straight lines meant it had to be human-made. As I drew nearer I saw that it was a boat landing. A small wooden jetty extending from the shore. Turning left had been the correct decision. Then again, it was possible that, in a world governed by connectivity, things would shift to accommodate whatever action I chose. Apparently, Menshiki's unconscious hint had helped steer me through to this point.

I could see the figure of a man, shrouded in the mist. He was tall. In fact, after the tiny Commendatore and Long Face, he looked like a giant. He was standing very still at the end of the jetty, as if lost in thought, leaning against some kind of dark machine. The swift-flowing river bubbled over his feet. He was the first human being I had encountered in this land. Or human-shaped being, perhaps. I approached him with trepidation.

I couldn't see him clearly, so I took a chance and called out, "Hello!"

through that cottony veil. But there was no reply. He just adjusted his posture slightly. I could see his dark silhouette shift in the mist. Perhaps my voice hadn't reached him. The sound of the river might have blotted it out. Or the air in these parts might not carry sound very well.

"Hello!" I said again, moving somewhat closer. In a louder voice this time. Still, he didn't speak. All I could hear was the unbroken rush of water. Perhaps he couldn't understand what I was saying.

"I can hear you. And I do understand," he said, as if reading my mind. His voice was deep and low, befitting his height. But it was also flat, utterly devoid of feeling. Just as the river was devoid of odor and taste.

54

ETERNITY IS A VERY LONG TIME

The tall man standing before me had no face. He did have a head, of course. It sat on his shoulders in a normal way. But the head lacked a face. Where a face should have been was blank. A milky blankness, like pale smoke. His voice emerged from within that emptiness like wind from a deep cavern.

The man was wearing what looked like a dark raincoat. The coat ended just short of the ground, so I could see the tips of his boots peeking out. Its buttons were fastened up to his neck. It was as if there was a storm on the horizon, and he had dressed for it.

I stood there, rooted to the spot, unable to speak. From a distance, he had reminded me of the man with the white Subaru Forester, or Tomohiko Amada the night he had visited my studio. Or again, the young man who slayed the Commendatore with his sword in *Killing Commendatore*. All were similarly tall. A closer look, however, told me he was none of them. He was just the *faceless man*. A broad-brimmed black hat was pulled low over his eyes. The brim half concealed the milky emptiness.

"I can hear you. And I do understand," he repeated. I didn't see his lips move, of course. He had none.

"Is this the boat landing?" I asked.

"Yes," the faceless man replied. "This is the boat landing. Only from here can one cross the river."

"I must travel to the other side."

"As must all."

"Do many come?"

The man did not reply. My question was sucked into the void. There followed an interminable silence.

"What is on the other side?" I asked. The white mist over the river concealed the far shore.

I could feel the faceless man studying my face from within the emptiness. "What is on the other side depends on what you are seeking. It is different for everyone."

"I am trying to locate the whereabouts of a young girl named Mariye Akikawa."

"So that is what you seek on the other side, correct?"

"Yes. That is what I seek. That is why I have come."

"And how was it, then, that you were able to find the entrance?"

"I killed an Idea that had taken the form of the Commendatore. I killed him with a carving knife in a nursing home in Izu Kogen. I did so with his permission. His death summoned Long Face, the Metaphor who opened the hole to the underground passageway. I forced him to let me in."

The man fixed his empty countenance on me for some time. He didn't speak. Had he understood me or not? I couldn't tell.

"Was there blood?"

"A great deal," I answered.

"Actual blood, I take it."

"So it seemed."

"Look at your hands."

I looked. But no trace of blood remained. Perhaps it had been washed away when I drank from the river. There ought to have been a lot, though.

"No matter," the faceless man said. "I have a boat, and I will ferry you across. But there is one condition."

I waited to be told what that might be.

"You must pay me an appropriate fee. That is the rule."

"And if I can't pay, am I unable to cross to the far shore?"

"Yes. You would have to remain here for eternity. The river is cold and deep, and the current is strong. And eternity is a very long time. That is no figure of speech, I assure you."

"But I have nothing to pay you with."

“Show me what is in your pockets,” the faceless man said, in a quiet voice.

I emptied my jacket and pants pockets. My wallet containing slightly less than 20,000 yen. My credit card, my bank card, my driver’s license, and a gas station discount coupon. My key ring with three keys on it. A cream-colored handkerchief and a disposable ballpoint pen. Five or six coins. And that was it. Minus the flashlight, of course.

The faceless man shook his head. “I’m sorry, but I see nothing that can pay for your passage. Money has no meaning here. Don’t you have something else?”

I had nothing more in my possession. A cheap watch was on my left wrist, but time had no value here either.

“If you give me paper, I can portray your likeness. My skill as a painter is the only other thing I carry with me.”

The faceless man laughed. At least I think he did. A faint trill echoed in the emptiness.

“In the first place, I have no face. How can you sketch the likeness of a man with no face? Can you draw a void?”

“I am a professional,” I said. “I have no need of a face to draw your portrait.”

I wasn’t at all sure I could pull it off. But I figured it was worth a shot.

“I would be most interested to see what you come up with,” the faceless man said. “Unfortunately there is no paper in these parts.”

I looked down at the ground. Perhaps I could scratch something on its surface with a stick. But it was solid rock. I shook my head.

“Are you certain that is all you carry with you?”

I carefully searched a second time. The pockets of my leather jacket were empty. Completely. I did find something small tucked in the bottom of one of my jeans pockets, though. A tiny plastic penguin. Menshiki had picked it up from the floor of the pit and given it to me. It had an even tinier strap, which Mariye had used to fasten it to her cell phone. It was her lucky charm. Somehow, it had fallen into the pit.

“Show me what is in your hand,” the faceless man said.

I opened my hand, revealing the figurine.

The faceless man stared at it with empty eyes.

“This will do,” he said after a moment. “I will accept this as payment.”

Should I hand it over or not? It was Mariye's precious lucky charm, after all. It wasn't mine. Could I just give it away? What if something bad happened to her as a result?

But I had no choice. If I failed to turn it over, I would never reach the opposite shore, and if I didn't reach the shore, then I would never find Mariye. The Commendatore's death would have been in vain.

"I will give you the penguin as my fare of passage," I said. "Please take me to the other side of the river."

The faceless man nodded. "The day may come when you can draw my likeness," he said. "If that day arrives, I will return the penguin to you."

The faceless man strode to the end of the wooden jetty and stepped down into the small boat moored there. It was a rectangular vessel, shaped like a pastry box. Barely six feet long and narrow, and made of heavy wooden boards. I doubted it could carry many passengers at a time. There was a thick mast in the middle of the boat, at the top of which stood a metal ring about four inches in diameter. A sturdy rope was threaded through that ring. The rope stretched across the river to the far shore in a straight line—it barely sagged at all. It appeared that the boat ran back and forth along that rope, which kept it from being swept away by the swift current. The boat looked as if it had been in use for ages. It had no visible means of propulsion, or even a proper prow. It was just a shallow wooden box floating on the water.

I followed the faceless man into the boat and seated myself on the horizontal plank that ran from side to side. He leaned against the thick mast with his eyes closed, as if waiting for something. Neither of us spoke. After a few minutes, as if it had made up its own mind, the boat began its slow departure. I had no idea what was propelling us, but we were moving silently toward the far shore. There was no sound of an engine, nor of any other machinery. All I could hear was the steady slapping of water against the hull. We moved at roughly the pace of someone walking. Our boat was dashed from side to side by the current, but the sturdy rope prevented us from being washed downstream. It was just as the faceless man had said—no one could cross the river without a boat. He leaned calmly against the mast, unperturbed even when it felt like our craft might capsize.

"Will I be able to find Mariye Akikawa when we reach the other side?" I asked, when we were about halfway across.

"I am here to ferry you across the river," the faceless man said. "To help you navigate the interstice between presence and absence. After that, it's up to you—my job is done."

Not long after, we hit the jetty on the far shore with a small bump. The faceless man's posture, however, did not change. He leaned against the mast, as if confirming some sort of internal process. When that was done, he expelled a great, empty breath and stepped up onto the jetty. I followed him out of the boat. The jetty and the winch-like mechanism attached to it were the same as those on the opposite bank. So similar, in fact, it felt as if we had made a round-trip, and ended back where we started. That feeling disappeared, however, the moment I stepped onshore. For the ground on this side was normal earth, not solid rock.

"You must proceed alone from here," the faceless man announced.

"But I don't know which path to take. Or which direction to go."

"Such things are inconsequential here," came the rumble from the milky void. "You have drunk from the river, have you not? Now each of your actions will generate an equivalent response, in accordance with the principle of connectivity. Such is the place you have come to."

With these words, the faceless man adjusted his wide-brimmed hat, turned on his heel, and walked back to his boat. Once he was aboard, it returned as it had come, following the rope to the other side. Slow and sure, like a well-trained animal. The faceless man and the boat were one as they vanished into the mist.

I decided to leave the jetty behind and walk downstream along the bank. I could have gone in any direction, but it seemed best to follow the river. That way, there was water to drink when I got thirsty. A short while later, I turned to look back at the jetty, but it was already cloaked in white mist. As though it had never existed.

The farther I walked, the wider the river became, and the gentler the current. There were no more whitecaps, and the sound of rushing water had practically disappeared. Why hadn't they put the pier here, instead of where the flow was so swift? True, the distance would have been greater, but the crossing would have been so much easier where the water was calm. All the same, this world probably operated according to its own principles, its own way of thinking. Even greater danger might lurk beneath the placid surface.

I searched my pockets. Sure enough, the penguin was gone. That the protective charm had been lost (most likely for all eternity) was hardly reassuring. Perhaps I had made the wrong choice. Yet what other option did I have? I could only hope Mariye would be all right without it. At this point, hope was all I had.

I made my way along the riverbank, the flashlight from Tomohiko Amada's bedside in one hand. I kept it turned off. This dusky world was not so dim as to require a light. I could see where I was walking, and for about twelve or fifteen feet ahead. The river flowed to my left, slow and silent. Once in a while, I could glimpse the far shore through the haze.

The farther on I pushed, the more the ground beneath my feet came to resemble a path. Not a well-defined path, yet something that fulfilled the function of a path. There were vague signs that people had passed this way before. Gradually, the path was leading me away from the river. At a certain point, I drew up short. Should I stick to the river? Or allow this *presumed path* to take me in another direction?

After some thought, I elected to follow the path and leave the river behind. I had a feeling it would lead me somewhere. *Now each of your actions will generate an equivalent response, in accordance with the principle of connectivity*, the ferryman had said. This path could well be an example. I decided to follow the plausible suggestion, if that's what it was, that had been presented to me.

The farther I moved from the river, the more the path turned uphill. Eventually, I realized I could no longer hear the rush of water. The slope was easy and the path almost straight, so my steps fell into a steady rhythm. The mist was melting away, but the light remained pale and somewhat opaque. There was no way to tell what lay ahead. I kept my eyes on my feet, and my breathing regular and systematic.

How long had I been walking? I had lost all sense of time. All sense of direction, too. And the thoughts running through my head were distracting me. I had so much to figure out, yet my thoughts had become so terribly fragmented. When I tried to focus on one thought, a new thought would appear to gulp it down, and my mind would careen in the wrong direction. Each time, I lost track of what I had just been thinking about.

I was so distracted, in fact, that I almost bumped right into *that*. I tripped on something, and raised my eyes as I was regaining my balance. In that instant, the air around me was transformed—I could feel it on my skin. I snapped back to reality. An enormous black mass loomed directly ahead. My jaw dropped in surprise. What was it? It took a moment to register that a huge forest stood in my path. It had materialized without warning in a terrain that, until that point, had had no vegetation, not a single leaf or blade of grass. No mystery, then, why I was so shocked.

It was a forest—no question there. A tangle of branches with thick leaves that formed a solid wall. Within the forest was darkness. More accurate than forest, perhaps, might have been "sea of trees." I stood before it and listened, but could hear nothing. No birdsongs, no branches rustling in the wind. A complete absence of sound.

I was afraid to step inside the forest. Instinctively. The trees were too dense, the darkness inside too deep. I had no way to gauge the scale, or how far the path would continue. It might well split into a labyrinth of side trails. If I got lost in that maze, my chances of escaping were practically zero. Still, I had no other real options. The path I had chosen headed straight into the forest (or, more accurately, was sucked into it, like train tracks are sucked into a tunnel). It made no sense, having come this far, to turn around and head back to the river. Who knows, the river might not even be there anymore. No, I had made my choice, and now I had to live with it. I would press on, at whatever cost.

Mustering my courage, I stepped into the trees. It was impossible to tell the time of day—it could have been dawn, or midday, or evening. The half-light never seemed to vary, no matter how much time passed. Then again, time might not exist in this world. In which case, this dusk could persist, day in and day out, forever.

Sure enough, it was dark inside. The layered branches above my head blocked out almost all light. Yet I left my flashlight off. Once my eyes adjusted, I could see enough to walk, and I didn't want to waste the batteries. I plunged through the forest, trying hard to empty my mind. Any thoughts would likely lead me to an even darker place. The path continued its gentle rise. All I could hear were my own footsteps, and those were more and more faint, as if their sound was slowly being sucked away. I hoped my thirst wouldn't return. By this time, the river would be far indeed. No chance of heading back for a drink, however thirsty I got.

How long did I walk? The forest was deep and dark, the view unchanging. The light never changed, either. My footsteps were all I could hear, and barely at that. The air was tasteless and odorless, as always. Thick trees walled both sides of the path. I could see nothing else. Did anything live here? Perhaps not. I had noticed no birds or insects.

Yet I could feel something watching me—the sensation was clear and very unpleasant. Sharp eyes were being trained in my direction from behind the wall of foliage. Every movement I made was under surveillance. My skin burned, as if under a magnifying glass in the sun. *What was I doing there?* they demanded. This was their domain, and I was a lone invader. Yet I never actually saw any of those eyes. I may have imagined them. Fear and suspicion can fashion eyes in the dark.

Then again, Mariye had felt Menshiki's eyes on her from across a valley, and through a telescope, no less. She had guessed that someone was keeping constant watch on her. And she was right. Those eyes were no fantasy.

Nevertheless, I decided to dismiss the eyes I felt scrutinizing me. There was no way that they were real. They had to be hallucinations, created by my fears. I needed to think that way. I had to make it through the great forest (though its actual size was a mystery). While retaining as much of my sanity as possible.

Luckily, there were no side trails. Thus I wasn't forced to make a choice that might take me into a maze that led nowhere. No thorny thickets blocked my way. All I had to do was push forward along a single path.

I couldn't tell how long I had been walking, yet I didn't feel especially tired. Perhaps I was under too much stress to register fatigue.

Just when my legs were getting a little heavy, however, I spied a yellow point of light in the distance. At first, I thought it was a firefly. But I was mistaken. The light didn't move, or flicker on and off. Its fixed position suggested that it was human-made. The farther I went, little by little, the light grew larger and brighter. There could be no doubt. *I was approaching something.*

Was it something good, or something bad? Would it help or harm me? Whichever, I was out of options. For better or for worse, I had to find out what that light was. If I didn't have the guts to do that, I never should have embarked on this journey in the first place. Step by step, I advanced toward the light.

Then, just as suddenly as it had appeared before me, the forest ended. The trees that had lined the path on both sides vanished, and before I knew it, I had stepped out into a broad clearing. The clearing was the shape of a half-moon, and perfectly level. Now I could see the sky once more, and view my surroundings in that dusky light. Directly across from me rose a sheer cliff, and at the base of that cliff was the open mouth of a dark cave. The yellow light I had been following streamed directly from that opening.

The gloomy sea of trees was behind me, the towering cliff (much too steep for me to climb) straight ahead. The mouth of the cave opened directly before me. I looked up at the sky a second time, then around at my surroundings. Nothing looked like a path. My next move had to be to enter the cave—there was no alternative. Before going in, I took several deep breaths, to brace myself. By moving forward, I would generate a new reality in accordance with the principle of connectivity. So the faceless man had said. I would navigate the interstice between presence and absence. I could only entrust myself to his words.

Warily, I stepped into the cave. Then it struck me—*I had been here before.* I knew this cave by sight. The air inside was familiar, too. Memories came flooding back. The wind cave on Mt. Fuji. The cave where our young uncle had taken Komichi and me during our summer break, back when we were kids. She had slipped into a narrow side tunnel and disappeared for a long while. I had been scared to death that she was gone for good. Had she been sucked into an underground maze for all eternity?

Eternity is a very long time, the faceless man had said.

I walked slowly through the cave toward the yellow light, deadening my footsteps and trying to quiet my pounding heart. I rounded a corner, and there it was: the source of the light. An old lantern with a black metal rim, the sort that coal miners once carried, hanging on a thick nail driven into the stone wall. A fat candle burned inside the lantern.

Lantern, I thought. The word had come up not long before. It was part of the name of the anti-Nazi underground student organization that Tomohiko Amada was presumed to have joined. Things seemed to be converging.

A woman was standing beneath the lantern. I didn't see her at first because she was so tiny. Less than two feet tall. Her black hair was coiled atop her head in a neat bun, and she wore a white gown from some ancient time. Its elegance was apparent at a glance. Another character lifted from *Killing Commendatore*. The beautiful maiden who looks on in horror, her hand over her mouth, as the Commendatore is slain. In Mozart's *Don Giovanni,* she is Donna Anna. The daughter of the Commendatore.

Magnified by the light of the lantern, her sharp black shadow trembled on the wall of the cave.

"I have been awaiting you," the miniature Donna Anna said.

55

A CLEAR CONTRAVENTION OF BASIC PRINCIPLES

"I have been awaiting you," said Donna Anna. She was tiny, but her voice was clear and bright.

Nothing could have surprised me by that point. It even seemed natural for her to be there waiting for me. She was a beautiful woman, with an innate elegance, and the way she spoke had a majestic ring. She might be only two feet tall, but she clearly had that special something that could captivate a man.

"I will be your guide," she said to me. "Please be so kind as to take that lantern."

I unhooked the lantern from the wall. I didn't know who had put it there, so far beyond her reach. Its circular metal handle allowed it to be hung on a nail or carried by hand.

"You were waiting for me?" I asked.

"Yes," she said. "For a very long time."

Could she be another form of Metaphor? I hesitated to pose such a bold question.

"Do you live in these parts?"

"Live here?" she said, casting a dubious glance in my direction. "No, I am *here* to meet you. And I'm afraid I don't understand what you mean by 'these parts.' "

I gave up asking questions after that. She was Donna Anna, and she had been waiting for me.

She wore the same sort of ancient garb as the Commendatore. In her case, a white garment, most likely made of fine silk. Draped in layers over the top half of her body, with loose-fitting pantaloons below. Though her shape was therefore hidden, I guessed she was slender but strong. Her small black shoes were fashioned of leather of some kind.

"Then let us commence," Donna Anna said to me. "Not much time remains. The path is narrowing as we speak. Please follow me. And be so good as to hold the lantern."

I followed in her wake, holding the lantern above her head. She walked toward the back of the cave with quick, practiced steps. The candle's flame fluttered as we moved, casting a dancing mosaic of shadows on the pitted walls.

"This looks like a wind cave on Mt. Fuji that I once visited," I said. "Is that possible?"

"All that is here *looks like* something," Donna Anna declaimed without turning around. As though she were addressing the darkness ahead.

"Do you mean to say nothing here is the real thing?"

"No one can tell what is or is not the real thing," she stated flatly. "All that we see is a product of connectivity. Light here is a metaphor for shadow, shadow a metaphor for light. You know this already, I believe."

I didn't think I knew, at least not all that well, but I refrained from inquiring further. That could only lead to more knotty abstractions.

The cave grew narrower the farther back we went. The roof became lower too, so that I had to stoop as I walked. Just as I had done in the Mt. Fuji wind cave. Finally, Donna Anna drew to a halt and turned to face me. Her small, flashing eyes stared up into mine.

"I can guide you this far. Now you must take the lead. I will follow, but only to a certain point. After that, you are on your own."

Take the lead? I shook my head in disbelief—from what I could see, we had reached the very back of the cave. A dark stone wall blocked our way. I passed the lantern across its face. But it appeared that we had hit a dead end.

"It seems we can't go any farther," I said.

"Please look again. There should be an opening in the corner to your left," Donna Anna said.

I shone the lantern on that section of the cave wall once more. When I stuck my head out and looked more closely, I could make out a dark depression on the far side of a large boulder. I squeezed myself between the wall and the boulder to inspect it. It certainly did appear to be an opening. I remembered my sister slipping into an even narrower crack.

I turned back to Donna Anna.

"You must enter there," the two-foot-tall woman said.

I looked at her lovely face, wondering what to say. On the wall, her elongated shadow flickered in the lantern's yellow light.

"I am fully aware," she said, "that you have been terrified of small, dark places all your life. In such places, you can no longer breathe normally. I am correct, am I not? Nevertheless, you must force yourself to enter. Only in such a manner can you grasp that which you seek."

"Where does this opening lead?"

"I do not know. The destination is something you yourself must determine by following your own heart."

"But fear is in my heart as well," I said. "That's what worries me. That my fear will distort what I see and push me in the wrong direction."

"Once again, it is you who determines the path. You are the one who chose the proper route to reach this world. You paid a great price for that, and have crossed the river by boat. You cannot turn back now."

I looked again at the opening. I shuddered to think I would have to crawl into that dark, cramped tunnel. Yet that was what I had to do. She was right—I couldn't turn back now. I placed the lantern on the ground and took the flashlight from my pocket. A lantern would be much too cumbersome in that tiny space.

"Believe in yourself," Donna Anna said, her voice small but penetrating. "You have drunk from the river, have you not?"

"Yes, I was very thirsty."

"It is good that you did so," Donna Anna said. "That river flows along the interstice between presence and absence. It is filled with hidden possibilities that only the finest metaphors can bring to the surface. Just as a great poet can use one scene to bring another new, unknown vista into view. It should be obvious, but the best metaphors make the best poems. Take good care not to avert your eyes from the new, unknown vistas you will encounter."

Tomohiko Amada's *Killing Commendatore* might be seen as one such "unknown vista." Like a great poem, the painting was a perfect metaphor, one that launched a new reality into the world.

I switched on the flashlight and checked its beam. It was bright and unwavering. The batteries should last for some time yet. I removed my leather jacket. It was too bulky to fit into such a tight space. That left me wearing a light sweater and jeans. The cave wasn't especially cold, but neither was it all that warm.

Bracing myself, I crouched until I was almost on all fours and squeezed headfirst into the opening. Inside I found what appeared to be a tunnel sunk into solid rock. It was smooth to the touch, as if worn by water over the course of many years. There were almost no jagged or protruding edges. As a result, despite its narrowness, I was able to progress more easily than I had expected. The rock was cool and slightly damp. I inched forward on my stomach like a worm, the flashlight illuminating my way. I figured that the tunnel must have functioned as a waterway at some point in the past.

The tunnel was about two feet high and three feet across. Crawling was the only option. It looked like it would go on forever, a dark, natural pipe that expanded and contracted by small degrees. Sometimes it curved to the side. At other times it sloped up or down. Thankfully, though, there were no abrupt rises or falls. Then it hit me. If this was an underground conduit, water could flood the tunnel at any moment, and I would surely drown. My legs stopped moving, paralyzed by fear.

I wanted to turn around and go back the way I had come. But it was impossible to reverse course in such a cramped space. The tunnel seemed to have grown even narrower. Crawling backward to where I had begun was out of the question. Terror engulfed me. I was literally nailed to the spot. I couldn't move forward, and I couldn't retreat. Every cell in my body cried out for fresh air. Forsaken by light, I felt powerless and alone.

"Do not stop. You must push on." Donna Anna's command was irrefutable. I couldn't tell if I was hearing things or if she was really behind me, urging me on.

"I can't move," I gasped, squeezing out the words. "And I can't breathe."

"Make fast your heart," said Donna Anna. "Do not let it flounder. Should that happen, you will surely fall prey to a Double Metaphor."

"What are Double Metaphors?" I asked.

"You should know the answer to that already."

"I should know?"

"That is because they are within you," said Donna Anna. "They grab hold of your true thoughts and feelings and devour them one after another, fattening themselves. That is what Double Metaphors are. They have been dwelling in the depths of your psyche since ancient times."

Unbidden, the man with the white Subaru Forester entered my mind. I didn't want him there. But there was no way around it. It was he who had pushed me to throttle that young woman, forcing me to look into the darkness of my own heart. He had reappeared more than once, to make sure I would remember that darkness.

I know where you were and what you were doing, he was announcing to me. Of course he knew everything. Because he lived inside me.

My heart was in chaos. I closed my eyes and tried to anchor it, to hold it in one place. I ground my teeth with the effort. But how should I go about securing my heart? Where was its true location, anyway? I looked within myself, searching one place after another. But it didn't turn up. Where could it be?

"Your true heart lives in your memory. It is nourished by the images it contains—that's how it lives," a woman said. This time, however, it was not Donna Anna speaking. It was Komi. My sister, dead at age twelve.

"Search your memory," said that dear voice. "Find something concrete. Something you can touch."

"Komi?" I said.

There was no answer.

"Komi, where are you?" I said.

Still no reply.

There in the dark, I searched my memory. Like rummaging through an old duffel bag. But it seemed to have been emptied. I couldn't even recall exactly what memory was.

"Turn off your light and listen to the wind," Komi said.

I switched off the flashlight. But I couldn't hear the wind, though

I tried. All I could make out was the restless pounding of my heart, a screen door banging in a gale.

"Listen to the wind," Komi repeated.

Once again, I held my breath and focused. This time, I could hear, lying beyond my heartbeat, a faint humming. A wind seemed to be blowing somewhere far away. A wisp of a breeze brushed my face. Air was entering the tunnel ahead. Air I could smell. The unmistakable odor of damp soil. The first odor I had encountered since setting foot in this Land of Metaphor. The tunnel was leading somewhere. To a place I could smell. In short, to the real world.

"All right then, on you go," said Donna Anna. "There isn't much time left."

With my flashlight turned off, I crawled on into the blackness. As I moved forward, I tried to draw even the slightest whiff of that real air into my lungs.

"Komi?" I asked again.

There was no answer.

I ransacked my store of memories. Komi and I had raised a pet cat. A smart black tomcat. We named it Koyasu, though why we gave it that name escapes me. Komi had picked it up as a kitten on her way home from school. One day, however, it disappeared. We scoured our neighborhood looking for it. We stopped countless people and showed them Koyasu's photograph. But in the end the cat never turned up.

I crawled on, the image of the black cat vivid in my mind. I tried to imagine my sister and me together, searching for it. I strained my eyes to catch a glimpse of the cat at the end of the dark tunnel. I pricked my ears to hear its mewing. The black cat was solid and concrete, something I could touch. I could feel its fur, its warmth, the firmness of its body—even hear it purr—as if it were yesterday.

"That's right," Komi said. "Just keep remembering like that."

I know where you were and what you were doing, the man with the white Subaru Forester called out of nowhere. He wore a black leather jacket and a golf cap with the Yonex logo. His voice was hoarse from the sea wind. Caught by surprise, I recoiled in fear.

I tried to find my memories of the cat. To draw the fragrance of damp earth into my lungs. I seemed to recall that smell from somewhere. From a time not so far away. But I couldn't remember, try as I might. Where had it been? As I struggled to recall, once again, my memories began to fade away.

Strangle me with this, the girl had said. Her pink tongue peeked out at me from between her lips. The belt of her bathrobe lay beside her pillow, ready to be used. Her pubic hair glistened like grass in the rain.

"Come on," Komi urged me. "Call up a favorite memory. Hurry!"

I tried to bring back the black cat. But Koyasu was gone. Why couldn't I remember him? Perhaps the darkness had snatched him away while I was distracted. Its power had devoured him. I had to come up with something else, and fast. I had the horrid sense that the tunnel was tightening around me. It seemed alive. *There is not much time*, Donna Anna had said. Cold sweat trickled from my armpits.

"Come on now, remember something," Komi's voice said behind me. "Something you can physically touch. Something you can draw."

Like a drowning man clutching a buoy, I latched onto my old Peugeot 205. My little French car. I remembered the feeling of the steering wheel as I toured northeastern Japan and Hokkaido. It felt like ages ago, yet I could still hear the rattle of that primitive four-cylinder engine, and the way the clutch growled when I shifted from second into third. For a month and a half, the car had been my constant comrade, my only friend. Now it was probably sitting in a scrap yard somewhere.

The tunnel was definitely narrowing. My head kept banging against the roof. I reached for the flashlight.

"Do not turn on the light," Donna Anna commanded.

"But I can't see where I'm going."

"You must not see," she said. *"Not with your eyes."*

"The hole is closing in. If I go on I won't be able to move."

There was no answer.

"I can't go any farther," I said. "What should I do?"

Again no answer.

I could no longer hear Donna Anna and Komi. I sensed they were gone. All that remained was a deep silence.

The tunnel continued to shrink, making it even harder for me to advance. Panic was setting in. My limbs felt paralyzed—just drawing a breath was growing difficult. A voice whispered in my ear. *You are trapped*, it said. *This is your coffin. You cannot move forward. You cannot move backward. You will lie buried here forever. Forsaken by humanity, in this dark and narrow tomb.*

I sensed something approaching from behind. A flattish thing, crawling toward me through the dark. It wasn't Donna Anna, nor was it Komi. In fact, it wasn't human. I could hear the scraping of its many feet and its ragged breathing. It stopped when it reached me. There followed a few moments of silence. It seemed to be holding its breath, planning its next move. Then something cold and slimy touched my bare ankle. The end of a long tentacle, it seemed. Sheer terror coursed up my back.

Could this be a Double Metaphor? That which stemmed from the darkness within me?

I know where you were and what you were doing.

I couldn't recall a thing. Not the black cat, not the Peugeot 205, not the Commendatore—everything was gone. My memory had been wiped clean a second time.

I squirmed and twisted, frantically trying to escape the tentacle. The tunnel had contracted even farther—I could barely move. I was trying to force myself into a space smaller than my body. That was a clear contravention of basic principles. It didn't take a genius to figure out it was physically impossible.

Nevertheless, I kept on thrusting, pushing myself forward. As Donna Anna had said, this was the path I had chosen, and it was too late to choose another. The Commendatore had died to make my quest possible. I had stabbed him with my own hands. His body had sunk in a pool of blood. I couldn't allow him to die for nothing. And the owner of that clammy tentacle was trying to get me in its grips.

Rallying my spirits, I pressed on. I could feel my sweater unravel as it caught and tore on the rock. I awkwardly squirmed ahead, loosening my joints like an escape artist slipping his bonds. My pace was no faster than that of a caterpillar. The narrow tunnel was squeezing me like a giant vise. My bones and muscles screamed. The slimy tentacle slithered farther up my ankle. Soon it would cover me, as I lay there in the impenetrable dark, unable to move. I would no longer be the person I was.

Jettisoning all reason, I mustered what strength I had left and forced myself into the ever-narrowing space. Every part of my body shrieked in pain. Yet I had to push forward, whatever the consequences. Even if I had to dislocate every joint. However agonizing that would be. For everything around me was the product of connectivity. Nothing was absolute. Pain was a metaphor. The tentacle clutching my leg was a metaphor. All was relative. Light was shadow, shadow was light. I had no choice but to believe. What else could I do?

The tunnel ended without warning, spitting me out like a clump of grass from a clogged drainpipe. I flew through the air, utterly defenseless. There was no time to think. I must have fallen at least six feet before I hit the ground. Luckily, it wasn't solid rock, but relatively soft earth. I curled and rolled as I fell, tucking in my head to protect it from the impact. A judo move, done without thinking. I whacked my shoulder and hip on landing, but I barely felt it.

Darkness surrounded me. And my flashlight was gone. I seemed to have dropped it when I tumbled out. I remained on all fours, not moving. I couldn't see anything. I couldn't think anything. I was only aware, and barely at that, of a growing pain in my joints. Every tendon, every bone wailed in protest at what it had been put through during my escape.

Yes—I had escaped that dreadful tunnel! The realization hit me at last. I could still feel the eerie tentacle sliding over my ankle. I was grateful to have eluded that thing, whatever it was.

But then, where was I now?

There was no breeze. But there was smell. The odor I had caught a whiff of in the tunnel was everywhere. I couldn't recall where I had encountered it before. Nevertheless, this place was dead quiet. Not a sound anywhere.

I needed to find my flashlight. I carefully searched the ground where I had fallen. On all fours, in a widening circle. The earth was moist. I was scared that I might touch something creepy in the dark, but there was nothing, not even a pebble. Just ground so perfectly flat it must have been leveled by human hands.

After a long search, I finally found the flashlight lying about three feet from where I had landed. The moment my hand touched its plastic casing was one of the happiest of my life.

But I didn't switch it on right away. Instead, I closed my eyes and took a number of deep breaths. As if I were patiently unraveling a stubborn knot. My breathing slowed. My heartbeat did, too, and my muscles began to return to normal. I slowly exhaled the last deep breath and switched on the flashlight. Its yellow light raced through the darkness. But I couldn't look yet. My eyes had grown too used to the dark—the tiniest light made my head split with pain.

I shielded my eyes with one hand until I could open my fingers enough to peer through the cracks. From what I could see, I had landed on the floor of a circular-shaped room. A room of modest size, with walls of stone. I shone the flashlight above my head. The room had a ceiling. No, not exactly that. Something more like a lid. No light seeped through.

I realized where I was: in the pit in the woods, behind the little shrine. I had crawled into the tunnel in Donna Anna's cave and tumbled out onto the floor of this stone chamber. I was in a real pit in the real world. I had no idea how that could have happened. But it had. I was back at the beginning, so to speak. But why was there no light? The lid was made of wooden boards. There were cracks between those boards, through which some light should enter. Yet none did.

I was stumped.

At least I knew where I was. The smell was a dead giveaway. Why had it taken me so long to figure out? I carefully examined my surroundings with my flashlight. The metal ladder that should have been standing there was gone. Someone must have pulled it out and carted it off. Which meant there was no means of escape.

What I found strange—it should have been strange, I guess—was that I could find no trace of the opening, no matter how hard I looked. I had exited the narrow tunnel and fallen onto the floor of this pit. Like a newborn baby pushed out in midair. Yet I couldn't find the aperture. It was as if it had closed after it spit me out.

Eventually, the flashlight's beam illuminated an object on the ground. Something I recognized. It was the old bell the Commendatore had rung—hearing it had led me to discover the pit. Everything had begun with this bell. I had left it on the shelf in the studio—then at some point it had vanished. I picked it up and examined it under the flashlight. It had an old wooden handle. There could be no doubt—it was *that bell.*

I stared at it for some time, trying to understand. Had someone brought it back? Had it returned under its own power? The Commendatore had told me the bell belonged to the pit. What did that mean—belonged to the pit? But I was too tired to figure out the principles that might explain what was taking place. And there was no pillar of logic I could lean on.

I sat down, back against the stone wall, and switched off the flashlight. I had to figure out how to escape from this pit. I didn't need light for that. And it was important to conserve the batteries.

So what should I do now?

56

IT APPEARS THAT SEVERAL BLANKS NEED FILLING IN

A number of things made no sense. Most troubling of all was the total absence of light. Someone had sealed the pit's opening. But who would do such a thing, and why?

I prayed that someone (whoever it was) hadn't piled boulders on top of the lid, returning it to how it had been in the beginning. That would mean my chances of getting out were practically zero.

A thought struck me—I clicked on the flashlight and checked my watch. It read 4:32. The second hand was circling the face, doing its job. Time was passing, no doubt about it. At least I was back where time flowed at a set pace, and in a single direction.

Yet what was time, when you got right down to it? We measured its passage with the hands of a clock for convenience's sake. But was that appropriate? Did time really flow in such a steady and linear way? Couldn't this be a mistaken way of thinking, an error of major proportions?

I clicked off the flashlight and, with a long sigh, returned to absolute darkness. Enough pondering time. Enough pondering space. Thinking about stuff like that led nowhere. It only added to my stress. I had to think about things that were concrete, things I could see and touch.

So I thought about Yuzu. She was certainly something I could see with my eyes and touch with my hands (if I was ever given that opportunity again). Now she was pregnant. This coming January, the child—not my child, but that of some other man—would be born. That situation continued without my involvement, in a place far removed from me. A new life with which I had no connection would enter this world. Yuzu had asked nothing of me. So why was she refusing to marry the father? I couldn't figure it out. If she planned to be a single mother, odds were she'd have to quit her job at the architectural firm. I doubted that a small business like that could extend a lengthy maternity leave to a new mother.

I could find no convincing answers to these questions, though I tried. I was stumped. And the darkness made me feel even more powerless.

If I ever got out of this pit, I would put aside my hesitations and go see Yuzu. No question about it, I was hurt when she left me for someone else. It angered me, too (although it took me a very long time to realize that). But why carry around my resentments for the rest of my life? I would go meet her and we could talk things out. I needed to know, from Yuzu herself, what she was thinking, and what she wanted. Before it was too late. Once I made that decision, I felt a little easier. If she wanted to be friends, well, maybe I could give it a shot. It wasn't beyond the realm of possibility, at least. Perhaps we could resolve things that way. If I managed to get out of the pit, that is.

After this I fell asleep. I had shed my leather jacket before entering the tunnel (what fate lay in store for that jacket of mine?), and the cold was starting to get to me. The thin sweater I had on over my T-shirt had been so shredded by the walls of the tunnel that it was a sweater in name only. Moreover, I had returned to the real world from the Land of Metaphor. In other words, I was back where time and temperature played their proper roles. Yet my need for sleep won out. I drifted off, sitting there on the ground, leaning against the hard stone wall. It was a pure sleep, free of dream or deception. A solitary sleep beyond anyone's reach, like the Spanish gold resting on the floor of the Irish Sea.

It was still pitch black when I woke up. I couldn't see my finger when I waved it in front of my face. The darkness blotted out the line between sleep and wakefulness as well. Where did one end and the other begin, and which side was I on? I dragged out my bag of memories and began flipping through them, as if counting a stack of gold coins: the black cat that had been our pet; my old Peugeot 205; Menshiki's white mansion; the record *Der Rosenkavalier;* the plastic penguin. I was able to call up memories of each, in great detail. My mind was working okay—the Double Metaphor hadn't devoured it. It's just that I had been in total darkness for so long that I was having trouble drawing a line between the world of sleep and the waking world.

I switched on the flashlight, covered it with my hand, and read my watch in the light leaking between my fingers: 1:18. Last time I looked, it was 4:32. Could I have been sleeping in such an uncomfortable position for nine hours? That was hard to believe. If that were true, I should be a lot stiffer. It seemed more reasonable to assume that, unbeknownst to me, time had traveled backward three hours. But I couldn't be certain either way. Being immersed in the dark for so long had obliterated my sense of time.

In any case, the cold had grown more penetrating. And I had to pee. Badly. Resigning myself, I shuffled to the other side of the pit and let it all out. It was a long pee that the ground quickly absorbed. A faint smell of ammonia lingered, but only for a moment. Once the need to pee had been taken care of, hunger stepped in to take its place. By slow and steady degrees, it seemed, my body was readapting to the real world. Perhaps the effects of the water I had drunk from the River of Metaphor were wearing off.

I had to get out of the pit as soon as possible. I felt that more urgently now. If I didn't, it wouldn't take long to starve to death. Human beings can only sustain life if provided with food and water—that was a basic rule of the real world. And my present location had neither. All I had was air (though the lid was closed, air seemed to be leaking in from somewhere). Air, love, and ideals were important, no argument there, but you couldn't survive on them alone.

I pulled myself off the ground and attempted to scale the pit's smooth stone wall. I tried from a number of spots, but, as I expected, it was a waste of energy. The wall was less than nine feet high, but it was straight up and down, with nothing at all to grab onto. It would take superhuman ability to climb, and even if I reached the top, there was still that heavy lid to deal with. I would need a solid foothold to push that aside.

I sat back down, resigned. Only one option presented itself. I could ring the bell. As the Commendatore had done. But there was one big difference between the Commendatore and me. He was an Idea, while

I was a flesh-and-blood human being. An Idea never felt hunger, while I did. An Idea wouldn't starve to death, whereas I would, relatively quickly. The Commendatore could ring the bell for a hundred years (though the concept of time was foreign to him) and not get tired, while my limit without food and water was probably three or four days. After that, I wouldn't have the strength, though the bell was light.

So I began ringing the bell there in the dark. There was nothing else to do. Of course I could call out for help. But the pit was in the middle of a deserted woods. Since the woods was the private property of the Amada family, under normal circumstances there would be no one around. To make matters worse, the cover of the pit had been sealed tight. I could shout at the top of my lungs and no one would hear. My voice would just grow hoarse, and I would become even thirstier. At least shaking the bell was better than nothing.

Moreover, there was something out of the ordinary about the bell's ring. It seemed to have some special power. In physical terms, it wasn't very loud. Yet I had heard it from my distant bed in the middle of the night. The autumn insects had fallen silent the moment they heard that ringing. As if commanded to stop their racket.

So I sat there at the bottom of the pit, my back against the stone wall, and rang the bell. I shook my wrist from side to side and emptied my mind as best I could. When I got tired, I took a break and then started again. As the Commendatore had done before me. It wasn't hard to clear my mind. When I listened to the bell I felt, quite naturally, that I didn't have to think about anything else. The ringing sounded different in the dark than in the light. I'm pretty sure that difference was real. I was stuck in a black hole with no way out, but as long as I was shaking the bell, I felt neither fear nor anxiety. I could forget cold and hunger, as well. For the most part, I could even set aside my need to analyze what was taking place. This was a welcome change, as you can imagine.

When I tired of ringing the bell, I dozed off leaning against the stone wall. When I awoke, I switched on the flashlight and checked my watch. Time, I discovered, was behaving in a very haphazard manner. Of course, this may have had more to do with me than the watch. No question there. But that haphazardness was fine with me. I just went on mindlessly ringing the bell, then falling asleep, then waking up to ring the bell again. An endless repetition. With the repetition, my consciousness grew ever more thin and rarified.

Not a single sound made its way into the pit. I couldn't hear the birds, or the wind. What could explain that? This was supposed to be the real world. I was back in a place where people felt hunger, and the need to pee. The real world ought to be filled with all kinds of noises.

I had no idea how much time had passed. I had given up checking my watch. The passing of days made even less sense than the passage of minutes and hours. How could it be otherwise in a place that lacked day and night? Not just time, either—I was losing contact with my own self. My body had become a stranger to me. I was finding it harder and harder to understand what my physical existence meant. Or perhaps I didn't care to understand. All I could do was keep ringing that bell. Until my wrist was almost numb.

After what felt like an eternity (or after time had surged and ebbed like waves pounding the shore), and my hunger became unbearable, finally I heard something above my head. It sounded as if someone had grabbed hold of a corner of the world and was trying to peel back its skin. But the sound didn't strike my ear as real. I mean, how could anyone do that? And if they succeeded, what would follow? A fresh new world, or an endless nothing? In truth, though, I didn't care one way or the other. The final result would probably be more or less the same.

There in the dark, I closed my eyes and waited for the peeling of the world to conclude. But the world wasn't to be peeled so easily, it seemed, and the din only mounted. Maybe it was real, after all. An actual object undergoing a process that produced an actual physical sound. Steeling myself, I opened my eyes and looked up. I trained the beam of my flashlight on the ceiling. Someone was up there making an awful racket. I didn't know why, but it was an ear-splitting grinding noise.

I couldn't tell if the sound threatened me, or was being made *on my behalf*. Whichever the case, I just sat there at the bottom of the pit shaking my bell, waiting to see how things would turn out. At last, a thin sheet of light shot through a crack between the boards and into the pit. Like the broad, sharp blade of a guillotine gliding through a mass of gelatin, it swept down through the darkness to land on my ankle. I dropped the bell and covered my face to protect my eyes.

Next, one of the boards was moved to the side and even more sunlight flooded in. Though my eyes were closed and my palms were pressed against them, I could feel the darkness turn to light. Then new air flowed in from above. It was fresh and cold, and filled with the fragrance of early winter. I loved that smell. I remembered how I had felt as a child wrapping a scarf around my neck on the first cold morning of the year. The softness of the wool against my skin.

Someone was calling my name from the top of the pit. At least, it seemed to be my name. I had forgotten I had one. Names possessed no meaning in the world where I had been for so long.

It took me a while to connect the *someone* calling my name with Wataru Menshiki. I shouted back. But no words emerged. All I could produce was a sort of growl, a signal that I was still alive. I wasn't sure my voice was strong enough to reach him, but at least I could hear it. The strange, harsh call of some imaginary beast.

"Are you all right?" Menshiki called down.

"Menshiki?"

"Yes, it's me," Menshiki said. "Are you hurt?"

"No, I'm all right," I said. My voice had returned. "I think," I added.

"How long have you been down there?"

"I don't know. It just happened."

"Can you climb the ladder if I lower it to you?"

"I think so," I said. Probably.

"Wait just a minute. I'll go get it."

My eyes began to adjust to the sunlight as I waited. I still couldn't open them all the way, but at least I didn't have to cover them with my hands. As luck would have it, it wasn't that bright. I could tell it was daytime, but the sky was probably blanketed with clouds. Or else dusk was approaching. At last, I heard the metal ladder being lowered.

"Please give me a little more time," I said. "My eyes aren't used to the light, so I have to be careful."

"Of course, take all the time you want," said Menshiki.

"Why was the pit so dark? There was no light at all."

"I covered it two days ago. It looked like someone had been monkeying with the lid, so I brought a heavy tarp from my house and tied it down with metal pegs and twine so it wouldn't budge. I didn't want a child to slip and fall in. I checked first to be sure no one was inside. It was empty then, I'm sure of it."

It made perfect sense. Menshiki had covered the lid. That's why it had been so dark.

"There were no signs that anyone had tampered with the tarp. It was just as I left it. So how did you get in? I don't understand," Menshiki said.

"I don't understand either," I said. "It just happened."

There was nothing more I could tell him. And I had no intention of trying to explain, either.

"Shall I come down?" Menshiki asked.

"No, please stay where you are. I'll come up."

I could keep my eyes half open now. Mysterious images were churning behind them, but at least my mind was functioning. I lined up the ladder against the wall, put my foot on the lowest rung, and tried to push myself up. But my legs were weak. They didn't feel like my legs at all. Still, I was able to gingerly climb up the ladder, one rung at a time. The air grew fresher the closer I got to the surface. I could hear birds chirping.

When I reached the top, Menshiki took my wrist in an iron grip and pulled me out. He was much stronger than I expected. Strong enough that I gave myself over to his hands without a second thought. Gratitude was all I felt. Out of the hole, I flopped onto my back and looked up at the dim sky. Sure enough, it was covered by gray clouds. I couldn't tell the time of day. Tiny pellets of rain struck my cheeks and forehead. I found the irregular way they landed on my face exhilarating. I had never realized what a blessing rain could be. It was so full of life. Even the first cold rain of winter.

"I'm starving. And thirsty. And cold. I'm freezing," I said. That's all I could get out. My teeth were chattering.

Menshiki guided me through the woods, his arm wrapped around my shoulder. I was having a hard time putting one foot in front of the other—by the end, he was pulling me along. He was a lot more powerful than he looked. Those daily workouts of his were paying off.

"Do you have the key?" Menshiki asked.

"It's under the potted plant to the right of the front door. Probably." The "probably" was necessary. Nothing in this world could be stated with absolute certainty. I was still shaking with cold. The chattering of my teeth was so loud I could barely hear myself talk.

"You'll be happy to hear Mariye returned home safe and sound early this afternoon," Menshiki said. "What a relief. I got a call from Shoko about an hour ago. I'd been calling you, but no one ever picked up. That worried me, so I came over. I could hear the faint ring of a bell coming from the woods. So on a hunch, I came out and removed the tarp."

The view opened up as we emerged from the trees. I could see Menshiki's silver Jaguar parked demurely in front of my house. It was as spotless as ever.

"Why is your car always so beautiful?" I asked Menshiki. Not a fitting question under the circumstances, perhaps, but something I had long wanted to ask.

"I don't know," he said in a disinterested tone. "Maybe it's because I wash it when I have nothing else to do. From front to back. Then once a month, a pro comes and waxes it. And my garage protects it from the elements. That's all."

That's all? If my poor Toyota Corolla wagon heard that, after six months spent languishing in wind and rain, its shoulders would sag in dismay. It might even pass out.

Menshiki took the key from under the flowerpot and opened the door.

"By the way, what day of the week is it?" I asked him.

"Today? Today is Tuesday."

"Tuesday? Are you sure?"

Menshiki double-checked his memory. "I put out the empty bottles and cans yesterday, so it must have been Monday. Therefore today is Tuesday, without a doubt."

It had been Saturday when I had visited Tomohiko Amada's room. So three days had passed. It wouldn't have surprised me had it been three weeks, or three months, or even three years. I made a mental note. I rubbed my jaw with my palm. But there was no three-day stubble. Instead, my chin was smooth. What explained that?

Menshiki took me to the bath straightaway. He put me in a hot shower and brought me a fresh change of clothes. The clothes I had been wearing were tattered and filthy. I rolled them up in a ball and threw them in the garbage. There were red contusions all over my body but no visible injuries. I wasn't bleeding.

Then he led me to the kitchen, sat me down, and slowly fed me water. By the end I had drained a big bottle of mineral water. While I was drinking he found several apples in the fridge and peeled them. I just sat there, admiring his skill with a knife. The plate of peeled apples looked beautiful, elegant even.

I ate three or four apples in all. It was a moving experience—I had never realized how delicious apples were. I wanted to thank their creator for inventing such a marvelous fruit. When I finished the apples, Menshiki dug up a carton of crackers and gave it to me. I emptied the box. The crackers were a bit soggy, but they still tasted like the best in the world. In the meantime, he boiled water, made tea, and mixed it with honey. I drank a number of cups. The tea and honey warmed me from the inside.

There wasn't much in my fridge. It was, however, well stocked with eggs.

"How about an omelet?" Menshiki asked.

"I'd love one," I said. I needed to fill my stomach—anything would do.

Menshiki took four eggs from the fridge, broke them in a bowl, whipped them with chopsticks, and added milk, salt, and pepper. Then he whipped them again. It was clear he knew what he was doing. Then he turned on the gas, chose a small frying pan, and melted some butter in it. He located a spatula in one of my drawers and deftly cooked the omelet.

His technique was remarkable, as I would have expected. He could have been featured on a TV cooking show. Housewives across the nation would have sighed with envy. When it came to omelets—when it came to *anything,* I should say—Menshiki was precise, efficient, and incredibly stylish. I could only look on in admiration. He slid the finished omelet onto a plate and gave it to me with a dollop of ketchup.

The finished omelet was so beautiful I wanted to sketch it. But instead

I grabbed my knife and started eating. The omelet wasn't just pretty to look at—it was delicious.

"This omelet is perfection," I said.

Menshiki laughed. "Not really. I've made better."

What sort of omelet could that have been? One that sprouted wings and flew from Tokyo to Osaka in under two hours?

When I had polished off the omelet, he took my plate to the sink. At last my stomach felt comfortable. Menshiki sat down across the table from me.

"Can we talk a little?" he asked me.

"Certainly," I said.

"Aren't you tired?"

"Maybe so. But we have lots to talk about."

Menshiki nodded. "It appears that several blanks need filling in."

If they can be filled in, I thought.

"Actually, I stopped by Sunday afternoon," Menshiki said. "I'd called many times but you never picked up, so I was a little worried. I got here around one."

I nodded. I had been *somewhere else* around then.

"I rang the bell and Tomohiko Amada's son came to the door. Masahiko, is that right?"

"Yes, Masahiko Amada. An old friend. He owns this house, and he's got a key so he can get in when I'm not here."

"He was—how should I put this—very worried about you. He said the two of you were visiting his father's room in the nursing home last Saturday when all of a sudden, you disappeared."

I nodded, but didn't say anything.

"He said you vanished into thin air while he was out of the room making a phone call. The nursing home is in Izu Kogen, so the nearest station is too far to reach on foot. But there were no signs that anyone had called a taxi. And the receptionist and the security guard hadn't seen you leave, either. Masahiko called your home later, but no one answered. He was so alarmed that he drove all the way here to check. He was concerned about your safety. Worried something bad had happened to you."

I sighed. "I'll try to explain things to Masahiko. His father's in bad shape, and I only added to his worries. How is his father, by the way? Did he say anything?"

"It seems he's been in a coma. Hasn't regained consciousness at all. His son has taken a room near the home. He was on his way back to Tokyo when he stopped by here."

"I should call him right away," I said, shaking my head.

"That's true," Menshiki said, placing his hands on the table. "But first I think you need to come up with a coherent story about where you've been and what you've been doing the past few days. Including an explanation of how you disappeared from the nursing home. No one's going to buy it if you tell them you just woke up and found yourself back here."

"You're right," I said. "But how about you? Can you buy my story?"

Menshiki thought for a moment. His brow was puckered, as if he was having trouble deciding what to say. "I've always been a man who thought along rational lines," he said at last. "That's how I was trained. To be honest, though, I can't be logical where the pit behind the shrine is concerned. Anything could happen there and it wouldn't feel strange in the least. Spending an hour inside the pit brought that home all the more. That place is more than just a hole in the ground. But I doubt anyone who hasn't experienced it could understand."

I couldn't find the right words to respond, so I stayed silent.

"I think you should take the position 'I don't remember anything' and then stick with it," Menshiki said. "I don't know how many people will believe you, but from what I can see, that's your only option."

I nodded. Yes, that could well be my only option.

"There are some things that can't be explained in this life," Menshiki went on, "and some others that probably *shouldn't* be explained. Especially when putting them into words ignores what is most crucial."

"You've experienced that, correct?"

"Of course," Menshiki said with a small smile. "More than once."

I drained what was left in my teacup.

"So Mariye wasn't hurt at all?" I asked.

"She was muddy and scratched up, but had no serious injuries. Not much more than a skinned knee. Just like you."

Just like me? "Where was she these past few days?"

Menshiki looked perplexed. "I'm pretty much in the dark about that, too. What I do know is that she returned home a short while ago. Dirty and banged up. That's all I was told. Shoko was in such a state she couldn't explain much over the phone. You should probably ask her yourself when things have settled down. Or, if possible, ask Mariye directly."

I nodded. "You're right. I'll do that."

"Don't you think you should get some sleep?" Menshiki asked.

No sooner had these words left his mouth than sleepiness hit me. I had slept deeply while I was in the pit (at least I think I had), but now I could barely keep my eyes open.

"Yes, you're right. I think I'll go lie down," I said, looking at the backs of his clasped hands, perfectly aligned on the table.

"Have a good sleep. That's what you need right now. Is there anything else I can do for you?"

I shook my head. "No, I can't think of anything. But thanks."

"Then I'll take off. Please don't hesitate to call me for whatever reason. I should be at home for the next little while." He slowly rose to his feet. "Thank goodness Mariye got home safely. And that I was able to help you out of a tough spot. To tell the truth, I haven't had much sleep these days either. So I think I'll go home and rest."

With that he left. As always, I heard the solid *thunk* of his car door slamming shut, and the engine starting up. I waited until the car was out of earshot before heading for bed. When my head hit the pillow, I remembered the old bell (I had left it and the flashlight in the pit!) for a split second. Then I descended into a deep sleep.

57

SOMETHING I HAVE TO DO EVENTUALLY

I awoke at two fifteen. Again surrounded by total darkness. For a split second, I was under the illusion that I was still in the pit, but I realized my mistake right away. There was a clear difference between the darkness here and there. Above ground, there was always a vestige of light, even on the blackest night. Not like underground, where no light could enter. It may have been two fifteen, but the sun was still in the sky, albeit on the other side of the planet. That was the size of it.

I turned on the light, went to the bathroom, and drank glass after glass of cold water. The house was hushed. Too hushed, in fact. I listened carefully, but could hear nothing. No breeze. No insect voices, since it was winter. No night birds. No bell. Come to think of it, I had first heard the bell ringing at precisely this time of night. The time when events outside the normal are most likely to occur.

I was no longer sleepy. I was wide awake. Draping a sweater over my pajamas, I headed for the studio. I hadn't set foot in there since returning home. And I was concerned about the paintings I had left. Especially *Killing Commendatore*. Menshiki had said that Masahiko had visited the house in my absence. If he had gone into the studio, he might have stumbled upon it. He would have known right away that it was his father's work. Fortunately, however, I had covered it. I'd worried about leaving it exposed, so I had taken it down from the wall and wrapped a sheet around it to hide it from inquisitive eyes. If the sheet hadn't been removed, Masahiko ought not to have seen it.

I walked in and flipped on the wall switch. The studio was dead quiet as well. Needless to say, no one was there. Not the Commendatore, not Tomohiko Amada. I was all alone.

Killing Commendatore was where I had left it on the floor, the sheet still in place. It didn't seem that anyone had touched it. I couldn't be sure, of course. But nothing suggested otherwise. I unwrapped the painting. It looked the same as always. There was the Commendatore. And Don Giovanni, who had run him through with his sword. And the shocked servant, Leporello. And the beautiful Donna Anna, covering her mouth in astonishment. And in the lower left-hand corner of the painting, poking his head through the square opening, the creepy-looking Long Face.

In truth, I had been harboring some misgivings. Might the painting have been altered by the series of events in which I had played a part? Long Face deleted from the scene, for example, because I had shut the lid? Or the Commendatore killed, not with a sword, but with a carving knife? Yet search as I might, I could find nothing changed. Long Face still poked his grotesque face out of his hole, the raised lid in one hand. His saucer eyes still surveyed the scene. The Commendatore was still impaled on a long sword, blood spewing from his heart. The painting remained a perfectly composed work of art. I admired it for a while, then put the sheet back over it.

I turned to look at the two paintings I was working on. They sat side by side on two easels. One, *The Pit in the Woods*, was wider than it was tall. The other, *A Portrait of Mariye Akikawa*, was taller than it was wide. I looked at them carefully. Both were exactly as I had left them. Nothing had been changed. One was finished, while the other awaited a final go-around.

Then I turned *The Man with the White Subaru Forester*, which had been facing the wall, sat on the floor, and took another good look at it. The man with the white Subaru Forester stared back at me from behind the thick layers of paint, which I had applied with my palette knife in several colors. He had no concrete shape, but I could see him there nonetheless. He was looking straight at me with the piercing eyes of a nocturnal bird of prey, his face empty of expression. He was dead set against the completion of his portrait—the exposure of his true form to the world. Against being hauled from the dark into the light.

But I was determined to reveal who he was. I had to drag him out into full view. However much he might resist. The time might not yet have come. But when it did, I had to be ready to follow through.

I returned to *A Portrait of Mariye Akikawa*. It was far enough along that I didn't need Mariye to model for me anymore. Only a series of final, technical operations remained. Then the portrait would be basically done. I thought it might turn out to be my most accomplished work to date. At the very least, it would capture the freshness of that beautiful thirteen-year-old girl. I was confident of that. But I knew I would never take those last steps. By leaving it unfinished I was shielding something within her, even though I didn't know what that something was. That much was clear.

I needed to look after a few things right away. I had to call Shoko and hear the full story of Mariye's return. I had to call Yuzu and tell her I wanted to see her to talk things out, as I'd resolved at the bottom of the pit. That it was time for us to meet. Then, of course, I had to talk to Masahiko. To explain how it was that I had vanished suddenly from his father's room at the nursing home, and tell him where I had been for the three days I was missing and unaccounted for (though what I would say—what was *possible* to say—escaped me).

Clearly, I couldn't call any of them now. I had to wait for a more appropriate time. That would come in due course—assuming, that is, that time was behaving normally. I drank a glass of warm milk that I heated on the stove and nibbled some biscuits as I sat and looked out the window. It was pitch black outside. No stars were out. Daybreak was still a while off. It was the time of year when nights were the longest.

How should I pass the time? The proper thing would be to climb back into bed. But I wasn't at all sleepy. I didn't feel like reading or working. With nothing better to do, I decided to run a bath. While the bathtub was filling, I lay on my back and stared at the ceiling.

Why had it been necessary to pass through that underground world? To make that trip, I had been forced to kill the Commendatore with my own hands. He had sacrificed his life, and I had been compelled to endure one ordeal after another in a world of darkness. There had to have been a reason. The underground realm was full of unmistakable danger, and real fear. Down there, the most outlandish occurrences weren't strange at all. By successfully navigating that realm, I seemed to have freed Mariye *from somewhere.* At least she had returned home safely. As the Commendatore had foretold. But what connected my experiences underground and her safe return? Were they somehow parallel?

Perhaps the river water I had ingested was an important piece of the puzzle. It could have altered something in me. I felt that at an intuitive and physical level, though it made no rational sense. Thanks to that change, I had passed through a tunnel clearly too small for my body. Cheered on by Donna Anna and Komi, I had managed to overcome my deep-rooted claustrophobia. No, Donna Anna and Komi could have been *a single entity,* Donna Anna at one moment, Komi at the next. Together, perhaps, they had shielded me from the dark powers, and protected Mariye Akikawa at the same time.

But where had Mariye been confined? Had she been confined in the first place? When I had given her penguin charm (though "given" didn't really cover it) to the faceless man, had I harmed her? Or, conversely, had the charm in some shape or form protected her in the end?

The questions only mounted.

Perhaps I would understand the events of the past few days better once I met Mariye in person. I would have to wait. True, things might be no clearer even after we talked. Mariye might recall nothing. Or she might remember, but (like me) be unwilling to share her story.

At any rate, I had to see her once more in this real world, and have a good long talk. We needed to share our stories about what had happened to us. If at all possible.

But was *this the real world?*

I looked around. So much was familiar. The breeze through the window carried a familiar smell, the sounds outside were familiar sounds.

Just because it looked like the real world at first glance, however, didn't mean that was necessarily the case. It might be no more than my assumption. I might well have descended through one hole in Izu and traveled the underworld only to be spit out three days later through the wrong hole in the mountains of Odawara. There was no guarantee that the world I had left and the world I had returned to were one and the same.

I rose from the sofa, stripped off my clothes, and stepped into the bathroom. Once again, I soaped and scrubbed every inch of my body. I thoroughly washed my hair. I brushed my teeth, swabbed my ears with cotton, trimmed my nails. I shaved (though there wasn't much beard to shave). I put on another set of clean underwear. A freshly ironed white cotton shirt and a pair of khaki pants with a sharp crease. I strove to make myself look as acceptable as I could to the real world. But the night still hadn't ended. Outside was pitch black. So black I felt morning might never arrive, not for all eternity.

But morning did come. I brewed some fresh coffee and made some buttered toast. The fridge was almost bare. Two eggs, some sour milk, and a few limp vegetables. I made a mental note to go shopping later.

I was washing the coffee cup when it struck me that I hadn't seen my girlfriend in some time. How long had it been? I couldn't count the exact number of days without checking my calendar. But I knew quite a while had passed. So many things had been going on—a number of them literally not in this world—that I hadn't noticed her failure to contact me.

Why was that? She called me at least twice every week. "How's it going?" she would say. I couldn't call her, though. She couldn't give me her cell phone number, and I didn't use email. When I wanted to see her, I had to wait for her call.

Sure enough, my girlfriend did call around nine that morning, when she was still in the back of my mind.

"I've got to talk to you about something," she said, skipping the pleasantries.

"Fine, let's talk," I said.

I leaned against the kitchen counter, phone to my ear. The clouds outside were starting to break up, and the early-winter sun was peeking through the gaps. The weather at least was improving. From the sound of it, though, what she had to say wasn't going to be all that pleasant.

"I think it's best if we don't see each other again," she said. "It's too bad, but . . ."

Her tone was flat and dispassionate. I couldn't tell if she really felt it was too bad or not.

"There are a number of reasons," she said.

"A number of reasons," I echoed.

"To begin with, I think my husband is catching on. He's noticed some signs."

"Signs," I repeated.

"Women leave certain signs in situations like this. Like they start paying more attention to their makeup and their clothes, or change their perfume, or start a serious diet. I've tried to be careful, but even so."

"I see."

"The main thing is, we can't go on like this."

"Like this," I repeated.

"With no future. No hope of resolution."

She had it there. Our relationship had no "future," no "hope of resolution." The risks were too large if we continued as we were. I didn't have all that much to lose, but she had a family and two teenage daughters attending private school.

"There's more," she went on. "I'm having a serious problem with my daughter. The older one."

Her elder daughter. If I remembered correctly, she was the obedient child who never talked back to her parents and got good grades.

"A serious problem?"

"She can't get out of bed in the morning."

"Can't get out of bed?"

"Hey, will you please stop repeating everything I say?"

"Sorry," I apologized. "But what is her specific problem? She can't get out of bed?"

"That's right. It's been going on for about two weeks. She doesn't try to get up. She doesn't go to school. She just lies in bed in her pajamas all day. Doesn't answer when spoken to. I take food to her, but she barely touches it."

"Has she seen a counselor?"

"Of course," she said. "There's a school counselor. No help at all."

I thought for a minute. But there was nothing I could say. I'd never even met the girl.

"So that's why I can't see you," she said.

"Because you have to stay home and look after her?"

"There's that. But that's not all."

She didn't go on, but I understood how she felt. She was terrified, and blaming herself as a mother for our affair.

"It's really too bad," I said.

"It's fine for you to say that, but it's even worse for me."

She could be right, I thought.

"There's one last thing I wanted to tell you," she said. She took a quick, deep breath.

"What's that?"

"I think you can become a really good artist. Even better than now."

"Thank you," I said. "That gives me some confidence."

"Goodbye."

"Take care," I said.

When our phone call ended, I went to the living room, stretched out on the sofa, and thought about her as I looked at the ceiling. We had been together so many times, yet never had I thought of painting her portrait. Somehow, that feeling had never arisen. Instead I had sketched her over and over again. In a small sketchbook with a thick pencil, so quickly I hardly removed pencil from paper. In most she was naked, and posing lewdly. Spreading her legs to show her vagina, for example. Or I sketched her in the act of making love. Simple drawings but still very real. And very vulgar. She loved looking at them.

"You're really good at drawing naughty pictures, huh? You toss them off, but they're super dirty."

"It's just for fun," I said.

I drew her again and again, then threw the drawings away. Someone might see them, and it didn't make sense to keep them. Still, maybe I should have secretly held on to at least one. To prove to myself she had really existed.

I got up slowly from the sofa. The day was only beginning. There were many conversations ahead.

58

LIKE HEARING ABOUT THE BEAUTIFUL CANALS OF MARS

I called Shoko Akikawa. It was just after nine thirty. A time when most people are already up and about. But no one picked up the phone. It rang on and on until the answering machine kicked in. *We're sorry, but we can't come to the phone right now. Please leave your message after the tone* . . . I left no message. She must be scrambling to deal with her niece's disappearance and sudden return. I kept calling at intervals, but no one answered.

I thought of calling Yuzu after that, but I didn't want to bother her while she was working. I could call during her lunch break. With luck, I would get to have a brief talk with her. It wasn't like our conversation would be a long one. I would simply ask if we could meet sometime soon—that was the gist of it. A yes-or-no question. If the answer was yes, we would set a date and a place to meet. If it was no, that was that.

Then, with a heavy heart, I called Masahiko. He picked up right away. He let out a huge sigh when he heard my voice.

"Are you home now?" he asked.

I told him I was.

"Can I call you back in a couple of minutes?"

Sure, I said. He called fifteen minutes later. He seemed to be using his cell phone on the roof of an office building, or someplace like that.

"Where the hell have you been?" he said, his voice uncharacteristically stern. "You disappeared from my father's room without a word—no one knew where you were. I drove all the way to Odawara looking for you."

"I'm really sorry," I said.

"When did you get home?"

"Last night."

"So you were traipsing around from Saturday afternoon until Tuesday night? Where did you go?"

"To be honest, I have no memory of where I was or what I was doing," I lied.

"So you just woke up and found yourself back home—is that it?"

"Yeah, that's it."

"For real? Are you serious?"

"There's no other way to explain it."

"Sorry, man. I can't buy it. Sounds fake to me."

"Come on, you've seen this sort of thing in movies and novels."

"Give me a break. Whenever they pull that amnesia bit I turn off the TV. It's so contrived."

"Alfred Hitchcock used it."

"You mean *Spellbound*? That's one of his second-rate films," Masahiko said. "So tell me what *really* happened."

"I don't know myself at this point. Like there are these fragments floating around, and I can't figure out how to piece them together. Maybe my memory will return in stages. I'll let you know if that happens. But I can't tell you anything right now. I'm sorry, but you'll have to wait a little longer."

Masahiko paused to digest what I had just said. "All right then, let's call it amnesia for now," he said in a resigned voice. "I gather your story doesn't involve drugs or alcohol or a mental breakdown or a femme fatale or abduction by aliens or anything along those lines."

"No. Nothing illegal or contrary to public morals."

"Public morals be damned," Masahiko said. "But clue me in on one thing, would you?"

"What's that?"

"How did you manage to slip out of the nursing home Saturday afternoon? They keep a really strict eye on who comes and goes. A number of famous people are staying there, so they're paranoid about leaks. They've got a receptionist stationed at the entrance, a guard on-site twenty-four seven, and security cameras. All the same, you managed to vanish in broad daylight without being spotted or caught on film. How?"

"There's a secret passage," I said.

"Secret passage?"

"An exit no one knows about."

"How did you find that? It was your first time there."

"Your father let me know. Or I should say, he gave me a hint. In a very indirect way."

"My father?" Masahiko said. "You must be kidding. His mind's as mushy as boiled cauliflower these days."

"That's one of the things I can't explain."

"What to do," Masahiko said with a sigh. "If it were anyone else I'd say, 'Cut the crap.' But it's you, so I guess I have to put up with it. Put up with this crazy, no-good bum who spends his whole life painting."

"Thanks," I said. "By the way, how's your father doing?"

"When I got back to the room after my phone call, you were nowhere to be seen and Dad was unconscious and barely breathing. I panicked, man. I couldn't figure out what was going on. I knew it wasn't your fault, but I couldn't help blaming you anyway."

"I really am sorry," I said. I wasn't kidding, either. Still, I felt a wave of relief that there was no trace of the Commendatore's body, or of the pool of blood on the floor.

"Yeah, you should be sorry. Anyway, I rented a room nearby to be with him, but his breathing stabilized and his condition improved slightly, so I came back to Tokyo the next afternoon. Work was piling up. I'm heading back this weekend, though."

"It's hard on you."

"There's nothing to be done. Like I told you, dying is a major undertaking. It's the person dying who has it hardest, though, so I really can't complain."

"Is there anything I can do?" I asked.

"No, there's nothing," Masahiko said. "But it would help if you didn't dump any more problems on me . . . Oh yeah, I almost forgot. When I was at your house on my way back to Tokyo your friend Menshiki stopped by. The handsome, white-haired guy in the snazzy silver Jaguar."

"Yes, I met him after that. He said you were there, and that you and he had talked."

"Just a few words at your doorstep. He seemed like an interesting guy."

"A *very* interesting guy," I said, putting it mildly.

"What does he do?"

"Not much of anything. He's so loaded he doesn't have to work. He trades stocks and plays the currency market online, but it's more like a hobby for him, a profitable way to kill time."

"That's really cool," Masahiko said, impressed. "It's like hearing about the beautiful canals of Mars. Where Martians row gondolas with golden oars. While imbibing honeyed tobacco through their ears. Warms my heart just hearing about it . . . Oh yeah, while we're at it, did you ever find the knife I left at your place?"

"Sorry, but no, I haven't come across it," I said. "I don't have a clue where it went. I'll buy you a new one."

"Don't sweat it. It probably had a bout of amnesia, just like you. It'll wander back before too long."

"Probably," I said. So the knife hadn't remained in Tomohiko Amada's room either. It had vanished somewhere, just like the Commendatore's corpse and the pool of blood. It might show up here, though, as Masahiko had said.

Our conversation ended there. We vowed to get together again soon and hung up.

After that, I drove my dusty old Corolla station wagon down the mountain to the shopping plaza. I went to the supermarket, where I toured the aisles with the neighborhood housewives. From the looks on their faces, they weren't thrilled by their morning shopping. Not a whole lot of excitement in their lives. No ferryboat rides in the Land of Metaphor, that's for sure.

I tossed what I needed—meat, fish, vegetables, milk, tofu, the whole lot—into my shopping cart and paid at the register. I saved five yen by bringing my own bag. Then I went to a discount liquor store and bought a twenty-four pack of Sapporo. Back home, I arranged most of what I had purchased in the fridge, including six cans of beer. I wrapped what needed to be frozen in plastic and stuck it in the freezer. I set a big pot of water on the stove and parboiled the asparagus and broccoli for salads. I boiled a few eggs, too. In the process, I managed to kill most of the morning. Nevertheless, there was still time to spare. I considered following Menshiki's example and washing my car, then realized it would get dirty again in no time flat, and tossed the idea. Parboiling vegetables was much more productive.

I called Yuzu's architectural firm shortly after noon. Actually, I wanted to wait until my feelings had settled down before talking to her, but at the same time I didn't want to delay acting on what I had decided in the darkness of the pit, even for a single day. Otherwise, something might cause my feelings to change. Yet the receiver weighed a ton in my hand. A cheerful-sounding young woman answered. I gave her my name, and asked to talk to Yuzu.

"Are you her husband?" she chirped.

Yes, I replied. To be precise I wasn't, of course, but there was no reason to go into details over the phone.

"Please hold on," she said.

I waited for quite a long time. I had nothing in particular to do, so I stood there leaning on the kitchen counter, receiver to my ear, biding my time until Yuzu came to the phone. A big black crow passed right in front of the window. Its glossy feathers gleamed in the sunlight.

"Hello," said Yuzu.

We exchanged a simple greeting. I had no idea how a just-divorced couple was supposed to address each other, how much distance was appropriate. So I kept it as brief and conventional as possible. How have you been? I've been fine. And you? Like a summer shower, our words were sucked up the moment they struck the parched soil of reality.

I mustered my courage. "I thought we should get together and talk about a number of things face-to-face," I said.

"What sorts of things are you talking about?" Yuzu asked. I hadn't expected that response (why hadn't I?), so I was at a loss for words. What did I mean by "things"?

"I . . . I haven't thought it through that far," I stammered.

"But you want to talk about a number of things, correct?"

"That's right. It occurred to me that we ended up like this without ever having talked."

She thought for a moment. "To tell the truth," she said, "I'm pregnant. I'm happy to see you, but don't be shocked to see how big my belly's grown."

"I know. Masahiko told me. He said you asked him to."

"That I did," she said.

"I don't know how big you've gotten, but I'd like to see you in any case. If it's not too much of an imposition."

"Can you wait a moment?" she asked.

I waited. She appeared to be leafing through her appointment book. Meanwhile, I tried hard to remember what kind of songs the Go-Go's sang. I doubted they were as good as Masahiko had claimed, but then maybe he was right, and my view was perverse.

"Next Monday evening is good for me," Yuzu said.

I did the calculation in my head. Today was Wednesday. So Monday was five days away. The day Menshiki took his empty bottles and cans to the pickup spot. A day I didn't have to teach drawing in town. That meant I was free—no need to check my schedule. What did Menshiki wear when he took out his garbage, I wondered.

"It's good for me too," I said. "Just give me a time and place and I'll be there."

She named a coffee shop not far from the Shinjuku Gyoen-mae Station. The name brought back memories. It was not far from her office, and we had met there often when we were still living together as a married couple. After she finished work, usually before we went out someplace for dinner. There was a little oyster bar a short distance away, which offered fresh oysters at a reasonable price. She loved eating their small oysters loaded with horseradish, and washed down with chilled Chablis. Was the restaurant still in the same spot?

"Can we meet there shortly after six?"

I said that'd be fine.

"I'll try not to be late."

"That's all right. I'll wait."

"Okay, see you then," she said, and hung up.

I stared at the receiver in my hand for a moment. So I would see Yuzu again. My estranged wife, soon to bear another man's child. The place and time had been set. Our conversation had gone without a hitch. Yet had I done the right thing? I wasn't at all sure. The receiver still weighed heavy in my hand. Like a phone built back in the Stone Age.

When it came down to it, though, could anything be completely correct, or completely incorrect? We lived in a world where rain might fall thirty percent, or seventy percent, of the time. Truth was probably no different. There could be thirty percent or seventy percent truth. Crows had it a lot easier. For them, it was either raining or not raining, one or the other. Percentages never crossed their minds.

Talking to Yuzu had left me at loose ends. I sat in the dining room for an hour, mostly looking at the clock on the wall. I would see her on Monday and we would talk about "a number of things." We hadn't seen each other since March. It had been a chilly Sunday afternoon then, rain quietly falling. Now she was seven months pregnant. A major change in her life. I, on the other hand, was still just me. True, I had drunk the water of the Land of Metaphor only a few days earlier, and had crossed the river that divided presence and absence, but I wasn't sure if the experience had changed me or not.

Finally, I called Shoko again. But no one came to the phone. Instead it switched to the answering machine. I gave up and sat down on the sofa. I had made all my calls, and nothing more needed to be done. I hadn't set foot in the studio in what felt like ages, and part of me wanted to get back to my easel, but I couldn't think of anything in particular that I wanted to paint.

I put Bruce Springsteen's *The River* on the turntable. Then I lay on the sofa, closed my eyes, and listened. When the A side of the first LP had finished, I turned it over and listened to the B side. Albums like

The River have to be heard in this fashion. After "Independence Day" wraps up the A side, you take the record in both hands, turn it over, and carefully lower the stylus. "Hungry Heart" fills the room. What was the point of listening to *The River* any other way? In my personal opinion, when CDs strung together the sides of records like *The River*, they spoiled the experience. The same was true of *Rubber Soul* and *Pet Sounds*. Great music should be presented in its proper form. And listened to in a proper manner.

Whatever the case, the E Street Band's performance was a knockout. The band revved up the singer, and the singer inspired the band. As I zoned in on the music, I could feel my worries fading.

I was lifting the needle from the first record when I realized that, perhaps, I should give Menshiki a call. We hadn't spoken since the day before, when he had rescued me from the pit. Yet somehow I didn't really feel like it. This happened on occasion. He was a fascinating guy, but there were times I really didn't want to talk to him. The gap between us was vast. Why should that be? At any rate, I didn't feel like hearing his voice at that particular moment.

So I gave up. I'd call him later. After all, the day had just begun. I put the second record of *The River* on the stereo. But just when I was settling back to listen to "Cadillac Ranch" ("All gonna meet down at the Cadillac Ranch"), the telephone rang. I lifted the needle and went into the dining room to answer it. I figured it was Menshiki. As it turned out, it was Shoko.

"Have you been trying to reach me this morning?" she began.

That's right, I replied, I had tried on several occasions. "I heard yesterday from Mr. Menshiki that Mariye had returned home, so I wondered how she was."

"Yes, she came back safe and sound. Yesterday afternoon. I called you a number of times to let you know but there was no answer, so I tried contacting Mr. Menshiki. Did you go somewhere?"

"Yes, I had to look after urgent business some distance from here. I got back last night. I wanted to contact you earlier, but there was no phone where I was, and I don't carry a cell phone," I said. It wasn't a complete lie.

"Mariye returned all by herself yesterday afternoon, covered in mud. But no serious injuries, thank goodness."

"Where was she all that time?"

"We don't know yet," she said in a hushed voice. As if afraid that her phone was tapped. "Mariye won't tell us what happened. We had filed a missing person's report, so the police came and asked her all sorts of questions, but she wouldn't tell them anything. Not a single word. So they gave up and left, saying that they'd come back when she'd had more time to recover. That at least she had made it home, and that she was safe. But she won't tell either her father or me anything. You know how stubborn she can be."

"But she was covered in mud, correct?"

"Yes, her whole body. Her school uniform was torn up too, and her arms and legs were scratched. We didn't have to take her to the hospital, though—none of her injuries was that serious."

Just like me, I thought. Muddy, clothing in tatters. Could we have wormed our way back to this world through the same narrow tunnel?

"And she won't speak?" I asked.

"No, not a single word since she came home. Not just words, either—she hasn't made a sound. As if someone had stolen her tongue."

"Do you think some kind of trauma might have left her in shock? Taken away her voice?"

"No, I don't think so. I think she's made up her mind not to say anything, a vow of silence, if you will. She's done this kind of thing before. When she's furious about something, for example. Once she's made up her mind like this she tends to stick to it—that's the sort of child she is."

"There's no question of criminal acts, right? Like kidnapping, or unlawful confinement?"

"I can't tell. The police say they'll come back to ask more questions once she's had a chance to calm down, so maybe we'll find out then," Shoko said. "But I do have a favor to ask, if it's not too much of an imposition."

"What might that be?"

"Would you try to talk to her? Just the two of you? There may be things she'll only open up to you about. She might reveal more about what happened if you're there."

I stood there with the receiver in my right hand, considering her suggestion. If Mariye and I were alone together, what was there to discuss? I couldn't begin to imagine. I had my own riddles to unravel and she (most likely) had hers. If we laid one set of riddles over the other, what answers could possibly emerge? Still, I had to see her. There were things we had to talk about.

"Of course. I'd be happy to," I said. "Where would you like me to go?"

"Oh no, please let us come to you, as always. I think that's best. If you don't mind, of course."

"No, that's fine with me," I said. "I'm free all day. Please come when it's convenient for you."

"Would it be all right if we came now? She's home from school today. If she's willing, of course."

"Please tell her she doesn't have to talk. That there are things on my end that I'd like to tell her," I said.

"Very well. I'll tell her exactly that. I'm dreadfully sorry to keep imposing on you like this," said the beautiful aunt. Then she quietly hung up the phone.

The phone rang again twenty minutes later. It was Shoko.

"We'll be coming at three o'clock," she said. "Mariye has said she's willing. Well, she gave a small nod, is more accurate."

I said I would expect them at three.

"Thank you so much," she said. "I'm at my wit's end. I don't understand what's going on, or what I should be doing."

I wanted to tell her I felt the same way, but I didn't. That's not the response she was seeking.

"I'll do what I can. I can't be sure if it will work, but I'll try my best," I said. Then I hung up.

I stole a look around the room as I put down the receiver. On the off chance that the Commendatore might be in the vicinity. But he was nowhere to be seen. I missed him. The way he looked, and his odd way of speaking. But I would never lay eyes on him again. With my own hand, I had driven a knife through his tiny heart. The razor-sharp carving knife Masahiko had brought to my house. All for the purpose of rescuing Mariye from someplace. I had to find out where that *someplace* was.

59

UNTIL DEATH SEPARATED US

Before Mariye arrived, I took another look at her portrait, so close to done. I could picture exactly what it would look like if I ever finished it. Sad to say, though, I never would. There was no way around that. I had no good explanation for why I couldn't complete the painting. No logical argument. Just the strong feeling that *it had to be that way*. The reason, I expected, would reveal itself in stages. What was clear now was that I was fighting a very dangerous opponent. I had to be on my toes every second.

I went out to the terrace, sat in a deck chair, and stared across the valley at Menshiki's white mansion. Handsome, colorless Menshiki, he of the white hair. "We only talked for a moment at your door, but he seemed like an interesting guy," Masahiko had said. "*A very* interesting guy," I had corrected him. At this stage of the game, though, I would have to say *a very, very, very* interesting guy.

A few minutes before three, the familiar blue Toyota Prius rolled up the slope and parked in its usual spot in front of my house. The engine stopped, the driver's door opened, and Shoko Akikawa got out. Most elegantly, pivoting in her seat, knees tight together. A moment later, Mariye emerged from the passenger's seat. Most reluctantly, her movements slow and sluggish. The morning clouds had sailed off somewhere, and the sky was the clear blue of early winter. The soft hair of the two women danced in the cold wind coming off the mountain. Mariye brushed the hair from her eyes in an impatient gesture.

Mariye was in a skirt, unusual for her. A wool skirt of navy blue, it reached her knees. Beneath was a pair of dark blue tights. Her white blouse was covered by a cashmere V-neck sweater. The sweater was a deep purple, the color of grapes. Her shoes were dark brown loafers. In that outfit, Mariye looked like a well-brought-up child from a well-off family, a healthy, pretty, utterly conventional girl. You could see nothing eccentric about her. Just that her chest was almost flat.

Shoko was wearing snug light-gray slacks. Gleaming black low-heeled shoes. A long white cardigan, fixed with a belt around her waist. Her breasts stood out proudly beneath the cardigan. She was carrying a black purse made of what looked like enamel. The sort women commonly carry, though their contents have always mystified me. Mariye appeared a bit at a loss with no pockets to plunge her hands into.

They were so different in age and stage of maturity, this young aunt and her niece, yet both were so lovely. I observed their approach through the parted curtains. When they walked side by side, the world brightened a little. As when Christmas and New Year's arrive in tandem each year.

The doorbell chimed, and I went to open the door. Shoko greeted me politely, and I ushered them inside. Mariye said nothing. Her lips were set in a straight line, as if someone had stitched them together. She was a strong-willed girl. Once she made up her mind about something, she never backed down.

As before, I led them to the living room. Shoko launched into a string of apologies, but I cut her off. This was no time for social niceties.

"If you don't mind, could you leave Mariye and me alone for a while?" I said, getting straight to the point. "I think that's best. Please come back in about two hours. Would that be possible?"

"Oh, well, certainly," the young aunt said. She seemed a little flustered. "If it's all right with Mariye, then it's all right with me."

Mariye gave a slight nod. It was all right with her.

Shoko Akikawa consulted her small silver watch.

"Then I'll come back at five o'clock. I'll be waiting at home, so please call if you need anything."

I told her we would.

Looking worried, Shoko paused uncertainly, clutching her black purse. Then she appeared to make up her mind, for she took a deep breath, smiled a bright smile, and left. There was the sound of the Prius's engine starting (I couldn't really hear it, but I assume it did), and the car disappeared down the slope. Mariye and I were left alone in the house.

The girl sat on the sofa and looked down at her lap, her lips still set in a stubborn line and her knees pressed together. Her pleated blouse was neatly ironed.

A deep silence followed. Finally, I spoke up.

"You don't have to say a word," I began. "You can stay quiet as long as you want. So try to relax. I'll do the talking—all you have to do is listen. All right?"

Mariye raised her eyes and looked at me. But she didn't speak. Nor did she nod or shake her head. She merely stared in my direction. Her face showed no emotion. I felt as if I were gazing at the full moon in winter. Perhaps she had made her heart like the moon for the time being. An icy mass of rock floating in the sky.

"First, I need your help with something," I said. "Can you come with me?"

I rose and headed to the studio. A moment later she got up and followed. The room was chilly, so I lit the kerosene stove. When I pulled back the curtains, the mountainside was bright in the sun. Mariye's portrait-in-progress was sitting on an easel, close to finished. She glanced at it but then quickly looked away, as if she had glimpsed something she shouldn't have.

I crouched down, removed the cloth I had draped over *Killing Commendatore*, and hung the painting on the wall. I asked Mariye to sit on the stool to observe it more closely.

"You've seen this painting before, right?"

Mariye gave a small nod.

"It's called *Killing Commendatore.* At least that's what was written on its wrapping. It's one of Tomohiko Amada's most perfect works, though we don't know exactly when he painted it. It's beautifully composed and masterfully drawn. Each character is fully realized and utterly convincing."

I paused for a moment, waiting for my words to sink in.

"Yet this painting was wrapped up and closeted away in the attic of this house," I went on, "where no one would ever see it. When I stumbled upon it and brought it downstairs, it had been gathering dust for a very long time. Apart from the artist, you and I are probably the only people who have ever looked at it. Your aunt could have too on your first visit, but for some reason it didn't catch her eye. I don't know what made Tomohiko Amada hide it in the attic. It's such a brilliant work, one of his true masterpieces, so why would he keep it from the world?"

Mariye didn't respond. She sat on the stool, her eyes fixed on *Killing Commendatore*.

I continued. "As if on cue, weird things have happened one after another since I stumbled on this painting. First, Mr. Menshiki went out of his way to make my acquaintance."

Mariye nodded slightly.

"Then I uncovered that strange hole behind the shrine in the woods. I heard a bell ringing in the middle of the night and traced it to that spot. It was coming from beneath a pile of stones. They couldn't be moved by hand—they were too big and too heavy. So Menshiki arranged for a landscaper to come in with his backhoe. I didn't understand why Menshiki would go to such lengths, and I still don't. At any rate, the stones were moved at great cost of time and money. Underneath them was a hole. A round pit about six feet across, made of smaller stones tightly set together in a perfect circle. Who built it, and for what purpose, is a mystery. Of course you know about the pit."

Mariye nodded.

"The Commendatore came out of that opened pit. This guy."

I went up to the painting and pointed to the figure. Mariye looked at him. But her expression didn't change.

"He looked exactly the same as you see here, same face, same clothes. But he was only two feet tall. Very compact. And with a peculiar way of speaking. For some reason, I seem to be the only person able to see him. He called himself an 'Idea.' And said he had been stuck in that pit. In other words, Mr. Menshiki and I had set him free. Do you get what he meant by 'Idea'?"

Mariye shook her head no.

"It's hard for me, too. The way I understand it, an idea is a type of concept. But not all concepts are ideas. Love, for example, is not an idea. But ideas are what make love possible. Without ideas, love cannot exist. This discussion can go on forever, though. And to tell you the truth, I'm not even sure of the correct definitions. Anyway, an idea is a concept, and concepts have no physical shape. They are pure abstractions. Nevertheless, this Idea temporarily borrowed the form of the Commendatore in the painting to make itself visible to me. Do you follow me so far?"

"Pretty much," Mariye broke her silence for the first time. "I met him too."

"You did?" I exclaimed. I looked at her in stunned silence. Then I recalled what the Commendatore had said to me in the Izu nursing home. *I met her not long ago*, he had told me. *We exchanged a few words.*

"So you met the Commendatore too."

Mariye nodded.

"When? Where?"

"At Mr. Menshiki's," she said.

"What did he say?"

Mariye clamped her lips together again. To signal, it seemed, that she didn't want to talk any more for the moment. I didn't push her further.

"Other characters in this painting have appeared as well," I said. "For example, the man in the lower left-hand corner of the painting, the bearded guy with the strangely shaped face. Right here."

I pointed to Long Face.

"I call him 'Long Face,' and he's a weird one, all right. He's about two and a half feet tall. He slipped out from the painting too—I caught him holding up the cover of his hole just as he is doing here, and he helped me reach the underground world. I had to get a bit rough, though, before he gave me directions."

Mariye looked at Long Face for some time. But she didn't say anything.

I continued. "I walked through that dim world, climbing hills, crossing a rapid river, until I met the pretty young woman you see right here. This person. I call her 'Donna Anna,' after the character in Mozart's opera *Don Giovanni*. She's also very small. She led me to a tunnel in the back of a cave. Then she and my dead sister helped me worm my way through to where it ended. If they hadn't cheered me on I never would have made it—I'd have been trapped in the underworld forever. My hunch—though of course it's pure guesswork—is that Donna Anna in this painting may be the young woman Tomohiko Amada loved when he was a student in Vienna. She was executed as a political prisoner seventy years ago."

Mariye looked at Donna Anna in the painting. Her face still as impassive as the white winter moon.

Then again, Donna Anna could have been Mariye's mother, stung to death by a swarm of hornets. Perhaps she was the one who had protected Mariye. Depending on who was looking at her, Donna Anna might embody many things. Of course, I didn't say this out loud.

"Then we have this man here," I said. I turned the painting leaning against the wall around so we could see its front. It was my portrait in progress, *The Man with the White Subaru Forester*. On the surface, it was just thick layers of paint, three colors in all. Behind those layers, though, was the Subaru Forester guy. I could see him. Though other people couldn't.

"I showed you this before, didn't I?"

Mariye gave a firm nod, but said nothing.

"You told me it was finished as it was."

Mariye nodded again.

"I call the person portrayed here—or the person I must eventually portray—'the man with the white Subaru Forester.' I ran across him in a small coastal village in Miyagi Prefecture. Our paths crossed twice. In a very mysterious and meaningful way. I have no idea what sort of person he is. I don't even know his name. But a moment came when I realized I had to paint him. I was compelled to. I started painting him from memory, but had to stop when I reached a certain point. So I painted over him like this."

Mariye's lips were still set in a straight line.

Then she shook her head from side to side.

"That man is really scary," she said.

"That man?" I said. I followed her eyes. They were fixed on *The Man with the White Subaru Forester*. "Do you mean the painting? Or the man?"

She gave another firm nod. Despite her fear, she seemed unable to look away.

"Can you see him?"

She nodded. “I can see him behind the paint. He’s standing there looking at me. Wearing a black cap.”

I turned it around and set it back, face against the wall.

“You have the ability to see the man with the Subaru Forester standing there. Most people don’t,” I said. “But I think it’s better if you don’t look at him anymore. There’s probably no need at this stage.”

Mariye nodded as if in agreement.

“I don’t know if the man with the white Subaru Forester is of this world or not. It’s possible that someone, or something, merely borrowed his form. In the same way an Idea borrowed the form of the Commendatore. Or it could be that I saw part of myself reflected in him. But when I was surrounded by real darkness, it was no mere reflection, believe me. It was a tangible, living, moving *thing*. The people in that land call it a ‘Double Metaphor.’ I do plan to finish the painting someday. But not yet—it’s still too early. And too dangerous. Some things shouldn’t be recklessly dragged into the light. But I may not be . . .”

Mariye was looking straight at me without saying a word. I found it difficult to continue.

“Anyway, thanks to the help of many people, I was somehow able to cross the underworld and squeeze through a narrow, black tunnel to make my way back to this world. At virtually the same moment, you were freed *from somewhere*. I can’t believe that was a mere stroke of luck. On Friday, you disappeared somewhere for four days. Then on Saturday I disappeared for three days. On Tuesday, we both *returned*. There has to be a connection. My guess is that the Commendatore connected us. And now he’s gone from this world. He fulfilled his role and moved on. Only you and I are left. We’re the only ones who can close the circle. Do you believe what I’m saying?”

Mariye nodded.

“That’s what I wanted to tell you. Why I asked to talk to you alone.”

Mariye’s eyes were trained on my face.

“No one else would believe me,” I went on, “even if I told the truth. They’d think I was nuts. I mean the story just doesn’t fly—it’s too far removed from reality—though I figured you’d believe me. And then I’d have to show them *Killing Commendatore*. Without that painting, nothing I said would make sense. But I don't want anyone else to see it. Only you."

Mariye kept looking at me. She didn't speak. But I could see the sparkle slowly returning to her eyes.

"Tomohiko Amada invested everything, all of himself, in this painting. It's filled with his emotion. As though he painted it with his own blood and flesh. Truly a once-in-a-lifetime work of art. He did it for himself, but also for those who were no longer of this world, a kind of requiem to their memory. To purify the blood they had shed."

"Requiem?"

"A work to bring peace to the spirits of the dead and heal their wounds. That's why he didn't expose it to public view. The critical reception, the accolades, the financial rewards—they had no meaning. He wanted none of those things for this painting. It was enough for him to know that he had created it, and that it existed somewhere. Even if it was wrapped up in paper and hidden in an attic where no one would ever see it. I want to respect his feelings."

The room was quiet for a while.

"You've played around here since you were small, right? Using that secret passageway of yours. Isn't that so?"

Mariye nodded.

"Did you ever meet Tomohiko Amada?"

"I saw the old guy. But I never talked to him. I just hid and looked at him from far away. When he was painting. I mean, I was trespassing, right?"

I nodded. The image was all too real. Mariye in the shrubbery, peeking into the studio. Tomohiko Amada on his stool, intently wielding his brush. The thought that he was being observed a million miles from his mind.

"You asked me to help you with something," Mariye said.

"So I did. There's one thing," I said. "I'd like you to help me wrap up these two paintings and hide them in the attic where no one can see them. *Killing Commendatore* and *The Man with the White Subaru Forester*. I don't think we need them right now. That's where I could use your help."

Mariye nodded but didn't say anything. Truth be told, this was a task I really didn't want to do alone. More than help, I needed someone to act as observer and witness. Someone tight-lipped, whom I could trust to share the secret.

I went to the kitchen and got some twine and a utility knife. Then Mariye and I packed up *Killing Commendatore*. We wrapped it carefully in the same brown washi, the traditional Japanese paper it had been in before, bound it with twine, draped it in a white cloth, and then tied it again. Firmly, to make it difficult for anyone to unwrap. The thick paint on *The Man with the White Subaru Forester* wasn't quite dry, so we wrapped it more loosely. Then we carried the two paintings to the closet of the guest bedroom. I climbed to the top of the stepladder, raised the trap door to the attic (much like Long Face had pushed up the square lid to his hole, come to think of it), and climbed up. The air was chilly there, but a pleasant kind of chilly. Mariye handed the paintings up to me. *Killing Commendatore* went first, followed by *The Man with the White Subaru Forester*. I leaned them next to each other against the wall.

All of a sudden, I sensed I had company. I gulped. Someone was there—I could feel a presence. Then I saw the horned owl. Probably the same owl I had seen the first time. The night bird was perched on the same beam as before, still as a statue. He didn't seem particularly concerned when I moved in his direction. Also like the first time.

"Hey. Come up and see something," I whispered to Mariye. "Something very cool. Try not to make any noise."

Looking curious, Mariye mounted the ladder and crawled through the opening into the attic. I pulled her up the last step with both hands. The floor of the attic was covered with a fine white dust, but she didn't show any concern that it would get on her wool skirt. I sat down and pointed out the horned owl to her. She knelt beside me and looked at the bird, entranced. It was very beautiful. Like a cat that had sprouted wings. "It's been living here the whole while," I whispered to her. "It goes out to hunt in the forest in the evening, and flies back in the morning to sleep. That's its entrance there."

I pointed at the air vent with the hole in its screen. Mariye nodded. I could hear the faint sound of her breathing.

We sat there side by side without speaking, looking at the owl. Showing little interest in us, the owl sat there quietly, a model of discretion. The owl and I had a tacit understanding that we would share the house. One of us was active during the day, the other at night—in that way, the domain of consciousness was shared equally, half and half.

Mariye reached over and took my hand in hers. Her head came to rest on my shoulder. I gently squeezed her hand back. Komi and I had spent long hours together like this. We were close as brother and sister. Our feelings had flowed back and forth in a very natural way. Until death separated us.

I could feel the tension drain from Mariye's body. Little by little, that part of her that had become so rigid was beginning to unclench. I stroked her head on my shoulder. Her soft, straight hair. When my hand touched her cheek, I realized she was crying. The tears were so warm it felt as if blood was spilling from her heart. I continued to hold her like that. The girl had needed to cry. But she hadn't been able to. Probably for a very long time. The horned owl and I kept watch over her as she wept.

The rays of the afternoon sun angled through the hole in the broken vent. White dust and silence surrounded us, nothing more. Dust and silence that seemed to have been passed down from antiquity. We could hear no wind. On his beam, the horned owl mutely preserved the wisdom of the forest. A wisdom also bequeathed from the distant past.

Mariye wept for a long time. She made no sound, but the trembling of her body told me she was still crying. I kept stroking her hair. As if she and I were heading upstream along the river of time.

60

IF THAT PERSON HAD PRETTY LONG ARMS

"I was at Mr. Menshiki's house," Mariye said. "The whole four days." She had stopped crying, and was talking again.

She and I were in the studio. Mariye was perched on the round stool, her knees touching as they peeked out from beneath her skirt. I was leaning on the windowsill. I could see how pretty her legs were. Her bulky tights couldn't hide that. When she matured a bit more, those legs would attract the gaze of many men. By then, her chest would have filled out too. Now, however, she was just a lost and confused girl, wavering on the threshold of adulthood.

"You were at Mr. Menshiki's?" I asked. "I'm not sure I understand. Can you fill me in a little?"

"I needed to know more about him, so I went to his house. I had to find out why he was watching our home through those binoculars every night. I think he bought the big house across the valley just to do that. To spy on us. I couldn't understand why he would do something like that. I mean, it was so not normal. I thought there had to be some kind of reason."

"So you went to pay him a visit?"

Mariye shook her head no. "I didn't pay him a visit. I snuck in. Secretly. And then I couldn't get out."

"You snuck in?"

"Yes, like a burglar. I didn't plan it like that, though."

When her morning classes ended on Friday, Mariye slipped out the back door of the school. If a student was unexpectedly absent in the morning, the school called their family. But no phone call was made when a student missed his or her afternoon classes. There was no clear reason for this policy—that's just the way things were done. Mariye had never skipped out before, so she figured if she got caught she could talk her way out of trouble. She hopped on a bus and got off close to where she lived. But instead of heading home, she turned up the opposite slope, toward Menshiki's house.

At first, Mariye had no intention of sneaking in. The idea never crossed her mind. Yet she wasn't planning to ring Menshiki's doorbell and invite herself in, either. The fact was, she went there with no plan in mind. She was simply drawn to the white mansion like a metal filing to a powerful magnet. She couldn't solve the mystery of Menshiki's behavior merely by standing outside his wall. She knew that much. Yet she couldn't stifle her curiosity. Her legs carried her to his gate under their own volition.

It was a very long climb. When she turned and looked back, she could see the ocean sparkling between the mountains. His house was surrounded by a high wall with a sturdy electrically operated gate positioned at the entrance. Security cameras were set on each side. One of the gate's pillars had a security company's logo stuck to it. She had to approach with care. She hid behind some bushes and took stock of the situation. She could spot no movement, either inside or outside the house. No one entered or left, and no noise of any kind came from within.

After wasting half an hour hanging around with nothing to do, she had given up and was preparing to leave when she saw a van roll up the hill. A minivan, from a parcel delivery service. It stopped in front of the gate, a door opened, and a uniformed young man jumped out, clipboard in hand. He walked to the gate and rang the bell. There was a brief exchange with someone over the intercom. When the big wooden gate started to slowly swing in, the young man hurried back to his van and drove inside.

Mariye had no time to think things through. The moment the van entered, she leapt from the bushes and sprinted as fast as she could through the closing gate. It was pretty close, but she managed to slip through a split second before it shut. The security cameras might have picked her up. But no one came out to challenge her. Dogs, though, were a scarier proposition. A guard dog might be prowling the grounds. She hadn't considered that before racing in. The instant the gate closed behind her, though, the possibility occurred to her. A property this extensive could easily have a Doberman or a German shepherd running loose. A big dog like that would be a problem. Mariye was afraid of dogs. But as luck would have it, none appeared. She heard no barking, either. Now that she thought of it, there had been no talk of a dog when she and her aunt had paid their visit.

Having made her way inside the wall, she hid behind some shrubs and appraised her situation. Her throat was dry. I stole in here like a burglar, she thought. I'm breaking the law—this is trespassing, no doubt about it. The cameras have recorded proof of my guilt.

Had she made the right move? She wasn't sure. When she had seen the delivery van pass through the gate, her response had been automatic. She'd had no time to consider the possible consequences. Now's my one and only chance, she'd thought, and acted on the spur of the moment. Her body had moved before her mind clicked in. Yet for some reason, even now, she had no second thoughts.

From her hiding place she saw the delivery van roll back up the driveway. Once again, the gate slowly swung open and the van passed through. If she was going to leave, now was the time. Just run out before the gate closed. Return to the world of safety. She wouldn't be a criminal. But she didn't move. Instead, she remained there, hidden in the shadows, and watched the gate close again. Intently biting her lower lip.

She waited there for precisely ten minutes, measuring the time on her small Casio G-Shock watch. When the ten minutes were up, she emerged from the shrubbery. Bending low so the cameras would have difficulty spotting her, she hurried down the gentle slope toward the front door of the house. It was two thirty.

What if Menshiki discovered her? She thought about that for a moment. Well, she decided, if that happened she'd wriggle out of it somehow. Menshiki seemed to have a keen interest (or something like that) in her. So if she told him she'd just come to say hi and, seeing the gate open, had walked in, and made it all seem like a kid's game, he would trust her. He wants to believe in something, she thought, so he'll swallow what I say. The problem was, where did his "keen interest" come from, and did he have good intentions, or was he dangerous?

The front door of the mansion was around the bend, at the bottom of the sloping driveway. There was a bell beside the door. Needless to say, she didn't push it. Instead, she moved clockwise around the building, hiding behind trees and shrubs, hugging the concrete wall and giving the roundabout where guests parked a wide berth. A two-car garage sat to the left of the entranceway. Its door was rolled down and locked. A little farther on sat a stylish little building that looked like a cottage. That must be the guesthouse, she thought. Beyond that was a tennis court. She had never seen a home with a tennis court before. Who did Mr. Menshiki play tennis with? The court, however, appeared to have been long ignored. It had no net, its all-weather surface was strewn with leaves, and the white lines were so faded they were almost invisible.

All the windows facing the mountainside were small and tightly shuttered, so nothing inside could be seen. As before, the house was absolutely quiet. No barking dogs. From time to time she could hear birds chirping high in the trees, but that was all. At the back of the house was another garage. Also with space for two cars. It seemed to have been added after the house was built. Menshiki sure could store an awful lot of cars!

The slope behind the house had been turned into a large Japanese-style garden. She could see a descending flight of steps, and below that a path weaving through a number of large rocks. The azalea bushes were pruned to perfection, the pine branches overhead an array of bright greens. What looked like an arbor lay just beyond. A reclining chair where one could stretch out and read sat under the arbor. Beside it was a coffee table. Lanterns and lights were scattered here and there.

Mariye worked her way around the house to the back. The house's broad deck looked from there out over the valley. She had walked out onto that deck on her first visit. It was from there that Menshiki kept watch on her home. The second she set foot on it she knew that was true. She felt it in her bones.

Mariye squinted as she looked over at her home. It was right across from her. So close it seemed a person could reach out and touch it (if that person had pretty long arms, that is). From this vantage point, the house looked utterly defenseless. At the time it was built, there had been no homes on this side of the valley. Only recently (though more than ten years ago) had building restrictions been eased and houses erected on this slope. That was why, when her home was designed, no attempt had been made to shield it from those across the way. That made it a sitting duck for prying eyes. A high-powered telescope or even a pair of good binoculars would give one a clear view of what was going on inside. The window to her bedroom was a perfect example. To be sure, she was a cautious girl. She always closed the curtain before taking off her clothes. But that didn't mean there were no unguarded moments. What had Menshiki seen?

Mariye descended the outside steps to the next floor where the study was, but the windows were shuttered there too. She couldn't peek in at all. So she kept walking down to the lowest level. Most of that floor was occupied by a large utility area. She could see a washing machine, a place for an ironing board, a room that seemed to be set aside for a live-in maid, and, on the far end, a sizable gym containing five or six exercise machines. Unlike the tennis court, these appeared to be well used. They all looked clean and well oiled. A heavy punching bag hung from the ceiling. Compared with the upper floors, this floor was less tightly guarded. Many of the windows lacked curtains, so she could peer inside. Nevertheless, both the windows and the sliding glass doors were securely locked from within. Here too the security company had pasted their stickers to scare off intruders. An alarm would sound in their offices if anyone tried to force their way in.

The mansion was huge. She found it impossible to believe that a single person could inhabit such a big space. It must be a lonely life. The concrete walls were thick, and every precaution had been taken to block anyone from gaining entry. True, there was no guard dog (maybe he didn't like dogs either), but apart from that every antiburglar device under the sun had been employed.

What should be her next step? Nothing came to mind. There was no way to get inside, and no way to breach the wall to get out. Menshiki was home, she knew that. He had pushed the button that opened the gate and taken delivery of the parcel. And he lived there by himself.

Once a week, a cleaning service came, but apart from that the house was off-limits to outsiders. That was his basic principle—he had told them that on their visit.

Since she couldn't gain access to the house, she had to find a place to hide outside. If she kept poking around she might locate a likely spot. After a long search, she finally came across what seemed to be a small storage shed at the far corner of the garden. The door was unlocked. Inside were a bunch of garden tools and stacked bags of fertilizer. She slipped in and sat down on the bags. The shed was far from inviting. But at least the security cameras wouldn't find her here. And it was unlikely anyone would show up. Sooner or later, things would change. All she could do was wait.

Although she was stuck in one place, she felt full of energy. After her shower that morning, she had noticed swellings on her chest in the mirror. It was an exciting development. Of course, she might be deluding herself. It could just be wishful thinking. She had inspected her chest from a number of angles, and touched it with her hands. There did seem to be two soft protuberances that had not been there before. Her nipples were still tiny (a far cry from her aunt's, which resembled olive pits), but there was a hint they might be about to sprout.

Mariye passed her time in the storage shed thinking about her budding breasts. She pictured how they might look when they grew. What would it feel like to live your life with really big ones? She imagined strapping on the kind of underwire bra her aunt used. That day was still miles away, however. After all, her periods had only begun that spring.

She was a little thirsty, but she could bear that. She consulted her chunky G-Shock watch. It was five minutes past three. Her painting class was on Fridays, but she'd been planning to skip that anyway. She hadn't brought her bag of painting supplies with her. Yet her aunt was sure to worry if she didn't get home by dinnertime. She could come up with a good excuse later.

She seemed to have fallen asleep. It was hard to believe that she could have slept in this place, and under these circumstances. Yet she had managed to drop off without realizing it. It hadn't been for very long.

Ten or fifteen minutes. Maybe less. But a deep sleep, nonetheless. She was disoriented when she awoke, her mind at loose ends. For a moment she didn't know where she was or what she was doing. It seemed she had been dreaming. A vague dream, something to do with full breasts and milk chocolate. Her mouth was filled with saliva. Then it hit her. I snuck into Menshiki's, she remembered, and now I'm hiding in his storage shed.

A noise had roused her. A repetitive, mechanical noise. To be more precise, a garage door clattering open. The door of the garage near the entrance. Menshiki was probably in his car and about to head off somewhere. Mariye hurried from the shed and ran around to the front, making as little sound as possible. When the door was fully open the clattering stopped. She heard a car start up, and then the front of Menshiki's silver Jaguar slowly emerged. Menshiki was sitting in the driver's seat. The driver's window was down, and his pure white hair glowed in the afternoon sun. She watched from behind the shrubbery.

Had Menshiki looked to his right, he could have glimpsed her there in the shadows. The shrubs were too small to provide full cover. But his eyes were trained straight ahead. Hands on the wheel, he seemed lost in thought. The Jaguar moved up the driveway, passed around the curve, and disappeared. The remote control–activated metal door began to clatter down again. The second before it closed, Mariye raced from her hiding place and slipped under the door. Like Indiana Jones in *Raiders of the Lost Ark*. Another reflex action. Without really thinking, she had decided to gain access to the house through the garage. The automatic door hesitated when it sensed her slide underneath, then resumed its descent until it was tightly shut.

Another car was in the garage. A stylish blue convertible with a beige hood, the sports car her aunt had admired on their previous visit. Mariye couldn't care less about cars, so she'd barely glanced at it then. It had a very long nose, and, here too, the Jaguar crest. Even someone who knew as little about cars as Mariye could tell it was worth a lot of money. A collector's piece, in all likelihood.

A person could pass into the house through a door in the garage. She tried the knob with some trepidation, but it turned easily. She sighed with relief. Few people would lock a door like that during the day, but Menshiki was such a cautious man she couldn't be sure. Perhaps something had been on his mind to make him forget. She'd been lucky.

She walked through the door and into the house. Should she take her shoes off or keep them on? In the end, she decided to carry them with her. Leaving them on the doorstep didn't seem like a good option. The house was hushed when she entered. As if everything in it was holding its breath. Menshiki was gone, and she was positive no one else was there. I'm alone in this huge house, she thought. For the next little while, I am free to go wherever, and do whatever, I want.

Menshiki had given them a basic guided tour on their first visit. She remembered it well enough. The general layout was fixed in her head. She entered the big living room that took up almost the entire first floor. From there, one could go out to the broad deck through a sliding glass door. She hesitated, though. Menshiki might have activated the security system before leaving. If he had, an alarm would go off when she tried to slide it open. A light would flash in the agency's office. They would phone the house to check. A password would be necessary to end the alert. Mariye stood before the sliding door, black loafers in hand, pondering the situation.

Finally, she reached the conclusion that Menshiki hadn't set the alarm. The fact that he had left the inner door in the garage unlocked suggested that he wasn't heading off on a long trip. Odds were he had gone shopping, or was running some sort of errand. Mariye made up her mind. She unlocked the door, slid it open, and waited to see what would happen. No alarm went off, and the security agency did not phone. She heaved a sigh of relief (had security guards found her there she couldn't have joked her way out of it) and stepped out onto the deck. Putting down her shoes, she went over to the binoculars and removed their plastic cover. They were too heavy to hold, so she tried balancing them on the railing, but that didn't work very well. Looking around, she noticed what looked like a stand leaning against the wall. It resembled a camera tripod and was the same olive color as the binoculars. The binoculars could be screwed onto the stand. She stuck them together, pulled up the low metal stool left nearby, sat down, and looked through them. Now using the binoculars was easy. Moreover, they were positioned so that she couldn't be observed from the other side of the valley. This had to be how Menshiki spent much of his time.

She was shocked at how clearly the inside of her house could be seen. Everything was a notch brighter—one of the binoculars' special features, she assumed. Some of the curtains in the rooms facing the valley hadn't been drawn. The view within was so distinct she felt she could reach out and touch what she was looking at. A vase of flowers, for example, or even a magazine on the table. Her aunt should be home at this hour. But she couldn't locate her anywhere.

It was weird to look inside her own house from such a distance, and in such naked detail. It felt as if she had become one of the dead (how was unclear) and now was viewing her home from their vantage point. She had belonged there for so long, yet it was hers no more. She knew it so intimately but could never go back. It was a strange, dissociated sensation.

She trained the binoculars on her own room. It faced in her direction, but the curtain was drawn. Shut tight, without a crack. Her familiar curtain, with its orange pattern. The orange bleached by the sun. She couldn't see behind it. But her shadow was probably visible at night, when the light was on. How visible, though, could only be known after dark. Mariye panned across the house, looking for her aunt. She ought to be there. But she was nowhere to be seen. Perhaps she was preparing dinner in the kitchen in the back. Or resting in her room. Wherever she was, she wasn't visible from this angle.

Mariye felt a powerful urge to go back to that house. Right away. She longed to sit in her familiar chair at the dining room table and sip hot tea in her very own cup. To watch her aunt preparing dinner in the kitchen. How wonderful that would be, she thought. Until that point, she had never imagined missing her home this way. Not for a second. To her, the house had always been an ugly, barren monstrosity. She had hated living there. In fact, she was impatient for the day when she was old enough to move into her own place, one that suited her. Yet now, looking at its interior from the other side of the valley through the clear lens, she wanted to return at any cost. *It was where she belonged.* Where she would be protected.

Just then she heard a faint droning sound. Prying her eyes from the binoculars, she saw something black circling above her. A large bee with a long body, probably a hornet. The kind of hostile, aggressive hornet with a sharp stinger that had killed her mother. Mariye ran back into the house, forcefully slid the door shut, and locked it. The hornet buzzed around the door for a while, as if to pen her in. It struck the glass several times, then finally gave up and flew away. Mariye gave a great sigh of relief. Her heart was pounding, her breathing ragged. Nothing scared her more than hornets. Her father had lectured her time and again how dangerous they were. Mariye had looked at many photographs so that she knew exactly how they looked. In the process, she had conceived the terrifying idea that she, like her mother, would be stung to death. She might well have the same allergic reaction. One couldn't escape death, but it should come later—she wanted to know what it felt like to have full breasts and a woman's nipples at least once before she died. It would really suck if hornets killed her before she had that chance.

It was better to stay in the house a while, for safety's sake. That savage insect would still be flying about. Moreover, it appeared to be targeting her. She decided to search inside the mansion and forget about going outside for the time being.

Her first step was to tour the sprawling living room. She could see no particular change since her first visit. There was the big Steinway grand piano. A small stack of musical scores was piled on top of it. A Bach invention, a Mozart sonata, one of Chopin's études, that sort of thing. Nothing that required advanced technical skill. Still, being able to play them at all was impressive. Mariye could tell that much. She had taken piano lessons when she was younger. (She hadn't gone very far—art was what had grabbed her.)

A number of books were scattered on the coffee table's marble top. Judging from the bookmarks stuck in them, all were in the process of being read. One was on philosophy, one was historical, and two were novels (one of which was in English). She recognized none of the titles and had heard of none of the authors' names. She flipped through several, but they weren't her thing. The master of the house loved difficult books and classical music. Between those pursuits, he looked into her home across the valley through high-powered binoculars.

Was he just a perv? Or was there a logical reason or purpose for his behavior? Did he have the hots for her aunt? Or for her? Or for both of them? (Was such a thing possible?)

Next she went to take a look at the lower levels. First she made her way to Menshiki's study. His portrait hung on the wall. She stood in the middle of the room and studied it for a moment. Of course, she had seen it before (that had been the purpose of their first visit). This time, though, the longer she looked at it, the more it felt as if Menshiki were there with her. So she turned away from the painting. Trying her best to ignore it, she went over to inspect his desk. There was a state-of-the-art Apple desktop computer, but she didn't switch it on. She knew without trying that it was secured. There would be no way she could gain access. Not much else was on the desk. There was a deskpad calendar with almost nothing written on it. Just a few incomprehensible symbols and numbers here and there. He would have input his daily schedule into the computer, and then shared it with his other devices. All would be locked. Mr. Menshiki was a cautious man. He would leave no traces.

The other things on the desk were the sort of work-related materials you would expect to find in anyone's study. The pencils were all of the same length, and sharpened to a fine point. Paper clips were arranged according to size. The white memo pad waited patiently for someone to write on it. The digital clock faithfully clicked off the time. The desk was in such perfect order it was frightening. Unless he's a well-made android, Mariye thought to herself, something sure is funny about Mr. Menshiki.

As she expected, every desk drawer was locked. That was only natural. No way he would neglect securing them. The study held little else that she wanted to see. She had no special interest in the shelves of books, or the CD collection, or the new, obviously expensive stereo system. Those did no more than reflect his range of tastes. They didn't help her understand who he was as a person. They had no connection to the secret he was (most likely) concealing.

Mariye left the study and walked down the dim hallway, checking the rooms as she went. All were unlocked. None had been included in the house tour. She and her aunt had only been shown the living room, the study, the dining room, and the kitchen (she had also used the guest bathroom on the first floor). Mariye opened the doors to these unknown rooms one by one. The first was Menshiki's bedroom. As the so-called master bedroom (she assumed), it was very big. It had a walk-in closet and a private bathroom. Its large bed was neatly turned out, with a quilted duvet. Since there was no live-in maid, she assumed Menshiki had made the bed. If so, its neatness didn't surprise her. A pair of plain dark brown pajamas lay next to the pillow, also neatly folded. A number of prints hung on the wall. A set by a single artist, from the looks of it. A half-read book rested on the bedside table. He certainly was an avid reader. The window faced the valley, but it wasn't very large and its blinds had been drawn.

She opened the door to the big walk-in closet. Rows of clothes were hanging there. Lots of jackets and blazers, but not many suits. Not many neckties, either. She guessed he seldom needed to dress for formal occasions. All the shirts had plastic covers, and appeared to have just come back from the cleaners. Shoes and sneakers were lined up on shelves in neat rows. Coats of varied thicknesses occupied another part of the closet. Everything in the closet was looked after with care and reflected the good taste of its owner. Indeed, the whole closet could have been featured as it was in a menswear magazine. There were not too many clothes, nor too few. Moderation governed everything.

His drawers contained socks, handkerchiefs, and underwear. All were pressed and folded, and arranged in perfect order. There were more drawers for his jeans, polo shirts, sweatshirts, and so forth. One large drawer had been entirely given over to a colorful array of beautiful sweaters. None had patterns. Yet Mariye could find nothing in any of these drawers to help her unravel Menshiki's secret. Everything was immaculate and divided according to its function. Not a speck of dust was on the floor, and all the picture frames were level on the walls.

Mariye did reach one clear conclusion about Menshiki, however: this man would be impossible to live with. No normal person could meet his standard. Her aunt was something of a neat freak, but even she wasn't this meticulous.

The next door opened onto what appeared to be the guest room. It had a double bed, made up and ready to be used. A writing desk and office chair sat near the window. There was also a small television set. But there was no sign that anyone had ever slept there—the room felt as if it had been forsaken for eternity. Mr. Menshiki was not in the habit of entertaining guests, it seemed. Instead, this room was apparently to be used in emergencies (though she couldn't imagine what those might be).

The room next door was more like a storeroom. It had no furniture, and at least ten cardboard boxes were stacked on the green carpet. Judging by their weight, they contained documents. Each had a label, with markings in ballpoint pen. All were carefully sealed with tape. Mariye imagined they were filled with work-related documents. Those might contain important secrets. But they were business secrets, not the sort of thing that she was after.

None of these rooms was locked. Though their windows faced the valley, their blinds were closed. No one was there to delight in the bright sunlight and the majestic view. They were dimly lit and smelled of abandonment.

The fourth room fascinated her. Not so much the room itself, though. The furnishings were sparse—just a single straight-backed chair and a small, plain wooden table. No pictures graced the bare walls. Without decoration of any kind, it felt barren and empty. A room no one ever used. Yet when she checked the walk-in closet, she found an assortment of women's clothes hanging there. Not a huge number. But everything a woman would need, more or less, for a stay of several days. Mariye guessed the clothes had been set aside for someone who came to visit Menshiki on a regular basis. She scowled. Did her aunt know a woman like that was in the picture?

She quickly realized her mistake, however. The clothes were all out of style, designs from a different era. The dresses and skirts and blouses sported name brands, and were very fashionable and expensive, but not the sort that women wore these days. Mariye wasn't that up-to-date on current trends, but even she could tell that much. They had probably been in style before she was born. And all were permeated with the smell of mothballs. It appeared that the clothes had been hanging there for quite some time. They were being well looked after, though. She saw no moth holes. And the colors hadn't faded, which meant that care had been taken not to expose them to extreme heat or cold. The dresses were size 5. That indicated that the woman was about five feet tall. And very slender, looking at the skirts. She wore a size 5 shoe.

An assortment of women's undergarments, socks, and nightgowns were stored in the closet drawers. All were in plastic bags to ward off dust. She pulled a few out to examine. The bras were a 32C. Mariye pictured the shape of the breasts they had held. Slightly smaller than her aunt's, she estimated (it was impossible to guess the shape of the nipples, of course). The panties were dainty and elegant. Some were on the sexy side. All in all, they spoke of a woman of some means, who shopped in lingerie boutiques while savoring the thought of embracing the man she loved. They were made of silk and lace and had to be washed by hand in lukewarm water. Not the sort of panties one wore to weed the garden. Here too the odor of mothballs was strong. She folded the panties up carefully, returned them to the plastic bag, and put it back in the drawer.

This was the wardrobe of a woman whom Menshiki had been seeing some time before—fifteen or twenty years ago, most likely. That was the conclusion Mariye drew. Then something had happened that caused the woman to leave her stylish clothes—her size 5 dresses, size 5 shoes, and 32C bras—behind. She had never come back. Why would she have left such an expensive collection behind? If they had separated for some reason, wouldn't the normal thing have been to take the clothes with her? Mariye couldn't figure it out. Moreover, Menshiki had preserved that small collection with such care. Like the river sprites of the Rhine, who took pains to preserve their legendary gold for posterity. He probably visited this room on occasion to look at the clothes and take them in his hands. When the seasons changed, he would replace the mothballs (she couldn't imagine him letting anyone else do this).

Where was that woman today? Perhaps she had married another man. Or died of illness, or in some kind of accident. Nevertheless, he held her in his memory, even now.

(Of course, Mariye had no way of knowing that woman was her

mother, and *I* could find no compelling reason to tell her. That right, I thought, belonged to Menshiki alone.)

Mariye pondered this new knowledge. Should she think more generously of a man who had treasured the memory of a woman for so long? Or was the fact that he had preserved her clothing with such care a little creepy?

Mariye was still thinking this through when, all at once, she heard the garage door clattering up. Menshiki had come home. She had been so absorbed in the clothes that she hadn't heard the front gate open, or the car in the driveway. She had to get away as quickly as possible. She needed to find a safe place to hide. Then she realized. Something of *vital importance*. Panic grabbed her.

She had forgotten her shoes on the deck. And the binoculars were out of their case and attached to their stand. The hornet had scared her so much that she had fled into the house without covering her tracks. Everything was out in the open. When Menshiki went out to the deck and saw those things (as he would sooner or later), he would know right away that someone had invaded his home in his absence. The black loafers would tell him that the invader was a girl. Menshiki was no dummy. It wouldn't take long for him to figure out it was Mariye. He would comb the house, searching every nook and cranny, until he found her hiding place. It would be child's play for him.

There wasn't time enough to run outside up to the deck, collect her shoes, and put the binoculars back where they belonged. She was certain to bump into Menshiki somewhere along the way. She couldn't think of a next step. Her heart pounded, her breathing became labored, her limbs froze with fear.

The car engine stopped and the garage door started clattering shut. Any minute now Menshiki would enter the house. What should she do? What should she . . . Her mind was a blank. She sat on the floor, her head in her hands and her eyes squeezed shut.

"It is best to remain where you are," someone said.

Was she hearing things? No, she wasn't. Pulling herself together, she opened her eyes. There was a little old man no more than two feet tall, perched on a low chest of drawers. His salt-and-pepper hair was tied in a bun on top of his head. He wore white garments from a bygone age and carried a tiny sword at his waist. Naturally, she thought she was hallucinating. Her panic was making her imagine things that weren't there.

"No, this is no hallucination," the little old man said in a small but resonant voice. "I am the Commendatore. And I am here to aid my young friends."

61

I HAVE TO BE A BRAVE, SMART GIRL

This is no hallucination," the Commendatore repeated. "There are sundry opinions as to whether I exist, but a hallucination I am not. I have come to aid my friends. You are in need of aid, are you not?"

"My friends" referred to her, Mariye assumed. She nodded. His manner of speech was strange indeed, but what he said was true. She needed help, no question there.

"My friends cannot retrieve your shoes from the deck," the Commendatore said. "And it is best to forget the binoculars as well. But quell your fears. I will strive my utmost to ensure that Menshiki does not go there. For the time being, at least. Once the sun sets, however, I cannot prevent him. When darkness falls, he will venture out to watch the home of my friends. This is his custom. We must fix the problem before that happens. Can my friends understand the import of my words?"

Mariye could only nod. Somehow, she did understand.

"My friends must hide in this closet awhile," said the Commendatore. "Be as quiet as a mouse. Give no sign that you are here. When the time is propitious I will let you know. Until then, do not move or make a sound. No matter what happens. Do my friends understand?"

Mariye nodded again. Was this a dream? Could he be an elf or sprite of some kind?

"I am neither dream nor sprite," the Commendatore read her thoughts. "I am an Idea, and thus lack shape of my own. It would be very inconvenient if my friends could not see me, so I have taken the form of the Commendatore for the time being."

Idea, the Commendatore . . . Mariye repeated the words in her mind without voicing them. He can tell what I am thinking. Then she remembered. He was a figure in that very wide Japanese-style painting by Tomohiko Amada that she had seen in his studio. Somehow he had slipped out of the painting and come here. That explained his tiny size.

"Affirmative," the Commendatore said. "I am borrowing the form of that character. The Commendatore—I myself do not know his significance. But I am called by that sobriquet now. Wait here in silence. I will come for my friends at the proper time. Do not fear. These raiments will shelter you."

These raiments will shelter me? What did that mean? But he did not respond to her unspoken question. A moment later he was gone. Vanished into thin air, like vapor.

Mariye did as the Commendatore said. She quieted her breathing and didn't move a muscle. Menshiki was home—she had heard him enter the house. He seemed to have been shopping, for she could make out the rustle of paper bags. Her breathing almost stopped when his slippered feet padded slowly past the room where she was hiding.

The closet door was a Venetian blind, so some light seeped upward through the slats. But only a tiny bit. The closet would grow very dark when the daylight faded. She could see only the carpeted floor through the cracks. The closet was cramped, and filled with the sharp odor of mothballs. With walls on all sides, there was nowhere to hide. And no way to escape. The lack of an escape route scared her to death.

The Commendatore had promised to come and get her when the right time came. She had no choice but to believe him. He had said, "These raiments will shelter you," too. He must have meant the clothes there in the closet. Old clothes worn by some unknown woman, likely before Mariye was even born. How could they protect her? She reached out and stroked a dress with a flower pattern. The pink cloth was soft to the touch. She let her fingertips linger for a while. She couldn't explain why, but there was something comforting about it.

I bet this dress would fit, Mariye thought. Its owner wasn't that much bigger than me. I can wear a size 5. Of course my chest hasn't filled out yet, so I'd have to figure a way to conceal that. But I could wear most of these clothes if I wanted to, or if I had to for some reason. The thought made her heart skip a beat.

Time was passing. Slowly but surely, the room was growing darker. Evening was approaching, minute by minute. She looked at her watch. But she couldn't read it in the gloom. She pressed a button and the face lit up. It was almost four thirty. The sun would be going down soon. The days were getting shorter. And when night did come, Menshiki would head out to the deck. It would take him but a second to realize that someone had invaded his home. She had to find some way to deal with the shoes and binoculars before that happened.

Mariye waited impatiently for the Commendatore to arrive, her heart in her mouth. Yet he never did. Perhaps there had been some kind of hitch. Menshiki might have left him no opening. She hadn't a clue how extensive the actual powers of a person—or an Idea—like the Commendatore were, in fact, or how far she could depend on him. Yet he was her only hope. She had nowhere else to turn. Mariye sat holding her knees on the floor of the closet, staring through the slats at the carpet. From time to time she reached up to stroke the flowery dress. As though it were a lifeline of some kind.

When the room had grown quite dark, she heard footsteps in the hall a second time. Once again, they were slow and soft. The footsteps came to an abrupt halt in front of the room where she was hiding. As if whoever it was had sniffed out something. A moment later she heard the door open. There could be no doubt. Her heart froze in her mouth. Then she heard the person (Menshiki, she presumed—no one else was in the house) step inside and gently close the door behind him. It clicked shut. *The man is in the room. For sure.* Like her, he held his breath and listened carefully, trying to pick up the slightest sign. She could tell. But the man did not turn on the light. Instead he carried out his search in the dark. Why? Anyone else would have switched on the light the moment they came in. It baffled her.

Mariye stared at the floor through the slats. If he came close enough, his toes would come into view. She couldn't see them yet. Yet his presence felt very real. It was definitely a man. Moreover, that man (it had to be Menshiki!) was staring at the closet door in the dark. He had picked up signs of something. Something different than usual. Next he would open the door. It couldn't be otherwise. It would be easy, since of course it wasn't locked. All he had to do was reach out, grab the knob, and pull.

The footsteps drew even closer. Fear gripped her. Cold sweat dripped from her armpits. I should never have come, she thought. I should have stayed home like a good girl. In my dear home across the valley. There is something really scary about this place. Something I should never have approached so recklessly. Some kind of consciousness operated here. The hornets were a part of it. Now she was within arm's reach of that *something*. She could see the toe of a slipper through the blinds. She could tell that the slipper was brown and made of leather, but it was too dark to see anything more.

Mariye instinctively reached up and grabbed the dress. The size 5 dress with the flower pattern. *Please help me! Protect me!* she prayed.

The man stood in front of the closet's double doors for some time. He didn't make a sound. She couldn't even hear him breathe. Still as a stone statue, he stood there gauging the situation. The silence grew heavier, the dark more impenetrable. She huddled on the floor, quivering. Her teeth chattered faintly. Mariye longed to shut her eyes and ears. To put her mind in a totally different place. But she didn't. She somehow knew how dangerous that would be. She must never give in to fear, however great. Never abandon her senses. Never stop thinking. With her ears pricked and her eyes fastened on the toes of the leather slippers, she fiercely clutched the hem of the soft pink dress.

The clothes would protect her. The whole wardrobe was her ally. The size 5 dresses, the size 5 shoes, the 32C bras—they would enfold her in a cloak of invisibility. I am not here, she told herself. *I am not here.*

How much time passed? She had no way of knowing. Time was no longer uniform, nor did it flow in sequence. Nevertheless, a fixed period seemed to have elapsed. At one point, the man had been on the verge of opening the door. Mariye felt that strongly. She braced herself. When it opened he would see her. She would see him. Then what? She had no clue. *Perhaps it's not Menshiki at all*—the thought popped into her head. *But then who could it be?*

Yet the man never opened the door. After some hesitation, he pulled back his hand and moved away. Why had he changed his mind at the last minute? *Something* must have held him back. He stepped out into the hallway and closed the door behind him. The room was empty again. For certain. It was no ruse. She was alone. She was certain of that. Mariye closed her eyes and expelled all the air she had been holding in a great sigh.

Her heart was still pounding. Like a tom-tom—that's how a novelist might describe it. What was a tom-tom, anyway? She had no clear picture. She had been in great peril. At the very last moment, however, something had intervened to protect her. Even so, this place was too dangerous—that much was obvious. Whoever it was, that *someone* had sensed her presence. Beyond a doubt. She couldn't hide in this room forever. This time, she had squeaked through. Next time she might not be so lucky.

She kept waiting. The room grew even darker. But she didn't make a sound. She was fearful, she was anxious, but she persevered. The Commendatore would not forget her. She believed what he had told her. She had no other options—she had to rely on the little guy with the funny way of talking.

Then, before she knew it, the Commendatore was there.

"My friends must leave immediately," he whispered. "Now, at this very moment. Wake up, it is now time."

Mariye was at a loss. It was hard to stand up. When she imagined leaving the closet she was assaulted by a new fear. Even greater dangers might await her in the world outside.

"Menshiki is in the shower," the Commendatore said. "You know what a clean person he is. So he should linger there awhile. But he will come out by and by. This is the one and only chance that my friends will have. Make haste!"

Marshaling her strength, Mariye pulled herself to her feet. She pushed the door of the closet open. The room was dark and empty.

Before she stepped out, she turned to take one last look at the clothes hanging there. She inhaled the smell of mothballs. She might never see these clothes again. For some reason, they had become so close to her, so dear.

"My friends must go now," said the Commendatore. "There is not much time. Go into the hallway and turn left."

With her bag over her shoulder, Mariye walked out the door and down the corridor. She ran up the stairs, cut across the big living room, and slid open the glass door to the deck terrace. The hornet might still be around. Or he might have retired for the night. He could be the kind of insect that wasn't fazed by the dark. But she couldn't dwell on that now. She stepped out, unscrewed the binoculars from their stand, and returned them to their plastic cover. She folded the stand and leaned it back against the wall. Her nerves made her hands fumble, so it took longer than she had expected. Then she picked her black loafers up off the deck. All the while, the Commendatore sat on the stool and watched her. The hornet never showed itself. To Mariye's great relief.

"Well done," said the Commendatore, with a nod. "Now go back inside, shut the door, and descend the stairs to the very bottom."

Down two flights of stairs? That would mean plunging into the depths of the house. Wasn't she trying to escape?

"There is no chance of escaping now," the Commendatore said, reading her mind. He shook his head from side to side. "The gate is strictly barred. My friends are constrained to hide a while longer. I beseech you to listen."

Mariye had no choice but to believe the Commendatore. She hurried through the living room and down the two flights of stairs.

The maid's room was at the bottom. Beside it was the laundry room and next to that a storeroom. At the end of the hallway was the gym with its row of exercise machines. The Commendatore pointed to the maid's room.

"This is your hiding place," he said. "Menshiki seldom ventures into that room. He descends once a day to do his laundry and to exercise, but he almost never enters there. It is unlikely he will find my friends, should you remain quiet. The room has a sink and a refrigerator. In case of earthquake, an ample store of food and mineral water has been set aside. So my friends will not starve. There is enough to live in relative safety for a number of days."

A number of days? Mariye asked (albeit without speaking) incredulously, her shoes in hand. I must remain *here* that long?

"Affirmative. It is a shame, but my friends are obliged to stay here for such a time," the Commendatore said, shaking his tiny head. "This house is kept under tight guard. In more than one way. This is a fact I cannot alter. An Idea's powers are limited, I am sad to say."

"How long will I have to stay here?" Mariye asked in a small voice. "I have to go home soon. My aunt will worry about me. If I'm missing too long, she'll have to report it to the police. Then there'll be a real mess."

The Commendatore shook his head. "A million pardons, but this is outside my control. My friends must wait here."

"Is Mr. Menshiki dangerous?"

"A very hard question to answer," the Commendatore said. He made an exaggerated frown. "Menshiki himself is not an evil man. He is a decent sort, one could say, with abilities that exceed those of most people. There is even a hint of nobility in him, if one looks hard enough. Yet there is a gap in his heart, an empty space that attracts the abnormal and the dangerous. It is there that the problem lies."

Mariye wasn't clear what all of this meant, of course. *The abnormal?*

"Who was the person standing outside the closet door?" she asked. "Was that Menshiki?"

"It was Menshiki, but at the same time it was not Menshiki."

"Is he aware of any of this?"

"Most likely," the Commendatore said. "Most likely. But there is nothing he can do about it."

The abnormal and the dangerous? Perhaps the hornet she had seen was one of the forms those things took, Mariye thought.

"Affirmative. Beware of those hornets. They are most virulent creatures," the Commendatore read her mind.

"Virulent?"

"They have the power to kill my friends," the Commendatore explained. "For now, my friends have no choice but to stay here. Do not go outside."

"Virulent," Mariye repeated in her mind. The word sure had a sinister ring.

Mariye opened the door of the maid's room and went in. It was little larger than Menshiki's bedroom closet. There was a kitchenette with a fridge, a hot plate, a small microwave oven, and a sink and faucet. There was also a bed and a tiny bathroom. The bed was bare, but there were blankets, quilts, and a pillow on the shelf, and a simple table and chair for meals. Only a single chair, though. A small window faced the valley. She could look out across it through a crack in the curtain.

"It is best to make as little noise as possible," the Commendatore said. "Do my friends understand?"

Mariye nodded.

"You are a brave girl, my friends," said the Commendatore. "A touch reckless, perhaps, but brave nonetheless. It is an admirable quality. But while you are here, you must be *very* alert. Never be caught off guard. This is no ordinary place. Sinister things are skulking out there that could cause you harm."

"Skulking?"

"Prowling about, in short."

Mariye nodded. In what way was this "no ordinary place," and what sort of sinister things were skulking? She wanted to know, but couldn't think how to ask. Where to begin? There was just so much she couldn't understand.

"I may not be able to come again," the Commendatore said, as if imparting a secret. "There is another place I must go, and another task I must look after. A very important task, if I may say. So I fear I cannot help my friends any further. Hereafter, my friends must manage on your own."

"But how can I escape this place by myself?"

The Commendatore narrowed his eyes and looked squarely at Mariye. "Be sure your ears are open and your eyes are peeled. And keep your wits about you. It is the only way. Then you will know when the right moment comes. As in, 'Aha, now is the time!' You are a brave, smart girl, my friends. Just stay alert."

Mariye nodded. I have to be a brave, smart girl, she thought.

"I wish my friends all the very best," the Commendatore said, encouraging her. Then, as if by afterthought, "And worry not, my friends. Your chest will soon fill out."

"Enough to fill a C-cup bra?"

The Commendatore gave an embarrassed shrug. "I fear I am a mere Idea. I know not how the undergarments of women are measured. But all the same, I can assure you that your breasts will grow. No need to worry. Time is the remedy for your concerns. It is the key for all things that possess form. True, time does not last forever, but as long as you have it, it is remarkably efficacious. So look forward to the future, my friends!"

"Thank you," Mariye said. It was certainly good to hear. She needed every bit of support to be the brave girl she knew she had to be.

Then the Commendatore vanished. Again, like vapor into thin air. The silence around her deepened the moment he was gone. The thought that she might never see him again left her sad and lonely. I have no one to rely on now, she thought. She sprawled out on the bare mattress and stared at the ceiling. It was low, and made of white plasterboard. In its exact center was a fluorescent light. But of course she couldn't turn it on. That was a definite no-brainer.

How long would she be stuck in this room? It was almost dinnertime. If she wasn't home by seven thirty, her aunt would call the arts-and-culture center. They would inform her that she'd been absent that day. The thought hurt. Her aunt would be hysterical, terrified that something bad had happened to her. Somehow, she needed to let her know she was all right. Then she remembered—there was a cell phone in the pocket of her school blazer. She had left it turned off.

She pulled it out and switched it on. The words "Low Battery" flashed on the screen. A split second later the screen went black. Her phone was dead. She could hardly blame the phone: she hadn't used it in ages (she seldom needed it in her daily life, and had little interest in—or affection for—cell phones), so no surprise the battery was drained.

She heaved a sigh. She should have recharged it once in a while at least. Just in case something happened. But there was no use crying over spilt milk. She stuck the cell phone back in her blazer pocket. But something had caught her attention, and she pulled it out again. The plastic penguin attached to it was gone! It had been her lucky charm since she had won it on points at a donut shop. The strap must have broken. But where on earth could she have dropped it? It was hard to imagine. She hardly ever took it out of her pocket.

At first, she felt uneasy without her lucky charm. Then she thought some more. Her own carelessness was probably to blame for losing it. But a new kind of talisman had appeared in its place—that closetful of clothes—and those clothes had protected her. And that little man with the funny way of talking, the Commendatore, had led her to this place. So *something*, she thought, is still looking out for me. No need to mope about the missing penguin.

Mariye wasn't carrying much. Wallet, handkerchief, change purse, house key, and a half a pack of Cool Mint gum—that was about it. Her shoulder bag contained pencils and pens and a few school textbooks. None were likely to be very useful.

She slipped out of the maid's room and went to check the storage room. As the Commendatore had said, it was stocked with provisions in case of earthquake. The ground was comparatively stable in this mountainous part of Odawara, so an earthquake shouldn't be that serious. The great Kanto earthquake of 1923 had devastated the city of Odawara, but here in the hills, the damage had been relatively minor (she'd done a summer project in grade school on the impact of the earthquake on the Odawara region). Nevertheless, it would be very difficult afterward to get food and water way up here. Thus Menshiki had taken pains to stock up on both. His caution knew no bounds.

She selected two bottles of mineral water, a box of crackers, and a bar of chocolate and carried them back to her room. She was pretty sure Menshiki wouldn't miss such a small amount. However meticulous he might be, he wouldn't keep tabs on how many bottles he had stored. The water was necessary because she didn't want to turn on the tap in her room if at all possible. That would make the pipes in the house gurgle. It is best to make as little noise as possible, the Commendatore had said. She had to be careful.

Mariye returned to the maid's room and locked the door from the inside. In a sense, it was a useless gesture, since Menshiki had keys to all the rooms in the house. Yet it might earn her a little time. At the very least, it eased her mind a bit.

She wasn't hungry at all, but she ate a few crackers and drank some of the water just to check. The crackers were mediocre, as was the water. She checked the labels—neither had reached its best-before date. I'm okay, she thought. I won't starve.

Outside was now completely dark. She pulled the curtain back a little farther and looked across the valley. She could see her house. She couldn't see what was going on inside without the binoculars, but she could tell lights were burning in some of the rooms. If she looked hard, she might be able to observe someone moving around. Her aunt was there, freaking out, she was sure, because she hadn't come home. Wasn't there a way to call her? Menshiki must have a phone somewhere. All she had to do was say, "Please don't worry. I'm all right," and hang up. If she kept it short, Menshiki probably wouldn't find out. But her room had no phone, nor had she seen one in that part of the house.

Could she escape under cover of darkness? Find a ladder somewhere and scale the wall to freedom? She recalled seeing a fold-up ladder in the garden shed. Then she recalled the Commendatore's words: *This place is kept under tight guard. In more than one way.* She was pretty sure that "tight guard" didn't refer to the security company's alarm system alone.

I should believe the Commendatore, Mariye thought. This is no normal place. Many things are lurking about. I have to be super cautious. Super patient. This is no time to be rash or willful. I should sit back and wait for the right opportunity, like the Commendatore said.

You will know when the right moment comes. As in, "Aha, now is the time!" You are a brave, smart girl, my friends. Just stay alert.

That's right, I have to be a brave, smart girl. Survive all this in good shape and then watch my breasts get bigger and bigger.

So she thought as she lay there on the bare mattress. All around was growing darker. She could tell that darkness of a different order was about to arrive.

62

ONE CAN STUMBLE INTO A LABYRINTH

Time followed its own principles, paying no heed to her thoughts. She lay there on the bare mattress in her little room, watching it sluggishly shuffle past. She had nothing else to do. It would be nice to have a book to read, she thought. But there were no books at hand, and even if there had been she couldn't switch on the light. All she could do was lie there in the dark. She had found flashlights and spare batteries in the storeroom but had decided to use those as little as possible.

The night deepened, and she fell asleep. She was nervous and apprehensive in such an unfamiliar place, and she wanted to stay awake, but at a certain point fatigue overcame her and she dropped off. She simply couldn't keep her eyes open. The coverless bed was cold, so she took a quilt and blankets from the closet, wrapped herself up in them like a Swiss Roll, and closed her eyes. There was no space heater in the room, and she couldn't use the central system for obvious reasons.

(A note here on the time frame: Menshiki would have left to visit me while Mariye was asleep. He stayed over and went back the following morning. In other words, he wasn't at home that night. The house was empty. But Mariye had no way of knowing that.)

Mariye woke up once that night to use the bathroom, but didn't flush the toilet. During the day was one thing, but in the still, wee hours of the morning the sound of running water could attract attention. Menshiki was without question a cautious and meticulous individual. He would notice even the slightest change. So why risk discovery?

Her watch said two in the morning. Saturday morning, that was. Friday had passed. When she peeped through the curtain she could see her home across the valley. The lights in the living room were blazing. It was after midnight and she still hadn't returned, so the people there—at night that would mean her father and her aunt—were unable to sleep. I've done an awful thing, Mariye thought. She even felt sorry for her father (very rare for her). I shouldn't have been so reckless—it wasn't my intention. This is what I get for acting so impulsively.

Yet whatever her regrets, however much she might blame herself, she couldn't transport herself across the valley. She was not a crow. She couldn't sprout wings and fly through the air. Nor could she disappear and reappear like the Commendatore. She was confined within her still-growing body, and shackled by time and space. Hers was a clumsy, awkward existence. Look at her chest—as flat as a board. Her breasts still pancakes that had failed to rise.

Naturally, Mariye was scared alone there in the dark. Her powerlessness pained her. She wished the Commendatore were there. She had so many things to ask him. Whether he answered them or not, at least she would have someone to talk to. To be sure, his way of speaking was odd, somewhat different from modern Japanese, but she could still understand his general meaning. But he might never come back. "There is another place I must go, and another task I must look after," he had told her. She was desolate to have lost him, perhaps forever.

From outside the window came the resonant cry of a night bird. It sounded like an owl, perhaps a horned owl. They were cloistered in the dark forests, honing their wisdom. I must be as wise as they are, she thought. Be a smart, brave girl. But sleep overtook her a second time. She couldn't keep her eyes open. Pulling the bedding around her once again, she lay down on the mattress and closed her eyes. It was a deep and dreamless sleep. When she woke up it was already growing light outside. Her watch said half past six.

The world was welcoming a new Saturday.

Mariye spent all that day holed up in the maid's room. In place of breakfast, she had more crackers, a few chocolates, and mineral water. She crept into the gym and borrowed several issues from a small mountain of Japanese editions of *National Geographic*. She guessed Menshiki read them when he was working out on his exercise bike, since they were stained here and there with what appeared to be his sweat. She read through them several times. There were articles on the habitat of the Alaskan wolf, the mysteries of the rising and ebbing of the tides, the life of the Inuit, and the gradual shrinking of the Amazon rain forest. Not Mariye's usual reading material by any means, but now, with nothing else to look at, she read them over and over until she had them practically memorized. She bored holes in the illustrations with her eyes.

When she tired of reading, she napped. On occasion, she looked through the curtain at her home across the valley. I wish I had that telescope now, she thought. Then I'd really be able to see inside, even watch people moving around. She wanted to be back inside her room with the orange curtains. Scrub every inch of her body in a nice hot bath, change into fresh pajamas, and curl up in her warm bed with her cat.

Just after nine in the morning, she heard the sound of someone coming down the stairs. The footsteps of a man in slippers. Menshiki, most likely. His way of walking was somehow distinctive. She wanted to peek through the keyhole, but the door didn't have one. She huddled over her knees in a corner of the room, her body rigid. Escape would be impossible if he opened the door and came in. The Commendatore had said that shouldn't happen, and she had taken him at his word. But nothing was a hundred percent sure thing in this world. Making herself as invisible as possible, she thought of the clothes in the closet and prayed, *Don't let anything happen to me.* Her throat was as dry as cotton.

Menshiki seemed to have brought down his dirty laundry. He probably washed a day's worth of clothes at this time each morning. He tossed them in, added detergent, set the timer and mode, and turned the washer on. She could tell by listening that his movements were practiced. She was surprised how well she could hear. The washer began to churn. Menshiki then moved to the gym and began working out on his exercise machines. That seemed to be his ritual—to work out while his clothes were spinning in the washer. While listening to classical music. She could hear strains of Baroque music coming from the speakers attached to the gym's ceiling. It sounded like Bach, or Handel, or Vivaldi. Mariye didn't know much about classical music, though, so it could have been any one of those three.

Mariye spent a full hour with her ears tuned to the churn of the washer, the systematic whirring of the exercise machines, and the music of either Bach, Handel, or Vivaldi. It was a nerve-wracking hour. True, Menshiki probably wouldn't notice that his pile of *National Geographic*s was short a few issues, or that his stash of crackers and chocolate in the storeroom was shrinking bit by bit. She had taken only a tiny fraction of what he had laid away. Nevertheless, there was no telling what might happen. She had to guard against carelessness. To stay on her toes.

Eventually, a buzzer went off and the washer stopped. Menshiki walked slowly back to the laundry room, took the clothes from the washer, put them in the dryer, and turned it on. The dryer began to turn. Satisfied that all was in order, Menshiki ambled up the stairs. It appeared that his workout had ended. Now he would probably take a long shower.

Mariye closed her eyes and sighed with relief. Menshiki would likely come back down in an hour or so. To remove his clothes from the dryer. Yet the most dangerous period had passed. At least it felt that way. He hadn't sensed her hiding there in the room. Hadn't felt her presence at all. She could breathe more freely now.

Then who had it been in front of the closet? The Commendatore had said it was Menshiki, but then again it wasn't him at all. What had that meant? She couldn't understand what he had been trying to say. It was just too difficult for her. Whatever the case, that *someone* had been able to tell that she (or at least a person) was in the closet. They had sensed her there, no doubt. Yet, *for some reason*, that someone was unable to open the closet door. What could that reason have been? Had that assembly of beautiful old clothes really protected her?

She longed to ask the Commendatore. But he had gone off somewhere. There was no one left who could explain things to her.

Menshiki did not set foot outside the house all that Saturday. As far as she knew, the garage door hadn't opened, nor had a car engine started up. He had come down to pick up his laundry, and then walked slowly back up the stairs. That was it. No one had visited the house at the top of the hill where the road came to an end. No parcels or registered documents had been delivered. The doorbell had remained silent. She had heard the telephone ring twice. The ring was faint and distant, but she could still make it out. It was picked up on the second ring the first time, and the third ring the time after that (that was how she knew Menshiki was in the house). The town garbage truck crawled up the slope to the melody of "Annie Laurie" and then crawled back down again (Saturday was garbage pickup day). Otherwise, she heard no sounds. The house was perfectly still.

The morning passed, afternoon rolled on, and soon evening was drawing near.

(A second note on the time frame: While Mariye was hiding in the maid's tiny room, I killed the Commendatore in the Izu nursing home, tied up Long Face, and descended into the underworld.)

But she never found the perfect time to escape. She had to be patient and wait for "the right moment," the Commendatore had told her. *You will know when the right moment comes. As in, "Aha, now is the time!"*

However, the "right moment" never came. Mariye grew more and more tired of waiting. Patience was not her strength. How long, she wondered, must I stay holed up here?

Menshiki began playing the piano not long before nightfall. Apparently, he kept the living room window open when he practiced, so Mariye could hear the music in her hiding place. It sounded like Mozart. One of his sonatas, in a major key. She had noticed the score on the piano. Menshiki ran through the slow-paced movement, then went back to repeat several sections, adjusting his fingering until he was satisfied. It was difficult, though, and he seemed to be having trouble balancing the sound. For the most part, Mozart's sonatas aren't all that hard, but a pianist who tries to master one can stumble into a labyrinth. That labyrinth, however, didn't seem to faze Menshiki in the least. Mariye listened to him patiently walk back and forth over the thorny passages. He practiced that way for about an hour. At the end, he closed the lid with a bang. She sensed he was frustrated. But not all that much. Rather, it was a moderate, elegant frustration. Even when he was alone (or at least, when he thought he was alone) in his sprawling mansion, he kept a tight rein on his feelings.

What followed was a repeat of the previous day. The sun set, the sky darkened, and the crows flew cawing back to their nests in the mountains. One by one, the lights of the houses across the valley went on.

The Akikawas' lights did too, and stayed lit even after midnight. Those lights signaled to Mariye just how worried her family was. At least it felt that way to her. It hurt not to be able to ease their pain.

In stark contrast, not a single light went on at Tomohiko Amada's house (in short, the house *I* inhabited). To all appearances, it looked abandoned. Night came, yet it remained black. It seemed that no one was home. Mariye thought it strange. Where had her teacher gone? Did he know that she was missing?

At a certain hour, sleep again attacked Mariye. The sandman showed no mercy. Shivering in her school blazer, she wrapped herself in blankets and quilts and closed her eyes. I wish my cat were here, she thought as she drifted off. For some reason, her cat—it was a she—seldom mewed or yowled. She only purred. Mariye could have kept her with her without fear of discovery. But of course she wasn't there. Mariye was all alone. In a small pitch-black room with no means of escape.

Sunday morning dawned. When Mariye opened her eyes it was still quite dark. Her watch said before six. The days were getting shorter. Rain was falling outside. A hushed, winter rain. She didn't realize it was raining until she noticed water dripping off the branches. The air in the room was chilly and damp. If only she had a sweater, she thought. All she was wearing under her blazer was a thin knitted vest, a cotton blouse, and beneath that a T-shirt. An outfit for a warm afternoon. A wool sweater would sure come in handy.

Then she remembered—she'd seen a sweater in *that closet*. An off-white cashmere that looked nice and warm. She could trot up the stairs and get it. Put it under her blazer, and she'd be warm as toast. But slipping out the door and climbing the stairs was just too dangerous. *Especially to that room.* She had to make do with what she had on. After all, this cold wasn't unbearable. Nothing like the brutal cold the Inuit had to deal with. This was the outskirts of Odawara, in early December.

Yet the rainy winter morning chilled her to the bone. She could feel the icy damp seep into her body. So Mariye closed her eyes and turned her thoughts to Hawaii instead. When she was small, she and her aunt, and her aunt's old school friend, had visited Hawaii. They rented a small surfboard for her on the beach at Waikiki, and she played in the waves—when she tired of that, she basked in the sun on the white sand. It was so warm, and so harmonious. High above her, the fronds of the palms swayed in the trade winds. White clouds sailed out to sea. She lay there and sipped a glass of lemonade, so cold her temples hurt. Mariye remembered the trip in detail. Would she ever see a place like that again? She'd give anything for that chance.

Once again, a little after nine, Menshiki came padding down the stairs in his slippers. The washer started, the classical music kicked in (this time it sounded like a Brahms symphony), and the rhythm of the exercise machines began. This lasted a full hour. A perfect repeat of the day before. Only the composer was different. The master of the house was certainly a creature of habit. He transferred the laundry from the washer to the dryer, and returned exactly an hour later to pick it up. He didn't come downstairs after that, and showed no interest at all in the maid's room.

(Another note on the time frame: Menshiki went to my home that afternoon, where he bumped into Masahiko and they had a brief conversation. For some reason, though, Mariye was again unaware that he had left the house.)

Menshiki's unwavering routine was useful to Mariye. She could prepare herself emotionally, and plan her movements in advance. Unexpected events would have made it much harder on her nerves. She had grown familiar with Menshiki's pattern, and adapted herself to it. He almost never went out (at least to her knowledge). He worked in his study, washed his own clothes, cooked his own meals, and, in the evening, sat down in front of his Steinway and practiced. Sometimes there was a phone call, but those were infrequent. She could count them on her fingers. For some reason, he didn't seem to like phones all that much. He appeared to take care of his work-related communications—she had no idea how extensive they were—on the computer in his study.

Menshiki took care of the basic cleaning, but once a week he had a cleaning service come to him. Mariye remembered him mentioning that on their previous visit. I don't mind doing it myself, he had said. Cleaning can cheer me up, just like cooking. But it was clearly beyond him to keep such a big house tidy on his own. Thus the need for professional help. He had said he left the house for half a day when they came. What day of the week would it be? Maybe that's when I can make my getaway, Mariye thought. People will be bringing equipment, so the gate should be opening and closing as their vehicles come and go. Menshiki should be absent. So getting out might not be all that hard. That could be my one and only chance.

Yet there was no sign that the cleaners were coming. Monday was much the same as Sunday. Menshiki was making good progress with Mozart: his mistakes were fewer, and the whole piece was coming together musically. He was a careful and patient man. Once he set a goal, he stuck to it. Mariye had to admit she was impressed. Even if he could make it through without a hitch, though, how pleasing would his Mozart be to the ear? Listening to what was coming from upstairs, she had her doubts.

She was surviving on crackers, chocolate, and mineral water. She also polished off an energy bar full of nuts. And a can of tuna fish. Since she had no toothbrush, she brushed her teeth with mineral water, using her finger. She read issue after issue of the Japanese version of *National Geographic*. In the process, she learned about a number of further topics: the man-eating tigers of Bengal; the lemurs of Madagascar; the shifting topography of the Grand Canyon; natural-gas extraction in Siberia; the life expectancy of the penguins of Antarctica; the world of the highland nomads of Afghanistan; the grueling initiation rituals of New Guinean youth. She learned the basics about AIDS, and Ebola. Such miscellaneous information about nature might prove useful one day. Then again, it might be entirely useless. Whatever the case, no other books were on hand. She devoured back issues of *National Geographic* like there was no tomorrow.

Once in a while, she would slip her hand under her T-shirt to check the status of her breasts. But they didn't appear to be growing at all. If anything, they seemed to be getting smaller. She was also concerned about her period. According to her calculations, the next was due in about ten days. She had found nothing related to that condition in the storeroom. (Plenty of toilet paper was stockpiled in case of earthquake, but no sanitary napkins or tampons. It seemed that women and their needs didn't register with the owner of the house.) She'd be in big trouble if it started while she was in hiding. Probably, though, she would have escaped by then. *Probably.* It was hard to imagine putting up with another ten days of this.

The cleaners finally showed up on Tuesday morning. She could hear the lively chatter of women in the upper garden as they unloaded equipment from the back of their van. Menshiki had not done his laundry that morning, nor performed his exercise routine. In fact, he hadn't come downstairs at all. She had wondered if this could be why (Menshiki wouldn't change his daily schedule without a reason), and, sure enough, it was as she had guessed. Menshiki had probably driven his Jaguar out the gate at the same moment the cleaners' big van pulled in.

Mariye rushed to tidy up the maid's room. She gathered the empty water bottles and cracker packets and put them in a garbage bag, which she set out in a visible place. The cleaners would look after it. She neatly folded the blanket and quilt and returned them to the closet. She took care to erase every trace of her presence. Now no one could tell that someone had been living there for days. Then she slung her bag over her shoulder and crept up the stairs. Timing her moves, she darted through the hallway without attracting the cleaners' attention. Her heart pounded at the thought of the dangers of *that room*. At the same time, though, she missed the clothes hanging in its closet. She wanted to go back for one last look. Touch them with her hands. But there was no time for that. She had to hurry.

She slipped through the front door undetected, and ran up the curved driveway. The gate had been left open, as she had anticipated. It made no sense for anyone working there to open and close it each time they passed through. Her face as she stepped out onto the road was a picture of normality.

Should I really be able to leave this easily? she thought outside the gate. Shouldn't I have to pay a higher price? Go through some sort of painful rite of passage, like the teenage tribesmen of New Guinea? Endure a ritual like that as a badge of courage? Those thoughts did not linger, however. They were dwarfed by the liberation she felt at having made her getaway.

The day was overcast, with low-lying clouds that threatened cold rain at any minute. But Mariye's face was raised to the sky. As if she were on the beach at Waikiki, gazing up at the swaying palm trees. She took several deep breaths, giddy with her good fortune. I am free, she thought. My feet will take me anywhere I want to go. My nights spent trembling in the dark are over. That fact alone made her grateful to be alive. It had been only four days, but now the world appeared so fresh, each tree, every blade of grass charged with such wonderful vitality. She found the smell of the wind exhilarating.

Yet this was no time to dawdle. Menshiki could have forgotten something and come driving back at any time. I should get away from here, she thought, and fast. Adopting what she hoped was a nonchalant expression, Mariye tried to smooth her wrinkled school uniform (she had been sleeping in it for days) and straighten her hair to avoid arousing suspicion as she trotted down the mountain.

At the foot of the slope, she turned up the road on the other side. But she did not take her usual route home—rather, she headed for my place. She had something in mind. But the house was empty. She rang the bell repeatedly, but no one came to the door.

Giving up, she went around to the back and took the path through the woods to the pit behind the little shrine. Now, however, a blue plastic sheet covered the pit. The sheet hadn't been there before. It was held firmly in place by cords attached to stakes driven into the ground. Stone weights were lined up on top. It was no longer possible to peek inside. In her absence, someone—who, she didn't know—had sealed it. Probably they considered it a safety hazard. She stood in front of the pit and listened for a while. But she heard nothing.

(My note: The fact she didn't hear the bell could have meant that I hadn't arrived yet. Or possibly that I had fallen asleep.)

Cold drops of rain began to fall. I should go home, she thought. My family is worried about me. But how could she explain the last four days? She had to think of something. She couldn't let on that she had been hiding at Menshiki's all that time—that was out of the question. It would create an even bigger mess. The police had probably been notified of her disappearance. If they knew that she had broken into Menshiki's home, she'd be charged with trespassing. She would be punished.

What if she claimed that she had fallen into the pit by accident, and had been unable to get out for four days? That only when her teacher—*me,* in other words—came by was she able to climb to safety. Mariye had expected me to play along with this scenario. But I hadn't been home, and the pit's opening had been secured with a plastic tarp. Thus her plan fell through. (Had that scenario unfolded, I would have had to explain to the police why Menshiki and I had brought in heavy equipment to uncover the pit, which might have led to even thornier problems.)

Claiming temporary amnesia was the only other story she could think of. Nothing else came to mind. She would say that those four days were a blank. That she couldn't remember a thing. That when she came to, she was lying alone on the mountain. She would stick with that—there was no other way. She had seen a TV show that hinged on that idea. She wasn't sure if people would swallow an excuse like that. The police and her family would grill her. They might send her to a psychiatrist or counselor of some kind. Even so, a claim of amnesia was the only option. She would have to mess up her hair, splatter mud on her legs and arms, and add a few scattered cuts and bruises to make it look as if she had spent all that time in the mountains. It would be an act she would have to carry through to the very end.

And in fact that was what she did. It was hardly a masterful performance, but she could come up with no alternative.

This was what Mariye revealed to me. She had just finished her account when Shoko Akikawa returned. I heard her Toyota Prius pull up in front of my house.

"I think you should keep quiet about what really happened," I said to Mariye. "Don't tell anyone but me. It will be our secret."

"Of course," Mariye said. "Of course I won't tell anyone. Even if I did, they wouldn't believe me."

"I believe you."

"Does this mean the circle is closed?"

"I don't know," I said. "Maybe not all the way. But I think we can rest easy. The dangerous part is over."

"The virulent part."

"That's right," I said. "The virulent part."

Mariye studied my face for a full ten seconds. "The Commendatore," she said in a small voice. "He really exists."

"That's right," I replied. "He really does." And I killed him with these hands. *Really.* But of course I couldn't tell her that.

Mariye gave a single nod. I knew she would keep our secret. It was a secret we would share forever.

I wished I could have told Mariye that the clothes that had protected her from that *something* had been worn by her late mother before she married. But I couldn't. I didn't have the right. Neither did the Commendatore. There was but one person in the world who did, and that was Menshiki. But he would never exercise it.

We all live our lives carrying secrets we cannot disclose.

63

BUT IT'S NOT WHAT YOU'RE THINKING

Mariye and I had a secret. An important secret shared by the two of us alone. I described my time in the underworld, and she told me exactly what had happened to her at Menshiki's mansion. We wrapped up the two paintings, *Killing Commendatore* and *The Man with the White Subaru Forester,* as tightly as we could and stored them in the attic of Tomohiko Amada's house. Nobody else knew about that, either. The owl did, of course, but it wasn't going to talk. It would hold our secret in perfect silence.

Mariye came to visit from time to time (she hid it from her aunt, using her secret passageway). We put our heads together to try to figure out what our experiences had in common, comparing the timelines right down to the smallest detail.

At first, I worried that Shoko would suspect that Mariye's four-day disappearance and my three-day "long-distance trip" were somehow related, but the idea seems never to have entered her head. Nor did the police direct their attention to that coincidence. They were ignorant of the passageway, so they dismissed my home as just another house on the next ridge over. Since I did not number among the Akikawas' "neighbors," they never came to interview me. Nor did it appear that Shoko had told them I was painting Mariye's portrait. She probably didn't see it as relevant. Had the police put Mariye's absence and my trip together, I could have been placed in a delicate situation.

. . .

I never completed my portrait of Mariye Akikawa. It was almost done, but I feared where finishing it might lead. Menshiki, for one, would move heaven and earth to put his hands on it. That much was clear, no matter what he might say to the contrary. I had no intention, however, of letting him install the painting in his private "sanctuary." That could be dangerous. So in the end I left it unfinished. Mariye, however, loved the painting ("It shows how I think these days," was how she put it), and wanted to keep it near her if possible. So I readily gave it to her in its unfinished state (along with the three sketches I had promised earlier).

"I think it's cool," Mariye said. "It's a work in progress, and I'm a work in progress too, now and forever."

"None of us are ever finished. Everyone is always a work in progress."

"How about Mr. Menshiki?" Mariye asked. "He looks very finished to me."

"I think he's a work in progress too," I said.

Menshiki was far from being a completed human being. From what I could tell, anyway. That is why, night after night, under cloak of darkness, he reached out to Mariye Akikawa across the valley on his high-powered binoculars. He couldn't help himself. That secret allowed him to maintain some sort of personal equilibrium. It was for him the equivalent of the long balancing pole that tightrope walkers carry.

Of course, Mariye was aware that Menshiki was peeking into her house. But she never revealed it to anyone (apart from me). She never told her aunt. What possessed him to do something like that? It mystified her. Yet for some reason she didn't feel like pursuing it any further. All she did was keep her curtain closed. The sun-bleached orange curtain stayed tightly shut at all times. She also made sure that the light in her room was off when she changed for bed at night. Elsewhere in the house, however, his voyeurism didn't bother her. Sometimes she even thought she enjoyed it. Perhaps she found some meaning in the fact that *she alone* knew what was going on.

According to Mariye, Shoko and Menshiki were still seeing each other. Her aunt would jump in the car and drive off to his house once or twice a week. Their relationship appeared to be sexual (Mariye hinted at this in a very roundabout way). Her young aunt never said where she was going, but Mariye knew. When she came back, her complexion was rosier than usual. In any case—whatever the nature of that peculiar void within Menshiki—Mariye was powerless to interfere in their affair. She could only let them continue on as they were. All she wished was not to be drawn into whatever was going on between the two of them. That she be allowed to stand at a safe distance, outside the whirlpool of their relationship.

I doubted that she could pull that off. Without realizing it, she would be sucked in sooner or later, to a greater or lesser degree. From the periphery, unavoidably toward the center. Menshiki was wooing Shoko Akikawa, but always with Mariye in mind. Whether he had planned it all from the start or not, he couldn't help himself—that's the kind of man he was. And, like it or not, I had brought them together. He had met Shoko in this house. That's what he had wanted. And when Menshiki wanted something, the guy knew how to put his hands on it.

Mariye wasn't sure what Menshiki would do with that closetful of shoes and size 5 dresses. She guessed he would keep them—whether they were stored in that closet or in another place. However his relationship with Shoko Akikawa turned out, he wouldn't be able to discard them, or burn them. That was because the wardrobe had become a part of his psyche. The clothes would be forever enshrined within his spiritual sanctuary.

I decided to quit teaching my painting class near Odawara Station. "I'm sorry, but I need to focus on my art," was how I put it to the director. He took it in stride. "It's a shame," he said. "Everyone says you're a wonderful teacher." His words didn't sound altogether false, either. I thanked him, and promised to stick it out till year's end. By then, he had located a good replacement, a retired high school art instructor in her mid-sixties. She struck me as a very nice woman, with eyes that resembled those of an elephant.

Menshiki called from time to time. No practical matter was ever involved—we just chatted. Each time he would ask if there had been any change in the pit behind the shrine, and each time I would tell him no, there hadn't. That was the honest truth. The blue plastic sheet was still stretched across the opening. I went to check sometimes when I was out for a walk, but never saw any sign that it had been tampered with. The stones holding it down hadn't been moved either. There were no more strange or suspicious events connected to the pit. I never heard the bell in the middle of the night, nor did the Commendatore (or anything else) emerge from it. It was just a big hole sitting quietly in the middle of the woods. The clump of tall pampas grass flattened by the backhoe was growing back, concealing the area around the pit once again.

As far as Menshiki knew, I had been in the pit the whole time I was missing. True, he couldn't explain how I had gotten inside. Yet he had found me there—that was an indisputable fact. As a result, he never connected Mariye's disappearance and mine. He could only see the overlap of the two events as some kind of strange coincidence.

Discreetly, I probed to see if he had an inkling that someone had been hiding in his house for four days. But he had seen no telltale signs. He was wholly in the dark. In which case, whoever had been standing outside the closet in the *forbidden chamber* was most likely not him. But then who had it been?

Although Menshiki called, he no longer came by for visits. Perhaps he no longer needed to hang out now that Shoko was in his grasp. Or maybe he had lost interest in me. Or both. It didn't matter to me one way or the other (though there were times I missed the sound of his Jaguar V8 purring up the slope).

Nevertheless, the occasional phone calls (always before eight in the evening) suggested that Menshiki felt we should stay connected in some way. Perhaps the fact that he had revealed to me that he *might* be Mariye's biological father weighed on his mind to some extent. I don't think he worried that I would blurt it out—to either Mariye or Shoko Akikawa—somewhere down the line. He was sure I would guard his secret. He could read me well enough to know that, like he could read all people. Yet it was *so foreign* to Menshiki to have bared his heart to anyone, whoever they might be. He had an iron will, but maybe even he found it exhausting to keep secrets to himself all the time. He must have really needed me on his side when he made his confession. And I had struck him as relatively harmless.

Whether or not he had exploited me from the beginning, however, I still owed him my gratitude. It was he who had rescued me from the pit. Had he not come along, if he hadn't lowered the ladder and then yanked me up to the surface, I would have become a dried-up corpse. In a sense, then, Menshiki and I had each placed our lives in the other's hands. That meant that our accounts were even.

Menshiki just nodded when I told him that I had given *A Portrait of Mariye Akikawa* to Mariye in its unfinished state. I guess he no longer needed the painting that much, though he had commissioned it. Or he saw no meaning in an unfinished work. Or his mind was on other things.

A few days after Menshiki and I had this conversation, I put a simple frame on *The Pit in the Woods*, placed the painting in the trunk of my Corolla, and took it to his house. This was the last time we would meet face-to-face.

"This is for saving my life. Please accept it," I said.

He seemed to like the painting a lot. (I thought it was pretty good myself.) He offered to pay me for it, but I turned him down. I had received too much money from him as it stood. There was no need for further obligations on either side. We had become neighbors who lived across the valley from each other, no more, and I wanted to keep it that way.

Tomohiko Amada passed away the Saturday of the week I was rescued from the pit. He had been in a coma for three days, and in the end his heart simply stopped beating. It shut down quietly and naturally, like a locomotive pulling into the last station. Masahiko was by his side throughout. He called me soon after.

"He went peacefully," he said. "That's the way I would like to go. I thought I could even detect a smile."

"A smile?" I asked.

"Maybe it wasn't a true smile, strictly speaking. But that's the way it looked. To me, anyway."

"I'm very sorry about your father," I said, choosing my words, "but I'm glad he went peacefully."

"He was semiconscious until midweek, but he didn't seem to want to leave any parting words," Masahiko said. "I guess he had no regrets—he lived his ninety years to the fullest, doing what he wanted to do."

You're wrong, I thought. He had regrets. In fact, he bore a very heavy burden. Yet only he knew what that burden was. Now there was no one left who knew, and it would remain like that forever.

"I'm afraid I'll be out of touch for a while," Masahiko said. "Dad was famous in his own way, which means I have to take care of all kinds of things. I'm the son and heir, so I can't say no. Let's get together and talk after things have settled down a little."

I thanked him for taking the trouble to let me know, and we hung up.

Tomohiko Amada's death cast an even deeper hush over my home. But that was only natural. He had lived there for a long time, after all. I shared the house with that silence for several days. It was intense, but not unpleasant. You could call it a pure silence, in that it was not connected to anything else. A chain of events had come to an end. That's how it felt, anyway. It was the kind of hush that comes when matters of major importance are finally resolved.

One night about two weeks after Tomohiko Amada's death, Mariye came to talk to me, stealing to my house in secret like a cautious cat. She didn't stay very long. Her family was keeping close watch on her, so she didn't have the freedom to come and go that she had enjoyed before.

"My breasts seem to be getting bigger," she said. "My aunt and I went shopping for a bra. The stores carry something called a 'beginner's bra.' Did you know that?"

No, I said, I didn't. I glanced at her chest but saw nothing new beneath her green Shetland sweater.

"I don't see much difference," I said.

"That's because the padding is thin. If it were any thicker, people would see the change right away and think you stuffed something inside. So you start thin and then work up from there. It's more complicated than I thought."

Mariye told me that a female police officer had questioned her at length about where she had been those four days. The questioning had been gentle most of the time, yet on occasion the woman had become very firm. But Mariye had stuck with her story: she could remember only that she'd been roaming the mountain and had gotten lost. The rest was a complete blank. She thought she'd survived on the mineral water and chocolate she always carried in her schoolbag. That was all she would say. Otherwise, she kept her mouth clamped shut. She was good at keeping quiet. Once the police were sure that she had not been kidnapped and held for ransom, they took her to a hospital to have her cuts and bruises examined. They wanted to know if she had been sexually abused in any way. When it was clear that no abuse had taken place, the police lost interest. She was just another runaway kid who had gone missing for a couple of days. Hardly a rare occurrence.

Mariye threw away everything she had been wearing during that time: her dark blue blazer, checked skirt, white blouse, knitted vest, loafers—everything. She bought a whole new set of school clothes to replace them. She wanted to start fresh. Then she went back to her life as if nothing had happened. The only difference was that she quit attending the painting class (she was too old for the children's class anyway). She hung my (unfinished) portrait of her on her wall.

It was hard to imagine what kind of woman she would grow up to be. Girls of that age can change in the blink of an eye, physically and emotionally. I might not even be able to recognize her in a few years. I was thus very happy to have painted her picture (unfinished though it was) as she was at thirteen, freezing her image in time. In this real world of ours, after all, nothing remains the same forever.

I called my former agent in Tokyo and told him I wanted to go back to portrait painting. He couldn't have been happier. They were always short of skilled artists.

"But you told me you were through with the business, didn't you?" he said.

"I changed my mind," I answered. Why exactly, I didn't say. He didn't ask, either.

I wanted to live without thinking about anything for a while, to let my hands move on their own, churning out normal, "commercial" portraits one after the other. In the process, I could gain some financial stability. I didn't know how long I could keep that up. I couldn't predict the future. But for the time being, at least, that's what I wanted. To use my hard-won skills without calling up any complicated thoughts. To avoid getting mixed up with Ideas, or Metaphors, or anything along those lines. To keep a safe distance from the messy private affairs of the wealthy, mysterious man who lived across the valley. Not to be dragged into any more dark tunnels for having brought hidden masterpieces into the light. More than anything, that's what I desired.

I met Yuzu. We talked over coffee and Perrier at a café not far from her office. Her belly wasn't as big as I had imagined.

"You're not planning to marry the father?" I asked her right off the bat.

She shook her head. "No, not at the present time."

"Why?"

"I just feel that's for the best."

"But you plan to have the child, right?"

She gave a little nod. "Of course. Can't turn back now."

"Are you living with him?"

"No, I'm not. Since you left I've lived alone."

"How come?"

"For one thing, we're not divorced yet."

"But I sent you the divorce papers a while ago, signed and sealed. So I assumed we were already divorced."

Yuzu was quiet for a moment. "To be honest, I never submitted them," she said at last. "I couldn't somehow, so I let them sit. You and I have been legally married all this time. That means the baby will legally be your child, whether we get divorced or not. You won't bear any responsibility for it, of course."

I couldn't grasp what she meant. "But biologically speaking, the baby is his, correct?"

Yuzu looked me in the eye. "It's not that simple," she said at last.

"What do you mean?"

"How can I put this? I'm not a hundred percent certain the baby is his."

Now it was my turn to look her in the eye. "Are you saying you don't know who got you pregnant?"

She nodded. *I don't know.*

"But it's not what you're thinking," she said. "I wasn't sleeping around. I can only have a sexual relationship with one man at a time. That's why I stopped sleeping with you. Right?"

I nodded.

"I felt sorry for you, though."

I nodded again.

"But I was careful to use protection with him. I didn't want a child. You know how I felt. I was ultra-cautious about those things. And yet I got pregnant, just like that."

"There can always be slipups, no matter how careful we try to be."

"Women know when something like that happens," Yuzu said, shaking her head. "We have a sixth sense that tells us. I don't think men have it."

Of course, I didn't.

"At any rate, you're planning to have the baby," I said.

Yuzu nodded.

"But you never wanted one. At least as long as we were together."

"That's true," she said. "I didn't want one with you. I didn't want one with anybody."

"And yet now you're going to go ahead and bring a child into the world without knowing who the father is. Why didn't you have an abortion? You could have done so earlier."

"I thought about it, of course. And part of me wanted one."

"But you didn't."

"This is how I think these days," Yuzu said. "This is my life, sure, but in the end almost all that happens in it may be decided arbitrarily, quite apart from me. In other words, although I may presume I have free will, in fact I may not be making any of the major decisions that affect me. I've come to think my pregnancy is an example of that."

I listened to her without saying anything.

"I know this sounds fatalistic, but it's what I have *truly* come to feel. Honestly and deeply. So then I thought, if that's how things work, why not have the child and raise it on my own. See it through, and find out what happens. That's come to seem terribly important."

"There's just one thing I need to ask," I said, diving in.

"What is it?"

"It's a simple question, one that requires a mere yes or no. I won't say anything more."

"No problem. Ask away."

"Can I return to you—would you take me back?"

Her brow furrowed slightly. She looked me hard in the face for a moment. "Do you mean you wish to live once more as husband and wife?"

"If that's possible."

"I'd like that," she said quietly. There was no hesitation in her voice. "You are still my husband, and your room is as you left it. You can come back anytime you wish."

"Are you still seeing the other man?" I inquired.

Yuzu quietly shook her head. "No, that's over."

"Why?"

"I didn't want to allow him parental rights—that's the main reason."

I said nothing.

"It seems to have come as a great shock to him. Only natural, I guess," she said. She rubbed her cheeks with her hands.

"But you would allow me?"

She rested her hands on the table and once again looked at me closely.

"You've changed a little, haven't you? Your features, or maybe your expression?"

"I don't know how I look, but I have learned a few things, I think."

"I may have learned a few things myself."

I picked up my cup and drained what was left of my coffee.

"Masahiko's father just passed away," I said, "so he's got a lot to deal with right now. When things have settled down for him, I'll pack my bags and return to our apartment in Hiroo, probably sometime early in the New Year. Assuming that's all right with you, of course."

She studied my face. As if gazing at a landscape she had missed for a very long time. Finally, she reached across the table and gently covered my hand with hers.

"I'd like to give it another try," she said. "In fact, I've been thinking that for a while."

"I've been thinking the same thing," I said.

"I don't know if it will work out or not."

"I don't know either. But it's worth a shot."

"I'm about to have a baby without knowing who the father is. Is that going to be all right with you?"

"I don't have a problem with that," I said. "I know you're going to think I'm crazy, but there's a possibility that I could be the baby's father—potentially. That's my feeling, anyway. I could have somehow gotten you pregnant, mentally, from a distance. As a concept, using a special route."

"As a concept?"

"That's one hypothesis."

Yuzu considered that for a minute. "If that's true," she said, "then that's one heck of a hypothesis."

"Perhaps nothing can be certain in this world," I said. "But at least we can believe in something."

She smiled. That was the end of our conversation that day. She took the subway home, while I climbed into my dusty old Toyota Corolla station wagon and drove back to my home on the mountain.

64

AS A FORM OF GRACE

It was several years after I moved back in with my wife that, on March 11, a huge earthquake devastated northeastern Japan. I sat in front of the television as, one after another, coastal villages and towns from Iwate all the way down to Miyagi were laid to waste before my eyes. That was the very same region I had driven through in my old Peugeot 205. I had encountered the man with the white Subaru Forester in one of those towns. Yet now all I could see were the remains of communities leveled by a tsunami that had fallen on them like some giant beast, leaving nothing in its wake but drowned wreckage. Try as I might, I could find no visible connection to *that town*. Since I couldn't remember the name of the place, I had no way of learning how much damage it had suffered, or how it had been changed.

I couldn't bring myself to do anything—I just sat staring at the TV screen for days on end in stunned silence. I was transfixed. I prayed to find something, anything, connected to my memories. If I failed, I feared, something stored within me, something very important, would be lost for good, carried off to some distant, unknown place. I wanted to hop in my car and drive to the stricken region. See for myself what had survived the disaster. That was out of the question, of course. The main roads had been torn to pieces, which meant that towns and villages were cut off from the world. Electricity, gas, water—all lifelines had been severed. Farther south, on the coast of Fukushima (where I had abandoned my Peugeot when it gave up the ghost), several nuclear reactors were in meltdown. It was impossible to venture into that part of the country.

I had not been a happy man when I had traveled there. It had been a lonely, painful, thoroughly wretched period in my life. I think I was lost in a number of ways. Nevertheless, the trip had allowed me to spend time among unfamiliar people, and witness their lives. I had not imagined then how valuable that would turn out to be. In the process—usually unconsciously—I had discarded some things and picked up others. By the time I passed through all those places I had become a somewhat different person.

I thought of *The Man with the White Subaru Forester* hidden in the attic of the Odawara house. Had that man—whether he belonged to the real world or not—still been living in the same town when disaster struck? What about the skinny young woman with whom I had spent that strange night. Had they and the other inhabitants been able to escape the earthquake and tsunami? Were they still alive? What was the fate of the love hotel and the roadside restaurant?

When five o'clock came around, I would go to pick up our daughter at the nursery school. This was my designated role (my wife having gone back to work at the architectural firm). On an adult's legs, the school was a ten-minute walk away. Then the two of us would slowly stroll home, hand in hand. If the weather was good, we would stop by a park on the way to sit on a bench and watch the neighborhood dogs pass by. Our daughter wanted a little dog of her own, but no pets were permitted in our apartment building, so she had to make do with looking at them in the park. Every so often, someone would let her pet their small, unthreatening dog.

Our daughter's name was Muro. Yuzu had chosen it. She had seen the name in a dream shortly before the baby was born. In the dream, she had been in a large Japanese-style room that looked out over a spacious and beautiful garden. There was a low, old-fashioned writing desk, and on top of that a sheet of white paper. On the paper a single character, 室 (Muro), had been written in bright black ink. The calligraphy was magnificent. That was Yuzu's dream. It stayed stuck in her mind even after she awoke. Thus, she decided, Muro had to be the baby's name. I was fine with that, of course. After all, she was the one having the baby.

The idea that the calligrapher might be Tomohiko Amada popped into my head. But that was just a passing thought. When you came right down to it, it was only a dream, nothing more.

I was happy the child was a girl. I had grown up with my younger sister Komi, so I found it relaxing to have a little girl around. It felt as natural as could be. I was happy, too, that she came into this world with her name already settled. Names are important, whatever one might say.

When we got home, Muro and I watched the news together. I tried to shield her from shots of towns being swallowed by the tsunami. I thought the images were too disturbing for a young child. I was quick to cover her eyes when they came on the screen.

"Why, Daddy?" Muro asked me.

"Because you're still too young."

"But it's real, isn't it?"

"Yes, it is. It's really happening somewhere far from here. But just because it's real doesn't mean you have to see it."

Muro thought about that for a while. But of course she couldn't wrap her head around what I had said. She couldn't understand tsunamis and earthquakes yet, or the meaning of death. All the same, I blocked her vision whenever the tsunami appeared on the screen. Understanding something and seeing it are two different things.

One time, I saw the man with the white Subaru Forester on TV. Or at least I thought I did. They were shooting a large fishing vessel stranded on a bluff some distance from shore, and *he* was standing nearby. Like an elephant keeper beside an elephant that had outlived its usefulness. But that shot was quickly followed by another. I couldn't be sure if it was really the man with the white Subaru Forester or not. But to me the tall fellow in the black windbreaker and black cap with a Yonex logo could be no one else.

His image came and went. There was only a brief second before the camera angle shifted.

Besides watching news about the earthquake, I painted "commercial" portraits on commission to shore up our finances. It was something I could do without thinking—when I sat before the canvas, my hands moved almost automatically. I had been seeking just that sort of life.

And that's what people had been seeking from me. The work provided a steady income. I needed that too. I had a family to take into account.

Two months after the earthquake, my old home in Odawara burned down. The house on the mountain where Tomohiko Amada had spent half his life. Masahiko called with the news. He had been tearing his hair out over how to look after it once I had left, and it turned out his fears were well founded. It had caught fire just before dawn at the end of the May holidays, and although firemen had rushed to the scene, the old wooden structure had almost burned to the ground by the time they arrived (the fire trucks had trouble navigating the steep and twisting road). Luckily, it had rained the night before, so flames hadn't spread to the surrounding trees. The fire department investigated, but to no avail. It might have been an electrical short circuit, but then again it could have been arson.

The first thing that came to mind when I heard the news was *Killing Commendatore*. It must have been incinerated along with the house. Same with *The Man with the White Subaru Forester*. And the record collection. Had the owl in the attic managed to escape?

Killing Commendatore was without a doubt one of Tomohiko Amada's best works, its demise a great loss to Japan's art world. Yet only a few people had laid eyes on it. Just Mariye Akikawa and me. Shoko Akikawa, very briefly. Its creator, Tomohiko Amada, of course. After that, possibly no one. Now it was gone forever, swallowed by the flames. I couldn't shake the feeling that I was somehow to blame. Shouldn't I have made public Tomohiko Amada's hidden masterpiece? Instead, I had bundled it up and stuck it back in the attic. Now it was just a pile of ashes. (I had carefully copied the characters who appeared in it in my sketchbook, all that remained of *Killing Commendatore*.) As a self-respecting artist myself, the idea pained me. The painting was so wonderful, I thought. Perhaps I had committed a crime against art itself.

Yet it also struck me that it might have been a work that *had to be lost*. Tomohiko Amada had poured just too much of his passion, his soul, into it for it to be exposed to public view. It was filled with his spirit. Thus, although it was a superb painting, it possessed some sort of vicious power—it could summon things from *the other side*. By discovering it, I had set a cycle of some kind in motion. Dragging a painting like that out into the light could well have been a big mistake. Wasn't that what the artist himself had thought? Wasn't that why he had hidden it in the attic, away from view? If so, then I had respected his wishes. Whichever the case, it had been lost to the flames, and there was no way anyone could turn back time to recover it.

I didn't regret the loss of *The Man with the White Subaru Forester* for a moment. I knew I would tackle that subject again in the future. By then, though, I would have become a more resolute man, and an artist of greater integrity. When it came time to create my own art again, I should be able to paint *The Man with the White Subaru Forester* from a whole new angle. Perhaps that work would become my own *Killing Commendatore*. If that happened, it would be the greatest legacy I could receive from Tomohiko Amada.

Mariye called me right after the fire, and we talked for half an hour about the little old house it had left in ashes. That house had been important to her. Not so much the building, perhaps, as the world it encompassed, and the time when it was an essential part of her life. That would include Tomohiko Amada, back in the days when he still lived there. Whenever she saw him, the painter was always immersed in his work. From Mariye's experience, an artist was someone who holed up for days painting in his studio. She had watched Amada through the window of that house. Now it was gone, and she had lost that world forever. I shared her sadness. That house held deep meaning for me as well, though I had lived there less than eight months.

At the end of our call, Mariye told me that her breasts were much bigger than before. By now, she was in her second year of high school. I had not seen her once since my departure. Our relationship consisted of an occasional phone call. I didn't particularly want to revisit the house, nor had I any compelling reason to go there. It was always Mariye who called me.

"They haven't filled out yet, but they're definitely growing," she whispered confidentially. It took me a while to register what she was talking about.

"Just as the Commendatore prophesied," she said.

That's wonderful, I said. I considered asking if she had a boyfriend, but decided against it.

Her aunt was still seeing Menshiki. She had revealed that to Mariye at some point. That they were *very close indeed*. And that they might get married before too long.

"Would you live with us if that happened?" her aunt had asked.

Mariye had pretended she hadn't heard. She was good at that.

I found the idea a bit unsettling. "Are you intending to live with Mr. Menshiki?" I asked her.

"I don't think so," she said. "But I'm not so sure."

Not so sure?

"I thought you had some pretty bad memories of his house," I said, my bafflement showing.

"All of that happened when I was a kid. It seems so long ago. And there's no way I'm going to live alone with my father."

So long ago?

It felt like yesterday to me. When I said that to Mariye, though, she didn't respond. Perhaps she wanted to forget those days, and what had taken place then. Or maybe she already had. Now that she was older, she might even have started to develop an interest in Menshiki, however slight. Maybe she had come to see something special in him, a blood tie of some sort.

"I really want to see what happened to that closetful of clothes," Mariye said.

"That room attracts you, doesn't it?"

"That's because those clothes protected me," she said. "But who knows, I may live on my own when I go to college."

Sounds good to me, I said.

"So what's the situation with the pit behind the shrine?" I asked.

"No change," Mariye replied. "The blue plastic sheet's still on it, even after the fire. Leaves will cover it eventually. Then maybe no one will know it's even there."

The little old bell would be lying on the floor of the pit. Together with the flashlight I had taken from Tomohiko Amada's room at the nursing home.

"Have you seen the Commendatore?" I asked.

"No, not once. It's hard to believe he really existed."

"He did, all right," I said. "You'd better believe it."

All the same, I figured that, little by little, that realm would disappear from Mariye's mind. Her life would grow busier and more complicated as she moved into her late teens. She would no longer have time to consider crazy things like Ideas and Metaphors.

Every so often, I found myself wondering about the plastic penguin. I had given it to the faceless man as payment for ferrying me across the river. There had been no alternative, given the swiftness of the current. I could only pray that little penguin was watching over Mariye from somewhere—probably as it shuttled back and forth between presence and absence.

I still can't be sure about the identity of Muro's father. A DNA test would tell me, but I have no desire to know the result. Perhaps we'll find out somewhere along the way. The truth may be revealed. But what meaning would that "truth" carry? Muro is my child in the legal sense, and I love her deeply. I treasure the time we spend together. I couldn't care less who her biological father is or isn't. The question is inconsequential. It can change nothing.

I went to Yuzu in a dream as I wandered from town to town in northeastern Japan. I made love to her while she was asleep, stealing into her dream and impregnating her, so that nine months and a few days later she bore a child. I love this idea (although I hold it in secret). That child's father is me as Idea, or perhaps me as Metaphor. Just as the Commendatore visited me, or as Donna Anna guided me through the dark, so did I, in some alternate world, deposit my seed in Yuzu's womb.

But I will not become like Menshiki. He has built his life by balancing the possibility that Mariye Akikawa is his child with the possibility that she isn't. It is through the subtle and unending oscillation between those two poles that he seeks to find the meaning of his own existence.

I have no need, though, to challenge my life in such a troublesome (or, at the least, unnatural) way. That is because I am endowed with the capacity *to believe*. I believe in all honesty that something will appear to guide me through the darkest and narrowest tunnel, or across the most desolate plain. That's what I learned from the strange events I experienced while living in that mountaintop house on the outskirts of Odawara.

Killing Commendatore may have been lost forever in the flames that hour before dawn, yet its beauty and power live within me even now. I can call up the images of the Commendatore, Donna Anna, the faceless man, and the rest with perfect clarity. They look so tangible, so real, I feel as though I could reach out and touch them. Contemplating them affords me perfect tranquility, as though I were watching raindrops fall on the surface of a broad reservoir. That soundless rain will fall forever in my heart.

I will probably live the rest of my life in their company. My little daughter Muro is their gift to me. A form of grace. I am convinced of this.

"The Commendatore was truly there," I say to Muro as she lies sleeping. "You'd better believe it."